A Complete Collection Of State-trials And Proceedings For High-treason And Other Crimes And Misdemeanours: Commencing With The Eleventh Year Of The Reign Of King Richard Ii. And Ending With The Sixteenth Year Of The Reign Of King George Iii. : With...

Francis Hargrave

A

Complete Collection

OF

STATE-TRIALS,

AND

PROCEEDINGS

FOR

HIGH-TREASON,

AND OTHER

CRIMES and MISDEMEANOURS;

THE FOURTH EDITION;

COMMENCING WITH

The Eleventh Year of the Reign of KING RICHARD II.

AND ENDING WITH

The Sixteenth Year of the Reign of KING GEORGE III.

WITH

TWO ALPHABETICAL TABLES TO THE WHOLE.

TO WHICH IS PREFIXED,

A NEW PREFACE,

By FRANCIS HARGRAVE, ESQUIRE.

VOLUME THE SEVENTH.

LONDON:

Printed by T. WRIGHT, Eſſex-Street, Strand;

For C. BATHURST, WILSON and NICHOLL, J. F. and C. RIVINGTON, L. DAVIS, T. LONGMAN, W. OWEN, T. CADELL, M. FOLINGSBY, T. LOWNDES, B. LAW, J. WILKIE, R. HORSFIELD, M. HINGESTON, S. BLADON, T. CARNAN, H. GARDNER, W. OTRIDGE, S. LEACROFT, T. EVANS, and the reſt of the Proprietors:

And Sold by G. KEARSLY, No. 46, near Serjeant's-Inn, Fleet-Street.

MDCCLXXVIII.

THE

PREFACE.

AFTER the Publication of a Collection of *State-Trials*, which confifts of Six Volumes in Folio; the Reader may poffibly be furpriz'd at the Appearance of two Volumes more of Collections on the fame Subject. For this Reafon it may be proper to premife fome Particulars prefatory to the Work, concerning the Inducements there were to it, and the Method wherein it has been purfued.

And here we would by no means be underftood to lay any Imputation on the Gentleman who prepar'd the laft Edition of that Work for the Prefs. The judicious Preface he prefix'd to it, plainly fhew'd him to be entirely Mafter of the Subject; and he perform'd, with eminent Sufficiency the Part he undertook, which was, to prepare and methodize fuch Tracts, Printed or Manufcript, as were brought to him; to infert them in their proper Places, and to make Remarks and References wherever there was Occafion. The Bufinefs of collecting the feveral Pieces was by no means his Province, nor was it to be expected from one who had daily Avocations in the way of his Profeffion.

And tho' it were admitted that the then Undertakers did every thing they poffibly could, to render the Work entire and complete, and fpared neither Pains nor Expence to procure Materials fit for the purpofe; yet it is no wonder, that in fo fruitful a Field, they fhould after all their Diligence leave fome Gleanings to reward the Induftry of thofe that came after them.

They proceeded in the firft Edition upon a very fcanty Plan, propofing to take in no Trials, but what were really *State-Trials*, and were taken at length and entire; and to this Plan they adhered ftrictly, except in a few Inftances: but in preparing the fecond Edition, by the Advice of feveral Gentlemen of Learning and Curiofity, a greater Latitude was taken, and as well feveral Cafes heard before the Court of *Star-Chamber* were inferted, as other Proceedings at Law, which could not properly be called *State-Trials*; and Trials which were well taken, tho' not of a Criminal Nature, were inferted, together with the dying Behaviour and Speeches of fuch unfortunate Perfons as fuffer'd Death upon their Convictions.

In almoft every of thefe Particulars, thefe Supplemental Volumes will appear to have received many Additions and Improvements. The Cafes here inferted, which were debated in the *Star-Chamber*, are fuch only as were confiderable for the Curiofity of the Fact enquired into; as the Cafe of *Davidfon* for fending down the Warrant for beheading the Queen of *Scots*, contrary to Queen *Elizabeth*'s Order; or for the Figure and Station of the Perfons concern'd, as Lord Chancellor *Bacon* and others. The Trial for a large Eftate in *Shadwell*, wherein the Lady *Ivy* was a Party; that of Mr. *Denew* and others, for affaulting Mr. *Colepepper*; the Proceedings between the Duke and Dutchefs of *Norfolk*, and his Grace's Trial with Mr. *Germaine*; and fome others were taken from printed Pieces, which, for their Price and Scarcity, were almoft equivalent to Manufcripts: and we can with Truth fay, that moft of the printed Tracts here made ufe of, coft above Ten times the Price, that an ordinary Piece of the fame Size is commonly fold for.

As for the Trials in thefe Volumes which were never before printed, we are not at liberty to give the Reafons why we believe them to be Authentick; but we conceive the intrinfick Marks they bear will be fo evident and convincing, to every one that reads them, of their being genuine, as to make any Proofs on that Head to be abfolutely unneceffary.

We have been oblig'd in a few Places to tranfcribe here and there fome Paffages from larger Works: but in this Particular we have been as fparing as poffible, having inferted no more than was abfolutely neceffary to preferve the Connexion, and to make the whole more intelligible. The greateft Freedom taken in that kind has been in the Collection of Arguments and Debates upon the *Habeas Corpus* Act and Liberty of the Subject, between the Years 1627 and 1640; in which we were obliged to be fometimes beholden (but as little as poffible) to Mr. *Rufhworth*'s Hiftorical Collections. As thefe Contefts, between the Crown and the Subject, were one of the greateft Caufes of the fatal Confufions which afterwards followed, and of that furprifing Revolution which was the Aftonifhment of all *Chriftendom*, every Proceeding in that Affair, warranted by fufficient Authority, was thought worth preferving; efpecially as it related to what, next to the Life of the Subject, is deemed moft precious in the Eye of the Law, his *Liberty*.

Some Gentlemen may perhaps think that Mr. *Rufhworth*'s Collection are fo full on this Head, that it would be a Prefumption to add any thing to them: but it will appear that moft of the Speeches and Proceedings here printed are not taken notice of by Mr. *Rufhworth*. How they came to be omitted, we will not pretend to determine; only we cannot forbear obferving, as a ftrange Inftance of Partiality in that Editor, that after inferting the Articles againft the Earl of *Strafford* at large in his Trial, he has abridg'd the Anfwer put in by him to his Articles, with this Introduction: *The Anfwer held three Hours, being above* 200 *Sheets of Paper, too long to be here inferted; yet take an Abftract of the faid Anfwer to the Articles exhibited againft him, which are as followeth.* Which Abftract is fo vaftly fhort, as not to contain above Ten Pages.

For fear of being thought prolix, in order to fwell the Price of the Book, we have omitted the Trial at large of the Earl of *Strafford*, it being to be had feparate at a moderate Price. We don't doubt but his Anfwer at large would have been a great Ornament to this Collection, and would have enabled the World to judge more clearly of his Cafe, than it is now likely to do. But as all the Proceedings againft him were ftrictly order'd to be obliterated; fo, with the utmoft Enquiry, we have been unable to find any Copy thereof remaining with the Defcendants of his Family, or in any other Hands.

The Cafe of *Monoplies*, between the *Eaft-India* Company and Mr. *Sandys*, does not, it muft be confeft, ftrictly fpeaking, come under the Defcription of a *State-Trial*; but as the publifhing the Proceedings between the King and the City of *London*, upon a *Quo Warranto*, in the laft Edition of the *State-Trials*, met with general Approbation, we hope the like candid Conftruction will be put upon the Step we have taken in this Cafe. The Queftion of the Power of the Crown to grant an exclufive Charter, and the Diftinction to be made between a criminal Monopoly, the regal Prerogative, and legal Property, are undoubtedly of the higheft Importance. The Point is debated upon this Occafion by the moft knowing and eminent Lawyers of the Time, and their Arguments are now firft publifhed from Manufcripts, which have not been taken notice of in any of the Law-Books now extant, (except a very fhort Abftract of fome of the Speeches, which is printed in Mr. Serjeant *Skinner*'s Reports) to which are added, the learned Arguments and Reafons of the Lord Chief-Juftice *Jeffreys*.

There are fome Inftances where we have not been able to procure complete Trials, and yet have obtained either Speeches made in them by Gentlemen of Note at that time, or large and particular Relations, though not in fo minute and exact a manner, as in Trials taken in Short-hand in Court. Where any thing of this kind has occur'd, which we judg'd worth notice, we have chofe to preferve them from the oblivion they would otherwife fink under, by inferting them in this Collection. And tho' they are not fo valuable as entire Trials, yet they may ferve to give a more clear Account of the Facts there tried, than is to be found in a general Hiftory; which, as the learned Editor of the *State-Trials* well obferves, is one confiderable Benefit arifing from Collections of this kind.

Concerning the other Pieces contained in this Collection, we need be the lefs particular in this place, as we have before moft of the Articles, or in Notes at the Bottom, given our Reafons for inferting them: Only left it fhould be thought that the remarkable Cafe of *Afhby* and *White*, in the laft Volume, contains no more than the fmall Book, publifhed under that Name in Octavo in the Year 1705, it may be proper to obferve, That the whole Proceedings and Debates of that memorable Affair are deduced in order of Time from the firft Complaint made in the Houfe of Commons; containing not only the Proceedings, Reports, Reprefentations, Conferences and Refolutions, of both Houfes, as publifh'd by their Order; but alfo the Proceedings and Arguments in the Court of *King's-Bench*.

In fine, as no Pains or Expence has been fpared to make this Collection complete, ufeful and inftructive, fo we muft fubmit the whole to the Judgment of the Publick, and rely upon the Candour of the Readers, for a kind Acceptance of our Endeavours.

THE

The ſeveral TRIALS, &c. contained in the SEVENTH VOLUME.

I.

1549. *PROCEEDINGS in Parliament againſt Sir* Thomas Seymour, *Knight, Lord* Sudley, *for High-Treaſon*, 2 & 3 Edw. VI. Page 1

II.

1550. *Proceedings againſt* Edward *Duke of* Somerſet, *in Parliament, for Miſdemeanours and High-Treaſon*, 3 *and* 4 Edw. VI. 12

III.

1551. *Proceedings before the Lords againſt* Edward *Duke of* Somerſet, *for High-Treaſon and Felony*, 5 Edw. VI. 15

IV.

1587. *The Arraignment of Mr.* Daviſon *in the* Star-Chamber, *for Miſpriſion and Contempt*, 30 Eliz. 20

V.

1588. *The Arraignment of Sir* Richard Knightly *and others, in the* Star-Chamber, *for maintaining ſeditious Perſons, Books, and Libels*, 31 Eliz. 29

VI.

1600. *Proceedings in Parliament againſt* John *Earl of* Gowrie, Alexander Ruthven, *his Brother*, Henry Ruthven, Hugh Montcrief, *and* Peter Eviot, *for High-Treaſon at* Edinburgh. 33

VII.

1600. *The Arraignment and Judgment of Capt.* Thomas Lee, *at the Seſſions-Houſe near* Newgate, *for High-Treaſon*, 43 Eliz. 44

VIII.

1600. *The Trial of Sir* Chriſtopher Blunt, *Sir* Charles Davers, *Sir* John Davis, *Sir* Gilly Merrick, *and* Henry Cuffe, *for High-Treaſon, at* Weſtminſter, 43 Eliz. 47

IX.

1603. *The Trial of Sir* Griffin Markham, *Knt. Sir* Edward Parham, *Knt.* George Brooke, *Eſq.* Bartholomew Brookeſby, *Eſq.* Anthony Copley, William Watſon, *Prieſt*, William Clarke, *Prieſt, for High-Treaſon, at* Wincheſter, 1 Jac. I. 63

X.

1603. *The Caſe between Sir* Francis Goodwin *and Sir* John Forteſcue, *in the Reign of King* James I. *as it ſtands upon the Journal of the Houſe of Commons*, 1 Jac. I. 67

XI.

1609. *The Proceſs and Trial of* Robert Logan *of* Reſtalrig, *for High-Treaſon, in conſpiring with* John *Earl of* Gowrie, *to murder King* James I. *at* Edinburgh, 7 Jac. I. 78

XII.

1609. *The Trial of the Lord* Balmerino, *for High-Treaſon, at* St. Andrew's, 7 Jac. I. 85

XIII.

1612. *The Arraignment and Confeſſion of the Lord* Sanquire (*who being a Baron of* Scotland, *was arraigned by the Name of* Robert Creighton, *Eſq.*), *at the* King's-Bench *Bar in* Weſtminſter-Hall, *for procuring the Murder of* John Turner, *a Maſter of Defence, whom he caus'd to be ſhot with a Piſtol, by one* Carliel *a* Scotiſhman, *for thruſting out one of his Eyes in playing at Rapier and Dagger*, 10 Jac. I. 86

XIV.

1615. *Proceedings againſt* John Ogilvie, *for High-Treaſon, at* Glaſgow, 13 Jac. I. 95

XV.

1618. *Proceedings againſt Mr.* Wraynham, *in the* Star-Chamber, *for ſlandering the Lord-Chancellor* Bacon *of Injuſtice*, 16 Jac. I. 102

XVI.

1627. *Proceedings on the* Habeas Corpus, *brought by Sir* Thomas Darnel, *Sir* John Corbet, *Sir* Walter Earl, *Sir* John Heveningham, *and Sir* Edmund Hampden, *at the* King's-Bench *in* Weſtminſter-Hall, 3 Car. I. 114

XVII.

1629. *Proceedings againſt* William Stroud, *Eſq.* Walter Long, *Eſq.* John Selden, *Eſq. and others, on an* Habeas Corpus, *in* Banco Regis, 5 Car. I. 217

XVIII.

1629. *Proceedings againſt Sir* John Elliot, Denzil Hollis, *and* Benjamin Valentine, *Eſqrs. for ſeditious Speeches in Parliament, in* Banco Regis, 5 Car. I. 242

XIX.

1631. *The Trial of* James *Lord* Uchiltrie, *for Calumnies and ſlanderous Speeches againſt* James *Marquis of* Hamilton, *the Earls of* Haddington, Roxburgh, *and* Buccleugh; *tending to ſowing Sedition betwixt his Majeſty and the ſaid Noblemen, at* Edinburgh, 6 Car. I. 260

XX.

1637. *The Trial of* John Lilburn *and* John Wharton, *for Printing and Publiſhing ſeditious Books, in the* Star-Chamber, 13 Car. I. 286

XXI.

1640. *Proceedings in Parliament againſt Sir* John Finch, *Baron of* Fordwich, *Lord-Keeper for High-Treaſon*, 16 Car. I. 309

XXII.

1647. *Two Judgments of the Lords aſſembled in Parliament, againſt* John Morris, *alias* Poyntz, Mary *his Wife*, Iſabel Smith, Leonard Darby, *and* John Harris; *for forging, framing, and publiſhing a Copy of a pretended Act of Parliament*, 23 Car. I. Page 317

XXIII.

1649. *The Trial of Col.* John Morris, *Governor of* Pontefract *Caſtle; at the Aſſizes at the Caſtle of* York, *before Mr.* John Puleſton, *and Mr. Baron* Thorpe, *Juſtices of Aſſize, for High-Treaſon*, 2 Car. II. 320

XXIV.

1650. *The Proceedings, Examination and Trial of Col.* Euſebius Andrewe, *before the High Court of Juſtice, for High-Treaſon*, 3 Car. II. 324

XXV.

1652. *The Trial of* Richard Faulconer, *for Perjury, at the* King's-Bench, 5 Car. II. 343

XXVI.

1653. *The Trial of Mr.* John Lilburn, *at the Seſſions-Houſe in the* Old-Bailey, *for returning into* England, *being baniſhed by Act of Parliament*, 6 Car. II. 354

XXVII.

1656. *The Trial of* Miles Sindercombe, *alias* Fiſh, *for High-Treaſon; at the Upper-Bench before the Lord Chief Juſtice* Glynn, *and Mr. Juſtice* Warburton, 8 Car. II. 371

XXVIII.

1661. *Proceedings againſt* Archibald *Marquis of* Argyle, *for High-Treaſon, in* Scotland, 13 Car. II. 379

XXIX.

1666. *The Trial of the Lord* Morley, *before the Houſe of Lords, for Murder*, 18 Car. II. 421

XXX.

1674. *The Proceedings in the Court of* King's-Bench, Exchequer, *and Houſe of Peers, in the Caſe of Sir* Samuel Barnardiſton, *Bart. againſt Sir* William Soame, *Sheriff of* Suffolk, *concerning the Election of Members to Parliament*, 26 Car. II. 428

XXXI.

1675. *Proceedings in the Houſe of Commons, on an Appeal being brought in the Houſe of Lords, by Dr.* Shirley, *againſt Sir* John Fagg, *and others, their Members*, 27 Car. II. 453

XXXII.

1676. *Proceedings againſt Mr.* Francis Jenks, *for a Speech made by him on the Huſtings at* Guildhall, *on* Midſummer-day, 27 Car. II. 468

XXXIII.

1679. *Articles of High-Miſdemeanours, humbly offer'd and preſented to the Conſideration of his moſt Sacred Majeſty, and his moſt Honourable Privy-Council, againſt Sir* William Scroggs, *Lord Chief-Juſtice of the* King's-Bench; *exhibited by Dr.* Oates *and Capt.* Bedloe, 31 Car. II. 476

XXXIV.

1680. *Proceedings againſt Sir* William Scroggs, *Knt. Lord Chief Juſtice of the* King's-Bench, *and other Judges, in Parliament*, 32 Car. II. 479

XXXV.

1680. *The Report from the Committee of the Commons in Parliament, appointed by the Honourable Houſe of Commons, to conſider the Petition of* Richard Thompſon *of* Briſtol, *Clerk, and to examine Complaints againſt him. And the Reſolution of the Commons in Parliament upon this Report for his Impeachment of High Crimes and Miſdemeanours*, 32 Car. II. 491

XXXVI.

1683. *The Great Caſe of Monopolies, between the* Eaſt-India *Company, Plaintiffs, and* Thomas Sandys, *Defendant; whether their Patent for Trading to the* Eaſt-Indies, *excluſive of all others, is good*, 35 Car. II. 493

XXXVII.

1684. *The Lady* Ivy's *Trial, for great Part of* Shadwell, *in the County of* Middleſex, *in* Banc. Reg. 36 Car. II. 571

XXXVIII.

1685. *The Trial of* William Diſney, *Eſq. by the King's Special Commiſſion of* Oyer *and* Terminer, *held at the* Marſhalſea *in* Southwark, *for High-Treaſon*, 2 Jac. II. 611

XXXIX.

1686. *The Trial with Sir* Edward Hales, *Bart. for neglecting to take the Oaths of Supremacy and Allegiance, with his Plea thereto, upon the King's diſpenſing with the Statute*, 25 Car. II. *and the Opinion of the Judges thereupon*, 2 Jac. II. 612

XL.

1686. *The Proceedings againſt Mr.* Samuel Johnſon, *who was tried at the* King's-Bench *Bar*, Weſtminſter, *for High Miſdemeanours, in writing and publiſhing ſeditious Libels*, 2 Jac. II. 645

XLI.

1688. *The Trial of* Rowland Walters, Dearing Bradſhaw, *and* Ambroſe Cave, *Gents. at the* Old-Bailey, *before Sir* John Shorter, *Knt. Lord-Mayor, and Sir* Batholomew Shower, *Knt. Recorder, with others of his Majeſty's Juſtices, for murdering Sir* Carles Pymm, *Bart.* 4 Jac. II. 648

A COMPLETE
COLLECTION
OF
TRIALS, &c.

I.

Proceedings in Parliament against Sir THOMAS SEYMOUR, Knt. Lord *Sudley*, for High-Treason, *Feb.* 25, 1549, 2 and 3 *Edw.* VI.

ABOUT the Year 1547 *, Sir *Thomas Seymour*, the Protector's brother, was brought to such a Share of his fortunes, that he was made a Baron, and Lord Admiral. But this not satisfying his ambition, he endeavoured to have linked himself into a nearer relation with the Crown, by marrying the King's Sister, the Lady *Elizabeth*. But finding he could not compass that, he made his addresses to *Catherine Parr*, the Queen Dowager, and they were married privately. Being by this match possessed of great wealth, he studied to engage all about the King to be his friends. His design was, that since he was the King's Uncle as well as his Brother, he ought to have a proportioned share with him in the Government. About *Easter* that year he first set about that design; and corrupted some about the King, who should bring him sometimes privately through the Gallery to the Queen Dowager's Lodgings; and he desired they would let him know when the King had occasion for Money, they should not trouble the Treasury, for he would furnish him. Thus he gained ground with the King.

When the Protector was that year in *Scotland*, the Admiral began to act more openly, and was for making a party for himself, of which *Paget* charged him in plain terms, yet all was ineffectual; for the Admiral was resolved to go on, and either get himself advanced higher, or perish in the attempt. During the Session, the Admiral got the King to write with his own hand a message to the House of Commons for making him Governor of his Person, and he intended to have gone with it to the House, and had a party there, by whose Interest he was confident to have carried his business: he dealt also with many of the Lords and Counsellors to assist him in it. When this was known, before he had gone with it to the House, some were sent in his Brother's name to see if they could prevail with him to go no further; he refused to hearken to them, and said, that if he were crossed in his attempt, he would make this the *blackest Parliament* that ever was in *England*. Upon that he was sent for by order from the Council, but refused to come, then they threatened him severely, and told him, the King's writing was nothing in Law, but that he who had procured it, was punishable for doing an act of such a nature, &c. so they resolved to have him sent to the *Tower*. But at last he submitted himself to the Protector and Council; and his Brother and he *seem'd* to be perfectly reconciled †, though it was visible he only put off his projects till a fitter conjuncture, and was on all occasions infusing into the King a dislike of every thing that was done, persuading him to assume the Government himself, and bribing his servants.

Thus he continued contriving and plotting for some time; the Protector had often been told of these things, and warned him of the danger into which he would throw himself. But his restless ambition seeming incurable, he was on the 19th of *January* (*Stow* sayeth the 16th) sent to the *Tower* ‡: and now many things broke out against him, particularly a conspiracy of his with Sir *William Sharington*, Vice-Treasurer of the *Mint* at *Bristol*, who was to have furnished him with 10,000 *l.* and had already coined about 12,000 *l.* false money ‖, and had clipt a great deal more, to the value of 40,000 *l.* in all; for which he was attainted by a process at common law, and that was confirmed in Parliament §. *Fowler* also, that waited in the Privy-Chamber, with others were sent to the *Tower*; many complaints being brought against him, the Lord *Russel*, the Earl of *Southampton* and Secretary *Petre* were ordered to receive their Examinations.

The Protector finding he could not persuade him to submit, on the 22d of *February* a report was made to the Council of all the informations against him; consisting not only of the particulars before-mentioned, but of many foul misdemeanours in the discharge of the Admiralty, several pirates being concerned with him, &c. The whole charge against him, consisting of 33 articles, is as followeth, *viz.*

Articles of High-Treason, and other Misdemeanours against the King's Majesty and his Crown, objected to Sir Thomas Seymour, *Knt. Lord* Seymour *of* Sudley, *and High Admiral of* England.

Ex libro Concilii, fol. 236. 1. WHEREAS the Duke of *Somerset* was made Governor of the King's Majesty's Person, and Protector of all his Realms, and Dominions, and Subjects, to the which you yourself did agree, and gave your consent in writing; it is objected and laid unto your charge, That this, notwithstanding you have attempted and gone about, by indirect means, to undo this Order, and to get into your hands the Government of the King's Majesty, to the great danger of his Highness's Person, and the Subversion of the State of the Realm.

2. It is objected, and laid to your charge, That by corrupting with Gifts, and fair Promises, divers of the Privy-Chamber, you went about to allure his Highness to condescend and agree to the same your most heinous and perilous purposes, to the great danger of his Highness's Person, and of the Subversion of the State of the Realm.

3. It is objected, and laid unto your charge, That you wrote a Letter with your own hand, which Letter the King's Majesty should have subscribed, or written again after that Copy, to the Parliament-House; and that you delivered the same to his Highness for that intent: With the which so written by his Highness, or subscribed, you have determined to have come into the Commons-House yourself; and there, with your fautors and adherents before prepared, to have made a broil, or tumult, or uproar, to the great danger of the King's Majesty's Person, and subversion of the State of this Realm.

4. It is objected, and laid unto your charge, That you yourself spake to divers of the Council, and laboured with divers of the Nobility of the Realm, to stick and adhere unto you for the alteration of the State, and order of the Realm, and to attain your other purposes, to the danger of the King's Majesty's Person, now in his tender years, and subversion of the State of the Realm.

5. It is objected, and laid unto your charge, That you did say openly and plainly, you would make the blackest Parliament that ever was in *England*.

6. It is objected, and laid to your charge, That being sent for by the authority, to answer to such things as were thought meet to be reformed in you, you refused to come; to a very evil example of disobedience, and danger thereby of the subversion of the State of the Realm.

7. It is objected, and laid to your charge, That since the last Sessions of this Parliament, notwithstanding much clemency shewed unto you, you have still continued in your former mischievous purposes; and continually, by yourself and others, studied and laboured to put into the King's Majesty's head and mind, a misliking of the Government of the Realm, and of the Lord Protector's doings, to the danger of his Person, and the great peril of the Realm.

8. It is objected, and laid to your charge, That the King's Majesty being of those tender years, and as yet by age unable to direct his own things, you have gone about to instil into his Grace's head, and as much as lieth in you, persuaded him to take upon himself the Government and managing of his own affairs, to the danger of his Highness's Person, and great peril of the whole Realm.

9. It is objected, and laid to your charge, That you had fully intended and appointed, to have taken the King's Majesty's Person into your own hands and custody, to the danger of his Subjects, and peril of the Realm.

10. It is objected, and laid to your charge, That you have corrupted, with money, certain of the Privy-Chamber, to persuade the King's Majesty to have a credit towards you; and so to insinuate you to his Grace, that when he lacked any thing, he should have it of you and none other body, to the intent he should mislike his ordering, and that you might the better, when you saw time, use the King's Highness for an instrument to this purpose, to the danger of his Royal Person, and subversion of the State of the Realm.

* *Burnet*'s History of the Reformation, vol. II.

† It is mentioned by some historians, that the first occasion of the quarrel betwen the two Brothers, arose from the envy and malice of the Duchess of *Somerset* against the Queen Dowager, wife to the Admiral, and that she claimed the Precedency as the Protector's Lady; but this is very unlikely, that she should be so ignorant of the customs of *England*, as to dispute precedency with the Queen Dowager. The whole story seems to be forg'd by *Saunders*, in his Treatise *de Schismat. Anglican.* and copied by *Hayward*, &c. See the complete History of *England*, vol II. p. 301. and *Burnet*'s History of the Reformation, vol. II. p 54. *Rapin* in *English*, 8vo. Edit. vol. VIII. p. 53. and *Strype*'s Memorials, vol. II. p. 124 and 475. But *Strype* in the same volume, p. 133, saith, King *Edward*, in his invaluable Journal, preserved in the *Cotton Library*, noteth, that the Protector was much offended with this marriage of his Brother to the Queen. See also *Strype*'s Animadversions on *Hayward* . Edw. the VI. *in his Memorials*, vol. II. p. 473. and *Burnet*'s Appendix to vol II. p. 392. concerning some errors and falshoods in *Saunders*'s Book of the *English* Schism.

‡ In *Bibliotheca Harleyana*, 4[illegible] B 19. 51. is the Duke of *Somerset*'s and Council's Letter to Sir *Philip Hoby*, [illegible] "The [illegible] proceedings of the Lord "High Admiral, the Duke's Brother, viz. That he attempted to take into his own hands the most [illegible] of the King's Majesty, [illegible] "with divers persons, to have moved [illegible] in the Parliament, and otherwise to have put the whole [illegible] "discovered, and he questioned [illegible] he seemed very penitent, whereupon he was forgiven, and his living advanced [illegible] That [illegible] "and had almost compassed a secret marriage between himself and the Lady *Eliz.* the King's Sister [illegible] "the King's Majesty, and the Lady *Mary*, and to have deposed of his Majesty's whole Council at his pleasure [illegible] into the *Tower* of *London*."

‖ See Sir *William Sharington*'s Confession in *Strype*'s Memorials, vol. II. pag 81. in the Repository.

§ See the Act for confirmation of the attainder of Sir *William Sharington*, Knt. in *Rastal*'s Statutes, [illegible] and the act for the restitution in blood of Sir *William Sharington*, Knt. ibid pag. 995.

11. It is objected, and laid unto your charge, That you promiſed the marriage of the King's Majeſty at your will and pleaſure.

12. It is objected, and laid unto your charge, That you have laboured, and gone about to combine and confederate yourſelf with ſome Perſons; and eſpecially moved thoſe Noblemen whom you thought not to be contented, to depart into their Countries, and make themſelves ſtrong; and otherwiſe, to allure them to ſerve your purpoſe by gentle promiſes and offers, to have a party and faction in readineſs to all your purpoſes, to the danger of the King's Majeſty's Perſon, and peril of the ſtate of the Realm.

13. It is objected, and laid unto your charge, That you have parted, as it were, in your imagination and intent, the Realm, to ſet Noblemen to countervail ſuch other Noblemen as you thought would lett your deviliſh purpoſes, and ſo laboured to be ſtrong to all your Devices; to the great danger of the King's Majeſty's Perſon, and great peril of the ſtate of the Realm.

14. It is objected, and laid unto your charge, That you had adviſed certain men to entertain and win the favour and good-wills of the head yeomen and ringleaders of certain countries, to the intent that they might bring the multitude and commons, when you ſhould think meet, to the furtherance of your purpoſes.

15. It is objected, and laid to your charge, That you have not only ſtudied and imagined how to have the rule of a number of men in your hands, but that you have attempted to get, and alſo gotten, divers ſtewardſhips of Noblemen's lands, and their mannoreds, to make your party ſtronger, for your purpoſes aforeſaid; to the danger of the King's Majeſty's Perſon, and great peril of the ſtate of the Realm.

16. It is objected, and laid to your charge, That you have retained young gentlemen, and hired yeomen, to a great multitude, and far above ſuch number as is permitted by the laws and ſtatutes of the Realm, or were otherwiſe neceſſary or convenient for your ſervice, place, or eſtate, to the fortifying of yourſelf towards all your evil intents and purpoſes; to the great danger of the King's Majeſty, and peril of the ſtate of the Realm.

17. It is objected, and laid to your charge, That you had ſo travailed in that matter, that you had made yourſelf able to make, of your own men, out of your lands and rules, and other your adherents, ten thouſand men, beſides your friends, to the advancement of all your intents and purpoſes; to the danger of the King's Majeſty's Perſon, and the great peril of the ſtate of the Realm.

18. It is objected, and laid unto your charge, That you had conferred, caſt, and weighed ſo much money as would find the ſaid ten thouſand men for a month; and that you knew how and where to have the ſame Sum; and that you had given warning to have and prepare the ſaid maſs of money in a readineſs; to the danger of the King's Majeſty's Perſon, and great peril to the ſtate of the Realm.

19. It is objected, and laid unto your charge, That you have not only, before you married the Queen, attempted and gone about to marry the King's Majeſty's Siſter, the Lady *Elizabeth*, ſecond Inheritor in remainder to the Crown, but alſo being then lett by the Lord Protector, and others of the Council, ſince that time, both in the life of the Queen, continued your old labour and love; and after her death, by ſecret and crafty means, practiſed to atchieve the ſaid purpoſe of marrying the ſaid Lady *Elizabeth*; to the danger of the King's Majeſty's Perſon, and peril of the ſtate of the ſame.

20. It is objected, and laid to your charge, That you married the late Queen ſo ſoon after the late King's death, that if ſhe had conceived ſtreight after, it ſhould have been a great doubt whether the child born ſhould have been accounted the late King's or yours; whereupon a marvellous danger and peril might, and was like to have enſued to the King's Majeſty's ſucceſſion and quiet of the Realm.

21. It is objected, and laid unto your charge, That you firſt married the Queen privately, and did diſſemble and keep cloſe the ſame; inſomuch, that a good ſpace after you had married her, you made labour to the King's Majeſty, and obtained a letter of his Majeſty's hand, to move and require the ſaid Queen to marry with you; and likewiſe procured the Lord Protector to ſpeak to the Queen to bear you her favour towards marriage: by the which colouring, not only your evil and diſſembling nature may be known, but alſo it is to be feared, that at this preſent you did intend to uſe the ſame practice in the marriage of the Lady *Elizabeth*'s Grace.

22. It is objected, and laid unto your charge, That you not only, ſo much as lay in you, did ſtop and lett all ſuch things as, either by Parliament or otherwiſe, ſhould tend to the advancement of the King's Majeſty's affairs, but did withdraw yourſelf from the King's Majeſty's ſervice; and being moved and ſpoken unto, for your own honour, and for the ability that was in you, to ſerve and aid the King's Majeſty's affairs, and the Lord Protector's, you would always draw back, and feign excuſes, and declare plainly that you would not do it.

Wherefore, upon the diſcourſe of all theſe foreſaid things, and of divers others, it muſt needs be intended, that all theſe preparations of men and money, the attempts and ſecret practices of the ſaid marriage; the abuſing and perſuading of the King's Majeſty to miſlike the Government, State, and Order of the Realm that now is, and to take the Government into his own hands, and to credit you; was to none other end and purpoſe, but after a title gotten to the Crown, and your party made ſtrong both by ſea and land, with furniture of men and money ſufficient to have aſpired to the Dignity Royal, by ſome heinous enterprize againſt the King's Majeſty's Perſon; to the ſubverſion of the whole ſtate of the Realm.

23. It is objected, and laid unto your charge, That you not only had gotten into your hands the ſtrong and dangerous iſles of *Scilly*, bought of divers men; but that ſo much as lay in your power, you travailed alſo to have *Londay*, and under pretence to have victualled the ſhips therewith, not only went about, but alſo moved the Lord Protector, and whole Council, that you might, by publick authority, have that, which by private fraud and falſhood, and confederating with *Sharington*, you had gotten; that is, the *Mint at Briſtol*, to be yours wholly, and only to ſerve your purpoſes, caſting, as may appear, that if theſe traitorous purpoſes had no good ſucceſs, yet you might thither convey a good maſs of money; where being aided with ſhips, and conſpiring at all evil events with pirates, you might at all times have a ſure and ſafe refuge, if any thing for your Demerits ſhould have been attempted againſt you.

24. It is alſo objected, and laid unto your charge, That having knowledge that Sir *William Sharington* Kt. had committed Treaſon, and otherwiſe wonderfully defrauded and deceived the King's Majeſty, nevertheleſs, you both by yourſelf, and by ſeeking Counſel for him, and by all means you could, did aid, aſſiſt, and bear him, contrary to your allegiance and duty to the King's Majeſty, and the good laws and orders of the Realm.

25. It is objected, and laid unto your charge, That where you owed to Sir *William Sharington* Kt. a great ſum of money, yet to abet, bear, and cloak the great falſhood of the ſaid *Sharington*, and to defraud the King's Majeſty, you were not afraid to ſay and affirm, before the Lord Protector and the Council, that the ſame *Sharington* did owe unto you a great ſum of money, *viz.* 2800*l.* and to conſpire with him in that falſhood, and take a bill of that feigned debt into your cuſtody.

26. It is objected, and laid unto your charge, That you by yourſelf and miniſters, have not only extorted and bribed great ſums of money of all ſuch ſhips as ſhould go into *Iſland*, but alſo as ſhould go any other where in merchandiſe, contrary to the liberty of this Realm, and to the great diſcouragement and deſtruction of the navy of the ſame, to the great danger of the King's Majeſty, and the ſtate of the Realm.

27. It is objected, and laid unto your charge, That where divers merchants, as well ſtrangers as *Engliſhmen*, have had their goods piratouſly robbed and taken, you have had their goods in your hands and cuſtody, daily ſeen in your houſe, and diſtributed among your ſervants and friends, without any reſtitution to the parties ſo injured and ſpoiled; ſo that thereby foreign Princes have in a manner been weary of the King's Majeſty's amity, and by their Ambaſſadors divers times complained, to the great ſlander of the King's Majeſty, and danger of the ſtate of the Realm.

28. It is objected, and laid unto your charge, That where certain men have taken certain Pirates, you have not only taken from the takers of the ſaid Pirates, all the goods and ſhips ſo taken, without any reward, but have caſt the ſaid takers, for their good ſervice done to the King's Majeſty, into Priſon, and there detained them a great time; ſome eight weeks, ſome more, ſome leſs, to the diſcouraging of ſuch as truly ſhould ſerve the King's Majeſty againſt his Pirates and Enemies.

29. It is objected, and laid unto your charge, That divers of the head Pirates being brought unto you, you have let the ſame Pirates go again free unto the ſeas; and taken away from the takers of them, not only all their commodity and profit, but from the true owners of the ſhips and goods, all ſuch as ever came into the Pirates hands, as though you were authorized to be the chief Pirate, and to have had all the advantages they could bring unto you.

30. It is objected, and laid unto your charge, That where order hath been taken, by the Lord Protector and the whole Council, that certain goods, piratically taken upon the ſeas, and otherwiſe known not to be wreck nor forfeited, ſhould be reſtored to the true owners, and Letters thereupon written by the Lord Protector and the Council; to the which Letters, you yourſelf, among the other, did ſet to your hand: Yet you, this notwithſtanding, have given commandment to your Officers, that no ſuch letters ſhould be obeyed; and written your private letters to the contrary, commanding the ſaid goods not to be reſtored, but kept to your own uſe and profit, contrary to your own hand before in the Council-Chamber written; and contrary to your duty and allegiance, and to the perilous example of others, and great ſlander and danger of the Realm.

31. It is objected, and laid unto your charge, That where certain ſtrangers, which were friends and allies to the King's Majeſty, had their ſhips, with wind and weather broken, and yet came unwrecked to the ſhore; when the Lord Protector and the Council had written for the reſtitution of the ſaid goods, and to the country to aid and ſave ſo much of the goods as might, you yourſelf ſubſcribing and conſenting thereto: yet this notwithſtanding, you have not only given contrary commandment to your Officers, but as a Pirate have written letters to ſome of your friends to help, that as much of theſe goods as they could, ſhould be conveyed away ſecretly by night farther off, upon hope that if the ſaid goods were aſſured, the owners would make no further labour for them, and then you might have enjoyed them, contrary to juſtice and your honour, and to the great ſlander of this Realm.

32. It is objected, and laid unto your charge, That you have not only diſcloſed the King's Majeſty's Secret Council, but alſo where you yourſelf, among the reſt, have conſented and agreed to certain things for the advancement of the King's affairs, you have ſpoken and laboured againſt the ſame.

33. It further is objected, and laid unto your charge, That your Deputy Steward, and other your Miniſters of the *Holt*, in the county of *Denbigh*, have now, againſt *Chriſtmas* laſt paſt, at the ſaid *Holt*, made ſuch proviſion of wheat, malt, beefs, and other ſuch things as be neceſſary for the ſuſtenance of a great number of men; making alſo, by all the means poſſible, a great maſs of money; inſomuch, that all the country doth greatly marvel at it, and the more, becauſe your ſervants have ſpread rumours abroad, that the King's Majeſty was dead; whereupon the country is in a great maze, doubt, and expectation, looking for ſome broil, and would have been more, if at this preſent, by your apprehenſion, it had not been ſtaied.

Theſe articles (as entered in the Council-Books) were ſo manifeſtly proved, not only by witneſſes, but by letters under his own hand, that it did not ſeem poſſible to deny them; yet he had been ſent to and examined by ſome of the Council, but refuſed to make a direct anſwer to them, or to ſign thoſe Anſwers that he had made. So it was ordered, that the next Day, all the Privy Council, except the Archbiſhop of *Canterbury*, and Sir *John Baker*, Speaker of the *Houſe of Commons*, who was engaged to attend in the Houſe, ſhould go to the *Tower*, and examine him. On the 23d the Lord Chancellor, with the other Counſellors, went to him, and read the Articles of his Charge, and earneſtly deſired him to make plain anſwers to them, excuſing himſelf where he could, and ſubmitting himſelf in other things; and that he would ſhew no obſtinacy of mind. He anſwered them, That he expected an open Trial, and his accuſers to be brought face to face. All the Counſellors endeavoured to perſuade him to be more tractable, but to no purpoſe. At laſt the Lord Chancellor required him, on his allegiance, to make his Anſwer. He deſired they would leave the Articles with him,

and

and he would consider of them, otherwise he would make no answer to them. But the Counsellors resolved not to leave them with him on those terms *. On the 24th of *February* it was resolved in Council, That the whole Board should after dinner acquaint the King with the state of that affair, and desire to know of him whether he would have the Law to take place? and since the thing had been before the Parliament, whether he would leave it to their determination? When the Counsellors waited on him, the Lord Chancellor opened the matter to the King, and delivered his opinion for leaving it to the Parliament; then every Counsellor by himself spoke his mind all to the same purpose. Last of all the Protector spake. He protested this was a most sorrowful business of him, that he had used all the means in his power to keep it from the coming to this extremity. But were it Son or Brother, he must prefer his Majesty's safety to them, for he weighed his allegiance more than his blood; and that therefore he was not against the request that the other Lords had made, and said, if he himself were guilty of such offences, he should not think he were worthy of life, and the rather, because he was of all men the most bound to his Majesty, and therefore he could not refuse Justice †. The King answered them in these words: "We perceive that there are great things objected and "laid to my Lord Admiral my Uncle, and they tend to Treason. And "we perceive that you require but justice to be done. We think it reason-"able, and we will, that you proceed according to your request." However, the Lords resolved that some of both Houses should be sent to the Admiral before the Bill should be put in against him, to see what he could or would say; so my Lord Chancellor, the Earl of *Shrewsbury*, *Warwick*, and *Southampton*, and Sir *John Baker*, Sir *Thomas Cheney*, and Sir *Anthony Denny* were sent to him. He was long obstinate, but after much persuasion was brought to give an answer to the first three Articles, *viz.*

The Lord Admiral's Answer to three of the former Articles.

TO the first, he saith, that about *Easter-Tide* was Twelve-months, he said to *Fowler*, as he supposeth it was, that if he might have the King in his custody, as Mr. *Page* had, he would be glad; and that he thought a man might bring him through the Gallery to his chamber, and so to his house: But this he said he spoke merrily, meaning no hurt. And that in the mean time after he heard, and upon that, sought out certain precedents, that there was in *England* at one time, one Protector, and another Regent of *France*, and the Duke of *Exeter*, and the Bishop of *Winchester*, Governors of the King's Person: Upon that, he had thought to have made suit to the Parliament-House for that purpose, and he had the names of all the Lords, and totted them whom he thought he might have to his purpose to labour them. But afterwards communing with Mr. Comptroller at *Ely-place*, being put in remembrance by him of his assenting and agreeing with his own Hand, that the Lord Protector should be Governour of the King's Person, he was ashamed of his doings, and left off that suit and labour.

To the second, he saith, he gave money to two or three of them which were about the King. To Mr. *Cheek*, he saith, he gave at *Christmas-Tide* was twelve months, when the Queen was at *Enfield* 40 *l.* whereof to himself 20 *l.* the other for the King, to bestow where it pleased his Grace amongst his servants. Mr. *Cheek* was very loth to take it, howbeit he would needs press that upon him; and to him he gave no more, at no time, as he remembreth, since the King's Majesty was crowned.

To the Grooms of the Chamber he hath at *New-Year's-Tides* given money, he doth not well remember what.

To *Fowler*, he saith, he gave money for the King, since the beginning of this Parliament now last at *London*, 20 *l.*

And divers times, he saith, the King hath sent to him for money, and he hath sent it. And what time Mr. *Latimer* preached before the King, the King sent to him to know what he should give Mr. *Latimer*; and he sent to him by *Fowler* 40 *l.* with this word, that 20 *l.* was a good reward for Mr. *Latimer*, and the other he might bestow amongst his Servants. Whether he hath given *Fowler* any money for himself, he doth not remember.

To the third, he saith, it is true, he drew such a Bill indeed himself, and proffered it to the King, or else to Mr. *Cheek*, he cannot well tell; and before that he saith, he caused the King to be moved by Mr. *Fowler*, whether he could be contented that he should have the Governance of him as Mr. *Stanhope* had. He knoweth not what Answer he had; but upon that he drew the said Bill to that effect, that his Majesty was content; but what Answer he had to the Bill, he cannot tell: Mr. *Cheek* can tell.

Then he on a sudden stopt short, and bade them be content, for he would go no further, and no intreaties would work on him, either to answer the rest, or to set his hand to the Answers he had made. On *February* the 25th, was read in the House of Lords the first time, The Bill for Attainder of the Lord Admiral: *Feb.* 26, read the second time: *Feb.* 27, read the third time; and concluded with the common assent of all the Peers **. The same day, being *Wednesday*, the Bill was sent down to the Commons; when it was thought good by them to send down certain Members of their House, to declare unto the Commons the manner after which the Lords had proceeded in that matter; and further to declare unto them, that in case they were minded to proceed in like sort, certain Noblemen who had given evidence against the said Lord Admiral, should be sent unto them to declare by mouth and presence such matters, as by their writing should in the mean time appear unto them. The Master of the Rolls, Sir *James Hales*, and Serjeant *Molineux*, were the persons sent by the Lords. *March* the 2d, they were sent again to the Lower House, with the like Commission in effect, as they were sent the *Wednesday* before. Answer was made, That they would consult together, and thereupon they would with speed send up their resolution. But no haste having been made therein by them of the Nether House, the Lords having sat so long, as it was thought the time now far spent, they concluded to depart; desiring the Lord Protector, that it would please him to receive such Answer as should be sent touching that purpose, and to make report thereof at their next Assembly, which should be the next *Monday*. *March* the 5th, the Bill was brought from the Commons for the attainder of the Lord *Sudley*. Thus it is related in the Journal of the House of Lords.

By the Journal of the House of Commons it appears, that this Bill was read there the last day of *February* the first time; *March* the 1st read again; and *March* the 2d the Master of the Rolls, Serjeant *Molineux*, Serjeant *Hales*, and the King's Sollicitor, were sent from the Lords to know the pleasure of this House, if it should be resolved there, to pass upon the attainder of the Admiral in such order as it passed in the higher House? Whereupon it was ordered, that advertisement thereof be sent to the Lords by some of that House: That it was resolved, that the Evidence should be heard orderly, as it was before the Lords: And also to require, that the Lords who affirmed that evidence, might come hither and declare it *viva Voce*. And this to be delivered to the Lord Protector by Mr. Speaker, and other the King's Privy Council of the House. *March* the 4th, the Master of the Rolls, *&c.* declared the King's pleasure to be, that the Admiral's presence was not necessary in this Court; and therefore not to be there. And further declared, That if the House would require to have the Lords to come and to satisfy the House for the evidence against the Admiral, the Lords would come. Then it it was ordered, that Master Comptroller, and others of the King's Privy Council, should hear the Lords; and require, that if it were judged necessary to have the Lords come down, that upon any further suit they might come down to the House. And the Bill for the attainder of High-Treason of Sir *Thomas Seymour*, Lord *Sudley*, was read the third time. Thus far the Journal of the House of Commons. On the 5th of *March* the Royal Assent was given to the Bill, which here followeth:

An Act for the Attainder of Sir Thomas Seymour, *Knt. Lord* Seymour *of* Sudley, *High Admiral of* England.

IN their most humble wise beseeching your most Excellent Majesty, the Lords Spiritual and Temporal, and the Commons in this present Parliament assembled; That where Sir *Thomas Seymour*, Lord *Seymour* of *Sudley*, High-Admiral of *England*, not having God before his Eyes, nor regarding the Duty which by Nature, Benefits, and Allegiance he ought to your Highness, nor being content with his honourable State and Condition, whereunto your Majesty hath called and indued him with; but replenished and filled with the most dangerous, insatiable, and fearful Vice of Ambition, and Greediness of Rule, Authority, and Dominion, did, in the first Year of your most noble and victorious Reign, determine and resolve with himself to take into his hands your most Noble Person, and the same either by violence, stealth or other undue means, to have in his possession, with the Order, Rule, and Government of your Majesty's Realms, Dominions, and Affairs, which were before that time, as well by your Royal Assent, as by the consent and liberate advice of all your Nobles and Council, whereof he the said Lord Admiral was one, otherwise ordered, decreed, and determined; by the means whereof, and by the most prudent foresight and direction of your Grace's dearest Uncle the Duke of *Somerset*, Governour of your Majesty's most Royal Person, and Protector of your Highness's Realms, Dominions and Subjects, being the said Admiral disappointed of his malicious Enterprise. The same Admiral continuing nevertheless his great Ambition, and most detestable, malicious, and traitorous Purpose, thinking by Tumult and Violence openly to atchieve that thing which by slight he could not secretly compass, travailed with your Majesty, being yet for your tender Years not able to conceive his falshood, by crafty, subtile and traitorous means and persuasions, having also prepared about your Grace, by corruption, sundry Persons to be Instruments to help forward all his naughty, traitorous purposes, to have caused your Grace at his contemplation, to have written a Bill or Letter of your Majesty's own Hand, to your High-Court of Parliament, desiring the same thereby to be good unto the said Lord *Seymour*, in such Suits and Matters as he should open and declare unto them; which Bill or Letter the said Lord Admiral thought and determined not only in his own Person to have brought into the Nether House of your said Court of Parliament, but also to have likewise opened the same in the Higher House, having in both the same Houses laboured, stirred, and moved a number of Persons to take part and join Cap. xviii.

* It is a strange thing, that as the particulars of his charge were manifestly proved, if any credit is to be given to the Council Book, not only by witnesses, but by letters under his own hand, they should refuse however to try him according to the laws of the land, and to bring his accusers face to face; and yet he was a Peer of the Realm, Lord High Admiral of *England*, and Uncle to the King. At last, finding he could not obtain this favour, or rather justice, he desired the Articles of his accusation might be left with him, and said he would answer to them when he had examined them; but even this was denied him: I don't know whether it was lawful then to leave with the party accused the Articles of his charge, and to allow him time to examine them: But as for the bringing his accusers face to face, it is evident that could not be denied him without injustice, though this pernicious custom had been introduced in the late Reign. *Rapin (English Oct. Edit.)* Vol. VIII. p. 50.

† It is a pretty hard task to justify the Duke of *Somerset* for prosecuting his own Brother to death, for crimes committed against his person only. But indeed it was never clearly proved, that he had formed any ill design either against the King or the State, as he protested to his last breath. But this is not the only time that Plots against the *Ministers* have been reckoned High-Treason. *Rapin (English)* Vol. VIII. p. 52.

** Bishop *Burnet*, in his *History of the Reformation*, Vol. II. p. 99. says, The Peers had been so accustomed to agree to such bills in King *Henry*'s time, that they did easily pass it. All the Judges and the King's Council delivered their opinions, That the Articles were Treason. Then the Evidence was brought: Many Lords gave it so fully, that all the rest, with one voice, consented to the Bill; only the Protector, *for natural pity's sake*, as in the Council Book, desired leave to withdraw. On the 27th, the Bill was sent down to the Commons, with a message, That if they desired to proceed as the Lords had done, those Lords that had given their Evidence in their own House, should come down and declare it to the Commons. But there was more opposition made in the House of Commons. Many argued against Attainders in absence, and thought it an odd way that some Peers should rise up in their places in their own House, and relate something to the slander of another, and that he should be thereupon attainted. Therefore it was pressed, that it might be done by a Trial, and that the Admiral should be brought to the bar, and be heard plead for himself. But on the 4th of *March* a message was sent from the King, That he thought it was not necessary to send for the Admiral; and that the Lords should come down and renew before them the Evidence they had given in their own House. This was done; and so the Bill was agreed to by the Commons in a full House, judged about four hundred, and there were not above ten or twelve that voted in the negative. The Bishop, in the next page says, But the way of proceeding was much condemned, since to attaint a man without bringing him to make his own defence, or to object what he could say to the Witnesses that were brought against him, was so illegal and unjust, that it could not be defended, or let this was to be said for it, That it was a little more regular than *Parliamentary Attainders* had been formerly; for here the Evidence, upon which it was founded, was given before both Houses.

with

with him in ſuch things as he would ſet forth and enterpriſe, whereby he thought to breed ſuch a Tumult, Uproar, and Sedition, as well in the ſaid Court, as in the whole Realm, as by the troubling of the whole State and Body of this your Realm, he might the more facily and eaſily bring to paſs his moſt fearful, deviliſh, and naughty Purpoſe: for the more ſure and certain compaſſing whereof, like as he feared not to ſay to certain Noblemen and others, that he would make the blackeſt Parliament that ever was ſeen here in *England*, ſo moſt traitorouſly, for the further Accompliſhment of his lewd Enterpriſe, he retained a great number of Men, and prepared a great furniture of Weapons and Habiliments of War, ready for the execution of his ſaid traitorous Attempts. And to colour and cloak his ſaid miſchievous purpoſes, did, by all ſuch ways and means as he could poſſibly deviſe and imagine, practiſe, as it were, for his entry towards the ſame, to ſeek and attain the Government of your moſt Noble Perſon, and thereby to have gotten into his hands the order of your Realms and Dominions, whereunto he aſpired in ſuch Sort, as he did even then travail expreſsly with the moſt part of your Highneſſes moſt Honourable Council to help him to the ſaid Government, doing likewiſe all he could in the Parliament by himſelf, his Servants and Miniſters, not only to hinder and lett all things there proponed, which touched the Honour, Surety, and Benefit of your Majeſty and the Realm; but alſo ſpreading abroad Slanders touching your Majeſty's Perſon, your deareſt Uncle the ſaid Lord Protector, and the whole State of your Council, over-vile, dangerous, and unmeet to be here recited: Which things being by the Goodneſs of God revealed, as your ſaid Uncle, the Lord Protector could not chuſe but heartily lament the ſaid Lord Admiral's evil, malicious, and corrupt Diſpoſition, chiefly in reſpect of the apparent and irrecuperable Danger which was like, by the ſame, preſently to have enſued to your Majeſty, and to your Reals and Dominions; and ſecondly, for that he was by proximity of Blood ſo nearly joined unto him. So hoping that by good Advertiſements and Counſels he might yet recover and ſave him, and by the Grace of God cauſe him to caſt away his naughty, vile, and ambitious Diſpoſition, and to have had a better Conſideration hereafter to his Duty, both to God and unto your Majeſty, whereunto he was moſt bounden; the ſaid Lord Protector laboured with the whole Councel and otherwiſe, to reconcile and reform him, which preſently muſt elſe have periſhed in his Folly and Outrage. And albeit, the ſaid Lord Protector had then perfect knowledge of the Attempts and Miſbehaviours of the ſaid Admiral before rehearſed; and that the ſaid Admiral had then ſaid, that he would not come at the ſaid Lord Protector and Council, altho' they ſent for him, and that he would not be committed to any ward for his doings by the beſt of them, whereby it appeared that he thought his Party ſtrong enough to reſiſt your Majeſty's Power and ordinary Authority; yet the ſaid Lord Protector, not ceaſing with all clemency to follow his godly and charitable purpoſe, did not only uſe all the good means he could deviſe by the perſuaſions of certain of your Grace's Council, and otherwiſe to frame him to the Amendment of his Evils, and ſo to bring him to the better remembrance of his Duty; but alſo conſidering, that if the matter ſhould have grown to extremity, being ſo near, and ſo much bound to your Majeſty, being new come to your Kingdom, your Subjects not altogether left in the beſt concord for matters of Religion, great ſlander, tumult, and danger might have enſued thereby as well here at home in your Realm, as from ſome outward parts with whom you were in the War, and in ſome ſecret enmity ready to enter the Wars, thought it, with the Advice of your whole Council, moſt meet and fureſt for your Majeſty to paſs his evil Doings over in ſilence, and in ſomewhat the more in reſpect of the better ſtay, for the time of your preſent Eſtate, to bridle him with your Liberality, and therefore to give unto him Lands to the yearly Value of eight hundred Pounds, truſting thereby, and by ſuch other good means as were uſed towards him, to encourage and move him to leave for ever that Ambition, and ſeditious Mind, and to live in ſuch order as might have pleaſed God, and ſerved your Majeſty, and your Publick Weal. But all this notwithſtanding, the Devil, who had before planted that vile and evil Weed ſo deeply in his Heart, that the Root of the ſame could not be clearly pulled out, but cauſed his Ambition eftſoons to ſpring, and ſhew itſelf more rankly than it had done before: For it plainly appeareth, that he tarried not long in his diſſembled good Mood and Promiſe, but began afreſh to imagine, compaſs and deviſe, for the ſatisfying of his traitorous deſire, to make a Party, Faction, and Confederation, whereof he would be the Head, and did not only get as many Rules and Offices into his hands of all Men, as he could poſſibly attain, and retained many Gentlemen and Yeomen into his Service, making a full account and reckoning, which he declared ſecretly to ſome of his familiars, that he was thereby able, of his own ruled Tenants and Servants, to make ten thouſand Men for the obtaining of his ſaid purpoſe; for whoſe Wages he had alſo deviſed after ten thouſand Pounds by the Month, out of your Majeſty's Mint at *Briſtol*, which he had obtained, with all your Treaſure in the ſame, by the means and conſent of Sir *William Sharington*, Knt. Vice-Treaſurer there, to be at his commandment, which Sir *William* now ſtandeth attainted of Treaſon; and alſo had put your Grace's Caſtle of the *Holt*, whereof he had the keeping, even now of late in a readineſs, and there cauſed to be prepared a great Furniture of Wheat, Malt, Beefs, and a great maſs of Money, for the feeding and entertainment of a number of Men: which Money he cauſed to be levied and taxed half the Year before the ſame was due; bruiting alſo for the better atchieving of his purpoſe, and to amaze therewith the more the people, that your Majeſty (whom God long preſerve to us) ſhould be dead; but alſo he laboured ſundry of your Nobles, and other your Grace's Subjects, to join with him, deviſing with divers of them, how and by what Policy, Ways, and Means they ſhould make themſelves ſtrong in their Countries for that purpoſe, and how they ſhould win unto them the head Yeomen, and Ringleaders of the common People; declaring how he meant to have matched, and ſet one Nobleman againſt another Nobleman, as he thought he could never compaſs and win to aſſent to this Faction and falſe Conſpiracy, promiſing to divers of them ſundry Benefits; yea, taking ſo much upon him, for the accompliſhment of his ſaid traitorous intent and purpoſe, as he ſpared not to promiſe your moſt excellent perſon in marriage to a Nobleman's Daughter of this your Realm. And yet not contented herewith, for the further advancement of his moſt naughty and traitorous purpoſe, did traitorouſly and unnaturally practiſe even with your Highneſs's own Perſon, to make your moſt Excellent Majeſty (for your tender years unable to underſtand his falſe and traitorous purpoſes) an inſtrument towards the undoing and deſtruction of your Highneſs, and the ſubverſion of the whole State of this your Grace's Realm: purſuing your Majeſty, as much as in him did lie, not only to take upon you, now in your young and tender age, the Rule and Order of yourſelf, intending and meaning by the colour thereof, to take in his hands your moſt Royal Perſon, the Rules and Orders of all the Affairs of your Realms and Dominions; being already by the ſaid Lord Protector, with the Advice of your Grace's moſt honourable Council, as well prudently and politically governed, as valiantly and nobly defended againſt our outward Enemies, to the increaſe of your immortal Fame and Honour; but alſo to receive and engender an hatred in your moſt noble Heart, both againſt your deareſt Uncle the ſaid Lord Protector, and all your true and faithful Councellors: To the which his deviliſh Perſuaſions and Aſſaults, God gave your Highneſs, even at this age, to the great rejoice of all us your faithful Subjects and Servants, a ſpecial Grace to reſiſt, above common reaſon and all expectation, and moſt graciouſly, without any Advice or Counſel, to refuſe and deny his evil advertiſements and perſuaſions. And further, the ſaid Admiral did moſt falſly and traitorouſly corrupt ſundry of your Highneſs's Privy-Chamber with many gifts, and otherwiſe, to the intent they ſhould move and procure your Majeſty to write ſundry Letters at his or their devices, and to put into your Grace's head a ſpecial and ſingular favour, affection, and truſt towards him, and a Diſpoſition to follow whatſoever he would have wrought towards all others, that he might the rather have compaſſed his moſt traitorous purpoſe, which muſt needs have tended to your Majeſty's Deſtruction (which God forbid), and to the utter ruin of all us, your Highneſs's moſt loving, faithful, and obedient Subjects. For, moſt gracious Sovereign Lord, beſides all this, it is moſt evident and apparent, that as immediately after the King your Father's Death, of moſt noble Memory, he bare a ſpecial love and favour to your Grace's Siſter the Lady *Elizabeth*, ſecond Perſon in the Remainder of the State of Succeſſion to the Crown of this Realm after your Majeſty, and the Heirs of your Body, whom the living God long preſerve unto us, with the increaſe of much Fruit; and would then of his great Preſumption and traitorous determination have married her, if he could by any means have brought to paſs the ſame, but that he was ſtayed by the ſaid Lord Protector, and other of your Grace's Council; ſo he did not only continue in his ſaid determination towards her, in the Queen his late Wife's time, but alſo by divers ſecret and crafty means and practices, continually ſought by atchieving of the ſame ſince the Queen's Death, as by ſundry ways is confeſſed, and appeareth. Inſomuch as the ſame being perceived by your ſaid deareſt Uncle, and ſome others beſide of your Council, and other Perſonages of Reputation; and the ſaid Admiral by them earneſtly adviſed to beware of it, and to forbear his pretenſed purpoſe, ſpecially for that it could not be but dangerous to your Grace's Perſon, he hath not been afraid to defend his naughty doings and purpoſes in it, and to aſk why he ſhould not continue his Suit towards the ſaid *Elizabeth?* with ſundry other words declaring his full intent and determinations to it; and neglecting all good Advices, Reaſons, and Admonitions made, given or alledged, contrary to his purpoſe, he hath ſecretly and earneſtly followed it, in ſuch ſort, as if ſundry other his miſchievous devices and practices had not appeared, and come to knowledge, it is evident that he would have done what he could ſecretly to have married her, as he did the late Queen, whom it may appear he married firſt, and after ſued to your Majeſty, and the Lord Protector, and your Council, for his preferment to it; whom nevertheleſs it hath been credibly declared, he holped to her end to haſte forwards his other purpoſe. But what this marriage of your ſaid Siſter, with his prepared forces and confederacies ſhould mean, and what the getting of the rule and order of your Majeſty's Mint at *Briſtol* into his hands with ten thouſand men, which beſides all his friends, and divers retainers, he accounted himſelf furniſhed of, and able to make all times within his own rules, and of his own ſervants and tenants, ſhould tend unto, for the wages and entertainments of whom he had prepared, as is aforeſaid, conſidering that the ſaid Admiral at all times, when occaſion of the ſervice of your Majeſty was neceſſary or requiſite, went always back, and refuſed to take it upon him, whether it were by ſea or land, as your Grace's Council both know, and divers times have lamented, and in that caſe travelled with him (in vain) to bring him unto it, whereby no good mind or will of him toward your Majeſty's ſafety or aſſurance can appear. And upon all theſe ſiniſter ways and means, what his corrupt and ſubtil attempts of getting your moſt noble Perſon into his hands, by colour whereof he might have wrought what he would, and whatſoever his ambitious intent could have deviſed with his preparation of victuals and money, and other his ſaid doings at your Grace's Caſtle of the *Holt*, and in the parts thereabouts, would have wrought in the end, eſpecially in this tender age of your Highneſs, and whilſt your Majeſty is in the Government of a Protector, it is fearful to conſider and think upon, and cannot otherwiſe be taken, but to be indeed more than a manifeſt declaration of a traitorous aſpiring to your Crown of this Realm, and to be King of the ſame, and an open deed and act, and a falſe and traitorous compaſs and imagination to depoſe and deprive your Majeſty from your Royal Eſtate and Title of your Realms, and to compaſs and imagine the Death of your moſt Noble Perſon, and moſt traitorouſly to take away and deſtroy all things which ſhould have founded to the lett and impediment of his moſt traitorous and ambitious enterprize.

And further, gracious Sovereign Lord, to declare the traitorous dipoſition of his nature, and how little he cared to offend your Grace's law, and how he did yet leſs regard his truth and duty towards your Grace, where *William Sharington*, Knight, late of *London*, the tenth day of *July*, in the firſt year of your Grace's Reign, hath in the County and City of *Briſtol* falſly and traitorouſly forged and counterfeited certain of your Grace's coin, and further imbezzled and purloined from your Majeſty, untruly and falſly at the leaſt, the ſum of forty thouſand pounds, for part whereof the ſame Sir *William Sharington* upon his own confeſſion is attainted of treaſon according to your Grace's laws; to which

ſaid

said traitorous Acts the said Lord Admiral did not only abet and procure the said Sir *William Sharington*, labouring him he should get as much money from time to time into his hands for his purpose as he could, so that he might ever have a good mass in a readiness; but also since the time of the said treasons and traitorous acts, so done by the said Sir *William Sharington*, the said Lord Admiral having perfect knowledge thereof, as well by the declaration of the most part of your Highness's Council, as by some of his own Counsel learned, hath traitorously comforted, aided, assisted, and maintained the same Sir *William Sharington* in his said traitorous acts and faults against your Grace's laws and statutes of this Realm; taking the patent, indentures, books and reckonings of the same Sir *William Sharington*, of his own authority, into his custody, and affirming both to sundry of your Grace's Council, and to divers of your subjects, that the said *Sharington* had wrong to be committed: devising all the ways he could possible, contrary to his duty and allegiance, traitorously to bear him in his evil and traitorous doings, and to deliver him, if he by any means might have come by him.

And for a further proof to induce, that the said Admiral did maintain and comfort the same *Sharington*, where the said Admiral owed to the said *Sharington* two thousand eight hundred pounds, the said *Sharington* upon a mistrust which he had before his apprehension, that he should for his fault and proceedings come one day to his trial and examination, communicating the same with the said Lord Admiral, and the said Admiral agreed and promised not only to aid and maintain and bear him to the uttermost of his power, as indeed he did both as is aforesaid, and in consulting with learned men for him, and otherwise, but also for his more assured aid, being indebted to the said *Sharington* the sum of two thousand eight hundred pounds, untruly conspired with the said *Sharington* upon a bill, whereby it appeared that the said *Sharington* should owe unto him the sum of two thousand pounds with interests, so as the said Admiral might help and relieve him with that two thousand pounds, with the interest at your Majesty's hand, as a debt unto himself; and also with two thousand eight hundred pounds which the said Admiral owed indeed to the said *Sharington*, amounting in the whole to five thousand and six hundred pounds: which bill most untruly, and to the maintenance and favour of the said *Sharington*, the said Lord Admiral affirmed before the said Lord Protector, and your Highness's Council, to be a true bill, and the same two thousand eight hundred pounds, with the interest, to be his just debt, and so was taken, until the said *Sharington* himself confessed and affirmed the truth, whereby the covin and falshood plainly appeared to the contrary.

Finally, most gracious Sovereign Lord, it were too much and over tedious to molest and trouble your excellent Majesty, either with the remembrance of his evil doings in his office of the Admiralty, wherein he hath so manifestly recited, maintained, aided and comforted sundry pirates, and taken to his own use the goods piratously taken against your laws, and expresly against the orders determined by the Lord Protector and the whole Council, whereunto his own hand hath been for the restitution of them; whereby he hath moved almost all Princes Christian to conceive a grudge and displeasure, and by open wars to seek remedies at their own hands, to the great trouble and danger of your Majesty, your realms and dominions; and to the great charge, loss and disquiet of your most loving and faithful subjects, and to the peril of breaking of the leagues and treaties of amity betwixt your Majesty and other foreign Princes, as their Ambassadors here have plainly declared, and, as present experience teacheth; or to express his innumerable untruths, falshoods, and deceitful practices, discovering and opening of your Majesty's Counsels, refusal to serve your Highness as he hath been commanded, oppression and manifest extortion of your Majesty's subjects, using *Island* and other voyages by the sea; and his determination of revenge towards all men with whom he was offended, which his own letters and other testimonies do declare against him; with a full resolution to have put the whole of his intent shortly in experience and execution (if God had not prevented it), to the destruction of your most Royal Person, and the subversion and alteration of the whole estate of your realms and dominions. Wherefore considering as well that he is a member so unnatural, unkind and corrupt, and such a heinous offender of your Majesty and your laws, as he cannot, nor may conveniently be suffered to remain in the body of your Grace's Commonwealth, but to the extream danger of your Highness, being Head, and of all the good members of the same, and is too pernicious and dangerous an example; that such a person so much bound and so forgetful of it, so mercifully heretofore intreated, and by sundry and great benefits allured and called, and so cruelly and ingrately continuing in his false and traitorous intents and purposes against your Highness, and the whole estate of your realm, should remain amongst us:

'It may therefore please your excellent Majesty, that it may be enacted with your Highness's assent, the Lords Spiritual and Temporal, and the Commons in this present Parliament assembled, and by authority of the same, That the said Sir *Thomas Seymour*, Knt. Lord *Seymour* of *Sudley*, High Admiral of *England*, for the said traitorous offences and deeds, shall be by the authority of this present Parliament adjudged and attainted of treason: And that the same Sir *Thomas Seymour*, Knt. Lord *Seymour* of *Sudley*, high Admiral of *England*, shall have, suffer, and sustain such pains of death, as in cases of High-Treason have been used and accustomed. And also, that the said Lord *Seymour* of *Sudley* shall forfeit and lose to your Majesty, and your Heirs, all such castles, manors, lands, tenements, leases, meadows, pastures, woods, waters, rents, reversions, services, offices, fees, annuities, and all other hereditaments, goods, chattels and debts whatsoever, the same Lord *Seymour* had, enjoyed, or was seized or possessed of at the seventeenth day of *January*, in the second year of your Grace's reign, or at any time since.

'And that all such castles, manors, lands, tenements, meadows, leases, pastures, woods, waters, rents, reversions, services, offices, fees, annuities, and other hereditaments, to be by authority of this present act adjudged, vested, and deemed in the actual and real possession of your Highness, from the said seventeenth day of *January*, without any office or inquisition to be thereof had or found. Saving to all and every person and persons, and bodies politick and corporate, and to their heirs, assigns, and successors; and to every of them (other than the said Lord *Seymour* of *Sudley* and his heirs) all such rights, titles, interests, uses, possessions, reversions, remainders, entries, conditions, leases, fees, offices, rents-services, rents-charges, rents-seck, annuities; commons, and all other commodities, profits, and hereditaments whatsoever, they or any of them had, might, or ought to have had, if this present act had never been had or made.

'Furthermore, the King's Majesty is pleased that it be enacted, That all person and persons, bodies politick and corporate, and their executors and administrators, shall be well and truly contented and paid, upon their humble suit and petition hereafter to be made unto his Highness of all such debts, which either by specialty, or by any other just and true contract, the said Lord Admiral did owe to them, or any of them, at any time before the said seventeenth day of *January*, in the said second year of his Majesty's reign*.'

On the tenth of *March* the Council resolved to press the King that justice might be done on the Admiral: and since the case was so heavy and lamentable to the Protector, (so it is in the Council-Book) though it was also sorrowful to them all, they resolv'd to proceed in it, so that neither the King, nor he, should be further troubled with it; after dinner they went to the King, the Protector being with them: the King, said he had well observed their proceeding, and thank'd them for their great care of his safety, and commanded them to proceed in it without further molesting him or the Protector; and ended, *I pray you, my Lords, do so.* Upon this they order'd the Bishop of *Ely* to go to the Admiral, and to instruct him in the things that related to another life, and to prepare him to take patiently his execution; and on the 17th of *March* he having made report to them of his attendance on the Admiral, the Council sign'd a Warrant for his execution, *viz.*

The Warrant for the Admiral's Execution.

THIS day, the 17th of *March*, the Lord Chancellor and the rest of the King's Council, meeting in his Highness's Palace of *Westminster*, heard the report of the Bishop of *Ely*, who by the said Lords, and others of the Council, was sent to instruct and comfort the Lord Admiral; after the hearing whereof, consulting and deliberating with themselves of the time most convenient for the execution of the said Lord Admiral, now attainted and condemned by the Parliament, they did condescend and agree, That the said Lord Admiral should be executed the *Wednesday* next following, betwixt the hours of nine and twelve in the forenoon the same day, upon *Tower-Hill*: His body and head to be buried within the *Tower*; the King's writ (as in such cases as heretofore hath been accustomed) being first directed and sent forth for that purpose and effect. Whereupon calling to the Council-Chamber the Bishop of *Ely*, they willed him to declare this their determination to the said Lord Admiral; and to instruct and teach him, the best he could, to the quiet and patient suffering of justice, and to prepare himself to Almighty God. *Ex Libro Concilii, fol. 141*

E. Somerset.

T. Cantuarien.	*William Paget.*
R. Rich, Cancel.	*Anthony Wingfield.*
W. St. John.	*William Petre.*
J. Russel.	*A. Denny.*
J. Warwick.	*Edward North.*
F. Shrewsbury.	*R. Sadler.*
Thomas Southampton.	

The said Bishop, after he had been with the Lord Admiral, repairing again to the Court, made report to Mr. Comptrollor and Secretary *Smith* of the Lord Admiral's requests †, the which were, that he required Mr. *Latimer* to come to him, the day of execution to be deferr'd, certain of his Servants to be with him, his Daughter to be with my Lady Duchess of *Suffolk* to be brought up, and such like. Touching which requests, the said Lords and the rest of the Council declar'd their minds to Mr. Secretary *Smith*, willing him to write their answer in a Letter to the Lieutenant of the *Tower*, who should shew in all those requests their resolute answer to the said Lord Admiral; which was done accordingly.

On the 20th of *March* he was brought to the Scaffold.

And in the fourth Sermon of Mayster *Hughe Latymer* ‡, whych he preached before the Kynge wythin hys Graces Palayce at *Westminster*, the xxix day of *Marche*, is the following account of the Lord Admiral ‖.

I knowe more of my Lord Admiral's death sith that tyme, then I did knowe before. O saye they, the man dyed very boldly, he woulde not have done so, hadde he not bene in a just quarell.

This is no good argument, my frendes. A man semeth not to feare death, therefore hys cause is good. Thys is a deceavable argumente. He went to hys death boldely: Ergo, he standeth in a just quarell.

If I should have saied al that I knewe, your ears woulde have yrked to have hearde it, and nowe God hath brought more to lyghte. And as touchyng the kynde of hys death, whether he be saved or no, I referre that to God onely. What God can do, I can not tell: I wyl not denye but that he maye in the twynkeling of an eye save a man, and turne hys harte. What he dyd, I cannot tell. And when a man hathe two strokes wyth an axe, whoo can tel that betwene two strokes he doth repent. It is very hard to judge; well, I wyl not go so nye to worke, but this I wyl say, if they aske me what I thinke of hys deathe, that he dyed very daungerously, yrkesomelye, horryblye.

The man beyng in the Tower, wrote certayne papers, whiche I sawe my selfe. Ther were two lyttle ones, one to my Ladye *Marye*'s Grace, and

* But in the 3 and 4 of *Edw.* VI. there pass'd an Act for restitution in blood of *Mary Seymour*, Daughter to Sir *Thomas Seymour*, Knt. Lord *Seymour* of *Sudley*, late Admiral of *England*. See *Rolls*, vol. I. pag. 996.

† *Strype*'s Memorials, vol. II. pag. 128.

‡ The Reverend Mr. *Wilson* in his translation of Monf. *De Thou*'s History of his Own Time, vol. I. pag. 272, says, 'The Duke of *Somerset*, the Protector, had conceiv'd a 'jealousy (which was fomented by the emulation of the women) of his Brother *Thomas* the Admiral, who had married *Catharine Parr*, the late King *Henry*'s widow; and had 'order'd him to be committed to prison, on suspicion of aiming at the Crown: and as it is the temper of that nation to be over-hasty and preposterously severe in matters 'which relate to the Commonwealth, after he had him put to the rack, he at last, by the suggestion of *Hugh Latimer*, procured him to be condemn'd to death; and on the '20th of *March* to be beheaded.'

‖ This is only to be found in the first Edition of *Latimer*'s Sermons in a small thick Octavo, for the later Editions are all castrated.

another to my Ladye *Elizabethe*'s Grace, tendynge to thys ende, that they shoulde conspyre agaynst my Lord Protectour's Grace.

Surely so seditiously as could be. Nowe what a kind of Death was thys, that when he was readye to laye his Head upon the Blocke, he turnes me to the Levetenantes Servaunte and sayeth, byd my Servaunte spede the Thyng that he wottes of: Wel, the Worde was over-heard.

Hys Servaunt confessed these two Papers, and they were found in a Shooe of hys. They were so sowen between the Soules of a velved Shooe. He made hys ynke so craftely, and wyth such Workmanship, as the lyke hath not bene sene.

I was Prisoner in the Tower miselfe, and I coulde never invente to make ynke so. It is a Wonder to hear of his Subtilitie. He made hys Pen of the Aglet of a Poynte that he plucked from hys Hose, and thus wrote these Letters soo seditiouslye, as ye have hearde, enforsynge many matters agaynst my Lord Protectour's Grace, and so fourth. God had lefte him to hymselfe, he hadde cleane forsaken hym. What woulde he have done if he had lived styll? that went about thys geare, when he layed hys head on the blocke at the ende of hys lyfe. Charity (they saye) worketh but godly, not after thys sorte. Well, he is gone, he knoweth hys fate by thys, he is eyther in joy or in payne. There is no repentance after thys lyfe, but if he dye in the state of damnacion, he shall ryse in the same. Yea, thoughe he have a whole Monkerye to synge for hym, he shall have hys fynal sentence when he dyeth.

And that servant of hys that confesseth and uttered thys gere, was an honest manne. He dyed honestlye in it. God put it in his herte. And as for the tother, whether he be saved or no, I leave it to God. But surelye, he was a wycked man, the Realme is well rydde of hym.

It hath a treasure, that he is gone, he knoweth hys fare by thys. A terrible example surelye, and to be noted of every man; nowe before he shoulde dye, I heard say he had commendations to the Kyng, and spake many wordes of his Majestye. All is the Kinge, the Kinge. Yea, *Bona Verba*. These were fayre wordes, the Kynge, the Kynge. It hath been the cast of all Traitours to pretend nothing against the Kynge's Person, they never pretend the matter to the Kynge, but to other. Subjects maye not resyste anye Magistrates, nor oughte to do nothinge contrarye to the Kinge's Lawes. And therefore these wordes, the Kynge, and so fourth, are of small effect. I have hearde muche wickednes of thys manne, and I have thought oft, Jesu, what wyl worth, what wyl be the ende of thys manne? Among others (that went to execution) I heard of a wanton woman, a naughtye lyer, a whore, a vayne bodye: and was ledde from *Newgate* to the place of execution, for a certain robberye that she had committed, and she hadde a wycked communication by the waye. This woman, I saye, as she wente by the waye, had wanton and folyshe talke, as thys: That yf good fellowes hadde kept touch wyth hyr, she hadde not been at thys time in that case; and amongste al other talke, she saied, That such a one, and named this manne, had hyr maidenhead fyrste; and heryinge thys of hym at that tyme, I loked ever what woulde be hys ende, what woulde become of hym.

He was a manne the fardest frome the feare of God that ever I knewe or hearde of in *Englande*. Fyrste he was author of all thys woman's whoredome. For if he had not had hyr maydenhead, she myghte have been maryed, and become an honeste womanne; whereas nowe beying nought with hym, shee fell afterwarde by that occasion to other: And they that were nought with hyr fel to robbery, and she folowed; and thus was he author of all thys. This geare came bi sequels, peradventure thys maye seeme to be a lyghte matter, but surelye it is a great matter: and he, by unrepentance, fel frome evyl to worse, and from worse to worste of all, tyll at the length he was made a spectacle to all the worlde. I have hearde saye, he was of the opinion that he believed not the immortalytye of the Soule, that he was not ryghte in the matter. And it mighte well appear by the takynge of hys death. But ye well say, What ye sclaunder, ye breake Charitye.

Nay, it is Charitie that I do, we canne have no better use of hym nowe, than to warne others to beware by hym.

Christ saith, *Remember* Lotte's *Wife!* she was a woman that would not be content with her good state, but wrestleled wyth God's callinge; and she was for that cause turned into a Salt Stone, *&c.* Thus may thys man be an example to us. Let us all subjects judge well of our Magistrates in suche matters, and be content wyth theyr doings, and loke not to be of the Counsaile.

And thus toke I occasion to speake of him, and to profit you thereby, and I beseech you so to take it, he may be a good warnyng to us, and this is the best use that wee can have of him now.

In his fifth Sermon he saieth, You will saye this, the Parliament House are wiser than I am; you might leave them to the defence of themselves: Although the men of the Parliament House can defende themselves, yet have I spoken thys of a good zeale, and a good ground of the Admiralle's wrytings: I have not fayned, nor lyed one jote. I will nowe leave the honourable Counsayle to answer for themselves. He confessed one fact, he would have hadde the Governaunce of the King's Majesty, and wot ye whye? He sayed, he would not in his minoritie have him brought up lyke a warde. I am sure he hath bene brought up so godly, with such Schole-masters, as never King was in *Englande*, *&c.*

And in his seventh Sermon he saieth thus: I have heard say, when that good Quene (meaning Queen *Cathrine*) that is gone, had ordained in her house dayly prayer both before none and after none, the Admyral gettes hym out of the waye, lyke a moule diggying in the earth. He shal be *Lotte*'s Wyfe to me as long as I lyve. He was a covetous man, an horrible covetous manne; I woulde there were no mo in *England*: He was an ambicious man; I woulde there were no mo in *Englande*: He was a sedicious man, a contemnar of Commune Prayer, I would there were no mo in *England*: He is gone, I wolde he had lefte none behind him. Remember you, my Lordes, that you pray in your houses, to the better mortification of your Fleshe.

II. Proceedings against *Edward*, Duke of Somerset, in Parliament, for *Misdemeanours* and *High-Treason*, *Jan.* 1550. 3 and 4 *Edw.* VI.

THE Duke of *Somerset* having taken the part of the common People against the Nobility in the business of inclosures, made himself many Enemies. He had also given great Grounds of Jealousy by entertaining foreign Troops in the King's Service; and the noble Palace he was raising in the *Strand* out of the Ruins of some Bishops Houses and Churches, drew as publick an Envy on him as any Thing he had done: And his acting by his own Authority, without asking the Advice of the Council, and often against it, was assuming a regal Power, and seemed not to be endured by those who thought they were in all Points his Equals. Thus, all *September*, there were great Heats between the Lords and him. The King was then at *Hampton-Court*, where the Protector also was, with some of his Retinue and Servants about him, which increased the Jealousies: for it was given out, he intended to carry away the King. On the 6th of *October*, some of the Council met, and sent to the Lord Mayor and Aldermen of *London* to obey no Letters from the Protector, and wrote to the Nobility to inform them how they were proceeding. The Protector hearing of these Things, removed the King to *Windsor* in all haste, and armed such as he could gather for his preservation: Whereupon several Letters passed between the Council at *London*, and those at *Windsor**; and at last a Proclamation was published against the Protector to the following effect: 1. "That the Protector, by his "malicious and evil Government, was the Occasion of all the Sedition "that of late happened within the Realm. 2. The Loss of the King's "Pieces in *France*. 3. That he was ambitious and sought his own "Glory, as appeared by building of most sumptuous and costly Houses "in the Time of the King's Wars. 4. That he esteemed nothing the "grave Counsel of the Councillors. 5. That he sowed Division between "the Nobles, the Gentlemen, and the Commons. 6. That the Nobles "assembled themselves together at *London*, for none other purpose but "to have caused the Protector to have lived within Limits, and to have "put such Order for the Surety of the King's Majesty as appertain-"ed: Whatsoever the Protector's Doings were, which they said were "unnatural, ungrate, and traitorous. 7. That the Protector slandered "the Council to the King, and did what in him lay to cause Variance "between the King and the Nobles. 8. That he was a great Traitor†, "and therefore the Lords desired the City and Commons to aid them to "take him from the King." This was signed by the Lord *Rich*, Lord Chancellor; the Lord *St. John*, President of the Council; the Marquis of *Northampton*; the Earl of *Warwick*, great Chamberlain; and most of the Council. On the 12th of *October* the whole Council went to *Windsor*, and coming to the King, they protested, that all they had done was only out of Zeal and Affection to his Person and Service. The King received them very kindly, and thanked them for their Care of him. On the 13th they sat in Council, and sent for those who were ordered to be kept in their Chambers, only *Cecil* (afterwards the famous Lord *Burleigh*) was let go; and, in the end, the Lord Protector was commanded from the King's Presence, and committed to Ward in a Tower within the Castle of *Windsor*, called *Beauchamp Tower*: and the next Day, being the 14th, they brought from thence the Protector, and conveyed him to the *Tower* of *London*. Some Time after, the Lords resorted to the *Tower*, and there charged the Protector with the following Articles of Misdemeanour and High-Treason**.

Articles objected to the Duke of Somerset.

1. THAT he took upon him the Office of Protector, upon express Condition, that he should do nothing in the King's Affairs, but by Assent of the late King's Executors, or the greatest Part of them.

2. That contrary to this Condition, he did hinder Justice, and subvert Laws of his own Authority, as well by Letters as by other Command.

3. That he caused divers Persons, arrested and imprisoned for Treason, Murder, Man-slaughter, and Felony, to be discharged, against the Laws and Statutes of the Realm.

4. That he appointed Lieutenants for Armies, and other Officers for the weighty Affairs of the King, under his own Writing and Seal.

5. That he communed with Ambassadors of other Realms alone, of the weighty Matters of the Realm.

6. That he would taunt and reprove divers of the King's most honourable Councillors, for declaring their Advice in the King's weighty Affairs against his Opinion; sometimes telling them, that they were not worthy to sit in Council; and sometimes, that he need not to open weighty Matters to them; and that if they were not agreeable to his Opinion, he would discharge them.

7. That against Law he held a Court of Request in his own House; and did enforce divers to answer there for their Freehold and Goods, and did determine of the same.

* See the Articles offered by the Protector, and the Letters that passed between the Lords and the King, in *Burnet's Reformation*, Vol. II. in the Collection of Records, p. 183, *&c.*

† This Proclamation, which had made him a Traitor, within three Days was called in again, with Commandment given none of them to be sold. *Fox's Book of Martyrs.* Vol. II. p. 1217. Old Edit.

** *Fox*, and *Hayward* (in his Life of King *Edward* the VI.) both say, the Duke was in the Tower a small Time before the Lords laid the Articles to his Charge: But *Burnet* and *Rapin* say, the *Duke* was called before the Council on the 14th, and that the Articles of his Accusation were then read to him.

8. That

8. That being no Officer, without the advice of the Council, or most part of them, he did dispose Offices of the King's gift for Money; grant leases and wards, and presentations of Benefices pertaining to the King; gave Bishopricks, and made sales of the King's Lands.

9. That he commanded alchimy and multiplication to be practised, thereby to abase the King's Coin.

10. That divers times he openly said, that the Nobility and Gentry were the only cause of dearth; whereupon the people rose to reform matters of themselves.

11. That against the mind of the whole council, he caused Proclamation to be made concerning inclosures; whereupon the people made divers insurrections, and destroyed many of the King's Subjects.

12. That he sent forth a Commission, with articles annexed, concerning inclosures, commons, highways, cottages, and such like matters, giving the Commissioners authority to hear and determine those causes, whereby the laws and statutes of the Realm were subverted, and much Rebellion raised.

13. That he suffered Rebels to assemble and lie armed in Camp, against the Nobility and Gentry of the Realm, without speedy repressing of them.

14. That he did comfort and encourage divers Rebels, by giving them money, and by promising them fees, rewards, and services.

15. That he caused a Proclamation to be made against law, and in favour of the Rebels, that none of them should be vexed or sued by any for their offences in their Rebellion.

16. That in time of Rebellion, he said, that he liked well the actions of the Rebels; and that the avarice of gentlemen gave occasion for the people to rise; and that it was better for them to die, than to perish for want.

17. That he said, the Lords of the Parliament were loth to reform inclosures and other things, therefore the people had a good cause to reform them themselves.

18. That after declaration of the defaults of *Bulloign*, and the pieces there, by such as did survey them, he would never amend the same.

19. That he would not suffer the King's pieces of *Newhaven*, and *Blackness*, to be furnished with men and provision; albeit he was advertised of the Defaults, and advised thereto by the King's Council; whereby the *French* King was emboldened to attempt upon them.

20. That he would neither give authority, nor suffer Noblemen and Gentlemen to suppress Rebels in time convenient; but wrote to them to speak the Rebels fair, and use them gently.

21. That upon the 5th of *October*, the present year, at *Hampton-Court*, for defence of his own private causes, he procured seditious Bills to be written in counterfeit hands, and secretly to be dispersed into divers parts of the Realm; beginning thus: *Good People*; intending thereby to raise the King's subjects to Rebellion and open War.

22. That the King's Privy Council did consult at *London* to come to him, and move him to reform his Government; but he hearing of their assembly, declared, by his letters in divers places, that they were high Traitors to the King.

23. That he declared untruly, as well to the King as to other young Lords attending his Person, that the Lords at *London* intended to destroy the King; and desired the King never to forget, but to revenge it, and desired the young Lords to put the King in remembrance thereof; with intent to make sedition and discord between the King and his Nobles.

24. That at divers times and places, he said, the Lords of the Council at *London* intended to kill me; but if I die, the King shall die: and if they famish me, they shall famish him.

25. That of his own head he removed the King so suddenly from *Hampton-Court* to *Windsor*, without any provision there made, that he was thereby not only in great fear, but cast thereby into a dangerous disease.

26. That by his Letters he caused the King's People to assemble in great numbers in armour, after the manner of War, to his aid and defence.

27. That he caused his servants and friends at *Hampton-Court* and *Windsor*, to be apparelled in the King's armour, when the King's servants and guards went unarmed.

28. * That he caused at *Windsor* his own person in the night-time to be guarded in harness by many persons, leaving the King's Majesty's person unguarded; and would not suffer his own guard and servants to be next the King's Person, but appointed his servants and friends to keep the gates.

29. That he intended to fly to *Jersey* or *Wales*, and laid post-horses and men, and a boat, to that purpose †.

After he had read and considered the above Articles, he sent the underwritten submission to the Lords.

Edward *Duke of* Somerset's *first Submission*.

I *Edward*, Duke of *Somerset*, have read and considered these saide twenty-nine Articles before specified, and do acknowledge my saide offences, faults, and crimes, doone and conteined in the same, and most humblie prostrate on my knees, do fullie and wholie submit myselfe to the most aboundant mercy and clemencie of the King's Majestie, for the moderation of my saide offences; having my full trust and confidence, that his Majestie, with the advice of his Highnesse most honourable Counsaile, will consider mine offences, faultes, wordes, and proceedings, that if anie of my saide offences be by his clemencie pardoned, remitted, or otherwise discharged, that I maie enjoye the benefite thereof, although the same become unknowne. And farther, I domost humblie beseech all my Lordes, and other his Majesties most honourable Counsayle, not onlie to be meanes to his Majestie, to take awaie and consider mine offences to have proceeded more of ignorance, negligence, follie, wilfulnes, and for lacke of good consideration, than of anie kankerd or malicious hart, evil intent or thought, tending to anie Treason to his Majestie or Realm: But that it may please his Majestie, by the charitable advise of their good Lordships, to have pity upon mee, my wife and children, and to take some mercifull waie with me, not according to the extremity of his lawes, but after his great goodnes and clemencie, whereunto whatsoever it shall bee, I doe most humblie with all my hart submit my selfe.

Written with mine owne hands the 23d Day of December (Burnet *says the 13th*) *in the 3d yeere of our Soveraigne Lord King* Edward *the Sixth.*

However, on the second of *January*, a Bill was put in against the Duke of *Somerset* of the Articles before-mentioned, with the above Confession. This he was prevailed with to do, upon assurance given, that he should be gently dealt with, if he would truly confess and submit himself to the King's mercy. But some of the Lords said, they did not know whether that Confession was not drawn from him by force; and that it might be an ill precedent to pass Acts upon such papers, without examining the party, whether he had subscribed them freely and uncompelled: Whereupon a Committee was appointed of four Temporal Lords and four Spiritual, who were sent to examine him concerning it. The day following the Bishop of *Coventry* and *Litchfield* made the Report. That he thanked them for their kind message, but that he had freely subscribed the Confession ‡ that lay before them. He made it on his knees before the King and Council, and signed it: and he protested his offences had flowed from rashness and indiscretion rather than malice; and that he had no treasonable design against the King or his Realms. So both Houses soon passed the Bill against him, and he was fined, by Act of Parliament, intitled, *An Act touching the Fine and Ransome of the Duke of Somerset*; that is, for the punishment of his late misdemeanors, whereby he was fined 2000*l.* a year of land, and lost all his goods and offices. Upon this, he sent another submission.

The second Submission of Edward *Duke of* Somerset, *Prisoner in the Tower.*

I AM most fearefull and full of heavinesse, my verie good Lordes, to understande that my last letter was no better accepted at your Lordships handes, to whom I am bounde during my life, for your most gentle and mercifull dealinge with me, that it pleased your goodnesse to bring my case to a fine. I truste your Lordshipes never think that ever I did, or woulde intende, to stand against the King's Majestie and youre Lordshipes Goodnes, or that I woulde goe about to justifie my cause, seeing his Majestie and your Lordshipes offereth clemencie, mercie, and pardon. Although the fine be to me importable, yet I doe commit my self wholie to his Highnesse and your Lordships mercies; I pray onlie the moderation of it, and did covet to declare to youre goodnesse mine inabilitie to beare it: And yet referred all to his Majestie, and your wisdome, goodnesse, and discretion. And I most humblie desire your Lordshipes not to think that I was about to contende with your Lordshipes, when I did speake of my conscience, I might erre, in that I thought I did for the best, as I doe acknowledge and confesse, that neither I am the wisest man in the worlde, nor yet if I were, I shoulde not escape without a most singular grace, but manie times I shoulde offende: But I leave all that, and most humblie, simplie, wholie, and lowlie, I submit my selfe to the King's Majestie and to your good Lordshipes; appealing from the rigour and extremitie of his Majestie's lawes, to his Majesty's great mercie and clemencie; praying your goodness to bee meanes to his Majestie, not to bee offended with mee, nor to exclude his Majestie's mercie and benignitie from me, for my rudeness and lack of discretion, but to accept my good minde as one that faine woulde doo that were well. And when I cannot or have not doone that things I ought to do, I would gladlie amende, and am readie at all times without condition to doo and suffer willinglie that thing that your honours will appoint mee, accepting what clemencie or mercie soever I obtayne to be of his Majestie's and your goodnesse. Most humbly on my knees praying his Majestie and your good Lordships to pardone mine offences, and to order me for them, as to his moste high mercifull clemencie shall appeere convenient. And finallie flying from extremitie of justice, desire mercie, as you bee, and are called, most mercifull Counsellors, not imputing my writings and doings hitherto as of stoutenesse or stubbornesse, but onlie for lack of discretion and wisdome. For the which once again I require pardon and favor to be shewed, and if it pleased your good Lordshipes to heare me, I trust you should find me lowly unto your honors, and so conformable unto your Lordships orders, that I trust to make amends, and obtaine pardon for my former folly. And thus I most humblie commit your good Lordships to Almighty God, to whom I shall alwaies pray that ye maie long continue in honor. *From the Tower, the second of* Februarie.

He came out of the *Tower* on the 6th of *February*, giving bond of 10000*l.* for his good behaviour, but limited that he should stay at the King's house at *Sheen*, or his own at *Sion*, and should not go four miles from them, nor come to the King or Council, unless he was called; and when he knew that the King was to come within four miles of these houses, he was to withdraw from them.

* This Article is in *Stow's Chronicle*, but omitted in *Hayward's* Life of *Edw.* VI. and *Burnet's* Reformation.

† *Rapin*, Vol. VIII. *Oct. Edit.* p. 72 says, Upon these accusations, to which it was then no time to answer, he was sent to the Tower; those whom he had taken so much pains to humble being become his proper Judges. He could not deny that most of the facts laid to his charge were true. But the question was, Whether they were crimes? for he was accused neither of fraud nor of rapine, nor of extortion. But that was to be decided only by the Peers of the Realm, or by the Parliament.

‡ Many thought his confession a very strange thing, and aggravated the abjectness of such a behaviour. But it was doubtless because they would have been glad he should have taken another course, which would not have failed to prove fatal to him. It is certain, that among the articles of his accusation, there were several which could be justified only by the intention, which would scarce have served his turn in the House of Peers the major part of whom were not inclined to favour him. For instance, to mention only the chief Article; could he deny that, *contrary to the condition on which he was made Protector, he had degraded, as it were, the other Regents, and reduced them to the state of bare counsellors?* It is true, he might have alledged the King's Patent. But it was the Patent of a minor King, between ten and eleven years old only, who looking upon him as his Governor, did every thing by his advice; wherefore the Duke could never have cleared himself upon this Article, any more than upon several others. Consequently his only remedy was to own himself guilty of all, and to cast himself upon the King's mercy. Besides, it concerned him highly to get out of prison if it was possible on any terms, since it was dangerous for him to continue any longer in the hands of his enemies. *Rapin* (8vo Edit.) Vol. VIII. p. 76

On

On the 16th he had his pardon, and carried himſelf ſo well, that on the 18th of *April* following he went by invitation to Court, to the King's Majeſty at *Greenwich*; where he was honourably received by the King and his Council, and dined with the King, and was ſworn of the Privy-Council; and the King of his ſpecial favour, and at the humble petition of the Council, by Patent dated *June* the 4th, gave him back almoſt all his eſtate that was forfeited.

III. *Proceedings againſt* EDWARD, *Duke of* SOMERSET, *for* High-Treaſon *and* Felony, Dec. 1, 1551, 5 Ed. VI. *at* Weſtminſter.

THE Duke of *Somerſet* had ſuch acceſs to the King, and ſuch freedoms with him (notwithſtanding the late judgment againſt him), that the Earl of *Warwick* had a mind to get rid of him. The Duke ſeemed alſo in *April* this year to have got the King again in his power, and dealt with the Lord *Strange* to perſuade the King to marry his daughter *Jane*; and that he would advertiſe him of all that paſſed about the King. The Earl of *Warwick* had got himſelf created Duke of *Northumberland*; and for ſeveral of his friends he procured a creation of new honours. The new Duke of *Northumberland* could no longer bear ſuch a Rival in greatneſs as the Duke of *Somerſet* was, who was the only perſon that he thought could take the King out of his hands: So a deſign being laid to deſtroy him, he was apprehended on the 17th of *October*, and ſent to the *Tower*, and with him the Lord *Gray*, Sir *Ralph Vane*, Sir *Thomas Palmer*, Sir *Thomas Arundell*, were alſo taken, and ſome of his followers, *Hamond*, *Newdigate*, and two of the *Seymours*, and were ſent to priſon. The Day after, the Dutcheſs of *Somerſet* was alſo ſent to the *Tower*, with one *Crane* and his wife, and two of her chamber-women; after theſe, Sir *Thomas Holdcroft*, Sir *Miles Patridge*, Sir *Michael Stanhope*, *Wingfield*, *Banniſter*, and *Vaughan*, were all made Priſoners.

But Sir *Thomas Palmer*, though impriſoned with him as an accomplice, was the perſon that ruined him. The evidence againſt the Duke was chiefly Sir *Thomas Palmer*'s Information; who being brought by the Duke of *Northumberland* privately to the King, related the whole conſpiracy.

Sir Thomas Palmer'*s Examination.*

HE declared, That upon St. *George's-Day* laſt, before the Duke of *Somerſet* being upon a journey towards the north, in caſe Sir *William Herbert*, Maſter of the Horſe, had not aſſured him that he ſhould receive no harm, would have raiſed the People; and that he had ſent the Lord *Gray* before to know who would be his friends: Alſo that the Duke of *Northumberland*, the Marquis of *Northampton*, the Earl of *Pembroke*, and other Lords, ſhould be invited to a banquet; and if they came with a bare company, to be ſet upon by the way; if ſtrongly, their heads ſhould have been cut off at the place of their feaſting. He declared farther, that Sir *Ralph Vane* had two thouſand men in readineſs: That Sir *Thomas Arundel* had aſſured the *Tower*, that *Patridge* ſhould raiſe *London*, and take the Great Seal; that *Seymour* and *Hamond* would wait upon him, and that all the Horſe of the Gendarmerie ſhould be ſlain.

The Earl of *Rutland* did affirm, that he had made a Party for getting himſelf declared Protector in the next Parliament.

The above-mentioned particulars were told the King, with ſuch circumſtances, that he was induced to believe them, and reſolved to leave him to the law.

Sir Thomas Palmer'*s ſecond Examination.*

THAT the Gendarmerie, upon the muſter-day, ſhould be aſſaulted by two thouſand men, under Sir *Ralph Vane*, and by an hundred horſes of the Duke of *Somerſet*'s, beſides his Friends, which ſhould ſtand by, and beſides the idle people, which were thought inclinable to take his part. That this done, he would run through the city and proclaim *Liberty, Liberty*, to raiſe the apprentices, *&c.* And in caſe his attempt did not ſucceed, he would go to the *Iſle of Wight*, or to *Poole*.

Crane'*s Examination.*

HE confeſſed all that *Palmer* had ſaid; to which he added, That the Lord *Paget*'s Houſe was the place, where the Nobility being invited to a banquet, ſhould have loſt their heads: And that the Earl of *Arundel* was made acquainted with the Conſpiracy by Sir *Michael Stanhope*, who was a meſſenger between them: And that the thing had been done, but that the greatneſs of the enterprize cauſed delays, and ſome diverſity of advice. And further, that the Duke of *Somerſet* once, feigning himſelf ſick, went to *London* to ſee what friends he could procure.

Hamond'*s Examination.*

HE confeſſed that the Duke of *Somerſet*'s chamber at *Greenwich* had been ſtrongly guarded in the night by many armed men.

All theſe were ſworn before the Council, and the greateſt part of the Nobility, that their Confeſſions were true; and they did ſay, that what was ſworn was without any kind of compulſion, force, or envy, or diſpleaſure, but as favourable to the Duke as they could ſwear to with ſafe Conſciences.

Lord Strange'*s Examination.*

HE voluntarily informed how the Duke deſired him to move the King to take to wife his third daughter the Lady *Jane*; and that he would be his ſpy about the King, to advertiſe him when any of the Council ſpake privately with him, and to acquaint him what they ſaid.

Hereupon the Lord Chancellor openly declared in the Star-Chamber theſe Accuſations againſt the Duke of *Somerſet*; and on the 22d of *October*, with much Shew and Ceremony, were all the Crafts and Corporations of *London* commanded to repair to their Halls, and there it was ſhewed them, That the Duke of *Somerſet* would have taken the Tower, ſeized on the Broad-Seal, and have deſtroyed the City, and then to have gone to the *Iſle of Wight*. After this Declaration, they were charged each Corporation to ward every Gate in *London*, and to have a walking Watch through the City. Towards the latter end of *November*, a Letter was ſent to the Lord Chancellor, to cauſe a ſufficient Commiſſion to be made, and ſealed with the Great Seal of *England*, of *Oyer* and *Terminer*, to the Lord Marquis of *Wincheſter*, that he may thereby be the King's Seneſchal, *hac unica vice tantum*, for the hearing and determining of the Treaſons and Felonies of the Duke of *Somerſet*, giving the Date of the ſaid Commiſſion the 28th of *November*; and the 1ſt of *December* was ordered for his Trial.

December 1. the Duke of *Somerſet* came to his Trial at *Weſtminſter-Hall*. The Lord Treaſurer ſat as High-Steward of *England*, under the Cloth of State, on a Bench between two Poſts, three degrees high. All the Lords to the number of twenty-ſeven, *viz.*

Dukes.	*Suſſex*,	*Bourough*,
Suffolk,	*Worceſter*,	*Zouch*,
Northumberland.	*Pembroke.*	*Stafford*,
Marquis.	Viſcount:	*Wentworth*,
Northampton.	*Hertford.*	*Darcy*,
Earls.	Barons:	*Sturton*,
Derby,	*Burgaveny*,	*Windſor*,
Bedford,	*Audley*,	*Cromwell*,
Huntington,	*Wharton*,	*Gobham*,
Rutland,	*Evers*,	*Bray*:
Bath;	*Latimer*;	

Theſe ſat a degree under, and heard the matter debated.

The Crime laids againſt him were caſt into five ſeveral Indictments, as King *Edward* VI. has it in his Journal; but the Record mentions only three, whether Indictments or Articles, is not ſo clear. 1. That he had deſigned to have ſeized on the King's Perſon, and ſo have governed all Affairs. 2. That he, with one hundred others, intended to have impriſoned the Earl of *Warwick*, afterwards Duke of *Northumberland*. And 3. That he had deſigned to have raiſed an Inſurrection in the City of *London*. But the Indictment which here follows, is only for deſigning to ſeize on and impriſon the Duke of *Northumberland*.

London' ſſ. 'INquiſitio capt' fuit apud Guihald' Civitat' London die Sabbathi, videlicet viceſimo primo die Novembris, anno 'regni domini Edwardi nuper Regis Anglie ſexti, quinto, coram Richardo Dobbes tunc Majore Civitat' London, ac aliis Juſticiariis, & 'Commiſſionariis per ſacramentum duodecim, &c. qui dixerunt ſuper ſacramentum ſuum, quod Edwardus Dux Somerſ' nuper de Sion in Comitat' Middleſex' Deum pre oculis ſuis non habens, ſed inſtigatione Diabolica ſeduct' & debit', legiantie ſue minime ponderans, 'apud Holborne, in parochia ſancta Andree infra Civit' London, viceſimo die Aprilis anno regni dicti nuper Regis Edwardi ſexti quinto ſupradicto, & diverſis diebus & vicibus antea & poſtea falſe, malitioſe, '& proditorie, per apertum factum circumivit, compaſſavit, & imaginavit, cum diverſis aliis perſonis predictum nuper Regem Edwardum ſextum de ſtatu ſuo Regali deponere & deprivare, necnon ex injuria ſua propria Perſona Regalem ipſius nuper Regnis natural' & ſupremi domini 'abſq; authoritate aliqua ſibi per ipſum nuper Regem dat', ſive conceſſa in ſolam gubernationem predicti nuper Ducis habere & retinere, ac ad voluntatem ejuſdem nuper Ducis regere & tractare, ac etiam omnia & ſingula dominia, negotia, authoritateſque Regias hujus regni Anglie ad libit' ipſius nuper Ducis, ordinare & uti, adtunc & ibidem arrogant', 'falſe, malitioſe, & proditorie compaſſavit & imaginavit: Et ulterius Juratores predicti preſentabant, quod idem nuper Dux Somerſ' ad ſuam proditoriam intentionem perimplend', & proficiend', ex malitia ſua precogitat' ſeipſum ſimul cum Michaele Stanhope nuper de Bedington in 'Comitat' Sur' Milit', Milone Patriche nuper de London, Milit', 'Thom' Holcroft nuper de London, Milit', Franciſco Newdigate nuper 'de London generoſ', ac cum diverſis aliis perſonis ad numerum centum perſonarum Jurator' predictis ignot' in forcibili modo ex eorum propriis authoritatibus ad intentionem capiend' & impriſonand' prenobilem 'Johannem nuper Ducem Northumberl' adtunc Comitem Warr', unum de Privat' Concilio dicti nuper Regis tunc exiſten' adtunc & ibidem illicite, falſe, malitioſe, & proditorie aſſemblaverunt, ipſiſque modo & forma predictis, illicite, voluntarie, & malitioſe aſſemblat', ad perimplend' '& exequend' falſam & proditoriam intentionem ſuam predictam, falſe, voluntarie, malitioſe, & proditorie, adtunc & ibidem per ſpatium duarum horarum & amplius inſimul continuaverunt & remanſerunt, contra legiantiam ſuam debitam, & contra pacem dicti nuper Regis coronam '& dignitatem ſuas, ac contra formam diverſorum ſtatutorum in hujuſmodi caſu nuper edit' & proviſ'. Et ulterius Juratores predicti preſentabant, quod predictus Edwardus nuper Dux Somers' Deum pre oculis ſuis non habens, ſed inſtigatione Diabolica ſeduct' viceſimo die 'Maii, anno regni dicti nuper Regis Edwardi ſexti quinto ſupradicto, & 'diverſis aliis diebus & vicibus antea, & poſtea apud Holborne, in predicta parochia ſancti Andree infra Civitat' London, & apud diverſa alia 'loca, infra Civitat' London predictam felonice, ut felo dicti nuper Regis per aperta verba & facta procuravit, movit & inſtigavit complurim' ſubdit' dicti nuper Regis ad inſurgend' & apertam rebellionem & 'inſurrectionem infra hoc regnum Anglie movend', contra ipſum nuper 'Regem, & adtunc & ibidem felonice ad capiend' & impriſonand' predictum prenobil' Johannem nuper Ducem Northumberland, tunc Comit' 'Warwic' de Privat' Concilio dicti nuper Regis adtunc exiſten' contra pacem ipſius nuper Regis coronam & dignitatem ſuas, ac contra formam ſtatuti in hujuſmodi caſu editi & proviſ'.

'Et poſtea ſcilicet die Mart's primo die Decembris, anno quinto ſupradicto, coram Willielmo Marchione Wynton, Theſaurar' Anglie, necnon Seneſchallo Anglie, hac vice apud Weſtmonaſterium ven' predictus Edwardus nuper Dux Somerſ', ſub cuſtod' Johannis Gage prenobil' ordinis

Garterii

‘ Garterii Milit’, Constabular’ dicti Turr’ London, in cujus custod’ preantea ex causa predicta, & aliis certis de causis commissus fuit ad barr’ apud Westmonasterium predictam duct’ in propria persona sua qui committebatur prefat’ Constabular’, &c. Et statim de omnibus & singulis seperalibus proditionibus, & feloniis predictis sibi superius imposit’ allocat’ qualit’ se voluisset inde acquietari, dixit quod ipse in nullo fuit culpabil’. Et inde de bono & malo pon’ se super pares suos, &c. Super quo Henric. Dux Suffolc’, Johannes Dux Northumberland, & ceteri Comit’ & Barones, predict’ Edwardi nuper Ducis Somers’ pares instant super eorum fidelitatibus & legianc’ dicto nuper Regi debit’ per prefat’ Seneschal’ Anglie de veritate inde dicend’ onerati, Et postea per eundem Seneschal’ ab inferiori pare, usque ad supremum parem illorum seperatim publice examinati quilibet eorum seperatim dixerunt, quod predictus Edwardus nuper Dux Somers’ de seperalibus proditionibus predictis sibi seperatim in forma predicta superius imposit’ in nullo fuit inde culpabil’. Et ulterius quilibet eorum seperatim dixerunt, quod predictus Edwardus nuper Dux Somers’ de feloniis predictis sibi seperatim in forma predicta superius imposit’ fuit culpabil’ modo & forma, prout per seperalia indictamenta inde superius supponebatur, super quo instant’ servien’ dicti nuper Regis ad legem, ac ipsius nuper Regis Attorn’ juxta debit’ legis formam pet’ versus eundem Edwardum nuper Ducem Somers’ judicium, & executionem super seperalibus feloniis predictis pro dicto nuper Rege habend’, &c.

Judgement que ferra ai quite pur le treason, & suspend pur le felonie.

‘ Et super hoc visis per Curiam predictam adtunc intellectis omnibus & singulis premissis, consideratum fuit quod predictus Edwardus nuper Dux Somers’ quoad seperales proditiones predictas sibi seperatim in forma predicta superius imposit’, & quamlibet eorum iret inde quiet’. Et quoad seperalis felonias predict’, eidem nuper Duci Somers’ in forma predicta superius imposit’ unde invent’ fuit culpabil’, ulterius consideratum fuit, quod idem Edwardus nuper Dux Somers’ suspenderetur, &c.’

Then were read the Depositions of *Palmer*, *Crane*, *Hamond*, *&c.* and the King’s Counsel opened the Indictment, and urged strongly *Palmer*’s voluntary Examination (as they called it) with *Crane*’s and the other Exminations.

The Duke of *Somerset* being, it seems, little acquainted with Law, did not desire Counsel to plead or assist him in Point of Law, but only answered to Matters of Fact; he desired no Advantage might be taken against him for any idle or angry Word that might at any time have fallen from him; he protested he never intended to have raised the Northern Parts, but had only, upon some Reports, sent to Sir *William Herbert* to be his Friend; that he had never determined to have killed the Duke of *Northumberland*, or any other Person, but had only talked of it, without any Intention of doing it. That for the Design of destroying the Gendarmery, it was ridiculous to think, that he with a small Troop could destroy so strong a Body, consisting of 900 Men; in which, though he had succeeded, it could have signified nothing. That he never designed to raise any Stirs in *London*, but had always looked upon it as a Place where he was most safe. That his having Men about him at *Greenwich* was with no ill Design, since when he could have done Mischief with them, he had not done it; but upon his Attachment rendered himself a Prisoner, without any Resistance. He objected also many things against the Witnesses, and desired they might be brought face to face. He particularly spoke against Sir *Thomas Palmer*, the chief Witness. But the Witnesses were not brought, only their Examinations before-mentioned read. Upon this the King’s Counsel replied, and avouched the Law to be, to assemble Men with Intent to kill the Duke of *Northumberland*, was Treason by a *Statute of the 3d and 4th of* Edw. VI. *made against unlawful Assemblies*, which enacts, ‘ That if twelve Persons should have assembled together to have killed any Privy-Counsellor, and upon Proclamation they had not dispersed themselves, it was Treason: Or, if such twelve had been by any malicious Artifice brought together for any Riot, and being warned, did not disperse themselves, it was Felony, without Benefit of Clergy or Sanctuary.’ That to raise *London*, or the North Parts of the Realm, was Treason. That to have Men about him to resist his Attachment was Felony. That to assault the Lords, and to devise their Deaths, was Felony. These Things were urged against him by the Counsel (as is their usual Way of Pleading) with much Bitterness. Then the Peers withdrew to debate the Matter. The Proofs about his Design of raising the North or the City, or of killing the Gendarmes, did not satisfy them, (for all these had been without Question treasonable) so they only held to that Point, *of conspiring to imprison the Duke of* Northumberland. The Duke of *Suffolk* was of Opinion, That no Contention among private Subjects should be on any Account screwed up to be Treason. The Duke of *Northumbeland* said, he would never consent that any Practice against him should be reputed Treason. Several of the Lords said, They held it unfit that the Duke of *Northumberland*, the Marquis of *Northampton*, and the Earl of *Pembroke*, should be on the Trial; because the Prisoner was chiefly charged with Practices intended against them. But Answer was made, That a Peer of the Realm might not be challenged. So after great Difference of Opinion, they all acquitted him of Treason. But the greater Number found him guilty of Felony*, and Judgment was given that he should be hanged †.

Then the Duke of *Northumberland* addressed himself to the Duke, and told him, That now, since by the Law he was condemned to die, as he had saved him formerly, so he would not now be wanting to serve him, how little soever he expected it from him; he desired him therefore to fly to the King’s Mercy, in which he promised him he would faithfully serve him. The Duke of *Somerset* then thanked the Lords for their Favour, and asked Pardon of the Duke of *Northumberland*, *Northampton*, and *Pembroke* for his ill Intentions against them; and made Suit for his Life, and for his Wife and Children: And from thence he was carried to the Tower, where he remained till *January* 22, when his Petition for Life having been rejected, he was brought to the Scaffold about eight o’Clock in the Morning.

Touching which Execution ‡, a few Words here would be bestowed in describing the wonderful Order and Manner thereof, according as it hath faithfully been suggested to us upon the Credit of a certain noble Personage, who not only was there present at the Deed doing, but also in Manner next unto him upon the Scaffold, beholding the Order of all Things with his Eyes, and with his Pen also reporting the same in Order and Manner as here followeth.

In the Year of our Lord 1552, the 22d Day of *January*, the noble Duke of *Somerset*, Uncle to King *Edward*, was brought out of the Tower of *London*, and delivered to the Sheriffs of the City, and compassed round about with a great Number of armed Men, both of the Guard and others, he was brought unto the Scaffold on *Tower-hill*; where as he nothing changing neither Voice nor Countenance, but in a Manner with the same Gesture which he commonly used at home, kneeling down upon both his Knees, and lifting up his Hands, commended himself unto God.

After that he had ended a few short Prayers, standing up again, and turning himself toward the East-side of the Scaffold, nothing at all abashed (as it seemed unto me standing about the Midst of the Scaffold, and diligently marking all Things), neither with the Sight of the Ax, neither yet of the Hangman, or of present Death §; but with the like Alacrity and Chearfulness of Mind and Countenance as beforetimes he was accustomed to hear the Causes and Supplications of others, and especially the Poor, he uttered these Words to the People:

Dearly beloved Friends,

I am brought hither to suffer Death, albeit that I never offended against the King, neither by Word nor Deed, and have been always as faithful and true unto this Realm, as any Man hath been. But forasmuch as I am by a Law condemned to die, I do acknowledge myself as well as others to be subject thereunto. Wherefore to testify my Obedience which I owe unto the Laws, I am come hither to suffer Death; whereunto I willingly offer myself, with most hearty Thanks unto God, that hath given me this Time of Repentance, who might through sudden Death have taken away my Life, that neither I should have acknowledg’d him nor myself.

Moreover (dearly beloved Friends), there is yet somewhat that I must put you in mind of, as touching Christian Religion; which, so long as I was in Authority, I always diligently set forth and furthered to my Power. Neither I repent me of my Doings, but rejoice therein, sith that now the State of Christian Religion cometh most near unto the Form and Order of the primitive Church. Which Thing I esteem as a great Benefit given of God both unto you and me: Most heartily exhorting you all, that this which is most purely set forth unto you, you will with like thankfulness accept and embrace, and set out the same in your living. Which Thing if you do not, without doubt greater Mischief and Calamity will follow.

When he had spoken these Words, suddenly there was a terrible Noise heard: Whereupon there came a great Fear on all Men. This Noise was as it had been the Noise of some great Storm or Tempest, which unto some seemed to be heard from above; like as if a great deal of Gunpowder being inclosed in an Armoury, and having caught Fire, had violently broken out. But unto some again, it seemed as though it had been a great Multitude of Horsemen running together, or coming upon them. Such a Noise then was in the Ears of all Men, albeit they saw nothing. Whereby it happened, that all the People being amazed without any evident Cause, without any Violence or Stroke stricken, or any Man seen, they ran away, some into the Ditches and Puddles, and some into the Houses thereabout; other some being afraid with the Horror and Noise, fell down groveling unto the Ground with their Pole-Axes and Halberts; and most of them cried out, Jesus, save us, Jesus, save us!

* One Attainder passed in *Edward* the Sixth’s Reign, when, tho’ the party was not heard, the witnesses were heard; but when the Duke of *Somerset* came to be tried both for Treason and Felony, he had not the benefit of the Accusers being brought face to face, but was proceeded against upon depositions read in the Court; he was acquitted of the Treason, but cast for Felony; and that occasioned the Act which the Commons grafted upon a Bill sent down by the Lords in the subsequent Sessions, *viz.* 5 and 6 *Edw.* VI. *State-Tracts*, vol. II. p. 554. By which Act, no Person shall be indicted, arraigned, *&c.* unless the offender be accused by two lawful Accusers; which Accusers, at the time of the Arraignment, shall be brought in Person before the Party so accused, *&c.* See *Rastal*, vol. I. p. 1023.

† *Thuanus*, translated by the Reverend Mr. *Wilson*, vol. II. p. 409. says, In *England* there were troubles of a most dangerous nature; for *John Dudley*, first created Earl of *Warwick*, and then Duke of *Northumberland*, an ambitious and sagacious Man, had accused the Duke of *Somerset*, Protector of the Realm, a Person of mean spirit, whose Patience he had long abused, of Male-administration, and had procured his imprisonment; after that, being reconciled to him, he put him upon beheading his brother, who was exceeding brave, and formidable to *Northumberland*. Which done, after he had gained his wish, and drawn the chief power into his own hands, he had nothing else to do, but to remove *Somerset* himself out of the way; towards whom he shewed such a contempt, as drove the other upon thought of killing *Dudley*, for the vindication of his own authority. *Somerset* therefore went to his house under pretence of a visit, covered with a coat of mail under his cloaths, and carrying with him a party of armed men, whom he left in the next chamber; but when he was introduced in the civilest manner to *Dudley*, who was naked and lying upon his bed, the good-natured Man repented him, would not execute his design, and departed without striking a stroke. The plot being afterwards discovered by the treachery of some of the accomplices, he was accused upon it, and, notwithstanding the unwillingness of the King, who had been brought up under his care, was condemned to death, because he had offended against a late Law, which had provided, That whoever was found contriving the death of a Privy-Counsellor, tho’ he did not accomplish it, should forfeit his head. Accordingly, in the beginning of the next year, he was, by the malignant sport of Fortune, beheaded at *London*. With him suffered Sir *Ralph Vane*, by whose advice *Somerset* was said to have held his unlawful cabals, and to have conspired against *Northumberland* and others.

‡ Taken from *Fox*’s Book of Martyrs, vol. II. p. 1247.

§ Bishop *Burnet*, in his second Volume of the *History of the Reformation*, p. 186. says, It was generally believed, that all this pretended conspiracy upon which he was condemned, was only a forgery; for both *Palmer* and *Crane*, the chief Witnesses, were soon after discharged, as were also *Bartvile* and *Hamond*, with all the rest that had been made prisoners on the pretence of this plot. And the Duke of *Northumberland* continued after that in so close friendship with *Palmer*, that it was generally believed he had been corrupted to betray him. And indeed, the not bringing witnesses into Court, but only the Depositions and the Parties sitting Judges, gave great occasion to condemn the Proceedings against him. For it was generally thought, that all was an artifice of *Palmer*’s, who had put the Duke of *Somerset* in fear of his life, and to get him to gather men about him for his own preservation; and that he afterwards being taken with him, seemed then to acknowledge all that which he had before contrived. This was more confirmed by the death of the other four, who were executed on the 26th of *February*, and did all protest they had never been guilty of any design, either against the King, or to kill the Lords. *Vane* added, That his blood would make *Northumberland*’s pillow uneasy to him. The people were generally much affected with this execution.

Those which tarried still in their Places, for fear knew not where they were. And I myself which was there present among the rest, being also afraid in this Hurly-burly, stood still altogether amazed, looking when any Man would knock me on the Head.

In the mean time, whilst these things were thus in doing, the People by Chance spied one Sir *Anthony Brown* riding unto the Scaffold, which was the occasion of a new noise; for when they saw him coming, they conjectured that which was not true, but notwithstanding which they all wish'd for, that the King by that Messenger had sent his Uncle pardon; and therefore with great rejoycing, and casting up their caps, they cried out, Pardon, pardon is come: God save the King! Thus this good Duke, altho' he was destitute of all Man's help, yet he saw before his departure, in how great love and favour he was with all Men. And truly I do not think, that in so great slaughter of Dukes as hath been in *England* within these few years, there were so many weeping eyes at one time; and not without cause: for all men did see in the decay of this Duke, the publick ruin of all *England*, except such as indeed did perceive nothing. But now to return from whence we have strayed, the duke in the mean time standing still in the same place, modestly, and with a grave countenance, made a sign to the people with his hand, that they would keep themselves quiet: Which thing being done, and silence obtained, he spake unto them in this manner.

Dearly beloved Friends, there is no such matter here in hand, as you vainly hope or believe. It seemeth thus good unto Almighty God, whose Ordinance it is meet and necessary that we all be obedient unto. Wherefore I pray you all to be quiet, and to be contented with my death, which I am most willing to suffer: and let us now join in prayer unto the Lord for the preservation of the King's Majesty, unto whom hitherto I have always shewed myself a most faithful and true subject. I have always been most diligent about his Majesty in his affairs, both at home and abroad, and no less diligent in seeking the common commodity of the whole Realm. At which words all the People cried out, and said, It was most true.

Then the Duke proceeding, said, Unto whose Majesty I wish continual health, with all felicity and all prosperous success. Whereunto the people again cried out, *Amen*.

Moreover, I do wish unto all his Counsellors the Grace and Favour of God, whereby they may rule in all things uprightly with justice. Unto whom I exhort you all in the Lord, to shew yourselves obedient, as it is your bounden duty, under the pain of condemnation, and also most profitable for the preservation and safeguard of the King's Majesty.

Moreover, forsomuch as heretofore I have had oftentimes affairs with divers Men, and hard it is to please every Man, therefore if there be any that hath been offended and injured by me, I most humbly require and ask him forgiveness; but especially Almighty God, whom throughout all my Life I have most grievously offended: and all other whatsoever they be that have offended me, I do with my whole heart forgive them. Now I once again require you, dearly beloved in the Lord, that you will keep yourselves quiet and still, lest through your tumult you might trouble me. For albeit the Spirit be willing and ready, the Flesh is frail and wavering; and thro' your quietness, I shall be much more quieter. Moreover, I desire you all to bear me witness, that I die here in the faith of Jesus Christ; desiring you to help me with your prayers, that I may persevere constant in the same unto my life's end.

After this, he turning himself again about like a meek Lamb, kneeled down upon his knees. Then Dr. *Cox*, who was there present to counsel and advertise him, delivered a certain Scroll into his hand, wherein was contained a brief confession unto God; which being read, he stood up again upon his feet, without any trouble of Mind, (as it appeared) and first bad the Sheriffs farewel, then the Lieutenant of the Tower and others, taking them all by the hands which were upon the Scaffold with him. Then he gave the Hangman certain money. Which done, he put off his gown, and kneeling down again in the straw, untied his shirt-strings. After that, the Hangman coming unto him, turned down his collar round about his neck, and all other things which did let or hinder him. Then lifting up his eyes to Heaven, where his only hope remained, and covering his face with his own handkerchief, he laid himself down along, shewing no manner of token of trouble or fear, neither did his countenance change, but that before his eyes were covered, there began to appear a red colour in the midst of his cheeks.

Thus this most meek and gentle Duke lying along, and looking for the stroke, because his doublet covered his neck, he was commanded to rise up and put it off; and then laying himself down again upon the block, and calling thrice upon the name of Jesus, saying, *Lord Jesu, save me!* As he was the third time repeating the same, even as the name of *Jesu* was in uttering, in a moment he was bereft both of head and life.

His Son continued in a disconsolate condition, deprived of all his titles; till Queen *Elizabeth*, in the first year of her reign, created him Earl of *Hertford*, and Baron *Seymour*; and his Grandson, *William* Earl of *Hertford*, was created Marquis of *Hertford*, 1640, and in the year 1660, he presented the following Case to the House of Peers: which giving a great light into that proceeding is here inserted.

The CASE *of the Marquis of* Hertford, *touching the Dukedom of* Somerset, *A. D.* 1660, *when the Bill was brought into Parliament to restore him to the Title of Duke of* Somerset.

EDWARD, Earl of *Hertford* (great Grandfather of the said Marquis) was by Letters Patents under the Great Seal of *England*, bearing date the 6th of *April*, 1 *Edw.* VI. created Duke of *Somerset*, to hold to him and the Heirs Males of his body, upon the body of the Lady *Anne* his then wife begotten, and to be begotten, for ever, with several other remainders over in tail.

The said Duke afterwards, viz. in *Michaelmas-Term*, 5 *Edw.* VI. was indicted of Felony, for procuring and stirring up others to take and imprison *John* Earl of *Warwick* (one of the King's Privy-Council); which Indictment (tho' void both in matter and form) was pretended to be grounded on the Statute of 3 and 4 *Edw.* VI. which makes it Felony to stir up and procure others to take away the Life of any of the King's Council; but this Indictment was only for stirring up others to imprison a Privy-Counsellor, (which was never reduced into act) and the same declared and branded in print to be void by learned Judges. Yet the said Duke was found guilty of Felony, and put to death for this fact, which was but a pretended Felony: and if true, yet no entail'd estate forfeitable thereby.

The malice of his enemies not satisfied with his blood, afterwards by their power (in the infancy of the Duke's Heir, who continued and was owned for Duke of *Somerset* for several months after his Father's death), procured an Act of Parliament in the same year, 5 *Edw.* VI. intitled, An Act touching the limitation of the late Duke of *Somerset*'s Lands, wherein there is a clause obliquely inserted *, to take away the said Honour so entailed as aforesaid; which, by no Felony (how notorious soever the same had been) could by law have been forfeited.

This being a case unprecedented, both in law and history, and so contrary to the rules of law, justice and reason, to have an attainder of Felony stand, for an offence, which apparently neither then, nor at any time after was Felony; and if a Felony, yet to have a forfeiture extended beyond the offence, (if there were any) and to be so maliciously prosecuted after the death of the said Duke, (who was mainly instrumental in bringing about the Blessed Reformation of Religion) it is humbly conceived to be most agreeable to justice to restore the said Marquis, who is Heir Male of the bodys of the said Duke and the Lady *Anne* his wife, to his ancient Honour, so illegally taken away as aforesaid.

Whereupon, in *September* 1660, the said Marquis of *Hertford* was restor'd to the Dukedom of *Somerset*, by a repeal of the Act of the 5th of *Edw.* VI.

* And be it farther enacted, That the said Duke and his Heirs Males, begotten upon the Body of the said Lady *Anne* for ever, shall, by authority of this Act, lose and forfeit unto your Highness, your Heirs and Successors for ever, and also be deprived from henceforth for ever, as well of the Names of Viscount *Beauchamp*, Earl of *Hertford*, and Duke of *Somerset*, and every of them, as also of all and every other his and their Honour or Honours, Degrees, Dignities, Estates, Preheminences, and Styles, by whatsoever Name or Names he the same Duke hath been called, named, or created, by any Letters Patents, Writs, or otherwise.

IV. The Arraignment of Mr. DAVISON in the *Star-Chamber*, upon *Tuesday* the 28th of *March*, 1587 †, 30 *Eliz.*

Before Sir *Christopher Wraye*, Chief Justice of *England*, who for the Time sate as Lord Privy-Seal; the Archbishop of *Canterbury*, and the Archbishop of *York*; the Earl of *Worcester*, the Earl of *Cumberland*, and the Earl of *Lincoln*; the Lord *Grey*, and Lord *Lumley*; Sir *James Croft*, the Comptroller; Sir *Gilbert Gerrard*, Master of the Rolls; the Lord Chief Justice of the Common-Pleas; *Edmund Anderson*; Sir *Roger Manwood*, the Lord Chief Baron; and Sir *Walter Mildmay*, the Chancellor of the Exchequer;

For hearing of a Matter of Misprision and Contempt against Mr. *Davison*, late one of her Majesty's Secretaries, and one of her Privy-Council, by Virtue of a Commission to them directed ‡.

WHereupon Mr. *Popham*, the Queen's Attorney-General, spake in form following:

My Lords, I am to inform your Lordships in her Majesty's behalf, of a certain great and grievous Contempt and Misprision against Mr. *Davison*, there Prisoner at the Bar, late one of her Majesty's Secretaries. The manifold and sundry practices committed by the *Scotish* Queen are not unknown unto your Honours, which were offences in the highest degree, and required to be looked unto with speed. It is well known unto your Lordships also, that thereupon, by earnest intreaty and intercession, her Majesty at length condescended that the matter should be heard and decided according unto law. Whereupon were those honourable proceedings had at *Fotheringhay*. But the residence which belonged thereunto, to-wit, the execution, her Majesty politiquely neither consented unto, nor denyed, esteeming no clemency in the former, nor wisdom in the latter. Which course, she held from the 25th of *October*, all *November*, *December* and *January*. During which time, most horrible conspiracies against her Majesty's Sacred Person were contrived, most false rumours that the *Scotish* Queen was escaped spread abroad, and bruited that foreigners were landed for invasion; all which, for preservation of the *Scotish* Queen, and prejudice of ours. Upon these considerations, her Majesty assented to sign the Warrant for her Execution, by whom such tumults were raised: Notwithstanding, being

† Copied from a MS. in *Caius* College, *Cambridge*, Class A. 1090. 8. p. 267.

‡ Queen *Elizabeth* undertook to make the Publick believe that the execution of the Queen of *Scots* was done against her will, and without her Knowledge; the way she went to work was this: *Davison* was the instrument she made use of, without his knowing any thing of the matter, to act this sort of [illegible]. A little before the Queen of *Scots'* sentence he was made Secretary of State; and it is very likely he was put into that post on purpose, that he might be drawn into the snare, and made accountable for Mary's death. *Rapin*, Vol. IX. (Oct. Edit.) pag. 105, 106. See also pag. 109, 110, 111, 112, 113 for more particulars of this affair.

being moved to mercy by her great wisdom, she thought it necessary to have it in readiness, if any attempt should be begun, and yet not in haste to execute the same: this so signed, she left with Mr. *Davison* to carry to the Great Seal, to have it in readiness as aforesaid. And he, after the sealing, and without her Majesty's commandment, presented it unto the Lords without her privity, contemptuously. Notwithstanding, upon the delivery thereof to him, her Majesty bid him use secrecy. And upon question made by the Lords whether her Majesty continued in that mind for execution of the *Scotish* Queen, he said, she held that course still; and upon farther question made, said her Majesty would not be farther troubled with that matter. Whereupon the Lords seeing no impediment, dispatched the execution, wherein Mr. *Davison* did break the secrecy her Majesty reposed in him, in delivering it unto the Lords, and dealt very contemptuously in not making her privy, knowing her mind to be to the contrary. For her Majesty sent Mr. *Killegrew* unto him, commanding him, if it were not sealed already, it should not be sealed; and after, when he told her Majesty it was sealed already, She asked him what haste? This act so done by him, he being but a particular Counsellor, her Majesty doth take it a matter of high indignity and abuse of her Counsellors, and a thing of the greatest moment that ever happened since her Reign, since which time never any Counsellor in matters of far less importance proceeded without her resolution or privity: which thing she leaves to your Honours consideration for punishment thereof.

Davison, with a comely countenance, replenished with gravity, a fine deliverance of speech, but a voice somewhat low (which he excused by late sickness) discreetly answered in sort ensuing:

My Lords, I am right sorry, that an action of this nature, for the honourable proceedings against the *Scotish* Queen, than which never was any thing more honourable, should after the full and laudable performance thereof be called into question. Again, my Lords, I am most sorry that her gracious Highness should conceive such an high displeasure against me, as to trouble your Honours with me at this present. But as in all mine actions heretofore, I have been most faithful and forward to do her Majesty's commandments; so in this, by your Honours favour, let me bear the testimony of my conscience, that I have done nothing either wittingly or willingly, but as became an honest man. And therefore, first, that I delivered it unto the Lords without her commandment, or against her commandment; let it be lawful for me with your Honours leave to protest the contrary. To that the Attorney answered, I said not that you delivered it unto the Lords against her commandment, but that you knowing her mind to be contrary to it. *Davison* to that replied, Well, then, I desire to have the proofs: whereupon the Sollicitor-General read his examination, wherein to the fixth point he sayeth, that after the signing and sealing he made her not privy to the sending down. Mr. *Davison* to that answered; My good Lords, the Warrant for the execution was signed and sealed by her Majesty's express commandment; which being so, I take it to be irrevocable in law. Whereupon, by the Advice of the Lords it was sent down, she not being privy to sending down, wherein I thought I dealt as beseemed me: for writs of execution do not use to come to her Majesty. That I was so forward, I thought it my duty, and for no other reason I protest; for I never had any private grudge or hatred against the Queen of *Scots*, but in respect of my Country and Common-Weal. The Warrant rested with me six Weeks before I presented it, and when I presented it, my Lord Admiral will witness I was sent for. The place I held, I protest I never sought for; it pleased her Majesty for some gracious opinion of me to prefer me thereunto. In which I am assured I have not committed any wilful error, but as an honest man should do; for nothing in the world is more dear to me than my reputation. I confess I said to some Lords, I took it to be her Majesty's pleasure to proceed therein, and I appeal to her Majesty's own conscience if I had not cause to think so. But she is my most gracious Sovereign, it is not my duty to say, if she gainsay; I will not stand in contestation with her, for it beseems me not, and therefore I submit myself to what punishment your Honours shall please to lay upon me.

To that the Sollicitor (*Egerton*) answered; Mr. *Davison*, you do well to extol the honour of the proceedings, for it beseems you, and so the truth was. But I must tell you the more honourable the proceedings were, the more is your contempt in not making her privy. In reserving the execution, I note her Majesty's magnanimity, who not regarded the dangers of her own self, to continue the other's life. And yet her wisdom is therein to be commended, who thought good to have it in a readiness, with intention to have clemency so long as might be. In not contesting with her Majesty you observe duty, but by your means was a great contempt; and farther, she said to you, you should use it with great secrecy.

To which Mr. *Davison* said, I confess it; and the Sollicitor replied, Why then that was a caution not to do it without her consent: so notwithstanding your intention was good, it was a foul error. Whereto *Davison* rejoined, She is my most gracious Sovereign, as good a Mistress unto me as ever any servant had, and what I have, I had it at her hands. I hope, therefore, my Lords think me not so unwise as to offend her, unless by oversight; but that I did it wittingly or willingly, I protest I did it not. And notwithstanding she sent Mr. *Killegrew* that it should not be sealed, if it were not sealed already; yet it proves not but that she had a mind to do it when it was sealed. She said unto me, What haste? Whereto I answered, I had done it by her Majesty's commandment, and that such a thing might not be dallied withal. Now, my Lords, the reasons to move me to think it was her Majesty's meaning, were sundry and divers: first, the honour and justice of the cause; next, I knew of advertisement from beyond the seas of her Majesty's imminent dangers. Also I was privy to the proceedings at *Fotheringhay*. I was not ignorant of the doings in Parliament. Last of all, the rumour of invasion, the cries and tumults in the Realm, which moved me, having no express commandment to the contrary, to do as I did. When he had said this, Mr. Sollicitor read his examination, where to the second he saith, when her Majesty bade him use secrecy, he said he would be as careful and secret as should need: to the third, he confesseth Mr. *Killegrew* came unto him, telling him, if it were not sealed already it should not be sealed. To the seventh, after the Warrant was sealed, her Majesty asked him, What haste? Whereto *Davison* answered, tho' her Majesty commanded me to keep it secret, and I told the Council of it, how can I be thought ill of for that? For her Majesty bade me expresly shew Mr. Secretary *Walsingham* thereof; my Lord-Chancellor must needs know it, forasmuch as he must seal it. And her Majesty made my Lord-Admiral privy thereunto, why then might I not make it known to some others that were chief Counsellors? To that, said Mr. Attorney, Though Mr. *Walsingham* should know it, yet it was not general. Mr. *Davison* answered, Neither was I verbally commanded to conceal it from the rest. Then said the Sollicitor, Another matter makes against you; my Lord-Treasurer did ask you, whether it was her Majesty's pleasure? And you answered, Yea. To that said *Davison*, I remember not that. The Sollicitor reply'd, It is my Lord-Treasurer's testimony. And *Davison* rejoined, I reverence his testimony; and proceeded, saying, my Lords, the cause is between her Majesty and me; she is my gracious Sovereign, and I her servant, it behoveth me not to say, if she gainsay, neither could I, as I said, contest against her; yet let me protest, that, in my own conceit, I have dealt as sincerely, soundly and honestly as any servant could do. Then spake the Lord Chief Justice of *England*, saying, By that, if she asked you, What haste? You might know it was her pleasure to defer it, and therefore you to do it without her commandment was a great offence. Then spake *Gawdie*, the Queen's Serjeant: My Lords, four things I note that Mr. *Davison* confesseth; first, that her Majesty bade him use secrecy; next, the Warrant being sealed, Mr. *Killegrew* was sent unto him, that were it not sealed already, it should not be sealed at all. Thirdly, he confesseth her Majesty was content he should shew it Mr. *Walsingham*, which proves she minded to keep it from the rest. And it had been his duty to have known her pleasure; and therefore for so much as he confesseth this,

Though the above Trial of Mr. *Davison* is very full, yet, as the underwritten one, copied from a MS. in the *Bodleian Library*, under the Title *Juridici*, 7843. 862. *pag.* 235. being something different, taken by an Eye-witness, and being short, we hope it will prove acceptable to the Reader, especially as it relates to the Treasons of *Mary* Queen of *Scots*; whose Trial in Vol. I. pag. 135. is very defective.

Ex MS. penes Robertus Sherrell, } 28 Martii 1587.

THE Proceedings against Mr *Davison* in the *Star-Chamber*, by Commission not read, but directed to these thirteen following

1. The Lord Chief Justice of *England*, as Lord Privy-Seal for that day.
2. The Lord Archbishop of *Canterbury*.
3. The Lord Archbishop of *York*.
4. The Earl of *Worcester*.
5. The Earl of *Cumberland*.
6. The Earl of *Lincoln*.
7. The Lord *Gray*.
8. The Lord *Lumley*
9. Sir *James A-Croft* *.

[* In the above Trial, called *Croft*. But in the Trial of the Earl of *Arundel*, 1589, he is called *A-Croft*. See State Trials, Vol. I. p. 157.]

10. Sir *Walter Mildmay*.
11. The Master of the Rolls.
12. The Lord Chief Baron
13. The Lord *Anderson*.

The sum of that which was proposed, and enforced against him by her Majesty's Counsellors at the Law

The matter laid against him is a great and heinous indignity, as her Majesty taketh it, committed by him in this last proceeding against the late *Scotish* Queen, which although it were in itself most just and honourable, yet in the manner of dealing concerning it, Mr. *Davison* is charged by her Majesty with want of Duty, &c. For whereas by the manifold defects of the said *S.* Queen, and that in the judgment of all the Realm in Parliament her life was now to satisfy the Law, and thus necessary for the preservation of the whole Realm, as was shewed; yet her Majesty, of her natural most gracious and merciful disposition, after the so honourable condition and proclamation of the *S.* Queen's guiltiness, notwithstanding so many important allegations and vehement intercessions, could not be brought to condescend to the execution; rather desiring by all means possible, if there were any hope of amendment and reclaim, to spare where she might honourably spill, than to spill where she might honourably spare; and in this mind she continued from *October* to the end of *January*. But when she saw that her malicious enemies daily increased their wicked attempts against her and the state, that rumours were spread and information given daily of attempts by invasion, by rebellions, by violence upon her Royal Person, to work a change and delivery of the said *S.* Queen, she most wisely resolved at length to have a bill or instrument, signed according to Law and Justice, in a readiness, whereby upon all occasions or occurrences, she might be executed: and this of special choice and trust, she thought good to commit to Mr. *Davison*, willing him to carry it to the Lord Chancellor, to have it under the Broad-Seal, but withal charged him to keep it very secret, and not to make any acquainted with it. The very same day he carried it to the seal, and the next day after having received charge from her Majesty, by the Lord-Admiral, that it should be stayed, if it was not sealed, but he declared it was sealed the day before, &c. whereto the Queen reply'd, What needs that haste? The next Day after this, (which was, I think, on *Candlemas*-Day) my Lord Treasurer asked him, If he knew what mind the Queen had towards the execution? He answered, To have it go forward; and so shewed it to him, and after to the rest of the Council, procuring their Warrant down to present execution, the Queen having

this, I take it to be a great Contempt, Indignity and Miſpriſion for him to ſay his Intent was good; he thought it ſo, is no Anſwer. Fourthly, Her Majeſty told him, ſhe thought of ſome other Courſe to be taken, and he gave her no Anſwer; beſides, he confeſſeth he told the Lords it was her Majeſty's Pleaſure upon ſuch a Demand made. *Daviſon* anſwered, that general Demand was made. *Gawdie* reply'd here, it is the Lord Treaſurer's Teſtimony. *Daviſon* rejoined, let me have right; it was but privately demanded between my Lord-Treaſurer and me. I will not ſpeak in Excuſe, but only to anſwer; I demand, whether the imparting of it to the Council be ſuch a Contempt: farther, there is Difference between an expreſs Commandment, and an imply'd Speech. The Loſs of my Place, I do not eſteem, neither weigh I this Diſgrace; only her Majeſty's Diſfavour is the Thing that grieves me. Then *Puckering* the Queen's Serjeant began to ſpeak, aggravating *Daviſon's* Offence, and forward to accuſe, and yet ſeemed more *pro forma tantum*, than of any matter he had to charge him withal, more than had been ſpoken of before. Whereupon *Daviſon* anſwered, All this ſpeech is anſwered, but that I made her not privy; whereto I ſay, I made her not privy in reſpect my Lords of the Council thought it not neceſſary, becauſe it was not fit ſhe ſhould be privy to the Execution. I will not ſtand upon Terms, as I ſay, for it becomes me not, but ſubmit myſelf to your Honours Cenſures.

Then ſaid *Wraye*, Mr. *Daviſon*, to ſay it was irrevocable you are deceived, for ſhe might do it at her Pleaſure. Then ſaid *Daviſon*, I beſeech you, my Lords, make Means to her Majeſty that I may have her Favour; and for the reſt, I wave it not. Whereupon *Wraye* willed Sir *Walter Mildmay* to deliver his Opinion; who began in Form following.

How honourable her Majeſty, our gracious Sovereign, hath dealt in all Juſtice, is known to all the World, againſt ſuch Traytors, by whom her Life ſhould have been taken away; whereupon ſhould enſue, Subverſion to the whole State, upon the Proceedings whereof it appeared that the *Scotiſh* Queen was chief Author, dealing moſt ingratefully againſt her, who before Time had ſaved her from them that vehemently ſought her Deſtruction. And notwithſtanding that her Majeſty might have proceeded againſt her as a private Perſon, yet ſhe granted her Commiſſion to great Perſons to hear what ſhe could alledge in her Defence. And albeit that upon the hearing thereof ſhe was declared to be guilty, yet none could think Execution might be done without her Majeſty's expreſs aſſent. Then he dilated of the Proceedings of Parliament, the Petition, her Anſwer thereunto, wherein he noted her Wiſdom in not being haſty in ſo high a Matter; he ſhewed farther, how ſhe was contented to hear Ambaſſadors, if they could propound any Thing in her Defence. Afterward followed the Proclamation to notify the Proceedings paſſed unto the People; for People, ſaid he, be deſirous to hear of State-matters, and I warrant you itch to underſtand what we do here: herein, ſaid he, was Juſtice, Mercy, and Diſcretion. Afterwards, upon the . . . . . and cries, ſhe thought it neceſſary to look unto it; upon this ſhe ſealed her Warrant, yet continuing her former clemency, not to put it in Execution; for as it was in her to grant that it ſhould be done, ſo ſhe might ſtay and defer it; which ſhe ſo meaning, it behoved her to truſt ſomebody, and ſo, ſaid he, ſhe did this Gentleman, called unto her ſervice upon Truſt, who, for the Acquaintance that I have had with him, was worthy of that Place. This Truſt ſhe committed unto him, and I am ſorry, ſaid he, he was not in this ſo good a Servant as in all other Things. Surely he had notable Cautions, not to have preſumed in ſo great a Matter to have done any Thing without her Commandment. His Offence, ſaid he, I interpret in two degrees; an abuſe to the Truſt, and the Contempt: for the firſt ſhe willed him to tell it Mr. *Walſingham*, and it is no Excuſe to ſay, ſhe forbad you not the reſt: for you ought not to have told it unto any but whom ſhe would. Alſo, which aggravates your Offence, you told the Lords ſhe was pleaſed. For the Contempt, the Writ was not delivered unto you, but had it not been delivered unto them to whom it was directed, then had it been a Commandment. Your good Intention was no Anſwer, neither ought my Lords to allow of it, albeit *per* Caſe I could allow it, becauſe I know you. Alſo your fault is the greater, which you know. Farther, you were near her, and had Time convenient to ſhew her; hereof ſaid he, hath followed a greater Miſchief to the Queen's Majeſty, which may turn to all our Hindrance, foraſmuch as our Welfare depends upon her well-doing. Next, ſaid he, hath followed a Diſhonour to her Majeſty, that ſhe having governed this Land ſo long Time in all Obedience, a Servant of hers in this Age, ſhould have ſo ſmall Regard. Now for my Opinion of the Offence, it reſteth to conſider what Puniſhment is behoveful in ſuch a Caſe. Puniſhments in this Court are either corporal, or pecuniary; pecuniary, by Fines impoſed upon Offenders; and corporal, by Puniſhments and ſuch like. Now, ſaid he, if the Fine ſhould be *ſecundum quantitatem delicti*, I think he ſhould not bear it; for I know his Eſtate. Surely leſs than ten thouſand Marks may not be ſufficient, which tho' it be too great for his Ability, yet is it too little for his Fault. The Qualification, wherefore, reſteth in them where I doubt not he ſhall find Favour; next he muſt ſuffer Impriſonment during her Majeſty's Pleaſure, which muſt be reſerved to her merciful Mitigation.

And after him ſpake *Manwood* the chief Baron, who in the Beginning of his Tale took ſo large a Scope, as many did judge he would be tedious, as he was indeed. Firſt, he declared how in the very Beginning the Queen of *Scots* bewrayed her Malice againſt the Crown of this Land when ſhe was Queen of *France*, at which Time ſhe made Letters Patents as Queen of *England*; ſhe uſurped her Majeſty's Stile, and ſhe quartered the Arms of *England*. Then he deſcended unto her doings when ſhe was Dowager; how ſhe excuſed her former offences by reaſon of coverture: then he declared her marriage with the Lord *Darnley*; the Murder of her Huſband, the Practices with the Biſhop of *Roſs*; her Conſpiracy with the Duke of *Norfolk*. To conclude, he couched the whole Hiſtory which any Way concerned her Life or Manners. At laſt he came to Mr. *Daviſon's* Offence, which he took in Law to be a Miſpriſion; and yet not every Commandment of the Prince tranſgreſſed, is a Miſpriſion: But, ſaid he, when one is put in Truſt in a Point of Juſtice, which is the Government of the Common-weal, there a Commandment tranſgreſſed is a Miſpriſion. For Example whereof, he cited a caſe there in that Place decided; meaning Sir *John Throgmorton's* Caſe, as many deemed. Alſo, ſaid he, if a Sheriff exerciſe his Office without an Oath, that is a Miſpriſion. And, ſaid he, if one have Power by Law to do a Thing, if he prevent the Time wherein it ought to be done, that is a Miſpriſion. And if a Judge for Expedition of Juſtice ſhould ſit in Judgment before the Term, that is Miſpriſion. Now, ſaid he, this is a Miſpriſion, becauſe you prevented the Time in doing it before you were commanded, altho' the Thing were lawful; for you did *juſtum*, but not *juſte*. Farther, by naming Mr. *Walſingham* in Specialty, it was a ſecluding the reſt in generality. And alſo, if the Warrant were ſealed, yet was it not lawful to kill her, becauſe the direction was ſpecial, and not general. So then he concluded, the contempt was great, and the puniſhment aſſeſſed by Sir *Walter Mildmay* worthily deſerved, whereunto he agreed.

After him, ſpake *Anderſon*, Chief Juſtice, who ſaid, The Proceeding had been honourable, which he would not ſpeak of, being known unto all men, and having been ſpoke to before. But to come to the caſe in queſtion; in the accuſation, ſaid he, be two parts, firſt, that Mr. *Daviſon*, without her Majeſty's commandment ſent it down; and the ſecond, that againſt her commandment he made the Lords privy. For the firſt, he confeſſed; to the ſecond he ſaith ſhe bade him uſe ſecrecy. The cauſes alledged by him are good, and yet the proceeding therein, that which cauſed the offence, the words, *uſe ſecrecy*, and not to cauſe it to be publiſhed or known to any. Then he being one of her Majeſty's Council,

---

having not notice nor knowledge of this; and after, when ſhe conferred with him about another courſe to be taken, he concealed from her what had been done therein. Theſe chief matters were proved by his own confeſſion in an examination before taken and urged againſt him, both in reſpect of himſelf being bound to eſpecial obedience, not only as a ſubject, but as a ſervant, a counſellor, a ſecretary ſo much truſted, and yet not to keep ſecret, where ſpecial charge was given him; and in reſpect of the Queen, ſo good and gracious a Prince, ſo well deſerving of him, the fountain and head of all juſtice and authority amongſt us, and yet not to be made privy of the doing of ſuch an act of ſo great a quality and importance as that was, wherein ſhe had ſhewed herſelf always, (and that moſt apparently) whereof Mr. *Daviſon* could not be ignorant, both backward and unwilling to yield to that which all her Realm deſired and ſued for at her Hands; yet Mr. *Daviſon*, contrary to her known mind, procured with ſuch haſte (of what good purpoſe in himſelf, this would not regard), but with apparent want of duty to his Sovereign, which did more appear in his concealing his proceedings when ſhe purpoſely talked with him of that matter as aforeſaid; all which they left to the Counſellors to judge of.

Mr. Daviſon's *Anſwer for himſelf.*

NOtwithſtanding at the bar, whither he was brought by his keeper, Sir *Owen Hopton*, being faint by reaſon of his late ſickneſs, and carrying his left arm in a ſcarf, benumbed I think by his late taken palſy, he ſpake ſomewhat faintly, unaudibly; tho' being required by his Commiſſioners to ſpeak higher, yet deſired favour to ſpeak as he could, which was to this effect: Firſt, proteſting that he was not guilty to himſelf of any wilful diſloyalty, or breach of duty, but that he did always ſince his firſt employment in her Majeſty's ſervice, endeavour to bear himſelf moſt ſerviceable and unblameable; and he took therein her Majeſty's own ſelf and God to witneſs; confeſſing alſo, that his ſkill and experience was not yet great in this latter kind of ſervice, whereto he was without his ſuit and above his expectation called; and for the matter proteſting alſo, that he would not for any danger, no not preſent death, in juſtifying himſelf, diſcloſe any private ſpeech or commandment that paſſed betwixt her Majeſty and him; nor would he by any means enter into any affirmation or avowing, which could not ſtand with his dutiful regard to her Majeſty's honour, &c. but would admit all that againſt him: and farther, that he would not in any part diſclaim my Lord Treaſurer's reports or teſtimony againſt him. But to the matters, he anſwered, firſt, That he was ſorry that a fact of that importance and neceſſity, ſo honourable and profitably for the Commonwealth, ſhould be ſo heavily taken againſt him; wherein he might take it on his ſoul, that he did nothing but that which in his underſtanding might be agreeable to her mind, neither did he otherwiſe conceive of her meaning and purpoſe; and that upon theſe inducements:

First, the conſideration of the thing itſelf, ſo juſt, ſo neceſſary, ſo honourable, ſo vehemently ſued for by the whole Realm. Secondly, in conſideration of her Majeſty, ſo gracious and wiſe a Prince, ſo loving and careful of her Subjects and Commonwealth; and more ſtrongly in conſideration of her words, which ſhe uſed at the firſt delivery of the bill, *Now you have it, let me be troubled no more with it.* Beſides the ſufficiency and perfectment of the ſaid inſtruments for the ſaid purpoſe, which was had by her directions, *viz.* as under the Great-Seal, all which were in his underſtanding proof enough what her meaning was, neither was there any apparent and direct countermand, without the which he took that inſtrument to be irrevocable. For the charge of ſecrecy, he conceived her meaning was, that it ſhould be kept from the common and publick knowledge only; for ſhe being a Prince ſo wiſe, did in his judgement conſider what violent attempts the favourites of the *S.* Queen might by likelihood offer in that deſperate plunge, if it ſhould be known that ſuch a Warrant was ſigned for her execution, and not from her Council. For her Majeſty's ſelf after willed in his way to the Lord Chancellor, to impart it to Sir *Francis Walſingham*, that then lay ſick at his houſe at *London*; herſelf made my Lord-Admiral privy to it, in ſending him to ſtay the Seal *ut ſupra*, and my Lord-Chancellor by ſealing muſt needs have ſome knowledge of it; and then why ſhould he think the Council ſhould not know it, being Privy-Counſellors and Counſellors of Eſtate, if he imparted it to none but to my Lord-Treaſurer, and he to the reſt, and that excuſably in regard of the great credit and truſt that her Majeſty uſually repoſeth in my Lord-Treaſurer for matter of greateſt moment and weight. Secondly, for ſending down the Warrant, he did it not without the opinion of the Council, and

cil, the fault is bad; and it is the worse, because by her saying what haste, he might gather what her intent was. Mr. *Davison* saith, he excuseth it by love to the Commonweal, which a man may term blind love, which is no excuse, but it remaineth a Contempt, and a Contempt is a Misprision; and yet is not every Misprision a Contempt? If a man do a thing without a warrant, it is a Contempt; and so he concluded this to be a great offence worthy the punishment inflicted upon him: and so ended.

After him spake the Master of the Rolls, agreeing with the censures of them that spake before; and that Mr. *Davison*'s great Zeal made him forget his duty. also saying, that the point did rest, whether he did know it was her Majesty's pleasure it should be stayed, which, said he, appeareth by his own confession; and therefore, in fine, he agreed with the former censures.

Next spake Sir *James Croft*, who said not very much, and yet spake somewhat: that he loved the man well, and so had cause, saying, that he had no lack of good-will; but yet had grievously offended. So he subscribed in opinion to the former judgement.

After him spake the Lord *Lumley*, who divided the offence into two parts. First, The neglect of his duty; and secondly, The breaking of his duty: saying further, that the Judges had told the law, and we must believe them, that it is within the compass of a Contempt. The matter, said he, is evident: for first, her unwillingness in the Parliament was a signification of her mind, which he let slip. And farther, in saying, that she was of that mind still, surely you spake without the book, which was a very bold part; for you ought to have told them how dutiful it was; yet, Sir, you took a worse course, that such a high matter by your persuasions, as it should seem, should be done without her privity. Why said he, what an abuse of the Counsellors was this? Surely a great abuse! and if it were a fault against them, much more against her Majesty: this is one of the highest offences, by my trowth, (for so he sware) that ever subject did against the Prince; and tho' you were my brother and heir (before God I speak it), I think the punishment too little; yet with no offence to you, but for the quality of your fault. But, I say, had a greater fine been imposed upon you, I would easily have agreed thereunto.

After him spake my Lord *Gray*; who said, Two points were spoken of: the first, touching the Queen of *Scots*; and the next, Mr. *Davison*'s offence. For the first, said he, it is largely discoursed: for the last, my good Lords, let me crave your farther examination. His offence is made the more for divers circumstances; the first circumstance is, for that it was for execution of a Queen; but what Queen? Surely such a Queen as practised most horrible treasons against our sovereign Queen! such a Queen, as conspired the overthrow of the whole State! yea, such a Queen, that sought the subversion of Christ's true Religion, to bring our souls headlong to the devil! So then, my Lords, the taking away such a Queen, can no way aggravate his fate. The second circumstance is, his breach of secrecy, which he excuseth, that he told it but to the chief Counsellors: whereas Mr. *Walsingham*, my Lord-Admiral and Lord-Chancellor, either by necessity, or commandment from her Majesty, did know it undoubtedly. Whatsoever my Lords before me have thought; his answer in the behalf doth satisfy me, so I am resolved. For the third point, she asking what haste? and he afterwards, to send it down without her privity, here, even here, is the full proof of the Contempt; here is that, that causes the offence, which he seemeth to acknowledge, yet with two considerations: the first, the seditious tumults within the Realm; the next, advertisements from *Ireland*, and beyond the seas. Now, my Lords, must not these considerations move him rather to put himself in her Majesty's mercy by dealing without her commandment, than commit her Majesty to the mercy of her foes by obeying her? For had that other thing happened (which God forbid), that her Majesty would have miscarried, and then this Warrant signed and sealed had been found in Mr. *Davison*'s hands, wanting nothing but execution, should we not then have judged him a traytor? should we not have torn and rent him asunder? Surely, my Lords, I should then have thought him more worthy of ten thousand deaths, than now of the least punishment that may be inflicted upon him; for each of us, in preservation of our Country, ought to lose our lands, our livings, and sacrifice our bodies; howbeit, I excuse not his offence, neither do I agree it as a Contempt, and I agree with the punishment; and yet I think his fault proceeded from a very good zeal he bore unto his Country: and I pray God, that that peculiar ornament of pity and compassion wherewith her Majesty is singular, may be so extended towards him, that all good subjects, by his example, may neglect their own private hindrance or disgrace in respect of the furtherance of the Weal publick.

After him spake the Earl of *Lincoln*, who, for his opinion, thought it was but negligently done, and not contemptuously; but had it been done in contempt, he would have then thought Fine and Imprisonment no sufficient punishment for an offence of that quality; yet the Offence being as it is, for company, said he, I agree to the Fine: but in mine opinion it is too much, saving that I know her Majesty is merciful: and for the rest, I agree with my Lord *Gray*.

The Earl of *Cumberland* repeated the case, neither aggravating nor denying the offence, but briefly concluded, he agreed in opinion with Sir *Walter Mildmay*.

And the Earl of *Worcester* said nothing, saving that he was of the same mind with Mr. Chancellor, that spake first.

After him spake the Archbishop of *York*, speaking, as he was, like a Bishop, rather than a Judge, to decide a matter which did concern the State; for he inveighed against Mr. *Davison*'s offence by places of Scripture: Obedience, said he, is the only virtue, and Disobedience the contrary, and God requireth nothing else but obedience. St. *Paul* saith, *Let every soul be subject unto the higher powers*, &c. And when *Joshua* was appointed Ruler over *Israel*, the People said, *They would obey him in all things.* If then they ought to obey a Prince in all things, much more in those things which be good. I am sorry, said he, for Mr *Davison*, for he did it neither wittingly nor willingly, as I think certainly, but of a good mind to cut off our common enemy: that it was a good deed, must needs be confessed; but that it was not well done, must needs be granted.

To

---

and therefore no presumption in him; and in his own judgment, he had sufficient warrant so to do by the first delivery of it from the Queen herself. Then considering the troublesome rumours that were then abroad, and that information came daily from *Ireland* and *Wales* of forces of people in arms, and the report scattered abroad that *Fotheringay-Castle* was broken, the prisoners gone, that *London* was fired, and her Majesty made away, amongst these terrors what should I do? Did I not that which any honest man and good subject would do in such a case? Further, it is not custom in court that particularities should trouble her Majesty in the execution of any such bills: but when she hath given, by her Royal assent, warrant, authority and life to it, the rest for the manner and means of execution is left to the Council; and for all other circumstances of time, when; of place, where; of persons, by whom; especially in this cause when her Majesty had said expresly that she would not be troubled any more with it. Thirdly, for the not imparting of it to her upon her communication with him, &c. 'I had it by me five or six Weeks before 'she spake any thing more of it, and was very unwilling to trouble her 'any more with it, especially remembring her words.'

This was the effect of his defence, not uttered continuately, as I have set it down, but interruptly to the particulars as they were objected, in much more forcibly large and choice terms; but I think that I have not left out any thing of weight. After this, the Commissioners began to speak *judiciously* unto the matter, whose Speeches I will by way of abridgement note, where any thing was spoken different from others, and especially notable; for most of them had the same beginning of the *Scotish* Queen's demerits, &c.

The first that spoke was Sir Walter Mildmay.

He handled eloquently the great causes the Queen had to deal severely with the *S.* Queen, and the importance of the Parliament thereto, and her Majesty's patience in forbearing, her wisdom in being willing, her natural and accustomable clemency in being slow; and compared her slackness with Mr. *Davison*'s haste, tho' he knew her mind herein very well. Then he shewed, that such things might not in any wise be extorted from Princes, and that persuasions and entreaties are the uttermost that subjects can offer, for the Prince's Heart is in God's hand to dispose of. As for the Council, it is known that no Prince's Counsellors are farther made privy to any thing, than that it pleaseth the Prince, and oftentimes that is imparted to one that is concealed from another with great cause; and therefore you should not presume farther than you had express leave, much less to have been an encouragement to the rest to proceed therein upon your own opinion. howsoever your desire was for the end good and honest, especially seeing there hath not been the like example. So he concluded that the punishment should not be in regard to the man's ability, but to the quantity of the Crime committed, (by his judgment) ten thousand marks, and imprisonment during her Majesty's pleasure. To which all after agreed.

2. *Sir* Roger Manhode, *Lord Chief-Baron.*

The second, shewed at large the *Scotish* Queen's perpetual evil mind to our Queen, to bereave her of her Crown in her life-time, as her usurping the Arms and Stile of *England* in possession, when she was first (out of the shell) married into *France*, her dissembling of it in her Widowhood, by laying the fault upon her late husband, and yet then seeking to be proclaimed Heir apparent in the life of her eldest sister, (for she never called her dear sister) which was a dangerous step to her purpose. After, in her second marriage, her bloodiness in consenting to her husband's murder, and upon that, flight and deprivation; her protection here by our Queen not only in life, but in honour, yet her assenting to the purposes of the Duke of *Norfolk*; and yet after that, tho' then our Queen would not suffer her for that to be touched, nor any way disabled, as many would have had her, not only agreeing to traitorous plots, but also complotting with them, and therein going beyond them all, so as we could never be in quiet, but we had a *Somervile*, and then an *Alden*, then a *Throckmorton*, then a *Parry*, and now lately *Abington* and *Babington*; her Majesty at length was forced to use a little severity with her accustomed mercy, and one ounce of one with ten of the other. For even in this proceeding against her, she might have been by the Statute of *Edward* III. by a Jury of Esquires and Gentlemen, attainted and burned, and her blood corrupt; yet her Majesty did chuse by a new order to deal more honourably with her. Then he came to this fact of Mr. *Davison*'s, which he amplified by the consideration of her Majesty's mind in all this, proceeding as the other did before: the thing he took to be Misprision and Contempt in our Law, punishable by Fine and Imprisonment; and he said, that Misprision and Contempt is to do any thing contrary to, or besides the Prince's commandment in point of Justice, not in other things; as Justices of *Westminster* to sit out of Term, to raze Indictments or Records; and so he gave other examples, as in the Ministers of the Law, *viz.* Sheriffs to execute their offices, to return Knights to the Parliament without their Oaths. So this thing then being so high a point of Justice, was not in any respect to be done otherwise than her Majesty's express commandment would bear, especially not with such haste, when she expresly declared her mind to the contrary; wherein Mr. *Davison* may seem by this haste, if her Majesty had any other purpose, to have prevented her, and God might otherwise have turned her mind; for it is not strange to hear of mutation in her Majesty in respect of this, as in the execution of the Duke of *Norfolk*, day and day was appointed, and often her Majesty declared her unwillingness and lothfulness to have put him to death, if otherwise the law might have been satisfied. The commandment to impart it to Sir *Francis Walsingham* in especiality, was an excluding the rest in generality; and farther, which he told my Lord-Treasurer could not be gathered of her Majesty's words, but rather the contrary; and the instrument was not so peremptory and irrevocable as he took it, nor a sufficient Warrant for any kind of proceeding against the S. Queen, neither for the associates, nor for any other: for that Statute, besides the condition and proclamation, doth require the Queen's direction,

and

To reveal secrets was bad: for her Majesty imparts not each part of her counsel to every Counsellor; so then his offence was a disobedience, and a great fault. He alledgeth in excuse, I think, a good intention, but that excuseth not the fault: for *obedientia est melior quam sacrificium.* And St. *Paul* saith, *Non facimus malum ut inde veniat bonum.* Therefore, said he, the offence was great, too dangerous; for, in such a case, one would be twice advised, if he were either honest or wise. Last of all, he concluded he agreed with the punishment assessed, and so ended his sermon.

Then spake the Archbishop of *Canterbury*, That the matter had been opened, first, concerning the doings of the *Scottish* Queen, whom he thought, living and dead, was ordained to disturb and trouble the state of *England*. Then concerning Mr. *Davison*'s offence, Albeit, said he, that which is done could be wished to be otherwise done, yet none I hope could wish it undone, whatsoever he did, in my opinion, said he, he did it in the superabundant zeal of Religion unto her Majesty, and love to the Commonwealth. These be great arguments, said he, and yet no excuse: for *modus non factum efficit culpam*; altho' the act were good, yet can I not excuse him in the circumstance, howbeit, said he, the mercy in the Prince in deferring it was severe, for there is a severe mercy, as well as a merciful severity: for it is written, *He slew* Og *the king of* Basan, *for his mercy endureth for ever.* Yet, said he, mercy in a Prince is not to be restrained; and therefore, because the example may be dangerous hereafter, that Counsellors may presume to do without the commandment of the Prince, which is a mischief more intolerable than an inconveniency; therefore I agree to that punishment which is before agreed.

Last of all spake *Wraye*, Chief Justice, who shewed the Cause, and said farther, That to every Contempt a commandment was not necessary, which in my opinion was needful to be proved; for, said he, the Bishop of *Winchester* came to the Parliament, and afterwards departed without licence, and therefore had a grievous Fine set upon him. Myself, said he, am a Justice of the King's Bench; in the Term we hear of matters of Treason, by the reason of our office; and out of the Term, by Commission of *Oyer* and *Terminer* associate with others: if, said he, a Commission should be directed unto me and others of *Oyer* and *Terminer* for a matter of Treason, and we should arraign the Person, and adjudge him to die, yet would I not put him to execution; and yet the Commission is to hear and determine. Surely, I think you meant well, and it was *bonum*, but not *bene*. Finally, he agreed the punishment should be as it was first of all assessed. But farther, said he, I must tell you, that forsomuch as the fault is yours, it declares her Majesty's sincerity, and not privity in this action, and that she is offended therewithal. Farther, my Lords, I must signify unto you from her Majesty, that forasmuch as the Lords of the Council were abused by Mr. *Davison*'s relation, in telling them she was pleased, and that which they did was for her safety, upon his wrong information, the Lords be sorrowful because they were abused by him; therefore her Majesty imputeth no fault to any of the Counsellors, but only to him; and the rest she doth disburthen of all blame.

This said; Mr. *Davison* craved leave to demand one question, and make one petition.

For your question, said *Wraye*, I think it was never the order in this Court, after the matter is heard judicially, to answer any question, (which Sir *Walter Mildmay* affirmed;) but for your petition you may speak.

Truly, my Lords, said *Davison*, my question shall be such as in your own conscience shall seem reasonable.

Whereat they neither gave him leave nor denied him.

Whereupon *Davison* said, If this Warrant, being signed and sealed, and left with me, and wanting nothing but execution, it should have fortuned her Majesty should have miscarried, whether then—

Nay, said *Wraye* and *Mildmay*, now you enter into that which is discussed already: yea, said *Manwood*, that question was moved by my Lord *Gray*.

Well then, said *Davison*, I will not seek for present enlargement of my liberty, nor release of my imprisonment, altho' my body be not well able to endure it; only let your Honours clear me, I beseech you, of all blemish of dishonesty, and be mediators for me, that I remain not in her Majesty's disfavour and disgrace: for I protest I shall be contented with any condition and state of life whatsoever, if I may have her Majesty's favour.

Whereunto the Lords universally answered, he spake like a good subject. And so the Court arose *.

---

and that must be either general, that all men may do it, which is not here granted; or particular, who, or by what means: neither is there here any such, especially her Majesty having no knowledge of the thing done. Further, she was the Queen's prisoner, and therefore no man might pretend to take her away, or deliver her without special privity from the Queen: and lastly, he shewed, that the good intent was no warrant to transgress duty; whereof he put a case or two, as where Judgment of death is given against one, and the Sheriff, for that he is a notorious thief or traytor, will hang him presently, before the Justice depart out of town.

3. Lord *Anderson*.

He noted a difference in law between Misprision and Contempt, that one was larger than the other, and both in point of Justice, and might be when the Warrant of a Justice, or a Commissioner's Letter in such matters is not directly and straitly observed; and urged, that a Secretary should be secret, and that it was his duty to have an express commandment.

4. Sir *Gibert Gerrard*, Master of the Rolls.

He handled the same matter that before is spoken by others, but somewhat otherwise.

5. Sir *James A-Croft*.

He shewed his mind indifferently, with protestations of his good-will and good-opinion of the man; that it was a rare example, and committed, as he thought, for want of experience more than for want of duty.

6. Lord *Lumley*.

He was somewhat sharp. Such Commissions of execution are sent to Sheriffs; you, no Sheriff, ought to be very particular for such great personages; you had no more Commission than I, *&c.* and of likelihood you have hereby prevented other good purposes, which God might have put into her Majesty's Mind, and herein you have seduced so many grave Counsellors, *&c.* If you were my brother, I would think ten times so much to be little enough, *&c.*

7. Lord *Gray*.

He proposed very vehemently the great exigence the good Gentleman was in at that time. My good Lords, consider, quoth he, and call to mind in what case we were daily, there came advertisement of forces come and arrived in *Ireland*, in *Wales*, advertisements from abroad, from our Provinces at home, even within fifteen miles of this City, of rising, firing, breaking up holders, yea of the destruction of her Majesty's Royal Person: if otherwise than well had come to her Majesty's Royal Person, which of us would not have run to him, and torn him with our hands? My Lords, why should *Davison* be more zealous and forward for his Prince than we? After he replyed to that of my Lord Chief Baron, that the telling of Sir *Francis Walsingham* did not exclude the rest, as he proved, but rather implied and presupposed that the rest should know it. for without this especial information, he being sick in his house, and so absent from the Court, could not in any due time have knowledge of it. After he agreed to the Punishment, but wish'd that her Majesty should have compassion on him to encourage others that were zealous to deserve well of her and the State, and so he ended. *Vulgique secutum ultima murmur erat.*

8. Earl of *Lincoln* said little to the purpose.

9. Earl of *Cumberland* was very short.

10. Earl of *Worcester* was short, and as before.

11. Archbishop of *York* discoursed theologically of the necessity and worthiness of the virtue of Obedience, even strictly to Princes in all things: and that *non faciendum malum ut inde veniat bonum*, adding the difference between *bonum* and *bene*, (as before my Lord Chief-Justice of *justum* and *juste*, which I forgot afore to relate) and good intents do not make the fact excusable, and that he ought to have a direct, express, and iterated command; whereto he cited a Rule out of Civil Law, (wherein he said he was so found and conversant) to this purpose, If the Prince commanded *aliquid magnum de libera, tenta si persistat, & habe secundam jussionem*: he concluded, he did agree to the punishment, but was sorry that Mr. *Davison*, of whom he had heard so well, should fall into this cause, he could not help it; a wiser man might have been led with zeal, and none of us would have it undone.

12. Archbishop of *Canterbury*, having said first somewhat of her who troubled us all both alive and dead, and theologically of *misericordia puniens*, as out of the *Psalm*, where God plagueth the enemy of his Church, for his mercy endureth for ever; for this present matter, he said, *non factum sed modus* was in question, a thing done, as he thought, unfeignedly of zeal, and that which might have been better done in consideration of her Majesty's purpose to forbear her death, which could not be unknown to Mr. *Davison*; for such things are by no means to be wrested from Princes, God will extraordinarily move their hearts, and when it shall be most for his glory. This example, he said, might be dangerous and inconvenient hereafter; and therefore he concluded it rather a mischief than an inconvenience, and so agreed to the punishment.

13. *Wraye*, Lord Chief-Justice. He, as Chief, concluded the matter, and pronounced Judgement judicially upon the grounds alledged before of others, which he enforced, *&c.* And after, as from her Majesty, spake somewhat to justify her proceedings in all these matters, and to declare that she did not for this impute any fault to her Council, for that they were misled by this man's undue suggestions.

Mr. *Davison* submitted himself to the Judgement of the Queen's mercy, and requested that he might propose a question, which he took upon his credit to be such as they would not dislike, and therefore he had leave; and a request. His question was, If this being in my hands, her Majesty had miscarried, what should have become of me? To this, Sir *Walter Mildmay* and my Lord Chief-Baron answered, that my Lord *Gray* had moved it already. His request was not for mitigation of his fine, nor for enlargement of prison, altho' he could never in all his life worse bear it than now; much less for his former estate: but only that he might, with her Majesty's favour, enjoy any condition whatsoever, requesting them to be intercessors for this. Nothing to this was said, but they arose and departed.

'These I am sure are the principal matters by any of them uttered, so 'far as by myself, or by my conference I could recall to mind.'

Ex Autographo Gulielmi Nutti, *qui oculatus testis adfuit.*

* *Davison* thus excused himself in an apologetical Discourse of his to *Walsingham*: The Queen, says he, after the departure of the *French* and *Scotish* Ambassadors, of her own motion, commanded me to deliver her the Warrant for executing the sentence against the Queen of *Scots*. When I had delivered it, she signed it readily with her own hand: when she had so done, she commanded it to be sealed with the Great Seal of *England*; and in jesting manner said, Go tell all this to *Walsingham*, who is now sick, altho' I fear he will die for sorrow when he hears it. She added also the reasons of her deferring it so long, namely, lest she might seem to have been violently or maliciously drawn thereto; whereas in the mean time she was not ignorant how necessary it was: moreover, she blamed *Pawlet* and *Drury*, that they had not eased her of this care, and wished that *Walsingham* would feel their pulses touching this matter. The next day after it was under the Great-Seal, she commanded me, by *Killegrew*, that it should not be done: and when I had informed her that it was done already, she found fault with such great haste; telling me, that in the judgment of some wise men, another course might be taken. I answered, that that course was always best and safest which was most just. But fearing lest she would lay the fault upon me, (as she had laid the putting of the Duke of *Norfolk* to death upon the Lord *Burleigh*) I acquainted *Hatton* with the whole matter, protesting that I would not plunge myself any deeper in so great a business. He presently imparted it to the Lord *Burleigh*, and the Lord [illegible] to the rest of the Council, who all consented to have the execution hastened, and every one of them vowed to bear an equal share in the blame, and sent *Beal* away with the Warrant and Letters. The third day after, when by a dream she was told of the Queen of *Scots'* death, I perceived that she wavered in her resolution, I asked her, whether she had changed her mind? She answered, No; but another course, said she, might have been devised. And withal she asked me, whether I had received any answer from *Pawlet*? Whose Letter when I had shewed her, wherein he flatly refused to undertake that which stood not with honour and justice, she waxing angry, accused him and others (who had bound themselves by the Association) of perjury and

and breach of their vow, as those that had promised great matters for their Prince's safety, but would perform nothing; yet there are, said she, who will do it for my sake. But I shewed her how dishonourable and unjust a thing this would be; and withal into how great danger she would bring *Pawlet* and *Drury* by it: for if she approved the fact, she would draw upon herself both danger and dishonour, not without censure of injustice; and if she disallowed it, she would utterly undo men of great desert, and their whole posterity. And afterwards she gave me a light check the same day that the Queen of *Scots* was executed, because she was not yet put to death. *Camden's Eliz.* in *Kennet's* Hist. of *England*, vol. II p. 538.

Freebairn, in his Life of *Mary* Queen of *Scots*, p. 269 says, Queen *Elizabeth* sent orders to *Pawlet*, on whose obedience she could reckon with certainty, for committing of any act of barbarity to make away with his prisoner, the Queen of *Scots*; and p. 270, 271 and 272. inserts a Letter from *Walsingham* and *Davison* (her two Secretaries) to Sir *Amias Pawlet*, with his answer, which were found among Sir *Amyas Pawlet*'s Papers; a copy of which, transcribed from the originals, were sent to Dr. *Mackenzie*, by Mr. *John Urry*, of *Christ-Church College*, *Oxford*.

The LETTER *wrote to Sir* Amias Pawlet *and Sir* Drew Drury.

'AFTER our hearty commendations, we find by a Speech lately made by her Majesty, That she doth note in you both a lack of that care and zeal for her service, that she looketh for at your hands, in that you have not in all this time (of yourselves without other provocation) found out some way to shorten the life of the *Scots* Queen, considering the great peril she is hourly subject to, so long as the said Queen should live; wherein, besides a kind of lack of love towards her, she wonders greatly that you have not that care of your own particular safeties, or rather the preservation of Religion, and the publick good and prosperity of your Countries that reason and policy commandeth; especially, having so good a warrant and ground for the satisfaction of your consciences toward God, and the discharge of your credit and reputation towards the world as the oath of association, which you both have so solemnly taken and vowed; especially the matter wherewith she standeth charged, being so clearly and manifestly proved against her: and therefore she taketh it most unkindly, that men professing that love towards her that you do, should in a kind of sort for lack of the discharge of your duties, cast the burden upon her, knowing, as you do, her indisposition to shed blood; especially, of one of that sex and quality, and so near to her in blood as the said Queen is. These respects, we find, do greatly trouble her Majesty; who, we assure you, hath sundry times protested, that if the regard of the danger of her good subjects, and faithful servants, did not more move her than her own peril, she would never be drawn to assent to the shedding of her blood. We thought it meet to acquaint you with these speeches lately passed from her Majesty, referring the same to your good judgments: And so we commit you to the protection of the Almighty.

London, February the 1st, 1586. *Your most assured Friends*, Fra. Walsingham, Will. Davison.

Directed thus:

To the Right Honourable Sir *Amias Pawlet*, Knight, one of his Majesty's Privy-Council.

This Letter was received at *Fothringay*, the 2d of *February*, at five in the afternoon, and in another Letter from Mr. *Davison*, of the 1st of *February*, to Sir *Amias*, he says, *I pray you let both this and the inclosed be committed to the fire, which measure shall be likewise met to your answer, after it hath been communicated to her Majesty for her satisfaction.* And in a Postscript of another Letter from Mr. *Davison* to him, dated the 3d of February, 1686, he says, *I intreated you in my last Letters, to burn both the Letters sent you for the argument's sake; which by your answer to Mr. Secretary (which I have seen) appeareth not to be done; I pray you let me intreat to make Hereticks of the one and the other, as I mean to use yours after her Majesty hath seen it.* And in the end of the Postscript, *I pray you let me know what you have done with my Letters because they are not to be kept, that I my satisfy her Majesty therein, who might otherwise take offence thereat; and if you treat this Postscript in the same kind, I shall care not a whit.* But it seems none of them observed this; for amongst the same papers, is the following Letter to Sir *Francis Walsingham*.

'SIR,

'YOUR Letters of yesterday coming to my hands this present day, at 5 *p. m.* I would not fail, according to your direction, to return my answer with all possible speed; which I shall deliver unto you with great grief and bitterness of mind, in that I am so unhappy, as living to see this unhappy day, in which I am required by Direction from my most gracious Sovereign, to do an act which God and the law forbiddeth. My Goods and Life are at her Majesty's disposition, and I am ready to lose the next morrow, if it shall please her; acknowledging, that I do hold them as of her meer and most gracious favour, and do not deign to enjoy them but with her Highness's good liking: but God forbid I should make so foul a shipwreck of my conscience, or leave so great a blot on my poor posterity, and shed blood without law or warrant; trusting, that her Majesty, of her accustomed clemency, and the rather by your good mediation, will take this my answer in good part, as proceeding from one who never will be inferior to any Christian Subject, living in honour, love and obedience towards his Sovereign; and thus I commit you to the mercy of the Almighty.

From *Fotheringay*, the 2d of *February*, 1586. *Your most assured poor Friend*, A. PAWLET.

P. S. Your Letters coming in the plural number, seem to be meant to Sir *Drew Drury*, as to myself; and yet because he is not named in them, neither the Letter directed unto him; he forbeareth to make any particular answer, but subscribeth in heart to my opinion. D. DRURY.

V. *The Arraignment of Sir* RICHARD KNIGHTLY, *and others, in the* Star-Chamber, *for maintaining seditious Persons, Books, and Libels*; Feb. 31, 1588. 31 Eliz. *

ON *Friday* the 13th of *February*, were brought as prisoners to the Bar, before the Lords in the High-Court of *Star-Chamber*, Sir *Richard Knightly*, Mr. *Hales*, Sir —— *Wickstone* †, and his wife, whose offences hereafter follow. And first, Mr. Attorney-General *Popham* began, That the prosperous and happy state of her Majesty was not unknown unto them all that were present, and so dilated thereon, *&c.* until two enemies had chosen to disturb this quietness, *viz.* the Papists abroad, who by foreign arms, *&c.* and the seditious Sectaries at home, whereof there are leud people; next the *Brownists* and their Fellows: but Justice had been done on these men, and the law executed. But there is another sort of sectary, that are of no settled state, but seek to transform and subvert all. These men would have . . . . Government in every several Congregation, severally in each Province, in every Diocess, yea, in every Parish; whereupon would ensue more mischief than any man by tongue can utter: they themselves cannot agree among themselves, but are full of envy and emulation; for what greater emulation than to fall to contention, and from contention proceed to violence? But they stay not here, nor contented with railing against the Church and the State thereof, but proceed to Court and the Common-Weal, that all things might contribute to preserve unity among the Brethren; no law, no order left, all propriety of things taken away and confounded.

But of what sort of People are these Sectaries? Of the very vilest and basest sort, and these must make confusion of all State, and so advance themselves in their Congregations, this their course and this their purpose; so the heel should govern the head, and not the head the heel, if these men be allowed. Her Majesty, in her great wisdom duly considered the great danger of these inconveniencies, took order that no pamphlets or treatises should be put in print, but such as should be first seen and allowed; and farther, lest that were not sufficient, she ordained that no printing should be used any where but in *London*, *Oxford*, and *Cambridge*. Notwithstanding, all this served not, but they would print in corners, and spread abroad things imprinted; wherefore her Majesty set forth a proclamation in *Anno* 25. that all *Brownists* books, and such other seditious books should be suppressed and burnt. Afterwards, when their new, seditious, and infamous Libels were spread abroad, her Majesty in *February* last set forth another Proclamation, that all her Subjects might take warning. but because no reformation is had, she now holds it necessary to proceed in justice: And therefore these men, now prisoners at the Bar, but answer to their offences, and receive according to their demerits: and first for their faults. Sir *Richard Knightly* being a great man in his country, a Deputy-Lieutenant, who had the government thereof, a seditious and leud rebel came unto him to have place and entertainment with him, and there Sir *Richard* received him to print: Sir *Richard* doth confess that *Penry* told him he would set forth such a like book as he had before-time set forth for the Government of *Wales*. That book contains sedition and slander most opprobrious; and yet Sir *Richard* was contented such a like book should be printed.

But farther, Sir *Richard* sent his man a ring for a token to receive the press into his house, who did so, and there they printed *The Epitome*, *Walgrave* himself being the printer; this is a most seditious and libellous pamphlet, fit for a vice in a play, and no other: but then the Parson of the Parish having found out the printing, told Sir *Richard* that it was very dangerous; whereupon Sir *Richard* caused him to take it down; but neither disliked nor discovered it, but kept it secret, and read the books himself. Again, when it was told him that his house would be searched for the press, he said he would course them that would come to search his house, beside, at his recommendation *Walgrave* was commended unto Mr *Hales*, and there had entertainment, and there *The Supplication to the Parliament* was printed by *Walgrave*, and published by *Newman*, Sir *Richard*'s man; and another book, viz. *Have you any Work for the Cooper?* was there printed likewise. Therein the Sectaries themselves confess, that inconvenience would ensue of this Government which they so sought to establish; but yet it must be brought in, because they were so determined. And from Mr. *Hales*'s house in *Coventry*, these books and this press must be conveyed to Sir —— *Wickstone*'s, where *Martyn senior*, and *Martyn junior* were both printed; wherein these libellers say, that all laws that any way impugn this doctrine of theirs are not to be obeyed in any cause. then if this be suffered, confusion and disorder must needs ensue. But farther, in these books they affirm that the time doth offer them a great opportunity, as though all things would be suffered in this so troublesome a time, rather than they should any way be disquieted. And for Sir —— *Wickstone*, albeit he knew the press was in his house, yet he kept secret, and would never discover it, but came many times, and did visit there at the Press; and his wife, by whose procurement and persuasions with her husband, they were first received into his house, did often relieve them with meat and drink, and gave them money in their purses. This is the substance and sum of their offence, which if they will deny, uncontestable and manifest proofs shall be produced against them. And so he concluded.

Hereupon Sir *Richard Knightly* began to answer, and most humbly besought their Lordships to consider of his simple wit, and weak capacity; not able to speak in such a place, and before so honourable an Assembly: and said, that these mishaps which were now so aggravated against them, were a punishment imposed by God, to put him in mind of other his grievous crimes committed against the Majesty of the Most Highest. He affirmed constantly that he was no Sectary, but of that religion, that self-same Religion, which he hoped all they which were then present were of, and so he trusted were all other her Majesty's loving Subjects. And if he should speak any thing amiss, he desired them not to impute it to his ill disposition, but to his wants, which were many, and the more, by reason of his late imprisonment: and said, he was right glad that their Honours were ordained by God, and appointed by her Majesty to be his Judges, at whose hands he was sure to receive nothing but justice: wherefore he besought them to be an intercessor and mediator to her Majesty in his behalf, against whom, for any offence committed, or against the State, to his knowledge, he was as clear as any present, and as good a Subject as ever came to that Bar. He utterly disclaimed the books, and denied to have any familiarity to his knowledge with those that were the writers of them; and shewed that the press was brought into his house upon this reason: There was a book that before-time was printed in *Oxford*, which to his knowledge was never called in; this book was written by one Mr. *Penry*, who requested Sir *Richard* that this book might be printed again in his house, and in respect of the want of learning, which he knew to be in the Ministry, he did the rather incline an ear unto. For although he must needs confess there were in the Ministry some good, yet to his thinking, for one good, there were forty bad; yea, so bad, as he thought them not worthy to sweep the Church; and therefore his zeal for the furtherance of God's Glory caused him to allow of this book. This, as he said, was about *St. James* tide was twelve-month, and he had heard nothing thereof again until *All-hallow-tide* following; and said, that the press was never in his own house, but in a house at the farther end of the town. And he said, at *Christmas* following *Walgrave* came to him and desired the press, and said that Mr. *Cartwright* had wrote a book against the Jesuits, which he hoped to print. This is the truth, saith he.

He wrote to Mr. *Hales* to defend a house for a poor man, and this was done before the Proclamation, since which time he never meddled

* Copied from a MS. in Caius College, *Cambridge*, Class A. 1090 8 p. 206. † Neale's Hist. of Puritans, Vol. I p. [illegible]

therein, as he said; for my Lord Chancellor most honourably gave him warning to look unto that, which he hath accomplished like a good Subject to her Majesty, to whom he confesseth himself most bounden, as he thinketh all the world is beside; and now hath learned of *David*, not so much as to touch the hem of the Lord's Anointed. He hopeth her Majesty will likewise forgive him, as she hath forgiven greater offences: And besought them all to be good unto him, and he for his part would say with *Moses* and *Paul*, that he would rather desire to be wiped out of the book of life, than not perform his duty to her Majesty. And so he concluded.

Mr. *Hales* began, That albeit it were a great grief unto him to be convented before their Lordships, yet in this he joyed that they were his Judges, that were the Governors and Judges of the Land, which could and would do him nothing else but justice; he confessed the blessing of God to be exceeding great unto the Commonwealth for placing her Majesty over the same, by whose means we enjoy that peace which other nations want, and we happy that live under her: he disclaimed the books; but he had great reason as he thought to gratify Sir *Richard Knightly* in any thing, to whom he owed much reverence, as him that had married his Aunt. Sir *Richard* desired him to lend his house for a poor man, to the which he condescended; but he knew not the man, nor his intent; he met with *Penry* in *Coventry*, at a Sermon, who desired him to direct him to his house, there he had *The Supplication to the Parliament* that was printed at *Oxford*; he told him he would print Mr. *Cartwright*'s book *against the Romish Testament*: he was privy that there was a press there, but nothing else.

It was an easy matter for a wiser man than himself to be thus overtaken; *Penry* himself was not indicted nor impeached. And he hoped, if a man ignorantly did receive a Traitor or Jesuit, that it was not treason, unless himself knew of it.

Attorney. You acknowledge you had a book of him?---*Hales.* I do.

Attorney. And you came to the maker of it?

Hales. It was before the Proclamation.

Attorney. It was after.

Hales. It was after the first, and before the second Proclamation. Hereupon was read the first Proclamation, made in 27 *Eliz.* against schismatical and seditious libels, Dr. *Brown*, and such others.

Hales. But Mr. *Penry*'s was no Libel, for he subscribed his name.

Attorney. There is no doubt but it is a Libel, tho' it be subscribed: whereunto *Hales* said nothing. And then was read the other Proclamation in 31 *Eliz.* And the Order in the *Star-Chamber*, made in 28 *Eliz.* whereby printing was allowed only in *London*, *Oxford* and *Cambridge*.

Wickstone said, he was an ignorant man, and craved he might answer by Counsel, which might direct him: whereunto the Lord Chancellor answered, that this was matter of fact which lay most properly within his own knowledge, and that he must provide to answer for himself, and that he needed no Counsel.

Whereupon *Wickstone* confessed, that his wife desired him to permit them a home in his house, which he consented unto, knowing the purpose of them, and that was all.

Lady *Wickstone* confessed that the zeal of reformation in the Church caused her to give them entertainment in her house, and she was the cause that they came thither, not thinking that it had been any way hurtful or dangerous to the State; and she humbly besought, that what fault soever she had committed, her husband might not be punished therefore, since he was not privy, but only by her means and request.

Hereupon Mr. *Puckering*, the Queen's Serjeant, began to lay open the enormities of those books, which they had in court, and divers clauses of them were read. First, he affirmed they tended to the ruin of the whole State, next to the abolishing of all ecclesiastical Government, to the removing of all manner of service, the overthrow of laws; and yet, say they, all laws which resist these men, are no more to be allowed than those which maintain stews. But *Penry* will never give that over, he says, though the *Spaniards* were overthrown and discomfited by famine and by hunger, yet the Lord will raise them up again, and make a weak and feeble generation to overthrow us. So here was read a great part of *The Epitome.*

Puckering. This is most scornful and seditious: But what is their conclusion? They conclude, our Parliament and Councils be assembled where no truth beareth sway; which is most false and scandalous: but if this their Government be not received, those of the Parliament-house nor their seed shall never prosper, nor they ever bear any more rule in *England.* And I *Penry* will never leave, till either this be performed, or that the Lord in vengeance and blood do plague and punish us.

For the other book [*Have you any work for the Cooper?*] therein is affirmed that our Church-Government is utterly unlawful: And albeit this form of theirs would be inconvenient in many points, yet every Christian is bound to receive pastors, doctors, elders and deacons.

For *Martin junior*, he affirms that it is unlawful to have any other Government, that all human laws maintaining any other form are ungodly and not to be obeyed; that the warrant that Bishops have to maintain their authority, is no better than that which did maintain the stews; that Antichrist is the head of their doctrine, and they part of his body.

For *Martin senior*, he loudly termeth the book of common service, the ...... Book at *Lambeth*, that 100,000 hands would sign to their positions and government which they seek. And farther, that they are the strength of the land, that it were no policy to reject their suit at such a time when the land was invaded.

After which, they read Sir *Richard*'s examination, wherein he confessed that *Penry* came unto him as before; but when *Sharp* the minister told him the books were leud and dangerous, he caused them to be pulled down, and that he knew of no book but *The Epitome.*

He sent a ring to his man *Jackson* by *Penry* to receive a load of stuff into his house, which was the press and other necessaries for printing.

Newman the Cobler wore his livery, and *Wastal* his man helped *Walgrave* away from his house, to Mr. *Hales* at *Coventry*: *Fox* his Schoolmaster, and *Wastal* his man, would commonly read the books in Sir *Richard*'s house, and scoff and scorn at *John of Canterbury.*

Sharp saith, that Sir *Richard* conferr'd with *Walgrave*, as *Newman* told him *The Epitome* was printed there: that when it was told Sir *Richard* his house would be searched, he answered, the knaves durst not search his house; and if they did he would have coursed them.

The printer's man saith, that the *Mind-Alls* were printed there; but Sir *Richard* answered, he never knew so much before. *Have you any work for the Cooper?* went in hand there, but they went away then to *Coventry.*

The printer's man would have submitted himself long before, but Sir *Richard* advised him not to do so in any case, for the Lords were so incensed, as he should be hanged if he were catched.

For *Hales*, *Have you any work for the Cooper?* was printed at his house, he came once to the press as they were printing it.

Mrs. *Wickstone* confesseth, *Martin junior* and *Martin senior* were printed in her house, she gave them entertainment, and placed them in a parlour; her husband knew it not till it was done: she told him, it was works of embroidering, and willed him to will his servants not to peep or pry into the parlour, since it pertained not to them: *Hodgskins* and two more printed them all. *Hodgskins* was desired to print more, but he refused. *Hodgskins* confesseth that he printed them two; and from Mr. *Wickstone*'s they were conveyed to *Warrington* in *Lancashire*: She gave them 2*s.* 6*d.* at their departure, and her husband 2*s.*

Upon this Mr. Sollicitor *Egerton* began to declare the danger of these books, that they tended to confusion of all states, to take away her Majesty's Prerogative Royal, to the diminution of her yearly revenue, where she at this time was forced to sell her revenues for maintenance of her Realm and People, to the disherison of a great number of their patronages and advowsons and appropriations, to the abrogating of the common law and the civil law in many points: Whereupon he desired their Lordships to proceed to sentence.

All the Lords agreed that the books were most leud, dangerous and seditious, and pernicious to the State, most scandalous in respect to our adversaries the Papists, who took occasion of our disagreement; that they were slanderous to her Majesty, in accusing her for not maintaining religion. Whereas she for defence of religion only hath scared all the enemies of the State; that the sword of war had been drawn out against her for that cause; nay, the sword of death had compassed her chair in her own chamber [Mr. *Parrie* and Mr. *Barnwell*]: Notwithstanding she, nothing dismayed, being of princely magnanimity and fortitude, hath not feared any of these dangers only for religion sake. That they took away her Majesty's regal Power, disinherited Noblemen and Gentlemen, took away all Property, abolished the reverend estate and calling of Bishops, which are one of the three ancient estates of this land; and so they meant to pick out one stone after another, till they pulled the whole house on their heads. That the faults of them there present were gross and grievous; Sir *Richard*, a man highly favoured of the Queen, and much bounden more than ordinarily any of his state.

Yet notwithstanding, said Mr. Vice-Chamberlain, you be beloved of all of us, yet justice must be done without affection or compassion; for *Puniantur hi, ne tu puniaris*; let the magistrate punish offenders, lest himself be punished. And again, *St. Augustine* saith, *pereat unus ne pereat unitas*; let the offender rather be punished, than the unity of the Church be confounded.

That their ignorance was no excuse, that ignorance which was wilful and malicious only to escape the punishment of law, which is as high an offence as any privity.

That it was a sillier answer of Mr. *Wickstone*, to say his wife desired him, a great folly to be ruled by her, and she passed the modesty of her sex to rule him. And Sir *John Perrot* said expresly, he thought him worthy of the greater punishment for giving such a foolish answer, as that he did it at his wife's desire.

The Lord Chancellor gave the assembly that stood by to note, that these prisoners were not the devisers and makers of these books; for if they had, another place had been fit for them, and not this: that the county of *Northampton* did swarm with these Sectaries, and in one place there was a Presbytery planted among them, till at length one of the brethren had offended, wherefore the other would have punished him; but he, when he should be punished, fled, and complained to a Justice of Peace, and so their power surceased, and all revealed; whereby he noted the vanity of their Government: yea, said he, it is proceeded so far in that Country, that the people were full of contention, and in some places had risen in arms about that quarrel; whereby he concluded it was necessary to prevent such mischief, and to make example of it, and desired the Judges to notify his action herein in their circuits abroad, to the end the whole Realm might have knowledge of it, and the people no more seduced with these leud libellers. For punishment, they all agreed that Sir *Richard* should be fined two thousand pounds*; Mr. *Hales*, a thousand marks; Mr. *Wickstone* for obeying his wife, and not discovering it, five hundred marks; Mrs. *Wickstone* a thousand pounds †; and all of them imprisonment at her Majesty's pleasure.

* This Sir *Richard Knightly* was divers times chosen Member of Parliament for the county of *Northampton*, in the reign of Queen *Elizabeth*. He was a great favourer of the Puritan party, and at the expence of printing their libels, as is reported, being influenced by *Snape*, and some other leading Ministers of this County; these libels were printed by one *Walgrave*, who had a travelling press for this purpose, which was once brought down to *Fawesley*, and from thence by several Stages removed to *Manchester*, where both the press and the workmen were seized by the Earl of *Derby*. For this offence Sir *Richard Knightly*, and his confederates, were cited into the *Star-Chamber*, and severely censured; but upon the intercession of Archbishop *Whitgift*, whom they had most insulted, they were set at liberty, and had their Fines remitted. But though thus zealous for the Puritan faction, he joined with Sir *Francis Hastings* in presenting a Petition to the House of Commons, for granting a Toleration to the Papists. *Bridges's Northamptonshire, by Whalley, fol. p.* 61.

† *Camden* says, That at this Time several scurrilous pamphlets were published against the Church of *England* by the Dissenters; their great patrons and abettors were Sir *Richard Knightly* and *Wickstone*, persons in other respects sober and pious, but drawn into the party by some instruments that were to make a private market of them. However the Knights had a pretty round fine laid on them in the *Star-Chamber*; but the Archbishop of *Canterbury* was so generously good-natured, as to procure a remission of it at her Majesty's hands. See *Camden's Eliz.* in the complete History of *England*, vol. II. pag. 556.

VI. Pro-

VI. Proceedings in Parliament against *John* Earl of *Gowrie*, *Alexander Ruthven* his Brother, *Henry Ruthven*, *Hugh Moncrief*, and *Peter Eviot*, for *High-Treason*, *Nov.* 15, 1600, at *Edinburgh* *.

WILLIAM, Earl of *Gowrie*, having been condemn'd at *Stirling*, and executed in the year 1584, with two others, for seditious practices, in seizing the King's Person at *Ruthven*-House, when in his minority, and banishing from him all others who were not of their party, making him condescend to what they propos'd, and levying forces to secure themselves and the King's Person in their custody; occasioned the hot Clergy of their party, both to preach and publish scandalous pamphlets against the King and Government: this did beget a strict friendship between young *Gowrie* and the factious Clergy. Albeit, the King did, with great benignity, restore the Earl of *Gowrie* to his Father's honour's and estate; yet, his two sons, the Earl, and Mr. *Alexander*, were nursed up in such malice against the King, by some of his relations, (but especially by the Clergy), that neither the King's restoring him to his Estate and Honour, conferring also other marks of favour and trust on him, (and placing his Sister as the first Lady of Honour to the Queen, and making his Brother *Alexander* one of his Bed-chamber) could allay his revenge; till at last, he resolv'd to bring his long-designed purpose to effect. For, in *August* 1600, he devis'd and contriv'd the bringing the King from *Falkland* to his house in *Perth*; and there, with his fellow-conspirators, to have murdered the King.

On account of this Treason †, and several disorders, a Parliament was indicted to meet at *Edinburgh* on the first of *November* that year 1600, albeit the printed Acts bear its meeting to be on the 15th.

Accordingly a Parliament was indicted, to be holden at *Edinburgh* on the 1st of *November* 1600, and (as is ordinary) it was adjourned to the 4th of *November*. On which day, Sir *Thomas Hamilton*, King's Advocate, produced a summons of Treason duly executed against *William Ruthven*, Brother and apparent Heir to *John* Earl of *Gowrie*, and Mr. *Alexander Ruthven*: calling also, in the summons, the tutors and curators of the said *William*, (if he had any) and all others, having pretence or interest in the matter, to hear it found; and declared, that the said Earl of *Gowrie*, and Mr. *Alexander* his Brother, had committed Treason, in attempting to bereave his Majesty of his Life, at *St. Johnstoun*, on the 5th day of *August* last by-past: The summons and executions being read, and the Heraulds and Messengers sworn to the veracity of the executions, both at their private houses, mercat-crosses, and Shoar and Peer of *Leith*, *&c.* (which are the most publick Intimations and Citations that can be given by the Law of *Scotland*); which Citations were given on the 28th day of *August* and 29th ditto, in their respective places and mercat-crosses, and the Parliament was declar'd current daily.

On the 9th day, the said summons and executions were read over again, another summons of treason was produc'd, with their executions and verifications, made on oath in the face of the Court, against *Alexander* and *Henry Ruthven*, sons to *Alexander Ruthven* of *Frieland*; and against *Hugh Moncrief*, brother to *William Moncrief* of that Ilk; *Patrick Eviot*, brother to *Colin Eviot* of *Balhousie*; to hear and see themselves decern'd, as guilty of High-Treason, and Lese-Majesty, against the King at *Perth*, the 5th day of *August* last past.

And likewise by warrant from the Parliament, one *Andrew Henderson*, who was prisoner in the Tolbooth of *Edinburgh*, on accusation for the said crime, was brought by the Baillie of *Edinburgh*, and sisted before the Parliament; he having receiv'd formal summons in the Tolbooth, on the 28th of *August* last past.

The summons being thrice called, the executions all verified, and none of the persons cited compearing, excepting *Andrew Henderson* the prisoner; the King's Advocate did take instruments: and likewise the King's Advocate did then, and there, produce before the Lords, our sovereign Lord's letters of relaxation, given under his Highness's signet at *Edinburgh*, relaxing all the persons so summoned from the horn, and from all the summons executed against them, at the instance of whatsoever persons; that so, they might have safety and freedom to compear: and which relaxations were promulgated, at the mercat-crosses of the shires where each person had his abode; and also at the mercat-cross at *Edinburgh*, and shoar and peer of *Leith*. And these executions and relaxations were registrated in the records of the shires where the accused did reside: on which production the King's Advocate did take instruments.

The Lords Commissioners in Parliament did remit the said *Andrew Henderson* to the Tolbooth for safe custody, and the Parliament adjourn'd until the 15th day of *November*: on which day, the Parliament having met, the said Sir *Thomas Hamilton*, Advocate, produc'd the said summons of Treason and Executions; and the Heraulds and Messengers having, of new, verified the executions upon oath formally, *&c.* neither *William*, nor none for him, nor the others cited, compearing; the King's Advocate did take instruments thereon, only Mr. *Thomas Henrison*, one of the Commissaries of *Edinburgh*, compeared for the foresaid *Andrew Henderson*, and produc'd the writ following, undersubscribed by the King's Advocate. "It is "our will, and we command you, that upon sight hereof, ye delete "*Andrew Henderson*, Chamberlain to umquhile *John* Earl of *Gowrie*, his "name furth of the summons of Treason and Forfaulture, raised and "executed against him, for being art, part, redd, counsel, and counselling, of the late Treason conspired by the said umquhile Earl, his "umquhile brother, and complices, against our Person; and as you will "answer to us hereupon; keeping thir presents for your warrant. Sub-"scribed with our hand at *Holy-rood-house*, the ninth of *November*, 1600. "Sic subscribitur, JACOBUS REX." Conform whereunto, the Advocate "did delete his Name."

The Heraulds and Messengers did, at that same time, again verify upon oath the executions given in; and the relaxations and executions against *William*, and *Alexander*, and *Henry Ruthven*, *Patrick Eviot*, and *Hugh Moncrief*; and the Parliament found the Dittay relevant: and then adjourned till the 15th Day of *November*, and remitted the examination of the witnesses to the Lords of Articles, which are a Committee of Parliament, according to the constant practice and custom in Parliament.

Nota, The Lords of the Articles in that Parliament, were two Bishops and four Abbots, all men of great worth and integrity; four Earls, *viz.* *Lennox*, *Errol*, *Marrischal*, and *Marr*; four Lords, *viz.* *Seton*, *Livingstoun*, *Newbottle*, and *Fivie*; seven Barons, and nine Commissioners of Burrows.

On the 15th of *November*, the Parliament did again meet, and the Advocate did again call the summons of Treason against all the forementioned Persons (except *Henderson*), for enterprizing the slaughter of the King, on the 5th of *August* last past. Being all three called, and none compearing, the hail Estates did find both the summons ‡, reasons and causes therein mentioned, relevant; and therefore admitted the same to the Advocate's probation. Whereupon the Advocate did produce the Letters of horning duly executed and endorsed, against *Alexander* and *Henry Ruthven*, *Hugh Moncrief*, and *Patrick Eviot*, bearing, that they were denounced Rebels, and put to the horn, for crimes of Treason therein mentioned.

And the oaths and depositions of the witnesses, let and adduc'd by the Advocate, for proving of the Treason against the defenders (taken before the Lords of Articles), *viz.* the deposition of umquhile Mr. *Thomas Cranstoun*, and *George Craigingelt*, when they were executed to death, for the foresaid crime of Treason: and likewise, the Advocate repeated the notoriety, with the circumstances of the matter of fact, to prove the points of the Libel; and produc'd the depositions of all the witnesses, which were all read, as follows:

The Depositions of the Witnesses, examined in presence of the Lords of Articles, for proving of the said two Summonses of Treason:

[Nota, *That the Words are printed as they were then written and spoke, for exactness sake.*]

THE Duke of *Lenox*, sworn and examined, depones, That upon the 5th day of *August* last by-past, this Deponent, for the time being in *Falkland* in company with his Majesty, he saw Mr. *Alexander Ruthven* speaking with his Grace before the stables, betwixt six and seven in the morning; and shortly thereafter, his Majesty passing to the hunting of the Buck, and having slain one in the Park of *Falkland*, his Highness spake to the Deponent, disyring him to accompany his Majesty to *Perth*, to speak to the Earl of *Gowrie*. And incontinent thereafter, this Deponent sent his servant for another horse, and for a sword, and lap on, and followed his Grace: and as this Deponent overtook his Grace, Mr. *Alexander Ruthven* was speaking with his Majesty; and shortly after the Deponent's coming to the King, his Highness rode a-part, and spake with this Deponent, saying, Ye cannot guess, man, what errand I am riding for; I am going to get a pose in *Perth*: and Mr. *Alexander Ruthven* has informed me, that he has fund a man, that has a pitchard full of coined Gold, of great sorts. And in the mean time, his Highness enquired of this Deponent, of what humour he thought Mr. *Alexander* to be of? Who answered, that he knew nothing of him, but as of an honest discreet Gentleman. And after that his Highness had declared to this Deponent, the hail circumstances of the man who had the said Gold, the place where it was found, and where it was kept; this Deponent answered, I like not that, Sir; for that is not likely. And they riding beside the bridge of *Erne*, his Majesty called to the Deponer, that Mr. *Alexander* disyred him to keep that matter of the pose secret, and take nobody with him; and then his Highness both at that time, and thereafter at *St. Johnstoun*, within the Earl of *Gowrie*'s hall, said to this Deponer, Take taint where I pass with Mr. *Alexander Ruthven*, and follow me. And as his Majesty was within a mile to *Perth*, after that Mr. *Alexander* had come a certain space with his Highness, he rod away and galloped to *Perth*, before the rest of the company, towards his brother's lodging, of purpose (as the Deponent believes), to advertise the Earl of *Gowrie* of his Majesty's coming there. And as his Majesty was within two pair of butt-langs to the town of *Perth*, the Earl of *Gowrie*, accompanied with diverse persons, all on foot, met his Highness in the *Inche*, and saluted him; and immediately thereafter, his Majesty

* Extracted from the authentick Records, and the principal Vouchers (which lie in publick custody in the Parliament-House, at *Edinburgh*), by *George*, Earl of *Cromerty*, Keeper of the Records, *Temp. Car.* 2.

† See *Spotswood's* History of the Church of *Scotland*, p. 457, 458, 459, 460.

‡ *N. B.* The Summonses and Executions are at full length recorded in the Books of Parliament; and being all exact in the Forms required by Law, it would not only be tedious, but useless, to repeat them here; they being patent in the Records.

accompanied with this Deponent, the Earl of *Mar*, *Inchechaffrey*, Sir *Thomas Erſkin*, Laird of *Urquhil*, *James Erſkin*, *William Stuart*, Sir *Hugh Herries*, Sir *John Ramſay*, *John Murray*, *John Hamilton* of the *Grange*, and *John Graham* of *Bagowie*, paſt all together, in the Earl of *Gowrie*'s Hall; the ſaid Earl of *Gowrie*, and the ſaid Mr. *Alexander Ruthven* being baith preſent with them. And after their Entry, his Majeſty cry'd for a drink, which was a long time a-coming: and it was an hour after his firſt coming, before his Majeſty got his dinner. And in the time that his Majeſty got his deſert, the Earl of *Gowrie* came to this Deponent, and to the Earl of *Mar*, and remanent perſons foreſaid, and deſired them to dine, which they did, in the Hall; and when they had near hand dined, the Earl of *Gowrie* came from his Majeſty's chamber to the Hall, and called for wine; and ſaid, that he was directed from his Majeſty's chamber, to drink his *Scoil* [the Word us'd then for drinking a health], to my Lord Duke, and the reſt of the company; which he did. And immediately after the Scoll had paſs'd about, this Deponent did raiſe from the table, to have waited upon his Majeſty, conform to his former direction, and then the Earl of *Gowrie* ſaid to the Deponent, that his Majeſty was gone up quietly, ſome quiet errand. And then, the ſaid Earl of *Gowrie* cry'd for the key of his garden, and paſs'd in company with this Deponent, to the garden, accompanied with *Lindores* and Sir *Hugh Herries*, and certain others: and ſhortly after their being in the garden, Mr. *Thomas Cranſtoun* came down to the garden, crying, the King's Majeſty is on horſeback, and riding through the *Inche*: and then the Earl of *Gowrie* cry'd, Horſe, Horſe. And the ſaid Mr. *Thomas Cranſtoun* anſwered to him, Your horſe is in town; to whilk the Earl of *Gowrie* made him no anſwer, but cry'd, Ay, Horſe, Horſe. And this Deponent and the Earl of *Gowrie* came firſt out of the garden, through the hall to the cloſs, and came to the oute gate; and this Deponent ſpeird at the porter, if the King was furth; who anſwer'd, that he was aſſured that his Majeſty was not come furth of the place. Then the Earl of *Gowrie* ſaid, I am ſure he is firſt always; ſtay, my Lord, drink, and I ſhall gang up, and get the verity and certainty thereof. And the ſaid Earl of *Gowrie* paſſed up, and incontinent came again to the cloſs, and he affirmed to this Deponent, that the King's Majeſty was furth at the back-gate, and away. Whereupon, this Deponent, the Earl of *Gowrie*, and *Mar*, and hail company, paſt furth at the fore-gate of the lodging; and ſtaid before the ſame gate, upon the ſtreet: and as they were ſtanding there, adviſing where to ſeek the King, incontinent, and in the mean time, this Deponent heard a voice, and ſaid to the Earl of *Mar*, This is the King's voice, that cryes, be where he will; and ſo they all looked up to the Lodging, and ſaw his Majeſty looking furth of the window, wanting his hat; his face being red, and an hand gripping his cheek and mouth; and the King cry'd, I am murder'd! Treaſon! My Lord *Mar*, help, help. And incontinent, this Deponent, the Earl of *Mar*, and their company, ran up the ſtair of the gallery-chamber, where his Majeſty was, to have relieved him: and as they paſſed up, they found the door of the chamber faſt; and ſeeing a ladder ſtanding beſide, they raſht at the door with the ladder, and the ſteps of the ladder brake: and ſyne, they ſend for hammers; and notwithſtanding large forcing with hammers, they got not entry at the ſaid chamber, while after the Earl of *Gowrie* and his brother were both ſlain. That *Robert Brown* paſt about be the back-door, and came to his Majeſty, and aſſured his Highneſs, that it was my Lord Duke and the Earl of *Mar*, that was ſtricking up the chamber-door; and the hammer was given through the hole of the door of the chamber: and they within brake the door and gave them entry: and, at their firſt entry, they ſaw the Earl of *Gowrie* lying dead in the chamber, Mr. *Alexander Ruthven* being ſlain, and taken down the ſtairs before their entry. And at their firſt entry within that chamber where the King's Majeſty was, the Deponent ſaw ſundry halberts and ſwords ſtricking under the door of the chamber, and ſides thereof, by reaſon the ſame was nae cloſs door; and knew none of the ſtrickers, except *Alexander Ruthven* one of the Defenders, who deſired to ſpeak with this Deponent thro' the door, and ſpeird at him, For God's ſake tell me how my Lord of *Gowrie* was. To whom this Deponent anſwered, He is well: and the ſaid Deponent bad *Alexander* to gang his way; and that he was ane fool; and that he would get little thanks for that labour. And, in the mean time, as they were continuing to ſtrick with halberts under the door, meikle *John Murray*, ſervant to *Tullibardin*, was ſtricken through the legg; and how ſoon the ſaid *Alexander Ruthven* had heard the ſaid Lord Duke ſpeak, he and his hail complices paſt from the foreſaid door, and made no more trouble thereafter thereat, and paſſed down to the cloſs, and ſtood there. And ſaw none of the remanent defenders preſent, at the doing of the violent turns that day, except by report, but the ſaid *Alexander Ruthven*: but ſays, that he ſaw *Hugh Moncrieſ*, *Earn*, and *Alexander Daithvenies*, and *Patrick Eviot*, with the Earl of *Gowrie*, at the King's dinner that day; and that before and thereafter, looking over the chamber window, he ſaw *George Craigingelt* and *Alexander Ruthven*; and did ſee others of the Earl of *Gowrie*'s ſervants, whom this Deponent knew not, ſtanding in arms within the cloſs: and alſo ſaw other perſons carrying ane Joiſt from the town, to the cloſs of the Earl of *Gowrie*'s lodging. and declares, that there abode ſundry perſons within the ſaid cloſe, and in the high-ſtreet, before the ſaid Earl's lodging, crying and making tumult, to the ſpace of two hours mair, next after the death of the ſaid Earl of *Gowrie*, and his brother.

Sic ſubſcribitur,
LENOX.

THE Earl of *Mar*, ſworn and examined, depones, conform to the Lord Duke of *Lenox*'s depoſition, in all things ſubſtantial, except that his Lordſhip ſaw not Mr. *Alexander Ruthven* in *Falkland*, while about ten hours the day libelled, ſhortly before the ſlaying of the buck: and alſo, overtook not his Majeſty that day, while his Majeſty was near the bridge of *Erne*: and, that after their dinner, my Lord of *Mar* paſſed not to the yeard, in company with the Earl of *Gowrie*, but paſſed to a chamber where the King dined, and ſaw nothing of the Joiſt.

Sic ſubſcribitur,
MAR.

ANdrew *Henderſon*, Chamberlain of *Scoon*, ſworn, depones, that he is of the age of thirty-eight years; declares, that upon *Monday* at night, the fourth day of *Auguſt* laſt by-paſt, this Deponent being, after ſupper, in company with the Earl of *Gowrie* and Mr. *Alexander Ruthven*, within my Lord's own chamber; the Earl of *Gowrie* inquired at this Deponent, What he had to do to-morrow? To whom this Deponent anſwered, That he had to do, to ride to *Ruthven*, to ſpeak with the Tenents. Then the Earl of *Gowrie* anſwered, Stay that journey, you muſt ride to *Falkland*, in company with my brother Mr. *Alexander*; and take *Andrew Ruthven* with you; and that ye be ready to ride be four hours in the morning: and haſte thou back with anſwer, as my brother orders you, by writ or otherways; and let *Andrew Ruthven* remain with my brother. And in the morning, after four hours, they rode all three together to *Falkland*; and coming to *Falkland*, they lighted at *John Barfour*'s houſe, and ſeeing that Colonel *Edmund* was there, they lodged in ane *Law*'s houſe; and the Maſter ſent this Deponent about ſeven hours in the morning, to ſee what the King's Majeſty was doing. And as he was within the place, he ſaw the King's Majeſty coming furth Mid-Cloſs, booted; and then he returned back again to the Maſter, and ſaid to him, Haſte you, the King's Majeſty is coming forth: and incontinent, the Maſter followed his Majeſty, and ſpake with his Majeſty foranent the Equirie; and the King laid his hand on his ſhoulder and clapped him, where they ſpake together be the ſpace of ane quarter of an hour. And thereafter, the Maſter directed this Deponent to ride to *Perth* in haſte, as he loved the Lord *Gowrie*'s and his honour, and advertiſe his brother, that his Majeſty will be there, with a few number incontinent; and cauſe make his dinner ready. Then this Deponent anſwered, Shall I ride preſently?. The Maſter anſwered, No, but ſtay a-while, and follow the King and me, while I ſpeak with his Majeſty again. And, as his Majeſty was riding through the Sloap of the Park-Dike, the Maſter ſpake to his Majeſty; and immediately thereafter, the Maſter bad this Deponent to paſs to *St. Johnſtoun*, with all poſſible diligence, according to his former directions. And, at this Deponent's coming to *Perth*, it was ſhortly after ten hours in the morning, he entered in the Lord of *Gowrie*'s chamber, where he ſaw his Lord ſpeak with *George Hay* and Mr. *Peter Hay*: and how ſoon my Lord of *Gowrie* ſaw this Deponent, he came aſide to this Deponent, and enquired ſecretly, What word he had brought from his brother? and if he had brought a letter? This Deponent anſwered, That he had brought no letter: What anſwer then, ſaid he, has he to me? This Deponent anſwered, That the Maſter his brother bad tell his Lordſhip, that the King's Majeſty would be there incontinent; and bad haſte his dinner. Then the Earl bad this Deponent to follow his lordſhip to the Cabinet, and ſpeird at him, how his Majeſty had tane with his brother? He anſwered, That he was well tane with; and when he did his courteſy, the King laid his hand upon his ſhoulder. The Earl ſpeird, what number of perſons [illegible] with the King at the hunting? who anſwered, That he knew not well, but that there were ſundry of his own with him, and ſome *Engliſh-men*. And then the Earl ſpeird, what Noblemen were with him? He anſwered, None [illegible] my Lord Duke. And thereafter, this Deponent paſſed to his own houſe in the town, and took off his boots, and returned to the Earl within an hour: and how ſoon the Earl ſaw him in his chamber, he called upon this Deponent, and bad him put on his Secret, [a coat of Mail] and Plate-Sleeves. The Deponent inquired to what effect? The Earl anſwered, I have an Highland-man to take in the *Shoegate*, and then the Deponent paſs'd to his own houſe, and put on his Secret, and Plate-Sleeves, came back again to the Earl of *Gowrie*'s houſe: and about half an hour to one, the Earl commanded this Deponent, Take up my dinner; and this Deponent paſs'd, and took up the firſt ſervice, by reaſon *Charles Craigingelt* was ſick. And in continent the ſaid Earl paſs'd to his dinner, accompanied with Mr. *John Moncrieſ*, Laird of *Petcrieſ*, Mr. *James Drummond*, *Alexander Peeples*, Baron of *Findowne*. And ſhortly after the firſt ſervice was ſet down, my Lord ſitting at the table with the foreſaid Company, *Andrew Ruthven* came in from the Maſter, and rounded to the Earl, but heard not what he ſaid; and ſhortly after, this Deponent paſſing down to take up the ſecond ſervice, Mr. *Alexander Ruthven* and *William Blair* came in to the Earl, my Lord ſitting at his dinner: and hown ſoon my Lord ſaw them, he and his hail company roſe from the table; and then this Deponent hearing my Lord on foot bid this Deponent ſend for his Steel-bonnet and Gantlet, believing that my Lord was going to take the ſaid Highland-man. And as this Deponent perceiv'd my Lord paſſing to the *Inche*, and not to the *Shoegate*, he ſent home his Steel-bonnet, and caſt his Gantlet in the pantry, and thereafter followed the Earl to the *Inche*, where he ſaw the ſaid Earl with his Majeſty, the Duke, and the Earl of *Mar*, and came in all together to the Earl's houſe. And after his Majeſty had come to the Earl's houſe, the Maſter of *Ruthven* ſpeird at this Deponent, where the key of the gallery-chamber was? Who anſwer'd, That he handled not the key ſince the Earl came in *Scotland*. Then the Maſter bid this Deponent ſpeak to Mr. *William Rynd* to give to him the ſaid key. And the Maſter paſſing up to the gallery, Mr. *William Rynd* followed him, and gave to him the ſaid key: and thereafter, immediately after his Majeſty's down-ſitting to his dinner, Mr. *Thomas Cranſtoun* came to this Deponent*, and bad him gang to the Earl of *Gowrie*; which this Deponent did. And the Earl of *Gowrie*, in the outer chamber, where the King dined, ſpake to this Deponent ſecretly, and bad him paſs to the gallery to his brother. So he paſſed up, and the Earl follows him; and they being all three together in the gallery-chamber, (whereof he had the key from Mr. *William Rynd*) the Earl ſaid to this Deponent, Tarry ſtill with my brother, and do any thing he bids you. Then this Deponent came to the Maſter, and ſpeird, What will you with me, Sir? Then the Maſter ſpoke to my Lord, Let *Andrew Henryſon* go into the round of the chamber, and I will lock him in, and take the key of the chamber with me, where this Deponent abode half an hour or thereby, locked his alane, having his Secret, Plate-Sleeves, Sword and Whinger with him, and wanting his ſteel bonnet. And all this time, this deponent feared ſome evil to be done: that, upon this, he kneel'd and pray'd to God; and about the end

* Upon the information of *Henderſon*, and other witneſſes, *Cranſtoun* and *Craigingelt* were pannelled before the Juſticiary at *Johnſtoun*; and upon clear teſtimonies, and on their own confeſſion at the bar (which they alſo adhered to on the Scaffold) they were both executed: Only alledging, that they did not know of the deſign to murder the King; but that they intended to force the King to make great reparations for the late Earl of *Gowrie*'s death: and that this Earl of *Gowrie* was to be made a great man.

end of the half hour, Mr. *Alexander* opens the door of the room, and entered first within the same, having the King's Majesty by the arm, and puts on his hat upon his head, draws forth this *Andrew Henderson* Deponent's whinger; and says to the King, having the drawn whinger in his hand, Sir, you must be my prisoner; remember on my father's death. And, as he held the whinger to his Majesty's breast, this Deponent threw the samen furth of Mr. *Alexander*'s hands. And the time that Mr. *Alexander* held the whinger to his Majesty's breast, the King was beginning to speak. The Master said, Hold your tongue, Sir, or, by *Christ*, ye shall die. Then his Majesty answered, Mr. *Alexander*, Ye and I were very great together; and as touching your father's death, Man, I was but a minor. My Council might have done any thing they pleased. And farther, Man, albeit ye bereave me of my life, ye will not be King of *Scotland*, for I have both sons and daughters, and there are Men in this town and friends that will not leave it unrevenged. Then Mr. *Alexander* answered, swearing with a great oath, that it was neither his life nor blood that he craved. And the King said, what traiks. [what then] albeit ye take off your hat; and then Mr. *Alexander* took off his hat. And the King said, What is it ye crave, Man, and ye crave not my life? who answered, Sir, it is but a promise. The King answered, What promise? The said Mr. *Alexander* answered, For, my Lord my brother will tell you. The King said, fetch hither your brother. And syne the said Mr. *Alexander* said to the King, Sir, you will not cry, nor open the window while I come again? and the King promised so to do. Then Mr. *Alexander* passed forth and locked, and passed not from the door, as he believes. In the mean time, the King entered in discourse with this Deponent, How came you in here, man? And this Deponent answered, as God lives, I am shot in here like a dog. The King answered, Will my Lord of *Gowrie* do me any evil, man? This Deponent answered, I vow to God I shall die first. And then the King bad this Deponent open the window and he opened the window that looked to the Spy-tower: and the King answered, Fy, the wrong window, man! And thereafter, this Deponent passing to the other window nearest his Majesty, to open the same; before he got to the window, Mr. *Alexander* opened the door, and came in again, and said to his Majesty, By God! there is no remedy, and then he loups to the King, and got him by both the hands, having ane garter in his hands. Then the King answered, I am a free prince, man; I will not be bound. so his Majesty cast loose his left hand from Mr. *Alexander*; and at that same time, this Deponent draws away the garter from Mr. *Alexander*, and his Majesty loups free from the said Mr. *Alexander*, and the said Mr. *Alexander* follows his Majesty, and with his left hand about his Majesty's craig, puts his right neeve [fist] in his Majesty's mouth: so his Majesty wrestling to be quite of him, this Deponent put his hand out of his Majesty's mouth. And thereafter, this Deponent did put his left hand over his Majesty's left shoulder, and pull'd up the broad of the window, whereunto the said Mr. *Alexander* had thrust his Majesty's head and shoulders; and with the force of the drawing up of the window, presses his Majesty's body about, his right side to the window: at which time his Majesty cries furth, Treason! treason! So the Master said to this Deponent, Is there no help with thee? Wo worth thee, thou villain! we all die. So twining his hand on the guard of his own sword; and, incontinent, the King's Majesty put his hand on the Master's hands, and staid him from drawing of his sword; and this ways they both being grasped together, come furth of the cabinet to the chamber: and, in the mean time, this Deponent threw about the key; then standing in the door of the head of the turnpike, which entred to the chamber, and opened the door thereof, to eschew [escape] himself, and to let his Majesty's servants in. And how soon he opened the door, *John Remsay* came in at the said door, with an haulk on his hand, and passed to the King's Majesty, and laid about him, and drew his whinger: and as he saw him minting with the whinger, this Deponent passed furth at the said door, and pass'd down the turnpike. And, as this Deponent pass'd through the close, and came to the fore-gate, this Deponent saw the Earl of *Gowrie* standing before the gate accompanied by sundry persons, of whom he remembers none; but remembers well, that the Earl had this Deponent's knapschaw, or head-piece, on his head, and two swords drawn in his hands: and incontinently thereafter, this Deponent pass'd to his own lodging, where he remained while the King passed furth of the town; and then the Deponent pass'd to the bridge, and walked up and down by the space of an hour, and returned not again to the Earl's lodging. And the time of his entry to his house that night, this Deponent's wife inquir'd at this Deponent, What trouble was within the place? To whom he answer'd, Well is me of one thing, that if I had not been there, the King had been twice sticked this night: but wo's me for the thing that is fallen out. And this Deponent being demanded by Mr. *John Moncrief*, after his returning from *Falkland*, where have you been with your boots on? answered, He had been two or three miles beyond *Erne*, and durst not tell him the verity, by reason the Earl of *Gowrie* had discharged him to tell the errand, he sent him, to any body. And farther, this Deponent declares, That when he saw the Earl of *Gowrie* standing with the drawn swords before the gate, this Deponent spoke not to the Earl, neither yet the Earl to him at that time, but he passed to his own house.

Sic subscribitur,
ANDREW HENDERSON.

THE Abbot of *Inchechaffrey*, sworn and examined, depones, That, upon the 5th day of *August* last by-past, this Deponent being in *Falkland*, about seven hours in the morning, he met Mr. *Alexander Ruthven* accompanied with *Andrew Ruthven*; and, at that time, only saluted the said Mr. *Alexander Ruthven*, without any conference farther at that time. And at that time, he saw the said Mr. *Alexander* enter into conference with his Majesty, upon the green, betwixt the stables and the park: which conference enduring for the space of a quarter of an hour, and the said Mr. *Alexander* accompanied his Majesty while they came to the Meadow; and, at his returning from his Majesty, this Deponent desired Mr. *Alexander* to disjune with him, by reason his own could not be so soon prepared. To whom Mr. *Alexander* answered, He might not tarry, by reason his Majesty had commanded him to await upon him. And, as this Deponent passed to *Falkland*, leaving Mr *Alexander* behind him, met his horse with his man, coming from *Falkland* to him; and then this Deponent, after he had disjuned in *Falkland*, he took his journey the high-way to *Inchechaffrey*, and the Deponent being but a mile be-north *Strameglo*, he's incompany'd with my Lord Duke, *Lindores*, the Laird of *Urquhill*, *John Hamilton* of the *Grange*, *Finlay Taixies*; and Mr. *Alexander Ruthven* came by this Deponent, riding the high-way to *Perth*. Then incontinent this Deponent horsed, and accompanied his Majesty to *Perth*, where he saw the Earl of *Gowrie* meet his Majesty in the *Inche*, and passed in company with his Majesty, and his Noblemen, and servants, to the Earl of *Gowrie*'s lodging, where they dined all together. And after dinner, this Deponent being in the chamber at the north-end of the hall, word passed thro' the hall, that his Majesty was passed away, and ridden towards *Falkland*; and then this Deponent, in company with the Lord of *Mar*, and remanent present for the time, passed to the close, and from that to the high-street; and the Earl of *Gowrie* being present with them, desired them to stay, while he returned and advertised them of the verity thereof. And incontinent the Earl of *Gowrie* passed up the stair, and returned back, and certified the Deponent and his colleagues of his Majesty's departure. Then the Lord Duke, this Deponent and remanent, cried for their horses to follow the King. Then, as they were standing upon the high-street, they heard ane cry, and a voice; and the Duke first declared, I am sure, yon is his Majesty's voice, be where he will himself. And immediately thereafter, this Deponent saw his Majesty looking forth of a window of the round, wanting his hat, and his face red, crying, Fy, help, my Lord *Mar*! Treason! treason! I am murder'd! And, at the same instant, to his judgment, was pulled *per* force in at that same window. And, incontinent thereafter this deponent passed in haste up with the Earl of *Mar* and my Lord Duke, to the chamber within the gallery, where he saw, heard, and did in all things conform to the Earl's deposition.

Sic subscribitur,
INCHECHAFFREY.

THE Abbot of *Lindores*, sworn and examined, depones, conform to the Lord Duke of *Lenox*, in all things; *addendo*, That after dinner, when word was of his Majesty's departure towards *Falkland*, and that they had all together came down to the Porter, and had inquired at him, Gif the King's Majesty was gone furth? the Porter answered, He was not passed furth; and the Earl of *Gowrie* affirmed, That he was passed furth at the back-gate: and the Porter said to the Earl of *Gowrie*, That cannot be, my Lord, because I have the key of the back-gate. And, after that his Majesty had cried furth of the window of the round, Treason! treason! *&c.* this Deponent saw *James Erskin* incontinently lay hands on the Earl of *Gowrie* upon the high-street; and immediately Sir *Thomas Erskin* gripped the Earl of *Gowrie*, Fy, Traitor! this is thy deed, thou shalt die. Then the Earl of *Gowrie* answered, I ken nothing of the matter. Then instantly the Earl of *Gowrie*'s men tugged the said Sir *Thomas Erskin* and *James Erskin* from the Earl of *Gowrie*: who incontinently ran the space of half ane pair of butt-lands from them, towards *Glenurchie*'s house, and drew furth his two swords, and cried, I will either be at my own house, or die by the gate. And incontinently thereafter the said Earl, accompanied with thirty persons, or thereby, passed within the said place, wherein his Majesty was for the time; and shortly after, the Deponent, as appeared to him, saw a multitude of people carrying a joist towards the place.

Sic subscribitur,
LINDORES.

SIR *Thomas Erskin*, of the age of thirty-six years, sworn, depones conform to the Lord *Inchechaffrey*, and Lord of *Lindores*; *addendo*, That immediately after this Deponent heard his Majesty cry furth of the window of the round, Fy, help! I am betrayed, they are murdering me! he ran with diligence towards the place, to have helpen his Majesty; and before his entry, seeing the Earl of *Gowrie*, this Deponent and his brother gripped him by the neck, and said to him, Traitor, this is thy deed. Whilk Earl answered, What is the matter? I ken nothing. Immediately the Earl's servants sever'd him from this Deponent and his brother. And this Deponent entered within the close, he forgathered with Sir *Hugh Herries*, who demanded of the Deponent what the matter meant; and, in the mean time, the Deponent heard Sir *John Ramsay* crying out at the turnpike-head, Fy, Sir *Thomas*, come up the turnpike, even to the head! And, as this Deponent had passed up five steps of the turnpike, he sees and meets with Mr. *Alexander Ruthven* blooded in two parts of his body, *viz.* in his face and in his neck; aud incontinent this Deponent cries to Sir *Hugh Herries*, and others that were with him, Fy, this is the Traitor, strike him! And incontinent he was stricken by them, and fell; and as he was fallen, he turn'd his face, and cried, Alas! I had not the wyte of it; this Deponent being standing above him in the turnpike. Thereafter, this Deponent pass'd to the head of the turnpike, and entered within the chamber at the head of the gallery, where the King and Sir *John Ramsay* were there alone present; and, at the first meeting, this Deponent said to his Majesty, I thought your Majesty would have concredited more to me, nor to have commanded me to await your Majesty at the door, gif ye thought it not meet to have taken men with you. Whereupon his Majesty answered to this Deponent, Alas! the traitor deceived me in that, as he did in the leave; for I commanded him expresly to bring you to me, which he promised to me to do; and returned back, as I thought, to fetch you; but he did nothing, but steiked the door. Shortly thereafter, Sir *Hugh Herries* followed the Deponent into the chamber, and *George Wilson*, servant to *James Erskin*: and immediately thereafter Mr. *Thomas Cranstoun*, with his sword drawn in his hand, entered within the said chamber; and the Earl of *Gowrie* followed him within the said chamber, with ane sword drawn in every one of his hands, and ane knapschaw on his head. who struck at this Deponent and his colleagues ane certain space. Likeas, they defended them and struke again: and that same time, this Deponent was hurt in the right hand be Mr. *Thomas Cranstoun*; and this Deponent heard my Lord of *Gowrie* speak some words at his entry, but understands them not. At last, Sir *John Ramsay* gave the Earl of *Gowrie* ane dead straik, and then the Earl leand him to his sword, and the Deponent saw a man had him up, whom he knew not, and how soon the Earl fell to the ground, Mr. *Thomas Cranstoun*, and the remanent who accompanied him, departed and pass'd down the turnpike. And the Deponent remembers, that

that at that time, there were more persons in the chamber with the Earl of *Gowrie* by Mr. *Thomas Cranstoun*, but knew nane of them, except that he believes that ane black man, that was there in company within the chamber, was *Hugh Moncrief*, brother to the Laird of *Moncrief*; but the Deponent knows not well, whether or not it was *Hugh Moncrief*.

Sic subscribitur,
Sir THOMAS ERSKIN.

SIR *John Ramsay*, of the age of twenty-three years, or thereby, sworn, depones, That immediately after he had dined, the day libelled, in the Earl of *Gowrie*'s house, he took his Majesty's haulk from *John Murray*, to the effect the said *John* might have dined: and the Deponent missing his Majesty, and forgathering with the Laird of *Pittencrief*, in the Earl of *Gowrie*'s hall; and demanding of *Pittencrief*, where his Majesty was? the said Laird first convoyed the Deponent to the chamber where the King dined, thereafter to the yaird, hoping that his Majesty had been there: and missing his Majesty in the yaird, convoy'd the Deponent up to ane fair gallery, where the Deponent was never before; where having remain'd a certain space beholding the gallery, they came both down to the closs; where they met with Mr. *Thomas Cranstoun* in the midst of the closs, who said to them, that his Majesty was away upon horseback, at the *Inche*: whereupon this Deponent and *Pittencrief* sindered; and the Deponent passed furth of the gate, to his stable, to have gotten his horse, and being standing at the stable door, he heard his Majesty cry, knew his Highness's voice, but understood not what he spake. Whereupon he comes immediately within the closs, and finding ane turnpike-door open, he enters within the samen, and runs up the turnpike, while he comes to the door upon the head thereof; and hearing ane struggling and din of mens feet, he ran with his hail force at the door of the turnpike-head, which enters to the chamber at the end of the gallery; the Deponent having in the mean time his haulk on his hand, and having dung open the door, he sees his Majesty and Mr. *Alexander Ruthven* in others arms, striving and wrestling together, his Majesty having Mr. *Alexander*'s head under his arm, and Mr. *Alexander* being almost on his knees, had his hand upon his Majesty's face and mouth: and his Majesty seeing the Deponent, cried, Fy! strike him laigh, because he has ane pyne doublet upon him. Whereupon the Deponent cast the haulk from him, and drew his whinger, wherewith he strake the said Mr. *Alexander*; and immediately after he was striken, his Majesty shot him down stairs whereat this Deponent had entered. Thereafter, this Deponent addresses himself to a window; and looking furth thereat, and saw Sir *Thomas Erskin*, the Deponent cried, Sir *Thomas* come up this turnpike, even to the head. In this mean time, his Majesty did put his foot upon the haulk-leash, and held her a lang time, while the Deponent came and took her up again: and then Sir *Thomas Erskin* entered. And in the rest depones conform to Sir *Thomas Erskin* in all points; and further says, That when the Deponent first entered within the chamber, he saw a man standing behind his Majesty's back, whom he no ways knew, nor remembers what apparelling he had on; but after that this Deponent had striken Mr. *Alexander*, he saw that man no more.

Sic subscribitur,
Sir JOHN RAMSAY.

JOhn Graham of *Urquhill*, sworn and examined, depones conform to the Lord Duke of *Lenox* and the Earl of *Mar* in all things, *reddens eandem causam scientiæ*; adding, That this deponent the time that he was at dinner in the hall, with my Lord Duke and Earl of *Mar*, he saw the King and Mr. *Alexander Ruthven* pass threw the hall up the turnpike, towards the gallery: and, as this Deponent, *John Hamilton*, and others, were following, Mr. *Alexander* cried Back, Gentlemen, stay, for so it is his Highness's will.

Sic subscribitur,
JOHN GRAHAM of *Urquhill*.

JOhn Graham of *Balgowne*, of the age of fifty years, or thereby, married, depones, conform to the Lord Duke in all things; adding, That this Deponent the day libelled, after the death of the Earl of *Gowrie* and his brother, and hearing his Majesty report, that Mr. *Alexander* pressed to have bound his Highness's hands with a garter; this Deponent found a garter at the cheek of the round door among the bent, and immediately thereafter this Deponent presented the garter to his Highness. and at the sight thereof, his Majesty said, That the same was the garter wherewith Mr. *Alexander* pressed to have bound his hands; and then, Sir *Thomas Erskin* gripped to the same garter, and said, That he would keep it, which he has yet in keeping.

Sic subscribitur,
JOHN GRAHAM of *Balgowne*.

I Mr. *John Moncrief* depones as follows, to-wit, That day I was still present with my Lord of *Gowrie*, unto the time I heard his Majesty cry, Treason! and saw him put his arm furth of the window of the room, and then left him: for I conceived in my heart it was plain treason, conspired against his Majesty, and was induced hereto, in respect of these presumptions following: *First*, I saw the King's Majesty and umquhile Mr. *Alexander Ruthven* my Lord's brother go furth at the hall-door their alanes; whereas his Majesty had no weapons, and Mr. *Alexander* had a sword. *Next*, I saw his Majesty come in a quiet and sober manner to the town, wherethrough appeared he would have no evil purpose in his mind. *Item*, He said, Mr. *Alexander* riding to *Falkland* in the morning, was obscured from me and my brother *Hugh* where he was; and I having enquired of my Brother *Hugh* where he was riding to, he knew nothing thereof; so that neither he nor I could get trial of the same. *Item*, I having enquired at *Andrew Henderson* himself, who rode to *Falkland*, and returned two hours before him, saluted me, and answered, That he had been two or three miles above the town; and says, the said *Andrew* had another doublet on, more than he used commonly, and was more bulksom; and, as appears, might have contain'd ane Secret. *Item*, That day being the Council-day of the town, my Lord excused himself, in respect of his advice. *Item*, I having pressed him to subscribe ane Confirmation of ane Lady's, first refused, in respect aforesaid; always passed it thereafter. *Item*, my Lord tarried longer from his dinner nor he used; and albeit *Andrew Ruthven*, who was with the Master, came and rounded my Lord at the board, he made him to misknow all things, unto the time that the said Mr. *Alexander* came himself, and then raise from the board, and met his Majesty. *Item*, My Lord obscured a together, that he knew of the coming of any man, while the Master came. *Item*, Mr. *Thomas Cranstoun* was the first that I heard cry, The King's Majesty is away. *Item*, After my Lord Duke and my Lord *Mar*, and his Majesty's servants were in the close, my Lord of *Gowrie* came back again to the hall, saying, The King was away: so that, as I thought, he would have each man thinking so. And I thought his Majesty was not received with that hearty complement as became. *Item*, After his Majesty's riding away, my brother *Hugh* came to my house, and I enquiring of him what he thought of this matters; answered, Before God, so far as I can perceive, I trow, it shall kyth ane plain treason on my Lord's part. And I speiring at him, If he knew any thing thereof? answered, he knew nothing; but he and *Henry Ruthven*, after all things were ended, fell in conference thereanent, and he thought things were likely. *Lastly*, *Andrew Henderson*'s Letter moves me most of all. And, upon my salvation and condemnation, I know no farther in this matter; nor yet can remember of any other circumstance or presumption, might have induced me to conceive the former, which I apprehend, in manner foresaid.

Sic subscribitur,
Mr. JOHN MONCRIEF.

I *Andrew Roy*, one of the Baillies of the Burgh of *Perth*, be thir Presents testifies upon my conscience, in the sight of God, as I shall answer to him in the Great Day, That upon the fifth day of *August*, one thousand and six hundred years, I being in the umquhile Earl of *Gowrie*'s Lodging, when his Majesty was there, saw his Majesty, after his dinner, accompanied with the Master of *Gowrie*, rise from the table, and gang furth of the chamber where he had dined; but, to what place, I know not; being beholding the said umquhile Earl of *Gowrie*'s entertainment of the Noblemen, in drinking his Majesty's Scoll to them; which, his Majesty, before his rising from the table, had commanded him to do. And after this, the Lords, viz. my Lord Duke, my Lord of *Mar*, my Lord *Lindores*, and my Lord of *Inchechaffrey*, with sundry of his Majesty's Gentlemen and Servants, accompanied with the Earl of *Gowrie* in person; and short space after dinner, had missed his Majesty, and enquired where he should be; they went to the fore-gate, and speir'd at the Porter, If he saw the King go furth at the fore-gate? and heard the Porter answer, That his Majesty was not gone furth that way. Also, that the Earl of *Gowrie* said to the Porter, Ye lie, knave, he is furth; and the Porter replied, That he should give his head, in case his Majesty were furth.

Yet, upon the Earl of *Gowrie*'s assurance, that his Majesty was furth to the *Inche*, the Lords issued out in haste at the fore-gate, and speiring where the King was, I saw ane ding up the long front-window, in the north-side of the turret, upon the high-gate; but who dang it up, I know not. And farther, saw clearly his Majesty shut furth his head and arm at the foresaid window, and heard his Majesty crying loudly, Fy, treason! treason! and murder! help, Earl of *Mar*! Whereupon, I being very agast, and wonderfully astonished, at that cruel and terrible sight, and pitiful and woful cry, I not knowing what the matter meant, but perceiving his Majesty in extream and great danger, ran with all possible diligence thro' the streets, crying loudly, Fy, treason; treason against the King! for God's sake, all honest men, haste and relieve the King: and commanded to ring the common bell, that all might come in haste to his Majesty's relief; and then I returned with all possible diligence, with a great number of the people with me, and came before the foresaid turret and window, where I saw his Majesty first cry out; and then I cried out, How is the King? But my Lord Duke and my Lord of *Mar* answered, The King is well, (praise be to God). Then I cried again up to his Majesty, and shew his Majesty, That the Baillies and Township were then come, in all haste, to supply and relieve his Majesty: and therefore besought his Majesty to command what was his Majesty's Will, and best to be done. And then his Majesty beckoned furth his hand to me and to the people, commanding me to cause the people retire them to their lodgings. Which commandment I incontinent obeyed, and commanded all manner of men to retire themselves to their lodgings; and likewise passed to the mercat-cross, and, by open proclamation commanded in his Highness's name, that all men should retire them to their lodgings, under the pain of treason, who obeyed not incontinent after my charge. And this I testify to be of verity, by the faith and truth of my body, so far as I justly can remember. In witness of which, I have subscribed these presents, with my hand, at *Perth*, the thirteenth day of *October*, one thousand and six hundred years, before these witnesses, Mr. *Patrick Gallowah*, Minister to his Majesty; *James Drummond* of *Letchel*; *Oliver Young*, *Constantine Wallace*, *Thomas Johnston*, Baillies; *Henry Elder*, Clerk; *Robert Anderson*, *Andrew Mowat*, and *William Jack*, Burgesses of *Perth*. *Sic subscribitur*, ANDREW ROY, Baillie, with my hand. Mr. *Patrick Gallowah* witness; *James Drummond* witness; *Oliver Young*, Baillie, witness; *Thomas Johnstoun*, Baillie, witness; *Robert Anderson* witness, *Andrew Arnolt* witness, *William Jack* witness, *Henry Elder*, Scribe, witness.

ROBert Christie, Porter to umquhile *John* Earl of *Gowrie*, of the age of thirty years, *solutus*, depones, That he was Porter to the Earl of *Gowrie*, the fifth day of *August* libelled: sicklike he was by the space of five weeks before. And shortly after the dinner, this Deponent saw my Lord Duke, the Earl of *Mar*, the Earl of *Gowrie*, come to the close: and my Lord Duke speird at this Deponent, if his Majesty was passed furth of the close? The Deponent answered, that he was not furth. Then the Lord of *Mar* said, Billy, tell me the verity, if his Majesty be furth or not? And he answered, in truth he is not furth. The Earl of *Gowrie* looking with an angry countenance, said, Thou lied, he is furth at the back-gate, and through the *Inche*. Then this Deponent answered, that cannot be, my Lord, for I have the key of the back-gate, and of all the gates of the place. Thereafter, this Deponent heard and saw his Majesty looking furth of the window of the round, and crying, Treason! Treason! fy, help, my Lord of *Mar*! And incontinent, my Lord Duke, the Earl of *Mar*, and others, ran up the stair of the turnpike to the gallery: and thereafter, the Lord of *Gowrie* came from the high-street, within the close, having a steel-bonnet on his head, and a drawn sword in his hand, accompanied with *Alexander* and *Harry Ruthven*, *Patrick Evict* and *Hugh Moncrief*, Mr. *Thomas Cranstoun*; all having drawn swords in their hands, and passed all together

together with my Lord, up the old turnpike; but what was done within the house and place thereafter, knows not, but by report: neither saw he any joist brought to the place, by any of the town. And knows no more of the matter.

Sic subscribitur,
ROBERT CHRISTIE.

ALexander Blair, younger of *Balthyik*, sworn and examined, depones, conform to *immediate præcedenti*; except, That he saw not my Lord of *Gowrie* pass with his company, and drawn swords, up the turnpike: but saw *Alexander* and *Hary Ruthven*, and *Hugh Moncrief*, come down the little turnpike, where they and my Lord had ascended; the saids three persons having drawn swords in their hands; but saw not *Patrick Eviot* there. And this Deponent says, that after the tumult was risen, and this Deponent pressing to enter within the place, he was a little staid by them in the place; but they yielded at once, and the Deponent got entry. Likewise he saw a joist brought from the town, and set up at the wall of the close; but who brought the samen in, he knows not.

Sic subscribitur,
ALEXANDER BLAIR,
Appearand of Balthyik.

GEorge Hay, prior of *Charterhouse*, of the age of twenty-eight years, or thereby, married; depones, conform to the Lord Duke of *Lenox*, in all things, after his Majesty's entry in *St. Johnstoun*, the day libelled: adding, that, samen day, the Deponent having ado in *St. Johnstoun* with the Earl of *Gowrie*, and speaking with him in his own place, he saw *Andrew Henderson* come in booted from *Falkland*, and heard the said Earl of *Gowrie* enquire of the said *Andrew*, who was with his Majesty in *Falkland*? And thereafter, the said Earl took the said *Andrew Henderson* to the cabinet, and, after a certain space, the Earl coming to the chamber, he gave this Deponent his dispatch; saying, That he had to do that day, and might not await of his errand, and bade him come another day.

Sic subscribitur,
GEORGE HAY.

MR. *Peter Hay*, of the age of thirty years, or thereby, married; depones, conform to *George Hay* in all things, the Witness immediately preceding.

Sic subscribitur,
PETER HAY.

RObert Graham of *Thorink*, sworn and examined, depones, conform to the Duke of *Lenox*, after that his Majesty entered in *Perth*.

Sic subscribitur, ROBERT GRAHAM.

OLiver Young, Baillie in *Perth*, sworn and examined, depones, That the day libelled, this Deponent was in the Earl of *Gowrie*'s lodging, where he saw the King dine, and after dinner, saw the King's Majesty and Mr. *Alexander Ruthven* pass their allanes through the hall, and up the turnpike; and immediately thereafter, this Deponent passed to his own lodging in the town, where he abode while the cry and tumult raise; and incontinent, this Deponent running to the place whereat his Majesty cryed out at the window; and commanded this Deponent, by name, to stay the tumult of the People: the which, this Deponent obeyed and did; and saw *Hugh Moncrief* coming furth of the place; but his face being bloody, and *Hary Ruthven*, one of the defenders, at the mouth of the Water-gate, with a drawn sword in his hand: and knows no more in the matter.

Sic subscribitur, OLIVER YOUNG.

JAmes Drummond of *Pitcarnis*, sworn and examined, depones, *conformis immediate præcedenti in omnibus*: adding, that as the Deponent, immediately after the cry raise, running to the place libelled, he meets upon the high-street *Alexander Ruthven* one of the defenders, having a drawn sword in his hand, and crying fire and powder! And he knows no more of the matter.

Sic subscribitur,
JAMES DRUMMOND.

WIlliam Reynd, flesher in St. *Johnstoun*, of the age of thirty years, or thereby, married, depones, That he saw within the close of *Perth*, after fray raise, *Patrick Eviot* and *Hugh Moncrief*, both bloody, having drawn swords in their hands.

Sic subscribitur,
WILLIAM REYND.

THomas burgess of *Perth*, sworn and examined, depones, conform to *James Drummond* and *William Reynd*; but he saw not *Patrick Eviot* there.

Sic subscribitur,
THOMAS

GEorge Wilson, servant to *James Erskin*, of the age of twenty-four years, or thereby, *solutus*, depones, conform to Sir *Thomas Erskin* in all things, by reason this Deponent was in company with the said Sir *Thomas*, after the first time, that he and *James Erskin* his brother had gripped the Earl of *Gowrie*, and were sindered from him be his servants; and immediately thereafter, this Deponent accompanied the said Sir *Thomas Erskin* up to the turnpike, into the chamber where his Majesty was, where he saw, as the said Sir *Thomas* has deponed, in all things.

Sic subscribitur,
GEORGE WILSON.

DAvid Reynd, flesher in *Perth*, sworn and examined, depones, conform to *James Drummond*, and heard *Alexander Ruthven* cry for powder; but saw not *Patrick Eviot*.

Sic subscribitur,
DAVID REYND.

GIlbert Hutchinson in *Perth*, of the age of twenty-four years, or thereby, *solutus*, depones, conform to *James Drummond* in all things, and *David Reynd*.

Sic subscribitur,
GILBERT HUTCHINSON.

JOhn Murray of *Arbany*, of the age of fifty-eight years, or thereby, married, depones, the day libelled, this Deponent came to *St. Johnstoun* after dinner, where he heard his Majesty crying furth of the window of the round, Fy, Treason, my Lord of *Mar*, help! Immediately thereafter, my Lord of *Mar* and the Duke ran up the broad turnpike; and the Deponent followed them in the close, where he saw the Lord of *Gowrie*, having ane steel bonnet on his head, and two drawn swords, ane in ilk hand, and saw the said Earl pass up the turnpike, accompanied with certain his servants, having drawn swords in their hands, of whom he knows none.

Sic subscribitur,
JOHN MURRAY.

THomas Burrell, burgess of *Perth*, sworn and examin'd, depones, conform to *James Drummond*, adding, That the time of the fray this Deponent entring within the close of the place, he saw standing in the close, with drawn swords in their hands, *Alexander* and *Harrie Ruthvens*, and *Hugh Moncrief* blooding in his face; and, at the same time, this Deponent saw Mr. *Thomas Cranstoun* come down the black turnpike, and he took forth of his hand his sword; and heard the said *Alexander Ruthven* cry for fire and powder; and saw not *Patrick Eviot* there.

Sic subscribitur,
THOMAS BURRELL.

ALexander Forrest, tailor in *Perth*, of the age of forty years, or thereby, married, depones, the day libelled, he saw *George Craigingelt*, and *Walter Crookshank* a laquey, standing in the yeard with drawn swords.

Sic subscribitur,
ALEXANDER FORREST.

WIlliam Robertson, notar in *Perth*, of the age of thirty-four years, or thereby, married, depones, the day libelled, this Deponent being within the close of the place, he saw the Lord of *Gowrie* standing in the close, accompanied with seven or eight Persons, of whom he knew none; the said Earl then having ane steel bonnet on his head, and ane drawn sword in ilk hand; at the whilk sight this Deponent being afraid, past furth of the place, and knows no more in the matter.

Sic subscribitur,
WILLIAM ROBERTSON.

RObert Calbraith, servant to the King's Majesty, of the age of thirty years, depones, conform to the Lord Duke of *Lenox* in all things, by reason this Deponent, all that Day, was in company with his Majesty, and after that his Majesty had cried out at the window, Treason! this Deponent followed the Duke and Earl of *Mar* up the turnpike, and depones, as they have deponed.

Sic subscribitur,
ROBERT CALBRAITH.

RObert Brown, servant to his Majesty, depones, conform *immediate præcedenti in omnibus*, because this Deponent, the time libelled, accompanied Sir *John Hamilton* to fetch the hammers up to the gallery; and this Deponent passed up the little black turnpike, and, at his first entry within the chamber, he saw the Earl of *Gowrie* lying dead, there being at that time in company with his Majesty, Sir *Thomas Erskin*, Sir *Hugh Herries*, Sir *John Ramsay*, and *George Wilson*.

Sic subscribitur,
ROBERT BROWN.

JAmes Bog, porter to his Majesty, sworn and examined, depones, That he saw the King's Majesty and Mr. *Alexander Ruthven* pass through the hall, and saw that day, *George Craigingelt* with ane drawn sword in his hand, accompanied with certain rascals; and, in others, depones, conform to the Lord Duke and Earl of *Mar* in all things.

Sic subscribitur,
JAMES BOG.

JOhn Bog, servant to his Majesty in the ale-cellar, sworn and examined, depones, conform to *James Bog*.

Sic subscribitur,
JOHN BOG.

ALexander Peebles, burgess of *Perth*, of the age of thirty years, or thereby, married, depones, the day libelled, this Deponent being within his own house foranent the Earl of *Gowrie*'s lodging; how soon his mother heard the common bell ring, she locked the door, and held him in all the time; and saw at that time, the Earl of *Gowrie* enter in at the gate with two drawn swords, ane in ilk hand, and ane lacquey put ane steel-bonnet one his head; and, ane certain space thereafter, the Deponent saw *Hugh Moncrief* come furth of the place with ane bloody head, and *Patrick Eviot*'s man likewise blooding; and also saw *Patrick Eviot* come furth of the hall; but remembers not if he had ane sword in his hand: and saw also *Alexander Ruthven* come furth with ane sword drawn in his hand.

Sic subscribitur,
ALEXANDER PEEBLES.

The Sentence and Doom pronounced by the Lords and Estates of Parliament for High-Treason, against John *Earl of* Gowrie, *and his Brother Mr.* Alexander Ruthven.

[To repeat the Libel and Executions, or the Libels *verbatim*, would be uselesly tedious to Readers, therefore I insert the Doom or Sentence *verbatim*, pronounced on the 15th Day of *November* 1600.]

'THE said Lords and Estates of Parliament finds, decerns and declares, that the said umquhill *John* Earl of *Gowrie*, and Mr. *Alexander Ruthven* his Brother, committed and did open and manifest Treason against our said Sovereign Lord, in all points, articles and matter contain'd in the said summons, and therefore it was given for doom, by the mouth of *David Lindsay* Dempster of Parliament, in manner and form as follows

'This Court of Parliament showes for law, that the said umquhil *John* 'Earl of *Gowrie*, and umquhil Mr. *Alexander Ruthven* his brother, com'mitted the foresaid crime of Treason and Lese-Majesty in their life'times, against our Sovereign Lord and his Authority Royal, in manner at 'length contain'd in the said summons: and therefore decerns and declares 'the name, memory and dignity of the said umquhil *John* Earl of *Gowrie*, 'and umquhil Mr. *Alexander Ruthven* his Brother, to be extinguish'd, and 'their arms to be cancell'd and deleted furth of the books of arms and no'bility; so that their posterity shall be unhabile, and uncapable in all time 'coming to bruik, possess or enjoy any offices, dignities, honours, suc'cessions, possessions, and all goods, moveables and immoveables, rights, 'titles, hope of succession, and others whatsomever within this Realm; 'and all goods, lands, rents, offices, benefits, honours, dignities, hope and 'appearance of succession, rights, titles, possessions, and other goods and 'gear, moveable and immoveable, and to theirs whatsomever, whilk is any 'ways pertain'd to the said umquhil *John* Earl of *Gowrie*, and umquhil 'Mr. *Alexander Ruthven* his Brother; or whilk is by any right, title, hope 'of succession, possession, or any other manner of way might have belong'd 'or pertain'd to them, to be confiscated, devolved in our Sovereign Lord, 'and to appertain to his Highness: and in all time coming, remain in 'property with his Majesty for ever. And farder, his Majesty and Estates 'foresaid, in detestation of the said horrible, unnatural and vile Treason, 'attempted by the said umquhil *John*, some time Earl of *Gowrie*, and um'quhil Mr. *Alexander Ruthven*, against his Highness's own life; decerns, 'statutes and ordains, that the said bodies of the saids Traitors shall be 'carried, upon *Monday* next, to the publick cross of *Edinburgh*: and 'there to be hang'd, quarter'd, and drawn, in presence of the hail People: 'and thereafter, the heads, quarters and carcasses, to be affix'd upon the 'most patent parts and places of the Burroughs of *Edinburgh*, *Perth*, '*Dundee* and *Stirling*. And this I give for doom.'

Besides the personal sentence given against the Earl of *Gowrie*, this Parliament did, by distinct Acts, disinherit and inhabilitate the brethren, and all the posterity of the Earl of *Gowrie*, from enjoying any heritage, place or office within *Scotland*; and discharging all Persons whatsoever to move or interceed for them, under high pains.

By another Act, the surname of *Ruthven* is appointed to be extinguish'd and abolish'd for ever; and such of them as were innocent of this Treason, were ordered to take other names, and to be inserted in publick Records.

By another Act, the 5th of *August* was appointed to be observed for thanksgiving, annually, and in all time coming, for the King's deliverance from the said Treason *.

By another Act, the lands and estate of *Ruthven* were annexed to the patrimony of the Crown. And, by several other particular Acts, Sir *Thomas Erskin*, (afterwards Earl of *Kelly*,) Sir *John Ramsay*, and Sir *Hugh Herries*, and some others, who did most immediately preserve the King's Person, had benefices and other favours conferr'd upon them in Parliament.

The Sentence and Doom pronounced by the Lords and Estates of Parliament, for High Treason, against Alexander *and* Harry Ruthvens, Hugh Moncreif *and* Patrick Eviot; *who were actors in the same crime, and judged by the same Parliament, on the 15th day of* November 1600.

'THE saids Lords and Estates of Parliament, finds, decerns, and de'clares, that the saids *Alexander* and *Harry Ruthven*, *Hugh Mon'creif*, and *Patrick Eviot*, and ilk ane of them, committed, and did open 'and manifest Treason against our Sovereign Lord in all points, articles, 'and manner contain'd in the said summons; and therefore it was given 'for doom by the mouth of *David Lindsay*, Dempster of Parliament, in 'manner and form as follows;

'This Court of Parliament shows for law, that the saids *Alexander* '*Ruthven*, *Harry Ruthven* his Brother, Sons lawful to umquhil *Alexander* '*Ruthven* of *Freeland*; *Hugh Moncreif*, Brother to *William Moncreif* of 'that ilk; and *Patrick Eviot*, Brother to *Colin Eviot* of *Balhousie*; com'mitted the crimes of Treason and Lese-Majesty against our Sovereign 'Lord and his Authority Royal, in manner at length contain'd in the said 'summons: and therefore decerns and declares their Persons to underly 'the pains of Treason and Lese-Majesty, and last punishment prescrib'd 'by the laws of this Realm; and all their goods, moveable and immove'able, as well heritages as offices, benefices, and others whatsomever per'taining to them, or whilk is, might any ways belong, or appertain to 'them, to be confiscated to his Majesty; and to remain with his Highness 'in property for ever; and their posterity to be now, and in all time 'coming, uncapable and unhabil to bruik and possess within this Realm, 'any honours, dignities, offices, benefices, successions, or other goods or 'gear, moveable or immoveable. And this I give for doom.'

* See *Rapin* (oct. Edit.) vol. IX. p. 251. for observations on this new Holiday.
Lord Chancellor *Bacon* in his Letter to the Marquis of *Buckingham*, dated *Aug.* 5, 1618. (See his Works, vol. IV. page. 670.) says, "I am here rejoicing with my neigh" bours the townsmen of *St. Albans* for this HAPPY DAY."
Mr. *Stephens* in his note on that passage in Lord *Bacon*'s Letter, says, "*The fifth of August* being the Anniversary of the King's deliverance from the Earl of *Gowrie*'s con" spiracy, was by some call'd the Court Holy-day, and ridicul'd as a fiction; though the truth thereof being deliver'd down by Archbishop *Spotiswood*, and other good " Historians, I see no great reason to call it into question."
In the Parliament which condemn'd *John* Earl of *Gowrie*, and his Brother Mr. *Alexander* in the year 1600, let it be considered, that a great part of the Nobility, and many of the Gentry, which did sit in that Parliament, were descended of *Gowrie*'s family, and nearly allied to it. As also the Lords of the Articles, who did examine the witnesses and evidences, several were of near relation to the Panel, particularly *Lenox* and *Levingston*; and the Barons and Burgesses being elected members, not by the King and Court, but by the Barons and Burroughs, and two Bishops and four Abbots, Church-men, being also of that number; what ground remains for doubting their impartiality and veracity, in making a report of what was asserted and sworn so publickly by the witnesses? And all the depositions, and written evidences, being then recorded, do yet remain in *publica custodia*, *Earl* Cromerty's *Account of the conspiracies of the Earls of* Gowrie, page 13.

VII. The Arraignment and Judgement of Captain THOMAS LEE, at the Sessions-house near *Newgate*, on *Monday* the 26th of *February*, 1600*. for *High Treason*, 43 *Eliz.*

The INDICTMENT.

"THAT he plotted and compassed to raise Sedition and Rebellion " to the Queen's Majesty's Person, to deprive her of her Crown " and Dignity, take away her life, commit her people to slaugh" ter, alter the form of Government and Religion; and upon this wicked " resolution, on the 12th day of *February*, 1600, in the afternoon about " the hours of four and five, he the said Captain *Lee* repaired to the " chamber of one Sir *Robert* † *Crosse*, Knt. (*sic MS.*) in the Parish of " *St. Giles* in the Fields, of purpose to discover his plot to him, and to " persuade the said Sir *Robert Crosse* to consent to join with him; namely " to go to the Royal Palace of our Sovereign Lady, being then at *Westminster*, and then and there to lay violent hands on her sacred Person, " and to take her prisoner; thinking by that means to set at liberty the " Earls of *Essex* and *Southampton*, and other Traitors now in prison. " But the said Sir *Robert Crosse* not consenting to that traitorous practice; " this *Thomas Lee* himself repaired to the said Royal Palace between the " hours of eight and nine in the same night, and pressed into the pre" sence, even to the Privy-chamber door, with purpose to have taken " the Person of our said Sovereign Lady, and performed his other trai" torous designs."

But there in that manner was apprehended, and examined, and so committed to prison.

To this being asked, whether he were guilty, or not?

He answered, Not guilty in manner and form as there set down.

And by whom he would be tried?

Said, by God and the Country, if he might see his Jury. He said farther, (protesting he was not guilty of any ill intent) that my Lord Admiral had long sought his life, and now he was like to have it.

The Jury called, he took exception to one, saying, he liked not his face; but urged to shew other reasons, he challenged him peremptorily.

But that, the Judges told him, could not be allowed in that case.

Capt. *Lee*. Then I am contented; proceed as you will.

My Lord Chief-Justice, at the end of the calling and impannelling, advertised the Jury what Treason was; namely, to intend to lay violent hands upon her Majesty, or to take away her life; to raise Rebellion even the intent was Treason, if it could be discovered by any overt-act.

Mr. Attorney-General. That he would prove him that stood at the bar, guilty of many foul Treasons.

Capt. *Lee*. Nay, for all your wit and learning, you shall never do that. I care not what you can say. I have lost a great deal of blood in her Majesty's service, and done good service in *Ireland*.

Mr. Attorney. That we shall see anon; and proceeded upon the Indictment: Where he shewed how, in the late Rebellion of that Arch-traitor *Essex*. For, said he, all the Nobility draw their Honour and Dignity of the Queen, as the Stars take their Light from the Sun; and so when they enter into any Rebellions and traitorous Practices against her Majesty, they deprive themselves of the Light, as it were, of that glory and honour which before-time they received from her, the chief and fountain of all their Light: and so he doubted not to call those persons Traitors, who, whilst they stood, were Noblemen; and now, failing of their allegiance, lost their Titles.

In the late Rebellion of this Traitor *Essex*, this *Lee* [illegible] and offered his service to the Lord-Admiral and Mr. Secretary, as he pretended, to kill the Earl, which he said he could do, as being well acquainted, and loved of the Earl: but they refusing, he would needs have offered so much to the Queen's Majesty; but with what mind, his practice will discover.

Capt. *Lee*. It is true, I would have been the first man should have gone against him whilst I thought him a traitor, and so would have adventured against any, to have defended the Queen.

Mr. Attorney-General. How you meant it, that will be plain anon.

After this, he came to Sir *Henry Nevil*, a Gentleman of noble blood, and uttered his mind to him concerning the practice in the Indictment; and after that came to Sir *Robert Crosse*, as you shall hear, and opened his vile purpose at large to persuade him. That these worthy men deserving all honour for their Loyalty, refused, and revealed his vile Plot in good time. And thus much he had confessed under his hand.

Capt. *Lee*. What I have set my hand to, I cannot tell; but I am sure I had never such intent as you would persuade the Jury I had.

Mr. Attorney. That is to be proved by Sir *Robert Crosse*, what you meant when you went about to persuade him.

Capt.

* From an authentic Manuscript, sent the Editor.
† Though the name in the MS. is *Crosse*, yet I take it to be *Crofts*, as *Camden* writes it.

Capt. *Lee.* I perswaded him not; and he will not say so.

Mr. Attorney. Well! he shall speak it before your face.

Then Sir *Robert Crosse* was sworn, and set in sight of the Prisoner; and began to tell,

That upon *Thursday* about five of the clock at night, Capt. *Lee* came to his lodging, he being ready to go abroad, and told him, he should not go out, yet he must speak with him; and so taking him aside, he spoke to him of these matters of Treason, and said, that half a dozen resolute men, &c.

Capt. *Lee* here interrupted him, saying; Nay, good *Robin Crosse* speak all the truth.

Mr. Attorney will'd Capt. *Lee* to give him leave to speak upon his oath.

Capt. *Lee* replied, I would nothing but put him in mind of the circumstance; and said, good *Robin*, remember how I began.

Sir *Robert* said he would. Thus then you spake to me:

I marvel what will become of these matters; a man might do a brave act to set those Lords at liberty. Why how? quoth I. Marry, Sir *Walter Rawleigh* might get him eternal honour and love more than ever he can otherwise, if he would procure her Majesty's warrant to free them, which he might compass by undertaking her person. I answered, You may be sure he will not do it. Then Capt. *Lee* reply'd, If half a dozen resolute men, such as might have access to the presence, would step unto the Queen, and kneel before her, and never rise till she had sign'd a warrant, and then send it by the Lord-Admiral, and never stir till the Earls of *Essex* and *Southampton* were brought to the Queen's presence, they might do it. And then he named Sir *Henry Nevil*, Sir *Jarvis Clifton*, Sir *George Gifford*, Sir *Richard Weston*, and themselves. I objected, how if some should offer to come upon us, and remove us from her Majesty. He answered, we might keep any body out by shutting the door, and telling them that offered to come in, that if any harm came to the Queen, if she should do otherwise than well, be it at their peril; and this was all. To which Sir *Robert* answered, he would sleep upon it.

Capt. *Lee.* But I did perswade you, Sir *Robert*, with protestation, saying, I never meant to be an actor myself, or perswade any other to it. And what a wretch am I, to be thought a villain for that I never meant? For my Lord of *Essex*, indeed, I loved and honoured him, so long as I thought him an honest man and a good subject. I spake these words with an *if*; *if* such a thing could be done.

Mr. Attorney. Why press'd you to the Privy-chamber door at such a time, where you were not wont to come?

And then was shewed the Examination of *William Poynes*, (who was himself in the *Fact*) to this purpose.

That he saw Capt. *Lee* press towards the Privy-chamber door, and stand very near, and mistrusting the worst, drew towards him. When he came near, he mark'd his colour, that was pale, his countenance stern, and his face having great drops of sweat standing on it *. When he came near to him, Capt. *Lee* lean'd hard upon him, and said, It was one of the wonders of God that I was not in this action with the Earl of *Essex*. Why? said Mr. *Poynes*. I was so well acquainted, and so much with my Lord of *Essex*, answered he. Then they paus'd. And Capt. *Lee* ask'd, Whether the Queen were at supper? Mr. *Poynes* answered, No.

Mr. Attorney. Mark, all the rest was but to bring in this.

Mr. *Poynes* told Capt *Lee* farther, perhaps he might do good service, if he were so well acquainted with the Earl, it was likely he knew somewhat of the Plot. Not I, answered Capt. *Lee*, but you shall hear more villanies and knaveries yet.

Mr. Attorney. Mark: What meant he by that speech?

To this. Capt. *Lee* could not deny but he spake it; but said, how was I there? had I any company? had I any dagger, or any thing about me, that might shew I meant to do the Queen any harm? No, I had not, neither did I mean any such thing; and for my being at the Privy-chamber door, I had been there five hundred times, and never was noted. And what reason had I for my Lord of *Essex*, to adventure any such thing. I have spent my blood in her Majesty's service, and so would again.

Mr. Attorney. You mark, there was love between him and the traitor *Essex*. And then Mr. Attorney caused a Letter to be read, which was written in the behalf of Capt. *Lee* to the now Deputy by the Earl of *Essex*: 'That he knew it was for one in place to do what he would; and further, What an unreasonable thing it was for any to require that at his friend's hands, that were out of time. He desired his Lordship to take notice of the Bearer Capt. *Lee*, one near allied to him, and that suffered for him, one that did as good service as any, when himself was in *Ireland*, and one that was as well seated for service as any; thus, whatsoever he did for the bearer, he would acknowledge as for himself. and so he concluded.'

Then likewise was read the confession of Capt. *Lee* to this purpose, That he loved and honoured the Earl of *Essex* as much as any man in *England*, saving Sir *Henry Lee*.

Mr. Attorney. This being but the prologue to an ensuing Tragedy, he would give a taste of the practices and treasons of the Earl of *Essex*, and his complices.

Capt. *Lee.* He doubted the treason would light on some of them that held the Earl a traitor.

Whereat a confused noise there was, that he was a villain to defend a traitor.

Mr. Attorney proceeded to shew the Queen's great grace in sending to him the said Earl, and the contempt and indignities offered to those honourable Persons and Counsellors sent to call him to his allegiance.

The Lord Chief-Justice spake to this point, confirming of his own knowledge what the Attorney said, much after the manner it was delivered at the Earl's arraignment. The Attorney, continued he, would of his own knowledge affirm, that all the associates and complices of the Earl in this practice, were of these three sorts; either *Atheists*, *Papists*, or *Men of broken Estates*: for he had looked into them all particularly. Then named he Sir *Christopher Blunt* and Sir *John Davis*, known Papists: *Catesby* and *Tresham* likewise; the last of which he said was a stock, that was *genere minax Dei*, and was he that abused the Lord-keeper in *Essex*-house; *Salisbury* also he named to be a notable villain, and these seven years together laid out for by the Lord Chief-Justice: and so of the rest he said he could speak.

Mr. Attorney. Besides in *Ireland*, it is plain to be proved, how he held intelligence with Seminaries and Priests, entertaining them to deal with the King of *Spain* and the Pope, to make himself King of *England*.

Capt. *Lee.* Who! my Lord of *Essex* deal with Seminaries and Priests? nay, it is well known he too much disliked those *Pater-noster* fellows to call them to a reckoning in any such matter.

Mr. Attorney said further, It is well known that the Earl of *Essex* used this Capt. *Lee* as a messenger to *Tyrone*, and *Tyrone* made him his bedfellow, and Capt. *Lee* brought a message back to the Earl of *Essex*, as he had confessed. Then there was some mention of a Letter between them; but I could not well hear what. Then was read Capt. *Lee's* confession to that point, how Sir *Christopher Blunt*, being Marshal, sent him to *Tyrone*, and when he came, he found him very peremptory, using insolent speeches, and condemning our nation as a base People, and said the Earl of *Essex* was sent to kill him, but he should not compass it; any of his slaves might easily kill the Earl, but he would not take the life of any. And further, if he would (meaning the Earl of *Essex*) follow his plot, he would make him the greatest in *England*. Capt. *Lee* had them read out all: they left out much matter that should be known.

Mr. Attorney would not have any further thing read, and pressed further, the circumstances that Capt. *Lee* had confessed, that made him think the Earl of *Essex* know of his going; namely, for that the Marshal was well known not to do such things, of far less consequence, without the Earl's privity and consent. Again, the Earl of *Essex* made a private sudden journey to the then house of the said Capt. *Lee*, where the said Sir *Christopher Blunt* lay sick, and within a day after, Sir *Christopher* sent him to *Tyrone*.

To these confessions read, Capt. *Lee* answered nothing, as not belonging to the matter of his Indictment.

Mr. Attorney urged, That it was very likely that this man had been made acquainted with these late practices; which Capt. *Lee* with protestation denied.

Mr. Attorney. Nay, it could not be but he must have an ill meaning, that he should offer, as he did, to kill the Earl of *Essex*, *flagrante crimine*, in that sort, and after enter into this plot and practice. Mark, said the Attorney, he said they might *force* her Majesty to do it: mark this word, *force*, (which, as I remember, was in some part of his own confession) *Go in unto her, and never leave her till she had done it.*

Capt. *Lee.* Why I did say, with an *If*; and then I am not a fool, but I know they must have been of a resolution that should have undertaken such a thing, and such as would not fear to displease her Majesty for half an hour, to please her all her life after: but I never meant to have been an actor myself.

The Court affirmed it was Treason to undertake to *force* her Majesty to do any thing against her will.

Capt. *Lee.* I never undertook it.

Mr. Attorney urged his words to Sir *Robert Mansfield* riding in his coach after he was apprehended, that shewed himself guilty, and so willed Sir *Robert Mansfield* should be sworn.

Sir *Robert Mansfield* affirmed, That Capt. *Lee* should say, that he had humbly sued to her Majesty this twelvemonth, that he might be employed in some service, wherein he might have some throats cut; and now he thought he had done somewhat to bring him to his end.

Captain *Lee* seemed to take some exceptions against Sir *Robert Mansfield*.

Sir *Robert Mansfield* protested he would neither wrong him, nor any man; and but for this cause, he had no reason to think otherwise than well of Capt. *Lee*.

Captain *Lee* confessed he had lived in misery, and cared not to live, his enemies were so many and so great.

Mr. Attorney urged her Majesty's pardon to him heretofore; for he said, he was a man many ways having passed the danger of the law, being full of cruelty and blood.

Capt *Lee* answered, it was the worst thing her Majesty did for him, to pardon him.

Mr. Attorney. Hark, how ungrateful he is!

Capt. *Lee.* Nay, I humbly thank her Majesty for that her Grace; but it had been better for me I had died then. I have lost a great deal of blood since, and now am like to end worse: and for that it is said I am a bloody man and cruel; I protest I have been in her Majesty's service forward, and indeed in fair fight I would do the worst against her Majesty's enemies: but when they submitted to my mercy, I ever used them but as became a Soldier and a Gentleman, as merciful as any.

My Lord of *London* told him, he knew it was a common thing in *Ireland*, they would not believe a man was dead till his head were off; and so you would not have any body perswaded that you were a traitor, unless her Majesty (God bless her) were dead.

Capt. *Lee.* No, my Lord, I never meant any such thing. You know, my Lord, it was ever my fault to be loose and lavish of my tongue; and that was my fault now, and I am like to pay for it.

Then the Jury were put together, who quickly found him guilty.

Upon Verdict given,

Mr. Attorney said, Now Capt. *Lee*, you may do well to confess this matter, what you know, and who set you on.

Capt. *Lee.* What? I am not a fool to be set on like a dog upon a bear; nobody set me on, for I endeavoured nothing.

* On the [illegible] of *February* *Thomas Lea* (a kinsman of Sir *Henry Lee*, who had wore the honour of the garter) told Sir *Robert Crofts*, Captain of a man of war, that it would be a glorious enterprize for [illegible] brave metled fellows to go to the Queen and compel her to discharge *Essex*, *Southampton*, and the rest that were in prison. He was a man himself of great assurance and resolution, had commanded a company in *Ireland*, was very intimate with *Tir-Oen*, and an absolute creature of the Earl of *Essex*. This did *Crofts* [illegible] discover to the Council; upon which this *Lea* was sought for, and found in the dusk of the evening about the door of the Queen's Privy-chamber. He seemed very thoughtful, was extreme pale, and in a great sweat, and frequently asked, *Whether her Majesty was ready to go to supper?* and, *whether the Council would be there?* In this posture he was seized, and examined, the next day had his trial, and by *Crofts's* evidence and his own confession, condemned, and carried away to *Tyburn*; where he owned that he had been indeed a great offender; but as to this design was very innocent, and having moreover protested, that he had never entertained the least ill thought against the Queen, he was there executed. And this, as the times went, appeared a very seasonable piece of justice. *Camden's Life* in the complete History of *England*, vol. [illegible] p. 6[illegible]. edit [illegible]

Mr.

Mr. Recorder with a very grave admonition to him, to make him see his fault and fly to God's mercy for pardon, pronounced Judgment; which he took patiently.

They asked him, what he had to say: he answered, nothing; but desired my Lord of *London*, that he might have one sent to him, fit for a man in his case.

Lord of *London*. What? you would not have a Jesuit or a Priest?

Capt. *Lee*. No, I am a Protestant: I never liked those *Pater-noster* fellows; but I desire a minister, and to receive the sacrament: and further I desire, my Lord-Chief-Justice, that my son may have no wrong, and that he may have that little that he had got together, and should leave behind him; for it was his by right, and his son might prove an honest man, and do his Country good service one day.

Lord-Chief-Justice. He should have his right; nobody should be wronged.

So the Court broke up.

Captain *Lee* still protesting he never intended any such thing against the Queen as was laid to his charge; which he continued to affirm afterwards to Mr. *Pasfield*, to whom he confessed his other sins very freely, even taking his death upon it.

He died the next day at *Tyburn* very christianly, confessing his other vices, but still denying this.

VIII. *The Trial of Sir* Christopher Blunt, *Sir* Charles Davers, *Sir* John Davis, *Sir* Gilly Merrick, *and* Henry Cuffe, March 5, 1600. 43 Eliz. *at* Westminster; *for* High-Treason *.

The Commissioners were,

The Earl of *Nottingham*, Lord High-Admiral.
The Lord *Hunsdon*, Lord-Chamberlain.
Mr. Secretary *Cecil*.
The Lord-Chief-Justice *Popham*.
Sir *John Fortescue*, Chancellor of the Exchequer.
Mr. Secretary *Herbert*.
With divers of the Judges.

THE Commission being read, the Court, proceeded to the Indictment, which was in substance as follows:

"That on the 8th day of *February* last, at *Essex-house*, they conspired the death and disinherison of the Queen's Majesty, and on that day caused an insurrection of the subjects, and made war in *London* against the Queen, and intended altering the Government, State, and Religion now established, and to surprize the Court at *Whitehall*. The Queen understanding of their intended Treasons, for preventing thereof, upon the 8th of *February*, sent the Lord-Keeper, the Earl of *Worcester*, Sir *William Knowles*, and the Lord-Chief-Justice, to *Essex-house*; they then commanded the Earls of *Essex* and *Southampton* upon their allegiance to desist from their purposes, to disperse their forces assembled, and to demean themselves as dutiful subjects. But they refused to obey their command; and committed them the said Lord-Keeper, Earl of *Worcester*, Sir *William Knowles*, and the Lord-Chief-Justice, to be strictly kept and detained in *Essex*-house, by the said Sir *John Davis*, keeping them in by force, and these words being used by some, Kill them! Kill them! And that the Earl of *Essex*, upon his going out of the house, commanded that if they should offer to deliver them out of their custody, or if the said Earl should miscarry in *London*, then they should kill the said Privy Councillors and the Earl of *Worcester*. And that the same day they, with the number of 300 men went into the City of *London*, seeking to stir up such citizens as they could move to their Rebellion. And that the said Sir *Charles Davers*, Sir *Christopher Blunt*, and Sir *John Davis*, on the said 8th day of *February*, together with the Earl of *Essex*, did fortify the said house, and armed themselves against the Earl of *Nottingham*, the Queen's Lieutenant, and against the Queen's Army and Forces sent for the suppressing of the said Rebels."

The Prisoners being demanded, whether they were guilty, or not guilty, of the several Treasons whereof they were indicted?

Sir *Christopher Blunt* confessed several of the things contained in the indictment, and would have pleaded not guilty to the rest ‡; but the Court told him he must plead general, either guilty or not guilty to the whole Indictment: and upon evidence excuse himself in what parts he can. Whereupon he pleaded to the Indictment, Not guilty; and put himself for his trial to God and his Country.

Sir *Charles Davers* made the like protestation, but was directed by the Court to plead to the Indictment and so he pleaded, Not guilty.

Sir *John Davis* said, his Case was different from the rest; but seeing he must plead negatively to all, he pleaded, Not Guilty.

Sir *Gilly Merrick* and Mr. *Cuffe* were arraigned upon another Indictment, but upon the points of the former Indictment, saving for levying of war in *London*, and assaulting the Queen's forces there, and conspiring and plotting at *Drury*-house.

Yelverton, the Queen's Serjeant, began the Evidence and opened the Indictment, shewed the act itself to be Treason by the Statute of 25 *Edw*. III. therefore for the prisoners to pretend an intent to another purpose, is no excuse.

To alter the State, change the Religion, inforce the Prince to settle power, and for subjects to sway things at their list, is *crimen læsæ majestatis*; and all Indictments term this Treason: for that subject that will rule his Prince, will never be ruled by his Prince, and to rule with his Prince, the world may as well bear two suns as the state suffer two such Governments.

For particular proofs and plain convincing of the parties, there need no other but their confessions; which he protested, as he would be credited in the world, came voluntarily from every man examin'd, no man being racked or tormented.

It is not unknown with what clemency the Queen let pass the offence committed by the Earl in *Ireland*: some of as great place as he, have suffered for less offence than was proved against him at his convention before the Lords. But such was her Majesty's clemency towards him, as not to suffer him to be brought to public trial for those offences; but he, to shew the mind he bore, impatient to expect the Queen's leisure and grace, gives himself wholly to think how he may wrest the Queen to his fancy. He being prisoner in the Lord-Keeper's house, the Queen was contented to let him take his choice of any Country in *England* where to live, only confined with this, that he should hold himself a subject under her Majesty's displeasure; yet left to be guarded only with his own discretion. This grace notwithstanding, he ceased not to plot with divers foreigners, he sends to the low Countries, practises in *Ireland*, raises spirits at home in *Drury*-house and *Essex*-house, for suppressing the Queen, calling of a Parliament, taking the Tower, possessing of *London*; and this cannot be intended without the destruction of her Majesty. and all these Plots, by all their own confessions, were conferred and disputed of divers times. Being sent for to come before the Lords of her Majesty's Privy-Council, the Earl refuses to come; and the same night sends for all his friends and followers to repair to him. The Queen hearing of this, sends the Lord-Keeper, the Earl of *Worcester*, Sir *William Knowles*, and the Lord-Chief-Justice unto him. These Councillors find the outward Court guarded; these Councillors coming to the Earl, commanded the Earl and all his accomplices to lay down force, and desiring private conference with the Earl; he refuseth, and saith he will go into *London*, and take order with the Mayor and Sheriffs of the City, and will then return to them again; so confident he was of his own strength and favour of the City. The other matters opened by Mr. Serjeant were the former points laid in the Indictment.

Mr. Attorney-General *Coke*, coming to urge the evidence, desired, because the bar was pestered, to have Sir *Gilly Merrick* and Mr. *Cuffe* removed for a time, which was done. Then Mr Attorney said, he was now to speak, not before common Judges, nor of common matters, but the greatest and the weightiest cause that ever he had to deal in, tho' he had now served the Queen some time.

The Queen's Serjeant hath generally delivered the matter, and he was now to prove what had been opened, wherewith he had striven with himself to have spoken nothing of him that dead is; but unavoidable necessity forced to name him, but it should be with these two cautions: first, to speak nothing but what the very matter enforceth; secondly, to say nothing but that without all contradiction was true, The question now is not to

* This is printed from a MS. purchased at the Sale of the MSS. of *Peter Le Neve*, Esq. *Norroy* King at Arms; and tho' in the MS. it is wrote to Sir *Charles Davers*, yet on the margin is wrote in Mr *Le Neve's* hand, Sir *Charles Danvers*; and so it is in *Camden's Eliz*. in the complete History of *England*, vol. II. p. 638.

‡ *Bacon*, who by command of Queen *Elizabeth*, published a declaration touching the Treasons of the Earl of *Essex* and his accomplices, (see his Works, vol. IV. p. 534) in that part which relates to what passed at the Arraignment of *Blunt*, &c. says, There were arraigned and tried by a Jury both of Aldermen of *London*, and other Gentlemen of good credit and sort, Sir *Christopher Blunt*, Sir *Charles Davers*, Sir *John Davis*, Sir *Gilly Merrick* and *Henry Cuffe*; the three first, whereof before they pleaded, asked this question of the Judges, *Whether they might not confess the Indictment in part, and plead Not guilty to it in the other part?* But being resolved by the Judges, that their pleading must be general; they pleaded Not guilty, as did likewise the other two, without any such question asked. The reason of that question was, as they confessed, in respect of the clause laid in the Indictment: *That they intended and compassed the death and destruction of the Queen's Majesty*; unto whose person (although they confessed at the bar, as they had done in their examinations, that their meaning was to come to her in such strength, as they should not be resisted, and to require of her divers conditions and alterations of Government, such as in their confessions are expressed), nevertheless they protested they intended no personal harm to herself. Whereupon, (as at the Arraignment of the two Earls) so, then again the Judges delivered the rule of the Law; that the wisdom and foresight of the laws of this land maketh this judgment, *That the subject that rebelleth or riseth in forcible manner to over-rule the royal will and power of the King, intendeth to deprive the King both of crown and life: and that the law judgeth not of the fact by the intent, but of the intent by the fact.* And the Queen's Council did again inforce that point, setting forth, that it was no mystery or quiddity of the common law, but it was a conclusion infallible of reason and experience: for that the crown was not a ceremony or garland, but consisted of pre-eminence and power.

And therefore, when the Subject will take upon him to give law to the King, and to make the power sovereign and commanding, to become subject and commanded; such subject layeth hold of the Crown, and taketh the sword out of the King's hands. And that the Crown was fastened to close upon the King's head, that it cannot be pulled off, but that head and life, and all will follow, as all examples, both in foreign stories, and here at home, do make manifest. And therefore, when their words did protest one thing, and their deeds did testify another, they were but like the precedent of the protestation used by *Manlius* the lieutenant of *Catiline*, that conspired against the state of *Rome*, who began his letter to the Senate with these words, *Deus hominesque testor, Patres conscripti, nos nihil aliud*, &c.

And it was said further, that admitting their protestations were so far true, that they had not at that time in their minds a formed and distinct cogitation to have destroyed the Queen's person; yet nothing was more variable and mutable than the mind of man, and especially *Honores mutant mores*: when they were once a-loft, and had the Queen in their hands, and were Peers in my Lord of *Essex's* Parliament, who could promise of what mind they would then be? Especially, when my Lord of *Essex*, at his arraignment, [illegible] of imprisoning the Privy-Councillors, by pretence that he was inforced to it by his unruly company. So that [illegible] extreme and [illegible] wickedness of mind, as to lay violent hands upon the Queen's sacred Person; yet, what [illegible] be done [illegible] Parts, must be then the question. [illegible] the example was remembered of *Richard* the Third, who though he were King [illegible] could never sleep quiet [illegible] till they were made away. Much less would a [illegible] that a Queen that had been their Sovereign, and had reigned so many years in such re[illegible] than make for their own turn.

[illegible] the chief part of what is [illegible]. The Trial of Sir *Christopher Blunt*, in State-Trials, vol. I. p. 20. [illegible] you, my Masters of the Jury, whether Sir *Christopher Blunt* is guilty of Treason, yea or no; for he confesses himself guilty of matter which is rebellion and insurrection, and that of itself is flat Treason.

Sir *Christopher Blunt* said hereupon, that he was now a man, what through weakness of his hurt, and through grief of his action, not himself, scarce *compos mentis*; therefore desired not to be concluded by what he said, for he hoped the Lords had call'd him thither rather to confess his faults, than to excuse or defend them.

Mr. Attorney said, they must now proceed, and Sir *Christopher Blunt* is not now alone in question: but as the Earl is concerned and interested in this cause, for order of proceeding, there was no man in the world but must be ruled by reason and by precedent; therefore if by these all men must, then would he so proceed against him.

Sir *Christopher Blunt* desired them to proceed against the others, for he would confess all that had been said. But Mr. Attorney desired to be heard against him, *ut pœna sit paucis culpa ab aliis*. Now, to shew this point of treason, the indictment containeth the matters touching the Queen's person. In private cases, if servants shall come to their masters with armed petitions, this is a shew of disobedience, and tendeth to destruction. To prove the point of *notiora*, 8 *Hen*. VIII. the Labourers of *Kent* made an insurrection against the Statute of Labourers, for the increasing of their wages. *Finieux*, and all the Judges then resolved this to be Treason. *Trin*. 37 *Eliz*. the Prentices in *London* making a rout in *Southwark*, upon information made against them in the *Star-Chamber*, some of them were sentenced to be whipped; whereupon others conspired to rise at *Bunhill*, and agree to whip the Mayor for suffering the Prentices to be whipped. And this intending to rise and make an insurrection; was resolved by all the Judges to be Treason.

39 *Eliz*. *Bradshaw*, and others in *Oxfordshire*, rising to overthrow closes, and to restore tillage; the rising was at *Inslow-hill*, the indictment was of Treason and conspiring the Queen's death, and adjudged treason against the Person of the Queen. Now, if the law make this construction of the acts of mechanical men, what shall be thought of the acts of Earls, and other strong Persons intending to surprize the *Tower*, to take the City, possess themselves of the Court, to call a Parliament, to change Government, to tolerate Religion? These intents of force must needs tend to Treason. The Prentices of *London*, the men of *Oxfordshire*, were hanged, drawn and quartered.

The Chief-Justice *Popham* delivered the reasons of all this to be, for that by force to compel the Prince in any government, is in itself Treason.

The *Attorney*. He that conspires to take *London*, and to surprize the Court, this doth merely concern the State: but this *Catiline* company, to conspire against the Queen herself, this concerns more! but the toleration of Religion, this of all things concerns most! for from before her coming to the Crown, her Majesty having holden so constant profession of the Religion now established, and since her reign so blessed of God in it; and for her now, by compulsion or otherwise, to be drawn to change it, what impiety and ingratitude against God were it to think it? This quarrel for the changing of Religion, was the great cause of the *Spanish* Invasion intended in 88, and the many treacheries against the Queen's Person, by poisoning her gloves, the Pomel of her saddle, and many other ways: therefore at the request or compulsion of a subject to change this true professed Religion, her Majesty would rather lose her Crown, and venture her Person itself in defence thereof, than ever suffer or endure it. *Adeo periculosum* is this to think? These things I have shewed for precedents. Now for story, see the Chronicles of our own Kingdoms. Queen *Isabel*, in the time of King *Edward* II. assembles great numbers, pretending for the good of the King and the Church; this was a glorious pretence! but she being upon the wings of her power, calling a Parliament in the name of the King, seeks the overthrow of the King, *ipse ipsaque nomina cujus imponit*. But the catastrophe, the conclusion was the smothering of the King, and putting to death the Treasurer and Chancellor: for, said she, the letter of the law is such, as we are all traitors, therefore so long as the King lives, we are all in danger. The story of *Richard* II. the Act of 1 *Henry* IV. calling a Parliament, putting the King in *Pomfret*-Castle, and the King's death following, are dangerous precedents, and too fitting these indictments. This treason's bud hath been long a-hatching, like unto an Elephant's whelp, long a-breeding, but bred in a hollow tree, and discovered before it was fledged.

It was forecast, that if they were few, it would not be acted; if they were many, it would not be concealed: therefore resolved few should know it. And upon the sudden, even when the matter was to be acted, then all to have notice of it. And for the tale of being to be murdered in his bed, or to be set upon by Sir *Walter Raleigh* going to the Lord-Treasurer's, this was but a buz, and so invented by them for a buz: but on the other side, it shall be proved directly, that they intended to kill Sir *Walter Raleigh*. It was objected, that the Queen's forces that would be suddenly raised would be an impediment to this action; but to prevent this, it was resolved to pretend that the State generally was with them now, where it may be some may think themselves excusable of Treason, because they knew not of the Treason intended, tho' they were present in the thing acted. For the clearing of this, Mr. Attorney referred himself to the opinion of the Judges in the point, whereupon it was delivered by my Lord-Chief-Justice,

That in case, where some pretended Treason, and others accompanied and assisted them in any action, tho' not knowing of the Treason intended, yet were they all guilty of Treason.

And for the honour of the Indictment, and manifesting the due of their proceedings, Mr. Secretary desired their judgments, whether in case, *when men were drawn into rebellion in such a matter, whether the law charged them not in this point with direct Treason against the Person of the Prince?* Which was affirmed by the Judges to be so, and the indictment must so charge them.

Now, for several proofs against every several person then arraigned, he would first begin with Sir *Christopher Blunt*, and with his own confession against him. The confession of Sir *Christopher Blunt* * contained this, That the 20th of *January*, he was sent for by the Earl of *Essex* to come up to *London*; whereupon he came, and was at *Drury*-house when the conference was there the *Sunday* or *Monday* sevennight before the going into *London*, but came when the conference was ended. The reason of their going into *London*, as they did on *Sunday* the 8th of *February*, was, because the alarm was given at the Court, and knowing into what hazard the Earl adventured, he went with him for safety of the Earl's life, as far as there might be power in him, and thought it lawful for subjects to use force for their safety, and the settling of true Religion. And being asked by Mr. Attorney, whether he was privy to the purpose of taking the Court? Said, he was privy to the conference of going to take the Court, but it was a thing first to be considered of, but not resolved. And being further asked by the Secretary, if in their conference it was not resolved, that if the Earl prevailed, and came to the authority he shot at, he would have suffered Toleration of Religion? answered, That he thought so; and said, he should be to blame to deny it; for the Earl had many times said to him, that he liked not the forcing of men's consciences; and in his usual talk would say, he misliked that any should be troubled for their conscience. And in a second confession, he set down, that the Earl, five days before his going into *London*, wrote down with his own hand certain articles to be disputed upon; whereof one was, whether they should take the *Tower*? another, touching the surprizing of the Court? and that the Earl usually spoke of this purpose to alter the government of the Realm. But the Examinant desired that might not have been set down, because it was no grace unto the rest.

Mr. Secretary desired to know the reason wherefore he would not have had this set down, which he understood to be, for that the confession was so liberal of matters so foul, as this being added, it would embroider the rest?

But Sir *Christopher Blunt* said, he was mistaken; but the altering of the Government being moved, and the removing of the Secretary, he desired forbearance to express any further matter, for gracing of himself. And in the said confession, Sir *Christopher Blunt* seemed to dissuade from the attempt intended, but utterly disliked the taking of the Court at that time of the night.

For a farther proof against Sir *Christopher Blunt*, that he had wrought with the Earl for a Toleration of Religion, and sought to seduce Sir *John Davis*; the confession of Sir *John Davis* was read, wherein it was set down, that Sir *John Davis* asking of Sir *Christopher Blunt*, if the Earl had promised Toleration of Religion, the Catholic Religion? Sir *Christopher Blunt* answered, that the Earl gave good hope of it. And *Davis* in his confession set down that principally by the persuasion of Sir *Christopher Blunt*, he became a Catholick; therefore being taken and committed to Mr. *Mompesson's*, he desired Mr. *Mompesson* to help him to a Priest. But at the Bar, *Davis* said, that many times he had conference with Sir *Christopher Blunt* touching Religion, but he was not the original persuader of him unto that Religion; but being bred up in *Oxford*, his Tutor, Mr. *Allen*, was a Catholick, and from him he took it, and hath ever lived free from giving offence by his profession; and saving this unhappy action, he hath always been loyal and obedient to law, hath accompanied the Earl ordinarily at summons, and communicated with him; and the reason of his words upon his first commitment, was supposing Mr. *Mompesson* to have been a Catholick, did request him to help him to a Priest, but grieved afterwards he was deceived in Mr. *Mompesson*. And the Lord-Admiral protested he knew that Mr. *Mompesson* was not affected to that Religion, which Sir *John Davis* thought to be true; but said, Mr. *Mompesson* had not kept word with him, for he promised upon his credit not to reveal his request.

And to prove Sir *Christopher Blunt* was an author, and a chief stirrer of the Rebellion in *London*, the confession of Lord *Sands* was read, wherein was set down, that he went with the Earl to Sheriff *Smith's*, but went not into the house: but being sent for by the Earl, went with him, and came back with him towards *Ludgate*; and Sir *Christopher Blunt* and the Lord *Sands*, at the chain before their coming to *Ludgate*, gave charge upon the Queen's forces, and were both hurt at that place.

Sir *Christopher Blunt* at the Bar confessed he was too forward in that action, and gave charge upon the Pikes, but denied the killing of .... at that place, which Mr. Attorney charged him withal; but he desired Mr. Attorney to think charitably of him, and not to charge him with that man's blood.

Then Mr. Attorney proceeded to prove, that where it was pretended and given out for a buz, that Sir *Walter Raleigh* should have sought to have murdered the Earl, that indeed they sought to murder Sir *Walter Raleigh*, to which purpose the confession of Sir *Ferdinando Gorge* was read; wherein was contained, that the Earl and Sir *Christopher Blunt*, that *Sunday*-morning that Sir *Walter Raleigh* had sent to speak with him, Sir *Christopher Blunt* advised *Gorge* to kill him; and to this end, Sir *Christopher Blunt* sent four shot after him when he went to speak with Sir *Walter Raleigh*.

But *Blunt* said, that Sir *Ferdinando Gorge* did much wrong him in so saying; but confessed, that in respect Sir *Ferdinando Gorge* was to be one of the principal executioners in this business, he wished *Gorge* not to go unto to Sir *Walter Raleigh*, nor to go home to him, but to meet him upon the water, and to take some pistols with him, that in case Sir *Walter Raleigh* should not suffer him to come off, that then he should be of force to come away, and bring Sir *Walter Raleigh* with him; and this was his advice.

And being asked by Mr. Secretary, whether he thought, or was persuaded that my Lord *Cobham*, or Sir *Walter Raleigh* intended any such thing against the Earl?

Sir *Christopher Blunt* answered, that he did not believe that they ever meant any such matter, nor the Earl himself feared it not, only it was a word cast out to colour other matters.

Gorge also confessed, that the Earl intended, after he had possessed himself of the Court, then to have gone into *London* with some principal officers of the State carried with him, and after a while to have called a Parliament, and settled things to his liking.

* See also B[illegible] Works Vol. IV. p. [illegible] for the several confessions relating to *Essex's* conspiracy, as signed before the Lords, and others of the Council.

And Mr. Secretary ſaid, that Sir *Ferdinando Gorge* being confronted with the Earl, had ſaid as much; and to ſatisfy thoſe queſtions, would have *Gorge* ſent for.

To prove that Sir *Chriſtopher Blunt* would not take notice of the Proclamation publiſhed in *London* by an Herald at Arms, the confeſſion of Capt. *Edward Bromley* was read, wherein was ſet down, that the Earl coming from Sheriff *Smith*'s houſe, ſaw in *Gracechurch-ſtreet* an Herald at Arms, and ſent Sir *Chriſtopher Blunt* to him, to tell him, that he ſhould not approach the Earl, for he would not hear him abuſe the Queen's name. And to prove that Sir *Chriſtopher Blunt* was a chief director of things done in the houſe that *Sunday*-morning the 8th of *February*, it was ſhewed, that *Mr.* Killegrew *of the Privy-chamber* coming that morning to *Eſſex*-houſe, Sir *Chriſtopher Blunt* meets him in the Court, and Mr. *Killegrew* told him, that he had a meſſage from the Queen to Sir *William Knowles*; and hearing by Sir *Chriſtopher Blunt* that Sir *William* was gone, he would have gone back again; but Sir *Chriſtopher Blunt* ſaid, he muſt not go; and ſmiling upon him, wiſhed him not to take it diſcourteouſly, for he muſt ſtay him.

But Sir *Chriſtopher Blunt* ſaid hereupon at the Bar, that the reaſon of the ſtaying of Mr. *Killegrew* was this; Mr. *Killegrew* being a Gentleman whom he knew the Queen truſted, he told him, he would deſire him to ſtay in the houſe, and hear the matter, and ſee their proceedings, that ſo he might truly inform the Queen of that which he knew would be diverſly and ſtrangely ſpoken of.

But againſt this, Mr. *Killegrew* himſelf ſaid, that he was ſtaid by Sir *Chriſtopher Blunt* by theſe words; "I muſt deal ſomewhat unmannerly "with you, and ſtay you now till you have ſpoken with my Lord;" and ſent Sir *John Davis* to go tell my Lord of *Eſſex*: whereupon the Earl, accompanied with divers others, came to Mr. *Killegrew*.

Mr. Attorney perceiving ſome ſhiftings in Sir *Chriſtopher Blunt*'s anſwers, willed him to confeſs things plainly, otherwiſe he would prove him guilty of the Earl's death.

Whereupon Sir *Chriſtopher Blunt* wiſhed that his death were worthy to reſtore the Earl to life again; but for his confeſſions, they had always been plain and true from the firſt, and plain to all he knew: wherein he appealed to Mr. Secretary, if he had found other by him.

Mr. Secretary acknowledged that he had always found him to deal honeſtly and plainly.

Now, to come to the great matter againſt Sir *Chriſtopher Blunt*, and the reſt. The Queen's Majeſty having intelligence of their intended treaſons; yet graciouſly diſpoſed to extenuate the offence of the Earl, commands her Privy-council to meet at the Lord-Treaſurer's houſe on *Saturday* at night, and that night ſends Mr. Secretary *Herbert* to the Earl, to ſignify unto him, that it was the Queen's pleaſure he ſhould repair unto her Council there; but the Earl refuſed to come. Mr. Secretary *Herbert*, the rather to invite his coming, offered to go in the coach with him alone without any light; or take boat and go by water, that they ſhould go and come without being diſcerned by any; but the Earl ſtill refuſed.

Sir *Chriſtopher Blunt* confeſſed he heard of Mr. Secretary *Herbert*'s coming, but wiſhed to God he had dealt more peremptorily with the Earl.

Mr. Secretary *Herbert* ſaid, he was not to be more peremptory with him than in the words of the Queen's own meſſage, which he delivered directly.

Mr. Secretary *Cecil* affirmed, that ſuch was the reſpect given to the Earl, and that nothing ſhould break out to the underſtanding of others; as it was once reſolved all the Council to have gone home to him to his own houſe.

Sir *Chriſtopher Blunt* ſaid, that the Earl kept very ſecret to himſelf the cauſe of his ſending for to the Lords of the Council, and what Mr. Secretary *Herbert*'s meſſage was; for being aſked what it was, he ſaid, that ſuch was the Queen's opinion of him, for all thoſe diſgraces, as her Council being to conſult of great matters, ſhe had ſent to have him amongſt them, and to have his opinion.

Mr. Attorney further urged, that the Queen's exceeding favour reſted not there; but even the ſame *Sunday*-morning before his going into *London*, the Queen ſent Mr. Secretary *Herbert* to him, to ſignify to him, that her pleaſure was he ſhould come before her Council, which he refuſed again; and thus was it true with him, that *conſuetudo peccandi*, did *tollere ſenſum peccati*. Her Majeſty notwithſtanding, after both theſe refuſals, vouchſafeth again the ſending unto him, maketh choice of his beſt friends and neareſt allies he had in the Court; the Lord-Keeper, the Lord-Chief-Juſtice, two that loved him exceedingly well while he ſtood a good ſervant and a true ſubject; the Earl of *Worceſter* and Sir *William Knowles* his near kinſmen. Theſe Lords valiantly, (for ſo I will term it, and to their honours I will ſpeak it, that it ſhall appear that in ſome gown-men there reſts as valiant minds, where the cauſe requires it, as in them that wear ſwords:) The Lord-Keeper ſtoutly, in the midſt of his armed troops, commands the Earl upon his allegiance to deſiſt from his purpoſe, and to lay down arms; when others in the tumult cried, My Lord, my Lord, you ſtay too long; others ſaid, Kill them! kill them! and, at this time, *Blunt* adviſed the Earl to impriſon them, which is Treaſon in itſelf.

But Sir *Chriſtopher Blunt* ſaid, that his advice to my Lord then was, that the place was unfit to talk in, being openly in the Court, and that therefore he would withdraw into ſome private place.

But my Lord-Chief-Juſtice *Popham* ſaid, that he himſelf hearing the company tumultuouſly cry, *Away, away, you loſe time*; hereupon he ſtept to the Earl, and perſuaded him to withdraw into ſome place private; and there to conſult with them. And to manifeſt in what manner the Lords were received and uſed, and how they found the houſe at their coming in, a Narrative was read, ſet down by my Lord-Keeper, all under his own hand-writing, which was thus: That coming to *Eſſex*-houſe the 8th of *February*, about ten of the clock in the morning, they found the gates ſhut. Upon their knocking, the wicket was opened, but none of their ſervants ſuffered to enter in with them, ſave only *J. Hughs*, who carried the Great Seal. From the gate to the houſe-door ſtood a guard of ſhot on both ſides; at their coming in, the company aſſembled tumultuouſly together; before their coming to the hall-door, the Earls of *Eſſex*, *Rutland*, and *Southampton* came and met them, and divers others flocked about the Earl. The Lord-Keeper ſtepping to the Earl of *Eſſex*, told him, that they were ſent to know the cauſe of their grievance; if there was any the Queen would hear it; but hearing that he had aſſembled ſo many into that houſe, and not knowing for what cauſe, the Queen had commanded them to command him to diſperſe thoſe companies. The Earl anſwered, that his life had been ſought; he had been preſidiouſly dealt with, and for his defence that company of his followers and friends were gathered together. The Lord-Keeper anſwered, if any ſuch matter was, he ſhould be heard and relieved. Hereupon the Earl of *Southampton* ſaid, *that he was aſſaulted in the ſtreet by the Lord* Gray. The Lord-Chief-Juſtice anſwered, he had Juſtice for that. The company gathering thick about them, the Lord-Keeper deſired the Earl of *Eſſex* to draw aſide; and they conferring ſecretly, the company cried, *All, All.* The Lord-Keeper told the Earl, that if he had any wrong done him, he ſhould be honourably righted. Then the company cried, *Away, away, my Lord, they betray you, they undo you.* All this while they were bare, but hereupon the Lord-Keeper put on his hat, and commanded the Earls upon their allegiance to deſiſt, and lay down their weapons: and private conference being again deſired, they were carried up into the great chamber, and as they went, ſome ſaid, *Throw the Great Seal out of the window*; ſome ſaid, *Kill them, kill them*; others cried, *Away, away.* Then they were led into one of the Earl's cloſets. The Lord-Keeper preſſing to ſpeak with the Earl, he ſaid, my Lord, be patient a-while; I will go take advice, ſpeak with my Lord-Mayor, and the Sheriffs of *London*, and will be with you again within this half hour. Then the Earl departed, and left them to the cuſtody of Sir *John Davis*, Sir *Chriſtopher Blunt*, and Sir *Gilly Merrick*. The Lords being thus in cuſtody, deſired leave to be gone, or that they might ſend one to the Queen to let her know how they were uſed; but this was denied them; and anſwered, that the Earl would return ſhortly, and till his return they muſt not let them go.

The Earl of *Rutland*'s confeſſion being read after the former narration of the Lord-Keeper's; thereby it appeared, that the Earls of *Eſſex* and *Southampton*, and Sir *Chriſtopher Blunt* of long time had been diſcontented, and that *Blunt* many times adviſed the Earl to ſtand upon his guard; and it was the advice of the Earl of *Southampton*, *Blunt*, and *Davis*, that the Lords ſhould be detained.

For the Earl of *Rutland* himſelf, Mr. Secretary ſaid, he thought him not to be acquainted with the plot; and the Earl of *Eſſex* himſelf had ſaid, that the Earl of *Rutland* was not privy to it: for his conceit of him was, and thus ſaid, that the Earl of *Rutland* knew it but two hours before. And, ſaid Mr. Secretary, if equality of Juſtice would ſuffer it, he wiſhed that no blood more might be ſpilt; for it was not the blood of any man that was required, and the Queen ſhould gain more by their lives than by their deaths; and doubted not but her Majeſty, in this lamentable accident, would triumph in mercy, but where and when there ſhould appear no other cauſe but merely her exceeding mercy. The Earl of *Rutland*'s confeſſion ſhewed further, that *Blunt*, when their going to the Court was intended, ſaid, O how fearful, and of how ſeveral humours ſhall we find them, when we come to the Court!

Further, to enforce the hard uſage of the Lords, the confeſſion of one *Whittington* was read, who ſaid, That after the Lord-Keeper and the other Lords were in the inner room, other company coming up towards the place, ſwore they would ſtab and kill the Councillors; whereupon *Whittington* ſent to the Earl of *Eſſex*, how violently ſome men preſſed, how cruelly they meant againſt the Councillors? Sir *Chriſtopher Blunt* hearing theſe words, ſaid, it was no time now to make orations. Whereupon the Earl of *Eſſex* preſently departed, and word left, that if the Earl of *Eſſex* miſcarried in *London*, or if they offered to eſcape before his return, then the Lord-Keeper and the Chief-Juſtice ſhould be killed.

The Lord-Chief-Juſtice hereupon aſked Sir *Chriſtopher Blunt*, Why they ſtood at the great chamber-door with muſkets charged and matches in their hands; which, thro' the key-hole, the Lord-Chief-Juſtice ſaid, he diſcerned?

Davis anſwered, and ſaid, he was charged with the cuſtody of the Lords, but againſt his will, for he much more deſired to have gone with the Earl into *London*, and that the Earl of *Southampton*, Sir *Charles Davers*, or ſome other might have kept them; but the Earl of *Eſſex* ſaid, No, he would but go take order with *London*, and come again within half an hour, in the mean time he ſhould keep them. Then Captain *Saliſbury* having the guard of the muſkets, was very violent and ſo diſordered, as he doubted what he would attempt, and, contrary to the will of others, brought up the ſhot ſo near the door: And Sir *John Davis* ſaid, that leſt the fury of *Saliſbury* ſhould attempt beyond that was meant, he ſometimes paſſed amongſt the ſhot, and to ſatisfy the Lords that no harm was meant them, he came in to them, whom when he perceived in ſome fear, he aſſured them that there ſhould be no force offered them.

But the Lord-Chief-Juſtice told Sir *John Davis* at the Bar, that he had no reaſon to think they were in fear, and bade him tell what words the Chief-Juſtice then uſed, which were theſe: If they did take their lives, it was but the cutting off of a few years, and when *Gorge* came, and would have let out the Lord-Chief-Juſtice only, he refuſed to go except they might all go; and ſaid, as they came together, ſo they would go together, or die together.

And Sir *John Davis* ſaid, that the better to aſſure the Lords that no harm was meant them, he went up to the Ladies, and intreated the Counteſs of *Eſſex* to come down, and be amongſt them: ſhe making ſome pauſe at it, ſaying, With what comfort can I go amongſt them? He perſuaded her to go and be amongſt them, the better to aſſure them that no barbarous uſage ſhould be offered unto them. And that he behaved himſelf reſpectfully towards them, being uncovered before them, when others ſtood covered by them: and ſuch proviſions as the houſe had, he prepared for them, and ſet them a dinner.

But the Lord-Chief-Juſtice ſaid, My Lord-Keeper and he told *Davis*, they would eat none of my Lord's meat.

But at the coming down of the Counteſs amongſt the Counſellors, Sir *John Davis* ſaid, that he perceiving the Lords in great doubt what the Earl meant, and hearing them ſay to my Lady, what a ſtrange courſe is this the Earl of *Eſſex* taketh? Thereupon Sir *John Davis* ſaid, that if he did perceive that the Earl intended any hurt unto the Queen, his ſword ſhould be the firſt that ſhould be drawn againſt him. And the Lord-Chief-Juſtice aſking

what

what was become of the Earl all that while, they having then staid from eleven of the clock till it was almost two, said, the Earl will be deceived of his purpose if he hope upon the City, for the Citizens are faithful to the Queen. Then *Davis* answered, the Earl had good hope of the City. It being replied, That perhaps some loose people might fall in to him, but he could have no good hopes of any that were substantial and good citizens; *Davis* said, my Lord is sure of the City, for of twenty-four Aldermen he is sure of twenty-one; and my Lord in this action will set such aids in the City in all places, as no spoil shall happen.

But to the honour of the City of *London*, Mr. Attorney often repeated, that of all the City, not one Man, save only one sorry prentice, was found to take part with with, and of Inns-of-Court-Men, not one man that followed him.

Sir *John Davis* being farther asked, when he first was made acquainted with this purpose of the Earl's? He said he knew not of it till the *Sunday* sevennight before their rising, and then their purpose was to surprize the Court at such a time as he should have small opposition; and that they met twice that *Sunday* or *Monday* before their rising, at *Drury*-house, when they consulted about surprizing the *Tower* and the Court. But debating long, they could not agree; whereupon breaking off, the Earl said, he would set order for all himself, since they could not agree on it; which were the Earl of *Southampton*, Sir *Christopher Blunt*, Sir *Charles Davers*, and Sir *John Davis*.

Hereupon Mr. Secretary told Sir *Christopher Blunt*, that the Earl had confessed that he had been a principal instigator of him to these acts, and a mover of him to plots more pernicious to the State than these.

Sir *Christopher Blunt* said, Hath my Lord that gone is, said so by me? Well, since I am so nearly touched in honour, and my reputation so far charged, I will tell you, Mr. Secretary, what I have counselled him, and what I have kept him from.

Mr. Secretary said, the Earl for part of his Sacrifice to God, had left it under his own hand all that he could disclose of all confederation in this matter.

Sir *Christopher Blunt* seemed ready at the Bar to have disclosed farther matter against the Earl, but referred to my Lord-Admiral and Mr. Secretary, whether he should there utter it, or privily deliver it to them two? Which afterwards he did, being brought into the Court of Wards to them after Judgment was given.

Mr. Attorney proceeding with his evidence, desired attention, saying, That the last day he gave evidence against the Earl, since which time it had been rumoured, that tho' the letter of the law was strong against the Earl, and his act expounded by the Law to be treason, yet his intention was not to touch the Queen's person or her State. But the Earl himself (whose Soul he doubted not but was with God, for his end was most penitent and Christian) before his death revoked all his Justifications made at his arraigning, save only one original purpose, not to lay hands upon the Queen; and took it upon his death, that he meant not to lay violent hands upon the Queen's person; yet remembring the tumultuous behaviour of them in his company at his house, said, that he feared he should have been forced to some wrong against the Queen's person.

Whereupon the Lord-Admiral affirmed, that the Earl of *Essex* said, It was fit he should die, for the Queen could not live and he too.

Mr. Secretary also delivered how clear a confession the Earl had made of all things, how long time four of them of her Majesty's Privy-Council at his intreaty had spent with him in the *Tower* upon *Saturday* before, and how he had revoked those imputations he had cast upon some men, and those asseverations he had in his own defence. Therefore, for his part, he must needs judge charitably of him, and forgive such wrongs as the Earl had done him; and if the diabolical imputation which the Earl at his arraignment cast upon him, further moved him to impatiency than his wont was, or was fit, he desired them that heard it to pardon him, for the provocation made him to forget all bands of speech.

Now was read some parts of the Earl's last confession, which contained four sheets of paper, all written with the Earl's hand; and it being shewed to *Cuffe* at the Bar, he acknowledged it to be the Earl's hand-writing. Out of the Earl's confession this was only read: That *Blunt*, *Cuffe*, *Temple*, and some others, tho' they were not present at *Drury*-house, yet they were privy to more dangerous practices and plots than these. And *Cuffe* being brought face to face before the Earl, the Earl charged him to call to God for mercy, and deal truly with the Queen; for he being to go out of the World, must deal truly with his soul. *Cuffe* said, it was long before he could be allowed pen and ink to write; else the Earl himself would have cleared him, as he did in these things, that in a few words he set down; which being read to the Earl, he said, true; and still as he read, he said true; out of which *Cuffe* would infer, that the Earl being truly remembred of things passed, would have cleared, and not left an accusation upon him. But these seemed to be other matters than such wherewith the Earl had charged him. And *Cuffe* denied not, but being confronted by the Earl, the words aforesaid were used to him. Then was read an abstract of the Earl's confession in these words:

He thanked God that he was thus prevented, for otherwise he knew not what misery might have befallen this land. He said, that men would wonder, if they knew how many motions had been made unto him, to remove the evils of the Common-wealth. He confessed that his rebellion was first plotted when he was prisoner at the Lord-Keeper's house; he intended to have surprized the Court with a power of men, and afterwards the *Tower*, to have countermined his actions, and been a bridle to the City, and then to have called a Parliament. He said, that *London* was a danger unto his soul, and the cause of his rebellion; for if he had not trusted to those of *London*, he had not taken this course. He called the men of *London* a base and cowardly people, saying, That he drove them from their barricadoes with two rapiers a-cross, and would undertake to sack *London* with four hundred men. He called himself a burden unto the Commonwealth to be spewed out. He called this his sin, a great sin, a bloody sin, a crying sin, and an infectious sin, infecting with a leprosy both far and near. He desired his life to be shortened, for that he knew the Queen could not be safe so long as he himself was living. He desired private death, to avoid the acclamations of the People.

This abstract read, Sir *Christopher Blunt* said, he must needs confess he was privy to the spleen that was carried against Mr. Secretary, and was too far consenting to his hurt; but never gave allowance, or was mover of the Earl to this plot.

Mr. Secretary interrupting him, wished him to conceal nothing that tended to the discovery of these treasons. For matter of injury intended against him, he wished not the naming of them, he did forgive them.

Sir *Christopher Blunt* said, that was favour out of his charitable disposition, more than he himself was worthy of.

Mr. Attorney proceeding, said, the Queen had charged those of her Council to say nothing in this business, but what might plainly be prov'd, if it were objected; for she would go with her justice untouched: therefore he would open matters, and which though they of the Jury need not to take as any part of their evidence; yet because they were true, and fortified the matter divulged and proclaimed through the Realm, for the honour of the Queen, though against an Earl that was executed, he would disclose unto them how this Treason had a deeper root than most were aware of: wherefore you shall plainly have it proved unto you, That there was a correspondence *betwixt the Earl of* Essex, *Sir* Christopher Blunt, *and the Arch Traytor* Tyrone; and this shall be proved unto you by the Earl's own creatures. Thus it fell out, after he had sixteen thousand foot, and thirteen hundred horse under his charge; such an army, as he himself said, should make the earth to tremble where he went. It was pretended by him that he would go into the North against the Rebel, but never intended; as appeared; for *Lee* must go to the Rebel, but the Earl must not know it, *and* Blunt *must suffer it, being Marshal, but give no warrant for it.* *Lee* goes to *Tyrone*, finds the Rebel up in proud terms against the *English* nation, railing against the Earl of *Essex*, as that he sought his life, and hired some about him to perform; which was a baser thing than ever he had offered to his father, or would do against him: but these terms were after qualified. *Lee* returning, brings answer from *Tyrone*, that he desired conference with the Earl, and would give his son for pledge; and sends word, that if the Earl would follow his counsel, he would make him the greatest man that ever was in *England*. *Lee* being returned, the Earl of *Essex* repairs to the place where Sir *Christopher Blunt* lay, where this being told him, he shook his head at it; but said nothing. Now the Earl of *Essex* gathers his army towards winter, takes his journey towards the North, goes with pretence to fight; but coming there, entertains a parley with the Rebel; being jealous lest any should hear it, takes order that the Earl of *Southampton* should keep all men from coming near, and he alone goes to parley with the Rebel. The effect of this was confessed by *Lee* while he lived, and to make it evident, the plotting of Treason between those two Earls, you shall understand it by an intelligence that passed, which, were it not the thing had been severally plotted, it had been impossible to have been advertised, for no bird upon her wing could have carried the news in that time. Sir *William Warren*, a man most trusted by the Rebel of any *Englishman*, he went to *Tyrone* the 28th of *September*; the Earl of *Essex* landed in *England* but the 26th of *September*; and *Tyrone* could then tell *Warren*, that he should see a strange alteration in *England* shortly, and it should not be long ere he should see him have a good share in *England*. This passed in the North of *Ireland*. In the South of *Ireland*, one *Mac Pueys*, Secretary, confessed, That it was agreed the *Earl of* Essex *should be King of* England, *and* Tyrone *Viceroy of* Ireland. In the middle of *Ireland*, *Fitz-Maurice*, sister's son to *Tyrone*, affirms the same, and says, that whensoever the Earl of *Essex* should need men; then it is agreed, that *Tyrone* shall find him a continual supply of 8000 men; and *Fitz-Maurice* hearing these things agreed betwixt the Earls, sends to know what he will have to do, lest he enter into attempt to the cross of their purposes. The Earl of *Essex* being commanded by express Letters that he should not come over, he notwithstanding comes over, brought all the strongest provisions away with him, left the Kingdom at all adventures, only trusts the rebel *Tyrone*'s word for the safety of that whole Kingdom. It may be thought these things more fitly should have been urged against the Earl himself; but the cause was, one, the shortness of time; another, because all the Lords were satisfied, and said there was Treason full enough proved against him, and it satisfied to condemn him. And when I was there entering into this matter, the Lord-Steward said to me, Mr. Attorney, I perceive you have more to say, but I enjoin you silence for the rest.

Now for proof of these things thus plotted in *Ireland*, the confession of *Lee* was read, who was a man the Earl had good opinion of, and he so devoted to the Earl, as he wished his own head might have suffered for him, *Lee* confessed, that on the *Sunday*, when he heard they were proclaimed Traitors, he was mightily discontented and grieved at the imprisonment of the Earls, and stuck not to profess unto some, that he could be contented to spend his life for their delivery, and thought it an easy matter to be performed, if six resolute Gentlemen would undertake it, and named them. And whereas the Earl denieth that ever he sent him to *Tyrone*, yet he thought the Earl knew when Sir *Christopher Blunt* sent him, for this reason, that the Marshal never did any great matter without the Earl's privity: And that this matter was such, as the Marshal would give him no warrant in writing for it. And when he was returned from *Tyrone*, the Earl of *Essex* then made a secret journey to Sir *Christopher Blunt*'s house, where Sir *Christopher Blunt* lay hurt. And *Lee* said, that at his coming to *Tyrone*, he found him proud, and railing at our nation, and said that the Earl had hired some to take his blood; but afterwards told *Lee* that he had sent *Essex* a message by *Snode* his Secretary; that if he would agree with him, he would make him the greatest that ever was in *England*. And *Lee* further confessed, that he knew *Essex*, *Blunt*, and *Tyrone* were all one, and all held one course.

Sir *Christopher Blunt* confessed, he knew of *Lee*'s going to *Tyrone*, but denied that he had ever notice what he said to *Tyrone*. It was true, he gave leave unto *Lee* to go to *Tyrone*, and the Earl of *Essex* was privy to it; yet the Earl in his life denied it.

But my Lord-Chief-Justice noted, That it was a thing agreed upon betwixt them, that *Lee* and *Blunt* should take this upon them, and for the fact, *Lee* and *Blunt* should have a pardon granted them, which was done by the Earl: this being about the 8th of *August*: yet the Earl of *Essex* wrote over hither to the Lords of the Privy-Council, the 14th of *August*, in these words: "Your

"Lor-

" ſhips would not think what cowardice theſe fellows are grown to ; yet " muſt theſe fellows be taught courage to fight, or elſe this Rebel will " never be ſubdued."

Further was read, a letter all of the Earl's own writing, dated the 8th of *October*, written to the Lord *Mountjoy*, after his being in *Ireland*, and the Earl here in *England*; ſignifying " that *Lee* is one ſo near to me, as " I muſt needs intreat your Lordſhip to do what you can for him, tho' " it is not in your power to do what you would ; you ſhall find him a " man of better ſervice than any is in *Ireland*. When I came thither, I " found him in good place, and ſometimes he entertained me to his great " charge ; which with your favour you muſt enable him to again. And " let it be my ſuit to you, to do him what good you can."

From out of theſe letters, it was urged by Mr. Attorney, that *Lee* was a man wholly plotted for him. The 26th of *September*, the Earl of *Eſſex* came to the Court ; the 28th of *September*, Captain *Warren* talks with *Tyrone*. *Warren* confeſſeth, that *Tyrone* ſware, that within two months he ſhould ſee the greateſt alteration, and the ſtrangeſt that ever he ſaw ; but *Warren* underſtood him not. Then ſaid *Tyrone*, I hope ere long to have a good ſhare in *England*.

The confeſſion of one *Knowd*, Secretary to *Owney Mac-Rorey*, taken the 16th of *February*, was read, wherein was ſet down, That *Owney Mac-Rorey* having ſecret intelligence of the plot betwixt the two Earls, *Eſſex* and *Tyrone*, wrote and ſent ſo twice, and deſired to be advertiſed thereof, that he might do nothing contrary to their deſigns. But *Tyrone* grew ſuſpicious, leſt the matter ſhould break out too ſoon : yet the effect of the anſwer was this, that the Earl of *Eſſex* ſhould be King of *England*, and he Viceroy of *Ireland*. And that for a while he ſhould attempt nothing upon the *Engliſh* ; and proved, that the Earl had left ſixteen barrels of powder in the North. And *Knowd* being aſked by a Gentleman, upon his returning out of the North, what news ? Said, it was agreed, that *Eſſex* ſhould be King of *England*, and *Tyrone* Viceroy of *Ireland*.

Turlagh Mac-Davy O Kelly, being a meſſenger from the M . . . . rebels, and brought the anſwer to . . . ſaid, the Earl of *Eſſex* was to go for *England*, and take that kingdom, and they to help him ; and among thoſe rebels it was reported, the Earl of *Eſſex* wrote a letter to the Earl of *Tyrone*, to follow his matter thoroughly : for now was the time.

The confeſſion of *Thomas Wood*, ſiſter's ſon to *James Fitz-Maurice*, Baron of *Lixnow*, and a man in great credit with this Baron, was read ; wherein he ſheweth, that being with *James Fitz-Maurice* at his houſe, about *Michaelmas*, when the Earl of *Eſſex* came over from *England*, *Fitz-Maurice* aſked him what friends the Earl of *Eſſex* had in *England* ? Who ſaid, he knew not ; but heard the Earl was well beloved in *England*. Then *Fitz-Maurice* told him, that the Earl of *Eſſex* was gone for *England* ; had diſcharged many of the forces, and that the Earl of *Deſmond* had ſent him word, that it was agreed the Earl of *Eſſex* ſhould be King of *England*, and *Tyrone* Viceroy of *Ireland*.

Hetherington's confeſſion, and ſome others, were ſpared reading, becauſe they only concerned the Earl of *Eſſex*.

Now Mr. Attorney opened, that notwithſtanding all thoſe plots, practices, and treaſons, were known to the Queen ; yet, after all this ſo graciouſly her Majeſty regarded him, and was pleaſed to cover his offences, as to have him privately to come before ſome of her Privy-Council only at the Lord-Treaſurer's, ſent one of her Secretaries twice to him, offered to paſs in all ſecrecy ; nay, Mr. Secretary ſaid, for ſaving his honour, that none ſhould take notice of any thing. They once all propoſed to have gone home to *Eſſex*-houſe to him, and during all the time of his reſtraint from Court, his letters have always had free paſſage to the Queen, and ſhe ever gave the reading to any thing he ſent. Wherefore, Mr. Attorney ſaid, the action of breaking out into that it did, it was a great mercy of the Queen's, that *in flagrante crimine* he was not, according to the martial law, preſently put to the ſword.

And here the evidence ended againſt Sir *Chriſtopher Blunt*.

And then Mr. Sollicitor General urged new evidence againſt Sir *Charles Davers*.

Mr. Sollicitor *Flemming* beginning, ſaid, He would prove Sir *Charles Davers* guilty of all the Treaſons charged againſt Sir *Chriſtopher Blunt*, and that he was a principal plotter, diſputer, officer and actor in all their treaſons. In fine, he was aſſigned to be keeper of the preſence-chamber, where, upon a ſignal given, all the Nobles to aſſemble, and paſſing to the privy-chamber to preſent themſelves to the Queen : and for making their way firſt, they ſhould apprehend Sir *Walter Raleigh*, captain of the guard ; and afterwards ſome of the privy-counſellors, and ſome other Lords. Theſe being ſeized upon, they ſhould afterwards have been put to an honourable tryal, and afterwards a Parliament ſhould be called, and government eſtabliſhed ; and ſo principally did the Earl of *Eſſex* count upon this gentleman, Sir *Charles Davers*, and ſo ſecret did he hold him to him, as that before *Chriſtmas* laſt the Earl diſcovered his intent to him, and told him he would lay ſuch a plot for taking the Court, as he ſhould not be reſiſted. And when Sir *Charles Davers* was in the Country, the Earl would not enter into conſultation about the buſineſs, until Sir *Charles Davers* came up ; and meſſengers were diſpatched preſently for him. Upon his coming up, a meeting was had at *Drury-houſe*, where divers projects were made, *Davis*, *Davers*, *Blunt*, *Gorge* and *Southampton* being preſent, amongſt whom it was agreed, the taking of the *Tower* to be very fit, for the better countenancing of the action.

The chiefeſt defence and pretence that Sir *Charles Davers* uſed, was the great love he bore to the Earl of *Southampton*, who heretofore had cauſed him his pardon, and having gained him his life, he thought he owed his life unto him in any thing he ſhould command him.

But Mr. Sollicitor ſaid, it behoved him rather to have been grateful and ſerviceable to the Queen, who gave him life, more than to him that ſued for his life. But this was the juſt revenge had of God, that followed for the foul murder he had committed.

Sir *Charles Davers* perceiving that his act had extended to Treaſon, altho' he intended no harm unto the Queen's perſon, ſaid he was ſorry he had ſo far forgotten himſelf as to plead Not guilty ; for it was not his purpoſe coming thither to defend, or deny any thing, but to confeſs all things that could be ſaid againſt him : Therefore confeſſed, that before *Chriſtmas* the Earl adviſed with him, how he might make his way to to the Queen, as that his acceſs to her ſhould not be reſiſted. But this was not reſolved till his return out of the country. When at *Drury-houſe*, they meeting, and *Littleton* coming thither ; at the laſt, it was reſolved, the plot ſet down by the Earl's own hand, were firſt, to take the Tower : for reaſon he yielded this, it would be a countenance to the action ; the taking of the Court, for which he would have ſo many able men, as they would at any time poſſeſs all the places of the Court. The manner to be this : Sir *Chriſtopher Blunt* to have the gate ; Sir *Gilly Merrick*, the hall ; Sir *John Davis*, the great chamber ; Sir *Charles Davers*, the privy-chamber ; the Earl himſelf ſhould come all along by land : at his coming into the great chamber, he ſhould put himſelf betwixt the halberts, (meaning, that he ſhould ſtep to the corner where the guard uſually ſet up their halberts againſt the wall) and poſſeſs himſelf of them, ſo as by them he would have no hurt ; and perhaps he ſhould find of the guard apt to take his part.

My Lord-Admiral ſaid, it was a fair warning to the guard, that they uſe not that faſhion of ſetting up their halberts in that manner.

When the Earl was thus come into the great chamber, divers of the Lords ſhould come out of the preſence thither, and ſaluting him, to welcome his coming to the Court ; then the Earl with ten or twelve Noblemen, to take their way into the Privy-Chamber.

It being aſked, what ſhould be done with them that ſhould make reſiſtance to this attempt ; it was anſwered, it was meant they ſhould be ſeized upon. And the Court being quieted, then to ſend to ſatisfy the City ; and then not long after, to call a Parliament.

A further confeſſion of Sir *Charles Davers* being read, there were ſet down the ſubſtance of the Earl's former articles, and theſe queſtions farther propounded ; as, whether the Court and Tower ſhould be attempted at one time ; and whether this attempt ſhould be with many, or with few ; if with many, where the number ſhould aſſemble ; and whether it ſhould not be fit for the Earl and ſome others to be armed with Privy-Coats ; and who were fitteſt Perſons to have cuſtody of the Lord-Admiral and the Secretaries ?

Theſe and ſome further matters alſo, Sir *Ferdinando Gorge* had confeſſed were diſputed upon.

And ſaid Mr. Secretary, ſince this is a World wherein Princes muſt be accountable for their doings to their Subjects, that men ſhould not marvel why like proceedings were not had againſt Sir *Ferdinando Gorge* as theſe, the reaſon of forbearance was not that he had deſerved better, or was otherwiſe conceited of, than to be an *Arch-Traitor* ; but becauſe he was *the inſtrument of ſaving and letting go thoſe that were ſent from the Queen to* Eſſex-*houſe* : and for this cauſe divers of her Majeſty's Privy-Council had been ſuitors to her Majeſty for ſparing his life for a time, though for their opinions of him, they held him an original and principal Traitor ; and that he adviſed more miſchievouſly than any other, for he would have had the Court fired upon the taking of it. Sir *Charles Davers* ſtill profeſſed, as he had done often, that he was privy and a diſputer of all theſe plots, but never was any deviſer of any, or inſtigator of my Lord in theſe things: Sir *Chriſtopher Blunt* for further clearing himſelf, ſays, he knew not of this plot till his coming to *London*, upon the Earl's ſending for him ; that they had allotted him to place, he knew ; but to what office, he knew not. And the more to be commiſerated, he beſought the Lords Commiſſioners to remember what natural conſiderations were to tie him to the *Earl*, *having married his Mother*. Now to how many adventures the obligations of love, and following of that Earl, had before carried him, the World did know ; and how liberal, prodigal and venturous I was of this life of mine, while it was my own, good Mr. Secretary, pleaſe to remember and report truly to the Queen. I beg it of you, becauſe I have moſt offended you, and have no cauſe to expect it, but from the bounty of your honour and charity.

Mr. Secretary told him he freely forgave whatſoever he conceived might give cauſe to him to be offended, and would truly perform for him what he deſired, and would deſire my Lord-Admiral to join with him in it ; though he ſaid he need not ſeek it of them, for the Queen would require it at their hands, to be truly informed of all their deſires.

Then ſaid Sir *Chriſtopher*, I muſt needs confeſs that heretofore, I having done much to her Majeſty's ſervice, adventured my life many times, as the marks of this my wretched carcaſe will ſhew ; hazarded my fortune when it was at the beſt, and all for the honour of her Majeſty, and in her ſervice, and yet ſhe never vouchſafed notice of me or my ſervice. it gave no little diſcontentment to me, but this never had the power to have an ill thought againſt her Majeſty. Therefore once again I beſeech you, that being as I was to that Earl, you pleaſe to relate to her Majeſty what you find by me, and what I have ſaid to you. And to ſtay any fury going upon me, I here confeſs myſelf guilty of all that can be ſaid againſt me, and moſt worthy to have deſerved death ; wherefore renouncing all juſtification or extenuation of my offence, I wholly caſt myſelf at her Majeſty's mercy. Sir *Charles Davers* made the like proteſtation.

And ſo ended the evidence againſt Sir *Charles Davers*.

Againſt Sir *John Davis*, Mr. *Francis Bacon* urged the evidence, beginning with diſcourſe upon the former ground of Mr. Attorney's, that every rebellion implied deſtruction of the Prince, and that in the precedents of *Edw.* II. and *Hen.* IV. the pretence in both was as in this, againſt certain Subjects, the *Spenſers* in one, and the Treaſurer in the other. And this ſtile of proteſtation that no harm was intended to the perſon of the Sovereign, was common in Traitors. *Manlius*, the lieutenant of *Catiline*, had that very proteſtation ; but the proceeding is ſuch in this, as no long diſcourſing needs to prove it Treaſon, the act itſelf was Treaſon. The principal offences charged upon Sir *John Davis* were two, one that he was a plotter, and of the Council at *Drury*-houſe : Another that in the inſurrection he had the cuſtody of the Privy-Counſellors in *Eſſex*-houſe, which had a correſpondence with the action in the ſtreet. The plot and inſurrection entered into, was to give laws to the Queen ; the preparation was to have a choice band of men for action ; men not met together by conſtellation, but aſſembled upon ſummons and letters ſent : for, ſaid Mr. *Bacon*, I will not charge Sir *John Davis*, although he be a man ſkilful in ſtrange arts, that he ſent ſpirits abroad, but letters were ſent about this matter. The things to be acted were the matters conſulted of, and then to deſign fit perſons for every action ; and for mutual encouragement there was a liſt of names drawn

drawn by the Earl, and these Councillors out of them were to elect fit persons to every office. The second plot was in taking of the Court, and in this consultation he was *penna Philosophi scribentis*; you were clerk of that Council-Table, and wrote all: and in the detaining of the Privy-Councillors, you were the man only trusted. And as the Earl of *Rutland* said, you held it a stratagem of war to detain pledges, and was meant to have carried the Lord-Keeper with the Great Seal into *London*; and to have had with you the Lord-Chief-Justice, a man for his integrity, honoured and well-beloved of the Citizens; and this *Achitophel* plot you thought to have followed.

Sir *John Davis* hereupon told Mr. *Bacon*, that, if with good manners I might, I would long since have interrupted you, and saved you a great part of labour; for my intent is not to deny any thing I have said, or excuse that I have done, but to confess myself guilty of all, and submit myself wholly to the Queen's mercy. But in that you call me Clerk of that Council, let me tell you, Sir *Charles Davers* was writing, but his hand being bad, I was desired to take the pen and write. But by and bye the Earl said he would speed it himself; therefore we being together so long, and doing so little, the Earl went to his house, and set down all with his own hand, which was formerly set forth, touching the taking and possessing of the Court.

The examination of Sir *John Davis* was read, which was to the effect as before is set down touching their consultations of taking of the Court; but added, it was agreed they should all come by land, and make their way to the Queen's own person, and hoped to find way in the Court indifferent.

The Lord-Admiral then charged Sir *John Davis* again with the detaining of the Lords in *Essex*-house, and his unwillingness to have let them go, though Sir *Ferdinando Gorge* came with a message, as he said, for letting them all go. And said the Lord-Admiral, the case was hard with these worthy Councillors: for by God he swore, though these Councillors had been in the house, yet being as he was, General of the Forces, and sent to force the house, he must and would have battered and blown it up, tho' it had been the death of them as well as the rest; and had all his own sons been there, he would have done it.

It was also charged against Sir *John Davis*, that not ten days before this action, Sir *John Davis* and Sir *Charles Davers* were seen upon the top of the *White Tower* within the *Tower*, viewing and surveying the place; but they said it was only for pleasure, to take view from thence, being there confessed, that they affirmed the *Tower* was a place of small strength.

And here ended the evidence against Sir *John Davis*.

Then Mr. Attorney took in hand the evidence against Sir *Gilly Merrick* and Mr. *Cuffe*. To *Cuffe*, Mr. Attorney said, that he was the arrantest Traitor that ever came to that Bar; he was *Poly* . . . . the very seducer of the Earl; and since he was a Scholar and a Sophister, he would frame him a syllogism, and bade *Cuffe* deny what part he would. The syllogism was this, *Whosoever commits rebellion, intends the Queen's death*; *but you committed rebellion*: Ergo, *you intended the Queen's death*. For the *polypragma*, this fellow, the cunning coiner of all plots, how to intrap a worthy gentleman, whom I am sorry to see so overtaken, I must name Sir *Henry Nevil*: This *Cuffe* hearing of Sir *Henry*'s landing out of *France*, watches his coming to *London*, presently comes to him, and tells him, he had commendations unto him from the Earl of *Essex*, and secretly lets him know what private intelligence my Lord had received from Court by some his inward friends; that much mislike was taken at Court with Sir *Henry*'s service in *France*; especially that at *Bullen*. Sir *Henry Nevil* said, it was more than he knew or had heard, but recommends his service with thanks to my Lord. Shortly after Sir *Henry Nevil* came to the Court, the Queen used him very graciously. The Lords interpreted very well of his service; now at his next meeting Mr. *Cuffe*, Sir *Henry* told *Cuffe*, he found no such matter at Court as he told him. Hereupon *Cuffe* replied, Oh, Sir, things are altered since I saw you last, and ere long you shall see a change: my Lord is like to come in favour again, and be restored to his greatness; and using one other verse, concluded with this, *Arma ferenti omnia dat, qui justa negat*. *Cuffe* still making resort to Sir *Henry Nevil*, finds opportunity when to disclose unto him all the Earl's plot of going to the Court; who hearing it, objects against it, that it was a thing could not be executed but by many, and all would not keep Counsel. *Cuffe* answered, that for execution they had so many come in to them, that they knew not to entertain all. A further objection being made, that tho' all places in the Court were possessed, yet *Westminster* would rise, and make force; *Cuffe* answered, we having the face of the State, all will follow and take with us.

For manifestation of all, the Narration penned by Sir *Henry Nevil* himself, was read in these words: "Their honours commanding him to disclose all, and his duty and conscience binding him to the same, he hath in that ill-couch'd Narration set down all his knowledge. *First*, at his arrival out of *France*, he was told that he had ill offices done him in Court by divers, and some of great place; and his actions at *Bullen*, and carriage there greatly blamed, as causing the ill success of the peace. And by *Cuffe* it was told him, the Earl would have him know he was wronged, because he was one that loved him. After this, *Cuffe* brought him a letter from the Earl, thereby desiring his love, and to hold it to him, besides many other words only of compliment. To which letter Sir *Henry* returns an answer suitable to so kind provocations. But all this while I never went to him; and being in the country within ten miles of the Earl, yet I never went to visit him. But *Cuffe* came to me from him, and told me the Earl was now at liberty, and all the World that would, might now freely come unto him: but still I put off my going, till at one time *Cuffe* came and told me my Lord expected my coming to him, and such a day he would stay supper for me; and if I came, and he chanced not to be in the way, a Gentleman of my Lord's should attend my coming, and bring me to my Lord's closet. About eight of the clock that night I came to my Lord, and was met by a Gentleman, and brought up to my Lord; who entertained me kindly, and after a while, after many questions of his hopes, but used no undutiful words of the Queen or State, I parted with my Lord, there having nothing but ordinary terms of Compliment passed us. Afterward Mr. *Cuffe* repairing often to me, I asked him at one time how his Lord's matters stood in Court. At one time he answered me, well; and told me of great hopes conceived; at some other time he answered me very discontentedly in these things, saying, it made no matter, it would cause my Lord to take other courses; and said, there was a pretext to lay up the Earl of *Southampton*, which was a warning that they meant to lay up the Lord of *Essex* after him: but my Lord was resolved they should never curb him up any more. Then told me, my Lord had in purpose some matters, but I should not embark myself further in them than I listed; and desired me to give a meeting to the Earl of *Southampton* and Sir *Charles Davers*. I said, I would, but with this limitation, that nothing was intended against the Queen's person: which was promised. But I detained them at two meetings, which caused them to make an ill judgment of my meaning towards them and the intendment. *Monday* on *Candlemas day* I standing in *Serjeants-Inn Gate*, the Earls of *Essex*, *Southampton*, and Sir *Christopher Blunt* passed by in a Coach, whom I saluted passing, and was the first time I had seen them of long. Anon after, *Cuffe* coming to me, told me he had a commission to deliver a secret unto me; which was, that my Lord finding his life sought by men potent about her Majesty, he was advised to make his appearance to the Queen, and go with strength for that purpose; describing the same manner of taking the Court, and making way to the Queen, as before is set down by others. This *Cuffe* said he was to impart to me, as one in whose love the Earl was confident. (But Mr. Secretary said, as he was grieved to think of this Gentleman's full respect, his worth and abilities to have done the Queen great service, so this right he would do him, that however the Earl was persuaded of him, yet he so far tendered his duty to the Queen, that I think the first suspicion given of the Earl's mind grew from this Gentleman.) The matters being propounded unto me, I made many objections, and put great difficulties in the execution; easy perfecting of things being promised, my answer was, *Multa sunt quæ non laudantur nisi cum aguntur*. When some persons were named for the actors, I objected, that if many knew it, it would not be concealed; if few were used, it would not be performed. The Earl of *Rutland* being named for one, said they would not trust him long aforehand; for if he knew it but two hours before, he would tell. In conclusion, I was desired to think of the things propounded in case they were shewed unto me. Afterward *Cuffe* came unto me, to whom I related all the speeches used in that conference, and told him I would not allow it, except they would conjure and take an oath to tempt nothing against the Queen's person; and against Mr. Secretary, I would never do nor consent to any thing, for he was nearer unto me, therefore they must *duce pudice*, spare me in that. *Cuffe* said to me, they would only have me present when things were doing; and if it fell out so, that I should be hastened to dispatch into *France* before that time, I might defer it by feigning sickness. By their appointment I should have been Secretary." (Here Mr. Secretary said, *Cuffe*, this was great presumption, for though to remove me had been no great matter, yet to take upon you to place another, this was high ambition.) "Further, it was required that Sir *Henry Nevil* should have sent a minister into *London*, to find how the City stood affected to the Earl."

(Mr. Attorney here said, it was in their plot, to have had two hundred ministers in the City and Country, to have blazed in pulpits the sincerity of this Earl's intentions.) "*Cuffe* further told Sir *Henry Nevil* of a buz in many men's mouths in *London*, and that there had been warning given to the Mayor and Aldermen to look to the City; but of twenty-four Aldermen he doubted not of twenty at the least."

Mr. Secretary here speaking, opened what he found had resolved the Earl to so free a confession and discovery of all things that he did. *Ashton*, who was his minister, and as I may term him his confessor, was a man much desired by the Earl; her Majesty was willing to yield any thing that might give comfort to the Earl's conscience, and be good for his Soul, sent Mr. Doctor *Dove*, a very worthy man, to confer with him, and prepare him to a christian end. He persuading confession as the way to repentance, and amongst other sins charging the Earl with this offence, his taking arms against his Prince, and refusing to come upon the command of his Prince, the Earl answered, he thought that refusal no fault; and for instance shewed, that *David* refused to come to *Saul* in the like case, being sent for. *Mr. Dove* so sufficiently answered the Earl in his arguments, and satisfied him in this example, how different it was from his case, and upon what ground that was, that the Earl in a kind relenting and falling from defences, desired earnestly confession with his own minister *Ashton*; which was yielded him. *Ashton*, like a godly and very learned man, and one deserving much for this service, dealt so roundly and feelingly with him, as that he made the Earl know that there was no salvation for him to hope for, if he dealt not clearly with his own conscience in the confessions of his sins, and high offences in this kind. His words so pierced and moved, as that to this man he disclosed the very secrets of his heart, to the purging of his soul and conscience, from the concealment of any thing he knew; and afterwards spent all the time he had to live in holy meditations, and revealing the secrets concerning the State, and discoursing of the mischief intended, and most penitently sorrowed for the accusations and imputations he had cast upon others touching the *conspiring with Spain* and the Infant of *Spain*.

And being asked touching some men supposed to be confederates in the taking of the City, he said that Captain *Bromley*, brother to Sir *Henry Bromley*, and Sir *John Scot* would assist him: and that Sheriff *Smith*, being a Colonel of a thousand men, would bring them in aid of him. And confessed by the Earl himself, that at such time as the Earl had purposed to lay down the thought of these ambitions, and had resolved contentedness in a private life, *Cuffe* comes to the Earl, and tells him he had indignities offered him, and his sufferance was such, as his friends said he had lost his courage with praying and hearing of sermons, and now was become a coward. Whereupon *Cuffe* persuaded him to let Sir *Charles Davers* come to him, who would let him know the mind of his friends; and after such time as the Earl had accused his confederates, being asked how he could prove the things discovered, answered, some of them have so much grace, as if I send but to them, they will confess it. Whereupon he wrote a ticket to the

Earl

Earl of *Southampton*, who upon veiw thereof confessed all to be true, and said my Lord had the start of him; for if I had had pen and paper, I had confessed these things first.

Whereupon Mr. Secretary said, that he must needs speak of a difference he found between Noble and Generous-minded Men, and others baser born; from the Earls and other the Gentlemen of birth and of good house, all their confessions came freely and liberally from them without concealment or covering any thing with untruths. By *Cuffe*, and some others of baser sort, nothing would be confessed, but what they were convinced of, and shadowed with untruths so far as their wits could do it. The Earl of *Essex* also in his life-time confessed to the Lords, that *Cuffe* was a principal instigator of him; and though of these plots himself had been a principal contriver, yet Sir *Christopher Blunt*, Sir *Charles Davers*, and Sir *John Davis* were privy to more dangerous and pernicious purposes than this action tended to, as might appear by their counsel given him that morning when he went into the City of *London*.

Cuffe being willed to speak for himself, said, The matters objected against him were many, and forced against him with all force of wit. therefore for the help of his weak memory, he would reduce all unto two heads: things plotted, and things acted. For the first, in them Mr. Attorney thinks he hath concluded me in mood and figure; but my answer is, that if a man may be excused of Treason by committing nothing, I am clear. Yet the number of matters heaped upon me, and the inferences and enforcements of the same used against me to make me odious, make me seem also as a monster of many heads in this business; but since by the law all accusations are to be believed, and facts weighed as by evidence they are proved; and things are best proved being singled; I will beseech Mr. Attorney that we may insist upon some point certain, and not as in a stream have all things at once brought upon me with violence. For my being in *Essex*-house the *Sunday*, I hope it shall be construed as in the case of others. Then if those who only had their being within the walls of that house, and no hand nor head in that action, were not Traitors; I hope that in favour and in charity you will accordingly judge of me, who spent all that day locked up in my chamber amongst my books, and never appeared unto any man till all was yielded up to my Lord-Admiral. To conclude me to be a Traitor, because I was in the house where Treason was committed; by the same reason if a lion had been there locked up in a grate, he had been in case of Treason. But whereas your argument, Mr. Attorney, is this, That whosoever intends Treason, and the same is afterwards acted by others, there the intender as well as the actor is a Traitor: But I intended Treason, and others acted it; *Ergo*, Mr. Attorney, it is not your *Major* that I deny, because my Lords the Judges have determined that; but I deny your *Minor*; for if the thing intended was the going to the Court; yet the thing acted was the going into *London*.

But Mr. Attorney General taking him short upon his own confession, concluded him a Traitor; for in Treason *the very intent is Treason*, if the same can be proved. Now, it is confessed by Mr. *Cuffe* that he intended the taking of the Court, which in itself is Treason.

Mr. *Cuffe* said, My Lords, the matters forced upon me so amaze me, as I know not what to say; but I beseech you, even as yourselves shall be judged, judge so of me both by my words and deeds, for this is the law both of God and man: and let not the accusations of others, or arguments now forced, so far have power against me, as to take from me my just defence. I am further charged with contriving plots for restoring the Earl to greatness. True, I must confess, as a servant that longed for the honour of his master, I have often wished to see his recalling to the Court, and restored to her Majesty's former favour; but beyond the limits of these desires, my thoughts never carried me, nor aspired to other greatness than to see him again in place of a servant and worthy subject, as before he had been. And whereas I stand accused to be as one that turned the wheel which else had stood, and to be the stirrer of his mind, which otherwise had settled to another course, to clear this, I had written two lines, which you Mr. Secretary, knew the Earl would have subscribed, if he might have been suffered.

But Mr. Secretary affirmed he perceived no such purpose in the Earl, neither remembred any such matter in that which is written.

Said *Cuffe*, You know, Mr. Secretary, my paper being read to the Earl, as he read, he said still as he went, *True, true.*

At the importunity of Mr. *Cuffe*, Mr. Secretary willed the paper should be read; but it tended only unto this, That if he knew of the Earl's intent to go to the Court, 'twas with such limitations as the Earl had propounded, otherwise not, for he had not suggested any of these new practices.

Mr. Attorney still following the matters strongly against him, told *Cuffe*, that he would give him a cuff that should set him down, and called to have read the Earl's confession, and some part of Sir *Henry Nevil*'s confession; which both were full plain and against him, as he had not to answer them. Only to the conference with Sir *Henry Nevil* he said, Whereas Mr. Attorney would make me the ... and a Messenger only from the Earl to Sir *Henry*, herein Mr. Attorney errs, not knowing, or not respecting the antient familiarity and love that for these many years space have been betwixt Sir *Henry Nevil* and me, for the delight we took together in conference of Learning, and discourses of Travels and States. And whereas I am charged with devising a lye, thereby to bind Sir *Henry Nevil* faster unto the Earl; it is well known to others, the Earl first sent me to Sir *Henry Killegrew* to tell him of it, and that from him it might come to Sir *Henry Nevil*'s ear. But Sir *Henry Killegrew* not being in town, and I afterwards meeting with Sir *Henry Nevil*, imparted it to him; therefore desired that he might not be wronged, and wished that *juramentum cal* .... might be forborn as a fault in any man. And for the speech used of twenty-one Aldermen in *London* that were sure to my Lord, there were some at the Bar as well as he, that had heard the Earl use the speech, and vouched Sir *Gilly Merrick*, but he denied it. For the buz that was given out, he said likewise, that Sir *John Davis* heard what my Lord said of this, but Sir *John Davis* being asked, denied the hearing of it.

And *Cuffe* being answered by Mr. Secretary, what he meant by having a Parliament? He answered, that it was conceived these things would work great alteration, and for settling of all things, they thought, that shortly would follow a Parliament.

Mr. Attorney said, that it was meant that *Cuffe* should have been Speaker of that Parliament.

And here ended the Evidence against *Cuffe*.

Against Sir *Gilly Merrick*, Mr. Attorney urged first, that he was the man who fortified *Essex*-house against the Queen's forces; and if God had not otherwise guided it, that day he had been the death of a noble person the Lord *Burleigh*, for he set one with a musket-shot to shoot at him, but missing the Lord *Burleigh*, Captain *Lovel*'s horse was killed under him at *Essex*-gate with that shot. And the same day that the Earl went, Sir *Gilly Merrick* comes to Mr. *Brown*'s house, being adjoining to the Tennis-Court, and shuts all his servants out of his house, and all that *Sunday* walked up and down the house, with musketeers following him. And the story of *Henry* IV. being set forth in a play, and in that play there being set forth the killing of the King upon a stage; the *Friday* before Sir *Gilly Merrick* and some others of the Earl's train having an humour to see a play, they must needs have the play of *Henry* IV.

The players told them that was stale, they should get nothing by playing of that, but no play else would serve; and Sir *Gilly Merrick* gives forty shillings to *Philips* the player to play this, besides whatsoever he could get.

It was urged also, that the Earl's purpose was to have against this time appointed men of his faction placed in all the houses near about him. To which end the confession of *Arthur Smith*, dwelling hard-by the Tennis-Court, was read; who said, that the week before, Sir *Gilly Merrick* came to his house, and enquired who lay there. It was told him of a lodging there that was kept for Sir *Walter Harcourt*; which being denied unto Sir *Gilly Merrick*, he railed and reviled the good man of the house with foul words, and willed him to discharge Sir *Walter Harcourt* of that lodging, for my Lord would have his friends to lie about him. Now the men that Sir *Gilly Merrick* would have lodged in that house, were *Owen Salisbury*, Capt. *Gwynne*, and *John Salisbury*.

Then was read a letter of Sir *Gilly Merrick* writ to his brother *John Merrick*; the effect was to pay money to Mr *Devereux*, and himself to come up to *London*, and Captain .... and Captain *Damnye*, to come up also, and my Lord would take it thankfully.

The confession of *Thomas Johnson* was read, who said he saw Sir *Gilly Merrick* all that day walk in his doublet and hose up and down the house, with muskets following him, and went down to the banqueting-house in the garden with his hat full of shot.

Sir *Gilly Merrick* said, his going with muskets after him, was to keep the Privy-Counsellors the safer from the fury of *Owen Salisbury*, who had sworn that if the house was forced, he would send them to go to the Devil. And *Johnson* said, that he saw one *Wever* follow Sir *Gilly Merrick* to the gate with a musket to have shot out there.

And by the confession of one *Watts*, it appeared that there was a watch in the house all *Saturday* at night, and none of the company went to bed, but for a while's rest threw themseves upon their beds in their clothes; and that Sir *Gilly Merrick* caused certain hogsheads to be broken up, to fortify against the Tennis-Court. That the Earl had a hundred muskets in the house, but wanted flaskets and much other furniture for them.

And here ended the evidence against Sir *Gilly Merrick* and the rest.

Now Mr. Attorney General desired to have a word unto all the prisoners at the Bar, and that he might not misreport, desired to have a paper read, subscribed by the hand of Mr. *Ashton*, Dr. *Mountford* and Dr. *Barlow*, for that it was spoken in their hearing. The Earl thanked God, that he had given him a deep insight into his sins, since his justifications used at the Bar then before; thanked God that his course was prevented; acknowledged that all confidence in man was vain; that he was worthily spewed out: and further, as in the Earl's confession. Now to conclude, at the Earl's arraignment I used a sentence, saying, *O tempora, O mores!* according to that against *Cataline*, *Hic tamen vivit*, for which saying, divers have since charged me, but I will say it again, and add this to it,

> *Dixerat O mores, O tempora! Tullius olim,*
> *Romanum strueret cum Catilina nefas.*
> *O tempora dicimus, &c.*
> *Et cur non dicimus, O mores!*

Now the jury went out to agree upon the Verdict, which after half an hour's time and more, they brought in, and found every of the five Prisoners severally guilty of High-Treason. The Verdict being entered, and the Jury discharged, the Queen's Serjeant prayed Judgment. The Chief-Justice then demanded of the Prisoners, what they had to say for themselves, why Judgment should not be given against them?

Sir *Christopher Blunt* then said, My Lords, for my high offence tending to Treason, in that I have risen in Rebellion against her Majesty, I have nothing to say to excuse myself, or extenuate my fault. But of any intention of Evil against her Majesty's person, my own thoughts cannot accuse me. My deserved, but unfatal fall, I must needs impute to my over-much love to that unhappy Earl. How I have followed him, how I have loved him, as being bewitched with too good an opinion of him, I now with grief feel it! But since this my too much fondness of him hath only led me into folly with him, and no other ambition, hope, or honour, I beseech your Lordships, and you my Lord-Admiral and Mr. Secretary especially, right me so much with your favours, as to relate truly to her Majesty what my heart and words are before you this day, and let her Majesty understand that it was the fair face of that Earl's pretences, and my near ties unto him, I having married his mother, that carried and allured me to that I did, and no disloyalty or undutifulness of mind towards her. What the services be that I have done, and adventures made in service for her Majesty, others have seen, and know what I have felt. This carcass of mine, when it shall be dissolved, will shew the marks, such was my readiness in all actions to the honour of her Majesty; as when my fortune was at the best, so good as that I enjoyed *two thousand pounds* a year at the least, beside other wealth by an honourable Lady whom you all know I married, yet when no commands enforced me, for her Majesty never commanded my going with the Earl in any journey, yet voluntarily I left all to adventure with the Earl in service for her Majesty into *Portugal*, at *Cales*, *the Islands*, and in *Ireland*,

Ireland, I was with him. And altho' all this be nothing to weigh against this present fact, and so I have nothing of desert that may plead mercy for me, yet if her Majesty, out of the abundance of her grace and mercy, shall afford me life, I doubt not but as I have done, so I may live to do; and if I live, I will be as ready as any subject the Queen hath to do the service for her Majesty which shall deserve my life. And this is all I wish, that since I have but a life to give unto her Majesty, that I might give it to the performance of some more acceptable service rather than to this end. But if it be resolved, as I have deserved, that die I must, it is not life I care for; for a death I owe unto her Majesty, and will yield it chearfully. And since the Earl that gone is, whose undue course hath brought us to this due punishment, hath left a blot upon me, and so far touched me in reputation and credit, as if I had been plotter and procurer of him to more dangerous practices than these, I must needs clear myself, that neither in foreign practices, which I count confederacies with *Spain*, nor in domestical dealings, which I count that with *Scotland*, in respect of their nearness to us, I have ever had to do so far, as to allow or advise any thing to the hurt of this State. Against you, Mr. Secretary, I cannot but confess I have assented to too great wrongs, and beyond that I am worthy, it pleaseth your Honour of your charitable disposition to forgive me; otherwise of the State I have never deserved evil. And for my further clearing, I desire humbly to be permitted to private conference with your honour, my Lord-Admiral, and with Mr. Secretary.

Which was yielded to. And that night he was brought into the Court of Wards, after the Court rose.

Sir *Charles Davers* being demanded what he had to say, why Judgment should not be given against him, used these words: I have nothing to say in stay of Judgment, for it is but just that I be adjudged to die: only this I say, my greatest fault was to consent unto things propounded, for my intention was far from thought of hurt unto her Majesty. I was never any persuader or instigator of the Earl in these things; nay, till I was sent for purposely by the Earl out of the country, I was a stranger to these purposes: then finding my Lord of *Southampton*, to whom I owed my love and life itself, that he was so far engaged in the business, and desired my assistance, I yielded advice to him, and gave consent to that I now repent; for there was no reason in me to seek changes, the present being better to me than alteration could promise. Ambition I had none, for my estate was good; discontentment could not trouble me, for I had been well used: but by all this my offence was the greater, in giving offence to the Queen, who had been so gracious unto me. Contrary to the resolution I came with, I have pleaded Not guilty, but this grew through the error of my understanding; but to the justifying of what is found, I also confess myself guilty. And though I have no cause to hope, yet do I not despair of her Majesty's mercy, and if it shall be her Majesty's pleasure to shew mercy, your Lordship and all here shall see, that none lives that shall better deserve life. But if her Majesty's pleasure be to execute Justice, I only request this with my best prayer, that I may die in her Majesty's favour. And these few requests I have to make, which I recommended unto your Lordships, my Lord-Admiral, and to your Honour, Mr. Secretary, that if I must die, that I may have some time given me to settle my conscience, and resolve my soul, because hitherto my hoping having been much, my care hath been the less this way; and if it may be thought fit, I desire to have one of my servants to repair to me for ordering of some things I have to do. And lastly, that your Honour, Mr. Secretary, remembring what your promise was to me, in respect of my descent and alliance to some noble blood, you will so far grace me, as to beg the favour of her Majesty, *that I may be beheaded*. And one request more, I beseech you, let me make suit to see the Earl of *Southampton* before I die.

Sir *Christopher Blunt* upon this said, My Lords, this weak, bruised head of mine made me forget that which I minded to have begged: That in respect I have always professed Arms, and been Marshal of the Field, a place of Honour, I may have so much grace as *to be beheaded*.

My Lord-Admiral and Mr. Secretary told them both, they would remember it to the Queen.

Sir *John Davis* said, I have nothing to say, but only to appeal to mercy. I confess I have highly offended, yet if it please her Majesty to extend mercy unto me, it shall not be to an unworthy servant: my former answers and discloses have not been to purchase favour, but to discover truth; and though by this I challenge no mercy, yet it intimates desert of favour. My great remorse and grief is for my poor *wife's estate*, to think that I being so much benefited and advanced by her, must now be the means to undo her; for I hear all her estate is seized on. Wherefore I beseech this favour, that she be not afflicted for my offence, but may enjoy what was her own.

Mr. Secretary, upon occasion of this speech of *Davis*, what he disclosed, said, Tho' his place did appropriate that to him to be the deliverer and restorer of requests; yet in this business nothing had been done or said by any, but three at least of the chief Counsellors of State have been privy to all that passed, and I only the Register of things moved unto them. And this I will say, that during all the time of the Earl's restraint from the court, his Letters have always had free passage to the Queen, and he might write what he listed, the Queen would ever read that.

Sir *Gilly Merrick*. I have little to say; but let what I have done be considered, and my offence will be found less than others. but the law hath adjudged it Treason, and I must die, and not unwillingly; for the tree being fallen, the branches must not stand. I did the office of a servant as my master bade me, but it was my fault to obey what was not just in him to command. My poor estate I pray you let be considered, it may be thought better of than it is. What it is, I shall set it down, and humbly pray that my poor wife and children may be pitied.

Cuffe confessed the Jury had done but right, in discharging their consciences; yet it was true that Divines held, *condemnatum eum aliquando faciunt quem dampnatum non faciunt*. The gracious proceeding afforded, and all reasonable requests yielded, emboldeneth me to make some small request: When I was restrained, I had not about me above two shillings. I had 350*l*. of ready money seized upon in my chamber. When I came into the *Tower*, I was put into a dark place; but afterwards Mr. Lieutenant pitying me, relieved me, and put me in a better place. Wherefore I pray to be returned unto the same prison, for there I am now provided of things necessary: otherwise perhaps I may be caring for things of this world for necessary succour of life, whenas I would now more willingly spend all my thoughts in other meditations.

This request was granted.

My second request is to you, Mr. Secretary, that I may have the company of some Divine repairing to me for the comfort of my soul, and crucifying of my flesh, that so at my farewell to this world with joyful arms I may embrace my Saviour; and for human respects, I desire the law may be satisfied with my life, without torturing or quartering my flesh; and the rather for favour's sake unto learning, though I have neither place nor great birth to speak for that. To plead for longer or other mercy I will not, but when my body shall be executed, sorrow be unto my soul, if ever I intended evil unto her Majesty's person. Alas! it was my too much love unto my Master that brought me unto this; but as that Earl, my Master, said, now the scales were taken from his eyes, and he saw his faults; so do I, but too late; heretofore in the course of my private state, things went so smoothly with me as I could desire; my religion was always sorting to the profession at this day. Some further things I would utter, but I desire to know whether now I must speak, or that I may be allowed pen and paper to write them hereafter.

It was allowed he should have means to write what he would.

Here ended all that passed before Judgment.

The Lord Chief Justice of *England*, Sir *John Popham*, being now to pronounce Judgment, used these words:

" I am sorry to see any so ill affected to this State as to become plotters and practisers against the State, and that so strongly as you and others in this action have done. And my grief is the more in this, men of worth, service and learning are the actors in that conspiracy! Shall it be said in the world abroad, that we *Englishmen*, now after forty-three years peace under so gracious and renowned a Prince, are become weary of the Government of such a Queen, whom all the world else admires for her government? Consider it well, whosoever had best hopes in this attempt of change, what would have followed upon it? Let me tell you of the smallest hurt, the blood of children, families and friends; for none of yourselves can otherwise think but this action would have cost much blood. And I am sorry to think, that *Englishmen* should seem to excuse themselves by ignorance of the law, which all subjects are bound to know, and are born to have the benefit of. Some of you now at the Bar are Christians; Where, I pray you, did you ever read or hear that it was lawful for the subject to command or constrain his Sovereign? It is a thing against the law of God, and all Nations. God forbid but that by actions men should be allowed to expound intents. Now your actions tending to a sovereignty, cannot but by yourselves be expounded Treason. But your intents, if they were otherwise, as you pretend, yet are not they to expound the law. For know this, that the law, which tends principally to the preserving of the Prince's person, is more tender and precise in this than in any other point.

" And although your Example be pitiful, yet by this, let all men know and learn how high all actions treasonable do touch, and what they tend to. To leave off from further discourse, I should now remember one thing to you all, but I see you all careful of it; that is, the care of your souls, to keep them from death, whereof sin is the cause; and sin is not removed but by repentance, which being truly and heartily performed, then follows what the Prophet *David* spake of, *Blessed are they to whom God imputeth no sin!* There will be a course taken to instruct you how to kill sin in this world, which otherwise shall not be killed in the world to come; for as you leave this world, so shall it be with you in the life to come."

And then pronounced Judgment against every of them, as in case of High-Treason *.

* For *Blunt's* and *Cuffe's* Speeches at Execution, see *State-Trials*, vol. I. p. 203, 204.

IX. The

IX. The Trial of Sir *Griffin Markham*, Knt. Sir *Edward Parham*, Knt. *George Brooke*, Esq. *Bartholomew Brookesby*, Esq. *Anthony Copley*; *William Watson*, Priest; *William Clarke*, Priest, for *High-Treason*, at *Winchester*, *November* the 15th, 1603. 1 *Jac.* 1*.

The Names of the Commissioners.

The Earl of *Suffolk*, Lord-Chamberlain.
Charles Earl of *Devonshire*.
Henry Lord *Howard*.
Robert Lord *Cecil*, Secretary.
Edward Lord *Wotton*, Comptroller.
John Stanhope, Knight and Chamberlain.
Lord-Chief-Justice of *England*.
Lord-Chief Justice of the *Common-Pleas*.
Justice *Gawdy*.
Justice *Walmesley*.
Justice *Warburton*.
Sir *William Wade*, Knight.

ON *Tuesday* the 15th of *November*, were arraigned at *Winchester*, *George Brooke*, Esq. Sir *Griffin Markham*, Knt. *Bartholomew Brookesby*, Esq. *Anthony Copley*, Gent. *William Watson*, Priest; *William Clarke*, Priest, and Sir *Edward Parham*, Knt.

The Effect of the INDICTMENT.

"FOR consulting with the Lord *Gray* and others, traitorously to surprise the King and young Prince at *Greenwich*, to carry them to the Tower guarded with some, that after the slaughter of many of the guards, should put on the guards coats, and so bring them, sending the Lord-Admiral before to signify the distress where the King was, and escape he made by the guards from *Greenwich*; and therefore desired to be taken in there for more safety. Which, if they could have effected, the treasures and jewels in the Tower should serve the turn for the effecting of their further purposes; that some of those of the Privy-Council, *viz.* the Lord-Chancellor, Treasurer *Cecil*, Chief-Justice, should be removed and cut off: and Mr. *Watson* should be Chancellor, *Brooke* Lord Treasurer, and *Markham* Secretary; *Gray* Lord-Marshal and Master of the Horse, if the now Master of the Horse were otherwise preferred, but for the Lord-Chief-Justice no man named. If their project for bringing them to the Tower failed, then to convey the King to *Dover*, where *George Brooke* presumed upon his interest with *Thomas Vardi*; but Mr. Attorney justified his Assurance of the Lord *Cobham*. In one of these places they meant to have kept the King for the space of three months, and at their first entrance, they should require three things. 1. A general pardon of all their purposes and intentions against the King and Prince. 2. The King should yield to a Toleration of religion; with an equality of all Counsellors and other Officers, as well Papists as Protestants, within his Court or otherwise. 3. That he should remove and cut off the fore-mentioned Counsellors, and others who should be thought to hinder this designment, for which purpose *Watson* named *Veale*, alias *Cole*, to alledge sufficient matter against them.

"And for the better effecting of this their purpose, *Watson* had devised under writing an oath should be administred for the preservation of the King's person, for the advancement of the Catholick religion, and for the concealing of all secrets that should be revealed unto them. That all the actions should be proceeded withal in the King's name, and they meant to send for the Lord-Mayor and Aldermen of *London*, that the King would speak with them: whom they meant to keep in safe custody, till they had delivered hostages to them not to withstand their assignments, and to furnish them with all such necessaries as they should require from them. *Watson* was the villainous hatcher of these Treasons; and *Brooke*, upon the learning of them, was as eager a prosecutor; and the Lord *Gray* more eager and violent than he, purposing to make a suit to the King for carrying over a regiment for the relief of *Ostend*, which he would have ready for the defence of his own person in this action, fearing the greatness of the catholick forces according to the promises of *George Brooke*, *Markham* and *Watson*, and knowing not how he might be dealt withal amongst them."

Mr. *George Brooke* said little or nothing in his own defence, only he made a ridiculous argument or two in the beginning: *viz.* that, that only could be the judge, and examiner of any action, which was the rule of the action: but the Common Law was not the rule of the action, *Ergo*, it could not be judge or ruler of the action: and therefore appealed to the person of the King. 2. That the Commissioners or Common Law had no authority over them; because it is a maxim in the law, *ejus esse condemnare, cujus est absolvere*: but the Common Law could not absolve him, being guilty, therefore could not condemn him.

Mr. Attorney to this would have answered particularly, but was by the Commissioners and Judges willed to reduce himself to his own element.

My Lord *Henry Howard* undertaking to have answered him, my Lord-Chief-Justice told him, that the King, by reason of his many causes, had many under him to execute the law of Justice; but he kept in his own hands the key of Mercy, either to bind or loose the proceedings, as in his own princely wisdom he should think fit.

Therefore said Mr. Attorney, you, Mr. *Brooke*, professing yourself to be learned, cannot be ignorant that both your ancestors have been, and you must be liable and subject yourself to the trial of the law of this nation, wherein you were born, and under which you live, & *ignorantia juris non excusat*. These treasons were term'd by the Lord *Cobham The Bye*, as Mr. *George Brooke* confessed to *Watson* and the Lord *Gray*; but, said he, *Walter Raleigh* † and I are chanced at the *Main*. Whereupon Mr. Attorney gave a touch of the treasons of the Lord *Cobham* and *Raleigh*, who had procured from *Aremberg* five or six hundred thousand Crowns, to be disposed by the Lord *Cobham*, who should therewith raise forces for the extirpation of the King and his Cubbes, and putting both *Scotland* and *England* in combustion; and so upon *Cobham*'s return out of *Spain*, to meet *Raleigh* at the isle of *Jersey*, and so to put on foot both titles, both within and without the land.

Mr. *George Brooke*, after his first arguments, spake little or nothing for himself, more than his own confession led him otherwhiles to excuse or qualify his own offence; only he gave cast of a letter, which, he said, he received from his Majesty, wherein he had liberty and authority to deal in the founding out of these practices; but neither at any time before nor at his arraignment, could shew the said letter. And the King being by some of the Lords Commissioners questioned withal on that point, requireth his letter to be produced, and denieth he wrote any such letter.

Sir *Griffin Markham* answered exceeding well, and truly to all things; denying nothing for his fault of Treason; but that he deserved death upon the persuasion of *Watson*, by whom he was misled, and assured that the King before his Coronation was not an actual, but a political King: only he desired to avoid the imputation of effusion of blood in that enterprize, and (if it were possible) the brand of a Traitor for his house and posterity, protesting how careless he was of his own life, which he desired to be exposed to any hazard or sacrifice (tho' it was never so desperate;) which if the King would not (in mercy) yield him, yet he desired their Lordships to be intercessors, that he might die under the Axe, and not by the Halter.

Watson spake very absurdly and deceivingly, without grace, or utterance, or good deliverance; which (added to his foresaid villainy) made him more odious and contemptible to all the hearers.

Clarke, the other Priest (an excellent nimble-tongu'd fellow), of good speech, more honest in the carriage of the business, of an excellent wit and memory, boldly, and in well-beseeming terms, uttering his mind, not unwilling to die, but desireth to avoid the imputation of a Traitor.

Copley, a man of a whining speech, but a shrewd invention and resolution.

Brookesby drawn in merely by *Watson* to take the oath before-mentioned, for some of the particularities, as the bringing the King to the Tower for the advancement of religion; but spake with nobody to incite them to the business, nor came himself according to his Time appointed by *Watson*, the 23d or 24th of *June*, but at that instant attended upon the Queen.

Sir *Edward Parham* was also by that villain *Watson* dealt withal after he had tendered him the oath to this purpose: that he understood the Lord *Gray* meant with forces to set upon the King, and to surprize him, that against that time, whether he would not draw his sword against the Lord *Gray* with the King's servants and friends? And if the King's servants were discomfited, whether with the rest of the Catholics he would not encounter the Lord *Gray*, and if he could bring him to the Tower for his relief and the advancement of the Catholick religion?

Parham told him, that he would so, if he was persuaded that his intendment of the Lord *Gray* were true, which at that time *Watson* could not assure him of; for he did but hear of so much: but said he, when I have better assurance thereof, which will be within these three days, you shall further hear of me. He staying the time, *Watson* came not, and so *Parham*'s proceedings went no further. but being urged in the point for bringing the King to the Tower, for the advancement of the catholick

* Copied from a MS in the *Bodleian* Library, *Rotulæ in Archivo*. A. 3033. 44. 8.

† Sir *John Hawles* (Sollicitor-General *Temp. Will.* III.) in his reply to Sir *Bartholomew Shower's Magistracy and Government of England Vindicated*, &c. pag. 32, says, the King came to *London* in *May*, and in *July* following was the pretended plot discovered; and in *November* following, the pretended delinquents were tried at *Winchester*, together with *Watson* and *Clarke*. Their accusations were in general.

First, To set the Crown on the Lady *Arabella*'s head, and to seize the King.

Secondly, To have a toleration of Religion.

Thirdly, To procure aid and assistance from foreign princes.

Fourthly, To turn out of Court such as they disliked, and place themselves in Offices.

Of these the first article is treason; what crimes the rest are, is doubtful. What of them was proved against the Lords *Cobham* and *Gray*, *Watson* and *Clarke*, or how their Trials were managed, doth not appear: but Sir *Walter Raleigh*'s Trial does appear, and is much like the Lord *Russel*'s, and therefore of some circumstances of it, I think, it is fit to take notice. Instead of conduits, &c. in the Lord *Russel*'s Trial, the cant words of the surprizing *the Bye*, and *the Main*, were made use of in Sir *Walter*'s, interpretable as the Council thought fit; which left it was astonishing to the Jury, which was all that was designed by the Council, and fatal to the Prisoners. I have no mind to run through all the parallel of Sir *Walter Raleigh*'s Trial, as it is printed before his History of the World, because the parallel is too exact, and sticks too close to the memory of Persons gone: only I will say, That if Sir *Walter Raleigh* was guilty of the thing he was accused of by the witnesses, though the accusation did not amount to a legal proof, it was High-Treason; but if the Lord *Russel* was guilty of the things he was accused of, he was not guilty of High-Treason.

And the same Author, says, pag. 35, I think it is plain at this day, that of Sir *Walter Raleigh*'s is thought a sham plot; what the Lord *Russel*'s is thought, let the Author say, I am loath to enumerate all, but if any person will give himself the trouble of reading and comparing the Trial of the Lord *Russel* with that of Sir *Walter Raleigh*, they will find them exactly parallel in a number of other particulars.

religion

Religion, he ſaid, he made no doubt, but that he with others, adventuring their lives for the reſcuing the King from the Lord *Gray*, and bringing him for his ſafety to the Tower, this then would not but merit ſome grace from the King, for the advancement of the Catholic religion.

Sir *Francis Darcy* being Foreman of the Jury, and excellently commended for this Day's carriage and behaviour, made two or three doubts concerning Sir *Edward Parham*'s caſe, and received reſolution from the Bench in ſome points, and the reſt left to his conſcience and underſtanding, went with the reſt of the Jury, and found all guilty, ſaving *Parham*, and ſo he was diſcharged; and upon the reſt ſentence of death was pronounced by the Lord-Chief-Juſtice.

The Copie of a *Letter* written from Maſter *T. M.* neere *Salisbury*, to Maſter *H. A.* at *London*, concerning the proceeding at *Wincheſter*; where the late Lord *Cobham*, Lord *Gray*, and Sir *Griffin Markham*, all attainted of hie Treaſon, were ready to be executed, on *Friday* the 9th of *December*, 1603.

At which time his Majeſties Warrant, *all written with his own hand*, (whereof the true Copie is here annexed) *was deliured to Sir* Benjamin Tichbourne, *High Sheriffe of* Hampſhire, *commanding him to ſuſpend their execution till further order.*

Imprinted at *London*, 1603.

SIR

I Haue receiued a letter from you; by which I perceiue howe much you deſire to be particularly enfourmed of the cauſe and manner of the ſtay of the late Lord *Cobham*'s, Lord *Graye*'s, and Sir *Griffin Markham*'s execution, appointed at *Wincheſter*; wherein, although there are many better able to diſcourſe at large of ſuch an action then myſelfe, yet I conceiue when you have peruſed this plaine and true relation, of that which all men there behelde that day, and many more ſince haue heard, from perſons of the beſt qualitie and knowledge, you will thanke me more, for ſuffering the trueth to ſhew itſelf vnclothed, then if I had laboured to haue deliuered you a tale well painted with curious words and fine phraſes.

You muſt therefore vnderſtand, that as ſoone as the arraignments were paſſed at *Wincheſter*, his Majeſties Priue-Counſel (to the number of fourteene or fifteene, of which companie all of them had either beene tryers of the Noblemen as their Peers, or ſitten as high Commiſſioners vpon the Gentlemen) were called before his Majeſtie (in his Priue-Chamber) at *Wilton*, where he commanded them to deliuer (without reſpect to any perſon) the true narration onely, of the order in the Triall of theſe perſons that had beene condemned by the lawe, and of the nature and degree of their offences, as had appeared in euery one of them, by their ſeueral anſweres.

All which being cleerely and juſtly reported by them (each ſpeaking in the hearing of the reſt) his Majeſtie, for his part, uſed himſelf ſo grauely and reſeruedly in all his ſpeeches, as well to themſelues at that time, as alſo to all other perſons after, in priuate or publique, as neither any of his Priue-Counſell, Nobilitie, or any that attended neereſt to his ſacred perſon, durſt preſume to mediate for any, or ſo much as to enquire what ſhould be the concluſion of this proceeding.

In the meane time, while the Court was full of uariety of diſcourſe, ſome ſpeaking out of probabilitie, others arguing out of deſire, what was like to be the fortune of all, or of any of theſe offendours, his Majeſtie hauing concluded onely in his own ſecret heart (which is the true oracle of grace and knowledge) in what manner to proceed; and that without aſking counſel of any earthly perſon; it pleaſed him to reſolue betweene God and himſelfe, that their execution ſhould be ſtayed, euen at the inſtant when the Axe ſhould be layde to the trees rootes. For the ſecret and orderly carriage whereof, his Majeſtie was careful to preuent all cauſe or colour of ſuſpicion, of that judicious, royall, and vnexpected courſe which followed. And therefore, after the two Prieſts were executed, on *Tueſday* the 29th of *November*, and Maſter *George Brooke* on *Monday* following, his Majeſtie on the ſame day, being the 1ſt of *December*, ſigned three Warrants, for the execution of the late Lord *Cobham*, Lord *Gray*, and Sir *Griffin Markham*, Knight, with particular direction to the Sheriffe, to performe it on *Friday* after, before ten a clocke in the morning.

All theſe directions being now become notorious, both by the writs of execution (which paſſed vnder the Great Seale) and by the making readie the Scaffolds at *Wincheſter*, his Majeſtie uery ſecretly (as now appeareth by the ſequele) drewe himſelfe into his cabinet, on *Wedneſday* before the day of execution, and there priuately framed a Warrant, written all with his own hand, to the Sheriffe, by vertue whereof he countermaunded all the former directions, alledging the reaſons therein mentioned. Of which ſeeing no man's pen can ſo well expreſſe, as his owne, I ſend you the Copie *verbatim*, as I took it out of the originall, which many read in my couſin Sir *Benjamin Tichbournes* hand.

And now to come to the ordering of this buſineſſe; among many other circumſtances, it is uery remarkable, with what diſcretion and foreſight that perſon was elected, which muſt be vſed in carriage of the Warrant. Firſt, his Majeſtie reſolved it ſhould be a *Scottiſhman*; being thereby like to be freeſt from particular dependencie vpon any Nobleman, Counſellors, or others, their friends or allyes. Next hee reſolued, to ſend a man of no extraordinarie ranke, becauſe the ſtanders-by ſhould not obſerue any alteration, nor the delinquents themſelves ſhould take any apprehenſion of ſuch a man's being there at that time: this being his Majeſties ſpeciall deſire, that euery one of them (being ſeuerally brought vpon the Scaffold) might quietly breath foorth their laſt wordes, and true confeſſion of his ſecreteſt conſcience. And ſo (to be ſhort) his Majeſtie made choice of Mr. *John Gibb*, a *Scottiſhman* (as aforeſaid) a man that had never dealt with any Counſellor, or other, for ſuite or buſineſſe, but one that had (within ſhort while after the King's firſt entrie) bene ſent backe into *Scotland*, from whence he was but freſhly arriued at *Wilton*, ſome fewe dayes before.

This party being by the King approoued for an ancient, truſtie, and ſecret ſeruant (as a Groome of his Majeſties bed-chamber) and a man (as is ſaid before) little knowen, and leſs bound to any Subject in *England* for any benefit, receiuing the Warrant ſecretly, on *Thurſday*, from the King's owne hand, and telling his fellowes (who would otherwiſe haue miſſed him) that he muſt lie that night at *Salisbury* vpon ſome priuate buſineſſe of his owne, he rode directly to *Wincheſter*, and there, keeping himſelfe priuate all night, roſe earely in the morning on *Friday*, and went obſcurely to the Caſtle-greene, where the people flocking in all the morning, as the time drewe neere, he put himſelfe with the throng, cloſe by the Scaffold, and there leaned till the Sheriffe brought up Sir *Griffin Markham* to the place, who was the man appointed firſt to die.

There the ſayd Sir *Griffin Markham*, hauing ended his prayer, and made himſelfe readie to kneele downe. Mr. *John Gibb* finding it fit time, while the axe was preparing, to giue ſome ſecret notice of his charge, called to my couſin *Tichbourne*, the Sheriffe, to ſpeake with him, and then deliuered him (priuately) his Majeſties Warrant, with further directions uerbally, how he ſhould vſe it.

Herevpon the Sheriffe, perceiuing fully his Majeſties intention, ſo warily and diſcreetly marſhalled the matter, as hee onely called Sir *Griffin Markham* vnto him on the Scaffold, and told him, that he muſt withdraw himſelfe into the hall, to be confronted (before his death) before thoſe two Lords, that were to follow him, about ſome points that did concern his Majeſties ſeruice; and ſo carrying *Markham* into the hall, he left him there, and went vp haſtily, for the Lord *Gray*, to the Caſtle, who being likewiſe brought vp to the Scaffold, and ſuffered to powre out his prayers to God (at great length) and to make his laſt confeſſion, as he would anſwere it upon his ſoule, when he was readie to kneele downe, to receiue the ſtroke of death, Maſter Sheriffe cauſed him to ſtay, and told him that he muſt goe downe for a while into the hall, where finding Sir *Griffin Markham*, he willed him to tarry there till he returned.

Laſt of all, he went for the Lord *Cobham*, who hauing alſo ended his deuotion to God, and making himſelfe ready to receiue the ſame blow, the Sheriffe finding the time come to publiſh the King's mercie to the worlde, and to reueale his myſterie, he cauſed both the Lord *Gray* and Sir *Griffin Markham* to be brought backe to the Scaffold, and there, before them all three that were condemned, and in the hearing of all the company, notified his Majeſties Warrant, by which he was authoriſed to ſtay the execution. Which ſtrange and vndeſerved Grace and Mercie, proceeding from a Prince, ſo deeply wounded without cauſe, or colour of cauſe giuen by himſelfe toward them in any thing, but meerely contrary (to both the Lords eſpecially) bred in the hearts, as well of the offenders as of the ſtanders-by, ſuch ſundry paſſions, according to the diuers tempers of their minds, as to ſome that ſhall receiue thoſe things by report, which others did behold with their eyes, my relation may rather ſeeme to be a deſcription of ſome ancient Hiſtory, expreſſed in a well-acted comedy, than that it was euer poſſible for any other man to repreſent, at one time, in a matter of this conſequence, ſo many liuely figures of Juſtice and Mercy in a King, of Terror and Penitence in Offenders, and of ſo great Admiration and Applauſe in all others, as appeared in this Action, carried only and wholy by his Majeſties owne direction.

The Lord *Cobham* (holding his hand to Heauen) applauded this incomparable Mercie of ſo gracious a Soueraigne, aggrauating his owne fault, by comparing it with the Princes Clemencie, wiſhing confuſion to all men aliue, that ſhould euer thinke a thought againſt ſuch a Prince, as neither gaue cauſe of offence, nor tooke reuenge of ingratitude.

The Lord *Gray*, finding in what meaſure this rare King had rewarded good for euill, and forborne to make him an example of diſcouragement and terror to all men that hereafter might attempt to break the bonds of loyalty, vpon the paſſions of any ambition, began to ſob and weep for a great while, with moſt deep contrition, proteſting now, that ſuch was his zeale and deſire to redeeme his fault by any meanes of ſatiſfaction, as he could eaſily ſacrifice his life, to preuent the loſſe of one finger of that royall hand, that had dealt ſo mercifully with him, when he leaſt looked for it.

Sir *Griffin Markham* (ſtanding like a man aſtoniſhed) did nothing but admire and pray. The people that were preſent witneſſed, by infinite applauſe and ſhouting, the joy and comfort which they took in theſe wonderfull effects of Grace and Mercy, from a Prince whome God had inſpired with ſo many royall gifts for their conſeruation, and would conſerue for his owne glorie.

The crie being carried out of the Caſtle-gates into the Town, was not onely ſounded with acclamation of all ſexes, qualities and affection, but the true report, diuulged ſince in all partes, hath bred in the worſt diſpoſed mindes, ſuch remorſe of iniquitie, in the beſt ſuch incouragement to loyaltie, and in thoſe that are indifferent ſuch feare to offend, and generally ſuch affection to his Majeſties Perſon, as perſwades the whole world, that Sathan himſelfe can neuer ſo far prevail with any, as to make them lift vp their hearts or hands againſt a Prince, from whom they receiue ſuch true effects of Juſtice and Goodneſs.

To conclude, therefore, I haue now done my beſt to ſatiſfy your deſire, though I feele (to my griefe) how ſhort I come to my own wiſh; becauſe I would haue expreſſed to the life (if it had been poſſible) both the matter and the forme of this proceeding, of both which the wiſeſt men, that haue ſeene and vnderſtoode all particular circumſtances, are at the ende of their wits, to giue an abſolute cenſure, whether of them both deſerue greater recommendation: this being moſt aſſured, that there is no Record extant, wherein ſo great wiſdome and vnderſtandinge, ſo ſolid judgement, ſo perfect a reſolution, to giue way to no requeſt, or mediation: ſo incrutable a heart, ſo royall and equal a tempered Mercie, after ſo clear and publike Juſtice, haue euer concurred ſo demonſtratiuely as in this late Action, wherein this bleſſed King hath not proceeded after the manner of men and of Kings, *Sed cœleſtis Judicis, æternique Regis more*, whereof he ſhall be moſt aſſured to reape theſe laſting fruites, of being beloued and feared of all men, obeyed with comfort, and ſerued with continuall joy and admiration. And ſo forbearing to hold you any longer at this time, I end. From my houſe, neere *Salisbury*, the 15th of *December*, 1603.

Your Lovin Couſin and Friend,

T. M.

His Majeſties *Warrant*, written with his own hand.

ALTHOUGH it be true, that all vell gouernid and flouriſhing Kingdomes and common Vealthis are eſtabliſhed by Iuſtice, and that theſe tuo Noblemen by birthe, that aire nou upon the point of Execution, aire for thair treaſonable practices condemnid by the Lawe, and adiudgit worthy of the

the execution thaireof, to the example and terror of otheris; the one of thaim hauing filthily practised the ouerthrow of the quhole kingdome, and the other for the surprise of our owin Personne, Yet it in regaird that this is the first yeere of our Reigne, in this Kingdome, and that neuer King was so farre obliished to his people as ve haue bene to this, by our entrie heere vith so hairtie and generall an applause of all sorts; Among quhom all the kinne, friendis, and allies of the saidis condemnit personnis vaire as forduart and duetifull as any other our good Subiectis, as also that at the very time of thair Arrainement none did more freely and reddily giue thair assent to thair conuiction, and to deliuer thaim to the handis of Iustice, then so many of thair neerest Kinsmen and Allies (as being Peiris) vaiere vpon thair Iurie, As likeuaise in regard that Iustice hath in some sort gottin course alreadie, by the execution of the tuo Priestis, and George Brooke, *that vaire the principall plotteris and intisairs of all the the rest, to the embracing of the saiddis treasonabill Machinations;* Vee *thairfore (being resolued to mix Clemencie with Iustice) aire contented, and by these Presentis command you, our Sheriffe of* Hampshire, *to superseide the Execution of the saidis tuo Noblemen, and to take thaim backe to thair prison againe, quhile our further pleasure be knowin. And since vee vill not haue our Lawis to haue respect to personnis, in spairing the great, and strikking the meaner sort; it is our pleasure, that the like course be also taken with* Markham, *being sorry from our hairt, that such is, not only the heynous nature of the saidis condemnid personnis crime, but euen the corruption is so great of thair naturall disposition, as the care vee haue for the safety and quiet of our State, and good Subiectis, vill not permit vs to vse that clemencie towardis thaim, quhich, in our owin naturall inclination, vee micht very easily be persuadit vnto.*

X. *The Case between Sir* Francis Goodwin *and Sir* John Fortescue, *in the Reign of King* James I. *as it stands upon the Journals of the* House of Commons.

[*Mercurii* 14 *die Martii*, 1604.

Ordered,

That what stands upon the Journal of this House, of King *James* I. in the Case between Sir *Francis Goodwin* and Sir *John Fortescue*, be printed.

Paul Jodrell, Cl' Dom' Com'.]

Die Jovis 22° *Martii*, 1603-4.

THE first motion was made by Sir *William Fleetwood*, one of the Knights returned for the County of *Bucks*, on the behalf of Sir *Francis Goodwin*, Knight, who, upon the first Writ of Summons directed to the Sheriff of *Bucks*, was elected the first Knight for that Shire: but the Return of his Election being made, it was refused by the Clerk of the Crown (*quia utlagatus*) and because Sir *John Fortescue*, upon a second Writ, was elected, and entered in that place, his desire was, that this Return might be examined, and Sir *Francis Goodwin* received as a Member of the House. The House gave way to the motion; and, for a more deliberate and judicial proceeding in a case of Privilege so important to the House,

Ordered, 'That the Serjeant (the proper Officer of the House) should 'give warning to the Clerk of the Crown to appear at the Bar at eight 'a-Clock the next morning, and to bring with him all the Writs of 'Summons, Indentures, and Returns of Election for the County of *Bucks*, 'made and returned for this Parliament; and to give warning also to Sir '*Francis Goodwin* to attend in person, whom their pleasure was to hear, '*ore tenus*, to deliver the state of his own cause, and the manner and rea-'sons of the proceeding in the Election of the Knights of the Shire for that 'County.'

This being a motion tending to matter of privilege, was seconded with another by Mr. Serjeant *Shirley*, touching an arrest of Sir *Thomas Riley*, &c.

Die Veneris, viz. 23° *Martii*, 1603-4.

SIR *George Copping*, Knight, Clerk of the Crown in the Chancery, this day, (according to former Order) being attended by the Serjeant of the House with his Mace, appeared at the Bar, and produced all the Writs of Summons, Indentures, and Returns made of the Knights for *Buckinghamshire* for this Parliament; which were severally read by the Clerk of the House, and then the Clerk of the Crown commanded to retire to the door: And after, Sir *Francis Goodwin* himself (whom it specially concerned) attending to know the pleasure of the House, was called in, to deliver the state of his own cause, *ore tenus*; wherein he was heard at large, and commanded again to retire until the House had determined what to do.

In this mean time the whole case was at large opened, and argued *pro & contra* by sundry learned and grave Members of the House, and after much dispute the question was agreed upon, and made.

Quest. 'Whether Sir *Francis Goodwin* were lawfully elected and re-'turned one of the Knights for *Bucks*; and ought to be admitted and 'received as a Member of this House?

Upon this Question it was

Resolved in the affirmative, That he was lawfully elected and returned, and (*de jure*) ought to be received.

Hereupon the Clerk of the Crown was commanded to file the first Indenture of Return: and order was given, that Sir *Francis* should presently take the oath of Supremacy usual, and his place in the House; which he did accordingly.

Die Martis, viz. 27° *die Martii*, 1604.

SIR *Francis Bacon*, in reporting a conference with the Lords, touching Wardship and other things, reported that a Lord touched the Case of Sir *Francis Goodwin* as a thing he had heard at large, but did not understand it; and therefore desired to know it more particularly from this House.

Answer was made, That they had no Warrant from the House to speak of it.

Sir *Edward Coke*, his Majesty's Attorney-General, and Mr. Doctor *Hone*, bring a Message from the Lords, expressing with what acceptation their Lordships entertained their motion yesterday, not only for the matter being of very great weight and consequence, but especially for the manner, namely, That, touching Wardship, they would not petition for ease in it as a matter of wrong, but of grief; and pray to be relieved by grace, and not by justice: And their Lordships for answer were desirous, and moved at that time to couple in the same petition the matter of grievance, of respite of homage, which his Majesty, out of his gracious favour and love to his people, had himself taken knowledge of "And as they con-"ceive it to be likely, that the conference may continue between "the two Houses, touching the said matters, as they are very zealous of "the furtherance of their purpose, so are they jealous of any impediment "that may breed let, or hindrance to them: therefore they desire, for a "more clear proceeding and removing of all stumbling-blocks, that the "former Committees may, in a second conference to be had, have autho-"rity to treat touching the Case of Sir *Francis Goodwin*, the Knight for "*Buckinghamshire* first of all, before any other matter were farther pro-"ceeded in."

A. The answer to this message, (as in such cases is for the more part usual) 'That they would return answer by messengers of their own.'

Upon this message it was argued by some, 'That in no sort they should 'give account to the Lords of their proceedings in the House; but that 'Mr. Speaker should from the House be a Suitor to his Majesty, to have 'access, and as their common mouth give his Highness satisfaction by 'direction from the House: That now the judgment of Sir *Francis Goodwin*'s case having passed the House, it could not, nor ought not, to be 'reversed by them. A precedent, *Anno* 27 *Eliz.* cited, where a bill 'brought down from the Lords, upon the first reading was rejected; the 'Lords sent messengers to demand a reason of their judgment. It was 'denied to yield any reason.'

This argument brought forth this question, which Mr. Speaker was ordered by the House presently to make, *viz*

Quest. 'Whether they should confer with the Lords, touching the case of Sir *Francis Goodwin* the Knight for *Buckinghamshire*?'

And *Resolved*, That they should not.

It was then considered as fit to return some answer of the message from the Lords; and Mr. Secretary *Herbert*, with some other of the Committees, were appointed to deliver to their Lordships, from the House,

That they did conceive it did not stand with the *Honour* and *Order* of the House, to give account of any their proceedings or doings: but if their Lordships have any purpose to confer for the residue, that then they will be ready at such time and place, and with such number as their Lordships shall think meet.

Upon the last message to the Lords, the messengers return, That their Lordships would presently send answer by messengers of their own.

Sir *Edward Coke*, his Majesty's Attorney-General, Mr D. *Carew*, Mr. D. *Hone*, and Mr. *Tyndall*, delivered from the Lords, That their Lordships taking notice in particular of the Return of the Sheriff of *Bucks*; and acquainting his Majesty with it, his Highness conceived himself ingaged and touched in honour that there might be some conference of it between the two Houses: and to that end, signified his pleasure unto them, and by them to this House.

Upon this message, so *extraordinary* and *unexpected*, the House entered in some consideration what were fit to be done; and

Resolved, That his Majesty might be moved for access the next day. And afterwards they understood his pleasure to be, That they should attend at *Whitehall* at eight a-clock the next morning. But because the time was then somewhat far spent, they

Ordered, That the House, with Mr. Speaker, should meet at six a-Clock the next morning in the House.

Yet afore their rising, they thought fit to name a Committee, to set down the effect of that which Mr. Speaker was to deliver from the House to the King, *viz.*

Sir *Francis Bacon*,	Mr. Serjeant *Hobbard*,	Sir *Robert Cotton*,
Mr. *Wentworth*,	Sir *Robert Wingfield*,	Sir *Thomas Lake*,
Mr. *Martin*,	Mr. *Hide*,	Sir *Oliver St. John*,
Mr. Serjeant *Sing*,	Mr. *Diet*,	Sir *Edward Stafford*,
Sir *Robert Wroth*,	Mr. *Winch*,	Mr. *Anthrobus*,
Mr. *Francis Moore*,	Sir *Edwyn Sandis*,	Mr Serjeant *Dodridge*.
Sir *Henry Mountague*,	Sir *Francis Hastings*,	Sir *Roger Wilbraham*,
Sir *Willam Fleetwood*,	Mr. *Wiseman*,	Mr. Sollicitor,
Mr. *Fuller*,	Sir *George Moore*,	Sir *Edward Tyrrel*,
Mr. Searjeant *Tanfield*,	Sir *Edward Hobby*,	

To meet at four a-clock this afternoon at the Parliament-Chamber in the *Middle-Temple*.

Die Mercurii, viz. 28° *die Martii*.

MR. Speaker, with a great number of the House, assembled at six a-clock this morning, with a purpose to treat and resolve what should be delivered to his Majesty, (being appointed to attend him the same morning at eight a-clock) touching the reasons of their proceeding in Sir *Francis Goodwin*'s case: but because the House was not then thought full enough for a matter of that consequence, they proceeded to the reading of Bills.

Upon motion touching Mr Speaker's attendance on the King, a Committee was named to accompany him, *viz.*

All the Privy-Council, being Members of the House.

Sir *George Carew*.	Sir *James Scudamore*.	Mr. *Nathanael Bacon*.
Vice-Chamberlain to the	Sir *Jerome Horsey*.	Sir *Richard Verney*.
Queen.	Sir *Edward Radcliffe*.	Sir *George Fane*.
Sir *Francis Bacon*.	Sir *Thomas Holcroft*.	Mr. *Toby Matthew*.
Mr. Serjeant *Dodridge*.	Sir *Anthony Rowse*.	Sir *Thomas Ridgway*.
Sir *Henry Mountague*.	Sir *Henry Nevill*.	Mr. *Edward Seymour*.
Mr. Serjeant *Hobbard*.	Sir *Edward Mountague*.	Sir *William Bourlacy*.
Mr. Serjeant *Lee*.	Sir *Thomas Hobby*.	Sir *Robert Moore*.
Mr. *Fuller*.	Sir *Michael Sandis*.	Sir *Jonathan Trelawney*.
Mr. *Hide*.	Mr. *Thomas Benson*.	Sir *Edward Denny*.
Mr. *Francis Moore*.	Sir *Francis Fane*.	Sir *Thomas Walsingham*.
Mr. *Winch*.	Sir *Francis Hastings*.	Sir *Francis Barrington*.
Mr. *Tate*.	Sir *George Moore*.	Sir *Robert Nappier*.
Mr. *Richard Martin*.	Sir *Edward Hobby*.	Sir *Valentine Knightley*.
Mr. Serjeant *Shirley*.	Sir *Robert Wingfield*.	Sir *George Carew*.
Mr. Serjeant *Tanfield*.	Sir *Maurice Berkley*.	Master of the *Chancery*.
Sir *John Hegham*.	Sir *Edward Tyrrell*.	Sir *Nicholas Halswell*.
Sir *Robert Oxenbridge*.	Sir *William Killegrew*.	Sir *John Thynne*.
Sir *William Fleetwood*.	Sir *Francis Popham*.	Sir *Thomas Freake*.
Sir *Edwyn Sandis*.	Mr. *Francis Clifford*.	Sir *Jerome Bowes*.
Sir *Robert Wroth*.	Sir *John Savill*.	Sir *Edward Herbert*.
Sir *George Fleetwood*.	Sir *Thomas Waller*.	Sir *John Leveson*.
Sir *John Scott*.	Sir *William Lower*.	Mr. *Dudley Carleton*.
Sir *Herbert Crofts*.		

Mr. Speaker, together with these Committees, were this day, at eight a-clock in the morning, appointed to attend his Majesty, and to relate the reasons of the proceeding of the House in Sir *Francis Goodwin's* case; where, upon answer or reply, such Lawyers as be of the Committee are to give their assistance.

Die Jovis, viz. 29° *die Martii*, 1604.

MR. Speaker relateth what he had delivered to the King by warrant from the House the day before, touching their proceeding in Sir *Francis Goodwin's* case, and his Majesty's answer; *whereof, because part was afterwards penned by select Committees*, read in the House, and offered in writing to the King, I have but touched the heads, omitting many circumstances. He said, he first delivered, 1. The manner and matter. 2. Then such precedents as had been vouched and stood upon. 3. He opened the body of the law for election.

The first writ of Summons, dated *ultimo Januarii* before the Parliament: the Writ issued duly; the liberty was free, by that writ, to chuse *in pleno comitatu*: the election was made according to that writ, and the indenture duly returned; *and therefore adjudged by the House*, That this first election being good, the second was consequently void.

For the matter of Utlawry against Sir *Francis Goodwin*, there was one prosecuted against him at the suit of *Johnson*, 31 *Eliz.* for 60*l.* and was laid and proceeded in the *Hustings, London*. Another, at the suit of one *Hacker*, for 16*l.* 39 *Eliz.* That Sir *Francis* had since been chosen, admitted, and served as a Member of this House, in the several Parliaments holden 39 and 43 *Eliz.*

That the Utlawry remained in the *Hustings*, so as the law could not take notice of it; neither was it pleadable.

1 *Eliz.* One *Smith* was found utlawed, and privileged by the House.

23 *Eliz.* One *Vaughan* utlawed; and, upon the question and division of the House, privileged: being carried with the difference of six voices.

35 *Eliz.* Three precedents vouched.

39 *Hen.* 6. *Fitz-Herbert.* The case not judged; but opinions delivered.

Mr. *John Killegrew* having fifty-two utlawries returned against him, was admitted to serve in the House.

Sir *William Harcourt* was found eighteen times utlawed, and yet was admitted to serve.

The manner of the Election is limited by the Statute.

The supposed utlawry, 31 *Eliz.* against Sir *Francis*, was no utlawry at all; for wheresoever a man is sued, the proclamation ought to go into the county where the party dwelleth; or else the utlawry is not good.

39 & 43 *Eliz.* The general pardon is good for utlawries, against all, saving the party at whose suit.

31 *Eliz.* It was *Franciscus Goodwin, Gen.*

39 *Eliz. Franciscus Goodwin Armig. The Sheriff is no judge* of the utlawry, neither could take notice it was the same man, and therefore could not properly return him utlawed.

His Majesty answered, He was loth he should be forced to alter his tune; and that he should now change it into matter of grief, by way of contestation. He did sample it to the murmur and contradiction of the people of *Israel*.

He did not attribute the cause of his grief to any purpose in the House to offend him; but only to a mistaking of the law. For matters of fact, he answered them all particularly. That, for his part, he was indifferent which of them were chosen, Sir *John*, or Sir *Francis*: that they could suspect no special affection in him, because this was a Councillor not brought in by himself.

That he had no purpose to impeach their privilege; but since they derived all matters of privilege *from him, and by his grant*, he expected they should not be turned against. That there was no precedent did suit this case fully. Precedents in the times of *Minors*, of *Tyrants*, of *Women*, of *Simple Kings*, not to be credited; because for some private ends. By the law this House ought not to meddle with Returns, being all made into the *Chancery*, and are to be corrected or reformed by that Court only, into which they are returned. 35 *Hen.* VI It was the Resolution of all the Judges, that matter of utlawry was a sufficient cause of dismission of any Member out of the House. *That the Judges have now resolved*, That Sir *Francis Goodwin* standeth utlawed according to the laws of this Land. In conclusion, it was his Majesty's special charge unto us,

That, 1. The course already taken should be truly reported. 2. That we should debate the matter, and resolve among ourselves. 3. That we should admit of conference with the Judges. 4. That we should make report of all the proceedings, unto the Council.

This relation being made, the House did not enter into any further consideration of the matter at that time; but

Resolved, and Ordered, That it should be the first matter moved the next morning.

Die Veneris, viz. 30° *die Martii*, 1604.

MOVED and urged by one, touching the difference now on foot between the King and the House, that there is just fear of some great abuse in the late election. That in his conscience the King hath been much misinformed; and that he had too many misinformers, which, he prayed God, might be removed or lessened in their number. That now the case of Sir *John Fortescue* and Sir *Francis Goodwin was become the case of the whole Kingdom*. That *old Lawyers forget, and commonly interpret the law according to the Time.*

That by this course the free election of the Country is taken away, and none shall be chosen but such as shall please the King and Council. Let us therefore, with fortitude, understanding and sincerity, seek to maintain our privilege; which cannot be taken or construed any contempt in us, but merely a maintenance of our common right, which our Ancestors have left us, and is just and fit for us to transfer to our posterity.

Another, for a law to be made, That never any man outlawed, should shew his face here again. The difference, he observed, was some unrespective carriage towards his Majesty in this matter; and therefore let our proceeding be dutiful and careful towards him, in advising of some speedy course to give his Majesty satisfaction; that is (as he conceived) according to the King's project, first, to advise amongst ourselves, and then to confer with the Judges, *not as Parliament-men, but as Counsellors*; not as tho' they were to reverse our errors, but that we might be better informed; not now the case of Sir *John* and Sir *Francis*, but a case of great difference between the King and us, wherein we are deeply to consider the consequence if this pique be bruited in the Country, abroad or beyond the seas. It is fit we let the King see how much we take to heart this matter, sithence our affections have so much appeared in the passing and present expediting of the Act of Recognition, &c.

Conclus. That we should tender our humble petition to his Majesty, for leave to make a law for the banishing of all Outlaws hereafter from the Parliament, and pray, that we may hold all our privileges entire.

A third, That we ought not to contest with the King; that it is fit to have a conference: that by it we shall lose no privilege, but rather gain; for the matters of the conference will be two, satisfaction of the King, and putting in certainty our privilege. All is not yet said that may be said; we are not to dispute with one that is Governor of thirty legions. *Confitendum est ne frustra interrogasset.* Let us deal plainly and freely with the Lords, and let them know all the reasons. They are jealous of the *honour of a Privy-Councillor, we of the freedom of Election.* It is fit great men maintain the Prerogative; so is it fit that we maintain our Privileges. *This is a Court of Record*, therefore ought we by all means seek to preserve the honour and dignity of it. If a Burgess be chosen for two places, the Burgess makes his choice for which he will serve, and a warrant shall be directed from Mr. Speaker, in the name of the House, to the Clerk of the Crown to send forth a writ for a new election for the other place left; which is a direct proof that it is a Court of *Power* and *Record*. We have a Clerk and a Register; all matters that pass here are entered of Record, and preserved. As they stand for the honour of a Councillor, so we for our Privileges. It is to be wished, that we had a law to declare our Privileges, that we have a Court of Record and a Register.

Obj. We (they say) *are but half of the body, and the Lords are the parts nearest the Head.*

Answ. Nothing ascends to the Head but by the Breasts, &c.

Concl. That we may pray it may be explained by a law what our Privileges are; and that no man outlawed may hereafter be admitted.

There must be a Judge of the Return before we sit; and this is now judged according to the positive Laws of the Realm by the King, which infringeth not our liberty, since we judge after the Court is set, according to discretion.

No precedent, that any man was put out of the House for utlawry; therefore it had been fit we should have desired to inform the King that he was misinformed.

Let us now leave this particular case to the King, and consider and resolve of the material questions that will fall out in the debate of it. 1. Whether this Court hath power to take notice of Returns made before we sit here? 2. Whether men utlawed may be of the House? 3. Whether a man pardoned, having not sued forth a writ of *Scire facias*, may be called in question? 4. Whether the Writ were returned the 17th of *February*, or no, upon Oath of the Sheriff?

Some others were strong in opinion, That we ought not to confer nor to commit, saying, That Majesty had conferred with Justice; yet Majesty had left the stopping of the wound to us. We should taint ourselves with three great Blemishes, if we should alter our Judgment, levity, cruelty and cowardice. There be three degrees of upright Judgment, motion; examination, judgment: all these have passed us. No Court can reform their own judgment. Every day a Term here. Every act that passeth this House is an Act of Parliament. Shall justice float up and down? Shall he be a Member to-day, and shall we tear him off to-morrow? If the Member be found, it is violence: if the hand tear the rest, it is cruelty. No part torn, but it may bleed to the ruin of the whole.

Let Sir *Francis Goodwin* stand as he is. duty and courage may stand together; let not the House be inveigled by suggestions. This may be called a *Quo Warranto* to seize our liberties.

There hath been three main Objections.

1. The King's Exception. *We can shew no precedent in this kind.*

Answ. "The King could shew no such writ before. Our hands were "never sought to be closed before, nor yet [illegible]! It opens a gap to "thrust us all into the [illegible]. A Chancellor may call a Parliament "of what persons he will by this course. Any suggestion by any person, "may be cause of sending a new writ."

2 Obj.

2. *Obj.* by the Lord-Chief-Justice. *By the Law we had nothing to do to examine Returns.*

Answ. "Judges cannot take notice of private customs or privileges: but we have a privilege which stands with the law." The Judges informed the King of the law, but not of a case of privilege. It is true, 35 *Hen.* VI. all the Judges resolved, That no outlawed man ought to be admitted; but that was controlled by Parliament. It is the same opinion now; let us controll it as then: we have done no offence to the State; let us therefore be constant in our own judgment.

3. *Obj.* Another, *The King's pleasure, that we should deliver the reasons of that we have done to be just.*

If we clear our contempt, we have discharged ourselves. The *King's Bench* cannot reverse their judgment the same Term; therefore not the Parliament. Let us send a message to the Lords, that we are ready so to do, as we do not undo this House.

Others, *Non coronabitur qui non legitime certaverit.* Not to be termed a difference between his Majesty and the Commons. *Rogamus, Auguste, non pugnamus.* The question is not of matter of privilege, but of judgment. Let us attend them as Lords of the Council, and not as Lords of Parliament.

We do no ways contest or contend with his Majesty. The King is no way bound in honour. If writs go forth unduly, they may be controlled without impeachment to the King's honour. It is the act of his inferiour officers It is now come to this question, "Whether the "Chancery or Parliament ought to have authority?"

Quest. *Whether we ought to satisfy the King in his commandment?*

The King's message was, that we should consider within ourselves, and resolve of ourselves; then no need to confer with the Judges: if we cannot, then it is fit to be resolved by the Judges.

The Judges have judged, and we have judged: What need then of conference? Let there be no spark of that grace taken from us, which we have had already from his Majesty. Let our reasons be put into articles, and delivered in all humbleness unto him. Upon the conclusion of this debate in this manner, the House proceeded to question; and the first was,

1. Quest. *Whether the House was resolved in the matter?*

And the question was answered by general voice, That the whole House was resolved.

2. Quest. *Whether the reasons of their proceeding shall be set down in writing?*

Resolved, That they shall be set down in writing: and ordered further, That a committee should be named for that purpose, and appointed first to set them down in writing, and to bring them to the House, there to be published, and to receive their allowance.

The Committees were instantly named, *viz.*

Sir *Robert Wingfield.*	Mr. *Martin.*
Sir *George Moore.*	Sir *Arthur Atye.*
Sir *Francis Bacon.*	Mr. *Francis Tate.*
Mr. *Yelverton.*	Sir *Roland Litton.*
Mr. *Dyett.*	Sir *Henry Nevill.*
Sir *Francis Hastings.*	Mr. Attorney of the Wards.
Mr. *Hedley.*	Sir *John Hollis.*
Mr. Recorder of *London.*	Sir *Robert Wreth.*
Sir *Edward Hobby.*	Sir *John Scott.*
Sir *Francis Barrington.*	Mr. *Hitcham.*
Mr. *Wiseman.*	Sir *Edward Stafford.*
Mr. *Hide.*	Sir *John Mallory.*
Mr. *Fuller.*	Sir *Herbert Crofts.*
Sir *Edward Mountague.*	Sir *Francis Fane.*
Mr. *Ravenscroft.*	Sir *Richard Molyneux.*
Sir *William Fleetwood.*	Sir *John Hungerford.*
Mr. *Winch.*	Sir *Edward Herbert.*
Sir *Thomas Challoner.*	All the Serjeants at Law.
Mr. Sollicitor.	Mr. *Nathaniel Bacon.*
Sir *Roger Wilbraham.*	Mr. *Hext.*
Sir *John Thynne.*	

To meet this afternoon at two a clock in the Exchequer-Chamber.

The authority given unto them by the House, was this:

The House being resolved upon the question, That the reasons of their precedent Resolution, touching the Return, Admittance and Retaining of Sir *Francis Goodwin* as a Member of this House, should be set down in writing; these Committees were specially appointed to perform that service, and have Warrant from the House to send for any Officer, to view and search any Record, or other thing of that kind, which may help their knowledge or memory in this particular service: And having deliberately by general consent set down all such reasons, they are to bring them in writing into the House, there to be read and approved, as shall be thought fit.

Die Lunæ, viz. 2° *die Aprilis*, 1604.

IT was then moved, That Committees might be named to take the examination of the Sheriff of *Buckinghamshire*, who was by former order sent for, and now come. And to that end were named,

Mr. Sollicitor.	Mr. Serjeant *Tanfield.*
Sir *Robert Wroth.*	Mr. Serjeant *Lee.*
Sir *William Fleetwood.*	Mr. *Yelverton.*
Sir *Thomas Challoner.*	Mr. *Francis Moore.*
Sir *Robert Wingfield.*	

Who were appointed to take his examination presently.

Sir *Charles Cornwallis* moveth in excuse of Sir *Francis Goodwin*'s absence from the House, and prayeth, That they would as well in their own judgment pardon it, as witness and affirm his care and modesty upon all occasions to the King, in that he hath forborn, during all the time of this question, to come into the House.

The examination was presently taken by these Committees, and returned in this form.

Interr. 1. *Why he removed the County from* Aylesbury *to* Brickhill?

He saith, it was by reason of the plague being at *Aylesbury*, the County being the 25th of *January*, at which time three were dead of the plague there. This was the only motive of removing his county.

Interr. *Whether he were present at the first Election?*

Saith, He was present, and was as faithful to wish this second place to Sir *Francis Goodwin*, as the first to Sir *John Fortescue*: sent Sir *Francis Goodwin* word, before the election, he should not need to bring any Freeholders, for the election he thought would be without scruple for them both; first to Sir *John*, second to Sir *Francis* About eight of the clock he came to *Brickhill*; was then told by Sir *George Throckmorton*, and others, that the first voice would be given for Sir *Francis*; he answered, He hoped it would not be so, and desired every Gentleman to deal with his Freeholders. After eight of the clock went to the election a great number, there being at the County . . . . After the Writ read, he first intimated the points of the Proclamation; then jointly propounded Sir *John Fortescue* and Sir *Francis Goodwin*. The Freeholders cried first, A *Goodwin*, a *Goodwin!* Every Justice of Peace on the Bench said, A *Fortescue*, a *Fortescue!* and came down from the Bench before they named any for a second place, and desired the Freeholders to name Sir *John Fortescue* for the first. Sir *Francis Goodwin* being in a chamber near, was sent for by the Sheriff and Justices, and he came down and earnestly persuaded with the Freeholders, saying, Sir *John* was his good Friend, had been his father's, and that they would not do Sir *John* that injury: notwithstanding the Freeholders would not desist, but all cried, A *Goodwin*, a *Goodwin!* Some crying, A *Fortescue*, to the number of sixty, or thereabouts; the other for Sir *Francis Goodwin*, being about two or three hundred: and Sir *Francis Goodwin*, to his thinking, dealt very plainly and earnestly in this matter for Sir *John Fortescue*; for that Sir *Francis Goodwin* did so earnestly protest it unto him.

Interr. 3. *Who laboured him to make the Return so long before the day of the Parliament?*

He being here in *London*, Mr. Attorney-General, the second of *March*, at his chamber in the *Inner-Temple*, delivered him two *Cap. Utlagat.* against Sir *Francis Goodwin*; and before he made his return, he went and advised with Mr. Attorney about his return, who penned it, and so it was done by his direction: and the return being written, upon *Friday* after the King's coming through *London*, near about my Lord Chancellor's gate, in the presence of Sir *John Fortescue*, he delivered the Writ to Sir *George Coppin*: and at this time (it being about four of the clock in the afternoon) and before they parted, Sir *John Fortescue* delivered him the second Writ sealed; Sir *John Fortescue*, Sir *George Coppin*, and himself, being not above an hour together at that time, and never had but this new Writ of Parliament to him delivered.

Subscribed, *Francis Cheyne.*

This was returned by the Committee to the hands of the Clerk, but not at all read in the House.

Mr. Speaker remembreth the matter of conference with the Judges, and offered to repeat and put again the questions that were formerly made; being before uncertainly and unperfectly left (as he said) in the case of *Buckinghamshire*, *viz.*

1. *Whether the House were resolved in the matter?*
2. *Whether they should confer with the Judges?*

And at length induced the House to entertain the latter question; and, being made, was carried by general voice in the negative, no conference.

Upon this passage, it was urged for a rule, That a question being once made, and carried in the affirmative or negative, cannot be questioned again; but must stand as a judgment of the house.

It was thought fit that Mr. Speaker should attend the Committee for penning the reasons in Sir *Francis Goodwin*'s case, not by commandment, but voluntary of himself.

Die Martis viz. 3° *die Aprilis*, 1604.

THE reasons of the proceeding of the House in Sir *Francis Goodwin's* case, penned by the Committee, were, according to former order, brought in by Mr. *Francis Moore*, and read by the Clerk, directed in form of a petition.

To the KING's most excellent Majesty,

The humble Answer of the Commons *House of Parliament to his Majesty's objections in Sir* Francis Goodwin's *case.*

MOST Gracious, our dear and dread Sovereign, relation being made to us by our Speaker, of your Majesty's royal clemency and patience in hearing us, and of your princely prudence in discerning; shewing affectionate desire rather to receive satisfaction to clear us, than cause to pardon us: we do in all humbleness render our most bounden thanks for the same; protesting, by the bond of our Allegiance, that we never had thought to offend your Majesty; at whose feet we shall ever lie prostrate, with loyal hearts, to sacrifice ourselves and all we have for your Majesty's service: and in this particular, we could find no quiet in our minds, that would suffer us to entertain other thoughts, until we had addressed our answer to your most excellent Majesty; for which nevertheless we have presumed of the longer time, in respect we have prepared some precedents, requiring search, to yield your Majesty better satisfaction.

There were objected against us, by your Majesty and your reverend Judges, four things, to impeach our proceedings, in receiving *Francis Goodwin*, Knight, into our House.

Objection 1ma, *The first, That we assume to ourselves power of examining of the elections and returns of Knights and Burgesses, which belonged to your Majesty's* Chancery, *and not to us. For that all returns of Writs were examinable in the Courts wherein they are returnable, and the Parliament Writs being returnable into the* Chancery, *the returns of them must needs be there examined, and not with us.*

Our

Our humble anfwer is, That, until the 7th year of King *Henry* IV. all Parliament-Writs were returnable into the Parliament; as appeareth by many precedents of record ready to be fhewed, and confequently the returns there examinable: In which year a Statute was made, That thenceforth every Parliament-Writ, containing the day and place where the Parliament fhall be holden, fhould have this claufe, *viz. Et electionem tuam in pleno comitatu factam diftincte & aperte fub figillo tuo & figillis eorum qui electioni illi interfuerint nobis in Cancellariam noftram ad diem & locum in brevi content' certifices indilate.*

By this, although the form of the Writ be fomewhat altered, yet the power of the Parliament, to examine and determine of elections remaineth; for fo the Statute hath been always expounded ever fithence, by ufe to this day: and for that purpofe, the Clerk of the Crown hath always ufed to attend all the Parliament-time, upon the Commons Houfe, with the Writs and Returns; and alfo the Commons, in the beginning of every Parliament, have ever ufed to appoint fpecial Committees, all the Parliament-time, for examining controverfies concerning elections and returns of Knights and Burgeffes: during which time, the Writs and Indentures remain with the Clerk of the Crown; and after the Parliament ended, and not before, are delivered to the Clerk of the Petty-bag in *Chancery*, to be kept there; which is warranted by reafon and precedents: Reafon, for that it is fit that the returns fhould be in that place examined, where the appearance and fervice of the writ is appointed. The appearance and fervice is in Parliament, therefore the return examinable in Parliament.

Precedents; One in the 29th year of the reign of the late Queen *Elizabeth*, where, after one Writ awarded into *Norfolk* for choice of Knights, and election made and returned, a fecond was before the Parliament-day awarded by the Lord-Chancellor, and thereupon another election and return made; and the Commons being attended with both Writs and Returns by the Clerk of the Crown, examined the caufe, allowed the firft, and rejected the fecond. So *Anno* 23 *Elizabethæ Reginæ*, a Burgefs was returned dead, and a new chofen, and returned by a new Writ: the party returned dead appeared, the Commons, notwithftanding the Sheriff's return, admitted the firft chofen, and rejected the fecond. Alfo, the faid 23d year, a Burgefs chofen for *Hull* was returned lunatick, and a new chofen upon a fecond Writ: the firft claimed his place; the Commons examined the caufe, and finding the return of lunacy to be true, they refufed him; but if it had been falfe, they would have received him. *Anno* 43 *Elizabethæ*, the Sheriff of *Rutlandfhire* returned himfelf elected. the Commons finding that he was not eligible by Law, fent a Warrant to the *Chancery* for a new Writ to choofe a new. *Anno* 43 *Eliz.* alfo a Burgefs was chofen for two Boroughs; the Commons, after he had made election which he would ferve for, fent Warrant to the *Chancery* for a Writ to choofe a new for the other Borough: Of which kind of precedents there are many other, wherewith we fpare to trouble your Majefty. All which together, *viz.* ufe, reafon and precedents, do concur to prove the *Chancery* to be a place appointed to receive the returns, as to keep them for the Parliament, but not to judge of them; and the inconvenience might be great, if the *Chancery* might, upon fuggeftions or Sheriffs returns, fend Writs for new elections, and thofe not fubject to examination in Parliament: for fo, when fit men were chofen by the Counties and Boroughs, the Lord-Chancellor, or the Sheriffs, might difplace them, and fend out new Writs, until fome were chofen to their liking; a thing dangerous in precedents for the time to come, howfoever we reft fecurely from it at this prefent by the now Lord-Chancellor's integrity.

Objection 2da *That we dealt in the caufe with too much precipitation, not feemly for a Council of gravity, and without refpect to your moft excellent Majefty, our Sovereign, who had directed the Writ to be made; and being but half a body, and no Court of Record alone, refufed conference with the Lords, the other half, notwithftanding they prayed it of us.*

Our humble anfwer is, to the precipitation, That we entered into this caufe, as in other Parliaments of like cafes hath been accuftomed, calling to us the Clerk of the Crown, and viewing both the Writs, and both returns; which in cafes of . . . . and motions, though not of bills requiring three readings, hath been Warrant by continual ufage amongft us: and thereupon, well finding that the latter Writ was awarded and fealed before the *Chancery* was repoffeffed of the former, which the Clerk of the Crown, and the Sheriff of the County, did both teftify, and well held to be a clear fault in law, proceeded to fentence with the lefs refpect of the latter election For our lack of refpect to your Majefty, we confefs, with grief of our hearts, we are right forry it fhall be fo conceived; protefting, that it was no way made known unto us before that time, that your Majefty had taken to yourfelf any fpecial notice, or directed any courfe in that caufe, other than the ordinary awarding Writs by your Highnefs's officers in that behalf: but if we had known as much as fome will have, by your Majefty's royal mouth, we would not, without your Majefty's privity, have proceeded in that manner. And further, it may pleafe your Majefty to give us leave to inform you, That in the examination of the caufe of the Sheriff avouched unto us, That *Goodwin* agreed to yield the firft place of the two Knights to Sir *John Fortefcue*, and in his own perfon, at the time of election, with extraordinary earneftnefs, entreated the electors it might fo be, and caufed the indentures to be made up to that purpofe; but the electors utterly refufed to feal them. Concerning our refufing conference with the Lords, there was none defired until after our fentence paffed; and then we thought, That in a matter private to our Houfe, which, by rules of order, might not be by us revoked, we might, without any imputation, refufe to confer. Yet underftanding by their Lordfhips, That your Majefty had been informed againft us, we made hafte (as in all duty we were bound) to lay open to your Majefty, our good and gracious Sovereign, the whole manner of our proceeding, "not doubting, though we were but part of a body, as to make new "laws, yet for any matter of privileges of our Houfe, we are and ever "have been a Court of ourfelves, of fufficient power to difcern and de- "termine without their Lordfhips, as their Lordfhips have ufed always "to do for theirs without us."

Objection 3tia. *That we have, by our fentence of receiving* Goodwin, *admitted, That Outlaws may be makers of laws; which is contrary to all laws.*

Our humble anfwer, That notwithftanding the precedents which we truly delivered, of admitting and retaining Outlaws in perfonal actions in the Commons Houfe, and none remitted for that caufe; yet we received fo great fatisfaction delivered from your royal Majefty's own mouth, with fuch excellent ftrength and light of reafon, more than before, in that point, we heard or did conceive, as we forthwith prepared an act to pafs our Houfe, That all Outlaws henceforth fhall ftand difabled to ferve in Parliament: but as concerning *Goodwin*'s particular, it could not appear unto us, having thoroughly examined all parts of the proceedings againft him, that he ftood an Outlaw, by the laws of *England*, at the time of the election made of him by the county; and that for two caufes: the firft is, That where the party outlawed ought to be five times proclaimed to appear in the Sheriff's County Court; and then not appearing, ought to be adjudged outlawed by the judgment of the Coroners of the County; there appeareth no record made in the *Huftings* of *London* that *Goodwin* was five times proclaimed, or that the Coroners gave judgment of outlawry againft him: but a Clerk, lately come to that office, hath now, many years after time, and fince this election, made entries, interlined with a new hand, that he was outlawed. to which new entries we could give no credit, for that the parties, at whofe fuit *Goodwin* was fued, have teftified in their writings of releafe, That they never proceeded further than to take out the Writ of *Exigent* for an outlawry; and being then paid their money defifted there: by which we find, That *Goodwin* was not five times proclaimed, nor adjudged outlawed, being a thing ufual in *London* to fpare that proclamation and judgment, if the party call not upon it; and no record being made for many years together, that either of them was done.

The fecond caufe was, for that the Writ of *Exigent*, by which the Sheriff was commanded to proclaim him five times, was never lawfully returned, nor certified by *Certiorari*; without which, we take it, That *Goodwin* ftood not difabled as an Outlaw.

To this, adding the two general pardons by Parliament, which had cleared the outlawry in truth and fubftance, (if any were) and that *Goodwin* could not apply the pardons by *Scire f.* for that no record nor return was extant of the outlawry, whereupon he might ground a *Scire fa.* we were of opinion, and fo your Majefty's moft reverend Judges would have been if they had known thus much, That *Goodwin* ftood not difabled by outlawry to be elected or ferve in Parliament: but when we confidered further, That the courfe taken againft *Goodwin* for drawing him into this outlawry of purpofe to difable him to ferve in this place, whereto the County had freely elected him, was unufual; we could not, with the reputation of our places, ferving as a Council of gravity, in allowance or continuance of that courfe, cenfure him to be rejected as an Outlaw: the particulars of which were thefe, *viz.*

Two Exigents awarded, . . . : . . . . . the other feven years paft to the *Huftings* in *London*; no entry made of five proclamations; nor of any judgment of the Coroners; nor any return of the Exigents made or endorfed; the party plaintiff fatisfied; the pretended outlawries being but upon a mean procefs; and as to your Majefty's duties and contempts pardoned now fince *Goodwin* was elected Knight, the Exigent now fought out fince the election procured to be returned in the name of the Sheriffs that then were, and are long fince dead, and new entry made of the five proclamations and Coroners judgment; and now a return made of that old Exigent, which could be of no ufe, but only for a purpofe to difable him for that place. Upon all which we could do no lefs in true difcretion than certify the election made *fecundum equum & bonum.*

Objection 4ta. *That we proceeded to examine the truth of the fact of outlawry, and gave our fentence upon that; whereas we ought to have been bound by the Sheriff's return of the outlawry from farther examining, whether the Party were outlawed or not.*

Our humble anfwer is, That the precedents cited before, in our anfwer to the firft objection, do prove the ufe of the Commons Houfe to examine *veritatem facti* in elections, and returns, and have not been tied peremptorily to allow the return; as if a Knight or Burgefs be untruly returned dead, or lunatick, yet when he appeareth to the Houfe to be living and found, they have, contrary to the return, received him into the Houfe, preferring the truth manifeft before the return. By which difcreet proceeding there is avoided that great inconvenience above-mentioned of giving liberty to Sheriffs, by untrue returns, to make and remove whom they lift to and from the Parliament fervice, how meet foever the parties be in the judgment of the County or Borough that elected them.

Thus, in all humility, we have prefented to your moft excellent Majefty the grounds and reafons of our late action, led with no affections, but guided by truth, warranted in our confciences, imitating precedents, maintaining our ancient privileges, honouring your excellent Majefty in all our fervices; to which in all loyalty and devotion we bind us and ours for ever, praying daily on the knees of our hearts, to the Majefty of the Almighty, that your Majefty and your pofterity may in all felicity reign over us and ours to the end of the world.

Thefe reafons fo fet down and publifhed to the Houfe, Mr. Secretary *Herbert* was fent with meffage to the Lords, That the Houfe had refolved of their anfwer to his Majefty, (in Sir *Francis Goodwin*'s cafe) and had fet it down in writing; and that it fhould be fent to their Lordfhips before four of the clock in the afternoon; who immediately returned their Lordfhips anfwer, That they would be ready at that time in the Council-Chamber at *Whitehall*, with thirty of the Lords, to receive what then fhould be delivered. Then were named threefcore to attend the delivery of the faid reafons at the time and place aforefaid.

Eodem die poft meridiem.

THE Houfe entering ferioufly into confultation what courfe was to be held with the Lords as alfo taking into more length of difputation, touching the bill of merchants, than were expected, fent fome meffengers to the Lords to excufe their long tarrying, *viz.*

Sir *Edward Hoby*.
Sir *Ro.* [illegible]
Sir *Henry* [illegible]
Sir *Francis Haftings*.
Mr *Martyn*.

This afternoon about five a-clock, the Committee appointed did attend to deliver the reasons aforesaid at the Council-Chamber, according to appointment and order of both Houses; and they were delivered by Sir *Francis Bacon*, one of the Committee, with desire, That their Lordships would be mediators in the behalf of the House, for his Majesty's satisfaction.

Die Mercurii, viz. 4° *die Aprilis*, 1604.

SIR *Francis Bacon* having the day before delivered to the Lords in the Council-Chamber of *Weitehall*, (according to the direction of the House) the reasons in writing, penned by the Committee, touching Sir *Francis Goodwin's* case, maketh report of what passed at the time of the said delivery.

First, That though the Committees imployed were a number specially deputed and selected; yet that the Lords admitted all Burgesses without distinction; that they offered it with testimony of their own speed and care in the business, so as they said no one thing had precedency, but only the bill of recognition; that they had such respect to the weight of it, as they had not committed it to any frailty of memory, or verbal relation, but put it into writing for more permanent memory of their duty and respect to his Majesty's grace and favour: that in conclusion they *prayed their Lordships, sithence they had nearer access, they would co-operate with them for the King's satisfaction*; and so delivered the writing to the hands of the Lord-Chancellor, who receiving it, demanded, whether they should send it to the King, or first peruse it? To which was answered, That since it was the King's pleasure they should concur; they desired their Lordships would first peruse. The Lord *Cecil* demanded, whether they had Warrant to amplify, explain, or debate any doubt or question made upon the reading? To which it was said, They had no Warrant. And so the writing was read, and no more done at that time.

Die Jovis, viz. 5° *die Aprilis*, 1604.

MR. Speaker by a private commandment attended the King this morning at eight a-clock, and there staid till ten.

Mr. Speaker excuseth his absence, by reason he was commanded to attend upon his Majesty. And bringeth message from his Majesty to this effect: That the King had received a parchment from the House. Whether it were an absolute resolution, or reason to give him satisfaction, he knew not: He thought it was rather intended for his satisfaction. His Majesty protested, by that love he bare to the House as his loving and loyal Subjects, and by the faith he did ever owe to God, he had as great a desire to maintain their privileges, as ever any Prince had, or as themselves. He had seen and considered of the manner and the matter; he had heard his Judges and Council; and that he was now distracted in judgment. Therefore, for his further satisfaction, he desired, and commanded, *as an absolute King*, that there might be a conference between the House and the Judges; and that for that purpose there might be a select Committee of grave and learned persons out of the House: That his Council might be present, *not as Umpires to determine, but to report indifferently on both sides*.

Upon this unexpected message there grew some amazement and silence. But at last one stood up and said: the Prince's command is like a thunderbolt; his command upon our Allegiance like the roaring of a Lion. To his command there is no contradiction; but how, or in what manner we should now proceed to perform obedience, that will be the question.

Another answered, let us petition to his Majesty, that he will be pleased to be present, to hear, moderate, and judge the case himself. Whereupon Mr. Speaker proceeded to this question.

Quest. Whether to confer with the Judges in the presence of the King and Council?

Which was resolved in the affirmative.

And a select Committee presently named for the conference, *viz.*

Lawyers.	Gentlemen.
Mr. Serjeant *Tanfield*.	Sir *George Carew*, Vice-Chamberlain to the Queen.
Mr. Serjeant *Hobbard*.	Sir *Francis Hastings*.
Mr. Serjeant *Leigh*.	Sir *Edward Hobby*.
Mr. Serjeant *Shirley*.	Sir *Robert Wroth*.
Mr. Serjeant *Dodridge*.	Sir *Henry Nevill*.
Sir *Thomas Hesketh*.	Sir *John Savile*.
Sir *Francis Bacon*.	Sir *George Moore*.
Mr. Recorder of *London*.	Mr. *Nathaniel Bacon*.
Mr. *Yelverton*.	Sir *Edward Stafford*.
Mr. *Crewe*.	Sir *William Fleetwood*.
Mr. *Lawrence Hide*.	Sir *Thomas Challoner*.
Mr. *Francis Moore*.	Sir *Roger Aston*.
Mr. *Richard Martin*.	Sir *Robert Wingfield*.
Mr. *Wincke*.	Sir *Edw. Mountague*.
Mr. *Dyett*.	Sir *Edwyn Sandis*.
Mr. *Fuller*.	Sir *Robert Cotton*.
Sir *Roger Wilbraham*.	
Mr. *Francis Tate*.	
Mr. Doctor *James*.	
Sir *Daniel Dunn*.	
Sir *John Bennet*.	

These Committees were selected and appointed to confer with the Judges of the Law, touching the reasons of proceeding in Sir *Francis Goodwin's* case, set down in writing, and delivered to his Majesty in the presence of the Lords of his Majesty's Council, according to his Highness's pleasure, signified by Mr. Speaker this day to the House.

It was further resolved and ordered by the House, (upon the motion to that end by Mr. *Lawrence Hide*) that the aforesaid Committee should insist upon the fortifications, and explaining of the reasons and answers delivered unto his Majesty; and not proceed to any other argument or answer, what occasion soever moved in the time of that debate.

Die Mercurii, viz. 11° *die Aprilis*, 1604.

Upon Adjournment.

SIR *Francis Bacon* was expected, and called to make a report of the late conference with the Judges in the presence of his Majesty and the Lords of the Council: but he made excuse, saying, he was not warranted to make any report; and *tantum permissum quantum commissum*: nevertheless, upon a question, he was over-ruled to make a report; and a motion thereupon made, That the Committees might first assemble in the Court of Wards, and confer among themselves, and then the report to be made.

Sir *Francis Bacon*, after the meeting of the Committees in the Court of Wards, reporteth what had passed in conference in the presence of his Majesty and his Council.

THE King said, He would be President himself. This attendance renewed the remembrance of the last, when we departed with such admiration. It was the voice of God in man: the good Spirit of God in the mouth of man. I do not say, the voice of God, and not of man. I am not one of *Herod's* flatterers. A curse fell upon him that said it: a curse on him that suffered it. We might say as was said to *Solomon*, We are glad, O King! that we give account to you, because you discern what is spoken.

We let pass no moment of time, until we had resolved and set down an answer in writing, which we now had ready.

That sithence we received a message from his Majesty by Mr. Speaker, of two parts: 1. The one Paternal. 2. The other Royal. 1. That we were as dear unto him as the safety of his person, or the preservation of his posterity. 2. Royal, that we should confer with his Judges, and that in the presence of himself and his Council. "That we did more now to King *James* "than ever was done since the Conquest, in giving account of our Judge-"ments." That we had no intent, in all our proceedings, to encounter his Majesty, or to impeach his Honour or Prerogative.

This was spoken by way of preamble by him you employed.

How to report his Majesty's Speeches; he knew the eloquence of a King was inimitable.

The King addressed himself to him as deputed by the House, and said, He would make three parts of what he had to say. The cause of the meeting was to draw to an end the difference in Sir *Francis Goodwin's* case.

If they required his absence, he was ready; because he feared he might be thought interested, and so breed an inequality on their part.

He said, That he would not hold his Prerogative or Honour, or receive any thing of any or all his subjects. This was his Magnanimity.

That he would confirm and ratify all just Privileges. This his Bounty and Amity. As a King, Royally: As King *James*, sweetly and kindly out of his good-nature.

One point was, Whether we were a Court of Record, and had power to judge of Returns. As our Court had power, so had the Chancery; and that the Court that first had passed their Judgment should not be controlled.

Upon a surmise, and upon the Sheriff's Return, there grew a difference.

That there are two powers. 1. Permanent: The other, Transitory. That *the* Chancery *was a confidenciary Court to the use of the Parliament during the time*.

Whatsoever the Sheriff inserts beyond the authority of his mandate, a nugation. The Parliaments of *England* not to be bound by a Sheriff's Return.

That our Privileges were not in question. That it was private jealousies without any kernel or substance. "He granted it was a Court of Record, "and a Judge of Returns." He moved, That neither Sir *John Fortescue*, nor Sir *Francis Goodwin* might have place; Sir *John* losing place, his Majesty did meet us half-way. That when there did arise a schism in the Church between a Pope and an Antipope, there could be no end of the difference until they were both put down.

Upon this Report, a motion was made, That it might be done by way of warrant; and therein to be inserted, That it was done at the request of the King: and was further said, (as anciently it hath been said) That we lose more at a Parliament than we gain at a Battle. That the authority of the Committee was only to fortify what was agreed on by the House for answer, and that they had no authority to consent.

It was further moved by another, That we should proceed to take away our dissention, and to preserve our liberties; and said, that in this we had exceeded our commission; and that we had drawn upon us a note of inconstancy and levity.

But the acclamation of the House, was, That it was testimony of our duty, and no levity.

So as the question was presently made,

Quest. Whether Sir *John Fortescue* and Sir *Francis Goodwin* shall both be secluded, and a warrant for a new writ directed? And upon the question resolved, That a writ should issue for a new choice, and a warrant directed accordingly.

A motion made, That thanks should be presented by Mr. Speaker to his Majesty, for his presence and direction in this matter; and thereupon Ordered, That his Majesty's pleasure should be known, by Sir *Roger Aston* for their attendance accordingly.

Because it hath been conceived by some, that Sir *Francis Goodwin* being the Member specially interested, it were fit he should give testimony of his liking and obedience in this course: being dealt withal to that end, he writ his letter to Mr. Speaker; which, before this question made, for better satisfaction of the House, was read in these words,

" *SIR*,

" I Am heartily sorry to have been the least occasion either of question be-" tween his Majesty and that honourable House, or of interruption to " those worthy and weighty causes, which by this time, in all likelihood, " had been in very good furtherance: wherefore, understanding very cre-" dibly, that it pleased his Majesty, when the Committees last attended " him, to take course with them for a third writ and election for the Knight-" ship of the County of *Buckingham*: I am so far from giving any impedi-" ment thereunto, that contrariwise, I humbly desire his Majesty's direc-" tion in that behalf to be accomplished and performed. So praying you, " according to such opportunity as will be ministred, to give furtherance " thereunto, I take my leave, and rest

Westm. *this* 11*th of April*, 1604.

Yours, most assured to be commanded,

FRA. GOODWIN."

Directed, *To the Right Worshipful Sir* Edward Phelips, *Knight, Speaker of the Honourable Court of Parliament.*

Die Jovis, viz. 12° *die Aprilis.*

A Motion made, That Mr. Speaker, in behalf of the House, should pray access to his Majesty, and present their humble thanks for his gratious presence and direction, upon the hearing of Sir *Francis Goodwin*'s cause; which was assented unto; and Sir *Roger Aston*, a servant of his Majesty's Bed-chamber, and one of the Members of the House, was presently appointed to know his Majesty's pleasure; which he did accordingly; and returned, That his Majesty was willing to give them access in the gallery at *Whitehall*, at two a-clock in the afternoon, the same day. Thereupon a Committee was named to attend Mr. Speaker to the King, with a general warrant to all others that should be pleased to accompany them.

The Committee especially named were,

All the Privy-Council of the House.

Sir *George Carew*, Vice Chamberlain to the Queen.	Sir *John Scott*.
The Lord *Buckhurst*.	Mr. *Edward Seymour*.
Sir *John Heigham*.	Sir *Thomas Holcroft*.
Sir *Robert Oxenbridge*.	Sir *Henry Nevill*.
Sir *William Fleetwood*.	Sir *Thomas Wolsingham*.
Sir *Edwyn Sandis*.	Sir *Thomas Benson*.
Sir *John Hollis*.	Sir *Francis Barrington*.
Mr. *John Sheffield*.	Sir *Robert Nappier*.
Sir *Francis Hastings*.	Sir *Valentine Knightley*.
Sir *George Moore*.	Sir *George Carew*, Master of the *Chancery*.
Sir *Robert Wingfield*.	Sir *Jerome Bowes*.
Sir *William Killegrew*.	Sir *John Thynne*.
Sir *Francis Popham*.	Sir *John Leveson*.
Mr. *Francis Clifford*.	Sir *William Burlacy*.
Sir *John Savile*.	Sir *Roger Aston*.
Sir *Richard Verney*.	Sir *Robert Moore*
Mr. *Toby Matthew*.	Mr. *Dudley Carleton*.
Sir *Thomas Ridgway*.	Sir *William Wray*.
Sir *Jonathan Trelawney*.	Sir *George St. Poll*.

Die Veneris, viz. 13° *die Aprilis*, 1604.

MR. Speaker returneth to the House the Effect of his message of thanks, delivered the last day in the name of the House to his Majesty; as also of his Majesty's answer, *viz.*

That he related to this House the humble and dutiful acceptation of what his Majesty had done, together with the humble thanks of the House for his zealous and paternal delivery of his Grace unto us, by his own mouth: what wonder they conceived in his Judgment, what Joy in his Grace, what comfort they had in his Justice, what approbation they made of his Prudence, and what obedience they yielded to his Power and Pleasure.

That his direction gave all men satisfaction. That they were determined to pursue the course he had prescribed. That now they were become suitors, he would be pleased to receive a representation of the humble thanks and service of the House.

His Majesty answered, That upon this second access, he was forced to reiterate what he had said before. That this question was unhappily cast upon him, for he carried as great a respect to our privileges as ever any Prince did; he was no ground-searcher; he was of the mind that our privileges were his strength: that he thought the ground of our proceeding was our not understanding that he had intermeddled before we had decided: that he thought also we had no wilful purpose to derogate any thing from him, for our answer was a grave, dutiful, and obedient answer.

But as the devil had unhappily cast this question between them, so he saw God had turned it to two good ends and purposes.

1. One, That he knew, and had approved our loyalty.
2. Another; That he had so good an occasion to make testimony of his bounty and grace.

That as we came to give him thanks, so did he redouble his thanks to us.

That he had rather be a King of his Subjects, than to be a king of many kingdoms.

The second part of his speech directed to the Lords and Us.

That this Parliament was not like to be long: that we would treat of such matters as most concerned the Commonwealth; and the last, of any thing that concerned himself.

Three main businesses in our hands.

1. The Union.
2. Sundry Publick and Commonwealth-Bills.
3. Matter of Religion, and reformation of Ecclesiastical Discipline.

For the Union, that it might be now prepared, and prosecuted the next Session.

That Union, which with the loss of much blood could never be brought to pass, as now it is. That the better to bring it to pass, we should be in affections united.

That we should first with all care proceed in such laws as concern the general good.

That all Heresies and Schisms might be rooted out, and care taken to plant and settle God's true Religion and Discipline in the Church.

That this wish above all things was at his death to leave,

1. One Worship to God.
   One Kingdom entirely governed.
   One Uniformity in Laws.

Lastly, That his occasions were infinite, and much beyond those of his Predecessors; and therefore that in this first Parliament we would not take from him that which we had yielded to others.

That in his affections he was noways inferior to others, nor in his desire to ease us.

The Warrant for a new Election of a Knight for *Bucks*, read and allowed in this form:

Whereas the Right Honourable Sir John Fortescue *Knight, Chancellor of his Majesty's Dutchy of* Lancaster, *and Sir* Francis Goodwin *Knight, have been severally elected and returned Knights of the Shire for the County of* Bucks, *to serve in this present Parliament: upon deliberate consultation, and for some special causes moving the Commons House of Parliament, It is this Day Ordered and Required by the said House, That a Writ be forthwith awarded for a new Election of another Knight for the said Shire: And this shall be your Warrant.*

Directed, To my very loving Friend, Sir *George Coppin* Knight, Clerk of the Crown in his Majesty's High Court of Chancery.

XI. The Process and Trial of ROBERT LOGAN, of *Restalrig*, for *High-Treason*, in conspiring with *John* Earl of *Gowrie*, to murder King *James* I. *June* 1609. 7 *Jac* 1.

IN the year 1608, the Earl of *Dunbar*, walking in his own Garden, and conversing with a country Gentleman, who lived near the place, falling accidentally to discourse on the matter of *Gowrie*'s forfeiture; this Gentleman told the Earl, that he being lately in company with one *Sprott*, a Notary, who lived in *Eyemouth*, who was ordinarily employ'd in the Laird of *Restalrig*'s service as a Notary and Trustee, and who was long acquainted with this Gentleman who was speaking to the Earl; told the Earl, that this *Sprott* had told him things concerning that Treason which he had never heard before; but that he had never told it, so long as those concern'd were alive. The Earl was curious to have the information, which the Gentleman told him, and was in short.

That umquhil *Robert Logan* of *Restalrig*, then dead, was a Co-partner and Contriver with the Earl of *Gowrie*, and his brother Mr. *Alexander*, in all that affair, and that *Sprott* had several letters, yet lying by him, which he had found amongst *Restalrig*'s papers, and some papers belonging to one, commonly call'd Laird *Bour*, the greatest confident of any man that *Restalrig* had, and who was also intimate with *Sprott* the Notary.

Whereupon the Earl of *Dunbar* acquainted the King's Advocate, and *Sprott* was seized and carried into *Edinburgh*, who, before several Lords of the Council, did, with great remorse of conscience, acknowledge,

That he knew perfectly that *Robert Logan*, late of *Restalrig*, was privy to, and upon the fore-knowledge of *Gowrie*'s treasonable conspiracy. and for the greater assurance of his knowledge, deponeth, That he knew, that there were divers letters interchanged betwixt them, anent the treasonable purposes aforesaid, in the beginning of the month of *July* 1600, which Letters, *James Bour*, called Laird *Bour*, servitour to *Restalrig* (who was employ'd mediator betwixt them, and privy to all that errand) had in keeping, and shewed the same to *Sprott*, in the place of *Fastcastle*.

And deponed, That he did abstract (*i. e.* steal) quietly from *James Bour*, the principal letter written by *Restalrig* to the Earl of *Gowrie*, which *Bour* had brought back from the Earl of *Gowrie* (as was the custom amongst them at that time); and that when *James Bour* employed him (*Sprott*) to look over his papers; that he did keep the same, and that it was yet in his keeping, and was in his chest, among his writings, where he left it when he was taken, (and accordingly, the letter was found there by the Sheriff-depute, who was ordered by Sir *William Hart*, Lord-Justice of *Scotland*, to seize the said chest, and search for this letter, which was found, and delivered to the King's Advocate).

Whereupon, the King's Advocate produced the summons of Treason, which was raised by warrant under the Seals, on the 5th of *February*, 1609; against all the defenders and others concerned, to compear before our sovereign Lord, or his Commissioner, and the Estates of Parliament, and Justice-General, on the 12th day of *April*, 1609, to answer, &c. And likewise produced the verifications of the executions, which were sworn to, by the Heralds, Messengers and Witnesses, in plain Parliament: all which are contained at length in the Records of Parliament; as are also the letters of relaxation and executions thereupon; relaxing *Robert Logan*, eldest son to umquhil *Robert Logan* the accused, from the horn, and all perils thereby; which relaxations were registrated in publick Records before the day of compearance. and then the Lord Advocate produced for verifying of the dittay and crimes, the principal letters, and did put them in the Clerk-Register's hands (where they lie among the publick Records); as likewise the depositions of the witnesses, taken by the Lords of the Articles, in common form.

All which being produced in presence of his Majesty's Commissioner, and the Estates of Parliament, upon the day of 1609, the defenders cited, and not compearing; the Advocate desired the Estates declaration on the relevancy: the true extracts whereof are as follow:

SIR *Thomas Hamilton* of *Binnie*, Knight, Advocate to our Sovereign Lord, in his Highness's name, for proving of the points of the said summons, and reason and cause of Treason and Lese Majesty contained therein, repeated divers missive bills, all written and subscribed by the said umquhil Laird of *Restalrig*. All the depositions of the witnesses, examined before the Lords of Articles before, and before the Lords of secret Council, *George Sprott*'s depositions, and conviction and execution to the death, for the same crime of Treason of *Gowrie*; together with divers writs and other probations, which were presently produced, before the said Estates, by the said Lord Advocate, in our sovereign Lord's Name, for proving of the foresaid summons of Treason, and the reason and cause of Lese Majesty contained therein; of the which missive bills and depositions produced by the said Advocate in our sovereign Lord's name, for proving the said summons of Treason,

Treason, and reasons therein contained, against the said *Robert Logan* and his foresaids; the tenour follows.

"RIGHT Honourable Sir, my duty, with service remembered: Please you understand, my Lord of *Gowrie*, and some others his Lordship's friends and well-wishers, who tenders his Lordship's preferment, are upon the resolution you know, for the revenge of that cause: and his Lordship has written to me anent that purpose; whereto I will accord in case ye will stand to, and bear a part; and before ye resolve, meet me and Mr. *Alexander Ruthven* in the *Cannongate*, on *Thursday* the next week, and be as wary as you can: indeed Mr. *Alexander Ruthven* spoke with me, four or five days since; and I have promised his Lordship an answer within ten days at farthest. As for the purpose, how Mr. *Alexander Ruthven* and I has set down the course, it will be a very easy done turn; and not far by that form, with the like stratagem, whereof we had conference in *T. S.* But in case you and Mr. *Alexander Ruthven* forgather, because he is somewhat uncautious; for God's sake beware with his racklessness as to this of *Padua*; for he told me one of the strangest tales of a Nobleman of *Padua* that ever I heard in my life, resembling the like purpose; I pray you, Sir, think nothing, altho' this bearer understand of it; for he is the special secretary of my life; his name is Laird *Bour*, and was old *Manderston's* man for dead and life, and even so now for me. And for my own part, he shall know of all that I do know in this world, so long as ever we live together; for I make him my houshold-man: he is well worthy of credit; and I recommend him to you. Always to the purpose I think best, for our plot, that we meet all at my house of *Fastcastle*: for I have concluded with Mr. *Alexander*, who I think shall be meetest to be conveyed quietly in a boat by sea; at which time, upon sure advertisement, I shall have the place very quiet and well provided; and as I receive your answer, I will post this bearer to my Lord: and I pray you, as you love your own life, (because it is not a matter of mows) be circumspect in all things, and take no fear but all shall be well. I have no will, that either my brother, or yet Mr. *N. R.* my Lord's old pedagogue, know any thing of the matter till all be done that we would have done; and then I care not who gets wit, that loves us. When ye have read, send this my letter back again with the bearer, that I may see it burnt myself; for so is the fashion in such errands: and if you please write your answer on the back hereof, in case ye will take my word for the credit of the bearer, and use all expedition; for the turn would not be long delayed. Ye know the King's hunting will be shortly; and then shall be best time, as Mr. *Alexander* has assured me, that my Lord has resolved to enterprize that matter. Looking for your answer, commits you to *Christ*'s holy protection. From *Fastcastle*, the 18th day of *July*, 1600.

Sic subscribitur,

Yours to utter power ready,

RESTALRIG.

"LAIRD *Bour*, I pray you haste you west to me about the errand I told you; and we shall confer at length of all things. I have received a new letter from my Lord of *Gowrie*, concerning the purpose that Mr. *Alexander* his Lordship's brother spoke to me before: and I perceive that I may have advantage of *Dirleton*; in case his other matter take effect; as we hope it shall. Always, I beseech you, be at me the morn and even; for I assured his Lordship's servant, that I shall send you over the water, within three days, with a full resolution of all my will, anent all purposes; and I shall indeed recommend you and your trustiness to his Lordship, as ye shall find an honest recompence for your pains in the end. I care not for all the land I have in this Kingdom, in case I can grip of *Dirleton*; for I esteem it the pleasantest dwelling in *Scotland*. For God's cause keep all things secret, that my Lord, my brother, get no knowledge of our purposes; for I rather be carded quick. And so looking for you, I rest till meeting."

From the Cannongate,
the 18th day of July.

P. S. I am very ill at ease, therefore speed you hither.

Sic subscribitur,

Yours to power ready,

RESTALRIG.

"RIGHT Honourable Sir, all my hearty with humble service remembred. Since I have taken in hand to enterprise with my Lord of *Gowrie*, your special and only best beloved; as we have set down the plat already, I will request you, that you will be very circumspect and wise, that no man get an advantage of us. I doubt not but you know the peril to be both life, lands and honour, in case the matter be not wisely used. And, for my own part, I shall have a special respect to my promise that I have made to his Lordship, and Mr. *Alexander* his Lordship's brother, altho' the Scaffold were set up. If I cannot come to *Falkland* the first night, I shall be timely in *St. Johnston* on the morn. Indeed, I lippened for my Lord himself, or else Mr. *Alexander* his Lordship's brother, at my house of *Fastcastle*, as I wrote to them both. Always I repose on your advertisement of the precise day, with credit to the bearer; for howbeit he be but ane sillie glyed old carle, I will answer for him, that he shall be very true. I pray you, Sir, read, and either burn or send again with the bearer; for I dare hazard my life, and all I have else in the world, on his message, I have such proof of his constant truth. So commits you to *Christ*'s holy protection."

From the Cannongate, *the 29th day of* July, 1600.

P. S. I use not to write on the back of any of my letters, concerning this errand.

Sic subscribitur,

Yours to all power, with humble service ready,

RESTALRIG.

"MY Lord, my most humble duty with service, in most hearty manner remembred: at the receipt of your Lordship's letter, I am so comforted, especially as your Lordship's purpose communicated to me therein, that I can utter my joy, nor find myself able how to encounter your Lordship with due thanks. Indeed, my Lord, at my being last in the town, Mr. *Alexander*, your Lordship's brother, imparted somewhat of your Lordship's intention, anent that matter, unto me. And, if I had not been busied about some turns of my own, I thought to have come over to *St. Johnston*, and spoken with your Lordship. Yet always, my Lord, I beseech your Lordship, both for the safety of your honour, credit, and more than that, that your life, my life, and the lives of many others, who may, perhaps, innocently smart for that turn afterwards, in case it be revealed by any, and likewise the utter wraking of our lands and houses, and extirpating of our name; look that we be all as sure as your Lordship, and I myself shall be, for my own part. And then, I doubt not, but with God's grace, we shall bring our matter to ane fine, which shall bring the contentment to us all, that ever wished for the revenge of *Machiavelian* massacring of our dearest friends. I doubt not, but Mr. *Alexander*, your Lordship's brother, has informed your Lordship what course I laid down, to bring all your co-associates to my house of *Fastcastle* by sea; where I should have all materials in readiness, for their safe receiving on land and into my house; making, as it were, but a manner of passing time in ane boat on the sea, in this fair summer-tide; and no other strangers to haunt my house, while we had concluded on the laying our plot; which is already devised by Mr. *Alexander* and me. And I would wish, that your Lordship would either come, or send Mr. *Alexander* to me; and thereafter, I would meet your Lordship in *Leith*, or quietly at *Restalrig*; where we should have prepar'd ane fine hatted kit, with sugar, and comfits, and wine; and thereafter confer on matters; and the sooner we brought our purpose to pass, it were the better, before harvest. Let not Mr. *W. R.* your old pedagogue, ken of your coming: but rather would I, if I durst be so bold to intreat your Lordship, once to come and see my own house, where I have kept my Lord *Bothwell* in his greatest extremities; say the King and his Council what they would: And in case GOD grant us happy success in this errand, I hope both to have your Lordship, and his Lordship, with many others of your lovers and his, at a good dinner before I die. Always I hope, that the King's Buck-hunting at *Falkland* this year, shall prepare some dainty chear for us, against that dinner, the next year, *jocose hoc* to animate your Lordship, at this time: but afterwards we will have better occasion to make merry. I protest, my Lord, before GOD, I wish nothing with a better heart, nor to atchieve to that which your Lordship would fain attain unto; and my continual prayer shall tend to that effect; and with the large spending of my lands, goods, yea, the hazarding of my life, shall not afray me from that, altho' the scaffold were already set up, before I should falsify my promise to your Lordship, and persuade your Lordship thereof: I trow, your Lordship has ane proof of my constancy already or now: but, my Lord, whereas your Lordship desires, in your letter, that I crave my Lord, my brother's mind anent this matter, I utterly dissent from that, that he ever should be ane Counsellor thereto; for in good faith, he will never help his friend, nor hurt his foe. Your Lordship may confide more in this old man, the bearer hereof, my man, Laird *Bour*, than in my brother; for I lippen my life, and all that I have else, in his hands: and I trow he would not spare to ride to Hell's-gate to pleasure me; and he is not beguiled of my part to him. Always, my Lord, when your Lordship has read my letter, deliver it to the bearer again, that I may see it burnt with my own eyes: as I have sent your Lordship's letter to your Lordship again; for so, it is the fashion I grant: and I pray your Lordship to rest fully persuaded of me, and all that I have promised; for I am resolved, howbeit it were to die in the morn. I must intreat your Lordship to expede *Bour*, and give him strait directions upon pain of his life, that he take never a wink of sleep, until he see me again; or else he will utterly undo us. I have already sent another letter to the Gentleman your Lordship knows, as the bearer will shew your Lordship, of his answer, and forwardness with your Lordship; and I shall shew your Lordship farther at meeting, when and where your Lordship shall think it meetest. Till which time, and ever, I commit your Lordship to the protection of Almighty God."

From Gunn's Green, *the 29th Day of* July, 1600.

POSTSCRIPT.

"Prays your Lordship hold me excused for my unseemly letter, which is not so well written, as mister were; for I durst not let any Writers ken of it; but took two sundry idle days, to do it myself. I will never forget the good sport that Mr. *Alexander*, your Lordship's brother, told me of a nobleman of *Padua*. It comes so oft to my memory; and indeed, it is Aparastur to this purpose we have in hand."

Your Lordship's own sworn and bunden man, to obey and serve with effold and ever ready service, to his utter power, to his life's end.

Sic subscribitur,

RESTALRIG.

"RIGHT Honourable, my hearty duty remembred, ye know, I told you, at our last meeting, in the *Cannongate*, that Mr. *Alexander* my Lord of *Gowrie*'s brother, had spoken with me anent the matter of our conclusion; and for my own part, I shall not be hindmost. And finsyne, I got a letter from his Lordship's self, for that same purpose. And upon the receipt thereof, understanding his Lordship's frankness and forwardness in it; GOD knows, if my heart was not lifted ten stages. I posted this same bearer to his Lordship, to whom you may concredit all your heart in that, as well as I: For, and it were my very soul, I durst make him messenger thereof, I have such experience of his truth, in many other

things,

" things. He is a filly old glved Carle, but wonder honest; and as he " has reported to me his Lordship's own answer, I think all matters shall " be concluded at my house of *Fastcastle*; for I, and Mr. *Alexander Ruthven*, concluded, That ye should come with him and his Lordship, and " only another man with you, being but only four in Company, intil one " of the great fishing-boats be sea to my house, where ye shall land als fately, as on *Leith*-shore, and the house against your Lordship's coming to " be quiet; and when you are about half a mile from shore, as it were passing by the house, to gar set forth a waff. But for God's sake, let neither any knowledge come to my Lord, my brother's ears, nor yet to Mr. " *W. R.* my Lord's old pedagogue; for my brother is kittle to shoe behind, and dare not enterprize for fear, and the other will dissuade us " from our purpose with reasons of Religion, which I can never abide. " I think there is none of a noble heart, or carries a stomach worth a penny, but they would be content and glad, to see ane contented revenge " of *Greysteil*'s death; and the sooner the better his Lordship be quick; " and bid Mr. *Alexander* remember on the sport he told me of *Padua*: for " I think with myself, that the cogitation on that should stimulate your " Lordship. And, for God's cause, use all your courses *cum discretione*. " Fail not, Sir, to send back again this letter; for Mr. *Alexander* learn'd " me that fashion, that I may see it destroyed myself. So, till your " coming, ever commits you heartily to *Christ*'s holy protection."

From Gun's Green, *the last Day of* July, 1600.

The Superscription is torn away from the last letter.

The Depositions of the Witnesses produced, are as follows:

MR. *Alexander Watson*, Minister at *Coldingham*, of the age of fifty years, married, depones, The five missive letters subscribed by the Laird *Restalrig*, and produced in process by the Lord Advocate, for proving of the reasons of Treason pursued against *Robert Logan*, son and apparent heir to *Robert Logan* of *Restalrig*, being shown to this deponent; and he having at length sighted and considered the same, depones, That he takes upon his conscience, that he verily believes, that the said five missive letters, and every one of them, are verily and truly written by the said umquhile *Robert Logan* of *Restalrig*, with his own hand: and proves this of some of his knowledge, that not only he thinks, that the character of every letter resembles perfectly the said umquhile *Robert*'s hand-writ every way; but also agrees with his fashion of spelling, which he has particularly remembred in every one of the said missive letters, in thir points following: *First*, That he never used to write ane *z* in the beginning of any word, such as *zou, zer's, zeld, zea*, and sick-like; but ever writ *y*, instead of the said *z*. That he writ all words beginning with *w*, with single *v*; and when that letter *w* fell to be in the midst or end, he put ane double *w*. That when he writ *quhan, quhair, qlk*, or any such words, whilk uses to be written and spelled by others, with which he wrote only *qh, quhen, quhair*, and sick-like. Whenever a word began with *con*, he never wrote *con* at length, but wrote with an *ly*. Whenever *t* fell to be in the end of a word, he wrote it without a stroke thro' *t*, and did the like whenever it fell in any part of ane word. And for farther confirmation of the premisses, he produced three letters written every word, and subscribed by the said umquhile *Robert Logan* of *Restalrig*, and comparing them to the five other Missives produced by the Advocate, show evidently the direct conformity of the samen, as well in the character and true resemblance of the hand-writ, as in the spelling and writing of divers writs, syllables and letter, according to the particulars above-specified.

Sic subscribitur,
Mr. Alexander Watson.

MR. *Alexander Smith*, Minister of *Chirnside*, of the age of thirty years, or thereby, married, depones, That he was well acquainted with the umquhile Laird of *Restalrig*, by reason he was pedagogue to his Bairns, and has seen very many of his hand-writs; and having seen, read, and at length considered the five missive letters produced by the Advocate; and inquir'd, if he knew the same to be the Laird of *Restalrig*'s proper hand-writ? declared, upon his great oath, That he certainly believes the saids five letters, and every word thereof, to be the Laird of *Restalrig*'s proper hand-writ; because he finds the character thereof to agree every way with the shape of his ordinary writing; and remarked very particularly the manner of *Restalrig*'s spelling of many words, otherwise nor other men commonly uses to write and spell, according to the hail particulars remarked of before, by Mr. *Alexander Watson*, the witness immediately preceding; and, in these points, and in all others, conform to the said Mr. *Alexander Watson*'s deposition in all things; *reddens causam scientiæ*, because he was perfectly acquainted with the Laird of *Restalrig*'s hand-writ in his lifetime; and was pedagogue to his Bairns many years, and in his company.

Sic subscribitur,
Mr. Alexander Smith.

SIR *John Arnott*, Provost of *Edinburgh*, of the age of threescore ten years, or thereby, married, depones, That he was well acquainted with *Robert Logan* of *Restalrig*, and with his hand-writ, because he had received divers of his letters himself, and seen many other letters written by him. And the five missive letters produc'd by the Advocate being shown to him; and he having seen and considered the same, remembred that he had seen, read, and perfectly considered the Laird of *Restalrig*'s hand-writ, as the letters written by the deponent at any time, or his own hand-writ. And so takes on his conscience, That the foresaids five missive Bills, produc'd by the Advocate, are the proper hand-writ and subscription of the said umquhile Laird of *Restalrig*, be his Judgment. And, for verification thereof, has produc'd four writs, all written be the said umquhile Laird of *Restalrig*, and sent to this deponent, to *Archibald Johnstoun*, agreeing perfectly in spelling and character, with the saids missives.

Sic subscribitur,
Sir John Arnott.

ALexander Cuik, Sheriff-Clerk of *Berwick*, of the age of fifty years, or thereby, married, depones, That he was well acquainted with the umquhile Laird of *Restalrig*, and has seen many and sundry of his writs, and receiv'd divers of his letters directed to himself, and being desired to see and consider the five letters produc'd by the Advocate, and to declare whether he knew and esteem'd to be all written by umquhile the Laird of *Restalrig*; depones, upon his Conscience, That he believes and esteems the saids hail letters to be all written by the Laird of *Restalrig*; *reddens causam scientiæ*, because, not only the character agrees every way with the shape of *Restalrig*'s hand-writ; but also the spelling in many particulars, wherein *Restalrig* differed from other men's form of writing. And in the particulars thereof, depones conform to the two first Witnesses, the Ministers of *Coldingham* and *Chirnside*; *reddens eandem causam scientiæ*.

Sic subscribitur,
Alexander Cuik.

William Home in *Aytoun*-Mill, of the age of thirty-three years, or thereby, married, depones, That all the five Missives above-written, being shown to this deponent, and having at length considered every one of them, takes upon his conscience, That to his knowledge, that the saids five missive letters are all written and subscribed by the umquhile Laird of *Restalrig*; for the special reasons contain'd in the depositions made by Mr. *Alexander Watson*, and Mr. *Alexander Smith*, Ministers; and *Alexander Cuik*, Sheriff-Clerk of *Berwick*; to whom he is conform in all things, *reddens eandem causam scientiæ*.

Sic subscribitur,
William Home.

John Horne, Notary in *Aymouth*, of the age of forty-two years, or thereby, *solutus*, depones, The foresaids five missive Bills, being at length sighted and considered by this deponent, depones and declares, upon conscience, to his knowledge, all the saids five Missives are the Laird of *Restalrig*'s proper hand-writ and subscription, for the reasons above-written in the deposition of *William Home*, *reddens eandem causam scientiæ*.

Sic subscribitur,
John Horne.

MR. *William Hogg*, Minister at *Aytoun*, of the age of thirty years, or thereby, married, depones, That he knew well the Laird of *Restalrig*, and has seen of his writs, and produc'd ane letter, written by *Restalrig* to the Laird of *Aytoun*, as written with *Restalrig*'s own hand-writ. And having considered the five writs produced by the Advocate; declares, That he thinks them likely to be his Writs; and that the same appears to be very like his writ, by the conformity of letters and spelling.

Sic subscribitur,
Mr. William Hogg.

The Deposition and Declaration of George Sprott, *as emitted by him, both before the Jury, judicially; and also upon the Scaffold, at the time of his Execution, on the 12th of* August, 1608. *Which Deposition and Declaration was made before the Council, on the* 10th *of* August, 1608, *written by the Clerk of Council,* James Primrose; *and subscribed by* Sprott's *own hand, in the presence of the Earl of* Dunbar, *the Earl of* Lothian, *the Bishop of* Ross, *the Lord* Holy-rood-house, *the Lord* Scoon, *the Lord* Blantyre, *Sir* William Hart *Lord-Justice, Mr.* John Hall, *Mr.* Patrick Galloway, *Mr.* Peter Hewart, *all three Ministers of the Kirks of* Edinburgh.

George Sprott, Notary in *Aymouth*, being brought to the scaffold and place of execution, he, in publick audience of the hail people, at the four nooks of the scaffold, ratified his former deposition, anent his knowledge, and concealing of *Restalrig*'s guiltiness of *Gowrie*'s Treason: for the which, he craved God and his Majesty humble forgiveness; being most sorry and grieved that he had offended God, and the King's Majesty, in concealing such a vile, detestable, and unnatural Treason, enterprized by the Earl of *Gowrie* and Laird of *Restalrig*, against his natural King, so good and so godly a Prince, who has ever been so gracious to his Subjects, and to this hail Island: protesting, That if he had a thousand lives to render, and were able to suffer ten thousand deaths, it is not sufficient satisfaction and recompence for his so foul and horrible offence; and that God had preserved him from many great perils, when his life was in extreme danger, to bring him to this publick declaration of that detestable and horrible fact, in testifying of the truth; as he said publickly, in presence of all the people, in these words following: *To my own shame, the shame of the devil, and the glory of God; for satisfying the consciences of all these, (if any be) that has, or can make any doubt of the truth of this so clear a matter*. And he acknowledges, that his haunting with *Restalrig*, who was a man without Religion, and subject to many other vices, and his thoughts of himself in thir matters, after the first sight of *Restalrig*'s letter written to *Gowrie*, and his continual bearing of company with *Restalrig* and Laird *Bour*, who was irreligious, and without fear of God, brought him from one sin to another, and consequently to this grievous crime, for the which, most justly, worthily and willingly, he is now to render his life. And he desired all the people to beware of ill company; and namely, of the company of those who are void of Religion. And he desired, that this his declaration might be inserted in his process as also, he desired the Ministers of God's word to publish this his declaration to their folks, from their pulpits; and took every one of them who were present by the hand, with their promise to do the same: saying unto them, That this was the most glorious day that ever his eyes did see; and with these words he prostrates himself, and falls upon his knees, in presence of the hail people, and made a very pithy prayer [as in Vol. I. p. 306.].

And so he continued a good space, in a most fervent prayer, to the great admiration and rejoicing of all the people; and in a better form and manner nor any of the beholders and hearers can be able to set down in writ, the same not being written in the present time, because there was no place of writing upon the scaffold, in respect of the prease and multitude of

People. And going up the ladder, he desired liberty to sing the sixth *Psalm*, and requested the people to acompany him in singing thereof; which being granted, and he being at the ladder-head, the same was tane up and sung by himself, with a very loud and mighty voice, and was assisted with above the number of five hundred persons, who with tears accompanied him in singing of that song. After the ending thereof, he repeated and ratified his former deposition. And, with that, recommending his soul to God, he was thrown over, and so ended his mortal life. In witness whereof, we Under-subscribers, who, for the most part, were all of us upon the scaffold with him, and remained with him unto the time of his death; and others of us in so convenient places near to the scaffold, that we did hear all that was spoken by him, have subscribed thir presents with our hands. *Sic subscribitur, Glasgow, B. Galloway, M. B. Brechin, Balfour of Burley, Holy-rood-house, John Preston, Thomas Regra, Peter Sharp,* Mr. *Patrick Galloway, John Hall, Walter Balcanquhal,* Mr. *Hewat,* Mr. *George Blyth, Charles Lumsden, Richard Tobie* Baillie of *Edinburgh, William Speir* Baillie, *James Ainsly* Baillie of *Edinburgh,* &c.

What is contained in this Speech being consonant to his deposition made before the Privy-Council, as also before the Inquest; here is added the deposition, as emitted by him.

This *Sprott*, after divers examinations, being moved with remorse of conscience, for the long concealing of the foreknowledge of this treasonable conspiracy; confesseth, declareth, and deponeth, with the peril of his own life,

" THAT he knew perfectly, that *Robert Logan* *, late of *Restalrig*, " was privy, and upon the foreknowledge of *Gowrie*'s treasonable " conspiracy. And for the greater assurance of his knowledge, deponeth, " that he knew that there were divers letters interchanged betwixt them, " anent the treasonable purpose aforesaid, in the beginning of the month " of *July*, 1600. Which letters, *James Bour*, called Laird *Bour*, servitor " to *Restalrig* (who was employed mediator betwixt them, and privy to " all that errand) had in keping, and shewed the same to *Sprott* in the " place of *Fastcastle*."

And producing the Earl of *Gowrie*'s letter to *Restalrig*;

" Which letter, written every word with *Restalrig*'s own hand, was " subscribed by him after his accustomed manner, RESTALRIG; and was " sent to the Earl of *Gowrie* by the said *James Bour*. After whose return, " within five days, with a new letter from *Gowrie*, he staid all night with " *Restalrig* in *Gun's Green* [a house of *Restalrig*'s]: and *Restalrig* rode to " *Lothian*, the morn thereafter, where he staid five or six days. Then " after his returning pass'd to *Fastcastle*, where he remained a certain " short space.

" And further deponeth, that he saw and heard *Restalrig* read the last " letter, which *Bour* brought back to him from *Gowrie*, and their confe- " rence thereanent. And heard *Bour* say, Sir, if you think to make any " commodity by this dealing, lay your hand to your heart. And *Restal-* " *rig* answered, that he would do as he thought best. And farther said to " *Bour*, howbeit he should sell all his own land that he had in the world, " he would pass through with the Earl of *Gowrie*; for that matter would " give him greater contentment, nor if he had the whole Kingdom: and " rather or he should falsify his promise, and recall his vow that he had " vowed to the Earl of *Gowrie*, he should spend all that he had in the world, " and hazard his life with his Lordship. To whom *Bour* answered, You " may do as you please, Sir; but it is not my counsel that ye should be " so sudden in that other matter. But for the condition of *Dirltoun*, I " would like very well of it. To whom *Restalrig* answered, Content your- " self, I am at my wit's end.

" And farther *Sprott* deponeth, That he entered himself thereafter in con- " ference with *Bour*, and demanded what was done bewixt the Laird and " the Earl of *Gowrie*? And *Bour* answered, That he believed that the Laird " should get *Dirltoun* without either gold or silver, but feared that it " should be as dear unto him. And *Sprott* enquiring how that could be; " *Bour* said, they had another Pye in hand nor the selling of any land; but " prayed *Sprott*, for God's sake, that he would let be, and not trouble him- " self with the Laird's business; for he feared, within few days, the Laird " would either be landless or lifeless."

And the said *George Sprott* being demanded, If this his Deposition was true, as he would answer upon the salvation and condemnation of his soul: and if he would go to death with it, seeing he knoweth the time and hour of his death to approach very near? deponeth for answer, " That " he hath not a desire to live, and that he knows the time to be short, " having care of no earthly thing, but only for clearing of his conscience " in the truth of all these things, to his own shame, before the world, and " to the honour of God, and safety of his own soul: That all the former " points and circumstances contained in this his Deposition, with the " Deposition made by him the 5th day of *July* last, and the whole re- " manent Depositions made by him sen that day, are true; which he will " take on his conscience, and as he hopeth to be saved of God, and " that he would seal the same with his blood."

And farther, being demanded, where this above-written letter, written by *Restalrig* to the Earl of *Gowrie*, which was returned again by *James Bour*, is now? deponeth, " That he abstracted it quietly from *Bour*, " in looking over and reading *Bour*'s letters, which he had in keeping of " *Restalrig*'s; and that he left the above-written letter in his chest among " his writings, when he was taken and brought away, and that it is closed " and folded within a piece of paper."

This foresaid Deposition was made by him the 10th *August*, 1608, written by *James Primrose*, Clerk of his Majesty's Privy-Council; and subscribed with the said *George Sprott*'s own hand; in the presence of the Earl of *Dunbar*, the Earl of *Lothian*, the Bishop of *Ross*, the Lord *Scoon*, the Lord *Holy-rood-house*, the Lord *Blantyre*, Sir *William Hart*, his Majesty's Justice, Mr. *John Hall*, Mr. *Patrick Galloway*, Mr. *Peter Hewart*, Ministers of the Kirks of *Edinburgh*.

Subscribed with all their hands.

And also the eleventh day of the foresaid month and year, the said *George Sprott* being examined in the presence of a number of the Council and Ministers aforesaid; and it being declared to him, That the time of his death now very near approached, and that therefore they desired him to clear his conscience with an upright declaration of the truth; and that he would not abuse the holy name of God, to make him, as it were, a witness to untruths: And specially being desired, that he would not take upon him the innocent blood of any person dead or quick, by making or forging lies and untruths against them:

" Deponeth, That he acknowledgeth his grievous offences to God, (who " hath made him a reasonable creature) in abusing his holy name with " many untruths, sen the beginning of this process: but now being resol- " ved to die, and attending the hour and time when it shall please God to " call him, he deponeth with many attestations, and as he wisheth to be " participant of the kingdom of Heaven, where he may be countable " and answerable upon the salvation and condemnation of his soul, for " all his doings and speeches in this earth, that all that he hath deponed " sen the fifth day of *July* last, in all his several depositions, were true " in every point and circumstance of the same; and that there is no " untruth in any point thereof."

And having desired Mr. *Patrick Galloway* to make a prayer, whereby he might be comforted now in his trouble; which was done:

" The said Deponer, with many tears after the prayer, affirmed this " his Deposition to be true; and for the confirmation thereof, declared, " that he would seal the same with his blood."

I had almost forgotten that, which in this action of his death was strange, and in a manner marvellous. For being urged by the Ministers and other of good Rank upon the scaffold, that now at his end he should declare nothing but the truth (touching the matter for which he suffered) on the peril of his own salvation and condemnation of his soul; he for the greater assurance of that his constant and true Deposition, promised (by the assistance of God) to give them an open and evident token before the yielding of his spirit. Which he accomplished thereafter: for before his last breath, when he had hung a pretty space; he lift up his hands a good height, and clapped them together aloud three several times, to the great wonder and admiration of all the beholders. And very soon thereafter he yielded his spirit.

As in the account of *Gowrie*'s and his brother's process, I did not insert the Libel and Summons, nor Executions, *verbatim*, as being very tedious and useless to Readers; on the same motives I do so here, but I insert the Doom and Sentence *verbatim*: the Libel, Summons and Autographons of these and others being at full in the public Records, and patent to all enquirers.

June 1609.

TO whilk Summons, with the Executions and Indorsations thereof respective foresaids, being this instant day read in presence of his Majesty's Commissioner and Estates of Parliament, first in Latin, *and thereafter in* Scots; *The said* Robert Logan *being oft times called of new, at the Tolbooth window of the said Court of* Edinburgh, *to have compeared and answered to the said Summons of Treason, and Reasons and Causes therein contained: And he not compearing to have defended in the said matter: and to have answered to the said Summons, The said Sir* Thomas Hamilton *of* Bynnie *Knight, Advocate to our Sovereign Lord, desired the said Estates Declaration, if the Reasons of the said Summons were relevant: the whilk Estates found the said Summons and Reasons and Causes therein contained relevant. Therefore the said Advocate, of new for proving of the foresaid Summons of Treason raised against the said* Robert Logan, *bearing and containing as is above-written; repeated all the foresaid missive Bills, and the saids Depositions of the said Witnesses examined before the saids Lords of Articles and Lords of Secret Council respective; and also* George Sprott's *Deposition, Conviction and Confession, in Judgment, and at his Execution to the death, for the said cause of Treason; with the hail other Writs and Probations produced and repeated by him of before; for proving of the foresaid Summons of Treason, and Reasons therein contained; and desired the saids Estates of Parliament yet, as of before, to advise the Probations foresaids, led and deduced in the said matter; and to pronounce their Sentence of Parliament thereuntil, according to the said Probations and their Consciences: And thereafter, the hail Depositions of the Witnesses, missive Bills, and hail Writs, and Probations, being read, seen, and considered by the foresaids hail Estates of Parliament; and they therewith being ripely advised, the said Lord Commissioner and Estates of Parliament finds, decerns, and declares, That the foresaid umquhil* Robert Logan *of* Restalrig, *committed and did in his life-time, open and manifest Treason, in all the Points, Articles, and Manners contained in the said Summons: and therefore it was given for Doom by the mouth of* David Lindsay, *Dempster of Parliament, in manner and form as follows:*

THIS Court of Parliament shews for Law, That the said umquhil Robert Logan *of* Restalrig, *in his life-time committed the foresaid crime of Treason and Lese Majesty; and that he was Art and Part guilty, and partaker thereof, against our Sovereign Lord and Authority Royal; and that the foresaids cruel, wicked and treasonable crimes were interprised, by his causing, persuasion, counsel and help. Likeas, the said umquhil* Robert Logan *of* Restalrig, *treasonably counselled the foresaid crime of Lese Majesty to his death, and in his death, in all manner, at length contained in the said Summons: and therefore, depones*

* Great part of this evidence is in the Trial of *George Sprott*, vol. I. p. 301, &c. tho' not so full. For the Earl of *Cromerty*, in his account of the Conspiracies of the Earl of *Gowrie*, (from whence this is taken) says p. 126. Mr. *Crawford* did bring a pamphlet printed at *London*, anno 1609, published by Dr. *George Abbot*, then Archbishop of *Canterbury*, who being providentially in *Scotland* in the year 1608, the Doctor's curiosity brought him in amongst the multitude of hearers of that Trial (of *G. Sprott*) whereby he was so convinced of the truth of *Gowrie*'s Treasons, and of the malice of the King's Calumniators, as moved the good Doctor to intreat for an extract and account of the whole process, attested by Sir *William Hart*, Lord Justice of *Scotland*, at that time (which the Doctor brought with him to *England*, and caused it to be printed, with a long preface, from which the Trial of *G. Sprott*, vol. I. is taken.) But that paper, printed at *London*, being drawn out as a memorial for Dr. *Abbot*'s own use, and not as a full Abstract of what is recorded, which I now publish from the original Depositions, Letters, and other Writs, lying in Record.

and declares the Name, Memory and Dignity of the said umquhil Robert Logan *of* Restalrig, *to be extinct and abolished, and his Arms cancelled, riven and delete furth of the books of Arms, and Nobility, so that his Posterity shall be excluded, and be unhabile to possess or enjoy any Offices, Honours, Dignities, Lands, Tenements, Rooms, Rents, Possessions or Goods, moveable or unmoveable, Rights and others whatsomever, within the Kingdom, in all time coming; and that all the saids Goods, Lands, Rooms, Tenements and other Goods, moveable and unmoveable, Rights and others whatsomever pertaining to the said umquhil* Robert Logan *of* Restalrig; *or which might otherways have pertained to him, at any time, since his conspiring of the said treasonable Crimes, to be escheat and forefaulted to our Sovereign Lord; to appertain and remain perpetually with his Majesty in property. And this I give for Doom.*

Note, Here, as in *Gowrie*'s Process, that the citing of dead Persons is among the legal Forms, prescribed both by our Laws, and Laws of several other Nations.

XII. The Trial of the Lord BALMERINOTH, at *St. Andrews*, the 10th of *March*, 1609. for *High-Treason*, 7 *Jac.* I *.

[The Lord *Balmerino* was a professed Protestant: But, upon what Motive is not known, he often pressed the King to write a Letter of Compliment to the Pope, which, it seems, his Majesty had as often refused to do. Hereupon, as the thing is related, *Balmerino* writ the Letter, and bringing the King several Dispatches at a time when his Majesty was in haste to be gone a-hunting, thrust it in among the rest; and the King, through inadvertency, in that hurry, signed it. The Letter thus signed, was sent away, and no more heard of it till some years after, Cardinal *Bellarmine* mentioning of it to the King's disadvantage, his Majesty was obliged to take notice of, and to question the Secretary about it.]

THE Lords being set, the Lord *Balmerinoth* was sent for: and being come, the Lord-Advocate told him, There was a Warrant come from his Majesty for his Trial, and therefore desired to know, whom he had entertained to speak for him.

He answered, He had great necessity to speak, the Cause being such as concern'd his Life and Estate; but he had greater necessity to hold his peace, by reason of his Offence, which was such as it admitted no excuse; and my grief for it so great, as it will not suffer me to extenuate my Crime: and therefore I will neither make any friend interested in that, whereunto myself fell without the advice of any; nor will I desire a Lawyer to make that seem less, which I would have all the world know to be such as it is.

Herein are two points in which I would have all men satisfied concerning his Majesty: First, for his Majesty's innocency in the writing of the letter; for I protest I could never draw him to hear with patience my motion. But he did utterly and absolutely refuse to take that course against conscience, which would neither satisfy me, who in a politick natural course had conceited it might be behoveful for his Majesty; and so applied myself to that crooked device, which hath worthily brought me to this estate wherein I now stand.

The second thing concerning his Majesty, is this: That whereas some in malice to his Majesty, or my Friends in commiseration of my estate, may think and report it too rigorous and cruel a course, which is held against me in a matter of this moment, the suggesting of a letter of recommendation, to proceed against my life and estate; I would have such know, that his Majesty's clemency is many ways testified unto the world, in cases that have seemed more nearly to concern him; and therefore men should not judge of his Majesty's disposition to mercy by this action; but rather cast their eyes upon my unhappiness, who have offended in such a point as his Majesty can extend no favour to me without the damage of his own honour, which being dearer to him than his life, it must needs be more tendered than twenty thousand such lives as mine. And therefore I desire not to be spared at so dear a rate as the impeachment of his Majesty's honour.

There are likewise two things concerning myself, which I desire all men to understand. First, That I had no aim at the alteration of Religion, or to bring in a Toleration, or what you will term it, by the writing of that letter: but merely a politick course, as I have said, which, as a natural man, I conceited might further his Majesty's Right. And this I protest to be true, as I shall answer God in the Day of Judgment, when the secrets of all hearts shall be disclosed.

Next, I would have no man think that it was gain or any private advantage that drew me to that; for I protest I never received or expected the least reward from any Prince in the world, save from the King my Master. And this, as I shall answer the great God in heaven.

This said, the Jury was called, and in their hearing was read the Indictment, which aggravated his crime by his Majesty's favours to him, which had deserved more regard; by his Majesty's refusal; by the dangers which did follow, or might have done; imputing all the Treasons which have been a-foot since, to be fruits of that letter; and lastly, charging him with having intelligence with foreign estates, and enemies of the Gospel, for the subversion of the state of Religion.

To all these he reply'd not one word.

Then was read his confession taken in *Frankland*, the effect of that which he made in *London*. Then was read the speech he uttered before the Council at *Whitehall*, containing his sorrow, his sins, the favours he had received, his unworthiness of them, his desire to give his Majesty satisfaction for his offence to the last drop of his blood. Last, was read a Letter from his Majesty to the Lord-Advocate, shewing his Majesty's refusal to listen to the Lord-President's motion, and setting down some circumstances which passed betwixt his Majesty and the Lord-President at the time of the refusal; against all which the President said nothing.

So the Jury going together, after a time returned, and found him guilty of all the parts of the Indictment.

Then the Lords conferring upon the Bench; my Lord Justice signified, That they were not to proceed further till they knew more of the King's pleasure. And so advising the Lord-President to fit himself for God; and giving the Jury thanks for their pains and care they had of his Majesty's Honour; the Court rose.

[" He was by order from Court detained a Prisoner for some time;
" and afterwards made a sort of Prisoner at large: till at last, in consi-
" deration of his submissive behaviour, and the sufferings he had under-
" gone; the King was pleased to pardon him, and to restore his blood
" and estate." †]

* Copied from a MS. in the *Bodleian* Library, *Rotulæ in Archivo*, A. 3033. 44, 10. And though short, is a more perfect Copy than that in the *Cotton* Library, *Julius*, F. 6. N. 34.

† His Son was tried for a Libel in the following Reign. *See* vol. I. p. 407.

XIII. The Arraignment and Confession of the Lord SANQUIRE, (who being a Baron of *Scotland*, was arraigned by the Name of *Robert Creighton*, Esq;) at the King's-Bench Bar, in *Westminster-hall*, on *Saturday* the 27th day of *June*, 1612. 10 *Jacobi Regis*, for procuring the Murder of *John Turner*, a Master of Defence, whom he caused to be shot with a Pistol by one *Carliel*, a *Scottishman*, for thrusting out one of his Eyes in playing at Rapier and Dagger *.

ALL things according to the usual form being prepared, and the Prisoner brought to the Bar, his Indictment was read.

Copia Indictamenti Roberti Creighton, *Armig.*

Middl. JUR' presentant pro Dom' Rege super sacr'm suum qd' cum Rob' Carliel nuper de Lond' Yeoman, et Jacob' Irweng nuper de Lond' præd' Yeoman, Deum præ oculis suis non habentes, sed instigatione diabolica seduct', undecimo die Maii anno regni Domini nostri Jacobi, Dei grat' Angl', Franc', et Hiberniæ Regis, fidei defensor', &c. decimo, et Scotiæ xlv. apud London, videl't, in parochia Sancti Dunstani in occident', in warda de Farringdon extra London præd', &c. vi et armis, &c. felonice ac ex maliciis suis præcogitat', in & super quendam Johan' Turner adtunc et ibidem in pace Dei et dicti Domini Regis existen', insultum et affraiam fecer', et præd' Robertus Carliel quoddam tormentum, Anglice vocat' *a Pistol*, valor' quinque solidorum adtunc et ibid' onerat' cum pulvere bombardico, et glandine plumbea, Anglice, *charged with Gun-powder and one leaden Bullet*, quod quidem torment' idem Robertus Carliel in manu sua dextra adtunc et ibid' habuit et tenuit in et super præfat' Johan' Turner adtunc et ibid' felonice, voluntarie, et ex malicia sua præcogitat', sagittavit, et exoneravit, Anglice, *did shoot off and discharge*, et præd' Ro. Carliel cum glandine plumbea præd', torment' præd', adtunc et ibid' emiss. præfatum Johan' Turner in et super sinistram partem pector' ipsius Johan' Turner prope sinistram mamillam ipsius Joh' Turner adtunc et ibid' felonice percussit, dans eidem Jo. Turner adtunc et ib' cum glandine plumbea præd' e torment' præd' adtunc et ib'm emiss. in et super præd' sinistram partem pector' ipsius Jo. Turner unam plagam mortal' latitud' dimid' unius pollic' et profunditat' quinq; pollic' de qua quid' plaga mortal' præd' J. Turner apud Lond' præd', in paroch' et ward' præd', instant' obiit: Et præd' Jac. Irwenge, felonice, et ex malicia

* From an authentic MS. lent the Editor.

malicia ſua præcogitat', adtunc & ib'm fuit præſens, auxilians, aſſiſtans, abettans, confortans, & manutenens, præfat' Robert' Carliel ad felon' & murdr' præd' in form' præd' felonice faciend' & perpetrand': Et ſic prædict' Robert' Carliel & Jacobus Irweng præfat' Johan' Turner apud Lond' præd', in paroch' & ward' præd', modo & forma præd', felon', voluntar', ac ex maliciis ſuis præcogit' interfecerunt & murdaverunt, contra pacem dicti Dom' Reg' nunc, coron' & dignitat' ſuas: Quidam Robert' Creighton nuper de paroch' Sanctæ Margaret' in Weſtm' in com' Middl' armig', Deum præ oculis ſuis non habens, ſed inſtigatione diabolica ſeduct' ante felon' & murdr' præd', per præfat' Rob. Carliel & Jacob. Irweng modo & forma præd' fact' & perpetrat', ſcil't, decimo die Maii, an' regni dicti Domini noſtri Jacobi, Dei grat' Angl', Franc', & Hibern' Regis decimo, & Scotiæ xiv. præd', Robert' Carliel apud prædict' paroch' Sanctæ Margaret' in Weſtm' præd', in com' Middl' præd', ad felon' & murdr' præd' modo & forma præd' faciend' & perpetrand', maliciof. felonic', voluntar', & ex malicia ſua præcogitata, incitavit, movit, abbettavit, conſuluit, & procuravit, contr' pacem dicti Domini Regis nunc, coron' & dignitat' ſuas, &c.

He then was demanded by the Clerk of the Crown, whether he was guilty of procuring the Murder of *John Turner*, or not guilty? He made anſwer to this effect:

My LORDS,

THAT which at my Arraignment the other day I pleaded to the contrary, was not that I could be ſo unworthy to deny any ſyllable of that I had formerly profeſſed before ſo honourable Perſonages, nor out of any deſire that the leaſt thing might be concealed, which might ſerve for evidence to convince me of this foul fact, whereof I now ſtand accus'd and indicted, and whereof I formerly have, and now do moſt willingly and penitently confeſs myſelf to be guilty; my purpoſe then was only to gain time for the diſpoſing of ſome temporal affairs, and for the better preparing of my Soul for her departure from this Body; for that I ſhould long live, I neither expect, nor much deſire. And now, my Lords, if that may ſtand with the courſe of the laws of the land (whereof I am altogether ignorant) I will eaſe this Jury, the King's Counſel, and your Lordſhips, and will confeſs myſelf guilty of this fact in the ſame manner as it is laid in the Indictment.

Or if that may not be permitted by law, yet ſhall I give ſuch evidence againſt myſelf, as I ſhall not leave it needful in any point to be aggravated; only in ſome circumſtances I will endeavour, if not to extenuate the fact, yet at leaſt to move your Lordſhips and this worthy Audience to pity my caſe; wherein as I know I can ſay nothing of ſubſtance that can help in a legal courſe of proceeding, ſo I much fear that thoſe circumſtances I would deliver, I ſhall not be able at full to expreſs my own thoughts, both by reaſon of my own imperfections, and alſo for that I lack the perfect uſe of the phraſe of this Country. But for that point, in ſuch paſſages as I ſhall not be underſtood in, I will humbly intreat your Lordſhips in your wiſdom, and this Audience in their Charity to conceive, that my meaning is, to make a full and true relation of all the paſſages of this buſineſs.

The firſt motive of this fatal accident was (as it is well known), that *Turner* playing with me at foils, now about ſeven years paſt at my Lord *Norris*'s houſe in *Oxfordſhire*, put out one of my eyes, and that (as my Soul and Conſcience was over-perſuaded) willingly and of ſet purpoſe. At the taking up of the foils, I proteſted unto him, I play'd but as a Scholar, and not as one that would contend with a Maſter in his own profeſſion, and thereupon requeſted him, That he would play as with a Scholar; the order whereof, tho' it be unknown to your Lordſhips, yet to divers honourable Perſonages that are preſent it is known to be, *to ſpare the Face*. After this loſs of mine eye, and with it the great hazard of the loſs of life, I muſt confeſs I ever kept a grudge of my Soul againſt him, but had no purpoſe to take ſo high a revenge; yet in the courſe of my revenge, I conſidered not my wrongs upon terms of Chriſtianity, for then I ſhould have ſought for other ſatisfaction; but being trained up in the Courts of Princes and in Arms, I ſtood upon the terms of Honour, and thence befel this Act of Diſhonour; whereby I have offended,

1. God.
2. My Prince.
3. My Native Country; and
4. This Country.
5. The Party murder'd.
6. His Wife, and
7. Poſterity.
8. *Carliel*, now executed; and laſtly,
9. My own Soul.

And am now to die for mine offence.

1. Firſt towards God; I hope that my earneſt prayer and ſupplications unto him, have (now at laſt) obtain'd his grace and pardon for this my horrible ſin, for at my return from this place, the people (of whom I expected ſcorn and diſgrace) did by their pity and clemency move that in me, which the pride of mine own heart would not till then ſuffer me to ſee; then I became to have a ſenſe and feeling of the foulneſs of my offence, which formerly I could not perſuade myſelf was any more than a juſt revenge for ſo foul a wrong, and ſince that time ſuch inward comfort and conſolation have I felt in my ſoul, that I doubt not but that my hearty contrition and true repentance is accepted before God, and that he of his mercy hath pardon'd mine offence.

2. For my offence unto the King's Majeſty; if I had more than my life to make ſatisfaction unto him, I would think myſelf happy: and this favour I requeſt of your Lordſhips, that the King may be truly informed of the ſincerity of my confeſſion, and of my hearty repentance, and if it pleaſe him not of his favour and clemency to pardon me this offence, yet I humbly deſire, That I may die in his grace and favour.

3. For mine own Country, let me intreat you that this my ſingular offence may not be laid as an aſperſion or blemiſh unto my Country, but that myſelf alone may bear the ſhame of it, and my Body the puniſhment.

4. On this Country, [illegible] I do deſerve no favour, I deſire that of Chriſtianity, you would be pleas'd to pity me as a repentant and ſorrowful man.

5. For the party murder'd, my blood muſt ſatisfy the law, to which I ſhall [illegible] ſuch true repentance and hearty ſorrowfulneſs, as I hope, by Chriſt's mercy, [illegible] for my offence.

6, 7. For his Wife and Poſterity, ſome relief I have given already, and more, God willing, I will add unto it.

8. For *Carliel*, his too much affection to me made him too forward an executioner of my will and wicked purpoſe; but I hope by his repentance, he is pardoned his offences to God: in him I muſt confeſs my ſin is doubled, and I pray God to pardon it me; for the manner of the murder, I neither commanded, nor gave allowance to piſtol him. But I confeſs, that at the requeſt of *Carliel* and *Graye*, I gave either of them a piſtol to bring themſelves off, after they ſhould kill him. For him who is now ſuſpected, I proteſt before God and all this company, I never knew him, nor ſpake with him, nor dealt either directly or indirectly with him in all my life.

9. Laſtly, For myſelf, I commit my Body to the King, and my Soul to God.

But, my Lords, beſides mine own offence, which in its own nature needs no aggravation, divers ſcandalous reports are given out, which blemiſh my reputation, which is more dear to me than my life.

Firſt, That I made ſhew of reconciliation with *Turner*, the which I proteſt is utterly untrue; for what I have formerly ſaid, I do again aſſure your good Lordſhips, That ever after my hurt received, I kept a grudge in my Soul againſt him, and never made the leaſt pretence of reconciliation with him, yet this, my Lords, I will ſay, that if he would have confeſſed and ſworn he did it not of purpoſe, and withal would have forſworn arms, I wou'd have pardoned him: for, my Lords, I conſidered that it muſt be done either of ſet purpoſe or ignorantly; if the firſt, I had no occaſion to pardon him; if the laſt, that is no excuſe in a maſter: and therefore for revenge of ſuch a wrong, I thought him unworthy to bear arms.

The ſecond obloquy is, That to defer the revenge ſo long, argues an inveterate malice, and an ill diſpoſition. For the deferring of my revenge, I anſwer, that at the receiving the hurt, I was ſo aſtoniſh'd that I thought I had been ſlain; and by the opinion of my Phyſicians from *Oxford* and other places, my life was then in much danger for many days after; yet after ſome months recovering my ſtrength, and getting ſome eaſe in mine eye, I went immediately over into *France*, and there continu'd two years, hoping of the recovery of mine eye again. At the King of *Denmark*'s coming hither, I came out of *France*, and then hearing at *Greenwich*, that *Turner* play'd there before the two Kings; I muſt confeſs, that after thoſe prizes done, I ſought for him up and down: and if I had met him in any place of the Court, I was then reſolved to have run him through; though I muſt confeſs the place had made my offence far greater. But miſſing him there that day, the next day I went after him to *London*, and there ſought after him for two days, but could not meet with him; the firſt news then I heard of him was, that he was gone into the Country unto the Lord *Norris*'s, and ſo for that time I was prevented of my purpoſe. Before his return I went into *Scotland*; and after my return again, I laid about for him, ever intending all this while, to have acted it myſelf. But ſeeing the difficulty of it, both for that I was well known about the *White-friers*, where he dwelt and kept ſchool, and yet did not myſelf know *Turner*, but carried others with me for my direction, I afterward agreed with two of my Countrymen, who undertook the acting of this tragedy; but nothing enſued upon it, and therefore I deſire I may conceal their names. After this, my occaſions call'd me over into *France* and other parts, ſo that my reſidence in this Country was very little, till now at laſt I dealt with this unfortunate *Carliel*, who took unto him one *Graye* for his partner, and brought him unto me; and thoſe two I directed to take a lodging in the *Fryers*, the better to diſcover how myſelf might come to revenge myſelf on the perſon of *Turner*. But after ſome delay they told me, I could with no conveniency come myſelf to do it; but they ſaid, they would undertake it: to which I aſſented, but preſcribed neither time nor manner how they could effect it. After this, *Graye* fell quite off, and went to the Ships for *Denmark*, which *Carliel* came and told me, and withal that *Turner* was then gone out of town; but ſince *Graye* had deceiv'd him, he would have nobody but himſelf, and would aſſuredly kill him at his return, tho' it were with the loſs of his own life. But I being long delay'd by two others whom formerly I ſpake of, and now alſo by theſe two, and ſeeing *Graye* gone, I thought that *Carliel* had ſpoken this but to give me content, and the more to inſinuate himſelf into my favour, ſo that I left him without any further direction, or much regard to his ſpeech; and never heard more of him till I heard that *Turner* was ſlain; the time whereof, and the manner, I proteſt before God and his Angels, I was altogether ignorant of; for had I expected it to have been done, I would not have ſtay'd myſelf here at the laſt caſt, for before that time I could with eaſe have gone over into *France*, for I had a licence to travel, and for tranſporting ſome horſes.

Another aſperſion is laid on me, that this was God's juſt judgment, for that I was an ill-natured fellow, ever revengeful and delighted in blood. To the firſt, I confeſs I was never willing to put up a wrong, where upon terms of honour I might right myſelf, nor never willing to pardon where I had a power to revenge. To the ſecond I ſay, that I was never guilty of blood till now, yet I have had occaſion to draw my ſword both in the field, and upon ſudden violences, and have both given and receiv'd hurts, and yet was never guilty of blood unto death till now, only I muſt confeſs that upon commiſſion from the King to ſuppreſs wrongs done me in my own Country, I put divers of the *Johnſons* to death; but for that, I hope, I ſhall need neither to aſk God nor man forgiveneſs.

Laſtly, The objection that ſince my Impriſonment I have attempted, by the means of my Countrymen, to break priſon and eſcape, a courſe which I proteſt upon my ſalvation was never moved unto me by any, nor did I ever lodge ſuch a thought in my breaſt; and for the further confirmation of that, I refer myſelf unto the Marſhal, and his Officers, who in the Priſon have ſeen and beſt know my deportment during my impriſonment.

Thus, my Lords, have I troubled you with [illegible], whereof I know no circumſtance can in any point of law do me any good, nor would I be thought all this while to plead for my life, my deſires only are, that my life might ſatisfy for mine offence, and that my reputation might not be left defamed.

Laſtly, my Lords, and the reſt of this honourable and worſhipful preſence, I deſire in Charity, that you will conſider theſe few circumſtances to move you to pity.

Firſt, The indignity I receiv'd from [illegible] mean a man.

Secondly,

Secondly, That it was done willingly, for I have been informed he bragged of it after it was done.

Thirdly, The perpetual loss of mine eye.

Fourthly, The want of law to give satisfaction for such a loss.

Fifthly, The continual blemish I received thereby.

Lastly, Unto this, I add my voluntary and free confession. Let me now add my last request to your Lordships, that the King may be truly inform'd of these things. Contrition, Confession, and Satisfaction are the means to obtain pardon from God for our sins; and these many times do move the mercy of Princes, which if his Highness shall extend to me, I shall desire my life may be spent to do him service; or if not, I shall most willingly submit myself to his Majesty's good pleasure, and yield to die.

The Lord *Sanquire* having ended his speech, Sir *Francis Bacon* spake as followeth:

In the case of life and death the Jury's part is in effect discharged; for after a frank and formal confession their labour is at an end: so that what hath been said by Mr. Attorney-General, and shall be by myself, is rather convenient than necessary.

My Lord *Sanquire*, your fault is great; it cannot be extenuated, and it needs not be aggravated; and (if it needed) you have made so full an anatomy of it, out of your own feeling, as it cannot be match'd by myself, or any man else out of a conceit.

This Christian and penitent course of yours, draws me thus far, that I agree, that even in extreme evils there are degrees: so this instance of your offence is not of the highest strain; for if you had sought to take away a man's life for his Vineyard as *Ahab* did, or for Envy as *Cain* did, or to possess his Bed as *David* did, surely this offence had been more odious. Your temptation was revenge, which the more natural it is to man, the more have laws, both divine and human, sought to repress it: (*mihi vindicta*.) But in one thing you and I shall never agree, that generous spirits (you say) are hard to forgive; no, contrariwise, generous and magnanimous spirits are readiest to forgive; and it is a weakness and impotency of mind to be unable to forgive.

But to the purpose; howsoever murder may arise upon several motives less or more odious, yet the law both of God and Man involves them in one degree; and therefore you may read that in *Joab's* case, which was a murder upon revenge, and match'd with your case; he for a dear brother, and you for a dear part of your own blood; yet there was a severe charge given, *it shall not pass unpunished*.

And certainly the circumstance of time is heavy unto you; it is now five years since this unfortunate man, *Turner*, be it upon accident or despight, gave the provocation, which was the seed of your malice. All passions are assuaged with time; love, hatred, grief, &c. all fire burns out with time, if no fewel be put to it: for you to have been in the gall of bitterness so long, and to have been in a restless case of his blood, is a strange example. And I must tell you plainly, that I conceive you have suck'd those affections of dwelling in malice rather out of *Italy*, and outlandish manners, where you have conversed, than out of any part of this Island of *England* and *Scotland*.

But now farther, my Lord, I would have you look a little upon this offence in the glass of God's judgment, that God may have the glory. You have friends and entertainment in foreign parts: it had been an easy thing for you to have set *Carliel*, or some other blood-hound on work, when your person had been beyond the seas; and so this news might have come to you in a pacquet, and you might have so looked on how the storm would pass. but God bereav'd you of this providence, and bound you here under the hand of a King, that is, though abundant in clemency, yet no less zealous of justice.

Again, when you came in at *Lambeth*, you might have persisted in the denial of the procurement of the fact, *Carliel* (a resolute man) might have cleared you: for they that are resolute in mischief, are commonly obstinate in concealing their procurers; and so nothing should be against you but presumption. But then God, to take away all obstruction of justice, gave you the Grace (which ought indeed to be more comfort unto you than any evasion, or device, whereby you might have escaped) to make a clear confession.

Other impediments there were not a few, which might have been an interruption to this day's justice, had not God in his providence removed them.

But now, that I have given God the honour, let me also give it where it's next due, which is to the King our Sovereign.

This murder was no sooner committed, and brought to his Majesty's ears, but his indignation (wherewith at first he was moved,) cast himself presently into a great deal of care and providence to have justice done.

First, came forth his proclamation, somewhat of a rare form, and devised and in effect directed by his Majesty himself, and with that he did prosecute the offenders (as it were) with the breath and blasts of his mouth. Then did his Majesty stretch forth his long arms, (for Kings you know have long arms) one of them to the sea, where he took *Gray* shipped for *Sweden*, who gave the first light of testimony; the other arm to *Scotland*, and took hold of *Carliel*, ere he was warm in his house, and brought him the length of this kingdom under such safe watch and custody, as he could have no means to escape, nor learn no lessons to stand mute, in which case perhaps this day's justice might have received a stop. So that I may conclude that his Majesty hath shew'd himself God's true Lieutenant, and that he is no respecter of persons, but *English*, *Scots*, Noblemen, Fencer, (which is but an ignoble trade) are all to him alike in respect of justice.

Nay, I may say further, that his Majesty hath had in this matter a kind of prophetical spirit; for at what time *Carliel* and *Gray*, and you, my Lord, yourself were fled no man knew whither, to the four winds; the King ever spake in a confident and undertaking manner, that wheresoever the offenders were in *Europe*, he would produce them forth to justice, of which words God hath made him master.

Lastly, To return to you, my Lord, though your offence hath been great, your confession hath been free, and your behaviour and speech full of discretion; and this sheweth, that though you could not resist the temptation, yet you bear a generous and Christian mind, answerable to your noble Family of which you are descended. This I commend to you, and take it to be an assured testimony of God's mercy and favour; in respect whereof all worldly things are but trash: and so it is fit for you, as your state now stands, to account them.

Then being demanded, whether he would speak any more for himself, he said, no; only desired that the King might be made acquainted with what he had already said.

Whereupon Judgment being required for the King;

Mr. Justice *Yelverton* gave Sentence of death against him as followeth:

My Lord Sanquire,

You are a Nobleman of *Scotland*, and (as I have heard yourself say) a Baron of above three hundred years antiquity; which I believe to be true. But now you have most wonderfully dishonoured the Nobility of your ancient House by this unhappy action; an action of murder so base and so barbarous, as the like I never heard of, nor scant the like a man shall never read of.

The manner of it is such, as is exceeding strange: done upon the sudden! done in an instant! done with a pistol! done with your own pistol! under the colour of kindness: As *Cain* talk'd with his brother *Abel*, he rose up and slew him.

Your executioners of the murder left the poor miserable man that was murdered no time to defend himself; no time to pray for himself; scant any time to breathe out these last words, *Lord have mercy upon me!*

The ground of this malice that you bore him, grew not out of any offence that he ever willingly gave you, but out of the pride and haughtiness of your own self; for that in the false conceit of your own skill, you would needs importune him to that action, the sequel whereof did most unhappily breed your blemish, the loss of your eye.

And you have prosecuted this malice very long; for you sollicited others, four or five years at the least, to have committed this foul and heinous murder. And this your fault is far greater than if you had committed the fact yourself; for then it had been but your own single murder *only*; but now have you made them who were the executioners of your malice, murderers also with you: so you have made their bodies subject to the justice of man, and their souls subject to the justice of God, which, without his great mercy, they must endure.

All these circumstances do exceedingly aggravate your offence.

This offence of yours is called one of the crying sins; for God said unto *Cain*, *The voice of thy brother's blood* (a strange phrase, a voice of blood!) *crieth unto me from the ground*.

And for the punishment of it, it is said elsewhere in the sacred Word of God, *That he that sheddeth man's blood, by man shall his blood be shed*. Again, *But this punishment of blood is not indeed to shed blood; for it is better that one should die by the law, than many without it*.

You are, my Lord, to take a serious consideration of the short estate of your life wherein presently you stand; for by the justice of the Law, you must suffer the pains of death, and be assuredly persuaded, the time is not far off: for tho' the King be exceeding merciful, yet is he also exceeding just. And he hath had such an extraordinary care of justice in this case, that tho' it were plotted by you, my Lord, that the murderer should escape, and fly into his own country of *Scotland*, far remote from the justice of the Law of *England*; yet his Majesty's care hath so pursued him, that there he was quickly apprehended, and that country could be no protection for him. Nay, his Majesty most religiously, and most like a just Prince, protested, that if he were in any part of Christendom to be found, he would surely have him; so zealous is he of justice in this so heinous an offence of murder. And in a matter that concerns justice, he respects not his own native nation of *Scotland*, more than he doth his own hereditary Realm of *England*.

Therefore, my Lord, prepare yourself to die; and tho' the manner of your death be by the Law of *England* unfitting (as you perhaps may think) for a man of your Honour and Blood, yet surely it is fit enough for a man of your merit and offence. And the Law of *England* makes no difference of subjects in matters of Felony for the manner of their deaths, when there is no difference of subjects in the manner of their offences; and not where; but how a man dieth, maketh to the purpose: for the way to Heaven is of like difference from all places. And, indeed, there is no death miserable, which the death of the soul doth not follow.

Death is the way of all the world, the passage of all the earth, and the end of all men; and not men alone, but all worldly things are mortal, the soul of man only excepted.

Therefore, my Lord, provide carefully that your soul may have a good and godly departure from the body, which will surely be by your unfeigned confession and earnest repentance of all your sins, and especially of this most bloody, this most heinous and crying sin, by your humble calling and crying upon God for his mercy and forgiveness, and by confident and stedfast faith in *Christ Jesus*, to receive and accept it.

For repentance is an act of all acts, and faith in the mercies of God is the *Star* that goeth before the face of repentance, and very exceeding available by these three syllables, *peccavi*.

And so with this short Exhortation I will end; and wish, whatsoever your life hath been heretofore, yet that your death may be happy now.

And so I will proceed to Judgment.

You have been indicted as accessary to wilful murder, as accessary in procuring the murder; and upon this Indictment you have been arraigned, and upon your arraignment you pleaded not guilty; but since, upon better advisement and judgment, you have confessed the fact. The Court therefore doth award, That you shall be led from hence to your former place of Imprisonment, and from thence to the place of execution, and there be hanged till you be dead. And God have mercy upon your soul.

And then the Judge speaking to the Sheriff, said, Mr. Sheriff, see execution be done *.

* The King had offered 1000l. for apprehending of him: the Archbishop of *Canterbury* and several great men interceded for him to no avail; nothing could move the King to pardon him, who thought the making him an example was necessary to curb the insolence of the Scots, who had already committed many outrages [illegible] the chief thing that contributed to this murder, was, the Lord *Sanquire's* being at the Court of *Henry* King of *France*, who asked him, [illegible] *done with a sword*. The King asked, *Doth the man live?* This question made such an impression upon the young Lord, that at his return to *England* he [illegible] be murdered in *Whitefriars* [illegible]. See *The Complete History of* England, vol. II. p. 686 and *Rapin*, vol. IX. p. [illegible].

On *Monday* following, being St. *Peter*'s Day, the 29th of *June*, 1612, the Lord *Sanquire* was brought from the Priſon ſomewhat early in the Morning, into the *Great Palace-Yard*, before *Weſtminſter-Hall* great Gate, there to ſuffer Death on a Gibbet erected for that Purpoſe; where being aſcended the Ladder, he ſpake to the People a good while, excuſing himſelf for the Fact no otherwiſe than formerly he had done at the *King's-Bench* Bar: Aſking God and the World Forgiveneſs for the ſame, proteſting his Deteſtation thereof, now that he truly underſtood the Foulneſs of it; affirming, that till he firſt was brought to his Trial, the Devil had ſo far blinded his Underſtanding, that he could not apprehend that he had done amiſs, or otherwiſe than was fitting for a Man of his Rank and Quality, having been trained up in the Wars, and lived the Life of a Soldier, which Sort of Men, he ſaid, ſtood more on Points of Honour than Religion. He humbly thanked God that had opened his Eyes, and given him the Grace to ſee his Offence, and truly to apprehend the Foulneſs of it. At length, he profeſſed himſelf to die a *Roman* Catholick, and deſired all *Roman* Catholicks there preſent to pray for him. He ſaid, that for worldly reſpects, he had long neglected the public Profeſſion of his Faith in that kind, and he thought God was angry with him for it; and he knew not but God might inflict this juſt Puniſhment upon him for that Neglect; and therefore he adviſed all Men that ſtood ſo affected in Heart, not to procraſtinate nor delay; for Delays, he ſaid, are dangerous. The Religion, he ſaid, was a good Religion, a ſaving Religion, and if he had been conſtant in that Religion, he was verily perſuaded he had never fallen into that Miſery.

So falling to his Prayers for a while in private, and after in publick praying for the King and Queen, their Royal Iſſue, and the State both of *England* and *Scotland*, with the Lords of the Council and Church, he ſubmitted himſelf to the Will of the Executioner; who caſting him off the Ladder, ſuffered him there to hang a long Time, that People in this great Man might take Notice of the King's greater Juſtice.

Note, That this Lord was tried by the Country, but challenged his Trial by Peers, which was denied him, becauſe though he were a Lord in *Scotland*, yet he was no Lord of the Parliament here in *England*, nor had any *Engliſh* Barony.

Note alſo, That *Carliel*, and another with him, but whether it were *Gray* or no, I cannot certainly affirm; but ſure I am, it was one that was with *Carliel* when he did the Fact (and I take it to be my Lord's Page), were hanging on two Gibbets ſet up in *Fleet-Street*, over againſt the great Gate of the *White-Friars*, very early in the Morning, before the Lord *Sanquire* had his Trial *.

Note alſo, That one of thoſe Gibbets was higher than the other by the Length of a Man, or thereabouts; and I demanding the Reaſon thereof, was anſwered by a Stander-by, that the Manner of *Scotland* is, that when a Gentleman is hanged with a Man of meaner Quality than himſelf, the Gentleman hath the Honour of the higher Gibbet, and thinks himſelf much wronged if he be not ſo diſpoſed of. Whether this Anſwer was ſerious, or by way of Scorn, let him that deſireth to be reſolved by Enquiry reſolve himſelf.

Sir *Edward Coke*, in his ninth Report, *p.* 117, *& ſeq.* gives the following Account of

The Lord *Sanchar*'s Caſe.

Robert Creighton, Lord *Sanchar* †, a Baron of *Scotland*, of his Malice prepenſe at *Weſtminſter*, in the County of *Middleſex*, incited and procured *Robert Carliel* to kill *John Turner*, who accordingly aſſociating himſelf with one *James Irweng*, the 11th of *May* now laſt paſt, killed the ſaid *John Turner* within the City of *London*. And the King in his Zeal to Juſtice in this Caſe, immediately ſent for the two Chief-Juſtices and Chief-Baron, and commanded there ſhould be ſpeedy proceeding againſt the Lord *Sanchar*, according to Law. To which the Juſtices anſwered, That the Lord *Sanchar* was but an Acceſſory in this Caſe, and therefore he (*a*) could not by Law be convicted before the principal is attainted; but if the principal could be apprehended, then both might be attainted with more Expedition than could be, if the principal ſhould be attainted by Utlagary. Then it was aſked, how the Lord *Sanchar*, being an ancient Baron of *Scotland*, ſhould be tried: And it was anſwered by them, That none within this Realm of *England* is accounted (*b*) a Peer of the Realm, but he who is a Lord of the Parliament of *England*; for every Subject either is a Lord of the Parliament, or one of the Commons, and the Lord *Sanchar* was not a Lord of the Parliament within this Kingdom, and therefore ſhould be tried by the Commons of the Realm, *viz.* Knights, Eſquires, or others of the Commons; and therewith agree our Books, as well ancient as others, (*c*) 11 *E.* III. *Brief* 473. 8 *R.* II. (*d*) *Proceſ. pl. ult.* (*e*) 20 *E.* IV. 6. *a. b.* 20 *El.* (*f*) 360. Then the King aſked, in what Court, after the principal is attainted, the Lord *Sanchar* ſhould be tried? And the Juſtices anſwered, that foraſmuch as the Procurement was in *Middleſex*, it was moſt convenient to try him in the King's-Bench. And thereupon the King reſolved, that he ſhould not be committed to the Tower, but to the Priſon of the King's-Bench, where he might be, if Occaſion required, ſooner and eaſier examined, than if he ſhould be committed to the Tower: And the King commanded the ſaid Juſtices, that all things ſhould be prepared for the legal Proceeding; and that he would endeavour to cauſe not only the principal, but others alſo who might diſcover the Truth of the Fact, to be apprehended. And thereupon the ſaid Chief-Juſtices conferred with the other Juſtices of the King's-Bench, before whom the Lord *Sanchar* ſhould be tried. And before them divers Queſtions were moved concerning the legal proceeding in this caſe. 1. Upon the Statute of (*g*) 2 *E.* VI. *c.* 24. by which it is enacted, as to this Point in this Manner: 'And farther be it enacted by 'the Authority aforeſaid, That where any Murder or Felony hereafter 'ſhall be committed or done in one County, and another Perſon or more 'ſhall be Acceſſory or Acceſſories by any manner of wiſe to any ſuch 'Murder or Felony in another County, that then an Indictment found or 'taken againſt ſuch Acceſſory, or Acceſſories, upon the Circumſtance of 'ſuch Matter before the Juſtices of the Peace, or other Juſtices or Com'miſſioners, to enquire of Felonies, where ſuch Offence of Acceſſory or 'Acceſſories in any manner of wiſe ſhall be committed or done, ſhall be 'as good and effectual in Law, as if the principal Offence had been com'mitted or done within the ſame County where ſuch Indictment ſhall be 'found: And that the Juſtices of Gaol-delivery, or Oyer and Terminer, 'or two of them, of or in ſuch County where the Offence of any ſuch 'Acceſſory ſhall be hereafter committed and done, upon ſuit to them 'made, ſhall write to the *Cuſtos Rotulorum*, or Keepers of the Records, 'where ſuch Principal ſhall be hereafter attainted or convicted, to cer'tify them whether ſuch principal be attainted, convicted, or otherwiſe 'diſcharged of ſuch principal Felony; who upon ſuch writing to them, or 'any of them directed, ſhall make ſufficient Certificate in writing, under 'their Seal or Seals, to the ſaid Juſtices, whether ſuch Principal be attainted, 'convicted, or otherwiſe diſcharged, or not. And after they that ſo 'ſhall have the Cuſtody of ſuch Records, do certify that ſuch Principal is 'attainted, convicted, or otherwiſe diſcharged of ſuch Offence by the 'Law; that then the Juſtices of Gaol-delivery, or of Oyer and Termi'ner, or other there authoriſed, ſhall proceed upon every ſuch Acceſſory, 'in the County or Counties where ſuch Acceſſory or Acceſſories became 'Acceſſory, in ſuch manner and form as if both the ſaid principal Of'fence and Acceſſory had been committed and done in the ſaid County 'where the Offence of the Acceſſory was or ſhall be committed or done. 'And that every ſuch Acceſſory, and other Offenders above expreſſed, 'ſhall anſwer upon their Arraignments, and receive ſuch Trial, Judg'ment, Order, and Execution, and ſuffer ſuch Forfeitures, Pains and 'Penalties, as is uſed in other Caſes of Felony: Any Law or Cuſtom 'to the contrary heretofore uſed in any wiſe notwithſtanding.' And upon this Statute, divers (*h*) Queſtions were moved; 1. If the Indictment in the County of *Middleſex* of the Acceſſory ſhould recite, that the principal was indicted before Commiſſioners of Oyer and Terminer in the City of *London*, (as in Truth he was) or if the Indictment ſhould recite *in facto*, that the principal committed the Murder in *London*, &c.? And it was reſolved, that the Indictment in *Middleſex* ſhould recite, *de facto*, that the Principal committed the Murder in *London*. For the recital, that the Principal is indicted of Murder in *London*, is no direct Affirmation that the Principal committed the Murder; for the Indictment is but an Accuſation, and in lieu of the King's Declaration, which may be true or falſe; and this agrees with former Precedents. And accordingly the Indictment was drawn; upon which the Acceſſory was convicted, as appears before by the Indictment itſelf.

2. The ſecond Queſtion moved upon the Statute, was, If the (*i*) Juſtices of the King's-Bench are within theſe Words, Juſtices of Gaol-delivery, or Oyer and Terminer? And it was objected, That the King's-Bench is the higheſt Court of ordinary Juſtice in criminal Cauſes within the Realm, and paramount the Authority of Juſtices of Gaol-delivery, and Commiſſioners of Oyer and Terminer; and as it is held in 27 *Aſſ.* 1. is (*k*) more than the Eyre; for they ſhall examine the Errors of the Juſtices in Eyre, Gaol-delivery, and Oyer and Terminer; and therefore inaſmuch as the Juſtices of the King's-Bench are paramount and ſuperiors over all the others, they cannot be included within their Inferiors, *viz.* Juſtices of Gaol-delivery, or of Oyer and Terminer. Alſo, the Juſtices of the King's-Bench have a diſtinct and ſupreme Court; and the Juſtices of Gaol-delivery, and Oyer and Terminer, other diſtinct and ſubordinate Courts. And therefore it was adjudged, *Hill.* 30 *El. Reg.* in the King's-Bench, that where *R.* (*l*) *Smith* was indicted of Forgery of a falſe Deed at the Seſſions of (*m*) Peace in the County of *Oxford*; and the Statute of 5 *El. c.* 14. which inflicts the Puniſhment, and upon which Act the Indictment was grounded, provides, that the Indictment ſhall be taken before Juſtices of Aſſize, and Juſtices of Oyer and Terminer: And although the Juſtices of Peace by their Commiſſion have Power to hear and determine Felonies, Treſpaſs, *&c.* and have an expreſs Clauſe *ad audiendum & terminand'*, ſo that they are, as it was urged, Juſtices of Oyer and Terminer; yet it was reſolved *per tot' cur'*, that becauſe there was a Commiſſion of Oyer and Terminer known diſtinctly by that Name, and the Commiſſion of the Peace known diſtinctly by another Name, that the ſaid Indictment was not well taken, and therefore was quaſhed. But it was reſolved, that the (*n*) Juſtices of the King's-Bench are the ſovereign Juſtices of Goal-delivery, and of Oyer and Terminer; and therefore they are included within the ſaid Words: And therefore it is held in 7 *E.* IV. 18. *a.* & 4 *H.* VII. 18. that if an Indictment of forcible Entry be removed into the King's-Bench, the Juſtices of the King's (*o*) Bench ſhall award Reſtitution; and yet the Statute of 8 *H.* VI. *c.* 9. ſpeaks only of Juſtices of the Peace; but the Reaſon is, becauſe they have the ſovereign and ſupreme Authority in ſuch Caſes. And according to this Reſolution, the Juſtices of the King's-Bench wrote according to the ſaid Act to the Juſtices of Goal-delivery in *London*, before whom the Principal was, *&c.* who certified the Record, *&c.* as appears before at large.

3. It was moved, if the Lord *Sanchar* could not in Term-time be indicted, arraigned, and convicted, at *Newgate* before Commiſſioners of (*p*) Oyer and Terminer for the County of *Middleſex*, and it was reſolved he could not; for the King's-Bench, as has been ſaid, is (*q*) more than Eyre, and therefore in (*r*) Term-time no Commiſſioner of Oyer and Terminer, or Gaol-delivery, by the Common Law, can ſit in the ſame County where the King's-Bench ſits; for (*s*) *in præſentia majoris ceſſat poteſt' minoris*, and therewith agrees 27 *Aſſ. p.* 1. But *Carliel* and *Irweng* were indicted and attainted in *London*, where the Murder was committed, before Juſtices of Oyer and Terminer in the (*t*) Term-time, becauſe in another County than where the King's-Bench ſits.

4. It was moved, if the Lord *Sanchar* being indicted in the King's-Bench, if there muſt be (*u*) fifteen Days for the return of the *ve. fa.* for if fifteen Days are requiſite, he cannot be arraigned this Term. And it was reſolved not, becauſe the Offence was committed in *Middleſex*, where the Court ſits; but if the Indictment had been taken in any other County,

* See the Record of the Conviction of *Carliel* and *Irweng*, in *Coke*'s ninth Report, p. 114.

† *Wilſon*'s Hiſt. p. 59, 60. (*a*) 4 Co. 43. b. (*b*) Co. Lit. 16. b. 7 Co. 15. a. Calvin's Caſe, 2 Inſt. 3 Inſt. 50. (*c*) 7 Co. 15. b. 16. a. Calvin's Caſe. (*d*) Fitz. Proceſs 224. 7 Co. 15. b. Calvin's Caſe. (*e*) 7 Co. 15. b. Calvin's Caſe. Br. Noſme de Dignity 29. (*f*) 7 Co. 15. b. 23. a. Calvin's Caſe. Dy. 360. pl. 6. Co. Lit. 261. b. (*g*) 2 & 3 E. VI. c. 24. 3 Inſt. 113. (*h*) 3 Inſt. 48, 49. (*i*) 3 Inſt. 103. 3 Mar. Br. Oyer and Termin. 8. 4 Inſt. 73. Cowley 66. Poſtea 112. b. (*k*) Stanf. Cor. 53. a. 4 Inſt. 73. Fitz. Aſſiſe 246. Br. Eſcape 21. Br. Juriſdict. 66. Poſtea 118. b. Br. Judges, Juſtices, &c. 16. (*l*) Cro. El. 78. 697. 3 Inſt. 103. Cawl. 258, 259. (*m*) Cr. El. 601. 697. Cawl. 258, 259. Savil 134. H. P. C. 165. (*n*) H. P. C. 165. Cawley 66. 3 Inſt. 103. Antea 118. a. 3 Mar. Br. Oyer & Terminer 8. 4 Inſt. 73. (*o*) Kelw. 159. a. b. Dy. 182. pl. 6. 11 Co. 59. a. b. 65. a. 1 Roll. Rep. 92. B. forcible Entre 27. Dalt. 25. pl. 8. Dalt. in Kelw. 204. pl. 2 Dalt. in Naſh. pl. 2. Fitz. Entre 24. Br. Reſtitut. 11. Dalt. Juſt. c. 314. Jenk. Cent. 197. 222. (*p*) H. P. C. 156. 3 Inſt. 27. 4 Inſt. 73. (*q*) Staunf. Cor. 53. a. 4 Inſt. 73. Fitz. Aſſiſe 246. Br. Eſcape 21. Br. Juriſdiction 66. 27. Aſſ. pl. 1. Br. Judges, Juſtices, &c. 16. Antea 114. a. (*r*) 10 Co. 73. b. 3 Inſt. 27. (*s*) 10 Co. 73. b. 2 Inſt. 26. 160. (*t*) Poſt. 121. a. (*u*) 2 Inſt. 550. 568. H. P. C. 157. Co. Lit. 124. b.

and

and removed thither, there ought to be fifteen days, *&c.* and therewith agree the precedents, and the continual uſage of the ſame Court.

5. It was reſolved, that foraſmuch as there was not any direct proof, that *James Irweng* was commanded or procured by the Lord *Sanchar* to commit the murder, but that he aſſociated himſelf to *Robert Carliel* who was procured by him, that the (*v*) beſt way is to indict the Lord *Sanchar*, as acceſſory to *Robert Carliel* only. for Indictments which concern the life of men ought to be framed as near the truth as may be, *& eo potius*, becauſe they are to be found by the oath of the Grand Inqueſt, which finding is called (*x*) ***veredictum, quaſi dictum veritatis***; and yet it was reſolved, that if one is indicted as acceſſory to (*y*) two, and he is found acceſſory to one, the verdict is good. *Vide* the Statute of *W.* I. *c.* (*z*) 14. by which it is enacted, ***That none be outlawed upon appeal of commandment, force, aid, or receit, until he that is appealed of the deed be attainted, ſo that one like law be uſed therein through the Realm.*** which is but an affirmance of the common Law: for there cannot be an acceſſory unleſs there be a principal, no more than there can be a ſhadow unleſs there be a body. But this word ***appeal*** has two ſignifications in law; one general, and that is taken for an accuſation, generally, and *accuſatio eſt duplex*, either by Inquiſition, *i.e.* by Indictment, and that is at the ſuit and in the name of the King; or by the party, and in his name, as in appeal by Writ or Bill: or by Appeal, *i.e.* accuſation of an approver; and therewith agree all our books, and *Stamf. l.* 2. *de Plac' cor' c.* 52. *f.* 142. *b.* where he ſaith, after the confeſſion of the Crime, the Felon may appeal, *ſ.* accuſe others coadjutors with him to do the Felony; and in this particular ſenſe for accuſation of the party it is oftner taken. And as there are two manner of Accuſations ſo there are two manner of attainders of Felony, *ſ.* by judgment given, *ſ.* one at the King's ſuit, and the other at the ſuit of the party; and both theſe attainders are in two manners, one after appearance, and the other upon default after appearance, two ways, *ſ.* either by verdict or confeſſion, and at the ſuit of the party, a third way. *ſ.* by battle, upon default by proceſs of outlawry, where judgment is given by the (*a*) Coroners, or by thoſe whom an act of Parliament and cuſtom have enabled. And in the Statute of *W.* (*b*) I. theſe words, ***upon appeal of commandment***, &c. are to be intended of an accuſation generally, *ſ.* by indictment, as by Writ or Bill, *&c.* and theſe words, ***until he that is appealed of the deed be attainted***, are meant of all manner of attainders, either at the King's ſuit, or at the ſuit of the party, and either upon appearance or upon default. And afterwards in the ſame Act, proviſion is made for the appeal of the party, which implies that the word ***appeal*** ſhall be taken in the general ſenſe.

6. It was reſolved, that if the principal is (*c*) erroneouſly attainted, either for error in the proceſs, or becauſe the principal being out of the Realm, *&c.* is outlawed, or that he was in priſon at the time of the outlawry, *&c.* yet the acceſſory ſhall be attainted, for the attainder againſt the principal ſtands till it is reverſed, and therewith agrees (*d*) 2 *R.* III. 12. the reſolution of all the Juſtices in the King's-Bench: And in 18 *E.* IV. 9. *b.* the (*e*) principal was erroneouſly outlawed for Felony, and the acceſſory taken, indicted, arraigned, convicted, attainted, and hanged; and afterwards the principal reverſed the outlawry, and was indicted and arraigned of the ſaid Felony, and found not guilty, by which he was acquitted, and all this appears in the ſaid book. Then it will be demanded, that foraſmuch as there cannot be an acceſſory, unleſs there is a principal, and in this caſe there is no principal, how the heir of the acceſſory ſhall be reſtored to the land which his father had forfeited by the ſaid unjuſt attainder? To that it is to be anſwered, that the heir may enter, or have his action; for now upon the matter by act in law, the attainder againſt his father is without any writ of error utterly annulled, for by the reverſal of the attainder againſt the principal, the attainder againſt the acceſſory, which depends upon the attainder of the principal, *ipſo facto* is utterly defeated and annulled; and this notably appears in an ancient book, in the time of *E.* I. tit. *Mort-daunceſt.* 46. where the caſe is, *A* was indicted of Felony, and *B.* of the receipt of *A.* *A.* eloined himſelf (and is outlawed): *B.* was taken, and put himſelf upon inqueſt, and found guilty, for which *B.* was attainted, and hanged, and the Lord entered, as into his eſcheat; and afterwards *A.* came, and reverſed the outlawry, and pleaded to the felony, and was found not guilty, by which he was acquitted; whereupon the heir of *B.* brought a (*f*) *Mort-daunceſter* againſt the Lord by eſcheat, who came and ſhewed all this matter, and there was a demur upon it; and it was awarded, that the heir of *B.* ſhould recover ſeiſin of the land; for if *B.* was now alive, he ſhould go quit by the acquittal of *A.* becauſe he could not be receiver of a felon, when *A.* is no felon; and all this appears in the ſaid book. *Vide* 4 *E.* III. 36. *b.* in *Dower* 43 *E.* III. 3. *a.* in *Aſſiſe & Reideſ.* 8 *H.* IV. 4. 11 *H.* IV. 4. 4 *E.* IV. 20. 6 *E.* IV. 9. 13 *E.* IV. 4. 9 *H.* VI. 38. *b.* 8 *H.* VII. 10. *& vide* the caſe of ſentence (*g*) of deprivation of one, and preſentment, inſtitution, and induction of another; and after by relation of a general pardon, *ipſo facto*, all are reſtored without appeal, or new preſentation, admiſſion, or inſtitution, *qd' vide* (*h*) *Dy. Nota* reader, to ouſt all queſt. to what gaol offenders ſhall be committed, it is enacted by the ſtatute of (*i*) 5 *H.* IV. *c.* 10. that none ſhall be impriſoned by any Juſtice of the Peace, but only in the common goal, ſaving to lords and others, who have gaols, their franchiſes in that caſe. By which it appears, how Juſtices of Peace offend, who commit felons, *&c.* to either of the Counters in *London*, and other priſons, which are not common goals.

But foraſmuch as ſeveral perſons have earneſtly deſired to know the circumſtances, as well of the proceeding, as of the fact itſelf, I will comply with their requeſt.

ROBert Creighton, Baron of *Sanchar*, a *Scotchman*, about five years ago play'd at Foils with *John Turner* a Fencing-maſter, and it happened that *Turner* in playing ſtruck out the Baron's eye with his Foil; upon which the Baron, finding himſelf impatient under ſo great an affront, and not able to bear the loſs of his eye without having his revenge, reſolved to procure ſomebody to kill *Turner*, and among his other ſervants, he prevailed upon *Gilbert Gray* and *Robert Carliel*, *Scotchmen*, two of his followers, to ſhoot *Turner* upon the firſt opportunity that ſhould offer. Theſe two then undertook to accompliſh this deſign, and induſtriouſly endeavoured to execute it, but the ninth day of *May* laſt, *Gray* repenting of a purpoſe and act ſo barbarous, vile and bloody, being touched with the Motion of the Holy Ghoſt, reſolved to proceed no farther; which the Baron of *Sanchar* being informed of, and that *Gray* ſlackened in his promiſe, *Robert Carliel*, as is aforeſaid, undertook to execute what he had promiſed: who, the eleventh of *May* following, aſſociating himſelf with *James Irweng* a *Scotchman*, of the frontiers, about ſeven o'clock in the evening came to a houſe in the *Friars*, which *Turner* uſed to frequent as he came from his ſchool, which was near that place; and finding *Turner* there, they ſaluted one another; and *Turner* with one of his friends ſat at the door, aſking them to drink, but *Carliel* and *Irweng* turning about to cock the piſtol, came back immediately, and *Carliel* drawing it from under his coat, diſcharged it upon *Turner*, and gave him a mortal wound near the left pap; ſo that *Turner*, after having ſaid theſe words, ***Lord have mercy upon me! I am killed***; immediately fell down. Whereupon *Carliel* and *Irweng* fled, *Carliel* to the town, and *Irweng* towards the River; but miſtaking his way, and entering into a court where they ſold wood, which was no thorough-fare, he was taken. *Carliel* likewiſe fled, and ſo did alſo the Baron of *Sanchar*. The ordinary Officers of Juſtice did their utmoſt, but could not take them: for in fact, as appeared afterwards, *Carliel* fled into *Scotland*, and *Gray* towards the Sea, thinking to go to *Sweden*, and *Sanchar* hid himſelf in *England*.

The impediments of Juſtice, difficulties of law, and impoſſibilities of legal Proceeding to take *Carliel*, the principal, which were in this caſe, are remarkable, and worthy of conſideration. The cure and remedy of the whole ought to be only and wholly attributed to the great care of his moſt excellent Majeſty, and to his perpetual love and zeal for Juſtice, as will clearly appear by what follows.

The impediments of Juſtice were two:

1. The truth of this fact, touching the Baron of *Sanchar*, could not appear, becauſe it conſiſted only in the words of his mouth by incitation and procurement; but by *Gray* and *Carliel*, who were fled, or by himſelf; and he was likewiſe gone.

2. It was not as yet known whither they were fled, and it could not be found out by all the ſearch and diligence which was uſed by the Officers and Magiſtrates of Juſtice.

The difficulties of Law are manifeſt by the foregoing reſolutions.

Impoſſibilities of legal proceeding.

1. It was impoſſible by legal proceſs to apprehend the body of *Carliel*, being in *Scotland*.

It was impoſſible alſo to proceed againſt the Baron of *Sanchar*, who was but an acceſſory, before the principal was attainted; a thing which would have required a very long proceeding, if he had not been taken.

Now therefore let us behold here the love and zeal which his Majeſty always had for Juſtice, who being informed by ſome of his principal Judges, with whom he had conſulted touching the nature of this preſent caſe, and finding if this fact ſhould be left to the ordinary proceeding of the Law, *Carliel* the aſſaſſin could not be taken, and that no ordinary power had been able to find *Gray* the witneſs, nor *Sanchar* the author; lo! the King by proclamation gives authority to any perſon whatſoever to apprehend theſe three, with a promiſe of great reward.

Upon this, the Baron of *Sanchar*, well knowing that the principal aſſaſſin and the witneſs were fled, ſurrendered himſelf, and denied that he incited or procured the fact: wherefore his Majeſty ſent poſt to the ſeaports (the gates of the Kingdom), as alſo into *Scotland*, and other places of his Dominions, where his admirable prudence had hopes of finding them; and the Lord ſo crowned his Royal thoughts, and gave ſuch a bleſſing to his zeal for juſtice, that ſome of his Couriers took *Gray* at the port of *Harwich*, ready to imbark for *Sweden*; and *Carliel* in *Scotland*, thinking to croſs the ſea for his greater ſafety. *Gray* then, being by his Majeſty's command examined, confeſs'd the whole truth of the fact againſt the Baron of *Sanchar*; who likewiſe by his Majeſty's direction being confronted with *Gray*, and particularly examined touching certain Articles, ſpecial and pertinent ſayings by his Majeſty himſelf, confeſs'd by writing under his own hand, that he had incited and procured this aſſaſſination; and being preſs'd thereupon by the queſtions, he diſcovered a long and inveterate malice which he had had, with all the occaſions and material circumſtances of this murder.

His Majeſty having regard to that which the Holy Ghoſt admoniſhes us of, (*quia non profertur cito contra malos ſententia, abſque timore ullo filii hominum perpetrant mala* (*k*) gave orders two days after, that *Carliel* the principal ſhould be brought to *London*; that he and *James Irweng*, in full term, (a thing not uſual) might be carried before the Juſtices at *Newgate*, and attainted and convicted. And a few days after the Baron of *Sanchar* was likewiſe attainted and convicted at the King's Bench in full term; and in a ſhort time after, to accompliſh his Majeſty's zeal for juſtice, the Baron *Sanchar* was (*l*) hanged publickly in Term-time at the Palace of *Weſtminſter*, according to the judgment and ſentence he had before received.

I have reported this caſe with all the circumſtances, becauſe this example has not its parallel: for altho' it is true, that the late Queen *Mary* is very famous on account of the examplary juſtice which ſhe cauſed to be executed upon Baron *Sturton*, for the barbarous murder of *Harquil*; yet this preſent example of the Baron of *Sanchar* very much ſurpaſſes that of the Baron of *Sturton*, and that for many conſiderations. 1. Becauſe the Baron of *Sturton* was taken by the ordinary courſe of the Law, even within the Kingdom; but the principal in this caſe could not be taken by any common power, but by the means of his Majeſty's royal and abſolute power only. 2. The Baron of *Sturton*'s offence was very apparent, and without any difficulty of Law: on the contrary, this of *Sanchar* was thereof (as appears) very full; but by his Majeſty's command, all theſe difficulties, with the conference and grave conſideration of his principal Judges, after ſearch of caſes precedent, were reſolved and cleared up, and notwithſtanding the impediments, difficulties and impoſſibilities in legal proceeding, greater expedition was uſed in this caſe than in that. In ſhort, the accompliſhment of the whole, the clearing up the truth of the fact in the caſe of the Baron of *Sanchar*, muſt be attributed to the great wiſdom, power and vigilance of his Majeſty, as appears by that which has been thereof ſaid before.

(*v*) 2 Inſt. 183. (*x*) Co. Lit. 226. a. (*y*) 2 Inſt. 183. H. P. C. 265. (*z*) 2 Inſt. 182, 138. 2 Inſt. 183. (*a*) 4 Co. 3[illegible] b. Co. Lit. [illegible]88. b. Cr. El. [illegible] (*b*) W. I. c. 14. 2 Inſt. 182, 183, 184. (*c*) Art. 6[illegible] [illegible] R. III. 21. b. (*d*) Ant. 68. b. 2 R. II. 21. b. (*e*) Br. Cor. 165. (*f*) H. P. C. [illegible] Rol. [illegible]7. (*g*) 6 Co. [illegible] 14. 2. 3 Inſt. 238. H. b. 82. 1, 3. Cr. El. 11. 789. Moor 131. Owen 87. Leach 22. 141. 1 Sid. 164, 168. Palm. 412. (*h*) Dy. 225. [illegible] 6 Co. [illegible] b. [illegible] 2 Brownl. 4[illegible] 2 Inſt. 43. Co. Lit. 230. (*k*) Eccleſiaſt. 8. 11. Ant. a 118. b. (*l*) 3 Inſt. 15.

The

The Baron of *Sanchar* was a man of a very ancient and noble family in *Scotland*; he was a man of great courage and wit, endowed with many excellent gifts, as well natural as acquired. The eloquence of his discourse, with the civility and discretion of his behaviour, when he came before and went from the Judges, compelled the people (who honoured him on account of his moral virtues, and those for his sake) to bewail his fall with great grief (altho' the occasion of it was this base and barbarous assassination, premeditated for five years together with a malice bloody and inveterate): this extraordinary affection of the people was, as he himself confessed, a very great consolation to him in his last troubles and afflictions. But at last their compassion abated, because they perceived he died a true Catholick.

XIV. Proceedings against JOHN OGILVIE, for *High-Treason*, on *Tuesday* the last Day of *February*, 1615, at *Glascow*, in *Scotland.*

JOHN *Ogilvie*, alias *Watson*, came into *Scotland*, in 1613; and making his residence for the most part of that winter in the north parts of *Scotland*; took his journey to *England* a little before *Easter*. Where, giving out to some of his Countrymen, that he had a supplication for some wrongs to present to his Majesty, he attended the Court some two months; and falling in acquaintance with a Gentleman of the West-country, after his pretended business was done, or the occasion disappointed, he returned into *Scotland* with the said Gentleman in the beginning of *June* thereafter. Upon this familiarity, and other intelligences given him, he came to *Glascow* in *August* following; and finding a kinder receipt by certain persons in that city, (who have since been justly condemned) he made some haunt and resort thither at sundry times, till at last he was detected, and by the direction of the Archbishop of *Glascow*, who at that time kept his residence within the city, apprehended and committed to prison on the 4th of *October*.

In his examination, which was the next morning, before the Archbishop of *Glascow*, the Bishop of *Argyle*, the Lords *Fleming*, *Boyde*, and *Kilsyth*, the Provost of the City of *Glascow*, Sir *Walter Stewart*, and Sir *George Elphingston*, Knights, he confessed his true name to be *John Ogilvie*, that he was born in the North of *Scotland*, and had been forth of the Country twenty-one years; that he lived at *Gratz*, in a college of the Jesuits, "*and was received in their order: that he returned into* Scotland *by the command of his Superior, and was to stay there until he was recalled, if no other impediment should offer.*" Being required to give his oath, that he should declare nothing but truth in such things as he should be demanded; he answered, "That he would take his oath, but with some exceptions, namely, if he were demanded any thing that touched his estate and life, or that might endanger these or any of them, he would not answer; likewise if the same tended to the prejudice of others." And when it was reply'd, that his exceptions being admitted, his oath was as good as no oath, seeing any questions that could be proposed would concern some of these; he was induced at last to give a simple oath, which he did upon his knees; and rising up from the ground, said, "I will neither lye nor equivocate, but what I say shall be truth; and what I am asked, if I find it impertinent for me to answer, I will say nothing, or declare plainly I will not tell."

Then being enquired of his coming into *Scotland*, the time and business he came to do, answered, his business was to save souls. Touching the time when he came into *Scotland*, answered in the *June* before: where he was apprehended to equivocate, notwithstanding of his protestation; for he meaned of his last coming, and was asked concerning the first. But the time at that examination was not understood. Being enquired of the places where he had been received, denied to tell; and if he had said Mass in any place, he answered, "he would not say any thing that might work prejudice to himself or others:" and because he had professed, that he would not lye, the reply he commonly made to such question was, "I will not tell you."

The Lords finding him thus obstinate, returned him to a chamber in the Castle, which was prepared for him.

The 12th of *December*, he was presented at *Edinburgh*, before the Lords Commissioners, appointed by his Majesty's missive for his examination and Trial: namely, The Lord of *Binning* Secretary, the Lord of *Kilsyth*, Sir *Gideon Murray* the Thesaurer-Deputy, and Sir *William Oliphant* his Majesty's Attorney-General: to whom he answered in all that was proponed, as of before at *Glascow*. There the letters intercepted with him were presented, which he acknowledged to be his: yet being demanded touching certain particulars contained in them, he denied to give their Lordships any satisfaction. So as their Lordships perceiving nothing but a pertinacious refusing in him to answer to points most reasonable, and withal apprehending his stay at Court in the last summer, to have been for some worse service than he could speed in, determined, according to the power given them, to extort by torments another confession; which being intimated to him, and he replying that he was ready to suffer what they pleased, it was thought fit to prove him with the easiest form of Trial that could be used.

It pleased his Majesty in this time, while he was remaining at *Glascow*, to send a commission to the Archbishop of *Glascow*, the Lord Bishop of *Argyle*, the Lord *Fleming*, Sir *George Elphingston*, and *James Hamilton* Provost of the city of *Glascow*, for trying the said *Ogilvie*.

His opinion touching his Highness's royal power, and the Pope's claimed jurisdiction, maintained by *Bellarmine*, *Suarez* and others of that sort: The questions were these.

1. "Whether the Pope be judge, and have power *in spiritualibus* over his Majesty, and whether that power will reach over his Majesty, even *in temporalibus*, if it be *in ordine ad spiritualia*, as *Bellarmine* affirmeth?

2. "Whether the Pope have power to excommunicate Kings, (especially such as are not of his Church) as his Majesty?

3. "Whether the Pope have power to depose Kings, by him excommunicated; and in particular, whether he have power to depose the King his Majesty?

4. "Whether it be no Murder to slay his Majesty, being so excommunicated and deposed by the Pope?

5. "Whether the Pope have power to assoil Subjects from the oath of their born and natural allegiance to his Majesty?

Upon the 18th day of *January*, the foresaid questions being read distinctly unto him, and he required to declare his opinion thereanent, answered as followeth:

"To the first, that he thought the Pope of Rome Judge to his Majesty, and to have power over him *in spiritualibus*, if the King be a Christian: and where it is asked, if that power will reach over his Majesty *in temporalibus*, he says, he is not obliged to declare his opinion therein, except to him that is Judge in controversies of Religion, which he acknowledges to be the Pope, or some one having authority from him.

"To the second he answered, That the Pope hath power to excommunicate his Majesty: and where it is said, that the King is not of the Pope's Church; he saith, that all who are baptized are under the Pope's power.

"To the third, where it is asked, if the Pope have power to depose his Majesty, being excommunicated; answered, that he will not declare his mind, except to him that is Judge in controversies of Religion.

"To the fourth, whether it be lawful to slay his Majesty, being excommunicated and deposed by the Pope: answered *ut supra*.

"To the fifth, whether the Pope hath power to assoil Subjects from their born and natural allegiance to his Majesty? answered, *ut supra*."

In all these articles he was particularly reasoned with, by the Archbishop of *Glascow*, Mr. *Robert Boyde* Principal of the College, (a man of rare erudition) and Mr. *Robert Scot*, one of the Ministers of the City; where it was also signified unto him, that it concerned him in no less than his life, what answer he should make; if he should stand obstinate in these he had given, he might know what favour was to be expected for his other crimes. Not the less ratifying all that formerly was said, he added this further, "that he condemned the oaths of supremacy and allegiance proponed to be sworn in *England*," and would needs have the writer to insert those words, to all which he put his hand, subscribing thus,

Johannes Ogilveus, societatis JESU.

These answers being sent to his Majesty, under the testification of the foresaid Commissioners, his Highness gave orders to the Lords of the Privy-Council for his Trial, which was appointed to be at *Glascow*, the last of *February*. Immediately after, the Archbishop of *Glascow* directed the Provost and Bailiffs of the city unto him, to signify, that *Tuesday* following was appointed for Arraignment, and that "he would not be accused for Mass-saying, or any thing else that concerned his profession, but for the answers that he had made to the demands proposed to him by his Majesty's Commissioners." They declared also, that if he should upon better resolution recal those answers, and apply himself to give his Majesty satisfaction in other points, which of duty he was obliged unto, the said Archbishop would use his credit with his Highness, and the Lords of the Privy Council for his safety. His answer was, "that he thanked his Lordship, for the good will and kindness offered, but he was so little minded to recal any thing he had said, as when he came to the place, he would make a commentary upon his answers."

The Arraignment of JOHN OGILVIE, Jesuit, on *Tuesday* the last of *February*, in the Town-house of *Glascow*, before *James Hamilton* Provost of *Glascow*, *James Bell*, *Colin Campbell*, and *James Bradwood*, Bailiffs of the City, Justices appointed by special Commission for that Business, by the Lords of the Privy-Council. The foresaid Judges being assisted by the honourable Lords there present:

John, Archbishop of *Glascow*.
James, Marquis of *Hamilton*.
Robert, Earl of *Lothian*.
W[illegible] Lord *Sanquhar*.
John, Lord *Fleming*.
Robert, Lord *Boyde*
And Sir *Walter Stewart*, Baily-deputy of the Regality of *Glascow*.

O[illegible] last of *February*, a little after eleven of the clock in [illegible] Court being set, Mr. *William Hay* of *Baro* com[illegible]ted by special commission from Sir *William Oli*[illegible] [illegible]y's Attorney General, produced the Indictment following: together with the citation used against those who were to pass upon the Jury, and the roll of their particular names, subscribed with his hand, according to the custom obse[illegible] in th[illegible].

The Indictment of John Ogilvie *Jeſuit, after the form of the Law of* Scotland.

John Ogilvie, by your ſubſcription, a prieſt of the late execrable order of Jeſuits, you are indicted and accuſed, That for as much as God, the Author of all righteous government, having eſtabliſhed Kings and Magiſtrates his Lieutenants upon earth, for repreſſing of violence, oppreſſion and vice, and the promoting of piety and juſtice, hath in his particular grace and favour, bleſſed this Country with a more ancient, juſt, and permanent Deſcent of lawful Kings than any other nation of the world, and extended our felicity beyond the happineſs of our anceſtors, by the juſtice, wiſdom and clemency of his Majeſty's proſperous reign; and hath not only rewarded his Majeſty's zeal and righteouſneſs with wealth and peace, but alſo honoured and ſtrengthened him with the acceſſion of the moſt mighty and flouriſhing Kingdoms of *England*, *France*, and *Ireland*. Which viſible favours proceeding directly from God's moſt bountiful hand, moved the whole Eſtates of this kingdom aſſembled in the Parliament holden at *Perth*, the 9th of *July*, 1606, to acknowledge his Majeſty's ſovereign authority, princely power, royal prerogative, and privilege of his Crown over all eſtates, perſons and cauſes whatſoever, within the kingdom: and all in one voice faithfully to promiſe, maintain, defend, obey and advance the life, ſafety, honour, dignity, ſovereign authority and prerogative royal of his ſacred Majeſty, and privileges of his Crown: and to withſtand all perſons, powers, and eſtates, who ſhould preſume, preſs, or intend any ways to impugn, hurt, or impair the ſame: As alſo his Majeſty, with advice of the whole eſtates of this kingdom, in the Parliament holden at *Edinburgh*, the 22d day of *May*, *Anno* 1584, ratified, approved, and perpetually confirmed, his Majeſty's royal power and authority over all eſtates, as well ſpiritual as temporal, within this Realm; and ſtatuted and ordained, that his Highneſs, his heirs and ſucceſſors, by themſelves and their Counſellors, were, and in all times coming ſhould be, Judges competent to all perſons his Highneſs's ſubjects, of whatſoever eſtate, degree, function, or condition, that ever they be of, ſpiritual or temporal, in all matters wherein they or any of them ſhould be apprehended, ſummoned, or charged to anſwer unto ſuch things as ſhould be inquired of them by our ſaid ſoverign Lord and his Council, and that none of them who ſhould be apprehended, called, or ſummoned, to the effect aforeſaid, ſhould preſume or take in hand to decline the judgment of his Highneſs, his heirs and ſucceſſors, or their Council in the premiſſes, under the pain of Treaſon. And likewiſe, by the 48th Act of King *James* I. his Parliament, and divers other Parliaments thereafter, it is ordained that all the King's lieges live and be governed under the King's laws and ſtatutes, and under no laws of other Countries and Realms, under the pain of Treaſon, and other, particularly expreſſed in the Acts before-mentioned, and other laws of this kingdom. Notwithſtanding whereof, it is of truth and verity, that you having renounced your natural allegiance and duty to your native and righteous King, and caſt off all reverence, reſpect, and obedience to his ſovereign authority and laws, and dedicated your mind and actions to the unlawful obedience of foreign powers, adverſaries to his Majeſty; and reſolving, ſo far as in you lieth, to ſeduce his Majeſty's ſubjects from the faith and allegiance due to his Majeſty, repaired to this Country in the month of *June* laſt paſt, or thereabout. And by your conferences, inticements, auricular confeſſions, Maſs-ſaying, and other ſubtle and crafty means, endeavoured yourſelf not only to corrupt many of his Majeſty's lieges in religion; but alſo to pervert them from their dutiful obedience due to his Majeſty, till you were diſcovered and apprehended by the Archbiſhop of *Glaſcow*, who, with divers his Majeſty's Counſellors and others, his good ſubjects, uſed all Chriſtian and charitable means to bring you to the ſenſe of your heinous offences, and deſire of amendment thereof: but they loſing all their well-intended labours, were (in reſpect of your perverſe obſtinacy) commanded by his Majeſty to enter to your examination, and the Trial of your heinous crimes and tranſgreſſions. And eſpecially the ſaid Archbiſhop of *Glaſcow*, and many others of good rank and quality adjoined to him, by his Majeſty, for your examination, having upon the 18th day of *January* laſt, called you before them, to examine you upon ſome particular interrogatories, preſcribed by his Majeſty to be demanded of you; as directly concerning his Majeſty's moſt ſacred perſon, life, crown, and eſtate: And chiefly you being demanded by them, whether the Pope hath power to depoſe Kings, being excommunicated? and in particular, if he have power to depoſe the King's Majeſty, our Sovereign, being excommunicated by him? You anſwered treaſonably, that you would not declare your mind, except to him that is Judge in the controverſies of Religion, whom (by your anſwer made to the latter part of the firſt interrogatory, demanded of you that day) you declared to be the Pope, or any having authority from him; albeit by the Acts of parliament and laws of this realm, made in the years of God 1560 and 1567, it is ſtatuted and ordained, that the Biſhop of *Rome* (called the Pope) ſhall have no Juriſdiction nor authority within this realm, in any time coming: and thereby not only declining treaſonably his Majeſty's Juriſdiction, allowing of the Pope's juriſdiction, which is diſcharged by Acts of Parliament, as ſaid is; but hath committed moſt damnable and High-Treaſon, in not acknowledging that the Pope hath no power to depoſe his Majeſty, who holding his Crown and Authority abſolutely, ſovereignly, and immediately of God, may not be depoſed by any earthly perſon, power, or authority. And thereafter you being demanded, if it be lawful to ſlay his Majeſty, being excommunicated and depoſed by the Pope? You anſwered *ut ſupra*: which was, that you would not declare your mind till you were before the Pope, or others having authority from him, thereby not only declining treaſonably his Majeſty's Juriſdiction and Authority Royal, but by your not anſwering clearly, that it is altogether unlawful, damnable, and diabolical, once to think that it is lawful to ſlay his moſt ſacred Majeſty, you have committed moſt heinous, pernicious, and unpardonable Treaſon. And laſtly, being demanded, if the Pope had power to aſſoil his Majeſty's born ſubjects from their natural allegiance? You anſwered, *ut ſupra*, and thereby both declined treaſonably his Highneſs's Juriſdiction and Authority-Royal, in refuſing to anſwer before his Majeſty's Counſellors and Commiſſioners aforeſaid, in one matter merely concerning his royal power over his people, and their ſubjection to his Majeſty, and alſo committed wilful and deteſtable Treaſon, in not acknowledging profeſſedly and preſently, that none on earth had power to aſſoil his Majeſty's ſubjects from their natural ſubjection and allegiance to him. But that it may be known that your Treaſon proceeded of fore-thought of felony, and obſtinate reſolution, you freely and unrequiredly did add to your foreſaid anſwers this damnable concluſion, that you condemned the oaths of ſupremacy and allegiance given to his Majeſty by his ſubjects in his Dominions: whereby it is apparent, that your errand to this Country, hath been to infect his Highneſs's ſubjects with the poiſon of your peſtilent and treaſonable opinion foreſaid, to the ſubverſion of Religion, overthrow of his Majeſty's authority and crown, and deſtruction of his moſt ſacred perſon. And albeit the courſe of all his Majeſty's life and reign hath manifeſted, how unwilling he hath ever been to uſe the ſeverity of his laws againſt thoſe who have ſaid and heard Maſs, and otherwiſe contravened the Acts of Parliament made againſt idolatrous Papiſtry, and practiſers thereof within this kingdom, deſiring rather to reclaim them by inſtruction, from their errors, to the knowledge and profeſſion of the truth: and when he found them obdurate, and of deſperate reſolution, relieving the Country of the dangerous progreſs of their courſes, by their impriſonment and baniſhment, whereof you had ſuch experience in the perſons of your own accomplices, condemned for their manifeſt crimes, as might very probably have made you to have expected the like, if any memory of your native duty and born allegiance had poſſeſſed your mind: but you being altogether deſtitute thereof, by the three laſt articles of your depoſitions above written, you have ſo plainly diſcovered, that you profeſſedly approve the means, and wiſh the effect of the overthrow of his Majeſty's eſtate, the deſtruction of his Highneſs's perſon, and ſeduction of his native ſubjects from their ſubjection and dutiful obedience: that thereby, and by every one of your foreſaid anſwers, you have committed moſt heinous, deteſtable, and unpardonable Treaſon, and deſervedly incurred the moſt rigorous pains thereof to be executed upon your body, lands, and goods, with all extremity, to the terror of others.

The Indictment being read, Mr. William Hay, *Subſtitute for his Majeſty's Attorney, opened the ſame, to the effect following:*

ALBEIT the Indictment of itſelf be clear enough, and repreſenteth ſufficiently to my Lords Juſtices, their honourable Lordſhips here aſſiſting, and to yourſelf *John Ogilvie*, who ſtands there accuſed, the weight and gravity of the crime by you committed, yet I ſhall reſume it to you in few words, that your anſwers may be the more diſtinct, and without miſtaking.

You are not accuſed of ſaying Maſs, nor of ſeducing his Majeſty's ſubjects to a contrary religion, nor of any point touching you in conſcience properly; but for declining his Majeſty's authority, againſt the laws and ſtatutes of the land, and for maintaining treaſonable opinions: ſuch as we of this realm have not heard by any avowed. The ſtatutes mentioned in your Indictment, make it Treaſon not to anſwer the King's Majeſty, or his Council in any matter which ſhall be demanded: you being examined by my Lord Archbiſhop of *Glaſcow*, and other honourable perſons adjoined to him by his Majeſty's ſpecial commiſſion, refuſed to anſwer to divers interrogatories proponed to you by their Lordſhips, and at the ſame time profeſſedly avouched the Pope of *Rome* his juriſdiction, which by the laws of the Country is many years ſince plainly diſcharged: therefore have you incurred the penalty contained in the ſtatutes, and the ſame ought and ſhould be executed upon you.

It is further laid unto your charge, that you being demanded in the particulars, namely, *Whether the Pope hath power to depoſe the King's Majeſty, our Sovereign?* Secondly, *Whether it be lawful to ſlay his Majeſty, being depoſed by the Pope?* Thirdly, *Whether the Pope hath power to aſſoil his Majeſty's ſubjects, from their natural allegiance, or not?* You denied to give any anſwer, touching any of theſe points, except ye were enquired thereof by the Pope, or others having authority from him: and ſo not acknowledging, that his Majeſty's Crown and Authority is held immediately and ſovereignly of God, the Author of all government; that it is deteſtable once to think, that his ſacred Majeſty may be lawfully killed, and that no man has power to aſſoil his Majeſty's ſubjects from their natural allegiance to his Highneſs: you have in theſe points, and every one of them, committed moſt heinous Treaſon; for the which what you ſay in your own defence I ſee not. And yet further that it may be ſeen, how deſperate your reſolution is in all theſe points, although you were not required concerning the oaths of ſupremacy and allegiance given to his Majeſty, by his ſubjects, ye freely, and out of your own motives, condemned theſe oaths as impious and unlawful; thereby hath it appeared what a wicked and treaſonable mind you foſter againſt his Majeſty, our Sovereign. If you ſhould deny it, here are your anſwers ſubſcribed with your own hand, which ye cannot but acknowledge; them I deſire to be read, as likewiſe the ſeveral Statutes of Parliament, which you are alledged to have tranſgreſſed, and thereafter, ſince his Majeſty is pleaſed, that the ordinary courſe of Trial be kept unto you; you ſhall have liberty to ſay for yourſelf, either againſt the relevancy of the Indictment, or verification produced, what you think beſt.

Then were read the Statutes of Parliament mentioned in the Indictment, and the ſaid John Ogilvie's *Anſwers to the demands propoſed unto him, which he acknowledged for his own, and the ſubſcription thereto ſubjoined, after which, having licenſe of the Court to ſay what he could for himſelf, he ſpake to this effect:*

FIRST under proteſtation, that I do no way acknowledge this judgment, nor receive you, that have that commiſſion there produced, for my Judges, I deny any point laid againſt me to be Treaſon: for if it were Treaſon, it would be Treaſon in all places, and in all kingdoms, but that, *ſaith he*, is known not to be ſo. As for your Acts of Parliament, they are made by a number of partial men, the beſt of the land not agreeing with them, and of matters not ſubject to their *Forum*, or Judicatory, for which I will not give a rotten fig.

Whereas I am thought an enemy to the King's Majeſty's authority, I know no other authority he hath, but that which he received from his predeceſſors, who acknowledged the Pope of *Rome's* juriſdiction. If the King, *ſaith he*, will be to me as his predeceſſors were to mine, I will obey and acknowledge him

him for my King; but if he do otherwise, and play the runnagate from God, as he and you all do, I will not acknowledge him more than this old hat.

Here the Archbishop of *Glascow* interrupted his speech, desiring him to deliver his mind in a greater calm, and with more reverend speeches of his Majesty (for he uttered those things in a vehement passion, and as one transported with fury). He remembered him, that he was accused upon his life, before Judges that were authorized by his Majesty's commission: to decline the judgment, or rail against his Majesty's authority, was bootless, and in a man of his profession, being an Ecclesiastick, very scandalous. He should rather take another course, to amend what he had offended in, and recall his former answers; if they had not proceeded from a deliberate purpose, or if he were resolute to maintain them, to do it with reason, and in a moderate sort; that this were his best, either for justifying himself, and the opinions he held, or for moving the Judges, and their Lordships that were assisting, to commiserate his case. He advertised him withal to be more temperate in his speeches concerning his Majesty, otherwise he would not be licensed thus to offend.

To this *Ogilvie* made some little answer, That he would take the advertisement, and speak more coolly; howbeit, he would never acknowledge the judgment, nor think they had power to sit on his life; but said, And for the reverence I do you, to stand bare-headed before you, I let you know it is, *Ad redemptionem vexationis, & non ad agnitionem judicii.*

The Advocate here insisted, that seeing all his answers tended to decline the judgment, and that he brought no reason why the Indictment should not go to a Trial, that the Jury should be chosen and sworn at the bar, according to the custom.

The Names of the Jury.

Sir *George Elphingston*, of *Blythswood.*
Sir *Thomas Boyd*, of *Bonshaw.*
Sir *James Edmeston*, of *Duntraith*, elder.
James Muirhead, of *Lachop.*
James Roberton, of *Ernock.*
Hugh Crawfurd, of *Jordan-Hill.*
John Carschore, of that Ilk.
Hugh Kennedy, Provost of *Aire.*
William Makarrel, of *Hill-house.*
James Blaire, Bailie of *Aire.*
James Dunlop, of *Pewmalne.*
John Steward, Burgess of *Aire.*
John Dunbar, Burgess there.
James Johnston, Burgess there.
John Cunningham, of *Rawes.*

It was allowed the prisoner to challenge any of the fore-named persons, and to oppose unto their admission: who said,

He had but one exception for them all: they were either enemies to his cause, or friends: if enemies, they could not be admitted upon his Trial; and if they were his friends, they should stand prisoners at the Bar with him.

The Jury were instantly sworn and admitted.

Then was the Indictment read again in the hearing of the Jury, and the evidences shewed them for verification thereof, which of before were produced. And the prisoner being of new remembered to say what he would for himself, for the better information of the Jury, spake these things following:

I wish these Gentlemen to consider well what they do. I cannot be tried nor judged by them, and whatever I suffer here, it is by way of injury, and not of judgment. *Injuria est, non judicium.* I am not accused of treason, but have done none offence, neither will I beg mercy.

Archbishop. This is strange, you have done none offence, and yet you are come in his Majesty's Kingdom, and have laboured to pervert his Highness's Subjects; both of these are against the Laws. In this have ye not offended?

Ogilvie. I came by commandment, and if I were even now forth of the Kingdom, I should return: neither do I repent any thing, but that I have not been so busy as I should, in that which ye call perverting. I hope to come to *Glascow* again, and to do more good; and if all the hairs of mine head were Priests, they should all come into the Kingdom.

Archbishop. And do you not esteem it a fault to go against the King's commandment, especially in this point of discharging you his Kingdom? If the King have any power within his Kingdom, it seems he may rid himself and his country of those with whom he is offended, and it savours of great Rebellion to say otherwise.

Ogilvie. I am a subject as free as the King is a King, he cannot discharge me if I be not an offender, which I am not.

And being asked for what offences he might be discharged by the King? answered, in the cases of theft and murder.

Archbishop. You come not to answer any thing to the points of your Indictment. Why did you decline his Majesty's authority, and refused to shew your opinion anent the Pope, his power in deposing Kings, and loosing subjects from their oath of allegiance? And when it was asked you, if it were lawful to slay the King, being deposed, and excommunicated by the Pope, which any loyal-hearted subject will abhor to think of, why did you not simply condemn it as unlawful? For in that you do not condemn it, you shew yourself of the opinion of the rest of your sect, who in their books maintain, that it is both lawful and commendable to slay Kings, if the Pope's Commission go forth once for it.

Ogilvie. For the declining of the King's authority, I will do it still in matter of Religion; for with such matters he hath nothing to do: neither have I done any other thing, but that which the Ministers did at *Dundee*, they would not acknowledge his Majesty's authority in spiritual matters more than I: and the best Ministers of the land are still of that mind, and if they be wise, will continue so.

The Archbishop reply'd, That he was mistaken, both in the place and matter, for it was not at *Dundee*, but *Aberdeen*, where eight Ministers meeting in a general assembly, contended not against the King's authority, but that the assembly called to that place and time could not be discharged by his Majesty's Commissioner: neither should the fault of a few, take it at the worst, be esteemed the deed of the whole. These have been punished for their offence, and some of them have confessed their error, and been graciously pardoned by his Majesty. All good and

profess otherwise, and our Religion teaches us to acknowledge his Majesty our only supreme Judge in all causes. The King is Keeper of both Tables, and his place bears him not only to the ruling of his subjects in justice, and preserving equity amongst them, but even to maintain Religion and God's pure Worship, of which he should have principal care. Your Lord the Pope hath not only denied this authority to Kings, which God giveth them, but usurpeth to himself a power of deposing and killing when he is displeased; and it were the less to be regarded, if this his usurpation had gone no further than your pens: but you have entered, by this pretended right, the throats of the greatest Kings, as your practice upon the two last *Henrys* of *France* bears witness. You are not able to lay such imputation upon us, nor our profession, which teaches, that next unto God Almighty, all men are bound to fear, serve, and honour their Kings. But what answer you touching these demands? Hath the Pope power to depose the King? or is it not murder to kill him, being deposed by the Pope?

Ogilvie. I refused before to answer such questions, because in answering, I should acknowledge you Judges in Controversies of Religion, which I do not. I will not cast holy things to dogs.

Archbishop. Is it a point of faith, that the Pope may depose his Majesty? or do you think it a controversy in Religion, Whether his Majesty (whom God save) may be lawfully killed, or not?

Ogilvie. It is a question amongst the Doctors of the Church, and many hold the affirmative not improbably. A Council hath not yet determined the point: and if it shall be concluded by the Church, that the Pope hath such power, I will give my life in defence of it, and if I had a thousand lives, I would bestow them that way, if they will make an article of faith of it.

Being urged by the Court to declare his own opinion, especially in that point, whether it were murder to kill his Majesty, being deposed by the Pope?

Ogilvie. I would not say it were unlawful, tho' I should save my life by it. That if the King offended against the Catholick Church, the Pope might punish him as well as a shepherd, or the poorest fellow in the country. That in abrogating the Pope's authority, the Estates of Parliament had gone beyond their limits, and that the King, in usurping the Pope's right, had lost his own. *Nam qui rapit jus alienum, perdit jus ad suum.*

Being asked touching the oath of allegiance, Why he did condemn it? and the same being read unto him; He said, It was a damnable oath against God and his truth, and that it was treason to swear it, because it brought the King's Person and State in danger. Since this Kingdom, said he, was Christian, the Pope's supreme power was always acknowledged: this being cast off (as we see in the Act of your Parliament) against all reason and conscience, and subjects forced to swear to a matter so unlawful, what marvel that attempts and dangerous courses be taken against him. *Justissima lex est, ut quæ agit aliquis, talia patiatur.* But would the King leave off his usurping upon the Pope, he might live without fear, as well as the King of *Spain*, or any other Christian Prince. Neither Bishop, nor Minister, nor all the Bishops and Ministers in his Majesty's Kingdoms had done, nor could do the like.

The Archbishop of *Glascow* did close all to the Jury, to this effect.

Gentlemen, and others, who are named upon this assize, tho' I minded to have said nothing, but sitten here a witness of the proceeding, I have been forced by his proud and impudent speeches, somewhat to reply, and must, with your patience, say a little more. It is this same day, two-and-twenty weeks past, that this prisoner fell into mine hands; since that time he hath had leisure to think enough what course was fittest for himself to take, for satisfying his Majesty whom he had offended, neither hath he lacked counsel and advice, the best that we could give him: besides, he hath found on our part nothing but courteous dealing, and better entertainment, than, I must now say it, he hath deserved. Mine own hopes were, that he would have followed another course than I see he hath taken, and not stand to the answers which he made to those demands which were moved unto him by his Majesty's Commissioners, and you have seen: but if his answers at the first were treasonable, they are now so little bettered, as in all your hearings, he hath uttered speeches most detestable, made a commentary worse than the text was, and shewed himself to carry the mind of an arrant and desperate traitor. You perceive he obscures not his affection towards the King's Majesty, our Sovereign, in all his speeches preferring the Pope to his Majesty: and which is more intolerable, affirmeth the King's Majesty to have lost the right of his Kingdom by usurping upon the Pope. He will not say, it is unlawful to kill his Majesty, he saith, it is treason for subjects to swear the oath of allegiance, and meaneth so much in his last words, as the King's Majesty's life and estate cannot be assured, except he renders himself the Pope's vassal.

Thus hath he left you little to do, except that his Majesty's pleasure is, the ordinary form be kept with him, you should never need once to remove: all his speeches have been so stuffed with Treason, that I am sure the patience of the Noblemen, and others here present, hath been much provoked.

In all that he hath said, I can mark but two things alledged by him for the Pope's authority over Kings; the words of our Saviour to St. *Peter*, *Pasce oves meas*, Feed my sheep: and the Subjection of Kings, especially of our Kings, since the Kingdom became Christian, to the Pope. For the words of our Saviour, how little they serve his purpose, I have no need to tell you. To feed the sheep of Christ, is not, I hope, to depose Kings from their estates, nor to enflame the hearts of subjects against Princes, much less to kill and dispatch them: we are better taught than to be deceived with such glosses. Saint *Peter* made never that sense of those words, and teacheth us a far other doctrine, in his first epistle, fifth chapter, and second and third verses.

I will not spend time with such purpose; only this I must say, that whatsoever was St. *Peter's* prerogative, the Pope of *Rome* hath nothing to do with it: for he cannot be St. *Peter's* successor that hath forsaken his doctrine, and gone against his practice directly, both in that and other points of Christian faith. And for the antiquity of his usurped power, I may justly say, that Mr *Ogilvie* is not well seen in antiquity, or then speaks against his knowledge, when he saith, that this power of the Pope was ever acknowledged by Christian Kings; the Bishops of *Rome* many years made no such claim, neither did the Kings ever dream of such subjection: long it was ere the Pope of *Rome* came to the height of commanding Kings, and not till he had oppressed the Church, under the pretext of St. *Peter*'s keys, bearing down all the Bishops within Christendom; which having done, then he made his invasion upon Princes, and that by degrees. The Histories of all ages make this plain, and the resisting he found by Kings in their Kingdoms, testified that they never acknowledged his superiority. Of our own, howbeit as we lie far from his seat, so had we less business and fewer occasions of contradiction; yet I can make it seen in divers particulars, when any question fell out anent the provision of Bishops and Archbishops to their places, the Bulls of *Rome* were so little respected, as the King's predecessors have always preferred and borne out their own choice; and the interdictions made upon the Realm, by these occasions, not without some imputation of weakness to the See Apostolick, have been recalled. The superstitions of *Rome* were amongst us last embraced, and with the first, by the mercies of God, shaken off. Whatsoever you brag of your antiquity, it is false both in this and in all the points of your profession else, which I could clear, if this time or place were fitting. But to you of this Jury, I have this only more to say, you are to enquire upon the verity of the Indictment, whether such and such things as are alledged to be committed by him, have been so or not: you have his subscription, which he acknowledgeth; you hear himself, and how he hath most treasonably disavowed his Majesty's authority: it concerns you only to pronounce as you shall find verified by the speeches that you have heard, and the testimonies produced. For the rest, the Justices know sufficiently what to do, and will serve God and his Majesty, according to the commission given them.

Master *William Hay*, Advocate for his Majesty, asked Instruments upon the prisoner's treasonable speeches, uttered in the hearing of the Jury, and his ratification of the former answers made to his Majesty's Commissioners: likewise, for the further clearing of the Indictment, repeated the Acts of Parliament mentioned in the said Indictment, with the Act of Privy-Council, made anent his Majesty's supremacy and the oath of allegiance. And desired the Jury deeply to weigh and consider the perverse and devilish disposition of the party accused; to the effect they might without scruple proceed in his conviction. And according to his place, protested for wilful error, if they should acquit him of any point contained in the said Indictment.

The persons named upon the Jury, removed to the higher House, which was prepared for them; and having elected Sir *George Elphingston*, Chancellor, all in one voice found the prisoner guilty of the whole treasonable crimes contained in the Indictment.

Which being reported by the said Sir *George Elphingston*, and confirmed by the whole Jury, then returned into the Court, judgment was given by direction of the Justices,

That the said *John Ogilvie*, for the treasons by him committed, should be hanged and quartered.

The Archbishop of *Glascow* demanded, if *Ogilvie* would say any thing else?

Ogilvie answered, No, my Lord. But I give your Lordship thanks for your kindness, and will desire your hand.

The Archbishop said, If you shall acknowledge your fault done to his Majesty, and crave God and his Highness's pardon, I will give you both hand and heart; for I wish you to die a good Christian.

Then *Ogilvie* asked, If he should be licensed to speak unto the people?

The Archbishop answered, If you will declare, that you suffer according to the Law, justly for your offence, and crave his Majesty's pardon for your treasonable speeches, you shall be licensed to say what you please; otherwise you ought not to be permitted.

Then said he, God have mercy upon me! And cried aloud, If there be here any hidden Catholicks, let them pray for me; but the prayers of Hereticks I will not have.

And so the Court arose.

A true Relation of such things as passed at the Execution of John Ogilvie, *upon the last day of* February, *Anno* 1615, *being* Tuesday *in the afternoon.*

AFTER judgment was given, by the space of some three hours, he remained in the place where he was convicted, having leisure granted him to prepare himself for death. He continued a while upon his knees at prayer, with a cold devotion; and when the hour of execution approached, his hands being tied by the Executioner, his spirits were perceived much to fail him. In going towards the scaffold, the throng of people was great, and he seemed much amazed; and when he was up, Mr. *Robert Scott*, and Mr. *William Struthers*, Ministers, very gravely and christianly exhorted him to an humble acknowledgment of his offence, and if any thing troubled his mind, to disburthen his conscience. In matters of Religion, they said, they would not then enter, but prayed him to resolve and settle his mind, and seek mercy and grace from God, through Jesus Christ, in whom only salvation is to be found.

Ogilvie answered, That he was prepared and resolved. Once he said, that he died for religion; but uttered this so weakly, as scarce he was heard by them that stood by upon the scaffold. Then addressing himself to execution, he kneeled at the ladder-foot, and prayed; Mr. *Robert Scott* in that while declaring to the people that his suffering was not for any matter of Religion, but for heinous treason against his Majesty, which he prayed God to forgive him. *Ogilvie* hearing this, said, He doth me wrong. One called *John Abircrumie*, a man of little wit, replied, No matter, *John*, the more wrongs the better. This man was seen to attend him carefully, and was ever heard asking of *Ogilvie* some token before his death; for which, and other business he made with him, he was put off the scaffold.

Ogilvie ending his prayer, arose to go up the ladder, but strength and courage, to the admiration of those who had seen him before, did quite forsake him: he trembled and shaked, saying, *he would fall*, and could hardly be helped up on the top of the ladder. He kissed the Hangman, and said, *Maria, mater gratiæ, ora pro me; omnes Angeli, orate pro me; omnes Sancti Sanctæque, orate pro me*: but with so low a voice, that they which stood at the ladder-foot had some difficulty to hear him.

The Executioner willed him to commend his soul to God, pronouncing these words unto him, Say *John, Lord, have mercy on me, Lord, receive my soul*: which he did with such feebleness of voice, that scarcely he could be heard. Then was he turned off, (his left foot for a space taking hold of the ladder, as a man unwilling to die) and hung till he was dead. His quartering, according to the judgment given, was, for some respects, not used; and his body buried in a place that is kept for malefactors.

We have understood, by some persons who visited him at times during his imprisonment, that amongst other his speeches with them, he said this, That if he had escaped his apprehension at this time, and lived till *Whitsunday* next, he should have done that which all the Bishops and Ministers both in *England* and *Scotland*, should never have helped. And if he might have lived at liberty unto that time, he would willingly have been drawn in pieces with horses, and have given his body to have been tormented.

XV. Proceedings against Mr. WRAYNHAM, in the *Star-Chamber*, for Slandering the Lord-Chancellor *Bacon* of Injustice, *Pasch.* 16 *Jac.* I. 1618.

BEFORE

The Duke of *Lenox*.
The Earl of *Suffolk*, Lord-Treasurer.
The Earl of *Worcester*, Lord-Privy-Seal.
The Earl of *Pembroke*, Lord-Chamberlain,
The Earl of *Arundel*.
Viscount *Wallingford*.
Sir *Fulke Greville*, Chancellor of the *Exchequer*.
Dr. *Abbot*, Lord Archbishop of *Canterbury*.
Dr. *King*, Bishop of *London*.
Dr. *Andrews*, Bishop of *Ely*.
Sir *Edward Montague*, Lord-Chief-Justice of the *King's-Bench*.
Sir *Henry Hobart*, Lord-Chief-Justice of the *Common-Pleas*.
Sir *Laurence Tanfield*, Lord-Chief-Baron of the *Exchequer*.
Sir *Edward Coke*.
Sir *Thomas Lake*, Principal Secretary.
Sir *Henry Cary*, Comptroller.

Sir Henry Yelverton, *Attorney-General*.

May it please your Lordships,

IT is the Honour of this Court, that it represents the highest earthly Majesty, and his presence; and it is his Majesty's Honour, that as himself is clothed with Justice, so you, as the greatest and highest next his Majesty, should put on the same garment.

Clemency and Justice are the two Lights of every Kingdom, without which your persons and estates would be exposed to violence, and without which great Monarchies would be but great Thefts; and as Justice is not to be recompensed in price, so ought not the scandal hereof to go unpunished; especially, when it toucheth so great a person, as, in the sacred seat of Justice, is next to the King; the Chief Judge in this Court, and the sole Judge in Chancery, who is much defamed by the Gentleman at the Bar, in the most precious point of all his virtues, his Justice: be it spoken without offence, basely and blamelesly is my Lord-Chancellor traduced, as if he deserved that all the thunderbolts of Heaven should fall upon him.

At my Lord's first coming into this place, he found a Cause in Chancery, between this Gentleman at the Bar, and one Mr. *Fisher*, not controverted in the title, but concerning the value of the lease, which *Fisher* held of *Wraynham*; in which, the Lord-Chancellor perused the proceedings of the cause, called the parties to give a summary end to so tedious a cause; and because the success answered not the desire of this Gentleman, therefore he kicks against authority, who before was not more grieved at the expence, than now impatient at the sentence; which was not want of justice in my Lord, but of equity in the cause.

I confess I was of Counsel with Mr. *Wraynham*, and pressed his cause as far as equity would suffer; but I know that Judges look with other eyes than Counsellors do; they go not by tale, but by weight. And therefore, their Judgment must answer the Counsel, and quiet the mind of the party; and tho' in gaming losers may speak, yet in judgment they must be silent; because it is presumed that nothing is taken from them but what is none of theirs. But this Gentleman being of an unquiet Spirit, after a secret murmuring, breaks out into a complaint to his Majesty; and not staying his return out of *Scotland*, but fancying himself, as if he saw some

Cloud ariſing over my Lord, wearying and tiring his Majeſty with infinite ſupplications in this caſe. And now, my Lords, as if all his former cauſe had been loſt, he preſents it no more in parts, or looſe papers, but compiling his undigeſted thoughts into a libel, though the volume was but in quarto, faſtens it on the King on *Good-Friday* laſt.

And his moſt princely Majeſty, finding it ſtuffed up with moſt bitter reviling ſpeeches againſt ſo great and worthy a Judge, hath of himſelf commanded me this Day to ſet forth and manifeſt his fault unto your Lordſhips, that ſo he might receive deſerved puniſhment.

In this *Velvet* pamphlet (for this Book is bound in *Velvet)* is ſet forth his cauſe, the work of this day; wherein Mr. *Wraynham* ſaith, he had two decrees in the firſt Lord-Chancellor's time, both under the Great Seal, and yet both are altered ſince the laſt Lord-Chancellor's death, and cancelled by this Lord-Chancellor in a prepoſterous manner; and Firſt, *without cauſe*; Secondly, *without matter*; Thirdly, *without any legal proceeding*; Fourthly, *without precedent*; Fifthly, *upon the Party's bare ſuggeſtions*; and Sixthly, *without calling Mr.* Wraynham *to anſwer*. And of this, my Lords, ſpitefully he imagines a threefold end: Firſt, *to reward* Fiſher's *fraud and perjuries*; Secondly, *to palliate his unjuſt Proceedings, and to rack things out of joint*; and Thirdly, *to confound* Wraynham's *eſtate*: and that my Lord was therein led by the rule of his own fancy. Yet he ſtayed not here; but, as if he would ſet ſpurs againſt my Lord, he aggravates my Lord's Injuſtice to be worſe than Murder; ſaying, That in his ſentence, he hath devoured him and his whole family. And ſecondly, as if one ſin ſhould follow upon another, he doubles it upon my Lord, and, in a manner, plainly gives my Lord the lye. And hearing that my Lord had ſatisfied his Majeſty in this caſe; he ſaith in his book, that he that did it unjuſtly, muſt, to maintain it, ſpeak untruly, adding falſhood to my Lord's Injuſtice; ſaying in his Book, it is given out my Lord hath begged *Wraynham*'s pardon. which, tho' it be the ſhew of a gentle heart, yet argues a guilty conſcience, and is but my Lord's cunning to avoid the hearing of the cauſe. And as if my Lord ſhould know his own diſeaſe to be foul, and were unwilling to have it ſearched or diſcovered; he charged my Lord with ſhifts, and tells him that he hath palliated oppreſſion with greatneſs, wit and eloquence; and that the height of authority makes men preſume. And to make this yet more ſharp, he urgeth, that my Lord, to maintain this, uſeth ſecret means, whereby the unſoundneſs of his actions may not be ſeen, and ſo to avoid cenſure; and, as if my Lord ſhould have ſkill in Magick, he ſaith, that my Lord hath raiſed a report from hell of the late Maſter of the Rolls, which was confuted before his face, and damned before his death; not content to ſcandalize the living, but ſo far, my Lords, doth his malice overſpread his wiſdom, that he doth not ceaſe, with his nails, to ſcrape the dead out of their graves again. When it is well known unto your Lordſhips, that the Maſter of the Rolls was a man of great underſtanding, great pains; great experience, great dexterity, and of great integrity, yet, becauſe this cauſe fell by caſualty into his hands, by reverence from the laſt Lord-Chancellor, and he followed not this man's humour in his report; therefore he brands him with theſe aſperſions, and adds this to the reſt, That he grounded this report upon Witneſſes, that ſwore impoſſibilities, groſs abſurdities, and apparent untruths. How can you but think, my Lords, but that this Gentleman's head is full of poiſon, ſeeing it fell out ſo faſt then into his pen, trampling upon the dead? And this is an addition unto his puniſhment, the injury of him that is dead, becauſe the State yet lives, wherein his juſtice is ſcandalized.

And now, my Lords, that you may the more deteſt his ſlanders, whereby he goeth about to ſlander my Lord-Chancellor's Juſtice; give me leave to open the plain and even way, wherein this great Judge walks in this particular caſe. The queſtions in Chancery at firſt were two, between *Wraynham* and *Fiſher*, upon croſs ſuits, either againſt the other: *Wraynham* complains of truſt broken, whereby he was defrauded; *Fiſher* upon a debt of a private reckoning detained by *Wraynham*. Upon proof of both theſe, it was by aſſent ordered, That *Fiſher* ſhould aſſign the Leaſe made unto him upon truſt, and *Wraynham* ſhould pay the Money, ſo well proved to be due to *Fiſher*: ſo by aſſent was the Decree had, which is the firſt Decree.

But Mr. *Wraynham*, wiſely ſuſpecting that Mr *Fiſher* had incumbred his Leaſe. and if it ſhould be aſſigned to him according to the Decree, it would be merely illuſory; he exhibits a new bill to diſcover what charge, and in what ſort, *Fiſher* had charged the land with incumbrances. And Mr. *Wraynham* finding the incumbrances greater, upon the reference of the Lord-Chancellor to the Maſter of the Rolls, a bargain was mediated between them, that *Fiſher* ſhould hold the Leaſe in queſtion, and *Wraynham* ſhould have after the rate of twelve years purchaſe, and to this both aſſented: ſo that your Lordſhips ſee that the firſt Decree was not cancell'd by my Lord Chancellor, but diſcharged by himſelf; for by the Decree he might have had the Leaſe; but he contented himſelf with twelve years purchaſe.

After this, the queſtion grew upon the value, which being referred to the laſt Maſter of the Rolls, how the value was at firſt, before the improvement, when it was in Leaſe to one *Harply*, and there, upon proof and oath of divers Witneſſes, the Maſter of the Rolls returned and certified the conſtant produce of the Leaſe to be worth 200*l.* by the year; whereupon *Wraynham* was to have it at twelve years purchaſe, amounting to 2400*l.* Mr. *Wraynham* ſeeing the land was much improved by a defence made againſt the ſea and other means, whereby the nature of the land was altered, and the profit much raiſed, moves the Lord-Chancellor not to recede from the bargain, but ſaith, that the Value returned was not the true value, for the land was worth 400*l.* by the year, and yet excepts by retainer in his hands, 2000 Marks which he owed to *Fiſher*, one thouſand and ſixty-ſix Pounds odd Money; whereby now Mr. *Wraynham* had received his 2400*l.* in his Purſe. And when he ſaw himſelf thus fleeced, having received 2400*l.* for that which coſt but 200*l.* now he ſtirs up new ſuits, and moves the Lord-Chancellor by a commiſſion to refer the value to two Knights that had been Farmers to the land, that they might certify the true value: the one, Sir *L'Eſtrange Mordaunt*, who certifies the value 318*l.* yearly; and the other, Sir *Henry Spillman*, certified the value to be 364*l.* yearly; and my Lord-Chancellor ſtrikes between them, and makes it 340*l.* So here is a difference of values, the firſt of 200*l.* upon oath yearly, and this at 340*l.* yearly, without oath. The firſt value is at the time of *Harply*'s Leaſe, the ſecond is at the time of the commiſſion granted; and after improvement of which, your Lordſhips well know in your wiſdom, the difference between land barren, and improved in value. The laſt Lord-Chancellor, according to the amounting value of 340*l.* a year, annexed the increaſe to *Wraynham*'s bargain, and that he ſhould have it, as if the lands were worth 340*l. per ann.* So that now, the 2400*l.* in his purſe, had been worth 1680*l.* annexed above 4000*l.* Mr. *Fiſher* finding this annexed to the bargain, and that he ſhou'd be preſs'd to pay the ſurpluſage, and that he had choice either to pay the Money, or to part with the Leaſe; *Fiſher* moved the Court, that he might give up the Leaſe, and deſires his firſt 2000 Marks with damages, which *Wraynham* aſſented to, ſo that he might have defalcation of that which *Fiſher* had received of the profits of the land. Upon this, upon conſent of parties, it was again decreed (and this is the ſecond Decree, which *Wraynham* ſo much triumphs upon, not being an abſolute and poſitive Decree, but qualified with this): Firſt, that *Wraynham* ſhould pay the 2400*l.* with damages to *Fiſher*: and, ſecondly, that *Wraynham* ſhou'd have defalcation of ſuch profits as Mr. *Fiſher* had received out of the land.

Mr. *Wraynham* ſtrives with this ſecond Decree, being willing to have the value of the land, not according as *Fiſher* had received, but what he might have recovered.

Now my Lord-Chancellor finding the caſe thus ſtanding, thought it no injuſtice againſt *Wraynham*'s own offer, not that *Fiſher* ſhou'd loſe his damages, having forborn 2400*l.* ten years, nor that *Wraynham* ſhou'd be allowed more defalcation than *Fiſher* cou'd receive, becauſe he was ty'd to a dry rent; and finding that *Wraynham* was neither willing nor able to return the 2400*l.* with damages unto *Fiſher*, my Lord-Chancellor thought fit to eſtabliſh the bargain, according to the firſt certificate of the Maſter of the Rolls upon oaths, becauſe the laſt certificate without oath, was not ſo equal in the balance of Juſtice, as that with oath, certified by the Maſter of the Rolls, upon the examination of divers Witneſſes.

Now, my good Lords, if this caſe ſtands thus, what Injuſtice is there committed? What unſoundneſs is there in this action? or, what cauſe is there for my Lord-Chancellor to hide himſelf, that this Gentleman ſhou'd in this caſe declaim againſt him this day? If it were, my Lords, to make my Lord-Chancellor, for fear, to take off his hand; he will let the World know he is more conſtant and couragious in the points of juſtice, than that which he did ſo juſtly, ſo ſlightly to revoke. And if it were to this end, to make my Lord-Chancellor to diſpute with Mr. *Wraynham*; I am to let you know from his Majeſty, he will not let him forego, nor forget his place, ſo much as to enter into debate with Mr. *Wraynham*, knowing that it were not fit for him to ſtand to wreſtle or wrangle with Mr. *Wraynham*, but rather to deſpiſe ſo mean an adverſary.

My Lords, you know, that wiſe and juſt men may walk the ſame way, though not the ſame paſſage; there are divers courſes and divers ways to the ſame end, Juſtice: for Juſtice ſake, they are both to be honour'd, neither to be blamed. For, my Lords, if Judges ſhould be traduc'd as unjuſt, becauſe they differ in opinion, they ſhou'd have thankleſs offices. Juſtice is the Harmony of Heaven, but *Lingua detractionis eſt lancea triplex.* Though this Gentleman hath ſweat hard to ſcoff and dare ſo high a Judge, yet the razor of his tongue cannot charge him that any thing came between God and his own conſcience, but the merits of the cauſe; though it be certainly true, whilſt a man carries this fleſh about him, his judgments and faculties will be imperfect. Yet, my Lords, I know that my Lord is the branch of ſuch a tree, who, though he bloſſom'd laſt, yet took more ſap from the root than any of the reſt: the ſon living in the memory of ſo worthy a father, the father living in the memory of ſo virtuous a ſon, who may ſay, as *Ageſilaus* once ſaid to his father, *I obey you in judging nothing contrary to law.*

I am glad this Gentleman is ſo naked of excuſe, yet heartily ſorry his defamation is ſo foul, as to draw ſuch a ſmart of puniſhment as this will be upon him; and here if neceſſity (the true defender of man's wickedneſs) ſhould ſtep in, I anſwer, Though neceſſity break through all laws, yet flying into the face of Juſtice, it muſt be broken by Juſtice; elſe no ſubject can be ſafe, nor no Court keep itſelf from infamy.

It is well, my Lord, that this fault falls out but ſeldom; for being exorbitant when it happens, it cannot but be foul. It is a pernicious example; for by this, when ſlanders are preſented inſtead of complaints, that is but to ſet diviſions between the King and his great Magiſtrates, to diſcourage Judges, and vilify Juſtice in the ſight and mouths of all the people.

Therefore I beſeech your Lordſhips to pardon me, if I be too long, and ſuffer me to ſhew your Lordſhips what this Court, in like caſes, hath done.

In the ſecond year of his Majeſty's reign, when Sir *Edward Coke*, according to his place, informed againſt *Foorth* in this Court, *ore tenus*, for petitioning his Majeſty againſt the laſt Lord-Chancellor, for granting an injunction for ſtaying of a ſuit at the Common Law, (which your Lordſhips know how neceſſary it is) he being convicted upon his own confeſſion, received a ſharp cenſure. I will conclude with this one, and I ſhall deſire your Lordſhips, in this place, to hear it read; and then do humbly beſeech your Lordſhips to hear the Gentleman at the Bar, either for his defence, or excuſe.

Then *Wraynham*'s Examinations were read in this Book and Epiſtle.

Then he was charged with theſe words following, in the end of his Epiſtle to his Majeſty: "He that judgeth unjuſtly, muſt, to maintain it, "ſpeak untruly; and the height of authority maketh men to preſume."

Alſo, in ſhewing of his Majeſty reaſons why the Maſter of the Rolls was faulty, he ſaid, *Firſt*, the Maſter of the Rolls had omitted many of his material proofs. *Secondly*, He ſhifted off other ſome. *Thirdly*, That he ſometimes wreſted the equity of his cauſe. *Fourthly*, That he did falſely cite *Fiſher*'s proofs. *Fifthly*, That he grounded the report upon the depoſition of Witneſſes that ſwore abſurdities, untruths, and mere impoſſibilities. And, *Laſtly*, as if the report had been condemned and damned before to the pit of hell, he ſaid it was raiſed as *ab inferno*.

In his Epiſtle to his Majeſty, he is charged with theſe words:

"I underſtand my Lord-Chancellor hath begged my pardon: it is outwardly the ſhew of a great heart, but inwardly it argueth a guilty "conſcience; otherwiſe, if firſt I had been found guilty, and his Lordſhip ſhould then have interceded with his Majeſty for me, it had been an "argu-

" argument of an indulgent nature; but to beg pardon where there is no " need, was manifestly done to avoid an hearing, and not in pity towards " me; for he that despoils me of my goods, I will not trust him with my " person. And therefore, far be it from me to hope, or trust in his good- " ness: I disclaim his favour, and infinitely deplore the judgment of his " Majesty."

And in the conclusion of his Epistle were these words: " I desire to " suffer at your gates, if I shall dare to slander so great and eminent a " Judge, unto so great and wise a King.

" If he should not desire to reward the *Fishers* for their fraud and per- " juries, I know not why he should have racked all out of joint.

" My Lord, with this his last cunning and rhetorick, hath palliated his " unjust proceedings against me; for my Lord's gesture and pronuncia- " tion in his speech is wanting in my writing, out of which a cloudy " mist may rise to hide the verity of your princely Judgment.

" I could never see by what reasons or words his Lordship hath co- " loured his dealings to excuse himself unto your Majesty, understanding " only a piece, and not the whole from your Majesty. This must move " me most humbly to beseech your Majesty to save my wife and children; " and out of your princely justice to appoint a day of hearing, whereby " there shall appear unto your Majesty, as well the sincerity of my affir- " mations, as the unsoundness of his Lordship's actions. For I never " sought corners, but openly, and sometimes in my Lord's presence, have " notified and complained of my wrongs, and desire a public hearing be- " fore your Majesty, which the greatest subject dares not do without " truth and justice."

And in another place, *Wraynham* saith, " My Lord Chancellor proves " nothing by record, nor delivers any thing by writing, to answer the " things objected against him; but would hide himself from the eyes of " your Majesty's justice."

His Majesty saith, though he receive petitions from his subjects against his highest Justices; yet he will have his Judges know, that they are subject to his account only, and to none else upon earth.

His Majesty received this petition on *Good-Friday* last, in which this Gentleman hath so far exceeded the measure of an humble complaint, that I must appeal to your Lordships against him.

Then was *Foorth's* precedent read, bearing date *Mercurii decimo quarto Novembr. termino Mich. 2 Jac.* I.

And likewise *Foorth's* two last petitions against my Lord-Chancellor, touching which reference is had. And the Lords asked Mr. *Wraynham* what he could say for himself.

Mr. WRAYNHAM.

Right Honourable, and my very good Lords,

FROM a man so perplexed with so many miseries, what can be expected? and what marvel, if I should faulter, or might let fall any speech that might seem uncomely?

My Lords, I know not how to behave myself, I will not willingly offend any, but especially the King's most excellent Majesty; yet nature commands me to defend myself, for it cannot be thought he can be faithful to another, that is not so to himself. And therefore I humbly desire, that what I offer in extenuation, or defence, that neither the meanest that hear it, nor your Lordships, which are to judge of it, would take it offensively.

My Book consisteth of three parts.

First, An Epistle to his Majesty.

Secondly, The body of the book, which relateth the truth of all the proceedings.

And, *Thirdly*, a conclusive speech in the nature of an epilogue.

Touching the body of the book, and the truth of the cause, I conceive it not now called in question, for I think your Lordships will not enter into the particulars; but because it hath pleased *Mr. Attorney* to speak something of it, I will not be silent.

My accusations, *my Lords*, are set forth in two things: *First*, that the complaint is of the Right-Honourable the Lord-Chancellor. *Secondly*, That it is in bitter and unreverend terms.

For the *first*, I must fly for succour and protection unto our dread Sovereign Lord the King; for it pleased his Majesty, sitting here in the sacred Seat of Justice, to declare, that if any were wronged in point of Justice, to him they might come and have redress; and for proof thereof, I humbly desire your Lordships to hear me read a sentence or two in his Majesty's Book.

" For, *saith he*, if any were wronged, their complaint should have come " unto me; none of you but will confess you have a King of a reason- " able understanding," *&c.*

And in another place, " Why then should you spare to complain unto " me, being the high-way; therefore as you come gaping to the Law for " Justice, *&c.*"

" But if you find bribery or corruption, then come boldly; but be- " ware of the justness of your cause."

First, therefore, in his Majesty's opinion, a man may be wronged in a Court of Justice.

Secondly, In that case, his Majesty is not only willing to receive a complaint, but to reform what is amiss: so that his Majesty publishing this much to all his subjects, I hope your Lordships will not conceive that barely to complain is a fault; especially seeing that his Majesty saith, " Why do you spare to complain?"

The *second* part of my accusation is, because I have used unreverend and bitter terms.

First, I divided the collections objected against me into two parts.

(1.) Into two sentences, which *Mr. Attorney* hath endeavoured to fasten on the Lord-Chancellor by inference

(2.) Into words, applied to his Lordship

My Lords, Touching the *first*, I hope general speeches shall have no such construction.

In the 116th *Psalm*, the Prophet saith of himself, *I have said in my fury, all men are lyars.* And in the 14th *Psalm* it is said of all men, *They have all gone out of the way, and are abominable; there is none that doth good, no not one.* And in the Epistle to the *Romans*, it is said, *Let God be just, and all men lyars.* And again it is said in Scripture, *That the poison of Asps is under their lips, that their throats were open sepulchres.* And yet it was never heard, that any of the Prophets and Apostles (godly men) found fault with *David*, saying, *You have said my throat is an open sepulchre; that I am a lyar, and abominable*; because they were but general speeches. And therefore, *my Lords*, I humbly pray, that any general speeches may not be applied to my Lord-Chancellor, for I had no such meaning.

For particular words, they are, as I take it, these, Unsoundness of his Lordship's actions; unjust proceedings, oppression, and injustice.

Now, *my Lords*, I must again fly to the King for succour, in these words for his Majesty points forth the things for which a subject may complain.

For his Majesty saith in his book, " If a man be wronged in the course " of Justice." What is it but injustice?

Secondly, His Majesty saith, " That if one find bribery, corruption, " injustice, *&c.*" and then we should come boldly.

First, For the word Injustice: he that proves the justice of his cause, proves the Judgment given against it injustice: for, *my Lords*, I conceive, under your Lordships favour, that this very word contains all the rest, and that all other words that I have used are but synonimies unto this; and I used them all, yea all, I protest, to avoid tautology, and to avoid always using of the same word, Injustice.

And that also which urged me to use it, was necessity; and that twofold necessity; *First*, For that unless I particularly accused his Lordship of injustice, I was out of hope ever to obtain an hearing of his Majesty.

Secondly, My miseries inforced me unto it: And therefore it may please your Lordships to understand, that in my first petition to his Majesty, there was no such word as Injustice, or that tended near unto it: but only it did set forth what the then Master of the Rolls, this Lord, and the last Lord Chancellor had done; and desired his Majesty to judge, whether the last Lord Chancellor, or the now Lord Keeper, had most justly distributed justice: It pleased his Majesty to give answer, " That he would take some " other course, when he came near *London*."

When his Majesty came to *Theobalds*, I framed two other petitions, and delivered the one to his Majesty, and the other to Secretary *Winwood*; and in neither of these petitions was there mention of injustice, or a word favouring of it.

And when I besought his Majesty, at that time, to hear the cause, or to refer the examination, he gave me this answer: " If myself, and the " Lords should trouble themselves about hearing of Sentences, no other " business would be done by us, for every man would be ready to com- " plain."

And thus I had fallen off, but that his Majesty said further unto me, " Will you charge my Lord Chancellor with injustice or bribery?" I blanched the matter again, and desired his Majesty would be pleased to grant me an hearing of the cause.

After which, when I had meditated again of his Majesty's question, I found great coherence between this question and the words in his Majesty's book, and thereupon was bold to use the word injustice. Unto which his Majesty was pleased to answer, " These accusations are too too com- " mon: but I will have relation of the cause from my Lord himself."

After all this, understanding that the Lord Chancellor had endeavoured to answer this matter unto his Majesty, and to this end had produced the Master of the Rolls, *Phillips*, his report; which, I confess, taken by itself, may not only satisfy my Lord Chancellor, but the King himself, or any man else living: and therefore, fearing that my Lord endeavoured to satisfy the King with that report, I saw there was no other course, but to give an answer unto it, which I could not do without the book. In making whereof, something was required, both before and after, which drew me to make the Epistle and the Epilogue.

In the making whereof, I mustered together all my miseries; I saw my Land taken away, which had been before established unto me; and after six-and-forty Orders, and twelve Reports, made in the Cause; nay, after Motions, Hearings, and Rehearings, fourscore in number, I beheld all overthrown in a moment, and all overthrown without a new bill preferred. I discerned the representation of a prison gaping for me, in which I must from thenceforth spend all the days of my life without release: for in this suit I have spent almost 3000*l.* and many of my friends were engaged for me, some damnified, others undone; and with this, did accompany many eminent miseries, likely to ensue upon me, my wife, and four children, the eldest of which being but five years old; so that we, that did every day formerly give bread to others, must now beg bread of others, or else starve, which is the miserablest of all deaths: and there being no means to move his Majesty to hear the Cause, but to accuse his Lordship of injustice; this, and all these, moved me to be sharp and bitter, and to use words, though dangerous in themselves, yet I hope pardonable in such extremities.

And now I hope, if this will not acquit me, yet your Honours will be pleased to move the King for his gracious pardon: for misery made patient *Job* break out and swell against God himself; and therefore, my Lords, how much more may it make me so compleatly miserable, to swell and transgress against man!

And if, my good Lords, you should hear all the passages of the cause, I should the better conceive your Lordships will not be troubled with it; and *Mr. Attorney* hath already set it forth in that fashion, as it makes much against me: but if your Lordships will vouchsafe me that favour, I hope I shall alter, or at least extenuate your Lordships opinions in this Cause.

In the year 1606, I preferred a bill in Chancery against *Edward Fisher*, for defrauding me of a Lease of sixty years: *Fisher* forswears the trust, and preferred another bill against me for debts; both bills came to be heard before *Kinglosse*: *Fisher* offered to purchase the Lease, and the debts were referred to two Masters. These took great pains concerning the debts; after which, the Lord Chancellor referred the whole business to those two Masters of the Chancery, and then having examined both Trust and Debts, they report the Trust proved, and for the Debts, they think fit that I should give *Fisher* [illegible] Marks, whereof [illegible] Marks were for damages. *Fisher*, not satisfied, moves my Lord Chancellor to hear the Cause himself, and this was in [illegible], and my Lord, upon an hearing, decreed, with the consent of *Fisher* and his Counsel, that he should assure the Land, and I pay [illegible] Marks within six Months.

After this, my Lord having made this decree by consent, I served *Fisher* with it; but his contempt was such, that after the commissions of Rebellion, I was entered to the [illegible] to attach him, and had a Commission awarded to the Sheriff of [illegible], to put me in possession.

Fisher perceiving that the hiding of his head could not keep me from having possession of the Land, takes another course by fraudulent conveyances between him and his brother, and others; and in a motion made in the name of Sir *Thomas Challoner*, (for they lodge the fast interest in him) they inform that this conveyance was before my bill exhibited, and therefore desire I might be put out of possession; and so it was ordered, that the possession should remain then as it was.

Then I, to discover those frauds, preferred a new Bill against *Fisher* the deceiver, and three others. They in their answer set forth matter sufficient to shew the fraud. For Sir *Thomas* saith, that this conveyance from Sir *Edward* his brother, was made and sealed when he never thought of it; that 1700 *l.* was to be paid; but yet he never saw the Land, he never bargain'd or condition'd for it, but hearing the trouble of it, assured it to *Richard*, the younger son of *Fisher*, the deceiver: and so because he also was unable to go on in the purchase, he lodged it in the hands of Sir *Thomas Challoner*.

Hobart, Attorney, informs my Lord Chancellor of these frauds; my Lord gave them a day, to shew cause why I should not have the Land till they could make better proofs. Then those witnesses, which were both *Fisher*'s men, were examined by my Lord Chancellor in open Court, and one of them swears that the conveyance, which must defeat the Decree, was sealed in the Hall; the other swears it was done in the Parlour; one, that it was read; the other, that it was not read: the one, that it was signed; the other, that it was not signed: one swears, that Sir *Edward Fisher* was present; the other, not present; and both, that it was done at such a time, when the Deed bears date twelve months after.

Then what remains after all this, but that I should have a confirmation of the old decree, or else a new? But I find it true, *Nemo læditur nisi à seipso*. For then the Lord Chancellor made a motion, that *Fisher* should buy the Land; against which, I not gainsaying, his Lordship referred the Mediation of the bargain to the Master of the Rolls, where it appeared, that Sir *Edward Fisher* had made a Lease of half the land for 200 *l.* the year; and therefore it was agreed, that *Fisher* should give 2400 *l.* out of the which, he was to deduct 2000 Marks for his Debts, due by the first Decree, and the residue about 1066 *l.* I received, because it did not appear what the Lands were worth. A Commission was awarded out to Sir *L'Estrange Mordaunt* and three others, to find out the true value of the land, and a bargain was not commanded, but propounded by the Court: And I beseech your Lordships to observe, that the Master of the Rolls being to consider of all the Examinations, lawfully taken in the Cause, nine Witnesses were taken by the Commission and duly examined; five Witnesses more were examined in the Examiner's Office, without my privity or consent, and contrary to an Order in Court: which Witnesses being examined, swore point-blank in all things; and according to those proofs, the Master of the Rolls made his Certificate, and found 200 *l.* a-year to be as much as the lands were worth.

Hereupon the Lord Chancellor gave a day to shew cause, why the cause should not be decreed, which was the Order, *quarto Maij*, 1610.

After this, the Lord *Hobart*, then Attorney, in the presence of the Master of the Rolls himself, did set down the defects of his own Report.

Lord-Treasurer. My Lords, this is contrary to all course, this must not be; for we mean not to enter into the merits of the cause.

Mr. At. *Yelverton.* Mr. *Wraynham*, for you to shift it off, doth but aggravate your offence; for when you say, you used the rest of your phrases as *synonymies* to Injustice, that implieth a taxation of his Lordship in point of justice; and so likewise do your words imply, when you say, by the greatness of his wit and eloquence, he doth palliate the injustice of the Cause: therefore tax my Lord particularly with one point of injustice.

Here Mr. *Wraynham* would not instance in any one particular.

Wrayn. Had I thought his Majesty would not have heard my cause, I would have sat down in silence, and have devoured my sorrow. I have formerly set down to your Lordships, that my Decree was reversed without a bill.

Mr. Att. That is, when the bill is absolute and constant, for there it must have a bill of revivor; but when it depends upon subsequent acts, and is qualified and conditional, there it may be reversed without bill.

Wrayn. I humbly submit myself in all things to your honourable and clement censure: for the manner, I beseech your Lordships pardon; and for the matter, I humbly crave compassion.

Mr. Serj. *Crew.* May it please your Lordships, the Prisoner at the Bar hath made a good submission at the last, I would he had begun with it.

My Lords, the Flux of foul mouths must be stopp'd, otherwise the greatest Magistrates will be traduced and slandered to Majesty himself; and though it be not Treason, yet I have heard it from a great and honourable Person sitting in this place, that it is *Crimen læsæ Majestatis*.

My Lords, for the two Lords, the one that lives, the other that is dead, and their demeanor in this case, in honour of him that is dead, and without flattery to him that is alive; I say, they both judged according to their consciences.

The Lord Chancellor that is dead, gave his judgment according to his conscience, and not according to the conscience of another man, but according to the integrity of his own heart: for Judges are to judge *secundum æquum & bonum in foro conscientiæ*. And this Lord also judged out of his noble conscience and integrity of his heart; for, my Lords, there was no binding decree.

As for the merits of the cause, it must not be examined of the one side, nor of the other, for both Lords have done according to conscience, *coram Deo & hominibus*. And each hath delivered his own sense according to their consciences.

The Lord which is dead, when he was alive, was one of the oracles of the wisdom of the time; and my living Lord attributes very much unto him, whom God hath also inriched with great ornaments of nature; for no Man, no Magistrate, hears with more attention, nor no Magistrate of Justice attends with more understanding and patience.

You then, Mr. *Wraynham*, thus to traduce my Lord, is a foul offence, with that black mouth of yours: you cannot traduce him of corruption, for, thanks be to God, he hath always despised riches, and set honour and justice before his eyes; and where the Magistrate is bribed, it is a sign of a corrupted estate.

For the justice of the Cause;

My Lords, I was of Counsel with *Fisher*, and I knew the merits of the cause; for my Lord Chancellor seeing what recompence *Fisher* ought in justice to have received, and finding a disability in *Wraynham* to perform it, was inforced to take the land from *Wraynham* to give it to *Fisher*, which is hardly of value to satisfy *Fisher*'s true debt and damages. And this, my Lords, was the true course of it; so it stands upon these parts your Lordships have heard.

I am glad at last, to hear Mr. *Wraynham*'s submission, and do humbly crave your Lordship's censure.

Sir *Edward Coke.* The cause before you, my Lords, is a very great cause, for a man must tread in this course upon a very slender bridge: I will single out, as near as I can, the state of the question, and then I will shew you in others, upon what words, and in what I shall ground my sentence: for a complaint to the King's Majesty, or a petition by any man that thinks himself wrong'd, I hold that regularly to be no offence. God forbid it should be so: I can make no hedge between the Sovereign and the Subject; nay, in some Kingdoms, *Querelas subditorum detrahere in principe deserentur capitale est:* And that would be derogation from a Monarch, that no subject should complain unto him; yet upon the Statute of *Westminster*, and at Common Law, I make no question but to shew you, that where petitions were made to the King in an unfit manner, they have been severely punished. Our case is now particularly in a sentence given by my Lord Chancellor, an eminent Judge in this Court, and a sole Judge in the highest Court of Equity that is in this Kingdom; yea, this case is after sentence, and against the sentence, and with many such scandalous and opprobrious terms against so high a Judge; and that not in paper, but in a book presented to the King; this book in my hand, which the King hath delivered to the Attorney General, that it might come before us for due punishment. Whether this book be justifiable, or no, that is the question.

It is a black book, *Est jam conveniens luctibus iste color*. And it is a strange book for some things that I will shew you, for it is no petition; and yet I will confirm every word I say by ancient and modern authorities; whereof, I am sorry, very sorry in good faith, for the excellent and worthy parts that are in you, Mr. *Wraynham*. Now mark your own words in your book; you call it a Review, or Revivor of the Report of the Master of the Rolls, *Phillips*, and the Decree of my Lord Chancellor: the High Commissioners have sometimes a Commission of Review, but it is very rare; and that is a Commission of Grace, not of Right: such a Review is presented unto his Majesty by *Wraynham*, in which he deals not like a petitioner, but like a censurer, censuring every man that deals in the cause.

Mark how the Common Law sets forth a Petitioner: It gives no ill words, it toucheth not men of injustice; for take this from me, that what grief soever a man hath, ill words work no good; and learned Counsel never use them.

And therefore the petitioner at the Common-Law, is, *Si placet majestati*, &c. & *quod justitia & rectum fiat*, &c. Now in your petition, see whether you have behaved yourself well: First, you make your major proposition; The unjust sentence of a Judge, is far worse than a particular murder: then your minor is, That my Lord-Chancellor hath satisfied his Majesty, that I have informed him falsely; but his Majesty knoweth, that he that judgeth unjustly, must, to maintain it, speak untruly; and that your Lordships and all Logicians know, the conclusion followeth necessarily.

First, he chargeth my Lord Chancellor with injustice, not complaining of any particular to be referred to examination; but saith in general, "He hath done unjustly, and is worse than a murderer; and that he hath "informed the King falsely."

My Lords, You know, if a man put false metal into the King's Coin, it is Treason; and if my Lord Chancellor shall infuse poison and false information into the King's ear, it was an heinous offence. Yet this contents not *Wraynham*; but he flieth at all, saying, "That the height of authority maketh Men presume." And hath a place of Scripture in his Book, *Woe be to them that write wicked Decrees:* and in another place he saith, "Oppression is palliated with wit and eloquence."

My Lords, ought these things to be in a petitioner? A petitioner must go meekly and humbly to work, without shew of touch of any man.

I will not omit a dead man; for, tho' spoken of him, it is a living fault.

As for this Master of the Rolls, never man in *England* was more excellent for the Chancery than that man; and for aught I heard, (that had reason to hear something of him) I never heard him taxed of corruption, being a man of excellent dexterity, diligent, early in the morning, ready to do justice: for him to be taxed in such a high degree, as to omit some of the material proofs, to shift off others, to wrest the equity of the cause, and such-like: and in another place, "That the Master of the Rolls made "an unjust and corrupt gloss upon a false text, &c." And in another place, he saith, "That Sir *Edward Phillips*'s report was raised *ab inferno*."

My Lords, You know that the slander of a dead man is punishable in this Court, as *Lewis Pickering* is able to tell you, whom I caused here to be censured for a slander against an Archbishop that is dead; for Justice lives, though the party be dead: and such slanders do wrong the living posterity and alliance of the man deceased.

But Mr. *Wraynham* spares not the King himself; for in one place of his Book he saith, *assurgat Rex*, &c. as if the King slept. And in another place he saith, "That the Decree is reversed without precedent." But that is not so, as I will satisfy you anon.

For Mr. *Wraynham*'s censure, I will never judge a man without authority and reason. 18 *E.* I. *in Rotulo Parliament.* 3. my Lord-Abbot there complained that *Solomon* of *Wragg*, and *Hugh Courtney* then *Chief-Justice*, had confederated to give Judgment against the Abbot. And the King answered, "Shall we, upon this petition, call a judgment in question?" And in the end, the answer is, *Rex rogabit, & aliter facere non potest per legem terræ*. And my Lord-Abbot, because he was a Lord, escaped punishment at that time.

Another precedent I will shew you, is, *Mich.* 18 *E.* III. *Rot.* 151. *coram Rege. Thomas Wilbraham* petitioned against the Justices of the King's-Bench, "That they had not done according to law and reason." And the petition was delivered to the representative body of the King and his Council; for

for the which the said *Wilbraham* was indicted, convicted, fined, and ransomed in the King's Bench.

19 *Ass. p.* 3. Between Sir *William Scott* and *Humphrey Hunney*, who complained to King *Edw.* III. "That Sir *William Scott*, Chief-Justice, had "awarded an assize contrary to law." And the King sent it to the Judges; whereupon *Hunney* was imprisoned, judged, fined, and ransomed: yet he had no remedy but in Parliament.

The Statute hath made a sharp law against such as speak scandalous news of the Chancellor, Justice of the King's-Bench, &c. And because divers were punished for slanders, in petitions to his Majesty; therefore, 13 *R.* II. *Rot. Parl. numb.* 45. the Commons desired they might not be troubled for any matter that should be contained in petitions to the King: and the King answered, "Let every man complain, so it be with law and reason."

Wraynham objected a place of Scripture for himself, where the Psalmist saith, *I have said in my fury, that all men are lyars.* The text is, *Dixi in excessu*: so *Wraynham* saith, "It was not in his fury, but in his excess."

And another thing that *Wraynham* offered in his defence, was the King's words, where he saith, in his Book, *Be bold to complain.* But of what? Of corruption? So likewise in *Rot. Parl.* 24 *Edw.* III. *Parl.* 3. *numb.* 16. *If any man mix corruption with his censures, Anathema sit.* So likewise it is extant in the Rolls of the Parliament *de la plbe*, that the great *de la Pole* was convicted of bribery, and put from his place; and Cardinal *Wolsey* was convicted of a foul corruption.

But if a man, according to sincerity, give judgment, though he differ from another Judge, this is no injustice. Famous *Dyer* gave judgment in the Common-Pleas, and this was reversed in the King's-Bench; yet he discharged his conscience: and altho' it was afterwards reversed, yet it was no Injustice. The like instance might be made of Sir *Christopher Wray*, and others. Now, in this case, my Lord-Chancellor that is living, differs from the Lord-Chancellor that is dead. This is not strange, it hath ever been, and ever will be; but if a Judge's conscience be oiled and moisten'd with corruption, then all is naught.

The King hath the Pleas of the Crown, and upon every Judgment one of the parties is angry and displeased: But this must not presently produce a new hearing, for that will hinder all other businesses. For I will put you a great case between a Nobleman here, and divers other Noblemen that were trusted by the Countess of *Southampton*, who were all Plaintiffs, and Sir *Moyle Finch* Defendant: and this was *Mich.* 42 & 43 *Eliz.* The main point that was controverted in the cause, was upon an exception of a Manor (as I remember) in the *Habendum* of the deed, which my Lord-Chancellor then thought void. And therefore decreed, "That my Lady "of *Southampton* should have all." Whereupon Sir *Moyle Finch* petitioned Queen *Elizabeth*, that she should refer the examination of the Decree to some of the Judges; but the Queen would never refer any thing to those that were named unto her, but she referred it to two other Judges not named in the petition, who attended my Lord-Chancellor; and they then resolved it against the Decree, and my Lord reversed his own Decree.

I know I have held your Lordships long; yet I cannot tell, in these critical days, whether men will be satisfied, which hath made me longer than I would have been. Therefore, to conclude, I agree, in all things, with the sentence given in *Foorth*'s case of 2 *Jac.*

Sir *Fulke Grevill*, Chancellor of the Exchequer. This Court hath no intent to discourage the meanest subject of his lawful appeal unto his Prince; for that were to disinherit the people of law, and the King of the intelligence of the oppression that might fall upon his people.

But this case I suppose not to be within the first. The matter in such cases, is but a review of an inferior sentence of a superior Magistate, my Lord-Chancellor of *England*! and that before he be heard, making the King his speedy executioner.

But examine the nature of these accusations, and you shall find them mere scandals, and impossibilities; as breaking Decrees, rewarding frauds and perjuries, palliating oppressions with greatness, wit, and eloquence.

Why, *my Lords*, if this liberty should spread, then I desire the indifferent hearers to see in what a miserable case the subject stands, when the right of every good man shall stand in the malignity, and unquiet nature of every turbulent spirit? And, my Lords the Judges, in what a case stand they, if by such clamours every delinquent shall be made Judge over them? and what privilege shall the King my Master have? For if this humour should take a little head, will it not carry both him and Justice into the field? And therefore I conclude, that this is severely to be punished; and is not a petition, but a presumptuous challenge, and of so far a worse nature beyond duels, as honour and universal Justice is beyond particular right: And therefore I agree with him that went before me, leaving his good parts to mercy, and his ill parts to the censure of *Foorth*'s case.

Lord Chief-Baron, Sir *Laurence Tanfield.* This cause is a cause of a high nature, being a scandal of a great and principal Officer of the Kingdom, and of one that is an high and eminent person: which scandal is set forth in this Book, which certainly I cannot call a petition; for the petitioner hath presumed too far, that it is a plain revise of a Decree. Every man knoweth, that the Chancellor hath the keeping of the Great-Seal, whereby is managed Mercy and Justice: and if this great person so trusted shall be thus traduced by every offender, how insufferable will this mischief be?

I doubt not but that by a right way, you may, by a petition in an humble course, and submissive manner, desire his Majesty that he would be pleased to review a sentence in Chancery, or else grant a commission to others to review the same. But doth this man observe this course? No, but he will be his own Judge, sentencing his own cause. I can call this Book no better, than a scandalous and malicious Invective against the Lord-Chancellor; and that not without great bitterness, as I have heard.

First, he taxeth him with injustice: then mark the circumstances; he saith, "My Lord-Chancellor hath reversed the Decree, without cause, "without new matter, without legal proceeding, without precedent, and "upon a bare suggestion."

Then he goeth further, saying, "Injustice is worse than murder; for "this Decree hath devoured him and his whole family."

And, not content with this, chargeth him with oppression, and palliating it with greatness, wit, and eloquence; than which, a greater and heavier scandal cannot be!

You shall not be barred of access to his Majesty, but that by a petition you may desire to have a Decree reviewed, and that his Majesty would grant a commission to review it. But these things must be done legally, and then the law protects us, tho' it be against a Nobleman. Sir *Richard Crofts* did sue an action for forgery of false deeds against the Lord *Beauchamp*; whereupon my Lord *Beauchamp* sued an action upon the Statute *de Scand. Magnat.* But that would bear no action, because it was done legally: for a man may suppose in his Writ such a fact, by the use of the said Writ; but he must beware that he prove it well, or else he shall be well fined in the same Court. But much more shall he deserve a fine, if he shall do it without Writ, or without ground or proof, as *Wraynham* hath done.

And therefore, because I must be short, I think him fully worthy of the censure before given, in all points.

Lord *Hobart*, Chief-Justice of the Common-Pleas. *Mr. Attorney* hath very worthily and like himself, according to his place, brought this man into this Court, to give answer for the greatest and most outrageous offence that of this kind hath been committed; in which case, I will first tell you, what I do not question, and then what I do question.

For the first, Petitions may be exhibited to the King without controversy; nay, in some cases they must be exhibited; and God forbid, that any man's way should be lock'd up, or that any Subject should be barred of access to his Majesty; for when appeals fail, and when ordinary remedy is wanting, so that there is no Judge above the highest Judge; yet, you may still resort unto your Sovereign for extreme remedy: this is proper to a King, *Cessas regnare, si cessas judicare*; for it is an inherent quality to his Crown. So that without controversy a man may petition against a sentence; for God forbid, that we that are Judges, should draw that privilege to ourselves, to give sentence, and not to hear it examin'd. But it is true, it must be presented as a supplication, and you must go formally to work: ordinarily you must go to the proper Courts of Justice; if that fails, the extraordinary course is open by the King: and this is no more than to shew to his Majesty, how you find yourself grieved, and then remit the cause and form to the King's wisdom.

But now see what this man hath done, he hath made neither the matter nor form of a petition.

First, for matter, he pretends, that is not saying that my Lord-Chancellor hath expresly infringed two Decrees, when he hath done nothing, only crossed an order, than which, there is nothing more common, for they are but interlocutory, and not definitive.

And for form, this is no Petition, no book, as he wou'd call it, but an express, peremptory and audacious libel. Then the manner offends yet more: for whereas a supplication imports, that a man shou'd speak it upon his knees, for as it is in some Realms, men attempt nothing against law, but they must do it with a rope about their necks: so that he that goeth about to attempt any thing against a Decree, he doth it with a rope of the King's censure about his neck: but mark the carriage of this man, how insolently he proceeds in this case!

First, for the King, as hath been well observed, he saith, *assurgat Rex*; as if he shou'd bid the King arise and take revenge.

Therefore for the Decree, he saith, that the foundation of it came from hell; if that be so, then this sentence must needs be hellish, when he falls upon a poor man, the Master of the Rolls: I call him poor man, because he is not living to answer for himself, but yet he was a worthy Minister of Justice, (for I had much cause to know him) and he was of as much dexterity and integrity, as ever man that sat in his place, and I believe the Chancery will find want of such a man. But not content with this, he scorns my Lord-Chancellor's courtesies, and carries himself, as if he wou'd trample all under foot.

So much for the manner: as for the matter, it is odious; the person with whom he hath to do, is the principal Officer and Magistrate of Justice in the Kingdom, one that hath the nomination of all the Justices of Peace, and the Principal that names all the Sheriffs; one that keeps and carries the Seal, and sits chief Judge in this Court, and sole Judge in the Chancery.

And shall we think that this man is bought and sold to Corruption, to Injustice, to Murder? What more tends to the King's dishonour, than that he shou'd place in the Judicature such an unworthy man? a man infinitely the more wrong'd, because he deserves his place, as well as any man that went before him; and yet his last Predecessor was very excellent, and deserved no small commendations. But *Wraynham* I condemn, as a man barbarous both toward the living and the dead; wherefore, there is a justice and tribute due to the Master of the Rolls deceased. I wou'd have mention made of it in the Decree, and with that addition to the sentence, I concur in all things with the President of the Court.

Sir *Edward Mountague*, Lord Chief-Justice. My Lords, it is a true saying, *Judicium non redditur nisi in invitum.* For I yet never saw any man sit down satisfied with a sentence that went against him.

I wou'd not so far have blamed *Wraynham* as to have censur'd him for complaining to the King; yet this restraint I find in law, which any man may see in King *Edgar*'s laws. "Let no man complain to the King in mat-"ters of variance, except he cannot have right at home, or that right be too "heavy for him. Then let him complain to the King." Whereby it is meant, that if the laws be so strict, he shall complain in a Court of Equity to the King himself. Then, to complain is not deny'd to any man, for all Justice comes from the King, and though he distribute his Justice to be ministered in several Courts, yet the primitive power resides still in his person. Therefore, to the Justice of his Majesty may any subject have resort; but this must be humbly as a Petitioner, not as Mr. *Wraynham* hath done here, who is not a suitor, but a censurer, and doth not complain, but proudly rails upon a high Judge.

Can you, Mr. *Wraynham*, charge your Judge with corruption, through fear or affection? (for I make them both alike.) Spare not the chief Judge nor highest Counsellor; I say, spare us not, wherever you can take us. But a judgment is pronounced from the sincerity of our consciences, and warranted

ranted by our judgment and learning: shall we then undergo the censure of every suitor? No State, at no time, ever suffered this.

My Lords, it lies upon us Judges as a duty, to restrain this boldness; our places as Judges, give us no privilege to do what we list, nor have suitors liberty to speak as they list of Judges: God, and Order, hath set bounds to both.

For the matter heretofore handled in the Chancery, it is not a work of this day to deal with that; we meddle not with your Decrees, we censure you only for your scandals. I saw in your Book a smooth Pen, and from your Tongue I have heard fair speeches; but in both I see a fiery spirit.

For you would raise up dissention between the two Lord-Keepers of the King's conscience, him that now is, and him that was, and now is with God: of these two Worthies I shall not say much; I will neither wrong the dead, nor flatter the living. The matter of difference, for any thing I can see, or you can say, is but an order against an order, wherein judgment may be varied by occasions, and through circumstances; true attributes are no flatteries.

This honour let me give to these two great men; of greater parts, better fitted for that place, never sat in this place: nay, a man may truly say, that the World hath scarce yielded two such men of so excellent gifts, in this latter age of the World.

But you, Mr. *Wraynham*, wronged both the living and the dead. Of the Master of the Rolls, that is dead, you spake your pleasure: but all that hear you, and know him, will be ready to give you the lye. You say that he should omit some of the proofs, and wrest other-some, and ground himself upon Witnesses that swore impossibilities, and absurdities, *&c.* Whoever knew that man, knows him to be a true Reporter, and a judicious Collector upon proofs, as ever was. I will not dissemble what others thought a fault in him, to be over-swift in judging: but this was the error of his greater experience, and riper judgment, than others had.

Now, for my Lord-Chancellor, by the words you use, you lay *four* of the greatest Crimes upon him, that can be laid upon a Judge: *Presumption, Oppression, Falsity,* and *Injustice*: all these you utter, with one breath, charging him with all in one sentence: for you say, "Height "of Authority makes great men presume." there is presumption and oppression. And in these words, "He that judges unjustly, must, to main-"tain it, speak untruly:" there you accuse him of falsity and injustice.

Ex ore tuo te judico, serve nequam. For in your book you say, "Let me "suffer as a Traitor, if all that I say prove not an entire truth, if I "should dare to slander so great a Judge to so wise a King." Therefore, out of your own mouth I pronounce sentence against you, *læsæ Majestatis*: and tho' not as a Traitor, yet as a great scandalizer. And if all were true that is said in your book, yet would I censure you for your quarrel with my Lord-Chancellor for form; and yet yourself use no form, no, not common civility. So that if it were against a common man, it were punishable, to offer such words to the eye of a King, as here you give to my Lord-Chancellor, calling him a rewarder of frauds and perjuries, an afflicter of the afflicted, a racker of things out of joint, a confounder of your estate, and the like.

These are not words fitting a Petitioner, to be spoken of a Lord-Chancellor, to be offered to a King.

And, *my Lords*, this man's fault goeth one step higher, touching the the Person of Majesty itself. I am a Judge of Crown-matters; and in this Libel, I think he hath scandalized the King in four things:

First, he saith, "The King is but a man, and so may err;" implying an error in the King.

Secondly, "That my Lord-Chancellor defends himself by secret "means, and that you are not called to answer." Than which, what greater tax unto so high a Majesty, to condemn and not to hear!

Thirdly, "That my Lord-Chancellor doth cover his injustice with "wit and eloquence." When we all know, that we have a Sovereign of those high and excellent gifts, that it is not rhetorick, or eloquence, that can cast dust in the King's eyes, or cause him any ways to turn aside from justice.

Lastly, you say, "That a man may distaste truth, and suspect judgment;" applying it unto his Majesty. Which offences reaching so high, my censure shall be the heavier upon you.

Now it will rest, what shall be done with this man? As I give my sentence from his own mouth, so I will take advice from himself; he saith, *State super viis antiquis*, Look what our ancestors have done of old, so let us do. In this then, you shall see what they did in like cases.

Mich. 13. of the Queen, *Rot.* 39. *Henry Blaunsford*, a Counsellor at Law, was committed to the *Fleet*, and fined for false reporting the opinion of the Lord *Leicester*, and Secretary *Cecil*, with these words, *Humanum est errare.*

So likewise, 19 *Hen.* VIII. my Lord *Stourton* was committed by the Court, and fined, for saying these words, "I am sorry to see Rhetorick "rule where Law should."

Sir *Rowland Flaxing* was committed, and fined, for reporting to the King, "That he could have no indifferency before the Lords of the Council:" For which he was deeply fined, 7 *Feb.* 18 *H.* VIII.

So likewise, in the time of *Hen.* VII. Sir *Richard Terres* was committed, fined, sent to the Pillory, and adjudged to lose both his ears for his slanderous complaint exhibited to the King in a written Book; and that against the Chief-Justice *Fitz-James*. the punishment of him that depraved the good Judge Sir *James Dyer*, is fresh in memory.

So that party which said Judge *Catlyne* was an unjust Judge, 8 *Eliz. Rot.* 10. whose name was *Thomas Welch*, of *London*, who was indicted in the King's-Bench for this, as for an offence against the Common-Law. His words that were delivered, were these: "My Lord-Chief-Justice "*Catlyne* is incensed against me, I cannot have Justice, nor can be "heard; for that Court now is made a Court of Conscience." This Indictment was found, and the record was, that it was *in magnum contempt. Dominæ Reginæ ac cur' suæ, ac in magn' scandalum, ac ignominiam leg. Angliæ, ac in scandalum capitalis Just. ac in malum exemplum omnium subditorum.*

So it is that this offence of *Wraynham's* is against the Law, the Commonwealth, and the Justice of the Kingdom; and therefore, according to [illegible] judgment in law, and with the sentence that was pronounced [illegible], I concur and pronounce the same against *Wraynham* in all things. And this right I would have done to the Lord-Chancellor living, the Lord-Chancellor and Master of the Rolls that are dead, that those things be fitly expressed to their honours, in the drawing up of the decree.

Sir *Thomas Lake*, Principal Secretary. *My Lords*, If I had been the first that had spoken in this case, I should have thought it the greatest difficulty how to walk evenly between the not discouraging the King's subjects, and in judging the prisoner at the bar.

But for that, my Lords before me have so well spoken, that no man may be discouraged to come to his Majesty in a discreet manner. And very good learning hath been delivered by all my Lords the Judges, such as may satisfy every man, yea, and not satisfy only, but direct them what to do in such cases: therefore I may be the shorter.

I will not be long in speaking of the honour due unto Magistrates; he that wades into that, shall have little of his own invention, nor of the offence that is now before us, for the King's Counsel hath so fully and perfectly delivered it, that perhaps by this time, he knows his own error. And my Lords the Judges have made it appear so, whereby I think it as great an offence, as ever was in this nature, and much more deserveth punishment, because it is against a man no less eminent in virtue, than in place.

Three things the Prisoner urgeth for himself.

First, for the word Injustice, he saith, "That admitting the thing "were unjust, then he might call it unjust."

But I answer, for a private man to call a publick sentence, Injustice, herein he sheweth his error.

Secondly, He urgeth, that it causeth a great loss unto him, and therefore he would be the rather excused.

It is true, I think, that man, by sentence, have loss, for *Judicium redditur in invitum*, but tho' it be a loss, it is *Damnum absque injuria.*

Thirdly, He went the wiser way, when he urgeth commiseration unto us. For my own part, I could commiserate the man, but I commiserate the Commonwealth much more; for if this should be suffered, tumults, and a multitude of other inconveniencies would arise. And therefore I judge him as the rest have done before me.

Sir *Henry Cary*, Comptroller. My Lords, before me have spoken so much, that I shall not need to speak, neither do I make any scruple of the said sentence.

When I consider how foully this man hath behaved himself, in Scandal and Invectives against so high a Magistrate, I must concur with the rest of the Lords that have gone before me.

Bishop of *Ely*, Dr. *Launcelot Andrews*. Tho' the ground of the complaint had been just, yet I believe my Lords the Judges, that the complaint being in so foul a manner, against so great a person, in so high a place, deserves sharp punishment: and therefore I agree with the former sentence.

Bishop of *London*, Dr. *John King*. I shall borrow a phrase of him, tho' spoke to another purpose: "That in a Senate, where many assistants "were, after two or three have well spoken, and well agitated a cause, "there is required nothing of the rest, but their assent."

It is a worthy saying, but when I find here before me an honourable person foully and despightfully spoke against, being one of the three vital parts of this Court, and without which it cannot have its subsistence; and of the three vital parts, the Principal, and also a Judge of another Court; and (as I learned of my Lords the Judges) of such a temporal Court, where if the edge of the law be too keen, the equity of the Chancery doth abate it:

In regard of this duty, it becometh me to speak, and because the party wrong'd is a great Counsellor and Officer of the State:

The first thing I say and lay hold of, is this, *interest reipublicæ*, it stands not with the honour of the King, with the safety and peace of the Kingdom, nor with the quiet of his Majesty, that Counsellors of State, and Judges in the Seat of Justice and Conscience, should be depraved, *anima & vita regnorum authoritas*, take it away from the Magistrate of State, take it away from the King himself, *& subversa jacet pristina sedes soliorum.*

For the place wherein this honourable person sits, is great between blood and blood, plea and plea, plague and plague, for the Judge shall end the controversy.

So that the first lesson which I shall make, is that which *Cambyses* made to another, *memento ex quo loco*, they sit in God's seat, and execute his, and not their own judgments: It is their art, their faculty, their profession, their learning to judge, and it is not open to every man, but it is *peregrina & unusquisque in arte sua artifex*; and therefore, for mine own part, I shall ever bend the best of my thoughts, the favourablest of my wishes, and the most of my prayers, that sitting in seats as they do, they may judge as they ought.

I know, that while they carry flesh about 'em, their faculties and judgments will be unperfect; they are but men, *& sic unusquisque insipiens*: so that I know not (amongst the number of mortal Wights) that man that can conceive every particularity of the law.

No marvel then, if one Judge differ from another, when the same man differs from himself; *Socrates puer differt a Socrate sene.* And though the Judges walk not in the same way, they tend to the same end; and tho' there be not *idem cursus*, yet there is the same, *idem portus*, *& non mutant, sed aptant legem*, according as the matter comes before them is varied, shaped, and fashioned.

It is unreasonable then to complain of a Judge, or unusual to go to the King with complaints; nay, it must be done with *calamo & atramento temperato*; and it must be done, *libello supp'sci, non famoso*, not as a sycophant and slanderer, but as a supplicant with a petition, not with a petulant invective declaration against a person of so great and honourable a place. This is a fact so unnatural, and unlawful, that all laws are broke both of God and Nations, and civility, and good manners, and all; nay, I know not how the laws of speech are kept, they are but three, *quid, de quo, cui*; the matter foul, spoken of so honourable a person, and to so transcendent a Magistrate.

Wraynham is a man, that did not only vent the bitterness of his soul, but [illegible] comes *virga* [illegible], God gives not blessing to their [illegible] and porcupine quills he shoots out, it enters deep, it wounds [illegible], it is not to be tolerated:

Let him keep his prison in [illegible] Book.

Wherein

Wherein, let me add for my last, the manner of presenting it, the writing itself; and then withal the defence now made, which, when I heard it, I was more offended than with the Book itself; and I may justly make a question, whether he were more foolish in writing it, or more vain in defending it?

His defence is a two-fold necessity: first, a necessity to induce the King to hear him; like *Absalom*, that would needs set *Tobias*'s fields on fire, to get his ear.

The other, a necessity of Estate, proceeding out of the Laws of necessity; *Gravissimi sunt morsus irritatæ necessitatis*. One part of speech was general; in that he meant not my Lord-Chancellor: but in the general there is a major, and in the particular there is the application, and then every man can make the conclusion, as hath been well observed by Sir *Edward Coke*.

You are a man of a private and profane spirit, and if you know not of what spirit you are, I can teach you; I say, of that spirit, that you compare yourself with Apostles and Prophets, and you misapply Scripture; your *dixi in excessu & trepidatione*, sheweth a difference between sinning upon passion, and deliberation. It comes fully home into your own bosom, & *pulchrum patet guttur in ore*.

The best part of this answer, was the last, and I wou'd it had been all in all; and so I agree with the sentence given before me.

Viscount *Wallingford*. I am sorry a man shou'd deserve so great a censure as this man's foul fault will make; yet I am very glad in this bold and quick-sighted age, that other men, by his example, may take heed not to exceed the bounds of modesty.

This humour, it seemeth self-love (which believes nothing but itself) hath begot that, that hath bred this Gentleman up so unmannerly, that he spares not to accuse the highest and greatest Judge of the Kingdom, of Oppression, Injustice, Murder, nay, of any thing; which is not only spoken by so ill a tongue, but aggravated by his answer.

For it seems, he wou'd encourage other men by the King's Book to do the like, wherein we may see the malice of this man, that will get poison from the fairest flower; yet every subject may take comfort in his Majesty's Book, and God forbid, that he which is wrong'd, shou'd be restrained to complain to his Sovereign; yet, this complaint is no Petition, but a very Libel, and deserves no better name.

The King's will is, that you should be bold, and that you should come to him; but yet you must be sure that your cause must be just and right. This is a good and gracious speech of a King; but 'tis pity Mr. *Wraynham* alledges Scripture to maintain an ill cause: and I do clear my Lord Chancellor dead, and alive, to be as worthy men as any in my time, and yet I have lived a long age; and God forbid their Consciences shou'd be led by private men's humours.

I say no more, but let every man that hears us this day, take heed, that their humours lead them not into these outrageous courses, but carry themselves with modesty. I shall not need to enlarge, but consent with my Lords before me.

Earl of *Arundel*. I shall not need to use many words for the matter; in brief, *Wraynham* hath forgot himself fully against a great and high instrument of Justice, renewing complaints upon complaints; after the King had told him in my hearing, that the Lord-Chancellor had done justly, as he himself would have done; and therefore I think him very much to blame, and well deserving the censure given. And the use is (as you see by him) for malicious men not to suck honey, but venom and poison out of the wholesome flowers; as his presumption is to be hated, so his humiliation and submission is to be pitied; yet I agree with my Lords in all things.

Pembroke, Lord-Chamberlain. No man's mouth is so stopp'd, but in case of grief he may seek redress. I think there is little scruple, that either the Master of the Rolls that is dead, or this Lord-Chancellor that is living, did proceed without Justice; because it is but an order against an order, a thing very frequent and usual in this, and in all other arbitrary Courts.

For the sentence, I agree with the Court, being sorry, since his last submission was humble, that before he hath abused this good part, and used his wit to his own confusion.

Duke of *Lenox*. I am sorry that *Wraynham* hath not the Grace of God to make use of his Majesty's Book, which is not to complain without just cause; and without he could make proof of his complaint. I will not repeat the worth of my Lord-Chancellor living, or dead: but I am sorry that a man of so great parts shou'd deserve so heavy a sentence; whereunto in all things I agree.

Worcester, Lord Privy-Seal. My Lords, I am of opinion, as formerly my Lords have been; I do hold this a very scandalous Libel, being against a person of such worth; the greater the person is, the more severe shou'd the punishment be for the offender: and so I concur in opinion with my Lords before me, and do think this offence to have exceeded his punishment; and therefore if a great fine had been laid upon him, I shou'd have agreed unto it.

Abbot, Lord Archbishop of *Canterbury*. The Lord, the Fountain of Wisdom, hath set this glorious work of the World in the order and beauty wherein it stands, and hath appointed Princes, Magistrates, and Judges to hear the causes of the people, not so much out of authority, as out of justice and reason: for if no such persons were to hear and determine other men's causes, every man must be his own Judge, which wou'd tend to nothing but ruin and preposterous confusion. God therefore, in his wisdom, order'd and ordain'd their bounds, in the Magistrate on the one side with instruction, and the Subject on the other side with protection; which instruction when he shewed them, the King's Throne is upheld by justice: and *David* was commanded to rule his people with justice and judgment; and the like commandment is given to others in subordinate places, not to pity the person of the poor, nor to stand in awe of the face of the mightiest, but to weigh the simplicity and integrity of Conscience. For mark the examples of the most holy and reverend Judges, *Moses*, *Samuel*, and the rest, to whom their greatest comfort was, that they could say, *Whose Ox or Ass have I taken? From whom have I received a reward?* And by the course of piety and divinity, we that sit sometimes to judge others, are at another time to stand at an higher bar, to receive judgment from Heaven.

With the great grace, and benefit of protection, God calls them by his own name, God's Children of the Highest; God being present amongst 'em to direct them, and defend them; God standeth in the Congregation of Princes, he is amongst all the People: thou shalt not detract nor slander the Judge, nor speak evil of the Princes of the people. And in two several Epistles, both in *Peter* and in *Jude*, it is said, "That in the latter "days there shall be wicked men, that shall speak evil of Magistrates, "and men of authority, blaspheming 'em;" as if it were blasphemy, tho' not against God, yet against those that are the Image of so great a God.

And therefore, since *Wraynham* hath blasphemed, spoken evil, and slander'd a chief Magistrate as any in the Kingdom; it remaineth, that in honour to God, and in duty and justice to the King and Kingdom, that he shou'd receive severe punishment; for it is his cause to-day, and it may be ours every day: and have not some, for justice sake, been inforc'd to endure the threatning of their heads? Wherefore, if greater punishment had been given him, I shou'd have assented; for Justice belongeth to us, but Mercy to our gracious Sovereign. Wherefore I agree in all things with the sentence before given.

Suffolk, Lord-Treasurer. I perceive, as the prisoner at the bar was charged at first, that he had foully offended, and ought to have yielded himself at the first, and not to have made his offence greater, by defending a bad cause.

My Lords who have heard his fault in part laid out, and censured him, I think they have done very worthily. For the party himself, I would I could come to him with a little better charity than I can, for his answer did more displease me, than his censure, for I see his spleen and his humour grows, rather to defame a worthy man, than to free himself, how unjustly, I appeal to the whole World, who came to his place with as much satisfaction to all hearts, and applause, with as good carriage as any man I ever heard came before him.

The thing that I would conclude with, is, that I would be glad that all that hear us might take us aright that are Judges; we desire not to be forborn by any Subject's tongue, that hath cause to complain, and therefore do it not for any particular respect to ourselves, but for the public course of justice, and for the care we have of the publick good, and for nothing else.

For the fault itself, it hath been so well opened by all the Lords, that I will spare to hold you longer in speaking of it. And for the sentence, I think it very fit and just: and therefore agree with the rest.

XVI. Proceedings on the *Habeas Corpus*, brought by Sir *Thomas Darnel*, Sir *John Corbet*, Sir *Walter Earl*, Sir *John Heveningham*, and Sir *Edmund Hampden*, *Nov.* 1627. 3 *Car.* I. at the *King's-Bench*, in *Westminster-Hall*.

THE King having deprived himself of the prospect of all parliamentary Aids, by dissolving the Parliament, and yet resolving to prosecute the war; it was necessary to project all possible ways and means of raising money; to which end letters were sent to the Lords-Lieutenants of the Counties, to return the names of the persons of ability, and what sums they could spare; and the Comptroller of the King's Houshold issued forth letters in the King's name, under the Privy Seal, to several persons returned for the Loan-money; some were assessed 20 *l.* some 15, and others 10 *l.* and Commissioners were appointed with private instructions how to behave themselves in this affair, and divers Lords of the Council were appointed to repair into their Counties to advance the Loan *. Collectors were also appointed to pay into the Exchequer the sums receiv'd, and to return the names of such as refus'd, or discovered a disposition to delay the payment of the sums impos'd. This assessment of the general-Loan did not pass currently with the people, for divers persons refus'd to subscribe or lend at the rate propos'd; the non-subscribers of high rank in all Counties were bound over by recognizances to tender their appearance at the Council-board, and perform'd the same accordingly, and divers of them committed to prison: which caus'd great murmuring. But amongst those many Gentlemen who were imprison'd throughout *England*, for refusing

* Sir *Randolf Crew* shewing no zeal for the advancement thereof, was then removed from his place of Lord Chief-Justice, and Sir *Nicholas Hyde* succeeded in his room: a person who, for his parts and abilities, was thought worthy of that preferment; yet nevertheless came to the same with a prejudice, coming in the place of one so well-beloved and so suddenly remov'd. *Rushworth.* Vol. I. Page 420.

[illegible] Sir *Randolf Crew*, Chief-Justice of the *King's Bench*, was discharged of his place by Writ under the Great Seal, for some cause of displeasure conceived against him, but for what, was not generally known.

to lend upon the Commission for Loans, only five of them brought their *Habeas Corpus*, viz. Sir *Thomas Darnel*, Sir *John Corbet*, Sir *Walter Earl*, Sir *John Heveningham*, and Sir *Edmund Hampden*.

Arguments upon the *Habeas Corpus*.

Sir Thomas Darnel *his Case*, Michaelis, 3° *Caroli*, *Banco Regis*.

SIR *Thomas Darnel*, Baronet, being imprisoned in the *Fleet*, by virtue of a warrant signed by the King's Attorney-General, upon the third of *November*, by Serjeant *Bramston*, his assigned Counsel, moved the Justices of the King's-Bench to grant him a Writ of *Habeas Corpus cum causa*, directed to the Warden of the *Fleet*, to shew that Court the cause of his imprisonment, that thereupon they might determine whether his restraint were legal or illegal; and it was granted by the Court returnable *Thursday* following, the 8*th* day of *November*.

On *Thursday*, Sir *Thomas Darnel* expected that his Writ should be returned, but it was delayed; and it was moved that the return should be on *Saturday*, the 10th of *November*, which made Sir *Thomas Darnel* the more remiss in suing out an *Alias* upon his *Habeas Corpus*.

On *Saturday* the Writ was not returned, and thereupon the King's Attorney-General gave order for an *Alias* upon the *Habeas Corpus* for Sir *Thomas Darnel*, returnable upon *Thursday* morning the 15th of *November*; by virtue of which Writ, the Warden of the *Fleet* brings Sir *Thomas Darnel* to the King's-Bench, and returneth as followeth:

Executio istius Brevis patet in quadam schedula annexat' huic brevi.

The return was this:

" Ego Henricus Liloe Miles guardianus prisonæ Domini Regis de " *le Fleet*, serenissimo domino Regi certifico quod dict' *Thomas Darnel* Baronet' detentus est in prisona prædict' sub custodia mea virtute cujusdam Warranti duorum de Privato Consilio mihi directi, cujus tenor " sequitur in his verbis, *viz.*

" *Whereas heretofore the Body of Sir* Thomas Darnel *hath been committed to your custody, these are to require you still to continue him; and to let you know that he was and is committed by the special command of his Majesty, &c.*"

Et hæc est causa detentionis prædict' Thomæ Darnel.

Serj. *Bramston.* MAY it please your Lordship, I did not expect this cause at this time, neither did I hear of it until I came now into the Hall; and therefore I shall now humbly shew you what my Client hath informed me since my coming hither. I understand by him that he expected not his coming to this place to-day; the Writ by which he was brought hither was not moved for by him, but was procured without his privity; and seeing his case is so, and that he perceives the cause of his coming, which before he knew not, his motion to your Lordship is, that you would be pleased to let him have the copy of the return, and give him time to speak unto it, and that this Writ being not sent out by his procurement, may not be filed.

Heath, Attorney-General. My Lords, it is true that this Gentleman, Sir *Thomas Darnel*, being imprisoned in the *Fleet*, did heretofore move your Lordships for a *Habeas Corpus*, &c. and it was granted him: and his Majesty being made acquainted therewith, was very willing that he and all his people might have equal justice; and when they desire that which seems to accord with the rules of the law, they should have it. But it fell out so, that on the day when the Writ should have been returned, the Warden of the *Fleet* did not return it, as it was his duty to have done; he did forbear to do it upon a commandment, because it was conceived, there being five at that time to appear, the Court would have been straitened for want of time: but I imagined that these Gentlemen who did desire the Writ before, should have again been earnest to renew them, which it seems they did not. This *Habeas Corpus* was sent out by special command, because these Gentlemen gave out in speeches, and in particular this Gentleman, That they did wonder why they should be hinder'd from Trial, and what should be the reason their Writs were not returned: nay, his Majesty did tell me, that they reported that the King did deny them the course of Justice, and therefore he commanded me to renew the Writ, which I did, and think I may do it *ex officio*.

Sir *Tho. Darnel.* My Lords, I knew not until now, but that I was committed by Mr *Attorney's* Warrant only, and thereupon I did desire a *Habeas Corpus* at the bar, which you were pleased to grant me; but now I understand that my restraint is by another means, and therefore I shall crave leave to have some time to speak to it. And as for the words alledged against me, as if I had spoken them, I humbly pray they may be no disparagement to my Cause, for I do patiently refer myself to your grave censures, as being accused of a fact whereof I am no ways guilty.

Hyde, L. C. Justice. You give a temperate and fair answer; and now you may perceive the upright and sincere proceedings that have been in this business. You did no sooner petition to have Counsel assigned you, but you had it granted to you, for indeed we cannot deny it; and I know not but that any Counsel might have moved for you, without having been assigned for you, and yet have had no blame; for it is the King's pleasure his laws should take place and be executed, and therefore do we sit here. When you made a motion for a *Habeas Corpus*, that was likewise granted; whether the commitment be by the King or others, this Court is a place where the King doth sit in person, and we have power to examine it; and if it appears that any man hath injury or wrong by his imprisonment, we have power to deliver and discharge him; if otherwise, he is to be remanded by us to prison again. Now it seems you are not ready to speak to this return, if you desire a further day, we ought to grant it.

Sir *Tho. Darnel.* My Lords, I humbly desire it.

L. C. J. I know no cause why it should be denied.

Serj. *Bramston.* My Lords, we shall desire the Writ may not be filed, and that we may have a copy of the return.

Attorn. Gen. You cannot deny the filing of the Writ, if you desi to have a copy of the return.

L. C. Justice. Although you be remanded at this time to prison, because you are not ready to speak to the return, we can adjourn you to a new day upon the Writ, and so you may prepare yourself; but if you will not have this filed, there must go out a new *Habeas Corpus*, and thereupon must be another return.

Serj. *Bramston.* My Lord, we desire some time, that we may be advised whether we may proceed or not.

L. C. Justice. Will you submit yourself to the King?

Sir *Tho. Darnel.* My Lord, I desire some time to advise of my proceedings: I have moved many men, and offered to retain them of my Counsel; but they refuse me, and I can get none to be of Counsel with me without your assistance.

L. C. Justice. You shall have what Counsel assigned you you will have or desire, for no offence will be taken against any man that shall advise you in your proceedings in Law.

Attorn. Gen. I will pass my word, they that do advise you, shall have no offence taken against them for it; and I shall give consent to any way that you shall desire, either that it may be filed, or that it may not be filed; for if you desire Justice, you shall have it, and the King will not deny it; but if it shall be conceived, as it is rumoured, that there was a denial of Justice on the King's part, you must know that his Majesty is very tender of that. And for the Gentleman, now he is brought hither, I conceive, but yet I leave it to your Lordship's judgment, that the Writ must be filed, and you must either deliver him, or remand him, or else it will be an escape in the Warden of the *Fleet*.

Sir *Tho. Darnel.* I would not have it thought that I should speak any thing against my Prince, and for those words I do deny them; for upon my conscience they never came into my thought: perhaps you shall find that they have been spoken by some other, but not by any of us.

L. C. Justice. Sir, you have made a fair answer, and I doubt not but Mr. *Attorney* will make the like relation of it; you move for the not filing of the Writ; if you refuse to have it filed, whereby it should not be of record, you must have no Copy of it; but if you will have it filed you shall have a Copy of it, and further time to speak to it; chuse whether of them you will.

Serj. *Bramston.* We desire to have the return read once more.

And it was read as before.

Serj. *Bramston.* So as the Writ may not be filed, we will desire no copy of the return.

L. C. Justice. Then the Gentleman must return back again into the custody of the Warden of the *Fleet*; and therefore I ask you, whether you desire to come hither again upon this Writ, or will you have a new one?

Sir *Tho. Darnel.* I desire your Lordship that I may have time to consider of it.

L. C. Justice. Then in God's name take your own time to think of it.

Michaelis, 3°. *Caroli Regis*. Thursday 22 November, 1627.

Sir *John Corbet*, Baronet, Sir *Walter Earl*, Sir *John Heveningham*, Sir *Edmund Hampden*, Knights, were brought to the Bar.

Serj. *Bramston* MAY it please your Lordship to hear the return read, or shall I open it?

L. C. Justice. Let it be read.

Mr. *Keeling* reads the return, being the same as that of Sir *Thomas Darnel*.

Serj. *Bramston.* May it please your Lordship, I shall humbly move upon this return in the behalf of Sir *John Heveningham*, with whom I am of Counsel; it is his petition, that he may be bailed from his imprisonment. it was but in vain for me to move that to a Court of Law, which by Law cannot be granted: and therefore in that regard, that upon this return it will be questioned, whether as this return is made, the Gentleman may be bailed or not? I shall humbly offer up to your Lordship the case, and some reasons out of mine understanding, arising out of the return itself, to satisfy your Lordship that these prisoners may, and, as their case is, ought to be bailed by your Lordship.

The exception that I take to this return, is as well to the matter and substance of the return, as to the manner and legal form thereof: the exception that I take to the matter, is in several respects.

That the return is too general, there is no sufficient cause shewn in special or in general of the commitment of this Gentleman; and as it is insufficient for the cause, so also in the time of the first imprisonment; for neither doth it appear a time upon the second Warrant from the Lords of the Council to detain him still in prison, yet by the return no time can appear when he was first imprisoned, tho' it be necessary it should be shewn, and if that time appear not, there is no cause your Lordship should remand him; and consequently he is to be delivered.

Touching the matter of the return, which is the cause of his imprisonment, it is expressed to be *per speciale mandatum domini Regis*: this is too general and uncertain, for that it is not manifest what kind of command this was.

Touching the legal form of the return, it is not, as it ought to be, fully and positively the return of the Keeper himself only, but it comes with a *significavit*, or *prout*, that he was committed *per speciale mandatum domini Regis*, as appeareth by Warrant from the Lords of the Council, not of the King himself; and that is not good in legal form.

For the matter and substance of the return, it is not good, because there ought to be a cause of that imprisonment.

This Writ is the means, and the only means that the subject hath in this and such-like case to obtain his liberty; there are other Writs by which men are delivered from restraint, as that *de homine replegiando*, but extends not to this cause, for it is particularly excepted in the body of the Writ *de manucaptione, & de cautione admittenda*, but they lie in other cases. but the Writ of *Habeas Corpus* is the only

means

means the subject hath to obtain his liberty, and the end of this Writ is to return the cause of the imprisonment, that it may be examined in this Court, whether the parties ought to be discharged or not: but that cannot be done upon this return: for the cause of the imprisonment of this Gentleman at first is so far from appearing particularly by it, that there is no cause at all expressed in it.

This Writ requires that the cause of the imprisonment should be returned, and if the cause be not specially certified by it, yet should it at the least be shewn in general, that it may appear to the Judges of the Court; and it must be expressed so far, as that it may appear to be none of those causes for which by law of the kingdom the subject ought not to be imprisoned; and it ought to be expressed that it was by presentment or indictment, and not upon petition or suggestion made to the King and Lords, which is against the Statute made in the 25 *Edw.* III. *c.* 4. 42 *Edw.* III. *c.* 3.

By the Statute 25 *Edw.* III. *cap.* 4. it is ordained and established, That no man from henceforth shall be taken by petition or suggestion made to the King or his Council, but by indictment or course of law; and accordingly it was enacted, 42 *Edw.* III. *cap.* 3. the title of which Statute is, None shall be put to answer an accusation made to the King without presentment. Then, my Lord, it being so, although the cause should not need to be expressed in such manner as that it may appear to be none of these causes mentioned in the Statute, or else the subject by this return loseth the benefit and advantage of these laws, which be their birth-right and inheritance; but in this return there is no cause at all appearing of the first commitment, and therefore it is plain, that there is no cause for your Lordship to remand him; but there is cause you should deliver him, since the Writ is to bring the body and the cause of the imprisonment before your Lordship.

But it may be objected, that this Writ of *Habeas Corpus* doth not demand the cause of the first commitment, but of the detaining only; and so the Writ is satisfied by the return; for though it shew no cause of the first commitment, but of detaining only, yet it declareth a cause why the Gentleman is detained in prison: this is no answer, nor can give any satisfaction; for the reason why the cause is to be returned, is for the subject's liberty, that if it shall appear a good and sufficient cause to your Lordship, then to be remanded; if your Lordship think and find it insufficient, he is to be enlarged.

This is the end of this Writ, and this cannot appear to your Lordship, unless the time of the first commitment be expressed in the return. I know that in some cases the time is not material, as when the cause of the commitment is (and that so especially) returned, as that the time is not material, it is enough to shew the cause without the time, as after a conviction or Trial had by Law, but when it is in this manner, that the time is the matter itself: for intend what cause you will of the commitment, yea though for the highest cause of Treason, there is no doubt but that upon the return thereof the time of it must appear; for it being before Trial and Conviction had by law, it is but an accusation, and he that is only accused ought by law to be let to bail.

But I beseech your Lordship to observe the consequence of this cause. If the law be, that upon this return this Gentleman should be remanded, I will not dispute whether or no, a man may be imprisoned before he be convicted according to the law; but if this return shall be good, then his imprisonment shall not continue on for a time, but for ever; and the subjects of this Kingdom may be restrained of their liberties perpetually, and by law there can be no remedy for the subject: and therefore this return cannot stand with the laws of the Realm, or that of *Magna Charta*; nor with the Statute of 28 *Edw.* III. *cap.* 3. for if a man be not bailable upon this return, they cannot have the benefit of these two laws, which are the inheritance of the subject.

If your Lordship shall think this to be a sufficient cause, then it goeth to a perpetual imprisonment of the subject: for in all those causes which may concern the King's subjects, and are applicable to all times and cases, we are not to reflect upon the present time and government, where justice and mercy floweth, but we are to look what may betide us in the time to come, hereafter.

It must be agreed on all sides, that the time of the first commitment doth not appear in this return, but by a latter warrant from the Lords of the Council, there is a time indeed expressed for the continuing of him in prison, and that appears; but if this shall be a good cause to remand these Gentlemen to prison, they may lie there these seven years longer, and seven years after them, nay, all the days of their lives. And if they sue out a Writ of *Habeas Corpus*, it is but making a new Warrant, and they shall be remanded, and shall never have the advantage of the laws which are the best inheritance of every subject.

And in *Edw.* VI. *fol.* 36. the laws are called the great inheritance of every subject, and the inheritance of inheritances, without which inheritance we have no inheritance.

These are the exceptions I desire to offer up to your Lordship touching the return, for the insufficiency of the cause returned, and the defect of the time of the first commitment, which should have been expressed.

I will not labour in objections till they be made against me, in regard the Statute of *Westminster primo* is so frequent in every man's mouth, that at the Common Law those men that were committed in four cases were not replevisable; *viz.* those that were taken for the death of a man, or the commandment of the King, or his Justices for the Forest. I shall speak something to it, though I intend not to spend much time about it, for it toucheth not this case we have in question.

For that is concerning a case of the Common Law, when men are taken by the King's Writs, and not by word of mouth, and it shall be so expounded, as Mr. *Stamford*, *fol.* 73. yet it is nothing to this case, for if you will take the true meaning of that Statute, it extends not at all to this Writ of *Habeas Corpus*, for the words are plain, they shall be replevisable by the common Writ, that is, by the Writ *de homine replegiando*, directed to the Sheriff to deliver them, if they were bailable: but this case is above the Sheriff, and he is not to be Judge there, whether the causes of the commitment be sufficient or not, as it appears in *Fitz-Herbert*, *de homine replegiando*, and many other places, and not of the very words of the Statute [illegible] clear, for there be many other causes mentioned, as the death of a man, the commandment of the Justices, &c. in which the Statute saith, men are not replevisable. But will a man conceive that the meaning is, that they shall not be bailed at all, but live in perpetual imprisonment? I think I shall not need to spend time, in that it is so plain; let me but make one instance.

A man is taken *de morte hominis*; he is not bailable by Writ; saith this Statute; that is, by the common Writ. there was a common Writ for this case, and that was called *de odio & atia*, as appeareth, *Bracton*, *Coron.* 34. This is the Writ intended by the Statute, which is a common Writ, and not a special Writ; but, my Lord, as this Writ *de odio & atia* was before this Statute, so it was afterwards taken away by the Statute of 28 *Edw.* III. *cap.* 9. But before that Statute, this Writ did lie in the special case, as is shewn in *Coke*'s 9th report, the *Poulterer*'s case; and the end of this Writ was, that the subject might not be too long detained in prison, as till the Justices of *Eyre* discharged them. So that the Law intended not that a man should suffer perpetual imprisonment, for they were very careful that men should not be kept too long in prison, which is also a liberty of the subject; and, my Lord, that this Court hath bailed upon a suspicion of High-Treason, I will offer it to your Lordship, when I shall shew you precedents in these cases of a commitment by the Privy-Council, or by the King himself: but before I offer these precedents unto your Lordship, of which there be many, I shall by your Lordship's favour speak a little to the next exception, and that is to the matter of the return, which I find to be *per speciale mandatum domini Regis*. And what is that? It appears by this Writ, there may be sundry commands by the King: we find a special command often in our Books, as in the Statute of *Marl. cap.* 8. they who were imprisoned *Red ss.* shall not be delivered without the special command of our Lord the King. And so in *Bracton*, *de Actionibus*, the last chapter, where it appears that the King's commandment for imprisonments is by special Writ, so by Writ again men are to be delivered, for in the case of *Redis.* or *Post Redis.* if it shall be removed by a *Certiorari*, that is by a special Writ to deliver parties. So that by this appears, that by the King's commandment to imprison, and to deliver in those cases, is understood this Writ, and so it may be in this case which we have heard.

And this return here is a special *Mandatum*; it may be understood to be under some of the King's Seals, 42 *Ass.* and ought to be delivered, and will you make a difference between the King's command under his seal, and his command by word of mouth? What difference there is, I leave it to your Lordship's judgment; but if there be any, it is the more material that it should be expressed what manner of command it was, which doth not here appear; and therefore it may be the King's command by Writ, or his command under his seal, or his command by word of mouth alone.

And if there is any of these commands of an higher nature than the other, doubtless, it is that by Writ, or under seal, for they are of record, and in these the person may be bailed, and why not in this? As to the legal form, admitting there were substances in the return, yet there wants legal form; for the Writ of *Habeas Corpus* is the commandment of the King to the Keeper of the prisons, and thereupon they are to make return both of the body, and of the cause of the commitment, and that cause is to appear of them who are the immediate Officers. And if he doth it by signification from another, that return is defective in law, and therefore this return cannot be good, for it must be from the Officer himself, and if the cause returned by him be good, it binds the prisoners.

The Warrant of the Lords was but a direction for him; he might have made his return to have been expressly by the King's commandment, there was Warrant for it, I shall not need to put you cases of it; for it is not enough that he returns that he was certified that the commitment was by the King's command, but he must of himself return this fact as it was done. And now, my Lord, I shall offer to your Lordship precedents of divers kinds, upon commitments by the special command of the King, and upon commitments both by the King and the Lords together. And howsoever I conceive, which I submit to your Lordship, that our case will not stand upon precedents, but upon the fundamental Laws and Statutes of this Realm; and though the precedents look the one way or the other, they are to be brought back unto the laws by which the Kingdom is governed. In the first of *Henry* VIII. *Rot. Parl.* 9. one *Harrison* was committed to the *Marshalsea* by the command of the King; and being removed by *Habeas Corpus* into the Court, the cause returned was, that he was committed *per mandatum Domini Regis*, and he was bailed.

In the fortieth of *Elizabeth*, *Thomas Wenden* was committed to the Gatehouse by the commandment of the Queen, and the Lords of the Council; and being removed by an *Habeas Corpus*, upon the general return he was bailed.

In 8 *Jacobi*, one *Caesar* was committed by the King's commandment, and this being returned upon his *Habeas Corpus*, upon the examination of this case it doth appear that it was over-ruled, that the return should be amended, or else the prisoner should be delivered.

The precedents concerning the commitment by the Lords of the Council, are in effect the same with these where the commitment is, by the reason why the cause of the commitment should not be shewn, holds in both cases, and that is the necessity of State; and therefore Mr. *Stamford* makes the command of the King, and that of the Lords of the Privy-Council, to be both as one; and to this purpose, if they speak, he speaks; and if he speaks, they speak.

The precedents that we can shew you, how the subject hath been delivered upon commitment by the Lords of the Council, as in the times of *Hen.* VIII. and in the times of Queen *Elizabeth*, and Queen *Mary*, are infinite, as in the 9th of *Elizabeth*, *Thomas Lawrence* was committed to the Tower by the Lords of the Council, and bailed upon an *Habeas Corpus*.

In the 43d of *Elizabeth*, *Catesby*'s case.

In the 3d of *Elizabeth*, *Lawson*'s case.

These were committed for High Treason, and yet bailed; for in all these cases there must be a conviction in one time, or a deliverance by law.

I have here divers other precedents that might be shewn to your Lordship. In 12 *Jacobi*. *Hus Reynolds*. In 12 *Jacobi*, *Rot.* 155. *Richard Beckwith*'s case. In 4 *Jacobi*, Sir *Thomas Monson* was committed for Treason to the Tower of *London*, and afterwards was brought hither, and bailed, and since our case stands upon this return, and yet there is no sufficient cause in law expressed in the return of the detaining this Gentleman, and since these precedents do warrant our proceedings; my humble suit to this Court is, that the Gentleman, Sir *John Heveningham*, who hath petitioned

tioned his Majesty, that he may have the benefit of the law, and his Majesty hath signified it; it is his pleasure that justice according to the law should be administered at all times in general to all his subjects; and particularly to these Gentlemen, which is their birth-right: my humble suit to your Lordship is, that these Gentlemen may have the Benefit of that law, and be delivered from their imprisonment.

Mr. Noye's *Argument of Counsel with Sir* Walter Earl *at that Time.*

May it please your Lordship, I am of Counsel with Sir *Walter Earl*, one of the prisoners at the bar; the return of this Writ is as those that have been before, they are much of one tenor, and as you have heard the tenor of that, so this Gentleman coming hither by an *Habeas Corpus*, I will by your Lordship's favour read the Writ.

"Carolus, Dei gratia, &c. Johanni Liloe Milit' Guardian' Prison' "nostræ de le Fleet salut', Præcipimus tibi quod corpus *Walteri Earl* "Milit' in prison' nostra sub custodia tua detent' ut dicit' una cum causa "detentionis suæ quocunque nomine prædict' *Walter'* censeat in eadem "Habeas Corpus, ad subjiciendum et recipiendum ea quæ curia nostra de "eo adtunc et ibidem ordin' conting' in hac parte et hæc nullatenus omit' "periculo incumbend' et habeas ibi hoc breve. Test' *Hyde*, apud *Westminster*, quarto die Novembris, Anno 8."

Executio istius Brevis patet in quadam schedula huic brevi annexat'.

Respons. Johan' Liloe Guardian' Prison' de le Fleet.

"Ego Johannes Liloe Mil' Guardian' Prison' domini Regis de le Fleet, "Serenissimo Domino Regi, apud *Westminster* 8. Post receptionem hu-"jus brevis quod in hac schedula est mentionat', Certifico quod *Walter* "*Earl* miles, in eodem brevium nominat' detentus est in Prisona de le "Fleet sub custodia mea prædict' per speciale mandatum domini Regis "mihi significatum per Warrantum duorum et aliorum de Privato Con-"cilio perhonorabilissimi dicti Domini Regis, cujus quidem tenor sequi-"tur in hæc verba."

Whereas Sir *Walter Earl*, Knight, was heretofore committed to your custody, these are to will and require you still to detain him, letting you know, that both his first commitment, and this direction for the continuance of him in prison, were and are by his Majesty's special commandment, from *Whitehall*, 7 *Novembris*, 1627.

Thomas Coventry, C. S. — *Marlborough.*
Henry Manchester. — *Pembroke.*
Thomas Suffolk. — *Salisbury.*
Bridgewater. — *Totness.*
Kelly. — *Grandison.*
R. Dunelm'. — *Guliel' Bath & Wells.*
Thomas Edmunds. — *Robert Nanton.*
John Cook. — *Richard Weston.*
Humphry Mayes.

To the Guardian of the Fleet or his Deputy.

"Et hæc est causa detentionis prædict' *Walteri Earl* sub custodia mea "in Prison' prædict'. Attamen corpus ejusdem *Walteri* coram Domino "Rege ad diem et locum prædictum, post receptionem brevis prædict' pa-"rat' habeo prout istud breve in se exiget et requirit."

Respons' Johan' Liloe Milit' Guardian' Prison' de le Fleet.

My Lord, the first *Habeas Corpus* bears date the 4th of *November*, then there is an *Alias Habeas* bears *Teste* after that, and the tenor thereof is a command to the Warden of the *Fleet*, *quod Habeas Corpus* Walteri Earl, *coram nobis ad subjiciendum & recipiendum ea quæ curia nostra de eo &c. ordin' conting'*. And the Warden of the *Fleet*, he certifies as your Lordship has heard. May it please your Lordship, I desire as before was desired for the other Gentlemen, that Sir *Walter Earl* may be also bailed, if there be no other cause of his imprisonment: for if there were a cause certified, and that cause were not sufficient to detain him still in prison, your Lordship would bail him; and if a man should be in a worse case, when there is no cause certified at all, that wou'd be very hard.

The Writ is, that he should bring the Prisoner *coram nobis*, before the King, the end of that is *ad subjiciendum & recipiendum*; now I conceive, that tho' there be a signification of the King's pleasure to have this Gentleman imprisoned, yet when the King grants this Writ to bring the prisoner hither, *ad subjiciendum & recipiendum*, his pleasure likewise is, to have the prisoner let go, if by law he be not chargeable; or otherwise to detain him still in prison, if the case so require it.

I will put your Lordship in mind of a case, and it was *Pasch.* 9 *Edw.* III. *M.* 3. I will cite by the *Placita*, because my Book is not paged as other Books are; it is in the case of a *Cessavit*.

In that case there were two things considerable: the one that there was a signification of the King's pleasure past, and that determined with him: the other, that though there was a signification of the King's pleasure before, yet there comes after that a Writ; and that was another signification of the King's pleasure, that the Prisoner shall be brought hither *ad subjiciendum*, to submit himself to punishment, if he have deserved it; or *ad recipiendum*, to receive his enlargement, and be delivered, if there be no cause of his imprisonment.

And if upon an *Habeas Corpus*, a cause of commitment be certified, that cause is to be tried here before your Lordship. But if no cause be shewn, then the proceedings must be *ut curia nostra ad man' contigerit*, the Court must do that which stands with Law and Justice, and that is to deliver him.

My Lord, I shall be bold to move one word more touching this return: I conceive that every Officer to a Court of Justice must make his return of his own act, or of the act of another, and not what he is certified of by another.

But in this case the Warden of the *Fleet* doth not certify himself, of himself, that this Gentleman was committed to him by the King, but that he was certified by the Lords of the Council, that it was the King's pleasure that he should detain him. But in our case the Warden of the *Fleet* must certify the immediate cause, and not the cause of the cause, as he doth by this return; *Detentus est sub custodia mea per speciale mandatum Domini Regis mihi significatum per Warrantum duorum de Privato Concilio*; that is not the use in law, but he ought to return the primary cause, and not the subsequent cause: as in 31 *Edw.* III. return, *Rex vicecom'* 87. in a Writ *de homine replegiando*, against an Abbot, the Sheriff returns, that he hath sent to the Bailiff of the Abbot, and he answered him, that the party was the Abbot's vil'ain, and so he cannot deliver him; that it is held an insufficient return, and a new *Alias* was granted. But if the Sheriff had returned, that the Abbot did certify him so, it had been good; but he must not return what is certified him by another.

In one of the precedents that hath been noted, as that of *Parker*, 22 *Hen.* VIII. there the Guardian of the prison certifies, that Parker *detentus est sub custodia mea per mandatum Domini Regis mihi nunciatum per* Robertum Pecke; now our case is by the nunciation of many, but in law *majus & minus non variant in speciem*, the certification of one and of many is of the same effect, although in moral understanding there may be a difference.

Trin. 2 *Edw.* III. *Rot.* 46. in this Court in 21 *Edw.* III in the printed Book there is a piece of it: the Abbot of *Bury* brings a prohibition out of this Court, the Bishop of *Norwich* pleaded in bar of that, *Quod mihi testificatum quod continetur in Archivis*, that he is excommunicated; there were two exceptions taken to this case in this precedent, and they are both in one case: the first was, that no cause appeareth, why he was excommunicated; there may be causes why he should be excommunicated, and then he should be barred, and there may be causes why the excommunication should not bar him: for it may be the excommunication was for bringing the action, which was the King's Writ; and therefore because there was no cause of the excommunication returned, it was ruled that it was not good. The other reason is that upon the Roll, which is *mihi testificatum*.

Now every man, when he will make a Certificate to the Court, *Proprium factum suum non alterius significare debet*, he must inform the Court of the immediate act done, and not that such things are told him, or that such things are signified unto him; but that was not done in this case, and therefore it was held insufficient, and so in this case of ours I conceive the Return is insufficient in the form. There is another cause, my Lord, for which I conceive this return is not good.

But first I will be bold to inform your Lordship, touching the Statute of *Magna Charta* 29. *Nullus liber homo capiatur vel imprisonetur, &c. nec super eum mittimus nisi per legale judicium parium suorum, vel per legem terræ.*

That in this Statute these words *in Carcerem* are omitted out of the printed Books: for it should be *nec eum in Carcerem mittimus*. For these words *per legem terræ*; what *Lex terræ* should be, I will not take upon me to expound, otherwise than I find them to be expounded by Acts of Parliament; and this is, that they are understood to be the process of the law, sometimes by Writ, sometimes by Attachment of the person: but whether *speciale mandatum Domini Regis* be intended by that or no, I leave it to your Lordship's exposition upon two petitions of the Commons, and answer of the King, in 36 *Edw.* III. N°. 9. and N°. 20.

In the first of them the Commons complain that the great Charter, the Charter of the Forest, and other Statutes were broken, and they desire that for the good of himself and of his people, they might be kept and put in execution, and that they might not be infringed by making an arrest by special command, or otherwise: and the answer was, that the assent of the Lords established and ordained, that the said Charter and other Statutes should be put in execution according to the petition, and that is without any disturbance by arrest by special command or otherwise; for it was granted, as it was petitioned.

In the same year, for they were very careful of this matter, and it was necessary it should be so, for it was then an usual thing to take men by Writs *quibusdam de causis*, and many of these words caused many Acts of Parliament; and it may be some of these Writs may be shewn: and I say in the same year they complained that men were imprisoned by special command, and without Indictment or other legal Course of law, and they desired that thing may not be done upon men by special command against the great Charter.

The King makes answer, that he is well pleased therewith: that was the first answer; and for the future he hath added farther, if any man be grieved, let him complain, and right shall be done unto him. This, my Lord, is an explanation of the great Charter, as also the Statute of 37 *Edward* III. *ch.* 18. is a Commentary upon it, that men would not be committed upon suggestion made to the King, without due proofs of law against them, and so it is enacted twice in one year.

We find more printed Books, as in *Hen.* VI. *Mon. de facts*, *Fitz.* 182. which is a strong case, under favour, in an action of trespass for cutting down trees. The Defendant saith, That the place where the trees are cut, is parcel of the Manor of *B.* whereof the King is seized in fee, and that the King did command him to cut them: and the opinion of the Court was, that this was no good plea, without shewing the specialty of the command; and they said, if the King command me to arrest a man, and I arrest him, he shall have an action of false imprisonment against me, although it were done in the King's presence.

In 1 *Joh cap.* 7. *fol.* 46. it is in print, and there we leave it.

Hussey Chief Justice saith, that Sir *John Markham* told King *Edw.* IV. that he could not arrest a man upon suspicion of Felony or Treason, as any of his subjects might; because if he should wrong a man by such arrest, the parties could have no remedy against him, if any man shall stand upon it. Here is a signification of the King's pleasure, not to have the cause of the commitment examined; he hath here another signification of his pleasure by Writ, whereby the party is brought hither *ad subjiciendum & recipiendum*, that he hath made your Lordship judge of that, which should be objected against this Gentleman, and either to punish him, or to deliver him; and if there be no cause shewn, it is to be intended that the party is to be delivered, and that it is the King's pleasure it should be so: and the Writ is a sufficient Warrant for the doing of it, there being no cause shewn of the imprisonment. And now, my Lord, I will speak a word to the Writ of *de homine replegiando*, and no other Writ, for that was the common Writ; and the four causes expressed in that Statute, to-wit, the death of a man, the command of the King, or his Justice, or Forest, were excepted in that Writ before that Statute made, as appears *Bracton* 133. so that the Writ was at the Common-Law before that Statute.

And

And it appears by our Books, that if a Man be brought hither by an *Habeas Corpus*, though he were imprisoned *de morte hominis*, as in the 21 *Edw.* IV. 7. *Winckfield* was bailed here, this Court bailed him, for he was brought hither *ad subjiciendum & recipiendum*, and not to lie in Prison God knows how long; and if the Statute should be expounded otherwise, there were no bailing Men outlawed, or Breakers of Prison, for they are not within this Statute, and yet this Court doth it at pleasure.

But plainly by the Statute itself, it appears, that it meant only the common Writ; for the Preamble recites, that the Sheriffs and others had taken and kept in Prison Persons detected of Felony, and let out to Plevin such as were not reprisable, to grieve the one Party, and to the Gain of the other; and forasmuch as before this time it was not determined what Prisoners were reprisable, and what not, but only in certain Cases were expressed, therefore it is ordained, &c.

Now this is no more than for Direction to the Keepers of the Prisons; for it leaves the Matter to the Discretion of the Judges, whether bailable or not; for when the Statute hath declared who are repleviable, who are not, as Men outlawed, those who have abjured the Realm, Breakers of Prison, Burners of Houses, Makers of false Money, counterfeiting of the King's Seal, and the like; it is then ordained, that if the Sheriff, or any other, let any go at large by Surety, that is not reprisable, whether he be Sheriff, Constable, or any other that hath the keeping of Prisons, and thereof be attainted, he shall lose his Office and Fee for ever; so that it extends to the common Gaolers and Keepers of Prisons, to direct them in what Cases they shall let men to bail, and in what Cases not: And that they shall not be Judges whom to let to replevin, and whom to keep in Prison; but it extends not to the Judges, for if the Makers of the Statute had meant them in it, they should have put a Pain or Penalty upon them also.

So then I conclude, under your Lordship's Favour, that as this Case is, there should have been a Cause of the Commitment expressed, for these Gentlemen are brought hither by Writ *ad subjiciendum*, if they be charged; and *ad recipiendum*, if they be not charged; and therefore in regard there is no Charge against them, whereupon they should be detained in Prison any longer, we desire that they may be bailed or discharged by your Lordship.

Mr. Selden's *Argument at the* King's-Bench *Bar the same Day.*

MY Lords, I am of Counsel with Sir *Edmund Hampden*; his case is the same with the other two Gentlemen. I cannot hope to say much, after That that hath been said; yet if it shall please your Lordship, I shall remember you of so much as is befallen my lot. Sir *Edward Hampden* is brought hither by a Writ of *Habeas Corpus*, and the Keeper of the Gatehouse hath returned upon the Writ, that Sir *Edmund Hampden* is detained in prison *per speciale mandatum domini Regis, mihi significatum per Warrantum duorum Privati Concilii dicti domini Regis*. And then he recites the Warrant of the Lords of the Council, which is, that they do will and require him to detain this Gentleman still in prison, letting him know that his first imprisonment, &c.

May it please your Lordship, I shall humbly move you that this Gentleman may also be bailed; for under favour, my Lord, there is no cause in the return, why he should be any farther imprisoned and restrained of his liberty.

My Lord, I shall say something to the form of the Writ, and of the return; but very little to them both, because there is a very little left for me to say.

My Lord, to the form, I say it expresseth nothing of the first caption, and therefore it is insufficient; I will add one reason, as hath been said: the *Habeas Corpus* hath only these words, *quod habeas corpus ejus una cum causa detentionis, & non captionis*. But, my Lord, because in all imprisonments, there is a cause of caption and detention, the caption is to be answered as well as the detention.

I have seen many Writs of this nature, and on them the caption is returned, that they might see the time of the caption, and thereby know whether the party should be delivered or no, and that in regard of the length of his imprisonment.

The next exception I take to the form is, that there is much uncertainty in it, so that no man can tell when the writ came to the Keeper of the prison, whether before the return or after; for it appears not when the King's command was for the commitment, or the signification of the Council came to him. It is true, that it appears that the Warrant was dated the 7th of *November*; but when it came to the Keeper of the prison, that appears not at all: and therefore, as for want of mentioning the same time of the caption, so for not expressing the same time when this warrant came, I think the return is faulty in form, and void.

And for apparent contradiction also, the return is insufficient; for in that part of the return which is before the Warrant, it is said, *Quod detentus est per speciale mandatum domini Regis*. The Warrant of the Lords of the Council, the very syllables of that Warrant are, that the Lords of the Council do will and require him still to detain him, which is contrary to the first part of the return.

Besides, my Lord, the Lords themselves say, in another place and passage of the Warrant, that the King commanded them to commit him, and so it is their commitment; so that upon the whole matter, there appears to be a clear contradiction in the return; and there being a contradiction in the return, it is void.

Now, my Lord, I will speak a word or two to the matter of the return; and that is touching the imprisonment, *per speciale mandatum domini Regis*, by the Lords of the Council, without any cause expressed: and admitting of any, or either, or both of these to be the return; I think that by the constant and settled Laws of this Kingdom, without which we have nothing, no man can be justly imprisoned by either of them, without a cause of the commitment expressed in the return. My Lord, in both the last Arguments the Statutes have been mentioned and fully expressed: yet I will add a little to that which hath been said.

The Statute of *Magna Charta*, *cap.* 29. that Statute if it were fully executed as it ought to be, every man would enjoy his liberty better than he doth.

The Law saith expresly, no Freeman shall be imprisoned without due process of the law; out of the very body of this Act of Parliament, besides the explanation of other Statutes, it appears, *Nullus liber homo capiatur vel imprisonatur nisi per legem terræ*. My Lord, I know these words *legem terræ*, do leave the question where it was, if the interpretation of the Statute were not. But I think under your Lordship's favour, there it must be intended by due course of law, to be either by presentment or by indictment.

My Lords, if the meaning of these words, *per legem terræ*, were but, as we use to say, according to the laws, which leaves the matter very uncertain; and *per speciale mandatum*, &c. be within the meaning of these words, according to the law; then this Act had done nothing. The Act is, No Freeman shall be imprisoned but by the law of the land. If you will understand these words, *per legem terræ*, in the first sense, this Statute shall extend to Villeins as well as to Freemen; for if I imprison another man's Villein, the Villein may have an action of false imprisonment: But the Lords and the King (for then they both had Villeins) might imprison them; and the Villein could have no remedy. But these words in the Statute, *per legem terræ*, were to the Freeman, which ought not to be imprisoned, but by due process of law: and unless the interpretation shall be this, the Freeman shall have no privilege above the Villein.

So that I conceive, my Lords, these words, *per legem terræ*, must be here so interpreted, as in 42 *Eliz.* The Bill is worth observing. It reciteth that divers persons without any writ or presentment were cast into prison, &c. that it might be enacted, that it should not be so done hereafter. The answer there is; that as this is an article of the great Charter, this should be granted: So that it seems the Statute is not taken to be an explanation of that of *Magna Charta*, but the very words of the Statute of *Magna Charta*.

I will conclude with a little observation upon these words, *nec super eum mittimus*; which words of themselves signify not so much, a man cannot find any fit sense for them.

But, my Lord, in the 7th year of King *John*, there was a great Charter, by which this Statute in the 9th of *Henry* III. whereby we are now regulated, was framed, and there the words are, *nec eum in carcerem mittimus*, We will not commit him to prison; that is, the King himself will not; and to justify this, there is a story of that time in *Matthew Paris*; and in that Book this Charter of King *John* is set down at large, which Book is very authentick, and there it is entered: and in the 9th of *Henry* III. he saith, that the Statute was renewed in the same words with the Charter of King *John*. And, my Lord, he might know it better than others, for he was the King's Chronologer in those times: and therefore, my Lord, since there be so many Reasons, and so many Precedents, and so many Statutes, which declare that no Freeman whatsoever ought to be imprisoned but according to the laws of the land; and that the liberty of the subject is the highest inheritance that he hath; my humble request is, that according to the ancient laws and privileges of this Realm, this Gentleman, my Client, may be bailed.

The Argument of Mr. Calthrop, *at the King's-Bench Bar*, 22 Novembris, Mich. 3 Caroli Regis.

SIR *John Corbet* being brought to the King's-Bench Bar, with Sir *Edmund Hampden*, Sir *Walter Earl*, and Sir *John Heveningham*, who were also brought thither by several writs of *Habeas Corpus*, with the same return; I being assigned by the Court of King's-Bench, upon a petition delivered, to be of Counsel with Sir *John Corbet*, did move that Sir *John Corbet* might be discharged of his imprisonment, and put in bail; for I did conceive that the return of this *Habeas Corpus* was insufficient, both in the matter of the return, and in the manner of the return, and so there ought not to be a longer detaining of Sir *John Corbet* in prison. For as to the manner of the return, it is not laid down precisely, that Sir *John Corbet* is detained in prison by the special commandment of the King, signified by the warrant of the Lords of the Council; the which is not a direct affirmation that he is detained by the special command of the King, but that the Lords of the Council, by their warrant, have signified unto him that he was committed and still detained by the special command of the King.

And howsoever the Lords of the Council had signified that he was detained by the commandment of the King, yet it may be he was not detained by the commandment of the King; for their signification of the same by warrant may be untrue, and the warrant of the Lords of the Council that is returned *in hæc verba*, importeth that the Keeper of the Gatehouse rather took upon him to return, that it was signified unto him by the warrant of the Lords of the Council, that Sir *John Corbet* was committed and detained by the special commandment of the King; because if the Keeper had taken upon him to affirm it upon his return, then needed he not to have returned the warrant of the Lords of the Council: and the warrant itself sheweth that he had only his information from the Lords of the Council. For their warrant is to let the Keeper know, that both the first commitment, and this direction for the continuing of him in prison, were and are by his Majesty's special commandment; and I do not see, as this return is made, that an accord upon the case can lie upon the Keeper of the Gatehouse, if Sir *John Corbet* was not committed nor detained by the special commandment of the King, so long as the warrant of the Lords of the Council be returned as it was made, because he doth return the same as the Significavit of the Lords by their warrant. *Register* 65. the writ of Excommunicat' *Capiend'* goeth, *Rex vicecom' Lincoln' S. significavit nob' venerabilis pater Henricus Lincolniensis Episcopus per Literas suas Patentes quod R. suus Parochial' propter suam manifestam contumac' authoritate ipsius Episc' ordin' excom' est, nec se vult per censuram Ecclesiasticam justiciar' &c. tibi præcipimus quod prædict' R. per corpus suum secundum consuetud' Angliæ Justic' &c.* And yet no man will say that there is an information of the King, that *R.* is excommunicated, but only that the Bishop of *Lincoln* had signified unto him that *R.* was excommunicated. And in *Fitz. Nat. Br.* 663. and *Register* 65. it appears that the form of the writ of Excommunication *deliberand'* is, *Rex Vicecom' London Salut'. Cum Thom' Jay allutar' London' qui nuper ad denuntiat. venerabil' patris Archiep' Eborum pro contumaciis suis ratione contractus in civitate nostra Eborum habit' ut dicebat. tanquam excom' & claves Ecclesiæ contemnent' per corp' suum secundum consuetud' Angliæ per te justic' præcepimus, donec &c. esset satisfact' eid' Archiepiscop. ad satisfaciendum Deo et sanctæ ecclesiæ, sufficientem exposuit cautionem, per quod eidem Archiepiscopus offic. Archidiac. London. mutuæ vicissitudin' obtentu scripsit ut ipsum absolvat ab excom' senten' memorata sicut idem Archiepiscopus per Literas suas patentes nob' significavit, tibi præcipimus quod præd' Thom. cum tibi constare poterit ipsum ab excom' prædict' per prædict' Official' absolvi a Prison' qua detinetur si ea occasione & non alia detineat' in eadem sine dilatione deliberari fac'.* And yet it can-

cannot be ſaid, that although the King recited in his writ that the Archbiſhop had ſignified unto him that he had written unto the Official of the Arch-deacon, that the King ſaid, that the Archbiſhop had written; for he doth not affirm ſo much preciſely, but only referreth himſelf unto the Certificate of the Archbiſhop.

Plowden 122. *Buckley* and *River*'s caſe, it is put, that if a man will bring an action of debt upon an obligation, and declare that it appears by the obligation that the defendant ſtood bound to the plaintiff in twenty pounds, the which he hath not paid, this declaration is not good; inſomuch as it is not alledged by matter in fact, that he was bound unto him in twenty pound, but the deed is alledged by recital only, 21 *Ed.* IV. 43.

Plowden Com' 126. & 145. *Browning* and *Beeſton*'s caſe.

The Abbot of *Waltham* being appointed collector of a Diſme granted unto the King in diſcharge of himſelf, in the Exchequer, pleadeth, *Quod inter recordat' Ter. Paſc. anno* 15. *domini Regis Edwardi* I. *inter alia continetur quod R.* II. had granted unto the predeceſſors of the ſaid Abbot, that he nor any of his ſucceſſors ſhould be any collectors of any Diſmes to be granted afterwards, and it was adjudged that this plea was ill.

For the ſaying [It was contained among the Records], it is no preciſe affirmation that the King had granted to his predeceſſors, that they ſhould be diſcharged of the collecting any Diſmes, but it is only an allegation by way of recital, and not by preciſe affirmation, the plea may not be good.

2 & 3 *Mar. Dyer* 117. & 118. the plaintiff's reply in bar of all pleadeth, that *John* Abbot of *W.* was ſeized of his lands in right of his Church, and ſo ſeized by the aſſent of the tenant by indenture, 14 *Hen.* IV. *teſtat' quod prædict' Abbat' & convent' demiſerunt & tradiderunt* unto the plaintiff; and ruled, that this form of pleading was ill, inſomuch as it was not alledged by preciſe affirmation, *quod demiſerunt, ſed indentura teſtatur, quod demiſerunt*; which is not ſufficient, inſomuch as it is only an allegation by way of recital, that the indenture doth witneſs, and the ſame indenture may witneſs ſo much, and yet not be a demiſe.

And if in pleading there muſt be direct affirmation of the matter alledged, then *à fortiori* in a return, which muſt be more preciſe than in pleading; and ſo by all the caſes I have formerly touched, it appeareth that this return is no expreſs affirmation of the Keeper of the Gatehouſe, that Sir *John Corbet* is detained in priſon by the ſpecial commandment of the King, but only an affirmation of the Lords of the Council, who had ſignified unto him that his detainment in priſon was by ſpecial command of the King.

The return, which ought to be certain, and punctual, and affirmative, and not by the way of information out of another man's mouth, may not be good, as appeareth by the ſeveral books of our Law.

23 *Ed.* III. *Rex vic'* 181. upon a *Homine replegiando*, againſt the Abbot of *C.* the Sheriff returneth that he had ſent to the Bailiff of the Abbot, that anſwered him, that he was the Villein of the Abbot, by which he might not make deliverance, and a *Sicut alias* was awarded, for his return was inſufficient; inſomuch that he had returned the anſwer of the Bailiff of the Abbot, where he ought to have returned the anſwer of the Abbot himſelf out of his own mouth.

Trin. 22 *Ed.* II. *Rot.* 46. *parent' vill' & Burg. Eveſque de Norwich, repl'* 68. *Nat. Br. Caſe* 34. *Fitz. Nat. Br.* 65. & 14 *Ed.* III. *Excom'* 29. the caſe appeareth to be ſuch in a treſpaſs; the defendant pleadeth, the plaintiff is excommunicate, and ſheweth forth the letter of the Biſhop of *Lincoln*, witneſſing that for divers contumacies, &c. and becauſe he had certified no *excommunic'* done by himſelf, but by another, the letter of Excommunication was annulled, for the Biſhop ought to have certified his own act, and not the act of another.

Hillarii 21 *Hen.* VIII. *Rot.* 37. it appeareth by the return of an *Habeas Corpus*, that *John Parker* was committed to priſon for ſecurity of the peace, and for ſuſpicion of felony, *as per mandatum domini Regis nunciatum per Robertum Peck, de Clifford's-Inn*; and upon his return, *John Parker* was bailed: for the return *Commiſſ. fuit per ſpeciale mandatum domini Regis, nunciatum per Robertum Peck*, was not good, inſomuch that it was not a direct return that he was committed *per mandatum domini Regis*.

And for the firſt point, I conclude, that this return is inſufficient in form, inſomuch, that it doth not make a preciſe and direct return, that he was committed and detained by the ſpecial command of the King, but only as it was ſignified by the warrant of the Lords of the Council, which will not ſerve the turn. And upon the book of 9 *Hen.* VI. 44. the return of the cauſe of a man's Impriſonment ought to be preciſe and direct upon the *Habeas Corpus*, inſomuch as thereby to be able to judge of the cauſe, whether it be ſufficient or not. for there may not any doubt be taken to the return, be it true or falſe, but the Court is to accept the ſame as true, and if it be falſe, the party muſt take his remedy by action upon the caſe.

And as concerning the matter of the return, it will reſt upon theſe parts:

Firſt, Whether the return, that he is detained in priſon by ſpecial commandment of our Lord the King, be good or not, without ſhewing the nature of the commandment, or the cauſe whereupon the commitment is grounded in the return?

The ſecond is, Whether the time of the firſt commitment by the commandment of the King, not appearing to the Court, is ſufficient to detain him in priſon?

Thirdly, Whether the impriſonment of the ſubjects without cauſe ſhewed, but only by the commandment of the King, be warrantable by the Laws and Statutes of this Realm?

As to the firſt part, I find by the books of our law, that commandments of the King are of ſeveral natures, by ſome of which the impriſonment of a man's body is utterly unlawful: and by others of them, although the impriſonment may be lawful, yet the continuance of him without bail or mainpriſe, will be utterly unlawful.

There is a verbal command of the King, which is by word of mouth of the King's only; and ſuch commandment by the King, by the books of our law, will not be ſufficient either to impriſon a man, or to continue him in priſon, 16. 6. *Monſtrans de faict ſi*, upon an action of treſpaſs brought for cutting of trees, the defendant pleadeth that the place where he cut them is parcel of the Manor of *D* whereof the King is ſeized in fee, and the King commanded him to cut the trees; and the opinion of the Court there, that the plea in bar was ill, becauſe he did not ſhew any ſpecial commandment of the King; and there it is agreed by the whole Court, that if the King commandeth one to arreſt another, and the party commanded did arreſt the other, an action of treſpaſs or falſe impriſonment is maintainable againſt the party that arreſted him, although it were done in the preſence of the King. 39 *H.* VI. 17. where one juſtifieth the ſeizure of the goods of a perſon that is outlawed by the commandment of the King, ſuch a party being no Officer, may not in an action brought againſt him have any aid of the King; for ſuch a commandment given to one that is not an Officer, will not any ways avail him, that is to juſtify himſelf by the return of that commandment.

37 *Hen.* VI. 10 If the King give me a thing, and I take the ſame by his commandment by word of mouth, it is not juſtified by law, nothing may paſs without matter of Record.

10 *Hen.* VII. 7. & 17. 18. it is agreed, that Juſtices may command one to arreſt another that is in their view or preſence, but not one that is out of their view or preſence. (1 *Croke. Hollinday V. Oxenbridge*)

And *Kebl.* 10 *Hen.* VII. 13. ſaid, that where one is arreſted by a parol command in their view or preſence, it is fitting that a record may be made of it, inſomuch, that without ſuch a record there can hardly be a juſtification in another Term.

Secondly, There is a commandment of the King by his Commiſſion, which, according to *Colvin*'s caſe in *Coke*'s ſeventh Report, it is called by him, *breve mandatum non remediabile*; and by virtue of ſuch a commandment, the King may neither ſeize the goods of his ſubject, nor impriſon his body, as it is reſolved in 42 *Aſſ. pl.* 5. where it is agreed by all the Juſtices, that a Commiſſion to take a man's goods, or impriſon his body without indictment or ſuit of the party, or other due proceſs, is againſt the law.

Thirdly, There is a commandment of the King, which is grounded upon a ſuggeſtion made to the King or to his Council; and if a man be committed to priſon by ſuch a ſuggeſtion, by commandment of the King, it is unlawful, and not warranted by the Law of the Realm.

The 25 of *Edw.* III. cap. 4. *de proviſionibus*, where it is contained in the great Charter of the *Franchiſes of England*, that none ſhall be impriſoned or arreſted of his Freehold or of his Franchiſes, nor of his free Cuſtoms, but by the law of the land.

It is awarded, conſented and eſtabliſhed, that from henceforth none ſhall be taken by petition or ſuggeſtion made to our Sovereign Lord the King, or to his Council, until it be by indictment or preſentment of his good and lawful neighbours, where ſuch deeds are done in due manner, or by proceſs made by writ original at the common law; nor that none ſhall be arreſted of his Franchiſes, nor of his Freehold, unleſs he be duly brought in, and anſwer, and forejudged of the ſame by way of law: and if any thing be done againſt the ſame, it ſhall be redreſſed and holden for nought.

37 *Ed.* III. *cap.* 10. although it be contained in the great Charter, that no man be taken or impriſoned or put out of his freehold, without due proceſs of the law; nevertheleſs, divers perſons make falſe ſuggeſtions to the King himſelf, as well for malice as otherwiſe, whereby the King is often grieved, and divers of the Realm put in great damages, contrary to the form of the ſame Statute.

Wherefore it is ordained, that all they that make ſuch ſuggeſtions, be ſent with their ſuggeſtions to the Chancellor or Treaſurer, and they and every of them find ſureties to purſue their ſuggeſtions, and endure the ſame pain as the other ſhould have had in caſe that his ſuggeſtion be found untrue; and that then proceſs of the law be made againſt them, without being taken or impriſoned, againſt the form of the ſame Charter, and other Statutes.

So that it appears by theſe ſeveral Statutes, that ſuch commandments of the King as are grounded upon ſuggeſtion, either made to himſelf or to his Council, for the impriſonment of a man, are againſt the law.

Fourthly, I find that there is a commandment of the King which is made under his hand, with his ſignet; for in the fourth and the fifth of *Philip* and *Mary*, *Dyer* 162. where the Statute of 1 *Ric.* II. *cap.* 11. reſtraineth the Warden of the Fleet for letting any man at large that is in upon judgment at the ſuit of any man, except it be by Writ or other commandment of the King; it was doubted, whether the Queen by letter under her hand and privy-ſignet doth give commandment to the Warden of the Fleet to ſuffer a man that is there in execution to go about his buſineſs, or the affairs of the Queen; whether this be a warrantable command or not within the Statute: and the Law hath always been conceived upon that book, that ſuch a commandment is not warrantable by Law. And if ſuch a command will not ſerve the turn, to give unto a man his liberty, which the law favoureth, and had the countenance of an Act of Parliament for the doing of it; then I conceive it ſhould be a more ſtrong caſe, the King ſhould not have power by his commandment to impriſon a man without due proceſs of the Law, and reſtrain him of his liberty, when there had been ſo many Acts of Parliament made for the liberty of the ſubjects.

Fifthly, I do find that there is the commandment of the King, which is by his Writ under the Great-Seal, or the Seal of the Court out of which it iſſueth, *Regiſt. f.* 69, & 70. In the Writ *de cautione admittenda*, I find the words, *mandatum Regis* expounded to be *breve Regis*, for the Writ goeth: *Rex vic' ſalutem. Cum nuper ad requiſitionem S. de Iſle canonici Lincolne venerabilis Patris H. Lincoln. Epiſcopi ipſo in remotis agente Vicarii general. per Literas ſuas Patentes nobis ſignificantes Nicho, B dict. Lincoln. Dioc. propter manifeſtam contumaciam Authoritate ipſius Epiſcopi Ordinar. excommunicat. eſſe nec ſi velle, &c. vobis præceperimus quod præfat. &c. ſatisfactum ex parte ipſius N. qui virtute mandati noſtri prædict per vos Capt. & in Priſon. noſtra de Newgate detent. exiſtit, &c. nos nolentes quod præfat. N. per breve noſtrum prædict. via præcludatur, &c. proſequi poſſit in forma Juris maxim. &c. integer eſſe debeat, vobis præcipimus quod ſcire &c. quod ſit &c. quare prædict. N. a Priſona prædict. deliberari non debeat. Rex juſticiar' ſuis de Banco ſalut. Cum nos nuper ad ſignificationem S. de Iſle &c. uſque ibi excommunicat. extitiſſe, nec ſe velle &c. eſſet ſatisfactum ex parte ipſius N. virtute mandati noſtri præd. cap. & in Priſona noſtra de Newgate tunc detenti, &c. et nolentes eo prætextu præfato N. per breve noſtrum præd. via præcludat. quo minus appellat. ſuæ negotium &c. proceſſerat. & appellant. ſtatut. &c. per breve noſtrum* [illegible] *conſuit.*

fult. & circumspect. in placitis per breve praedict. coram vobis pendentibus procedere valeatis secundum legem & consuetudinem Regni nostri.

Stauf. 72. 5 *E.* III. *c.* 8. 1 *E.* III. *c.* 9. saith, that every *Capias* in a personal action is a commandment of the King, for it is *Praecipimus tibi quod capias, &c.* and yet the defendant, as there it is said, is replevisable by the Common Law. 7 *R.* 20. *a. Calvin's* case, saith, that there are two kind of Writs, *viz. brevia mandatoria & remedialia, & brevia mandatoria & non remedialia. Brevia mandatoria & remedialia*, are Writs of right, formed on, *&c.* debts, trespasses, and shortly all Writs real and personal, whereby the party wronged is to recover somewhat, and to be remedied for that wrong which is done unto him.

Sixthly, I do find by our books of Law, and by the *Register*, that this special *mandatum domini Regis*, is expounded to be this Writ, and that the law taketh no notice of any other *speciale mandatum*, than by this Writ. The which being so, when the return is made, that he is imprisoned and detained in prison by the special commandment of the King, how can the Court adjudge upon this return, that Sir *John Corbet* ought to be kept in prison, and not to be bailed; when the nature of the special commandment is not set forth in the return, whereby it may appear unto the Court that he is not bailable? In *Bracton*, *c.* 12. 117. you shall see a Writ reciting, *Praecipimus tibi quod non implacites nec implacitari permittas talem de libero tenemento suo tali villa, sine speciali praecepto nostro vel Capitalis Justiciar' nostri.*

And the reason of it there is given, *quia nemo de libero tenemento sine brevi sive libello conventionali nisi gratis voluerit respondebit.* So as the exception of special commandment by the very book, appeareth to be *breve sive libellus conventionalis. Regist.* 271. the Writ of Manucaption goeth in this manner. *Rex vic. Salut. Cum nuper assignavertmus dilectos & fideles nostros A. B. & C. D. ad inquisitiones de forstallariis. & transgressionibus contra formam statuti dudum apud Winton. editi in com. tuo faciend & ad illos quos inde culpabiles invenirent. capiend. & in Prisona nostra salvo custod. faciend. donec aliud inde praecipissemus quod C. D. & E. pro hujusmodi forstallamentis & transgressionibus unde coram praefat. A. B. & C. D. indict fuerint, capt. & in prisona de L. detent. exist. a qua deliberari non possunt, sine mandato nostro speciali, nos volentes eisdem C. D. & E. gratiam in hac parte facere specialem, tibi praecipimus quod si praedict. C. D. & E. occasione praedict. & non alia in Prisona praedict. detineantur, & pro transgressionibus illis secundum legem & consuetudinem Regni nostri Angliae replegiabiles existunt &c. tunc impos' C. D & E a Prisona praedict. si ea occasione, & non alia detineantur in eadem, interim deliberari facias per manucapt. supradict. & habeas ibi tunc coram praefat. Justiciar. nomina manucapt. illorum & hoc breve.*

And the exposition of this *speciale mandatum domini Regis*, mentioned in the Writ, is expounded to be *breve domini Regis*, and thereupon is this Writ directed unto the Sheriff for the delivery of them.

And so much for the first branch of the first part: I conclude, that the special command of the King, without shewing the nature of the commandment of the King, is too general, and therefore insufficient; for he ought to have returned the nature of the commandment of the King, whereby the Court might have adjudged upon it, whether it were such a commandment that the imprisonment of Sir *John Corbet* be lawful or not; and whether it were such a commandment of the King, that although the imprisonment were lawful at the first, yet he might be bailed by law.

And as for the general return of *speciale mandatum domini Regis*, without shewing the cause of the imprisonment either special or general, I hold, that for that cause also the return is insufficient,

First, in regard of the *Habeas Corpus*, which is the commandment of the King only, made the 15th of *November*.

According to the *Teste* of the Writ, commanding the Keeper of the Gatehouse to have the body of Sir *John Corbet, una cum causa detentionis, & ad subjiciendum & recipiendum ea quae curia nostra de eo ad tunc ibid. ordinar. contingat'*; so as the commandment of the Writ being to shew the cause of his detaining in prison, the Keeper of the Gatehouse doth not give a full answer unto the Writ, unless the cause of the detainment in prison be returned; and the Court doth not know how to give their judgment upon him, either for his imprisonment, or for his discharge, according to the purport of the Writ, when there is not a cause returned. And forasmuch as upon an *Excommengement* certified, it hath been adjudged oftentimes that Certificates were insufficient, where the cause of the commitment hath not been certified, that the Court might adjudge whether the Ecclesiastical Judges, who pronounced the excommunication, had power over the original cause according to the Book of 14 *Hen.* IV. 14. 8. *Rep.* 68. *Trollop's* case, and 20 *Edw.* III *Excommengement* 9.

So upon an *Habeas Corpus* in this Court, where a man hath been committed by the Chancellor of *England*, by the Council of *England*, Marches of *Wales*, Warden of the Stanneries, High-Commission, Admiralty, Dutchy, Court of Request, Commission of Sewers or Bankrupts, it hath several times been adjudged that the return was insufficient, where the particular cause of imprisonment hath not been shewn, to the intent that it might appear, that those that committed him had jurisdiction over the cause, otherwise he ought to be discharged by the law. And I spare to recite particular causes in every kind of these, because there are so many precedents of them in several ages of every King of this Realm: and it is an infallible maxim of the law, That as the Court of the Kings-Bench, and Judges, ought not to deny an *Habeas Corpus* unto any prisoner that shall demand the same, by whomsoever he be committed, so ought the cause of his imprisonment to be shewn upon the return, so that the Court may adjudge of the cause, whether the cause of the imprisonment be lawful or not. And because I will not trouble the Court with so many precedents, but such as shall suit with the cause in question, I will only produce and touch such precedents, where the party was committed either by the commandment of the King, or otherwise by the commandment of the Privy-Council, which *Stanford fol.* 72. termeth the mouth of the King, such Acts as are done by the Privy-Council, being as Acts done by the King himself.

And in all these causes you shall find that there is a cause returned as well as a *speciale mandatum domini Regis* [illegible] *mandatum Privati Concilii domini Regis*, whereby the Court may adjudge of the cause, and bail them if they shall see cause.

In the 8th of *Hen.* VII. upon return of an *Habeas Corpus* awarded for the body of one [illegible], it appeareth that he was committed by the Mayor of *Windsor* for suspicion of felony, and *ad sectam ipsius Regis pro quibusdam feloniis & transgressionibus ac per mandatum domini Regis* 21 *Hen.* VII. upon the return of an *Habeas Corpus* sent for the body of *Hugh Pain*, it appeared that he was committed to prison, *per mandatum dominorum Privati Concilii domini Regis pro suspicione feloniae.*

Primo Henrici Octavi, Rot. 9. upon the return of an *Habeas Corpus* sent for the body of one *Thomas Harrison* and others, it appears that they were committed to the Earl of *Shrewsbury*, being Marshal of the Houshold, *per mandatum domini Regis, & pro suspicione feloniae, & pro homicidio facto super Mare.*

3 & 4 *Philip. & Mariae*, upon a return of an *Habeas Corpus*, sent for the body of one *Peter Man*, it appeareth that he was committed *pro suspicione feloniae, ac per mandatum domini Regis & Reginae.*

4 & 5 *Philippi & Mariae*, upon the return of an *Habeas Corpus* sent for the body of one *Thomas Newport*, it appeared that he was committed to the Tower, *pro suspicione contrafact' monetae per privatum Concilium domini Regis & Reginae.*

33 *Elizabethae*, upon the return of an *Habeas Corpus* for the body of one *Laurence Brown*, it appeareth that he was committed, *per mandatum Privati Concilii dominae Reginae pro diversis causis ipsam Reginam tangent' ac etiam pro suspicione proditionis.*

So as by all these precedents it appeareth where the return is either, *per mandatum domini Regis*, or *per mandatum dominorum Privati Concilii domini Regis*, there is also a cause over and besides the *mandatum* returned. As to that which may be objected, that *per mandatum domini Regis*, or *Privati Concilii domini Regis*, is a good return of his imprisonment, I answer,

First, That there is a cause: for it is not to be presumed that the King or Council would commit one to prison without some offence; and therefore this *mandatum* being occasion'd by the offence or fault, the offence or fault must be the cause, and not the command of the King or Council, which is occasion'd by the cause.

Secondly, It appears that the jurisdiction of the Privy-Council is a limited jurisdiction, for they have no power in all causes, their power being restrained in certain causes by several Acts of Parliament, as it appeareth by the Statute of 20 *E.* III. *c.* 11. 25 *E.* III. *c.* 1. *Stat.* 4. (*vide* 4 *Instit. p* 53.) the private petition in Parliament permitted in the 1 *R.* II. where the Commons petition that the Privy-Council might not make any ordinance against the Common Law, Customs or Statutes of the Realm; the 4 *Hen.* IV. *cap.* 3. 13 *Hen.* IV. 7. 31 *Hen.* VI. And their jurisdiction being a limited jurisdiction, the cause and grounds of their commitment ought to appear, whereby it may appear if the Lords of the Council did commit him for such a cause as was within their jurisdiction: for if they did command me to be committed to prison for a cause whereof they had not jurisdiction, the Court ought to discharge me of this imprisonment. And howsoever the King is *Vicarius Dei in terra*, yet *Bracton, cap* 8 *fol.* 107. saith, *quod nihil aliud potest Rex in terris cum sit Minister Dei & Vicarius, quam solum quod de jure potest, nec obstat, quod dicitur quod principi placet, legis habet vigorem, quia sequitur in fine legis cum lege Regia quae de ejus imperio lata est; id est, non quicquid de voluntate Regis temere praesumptum est, sed animo condendi Jura, sed quod consilio Magistratuum suorum Rege author. praestant. & habita super hoc deliberatione & tract. rect. fuer. definit. Potestat. itaque sua juris est, & non injuriae.* The which being so, then also it ought to appear upon what cause the King committeth one to prison, whereby the Judges which are indifferent between the King and his Subjects, may judge whether his commitment be against the Laws and Statutes of this Realm, or not.

Thirdly, It is to be observed, that the King's command by his writ of *Habeas Corpus*, is since the commandment of the King for his commitment; and this being the latter commandment, ought to be obeyed, wherefore that commanding a return of the body *cum causa detentionis*, there must be a return of some other cause than *per mandatum domini Regis*, the same commandment being before the return of the Writ.

Pasch. 9. *E.* III. *pl.* 30. *fol.* 56. upon a Writ of *Cessavit* brought in the County of *Northumberland*, the Defendants plead, That by reason of the Country being destroyed by wars with the *Scots*, King *Ed.* II. gave command that no Writ of *Cessavit* should be brought during the wars with *Scotland*, and that the King had sent his Writ to surcease the plea, and he averreth that the wars with *Scotland* did continue.

Hearle that giveth the rule saith, That we have command by the King that now is, to hold this plea, wherefore we will not surcease for any Writ of the King that is dead. And so upon all these reasons and precedents formerly alledged, I conclude, that the return that Sir *John Corbet* was committed and detained in prison, *per speciale mandatum domini Regis*, without shewing the nature of the commandment, by which the Court may judge whether the commandment be of such a nature as he ought to be detained in prison, and that without shewing the cause upon which the commandment of the King is grounded, is not good. As to the second part, which is, whether the time of the commitment by the return of the Writ, not appearing unto the Court, the Court ought to detain him in prison, or not: I conceive that he ought not to be continued in prison, admitting that the first commitment by the command of the King was lawful; yet when he hath continued in prison by such a convenient time, as may be thought fit for that offence for which he is committed, he ought to be brought to answer, and not to continue still in prison without being brought to answer.

For it appears by the books of our laws, that liberty is a thing so favoured by the law, that the law will not suffer the continuance of a man in prison for any longer time than of necessity it must; and therefore the law will neither suffer the Party, Sheriffs or Judges to continue a man in prison by their power and their pleasure, but doth speed the delivery of a man out of prison, with [illegible] expedition as [illegible].

And upon this reason it [illegible] in [illegible] *El. Pro* [illegible] 8 *Ed.* IV. 13. That [illegible] the law [illegible] that there [illegible] be a term between the tede of an original Writ and the return of the same, where there is only a summons, and no imprisonment of the body, yet it will not allow that there shall be a term between the teste of a Writ of *Capias*, and the return of the [illegible] where the body [illegible] imprisoned [illegible] the [illegible] power [illegible] man [illegible] III. [illegible] *H.* VII. [illegible] *E.* IV. [illegible] III. [illegible] *Hen.* VII

Bracton's

Keilaway's Reports do all agree, that if a *Capias* shall be awarded against a man for the apprehending of his body, and the Sheriff will return the *Capias* that is awarded against the party, a *non est inventus*, or that *languidus est in prisona*, yet the law will allow the party against whom it is awarded, for the avoiding of his corporal penance and duress of imprisonment, to appear *gratis*, and for to answer.

For the law will not allow the Sheriff by his false return to keep one in prison longer than needs must, 38 *Ass. pl.* 22. *Brooks* imprisonment 100. saith, That it was determined in Parliament that a man is not to be detained in prison, after he hath made tender of his fine for his imprisonment; therefore I desire your Lordship that Sir *John Corbet* may not be longer kept in durance, but be discharged according to the law.

L. C. Justice. Mr. Attorney, you have heard many learned arguments; if you be provided to answer presently, we will hear you; but if you will have a longer day, for that you are not provided to argue, you may, we will give it you.

Doderidge. If you will, you may see the precedents; it may be you have not seen some of them, and we must see them too.

Attorn. Gen. *Heath.* May it please your Lordship, the Gentlemen that be of Counsel with the Knights at the Bar, they have said much, and spoken very long for their Clients, and to good purpose and pertinently. It is a cause that carrieth with it a great deal of weight, both towards the King and his Subjects also, and I am not so hasty to put myself upon the main point of this cause, when it is almost time for your Lordship to rise.

My Lord, the Gentlemen have severally spoken, and given and insisted upon several reasons, and they have cited many precedents. I could say something of them at this present, and that some of them have been mistaken; and therefore I beseech your Lordship, that I may have time to answer, that I may not wrong the cause of the King's part, or slight the cause on the Subject's part.

But that which I desire to say now is, that these Gentlemen have all of them gone in one form, to divide the cause into two parts:

The first, the form of the return.

The second, the matter of the return.

For the form, methinks we may put an end to that now, if your Lordship please, that we may have no return to that another day, but I may apply myself unto the matter of the return.

To the form of the return they have taken divers exceptions, but they especially insisted upon two main heads:

First, That the return is not good, because it is not an absolute return. I confess the ground is well laid, and the major is good, that if this return be not positively the return of the Warden of the *Fleet* himself, but the relation of another, it is no good return, therefore I need spend no time in that, the ground being well laid. But under your Lordship's favour, the minor proposition I deny, we differ only in that; for I say that this return is certain, and that it is not the words of any man else, but the express words of the Warden himself, and that this is added *ex abundanti* to give satisfaction to the Court, that he had order to make the return: therefore I desire your Lordship to cast your eyes upon the substance of the return, and distinguish it into parts.

The words are, *Detentus est in prisona sub custodia mea per speciale mandatum domini Regis, mibi significatum per Warrantum duorum Privati Concilii dicti domini Regis, &c.* If he had turned these words, and said, *Detent' est prout mibi significat' per Warrantum duorum Privati Concilii per speciale mandatum domini Regis*, then it might be taken to be the words of the Lords of the Council: but the first words being positive, *Detentus est per speciale mandatum domini Regis*, that is sufficient, and the rest is surplusage, and he doth not say, *prout mibi significat'*, but *mibi significat'* only; which is absolute, and the resolution thereof resteth more in your Lordship's expounding of the words; than in putting any case upon them.

The second exception is taken to the form of the return, for that there is not the cause of the imprisonment returned, but of the detaining alone.

My Lord, I say no more at present to that, but this: No man is bound to answer more than that which is the contents of the Writ. But the Writ it may be to know specially the cause of the detaining, or what the cause of the caption is only, and if the Officer make answer to that which is required of him in the Writ, it is sufficient. It may be, there be precedents both ways, I am sure there are for detentions, and there is no cause why the Officer shall shew the time of his commitment: but if the prisoner shall desire it, your Lordship may grant him a Writ, to shew the cause both of his caption and detention also.

Thirdly, They say that this return is uncertain, and that it is the Warrant of the Lords of the Council, and not of the King, by which he is committed.

For that, my Lord, I say, that if it had all been left out, and he had only said, *Detentus fuit per speciale mandatum domini Regis*, it had been sufficient: but when he doth more, it is superfluous, and not necessary, for it appeared before by whom he was committed; and when he returns the Warrant of the Lords of the Council, it is not their words that commit him: But they being the representative body of the King, they do express what the King's command is, but they signify nothing of their own; and therefore I desire your Lordship to deliver your opinion in that point of the return, whether it be positive or no.

This cause, as it greatly concerns the Subjects, so it much concerns the King too. I am sorry there should be any occasion to bring these things in question; but since it is now here, I hope I shall give satisfaction to your Lordship, and to the parties too, and I desire that I may have till *Monday* for it.

L. C. Justice. I think it is not best for us to declare our opinions by piece-meals, but upon all the case together, and as you are a stranger to the return, so are we; and there be many Precedents and Acts of Parliament not printed, which we must see.

Doderidge. This is the greatest cause that ever I knew in this Court; our judgments that we give between party and party, between the King and the meanest subject, ought to be maturely advised on, for so are the entries of our judgments, *Quod matura deliberatione habita*, It was judged, *&c.* And we must see the Precedents and Acts of Parliament that we hear mentioned.

Justice *Jones.* Mr. Attorney, if it be so that the Law of *Magna Charta* and other Statutes be now in force, and the Gentlemen be not delivered by this Court, how shall they be delivered? Apply yourself to shew us any other way to deliver them.

Doderidge. Yea, or else they shall have a perpetual imprisonment.

Per Curiam. Monday was appointed for the Attorney's argument, and in the interim the Counsel for the Gentlemen were by order appointed to attend the Judges with all the precedents and unprinted Statutes which they mentioned, and that they should let the Attorney see them also.

And the Gentlemen being asked if they desired to come again, answered they did, and a rule was entered for it.

Monday, 26 November 1627. *Tertio Michaelis, 38 Caroli Regis, in Banco Regis.*

Sir *John Corbet*, Sir *Walter Earl*, Sir *John Heveningham*, Sir *Edmund Hampden*, Knights, were brought to the Bar.

Attorn. Gen. *Heath.* MAY it please your Lordship, these Gentlemen, Sir *John Corbet*, Sir *Walter Earl*, Sir *John Heveningham*, and Sir *Edmund Hampden*, upon their motion to this Court to have their *Habeas Corpus*, and that themselves, and the cause of their detaining them in their several prisons, might be brought before your Lordship, had it granted to them.

My Lord, at the first motion of it, the knowledge thereof coming, and that they had such a desire, his Majesty was very willing to grant unto them (as to all his subjects) this common case of Justice; and tho' it be a case which concerns himself in a high degree, yet he hath been so gracious and so just, as not to refuse to leave the examination and determination thereof to the laws of this kingdom.

My Lord, it is very true that this is a very great cause, and hath raised a great expectation, and for the manner of it, more than was necessary; but, my Lord, I am afraid these Gentlemen whom it concerns, have rather advised their Counsel, than their Counsel them: but I shall take the case as now I find it, and as the Gentlemen's Counsel, on the other side, have led me the way to it.

My Lord, the exceptions that have been taken by the Counsel on the other side, to the return made by the Warden of the *Fleet*, and the rest of the Guardians of several prisons, have been two. For renewing of your Lordship's memory, we will read one of the returns, they are all alike.

Then the return was read for Sir *John Heveningham*, by Mr. *Keeling*.

Attorn. Gen. May it please your Lordship, against this return the Counsel of the Gentlemen have taken some exceptions, and have divided their objections into two main points, the one the form, the other the matter. To the form they have objected four several things:

First, That the return is not positive, but referred to the signification made by another, as the Lords of the Council.

Secondly, That the keepers of the prisons have not returned the cause of the commitment, but the cause of the cause, which is not good.

Thirdly, That the return is imperfect, for that it shews only the cause of the detaining in prison, and not the cause of the first commitment.

And *lastly*, That the return is contradictory in itself, for that in the first part thereof there is a certification that the detaining of these Gentlemen in prison, is *per speciale mandatum domini Regis*; and when the Warrant of the Lords of the Council is shewed, it appears that the commitment is by the command of the King, signified by the Lords of the Council: and by your Lordship's favour, I will give a several answer to every of these several objections. And for the first, that the return is not positive and affirmative, but depends upon and hath relation to some other, and therefore it is not good, I do agree that the ground is true, that if the return be not positive, it is not good: we differ only in the minor, that the return is not positive and affirmative; for I agree that these Book-cases, that have been put, are good law: as 27 *Ass. pl.* 65. that if the Sheriff return that he had sent to the Bailiff of the Hundred, and he gives him that answer, that is no good return; for the Sheriff ought to make the return as of his own act, without naming of the Bailiff of the Hundred in his return: for if he return, *Quod mandavi Ballivo itineranti qui habet retorn' omnium brevium & executionem eorund' per Cartam domini Regis qui mibi dedit nullum responsum*; this is not good, if he were not Bailiff of a franchise or signiory, for so is 21 *H.* VII. *fol.* 4.

There hath been cited to maintain these objections, 20 *Ed.* III. The record I have perused, and there I find that the Bishop said, that it is found *in Archivis*, in the record, *&c.* that he was excommunicated; but it was found to be *in Archivis*, *&c.* and that is no positive return that it is so. I will oppugn what hath been said by the Counsel on the other side; it must be granted that if the return here be not positive, it is imperfect, and in 5 *H.* VII. 28. it is said, that an imperfect return is no return at all, it is all one; but if the return was so, that was not much material, for then it were but temporary, and it might be amended: but, my Lord, they have mistaken the minor proposition, for they have taken it as granted that there is an imperfect return from the Lords of the Council. My Lord, I shall intreat you to cast your eyes upon the return, and you shall find the first words positive and affirmative: the words are, *Quod detentus est sub custodia mea per speciale mandatum domini Regis*: the other words, *mibi significatum*, follow after, but are not part of the affirmation made before it. But if they will have it as they seem to understand it, then they must turn the words thus: *Quod testificatum*, or *significatum est mibi per dominos Privati Concilii quod detentus est per speciale mandatum domini Regis*; and then indeed it had not been their own proper return, but the signification of another, the Lords of the Council: the turning of the sentence will resolve this point; the thing itself must speak for itself. I conceive by your Lordship's favour, that it is plain and clear, here is a positive return, that the detaining is by the commandment of the King: and the rest of the return is rather for satisfaction to myself and the Court, than otherwise any part of the return.

The

The second objection hath dependance upon this, as that he hath returned the cause of the cause, and not the cause itself, wherein, under your Lordship's favour, they are utterly mistaken; for the return is affirmative, *Ego Johannes Liloe testifico, &c.* I know that among the Logicians there are two causes, there is *Causa causans*, and *Causa causata*: the *Causa causans* here in this case is not the warrant from the Lords of the Council, for that is *Causa causata*: but the primary and original cause, which is *Causa causans*, is *speciale mandatum domini Regis*; the other is but the Council's signification or testification, or warrant for him that made the return.

To the third objection, that the return is imperfect, because it shews only the cause of the detaining in prison, and not the cause of the first commitment:

My Lords, for that I shall not insist much upon it, for that I did say the last day, which I must say again, it is sufficient for an Officer of the Law to answer that point of the Writ which is in command.

Will your Lordship please to hear the Writ read, and then to see, whether the Wardens of the Prisons have not made answer to so much as was in command?——Then the Writ was read by Mr. *Keeling*.

Att. Gen. My Lord, the Writ itself clears the objection; for it is to have the Party mentioned in it, and the cause of his Detention, returned into this Court; and therefore the answer to that is sufficient. Only, my Lord, the Warden of the *Fleet*, and the rest of the Keepers of the Prisons, had dealt prudently in their Proceedings, if they had only said, that they were detained *per speciale mandatum Domini Regis*, and it had been good, and they might have omitted the rest: but because, if they should make a false return, they were liable to the Actions of the Party, they did discreetly to have the Certification of the Lords of the Council, in suspicion that if this return was not true, they were liable to the Actions of these Gentlemen.

In 9 *H.* VI. 40, 44. it is said, that whatsoever the cause be that is returned, it must be accepted by the Court; they must not doubt of the truth of the Return, and the Officer that shall return it is liable to an Action if the Return is false, and therefore the Guardians of the Prisons did wisely, because they knew this was a case of great expectation, to shew from whom they had their warrant, and so to see whether the cause be true or not.

The last Objection to the Return is, that it is contradictory in itself, as that the first Part of it is, that they are detained in prison *per speciale mandatum Domini Regis*; but in this relation of it, it shews that they are detained by the command of the Lords of the Council; for the words of their Warrant are, to require you still to detain him, *&c.*

But, my Lord, if they will be pleased to see the whole Warrant together, they shall find that the Lords of the Council speak not their own words or command in that Warrant, but they say that you are to take notice of it, as the words and command of the King; for, my Lord, the Lords of the Council are the Servants to the King, they signify his Majesty's pleasure to your Lordship and they say it is his Majesty's Pleasure you should know that the first commitment, and this present detaining him in Prison, are by his Majesty's special Commandment.

And this, my Lord, is all that I will say for the sufficiency of the Form of the Return, to prove that it is sufficient.

Touching the matter of the Return, the main Point thereof, it is but a single question, and I hope, my Lord, of no great difficulty; and that is, whether they be replevisable, or not replevisable? It appears that the commitment is not in a legal and ordinary way, but that it is *per speciale mandatum Domini Regis*; which implies, not only the fact done, but so extraordinarily done, that it is notorious to be his Majesty's immediate Act and Will it should be so, whether in this case they should be bailable or not in this Court, which I acknowledge to be the highest Court of Judicature for such a Case as is in Question.

The Counsel on the other side desire, that they may be bailed, and have concluded that they may not be remanded; their grounds of Argument (though they were many that did speak) I have in my Collection divided into five Points:

The first was, reasons that they must be so, arising from the inconveniences that would fall to the Subjects, if it should not be so in the main points of their liberty.

The second was, they shewed divers Authorities out of their Law-books, which they endeavoured to apply.

The third was, The Petition of the Commons answered by several Kings in Parliament.

The fourth was, Acts of Parliament in print.

The last was, Precedents of divers times, which they alledged to prove, that men committed by the King's commandment, and by the commandment of the Lords of the Privy-Council, (which I conceive to be all one, for the body of the Privy-Council represents the King himself) that upon such commitment in such causes men had been bailed.

In the course of my arguments I will follow their method, first, to answer their reasons, and then those Books which they have cited, which I conceive to be pertinent to this question, and then the Petition and Answer made in Parliament, and then their Acts of Parliament, next their Precedents; and lastly, I will give your Lordship some reasons of my own, which I hope shall sufficiently satisfy your Lordship and all others, but the parties themselves, for I except them.

My Lord, the great and mighty reason that they insisted upon, was the inconveniences that might come to the subjects in their liberties, if this return should be good; and this reason they inferred out of records and books of the Common Law, which gives the liberty of the subjects; I do acknowledge that the liberty of the subject is just, and that it is the inheritance of the subject, but yet it is their inheritance *secundum legem terræ*.

My Lords, they put many cases likewise to enforce it, 1 & 2 *Eliz. Dyer, fo.* 175. that the continuance of a *Capias* shall be from term to term, without a term betwixt, because otherwise the party defendant may be kept too long in prison; and 38. *Ass. pl.* 22. *Broke tit.* Imprisonment 100. that imprisonment is but to detain the party till he have made fine to the King, and therefore the King cannot justly detain him in prison after the fine tendered; and 16 *H.* VI. *monstrans de fait* 182. if the King command me to arrest a man, and thereupon I do arrest him, he may have an action of false imprisonment, or of trespass against me, though it be done in the King's presence: and 1 *H* VII. 4. the discourse of *Hussey*, where he saith, that Sir *John Markham* delivered unto King *Edward* the Fourth, that he should not arrest upon treason or felony any of his Subjects because he could not wrong his subjects by such arrest, for they could not have remedy against him.

These, my Lord, are the causes that they insisted upon for this purpose.

To the two first, I shall give but one answer; which is, that the restraint in these two cases, and most of the other cases before cited, appears to be in the ordinary course of Judicature fit for *Westminster-Hall*, and not for the King's Council-Table. A Writ of *Capias* was the first original of it, and therefore not to be applied to the cause of ours.

And for the other two cases, the law presumeth that the active part of them is not so proper for the Majesty of a King, whoever doth these things by his subordinate Officers; but that the subject should not be committed by the King, was never heard of, for the King may commit any man at his pleasure; but that is not our case: but whether when the King hath committed one, he must render a cause of that commitment, that it may appear whether the party be bailable or not, or else the party must be delivered.

The Book 9 *E.* III. *fol.* 16. *pl.* 30. cited of a *Cessavit*, the King having by Proclamation commanded, that in the County of *Northumberland* no *Cessavit* should be brought, *&c.* during the war; the tenant pleaded this command, and it was denied him, and he, notwithstanding that, was commanded to plead; but the reason thereof was, because the commandment thereof was given by *E.* II. who being dead, the commandment was determined.

The Book of *Edward* the Third, 4 *fol.* 16. is indeed, where the commandment was given by the same King, and that was likewise denied him; for the King cannot command your Lordship, or any other Court of Justice, to proceed otherwise than according to the Laws of this Kingdom; for it is part of your Lordship's oath, to judge according to the Law of the Kingdom. But, my Lord, there is a great difference between those legal commands, and that *absoluta Potestas* that a Sovereign hath, by which a King commands; but when I call it *absoluta potestas*, I do not mean that it is such a power as that a King may do what he pleaseth, for he hath rules to govern himself by, as well as your Lordships, who are subordinate Judges under him. The difference is, the King is the Head of the same fountain of Justice, which your Lordship administers to all his subjects; all Justice is derived from him, and what he doth, he doth not as a private person, but as the Head of the Commonwealth, as *Justiciarius Regni*, yea, the very essence of Justice under God upon earth is in him: and shall not we generally, not as subjects only, but as Lawyers, who govern themselves by the rules of the Law, submit to his commands, but make inquiries whether they be lawful, and say that the King doth not this or that in course of Justice?

If your Lordship sitting here shall proceed according to Justice, who calleth your actions in question, except there are some errors in the proceeding? and then you are subject to a Writ of Error.

But who shall call in question the Actions or the Justice of the King, who is not to give any account for them? as in this our case, that he commits a subject, and shews no cause for it.

The King commits and often shews no cause, for it is sometimes generally, *Per speciale mandatum domini Regis*, sometimes *Pro certis causis ipsum dominum Regem moventibus*; but if the King do this, shall it not be good? It is all one when the commitment is *Per speciale mandatum domini Regis*, and when it is *Pro certis causis ipsum dominum Regem moventibus*; and it is the same if the commitment be *Certis de causis ipsum dominum Regem tangentibus*.

And, my Lord, unless the Return to you doth open the secrets of the commitment, your Lordship cannot judge whether the party ought by Law to be remanded, or delivered: and therefore if the King allow and give warrant to those that make the return, that they shall express the cause of the commitment, as many times he doth, either for suspicion of felony, or making money, or the like; we shall shew your Lordship that in these causes this Court in its Jurisdiction were proper to try these criminal causes, and your Lordship doth proceed in them although the commitment be *Per speciale mandatum domini Regis*, which hath not a secret in it in these causes, for with the warrant he sendeth your Lordship the cause of the committing; and when these warrants are made and brought into this Court, your Lordship may proceed: but if there be no cause expressed, this Court hath always used to remand them; for it hath been used, and it is to be intended a matter of State, and that it is not ripe nor timely for it to appear.

My Lord, the main fundamental grounds of Arguments upon this case begins with *Magna Charta*, from thence have grown Statutes for explanation thereof, several Petitions of Parliament, and Precedents for expedition; I shall give answers to them all.

For *Magna Charta*, in the 29th Chapter, hath these words; No Freeman shall be taken or imprisoned, or disseised, of his freehold liberties, nor free customs, nor be outlawed, or exiled, nor any other way destroyed, nor we will not pass upon him nor condemn him, but by lawful Judgment of his Peers, or by the Law of the Realm.

My Lord, this Statute hath been many times confirmed; the Lord *Coke* numbered up the number to be about twenty; and we are to conclude on this, it is the foundation of our liberties.

No Freeman can be imprisoned but by *legale judicium Parium suorum, aut per legem terræ*. But will they have it understood that no man should be committed, but first he shall be indicted or presented? I think that no learned man will offer that; for certainly there is no Justice of Peace in a County, nor Constable within a Town, but he doth otherwise, and might commit before an Indictment can be drawn or a Presentment can be made: what then is meant by these words, *Per legem terræ*? If any man shall say, this doth not warrant that the King may for reasons moving him commit a man, and not be answerable for it, neither to the party, nor (under your Lordship's favour) unto any Court of Justice, but to the High Court of Heaven; I do deny it, and will prove it by our Statutes.

My Lord, it was urged by the Counsel on the other side, that our printed *Magna Charta*, which saith *nec super eum mittimus*, is mistaken; and that in divers Manuscripts it is expressly set down to be, *nec eum in carcerem mittimus*. I cannot judge of the Manuscripts that I have not seen; but, my Lord, I have one here by me, which was written many Ages ago, and the words in print are word for word as that which is here written.

Then they ſay, that *Matthew Paris* ſets it down ſo in his Hiſtory: My Lord, we do not govern ourſelves by Chronicle, but to anſwer that of *Matthew Paris*, he reports a Thing done in King *John*'s Time, but it was then but thought on, and it was enacted in the Time of *Henry* the Third; and there be many Things ſaid to be done in *Matthew Paris* which were not, and many Things omitted by him which were done.

This Charter was but in Election in the Time of King *John*, and then it might be, *nec eum in carcerem mittimus*; but it was not enacted till the Time of *Henry* the Third, and then that was omitted, and the Charter granted as now we have it.

But if they do ſee no more than I in this Clauſe, I know not why we ſhould contend about theſe Words, ſeeing the firſt Part of this Statute ſaith, *Nemo imprisonetur*, why then may not I ſay as well, *nec eum in carcerem mittimus?* I ſee no Difference in the Words, and therefore, my Lord, I ſhall not inſiſt any longer upon the literal Expoſition of the Words of *Magna Charta*, but I will reſort to the reſt of it, which is expreſt in the ſubſequent Statute and in common Practice.

The Counſel on the other Side ſaid, that the Statute of 28 *E.* III. *c.* 3. expreſſeth and giveth Life to this Charter; I ſhall deſire to have that Statute read.

Keeling, Clerk. *Item*, Whereas it is contained in the great Charter, *&c.* *Vide* all theſe Statutes in *Littleton*'s Argument in Parliament *poſtea*.

Attorney Gen. My Lord, the reading of this Statute will give Anſwer to it; for it is apparent by the Words thereof, none ſhall be taken by Petition, *&c.* and that the Court be extended to the firſt Arreſt, but they are to be underſtood that none ſhall be condemned, but he ſhall be brought to anſwer and be tried.

And if it be expounded otherwiſe, it will be contrary to that Practice which was then in uſe.

But it is utterly forbidden by this Statute, that any Man ſhould be condemned upon Suggeſtions or Petitions made to the King or Council, without due Trial by Law.

The next Statute they cited was 25 *E.* III. *cap.* 4. My Lord, I deſire that That may be read.

Keeling, Clerk. *Item*, That no Man, of what Eſtate or Condition ſoever he be, ſhall be put out of Land or Tenement, nor taken, nor impriſoned, nor diſinherited, nor put to Death, without being brought to anſwer by due Proceſs of Law.

Attorney Gen. My Lord, this Statute is intended to be a final Proſecution: For if a Man ſhall be impriſoned without due Proceſs, and never be brought to anſwer, that is unjuſt, and forbidden by this Statute; but when a Man is taken in Cauſes that are unknown to us, (who walk below Stairs) we are not privy to the Circumſtances which may cauſe the Trial to be delayed; and peradventure it is not time to bring the Matter to Trial, becauſe it is not yet come to Maturity, and therefore this is not within the meaning of the Statute.

Another Statute that they mention is in the ſame Year, and it is Page 9 *chap.* 9. I deſire it may be read.

Keeling, Clerk. *Item*, Becauſe the People of the Realm, *&c.* *Vide Littleton*'s Argument *poſtea*.

Attorney Gen. My Lord, it is very clear that this Statute had no manner of Thought of this Cauſe in Queſtion; but whereas Sheriffs did procure Commiſſions to be awarded to themſelves for their private Gain, to the Prejudice of the Subject, the Statute condemneth thoſe Commiſſions, but it maketh nothing to this Queſtion which we have now in Hand. The next Statute which they cited, was 37 *Ed.* III. *cap.* 18. I beſeech it may be read.

Keeling, Clerk. *Item*, Though it be contained in the great Charter, *&c.* *Vide* as aforeſaid.

Attorney Gen. My Lord, this Statute ſeems to be a Commentary and Light to the other Statutes, the Scope whereof is againſt private Suggeſtions made to the King or his Council, and not in a legal Way, and therefore it condemns them; and this is more fully expreſſed in the Statute of 38 *Ed.* III. *cap.* 9. which they likewiſe mentioned: By which Statute Direction is given what Security, thoſe Perſons which make ſuch Suggeſtions are to give, that they ſhould proſecute their Suggeſtions, and what Puniſhment they ſhall undergo, if their Suggeſtions be found falſe.

Keeling, Clerk. *Item*, As to the Article made at the laſt Parliament, *&c.* *Vide* as before ſaid.

Attorney Gen. My Lord, this and the laſt Statute ſeem to conduce both to one Purpoſe, that they that in their Accuſations went not in a legal Way to bring the Party to his Anſwer, it was directed by this Statute, that they ſhould go a legal Way.

The laſt Act of Parliament in Print, the Counſel on the other Side produced, was the Statute of 1 *R.* II. *cap.* 12. which I deſire may be read.

Keeling, Clerk. *Item*, Whereas divers People at the Suit of Parties were committed to the *Fleet*, *&c.* *Vide* as before.

Attorney Gen. My Lord, it appeareth that the Scope of this Statute is againſt the Wardens of the *Fleet*, for ſome Miſcarriages in them; but there is one thing in this Statute which I ſhall deſire your Lordſhip to obſerve; and that is, for thoſe Miſdemeanors he ſhall forfeit his Office, except it be by Writ from the King or his Commandment; ſo that it was no new Doctrine in theſe Times, that the King might then give ſuch Commandment for committing. The Scope of this Statute had two Hands: Firſt, That the Warden ſhould forfeit his Office; and, ſecondly, that he ſhould recompenſe the Party.

In the fourth and fifth of *Phil.* & *Mar. Dyer* 162. it was reſolved, That if the Warden ſhall deliver a Man out of Priſon without Command, he forfeiteth his Office, and Damage unto the Party, but if he have the Command of the King, that ſhall excuſe the Forfeiture of his Office: [illegible] theſe Gentlemen are now, [illegible]

[illegible] the Court from whence [illegible] Warden, it [illegible] the Forfeiture of his Office, but [illegible] the Party.

[illegible] the Statute, which the other [illegible] which were all the private Statutes cited by the Counſel on the other Side.

[illegible] Statutes, I thought it equal [illegible] Lordſhip that they might be read.

[illegible] mentioned Petitions of the Commons, and the Anſwers to them of ſeveral Kings in Parliament. The firſt is, *Rot. pl.* 6 *Ed.* III. *numero primo & numero viceſimo:* Beſides theſe two, there is one other of 28 *Ed.* III. *num.* 18.

My Lord, of theſe three Petitions and their Anſwers, the two firſt were mentioned by the Counſel on the other Side; and that in 28 *Ed.* III. 28. I have produced, all of them even to one Purpoſe.

The Commons then petitioned the King, that all the Statutes made in Expoſition of *Magna Charta*, and of the Foreſt, may be kept and obſerved. The King makes Anſwer, that it ſhall be done. And in one of the Anſwers it is ſaid, If any Man be grieved, he may complain. But what is all this to the Point in Queſtion? Could there be any other Anſwer to give Life to theſe Requeſts?

The King he is petitioned that ſome are injured, he anſwers, That if they complain, they ſhall be relieved.

And now, my Lord, we are where we were, to find out the true Meaning of *Magna Charta*, for there is the Foundation of our Caſe; all this that hath been ſaid concerneth other things, and is nothing to the thing in Queſtion.

There is not a Word either of the Commitment of the King, or Commandment of the Council, in all the Statutes and Records.

And now, my Lord, I am at an End of thoſe Statutes, and come to That that was alledged and mentioned to be in 3 *H.* VI. 46. and if I could have found it, I would have brought it, but I could not find it; therefore if they have it, I deſire that they will ſhew it, but I think they have it not, and therefore I will let that go.

My Lord, I come to that which I inſiſted upon, the Queſtion as it was at firſt, not whether the King or the Lords of the Council can commit a Man, and ſhew no Cauſe wherefore they do commit him; but whether the ordinary Courts of Juſtice have Power to bail him or no; for that I will inſiſt upon the Statute of *Weſtm. primo*, which I deſire your Lordſhip may be read, and then I will apply. *Vide Weſtm. primo.*

My Lord, this Statute, if I miſunderſtand it not, is a full Expreſſion to the Purpoſe of *Magna Charta*; the Scope whereof is to direct us in what Caſes Men impriſoned were to be bailed.

It was eſpecially for Direction to the Sheriffs and others; but to ſay Courts of Juſtice are excluded from this Statute, I conceive it cannot be.

It recites, That whereas heretofore it was not reſolved in what Caſes Men were repleviſable, and in what Caſes not, but only in theſe four Caſes; for the Death of a Man, or by the Commandment of the King, or of his Juſtices, or of the Foreſt.

My Lord, I ſay that this Statute expreſſeth not the Law was made by this Statute, that in theſe Caſes Men were not repleviſable; but it expreſſeth that the Law was clear in theſe Caſes; in theſe four Caſes it was clearly reſolved before.

I pray you, my Lord, obſerve the Time of the making of this Statute; that of *Magna Charta* was made in the Time of *Henry* III. and this of *Weſtminſter* in the Time of *Edw.* I. ſo that it was made in the Time of the ſame.

And, my Lord, if they had underſtood the Statute of *Magna Charta* in another Senſe, would they not have expreſſed it ſo in this Statute? Was it not better for them than for us, they being nearer the firſt making of *Magna Charta* than we are? But certainly the Statute of *Magna Charta* was expounded at the Time, as I have ſhewed before, if not, without all doubt at the Time of making of *Weſtm. primo*.

The Parliament would not have been ſo careful to provide for Things of leſſer Moment, and omit this of ſo great Conſequence, if there had been any Queſtion of it. In all Times and Ages, *Magna Charta* hath been confirmed, but they ſhew not any one Law that doth except againſt this poſitive Law of *Weſtminſter* the firſt, or any Acts of Parliament; nay more, in any printed Books, that in this caſe Men ſhould be repleviable.

My Lord, if you know nothing printed or unprinted, if any will deſire to alter a Courſe that always hath been held, you will ſeek for Precedents, for the conſtant Uſe and Courſe is the beſt Expoſition of the Law; it is not enough for me to ſay, This it is, unleſs I make it good.

Firſt then, I ſay, they on the other Side cannot cite one Book, Statute, or other Thing, to prove, that they that have been committed *per ſpeciale mandatum domini Regis*, are bailable.

But, my Lord, I find ſome to the contrary, that they are not bailable, and I will cite ſome of them, and read of others; for I would not in a Caſe of that Expectation, that it ſhould be thought that any thing ſhould be miſinterpreted.

In the 33 *Hen.* VI. *folio viceſimo tertio*, *Robert Poyning*'s Caſe, he was committed *pro diverſis cauſis ipſum dominum Regem tangent'*; this alters not the Caſe, for it was as good as no Cauſe, for it was the Warrant *domini Regis*, and there is no Queſtion upon this; But, my Lord, I know this is not the Point in Queſtion.

The next Thing I ſhall ſhew unto your Lordſhip, is *Paſch.* 21 *Edwardi primi*, *Rot. cla. ſecund.* and this, my Lord, was near the time of making of the Statute of *Weſtm. prim.* and this Precedent is to this Purpoſe:

The Sheriff of *Leiceſterſhire* and *Warwickſhire* (for then there was but one Sheriff to both thoſe Shires) did receive Commandment by Letters from the King, That whereas the Earl of *Warwick* had commanded divers Perſons to the Cuſtody of the ſaid Sheriff, the King ſent a Letter to the ſaid Sheriff, commanding, that to thoſe who were committed to his Cuſtody by the Earl of *Warwick*, he ſhould ſhew no Grace to them; that is, they ſhould not be bailed.

The Sheriff, notwithſtanding this Command, lets ſome of thoſe Priſoners to bail; whereupon he was complained of in Parliament, that he had done againſt the King's Commandment, and he was condemned for it.

This was in Parliament; I wonder this ſhould be done in Parliament, and that it was not ſaid there, that this Commitment, being done by the King's Commandment, was not good; no, he was condemned in Parliament, for it was one that did break the Statute of *Weſtm. prim.*

My Lord, the Uſe that I make of this Record is this. It recites, that the Earl of *Warwick* committed divers, it might be that he did commit them by Direction from the King, but the Record mentioneth not ſo much, but it ſhews, that the King by Letters commanded the Sheriff, that he ſhould ſhew ſome Perſons no Grace, and yet he did; he was examined upon this, and by Parliament committed.

The next Matter I will offer to your Lordſhip's Judgment for the true Expoſition of the Law in this Caſe, is the Book we call The *Regiſter*, an

Authority

respected, it is the foundation of all our Writs at the Common Law; I bring not the Book.

In this Book there is one Writ saith thus, *Rex, &c. Quod repiar' fac' A. nisi fuerit per speciale mandatum domini Regis.*

Justice *Doderidge.* In what Writ is that, *de homine replegiando?*

Attorn. Gen. Yes, in the Writ *de homine replegiando*; and there is another Writ directed to the Constable of *Dover*, in the very same words; by which it appears that they that are imprisoned by the King's command, *non sunt replegiabiles.*

Mr. *Fitzherbert*, a grave Judge, and is in authority with us, perusing these Writs, expressed it in these words plainly: "There are some cases "wherein a man cannot have this Writ, although he be taken and de-"tained in prison; as if he be taken by the death of a man, or if he be "taken by the commandment of the King's Justices;" and mentions not Chief Justice: which I believe is to be intended not of the Chief of the Court of Judicature, but of the Chief Justice of *England*, for there was such a one in those days. Thus, my Lord, you see the opinion of Mr. *Fitzherbert* in this case.

The next thing, that I will shew your Lordship is the opinion of Mr. *Stamford*, in his Pleas of the Crown, *fol.* 72. where he sets down the Statute of *Westminster primo*, and then he adds, that by this it appears, that in four cases at the Common Law a man is not replevisable; in those that were taken for the death of a man, or by the commandment of the King, or of his Justices, or of the Forest: and there he saith, that the commandment of the King is to be intended, either the commandment of his mouth or of his Council, which is incorporated to him, and speak with the mouth of the King.

My Lord, I shall desire no better Commentaries upon a Law, than these reverend grave Judges, who have put Books of Law in print, and such Books as none, I believe, will say their judgments are weak.

The next thing, I shall offer unto your Lordship is this, that I cannot shew with so great authority as I have done the rest, because I have not the thing itself by me; but I will put it to your Lordship's memory, I presume you may well remember it; it is the resolution of all the Judges, which was given in the four-and-thirtieth of Queen *Elizabeth*, it fell out upon an unhappy occasion, which was thus: the Judges they complain that Sheriffs and other Officers could not execute the process of the Law as they ought, for that the parties on whom such process shall be executed were sent away by some of the Queen's Council, that they could not be found: the Judges hereupon petitioned the Lord-Chancellor, that he would be a suitor to her Majesty that nothing be done hereafter. And thereupon the Judges were desired to shew in what cases men that were committed were not bailable, whether upon the commitment of the Queen or any other.

The Judges make answer, that if a man shall be committed by the Queen, by her command, or by the Privy-Council, he is not bailable: if your Lordship ask me what authority I have for this, I can only say, I have it out of the Book of the Lord *Anderson*, written with his own hand.

My Lord, I pray you give me leave to observe the time when this was done; it was in a time, and we may truly call it a good time, in the time of good Queen *Elizabeth*, and yet we see there was then cause of complaint: and therefore I would not have men think that we are now grown so bad (as the opinion is we are), for we see that then in those times there was cause of complaint, and it may be more than is now.

This, my Lord, was the resolution of all the Judges and Barons of the Exchequer, and not by some Great one.

Now I will apply myself to that, which has been enforced by the Counsel on the other side, which was the reason that the subject hath interest in this case.

My Lord, I do acknowledge it, but I must say that the Sovereign hath great interest in it too. And sure I am, that the first stone of Sovereignty was no sooner laid, but this power was given to the Sovereign: if you ask me whether it be unlimited; my Lord, I say it is not the question now in hand: but the Common Law, which hath long flourished under the Government of our King and his Progenitors Kings of this Realm, hath ever had that reverend respect of their Sovereign, as that it hath concluded the King can do no wrong: and as it is in the Lord *Berkley*'s case in *Plowden*'s *Com.* 246 *b.* it is part of the King's prerogative that he can do no wrong.

In the fourth of *Edw.* IV. *fol.* 25. the King cannot be a Disseisor; and so it is also in the Lord *Berkley*'s case in 32 *Hen.* VIII. *Dyer, fol.* 8.

The King cannot usurp upon a Patron, for the Common Law hath that reverend respect to him, as that it cannot conceive he will do any injury.

But the King commits a subject, and expresseth no cause of the commitment: What then? Shall it be thought that there is no cause why he should be committed?

Nay, my Lord, the course of all times hath been, to say there is no cause expressed, and therefore the matter is not ripe, and thereupon the Courts of Judicature have ever rested satisfied therewith, they would not search into it.

My Lords, there be *Arcana Dei, & Arcana Imperii*; and they that search too far into them, and make themselves busier with them than their places do require, they will make themselves, *&c.* I will say no more; but I shall be able to shew that there shall as much prejudice come to the Kingdom, if God direct not the heart of the King, which is in the hand of God, as the rivers of waters: I say, there may as much hazard come to the Commonwealth in many other things, with which the King is trusted, as in this particular there can accrue to the subject.

If a Treason be committed, as it was not long ago, not far removed from our memories; since there was a Treason, and the actors thereof fled, some to the Court of *Rome*, some to *Brussels*, when it was to be put in execution; the Treason being discovered, one is apprehended upon suspicion of it, and is put into the Tower, and there he lieth, and thinketh the time very long; and I cannot blame him.

It may be he is innocent, and thereupon he brings a *Habeas Corpus*, and by virtue of that writ he is brought hither; and will your Lordship think it fit or convenient to bail him, when the accusation against him must come from beyond the sea? I think you will rather to respect the proceedings of the State, as that you will believe these things are done with a cause, than inquire further of them.

Peradventure some great misdemeanor may be committed, and some of the parties make away, so as Proclamation cannot overtake them, and some are taken, is it fit that they that are in prison should be tried before the principal be taken?

I will give you an instance, that lately was put into my mind; there be some prisoners in the Tower at this present, which were put in thither when they were very young: if they should bring an *Habeas Corpus*, they were imprisoned for State-matters, will your Lordship deliver them? No, in that the State doth not think it fit to send them back into their own Countries, you will esteem so reverendly of the State for committing children, that you will believe that there is great reason of State so to do, or else they would not do it: many inconveniences may follow, if it should be otherwise. It may be, divers men do suffer wrongfully in prison, but therefore shall all prisoners be delivered? That were a great mischief.

No doubt but the King's power is absolutely over his coins; if then he shall command his coin shall be turned to brass or leather, I confess it were inconvenient; but if the King would do it, the answer that I can make is, that he would not undo the Kingdom: but can your Lordship hinder it, as being an inconvenience, if he would do it? The Cinque Ports are free for traffick for all his subjects; but the King in his Cabinet understands there is danger of War to come upon this Kingdom, thereupon he shuts the Ports, that no man can go out; shall the Merchant say this is injustice in the King? And as in this, so in many other particulars this may appear, but I will not go too high: and therefore we are too wise, nay, we are too foolish, in undertaking to examine matters of State, to which we are not born. Now, my Lord, I come to our Book-Cases, by which it appears what our King may do, and nothing can be said against it, but he will not do it; the King may pardon all Traitors and Felons, and if he should do it, may not the subjects say, If the King do this, the bad will overcome the good? But shall any say, The King cannot do this? No, we may only say, He will not do this.

The King may exempt men from the office of Sheriff, is not this inconvenient? And may it not be said, he may exempt ten in a Shire, and then the burden of the Country shall rest upon the meaner sort of people? Can any man say more to this, than that he will not do it?

Inheritances are to be decided upon Trial, the King may exempt private men from being of a Jury; but if he exempt all men who shall try our causes? for it is to be presumed, that he will not do it.

But to our case: By the Statute of *Magna Charta*, no man shall be put out of his Freehold, *&c.* But if the King will do it, must not the party that is so put out go to the King by petition? But you will say, It is a petition of right; and it may be these Gentlemen's is so; admit it be, yet when such a petition comes to the King, must it not be answered with these words, *Soit droit fait al parte?* And when the King will give that Warrant for it, then they must have it done, and not before.

And this may answer a perpetual imprisonment, and God forbid that this should be so; and now, my Lord, I will trouble you no longer, but I will go to precedents. Precedents I know prevail much, and rule in many cases; and if the precedents they cite were not misinterpreted, I should think they had said a great deal.

But, my Lord, I will answer their precedents with precedents; nay, I will shew your Lordship that the precedents which they have cited are no precedents for them.

And, my Lord, it is a dangerous thing for men in matters of weight to avouch precedents with confidence, when they make nothing for them: for, my Lord, precedents are now become almost proclamations, for they already run up and down the Town; and yet they know but part of them, and not all, and I think if they knew all, men would be more modest.

But, my Lord, I will now come to these precedents, where I may say they have not dealt freely with me, for they have shewed me many precedents more than they mentioned here, and it may be they have done the like unto your Lordship.

They alledged but eight precedents before your Lordship, but they have brought sixteen unto me: for these eight mentioned here, I will take them in order as they were cited, and answer.

The first precedent they cited was in *Hen.* VIII. *Rot.* 9. of one *Harison:* we have the Record here to shew your Lordship, that he was committed for suspicion of Felony, which was expressed in the Warrant; and then, my Lord, this is clear, if the King, or the Lords of the Council, will express any thing within your Lordship's jurisdiction, there is good ground for your proceedings; but when there is nothing expressed, whether you will judge what the cause of the Warrant is, I will leave to your Lordship's judgment; but it appears this was the cause, and that he was delivered.

The next precedent was 22 *H.* VIII. *Rot.* 57. and it was *Parker*'s case; and it is true that his commitment appeared to be *per speciale mandatum domini Regis*, but it was also proposed to be *pro pace & suspicione feloniæ*; and the signification of the command was given by Mr. *Peck* of *Clifford's-Inn:* but there the Warrant shews the cause of the commitment was for the peace and suspicion of Felony, and therefore he was bailed.

The next was in 40 *Eliz. Wendon*'s case; but, my Lord, that commitment was out of the Star-Chamber by an ordinary course: then they cited 8 *Jac. Thomas Cæsar*'s case; he indeed was committed by *speciale mandatum domini Regis*, and brought his *Habeas Corpus*, but the Roll saith *remittitur;* and is that a Warrant for them to say that he was delivered?

Then Sir *Thomas Fermor*'s case was cited; and, my Lord, when we looked into the Records, we found that he was committed for suspicion of Treason; and he was tried for it and discharged.

The next precedent was Sir *Thomas Monson*'s case; I wonder that they did cite that, for he was committed by the Lords of the Council indeed; but the ground of it was suspicion of the death of Sir *Thomas Overbury*, and he was discharged again by the Lords of the Council. Certainly if they had known this, they would not have named this as a precedent.

The next was *Reynor*'s case; he, my Lord, was one of the Gun-Powder-Treason, and yet there was a Warrant to discharge him too. And therefore what these precedents are, I shall submit to your Lordship: I must confess, when they are cited together, they make a great noise; but when they are examined severally, they prove nothing.

My Lord, there is one more precedent that was cited here before your Lordship, and I hope that one shall be as none.

It was mentioned to be *Laurence Brown*'s case, 30 *Eliz.* I know not what it is, but it is like to be of the same value as the rest; *Pro certis causis eos moventibus*, &c.

And thus, my Lord, I have gone through those precedents that were alledged here before your Lordship; and now I will come to those precedents that were brought to me, and not mentioned here.

The first was *John Browning*'s case, in 21 *H.* VIII. My Lord, these precedents came not to me before *Saturday* last, about candle-lighting; and yesterday was no time fitting to search out precedents, and how could I then search for this?

The next was *William Rogers*'s case, of the same time. But the cause is expressed to be for suspicion of Felony, which is a cause within the jurisdiction of this Court.

Newport's case was the like, in 4 & 5 *Phil.* & *Mar.* and so was *Thomas Lawrence*'s case, 9 *Eliz.* and *Edw. Harcourt*'s case, 5 *Eliz.* which was for suspicion of Felony. *Richard Beckwith*, and not *Bartwith*, as was cited, for they have mistaken both names and matters, was committed *per speciale mandatum domini Regis*; and the Record saith he was bailed. But it was by reason of a letter from the Lords of the Council.

The cause of *Peter Man*'s commitment in the 4 and 5 of *Philip* and *Mary*, appears to be for suspicion of Felony and Robbery.

For *Reynor*'s case, it is the same with *Beckwith*, and were both for one thing.

In the 8 *Hen.* VII. one *Roger Cherry* was committed *per mandatum domini Regis*, and it was for a criminal case; and he was afterwards indicted, and acquitted and delivered.

And there is another precedent thereof, that saith, he was afterwards arraigned, condemned, and hanged; we have the Record of it.

And now, my Lord, I will shew some precedents on the other side, where men have been committed by the commandment of the King, and by the commandment of the Council, and have been delivered again by their directions: and of this kind there be two in the Tower, that as they were committed by Warrant, so by Warrants again for their bailing they were delivered; the offences were against the Forest, and for Murder.

In the 4th *Edw.* III. *M.* 4. *Edmund de Newport* in *Essex* was indicted for an offence committed by him in the Forest. And *M.* 7. *John Fox* was likewise indicted for an offence by him done in the Forest: and there be two Warrants to bail them.

M. 20. *John Cobb* was the like, and there was a letter from the King, *Quod ponatur in Ballium usque ad proximam Assisam.*

These were offences within *Westminster primo*, and there be several Warrants to bail them.

The Clerk of this Court hath many Records, by which it appeareth, that many have been committed by the command of the King and of the Queen, and of the Council, and brought their *Habeas Corpus*; and the success was, that many of them were committed to the same prisons, and divers were committed to the Marshal of this Court: the reason was, for that many of them were to appear here, their causes being triable here; and it would have been a great trouble to send them back so far to prison as into the Countries, and therefore they were delivered to the Marshal of the King's houshold: again, many had their trials in this Court, and some suffered, and some were delivered by special command, as they were committed by special command.

The number of these of this nature are infinite that have been in our times; we have found some forty precedents of men committed out of the Chancery, and by the High-Commission, for contempts, and some by the Barons of the Exchequer, and some in *London*, that have been brought hither by *Habeas Corpus*.

Of this I shall observe, that in the 11 *Jacobi*, there was a private constitution in *London*, made between the white Bakers, that they might live one by another, and the one not to invade the other's liberties; and for contempt against this ordinance, some were committed to prison; as *Thomas Heaning*, and *Littlepage*: they had a *Habeas Corpus*, and the cause was shewn to be by reason of the said Constitution, and thereupon the prisoners were sent back to *London*, to abide the order of the Mayor. For, my Lord, this Court hath been ever careful not to examine the Decrees of the Chancery, or Court of Requests, but have only looked whether the cause returned be within the jurisdiction of this Court; nor have they called in question the by-laws and constitutions of *London*, but they send them back to the Court of Justice that committeth them.

And hath this Court been so careful of these inferiour Courts to this which is the chief? and when the King, who is the Head of Justice, shall commit a man, shall not they be as careful to do the like Justice to him? But when the King saith to them, The commitment was by my Warrant and Commandment, will you question this, and whether this commitment be good or no? I hope you will not.

And now, my Lord, touching some precedents which have been taken out of their own shewing, I shall make it appear, that as they have been committed by the King or Council, so they had Warrants also to discharge them: and they, my Lord, are two ancient Records; the first is 7 *H.* VII. *Rot.* 6. the other, *Rot.* 73. The first was *Thomas Brown*, he was committed to the *Marshalsea, per mandatum domini Regis, & aliis certis de causis*: and afterwards the Records say, *Dominus Rex quoad* Chaie *relaxavit mandatum suum*, and he was bailed, and the rest lay by it.

My Lord, I will conclude; I could be infinite in this case in precedents, but enough is enough, your Lordship knoweth the weight of precedents; it is not enough to shew this was done, but also to shew the reason why it was done. I will trouble your Lordship no longer, but if any man shall doubt whether that or any part thereof be truly recited which hath been said touching the Records or Statutes, I can say no more, but that the Statutes have been read, and the Records are ready sorted out to be seen by your Lordship.

I shall conclude (what I shall say) in this case, to answer the fear rather than the just ground of them that say, this may be a cause of great danger, with the words of *Bracton*, who spake not to flatter the present age; *lib.* 1. *cap.* 8. in the end, speaking of a writ for wrong done by the King to the Subject touching land, he hath these words: *Si judicium a Rege petatur (cum breve non currat contra ipsum) locus erit supplicationi quod factum suum corrigat & emendet, quod quidem si non fecerit, satis sufficit ei ad pœnam quod dominum expectet ultorem, nemo quidem de factis suis præsumat disputare, multo fortius contra factum suum venire.*

My Lord, I English it not, for I apply it not, any man may make use of it as he pleaseth; and so I conclude both for the point of exception, and matter of the return, which I refer to your Lordship's judgment, whether all in the return but these words, *per speciale mandatum domini Regis*, be not superfluous. And for the matter, whether these Gentlemen be bailable or not bailable, I have shewed your Lordship, that by the practice of all ages they are not bailable, but have been remanded back.

And therefore I pray your Lordship, that these Gentlemen may be remitted, and left to go the right way for their delivery, which is by a petition to the King. Whether it be a Petition of right or of grace, I know not; it must be, I am sure, to the King, from whom I do personally understand that these Gentlemen did never yet present any Petition to him that came to his knowledge.

L. C. Justice. Mr. Attorney, thus much we must say to you, you have taken a great deal of pains, you having had so short a time to consider of this case; it is a case of very great weight and expectation, and we do not intend that you shall expect long for our resolution, for that these Gentlemen are in prison, and desire no doubt to know where they must trust; I hope we shall resolve according to the reason of former times, and according to our consciences: but this I must tell you, as I did those that argued, you must bring in your precedents; for though we have seen some of them, yet some of them we have not seen, therefore we desire that your servants or yourselves do attend, and bring unto us after dinner those precedents you have mentioned on the King's part, for we intend to meet this afternoon, and you shall have our opinions to-morrow: and I must tell you on the other side, that this cause being of such weight, Counsel should be wary how they speak any thing to inveigle the Court.

Touching such precedents as you urged in some of them, we know there is something urged which makes not for you, so you have omitted some material things to be shewn; I speak it to this purpose, not to prejudice the cause, or to deliver my opinion, which becomes me not, but to shew, that Counsellors should be careful: and this I dare say, there is matter in some of the precedents themselves that leads to another case, if they were entirely cited.

The Term grows away, you shall not be long in expectation, we will meet this afternoon, and give you our opinions to-morrow morning.

Mr. *Noye.* We desire that Mr. *Attorney* may bring the precedents of 34 *Elizabeth* with him.

Mr. *Attorney.* I will shew you any thing; but, my Lord, I shall be bold to claim the privilege of my place, as the King's Counsel; when the King's Attorney hath spoken, there ought to be no Arguments after that; but if you ask to see any thing, you shall have it.

L. C. Justice. It is that we aim at, that truth and right may appear, and not to satisfy the one or the other part; but it is not desired to make use of it by way of reply, but for satisfaction only.

Serj. *Bramston.* My Lord, for the precedents I cited, I did think they should have been brought and read in the Court, that your Lordship might see them.

L. C. Justice. You shall need no Apology, the Records and Precedents shall be brought to the Court, and read openly, for the Court will not wrong you, and you shall see the difference between them, and your relation of them; nor you must not wrong us with your written verities.

ON *Thursday* the twenty-eighth of *November*, *Michaelis*, 3 *Caroli Regis*, Chief-Justice-*Hyde*, Justice *Doderidge*, Justice *Jones*, and Justice *Whitlock* on the Bench: Sir *John Corbet*, Sir *Walter Earl*, Sir *John Heveningham*, and Sir *Edmund Hampden* at the Bar.

L. C. Justice. I am sure you here expect the resolution of the whole Court, as accordingly yesterday we told you you should have.

This is a case of very great weight and great expectation, and it had been fit we should have used more solemn arguments of it than now for the shortness of the time we can do; for you have been long in prison, and it is fit you should know whereunto you should trust: I am sure you expect justice from hence, and God forbid we should sit here but to do Justice to all men according to our best skill and knowledge, for it is our oaths and duties so to do, and I am sure there is nothing else expected of us. We are sworn to maintain all Prerogatives of the King, that is one branch of our oath; and we are likewise sworn to administer Justice equally to all people.

We cannot, I tell you, deliver in solemn arguments, and give the judgments of every one of us touching this case, as the weight thereof requireth; but we have met together, and we have duly and seriously considered of it, and of all that which has been spoken of on either side, and we are grown to a resolution, and my Brothers have enjoined me to deliver to you the resolution of the whole Court; and therefore though it be delivered by my mouth, it is the resolution of us all: I hope I shall not mistake any thing of their intention in my delivery; but if I do, they sit here by me, and I shall not take it ill if they right me.

Therefore I must tell you, there hath been many points learnedly argued at the Bar, which we shall not touch, or give our Resolution upon, but bend ourselves to the point in judgment here.

These three Statutes, as for example, the Statute of *Magna Charta*, 25 *E.* III. and 36 *E.* III. and the Statute of *Westminster primo*, and divers other Statutes that have been alledged, and particularly disputed of, we all acknowledge and resolve, that they are good Laws, and that they be in force: but the interpretation of them at this time belongs not to us, for we are driven to another point: and though the meaning of them belongs to the one way or the other, yet our judgment must be the same; for that which is now to be judged by us is this, Whether one that is committed by the King's authority, and no cause declared of his commitment, according as here it is upon this return, whether we ought to deliver him by bail, or to remand him back again? Wherein you must know this which your Counsel will tell you, we can take notice only of this return; and when the case appears to come to us no otherwise than by the return, we are not bound to examine the truth of the return, but the sufficiency of it, for there is a great difference between the sufficiency and the truth.

We cannot judge upon rumors nor reports, but upon that which is before us on record; and therefore the Return is examinable by us, whether it be sufficient or not.

3 The

The exceptions which have been taken to this Return were two: the one for the form, the other for the substance.

For the form, whether it be formally returned or no, for it is not returned (as it is said) positively and absolutely, that they were committed by the King, but as it appears by a warrant from the Lords of the Council, and then there seems to be a contradiction in the Return.

For first it saith, they were committed by the King's command, and afterwards it alledgeth it to be by a warrant of the Lords of the Council, and so it is repugnant.

Now we conceive that this is a positive and an absolute return, and so the reason is, that he first returns that they are detained by the special command of the King, and if he had ceased there it had been positive; now there follows, that this was signified to them by the Lords of the Council. This is returned, to ascertain the Court that he returned the cause truly, and to shew us that we should not doubt the verity of this return; and not to shew to us that he hath no knowledge of the cause but by the signification of the Lords of the Council: according to that case of the Bishop of *Norwich*, touching the excommunication, he must testify his own knowledge, and not *continetur in Archivis*: so a Sheriff must not return *quod mandavi ball'*, &c. and he gives this answer, unless it be a Bailiff of a Liberty that hath return of Writs.

And so here if the Warden of the Fleet had returned, that the Lords of the Council had signified unto him that his prisoner was detained by the King's commandment, that had been sufficient: but when he returns positively at the first, that it is done by the King's direction, he shews afterwards that which should make it appear that he deals not falsely; which might have been omitted, but being mentioned that That is the scope of it, and not otherwise, the Return is good and positive.

Now then to the other objections, because he speaks nothing of the caption why they were taken, you know it is the usual return of all Officers to answer the point in question; there is not one word in the Writ that demands the cause why they were taken, but why they are detained: so that the point in the Writ is sufficiently answered; for though sometimes it is necessary that the cause of the caption should be certified, yet sometimes it is superfluous: but in our case the cause of the detention is sufficiently answered, which is the demand of the Writ, and therefore we resolve that the form of this return is good. The next thing is the main point in Law, whether the substance or matter of the return be good or no, wherein the substance is this, he doth certify that they are detained in prison by the special command of the King; and whether this be good in Law or no, that is the question.

To this purpose, if you remember this point, I say you did not cite any Book or Case in print, but many precedents, which, I confess, are as strong as any Book-Cases; for Book-Cases, I confess, are taken and selected out of the Records and Resolutions of Judges, and that is it which is in our Books, though they be not so obvious for every eye, but are found out by pains and diligent search, and being produced, are of the same and equal authority with our Book-Cases; but this must be when Records are brought faithfully and entirely, so that the Court may judge of them.

Now the precedents, you urged them to be so many, and so fully to the point, that we may thereby see that it is good to hear what can be said on both sides, and for to hear all, and view the Records themselves; and therefore we required you to bring the Records to us, and you did so, and you brought us more than you mentioned here; and we have perused them all, that thereby we might see whether the Court be faithfully dealt withal or no; for though Counsellors may urge a Book for their own advantage, yet it is the duty of the Court to see and distinguish of their allegations as the truth may appear.

This I told you yesterday, when I told you your precedents warranted not so much as you urged them for; for if you remember, you urged some precedents to be, that where men were committed by the King, or by the Lords of the Council, and no cause expressed why they were committed, they were delivered.

This is in effect our case, if the precedents affirm that when a man is committed by the King's command, and no just cause is shewn, that upon such a general return the party shall *ipso facto* be delivered; for if the return be not amended, then he shall be discharged.

For altho' men come with prepared minds, yet the preparation of every man's heart ought to submit to the truth, and by the precedents, you shall see if it be so as you have alledged; but this I dare affirm, that no one of the Records that you have cited, doth inforce what you have concluded out of them, no not one; and therefore as you have cited Records and Precedents, Precedents shall judge this case.

I will shew you how they differ from the Records: you have concluded, when the King hath committed one, and expresseth not the cause, the Court hath delivered the party; but you shall see the contrary concluded in every case that you have put: where the cause of the commitment hath been expressed, there the party hath been delivered by the Court, if the case so required; but where there hath been no cause expressed, they have ever been remanded; or if they have been delivered, they have been delivered by the King's direction, or by the Lords of the Council: If this fall now in proof, you see you have gathered fair conclusions out of the Records, and that you may see that this is so, I have brought the Records with me of your own propounding, and I will go through them from point to point, and then judge yourselves of the case.

It is not material whether I call for them in that order as you produced them or no, and therefore I will take them as they are, first or last in the King's Reign. They are in number many, in the time of *Henry* VII. *Henry* VIII. Queen *Mary*, Queen *Elizabeth*, and King *James*'s time.

I will shew you Sir *Thomas Monson*'s Case in 14 *Jacobi*, which was in all our memories.

I will begin with *Hill.* 8 *H* VII. *R. Cherry*'s case; you vouched it to this purpose, That *Cherry* being committed by the Mayor of *Windsor*, was brought hither by a *Habeas Corpus*, and the Mayor returns that he was committed *per mandatum domini Regis* and that thereupon he was delivered; but you shall find by the Record, that he was committed by the Mayor at the suit of the King for Felony, for which he was afterwards indicted, brought to a trial, and then discharged.

Vide this Record in Mr *Selden*'s Argument in the Parliament, 3 & 4 *Caroli Regis*, and so all the rest *postea*.

The next was 19 *H.* VII. *Urswick*'s case; and you say he was brought hither by the Warden of the *Fleet*, who, as you said, returned that he was committed *per mandatum domini Regis*, and you said he was discharged, but he was bailed upon the Lord's Letter, and brought hither to record his return, for he was bound to appear here, and then he was discharged, but that was the cause of his bringing hither. *Vide* the Records as aforesaid.

The next was *Hugh Pain*'s case, in 21 *H.* VII. and that you urged thus: You say that he was brought hither by a *Habeas Corpus* by the Warden of the *Fleet*, who returned that he was committed by the King's Council, and he was bailed: now we find that he was committed by them for suspicion of felony; and that cause was declared, and he was bailed: so that you see there was a cause expressed. *Vide* the Records aforesaid.

The next is 2 *H.* VIII. *Thomas Beckley* and *Robert Harrison*'s case; these you said were brought in hither by *George* Earl of *Shrewsbury*, and *Thomas* Earl of *Surrey*; and the return was, that they were committed by the command of *Hen.* VII. and that they were bailed; but you shall find that they were committed for suspicion of felony; and that *Harrison* was committed by *Hen.* VII. but it was for Homicide upon the Sea, and so the cause is expressed, and afterwards he was bailed. The next was in 22 *H.* VIII. *John Parker*'s case: you urged it to this purpose, That he was brought hither by a *Habeas Corpus* by the Sheriffs of *London*, and they you said returned, that he was committed *per speciale mandatum domini Regis nunciatum*, &c by *Robert Peck*, &c. The cause why you urged this was two-fold; first, that he was committed by the King's command, and yet he was bailed; secondly, That he was committed *per mandatum domini Regis nunciat' per* such a one: but you shall find by the Record that he was committed for the security of the peace, and for suspicion of felony, and that was the cause for which he was bailed, for he is bailable by Law when such a cause appears. *Vide* the Record as afore.

Go on to the next, and that is *Peter Man*'s case, in the 3 and 4 *Philip* and *Mary*; you urged that to this purpose, you say, that he was brought by the Keeper of the *Gate-House*, and you say, that he returned, that he was committed by the command of the King and Queen's Council, and thereupon he was bailed; but you shall find that he was committed for suspicion of felony and robbery, and thereupon he was bailed.

The next is in the 4 and 5 *Phil.* & *Mar. Edward Newport*'s case; you said that the Constable of the *Tower* brought him hither, and returned that he was committed by the Council of the King and Queen, and that he was bailed: but you see by the Records, that he was committed for suspicion of coining, which is bailable only in this Court, and therefore it was removed hither. Yet this I must tell you, that it is true, in one Record it appears not but as you have cited it, but you may see how it is supplied by another Record, and the cause, and he was delivered by a proclamation. *Vide* both Records in Mr. *Selden*'s Argument.

Doderidge. He could not be delivered by proclamation, unless it was for a criminal cause.

L. C. J. *Hyde.* Observe another thing in the Book, he is brought hither by the special command of the Council: so that although it appears not in the Record, yet if the King or Lords mean to have him tried for his life, he is brought hither. Then you cited *Robert Constable*'s case, 9 *Eliz.* and you said he was brought hither by the Lieutenant of the *Tower*, who returned that he was committed by the Lords of the Council, and thereupon he was bailed; but you shall find that he came hither to plead his pardon, and he was pardoned. *Vide* the Record as aforesaid.

Thomas Lawrence's case in 9 *Eliz.* is the same with *Constable*'s, for it appears that he was brought hither to plead his pardon, and he was pardoned, and that was the cause he was brought hither.

The next was in the 21 *Eliz. John Browning*'s case; it is true he was committed by the Lords of the Council, and he was brought by a *Habeas Corpus* to the Chamber hf Sir *Christopher Wray*, Chief-Justice, and he was there bailed.

The next was 33 *Eliz. William Rogers*; and he, you said, was brought hither by the Keeper of the *Gate-house*, who returned, that he was committed to him by the Lords of the Council, yet there was a cause expressed, and that was for suspicion of coining of money.

The next was in 39 *Eliz. Laurence Broome*; you say that he was brought hither by the Keeper of the *Gate-house*, who returned, that he was committed for divers causes, moving the Lords of the Council, and thereupon he was delivered; but the Record is, that the return also was for suspicion of Treason; and although the suspicion of Treason appears not in one Record, yet there is another for it. Here you see the cause of his commitment, and that he was bailed, but it was by the King's command, *usque Oct. Michaelis*. *Vide* the Record.

I blame not you that are of Counsel with these Gentlemen for urging this Record, for this cause is not expressed in your Record; but that he was committed by the command of the Council only; but he was committed for suspicion of Felony with Sir *Thomas Smith*. *Vide* the Record.

The next is in 40 *Eliz. Edward Harcourt*'s case, and *Thomas Wenden*'s case; I bring them together, because they are both in one year. In the 40 of *Eliz. Edward Harcourt*, you say, was committed to the *Gate-house* by the Lords of the Council; and the return was, that he was committed by them, *Certis de causis ipsos moventibus ignotis*, and he was bailed.

Here is another in the same time committed to the same prison by the Lords in the Star-Chamber, it was *Thomas Wenden*'s case; and he, you say, was committed by them, *certis de causis*, (as the other was) and that he was bailed, but you shall find in the margin of the Roll, *Traditur in ball' ex assensu Concilii dominæ Reginæ*; and that was the relation of the Queen's Attorney, so that you see how the precedent fits you.

The next are two more Commitments to the *Gate-house*, *Beckwith* and *Reyner*, they, you said, were committed to the *Gate-house*, brought their *Habeas Corpus*, and the Keeper of the *Gate-house* returned, that they were committed by virtue of a Warrant from the Archbishop of *Canterbury*, *Henry* Earl of *Northampton*, Lord Warden of the Cinque Ports, and others of the Privy-Council; requiring the said Keeper to receive the said *Beckwith* and *Reyner* into his charge, until they ſhould have further order from them in that behalf; and you ſay they were bailed.

Vide the Record in Mr. *Selden* aforeſaid.

Now you ſhall ſee the direction to bail him; he was bailed by the direction from the Lords of the Council, as appears by their letter. *Vide* as aforeſaid.

Now we come to *Cæſar*'s caſe, in 8 *Jacobi*; you urged that to this purpoſe: you ſay he was committed to the *Marſhalſea*, who upon a *Habeas Corpus* returned, that he was committed *per ſpeciale mandatum domini Regis*, and you ſay, becauſe the return was ſo general, the rule of the Court was, that it ſhould be amended, or elſe he ſhould be diſcharged. I will open to you what the reaſon of that rule was, for that notice was taken, that the Keeper of the priſon had uſed a falſe return, and had uſurped the name of the King; I know not how, but the commitment was not by the King's command; and that was the cauſe that he had a day given him to amend his return, but his body was remanded to priſon, as you ſhall ſee by the Record. *Vide* the Record, &c.

The laſt precedent that you uſed, was that of Sir *Thomas Monſon*; and that was ſo notorious, and ſo late, that I marvel that was offered at all, it made me jealous of all the reſt, that was ſo notorious; and now I have omitted none you brought me. *Vide* the Record.

By this Record you may ſee that he was committed by divers Lords of the Council; and it was for the ſuſpicion of the death of Sir *Tho. Overbury*, and it is notoriouſly known, that he was brought hither to plead his pardon.

I will not tell you that you read all theſe precedents, for you read none, but urged them here before us; but we required you to bring them to us, and they were brought to us, Mr. *Corbet* brought them all but one, and that Mr. *Noye* brought, it was in the 22 *Hen.* VIII. *Parker*'s caſe; and one Mr. *Holborn*, a man whoſe face I never ſaw before, nor is he now in mine eye, did yeſterday bring us one precedent to this purpoſe, and it was Sir *John Brocket*'s caſe in 1 *Jac.* he was committed to the *Gatehouſe*, and upon a *Habeas Corpus*, the Keeper returned that *Commiſſ' fuit per Warrantum Dominorum de Privat' Concilio, cujus tenor ſequitur in hæc verba, viz.* To the Keeper of the *Gatehouſe*, &c. *Vide* Mr. *Selden*'s precedents; but ſee upon what ground he was bailed, it was a ſpecial command of the Lords of the Council. *Vide* the Record.

Theſe are all the Records and Precedents that you miniſtred unto us in your argument, and that were delivered unto us, for I have dealt faithfully with you; and now you have ſeen them in the caſes, I would have any man judge of the concluſion which you made the laſt day, that when a man is committed, and the caſe not known, but it is certified to be by the King's ſpecial commandment, and the *Habeas Corpus* is procured by yourſelves and ſpeeded by the King, that we can diſcharge or bail them.

Then the precedents are all againſt you every one of them, and what ſhall guide our judgments, ſince there is nothing alledged in this caſe but precedents? That if no cauſe of the commitment be expreſſed, it is to be preſumed to be for matter of State, which we cannot take notice of; you ſee we find none, no not one, that hath been delivered by bail in the like caſes, but by the hand of the King or his direction.

If we ſhould ceaſe here, you ſee you have ſhewn nothing to ſatisfy us, and we know that you that be of their Counſel, will ſatisfy your Clients therein.

But you ſhall ſee that we have taken a little pains in this caſe, and we will ſhew you ſome precedents on the other ſide; and I believe there be five hundred of this nature, that may be cited to this purpoſe. I ſhall go retrograde, and go backwards in citing the years of the precedents that I ſhall mention.

I will begin with 7 *H.* VIII. *Edward Page*, he was brought hither by the Steward of the *Marſhalſea*, who returned that he was committed *per mandatum domini Regis*, and he was remitted, ſo that he was not delivered upon this general return, but he was remanded.

The next was 12 *H.* VII. there you ſhall ſee a precedent where one was committed, his name was *Thomas Tew*, he was committed for felony, and alſo *per mandatum domini Regis*, and the King's Attorney came hither and releaſed the King's command, and thereupon he was bailed.

Mr. *Noye*. It is all one with *Parker*'s caſe.

L. C. Juſt. No; for here were two cauſes of the commitment, *Hobart* was then the King's Attorney, and he ſignified in open Court that he was diſcharged by the King's command, and *Poſtea traditur in ball' pro ſuſpicione feloniæ*.

The next was *Humphrey Broch*, 9 *H.* VII. *Rot.* 14. you ſhall find it much to that purpoſe as the other was before; he was impriſoned for an outlawry, and by the commandment of the King alſo, and after that the releaſe of the King's commandment was certified to the Chief-Juſtice, he was thereupon diſcharged. *Vide* the Record.

The next is 7 *H.* VII. *Thomas Brown*, *John Rawlings*, *Robert Sherman* and others, were committed *per mandatum domini Regis*, and for felony, outlawry, and other cauſes, as appears by the Records, and after the King releaſeth his commandment, and that the outlawry ſhould be reverſed, and for the felony he was bailed. *Vide* the Record.

So that you may ſee the offences mentioned in the Warrant for the commitment were triable here, and when the King releaſes his commandment they were bailed for the reſt, but they that were committed by the commandment of the King were releaſed by the King.

In 7. *H.* VII. the caſes of *William Bartholomew*, *Henry Carre*, *William Chaſe*, and others, is to the ſame effect, by all which you may ſee, that when the King releaſeth his commandment, they were bailed for the reſt, and as they were committed by the King's commandment, ſo they were releaſed by the King's command.

Now here I ſhall trouble you with no more precedents, and you ſee your own what concluſion they produce. And as to thoſe ſtrong precedents alledged on the other ſide, we are not wiſer than they that went before us; and the common cuſtom of the law is, the Common Law of the land, and that hath been the continual common cuſtom of the law, to which we are to ſubmit, for we come not to change the law, but to ſubmit to it.

We have looked upon that precedent that was mentioned by Mr. Attorney; the reſolution of all the Judges of *England*, in 34 *Eliz.* We have conſidered of the time, and I think there were not before, nor have been ſince, more upright Judges than they were, *Wray* was one, and *Anderſon* another: in *Eaſter* Term this was certified under the hands of all the Judges of *England*, and Barons of the Exchequer in a duplicate, whereof the one was delivered to the Lord-Chancellor, and the other to the Lord-Treaſurer, to be delivered to the Queen. We have compared our copies, not taking them the one from the other, but bringing them: we have long had them by us together, and they all agree word for word, and that which Mr. Attorney ſaid, he had out of Judge *Anderſon*'s Book, and it is to this purpoſe, to omit other things, that if a man be committed by the commandment of the King, he is not to be delivered by a *Habeas Corpus* in this Court, for we know not the cauſe of the commitment. *Vide* this at the latter end of the firſt part of Mr. *Selden*'s argument, as aforeſaid.

But the queſtion now is, Whether we may deliver this Gentleman or not? You ſee what hath been the practice in all the Kings times heretofore, and your own Records; and this reſolution of all the Judges teacheth us, and what can we do but walk in the ſteps of our forefathers? If you aſk me which way you ſhould be delivered, we ſhall tell you, we muſt not counſel you.

Mr. Attorney hath told you that the King hath done it, and we truſt him in great matters, and he is bound by Law, and he bids us proceed by Law, as we are ſworn to do, and ſo is the King; and we make no doubt but the King, if you ſeek to him, he knowing the cauſe why you are impriſoned, he will have mercy; but we leave that. If in Juſtice we ought to deliver you, we would do it; but upon theſe grounds, and theſe Records, and the precedents and reſolutions, we cannot deliver you, but you muſt be remanded. Now if I have miſtaken any thing, I deſire to be righted by my Brethren, I have endeavoured to give the reſolutions of us all *.

They continued in cuſtody till the 29th of *January* following, when his Majeſty in Council order'd all the impriſon'd Gentlemen to be releas'd; and Writs being iſſued about this time for electing Members of Parliament, to meet *March* the 17th, thoſe Gentlemen who ſuffer'd for the Loan, were elected in many places. On the 17th of *March* the Houſe met, and Sir *John Finch* was choſen Speaker. On the 20th, the Houſe ſettled their Committees; and the 22d was ſpent in opening the Grievances, as *Billeting of Soldiers, Loans by Benevolence and Privy-Seal, and the impriſoning certain Gentlemen who refus'd to lend upon that Account, who afterwards bringing their* Habeas Corpus, *were notwithſtanding remanded to priſon*; nor did the Houſe incline to ſupply his Majeſty till theſe Grievances were redreſſed.

To which purpoſe Sir *Francis Seymour* ſpoke thus:

THIS is the great Council of the Kingdom, and here (if not here alone) his Majeſty may ſee as in a true glaſs the State of the Kingdom; we are called hither by his Majeſty's Writs to give him faithful counſel, ſuch as may ſtand with his honour; but this we muſt do without flattery: we are ſent hither by the Commons to diſcharge that truſt repoſed in us, by delivering up their juſt grievances, and this we muſt do without fear: let us not therefore be like *Cambyſes*'s Judges, who being demanded of their King whether it were not lawful for him to do what in itſelf was unlawful? They, rather to pleaſe the King, than to diſcharge their own conſciences, anſwered, That the *Perſian* Kings might do what they liſted. This baſe flattery tends to miſchief, being fitter for reproof than imitation; and as flattery, ſo fear taketh away the judgment: let us not then be poſſeſſed with fear or flattery, of corruptions the baſeſt. For my own part, I ſhall ſhun both theſe, and ſpeak my conſcience with as much duty to his Majeſty as any man, but not neglecting the Public, in which his Majeſty and the Commonwealth have an Intereſt: but how can we ſhew our affections, whilſt we retain our fears? or how can we think of giving of Subſidies, till we know whether we have any thing to give or no? For if his Majeſty be perſuaded by any to take from his ſubjects what he will, and where it pleaſeth him; I would gladly know what we have to give? It's true, it is ill with thoſe ſubjects that ſhall give laws to their Princes, and as ill with thoſe Princes which ſhall uſe force with thoſe laws; that this hath been done, appeareth by the billeting of Soldiers, a thing no way advantageous to his Majeſty's ſervice, but a burden to the Commonwealth; this alſo appeareth by the laſt *Levy of Money againſt an Act of Parliament*. Again, Mr. Speaker, what greater proof can there be of this, than *the impriſonment of divers Gentlemen for the Loan*, who if they had done the contrary for fear, their fault had been as great as theirs that were the projectors in it; and to countenance theſe proceedings, hath it not been preached (or rather prated) in our Pulpits, that all we have is the King's, *Jure Divino*, ſay theſe time ſervers; they forſake their own function, and turn ignorant Stateſmen: we ſee how willing they will be to change a good Conſcience for a Biſhoprick; and (Mr. Speaker) we ſee how eaſy it is for a Prince, how juſt and good ſoever, to be abuſed, in regard he muſt ſee with other men's eyes, and hear with other men's ears. Let us not flatter his Majeſty, it is too apparent to all the World, the King and People ſuffer more now than ever, his Majeſty in his affairs abroad, and his People in their eſtates at home: but will you know the reaſon of all this? Let us look back to the actions of former Princes, and we ſhall find that thoſe Princes have been in greateſt want and extremity that exacted moſt of their ſubjects, and moſt unfortunate in the choice of their Miniſters, and to have failed moſt in their undertakings, happy is that Prince that hath thoſe that are faithful of his Council. That which his Majeſty wanted in the management of his affairs concerning *France* and *Spain*, I am clear, was his want of faithful Council to adviſe: the reaſon is plain, a Prince is ſtrongeſt by faithful and wiſe Council; I would I could truly ſay, ſuch have been employed abroad. I will con-

* Mr. *Whitlock* in his *Memorials of the Engliſh Affairs*, Page 8 (Edit. 1732.) ſays, "Five of the impriſon'd Gentlemen, by *Habeas Corpus* were brought to the *King's-Bench*; "and (by their Counſel aſſign'd) took exceptions to the Return, *For that it had not the cauſe of their Commitment, but of their Detainer in Priſon* per ſpeciale mandatum Regis, *which is no particular cauſe*; and the Law being moſt tender of the ſubjects liberty." *Noye*, *Selden*, *Bramſton*, *Calthorpe* and others, who were of Counſel for the Priſoners, prayed they might be releaſed and diſcharged.

Heath, the King's Attorney, at another day argued in maintenance of the Return. *Hyde*, Chief-Juſtice, declared the opinion of the Court, *That the Return was poſitive and abſolute, by the King's ſpecial command, and the ſignification of it by the Lords of the Council is only to inform the Court: And that the* Habeas Corpus *is not to return the cauſe of the Impriſonment, but of the detention in Priſon; that the matter of this Return is ſufficient, and the Court is not to examine the truth of the Return, but muſt take it as it is.* So the Priſoners were remanded.

feſs,

ſeſs, and ſtill ſhall from my heart, he is no good ſubject, nor well affected to his Majeſty and the State, that will not willingly and freely lay down his Life, when the end may be the ſervice of his Majeſty, and the good of the Common-weal. But on the contrary, when againſt a Parliament-Law, the ſubject ſhall have taken from him his goods againſt his will, and his liberty againſt the laws of the land; ſhall it be accounted want of duty in us to ſtand upon our privileges, hereditary to us, and confirmed by ſo many Acts of Parliament?

In doing this we ſhall but tread the ſteps of our forefathers, who ever preferred the publick Intereſt before their own right, nay, before their own lives; nor can it be any wrong to his Majeſty to ſtand upon them, ſo as thereby we may be the better enabled to do his Majeſty ſervice. But it will be a wrong to us and our poſterity, and our conſciences, if we willingly forego that which belongs unto us by the law of God, and of the Land, and this we ſhall do well to preſent to his Majeſty; we have no cauſe to doubt of his Majeſty's gracious acceptation.

Sir *Thomas Wentworth.*

THIS debate carries a double aſpect towards the Sovereign and the Subject, though both be innocent, both are injured and both to be cured. Surely, in the greateſt humility I ſpeak it, theſe illegal ways are puniſhment and marks of indignation, *the raiſing of Loans* ſtrengthened by commiſſion, with unheard-of inſtructions and oaths; the billeting of Soldiers by the Lieutenants, and Deputy-Lieutenants, have been as if they could have perſuaded Chriſtian Princes, yea Worlds, that the right of Empires had been to take away by ſtrong hands, and they have endeavoured, as far as poſſible for them, to do it. This hath not been done by the King (under the pleaſing ſhade of whoſe Crown I hope we ſhall ever gather the fruits of Juſtice), but by projectors, who have extended the prerogative of the King beyond the juſt ſymmetry, which maketh a ſweet harmony of the whole: they have brought the Crown into greater want than ever, by anticipating the Revenues; and can the ſhepherd be thus ſmitten, and the ſheep not ſcattered? They have introduced a Privy-Council, raviſhing at once the ſpheres of all ancient government, *impriſoning us without either bail or bond*; they have taken from us, what? What ſhall I ſay indeed, what have they left us? All means of ſupplying the King, and ingratiating ourſelves with him, taking up the root of all propriety, which if it be not ſeaſonably ſet again into the ground by his Majeſty' own hands, we ſhall have, inſtead of beauty, baldneſs. To the making of thoſe whole, I ſhall apply myſelf, and propound a remedy to all theſe diſeaſes. By one and the ſame thing have King and People been hurt, and by the ſame muſt they be cured; to vindicate, what, new things? No, our ancient vital liberties, by re-inforcing the ancient laws made by our anceſtors, by ſetting forth ſuch a character of them, as no licentious ſpirit ſhall dare to enter upon them. And ſhall we think this is a way to break a Parliament? No, our deſires are modeſt and juſt, I ſpeak truly, both for the Intereſt of the King and People; if we enjoy not theſe, it will be impoſſible for us to relieve him.

Therefore let us never fear they ſhall not be accepted by his goodneſs; wherefore I ſhall ſhortly deſcend to my motions, conſiſting of four parts; two of which have relation to our perſons, two to the propriety of goods. For our perſons; firſt, the freedom of them from impriſonment: ſecondly, from employment abroad, contrary to the ancient cuſtoms. For our goods, that no Levies be made, but by Parliament: ſecondly, no billetting of Soldiers. It is moſt neceſſary that theſe be reſolved, that the ſubject may be ſecured in both.

Sir *Benjamin Rudyard.*

THIS is the criſis of Parliaments; we ſhall know by this if Parliaments live or die, the King will be valued by the ſucceſs of us, the Counſels of this Houſe will have operations in all, 'tis fit we be wiſe; his Majeſty begins to us with affection, proclaiming, that he will rely upon his People's love. Preſervation is natural, we are not now on the *bene eſſe*, but on the *eſſe*; be ſure *England* is ours, and then prune it. Is it no ſmall matter that we have provoked two moſt potent Kings? We have united them, and have betrayed ourſelves more than our Enemies could. Men and Brethren, what ſhall we do? Is there no Balm in *Gilead*? If the King draw one way, and the Parliament another, we muſt all ſink. I reſpect no particular, I am not ſo wiſe to contemn what is determined by the major part; one day tells another, and one Parliament inſtructs another. I deſire this Houſe to avoid all conteſtations, the hearts of Kings are great, 'tis comely that Kings have the better of their ſubjects. Give the King leave to come off, I believe his Majeſty expects but the occaſion. 'Tis lawful, and our duty to adviſe his Majeſty, but the way is to take a right courſe to attain the right end; which I think may be thus: by truſting the King, and to breed a truſt in him; by giving him a large ſupply according to his wants, by proſtrating our grievances humbly at his feet, from thence they will have the beſt way to his heart, that is done in duty to his Majeſty. And to ſay all at once, let us all labour to get the King on our ſide, and this may be no hard matter, conſidering the near ſubſiſtence between the King and People

Sir *Edward Coke.*

DUM *tempus habemus, bonum operemur.* I am abſolutely for giving a ſupply to his Majeſty; yet with ſome caution. To tell you of foreign dangers and inbred evils, I will not do it, the State is inclining to a conſumption, yet not incurable: I fear not foreign Enemies, God ſend us peace at home for this diſeaſe I will propound remedies, I will ſeek nothing out of mine own head, but from my heart, and out of Acts of Parliament. I am not able to fly at all grievances, *but only at Loans.* Let us not flatter ourſelves; who will give Subſidies, if the King may impoſe what he will? and if, after Parliament, the King may inhaunce what he pleaſeth? I know the King will not do it, I know he is a religious King, free from perſonal vices, but he deals with other men's hands, and ſees with other men's eyes. Will any give a Subſidy that will be taxed after Parliament at pleaſure? The King cannot tax any by way of Loans: I differ from them, who would have this of Loans go amongſt Grievances, but I would have it go alone.

I'll begin with a noble Record, it chears me to think of it, 25 *E.* III. it is worthy to be written in letters of gold; *Loans againſt the will of the Subject, are againſt Reaſon, and the Franchiſes of the Land*, and they deſire reſtitution What a word is that *Franchiſe*? The Lord may tax his Villein high or low, but it is againſt the Franchiſes of the Land, for Freemen to be taxed but by their conſent in Parliament. *Franchiſe* is a *French* word, and in *Latin* it is *Libertas.* In *Magna Charta* it is provided, that, *Nullus liber homo capiatur vel impriſonetur aut diſſeiſietur de libero tenemento ſuo,* &c. *niſi per legale judicium parium ſuorum vel per legem terræ*, which Charter hath been confirmed by good Kings above thirty times.

When theſe Gentlemen had ſpoken, Sir *John Cook*, Secretary of State, took up the matter for the King, and concluded for redreſs of Grievances, ſo that ſupplies take the precedency; and ſaid:

Mr. Secretary *Cook.*

I Had rather you would hear any than me; I will not anſwer what hath been already ſpoken; my intent is not to ſtir, but to quiet; not to provoke, but to appeaſe: my deſire is, that every one reſort to his own heart to reunite the King and his State, and to take away the ſcandal from us; every one ſpeaks from the abundance of his heart. I do conclude out of every one's concluſion, to give to the King, to redreſs grievances; all the difference is about the manner. We all are Inhabitants in one Houſe, the Commonwealth, let every one in ſomewhat amend his Houſe, ſomewhat is amiſs. but if all the Houſe be on fire, will we then think of mending what is amiſs? will you not rather quench the fire? the danger all apprehend. The way that is propounded, I ſeek not to decline, illegal courſes have been taken, it muſt be confeſs'd, the redreſs muſt be by Laws and Puniſhment: but withal, add the Law of neceſſity; neceſſity hath no law, you muſt abilitate the State to do, what you do by petition require. It is wiſhed we begin with grievances; I deny not that we prepare them, but ſhall we offer them firſt? Will not this ſeem a condition with his Majeſty? Do we not deal with a wiſe King, jealous of his honour? All ſubſidies cannot advantage his Majeſty ſo much, as that his ſubjects do agree to ſupply him; this will amaze the Enemy more than ten Subſidies: begin therefore with the King, and not with ourſelves.

Sir *Robert Phillips.*

THIS day's debate makes me call to mind the cuſtom of the *Romans*, who had a ſolemn Feaſt once a year for their Slaves, at which time they had liberty (without exception) to ſpeak what they would, whereby to eaſe their afflicted minds, which being finiſhed, they ſeverally returned to their former ſervitude. This may, with ſome reſemblance and diſtinction, well ſet forth our preſent ſtate; where now, after the revolution of ſome time, and grievous ſufferings of many violent oppreſſions, we have (as thoſe Slaves had) a day of liberty of ſpeech; but ſhall not, I truſt, be herein Slaves, for we are free, we are not Bondmen, but Subjects: theſe, after their feaſts, were Slaves again; but 'tis our hope to return Freemen. I am glad to ſee this morning's work, to ſee ſuch a ſenſe of the grievances under which we groan. I ſee a concurrence of grief from all parts, to ſee the Subject wronged, and a fit way to ſee the Subject righted: I expected to ſee a diviſion, but I ſee an honourable conjunction, and I take it a good omen. It was wiſhed by one, that there were a forgetfulneſs of all; let him not proſper that wiſheth it not. No, there is no ſuch ways to perfect remedy, as to forget injuries; but not ſo to forget, as not to recover them. It was uſual in *Rome* to bury all injuries on purpoſe to recover them. It was ſaid by a Gentleman, that ever ſpeaks freely, *We muſt ſo govern ourſelves, as if this Parliament muſt be the Criſis of all Parliaments, and this is the laſt.* I hope well, and there will be no cauſe for the King, our Head, to except againſt us, or we againſt him. The dangers abroad are preſented to us; he is no *Engliſhman* that is not apprehenſive of them.

We have provoked two potent Kings (the one too near), who are too ſtrongly joined together; the dangers are not chimerical, but real, I acknowledge it, but it muſt be done in proportion of our dangers at home: I more fear the violation of publick Rights at home, than a foreign Enemy. Muſt it be our duties and direction to defend foreign dangers, and eſtabliſh ſecurity againſt them, and ſhall we not look at that which ſhall make us able and willing thereunto? We ſhall not omit to confide and truſt his Majeſty, otherwiſe our Counſels will be with fears, and that becomes not *Engliſhmen*. The unaccuſtomed violences (I have nothing but a good meaning) trench into all we have. To the four particulars already mentioned, wherein we ſuffer, one more may be added, leſt God forbear to hear me in the day of my trouble, our Religion is made vendible by Commiſſions: Alas! now a toleration is granted (little leſs), and men for pecuniary annual rates diſpenſed withal, whereby Papiſts, without fear of law, practiſe Idolatry, and ſcoff at Parliaments, at Laws, and all. It is well known, the people of this State are under no other ſubjection, than what they did voluntarily conſent unto, by the original contract between King and People; and as there are many Prerogatives and Privileges conferred on the King, ſo there are left to the Subject many neceſſary Liberties and Privileges, as appears by the common Laws and Acts of Parliament, notwithſtanding what theſe two *Sycophants (Sibthorp and Manwaring)* have prated in the Pulpit to the contrary. Was there ever yet King of *England* that directly violated the Subjects Liberty and Property, but their actions were ever complained of in Parliament, and no ſooner complained of than redreſſed? 21 *E.* III. there went out a Commiſſion to raiſe money in a ſtrange manner; the ſucceeding Parliament craved redreſs, and, till *H.* VIII. we never heard of the ſaid Commiſſions again.

Another way was by Loan, a Worm that canker'd the Law, the Parliament did redreſs it, and that money was paid again. The next little Engine was *Benevolence*; what the force of that was, look into the Statute of *R.* III. which damned that particular way, and all other indirect ways.

Since the Right of the Subject is thus bulwark'd by the Law of the Kingdom, and Princes upon complaint have rectified them, I am confident we ſhall have the like cauſe of joy from his Majeſty.

I will here make a little digreſſion: The County *(Somerſetſhire)* I ſerve for, were pleaſed to command me to ſeek the removal from them of the greateſt burthen that ever people ſuffered. It was excellently ſaid, Commiſſionary Lieutenants do deprive us of all Liberty. If ever the like was ſeen of the Lieutenancy that now is, I will never be believed more. They tell the people they muſt pay ſo much upon warrant from a Deputy-Lieutenant, or be bound to the good behaviour, are ſent up to the Lords of the Council, it is the ſtrangeſt Engine to rend the liberty of the Subject that ever was. There is now a *Decemvirat* in every County, and amongſt that *Decemviri*, there is ſome *Claudius Appius* that ſeek their own revenges. We complain of *Loans* and *Impoſitions*, but when Deputy-Lieutenants may ſend Warrants to impriſon our Perſons at pleaſure, fure, if we pay not what they fent for, it concerns us to preferve the Country in freedom, and to confider of this kind of people. There is now *Neceffity* brought in for an argument; all know that *Neceffity* is an armed man, and that *Neceffity* is an *evil Counfellor*, I would we had never known that Counfel; we are almoft grown like the *Turks*, who fend their *Janizaries*, who place the Halbert at the door, and there he is Mafter of the houfe. We have Soldiers billetted, and Warrants to collect money, which if they do not, the Soldiers muft come and rifle. The *Romans* fending one into *Spain*, found no greater complaint, than the difcontent that did arife, from Soldiers placed amongft them. I would you would look into *Fortefcue*, where he puts the Prince in mind, what mifery he faw, where Soldiers were put upon the people: But, faith he, no man is forced to take Soldiers but Inns, and they are to be paid by them. I defire we refort to his Majefty for redrefs, and to reduce all into bounds.

The other way of Grievance is a Judgment in a legal courfe of proceeding; we have had three Judgments of late times, all exceeding one another in prejudice of the Subject: The firft was, that which was judged in all formality, the *Poftnati (Scots)* cafe, which People I honour; for we find many of them love us more than we do ourfelves: I do not complain of it, but only mention it.

The other Judgment was for Impofitions, which was given in the Exchequer, and this Houfe twice afterwards damned that Judgment. How remifs our eyes are upon that, I grieve to fee.

There is a Judgment, if I may fo call it, a fatal Judgment againft the Liberty of the Subject, *Mich.* 3 *Car.* in Sir *John Heveningham*'s cafe, argued at the Bar, and pronounced but by one alone. I can live, although another without Title be put to live with me; nay, I can live, although I pay Excifes and Impofitions for more than I do: but to have my liberty, which is the foul of my life, taken from me by power, and to be pent up in a Gaol without remedy by Law, and this to be fo adjudged to perifh in Gaol; O improvident Anceftors! O unwife Forefathers! to be fo curious in providing for the quiet poffeffion of our Lands and Liberties of Parliament, and to neglect our Perfons and Bodies, and to let them die in prifon, and that *durante bene placito*, remedilefs. If this be Law, what do we talk of our Liberties? Why do we trouble ourfelves with the difpute of Law, Franchifes, Propriety of Goods? It is the *Summa totalis* of all miferies; I will not fay it was erroneous, but I hope we fhall fpeak our minds, when that Judgment comes here to be debated. What may a man call this? it not Liberty. Having paffed in fome confufion in the fafhion of my delivery, I conclude: We will confider two particulars, his Majefty, and his People. His Majefty calls to us, and craves our affiftance to revive again his honour, and the honour of the Nation: The People fend us, as we hope, with that direction, that we fhall return to them with that Olive-branch, that affurance of being free from thofe calamities, under which they can hardly breathe. Our fins have brought on us thofe miferies, let us all bring our Portion to make up the wall: we come with loyal hearts; his Majefty fhall find, that it is we that are his faithful Counfellors; let all Sycophants be far removed from his Majefty, fince we cannot help his Majefty without opening our grievances; let us difcharge our duties therein: yet while we feek Liberty, we will not forget Subjection. All things a State can be capable of, either bleffings or punifhments, depend on this meeting: if any think the King may be fupplied, and the Commonwealth preferved without redrefs of grievances, he is deceived. The Kings of *England* were never more glorious than when they trufted their Subjects; let us make all hafte to do the Errand for which we came; let the Houfe confider to prepare our Grievances fit for his Majefty's view, not to make a Law to give us new Liberties, but declaratory, with refpective Penalties; fo that thofe which violate them, if they would be vile, they fhould fear infamy with men; and then we fhall think of fuch a Supply as never Prince received, and with our money we fhall give him our hearts, and give him a new people rais'd from the dead: Then I hope this Parliament will been titled, The Parliament of Wonders, and God's Judgments diverted, and thefe beams of goodnefs fhall give us life, and we fhall go home to our own Countries, and leave our Pofterities as free as our Anceftors left us.

But this day, as alfo the two next days Debate, produced no Refolutions.

Monday, 24 *March*, Secretary *Cook* renewed the motion of Supplies for his Majefty, yet fo, that Grievances be likewife taken into confideration.

Then he made a motion, That the fame Committee may hear Propofitions of general heads of Supply, and afterwards go to other bufineffes of the day for Grievances. Others preferred the confideration of Grievances, as a particular root that invaded the main Liberty of the Subject. It is the Law (faid they), that glorious fundamental Right, whereby we have power to give; we defire but that his Majefty may let us have that Right therein, which, next to God, we all defire, and then we doubt not, but we fhall give his Majefty all fupply we can. The time was, when it was ufual to defire favours for fowing of difcords, as *Gondomar* did for *Raleigh*'s head. But the debates of this day came to no Refolution.

The day following, being the 25th, Mr. Secretary *Cook* tendered the Houfe certain Propofitions from the King, touching Supply; and told them, That his Majefty, finding time precious, expects that they fhould begin fpeedily, left they fpend that time in deliberation, which fhould be fpent in action; that he efteems the Grievances of the Houfe his own, and ftands not on Precedents in point of Honour. Therefore, to fatisfy his Majefty, let the fame Committee take his Majefty's Propofitions into confideration, and let both concur, whether to fit on one in the forenoon, or the other in the afternoon, it is all one to his Majefty.

Hereupon the Houfe turned themfelves into a Committee, and commanded *Edward Littleton*, Efq; unto the Chair, and ordered the Committee to take into confideration the Liberty of the Subject, in his Perfon, and in his Goods, and alfo to take into confideration his Majefty's Supply. In this Debate the Grievances were reduced to fix heads, as to our Perfons.

1. Attendance at the Council-board.
2. Imprifonment.
3. Confinement.
4. Defignation for foreign Employment.
5. Martial Law.
6. Undue Proceedings in matter of Judicature.

The firft matter debated, was the Subject's Liberty in his perfon; the particular inftance was in the cafe of Sir *John Heveningham*, and thofe other Gentlemen who were imprifoned about Loan-money, and thereupon had brought their *Habeas Corpus*, had their Cafe argued, and were neverthelefs remanded to Prifon, and a Judgment, as it was then faid, was entered.

Then Sir *Edward Coke* fpoke as follows.

IT is true, that the King's Prerogative is a part of the Law of this Kingdom, and a fupreme part, for the Prerogative is highly tendered and refpected of the Law; yet it hath bounds fet unto it by the Laws of *England*. But fome worthy Members of this Houfe have fpoken of foreign States, which I conceive to be a foreign Speech, and not able to weaken the fide I fhall maintain.

That Mr. *Attorney (Sir Robert Heath)* may have fomething to anfwer unto, I will fpeak, without taking another day, to the body of the Caufe, yet keeping fomething in ftore for another time. I have not my *Vade mecum* here, yet I will endeavour to recite my Authorities truly; I fhall begin with an old Authority, for *Errorem ad fua principia referre, eft refellere*.

The ground of this error was the Statute of *Weft.* 1. *cap.* 15. which faith, That thofe are not repleviable, who are committed for the death of a man, or by the commandment of the King, or his Juftices, or for the Foreft (for fo it was cited;) and *Stamford* 72. expounding hereof, the commandment of the King to be the commandment of the King's mouth, or of his Council, but it is clear that by *præceptum* is underftood the commandment of the Juftices of the *King's Bench*, and *Common-Pleas*; and this is *contemporanea expofitio, quæ eft fortiffima in lege*.

To this purpofe *vide Weftm.* 1. *cap.* 9. the Book of 2 *R.* II. *item, cap.* 20. *de malè acceptibus in parc.* the Book of 8 *Hen.* IV. 5. *item*, 25. 26. 29. *cap. ejufdem ftatuti*, whereby it may appear that the commandment here fpoken of to be the commandment of the King, is his commandment by the Judges, *Præceptum Domini Regis in Curia, non in Camera*. So it is likewife taken 1 *R.* II. *cap.* 12. in a Statute made in the next King's Reign, and exprefly in *Dyer, fol.* 162. §. 50. & *fol.* 192. §. 24. Shall I further prove it by matter of Record? *Fac hoc & vives*; it is 18 *E.* III. *Rot.* 33 *coram Rege*, *John Bilfton*'s cafe, who being committed and detained in prifon by the commandment of the King, was difcharged by *Habeas Corpus, eo quod Breve Domini Regis non fuit fufficiens caufa*.

All the Acts of Parliament in title of *Accufation* are direct to the point, and alfo the 16 *Hen.* VI. *Brooke* and *Littleton*, 2. 8. *monftrans de fait* 182. *per Cur.* The King cannot command a man to be arrefted in his prefence: the King can arreft no man, becaufe there is no remedy againft him, 1 *Hen.* VII. 4. likewife *prædict. ftat. cap.* 18. the King's pleafure is not binding without the affent of the Realm.

I never read any opinion againft what I have faid, but that of *Stamford*, miftaken (as you fee) in the ground: yet I fay not that a man may not be committed without precife fhewing the caufe in particular; for it is fufficient if the caufe in general be fhewed, as for Treafon, &c. 1. *E.* II. *ftat. de fran gend. prifon. nullus habeat judicium*, &c. there the caufe of imprifonment muft be known, elfe the Statute will be of little force; the words thereof do plainly demonftrate the intent of the Statute to be accordingly.

I will conclude with the higheft authority, that is, 25 chap. of the *Acts* of the Apoftles, the laft verfe, where Saint *Paul* faith, *It is againft reafon to fend a man to prifon without fhewing a caufe.*

Thus, Mr. *Attorney*, according to the rules of Phyfick, I have given you a Preparative, which doth precede a purge. I have much more in ftore *.

Mr. *Creffwell*'s Speech.

I Stand up to fpeak fomewhat concerning the point of the Subjects grievances by imprifonment of their perfons without any declaration of the caufe, contrary unto, and in derogation of, the fundamental Laws and Liberties of this Kingdom.

I think I am one of the *Puifnes* of our profeffion, which are of the Members of this Houfe; but howfoever fure I am in that refpect of my own inabilities, I am the *Puifne* of all the whole Houfe; therefore, according to the ufual courfe of Students in our profeffion, I (as the *Puifne*) fpeak firft in time, becaufe I can fpeak leaft in matter.

In purfuance of which courfe I fhall rather put the cafe than argue it: and therefore I fhall humbly defire firft of all, of this honourable Houfe in general, that the goodnefs of the caufe may receive no prejudice by the weaknefs of my argument, and next of all, of my Mafters here of the fame profeffion in particular, that they by their learned judgments will fupply the great defects I fhall difcover by declaring of my unlearned opinion.

Before I fpeak of the queftion, give me leave, as an entrance thereunto, to fpeak firft of the occafion.

You fhall know, *Juftice* is the life and the heart's-blood of the Common-wealth, and if the Common-wealth bleed in the mafter-vein, all the balm in *Gilead* is but in vain to preferve this our body of policy from ruin and deftruction. Juftice is both *Columna & Corona Reipublicæ*, fhe is both the Column and the Pillar, the Crown and the Glory of the Common-wealth. This is made good in Scripture by the judgment of *Solomon*, the wifeft King that ever reigned on earth. For firft, fhe is the Pillar, for he faith, that by Juftice the Throne fhall be eftablifhed. Secondly, fhe is the Crown; for he faith, that by Juftice a Nation is exalted.

Our Laws, which are the rules of this Juftice, they are the *ne plus ultra* to both the King and the Subject; and as they are the *Hercules* Pillar, fo are they the Pillar to every *Hercules*, to every *Prince*, which he muft not pafs.

Give me leave to refemble her to *Nebuchadnezzar*'s tree: for fhe is fo great, that fhe doth fhade not only the Palace of the King, and the Houfe of the Nobles, but doth alfo fhelter the cottage of the pooreft beggar.

* I [illegible] not to make an argument in this point, the greateft that ever was in this place, or elfewhere. This Liberty, which all men, as well Lawyers as others, believe, as I [illegible] hath been violated, tho' not without complaint: but except in this late cafe, I am confident, was never adjudged before. The *Habeas Corpus* was brought, the caufe was returned by commandment of the King, intimated by the Lords of the Council, Argument was made, feven Acts of Parliament were mentioned, [illegible] over, and [illegible]; and upon that a Declaration of Judgment was given, and so adjudged, *That upon any commitment of the King or the Council* [illegible] I ever obferved in any great caufe, [illegible] arguments ufed to be made. We fee his Majefty and his Council are both interefted in this. I do defire that fome of the King's Council may fpeak what they can to fatisfy us of this great power. MSS. Pymmi apud virum honoratum Thomam Hales Baronettum. See Selden's Life in his Works, Vol. I. p. 12.

Where-

Wherefore, if either now the blasts of indignation, or the unresistable violator of laws, Necessity, hath so bruised any of the branches of this tree, that either our persons, or goods, or possessions have not the same shelter as before; yet let us not therefore neglect the root of this great tree, but rather with all our possible endeavour and unfeigned duty, both apply fresh and fertile mould unto it, and also water it even with our own tears, that so these bruised branches may be recover'd, and the whole tree again prosper and flourish. For this I have learned from an ancient Father of the Church, that though *preces Regum sunt armatæ*, yet *arma subditorum* are but only *preces & lachrymæ*.

I know well that *Cor Regis inscrutabile*; and that Kings, although they are but men before God, yet are they Gods before men. And therefore to my gracious and dread Sovereign, (whose virtues are true qualities ingenerate both in his judgment and nature) let my arm be cut off, nay, let my soul not live that day, that I shall dare to lift up my arm to touch that forbidden fruit, those flowers of his princely Crown and Diadem.

But yet in our *Eden*, in this garden of the Commonwealth, as there are the *flowers of the Sun*, which are so glorious that they are to be handled only by royal Majesty; so are there also some daisies and wholesome herbs, which every common hand that lives and labours in this garden may pick and gather up, and take comfort and repose in them. Amongst all which this *oculus diei*, this *bona libertas* is one, and the chief one.

Thus much in all humbleness I presume to speak for the occasion. I will now descend to the question: wherein I hold, (with all dutiful submission to better Judgments) that these Acts of power in imprisoning and confining of his Majesty's Subjects in such manner, without any declaration of the cause, are against the fundamental Laws and liberties of this Kingdom.

And for these reasons thus briefly drawn, I conclude,

1. The first, from the great favour which the Law doth give unto, and the great care which it hath ever taken of the Liberty and Safety of this Kingdom.

I should not need to take the question in pieces, nor handle it in parts dividedly, but as one entire; because I hold no other difference between imprisonment and confinement than only this, that one hath a less and straiter, the other a greater and larger prison. And this word confinement not being to be found in any one case of our Law, if therefore it is become the language of State, it is too difficult for me to define.

To proceed therefore in maintenance of my first reason; I find our Law doth so much favour the Subject's Liberty of his person, that the body of a man was not liable to be arrested or imprisoned for any other cause at the Common-Law, but for force, and things done against the peace. For the Common-Law (being the preserver of the land) so abhorreth force, that those that commit it she accounts her capital enemies, and therefore did subject their bodies to imprisonment. But by the Statute of *Marlebridge*, *Cap.* 24. which was made 35 *Hen* III. who was the eighth King from the Conquest, because Bailiffs would not render accounts to their Lords, it was enacted, that their bodies should be attached: And afterwards by the Statute 23 *Ed.* III. 17. who was the eleventh King after the Conquest, because men made no conscience to pay their debts; it was enacted that their bodies should likewise be attached. But before those statutes no man's body was subject to be taken or imprisoned otherwise than as aforesaid. Whereby it is evident, how much the Common-Law favoured the Liberty of the Subject, and protected his body from imprisonment.

I will inforce the reason further by a rule in Law, and some cases in Law upon that rule.

The rule is this, That *Corporalis injuria non recipit æstimationem è futuro*: So as if the question be not for a wrong done to the person, the Law will not compel him to sustain it, and afterwards accept a remedy; for the Law holds no damage a sufficient recompence for a wrong which is corporal.

The cases in Law to prove this, shall be these.

If one menace me in my goods, or that he will burn the evidence of my land, which he hath in his custody, unless I make unto him a bond; there I cannot avoid the bond, by pleading of this menace. But if he restrains my person, or threatens me with battery, or with burning my house, which is a protection for my person, or with burning an instrument of manumission, which is an evidence of my enfranchisement; upon these menaces or dares, I shall avoid the bond by plea.

So if a Trespasser drives my beast over another man's ground, and I pursue to rescue it, there I am a Trespasser to him on whose ground I am. But if a man assault my person, and I for my safety fly over into another man's ground, there I am no Trespasser to him, for *Quod quis in tuitione sui corporis fecerit, jure id fecisse existimatur*.

Nay, which is more, the Common-Law did favour the Liberty not only of Freemen, but even of the persons of Bondmen, and Villeins, who have no propriety either in Lands or Goods, as Freemen have; and therefore by the Law, the Lord could not maim his Villein, nay, if the Lord commanded another to beat his Villein, and he did it, the Villein should have his action of battery against him for it.

If the Lord made a lease for years to his Villein, if he did plead with his Villein, if he tendered his Villein to be Champion for him in a Writ of Right; any of these Acts, and many other, which I omit, were in Law enfranchisements, and made these Villeins Freemen. Nay, in a suit brought against one, if he by Attorney will plead that he is a Villein, the Law is so careful of Freedom, that it disallows this Plea by Attorney, but he must do it *propria persona*, because it binds his posterity and blood to the Villein's also. And thus much in the general for my first reason.

2. My next reason is drawn by an argument *à majori ad minus*; I frame it thus: If the King have no absolute power over our lands or goods, then *à fortiori* not over our persons, to imprison them without declaring the cause, for our persons are much more worth than either lands or goods, which is proved by what I have said already, and *Christ* himself makes it clear, where he saith, *Annon est corpus supra vestimentum?* Is not the body of more worth than the raiment? Where the *Canonists* say, that *vestimentum* comprehendeth all outward things which are not in the same degree with that which is corporal. And our Law maketh it also plain, for if a Villein purchaseth frank-land, this makes it Villein-land according to the nature of his person; but it holds not *è converso*, frank-land shall not free the person. Now that the King hath no absolute power either over our lands or goods, I will only at this time but put a case or two: for without proof of the premisses, my conclusion would not follow.

First for land: The King cannot by his Letters-Patent make the son of an Alien heir to his father, nor to any other, for he cannot disinherit the right heir, saith the book, nor do no prejudice to the Lord of his Escheat. The King by his Prerogative shall pay no toll for things bought in fairs and markets; but a custom for paying toll to go over the soil and freeholds of another shall bind the King. for this toucheth the inheritance of the Subject, and therefore the King shall not have so much as a way over his lands without paying; and if not a way, then certainly not the land itself.

Next for goods: if a man hath a jewel in gage for ten pound, &c and is attainted for Treason, the King shall not have this jewel, if he pays not the ten pound. So if Cattle be distreined, and the owner of them afterwards be attainted, yet the King shall not have them until he have satisfied that for which they were distreined. And if in these cases, where the owners of the goods are such capital offenders, the King cannot have them; much less shall he have them when the owner is innocent, and no offender.

Nay, I may well say that almost every leaf and page of all the volumes of our Common-Law prove this right of propriety, this distinction of *meum* and *tuum*, as well between King and Subject, as one Subject and another: and therefore my conclusion follows, That if the prerogative extend not neither to lands nor to goods, then *à fortiori* not to the person, which is more worth than either lands or goods, as I said. And yet I agree, that by the very law of nature, service of the person of the subject is due to his Sovereign; but this must be in such things which are not against the law of nature: but to have the body imprisoned without any cause declared, and so to become in bondage, I am sure is contrary unto, and against the law of nature, and therefore not to be inforced by the Sovereign upon his Subjects.

3. My next reason is drawn *ab inutili & incommodo*. For the Statute *de frangentibus prisonam*, made 1 E. II. is, *quod nullus qui prisonam fregerit, subeat judicium vitæ vel membrorum pro fractione prisonæ tantum, nisi causa pro qua captus imprisonetur tale judicium requirat*. Whence this conclusion is clearly gathered, That if a man be committed to prison without declaring what cause, and then if either Malefactor do break the prison, or the Gaoler suffer him to escape, albeit the prisoner so escaping had committed *Crimen læsæ majestatis*, yet neither the Gaoler nor any other that procured his escape, by the Law suffer any corporal punishment for setting him at large; which, if admitted, might prove in consequence a matter of great danger to the Commonwealth.

4. My next reason is drawn *ab Regis honore*, from that great honour the Law doth attribute unto sovereign Majesty: and therefore the rule of law is, that *Solum Rex hoc non potest facere, quod non potest injuste agere*. And therefore if a subject hath the donation, and the King the presentation to a Church, whereunto the King presents without the subject's nomination, here the *quare impedit* lies against the Incumbent, and the King is in law no disturber.

And *Hussey*, Chief-Justice, in 1 *Hen.* VII. *fol.* 4. saith, that Sir *John Markham* told King *Edw.* IV. he could not arrest a man either for Treason or Felony, as a subject might, because that if the King did wrong, the party could not have his action against him.

What is the reason that an action of false imprisonment lies against the Sheriff, if he doth not return the King's Writ, by which he hath taken the body of the subject, but this, because the Writ doth *breviter enarrare causam captionis*, (which if it doth not, it shall abate, and is void in law) and being returned, the party when he appears may know what to answer, and the Court upon what to judge? And if the King's Writ under his Great Seal cannot imprison the subject, unless it contains the cause, shall then the King's warrant otherwise do it without containing the cause; that his Judges upon return thereof may likewise judge of the same, either to remain, or judge the party imprisoned?

I should argue this point more closely upon the Statute of *Magna Charta* 29. *quod nullus liber homo imprisonetur*; the Statute of *West.* 1. *cap.* 15. for letting persons to bail; and the judgments lately given in the *King's-Bench*: but the latter of these Statutes having been by that honourable Gentleman Sir *Edward Coke* (to whom the professors of the law both in this and all succeeding ages, are, and will be much bound) already expounded unto us, and that also fortified by those many cotemporary expositions and judgments by him learnedly cited; and there being many learned Lawyers here, whose time I will not waste, who were present; and some of them perhaps of Counsel in the late cause adjudged in the *King's-Bench*, where you (to whose person I now speak) do well know I was absent, being then of Counsel in a cause in another Court, and my practice being in the Country, far remote from the Treasure of Antiquity, and Records conducing to the clearing of this point; therefore the narrowness of my understanding commends unto me sober ignorance, rather than presumptuous knowledge, and also commands me no further to trouble your patience.

But I will conclude with that which I find reported by Sir *John Davis*, who was the King's Serjeant, and so, by the duty of his place, would no doubt maintain to his uttermost the prerogatives of the King his royal Master, and yet it was by him thus said in those Reports of his upon the case of Tanistry Customs, *p.* 29. That the Kings of *England* always have had a monarchy-royal, and not a monarchy-seignoral: where, under the first (saith he), "the subjects are freemen, and have propriety in their "goods, and free-hold, and inheritance in their lands; but under the lat-"ter they are as Villeins and Slaves, and have propriety in nothing. And "therefore (saith he) when a Royal Monarch makes a new Conquest, yet "if he receives any of his Nation's ancient Inhabitants into his protec-"tion, they and their heirs after them shall enjoy their lands and liberties "according to the law." And there he voucheth this precedent and judgment following, given before *William* the *Conqueror* himself, *viz.*

"That one *Sherborn* a *Saxon*, at the time of the Conquest being owner "of a castle and lands in *Norfolk*, the Conqueror gave the same to one "*Warren* a *Norman*, and *Sherborn* dying, the heir claiming the same by "descent according to the law, it was before the Conqueror himself ad-"judged

"judged for the heir, and that the gift thereof by the Conqueror was void."

If then it were thus in the Conqueror's time, and by his own sentence and judgment, and hath so continued in all the successions of our Kings ever since, what doubt need we have, but that his most excellent Majesty, upon our humble petition prostrated at his feet, (which, as was well said, is the best passage to his heart) will vouchsafe unto us our ancient liberties and birth-rights, with a thorough reformation of this and other just grievances? And so I humbly crave pardon of this honourable House, that I have made a short lesson long

Upon this and other arguments made in this case of the *Habeas Corpus*, the House referred the whole business to a Committee, to examine all the proceedings: concerning which, Mr. *Selden* afterwards made report to the House, that Mr. *Waterhouse*, a Clerk in the Crown-Office, being examined before the Committee, did confess, that by direction from Sir *Robert Heath*, the King's Attorney-General, he did write the draught of a judgment in the case before-mentioned, which was delivered to Mr. Attorney. And Mr. *Keeling* being examined before the Committee did confess, that after *Mich.* term last, the Attorney-General wished him to make a special entry of the *Habeas Corpus*: to which he answered, he knew no special entry in those cases, but only a *Remittitur*: but said to Mr. Attorney, that if he pleased to draw one, and the Court after assented to it, he would then enter it. The Attorney did accordingly make a draught, and the Copy thereof Mr. *Keeling* produced to the Committee. And further said, that he carried this draught to the Judges, but they would not assent to a special entry: nevertheless, the Attorney-General divers times sent to him, and told him there was no remedy, but he must enter it. Yet a week before the Parliament met, the Attorney-General called for the draught again, which accordingly he gave unto him, and never heard of it more.

Sir *Robert Philips*, upon this report, gave his opinion, "That this intended judgment in the *Habeas Corpus*, was a draught made by some man "that desired to strike us from all our liberties: but the Judges justly "refused it. But if the Judges did intend it, we sit not here (said he) "to answer the trust we are sent for, if we present not this matter to his "Majesty. Let this business be further searched into, and see how this "judgment lies against us, and what the Judges do say concerning "the same."

March 27. The House proceeded in further debate of the liberty of the subject. When

Mr. *Hackwell* resumed the debate of the matter concerning the *Habeas Corpus*.

"The late judgment (said he) which lies in bar, is only an award, "and no judgment; and in the Lord Chief-Justice's argument, there was "no word spoken, that the King might commit or detain without cause.

"For the King to commit a man, is *indignum Rege*: Mercy and Ho- "nour flow immediately from the King, Judgment and Justice are his too, "but they flow from his Ministers; the Sword is carried before him, "but the Sceptre is in his hands. These are true emblems of a good King.

"The Law admits not the King's power of detaining in prison at plea- "sure. In ancient times prisons were but *pro custodia, carceres non ad pœnam, sed ad custodiam*. Admit the King may commit a man, yet to de- "tain him as long as he pleaseth is dangerous, and then a man shall be "punished before his offence: Imprisonment is a maceration of the body, "and horror to the mind; it is *vita pejor morte*."

Then the House commanded that case in the Lord Chief-Justice *Anderson*'s Book, all of his own hand-writing, to be openly read. The words of the Report were these:

"Divers persons fueront committes a several temps a several prisons, "sur pleasure sans bon cause parte de queux estiant amesnes en banck le "Roy. Et parte en se Commune banck fueront accordant a la ley de la "terre mise a large & discharge de le imprisonment, pur que aucuns grants "fueront ostendus & procure un commandment a les Judges que ils ne fera "issent apres. Ceo nient meens les Judges ne surcease mes per advise "enter eux ils fesoient certain Articles le tenour de queux ensue, & deli- "ver eux al seigneurs Chauncelor & Treasurer & eux subscribe avec "toute lour maines, les Articles sont come ensuont."

[We her Majesty's Justices of both Benches, and Barons of the Exchequer, desire your Lordships, that by some good means some order may be taken, that her Highness's Subjects may not be committed or detain'd in prison by commandment of any Nobleman or Counsellor against the laws of the Realm; either else help us to have access to her Majesty, to the end to become suitors to her for the same; for divers have been imprisoned for suing ordinary actions and suits at the Common Law, until they have been constrained to leave the same against their wills, and put the same to order, albeit judgment and execution have been had therein, to their great losses and griefs for the aid of which persons, her Majesty's Writs have sundry times been directed to sundry persons, having the custody of such persons unlawfully imprisoned, upon which Writs, no good or lawful cause of imprisonment hath been returned or certified. Whereupon, according to the laws, they have been discharged of their imprisonment; some of which persons so delivered, have been again committed to prison in secret places, and not to any common or ordinary prison, or lawful Officer or Sheriff, or other lawfully authorized, to have or keep a Gaol; so that upon complaint made for their delivery, the Queen's Courts cannot tell to whom to direct her Majesty's Writs; and by this means Justice cannot be done. And moreover, divers Officers and Serjeants of *London* have been many times committed to prison for lawful executing of her Majesty's Writs, sued forth of her Majesty's Courts at *Westminster*; and thereby her Majesty's Subjects and Officers are so terrified, that they dare not sue or execute her Majesty's Laws, her Writs and Commandments: divers others have been sent for by Pursivants, and brought to *London* from their dwellings, and by unlawful imprisonment have been constrained, not only to withdraw their lawful suits, but have also been compelled to pay the Pursivants, so bringing such persons, great sums of money. All which, upon complaint the Judges are bound by office and oath to relieve and help, by and according to her Majesty's laws. And when it pleaseth your Lordships to will divers of us to set down in what cases a prisoner, sent to custody by her Majesty or her Council, are to be detained in prison, and not to be delivered by her Majesty's Court or Judges; we think, that if any person be committed by her Majesty's command, from her person, or by order from the Council-board; and if any one or two of her Council commit one for High-Treason, such persons so in the cases before committed, may not be delivered by any of her Courts, without due trial by the law, and judgment of acquittal had: Nevertheless the Judges may award the Queen's Writ to bring the bodies of such prisoners before them; and if upon return thereof, the causes of their commitment be certified to the Judges as it ought to be; then the Judges in the cases before, ought not to deliver him; but to remand him to the place from whence he came, which cannot be conveniently done, unless notice of the cause in general, or else in special, be given to the Keeper or Gaoler that shall have the custody of such prisoner. All the Judges and Barons did subscribe their names to these Articles, *Ter Paschæ* 34 *Eliz.* and delivered one to the Lord-Chancellor, and another to the Lord-Treasurer: after which time there did follow more quietness than before, in the cause before-mentioned.]

After the reading of this Report, Sir *Edward Coke* said, That of my own knowledge this Book was written with my Lord *Anderson*'s own hand, it is no flying report of a young Student. I was Solicitor then, and Treasurer *Burleigh* was as much against commitment as any of this Kingdom; it was the *White Staves* that made this stir. Let us draw towards a conclusion: the question is, Whether a Freeman can be imprisoned by the King, without setting down the cause? I leave it as bare as *Æsop*'s Crow, they that argue against it, *Humores moti & non remoti corpus destruunt*. It is a maxim, the Common Law has admeasured the King's Prerogative, that in no case it can prejudice the inheritance of the subjects; had the Law given the Prerogative to that which is taken, it would have set some time to it, else mark what would follow. I shall have an Estate of Inheritance for life, or for years in my land, or propriety in my goods, and I shall be a tenant at will for my liberty; I shall have propriety in my own house, and not liberty in my person, *Perspicue vera non sunt probanda*. The King hath distributed his Judicial Power to Courts of Justice, and to Ministers of Justice; it is too low for so great a Monarch as the King is, to commit men to prison; and it is against law, that men should be committed, and no cause shewed. I would not speak this, but that I hope my gracious King will hear of it; yet it is not I *Edward Coke* that speaks it, but the Records that speak it; we have a national appropriate Law to this Nation, *divisi. ab orbe Britannis*.

Mr. *Selden*.

I Was sent hither, and trusted with the lives and liberties of them that sent me. Since I came, I took here an oath to defend the King's prerogatives and rights. I profess, tho' once I was of Counsel, and then I spoke for my fee, for the Gentlemen in their *Habeas Corpus*; yet now I speak according to my knowledge and conscience.

The question is, whether any subject or freeman, that is committed to prison, and the cause not shewn in the Warrant, he ought to be bailed or delivered? I think, confidently it belongs to every subject that is not a Villein that he ought to be bailed, or delivered.

I shall speak in this course. 1. I will shew the reasons. 2. Acts of Parliament. 3. Precedents. 4. Answer objections.

I. Reasons drawn from three heads:

1. From remedies provided by the Common Law against imprisonment. For that precious thing of liberty there are divers remedies, by which it appears, if no known cause be of further detainment, he is to be delivered. I will not mention the action of false imprisonment, but the Writ *de odio & atia*, which is not taken away, for that it is in *Magna Charta*. That Writ was sent to know, if the party imprisoned were committed for any cause of malice and hatred, and this was to be enquired of in Jury. For the Writ *de homine replegiando*, if one be imprisoned under the Sheriff, he must be delivered, if he be not detained for a cause for which he is not replevisable. For the *Habeas Corpus*, the Keeper is to bring the body *ad subjiciendum & recipiendum*. If there be no cause, how can the Court consider of the cause? For appeal, by the old law in the time of *Hen.* I. one imprisoned might have his appeal, as appears by *Bracton*, *c.* 25. *lib. de corona*. *Fleta*, *c.* 42.

2. The second reason is from the consideration of Freemen and Villeins. All admit we are *liberi homines*; but do but consider the difference of Villeins and Freemen, and I know no difference in their persons, but only the one cannot be imprisoned, as the other may. Whoever can say I can imprison him, I will say he is my Villein. It is the sole distinction of Freemen, that they cannot be imprisoned at pleasure.

In old time none but *Jews* and Villeins could be imprisoned, and confined. The *Jews* were as demesne Villeins of the King; he could send to them to lend money, and if they did not, he imprisoned them.

3. From matter of punishment. When any thing is declared by any new Statute to be an offence, it goes, That he shall be fined and imprisoned. To what end were this in any Act of Parliament, if imprisonment was at the King's will?

II. For Acts of Parliament, *Magna Charta*, *c.* 19. In that Act when it was first made, it was *nec eum in carcere mittimus*, 17 *Joh.* that Statute was made, and then it had those words. The course then was to send down all Acts of Parliament and Charters to the Abbeys to be enrolled. *Matthew Paris*, 345. & 342 recites that Charter of 17 *John*.

They object in *Magna Charta*, there is *lex terræ*, and by the law one may be imprisoned.

Lex terræ is the process of law, for the law imprisons no man at all, but it is meant the process of law, 5 *Edw.* III. Upon some occasion it was enacted, That none be attached contrary to the great Charter and the law of the land. 25 *Edw.* III. divers were committed to the Tower, and no man knew wherefore, whereupon was 25 *Edw.* III made, 28 *Edw* III. *c.* 3. 36 *Edw.* III. *n.* 9. is against imprisonment, *per speciale mandatum*.

III. For Precedents, 18 *Edw.* III. *rot.* 33 *Hen.* I. *Hen.* VIII. *rot.* 9. 12 *Jac. rot.* 153.

IV. Objections against it. *First*, Against the reason; a man may be committed for a point of State that may not be known: I understand not matters of State; I expected not the objection in a Court of Justice; and it may be a word for any King to try the courage of his Judges, and to suppose there is a cause of State, when perhaps there is no cause appears to them. It is as if they sent him back to prison, they knew not wherefore; which cannot be in a Court of Justice, where they are sworn to do justice.

Secondly,

Secondly, As to the Acts of Parliament, the Judges gave no answer, but only commended them; but the Attorney answered them with one blow to strike them all; that they are to be considered for common and ordinary causes, that happen in *Westminster-hall* only. But do but consider *Magna Charta*, which reflects upon the King; *nec super eum ibimus*. By the Law, if I bring an Appeal of Murder against a Nobleman, which is my suit, he shall not be tried by his Peers; but if he be indicted for that murder, which is the King's suit, he shall; which shews, that that which is in *Magna Charta* is meant of the King, though it be not in the third Person.

Third Objection is against the Statute of *Westminster* 1. c. 15. But the King's command is the command of the King by his Justices; and also the word, Replevisable, never signifies bailable; bailable, is in a Court of Record, by the King's Justices: but replevisable, is by the Sheriff. The Statute is to the Sheriff, and it shews the particular causes, and concludes that the Sheriff shall lose his bailiwick. The Sheriff could never replevy one for Murder, or matters of the Forest: but in the *King's-Bench* for Murder, or matters of the Forest they may, 3. *assis.* 19. 21 *Edw.* IV. 25. 22 *Hen.* VI. 48. *Newton*. If any man be taken by our command, or by the command of the King, if the Sheriff take the party, he must come to us, we will grant a *Supersedeas*.

Fourthly, They object against the precedents cited; they are all of this kind, they were imprisoned *per mandatum domini Regis*, or *Concilii*, without cause, or the cause is expressed. When the cause is expressed, and is within the cognizance of the Court, there they bailed them, but when it is for Felony or Treason, it may be done beyond the seas, and then the Court has no cognizance of them. When no cause is set, yet bailment is alledged; then they answer divers were so bailed, but the cause appears by Paper-Books; but I never saw these Books to be Records, and Judges of Record made their judgment in Records, and the cause only appears by Record.

For the Resolution cited 34 *Eliz.* all precedents were read, Acts of Parliament indeed were passed over, and yet that was not read. As we have that liberty here, so I dare say, no Prince in *Christendom* doth assume this power to imprison any without any cause. I find no steps or *vestigium* of any such power *.

Saturday, *March* 29, 1628. Mr. Sollicitor spake as followeth:

My care when I spake last was to give satisfaction that the Judges did not err in their late Resolutions; but if they did, it was *cum patribus*: the Judges knew nothing of the cause of the Gentlemen's imprisonment; if they had known the cause of their Imprisonment in private, they would have appealed to his Majesty for his Grace. For to reiterate all the authorities I will not, I have something to say in the point, to put into the scale, which might have been then said, had it not been for the unhappy difference that might have been between the two Courts in *Westminster-hall*, the *King's-Bench* and the *Chancery Court*.

In 13 *Jac.* divers were committed for disobedience to the Decree of the Court of Chancery, as namely *Rosswell* and others, and it was resolved, That the Judges could not deliver such; and at the same time some were committed by Warrant from the King and the Lords of the Council, and this came in Question, *Mich.* 13 *Jac.* and so continued divers Terms. There was then recourse had to those arguments, and I have a report here of that time what the Judges did then, part whereof I will read.

It was resolved by † *Coke*, *Crook*, *Doderidge* and *Houghton*, that the return was good, and that the cause need not to be disclosed, being *per mandatum Concilii*, as *Arcana Regni* (and the report further saith, that in 34 *Eliz.* it was resolved accordingly), and by *Coke* 'twas said, That if the Privy-Council commit one, he is not bailable by any Court of Justice, and *Stamford's* opinion is so, *fol.* 72. See what opinion the Judge had of the resolution in 34 *Eliz.* and of *Stamford*.

To this Sir *Edward Coke* replied: This report moves not me at all; that report is not yet twenty-one years old, but under age, being in 13 *Jac.* In truth, when I read *Stamford*, I was of his opinion at the first, but since, looking into those Records before-mentioned, I was of another mind ‡. He brings in an ill time 13 *Jac.* when there was clashing between the Court of *King's-Bench* and *Chancery*, as also there were then many of the Traitors that were of the Powder-Treason, committed *per mandatum Concilii*.

Upon *Monday*, *April* 1, the debate being re-assumed, Sir *Robert Philips* moved, That considering the House was now ready for the Question, they might hear the resolution read of all the Judges in 34 *Eliz.* about this matter.

Then Sir *Edward Coke* stood up and said, The Glass of Time runs out, and something cast upon us hath retarded us; when I spake against the Loans and this matter, I expected blows, and somewhat was spoken, though not to the matter.

Concerning that (that hath been objected) I did when I was a Judge, I will say somewhat. Indeed a motion was made, but no argument or debate, or resolution upon advice; I will never palliate with this House, there is no Judge that hath an upright heart to God, and a clear heart to the world, but he hath some Warrant for every thing that he doth. I confess when I read *Stamford* then, and had it in my hands, I was of that opinion at the Council-Table; but when I perceived that some Members of this House were taken away, even in the face of this House, and sent to prison, and when I was not far off from that place myself. I went to my books, and would not be quiet till I had satisfied myself. *Stamford* at the first was my guide, but my guide had deceived me, therefore I swerved from it: I have now better guides, Acts of Parliament and other precedents, these are now my guides. I desire to be free from the imputation that hath been laid upon me.

As for the copy of the intended Judgment, I fear, had it not been for this Parliament, it had been entered ere this time; a Parliament brings Judges and all other men into good order: if any Clerk had drawn this draught, he would have done it by a precedent, and there can be no precedent found that warrants it, and therefore I believe that some other did it.

This draught of the judgment, should it be entered, will sting us to death, *quia nulla causa fuit ostenta, ideo ne fuit baileabile*, and that it appears to be so by the Records. I persuade myself Mr. Attorney drew it; I had a copy of my Lord *Anderson's* report of the Judges resolution, 34 *Eliz.* long ago; but I durst not vouch it (and it was so in that copy) for that it was Apocrypha, and did not answer his gravity that made it, and yet it was cited in the King's-Bench, *That all the Judges of* England *ruled it so*.

Then the House of Commons came to the following Resolutions.

Resolved upon the question, *Nemine contradicente*,

I. That no Freeman ought to be detained or kept in prison, or otherwise restrained by the command of the King or Privy-Council, or any other, unless some cause of the commitment, detainer or restraint be expressed, for which by Law he ought to be committed, detained or restrained.

II. That the Writ of *Habeas Corpus* may not be denied, but ought to be granted to every man that is committed or detained in prison, or otherwise restrained, though it be by the command of the King, the Privy-Council, or any other, he praying the same.

III. That if a Freeman be committed or detained in prison, or otherwise restrained by the command of the King, the Privy-Council, or any other, no cause of such commitment, detainer, or restraint being expressed, for which by Law he ought to be committed, detained, or restrained, and the same be returned upon an *Habeas Corpus*, granted for the said party; then he ought to be delivered or bailed.

And then taking into consideration the Property of the Subject in his goods, they came to this Resolution, to which there was not a negative; *viz.*

That it is the antient and indubitable Right of every Freeman, that he hath a full and absolute property in his goods and estate; that no Tax, Taillage, Loan, Benevolence, or other like charge ought to be commanded, or levied by the King, or any of his Ministers, without common consent by Act of Parliament.

The Commons having shewed their Care of the Subjects in the Liberty of their Persons, and Propriety in their Goods, did now prepare to transmit their resolutions to the Lords for their concurrence; and several Members were appointed to manage a conference with the Lords concerning the same; and *Monday*, *April* the 7th, the conference was held, and opened by Sir *Dudley Diggs*.

A CONFERENCE *desired by the Lords, and had by a Committee of both Houses, concerning the Rights and Privileges of the Subjects.*

Sir *Dudley Diggs*.

MY LORDS,

I Shall, I hope, auspiciously begin this conference this day, with an observation out of an Holy Story, in the days of good King *Josiah*, (2 *Chron.* 34.) when the land was purged of Idolatry, and the great men went about to repair the House of God; while money was sought for, there was found a Book of the Law which had been neglected, and afterwards being presented to the good King, procured the blessing, which your Lordship may read in the Scriptures. (2 *Kings* 22.)

My good Lords, I am confident your Lordships will as chearfully join with the Commons, in acknowledgement of God's great blessing in our good King *Josiah*, as the Knights, Citizens, and Burgesses of the House of Commons, by me their unworthiest servant, do thankfully remember your most religious and truly honourable invitation of them to the late petition, for cleansing this land from Popish abominations; which I may truly call a necessary and a happy repairing of the House of God. And, to go on with the parallel, whilst we the Commons, out of our good affections, were seeking for money, we found, I cannot say a book of the Law, but many, and those fundamental points thereof neglected and broken, which hath occasioned our desire of this conference: wherein I am first commanded to shew to your Lordships in general, that the Laws of *England* are grounded on reason, more ancient than books, consisting much in unwritten customs, yet so full of justice and true equity, that your most honourable Predecessors and Ancestors many times propugned them with a *nolumus mutari*; and so ancient, that from the *Saxon* days, notwithstanding the injuries and ruins of time, they have continued in most parts the same, as may appear in old remaining monuments of the Laws of *Ethelbert*, the first Christian King of *Kent*, *Ina* the King of the *West-Saxons*, *Offa* of the *Mercians*, and of *Alfred* the great Monarch, who united the *Saxon Heptarchy*, whose Laws are yet to be seen, published, as some think, by Parliament, as he says to that end, *Ut qui sub uno rege, sub una lege regerentur*. And though the book of *Litchfield*, speaking of the troublesome times of the *Danes*, says that then *Jus sopitum erat in regno, leges & consuetudines sopitae sunt*, and *prava voluntas, vis, & violentia magis regnabant quam judicia vel justitia*, yet, by the blessing of God, a good King, *Edward*, commonly called St. *Edward*, did awaken those Laws, and as the old words are, *Excitatas reparavit, reparatas decoravit, decoratas confirmavit*. Which *confirmavit* shews, that good King *Edward* did not give those Laws, which *William* the Conqueror, and all his Successors, since that time have sworn unto.

And here, my Lords, by many cases frequent in our modern Laws, strongly concurring with those of the ancient *Saxon* Kings, I might, if time were not precious, demonstrate that our Laws and Customs were the same.

* *Die Veneris*, *Mar* 28. I rise to make a Motion. Yesterday a learned Argument was made by Mr Sollicitor, and 21 *Edw.* I. was cited by him, which makes clearly for the Subject, also for that *salus populi*. I am sure that *libertas populi est salus populi*. And *Festus* himself that sent *Paul* to *Agrippa* was a Lawyer of the Empire; and to send a Prisoner without signifying the Crimes laid against him, seem'd unreasonable to *Festus* to do. By the Law of the Empire none were to be committed above thirty days, and the Gaoler is under a penalty to certify the cause of the Prisoner's commitment: and if the Gaoler be slack, he is to be freed. When they speak here of the Judgment given in the *King's-Bench*, they say the Precedents were mis-recited. Let a Sub-committee search into those Judgments and Precedents. I heard here a *quousque*, and there is nothing but a *remittitur*. The Course of the Officer is to enter *quousque*, &c. and that is till they be delivered by Law, and is all the Judgment that can be. *Ex MSS. Pymmii.* See *Selden's* Life in his Works.

† *Coke* was then a Judge, and in Favour at Court.

‡ *Coke* of one mind, when a Judge, and in favour; of another, when out of Court, and discontented.

I will

I will only intreat your Lordſhips Leave to tell you, that as we have now, even in thoſe *Saxon* times they had their Courts-Baron and Courts-Leet, and Sheriffs-Courts, by which, as *Tacitus* ſays of the *Germans* their Anceſtors, *Jura reddebunt per pagos & vicos*; and, I do believe, as we have now, they had their Parliaments, where new Laws were made *cum conſenſu prælatorum, magnatum & totius communitatis*; or, as another writes, *cum conſilio prælatorum, nobilium, & ſapientium laicorum*. I will add nothing out of *Glanvile* that wrote in the time of *H.* II. or *Bracton* that wrote in the days of *H.* III. only give me leave to cite that of *Forteſcue*, the learned Chancellor to *H.* VI. who writing of this kingdom, ſays, *Regnum illud in omnibus nationum, & Regum temporibus, eiſdem quibus nunc regitur legibus & conſuetudinibus, regebatur*. But, my good Lords, as the Poet ſaid of Fame, I may ſay of our Common-Law;

Ingrediturque ſolo caput inter nubila condit.

Wherefore the cloudy part being mine, I will make haſte to open way for your Lordſhips to hear more certain arguments, and ſuch as go on more ſure grounds.

Be pleaſed then to know, that it is an undoubted and fundamental point of this ſo ancient Common-Law of *England*, that the Subject hath a true property in his Goods and Poſſeſſions, which doth preſerve, as ſacred, that *meum & tuum*, that is the nurſe of induſtry, and mother of courage, and without which, there can be no juſtice, of which *meum & tuum* is the proper object. But the undoubted birthright of free Subjects, hath lately not a little been invaded and prejudiced by preſſures, the more grievous, becauſe they have been purſued by impriſonment, contrary to the Franchiſes of this land; and when, according to the Laws and Statutes of this Realm, redreſs hath been ſought for in a legal way, by demanding *Habeas Corpus* from the Judges, and a diſcharge or trial according to the Law of the land, ſucceſs hath failed; that now inforceth the Commons, in this preſent Parliament aſſembled, to examine by Acts of Parliament, precedents and reaſons, the truth of the *Engliſh* Subjects Liberty, which I ſhall leave to learned Gentlemen, whoſe weighty arguments, I hope, will leave no place in your Lordſhips memories, for the errours and infirmities of your humbleſt ſervant, that doth thankfully acknowledge the great favour of your honourable and patient attention.

Mr. Littleton's *Argument, made by the command of the Houſe of Commons out of Acts of Parliament, and Authorities of Law, expounding the ſame, at the firſt Conference with the Lords, concerning the Liberty of the perſon of every Freeman* *.

My Lords,

UPON the occaſions delivered by the Gentleman that laſt ſpake, your Lordſhips have heard the Commons have taken into their ſerious conſideration the matter of perſonal Liberty, and after long debate thereof on divers days, as well by ſolemn arguments, as ſingle propoſitions of doubts and anſwers, to the end no ſcruple might remain in any man's breaſt unſatisfied, they have upon a full ſearch, and clear underſtanding of all things pertinent to the queſtion, unanimouſly declared, That no Freeman ought to be committed or detained in priſon by the command of the King or Privy-Council, or any other, unleſs ſome cauſe of the commitment, detainer, or reſtraint be expreſſed, for which by Law he ought to be committed, detained, or reſtrained. And they have ſent me, with other of their Members, to repreſent unto your Lordſhips the true grounds of ſuch their reſolution, and have charged me particularly, leaving the reaſons of Law and precedents, for others, to give your Lordſhips ſatisfaction, that this Liberty is eſtabliſhed and confirmed by the whole State, the King, the Lords Spiritual and Temporal, and Commons, by ſeveral Acts of Parliament; the authority whereof is ſo great, that it can receive no anſwer, ſave by interpretation or repeal by future Statutes. And thoſe that I ſhall mind your Lordſhips of, are ſo direct in point, that they can bear no other expoſition at all, and ſure I am they are ſtill in force.

The firſt of them is the Grand Charter or the Liberties of *England*, firſt granted in the ſeventeenth year of King *John*, and renewed in the ninth year of *Henry* the third, and ſince confirmed in Parliament above thirty times. The words are theſe, ch. 29. *Nullus liber homo capiatur, vel impriſonetur, aut diſſeiſetur de libero tenemento ſuo, vel libertatibus, vel liberis conſuetudinibus ſuis, aut utlagetur, aut exuletur, aut aliquo modo deſtruatur, nec ſuper eum ibimus, nec ſuper eum mittemus, niſi per legale judicium parium ſuorum, vel per legem terræ.*

Theſe words, *nullus liber homo*, &c. are expreſs enough, yet it is remarkable that *Mathew Paris*, an Author of ſpecial credit, doth obſerve, *fol.* 432 that the Charter of 9 *Hen.* III. was the very ſame as that of 17 King *John*, [illegible] are his words and that of King *John* he ſetteth down [illegible], *fol.* 342. and there the words are directly [illegible] and ſuch a corruption as is now in the print, might eaſily happen betwixt 9 *Hen.* III. and 28 *Edw.* I. when this Charter was firſt exemplified, but certainly there is ſufficient left in that which is extant to [illegible]. For the words are that no Freeman ſhall be taken or impriſoned, but by the lawful judgment of his Peers, which is by a Jury of Peers, ordinary Juries for others, who are their Peers, or by the Law of the land; which words, Law of the Land, muſt of neceſſity be underſtood in this Nation, to be by due proceſs of the law, and not the law of the land generally, for otherwiſe it would comprehend Bond-men (whom we call Villeins) who are excluded by the word *Liber*, for the general law of the land doth allow their Lords to impriſon them at their pleaſure without cauſe, wherein they only differ from the Freemen in reſpect of their perſons, who cannot be impriſoned without a cauſe. And that this is the true underſtanding of theſe words, *Per legem terræ*, will more plainly appear [illegible] other Statutes that I ſhall uſe, which do expound the law accordingly. And though the words of this grand Charter be ſpoken in [illegible] perſon, yet they are not to be underſtood of ſuits betwixt party and party, [illegible], but even of the King's ſuits againſt [illegible] the occaſion of getting of that Charter, [illegible] betwixt thoſe Kings and their people [illegible] upon their power over them, and [illegible] ſubject and ſubject.

Secondly, The words *per legale judicium parium ſuorum*, immediately preceding the other of *per legem terræ*, are meant of Trials at the King's ſuit, and not at the proſecution of a ſubject. And therefore, if a Peer of the Realm be arraigned, at the ſuit of the King, upon an Indictment of murder, he ſhall be tried by his Peers, that is Nobles; but if he be appealed of murder by a ſubject, his Trial ſhall be by an ordinary Jury of twelve Freeholders, as appeareth in 10 *Edw.* IV. 6. 33 *Hen.* VIII. *Brooke* Title, *Trials* 142. *Stan. Cor. li.* 3. *ca.* 1. *fol.* 152. and in 10 *Edw.* IV. 6. it is ſaid, ſuch is the meaning of *Magna Charta*, for the ſame reaſon; therefore as *per judicium parium ſuorum* extends to the King's ſuit, ſo ſhall theſe words *per legem terræ*.

And in 8 *Ed.* II. *rot. parliament. numb.* 7. there is a petition that a Writ under the Privy-Seal went to the Guardians of the great Seals, to cauſe lands to be ſeized into the King's hands, by force of which there went a Writ out of the Chancery to the Eſcheator, to ſeize, againſt the form of the grand Charter, that the King nor his Miniſters ſhall out no man of his Freehold without reaſonable judgment, and the party was reſtored to his land; which ſhewed the Statute did extend to the King.

There was no invaſion upon this perſonal liberty, till the time of King *Edw.* III. which was ſoon reſented by the ſubject; for in 5 *Edw.* III. *cap.* 9. it is ordained in theſe words It is enacted that no man from henceforth ſhall be attached by any accuſation, nor fore-judged of life or limb, nor his lands, tenements, goods, nor chattels ſeized into the King's hands, againſt the form of the great Charter, and the law of the land. 25 *Edw.* III. *cap.* 4. it is more full, and doth expound the words of the grand Charter, and is thus; Whereas it is contained in the grand Charter of the Franchiſes of *England*, that no Freeman ſhall be impriſoned, nor put out of his Freehold, nor free cuſtom, unleſs it be by the law of the land; it is awarded, aſſented, and eſtabliſhed, that from hence none ſhall be taken by petition or ſuggeſtion, made to our Lord the King, or to his Council, unleſs it be by Indictment, or preſentment of his good and lawful people of the ſame neighbourhood; which ſuch deeds ſhall be done in due manner, or by proceſs made by Writ original at the Common Law, nor that none be outed of his Franchiſes, nor of his Freehold, unleſs he be duly brought in to anſwer, and fore-judged of the ſame by the courſe of the law; and if any thing be done againſt the ſame, it ſhall be redreſſed and holden for nought.

Out of this Statute I obſerve, that what in *Magna Charta*, and the preamble of the Statute is termed *by the Law of the Land*, is in the body of the Act expounded to be by proceſs made by the Writ original at the Common Law, which is a plain interpretation of the words (law of the land) in the grand Charter. And I note that this law was made upon the commitment of divers to the Tower, no man yet knoweth for what.

28 *Edw.* III. *cap.* 3. it is more direct, this liberty being followed with freſh [illegible] the ſubject, where the words are not many, but very full and ſignificant, that no man of what ſtate or condition ſoever he be, ſhall be put out of his lands or tenements, nor taken, nor impriſoned, nor diſinherited, nor put to death, without he be brought in to anſwer by due proceſs of law.

Here your Lordſhips ſee the uſual words, the law of the land, are rendered by due proceſs of the law.

36 *Edw.* III. *rot. parliament. numero* 9. Amongſt the petitions of the Commons, one of them being tranſlated into *Engliſh* out of *French*, is thus, firſt, that the great Charter, and the Charter of the Foreſt, and other Statutes made in his time, and the time of his Progenitors, for the profit of him, and his Commonalty, be well and firmly kept, and put in due execution, without putting diſturbance, or making arreſt contrary to them by ſpecial command, or in other manner.

The anſwer to the petition, which makes it an Act of Parliament, is, 'Our Lord the King, by the aſſent of the Prelates, Dukes, Earls, Barons, and the Commonalty, hath ordained and eſtabliſhed, that the ſaid Charters and Statutes be held, and put in execution, according to the ſaid petition.' It is obſervable, that the Statutes were to be put in execution according to the ſaid petition, which is, that no arreſt ſhould be made contrary to the Statutes, by ſpecial command. This concludes the queſtion, and is of as great force as if it were printed, for the Parliament-Roll is the true Warrant of an Act, and many are omitted out of the Books, that are extant in the Roll.

36 *Edw.* III. *Rot. Parliament. num.* 22. explaineth it further; for there the petition is, Whereas it is contained in the grand Charter and other Statutes, that no man be taken or impriſoned by ſpecial command without Indictment, or other due proceſs to be made by the law, and oftentimes it hath been, and yet is, many are hindred, taken and impriſoned without Indictment, or other proceſs made by the law upon them, as well of things done out of the Foreſt of the King, as for other things, that it would therefore pleaſe our ſaid Lord to command them to be delivered, which are ſo taken by ſpecial command, againſt the form of the Charter and Statutes as aforeſaid.

The Anſwer is,

The King is pleaſed, that if any man find himſelf grieved, that he come and make his complaint, and right ſhall be done unto him. 37 *Edw.* III. *cap.* 18. agreeth in ſubſtance with the [illegible], though it be contained in the great Charter, that no man be taken nor impriſoned, nor put out of his Freehold without proceſs of the law, nevertheleſs divers people make falſe ſuggeſtions to the King himſelf, as well for malice as otherwiſe, whereat the King is often grieved, and divers of the Realm put in damage, againſt the form of the ſame Charter; wherefore it is ordained, that all they which make ſuch ſuggeſtions, ſhall be ſent with the ſame ſuggeſtions to the Chancellor, Treaſurer, and his grand Council, and that they there find ſurety to purſue their ſuggeſtions, and incur the ſame pain that the other ſhould have had, if he were attainted, in caſe that the ſuggeſtion be found evil, and that then proceſs of law be made againſt them without being taken or impriſoned, againſt the form of the ſaid Charter, and other Statutes. Here the law of the land in the grand Charter is explained to be without proceſs of law.

42 *Edw.* III. *cap.* 13. At the requeſt of the Commons by their petition put forth in this Parliament, to eſchew miſchief and damage done to divers

* [illegible] Argument [illegible] printed in *Cotton. Poſthuma* [illegible] by Sir [illegible] Bart. But whoever conſults the [illegible] will find, that [illegible] the four Lawyers appointed by the Houſe of Commons to manage that [illegible] Conference.

of

of his Commons by false Accusers, which oftentimes have made their Accusations, more for Revenge and singular Benefit, than for the Profit of the King, or of his People; of which accused Persons some have been taken and caused to come before the King's Council by Writ, and otherwise upon grievous Pains against the Law; it is assented and accorded for the good Governance of the Commons, that no Man be put to answer without Presentment before Justices or Matter of Record, or by due Process and Writ original, according to the old Law of the Land: and if any thing from hence be done to the contrary, it shall be void in the Law, and holden for Error.

But this is better in the Parlament Roll, where the Petition and Answer, which makes the Act, are set down at large, 42 *Edw.* III *Rot. Parliamenti, numero* 12.

The Petition

" *Item*, Because that many of your Commons are hurt and destroyed " by false Accusers, who make their Accusations more for their Revenge " and particular Gain, than for the Profit of the King, or of his People: " And those that are accused by them, some are taken, and others are " made to come before the King's Council by Writ, or other Commandment of the King, upon grievous Pains contrary to the Law. That it " would please our Lord the King, and his good Council, for the just " Government of his People, to ordain, that if hereafter any Accuser " propose any Matter for the Profit of the King, that the same Matter be " sent to the Justices of the one Bench or of the other, or the Assizes, to " be enquired and determined according to the Law; and if it concern " the Accuser or Party, that he take his Suit at the Common Law; and " that no Man be put to answer without Presentment before the Justices " or Matter of Record, and by due Process and original Writ, according " to the ancient Law of the Land. And if any thing henceforward be " done to the contrary, that it be void in Law, and held for Error."

Here by due Process and original Writ, according to the ancient Law of the Land, is meant the same thing, as *per legem terræ*, in *Magna Charta*; and the Abuse was, they were put to answer by the Commandment of the King.

The King's Answer is thus:

" Because that this Article is an Article of the grand Charter, the King " willeth that this be done, as the Petition doth demand." By this appeareth that *per legem terræ*, in *Magna Charta*, is meant by due Process of the Law.

Thus your Lordships have heard Acts of Parliament in the Point. But the Statute of *Westminst.* 1. *cap.* 15. is urged to disprove this Opinion, where it is expresly said, that a Man is not repleviable, who is committed by the Command of the King; therefore the Command of the King, without any Cause shewed, is sufficient to commit a Man to Prison. And because the Strength of the Argument may appear, and the Answer be better understood, I will read the Words of the Statute, which are thus:

[And forasmuch as Sheriffs and others, which have taken and kept in Prison Persons detected for Felony, and oftentimes have let out by Replevin such as were not repleviable, and have kept in Prison such as were repleviable, because they would gain of the one Party, and grieve the other; and forasmuch as before this time it was not certainly determined what Persons were repleviable, and what not, but only those that were taken for the Death of a Man, or by the Commandment of the King, or of his Justices, or for the Forest; it is provided, and by the King commanded, that such Prisoners as were before outlawed, and they which have abjured the Realm, Provers, and such as be taken with the Manner, and those which have broken the King's Prison, Thieves openly defamed and known, and such as be appealed by Approvers; so long as the Approvers are living, if they be not of good Name, and such as be taken for burning of Houses feloniously done, or for false Money, or for counterfeiting the King's [illegible] taken at the Request of the [illegible] or for treason touching the King himself, shall be in no wise replevisable by the common Writ, or without Writ.]

[illegible] Sheriffs or [illegible] Suspicion, or of petty Larceny, that [illegible] guilty of [illegible] Receipt of Felons, or of Commandment, [illegible] of Felony done, or guilty of some other [illegible] either Life or Member [illegible] the Death of the Approver, [illegible] from henceforth be let out [illegible] and that [illegible] Sheriff, or any other, [illegible] if he be Sheriff or Constable, or [illegible] which hath keeping of Prisons [illegible] his Office and Fee [illegible] or Bailiff, or such as hath [illegible] Will of his Lord, or any other Bailiff [illegible] three Years Imprisonment and to take a Fine [illegible] any Man with-hold Prisoners [illegible] sufficient Surety, he shall pay [illegible] King [illegible] take any Reward for the [illegible] Prisoner, and also shall pay [illegible]

[illegible]

It [illegible] by the Commandment of the King [illegible] Words of the Statute. But [illegible] the House of Commons [illegible] King's Court [illegible] For the [illegible] to be known, the [illegible] by the Sheriff [illegible] Pleas [illegible] Court of Record, [illegible]

[illegible] Sheriff and other [illegible] Officers, and [illegible] Judges.]

The Preamble, which is the Key that openeth the Entrance into the Meaning of the Makers of the Law, is, " For as much as Sheriffs and " others have taken and kept in Prison Persons detected of Felony." Out of these Words I observe that it nominateth Sheriffs, and then if the Judges should be included, they must be comprehended under that general Word, *others*; which doth not extend to those of an higher Rank, but to inferiors, for the best by all Courses is first to be named. And therefore if a Man bring a Writ of Customs and Services, and name Rents and other things, the general shall not include Homage, which is a personal Service, and of an higher Nature, but it shall extend to ordinary annual Service, 31 *Edw.* I. *Droit* 67. So the Statute of 13 *Eliz. cap.* 10. which beginneth with Colleges, Deans and Chapters, Parsons, Vicars, and concludes with these Words, " and others having spiritual Promotions," shall not comprehend Bishops that are of an higher Degree, as appeareth in the Archbishop of *Canterbury*'s Case, reported by Sir *Edward Coke*, *lib.* 2. *fol.* 46. *B.*

And thus much is explained in the very Statute towards the End, when it doth enumerate those who were meant by the Word, *others*, namely, Under-Sheriffs, Constables, Bailiffs, *&c.*

Again, the Words are, *Sheriffs and others which have taken and kept in Prison.* Now every Man knoweth, Judges do neither arrest, nor keep Men in Prison; that is the Office of Sheriffs and other inferior Ministers. Therefore this Statute meant such only, and not Judges.

The Words are further, that they let out by Replevin such as are not repleviable, that is the proper Language for a Sheriff; nay, more express afterward in the Body of the Statute, that such as are there mentioned, shall in nowise be repleviable by the common Writ, which is *de homine replegiando*, and is directed to the Sheriff, nor without Writ, which is by the Sheriff *ex officio*. But that which receives no Answer is this, that the Command of the Justices, who derive their Authority from the Crown, is there equal as to this Purpose with the Command of the King. And therefore by all reasonable Construction, it must needs relate to Officers that are subordinate to both, as Sheriffs, Under-Sheriffs, Bailiffs, Constables, and the like. And it were a harsh Exposition to say, that the Justices might not discharge their own Command, and yet that reason would conclude as much; and that this was meant of the Sheriff and other Ministers of Justice, appears by the Recital, 27 *Edw.* I. *cap.* 3. and likewise by *Fleta*, a Manuscript, so called, because the Author lay in the *Fleet* when he made the Book: For he, *lib.* 2. *cap.* 52. in his Chapter of Turns, and the Views of the Hundred Courts in the Country, setteth down the Articles of the Charges that are there to be inquired of, amongst which, one of them is *de replegiabilibus injuste detentis & irreplegiabilibus dimissis*; which cannot be meant of not bailing by the Justices; for what have the inferior Courts in the Country to do with the Acts of the Justices?

And to make that more plain, he setteth down in that Chapter, that concerneth Sheriffs only, the very Statute of *Westminster* 1. which he translates *verbatim* out of the *French* into the *Latin*; save that he renders taken by the Command of the Justices, thus, *per judicium Justiciariorum*; and his Preface to the Statute plainly sheweth, that he understood it of Replevin by Sheriffs; for he saith, *Qui debent per plegios dimitti, qui non declarat hoc Statutum*; and *per plegios* is before the Sheriff.

But for direct Authority, It is the Opinion of *Newton*, Chief Justice, 22 *Hen.* VI. 46. where his Words are these: " It cannot be intended " that the Sheriff did suffer him to go at large by Mainprize; for where " one is taken by the Writ of the King, or the Commandment of the " King, he is irrepleviable; but in such Case his Friends may come to " the Justices from him if he be arrested, and purchase a *Supersedeas*." This Judge concludes, that the Sheriff cannot deliver him that is taken by the Command of the King, for that he is irrepleviable, which is the very Word of the Statute. But, saith he, his Friends may come to the Justices, and purchase a *Supersedeas* [illegible] very Question, that the Sheriff had no Power, but the Justices had Power to deliver him that is committed by the King's Command, and both the ancient and modern Practice maketh it [illegible] for he that is taken for the Death of a Man, or for the Forest, is not repleviable by the Sheriff, yet they are ordinarily bailed by the Justices [illegible] the King's Writs directed to the Sheriffs in the Times of [illegible] in the close Rolls, which could not be done [illegible] And it is every Day's Experience, that the Justices [illegible] for Murder and Offences done in the Forest, which they could not do, if the Word *repleviable*, in *Westm.* 1. were [illegible] the Justices, as well as of the Sheriffs.

For Authorities that [illegible] to prove the contrary, they are in Number three. The first is 2 [illegible] III. [illegible] which [illegible] is in the Book of Pleas in Parliament at the Tower, upon an Action [illegible] brought. *Fol.* 44. It is [illegible] that the Action in Parliament upon an [illegible] which was usual in those times! And the Case is, that [illegible] the Sheriff of the Counties of *Leicester* and *Warwick*, [illegible] for that [illegible] at large [illegible] the Son of [illegible] the Will and Command of the King, whereas [illegible] commanded him by Letters under the [illegible] to [illegible] that was committed by the [illegible] of [illegible] as that [illegible] whereunto the Sheriff [illegible] the King's Houshold [illegible] Letters; and [illegible] the Sheriff [illegible] the Receipt of the King's Letters, thereupon he was committed to Prison [illegible] the Statute.

To this I answer, the Sheriff was justly punished, for that he was expressly bound by the Statute of *Westm.* 1. which was agreed [illegible] but this is no Proof that the Judges had no Power to bail the Man.

The next Authority is 22 *Hen.* VI. in the Court of Common Pleas, [illegible] 28 [illegible] *Robert* [illegible] [illegible] he were delivered, or bailed, or not. 2. It appears expresly, that he was brought thither to be charged in an Action of debt, at another Man's suit, no desire of his own to be delivered, or bailed; and then if he were remanded, it is no way material to the question in hand. But that which is most relied upon, is the opinion of *Stamf.* in his Book of Pleas of the Crown, *lib.* 2. *cap.* 18 *fol.* 72, 73. in his Chapter of Mainprize, where he reciteth the Statute of *Westm.* 1. *cap.* 15. and then saith thus: "By this Statute it appears, that in four cases at the Common Law a Man was not repleviable; to-wit, those that were taken for the death of a man, by the command of the King, or his Justices, or for the Forest;" thus far he is most right. Then he goeth on, and saith, "As to the command of the King, that is understood by the command of his own mouth, or his Council, which is incorporated unto him, and spake with his mouth, or otherwise every Writ or *Capias* to take a man, which is the King's command, would be as much; and as to the command of the Justices, that is meant their absolute commandment, for if it be by their ordinary commandment, he is repleviable by the Sheriff, if it be not in some of the cases prohibited by the Statute."

The answer that I give unto this is, that *Stamford* had said nothing whether a man may be committed without cause by the King's command, or whether the Judges ought not to bail him in such case, only that such a one is not repleviable; which is agreed, for that belongs to the Sheriff. And because no man should think he meant any such thing, he concludes the whole sentence touching the command of the King and the Justices, that one committed by the ordinary command of the Justice, is repleviable by the Sheriff; or at least it appears not that he meant that a man committed by the King, or by the Privy-Council without cause, should not be bailable by the Justices, and he hath given no opinion in this case; what he would have said, if he had been asked the question, cannot be known, neither doth it appear, that, by any thing that he hath said, he meant any such thing as would be inferred out of him. And now, my Lords, I have performed the commands of the Commons, and as I conceive shall clear the declaration of personal liberty, an ancient and undoubted truth, fortified with seven Acts of Parliament, and not opposed by any Statute or Authority of Law whatsoever. *See* Littleton's *Precedents after Mr.* Selden's.

Mr. Selden's *Argument.*

MY LORDS,

YOUR Lordships have heard from the Gentleman that last spake, a great part of the grounds upon which the House of Commons, upon mature deliberation, proceeded to that clear resolution touching the right of the liberty of their persons. The many Acts of Parliament, which are the written Laws of the Land, and are expresly in the point, have been read and opened, and such objections as have been by some made to them, and some objections also made out of another Act of Parliament, have been cleared and answered. It may seem now perhaps (my Lords) that little remains needful to be further added, for the inforcement and maintenance of so fundamental and established a right and liberty belonging to every Freeman of the Kingdom. But in the examination of questions of Law of Right, besides the Laws or Acts of Parliament, that ought chiefly to direct and regulate every man's judgment, whatsoever hath been put in practice to the contrary, there are commonly used also former Judgments, or Precedents, and indeed have been so used sometimes, that the weight of reason, of Law, and of Acts of Parliament, hath been laid by, and resolutions have been made, and that in this very point, only upon the interpretation and apprehension of precedents. Precedents, my Lords, are good *media*, or proofs of illustration or confirmation where they agree with the express Law; but they can never be proof enough to overthrow any one Law, much less seven several Acts of Parliament, as the number of them is for the point. The House of Commons therefore taking into consideration, that in this question, being of so high a nature, that never any exceeded it in any Court of Justice whatsoever, all the several ways of just examination of the truth should be used, have also most carefully informed themselves of all former judgments and precedents concerning this great point either way, and have been no less careful of the due preservation of his Majesty's just Prerogative than of their own Rights. The precedents here are of two kinds, either merely matter of Record, or else the former resolutions of the Judges, after solemn debate in the point.

This point that concerns precedents, the House of Commons have commanded me to present to your Lordships, which I shall as briefly as I may, so I do it faithfully and perspicuously. To that end, my Lords, before I come to the particulars of any of those precedents, I shall first remember to your Lordships, that which will seem as a general key for the opening and true apprehension of all them of Record, without which key, no man, unless he be vers'd in the entries and course of the King's-Bench, can possibly understand them.

In all cases, my Lords, where any Right or Liberty belongs to the Subjects by any positive Law written or unwritten, if there were not also a remedy by Law, for the enjoying or regaining this Right or Liberty, when it is violated or taken from him, the positive Law were most vain, and to no purpose; and it were to no purpose for any man to have any Right in any land or other inheritance if there were not a known remedy, that is, an Action or Writ, by which, in some Court of ordinary Justice, he might recover it. And in this case of Right of Liberty of Person, if there were not a remedy in the Law for regaining it, when it is restrained, it were of no purpose to speak of Laws, that ordain it should not be restrained. Therefore in this case also, I shall first shew you the remedy that every Freeman is to use for the regaining of his Liberty, when he is against Law imprisoned, that so upon the legal course and form to be held in using that remedy, the precedents or judgments upon it, for all Judgments of Record rise out of this remedy, may be easily understood. There are in Law divers remedies for inlarging of a Freeman imprisoned, as the Writs of *Odio & atia*, and of *Homine replegiando*, besides the common or most known Writs of *Habeas Corpus*, or *Corpus cum causa*, as it is also called.

The first two Writs are to be directed to the Sheriff of the County, and lie in some particular cases, with which it would be untimely for me to trouble your Lordships, because they concern not that which is committed to my charge. But that Writ of *Habeas Corpus*, or *Corpus cum causa*, is the highest remedy in Law, for any man that is imprisoned, and the only remedy for him that is imprisoned by the special command of the King, or the Lords of the Privy-Council, without shewing cause of the commitment: neither is there in the Law any such thing, nor was there ever mention of any such thing in the Laws of this land, as a Petition of Right to be used in such cases for Liberty of the Person, nor is there any legal course for inlargement to be taken in such cases; howsoever the contrary hath upon no ground or colour of Law been pretended. Now, my Lords, if any man be so imprisoned by any such command, or otherwise, in any prison whatsoever through *England*, and desire by himself, or any other in his behalf, this Writ of *Habeas Corpus* for the purpose in the Court of King's-Bench, the Writ is to be granted to him, and ought not to be denied him, no otherwise than another ordinary original Writ in the Chancery, or other common process of Law may be denied; which amongst other things the House resolved also, upon mature deliberation, and I was commanded to let your Lordships know so much. This Writ is directed to the Keeper of the prison, in whose custody the prisoner remains, commanding him that after a certain day, he bring in the body of the prisoner, *ad subjiciend. & recipiend juxta quod curia consideraverit, &c. una cum causa captionis & detentionis*; and oftentimes *una cum causa detentionis* only, *captionis* being omitted.

The keeper of the prison thereupon returns by what Warrant he detains the prisoner, and with his return filed to his Writ, brings the Prisoner to the Bar at the time appointed; when the return is thus made, the Court judgeth of the sufficiency or insufficiency of it, only out of the body of it, without having respect unto any other thing whatsoever; that is, they suppose the return to be true whatsoever it be: if it be false, the prisoner may have his action on the Case against the Goaler that brought him. Now, my Lords, when the prisoner comes thus to the Bar, if he desire to be bailed, and that the Court upon the view of the return think him in Law to be bailable, then he is always first taken from the Keeper of the prison that brings him, and committed to the Marshal of the King's-Bench, and afterwards bailed, and the entry perpetually is *Committitur Mariscallo & postea traditur in Ball'*; for the Court never bails any man, until he first becomes their own prisoner, and be *in Custodia Mariscall'* of that Court. But if upon the return of the *Habeas Corpus*, it appear to the Court, that the prisoner ought not to be bailed, nor discharged from the prison whence he is brought, then he is remanded or sent back again, there to continue, until by course of Law he may be delivered; and the entry in this case is *Remittitur quousque secundum legem deliberatus fuerit*, or *Remittitur quousque, &c.* which is all one, and the highest award or judgment that ever was or can be given upon an *Habeas Corpus*. But if the Judges doubt only whether in Law they ought to take him from the prison whence he came, or give a day to the Sheriff to amend his Writ, as often they do, then they remand him only during the time of their doubt, or until the Sheriff hath amended his return, and the entry upon that is *Remittitur* only, or *Remittitur prisonæ præd.* without any more. And so *remittitur* generally is of far less moment in the award upon the *Habeas Corpus*, than *remittitur quousque, &c.* howsoever the vulgar opinions raised out of the late Judgment be to the contrary. All these things are of most known and constant use in the Court of King's-Bench, as it cannot be doubted but your Lordships will easily know from the grave and learned my Lords the Judges.

These two courses, the one of the entry of *Comititur Mariscall. & postea traditur in Ballium*, and the other *remittitur quousque, &c. & remittitur* generally, or *remittitur prisonæ præd* together with the nature of the *Habeas Corpus*, thus stated; it will be easier for me to open, and your Lordships to observe, whatsoever shall occur to the purpose in the precedents of Record, to which I shall come now in the particular. But before I come to the precedents, I am to let you know the resolutions of the House of Commons touching the enlargement of a man committed by the command of the King, or the Privy-Council, or any other, without cause shewed of such commitment: it is thus; That if a Freeman be committed or detained in prison, or otherwise restrained by the command of the King, the Privy-Council, or any other, and no cause of such commitment, detainer, or restraint be expressed, for which by Law he ought to be committed, detained or restrained; and the same be returned upon an *Habeas Corpus* granted for the party, then he ought to be delivered and bailed.

This resolution, as it is grounded upon the Acts of Parliament already shewn, and the reason of the Law of the Land, which is committed to the charge of another, and anon also to be opened to you, is strengthened also by many Precedents of Record.

But the Precedents of Record that concern this point are of two kinds, for the House of Commons hath informed itself of such as concern it either way. The first, such as shew expresly, that Persons committed by the command of the King, or of the Privy-Council, without other cause shewed, have been enlarged upon bail when they prayed it, whence it appears clearly, that by the Law, they are bailable, and so by *Habeas Corpus* to be set at liberty: for tho' they ought not to have been committed without a cause shewed of the commitment, yet it is true that the reverend Judges of this Land did pay such respect to such commitments, by the command of the King, or of the Lords of the Council, (as also to the commitment sometimes of inferior persons) that upon the *Habeas Corpus*, they rarely used absolutely to discharge the persons instantly, but only to enlarge them upon bail; which sufficiently secures and preserves the Liberty of the Subject, according to the Laws that your Lordships have already heard, nor in any of the cases is there any difference made between such commitments by the Lords of the Council, that are incorporated with him. The second kind of precedents of Record are, such as have been pretended to prove the Law to be contrary, and that persons so committed ought not to be set at liberty upon bail, and are in the nature of objections out of Record.

I shall deliver them summarily to your Lordships with all faith, and also true copies of them; out of which it shall appear clearly to your Lordships, that of those of the first kind, there are no less than twelve, most full and directly in the point, to prove that persons so committed are to be delivered upon bail: and amongst those of the other kind, there is not so much as one, not one, that proves at all any thing to the contrary. I shall first, my Lords, go through them of the first kind, and so observe them to your Lordships, that such scruples as have been made upon them by some that have

have excepted againſt them; ſhall be cleared alſo according as I ſhall open them ſeverally.

The firſt of the firſt kind is of *Ed.* IIId's time, it is in *Paſchæ* 18 *Ed.* III. *Rot.* 33. The caſe was thus:

King *Ed.* III. had committed by Writ, and that under his great Seal (as moſt of the King's commands in thoſe times were) one *John de Bildeſton*, a Clergyman, to the priſon of the Tower, without any cauſe ſhewed of the commitment. The Lieutenant of the Tower is commanded to bring him to the King's-Bench, where he is committed to the Marſhal; but the Court aſks of the Lieutenant, if there were any cauſe to keep this *Bildeſton* in priſon, beſides that commitment of the King; he anſwered no: whereupon the Roll ſays, *quia videtur cur. bre. præd. ſufficient. non eſſe cauſam præd. Johan. de Bildeſton in priſona Dom. Regis hic detinend. idem Johannes admittitur per manucaptionem Willielmi de Wakefield*, and ſome others, where the Judgment of the point is fully declared in the very point.

The ſecond, in the firſt kind of precedents of Record, is in the time of *H.* VIII. one *John Parker*'s Caſe, who was committed to the Sheriff of *London*, *pro ſecuritate pacis*, at the ſuit of one *Brinton*, *ac pro ſuſpicione feloniæ* committed by him in *Glouceſterſhire*, *ac per mandatum Dom. Rs.* he is committed to the Marſhal of the King's-Bench, *& poſtea iſto eodem termino traditur in Ball'.* Here were other cauſes of the commitment, but plainly one was by the command of the King, ſignified to the Sheriffs of *London*, of which they took notice; but ſome have interpreted this, as if the commitment had been for ſuſpicion of felony by the command of the King, in which caſe it is agreed of all hands, that the priſoner is bailable; but no man can think ſo of this precedent, that obſerves the context, and underſtands the Grammar of it, wherein moſt plainly *ac per mandatum dom. Regis* hath no reference to any other cauſe whatſoever, but is a ſingle cauſe enumerated in the return by itſelf, as the Record clearly ſheweth; it is in 22 *H* VIII. *Rot.* 37.

The third is of the ſame King's time, it is 35 *H.* VIII. *Rot.* 33. *John Binck*'s Caſe; he was committed by the Lords of the Council *pro ſuſpicione feloniæ ac pro aliis cauſis illos moventibus, qui committitur Mariſcallo et immediate ex gratia curiæ ſpeciale traditur in Ball'.* They committed him for ſuſpicion of felony, and other cauſes them thereunto moving, wherein there might be matter of State, or whatſoever elſe can be ſuppoſed, and plainly the cauſe of their commitment is not expreſſed; yet the Court bailed him without having regard to theſe unknown cauſes that moved the Lords of the Council. But it has indeed ſome difference from either of thoſe other two that precede, and from the other nine alſo that follow; for it is agreed, that if a cauſe be expreſſed in the return, inſomuch that the Court can know why he is committed, that then he may be bailed, but not if they know not the cauſe. Now if a man is committed for a cauſe expreſſed, *et pro aliis cauſis Dominos de Concilio moventibus*; certainly the Court can no more know in ſuch a caſe what the cauſe is than any other.

The fourth of theſe is in the time of Queen *Mary*, it is *Paſch.* 2 & 3. *P. & Mar. Rot.* 58. *Overton*'s caſe: *Richard Overton* was returned upon an *Habeas Corpus*, directed to the Sheriffs of *London*, to have been committed and detained *per mandatum prænobilium Dominorum honorabilis Concilii Dominorum Regis et Reginæ, qui committitur Marr. & immedia tetraditur in Ball'.* In anſwer to this precedent, or by way of objection to the force of it, it hath been ſaid, that this *Overton* at this time ſtood indicted of High-Treaſon. It is true, he was ſo indicted, but that appears in another Roll, that hath no reference to the Return, as the Return hath no reference to that Roll; yet they that object this againſt the force of this precedent, ſay, that becauſe he was indicted of Treaſon, therefore though he was committed by the command of the Lords of the Council, without cauſe ſhewed, yet he was bailable for the Treaſon, and upon that was here bailed: than which objection nothing is more contrary, either to law or common reaſon. It is moſt contrary to Law, for that clearly every Return is to be adjudged by the Court out of the body of itſelf, and not by any other collateral or foreign Record whatſoever. Therefore the matter of the Indictment here, cannot in Law be cauſe of bailing of the priſoner; and ſo it is adverſe to all common reaſon, that if the objection be admitted, it muſt of neceſſity follow, that whoſoever ſhall be committed by the King, or Privy-Council, without cauſe ſhewed, and be not indicted of Treaſon, or ſome other Offence, may not be enlarged, by reaſon of ſuppoſition of matter of State. But that whoſoever is ſo committed, and withal ſtands ſo indicted, though in another Record, may be enlarged, whatſoever the matter of State be for which he was committed. The abſurdity of which aſſertion needs not a word for further confutation, as if any of the Gentlemen in the laſt judgment, ought to have been the ſooner delivered, if he had been alſo indicted of Treaſon; if ſo, Traytors and Felons have the higheſt privilege in perſonal liberty, and that above all other ſubjects of the Kingdom.

The fifth of this kind is of Queen *Mary*'s time alſo, it is *Paſch.* 4 & 5 *P. & Mar. Rot.* 45. the Caſe of *Edward Newport:* He was brought into the King's-Bench by *Habeas Corpus* out of the Tower of *London*, *Cum cauſa, viz. quod commiſſus fuit per mandatum Concilii Dominæ Reginæ, qui committitur Marr. & immediate traditur in Ballium.*

To this the like anſwer has been made, as to that other caſe of *Overton*'s next before cited; they ſay that in another Roll of another Term of the ſame year, it appears he was in queſtion for ſuſpicion of coining, and it is true he was ſo; but the return, and his commitment mentioned in it, have no reference to any ſuch offence, nor hath the bailment of him relation to any thing, but to the abſolute commitment by the Privy-Council: So that the anſwer to the like objection made againſt *Overton*'s caſe, ſatisfies this alſo.

The ſixth of theſe is of Queen *Elizabeth*'s time, *Mich.* 9 *El. Rot.* 35. the caſe of *Tho. Laurence*; this *Laurence* came in by *Habeas Corpus*, returned by the Sheriffs of *London*, to be detained in priſon *per mandat. Concilii Dominæ Reginæ, qui committitur Marr. & ſuper hoc traditur in Ballium.*

An objection hath been invented againſt this alſo; it hath been ſaid, that this man was pardoned, and indeed it appears ſo in the margin of the Roll, where the word *pardonatur* is entered: but clearly his enlargement by bail was upon the body of the return only, unto which that note of pardon in the margin of the Roll hath no relation at all; and can any man think, that a man pardoned (for what offence ſoever it be) might not as well be committed for ſome *Arcanum*, or matter of State, as one that is not pardoned, or out of his innocency wants no pardon?

The ſeventh of theſe is in the ſame year, and of *Eaſter*-Term following: it is *P.* 9. *Rot.* 68. *Rob. Conſtable*'s caſe: He was brought by *Habeas Corpus* out of the Tower; and in the return it appeareth he was committed there, *per mandatum privati Concilii Dominæ Reginæ, qui committitur Marr. & poſtea iſto eodem ter' traditur in Ball'.* The like objection hath been made to this, as that before of *Laurence*, but the ſelf-ſame anſwer clearly ſatisfies for them both.

The eighth is of the ſame Queen's time, in *Paſch* 20 *El. Rot* 72. *John Browning*'s caſe. This *Browning* came by *Habeas Corpus* out of the Tower, whither he had been committed, and was returned to have been committed, *per privat. Concil. Dominæ Reginæ, qui committitur Marr. & poſtea iſto eodem termino traditur in Ball.* To this it hath been ſaid, that it was done at the Chief-Juſtice *Wray*'s Chamber, and not in the Court: and thus the authority of the precedent hath been leſſened or ſlighted. If it had been done at his Chamber, it would have proved at leaſt this much, that Sir *Chriſtopher Wray*, then Chief-Juſtice of the King's-Bench, being a grave, learned, and upright Judge, knowing the law to be ſo, did bail this *Browning*, and enlarge him, and even ſo far the precedent were of value enough; but it is plain, that though the *Habeas Corpus* were returnable, as indeed it appears in the Record itſelf, at his Chamber in *Serjeants-Inn*, yet he only committed him to the King's-Bench preſently, and referred the conſideration of enlarging him to the Court, who afterward did it: For the Record ſays, *Et poſtea iſto eodem termino traditur in Ball.* which cannot be of an enlargement at the Chief-Juſtice's Chamber.

The ninth of this firſt kind is *Hill.* 40 *El. Rot.* 62. *Edward Harecourt*'s caſe; he was impriſoned in the *Gatehouſe*, and that *per Dominos de privato Concilio Dominæ Reginæ pro certis cauſis eos moventibus & ei ignotis:* and upon his *Habeas Corpus* was returned to be therefore only detained, *Qui committitur Marr. & poſtea iſto eodem termino traditur in Ball.* To this never any Colour of anſwer hath been yet offered.

The tenth is *Cateſbie*'s caſe in the Vacation after *Hill.* Term, 43 *El. Rot.* *Robert Cateſbie* was committed to the *Fleet per warrantum diverſor. prænobilium viror. de privato concilio Dominæ Reginæ*; he was brought before Juſtice *Fenner*, one of the then Juſtices of the King's-Bench by *Habeas Corpus* at *Wincheſter-houſe*, *Southwark*; *Et commiſſ. fuit Marr. per præfat. Edwardum Fenner, & ſtatim traditur in Ball.*

The eleventh is *Rich. Beckwith*'s caſe, which was in *Hil.* twelfth of King *James*, *Rot.* 153. He was returned upon his *Habeas Corpus* to have been committed to the *Gatehouſe* by divers Lords of the Privy-Council; *Qui committitur Marr. & poſtea iſto eodem termino traditur in Ball.*

To this it hath been ſaid by ſome, that *Beckwith* was bailed upon a letter, written by the Lords of the Council to that purpoſe to the Judges; but it appears not that there was ever any letter written to them to that purpoſe: which though it had been, would have proved nothing againſt the authority of the Record; for it was never heard of, that Judges were to be directed in point of Law by letters from the Lords of the Council, although it cannot be doubted, but that by ſuch letters ſometimes they have been moved to bail men, that would or did not aſk their enlargement without ſuch letters, as in ſome examples I ſhall ſhew your Lordſhips among the precedents of the ſecond kind.

The twelfth and laſt of theſe is that of Sir *Tho. Monſon*'s caſe; it is *Mich.* 14 *Jac. Rot.* 147. He was committed to the Tower *per warrantum à diverſis Dominis de privato Concilio Domini Regis locum tenenti directum*; and he was returned by the Lieutenant to be therefore detained in priſon, *qui committitur Marr. & ſuper traditur hoc in Ball.*

To this it hath been anſwered, that every body knows by common fame, that this Gentleman was committed for ſuſpicion of the death of Sir *Tho. Overbury*, and that he was therefore bailable: a moſt ſtrange interpretation, as if the body of the Return and the Warrant of the Privy-Council ſhould be underſtood, and adjudged out of fame only. Was there not as much a fame, why the Gentlemen, that were remanded in the laſt judgment, were committed, and might not the ſelf-ſame reaſon have ſerved to enlarge them, their offence (if any were) being I think much leſs than that for which this Gentleman was ſuſpected?

And thus I have faithfully opened the number of twelve precedents, moſt expreſs in the very point in queſtion, and cleared the objections that have been made againſt them.

And of ſuch precedents of Record as are of the firſt kind, which prove plainly the practice of former ages, and judgment of the Court of King's Bench, in the very point, on the behalf of the Subject, my Lords, hitherto.

I come next to thoſe of the ſecond kind, or ſuch as are pretended, that perſons ſo committed are not to be enlarged by the Judges upon the *Habeas Corpus* brought, but to remain in priſon ſtill at the command of the King or the Privy-Council.

Theſe are of two natures; the firſt of theſe are, where ſome aſſent of the King or the Privy-Council appears upon the enlargement of a priſoner ſo committed; as if, that becauſe ſuch aſſent appears, the enlargement could not have been without ſuch aſſent.

The ſecond of this kind, are thoſe which have been urged as expreſs teſtimonies of the Judges denying bail; and in ſuch caſes, I ſhall open theſe alſo to your Lordſhips: which being done, it will moſt clearly appear, that there is nothing at all in any of theſe, that makes any thing at all againſt the Reſolution of the Houſe of Commons, touching this point; nay, it is ſo far from their making any thing againſt it, that ſome of them add good weight alſo to the proof of that reſolution.

For thoſe of the firſt nature of this ſecond kind of precedents, they begun in the time of *H.* VII. *Tho. Brugge*, and divers others were impriſoned in the King's-Bench *ad mandatum Dom. Regis*, they never ſought remedy by *Habeas Corpus*, or otherwiſe, for aught appears: But the Roll ſays, that *Dominus Rex relaxavit mandatum*, and ſo they were bailed. But can any man think, that this is an Argument either in Law or common reaſon, that therefore they could not have been bailed without ſuch aſſent? It is common in caſes of common perſons, that one being in priſon for ſurety of the peace or the like, at the ſuit of another, is bailed upon the releaſe of the party plaintiff; can it follow, that therefore he could not have been bailed without ſuch releaſe? Nothing is more plain than the contrary. It were the ſame thing to ſay, that if it

ap-

appear, that if a plaintiff be non-suit, therefore unless he had been non-suit, he could not have been barr'd in the suit. The case last cited is *Mich.* 7 *H* VII. *rot.* 6.

The very like is in the same year, *Hil.* 7 *H.* VII. *Rot.* 13. The case of *Will. B[illegible]*, *W[illegible]. C[illegible]*, and divers others, and the self-same answer, that is given to the other, clears this.

So in the same year, *Pasch.* 7 *H.* VII. *Rot.* 18. *John Beomond's* case is the same in substance with those other two, and the self-same answer also satisfies, that clears them.

The next case is, *Mich.* 22 *H.* VII. *Rot.* 8. *Tho' Yew's* case; he was committed *ad se. pacis*, for the security of the peace, at the suit of one *Freeman*, and besides, *ad mandatum Dom. Regis.* Afterwards, *Freeman relaxavit sec. pacis*, and then Sir *J[illegible]. Hobbard*, the then King's Attorney General, *relaxavit mandatum Dom. Regis*, and thereupon he is bailed. The release of the King's Attorney no more proves that he could not have been enlarged without such release or assent, than that he could not have been bailed without release of surety of the peace by *Freeman*.

The very like is in *Hil.* 9 *H.* VII. *Rot.* 14. The case of *Humphry Broche*, which proves no more here than the rest of this kind already cited.

Then for this point also, *Broome's* case of Queen *Elizabeth's* time, is *Trin.* 29 *El. Rot.* 128. *Laurence Broome* was committed to the Gatehouse *per mandatum Dom. Concilii Dominæ Reginæ*, and being returned so upon the *Habeas Corpus*, is first committed to the Marshalsea as the course is, and then bailed by the Court, which indeed is an express precedent, that might perhaps well have been added to the number of the first twelve: which so plainly shews the practice of enlarging prisoners in this case, by judgment of the Court upon the *Habeas Corpus*. But it is true, that in the Scrolls of that year, where the bails are entered, but not in the Record of the *Habeas Corpus*, there was a note, that this *Broome* was bailed *per mandatum privati Concilii*; but plainly this is not any kind of Argument, that therefore in law he might not have been otherwise bailed.

The self-same is to be said of another of this kind, in *Mich* 40 *El. Rot.* 37. *Wenden's* case. *Tho. Wenden* was committed to the Gatehouse by the Queen and the Lords of the Council *pro certis causis* generally; he is brought by *Habeas Corpus* into the King's-Bench, and bailed by the Court. But it is said, that in the Scrolls of that year, it appears that his enlargement was *per consensum Dom. privati Concilii*; and it is true that the Queen's Attorney did tell the Court, that the Lords of the Council did assent to it. Follows it therefore, that it could not have been without such assent?

Next is *Hil.* 43 *El. Rot.* 89. when divers Gentlemen of special Quality were imprisoned by the command of the Privy-Council; the Queen being graciously pleased to enlarge them, sends a commandment to the Judges of the King's-Bench, that they should take such a course, for delivering them upon bail as they should think fit: and they did so, and enlarged them upon Writs of *Habeas Corpus*. Follows it therefore, that this might not have been done by Law, if the parties themselves had desired it?

So in *Trin.* 1 *Jac. rot.* 30. Sir *John Brocket* being committed to the Gatehouse, is returned to stand committed *per mandatum privati Concilii*, and he is inlarged *virtute warranti a Concilio prædicto*. But the same answer that satisfies for the rest before cited, serves for this also.

The last of these, is *Reyner's* case, in *Mich.* 12 *Jac. rot.* 119. He was committed to the Gatehouse by the Lords of the Council, and being brought into the King's-Bench by *Habeas Corpus*, is inlarged upon bail; but this they say was upon a letter written from one of the Lords of the Council to the Judges. It is true, that such a letter was written, but the answer to the former precedents of this nature, are sufficient to clear this also.

And in all these observe,

1. That it appears not, that the party ever desired to be inlarged by the Court, or was denied it.

2. Letters either from the King or Council cannot alter the law in any case: so that hitherto nothing hath been brought on the contrary part, that hath any force or colour of reason in it.

We come now, my Lords, to those precedents of the other nature cited against the liberty of the subject: that is, such as have been used to make like the persons so committed may not be inlarged by the Court.

They are in number eight, but there is not one of them that proves any such thing, as your Lordships will plainly see upon opening them. [illegible]

The [illegible] the [illegible] the persons and [illegible]; I shall therefore recite them all [illegible] and the rest [illegible] together.

The first is *Richard [illegible]'s* case, *Hil.* 7 *Hen.* VII. *Rot.* 8. He and [illegible] to the [illegible] the Houshold, [illegible] *Regis*, [illegible] upon a *Habeas Corpus* into the King's-Bench where [illegible] &c.

The second is [illegible] VII. [illegible] committed to the [illegible] *Regis*, and so returned upon a *Habeas Corpus*, [illegible] &c.

The third [illegible] VIII. [illegible] who was committed to the *Marshalsea* of the Houshold, *per mandatum* [illegible] *Regis*, [illegible] returned upon his *Habeas Corpus*, and the entry is [illegible] &c.

The fourth is *George [illegible]'s* case, *Pasc.* 19. *Hen* VIII. *rot.* 19. He was committed to the [illegible] *per mandatum* [illegible], and returned so upon his *Habeas Corpus*, [illegible] *committitur Marr.* &c.

[illegible] these four have been used principally, as express precedents, to prove that a prisoner so committed cannot be enlarged [illegible] at the first sight, [illegible] the course and entries of the Court of King's-Bench, they may be supposed to prove as much; but in truth they rather prove the contrary, [illegible] there is no colour in them [illegible] as they have been used for. To which purpose I beseech your Lordships to call to your memories, that which I first observed to you touching the course of that Court. Where a prisoner is brought in by *Habeas Corpus*, he is [illegible] to be remanded, but committed to the Marshal of the Court, and then bailed as his case requires. This is [illegible] the entry, [illegible] by the special command of the King, are first remanded, taken from the prison [illegible]; wherein you may observe, my Lords, that if a general suspicion or matter of State were of force in such a case, it might be as needful in point of State, to have the prisoner remain in the prison, where the King by such an absolute command committed him, as to have him at all committed. When they have taken them from the prisons where before they were, they commit them to the Marshal of their own Court, which is but the first step to bailing them. Now it appears not indeed that they were bailed, for then *Traditur in Ball.* had followed, but nothing at all appears that they were denied it; perhaps they never ask'd it, perhaps they could not find such as were sufficient to bail them. And in truth, whensoever any man is but removed from any prison in *England* (though it be for debt or trespass only) into that Court, the entry is but in the self-same syllables as in these four cases.

And in truth if these proceedings did prove, that any of the prisoners named in them were not bailable, or had been thought by the Court not to have been bailable; it will necessarily follow, that no man living that is ordinarily removed from any prison into the King's Bench; or that is there upon any ordinary action of debt, or action of trespass, could be bailed, for every man that is brought thither, and not remanded, and every man that is arrested but for a debt or trespass, and was returned into that Court, is likewise committed to the Marshal of that Court, and by the self-same entry, and not otherwise, yet these four have been much stood on, and have strangely misled the judgment of some that did not, or would not seem to understand the course of that Court.

The fifth of this nature is *Edward Page's* case; it is *Tr.* 7 *Hen.* VIII. This might have been well reckoned with the former four, had not the misentry of the Clerk only made it vary from them. *Edward Page* was committed to the *Marshalsea* of the Houshold, and that *per mandatum domini Regis*, and returned to be therefore detained, and the entry, is *Qui committitur Marr. Hospitii Dom. Regis.* This word *Marr.* is written in the Margin of the roll; this hath been used to prove, that the Judges remanded this prisoner, if they had done so, the remanding had been only while they advised, and not any such award which is given when they adjudge him not bailable. But in truth the word *Committitur* shews, that there was not any remanding of him, nor doth that Court ever commit any man to the *Marshalsea* of the Houshold: and besides, the word *Marr* for *Marescallo* in the margin, shews plainly that he was committed to the Marshal of the King's-Bench, and not remanded to the *Marshalsea* of the Houshold; for such entry of that word in the margin, is perpetually in cases of that nature, when they commit a man to their own prison, and so give him the first step to bailment, which he may have if he ask it, and can find bail. And doubtless these words of *Hospitii præd.* were added by the error of the Clerk, for want of distinction in his understanding, from the *Marr.* of the King's-Bench, to the Marshal of the Houshold.

The sixth of these is *Thomas Cæsar's* case; it is 8 *Jac. rot.* 99. This *Cæsar* was committed to the *Marshalsea* of the Houshold, *per mandatum domini Regis*, and returned to be therefore detained, and indeed a *remittitur* is in the roll, but not a *remittitur quousque*, but only that kind of *remittitur* which is only used while the Court advises. And in truth this is so far from proving any thing against the resolution of the House of Commons, that it appears that the opinion of the reverend Judges of that time was, that the return was insufficient, and that if it were not amended, the prisoner shall be discharged. For in the Book of Rules in the Court of *Mich.* Term (when *Cæsar's* case was in question), they expressly ordered, that if the Steward's Marshal did not amend their return, the prisoner should be absolutely discharged: the words of the rule are, *Nisi Senescallus & Marescal. Hospitii domini Regis sufficienter returnaverint breve de Habeas Corpus Thomæ Cæsar dier. mercur prox. post quindenam sci. et Martin def. exonerabitur.* And this is also the force of that precedent, but yet there hath been an interpretation upon this rule. It hath been said that the Judges gave this rule, because the truth was, that the return was false, and that it was well known, that the prisoner was not committed by the immediate command of the King, but by the command of the Lord-Chamberlain, and thence (as it was said) they made this rule; but this kind of interpretation is the first that ever was supposed, that Judges should take notice of the truth or falshood of the return, otherwise than the body of the return could inform them. And the rule itself speaks plainly of the sufficiency only, and not of the truth or falshood of it.

The seventh [illegible] *Dan[illegible]*, *Edward [illegible]*, [illegible] committed [illegible] *Marshalsea* of the [illegible] upon *Habeas Corpus* [illegible] returned, but [illegible] posterity [illegible] this word [illegible] with the roll [illegible] only, [illegible] of this kind [illegible].

The eighth [illegible] the case of [illegible] *Sal[illegible]*; it is [illegible] *Jac.* Sir [illegible] *Regis*; [illegible] of the Court [illegible] of that Court, [illegible] detained. [illegible] only a *remittitur* [illegible] and [illegible] the Court [illegible] and in the [illegible] the Court had thought that the return had [illegible] good, they would [illegible] have given so many several days to have [illegible] it, [illegible] been sufficient in that case, why [illegible]?

The ninth and last of these is, [illegible] *Salvo[illegible]*, [illegible] returned [illegible] therefore, only generally, [illegible] thereof [illegible] the Court [illegible] *Corpus*,

These are all that [illegible] to the contrary [illegible] upon the view of them [illegible] to your Lordships, it is plain that

that there is not one, not so much as one at all, that proveth any such thing, as that persons committed by the command of the King, or the Lords of the Council without cause shewed, might not be enlarged; but indeed the most of them expressly prove rather the contrary.

Now, my Lords, having thus gone through the precedents of Record, that concern the point of either side, before I come to the other kind of precedents, which are the solemn resolutions of Judges in former times, I shall (as I am commanded also by the House of Commons) represent unto your Lordships somewhat else they have thought very considerable; with which they met, whilst they were in a most careful enquiry of whatsoever concerned them in this great question.

It is, my Lords, a draught of an entry of a judgment in that great case lately adjudged in the Court of *King's-Bench*, when divers Gentlemen imprisoned *per speciale mandatum domini Regis*, were by the award and order of the Court, after solemn debate, sent back to prison, because it was expressly said, they could not in Justice deliver them, tho' they prayed to be bailed. The case is famous, and well known to your Lordships, therefore I need not further to mention it. as yet indeed there is no judgment entered upon the roll, but there is room enough for any kind of judgment to be entered. But, my Lords, there is a form of a judgment, a most unusual one; such a one as never was in any such case before (for indeed there was never before any case so adjudged), and thus drawn on by a chief Clerk of that Court (by direction of Mr. Attorney-General), as the House was informed by the Clerk, in which the reason of the judgment, and remanding of those Gentlemen, is expressed in such sort, as if it should be declared upon Record for ever, that the laws were, that no man could ever be inlarged from imprisonment that stood committed by such an absolute command.

The draught is only in Sir *John Heveningham*'s case, being one of the Gentlemen that was remanded, and it was made for a form for all the rest. The words of it are after the usual entry of a *Curia advisare vult* for a time; That *visis retur. prædict. nec non diversis antiquis recordis in Curia hic remanent. consimiles casus continentibus, maturaq; deliberatione, inde prius habita, eo quod nulla specialis causa captionis sive detentionis præd. Johannis exprimitur, sed generaliter quod detentus est in prisona præd'. per speciale mandatum domini Regis, ideo præd'. Johannes remittitur præfat. custodi Mar. Hospitii præd salvo custodiend. quousq;* &c. that is, *quousque secundum legem deliberatus fuerit.* And if that Court, that is the highest for ordinary Justice, cannot deliver him *secundum legem*; what law is there, I beseech you, my Lords, that can be sought for in any other inferior Court to deliver him? Now, my Lords, because this draught, if it were entered in the roll, (as it was prepared for no other purpose) would be as great a declaration, contrary to the many Acts of Parliament already cited, contrary to all precedents of former times, and to all reason of law; to the utter subversion of the highest liberty and right belonging to every Freeman of this Kingdom, and for that especially also it supposes, that divers ancient records had been looked into by the Court in like cases, by which records their judgments were directed; whereas in truth, there is not any one record at all extant that with any colour (not so much indeed as with any colour) warrants the judgment: therefore the House of Commons thought fit also, that I should, with the rest that hath been said, shew this draught also to your Lordships.

I come now to the other kind of precedents, that is, solemn resolutions of Judges, which being not of record, remain only in authentick copies: but of this kind there is but one in this case, that is the resolution of all the Judges in the time of Queen *Elizabeth*. It was in the 34th of her reign, when divers persons had been committed by absolute command, and delivered by the Justices of the one Bench or the other; whereupon it was desired, that the Judges would declare in what cases persons committed by such command were to be inlarged, which hath been variously cited, and variously apprehended.

The House of Commons, therefore, desiring with all care to inform themselves as fully of the truth of it as possibly they might, got into their hands from a Member of their House, a Book of selected cases, collected by a reverend and learned Chief-Justice of the Common-Pleas, that was one of them that gave the resolution, which is entered at large in that Book: I mean the Lord Chief-Justice *Anderson*, it is written in the Book with his own hand, as the rest of the Book is, and howsoever it hath been cited, and was cited in that great judgment upon the *Habeas Corpus* in the *King's-Bench*, as if it had been, that upon such commitments the Judges might not bail the prisoners; yet it is most plain, that in the resolution itself no such thing is contained, but rather expressed the contrary. I shall better represent it to your Lordships by reading it, than by opening it.

Then it was read here. [*See* ante 147, 148.]

If this resolution doth resolve any thing, it doth indeed upon the enquiry resolve fully the contrary to that which hath been pretended, and enough for the maintenance of the ancient and fundamental point of liberty of the person, to be regained by *Habeas Corpus* when any is imprisoned. And I the rather thought it fit now to read it to your Lordships, that it might be at large heard, because in the great judgment in the *King's-Bench*, though it was cited at the bar, as against this point of personal liberty, as also at the Bench, yet though every thing else of record that was used, were at large read openly, this was not read either at Bar or Bench, for indeed if it had, every hearer would easily have known the force of it to have been mistaken contrary to the judgment.

My Lords, having thus gone through the charge committed to me by the House of Commons, and having thus mentioned to your Lordships, and opened the many precedents of records, and that draught of the judgment in this like case, as also this resolution; I shall now (as I have [illegible] and direction given me,) lest your Lordships should be put to much trouble and expence of time in finding or getting Copies at large of those things which I have cited, offer also to your Lordships authentick Copies of them all, and so leave them, and whatsoever else I have said, to your Lordships further consideration.

The true Copy of the Precedents of Record.

Inter Record. Dom. Regis Caroli in Thesauro Recept. Scaccarii sui sub custodia Dom. Thesaurar. & Camerar. ibidem remanen. viz. Placita coram Domino Rege apud Westmonast. de Ter' Pasche anno Regi Edwardi III. post conquest. Angliæ 18. inter alia sic continetur ut sequitur.

Rot. 33. Adhuc de termino Pasch.

DOMINUS Rex mandavit dilecto & fideli suo Roberto de Dalton Constabular' Turris suæ London vel ejus locum tenent' bre. suum in hæc verba: Edwardus Dei gratia Rex Angliæ, Franciæ, & Dominus Hiberniæ dilecto et fideli suo Roberto de Dalton Constabular' Turris suæ London vel ejus locum tenent. salutem. Mandamus quod Johannem Bildeston capellan' quem vic. nostr. London ad mandatum nostrum apud pred. Turrim vobis liberavit ab eisdem recipiatis & in prisona nostra Turris London pred salvo custodir' fac' quousque aliud super hoc duxerimus demandand. teste meipso apud Turrim nostram London 30 die Martii Anno regni nostri Angliæ 16. Regni vero nostri Franciæ 30. Et modo scilt. in Crast. Ascen. Dom. anno Regis nunc 8. coram Domino Rege apud Westminst. venit Johannes de Wynwick locum tenens pred. Constabular. & adduxit coram Justiciar' hic in Cur. pred. Johannem de Bildeston quem ille a prefat. Vicecomit. virtute brevis pred. recepit. &c. Et dicit quod ipse a Domino Rege habuit mandat. ducend. & liberand. corpus ipsius Johannis de Bildeston prefat. Justiciar. hic, &c. Et quesitum est de pred. Johanne de Wynwick si quam aliam detentionis prefat. Johannis de Bildeston habeat Causam. Qui dicit quod non nisi bre. pred. tantum. Et quia videtur cur. bre. pred. sufficien. non esse predict. Johannis de Bildeston prison. Marr' Regis hic retinen. &c. Idem Johannes dimittitur per manus Willielm. de Wakefield rectoris Eccle. de Willingham, Johannis de Wynwick in Com. Kanc. Johannis de Norton in Com. Norff. Nicolai de Blandefford in Com. Middl. & Rogeri de Bromley in Com. Stafford, qui eum manuceperunt habend. eum coram Domino Rege in Octabis Sancti Trin. ubicunque &c. viz. Corpus pro corpore &c. Ad quas Octabis Sanct. Trin. coram Domino Rege apud Westm. ven. pred, per manus pred' Et super hoc mandavit Justiciar. suis hic quoddam bre. suum Claus. in hæc verba, Edwardus Dei gratia Rex Angliæ, & Franciæ, & Dominus Hiberniæ, dilectis & fidel. suis Willielmo Scot, & sociis suis justiciar' ad placita coram nobis tenend. assignat. saltem cum nuper mandaverimus dilecto & fideli nostro Roberto de Dalton Constabular' Turris nostræ London vel ejus locum tenen. quod Johannem de Bildeston Capellanum capt. & detent. in prisona Turris pred. per preceptum nostrum pro suspicione contrafactionis magni Sigilli nostri cum Attachiat. & aliis causis caption. & detentionem pred. tangent. salvo & secur' duci fac' coram nobis in Crast. Ascen. Dom. ubicunque tunc fuissemus in Anglia prisonæ Marescall. nostr. coram nobis liberand. in eadem quousque per quendam informatorem essemus plenius informat. custod. & tuta inde informatione pred. ulterius pred. super hoc fieri fecerimus quod fore viderimus faciend. secundum legem, & consuetudinem Regni nostri Angliæ, nos in casu quod dictus Informator non ven. coram nobis ad informand. nos plenius super premiss. volentes eadem Johannem ea de causa Justiciar' deferre in hac parte vobis mandamus quod si pred. Informator in Quinden. Sanct. Trin. prox. futur. vel circa non venit super hoc plenius informat. tunc advent. ejusdem informator is minime expectat. eidem Johanni super hoc fieri fac. Justic. complement. prout fore videritis faciend. secundum legem & consuetudinem Regni nostri Angliæ, teste meipso apud Westminst. 12 Maii Anno Regni nostri Angliæ 18. Regni vero nostri Franc' quinto. Quo quidem bre. respect. fact. est proclamatio quod siquis dictum regem super premiss. informare vel erga ipsum Johannem prosequi voluerit, quod veniat. Et super hoc venit pred. W. de Wakefield, Nicholas de Wandsworth, Johannes Brynwyn, Johannes de Longham, Johannes de Norton, & Rogerus de Bromley omnes de Com' Midd' & man' pred. Johannem de Bildeston habend. eum coram Domino Rege de die in diem usque ad prefat' quinden. Sanct. Trin. ubicunque, &c. Ad quem diem Anno 18. coram Domino Rege apud Westminst. venit pred. Johannes de Bildeston per manus pred. & iterata facta est proclam. in forma qua superius, &c. et nullus venit ad dictum Regem informand' &c. per quod concess. est quod pred. Johannes de Bildeston eat inde sine die salva semper actione Dom. Regis si qua, &c.

De Ter' Sanct. Hillar' Anno 22 H. VIII. *& per cont. Rot. ejusdem Rotul.* 38.

Johannes Parker per Ricardum Choppin, &. W. Daunsey Vic' London virtute brevis Dom. Regis de Latitat, pro pace versus ipsum Johannem Parker ad sect. Johannis Bruton eis inde direct. & coram Rege duct. cum causa, viz. quod idem Johannes Parker capt. fuit in civitate pred. pro secu' pacis pred. & pro suspicione feloniæ per ipsum apud Croweall in Com. Glocest. perpetrat. per nomen Johannis Parker de Thornbury in Com. Glocest. Corser, alias dict. Johan. Charbs de eodem Com' Surgeon, ac per mandatum Dom. Regis nunciat' per Robertum Peck gen' de Cliffords-Inn, qui committitur Marr' &c. & postea iste eodem termino traditur in Ballium Thomæ Atkins de Thornbury pred. Weaver, & Willi. Nole de eadem villa & Dom. usque a die Pasche in unum men. Weaver ubicunque &c. Et quod idem Johannis Parker citra eundem diem personaliter comparuit coram Justiciar' Dom. Regis ad prox. general. Gaol deliberation' in Com. Glocest. prox. tenend. ad subjiciend. & recipiend. ea omnia, & singula quæ pertinet. Justiciar' de eo tunc ordinare contigerit, &c. viz. Corpus pro corpore &c. Ad quem diem pred. Johannis Parker licet ipsi 4. placit. solemniter exact. ad comparend. non ven. ideo caperet cum plur' Trin. ad quem diem ex Octab. Trin. postea Trin. 24 H. VIII. ex Crast. quinden. Pasch. Ad quem diem bre. & vic' return' quod ad Hull. tent. apud London die lune prox' post fest. Sanctæ Scholasticæ Anno Regis H. VIII. 25. Johannes Parker, & W. Nole utl' fuer. prout patet per bre. Regis de Ter' Paschæ Anno 25 Rs pred.

De Ter. Sanct. Mich. anno 25 H. VIII. *& per cont. ejusdem Rot.* 33.

Johannem Bricks per Ro. Baker Ar. Senescall Cur. Marr. & Radum Hapton Mar' ejusdem Cur. virtute brevis Dom. Regis de Hab. as Corpus ad sub-

subjiciend. & recipiend. &c. eis inde direct. coram Domino Rege duct' cum causa, viz. quod ante adventum brevis pred. Johannes Byncks captus fuit per mandatum privati Concilii Dom. Regis pro suspicione feloniæ, & pro aliis causis illos movent. & duc' ad Gaol. Marr. & ibidem detent. virtute Gaol' pred. qui committitur Marr. &c. Et immediate ex gra' cur. special' pred. Johannes Byncks de Magn Marlow in Com. Buck. Weaver traditur in Ball. Thomæ Bigham de London Gent. & Johannis Woodward de Marlow pred. Taylor, usque in craft. Sanct. Martin. ubicunque &c utque pleg. corpus pro corpore, &c. Ad quem diem comperuit & Robertus Drury Ar' & Johannes Bosse gen. Domino Justiciar' Dom. Regis ad pacem in Com. Buck. virtute brevis Dom. Regis eis direct. Domino Regi certificaverunt quod nullum indictamentum de aliquibus feloniis & transg. versus ipsum Johannem Byncks coram eis ad presens resident. Et ulterius de fama et gestu ipsius Johannis Byncks per sacram. proborum & legalium homin. Com. Buck. diligenter inquiri fecerunt, & nihil aliud preter bonum de eo coram eis est compertum. Ideo concess. est quod pred. Jo. Byncks de premissis eat inde fine die deliberatur per proclamationem & Jur. prout moris est.

De Ter. Paf. Anno 2 & 3 Ph. & Mar. Rot. 58.

Ricardus Overton nuper de London gen. per Tho. Leigh, & Johannem Machell vic' London virtute brevis Dom. Regis & Reginæ de Habeas Corpus ad stand. rect. &c. eis inde direct. coram Willielmo Portman mil' capital. Justiciar. &c. duct. cum causa, viz. quod pred. Ricardus Overton 9. die Octobr. ult. preter commiss. fuit prison. de Newgate, & ibidem in eadem prisona sub custod. dict. Vic. detent. ad mandatum pernobilium duorum honorabilis concil. pred. Regis & Reginæ qui committit. Marr. &c. et immediate traditur in Ball. Willielmo Overton de London gen. & Johanni Tayler de parochia Sanct. Martini apud Ludgate London merc. usque Octab. Trin. viz. uterque manucaptor. pred. corpus pro corpore & postea Tr. 2. El. Reginæ, corpus Overton & pleg. suos Octabis Michael. ad quem diem ex mens. Pasch. ad quem diem vic. ret. quod ad Hust. suum tent. Guildhal' Civitatis London die Lunæ post festum Sanct. Gregor. Epi. pred. W. Overton utl' est & per brc. Pas. Anno suprad.

De Ter. Sanct. Mich. Anno 2 & 3 P. & Mar. Rot. 16. *habet Chart. allocat. Trin.* 2 & 3 *Phil. & M.*

Ricardus Overton nuper de Lond. gen. capt. Octab Hill. pro quibusdam altis prodic. unde indictat. est, ad quem diem Pasc. ad quem diem ex Ct. Animarum.

De Termino Pasch. 4 & 5 *P. & Mar & per cont. ejusdem Rot.* 45.

Edwardus Newport gen. per Robertum Oxenbridge mil' Constabular' Turris pred. virtute bre. Dominor. Regis & Reginæ de Habeas Corpus ad subjiciend. &c. ei inde direct. ad Barr. coram Domino Rege & Regina duct. cum causa, viz. quod ipse sibi commiss. fuit per mandat. concilii Dominæ Reginæ, qui committitur Marr. & immediate traditur in Ball. prout, &c. Et postea fine die per proclamation. virtute brevis de gestu & fama prout, &c. Rot. 17. ejusdem anni.

De Ter. Mich. Anno 4 & 5 P. & Mar. per Cont: ejusdem Rotul. 17.

Memorand. quod 14. die Octobr. Anno 4 & 5 Phil. & Mar. Edwardus Newport de Hanley in Com. Wigorn. ac capt. fuit per Uxbridge in Com. pred. pro suspicione contra factionis quarundem pec. auri vocat. *French crowns*, per ipsum & alibi in Com. Wigor. fier. supposit. & ea de causa per mandatum Concil' Dominor. Regis & Reginæ commiss. ad Barr. tunc duct. fuit, qui committitur Marr. &c. et super hoc idem Edwardus Newport traditur in Ball. Thomæ Charge de Latton in Com. Essex gener' Edwardo Hales de Parochia Sancti Olavi, London, gen. Johanni Baker, Clerico Ordinar. London, Johanni Gill de Parochia Sanct. Tho. Apostoli London, Clothworker, & Richardo Parks de Brownsgrave in Com. Wigorn. Yeoman, usque Octabis Hill. ubicunque &c. viz. quilibt. pleg. proced. sub pœna 100l. & pred. Edwardus sub pœna 200l. quas, &c. Ad quem diem comperuit & committitur Constabular. Turris London per mandatum Concil. Dom. Regis & Reginæ ibid. salvo custodiend. quousque, &c. Et postea Pas 4 & 5 P. & M. traditur in Ball. prout patet per Scrivect. finium istius ter. & postea M. 5 & 6 P. & M. exonerat. per cur. eo quod tam per Sacram. 12 probor. & legalium hominum de pred. Com. Midd. coram Dom. Rege & Domina Regina hic in cur. mea parte jurat. & onerat. quam per Sacrament. 12. probor. legal homin. de pred. Com. Wigor. coram Edwardo Saunders, & Johanne Whiddon mil. & aliis Justiciar' dictor' Dom. Regis & Reginæ ad pacem ac de diversis feloniis transgress. & aliis malefact. in eodem com' perpetrat audiend. & terminand. assignat. virtute brevis dictor. Dominor. Regis & Reginæ eis inde direct. in ea parte jurat. & onerat ad inquirend de gestu & fama ipsius Edwardi comperti existit quod idem Edwardus est de bonis gestu & fama, ideo proclamatio est inde facta prout moris est secund. legem & consuetudinem Reg. Angliæ, &c. concess. est, quod pred. Edwardus eat inde sine die.

De Ter. Paf. 9. *El. Rot.* 35.

Tho. Lawrence per Christopher' Drap. Majorem civitatis London' Ambrosium Nicholas & Rcu' Lambert vic. ejusdem civitatis virtute brevis Dom Reginæ de Habeas Corpus, &c. eis inde direct. & coram Domina Regina dict. cum causa, viz. quod 7 die Novembr. Anno regni Dom. El. nunc Reginæ Angliæ 8. pred. Thomas Lawrence indicto brevi nominat. captus fuit in civitate pred. & in prisona Dom. Reginæ sub custod. pred. [illegible] Reginæ qui committitur Marr. [illegible] per Scrivect finium istius ter.

De [illegible] Rot [illegible]

[illegible] locum tenend. Turris [illegible] Habeas Corpus ei inde direct. & coram Domina [illegible] quod idem Robert- [illegible] commissus fuit per mandatum [illegible] qui committitur Marr. [illegible] in Ball' prout patet [illegible]

Ter Paf. Anno 20 *El. & per cont. ejusdem Rot.* 72.

Johannes Browning per Owen Hopton mil' locum tenen' Turris Dominæ Reginæ London virtute brevis Habeas Corpus ad subjiciend. ei inde direct. & coram dilecto & fideli Ch. Wray mil. capit. Justiciar. Dom Reginæ ad placita coram nobis tenend. assignat. apud hospitium suum in Serjeants-Inn Fleet-street London' die lunæ, viz. 12 die Maii duct. cum causa viz. quod pred. Johannes Browning commissus fuit eidem locum tenend. per mandatum privati concil' Reginæ salvo custodiend. &c. qui com. Marr. &c. & postea isto eodem Ter. traditur in Ball' prout pat. per Scrivect. finium istius Ter.

De Ter. Sanct. Hillar. Anno 40 *El. Reginæ & per cont. ejusdem Rot.* 62.

Edwardus Harecourt per Hugonem Parlour custod. prisonæ Dominæ Reginæ de Gatehouse intra civitatem Westminst. in Com. Middl. virtute brevis Dominæ Reginæ de Habeas Corpus ad subjiciend. &c. ei inde direct. & coram Domina Regina apud Westminst. dicta cum causa, viz. quod ante advent. brevis pred. scil. 7. die Octobr. an. Regni Dom. Regin. nunc 39 corpus Edw. Harecourt, per duos privat. Concil. dictæ Dominæ Reginæ ei commiss. fuit salvo & secure custodiend. certis de causis ipsos movent. & ei ignotis, qui committitur Marr. &c. et postea isto eodem Ter. traditur in Ball. prout patet per Scrivect. finium istius Termini.

De Vacatione Hillar. Anno 43 *El.*

Robertus Catesbie per Johannem Phillips Guardian' de le Fleet virtute brevis Dominæ Reginæ de Habeas Corpus ad subjiciend. &c. ei inde direct. & coram Edwardo Fenner uno Justiciar. Dominæ Reginæ ad placita coram ipsa Regina tenend. assignat. apud Winchester-House in Burgo de Southwark in Com. Surr. dict. cum causa, viz. quod pred. Robertus commissus fuit prisonæ pred. primo die Martii Anno 43 El. War. diversorum prænobilium virorum de privato Concilio Dominæ Reginæ in hæc verba:

To the Warden of the Fleet, or his Deputy: These shall be to will and require you, to receive at the hands of the Keeper of the Compter of Woodstreet, *the person of* Robert Catesbie, *Esquire, and him to detain, and keep safely in that prison under your charge, until you shall have other direction to the contrary, whereof this shall be your Warrant.*

Et prefat. Robertus commissus fuit Marr. per prefat. Edwardum Fenner, & statim traditur in Ball' prout patet, &c.

Ter. Hill. Anno 43 *Eliz. Reginæ* 12 *Jac. Regis.*

Ricardus Beckwith gen' per Aquilam Wykes custod. prisonæ de Gatehouse in Com. Midd. virtute brevis Dom Regis de Habeas Corpus ad subjiciend. ei inde direct. & coram Domino Rege duct. cum causa, viz. quod ante advent brevis predict. scilicet 10 die Julii Anno Regni Dom. Jac. Regis Dei gratia Angliæ, Franc. & Hiberniæ fidei defensor. &c. 11 & Scot. 47. predict. Ricardus Beckwith sibi commissus fuit prisonæ predict. sub custod. sua virtute cujusdem Warrant. sibi fact. & direct. per Georgium divina providentia Cant. Archiepiscopum totius Angliæ Primat. & Metropolitan. Henric. Com. Northampton Dominum Guardian. 5 portuum & un. de privato Concil. Regis, Tho. Com. Suffolk Dom. Camerar' Regiæ Familiæ ac facr' Concil. Dom. Regis Edwardum Domini Wooton gubernator Regiæ familiæ, Johannem Dom. Stanhope Vice-Camerar' Regiæ familiæ, cujus Warrant. tenor sequitur in hæc verba:

To Aquila Wykes, *Keeper of the Gatehouse in* Westminster, *or his Deputy: Whereas it is thought meet that* Miles Rayner *and* Richard Beckwith *be restrained of their Liberty, and committed to the prison of the Gatehouse; These shall be to will and require you to receive the persons of the said* Rayner *and* Beckwith *into your charge, and safe keeping in that prison, there to remain until you shall have further order from us in that behalf, for which this shall be your Warrant. Dated at* Whitehall *the* 10*th of* July, 1613. Et postea isto eodem termino.

De Ter. Mich. An. 14 *Jac. per cont. ejusd. Rot.* 147.

Thomas Mounson miles per Georgium More locum tenent' Turris Dom. Regis London' virtute brevis Dom. Regis de Habeas Corpus ad subjiciend. &c. ei inde direct. coram Domino Rege apud West. duct. cum causa, viz. quod ante adventum brevis predict. Thomas sibi commissus fuit per Warrant. advers. Dominis de privato Concilio Regis sibi direct &c. Qui committitur Marr. &c. & super hoc traditur in Ball' prout patet per Scrivect. fin. istius Termini.

De Ter. Mich. 7 *H.* VII. *& per cont. ejusdem Rot.* 6.

Tho. Brugg junior, nuper de Yanington in Com' Hertford gen', Johannes Rawleus nuper de Lemster in Com' pred' Yeoman, Rob. Sherman nuper de Lemster in Com. predict. Walter Thomas nuper de eadem in Com. predict. Hosier, Tho Baliard nuper de eadem in eodem Com. Smith Cadwallader ap John Duy nuper de Kerry in Marchia Walliæ in Com. Salop adjacen. gen. Reginald ap Breingham, alias Sherman, nuper de Lemster in Com. Hereford Sherman, & Thomas Turner nuper de Kingsland in Com. Hereford Courser, sunt in custod. Marr. ad mandatum Dom. Regis, &c. ac pro aliis certis de causis prout patet alibi de Record. &c. per Record. istius Ter. postea isto Termin. Dominus relaxavit mandatum suum & prosecut. predict. comparuerint per Attorn. &c. Et quod utlag. versus prefat. Thomam Brugg revocatur isto termino & predict. Johannes Rawleus pro selon. & murdro predict. traditur in Ball' prout patet alibi, &c. ideo hic Marr. de ejus corpore per cur. exoneratur, &c.

Ter. Hillar. 7 *H.* VII. *& per cont. ejusdem Rot.* 18.

W. Bartholomew, Johannes Bartholomew, Willelmus Chace, Henr. Cart. Tho Rotel[illegible], Tho. Street, Robertus [illegible], & Henr. Bancks sunt in custod. Marr. ad cust. mandat. dom. Regis, &c. per record. istius termini ac predict. Willelmus Chace pro [illegible] Randulphi [illegible] [illegible] &c. Patche sequen [illegible] postea termin sequen. dict. Dominus Rex mandatum suum predict. quoad Willelmus Chace [illegible] per Regis Attornat & pro pace & pro selon. & murdro traditur in Ball.

De Ter. Paf. 7 *H.* VII *& per cont. Rot ejusdem* [illegible]

Thomas Bermond de Wednesbury in Com' Staff [illegible] in custod. Marr. ad mandatum Dom. Regis, &c. per record. [illegible] Pasch' 7 Hen. VII sequen' predict. Johannes Bermond de [illegible]- date dato prediſt. exoneratus exiſtit ideo Mar' de eo per eandem Cur' exoneratus exiſt.

De Ter. Mich. Anno 12 *H.* VII. *Rot.* 8.

Thomas Yewe de villa de Staff. in com' Stafford Yeoman, per Johannem Shawe & Ricardum Haddon vic' London virtute brevis Dom. Regis de Habeas Corpus, ad Sect. ipſius Regis eis inde direct. coram Rege duct. cum cauſa quod idem Thomas Yewe attachiatus fuit per Ricardum Whittington Serjeant apud Baynard's Caſtle Civitatis prediſt. & priſona dicti Dom. Regis infra eandem Civitatem ſalvo cuſtodiend cauſa pro ſuſpicione felon. apud Coventrie in com' War' perpetrat. ad Suggeſtionem Willielmi King Innholder, ac inſuper idem Tho. Yewe detinetur in priſona prediſt. virtute cujuſdem alterius querel. verſus ipſum ad ſectam Johannes Freeman Serjeant de eo quod inveniat. ei inſufficiend. ſecur. pacis indicta cur. coram Johanne Waiger nuper vic. Ac ulterius idem Tho. Yewe detent. eſt in dicta priſona pro 23*l.* debit. & 21. 8*d.* dampnis & cuſtag. quos Robertus Corbet Mercer, ex cognitione ipſius defend. verſus eum recuperavit in eadem cur. coram eodem Johanne Waiger nuper vic. Ac etiam idem Tho. detinetur in dicta priſona ad mandatum domini Regis, per Johannem Shawe, Alderman, Civitatis London, qui committitur Marr. &c. poſtea ſcilicet ter. Sanct. Trin. Anno 19 Regis H. VII. prediſt. Johannes Freeman relaxavit ſecur. pacis verſus eundem Tho. Yewe dictuſq, Robertus Corbet cognovit ſe fore ſatisfact. de debito & dampnis prediſt. Ac Jacobus Hubberd Attornat. General. dom. Regis relaxavit mandatum dom. Regis, ac pro ſuſpicione feloniæ prediſt. traditur in Ball. Symon Little de London Taylor, & Johanni Aſhe de London Skinner, uſque Octabis Mich. ubicunq; &c. Ad qui diem comperuit & Robertus Throgmorton miles unus cuſtod. pacis prediſt. com' Warr' return' quod null. Indictament. de aliquibus felon' ſive tranſgreſſ. verſus pretat Tho. Yewe coram eo & Sociis ad preſens reſidet. et ulter. virtute brevis dom. Regis ſibi & Sociis ſuis direct. per Sacrament. 12 probor. & legal. hominum de villa de Coventry prediſt. de geſtu & fama prediſt. Thome diligenter inquiſitionem fecerunt, & nihil de eo preter bonum coram eo & Sociis ſuis eſt compertum ſed de bono geſtu & fama, ideo conceſſ. eſt quod prediſt. Tho. eat inde ſine die,

Ter. Hillar. Anno 9 *H* VII. *& per cont. ejuſdem Rot.* 14.

Humfridus Broche nuper de Canterbrig. in Cantabr. Scholar. per Robertum Willoughbie dom' Brook mil. Seneſchall. Hoſpitii dom. Regis, ac Johannem Digbie mil. Marr' cur' Marr' Hoſpitii prediſt' virtute cujuſdem brevis dom. Regis de Habeas Corpus ad ſectam ipſius Regis ad ſtand. rect', &c. ad ſect. partis utlag. eis inde direct. coram Rege duct. cum cauſa viz. quod idem Humfridus commiſſus fuit Gaol. Mart' Hoſpitii dom. Regis & hac de cauſa & non alia idem Humfridus in priſona pred detinetur, qui committitur Marr' &c. poſtea Paſ. ſequen' Rex relinquit mandatum ſuum Capit.l. Juſticiar' per Tho. Lovett mil. oſten' & pro utlag pred. traditur in Ball. prout patet alibi.

De Ter' Sct. Trinit' anno 39 *El. & per cont. Rot. ejuſdem* 113.

Lawrence Broome per Hugonem Parlour cuſtod. priſone Domine Regine de la Gatehouſe, virtute brevis Domine Regine de Habeas Corpus ad ſubjiciend. &c. ei inde direct. & coram Domina Regina apud Weſtminſt' duct. cum cauſa viz. quod prediſt Lawrence Broome in arcta cuſtod. ſua remanſet per mandatum duorum de Concilio dicte Domin. Regine pro certis cauſis eos movent' qui committitur Marr' & poſtea iſte eodem termino traditur in Ball. prout patet, &c.

Per Scrtveſt. Fin. Ter' Sct' Trin. anno 39 *El. Regine.*

Lawrence Broome de Parva Baddow in Com. pred. huſband. traditur in Ball' ad ſubjiciend. &c. ad mandat. privat. Concil. Domine Regine ſuper Habeas Corpus,

Verſus Rando. Mayall de Hatfield Beverell in Com' pred' Gener.
Verſus Henrico Odall de eadem Gen.
Verſus Will. Eckaſden de Weſtminſt' Bricklayer.
Verſus Ric Morgan de Weſtminſt' Labourer.
Uterq; ſub pena 40*l.* & princeps ſub pena 100 marcarum.
Pro ſuſpicione proditionis cum Johanne Smith mil.

De Ter' Sct' Michaelis anno 4 *El. & per cont. Rot. ejuſdem* 37.

Tho. Wenden per Hugonem Parlour gen' cuſtod. priſone Domine Regine de le Gatehouſe, virtute brevis Domine Regine de Habeas Corpus ad ſubjiciend. &c. ei inde direct' & coram Domina Regina apud Weſtm' duct cum cauſa, viz. quod 18 die Junii, Anno Regni Domine El. nunc Regine Anglie 38. corpus, &c. infra nominat. Tho' Wenden extra cur' ejuſdem Domine Regine coram ipſa Domina Regina privati Concilii Dom. Regis cujus tenor ſequitur in hæc verba, ſcilicet; *Theſe are to will and require you to receive into your charge and cuſtody, the perſon of* John Brocket, *Knight, and him to retain in ſafe keeping under your charge until you ſhall have further order for his inlargement; whoſe commitment being for ſome ſpecial matter concerning the ſervice of our ſovereign Lord the King, you may not fail to regard this Warrant accordingly. From the King's Palace at* Whitehall, *the laſt of* March, 1605. Eaq; fuit cauſa detentionis pred. Johannis in priſona pred. qui committitur Marr. &c. & poſtea traditur in Ball' prout patet, &c.

Ter. Mich. anno 12 *Jac. Regis, Rot* 110.

Milo Reyner per Aquilam Wykes cuſtod. priſone de le Gatehouſe, virtute brevis dom. Regis de Habeas Corpus ad ſubjiciend &c. coram Domino Rege duct. cum cauſa viz. quod ante advent. brevis pred. ſcilt. 10 Julii Anno Dom. 1613 pred. Milo Reyner commiſſus fuit priſonæ pred' & huc uſq; detent. virtute Warr' cujuſdem fact. & direct. per Georgium Archiepiſcopum Cant. Henr. Com. Northampton. Tho. Com. Suffolk, Wilhelm. Dom. Knolles, Edwardum, Dom. Wooton, & Edwardum Dom. Stanhope, cujus Warranti tenor ſequitur in hæc verba. *To* Aquila Wykes, *Keeper of the Gatehouſe in* Weſtminſter, *or his Deputy: Whereas it is thought meet that* Miles Reyner *and* Richard Beckwith *be reſtrained of their liberty, and committed to the priſon of the Gatehouſe: These ſhall be to will and require you, to receive the perſons of* Reyner *and* Beckwith *into your charge and keeping, until you ſhall have further order from us in that behalf, for which this ſhall be your ſufficient Warrant, dated at* Whitehall, *the* 10th of July, 1613. Et hæc eſt cauſa detentionis ſue in priſona pred. qui committitur Marr' &c. & poſtea iſto eodem ter' traditur in Ball' prout patet, &c.

Ter. Hill. 5 *H.* VII. *& per Cont. ejuſdem Rot.* 18.

Ric'us Everard nuper de Colcheſter in Com. Eſſex Clericus, & Robertus Wight nuper de Norwico Smith, per Robertum Willoughbie mil. Dom. de Brooke, Seneſchall' Hoſpitii Dom. Regis, & Johannem Turberville mil' Marr' Hoſpitii pred. virtute bre. de Habeas Corpus ad ſectam ipſius Regis pro quibuſdam proditionibus, & felon' unde indicto Com. Eſſex indictat. ſunt eis inde direct. coram Domino Rege duct cum cauſa, viz. quod idem Ricardus Everard & Robertus Wight commiſſ. fuer' cuſtod. Marr. pred. per mandat. Dom. Regis, qui committitur Marr. &c.

Ter. Hill. 8 *H.* VII. *& per Cont. ejuſdem Rot.* 14.

Roger Cherrie nuper de Nova Windſor in Com' pred. Yeoman, alias dict. Rogerus Stearries nuper de eadem in eodem Com' Yeom. per Johan. Baker, Majorem villæ Dom. Regis de Nova Windſor in Com. pred. virtute brevis Dom. Regis de Habeas Corpus ad ſect. ipſius Regis pro quibuſdam feloniis & tranſgr. unde in Com. Midd. indictatus eſt ſibi inde direct. coram Domino Rege duct. cum cauſa, viz. quod idem Roger' commiſſus fuit Gaol. Dom. Regis infra villa pred. per mandat. Dom. Regis qui committitur Marr. &c.

Ter. Hill. 9 *H.* VII. *& per Cont. ejuſdem Rot.* 14.

Chriſtophorus Burton nuper de Rocheſter in Com' Cantii Hackneyman, per Robertum Willoughbie Dom. Brooke, mil' Seneſchall' Hoſpitii Dom: Regis, & Johannem Digbie mil' Marr. cur. Marr. Hoſpitii pred. per mandatum Dom. Regis. Et hæc eſt cauſa & non alia, qui committitur Marr. &c.

Ter. Paſ. Anno 19 *H.* VII. *& per Cont. ejuſdem Rot.* 23.

Georgius Urſewicke de London, Mercer, per Oliverum Wood locum tenen. priſone Dom. Regis de le Fleet, virtute brevis Dom Regis de conſervand. diem, &c. ei inde direct. coram Rege duct. cum cauſa, viz. quod idem Georgius, 13 Maii, Anno 19. Regis commiſſus fuit priſone de le Fleet, per mandatum ipſius Dom. Regis ſalvo cuſtodiend. ſub pena 40*l.* qui committitur Marr. &c

Ter. Trin. Anno 8 *H.* VIII. *per Cont. ejuſdem Rot.* 23.

Edwardus Page nuper de London, Gent. per Georgium Com. Salopiæ Seneſchall. Hoſpitii Dom. Regis & Henricum Shamburne Marr. cur. Mar. Hoſpitii pred. virtute brevis Dom. Regis de Habeas Corpus, ad ſect. ipſius Regis ad conſervand. diem, &c. eis inde direct. & coram Rege duct. cum cauſa, viz. quod idem Edwardus captus & detentus in priſona Regis Marr. pred. per mandatum Dom. Regis ibidem ſalvo cuſtodiend. &c. qui committitur Marr. Hoſpitii Dom. Regis.

Ter. Mich. Anno 8 *Jac. & per Cont. ejuſdem Rot.* 99.

Tho. Cæſar per Tho. Vavaſour mil' Mar Hoſpitii Dom. Regis & Marr. ejuſdem Hoſpitii Dom. Regis, virtute brevis Domini Regis de Habeas Corpus ad ſubjiciend. &c. ei inde direct. & coram Rege apud Weſtminſt. duct. cum cauſa, viz. quod ante adventum brevis pred. ſcil. 18 Julii Anno Regni dicti Dom. Regis nunc Angliæ; &c. 7. Tho. Cæſar, in brevi fuit pred. nominat. captus apud Whitehall in Com' Middl. per ſpeciale mandatum Dom. Regis ac per eundem Regem adtunc & ibidem commiſſ. fuit priſon. Marr. ibidem ſalvo cuſtodiend. quouſq; &c Et ea fuit cauſa captionis & detentionis ejuſdem Tho. Cæſar, qui committitur priſonæ Marr. pred.

Ter. Sancti Mich. 8 *Jac Regis*

Niſi pred. Seneſchall. & Marr. Hoſpitii Dom. Regis ſufficienter return' bre. de Habeas Corpus, Tho. Cæſar die Mercur. per quinden. Sanct. Martini defendens exonerabitur.

Ter. Hill. 12 *Jac. Rot.* 153.

Jacobus Demaiſtres, Edwardus Emerſon, Georgius Brookeſhall & W. Stephens, per Tho. Vavaſour mil' Marr. Marr Hoſpitii Regis virtute bre. Dom. Regis de Habeas Corpus ad ſubjiciend. &c. ei inde direct. coram Domino Rege apud Weſtminſt. duct. cum cauſa, viz. quod ante adventum brevis pred. ſcilt. 22 Januar. Anno Regis Jacobi Angliæ, &c. 12. & Scot. 48. pred. Jacobus Demaiſtres, Edwardus Emerſon, Georgius Brookeſhall, & W. Stephens in brevi huic Schedul' annex. nominat. commiſſ. fuer' Gaol' Marr. Hoſpitii Dom. Regis, pro cauſis ipſum Regem & ſervic' ſuum tangen. & concernen. Et hæc eſt cauſa Captionis pred. Jacobi, Edwardi, Georgii & Willielmi, & poſtea immediate remittitur præfat. Marr. Hoſpitii pred.

Ter. Hill. 12 *Jac Regis.*

Samuel Saltonſtall miles per Johannem Wilkinſon arm' guard. de le Fleet, virtute brevis Dom. Regis de Habeas Corpus ad ſubjiciend. &c. ei inde direct. & coram Domino Rege apud Weſtminſt. duct. cum cauſa, viz quod pred. Samuel commiſſ. fuit priſonæ pred. 11 Martii, 1608. per Warrant. a Dominis de privato concilio Dom. Regis & quod detentus fuit etiam idem Samuel in priſona pred. virtute cujuſdem ordinis in cur. Can' Dom. Regis fact. cujus ordinis tenor patet per Rot. Record. iſtius Termini ad quem diem pred. Samuel remittitur priſonæ pred. Et ſecundus dies prox. ter' datus eſt guardian. priſonæ pred. ad emendand. return. ſuum ſufficien. ſuper pred. bre. de Habeas Corpus, & quod tunc intulerit hic in cur corpus pred. Samuel Saltonſtall mil'. Ad quem quidem diem prefat. Guardian. priſonæ pred. ſuper pred. bre. de Habeas Corpus retorn. quod pred. Samuel commiſſus fuit priſonæ pred. 11 die Martii 1608. per Warrant. a Dom. de privat' Concil. dict Dom. Regis apud Whitehall tunc ſeden. & quod poſtea 11 die Febr. 1610. commiſſ. fuit extra cur. Canc. Dom. Regis apud Weſtminſt. pro contemptu ſuo eidem cur. illat. Et quod detent. fuit etiam idem Samuel in priſona pred. per mandat. Dom. Cancellar' Angliæ ſuper quo pred. Samuel iterum remittitur priſonæ pred. & ulterius dies dat. eſt prefat. Guardian. ad emendand. retorn. ſuum ſuper Habeas Corpus ver. defend prout ſtat. voluit uſq; diem Jovis prox. Ment. Paſch. Et tunc ad habend. Corpus &c. Ad quam diem prefat. guardian. intulit corpus hic in cur. & return' ſuper Habeas Corpus quod pred. Samuel commiſſ. fuit priſonæ pred. 11 die Martii, 1608. virtute cujuſdem Warranti a Dominis de privato Concil. Dom. Regis tunc ſeden. apud Whitehall, & quod etiam idem Sam.

Sam. commiff. fuit prifonæ 11 Febr. Anno Regis Jac. 8. per cur. Canc. Dom. Regis apud Weftminft. tunc exiften. pro quadam contempt. per eundem Samuel eidem cur. illat. & perpetrat. proinde falvo cuftodiend. qui remittitur prifonæ pred.

Ter. Tr. anno 13 *Jac. & per Cont. ejufdem Rot.* 17.

Samuel Saltonftall miles per Johannem Wilkinfon Guardian. prifonæ de le Fleet, virtute brevis Dom. Regis de Habeas Corpus ad fubjiciend. & recipiend. &c. ei inde direct & coram Domino Rege apud Weftminft. duct. cum caufa, viz. quod pred. Samuel Saltonftall commiffus fuit prifonæ pred. 12 die Martii Anno Regis Jacob. Angliæ, &c. fexto, virtute cujufdam Warrant. a dominis de privat. Concilio Dom. Regis tunc feden. apud Whitehall commiffus fuit etiam idem Samuel Saltonftall miles prifonæ pred. 12 die Febr. Anno 1610. & Anno Reg. Jac. Angliæ, &c. 8. per confiderat. cur. Cancell' dicti Dom. Regis apud Weftminft. pro contempt. eidem cur. adtunc per pred. Samuel illat. ibidem proind. falvo cuftodiend. Et hæc funt caufæ captionis & detentionis pred. Sam. Saltonftall mil. in prifona pred. cujus tamen corpus ad diem & locum infra content. parat. habeo prout mihi precipitur.

True Copies of the Records not printed, which were ufed by Sir Edward Littleton.

Inter Record. Domini Regis Caroli in Thefaur. Recept. Scaccarii fui fub cuftodia Thefaurar. & Camerar. ibidem remanent. viz. Pl coram ipfo Domino Rege, & Concilio fuo, ad Parliamentum fuum poft Pafch. apud London in Maner' Arch-Epifcopi Ebor', anno Regni Domini Regis Ed. III. 21. Inter alia fic continetur ut fequitur, Rot. 2. in-corfo.

STephanus Rabaz Vicecomes Leic & Warw. coram ipfo Domino Rege & ejus Concilio arenatus & ad Rationem pofitus de hoc quod cum J. B. E. H. & W. H. nuper Balliv' ipfius Vicecomitis per Dom. Regem fuiffent affign' ad Gaolas Domini Regis deliberand. eidem vic' quendam W. P. per quendam appellatorem ante adventum eorum Jufticiariorum ibidem appellat. & capt. vivente ipfo appellatore ufque diem deliberationis coram eis fact. demiff. per pleviam contra formam Statuti, &c. Et etiam quendam R. de C. qui de morte hominis judicatus fuit, & per eundem Vicecomit' captus, idem R. fine ferris coram eifdem Jufticiar' ad deliberationem præd' produxit contra confuetudinem Regni, & fimiliter quendam Walterum filium Walteri le Perfone qui per præceptum Comitis Warwici captus fuit, dimifit per pleviam contra vocem & preceptum Domini Regis; cum idem Dominus Rex per literas fuas fub privato Sigillo fuo eidem Vicecomit. precipiet quod nulli per preceptum pred. Com. Warwici capt. aliquam gratiam vel favorem fac. &c. Et fuper hoc prefat. J. B qui prefens eft, & qui fuit primus Jufticiar. pred. premiff. recordatur & pred. vicecomes dicit quoad pred. W. P. ipfe nunquam a tempore captionis ipfius W. per pred. appellatorem demiff. fuit per pleviam aliquam ante advent. pred. Jufticiar. Imo dicit quod per dimid. Anni ante adventum eorum Jufticiar. captus fuit. Et quoad pred. R. bene cognofcit quod ipfe dimifit eum per pleviam, & hoc bene facere potuit ratione ac authoritate officii fui, eo quod captus fuit pro quadam fimplici tranfgreffione, & non pro aliqua felonia, pro qua replegiari non potuit. Et quoad 3. viz W. filium Perfone bene cognofcit quod ipfe captus fuit per preceptum pred. Com. Warwici & quod dimifit eum per pleviam. Sed dicit quod hoc fecit ad rogatum quorundam de Hofpitio & Curia Dom Regis, qui eum fpecialiter inde rogaverint per literas fuas. Et fuper hoc idem vicecom. quefivit per Dom. Regem quis eum rogavit, & literas fuas ei direxit, & ubi literæ illæ funt, dicit quod Walterus de Langton eum per literas fuas inde rogavit, fed dicit quod literæ illæ funt in partibus fuis Leic. Et fuper hoc idem Vicecomes profert bre. Dom. Regis de privato figillo eidem vic direct. quod teftatur quod Dominus Rex eidem Vic. precipit, quod omnes illos tranf. contra pacem & de quibus Comes Warwici ei fcire fecit, caperet, & falvo cuftodir. abfque aliqua gratia eis facienda. Et quia pred. Jufticiar' expreffe recordat. quod ipfi & focii fui per bonam & legalem inquifitionem de militibus & aliis communibus coram eis fact. invenerunt quod pred. W. de Petling dimiffus fuit per pleviam per magnum tempus ante adventum eorundem Juftic. ufq; adventum eorundem & per vic. pred. Et etiam quia pred. vic. cognofcit quod pred. R. dimiffus fuit per pleviam per ipfum vic. & hoc dic. quod bene facere potuit, eo quod captus fuit pro levi tranfgreffion. & per record. ejufdem Jufticiar. compert. eft quod captus fuit pro morte hominis quod eft contrar. dict. pred. vicecom. & fimiliter quod idem vicecom. cognovit, quod recepit literam Dom. Regis per quam Rex ei precepit, quod nullam gratiam fecerit illis qui capt. fuer. per precept. pred. Com. & idem vicecomes contra preceptum illud dimifit pred. Willielmum filium Walteri per pleviam qui captus fuit per preceptum pred. Comitis prout idem vicecomes fatetur. Et fic tam ratione ipfius tranfgr. quam aliarum pred. incidit in penam Stat. Conf. eft quod pred. vicecomes committatur prifonæ juxta formam Statuti, &c.

Ex Rot. Parliamenti de anno 35 *Regis Ed.* III. *Numero* 9.

Primerement que le grand Chartre, & le Chartre de Foreft, & les autres Statuts fait en fon temps & de fes Progenitors per profits de lui, & de la Commenalty foient bien & ferment gardes, & mife en due execution fauns difturbance mettre ou arreft faire le contre par fpecial mandement, ou en autre manere. Noftre Seignior le Roy per affent Prelates, Dukes, Comites, Barons, & la Commenaltie ad ordeine & eftabili que les dits Chartres & Statuts foient tenus & mife en execution felon le dit Petition.

Stat 30 *Ed.* III. *Num.* 22.

Item, come il foit contenus en le grand Chartre & autres Stat[illegible] que nul [illegible] ne impriſon per fpecial mandement fauns [illegible], [illegible] faire par le ley, & foient foits [illegible], & uncore eft que [illegible] font [illegible] pris, & imprifon fauns indictment ou [illegible] procès fait per le ley [illegible], [illegible] hors de le foreft [illegible], [illegible] plefe a noftre dit Sr. commaund. & [illegible] per del fpecial mandement contre le [illegible] Chartres & Statuts avant dits.

Item, [illegible] Roy & fon Conceil de fort grande [illegible], & fait le [illegible] droit [illegible] la ley.

Parliament. Anno 42 *Ed.* III. *Numero* 12.

Item, pur ceo que plufours de voftre come font amerce & difturbes per faulx accufors queux font lour accufements plus pur lour vengeances & fingulers profits que pur le profit de Roy ou de fon peuple, & les accufes per eux afcuns ont eft pris & afcuns font faire ven. de le Conceil Roy per brief ou autre mandement de Roy fub grande pain encountre la ley, Plefe a noftre Sr. le Roy & fon Conceil pur droit gouvernment de fon peuple ordeign que fi defire afcun accufors purpofe afcun matire pur profit du Roy que cele matire foit mander a fes Juftices del' un Banke ou del' autre, ou d'Affifes deut enquere & terminere felonque la ley, & fi le touche la onfour ou partie eit la font a la come ley, & que null home foit mis a refpondere fans prefentment deut Juftices, ou chofe de Record, ou per due proces & briefe original, felon l'ancient ley de la terre, & fi rien defire enovant foit fait a l'encontre, foit voide en ley, & tenu pur error. Pur ceo que cefte Article eft Article de le grande Chartre le Roy voet que ceo foit fait come la Petition demande.

Ex Rot. clauf. de Anno Regni Regis, Ed. I. *primo, Membrano* 1.

Thomas de Clere de Beckwith captus & detent. in prifona de Northampton pro tranfgreffione foreft. habet literas Rogero de Clifford, Jufticiar' Foreft. citra Trent. quod ponatur per ball' Dat. apud Sanct. Martin. Magn. London 20 die Octobr.

Membrano 7.

Stephanus de Lindley capt & detent. in prifona pro tranfgref. per ipfum fact. in foreft. Regis de Lindley habet literas Regis Galfrido de Nevill, Jufticiar. ultra Trent. quod ponatur per ballium.

Membrano 8.

Tho. Spademan capt. & detent. in prifona de Oxon. pro morte Willielmi Wanne unde rectat. eft, habet literas Regis Vicec. Oxon. quod ponatur per ball'.

Membrano 9.

Willielmus de Deane, Matheus Cruit, Roger de Bedell, W. Halfrench, Robertus Wyat, Alexander Hareing, Harry de Shorne, Nicolas de Snodilonde, Turgefius de Hertfield, Robertus de Pole, & Ricardus Galiot, capti & detent. in prifona de Cant. pro morte Galfridi de Cottiller unde appellati funt, habent literas Regis Vic' Kan. quod ponantur per ball' Dat. 23 Martii.

Clauf. Anno 2 *Ed.* I *Membr.* 12.

Rex Rogero de Clifford, Jufticiar. Foreft. citra Trent. mandamus vobis quod fi Robertus Unwin, capt. & detent. in prifona noftra de Aylefbury pro tranfgref. Foreft. noftr. invenerit vobis 12 probos & legales homines de Ball. veftra qui manucapiant eum habere coram Jufticiar. noftr. ad placita Foreft. cum in partes, &c. ad Stand. inde rectat. tunc apud Robertum fi fecundum Affifam Foreft. fuer. repleg. per dictos duodecim, interim traditur in Ball. ficut pred. eft & habeatis nomina illorum 12 hominum. Et hoc bre. &c. Dat. 27 Februar.

Clauf. Anne 2 *Ed.* I. *Num.* 14.

Unwynus de Boycot, Galfridus de Wickeram, & Hugo de Stone, detent. in prifona Regis de Aylefbury pro tranfgr. venationis habuit bre. direct. Rogero de Clifford Jufticiar. Foreft. quod fi fecundum Affif. Foreftæ erunt repleg. ufque advent. Jufticiar. Regis ad placita Foreft. cum in partes illas venerint. Dat. apud Coddington, 28 die Decembr.

Numero 15.

Guilbert Conray de Keddington, & Hugo le Taylor de Keddington capt. & detent. in prifona fancti Edmundi pro morte Edmundi Bunting unde rectati funt habuerint literas Regis vic' Suff. quod ponantur per Ball.

Clauf. Anno 3 *Ed.* I. *Num.* 11.

Galfridus de Hairton captus & detentus in prifona Regis Ebor' pro morte Adel' Clerke, unde rectatus eft habet literas Regis vic' Ebor. quod ponatur per Ball' Dat. apud Weftminft. 15 Junii.

Numero 20.

Robertus Belbarbe captus & detentus in prifona de Newgate pro morte Thomæ Pollard, unde rectatus eft habet literas Regis vic. Midd. quod ponatur per Ball' Dat. 28 Februar.

Clauf. num. 4 *Ed.* I. *Membr.* 5.

Mandatum eft Rado de Sandwico quod fi W. de Pattare, & Johannes filius ejus, Walterus Home, Walterus Corwen, Henricus Path, & W. Cadegan, capt. & detent. in prifona Regis de Sanct Brionell pro tranfgr. For. unde rectati funt, invenerint fibi 12 probos & legales homines de Ball. fua, viz. quilibet eorum 12 qui eos manucap' habere coram Jufticiar. Regis ad placita Foreft. cum in partes illas venerint ad ftand. inde rectat. tunc ipfos Willielm. Johannem, Walterum, Walterum, Henricum, & Willielm. pred. 12 fi fecundum Affif. fuer. repleg. tradantur in Ball' ut pred. eft, & habeant ibi nomina illorum 12 hominum & hoc bre. Teft. Rege apud Ball' locum Regis 29 die Augufti.

Clauf. Anno 4 *Ed.* I. *Membr* 16.

Henricus filius Rogeri de Kenn de Cotiefbrooke capt. & detent. in prifona noftra Northampton pro morte Simonis de Charrettell, unde appellatus eft, habet literas Regis vic' Northampton quod ponatur per ballium.

Clauf. Anno 5 *Ed.* I. *Memb.* 1.

Mandatum eft Galfrid. de Nevil Jufticiar. Foreft. ultr. Trent. quod S. Walterus de le Greene captus & detentus in prifona de Nottingham pro tranfgr. For' invenerit fibi 12 probos & legales homines qui eum manucapiant, &c ad ftand. inde rectat. fecundum Affif. For' Regis tunc ibidem Walter pred. 12 traditur in ballium ficut pred. eft. Dat. 16 Nov.

Membrano 2.

Thomas de Upwell & Juliana uxor ejus capt. & detent. in prifona de [illegible] pro morte Stephani [illegible], unde [illegible] habent literas [illegible] Nott. quod ponantur per Ballium. Dat apud Rothelm 28 die Septembr.

Clauf. Anno [illegible] *Ed.* I. *Num.* [illegible]

[illegible] Peffle captus & detentus [illegible] Regis [illegible] Norwic. pro [illegible] Julianæ quondam uxoris fuæ, unde [illegible] habet literas [illegible] quod ponatur per Ball' Tefte Rege apud [illegible] Novemb.

M[illegible]

Membrano 4.

Mandatum est vic' Nottingham quod si Tho. de Cudart rectat. de transgr. Forest. quod fecisse dicebatur in Forest. de Sherwood, invenerit sibi sex probos & legales homines de Balliva sua qui eum manucap' habere coram rege ad mandatum regis ad stand. rect. coram rege cum Rex inde cum eo loqui voluerit, tunc pred. Tho. pred. sex hominib. tradat in ballium juxta manucapt. supradict. Dat. 15. die Decembr.

Membrano 4.

Tho. Burrell captus & detent. in prisona Regis Exon. pro morte Galfrid. Geffard unde rectat. est habet literas Dom. Regis vic' Devon. quod ponatur per ball'.

Claus. Anno 1 Ed. II. *Membr.* 1.

Johannes Brynn de Rollinwsith capt. & detent. in prisona Regis Oxon. pro morte Johannis de Sutton, unde rectat. est habet literas Regis vic. Oxon. quod ponatur per Ball. usque prim. Assis. si ea occasione, &c. Teste Rege apud Bristol, 28 Junii.

Membrano 2.

W. Spore Capell. capt. & detent. in prisona Regis Oxon. pro morte Johannis Spore unde indictatus est, & habet literas Regis vic' Devon. quod ponatur per ballium usque ad prox. Assis. si ea occasione, &c. Teste rege apud Windsor 28 die Maii.

Numero 10.

Gilbertus Fairchild capt. & detent. in Gaole Regis Dorcester pro morte Henrici de Langton, unde indictat. est habet literas quod ponatur per ballium usque ad prim' assis. Teste Rege apud Westminst. 28. Februar'.

Claus. Anno 2 *Ed.* II. *Membr.* 1.

Willielmus Sandie de Cobham capt. & detent. in prisona Regis Cant. pro morte Johannis de Sprink, Johannis Ermona de Dunberke, unde rectatus est habet literas Regis vic' Kanc' quod ponatur per Ball' usque ad primum Assis. si ea occasione, &c. Teste rege apud Cestre. 29 Junii.

Radulph. Corynn capt. & detentus in Gaole Regis de Lincolne pro morte Willielmi filii Symonis Porter unde rect. est & habet literas Regis vic' Lincolne quod ponatur per Ball' usque ad primam Assis. si ea occasione, &c. Teste rege apud Sheene 3 diei Junii.

Membrano 7.

Johannes de Githerd capt' & detent. in prisona Regis Ebor' pro morte Mathei Sampson de Ebor' unde rectatus est habet literas Regis vic' Ebor' quod ponatur per Ball' usque ad prim' Assis. Dat. apud Langele 30 die Aprilis.

Claus. 3 *Ed.* II. *Membr.* 13.

Adam de Pepper captus & detent. in Gaole Regis Ebor' pro morte Henrici le Symer' de Eastrick unde rectatus est habet literas Regis vic' Ebor' quod ponat' per Ball' usque ad primam assis. Teste rege apud Westminst. 7 die Febr.

Numero 14.

Margareta uxor Willielmi Calbot capta & detenta in Gaole Regis Norwici pro morte Agnetis filiæ Willielmi Calbot, & Matildæ sororis ejusdem Agnetis, unde rectata est habet literas Regis vic' Norff. quod ponatur per Ball'. Teste rege apud Sheene 22 Jan.

Numero 18.

Johannes Frere captus & detent. in Gaole Regis Oxon. pro morte Adæ de Egeleigh unde rectat. est habet literas Regis vic' Devon. quod ponatur per Ball'. Teste apud Westminst. 8 Decembr.

Claus. Anno 4. *Ed.* II. *Membr.* 7.

Robertus Shereve capt. & detent. in Gaole Regis de Colcestr. pro morte Roberti le Moigne, unde rectat. est habet literas Regis vic' Essex quod ponatur per Ball' usque ad prim' Assis. Dat. 22 die Maii.

Numero 8.

W. Filius Roberti le Fishere de Shirborne capt. & detent. in Gaole Regis Ebor' pro morte Roberti le Monus de Norton, unde rectatus est habet literas Regis vic. Ebor. quod ponatur per Ball. usque ad primam Assis. Dat. 25 April.

Claus. Anno 4 *Ed.* II. *Numero* 22.

Thomas Ellis de Stanford capt. & detent. in prisona Regis Lincolne pro morte Michaelis filii Willielmi de Fodering, unde rectat. est habet literas Regis vic. Lincolne quod ponatur per Ball' usque ad prim. Assis. Teste Rege apud novam Westmonast. 8 die Septembr.

Sir Edward Coke *took up the Argument, as to the rational part of the Law, and began with this Introduction* *.

YOUR Lordships have heard seven Acts of Parliament in point, and thirty-one precedents summarily collected, and with great understanding delivered; which I have perused, and understand them all thoroughly, and that there was not one of them against the resolution of the House of Commons. Twelve of the precedents are *in terminis terminantibus*, a whole Jury of precedents, and all in point; and to my understanding, they admit of no answer: but I am persuaded in my conscience, that a number of them was never shewed at the *King's-Bench*, because I know out of whose quiver two of them came, and that they were not known before. I am much transported with joy, because of the hopes to proceed with good success in this weighty business, your Lordships being so full of Justice, and the very theme and subject doth promise success, which was, *Corpus cum causa*, the freedom of an *Englishman*, not to be imprisoned without cause shewn; which is my part to shew, and the reason and the cause why it should be so. And I doubt not but we shall go on happily; and, my Lords, it would be unseasonable to be prolix and copious, because, *quod intempestum injucundum*. I would speak here a little to some points which are not so clear and obvious, for otherwise *perspicua vera non sunt probanda*, and to gild gold were idle and superfluous; therefore shall briefly clear to your Lordships some doubts made of the Statute of *Westminster*, which says, Sheriffs and others may not replevy men in prison for four causes;

1. For Death of a Man.
2. Commandment of the King.
3. Absolute Command from the Justices.
4. For Matters of the Forest.

I was once a Judge of the *King's-Bench*, and did wonder how the Judges of these times thus interpret the Statute. The Statute only shews what Sheriffs can only do, by way of replevin; the Sheriffs Court is a petty and base Court, and not of Record, where the Sheriff is not the Judge, but the Jurors, that is, *John a Noke*, and *John a Stiles*, *William Roe*, and *John Doe*, and such worthies as these. Again, the Statute saith there, he cannot be replevied if he be taken for the death of a man; and no marvel, whoever thought it; for the Scripture saith, *Sanguis nullo modo expiari potest nisi Sanguine*. But if he cannot be there replevied, at the *King's-Bench* he may, it is there done every day. Mr. Sheriff, you should replevy a man in such a case, *Ergo*, not bail him, my Lords the Judges, *(non sequitur)*: What not Judges bail? What not the *King's-Bench*, the highest Court of Record of ordinary jurisdiction? for the *King's-Bench* is higher than the *Chancery*. And this he prov'd by Heraldry, *Additio probat minoritatem*, that addition proves the younger Brother. Now the *Teste* of the *King's-Bench* is *coram Dom. Rege*, without any addition, but that of the *Chancery*, *coram Dom. Rege in Cancellario*, with that addition of a Cadet, a younger Brother. I am very sorry I am so much straitned for want of time, for I am much delighted with these things. What, may not the Judges meddle with any thing in the Forest? If that were so, I would never dwell in a Forest, to be wholly under the jurisdiction of the Wardens and Regarders. These glosses and interpretations are very strange to me, and others who have been Judges. My Lords, all those arguments offered unto your Lordships in this last conference, are of a double nature. 1. Acts of Parliament. 2. Judicial Precedents. For the first, I hold it a proper argument for your Lordships, because you, my Lords Temporal, and you, my Lords Spiritual, gave your assent unto those Acts of Parliament; and therefore if these cannot persuade you, nothing can. For the second, which are judicial precedents, it is *Argumentum ab authoritate*, and *Argumentum ab authoritate valet affirmativè*: that is, I conceive, tho' it be no good argument to say negatively, the Judges have given no opinion in the point, *Ergo*, that is not law; yet affirmatively it concludes well: the Judges have clearly delivered their opinions in the point, *Ergo*, it is good law; which I fortify with a strong axiom, *Neminem oportet sapientiorem esse legibus*, as long as these laws stand unrepealed. Now, these two arguments being so well pressed to your Lordships by my Colleagues, I think your Lordships may wonder what my part may be; it is short, but sweet: it is the reason of all those laws and precedents, and reason must needs be welcome to all men; for all men are not capable of the understanding of the law, but every man is capable of reason. And those reasons I offer to your Lordships, in affirmance of the ancient laws and precedents made for the liberty of the subject, against imprisonment without cause expressed, and shall shew them in order and method, to confirm the same.

1. *A re ipsa.*
2. *A minori ad majus.*
3. From the remedies provided.
4. From the extent and universality of the same.
5. From the infiniteness of the time.
6. *A Fine.*

The first general reason is, *à re ipsa*, even from the nature of imprisonment, *ex visceribus causæ*; for I will speak nothing but *ad idem*, be it close or other imprisonment: and this argument is threefold, because an imprisoned man upon will and pleasure is,

1. A Bondman.
2. Worse than a Bondman.
3. Not so much as a man; for *mortuus homo non est homo*, a prisoner is a dead man.

1. No man can be imprisoned upon will and pleasure of any, but he that is a Bondman and Villein, for that imprisonment and bondage are *propria quarto modo* to Villeins †. Now *propria quarto modo*, and the *species*, are convertible; whosoever is a Bondman, may be imprisoned upon will and pleasure, and whosoever may be imprisoned upon will and pleasure, is a Bondman.

2. If a Freeman of *England* might be imprisoned at the will and pleasure of the King or his commandment, then were they in worse case than Bondmen or Villeins; for the Lord of a Villein cannot command another to imprison his Villein without cause, as of disobedience, or refusing to serve, as it is agreed in the Year-books. And here he said, that no man should reprehend any thing that he said out of the Books or Records: he said §, he would prove a Freeman imprisonable upon command or pleasure, without cause expressed, to be absolutely in worse case than a Villein; and if he did not make this plain, he desired their Lordships not to believe him in any thing else: and then produced two Book-cases, 7 *E.* III. *fol.* 50. in the new print, 348 old print. "A Prior had commanded one to imprison his Villein, the Judges were ready to bail him, "till the Prior gave his reason, that he refused to be Bailiff of his Manor; and that satisfied the Judges. 2d Case, 33 *Ed.* III. title *Tresp.* "253. in *Faux imprisonment*, it was of an Abbot, who commanded one "to take and detain his Villein, but demanded his cause, he gives it, "because he refused, being thereunto required, to drive his Cattle.

"*Ergo*, Freemen imprisoned, without cause shewn, are in worse case than "Villeins, that must have a cause shewn them why they are imprisoned.

* The Lord-President, who reported the Conference to the House, begun thus: The Conference upon *Monday* last with the Lower House, was about the Liberty of the Subject, to set this forth, they employed four Speakers: the first was Sir *Dudley Diggs*, a Man of a voluble and eloquent Speech, his part was the Introduction; the second was Mr. *Littleton*, a grave and learned Lawyer; whose part was to represent the resolution of the House, and their Grounds whereupon they went; the third was Mr. *Selden*, a great Antiquary and a pregnant Man, his part was to shew the Law, and the precedents in point; the fourth was the Lord *Coke*, that famous reporter of the Law, whose part was to shew the reason of all that the others had said, and all that which was said was but an affirmance of the Common-Law. *From a MS. belonging to the late* Peter le Neve, *Esq; and wrote at that time, wherein the Conference is related.*

† *Vide* the Writ *de Nativo habendo.* § *Fitz-Herbert fait ut non de ceo.*

"3. A Freeman imprisoned without Cause, is so far from being a "Bondman, that he is not so much as a Man, but is indeed a dead Man, "and so no Man: Imprisonment is accounted in Law a civil Death, *per-"dit domum, familiam, vicinos, patriam,* and is to live amongst wretched "and wicked Men, Malefactors, and the like." And that Death and Imprisonment was the same, he proved by an Argument *ab effectis*, because they both produce the like immediate Effects; he quoted a Book for this: If a Man be threatened to be killed, he may avoid a Feoffment of Lands, Gifts of Goods, *&c.* 39 *H.* I. 65, *&c.* so it is if he be threatened to be imprisoned; the one is an actual, the other is a civil Death. And this is the first general Argument, drawn *à re ipsa*, from the Nature of Imprisonment, to which *res ipsa consilium dedit.*

The second general Reason he took also from his Books; for he said he had no Law, but what by great Pains and Industry he learnt at his Book; for at ten Years of Age, he had no more Law than other Men of like Age: And this second Reason is, *à minori ad majus*; he takes it from *Bracton, fol.* 105, *minima pœna corporalis, est major qualibet pecuniaria.*

But the King himself cannot impose a Fine upon any Man, but it must be done judicially by his Judges, *per Justiciarios in Curia, non per Regem in Camera*; and so it hath been resolved by all the Judges of *England*: He quoted 3 R. II. *fol.* 11.

The third general Reason is taken from the Number and Diversity of Remedies, which the Laws give against Imprisonment, *viz.*

Breve de homine replegiando.
De odio & atia.
De Habeas Corpus.
An Appeal of Imprisonment.
Breve de manucaptione.

Two of these are antiquated, but the Writ *de odio & atia* is revived, for that was given by the Statute of *Magna Charta, chap.* 26. and therefore though it were repealed by the Statute of 28 *E.* III. *cap.* 9. yet it is revived again by the Statute 42 *E.* III. *cap.* 1. by which it is provided, that all Statutes made against *Magna Charta* are void. Now the Law would never have given so many Remedies, if the Freemen of *England* might have been imprisoned at free Will and Pleasure.

The fourth general Reason is from the Extent and Universality of the pretended Power to imprison: For it should extend not only to the Commons of this Realm, and their Posterities, but to the Nobles of the Land, and their Progenies, to the Bishops and Clergy of the Realm, and their Successors. And he gave a Cause why the Commons came to their Lordships, *Commune periculum commune requirit auxilium.* Nay, it reacheth to all Persons, of what Condition, or Sex, or Age soever; to all Judges and Officers, whose Attendance is necessary, *&c.* without Exception; and therefore an Imprisonment of such an Extent, without Reason, is against Reason.

The fifth general Reason is drawn from the Indefiniteness of Time; the pretended Power being limited to no Time, it may be perpetual during Life; and this is very hard: To cast an old Man into Prison, nay, to close Prison, and no Time allotted for his coming forth, is a hard Case, as any Man would think that had been so used. And here he held it an unreasonable Thing, that a Man had a Remedy for his Horse or Cattle, if detained, and none for his Body thus indefinitely imprisoned; for a Prison without a prefixed time, is a Kind of Hell.

The sixth and last Argument is *à Fine*; and *sapiens incipit à Fine*, and he wished he had begun there also; and this Argument he made threefold.

Ab honesto.	This being less honourable.
Ab utili.	This being less profitable.
A tuto.	This Imprisonment by Will and Pleasure, being very dangerous for the King and Kingdom.

1. *Ab honesto.* It would be no Honour to a King or Kingdom, to be a King of Bondmen or Slaves; the End of this would be both *dedecus & damnum*, both to King and Kingdom, that in former Times hath been so renowned.

2. *Ab utili.* It would be against the Profit of the King and Kingdom, for the Execution of those Laws before remembered, *Magna Charta*, 5 *Edw.* III. 25 *Edw.* III. 28 *Edw.* III. whereby the King was inhibited to imprison upon Pleasure: You see (quoth he) that this was *vetus querela*, an old Question, and now brought in again, after seven Acts of Parliament: I say, the Execution of all these Laws are adjudged in Parliament to be for the common Profit of the King and People; (and he quoted the Roll) this pretended Power being against the Profit of the King, can be no Part of his Prerogative.

He was pleased to call this a binding Reason, and to say, that the Wit of Man could not answer it; indeed the great Men kept this Roll from being printed, but that it was equivalent in Force to the printed Rolls.

3. A Reason *à tuto.* It is dangerous to the King for two Respects; first, of Loss; secondly, of destroying the Endeavours of Men. First, If he be committed without the Expression of the Cause, though he escape, albeit in Truth it were for Treason or Felony, yet this Escape is neither Felony nor Treason; but if the Cause be expressed for Suspicion of Treason or Felony, then the Escape, though it be innocent, is Treason or Felony. [The Act, which is in *Latin*, is, *nisi causa pro qua captus, & imprisonat. fuit tale judicium requirat, si de illa pro legem & consuetudinem terræ fuisset convictus.*] He quoted a Cause in Print like a Reason of the Law, not like *remittitur* at the rising of the Court; for there the Prisoner *traditur in Ballium quod breve Regis non fuit sufficiens causa*: The King's Command. He quoted another famous Cause; the Commons in Parliament, incensed against the Duke of *Suffolk*, desire he should be committed: The Lords and all the Judges, whereof those great Worthies, *Prescot* and *Fortescue*, were two, delivered a flat Opinion, that he ought not to be committed without an especial Cause. He questioned also the Name and Etymology of the Writ in question, *Corpus cum causa*; *Ergo*, the Cause must be brought before the Judge, else how can he take Notice hereof?

Lastly, He pressed a Place in the Gospel, *Acts* 25. last Verse, where *Festus* conceives it an absurd and unreasonable Thing, to send a Prisoner to a *Roman* Emperor, and not to write along with him the Cause alledged against him: Send therefore no Man a Prisoner without his Causes along with him, *hoc fac & vives.* And that was the first Reason, *à tuto*, that it was not safe for the King, in regard of Loss, to commit Men without a Cause.

The second Reason is, that such Commitments will destroy the Endeavours of all Men. Who will endeavour to employ himself in any Profession, either of War, Merchandize, or of any liberal Knowledge, if he be but a Tenant at Will of his Liberty? For no Tenant at Will will support or improve any Thing, because he hath no certain Estate; *Ergo*, to make Men Tenants at Will of their Liberties destroys all Industry and Endeavours whatsoever. And so much for these six principal Reasons: Taken,

1. *A re ipsa.*
2. *A minori ad majus.*
3. *A remediis.*
4. From the Extent and Universality.
5. From the Infiniteness of the Time.
6. *A fine.*

Loss of { Honour. Profit. Security. Industry.

These were his Reasons.

Here he made another Protestation, That if a Remedy had been given in this Case, they would not have meddled therewith by no Means; but now that remedy being not obtained in the *King's-Bench*, without looking back upon any thing that hath been done or omitted, they desire some Provision for the future only. And here he took Occasion to add four Book-cases and Authorities, all in the Point; saying, that if the learned Counsel on the other Side could produce but one against the Liberties, so pat and pertinent, oh! how they could hug and cull it! 16 *H.* VI. *tit. Monstrance de fait* 82. by the whole Court, the King in his Presence cannot command a Man to be arrested, but an Action of false Imprisonment lieth against him that arresteth: If not the King in his Royal Presence, then none others can do it. *Non sic itur ad astra.* 1 *Hen.* VII. 4. *Hussey* reports the Opinion of *Markham*, Chief-Justice to *Edw.* IV. that he could not imprison by Word of Mouth; and the Reason, because the Party hath no Remedy; for the Law leaves every Man a Remedy of causeless Imprisonment. He added, that *Markham* was a worthy Judge, though he fell into Adversities at last by the Lord *Rivers*'s Means. *Fortescue*, chap. 8. *Proprio ore nullus Regum usus est*, to imprison any Man, *&c.* 4 *Eliz.* Times blessed and renowned for Justice and Religion, in *Plowden*, 235. the Common Law hath so admeasured the King's Prerogative, as he cannot prejudice any Man in his Inheritance; and the greatest Inheritance a Man hath, is the Liberty of his Person, for all others are accessary to it: For thus he quoted the Orator *Cicero*, *Major hæreditas venit unicuique nostrum à Jure legibus quam à parentibus.*

And these are the Authorities he cited in this Point.

Now he propounded and answered two Objections: First, in Point of State; Secondly, in the Course held by the House of Commons.

May not the Privy Council commit, without Cause shewed, in no Matter of State where Secrecy is required? Would not this be an Hindrance to his Majesty's Service?

It can be no Prejudice to the King by reason of Matter of State, for the Cause must be of higher or lower Nature. If it be for Suspicion of Treason, Misprision of Treason, or Felony, it may be by general Words couched; if it be for any other thing of smaller Nature, as Contempt, and the like, the particular Cause must be shewed, and no *individuum vagum*, or uncertain Cause to be admitted.

Again, if the Law be so clear as you make it, why needs the Declaration and Remonstrance in Parliament?

The Subject hath in this Case sued for Remedy in *King's-Bench* by *Habeas Corpus*, and found none; therefore it is necessary to be cleared in Parliament. And here ended his Discourse. And then he made a Recapitulation of all that had been offered unto their Lordships, that generally their Lordships had been advised by the most faithful Counsellors that can be; dead Men, these can't be daunted by Fear, nor misled by Affection, Reward, or Hope of Preferment, and therefore your Lordships might safely believe them: Particularly their Lordships had three several Kinds of Proofs.

1. Acts of Parliament, judicial Precedents, good Reasons. First, You have had many ancient Acts of Parliament in the Point, besides *Magna Charta*; that is, seven Acts of Parliament, which indeed are thirty-seven, *Magna Charta* being confirmed thirty times, for so often have the Kings of *England* given their Royal Assent thereto.

2. Judicial Precedents of grave and reverend Judges, *in terminis terminantibus*, that long since departed the World, and they were many in Number. Precedents being twelve, and the Judges four of a Bench, made four times twelve, and that is forty-eight Judges.

3. You have, as he termed them, *vividas rationes*, manifest and apparent Reasons: towards the Conclusion he declareth to their Lordships, that they of the House of Commons have, upon great Study and serious Consideration, made a great Manifestation unanimously, *Nullo contradicente*, concerning this great Liberty of the Subject, and have vindicated and recovered the Body of this fundamental Liberty, both of their Lordships and themselves, from Shadows, which some times of the Day are long, some times short, and some times long again; and therefore we must not be guided by Shadows: And they have transmitted to their Lordships, not *capita rerum*, Heads or Briefs, for these *compendia are dispendia*; but the Records at large, *in terminis terminantibus.* And so he concluded, that their Lordships are involved in the same Danger, and therefore *ex congruo & condigno*, they desired a Conference, to the End their Lordships might make the like Declaration as they had done; *Commune periculum requirit commune auxilium*; and thereupon take such further Course as may secure their Lordships and them, and all their Posterity, in enjoying of their ancient, undoubted, and fundamental Liberties.

The Substance of the Objections made by Mr. Attorney-General (Sir Robert Heath) *before a Committee of both Houses, to the Argument that was made by the House of Commons, at the first Conference with the Lords.*

AFTER the first Conference, which was desired by the Lords, and had by a Committee of both Houses in the Painted Chamber, touching the Reasons, Laws, Acts of Parliament, and Precedents concerning the Liberty of the Person of every Freeman; Mr. Attorney-General being heard before the Committee of both Houses, as it was assented to by the House of Commons, that he might be, before they went up to the conference; after some preamble made, wherein he declined the answering all Reasons of Law, and Acts of Parliament, came only to the precedents used in the argument before delivered; and so endeavoured to weaken the strength of them, that had been brought in behalf of the subjects, and to shew that some other were directly contrary to the Law, comprehended in the resolutions of the House of Commons, touching the bailing of prisoners, returned upon the Writ of *Habeas Corpus* to be committed by the special command of the King, or the Council, without any cause shewed, for which by Law they ought to be committed. And the course which was taken (it pleased the Committee of both Houses to allow of) was, that Mr. Attorney should make his objections to every particular precedent, and that the Gentlemen appointed, and trusted herein by the House of Commons, by several replies should satisfy the Lords touching the objections made by him, against, or upon every particular, as the order of the precedents should lead them. He began with the first twelve precedents that were used by the House of Commons at the conference desired by them, to prove that prisoners returned to stand so committed, were delivered upon bail by the Court of King's-Bench.

The first was that of *Bildeston*'s case, in the 18 *Edw.* III. *Rot.* 33.

To this he objected; first, that in the return of him into the Court, it did not appear, that this *Bildeston* was committed by the King's command; and secondly, that in the Record it did appear also that he had been committed for suspicion of counterfeiting the great Seal, and so by consequence was bailable by the Law, in regard there appeared a cause why he was committed: in which case it was granted by him (as indeed it was plain and agreed of all hands) that the prisoner is bailable, though committed by command of the King. And he said that this part of the Record, by which it appeared he had been committed for suspicion of Treason, was not observed to the Lords in the Argument before used; and he shewed also to the Lords, that there were three several kinds of Records, by which the full truth of every award, or bailing upon an *Habeas Corpus* is known. First, the Remembrance-Roll, wherein the award is given; secondly, the File of the Writ and the Return; and thirdly, the Scruet-Roll or Scruet *finium*, wherein the bail is entered, and that only the Remembrance-Roll of this case was to be found: and that if the other two of it were extant, he doubted not but that it would appear also, that upon the return itself the cause of the commitment had been expressed. And so he concluded, that this proved not for the Resolution of the House of Commons, touching the matter of bail, where a prisoner was committed by the King's special command without cause shewed.

To these objections the reply was, First, that it was plain that *Bildeston* was committed by the King's express command. For so the very words of the Writ are to the Constable of the Tower, *quod eum teneri & custodiri facias, &c.* than which nothing can more fully express a commitment by the King's command. Secondly, however it be true, that in the latter part of the Record it doth appear, that *Bildeston* had been committed for suspicion of Treason, yet if the times of the proceeding, expressed in the Record, were observed, it would be plain that the objection was of no force; for this one ground, both in this case and in all the rest, is infallible, and never to be doubted of in the Law, That Justices of every Court adjudge of the force and strength of a return out of the body of itself only, and as therein it appears. Now in *Easter* Term in the 18 *Edward* III. he was returned and brought before them, as committed only by the Writ; wherein no cause is expressed, and the Lieutenant and the Constable of the Tower, that brought him into the Court, says, that he had no other Warrant to detain him *nisi breve predictum*, wherein there was no mention of any cause; and the Court thereupon adjudged, that *breve predictum*, or that special command, was not sufficient cause to detain him in prison, and thereupon he is by judgment of the Court in *Easter* Term let to Mainprise. But that part of the Record wherein it appears, that he had indeed been committed for suspicion of Treason, is of *Trinity* Term following, when the King, after the letting of him to Mainprise, sent to the Judges that they should discharge his Mainprise, because no man prosecuted him. And at that time it appears (but not before) that he had been in for suspicion of Treason; so that he was returned to stand committed by the King's special command only, without cause shewed, in *Easter* Term, and then by judgment of the Court let to Mainprise, (which to this purpose is but the same with bail, though otherwise it differ). And in the Term following upon another occasion the Court knew, that he had been committed for suspicion of Treason, which has no relation at all to the letting of him to Mainprise, nor to the judgment of the Court then given; when they did not, nor could possibly know any cause for which the King had committed him. And it was said, in behalf of the House of Commons, that they had not indeed in their Argument expressly used this latter part of the Record of *Bildeston*'s case, because it being only of *Trinity* Term following, could not concern the Reason of an award given by the Court in *Easter* Term next before; yet notwithstanding that they had most faithfully, at the time of their argument, delivered in to the Lords, as indeed they had, a perfect copy at large of the whole Record of this case; as they had done also of all other precedents whatsoever cited by them; insomuch as in truth there was not one precedent of Record on either side, the copy whereof they had not delivered in likewise, nor did Mr. Attorney mention any one besides those that were so delivered in by them. And as touching those three kinds of Records, the Remembrance-Roll, the Return and File of the Writ, and Scruets; it was answered by the Gentlemen employed by the House of Commons, that it was true, that the Scruet and the Return of this case of *Bildeston* was not to be found; but that did not lessen the weight of the precedent, because always in the award or judgment drawn up in the Remembrance-Roll, the cause (whatsoever it be) when any is shewed, upon the Return is always expressed, as it appears clearly by the constant entries of the King's-Bench-Court. So that if any cause had appeared unto the Court, it must have appeared plainly in that part of the Roll which belongs to *Easter*-Term, wherein the judgment was given: but the return of the commitment by the King's command without cause shewed, and the judgment of the Court, that the prisoner was to be let to mainprise, appears therein only. And so, notwithstanding any objection made by Mr. Attorney, the cause was maintained to be a clear proof, among many others, touching that resolution of the House of Commons.

To the second of these twelve, which is *Parker*'s case, in the 22 *H.* VIII. *Rot.* 37. his objections were two; first, that it is true, that he was returned to be committed *per mandatum Domini Regis*; but it appeared that this command was certified to the Sherifs of *London* by one *Robert Peck* gentleman; and that in regard that the command came no otherwise, the return was held insufficient, and that therefore he was bailed. Secondly, that it appears also in the Record, that he was committed *pro suspicione feloniæ ac per mandatum Domini Regis*: so that in regard that the expression of the cause of his commitment, suspicion of felony, precedes the command of the King, therefore it must be intended that the Court took the cause why the King committed him to be of less moment than felony, and therefore bailed him. For he objected, that even the House of Commons themselves, in some arguments used by them, touching the interpretation of the Statute of *Westminster* the first, *cap.* 15. about this point, had affirmed, that in enumeration of particulars, those of greatest nature were first mentioned, and that it was supposed, that such as followed were usually of less nature or moment.

But the reply was to the first objection, that the addition of the certifying of the King's command by *Robert Peck*, altered not the case: First, because the Sheriffs in their return took notice of the command as what they were assured of; and then howsoever it came to them, it was of equal force, as if it had been mentioned without reference to *Peck*. Secondly, As divers Patents pass the great Seal by Writ of Privy-Seal, and are subscribed *per breve de privato sigillo*; so divers *per ipsum Regem*, are so subscribed; and oftentimes in the Roll of former times, to the words *per ipsum Regem*, are added *nunciante A. B.* So that the King's command generally, and the King's command related or certified by such a man, is to this purpose of like nature. Thirdly, in the late great case of *Habeas Corpus*, where the return of the commitment was *per speciale mandatum Domini Regis mihi significatum per Dominos de privato Concilio*; the Court of King's-Bench did agree, that it was the same, and of like force as if *mihi significatum, &c.* had not followed, and that those words were void. According whereunto, here also *per mandatum Dom. Regis nunciatum per Robert Peck*, had been wholly omitted and void likewise. And in truth in that late case, this case of *Parker* was cited both at the Bar and Bench: and at the Bench it was interpreted by the Judges no otherwise, than if it had been only *per mandatum Domini Regis* in place of it: but the objection there was made of another kind, as was delivered in the first argument, made out of precedents in behalf of the House of Commons. Therefore to the second objection, touching the course of enumeration of the causes in the return, it was said, that howsoever in some Acts of Parliament, and elsewhere in the solemn expressions used in the Law, things of greater nature preceded, and the less follow; yet in this case, the contrary was most plain, for in the return it appears, that there were three causes for detaining the prisoners; Surety of the peace, suspicion of felony, and the King's command: and Surety of the peace is first mentioned, which is plainly less than felony. And therefore it is plain, if any force of argument be taken from this enumeration, that the contrary to that which Mr. Attorney inferred is to be concluded; that is, that as felony is a greater cause than Surety of the peace, so the matter whereupon the King's command was grounded, was greater than Felony. But in truth this kind of argument holds neither way here, and whatsoever the cause were, why the King committed him, it was impossible for the Court to know it: and it also might be of very high moment in matter of State, and yet of far less nature than felony. All which shews, that this precedent hath its full force also, according as it was first used in argument by the House of Commons.

To the third of these, which is *Binck*'s case in the 35 *H.* VIII. *Rot.* 33. the objection was, that there was a cause expressed *pro suspicione feloniæ*: and though *pro aliis causis illos moventibus* were added in the return, yet because in the course of enumeration, the general name of *aliis* coming after particulars, includes things of less nature than the particular doth, therefore in this case suspicion of felony being the first, the other causes afterwards generally mentioned must be intended of less nature, for which the prisoner was bailable, because he was bailable for the greater, which was suspicion of felony. Hereunto it was replied, that the argument of enumeration in these cases is of no moment, as is next before shewed: and that although it were of any moment, yet *aliæ causæ*, though less than felony, might be of very great consequence in matter of State, which is pretended usually upon general returns of command, without cause shewed; and it is most plain, that the Court could not possibly know the reasons, why the prisoner here was committed, and yet they bailed him, without looking further after any unknown thing under that title of matter of State, which might as well have been in this case as in any other whatsoever.

To the fourth of these, which is *Overton*'s case, in *Pasch.* 2. & 3. *Phil. & Mar. Rot.* 58. And to the fifth, which is *Newport*'s case, *Pasch. Phil. & Mar.* 4 & 5 *Rot.* 45. only these objections were said over again by Mr. Attorney, which are mentioned in the argument made out of the precedents in behalf of the House of Commons at the first conference; and in the same argument are fully and clearly satisfied, as they were in like manner now again.

To the sixth of these, which was *Lawrence*'s case, 9 *Eliz. Rot.* 35. and the seventh, which is *Constable*'s, *Pasch.* 9 *Eliz. Rot.* 68. the same objections were likewise said over again by Mr. Attorney, that are mentioned, and are clearly and fully answered in the argument made at the conference out of precedents in behalf of the House of Commons; the force of the objection being only, that it appeared in the margin of the Roll, that the word *Pardon* was written: but it is plain that the word there hath no reference at all to the reason why they were bailed, nor could it have reference to the cause why they were committed, in regard the cause why they were committed is utterly unknown, and was not shewed.

To the eighth of these precedents, which was *Browning*'s case, *Pasch.* 20 *Eliz. Rot.* 72. it was said by Mr. Attorney, that he was bailed by a letter from the Lords of the Council, directed to the Judges of the Court; but ut being asked for that letter, or any testimony of it, he could produce none at all; but said, he thought the testimony of it was burnt, among many other things of the Council-table at the burning of the Banqueting-House.

To the 9th, being *Harecourt's* case, *Pasch.* 40 *Eliz. Rot.* 62. the selfsame objection was made by him, but no warrant was shewed to maintain his objection.

To the 10th, which is *Catesby's* case, *in vacatione Hill.* 43 *Eliz.* he said, that it was by direction of a Privy-Seal from the Queen; and to that purpose he shewed the Privy-Seal of 43 *Eliz.* which is at large among the transcripts of the Records concerning bails taken in cases, where the King or the Lords assented. But it was replied, That the Privy-Seal was made only for some particular Gentlemen mentioned in it, and for none other, as indeed appears in it: and then he said, that it was likely that *Catesby* here had a Privy-Seal in this behalf, because those other had so; which was all the force of his objection.

To the 11th of these, which is *Beckwith's* case in *Hill.* 12 *Jac. Rot.* 153. he said, that the Lords of the Council sent a letter to the Court of King's-Bench to bail him. And indeed he produced a letter, which could not by any means be found when the arguments were made at the first conference: and this letter, and a copy of an obscure report made by a young student (which was brought to another purpose, as is hereafter shewed), were the only things written of any kind that Mr. Attorney produced, besides the particulars shewed by the House of Commons at the first conference. To this it was replied, That the letter was of no moment, being only a direction to the Chief-Justice, and no matter of Record, nor any way concerning the rest of the Judges: and besides, either the prisoner was bailable by the Law, or not bailable: if bailable by the Law, then he was to be bailed without any such letter; if not bailable by the Law, then plainly the Judges could not have bailed him upon the letter, without breach of their oath, which is, *That they are to do justice according to the Law, without having respect to any command whatsoever.* So that the letter in this case, or the like in any other case, is for point of Law to no purpose, nor hath any weight at all by way of objection against what the Record and the Judgment of the Court shew us.

To the 12th and last of these, which is Sir *Thomas Monson's* case in the 14 *Jac. Rot.* 147. the same objection only was said over by him, which was mentioned and clearly answered in the argument; and that one ground which is infallible, *That the judgment upon a return is to be made only out of what appears in the body of the return itself*, was again insisted upon in this case, as it was also in most of the the rest. And indeed that alone which is most clear Law, fully satisfies almost all kind of objections that have been made to any of these precedents; which, thus rightly understood, are many ample testimonies of the Judgment of the Court of King's-Bench, touching this great point, in the several ages, and reigns of the several princes under which they fall.

After his objections to the twelve, and the replies and satisfactions given to these objections, he came next to those wherein the assent of the King and Privy-Council appears to have been upon the enlargement: but he made not to any of these any other kind of objections whatsoever, than such as are mentioned and clearly answered (as they were now again) in the argument made at the first conference. And for so much as concerns letters of assent or direction, the same was here said again by way of reply to him, as is before said touching the letter in *Beckwith's* case.

After these were dispatched, he came to urge the eight precedents, which seemed to make for the other side against the resolution of the House of Commons: which eight were used, and copies of them also were given in to the Lords at the first conference.

Of these eight, the first four were urged by him, as being of one kind; the difference of them only being such, that, save only in the names of prisons and of persons, they are but the self-same.

To the force of these four he objected thus: that *Richard Everard* (for the purpose) in the first of them, which is 5 *H.* VII. *Rot.* 18. *Roger Cherry* in the second of them, which is 8 *H.* VII. *Rot.* 12. *Christopher Burton*, in the third of them, which is 9 *H.* VII *Rot.* 14. and *George Urswick* in the fourth of them, which is 19 *H.* VII. *Rot.* 13. were returned into the King's-Bench upon several Writs of *Habeas Corpus*, to have been committed and detained in the several prisons whence they came *per mandatum Domini Regis*, and that upon that return they were committed to the Marshal of the King's-Bench; and that however it had been objected against those precedents, that this kind of commitment was by the course of that Court, always done before the bailing of the prisoner, yet that it did not appear that they were bailed.

The Reply to this objection was, That by constant course of King's-Bench, whosoever came in upon *Habeas Corpus*, or otherwise upon any Writ in that Court, cannot be bailed until he be first committed to the Marshal of that Court; and that thence it was, that all those four were committed to the Marshal, as appears by the entry, *Qui committitur Marescallo, &c.* which is the usual entry in such a case, and that the Clerks of that Court acknowledge this course and entry to be most constant. So that all the inference, that can be made out of these four is, that four prisoners being brought from four several prisons by *Habeas Corpus* into the King's-Bench, and returned to stand committed *per mandatum Domini Regis*, were so far from being remanded by the Law, that in all these four cases, they were first taken from the several prisons, wherein they had been detained, by such a general command (which could not have been if they had not been adjudged in every one of the cases to have been bailable by the Court), and that this commitment of them to the Marshal of the King's-Bench, was the first step towards the bailing of them, as in all other cases. But that it appears not, that either they ever demanded to be bailed, or that they were able to find sufficient bail: and if they did not the one, or could not do the other, it may follow indeed that they were not bailed. But this commitment to the King's-Bench being the first step to the bailing of them (as by the constant course it is) shews most plainly that they were bailable by the Law, which is the only thing in question. So that altho' these four precedents were ranked among them, that may seem to make against the resolution of the House of Commons, which was done, both because they have this small colour in them for the other side, to any man that is not acquainted with the nature and reasons of the entries, and courses of the Court of King's-Bench, and also because all or some of them had been used in the late great case in the King's-Bench, as precedents that made against the liberty claimed by the subject; yet, in truth, all four of them do fully prove their resolution: that is, they plainly shew that the Court of King's-Bench in every one of them resolved, that the prisoners so committed were bailable, otherwise they had been remanded, and not committed to the Marshal of the King's-Bench. And this was the answer to the objection made by Mr. Attorney upon those four precedents, being all of the time of King *Henry* the seventh.

To the fifth of these eight, being *Edward Page's* Case, in 7 *H.* VIII. *Rot.* 23. Mr. Attorney objected thus: He said, that *Edward Page* was committed to the Marshalsea of the Houshold, *per mandatum Domini Regis ibidem salvo custodiend.* &c. *Qui committitur Marescallo, &c. Hospitii Domini Regis.* By which it appeareth, as he said, that the Court remanded him back to the prison of the Marshalsea of the Houshold: and he said, that whereas it had been objected at the first conference, that there was some mistaking in the entry; he conceived, indeed, that there was a mistaking, but it was that the Clerk had entred *committitur* for *remittitur*, and that it should have been *Qui remittitur Marescallo Hospitii Domini Regis*: for whenever they remanded the prisoner, *remittitur*, and not *committitur* should be entered. And that mistaking being so rectified and understood, he conceived it was a direct precedent against the resolution of the House of Commons.

To this it was answered by the Gentlemen of the House of Commons, That there was no doubt, indeed, but that a mistake was in the entry by the Clerk, but that the mistaking was quite of another nature. The addition of those words, *hospitii Dom. Regis*, was the mistaking, and the entry should have been, *qui committitur Marescallo, &c.* only; that is, he was committed to the Marshal of the King's-Bench; and so indeed the force of this precedent should be but just the same with the first four: but the ignorance of the Clerk that entered it, knowing not how to distinguish between the Marshal of the Houshold and the Marshal of the King's-Bench, was the cause of the addition of these words, *hospitii Dom. Regis.*

And to confirm fully this kind of interpretation of that precedent, and of the mistaking of it, it was observed by the Gentlemen of the House of Commons, that there is in the margin of the Roll an infallible character that justifies so much. For by the course of that Court, whensoever a prisoner is committed to the Marshal of the King's-Bench and not remanded, the word *Marescallo* is written in the margin short by *Marr'* turned up, and that is never written there, but when the meaning and sense of the entry is, that the prisoner is committed to the prison of the same Court. Now in this case *Marr'* in the Margin is likewise written: which most clearly shews that the truth of this case was, that this *Page* was committed to the Marshal of the King's-Bench, and not remanded; which if it had been, neither could the entry have been *committitur*, nor should the margin of the Roll have had *Marr'* written in it.

And thus they have answered Mr. Attorney's objections touching this precedent, and concluded that now, besides the first four of the eight, they had another, and so five to prove that a prisoner committed *per mandatum Domini Regis*, generally was bailable by the judgment of the Court. However, it appears not in these particulars that they were bailed; which perhaps they were not, either because they prayed it not, or because they could not find sufficient bail.

The sixth of these precedents, being the case of *Thomas Cæsar*, in the 8 *Jac. Regis Rot.* 99. Mr. Attorney objected to it thus: That *Cæsar* being committed *per mandatum Domini Regis* to the Marshalsea of the Household, was returned upon *Habeas Corpus* to be so committed, and therefore detained in prison, and that the entry is, *Qui committitur prisonæ Marescal. prædict.* by which it appears clearly, that he was remanded to the same prison from whence he came.

To this the Gentlemen of the House of Commons gave this answer: They said, that the usual entry of a *remittitur*, when it is to shew that the Court by way of judgment, or award upon a resolution, or debate, remands the prisoner, is, *remittitur quousque secundum legem deliberatus fuerit*: but when they advise, or give way to the Keeper of the prison to amend his return, or the like, then the entry is only *remittitur* generally, or *remittitur prisonæ prædict.* But it was indeed affirmed by Mr. *Keeling*, a Clerk of great experience in that Court, that the entry of a *Remittitur* generally, or *remittitur prisonæ prædictæ* was indifferently used for the same, as *remittitur quousque*, &c. Yet it was expresly shewed by the Gentlemen of the House of Commons, that there was sometimes a difference, and that so it might well be in this case. For in the last of these eight precedents, which is *Saltonstall's* case, they observed that *remittitur prisonæ prædictæ* is often used; and that it is twice used only for a remanding, during the time that the Court gave leave to the Warden of the Fleet to amend his return; which shews plainly, that tho' sometimes *remittitur* generally, and *remittitur quousque*, &c. may mean the same, yet sometimes it doth not. And that, in this case of *Cæsar* it doth not mean any other, but only so much as it doth twice in that of *Saltonstall's* case, was proved also by a rule of the Court, which was cited out of the rule-book of the Court of King's-Bench, by which rule the Court expresly ordered, that unless the Steward and Marshal of the Houshold did sufficiently return the Writ of *Habeas Corpus* for *Cæsar*, that he should be discharged. The words of the rule are, *Nisi prædicti Senescallus & Marescallus hospitii Domini Regis sufficienter retornaverint breve de Habeas Corpus, Tho. Cæsar die Mercurii proximæ post quindenam Sancti Martini de prisona exonerabitur.* And this was the opinion of the Court; which shews that the Court was so far from remanding him upon the return, that they resolved, that unless some better return were made, the prisoner should be discharged of his first imprisonment, though it appeared to them out of the body of the return (upon which they were only to judge), that he was committed *per mandatum Domini Regis* only. And the rule not only shews the opinion of the Court then to have been agreeable with the resolution of the House of Commons, but also proves that *Remittitur* generally, or *Remittitur prisonæ prædictæ*, doth not always imply a remanding upon judgment or debate. And this answer was given to this of *Cæsar's* case, that is the sixth of this number.

The

The ſeventh is the caſe of *James Demetrius*. It was 12 *Jac. Rot.* 153. Mr. Attorney objected that this *Demetrius* and divers others being Brewers, were committed *per concilium Domini Regis* to the Marſhalſea of the Houſhold, and that upon the commitment ſo generally returned, they were remanded, and that the entry was *immediate remittitur præfato Mareſcallo hoſpitii prædicti*; where he obſerved, that *immediate* ſhews that the Judges of that time were ſo reſolved of this Queſtion, that they remanded them preſently, as men that well knew what the Law was herein.

Hereunto the Gentlemen of the Houſe of Commons gave theſe anſwers. Firſt, That the *Remittitur* in this caſe is but as the other in *Cæſar*'s, and ſo proves nothing againſt them. Secondly, That *immediate* being added to it, ſhews plainly that it was done without debate, or any argument or conſideration had of it, which makes the authority of the precedents to be of no force in point of Law, for judgments and awards given upon deliberation only and debate are proofs and arguments of weight, and not any ſudden Act of the Court without debate or deliberation. And the entry of *immediate* being propoſed by Mr. *Keeling*, it was confirmed by him, that by that entry it appears by this courſe, that the remanding of him was the ſelf-ſame day he was brought, which, as it was ſaid by the Gentlemen of the Houſe of Commons, might be at the riſing of the Court, or upon adviſement, and the like. And this anſwer was given to this precedent of the Brewers.

The laſt of the eight, to which Mr. Attorney objected, is *Saltonſtall*'s caſe, in the 13 *Jac Regis*. He was committed *per mandatum Dominorum Regis de privato Concilio*: and being returned by the Warden of the Fleet to be ſo, *Remittitur priſonæ prædictæ*; and in the 13 *Jac.* in the ſame caſe there is *remittitur* generally in the Roll. And theſe two make but one caſe, and are as one precedent.

To this the Gentlemen of the Houſe of Commons anſwered, That it is true, the Rolls have ſuch entries of *remittitur* in them generally, but that proves nothing upon the reaſon before uſed by them in *Cæſar*'s caſe. But alſo *Saltonſtall* was committed for another cauſe beſides *per mandatum Dom. Regis*, a contempt againſt an order in the Chancery, and that was in the return alſo. And beſides the Court, as it appears in the Record, gave ſeveral days to the Warden of the Fleet to amend his return, which they would not have done, if they had conceived it ſufficient, for that which is ſufficient needs not amendment.

To this Mr. Attorney replied, That they gave him a day to amend his return, in reſpect of that part of it which concerns the order in Chancery, and not in reſpect of that which was *per mandatum Dom. Regis*. But the Gentlemen of the Houſe of Commons anſwered, That that appeared not any where, nor indeed is it likely at all, nor can be reaſonably ſo underſtood, becauſe if the other return *per mandatum Dom. Regis* had been ſufficient by itſelf, then doubtleſs they would have remanded him upon that alone, for then they needed not at all to have ſtood upon the other part of the return in this caſe. So that out of the Record itſelf it appears fully, that the Court conceived the return to be inſufficient.

So the Gentlemen of the Houſe of Commons concluded, that they had a great number of precedents beſides divers Acts of Parliament, and Reaſons of Common Law, agreeable to their reſolution, and that there was not one precedent at all that made againſt them, but indeed, that almoſt all that were brought, as well againſt them as for them, if rightly underſtood, made fully for the maintenance of their reſolution: and that there was not one example or precedent of a *Remittitur* in any kind upon the point before that of *Cæſar*'s caſe, which is before cleared with the reſt, and is but of late time, and of no moment againſt the reſolution of the Houſe of Commons.

And thus, for ſo much as concerned the precedents of Record, the firſt day of the conference deſired by the Lords ended.

The next day they deſired another conference with the Houſe of Commons, at which it pleaſed the Committee of both Houſes to hear Mr. Attorney again make what objections he could againſt other parts of the argument formerly delivered from the Houſe of Commons. He then objected againſt the Acts of Parliament, and againſt the Reaſons of Law, and his objections to thoſe parts were anſwered, as it appears by the anſwers by order given into the Houſe of Commons by the Gentlemen that made them. [*Vide poſtea*, p. 180.] He objected alſo upon the ſecond day againſt the ſecond kind of precedents, which are reſolutions of Judges in former times, and not of Record, and brought alſo ſome other teſtimonies of the opinions of Judges in former times, touching this point.

Firſt, for that reſolution of all the Judges of *England* in 34 *Eliz.* mentioned and read in the arguments at the firſt conference, he ſaid, That it was directly againſt the reſolution of the Houſe of Commons, and obſerved the words of it in one place to be, that perſons ſo committed by the King, or by the Council, may not be delivered by any of the Courts, &c. And in another, that if the cauſe were expreſſed, either in general or in ſpecialty, it was ſufficient; and he ſaid that the expreſſing of a cauſe in generality was to ſhew the King or the Council's command: and to this purpoſe, he read the whole words of that reſolution of the Judges. Then he objected alſo, that in the report of one *Roſwell*'s caſe in the King's-Bench, in 13 *Jac.* he found that the opinion of the Judges of that Court (Sir *Edward Coke* being then chief Judge and one of them) was, that a priſoner being committed *per mandatum Dom. Regi*, or *privati Concilii*, without cauſe ſhewed, and ſo returned, could not be bailed becauſe it might be matter of State, or *Arcana Imperii*, for which he ſtood committed. And to this alſo he added, an opinion he found in a Journal in the Houſe of Commons of 13 *Jac.* wherein Sir *Edward Coke* ſpeaking to a bill preferred for the explanation of *Magna Charta* touching impriſonment, ſaid in the ſame Houſe, That one ſo committed could not be inlarged by the Law, becauſe it might be matter of State for which he was committed. And amongſt theſe objections of the other nature alſo, he ſpake of the confidence that was ſhewed in behalf of the Houſe of Commons: and he ſaid, it was not confidence of either part could add any thing to the determination of the queſtion, but if it could, that he had as much reaſon of confidence for the other ſide againſt the reſolution of the Houſe of Commons, grounding himſelf upon the force of his objections, which, as he conceived, had ſo weakened the arguments of the Houſe of Commons.

To this a reply was made; and firſt it was ſaid to the Lords on the behalf of the Houſe of Commons, That notwithſtanding any thing yet objected, they were upon clear reaſon ſtill confident of the truth of their firſt reſolution, grounded upon ſo juſt examination, and deliberation taken by them. And it was obſerved to the Lords alſo, that their confidence herein was of another nature, and of greater weight, than any confidence that could be expreſſed by Mr. Attorney, or whomſoever elſe being of his Majeſty's Counſel learned.

To which purpoſe the Lords were deſired to take into their memories the difference between the preſent qualities of the Gentlemen that ſpake in behalf of the Houſe of Commons, and of the King's learned Counſel in their ſpeaking there, howſoever accidentally they were both men of the ſame profeſſion: for the King's Counſel ſpake as Counſel perpetually retained by Fee, and if they made gloſſes or what advantageous interpretation ſoever for their own part, they did but what belonged to their place and quality, as Mr. Attorney had done. But the Gentlemen that ſpake in behalf of the Houſe of Commons, came there, bound on the one ſide by the truſt repoſed in them by their Country that ſent them, and on the other ſide by an oath taken by every of them before he ſit in the Houſe, to maintain and defend the Rights and Prerogatives of the Crown: ſo that even in the point of confidence alone, thoſe of them that ſpeak as retained Counſel by perpetual Fee, and thoſe that by their place being admitted to ſpeak, are bound to utter nothing but truth, both by ſuch a truſt and ſuch an oath, were no way to be ſo compared or counterpoiſed, as if the one were of no more weight than the other.

And then the objections before mentioned were alſo anſwered.

For that of the reſolution of all the Judges in *England* in 34 *Eliz.* it was ſhewed, that plainly it agreed with the reſolution of the Houſe of Commons: for although indeed it might have been expreſſed with more perſpicuity, yet the words of it, as they are, ſufficiently ſhew the meaning of it to be no otherwiſe. To that purpoſe, beſides the words of the whole frame of this reſolution of the Judges, as it is in the copy tranſcribed out of the Lord Chief Juſtice *Anderſon*'s Book, written in his own hand, which book was here offered to be ſhewed in the behalf of the Houſe of Commons; it was obſerved, that the words of the firſt part of it ſhew plainly, that all the Judges of *England* then reſolved, that the priſoners ſpoken of in the firſt part of their reſolution were only priſoners committed with cauſe ſhewed; for they only ſay they might not be delivered by any Court without due trial by Law, and judgment of acquittal had; which ſhews plainly they meant that by trial and acquittal they might be delivered. But it is clear that no trial or acquittal can be had, where there is not ſome cauſe laid to their charge, for which they ought to ſtand committed. Therefore in that part of the reſolution ſuch priſoners are only meant as are committed with cauſe ſhewed, which alſo the Judges in that reſolution expreſly thought neceſſary, as appears in the ſecond part of their reſolution, wherein they have theſe words: " If upon the return of " their *Habeas Corpus*, the cauſe of their commitment be certified to the " Judges, as it ought to be, &c." By which words they ſhew plainly, that every return of a commitment is inſufficient that hath not a cauſe ſhewed of it. And to that which Mr. Attorney ſaid, as if the cauſe were ſufficiently expreſſed in generality, if the King's command or the Council's were expreſſed in it, as if that were meant in the reſolution for a ſufficient general cauſe; it was anſwered, That it was never heard of in Law, that the power or perſon that committed the priſoner was underſtood for the *cauſa captionis* or *cauſa detentionis*, but only the reaſon why that power or perſon committed the priſoner. As alſo in common ſpeech, if any man aſk why or for what cauſe a man ſtands committed, the anſwer is not, that ſuch a one committed him, but his offence or ſome other cauſe is underſtood in the queſtion, and is to be ſhewed in the anſwer. But to ſay that ſuch a one committed the priſoner, is an anſwer only to the queſtion, who committed him? and not why, or for what cauſe he ſtands ſo committed?

Then for that of the copy of the report, in 13 *Jac.* ſhewed forth by Mr. Attorney, it was anſwered by the Gentlemen of the Houſe of Commons, That the report itſelf which had been before ſeen, and peruſed among many other things at a Committee made by the Houſe, was of ſlight or no authority, for that it was taken by one, who was at that time a young ſtudent, and as a reporter in the King's Bench, and there was not any other report to be found that agreed with it. Secondly, Although the reports of young ſtudents, when they take the words of Judges as they fall from their mouths at the Bench, and in the ſame perſon and form as they have ſpoken, may be of good credit, yet in this caſe there was not one word ſo reported: but in truth there being three caſes at a time in the *King's-Bench*, one *Roſwell*'s caſe, *Allen*'s, and *Saltonſtall*'s caſe, every of which had ſomething of like nature in it, the ſtudent having been preſent in the Court, made up the frame of one report or caſe out of all three in his own words, and ſo put it into his Book. ſo that there is not a word in the report, but it is framed according to the ſtudent's fancy, as it is written; and nothing is expreſſed in it, as it came from the mouth of the Judges, otherwiſe than his fancy directed him.

Thirdly, There are in the report plain falſhoods of matter of fact, which are to be attributed either to the Judges or to the Reporter. It is moſt likely by all reaſon, that they proceeded from the Reporter's fault; howſoever, theſe matters of falſhood ſhew ſufficiently that the credit of the reſt is of light value. It is ſaid in the report, that *Harcourt* being committed by the Council, was bailed, in 40 *Eliz.* upon a Privy-Seal or a Letter, whereas in truth there is no ſuch thing. And it is ſaid there, that kind of Letters are filed in the Crown-Office, whereas in truth there was not any ſuch kind of Letters filed there in any office whatſoever. That Reſolution of the Judges in 34 *Eliz.* is miſ-cited there, and made in 35 *Eliz.* And it is ſaid there, that by that Reſolution a priſoner committed by the command of the King might not at all be delivered by the Court, whereas no ſuch thing is comprehended in that Reſolution.

But that which is of moſt moment is, that howſoever [illegible] the report were, yet the opinion of the Judges [illegible] the Judges late had of the caſe, is of light moment [illegible] points eſpecially, the moſt grave and learned men living may on a ſudden let fall (and

that

that without any diſparagement to them) ſuch opinions as they may well, and ought to change upon further inquiry, examination, and full debate had before them, and mature deliberation taken by them. Now plainly in that of 13 *Jac.* there is not ſo much as a pretence of any debate at the Bar or Bench. All that is reported to have been, is reported as ſpoken of the ſudden. And can any man take ſuch a ſudden opinion to be of value againſt ſolemn debates and mature deliberations ſince had of the point? And indeed this great point, and all circumſtances belonging to it, have within this half year, been ſo fully examined and ſearched into, that it may well be affirmed, that the moſt learned man whatſoever that hath now conſidered of it, hath within that time, or might have, learned more reaſon of ſatisfaction in it, than ever before he met with. Therefore the ſudden opinion of the Judges to the contrary is of no value here, which alſo is to be ſaid of that opinion obviouſly delivered in the Commons Houſe in 18 *Jac.* as Mr. Attorney objected out of the Journal of the Houſe. But beſides, neither was the truth of that report of that opinion in the Journal any way acknowledged, for it was ſaid in behalf of the Houſe of Commons, that their Journals were for matters of Orders and Reſolutions of the Houſe of ſuch authority, as that they were as their Records. But for any particular man's opinion, noted in any of them, it was ſo far from being of any authority with them, that in truth no particular opinion is at all to be entered in them, and that their Clerk offends, whenever he doth to the contrary. And to conclude, no ſuch opinion whatſoever can be ſufficient to weaken the clear Law comprehended in theſe Reſolutions of the Houſe of Commons, grounded upon ſo many Acts of Parliament, ſo much Reaſon of the Common-Law, and ſo many Precedents of Record, and the Reſolution of all the Judges of *England*; and againſt which not one Law, written or unwritten, not one Precedent, not one Reaſon hath been brought, that makes any thing to the contrary

And thus ended the next day of the Conference deſired by the Lords, and had by a Committee of both Houſes.

Serjeant Aſhley's *Argument, ſeconding Mr.* Attorney, *in the behalf of his Majeſty.*

I Hope it will be neither offenſive nor tedious to your Lordſhips, if I ſaid ſomewhat to ſecond Mr. Attorney: which I the rather deſire, becauſe yeſterday it was taken by the Gentlemen, and argued on the behalf of the Commons, that the cauſe was as good as gained by them, and yielded by us, in that we acknowledged the Statute of *Magna Charta*, and the other ſubſequent Statutes to be yet in force: for on that they inforced this general concluſion:

That therefore no man could be committed, or impriſoned, but by due proceſs, preſentment or indictment.

Which we ſay is a *Non ſequitur* upon ſuch our acknowledgement; for then it would follow by neceſſary conſequence, that no impriſonment could be juſtified but by proceſs of law, which we utterly deny. For in the cauſe of the Conſtable cited by Mr. Attorney, it is moſt clear, that by the ancient law of the land a Conſtable might, *ex officio*, without any Warrant, arreſt and reſtrain a man to prevent an affray, or to ſuppreſs it. And ſo is the authority 38 *Hen.* VIII. *Brook's abſtract.* So may he, after the affray, apprehend and commit to priſon the perſon that hath wounded a man that is in peril of death, and that without warrant or proceſs; as it is in 38 *Edw.* III. *fol.* 6.

Alſo any man that is no Officer may apprehend a Felon without Writ, or Warrant, or purſue him as a Wolf, and as a common enemy to the Commonwealth, as the Book is 14 *Hen.* VIII. *fol.* 16. So might any one arreſt a Night-walker, becauſe it is for the common profit, as the reaſon is given 4 *Hen.* VII. *fol.* 7.

In like manner the Judges in theſe ſeveral Courts may commit a man, either for contempt, or miſdemeanor, without either Proceſs or Warrant, other than Take him Sheriff, or Take him Marſhal, or Warden of the *Fleet*. And the adverſaries will not deny, but if the King will alledge cauſe, he may commit a man *per mandatum* as the Judges do, without Proceſs or Warrant.

And various are the caſes that may be inſtanced, wherein there may be a lawful commitment without proceſs. Wherefore I do poſitively and with confidence affirm, that if the impriſonment be lawful, whether it be by proceſs, or without proceſs, it is not prohibited by the law.

Which being granted, then the queſtion will aptly be made, Whether the King or Council may commit to priſon *per legem terræ*, were only that a part of the Municipal Law of this Realm, which we call the Common-Law? For there are alſo divers juriſdictions in this Kingdom, which are alſo reckoned the law of the land.

As in *Cawdry's* caſe in *Coke's* 5th report, *fol.* 1. the firſt *Eccleſiaſtical* Law is held the law of the land, to puniſh Blaſphemies, Schiſms, Hereſies, Simony, Inceſt, and the like, for a good reaſon there rendered, *viz.* That otherwiſe the King ſhould not have power to do Juſtice to his Subjects in all caſes, nor to puniſh all crimes within his Kingdom.

The Admiral's juriſdiction is alſo *lex terræ*, or things done upon the Sea: but if they exceed their juriſdiction, a prohibition is awarded upon the Statute of *nullus liber homo*; by which appears that the Statute is in force, as we have acknowledged.

The Martial Law likewiſe, though not to be exerciſed in times of peace, when recourſe may be had to the King's Courts, yet in times of invaſion, or other times of Hoſtility, when an Army-Royal is in the field, and offences are committed, which require ſpeedy reformation, and cannot expect the ſolemnity of legal Trials; then ſuch impriſonment, execution, or other juſtice done by the Law Martial is warrantable, for it is then the law of the land, and is *jus gentium*, which ever ſerves for a ſupply in the defect of the Common Law, when ordinary proceeding cannot be had.

And ſo it is alſo in the caſe of the Law of the Merchant, which is mentioned 13 *Edw.* IV. *fol.* 9, 10. where a Merchant-ſtranger was wronged in his goods, which he had committed to a Carrier to convey to *Southampton*, and the Carrier imbezzled ſome of the goods: for remedy whereof the Merchant ſued before the Council in the *Star-Chamber* for redreſs. It is there ſaid thus: Merchant-ſtrangers have by the King ſafe-conduct for coming into this Realm; therefore they ſhall not be compelled to attend the ordinary Trial of the Common Law, but, for expedition, ſhall ſue before the King's Council, or in Chancery, *de die in diem & de horâ in horam*; where the caſe ſhall be determined by the Law of Merchants.

In the like manner it is in the Law of State; when the neceſſity of State requires it, they do and may proceed to natural equity; as in thoſe other caſes where the law of the land provides not, there the proceeding may be by the law of natural equity: and infinite are the occurrences of State, unto which the Common Law extends not. And if theſe proceedings of State ſhould not alſo be accounted the law of the land, then we do fall into the ſame inconveniency mentioned in *Cawdry's* caſe, that the King ſhould not be able to do Juſtice in all caſes within his own Dominions.

If then the King nor his Council may not commit, it muſt needs follow, that either the King muſt have no Council of State, or having ſuch a Council, they muſt have no power to make Orders, or Acts of State; or if they may, they muſt be without means to compel obedience to thoſe Acts: and ſo we ſhall allow them juriſdiction, but not compel obedience to thoſe Acts; but not correction, which will be then as fruitleſs as the command. *Fruſtra potentia quæ nunquam redigitur in ſtatutum.* Whereas the very Act of *Weſtminſter* the firſt, ſhews plainly that the King may commit, and that his commitment is lawful, or elſe that Act would never have declared a man to be irrepleviable when he is committed by the command of the King, if the Law-makers had conceived that his commitment had been unlawful. And Divine Truth informs us, that the Kings have their power from God, the *Pſalmiſt* calling them *the Children of the Moſt High*; which is in a more ſpecial manner underſtood than of other men: for all the ſons of *Adam* are by election the ſons of God, and all the ſons of *Abraham* by recreation, or regeneration, the children of the Moſt High, in reſpect of the power which is committed unto them; who hath alſo furniſhed them with ornaments and arms fit for the exerciſing of that power, and hath given them Scepters, Swords, and Crowns; Scepters to inſtitute, and Swords to execute laws; and Crowns as Enſigns of that power and dignity, with which they are inveſted. Shall we then conceive that our King hath ſo far tranſmitted the power of his Sword to inferior Magiſtrates, that he hath not reſerved ſo much ſupreme power as to commit an offender to priſon? 10 *Hen.* VI. *fol.* 7. it appears that a Steward of a Court-Leet may commit a man to priſon, and ſhall not the King, from whom all inferior power is deduced, have power to commit? We call him the Fountain of Juſtice, yet when theſe ſtreams and rivulets, which flow from that fountain, come freſh and full, we would ſo far exhauſt that fountain, as to leave it dry. But they that will admit him ſo much power, do require the expreſſion of the cauſe; I demand whether they will have a general cauſe alledged, or a ſpecial? If general, as they have inſtances for Treaſon, Felony, or for Contempt, (for to leave fencing, and to ſpeak plainly as they intend it) *viz.* If Loan of money ſhould be required and refuſed, and thereupon a commitment enſue, and the cauſe ſignified to be for Contempt, this being unequal inconvenience from yielding, the remedy is ſought; in the next Parliament would be required the expreſſion of the particular cauſe of the commitment. Then how unfit would it be for King or Council in caſes to expreſs the particular cauſe, it's eaſily to be adjudged, when there is no State, or Policy of Government, whether it be Monarchical, or of any other frame, which have not ſome Secrets of State, not communicable to vulgar underſtanding.

I will inſtance but one; if a King imploy an Ambaſſador to a Foreign Country or State, with inſtructions for his Negotiation, and he purſue not his inſtructions, whereby diſhonour and damage may enſue to the Kingdom, is not this committable?

And yet the particular of his inſtruction, and the manner of his miſcarrying, is not fit to be declared to his Keeper, or by him to be certified to the Judges, where it is to be opened and debated in the preſence of a great audience.

I therefore conclude, for offences againſt the State, in caſe of State Government, the King and his Council have lawful power to puniſh by impriſonment, without ſhewing particular cauſe, where it may tend to the diſcloſing of State-Government. It is well known to many that know me, how much I have laboured in this law of the ſubjects liberty very many years before I was in the King's ſervice, and had no cauſe then to ſpeak, but to ſpeak *ex animo*; yet did I then maintain and publiſh the ſame opinion which now I have declared concerning the King's ſupreme power in matters of State, and therefore cannot juſtly be cenſured to ſpeak at this preſent only to merit of my Maſter. But if I may freely ſpeak my own underſtanding, I conceive it to be a queſtion too high to be determined by any legal direction; for it muſt needs be an hard caſe of contention, when the Conqueror muſt ſit down with irreparable loſſes, as in this caſe. If the Subject prevails, he gains liberty, but loſeth the benefit of that State-Government, by which a Monarchy may ſoon become an Anarchy; or if the State prevails, it gains abſolute Sovereignty, but loſeth Subjects: not their ſubjection, for obedience we muſt yield, tho' nothing be left us but prayers and tears, but yet loſeth the beſt part of them, which is their affections, whereby Sovereignty is eſtabliſhed, and the Crown firmly fixt on his royal head. Between two ſuch extremes there is no way to moderate, but to find a *medium* for the accommodation of the difference; which is not for me to preſcribe, but only to move your Lordſhips, to whom I ſubmit.

After Mr. Serjeant's ſpeech ended, my Lord-Preſident ſaid thus to the Gentlemen of the Houſe of Commons; That though at this free conference, liberty was given by the Lords to the King's Counſel to ſpeak what they thought fit for his Majeſty, *yet Mr. Serjeant* Aſhley *had no authority, or direction from them to ſpeak in that manner he had done.* And he was committed into cuſtody, and afterwards, being ſorry for any haſty expreſſion he might have uſed, was diſcharged

The Objections of the King's Counſel, with the Anſwers made thereunto, at the two Conferences touching the ſame matter.

IT was agreed by the Attorney-General, Sir *Robert Heath*, that the ſeven Statutes urged by the Commons were in force, and that *Magna Charta* did extend not properly to the King But he ſaid, 1. That ſome of them are in general words, and therefore conclude nothing, but are to be expounded by the precedents; and others that be more particular, are applied to the ſuggeſtions of ſubjects, and not to the King's command ſimply of itſelf. Hereunto it was anſwered, That the Statutes were as direct as could be, which appeareth by the reading of them, and that though ſome of them ſpeak

ſpeak of ſuggeſtions of the ſubjects, yet others do not: and they that do, are as effectual, for that they are in equal reaſon, a commitment by the command of the King, being of as great force, when it moveth by a ſuggeſtion from a ſubject, as when the King taketh notice of it himſelf; the rather for that Kings ſeldom intermeddle with matters of this nature, but by information from ſome of their people.

2. Mr. Attorney objected, that *per legem terræ* in *Magna Charta* (which is the foundation of this queſtion) cannot be underſtood for proceſs of the law and original writs; for that in all criminal proceedings no original writ is uſed at all; but every Conſtable either for Felony or Breach of the Peace, or to prevent the Breach of the Peace, may commit without proceſs or original writ, and it were hard the King ſhould not have the power of a Conſtable. And the Statute cited by the Commons, makes proceſs of the law and writ original, to be all one.

The anſwer of the Commons to this objection was, that they do not intend original writs only by law of the land, but all other legal proceſs, which comprehends the whole proceedings of law upon cauſe, other than trial by Jury, *Judicium parium*, unto which it is oppoſed. Thus much is imported *ex vi termini* out of the word Proceſs; and by the true acceptation thereof in the Statutes that have been uſed by the Commons to maintain the declaration, and moſt eſpecially the Statutes of 25 *Ed.* III. *cap.* 4. where it appeareth that a man ought to be brought in to anſwer by the courſe of the law, having former mention of proceſs made by original writ.

And in 28 *Ed.* III. *cap.* 3. by the courſe of the law is rendered by due proceſs of the law. And 36 *Ed.* III. *Rot. Parliamenti*, *num.* 20. the petition of the Commons ſaith, that no man ought to be impriſoned by ſpecial command without indictment or other due proceſs to be made by the law. 37 *Ed.* III. *cap.* 18. calleth the ſame thing proceſs of the law; and 42 *Ed.* III. *cap.* 3. ſtileth it by due proceſs and writ original; where the conjunctive muſt be taken for a diſ-junctive, which change is ordinary in an expoſition of Statutes and Deeds, to avoid inconveniences, to make it ſtand with the reſt; and with reaſon, as it may be collected, by the law of the land in *Magna Charta*, by the courſe of the law in 25 *Ed.* III. by the due proceſs of law in 28 *Ed.* III. other due proceſs to be made by the law in 36 *Ed.* III. proceſs of the law in 37 *Ed.* III. and by due proceſs and writ original in 42 *Ed.* III. are meant one and the ſame thing; the latter of theſe Statutes referring always to the former, and that all of them import any due and regular proceedings of law upon a cauſe other than the Trial by Jury. And this appeareth 10 *Rep.* 74. in the caſe of the *Marſhalſea*, and 11 *Rep.* 99. *James Bagg*'s caſe, where it is underſtood of giving juriſdiction by Charter or Preſcription, which is the ground of a proceeding by courſe of law. And in *Selden*'s Notes on *Forteſcue*, *fol.* 29. where it is expounded for law-wager, which is likewiſe a Trial at law by the oath of the parties differing from that by Jury. And it doth truly comprehend theſe and all other regular proceedings in law upon cauſe, which gives authority to the Conſtable to arreſt upon cauſe. And if this be not the true expoſition of theſe words *per legem terræ*, the King's Counſel were deſired to declare their meaning, which they never offered to do; and yet certainly theſe words were not put into the Statute without ſome intention of conſequence.

And thereupon Mr. Serjeant *Aſhley* offered an interpretation of them thus: namely, That there were divers laws of this Realm, as the Common Law, the Law of the Chancery, the Eccleſiaſtical Law, the Law of the Admiralty or Marine Law, the Law of Merchants, the Martial Law, and the Law of State; and that theſe words *per legem terræ* do extend to all theſe Laws.

To this it was anſwered, that we read of no law of State, and that none of theſe Laws can be meant there, ſave the Common Law, which is the principal and general law, and is always underſtood by way of excellency, when mention is made of the law of the land generally: and that though each of the other laws, which are admitted into this Kingdom by Cuſtom or Act of Parliament, may juſtly be called *a* law of the land, yet none of them can have the preheminence to be ſtiled *the* law of the land. And no Statute, Law-Book, or other Authority, printed or unprinted could be ſhewn, to prove that the law of the land, being generally mentioned, was ever intended of any other than the Common Law; and yet even by theſe other laws, a man may not be committed without a cauſe expreſſed.

But it ſtandeth with the rule of other legal expoſitions, that *per legem terræ* muſt be meant the Common Law, which is the general and univerſal Law by which men hold their Inheritances; and therefore if a man ſpeak of eſcuage generally, it is underſtood, as *Littleton* obſerveth, *Sect.* 99. of the incertain eſcuage, which is a Knight's ſervice tenure, for the defence of the Realm, by the body of the tenant in time of war, and not of certain eſcuage, which giveth only a contribution in money, and no perſonal ſervice.

And if a Statute ſpeak of the King's Courts of Record, it is meant only of the four at *Weſtminſter* by way of excellency, *Coke*'s 6. *Rep.* 20. *Gregory*'s caſe. So the Canoniſts by the Excommunication ſimply ſpoken, do intend the greater Excommunication. And the Emperor in his Inſtitutions ſaith, that the Civil Law being ſpoken generally, is meant of the Civil Law of *Rome*, though the Law of every City is a Civil Law; as when a man names the Poet, the *Grecians* underſtand *Homer*, the *Latiniſts Virgil*.

2. Admit *per legem terræ* extend to all the laws of the land, yet a man muſt not be committed by any of them, but by the due proceedings that are executed by thoſe laws, and upon a cauſe declared.

Again, it was urged, That the King was not bound to expreſs a cauſe of impriſonment, becauſe there may be in it matter of State, not fit to be revealed for a time, leſt the confederates thereupon make means to eſcape the hands of Juſtice. And therefore the Statutes cannot be intended to reſtrain all commitments, unleſs a cauſe be expreſſed; for that it would be very inconvenient and dangerous to the State, to publiſh the cauſe at the very firſt.

Hereunto it was replied by the Commons, That all danger and inconvenience may be avoided by declaring a general cauſe, as for Treaſon, Suſpicion of Treaſon, Miſpriſion of Treaſon, or Felony, without ſpecifying the particular; which can give no greater light to a confederate, than will be conjectured by the very apprehenſion upon the impriſonment, if nothing at all were expreſſed.

It was further alledged, That there was a kind of contradiction in the poſition of the Commons, when they ſay, a party committed without a cauſe ſhewed, ought to be delivered or bailed; bailing being a kind of impriſonment; delivery, a total freeing.

To this it hath been anſwered, that it hath always been the diſcretion of the Judges, to give ſo much reſpect to a commitment by the command of the King, or the Privy-Council, (which are ever intended to be done in juſt and weighty cauſes) that they will not preſently ſet them free, but bail them to anſwer what ſhall be objected againſt them on his Majeſty's behalf; but if any other inferiour Officer do commit a man without ſhewing cauſe, they do inſtantly deliver him, as having no cauſe to expect their leiſure. So the delivery is applied to an impriſonment by the command of ſome mean Miniſter of Juſtice; bailing, when it is done by the command of the King or his Council.

It was argued by Mr. Attorney, that bailing was a grace and favour of a Court of Juſtice, and that they may refuſe to do it.

This was agreed to be true in divers caſes, as where the cauſe appears to be for Felony, or other crimes expreſſed, for that there is another way to diſcharge them in ſome convenient time by their Trial; and yet in theſe caſes, the conſtant practice hath been anciently and modernly to bail men: but where no cauſe of the impriſonment is returned, but the command of the King, there is no way to deliver ſuch perſon by Trial or otherwiſe, but that of the *Habeas Corpus*. And if they ſhould be then remanded, they might be perpetually impriſoned, without any remedy at all, and conſequently a man that had committed no offence, might be in a worſe caſe than a great offender, for the latter ſhould have an ordinary Trial to diſcharge him, the other ſhould never be delivered.

It was further ſaid, that though the Statute of *Weſtminſter* 1. *cap.* 15. be a Statute which by way of proviſion did extend only to the Sheriff, yet the recital of that Statute touching the four caſes, wherein a man was not repleviable at the Common Law, namely, thoſe that were committed for the death of a man, by the command of the King, or of his Juſtices, or for the Foreſt; did declare that the Juſtices could not bail ſuch a one, and that repleviable and bailable were ſynonimous or all one. and that *Stamford*, a Judge of great authority, doth expound it accordingly (*Stam. pl. Cor.* 72.) and that neither the Statute nor he ſay repleviable by the Sheriff, but generally without reſtraint, and that if the Chief Juſtice commits a man, he is not to be inlarged by any other Court, as appeareth in the *Regiſter*.

To this it was anſwered, 1. That the recital of the body of the Statute, relateth to the Sheriff only, as appeareth by the very words. 2. That repleviable is to the Sheriff, for that the word imports no more; but a man committed by the Chief-Juſtice, is bailable by the Court of *King's-Bench*. 3. That *Stamford* meaneth all of the Sheriff, or at leaſt he hath not ſufficiently expreſſed that he intended the Juſtices. 4. It was denied that repleviable and bailable were the ſame, for they differ in reſpect of the place where they are uſed, bail being in the King's Court of Record, repleviable before the Sheriff; and they are of ſeveral natures, repleviable being a letting at large upon ſureties, bailing being when one *traditur in ballium*, the bail are his Gaolers, and may impriſon him, and ſhall ſuffer body for body; which is not true of replevying by ſureties: and bail differeth from mainprize in this, that mainprize is an undertaking in a ſum certain, bailing is to anſwer the condemnation in civil cauſes, and in criminal, body for body.

The reaſons and authorities in the firſt conference were then renewed, and no exceptions taken to any, ſave that in 22 *Hen.* VI. it doth not appear that the command of the King was by his mouth, which muſt be intended, or by his Council, which is all one, as is obſerved by *Stamford*; for the two words are, that a man is not repleviable by the Sheriff, who is committed by the Writ or the commandment of the King.

21 *Ed.* I. *Rot.* 2, *dorſ* was cited by the King's Counſel; but it was anſwered, that it concerned the Sheriff of *Leiceſterſhire* only, and not the power of the Judges. 33 *Hen.* VI. the King's Attorney confeſſed, was nothing to the purpoſe, and yet that Book hath been uſually cited by thoſe that maintain the contrary to the declaration of the Commons. And therefore ſuch ſudden opinions as have been given thereupon, are not to be regarded, the foundation failing

And where it was ſaid that the *French* of 36 *Ed.* III. *Rot. Parliamenti*, *num.* 9. which can receive no anſwer, did not warrant what was inferred thence; but that theſe words, *ſans diſturbance mettre, ou arreſt faire, & le contre per ſpecial mandement ou en autre maniare*, muſt be underſtood, that the Statutes ſhould be put in execution. without putting diſturbance, or making arreſt to the contrary by ſpecial command or in other manner; the Commons did utterly deny the interpretation given by the King's Counſel: and to juſtify their own did appeal to all men that underſtood *French*. And upon the ſeven Statutes did conclude, that their declaration remained an undoubted truth, not controlled by any thing ſaid to the contrary.

[*The Proceedings against the Earl of* Suffolk, 14 April, 1628 *.

MR *Kerton* acquainted the Houſe, that the Earl of *Suffolk* had ſaid to ſome Gentlemen, *That Mr.* Selden *had razed a Record, and deſerved to be hanged, for going about to ſet diviſion betwixt the King and his Subjects*. And being demanded to whom the words were ſpoken, he was unwilling to name any, till upon the queſtion it was reſolved he ſhould nominate him. He then named Sir *John Strangways*; who was unwilling to ſpeak what he had heard from the Earl: but being commanded by the Houſe, and reſolved upon the queſtion, he confeſſed,

That upon *Saturday* laſt, he being in the Committee-Chamber of the Lords, the Earl of *Suffolk* called to him, and ſaid, *Sir* John, *will you not hang* Selden? To whom he ſaid, For what? The Earl replied, *By God he hath razed a Record, and deſerves to be hanged* †.

This the Houſe of Commons took as a great injury done to the whole Houſe, Mr. *Selden* being employed by them in the Conference with the Lords in the great cauſe concerning the Liberty of the perſons of the ſubjects.

The

* This was *Theophilus* Earl of *Suffolk*, Son to *James* Earl of *Suffolk*, Lord-Treaſurer, *Temp. Jac.* I.

† Mr. *Selden*.] I am called up to juſtify myſelf. I ſee the words charge me to have razed Records. I hope no man believes I ever did it. I cannot gueſs what this Lord means. I did deliver in whole Copies of divers Records examined by myſelf, and divers other Gentlemen of this Houſe These I delivered in to the Lords Houſe; and the Clerk of the Crown brought in the Records of the Office before the Lords: I deſire that there may be a meſſage from this Houſe to the Lords, to make at the Bar there a Charge againſt the Lord that ſpoke thus; and I hope we ſhall have Juſtice. *Ex MSS. Pymmis in* Selden's *Life, in his Works*, Vol. p. 16.

The House presently sent Sir *Robert Phillips* with a message to the Lords to this effect, he expressed the great care the Commons had upon all occasions to maintain all mutual respect and correspondency betwixt both Houses: then he informed them of a great injury done by the Earl of *Suffolk* to the whole House, and to Mr. *Selden*, a particular Member thereof, who by their command had been employed in the late conference with their Lordships: that the House was very sensible thereof, and according to former precedents, made them truly acquainted with it, and demanded Justice against the Earl of *Suffolk*. He read the words, saying they were spoken to Sir *John Strangways*, a Member of their House.

After a short stay, the Lords called for the Messenger, to whom the Lord-Keeper gave this answer; he signified the great desire and care of their Lordships to maintain and increase the correspondencies betwixt both Houses, and as a testimony thereof they had partly taken into consideration the charge: that the Earl of *Suffolk*, being a man of great place and honour, had voluntarily protested upon his Honour and Soul, that there passed no such words as those from him to Sir *John Strangways*: and the Lord-Keeper wished that their Lordships speedy proceedings in this business might testify their love and good-will to the Commons House.

The next day, being the 15th of *April*, Sir *John Strangways* made a protestation openly in the House, wherein he avowed that (notwithstanding the Earl's denial) he did speak those words positively unto him, and would maintain it any way fitting a Member of that House, or a Gentleman of Honour.

They ordered that this protestation should be entered into the Journal-book, and that a Committee should take into consideration what was fit for the House to proceed to, for the justification of Sir *John Strangways*, and what was fitting to be done in this case, and to examine witnesses of the proof the words.

Upon the 17th day Sir *John Elliot* reported what the Committee had done; That they had sent for and examined Sir *Christopher Nevil*; who related, that upon *Saturday* being in the Lords Committee-Chamber, the Earl of *Suffolk* said thus to him: Mr. Attorney hath cleared the business, and hath made the cause plain on the King's side; and further said, Mr. *Selden* hath razed a Record, and hath deserved to be hanged, and the Lower House should do well to join with the higher in a petition to the King to hang him, and added as a reason, for Mr. *Selden* went about, and took a course to divide the King from his people, or words to that effect. And being asked, whether he conceived that those words of dividing the King from his people, had relation to the whole and general action of Mr. *Selden* before the Lords, or to the particular of razing a record? He conceived they were referred to the general action.

They had examined one Mr *Littleton*, who confessed he heard the Earl of *Suffolk* speak to a Gentleman, whom he knew not, words to this effect, *viz.* That he would not be in Mr. *Selden*'s coat for 10,000*l.* and that Mr. *Selden* deserved to be hanged.

The second part of this report concerned the particular of Sir *John Strangways*, wherein though the Committee found no witness to prove the words spoken to Sir *John Strangways*, yet there were many circumstances which persuaded them of the truth thereof.

1. That the same words in the same syllables were spoken to Sir *Christopher Nevil*, and that the Earl as he called to him Sir *John Strangways*, so he called to him Sir *Christopher Nevil*.

2. That the Earl of *Suffolk* called Sir *John Strangways* to him, and spake to him, was proved by Sir *George Fane*, and Sir *Alexander St. John*, at which time the Earl seemed full of that which he delivered.

3. That Sir *John Strangways* instantly after his discourse with the Earl of *Suffolk* went to the Earl of *Hertford*, and delivered him the passages betwixt them, being the same related in the House.

4. From the unwillingness of Sir *John Strangways*, though called upon by the House, to testify against the Earl, till it was resolved by question he should do it: from a probability, that had not these words been spoken to himself, it is like he would have produced Sir *Christopher Nevil*, from whom he also heard the same.

5. From the worth of the Gentleman, and his ingenuous protestation in the House, That he was ready to justify the truth of what he said in any course the House should think meet, or was fit for a Gentleman of Honour.

Hereupon the House resolved upon the Question;

1. That the Earl of *Suffolk*, notwithstanding his denial, had laid a most unjust and scandalous imputation upon Mr. *Selden*, a Member of the House, being imployed in the service of the House, and therein upon the whole House of Commons.

2. That this House, upon due examination, is fully satisfied that Sir *John Strangways* (notwithstanding the Earl of *Suffolk*'s denial) hath affirmed nothing but what is most true and certain.

3. That these particulars and additions be again presented to the Lords, and the Earl of *Suffolk* be newly charged at the bar, and the Lords desired to proceed in Justice against the Earl, and to inflict such punishment upon him as an offence of so high a nature, being against the House of Commons, doth deserve.

Sir *John Elliot* was sent with a message to the Lords; who after a while returned this answer, That they had taken the message into consideration, and would further take it into due consultation, and in convenient time would return an answer by Messengers of their own. *But what was done in this affair does not appear.*

MR. *Noye*, on the 16th of *April*, offered an answer to the inconveniencies presented by Mr. Attorney, which were four in number.

First, where it was objected, that it was inconvenient to express the cause, for fear of divulging the *Arcana imperii*, for hereby all may be discovered, and abundance of Traitors never brought to Justice:

To this that learned man answered,

That the Judges by the intention of the Law were the King's Council, and the secrets may safely be committed to all or some of them, who might advise whether they will bail him, and hence no danger to King, or subjects, for their oath will not permit them to reveal the secrets of the King, nor yet to detain the subject long, if by law he be to be delivered.

Secondly, For that objection of the children of *[illegible]*, he had this for a ground, that the King can do no wrong; but in cases of extreme necessity, we must yield sometimes for the preservation of the State, *ubi unius damnum utilitate publica rependitur*: he said there was no trust in the children of Traitors, no wrong done if they did *tabescere*, or *marcescere in carcere*. It is the same case of necessity, as when to avoid the burning of a Town, we are forced to pull down an honest man's house, or to compel a man to dwell by the sea-side for defence or fortitude. Yet the King can do no wrong, for *potentia juris est non injuria*: *Ergo* the Act of the King, tho' to the wrong of another, is by the Law made no wrong; as if he commanded a person to be kept in prison, yet he is responsible for his wrong: he quoted a book, 42. 6. *Ass. Port.*

Thirdly, The instance made of *Westminst.* first, he said there was a great difference between those three, Mainprise, Bail, and Replevin. The Statute says, a man cannot be replevied. *Ergo*, not bailed *non sequitur*. Mainprise is under pain; Bail is body for body: but no pain is ever in Court to be declared, unless the party appears. Replevin is neither by surety nor bail; and Replevin is never in Court.

Fourthly, Where it is said that Bail is *ex gratia*, he answers, That if the prisoner comes to *Habeas Corpus*, then it is not *ex gratia*, yet the Court may advise, but mark the words *ad subjiciendum & recipiendum prout curia consideraverit*. Now it is impossible the Judges should do so, if no cause be expressed; for if they know no cause, he may bring the first, second, third, and fourth *Habeas Corpus*, and so infinite till he find himself a perpetual prisoner: so that no cause expressed, is worse for a man than the greatest cause or villainy that can be imagined. And thus far proceeded that learned Gentleman.

MR. *Glanvile* said, That by favour of the House of Commons he had liberty to speak, if opportunity were offered. He applied his answer to one particular of Mr. Attorney, who assigned to the King four great trusts: 1. War, 2 Coins, 3. Denizens, 4 Pardons, it is assented to, that the King is trusted with all these four legal Prerogatives, but the argument followeth not, the King is trusted with many Prerogatives: *Ergo*, in this *non sequitur non est sufficiens enumeratio partium*. He said he could answer these particulars with two rules, whereof the first should wipe off the first and the second; and the other, the third and fourth.

The first rule is this: there is no fear of trusting the King with any thing, but the fear of ill Counsel. the King may easily there be trusted, where ill Counsel doth not engage both the King and subjects, as it doth in matter of War and Coin. If he miscarry in the Wars, it is not always *plectuntur Archivi*, but he smarts equally with the people; if he abase his Coin, he loseth more than any of his people; *Ergo*, he may safely be trusted with the flowers of the Crown, War and Coin.

The second rule he began was this, When the King is trusted to confer grace, it is one thing; but when he is trusted to infer an injury, it is another matter. The former power cannot, by miscounselling, be brought to prejudice another, the latter may; if the King pardoneth a guilty man, he punisheth not a good subject; if he denizen never so many strangers, it is but *damnum sine injuria*: we allow him a liberty to confer grace, but not without cause to infer punishment; and indeed he cannot do injury, for if he command to do a man wrong, the command is void, *& actor fit author*, and the actor becomes the wrong doer. Therefore the King may safely be trusted with War, Coin, Denizens, and Pardons, but not with a power to imprison without expression of cause, or limitation of time; as the Poet tells us, because *Libertas potius auro*

After these Debates, the House of Peers called upon the Judges to answer the Charge of the House of Commons, for their Judgment on the *Habeas Corpus*, brought in *Mich.* Term by the Gentlemen imprisoned for refusing to subscribe to the *Loan*.

The Answer of the Judges for Matter of Fact upon the Habeas Corpus, 21 April.

THE Chief-Justice saith, They are prepared to obey our command, but they desire to be advised by us, whether they being sworn upon penalty of forfeiting Body, Lands, and Goods, into the King's hands to give an account to him, may without Warrant do this.

The Duke said, He had acquainted the King with the business, and for aught he knew he is well content therewith; but for better assurance, he hath sent his brother of *Anglesey* to know his pleasure.

Devonshire. If a complaint be made by a mean man against the greatest Officer in this place, he is to give an account of his doings to this House.

Bishop of *Lincoln.* This motion proceeded from him, and so took it for clear, that there was an appeal from the Chancery to a higher Court than the King's-Bench, and that Court hath ever given an account of their doings.

The Lord *Say.* He wondered there should be any question made of this business, because in his opinion this being the highest Court, did admit of no appeal.

The President. The Judges did not do this by way of appeal, but as the most common way for them, this being a matter concerning the King's Prerogative.

Lord *Say* If they will not declare themselves, we must take into consideration the point of our privilege.

The Duke. This was not done by the Judges, as fearing to answer, but respect to the King. And now his brother was come with answer from the King, that they might proceed.

Order was taken that this passage should not be entered into the Journal-Book. And so Judge WHITLOCK *spake.*

MY Lords, we are by your appointment here ready to clear any aspersion of the House of Commons in their last presentment upon the King's-Bench, that the Subject was wounded in this judgment there being given. If such a thing were, my Lords, your Lordships, not they, have the power to question and judge the same. But, my Lords, I say there was no judgment given, whereby either the Prerogative might be enlarged, or the right of the Subject trenched upon. It is true, my Lords, in *Michaelmas* Term last, four Gentlemen petitioned for an *Habeas Corpus*, which they obtained, and Counsel was assigned unto them, the return was *per speciale mandatum Domini Regis*, which likewise was made unto us in the hearing of eighteen Privy Councillors. Now, my Lords, if we had delivered them presently upon this, it must

I

muſt have been, becauſe the King did not ſhew the cauſe, wherein we ſhould have judged the King had done wrong; and this is beyond our knowledge, for he might have committed them for other matters than we could have imagined. But they might ſay, thus they might have been kept in priſon all their days; I anſwer no, but we did remit them, that we might better adviſe of the matter: and they the next day might have had a new Writ, if they had pleaſed. But they ſay, we ought not to have denied bail. I anſwer, if we had done ſo, it muſt needs have reflected upon the King, that he had unjuſtly impriſoned them. And it appears in *Dyer*, 2 *Eliz.* that divers Gentlemen being committed, and requiring *Habeas Corpus*, ſome were bailed, others remitted; whereby it appears, much is left to the diſcretion of the Judges.

For that which troubled ſo much, *remittitur quouſque*, this, my Lords, was only (as I ſaid before) to take time what to do; and whereas they will have a difference betwixt *remittitur* and *remittitur quouſque*, my Lords, I confeſs I can find none; but theſe are new inventions to trouble old Records. And herein, my Lords, we have dealt with knowledge and underſtanding; for had we given a Judgment, the party muſt thereupon have reſted. Every Judgment muſt come to an iſſue in matter of fact, or demur in point of Law; here is neither, therefore no Judgment.

As to endeavouring to have a Judgment entered; it is true, Mr. Attorney preſſed the ſame for his Maſter's ſervice; but we being ſworn to do right betwixt the King and his Subjects, commanded the Clerk to make no entry, but according to the old form; and the rule was given by the Chief Juſtice alone. I have ſpent my time in this Court, and I ſpeak confidently, I did never ſee nor know by any Record, that upon ſuch a return as this, a man was bailed, the King not firſt conſulted with in ſuch a caſe as this.

The Commons Houſe do not know what letters and commands we received, for theſe remain in our Court, and were not viewed by them: for the reſt of the matters preſented by the Houſe of Commons, they were not in agitation before us, whether the King may commit, and how long he may detain a man committed. Therefore having anſwered ſo much as concerneth us, I deſire your Lordſhips good conſtructions of what hath been ſaid.

JUDGE *Jones* ſaid, he was here to deliver before us, what Judgment was given before them concerning the *Habeas Corpus*: he anſwered, No judgment was given, and the matter of fact was ſuch as my brother delivered unto you yeſterday. Theſe four Gentlemen were committed to the Fleet, Gate-houſe, and Marſhal of the Houſhold. Four returns were made upon the Writs, and every one of them had a Counſellor appointed, who had copies of the returns. A rule was granted, their Council heard, and exception taken to the return, becauſe it did not ſhew cauſe of their caption.

Theſe were of no force, in the opinion of the Judges. The next exception was, becauſe no cauſe of their commitment was ſhewed, which the Judges held to be all one in point of Law. Then, my Lords, they alledged many Precedents and Statutes of themſelves, which the King's Attorney anſwered, That perſons committed by the King, or Council, were never bailed, but his pleaſure was firſt known.

We agreed at the Chamber of the Chief-Juſtice, that all the Statutes alledged are in force; but whether we ſhould bail them or no, was the queſtion, therefore we remitted them *quouſque*. After which Mr. Attorney required a Judgment might be entered: I commanded the Clerk, he ſhould not ſuffer any ſuch thing to be done, becauſe we would be better adviſed.

But ſome will ſay, our Act is otherwiſe: I anſwer, No; for we have done no more than we do upon an ordinary Writ, when we purpoſe to be better adviſed, and that was only an interlocutory order. But, my Lords, put the caſe a *Habeas Corpus* ſhould be granted for one that is committed by the Houſe of Commons, would they (think you) take it well he ſhould be bailed at his firſt coming to the Court? I think they would not, and I think the King would have done ſo in this caſe. Now, my Lords, there is a petition of Right, and a petition of Grace: to be bailed, is a matter of Grace; therefore if a man be brought upon an *Habeas Corpus*, and not bailed, he cannot ſay the Court hath done him any wrong. I have now ſerved ſeven years a Judge in this Court, and my conſcience beareth me witneſs, that I have not wronged the ſame; I have been thought ſometimes too forward for the Liberty of the Subject. I am myſelf *Liber Homo*, my Anceſtors gave their voice for *Magna Charta*. I enjoy that Houſe ſtill, which they did, I do not now mean to draw God's wrath upon my poſterity; and therefore I will neither advance the King's Prerogative, nor leſſen the Liberty of the Subject, to the danger of either King or People. This is my profeſſion before God and your Lordſhips.

JUDGE *Dodderidge* ſaid, It is no more fit for a Judge to decline to give an account of his Doings, than for a Chriſtian of his Faith. God knoweth, I have endeavoured always to keep a good conſcience; for a troubled one, who can bear? The Kingdom holds of none but God, and Judgments do not paſs privately in Chambers, but publickly in Court, where every one may hear, which cauſeth Judgment to be given with maturity. Your Lordſhips have heard the particulars delivered by my Brethren, how that Council being aſſigned to thoſe four Gentlemen, in the latter end of *Michaelmas* Term their cauſe received hearing; and upon conſideration of the Statutes and Records, we found ſome of them to be according to the good old Law of *Magna Charta*: but we thought, that they did not come ſo cloſe to this caſe, as that bail ſhould be thereupon preſently granted. My Lords, the *Habeas Corpus* conſiſts of three parts, the Writ, the Return upon the Writ or Schedule, and the Entry or Rule reciting the *Habeas Corpus*; and the Return, together with the opinion of the Court, either a *remittitur*, or *traditur in Ballium*. In this caſe a *remittitur* was granted, which we did, that we might take better adviſement upon the caſe, and upon the *remittitur* (my Lords) they might have had a new Writ the next day; and I wiſh they had, becauſe it may be they had been more, and we had been [illegible] of a great [illegible]. And, my Lords, when the Attorney, upon the *remittitur*, preſſed an entry, we all ſtraitly charged the Clerk that he ſhould make no other entry than ſuch as our Predeceſſors had uſually made in like caſes: for the difference (my Lords) betwixt *remittitur* and *remittitur quouſque*, I could never yet find any. I have now ſat in this Court fifteen years, and I ſhould know ſomething; ſurely, if I had gone in a mill ſo long, ſome duſt would cleave to my cloaths. I am old, and have one foot in the grave, therefore I will look to the better part, as near as I can. But *omnia habere in memoria, & in nullo errare, divinum potius eſt quam humanum.*

THE Lord-Chief-Juſtice, Sir *Nicholas Hyde*, ſaid, He ſhould not ſpeak with confidence, unleſs he might ſtand right in the opinion of the Houſe; and proteſted what he ſpake the day before, was not ſaid by him with any purpoſe to trench upon the Privileges of this Houſe, but out of that reſpect which by his place he thought he owed to the King. He ſaid, concerning the point he was to ſpeak of, that he would not trouble the Lords with things formerly repeated, wherein he concurred with his Brethren. He ſaid, if it were true the King might not commit, they had done wrong in not partly delivering; for, my Lords (ſaith he), theſe Statutes and good Laws being all in force, we meant not to trench upon any of them; moſt of them being Commentaries upon *Magna Charta*: but I know not any Statute that goeth ſo far, that the King may not commit. Therefore juſtly we think, we delivered the interpretation thereof to that purpoſe: for, my Lords, *Lex terræ* is not to be found in this Statute, they gave me no example, neither was there any cauſe ſhewed in the Return. A precedent (my Lords) that hath run in a ſtorm, doth not much direct us in point of Law, and Records are the beſt Teſtimonies. Thoſe precedents they brought being read, we ſhewed them wherein they were miſtaken; if we have erred, *erramus cum patribus*, and they can ſhew no precedent, but that our Predeceſſors have done as we have done, ſometimes bailing, ſometimes remitting, ſometimes diſcharging. Yet we do never bail any committed by the King, or his Council, till his pleaſure be firſt known. Thus did the Lord-Chief-Juſtice *Coke* in *Rayner*'s caſe. They ſay, this would have been done if the King had not written, but why then was the letter read and publiſhed, and kept, and why was the Town-Clerk ſent carefully to enquire (becauſe the letter ſo directed) whether theſe men offered for bail were Subſidy Men? The letter ſheweth alſo, that *Beckwith* was committed for ſuſpicion of being acquainted with the Gunpowder-Treaſon; but no proof being produced, the King left him to be bailed.

*The Earl * of* WARWICK'*s Speech*, 21 *April*, 1628.

MY Lords, I will obſerve ſomething out of the law wherein this Liberty of the Subject's Perſon is founded, and ſome things out of precedents which have been alledged. For the law of *Magna Charta*, and the reſt concerning theſe points, they are acknowledged by all to be of force; and that they were to ſecure the ſubjects from wrongful impriſonment, as well, or rather more concerning the King, than the ſubject. Why then, beſides the grand Charter, and thoſe ſix other Acts of Parliament, in the very point, we know that *Magna Charta* hath been at leaſt thirty times confirmed; ſo that upon the matter we have ſix or ſeven-and-thirty Acts of Parliament to confirm this Liberty, although it was made matter of deriſion the other day in this Houſe.

One is that of 36 *E.* III. Nº. 9. and another in the ſame year, Nº. 20. not printed, but yet as good as thoſe that are; and that of 42 *E.* III. *cap.* 3. ſo expreſs in the point, eſpecially the Petition of the Commons that year; which was read by Mr *Littleton* with the King's anſwer ſo full, and free from all exception, to which I refer your Lordſhips, that I know not how any thing in the world can be more plain. And therefore, if in Parliament ye ſhould make any doubt of that which is ſo fully confirmed in Parliament, and in a caſe ſo clear go about by new gloſſes to alter the old and good Law, we ſhall not only forſake the ſteps of our Anceſtors, who in caſes of ſmall importance would anſwer, *nolumus mutare leges Angliæ*; but we ſhall yield up and betray our Right in the greateſt inheritance the ſubjects of *England* have, and that is the Laws of *England*. And truly I wonder how any man can admit of ſuch a gloſs upon the plain Text, as ſhould overthrow the force of the Law; for whereas the Law of *Magna Charta* is, that no Freeman ſhall be impriſoned but by lawful Judgment of his Peers, or the Law of the Land; therefore that the King hath power to commit without cauſe, is a ſenſe not only expreſſly contrary to other Acts of Parliament, and thoſe eſpecially formerly cited, but againſt common ſenſe. For Mr. Attorney confeſſeth this Law concerns the King; why then, where the Law ſaith the King ſhall not commit, but by the Law of the Land, the meaning muſt be, as Mr. Attorney would have it, that the King muſt not commit but at his own pleaſure. And ſhall we think that our Anceſtors were ſo fooliſh, to hazard their perſons and eſtates, and labour ſo much to get a Law, and to have it thirty times confirmed, that the King might not commit his Subjects but at his own pleaſure? And if he did commit any of his Subjects without a cauſe ſhewn, then he muſt lie during pleaſure, than which nothing can be imagined more ridiculous, and contrary to true reaſon.

For the precedents, I obſerve, that there hath been many ſhewn, by which it appears to me evidently, that ſuch as have been committed by the King's Council, they have been delivered upon *Habeas Corpus*, and that conſtantly. It is true, that ſome precedents were brought on the King's part, that when ſome of theſe perſons deſired to be delivered by *Habeas Corpus*, the King, or his Council ſignified his Majeſty's pleaſure that they ſhould be delivered, or the King's Attorney hath come into the Court, and related the King's command: but this ſeems to make for the Subject; for it being in his Majeſty's power to deliver them, who by his ſpecial command were impriſoned, may not we well think, that his Majeſty would rather at that time have ſtayed their deliverance by Law, than furthered it with his letters; and made the priſoners rather beholden to him for his grace and mercy, than to the Judges for Juſtice, had not his Majeſty known that at that time they ought to have been delivered by Law? I think no man would imagine a wiſe King would have ſuffered his Grace and Prerogative (if any ſuch Prerogative were) to be ſo continually queſtioned, and his Majeſty and his Council ſo far from commanding the Judges not to proceed to deliver the priſoner by them committed,

* This was *Robert* Earl of *Warwick*, afterwards Admiral for the Long Parliament.

without cause shewn, as that on the other side, which is all the force of these precedents, the King and the Council signified to the Judges, that they should proceed to deliver the parties. Certainly if the King had challenged any such Prerogative, that a person committed, without any cause shewn, ought not to be delivered by the Judges without his consent, it would have appeared, by one precedent or other amongst all that have been produced, that his Majesty would have made some claim to such a Prerogative. But it appears to the contrary, that, in many of these cases, the King or his Council did never interpose; and where they did, it was always in affirmation and encouragement to that Court to proceed. And besides, the writing of letters from his Majesty to the Judges to do Justice to his Majesty's Subjects, may with as good reason be interpreted, that without those Letters they might not do Justice: also the King signified his willingness, that such and such persons, which were committed by him, should be delivered; therefore they could not be delivered without it, which is a strange reason. So that finding the Laws so full, so many, and so plain in the point, and finding, that whenever any were committed, without cause shewn, and brought their *Habeas Corpus*, they were delivered, and no command ever given to the contrary, or claim made on the King's part to any such Prerogative: I may safely conclude, as the House of Commons have done; and if any one precedent or two of late can be shewn, that the Judges have not delivered the prisoners so committed, I think it is their fault, and to be inquired of. But contrary, it seems to me to be an undoubted Liberty of the Subject, that if he be committed without cause, or without cause shewn, yet he may have some speedy course to bring himself to trial, either to justify his own innocency, or to receive punishment according to his fault. for God forbid, that an innocent man, by the Laws of *England*, should be put in worse case than the most grievous malefactors are; which must needs be, if this should be, that if a cause be shewed, he may have his trial, but if none, he must lie and pine in prison during pleasure. Mr. Serjeant *Ashley*, the other day, told your Lordships of the Emblem of a King, but by his leave made wrong use of it. For a King bears in one hand the Globe, and in the other the golden Scepter, the types of Sovereignty and Mercy, but the Sword of Justice is ever carried before him by a Minister of Justice; which shews, Subjects may have their remedies for injustice done, and appeals to higher powers: for the Laws of *England* are so favourable to their Princes, as they can do no Injustice.

Therefore I will conclude, as all disputes I hold do, *Magna est veritas & prævalebit*; so I make no doubt, we living under so good a Prince as we do, when this is represented unto him, he will answer us, *Magna est Charta & prævalebit*.

From this time to the 25th of the same month, the House of Commons in a grand Committee spent most of their time in debate about Martial Law, and part thereof in giving the Lords a meeting at two conferences, concerning their resolves, in order to a Petition of Right, transmitted by the Commons to their Lordships.

Friday, 25th *of* April, 1628, *the Lords had a conference with the Commons, where the Lord Archbishop of* Canterbury, *(Dr.* George Abbot*) spake as follows:*

Gentlemen of the House of Commons,

THE service of the King and safety of the Kingdom do call on us my Lords, to give all convenient expedition, to dispatch some of these great and weighty businesses before us. For the better effecting whereof, my Lords have thought fit to let you know, that they do in general agree with you, and doubt not, but you will agree with us, to the best of your power, to maintain and support the fundamental Laws of the Kingdom, and the fundamental Liberties of the Subject: for the particulars which may hereafter fall in debate, they have given me in charge to let you know, That what hath been presented by you unto their Lordships, they have laid nothing of it by, they are not out of love with any thing that you have tendered unto them; they have voted nothing, neither are they in love with any thing proceeding from themselves: for that which we shall say and propose unto you, is out of an intendment to invite you to a mutual and free conference, that you with confidence may come to us, and we with confidence may speak with you; so that we may come to a conclusion of those things, which we both unanimously desire.

We have resolved of nothing, designed or determined nothing, but desire to take you with us, praying help from you as you have done from us.

My Lords have thought of some Propositions, which they have ordered to be read here, and then left with you in writing, that if it seem good to you, we may uniformly concur for the substance; and if you differ, that you would be pleased to put out, add, alter, or diminish, as you shall think fit, that so we may come the better to the end that we do both so desirously embrace.

Then the five Propositions following were read by the Clerk of the Upper House.

1. THAT his Majesty would be pleased graciously to declare, That the good old Law called *Magna Charta*, and the six Statutes conceived to be declarations and explanations of that Law, do still stand in force to all intents and purposes.

2. That his Majesty would be pleased graciously to declare, That according to *Magna Charta*, and the Statutes afore-named, as also according to the most ancient Customs and Laws of this Land, every free Subject of this Realm hath a fundamental Propriety in his Goods, and a fundamental Liberty of his Person.

3. That his Majesty would be graciously pleased to declare, That it is his royal pleasure to ratify and confirm unto all and every his loyal and faithful Subjects, all their ancient, several, just Liberties, Privileges, and Rights, in as ample and beneficial manner, to all intents and purposes, as their Ancestors did enjoy the same, under the Government of the best of his noble Progenitors.

4. That his Majesty would be pleased graciously to declare, for the good content of his Loyal Subjects, and for the securing them from future fear, That in all cases within the cognizance of the Common Law concerning the Liberties of the Subject, his Majesty would proceed according to the Common Law of this Land, and according to the Laws established in the Kingdom, and in no other manner or wise.

5. As touching his Majesty's Royal Prerogative, intrinsical to his Sovereignty, and intrusted him withal from God, *ad communem totius populi salutem, & non ad destructionem*, his Majesty would resolve not to use or divert the same, to the prejudice of any of his loyal people, in the propriety of their goods, or liberty of their Persons. And in case, for the security of his Majesty's Royal Person, the common safety of his People, or the peaceable government of this Kingdom, his Majesty shall find just cause for reason of State to imprison or restrain any man's person, his Majesty would graciously declare, That within a convenient time he shall, and will express the cause of the commitment or restraint, either general or special; and upon a cause so expressed will leave him immediately to be tried according to the common justice of the Kingdom.

After the reading of the Propositions, the Archbishop said:

This is but a Model to be added unto, altered, or diminished, as in your reasons and wisdoms ye shall think fit, after ye have communicated the same to the rest of the Members of the House.

To this Speech, Sir Dudley Diggs, *it being at a free conference in behalf of the Commons, made this Reply:*

MY Lords, it hath pleased Almighty God many ways to bless the Knights, Citizens and Burgesses, now assembled in Parliament, with great comfort, and strong hopes, that this will prove as happy a Parliament as ever was in *England*. And in their consultations for the service of his Majesty, and the safety of this Kingdom, our special comfort and strong hopes have risen from the continued good respect, which your Lordships so nobly have been pleased to shew unto them; particularly at this present, in your so honourable profession to agree with them in general, in desiring to maintain and support the fundamental Laws and Liberties of *England*.

The Commons have commanded me in like sort, to assure your Lordships they have been, are, and will be, as ready to propugn the just Prerogative of his Majesty, of which in all their Arguments, Searches of Records, and Resolutions, they have been most careful, according to that which formerly was, and now again is, protected by them.

Another noble argument of your honourable disposition towards them is expressed in this, That you are pleased to expect no present answer from them, who are (as your Lordships in your great wisdoms, they doubt not, have considered) a great Body, that must advise upon all new propositions, and resolve upon them before they can give answer, according to the antient order of their House. But it is manifest in general (God be thanked for it) there is a great concurrence of affection to the same end in both Houses, and such good harmony, that I intreat your Lordships leave to borrow a comparison from nature, or natural philosophy: As two Lutes well strung and tuned brought together, if one be played on, little straws and sticks will stir upon the other, though it lie still, so though we have no power to reply, yet these things said and propounded cannot but work in our hearts, and we will faithfully report these passages to our House, from whence in due time (we hope) your Lordships shall receive a contentful answer.

Mr. Selden's *Speech, about the five Propositions sent from the Lords to the House of Commons,* April 26, 1628.

OUR Debate is now, how we like of the Propositions. Ours were resolutions of Law, and no man can make question of them. And as we are constant, so I hope they of other places that have weighed them, are of the same mind with us. But now their Lordships laying them by, propound what they would have to be Law. As they may speak to what comes from us, so may we to what comes from them, and they did invite us thereto. I think there is not one of the five fit to be desired and asked. The first three are not fit, for there is no use of them in these great questions. The fourth we have already, and the fifth is not fit to be had at all. The first is, to declare that *Magna Charta* and the six Statutes, conceived to be declarations and explanations of that Law, do still stand in force to all intents and purposes. Consider what it is we ask: Who doubts whether they stand in force or no? Indeed some have published that *Magna Charta* is but a Charter, and no Law. But it is an Act of Parliament; and let men speak what they will, that was the fashion of Statutes till printing came in. The Statutes were sent down in the King's name to be proclaimed, and he prefixed his name, and this was till about *Hen.* VI. Also the body of *Magna Charta* is, that it is consented to by all the Earls, &c. and for the assent there was a fifteenth granted, and clearly that cannot be without an Act of Parliament: and so constant it is, that all else in it is to this day put in execution. In former Parliaments, by thirty at least, it was confirmed, but it was not of necessity, and yet they are surer than this declaration you will now add. For the second, that his Majesty will declare that every Subject hath a Propriety in his goods, and Liberty of his person; they that drew this might mean somewhat more than I understand: I know not what we gain. Who doubts of our propriety? I never heard it denied, but in the pulpit, which is of no weight. For the third, that his Majesty will confirm all just liberties, none can tell what this will produce. It is not fit we trouble his Majesty with it. The fourth is not fit to be asked; That in all cases within the cognizance of the Common Law concerning the Liberties of his subjects, his Majesty would proceed according to the Common Law. I conceive his Majesty never proceeded but according to Law. It may be there were commitments, yet the Courts of Justice were open for the parties to seek Justice. And if any thing be done against the Law, there, it is the fault of them that sit there. So we shall take it. But yet his Majesty hath done nothing against the Law. For the fifth, it is not fit to be had, and therefore not fit to be asked. If we ask it parliamentarily, we shall have a Law to that Sense and so we shall destroy our fundamental Liberties, which we have already resolved. Now a *convenient time* must be set down. In former Times there was no need of such Innovations; for such Law of State, in a *convenient time* every Man was to be delivered by Law. If they were so wise then to hold it needless, why is it now necessary? And for *convenient time*; what is *convenient time?* Who shall judge of it but the Judges? And so they now shall have the Power of the Lords, and of the Council. Also now we desire in some Cases the Prerogative, *&c.* I would fain see if any Person may not be committed at Pleasure by this Clause, and no Man is exempted. At this little Gap every Man's Liberty may in Time go out.

The Commons were not satisfied with these Propositions, which were conceived to weaken the Petition of Right, then under Consideration, but demurred upon them.

Monday, 28 April. *The Lord Keeper spake to both Houses of Parliament by the King's Command, who was then present.*

MY Lords, and ye the Knights, Citizens, and Burgesses of the House of Commons, ye cannot but remember the great and important Affairs, concerning the Safety both of State and Religion, declared first from his Majesty's own Mouth, to be the Causes of the assembling of this Parliament; the Sense whereof, as it doth daily increase with his Majesty, so it ought to do, and his Majesty doubts not but it doth so with you, since the Danger increaseth every Day, both by Effluxion of Time, and Preparations of the Enemy.

Yet his Majesty doth well weigh, that this Expence of Time hath been occasioned by the Debate which hath arisen in both Houses touching the Liberty of the Subject; in which, as his Majesty takes in good part the Purpose and Intent of the Houses, so clearly and frequently professed, that they would not diminish or blemish his Royal and just Prerogative, so he presumes, that ye will all confess it a Point of extraordinary Grace and Justice in him, to suffer it to rest so long in Dispute without Interruption. But now his Majesty, considering the Length of Time which it hath already taken, and fearing nothing so much as any future Loss of that, whereof every Hour and Minute is so precious, and foreseeing that the ordinary way of Debate, though never so carefully husbanded, must, in regard of the Form of both Houses, necessarily take more time than the Affairs of Christendom can permit; his Majesty, out of his great princely Care, hath thought of this Expedient to shorten the Business, by declaring the Clearness of his own Heart and Intention: And therefore hath commanded me to let you know, *That he holdeth the Statute of* Magna Charta, *and the other six Statutes insisted upon for the Subject's Liberty, to be all in force, and assures you, that he will maintain all his Subjects in the just Freedom of their Persons, and Safety of their Estates; and that he will govern according to the Laws and Statutes of this Realm; and that ye shall find as much Security in his Majesty's Royal Word and Promise, as in the Strength of any Law ye can make; so that hereafter ye shall never have Cause to complain.* The Conclusion is, That his Majesty prayeth God, who hath hitherto blessed this Kingdom, and put into his Heart to come to you this Day, to make the Success thereof happy, both to King and People. And therefore he desires, that no Doubt or Distrust may possess any Man, but that ye will all proceed speedily and unanimously to the Business.

The Commons being returned from the Lords House, Mr. Secretary *Cook* persuaded them to comply with the King.

His Majesty, said he, puts us in Mind of the great important Affairs of the State, and of his Sense thereof, that the Effluxion of Time increaseth in him, and he doubts not but that it doth increase in us. Ye see his Majesty's Moderation in the Interpretation of all our Actions, he saith, that he hopes we have the same Sense he hath, he is pleased to consider of the Occasion of Expence of Time that grew from the Debates in both Houses. We see how indulgent he is, that however the Affairs of Christendom are great, yet he counts not this, nay, he takes in good Part our Proceedings and our Declarations, that we will not impeach the Prerogative. Also his Majesty presumes, that we will confess, that he hath used extraordinary Grace, in that he hath endured dispute so long, he acknowledgeth it Justice to stand as we have done.

Further, Out of a princely Care of the Publick, he is careful no more Time be lost, and because he sees some extraordinary Course to be taken to satisfy us, he observes, that in the Form of the Debate, such length is required as the Nature of the Business will not endure. It is to be presumed, that his Government will be according to the Law. We cannot but remember what his Father said, *He is no King, but a Tyrant, that governs not by Law*; but this Kingdom is to be governed by the Common Law, and his Majesty assures us so much; the Interpretation is left to the Judges, and to his great Council, and all is to be guided by the Common Law. I mean not *Magna Charta* only, for that *Magna Charta* was part of the Common Law, and the ancient Law of this Kingdom, all our Difference is in the Application of this Law, and how this Law, with Difference, is derived into every Court. I conceive there are two Rules, the one of this, that is rigid, and will not bend, and this is the Law of the Kings-Bench; this Law will not bend, and when it lights on Subjects strongly, if it do not bend, it is unjust, and there comes in the Law of Chancery and Equity: This is Application of Law in private Men's Cases, when it comes to *Meum & Tuum*. And thus the general Government of Cases, with relation to the common State of the Kingdom, is from the Council-Board, and there they are to carry [illegible] of the Kingdom; suppose it be in Time of Dearth, Pestilence, [illegible] may in that Time be forced, and be brought to the Market. We [illegible] Experience of it of Coals in *London*, and the Council-Board commanded [illegible] to be brought forth and sold. In a Time of Pestilence Men may be restrained. If a Schism be like to grow in a Church, the State will enquire after the Favourers of it. If there be fear of an Invasion, and it be encouraged by hope of a Party among us, it is in the Power of the Government to restrain Men to their Houses.

In the Composure of these things, there is great Difference: What Differences have been between the Courts of Chancery and King's-Bench? It is hard to put true Difference between the King's Prerogative and our Liberties. His Majesty saw Expence of Time would be prejudicial; it pleased God to move his Majesty by a Divine Hand to shew us a Way to clear all our Difficulties, let us attend to all the Parts of it; there be five Degrees, and there is more Assurance than we could have by any Law whatsoever. His Majesty declares, that *Magna Charta* and the other Statutes are in Force: This is not the first time that the Liberty of the Subject was infringed, or was in debate and confirmed; all Times thought it safe, that when they came to a Negative of Power, it was hard to keep Government and Liberty together; but his Majesty stopped not there; but according to the Sense of these Laws, that he will govern his Subjects in their just Liberties, he assures us our Liberties are just, they are not of Grace, but of Right; nay, he assures us, he will govern us according to the Laws of the Realm, and that we shall find as much Security in his Majesty's Promise, as in any Law we can make; and whatsoever Law we shall make, it must come to his Majesty's Allowance; and if his Majesty find Cause in his Government, he may not put Life to it. We daily see all Laws are broken, and all Laws will be broke for the publick Good, and the King may pardon all Offenders; his Majesty did see, that the best way to settle all at Unity, is to express his own Heart: The King's Heart is the best Guider of his own Promise, his Promise is bound with his own Heart. What Prince can express more Care and Wisdom?

Lastly, he saith, That hereafter ye shall never have the like Cause to complain. May we not think the Breach is made up? Is not his Majesty engaged in his Royal Word?

The Conclusion is full of Weight: And he prays God, that as God hath blessed this Kingdom, and put it into his Heart to come amongst us, so to make this Day successful. *The Wrath of a King is like the roaring of a Lion*, and all Laws with his Wrath are to no Effect; but *the King's Favour is like the Dew upon the Grass*, there all will prosper; and God made the Instruments to unite all Hearts.

His Majesty having thus discharged himself, he prays us to proceed to the Business that so much concerns him. As his Majesty hath now shewed himself the best of Kings, let us acknowledge his Majesty's Goodness, and return to that Union which we all desire.

But this Motion was not received with general Acceptation; and Sir *Benjamin Rudyard* replied to it.

WE are now upon a great Business, and the Manner of handling it may be as great as the Business itself. I need not tell you, that Liberty is a precious Thing, for every Man may set his own Price upon it, and he that doth not value it, deserves to be valued accordingly. For my own Part, I am clear without Scruple, that what we have resolved, is according to the Law; and if any Judge in *England* were of a contrary Opinion, I am sure we should have heard of him ere now. Without all Question, the very Point, Scope, and Drift of *Magna Charta* was, to reduce the Regal to a Legal Power, in Matter of Imprisonment, or else it had not been worthy so much contending for.

But there have been Precedents brought to prove the Practice and Interpretation of the Law. I confess I have heard many Precedents of Utility and Respect, but none at all of Truth, or of Law: Certainly there is no Court of Justice in *England*, that will discharge a Prisoner committed by the King, *Rege inconsulto*, without acquainting the King, yet this good Manners was never made, or mentioned as a legal Part of the Delivery.

It is objected, That the King ought to have a Trust left and deposited in him, God forbid but he should. And I say, that it is impossible to take it from him, for it is not in the Wit of Man to devise such a Law as should be able to comprehend all Particulars, all Accidents, but that extraordinary Cases must happen, which, when they come, if they be disposed of for the common Good, there will be no Law against them, yet must the Law be general, for otherwise Admissions and Exceptions will fret, and eat out the Law to nothing. God himself has constituted a general Law of Nature, to govern the ordinary Course of Things, he hath made no Law for Miracles, yet there is this Observation of them, that they are rather *praeter naturam*, than *contra naturam*, and always *propter bonum finem*. For Kings Prerogatives are rather besides the Law, than against it; and when they are directed to right Ends for the publick Good, they are not only concurring Laws, but even Laws in Singularity and Excellence.

But to come nearer, Mr. Speaker, let us consider where we are now, what Steps we have gone and gained; the King's learned Counsel have acknowledged all the Laws to be still in Force, the Judges have not allowed any Judgment against these Laws; the Lords also have confessed, that the Laws are in full Strength, they have further retained our Resolutions entire, and without Prejudice.

All this hitherto is for our Advantage; but above all, his Majesty has this Day (himself been publickly present) declared by the Mouth of the Lord Keeper, before both the Houses, That *Magna Charta*, and the other six Statutes are still in Force, that he will maintain his Subjects in the Liberties of their Persons, and Propriety of their Goods; that he will govern them according to the Laws of the Kingdom: this is a solemn and binding Satisfaction, expressing his gracious Readiness to comply with his People in all their reasonable and just Desires. The King is a good Man, and it is no Diminution to a King to be called so; for whosoever is a good Man, shall be greater than a King that is not so. The King certainly is very tender of his present Honour, and of his Fame hereafter: He will think it hard to have a worse Mark set upon his Government than upon any of his Ancestors, by extraordinary Restraints: His Majesty hath already intimated unto us by a Message, That he doth willingly give way to have the Abuse of Power reformed. By which I do verily believe, that he doth very well understand what a miserable Power it is, which hath produced so much Weakness to himself, and to the Kingdom, and it is our Happiness, that he is so really sensible of it.

For my own Part, I shall be very glad to see that good old decrepid Law of *Magna Charta*, which hath been kept so long, and lain Bed-rid as it were, I shall be glad to see it walk abroad again with new Vigour and Lustre, attended and followed with the other six Statutes. Questionless it will be a great Heartening to all the People. I doubt not, but upon a debating Conference with the Lords, we shall happily fall upon a fair and fit accommodation,

accommodation, concerning the Liberty of our Persons and propriety of our Goods. I hope we may have a Bill, to agree in the point, against imprisonment for Loans or *Privy*-Seals. As for intrinsical power and reason of State, they are matters in the clouds, where I desire we may leave them, and not meddle with them at all; lest by the way of admittance, we may lose somewhat of that which is our own already. Yet this by the way I will say of Reason of State, That, in the latitude by which 'tis used, it hath eaten out almost, not only the Laws, but all the Religion of Christendom.

Now, Mr. Speaker, I will only remember you of one precept, and that of the wisest man; *Be not over-wise, be not over-just:* and he gives this reason, *for why wilt thou be desolate?*

Sir, if Justice and Wisdom may be stretch'd to desolation, let us thereby learn, that Moderation is the Virtue of Virtues, and the Wisdom of Wisdoms. Let it be our Master-piece so to carry our business, that we may keep Parliaments on foot: For as long as they are frequent, there will be no irregular power; which though it cannot be broken at once, yet in short time it will fade and moulder away: there can be no total or final loss of Liberties, but by loss of Parliaments. As long as they last, what we cannot get at one time, we may have at another.

Let no man think, that what I have said is the Language of a private End, my aim is upon the good success of the whole, for, I thank God, my mind stands above any fortune that is to be got by base and unworthy means: no man is bound to be rich or great, no, nor to be wise; but every man is bound to be honest, out of which heart I have spoken.

The Bishop of Exeter's [*Dr. Joseph Hall*] *Letter sent to the House of Commons,* 28 *April,* 1628.

Gentlemen,

FOR God's sake be wise in your well-meant Zeal: why do you argue away precious time that can never be revoked, or repaired? Wo is me! while we dispute, our friends perish, and we must follow them. Where are we, if we break; and (I tremble to think) we cannot but break, if we hold so stiff. Our liberties and proprieties are sufficiently declared to be sure and legal, our remedies are clear and irrefragable; what do we fear, every subject sees the way now chalked out for future Justice, and who dares henceforth tread besides it? Certainly whilst Parliaments live, we need not misdoubt the violations of our Freedoms and Rights; may we be but where the Law found us, we shall sufficiently enjoy ourselves and ours; it is no season to search for more! O let us not, whilst we over-rigidly plead for an higher strain of safety, put ourselves into a necessity of ruin and utter despair of redress: let us not, in the suspicion of Evils that may be, cast ourselves into a present confusion. If you love yourselves and your Country, remit something of your own terms; and since the substance is yielded by your Noble Patriots, stand not too rigorously upon points of circumstance: fear not to trust a good King, who, after the strict Laws made, must be trusted with the execution. Think that your Country, nay Christendom, lies on the mercy of your present Resolutions. Relent, or farewel welfare.

From him whose faithful heart bleeds in a vowed sacrifice for his King and Country,

EXETER.

Upon this debate it was ordered, That a Committee of Lawyers do draw a Bill, containing the substance of *Magna Charta*, and the other Statutes, that do concern the Liberty of the Subject; which business took up two whole days.

Mr. Selden's *Speech at the Committee about the Bill for* Magna Charta, *and the Liberties of the Subject.*

April 28, 1628.

I Would have the violation tenderly mentioned. Let us set down the Statute of *Magna Charta*. 13 *Hen.* IV. it is adjudged in the Parliament-Roll, that the Statute of Tallage is an Act of Parliament. It is not entered in the Statute-Roll, and it was 34 *Ed.* I. 19 *Ed.* II. *rot. claus. mem.* 1[illegible]. *Les Comens priont lou divers suer' prise & imprison per accusement de persons malevoient lou ne suer' indict acc' al ley nel terre, ils priont que ils que sont pris sans indictment veignont en Chancery, & que droit serra fait. Et roy vult que nul serra pris.* But this is not in the Parliament-Roll 5 *Ed.* III. c. 9. 14 *Ed.* III c. 1. that there shall be no aid nor charge but by Parliament. 25 *Ed.* III. *c.* 4 None shall be attached by petition without presentment, or an original Writ. 25 *Ed* III. *no.* 16. *Item, priont les Comens que les loans soient relesse, & nul serra compell de faire arrere encontre les franchises del terre. Le roy le plest.* 28 Ed III. *c.* 3 *Nul serra ouste de terre ou tenements sans due proces del ley.* 36 Ed III. no. 9. *Que le grand Charter serra duly observe, & null serra imprison sur special command.* 36 Ed III. no 20. *Que nul serra imprison per special command.* 36 Ed. III. no. 2[illegible] *Si ascun home soit grieve contre les articles, avant dit veigne en Chancery & droit serra fait.* 37 Ed. III. no 10. *Ils la desire que le grand Charter & specialment les articles darrein stat. soient execute.* 37 Ed. III. c 18. *Il est contenu en le grand Charter que nul serra imprison,* &c. *tis que sont tiel,* &c. 38 Ed. III. no. 10. *Les Comens priont que le grand Charter & les autres statuts soient execute & que breves serront grauntez al cestuy que sue pur ceo, & si ascun jugement soit fait, il serra void.*

THursday the first of *May*, Mr. Secretary *Cook* delivered a Message from his Majesty, *viz.* to know whether the House will rest on his Royal Word, or no, declared to them by the Lord-Keeper; which if they do, he assures them it shall be royally performed.

Upon this there was a silence for a good space: then Mr. Secretary *Cook* proceeded: This silence invites [illegible] a further speech, and farther to address myself, now we see we must grow towards an issue. For my part, how confident I have been of the good issue of this Parliament, I have certified in this place, and elsewhere, and I am still confident thereof; I know his Majesty is resolved to do as much as ever King did for his Subjects: all this debate hath grown out of a sense of our sufferings, and a de[illegible] been made.

[illegible] Parliament [illegible] of that [illegible] King and [illegible] his Crown, which [illegible] War, [illegible] His Majesty called this Parliament to make up the breach: his Majesty assures us we shall not have the like cause to complain; he assures, the Laws shall be established, what can we desire more? All is, that we provide for Posterity, and that we do prevent the like suffering for the future. Were not the same means provided by them before us? Can we do more? We are come to the Liberty of the Subjects, and the Prerogative of the King, I hope we shall not add any thing to ourselves, to depress him. I will not divine I think we shall find difficulty with the King, or with the Lords, I shall not deliver my opinion as a Counsellor to his Majesty, which I will not justify and say here, or at the Council-Board. Will we in this necessity strive to bring ourselves into a better condition, and greater Liberty than our Fathers had, and the Crown into a worse than ever? I dare not advise his Majesty to admit of that: If this that we now desire be no Innovation, it is all contained in those Acts and Statutes, and whatsoever else we would add more, is a diminution to the King's power, and an addition to our own. We deal with a wise and prudent Prince, that hath a sword in his hand for our good, and this good is supported by power. Do not think, that by cases of Law and Debate we can make that not to be Law, which in experience we every day find necessary.

Give me leave freely to tell you, that I know by experience, that by the place I hold under his Majesty, if I will discharge the duty of my place and the oath I have taken to his Majesty, I must commit, and neither express the cause to the Gaoler, nor to the Judges, nor to any Counsellor in *England*, but to the King himself; yet do not think I go without ground of reason, or take this power committed to me to be unlimited; yea, rather it is to me a charge, burthen, and danger: for if I by this power shall commit the poorest porter, if I do it not upon a just cause, if it may appear, the burthen will fall upon me heavier than the Law can inflict, for I shall lose my credit with his Majesty, and my place. And I beseech you consider whether those that have been in the same place have not committed freely, and not any doubt made of it, nor any complaint made by the Subject.

SIR *Robert Phillips* hereupon spake thus: That if the words of Kings strike impressions in the hearts of subjects, then do these words upon this occasion strike an impression in the hearts of us all: to speak in a plain language, we are now come to the end of our Journey, and the well-disposing of an answer to this message, will give happiness or misery to this Kingdom. Let us set the Commonwealth of *England* before the eyes of his Majesty, that we may justify ourselves, that we have demeaned ourselves dutifully to his Majesty.

Mr. *Hackwell* of *Lincoln's-Inn*, 1 *May*, 1628.

SIR,

I Chose rather to discover my weakness by speaking, than to betray my conscience by silence: my opinion is, that we shall do well totally to omit our resolution out of this Bill, and rely only upon a confirmation of the Laws.

The Objections made against this Opinion are two.

The first is, that we shall thereby recede from our own resolution.

The second, that by a bare confirmation of the old Laws, without inserting of our resolution, by way of explanation, we shall be but in the same case as before.

For the first, that though we desire only a confirmation without adding of our resolution, we do not thereby recede from our resolution, I reason thus:

Our resolution was drawn out of the sense of those Laws, which are now desired to be confirmed, so that no question can be made by any of us that have thus declared ourselves, but that our resolution is virtually contained in those Laws. If that be so, how can our acceptance of a confirmation of these Laws be a departure from our resolution?

Nay, rather we think the contrary is true, he that doubts, that by confirmation of these Laws our resolution is not hereby confirmed, doubts whether we have justly deduced our resolutions out of those Laws, and so calls our resolution into question.

This argument alone is, in my opinion, a full answer to that first objection, that in desiring a bare confirmation of those Laws, we depart from our resolutions.

The second Objection is, that if we have nothing but a confirmation, we are in no better case than we were before those late violations of the Law.

This I deny, and do confidently affirm, that although we have no more than a confirmation of those Laws which are recited in the Bill that is now before us, we shall depart hence in far better case than we came, and that in divers respects.

First, Some of the Laws recited in this Bill, and desired to be confirmed, are not printed Laws, and are known to few professors of the Law, and much less to others; and yet they are Laws of as great consequence for the Liberty of the Subject, if not of greater, than any that are printed [illegible] namely 25 *Ed* III. *no* 1. That Loans against the will of the lender are against reason and the freedom of the Realm. 36 *Ed.* III. *no.* 9 by which Imprisonments by special commandment without due process are forbidden. These two are not printed.

That excellent Law *de Tallagio non concedendo* in print, hath in a publick Court been by a great Counsellor said to be but a Charter, and no Law.

The Statute 1 *Rich.* III. against Benevolences, is by some opinions in print an absolute Law. If we can get all these good Laws, besides those six other, which are expositions of *Magna Charta*, in the point of the freedom of our persons, to be confirmed and put in one Law, to the easy view of all men, is not our case far better than when we came hither?

Secondly, Will not the occasion of the making of this Law of confirmation, so notoriously known, be transmitted to all posterity? Certainly it will never be forgotten, that the occasion thereof was the imprisonment of those worthy Gentlemen for not lending, and the resolution in the *King's-Bench* in denying to bail them; and is not the occasion of the making of [illegible] it? If so, then by having a confirmation upon this occasion, we have bettered our case very much.

Thirdly, Have not the Judges in the *King's-Bench* in open Parliament, upon our complaint disclaimed to have given any judgment in this point?

Which generally before by the Parliament was otherwise conceived; for now they say, it was but an award and no judgment, will such a notorious Act upon so important an occasion in so publick a place be quickly forgotten? Nay, will not the memory of it for ever remain upon record? Is not our case then much better than when we came hither?

Fourthly, Will not the resolution of this House, and all our arguments and reasons against imprisonment without a cause expressed (which no doubt by the course we have taken will be transferred to posterity) be a great means to stay any Judge hereafter from declaring any judgment to the contrary, especially if there be likelihood of a Parliament? Is not our case in this very much amended?

Lastly, Have we not received Propositions from the Lords, wherein (amongst other things) they declared, that they are not out of love with our proceedings? Is not this a great strengthening to it? But after so long debate amongst them about it, they cannot take any just exception to it; and doth not this also much amend our case?

From all these reasons, I conclude that the second objection, that by a confirmation we are in no better case than when we came together, is also a weak objection.

Now for reasons to move us to proceed in this course of accepting a confirmation: First, We have his Majesty's gracious Promise to yield to a confirmation of the old Laws, from which we may rest most assured he will not depart; if we tender him, withal, our Proposition to be enacted, we have cause to doubt that we shall lose both the one and the other.

Secondly, We are no less assured of the Lords joining with us, for in their Propositions sent to us they have delivered themselves to that purpose: this is then a secure way of getting somewhat of great advantage to us; as we have great hopes, and in a manner assurance on this side; so on the other side we have great doubts and fears, that by offering our resolution to be enacted, we shall lose all.

For first we have had already experience of the Lords, that they are not very forward to join with us in a declaration of our Proposition to be Law; if they stumble at a declaration, much more will they, in yielding to make a Law in the same point.

And have we not much more cause to doubt that his Majesty will not yield unto it, seeing it toucheth him so near? Is it not the notice of his pleasure that hath wrought thus with the Lords?

If we should clog our Bill with our Proposition, and it should be rejected by the Lords, or by the King, is not our resolution much weakened by it; and are we not then in far worse case than before we made it? Our resolution for the rejecting of our Proposition, will tend to a justification of all that hath been done against us in this great point of our Liberty.

Let us then, like wise men, conform our desire to our hopes, and guide our hopes by probabilities; other desires and other hopes are but vain.

This is my poor opinion in this weighty business.

And so the day following they had further debate upon that matter, the House being turned into a Grand Committee, and Mr. *Herbert* in the chair.

Some said that the subject has suffered more in the violation of ancient Liberties within these few years, than in three hundred years before, and therefore care ought to be taken for the time to come.

Sir *Edward Coke* said, That that *Royal Word* had reference to some message formerly sent; his Majesty's word was, that they may secure themselves any way, by Bill or otherwise, he promised to give way to it. And to the end that this might not touch his Majesty's honour, it was proposed, that the Bill come not from the House, but from the King: We will and grant for us and our successors, and that we and our successors will do thus and thus; and it is the King's honour, he cannot speak but by Record.

Others desired the House to consider, when and where the late promise was made; was it not in the face of both Houses? Cruel Kings have been careful to perform their promises, yea, though they have been unlawful, as *Herod*. Therefore if we rest upon his Majesty's promise, we may assure ourselves of the performance of it; besides, we bind his Majesty, by relying on his word: we have laws enough, it is the execution of them that is our life, and it is the King that gives life and execution.

Sir *Thomas Wentworth* concluded the debate, saying, That never House of Parliament trusted more in the goodness of their King, for their own private account, than the present; but we are ambitious that his Majesty's goodness may remain to Posterity, and we are accountable to a publick trust: and therefore seeing there hath been a publick violation of the laws by his Ministers, nothing will satisfy him but a publick amends; and our desires to vindicate the subjects right by Bill, are no more than are laid down in former Laws, with some modest provision for instruction, performance and execution.

Which so well agreed with the sense of the House, that they made it the subject of a message to be delivered by the Speaker to his Majesty.

Amidst those deliberations, another message was delivered *May* 2. from his Majesty by Mr. Secretary *Cook*, That howsoever we proceed in this business we have in hand, which his Majesty will not doubt, but to be according to our constant profession, and so as he may have cause to give us thanks; yet his resolution is, that both his royal care, and hearty and tender affection towards all his loving subjects, shall appear to the whole Kingdom, and all the World, that he will govern us according to the laws and customs of this Realm; that he will maintain us in the liberties of our persons, and proprieties of our goods, so as we may enjoy as much happiness as our fore-fathers in their best times; and that he will rectify what hath been, or may be found amiss amongst us, so that hereafter there may be no just cause to complain. Wherein as his Majesty will rank himself amongst the best of our Kings, and shew he hath no intention to invade or impeach our lawful liberties, or right; so he will have us match ourselves with the best subjects, not by incroaching upon that sovereignty and prerogative, which God hath put into his hands for our good, but by containing ourselves within the bounds and laws of our forefathers, without restraining them, or enlarging them by new explanations, interpretations, expositions, or additions in any sort, which, he telleth us, he will not give way unto.

That the weight of the affairs of the Kingdom, and *Christendom*, do press him more and more, and that the time is now grown to that point of maturity, that it cannot endure long debate or delay; so as this Session of Parliament must continue no longer than *Tuesday* come seven-night at furthest: in which time his Majesty, for his part, will be ready to perform what he promised; and if the House be not ready to do that is fit for themselves, it shall be their own faults.

And upon assurance of our good dispatch and correspondence, his Majesty declareth, that his royal intention is to have another Session of Parliament at *Michaelmas* next, for the perfecting of such things as cannot now be done.

This message was debated the next day, being *Saturday*, *May* 3, whereupon Sir *John Elliot* spake to this effect:

The King, saith he, will rank himself with the best of Kings, and therefore he would have us rank ourselves with the best subjects; we will not incroach upon that Sovereignty that God hath put into his hands; this makes me fear his Majesty is mis-informed in what we go about; let us make some enlargement, and put it before him, that we will not make any thing new. As for the time of this Session, it is but short; and look how many messages we have, so many interruptions, and mis-reports, and mis-representations to his Majesty produce those messages.

Sir *Miles Fleetwood* continued the debate, and said, That this business is of great importance, we are to accommodate this: the breach of this Parliament will be the greatest misery that ever befell us: the eyes of *Christendom* are upon this Parliament, the State of all our Protestant Friends are ready to be swallowed up by the Emperor's Forces, and our own Kingdom is in a miserable strait, for the defence of our Religion that is invaded by the Roman Catholicks, by the colour of a commission, which is intolerable; the defence of our Realm by Shipping is decayed, the King's revenue is sold and gone; where shall the relief be obtained but in Parliament? Now we are in the way, let us proceed by way of Bill, in pursuance of the King's message, to establish the fundamental Laws in propriety of our goods, and liberty of our persons: It was declared to us, *that courses by Loan and Imprisonment were not lawful*; let us touch them in our Bill, and that all precedents and judgments seeming to the contrary, be void; and that all commitments against the Law be remedied, and that we be protected against the fear of commitments.

Mr. Mason's *Speech*.

I AM of opinion with the Gentleman that spake first, that, in our proceedings in the matter now in debate, we should have use of the title of the Statute, called *circumspecte agatis*; for it concerns the liberty of our persons, without which we do not enjoy our lives.

The Question is:

Whether in this Bill for the explanation of *Magna Charta*, and the rest of the Statutes, we shall provide that the cause of the commitment must be expressed upon the commitment, or upon return of the *Habeas Corpus*?

Before I speak to the question itself, I shall propose some observations, in my conceit, necessarily conducing to the debate of the matter.

1. That we ought to take care, and to provide for posterity, as our predecessors have done for us, and that this provident care cannot be expounded to be any distrust of the performance of his Majesty's gracious declaration, this Act providing for perpetuity, to which his Highness's promise, unless it were by Act of Parliament, cannot extend.

2. That we having long debated and solemnly resolved our rights and privileges by virtue of these Statutes, and if now we shall reduce those declarations and those resolutions into an Act, we must ever hereafter expect to be confined within the bounds of that Act, being made at our suit, and to be the limits of the Prerogative in that respect, and it being an Act of explanation, which shall receive no further explanation than itself contains.

3. That by this Act we must provide a remedy against the persons which detain us in prison, for as to the commander, there can be no certainty.

Concerning the Question itself:

It hath been solemnly and clearly resolved by the House, that the commitment of a Freeman, without expressing the cause at the time of the commitment, is against the Law: If by this Act of explanation we shall provide only that the cause ought to be expressed upon the return of the *Habeas Corpus*, then out of the words of the Statute, it will necessarily be inferred, that before the return of the *Habeas Corpus* the cause need not to be expressed, because the Statute hath appointed the time of the expression of the cause; and it will be construed, that if the makers of the Statutes had intended that the cause should have been sooner shewn, they would have provided for it by the Act, and then the Act, which we term an Act of explanation, will be an Act of the abridging of *Magna Charta*, and the rest of the Statutes: or if this Act do not make the commitment without expressing the cause, to be lawful, yet it will clearly amount to a toleration of the commitment, without expressing the cause, until the *Habeas Corpus*, or to a general or perpetual dispensation, beginning with, and continuing as long as the Law itself. And in my understanding the words in this intended Law, that no Freeman can be committed without cause, can no ways advantage us, or satisfy this objection; for till the return of the *Habeas Corpus*, he that commits is Judge of the cause, or at least hath a licence by this Law till that time to conceal the cause, and the Gaoler is not subject to any action for the detaining of the Prisoner upon such command. For if the prisoner demanded the cause of his imprisonment of the Gaoler, it will be a safe answer for him to say that he detains a prisoner by warrant, and that it belongs not unto him to desire those which commit the prisoner to shew the cause until he returns the *Habeas Corpus*. And if the prisoner be a Suitor to know the cause from those that committed him, it will be a sufficient answer for them to say, they will express the cause at the return of the *Habeas Corpus*. In this case there will be a wrong, because the commitment is without cause expressed, and one that suffers that wrong, *viz.* the party imprisoned; and yet no such wrong-doer but may excuse, if not justify himself by this Law.

In making of Laws, we must consider the inconveniences which may ensue, and provide for the prevention of them, *lex caveat de futuris*. I have taken into my thoughts some inconveniences which I shall expose to your consideration, not imagining that they can happen in the time of our gracious Sovereign; but in an Act of Parliament, we must provide for the prevention of all inconveniences in future times.

1. If a man be in danger to be imprisoned in the beginning of a long vacation for refusing to pay some sm.* sum of money, and knows that by this Act he can have no inlargement till the return of the *Habeas Corpus* in the Term, and that the charge of his being in Prison, and of his inlargement by *Habeas Corpus* will amount to more than the sum, he will part with money to prevent his imprisonment, or to redeem himself thence, because he cannot say any man doth him wrong, until the return of the *Habeas Corpus*, and the Law resolves. A man will pay a fine rather than be imprisoned, for the judgment which is given when one is fined, is *ideo capiatur*, and the execution for debt is a *capias ad satisfaciendum*, the Law presuming any man will part with his money to gain his Liberty. And if the prisoner procure an *Habeas Corpus*, and be brought into the King's-Bench by virtue of it, yet the cause need not to be then expressed; the provision of this Law being, that if no cause be then expressed, he shall be bailed, and no cause being shewn upon the return of the *Habeas Corpus*, yet it may be pretended, that at the time of his commitment there were strong presumptions of some great offence, but upon examination they are cleared: or it may be said, that the offence was of that nature, that the time of his imprisonment before the return was a sufficient punishment. And we may be frequently imprisoned in this manner, and never understand the cause, and have often such punishment, and have no means to justify ourselves; and for all these proceedings this Law will be the justification, or colour.

2. If by this Act there be a toleration of imprisonment without shewing cause, until the return of the *Habeas Corpus*; yet it is possible to accompany that imprisonment with such circumstances of close restraint, and other hardships, which I forbear to express, as may make an imprisonment for that short time, as great a punishment, as a perpetual imprisonment in an ordinary manner.

3. The party may be imprisoned a long time before he shall come to be delivered by this Law; the place of his imprisonment may be in the furthest part of this Kingdom; the Judges always make the return of the *Habeas Corpus* answerable to the distance of the prison from *Westminster*; the Gaoler may neglect the return of the first process, and then the party must procure an *Alias*, and the Gaoler may be then in some other imployment for the King, and excuse the not returning the body upon that process; and this may make the imprisonment for a year. And in the end no cause being returned, the party may be discharged; but in the mean time he shall have imprisonment, he shall never know the cause, he shall have no remedy for it, nor be able to question any for injustice, which have not a justification, or excuse by this Law.

4. The party may be imprisoned during his life, and yet there shall be no cause ever shewn. I will instance in this manner: a man may be committed to the furthest part of the Kingdom Westward; he obtains an *Habeas Corpus*; before the Gaoler receives the *Habeas Corpus*, or before he returns it, the prisoner by Warrant is removed from that prison to another, it may be the furthest Northern part of the Realm. The first Gaoler returns the special matter, which will be sufficient to free himself, and in like manner the prisoner may be translated from one prison to another, and his whole life shall be a peregrination, or wayfaring from one Gaol to another, and he shall never know the cause, nor be able to complain of any, who cannot defend their actions by this Bill.

5. If the prisoner be brought into the Court by *Habeas Corpus*, and no cause expressed, and thereupon he be inlarged, he may be partly committed again, and then his enlargement shall only make way for his commitment: and this may continue during his life, and he shall never know the cause; and this not remedied, but rather permitted by this Act.

And there are also some things remarkably considerable in this matter, the expence of the party in prison; his fees to the Gaoler, his costs in obtaining and prosecuting an *Habeas Corpus*, and his charges in removing himself, attended with such as have the charge of his conduct: and that the prisoner must sustain all this without satisfaction, or knowing the cause.

The only reason given by those of the other opinion is, That it is requisite, the King and Council should have power to command the detainer of a man in prison for some time, without expressing the cause; because it is supposed, that the manifestation of the cause at first may prevent the discovery of a Treason. The reason is answered by the remedy proposed; by this Act it being proposed, that it shall be provided by this Bill, that upon our commitment, we may instantly have recourse to the Chancery for an *Habeas Corpus*, returnable in that Court, which is always open; and that upon the receipt thereof, the Writ must be returned, and the cause thereupon expressed. If then this remedy be really the cause of commitment, it must partly appear; which contradicts the former reason of State.

And in my own opinion, we ought not only to take care, that the Subject should be delivered out of prison, but to prevent his imprisonment; the Statute of *Magna Charta*, and the rest of the Acts, providing that no man should be imprisoned, but by the Law of the Land. And although the King, or Council, as it hath been objected, by force may commit us without cause, notwithstanding any Laws we can make; yet I am sure without such an Act of Parliament, such commitment can have no legal colour, and I would be loth we should make a Law to endanger ourselves. For which reasons I conceive, that there being so many ways to evade this Act, we shall be in a worse case by it, than without it; as it provides no remedy to prevent our imprisonment without expressing the cause to be lawful, and administers excuses for continuing us in prison, as I have before declared. And thus for providing for one particular out of reason of State, which possibly may fall out in an age or two, we shall spring a leak, which may sink all our Liberties, and open a gap, through which *Magna Charta*, and the rest of the Statutes, may issue out and vanish. I therefore conclude, that in my poor understanding (which I submit to better Judgments), I had rather depend upon our former resolutions, and the King's gracious declarations, than to pass an Act in such manner as hath been proposed.

In conclusion, the Commons agreed to an answer to all the preceding messages, and presented it to the King by the mouth of their Speaker.

The Speaker's Speech (Sir John Finch) *to the King, in answer to several Messages, in the Banqueting-House*, May 5.

Most Gracious and Dread Sovereign,

YOUR Loyal and Obedient Subjects, the Commons now assembled in Parliament, by several messages from your Majesty, and especially by that your declaration delivered by the Lord-Keeper before both Houses, have, to their exceeding great joy and comfort, received many ample expressions of your princely care and tender affections towards them, with a gracious promise and assurance, that your Majesty will govern according to the Laws of this Realm, and so maintain all your Subjects, in the just freedom of their persons, and safety of their estates, that all their Rights and Liberties may be by them enjoyed, with as much freedom and security in their time, as in any age heretofore by their Ancestors, under the best of your Progenitors: For this so great a favour, enlarged by a comfortable intimation of your Majesty's confidence in the proceedings of this House, they do, by me, their Speaker, make a full return of most humble thanks to your Majesty, with all dutiful acknowledgment of your grace and goodness herein extended unto them.

And whereas in one of those messages delivered from your Majesty, there was an expression of your desire to know, whether this House would rest upon your Royal word and promise, assuring them, that if they would, it should be royally and really performed: As they again present their humble thanks for the seconding and strengthening of your former Royal expressions, so in all humbleness they assure your Majesty, that their greatest confidence is, and ever must be, in your grace and goodness, without which, they well know, nothing they can frame or desire, will be of safety or value to them; therefore are all humble suitors to your Majesty, that your Royal heart will graciously accept and believe the truth of theirs, which they humbly present, as full of truth and confidence in your Royal word and promise, as ever House of Commons reposed in any of their best Kings.

True it is, they cannot but remember the publick trust, for which they are accountable to present and future times, and their desires are, That your Majesty's goodness might, in fruit and memory, be the blessing and joy of Posterity.

They say also, That of late, there hath been publick violation of the Laws, and the Subjects Liberties, by some of your Majesty's Ministers; and thence conceive, that no less than a publick remedy will raise the dejected hearts of your loving Subjects to a chearful supply of your Majesty, or make them receive content in the proceedings of this House.

From these considerations, they most humbly beg your Majesty's leave to lay hold of that gracious offer of yours, which gave them assurance, that if they thought fit to secure themselves in their Rights and Liberties, by way of Bill or otherwise, so it might be provided with due respect to God's honour, and the publick good, you would be graciously pleased to give way unto it. Far from their intentions it is, any way to encroach upon your Sovereignty or Prerogative; nor have they the least thought of stretching or enlarging the Laws in any sort, by any new interpretations or additions; the bounds of their desires extend no further, than to some necessary explanation of that, which is truly comprehended within the just sense and meaning of those Laws, with some moderate provision for execution and performance, as in times past, upon like occasion hath been used.

The way how to accomplish these their humble desires, is now in serious consideration with them, wherein they humbly assure your Majesty, they will neither lose time, nor seek any thing of your Majesty, but that they hope may be fit for dutiful and loyal Subjects to ask, and for a gracious and just King to grant.

His Majesty's Answer was delivered by the Lord-Keeper, Thomas *Lord* Coventry.

MR. Speaker, and you Gentlemen of the House of Commons, his Majesty has commanded me to tell you, that he expected an answer by your actions, and not delay by discourse: ye acknowledge his trust and confidence in your proceedings, but his Majesty sees not how you requite him by your confidence of his word and actions: for what need explanations, if ye doubted not the performance of the true meaning? for explanations will hazard an incroachment upon his Prerogative. And it may well be said, What need a new Law to confirm an old, if you repose confidence in the declaration his Majesty made by me to both Houses? And yourselves acknowledge, that your greatest trust and confidence must be in his Majesty's grace and goodness, without which nothing that you can frame will be of safety, or available to you. Yet, to shew clearly the sincerity of his Majesty's intentions, he is content, that a Bill be drawn for a confirmation of *Magna Charta*, and the six other Statutes insisted upon for the Subjects Liberties, if ye shall chuse that to be the best way; but so, as it may be without additions, paraphrases, or explanations.

Thus, if you please, you may be secured from your needless fears, and this Parliament may have a happy wished-for end; whereas by the contrary, if you seek to tie your King by new, and indeed impossible bonds, you must be accountable to God and your Country for the ill success of this meeting: His Majesty having given his Royal word, that you shall have no cause to complain hereafter; less than which, hath been enough to reconcile great Princes, and therefore ought much more to prevail between a King and his Subjects.

Lastly, I am commanded to tell you, that his Majesty's pleasure is, That without further replies or messages, or other unnecessary delays, you do what you mean to do speedily, remembering the last message, which his Majesty sent you by Secretary *Cook*, in point of time: his Majesty always intending to perform his promise to his people.

NOtwithstanding the intimation of his Majesty's good pleasure for a Bill, Mr. Secretary *Cook*, *Tuesday, May* 6, again pressed the House to rely upon the King's word, saying, That he had rather follow others, than begin to enter into this business: loss of time hath been the greatest complaint; the matter fallen now into consideration, is, what way to take, whether to rely on his Majesty's word, or on a Bill? If we will consider the advantage we have in taking his Majesty's word, it will be of the largest extent, and we shall chuse that that hath most assurance; an Act of Par-

Parliament is by the consent of the King and Parliament; but this assurance by word is, that he will govern us by the Laws; the King promises that, and also that they shall be so executed, that we shall enjoy as much freedom as ever. This contains many Laws, and a grant of all good Laws; nay, it contains a confirmation of those very Laws, assurance, which binds further than the Law can: first, it binds his affection, which is the greatest bond between King and Subject, and that binds his judgment also, nay, his honour, and that not at home, but abroad; the Royal word of a King is the ground of all treaty; nay, it binds his conscience. This confirmation between both Houses is in nature of a vow; for my part, I think it is the greatest advantage to rely on his Majesty's word. He further added, this debate was fitter to be done before the House, and not before the Committee; and that it was a new course to go to a Committee of the whole House.

Sir *John Elliott* replied, That the proceeding in a Committee is more honourable and advantageous to the King and the House, for that way leads most to truth, and it is a more open way, and where every man may add his reason, and make answer upon the hearing of other men's reasons and arguments.

This being the general sense, the House was turned into a Committee, to take into consideration what was delivered to the King by the Speaker, and what was delivered to them by the Lord-Keeper, and all other messages, and the Committee was not to be bounded by any order: the key was brought up, and none were to go out without leave first asked.

In the debate of this business at the Committee, some were for letting the Bill rest: but Sir *Edward Coke*'s reasons prevailed to the contrary. Was it ever known (said he) that general words were a sufficient satisfaction to particular grievances? Was ever a verbal declaration of the King *Verbum Regni*? When Grievances be, the Parliament is to redress them. Did ever Parliament rely on messages? They put up Petitions of their Grievances, and the King ever answered them: the King's answer is very gracious, but what is the Law of the Realm, that is the question? I put no diffidence in his Majesty, the King must speak by a Record, and in particulars, and not in general: did you ever know the King's message come into a Bill of Subsidies? All succeeding Kings will say, Ye must trust me as you did my Predecessors, and trust my messages; but messages of love never came into a Parliament. Let us put up a Petition of Right: not that I distrust the King, but that I cannot take his trust, but in a Parliamentary way.

On *Thursday* 8 *May*, the Petition of Right was finished, and the Clause of Martial Law was added unto it, and it was delivered to the Lords at a conference in the Painted Chamber for their concurrence; which conference was managed by Sir *Edward Coke*, who thus expressed himself: I pray your Lordships to excuse us, for we have been till one of clock about the great business, and (blessed be God) we have dispatch'd it in some measure, and before this time we were not able to attend your Lordships, but I hope that this will prove a great blessing to us. My Lords, I am commanded from the House of Commons to express their singular care and affection they have of concurrence with your Lordships, in these urging affairs and proceedings of this Parliament; both for the good of the Commonwealth, and principally for his Majesty's. And this I may say in this particular, if we had hundreds of tongues, we were not able to express this desire which we have of that concurrence with your Lordships: but I will leave it without any further expression. My Lords, it is evident what necessity there is, both in respect of yourselves, and your Posterities, to have good success in this business. We have acquainted your Lordships with the reasons and arguments, and after we have had some conference, we have received from your Lordships five propositions; and it behoves me to give your Lordships some reasons why you have not heard from us before now; for in the mean time, as we were consulting of this weighty business, we have received divers messages from our great Sovereign the King, and they consisted of five parts:

1. That his Majesty would maintain all his Subjects in their just freedom, both of their persons and estates.
2. That he will govern according to his Laws and Statutes.
3. That we should find much confidence in his Royal word; I pray observe that.
4. That we shall enjoy all our Rights and Liberties, with as much freedom and liberty as ever any Subjects have done in former times.
5. That whether we shall think it fit, either by way of Bill or otherwise, to go on in this great business, his Majesty would be pleased to give way to it.

These gracious messages did so work upon our affections, that we have taken them into consideration. My Lords, when we had these messages, (I deal plainly, for so I am commanded by the House of Commons) we did consider, what way we might go for our more secure way, nay, yours; we did think it the safest way to go in a Parliamentary course, for we have a maxim in the House of Commons, and written on the walls of our House, That old ways are the safest and surest ways: And at last we fell upon that which we did think (if that your Lordships did consent with us) it is the most ancient way of all, and that is, my Lords, *via fausta*, both to his Majesty, to your Lordships, and to ourselves. For, my Lords, this is the greatest Bond, that any Subject can have in Parliament, *Verbum Regis*, this is an high point of honour, but this shall be done by the Lords and Commons, and assented to by the King in Parliament; this is the greatest obligation of all; and this is for the King's honour and our safety. Therefore, my Lords, we have drawn a form of a Petition, desiring your Lordships to concur with us therein; for we come with an unanimous consent of all the House of Commons, and there is great reason your Lordships should do so, for your Lordships are involved in the same condition, *Commune Periculum*. So I have done with the first part: And now I shall be bold to read that which we have so agreed on, and I shall desire your Lordships leave that I may read it.

Here the Petition of Right was read; but we forbear to insert it as yet, because there were propositions for alteration; and it is not perfect, till the Royal assent be given to it.

From the eighth to the twelfth of *May*, all publick business was laid aside. On *Monday* the twelfth, the Lords had a conference with the Commons, where the Lord-Keeper made this Speech:

Gentlemen of the House of Commons,

MY Lords, having a most affectionate desire to maintain that good concurrence, that in this Parliament and others have been of late between both Houses, desired this Conference, to acquaint you, how, and in what manner, they have proceeded in the Petition of Right that came from this House, and to let you know, that as soon as they had received it, they, with all care and expedition they possibly could, addressed themselves to consider thereof; and after good time spent in Debate in the whole House, they made a Committee to consider, whether retaining the substance of the Petition, there might not be some words altered, or put in to make it more sweet, to procure it a passable way to his Majesty: we know this must be crowned by the King, and good must come to all the Kingdom by this course now taken. The Committee hath met, and hath propounded some small matters to be altered in some few words, to make it passable, and not in substance. And the Lords having this reported from their Committee, and heard it read in their House, resolved of nothing till they have your consent; yet they think it fitter to have it propounded to you, to consider, whether there should be any alteration or no, and how the propounded alterations may stand with your liking.

Concerning the commitment by the King and the Council, without expressing the cause, it was resolved by the Lords to debate it this morning, and as soon as they should have debated it, they purposed to have your concurrence with them before they resolved it; but at the instant when they thought to have debated it, they received a Letter from his Majesty, which, they conceive, will give a satisfaction to both Houses in the main point. My Lords desiring to keep that good concurrence begun, desired to communicate that Letter unto you, that you might take the same into your considerations, as they mean to do themselves: This Letter is to be read unto you.

To our Right Trusty and Well-beloved, the Lords Spiritual and Temporal of the Higher House of Parliament.

Carolus Rex.

"WE being desirous of nothing more than the advancement of the "peace and prosperity of our People, have given leave to free "Debate upon the highest points of our Prerogative Royal, which in the "time of our Predecessors, Kings and Queens of this Realm, were ever "restrained as matters that they would not have discussed; and in other "things we have been willing so far to descend to the desires of our good "Subjects, as might fully satisfy all moderate minds, and free them from "all just fears and jealousies, which those messages, which we have hitherto "sent into the Commons House, will well demonstrate unto the World. "Yet we find it still insisted upon, that in no case whatsoever, should it "never so nearly concern matters of State or Government, we, or our "Privy-Council, have no power to commit any man without the cause "shewed; whereas it often happens, that should the cause be shewed, "the service itself would thereby be destroyed and defeated, and the "cause alledged must be such, as may be determined by our Judges of "our Courts of *Westminster*, in a legal and ordinary way of justice; "whereas the causes may be such, whereof the Judges have no capacity "of judicature, nor rules of Law to direct and guide their judgment in "cases of that transcendent nature; which happening so often, the very "intermitting the constant rule of Government, for so many ages, with-"in this Kingdom practised, would soon dissolve the very foundation and "frame of our Monarchy. Wherefore, as to our Commons we have made "fair propositions, which might equally preserve the just Liberty of the "Subject; so, my Lords, we have thought good to let you know, that "without the overthrow of Sovereignty, we cannot suffer this power to "be impeached; notwithstanding, to clear our conscience and just inten-"tions, this we publish, That it is not in our heart, nor will we ever extend "our Royal power, lent unto us from God, beyond the just rule of Mode-"ration, in any thing which shall be contrary to our Laws and Customs, "wherein the safety of our people shall be our only aim. And we do "hereby declare our Royal pleasure and resolution to be, which, God "willing, we shall ever constantly continue and maintain, That neither "we, nor our Privy-Council, shall or will, at any time hereafter, com-"mit or command to prison, or otherwise restrain the person of any for "not lending money to us, nor for any cause, which in our conscience "doth not concern the publick good and safety of us and our people; "we will not be drawn to pretend any cause, wherein our judgment and "conscience is not satisfied with; which base thoughts, we hope, no man "can imagine will fall into our Royal breast; and that in all cases of "this nature, which shall hereafter happen, we shall, upon the humble "Petition of the Party, or address of our Judges unto us, readily and "really express the true cause of their commitment or restraint, so soon "as with conveniency and safety the same is fit to be disclosed and ex-"pressed. And that in all causes criminal of ordinary jurisdiction, our "Judges shall proceed to the deliverance or bailment of the prisoner, ac-"cording to the known and ordinary rules of the Laws of this Land, and "according to the Statutes of *Magna Charta*, and those other six Statutes "insisted upon, which we do take knowledge stand in full force, and which "we intend not to abrogate and weaken, against the true intention there-"of. This we have thought fit to signify unto you, the rather to shorten "any long Debate upon this great question, the season of the year being "so far advanced, and our great occasions of State not lending us many "more days for longer continuance of this Session of Parliament."

Given under our Signet at our Palace at Westminster, 12 Maii, *the fourth year of our Reign.*

The same day the King's Letter was communicated to the House of Commons, they laid it aside, and Sir *Thomas Wentworth* said, It was a Letter of Grace; but the people will only like of that which is done in a Parliamentary way: besides, the debate of it would spend much time, neither was it directed

directed to the House of Commons; and the Petition of Right would clear all mistakes: For (said he) some give it out, as if the House went about to pinch the King's Prerogative. But the further debate of this matter took up several days.

May 17. The Lords propounded, at a conference, an addition to be made to the Petition of Right, which was delivered by the Lord-Keeper, to this purpose:

YOU the Knights, Citizens, and Burgesses of the House of Commons, my Lords have commanded me to present unto you the singular care and affection they have to preserve that correspondency and order, which the two Houses (both in this and former Parliaments, to the happiness of this Kingdom) have heretofore enjoyed.

They command me also to let you know, that they have no less care and affection to bring that great business, *the Liberty of the Subject*, to an happy issue. And whereas at the last conference of both Houses, there were some things propounded, that came from their Lordships, out of a desire the Petition might have the easier passage with his Majesty, not intending to alter in any manner the substance of the Petition; but it was then thought fit, that there was another part of the Petition, of as great importance and weight: my Lords, since the time of that conference, have imploy'd themselves wholly to reduce the Petition to such a frame and order, that may give both to you and them hope of acceptance.

And after many deliberations, and much advice taken, my Lords have resolved to represent to you something which they have thought upon, yet not as a thing conclusive to them or you; and according to their desires (having mentioned it in the beginning) have held it fit to conclude of nothing, till that you be made acquainted with it, and that there may be a mature advisement between you and them, so that there may be the happier conclusion in all their business.

This being the determination of the Lords, that nothing, that is now offered unto you, should be conclusive, yet they thought it convenient to present it unto you.

This alteration (and not alteration, but addition) which they shall propound unto you, to be advised and conferred upon, which is no breach of the same, they think it meet, if it shall stand with your liking, to be put in the conclusion of the Petition which I shall now read unto you.

We present this our humble Petition to your Majesty, with the care not only of preserving our own Liberties, but with due regard to leave intire that Sovereign Power, wherewith your Majesty is trusted for the Protection, Safety, and Happiness of the People.

This is the thing the Lords do present unto you, the Subject of this conference, concerning the adding of this in the conclusion of the Petition; and as they know, that this is no small thing, and that you cannot presently give an answer to it; therefore they desire you, that you do with some speed consider of it, and their Lordships will be ready this afternoon.

This addition produced several speeches.

Mr. *Alford.*] Let us look (said he) into the Records, and see what they are, what is *Sovereign Power?* *Bodin* saith, That it is free from any condition, by this we shall acknowledge a Regal, as well as a Legal Power: Let us give that to the King, that the Law gives him, and no more.

Mr. *Pymm.*] I am not able to speak to this question, I know not what it is All our Petition is for the Laws of *England*, and this power seems to be another distinct power from the power of the Law. I know how to add Sovereign to his Person, but not to his Power And we cannot leave to him a Sovereign Power, when we never were possessed of it.

Mr *Hackwell.*] We cannot admit of those words with safety, they are applicable to all the parts of our Petition: It is in the nature of a Saving, and by it we shall imply, as if we had incroached on his Prerogative, all the Laws we cite are without a Saving and yet now after the violation of them we must add a Saving. I have seen divers Petitions, and where the Subject claimed a Right, there I never saw a Saving of this nature.

Sir *Edward Coke*] This is *magnum in parvo*, this is propounded to be a conclusion of our Petition: It is a matter of great weight, and, to speak plainly, it will overthrow all our Petition, it trenches to all parts of it. It flies at Loans, and at the Oath, and at Imprisonment, and Billeting of Soldiers, this turns all about again. Look into all the Petitions of former times, they never petitioned, wherein there was a saving of the King's Sovereignty I know that Prerogative is part of the Law, but sovereign Power is no Parliamentary word. In my opinion, it weakens *Magna Charta*, and all our Statutes, for they are absolute, without any saving of sovereign Power. And shall we now add it, we shall weaken the foundation of Law, and then the building must needs fall, let us take heed what we yield unto: *Magna Charta* is such a fellow, that he will have no sovereign. I wonder this sovereign was not in *Magna Charta*, or in the confirmations of it: If we grant this, by implication we give a sovereign power above all these Laws. power in Law, is taken for a power with force: The Sheriff shall take the power of the County, what it means here, God only knows. It is repugnant to our petition, that is a *Petition of Right*, grounded on Acts of Parliament. Our Predecessors could never endure a *salvo jure suo*, no more than the Kings of old could endure for the Church, *salvo honore Dei & Ecclesiæ*. We must not admit of it, and to qualify it, is impossible. Let us hold our privileges according to the Law; that power, that is above this, is not fit for the King and People to have it disputed further. I had rather, for my part, have the prerogative acted, and I myself to lie under it, than to have it disputed.

Sir *Thomas Wentworth.*] If we do admit of this addition, we shall leave the Subject worse than we found him, and we shall have little thanks for our labour, when we come home. Let us leave all power to his Majesty to punish malefactors; but our Laws are not acquainted with sovereign power: we desire no new thing, nor do we offer to trench on his Majesty's prerogative; we must not recede from this petition, either in part or whole.

Mr. *Noye.*] To add a Saving, is not safe; doubtful words may beget ill construction: and the words are not only doubtful words, but words unknown to us, and never used in any act or Petition before.

Mr. *Selden.*] Let us not go too hastily to the question. If there be any objections, let any propound them, and let others answer them as they think good. I will not touch the reasons already given. The sum of this addition is, that our right is not to be subject to Loans or Imprisonment without cause, or martial law, but by sovereign power. If it hath no reference to our Petition, what doth it here? I am sure all others will say it hath reference, and so must we. How far it doth exceed all examples of former times, no man can shew me the like. I have made that search that fully satisfies me, and I find not another besides 28 *Ed.* I. We have a great many petitions and bills of parliament in all ages, in all which we are sure no such thing is added. That clause of the 28 *Edw.* I. it was not in the petition, but in the King's answer.

In *Magna Charta* there were no such clauses; the articles themselves are to be seen in a library at *Lambeth*, in a book of that time, upon which the law was made. There was none in the Statutes in King *John*'s time, for these I have seen, there is no saving. In the articles of *confirmatio chartarum*, is a saving, *les ancients aids*, that is, for *file maryer*, & *pur fair fitz chivalier*, and for ransom. And in the articles of King *John*, in the original charter, which I can shew, there those three aids were named therein, and they were all known. In the 25 *Edw.* III. there is a petition against Loans, there is no saving, and so in others. As for that addition in the 28 *Edw.* I. do but observe the petitions after *Magna Charta*; as 5 *Edw.* III. they put up a petition: whereas in *Magna Charta* it is contained, that none be imprisoned but by due process of law; those words are not in *Magna Charta*, and yet there is no saving. And so in the 28 *Edw.* III. and 36, 37, and 42 of *Edw.* III. all which pass by petition, and yet there is no saving in them. And there are in them other words that are not in *Magna Charta*, and yet no saving. For that that Mr. Speaker said to the King, it was our heart, and ever shall be; but we then spoke of the King's prerogative by itself, and we are bound to say so: but speaking of our rights, shall we say we are not to be imprisoned, saving but by the King's sovereign power? Say my Lands, without any title, be seized in the King's hand, and I bring a petition of right, and I go to the King, and say, I do by no means seek your Majesty's right and title; and after that, I bring a petition or *monstrance de droit*, setting forth my own right and title, and withal set down a saving, that I leave intire his Majesty's right, it would be improper. It was objected, that in the 28 of *Edw.* I. in the end of *articuli super chartas*, which was a confirmation of *Magna Charta*, and *Charta de Foresta*, in the end there is a clause, *savant le droit & signiory*; the words are extant in that roll that is now extant, but the original roll is not extant.

In the 25 *Edw.* I. there was a confirmation of the Charter; in the 27 *Edw.* I. the Parliament was called, and much stir there was about the Charter, and renewing the Articles, but then little was done. In 28 *Edw.* I. the Commons by petition or bill, did obtain the liberties and articles at the end of the Parliament; they were extracted out of the roll, and proclaimed abroad. The addition was added in the proclamation: In the bill there was no *savant*, but afterwards it was put in; and to prove this, it is true, there is no Parliament-roll of that year, yet we have historics of that time. In the library at *Oxford*, there is a journal of a parliament of that very year, which mentions so much; also in the publick library at *Cambridge*, there is a manuscript that belonged to an Abbey, it was of the same year 28 *Edw.* I. and it mentions the parliament and the petitions, and *articulos quos petierunt sic confirmaverat rex ut in fine audiret, Salvo jure coronæ regis*; and they came by proclamation in *London*. When the people heard this clause added in the end, they fell into execration for that addition, and the great Earls that went away dissatisfied from the Parliament, hearing of this, went to the King, and afterwards it was cleared at the next Parliament. Now there is no Parliament-roll of this at that time, only in one roll in the end of *Edw.* III. there is a roll, that recites not the Parliament bill, but the Statute that was the effect of the roll, that was proclaimed.

The Lords afterwards, at a conference, tendered reasons to fortify their addition, which were briefly reported by the Lord Keeper.

THAT the Lords were all agreed to defend and maintain the just liberties of the Subject, and of the Crown; and that the word, *leave*, was debated amongst them; and thereby they meant to give no new, but what was before. For the words, *Sovereign Power*, as he is a King, he is a Sovereign, and must have power; and he said, the words were easier than the *Prerogative*. As for the word, *that*, which is a relative, and referred to *that power*, that is for the safety of the people, and this, said he, can never grieve any man. Being thus published, it is not sovereign power in general, but now in confutation of our reasons, *Magna Charta* was not with a saving; but, said he, you pursue not the words in *Magna Charta*, and therefore it needs an addition

As for the 28 of *Edw.* III. he said, there was a saving; and an ill exposition cannot be made of this, and both Houses have agreed it in substance already; the Commons did it in a speech delivered by the Speaker, and that we say we have not a thought to incroach on the King's sovereignty; and why may you not add it in your petition?

Upon this report, Mr. *Mason* spake his opinion in manner following:

IN our Petition of Right to the King's Majesty, we mention the laws and statutes, by which it appear'd, That no tax, loan, or the like, ought to be levied by the King, but by common assent in Parliament: that no freeman ought to be imprisoned but by the law of the land; that no freeman ought to be compell'd to suffer soldiers in his house. In the petition we have expressed the breach of these laws, and desire we may not suffer the like; all which we pray as our rights and liberties.

The Lords have proposed an addition to this Petition, in these words:

We humbly present this Petition to your Majesty, not only with a care of our own Liberties, but with a due regard to leave entire that Sovereign Power *where-*

wherewith your Majeſty is intruſted for the protection, ſafety, and happineſs of your people.

And whether we ſhall conſent unto this addition, is the ſubject of this day's diſcourſe: and becauſe my Lord-Keeper, at the laſt conference, declared their Lordſhips had taken the words of the petition apart, I ſhall do ſo too. The word, *leave*, in a petition, is of the ſame nature as *ſaving* in a grant, or act of parliament: when a man grants but part of a thing, he ſaves the reſt; when he petitions to be reſtored but to part, he leaveth the reſt: then in the end of our petition, the word, *leave*, will imply, that ſomething is to be left of that, or at leaſt with a reference to what we deſire.

The word, *intire*, is very conſiderable; a Conqueror is bound by no Law, but hath power *dare leges*, his Will is a Law; and although *William* the Conqueror, at firſt, to make his way to the Crown of *England* the more eaſy, and the poſſeſſion of it more ſure, claimed it by title; but afterwards when there were no powerful pretenders to the Crown, the title of conqueſt (to introduce that abſolute power of a Conqueror) was claimed, and that Statute of *Magna Charta*, and other Statutes mentioned in our petition, do principally limit that power. I hope it is as lawful for me to cite a Jeſuit, as it is for Dr. *Manwaring* to falſify him; *Suares*, in his firſt book, *de Legibus, cap.* 17. delivered his opinion in theſe words, *Amplitudo & reſtrictio poteſtatis Regum circa ea quæ per ſe mala vel injuſta non ſunt, pendet ex arbitrio hominum & ex ambigua conventione vel pacto inter reges & regnum.* And he farther expreſſeth his opinion, That the King of *Spain* was ſo abſolute a Monarch, that he might lawfully impoſe tribute without conſent of his people, until about two hundred years ſince, when it was concluded between him and his people, that without conſent of his people by proxies, he ſhould not impoſe any tribute. And *Suares*'s opinion is, That by that agreement, the Kings of *Spain* are bound to impoſe no tribute without conſent.

And this agreement that author calls a reſtraining of that ſovereign power; the Statutes then mentioned in our Petition, reſtraining that abſolute power of a Conqueror: if we recite thoſe Statutes, and ſay, we leave the ſovereign power intire, we do take away that reſtraint which is the virtue and ſtrength of thoſe Statutes, and ſet at liberty the claim of the ſovereign power of a Conqueror, which is to be limited and reſtrained by no laws: this may be the danger of the word, *intire*.

The next word delivered by the Lords as obſervable, is the particle, *That*; becauſe it was ſaid, that all ſovereign power is not mentioned to be left, but only (that) with which the King is truſted for our protection, ſafety, and happineſs: But I conceive this to be an exception of all ſovereign power; for all ſovereign power in a King, is for the protection, ſafety, and happineſs of his people. If all ſovereign power be excepted, you may eaſily judge the conſequence, all Loans and Taxes being impoſed by colour of that ſovereign power.

The next word is, *Truſted*; which is very ambiguous, whether it be meant, truſted by God only as a Conqueror, or by the people alſo, as King, which are to govern alſo according to laws, *ex pacto*. In this point I will not preſume to adventure further; only I like it not, by reaſon of the doubtful expoſition it admits. I have likewiſe conſidered the propoſition itſelf, and therein I have fallen upon the dilemma, that this addition ſhall be conſtrued either to refer unto the petition, or not; if it doth refer unto the petition, it is merely uſeleſs and unneceſſary, and unbefitting the judgment of this grave and great aſſembly to add to a petition of this weight. If it hath reference unto it, then it deſtroys not only the virtue and ſtrength of our petition of Right, but our Rights themſelves; for the addition being referred to each part of the petition, will neceſſarily receive this conſtruction: That none ought to be compelled to make any Gift, Loan, or ſuch like charge, without common conſent, or Act of Parliament, unleſs it be by the ſovereign power, with which the King is truſted for the protection, ſafety, and happineſs of his people.

That none ought to be compelled to ſojourn or billet ſoldiers, unleſs by the ſame ſovereign power; and ſo of the reſt of the Rights contained in the petition: and then the moſt favourable conſtruction will be, that the King hath an ordinary prerogative, and by that he cannot impoſe Taxes, or impriſon, that is, he cannot impoſe Taxes at his Will to employ them as he pleaſeth; but that he hath an extraordinary and tranſcendent ſovereign power for the protection and happineſs of his people, and for ſuch purpoſe he may impoſe Taxes, or billet ſoldiers as he pleaſeth, and we may aſſure ourſelves, that hereafter all Loans, Taxes, and billetting of ſoldiers, will be ſaid to be for the protection, ſafety, and happineſs of the people. Certainly hereafter it will be conceived, That an Houſe of Parliament would not have made an unneceſſary addition to this Petition of Right; and therefore it will be reſolved, That the addition hath relation to the Petition, which will have ſuch operation as I have formerly declared; and I the rather fear it, becauſe the late Loan and Billetting have been declared to have been by ſovereign power for the good of ourſelves; and if it be doubtful whether this propoſition hath reference to the petition or not, I knew not who ſhall judge whether Loans or Impriſonments hereafter be by that ſovereign power or not?

A Parliament, which is made a Body of ſeveral Writs, and may be diſſolved by one Commiſſion, cannot be certain to decide this queſtion. We cannot reſolve that the Judges ſhall determine the words of the King's Letter read in this Houſe, expreſſing the cauſe of commitment may be ſuch, that the Judges have not capacity of judicature, no Rules of Law to direct and guide their judgments in caſes of that tranſcendent nature; the Judges then, and the judgments, are eaſily conjectured. It hath been confeſſed by the King's Counſel, that the ſtatute of *Magna Charta* binds the King, and his ſovereign power cannot be divided from himſelf. If then the ſtatute of *Magna Charta* binds the King, it binds his ſovereign power. If to the petition theſe words be added, the expoſition muſt be, that the ſtatute of *Magna Charta* binds the King's ſovereign power; ſaving the King's ſovereign power, I ſhall endeavour to give ſome anſwer to the reaſons given by the Lords.

The firſt is, That it is the intention of both Houſes, to maintain the juſt liberty of the Subject, and not to diminiſh the juſt power of the King; and therefore the expreſſion of that intention in this petition, cannot prejudice us. To which I anſwer,

Firſt, That our intention was, and is, as we then profeſſed, and no man can aſſign any particular in which we have done to the contrary; neither have we any way tranſgreſſed in that kind in this petition: and if we make this addition to the petition, it would give ſome intimation, that we have given cauſe or colour of offence therein; which we deny: and which if any man conceive ſo, let him aſſign the particular, that we may give anſwer thereunto.

By our petition, we only deſire our particular Rights and Liberties to be confirmed to us; and therefore it is not proper for us in it to mention ſovereign power in general, being altogether impertinent to the matter of the petition.

There is a great difference between the words of the addition, and the words propoſed therein, *viz.* between juſt Power, which may be conceived to be limited by Laws, and ſovereign Power, which is ſuppoſed to be tranſcendent and boundleſs.

The ſecond reaſon delivered by their Lordſhips, was, That the King is ſovereign; that as he is ſovereign, he hath power, and that that ſovereign power is to be left: for my part, I would leave it ſo, as not to mention it; but if it ſhould be expreſſed to be left in this petition, as it is propoſed, it muſt admit ſomething to be left in the King of what we pray, or at leaſt admit ſome ſovereign power in his Majeſty, in theſe privileges which we claim to be our right, which would fruſtrate our petition, and deſtroy our right; as I have formerly ſhewed.

The third reaſon given for this addition, was, That in the ſtatute of *Articuli ſuper Chartas*, there is a ſaving of the *Right* and *Seigniory* of the Crown.

To which I give theſe anſwers: That *Magna Charta* was confirmed above thirty times, and a general ſaving was in none of theſe Acts of confirmation, but in this only; and I ſee no cauſe we ſhould follow one ill, and not thirty good precedents; and the rather, becauſe that ſaving produced ill effects, that are well known.

That ſaving was by Act of Parliament; the concluſion of which Act is, That in all thoſe caſes the King did will, and all thoſe that were at the making of that ordinance did intend, that the *Right* and *Seigniory* of the Crown ſhould be ſaved: by which it appears, that the ſaving was not in the Petition of the Commons, but added by the King; for in the petition, the King's will is not expreſſed.

In that Act the King did grant, and part with, to his people, divers rights belonging to his prerogative, as in the firſt chapter he granted, That the people might chuſe three men, which might have power to hear and determine complaints, made againſt thoſe that offended in any point of *Magna Charta*, though they were the King's Officers, and to fine and ranſom them. And in the 8, 12, and 19 Chapters of that Statute, the King parted with other prerogatives, and therefore there might be ſome reaſon of the adding of that Sovereign Power, by the King's Counſel: But in this petition, we deſire nothing of the King's Prerogative, but pray the enjoying of our proper and undoubted rights and privileges; therefore there is no cauſe to add any words, which may imply a ſaving of that which concerns not the matter in the petition.

The fourth reaſon given by their Lordſhips, was, That by the mouth of our Speaker, we have this Parliament declared, That it was far from our intention to incroach upon his Majeſty's prerogative, and that therefore it could not prejudice us, to mention the ſame reſolution in an addition to this Petition.

To which I anſwer, That that declaration was a general anſwer to a meſſage from his Majeſty to us, by which his Majeſty expreſſed that he would not have his prerogative ſtraitened by any new explanation of *Magna Charta*, or the reſt of the Statutes; and therefore that expreſſion of our Speaker's was then proper, to make it have reference to this petition, there being nothing therein contained, but particular rights of the Subject, and nothing at all concerning his Majeſty's prerogative.

Secondly, That anſwer was to give his Majeſty ſatisfaction of all our proceedings in general, and no man can aſſign any particular, in which we have broken it, and this Petition juſtifies itſelf, that in it we have not offended againſt the proteſtation: And I know no reaſon, but that this declaration ſhould be added to all our Laws we ſhall agree on this Parliament, as well as to this petition.

The laſt reaſon given, was, That we have varied in our petition from the words of *Magna Charta*, and therefore it was very neceſſary that a ſaving ſhould be added to this petition.

I anſwer, that in the Statute 5 *E.* III. 25 *E.* III. 28 *E.* III. and other Statutes, with which *Magna Charta* is confirmed. The words of the Statute of explanation differ from the words of *Magna Charta* itſelf; the words of ſome of the Statutes of explanation, being, *That no man ought to be apprehended, unleſs by indictment, or due proceſs of Law*; and the other Statutes differing from the words of *Magna Charta*, in many other particulars, and yet there is no ſaving in thoſe Statutes, much leſs ſhould there be any in a *Petition of Right*. Theſe are the anſwers I have conceived to the reaſons of their Lordſhips, and the expoſition, I apprehend, muſt be made of the propoſed words, being added to our petition. And therefore, I conclude, that, in my opinion, we may not conſent to this addition, which I ſubmit to better judgments.

The Commons afterwards appointed Mr. *Glanvile* and Sir *Henry Martin* to manage another conference to be had with the Lords, concerning the ſaid matter, and to clear the ſenſe of the Commons in that point: The one argues the legal, the other the rational part.

Mr. Glanvile's *Speech in a full Committee of both Houſes of Parliament,* May 23, *in the Painted Chamber at* Weſtminſter.

MY Lords, I have in charge, from the Commons Houſe of Parliament (whereof I am a Member) to expreſs this day before your Lordſhips ſome part of their clear ſenſe, touching one point that hath occurred in the great debate, which hath ſo long depended in both Houſes.

I ſhall not need many words to induce or ſtate the queſtion, which I am to handle in this free conference. The ſubject matter of our meeting is well known to your Lordſhips, I will therefore only look ſo far back upon it, and ſo far recollect ſummarily the proceedings it hath had, as may be requiſite to preſent clearly to your Lordſhips conſiderations, the nature and conſequence of the particular wherein I muſt inſiſt.

Your Lordships may be pleased to remember, now that the Commons in this Parliament have framed a petition to be presented to his Majesty, a petition of Right rightly composed, relating nothing but truth, desiring nothing but justice; a petition justly occasioned, a petition necessary and fit for these times, a petition founded upon solid and substantial grounds, the Laws and Statutes of this Realm, sure rocks to build upon; a petition bounded within due limits, and directed upon right ends, to vindicate some lawful and just Liberties of the free Subjects of this Kingdom from the prejudice of violations past, and to secure them from future innovations.

And because my following discourse must reflect chiefly, if not wholly, upon the matter of this petition, I shall here crave leave shortly to open to your Lordships the distinct parts whereof it doth consist, and those are four.

The first concerns levies of monies, by way of Loans or otherwise, for his Majesty's supply; declaring, that no man ought, and praying that no man hereafter be compelled to make or yield any gift, loan, benevolence, tax, or such like charge, without common consent by Act of Parliament.

2. The second is concerning that liberty of person, which rightfully belongs to the free Subjects of this Realm, expressing it to be against the tenure of the Laws and Statutes of the land, that any Freeman should be imprisoned without cause shewed; and then reciting how this Liberty, amongst others, hath lately been infringed, it concludeth with a just and necessary desire, for the better clearing and allowance of this privilege for the future.

3. The third declareth the unlawfulness of billetting or placing Soldiers or Mariners, to sojourn in free Subjects houses against their wills, and prayeth remedy against that grievance.

4. The fourth and last aimeth at redress touching Commissions, to proceed to the trial and condemnation of offenders, and causing them to be executed and put to death by the Law Martial, in times and places, when and where, if by the Laws and Statutes of the Land they had deserved death, by the same Laws and Statutes also they might, and by none other ought to be, adjudged and executed.

This petition, the careful House of Commons, not willing to omit any thing pertaining to their duties, or which might advance their moderate and just ends, did heretofore offer up unto your Lordships consideration, accompanied with an humble desire, That in your nobleness and justice, you would be pleased to join with them in presenting it to his Majesty, that so coming from the whole body of the Realm, the Peers and People, to him that is the Head of both, our gracious Sovereign, who must crown the work, or else all our labour is in vain; it might, by your Lordships concurrence and assistance, find the more easy passage, and obtain the better answer.

Your Lordships, as your manner is in cases of so great importance, were pleased to debate and weigh it well, and thereupon you propounded to us some few amendments (as you termed them) by way of alteration, alledging, that they were only in matters of form, and not of substance; and that they were intended to no other end, but to sweeten the petition, and make it the more passable with his Majesty.

In this the House of Commons cannot but observe, that fair and good respect which your Lordships have used in your proceedings with them, by your concluding or voting nothing in your House, until you had imparted it unto them; whereby our meetings about this business have been justly stiled free conferences, either party repairing hither disengaged to hear and weigh the other's reasons, and both Houses coming with a full intention, upon due consideration of all that can be said on the other side, to join at last in resolving and acting that which shall be found most just and necessary for the honour and safety of his Majesty and the whole Kingdom.

And touching those propounded alterations, which were not many, your Lordships cannot but remember, that the House of Commons have yielded to an accommodation, or change of their petition in two particulars; whereby they hope your Lordships have observed, as well as you may, they have not been affected unto words and phrases, nor overmuch abounding in their own sense; but rather willing to comply with your Lordships in all indifferent things.

For the rest of your proposed amendments, if we do not misconceive your Lordships, as we are confident we do not, your Lordships, of yourselves, have been pleased to relinquish them with a new overture, for one only clause to be added in the end or foot of the petition, whereby the work of this day is reduced to one simple head, whether that clause shall be received or not?

This yielding of the Commons in part unto your Lordships, of other points by you somewhat insisted upon, giveth us great assurance, that our ends are one; and putteth us in hope, that, in conclusion, we shall concur, and proceed unanimously to seek the same ends, by the same means.

The clause propounded by your Lordships to be added to the petition, is this:

We humbly present this petition to your Majesty, not only with a care for preservation of Liberties, but with a due regard to leave intire that Sovereign Power, wherewith your Majesty is intrusted for the protection, safety, and happiness of your People.

A clause specious in shew, and smooth in words, but in effect and consequence most dangerous, as I hope to make most evident: however, coming from your Lordships, the House of Commons took it into their considerations, as becomes them, and apprehending upon the first debate, that it threatened ruin to the whole petition, they did heretofore deliver some reasons to your Lordships, for which they then desired to be spared from admitting it.

To these reasons, your Lordships offered some answers at the last meeting; which having been faithfully reported to our House, and there debated as was requisite for a business of such weight and importance, I must say truly to your Lordships, yet with due reverence to your opinions, the Commons are not satisfied with your arguments; and therefore they have commanded me to recollect your Lordships reasons for this clause, and in a fair reply to let you see the causes why they differ from you in opinion.

But before I come to handle the particulars wherein we dissent from your Lordships, I will in the first place take notice yet a little further, of that general wherein we all concur; which is, that we desire not (neither do your Lordships) to augment or dilate the Liberties and Privileges of the Subjects beyond the just and due bounds, nor to encroach upon the limits of his Majesty's Prerogative Royal. And as in this, your Lordships at the last meeting expressed clearly your own senses, so were your Lordships not mistaken in collecting the concurrent sense and meaning of the House of Commons; they often have protested they do, and ever must protest, That these have been, and shall be the bounds of their desires, to demand and seek nothing but that which may be fit for dutiful and loyal Subjects to ask, and for a gracious and just King to grant: for as they claim by Laws some Liberties for themselves, so do they acknowledge a Prerogative, a high and just Prerogative belonging to the King, which they intend not to diminish. And now, my Lords, being assured, not by strained inferences, or obscure collections, but by the express and clear declarations of both Houses, that our ends are the same; it were a miserable unhappiness, if we should fail in finding out the means to accomplish our desires.

My Lords, the heads of those particular reasons which you insisted upon the last day, were only these:

First, you told us, that the word [leave] was of such a nature, that it could give no new thing to his Majesty.

2. That no just exception could be taken to the words [Sovereign Power]; for that as his Majesty is a King, so he is a Sovereign; and as he is a Sovereign, so he hath power.

3. That the sovereign power mentioned in this clause is not absolute, or indefinite, but limited and regulated by the particle [that]; and he word [subsequent] which restrains it to be applied only for protection, safety, and happiness of the people, whereby ye inferred, there could be no danger in the allowance of such power.

4. That this clause contained no more in substance, but the like expressions of our meanings in this petition, which we had formerly signified unto his Majesty by the mouth of Mr Speaker, that we no way intended to incroach upon his Majesty's sovereign power or prerogative.

5. That in our petition we have used other words, and of larger extent, touching our Liberties, than are contained in the statutes whereon it is grounded. In respect of which enlargement, it was fit to have some express, or implied saving, or narrative declaratory for the King's sovereign power, of which narrative you alledge this clause to be.

Lastly, Whereas the Commons, as a main argument against the clause, had much insisted upon this, that it was unprecedented, and unparliamentary in a petition from the Subject, to insert a saving for the Crown; your Lordships brought for instance to the contrary, the two Statutes of the 25 *E.* I. commonly called *confirmatio chartarum*, and 28 *E.* I. known by this name of *Articuli super Chartas*; in both which Statutes there are savings for the King.

Having thus reduced to your Lordships memories, the effects of your own reasons; I will now, with your Lordships favour, come to the points of our reply, wherein I most humbly beseech your Lordships to weigh the reasons which I shall present, not as the sense of myself, the weakest Member of our House, but as the genuine and true sense of the whole House of Commons, conceived in a business there debated with the greatest gravity and solemnity, with the greatest concurrence of opinions, and unanimity that ever was in any business maturely agitated in that House. I shall not, peradventure, follow the method of your Lordships recollected reasons in my answering to them, nor labour to urge many reasons. It is the desire of the Commons, that the weight of their arguments should recompense (if need be) the smallness of their number. And, in conclusion, when you have heard me through, I hope your Lordships shall be enabled to collect clearly, out of the frame of what I shall deliver, that in some part or other of my discourse there is a full and satisfactory answer given to every particular reason or objection of your Lordships.

The reasons that are now appointed to be presented to your Lordships, are of two kinds, legal and rational, of which those of the former sort are allotted to my charge; and the first of them is thus:

The clause now under question, if it be added to the petition, then either it must refer or relate unto it, or else not; if it have no such reference, is it not clear that it is needless and superfluous? And if it have such reference, is it not clear, that then it must needs have an operation upon the whole petition, and upon all the parts of it?

We cannot think that your Lordships would offer us a vain thing; and therefore taking it for granted, that if it be added, it would refer to the petition; let me beseech your Lordships to observe with me, and with the House of Commons, what alteration and qualification of the same it will introduce.

The petition of itself, simply, and without this clause, declareth absolutely the rights and privileges of the Subject, in divers points; and among the rest touching the levies of monies, by way of Loans or otherwise, for his Majesty's supply, That such loans and other charges of the like nature, by the Laws and Statutes of this Land, ought not to be made or laid without common consent by Act of Parliament: But admit this clause to be annexed with reference (to the petition), and it must necessarily conclude and have this exposition, That Loans and the like charges (true it is, ordinarily) are against the Laws and Statutes of the Realm, *unless they be warranted by sovereign Power*, and that they cannot be commanded or raised without assent of Parliament, *unless it be by sovereign Power*. What were this but to admit a sovereign Power in the King above the Laws and Statutes of the Kingdom?

Another part of this petition is, That the free Subjects of this Realm ought not to be imprisoned without cause shewed: But by this clause a sovereign Power will be admitted, and left entire to his Majesty, sufficient to controul the force of Law, and to bring in this new and dangerous interpretation, That the free Subjects of this Realm ought not by Law to be imprisoned without cause shewed, *unless it be by sovereign Power*.

In a word, This clause, if it should be admitted, would take away the effect of every part of the petition, and become destructive to the whole: for thence will be the exposition touching the billetting of Soldiers and Mariners in Freemen's houses against their wills, and thence will be the expo-

expoſition touching the times and places for execution of the Law Martial, contrary to the Laws and Statutes of the Realm.

The ſcope of this petition, as I have before obſerved, is not to amend our caſe, but to reſtore us to the ſame ſtate we were in before; whereas, if this clauſe be received, inſtead of mending the condition of the poor Subjects, whoſe Liberties of late have been miſerably violated by ſome Miniſters, we ſhall leave them worſe than we found them; inſtead of curing their wounds, we ſhall make them deeper. We have ſet bounds to our deſires in this great buſineſs, whereof one is not to diminiſh the Prerogative of the King, by mounting it too high; and if we bound ourſelves on the other ſide with this limit, not to abridge the lawful privileges of the Subject, by deſcending beneath that which is meet, no man, we hope, can blame us.

My Lords, as there is mention made in the additional *clauſe of ſovereign Power*, ſo is there likewiſe of a truſt repoſed in his Majeſty, touching the uſe of ſovereign Power.

The word *Truſt* is of great latitude and large extent, and therefore ought to be well and warily applied and reſtrained, eſpecially in the caſe of a King: there is a truſt inſeparably repoſed in the perſons of the Kings of *England*, but that truſt is regulated by Law. For example, when Statutes are made to prohibit things not *mala in ſe*, but only *mala quia probibita*, under certain forfeitures and penalties, to accrue to the King, and to the informers that ſhall ſue for the breach of them; the Commons muſt and ever will acknowledge a regal and ſovereign prerogative in the King, touching ſuch Statutes, that it is in his Majeſty's abſolute and undoubted power, to grant diſpenſations to particular perſons, with the clauſes of *non obſtante*, to do as they might have done before thoſe Statutes, wherein his Majeſty conferring grace and favour upon ſome, doth not do wrong to others. But there is a difference between thoſe Statutes, and the Laws and Statutes whereon the petition is grounded: by thoſe Statutes the Subject has no intereſt in the penalties, which are all the fruit ſuch Statutes can produce, until by ſuit or information commenced he become intitled to the particular forfeitures: whereas the Laws and Statutes mentioned in our petition are of another nature; there ſhall your Lordſhips find us rely upon the good old Statute, called *Magna Charta*, which declareth and confirmeth the antient common Laws of the Liberties of *England*: There ſhall your Lordſhips alſo find us to inſiſt upon divers other moſt material Statutes, made in the time of King *Edward* III. and *Edward* IV. and other famous Kings, for explanation and ratification of the lawful rights and privileges belonging to the Subjects of this Realm: Laws not inflicting penalties upon offenders, *in malis prohibitis*, but Laws declarative or poſitive, conferring or confirming, *ipſo facto*, an inherent right and intereſt of Liberty and Freedom in the Subjects of this Realm, as their birthrights and inheritance deſcendable to their heirs and poſterity; Statutes incorporate into the body of the Common Law, over which (with reverence be it ſpoken) there is no truſt repoſed in the King's *Sovereign Power*, or *Prerogative Royal*, to enable him to diſpenſe with them, or to take from his Subjects that birthright or inheritance which they have in their Liberties, by virtue of the Common Law and of theſe Statutes.

But if this clauſe be added to our petition, we ſhall then make a dangerous overture to confound this good deſtination touching what Statutes the King is truſted to controul by diſpenſations, and what not; and ſhall give an intimation to poſterity, as if it were the opinion both of the Lords and Commons aſſembled in this Parliament, that there is a truſt repoſed in the King, to lay aſide by his *ſovereign Power*, in ſome emergent caſes, as well the Common-Law, and ſuch Statutes as declare or ratify the Subjects liberty, or confer intereſt upon their perſons, as thoſe other penal ſtatutes of ſuch nature as I have mentioned before; which, as we can by no means admit, ſo we believe aſſuredly, that it is far from the deſire of our moſt gracious Sovereign, to affect ſo vaſt a truſt, which being tranſmitted to a ſucceſſor of a different temper, might enable him to alter the whole frame and fabrick of the Commonwealth, and to diſſolve that Government whereby this Kingdom hath flouriſhed for ſo many years and ages, under his Majeſty's moſt Royal Anceſtors and Predeceſſors.

Our next reaſon is, that we hold it contrary to all courſe of Parliament, and abſolutely repugnant to the very nature of a petition of Right, conſiſting of particulars, as ours doth, to clog it with a general *Saving* or Declaration, to the weakening of the Right demanded; and we are bold to renew with ſome confidence our allegation, that there can be no precedent ſhewed of any ſuch clauſe in any ſuch petitions in times paſt.

I ſhall inſiſt the longer upon this particular, and labour the more carefully to clear it, becauſe your Lordſhips were pleaſed the laſt day to urge againſt us the ſtatutes of 25 and 28 of *Edw*. I. as arguments to prove the contrary, and ſeemed not to be ſatiſfied with that which in this point we had affirmed. True it is, that in thoſe ſtatutes there are ſuch *Savings* as your Lordſhips have obſerved; but I ſhall offer you a clear anſwer to them, and to all other *Savings* of like nature that can be found in any ſtatutes whatſoever.

Firſt, in the general, and then I ſhall apply particular anſwers to the particulars of thoſe two ſtatutes; whereby it will be moſt evident, that thoſe examples can no ways ſuit with the matter now in hand. To this end it will be neceſſary, that we conſider duly what that queſtion is, which indeed concerneth a petition, and not an Act of Parliament. This being well obſerved, by ſhewing unto your Lordſhips the difference between a petition for the Law, and the Law ordained upon ſuch a petition, and open truly and perſpicuouſly the courſe that was holden in framing of ſtatutes before 2 *Hen*. V. different from that which ever ſince then hath been uſed, and is ſtill in uſe amongſt us, and by noting the times wherein theſe ſtatutes were made, which was about one hundred years before 2 *Hen*. V. beſides the differences between theſe *Savings* and this clauſe; I doubt not but I ſhall give ample ſatiſfaction to your Lordſhips, that the Commons, as well in this as in all their other reaſons, have been moſt careful to rely upon nothing but that which is moſt true and pertinent.

Before the ſecond year of King *Henry* V. the courſe was thus: when the Commons were ſuitors for a Law, either the Speaker of their Houſe by word of mouth from them, the Lords Houſe joining with them, or by ſome bill in writing, which was uſually called their petition, moved the King, to ordain Laws for the redreſs of ſuch miſchiefs or inconveniences, as were found grievous unto the people.

To theſe petitions the King made anſwer as he pleaſed, ſometimes to part, ſometimes to the whole, ſometimes by denial, ſometimes by aſſent, ſometimes abſolutely, and ſometimes by qualification. Upon theſe motions and petitions, and the King's anſwers to them, was the Law drawn up and ingroſſed in the Statute-Roll to bind the Kingdom; but this inconvenience was found in this courſe, that oftentimes the ſtatutes thus framed, were againſt the ſenſe and meaning of the Commons, at whoſe deſires they were ordained; and therefore in the 2 *Hen*. V. finding that it tended to the violation of their liberty and freedom, whoſe right it was, and ever had been, that no Law ſhould be made without their aſſent; they then exhibited a petition to the King, declaring their right in this particular: praying, that from thenceforth no Law might be made or ingroſſed as Statutes, by additions or diminutions to their motions or petitions, that ſhould change their ſenſe, or intent, without their aſſent; which was accordingly eſtabliſhed by Act of Parliament. Ever ſince then, the Right hath been, as the uſe was before, that the King taketh the whole, or leaveth the whole of all Bills or Petitions, exhibited for the obtaining of Laws.

From this courſe, and from the time when firſt it became conſtant and ſettled, we conclude ſtrongly, that it is no good argument, becauſe ye find *Savings* in Acts of Parliament before the ſecond of *Hen*. V. that thoſe *Savings* were before in the petitions that begat thoſe ſtatutes: for if the petitions for the two Loans ſo much inſiſted upon (which petitions, for any thing we know, are not now extant) were never ſo abſolute, yet might the King, according to the uſage of thoſe times, inſert the *Savings* in his anſwers; which paſſing from thence into the Statute-Roll, do only give ſome little colour, but are not proof at all that the petitions alſo were with *Savings*.

Thus much for the general; to come now to the particular ſtatute of 25 of *Edw*. I. which was a confirmation of *Magna Charta*, with ſome proviſion for the better execution of it, as Common Law, which words are worth the noting.

It is true, that Statute hath alſo a clauſe to this effect, That the King, or his Heirs, from thenceforth ſhould take no Aids, Taxes, or Priſage of his Subjects, but by common aſſent of all the Realm, ſaving the antient Aids and Priſage due and accuſtomed.

This *Saving*, if it were granted, (which is not, nor cannot be proved) that it was as well in the Petition as in the Act; yet can it no way imply, that it is either fit or ſafe, that the clauſe now in queſtion ſhould be added to our petition: for the nature and office of a *Saving*, or exception, is to exempt particulars out of a general, and to ratify the rule in things not exempted, but in no ſort to weaken or deſtroy the general rule itſelf.

The body of that Law was againſt all Aids, and Taxes, and Priſage in general, and was a confirmation of the Common Law, formerly declared by *Magna Charta*; the *Saving* was only of Aids and Priſage in particular, ſo well deſcribed and reſtrained by the words, *ancient and accuſtomed*, that there could be no doubt what could be the clear meaning and extent of that exception; for the King's Right to thoſe ancient Aids, intended by that Statute to be ſaved to him, was well known in thoſe days, and is not yet forgotten.

Theſe Aids were three; from the King's Tenants by Knights ſervice, due by the Common Law, or general cuſtom of the Realm: Aid to ranſom the King's Royal perſon, if unhappily he ſhould be taken priſoner in the wars: Aid to make the King's eldeſt ſon a Knight, and Aid to marry the King's eldeſt daughter once, but no more: and that thoſe were the only Aids intended to be ſaved to the Crown by that Statute, appeareth in ſome clearneſs by the Charter of King *John*, dated at *Running-Mead* the 15th of *June*, in the fifth year of his Reign, wherein they are enumerated with an excluſion of all other Aids whatſoever. Of this Charter I have here one of the Originals, whereon I beſeech your Lordſhips to caſt your eyes, and give me leave to read the very words which concern this point. Theſe words (my Lords) are thus: *Nullum ſcutagium vel auxilium ponatur in regno noſtro, niſi per commune conſilium regni noſtri, niſi ad corpus noſtrum redimendum, & primogenitum filium noſtrum militem faciendum, & ad filiam noſtram primogenitam ſemel maritandam, & ad hoc non fiat niſi rationabile auxilium.*

Touching priſage, the other thing excepted by this Statute, it is alſo of a particular right to the Crown ſo well known, that it needeth no deſcription, the King being in poſſeſſion of it by every day's uſage.

It is to take one tun of wine before the maſt, and another behind the maſt, of every ſhip bringing in above twenty tuns of wine, and here diſcharging them by way of Merchandiſe.

But our petition conſiſteth altogether in particulars, to which if any general *Saving*, or words amounting to one, ſhould be annexed, it cannot work to confirm things not excepted, which are none, but to confound things included, which are all the parts of the petition; and it muſt needs beget this dangerous expoſition, that the Rights and Liberties of the Subject, declared and demanded by this petition, are not theirs abſolutely, but *ſub modo*; not to continue always, but only to take place, when the King is pleaſed not to exerciſe that *ſovereign Power*, wherewith, this clauſe admitted, he is truſted for the protection, ſafety, and happineſs of his people. And thus that birthright and inheritance, which we have in our Liberties, ſhall by our own aſſents be turned into a mere tenancy at will and ſufferance.

Touching the Statute of 28 *Edw*. I. *Articuli ſuper Chartas*, the ſcope of that Statute, among other things, being to provide for the better obſerving and maintaining of *Magna Charta*, hath in it nevertheleſs two *Savings* for the King; the one particular, as I take it, to preſerve the antient priſage, due and accuſtomed, as of wines and other goods; the other general, ſeigniory of the Crown in all things.

To theſe two *Savings*, beſides the former anſwers, which may be for the moſt part applied to this Statute as well as to the former, I add theſe further anſwers: the firſt of theſe two *Savings*, is of the ſame priſage of wines, which is excepted in the 25 *Edw*. I. but in ſome more clearneſs; for that here the word (*wines*) is expreſsly annexed to the word (*priſage*) which I take to ſo much to be in expoſition of the former Law. And albeit theſe words (*and of other goods*) be added, yet do I take it to be but a particular *Saving*, or exception, which being qualified with the words (*antient, due, and accuſ-*

accustomed) is not very dangerous, nor can be understood of Prisage or Levies upon Goods of all Sorts at the King's Will and Pleasure; but only of the old and certain Customs upon Wool, Woolfels, and Leather, which were due to the Crown, long before the making of this Statute.

For the latter of the two *savings* in this Act, which is of the more unusual Nature, and subject to the more Exception; it is indeed general, and if we may believe the concurrent Relations of the Histories of those Times, as well those that are now printed, as those that remain only in Manuscripts, it gave Distaste from the Beginning, and wrought no good Effect, but produced such Distempers and Troubles in the State, as we wish may be buried in perpetual Oblivion; and that the like *saving* in these and future Times may never breed the like Disturbance: For from hence arose a Jealousy, that *Magna Charta*, which declared the ancient Right of the Subject, and was an absolute Law in itself, being now confirmed by a latter Act, with this Addition of a general *saving*; for the King's Right in all Things by the *saving* was weakened, and that made doubtful, which was clear before. But not to depart from our main Ground, which is, that *savings* in old Acts of Parliament, before the 2 *H.* V. are no Proof that there were the like *savings* in the Petitions for those Acts; let me observe unto your Lordships, and so leave this Point, that albeit this Petition, whereon this Act of 28 *Ed.* I. was grounded, be perished; yet hath it pleased God, that the very Frame and Context of the Act itself, as it is drawn up, and entered upon the Statute-roll, and printed in our Book, doth manifestly import, that this *saving* came in by the King's Answer, and was not in the original Petition of the Lords and Commons; for it cometh in at the End of the Act after the Words *(le Roy le veut)* which commonly are the Words of the Royal Assent to an Act of Parliament. And though they be mixed and followed with other Words, as though the King's Counsel, and the rest who were present at the making of this Ordinance, did intend the same *saving*; yet is not that conclusive, so long as by the Form of those Times, the King's Answer working upon the Materials of the Petition, might be conceived by some to make the Law effectual, though varying from the Frame of the Petition.

The next Reason which the Commons have commanded me to use, for which they still desire to be spared from adding this Clause to their Petition, is this: This offensive Law of 28 *E.* I. which confirmed *Magna Charta*, with a *saving*, rested not long in Peace, for it gave not that Satisfaction to the Lords or People, as was requisite they should have in a Case so nearly concerning them: And therefore about thirty-three or thirty-four of the same King's Reign, a latter Act of Parliament was made, whereby it was enacted, that all Men should have their Laws, and Liberties, and free Customs, as largely and wholly as they had used to have at any time when they had them best; and if any Statutes had been made, or any Customs brought in to the contrary, that all such Statutes and Customs should be void.

This was the first Law which I call now to mind, that restored *Magna Charta* to the original Purity wherein it was first moulded, albeit it hath since been confirmed above twenty times more by several Acts of Parliament, in the Reigns of divers most just and gracious Kings, who were most apprehensive of their Rights, and jealous of their Honours, and always without *savings*; so as if between 22 and 34 *Edw* I. *Magna Charta* stood blemished with many *savings* of the King's Rights or Seigniory, which might be conceived to be above the Law; that Stain and Blemish was long since taken away, and cleared by those many absolute Declarations and Confirmations of that excellent Law which followed in after Ages, and so it standeth at this day purged and exempted now from any such *saving* whatsoever.

I beseech your Lordships therefore to observe the Circumstance of Time, wherein we offer this Petition to be presented to your Lordships, and by us unto his Majesty: Do we offer it when *Magna Charta* stands clogged with *savings*? No, my Lords, but at this Day, when latter and better Confirmations have vindicated and set free that Law from all Exceptions; and shall we now annex another and worse *saving* to it, by an unnecessary Clause in that Petition, which we expect should have the Fruits and Effects of a Law? Shall we ourselves relinquish or adulterate that, which cost our Ancestors such Care and Trouble to purchase and refine? No, my Lords, but as we should hold ourselves unhappy, if we should not amend the wretched Estate of the poor Subject, so let us hold it a Wickedness to impair it.

Whereas it was further urged by your Lordships, That to insert this Clause into our Petition, would be no more than to do that again at your Lordships Motion and Request, which we had formerly done by the Mouth of our Speaker; and that there is no Cause why we should recede from that which so solemnly we have professed · To this I answer and confess, it was then in our Hearts, and it is now, and shall be ever, not to encroach on his Majesty's sovereign Power. But I beseech your Lordships to observe the different Occasion and Reference of that Protestation, and of this Clause.

That was a general Answer to a general Message, which we received from his Majesty, warning us not to encroach upon his Prerogative; to which, like dutiful and loving Subjects, we answered at full, according to the Integrity of our own Hearts; nor was there any Danger in making such an Answer to such a Message, nor could we answer more truly or more properly: But did that Answer extend to acknowledge a *sovereign Power* in the King, above the Laws and Statutes mentioned in our Petition, or controul the Liberties of the Subjects, therein declared and demanded? No, my Lords, it hath no Reference to any such Particulars; and the same Words which in some Cases may be fit to be used, and were unmannerly to be omitted, cannot in other Cases be spoken, but with Impertinency at the least, if not with Danger. I have formerly opened my Reasons, proving the Danger of this Clause, and am commanded to illustrate the Impertinency of adding it to the Petition by a familiar Case, which was put in our House by a learned Gentleman, and of my own Robe. The Case is this, Two Manours or Lordships lie adjoining together, and perchance intermixed, so as there is some difficulty to discern the true Bounds of either; as it may be touching the Confines where the Liberty of the Subject, and the Prerogative of the Crown do border each upon the other; to the one of the Manours the King hath clear right, and is in actual Possession of it, but the other is the Subject's. The King being misinformed, that the Subject hath intruded upon his Majesty's Manour, asketh his Subject, whether he doth enter upon his Majesty's Manour, or pretendeth any Title to it, or any Part of it. The Subject being now justly occasioned, maketh Answer truly to the King, that he hath not intruded, nor will intrude upon his Majesty's Manour, nor doth make any Claim or Title to it, or any Part of it. This Answer is proper and fair; nay, it were unmannerly and ill done of the Subject not to answer upon this Occasion. Afterwards the King, upon Colour of some double or single Matter of Record, seizeth into his Highness's Hands, upon a pretended Title, the Subject's Manour: The Subject then exhibiteth his Petition of Right to his Majesty, to retain Restitution of his own Manour, and therein layeth down Title to his own Manour only: Were it not improper and absurd in this Case for him to tell the King, that he did not intend to make any Claim or Title to his Majesty's Manour, which is not questioned? Doubtless it were. This Case, rightly applyed, will fit our Purpose well, and notably explain the Nature of our Petition.

Why should we speak of leaving entire the *King's Sovereign Power*, whereon we encroach not, while we only seek to recover our own Liberties and Privileges, which have been seized upon by some of the King's Ministers? If our Petition did trench actually upon his Majesty's Prerogative, would our saying, that we intended it not, make the thing otherwise than the Truth?

My Lords, there needeth no Protestation or Declaration to the contrary of that which we have not done; and to put in such a Clause, cannot argue less than a fear in us, as if we had invaded it: which we hold sacred, and are assured, that we have not touched either in our Words or in our Intentions. And touching your Lordships Observation upon the Word *(leave)*, if it be not a proper Word to give any new thing to the King, sure we are, it is a Word dangerous in another Sense; for it may amount, without all question, to acknowledge an old Right of *sovereign Power* in his Majesty, above those Laws and Statutes whereon only our Liberties are founded; a Doctrine which we most humbly crave your Lordships Leave freely to protest against. And for your Lordships proffering, that some *saving* should be requisite for Preservation of his Majesty's *sovereign Power*, in respect our Petition runneth in larger Words than our Laws and Statutes whereon we ground it; what is this but a clear Confession by your Lordships, that this Clause was intended by you to be that *saving*? For other *saving* than this we find not tendered by you: And if it be such a *saving*, how can it stand with your Lordships other Arguments, that it should be of no other Effect than our former Expression to his Majesty by the Mouth of our Speaker? But I will not insist upon Collections of this Kind; I will only shew you the Reasons of the Commons, why this Petition needeth no such saying, albeit the Words of these Statutes be exceeded in the declaratory Part of our Petition: those things that are within the Equity and true Meaning of a Statute, are as good Laws as those which are contained in the express Letter, and therefore the Statutes of the 42 *Ed.* III. 36 *H.* III. *Rot. Par. N.* 12. and other the Statutes made in this Time of King *Edw.* III. for the Explanation of *Magna Charta*, which hath been so often vouched in this Parliament, though they differ in Words from *Magna Charta*, had no *saving* annexed to any of them, because they enacted more than was contained in effect in that good Law, under the Words, *per legale judicium parium suorum, aut per legem terræ*; which by these latter Laws are expounded to import, that none should be put to answer without Presentment, or Matter of Record, or by due Process, or Writ Original: and if otherwise, it should be void, and holden for Error.

It hath not been yet shewn unto us from your Lordships, that we have in any of our Expressions or Applications strained or misapplied any of the Laws or Statutes whereon we do insist; and we are very confident and well assured, that no such mistaking can be assigned in any Point of our Petition now under question: If therefore it do not exceed the true Sense and Construction of *Magna Charta* in the subsequent Laws of Explanation, whereon it is grounded, what Reason is there to add a *saving* to this Petition more than to those Laws; since we desire to transmit the Fruits of these our Labours to Posterity, not only for the Justification of ourselves, in Right of our present and their future Liberties, but also for a brave Expression and perpetual Testimony of that Grace and Justice, which we assure ourselves we shall receive in his Majesty's speedy and clear Answer? This is the Thing we seek for, and this is the Thing we hoped for, and this is the Thing only will settle such an Unity and Confidence betwixt his Majesty and us, and raise such a Chearfulness in the Hearts of all his loving Subjects, as will make us proceed unanimously, and with all Expedition to supply him for his great Occasions in such Measure, and in such Way, as may make him safe at home, and feared abroad.

Sir *Henry Martin.* My Lords, the Work of this Day, wherein the House of Commons hath employed the Gentleman that spoke last, and myself, was to reply to the Answer, which it hath pleased the Lord-Keeper to make to those Reasons, which we had offered to your Lordships Consideration, in Justification of our Refusal, not to admit into our Petition the Addition commended by your Lordships. Which Reasons of ours, since they have not given such Satisfaction as we desired, and well hoped, as by the Lord-Keeper's Answer appeared; it was thought fit, for our better Order and Method in replying, to divide the Lord-Keeper's Answer into two Parts, a legal and a rational: The Reply to the legal your Lordships have heard, myself comes intrusted to reply to the rational, which also consisted of two Branches, the first deduced from the whole Context of the additional Clause, the second enforced out of some Part.

In the first were these Reasons, That the same deserved our Acceptance. First, as satisfactory to the King; secondly, to your Lordships; thirdly, agreeable to what ourselves had often protested, and professed expresly by the Mouth of our Speaker.

I must confess these Motives were weighty and of great Force; and therefore, to avoid misunderstanding and misconceit, which otherwise might be taken against the House of Commons upon the Refusal of the propounded Addition, it is necessary to state the Question rightly, and to set down the true Difference between your Lordships and us. Now, indeed, there is no Difference or Question between your Lordships and us, concerning this additional Clause in the Nature and Quality of a Proposition. For so considered, we say it is most true, and to be received and embraced by us, *in toto & quolibet parte & qualibet syllaba*; yea, and were that the Question, we should add to the Addition, and instead of due regard, say, we have had, have, and ever will have, a special and singular regard, where

where to leave entire Sovereign Power. But this were to intimate, as if we had first cropt, and then left it; but our Regard was to acknowledge and confess it sincerely, and to maintain it constantly, even to the hazard of our goods and lives, if need be.

To which purpose your Lordships may be pleased to remember that strict oath every Member of our House hath taken this very session, in these words: *I* (A. B.) *do utterly testify and declare in my conscience, That the King's Highness is the supreme sovereign Governour of this Realm in all causes, &c. and to my utmost power will assist and defend all Jurisdictions, Privileges, Preheminences and Authorities, granted or belonging to the King's Highness, or united or annexed to the imperial Crown of this Realm, &c.*

So that your Lordships need not to borrow from our protestations any exhortations to us, to entertain a writing in assistance of the King's sovereign Power, since we stand obliged by the most sacred bond of a solemn oath, to assist and defend the same, if cause or occasion so required. So that the only question between your Lordships and us, is, whether this clause should be added to our petition, and received into it as part thereof? Which to do; your Lordships reasons have not persuaded us, because so to admit it, were to overthrow the fabrick and substance of our Petition of Right, and to anninilate the right pretended by us, and the petition itself in effect: For these words being added to our Petition, *viz.* "We humbly present "this petition, &c. with due regard to leave entire your sovereign Pow-"er, &c." do include manifestly an exception to our Petition; and an exception being of the nature of the thing whereunto it is an exception, *exceptio est de regula*, must of necessity destroy the Rule or Petition, so far as to the case excepted; *Exceptio firmat regulam in casibus non exceptis, in casibus exceptis destruit regulam.* Then this construction followeth upon our petition thus inlarged, that after we have petitioned, that no freeman should be compelled by imprisonment to lend or contribute money to his Majesty without his assent in Parliament, nor receive, against his will, Soldiers into his House, or undergo a commission of Martial Law for Life or Member in time of peace; we should add, Except his Majesty be pleased to require our moneys, and imprison us for not lending, and send Soldiers into our Houses, and execute us by Martial Law, in time of peace, by virtue of his sovereign Power: which construction, as it followeth necessarily upon this enlargement, so it concludeth against our right in the premisses, and utterly frustrateth all our petition; neither may it seem strange, if this clause additional (which of itself is in quality of a proposition we confess) being added to our petition (which also is true) should overthrow the very frame and fabrick of it, seeing the Logicians take knowledge of such a fallacy, called by them, *Fallacia à bene divisis ad mala conjuncta. Horace* the Poet giveth an instance to this purpose, in a Painter, who when he had painted the head of a man according to art, would then join to it the neck of a horse, and so marr the one and the other; whereas each by itself might have been a piece of right good workmanship.

The second branch of my Lord-Keeper's rational part was enforced out of the last words of this addition, by which his Lordship said, that they did not leave intire all sovereign Power, but that wherewith his Majesty is trusted, for the protection, safety, and happiness of the people; as if his Lordship would infer, that sovereign Power wherewith, &c. in this place to be *Terminum diminuentem*, a term of diminution or qualification, and in that consideration might induce us to accept it. But under his Lordship's correction, we cannot so interpret it: For first we are assured, that there is no sovereign Power wherewith his Majesty is trusted, either by God, or Man, but only that which is for the protection, safety, and happiness of his people; and therefore, that limitation can make no impression upon us: but we conceive it rather in this place to have the force *Termini adaugentis*, to be a term of important advantage against our petition, a term of restriction, and that wheresoever his Majesty's sovereign Power should be exercised upon us in all or any the particulars mentioned in the Petition, we should, without further enquiry, submit thereunto, as assuming and taking it *prò concesso*, it conduced to our safety and happiness, &c. Since therefore (as the petition is now conceived) it carrieth the form and face of a picture, which representeth to the life the pressures and grievances of the people, with the easy remedies; and therefore we hope that his Majesty, casting upon it a gracious eye, will compassionate his poor loyal Subjects, and afford a comfortable answer.

I do humbly praise your Lordships not to marr or blemish the grace and face of this picture with this unnecessary addition; and unnecessary I prove it to be, according to that rule, *Expressio ejus quod tacite inest nihil operatur.* And sovereign Power, in cases where it hath place, and ought to be used, is always necessarily understood, and though not expressed, yet supplied by reasonable intendment, or by the opinion of all learned men.

And therefore it neither is nor can be by us expresly included, especially in this petition, where the addition thereof would make such a confusion of the whole sense and substance.

The King's sovereign Power and Prerogative is always able to save itself; and if it were not, we must, without this addition, save it to our utmost powers, if we will save our oath, and save ourselves. The true state of the cause thus standing between your Lordships and us, the House of Commons doth not a little marvel upon what grounds your Lordships are so earnest to urge upon them this addition to be inserted into their petition; they nothing doubt, but the same proceeded out of a sollicitude and fear, which your Lordships have, lest otherwise the simple and absolute passage of this petition might be construed hereafter in prejudice of his Majesty's sovereign Power: And this your Lordships sollicitude and fear proceedeth from your love, as the Poet saith,

Res est solliciti plena timoris Amor.

But I humbly pray your Lordships to examine with us, the grounds of this your sollicitude and fear; which grounds must needs be laid either upon the words of the petition, or the intention of the petitioners.

Upon the words there is no possibility to lay them, for therein is no mention made of the sovereign Power; and were the words doubtful, as thus, We pray the like things be not done hereafter, under pretext of your Majesty's sovereign Power; yet in respect of the protestations preceding, concomitant and subsequent to the petition, such doubtful words ought reasonably to be interpreted only of such sovereign Power as was applicable to the cases wherein it was exercised; and of such sovereign Power as should be justly practised. But there are no such doubtful words, and therefore it followeth, that your Lordships fear and sollicitude must be grounded upon the intention of the petitioners. Now your Lordships will know, that the House of Commons is not ignorant, that in a Session of Parliament, though it continue so many weeks, as this hath done days, yet there is nothing *prius & posterius*, but all things are held and taken as done at one time. If so, what a strange collection was this, that at the same time the House of Commons should oblige themselves, by a fearful adjuration, to assist and defend all privileges and prerogatives belonging to the King, and at the same time by a petition (cautiously conveyed) endeavour or intend to divest and deprive the King of some prerogatives belonging to his Crown? If therefore such fear and sollicitude can neither be grounded upon the words of the petition, nor intention of the petitioners, I humbly pray your Lordships to lay them aside. As we do believe that the proposition of this addition from your Lordships was not only excusable, but commendable, as proceeding from your Love; so now having heard our reasons, your Lordships would rest satisfied, that our refusal to admit them into our petition, proceedeth from the conscience of the integrity and uprightness of our own hearts, that we in all this petition have no such end to abate or diminish the King's just prerogative. And so much in reply to that rational part, whereby my Lord-Keeper laboured to persuade the entertainment of this addition.

This being done, it pleased the House of Commons to instruct and furnish me with certain reasons, which I shall use to your Lordships, to procure your absolute conjunction with us in presenting this petition; which albeit I cannot set forth according to their worth, and the instructions given me by the House, yet, I hope, their own weight will so press down into your Lordships consciences and judgments, that without farther scruple, you will chearfully vouchsafe to accompany this petition with your right noble presence.

A personis. The first argument wherewith I was commanded to move your Lordships, was drawn from the consideration of the persons, which are petitioners, the *House of Commons*; a House, whose temper, mildness, and moderation in this Parliament hath been such, as we should be unthankful and injurious to Almighty God, if we should not acknowledge his good hand upon us, upon our tongues, upon our hearts, procured, no doubt, by our late solemn and publick Humiliation and Prayers.

This moderation will the better appear, if, in the first place, it may be remembered, in what passion and distemper many Members of this House arrived thither, what bosoms, what pockets full of complaints and lamentable grievances the most part brought thither, and those every day renewed by letters and packets from all parts and quarters: You know the old proverb, *Ubi dolor ibi digitus, ubi amor ibi oculus*: it is hard to keep our fingers from often handling the parts ill affected; but yet our moderation overcame our passion, our discretion overcame our affection.

This moderation also will the better appear, if in the second place it be not forgotten, how our ancestors and predecessors carried themselves in Parliaments, when upon lighter provocations, less would not serve their turns, but new severe commissions to hear and determine offences against their Liberties, publick ecclesiastical curses, or excommunications against the authors or actors of such violations, accusations, condemnations, executions, banishments. But what have we said all this Parliament? We only look forward, not backward: we desire amendment hereafter, no man's punishment for aught done heretofore; nothing written by us in blood, nay, not one word spoken against any man's person in displeasure. The conclusion of our petition is, that we may be better intreated in time to come: and doth not this moderate petition deserve your Lordships chearful conjunction, *ex congruo & condigno*? If a worm being trodden upon, could speak, a worm would say, Tread upon me no more, I pray you: Higher we rise not, lower we cannot descend; and thus much we think in modesty may well be spoken in our own commendation, thence to move your Lordships to vouchsafe us your noble company in this petition without surcharging it with this addition.

A tempore. Our next argument is drawn *a tempore*, from the unseasonableness of the time. The Wiseman saith, *There is a time for all things under the Sun; Tempus suum.* And if, in the Wiseman's judgment, a word spoken in its due time be precious as Gold and Silver, then an unseasonable time detracts as much from the thing or word done or spoken: We hold (under your favours) that the time is not seasonable now for this addition. It is true, that of itself, sovereign Power is a thing always so sacred, that to handle it otherwise than tenderly, is a kind of Sacrilege, and to speak of it otherwise than reverently, is a kind of Blasphemy. But every vulgar capacity is not so affected the most part of men; nay, almost all men, judge and esteem all things, not according to their own intrinsick virtue and quality, but according to their immediate effects and operations, which the same things have upon them. Hence it is, that Religion itself receiveth more or less credit or approbation, as the teachers or professors are worse or better; yea, if God himself send a very wet harvest or seed-time, men are apt enough to censure divine Power. The sovereign Power hath not now, for the present, the ancient amiable aspect, in respect of some late sad influences; but by God's grace it will soon recover.

To intermix with this petition any mention of sovereign Power, *rebus sic stantibus*, when angry men say, sovereign Power hath been abused, and the most moderate wish it had not been so used; we hold it not seasonable, under your Lordships correction.

A loco. Our next Argument is drawn *a loco*: we think *the Place* where your Lordships would have this addition inserted, viz. in the petition, no convenient or seasonable place. Your Lordships will easily believe, that this petition will run through many hands, every man will be desirous to see and to read what their Knights and Burgesses have done in Parliament upon their complaints, what they have brought home for their five Subsidies: If, in perusing of this petition, they fall upon the mention of sovereign Power, they presently fall to arguing, and reasoning, and descanting, what sovereign Power is, what is the Latitude, whence the Original, and where the bounds? with many such curious and capricious questions; by which course, sovereign Power is little advanced or advantaged: for I have ever been of opinion, that it is then best with sovereign Power, when it is had in tacit veneration, not when it is profaned by publick hearings or examinations.

Our last Argument is drawn from our *Duty* and *Loyalty* to his Majesty, in consideration whereof, we are fearful at this time to take this addition into our petition, lest we should do his Majesty herein some disservice: with your Lordships, we make the great Council of the King and Kingdom; and tho' your Lordships, having the happiness to be near his Majesty, know other things better, yet certainly the state and condition of the several parts for which we serve, their dispositions and inclinations, their apprehensions, their fears and jealousies, are best known unto us. And here I pray your Lordships to give me leave to use the figure called *Reticentia*, that is, to insinuate and intimate more than I mean to speak. Our chief and principal end in this Parliament, is, to make up all rents and breaches between the King and his Subjects, to draw them, and knit them together, from that distance, whereof the world abroad takes too much notice, to work a perfect union and reconciliation. How unproperly and unapt at this time this addition will be in respect of this end, we cannot but foresee, and therefore shun it; and do resolve, that it is neither agreeable to the persons of such Counsellors, of whom we are, not answerable to that love and duty which we owe to his Majesty, to hazard an end of such unspeakable consequence, upon the admittance of this addition into our petition, whereof (as we have shewed) the omission at this time can by no means harm the King's prerogative, the expression may produce manifold inconveniencies. And therefore, since the admittance of your Lordships addition into our petition is incoherent and incompatible with the body of the same; since there is no necessary use of it for the saving of the King's Prerogative; since the moderation of our petition deserveth your Lordships chearful conjunction with us; since this addition is unseasonable for the time, and inconvenient in respect of the place where your Lordships would have it inserted; and lastly, may prove a disservice to his Majesty; I conclude with a most affectionate prayer to your Lordships, to join with the House of Commons, in presenting this petition unto his Sacred Majesty, as it is, without this addition.

Monday, *26th of* May, *the Lord Keeper made this Speech at a Conference.*

Gentlemen,

YE that are Knights, Citizens and Burgesses of the House of Commons, I have many times this Parliament, by command from my Lords, declared the great zeal and affection which my Lords have to maintain and nourish the good concurrence and correspondency which hath hitherto continued between both Houses, that there might be a happy issue in this great business, for the common good of the King and Kingdom. Now that which I have to say this day from my Lords, is, to let you know, this fair proceeding is not a profession of words only, but really and indeed concerning the petition, which hath been long in agitation, as the weight of the cause required. Since the last conference, my Lords have taken it into their serious and instant consideration, and at length are fallen upon a resolution, which I am to acquaint you with.

The Lords have unanimously agreed with you *in omnibus*, and have voted, that they will join with you in your petition, with the only alteration of the word [*means*] to be put instead of the word [*pretext*,] and for the word [*unlawful*] to be put out, and in place thereof to add [*not warrantable* by the laws and statutes of the Realm]. Which two alterations yourselves consented unto.

So that concerning this business there remains nothing now, but that having the petition in your hands, ye will (if ye have not already) vote it as they have done, and so prepare it for his Majesty; and my Lords will take order, that the King be moved for a speedy access to present the same to his Majesty.

And, after some pause, he said, There rests one thing which my Lords have commanded me to add, That in regard this petition toucheth upon certain charges raised by the Lords Lieutenants, and other persons, many times for good use, for the service and safety of the Kingdom, that ye take it into your care and consideration, and to provide a law for assessing of such charges, as the occasion of the time shall require.

The Lords and Commons being thus happily accorded, the petition, with the aforesaid amendments, was read in the House two several times together: then it was voted upon the question, and that it should be ingrossed, and read the third time, and the House to sit in the afternoon till it was ingrossed, and read, and ordered to be presented to the King; to which there was not a negative vote.

Wednesday, 28 *May*, the Lords and Commons had a conference about the manner of delivery of the petition; and Sir *Ed. Coke* reported, that their Lordships were agreed, That no addition or preface be used to the King, but that the petition be preferred to his Majesty by command of the Lords and Commons; and his Majesty be desired, that to content his people, he would be pleased to give his gracious answer in full Parliament.

Monday, 2d June, *the King came to the Parliament, and spake thus in brief to both Houses:*

Gentlemen,

I AM come hither to perform my duty; I think no man can think it long, since I have not taken so many days in answering the petition, as you spent weeks in framing it: and I am come hither to shew you, that as well in formal things as in essential, I desire to give you as much content as in me lies.

After this, the Lord Keeper spake as followeth:

MY Lords, and you the Knights, Citizens, and Burgesses of the House of Commons, his Majesty hath commanded me to say unto you, that he takes it in good part, that in consideration of settling your own Liberties, you have generally professed in both Houses, that you have no intention to lessen or diminish his Majesty's Prerogative; wherein as you have cleared your own intentions, so now his Majesty comes to clear his, and to subscribe a firm league with his people, which is ever likely to be most constant and perpetual, when the conditions are equal, and known to be so. these cannot be in a more happy estate, than when your Liberties shall be an ornament and a strength to his Majesty's Prerogative, and his Prerogative a defence of your Liberties; in this his Majesty doubts not, but both he and you shall take a mutual comfort hereafter; and, for his part, he is resolved to give an example, in the using of his power for the preservation of your Liberties, that hereafter ye shall have no cause to complain. This is the sum of that which I am to say to you from his Majesty: and that which farther remains, is, that you here read your own petition, and his Majesty's gracious answer.

The Petition exhibited to his Majesty by the Lords Spiritual and Temporal, and Commons in this present Parliament assembled, concerning divers Rights and Liberties of the Subjects.

To the King's most Excellent Majesty.

I. *HUmbly shew unto our Sovereign Lord the King, the Lords Spiritual and Temporal, and Commons in Parliament assembled, that whereas it is declared and enacted by a Statute made in the time of the Reign of K* Edward *the First, commonly called,* Statutum de Tallagio non concedendo *, *that no tallage or aid shall be laid or levied, by the King or his Heirs, in this Realm, without the good will and assent of the Archbishops, Bishops, Earls, Barons, Knights, Burgesses, and other the Freemen of the Commonalty of this Realm: and by authority of Parliament holden in the five-and-twentieth year of the Reign of King* Edward *the Third* †, *it is declared and enacted, That from thenceforth no person shall be compelled to make any Loans to the King against his will, because such Loans were against reason, and the Franchise of the Land; and by other* § *Laws of this Realm it is provided, that none should be charged by any charge or imposition, called a* Benevolence, *nor by such like charge, by which the Statutes before-mentioned, and other the good Laws and Statutes of this Realm, your Subjects have inherited this freedom, that they should not be compelled to contribute to any tax, tallage, aid, or other like charge, not set by common consent in Parliament.*

II. *Yet nevertheless, of late, divers Commissions, directed to sundry Commissioners in several Counties, with instructions, have issued; by means whereof your people have been in divers places assembled, and required to lend certain sums of money unto your Majesty, and many of them, upon their refusal so to do, have had an oath administered unto them, not warrantable by the Laws or Statutes of this Realm, and have been constrained to become bound to make appearance, and give attendance before your Privy-Council, and in other places; and others of them have been therefore imprisoned, confined, and sundry other ways molested and disquieted. And divers other charges have been laid and levied upon your people in several Counties, by Lords Lieutenants, Deputy Lieutenants, Commissioners for musters, Justices of Peace, and others, by command and direction from your Majesty, or your Privy-Council, against the Laws and free Customs of this Realm.*

III. *And whereas also by the Statute called* ‖, The great Charter of the Liberties of England, *it is declared and enacted, That no Freeman may be taken or imprisoned, or be disseised of his Freehold or Liberties, or his free Customs, or be outlawed or exiled, or in any manner destroyed, but by the lawful judgment of his Peers, or by the Law of the Land.*

IV. *And in the eight-and-twentieth year of the Reign of King* Edward *the Third* **, *it was declared and enacted by authority of Parliament, that no man, of what estate or condition he be, should be put out of his Land or Tenements, nor taken, nor imprisoned, nor disherited, nor put to death, without being brought to answer by due process of Law.*

V. *Nevertheless, against the tenor of the said Statutes* ††, *and other the good Laws and Statutes of your Realm, to that end provided, divers of your Subjects have of late been imprisoned, without any cause shewed, and when for their deliverance they were brought before your Justices, by your Majesty's Writs of* Habeas Corpus, *there to undergo and receive as the Court should order, and their keepers commanded to certify the causes of their detainer, no cause was certified, but that they were detained by your Majesty's special Command, signified by the Lords of your Privy-Council, and yet were returned back to several prisons, without being charged with any thing to which they might make answer according to the Law.*

[*The sixth, seventh, eighth, and ninth Clauses, relating to billeting of Soldiers and martial Law, are not here inserted.*]

X. *They do therefore humbly pray your most excellent Majesty* §§, 1. *That no man hereafter be compelled to make or yield any Gift, Loan, Benevolence, Tax, or such like charge, without common consent by Act of Parliament*, 2. *and that none be called to make answer, or take such oath, or to give attendance, or be confined, or otherwise molested or disquieted concerning the same, or for refusal thereof:* 3. *and that no Freeman in any such manner as is before-mentioned, be imprisoned or detained.*

XI. *All which they most humbly pray of your most excellent Majesty, as their Rights and Liberties, according to the Laws and Statutes of this Realm: and that your Majesty would also vouchsafe to declare, that the awards, doings, and proceedings, to the prejudice of your people, in any of the premisses, shall not be drawn hereafter into consequence or example: and that your Majesty would be also graciously pleased, for the further comfort and safety of your people, to declare your Royal will and pleasure, that in the things aforesaid, all your Officers and Ministers shall serve you, according to the Laws and Statutes of this Realm, as they tender the Honour of your Majesty, and the Prosperity of this Kingdom.* [See Statutes at large, 3, 4 *Car.* I.]

Which petition being read the 2d of *Jun.*, 1628. the King's answer was thus delivered by the Lord Keeper:

The King willeth, that right be done according to the Laws and Customs of the Realm; and that the Statutes be put in due execution, that his Subjects may have no cause to complain of any wrong or oppressions, contrary to their just Rights and Liberties: to the preservation whereof, he holds himself in conscience as well obliged, as of his Prerogative.

On *Tuesday, June* 3. the King's answer was read in the House of Commons, and seemed not full enough, in regard of so much expence of time and labour, as had been imployed in contriving the petition.

June 3. *A Message was brought from the King by the Speaker,*

THAT his Majesty having, upon the petition, exhibited by both Houses, given an answer full of justice and grace, for which we and our posterity have just cause to bless his Majesty, it is now time

* 34 *Edw.* I. † 25 *Edw.* III. *Rot. Parl.* § 1 *Edw.* III. 6. 11 *R.* II. 9. 1 *R.* III. 2. ‖ 9 *Hen.* III. 29. ** 28 *Edw.* III. 3. †† 37 *Edw.* III. 18. 38 *Edw.* III. 9. 42 *Edw.* III. 3. 17 *Ric.* II. 6. §§ 25 *Edw.* I. 6.

to grow to a conclusion of the Session; and therefore his Majesty thinks fit to let you know, that as he doth resolve to abide by that answer, without further change or alteration, so he will Royally and Really perform unto you what he hath thereby promised: and further, that he resolves to end this Session upon *Wednesday* the 11*th* of this month. And therefore wisheth, that the House will seriously attend those businesses, which may best bring the Session to a happy conclusion, without entertaining new matters; and so husband the time, that his Majesty may with the more comfort bring us speedily together again: at which time, if there be any further grievances not contained, or expressed in the petition, they may be more maturely considered than the time will now permit.

Another Message was brought from his Majesty by the Speaker, Thursday *5th of June.*

HIS Majesty wished them to remember the Message he last sent them, by which he set a day for the end of this Session, and he commanded the Speaker to let them know, that he will certainly hold that day prefix'd without alteration; and because that cannot be, if the House entertain more business of length, he requires them, that they enter not into, or proceed with any new business, which may spend greater time, or which may lay any scandal or aspersion upon the State-government or Ministers thereof.

Sir *Robert Philips*, upon this occasion, expressed himself thus: I perceive, that towards God, and towards man, there is little hope, after our humble and careful endeavours, seeing our sins are many and so great. I consider my own infirmities, and if ever my passions were wrought upon, that now this Message stirs me up especially; when I remember with what moderation we have proceeded, I cannot but wonder to see the miserable straight we are now in: What have we not done, to have merited? Former times have given wounds enough to the people's Liberty, we came hither full of wounds, and we have cured what we could; and what is the return of all but misery and desolation? What did we aim at, but to have served his Majesty, and to have done that which would have made him Great and Glorious? If this be a fault, then we are all criminous. What shall we do, since our humble purposes are thus prevented, which were not to have laid any aspersion on the Government, since it tended to no other end, but to give his Majesty true information of his and our danger? And to this we are enforced out of a Necessity of duty to the King, our Country, and to Posterity; but we being stopped, and stopped in such manner, as we are enjoined, so we must now leave to be a Council. I hear this with that grief, as the saddest Message of the greatest loss in the world. But let us still be wise, be humble; let us make a fair Declaration to the King.

Sir *John Elliot*.] Our sins are so exceeding great, that unless we speedily return to God, God will remove himself further from us; ye know with what affection and integrity we have proceeded hitherto to have gained his Majesty's heart, and out of a necessity of our duty, were brought to that course we were in: I doubt, a misrepresentation to his Majesty hath drawn this mark of his displeasure upon us: I observe in the Message, amongst other sad particulars, it is conceived, that we were about to lay some aspersions on the Government; give me leave to protest, that so clear were our intentions, that we desire only to vindicate those dishonours to our King and Country, *&c.* It is said also, as if we cast some aspersions on his Majesty's Ministers; I am confident no Minister, how dear soever can—

Here the Speaker started up from the seat of the Chair, apprehending Sir *John Elliot* intended to fall upon the Duke, and some of the Ministers of State; and said, There is a command laid upon me, that I must command you not to proceed. Whereupon Sir *John Elliot* sate down.

Sir *Dudley Diggs*.] I am as much grieved as ever. Must we not proceed? Let us sit in silence, we are miserable, we know not what to do.

Hereupon there was a silence in the House for a while, which was broken by Sir *Nathaniel Rich*, in these words:

Sir *Nathaniel Rich*.] We must now speak, or for ever hold our peace; for us to be silent when King and Kingdom are in this calamity, is not fit. The question is, Whether we shall secure ourselves by silence, yea or no? I know it is more for our own security, but it is not for the security of those for whom we serve, let us think on them: some instruments desire a change, we fear his Majesty's safety, and the safety of the Kingdom, I do not say we now see it; and shall we now sit still and do nothing, and so be scattered? Let us go together to the Lords, and shew our dangers, that we may then go to the King together.

Others said, that the Speech lately spoken by Sir *John Elliot*, had given offence (as they feared) to his Majesty.

Whereupon the House declared, *That every Member of the House is free from any undutiful Speech, from the beginning of the Parliament to that day; and ordered, that the House be turned into a Committee, to consider what is fit to be done for the safety of the Kingdom; and that no man go out upon pain of going to the* Tower. But before the Speaker left the Chair, he desired leave to go forth; and the House ordered that he may go forth, if he please. And the House was hereupon turned into a Grand Committee; Mr. *Whitby* in the Chair.

Mr. *Wandesford*.] I am as full of grief as others, let us recollect our *English* Hearts, and not sit still, but do our duties: two ways are propounded, to go to the Lords, or to the King, I think it is fit we go to the King, for this doth concern our Liberties, and let us not fear to make a Remonstrance of our Rights; we are his Counsellors. There are some men which call evil good, and good evil, and bitter sweet; Justice is now called popularity and faction.

Sir *Edward Coke*.] We have dealt with that duty and moderation that never was the like, *Rebus sic stantibus*, after such a violation of the Liberties of the Subject; let us take this to heart. In 30 *E.* III. were they then in doubt in Parliament to name men that misled the King? They accused *John de Gaunt*, the King's Son, and Lord *Latimer*, and Lord *Nevil*, for misadvising the King, and they went to the *Tower* for it; now when there is such a downfal of the State, shall we hold our tongues? How shall we answer our duties to God and men? 7 *H.* IV. *Parl. Rot. numb.* 31, & 32. 11 *H.* IV. *numb.* 13. there the Council are complained of, and are removed from the King; they mewed up the King, and dissuaded him from the common good; and why are we now retired from that way we were in? Why may we not name those that are the cause of all our evils? In 4 *H.* III. & 27 *E.* III. & 13 *R.* II. the Parliament moderated the King's Prerogative; and nothing grows to abuse, but this House hath power to treat of it. What shall we do? Let us palliate no longer; if we do, God will not prosper us. I think the Duke of *Buckingham* is the cause of all our miseries, and till the King be informed thereof, we shall never go out with honour, or sit with honour here, that man is the grievance of grievances: let us set down the causes of all our disasters, and all will reflect upon him. As for going to the Lords, that is not *via Regia*; our Liberties are now impeached, we are concerned, it is not *via Regia*, the Lords are not participant with our Liberties.

Mr. *Selden* advised, That a Declaration be drawn under four Heads: 1. To express the House's dutiful carriage towards his Majesty. 2. To tender their Liberties that are violated. 3. To present what the purpose of the House was to have dealt in. 4. That that great person, *viz.* the *Duke*, fearing himself to be questioned, did interpose and cause this distraction. All this time, (said he) we have cast a mantle on what was done last Parliament; but now being driven again to look on that man, let us proceed with that which was then well begun, and let the charge be renewed that was last Parliament against him, to which he made an answer, but the particulars were sufficient, that we might demand judgment on that answer only.

In conclusion, the House agreed upon several Heads for a Remonstrance. But the Speaker (who, after he had leave to go forth, went privately to the King) brought this Message:

That his Majesty commands for the present they adjourn the House till to-morrow morning, and that all Committees cease in the mean time. And the House was accordingly adjourned.

At the same time the King sent for the Lord-Keeper to attend him presently; the House of Lords was adjourned *ad libitum*. The Lord-Keeper being returned, and the House resumed, his Lordship signified his Majesty's desire, that the House and all Committees be adjourned till to-morrow morning.

Friday, *6th of* June, *Mr. Speaker brings another Message from the King.*

IN my service to this House I have had many undeserved favours from you, which I shall ever with all humbleness acknowledge, but none can be greater than that testimony of your confidence yesterday shewed unto me, whereby I hope I have done nothing, or made any representation to his Majesty, but what is for the honour and service of this House, and I will have my tongue cleave to my mouth, before I will speak to the disadvantage of any Member thereof: I have now a Message to deliver unto you;

Whereas his Majesty understanding, that you did conceive his last Message to restrain you in your just Privileges, these are to declare his intentions, That he had no meaning of barring you from what hath been your Right, but only to avoid all scandals on his Council and Actions past, and that his Ministers might not be, nor himself, under their names, taxed for their Counsel unto his Majesty, and that no such particulars should be taken in hand, as would ask a longer time of consideration than what he hath already prefixed, and still resolves to hold; that so, for this time, Christendom might take notice of a sweet parting between him and his people: Which if it fall out, his Majesty will not be long from another meeting, when such grievances (if there be any) at their leisure and convenience may be considered.

Mr. Speaker proceeded:

I will observe somewhat out of this Message; ye may observe a great inclination in his Majesty to meet in this House. I was bold yesterday to take notice of that liberty ye gave me to go to his Majesty: I know there are none here but did imagine whither I went, and but that I knew you were desirous and content that I should leave you, I would not have desired it: give me leave to say, This Message bars you not of your Right in matter, nay, not in manner; but it reacheth to his Counsels past, and for giving him counsel in those things which he commanded.

The House of Lords likewise received this Message by the Lord-Keeper.

MY Lords, his Majesty takes notice, to your great advantage, of the proceedings of this House upon the hearing of his Majesty's Message yesterday; he accounts it a fair respect, that ye would neither agree on any Committee, or send any Message to his Majesty, though it were in your own hearts, but yield yourselves to his Majesty's Message, and defer your own resolutions till you meet again at the time appointed by his Majesty. Yet his Majesty takes it in extreme good part to hear what was in your heart, and especially that you were so sensible of the inconvenience that might ensue upon the breach of this Parliament: which if it had happen'd or shall hereafter happen, his Majesty assures himself, that he shall stand clear before God and men of the occasion.

But his Majesty saith, Ye had just cause to be sensible of the danger, considering how the state of Christendom now stands in respect of the multitude and strength of our enemies, and weakness on our part. All which his Majesty knows very exactly, and in respect thereof, called this Parliament. the particulars his Majesty holds it needless to recite, especially to your Lordships, since they are apparent to all men; neither will it be needful to reiterate them to his Majesty, whose cares are most attentive upon them, and the best remedy that can be thought on thereon, is, if his Subjects do their parts. Therefore his Majesty gives you hearty thanks, and bids me tell you, that nothing hath been more acceptable to him all the time of this Parliament, than this dutiful and discreet carriage of your Lordships, which he professeth hath been a chief motive to his Majesty, to suspend those intentions that were not far from a resolution.

Sir

Sir *Robert Philips* assumed the debate, upon the Message delivered by the Speaker, and said; I rise up with a disposition, somewhat in more hope of comfort than yesterday; yet, in regard of the uncertainty of Counsels, I shall not change much. In the first place, I must be bold without flattering, a thing not incident to me, to tell you (Mr. Speaker) you have not only at all times discharged the duty of a good Speaker, but of a good man; for which I render you many thanks.

Another respect touching his Majesty's answer to our petition; first, if that answer fall out to be short, I free his Majesty, and I believe his resolution was to give that which we all expected: but in that, as in others, we have suffered, by reason of interposed persons between his Majesty and us. But this day is by intervenient accidents diverted from that, but so, as in time we go to his Majesty: therefore let us remove those jealousies in his Majesty of our proceedings, that by some men overgrown have been misrepresented. We have proceeded with temper, in confidence of his Majesty's goodness to us, and our fidelity to him; and if any have construed, that what we have done hath been out of fear, let him know we came hither Freemen, and will ever resolve to endure the worst; and they are poor men that make such interpretations of Parliaments. In this way and method we proceeded, and if any thing fall out unhappily, it is not King *Charles* that advised himself, but King *Charles* misadvised by others, and misled by mis-ordered Counsel; it becomes us to consider what we were doing, and now to advise what is fit to be done. We were taking consideration of the State of the Kingdom, and to present to his Majesty the danger he and we are in, if since any man hath been named in particular, (though I love to speak of my betters with humility) let him thank himself and his Counsels, but those necessary jealousies give us occasion to name him; I assure myself we shall proceed with temper, and give his Majesty satisfaction, if we proceed in that way. His Majesty's Message is now explanatory in point of our Liberties, that he intends not to bar us of our Rights, and that he would not have any aspersion cast on the Counsels past; let us present to his Majesty shortly and faithfully, and declare our intentions, that we intend not to lay any aspersions upon him, but out of a necessity to prevent the imminent dangers we are surrounded with, and to present to him the affairs at home and abroad, and to desire his Majesty, that no interposition or mis-information of men in fault may prevail, but to expect the issue that shall be full of duty and loyalty.

The Commons sent a Message to the Lords, that they would join in an humble request to the King, that a clear and satisfactory answer be given by his Majesty in full Parliament to the Petition of Right; whereunto the Lords did agree.

June the seventh, the King came to the Lords House, and the House of Commons were sent for. And the Lord-Keeper presented the humble Petition of both Houses, and said,

MAY it please your most excellent Majesty, the Lords Spiritual and Temporal, and Commons in Parliament assembled, taking into consideration that the good intelligence between your Majesty and your people doth much depend upon your Majesty's answer unto their Petition of Right formerly presented; with unanimous consent do now become most humble Suitors unto your Majesty, that you would be graciously pleased to give a clear and satisfactory answer thereunto in full Parliament.

Whereunto the King replied,

The answer I have already given you was made with so good deliberation, and approved by the judgments of so many wise men, that I could not have imagined but it should have given you full satisfaction; but to avoid all ambiguous interpretations, and to shew you that there is no doubleness in my meaning, I am willing to please you as well in words as in substance; read your petition, and you shall have an answer that I am sure will please you.

The petition was read, and this answer was returned: *Soit droit fait come il est desire par le petition.* C. R.

This I am sure (said his Majesty) is full, yet no more than I granted you in my first answer; for the meaning of that was to confirm all your Liberties, knowing, according to your own protestations, that you neither mean nor can hurt my Prerogative. And I assure you, my maxim is, that the People's Liberties strengthen the King's Prerogative, and the King's Prerogative is to defend the People's Liberties.

You see how ready I have shewed myself to satisfy your demands, so that I have done my part; wherefore, if this Parliament have not a happy conclusion, the sin is yours, I am free from it.

Whereupon the Commons returned to their own House with unspeakable joy, and resolved so to proceed as to express their thankfulness.

The King's Message to the Lower House, by Sir Humfrey May, *10th of June* 1628.

HIS Majesty is well pleased that your Petition of Right, and his Answer, be not only recorded in both Houses of Parliament, but also in all the Courts of *Westminster*; and that his pleasure is, it be put in print for his honour, and the content and satisfaction of his people, and that you proceed cheerfully to settle businesses for the good and reformation of the Commonwealth.

June 26. The Speaker being sent for to the King at *Whitehall*, came not into the House till about nine a-clock. And after prayers, the Remonstrance concerning tunnage and poundage being ingrossed, was a reading in the House; and while it was a reading, the King sent for the Speaker and the whole House, and the King made a Speech as followeth:

IT may seem strange, that I came so suddenly to end this Session; before I give my assent to the Bills. I will tell you the cause, though I must avow, that I owe the account of my actions to God alone. It is known to every one, that a while ago the House of Commons gave me a Remonstrance; how acceptable, every man may judge; and for the merit of it, I will not call that in question, for I am sure no wise man can justify it.

Now, since I am truly informed that a second Remonstrance is preparing for me to take away the profit of my tunnage and poundage, one of the chief maintenances of my Crown, by alledging I have given away my Right thereto by my answer to your petition:

This is so prejudicial unto me, that I am forced to end this Session some few hours before I meant, being not willing to receive any more Remonstrances, to which I must give a harsh answer. And since I see, that even the House of Commons begins already to make false constructions of what I granted in your petition, lest it be worse interpreted in the Country, I will now make a Declaration concerning the true intent thereof.

The profession of both Houses in the time of hammering this petition, was no way to trench upon my Prerogative, saying, they had neither intention or power to hurt it. Therefore it must needs be conceived, that I have granted no new, but only confirmed the antient Liberties of my Subjects. Yet to shew the clearness of my intentions, that I neither repent, nor mean to recede from any thing I have promised you, I do here declare myself, That those things which have been done, whereby many have had some cause to suspect the Liberties of the Subjects to be trenched upon, which indeed was the first and true ground of the petition, shall not hereafter be drawn into example for your prejudice; and from time to time, in the word of a King, ye shall not have the like cause to complain. But as for tunnage and poundage, it is a thing I cannot want, and was never intended by you to ask, nor meant by me, I am sure, to grant.

To conclude, I command you all that are here to take notice of what I have spoken at this time, to be the true intent and meaning of what I granted you in your petition; but especially you, my Lords the Judges, for to you only, under me, belongs the interpretation of Laws: for none of the Houses of Parliament, either joint or separate, (what new Doctrine soever may be raised) have any power either to make or declare a Law without my consent.

Then the Lord Keeper said, It is his Majesty's pleasure that this Session now end, and that the Parliament be prorogued till the 20*th* of *October* next.

In the following Sessions, *viz. Wednesday, January* 21*st*, it was ordered that Mr. *Selden* and others should see if the *Petition of Right* and his Majesty's answer thereunto were inrolled in the Parliament Rolls, and the Courts at *Westminster*, as his Majesty sent them word the last Session they should be; and also in what manner they were entered; which was done accordingly: and Mr. *Selden* made report to the House, that his Majesty's Speech made the last day of the Session in the Upper House is also entered by his Majesty's command.

Hereupon Mr. *Pym* moved, that the debate hereof should be deferred till *Tuesday* next, by reason of the fewness of the House.

Sir *John Elliot*.] This which is now mentioned, concerns the honour of the House, and the Liberty of the Kingdom; it is true, it deserves to be deferred till there be a full House, but it is good to prepare things. I find it is a great point; I desire a select Committee may enter into consideration thereof, and also how other Liberties of the Kingdom be invaded. I find in the country *the Petition of Right* printed indeed, but with an answer that never gave any satisfaction: I desire a Committee may consider thereof, and present it to the House, and that the Printer be sent for, to give satisfaction to the House, by what warrant it was printed. Which was ordered.

Mr. *Selden*.] For this Petition of Right, it is known how lately it hath been violated since our last meeting; the Liberties for life, person and freehold, how they have been invaded; and have not some been committed, contrary to that? Now we, knowing these invasions, must take notice of it. For Liberties, for State, we know of an order made in the *Exchequer*, that a Sheriff was commanded not to execute a replevin, and men's goods are taken and must not be restored. Whereas no man ought to lose life, or limb, but by Law; hath not one lately lost his ears (meaning *Savage*) that was censured in the *Star-Chamber* by an arbitrary sentence and judgment? Next, they will take away our arms, and then our lives. Let all see we are sensible of these customs creeping upon us: let us make a just presentation hereof to his Majesty.

Norton the King's Printer was brought to the Bar, and asked by what warrant the additions to the Petition were printed? He answered, that there was a warrant (as he thought) from the King himself. And being asked whether there were not some copies printed without additions, he answered, there were some, but they were suppressed by warrant.

Sir *John Elliot* desired some clearer satisfaction might be made, and that he might answer directly by what warrant. Whereupon he was called in again: who said, he did not remember the particular, but sure he was there was a warrant.

Mr. *Selden* reported from the Committee concerning the printing of the Petition of Right, that there were printed 1500 without any addition at all, which were published in the time of the last Parliament: but since the Parliament, other copies have been printed, and these supprest and made waste paper; which the Printer did, as he said, by command from Mr. *Attorney*, which he received from his Majesty. And the Printer further said, That the *Attorney* was with the Lord Privy-Seal at *Whitehall*, and there delivered unto the Printer sundry papers, with divers hands to them, and on the backside was endorsed thus, *We will and command you, that these copies be printed.*

Which put an end to this grand affair.

XVII. *Pre-*

XVII. Proceedings against *William Stroud*, Esq; *Walter Long*, Esq; *John Selden*, Esq; and others, on an *Habeas Corpus*, in *Banco Regis*. 1629. 5 *Car*. I.

ON *February* 23*d*, the House of Commons being upon the debate of the business of the customers, who had seized goods belonging to Mr. *Rolls*, a Member of the House, dissolved themselves into a grand Committee, and at last resolv'd,

That Mr. Rolls, *a Member of the House, ought to have privilege of person and goods, but the command of the King is so great, that they leave it to the House.*

After which, the King's message, in justification of the farmers and officers of the customs, was taken into consideration; which occasioned warm debates, and the Speaker being moved to put the question then propos'd, refus'd to do it, and said, *That he was otherwise commanded by the King.*

Then said Mr. *Selden, Dare not you, Mr.* Speaker, *put the Question when we command you? If you will not put it, we must sit still; thus we shall never be able to do any thing. They that come after you, may say, They have the King's command not to do it. We sit here by the command of the King under the Great Seal, and you are, by his Majesty, sitting in this Royal Chair, before both Houses, appointed for our Speaker; and now you refuse to perform your Office.*

Hereupon the House (in some heat) adjourned till *Wednesday* next.

On *Wednesday* the 25th of *February*, both Houses, by his Majesty's command, were adjourned until *Monday* morning the 2d of *March*.

Monday the 2d of *March*, the Commons met, and urged the Speaker to put the Question; who said, *I have a command from the King to adjourn till* March *the* 10*th*; *and put no Question*. And endeavouring to go out of the Chair, was notwithstanding held by some Members (the House foreseeing a dissolution) till a protestation was published in the House; 1. Against Popery and Arminianism. 2. Against tunnage and poundage not granted by Parliament. 3. If any Merchant yield or pay tunnage and poundage not granted by Parliament, he should be reputed a betrayer of the Liberties of *England*.

Hereupon the King sent for the Serjeant of the House; but he was detained, the door being lock'd: Then he sent the Gentleman-Usher of the Lords House, with a message; and he was refused admittance, till the said Votes were read. And then in much confusion the House was adjourned to the 10*th* of *March*. Nevertheless his Majesty, by Proclamation, dated the 2d of *March*, declares the Parliament to be dissolved.

(Though the Proclamation was not published till the 10th) and the day following, (the 3d) Warrants were directed from the Council to *Denzil Holles*, Esq; Sir *Miles Hobart*, Sir *John Elliot*, Sir *Peter Hayman*, *John Selden*, *William Coriton*, *Walter Long*, *William Stroud*, *Benjamin Valentine*, Esqrs; commanding their personal appearance on the morrow. At which time, Mr. *Holles*, Sir *John Elliot*, Mr. *Coriton*, Mr. *Valentine* appearing, and refusing to answer out of Parliament what was said and done in Parliament, were committed close prisoners to the *Tower*; and Warrants were given (the Parliament being still in being) for the sealing up of the Studies of Mr. *Holles*, Mr. *Selden*, and Sir *John Elliot*. But Mr. *Long* and Mr. *Stroud* not then, nor for some time after appearing, a Proclamation issued forth for the apprehending of them.

The King purposing to proceed against the Members of the House of Commons, who were committed to prison by him in the *Star-Chamber*, caused certain questions to be proposed to the Judges upon the 25*th* of *April*.

Whereupon all the Judges met at *Serjeants-Inn* by command from his Majesty, where Mr. Attorney proposed certain questions concerning the offences of some of the Parliament-men committed to the *Tower*, and other prisons: At which time, one question was proposed and resolved, *viz. That the Statute of* 4. H. VIII. *intitled*, An Act concerning *Richard Strode*, *was a particular Act of Parliament, and extended only to* Richard Strode, *and to those persons that had joined with him to prefer a Bill to the House of Commons concerning Tinners: And although the Act be private, and extendeth to them alone, yet it was no more than all other Parliament-men, by privilege of the House, ought to have,* viz. *Freedom of Speech concerning those matters debated in Parliament by a Parliamentary course.*

The rest of the questions Mr. Attorney was wished to set down in writing against another day.

Upon *Monday* following, all the Judges met again, and then Mr. Attorney proposed these questions:

1. *Whether if any Subject hath received probable information of any Treason or treacherous attempt or intention against the King or State, that Subject ought not to make known to the King, or his Majesty's Commissioners, when thereunto he shall be required, what information he hath received, and the grounds thereof; to the end the King being truly informed, may prevent the danger? And if the said Subject in such case shall refuse to be examined, or to answer the questions which shall be demanded of him for further inquiry and discovery of the truth, whether it be not a high contempt in him, punishable in the Star-Chamber, as an offence against the general Justice and Government of the Kingdom?*

Sol. The resolution and answer of all the Justices, That it is an offence punishable as aforesaid, so that this do not concern himself, but another, nor draw him to danger of Treason or Contempt by his answer.

2. *Whether it be a good answer or excuse, being thus interrogated, and refusing to answer, to say,* That he was a Parliament-man when he received the information, and that he spake thereof in the Parliament-house: and therefore the Parliament being now ended, he refused to answer to any such questions but in the Parliament-house, and not in any other place?

Sol. To this the Judges, by advice privately to Mr. Attorney, gave this answer, That this excuse being in nature of a Plea, and an errour in judgment, was not punishable, until he were over-ruled in an orderly manner to make another answer; and whether the party were brought in *Ore tenus*, or by information, for this Plea he was not to be punished.

3. *Whether a Parliament-man, committing an offence against the King or Council not in a Parliament way, might, after the Parliament ended, be punished or not?*

Sol. All the Judges, *una voce*, answered, he might, if he be not punished for it in Parliament; for the Parliament shall not give privilege to any *contra morem Parliamentarium*, to exceed the bounds and limits of his place and duty. And all agreed, That regularly he cannot be compelled out of Parliament to answer things done in Parliament in a Parliamentary course; but it is otherwise where things are done exorbitantly, for those are not the acts of a Court.

4. *Whether if one Parliament-man alone shall resolve, or two or three shall covertly conspire to raise false slanders and rumours against the Lords of the Council and Judges, not with intent to question them in a legal course, or in a Parliamentary way, but to blast them, and to bring them to hatred of the people, and the Government in contempt, be punishable in the Star-Chamber after the Parliament is ended?*

Sol. The Judges resolve, That the same was punishable out of Parliament, as an offence exorbitant committed in Parliament, beyond the office, and besides the duty of a Parliament-man.

There was another question put by Mr. Attorney, viz.

Whether if a man in Parliament, by way of digression, and not upon any occasion arising concerning the same in Parliament, shall say, The Lords of the Council and the Judges had agreed to trample upon the Liberty of the Subject, and the Privileges of Parliament, he were punishable or not?

The Judges desired to be spared to make any answer thereunto, because it concerned themselves in particular *.

The

* *Nalson* in his Collections, Vol. II. p. 374, says, There were several questions propos'd to the three Chief-Judges about matters in Parliament, to which they gave these answers; which being something different from what is above, are here inserted.

Quære I. *Whether a Parliament-man, offending the King criminally or contemptuously in the Parliament-house (and not then punished), may not be punished out of Parliament?*

Answer. We conceive, That if a Parliament-man, exceeding the privilege of Parliament, do criminally or contemptuously offend the King in the Parliament-house (and not there punished) may be punished out of Parliament.

Quære II. *Whether the King, as he hath the power of calling and dissolving a Parliament, have not also an absolute power to cause it to be adjourned at his pleasure?*

Answer. We conceive, That the King hath the power of commanding of adjournments of Parliaments, as well as of calling, proroguing and dissolving of Parliaments: But for the manner thereof, or the more particular answer to this, and the next subsequent question, we refer ourselves to the precedents of both Houses.

Quære III. *Whether, if the King do command an adjournment to be made, he hath not also power to command all further proceedings in Parliament to cease at that time?*

Quære IV. *Whether it be not a high contempt in a Member of the House, contrary to the King's express commandment, contemptuously to oppose the adjournment?*

Answer. The King's express commandment being signified for an adjournment, if any after that shall contemptuously oppose it, further, or otherwise than the privilege of the House will warrant; this we conceive to be a great Contempt.

Quære V. *Whether, if a few Parliament-men do conspire together, to stir up ill affections in the People against the King, and the Government, and to leave the Parliament with such a loose, and by words or writings put it in execution, and this not punished in Parliament, it be an offence punishable out of Parliament?*

Answer. We conceive this offence to be punishable out of Parliament.

Quære VI. *Whether, if some Parliament-men shall conspire together to publish papers containing false and scandalous rumours against the Lords of the Privy-Council, or any one or more of them, not to the end to question them in a legal or Parliamentary way, but to bring them into hatred of the People, and the Government into Contempt, and to make discord between the Lords and Commons; is not this an offence punishable out of Parliament?*

Answer. We conceive this also to be an offence punishable out of Parliament.

Quære VII. *If two or three or more of the Parliament shall conspire to defame the King's Government, and to deter his Subjects from obeying or assisting the King; of what nature this offence is?*

Answer. The nature and quality of this offence will be greater or lesser, as the circumstances shall fall out, upon the truth of the fact.

Quære VIII. *Can any privilege of the House warrant a tumultuous Proceeding?*

Answer. We humbly conceive, that an earnest, though a disorderly and confused proceeding in such a multitude, may be called tumultuous, and yet the privilege of the House may warrant it.

We in all humbleness are willing to satisfy your Majesty's Command, but until the particulars of the fact do appear, we can give no directer answers than before.

And particularly as to the second Quære, about the King's power of adjourning as well as calling and dissolving of Parliaments, these following Parliamentary precedents were given in.

Mercur. 4. *Aprilis*, 1 *Jac. Seff.* 1. Mr. Speaker pronounceth his Majesty's pleasure of adjourning the House till the 11*th* of *April* (and it was so done).

Jovis 18 *Dec.* 1606. The Lords by their Messengers signified the King's Pleasure, that the Session should be adjourned till the 10*th* of *February* following.

Upon this Message Mr. Speaker adjourned the House according to his Majesty's said Pleasure.

Martis [illegible] *Martii* [illegible]. The Speaker delivered the King's Pleasure, that the House should be adjourned till *Monday* the 20*th* of *April* following.

Mercurii 20 *Maii* 1607. Mr Speaker signified the King's Pleasure about nine o'Clock to adjourn the House till the [illegible] of the same month.

And the [illegible] of *May*, he being challenged for adjourning without the privity of the House, he excuseth it, and saith, as the House had power to adjourn themselves, so the King had a superior power, and by his command he did it.

The next day Mr. *Attorney* put the Judges another Caſe.

It is demanded of a Parliament-man, being called *Ore tenus*, before the Court of *Star-Chamber*, being charged, that he did not ſubmit himſelf to examination for ſuch things as did concern the King and the Government of the State, and were affirmed to be done by a third perſon, and not by himſelf; if he confeſſes his hand to that refuſal, and make his excuſe, and plead becauſe he had privilege of Parliament;

Whether the Court will not over-rule this Plea as erroneous, and that he ought to make a further anſwer?

Anſ. It is the juſteſt way for the King and the Party not to proceed *Ore tenus*, becauſe it being a point in Law, it is fit to hear Counſel before it be over-ruled; and upon an *Ore tenus*, by the Rules of *Star-Chamber*, Counſel ought not to be admitted; and that it would not be for the honour of the King, nor the ſafety of the Subject, to proceed in that manner.

[But the King dropped the Proceedings againſt them in the *Star-Chamber*.]

Paſch. 5 *Car.* upon an *Habeas Corpus* of this Court to bring the body of *William Stroud*, Eſq. with the cauſe of his impriſonment, to the Marſhal of the *King's Bench*; it was returned in this manner:

That Mr. William Stroud *was committed under my cuſtody by virtue of a certain Warrant under the hands of twelve the Lords of the Privy-Council of the King.* The tenour of which Warrant followeth in theſe words:

You are to take knowledge, That it is his Majeſty's pleaſure and commandment, that you take into your cuſtody the body of William Stroud, *Eſq; and keep him cloſe priſoner till you ſhall receive other order, either from his Majeſty, or this Board: for ſo doing, this ſhall be your Warrant.* Dated this 2d of *April*, 1629. And the direction of the Warrant was, *To the Marſhal of the* King's Bench, *or his Deputy.*

He is alſo detained in priſon by virtue of a Warrant under his Majeſty's hand; the tenour of which Warrant followeth in theſe words:

C. R.

Whereas you have in your cuſtody the body of William Stroud, *Eſq. by Warrant of our Lords of our Privy-Council, by our ſpecial command, you are to take notice, that this Commitment was for notable Contempts by him committed againſt our Self and our Government, and for ſtirring up Sedition againſt us; for which you are to detain him in your cuſtody, and to keep him cloſe priſoner, until our pleaſure be further known concerning his deliverance.*

Given at *Greenwich*, the 7th of *May*, 1629. in the fifth year of our Reign.

The direction being, *To the Marſhal of our Bench* for the time being, *& hæ ſunt cauſæ captionis & detentionis prædicti* Gulielmi Stroud.

And upon another *Habeas Corpus* to the Marſhal of the Houſhold, to have the body of *Walter Long*, Eſq. in Court, it was returned according as the return of Mr. *Stroud* was.

Mr. *Aſk*, of the *Inner-Temple*, of Counſel for Mr. *Stroud*; and Mr. *Maſon* of *Lincoln's-Inn*, of Counſel for Mr. *Long*; argued againſt the inſufficiency of the Return.

Mr. *Aſk*. That the Return was inſufficient. The Return conſiſts upon two Warrants, bearing ſeveral dates, which are the cauſes of the taking and detaining of the priſoner. For the firſt Warrant, which is of the Lords of the Council, that is inſufficient: becauſe no cauſe is ſhewn of his commitment, which is expreſly againſt the reſolution of the Parliament, and their Petition of Right, in the time of this King, which now is, to which he had likewiſe given his aſſent; ſo his taking by virtue of the ſaid Warrant is wrongful. And for the ſecond Warrant, it is inſufficient alſo, and that notwithſtanding it be the King's own; for the King himſelf cannot impriſon any man, as our Books are, to wit, 16 *H.* VI. *F. Monſtrance de faits.* 1. *H.* VII. 4. *Huſſey* reports it to be the opinion of *Markham*, in the time of *Edw.* IV. and *Forteſcue* in his Book, *de laudibus Legum Angliæ, cap.* 18. And the reaſon given, is, becauſe no action of falſe impriſonment lies againſt the King, if the impriſonment be wrongful; and the King cannot be a wrong doer. The Statute of *Magna Charta* is, That no Freeman be impriſoned but by the Law of the Land. And it appears by theſe Books, that it is againſt the Law of the Land that the King ſhould impriſon any one.

2. Admit that this be only a ſignification and notification given by the King himſelf, of the commitment of the priſoner; yet it ſeems that that ſignification is of no force, 1. Becauſe the words are general and uncertain——*for notable contempts.*——There are in the Law many contempts of ſeveral natures; there are contempts againſt the Common Law, againſt the Statute Law; contempts in words, geſtures, or actions. And it appears not to the Court of what nature theſe contempts were.——*Notable*——Every contempt which is made to the King is notable.——*Againſt our Government*——Contempt which is committed in a Court of Record or Chancery, is a contempt againſt the Government of the King, to wit, becauſe they diſobey the King when he commands them by his Writs, *Coke* 8. 60. *a. Beecher*'s Caſe. The laſt words of the Return are, ——*For ſtirring up of ſedition againſt us*----which words likewiſe are indefinite and general. I find not the word *Sedition* in our Books, but taken adjectively, as ſeditious Books, ſeditious News, *&c.* In the Statute of the 1*ſt* and 2*d Phil.* and *Mary, cap.* 3. the words are, *If any perſon ſhall be convicted*, &c. *for ſpeaking*, &c. *any falſe, ſeditious, or ſlanderous news, ſaying of tales of the Queen*, &c. *he ſhall loſe his ears, or pay* 100l. There the penalty impoſed upon ſuch ſedition is but a fine. *Coke* 4. Lord *Cromwel*'s Caſe, *p.* 13. where ſedition is defined to be *ſeorſum itio*, when a man takes a courſe of his own. And there it is ſaid, that the words,---*maintain ſedition againſt the Queen's proceedings*----ſhall be expounded according to the coherence of all the words, and the intent of the parties. So that it is plain, that there is a ſedition that is only fineable, and which is no cauſe of impriſonment without Bail: And what the ſedition is that is here intended, cannot be gathered out of the words, they are ſo general.-----*againſt Us*---thoſe words are redundant, for every ſedition is againſt the King.

Upon the generality and incertainty of all the words in the Return, he put theſe Caſes: 18 *E.* III. A man was indicted, *quia furatus eſt equum*, and doth not ſay, *Felonicè*, and therefore ill. 29 *Aſſ.* 45. A man was indicted that he was *communis latro*, and the indictment held vicious, becauſe too general. So here the offences are returned generally. But there ought to be ſomething individual, *Coke* 5. 57. *Specot*'s Caſe, *quia ſchiſmaticus inveteratus*, is no good cauſe for the Biſhop to refuſe a Clerk, for it is too general, and there are ſchiſms of divers kinds. 38 *E.* III. 2. Becauſe the Clerk is *criminoſus*, it is no good cauſe for the Biſhop to refuſe him. 8 and 9 *Eliz. Dy.* 254. The Biſhop of *N.* refuſeth one, becauſe he was a haunter of taverns, &c. for which, and divers other crimes, he was unfit; held that the laſt words are too general and incertain. 40 *E.* III. 6. In the tender of a marriage, and refuſal of the heir, he ought to alledge a certain cauſe of refuſal, whereupon iſſue may be taken. *Coke* 8. 68. *Trollop*'s Caſe, to ſay, That the plaintiff is excommunicated for divers contumacies, ſhall not diſable him, without ſhewing ſome cauſe in ſpecial of the excommunication, upon which the Court may judge whether it were juſt or no: ſo here. And he concluded with a Caſe that was reſolved, *Hill.* 33 *Eliz. Peak* and *Paul* the Defendants ſaid of the Plaintiff, Thou art a mutinous and ſeditious man, and maintaineſt ſedition againſt the Queen; and the words adjudged not actionable.

Mr. *Maſon* (afterwards Recorder of *London*) moved alſo, That the Return was inſufficient. For the firſt Warrant, That he was committed by command of the King, ſignified by the Privy-Council, I will not argue that, becauſe it was claimed as an ancient Right pertaining to the Subject in the Petition of Right, whereto the King himſelf hath given his conſent. For the ſecond Warrant, the Return is,------*for ſtirring up ſedition againſt us and our Government.* Sedition is not any determined offence within our Law; our Law gives definitions or deſcriptions of other offences, to wit, of Treaſon, Murder, Felony, &c. but there is no crime in our Law called Sedition. It is defined by a *Civilian* to be *Seditio*, or *Seceſſio, cum pars Reipublicæ contra partem inſurgit*; ſo that Sedition is nothing but diviſion. *Bracton* and *Glanvile* have the word *Seditio* generally. Before the Statute of 25 *E.* III. *cap.* 2. it was not clear enough what thing was Treaſon, what not; by which Statute it is declared what ſhall be called Treaſon, and that the Judges ſhall not declare any thing to be Treaſon, that is not contained within the ſaid Statute, but it ſhall be declared only by Parliament. And that Statute ſpeaks not of Sedition, nor the Statute of 1 *H.* IV. *cap.* 10. which makes ſome things Treaſon, which are not contained within the ſaid Statute of 25 *E.* III. The Statute of 1 *E.* VI. *cap.* 12. takes away all intervenient Statutes, which declared new Treaſons; and the ſaid Act declares other things to be Treaſon, but mentions not Sedition. Sedition is the quality of an offence, and is oftentimes taken adverbially, or adjectively. To raiſe tumults or treſpaſſes is Sedition, *Trin.* 21 *E.* III. *rot.* 23. *B. R. Gerbert*'s Caſe; a man was indicted, becauſe in the high-ſtreet he took *J. S.* there, being in hoſtile manner, and uſurped over him royal power, which is manifeſt Sedition; and there it was but an indictment of treſpaſs. *Mich.* 20 *E.* I. *rot.* 27. One that was Surveyor of the wood-work for the King, was indicted for ſtealing of timber, and detaining wages (*ridding* Carpenters wages) by one that was but a boy; and this is there termed ſedition, and yet it was but a petty felony. *Mich.* 42 *E.* III. *rot.*65. *B. R. R. Pope* was appealed by the wife of *J. S.* becauſe he feloniouſly and ſeditiouſly murdered *J. S.* and *ſeditiouſly* was there put in, becauſe it was done privily. By which caſes it appears, that Sedition is not taken as a ſubſtantive, ſo that it may be applied to treaſon, treſpaſs, or other offences. By the Statute of 2 *H.* IV. *cap.* 15. there is a puniſhment inflicted for the raiſing of ſeditious doctrine, and yet no puniſhment could have been inflicted for it until the ſaid Statute; and yet it was ſeditious, as well before the ſaid Statute as after. And this appears alſo by the Statute of 1*ſt* and 2*d* of *Philip* and *Mary, cap.* 3. which hath been cited. The Statute 13 *Eliz. cap.* 2. recites, that divers ſeditious and evil-diſpoſed perſons, *&c.* obtained bulls of reconciliation from the Pope, which offence was made Treaſon by the ſaid Statute, (for it was not before, and yet there was ſedition) and by the ſaid Statute, the aiders and abettors are but in the caſe of *Premunire.* By the Statute of 13 *Eliz. cap.* 1. for the avoiding of contentious and ſeditious titles to the Crown, it is enacted by the ſaid Statute, That he that ſhall declare the ſucceſſor of the King, ſhall forfeit the moiety of his goods, *&c.* ſo that the ſaid offence, although it be ſeditious, is not treaſon by the Common Law, nor is it made treaſon by the Statute of 25 *E.* III. nor by the Statute of 13 *Eliz.* By the Statute of 23 *Eliz. cap.* 2. he that ſpeaks ſeditious or ſlanderous news of the Queen ſhall loſe his ears, or pay 200*l.* and the ſecond offence is made felony. The Statute of 35 *Eliz. cap.* 1. is againſt ſeditious ſectaries, which abſent themſelves from the Church; they are to be puniſhed 10*l.* by the month. Out of all which Statutes it may be collected, that the word *Sedition* is taken variouſly, according to the ſubject in hand. And *Coke* 4. 13. Lord *Cromwel*'s Caſe, *Seditious* is referred to doctrine. There are offences more high in their nature than Sedition, which were not treaſon, unleſs ſo declared by Act of Parliament. Every rebellious Act is Sedition, yet if ſuch Acts be not within the Statute of 25 *E.* III. they are not treaſon. 17 *R.* II. *cap.* 8. Inſurrection of villeins and others is made treaſon; which proves, that before this Act it was not treaſon. And this Act of 17 *R.* II. is repealed by the Statute of 1 *H.* IV. By the Statute of 3 and 4 *E.* VI. *cap.* 5. to aſſemble people to alter the Laws, is made treaſon, if they continue together an hour after Proclamation made. This aſſembly of people was Sedition at the Common Law; and the very aſſembly, if they after diſſolve upon Proclamation made, is not treaſon by the ſaid Statute. By the Statute of 14 *Eliz.cap.*1. it is made felony, maliciouſly and rebelliouſly to hold from the Queen any Caſtles, *&c.* but becauſe this relates not to the Statute of 25 *E.* III. it is not treaſon. 2. It ſeems clearly, that this caſe is within the Petition of Right, in which *Magna Charta*, and the Statutes of 25 and 28 *E.* III. are recited. The grievance there was, that divers have been impriſoned without any cauſe ſhewed, to which they might make anſwer according to the law. And upon this return, nothing appears to be objected to which he might anſwer. It appears not what that Act, which is called *Sedition*, was. This is

Veneris 30 *Martii* 1610. His Majeſty's Pleaſure to adjourn from *Tueſday* till *Monday* ſevennight,

11 *July.* The King by Commiſſion adjourneth the Lords Houſe. Meſſengers ſent to the Commons. They ſend by Meſſengers of their own to the Lords, that they uſe to adjourn themſelves.

The Commiſſion is ſent down, Mr. *Speaker* adjourneth the Houſe till the firſt of *Auguſt.*

26 *Febr.* 4 *Car.* Mr. *Speaker* ſignifieth his Majeſty's Pleaſure, that the Houſe be preſently adjourned till *Monday* next, and in the mean time all Committees and other proceedings to ceaſe.

And thereupon Mr. *Speaker* in the name of the Houſe adjourned the ſame accordingly.

the

the very grief intended to be remedied by this Statute: to this he cannot answer according to Law. It appears not whether this were a seditious Act, trespass, or slander, or what it was at all. The words are,——*Sedition against the King*;——this helps not, for every offence is against the King, against his Crown and Dignity; that which disturbs the Commonwealth is against the King; seditious Doctrine is sedition against the King, as is beforesaid. In 28 *H* VI. *vide prostrat. fol.* 19. the Lords and Commons desire the King, that *William de la Pool* may be committed for divers Treasons, and sundry other heinous crimes, and the petition held not good, because too general: whereupon they exhibit particular Articles against him. And therefore upon the whole matter prayed, that Mr. *Long* might be discharged from his imprisonment.

On another day, *Berkley* and *Davenport*, the King's Serjeants, argued for the King, that this Return was sufficient in Law to detain them in prison. *Berkley* began, and said, That the case is new, and of great weight and consequence; and yet, under favour, the Prerogative of the King, and the Liberty of the Subject, are not mainly touched therein; for the case is not so general as it hath been made, but particular upon this particular return. The Liberty of the Subject is a tender point, the right whereof is great, just, and inviolable. The Prerogative of the King is an high point, to which every Subject ought to submit. I intend not to make any discourse of the one or the other, I will only remember what the King hath determined upon them both, in his speech which he made upon the Petition of Right; to wit, that the People's Liberties strengthen the King's Prerogative, and that the King's Prerogative is to defend the People's Liberties. This may settle the hearts of the people concerning their Liberty. The way which I intend to treat in my Argument, is, to answer the objections and reasons which have been made, and to give some reasons, whereby this Return shall be sufficient.

The objections which have been made are reducible to four heads:

1. By what the Prisoner here shall be said to be committed and detained.
2. That this Commitment is against the Petition of Right.
3. That the cause which is here returned is general and incertain.
4. That the offences mentioned in the Return are but fineable; and therefore, notwithstanding them, the party is bailable.

For the first, it hath been objected, That the Commitment here was by the Lords of the Privy-Council, and the signification of this cause is by the King himself. But I say, that there is a further matter in the Return; for the Lords of the Council do it by the command of the King, and they only pursue this command. I will not dispute whether the Lords of the Council have power to commit an offender or no, it is common in experience, 33 *H.* VI. 28. *Poigne*'s case is express in it. And in the Petition of Right it is admitted, that they may commit. And this is not alledged there for a grievance, but the grievance there, was, because the particular charge of commitment was not shewed. Some Books have been objected to prove, that the King, though in person, cannot commit any person; 16 *H.* VI. *F. Monstrance de faits* 182. But the authority of that Book vanisheth, if the case be put at large, which was in trespass for cutting of trees. The Defendant said, That the place where, &c. is parcel of the Manor of *D.* whereof the King is seized in Fee, and the King commands us to cut. And the opinion of the Court was, that this is no plea, without shewing a specialty of the command of the King. And there the whole Court says, That if the King command me to arrest a man, whereby I arrest him, he shall have trespass or imprisonment against me, altho' it be done in the presence of the King. That the following words are to be understood, that the principal case was of one command of the King by word, and then such command by word to arrest a man is void. And 1 *H.* VII. 4. was objected; *Hussey* says, that *Markham* said to King *Edw.* IV. that he cannot arrest a man for suspicion of Treason or Felony, because if he do wrong, the party cannot have his action. To this I say, That the Book there is to be understood of a wrongful arrest, for there it is spoken of an action of false imprisonment; and a wrongful arrest cannot be made by the King.

2. It stands not with the dignity of the King to arrest any man. *Coke*, 4. 73. The King makes a lease for years, rendering rent, with condition of re-entry for non-payment; he shall take advantage of the condition without any demand; and the reason there given, is, that a *decorum* and conveniency might be observed. So it is not befitting for the King in person to arrest any man, but the King may command another to do it. *Bratton lib.* 2. *de acquirendo rerum Dominio, fol.* 55. says, That the Crown of the King is to do justice and judgment, and *facere pacem*, without which the Crown itself cannot subsist. Several constructions are to be made upon those several words,——and the last words——*facere pacem*——imply, that the King hath a coercive power. *Britton f.* 1. amongst the *Errata*. The King said, Because we are not sufficient in person to do every thing, we divide the charge into many parts. We are the people's Justice, and a Justice implies one that hath power to do Justice in every kind, to wit, by imprisonment, or otherwise. 20 *H.* VII. 7 *Coke* 11. 85. it is said, That the King is the Chief-Justice. And *Lambert*, in his *Justice of Peace, fol.* 3. says, That in ancient histories, the Chief-Justice of *England* is called *Capitalis Justiciarius & Prima Justicia*, after the King in *England*. So that the King hath the same power of Justice, as the Chief-Justice had. This imprisonment here, which is before conviction for any offence, is not used toward the Subject as imprisonment for any fault, but is rather an arrest or restraint to avoid further inconveniencies. 14 *H.* VII. 8. A Justice of Peace may arrest 'men riotously assembled, for prevention of further mischief. And the Book also says, That he may leave his servants there to arrest men, for safeguard of the Peace. It is a case well known, that if a house be set on fire, every man may pull down the next house, for prevention of a greater mischief, so it seems concerning the Incendiaries of State, they ought to be restrained and supprest, lest others should be stirred up by them to the same combustion. 22. *Ass.* 56. and 22 *E.* IV. 45. in false imprisonment the Defendant justifies, because the Plaintiff was mad and out of his wits, and that he had done some harm, and that he had bound and beat him to avoid further harm, which might have happened by his madness; and the justification was held good. So is it in matter of Government; to avoid commotions, the King ought to use his coercive power against those that are enraged. The objection was, that this course was against the Petition of Right. But I answer, That this case is out of the words of that petition; the words of the petition were, —Whereas by the Statute called, the great Charter, and by the Statute of 28 *E.* III. no Freeman may be taken or imprisoned;—yet against the tenour of the said Statute, &c. divers of your Subjects have of late been imprisoned, without any cause shewed; and when for their deliverance, &c. they were brought before the Justices by Writs of *Habeas Corpus*, there to undergo and receive as the Court should order, and their Keepers commanded to certify the cause of their detainer, and no cause was certified, but that they were detained by your Majesty's special command, signified by the Lords of your Council; and yet were returned back to several prisons, without being charged with any thing to which they might make answer according to Law. These last words are observable,——without being charged with any thing to which they might make answer——these words do not refer to the return of the *Habeas Corpus*; for the cause returned therein cannot be traversed, 9 *H.* VI. 54. but the Court took it as true. But the setting forth of the cause, and the answer to the same cause, is to be upon other proceedings, to wit, upon the Indictment for the offence, or otherwise. And there is a great difference between the return of a Writ to which a man may answer, and the return of an *Habeas Corpus*, 10 *E.* IV. &. 3 *H* VII. 11. are, that if the Sheriff return *Rescous*, all certainties of every circumstance ought to be shewed; because it is fitting, that a thing certain be brought into judgment. And upon shewing of the grievance, as above, the Petition is, that no Freeman, in any such manner as before is mentioned, be imprisoned or detained; *scil.* and it hath relation to such imprisonment, which is mentioned in the premisses. And imprisonment mentioned in the Premisses of the Petition, is, where no cause at all was mentioned; then where any cause is shewed, is out of the Petition, and that *such* is the word relative, appears by *Coke* 11. 62. where many cases are put to the same purpose, which see.

The third objection was, That the Return was general and uncertain. The Counsel on the other side had divided the words of the Return, but that is to offer violence thereto; for an exposition shall not be made by fractions, but upon the whole matter. For the first words,—*notable contempts*—it hath been said, that the addition of the word *notable* is but to make a flourish But I say, That *notable* is not the emphasis of the Return, but it only expresseth the nature of the offence; and yet *notable* is a word observable by itself in the Law, and implies, that the thing is known and noted. By 27 *E.* I. Sheriffs shall be punished, that let notorious offenders to bail; and by the Statute of 4 *H.* IV. *cap.* 3. a notorious or common Thief shall not make his purgation: and 26 *E.* III. 71. in a trespass for false imprisonment, the Defendant said, That the Plaintiff came into the Town of *Huntington*, and because he was seen in the company of *R. de Thorby*, who was a notorious Thief, he, as Bailiff of *Huntington*, took him upon suspicion. I confess, that—*for contempts*—is general, yea, it is *genus generalissimum*, and within the Petition of Right; but the words are,——*against ourself.*——It hath been said, that this might be by irreverent words or gestures.——*And our Government*——it hath been said, that this might be by contempt to the King's Writ, or by *Retraxit*, as *Beecher's* case is. To this I answer, that those words which are spoken to one purpose, ought not to be wrested to another; and this is against the common meaning of the words. *Coke* 4. Thou art a murderer, the Defendant shall not afterwards explain it to be a murderer of Hares, for the highest murder is intended. So here, the highest Government is intended.

4. It hath been objected, that——*for stirring up of sedition against us*——may perhaps be but an offence fineable: but those words joined with the former words, shew this to be an offence of the highest nature; sedition is a special contempt. And although sedition in itself may be but a general offence, yet here it is,——*sedition against us and our Government*——which makes it particular. It hath been confessed by one, that argued on the other side, that there is a general in a particular. *Coke* 4. *p.* 75. *Holland*'s case, there is the most general, and there is a general in particular, as the State Ecclesiastical. *Thirdly*, There is more particular, as the Colleges, Deans, and Chapters. This being in a case of Return upon *Habeas Corpus*, no precise certainty is required. In an Indictment, a certainty of all circumstances is requisite; in Pleading, a certainty is required; in Counts, a more precise certainty; in Bars, a certainty to a common intent is enough. There is not such precise certainty required here as in Indictment or Count, because the party ought to answer unto them; nor so much certainty required in this as in a Bar. And the Return is not incertain; for, as it is said in *Plowden* 202. and 193. a thing is incertain, where it may be taken indifferently one way or the other. But where the intendment the one way exceeds the intendment the other way, it is not uncertain as it is here. The words are,——*for notable contempts against us and our Government, and for stirring up of sedition against us*——here is a certainty of intendment one way. There are many Writs which are more uncertain than this Return here is, and yet good. The Writ concerning the taking of an Apostate is general, *quod spreto habitu ordinis*; and yet there are more sorts of Apostacies. In the Writ concerning the amoving of a Leper, the words are general, and yet it appears by *F. N. B.* that there are two kinds of Lepers, one outward, and the other inward; and for the latter, the Writ concerning amoving a Leper. So the Writs concerning the burning of an Heretick, and concerning the burning of an Ideot, are general; and yet there are sundry kinds of Hereticks and Ideots also. But it hath been objected, that *Sedition* is not a law-term, nor known in the Law, of which the Judges can take no notice; but the words to express offences of this nature, are Murder, Treason, Felony, &c. and that no Indictment of sedition generally was ever seen. To this I answer, perhaps it is true, that no Indictment was ever seen made, because the form of an Indictment is precise; words of art are required therein, as appears in *Dyer* 69. 261. *Coke* 4. *p.* 39. *Vaux's* case; yet in 5. *E.* VI. *Dyer* 69 it is said, that *Furatus* implies *felonice cepit*, altho' the contrary hath been objected. In a Return, words by periphrasis are sufficient. The Warrant of a Justice of Peace to apprehend *J. S.* because of prepense malice, *interfecit J. D.* is good enough, although there wants the word *murdravit*. In 5 *R.* II. *F. Trial* 54. *Belknap* says, That a miscreant shall forfeit his land. Out of which it may be gathered, that a man may be indicted for miscreancy. And it seems likewise, that an Indictment of sedition may be good, for in

4 some

some cases it is Treason. I agree, *Peake*'s case, which hath been objected, that for these words [*seditious fellow*] no action lies, and so is, *Coke* 4. 19. because those words do not import an Act to be done, but only an inclination to do it; but if a man say such words of another, which import that he hath made sedition, they are actionable, as it was resolved in *Phillips*'s and *Badby*'s case, 24 *Eliz. Coke* 4. 19. *Thou hast made a seditious Sermon, and moved the people to sedition this day*, adjudged actionable. So in the Lord *Cromwel*'s, *Coke* 4. 12, 13. the action would have lain for those words, *You like of those that maintain sedition against the Queen's proceedings*, if there had not been another matter in the case. I agree, the case of 21 *E.* III. Sir *John Garbyol*'s case, and 42 *E.* III. for in those cases, sedition was only taken adjectively, and shews an inclination only to do a seditious Act; and in such sense, sedition may be applied to other offences than Treason. In 31 *E.* I. *f. Gard.* 157. *Gardein* in *Socage* made feofment of land which he had in ward, this is forfeiture, says the Book, for the Treason which he did to the ward; so there, one thing is called Treason, which is only a breach of trust. In an appeal of *Mayhem*, it is *felonice*, and yet 6 *H.* VII. 1. it is not Felony; but Felony is there only put to express the heinousness of the offence; it is, as it were, a Felony. The Statute of 2 *H.* IV. 1 *Mar.* 13 *Eliz.* 35 *Eliz.* 17 *R.* II. 3 & 4 *E.* VI. 14 *Eliz.* which have been objected, have the word *sedition*, but not applicable to this case. *Bracton* in his Book *de Corona*, says, *si quis, &c.* If any by rash attempt, plotting the King's death, should act, or cause any to act, to the sedition of the Lord the King, or of his army, it is Treason. And *Glanvile*, in as many words, says, That to do any thing in sedition of the Kingdom, or of the army, is High-Treason. And *Britton, fol.* 16. it is High-Treason to disinherit the King of the Realm, and sedition tendeth to the disinheritance of the King; for, as it hath been said, *Seditio est quasi seorsum-itio*, when the people are sever'd from the King: or it is, *Separans à ditione*, when the people are sever'd from the power of the King. And in this sense sedition is no stranger in our Law, and such sedition which severs the people from the King, is Treason.

But it hath been objected, That by the Statute of 25 *E.* III. the Parliament ought only to determine what is Treason, what not. To this I answer, That upon the said Statute, the positive Law had always made explication and exposition. *Br. Treason* 24. the words are *Compass or imagine the death of the King*; and there it is taken, that he that maliciously deviseth how the King may come to death, by words or otherwise, and does an act to explain it, as, in assaying harness, this is Treason. 13 *El. Dy.* 298. Doctor *Story*'s case, he being beyond sea, practised with a foreign Prince to invade the Realm, and held Treason, because invasion is to the peril of the Prince, and so within the Statute of 24 *E.* III. *Mar. Dy.* 144. The taking of the Castle of *Scarborough* was Treason in *Stafford*, by 30 *ass. p.* 19. which was presently after the making of the Statute of 25 *E.* III. A man ought to have been hanged and drawn, that brought letters of Excommengement from the Pope, and published them in *England*: and it is to be noted, that at the same time there was no Statute to make it Treason, but upon construction of the said Statute of 25 *E.* III. though now it be made Treason by the Statute of 13 *Eliz.* if it be with intention to advance foreign Power. Perhaps the sedition mentioned in this Return is High-Treason; and yet the King may make it an offence finable, for he may prosecute the offender in what course he pleaseth; and if it be Treason, then the prisoners are not bailable by the Statute of *Westminster*. But, suppose that it is but a finable offence, yet by the said Statute, those who are imprisoned for open and notorious naughtiness, shall not be bailed; the same naughtiness is there intended high and exorbitant offence.

2. It is fit to restrain the prisoners of their liberty, that the Commonwealth be not damnified. It is lawful to pull down a house, to prevent the spreading mischief of fire; it is lawful to restrain a furious man. And by the 14 *H.* VII. a Justice of Peace may restrain a rout. Then the restraint of dangerous men to the Commonwealth is justifiable and necessary. 24 *E.* III. 33. *p.* 25. Sir *Thomas Figet* went armed in the Palace, which was shewed to the King's Council. wherefore he was taken and disarmed before the Chief-Justice, and committed to the prison, and he could not be bailed till the King sent his pleasure; and yet it was shewed, that the Lord of *T.* threatened him. Out of which case I observe two things: 1. That the Judge of this Court did cause a man to be apprehended, upon complaint made to the Council, that is, to the Lords of the Privy-Council. 2. That although he did nothing, he is not mainpernable until the King sent his pleasure, because he was armed and furiously disposed. So here. Wherefore I pray, that the prisoners may be sent back again.

Davenport argued to the same intent and purpose, and therefore I will report his argument briefly.

1. He said, That the Return here is sufficient. The Counsel on the other side have made fractions of this Return, and divided it into several parts, whereas the genuine construction ought to have been made upon the entire Return; for no violence ought to be offered to the Text. 7 *E.* IV. 20. In false imprisonment, the Defendant did justify, and alledged several reasons of his justification; to wit, because a man was killed, and that this was in the County of *S.* and that the common voice and fame was, that the Plaintiff was culpable. And this was held a good plea, although *Bryan* did there object, That the plea was double or treble; and the reason was, because twenty causes of suspicion make but one entire cause; and indivisible unity in this ought not to be divided: so *Coke* 8. 66. *Crogate*'s case. In an action of trespass, the Defendant justifies for several causes, and held good, because upon the matter, all of them make but one cause. *Coke* 8. 1. 17, It is said, That it is an unjust thing, unless the whole Law be looked into, to judge and answer, by propounding any one particular thereof; and if it be unjust in the exposition of a Law, it is uncivil in a Return to make fractions of it, in the construction thereof especially, it being a Return for information, and not for accusation.

2. Although the Counsel on the other side have taken this case to be within the Petition of Right, yet this is *Petitio principii*, to take that for granted which is the question in debate. He said, That he would not offer violence to the Petition of Right, to which the King had assented, and which shall really be performed. But the question here is, whether this Return be within it? And the Judges are keepers, not masters of this pledge; and it seems, that this Return is out of the letter and meaning of the said Statute.

3. He said, That this was the actual commitment of the Lords of the Privy-Council, and the habitual or virtual commitment of the King. [But because upon these two matters he put no case, nor gave any reason, but what had been put or given in the argument of the grand *Habeas Corpus, Mich.* 3 *Caroli*, and afterwards in the House of Commons, (*vide pag.* 115, *&c. ante*) which was reported to the Lords in the Painted Chamber, I have here omitted them.] And for the great respect which the Law gives to the commands of the King, he put these cases: 7 *H.* III. attachment of waste against the tenant in dower, and the waste was assigned in the taking of Fish out of a pond, and the carrying them away. And the Defendant pleaded, That her second Husband, by the command of the Lord the King, took all the Fish out of the said pond to the use of the Lord the King, and held a good justification; which proves, that the command of the King there to her Husband, excused her of the said waste. And yet it is clear, that a tenant in dower is liable to an action of waste, for waste done in the time of her second Husband: but contrary is it, where a woman is tenant for life, and took a Husband, who made waste and died, no action lies against the wife for that waste. And *F. N. B.* 17 *A.* If the tenant *in præcipe* at the *grand cape* makes default, the King may send a Writ to the Justices, rehearsing that he was in his service, *&c.* commanding them, that that default be not prejudicial to him; and this command of the King excuseth his default, be the cause true or no.

4. For the particulars of the Return, it is——*for notable contempts against the Government*;—but as to that, it hath been said, that the King hath sundry Governments, to wit, Ecclesiastical, Political, *&c.* and it is not shewn against which of them. This is but a cavilling exception; they might as well have excepted to this Return, because it is not shewn, that these contempts were after the last general pardon; that had been a better exception. The last words of the Return are,——*raising sedition against us*;——but as to this, it has been said, That *seditio* is not a word known in the Law, and is always taken either adverbially, or adjectively, and is not a substantive. To this he said, That although it is not a substantive for the preservation, yet it is a substantive for the destruction of a Kingdom. And he said, That he found the word *seditio* in the Law, and the consequent of it likewise, which *is seductio populi*. But it is not ever found to be taken in a good sense, it's always ranked and coupled with Treason, Rebellion, Insurrection, or such like, as it appears by all those Statutes which have been remembered on the other side. Therefore he prayed that the prisoners might be sent back.

Trin. 5 *Car.* I. B. R.

THE first day of the Term, upon *Habeas Corpus* to Sir *Allen Apsley*, the Lieutenant of the *Tower*, to bring here the body of *John Selden*, Esq; with the cause of detention; he returned the same cause as in Mr. *Stroud*'s case: and Mr. *Littleton* (afterwards Sir *Edward*, and Chief-Justice of the *Common-Pleas*, and Keeper of the Great Seal) of Counsel with him, moved, That the Return was insufficient in substance, therefore he prayed that he might be bailed. It is true, that it is of great consequence, both to the Crown of the King, and to the Liberty of the Subject. But, under favour, for the difficulty of Law contained in it, the case cannot be called grand. In my argument, I will offer nothing to the Court, but that which I have seen with these eyes, and that which in my understanding (which is much subject to mistakes) can receive no sufficient answer.

I will divide my argument into four several heads:

1. To point out those matters which I think unnecessary, and not conducible to the matter in question.
2. I will consider the Warrant of the Privy-Council in this case.
3. The Warrant of the King himself.
4. The objections which have been made by the contrary side, the strength of them, and give answer to them.

For the first of these heads, 1. I will admit, that the King may commit a man. 2. That a man committed by the King is not replevisable by the Sheriff, but he is bailable by this Court, notwithstanding the Statute of *Westm.* 1. *C.* 15. And that he shall not be bailable, is against the Petition of Right; I will not dispute it, for it is established by the answer of the King to the said petition. And the arguments made to this purpose in the said Parliament, and in the Painted Chamber before both the Houses, are recorded in Parliament, to which every one may resort. But I will lay as a ground of my following argument, that as offences are of two natures, capital, or as trespasses; so they are punished in two manners, to wit, capitally, or by fine, or imprisonment. For the offences of the first nature, as Treasons, and the like, imprisonment is imposed upon the offender, only for custody; but for misdemeanors of the second nature, imprisonment is imposed upon him for a punishment. Then this is my ground, That no Freeman that is imprisoned, only for misdemeanors before conviction, may be detained in prison without bail, if it be offered, unless it be in some particular cases, in which the contrary is ordained by any particular Statute.

2. For the Warrant of the Privy-Council, which signifies the pleasure of the King to commit the prisoner; perhaps this was a good ground of the commitment, but it is no ground for the detaining of the prisoner without bail; and this the King himself hath acknowledged, as the ancient right of the Subject, in the Petition of Right; wherefore it is not now to be disputed.

3. For the Warrant of the King, as it is certified by this Return, there is not any sufficient cause contained within it, for the detaining of the prisoner in prison; for the Law being, as I have declared above, that for a misdemeanor before conviction, no Freeman may be imprisoned before conviction, without bail or mainprize, the sole question now is, if this return contain within it any capital offence; or if only a trespass or misdemeanor, and then the party is bailable: and for the disquisition hereof, I will consider the Return, 1. As it is divided in several parts: 2. I will consider all those parts of it together. 1. As it is severed in parts. The first part of it, *for notable contempts by him committed against ourself and our Government*. For *contempts*, all contempts are against the King, mediately, or immediately, and against his Government. *Notable*, this is all one with notorious and manifest, as appears by the Statute of *Westm.* 1. *cap.* 15. and 26 *E.* III. 71. which hath been remembered. And *notable* is

but an emphatical expression of the nature of the thing, and alters it not. [*Against us*] all riots, routs, batteries, and trespasses, are against us, and against our Crown and Dignity, contempt against our Court of Justice is a contempt against us. But if the Return were made here, that he was committed for a contempt made in *Chancery*, the party shall be bailed, as it was resolved in this Court in *Michael Apsley's* case, and in *Russwell's* case, 13 *Jac.* for the Return is too general. In it the nature of the offence ought to be expressed, that the Court may judge thereof. And *contempts* here is *individuum vagum*: therefore for them, before conviction, the party cannot be imprisoned without bail or mainprize.

The second part of the Return is [*and for stirring up of sedition against us*]: the other side said, That *seditio* is ever taken in the worse sense: that is true. But hence it follows not, that the Party that commits it is not bailable. Every small offence is taken in the worst sense, as the stealing of an Apple, and the like; but such kind of offenders shall not be committed without bail. To examine the nature of this offence, which is called *sedition*, it ought to be understood, as this Return is, either as Trespass, or as High-Treason; for it cannot be intended to be Petty-Treason: for Petty-Treason is so called in respect of the offence done to any particular Subject; but in respect of the King, it is but a Felony, therefore the Indictments for the same are feloniously and traitorously. And here the words are,---*sedition against us*---so of necessity it ought to be intended of an offence, that more immediately concerns the same King. For the discussing of this matter,

1. I will consider in what sense and signification this word *seditio* is used.
2. How it shall be expounded here by relation thereof to the King.
3. What sense these words [*against us*] shall have here.

1. For sedition; it is not found in the division of offences in our Law, but as it is mingled and coupled with other offences. No Indictment of sedition only was ever seen, nor can be shewn; routs, riots, and unlawful Assemblies, are much of the same nature with it, and do well express the nature of sedition. The *English* word is drawn from the word *seditio* in *Latin*, and the derivation of it is, as hath been observed, *Se-itio*, or *Seorsum-itio*; and the seditious (as one says) take a diversion, and draw others: it is used in the Bible, in Poets, Histories, and Orators, for tumult, or hurly-burly, or uproar, or confused noise,---*Seditioque recens dubiusque fusur..., in Liv. lib.* 2. *cap.* 44. And in *Tacitus* it is taken for mutiny in an army, when the army is always repining at the Captain. In the *Italian* Language, which is the elder son of *Latin*, sedition and discord is all one. *Numb. cap.* 20. 3. the *Latin* translation is, *Versi in seditione*; the *English* is, *chode*, or *murmured*. *Numb.* 26. 9. the *Latin* is, *In seditione Corah*; the *English* is, *In the Company of Corah*. *Numb.* 27. 3. the *Latin* is, *Nec fuit in seditione eorum*; the *English* is, *In the company or assembly of them*. *Judg.* 12. 1. the *Latin* Translation is, *Facta est ergo seditio in Ephraim*; the *English* Translation is, *The men of Ephraim gathered themselves together*. In the New Testament, *Acts* 19. 40. *Seditio* in the *Latin* is translated *uproar* or *meeting*. *Acts* 15. 2. *Facta est ergo seditio, &c.* and it is translated *dissension* and *disputation*. *Acts* 24. 5. *Tertullus* the Orator accuseth *Paul* for moving *sedition*, and the subsequent words are, *A ring-leader of the sect of the Pharisees*; so that his sedition there was but a schism: and the words there are in a manner the very same with our's here; there it was, *for moving*, here, *for stirring of sedition*. *Seditio*, as an approved Author says, imports *discordiam*, to-wit, when the members of one body fight one against another. The Lord of *St. Albans*, who was lately the Lord-Chancellor of *England*, and was a Lawyer and great Statesman likewise, and well knew the acceptation of this word *sedition* in our Law, hath made an essay of sedition, and the title of the essay is, *Of Seditions and Tumults*: the whole essay deserves the reading. (See *Bacon's* Works, Vol. III. *p.* 320.) And there is a Prayer in the Litany,---*from sedition and heresy, &c.* So that here sedition is taken as a kind of sect.

This being the natural signification of the word, then the next labour shall be to see, if any thing in our Law cross this exposition. And it seems clearly, that there is not, 2 *H.* IV. *cap.* 15. And it is in the Parliament-roll, *numb.* 48. against *Lollards*, who at that time were taken as heretics, and says, That such Preachers which excite and stir up to sedition, shall be convented before the Ordinary, *&c.* There, sedition is taken for dissention and division in doctrine. And this is not made Treason by the said Statute, although the said Statute be now repealed by the Statute of 25 *H* VIII. *c.* 4. 1 and 2 *Phil. & Mar. c.* 3. which is in *Rastal*, *News* 4 which is an act against seditious words and news of the King and Queen, which is a great misdemeanour; and yet the punishment appointed to be inflicted by the said Statute, is but the Pillory, or a fine of 100 *l.* And the said Statute, by the Statute of 1 *Eliz. c.* 16. was extended to her also, which Statute now by her death is expired: which I pray may be observed, 13 *Eliz. cap.* 1. against those, who seditiously publish who are the true heirs of the Crown, that they shall be imprisoned for a year, *&c.* And 13 *Eliz. c.* 2. the seditious bringing in of the Pope's Bulls is made Treason, which implies, that it was not so at the Common Law. 23 *Eliz. c.* 2. If any person shall devise, write, or print any Book, containing any false, seditious and slanderous matter, to the stirring up or moving of any rebellion, *&c.* every such offence shall be judged felony. And in an Indictment upon the said Statute (which see *Coke's Entries*, *f.* 352, 353.) there are the words---*rebellionem & seditionem movere*; and yet it is but felony, 35 *Eliz. c.* 1. made against seditious sectaries. Also there are certain Books and Authorities in Law, which express the nature of this word sedition. *Coke's* [illegible] *Rep. f.* 13. the Lord *Cromwell's* case. In an action for those words [illegible] *of those that maintain sermons against the Queen's proceedings*, the Defendant pleaded, That he intended the maintenance of a seditious sermon; and this was adjudged a good plea and justification. From whence it follows, that the seditious sermon mentioned in the declaration, and the maintaining of sedition against the Queen, is all of one signification, for if they might have been taken in a different sense, the justification had not been good. *Philips* and *Badby's* case, which is in *Coke's* 4. *Rep. p.* 19. *a.* which was objected by Serjeant *Berkley*, makes strongly for me, for there an action upon the case was brought by a person for those words, *Thou hast made a seditious sermon, and moved the people*

to sedition this day. And although it were there adjudged, that the action lay, yet the reason of the judgment is observable, which was, because the words scandalize the Plaintiff in his profession; which imply, that if they had not scandalized him in his profession, no action would have lain. And ordinary words, if they scandalize a man in his profession, are actionable, as to say to a Judge, that he is a corrupt man; or to a Merchant, that he is a Bankrupt; although if they were spoken to another man, they would not bear an action. And although the Book say, that no Act followed there, yet if the matter objected had been treason, the very will had been punishable, and, by consequence, a great slander. But it is observed, that words which imply an inclination only to sedition, are not actionable, as, *seditious knave*, but inclination to treason is treason, therefore words which imply it are actionable. And also for divers words, an action upon the case will lie, which induce not treason or felony; as for calling a woman whore, by which she loseth her marriage, and such like. Then sedition is no offence in itself, but the aggravation of an offence, and no indictment (as I have said afore) was ever seen of this singly by itself. *Trin.* 21 *E.* III. *rot.* 23. Sir *John Gurbut's* Case, which was put before by Mr. *Mason*, the indictment was in prejudice of his Crown, and in manifest sedition; and yet the offence there was but a robbery. It is true, that upon his arraignment he stood mute, therefore the Roll is, that he was put to penance, that is, to strong and hard pain; and this proves, that it was not Treason; for if a man arraigned of Treason stand mute, yet the usual judgment of Treason shall be given on him. And it is true also, that he cannot have his Clergy, because *insidiator viarum* was in the indictment; which if it was, outs the party of its Clergy, until the Statute of 4 *H.* IV. *cap.* 2. as is observed in *Coke's* 11 *Rep. p.* 29. *Alexander Poulter's* Case. And upon the same *Roll* of 21 *E.* III. there are four other indictments of the same nature, where *seditiose* is contained in them. *Anno* 1585. Queen *Elizabeth* sent a Letter (which I have seen by the hands of the noble Antiquary Sir *Robert Cotton*) to the Mayor of *London*, for the suppressing of divers seditious Libels which were published against her Princely Government; and yet in the conclusion of the Letter it appears, that they were only against the Earl of *Leicester*, and this was to be published only by Proclamation in *London*.

5 *H.* IV. *numb.* 11. and 13. the Earl of *Northumberland* preferred a Petition to the King in Parliament, in which he confesseth, that he had not kept his Majesty's Laws as a liege Subject; and also confesseth the gathering of Power, and the giving of Liberties: wherefore he petitioned the worship of the King (for so are the words) for his grace. The King, upon this Petition, demanded the opinion of the Lords of Parliament, and of the Judges assistant, if any thing contained within the said Petition were Treason, or no; and it was resolved by them all, that nothing, as it is mentioned in the said Petition, was Treason, but great Misdemeanors; and yet truly, though not fully there mentioned, it was a great rebellion and insurrection. But they adjudged according to the said Petition, as you are now to judge upon the Return as it is made here. In *Mich.* 33 *Eliz. Cawdry's* Case, *Coke's* fifth Report, *p.* 1. Sedition and Schism were described; as Schism is a separation from the unity of the Church, so Sedition is a separation from the unity of the Commonwealth. And an Author says, That a seditious person differs from a Schismatick, because the one opposeth the spiritual truth, the other the temporal: And as Schism of itself is not Heresy, so Sedition without other adjuncts is not Treason. *Bracton*, *f.* 112, 113, 118. hath been objected, that he makes Sedition Treason: I will grant to them, *Hengham* also, who is to the same purpose, for in those Books it is called, *Seditio Regis & Regni*. To them I answer, 1. That they are obscure. For what signifies *seditio Regis*, or *tumultus Regis*? Shall it be the same thing in sense with *seditio contra Regem*? It seems that the said Authors neither remember Law nor Language. 2. Although they reckon Sedition amongst the crime *læsæ Majestatis*, yet that is not to be regarded; for they are obsolete Authors, and are not esteemed as Authors in our Law, as it is in *Pl.* 356. and *Coke* 8. 35. but they may be used for ornament, and they are good marks to shew to us how the Law was then taken, but not to declare how the Law is at this day, they are no binding authority; and if they be, yet we have them on our side likewise: For in his 14*th* Book, *Glanvile* says, That a man accused of such a crime shall be bailed, and that the accuser shall give pledges. And *Bracton* says, That if no accuser appears, they shall be set at liberty. And *Hengham* reckons amongst the crimes *læsæ Majestatis*, the breach of the Peace, and so does *Glanvile* also. *Fleta*, who was a follower of *Bracton*, and transcribes much *verbatim* out of him, calls Sedition, *Seductionem* of the Lord the King. And 12 *Edw.* I. the Statute of *Rutland*, which prescribes Laws for *Wales*, enacts, that the Sheriff shall inquire in his turn, *de seductoribus Domini Regis*; and it is not apparent, whether he intended those which seduce the King or his People. And in latter times, *Seditio* is called *Seductio*. In the time of *Henry* the seventh, the Earl of *Northumberland*, being a great and potent Peer, and the King standing in awe of him, caused him, with twenty-four others of great quality, to enter into an obligation of twenty thousand pounds (which obligation is in the hands of Sir *Robert Cotton*) unto him, That if the said Earl knew Treason, Seduction, Loss, *&c.* to be intended to the King, that he should reveal it. 3. Also *Crimen læsæ Majestatis*, which is the phrase of the Civil Law, is more general than Treason; and the old Authors, which have been cited much, follow the Civil-Law, which hath this expression; and Sedition by the Civil-Law is Treason. But it was resolved 11 *R.* II *n.* 14 we are not governed by the Civil-Law*. And the *Mirrour of Justices*, the principal copy whereof is in *Bennet-College* Library in *Cambridge*, and there is also a copy in *Lincoln's-Inn* Library, nor *Britton* in his Book, who writ in the name of the King, have not the word *Sedition* in them. And I affirm confidently, that there cannot be shewn any Record, Book, or Statute, after the making the Statute of 25 *Edw.* III. in which *Sedition* is taken as a capital offence. And yet the *Mirrour of Justices* reckons up several kinds of Treasons, which he divides into Treasons against the celestial or terrestrial Majesty; against the celestial Majesty, as Schism, Heresy, Misereancy (and according to this, the Book of 5 *R.* II. *Trial* 54. is to be understood, which says, That a miscreant

* See [illegible], *f.* 115. the which was not cited; there, never Sedition, Strife, or [illegible] Lord.

shall forfeit his Lands, because it is a kind of Treason). And also he shews divers Treasons against the King, as, The deflowering of the King's eldest Daughter, *&c.* but not a word of Sedition. But admit, that Sedition imports a greater offence than Tumult, yet there is no colour to say, that it is Treason, for 25 *Edw.* III. is a flat bar (that I may use the *Inner-Temple* phrase) to any thing to be Treason, which is not contained in it, unless it be made Treason by any special Act afterwards; and 25 *Edw.* III. does not make it Treason. *Stamford* cites *Glanville*, and *Bracton*, and other ancient Books, to shew what was Treason before the said Statute, and what not: And he says, That it was a great doubt what shall be called Treason; saving that all agree, that any thing that tends to the death of the King was Treason. *3dly*, Now examine the words, ——*against Us*—— those words make not the crime more heinous, as the case is. I agree, that if the words had been,----*Sedition to take away the Life of the King*---it would have been Treason; yea, the very thought of Treason is Treason, (though none can judge thereof till it be produc'd in Act) 19 *H.* VI. 47. *b.* by *Newton*, 13 *Jac. B. R. John Owen*'s Case, the writing of a Letter, whereby he intended the death of the King, was Treason; but it is not expressed, that the raising of this Sedition was with such intent; whereby this differs from all the cases which can be put, in which there is such an intent of the death of the King. Also this raising of Sedition against Us, shall not be intended Treason; for if it had been so, the King would have so expressed it by the word Treason: For, as in his gracious disposition, he will not extend a fault beyond the magnitude thereof, so he will give to every offence the true and genuine name. If the Return had been---*against Our Person*---it had been more certain, that it concerned the King immediately; this may be against any point of his Government. And the proper and natural signification of the words,- - *against Us*---is as much as, against our Authority, our Superintendency, against our Peace, Crown and Dignity, which are the usual words in every Indictment of Felony. Every breach of the Peace is against the King. The usual Return upon every ordinary Writ out of this Court is, That the party be before Us, and Contempt to this Court is, Contempt against Us; and it is in the nature of Sedition to the King. Contempts to the Court of *Star-Chamber* are Contempts against Us; and upon them, Commissions of Rebellion issue: and if the parties are brought in upon such Commissions, yet they are bailable until their conviction. The King stiles himself, *Us*, in Writs; and every disobedience to any Writ may be said, *Sedition against Us.* Routs, riots, illegal assemblies, may well be said and called, *Sedition against Us*: And for such offences, a man shall not be restrained of his Liberty upon an *it may be*. Such a Return is necessary, by which the Court may be truly informed of the offence. For the Writ of *Habeas Corpus* is, to submit and receive what the Court shall ordain. And this Return of this nature is not to be compared to Writs which are general, and make a brief narration of the matter, and are pursued and explained by subsequent declarations. And yet I urge not, that the Return ought to be as certain as an Indictment; for an Indictment of Murder is not good, if it lack the word *Murdravit*. But the Return upon an *Habeas Corpus*, *q. d. interfecit I. S.* upon prepensed malice, is good; for the nature of the thing is expressed, although the formal word be wanting; but out of the Return, the substance of the offence ought always to appear, which appears not here. But it hath been said by the other side, That, let the cause in the Return be as it will, yet it is not traversable, 9 *H.* VI. 54. and I confess it. But as *Coke*'s 11. *Rep. P.* 93. *James Bagg*'s Case is, the Return ought to have certainly so much in it, that, if it be false, the party grieved may have his action upon the case. And the grievance complained of in the Petition of Right is, That upon such Return no cause was certified, that is, no such cause upon which any Indictment might be drawn up; for we never understand, that the party shall be tried upon the *Habeas Corpus*, but that upon the matter contained within it an Indictment shall be made, and he shall have his trial upon it. And yet it is clear, and it hath been agreed of all hands, in the argument of the grand *Habeas Corpus*, *Mich.* 3 *Car.* in this Court, that if the cause be certified upon the Return of the *Habeas Corpus*, that the Court may judge of the legality of that cause. 2. Consider the parts of this Return, as they are coupled together,-----*for notable Contempts by him committed against Our Self and Our Government, and for stirring up of Sedition against Us.*---Upon the entire Return, the King joins Sedition with notable Contempts; so that it is as much as if he had said, that *Sedition* is one of the notable Contempts mentioned in the first part of the Return, so that he makes it but a Contempt. For the generality and incertainty of the Return, I refer my self to the cases put by Mr. *Ask*, and I will not wave any of them. True it is, if the Return had been, that it was for Treason, he had not been bailable but by the discretion of the Court, and such Return would have been good, but it is not so of Sedition. *Gard.* 157. Treason is applied to a petty offence, to the breach of Trust by a Guardian in *Socage*, but it is not Treason. And so Sedition is of an inferior nature than Treason, and is oftentimes taken of a Trespass; it is not Treason of itself, nor *seditiose* was never used in an Indictment of Treason. It was not Treason before the 25 of *Edw.* III. nor can it be Treason: for 25 *Edw.* III. is a flat Bar (as I have said before) to all other offences to be Treason, which are not contained within the said Act, or declared by any Statute afterwards. And there are offences which are more heinous in their nature than Sedition is, which are no Treason, as Insurrections, *&c.* which see in the Statute 11 *H.* VII. *cap.* 7. 2 *H.* V. *cap.* 9. 8 *H.* VI. *cap.* 14. 5 *R.* II. *cap.* 6. 17 *R.* II. *cap.* 8. And by 3 and 4 *E.* VI. *cap.* 5. the assembly of twelve persons to attempt the alteration of any Law, and the continuance together by the space of an hour, being commanded to return, is made Treason; which Act was continued by the Statute of 1 *Mar. cap.* 12. and 1 *Eliz. cap.* 16. but now is expired by her death, and is not now in force, (although the contrary be conceived by some) which I pray may be well observed. By the Statute of 14 *Eliz. cap.* 1. rebellious taking of the Castles of the King is made Treason, if they be not delivered, *&c.* which shews clearly, that such taking of Castles in its nature was not Treason. But the said Statute is now expired, and also all Statutes, creating new Treasons, are now repealed. But, for a conclusion of this part of my argument, I will cite a case, which I think express in the point, or more strong than the case in question; and it was *M.* 9. *E.* III. *roll* 39. *B. R. Peter Russel*'s Case; he was committed to prison by the Deputy-Justice of *North-Wales*, because he was accused by one *William Solyman* of Sedition, and other things touching the King: And hereupon a Commission issued out of the Chancery, to enquire, if the said *Peter Russel* behaved himself well or seditiously against the King; and by the inquisition it was found, that he behaved himself well. And upon an *Habeas Corpus* out of this Court, his body was returned, but no Cause. But the said inquisition was brought hither out of Chancery, and for that no cause of his caption was returned, he prayed delivery; but the Court would not deliver him, till it knew the cause of his commitment: Therefore (taking no regard of the said Inquisition) they now send a Writ to the now Justice of *Wales*, to certify the cause of his commitment. And thereupon he made this Return, That the aforesaid *Peter Russel* was taken, because one *William Solyman* charged him, that he had committed divers Seditions against the Lord the King, and for that cause he was detained, and for no other. And because the Return mentions not what Sedition in special, he was bailed, but not discharged. And I desire the bailment of the prisoner only, and not his deliverance. I desire that the Case be well observed. In the said Case, there was an actual Sedition against the King, here is only a stirring up of Sedition. The words of the said Award are, *Videtur curia*; which are the solemn words of a Judgment, given upon great deliberation. There it was,----*for other things concerning Us*----This is all one as if he had said,----*for other things against Us*---Concerning the King, and, against the King, are all one, as appears by 25 *E.* III. *c.* 4. *de Clero*, *Stamf.* 124. *Westm.* 1. *c.* 15. *Bracton*, *f.* 119. 14 *Eliz. c.* 2. And the words of the Judgment in the said Case, were not----*dimitt'tur*---but, *ideo dimittendus*----which imply the right of the party to be bailed. The said case in some things was more particular than our case, and more strong; for there was an accuser to boot, which wants in our case. There, true it is, that he was committed by the Justice of *Wales*, and here by the King himself; but this makes no difference, as to this Court: for, be the commitment by the King himself, or by any other, if it be not upon just cause, the party may be bailed in this Court. And for the inquisition, which is mentioned, it was no trial in the case; nor did the Court give any regard thereto. To detain the prisoner by the command of the King singly, is against the Petition of Right; but it being coupled with the cause, the cause is to be considered, and the truth of the cause is to be intended, as well where it is mentioned to be by an inferiour Judge, as where by the King himself, for it is traversable neither in the one nor other. And 22 *H.* VIII. *roll* 37. *B. R.* and 1 *H.* VIII. *roll* 8. *Harrison*'s Case, resolved, That a man committed by the command of the King is bailable. And 33 *Eliz.* it was resolved by all the Justices of *England*, which I have viewed in Chief-Justice *Anderson*'s Book, under his own hand, and it was produced in Parliament, That all men committed by the Privy-Council are bailable, if the commitment be not for High-Treason. In all cases of commitment, an accuser is understood. Suppose that the accusation mentioned in *Russel*'s Case of Sedition, had been an accusation of Treason, then the Judges ought not to have bailed him of right, and no man will say, but that the said accusation was a good cause to commit him. But the discovery of the offence ought to be afterward in an Indictment.

Fourthly, I come to the objections which have been made on the contrary.

1. It was objected, That this was a case of great consequence; I confess it, but this consequence is not to the King; for if it be truly Treason, then they might have returned Treason, and then the party was not to be bailed of right, till there should be a failure of prosecution; as was lately in *Melvin*'s Case, who was bailed for lack of prosecution; the Return being for High-Treason.

2. It was objected that there can be no conviction, as this case is, therefore there ought to be coercive power to restrain the prisoner. This is strange news to me, that there shall be any offence for which a man cannot be convicted. And if there can be no conviction, it hence follows, that there is no offence, and if there be no offence, there ought by consequence to be no imprisonment.

3. The case of 14 *H.* VII. VIII. hath been objected, that a Justice of Peace may commit Rioters without bail. I confess it, for this is by force of a Statute which ordains it.

4. It hath been objected, That if an house be on fire, it is lawful to pull down the neighbour's house, for the prevention of further mischief; and the cases of 22 *ass.* and 27 *E.* IV. that every man may justify the coercion of a mad-man. I answer, That these cases are true, as of necessity, and no other evasion; but here, bail is proffered, which is, body for body. Fire is swift, and cannot be punished, and no caution can be obtained thereof. But observe the true inference and consequence of this argument, If my house be on fire, my neighbour's house must be pulled down: Mr. *Selden* is committed, *ergo* Mr. *Hobart*, his neighbour, must be imprisoned.

5. It hath been objected out of *Br. Treason*, 24. 1 *Mar.* that the said Statute of 25 *E.* III. is taken largely, and that the detaining of a Castle or Fortress is Treason. To this I answer, that the bare detaining of a Castle is not Treason, unless it be with intention of the death of the King; but the taking of a Castle is Treason. And the case there meant by *Brook*, is *Constable*'s Case, *Dy.* 128. And I confess, 13 *Eliz. Dy.* 298. Dr. *Story*'s Case *, that conspiracy to invade the Kingdom, is Treason; for this cannot be without great danger of the death of the King; for,---*arma tenenti, omnia dat qui justa negat.*---And all their Indictments were, that they intended the death of the King, but no such intention is expressed here.

6. It hath been objected, That this case is out of the Petition of Right, because in this return there is a cause shewed. But the grievance whereupon the Petition of Right was framed, was, where no cause was returned. It is true, that the grievance goes no further, but where no cause was returned; for that was the grievance at that time. But the words of the Petition of Right are further,---*to be charged with any thing, to which they might make answer by the Law*---which implies, that such cause ought to be contained in the Return, which being put into an Indictment, the party may have his answer thereto.

* See [illegible] of *England* [illegible], in vol. III. *p.* 684.
See also Sir *Jo. Hawles*'s Reply to the Magistracy of *England* vindicated, (a Folio Pamphlet) *p.* 26.

7. It

7. It was objected, That the Return ſhall not be conſtrued and expounded by fractions. I anſwer, That we need not make ſuch an expoſition; for the joint conſtruction thereof makes more for us, than the ſeveral, as is ſhewed before.

8. That a general Return is ſufficient, and it need not have terms of art in it, as an Indictment ought to have. For anſwer, I confeſs it; but I affirm, as above, that a Return ought to be ſo particular, that the nature of the offence ought to appear out of it: and it is not to be compared to general Writs, as *Apoſtatâ capiendo, Idiotâ examinando, Leproſo amovendo*, and the like: for thoſe Writs are good enough, becauſe they contain the very matter. And although it hath been ſaid, that there are two kinds of Lepers, yet I never heard but of one: and the Writ, *de Hæretico comburendo*, is general, and good, becauſe it is but a Writ of execution upon a Judgment given by the ſpiritual Power. But becauſe they might not meddle with the blood of any man, the execution is by the ſecular Power.

9. It hath been objected out of 30 *aſſ. p.* 19. that the King would have one drawn and hanged for bringing into *England* the Bulls of the Pope. But the Book anſwers itſelf, for he was not drawn and hanged.

10. The Statute of *Weſtmin.* 1. *cap.* 15. was objected. But as oft as that Statute is objected, I will always cry out, *The Petition of Right, The Petition of Right!* as the King of *France* cried out nothing but *France, France!* when all the ſeveral Dominions of the King of *Spain* were objected to him.

11. A curious diſtinction hath been taken by Serjeant *Davenport*, between ſtirring *To* Sedition, and ſtirring *Up* Sedition; for the firſt implies an inclination only to do it, the ſecond implies an act done. But this is too nice, for if a man ſtir up Sedition, or to Sedition, if it be with intention of the death of the King, the one and the other is Treaſon.

12. The opinion of *Forteſcue* in 31 *H.* VI. 10. *b.* hath been objected, That for an offence done to the Court, a man may be committed before conviction. To this I anſwer, 1. That the Book does not ſay, That he ſhall be committed without Bail. 2. The offence being done in face of the Court, the very view of the Court is a conviction in Law.

13. There was objected the 24 of *Edw.* III. 23. Sir *Thomas Fitchet*'s Caſe, who, for going armed in the Palace, was committed by this Court without bail or mainprize, which ſeems to be the ſtrongeſt and hardeſt caſe that hath been objected. But the anſwer to it is clear, and undeniable; for the Statute of 2 *E.* III. *cap.* 3. is, That if any one come armed before the Juſtices, he ſhall forfeit his armour, and ſhall be impriſoned during the King's pleaſure; ſo that by the expreſs purview of the Statute, ſuch a man is not bailable. So my concluſion remains firm, notwithſtanding any of thoſe objections. That the priſoner here, being committed before conviction of any offence, (it being not poſſible to underſtand this offence Treaſon) is bailable; and that he is bailable here, I will offer two other reaſons: 1. The return is here for Sedition; and there is an information in the *Star-chamber* againſt the priſoner, for ſeditious Practices againſt the King and his Government. I will not affirm, that they are the ſame offence, but there is ſome probability that they are the ſelf-ſame; and if they be the ſame offence, then the ſedition here intended is not Treaſon, and ſo the party is bailable. 2. This priſoner was ready at this Bar the laſt Term, and here was a Grand-Jury at Bar the laſt Term, and here was the King's Counſel preſent, who are moſt watchful for the King; and yet an Indictment was not preferred to them againſt this priſoner. Which things induce me to be of opinion, that the offence here mentioned in this Return is not Treaſon, or ſo great as is pretended on the other ſide. I will remember one caſe which perhaps may be objected, (and yet I think they will not object it) and ſo conclude. 11 *R.* II. Parliament Roll 14. in the printed Statute, *cap.* 3. and 5. where it appears, that divers queſtions were propounded by the King to *Treſilian* and *Belknap*, the two Chief-Juſtices, and to the other Juſtices: one of which queſtions was, how they are to be puniſhed, who reſiſted the King in exerciſing his Royal Power, *&c.*? And the anſwer of the Judges was, *una voce*, that they are to be puniſhed as traitors; and 21 *R.* II. *cap.* 21. this opinion was confirmed. But afterwards in 1 *H.* IV. *cap.* 3. and 4. and 1 *H.* IV. in the Parliament-Roll, *numb.* 66, 67. the Judges were queſtioned, for their opinion, in Parliament. They anſwered, That they were threatened and enforced to give this opinion, and that they were in truth of the contrary opinion. And *Belknap* ſaid, That he acquainted and proteſted to the Earl of *Kent* aforehand, that his opinion was always to the contrary. But the Parliament was not content with theſe excuſes, but they were all adjudged Traitors; and *Treſilian*'s end is known to all, and *Belknap* was baniſhed; for his wife, in 2 *H.* IV. brought a Writ, without naming her huſband, becauſe he was baniſhed. And the ſaid Statute of 21 *R.* II. was repealed. Therefore upon the whole matter I conclude, that the priſoner ought to be bailed.

On the ſame day, Sir *Miles Hobart*, and *Benjamin Valentine*, and *Denzil Holles*, Eſquires, were at the Bar, upon an *Habeas Corpus* directed to the ſeveral priſons; and their Counſel was ready at the Bar to have argued the caſe for them alſo: But becauſe the ſame Return was made as above, they ſaid, That all of them would rely upon this argument made by Mr. *Littleton*.

Mr. Selden's *Argument* *.

UPON the Writ of *Habeas Corpus ad ſubjiciendum & recipiendum*, directed out of the *King's-Bench* to the Lieutenant of the *Tower*, he returns, that the priſoner was firſt committed to his cuſtody by a warrant of the Lords of the Privy-Council, dated 4 *Martii* 5 *Caroli Regis*, and recites the warrant wherein the King's pleaſure for the commitment is alſo ſignified. And farther, he returns, that the priſoner is detained by him, by virtue of another warrant, afterward directed to him, under the King's own hand, dated the 7th of *May* following; wherein it is ſignified, that he was to take knowledge, that the commitment was *for notable contempts committed againſt Our Self and Our Government, and for ſtirring up of Sedition againſt Us*, with a command to detain him until his Majeſty's pleaſure were farther known, *&c.* And ſo certifies the Court, that theſe are the cauſes of taking and detaining him, and brings in his Body according to the Writ. And, whether upon this Return, the priſoner ought to be delivered by the Court, upon ſufficient bail, or remanded to the *Tower*, is the queſtion? That is, ſuppoſing the Return to be every way true (as in all caſes it muſt be ſuppoſed, when the queſtion ariſes upon a Return), whether there be ſufficient cauſe expreſſed in it, for which the priſoner ought to be remanded? Or, that the cauſe of the commitment be ſuch (as it is expreſſed in the Return) that he ought to be bailed? If there were no more in the caſe, but the Lords, or the King's command only, without farther cauſe ſhewed of the commitment, then it were clear, by the declaration of both Houſes of Parliament, and the anſwer of his Majeſty to that declaration, in the late *Petition of Right*, that the priſoners were to be remanded. And the objections that ſome have made, out of the Statute of *Weſtminſter*, the firſt, *cap.* 15. That perſons committed by command of the King, are not *replevisable*, and out of *Stamford*, fol. 73. as if he interpreted *bailable* (which indeed he doth not, if he be obſerved) to be underſtood in that Statute by *repleviſable*, and the like, are directly againſt the very body of the *Petition of Right*, and were ſo fully cleared in the debates, out of which the *Petition of Right* was framed, that to diſpute them again, were but to queſtion what the whole Parliament had already reſolved on, as the certain and eſtabliſhed Law of the Kingdom. Nor is it timely to diſpute here again the general power of commitment, by the Lords or by the King himſelf. There is a commitment in the caſe, and there is a cauſe ſhewed of that commitment, and of the detainer in priſon; and the quality of that cauſe only is truly the ſole queſtion; to the ſtating of which, the nature and courſe of bails upon offences, either returned generally upon *Habeas Corpus*, or appearing more ſpecially upon Indictments, is ſhortly to be firſt opened. All offences, by the Laws of the Realm, being of two kinds: The firſt, puniſhable by loſs of life or limb; the ſecond, by fine, or ſome pecuniary mulct, or damage and impriſonment, or by one of them; and thoſe of the firſt kind being Treaſon, Murder, Felonies of leſs nature, and ſome more; and of the ſecond kind, bloodſheds, affrays, and other treſpaſſes: If any priſoner ſtand committed (though before conviction) for Treaſon or Murder; the Judges, for aught appears in the Books, have not often uſed to let him to bail, unleſs it have appeared to them, that there hath been either want of proſecution, or of evidence to proceed, or that the proceeding through diſability of the appellant (in caſe of appeals), as when he is excommunicate, is delayed; or that the evidence is ſlight, or ſome ſuch like cauſe. So that in the bailing upon ſuch offences of the higheſt nature, a kind of diſcretion, rather than a conſtant Law hath been exerciſed, when it ſtands wholly indifferent in the eye of the Court, whether the priſoner be guilty or not †. And according to that, they often let to bail, detain in priſon, or remand the priſoner. Alſo in Felonies of leſs nature, which being all, as thoſe of the greateſt nature capital, and ſo the puniſhment of the ſame above impriſonment, the impriſonment of the offenders without bail, is only uſed *ad ſalvam cuſtodiam*, and cannot be uſed *ad pœnam*. But if a priſoner before conviction, or ſomewhat that ſupplies a conviction, (ſo therefore alſo fit enough before conviction) ſtand committed for treſpaſſes only, as all offences of the ſecond kind are, and are puniſhable only by fine and impriſonment, or by one of them (in which caſe impriſonment is to be the higheſt part of his puniſhment, after conviction) there, by the conſtant courſe (unleſs ſome ſpecial Act of Parliament be to the contrary in ſome particular caſe) upon offer of good bail to the Court, he is to be bailed, which agrees alſo with all juſtice and exactneſs of reaſon, that ſo both the Court may, by his ſureties and bail (to whoſe care he is a-new committed) be aſſured to have him ready at the day given him upon the bail, to anſwer all proceeding againſt him; and he himſelf, having ſureties that ſo undertake for his appearance, may not be compelled, before conviction, to endure that continually, *ad cuſtodiam* only, which is the higheſt part of what he is to ſuffer, after conviction, *ad pœnam*. So that in caſes of impriſonment for offences of the firſt kind, divers circumſtances might be, for which ſufficient bail offered might, according to the uſe, be refuſed by the Court. But in caſes of impriſonment for offences of the ſecond kind, ſufficient bail, offered before conviction, ought of common right to be accepted; ſaving ſtill, where a ſpecial Act of Parliament alters the Law in ſome particular caſe: but there is no colour or pretence of any ſuch Act concerning the caſe in queſtion; ſo that we are to examine it (for the point of bailing) only at the Common Law.

The ſtate then of the queſtion is but this: Whether that expreſſion, *for notable Contempts againſt Our Self, and Our Government, and for ſtirring up of Sedition againſt Us*, do denote any offence of the firſt kind? Which, if it do not, or ſo do not, as that the Court may by the words of it be ſufficiently informed that it is ſome offence, at leaſt, of the firſt kind; the bail, in this caſe, ought to be accepted. The offences in the Return being two; firſt, *notable Contempts*, and then *ſtirring of Sedition*, and both *againſt the King*.

There can be no queſtion made of it, but that all *Contempts*, of what kind ſoever, that are puniſhable by the Laws of the Realm, are *againſt the King and his Government*, immediately or mediately. And altho' the latitude of them be ſuch, as that ſome may vaſtly exceed others; yet they are all, as *Contempts*, only treſpaſſes, *&c.* puniſhable only by fine or impriſonment, or by both, but not until conviction of the parties (as neither are other like offences), unleſs the Contempt be in the face of ſome Court, againſt which it is committed, which ſupplies a conviction. Now in this caſe, the Contempts are only expreſſed in a generality, and no conviction appears of them. So that for that part of the Return, there can be no colour why the bail ought not to be accepted. But all the doubt of the caſe depends upon the ſecond offence; that is, *the ſtirring up of Sedition againſt the King*. Which if it be an offence only of the ſame kind as *Contempts* are, or a mere treſpaſs only to the King; or, if by the words of the Return, it appears not to the Court to be an offence of the firſt kind, that is, either Treaſon, or Felony

* The Editor of Mr. *Selden*'s Works, in his Preface to the third Volume, says, "This is the Subſtance of an Argument made in his (Mr. *Selden*'s) own Caſe, and which was "pronounced by Mr. *Littleton*." But as there is ſo great a difference between them, we leave the Reader to judge of that; and, as it concerns ſo grand a point as the Liberty of the Subject, have therefore given both.

† Vide 2 aſſiſ. pl. 3. 3 aſſiſ. pl. 12. 43 aſſiſ. pl. 40. 26 aſſiſ. pl. 47. 41 aſſiſ. pl. 14. 21 *Edw.* IV. fol. 25. and 71. b. Brooke, tit. Mainpriſe 60 & 61. 2 *Eliz.* *Dyer*, fol. 179. a.

at least. (there being no conviction in the case) the prisoner ought to be bailed. For, unless the Court be assured, out of the words of the Return, that the prisoner stands committed for some such cause, for which he might not of right, demand his bail; it is clear they ought to bail him. It rests therefore to examine the nature of the offence comprehended in those words, *stirring up sedition against us.* If it be any thing above what is trespass only, plainly it must be either Treason or Felony. For Felony, no man pretends that by those words, any kind of Felony is to be understood! The question then must be, whether the *stirring up sedition against the King* be Treason or no; that is High-Treason, as all Treason is that toucheth the King, as Treason? For Petit-Treason, by the Common Law, is Felony, in regard of the King, and Treason only with respect to persons slain, against the faith and obedience due from the offender; and therefore the indictments of it say, *felonice & proditorie.*

In the consideration of the question thus stated, first, the use of the word *sedition*, and the sense of it in our Language, and in our Laws, that received it out of that language, is to be examined, and then what those words, *against us*, import. Out of both which, it will be easily concluded, that the offence, as it is expressed in the Return, although it be a great one, yet it is only a trespass, and punishable by fine only or imprisonment, or both of them. For *sedition*, and the general notion of it; we have not either in the division or explication of offences that occur in our Books, an express definition, description or declaration of it, though it occurs sometimes, as mingled with some other offences, and the adjective of it oftener than the substantive. Nor hath there been yet found any indictment or proceeding upon the crime of *sedition*, by that name singly, as an offence in Law, clearly enough known by itself. *Unlawful assemblies, routs, riots, commotions*, are the nearest, if not the very things that by other names do, for the most part, express what sedition is in our Laws. *Vid.* 3 *Hen.* VII. *fol* 1. & *Brook, riots* 4 & 5. But our language, rather than our Laws, hath received the word from *Latin*, and thence hath in preambles of Statutes, and of indictments, sometimes inserted it; so that missing an express exposition of the word in our Law, we have reason to seek for it first in the language whence we received it, and then in the use of it in our own.

In *Latin*, that which is mutiny, raising of tumult, assembling of any armed power, or conventicles, or the like, is *sedition*. Whence it is, that in the Civil-Law, *seditio & tumultus* are frequently joined: and *concitatores seditionis*, and *auctores seditionis*, occur in the text of that Law *, for such as stir up *sedition*. And thence also *seditio militaris* is used for a mutiny of the Soldiers in the Army, in *Tacitus* and others, and that for no more than the professing themselves against any command whatsoever given by the General. In this sense it is used also by a Lawyer of *Ephesus*, in the holy text, where *Demetrius* the silver-smith assembled the rest of his company against St. *Paul*, for preaching against *Diana*. "For we are (saith he, "speaking to appease the assembly) even in jeopardy to be accused of this "day's *sedition*, forasmuch as there is no cause whereby we may give a "reason of this concourse of people," Acts xix. 40. In the same sense *Tertullus*, an Orator and Lawyer, pleading against St. *Paul* at *Cæsarea*, before *Felix* the Governor there, "We have found this man a mover of *se*-"*dition* amongst all the Jews throughout the World, and a chief main-"tainer of the sect of the *Nazarenes*," Acts xxiv 5. And such like testimonies are very obvious. In the self-same sense the word was received into our language, as we may see in that Act of Parliament against the *Lollards*, under *Hen.* IV. 2 *Hen.* IV. *c.* 15. The words there are, "That they taught openly and privily divers new doctrines, contrary to "the faith and determinations of the Holy Church; and of such sect and "wicked doctrine and opinions they make unlawful conventicles and "confederacies, they hold and exercise schools, they make and write "books, they do wickedly instruct and inform people." Et ad *seditionem* seu insurrectionem excitant quantum possunt, & magnas dissentiones & divisiones in populo faciunt. *Rot. Parl.* 2 H. IV. *n.* 48. "And, as much as they "may, incite and stir them to *sedition* and *insurrection*, and maketh great "strife and division among the people, &c." And about the beginning of Queen *Mary*, an Act of Parliament was made against *seditious words and rumours*; in the preamble whereof, *seditious and slanderous news* is mentioned, and *seditious and slanderous writings, and persons intending and practising to move and stir seditions* (so it is in *Rastall* and the Roll of Parliament, not *seditious*, as in the Statutes at large), *discord, dissension, and Rebellion within this Realm*, 1 & 2 *Phil.* & *Mar.* 3. And to the same purpose, an Act of Explanation of the said Act of Queen *Mary*, was made in the beginning of Queen *Elizabeth*, 1 *Eliz. cap.* 6. wherein mention also is of *false, seditious, and slanderous news, or tales*, against the Queen. As also in her 13th year, *cap.* 1. a provision is made against *contentious and seditious spreading abroad of titles to the succession of the Crown.* And in another Act of the same year, *c.* 2. also the bringing Bulls from *Rome, to raise and stir sedition*, is mentioned in the preamble. And in the 23d year, another Act 23 *Eliz. cap.* 2. was made with this title, "Against seditious words and "rumours uttered against the Queen's most excellent Majesty." And in indictments upon that Statute of the 1*st* and 2*d* of *Philip* and *Mary*, as it was continued in the Act of the 23*d* of *Elizabeth*; the party indicted for slanderous words, in defamation of the Queen, is said to have been "ma-"chinans & intendens *seditionem* & rebellionem infra hoc regnum An-"gliæ movere & suscitare, *and that* advisate, & cum malitiosa intentione, "contra dictam dominam reginam, & felonice ut felo dicte domine re-"gine nunc, devisavit & scripsit quasdam falsas, seditiosas, & scandalosas "materias, &c." 34 Eliz. Coke, *lib. intrat. tit. indictment. fol.* 352. *col.* 3 & 353. where the title is misreferred to the Act of 1 *Eliz. cap.* 2.

In the Lord *Cromwell's* case also, 20 *Eliz* Coke 4. *in act. de scandalis*, *seditio* is mentioned *against the Queen's proceedings*; and *seditio domini regis*, [illegible] in *Bracton*, *fol.* 118 and *seditio regni, vel exercitus*, in [illegible] 1. and *seditio personæ domini regis vel exercitus*, in [illegible]

Now, [illegible] the sense of the words *sedition* and [illegible], it will be [illegible] plain, [illegible] these places, except those old Books of *Bracton*, *Glanvile*, [illegible], the interpretation of whom hath fittest place after the examination of the objections made to prove *sedition* to be *treason*, [illegible] in [illegible] language, and in the use of our Laws, that received the [illegible], [illegible] an offence as was not punishable (without some special provision by Act of Parliament) otherwise than by fine and imprisonment

at the utmost; and were reputed singly, but as words or names designing *tumults, unlawful assemblies, routs, factions or rebellions* against any part of the established Laws, or publick commands. Therefore in that Act of 2 *Hen.* IV. concerning the *Lollards*, the punishment of them that offended against the Acts, and *were such stirrers of sedition and insurrection*, was, that they should be imprisoned only by virtue of that Act, until purgation, if they purged themselves; and imprisoned and fined after conviction; and detained in prison till abjuration: and upon refusal to abjure, or upon relapse, to be burnt for Hereticks: But that Act is repealed by the 25 *Hen.* VIII. *cap.* 14. So, by the Act of the 1*st* and 2*d* of *Philip* and *Mary*, the first offence of *speaking seditious and slanderous words*, or rumours of the King or Queen, was after conviction, standing on the Pillory, and loss of Ears, (unless he redeemed them by the fine of 100*l.*) and three months imprisonment. And if any, from another's report, shall speak any seditious and slanderous news of the King and Queen, he should, after conviction, lose one Ear (or redeem it by 100 Marks) and have one month's imprisonment: And that 'if any should maliciously devise, or 'write any book or writing, containing any false matter, clause or sen-'tence, of slander, reproach, and dishonour of the King or Queen, to 'alienate the minds of the subjects from their dutiful obedience, or to the 'encouraging, stirring, or moving of any insurrection or rebellion within 'this realm, or, if any procure any such thing to be done (the said of-'fence being not punishable by the Statute of 25 of *Edw.* III. of treason) 'he should lose his right hand. And that the second offence of them 'that were punishable by loss of Ear, or Ears, should be imprisoned du-'ring life, and loss of all their goods and chattels." This Act of Queen *Mary* expired at her death, and agreeable to it was that provision of the Act of 1 *Eliz. c.* 6. which extended the same to Queen *Elizabeth*, during her life; but there is no such law at this day in being. So, in that of the 13 of *Eliz cap.* 1. the first offence of *contentious and seditious spreading abroad of titles to the succession of the Crown*, is punished by the imprisonment of one whole year, and the loss of half the offender's goods, and the second offence by the pains of a *præmunire.* The bringing in of Bulls also from *Rome*, to alienate the minds of the subjects from their dutiful obedience, and to raise and stir *sedition* and *rebellion*, is made High-Treason by that other Act of the same year. By which it appears, that *stirring to sedition* alone is in that very Act clearly supposed of far less nature. But that Act is also expired. In that also of the 23 of *Eliz. cap.* 2. the reporters of *seditious news or rumours* against the Queen, was made loss of Ears (as before;) or, that to be redeemed at 200*l.* besides imprisonment of six months: and the reporters from another's mouth, to be punished according to that of 1 and 2 of *Philip* and *Mary*, saving, that the imprisonment, by this Act, is three months, and the second offence is made Felony, and writing of any seditious matter, to the purposes in that Act of Queen *Mary*, is made Felony, upon which Act the indictments of Felony, before-mentioned, are grounded; but that Act also expired by the death of Queen *Elizabeth*. And in that case of the Lord *Cromwell*, who brought a *Scandalum Magnatum* against the Parson of *Northelenham* in *Norfolk*, for saying, *That you like not of me, but you like of them that maintain seditions against the Queen's proceedings.* Although, in the report of the case, *sedition* generally be called an open and heinous crime, and described to be as in the nature of some great factious assembly, or riot; yet the defendant justifies the words, by this, that the plaintiff and he had discourse of one that preached against the Book of Common-Prayer, and that in their discourse the plaintiff said to the defendant, *I like not of thee:* To which he replied, *It is no marvel, for you like of them that maintain sedition* (prædict' *seditiosam* doctrinam innuendo) *against the Queen's proceedings*; and the justification allowed good. Whence it appears clearly, that *maintaining sedition* generally may be, such preaching of seditious doctrine which is punishable only by the Statute of 1 *Eliz cap.* 1. by fine and imprisonment. Out of all which examples, it appears, that *sedition*, and Acts *seditiously* done, are of themselves singly no capital crimes, or otherwise punishable than by fine or imprisonment, or both; unless by some special Act of Parliament it be ordained otherwise. And to confirm this also, we may observe divers other Statutes; where *routs, riots, rebellions*, and *insurrections* (all which, of themselves, if no traitorous attempt appear, by some overt Act, are punishable but by fine or imprisonment, unless some Act of Parliament especially ordain a greater punishment) have special punishments appointed for them; being at the Common Law but in the nature of trespasses. As in the 17 *Rich.* II. *c.* 8. it appears, that in the 5*th* year of the same King (which is 5 *Rich.* II. *c.* 6. *Stat.* 1.) *outrageous assemblies* of the people *against the King's dignity, and his Crown, and the Laws of the land* (as every great riot is) were made *Treason*; which Act is long since repealed. Whence it is also very observable to this purpose, that in two Acts of Parliament, the one of the 2 *Hen.* V. *c.* 9. *Stat.* 1. and the other of the 8 *Hen.* VI. *c.* 14. the simple word *riote* (which is most known in the Law, to this day, for *seditious* assemblies) is taken plainly as an expression sufficiently comprehending assemblies of people, in great number, in manner of insurrection, and also rebellions, as will appear plainly, by comparing the preambles with the bodies of the same Acts. And in 11 *Hen.* VII. *c.* 7. for the punishment of *unlawful raising and leading of people, riots, routs, and other unlawful assemblies*, a form of proceeding is appointed; wherein appears most plainly and expressly, that the punishment was only by fine and imprisonment, and the Act was to continue but till the next Parliament, when it expired. Therefore also by the Act of 3 & 4 *Edw.* VI. *c.* 5. entitled, 'An Act for the punishment of unlawful assemblies, and rising of the 'King's Subjects,' it was ordained, 'That if any persons, to the number 'of twelve, or above, being assembled together, shall intend, with force 'of arms, unlawfully, and of their own authority, to kill or imprison any 'of the King's Privy-Council, or to alter or change any Laws established 'by Parliament, and shall not depart and return to their own habitations, 'within one hour after commandment made by the Sheriff, some Justice of the 'Peace, or other such Officer, in that behalf, the offence should be High-'Treason. And if such Persons assembled, to the pulling down of ditches, 'or laying open inclosures, or to the committing of some such more 'offences, retire not within that space, that it shall be felony in them. 'And if any should incite such persons to any such act, by speaking, 'ringing a bell, sounding a trumpet, firing of beacons, or the like; inso-'much that they remained together after any such command as aforesaid

* [illegible] lib. 1. & [illegible] Cod. de [illegible]

'by the space of an hour, and commit any such Act, as aforesaid, it 'should be Felony also. And the persons so assembled, and remaining 'together, to the number of forty, by the space of two hours, are by the 'same made Traitors. And that if the number be above two, and under 'twelve, that with force of arms, unlawfully, and of their own autho'rity, assembled for the casting down of ditches, inclosures, and divers 'such other things, their staying together after such command by the 'space of an hour, should be punished by a year's imprisonment, and fine 'and ransom at the King's pleasure.' And it is also in the same Act ordained, 'That if any person shall procure, move, or stir any other per'son, or persons, to arise, or make any traiterous or rebellious assembly, to 'the intent to do any of the things before-mentioned, it should be Fe'lony. And further, that if any person were spoken to, moved, or stir'red to make any commotion, insurrection, or unlawful assembly for 'any of the intents before-mentioned, and did not tell it within twenty'four hours afterward, unless he have sufficient excuse, to some head 'Officer where such speaking were had, should suffer imprisonment, 'until he were discharged by three Justices of the Peace, whereof one to 'be of the *quorum*.' This Act was to endure till the end of the next Parliament only, which was in 7 *Edw.* VI. and then, *cap.* 11. it was continued till the end of the next, which was in 1 *Mar. sess.* 2 wherein, *c.* 12. it is repealed, and another of the same nature made. Both which shew most evidently, that those unlawful assemblies, insurrections, commotions, and the like, which are plainly *Seditions*, provided for by those Acts, were before but trespasses, punishable only by fine and imprisonment. That of the 1 *Mar. sess.* 2. *c.* 12. is intituled, *An Act against unlawful and rebellious assemblies*, where the clause of the Privy-Councillors (that was in the 3 & 4 *Edw.* VI.) is omitted; and the rest of the offence touching the altering of Laws, is expressed, as in that of *Ed.* VI. saving that the crime is made Felony, whereas it was Treason by that of *Ed.* VI. The rest of that Act of 1 *Mar.* is, for the most part, agreeable with that of *Ed.* VI. saving, that none of the offences are Treason by this Act, but Felony at the most. And for the being *spoken to, or stirred to make any commotion, and not discovering it*, here, in this of Queen *Mary*, the offender is to suffer imprisonment only for three months, unless he be discharged by three Justices of the Peace, as in that of *Ed.* VI. This of Queen *Mary*, was kept on by continuance only, from one Parliament to another, during her time; and in 1 *Eliz. c.* 16. it was made to continue during the life of Queen *Elizabeth*, and at her death expired. To this purpose also the Act of 14 *Eliz. c.* 1. is observable; where, 'unlawful 'practices, secret conspiracies and devices, to take or surprize any of 'the Queen's fortified Castles, and the malicious and rebellious intent 'of surprizing, or taking them, being expressed by overt-act, or word,' are made Felony; 'and the not giving them up within six days after 'command from her, is made Treason,' which Act also expired with her life. Here the offences made Treason and Felony by the Act, were both *Seditions* of a high nature, and yet but trespasses before the Act made, nor are they other now the Act is expired. For the surprizing or detaining of a Castle, without levying a war, or some other Act of Treason (as in *Sherley*'s case in *Dyer*) it is not Treason, but by that Act. To these we may justly add that case of the Earl of *Northumberland* in 5 *Hen.* IV. *rot. parl. n.* 11, 12. *&c.* He acknowledged by writing, in Parliament, that he was guilty of not *keeping the Laws as ligeance asketh, and of gathering power, and giving of liveries* (which are the words of the Parliament-Roll), and upon special consideration had, by the Lords and Judges in Parliament, of the nature of the offence thus set forth, they adjudged it was neither Felony nor Treason, but only Trespass; and so are the express words of the Roll. Yet the *gathering of power, and giving liveries, and breaking of allegiance*, are large expressions of that, which in itself was truly *sedition*, and that of a high nature. And thus, both by the use of the word, and the punishment provided, in some cases in Parliament, for remedy of the offence (without which special provision it is never found capital) it appears clearly that *sedition*, or the *stirring of sedition*, alone, at the Common Law, (and no Statute, now in force, hath ordained otherwise) is but trespass, and punishable only by fine and imprisonment.

Now for the words *against us*, that is, against the King. There is no doubt at all, but that all offences are against the King. Every slight trespass, by the Law, is *contra pacem domini Regis*, and whatsoever is against his *peace* is against him; as also divers indictments of mere trespasses conclude with *in contemptum Domini Regis*, and *contra coronam & dignitatem suas*: As in an indictment for hearing of mass, is *contra pacem, dignitatem & coronam domini regis*. All which import *against the King*. And that Act of 23 *Eliz.* is made *against seditious words against the Queen's most excellent Majesty*, which, even after the Act, remained not capital, being before but trespass. And in the preamble of that of 14 *Eliz.* it appears, the Act was made against 'unlawful practice, secret conspiracies 'and devices, stirred and moved against our sovereign Lady the Queen, in 'seeking unlawfully to take her Castles, Fortresses, and the like.' And in *Bracton*, *fol.* 119. *b.* §. 3. & 120. *b.* § 6. the concealing of treasure, which is punishable by fine and imprisonment, is expressly said to be *gravis præsumptio contra regem & dignitatem, & coronam suam*, as also the not keeping the assises of bread and ale, and the like. Neither is there any doubt of this, but that the words, *against the King*, may be applicable to any kind, and as well to the least as the greatest kind of offences, and imply nothing that increases the offence above trespass.

It follows then, for the last part of the consideration, that (*sedition* being but that which we otherwise call *unlawful assemblies, riot, mutiny, rebellion*, or the like, and every offence punishable, being *against the King*) the *stirring up of sedition against the King*, which is or may be the *stirring up of a rout, unlawful assembly, mutiny, rebellion*, or the like, against some ordinary, or extraordinary command, process, writ, or execution of some established Law, is no other offence, by the expression in the return, nor can thereby be understood to be other (without some special Act of Parliament have altered the Law) than trespass, and punishable only by fine and imprisonment, and so, by consequence, no *Treason*. As for a special Act of Parliament, that maketh *sedition against the King*, to be higher than *trespass*, there is none such extant. Among all the Acts of Parliament that are in force, there is none gives any colour here, but that of 25 *Ed.* III. wherein Treason is declared. And in that Act, only these words; 'If any one levy War 'against our Lord the King, in his Realm, or be adhering to the enemies 'of our Lord the King in his Realm, giving to them aid or comfort in 'his Realm, or elsewhere, and hereof be attainted of overt Act, it is 'High-Treason.' The other words concerning other and higher Treasons, in that Act, have nothing that can so much as of themselves suppose a *sedition against the King*; but it is true, that in those before recited there may be a *sedition against the King*; that is, the *levying of War against the King* may be by *sedition*, or the *adhering to the King's enemies*, or the *levying of War against him*, may be, by a low expression, perhaps stiled *sedition against the King*; as in every greater crime, as in theft, *trespass* may be included, or understood. Now, unless on the other side, in that which is *sedition* against the King, Treason must necessarily be understood, these words of the 25 *Ed.* III. make no more to prove that *sedition* is Treason, than any Act against theft can prove that *trespass* is Felony. Therefore also, in that very Act of 25 *Ed.* III. the riding openly or secretly with armed men to kill or rob another man, or to take him, and keep him 'till he make fine and ransom for his deliverance (though it be plainly *sedition against the King*, it being against his Peace, his Laws, and his Crown and Dignity) is but Felony, if robbery be committed with it, and trespass only if imprisonment till fine and ransom. And so it is declared expresly in that Act. And though there have been divers Acts of Parliament since that of the 25 *Ed.* III. that have made divers other facts Treason, yet there is none of them that remain unrepealed, or not expired, that make any such fact Treason, as is of the nature of *sedition against the King*: And except only the Treasons made by those special Acts of Parliament that remain in force (as those concerning Bulls from *Rome*, Jesuits, clipping of Coin, and some few more), there is nothing at this day treason, saving what is comprised in that Act of 25 *Ed.* III. to which some special Laws* have, in the ages since *Ed* III. now and then reduced all Treason, by abrogating all intervenient Laws of Treason. And by that Act, if there be a doubt that happens before the Judges, by reason of any new case that comes before them, they ought not to judge it Treason, until it be enacted by Parliament to be so. And it doth, in the same Act, appear, that before that time, there was a greater latitude of Treason, than at any time since. Now, even in that time, there is an express judgment of the very point in question; though not in the same terms with this case, yet in the self-same sense, as if this case had then been before the Judges. It was the case of one *Russel*, he was imprisoned by the Justice of *North Wales*, in 9 *Ed.* III. and returned to be so, *eo quod A. B. imposuit ei fecisse debuisse diversas seditiones, &c. dominum regem tangentes.* Upon this return, the Court adjudged, that the offences contained in the Return, and as they could thereby be understood, were such for which he ought to be bailed; and they give their reason with the judgment, *because it did not appear what kind of sedition against the King was meant by it. Eo quod non specificatur quales seditiones, &c. ideo dimittendus*, by mainprize or bail, which to this purpose are all one. For if the *sedition* had been with traitorous intents, and so expressed, then it had been Treason, for which they would not have let him to mainprize. But because *sedition* against the King might be of divers other natures, and mere trespasses, therefore they said, *ideo dimittendus est*; expressing therein the right of the prisoner, that he might justly claim to be bailed, and by law ought to be bailed, and not only that he was bailable. But three objections may, perhaps, be made to this judgment, to make it differ in substance from the case in question. The first, that *A. B. imposuit ei fecisse debuisse diversas seditiones, &c.* which being as an accusation in so general terms, was not certain enough to make him answer to it, and thence might be cause of the judgment. The second, that it is not *contra Dominum Regem*, or *against the King*, as the case here is, but *tangentes*, or *touching* the King. And the third, that here is the King's Warrant witnessing the offence, and command for imprisonment, and in that of 9 *Ed.* III. only the charge of a Subject and the commitment of a Subject. To all three, the reply is easy. For the first, it is plain, that the Justice of *North Wales* shews the reason of the imprisonment to be, because *Russel* was charged by *A. B.* to have committed *sedition touching the King*, as every one that is returned to stand committed for any offence, is supposed to stand so committed, because somebody charged him, or accused him, or can testify against him; and that is here more particularly expressed, which in every Return is supposed to be understood in the general words. As, suppose the Return were, that such a one stands committed for Treason, or Murder, upon the accusation, testimony, or examination of *A. B.* taken thus, or thus: would the Court bail him the sooner for that addition? And in Returns, it was never expected that there should be such certainty as that the prisoner might plead and be tried. Which can never be done from Returns, but only by Appeals or Indictments, wherein the offence is in special set forth by time, place, and all circumstances. Or, if they had, in this case of *Russel*, expected or considered such a certainty, they ought not to have let him into mainprize, or bailed him; but clearly dismissed him. For, if an appeal, which is an accusation, were brought against a man, or an indictment put in *de diversis murdris*, or *de murdro*, generally, or, *de proditione* generally, clearly, upon such an appeal or indictment, the Court would not put the party neither to answer, nor so much as to the trouble of bail or mainprize, because such a charge that way, were merely void. For in appeals and indictments, the particular circumstance, and the special offence must always be set forth, or else they are void, but, in Returns, the general expression is sufficient for the Court to judge, whether the offence be such, as that the prisoner ought to be bailed or no, as the common and most known practice is. So that the first objection is of no force. For the second, it is certain, that the words *tangentes regem*, and *contra regem*, in matter of offences, occurring in our Laws, are taken as synonimous. As in 25 *Ed.* III. *Stat. de clero*, *cap.* 4. we have *Treasons* or *Felonies*, touchants autres persons que le roy mesme ou son royal majestie, *touching others than the King*, which is the same with, *being against others than the King*, or *lesser than the King*; that is, *petit Treasons* (which are both Treasons and Felonies) as it appears in *Stanford*, *l.* 2 *c.* 43 *fol.* 124 *b.* High Treason being *touching the King*, or *against the King*, or *extending to the King*; which is the same in 25 *Ed.* III. *de proditoribus*. Where the sense of the words appears by a Law made but few years after this very case of *Russel*. So in *Westmin.* 1. *c.* 15. *Treason que touche le roy mesme*, is expressly for *Treason against the King*,

* Vid. 12 Rich. II. c. [illegible] 5 Hen. IV. [illegible] 1 Ed. VI. [illegible] 1 Mar. [illegible] c. 6.

King; that is, High-Treason. And *Bracton, fol.* 119 *b.* §. 2. calls the counterfeiting the Great Seal, which is High-Treason to this day, *Crimen læsæ majestatis, quod tangit coronam Regis*, or *Treason against the King*. And, in this latter age, we see in the Statute of 14 *Eliz. cap.* 2. that *Treason touching the person of the Queen*, and *Treason concerning the person of the Queen*, are both as the same, and both for *Treasons against the Queen's person*. So that *tangentes regem*, and *contra regem*, denote the self-same thing in the Law, and for that matter, *Russel's* case and this Return are of the self-same nature. Now for the third objection concerning the King's warrant and command in this present case, which is not in that of *Russel's*, but only the accusation, or charge, and command of a Subject. For the command singly considered, it is clearly against the Petition of Right: But if it be considered here (as it ought) joined with the cause of commitment, then the cause is only considerable by itself, as expressed by the warrant. But there is no Book-case, Act of Parliament, or other testimony of Law with us, that in this kind of consideration makes any difference between the expression of an offence, in a Return of the King's warrant, and the expression of it in a Return of a Subject. For all Returns of this kind, in judgment of Law, are supposed true; and the sole point examinable, for matter of bail, is the nature of the offence; unless the commitment were by one that might not commit, or that some other circumstance, not concerning these matters, were in the case. And besides, in 27 *Hen.* VIII. *rot.* 38. Parker's *case*, & 1 *Hen.* VIII. *rot* .... the King's command for commitment for Murder, and other offences of high nature, hath been in the Return, where the Prisoner was bailed. Nor will there remain any colour of testimony to maintain this last objection.

And as against this case of *Russel* (which is so fully in the point) these objections may be made; so against the main, the conclusion, it may be objected out of those old Authors, *Bracton, Glanville* and *Hengham*; that *Bracton*, in express words, makes *seditio domini Regis* to be Treason: *Si quis aliquid egerit* (saith he, fol. 118. b.) *ad seditionem domini Regis, vel exercitus sui, vel procurantibus auxilium & consilium præbuerit vel consensum*, it is *crimen læsæ majestatis*, to be punished with death, and so supposes it High-Treason. So *Glanville, Si quis machinatus fuerit, vel aliquid fecerit, in mortem Regis, vel seditionem regni, vel exercitus*; he saith it is likewise Treason. And *Hengham* bringing examples of the *Placita de crimine læsæ majestatis*, adds, *ut de nece vel seditione personæ domini Regis, vel regni, vel exercitus*. Where we see, *seditio Regis*, or *regni*, or *exercitus*, is supposed Treason. But the answers to the authority of these old Authors is various. *First*, However they were all three (if at least that of *Glanville* be the work of Sir *Randal Glanvile*, Chief-Justice of *England* under *Hen.* II.) learned and famous Judges in their ages, yet they lived so long since, and the rest of the particulars of which they write, are so different (whether we observe the Pleas of the Crown in them, or the Pleas between party and party) from the practice and established Laws of the ensuing ages, that their authority is of slight or no moment, for direction in judgment of the Law at this day, though it be very considerable in examination what the Law was in their times; and that way it sometimes is used as an ornament in argument only, as it is said in the *commentaries* of them. The first of them died about 400 years since; the second, about 350; and *Hengham* about 300 years past. Secondly, The words of *seditio Regis*, or *regni*, are an obscure expression, and hardly so intelligible as that we may know what they meant. For what can *sedition of the King* mean, in *English* or in *Latin*, as they express it? And if it be taken for *sedition against the King* (as indeed the like words are interpreted in *Scottish*, out of the *Regiam majestatem*, by Mr. *Skene*) it must be so taken against all Grammar, and usual context of words; for no more than *tumultus Regis, rebellio Regis, insurrectio Regis*, is *tumult against the King*, or *rebellion against the King*, or *insurrection against the King*, is *seditio Regis*, in force of Language, *sedition against the King*. Thirdly, Admit it be rightly taken for *sedition against the King*, in those old Authors, yet the Statute of 25 *Edw.* III. *de proditionibus*, so settles the Law for Treason, that whatsoever was Treason before that Act, and is not comprised within that Act, is no Treason at this day, unless some special Act of Parliament have ordained it. Fourthly, The constant course of testimonies, as they are before shewed, since the 25th of Ed. III. prove expressly, that only *sedition against the King* is taken for a less offence, and mere trespass. Fifthly, In particular offences, we see *Bracton* (whose authority is the chief of the three, whether we regard the expression, or the quality of the writer) differs much from the Common Law of the later ages: and so much, that he is directly, in some things of great moment, contrary to the clear known Law, both of the present and of ancient times. As he allows no killing of a man to be Murder, but what is done so secretly, that it is not known who doth it. *Bracton, l.* 3. *de Corona, fol.* 134. *b.* & 135. And that if the offender be taken, or, if the party hurt live long enough to discover him that hurt him, though he die afterward, it is (saith he) no Murder. Which is directly contrary to the Law, yet altered by no special Act of Parliament. So, *Si quis alterius virilia absciderit, & libidinis causa, vel commercii castraverit, sequitur* (saith he, p. 144. *b.* §. 3.) *pœna aliquando capitalis, aliquando perpetuum exilium, cum omnium bonorum ademptione*; whereas there is no such thing in the Laws of *England*. But indeed, by the Civil Law, *Qui hominem libidinis, vel promercii causa castraverit, pœna legis Corneliæ de sicariis punitur*; that is, is punishable capitally. *ff. ad leg. Cornel. de sicariis, l.* 3. §. 4. & *l.* 4. §. *ult.* Whence, doubtless, *Bracton* (who cites often, to other purposes, the very texts and words, and quotes the places of the *Digests*, and the *Code*) had that punishment for such as gelded men. And thence also had, by all likelihood, that touching *sedition*. For, by the Civil Law, all *sedition*, publick raising of tumults, gathering armed men without publick authority, and whatsoever is but with us as a commotion or riot, is Treason (*crimen læsæ majestatis*) and capital. To which purpose there be divers texts in that Law *ff. ad leg. Juliam majest. l.* 1. & *de pœnis, l.* 38. §. 2. *de appellationibus, l.* 16. *C. de seditiosis, l.* 1. & 2. &c. which doubtless he both read, and often followed: and by *concitatores seditionis*, or *stirrers up of sedition*, by that very name were condemned as capital Traitors. But this was never, for aught appears, Law in *England*; but the contrary appears plain enough by what is already said. Sixthly, For answer to the objections out of *Bracton* and *Glanville*, if their authority shall be taken sufficient to maintain *sedition* to be Treason; then will it be as reasonable to prove, that in such a case bail also should be taken. For *Bracton* saith expresly of that, and other Treasons, that he joins with it, that the prisoner ought to be bailed, unless an accuser be present. *Si quis*, saith he, *de hoc crimine defamatus fuerit, tunc videndum erat utrum appareat accusator, vel non*; *si autem nullus appareat, nisi sola fama quæ tantum apud bonos & graves oriatur. hic salvo attachiabitur per salvos & securos plegios*; *vel si plegios non habuerit, per carcer is inclusionem, donec de crimine sibi imposito veritas inquiratur*. And *Glanville* saith expressly, that although an accuser be present, yet he is to be bailed. *Etiamsi accusator fuerit* (saith he) *accusatus dimittitur per plegios*; *aut si non fuerit, in carcerem dimittitur*. So that either the authority of these old Authors is of no moment, for the reasons before shewed, or if it be valuable, and that advantage must be taken from them, it is as reasonable that their other opinion, for the bail, be as well accepted and allowed of in this case. But there remains, perhaps, one objection, out of the opinions of *Tresilian* and *Belknap*, the two Chief-Justices; and of *Holt, Fulthorp*, and *Burgh*, Justices of the Common-Pleas, and *Lockton*, one of the King's Serjeants in 11 *Rich.* II. (*Vide* 21 *Rich.* II. *c.* 11. see the Roll:) Who being, among other things, demanded at *Nottingham* by the King, and charged to answer, upon their faith and legiance to the King, how they ought to be punished that did interrupt the King, so that he might not exercise those things that pertaineth to his regality and prerogative; (in which words, perhaps, may be included all kind of sedition against any proceeding, process, or ordinary command of the King) with one assent they answered, That they ought to be punished as Traitors. And if that were Law, it were hard to find a sedition against the King, but that it were Treason. For all his proceedings, process, and ordinary commands, belong to his regality and prerogative; and every sedition against him, is a kind of interruption of the exercise, at least, of those proceedings, process, and ordinary commands.

It is true, that in the 11th of *Rich.* II. such an answer, among divers others of like nature, were given by those Judges, and that Serjeant; and they put their Seals also to them. But it is as true, that for these very answers they were accused by the Commons in Parliament, the self-same year, where they answered upon the accusation: First, That the answers were written in the original to which their Seals were put, otherwise than their meaning was, in some part. Secondly, That they had been threatened to make no other answer than what might agree with the King's liking. Thirdly, That their answers proceeded not of their free-will, but for fear of death; and that some of them had revealed as much to the Earl of *Kent*, desiring him to witness as much hereafter if time served. *Rot. Parl.* 11. *Rich.* II. *n.* 14. & *vide Stat.* 11 *Rich.* II. *c.* 3, 5, &c. Notwithstanding all which, at the instance of the Commons, they were judged all by Declaration in Parliament made by the King and Commons (which was according to the Act of 25 *Edw.* III. and so by Act of Parliament) to be Traitors, and to suffer as in case of Treason; good part of which proceeding is remembred in the Statutes of that year, but much more in the Rolls of that Parliament. And although in the Parliament of 21 of *Rich.* II. that Parliament, and in particular, this proceeding against the Judges, were wholly annulled, and their answers adjudged good; as appears in the printed Statutes of that year, 21 *Rich.* II. *c.* 12. yet in the 1st of *Hen.* IV. it was declared by Parliament, 1 *Hen.* IV. *c.* 3. that this proceeding of Parliament of 21 of *Rich* II. being caused by a certain number only, of the Members of Parliament, and that the *Statutes, Judgments, Ordinances, and Establishments, were made, ordained, and given erroneously and deceitfully in great disherison and final destruction, and undoing of the liege people of the realm.* Where also it was further declared and adjudged, in the same Parliament, that all the Parliament of 21 *Rich.* II. and all *circumstances and dependents thereupon to be of no force or value, but annulled.* And besides, that *the Parliament of the* 11*th of Rich.* II. wherein those Judges were condemned as Traitors, for that answer, and all the rest of that kind, should *be firmly holden and kept, after the purport and effect of the same, as a thing made for the great honour and common profit of the Realm.* So that that answer of the Judges, in the 11 of *Rich* II. so highly condemned as false and erroneous, by two Parliaments, both which have to this day continued in firm strength, is of no weight to prove that *sedition against the King is Treason*. Nor doth any thing else prove it, but the contrary is manifested by the arguments before urged. And by consequence, it is only trespass against the King, and punishable by fine and imprisonment, and therefore the prisoner returned to stand committed *for stirring it up against the King* ought to be bailed.

Some days after Sir *Rob. Heath*, the King's Attorney-General, argued, That this return was good, and that the parties ought not to be bailed: And that within the return there appears good cause of their commitment, and of their detaining also. The case is great in expectation and consequence: and concerns the liberty of the subject on the one part, whereof the argument is plausible; and on the other part, it concerns the safety and sovereignty of the King, which is a thing of great weight. The consideration of both pertains to you the Judges, without slighting the one, or too much elevating the other. The Return, which now is before you, is entire; but I will first consider it as divided in parts. First, the first Warrant, which is that of the Lords of the Privy-Council, is general, that it was by the command of the Lord the King: and this in former times was held a very good return, when due respect and reverence was given to government; but, *Tempora mutantur*. And this return is no way weakned by any latter opinion; for notwithstanding that, the first commitment of a man may be general: for if upon the return, the true cause should be reveal'd to the Gaoler, by this means, faults should be published and divulged before their punishment, and so the complices of the fact will escape, and it is not fit that the Gaoler, which is but a ministerial Officer, should be acquainted with the secrets of the cause. But when the cause is returned in court, more certainty is requisite; for then (as it hath been objected) something ought to be expressed to which the party may answer, and upon which the Court may ground their judgment. And to this purpose, the Petition of Right hath been much insisted upon; but the Law is not altered by it, but remains as it was before. And this will appear upon the view of all the parts of the Petition. 1. The occasion of the Petition, and the grievance, is shewed in these words: *Divers of your Subjects have been of late imprisoned, without any cause shewed*, &c. But

in

in this return there is a cause shewed, to which the parties may answer. Then, 2. The prayer of the Petition is, That no freeman, in any such manner as before is mentioned, be imprisoned or detained; that is, such manner of imprisonment, the ground whereof doth not appear. Then the answer of the King to the Petition was in sundry words: 2 *June* 1628, in these words, *The King willeth, that right be done according to the Laws and Customs of the Realm, &c.* Which answer gave not satisfaction. And afterwards his answer was in a Parliamentary Phrase, *Soit droit fait come est desire*. But afterwards, on the 26 of *June*, 1628, the King expressed his intention and meaning in the said answer. "It must be conceived, that "I have granted no new, but only confirmed the ancient Liberties of my "subjects, *&c.*" A Petition in Parliament is not a Law, yet it is for the honour and dignity of the King, to observe and keep it faithfully; but it is the duty of the people not to stretch it beyond the words and intention of the King. And no other construction can be made of the Petition, than to take it as a confirmation of the antient liberties and rights of the subjects. So that now the case remains in the same quality and degree, as it was before the Petition Therefore we will now consider, how the Law was taken before the Petition; and for the discussing thereof, we will examine the second Part of the Return, and in it two things: 1. If the Return, as it is now made, shall be intended for true. 2. Admit that it is true, if there be any offence contained within it, which is good to detain the prisoners. For the 1. it is clear, that the cause shall be intended true which is returned, though in truth it be false; and so are 9 *H.* VI. 44. and *F. Corpus cum causa*, an 12 *Coke's Rep.* 11 *p.* 93 *Bagg's* case. 2. It seems that there is such a crime contain'd in this return, which is a good cause for detaining the Prisoners. It is true, that it was confidently urged in Parliament, in 3 *Car.* that general returns, that were committed by the command of the Lord the King, are not good: and that those arguments remain as monuments on record, in the Upper House of Parliament; but I will not admit them for Law. But I will remember what was the opinion of former times, 22 *H.* VI. 52. by *Newton*; a man committed by the command of the King, is not repleviable. And the opinion cannot be intended of a replevin made by the Sheriff, because the principal case there is upon a return in this Court. 33 *Hen.* VI. 28. *Poyning's* case, where the return was, That he was committed by the Lords of the Council, and it was admitted good. It is true, that this opinion is grounded upon *West.* 1. *c.* 15. but I will not insist upon it. But the constant opinion hath always been, that a man committed by the command of the King is not bailable. In 9 *H.* VI. 44. it is said, That if one be taken upon the King's suit, the Court will not grant a *supersedeas*. The contrary opinion is grounded upon *Magna Charta*, which is a general Law, and literally hath no sense to that purpose, and it is contrary to the usual practice in criminal causes, in which the imprisonment is always lawful until the Trial, altho' it be made by a Justice of Peace, or Constable. And that a man committed by the command of the King or Privy-Council, is not bailable, he cited 1 *Jacobi*, Sir *John Brocket's* case, 8 *Jacobi*, *Thomas Caesar's* case 12 *Jac.* *James Demaistres's* case; 43 *Eliz.* *William Kinch's* case; and in the case of *M.* 36 *Eliz.* and 4 and 5 *Eliz.* *Richard Thimelby's* case; and said, that there are innumerable precedents to this purpose. *M.* 21 & 22 *Eliz.* upon the return of an *Habeas Corpus* it appears, that *Michael Page* was committed by the command of the Lord the King, but was not delivered, and after was arraigned in this Court, and lost his hand. And at the same time *Stubbs* was committed by the command of the Lord the King, for seditious words and rumours, and he lost his hand also upon the same Trial *M.* 17 & 18 *Eliz.* upon *Habeas Corpus* for *John Loan*, it was returned, That he was committed for divulging sundry seditious writings, and he was remanded And 7 *H.* VII. *roll* 6. *Rug's* case; and *roll* 13. *Chase's* case, where the return was, That they were committed by the command of the Lord the King, and they were not delivered, and this was also the opinion in this Court, *M.* 3 *Car.* and after the said time the Law is not altered, and so, I hope, neither are your opinions.

But to consider the particular cause mentioned in the return, I will not rely upon the first part of the words, although they be of great weight, but only upon the last words,——*for stirring up of sedition against Us.*—— But it hath been objected, that *Sedition* is not a word known in the Law: But I marvel that the signification of the word is not understood, when it is joined with the words——*against Us*,——this ought to be understood, Sedition against the King, in his politick capacity *Sedition* hath sundry acceptations, according to the subject handled, as it appears *Coke's* 4 *Rep.* *p.* 13. Lord *Cromwell's* case, which hath been cited If it be spoken of a man, that he is seditious, if it be of a Company in *London*, it shall be understood sedition in the Company, if it be spoken of a Soldier, it shall be taken for mutinous. Mr. *Littleton*, who argued this case, very well said, That *Tacitus* used this word, and it is true, and he says, That there are two manners of sedition, *Seditio armata & togata*, and the last is more dangerous than the former But couple it with the subsequent words here, [*against us*] the interpretation and sense thereof is easy, and *loquendum ut vulgus*. Mr. *Littleton* shews the acceptation of this word in divers places of Scripture, and I will not reject them, for they make for me; 20 *Numb.* [illegible] the Latin is,—*populi [illegible] in seditionem*,—and it is englished—[illegible]—but clearly it was High-Treason against the Government, and God himself 26 *Numb.* [illegible] *in seditione* [illegible]—it is manifest, that that was a great Insurrection. 12 *Jud.* 1 *[illegible]*, *The Ephraimites [illegible] against Jephtha*, and he at the same time was their Judge and Governor, so it was the height of Insurrection. It is true, that in [illegible] and in some translations it is, *[illegible] repugnat* [illegible], for it may be taken in several senses. 19 *Acts* 40. the Town-Clerk there knew not how to answer for *this days sedition*, or insurrection, and no doubt he was in great peril, for it was a great insurrection, and I wish the greater ones were as circumspect as he was. 24 *Acts* 5. *Tertullus accused Paul of sedition*, and doubtless it was conceived a great offence, if you consider the time and other circumstances, for they were Heathens and Romans And although he in very truth taught the Gospel of Christ, yet he was taken for a pestilent fellow, and as a persuader to shake off Government *Bracton, lib.* 3. *de Corona, c.* 2 ranks sedition amongst the crimes *Laesae Majestatis*. But it hath been objected, that if it be a capital offence, it ought to be Felony or Treason. To this I say, that it cannot be Felony, but it may be Treason, for any thing that appears. It is true, that by the Statute of 25 *E.* III. Treasons are declared, and nothing shall be called Treason, which is not comprised within the said Statute, unless it be declared so by Act of Parliament. But upon Indictment of Treason, such Sedition as this may be given in evidence, and perhaps will prove Treason And the return is not, that he was seditious, which shews only an inclination; but that he stirred up sedition, which may be Treason, if the evidence will bear it. In divers Acts of Parliament, notice is taken of this word [*Seditio*], and it is always coupled with Insurrection or Rebellion, as appears by the Statutes of 5 *R.* II. *c.* 6. 17 *R.* II. *c.* 8. 2 *H.* V. *c.* 9. 8 *H.* VI. *c.* 14. 3 & 4 *E.* VI. *c.* 5. 2 *R.* II. *c.* 5. 1 & 2 *Phil.* & *Mar.* *c.* 2. 1 *Eliz.* *c.* 7. 13 *Eliz.* *c.* 2. 23 *Eliz.* *c.* 2. 27 *Eliz.* *c.* 2. and 35 *Eliz.* *c.* 1. all which were cited before; and they prove, that *Sedition* is a word well known in the Law, and of dangerous consequence, and which cannot be expounded in good sense. Wherefore, as to the nature of the offence, I leave it to the Court. But out of these Statutes it appears, that there is a narrow difference between it and Treason, if there be any at all.

3dly, As to the Objections which have been made, I will give a short answer to them.

1. It was objected, That every imprisonment is either for custody, or punishment; the last is always after the Judgment given for the offence; and if it be but for custody, the Party upon tender of sufficient Mainpernors is bailable. I confess, that this difference is true, but not in all respects; for I deny, that a man is always bailable, when imprisonment is imposed upon him for custody: For imprisonment is for two intents; the one is, that the Party which had offended, should not avoid the judgment of Law; the second is, that he shall not do harm in the interim during his Trial; and the Law is careful in this point. But it hath been said, That although the party be bailed, yet he is imprisoned. I deny that, for so is 1 *H.* IV. 6. If the Party come not at the day, the Bail shall be imprisoned; but yet the Bail shall not suffer the same punishment which ought to have been inflicted upon the Party; as if it were for Treason, the Bail shall not answer for the fault, but only for the body. Serjeant *Berkley* did well call a seditious man an Incendiary to the Government, and, as *commune incendium*, is to be restrained of his Liberty. And he put 22 *E.* IV. and 22 *ass.* 56. that a mad-man may be restrained, to prevent the hurt he would otherwise do himself and others. A seditious man is as a mad-man, in the publick state of the Commonwealth, and therefore ought to be restrained. And it appears by the Writ *de Leproso amovendo*, that a Leper is to be removed, and, in a manner, imprisoned, for the contagion of the disease; and this is for the Safeguard of others, lest his Leprosy infect others. The application is easy, and by the Statute of 1 *Jac.* *c.* 33. is restrained to keep within doors; and if he go abroad, any man may justify the killing of him. The infection of Sedition is as dangerous as any of these diseases, therefore it is not safe to let seditious men to bail, or at liberty; and in dangerous cases, the wisest way is to make all safe. In all cases of this nature, much is left to the discretion of the Court. The case of *M.* 9. *E.* III *roll.* 39 *Russell*, hath been objected, to be in the point; I have viewed the record of that case, and although it be verbally, yet it is not materially to this purpose for the commitment was by a Justice of *North Wales*, upon the accusation of an accuser, and it was within a short time after the Statute of 5 *E.* III. by which it was ordained, That none should be imprisoned upon the accusation of one accuser: but here the detainment is by the King himself, for stirring up of sedition. And there the return was, That he was accused of seditions and indecencies, where the latter word doth qualify the former And there issued a Writ of good behaviour (as the Use was) to enquire of the truth of the offence, and it was found, that there was no such offence and then upon the same return again he was set at liberty; so that the case there was special, and the manner of proceedings special. And I desire that one thing may be observed, that *Russell* came in here upon the *Habeas Corpus*, 20 *Sept.* but was not delivered until *Hillary* Term following And for 28 *H* VI. the Duke of *Suffolk's* case, which was objected, that the general accusation of divers Treasons was not legal. That is true, because it was in Parliament, and in the nature of an accusation; and being in a Court of Justice, it had been unjust to condemn a man before his Trial; and yet this Court, upon probability of a fault, does oft-times restrain a man before conviction. But it hath been objected in this case, They have been a long time imprisoned, and no proceedings against them It is well known, there have been some proceedings against them, and they declined them, and also more than three months is requisite for the preparation of such proceedings, and the King intends to proceed against them in convenient time. And some that were offenders in the same kind are already delivered, to wit, Mr. *Coriton* and Sir *Peter Hayman* Therefore, if any injury be done to the Prisoners, they themselves are the cause of it, for not submitting themselves to the King And for the instance which Mr *Littleton* used of the Judges in 11 *R* II altho' they suffered for their opinions given to the King, I desire, that the time when their opinion was delivered, may be considered, to wit, in the time of *R.* II and the time when they suffered, to wit, in the time of *H* IV. And it was the saying of a Noble Gentleman, the Lord *Egerton*, That *Belknap* suffered rather by the potency of his enemies, than the greatness of his offence: And yet it is to be confessed, that they might have given better counsel; but there was no time to dispute of the justness of their counsel, when the sword was in the hands of the Conqueror.

What hath been relied upon is the resolution of all the Justices of *England* in 34 *Eliz* which resolution is now registered in the Upper House of Parliament, at the request of the Commons, in *Tertio Caroli Regis*; but I leave it to you, as that resolution shall sway your Judgments. The said resolution is, That the cause ought to be certified in the general, or specialty, and here the general cause is certified at least, if the special be not so: and upon the whole matter the bailment of these prisoners is left to your discretion; [illegible] I have shewed to you the direction of your predecessors. And if any danger appear to you in their bailment, I am confident that you will not bail them, if any danger may ensue; but first you are to consult with the King, and he will shew you where the danger rests. Therefore upon the whole matter I pray, that they be remanded

When the Court was ready to have delivered their Opinions in this great Business, the Prisoners were not brought to the Bar, according to the Rule of the Court. Therefore Proclamation was made for the Keepers of the several Prisons to bring in their Prisoners; but none of them appeared, except the Marshal of the King's-Bench, who informed the Court, that Mr. *Stroud*, who was in his Custody, was removed Yesterday, and put in the *Tower* of *London* by the King's own Warrant: And so it was done with the other Prisoners; for each of them was removed out of his Prison in which he was before. But notwithstanding, it was prayed by the Counsel for the Prisoners, that the Court would deliver their Opinion as to the Matter in Law: But the Court refused to do that, because it was to no Purpose; for the Prisoners being absent, they could not be bailed, delivered, or remanded.

The Evening before, there came a Letter to the Judges of this Court from the King himself, informing the Court with the Reasons, wherefore the Prisoners were not suffered to come at the Day appointed for the Resolution of the Judges.

To our Trusty and Well-beloved, our Chief-Justice, and the rest of our Justices of our Bench.

" C. R.

" TRUSTY and Well-beloved, we greet you well. Whereas by " our special Commandment we have lately removed Sir *Miles Hobart*, *Walter Long*, and *Will. Stroud*, from the several Prisons where " they were formerly committed, and have now sent them to our *Tower* " of *London*; understanding there are various Constructions made thereof, " according to the several Apprehensions of those who discourse of it, as " if we had done it to decline the Course of Justice; we have therefore " thought fit to let you know the true Reason and Occasion thereof; as " also, why we commanded those and the other Prisoners should not " come before you the last Day. We (having heard how most of them " a while since did carry themselves insolently and unmannerly both to- " wards us and your Lordships) were and are very sensible thereof; and " though we hear yourselves gave them some Admonition for that Miscar- " riage, yet we could not but resent our Honour, and the Honour of so " great a Court of Justice so far, as to let the World know how much " we dislike the same: And having understood that your Lordships, and " the rest of our Judges and Barons of our Court of Common Pleas and " Exchequer, (whose Advices and Judgements we have desired in this " great Business, so much concerning our Government), have not yet " resolved the main Question; we did not think the Presence of those " Prisoners necessary; and until we should find their Temper and Discre- " tions to be such as may deserve it, we were not willing to afford them " Favour. Nevertheless, the Respect we bear to the Proceedings of that " Court, hath caused us to give Way, that *Selden* and *Valentine* should at- " tend you To-morrow, they being sufficient to appear before you, since " you cannot as yet give any resolute Opinion in the main Point in ques- " tion."

Given under our Signet, at our Manour at *Greenwich*, this 24 *Junii*, in the fifth Year of our Reign.

Within three Hours after the Receipt of those Letters, other Letters were brought unto the said Judges, as followeth:

To our Trusty and Well-beloved, our Chief-Justice, and the rest of our Justices of our Bench.

" C. R.

" TRUSTY and Well-beloved, We greet you well. Whereas by " our Letters of this Day's Date, we gave you to understand our " Pleasure, That of those Prisoners which, by our Commandment, are " kept in our *Tower* of *London*, *Selden* and *Valentine* should be brought " To-morrow before you; now, upon more mature Deliberation, we " have resolved, That all of them shall receive the same Treatment, and " that none shall come before you, until we have Cause given us to believe " they will make a better Demonstration of their Modesty and Civility, " both towards us and your Lordships, than at their last Appearance they " did."

Given under our Signet, at *Greenwich*, this 24th Day of *June*, in the fifth Year of our Reign.

So the Court this Term delivered no Opinion, and the imprisoned Gentlemen continued in restraint all the long Vacation.

Towards the latter End of this Vacation, all the Justices of the King's-Bench being then in the Country, received every one of them a Letter to be at *Serjeant's Inn* upon *Michaelmas-Day*. These Letters were from the Council-Table; and the Cause expressed in them was, *That his Majesty had present and urgent Occasion to use their Service.* The Judges came up accordingly on *Tuesday*, being *Michaelmas-Day*. The next Morning about four o'Clock, Letters were brought to the Chief-Justice from Mr. *Trumbal*, Clerk of the Council then attending, that he and Judge *Whitelocke*, one of the Judges of that Court, should attend the King that Morning so soon as conveniently they could; which the Chief-Justice and that Judge did at *Hampton* that Morning; where the King taking them apart from the Council, fell upon the Business of the Gentlemen in the *Tower*, and was contented they should be bailed, notwithstanding their Obstinacy, in that they would not give the King a Petition, expressing, *That they were sorry he was offended with them.* He shewed his Purpose to proceed against them by the Common Law in the *King's-Bench*, and to leave his proceeding in the *Star-Chamber*. Divers other Matters he proposed to the said Judges by way of Advice*, and seemed well contented with what they answered, though it was not to his Mind; which was, That the Offences were not capital, and that by the Law the Prisoners ought to be bailed, giving Security for their good Behaviour. Whereupon the King told them, *That he would never be offended with his Judges, so they dealt plainly with him, and did not answer him by Oracles and Riddles* †.

The first Day of *Michaelmas* Term it was moved by Mr. *Mason*, to have the Resolution of the Judges; and the Court with one Voice said, That they are now content that they should be bailed, but that they ought to find Sureties also for the good Behaviour. And Justice *Jones* said, That so it was done in the Case which had been often remembered to another Purpose, to wit, *Russel's* Case, in 9 *E. III.* To which Mr. *Selden* answered (with whom all the other Prisoners agreed in Opinion), That they have their Sureties ready for the Bail, but not for the good Behaviour; and desire, that the Bail might first be accepted, and that they be not urged to the other; and that for these Reasons:

First, The Case here hath long depended in Court (and they have been imprisoned for these thirty Weeks), and it had been oftentimes argued on the one Side and the other; and those that argued for the King, always demanded that we should be remanded; and those which argued on our Side, desired that we might be bailed or discharged; but it was never the Desire of the one Side or the other, that we should be bound to the good Behaviour. And in the last Term four several Days were appointed for the Resolution of the Court, and the sole Point in question was, *If bailable or not?* Therefore he now desires, that the Matter of Bail and of good Behaviour may be severed, and not confounded.

Secondly, Because the finding of Sureties of good Behaviour is seldom urged upon Returns of Felonies or Treasons. And it is but an Implication upon the Return, that we are culpable of those Matters which are objected.

Thirdly, We demand to be bailed in point of Right; and if it be not grantable of Right, we do not demand it: But the finding of Sureties for the good Behaviour, is a Point of Discretion merely; and we cannot assent to it without great Offence to the Parliament, where these Matters which are surmised by Return were acted; and by the Statute of 4 *H. VIII.* all Punishments of such Nature are made void, and of none Effect. Therefore, &c.

Court. The Return doth not make Mention of any thing done in Parliament, and we cannot in a judicial Way take Notice that these Things were done in Parliament. And by *Whitelocke*, the Surety of good Behaviour, is a preventing Medicine of the Damage that may fall out to the Commonwealth, and it is an Act of Government and Jurisdiction, and not of Law. And by *Croke*, it is no Inconvenience to the Prisoners; for the same Bail sufficeth, and all shall be written upon one Piece of Parchment. And *Heath*, Attorney General, said, That by the Command of the King, he had an Information ready in his Hand to deliver in the Court against them.

Hyde, Chief-Justice. If now you refuse to find Sureties for the good Behaviour, and be for that Cause remanded, perhaps we afterwards will not grant a *Habeas Corpus* for you, inasmuch as we are made acquainted with the Cause of your Imprisonment.

Ashley, the King's Serjeant, offered his own Bail for Mr. *Holles*, one of the Prisoners, (who had married his Daughter and Heir) but the Court refused it; for it is contrary to the Course of the Court, unless the Prisoner himself will become bound also ‡.

And Mr. *Long*, that had found Sureties in the Chief-Justice's Chamber, for the good Behaviour, refused to continue his Sureties any longer, inasmuch as they were bound in a great Sum of 2000 *l.* and the good Behaviour was a ticklish Point. Therefore he was committed to the Custody of the Marshal, and all the other Prisoners were remanded to Prison, because they would not find Sureties for the good Behaviour.

Mich. 6 *Car. B. R.*

John Selden was committed to the *Marshalsea* of the *King's Bench*, for not putting in Sureties for his good Behaviour. There were with him in the same Prison, *Hobart*, *Stroud*, and *Valentine*. In the End of *Trinity Term*, 6 *Car.* the Sickness increasing in *Southwark*, the three last named made Suit unto the Judges of the *King's-Bench*, to be delivered over to the *Gatehouse* in *Westminster*, to avoid the Danger. The Judges thought it Charity, and by Writ to the Marshal of the *King's-Bench*, commanded him to deliver them to the Keeper of the *Gatehouse*, and sent him a Writ to receive them. Mr. *Selden* never sent unto them whilst they were in Town, but when they were all gone, made Suit to the Lord-Treasurer to move the King, that, to avoid this Danger, he might be removed to the *Gatehouse*; which he did, and sent a Warrant under his Hand to the Marshal, signifying his Majesty's Pleasure to remove him to the *Gatehouse*; accordingly he was removed. Thereupon, when the Judges came to Town in *Michaelmas Term*, they called the Marshal to Account for his Prisoner, Mr. *Selden*; and he presenting unto them the Lord Treasurer's Warrant by the King's Direction, the Judges told him it would not serve, for he could not be removed but by Writ; and upon his Majesty's Pleasure signified, it might so have been done. And although the Judges were out of Town, yet the Clerk of the Crown would have made the Writ upon so good a Warrant, and it might have been subscribed by the Judges at their Return. And to avoid the like Error hereafter, the Court sent Justice *Whitelocke* to the Lord Treasurer, to let him know, that Mr. *Selden*

* Mr. *Whitelocke* in his Memorials, page 13. says, My Father did often and highly complain against this way of sending to the Judges for their Opinions beforehand; and said, *That if Bp.* Laud *went on in his way, he would kindle a Flame in the Nation.*

† Mr. *Whitelocke*, in his Memorials of the *English* Affairs, p. 14. (Edit. 1732.) The Judges were somewhat perplexed about the *Habeas Corpus* for the Parliament-men, and wrote an humble and stout Letter to the King, *That by their Oaths they were to bail the Prisoners; but thought fit, before they did it, or published their Opinions therein, to inform his Majesty thereof, and humbly to advise him (as had been done by his noble Progenitors in like Case) to send a Direction to his Justices of his Bench, to bail the Prisoners.* But the Lord-Keeper would not acknowledge to my Father, who was sent to him from the rest of his Brethren about this Business, that he had shewed the Judges Letter to the King, but dissembled the Matter, and told him, that he and his Brethren must attend the King at *Greenwich*, at a Day appointed by him.

Accordingly the Judges attended the King, who was not pleased with their Determination, but commanded them not to deliver any Opinion in this Case without consulting with the rest of the Judges; who delayed the Business, and would hear Arguments in the Case as well as the Judges of the King's-Bench had done; and so the Business was put off to the End of the Term. Then the Court of King's-Bench being ready to deliver their Opinions, the Prisoners were removed to other Prisons, and a Letter came to the Judges from the King, *That this was done because of their insolent Carriage at the Bar.* And so they did not appear.

The Justices of the King's-Bench were sent for by the Lord-Keeper to be in *London* on *Michaelmas*-day. The Chief-Justice *Hyde*, and my Father, were sent for to the King at *Hampton Court*, who advised with them about the imprisoned Parliament-men; and both these Judges did what good Offices they could, to bring on the King to heal these Breaches.

‡ This Motion of discharging proceeded from the King himself, who had conferred with the Judges, and had declared his Content the Prisoners should be bailed, notwithstanding their Obstinacy, that they would not so much as present a Petition to him to express that *they were sorry he was offended with them.* But the Prisoners began now to value themselves upon their Sufferings, and had so much Countenance from several of their late Fellow-members, that they would not now accept of a Deliverance, but unanimously refused to find Sureties for their Behaviour. Nay, Mr *Holis* was so industrious to be continued in Custody that when one offered his own Bail, he would not yield to the Course of the Court, to be bound himself with him. And even Mr. *Long*, who had actually found Sureties in the Chief-Justice's Chamber, declared in Court, that his Sureties should no longer continue. Such a Merit did they now place in Confinement, as to labour against their own Liberty, and by such glorying in Persecution to raise a Popularity to themselves, and cast an Odium on the King. *Kennet's* Hist. of *England* Vol III. page 40.

never

never looked after any of the Court, but fought a new and irregular way to be removed without them. The Lord Treasurer made a very honourable anfwer, That he would not move the King for Mr *Selden* to be removed by this means, until he fent him word, on his credit, that it was a legal way; and told that Judge, that Mr. *Selden* was at the Judges difpofe, to remove back when they would, for it was not the King's meaning to do any thing contrary to the order of the Court, or their formal proceedings. fo Writs were fent this *Michaelmas Term* to remove the four prifoners back again to the *Marfhalfea*.

The Cafe of Sir *Miles Hobart*, and *William Stroud*, Efq.

ON the 23d of *January*, the Attorney-General exhibited two feveral Informations, the one againft *William Stroud*, Efq; the other againft Sir *Miles Hobart*, Knight. The charge againft both of them therein, was for feveral efcapes out of the prifon of the *Gatehoufe*: they both pleaded, Not Guilty. And their Cafes appeared to be as followeth: The faid *William Stroud*, and Sir *Miles Hobart*, were by the King's command committed to prifon, for mifdemeanors alledged againft them, in their carriage in the Houfe of Commons at the laft Parliament. Afterwards in *Trinity Term*, *Anno* 6 *Caroli*, both of them being by order of this Court, and by a Warrant from the Attorney-General to be removed unto the *Gatehoufe*; the Warden of the *Marfhalfea* (where they were before imprifoned) fent the faid *Stroud* to the Keeper of the *Gatehoufe*, who received him into his Houfe lately built, and adjoining to the prifon of the *Gatehoufe*, but being no part thereof. After which receipt, the fame night, he licenfed the faid *Stroud* to go with his Keeper unto his Chamber in *Gray's-Inn*, and there to refide. Sir *Miles Hobart* was alfo by the faid Warden of the *Marfhalfea*, delivered to the Keeper of the *Gatehoufe*, but being fick, and abiding at his Chamber in *Fleet-ftreet*, he could not be removed to the prifon of the *Gatehoufe*, but there continued with his Keeper alfo. Afterwards the Sicknefs increafing in *London*, they (with the licence of the Keeper of the *Gatehoufe*, as it was proved) retired with their Under-keepers to their feveral Houfes in the Country for the fpace of fix weeks, until *Michaelmas Term* then next following, when by direction of the faid Keeper they returned to his Houfe; but in all that fpace it could not be proved, that they were in any part of the old Prifon of the *Gatehoufe*, but in the new building thereto adjoining, unlefs when they once withdrew themfelves to a Clofe-ftool, which was placed near to the Parlour, and was part of the old Prifon of the *Gatehoufe*. This Evidence was given to both the Juries, and both of them returned their Verdicts feverally, *That they were not Guilty*, according to the information exhibited againft them. And in this cafe it was debated at the Bar and Bench, whether by this receipt and continuance in the new houfe only, it may be faid, That they ever had been imprifoned? And the Judges held, *That their voluntary retirement to the Clofe-ftool made them to be prifoners*. They refolved alfo, that in this and all other cafes, although a Prifoner depart from Prifon with his Keeper's licence, yet it is an offence as well punifhable in the Prifoner as in the Keeper. And *Calthorpe* made this difference between breach of Prifon and efcape; the firft is *againft the Gaoler's will*, the other is *with his confent, but in both the Prifoner is punifhable*: whereunto the whole Court agreed. It was alfo refolved that the Prifon of the *King's-Bench* is not any local Prifon, confined only to one place, and that every place where any Perfon is reftrained of his Liberty is a Prifon: As, if one take fanctuary and depart thence, he fhall be faid to break Prifon *.

In the next Parliament, which met *April* 13, 1640, it was referr'd to a Committee, to confider of the breach of privilege by Sir *John Finch* (the Speaker), 5 *Car.* I. who refus'd to put the queftion by command of the Houfe; and the Committee order'd to ftate matter of fact, and fo report.

Monday, *April* 20. Mr. Treafurer reported, that Sir *John Finch* late Speaker did not fay, *He would not put the queftion*; but that, *He durft not put it*: That *he left the Chair not to difobey the Houfe*, but *to obey his Majefty*.

The Houfe thereupon *refolv'd*, That it was a breach of Privilege of the Houfe, for the Speaker not to obey the commands of the Houfe; and that it appear'd the Speaker did adjourn the Houfe by command of the King, without confent of the Houfe, which is alfo a breach of Privilege; it was therefore order'd, that this fhould be humbly reprefented to his Majefty.

But this Parliament being foon diffolved, *viz.* *May* 5. 1640. nothing was done for thefe Gentlemen, but in the next Parliament, which met *Nov.* 3. 1640. reparation was ordered them; as will be fhewn in the following Proceeding.

XVIII. Proceedings againft Sir JOHN ELLIOT, DENZIL HOLLES, Efq. and BENJAMIN VALENTINE, Efq. for feditious Speeches in Parliament; in *B. R. Mich.* 5 *Car.* I. 1629 †.

SIR *Robert Heath*, the King's Attorney-General, exhibited informations in this Court againft Sir *John Elliot*, Knight, *Denzil Holles*, and *Benjamin Valentine*, Efqrs. the effect of which was, ‡ That the King that now is, for weighty caufes, fuch a day and year, did fummon a Parliament, and to that purpofe fent his Writ to the Sheriff of *Cornwall* to chufe two Knights: by virtue whereof Sir *John Elliot* was chofen and returned Knight for *Cornwall*. And that in the fame manner, the other Defendants were elected Burgeffes of other places, for the fame Parliament. And fhewed further, that Sir *John Finch* was chofen for one of the Citizens of *Canterbury*, and was Speaker of the Houfe of Commons. And that the faid *Elliot* publickly and malicioufly in the Houfe of Commons, to raife fedition between the King, his Nobles, and People, uttered thefe words, *That the Council and Judges had all confpired to trample under foot the Liberties of the Subjects*. He further fhewed, that the King had power to call, adjourn, and diffolve Parliaments: and that the King, for divers reafons, had a purpofe to have the Houfe of Commons adjourned, and gave direction to Sir *John Finch*, then the Speaker, to move an adjournment; and if it fhould not be obeyed, that he fhould forthwith come from the Houfe to the King. And that the Defendants, by confederacy aforehand, fpake a long and continued fpeech, which was recited *verbatim*, in which were divers malicious and feditious words, of dangerous confequence. And to the intent that they might not be prevented of uttering their premeditate Speeches, their intention was, that the Speaker fhould not go out of the Chair till they had fpoken them; the Defendants, *Holles* and *Valentine*, laid violent hands upon the Speaker, to the great affrightment and difturbance of the Houfe. And the Speaker being got out of the Chair, they by violence fet him in the Chair again, fo that there was a great tumult in the Houfe. And after the faid fpeeches pronounced by Sir *John Elliot*, *Holles* did recapitulate them.

And to this information,

The Defendants put in a plea to the jurifdiction of the Court, becaufe *thefe offences are fuppofed to be done in Parliament, and ought not to be punifhed in this Court, or in any other, but in Parliament*.

And the Attorney-General moved the Court, to over-rule the plea to the jurifdiction. And that, he faid, the Court might do, although he had not demurred upon the Plea.

But the Court would not over-rule the plea, but gave day to join in demurrer this Term. And on the firft Day of the next Term, the record fhall be read, and within a day after fhall be argued at bar.

Hyde, Chief-Juftice, faid to the Counfel of the Defendants; So far light we will give you: this is no new queftion, but all the Judges in *England*, and Barons of the *Exchequer*, before now, have oft been affembled on this occafion, and have, with great patience, heard the arguments on both fides, and it was refolved by them all with one voice, That an offence committed in Parliament, criminally or contemptuoufly, the Parliament being ended, refts punifhable in another Court.

Jones. It is true, that we all refolved, That an offence committed in Parliament againft the Crown, is punifhable after the Parliament in another Court; and what Court fhall that be, but the Court of the *King's-Bench*, in which the King, by intendment, fitteth?

Whitlocke. The queftion is now reduced to a narrow room, for all the Judges are agreed, That an offence committed in Parliament againft the King or his Government, may be punifhed out of Parliament. So that the fole doubt which now remains, is, whether this Court can punifh it.

Croke agreed, That fo it had been refolved by all the Judges, becaufe otherwife there would be a failure of Juftice. And by him, if fuch an offence be punifhable in another Court, what Court fhall punifh it but this Court, which is the higheft Court in the Realm for criminal offences? And perhaps not only criminal actions committed in Parliament are punifhable here, but words alfo.

Mr. *Mafon* of *Lincoln's-Inn* argued for Sir *John Elliot*, one of the Defendants. The charges in the information againft him are three:

1 For Speeches.

2. For Contempts to the King, in refifting the Adjournment.

* Mr. *Whitlocke*, in his Memorials, *p.* 16. fays, In the Year 1631. fome of the imprifoned Parliament-men, upon their Petition, were removed from the Prifons wherein they then were, to other Prifons, to prevent the danger of the Sicknefs then increafing. Sir *Miles Hobart* put in fureties for his good behaviour, and fo was difcharged from his Imprifonment.

Anno 1631. Sir *John Walter* died, a grave and learned Judge; he fell into the King's difpleafure, charged by his Majefty *for dealing cauteloufly, and not plainly*, with him, *in the bufinefs concerning the Parliament-men*: as if he had given his opinion to the King privately one way, and thereby brought him on the Stage, and there left him, and then was of another Judgment.

His opinion was contrary to all the reft of the Judges, *That a Parliament-man for Mifdemeanor in the Houfe, criminally, out of his Office and Duty, might be only imprifoned, and not farther proceeded againft*: which feemed very ftrange to the other Judges, becaufe it could not appear, whether the Party had committed an offence, unlefs he might be admitted to his anfwer.

The King difcharged him of his fervice by meffage, yet he kept his place of Chief-Baron, and would not leave it but by legal Proceeding; becaufe his Patent of it was, *Quam diu fe bene gefferit*, and it muft be tried whether he did *bene fe geffere*, or not: He never fat in Court after the King forbad him, yet held his place till he died.

† The King at firft intended to proceed againft the above Gentlemen in the *Star-Chamber*, to which end an Information was exhibited againft them in that Court, on the 7th of *May*; but that being dropped, they were proceeded againft in the *King's-Bench*, and the fame matters in effect were fet forth as in the Information in the *Star-Chamber*.

‡ See the Information in the *King's Bench*, the Defendant's Plea, the Attorney-General's Demurrer, &c. at large, *poftea*

3. For Conſpiracy with the other Defendants, to detain Mr. Speaker in the Chair.

In the diſcuſſion of theſe matters, he argued much to the ſame intent he had argued before, therefore his argument is reported here very briefly.

1. For his Speeches, they contain matter of accuſation againſt ſome great Peers of the Realm; and as to them, he ſaid, that the King cannot take notice of them. The Parliament is a Council, and the Grand Council of the King, and Councils are ſecret and cloſe, none other have acceſs to thoſe Councils of Parliament, and they themſelves ought not to impart them without the conſent of the whole Houſe. A Jury in a Leet, which is ſworn to inquire of offences within the ſaid juriſdiction, are ſworn to keep their own counſel; ſo the Houſe of Commons inquire of all grievances within the Kingdom, and their Counſels are not to be revealed. And to this purpoſe was a petition, 2 *H.* IV. *numb.* 10. That the King ſhall not give credit to any private reports of their proceedings, to which the King aſſents: therefore the King ought not to give credit to the information of theſe offences in this caſe. 2. The words themſelves contain ſeveral accuſations of great men, and the liberty of accuſation hath always been Parliamentary. 50 *E.* III. Parliament-Roll, *numb.* 21. the Lord *Latimer* was impeached in Parliament for ſundry offences. 11 *R.* II. the Archbiſhop of *York*; 18 *H.* VI. *numb.* 18. the Duke of *Suffolk*; 1 *Mar. Dy.* 93. the Duke of *Norfolk*; 36 *H.* VI. *numb.* 60. un Vicar General; 2 & 3 *E.* VI. *c.* 18. the Lord *Seymour*, 18 of King *James*, the Lord of *St. Albans*, Chancellor of *England*; and 21 of King *James*, *Cranfield*, Lord Treaſurer; and 1 *Car.* the Duke of *Buckingham*. 3. This is a privilege of Parliament which is determinable in Parliament, and not elſewhere; 11 *R.* II. *numb.* 7. the Parliament-Roll, A Petition exhibited in Parliament, and allowed by the King, That the liberties and privileges of Parliament ſhall only be diſcuſſed there, and not in other Courts, nor by the Common, nor Civil Law; (ſee this caſe more at large in *Selden*'s notes upon *Forteſcue*, *f.* 42.) 11 *R.* II. Roll of the proceſs and judgment. An appeal of Treaſon was exhibited againſt the Archbiſhop of *Canterbury* and others, and there the advice of the ſages of the one Law and the other being required; but becauſe the appeal concerned perſons which are Peers of the Realm, which are not tried elſewhere than in Parliament, and not in an inferior Court. 28 *H.* VI. *numb* 18. There being a queſtion in Parliament concerning precedency, between the Earl of *Arundel*, and the Earl of *Devon*, the opinion of the Judges being demanded, they anſwered, That this queſtion ought to be determined by the Parliament, and by no other. 31 *H.* VI. *numb.* 25, 26. During the prorogation of the Parliament, *Thorp* that was the Speaker, was out in execution at the ſuit of the Duke of *York*, and upon the re-aſſembly of the Parliament, the Commons made ſuit to the King and Lords to have their Speaker delivered. Upon this, the Lords demand the opinion of the Judges; who anſwer, That they ought not to determine the privileges of the High-Court of Parliament. 4. This accuſation in Parliament is in legal courſe of Juſtice, and therefore the accuſer ſhall never be impeached, 13 *H.* VII. and 11 *Eliz. Dy.* 285. Forging of falſe Deeds brought againſt a Peer of the Realm, action *de ſcandalis magnatum*, doth not lie. *Coke*'s *Rep.* 4. 14. *Cutler* and *Dixy*'s caſe, where divers caſes are likewiſe put to this purpoſe. 35 *H.* VI. 15. If upon the view of the body the ſlayer cannot be found, the *Coroner* ought to enquire, Who firſt found the dead body? And if the firſt finder accuſe another of the murder, that is afterward acquit, he ſhall not have an action upon the caſe, for it was done in legal manner. So it is the duty of the Commons to enquire of the grievances of the Subjects, and the cauſes thereof, and doing it in a legal manner, 19 *H.* VI. 19. 8 *H.* IV. 6. in conſpiracy it is a good plea, that he was one of the indictors. And 20 *H.* VI. 5. that he was a grand Jury-man, and informed his Companions. And 21 *E.* IV. 6, 7. and 35 *H.* VI. 14. that he was a Juſtice of Peace, and informed the Jury, 27 *aſſ. p.* 12. is to the ſame purpoſe. And if a Juſtice of Peace, the firſt Finder, a Juror, or Indictor, ſhall not be puniſhed in ſuch caſes; *à fortiori*, a Member of the Houſe of Commons ſhall not, who, as 1 *H* VII. is a Judge. 27 *aſſ. p.* 44. may be objected, where two were indicted of a conſpiracy, becauſe they maintained one another, but the reaſon of the ſaid caſe was, becauſe maintenance is a matter forbidden by the Law; but Parliamentary accuſation, which is our matter, is not forbidden by any Law. *Coke*'s *Rep.* 9. 56. there was a conſpiracy, in procuring others to be indicted. And it is true, for there it was not his duty to prefer ſuch accuſation. (2) The accuſation was extra-judicial, and out of Court; but it was not ſo in our caſe. (3) Words ſpoken in Parliament, which is a ſuperiour Court, cannot be queſtioned in this Court, which is inferiour. 3 *E.* III. 19. and *Stamford* 153. will be objected, where the Biſhop of *Wincheſter* was arraigned in this Court, becauſe he departed the Parliament without licence; there is but the opinion of *Scroop*, and the caſe was entered, *P.* 3 *E.* 19. And it is to be obſerved, that the plea of the Biſhop there, was never over-ruled. From this I gather, that *Scroop* was not conſtant to his opinion, which was ſudden, being in the ſame Term in which the plea was entered; or if he were, yet the other Judges agree not with him, and alſo at laſt the Biſhop was diſcharged by the King's Writ. From this I gather, that the opinion of the Court was againſt the King, as in *Pl.* 20. in *Fogaſſa*'s caſe, where the opinion of the Court was againſt the King, the party was diſcharged by Privy-Seal. 1 and 2 *Phil. & Mar.* hath been objected, where an information in this Court was preferred againſt Mr. *Plowden*, and other Members of the Houſe of Commons, for departing from the Houſe without licence. But in that caſe I obſerve theſe matters. (1) That this information depended during all the life of the Queen, and at laſt was *ſine die*, by the death of the Queen. (2) In the ſaid caſe, no plea was made to the juriſdiction of the Court, as here it is. (3) Some of them ſubmitted themſelves to the fine, becauſe it was eaſy, for it was but 53*s.* 4*d.* But this cannot be urged as a precedent, becauſe it never came in judgment, and no opinion of the Court was delivered therein. And it is no argument, that becauſe at that time they would not plead to the juriſdiction, therefore we now cannot if we would. (4) Theſe offences were not done in the Parliament-Houſe, but elſewhere by their abſence, of which the Country may take notice; but not of our matters done in Parliament. And abſence from Parliament, is an offence againſt the King's ſummons to Parliament. 20 *R.* II. Parliament-Roll 12. *Thomas Hackſey* was indicted of High-Treaſon in this Court, for preferring Petition in Parliament; but 1 *H.* IV. *numb.* 90. he preferred a Petition to have this judgment voided, and ſo it was, although the King had pardoned him before. And 1 *H.* IV. *numb.* 104. all the Commons made petition to the ſame purpoſe, becauſe this tends to the deſtruction of their privileges. And this was likewiſe granted. 4 *H.* VIII. *c.* 8. *Strode's* caſe, That all condemnations impoſed upon one, for preferring of any Bill, ſpeaking, or reaſoning in Parliament, are void. And this hath always been conceived to be a general Act, becauſe the prayers, time, words, and perſons are general, and the anſwer to it is general; for a general Act is always anſwered with, *Le Roy veut*, and a particular Act with *Soit droit fait al partyes.* And 33 *H.* VI. 17, 18. a general Act is always inrolled, and ſo this is.

Secondly, For the ſecond matter, the contempt to the command of the adjournment, *Jac.* 18. it was queſtioned in Parliament, whether the King can adjourn the Parliament, (although it be without doubt that the King can prorogue it). And the Judges reſolve, that the King may adjourn the Houſe by commiſſion; and 27 *Eliz.* it was reſolved accordingly. But it is to be obſerved, that none was then impeached for moving that queſtion. (2) It is to be obſerved, that they reſolve, that the adjournment may be by commiſſion, but not reſolved that it may be by a verbal command, ſignified by another; and it derogates not from the King's Prerogative, that he cannot ſo do, no more than in the caſe of 26 *H.* VIII. 8. that he cannot grant one acre of land by parol. The King himſelf may adjourn the Houſe in perſon, or under the Great Seal, but not by verbal Meſſage, for none is bound to give credit to ſuch Meſſage; but when it is under the Great Seal, it is *Teſte Meipſo.* And if there was no command, then there can be no contempt in the diſobedience of that command. (3) In this, no contempt appears by the information; for the information is, That the King had power to adjourn Parliaments. Then put the caſe, the command be, that they ſhould adjourn themſelves: this is no purſuance of the Power which he is ſuppoſed to have. The Houſe may be adjourned two ways, to wit, by the King, or by the Houſe itſelf, the laſt is their own voluntary act, which the King cannot compel, for, *Voluntas non cogitur.*

Thirdly, For the third matter, which is the conſpiracy: although this be ſuppoſed to be out of the Houſe, yet the Act is legal; for Members of the Houſe may adviſe of matters out of the Houſe; for the Houſe itſelf is not ſo much for conſultations, as for propoſition of them. And 20 *H.* VI. 34. is, that inqueſts which are ſworn for the King, may enquire of matters elſewhere. (2) For the conſpiracy to lay violent hands upon the Speaker, to keep him in the chair; the Houſe hath privilege to detain him in the chair, and it was but lightly and ſoftly, and other Speakers have been ſo ſerved. (3) The King cannot prefer an information for treſpaſs, for it is ſaid, the King ought to be informed by a Jury, to wit, by indictment, or preſentment. (4) This cannot be any contempt, becauſe it appears not that the Houſe was adjourned; and if ſo, then the Speaker ought to remain in the chair; for without him, the Houſe cannot be adjourned. But it may be objected, that the information is, That all theſe matters were done maliciouſly and ſeditiouſly. But to this I anſwer, That this is always to be underſtood according to the ſubject matter, 15 *E.* IV. 4. and 18 *H.* VIII. 5. A wife that hath title to have Dower, agrees with another to enter, (which hath right) that ſhe againſt him may recover her dower. This ſhall not be called *Covin*, becauſe both the parties have right and titles. (2) It will be objected, That if theſe matters ſhall not be puniſhable here; they ſhall be unpuniſhed altogether, becauſe the Parliament is determined. To this I ſay, That they may be puniſhed in the ſubſequent Parliament, and ſo there ſhall be no failure of right. And many times matters in one Parliament have been continued to another, as 4 *E.* III. *numb.* 16. the Lord *Berkley*'s caſe, 50 *E.* III. *numb.* 185. 21 *R.* II. *c.* 16. 6 *H.* VI. *numb.* 45, 46. 8 *H.* IV. *numb.* 12. offence in the foreſt ought to be puniſhed in Eyre, and Eyres oftentimes were not held but every third year. *C.* 9. *Epiſtle*, and 36 *E.* III. *c.* 10. A Parliament may be every year. Error in this Court cannot be reverſed but in Parliament, and yet it was never objected, that therefore there ſhall be a failure of right. 25 *E.* III. *c.* 2. If a new caſe of Treaſon happen, which is doubtful, it ſhall not be determined till the next Parliament. So in *Weſtm.* 2. *c.* 28. where a new caſe happens, in which there is no Writ, ſtay ſhall be made till the next Parliament. And yet in theſe caſes, there is no failure of right. And ſo the Judges have always done in all difficult caſes, they have referred the determination of them to the next Parliament, as appears by 2 *E.* III. 6, 7. 1 *E.* III. 8. 33 *H.* VI. 18. 5 *E.* II. *Dower* 145. the caſe of dower of a rent-charge. And 1 *Jac.* the Judges refuſe to deliver their opinions concerning the union of the two Kingdoms. The preſent caſe is great, rare, and without precedent, therefore, not determinable but in Parliament. And it is of dangerous conſequence; for (1) by the ſame reaſon, all the Members of the Houſe of Commons may be queſtioned. (2) The parties ſhall be diſabled to make their defence, and the Clerk of Parliament is not bound to diſcloſe thoſe particulars. And by this means, the debates of a great Council ſhall be referred to a petty Jury. And the parties cannot make juſtification, for they cannot ſpeak thoſe words here, which were ſpoken in the Parliament, without ſlander. And the Defendants have not means to compel any to be witneſſes for them; for the Members of the Houſe ought not to diſcover the Counſel of the Houſe: ſo that they are debarred of juſtification, evidence, and witneſs. *Laſtly*, By this means, none will adventure to accuſe any offender in Parliament, but will rather ſubmit himſelf to the common danger; for, for his pains he ſhall be impriſoned, and perhaps greatly fined: and if both theſe be unjuſt, yet the party ſo vexed can have no recompence. Therefore, &c.

The Court. The queſtion is not now, whether theſe matters be offences, and whether true or falſe. But, admitting them to be offences, the ſole queſtion is, whether this Court may puniſh them; ſo that a great part of your argument is nothing to the preſent queſtion.

At another day, being the next, Mr. *Calthrope* (who ſucceeded Mr. *Maſon*, as Recorder of *London*) argued for Mr. *Valentine*, another of the Defendants.

1. In general, he ſaid, for the nature of the crimes, that they are of four ſorts:

1. In Matter.
2. In Words.
3. By Conſent.
4. By Letters.

1

Two

Two of them are laid to the charge of this Defendant, to wit, the crime of the Matter, and of Consent. And of offences, *Bracton* makes some publick, some private. The offences here are publick. And of them, some are capital, some not capital; as assault, conspiracy, and such like, which have not the punishment of life and death. Publick crimes capital are such as are against the Law of Nature, as Treason, Murder; I will agree, that if they be committed in Parliament, they may be questioned elsewhere out of Parliament. But in our case, the crimes are not capital, for they are assault and conspiracy, which in many cases may be justified, as appears by 22 *H.* VII. *Keilw.* 92. 2. *ass.* 3 *H.* IV. 10. 22 *E.* IV. 43. Therefore this Court shall not have jurisdiction of them, for they are not against the Law of Nations, of God, or Nature; and if these matters shall be examinable here, by consequence all actions of Parliament-men may be drawn in question in this Court. But it seems by these reasons, that this Court shall not have jurisdiction, as this case is:

1. Because these offences are justifiable, being but the bringing the Speaker to the Chair, which also perhaps was done by the Votes of the Commons; but if these matters shall be justified in this Court, no trial can be, for upon issue of his own wrong, he cannot be tried, because acts done in the House of Commons are of record, as it was resolved in the Parliament, 1 *Jac.* and 16 *H.* VII. 3. *C.* 9. 31. are, that such matters cannot be tried by the Country. And now they cannot be tried by record, because, as 22 *H.* VIII. *Dy.* 32. is, an inferior Court cannot write to a superior. And no *Certiorari* lies out of the *Chancery*, to send this here by *Mittimus*, for there was never any precedent thereof; and the Book of the House of Commons, which is with their Clerk, ought not to be divulged. And *C. Little.* is, that if a Man be indicted in this Court for Piracy committed upon the Sea, he may well plead to the jurisdiction of this Court, because this Court cannot try it.

2. It appears by the old Treatise, *de modo tenendi Parliamentum*, that the Judges are but assistants in the Parliament; and if any words or acts are made there, they have no power to contradict or controul them. Then it is incongruous that they, after the Parliament dissolved, shall have power to punish such words or acts, which at the time of the speaking or doing, they had not power to contradict. There are superior, middle, and more inferior Magistrates; and the superior shall not be subject to the controul of the inferior. It is a position, that *in pares est nullum imperium, multo minus in eos, qui magis imperium habent. C. Littl.* says, That the Parliament is the supreme Tribunal of the Kingdom, and they are Judges of the supreme Tribunal; therefore they ought not to be questioned by their inferiors. (3.) The offences objected do concern the privileges of Parliament, which privileges are determinable in Parliament, and not elsewhere, as appears by the precedents which have been cited before. (4.) The Common Law hath assigned proper Courts for matters, in respect of the place and persons: 1. For the place, it appears by 11 *E.* IV. 3. and *old Entries*, 101. that in an *ejectione firmae*, it is a good plea, that the Land is ancient demesne, and this excludes all other Courts. So it is for Land in *Durham*, *old Entries*, 419. for it is questionable there, and not out of the County. 2. For Persons, *H.* 15 *H.* VII. *rol.* 93. *old Entries*, 47. If a Clerk of the *Chancery* be impleaded in this Court, he may plead his privilege, and shall not answer. So it is of a Clerk of the *Exchequer*, *old Entries*, 473. then much more when offences are done in Parliament, which is exempt in ordinary jurisdiction, they shall not be drawn into question in this Court. And if a man be indicted in this Court, he may plead sanctuary, 22 *H.* VII. *Keilw.* 91. & 22. and shall be restored, 21 *E.* III. 60. The Abbot of *Bury*'s case is to the same purpose. (5.) For any thing that appears, the House of Commons had approved of these matters, therefore they ought not to be questioned in this Court. And if they be offences, and the said House hath not punished them, this will be a casting of imputation upon them. (6.) It appears by the *old Entries*, 446, 447. that such an one ought to represent the Borough of *St. Germains*, from whence he was sent; therefore he is in nature of an Ambassador, and he shall not be questioned for any thing in the execution of his Office, if he do nothing against the Law of Nature or Nations, as it is the case of an Ambassador. In the time of Queen *Elizabeth*, (*Camden*'s Brit. 449.) the Bishop of *Ross*, in *Scotland*, being Ambassador here, attempted divers matters against the State; and by the opinion of all the Civilians of the said time, he may be questioned for those offences, because they are against the Law of Nations and Nature; and in such matters, he shall not enjoy the privileges of an Ambassador. But if he commit a civil offence, which is against the Municipal Law only, he cannot be questioned for it, as *Bodin. de Republica*, agrees the case. Upon the Statute of 28 *H.* VIII. *c.* 15. for Trial of Pirates, 13 *Jac.* the case fell out to be thus: A Jew came Ambassador to the *United Provinces*, and in his journey he took some *Spanish* Ships, and after was driven upon this Coast; and agreed upon the said Statute, that he cannot be tried as a Pirate here by commission, but he may be questioned *civiliter* in the Admiralty, for, *Legati sua Regi sub judicium faciunt*. So Ambassadors of Parliament, *sub Parliamento*, to wit, in such things, which of themselves are justifiable. (7.) There was never any precedent, that this Court hath punished offences of this nature, committed in Parliament, where any plea was put in, as here it is to the jurisdiction of the Court, and where there is no precedent, non-usage is a good expositor of the Law. Lord *Litt.* [illegible] *Co. Litt. f.* 81. says, as usage is good interpreter of the Laws, so non-usage, where there is no example, is a great intendment that the Law will not bear it. [illegible] *Eliz. Dy.* 22[illegible], upon the Statute of 27 *H.* VIII. of Inrollments, that bargain and sale of a House in [illegible] ought not to be enrolled there [illegible] because it is not used. [illegible] 3 *Eliz. Dy.* 37[illegible]. no error lies here of a judgment given in the five Ports, because such Writ was never seen, [illegible] in the diversity of Courts it is said, that error lies of a judgment given in the five Ports. 39 *H.* VI. 39. by [illegible] that a protection to go to *Rome* was never seen, therefore he disallowed it. (8.) If this Court shall have jurisdiction, the Court may give judgment according to Law, and yet contrary to Parliament Law, for the Parliament in divers cases hath a peculiar Law. Notwithstanding the Statute of 1 *H.* V. c. 1. that every Burgess ought to be resident within the Borough of which he is Burgess, yet the constant usage of Parliament is contrary thereunto; and if such matter shall be in question before you, ye ought to adjudge according to the Statute, and not according to the usage. So the House of Lords hath a special Law also, as appears by 11 *R.* II. the roll of the process and judgment, (which hath been cited before to another purpose) where an appeal was not according to the one Law or the other, yet it was good according to the course of Parliament. (9.) Because this matter is brought in this Court by way of information, where it ought to be by way of indictment. And it appears by 41 *ass.* *p.* 12. that if a bill of Deceit be brought in this Court, where it ought to be by Writ, this matter may be pleaded to the jurisdiction of the Court, because it is *vi & armis*, and *contra pacem*. It appears by all our Books, that informations ought not to be grounded upon surmises, but upon matter of Record, 4 *H.* VII. 5. 6 *E.* VI. *Dy.* 74. Information in the *Exchequer*, and 11 *H.* VIII. *Keilw* 101. are to this purpose. And if the matter be *vi & armis*, then it ought to be found by Inquest. 2 *E.* III. 1, 2. Appeal shall not be granted upon the return of the Sheriff, but the King ought to be certified of it by indictment. 1 *H.* VII. 6. and *Stamf. f.* 95. *a.* upon the Statute of 25 *E.* III. *c.* 4. that none shall be imprisoned but upon indictment or presentment; and 28 *E.* III. *c.* 3. 42 *E.* III. *c.* 3. are to the same purpose. So here, this information ought to have been grounded upon indictment, or other matter of Record, and not upon bare intelligence given to the King. (10.) The present case is great and difficult, and in such cases, the Judges have always outed themselves of jurisdiction, as appears by *Bracton, Book* II. *f.* 1. *Si aliquid novi non usitatum in Regno acciderit*, 2 *E.* III. 6, 7. and *Dover* 242.

Now I will remove some objections which may be made.

Where the King is Plaintiff, it is in his election to bring his action in what Court he pleases. This is true in some sense, to wit, That the King is not restrained by the Statute of *Magna Charta*, *Quod communia placita non sequantur curiam nostram*, for he may bring his *Quare impedit* in *B. R.* And if it concerns *Durham*, or other County Palatine, yet the King may have his action here: for the said Courts are created by Patent, and the King may not be restrained by Parliament, or by his own Patent, to bring his action where he pleaseth. But the King shall not have his action where he pleaseth against a prohibition of the Common Law, as 12 *H.* VII. *Keilw.* 6. the King shall not have a *Formedon* in *Chancery*. And *C.* 6. 20. *Gregory's* case, if the King will bring an information in an inferior Court, the party may plead to the jurisdiction. So where the Common Law makes a prohibition, the King hath not election of his Court.

The information is *contra formam Statuti*, which Statute, as I conceive, is intended the Statute of 5 *H.* IV. *c.* 6 and 11 *H.* VI. *c.* 11. which gives power to this Court to punish an assault made upon the servant of a Knight of Parliament. But our case is not within those Statutes, nor the intent of them; for it is not intendible, that the Parliament should disadvantage themselves in point of their privilege. And this was a Trespass done within the House, by Parliament-men amongst themselves. And *Crompton's Jurisdiction of Courts, f.* 8. saith, That the Parliament may punish trespasses done there.

Precedents have been cited of Parliament-men imprisoned and punished for matters done in Parliament. To this I say, That there is *Via juris*, and *Via facti*; and *Via facti* is not always *Via juris*. *C.* 4. 93. precedents are no good directions, unless they be judicial.

Otherwise there will be a failure of Justice, wrongs shall be unpunished. To this I answer, That a mischief is oft-times rather sufferable than an inconvenience, to draw in question the privileges of Parliament. By the antient Common Law, as it appears by 21 *E.* III. 23. and 21 *ass.* if an Infant bring an Appeal, the suit shall be staid during his infancy; because the party cannot have his Trial by battle against the Infant; but the Law is now held otherwise in the said case. And in some cases, criminal offences shall be dispunished, 29 *H.* VIII. *Dy.* 40. Appeal of Murder lies not for Murder done in several Counties.

This Court of *B. R* is *coram ipso Rege*; the King himself, by intendment, is here in person. And as it is said, *C.* 9. 118. it is *Supremum Regni Tribunal*, of ordinary jurisdiction. But to this I say, That the Parliament is a transcendent Court, and of transcendent jurisdiction: it appears by 28 *ass. p.* 52. that the stile of other Courts is *coram Rege*, as well as this is; as *coram Rege in Cancellaria*, *coram Rege in Camera*; and though it be *coram Rege*, yet the Judges give the judgment. And in the time of *H.* III. in this Court, some Entries were *coram Rege*, others, *coram Hugone de Bigod*.

The privileges of Parliament are not questioned, but the conspiracies and misdemeanors of some of them. But to this I say, that the distinction is difficult and narrow in this case, where the offences objected are justifiable, and if they be offences, this reflects upon the House, which hath not punished them.

The cases of 3 *E.* III. 19. and 1 and 2 *Phil. & Mar.* have been objected. But for the last it is observable, That no plea was pleaded to the jurisdiction, as it is in our case. And if a Parliament-man, or other which hath privilege, be impleaded in another Court, and neglect his plea to the jurisdiction, the Court may well proceed, 9 *H.* VII. 14. 35 *H.* VI. [illegible] *H.* 13 *Jac.* In this Court, the Lord *Neville*, that was a Peer of Parliament, was indicted for the [illegible] of one *Egod*, and pleaded his pardon. And there it was doubted, how the Court should proceed against him (for he, by Law, ought to have his Trial by his Peers). And it was resolved, that when he pleads his pardon, or confesseth his fault, then he gives jurisdiction to the Court, and the Court may give judgment against him. So that these cases, where it was not pleaded to the jurisdiction, can be no precedent in our case.

The privilege here is not claimed by Prescription, or Custom, [illegible] it is [illegible]. But I say, that [illegible] good, [illegible] where the Common Law [illegible] Court [illegible] needs no Custom or Prescription, 10 *H.* VI. 13. 8 *H.* VIII. *Keilw.* 189. *Br*[illegible] 515. When Institution to a Church is pleaded, there is no need to [illegible] prescription, because every Church is a Sanctuary by the Common Law. Therefore, &c.

[illegible] *Robert Heath*, the King's Attorney, the [illegible] day replied on the other side, but briefly. *First*, he answered the objections [illegible]

First, He said, That informations might well be [illegible] which are not capital, and [illegible] such informations. But [illegible]

[illegible]

Secondly, It hath been objected, That they are a Council, therefore they ought to speak freely. But such speeches which are here pronounced, prove them not Councillors of State, but *Bedlams*; the addition of one word would have made it Treason, to wit, *proditorie*. But it is the pleasure of the King to proceed in this manner, as now it is. And there is great difference between Bills and Libels, and between their proceedings, as Council and as mutinous.

Thirdly, That it would be of dangerous consequence; for by this means none would adventure to complain of grievances. I answer, they may make their complaints in a parliamentary manner; but they may not move things, which tend to distraction of the King and his Government.

Fourthly, These matters may be punished in following Parliaments But this is impossible, for following Parliaments cannot know with what mind these matters were done. Also the House of Commons is not a Court of Justice of itself. The two Houses are but one body, and they cannot proceed criminally to punish crimes, but only their Members by way of imprisonment; and also they are not a Court of Record. And they have forbid their Clerk to make entry of their speeches, but only of matters of course; for many times they speak upon the sudden, as occasion is offered. And there is no necessity that the King should expect a new Parliament. The Lords may grant Commissions to determine matters after the Parliament ended: but the House of Commons cannot do so. And also a new House of Commons consists of new men, which have no cognizance of these offences. 1 *H.* IV. The Bishop of *Carlisle*, for words spoken in the Parliament, that the King had not right to the Crown, was arraigned in this Court of High-Treason; and then he did not plead his privilege of Parliament, but said, That he was *Episcopus unctus*, &c.

Fifthly, 4 *H.* VIII. *Strode*'s case hath been objected. But this is but a particular Act, although it be in print; for *Rastal* entitles it by the name of *Strode*. so the title, body, and proviso of the Act are particular.

Sixthly, That this is an inferiour Court to the Parliament, therefore, *&c.* To this I say, That, even sitting the Parliament, this Court of *B. R.* and other Courts, may judge of their privileges, as of a Parliament-man put in execution, *&c.* and other cases. It is true that the Judges have oft-times declined to give their judgment upon the privileges of Parliament, sitting the Court. But from this it follows not, that when the offence is committed there, and not punished, and the said Court dissolved, that therefore the said matter shall not be questioned in this Court.

Seventhly, By this means the privileges of Parliament shall be in great danger, if this Court may judge of them. But I answer, That there is no danger at all, for this Court may judge of Acts of Parliament.

Eighthly, Perhaps these matters were done by the Votes of the House; or, if they be offences, it is an imputation to the House to say, That they had neglected to punish them; but this matter doth not appear. And if the truth were so, these matters might be given in evidence.

Ninthly. There is no precedent in the case, which is a great presumption of Law. But to this I answer, That there was never any precedent of such a fact, therefore there cannot be a precedent of such a judgment. And yet in the time of Queen *Elizabeth*, it was resolved by *Brown*, and many other Justices, that offences done in Parliament may be punished out of Parliament, by imprisonment or otherwise. And the case of 3 *E.* III. 19. is taken for good Law by *Stamf.* and *Fitzh.* And 22 *E.* III. and 1 *Mar.* accord directly with it. But it hath been objected, that there was no plea made to the jurisdiction. But it is to be observed, that *Plowden*, that was a learned man, was one of the Defendants, and he pleaded not to the jurisdiction, but pleaded licence to depart. And the said information depended during all the Reign of Queen *Mary*, during which time there were four Parliaments, and they never questioned this matter.

But it hath been further objected, That the said case differs from our case, because that there the offence was done out of the House, and this was done within the House. But in the said case, if licence to depart be pleaded, it ought to be tried in Parliament, as well as these offences here. Therefore, *&c.*

The Judges also the same day spake briefly to the case, and agreed with one voice, *That the Court, as this case is, shall have jurisdiction, although that these offences were committed in Parliament, and that the imprisoned Members ought to answer.*

Jones began and said, That though this question be now newly moved, yet it is an ancient question with him; for it had been in his thoughts these eighteen years. For this information there are three questions in it:

1 *Whether the matters informed be true or false? And this ought to be determined by Jury or Demurrer.*

2. *When the matters of the information are found or confessed to be true, if the information be good in substance?*

3 *Admit that the offences are truly charged, if this Court hath power to punish them? And that is the sole question of this day.*

And it seems to me, that of these offences, although committed in Parliament, this Court shall have jurisdiction to punish them. The Plea of the Defendants here to the jurisdiction being concluded with a demurrer, is not peremptory unto them, although it be adjudged against them; but if the plea be pleaded to the jurisdiction, which is found against the Defendant by Verdict, this is peremptory.

In the discussion of this point, I decline these questions.

1. *If the matter be voted in Parliament, when it is finished, it can be punished and examined in another Court?*

2. *If the matter be commenced in Parliament, and that ended, if afterward it may be questioned in another Court?*

I question not these matters, but I hold, that an offence committed criminally in Parliament, may be questioned elsewhere, as in this Court; and that for these reasons:

First, Quia interest Reipublicæ ut maleficia non maneant impunita: *and there ought to be a fresh punishment of them. Parliaments are called at the King's pleasure, and the King is not compellable to call his Parliament; and if before the next Parliament, the party offending, or the witnesses die, then there will be a failure of Justice.*

Secondly, *The Parliament is no constant Court every Parliament mostly consists of several men, and, by consequence, they cannot take notice of matters done in the foregoing Parliament; and there they do not examine by oath, unless it be in* Chancery, *as it is used of late time.*

Thirdly, *The Parliament cannot send Process to make the offenders to appear at the next Parliament; and being at large, if they hear a noise of a Parliament, they will* fugam facere, *and so prevent their punishment.*

Fourthly, *Put the case, that one of the Defendants be made a Baron of Parliament, now he cannot be punished in the House of Commons, and so he shall be unpunished.*

It hath been objected, *That the Parliament is the superiour Court to this, therefore this Court cannot examine their proceedings.*

To this I say, That this Court of the *King's-Bench* is a higher Court than the Justices of Oyer and Terminer, or the Justices of Assize: but if an offence be done where the *King's-Bench* is, after it is removed, this offence may be examined by the Justices of Oyer and Terminer, or by the Justices of Assize. We cannot question the judgments of Parliaments, but their particular offences.

2 Object. *It is a privilege of Parliament, whereof we are not competent Judges.*

To this I say, That *privilegium est privata Lex & privat. legem.* And this ought to be by grant or prescription in Parliament: and then it ought to be pleaded for the manner, as is in 33 *H.* VIII. *Dy.* as it is not here pleaded. Also we are Judges of all Acts of Parliament: as 4 *H.* VII. Ordinance made by the King and Commons is not good, and we are Judges what shall be a Session of Parliament, as it is in *Plowden*, in *Partridge*'s case. We are Judges of their lives and lands, therefore of their liberties. And 8 *Eliz.* (which was cited by Mr. Attorney) it was the opinion of *Dyer*, *Oatlyn*, *Welsh*, *Brown*, and *Southcot*, Justices, That offences committed in Parliament may be punished out of Parliament. And 3 *Ed.* V. 19. it is good Law. And it is usual near the end of Parliaments to set down some petty punishment upon offenders in Parliament, to prevent other Courts. And I have seen a Roll in this Court, in 6 *H.* VI. where judgment was given in a Writ of Annuity in *Ireland*, and afterward the said judgment was reversed in Parliament in *Ireland*; upon which judgment Writ of Error was brought in this Court, and reversed.

Hyde Chief-Justice, to the same intent: No new matter hath been offered to us now by them that argue for the Defendants, but the same reasons and authorities in substance, which were objected before all the Justices of *England*, and Barons of the *Exchequer*, at *Serjeants-Inn* in *Fleet-street*, upon an information in the *Star-Chamber* for the same matter. At which time, after great deliberation, it was resolved by all of them, *That no offence committed in Parliament, that being ended, may be punished out of Parliament.* And no Court more apt for that purpose than this Court in which we are. and it cannot be punished in a future Parliament, because it cannot take notice of matters done in a foregoing Parliament.

As to what was said, That an inferiour Court cannot meddle with matters done in a superiour; true it is, that an inferiour Court cannot meddle with judgments of a superiour Court; but if particular Members of a superiour Court offend, they are oft-times punishable in an inferiour Court. as, if a Judge shall commit a capital offence in this Court, he may be arraigned thereof at *Newgate.* 3 *E.* III. 19. and 1 *Mar.* which have been cited, over-rule this case. Therefore, *&c.*

Justice *Whitlocke.* 1. *I say in this case*, Nihil dictum quod non dictum prius.

2. *That all the Judges of* England *have resolved this very point.*

3. *That now we are but upon the brink and skirts of the cause for it is not now in question, if these be offences or no; or, if true or false, but only if this Court have jurisdiction.*

But it hath been objected, *That the offence is not capital, therefore it is not examinable in this Court.*

But though it be not capital, yet it is criminal, for it is sowing of sedition to the destruction of the Commonwealth. The question now is not between us that are Judges of this Court, and the Parliament, or between the King and the Parliament; but between some private Members of the House of Commons and the King himself. for here the King himself questions them for those offences, as well he may. In every Commonwealth there is one super-eminent power, which is not subject to be questioned by any other; and that is the King in this Commonwealth, who, as *Bracton* saith, *Solum Deum habet ultorem.* But no other within the Realm hath this privilege. It is true, that that which is done in Parliament by consent of all the House, shall not be questioned elsewhere; but if any private Members, *exuunt personas judicum, & induunt malefacientium personas, & sunt seditiosi*; is there such sanctimony in the place, that they may not be questioned for it elsewhere? The Bishop of *Ross*, as the case hath been put, being Ambassador here, practised matters against the State: and it was resolved, That although *Legatus sit Rex in alieno sol.* yet when he goes out of the bounds of his office, and complots with Traitors in this Kingdom, that he shall be punished as an offender here. A Minister hath a great privilege when he is in the Pulpit; but yet, if in the Pulpit he utter speeches which are scandalous to the State, he is punishable. So in this case, when a Burgess of Parliament becomes mutinous, he shall not have the privilege of Parliament. In my opinion, the Realm cannot consist without Parliaments, but the behaviour of Parliament-men ought to be Parliamentary. No outrageous speeches were ever used against a great Minister of State in Parliament, which have not been punished. If a Judge of this Court utter scandalous speeches to the State, he may be questioned for them before Commissioners of Oyer and Terminer, because this is no judicial act of the Court.

But it hath been objected, *That we cannot examine Acts done by a higher Power.*

To this I put this case. when a Peer of the Realm is arraigned of Treason, we are not his Judges, but the High Steward, and he shall be tried by his Peers: but if error be committed in this proceeding, that shall be reversed by error in this Court. for that which we do is *coram ipso Rege.*

It hath been objected, *That the Parliament-Law differs from the Law by which we judge in this Court in sundry cases.* And for the instance which hath been made, *That by the Statute, none ought to be chosen Burgess of a Town in which he doth not inhabit, but that the usage of Parliament is contrary:* But

if

if information be brought upon the said Statute against such a Burgess, I think that the Statute is a good warrant for us to give judgment against him.

And it hath been objected, *That there is no precedent in this matter.*

But there are sundry precedents, by which it appears, that the Parliament hath transmitted matters to this Court; as 2 *R.* II. there being a question between a great Peer and a Bishop, it was transmitted to this Court, being for matter of behaviour: and although the Judges of this Court are but inferiour men, yet the Court is higher. For it appears by the 11 *Eliz. Dy.* That the Earl Marshal of *England* is an Officer of this Court, and it is always admitted in Parliament, That the Privileges of Parliament hold not in three cases, to wit, *First, in case of Treason. Secondly, in case of Felony. And thirdly, in suit for the Peace.* And the last is our very case Therefore, *&c.*

Croke argued to the same intent: he said, *That these offences ought to be punished in the Court, or no where; and all manner of offences which are against the Crown, are examinable in this Court.*

It hath been objected, *That by this means, none will adventure to make complaints in Parliament.*

That is not so; for he may complain in a Parliamentary course, but not falsely and unlawfully, as here is pretended; for that which is unlawfully, cannot be in a Parliamentary course.

It hath been objected, *That the Parliament is a higher Court than this.*

And it is true. But every Member is not a Court; and if he commit offence, he is punishable here. Our Court is a Court of high Jurisdiction, it cannot take cognizance of real Pleas; but if a real Plea comes by Error in this Court, it shall never be transmitted. But this Court may award a *Grand Cape*, and other Process usual in real actions: but of all capital and criminal Causes, we are originally competent Judges, and by consequence of this matter. But I am not of the opinion of Mr. Attorney-General, that the word *proditorie* would have made this Treason. And for the other matters, he agreed with the Judges. Therefore by the Court, the Defendants were ruled to plead further: and Mr. *Lenthal* of *Lincoln's-Inn* was assigned of Counsel for them.

But inasmuch as the Defendants would not put in any other Plea, the last day of the Term Judgment was given against them upon a *Nihil dicit*; which Judgment was pronounced by *Jones* to this effect:

"The matter of the information now, by the confession of the Defendants, is admitted to be true, and we think their Plea to the jurisdiction insufficient for the matter and manner of it. And we hereby will not draw the true Liberties of Parliament-men into question; to wit, for such matters which they do or speak in a Parliamentary manner. But in this case there was a conspiracy between the Defendants to slander the State, and to raise sedition and discord between the King, his Peers, and People; and this was not a Parliamentary course. All the Judges of *England*, except one, have resolved the Statute of 4 *H.* VIII. to be a private Act, and to extend to *Strode* only. But every Member of the Parliament shall have such Privileges as are there mentioned; but they have no Privilege to speak at their pleasure. The Parliament is an high Court, therefore it ought not to be disorderly, but ought to give good example to other Courts. If a Judge of our Court should rail upon the State, or Clergy, he is punishable for it. A Member of the Parliament may charge any great Officer of the State with any particular offence; but this was a malevolous accusation in the generality of all the Officers of State, therefore the matter contained within the information is a great offence, and punishable in this Court.

2. For the punishment, although the offence be great, yet that shall be with a light hand, and shall be in this manner."

1. *That every of the Defendants shall be imprisoned during the King's pleasure: Sir* John Elliot *to be imprisoned in the* Tower of London, *and the other Defendants in other prisons.*

2. *That none of them shall be delivered out of prison until he give security in this Court for his good behaviour, and have made submission and acknowledgment of his offence.*

3. *Sir* John Elliot, *inasmuch as we think him the greatest Offender, and the Ringleader, shall pay to the King a Fine of* 2000l. *and Mr* Holles, *a Fine of* 1000 Marks: *and Mr.* Valentine, *because he is of less ability than the rest, shall pay a Fine of* 500l. And to all this, all the other Justices with one voice accorded.

Afterwards the Parliament which met the third of *November*, 1640. upon report made by Mr. Recorder *Glyn*, of the state of the several and respective cases of Mr. *Holles*, Mr. *Selden*, and the rest of the imprisoned Members of the Parliament, in *Tertio Caroli*, touching their extraordinary sufferings, for their constant affections to the Liberties of the Kingdom, expressed in that Parliament; and upon arguments made in the House thereupon, did, upon the sixth of *July*, 1641, pass these ensuing votes; which, in respect of the reference they have to these last mentioned proceedings, we have thought fit to insert. *viz.*

July 6. 1641.

1. RESolved upon the question, That the issuing out of the Warrants from the Lords and others of the Privy-Council, compelling Mr. *Holles*, and the rest of the Members of that Parliament, 3 *Car.* during the Parliament, to appear before them, is a breach of the Privilege of Parliament by those Privy Councellors.

2. *Resolved, &c.* That the committing of Mr. *Holles* and the rest, by the Lords and others of the Privy-Council, during the Parliament, is a breach of the Privilege of Parliament by those Lords, and others.

3. *Resolved, &c.* That the [illegible] and [illegible] Chamber, Study, and Papers of Mr. *Holles*, Mr. *Selden*, and Sir *John Elliot*, [illegible] Members of this House, and during the Parliament, and [illegible] of Warrants to that purpose, was a breach of the Privilege of Parliament, by those that executed the same.

4. *Resolved, &c.* That the exhibiting of an information in the Court of *Star-Chamber*, against Mr. *Holles* and the rest, for matters done by them in Parliament, being Members of Parliament, and the same so appearing in the information, is a breach of the Privilege of Parliament.

5. *Resolved, &c.* That Sir *Robert Heath*, and Sir *Humphrey Davenport*, Sir *Heneage Finch*, Mr. *Hudson*, and Sir *Robert Berkley*, that subscribed their names to the information, are guilty thereby of the breach of Privilege of Parliament.

6. *Resolved, &c.* That there was a delay of Justice towards Mr. *Holles*, and the rest that appeared upon the *Habeas Corpus*, in that they were not bailed in *Easter* and *Trinity*-Term, 5 *Car.*

7. *Resolved, &c.* That Sir *Nicholas Hyde*, then Chief Justice of the King's-Bench, is guilty of this delay.

8. *Resolved, &c.* That Sir *William Jones*, being then one of the Justices of the Court of King's-Bench, is guilty of this delay.

9. *Resolved, &c.* That Sir *James Whitlocke*, Knt. then one of the Justices of the Court of King's-Bench, is not guilty of this delay*.

Ordered, That the further debate of this shall be taken into consideration on to-morrow morning.

July 8. 1641.

10. RESolved upon the Question, That Sir *George Croke* Knight, then one of the Judges of the King's-Bench, is not guilty of this delay.

11. That the continuance of Mr. *Holles*, and the rest of the Members of Parliament, 3 *Car.* in prison, by the then Judges of the King's-Bench, for not putting in Sureties for their good behaviour, was without just or legal cause.

12. That the exhibiting of the information against Mr. *Holles*, Sir *John Elliot*, and Mr. *Valentine*, in the King's-Bench, being Members of Parliament, for matters done in Parliament, was a breach of the Privilege of Parliament.

13. That the over-ruling of the Plea, pleaded by Mr. *Holles*, Sir *John Elliot*, and Mr. *Valentine*, upon the information to the jurisdiction of the Court, was against the Law and Privilege of Parliament.

14. That the judgment given upon a *Nihil dicit*, against Mr. *Holles*, Sir *John Elliot*, and Mr *Valentine*, and Fine thereupon imposed, and their several imprisonments thereupon, was against the Law and Privilege of Parliament.

15. That the several proceedings against Mr. *Holles*, and the rest, by committing them, and prosecuting them in the *Star-Chamber*, and in the King's-Bench, is a grievance.

16. That Mr *Holles*, Mr. *Stroud*, Mr. *Valentine*, and Mr. *Long*, and the Heirs and Executors of Sir *John Elliot*, Sir *Miles Hobart*, and Sir *Peter Heyman*, respectively, ought to have reparation for their respective damages and sufferings, against the Lords and others of the Council, by whose warrants they were apprehended and committed, and against the Council that put their hands to the information in the *Star-Chamber*, and against the Judges of the King's-Bench.

17. That Mr. *Lawrence Whitaker*, being a Member of the Parliament 3 *Car.* entering into the Chamber of Sir *John Elliot*, being likewise a Member of the Parliament, searching of his trunks and papers, and sealing of them, is guilty of the breach of the Privilege of Parliament, this being done before the dissolution of Parliament.

18. *Resolved upon the Question*, That Mr. *Lawrence Whitaker* being guilty of the breach of the Privileges as aforesaid, shall be sent forthwith to the *Tower*, there to remain a prisoner during the pleasure of the House.

Mr. *Whitaker* was called down, and kneeling at the Bar, Mr. Speaker pronounced this sentence against him accordingly.

Mr. *Whitaker* being at the Bar, did not deny, but that he did search and seal up the Chamber, and Trunk, and Study of Sir *John Elliot*, between the second and tenth of *March*, during which time the Parliament was adjourned: But endeavoured to extenuate it, by the confusion of the times, at that time; the length of the time since that crime was committed being thirteen years; the command that lay upon him, being commanded by the King and twenty-three Privy-Counsellors.

Afterwards Mr. Recorder *Glyn* made a farther Report to the House of Commons, *viz.*

The Warrant, which issued and was subscribed by twelve Privy-Counsellors, to summon nine of the Members of the House of Commons, in the Parliament of *Tertio Caroli*, to appear before them during the Parliament; *viz.* Mr. *William Stroud*, Mr. *Benjamin Valentine*, Mr. *Holles*, Sir *John Elliot*, Mr. *Selden*, Sir *Miles Hobart*, Sir *Peter Heyman*, Mr. *Walter Long*, and Mr. *William Coriton*, bearing date *Tertio Martii*, *Quarto Caroli*; and the names of the twelve Privy-Counsellors that signed this warrant were read: the Parliament being adjourned the second of *March*, to the tenth of *March*, and then dissolved.

The Warrants under the hands of sixteen Privy-Counsellors, for committing of Mr *Denzil Holles*, Sir *John Elliot*, Mr. *John Selden*, Mr. *Benjamin Valentine*, and Mr. *William Coriton*, close Prisoners to the *Tower*, bearing date, *Quarto Martii*, *Quarto Caroli*, during the Parliament; were read; and the names of the Privy-Counsellors that subscribed them, were read. The Warrants under the hands of twenty-two Privy-Counsellors, directed to *William B[illegible]well* Esq. to repair to the Lodgings of *Denzil Holles* Esq. and [illegible] to repair to the Lodgings of Mr. *John Selden*, and to *Lawrence Whitaker* Esq. [illegible] Lodgings of Sir *John Elliot*, requiring them to [illegible] up the trunks, studies, and cabinets, or any other thing that had any papers in them, of the said Mr. *Holles*, Mr *John*

* Mr. *Whitlocke* in his *Memorials* [illegible], In the House there fell out a Debate touching the Writs of *Habeas Corpus*, upon which Selden and the rest of his fellow-prisoners [illegible] to be bailed; and the Judges of the King's-Bench did not [illegible] *their good behaviour*. This was so far aggravated by some, that they moved, [illegible] *Bench whether they were* [illegible] *to prison*; which Judges they named to be [illegible] *Jones*, and my Father [illegible] Judge [illegible], who was [illegible] Court, they excused him, as differing in Opinion from the rest.

I being a Member of the House, [illegible] to be mistaken, as to the Fact, and [illegible] behalf of my Father, to this effect:

"[illegible] it was not [illegible] to divert [illegible] Members of the House, [illegible] the "free-born Subjects of this Kingdom [illegible] "Member of this Honourable House [illegible] Parliament: and he appeals to that [illegible] Gentlemen, [illegible] "then Sufferers with him. And for his Opinion, and Carriage in the Case of the *Habeas Corpus*, [illegible] "years for it, to the honourable Gentlemen, who were concerned in it; and others, who [illegible] [illegible] who seemed very much of the Matter of Fact, and expressed themselves with great Respect and Honour to the Memory of the deceased Judge, [illegible] reckoned by the House in the same degree with Judge *Croke*, as to their Censure and Proceedings.

Selden

Selden, and Sir *John Elliot*, were read, and likewife the names of the Privy-Councillors that fubfcribed the faid Warrants. A Warrant under the hands of thirteen Privy-Councillors, for the commitment of Mr. *William Stroud* clofe Prifoner to the King's-Bench, bearing date 2d *April*, 1628, was read, and the Names of the Privy-Councillors that fubfcribed it: The like Warrant was for the Commitment of Mr. *Walter Long*, clofe Prifoner to the Marfhalfea.

Refolved, &c. That Mr. *Holles* fhall have the Sum of five thoufand Pounds for his Damages, Loffes, Imprifonments, and Sufferings, fuftained and undergone by him, for his Service done to the Commonwealth in the Parliament of *Tertio Caroli*.

Refolved, &c. That Mr. *John Selden* fhall have the Sum of five thoufand Pounds for his Damages, Loffes, Imprifonments, and Sufferings, fuftained and undergone by him, for his Service done to the Commonwealth in the Parliament of *Tertio Caroli*.

Refolved, &c. That the Sum of five thoufand Pounds be affigned for the Damages, Loffes, Imprifonments, and Sufferings, fuftained and undergone by Sir *John Elliot*, for his Service done to the Commonwealth in the Parliament of *Tertio Caroli*, to be difpofed of in fuch Manner as this Houfe fhall appoint.

Refolved, &c. That the Sum of two thoufand Pounds, Part of four thoufand Pounds, paid into the late Court of *Wards and Liveries*, by the Heirs of Sir *John Elliot*, by reafon of his Marriage with Sir *Daniel Norton*'s Daughter, fhall be repaid to Mr. *Elliot*, out of the Arrears of Monies payable into the late Court of *Wards and Liveries*, before the taking away of the faid late Court.

Ordered, That it be referred to the Committee who brought in this Report, to examine the Decree made in the late Court of *Wards and Liveries*, concerning the Marriage of Sir *John Elliot*'s Heir with Sir *Daniel Norton*'s Daughter; and what Monies were paid by reafon of the faid Decree, and by whom; and to report their Opinion thereupon to the Houfe.

Ordered, That it be referred to the Committee, to examine after what Manner Sir *John Elliot* came to his Death, his Ufage in the *Tower*, and to view the Rooms and Places where he was imprifoned, and where he died, and to report the fame to the Houfe.

Refolved, &c. That the Sum of five thoufand Pounds fhall be paid unto the . . . . . . of Sir *Peter Heyman*, for the Damages, Loffes, Sufferings, and Imprifonments, fuftained and undergone by Sir *Peter Heyman*, for his Service done to the Commonwealth in the Parliament of *Tertio Caroli*.

Refolved, &c. That Mr. *Walter Long* fhall have the Sum of five thoufand Pounds paid unto him, for the Damages, Loffes, Sufferings, and Imprifonment, fuftained and undergone by him, for his Service done to the Commonwealth in the Parliament *Tertio Caroli*.

Refolved, &c. That the Sum of five thoufand Pounds fhall be affigned for the Damages, Loffes, Sufferings, and Imprifonment, fuftained and undergone by Mr. *Stroud* (late a Member of this Houfe), deceafed, for Service done by him to the Commonwealth in the Parliament of *Tertio Caroli*.

Refolved, &c. That Mr. *Benjamin Valentine* fhall have the Sum of five thoufand Pounds paid unto him, for the Damages, Loffes, Sufferings, and Imprifonments, fuftained and undergone by him, for his Service to the Commonwealth in the Parliament of *Tertio Caroli*.

Refolved, &c. That the Sum of five hundred Pounds fhall be beftowed and difpofed of, for the erecting a Monument to Sir *Miles Hobart*, a Member of the Parliament of *Tertio Caroli*, in Memory of his Sufferings for his Service to the Commonwealth in the Parliament of *Tertio Caroli*.

Ordered, That it be recommitted to the Committee, who brought in this Report, to confider how the feveral Sums of Money this Day ordered to be paid for Damages to the feveral Members before-named, for their Sufferings in the Service of the Commonwealth, may be raifed.

In the Reign of King *Charles* II. this Affair was taken into Confideration, and the Houfe of Commons came to feveral Refolutions.

Die Martis, 12 *Novembris* 1667.

Upon a Report made by Mr. *Vaughan* from the Committee concerning Freedom of Speech in Parliament,

Refolved, &c. That the Houfe do agree with the Committee, That the Act of Parliament in 4 *Hen.* VIII. commonly intitled, An Act concerning *Richard Strode*, is a general Law, extending to indemnify all and every the Members of both Houfes of Parliament, in all Parliaments, for and touching any Bills, fpeaking, reafoning, or declaring of any Matter or Matters, in and concerning the Parliament to be communed and treated of, and is a declaratory Law of the ancient and neceffary Rights and Privileges of Parliament.

Die Sabbati, 23 *Novembris* 1667.

Refolved, &c. That the Judgment given 5 *Car.* againft Sir *John Elliot*, *Denzil Holles*, and *Benj. Valentine*, in the King's-Bench, is an illegal Judgment, and againft the Freedom and Privilege of Parliament.

Die Sabbati, 7 *Decembris* 1667.

Refolved, &c. That the Concurrence of the Lords be defired to the Votes of this Houfe concerning Freedom of Speech in Parliament; and that a Conference be on *Monday* next defired to be had with the Lords, at which time the Votes may be delivered, and Reafons for them given.

Die Jovis, 12 *Decembris* 1667.

A Meffage from the Lords by Sir *William Child* and Sir *Thomas Eftcourt*:

Mr. Speaker,

The Lords have commanded us to acquaint you, that they agree with this Houfe in the Votes delivered them at the laft Conference concerning Freedom of Speech in Parliament.

Die Mercurii, 11 *Decembris* 1667.

Next the Lord Chamberlain and the Lord *Afhley* reported the Effect of the Conference with the Houfe of Commons Yefterday, which was managed by Mr. *Vaughan*, who faid he was commanded by the Houfe of Commons to acquaint their Lordfhips with fome Refolves of their Houfe concerning the Freedom of Speech in Parliament, and to defire their Lordfhips Concurrence therein.

In order to which, he was to acquaint their Lordfhips with the Reafons that induced the Houfe of Commons to pafs thofe Refolves.

He faid the Houfe of Commons was accidentally informed of certain Books publifhed under the Name of Sir *George Croke*'s *Reports*, in one of which there was a Cafe publifhed, which did very much concern this great Privilege of Parliament; and which paffing from Hand to Hand amongft the Men of the Long Robe, might come in time to be a received Opinion as good Law.

The Houfe of Commons confidering the Confequence, did take care that this Cafe might be enquired into, and caufed the Book to be produced and read in their Houfe, and he thought it the next and cleareft Way to inform their Lordfhips, is to read the Cafe itfelf, which is *Quinto Caroli primi Michaelmas Term*, which Cafe was read as followeth:

The King verfus *Sir* John Elliot, Denzil Holles, *and* Benjamin Valentine.

AN Information was exhibited againft them by the Attorney-General, reciting, that a Parliament was fummoned to be held at *Weftminfter*, 17 *Martii* 3 *Caroli Regis ibidem incboat.* And that Sir *John Elliot* was duly elected and returned Knight for the County of *Cornwall*, and the other two Burgeffes of Parliament for other Places; and Sir *John Finch* chofen Speaker. That Sir *John Elliot*, *machinans & intendens omnibus viis & modis feminare & excitare* Difcord, evil Will, Murmurings, and Seditions, as well *verfus Regem, magnates, prælatos, proceres & jufticiarios, & reliquos fubjectos Regis, & totaliter deprivare & fubvertere regimen & gubernationem Regni* Angliæ, *tam in domino Rege quam in conciliariis & miniftris fuis cujufcunque generis, & introducere tumultum & confufionem* in all Eftates and Parts, & *ad intentionem*, that all the King's Subjects fhould withdraw their Affections from the King, the 23d of *Febr. Anno* 4 *Car.* in the Parliament, and hearing of the Commons, *falfo, malitiofe, & feditiofe*, ufed thefe Words, *The King's Privy Council, his Judges, and his Counfel learned, have confpired together to trample under their Feet the Liberties of the Subjects of this Realm, and the Liberties of this Houfe.*

And afterwards, upon the fecond of *March*, *Anno* 4. aforefaid, the King appointed the Parliament to be adjourned until the 10th of *March* next following, and fo fignified his Pleafure to the Houfe of Commons; and that the three Defendants the faid 2d Day of *March*, 4 *Car. malitiofe* agreed, and amongft themfelves confpired to difturb and diftract the Commons, that they fhould not adjourn themfelves according to the King's Pleafure before fignified; and that the faid Sir *John Elliot*, according to the Agreement and Confpiracy aforefaid, had malicioufly *in propofitum & intentionem prædictam* in the Houfe of Commons aforefaid, fpoken thefe falfe, pernicious, and feditious Words precedent, &c. And that the faid *Denzil Holles*, according to the Agreement and Confpiracy aforefaid, between him and the other Defendants, then and there *falfo, malitiofe, & feditiofe* uttered *hæc falfa, malitiofa & fcandalofa verba præcedentia*, &c. And that the faid *Denzil Holles*, and *Benjamin Valentine*, *fecundum agreamentum & confpirationem prædict. &c. ad intentionem & propofitum prædict.* uttered the faid Words upon the faid 2d Day of *March*, after the fignifying the King's Pleafure to adjourn; and the faid Sir *John Finch*, the Speaker, endeavouring to get out of the Chair, according to the King's Command, they *vi & armis manu forti & illicito* affaulted, evil intreated, and forcibly detain'd him in the Chair; and afterwards being out of the Chair, they affaulted him in the Houfe, and evil entreated him, *& violenter manu forti & illicito* drew him to the Chair, and thruft him into it. Whereupon there was great Tumult and Commotion in the Houfe, to the great Terror of the Commons there affembled, againft their Allegiance, in *maximum contemptum*, and to the Difherifon of the King, his Crown and Dignity, for which, &c. To this Information the Defendants appearing, pleaded to the Jurifdiction of this Court, that the Court ought not to have Cognizance thereof, becaufe it is for Offences done in Parliament, and ought to be there examined and punifhed, and not elfewhere. It was thereupon demurred, and after Argument adjudged, that they ought to anfwer; for the Charge is for Confpiracy, feditious Acts and Practices, to ftop the Adjournment of the Parliament, which may be examined out of Parliament, being feditious and unlawful Acts; and this Court may take cognizance and punifh them: Afterwards divers Rules being given againft them, *viz.* Sir *John Elliot*, that he fhould be committed to the *Tower*, and fhould pay 2000*l.* Fine, and upon his Enlargement fhould find Sureties for his good Behaviour; and againft *Holles*, that he fhould pay a thoufand Marks, and fhould be imprifoned, and find Sureties, &c. and againft *Valentine*, that he fhould pay 500*l.* Fine, be imprifoned, and find Sureties.

Then Mr. *Vaughan* laid much Emphafis upon the Words *machinans & intendens*, &c. and then went on, That the Houfe of Commons had not only read the Cafe as it was in the Book, but did look into the Record, where, in the Information itfelf, they found fome confiderable Differences from the Print; as that the Crime alledged confifting partly of Words fpoken in the Houfe, partly of criminal Actions pretended to be committed; the Gentlemen accufed pleaded feverally, namely, fpecially to the Words, and a feveral Plea apart to the criminal Actions: But the Court dealt fo craftily, that they over-ruled the whole Plea, mingled together, and took it in general, fo that perhaps whatfoever was criminal in the Actions might ferve for a Juftification of their Rule, and might make it feem in time to become a Precedent, and a ruled Cafe againft the Liberty of Speech in Parliament, which they durft not fingly and barefaced have done.

The Houfe of Commons did take care to enquire what ancient Laws did fortify this the greateft Privilege of both Houfes; and they found in the 4th Year of *Henry* VIII. an Act concerning one *Richard Strode*, who was a Member of Parliament, and was fined at the Stannary Courts in the *Weft*, for condefcending and agreeing with other Members of the Houfe to pafs certain Acts to the Prejudice of the *Stannaries*; this Act was made occafionally for him, but did reach to every Member of Parliament that then was, or fhall be; the very Words being, *viz.*

[And over that, it be enacted by the fame Authority, that all Suits, Accufements, Condemnations, Executions, Fines, Amercements, Punifhments, Corrections, Grievances, Charges and Impofitions, put or had, or hereafter to be put or had unto, or upon the faid *Richard*, and to every other Perfon or Perfons afore-fpecified, that now be of this prefent Parliament, or that of any Parliament hereafter fhall be, for any Bill, fpeaking, reafoning, or declaring of any Matter or Matters concerning the Parliament to be commenced and treated of, be utterly void, and of none Effect. And over that, be it enacted by the faid Authority, that if the faid *Richard Strode*, or any of the faid other Perfon or Perfons hereafter be vexed, troubled, or otherwife charged for any Caufes as is aforefaid, that then he or they, and every of them fo vexed or troubled of, or for the

fame,

same, to have action upon the Case against every such person or persons so vexing or troubling any, contrary to this ordinance and provision; in the which action the party grieved shall recover treble damages and costs; and that no protection, essoyne, nor wager of Law in the said action in any wise be admitted nor received.]

He said, 'tis very possible the Plea of those worthy persons, *Denzil Holles*, Sir *John Elliot*, and the rest, was not sufficient to the Jurisdiction of the Court, if you take in their criminal actions all together; but, as to the words spoken in Parliament, the Court could have no Jurisdiction while this Act of 4 *Hen.* VIII. is in force, which extends to all Members that then were (or ever should be), as well as *Strode*; and was a publick general Law, though made upon a private and a particular occasion.

He recommended to their Lordships the consideration of the time when these words in the case of Sir *George Croke*'s Reports were spoken, which was the second of *March*, 4 *Caroli primi*, being in that Parliament which began in the precedent *March*, 3 *Car.* at which time the Judgment given in the King's-Bench about the *Habeas Corpus* was newly reversed, which concerned the freedom of our persons, the liberty of Speech invaded in this case; and not long after the same Judges (with some others) joined with them in the cases of Ship-money, invaded the Propriety of our Goods and Estates; so that their Lordships find every part of these words for which those worthy persons were accused, justified.

If any man should speak against any of the great Officers, as the Chancellor or Treasurer, or any of the rest recited in those Acts, as by accusing them of Corruption, ill Counsel, or the like, he might possibly justify himself by proving of it; but in this case it was impossible to do it, because those Judgments had preceded and concluded him, for he could make none, but by alledging their own Judgments which they themselves had resolved, and would not therefore allow to be Crimes, which they had made for Laws.

He did inform their Lordships, that the Bill in the Rolls hath another title than that he did mention; this being that, that the Clerks knew it by, rather than the proper Title.

The words in the case are charged *ea intentione*, which ought not to be; for it is clear, and undoubted Law, that whatever is in itself lawful, cannot have an unlawful intent annexed to it. Things unlawful may be made a higher crime by the illness of the intent; for instance, taking away my Horse is a Trespass only, but intending to steal him makes it Felony; borrowing my Horse, though intending to steal him, is not Felony, because borrowing is lawful; and there were no use of freedom of Speech otherwise, for a depraved intention may be annexed to any the most justifiable action. If a man eat no flesh, he may be accused for the depraved intention of bringing in the *Pythagorean* religion, and subverting the *Christian*: If a man drink water, he may be accused of the depraved intention of subverting the King's Government, by destroying his Revenue both of Excise and Custom.

No man can make a doubt, but whatsoever is once enacted is lawful; but nothing can come into an Act of Parliament, but it must be first offered or propounded by somebody, so that if the Act can wrong nobody, no more can the first propounding; the Members must be as free as the Houses. An Act of Parliament cannot disturb the State, therefore the Debate that tends to it cannot, for it must be propounded and debated before it can be enacted.

In the reign of *Henry* the Eighth, when there were so many Persons taken by Act of Parliament out of the Lords House, as the Abbots and Priors, and all the Religious Houses and Lands taken away; it had been a strange information against any Member of Parliament then, for propounding so great an alteration in Church and State.

Besides, Religion itself began then to be altered, and was perfected in the beginning of *Edward* the Sixth's reign, and returned again to Popery in the beginning of Queen *Mary*'s; and the Protestant Religion restored again in the beginning of Queen *Elizabeth*'s.

Should a Member of Parliament, in any of these times, have been justly informed against in the King's-Bench for propounding or debating any of these alterations; so that their Lordships perceive the reasons and inducements the House of Commons had to pass these Votes now presented to their Lordships?

Afterwards these Votes were read, *viz.*

Resolved, &c. That the Act of Parliament 4 *Hen.* VIII. commonly intitled, An Act concerning *Richard Strode*, is a general Law, extending to indemnify all and every the Members of both Houses of Parliament, in all Parliaments, for and touching any Bills, speaking, reasoning, or declaring of any matter or matters in and concerning the Parliament, to be communed and treated of; and is a declaratory Law of the antient and necessary Rights and Privileges of Parliament.

Resolved, &c. That the Judgment given 5 *Car.* against Sir *John Elliot*, *Denzil Holles*, and *Benjamin Valentine* Esquires, in the King's Bench, was an illegal Judgment, and against the Freedom and Privilege of Parliament.

To both which Votes the Lords agree with the House of Commons.

Upon consideration had this day of a Judgment given in the Court of King's-Bench in *Michaelmas*-Term, in the fifth year of King *Charles* the First, against Sir *John Elliot* Knt. *Denzil Holles*, and *Benjamin Valentine* Esquires, which Judgment is found to be erroneous. It is ordered by the Lords Spiritual and Temporal in Parliament assembled, That the said *Denzil Holles* Esq; (now Lord *Holles*, Baron of *Ifeild*) be desired to cause the Roll of the Court of King's-Bench, wherein the said Judgment is recorded, to be brought before the Lords in Parliament by a Writ of Error, to the end that such further Judgment may be given upon the said case, as this House shall find meet.

Attorn Gen. & *al.* versus Holles & *al.*

Mich. 10 Car. secundi Regis. Rot. 75.

An Information in the King's Bench against Sir John Elliot,

Memorandum, quod Rob Heath Mil. Attorn. Dom. Regis nunc General. qui pro eodem Dom Rege in hac parte sequitur in propr. persona sua ven. hic in Cur. dicti Dom. Regis coram Rege apud Westm. die Mercur. prox. post Crastin. animar. isto eodem Term. & pro eodem Domino Rege protulit hic in Cur. dicti Domin. Regis coram ipso Rege tunc ibidem quandam informationem versus Johan. Elliot nuper de London Mil. Benjamin Valentine nuper de London Ar. & Denzil Holles nuper de London Ar. que sequitur in hec verba scilicet Midd ss. Memorandum quod Robertus Heath Mil. Attorn. Dom. Regis nunc General. qui pro eodem Dom. Rege in hac parte sequitur in propria persona sua ven. hic in Cur. dicti Dom. Regis coram ipso Rege apud Westm. die Mercur. prox. post Crastin. Animar. isto eodem Termino. Et pro eodem Dom. Rege dat Cur. hic intelligi & informari. Quod cum dictus Dom. Rex pro diversis arduis & urgentibus negotiis ipsum Regem & statum & defension. Regn. Angl. & Ecclesiæ Anglican. concernen. quoddam Parliament. suum apud Civit. suam Westm. pred. teneri ordinavit. Cumque superinde quoddam Parliamentum suum debito modo inchoat. & tent. fuit apud Westm. pred. decimo septimo die Martii Anno Regni dicti Dom. Regis 3 & ibidem per diversas prorogationes continuat. usque 10 diem Martii Anno regni dicti Dom. Regis 4°. quo quidem 10 die Martii idem Parliament. dissolut. fuit. Cumque antea pred. 17 diem Martii Anno 3° suprad. scilicet 16 die ejusdem mensis Mar. Anno 3° suprad. Johannes Elliot nuper de London Mil. debito modo elect. & retorn. fuit un. Mil. pro Com. Cornub. in eodem Parliament. deservitur. Cumque etiam Benjamin Valentine nuper de London Ar. eodem 16 die Martii Anno 3° suprad. debito modo elect. & retornat. fuit un. Burgens. pro Burgo de St. Germans in pred. Com. Cornub. in eodem Parliament. deservitur. Cumque etiam Denzil Holles nuper de London Ar. eodem 16 die Martii Anno 3° suprad. debito modo elect. & retornat. fuit un. Burgens. pro Burgo de Dorchester in Com. Dors. in eodem Parliament. deservitur. Cumque etiam Johannes Finch Mil. eodem 16 die Martii Anno 3° suprad. debito modo elect. & retornat. fuit un. Civium pro Civitat. Cantuar. in eodem Parliament. deservitur. Cumque pred. 16° die Martii Anno 3 suprad. prefat. J. Finch apud Westm. pred. debito modo electus & constitut. fuit prolocutor. per Commun. in eodem Parliament. Et sic Prolocutor pro Commun. continuavit usque dissolution. ejusdem Parliament. Quod prefat. J. E. machinans & intendens omnibus viis & modis quibus poterit discord. malevolenc. murmuraciones & seditiones tam inter pred. Dom. Regem & magnati prælatos, proceres & justic. suos hujus Regni quam int. pred. magnat. prælat. proceres & justiciar. dicti Dom. Regis & reliquos subdit. suos seminare & excitare & Regimen & gubernation. hujus Regni Angl. tam in pred. Dom. Rege quam in consiliar. & ministris suis cujuscunque generis totalit. deprivare & enervare & tumult. & confusion. in omnibus statibus & partibus hujus Regni Angl. introducere & ad intention. quod veri & ligei subditi dicti domini Regis cordialem suum amorem ab ipso Rege retraherent in & duran. Parliament. pred. scilicet 23 die Febr. Anno 4° suprad. apud Westm. pred. in Domo Commun. Parliament. ibidem & sedente eadem domo Militib. Civib. & Burgens. adtunc & ibidem assemblat. & in eor. presentia & auditu falso & malitiose & seditiose hec falsa ficta malitiosa & scandalosa verba Anglicana alta voce dixit & propalavit, videlicet, *The King's Privy Council, all his Judges and his Counsel learned, have conspired together to trample under their feet the Liberty of the Subjects of this Realm, and the Privileges of this House.* (Privileg. pred. Domus Commun. Parliament. innuendo) Cumque potestas summonend. Parliament. ejusdemque continuand. adjornand. prorogand. & dissolvend. Dom. Regi spectat & de jure pertinet ad libitum & beneplacitum suum. Cumque dictus Dom. Rex pro divers. urgent. causis ipsum ad hoc specialit. moven. secundo die Martii Anno 4° suprad. Parliament. pred. adjornari ordinavit eodem secundo die Martii usque 10 diem ejusdem mensis Martii adtunc prox. futur. Et dictus Dom. Rex pred. secundo die Martii Anno 4° suprad. apud Westm. pred. mandavit prefat Johanni Finch adtunc prolocutori pred quod ipse eodem secundo die Martii Militibus Civibus & Burgens. in Domo Commun Parliament. adtunc & ibidem assemblat beneplacitum dicti Dom. Regis significaret & notum faceret quod immediate post signification. ill. sic fact. pred. domus Commun. per ipsos Mil Cives & Burgens adjornaretur usque 10 diem Martii adtunc prox. futur. Et superinde prefat. Johannes Finch eodem secundo die Martii apud Westm. pred. Militib. Civib & Burgens. in dicta domo Commun. Parliament adtunc & ibidem assemblat. seden. eadem domo publice significavit & notum fecit pred. beneplacitum dicti Dom. Regis quod pred. domus immediate post signification. ill. fact. usque ad pred. 10 diem Martii per seipsos adjornaretur & quod pred. Johannes Elliot B. Valentine & Denzil Holles tempore signification pred. per pred. prolocutor in forma pred. fact. presentes fuer. in domo Commun. pred & adtunc & ibidem audiverunt eandem signification. & ill. bene intellexer. pred. tamen J. F B V & D. H. eodem secundo die Martii Anno quarto suprad. apud Westm. pred malitiose agreaver. & inter eos conspiraver. ad disturband. Milites Cives & Burgens. de pred. domo Commun. Parliament. in eadem domo apud Westm. pred. adtunc & ibidem assemblat. ne illi secundum beneplacitum dicti Dom. Regis eis ut prefertur significat. seipsos adjornarent [illegible]. Et pred. J E. secundum agreament. & conspiration. pred. ad malitiosa proposita & intention. pred. postea scilicet eodem secundo die Martii Anno 4° suprad. apud Westm pred. in eadem dom. Commun. Parliament. in presenti[illegible] & [illegible] pred Milit. Civium & Burgens. adtunc & ibidem assemblat. alta voce falso malitiose & seditiose dixit & propalavit hec falsa ficta scandalosa malitiosa & seditiosa Anglicana verba sequen. *The miserable Condition we are in, both in Matters of Religion and Policy, makes me look with a tender eye both to the person of the King and the Subject. You know how Arminianism doth undermine us, and how Popery comes upon us [illegible] as it gives a Terror to the Law, that particularly concerning the Plantation of Jesuits amongst us, and other things incident thereto, do manifestly shew it. [illegible] not only these men who are actors themselves, I mean the Jesuits, but those that are their great Masters and Fautors, they [illegible] the power of the Law, and dare check Magistrates in the Execution of their duties; from them it comes that we suffer their guilt, and the fear of punishment [illegible] befall them, brings us upon these Rocks. [illegible] the same Prelates of the Church, the great Bishop of Winchester and [illegible], [illegible] apparent what they have done to cast an aspersion upon the Honour, Piety and Goodness of*

Benjamin Valentine, and Denzil Holles Esqs; Members of the House of Commons, for several seditious Speeches in the said House, and assaulting the Speaker, and forcing him to sit in the chair after the King had signified his Pleasure that the House should be adjourned.

of the King. These are not all: but it is extended to some others, who, I fear, in guilt and conscience of their own ill deserts, do join their power with that Bishop, and the rest, to draw his Majesty into a jealousy of the Parliament; amongst them I shall not fear to name the Great Lord Treasurer, in whose person is, I fear, contracted all that which we suffer. If we look into religion and policy, I find him building upon the ground laid by the Duke of Bucks, *his great Master; from him, I fear, came those ill Counsels which contracted that unhappy conclusion of the last Session of Parliament. And whosoever shall go about to break Parliaments, Parliaments will break him! I find that not only in the affections of his Heart, but also in relation to him, he is the head of the Papists. They and their Priests and Jesuits have all relation to him, and I doubt not to fix it indubitably upon him; and so far from the greatness and power of him comes the danger of our Religion. For policy in that great Question of Tonnage and Poundage; that interest that is pretended to be the King's, is but the interest of that person to undermine the policy of this Government, and thereby to weaken the Kingdom. It was the Counsel of* Hospitales, *Chancellor to* Charles *the Ninth, King of* France, *that the way to weaken this Kingdom was to impeach the Trade of it, and so to lay our walls waste and open. And I doubt not, but by the disquisition of a few days to prove that his labours are to undermine us; That he invites Strangers to come in to drive our Trade, or at least our Merchants to trade in strange bottoms, which is as dangerous, and this is that which imprints this fear in his person, and makes him to misinterpret our proceedings to his Majesty. Now therefore it will be fit for true* Englishmen *to perform their duties, and to shew their desire of the safety both of the King and Kingdom, and to resolve to defend the sincerity of our Religion, and to declare our resolutions also for the defence of the right of the Subject, whereby we may declare ourselves to be Freemen, and so the more wealthy and able to supply his Majesty upon all occasions. And that we should declare all that we have suffered, to be the effect of new Counsels, to the ruin of the Government of this State, and to make a protestation against all those men, whether greater or subordinate, that they shall all be declared as capital enemies to the King and Kingdom, that will persuade the King to take Tonnage and Poundage without Grant of Parliament. And that if any Merchants shall willingly pay those Duties without consent of Parliament, they shall be declared as Accessaries to the rest.* Quodque pred. D. H. secundum agreament. & conspiration. inde inter ipsum & prefat. J E. & B. V. ut prefertur prehabit. postea scilicet eodem secundo die Martii Anno 4° suprad. apud Westm. pred. in eadem domo Commun. Parliament. militib. civib. & burgent. adtunc & ibidem assemblat. & in eor. presentia & auditu alta voce falso malitiose & seditiose dixit & propalavit hec falsa ficta malitiosa perniciosa & seditiosa verba Anglican. sequen. videlicet, *Whosoever shall counsel the taking up of Tonnage and Poundage without an Act of Parliament, let him be accounted a capital enemy to the King and Kingdom; and what Merchant soever shall pay Tonnage and Poundage, without an Act of Parliament, let him be accounted a betrayer of the Liberties of the Subject, and a capital enemy to the King and Kingdom.* Quodque prefat. B. V. & D. H. secundum agreament. & conspiration. pred. inde inter eos & prefat. J. E. prehabit. ad intention. & proposit. pred. & ad intention. quod. prefat. J. E. & D. H. pred. falsa malitiosa scandalosa & seditiosa verba pred. in forma pred. & ad intention. & proposita pred. per eos pred. secundo die Martii Anno 4° suprad. dict. & propalat. ut prefertur dicerent & propalarent eodem secundo die Martii post signification. pred. pred. beneplaciti dicti Dom. Regis pro adjornament. dict. domus Commun Parliament. ut prefertur. fiend. per prefat. prolocutorem fact. & ante dictionem & propalationem aliquor. verbor. pred. prefat. J. E. & D. H. eodem secundo die Martii ut prefertur dict. & propalat. prefat. Johanne Finch prolocutor. pred. adtunc & ibidem in quadam Cathedra Anglice vocat. *the Speaker's Chair* in domo pred. existen. & extra pred. secundum mandat. dicti dom. Regis ei in hac parte prius dat. ire conan. in & super prefat. Johannem Finch adtunc & ibidem in pace Dei & dict Dom. Regis existen. vi & armis & manu forti & illicite insult. fecer. & eundem J. Finch maletractaver. & eundem J F. in Cathedra pred contra voluntat. suam manu forti & illicite detinuer. Quodque postea eodem secundo die Martii & ante diction. propalation. aliquor verbor. pred. per pred. J. E. & D. H dict. & propalat. secundo die Martii Anno 4° suprad. prefat. J. F. prolocutor. pred. apud Westm. pred. in domo pred. extra Cathedram pred. adtunc existen. in & super prefat. J. F. adtunc & ibidem in pace Dei & dict. Domini Regis insult. fecer. & prefat. J. Finch maletractaver. & violent. manu forti & illicite contra voluntat. suam in Cathedram pred. traxer. truser. & impuler. per quod magn. tumult. & periculosa commotio & confusio in dom. Commun. pred. & maximi terror. pred. Militib. Civib & Burgens. adtunc & ibidem assemblat. adtunc & ibidem mot. & excitat fuer. contra ligeanc. suar. debit. in magn. contempt. & manifest exheredationem dicti Domini Regis & derogation. persone regiminis & prerogative sue Regie & in legum & statut. hujus regni Angl. subversion & in magn. scandal. & ignominiam Consiliar. de privato Concilio dicti Dom. Regis & al. magnat. prelator. & [illegible]

nes dic. quod ipse pred. 16 die Martii Anno 3° suprad. in informatione pred. mentionat. debito modo elect & retorn. fuit un. Mil. pro pred. Com. Cornub. in Parliament. pred. deservitur. prout in informatione pred. superius mentionat. Quodque idem. J. tempore supposit. offens. transgr. & contempt. pred. in dicend. & propaland. Anglicana verba pred. eidem J. in forma pred. imposit. ac duran. toto tempore Parliament. pred. apud Westm pred. fuit & remansit un. mil. pro Com. Cornub. pred. pro eodem Parliament. Et hoc parat. est verificare unde ex quo in informatione pred. evidenter apparet & plene liquet quod supposit. offens. transgr. & contempt. pred. in dicend. & propaland. Anglicana verba pred. eidem J. in forma pred. imposit. & per information. pred. supposit. commiss. fore commiss. fuit in pred. domo Commun. Parliament. pred. in Parliament. pred. idem J. pet. Judic. si pred. Dom. Rex nunc hic de offens. transgr. & contempt. pred. quoad Anglicana verba pred. per ipsum J. in Parliament. pred. in forma pred. dici & propalari supposit. in Cur. dicti Dom. Regis nunc hic responderi velit aut debeat. Et quoad tot. resid. supposit. offens. transgr. & contempt in informatione pred. mentionat. eidem J. in forma pred. imposit. eidem J. dic. quod ipse non intendit quod dictus Dom. Rex nunc de aut pro pred. resid. offens. transgr. & contempt. pred. in eadem informatione mentionat. eidem J. superius in forma pred. imposit. in Cur. dicti Dom. Regis nunc hic responderi velit aut debeat quia dic. quod resid. pred. supposit. offens transgr. & contempt. in informatione pred superius spec. eidem Johanni per information. pred. in forma pred. imposit. in Parliament. & non in Cur. Dom. Regis nunc hic audiri & terminari debent. Et idem J ulterius dic. quod ipse pred. 16 die Martii Anno 3° suprad. in informatione pred. mentionat. debito modo elect & retornat. fuit un. Mil. pro pred. Com. Cornub. in pred. Parliament. deservitur, prout per information. pred. superius mentionat. Quodque idem J. tempore resid. supposit. offens transgr. & contempt. pred. ei in forma pred. imposit. Ac duran. toto tempore Parliament. pred. apud Westm. pred. fuit & remansit un. Mil. pro pred. Com. Cornub. in Parliament. pred. Et hoc parat. est verificare. Unde & ex quo in informatione pred. evident. apparet & plene liquet quod pred. resid. pred. supposit. transgr. offens. & contempt. pred. in informatione pred. mentionat eidem J. in forma pred. imposit. per eandem information. supposit. fore commiss. fuit commiss. in pred. domo Commun. Parliament. pred. in Parliament. pred. idem J. pet. Judic. si dictus Dom. Rex nunc de resid. pred. supposit. offens. transgr. & contempt. in informatione pred. mentionat. eidem J. in forma pred. imposit. in Parliament. pred. in forma pred. fieri supposit. in Cur. Dom. Regis nunc hic responderi velit aut debeat, &c.

Et pred. Benjamin. Valentine habit. audit. information. pred. idem B. dic. quod ipse non intendit quod dictus Dom. Rex nunc de aut pro supposit. offens. & contempt. pred. in informatione pred. mentionat. eidem B. per eandem information. imposit. in Cur. dicti Dom. Regis nunc hic responderi velit aut debeat. Quia dic. quod pred. supposit. offens. transgr. & contempt. in informatione pred. mentionat. eidem B. per eandem informationem in forma pred. imposit. in Parliament. & non in Cur. Domini Regis nunc hic audiri & terminari debent. Et idem B. ulterius dicit quod ipse pred. 16 die Martii Anno 3° suprad. in informatione pred. mentionat. debito modo elect. & retorn. fuit un. Burgens. pro predicto Burgo de St. Germans in pred. Com. Cornub. in pred. Parliament. deservitur, prout per information. pred. superius mentionat. Quodq; idem B. tempore supposit. offens. transgr. & contempt. pred. ei in forma pred. imposit. Ac duran. toto tempore Parliament. pred. apud Westm. pred. fuit & remansit. un. Burgens. pro pred. Burgo de St. Germans in eodem Parliament. Et hoc parat. est verificare. Unde & ex quo in informatione pred. evident. apparet & bene liquet quod supposit. offens. transgr. & contempt. pred. in informatione pred. mentionat. eidem B. in forma pred. imposit. per information. pred. supposit. fore commiss. fuit commiss. in pred. domo Commun. Parliamenti pred. Idem B. pet. Judic. si dictus Dominus Rex nunc de offens. transgr. & contempt. pred. sic sibi imposit. per ipsum B. in Parliament. predict. fieri supposit. in Cur. dicti Dom. Regis nunc hic responderi velit aut debeat, &c.

Et pred. Denzil Holles habit. audit. information. idem D. quoad supposit. transgr. offens. & contempt. pred. in informatione pred. mentionat. in dicend. & propaland. pred. Anglicana verba in informatione pred. superius recitat. Ac eidem D. per information. pred. in forma pred. imposit. dic. quod ipse non intendit quod Dominus Rex nunc de aut pro supposit transgr. offens. & contempt. ill eidem. D sic imposit. in Cur. dicti Domini Regis nunc hic responderi velit aut debeat. Quia dic. quod pred. supposit offens. transf. & contempt. in dicend. & propaland. pred. Anglicana verba in informatione pred. mentionat. eidem D. in forma pred. imposit. in Parliament. & non in Cur. Dom. Regis nunc hic audiri & terminari debeant, &c. Et ulterius idem D. dic. quod ipse pred. 16 die Martii Anno 2° suprad in informatione pred. mentionat debito modo [illegible] in Cur. Dom. Regis nunc hic audiri & terminari debent. Et idem D. ulterius dic. quod ipse pred. 16 die Martii Anno 3° suprad. in informatione pred. mentionat. debito modo elect. & retornat. fuit un. Burgens. pro pred. Burgo de Dorchester in pred. Com. Dorf. in pred. Parliament. deservitur, prout per information. pred. superius mentionatur. Quodque idem D. tempore resid. suppofit. offens. transgr. & contempt. pred. ei in forma pred. impofit. ac duran. toto tempore Parliament. pred. apud Westm. pred. fuit & remansit un. Burgens. pro pred. Burgo de Dorchester in pred. Com. Dorf. in Parliament. pred. Et hoc parat est verificare. Unde & ex quo in Informatione pred. evident. apparet & plene liquet quod pred. resid. suppofit. offens. transgr. & contempt. pred in Informatione pred. mentionat. eidem D. in forma pred. impofit. per eandem Informationem suppon. fore commiss. in pred. domo Commun Parliament pred. in Parliament. pred. idem D. pet. Judic. si dictus Dom. Rex nunc de resid. predict. suppofit. offens. transgr. & contempt. in Informatione pred. mentionat. eidem D. in forma pred. impofit. in Parliament. pred. in forma pred. fieri suppofit. in Cur. Dom. Regis hic responderi velit aut debeat, &c.

The Attorney-General demurs to the Pleas severally.

Et prefat. Robertus Heath Mil. qui sequitur, &c. quoad pred. placitum pred. J. Elliot pro eodem Dom. Rege dic. quod placitum ill. prefat. J. in forma pred. superius placitat. materiaque in placito pred. content minus sufficien. in lege existunt ad precludend. Cur hic a Jurisdiction. sua audiend. & terminand. offens. transgr. & contempt. in informatione pred. mentionat eidem J. per eandem informationem in forma pred. impofit. Unde pro defectu sufficien. respon. in hac parte pet. Judic. Et quod prefat. J. dicto Dom. Regi in Cur. hic respondeat de & in premiss. &c.

Et prefat. R. H. Mil. qui sequitur, &c. quoad pred. placitum prefat. B. V. pro eodem Domino Rege dic. quod placitum ill. prefat. B. in forma pred superius placitat. materiaque in eodem content. minus sufficien. in lege exist. ad precludend. Cur. hic a Jurisdiction. sua audiend. & terminand. offens transgr. & contempt pred. in Informatione pred. mentionat. eidem B. per eandem Information. in forma pred. impofit. Unde pro defectu sufficien. Respons. in hac parte pet. Judic. & quod prefat. B. dicto Dom. Regi in Cur. hic respondeat de & in premiss. &c. Et simile quoad placitum Denzil Holles.

The Defendants severally join in Demurrer.

Et pred. J. Elliot Mil. ut prius dic. quod placitum pred. per ipsum J. superius in forma pred. placitat. materiaque in placito pred content. bon. & sufficien in lege existunt ad precludend. Cur. hic a Jurisdiction. sua audiend. & terminand. offens. transgr. & contempt. pred. in Informatione pred. mentionat. eidem Johanni per eandem Informationem in forma pred. impofit. Quod quidem placitum materiamque in eodem placito content. idem J. E. Mil. parat. est verificare. Unde ex quo idem Attorn. dicti Dom. Regis pro eodem Dom. Rege ad placitum ill. non respond. nec ill. aliqualit. dedic. sed verification ill. admittere omnino recusat pet. Judic. & quod ipse idem J de offens. transgr. & contempt. pred. in Informatione pred. mentionat. eidem J. per eandem Informationem in forma pred impofit. per Cur hic dimittatur, &c. Et sic de verbo in verbum pro Valentine & Holles separatim.

Cur. advisare vult.

Et quia Cur Dom. Regis hic de Judic. suo inde reddend. nondum advisatur dies inde dat. est tam prefat Roberto Heath Mil qui sequitur, &c. quam pred. J E. B. V. & D H. in statu quo nunc, &c. usque Octab. Sancti Hillar. coram Dom. Rege ubicunque, &c. de Judicio suo inde audiend. eo quod Cur nondum, &c. Ad quas quidem Octab. Sancti Hillar. coram Dom. Rege apud Westm ven tam prefat. R. H qui sequitur, &c. quam pred J. E. B. V & D. H. in propr. person. suis Et prefat R. H qui sequitur, &c. pro eodem Dom. Rege pet. Judic. Et quod pred. J E. B. V D H. dicto Dom. Regi in Cur. hic respondeant & eor. quilibet respondeat de & in premiss. &c. Super quo visis lectis & audit omnibus & singulis premiss. pro eo quod videtur Cur. hic quod separal placita pred. per prefat. J. E B V. & D. H. in forma pred superius placitat materiaque in separal. placitis pred. content. minus sufficien. in lege existunt ad precludend. Cur. hic a Jurisdictione sua audiend. & terminand. offens. transgr. & contempt. pred. in informatione pred. mentionat. eisdem J. E. B. V. & D. H. per eandem Information. in forma pred. impofit. dictum est eisdem J E. B. V. & D H quod ipsi iidem J E. B. V & D H. dicto Dom Regi in Cur. hic respondeant & eor. quilibet respondeat de & in premiss. in informatione pred superius content. &c. Et super hoc dies dat. est per Cur. eisdem J. E. B. V & D. H. coram Dom Rege ubicunque, &c. usque diem Veneris prox. post Octab. Pur. beate Marie Virgin. ad Information. predict. interloquend. & ad respond periculi. suis. Ad quem diem coram Dom Rege apud Westm. ven tam prefat. R. H. qui sequitur, &c. quam prefat. J E B V. & D. H in propr. personis suis. Et prefat. J. E. B V. & D H. licet ipsi sepius premonit. & solempnit. exact. ad respond. nihil dicunt in Barr. sive exoneration. Information. pred. per quod idem Dominus Rex remanet versus eos inde indefens. Ideo consid. est quod pred. J. E. B. V. & D H. capiantur ad satisfaciend. Dom. Regi de finib. suis occasione transgr. & contempt. pred. Ac quod habeant Imprisonament. corpor. suor ad voluntat. ipsius Dom Regis. & quod antequam deliberentur quilibet eor. inveniat. suffic. secur. de se bene gerend. erga dictum Dominum Regem & cunctum populum suum Et quod pred J. E committatur locum custodi Turris Domini Regis London. salvo custodiend. quousque, &c. Quodque pred. B. V & D H committantur Mar. marescal Domini Regis coram ipso Rege salvo custodiend. quousque, &c.

The Attorney-General prays that the Defendants may answer.

Judgment that the Pleas to the Jurisdiction of the King's-bench are insufficient.

The Defendants ordered to answer over.

Day given to the Defendants to answer *periculo suo*.

Judgment against them for want of Pleas in Chief.

Quod cap. ad satisfaciend. de finibus.

That they be imprisoned during the King's Pleasure, and find Sureties for the Good Behaviour before they be discharged. Sir John Eliot committed to the Tower, the other to the King's-Bench Prison.

The Afferments of their Fines by the Court.

Et finis ejusdem J. E. afferatur per Cur. occasione pred. ad 2000*l.*

Et finis ejusdem B. V. afferatur per Cur. occasione pred. ad 500*l.*

Et finis ejusdem D. H. afferatur per Cur. ad 1000 mercas.

Postea scilicet die Lune prox. post Octab. Pur. beate Marie Virgin. Anno Regni Dom. Caroli nunc Regis Angl. &c. 12. coram Dom. Rege apud West. ven. Johannes Banks Mil. Attorn. Dom. Regis nunc General. qui pro eodem Dom. Rege modo in hac parte sequitur & pro eodem Dom. Rege dic. & cognovit quod pred. D. H. solvit & satisfecit pred. 1000 mercas recept. ad Scaccarii dicti Dom. Regis ad usum dicti Dom. Regis in plen. satisfaction. pred. finis super ipsum D. pro offens. pred. in informatione pred. superius nominat. per Cur. hic in ipsum impofit. prout per constat. sub manu Edwardi Wardour Mil. Clerici pell. um recept. Scaccarii dicti Dom. Regis hic in Cur. ostens. plene liquet. Et pro eodem Dom. Rege idem Attorn. dicti Dom. Regis general. cognovit dictum Dom. Regem inde fore satisfactum. Ideo idem D. H. de eisdem 1000 merc.s eat inde quiet. Postea scilicet die Mercur. prox. post Quinden. Pasche Anno Regni dicti Dom. Regis nunc Angl. &c. 16 coram Dom. Rege apud Westm. ven. Johannes Banks Mil. Attorn. Dom. Regis nunc general. in propr. persona sua. Et protulit in Cur. dicti Dom. Regis coram Dom. Rege tunc ibidem quoddam breve ipsius Dom. Regis de privat. sigillo sibi & al. direct. & petiit illud irrotulari & allocari, cujus quidem brevis tenor sequitur in hec verba: Charles, *by the Grace of God, King of* England, Scotland, France, *and* Ireland, *Defender of the Faith*, &c. *To the Lord High-Treasurer of* England, *Chancellor, Under-Treasurer, and Barons of our Exchequer, and all other Officers and Ministers of the same Court for the Time being, and to the Chief-Justice, and the rest of our Justices of our Court of King's-Bench, and to our Attorney-General, and all other Officers and Ministers of the same Court for the Time being, Greeting. Whereas in* Michaelmas *Term, in the tenth year of our Reign, upon an Information in our Name exhibited in our Court of King's-Bench, against* Benjamin Valentine, *Esq; and others, for divers Offences, Trespasses, and Contempts therein mentioned, the said* Benjamin Valentine, *by Judgment of the same Court, was fined to us in the Sum of* 500l. *and to be committed to our Prison of our Marshalsea during our Pleasure; and that he shall find sufficient security for his good behaviour to us and our People, as by the said Information and Judgment thereupon remaining upon Record in our said Court of King's-Bench, more at large may appear. And whereas the said* B. V. *hath been restrained of his Liberty since the last Parliament for not satisfying the said Fine so imposed on him, as aforesaid.* Now know ye, *That we of our special Grace have remised, released, and quit-claimed, and by these presents, for us, our Heirs and Successors, do remise, release, and quit-claim unto the said* B. V. *the said fine or Sum of* 500l *by the Judgment of our said Court on him the said* B. V. *imposed as aforesaid. And all Commitment, Imprisonment, and other Matters whatsoever adjudged or inflicted upon him in our said Court, for or by reason of the Trespasses, Offences or Contempts aforesaid. Wherefore we do by these Presents will and require, as well the Lord Treasurer, Chancellor, Under-Treasurer, and Barons of our Exchequer, as the Justices of our Court of King's-Bench, and the Officers and Ministers of the said several Courts respectively, to whom it shall or may appertain, that they, and every of them respectively, at all times hereafter do forbear, and utterly surcease to make or grant forth any Extents, Seizures, Executions, or other Process whatsoever, against the said* B. V. *his Heirs, Executors or Administrators, or his or their Lands, Tenements, Hereditaments, Goods or Chattels for or concerning the levying of the said Fine or Sum of* 500l. *or any Part thereof. And that they take Order as well for his full and clear Discharge thereof, as of and from his Commitment and Imprisonment as aforesaid. And these Presents, or the Inrollment thereof, shall be unto them, and every of them to whom it shall or may appertain, a sufficient Warrant and Discharge in that behalf. And lastly, we will, and by these Presents authorise and require our Attorney-General for the Time being, for us, and in our Behalf, to acknowledge Satisfaction upon Record of and for the said Fine of* 500l *on the said* B. V. *by Judgment of our said Court so imposed as aforesaid. Whereby he may be fully and absolutely acquitted and discharged thereof against us, our Heirs and Successors, and these Presents, or the Inrollment thereof, shall be unto our said Attorney-General for the Time being a good and sufficient Warrant in that Behalf. Given under our Privy-Seal at our Palace of Westm. the 7th day of* March, *in the fifteenth Year of our Reign.* Et super hoc idem J. B. Miles Attorn dicti Dom. Regis General pro eodem Dom. Rege virtute brevis de privat. sigillo predict. dicit & cognovit ipsum Dominum Regem fore plenar satisfact de pred. fin. 500*l.* super ipsum. B. V. pro offens. predict. in Informatione predict. mentionat. per Cur. hic ut prefertur impofit. & pet. quod pred. B V. virtute brevis pred. de Imprisonament. suo ads ipsum Dom Regis & de Judic. pred exoneretur & dimittatur super quo vis. & per Cur. hic intellect omnibus & singulis premiss. consid est per Cur. quod pred. B. V. pro offens. pred. in Informatione pred superius mentionat. per Cur. hic ut prefertur impofit. sit inde quiet. & eat inde sine die, & quod ipse idem B V de Imprisonament. suo ad sect. Dom. Regis & de Judic. pred. versus ipsum B in forma pred. reddit exoneretur & dimittatur, &c. Postea scilicet 1?° die Febr' Anno Regni Dom. nostri Caroli secundi nunc Regis Angl. &c. 20° Dominus Rex mandavit dilecto & fidel. suo Johanni Kelynge Mil. Capital Justic. dicti Dom. Regis ad placita coram ipso Rege tenend. assign. breve suum clausum in hec verba, Carolus secundus, &c. dilecto & fidel. nostro Johanni Kelynge Mil Capital. Justic. nostro ad placita coram nobis tenend assign. salutem Quia in record. process. ac etiam in redditione Judicii super quandam Informationem in Cur. Dom. Caroli primi nuper Regis Angl. patris nostri precharissimi coram ipso nuper Dom. Rege exhibit. per Robertum Heath Mil. tunc Attorn. General. ipsius nuper Dom. Regis, qui pro eodem Domino Rege in ea parte sequebatur versus Johannem Elliot nuper de London Mil. B Valentine nuper de London pred. Ar & D. Holles nuper de Lond. pred. Ar de divers. misdemeanors, ut dicitur Error intervenit manifestus de grave dampn ipsius D. H. nunc Dom Hollis Baron. de Ifeld sicut ex querela sua accepimus. Nos errorem siquis fuerit modo debito corrigi & eidem D. H. modo Do-

Afterwards the Attorney-General comes into Court, and acknowledges that *Holles* has paid his Fine.

At another Time after the Attorney brings into Court the King's Letters Patents under his Privy-Seal, whereby the King remits to *Valentine* his Fine, and all the rest of the Judgment; and prays the same may be inrolled and allowed.

Judgment of the Court at the Attorney's prayer, that *Valentine* be discharged.

D. Holles, now Lord Holles, brings a Writ of Error upon the said Judgment, returnable in Parliament.

mino

mino Holles Baron. de Ifeild plenam & celerem Juftic. fieri volen. in hac parte vobis mandamus quod fi Judic. inde reddit. fit tunc record. & proceff. pred. cum omnibus ea tangen. nobis in prefent. Parliament. noftrum diftincte & aperte mittatis & hoc breve ut infpect. record. & procefs. pred. ulterius inde affenfu Dominor. Spiritual. & Temporal. in eodem Parliament. exiften. pro Error. ill. corrigend. quod de Jure & fecundum legem & conf. Regni noftri Angl. fuerit faciend. T. meipfo apud Weftm. 12° die Febr. Anno Regni noftri 20.

Norbury.

The Lord Chief-Juftice delivers the Record.

Virtute cujus quidem brevis dictus Capital. Juftic. record. pred. Dom. Regi in prefent Parliament. propr. manibus protulit fecundum exigenc. ejufdem brevis & poftea fcilt. 8° die Martii Anno Regni Dom. Regis nunc Caroli fecundi 20 coram ipfo Rege in prefenti Parliament. ven. pred' D. H. modo Dom. Holles Baro de Ifeild per Samuel. Aftry Attorn. fuum & dicit quod in Record. & proceff. pred. ac etiam in redditione Judicii pred. manifeft. eft Errat. videlicet in hæc verba in Informatione pred. mentionat. fore dicti & propalat. in domo Commun. Parliament. per pred. D. H. modo Dominum Holles tunc exiften. Burgenf. pro Burgo de Dorchefter in tunc prefen. Parliament. defervien' audiri & terminari in domo Commun Parliament. debeant per legem terre & non in Cur. Domini Regis & in hoc quod per Information. in dicto Record. mentionat. idem D. H. modo Dominus Holles oneratur cum dictione & propalatione quorundam verbor. in domo Commun. Parliament. ac etiam cum tranfgrf. & infult. fact. vi & armis fuper Johannem Finch prolocutor. ejufdem tunc domus Commun. Parliament. Ad que idem D. H. modo Dominus H. duo feparal. placita placitabat tamen unicum tantum Judic. reddit. eft de utroque per Cur. & unicus finis ubi duo Judicia reddi & duo fines imponi debuiffent quia fi forte tranfgr. & infult. audirj & terminari forte poffit aut debeat in Cur. Dom. Regis coram ipfo Rege tamen dictio & propalatio verbor. quorumcunque in domo Commun. Parliament. per Burgenf. in eodem Parliament. defervien. alibi quam in Parliament. audiri feu terminari non debent, &c.

Errors affigned.

In nullo eft Errat' by the Attorney-General.

Et Galfridus Palmer Mil. & Bar. Attorn. Domini Regis nunc General. qui per eodem Dom. Rege in hac parte fequitur prefen. in propr. perfona fua pro eodem Dom. Rege dicti quod nec in Record. & Procefs. pred. nec in redditione Judicii pred. in ullo eft Errat. & pet. &c.

A Meffage was fent to the Houfe of Commons by Sir *William Child* and Sir *Juftinian Lewin*, to acquaint them, that the Lords do agree to thofe Votes which were delivered at the Conference yefterday.

Die Mercurii, 15 *April,* 1668.

"WHereas Counfel have been this day heard at the Bar, as well to argue "the Errors affigned by the Lord *Holles*, Baron of *Ifeild*, upon a Writ "of Error depending in this Houfe, brought againft a Judgment given in "the Court of King's-Bench in 5 *Car.* I againft the faid Lord *Holles*, by "the name of *Denzil Holles*, Efq. and others; as alfo to maintain and "defend the faid Judgment on his Majefty's behalf: Upon due confidera-"tion had of what hath been offered on both parts thereupon, the Lords "Spiritual and Temporal in Parliament do order and adjudge, That the "faid Judgment given in the Court of King's-Bench in 5 *Car.* I. againft "the faid *Denzil Holles*, and others, fhall be reverfed."

The Form whereof (to be affixed to the Tranfcript of the Record) followeth:

ET quia Curia Parliamenti de judicio fuo de & fuper præmiffis reddend' nondum advifatur, dies datus eft tam prædict' Galfrido Palmer *Militi & Baronet' qui fequitur, &c. quam prædict'* Denzil *Dom no* Holles *coram eadem Curia ufque ad diem* Mercurii *decimum quintum diem* Aprilis *tunc proximum fequentem apud* Weftmonaft. *in Comitat'* Midd' *de judicio fuo inde audiend' eo quod Curia prædict' nondum, &c. Ad quem diem coram Curia prædict' venit tam prædict'* Galfridus Palmer *qui fequitur, &c. quam prædictus* Denzil *Dominus* Holles *in propriis perfonis fuis. Super quo, vifis, & per eandem Curiam nunc hic plenius intellectis omnibus & fingulis præmiffis, maturaque deliberatione inde habita, confideratum eft per Curiam prædictam, quod Judicium prædict' ob errores prædictos & alios in Recordo & Proceffu prædictis compertos, revocetur, adnulletur & penitus pro nullo habeatur. Et quod prædict'* Denzil *Dominus* Holles *ad omnia quæ idem* Denzil *Dominus* Holles *occafione Judicii prædict. amifit, reftituatur.*

Jo. Browne, *Cleric. Parliamentorum.*

XIX. The Trial of *James* Lord *Uchiltrie*, for Calumnies and flanderous Speeches againft *James* Marquis of *Hamilton*; the Earls of *Haddington*, *Roxburgh*, and *Buccleugh*, tending to the fowing of Sedition betwixt his Majefty and the faid Noblemen; at *Edinburgh*, *Nov.* 30, 1631. 6 *Car.* I.

[From an Authentic MS.]

Curia Jufticiariæ S. D. N. Regis tenta in pretorio burgi de Edinburgh, *ultimo die menfis* Novembris, *Anno Dom. Millefimo, Sexcentefimo, Trigefimo primo, per Honorabiles & Difcretos Viros, Magiftros* Alexandrum Colville *de* Blair, *&* Jacobum Robertoun *Advocatum, Jufticiarios deputatos nobilis & potentis domini* Willielmi *Comitis de* Stratherne *&* Monteith, *Dom.* Grahame, Kilbryde, *&* Kynpont, *præfidis fecreti Concilii & Jufticiarii generalis Dom. S. D. N. Regis totius Regni fui* Scotiæ, *ubilibet conftitut. Sectis vocatis & Curia legitime affirmata.*

Intran'

JAMES Lord *Uchiltrie* delated of the making of Leafings, Calumnies and flanderous Speeches againft *James* Marquis of *Hamilton*, the Earls of *Haddington*, *Roxburgh*, and *Buccleugh*; tending to the fowing of fedition betwixt his Majefty and the faid Noblemen, his Majefty's loyal Subjects, in form and manner fpecify'd and fet down in his Dittay.

Purfuer, Sir *Thomas Hope* of *Craighall*, Knight and Baronet, Advocate to our Sovereign Lord for his Highnefs's entries.

My Lord Advocate produced an Act of fecret Council, commanding him to purfue *James* Lord *Uchiltrie*, now entered upon pannel for the Crimes contained in his Dittay, of the which Act of Council the tenor follows. *Apud* Halyrudhoufe *Vicefimo 2do die menfis* Novembris *Anno Dom. Millefimo, Sexcentefimo, Trigefimo primo.* Forafmekill as the King's Majefty, by his Letter directed to the Lords of his Privy-Council, having fignified his royal pleafure and direction, that *James* Lord *Uchiltrie*, whom his Majefty has fent home to be kept in clofe ward, fhall be try'd and cenfur'd according to the Laws of this Kingdom, for fome Informations given by him, reflecting upon fome Noblemen and Counfellors of the fame, before what Judicatory and Judges the faid Lords fhould think fit and competent for that purpofe; and his Majefty having, to that end, fent down to the faid Lords fome depofitions under the Lord *Uchiltrie*'s own hand, and the authentick copies of others, whereof the principals are retained by his Majefty, becaufe they likewife concern other perfons. And the faid Lords having read and confidered the fame depofitions, and having taken into their confideration, which is the moft proper judgment for trying and cenfuring of matters of this kind, they have all with one voice found, and by the tenor of this Act, finds and declares, that the Trial and Cenfuring of the faid Lord upon the particular aforefaid, is moft proper and competent to be followed out before his Majefty's Juftice; and therefore ordains Sir *Thomas Hope* of *Craighall*, Knt. his Majefty's Advocate, to form and draw up the faid Lord *Uchiltrie*'s Dittay; and to purfue him criminally thereupon, before his Majefty's Juftice, upon the laft day of *November* inftant; and ordains his Majefty's faid Advocate to give a juft copy of the Dittay to the faid Lord *Uchiltrie*, betwixt and the 24th of *November* at night, to the intent he may have time to be advifed therewith, and to confult his Advocates, anent his lawful [illegible] competent to him againft the fame. Anent the doing whereof, [illegible] of this Act, fhall be unto his Majefty's faid Advocate [illegible] *ex* [illegible] *de Libris actorum fecreti Concilii S. D. N. Regis, per* [illegible] *Clericum ejufdem fub meis figno & fubfcriptione* [illegible] James Prymrois. After production and reading of the [illegible] Act of Council, my Lord Advocate alfo produced his Majefty's Letter [illegible] to the Lords of his Majefty's Privy-Council of this Kingdom, dated the 24th of *September* 1631, together with two depofitions of the Lord *Uchiltrie*'s, the one dated the 20th of *June* 1631, the other upon the [illegible] of *June* 1631. Then three feveral depofitions made by *D*[illegible] Lord *R*[illegible] whereof two thereof dated upon the 21ft of *June* 1631, and the third upon the 24th of *June* 1631, all true copies thereof under the hand and fubfcription of the Committee of the Council of *England*. Of the which depofitions and Letter above-written, directed by his Majefty to the Council, the tenor follows. In the firft, the depofition made by *James* Lord *Uchiltrie* upon the 20th of *June* 1631.

Copia vera. The Examination of James *Lord* Uchiltrie, *taken the* 20th *of* June 1631.

THE faid Examinant faith, That on or about the 6th [illegible] of *May* laft, at the fign of the *Bear* near the *Bridge-foot*, the Lord *Rea* told this Examinant, that foldiers and travellers did often hear thofe things, whereof thofe that ftaid at home had no notice; and faid, he did believe there was a plot againft this Land. This Examinant wifh'd him, if he had any good grounds fo to think, that he fhould not fail to difcover it. The Lord *Rea* faid, he had no certain ground, but if he had ftay'd but [illegible] longer in the *Low Countries*, he would have known the certainty, and that he would have hazarded his life but he would have had the certainty.

The

The 13th of *May* the Lord *Rea* came to this Examinant's Chamber, and there putting this Examinant in mind of the former Speech between them, he told this Examinant, that he had learned more certainty than ever he had before ſince the Time of their laſt Speech; whereupon divers Paſſages were between his Lordſhip and this Examinant about the Diſcovery of it, and the Manner. In the End his Lordſhip told this Examinant, that the Purpoſe of the Marquis of *Hamilton*'s Levies (as divers of his Commanders and Followers had informed him the ſaid Lord *Rea*) was, that either they ſhould not go out of *England* and *Scotland*, or if they did, they ſhould return to *England* or *Scotland*, and ſurprize the King's Houſes in *Scotland*, *viz.* the Caſtles of *Edinburgh*, *Striveling*, and *Dunbarton*; and fortify themſelves in *Leith*, under Pretence of training; and ſhould take *Berwick*, and ſo march forward into *England*. And this Examinant aſking what could be their Intention ſo to do; the Lord *Rea* ſaid, that he was informed they meaned to take the King's Perſon, and to immurate him, to ſend the Queen into a Cloiſter, and to captivate the young Prince with his Father, and to ſtrike off the Heads of all the Principal Men about the King, both *Engliſh* and *Scots*: And in particular the Lord-Treaſurer of *England*, the Earl of *Monteith*, Sir *William Alexander*, and Sir *Thomas Hope*. And this Examinant ſaith, That before the Lord *Rea* diſcovered the Particularities aforeſaid to this Examinant, this Examinant uſing Perſuaſions to him to reveal it, aſked the Lord *Rea* what it might be, ſaying, it was either a *French* or a *Spaniſh* Faction. To which the Lord *Rea* ſaid, It was neither; but told this Examinant what it was, and ſo revealed the Particulars above-mentioned. Whereupon the Lord *Rea* being fully reſolved to proceed to a further Diſcovery, and thinking it fitter to be done by this Examinant than by himſelf, leſt thoſe whom it concerned might ſooner ſuſpect it, deſired this Examinant to acquaint his Majeſty or the Lord-Treaſurer therewith.

On the Morrow, being *Saturday* the 14th of *May* at Night, this Examinant came to have ſpoken with the Lord-Treaſurer; but his Lordſhip being gone to Bed, by his Appointment, this Examinant came the next Morning, and told him, he had ſomewhat to reveal that concerned his Majeſty, and all his Kingdoms and Poſterity. The Lord-Treaſurer thereupon went inſtantly up to the King, and after, the ſame Day, told this Examinant, that his Majeſty had given him Commiſſion to hear this Examinant's Relation. This Examinant further ſaith, That the Lord *Rea* told this Examinant, that he had much of this beyond Sea from *Robert Meldrum* and *David Ramſay*. But ſince his coming into *England* (as he ſaid) he had ſpoken with Sir *James Ramſay*, Sir *James Hamilton*, Colonel *Alexander Hamilton* and Captain *Douglas*, and had gotten ſomewhat out of every one of them: He alſo ſaid, he had ſpoken with the Lord *Seaforth*, and underſtood ſomewhat from him.

On *Monday* the 16th of *May*, this Examinant attended the Lord-Treaſurer at *Whitehall*; and entering into a Relation, in the very Beginning diſcovered, that the Matter which he was to relate concerned the Lord Marquis of *Hamilton* and his Actions; which ſo ſoon as he had named, the Lord-Treaſurer commanded him to ſay no more, until he had acquainted the King again; but wiſhed this Examinant that he and the Lord *Rea* ſhould go preſently to *Greenwich*, where the Lord-Treaſurer would meet them. But the King being come towards *Whitehall*, this Examinant and the Lord *Rea* came back again, and were then appointed by the Lord-Treaſurer to attend his Majeſty on *Thurſday* at ten o'Clock, which they did. The Examinant further ſaith, That on *Monday* the 16th of *May*, this Examinant delivered to the Lord-Treaſurer a Liſt of Names, to repreſent to his Majeſty the Strength of the Lord *Hamilton*'s Party and Adherents in *Scotland*. At this Examinant's coming to his Majeſty, this Examinant told the King, that the Buſineſs was a Treaſon intended againſt his Majeſty, and the Party was the Marquis of *Hamilton*, as this Examinant was informed; and that it was the filthieſt Treaſon that ever was intended, and was ſorry that any *Scottiſh* Man ſhould have a Hand in it, for it was a Shame to the whole Nation. And then the Lord *Rea* himſelf coming in, made relation to his Majeſty, who remitted him to the Lord-Treaſurer; whereupon this Examinant coming to the Lord-Treaſurer, and telling him the King had remitted the Lord *Rea* unto him; the Lord Treaſurer wiſhed, that the Lord *Rea* would put his Relation in writing. Whereupon the Lord *Rea* and this Examinant went together, and ſat up all Night; and the Lord *Rea* firſt putting it into writing, this Examinant wrote it out of the Lord *Rea*'s Papers, who on the Morrow brought the ſame to the Lord-Treaſurer: But this Examinant was not then preſent, but the next Time that he came to the Lord-Treaſurer's, being aſked by him whoſe the Hand-writing was, this Examinant ſaid, it was his own Hand; and the Lord-Treaſurer telling him that the Lord *Rea* had not ſubſcribed it, this Examinant ſaid, he would without doubt ſubſcribe it. And about two Days after he brought the Lord *Rea* to the Lord-Treaſurer, who read over the whole writing, and ſubſcribed his Name to it, ſaying, he would ſeal it with his Blood.

This Examinant further confeſſeth, That he told the Lord-Treaſurer, that the Lord *Rea* told him he had yet more, and would ſay ſo much, that the Marquis ſhould not have the Face to deny it: which the Lord *Rea* then preſent affirmed; inſomuch as the Lord Treaſurer ſaid, Then is the Buſineſs at an End, there needs no writing.

This Examinant further ſaith, That on the *Sunday* Morning, when the Marquis of *Hamilton* came out of *Scotland*, the Lord *Rea* told this Examinant, that he had ſpoken with the Lord *Seaforth*, who aſſured him their Purpoſe was to take the King, the Queen, and the Prince; and this Examinant aſking how they ſhould effect it, the Lord *Rea* replied, the Lord *Seaforth* had told him, they were great with the Earl of *Dorſet*, who had the Cuſtody of the Prince. And this Examinant further ſaith, That the Lord *Rea* told him, that he was aſſured by my Lord of *Roxburgh*, that the Marquis and his Company would haſten their Purpoſe; and the Lord *Rea* ſaid, that ſurely the *Hamiltons* had taken ſome Vent of the Buſineſs, and that Sir *James Ramſay* had told him, he had 1500 Men in Readineſs upon an Hour's Warning, but they ſhould not come about *London* till their Buſineſs was ready withal; which this Examinant the ſame Morning acquainted the Lord-Treaſurer, to the Intent that his Majeſty might know thereof.

And further ſaith, That ſhortly after the Lord *Rea* told him he had ſpoken with the Lord *Seaforth*, who told him, that the Matter which he had formerly told him concerning the Earl of *Dorſet*, was but a diſguis'd thing.

This Examinant further ſaith, That on that *Sunday* Morning he wiſhed the Lord-Treaſurer to adviſe the King, that he ſhould go to *London* for more Safety; and underſtanding the King had ſent for the Lord *Rea*, this Examinant wiſhed the Lord *Rea* were not ſent for, becauſe the Lord *Rea* was gone to the Lord *Seaforth*'s to learn more: And further ſaith, That the ſame time being in the End of the King's Dinner, this Examinant told the King in theſe Words: *Sir, now we know the Buſineſs, but know not the Time; and therefore, Sir, either do or die.*

Copia Vera, my Lord Rea's *firſt Examination, 21ſt of June, 1631* *.

IN the Examination of *Donald* Lord *Rea*, taken the 21ſt of *June*, 1631, the ſaid Examinant ſaith, that having heard in *Sweden* from *David Ramſay*, ſuch things as are contained in the written Relation which hath been delivered to his Majeſty; and before having heard in *Pomerland* thoſe Paſſages from *Robert Meldrum* which are in the ſame Relation, this Examinant having a Reſolution to come for *England* about *December* laſt, was ſtayed in *Denmark* by Reaſon of the Ice, ſo as he came not to *Holland* till about *March* laſt, where he had Conference with *David Ramſay*, and heard from him ſuch other Paſſages as are contained in the ſame Relation. And after coming into *England*, becauſe *David Ramſay* had told this Examinant, that he would write to the Marquis of *Hamilton*, how far forth the ſaid *David Ramſay* had treated with this Examinant, this Examinant expected that the Marquis would have ſpoken thereof unto him; he did therefore forbear to ſay any thing thereof; yet about two or three Days before the Lord Marquis went into *Scotland*, this Examinant did ſpeak to the Lord *Uchiltrie* to this Purpoſe: That his Lordſhip was better acquainted than this Examinant with the Faſhions and Laws of this Land; and deſired to know what Danger it was, if any Man hearing beyond Sea of Things that might be dangerous to the King or State, ſhould not ſpeak of it. To which the Lord *Uchiltrie* anſwered, No leſs than your Head and Eſtate. And this was all that paſſed between them at that Time, being the firſt Time they ſpake thereof; and the Place was (as he thinketh) at the Lord *Uchiltrie*'s own Lodgings.

He further ſaith, That about eight or ten Days after, this Examinant coming to the Lord *Uchiltrie*'s Lodgings to talk of ſome other Buſineſs, after Speech thereof, ſpake to this Effect: My Lord, you remember I aſked you a Queſtion a while ſince, what the Danger might be, not to ſpeak of Matters dangerous to the King or State, which he had heard beyond the Seas, and I would now again have your Advice therein: And the Lord *Uchiltrie* promiſing his readineſs to adviſe him, ſo as he might be acquainted with the particular, this Examinant told him, he would acquaint him with the particular, if he would ſwear not to diſcover it but as he ſhould direct; adding, That if he did otherwiſe, this Examinant would pay him. The Lord *Uchiltrie* then ſaid, and proteſted, That he would not diſcover any thing but as this Examinant ſhould appoint, whereupon this Examinant declared the particular to him, who hearing it, told this Examinant it was neceſſary to be revealed, and doubted leſt this Examinant had kept it too long already. But then this Examinant ſaid, Conſidering it concerned one ſo near the King as the Marquis of *Hamilton*, he thought it not fit that this Examinant ſhould himſelf break it to the King, leſt the King ſhould at firſt reject it; but it would be fitter for ſome other to do it, and therefore deſired his Opinion how to diſcover it. The Lord *Uchiltrie* adviſing a while, ſaid, He thought it beſt it were diſcovered to ſome of the Privy-Council; whereupon this Examinant ſaid, That he would not diſcover it to any *Scotſman*, but thought it beſt to reveal it to the Lord-Treaſurer, becauſe he thought the Lord Treaſurer was no way in the Plot.

According to which Reſolution the Lord *Uchiltrie* (as he after told this Examinant) did, according as was agreed between him and this Examinant, repair to the Lord-Treaſurer the ſame Night; but failing then to ſpeak with him, he went the next Morning, before this Examinant ſaw him, and returning, told this Examinant he had been with the Lord-Treaſurer, and in general imparted to him, that he had a Matter to diſcover which nearly concerned his Majeſty: And ſaid further, it was no *Engliſh* Buſineſs, but it was (to his own Shame he ſpake it) a *Scottiſh* Buſineſs, neither was it any Popiſh Plot: And the Lord-Treaſurer then refuſed to hear it, till he had Warrant from the King.

After the Lord *Uchiltrie* and this Examinant were appointed to wait on the King at *Greenwich*, whither this Examinant coming, found the Lord *Uchiltrie* within with his Majeſty, and then this Examinant coming in, made a full Relation to his Majeſty; who aſking this Examinant wherefore he had not himſelf told his Majeſty ſooner of it, this Examinant anſwered, That conſidering the nearneſs of the Marquis of *Hamilton* to his Majeſty, this Examinant was afraid leſt his Majeſty would have been impatient towards this Examinant; and beſought his Majeſty to forgive this Examinant, if he had thought he had done amiſs therein. His Majeſty thereupon referred this Examinant to the Lord-Treaſurer, and bid this Examinant put the Relation in Writing. Whereupon that Night this Examinant and the Lord *Uchiltrie* ſat up all Night, and this Examinant writing it firſt down, the Lord *Uchiltrie* wrote it Sheet after Sheet, out of this Examinant's Paper. And this Examinant brought the ſame written Relation to the Lord-Treaſurer, and read it unto him, and left it with him. And a Day or two after, this Examinant and the Lord *Uchiltrie* came again together to the Lord-Treaſurer; the Lord *Uchiltrie* having told him, that this Examinant had forgotten to ſign it; and then this Examinant ſigned it, ſaying, he would make it good with his Blood.

At which Time this Examinant remembers the Lord *Uchiltrie* told the Lord-Treaſurer, that this Examinant had more to ſay yet, which this Examinant did then alſo affirm; and the Cauſe wherefore he did affirm it, was, becauſe this Examinant had ſpoken with the Lord *Seaforth*, and had ſome Particulars from him, which he did not particularly tell to the Lord *Uchiltrie*, but affirmed to him in the general, that he could ſay no more; but a Day or two after, this Examinant went again to the Lord *Seaforth*, and ſpake with him, and then he told the ſame, firſt to the Lord *Uchiltrie*.

He further ſaith, That the Lord *Uchiltrie*, on *Sunday* Morning, told this Examinant, that he had been with the Lord-Treaſurer, and had told him of the Paſſages with the Lord *Seaforth*, and of the Marquis's Return, and that he conceived it might be dangerous at that time for his Majeſty. But this Examinant told him, he had done evil therein, for there was no ſuch ſuddenneſs to be feared: And on the

* See the Trial of *Rea* and *Ramſay* by Combat, in *Ruſhworth*'s Collections, Vol. II. page 113. which Method of Trial being now diſuſed, is not inſerted in this Work.

ſame

fame *Sunday* in the afternoon, this Examinant coming to his Majesty, and hearing from him, that he had been advertis'd of fomewhat importing matter of prefent danger; this Examinant faid, he had been with the Lord *Seaforth*, but had not the certainty of things, but pray'd his Majesty to give him leave to go again to the Lord *Seaforth*'s, and then he would learn all. And at the fame time his Majefty telling what danger had been fuggefted to him, now upon the Marquis's return; this Examinant protefted he knew nothing againft the perfon of the Marquis; but that he was, for aught this Examinant knew, as good a fubject as any the King had.

Copia Vera. My Lord Rea's *fecond Examination, the 21ft of* June 1631.

THE Examination of *Donald* Lord *Rea*, taken the 21ft of *June* 1631.

The faid Lord *Rea*, having deliberately heard read the Examination of *James* Lord *Uchiltrie*, taken the 20th of this inftant month, doth acknowledge the fame to be true in all points, fo far as the fame concerneth the knowledge, words or acts of this Examinant, faving the explanations hereafter following. He faith, that as touching the conference between the Lord *Uchiltrie* and this Examinant the 13th of *May* laft, where it is therein mentioned that this Examinant told him, that fince the time of their laft fpeech, he had learned more certainty than ever he had before; this Examinant did not fay, that he had learned more certainty fince their laft fpeech, for in truth he had not learned any thing within that time. But thinks he might fay, that he had learned more certainty fince he came to *England*, than he had before; and therefore takes it, that the Lord *Uchiltrie* did miftake in that point.

And whereas in the fame conference it is fet down, that this Examinant fhould fay that he was inform'd, that they meant to ftrike off the heads of all the principal men about the King; this Examinant faid, that he was inform'd they would ftrike off the heads of the *Spanifh* faction; and that he named the Lord-Treafurer, the two Bifhops, the Earl-Marfhal, the Earl of *Carlifle*, Sir *Francis Cottington*, the Lord *Monteith*, Sir *William Alexander*, and Sir *Thomas Hope*, and likewife Sir *Kenelm Digby*, and fpake of none other, neither in general nor particular; and faith, that he was fo inform'd touching the *Spanifh* faction by Mr. *Meldrum*, and *David Ramfay*; and touching the *Scots* by the Earl of *Seaforth*. And faith, that *Meldrum* and *David Ramfay* did name the aforefaid *Englifhmen* to be of the *Spanifh* faction. And whereas it is faid, that this Examinant defired the Lord *Uchiltrie* to acquaint his Majefty or the Lord-Treafurer with the matter; this Examinant did defire him to acquaint the Lord-Treafurer, but did not mention his Majefty, but that it fhould come by the Lord-Treafurer to his Majefty.

He confeffed, he faid, that fince his coming into *England*, he had fpoken with Sir *James Ramfay*, Sir *James Hamilton*, and Capt. *Douglas*, and gotten fomewhat out of every one of them; but did not fay he had fpoken with *Alexander Hamilton*, or gotten any thing out of him fince this Examinant's coming into *England*.

This Examinant denieth, that he either faid himfelf, or affirm'd its being faid by the Lord *Uchiltrie*, that he could fay fo much as the Marquis fhould not have the face to deny it; but faid, he could bring as honeft a man as this Examinant, that would tell to the Marquis's face more than this Examinant would do: and thus he meant by the Lord *Seaforth*.

He confeffed that he faid, Sir *James Ramfay* told him he had fifteen hundred men in readinefs, but would not bring them together, till the parties in *Scotland* were firft ready; and faith, Sir *James* told him as much, and that there were good officers, and the Earl of *Effex*, and the Archbifhop of *Canterbury* were fureties for fome of them; and other than this, he fpake not touching the 1500 men.

He faith, he was not acquainted with the lift of the Names delivered by the Lord *Uchiltrie* to the Lord-Treafurer, nor had any thing to do therein.

Copia vera. The fecond Examination of James *Lord* Uchiltrie, *taken the 24th of* June 1631.

THE faid Examinant confeffeth, that the underftanding which he had of the bufinefs, concerning the Marquis of *Hamilton*, whereof he hath been fo often examined, came to him from the Lord *Rea*.

He confeffeth further, that the paper of Names which he did deliver to the Lord-Treafurer, was made by this Examinant himfelf, and the Lord *Rea* was not privy to the making of it, or to the delivery thereof to the Lord-Treafurer, till after it was done.

He faith, that the caufe wherefore he did in that paper mention the Lord Marquis to be prime Agent, was, for that the Lord *Rea* had told him, the Lord Marquis's followers had faid, the intent of the Marquis's levies was to invade *Scotland*. Being told, that the Lord *Rea* hath been fo far from charging the Marquis, that he hath affirm'd before his Majefty, that for aught he knows, the Marquis is as good a fubject as any the King hath; he anfwereth, that in tendernefs and care of the King's fafety, and upon ground of the Lord *Rea*'s relation, for the Lord Marquis's followers, he have gone any thing too far, he trufteth his Majefty will impute it to his duty.

Being afked, why, in the aforefaid paper, he makes the Earl of *Melros*, the Earl of *Roxburgh*, and the Earl of *Buccleugh* to be plotters, faith, that the Lord *Rea* told him, the Lord *Seaforth* had affirm'd it to him, that the Earls of *Melros* and *Roxburgh* were acquainted with the particulars and fecrets of the bufinefs. And further faith, the Lord *Rea* had told him, he could not guefs who elfe fhould be in the plot, unlefs it were the Lord *Buccleugh*; of whom the Lord *Rea* faid, he heard him fpeak terrible and prefumptuous words againft the King, at his own table in *Holland*.

He faith, the Lord *Rea* did affirm to this Examinant, that he had the aforefaid report of the Earls of *Melros* and *Roxburgh* from the Lord *Seaforth*, before he, this Examinant, made or delivered the faid Paper to the Lord-Treafurer. The faid Examinant doth avow, that on the 13th of *May*, the Lord *Rea* had affirm'd to him, that fince their former fpeech, (which was the 6th or 7th of *May*) he had learned more certainty than ever he had before.

He confeffeth, that whereas in his former Examination, he faid, the Lord *Rea* told him, he was inform'd that they meant to ftrike off the heads of all the principal men about the King, he was miftaken in mentioning all, and did not well mark himfelf when he fo expreffed it; his purpofe being to have faid, they would ftrike off the heads of many; for fo, he takes it, was the fcope of the Lord *Rea*'s fpeech.

Being told that the Lord *Rea* denieth, that he fpake with Col. *Alexander Hamilton* fince his coming into *England*, he faith, it is poffible that this Examinant might miftake in adding that name to the reft, and therefore will not conteft about that. He doth avow, that in the prefence of the Lord *Rea*, before the Lord-Treafurer, this Examinant faid, the Lord *Rea* could fay fo much as the Marquis fhould not have the face to deny it; and what this Examinant faid, the Lord *Rea* being then prefent, and hearing it, did not gainfay.

He faith, the Lord *Rea* told him, Sir *James Ramfay* faid to him, that he had 1500 men in readinefs, and the firft time faid, upon an hour's warning. But at a fecond time, the Lord *Rea* fpoke of eight days warning; and further, that he would not bring them to *London* till their bufinefs was ready.

Being acquainted with what *John Macky*, fon to the Lord *Rea*, had confeffed to have been told him by this Examinant, he doth acknowledge it, and that he faid it to *John Macky*, after the Lord *Rea* and this Examinant had attended his Majefty about the fame bufinefs, but did not think his fpeech thereof to *John Macky* fhould have done any hurt to the bufinefs.

Copia vera. The third Examination of Donald *Lord* Rea, *taken the 24th of* June 1631.

HE faith, that the firft time that the Lord *Seaforth* had any fpeech with this Examinant, touching the Earls of *Melros* and *Roxburgh*, being privy to the particulars and fecrets of the Lord *Hamilton*'s bufinefs, was on *Monday* after the Marquis's coming out of *Scotland*, and not before.

He further faith, that the Lord *Uchiltrie* having fome fpeech with this Examinant, who might be like in *Scotland* to take arms, if the Marquis of *Hamilton* fhould take up arms; the faid Lord *Uchiltrie*, and not this Examinant, named the Lord *Buccleugh*: whereupon this Examinant told him, that at the fiege of the *Buffe*, this Examinant heard the Lord *Buccleugh* ufe fome words, whereby this Examinant took him to come male-content out of *England*.

The Tenor of his Majefty's Letter directed to the Lords of his Majefty's Council of Scotland.

Charles R.

"RIGHT trufty and right well-beloved Coufins and Counfellors, right
" trufty and well-beloved Coufins and Counfellors; and right trufty
" and well-beloved Counfellors, we greet you well. The Lord *Uchiltrie*
" having been examined before our Council here, touching fome infor-
" mations given by him, reflecting upon fome of the Nobility of that our
" Kingdom; we have been pleas'd to remit him thither, to be try'd ac-
" cording to the Laws thereof; having to that purpofe fent you herewith
" inclos'd fome depofitions under his own hand, and the authentick co-
" pies of others, whereof the principals we caufe to be referved here, be-
" caufe they likewife concern other perfons. Our pleafure is, that having
" given order for receiving and committing him to fafe cuftody, you caufe
" try and cenfure him according to our faid Laws, before what Judicature
" and Judges you fhall think fit and competent for that purpofe, and for
" your fo doing thefe fhall be fufficient Warrant. Given at our Honour
" of *Hampton-Court*, the 24th of *September* 1631."

After this, my Lord Advocate produced the lift of Names, or reprefentation written and given in by him to the Lord-Treafurer of *England*, upon the 16th of *May* 1631. together with the Lord *Uchiltrie*'s dittay, of the which lift or reprefentation and dittay aforefaid, the tenor followeth:

The tenor of the Lift.

Reprefentation for my Lord-Treafurer.

The Marquis of *Hamilton* is prime Agent.

Plotters.

The Earl of *Melros*.
The Earl of *Roxburgh*.
The Earl of *Buccleugh*.

Adherents to *Hamilton*, by new blood and affinity, and dependance.

The Earl of *Kinghorne*.
The Earl of *Abercorne*.
The Earl of *Glencairne*.
The Vifcount *Lauderdale*.
The Marquis of *Huntley*.
The Earl of *Wigton*.

By near Alliance by his two Sifters.

The Earl of *Eglington*.
The Vifcount *Drumlangrig*.

The Earl of *Melros* hath Alliance and Affinity.

The Earl of *Caffils* his Son-in-Law.
The Lord *Carnegie* his Son-in-Law.
The Lord *Lyndefay* his Grandchild by his Daughter.
The Lord *Boyd* his Grandchild by his Daughter.
The Lord *Ogilvie* his Son-in-Law.
His eldeft Son married to the Earl of *Mar*'s Daughter;

And fo Brother-in-Law to the Lord *Erfkyne*, now Keeper of his Majefty's two principal Caftles of *Striveling* and *Edinburgh*, and fo Commander of all almoft of his Majefty's Ordnance in *Scotland*.

The Earl of *Melros*'s fon, likewife Brother-in-Law to the Earl-Marfhal, and to the Earls of *Rothes* and *Kinghorne*

The Earl of *Melros*'s fecond Son, married to the Lord *Wanchton*'s Daughter.

The Earl of *Melros* himfelf Brother-in-Law to the Earl of *Somerfet*, and to the Lord *Balmerinoch*.

The Earl of *Roxburgh*,

Brother-in-Law to the Earl of *Perth*.
Father-in-Law to the Conftable of *Dundee*.
Father-in-Law to the Lord *Pitcairn*

And the faid Lord *Roxburgh* able to raife of his own friends and followers above 1000 Gentlemen in two days.

The Earl of *Buccleugh*.

The Earl of *Buccleugh*, Nephew to *Roxburgh*
The Earl of *Buccleugh*, Brother-in-Law to the Lord *Erfkyne*.
The Lord *Hayes*.
The Earl of *Winton*.
The Lord *Sempill*.
The Lord *Rofs*.

Apud Edinburgh Vigefimo nono Novembris 1631.

In prefence of the Bifhop of Dunblane, *my Lord of* Carnegie, *my Lord Juftice Clerk, and Juftice Depute*

The whilk day *James* Lord *Uchiltrie* being prefent before the Lords Examinators above-named; and the lift of Names before mentioned being

fhew'd

shew'd unto him, and he required to declare if he would recognize and acknowledge the same to be his own hand-writing; the said Lord *Uchiltrie*, after inspection and consideration thereof, declar'd that list of Names was written with his own hand, and delivered by him to the Lord-Treasurer of *England*; *sic subscribitur* J. Uchiltrie; *ad B. of* Dumblane, Carnegie, Geo. Elphinston, A. Colville.

The Tenor of the Lord Uchiltrie'*s Dittoy or Indictment.*

James Lord *Uchiltrie*,

YE are indicted and accused forasmekill as by divers Acts, Statutes and Constitutions of Parliament, made and published in the days of our sovereign Lord's most royal Progenitors; specially by the 43d Act of the second Parliament of King *James* I. of worthy memory, it is enacted, statute and ordained, That all Leasing-makers and tellers of them, whilk may engender discord betwixt the King and his People, wherever they may be gotten, shall be challenged by them that power has, and tyne life and goods to the King. And likewise by the 83d Act of the sixth Parliament of King *James* I. of eternal memory, bearing touching the article of Leasing-makers to the King's Grace, of his Barons, great Men and Lieges, and for punishment to be put to them; therefore it is thereby declared, that the King's Grace, with advice of his three Estates, ratifies and approves the Acts and Statutes made thereupon of before, and ordains the same to be put to due execution in all points; whilks Acts of Parliament, in the 205th Act of the 14th Parliament of our sovereign Lord's dearest Father King *James* the VI. of happy and never-dying memory, and with advice of his Highness's Estates in that Parliament ratify'd, approveh, and confirm'd, and ordain'd to be put in execution in all time thereafter following, as in the said Laws and Acts of Parliament, at length is contain'd. Notwithstanding whereof, it is of verity, that he the said *James* Lord *Uchiltrie*, having in the month of *May*, the year of God 1631, last past, heard by relation of *Donald* Lord *Rea*, that certain speeches, surmises and informations were made to him by *David Ramsay*, with the head of Mr. *Robert Meldrum*, and certain other persons beyond sea, in *Sweden*, *Pomerland* and *Holland* respectively; and by the said *David Ramsay* and certain other persons within the Kingdom of *England*, anent some plot and dangerous purpose intended against the sacred person of our gracious Lord and Sovereign, the King's most excellent Majesty, his gracious Queen, and their dearest son the Prince, and against the Land, by surprizing the King's Majesty's Houses and Castles of *Edinburgh*, *Striveling*, and *Dumbarton*, and for seizing of the Town of *Leith*. Ye not being content to retain yourself within the bounds of a faithful subject, by revealing of that, whereof ye had received information from the said Lord *Rea*, out of a malicious policy and design, tending to the sowing of discord and sedition betwixt his Majesty and his most loyal subjects, the Lord Marquis of *Hamilton*, the Earl of *Haddington*, the Earl of *Roxburgh*, and the Earl of *Buccleugh*; did at your first meeting with his Majesty, which was upon the 17th of *May* last past, signify to his Highness, that the business was a Treason intended against his Majesty; and that the party was the Marquis of *Hamilton*, as ye was inform'd. And to the effect his Majesty might be put in better assurance of the truth of your said speeches, ye upon the 16th of *May* preceding, delivered to the Lord-Treasurer of *England*, a List of Names, to represent to his Majesty, the strength of the said Marquis of *Hamilton*'s Party and adherents in *Scotland*. Whilk is all written with your own hand, and intitled, *Representation for my Lord-Treasurer*. Wherein ye name the Marquis of *Hamilton* to be the prime Agent, and names the Earl of *Melros*, now Earl of *Haddington*, the Earl of *Roxburgh*, and the Earl of *Buccleugh*, to be Plotters. Likewise upon *Sunday*, being the 22d of *May* last past, at which day the Marquis of *Hamilton* (having come post from *Scotland* in three days) was to present himself to his Majesty. And ye thinking that ye had possess'd his Majesty sufficiently with your malicious Leasings and Calumnies against the said Lord Marquis; and that his Majesty being so instigate and irritate against him, would follow your cruel and malicious Counsel; ye came to his Majesty about the end of his dinner, and most boldly and male-pertly spake to his Majesty these words, 'Sir, now ye know the 'business, but knows not the time, and therefore, Sir, either do or die.' By the whilk malicious Counsel (if God by his Grace had not rul'd and directed the heart of our gracious Sovereign to proceed in the business with greater wisdom, calmness and moderation, ye by your former wicked Counsel intended) ye thereby did what in you lay, to move and cause his Majesty, to put in practice some sudden and violent course, for subversion of the life and honour of the said Lord Marquis, his Majesty's most loyal subject. Like as all the present articles and passages in your proceedings, in the premises, were maliciously forged, invented and practised by yourself; without any warrant arising to you from the relation of the said Lord *Rea*'s; whilk is manifest by your own deposition, made in the presence of a number of the Council of *England*, deputed by his Majesty for your examination, upon the 20th and 24th of *June* last past: By the which ye have granted and confessed the premises laid to your charge to be of verity: and also does grant, that the paper of Names which ye did deliver to my Lord-Treasurer, as said is, was made by yourself. And that the Lord *Rea* was not privy to the making thereof, nor to the delivery of the same, to the said Lord-Treasurer. And siclike in your examination, ye being inquired for what cause, ye did name the said Lord Marquis to be prime agent, ye could assign no true reason, nor cause, by any warrant of the Lord *Rea* against the Marquis. But by the contrary, the said Lord *Rea* being examined upon the 21st of *June*, in presence of his Majesty's Council, declared that he knew nothing against the person of the Lord Marquis; but that the said Lord Marquis was as good a Subject as any the King's Majesty had. And likewise ye being ask'd by what warrant ye did call the Earls of *Melros*, *Roxburgh*, and *Buccleugh* to be Plotters; ye answered thereto, that the Lord *Rea* had told you, that the Lord *Seaforth* had affirm'd to him, that the Earls of *Melros* and *Roxburgh* were acquainted with the particulars and secrets of that business, declaring thereby that the Lord *Rea* had affirm'd that to you, before you gave in, and delivered your paper of representation to the Lord-Treasurer. And further, ye declar'd, that the Lord *Rea* had told you, that he could not guess who else should have been upon the plot, unless it were the Lord *Buccleugh*. Albeit the Lord *Rea* being examined in presence of his Majesty's Council upon the 24th of *June* last past, declar'd, that the first time the Lord *Seaforth* had any speech with him, anent the Earls of *Melros* and *Roxburgh*, and their being privy to the Marquis of *Hamilton*'s business, was upon the *Monday* after the Marquis of *Hamilton*'s coming out of *Scotland*, and not before: and the Marquis having come to Court from *Scotland* upon *Saturday* the 21st of *May*, and the representation given by you to the Lord-Treasurer, containing the list of the plotters and actors, being given in by you to the said Lord-Treasurer, upon the 16th of *May* before; ye could never truly affirm, that ye had named the said Earls to be plotters, upon pretence of any information received from my Lord *Rea*; who did not speak to you anent them, at the time of the giving of the said representation; but eight days thereafter, and such like. The said Lord *Rea* depon'd upon the said 24th of *June*, that ye, and not he, did name the Earl of *Buccleugh*, as one who would take arms in *Scotland* to assist the Marquis; by the whilk Leasings, Calumnies and slanderous Speeches, untruly plotted, devised and vented by you, against the said Marquis of *Hamilton*, the Earls of *Haddington*, *Roxburgh*, and *Buccleugh* in manner foresaid; all of them being his Majesty's faithful Councillors and loyal Subjects; ye have manifestly controverted the tenor of the said Laws, and Acts of Parliament, and incurr'd the pains and punishment mention'd therein, *viz.* the deserv'd punishment of death, which ought and should be execute upon you with all rigour, to the terror and example of others.

The Justice at command of a warrant and direction of the Lords of the secret Council, whereof the tenor follows, *Apud* Halyrudhouse, *Vicesimo quinto die mensis* Novembris 1631. The Lords of the secret Council, for some special cause, and considerations moving them, ordains and commands his Majesty's Justice, Justice-Clerk and their Deputes, to prorogat and continue the Dyet appointed for the Trial of *James* Lord *Uchiltrie*, until *Thursday* next, the 1st of *December* next to come: whereanent this extract of the Act shall be unto the said Justice, Justice-Clerk and their Deputes, *a Warrant extractum de libris Actorum secreti Concilii S. D. N. Regis, per me* Jacobum Prymrose, *Clericum ejusdem, sub meis signo & subscriptione manualibus, sic subscribitur* Jacobus Prymrose. Prorogates and continues the Trial of *James* Lord *Uchiltrie*, now impannell'd, to the Morn the 1st of *December* next to come, and ordain'd him to be return'd back to Ward, to be kept in sure firmance, in the mean time: the Jury or Persons of Assize summon'd to this day, are warn'd, *apud acta* to compear the said first day of *December* next to come: ilk person under the pain of six Marks. Whereupon the Advocate asked Instruments.

Curia Justiciaria S. D. N. Regis tent' in pretorio burgi de Edinburgh, *primo die mensis* Decembris, *Anno Dom. Millesimo, Sexcentesimo, Tricesimo primo, per Honorabiles & Discretos Viros, Magistros,* Alexander Colville *de* Blair, & Jacobum Robertoun, *Advocatum, Justiciarios deputatos nobilis & potentis Comitis* Willielmi *Comitis de* Stratherne & Monteith, *Dom.* Grahame, Killbryde, & Kynpont, *praesidis secreti Concilii & Justiciarii generalis dict. S. D. N. Regis, totius sui Regni* Scotiae, *ubilibet constitut. Sectis vocatis & Curia legitime affirmata.*

Intran'

JAMES Lord *Uchiltrie*, delated of the Crimes foresaids, contained in his Indictment preceding.

Pursuer.

Sir *Thomas Hope* of *Craighall*, Knight and Baronet; his Majesty's Advocate for his Highness's Entries.

Prolocutors in Defence.

Mr. *Robert Nairne*, Mr. *Alexander Pierson*, *Gilbert Neilson*, } Advocates.

The Prolocutors for the impannell'd, produc'd an Act of the Lords of secret Council; ordaining and commanding them to compear and assist him, by proponing of all lawful defence, competent to him on his Trial, and desired the same might be insert and remain on process, whereof the tenor follows. *Apud* Halyrudhouse *Vigesimo quinto die mensis* Novembris, 1631. Whereas *James* Lord *Uchiltrie* has made choice of Mr. *Robert Nairne*, Mr. *Alexander Pierson* and *Gilbert Neilson*, Advocates, to concur and join with him, for proponing of his lawful defences, competent to him against the Dittay, whereupon he is to be accus'd before his Majesty's Justice, upon the 1st of *December* next: therefore the Lords of secret Council ordains and commands the said three Advocates to confer and meet with the said Lord *Uchiltrie*, to receive his informations; to accompany and assist him at the Bar; and to do their duty and office in all and every thing lying to their charge, concerning the proponing of all lawful defences, competent to the said Lord in his Trial. Whereanent the extract of this Act shall be to them a Warrant *extractum de libris Actorum secreti Concilii S. D. N. Regis per me, Magistrum* Gilbertum Prymrose, *Clericum ejusdem, sub meis signo & subscriptione manualibus, sic subscribitur* M. Prymrose. After reading of the whilk Act of Council, the said Prolocutors protested, because the present matter of disputation *est res ardua*, anent Treason and Relations thereof, from party to party; that whatever the exigence of the cause requires from them, as proofs to speak herein, for clearing of the Nobleman impannelled, his innocence, and of the warrants of his information; that it is not with any thought of wronging, or tasking of any parties, Noblemen or others; but to do that whilk their duty, as Prolocutors craves of them to be done, being commanded hereto by the Lords of his Majesty's secret Council: and that the purpose and speeches that [illegible] by God's assistance be uttered and [illegible] by them in this matter, may be so accepted of my Lord Justice.

Thereafter the Indictment of the [illegible], being [illegible] judicially, and [illegible] of the Crimes therein contained; my Lord Advocate asked Instruments strument, of the reading thereof, and of the Acts of Parliament set down in the proposition of the said Indictment. And because the subsumption of the said Indictment is founded upon certain depositions made in *England*, in presence of five of his Majesty's Councillors, deputed by his Majesty to that effect; he therefore repeats the examinations of the Lord *Uchiltrie* produced yesterday in process, dated the 20th and 24th of *June* last; with the three Examinations of my Lord *Rea's*, whereof two are dated the 21st of *June*, and the third upon the 24th of *June*: And declared, that he used these depositions under the hands and subscriptions of the five Councillors of *England*, as authentick copies, whilk should make as good faith, as if the principal were produced.

It is alledged by Mr. *Alexander Pierson*, as Prolocutor for the Pannel, that it cannot, nor should not be proceeded against the Impanelled here in *Scotland*, but conform to the Laws and Statutes of *England*; the place of the Pannel his offence, (if any be) and not conform to the municipal Laws of *Scotland*. 'Quia de jure Judex originis vel domicilii non potest punire subditum delinquentem extra territorium, nisi secundum pœnam impositam a jure communi, vel secundum statuta Loci in quo deliquit non; autem secundum statuta ipsius loci originis, vel domicilii.' Julius Clarus, Quest. 85. Numb. quarto.

It is answered by my Lord Advocate, that the Alledgente is no ways relevant, except the Pannel will condescend to the relevance of the dittay; and of his own consent be content, that the same pass to the knowledge of an Assize. Next, it is answered by his Majesty's Advocates that he oppones his Majesty's Letter direct to the Council, bearing, that the Impannelled shall be tried according to the Laws of this Kingdom. And in the one place it shall be justified, that his Majesty's Letter shall be grounded upon the Civil and Common Law.

It is answered thereto by the Lord *Uchiltrie* and his Prolocutors; that the King's Majesty's Letter is, and must be understood, without prejudice, of the Pannel's lawful defences.

Item, That the alledged Crimes contained in the dittay are, or perchance may be, lawful in *England*, and yet criminal in *Scotland*; and it carries no reason that the Pannel should be punished here in *Scotland*, for any fact committed in *England*, not punishable by the Laws of *England*, where the Pannel is *tutus ratione Loci*.

Secundo, It is alledged by the Pannel, that the subsumption of the Indictment has no dependance upon the proposition thereof; because the particulars contained in the subsumption are no ways the Leasings mentioned in the said Acts of Parliament, whereupon the proposition is founded, especially seeing the Leasings mentioned in the said Acts, are Leasings tending to discord betwixt the King and his people; and the telling whereof is unlawful and prohibit. But the particulars of the Dittay or Indictment are no ways such. But by the contrary, the matter thereof being an heinous Treason against the King's Majesty and Estate; in favour of both, *propter publicam utilitatem*, it is incumbent to every subject that shall hear speeches of such matter, though the matter itself be a lie and untruth, whilk is alike to the hearer, neither does it belong to him, to judge or discern therein; it is incumbent, I say, to every subject incontinently to tell the same; the telling whereof tends not to discord between the King and his People; but to suppress and prevent the same, and the chief cause thereof, which is Treason; and the not telling and revealing whereof is punishable by the Law of all Nations, by our municipal Laws and Acts of Parliament; yea, by the same Acts, whereupon the dittay is founded, *viz. James* VI. Parliament 14. *cap.* 205. And therefore the telling thereof is no ways prohibited and punishable by the said Acts, neither are these particulars in the Indictment, the Leasings mentioned in the said Acts, whilk is *medium concludendi* in the dittay. And whilk last Act being the last in time, as it ratifies, so it explains the true sense of the former.

And further, it is alledged by *Gilbert Neilson*, Prolocutor for the Pannel, that not only by the foresaid Act, of the 14th Parliament of King *James* VI. whereupon the dittay is founded, is there a necessity laid upon the Impannelled, and all his Majesty's Lieges to reveal what they hear, concerning his Majesty's prejudice; but likewise by the 134th Act of *James* VI's 8th Parliament, it is specially statute, that whosoever hears any speeches to the harm or prejudice of the King's Majesty's Estate, shall with all diligence reveal the same to his Majesty, or to some other, the King's Majesty's Officers, that may make the same manifest to his Majesty, with this special addition, that in case the same be not done, the person concealer, and not teller or revealer, shall incur the like punishment, contained in the said Acts, set down against the principal Leasing-makers. And so the Impannelled was necessitate, upon no less pain than his life and estate, to reveal the same. It is answered by his Majesty's Advocate, That this preceding defence can elude no part of the dittay: because the first part thereof anent the lawfulness or necessity of revealing of Treason is granted in the Dittay or Indictment. And if the Pannel had contained himself within the duty of revealing, albeit the Plot and Treason revealed had been false, yet he would have deserved commendation and reward from his Master. But the Indictment is founded upon three particulars, to the whilk no answer is made, and whilks three particulars agrees and quadrates with the natural quality of the Leasings, contained in the Act of Parliament, whereupon the dittay is founded. Because they are such, as might have engendered discord betwixt his Majesty and his loyal subjects: in so far as it is qualified in the dittay, that the Impannelled having only had his relations from the Lord *Rea*, and whilk relations had no warrant against the Marquis of *Hamilton's* person, as author or actor of the Treason, nor against the three Noblemen as Plotters, but depended *ex auditu auditus, vel relatione relati ab altero*, that is, from *David Ramsay*, and Mr. *Robert Meldrum*, of whom neither of them did relate any thing that could prove against the Marquis; but simply upon the speeches and report of some, whom they call his followers, or upon their imagination, or possibly foolish and perverse wishes, that the Nobleman who was imployed for the levying of an army for aiding the King of *Sweden*, should employ his forces to the destruction of the King, his Queen, the Prince their eldest Son, and Kingdom. Yet the Impannelled, when [illegible] might have [illegible] expressed his loyal duty to his [illegible] by [illegible] the Lord *Rea* to his Majesty, [illegible] his own [illegible], did [illegible] appearance before his Majesty [illegible] uncertain report and relation [illegible] Treason, and the

party the Marquis of *Hamilton*. Next, the Pannel, by his representation all written with his own hand, and delivered to my Lord-Treasurer of *England*, to be shewn to his Majesty, he has expressed the Lord Marquis to be prime Agent; and the Earls of *Haddington*, *Roxburgh*, and *Buccleugh* to be plotters; and hath added to the number of twenty or thirty Noblemen, as adherents to them. And last, when his Majesty had received this positive information, and was possessed with appearance of the truth thereof; to add a spark to the fuel, the Motto was given, *Sir, now either do or die*; whilk words could not contain any other intention or event (if his Majesty had not been graciously and wisely disposed), but either to have used some violent course against the Marquis's person and life, or to commit him to prison, and to cause him to make answer as to Treason, *ex Vinculis*; whilk is the condition of Traytors, both by the Common Law and by the Act of Parliament, made by King *James* II. Parliament 12. *cap.* 49. whereby it is ordained, that persons slandered of Treason, shall be taken and remain in firmance, while they thole an Assize. And all thir proceedings are directly contrary to the Act of Parliament, whereupon the dittay is founded, especially seeing the Pannel, by his deposition made the 20th of *June*, *Articulo primo*, in relating the Lord *Rea's* first speeches, declared that the Lord *Rea* granted that he had no certain ground for the Treason alledged by him; and it is an heinous and odious fact, punishable by all laws, to turn relation into delation, and to be an author or adviser to a sovereign Prince, to begin at execution before Trial. And all the particular points of the dittay are clear, and evident by the deposition of the Impannelled, made upon the 20th and 24th days of *June*; whilk are the true copies of the original and authentick depositions, made in the presence of five of his Majesty's Council in *England*; like as the copies produced and read in presence of the Pannel, and his Prolocutors, are subscribed by the said five Councillors; and also are declared by his Majesty's Letter, directed to his Council the 24th of *September*, to be true copies of the said depositions; whereof the principals are retained by his Majesty, for the causes mentioned in the said Letter. And therefore ought to have full faith, as if the principals were produced; like as the Pannel by his Acts *de calumnia* will not refuse, but that the representation containing the list of the names was given in by him, without the privity of the Lord *Rea*, and also that he spake these words to his Majesty upon the *Sunday* after dinner, being the 22d of *May*; which was the self same day that the Marquis came from *Scotland* to *England*, and was to present himself to his Majesty, *viz.* the purpose is known, the time not known; *Sir, either do or die*, in respect whereof the alledgente ought to be repelled.

'Tis duplyed for the Pannel by his Prolocutors, as to the particulars contained in my Lord Advocate's answer, they cease to answer him now in the general, seeing they are upon the relevancy of the Dittay and Indictment, and shall answer every one, *singulatim*, as they lie in the Indictment, *suo loco*.

Tertio, It is alledged for the Pannel, that the Particulars contained in the Indictment are not Leasings, 'quoad referentem neque id genus referens mentitur, quoniam quantum in ipso est non fallit, sed fallitur, & quicquid falsitatis vel mendacii in relatis inest, id ad suos authores referendum, cap. Is autem 22 Quest. 2. & cap. 55. Beatus Paulus ibidem, ubi dicitur, non mentiri eum qui animum fallendi non habet quod est essentiale & formale mendacii, impostura scilicet & intentio fallendi.' And the telling and revealing of the whilks matters aforesaid, 'nullum habet in se delictum, sed est de natura boni,' being commanded, and therefore in the hearer and relater. 'presumitur omnis dolus abesse, quia parere necesse habet.' And specially in such a business as this, whilk so highly concerns the King's Majesty and Estate. Whereof there was so great appearance, by the relation made by the Lord *Rea*, whilk the Pannel craves may be read to the Judge.

It is answered by my Lord Advocate, that if the defence means of the Treason related by the Lord *Rea*, the Pannel cannot be quarrelled for it, nor for telling thereof, albeit it were a lye. But the Leasings and Calumnies assumed upon in the dittay, arises upon the contradiction, betwixt that which was related by the Lord *Rea*, and that whilk was spoken and affirmed positive to his Majesty. And where it is alledged, that 'mendacium est semper cum animo fallendi,' that is, 'in discrepantia inter intellectum & vocem ejusdem personæ;' where he thinks one thing, and speaks another, whilk is not our case. But *mendacium vel falsitas*, whereupon we dispute, is the discrepance and the contrariety betwixt the relation made by the Lord *Rea*, and that which is related by the Pannel: wherein the Pannel was obliged, as a faithful subject, to make a simple or true relation, 'sine Paraphrasi, vel Periphrasi, sine Interpretatione, vel Circumlocutione, & ut in Apographa vel exemplari committitur falsitas, si transcriptio differt ab exemplari, ita committitur falsitas ubi relatio positive refertur;' whilk is the Leasings, whereupon the dittay subsumes. And where it is desired that the Lord *Rea's* relation may be produced and read to the Judge, if it be meant of that relation whilk is subscribed by the five Councillors of *England*; and if the Pannel will acknowledge it, to make faith as the principal, together with the remanent depositions of the Pannel, and the Lord *Rea*, whilk are all subscribed by the said five Councillors, and already produced and read to the Judge; the Pannel shall receive satisfaction of his desires, otherways not.

It is duplyed for the Pannel, that the foresaid alledgeance is to answer that part of the dittay, bearing the heads thereof to be forged and vented by the Pannel.

Quarto, It is alledged by the Pannel, that as to the subsumption of the dittay, bearing, that all the articles and passages of proceeding therein mentioned, were maliciously invented and practised by the Pannel, whilk is qualifyed by the Pannel's own deposition and alledged confession against himself, and by the Pannel's deposition freeing the Lord *Rea*, and the Lord *Rea's* deposition freeing himself thereof; the qualification inforces not the Pannel in the particulars to be a Leasing-maker, and to have forged lyes.

First, For the Pannel's own deposition, it inforces the just contrary, to wit, that the Lord *Rea* was the Pannel's informer in all. As for the Lord *Rea's* deposition against the Pannel, proported in the dittay, that inforces not forging of lyes against the Pannel, neither can the Lord *Rea's* deposition have any force against him, first, because the Lord *Rea* is party, and the Pannel [illegible] witness [illegible] for the King, and whose deposition [illegible] be respected

ſpected againſt the teſtimony, made againſt himſelf, for the King's Majeſty: and in effect is but a denial, whilk can neither liberate himſelf, nor weaken the Pannel's depoſition. *Et omnibus in re propria dicendi teſtimonii facultatem jura ſubmoverunt, lege* 10. *Cod. de teſtibus. Item,* The Lord *Rea*'s depoſition made by him, not being ſworn, and ſo is null of the Law; *Quia teſtis injuratus examinatus non probat nec fidem faciat, Lege Juris-Jurandi, nona Cod. de teſtibus & Lege teſtium* xviii. *Cod. eodem.*

Item, The Lord *Rea*'s depoſition not made in the preſence of the Pannel, and ſo *non valeat authentica, ſed etſi, Cod de teſtibus. Item,* Although the Lord *Rea* were not party, he is but *teſtis ſingularis & nihil probat. Item,* The Lord *Rea*'s depoſitions produced cannot be reſpected, becauſe they are not the principal ſubſcribed by my Lord *Rea*, but relations, and doubtleſs from the Council. *Et in criminalibus aliorum Judicum relationibus credere non oportet, Lege ſingul.* xiv. *Cod. de accuſationibus & inſcriptionibus.*

It is declared by the Lord *Uchiltrie* himſelf, now upon Pannel, that the depoſitions whilk he made in *England*, and ſubſcribed with his hand, are true in themſelves, as he there depon'd, according to the relations and grounds of Information, which he received from the Lord *Rea*. The reconciliations which are ingroſſed in the ſeveral depoſitions, being allowed and admitted for reconciling of any apparent contrariety, without prejudice of what explanation of the ſame depoſitions he may juſtly make further, he declares, that the alledged copies of the Pannel's own depoſitions, under the hand of the five Councillors, ſo far as his memory can ſerve him, are not different in the ſubſtance of them, from the original. But that there is no more in his depoſitions, nor that whilk the ſubſcribed copies contain, that he cannot ſay. And this his Lordſhip does according to his memory, and in reverence of his Majeſty's Letter, and Noblemen's hands thereat.

My Lord Advocate takes Inſtruments of the Impannell'd's declaration in that part, whereby he grants that the copies of his depoſitions made by him, under the hand of the five Councillors, is not different in ſubſtance, according to the Pannel's memory.

Thereafter, my Lord *Uchiltrie* and his Prolocutors craved that the Lord *Rea*'s relation made upon the 18th of *May*, whilk is under the hand of the five Councillors, might be read to him, becauſe he minds to found exceptions thereupon.

To the whilk, it is anſwered by his Majeſty's Advocate, that he cannot be compelled to produce the ſaid relation, in reſpect no part of the qualification of the Dittay is founded thereupon. And yet according to his former anſwer, ſays, if the Pannel will acknowledge the ſame, as it is under the hands of the five Councillors, to make as great faith as the principal, he is content, that the ſaid relation be read; of the whilk relation the tenor follows.

The true Relation of ſuch paſſages, as I Donald *Lord* Rea *have heard or learned, which may concern my moſt dread Sovereign, or his Eſtate, beyond Seas and elſe-where,* as I will be ready to take my Oath upon, and ſeal with my blood againſt all opponents. *Written this 18th of* May, 1631.

IN the month of *April*, 1630, or thereby, at my coming from *Stockholm*, I found Colonel *Alexander Hamilton*, Brother to the Earl of *Haddington*, Sir *James Hamilton*, Son to the ſaid Earl, Sir *James Hamilton* of *Reidhall*, Nephew to the ſaid Earl, and one *Hamilton* the Lord of . . . . . . ; who were all Officers under the King of *Sweden* then. But before my coming there, they had all caſhier'd themſelves, not having ſerved one year.

At this time the Laird of *Benſho, Lyndeſay*, my Lieutenant-Colonel, being Bed-fellow and Comrade to Sir *James Hamilton* Son to the Earl of *Haddington*, keeping a chamber in *James Muckleane*'s a *Scotſman*'s Houſe in *Stockholm*, *Lyndeſay* did inform me, that the reaſon why the *Hamiltons* had caſhier'd themſelves, was becauſe their Chief, the Marquis of *Hamilton*, was to be a Soldier, and they would follow his fortunes. I aſked *Lyndeſay* who had told him ſo much; he told me, Sir *James Hamilton* of *Priestfield*, *Haddington*'s Son: and *Lyndeſay* told me withal, that all theſe *Hamiltons*, and Sir *John Hamilton*, another Son of *Haddington*'s, had denuded themſelves of their Fortunes and Eſtates, ſome of them to their friends, but the Earl of *Haddington*'s children to their father.

Moreover, *Lyndeſay* told me, that Sir *James Hamilton*, *Haddington*'s ſecond Son, had told him, that Sir *James Spence*, now Lord *Spence*, had directed Mr. *Robert Meldrum* with Letters into *England*, and that thereafter they did expect *David Ramſay* with the bead Couſin to the Lord *Spence*, as Ambaſſador from the Marquis of *Hamilton*. And all the *Hamiltons* did expect *David Ramſay*'s coming.

Alſo *Lyndeſay* did inform me, that Sir *James Hamilton* did deſire him to join with them, and that they would give him a Regiment; which he did accept, and did deſire my conſent, which I did yield unto.

Alſo ten or twelve days after we did hear from *Denmark*, that there was an Ambaſſador coming from *England*, who proves to be *David Ramſay*; who did give himſelf out, all the way as he came, to be an Ambaſſador: which to prove, he did ſtand in competition with his Majeſty, our dread Sovereign's extraordinary Ambaſſador Sir *Thomas Roe*; both the ſaid Sir *Thomas* and *David Ramſay* encountring in the Town of . . . . in *Denmark*: yet *David Ramſay* would never do ſo much as viſit the other Ambaſſador. Upon which overſight I did queſtion *David Ramſay*, whoſe anſwer was, he did not deſire to be ſeen of any man that would diſcover him; affirming to his Couſin Sir *Robert Anſtruther* (as *David Ramſay* told me) that no honeſt man could live at home. *David Ramſay*, Colonel *Alexander Hamilton*, and Sir *James Hamilton*, attending their diſpatch from the King of *Sweden* at *Elſmeby*, were forc'd to reſide with me in my ſhip, for at this time we were all on ſhip-board.

And one night drinking ſome healths, amongſt the reſt, the Marquis's health coming by courſe, I aſk'd Col *Alexander Hamilton*, the Marquis's Chriſtian name; he anſwer'd me, *James, by the Grace of God*, Sir *James* added, *King of Scotland*: therefore his health paſſed under that name, till I did take exceptions, and did deſire them to alter their title; Sir *James Hamilton* anſwered *nolens, volens*, it ſhould be ſo, and did laugh. I did deſire them to drink it more covertly, thus, *To the happy event of all Good Intentions*, ſo *David Ramſay* ſaid it ſhould be ſo.

That night, after the two Colonels *Hamiltons* went to bed, *David Ramſay* and I being alone on the hatches above, *David Ramſay* and I drinking and ſmoaking a Pipe of Tobacco, told me many abuſes in the Court of *England*; laying the whole blame upon the Lord-Treaſurer. He told me, that the Marquis had ſent him with a Challenge to the Treaſurer, and that *Popery* and *Arminianiſm* had ever come the moſt part from the Biſhops; and that there was nothing look'd for but deſolation and change of Religion, and that the poor ſoul the King was blinded to his ruin; and that he had been plain with the King, till he did give him no ear; therefore he ſaid, he had retir'd himſelf from thence, ſince no honeſt man could live there, and with many ſuch diſcourſes he laboured to poſſeſs me. My anſwer was, The Lord amend thoſe evils, and no remedy but patience. By God, *Donald*, (ſaid he) I will uſe your own phraſe, We muſt help God to amend it. He told me, he had brought as much Gold with him, as would maintain him at the rate of ſix pound a-day for three years, and did aſſure me that before that time would expire, that God would raiſe up ſome men to defend his Church, and liberate honeſt men from ſlavery. Withal he told me, that his Majeſty at his parting with him, told him, that he would do with him as King *Henry* IV. ſaid to *Colvil*, I will think on thee in abſence as preſent.

Thereafter I did deſire one favour of him, that he would tell me if the Marquis of *Hamilton* would come over; he ſaid, he would tell me to-morrow. The next night after, I did renew my former queſtion of the Marquis's coming over, and he ſaid he would. I aſk'd him what content my Lord Marquis had at Home? He ſaid none, for the King had forced him to marry a Wife, and to acknowledge her, who he ſaid was a very beaſt.

I aſk'd him of what Religion my Lord Marquis was? He ſaid, a good Proteſtant, and before it were long, he would let the world ſee his aim was the defence of his Religion. I told him, it did avail us little to make the Goſpel a fair paſſage in *Germany*, if we loſt it at home. He ſaid, there were many honeſt men in our land, and that the Marquis would uſe his army to protect them, which was his only aim. I deſir'd him to go no further on with me; for I would not deſire more truſt of it, but that I would ſpend my blood in my Lord Marquis's quarrel. Well, my Lord, I will go no further, for my Maſter's ſecret no Man ſhall get.

The third night, on land in an Iſle, he told me, that *Alexander Hamilton* and Sir *James* were to go for *England*, and he to *Holland*, yet if I had any thing to do in *England*, that he would be willing to do me [illegible] I told him I had a mind to ſeek the reverſion of *Orkney* from the King my Maſter, if the Marquis would mediate with my Maſter; for it were good for my Lord to have a friend in that place for his ends. He ſaid, By God it was to be thought upon; and he did deſire me to give him leave to think upon it that night. On the morrow, he and *Alexander Hamilton* did deſire me to write a general Letter to the Marquis, with the two Colonel *Hamiltons*, with great aſſurances of true friendſhip from their Maſter, if I would continue conſtant in reſolution; I did give them my Letter, and ſo we parted.

In the month of *July*, a day or two after the taking of *Stetin*, I did encounter Mr *Meldrum* who came from *England*: after Salutations, I did aſk him what news? He anſwered me, matters are worſe and worſe; the King giveth greater way to *Papiſts* and *Arminians* than before; that *Cottingham* was gone to beg peace with *Spain*, that *Pembroke* was dead; that the Marquis govern'd all, and was made Keeper of *Windſor*, and was made Knight of the Garter, and was to be Admiral of *England*. He did aſk me where his Couſin *David Ramſay* was: I told him he was gone for *Holland*; he did aſk me, what he had done: I did anſwer, that all was ended to his mind, and that *Alexander Hamilton* was to get Powder, Arms, and Munition with him from *Sweden*, to the Marquis. At theſe news, he did throw his Cap to the ground, and cut a caper, calling aloud, Good news! good news! I am a happy man! I am happy and made for ever! I thank God my five years pains is not for nothing; good my Lord *Rea*, is this true? Yes, ſaid I, for I have one double of the Contract, I am ingaged in the buſineſs to *David Ramſay*, and *Alexander Hamilton* and Sir *James Hamilton*, and by Writ to my Lord *Hamilton*. O my Lord, (ſaith he) that was the work of God and not man, to inſpire your Lordſhip to go with us!

At that time I caſt *Lyndeſay* looſe, to find more of *Meldrum*; who told *Lyndſay* that ſix thouſand trained Soldiers would do the turn with their own faction in the Country.

The next day at Colonel *Leſlie*'s Tent, I encountered *Meldrum*, whom I did call out, and he told me that King *Charles* was good and created for nothing, but for deſolations and undoing of Kingdoms, Religion, and People. There was no way but to immurate him within a Wall or Dungeon for ever. I aſked what way we might do that? He ſaid the way was eaſy: firſt, after the men were liſted in *Scotland*, that they might take one month's time to learn to handle their arms at *Leith*, without any ſuſpicion: then they might ſeize on the Caſtles of *Edinburgh*, *Sterling*, and *Dumbarton* in one night, and upon *Berwick*; and having the Caſtle of *Edinburgh*, the Town durſt not ſtir; then to fortify *Leith*; thereafter into *England* per force. I anſwered, the Plot was good if it held.

He told me further, that he was writing a declaration of the Juſtneſs of the Marquis's quarrel, with the tyrannical uſing and ſuffering of the Church under King *James* in his laſt days, and now worſe groaning under his Son; with the *Hamiltons* clear title to the Crown. I allowed of all. But I did demand who I thought would take our parts; he ſaid, he did know nine of the beſt Earls in *Scotland* that would live and die with us. As alſo that the body of *England* was with us, and ſome of the Nobility for evil will of the Treaſurer. The next day there came news of the birth of the Prince; I did aſk *Meldrum* if that would cool the Marquis's intentions: he ſighed and ſaid, not if the King and Queen of *Bohemia* will give their Daughter to the Marquis, as they had promiſed. Is that true, ſaid I? He anſwered, I ſhould ſee ere it were long. That night I did deſire *Lyndeſay* to drink with *Meldrum*, which he did, and *Harry Muſchamp* an *Engliſh* Gentleman was with them. *Lyndeſay* told me on the morrow, he did think *Meldrum* to be the worſt Secretary in the world, for he did reveal this laſt night all he did think. I do not remember the night's diſcourſe; but do remit to *Muſchamp*'s relation.

A week after, I did ſpeak with *Meldrum* again at *Leſlie*'s tent; ſo he did deſire me to walk forth, and told me he had been with Secretary *Sadeler*, to whom

whom *Meldrum* did deliver a private packet of Letters, and did require answer. But the Secretary told him, that the King of *Sweden* would write none, till he heard from the Marquis of his last Letters, sent with *David Ramsay*.

Meldrum went further with the Secretary of *Sweden*, telling him, that it was greatly for the advantage of the King of *Sweden*, whose ambition was without limits, that the Marquis did raise war in *Britain*, for if the King of *Sweden* had a mind to take *Denmark*, the King of *Britain* should not be able to help his Uncle. The Secretary of *Sweden* did answer, that we care not for, neither do we fear your King; for he that would not help his own Sister, will never help his Uncle.

I did ask *Meldrum*, what they did intend to do with the Prince and Queen of *Britain*? He answered, the Child should be cast in with his Father, and the Queen sent home to her Mother to be put in a Monastery.

I did ask him, what charge he would have in those employments? He said, he should be Secretary of State, and have a Horse-Troop.

Meldrum did shew me also, that all who would not take our part, of *Scotsmen* in *Scotland*, should be put in the *Bass*, or some other prison, till all were ours; and that the Marquis would take pledges of all who in *Scotland* did lie by as neutrals at the first.

At my coming to *Holland* in *March* last, *David Ramsay* did leave word at *Amsterdam*, when I did come, to send him word; which I did: he came from the *Hague* to *Amsterdam*, and stayed with me eight days, where he did deliver me a Letter from the Marquis only of compliment and thanks. He told me all went right with the Marquis; that he had gotten from his Majesty 10,000*l.* in *England*, and the Wine-Customs of *Scotland* for fifteen years; which the Marquis would sell, and that all things went on without any obstacle; and that the only stay was for want of Arms and Munition, and especially Powder; and desired me to put on hard for this, with the *Swedish* Ambassador, which I did. Thereafter he told me, he had evil news to tell me, that the Marquis's wife was brought to bed of a child.

I did ask him, where our forces should meet; he said upon the Sea, and thereafter land in *Scotland* or *England*, he would tell me no more. but that for my business of *Orkney*, I might have it better cheap than to pay the duties of it, and he told me, that when I should meet with the Marquis, he would infuse in me that which he durst not; since he would have the Marquis to take the thanks to himself. And withal he did desire me, that I should not tell the Marquis what had past between him and me.

I did ask him, what part of *England* we should best land at? He said at *Yarmouth* or *Harwich*, or thereby. He told me that *England* had made a peace with *Spain* very prejudicial to *Holland*, and that the Treasurer and such of the *Spanish* faction, as *Carlisle*, and *Cottington*, and *Kenelm Digby*, had mussled the King to bar the *Hollander* from the fishing; which he said might fall out happily for them, and he did desire me to assist them at the Prince of *Orange*'s hand, as a special service to the Marquis, to make the States contribute with the Marquis: and I did speak to the Prince of *Orange*, and his Excellency told me, that he would do his best therein.

He told me, that *Spain* and *France* were striving who should first drink up *England* in their ambition; but he hoped the Marquis should prevent them both. He did ask my advice, whether it were best to cross the Seas once, or to go on bravely? I answered, delays were not good, which he did subscribe to; and so we concluded, and I came for *England*.

At my coming to *England*, my Lord *Hamilton* did give me many thanks, assuring me, that he would not want me; and that I should have what conditions I would desire, for he said, that should not separate us.

I did desire his Lordship to go on with me really, if he meant to have my service, he should have it without conditions; he did answer, My Lord, I will not want you, for I have written to the King of *Sweden*, with *[illegible]* and *Meldrum*, that I will detain you with me, and assure your Lordship, that he that will hazard with me now in this business, it shall be a tye to me and my posterity, to hazard my fortune and estate with him and his. The same word the next day he sent to me, with Sir *James Hamilton*, the Earl of *Heddington*'s son.

The said Sir *James Hamilton* and I being together, I did much commend a suit of apparel which Sir *James* had, his answer was, I have them on, pay them who will. I have taken them up, it may be a Merchant of *London* will pay for them, ere it be long, my Lord, take one also on [illegible]'s head.

The first day, my Lord Marquis went down to *Greenwich* in a barge, accompany'd with Sir *[illegible] Ramsay*, Sir *James Hamilton*, Sir *Robert Balfour*, Capt. *Douglas* and (I do think) *Lieutenant Lisle*, the King our master having gone before; the discourse was moved, if they were to make an insurrection, where would they begin? The Marquis answered, he would march to *London* directly, and one of them (I think Capt. *Douglas*) said, that [illegible] house in *London* should make them up for ever.

That day my Lord Marquis told me, he would sell the Wine Customs, for he expected no more from *Scotland*.

Capt. *Douglas* told me, that they would have from the King an hundred barrels of Powder, and that they would make shift for arms.

Sir *James Ramsay* told me, on *Sunday* last at *Greenwich*, that he had 1500 men in readiness on a week or less advertisement, and that his stay only was here, till he heard the men in *Scotland* were ready, and that his rendezvous would be at *Norwich*, and meet the rest. Sir *James Hamilton* told me that the *English* rendezvous should ship at *Harwich*, for he said, the Devil have his part of the river of *Thames*, he did not like it.

The Earl of *Roxburgh* told me, that he and others the Marquis's friends, were at first against the Marquis's course, but now since they saw his Lordship so far engaged, and that he only aim'd at the glory of God, that he and all others his friends would put to their helping hand.

On *Thursday* last, the Earl of *Roxburgh* told me, that the Marquis would listen to his relation, and said, that he would assure me, my Lord Marquis thinks himself for ever bound to me, and so do all his friends, for his Lordship's cause; and I will assure your Lordship he trusts you, and that you never took a more [illegible] and real friend by the hand.

My Lord *Roxburgh*, Sir *James Ramsay*, and Capt. *Douglas* questioned me, what was the reason, that I had taken on Sir *Pierce Crosby* since the Marquis had cast him off? This day, severally, I told them, I was forced, in [illegible] and [illegible], to [illegible] to the King of *Sweden*, to that I did take on Sir *Pierce Crosby*, to send him thither with *Irish* and *English*, and that myself was minded with all the *Scots* that I could get, to follow the Marquis's fortunes; the which answer severally given, gave them all content.

In witness of the truth of these, I have sign'd it with my hand, day and year aforesaid.

Sic subscribitur, D. Rea.

After reading of the whilk relation judicially, the said Lord *Uchiltrie* declared, that so far as his memory serves him, there is no difference betwixt the foresaid copy of relation, subscrib'd by the five Councillors, and the principal, or original, set down and subscrib'd by the said *Donald* Lord *Rea*: upon the making of the whilk declaration, his Majesty's Advocate ask'd instruments.

Thereafter his Majesty's Advocate answering to the former alledgeances proponed by the Pannel, and to the first part thereof, he opponed the Pannel's own depositions, made upon the 20th and 24th of *June*, subscribed by the five Councillors; and whilk are granted by the Pannel to be true copies, together with the representation subscrib'd and written with the Pannel's own hand, whilk verifies the first and last points of the particulars concerning the Pannel's positive affirmation of the Treason. And that the Marquis was prime Agent thereof, together with the speeches spoken to his Majesty, upon the *Sunday* after dinner; and as to the third particular point of the Dittay, anent the Earls of *Haddington*, *Roxburgh*, and *Buccleugh*, who are called Plotters; that is verified by the relations made by the Lord *Rea* the 18th of *May*, acknowledg'd also by the Pannel, and by the Lord *Rea*'s depositions, whilks are used conjunctly, for verifying the second particular point of the Judgment, anent the three Noblemen who are call'd Plotters, the one thereof, *viz.* the relation to prove the negative part of the Dittay, and that the Pannel had no warrant from the Lord *Rea*: and for verifying the affirmative, that the Lord *Rea* disclaimed the same uses, the said Lord *Rea*'s depositions. And where it is alledged, that the Dittay, so far as it is founded upon the Lord *Rea*'s deposition, is not relevant against the Pannel, because he is the Pannel's party, and because he was not sworn, and not in presence of parties, *quod est testis singularis*, and not subscribed by him; it is answered, first, That the negative point *per se* is sufficient to infer the relevancy of the Dittay in this point; that he gave them up as Plotters, without any warrant of the relation from the Lord *Rea*. whilk is clear, by conferring the list of representation, given in by the Pannel (wherein they are called Plotters), with the said Lord *Rea*'s relation. Whereby it is evident that the representation, given in upon the 16th of *May*, could have no warrant of the relation, whilk in the Pannel's depositions is affirmed to have begun upon the 13th of *May*, and closed the 18th of *May*, and deliver'd to the Lord-Treasurer to be given in to his Majesty. Within the whilk relation there is not a word of the said three Earls; neither can the Pannel pretend ignorance hereof, in respect he in his own deposition grants and confesseth, that the Lord-Treasurer, to whom they were remitted by his Majesty, desired to give in the relation in writing, conform to the whilk the Pannel and the Lord *Rea* went together and consumed the whole night in drawing the said relation; whilk night was the night or evening of the said 17th of *May*, whereupon first they appeared before his Majesty. And the Pannel having given in the representation of the prime Agent and the Plotters upon the 16th day preceding, he could not have omitted such a substantial point of the relation, which so nearly touch'd the Marquis and the three Noblemen aforesaid, and the Pannel's own exoneration. Like as the Pannel himself with his own hand wrote up and drew off the said Lord *Rea*'s Papers the said relation of the 18th of *May*: So that the Pannel can never affirm, that he had any Warrant from the said relation for branding the Marquis as prime Agent, and the said three Noblemen as Plotters. And as to the Arguments made against the Lord *Rea*'s deposition;

First, the same is not used *per se*, but jointly with the other, *Et juncta [illegible] faciunt fidem*. Next the Lord *Rea* is not the Pannel his party, *sed est [illegible] & mandator quem tenebatur [illegible]*, otherways he would have been himself culpable of Treason, or, a delator of Treason against the said Noblemen, *[illegible]*, by Act of Parliament, made by King *James* VI. *Par.* 11. *Cap.* 42. Next, *Nulla necessitas jurisjurandi quia non [illegible] a reo nuncupatus.* And the singularity cannot be objected, because he used him *tanquam [illegible]*, to warrant his declaration; and for present he could not be, if the Lord *Rea* had been examined *tanquam testis*, as the Pannel alledges: and as to the authenticknefs of the Copy of the Relation, it is approven by the Pannel, and he cannot be heard to object against the authenticknefs thereof, nor of the other Copies; because they are subscribed by the said five Councillors, and have the Warrant of his Majesty's missive Letter directed to the Council: which the Pannel for reverence of his Majesty's Letter, and of the Councillors subscribers of the said Copies, has acknowledged as true. And therefore cannot be heard to object against the remanent, whilk has the like solemnity of his Majesty's Letter, and consequently the fourth Alledgeance ought to be repelled.

Quarto, It is alledged for the Pannel by his Prolocutors, That as to the particulars of his Dittay, the Pannel purges every one of them in manner following; *viz.* The first particular point is not relevant, because that the Pannel at his first meeting with his Majesty upon the 17th of *May* did signify to his Majesty, that the business was a Treason against his Majesty, and that the Party was the Marquis of *Hamilton*, as he was informed. This Article enforces not against the Pannel, that he is a Leasing-maker and [illegible], but clearly frees him thereof, bearing *as he was informed*. Whilk Article being the [illegible] and Substance of the whole Dittay, having the aforesaid Clause (as he was informed) annex'd thereto, it forces of necessity the same Clause to all the particulars of the Dittay comprehended [illegible] Generals, *[illegible] semper specialia generalibus insunt.* And that the Pannel [illegible] information, it is clear by the Pannel's Depositions upon the 20 and 24 Days of *June*, and by the Lord *Rea*'s Deposition the [illegible] of *June*, acknowledging the Pannel's Examination to be true in all Points, in so far as the same concerns the Knowledge, Words and Acts of the Lord *Rea*, and by the Relations made by the Lord *Rea* and subscribed by him, and other Relations made by the said Lord *Rea* to the Pannel by Word, as the Pannel's own Deposition bears. Neither was it ever

heard

heard or practis'd, that any Subject being neceſſitated by the Law to reveal what may concern the King's Majeſty or the State, and revealing the ſame with his informer therein, and conſtantly abiding thereat, and willing to maintain the ſame upon any Torture or Trial whatſomever; that the Revealer, upon the Party's denial, ſhould be call'd in queſtion of his Life, as the Deviſer and Forger, or the ſame to work any ways againſt the Revealer, and which if it ſhould now take place, and begin to be a preparative againſt the Pannel; it were to give way and occaſion to all treaſonable Exploits, and that ſecurely, becauſe none would or durſt reveal the ſame.

Next, as for the Liſt of Names of the principal Agent and Plotters repreſented to the Lord-Treaſurer the 16th of *May*, affirmed to be forged and invented by the Pannel himſelf without any Warrant from my Lord *Rea*, conform to the Pannel's depoſition upon the 20th and 24th days of *June* laſt, none of the Pannel's depoſitions foreſaid, to the whilk the Dittay remits, bear any ſuch Confeſſion or Forging by the Pannel; but bears expreſsly the Lord *Rea*'s relation to him in both the Pannel's depoſitions, which is ſufficient for an informer.

It is aſked by the Pannel, That whereas it is alledged by my Lord Advocate, that the Pannel could never aſcribe any true Cauſe or Knowledge in the Liſt or Repreſentation where the Lord Marquis is named prime Agent, and the ſaid Earls of *Haddington*, *Roxburgh*, and *Buccleugh*, Plotters; becauſe the Lord Advocate affirms, that the relation was given in upon the 18th day, and the Liſt preſented to the Treaſurer the 16th day; and ſo the Pannel could have no juſt reaſon why theſe contained in the Liſt, were not contain'd in the relation, which was poſterior. The Pannel affirms, that howſoever the Liſt was given in before, the reaſon thereof is thus: The Lord Advocate making mention of his relation, diſtinguiſhes not betwixt a relation by Word, and another by Writ; but ſo it is, that my Lord *Rea* made relation to the Pannel upon the 13th of *May* of the whole things contain'd in the Relation upon the 18th of *May*, as appears evidently by the Pannel's 1ſt and 2d Depoſitions, and upon the 14th and 15th days my Lord *Rea* renewed the diſcourſe concerning my Lord *Seaforth*, and explains himſelf in theſe particulars concerning the Earls of *Haddington* and *Roxburgh*, anent their being upon the Secret and Counſel of the Marquis's courſes; That it was repreſented upon the 14th and 15th days, the Lord *Rea* and the Pannel being both at *Greenwich*, return'd upon *Monday* morning, being the 16th day, to *London*; at which time the Pannel went unto the Lord-Treaſurer, and there fell in diſcourſe with the Treaſurer on the Buſineſs concerning the Marquis's Power in *Scotland*, and Friendſhip with the Pannel, and to ſhew his Lordſhip he would let him know was very great; and ſo came forward to the Pannel's own Houſe, and wrote the Repreſentation, and delivered the ſame to the Lord-Treaſurer, which was done upon the 16th day, being *Monday*. And where my Lord Advocate alledges, that there could be no ground for this repreſentation before the giving in thereof from my Lord *Rea*'s written relation, becauſe the repreſentation preceded it in time, and the Plotters were not nam'd in the relation, whilk therefore followed upon the 18th of *May*, anſwers the verbal relations concerning the Plotters made by the Lord *Rea* to the Pannel preceded the ſcriptural relations given in to the Treaſurer; yea and the repreſentation both, becauſe done upon the 14th and 15th days of *May*, the repreſentation being upon the 16th, and the written relation upon the 18th. Neither was it needful to the Lord *Rea* to make that relation in this paper, which he had made to the Pannel before by word, like as there are ſundry other things in the Pannel's depoſitions, whilk are not ſet down in that written relation. Firſt, becauſe in all the written relation, no mention is made of my Lord *Seaforth*, or any thing proceeding from him; if of nothing from him, why then of the Grounds of the Pannel's repreſentation, whilk was had from my Lord of *Seaforth*?

The Juſtice continues all farther diſputation and reaſoning in this matter (by reaſon of the lateneſs of the Night) to the Morn the 2d of this Month of *December*, and ordains the Pannel to be returned to Ward, to remain therein in the mean time; the Perſons alſo warn'd *apud Acta* to the morn, all Perſons under the pain of a thouſand Marks.

Curia Juſticiaria S. D. N. Regis tent' in prætorio burgi de Edinburgh, *ſecundo die menſis* Decembris, *Anno Dom. Milleſimo, Sexценteſimo, Triceſimo primo, per Honorabiles & Diſcretos Viros, Magiſtros,* Alexandrum Colville *de* Blair, *&* Jacobum Robertoun, *Advocatum, Juſticiarios deputatos nobilis & potentis Comitis Willielmi Comitis de* Stratherne, *&* Monteith, *Dom.* Grahame, Kilbryde, *&* Kynpont, *præſidis ſecreti Concilii & Juſticiarii generalis dict. S. D. N. Regis, totius ſui Regni* Scotiæ, *ubilibet conſtitut. Sectis vocatis & Curia legitime affirmata.*

Intran'

JAMES Lord *Uchiltrie*, delated of the Crimes foreſaids, contained in his Dittay.

Purſuer.

Sir *Thomas Hope* of *Craighall*, Knight and Baronet; his Majeſty's Advocate for his Highneſs's Entries.

Prolocutors in Defence.

Mr. *Robert Nairne*,
Mr. *Alexander Pierſon*, } Advocates.
Gilbert Neilſon,

The ſaid *James* Lord *Uchiltrie* by himſelf repeats the former firſt alledgeance, word by word, as it ſtands, and eikis thereto, that he can no ways be in *mala fide*: That the Grounds of his repreſentation preceded not his written repreſentation *hoc Argumento*, as it is alledged, becauſe the Lord *Rea* had omitted in his relation to make mention thereof; whereas my Lord *Rea*'s facts cannot make the Pannel guilty ſimply; neither can his omiſſions take away the ſtrength of the Pannel's Arguments of his innocency: For it was the Pannel's part to follow him, and not to lead him; to reveal aſſertions, and not to indite aſſertions to him. Neither was the Pannel under any juſt cauſe of fear that his omiſſion could endanger him in the point; becauſe he was conſcious to himſelf, that my Lord *Rea* had told him the grounds of his repreſentation of befor., *viz.* upon the 14th and 15th days of *May*, by verbal relations thereof upon the ſaid days. The Pannel likewiſe knew that there was a ſecond relation wrote of ſundry other particulars to be made by my Lord *Rea* ſubſequent; among the whilk he knew the Grounds of his preceding verbal relations of his repreſentation was to be juſtified and cleared. So by theſe reaſons the Lord *Rea*'s omiſſion of the grounds of the Pannel's repreſentation out of his ſcriptural relation, *eo tempore*, can give no juſt ground to invalid or infringe the truth of the Pannel's aſſertion. That my Lord *Rea* by verbal relation preceding both the repreſentation and that written relation, had told him, that the Earls of *Haddington* and *Roxburgh* were upon the Council and ſecret of the buſineſs informed againſt the Lord Marquis. The ſame laſt Argument holds good likewiſe for my Lord *Buccleugh*; and as to the repreſentation in general, the Pannel declares, That it was written and given in upon a Diſcourſe of my Lord Treaſurer's inquiry for the Friendſhip of the Marquis in *Scotland* by Blood or Intereſt; whereby conjecture might be made of his power ſuppoſitive, if his Friends had joined to him. And this is clear by the very Writ itſelf, in naming it a repreſentation, and not an information, accuſation, nor relation. The general ſtrain of the Writ likewiſe evidences, that there was no intent by that Writ to reflect in any thing concerning the Lord Marquis or thoſe three Noblemen. Becauſe the repreſentation containing one ſide and a half of paper, that whilk concerns theſe Noblemen originally will ſcarce take up two long lines. Whereby it is manifeſt, that the intent of the Pannel was more to illuſtrate other things, *viz.* The alliance and intereſt in blood of the Noblemen to theſe firſt four, than any intent of either delating or inſerting any crime or fact againſt theſe firſt four; but to diſtinguiſh by way of narration betwixt the one and the other. And altho' this be ſaid, the Pannel atteſts, that the mentioning of theſe Noblemen ſucceeding the firſt four, be taken in no evil part, for he atteſts no meaning to that effect, whilk the Pannel thinks Chriſtian Charity will not preſume; his Wife's Son, his Children's Brother, the prop of his providence under God, and of his Wife and Children, the Earl of *Caſſils* being one; and the Marquis of *Huntley* his Chief by his Mother, his good Dame, Brother's Son, who ſaved the Pannel's life, and for whom the Pannel has ventur'd his life, or any of his; can it be preſumed that the Impannelled would have intended malice to that Maſs, wherein theſe two helped to make up the conſtruction? Neither doth it appear by any intent, that any thing was meant by the repreſentation, but an explanation of Noblemen's power in *Scotland*. Neither let this be thought any new invention, or new explanation; becauſe it is mentioned before that alledged by my Lord Advocate in the Dittay, and acknowledged thereby; neither can it be preſumed, that theſe words, prime Agent and Plotters, can import an information of any thing, becauſe all direct affirmations muſt be enunciation, and muſt have *ſuum vinculum* to join the Subject and the Attribute together. Which *Vinculum* and connection of it want no enunciation; if no enunciation, no affirmation, nor lye. But ſo it is, the Words prime Agent have no *Vinculum*, nor the word Plotters ſimply has no *Vinculum* betwixt them as Attributes, and the perſons named as the Subject, and therefore no enunciation, nor affirmation, nor lye. And where my Lord Advocate in his Dittay affirms, that it is manifeſt by the Pannel's own depoſition, the truth of the Dittay; and in the diſpute yeſterday, produces a particular, that the Pannel ſhould have deponed, that the Lord *Rea* ſaid, that he had no certainty of the buſineſs; this can no ways fortify the aſſumption of the Dittay. Becauſe the Pannel's depoſition ſays not that the Lord *Rea* had certainty, but whether he had certainty or no, the words whilk the Pannel alledges was told to him by the Lord *Rea*; for the Pannel's depoſition depends not upon a *ſcientia certa*, but *relatio certa*, that he ſpake it to the Pannel as he has deponed. As to the third Article of the Dittay, anent the Pannel's proceeding and ſpeeches to his Majeſty the 23d of *May*, to-wit, *Sir, ye know the buſineſs, but know not the time*; *Sir, either do, or die*; this Article enforces not upon the Pannel lying to his Majeſty. For the Lord *Rea*, and the Pannel upon his information, both had acquainted his Majeſty with the buſineſs, ſo that the Pannel might truly ſay, *Sir, ye know the buſineſs*; and it is as true, that the Pannel knew not the time. As to the words *do or die*, that is a uſual phraſe of ſpeech, and imports, *Sir, ſee to your ſafety*, till theſe informations had been clear'd, and is of itſelf a faithful advice to his Majeſty, and not a malicious Counſel; and advice for to prevent the King's Majeſty his harm, and not to draw harm upon any other: like as the words themſelves inforces not againſt the Pannel, as the Dittay bears; but does very well admit a harmleſs ſenſe, and ſhould be interpret to the beſt meaning the words may admit. *Quia de jure etiam in dubiis & obſcuris quod minimum & benignius ſequitur. Lege nona & 56 de Regulis juris; & in ambiguis orationibus maxima ſententia ſpectanda eſt ejus qui eas protulet. Lege 96. ibidem; & quoties idem ſermo duas ſententias exprimit, ea potiſſimum accipienda eſt, quæ rei gerendæ aptior eſt, dabit autem operam exprimi reus dicta verba at cui licito*; to-wit, the revealing of purpoſes, he heard againſt the King and State. *Denique in pœnalibus cauſis ſemper benignius interpretandum eſt.* And therefore the Pannel's ſpeaking and inſiſting with the King's Majeſty to ſee to his own ſafety, ſhould be referred to its own cauſe; to-wit, the Pannel's moſt bounden duty and tender love to the King's Majeſty, his welfare, and to the State of the Kingdom, fearing their faith, upon that relation that had been made to him. And alſo fearing his own faith, if that he ſhould have been found any ways remiſs or ſlack in not inſiſting with his Majeſty to prevent thoſe evils and treaſonable plots, ſo often related and repeated to him; and whilk the Pannel then feared to have been Treaſon, and to have come beyond Sea. And ſhould not be attributed, as the Dittay bears, to any malicious Counſel, or Purpoſe of the Pannel, for inſtigating, or ſtirring up of his Majeſty, to any ſudden and violent courſe againſt the Marquis's life and honour; as the Pannel atteſted before God, to have been his true meaning. Like as he in his Examination in *June*, upon the 21ſt thereof, depones, that upon *Sunday* Morning, whilk was that day he adviſed the King's Majeſty with theſe former words, was, that he ſhould go to *London* for more ſafety, and that the Pannel had no other end of ſpeaking of the words foreſaid.

Item, The words *do or die*, can be no Leaſing, becauſe they are not words of affirmation, but of counſel or advice.

As to the Paper of Names, whilk the Dittay affirms; the Pannel has confeſſed to be made by himſelf, and that the Lord *Rea* was not privy to the

the making thereof nor delivery of the ſame to the Lord-Treaſurer; it is anſwered, theſe words made by yourſelf, is written with your own hand, ſo purported to be by the Dittay itſelf, in that article anent the liſt of names delivered to the Treaſurer. To the writing of the whilk paper with Pen and Ink, and to the inſtant delivery thereof, by the Pannel to the ſaid Lord-Treaſurer, the Lord *Rea* was not privy, he not being preſent with the Pannel at that time; but does no ways enforce, that the names and matter of that written paper was forged and deviſed by the Pannel. But by the contrary, the Pannel by this depoſition, made the 20th of *June*, whilk bears, that after the Lord *Rea* had revealed to him the particulars, he deſired the Pannel to acquaint his Majeſty, or the Lord-Treaſurer therewith; leaving to the Pannel his own free-will, whether he ſhould acquaint him therewith by word or writ. *Et hic maxime ſpectanda eſt ſententia proferentis*, who is no ways contrary to himſelf in his depoſitions; but whilks both ſubſiſts in their own true ſenſe.

As to the Article bearing the Pannel in his Examination, being inquired for what cauſe he did name the Lord Marquis to be prime Agent; and that the Pannel affirmed, that he could aſſign no true reaſon nor warrant from the Lord *Rea*: it is anſwered, that the Pannel is not obliged to give any true cauſe. But that the Lord *Rea*'s relation to him *qualis qualis* is a ſufficient Warrant.

Secundo, The Pannel's depoſition upon the 24th of *June* bears the contrary of the ſaid Article, and aſſigns the cauſe to be, that the Lord *Rea* had told him, that the Lord Marquis's followers had ſaid, the intent of the Marquis's Levies was to invade *Scotland* or *England*. As alſo the Pannel's Examination upon the 20th of *June* purports, that upon the 13th of *May*, the Lord *Rea* came to the Pannel's chamber, and there putting the Pannel in mind of their former ſpeeches, told the Pannel that the purpoſe of the Marquis of *Hamilton*'s Levies, as divers of his Commanders and Followers had inform'd him, was, that either they ſhould not go out of *England* or *Scotland*, or if they did, they ſhould return to *England* or *Scotland*, and ſurprize the King's Houſes in *Scotland*, *viz.* the Caſtles of *Edinburgh*, *Striveling* and *Dumbarton*, and fortify themſelves in *Leith*, under the pretence of training, and ſhould take *Berwick*, and ſo march forward into *England*: and that the intention ſo to do, was, as the Lord *Rea* ſaid, that he was ſo informed, and as the depoſition in itſelf bears.

Tertio, The Lord *Rea*'s written relations of divers perſons diſcourſes to the ſame purpoſe, of the whilk he was informed by themſelves, whilks written relations, although they be written on the 18th of *May* laſt, yet are of matters and purpoſes that paſſed long before, and related of before to the Pannel by word, by the ſaid Lord *Rea*.

Quarto, The Lord *Rea* at his firſt coming to his Majeſty in this buſineſs, in the Pannel's hearing, being aſked of the King's Majeſty, why he had not told his Majeſty ſooner of it; the ſaid Lord *Rea* anſwered, becauſe it concerned ſo near the Marquis of *Hamilton*, who was ſo near to his Majeſty; he was afraid to communicate the ſame to his Majeſty immediately, as the ſaid Lord *Rea*'s depoſition taken upon the 21ſt of *June* purports.

Item, The Lord *Rea*'s depoſition made upon the 21ſt of *June*, wherein he depones, that he ſaid he ſhould bring as honeſt a man as himſelf, that would tell to the Lord Marquis's face more nor the Lord *Rea* would do; ſo all that the Pannel ſpake herein, was by Information, and ſo therein is no Forger, nor maker of Leaſings.

Item, The Pannel's depoſition, taken upon the 20th of *June*, bearing that the Pannel told the Lord-Treaſurer, That the Lord *Rea* told him, he had yet more, and would ſay ſo much, as the Lord Marquis would not have a face to deny it; whilk the Lord *Rea* then preſent affirmed, in ſo much as the Lord-Treaſurer ſaid, then is the buſineſs at an end, there needs no more writing. And this Article before repeated, the Pannel affirms, that the Lord-Treaſurer of *England* heard theſe words, and did affirm the ſame before the King's Majeſty and Council of *England*, upon the peril of the Pannel's head.

Item, As to the Article bearing the Lord *Rea*'s declaration upon the 21ſt of *June*, that he knows nothing againſt the perſon of the Lord Marquis, but that the Marquis was as good a Subject as any the King had: it is anſwered thereto by the Pannel, that his depoſition and repreſentation depends not upon the Lord *Rea*'s knowledge, but upon his relation made to the Pannel. And that declaration of the Lord *Rea*'s takes not away the relation made by him to the Pannel, and doth not infer making and forging of Leaſings in the Pannel without warrant from him; this ſpecially being conſidered, for weakening and infringing of the Lord *Rea*'s oppoſitions to the Pannel's depoſitions, that my Lord *Rea* having ſaid theſe words in preſence of the Treaſurer of *England*, and juſtified by the Lord-Treaſurer of *England*, in preſence of his Majeſty and Council of *England*, that the Lord *Rea* would ſay ſo much, as the Marquis ſhould not have the face to deny it; and now he ſays that he knows nothing anent the Marquis's perſon: whilk are contradictory to himſelf, and renders himſelf not ſufficient to improve the Pannel's depoſitions.

Item, Here the Pannel, in this place, repeats the objections of the nullities, made againſt the Lord *Rea*'s depoſitions, ſo far as the ſame may be prejudicial to the Pannel.

Item, As to the Article, bearing that the Pannel being aſk'd, by what warrant, he call'd the three Earls Plotters; and that he anſwer'd that the Lord *Rea* had told him, that the Lord *Seaforth* had affirm'd to him, that the Earls of *Melros* and *Roxburgh* were acquainted with the particulars and ſecrets of that buſineſs; declaring therewith, that the Lord *Rea* had affirm'd the ſame to him, before he gave in the paper of repreſentation to my Lord-Treaſurer. Albeit the Lord *Rea*, by his depoſition the 24th of *June*, declar'd, that the firſt time the Lord *Seaforth* had ſpeech with him, anent the ſaid two Earls, and their being privy to the Marquis's buſineſs, was upon the *Monday* after the Marquis's coming out of *Scotland*, and not before, and ſo after the repreſentation given in to the Treaſurer upon the 18th of *May*, containing the names of the Plotters and Actors; at whilk time the Pannel could not truly affirm any information from my Lord *Rea* to the whilk it is anſwer'd by the Pannel, that he, by his depoſition made the 24th of *June*, has declar'd, that all the underſtanding the Pannel had in the buſineſs, came to him from the Lord *Rea*, alſo by his depoſition the 20th of *June*.

Item, The Lord *Rea*'s granting of the ſpeech himſelf, anent the two Earls, makes preſumption againſt the ſaid Lord *Rea*, likewiſe for the time, *Quia dicta facta preſupponunt & trahunt ſe cum ſuis circumſtantiis*: neither is it probable nor ordinary, that there ſhould be that ſagacity of ſpirit in the Pannel, as to preſs what the Lord *Rea* ſhould make to him ſo long before, *Quod non præſumitur, ſed præſumptio, pro eo eſt, quod maxime eſt, ſecundum naturam toto; titulo de preſumptionibus*. And ſo this article enforces not againſt the Pannel, that he is maker and forger, becauſe the Lord *Rea* denies not ſimply, but the time of the Pannel's depoſition thereanent, whilk is no Leaſing.

Item, The Pannel in his Examination upon the 20th of *June*, in the courſe and order of the depoſitions thereof, whilk is the order of time, before the article anent the repreſentation of the liſt of names to the Lord-Treaſurer; he depones, that the Lord *Rea* had told him, that he had ſpoken with the Lord *Seaforth*, and had underſtood that from him; whilk general has no other meaning but that whilk is particulariz'd, by the ſaid Lord *Rea*'s Examination upon the 24th of *June*; in that article thereof, bearing that the Lord *Rea* did affirm to the Pannel, that he heard the aforeſaid report of the two Earls, before the Pannel made or deliver'd the paper of repreſentation.

Item, The Lord *Rea*'s depoſition upon the 24th of *June*, bears not the Lord *Rea* to deny, that he did affirm to the Pannel, that he heard the report of the ſaid two Earls from the Lord *Seaforth*, before the Pannel made or deliver'd the paper of repreſentation to the Treaſurer. But purports, that the firſt time that the Lord *Seaforth* had any ſpeech with the Lord *Rea*, touching the two Earls, their being privy to the particulars and ſecrets of the Lord *Hamilton*'s buſineſs, was upon *Monday* after the Marquis's coming from *Scotland*. And ſo that the Lord *Seaforth* had not ſpoken with the Lord *Rea* thereanent at that time; whilk is nothing to the Pannel, whether the Lord *Seaforth* had ſpoken with the Lord *Rea* or not. But denies not the foreſaid report of the two Earls made by the Lord *Rea* to the Pannel, whilk the Lord *Rea* did then affirm, that he had the ſame by information of the Lord *Seaforth*; neither is the Pannel obliged to make good the Lord *Rea*'s warrant herein, that the Lord *Rea* had the ſame by information of the Lord *Seaforth*, but the queſtion is, if the Pannel heard the ſame from the Lord *Rea*, before the giving in of the repreſentation to the Treaſurer. Whilk the Pannel affirms and abides at, conform to his depoſitions, made upon the 20th and 24th of *June*, as ſaid is.

Item, The Pannel here alſo repeats all the objections againſt the Lord *Rea*'s depoſitions, *ut ſupra*.

Item, Anent the Article, bearing, the Lord *Rea* to have told the Pannel, that he could not gueſs who elſe ſhould have been in the plot, unleſs it were the Lord *Buccleugh*; and that the Lord *Rea*, who by his depoſition upon the 24th of *June* depones, that the Pannel, and not he, did name the Earl of *Buccleugh*, as one would take arms in *Scotland* to aſſiſt the Marquis: It is anſwered thereto, *ut ſupra*, that the Pannel by his depoſition has declared, that all the underſtanding he had in the buſineſs, came to him from the Lord *Rea*, as the Pannel's Examination bears, and whilk he abides at as moſt true.

Item, The Pannel's depoſition upon the 24th of *June*, bearing the Lord *Rea* told him, anent the Earl of *Buccleugh*, is not ſimply, but *cum cauſa*, bearing the Lord *Rea*'s reaſon, wherefore he named him: and whilk reaſon in ſubſtance is granted by the Lord *Rea*, although with ſome diverſity of words, at the leaſt not denied in his Examination upon the 24th of *June*. And therefore, the ſaid Lord *Rea*'s depoſition affirming the reaſon, but denying the naming the ſaid Lord *Buccleugh*, ought not to be credited in his denial; but the Lord *Rea*'s affirming of the reaſon, inforces upon him the naming of the ſaid Earl. *Quia ratio confeſſa dicti præponderat & præſumit contra proferentem.*

Item, The Lord *Rea*'s ſpeeches to the Pannel, anent the Lord *Buccleugh*, though conjectural, neceſſitate the Pannel to the repreſentation, and revealing of the ſame to his Majeſty; eſpecially ſeeing the Lord *Rea* ſtrengtheneth the ſame with reaſon wherefore he ſo ſpake, to wit, that he heard the Lord *Buccleugh* ſpeak terrible and preſumptuous words againſt the King's Majeſty, at his own table in *Holland*; as the Pannel's depoſition upon the 24th of *June* purports, and whilk is granted by the Lord *Rea* himſelf in ſubſtance, at the leaſt not denied.

Item, The Pannel repeats here again all his objections againſt the Lord *Rea*'s depoſitions; and alledges that it was never heard nor practis'd, that a ſubject being neceſſitate by the Law, to reveal what may concern the King or State, and revealing the ſame with his informer therein, and conſtantly abiding thereat, and willing to maintain the ſame by any trial or torture, that the revealer, upon the party's denial, ſhould be called in queſtion of his life, or the ſame any ways work againſt the revealer. And whilk if it ſhould now take place, and begin a preparative againſt the Pannel, the ſame were to give way and occaſion to all treaſonable exploits; and that ſecurely, becauſe none would or durſt reveal the ſame.

And further, where it is affirm'd by the Dittay, that in the liſt preſented by the Pannel to the Lord Treaſurer, there is deſign'd the Earls of *Haddington*, *Roxburgh* and *Buccleugh* to be Plotters; the Pannel had ground to make the relation, no ways affirming any thing poſitive; becauſe in the Pannel's depoſition made the 24th of *June*, being examined and aſked why in the aforeſaid paper, he makes the ſaid Earls plotters;

It is anſwered in the depoſition, that the Lord *Rea* had told the Pannel, he could not gueſs who elſe ſhould be in the Plot, unleſs it were the Earl of *Buccleugh*; whilk word Plot, having had relation to the Earl's buſineſs, muſt alſo have relation to the other two Earls, ſeeing they were ſpoken of all at one time.

It is anſwered by his Majeſty's Advocate, firſt, to the firſt Article of the fifth exception, anent the purging of the Pannel's ſpeech to his Majeſty, upon the 17th of *May*. By this word that is ſubjoin'd, as the Pannel is inform'd, whilk the proponer for the Pannel will have to be repeated in all the ſubſequent paſſages concerning the buſineſs; firſt, that this word, *as he is inform'd*, cannot purge him, becauſe he received no poſitive information from the Lord *Rea* againſt the Marquis, nor no warrant to call him Party, Prime Agent, and to affirm to his Majeſty the buſineſs was known; to whilk laſt he ſubjoins his Counſel, very dangerous for the life and eſtate of the Marquis; whilks three are conjoin'd to infer againſt the Pannel, an exceeding of the relation made to him by the Lord *Rea*, and the exceeding of it, with the Peril of the Nobleman,

man, his life and estate; there being neither word nor passage in the Lord *Rea*'s written relation, whilk may either warrant their speeches, or infer them by consequence. And in matters of this high strain, as of Treason, no illation by consequence is permissable, but upon the peril of him that infers. For in all the written relation there is not a direct word spoken against the Marquis, neither by *David Ramsay*, nor by Mr. *Robert Meldrum*; but allanerly some mad and frantick speeches utter'd by *Meldrum* upon his own imagination, or wish to have it so, for disturbance of the estate, by expressing the manner how such an enterprize, according to his foolish opinion, might be performed; but not one word or syllable, that *Meldrum* heard it from the Lord Marquis, or from any who declar'd they heard the Marquis speak it. And as to *David Ramsay*, the worst word that is in his relation, is anent the Marquis's miscontentment, and all the Marquis's aim was to use his Levy for the protection of Religion, whilk aim and intention the Lord *Rea*, after his coming to *England*, clearly understood by the Lord Marquis himself; who employ'd him to be a Colonel in his company, and gave him this assurance, that he that would hazard with him in that glorious business for assistance of the King of *Sweden*, should make use of him, with the hazard of his fortune and estate: and none of these passages will quadrate with those speeches spoken by the Pannel to his Majesty; That it was a Treason, an odious Treason, and the Lord Marquis Party, as the Pannel was inform'd, and that it was the filthiest Treason that ever was intended, and that the Pannel was sorry that any *Scotsman* should have fallen into it, it being a shame to the whole Nation: whilk is a positive affirmation, not as the Pannel was informed, but as he himself did infer, upon the relation made to him by my Lord *Rea*, who would give the Pannel no assurance he had any certain ground, whilk is manifest by the Pannel's deposition upon the 20th of *June* last. And as to the relation, albeit it avow'd with these words (as he is inform'd) could give the Pannel no warrant to express these positive speeches to his Majesty, upon the 17th of *May*; so far less to the other of prime Agent, and known business, with the subsequent counsel. *First*, Because they are positively spoken without adjection, (as he is inform'd), and where the proponer for the Pannel urges that these words *as he is informed*, must be repeal'd in all subsequent passages; that has some probability, *in unico continuo actu, vel unica scriptura*. But here the Acts are diverse, the days diverse, the expression of writing diverse, the list being upon the 16th of *May*; the speech with the King, as he is inform'd, upon the 17th of *May*; and the speech of the known business with the Council being upon the 22d of *May*: and these three taken *conjunctim* evidently charges the Pannel with the excess of his duty. For he did all his duty that was required of him, as a faithful subject, when upon the 15th of *May*, whilk preceded all the expressions, he came to the Lord-Treasurer and told him, that he had a business to reveal concerning his Majesty, and whilk (as he said) concern'd the Marquis of *Hamilton*'s actions, and that he had the same of the Lord *Rea*; after the whilk, he had no necessity as a loyal subject, to go further. And yet he goes on to the expression of all these speeches, and adds thereto his dangerous Counsel to his Majesty; whilk can have no respect to the Lord *Rea*'s relation, nor to the Pannels' duty in revealing of it. And where the Pannel would purge his giving in of the lists first, because it is not an enunciative speech, *qua caret vinculo*, this is contrary to the representation, bearing the *vinculum* is the Marquis of *Hamilton* as prime Agent; and this word *is* must be repeated in the subsequent word Plotters; the sentence being, the Earls of *Melros*, *Roxburgh*, and *Buccleugh* Plotters. Whilk is a sentence that has a clear signification, affirming the attribute Plotters upon them three, in as evident and clear signification, as the clause subsequent, whilk names the whole Noblemen adherent by blood.

And where it is alledg'd, that albeit the Pannel named the Lord Marquis prime Agent, he did allanerly upon intention to distinguish the Marquis, and the other three Earls from these of their Adherents in blood; and urges that this intention should be charitably expounded.

It is answered, that *crimen vel delictum non potest purgari bona intentione*. And if the points contained in the Dittay, whereupon the Pannel is accused, be in their own nature criminal, they cannot be purged by a good intention, nor yet by a protestation adjected, the time of the doing it. But the intention, with the fact and deed, are both alike judged odious, and punishable. *Et nunquam præsumitur bona intentio nisi probetur, ad eluendum crimen*; as it is instanced, by *Jul. Clarus de injuriis, tu mentiris salva reverentia*. This instance being adduced, whilk by the opinions of all the Doctors cannot excuse the committers of the injury, and much less in this Dittay; whilk contains *Injuriam capitalem*, striking upon the life and fame of the Noblemen. *Nam qui defamat, jugulat plusquam maledicto quam in manu injuria est qui sic incidiatur, ut nota et iamad posteros transeat, quod est sæpe eundem occidere:* and charity can have no place here, without the offence of Justice, whilk craves the due punishment from the offender. And where it is alledged, that the Pannel had no warrant, both to name the Marquis prime Agent, and the Earls Plotters, by a verbal relation from the Lord *Rea*, there can be no respect had to a verbal relation, except it were proven to the Judge, especially in a matter *tantæ atrocitatis* Neither can the Pannel alledge to a verbal relation, to colour his behaviour therewith, because the Pannel affirms, that thir verbal relations were made upon the 14th and 15th of *May*, whilk preceded the relation exhibited in Writ, upon the 18th of *May*. In the whilk relation there is not a syllable of the three Earls as Plotters, albeit in the relation there is mention made of the speeches spoken by the Earl of *Roxburgh* to the Lord *Rea*. And the Pannel having given in his list upon the 16th of *May*, and knowing the peril of adding or paring to that, whilk was related to him in a matter of this importance; whilk should have been as tenderly handled, as the life, honour and safety of our gracious Sovereign upon the one side, and the care to eschew the branding of Noblemen with the odious aspersion of his Treason, did require of him, on the other part: he cannot pretend a colour of excuse by the omission of the name of the said three Earls in the relation given in upon the 18th of *May*, thereafter, specially seeing the relation in effect was his own deed, because he brought the Lord *Rea* to his Majesty, to make the relation. And the Lord *Rea*, in his relation to his Majesty spake never a word of the three Earls; nor yet the Pannel in his relation to the King's Majesty, and the Lord-Treasurer, spake not a syllable thereof: whilk is clear by the Pannel's depositions upon the 20th of *June*, which bears his relation, made in presence of the Councillors his Examinators; wherein is no word of the three Earls. And likewise by the Examination of the Lord *Rea* upon the 21st of *June*, which is such like; and when his Majesty had remitted the Pannel and the Lord *Rea* to the Treasurer, who directed them to draw up the Lord *Rea*'s relation in Writ; the Pannel confesseth, that he and the Lord *Rea* went home, and sat up all night, and that the Pannel, after the Lord *Rea* had put the relation in writ, did write the same over with his own hand, out of the Lord *Rea*'s papers. And yet not a word of the relation of the three Earls; which would not have been omitted, if it had been truly done. And where the Pannel pretends, that the omission thereof was in respect that the relation contains allanerly that which was related by the Lord *Rea* upon the 13th of *May*; but not that which was upon 14th and 15th of *May*; which was learned of the Lord *Seaforth*; that alledgeance hath no warrant of the relation, nor yet any appearance at all; because in the Pannel's Examination upon the 20th of *June*, the Pannel doth condescend of that which was done upon the 14th and 15th of *May*; but not one word of the Earls, albeit in that same Examination he makes mention, that the Lord *Rea* had spoken with the Lord *Seaforth*. And sic-like, in the Examination of *Donald* Lord *Rea*, upon the 21st of *June*, 1631, and also the Pannel's own deposition foresaid, that the Pannel two days after the relation, which behoved to be upon the 20th of *May* (relation being upon the 18th), the Pannel brought the Lord *Rea* to the Treasurer, and caused him to subscribe his relation; at which time the Pannel told the Lord-Treasurer, that the Lord *Rea* had more to say, whereupon the Lord *Rea* being ask'd what it was, and wherefore detained, the Lord *Rea* answered, that he had spoken with the Lord *Seaforth*, and had sundry particulars from him, which he did not tell to the Lord *Uchiltrie* in particular, but generally affirmed to him he would say more. But one or two days after, the Lord *Rea* went to the Earl of *Seaforth*, and then told the same, first to the Pannel. And that the Pannel, upon the *Sunday* of the Morning (which was the day of the Marquis's returning from *Scotland*) he had told the Lord-Treasurer these particulars spoken by the Lord *Seaforth*, and therewith also of the Marquis's return; whereby it is clear, that as nothing is contained in the relation touching the three Earls, neither in the verbal relation to his Majesty and Lord-Treasurer, nor in the subscribed relation; so the speeches thereanent spoken by the Lord *Rea* to the Pannel, was not till eight days after giving in of the list.

And where it is alledged by the Pannel, that as the Lord *Rea*'s fact cannot burden him, far less his omission; it is answered, first, it must bind him, because he has named him to be his Author: and wherein he is not his Author, the Pannel himself must needs be the forger. And next, because the relation in effect is the Pannel's own deed, as said is, and as to the purgation of the speeches, that the business is known, *Sir, either do or die*; that the same must be interpret *secundum communem usum loquendi*; and to mean as mickel as, see to your own safety: it is answered, that they must be taken properly, and not improperly, and must be ruled by the preceding speeches of the party and prime Agent; as if the Pannel had said to any person, this man slew your father, *do or die*. In the which case, the words would not be exponed safety, but revenge: and where it is alledg'd *quod in dubiis benignior fieri debet interpretatio*; this rule of law has only place *in contradictiosus, sed non in criminosus, præcipue atrocioribus*, as this is. But it is urged, *hic sumus in facto lic to*; but it is answered, *hic in maxime illicito*. Because there was nothing required of the Pannel, but to reveal (whilk was done of before); and whatever was done after the revealing, that might tend to the hurt of the reputation of the Noblemen, or touch them in their life and estate, was altogether unlawful and capital; and the unlawfulness is manifest, by the subjoining of that pernicious Counsel, *to do or die*: whilk is not of the nature of a relation, but of the nature of the instigation, of a sovereign Prince to a dangerous act, tending to the destruction of the life and honour of them, against whom the Counsel is given; and by their answers, the whole objections made against the particulars of the libel are solved. To the which is added, the Lord *Rea*'s declaration by Oath, freeing the Marquis, his Majesty's Letter of the 29th of *June*, sent down to the Council, declaring the Lord Marquis, and the said three Earls of *Haddington*, *Roxburgh* and *Buccleugh* (to be as his Majesty knows them to be) as good and faithful Subjects as any within his Majesty's Kingdoms; and declaring his Majesty's resolution, to have those who have given false information against them, to be punished. After the which, did follow his Majesty's Letter of the date of the 24th of *September*, for trying and censuring the Pannel, upon the particulars given forth by him against the Noblemen: wherein the Pannel, notwithstanding of all his purgations, can have no just warrant against the Marquis, specially in the two last points of prime Agent, and known business; nor pretext against the Earls of *Haddington* and *Roxburgh*, but (by the Pannel's confession) least of all against the Earl of *Buccleugh*, against whom he had nothing but a guess by his own confession, and yet he makes him Plotter.

It is duplyed by Mr. *Robert Nairne* for the Pannel, that this Dittay consists upon three deeds done and committed by the Pannel, together with his intention in the doing of them. As to the Pannel's intention, that it was not of purpose of making any Leasing, against the Act of Parliament, but to the revealing of an alledged Treason against his Majesty, the revealing whereof was necessitate by that addition adjoined to the said Act of Parliament libelled; for obedience of the which Act, the Pannel [illegible] ever was done in this business by him, and that the first part of the Dittay is not relevant against the Pannel, to infer the [illegible] against him, is clear, [illegible] the argument [illegible] A deed commanded by the Act of Parliament, cannot infer a [illegible] the same Act of Parliament; true it is, that the first deed contained in the [illegible] of this Dittay was commanded by the Act of Parliament, [illegible] enjoining a necessity to all hearers of treasonable speeches [illegible] the King [illegible] to reveal the [illegible], he did the same [illegible]. Whereas it is alledged in the Dittay, that by and after the information which the Pannel had by relation, he has exceeded in the particulars contained in the Dittay. And first, in the first particular, at the doing and speaking whereof by and after the anterior information, which the Pannel had received, the Lord *Rea* the Author was present, who being inquired of by by his Majesty, why he was so long in revealing of the alledged Treasons; he answered, That he was afraid to do the same, in respect of the nearness betwixt his Majesty and the Marquis. So that that which the Pannel did for Obedience to the Law, and his Author being present beside him, is no ways relevant to infer the Punishment of Leasing-makers against him contained in the Act of Parliament. Like as also the said Lord *Rea*, after the said Relation to his Majesty being remitted to the Lord-Treasurer, declared that the Marquis was Party; and further said, That he would cause as honest Men as the Lord *Rea* himself to affirm the same.

Whereas my Lord Advocate, in his Reply, quarrels the former Words positively set down, and not by Relation; it is duplyed, That the Form of the Speech is not in question here, but the Matter; for albeit, that the Pannel had reported in other Words, or by a Description, or Paraphrase, that which my Lord *Rea* related unto him, without changing or altering of the Substance, commits no Fault, nor cannot be accounted therefore a Leasing-maker. And here the Proponer repeats the Words contained in the Relation and Depositions, which he remits to the Judges Consideration. And to the second Part of the Subsumption, anent the Delivery of the List of Names to the Treasurer, it is answered, That that Part of the Dittay is most irrelevant, and cannot be subsumed upon the Proposition of the Indictment; for to reason thus, all Leasing-makers should be punished. True it is, that the Pannel has written, and delivered a List of Names to the Treasurer: *Ergo*, he ought to be punished, is an evil Argument, which is remitted to the Judge, except it had libelled, that the said List contained Leasings, which is not libelled. And albeit it had been libelled, it is alledged, that the said List of Names as it is set down, contains no Purpose, for it is not written therein, prime Agent and Plotters in such a Treason; not only indefinite prime Agent and Plotters. And if the Pursuer will force these Words, to this alledged Treason contained in the Relation, the Pannel then will repeat the Word used of before (as he is informed). And here alledges, that it is as lesome, or rather more lesome to the Pannel, to eik true Words for the Pannel's good, nor to the Pursuer of the Dittay, to eik others for his Accusation. And albeit the said Words had been adjected, whereby the Sentence might have been filled against the Pannel; yet he closes himself with the Relation made by the said Lord *Rea* verbally, before making of the written Relation. And where it is disputed, that there cannot be a verbal Relation here respected; it is answered for the Pannel, that it is clear, that the written Relation we learned of the Marquis's Servants and Followers *tantum*.

And further alledges, That the Disputation of the Time of the giving in of the List upon the 16th Day, and the Time of the speaking of the Lord *Rea* with the Lord *Seaforth*, upon the 21st Day, is no ways relevant nor material; it being confessed, at the least not denied by my Lord *Rea*, that he had related of the three Earls to the Pannel: For the Deed being constant, the Circumstance of Time is not so material, and cannot be presumed that the Pannel should have any Knowledge thereof; who had of before been very long absent, and no ways interested in their Advice, and altogether ignorant of them; could of himself without any Information, named the same Persons whom the Revealer was to name, and none other.

It is answered by his Majesty's Advocate, That he oppones the Dittay, with the Reply made to the former Defences.

Lastly, It is alledged for the Pannel, That as it cannot be proceeded against the Pannel here in *Scotland*, but conform to the Laws and Statutes of *England*, the Place of the Pannel's alledged Offence, and according as the Fact is punishable, or not punishable, and more and less punishable in the Kingdom of *England*; so there can be no legal Accusation institute or laid against the Pannel here in *Scotland* for the said Facts and Deed, but upon the Laws of *England*, or at least upon the Common Law. And true it is, that the Dittay is not founded upon the Laws of *England*, nor yet upon the Common Law; but upon the municipal Laws of *Scotland*, and Acts of Parliament thereof: And therefore the Dittay is no ways relevant, subsuming and concluding upon the Acts of Parliament, mentioned in the Proposition of the Dittay.

Item, If the Relevancy of the Dittay all be sustained, it is alledged, that there can be no Pain inflicted, but that whereby the said Facts and Deeds are punishable by the Laws and Statutes of *England*, or by the Common Law, and no ways by the Pains mentioned in the said Acts of Parliament. *Quia judex originis vel domicilii non potest punire subditum delinquentem extra territorium, nisi secundum pœnam impositam a jure communi vel statutis Loci in quo deliquit, non autem secundum statuta ipsius Loci originis vel domicilii. Jul. Clarus, Quæstio* 85.

To the whilk it is answered by his Majesty's Advocate, That the first Part of the Alledgeance is altogether unreasonable and absurd; and as to the second Part of the Alledgeance, it is answered, That the Pannel, being a *Scotsman* by Birth, and also *quoad domicilium* being resident, by his Lady and Children in *Scotland*; and having committed the Crime libelled against four Noblemen in *Scotland*; he must be subject not only to the Laws of the Kingdom, but to the Pain and Punishment contained in the Laws: like as his Majesty by his missive Letter has ordained him to be tried and censured by the Laws of the Kingdom. And where it is alledged, that he is only punishable by the Pain inflicted in *England*, where the Crime is committed; and for this alledges *Jul. Cl.* in his 85th Question; first *Julius Clarus* in that Place calls the Matter disputable, *& egere decisione Cæsarea*: Next, he adduces the Number of Doctors, conflicting in divers Opinions *pro & contra*. And in the End he seems himself to incline to the punishment *Loci delicti*. And after it, cites *Marianus in cap. Postulasti extra de foro competenti: qui dicit generaliter esse communem conclusionem, quod delinquens debeat punire pœna imposita a Statutis Loci in quo delinquens punitur*. And this last Speech after his own carries *communem opinionem*, for his own is only given, *ad cautionem*, to free the Judges from Inquisition of Law. From whilk the Justice-General is well warranted, by his Majesty's Letter commanding the Pannel to be judged, conform to the Laws of the Kingdom.

And further, it is granted by *Jul. Clar.* to the which the Proponer assents in his Acceptation, *quod posset delinquens punire pœna juris communis vel pœna loci ubi delinquitur*. But so it is, that by the Common Law, *Calumniatores puniuntur pœna talionis, lege quisvis Cod. de Calumniatoribus, novella Leonis* 77. *Lege finali Cod. de accusationibus Leg.* 38. *digest. de pœnis.* And *Cicero* in his Fragments cites the Law in his Twelve Tables, in these Words: *Nostræ inquit, doudecim tabulæ cum per paucas res copite sanxissent in his banc sanxiendam putaverint; si quis actitavisset quod infamiam faterет flagitiumve alteri, & præterea atrox injuria, de jure communi punibilis est pœna mortis. Jul. Clar. Quæstione* 83. *numero* 9. The Justice continues this Diet with all further Disputation and Reasoning in this Matter, to the Morn the third Day of *December* instant; and ordains the Pannel to be returned back to his Ward, therein to remain in the mean time. The Persons of Assize warned thereto, *apud acta*, as of before, ilk Person under the pain of one thousand Marks.

Curia Justiciaria S. D. N. Regis tent' in prætorio burgi de Edinburgh, *tertio die mensis* Decembris, *Anno Dom. Millesimo, Sexcentesimo, Trigesimo primo, per Honorabiles & Discretos Viros, Magistros* Alexandrum Colville *de* Blair, *&* Jacobum Robertoun, *Advocatum, Justiciarios deputatos nobilis & potentis Comitis* Willielmi *Comitis de* Stratherne *&* Monteith, *Dom.* Grahame, Kilbryde, *&* Kynpont, *præsidis secreti Concilii ac Justiciarii generalis dict. S. D. N. Regis, totius sui Regni* Scotiæ, *ubilibet constitut. Sectis vocatis & Curia legitime affirmata.*

Intran'

JAMES Lord *Uchiltrie*, delated in the Crimes foresaid, specified in his Dittay.

Pursuer,

Sir *Thomas Hope* of *Craighall*, Knight and Baronet; Advocate to our Sovereign Lord for his Highness's Entries.

Prolocutors in Defence.

Mr. *Robert Nairne*,
Mr. *Alexander Pierson*, } Advocates.
Gilbert Neilson,

It is duplyed by the said *James* Lord *Uchiltrie* himself, being entered upon Pannel anent the first Part of my Lord Advocate's Reply, bearing, that the Clausule, as he was informed, can no ways be repeated in the Particulars. And although the Pannel so said, yet he has no positive Information from the Lord *Rea*; it is answered, the same ought to be repelled, because of the Clause *(as the Pannel was informed)* purported in the Dittay itself: For the Pannel in that whilk is the same, and Strength of the whole Dittay, is necessarily understood, and should be repeated in all the subsequent Passages of the Dittay; because it is *unicus actus continuatus*. And whilks whole three Parts of the Subsumption, as they are used conjunctly by my Lord Advocate against the Pannel; so the Pannel alledges that these Words, as he is informed, contained in the general, must be understood and repeated in all the three several Parts of the Subsumption; as being the Sum of all, whilk is after alledged, or was after imparted by the Pannel, and ought so to be understood. And where it is alledged, that where the Pannel, although he said, *as he was informed*, yet it is no positive Information from my Lord *Rea*, to ground a positive Assertion of the whole, contained in the Dittay.

It is answered thereto, He had positive Assertions and Information *quoad relationem*; *sed quoad veritatem* he was not bound to have it; sic-like many Parts of his Affirmations would be best cleared by the confronting of the Pannel and his Informer, whilk was never yet done. Neither are the chief of the Pannel's Affirmations, alledged by my Lord Advocate, simply taken, positive Affirmations, but with Interpretations, Constructions and Glosses, dipping *in mentem* of the Pannel: To which God is his only Judge, and it is an hard Matter by presumed Constructions, to draw the Pannel to the Question of his Life; *Nam non presumuntur delicta, sed probantur*. The Pannel refers himself to his Deposition, *in substantialibus*, undenied by the Lord *Rea*, as is clear by the Pannel's former Exceptions. Whereas my Lord Advocate mentions the Madness and foolish Imagination of *Meldrum*, as the Lord *Rea*'s Author of the Speeches; first, the Pannel protests, he urges nothing against those Noblemen from himself, *ab origine*. But he adheres to the Relations of the Lord *Rea*, verbal and by Writ; neither disputes he against *Meldrum*'s Sufficiency, or for it; but that *Meldrum*'s Words, related to him by the Lord *Rea*, gave him just Ground of revealing. And as to the Words alledged, related by the Pannel to the King, anent the odiousness of the Matter, and the Lord Marquis as Party; this can no ways be laid to the Pannel's Charge as a Fault, much less as a Crime capital, because the Informer, *viz.* the Lord *Rea*, was present at the Discourse; and related himself to the King, *eodem tempore*, the Particulars of what the Pannel had spoken; neither did he at that time oppose him, or contradict him in one Circumstance, whereby the Pannel was *bona fide* [illegible], and therefore ought not now to be laid to his Charge. And further, in the Time of the Pannel's relating his own Words, the Pannel affirms, that he did it with Tears coming over his Cheeks, no Sign of Malice, or sowing Sedition, in expressing these Words to the King, like as his Majesty bare record thereof, before the Council of *England*, the Impannelled being present.

And to that Part of my Lord Advocate's Reply, anent the Lord Marquis to be prime Agent; the Pannel repeats the first Member of his Duply, together with the Impannelled's former Exceptions thereanent.

And where my Lord Advocate affirms, that the Pannel did his Duty sufficiently in the first Discourse, and might have acquiesced there with Duty; the Pannel affirms, that he could not, because all the time, from the 13th of *May* to the 20th, it was *actus continuatus*, by constant Information running from the Informer to the Pannel; and so required a constant Duty, whilk he durst not omit, neither with Safety nor Duty. And this is clearly by my Lord *Rea*'s own Deposition; who affirms the relating of several things, in several Days and Times, and is manifestly proven by the Pannel's own Depositions.

And where my Lord Advocate refuses to the Pannel the Exception of Charity, answering, That *crimen non potest purgari bona intentione, transeat*, where there is *crimen simplex*. But where there is *tantum crimen*, by Constructions, Periphrases, and Glosses, *supra mentem*, yea, *contra mentem* of the Pannel; there Charity justly may be admitted: For a good Intention, as it will not purge a manifest Crime, neither should the wresting of the Pannel's Intention inforce a Crime, and so not debar Charity.

And

And where my Lord Advocate doth urge against the Pannel's defaming of the Noblemen, it is answered by the Pannel, that the first Author must be the defamer, and not the revealer; the whole matter of the pretended defamation, being original acts of the Lord *Rea*'s *quod defensorem*, upon Pannel, and not Acts of the Pannel; as it is evident, by the Pannel's two depositions, the Lord *Rea*'s first deposition the 21st of *May*, where the said Lord *Rea* doth acknowledge the examination of the Pannel, taken the 20th of *June*, to be true in all points, so far as the same concerns the knowledge, words and acts of the said Lord *Rea*; upon the explanations then following. By which explanations, and notwithstanding thereof, there is substance enough in the Pannel's deposition, to prove that the Lord *Rea*, and not the Pannel, was Author to the whole matter of the pretended defamation. And whereas my Lord Advocate would in his reply seem to question the verbal relations, flowing from the Lord *Rea* to the Pannel, to this the Pannel opposes his own deposition, and the first article of my Lord *Rea*'s examination formerly cited, wherein the Lord *Rea* ratifies the Pannel's verbal assertions: if he ratifies them, they must be in *rerum natura*; if they be, my Lord Advocate's assertion is not relevant. And where my Lord Advocate alledges the leaving forth of the Lord *Rea*'s verbal relation, out of his representation in writ, given in to the Lord-Treasurer; the Pannel repeats his exception made thereanent of before. And to all my Lord Advocate's discourse to that effect, containing one side of paper, the Pannel opposes his first answer, and his depositions, and the Lord *Rea*'s relations, and his examinations agreeing thereto. And whereas my Lord Advocate would bind the Pannel to answer for the Lord *Rea*'s omissions, because the Lord *Rea* is his Author; the Pannel being sitting behind at the time of the expression, can hardly find means to be persuaded that it came from his Majesty's Advocate; and opposes and repeats the Pannel's exception herein. And where my Lord Advocate, upon these words, ye know the business, and not the time (*do or die*), says, that these words should have a proper interpretation; which is, says he, to be a Counsel given by the Pannel, for subversion of the Marquis's honour and estate: the Pannel answers thereto, that he adheres to his exception already alledged; and further adds, that the Lord *Rea* said to the Pannel that *Sunday* morning, that the Lord *Seaforth* had said to the Lord *Rea*, their purpose was to take the King, the Queen, and the Prince: and so the information being given to the Pannel, furnished to the Pannel great cause of fear, and his fear the reason of the expression of these words, of advising the King to prevent his danger; as the Pannel had formerly advised my Lord-Treasurer of *England*, to advise his Majesty to retire to *Whitehall* from *Greenwich*, as to a place of more safety. And this is clear, by the Pannel's deposition the 20th of *June*, ratified by the Lord *Rea* in the first Article of his Examination the 21st of *June*.

And where my Lord Advocate alledges, that the Lord *Rea* and his Majesty's Letter frees the Marquis of *Hamilton*, and the other Noblemen, by the Lord *Rea*'s Oath:

It is answered thereto by the Pannel, that the Pannel doth not charge them; he only charges the Lord *Rea* as his Informer and Author, humbly attesting, that in what essential points the Lord *Rea* is contrary to the Pannel, he does the Pannel wrong: and therefore the Pannel declares, that whensoever it shall please his Majesty to permit the Pannel and the Lord *Rea* to be confronted, or if then upon difference, the matter be not cleared of the Pannel's innocency; the Pannel is ready to hazard his life in a duel, to the glory of God, and to the clearing of the truth of this business, his Majesty commanding the same, with a protestation, that he carries no malice to the said Lord *Rea*. If the business be not decided by this, or that if his Majesty is pleased to admit torture before a duel-trial, the Pannel is ready with him to bear out the torture, and to be try'd thereby, with the said Lord *Rea*, and let the truth then appear: which if it be not then, whenever it shall please God to call the Pannel to bear testimony thereof with his blood, if God be not graciously pleased to bear him up in it, let men so conceive: and if God bear him out in it, then will he be found meet after his death, to have been an honest man, and his Blood shall be required of the takers thereof.

My Lord Advocate, before any answer to be made by him to the Pannel's former duply, produced his Majesty's Letter sent down to the Lords of his Majesty's Privy-Council, of the date of the 29th of *June*, 1631, and desired the same to be judicially read, of the whilk the tenor follows.

"To our right trusty and right well-beloved Cousin and Counsellor; "to our right trusty and well-beloved Cousins and Counsellors; to our "right trusty and well-beloved Counsellors, the Viscount of *Duplin*, our "Chancellor, the Earl of *Menteith*, President of our Privy-Council, "and to the remanent Earls, Lords, and other of our Privy-Council, of "our Kingdom of *Scotland*."

Sic supra scribitur,

Charles R.

"RIght trusty and right well-beloved Cousin and Counsellor, and right "trusty and right well-beloved Cousins and Counsellors, and right "trusty and well-beloved Counsellors, we greet you well. Whereas we "are informed of a practice in appearance so pernicious, and nearly "concerning us, as we would not but take some trial thereof, both "by ourself, and some of our Council, appointed by us for that "purpose. But in the mean time, because of some [illegible] rumours "maliciously dispersed thereupon, to the prejudice of our right trusty "and right well-beloved Cousin and Counsellors, the Marquis of *Hamilton*, and the Earls of *Haddington*, *Roxburgh*, and *Buccleugh*, and "some others, lest the like reports be brought unto your ears, we "have thought good hereby to declare, that not only we have found by "the trial we ourselves have taken, that they are altogether innocent and "clear thereof, but likewise that the prime informer thereof hath now "cleared them upon Oath, testifying them (as we know them to be) as "good and faithful Subjects, as we have in any of our Kingdoms. And "for the business itself, whensoever it shall be fully tried, we will thereafter express our further pleasure concerning others interested therein, "according as we shall find just cause, either in punishing any person "that shall be found guilty, or in punishing any person that shall be "found to have given false information. And whereas we have formerly "by our Letters recommended unto you, our right trusty and right well-beloved Cousin the Marquis of *Hamilton*, for furthering the speedy levy "and transportation of his men with all possible diligence, these are again "to require you to contribute the best help that your authority or endeavours can afford for that effect. Whereof, both out of the regard we "have to him, and to that employment, being very confident of your "best care; we bid you farewel. From our Court, at *Greenwich*, the "29th of *June*, 1631."

After reading of the which Letter of his Majesty, it is answered by my Lord Advocate, that the urging of the Pannel to have the words (*as he is informed*) to be repeated in all the rest of the Dittay, wants all reason; the points of the Dittay bearing relation of several deeds done in several times. And where it is alledged by the Pannel, that these words, *as he was informed*, were true, *quoad relationem & quoad veritatem*, there was no necessity: If this were true, the Dittay were eluded, for the Pannel is not accused of a Leesing in respect of the verity of the matter related, but in respect of his discrepance from his Author, and that he affirms more than his Author, and with greater certainty than his Author: and that, not content with both these two excesses, he follows it out to the very point of execution, which is evident in the point of certainty, by these words spoken to his Majesty, *the business is known*, whilk is more certain by the opposition of the uncertainty of time only, which redoubles the certainty of the business. And in the point of execution, by that pernicious and cruel Counsel, *do or die*: the effect of which pernicious Counsel, if God in mercy had not disposed the royal heart of our wise and gracious Sovereign, would have produced more lamentable effects, nor could be quenched with the pity of tears shed by the Pannel. And the conferring of the Lord *Rea* (whom the Pannel calls the prime Author) with himself, in the progress of his behaviour, will manifest the Pannel's guiltiness of the points of the Dittay, wherein he is accused for the Lord *Rea*, who behoved to have greater certainty than the Pannel, never proceeded to the points of positive Party, prime Agent, Plotters; and to say to the supreme sovereign Prince, that the business was known, in all which points the Pannel has involved himself; but the Lord *Rea* was content to reveal the reports made to him by *David Ramsay*, and Mr. *Robert Meldrum*, to the Pannel, without adding or paring. And when the Pannel, upon the 22d of *May*, which was the day of the Marquis's returning from *Scotland* to *England*, came to the Lord *Rea*, and told him, that he had been with the Lord-Treasurer, and acquainted him with the passages, which he had from the Lord *Seaforth*, and of the Lord Marquis's return, and that he had conceived, that it might be dangerous at that time for his Majesty, for the which cause the Pannel in his deposition saith, that he did advise the King to remove from *Greenwich*, to *Whitehall* or *London*, my Lord *Rea* answered, that the Pannel had done evil therein, for there was no such suddenness to be feared: yet notwithstanding hereof, and that his Author had reproved his rashness, the Pannel went thereafter and attended his Majesty at dinner, and at the end of dinner spake these words of the certainty of the plot, uncertainty of the time, and added the Counsel. Like as the Pannel being asked, hereupon granted that he met with the Lord *Rea* upon that *Sunday* the Marquis came to Court, and also that he met with the Lord-Treasurer; and counsell'd his Majesty's removing from *Greenwich* to *London*. But denies that the Lord *Rea* said, that he thought it was evil done. Notwithstanding hereof, the Pannel went thereafter and attended his Majesty at dinner, spake the words and gave the Counsel; like as his Majesty being something wakened by that fearful Counsel, sent for the Lord *Rea*, and did acquaint him, that some present danger was suggested to his Majesty, upon the Marquis's returning. To the which the Lord *Rea* answered by Oath, that he knew nothing against the Marquis, for any thing he knew, but that he was as good a subject as any his Majesty had.

And where the Pannel would seem to free himself, by denying the Counsel given to him by the Lord *Rea*, it cannot be [illegible] to execute, except he would prove that his Author advised him to do it: which is improbable, seeing the Lord *Rea*, his Author, neither did it, nor allowed of its being done by the Pannel. And where it is alledged by the Pannel, that he had sufficient warrant from his Informer, he cannot affirm it, as being contrary to the relation made by his Author: which is not a syllable of the Marquis as prime Agent, nor of the three Noblemen as Plotters. And whatever the Pannel did after the discovery of the business to the Lord-Treasurer, which was upon the 15th of *May*; it was the Pannel's own word, work and deed, as the giving in of the Bill, expressing the certainty of the plot, and urging the putting in execution. And where the Pannel alledges, that all was done upon a good intention, and that God is only Judge of the mind; it is true, where the mind is not revealed by speech or act punishable of the Law: but if either speech or deed be done against the Law, the pretext of the mind will never excuse it.

And albeit it be true, as the Pannel alledges, *Quod delicta non praesumuntur sed probantur*: yet it is as true, *Quod in [illegible] praesumitur dolus nisi probetur contrarium*. And in the case of this Dittay, we have a Law prohibiting Leasings and Calumnies under the pain of death, and seeing by the Dittay, there are three particulars libelled, which his Majesty in his Letter of the date of the 29th of *June*, has called false informations, and which directly fall within the compass of the Law, as reflecting upon the life, honour and estate of the Noblemen, the Pannel's excuse [illegible] is too slender, to free him from the punishment of the Law. And where it is alledged by the Pannel, that he has named his Authors, and that he was present the time of his relation, and did not contradict him therein, which the Pannel alledges for a sufficient ground of his exoneration, the contrary is found, for the Lord *Rea*, in his examination upon the 21st of *June*, doth acknowledge the Pannel's examination to be true in all points, saving the explanations thereafter subjoined: But this approbation cannot exceed the subject, and [illegible] the subject must be restricted according to the conditions of the [illegible], but so it is, that in the Pannel's examination, which is approven by the Lord *Rea*, there is not one syllable of the Lord Marquis as Party or prime Agent, or of the three Noblemen as Plotters.

And therefore that falls not within the compaſs of the approbation, and where it may appear that in the Pannel's examination upon the 20th of *June*, 'tis granted, that on *Monday* the 16th of *May*, he deliver'd to the Lord-Treaſurer the liſt of names; that is not a part of the Pannel's relation approven by the Lord *Rea:* but it is the Pannel's anſwer to an interrogatory, aſked of him by the Counſel, which could have no reſpect to the Lord *Rea*'s relation. Like as the Pannel being examin'd thereupon the 24th of *June*, grants that the liſt was made by himſelf: and that the Lord *Rea* was not privy to the making thereof, which is alſo confeſſed by the Lord *Rea* himſelf in his examination the 21ſt of *June*, 1631, and laſt article thereof. Wherein he depones, not only that he was not acquainted with the liſt of names deliver'd to the Lord-Treaſurer, but that he had nothing to do therein; which both excludes the concourſe of the making of the liſt, and his knowledge of the purpoſe of it. And where it is alledged by the Pannel that after the revealing to the Lord-Treaſurer, he could not abſtain from the remanent paſſages of his behaviour, becauſe it was *actus continuatus* by the Lord *Rea* to the Pannel, from the 13th of *May* to the 20th of *May*; it is anſwered, that after the firſt revealing, the Pannel had no more to do in the neceſſity of duty, becauſe his Author was revealed: and whatever followed after diſcovery made by the Pannel, would have tied the Author and not the Pannel; there being no Law that might have puniſhed the Pannel for ſhifting his courſe after the revealing. But there being manifeſt hazard and danger in Law, to follow further after the revealing of the buſineſs, which the Author thought neither clear nor certain; and the Pannel not being conſcious upon what mind the Lord *Rea* made his firſt Information to him, which might very readily have been upon malecontentment, grudging and malice, his credulity to him was cruelty aginſt the Noblemen. And his going forwards after the revealing, was a manifeſt engagement of himſelf, in the malice of the Author, and drawing upon himſelf the opinion of greater.

And where it is alledged by the Pannel, that his Behaviour cannot be counted in the nature of Leaſings, puniſhed by Act of Parliament, but allanerly by way of illation and ſiniſter conſtruction; the contrary is clear, by the three points of the Dittay. And the Purſuer, in his reply, has moſt juſtly challenged the Pannel as a defamer of Noblemen; becauſe their fame, honour and credit was unblameable before it was taxed by the Pannel; and the Lord Marquis brought under danger of the loſs of life, honour and eſtate.

And where it is pretended by the Pannel, that the cauſe of his ſpeaking of theſe words to his Majeſty, upon the *Sunday* of the Marquis's coming to Court, was becauſe the Lord *Rea* told the Pannel that the Lord *Seaforth* had aſſured him, that the Plot was for taking off the King and the Queen; firſt, that excuſe has no warrant from the Lord *Rea*'s depoſition; next, in that ſame conference betwixt the Pannel and the Lord *Rea* upon the ſaid *Sunday*, the Lord *Rea* told him it was an idle fear; and thirdly, it cannot be a pretext, becauſe that paſſage of the taking the King and Queen, is contained in the relation made by the Lord *Rea* upon the 18th of *May*; and ſo cannot be pretended as a new information lately come to his knowledge, to waken the Pannel to ſuch a pernicious Counſel. And this ſhall ſuffice for anſwer to the Duply, which is cloſed with that which is contained in the Reply; that the Pannel had no warrant of his ſpeeches and proceedings poſitive againſt the Marquis; nor colour of warrant againſt the three Earls, and neither warrant nor colour at all againſt the Earl of *Buccleugh*, againſt whom the Pannel, by his own confeſſion, had nothing but the gueſs of the Lord *Rea*; which the Lord *Rea* not the leſs refuſes, and affirms to be the nomination of the Pannel. But howſoever it is only a gueſs, by his own confeſſion, from his Author, and yet in his liſt he makes him a Plotter. And albeit the like evidence of the Pannel's Calumnies againſt the other two Earls being undoubted, as having no warrant at all from the Lord *Rea*'s relation, wherein there is no ſyllable of theſe Noblemen; and that the excuſe made by the Pannel of a verbal relation by the Lord *Rea*, has no probability, and alſo is contradicted by the Lord *Rea*, being poiſed thereupon: Yet in theſe two Noblemen the Pannel covers himſelf under the ſhadow of a verbal relation, againſt that which himſelf drew up in writing; but in the Lord *Buccleugh*'s he is excluded from all verbal relation, in reſpect of his own depoſition, whereby he is manifeſtly convinced of incurring the puniſhment of the Acts of Parliament, whereupon the Dittay is formed, as having named him Plotter, when by his own depoſition he grants it to be a gueſs of the Lord *Rea*.

It is quadruply'd by the Pannel, that for anſwer to the Triply, made by the Lord Advocate his Purſuer, he repeats and oppones his defences contained in the former exception and duply. And further the Pannel adds, that where it is objected by my Lord Advocate againſt the Pannel, that he had no ground nor cauſe from the Lord *Rea*'s relation, from the Pannel by word, to call the two Earls of *Haddington* and *Roxburgh* Plotters; but by the contrary, that the Lord *Rea* refuſes and denies the ſame; again the which objection, the Pannel does repeat and adhere to that article of his ſecond depoſition, dated the 24th of *June* in theſe words following: he ſaith, the Lord *Rea* did affirm to the Examinant, that he had the foreſaid Report, anent the Earls of *Melros* and *Roxburgh*, from the Lord *Seaforth*, before the Pannel then examined, made or delivered this ſaid Paper or Liſt to the Treaſurer. And in the article preceding, in the ſame depoſition, the Pannel affirms the Lord *Rea* told him this; whereby it evidently appears by the two articles joined together, that the Pannel had ground for that part of his repreſentation.

And whereas it is affirmed by my Lord Advocate, that the Lord *Rea* denies the ſame, this comparing of the Pannel's aſſertion, and the words of the Lord *Rea*'s denial together, the Lord *Rea*'s words will be found to import no direct nor clear denial; the Pannel affirms that the Lord *Rea* told him, that the Earl of *Seaforth* told him, that the ſaid two Earls were upon the ſecrets of the buſineſs of the Marquis; my Lord *Rea*'s words in his denial bearing, that the firſt time the Lord *Seaforth* had any ſpeech with him, touching the ſaid Earls of *Haddington* and *Roxburgh*, their being privy to the particulars and ſecrets of the Lord *Hamilton*'s buſineſs, was on the *Monday* after the Marquis's coming out of *Scotland*. The Pannel affirms, that the Lord *Rea* told him ſuch a thing; the Lord *Rea* ſays, the Lord *Seaforth* ſpake not to him any ſuch matter before ſuch a day: how do theſe two agree, or contradict one another? The Pannel affirms the Lord *Rea* told him; my Lord *Rea* affirms my Lord *Seaforth* told him not ſuch a thing, before ſuch a day: what is that to the Pannel, if the Lord *Seaforth* had never told that to the Lord *Rea*, the Lord *Rea* might have told it to the Pannel for all that? And where it is alledged for the fortifying of the Triply by my Lord Advocate, that the Lord *Rea* in his depoſition, denieth that he was acquainted with the liſt of names, delivered by the Pannel, or had any thing to do therein; the Pannel affirms, that this eludes not the particular words concerning the two Earls; becauſe of the denial of the general liſt, wherein they were ingroſſed: for the manner of the diſcovery was left to the Pannel, when the direction of the diſcovery was given him. And ſo it was not needful that the Lord *Rea* ſhould be acquainted with the Papers, with the Pen, the Ink, the Hour and the Manner of the writing; becauſe that was left to the Pannel. Neither can the general denial of one piece of Paper take away the Pannel's teſtimony of the certain, determined, condeſcended upon by word. And for his word that he had no hand therein, is not meant *de materia*, affirmed by the Pannel, reported to him againſt the ſaid two Earls; becauſe he grants the ſubſtance in the preceding depoſition made by him thereanent. And as to that relation by that liſt, concerning the Earl of *Buccleugh* as Plotter, for defence of the Pannel's depoſition, it is produced in theſe words, bearing, 'And further ſaith (to wit, the Pannel), that the Lord *Rea* had told him, he could not gueſs who alſo ſhould be in the plot, unleſs it were the Lord *Buccleugh*; of whom the Lord *Rea* ſaid, he heard him ſpeak terrible words againſt the King, at his own table in *Holland*.' There it is affirmed, that he ſuſpected the Lord *Buccleugh* to be upon the Plot: if ſuſpected to be on the Plot by the Lord *Rea*, and told by him to the Pannel; the Pannel was neceſſitated to reveal the ſame, yea *in iiſdem terminis*, to reveal him to be a Plotter; whom he ſaid, he ſuſpected to be upon the Plot. To this my Lord Advocate objected, my Lord *Rea*'s denial, which are in theſe Words: That the Pannel and Lord *Rea* having ſome ſpeech together, who might be look'd for in *Scotland* to take arms; the Pannel, and not the Lord *Rea*, named the Lord *Buccleugh*. Whereupon the Lord *Rea* told, that at the ſiege of the *Buſſe*, the Lord *Rea* heard the Lord *Buccleugh* uſe ſome words, whereby the Lord *Rea* took the Lord *Buccleugh* to have come malecontent out of *England*. In this preſumed denial, there is contained a diſcourſe betwixt the Pannel and the Lord *Rea*, as the Lord *Rea* alledges. And in this diſcourſe, that the Pannel ſhould have named the Lord *Buccleugh*, and not the Lord *Rea*; this naming, is a naming in the reſpect of time firſt or laſt; for the Lord *Rea* grants that he did name the Lord *Buccleugh*, becauſe of the laſt words of that clauſe; ſo that his denial reſpects only priority of time, but no ways the Pannel's aſſertion; for not a word of his aſſertion is denied. But by the contrary, for corroboration of the Pannel's juſt ground, concerning the Earl of *Buccleugh*; the Lord *Rea* makes addition of more nor the Pannel had remembrance of; and ſo fortifies his affirmation, and proves no denial thereof.

The Pannel adds further, for eluding of the miſtaking of theſe his words, *Sir, we know the buſineſs, but not the time, therefore do or die.* It is affirmed by the Lord *Rea*, that he did hear of his Majeſty, that there was a danger ſuggeſted to him; which danger my Lord Advocate alledges to have come from the Pannel's words. If a danger but by the King's ſelf apprehended, then not a perſecution, for a danger imports defenſive remedies, and not violent and malicious attempts; yea, it imports and implies a preventing, and not a perſecuting. And laſtly, it clearly confirms the mentioned intention of the Pannel's expreſſing of thoſe words, which was to prevent his Majeſty's danger. This the Pannel's alledgeance, is cleared in the Lord *Rea*'s depoſition, made the 21ſt of *June*; yea, this is my Lord *Rea*'s relation, to whom the Pannel never ſpake, ſince the Pannel and he entered to their Trial. As for the words, *Sir, we know the buſineſs infallibly, this is no lye*; becauſe the Pannel and the Lord *Rea* was at his Majeſty's ten days before, and affirmed the ſame: the Pannel by relation from the Lord *Rea*, and the Lord *Rea* from others, and *ſo that is no lye*. And that the Pannel did not know the time, it is alledged in the contrary, *Ergo*, not no lye. As for the words *do or die*, by my Lord Advocate's declaration, it is but *concilium perniciofum*. And that it is not *mendacium*, neither can it be made nor interpreted *mendacium*, by any probability or ſenſe, and no malicious Counſel, as is alledged againſt the Pannel; conſidering the Pannel's declared intent, and the Lord *Rea*'s before-mentioned examination, wherein it is called a danger, *ſo not a lye*, and therefore not rightly ſubſumed.

My Lord Advocate repeats his former replies and triplies, and deſires my Lord Juſtice to cloſe this proceſs, ſo that there be no further diſpenſation or reaſoning herein, till anent the relevance or irrevelance of the Indictment. The Juſtice by *Interloquitor* declares the proceſs to be cloſed; and continues *Interloquitor* upon the alledgeances proponed by the Pannel againſt the Dittay, and Anſwers made thereto by his Majeſty's Advocate, to *Wedneſday* next, the ſeventh of *December* inſtant; the perſons of Aſſize warned *apud Acta*, to compear the ſaid day in the hour of cauſe, ilk perſon under the pain of a thouſand Marks. And ordained the Pannel to be returned to Ward, therein to remain in the mean time: whereupon my Lord Advocate aſked Inſtruments.

Curia Justiciaria S. D. N. Regis teni' in prætorio burgi de Edinburgh, *septimo die mensis* Decembris, *Anno Dom. Millesimo, Sexcentesimo, Trigesimo primo, per Honorabiles & Discretos Viros, Magistros* Alexandrum Colville *de* Blair, & Jacobum Robertoun *Advocatum, Justiciarios deputatos nobilis & potentis Comitis* Willielmi *Comitis de* Stratherne & Menteith, *Dom.* Graham, Kilbryde, & Kynpont, & *Præsidis secreti Concilii & Justiciarii generalis dict. S. D. N. Regis totius Regni sui* Scotiæ, *ubilibet constitut. Sectis vocatis & Curia legitime affirmata.*

Intran'

JAMES Lord *Uchiltrie*, delated of the Crimes foresaid, mentioned in his indictment.

Pursuer.

Sir *Thomas Hope* of *Craighall*, Knight and Baronet; his Majesty's Advocate for his Highness's Entries.

Prolocutors in Defence.

Mr. *Robert Nairne*.
Mr. *Alexander Pierson*. } Advocates.
Gilbert Neilson.

The Lord *Uchiltrie* being entered upon Pannel, produced to my Lord Justice, an Act of the Lords of his Majesty's secret Council, for continuation of this Diet, and of all further Trial or Proceeding against him, for the Crimes contained in his Dittay, to the first day of *February* next to come; of the whilk Act of Council the tenor follows: *Apud* Halyrudhouse *sexto die mensis* Decembris, *Anno Dom. Millesimo, Sexcentesimo, Tricesimo primo.* The Lords of the secret Council, for some special causes and considerations, ordains and commands his Majesty's Justice, Justice-Clerk and their Deputies, to continue all farther Trial and Proceeding against *James* Lord *Uchiltrie*, upon the Crimes whereof he has been accused before them, till the first day of *February* next. Whereanent the extract of this Act shall be unto them a Warrant, *extractum de libris actorum secreti Consilii S. D. N. Regis, per me* Jacobum Prymrose *Clericum ejusdem, sub meis signo & subscriptione manualibus, sic subscribitur* Jacobus Prymrose. According to the which Act of Council, Warrant and Command aforesaid, therein contained, the Justice continues all further Trial and Proceeding against the said *James* Lord *Uchiltrie*, upon the Crimes aforesaid, unto the said first day of *February* next to come: And ordained him to be taken back again to his Ward, therein to remain in sure firmance, till the said day. The whole persons of Assize, called upon by their names, are of new warned, *apud Acta*, to compear before his Majesty's Justice, the said first day of *February* next to come, in the hour of Cause; ilk person under the pain of one thousand Marks. Whereupon my Lord Advocate asked Instruments, *Extractum de libris actorum adjournalis S. D. N. Regis, per me* Johannem Bannatyne, *Clericum deputatum honorabilis viri, Dom.* Georgii Elphingston *de* Blythiswood, *militis, Clerici Justiciarii principalis dicti S. D. N. Regis, & dictorum Curiarum, Testan. bis meo signo & subscriptione manualibus.*

Sic Subscribitur,

Johannis Bannatyne *Clericus deputatus Clerici Justiciariæ Generalis S. D. N. Regis, Testan. bis meis signo & subscriptione.*

The Lord *Uchiltrie* appearing on the said 1st of *Feb.* was sentenced to perpetual Imprisonment *.

" * The Lord *Uchiltrie*, a Man of a subtil Spirit and good Parts, had not those endowments of his mind been stained with some ill Qualities; his Malice against the Marquis " of *Hamilton* was hereditary, he being the Son of Capt. *James Stewart*, who in King *James*'s minority, when the *Hamiltons* were groundlesly and in a mock Parliament at- " tainted, carried the Title of Earl of *Arran*, and possessed their Fortunes." *Burnet*'s Memoirs of the Dukes of *Hamilton*, p. 11, and 12. where he relates the whole business; and *page* 12. says, " This was a Calumny, than which Hell could not have forged a fouler, for Lord *Uchiltrie* judged that this would infallibly have produced one of two ef- " fects, either raised such a Jealousy in the King's thoughts, as to have quite ruin'd the Marquis, since few Ministers are proof against such whispers, or at least it would have " stopp'd his Voyage for a while, till he was tried, and the smallest delay in that would have scatter'd his Soldiers, (which the King was to send under the Marquis's com- " mand, to assist the King of *Sweden* to recover the *Palatinate*) so that this design failing, in which his Honour was now so far engag'd, a stain should lie on him through all " *Europe*. Lord *Weston* carried this story to the King, whether provoked to it out of hatred to the Marquis, or mov'd from his zeal and duty to the King, shall not be de- " termined; though the last was pretended by him, in many of his Letters to the Marquis. But his Majesty knew the Marquis too well, and understood all his motions and " the progress of this Affair, too exactly, to give any credit to this Forgery. And *page* 13. " But the Marquis was not able to lie under such terrible Imputations, where- " fore he pressed that *Uchiltrie* might be put to it, to prove what he had alledg'd: but all he offered against *Ramsay* was only a presumption, which *Ramsay* denied, and *Rea* " affirm'd; so that they were both put under Bail, and nothing appear'd that did touch the Marquis: for though *Ramsay* had been as guilty as the Lord *Rea* call'd him, that " left no Imputation on him, since none can be made answerable for those they employ, unless it appear that they followed the Instructions given them. So the Marquis was " dispatched to *Germany*. Lord *Uchiltrie* had charged the Marquis with Treason, and failing so totally in his Probation, was sent down to *Scotland* to be tried, where he had " a legal and free Trial for his false Charge before the Justice-General, and such Assessors as were appointed to sit with him, by the Privy-Council: and had the Marquis " repaid him in his own Coin, he could not have escap'd capital Punishment. But he was satisfied with his own justification, and such a Censure put on the Calumniator, " as might deter others from the like Attempts. Wherefore he was condemn'd to perpetual Imprisonment in *Blackness* Castle, and he continued there for twenty Years."

XX. The Trial of *John Lilburn* and *John Wharton*, for Printing and Publishing Seditious Books. In the *Star-Chamber*, *Feb.* 9. 1637. 13. *Car.* I.

B E F O R E

The Lord Archbishop of *Canterbury*.
The Lord-Keeper, Lord *Coventry*.
The Lord-Treasurer, Bishop of *London*.
The Lord Privy-Seal, Earl of *Manchester*.
The Earl-Marshal, Earl of *Arundel*.
The Earl of *Salisbury*.
The Earl of *Dorset*.
Lord *Cottington*.
Lord *Newburgh*.
Lord Chief-Justice *Bramston*.
Sir *Henry Vane*.
Mr. Secretary *Cooke*.
Mr. Secretary *Windebank*.
Judge *Jones*, and others.

[Written by *John Lilburn*.]

UPON *Tuesday* the 11th or 12th of *December*, 1637, I was treacherously and Judasly betrayed (by one that I supposed to be my friend) into the hands of the Pursuivant, with four of his assistants, as I was walking in *Soper lane* with one *John Chilburne*, servant to old Mr. *John Wharton*, in *Bow-lane*, a Hot-presser.

And about twelve of the Clock the next day, I was committed to the *Gatehouse*, by Sir *John Lamb*, the Prelate of *Canterbury*'s Chancellor, with others, without any examination at all, for sending of factious and scandalous Books out of *Holland* into *England*. And having not been at the foresaid prison above three days, I was removed, by a warrant from the Lords of the Council, to the *Fleet*, where I now remain. And after my being there some time, I drew a Petition to the Lords of the Council for my liberty: and their answer to it was, that I should be examined before Sir *John Banks*, the King's Attorney: The copy of which examination thus follows.

Upon *Tuesday* the 14th of *January*, 1637, I was had to Sir *John Banks* the Attorney-General's Chamber, (now Lord Chief-Justice of the Court of Pleas) and was referred to be examined by Mr. *Cockshey* his chief Clerk; and at our first coming together, he did kindly intreat me, and made me sit down by him, and put on my hat, and began with me after this manner: Mr. *Lilburn*, what is your Christian name? I said *John*. Did you live in *London* before you went into *Holland*? Yes, that I did. Where? Near *London-stone*? With whom there? With Mr. *Thomas Hewson*. What Trade is he? A dealer in Cloth, I told him. How long did you serve him? About five years. How came you to part? After this manner. I perceiving my Master had an intention to leave off his Trade, I often moved him that I might have my liberty, to provide for myself, and at the last he condescended unto it; and so I went into the Country, to have the content of my friends; and after that went into *Holland*. Where were you there? At *Rotterdam*. And from thence you went to *Amsterdam*? Yes, I was at *Amsterdam*. What Books did you see in *Holland*? Great store of Books, for in every Bookseller's shop as I came in, there were great store of Books. I know that, but I ask you, if you did see Dr. *Bastwick*'s Answer to my Master's Information, and a Book called his Litany? Yes, I saw them there; and if you please to go thither, you may buy an hundred of them at the Booksellers, if you have a mind to them. Have you seen the *Unbishoping of Timothy* and *Titus*, the *Looking-glass*, and a *Breviate of the Bishop's late Proceedings*? Yes, I have, and those also you may have there, if you please to send for them. Who printed all those Books? I do not know. Who was at the charges of printing them? Of that I am ignorant. But did you not send over some of these Books?

Lilburn. I sent not any of them over. Do you know one *Hargust* there? Yes, I did see such a man. Where did you see him? I met with him one day accidentally at *Amsterdam*. How oft did you see him there? Twice upon one day. But did not he send over Books? If he did, it is nothing to me, for his doings are unknown to me. But he wrote a Letter, by your directions, did he not? What he writ over I know no more than you: But did you see him no where else there? Yes, I saw him at *Rotterdam*. What conference had you with him? Very little. But why do you ask me all these questions? These are beside the matter of my imprisonment; I pray come to the thing for which I am accused, and imprisoned. No, these are not beside the business, but do belong to the thing for which you are imprisoned. But do you know of any that sent over any Books?

Lilburn. What other men did, doth not belong to me to know or search into; sufficient it is for me to look well to my own occasions. Well, here is the examination of one *Edmund Chillington*, do you know such a one? Yes. How long have you been acquainted with him? A little before I went away, but how long, I do not certainly know. Do you know one *John Wharton*? No. Do you not? He is a Hot-presser. I know him, but I do not well remember his other name. How long have you been acquainted with him, and how came you acquainted? I cannot well tell you. How long do you think? I do not know. What Speeches had you with *Chillington* since you came to town? I am not bound to tell you: but Sir (as I said before) why do you ask me all these questions? These are nothing pertinent to my imprisonment, for I am not imprisoned for knowing and talking with such and such men, but for sending over Books, and therefore I am not willing to answer you to any more of these questions, because I see you

you go about by this examination to insnare me: for seeing the things for which I am imprisoned cannot be proved against me, you will get other matter out of my examination; and therefore if you will not ask me about the thing laid to my charge, I shall answer no more. But if you will ask of that, I shall then answer you, and do answer, that for the thing for which I am imprisoned, which is for sending over Books, I am clear, for I sent none: and of any other matter that you have to accuse me of, I know it is warrantable by the Law of God, and I think by the Law of the Land, that I may stand upon my just defence, and not answer to your interrogatories; and that my accusers ought to be brought face to face, to justify what they accuse me of. And this is all the answer that for the present I am willing to make. and if you ask me of any more things, I shall answer you with silence. At this he was exceeding angry, and said, there would be a course taken with me to make me answer. I told him, I did not regard what course they would take with me, only this I desire you to take notice of, that I do not refuse to answer out of any contempt, but only because I am ignorant of what belongs to an examination, (for this is the first time that ever I was examined;) and therefore I am unwilling to answer to any impertinent questions, for fear that with my answer I may do myself hurt

This is not the way to get liberty: I had thought you would have answered punctually, that so you might have been dispatched as shortly as might be.

Lilburn. I have answered punctually to the thing for which I am imprisoned, and more I am not bound to answer, and for my liberty I must wait God's time.

You had better answer, for I have two examinations wherein you are accused. *Lilburn.* Of what am I accused? *Chillington* hath accused you for printing ten or twelve thousand of Books in *Holland*, and that they stand you in about eighty pound, and that you had a Chamber at Mr. *John Foot's*, at *Delft*, where he thinks the Books were kept, and that you would have printed the *Unmasking of the Mystery of Iniquity*, if you could have got a true copy of it. I do not believe that *Chillington* said any such things; and if he did, I know and am sure, that they are all of them lyes. You received money of Mr. *Wharton* since you came to Town, did you not? What if I did? It was for Books? I do not say so. For what sort of Books was it? I do not say it was for any, and I have already answered you all that for the present I have to answer; and if that will give you content, well and good; if not, do what you please. If you will not answer no more (here I told him, if I had thought he would have insisted upon such impertinent questions, I would not have given him so many answers) we have power to send you to the place from whence you came. You may do your pleasure, said I. So he called in anger for my Keeper, and gave him a strict charge to look well to me. I said, they should not fear my running away. And so I was sent down to Sir *John Banks* himself. And after he had read over what his man had writ, he called me in, and said, I perceive you are unwilling to confess the truth.

Lilburn. No, Sir, I have spoken the truth. Sir *John Banks.* This is your examination, is it not? What your man hath writ, I do not know. Come near, and see that I read it right. Sir, I do not own it for my examination, for your man hath writ what it pleased him, and hath not writ my answer; for my answer was to him, and so it is to you, that for the thing for which I am imprisoned (which is for sending over Books) I am clear, for I did not send any, and for any other matter that is laid to my charge, I know it is warrantable by the Law of God, and I think by the Law of the Land, for me to stand upon my just defence, and that my accusers ought to be brought face to face, to justify what they accuse me of: and this is all that I have to say for the present. You must set your hand to this your examination. I beseech you, Sir, pardon me, I will set my hand to nothing but what I have now said. So he took the pen and writ, "The "examined is unwilling to answer to any thing but that for which he is "imprisoned." Now you will set your hand to it? I am not willing, in regard I do not own that which your man hath writ; but if it please you to lend me the pen, I will write my answer, and set my hand to it. So he gave me the pen, and I begun to write thus: "The answer of me *John* "*Lilburn* is," and here he took the pen from me, and said he could not stay, that was sufficient. Then one of my Keepers asked him if they might have me back again? And he said yea: for he had no order for my inlargement.

And about ten or twelve days after, I was had forth to *Grays-Inn* again; and when I came there, I was had to the *Star-Chamber* office, and being there, as the order is, I must enter my appearance, they told me. I said, To what? For I was never served with any *Subpœna*; neither was there any Bill preferred against me, that I did hear of. One of the Clerks told me, I must first be examined, and then Sir *John* would make the Bill. It seems they had no grounded matter against me for to write a Bill, and therefore they went about to make me betray my own innocency, that so they might ground the Bill upon my own words. and, at the entrance of my appearance, the Clerk and I had a deal of discourse, (the particulars whereof for brevity sake I now omit;) but in the conclusion he demanded money of me, for entering of my appearance: and I told him I was but a young man, and a prisoner, and money was not very plentiful with me, and therefore I would not part with any money upon such terms. Well (said he) if you will not pay your fee, I will dash out your name again. Do what you please (said I) I care not if you do; so he made complaint to Mr. *Goad*, the Master of the Office, that I refused to enter my appearance. And then I was brought before him, and he demanded of me what my business was? I told him, I had no business with him, but I was a prisoner in the *Fleet*, and was sent for, but to whom and to what end I do not know, and therefore if he had nothing to say to me, I had no business with him. And then one of the Clerks said, I was to be examined. Then Mr. *Goad* said, Tender him the Book: so I looked another way, as though I did not give ear to what he said; and then he bid me pull off my Glove, and lay my hand upon the Book. What to do, Sir? said I. You must swear, said he. To what? *That you shall make true answer to all things that are asked you.* Must I so, Sir? But before I swear, I will know to what I must swear. As soon as you have sworn, you shall, but not before. To that I answered, Sir, I am but a young man, and do not well know what belongs to the nature of an Oath, and therefore before I swear, I will be better advised. Saith he, how old are you? About twenty years old, I told him. You have received the Sacrament, have you not? Yes, that I have. And you have heard the Ministers deliver God's word, have you not? I have heard Sermons. Well then, you know the holy Evangelists? Yes, that I do. But, Sir, though I have received the Sacrament, and have heard Sermons, yet it doth not therefore follow that I am bound to take an Oath, which I doubt of the lawfulness of. Look you here, said he (and with that he opened the Book), we desire you to swear by no foreign thing, but to swear by the holy Evangelists. Sir, I do not doubt or question that; I question how lawful it is for me to swear to I do not know what. So some of the Clerks began to reason with me, and told me every one took that Oath; and would I be wiser than all other men? I told them, it made no matter to me what other men do; but before I swear, I will know better grounds and reasons than other men's practices, to convince me of the lawfulness of such an Oath, to swear I do not know to what. So Mr. *Goad* bid them hold their peace, he was not to convince any man's conscience of the lawfulness of it, but only to offer and tender it. Will you take it or no, saith he? Sir, I will be better advised first. Whereupon there was a Messenger sent to Sir *John Banks*, to certify him, that I would not take the *Star-Chamber* Oath; and also to know of him what should be done with me. So I looked I should be committed close prisoner, or worse. And about an hour after came Mr. *Cockshey*, Sir *John's* chief Clerk: What (said he) Mr. *Lilburn*, it seems you will not take your Oath, to make true answer? I told him, I would be better advised before I took such an Oath. Well then (saith he) you must go from whence you came.

Upon *Friday* the 9th of *February*, in the morning, one of the Officers of the *Fleet* came to my Chamber, and bid me get up and make me ready to go to the *Star-Chamber-Bar* forthwith. I having no time to fit myself, made me ready in all haste to go. And being at the bar, Sir *John Banks* laid a verbal accusation against me; which was, that I refused to answer, and also to enter my appearance, and that I refused to take the *Star-Chamber* Oath: and then was read the affidavit of one *Edmond Chillington*, Button-seller, made against Mr. *John Wharton* and myself. the sum of which was, that he and I had printed at *Rotterdam*, in *Holland*, Dr. *Bastwick's* Answer, and his Litany, and divers other scandalous Books. And then after I had obtained leave to speak, I said, My noble Lords, as for that Affidavit, it is a most false lye and untrue.

Lord-Keeper. Why will you not answer? *Lilburn.* My honourable Lord, I have answered fully before Sir *John Banks* to all things that belong to me to answer unto; and for other things, which concern other men, I have nothing to do with them. But why do you refuse to take the *Star-Chamber* Oath? Most noble Lord, I refused upon this ground, because that when I was examined, though I had fully answered all things that belonged to me to answer unto, and had cleared myself of the thing for which I am imprisoned, which was for sending Books out of *Holland*, yet that would not satisfy and give content, but other things were put unto me, concerning other men, to insnare me, and get further matter against me; which I perceiving refused, being not bound to answer to such things as do not belong unto me. And withal I perceived the Oath to be an Oath of inquiry, and for the lawfulness of which Oath, I have no warrant; and upon these grounds I did and do still refuse the Oath. Upon this some of the King's Counsel and some of the Lords spoke: Would I condemn and contradict the laws of the land, and be wiser than all other men, to refuse that which is the Oath of the Court, administred unto all that come there? *Lord Keeper.* Well; tender him the Book. I standing against the Prelate of *Canterbury's* back, he looked over his shoulder at me, and bid me pull off my glove, and lay my hand upon the Book. Unto whom I replied, Sir, I will not swear, and then directing my speech unto the Lords, I said, Most honourable and noble Lords, with all reverence and submission unto your Honours, submitting my body unto your Lordships pleasure, and whatsoever you please to inflict upon it, yet must I refuse the Oath. My Lords, said the *Arch-Prelate*, (in a deriding manner) do you hear him? He saith, with all reverence and submission he refuseth the Oath. Well, come, come (said my *Lord-Keeper)*, submit yourself unto the Court.

Lilburn. Most noble Lords, with all willingness, I submit my body unto your Honours pleasure; but for any other submission, most Honourable Lords, I am conscious unto myself, that I have done nothing that doth deserve a convention before this illustrious Assembly; and therefore for me to submit, is to submit I do not know wherefore.

Earl of *Dorset.* My Lords, this is one of their private spirits; do you hear him, how he stands in his own justification? Well, my Lords, said the great Prelate, this fellow (meaning me) hath been one of the notoriousest dispersers of libellous Books that is in the Kingdom; and that is the Father of them all (pointing to old Mr. *Wharton)*.

Lilburn. Sir, I know you are not able to prove, and to make that good which you have said. I have testimony of it, said he. Then, said I, produce them in the face of the open Court, that we may see what they have to accuse me of; and I am ready here to answer for myself, and to make my just defence. With this he was silent, and said not one word more to me, and then they asked my Fellow Soldier, old Mr. *Wharton*, whether he would take the Oath; which he refused, and began to tell them of the Bishops cruelty towards him; and that they had had him in five several Prisons within these two years, for refusing the Oath. And then there was silence; after which was read how the Court had proceeded against some that had harboured Jesuits and Seminary-priests (those Traitors) who refused to be examined upon Oath; and in regard that we refused likewise to be examined upon Oath, it was fit, they said, that we should be proceeded against, as they were. So they were the precedent by which we were censured, though their cause and ours be much unlike, in regard theirs were little better than Treason; but our crime was so far from Treason, that it was neither against the glory of God, the honour of the King, the laws of the land, nor the good of the Commonwealth. but rather for the maintaining of the honour of them all, as all those that read the Books without partial affections and prejudicate hearts can witness and declare; and if the Books had had any Treason, or any thing against the Law of the Land in them, yet we were but supposedly guilty; for the things were never fully proved against us. Indeed there were two Oaths read in Court, which they said were sworn against us by one man, but he was never brought face to face, and in both his Oaths he hath forsworn himself, as in many particulars thereof we are both able to make good. In the conclusion, my *Lord Keeper* stood up, and said,

My

My Lords, I hold it fit, that they should be both for their contempt committed close Prisoners till *Tuesday* next; and if they do not conform themselves betwixt this and then to take the Oath, and yield to be examined before Mr. *Goad*, then that they shall be brought hither again, and censured, and made an example. Unto which they all agreed; and so we were committed close Prisoners, and no Friends admitted to come unto us.

In Camera Stellat' coram Concilio ibidem 9. *die* Febr. Anno 13 Car. *Regis.*

'UPon Information this day to this Honourable Court, by Sir *John Banks* Knight, his Majesty's Attorney-General, That *John Lilburn* and *John Wharton*, who are now at the Bar of this Court, were the 24th of *January* last ordered to be examined upon Interrogatories touching their unlawful printing, publishing, and dispersing of libellous and seditious Books, contrary to the decree of this Court, which was verified by affidavit; and being brought up to the Office to appear and be examined accordingly, the said *Lilburn* refused to appear, and both of them denied to take an Oath to make answer to Interrogatories, as appears by Certificate of Mr. *Goad*: it was humbly prayed that their appearance may be recorded, they being now present in Court, and that they may now have their Oaths tendered unto them; which if they shall refuse to take, that then this Court will proceed to a censure against them for their high contempt therein, as hath been used in like cases, which the Court held fit: And hath therefore ordered, That their appearance shall be recorded, as is desired. And for that the said Delinquents do now again most contemptuously refuse to take their Oaths now tendered to them in open Court, their Lordships have further ordered, That the said *Lilburn* and *Wharton* shall be remanded to the prison of the *Fleet*, there to remain close Prisoners until they conform themselves in obedience to take their Oaths, and be examined; and that unless they do take their Oaths, and yield to be examined by *Monday*-night next, their Lordships will, on the last sitting of this Term, proceed to censure against them for their contempts therein, as is desired.'

And upon *Monday* after we were had to *Gray's-Inn*, and I being the first there, Mr. *Goad* said to me, according to the Lords order upon *Friday* last, I have sent for you to tender the Oath unto you. Sir, I beseech you, let me hear the Lords order. So he caused it to be read unto me, and then tendered me the Book. Well, Sir, said I, I am of the same mind I was; and withal I understand, that this Oath is one and the same with the *High Commission Oath*, which Oath I know to be both against the Law of God, and the Law of the Land; and therefore in brief I dare not take the Oath, though I suffer death for the refusal of it. Well, said he, I did not send for you to dispute with you about the lawfulness of it, but only according to my place to tender it unto you. Sir, I dare not take it, though I lose my life for the refusal of it. So he said, he had no more to say to me; and I took my leave of him, and came away. And after that, came the old man, Mr. *Wharton*, and it was tendered unto him, which he refused to take: and (as he hath told me) he declared unto him how the Bishops had him eight times in prison for the refusal of it, and he had suffered the Bishops merciless cruelty for many years together, and he would now never take it as long as he lived; and withal told him, that if there were a Cart ready at the door to carry him to *Tyburn*, he would be hanged, before ever he would take it. And this was that day's business.

Upon the next morning, *Feb.* 13. about seven a-clock, we were had to the *Star-Chamber* Bar again, to receive our censure; and stood at the Bar about two hours before Sir *John Banks* came: but at last he began his accusation against us, that we did still continue in our former stubbornness. And also there was another Affidavit of the foresaid *Edmund Chillington's* read against us; the sum of which was, that I had confessed to him, that I had printed Dr. *Bastwick's Answer* to Sir *John Banks's Information*, and his *Litany*; and another Book, *An Answer unto certain Objections*; and another Book of his called, *The Vanity and Impiety of the old Litany*; and that I had divers other Books of Dr. *Bastwick's* a-printing. And that Mr. *John Wharton* had been at the charges of Printing a Book called, *A Breviate of the Bishops late Proceedings*; and another Book, called *Sixteen new Queries*, and divers other factious Books: and that one *James Ouldam*, a Turner in *Westminster-hall*, had dispersed divers of these Books. Then I said after this manner: Most noble Lords, I beseech your Honours, that you would be pleased to give me leave to speak for myself, and to make my just defence; and I shall labour so to order my speeches, that I shall not give your Honours any just distaste; and withal shall do it with as much brevity as I can. So having obtained my desire, I began and said, My Lords, it seems there were divers Books sent out of *Holland*, which came to the hands of one *Edmund Chillington*, who made this Affidavit against us; and, as I understand, he delivered divers of these Books unto one *John Chilburne*, servant to this old man Mr. *Wharton*; and his master being in prison, he dispersed divers of them for the foresaid *Chillington's* use; whereupon the Books were taken in his custody. he being found dispersing of them, goes to one *Smith*, a Taylor, in *Bridewell*, (as I am informed) and desires him to get his peace made with the Bishops. Whereupon he covenants with some of the Bishops creatures to betray me into their hands, being newly come out of *Holland*, which (as he said) did send over these Books. So, my Lords, he having purchased his own liberty, lays the plot for betraying me, and I was taken by a Pursuivant and four others of his assistants, walking in the streets with the foresaid *John Chilburne*, who had laid and contrived the plot before (as I am able to make good), and the next morning I was committed by Sir *John Lamb* to the *Gate-house*. Now, my Lords, I do protest before your Honours on the word of a Christian, that I did not send over these Books, neither did I know the Ship that brought them, nor any that belongs to the Ship, nor to my knowledge did never see with my eyes, either the Ship, or any that belongs unto it.

And being at the *Gate-house*, I was removed (by six of your Honours) to the *Fleet*, at which time the said *Chillington* was removed from *Bridewell* to *Newgate*; and being kept close there, he, by their threats and persuasions, and the procuring of his own liberty, goes and accuses me for printing ten or twelve thousand Books in *Holland*. And at my examination before Sir *John Banks*, I cleared myself of that; and upon *Friday* last he made an Affidavit against me, in which he hath most falsly forsworn himself, and to-day he hath made another; which is also a most false untruth: and withal, my Lords, he is known to be a notorious lying fellow, and hath accused me for the purchasing of his own liberty, which he hath got. And therefore, I beseech your Honours, to take it into your serious consideration, whether I am to be censured upon such a fellow's Affidavit or no. Then said the Lord-Keeper, Thou art a mad fellow, seeing things are thus, that thou wilt not take thine Oath, and answer truly.

My honourable Lord, I have declared unto you the real truth; but for the Oath, it is an Oath of Inquiry, and of the same nature as the High-Commission Oath; which Oath I know to be unlawful; and withal I find no warrant in the word of God for an Oath of Inquiry, and it ought to be the director of me in all things that I do: and therefore, my Lords, at no hand, I dare not take the Oath. (When I named the word of God, the Court began to laugh, as though they had had nothing to do with it.) My Lords (said Mr. *Goad*) he told me yesterday, he durst not take the Oath, though he suffered death for the refusal of it. And with that my Lord Privy-Seal spoke: Will you (said he) take your Oath, that that which you have said is true? My Lord (said I) I am but a young man, and do not well know what belongs to the nature of an Oath, (but that which I have said, is a real truth) but thus much; by God's appointment, I know an Oath ought to be the end of all controversy and strife, *Heb.* vi. 16. and if it might be so in this my present cause, I would safely take my Oath, that what I have said is true. So they spoke to the old man, my fellow-partner, and asked him whether he would take the Oath? So he desired them to give him leave to speak; and he began to thunder it out against the Bishops, and told them, they required three Oaths of the King's Subjects; namely, the Oath of Churchwardenship, and the Oath of Canonical Obedience, and the Oath *ex Officio*; which (said he) are all against the Law of the Land, and by which they deceive and perjure thousands of the King's Subjects in a year. And withal, my Lords, (said he) there is a maxim in Divinity, that we should prefer the glory of God, and the Good of our King and Country, before our own lives. But the Lords wondering to hear the old man begin to talk after this manner, commanded him to hold his peace, and to answer them, whether he would take the Oath or no? To which he replied, and desired them to let him talk a little, and he would tell them by and bye. At which all the Court burst out a-laughing; but they would not let him go on, but commanded silence (which if they would have let him proceed, he would have so pepper'd the Bishops, as they were never in their lives in an open Court of Judicature). So they asked us again, whether we would take the Oath? Which we both again refused; and withal I told them, that for the reasons before I durst not take it. Then they said, they would proceed to censure. I bid them do as they pleased, for I knew myself innocent of the thing for which I was imprisoned and accused, but yet, notwithstanding, did submit my body to their Honours pleasure. So they censured us 500*l.* a-piece; and then stood up Judge *Jones*, and said, It was fit, that I being a young man, for example sake, should have some corporal punishment inflicted upon me. So my censure was to be whipt, but neither time nor place allotted. And for the old man, in regard of his age, being eighty-five years old, they would spare his corporal punishment, though (said they) he deserves it as well as the other (meaning me), yet he should stand upon the Pillory: but I could not understand or perceive by my censure, that I was to stand upon the Pillory. And when I came from the Bar, I spoke in an audible voice, and said, My Lords, I beseech God to bless your Honours, and to discover and make known unto you the wickedness and cruelty of the Prelates.

In Camera Stellata coram Concilio ibidem 13 *die* Febr. *Anno decimo tertio* Car. *Regis.*

'WHereas, upon Information to this Court the ninth of this instant *February*, by Sir *John Banks* Knight, his Majesty's Attorney-General, that *John Lilburn* and *John Wharton* (then present at the Bar) were the 24th of *January* last ordered to be examined upon Interrogatories touching their unlawful printing, importing, publishing, and dispersing of libellous and seditious Books, contrary to the Decree of this Court, which was verified by Affidavit, and being brought up to the Office to appear and be examined, the said *Lilburn* refused to appear, and both of them denied to take an Oath to make some answer to Interrogatories, as appeared by the certificate of Mr. *Goad*, Deputy Clerk of this Court: the Court did on that day order, that their appearances should be recorded, they being present in Court as aforesaid; and that in respect the said Delinquents did then again contemptuously refuse to take their Oaths tendered to them in open Court, they should be remanded to the prison of the *Fleet*, there to remain close prisoners, until they conformed themselves in obedience to take their Oaths and be examined; and that unless they did take their Oaths, and yield to be examined by *Monday*-night next then next following, and now last past, their Lordships would on this sitting-day proceed to a censure against them for their contempts therein. Now this day the said *Lilburn* and *Wharton* being again brought to the Bar, his Majesty's said Attorney informed this honourable Court, that they still continued in their former obstinacy, and contemptuously refused to take their Oaths, to make true answer to the Interrogatories, although they had been sent for, and their Oaths assented to be given unto them by Mr. *Goad*, Deputy Clerk of this Court, who now certified the same in Court: and therefore his Majesty's said Attorney humbly pleaded on his Majesty's behalf, that their Lordships would now proceed to censure against the said Delinquents, for their great contempts and disobedience therein. Whereupon their Lordships endeavoured, by fair persuasions, to draw them to conformity and obedience, and withal offered, that if they yet would submit and take their Oaths, their Lordships would accept thereof, and not proceed to censure against them. But such was the insufferable disobedience and contempt of the said Delinquents, that they still persisted in their former obstinacy, and wilfully refused to take their Oaths. In respect whereof the whole Court did with an unanimous consent, declare and adjudge the said *Lilburn* and *Wharton* guilty of a very high contempt and offence, of dangerous consequence and evil example, and worthy to undergo very sharp, severe, and exemplary censure, which might deter others from the like presumptuous boldness in refusing 'to take a legal Oath; without which, many great and exorbitant offences, to the prejudice and danger of his Majesty, his Kingdoms, and loving Subjects, might go away undiscovered, and unpunished. And therefore their Lordships have now ordered, adjudged and decreed, That the said *Lilburn* and *Wharton* shall be remanded to the *Fleet*, there to remain until they conform themselves in obedience to the orders of this Court, and that they shall pay five hundred pounds a-piece for their several fines to his Majesty's use; and before their enlargements out of the *Fleet*, become bound with good sureties for their good behaviour. And to the end that others may be the more deterred from daring to offend in the like kind hereafter, the Court hath further ordered and decreed, That the said *John Lilburn* shall be whipt through the Streets, from the prison of the *Fleet* unto the * Pillory, to be erected in such time, and place, as this Court shall hold fit and direct; and that both he and the said *Wharton* shall be both of them set in the said Pillory, and from thence be returned to the *Fleet*, there to remain according to this Decree.'

After our censure, we had the liberty of the prison for a few days; but the old man, my fellow-partner, went to the Warden of the *Fleet*, and told him the sum of that which he intended in the *Star-Chamber*, to have spoken against the Bishops, if the Lords would have let him. He told the Warden, how the Bishops were the greatest Tyrants that ever were since *Adam's* creation; and that they were more cruel than the *Cannibals*, those Men-eaters, for (said he) they presently devour men, and put an end to their pain, but the Bishops do it by degrees, and are many years in exercising their cruelty and tyranny upon those that stand out against them; and therefore are worse than the very *Cannibals*, &c.

This came to the Lords of the Council's ears, whereupon we were the next *Monday* after brought both together, and locked up close prisoners in one Chamber, without any order or warrant at all, but only Warden *Ingram's* bare command and pleasure. But the old man, about three weeks after, made a Petition to the Lords of the Council, that he might have some liberty; and being very weak, more likely to die than to live, he had his liberty granted till the Term: but I do still remain close prisoner.

Upon *Wednesday* the 18*th* of *April*, 1638, I was cruelly whipp'd through the Streets to *Westminster* †, and at the last came to the Pillory, where I was unloosed from the Cart, and having put on some of my clothes, went to the Tavern, where I staid a pretty while waiting for my Surgeon, who was not yet come to dress me; where were many of my friends, who exceedingly rejoiced to see my courage, that the Lord had enabled me to undergo my punishment so willingly.

I having a desire to retire into a private room from the multitude of people that were about me, which made me like to faint; I had not been there long, but Mr. *Lightbourne*, the Tipstaff of the *Star-Chamber*, came unto me, saying, the Lords sent him to me, to know if I would acknowledge myself to be in a fault, and then he knew what to say unto me. To whom I replied, Have their Honours caused me to be whipt from the *Fleet* to *Westminster*, and do they now send to know if I will acknowledge a fault? They should have done this before I had been whipt; for now, seeing I have undergone the greatest part of my punishment, I hope the Lord will assist me to go through it all: and beside, if I would have done this at the first, I needed not to have come to this: But as I told the Lords when I was before them at the Bar, so I desire you to tell them again, that I am not conscious to myself of doing any thing that deserves a submission, but yet I do willingly submit to their Lordships pleasures in my censure. He told me, if I would confess my fault, it would save me a standing in the Pillory; otherwise, I must undergo the burthen of it.

Well (said I) I regard not a little outward disgrace for the cause of my God, I have found already that sweetness in him, in whom I have believed, that through his strength, I am able to undergo any thing that shall be inflicted on me; but methinks that I had very hard measure, that I should be condemned and thus punished upon two Oaths, in which the party has most falsly forsworn himself, and because I would not take an Oath to betray mine own innocence. Why, *Paul* found more mercy from the Heathen *Roman Governors*, for they would not put him to an Oath to accuse himself, but suffered him to make the best defence he could for himself; neither would they condemn him, before his accusers and he were brought face to face, to justify, and fully to prove their accusation; but the Lords have not dealt so with me, for my accusers and I were never brought face to face, to justify their accusation against me. It is true, two false Oaths were sworn against me, and I was thereupon condemned, and because I would not accuse myself. And so he went away, and I prepared myself for the Pillory, to which I went with a joyful courage, and when I was upon it, I made obeisance to the Lords, some of them (as I suppose) looking out at the *Star-Chamber* window towards me. And so I put my neck into the hole, which being a great deal too low for me, it was very painful to me, in regard of continuance of the time that I stood on the Pillory, which was about two hours; my back being also very sore, and the Sun shining so exceeding hot, and the *Tipstaff-man* not suffering me to keep on my hat to defend my head from the heat of the Sun, so that I stood there in great pain; yet through the strength of my God I underwent it with courage, to the very last minute; and lifting up my heart and spirit unto my God, I began to speak after this manner:

My Christian Brethren,

TO all you that love the Lord *Jesus Christ*, and desire that he should reign and rule in your hearts and lives, to you especially, and to as many as hear me this day, I direct my Speech.

I stand here in the place of ignominy and shame, yet to me it is not so, but I own and embrace it, as the *Welcome Cross of Christ*, and as a badge of my *Christian Profession*. I have been already whipt from the *Fleet* to this place, by virtue of a censure from the honourable Lords of the *Star-Chamber*; the cause of my censure I shall declare unto you as briefly as I can.

The Lord, by his special hand of Providence, so ordered it, that not long ago I was in *Holland*, where I was like to have settled myself in the course of Trading, that might have brought me in a pretty large portion of earthly things, (after which my heart did too much run) but the Lord having a better portion in store for me, and more durable riches to bestow upon my Soul, by the same hand of Providence, brought me back again, and cast me into easy affliction, that thereby I might be weaned from the World, and see the vanity and emptiness of all things therein. And he hath now pitched my soul upon such an object of beauty, amiableness, and excellency, as is as permanent and endurable, as eternity itself; namely, the personal excellency of the Lord *Jesus Christ*, the sweetness of whose presence no affliction can ever be able to wrest out of my Soul.

Now, while I was in *Holland*, it seems there were divers Books of that noble and renowned Doctor *John Bastwick* sent into *England*, which came into the hands of one *Edmund Chillington*; for the sending over of which I was taken and apprehended, the plot being before laid by one *John Chilburne* (whom I supposed, and took to be my Friend), servant to my old fellow-soldier, Mr. *John Wharton*, living in *Bow-lane*, after this manner:

I walking in the street with the said *John Chilburne*, was taken by the Pursuivant and his men; the said *John*, as I verily believe, having given direction to them where to stand, and he himself was the third man that laid hands on me to hold me.

Now, at my censure before the Lords, I there declared upon the word of a Christian, that I sent not over those Books, neither did I know the Ship that brought them, nor any of the men that belonged to the Ship, nor to my knowledge did I ever see either ship, or any appertaining to it in all my days.

Besides this, I was accused at my examination before the King's Attorney, at his chamber, by the said *Edmund Chillington*, Button-seller, living in *Cannon-street*, near *Abchurch-lane*, and late prisoner in *Bridewell* and *Newgate*, for printing ten or twelve thousand Books in *Holland*; and that I would have printed the *Unmasking the Mystery of Iniquity*, if I could have gotten a true copy of it, and that I had a Chamber in Mr. *John Foot's* house at *Delft*, where he thinks the books were kept.

Now, here I declare before you all, upon the word of a suffering Christian, that he might as well have accused me of printing a hundred thousand books, and the one been as true as the other. And for the printing the *Unmasking the Mystery of Iniquity*, upon the word of an honest man, I never saw, nor to my knowledge heard of the book, till I came back again into *England*. And for my having a Chamber at Mr. *John Foot's* house at *Delft*, where he thinks the books were kept; I was so far from having a Chamber there, as I never lay in his house but twice or thrice at the most: and upon the last *Friday* of the last Term, I was brought to the *Star-Chamber-Bar*, where before me was read the said *Edmund Chillington's Affidavit*, upon oath against Mr *John Wharton* and myself; the sum of which oath was, That he and I had printed (at *Rotterdam*, in *Holland*) Dr. *Bastwick's Answer*, and his *Litany*, with divers other scandalous books.

Now, here again I speak it in the presence of God, and all you that hear me, that Mr. *Wharton* and I never joined together in printing either these, or any other books whatsoever, neither did I receive any money from him toward the printing any.

Withal, in his first Oath, he peremptorily swore, that we had printed them at *Rotterdam*: unto which I likewise say, That he hath in this particular forswore himself: for mine own part, I never in all my days either printed, or caused to be printed, either for myself, or for Mr. *Wharton*, any books at *Rotterdam*; neither did I come into any Printing-house there, all the time that I was in the City.

And then upon the *Tuesday* after, he swore against both of us again. The sum of which oaths was, that I had confessed to him (which is most false) that I had printed Dr. *Bastwick's* Answer to Sir *John Banks's Information*, and his *Litany*; and another Book, called, *Certain Answers to certain Objections*: and another Book, called, *The Vanity and Impiety of the Old Litany*. And that I had divers other Books of the said Dr. *Bastwick's* in printing, and that Mr. *Wharton* had been at the charges of printing a Book, called, *A Breviate of the Bishops late Proceedings*; and another Book, called, *Sixteen New Queries*, and in this his oath hath sworn they were printed at *Rotterdam*, or somewhere else in *Holland*; and that one *James Oldham*, a Turner, keeping Shop at *Westminster-hall* Gate, dispersed divers of these Books. Now, in this oath he hath [illegible] himself in a high degree; for whereas he took his oath that I had printed the Book, called, *The Vanity and Impiety of the Old Litany*, [illegible] speak it before you all, that I never in all my days [illegible] in print; but I must confess, I have seen and read it [illegible], before the Doctor was censured. And as for other Books, [illegible] saith I have divers in printing, to that I answer, that [illegible], I never read nor saw any of the Doctor's Books, but [illegible] in *English*, and one little thing more of about [illegible] of paper, which is annexed to the *Vanity of the Old Litany*. And as for his *Latin* Books, I never saw any but two, namely, his *Flagellum*, for which he was first censured in the High-Commission-Court, and his [illegible], which were both in print long before I knew the Doctor: but it is true, there is a second edition of his *Flagellum*, but that was at the press above two years ago; namely, *Anno* 1634, and some of this impression was in *England* before I came out of *Holland*.

And these are the main things for which I was censured and condemned, being two oaths in which the said *Chillington* hath [illegible] to [illegible] himself, and if he had not forsworn himself, yet [illegible] I am given to understand) I might have excepted against him, being [illegible] person himself, and a prisoner, and did that which he did against me for purchasing his own Liberty, which he hath by such *Judas*-like means got and obtained, who is also known to be a lying fellow, as I told the Lords I was able to prove and make good.

But besides all this, there was an inquisition-oath tendered unto me (which I refused to take) on four several days, the Sum of which oath is thus much: 'You shall swear that you shall make true 'answer to all things that shall be asked of you: so help you God.' Now this oath I refused as a sinful and unlawful oath, it being the High-Commission oath, with which the Prelates ever have, and still do, so butcherly torment, afflict and undo, the dear Saints and Servants of God. It is an oath against the Law of the Land (as Mr. *Nathaniel Fiennes* in his Argument doth prove): And also it is expressly against

* The Pillory was placed between *Westminster-Hall Gate* and the *Star-Chamber*.

† And as the Cart drew him along, he repeated several Texts of Scripture, and talk'd enthusiastically to the People, which for brevity's sake is here omitted.

the Petition of Right, an Act of Parliament enacted in the 3 and 4 year of our King. Again, it is absolutely against the Law of God; for that Law requires no man to accuse himself; but if any thing be laid to his charge, there must come two or three witnesses at least to prove it. It is also against the practice of Christ himself, who, in all his examinations before the High Priest, would not accuse himself, but upon their demands, returned this answer, *Why ask you me? Go to them that heard me.*

Withal, this Oath is against the very Law of Nature; for Nature is always a preserver of itself, and not a destroyer: But if a man takes this wicked Oath, he destroys and undoes himself, as daily Experience doth witness. Nay, it is worse than the Law of the Heathen *Romans*, as we may read, *Acts* xxv. 16. *For when* Paul *stood before the Pagan Governors, and the Jews required Judgement against him, the Governor replyed, It is not the manner of the* Romans *to condemn any man, before he and his accusers be brought face to face, to justify their accusation.* But for my own part, if I had been proceeded against by a Bill, I would have answered and justified all that they could have proved against me; and by the strength of my God, would have sealed whatsoever I have done with my blood: for I am privy to mine own actions, and my conscience bears me witness, that I have laboured, ever since the Lord in mercy made the riches of his grace known to my soul, to keep a good conscience, and to walk inoffensively both towards God and man. But as for that Oath that was put upon me, I did refuse to take it as a sinful and unlawful Oath, and by the strength of my God enabling me, I will never take it, though I be pulled in pieces by wild Horses, as the antient Christians were by the bloody Tyrants in the *Primitive Church*; neither shall I think that man a faithful subject of Christ's Kingdom, that shall at any time hereafter take it, seeing the wickedness of it hath been so apparently laid open by so many, for the refusal whereof many do suffer cruel persecution to this day.

Thus have I, as briefly as I could, declared unto you, the whole cause of my standing here this day; I being upon these grounds censured by the Lords at the *Star-Chamber* on the last Court-day of the last Term, to pay 500*l.* to the King, and to receive the punishment, which with rejoicing I have undergone, unto whose censure I do with willingness and cheerfulness submit myself.

But seeing I now stand here at this present, I intend, the Lord assisting me with his power, and guiding me by his Spirit, to declare my mind unto you.

I have nothing to say to any man's person, and therefore will not meddle with that; only the things that I have to say, in the first place are concerning the Bishops and their calling: They challenge their callings to be *Jure Divino*; and for the oppugning of which, those three renowned living martyrs of the Lord, Dr. *Bastwick*, Mr. *Burton*, and Mr. *Prynne*, did suffer in this place, and they have sufficiently proved, that their calling is not from God: which men I love and honour, and do persuade myself that their souls are dear and precious in the sight of God, tho' they were so cruelly and butcherly dealt with by the Prelates. And as for Mr. *Burton* and Mr. *Prynne*, they are worthy and learned men, but yet did not in many things write so fully as the Doctor did, who hath sufficiently and plentifully set forth the wickedness, both of the Prelates themselves, and of their callings (as you may read in his Books), that they are not *Jure Divino*; which noble and reverend Doctor I love with all my soul: and as he is a man that stands for the truth and glory of God, my very life and heart-blood I will lay down to his honour, and the maintaining of his cause for which he suffered, it being God's cause. As for the Bishops, they used in former times to challenge their jurisdiction, callings and power from the King: but they have now openly, in the *High Commission-Court*, renounced that, as was heard by many, at the censure of that noble Doctor: and as you may further read in his *Apologeticus*; and in his *Answer* to Sir *John Banks's Information*. Now I will here maintain it before them all, that their calling is so far from being *Jure Divino* (as they say they are), that they are rather *Jure Diabolico*, which if I am not able to prove, let me be hanged up at the Hall-gate. But, my Brethren, for your better satisfaction, read the ixth and sixth Chapters of the *Revelation*, and there you shall see, that there came *Locusts* out of the *Bottomless Pitt* part of whom they are, and they are there lively described. Also you shall there find, that the Beast (which is the Pope, or *Roman* State and Government) hath given to him by the *Dragon* (the *Devil*) his power, seat, and great authority. So that the Pope's authority comes from the *Devil*; and the Prelates, and their Creatures, in their printed Books, do challenge their authority, jurisdiction and power (that they exercise over all sorts of people) is from *Rome*.

And for proving the Church of *England* to be a true Church, their best and strongest argument is, that the Bishops are lineally descended from his Holiness (or Impiousness) of *Rome*, as you may read in *Pocklington's* Book, called *Sunday no Sabbath*. So that by their own confession they stand by that same power and authority, that they have received from the Pope: so that their calling is not from God, but from the Devil. For the Pope cannot give a better authority or calling to them than he himself hath; but his authority and calling is from the Devil, therefore the Prelate's calling and authority is from the Devil also, *Revel.* ix. 3. *And there came out of the smoke, Locusts upon the earth, and unto them was given power, as the Scorpions of the earth have power to hurt and undo men*, as the Prelates daily do: and also, *Revel.* xiii. 2. *And the Beast which I saw* (saith St. *John*) *was like unto a Leopard, and his feet were as the feet of a Bear, and his mouth as the mouth of a Lion; and the Dragon* (that is to say, the Devil) *gave him his power, his seat and great authority*; and verse 15, 16, 17. And whether the Prelates as well as the Pope, do not daily the same things, let every man that hath but common reason judge.

For do not their daily practices and cruel burthens imposed on all sorts of people, high and low, rich and poor, witness that their descent is from the Beast, part of his state and kingdom? so also *Revel.* xvi. 13, 14. all which places do declare, that their power and authority being from the Pope (as they themselves [illegible]) therefore it must originally come from the Devil. For their power and callings must of necessity proceed either from God, or else from the Devil; but it proceeds not from God, as the Scriptures sufficiently declare, therefore their calling and power proceeds from the Devil, as both Scripture and their own daily practices do demonstrate and prove. And as for that last place cited, *Rev.* xvi. 13, 14. if you please to read the second and third parts of Dr. *Bastwick*'s Litany, you shall find, he there proves, that the Prelates practices do every way suit with, and make good that portion of Scripture to the utmost. For in their Sermons that they preach before his Majesty, how do they incense the King and Nobles against the people of God, labouring to make them odious in his sight, and stirring him up to execute vengeance upon them, though they be the most harmless generation of all others?

And as for all these officers that are under them, and made by them, for mine own particular, I cannot see but that their callings are as unlawful as the Bishops themselves; and in particular, for the callings of the Ministers, I do not, nor will not speak against their persons, for I know some of them to be very able men, and men of excellent gifts and qualifications; and I persuade myself, their souls are very dear and precious in the sight of God.

Yet notwithstanding, this proves not their callings to be ever the better, as it is in civil government: If the King (whom God hath made a lawful Magistrate) make a wicked man an officer, he is as true an officer, and as well to be obeyed, coming in the King's name, as the best man in the world coming with the same authority; for in such a case, he that is a wicked man, hath his calling from as good authority as the godliest man hath; and therefore his calling is as good as the other's.

But on the other side, if he that hath no authority make officers, tho' the men themselves be ever so good and holy, yet their holiness makes their calling never a whit the truer; but still is a false calling, in regard his authority was not good nor lawful that made them. And even so the Ministers, be they ever so holy men, yet they have one and the same calling with the wickedest that is amongst them; their holiness proves not their callings to be ever the truer, seeing their authority that made them Ministers is false: and therefore they have more to answer for than any of the rest, by how much the more God hath bestowed greater gifts upon them than upon others, and yet they detain the truth in unrighteousness from God's people, and do not make known to them, as they ought, the whole will and counsel of God.

And again, the greater is their sin, if their callings be unlawful (as I verily believe they are), in that they still hold them, and do not willingly lay down and renounce them; or they do but deceive the people, and highly dishonour God, and sin against their own souls, while they preach unto the people by virtue of an *Antichristian* and unlawful calling. And the more godly and able the Minister is, that still preaches by virtue of this calling, the more hurt he doth; for the people that have such a Minister will not be persuaded of the truth of things, though one speak, and inform them in the name of the Lord; but will be ready to reply, Our Minister that preaches still by virtue of this calling, is so holy a man, that were not his calling right and good, I do assure myself he would no longer preach by virtue thereof. And thus the holiness of the Minister is a cloak to cover the unlawfulness of his calling, and make the people continue rebels against Christ, his Sceptre and Kingdom, which is an aggravation of his sin: for by this means the people are kept off from receiving the whole truth into their souls, and rest in being but almost Christians, or but Christians in part. But, O my Brethren, it becomes all you that fear God, and tender the salvation of your own souls, to look about you, and to shake off that long security and formality in Religion that you have been in: for God, of all things, cannot endure *Lukewarmness*, *Rev.* iii. 16. and search out diligently the truth of things, and try them in the balance of the Sanctuary. I beseech you take things no more upon trust, as hitherto you have done, but take pains to search and find out those spiritual and hidden truths that God hath enwrapped in his sacred Book, and find out a bottom for your own souls: for if you will have the comforts of them, you must bestow some labour for the getting of them, and you must search diligently before you find them, *Prov.* ii. Labour also to withdraw your necks from under that spiritual and *Antichristian* bondage (unto which you have for a long time subjected your souls), lest the Lord cast his plagues, and the heaviness of his wrath, to seize both upon your bodies and souls, seeing you are now warned of the danger of these things.

For he himself hath said, *Rev.* xiv. 9, 10, 11. *That if any man worship the Beast and his Image, and receive his mark in his forehead, or in his hand, the same shall drink of the wine of his wrath, which is poured out without mixture, into the cup of his indignation, and he shall be tormented with fire and brimstone, in the presence of the holy Angels, and in the presence of the Lamb; and the smoke of their torment ascended up for ever and ever, and they have no rest, day nor night, who worship the Beast and his Image, and whosoever receiveth the mark of his name.* Therefore as you love your own souls, and look for that immortal Crown of happiness in the world to come, look that you withdraw yourselves from that *Antichristian* power and slavery that you are now under, even as God himself hath commanded and enjoined you, in *Rev* xviii. 4. *Come out of her, my people, that you be not partakers of her sins, and that you receive not of her plagues, for her sins have reached unto Heaven, and God hath remembered her iniquities.* Here is the voice of God himself, commanding all his chosen ones, though they have lived under this *Antichristian* slavish power and state a long time, yet at last to withdraw their obedience and subjection from it. My brethren, we are all at this present, in a very dangerous and fearful condition, under the idolatrous and spiritual bondage of the Prelates, in regard we have turned the [illegible] unto our God, in seeing his almighty great name, and his heavenly truth trodden under foot, and so highly dishonoured by them, and yet we not only let them alone in holding our peace, but most slavishly and wickedly subject ourselves unto them, fearing the face of a piece of dirt, more than the Almighty great God of heaven and earth, who is able to cast both body and soul into everlasting damnation.

Oh repent, I beseech you therefore repent, for that great dishonour you have suffered to be done unto God by your fearfulness and cowardliness, and for the time to come put on courageous resolutions like valiant soldiers of *Jesus Christ*, and fight manfully in this his spiritual battle. In which battle some of his soldiers have already lost part of their blood, and withal, study this Book of the *Revelation*, and there you shall see the mystery of iniquity fully unfolded and explained, [illegible] what great spiritual battles have been fought betwixt the Lamb and his servants, and the *Dragon* (the *Devil*) and his vassals; and [illegible]

Therefore gird on your spiritual armour, spoken of, *Ephes.* vi. that you may quit yourselves like good and faithful soldiers, and fear no Colours, [illegible] victory and conquest is ours already; [illegible] of any bodily and temporal battle, [illegible]

4

not discouraged and knock'd off from the study of it, because of the obscurity and darkness of it; for the Lord hath promised his enlightening Spirit unto all his people that are laborious and studious to know him a-right, and also he hath promised a blessing, and pronounced a blessedness unto all that read and labour to keep the things contained in this Book, *Rev.* i. 3. My Christian Brethren, in the bowels of *Jesus Christ*, I beseech you do not contemn the things that are deliver'd to you, in regard of the meanness and weakness of me the instrument, being but one of the meanest and unworthiest of the servants of *Jesus Christ*, for the Lord many times doth great things by weak means, that his power may be more seen; for we are too ready to cast our eye upon the means and instrument, not looking up unto that Almighty power that is in God, who is able to do the greatest things by the weakest means, and therefore out of the mouths of *Babes* and *Sucklings* he hath ordained strength, *Psal.* viii. 2. And he hath chosen the foolish things of the world to confound the wise, and God hath chosen the weak things of the world to confound the things which are mighty, and base things of the world, and things which are depised, hath God chosen; yea, things which are not, to bring to nought the things that are, 1 *Cor.* i. 27, 28. And he gives the reason wherefore he is pleased so to do, *That no flesh should glory in his presence.*

So you see God is not tyed to any instrument and means to effect his own glory, but he by the least instrument is able to bring to pass the greatest things.

It is true, I am a young man, and no Scholar, according to that which the World counts Scholarship, yet I have obtained mercy of the Lord to be faithful, and he, by a Divine Providence, hath brought me hither this day; and I speak to you in the name of the Lord, being assisted with the Spirit and Power of the God of Heaven and Earth: and I speak not the words of rashness or inconsiderateness, but the words of soberness, and mature deliberation, for I did consult with my God, before I came hither, and desired him that he would direct and enable me to speak that, which might be for his glory and the good of his people. And as I am a soldier, fighting under the banner of the great and mighty Captain, the Lord *Jesus Christ*; and as I look for that Crown of immortality, which one day I know shall be set upon my temples, being in the condition that I am in, I dare not hold my peace, but speak unto you with boldness in the might and strength of my God, the things which the Lord in mercy hath made known unto my soul, come life, come death.

[When I was hereabout, there came a fat Lawyer, I do not know his name, and commanded me to hold my peace, and leave my preaching. To whom I replied and said, Sir, I will not hold my peace, but speak my mind freely, though I be hanged at *Tyburn* for my pains. It seems he himself was galled and touched, as the Lawyers were in Christ's time, when he spake against the *Scribes* and *Pharisees*, which made them say, *Master, in saying thus thou revilest us also.* So he went his way, and (I think) complained to the Lords, but I went on with my speech, and said:]

My Brethren, be not discouraged at the ways of God for the affliction and cross that doth accompany them, for it is sweet and comfortable drawing in the yoke of Christ for all that, and I have found it so by experience; for my soul is fill'd so full of spiritual and heavenly joy, that with my tongue I am not able to express it, neither are any capable (I think) to partake of so great a degree of consolation, but only those upon whom the Lord's gracious afflicting hand is.

And for mine own part, I stand this day in the place of an evil doer, but my conscience witnesseth that I am not so. [And hereabout I put my hand into my pocket, and pull'd out three of worthy Dr. *Bastwick*'s Books, and threw them among the people, and said,] There is part of the Books for which I suffer, take them among you, and read them, and see if you find any thing in them against the Law of God, the Law of the Land, the Glory of God, the Honour of the King or State.

I am the son of a Gentleman, and my friends are of rank and quality in the Country where they live, which is two hundred miles from this place, and I am in my present condition deserted of them all; for I know, not one of them dare meddle with me in my present estate, being I am stung by the *Scorpions*, (the *Prelates*) and for any thing that I know, it may be I shall never have a favourable countenance from any of them again: and withal, am a young man, and likely to have lived well, and in plenty, according to the fashion of the world; yet notwithstanding, for the cause of Christ and to do him service, I have and do bid adieu to father, friends, and riches, pleasures, ease, contented life and blood, and lay all down at the foot stool of *Jesus Christ*, being willing to part with all, rather than I will dishonour him, or in the least measure part with the peace of a good conscience, and that sweetness and joy which I have found in him. For in naked Christ is the quintessence of sweetness, and I am so far from thinking my affliction and punishment, which I have this day endured, and still do endure and groan under, a disgrace, that I receive it as the welcome *Cross of Christ*, do think myself this day more honoured by my sufferings, than if a crown of gold had been set upon my head: for I have in some part been made conformable to my Lord and Master, and have in some measure drank of the same Cup, which he himself drank of, while he was in this sinful world. For he shed his most precious blood for the salvation of my poor soul, that so I might be reconciled to his Father; therefore am I willing to undergo any thing for his sake, and that inward joy and consolation within me, that carries me high above all my pains and torments. And you, (*my Brethren*) if you be willing to have Christ, you must own him, and take him upon his own terms, and know that Christ and the Cross is inseparable; for he that will live godly in *Christ Jesus*, must suffer persecution and affliction; it is the lot and portion of all his chosen ones, through many afflictions and trials we must enter into glory; and the *Apostle* saith, *That if ye be without affliction, whereof all are partakers, then are ye bastards, and not sons.* And therefore, if you will have Christ, sit down and reckon before ever you make profession of him, what he will cost you; lest when you come to the trial, you dishonour him; and if you be not willing and contented withal, and let all go for his sake, you are not worthy of him.

If parents, husband, wife or children, lands or livings, riches or honours, pleasure or ease, life or blood, stand in the way, you must be willing to part with all these, and to entertain Christ naked and alone, though you have nothing but the Cross, or else you are not worthy of him; *Math.* x. 37, 38.

Oh, my Brethren, there is such sweetness and contentedness in enjoying the *Lord Jesus* alone, that it is able, where it is felt, to make a man go thro' all difficulties, and endure all hardships that may possibly come upon him. Therefore, if he call you to it, do not deny him, nor his truth in the least manner; for he hath said, *He that denies him before men, him will he deny before his Father, which is in Heaven.* And now is the time that we must shew ourselves good soldiers of *Jesus Christ*, for his truth, his cause and glory lies at stake in a high degree, therefore put on courageous resolutions, and withdraw your necks and souls from all false power and worship, and fight with courage and boldness in this spiritual battle, in which battle, the Lord before your eyes hath raised up some valiant Champions that fought up to the ears in blood: therefore be courageous soldiers, and fight it out bravely, that your God may be glorified by you, and let him only have the service, both of your inward and outward man, and stand to his cause, and love your own souls, and fear not the face of any mortal man; for God hath promised to be with you, and uphold you, that they shall not prevail against you, *Isa.* xli 10, 11. But alas, how few are there that dare shew any courage for God and his cause, though his glory lies at the stake, but think themselves happy and well, and count themselves wise men, if they can sleep in a whole skin; when Christ hath said, *He that will save his life shall lose it; and he that will lose his life for his sake, shall find it. What shall it profit a man, if he gain the whole world, and lose his own soul?*

Therefore it is better for a man to be willing and contented to let all go for the enjoying of Christ, and doing him service, than to sit down and sleep in a whole skin, though in so doing he gain all the world, and see him dishonoured, his glory and truth trodden under foot, and the blood of his servants shed and spilt.

Yes, without doubt, it is; but many are in these times, so far from suffering valiantly for Christ, that they rather dissuade men from it, and count it a point of singularity and pride, and self-ends, for a man to put himself forward to do God service; asking, what calling and warrant any private man hath thereunto, seeing it belongs to the Ministers to speak of these things? Yes, so it doth; but alas, they are so cowardly and fearful, that they dare not speak.

And therefore it belongs also to thee, or me, or any other man, if thou be'st a soldier of *Jesus Christ*, whatsoever by place or calling thy rank or degree be, be it higher or lower, yet if he call for thy service, thou art bound, though others stand still, to maintain his power and glory to the utmost of thy power and strength, yea, to the shedding the last drop of thy blood; for he hath not loved his life unto the death for thy sake, but shed his precious blood for the redemption of thy soul. Hath he done this for thee, and darest thou see him dishonoured, and his glory lie at the stake, and not speak in his behalf, or do him the best service thou canst?

If out of a base and cowardly spirit thus thou doest, let me tell thee here, and that truly to thy face, thou hast a *Dalilah* in thy heart, which thou lovest more than God, and that thou shalt one day certainly find by woful experience. Alas, if men should hold their peace in such times as these, the Lord would cause the very stones to speak, to convince man of his cowardly baseness.

Having proceeded in a manner thus far by the strength of my God, with boldness and courage in my speech, the *Warden of the Fleet* came with the fat *Lawyer*, and commanded me to hold my peace. To whom I replied, I would speak and declare my cause and mind, though I were to be hanged at the gate for my speaking. And he caused proclamation to be made upon the Pillory, for bringing to him the Books. so then he commanded me to be gagged, and if I spake any more, that then I should be whipt again upon the Pillory.

So I remained about an hour and a half gagged, being intercepted of much matter, which by God's assistance I intended to have spoken; but yet with their cruelty I was nothing at all daunted, for I was full of comfort and courage, being mightily strengthened with the power of the Almighty, which made me with chearfulness triumph over all my sufferings, not shewing one sad countenance or discontented heart.

And when I was to come down, having taken out my head out of the Pillory, I looked about me upon the people, and said, *I am more than a conqueror through him that hath loved me. Vivat Rex*, Let the King live for ever; and so I came down, and was had back again to the Tavern, where I, together with Mr. *Wharton*, staid a while, till one went to the Warden to know what should be done with me, who gave order we should be carried back again to the *Fleet*.

After I came back to the prison, none were suffered to come to me, but the Surgeon to dress me.

[*Here* Lilburn *gives an account of his cruel Whipping, &c. but as it is afterwards mentioned in the depositions before the Lords, is here omitted.*]

The rest that I intended by the strength of my God to have spoken (if I had not been prevented by the Gag), I now forbear to set down, in regard I hear I am to come into the Field again to fight a second Battle, unto which time I reserve it: if the Lord so order it that I may have liberty to speak, I doubt not but by the might and power of my God, in whom I rest and trust, valiantly to display the weapons of a good Soldier of *Jesus Christ*, come life, come death. and in the mean time, to what I have here said and written, I set to my name, by me, *John Lilburn*, being written with part of mine own blood.

John Lilburn.

At the Inner Star-Chamber, *the* 18*th of* April, Anno Dom. 1638.

P R E S E N T.

Lord Archbishop of *Canterbury*, Lord-Treasurer, Earl-Marshal, Lord *Cottington*, Mr. Secretary *Cooke*,
Lord-Keeper, Lord-Privy-Seal, Earl of *Salisbury*, Lord *Newburgh*, Mr. Secretary *Windeback*.

WHEREAS *John Lilburn*, Prisoner in the *Fleet*, by sentence in the *Star-Chamber*, did this day suffer condign punishment for his several Offences, by whipping at a cart, and standing in the pillory; and as their Lordships were this day informed, during the time that his body was under the said execution, audaciously and wickedly did not only utter sundry scandalous speeches, but likewise scattered divers copies of seditious books among the people, that beheld the said execution; for which very thing, among other offences of like nature, he hath been censured in the said Court by the aforesaid Sentence: It is therefore, by their Lordships ordered, That the said *John Lilburn* should be laid alone, with irons on his hands and legs in the Wards of the *Fleet*, where the basest and meanest sort of prisoners are used to be put; and that the Warden of the Fleet take special care to hinder the resort of any Persons whatsoever unto him. And particularly, that he be not supplied with money from any friend, and that he take special notice of all letters, writings, and books brought unto him, and seize and deliver the same unto their Lordships; and take notice from time to time, who they be that resort unto the said prison to visit the said *Lilburn*, or to speak with him, and inform the Board thereof. And it was lastly ordered, that all persons that shall be hereafter produced to receive corporal punishment according to sentence of that Court, or by order of the Board, shall have their garments searched before they be brought forth, and neither writing, nor other thing suffered to be about them; and their hands likewise to be bound, during the time they are under punishment. Whereof, together with the other premisses, the said Warden of the Fleet is hereby required to take notice, and to have special care, that this their Lordships order be accordingly observed.

Examined per Dudley Carleton.

And on the said 18th of *April*, it was further ordered by the said Court of *Star-Chamber*,

'That his Majesty's Attorney and Sollicitor-General should be hereby 'prayed and required, to take strict examination of *John Lilburn* Prisoner 'in the Fleet, touching the Demeanour and Speeches of him the said *Lilburn*, during the time of his whipping and standing in the Pillory this 'day, according to the Sentence of his Majesty's Court of *Star-Chamber*; 'particularly, whether the said *Lilburn* did at that time utter any speeches 'tending to Sedition, or to the dishonour of the said Court of *Star-Chamber*, or any Member of the said Court? and whether he did throw 'about and disperse at the same time any seditious Pamphlets and Books, 'either of that sort for which he was formerly censured, or any other of 'like nature? What the Speeches were, and who heard them? What 'the said Books were, and whence and of whom the said *Lilburn* had 'them? And what other material Circumstances they should think fit to 'examine, either the said *Lilburn* upon, or any other Person by whom 'they shall think good to inform themselves for the better finding out the 'truth. and thereupon to make certificate to the Board what they find, 'together with their opinions.'

The third of *November*, 1640, being the first day the late dissolved Parliament sate, I according to Law and Justice preferred my Petition and Complaint to them; who upon the reading of my Petition, immediately ordered me my Liberty [being, as I remember, the first prisoner in *England* set at liberty by them] to follow my Petition, and according to the legal custom of Parliaments make it good by proof, before a select Committee appointed by them to that purpose, Mr. *Francis Rouse* having the Chair; before whom many particular days one after another I appeared with my Counsel and my Witnesses, and fully proved all my Petition. Upon the report of all which by Mr. *Rouse* the Chairman, the House of Commons upon the fourth of *May*, 1641, [being the very same day that the King himself caused me to be arraigned for High Treason at the Bar of the House of Peers] voted and resolved upon the question,

That the Sentence of the *Star-Chamber* given against *John Lilburn* is illegal, and against the Liberty of the Subject; and also bloody, cruel, wicked, barbarous, and tyrannical.

Resolved upon the Question, That reparation ought to be given to Mr. *Lilburn* for his imprisonment, sufferings, and losses sustained by that illegal Sentence.

Ordered, That the Committee shall prepare this case of Mr. *Lilburn*'s to be transmitted to the Lords, with those other of Dr. *Bastwick*, Dr. *Leighton*, Mr. *Burton*, and Mr. *Prynne*.

H. Elsinge, Cler. Parl. Dom. Com.

After which Votes (being in a full, free, unravish'd, or unforc'd, legal, and unquestionable Parliament, after a full, open, free*, and fair hearing, and examining of all my aforesaid sufferings and complaints) troubles and the wars came on, and being in my own conscience fully satisfied of the justness of the Parliament's than cause, in the height of zeal, accompanied with judgment and conscience, "upon the principles I have largely laid "down in the 26, 27, 75, 76th pages of my Book of the 8th of *June*, "1649, intitled *England*'s legal, fundamental, &c." I took up arms for them, and fought heartily and faithfully in their quarrel, (for maintaining of which I had like to have been hang'd at *Oxford*, while during my imprisonment there, I lost 5 or 600 *l.* out of my estate at *London*,) till the present Earl of *Manchester* had like to have hanged me, for being a little too quick in taking in *Tickell Castle*, which spoiled a soldier of me ever since. After which, in the year 1645, I followed the House of Commons close, to transmit my foresaid Votes to the Lords, as appears by the following Petition:

To the Honourable the House of Commons now assembled in the High-Court of Parliament;

The humble Petition of John Lilburn, *Lieut. Col.*

In all humility sheweth,

THAT your petitioner having suffered abundance of inhuman, barbarous cruelty, by virtue of an illegal decree made against him, in the *Star-Chamber*, 1637. as by the copy of his petition hereunto annexed, formerly presented to this honourable House, and by your own Votes made the 4th of *May*, 1641. (upon the examination of the petition) will appear: Which Votes are as followeth; First, That the sentence of the *Star-Chamber* given against him is illegal, against the liberty of the Subject, and also Bloody, Wicked, Cruel, Barbarous, and Tyrannical. Secondly, That reparation ought to be given to him for his imprisonment, sufferings and losses, sustained by that illegal sentence. And then also it was ordered, that care should be taken to draw up his case, and transmit it to the Lords: but by reason of multitude of business in this honourable House, there hath been no further proceedings in it since. And these distractions coming on, your petitioner took command under the Right Honourable *Robert* Lord *Brook*, with whose Regiment he adventured his life freely and resolutely, both at *Kenton* field, and *Brentford*, where he was taken prisoner and carried away to *Oxford*: where, within a short time after his coming, the King sent to the castle to your petitioner, the now Earl of *Kingston*, the Lord *Dunsmore*, the Lord *Maltrevers*, and the Lord *Andover*, to woo your petitioner with large proffers of the honour and glory of Court-preferment, to forsake the Parliament's party, and to ingage on his party. Upon the slighting and contemning of which, your petitioner was within few days after laid in irons, and kept an exceeding close prisoner, and forced several times to march into *Oxford* in irons, to Judge *Heath*, before whom he was arraigned for High-Treason, for drawing his sword in the cause of the Commonwealth, and suffered multitude of miseries, in his almost twelve-months captivity there: in which time he lost above 600 *l* in his estate that he left behind him at *London*, (as he is clearly able to make appear). And immediately after his coming from thence, he took command in the Earl of *Manchester*'s army, his commission as *Major* of foot, bearing date the 7th of *October*, 1643. which lasted till the 16th of *May*, 1644. at which time he was authorised by Commission as Lieut. Col. to command a Regiment of Dragoons; in which services having been in many engagements, he hopes it will easily appear, that he hath not only behaved himself honestly and faithfully, but also valiantly and stoutly, in the midst of many discouragements, God crowning some of his endeavours with success; especially at the taking of *Tickell-Castle*, and Sir *Francis Wortbley*'s garrison, at which place your petitioner was shot through his arm. The premises considered, he humbly beseecheth this Honourable Assembly to perfect that Justice, which you so happily began for your petitioner, and to give him reparation for his large and tedious imprisonment, and heavy sufferings by the *Star-Chamber* decree; he having waited four years with patience for that end, though he lost by his imprisonment all that he had, and was deprived of a profitable calling, being then in the way of a Factor in the *Low Countries*; and also to take off the King's fine, and to consider his service with the Earl of *Manchester*, wherein he faithfully adventured his life, spent a great deal of his own money, and lost at *Newark*, when Prince *Rupert* raised the siege, almost 100 *l.* being stripp'd from the crown of the head to the sole of the foot, besides his former losses at *Kenton* and *Brentford*: And that you will be pleased, for his present subsistence, to appoint the payment of so much of his present arrears, as you in your great wisdoms shall think fit, to supply his urgent and pressing necessities, there being now due to them 600 *l.* and upwards. And that Col. *King* may be commanded to account with the petitioner, which formerly he hath refused to do (though commanded by his General), and to give him debentures for what is due by the State in his service, and to pay him what he hath received for the petitioner, and detained from him.

And he shall pray, &c.

JOHN LILBURN.

The annex'd Petition thus followeth.

To the House of Commons now assembled in the High-Court of Parliament;

The humble Petition of John Lilburn *prisoner in the* Fleet;

In all humility sheweth,

THAT in *December* next will be three years, your petitioner, upon supposal of sending over certain Books of Dr. *Bastwick*'s, from *Holland* into *England*, was by Dr. *Lamb*'s warrant without any examination at all sent to the *Gatehorse* prison, and from thence within three days removed to the *Fleet*, where he abiding prisoner, in *Candlemas-Term* following, was proceeded against in the Honourable Court of *Star-Chamber*: where your petitioner appearing (and entering of his name, for want of money his name was struck out again), and he refusing to take an Oath to answer to all things that should be demanded of him (for that your petitioner conceived that Oath to be dangerous and illegal) without any interrogatory tendered him, for his refusing the said Oath, he was prosecuted and censured in the said Court most heavily, being fined 500 *l.* to the King, and sent prisoner to the *Fleet*. And in *Easter-Term* following, was whipped from the *Fleet* to *Westminster*, with a three-fold knotted cord, receiving at least 200 stripes; and then at *Westminster*, he was set on the Pillory the space of two hours, and (over and above the censure of the Court) at the Warden of the *Fleet*'s command, was gagged about an hour and a half; after which most cruel sufferings, was again returned to the *Fleet* close prisoner. When through his said sufferings, the next morning he being sick of an extream fever, could not have admittance for his Surgeon to let him blood, or dress his sores, till the afternoon of the said day; tho' the Surgeon, in pity to the prisoner, went to *Westminster* to the Warden himself; and your petitioner hath been close prisoner in the *Fleet* ever since, where in a most cruel manner he hath been put into iron fetters, both hands and legs, which caused a most dangerous sickness that continued six months; and after some small recovery, was again laid in irons, which caused at least five months sickness, more dangerous than the former. During which time of sickness, they most inhumanly denied his friends to come and see him, until they would give them money for their admittance, and they have denied many to come at all; and have beaten and kicked, and otherwise most shamefully abused such his friends as came to see him in his great distress, and to bring him food and necessaries to sustain his life, and also have kept his servant from him, and his food. So that if he had not been relieved by stealth of his fellow-prisoners, he had been kept from any food at all, for above the space of 10 days together: and the prisoners that out of

* Where, (I very well remember,) Sir *Arthur Haslerig* was one of my zealous and forward Judges; and when Warden *James Ingram* came to the Bar of the Court of Wards, and brought Mr *Herne* the Counsellor to plead for the Lords, and in excuse of himself, who stiffly insisted in a high manner upon the orders and decrees of Star-Chamber, upon which I very well remember Sir *Artour*, with a great deal of indignation, said unto *Herne*, I value not a Decree of the Lords in Star-Chamber a rush, if it be not expresly according to the tenor of their Commission, the Law: and I further tell you, it is a ridiculous thing, Sir, to summon Parliaments to meet together to make Laws, if the Lords Decrees in Star-Chamber against Law should be binding. And therefore, although you have proved for your Client Mr. *Ingram*, that the Lords in open Court (the Court sitting) commanded him on the Pillory to gag Mr. *Lilburn*, for speaking against them, yet I tell you by Law that order ought to have been in writing according to the custom of the Court, which you confess it was not, and therefore Mr *Ingram* must smart for his executing of orders on Mr *Lilburn* made illegally.

Pity have relieved him, have been most cruelly punished, and the Keepers have not forborn to confess themselves, that they should have starved him long ago, had not the prisoners relieved him. And besides all this, they have most cruelly beaten and wounded him, to the hazard of his limbs, and danger of his life, had he not been rescued and saved by the prisoners of the same house. In which most miserable condition, your poor petitioner hath continued a prisoner for the space of about two years and a half, and is like still to continue in the same, under the merciless hands of the Warden of the *Fleet*, who hath denied lawful liberty to his prisoner, for that he hath said, he must observe the man that hath so great a sway in the Kingdom, intimating the Archbishop.

All which his deplored condition, and lamentable miseries, he most humbly presenteth to this most Honourable Assembly, beseeching them to be pleased to cast an eye of compassion towards him, and to afford him such relief from his censure and hard imprisonment, as may seem good to your wisdoms, who otherwise is like to perish under the hands of merciless men.

And your Petitioner shall ever pray (as in duty he is bound) to the Lord to bless and prosper this Honourable Assembly. JOHN LILBURN.

At the debate of which, there was not a little opposition by some, who (as I conceive) thought I was not capable of enjoying justice, although to my knowledge I never did an act in all my life that put me out of the protection of the law, or that tended to the disfranchising me of being a Denizen and Freeman of *England*; and therefore ought to enjoy as great a privilege in the enjoyment of the benefit of the Law of *England*, as any free Denizen of *England* whatsoever, by what name or title soever he be called. The issue of which debate, so much as I have under the Clerk's hand, thus followeth.

Die Lunæ, 10 *Nov.* 1645.

Ordered, &c. That the Vote formerly passed in this House, concerning the proceedings against Lieut. Col. *Lilburn* in the *Star-Chamber*, be forthwith transmitted to the Lords.

Ordered, &c. That it be referred to the Committee of accounts to cast up and state the accounts of Lieut. Col. *Lilburn*, and to certify what is due to him, to this House. *H. Elsynge, Cler. Parl. D. Com.*

After passing these Votes, I found quick dispatch to the Lords; and upon the first of *December*, 1645, by special decree, they took off the fine set upon me by the *Star-Chamber*; and afterwards at their open Bar judicially, upon the 13th of *February*, 1645, appointed me a solemn hearing *de novo* of the whole matter, and assigned Mr. *John Bradshaw* and Mr. *John Cook* for my Counsel.

Lieut. Col. John Lilburn's *Sufferings, as they were represented and proved before the Right Honourable the* House of Peers, *in Parliament assembled, the 13th day of* February, 1645.

MR. *Bradshaw* and Mr. *Cook* being assigned for Counsel with the said Mr. *Lilburn*; Mr. *Bradshaw* having succinctly, and so truly opened the case, as if he had been an eye-witness of his Client's sufferings, acquainted their Lordships, that the same had received a full and solemn hearing before a Committee of the honourable House of Commons: upon whose report it was by that honourable House, *May* 4, 1641, resolved upon the question, *That the sentence of the* Star-Chamber *given against* John Lilburn *is illegal, and against the liberty of the subject*; and also Bloody, Wicked, Cruel, Barbarous, and Tyrannical; and likewise further resolved upon the question, *That reparation ought to be given to Mr.* Lilburn, *for his imprisonment, sufferings and losses, sustained by that illegal sentence.* And now, my Lords, they have transmitted them to your Lordships, by whose noble favour and justice we are now before your Honours, to lay open the illegality of that sentence, and all the proceedings thereupon, and to crave your Lordships justice for reparations, proportionable to our Client's sufferings.

And in the first place he presented an Order, whereby Mr. *Lilburn* was first illegally attached, and committed to the prison of the *Gatehouse*, which was read in these words.

Sexto Decemb. Anno Dom. 1637.

Emanavit Attach. Direct. Wragge, & Flamsteed, pro Corporis Capt. Johannis Lilburn de Civitate London, ad immediate admittend. &c. Signat. per Lambe, Gwynn, & Aylett. — *Ex directione Baker Cler. Cappellani Lond.*

Exam. *Edwardus Latham Reg. Regi Deput.*

The *English* of which thus followeth:

The 6th of *Decemb.* 1637.

There issued an attachment directed to *Wragge* and *Flamsteed*, for the taking of the body of *John Lilburn*, of the City of *London*, and to bring immediately, *&c.* Signed by *Lambe*, *Gwynn*, and *Aylett*. — By direction of the Court, *Baker*, Clerk Chaplain.

Examined by *Edward Latham*, Deputy of the Register.

Which Order being read, Mr. *Bradshaw* observed, that the original imprisonment itself was illegal, because they never convented Mr. *Lilburn* to speak for himself, nor examined him upon any crime. But, my Lords, it is no marvel that such kind of injustice as this proceeded from those High Commissioners, because it was their usual practice to be attachers, judges, gaolers and executioners themselves, without regard of any legal way of proceedings. He then desired their Lordships, that the sentence against Mr. *Lilburn* in the *Star-Chamber* might also be read, which was accordingly done; *viz.*

In Cam. Stel. coram Canc. ibidem 13 *Die Febr. Anno Decimo tertio Car. Reg.* Lord *Coventry*, Lord Keeper, *&c.*

WHereas upon information to this Court, the 9th of *February*, by Sir *John Banks* Knt. his Majesty's Attorney-General, that *John Lilburn* and *John Wharton*, then present at the Bar, were the 24th of *Jan.* last, ordered to be examined upon interrogatories, touching their unlawful printing, importing, publishing and dispersing of libellous and seditious Books*, contrary to the decree of this Court, which was verified by Affidavit, and being brought up to the Office to appear and be examined, the said *Lilburn* refused to * appear; and both of them denied to take an Oath to make true answer to Interrogatories, as appeared by the certificate of Mr. *Good*, Deputy-Clerk of this Court. The Court did on that day order, that their appearances should then be recorded, they being present in Court as aforesaid; and that in respect the said delinquents did then again contemptuously refuse to take their Oaths, tendered unto them in open Court, they should be remanded to the Prison of the *Fleet*, there to remain close prisoners, until they conform themselves in obedience to take their Oaths, and be examined; and that unless they did take their Oaths, and yield to be examined by *Monday* night then next following, and now last past, their Lordships would on this sitting day proceed to a censure against them for their contempts therein.

Now this day the said *Lilburn* and *Wharton* being again brought unto the Bar, his Majesty's said Attorney informed this Honourable Court, that they still continued in their former obstinacy, and contemptuously refused to take their Oaths, to make true answer to the † Interrogatories, although they had been sent for, and their Oaths offered to be given unto them by Mr. *Good*, Deputy Clerk of this Court, who now certified the same in Court. And therefore his Majesty's said Attorney humbly prayed on his Majesty's behalf, that their Lordships would now proceed to censure against the said delinquents for their great contempts and disobedience therein. Whereupon their Lordships endeavoured by fair persuasions to draw them to conformity and obedience; and withal offered, that if yet they would submit and take their Oaths, their Lordships would accept thereof, and not proceed to censure against them. But such was the insufferable disobedience and contempt of the said delinquents, that they still persisted in their former obstinacy, and wilfully refused to take their Oaths. In respect whereof the whole Court did, with an unanimous consent, declare and adjudge the said *Lilburn* and *Wharton* guilty of a very high contempt, and offence of dangerous consequence and evil example, and worthy to undergo a very sharp, exemplary and severe censure, which may deter others from the like presumptuous boldness, in refusing to take a legal ** Oath; without which, many great and exorbitant offences to the prejudice and danger of his Majesty, his Kingdoms, and loving Subjects, might go away undiscovered and unpunished. And therefore their Lordships have now ordered, adjudged and decreed, that the said *Lilburn* and *Wharton* shall be remanded to the *Fleet*, there to remain until they conform themselves in obedience to the orders of this Court, and that they shall pay 500*l.* a-piece for their several fines to his Majesty's use; and before their enlargements out of the *Fleet*, become bound with good sureties for their good behaviour. And to the end that others may be more deterred from daring to offend in the like kind hereafter, the Court hath further ordered and decreed, That the said *John Lilburn* shall be whipped through the street, from the Prison of the *Fleet* unto the Pillory, to be erected at such time and in such place as this Court shall hold fit and direct; and that both he and the said *Wharton* shall be both then set in the said Pillory, and from thence be returned to the *Fleet*, there to remain according to this Decree.

John Arthur, Dep.

At the concluding of which, Mr. *Bradshaw* observed, that this sentence was *felo de se*, guilty of its own death; the ground whereof being, because Mr. *Lilburn refused* to take an Oath, to answer to all such questions as should be demanded of him, it being contrary to the laws of God, Nature, and the Kingdom, for any man to be his own accuser: the execution of which cruel and bloody sentence was proved by several witnesses of quality and good repute upon Oath at their Lordships bar, the substance of whose testimony was:

In the first place,

Mr. *Thomas Smith* Merchant, upon his Oath declared to their Lordships, that he saw Mr. *Lilburn* tied to a Cart at *Fleet-bridge*, being stripped from the waist upward, and whipped from thence to *Westminster*; and that so near as he was able to judge, every two, three or four steps he had a lash, with a whip that he was sure had two or three cords tied full of knots; and for the number he did not judge them so few as 500, and he thought that if he should say 500 and 500, he should not say amiss: but 500 he was confident was the least. And that he saw him set upon the Pillory, *&c.* the Officers being very cruel towards him, or any that spoke unto him.

The next witness was Mrs. *Mary Dorman*; the substance of whose testimony upon Oath was, that she saw Mr. *Lilburn* whipped from *Fleet-bridge* to *Westminster*, in such a barbarous and cruel manner, that she was not able to express it, and that she did believe that both his shoulders were swelled almost as big as a penny-loaf, with the bruises of the knotted cords; and that she did see him set upon the Pillory immediately, above the space of two hours bare-headed, the sun shining very hot, and he took occasion to declare the unjustness of his sentence, upon which the Warden of the *Fleet* caused him to be gagged above an hour, and did it with such cruelty, that he made his mouth to bleed.

Mr. *Higgs* his Surgeon testified upon Oath to this effect; that he did not see his patient Mr. *Lilburn* whipped, but being desired to perform the office of a Surgeon to him, he that day drest his back, which was one of the miserablest that ever he did see; for the wales in his back, made by his cruel whipping, were bigger than Tobacco-pipes, and that he saw him set in the Pillory, and gagged.

And Mr. *Thomas Hawes* upon Oath testified to this effect; that he did see Mr. *Lilburn* set upon the Pillory, above (as he judged) the space of two hours, the Sun shining very hot, and they would not suffer him to have any cover upon his head: and he taking occasion to speak of the Bishops cruelty towards him, and how unjustly they had caused him to be dealt with, the Warden of the *Fleet* caused him to be gagged in such a cruel manner, as if he would have torn his jaws in pieces, insomuch that the blood came out of his mouth.

In the next place, *A second sentence made in the Inner Star-Chamber* was read, which thus followeth.

* *Lilburn* did enter his Name, but refusing to give them Money they put out his Name again.

† They never shewed the Interrogatories to *Lilburn*, though he desired the sight of them, that so he might know what he did swear to.

** The sum of which was, You shall swear to make true answer to all things that are asked you, so help you God.

At the Inner Star-Chamber, the 18th of April, *Anno Dom.* 1638.

Present Lord Archbishop of Canterbury, *Lord-Keeper, Lord-Treasurer,* &c.

WHereas *John Lilburn* prisoner in the *Fleet*, by sentence in the *Star-Chamber*, did this day suffer condign punishment for his several offences, by whipping at a Cart, and standing in the Pillory; and as their Lordships were this day informed, during the time that his body was under the said execution, audaciously and wickedly did not only utter sundry scandalous speeches, but likewise scattered divers copies of seditious Books amongst the people that beheld the said execution, for which very thing, amongst other offences of like nature, he hath been censured in the said Court, by the aforesaid sentence: it is therefore by their Lordships ordered, that the said *John Lilburn* should be laid alone with irons on his hands and legs, in the Wards of the *Fleet*, where the basest and meanest sort of prisoners are used to be put; and that the Warden of the *Fleet* take special care to hinder the resort of any persons whatsoever unto him; and particularly, that he be not supplied with money from any friend: and that he take special notice of all Letters, Writings, and Books brought unto him, and seize and deliver the same unto their Lordships: and take notice from time to time who they be that resort unto the said prison, to visit the said *Lilburn*, or to speak with him, and inform the Board thereof. And it was lastly ordered, that all persons that shall be hereafter produced to receive corporal punishment, according to sentence of that Court, or by order of the Board, shall have their garments searched before they be brought forth, and neither writing nor other thing suffered to be about them; and their hands likewise to be bound, during the time they are under punishment. Whereof, together with the other premises, the said Warden of the *Fleet* is hereby required to take notice, and to have especial care, that this their Lordships order be accordingly observed.

Examined per Dudley Carleton.

And the execution of this latter sentence in a most barbarous and inhuman manner, was punctually proved by sufficient witnesses, as followeth; *viz.* Mr. *Higgs* his Surgeon again testified, that that night Mr. *Lilburn* suffered, he was had back to the *Fleet*, and he repairing to Dr. *Gran*, to crave his advice, he advised him to let his patient blood, to prevent a fever; and he accordingly came the next morning to the *Fleet* to let his patient blood, and dress his sores, but he found him locked up close in a room, and was by the Officers of the *Fleet* denied access unto him. Whereupon he immediately went to the Warden, being then at *Westminster*, who denied him access to the said Mr. *Lilburn*, till the afternoon that he came home; which was a great act of cruelty, and much to the danger of Mr. *Lilburn*'s health, and welfare: and the next day they removed him down to the Common Gaol, where they laid him in irons, and several times wounded him, to the extreme hazard of his life, and several times denied me access to him in his extremity.

Dr. *Hubbard*, Justice of the Peace, made Oath to this effect; that when Mr. *Lilburn* was prisoner in the *Fleet*, he was desired as a Physician to visit him: and going so to do, he was again and again denied access to him: but upon much importunity to the Warden, he was admitted to him, whom he found in an extream violent fever, lying in irons upon both hands and legs, to the extreme hazard of his life.

Mrs. *Mary Dorman* further declared, that after Mr. *Lilburn* had suffered, she went often to visit him, who was laid in irons, and his friends denied access to him; and that the Officers of the *Fleet* strongly endeavoured to starve him: so that many times his friends were forced to bring his meat to the poor men's bag, and give them money to convey it to him through a hole in a wall betwixt them and him. Mr. *Thomas Hawes* further declared, that after Mr. *Lilburn* suffered, he often went to visit him, and was beat by the Gaolers, and was in danger to have lost his life for so doing; and that they so strongly laboured to starve Mr. *Lilburn*, that they were forced to convey his diet to him by the poor men that begged at the grate: but the Gaolers finding out that Mr. *Lilburn* got his diet that way, they dealt so cruelly with the poor men, that Mr. *Lilburn* was deprived of that way of relief, and then his friends got the son of one *Archer* that was prisoner in the next room to him, for accusing the Deputy of *Ireland* for murdering one *Esmond*, to convey his victuals to him: which was done by stealth, through a hole where a board was pulled up in his floor, when the rest of the prisoners were at the Chapel at service; and, my Lords, divers times the conveying of his meat to him, cost him and his friends, upon the prisoners, &c. more than the meat itself.

Robert Ellis, some time a fellow-prisoner with Mr *Lilburn* in the *Fleet*, upon Oath declared before their Lordships, that the Officers of the *Fleet* after they brought Mr. *Lilburn* into the common Wards, used him very barbarously and cruelly, laying him for a long time in irons, keeping his friends from him, and his victuals, and several times had like to have slain and murdered him, and he verily believes had effected it, if he had not help'd him, for which they took his bed from him, and put him off the charity, and kept him five weeks in a dungeon, and had like to have murdered him, and afterwards removed him to the King's-Bench, that so they might the more easily have their wills of Mr. *Lilburn*, &c.

Their Lordships being satisfied of the Injustice and Illegality of the proceedings, Mr. *Bradshaw* said, that he conceived no man's sufferings in the Kingdom had been so great as his Client's were for a Gentleman to be so cruelly tortured and whipped, pillory'd, gagged, close imprisoned, ironed, beat and wounded, and that contrary to Law, is a cruelty unheard of, and therefore hoped that for such unparalleled sufferings, and oppressions, the fair hand of their Lordships honourable Justice would give and reach him forth unparalleled damages; and though many of his Judges that did him injustice be dead, yet he hoped the hand of Justice of their Honours, joined with the honourable House of Commons, will be so long, as to reach their living and surviving estates, and cut of them, &c. make him timely, large and unparalleled reparations.

Mr. *Cook* [illegible] spoke in the behalf of Mr *Lilburn* (and afterwards printed his argument), and said the punishment inflicted upon him may be reduced to four heads:

(1.) Imprisonment, whereby a man is buried alive, loses the comfort and benefit of his five senses, and [illegible], the unmoveable subject of the law, or as a dead carcase. 'Tis true, that in itself it is the easiest of all corporal punishments: but the continuance of it, makes it such a lingering consumption, that it is better to be upon the rack an hour, than to be imprisoned a year. as it is better to be once wet to the skin, than to be subject to a perpetual dropping: especially for an active spirit, there is no such torment as to deprive him of liberty; for active *Theseus* was condemned only to sit still. there is no end of such a misery, as the *Heathen* persecuting Tyrant said, *Nondum tibi redii in gratiam*; to put a man out of his pain, was always counted a favour. But Mr. *Lilburn*'s imprisonment was aggravated by three steps or gradations.

1. A close imprisonment, not the dearest friend to come to him; we do not find that any of the primitive *Christians* were used so by the Tyrants, for then that heavy charge might be answered in the Scripture, *I was in prison, and ye visited me not*; extraordinary matters of state and high concernments always excepted: but the Surgeon was not permitted some time to come to Mr. *Lilburn* to dress him, nor the Physician when he was in a fever; a cruelty unheard of amongst the *Turks*: for they are careful of their slaves in their sickness, and fatten them, that they may endure their blows, but it is too probable that those which were Mr. *Lilburn*'s malicious enemies, did too much thirst after his blood.

2. The Keepers were ordered to take care that no money be conveyed to him, which argues that they had a desire to starve him: the Prophet saith, *It is better to die by the sword, than famine*, which is the greatest of all torments; for all punishments may be undergone by patience, but only hunger: which the more any man thinks by patience to overcome, the more violent it is. Undoubtedly, had it not been for the pity of some poor resolute fellow-prisoners, Mr. *Lilburn* had been starved to death: far worse than any of the four *Roman* punishments, which were *lapidatio, combustio, decollatio, strangulatio*, stoning, burning, beheading, and strangling. How severely, yet most justly, did the same Judges several times punish the intent to poison or destroy another man? The going about to murder, nay the giving of the lye, because it is preparatory to murder, by provoking quarrels, was censurable in that Court; *à multo fortiori*, much more from the stronger, then in this case used, where there was so much cruelty inflicted, that death might probably have ensued, had not God by his extraordinary mercy supported him in those sad afflictions, those unjust Judges for transgressing not only the bounds of humanity, but all the rules of their own ordinary Justice, ought to make Mr *Lilburn* answerable satisfaction.

3. This imprisonment was for about three years, until he petitioned the Parliament. Many times the first motions of anger are not in a man's own power; because he would not accuse himself as they desired, they might have in a passion committed him, and the Sun might have gone down upon their wrath; nay, the Moon might have made her peragration, or the summer season might have melted their frozen consciences, or the winter cold have allayed the heat of their malice, or the Sun might have made his revolution, but their malice continued three years; and had not he been delivered by the Justice of the Parliament, in probability might have continued for ever.

(2.) Whipping, a most painful and shameful punishment; Flagellations and Scourgings being for slaves and incorrigible rogues, and hedge-robbers. *In undecimo Elizab.* one *Cartwright* brought a slave from *Russia*, and would scourge him cruelly, for which he was questioned; and it was resolved, that *England* was too pure an air for slaves to breathe in; and it was often resolved in the *Star-Chamber*, that no Gentleman was to be whipp'd for any offence whatsoever: it being well known that *John Lilburn*'s ancestors have been ancient Gentlemen, and that which these Judges could not be ignorant of, especially the Earl-Marshal, who is presumed to know all the ancient Gentry in the Kingdom. But the like whipping was never read of amongst the *Assyrians, Persians, Grecians*, or *Romans*. For,

1. It was from the *Fleet* to *Westminster* (above a mile distance) a great concourse and confluence of people looking upon him, as if he had been some miserable slave.

2. He received every two or three steps a blow, 500 strokes at the least; for one Mr. *Smith*, a Merchant, that went along with him, testified that so far as he was able to judge, he received 500 or 1000, but of the first he was most certain; and this was with a treble-corded whip, with at least twenty knots upon it.

Amongst the *Romans* no malefactor had ever above forty stripes, and every stroke stood for three stripes, for the whip was of three thongs; and but one knot at the end of every thong. St. *Paul* received thirty-nine stripes, which was but thirteen blows. Not long since in *Orleans*, a Priest was sentenced to be whipp'd for fornication, having abused a poor maid, telling her that their popish St. *Francis* would come and lie with her such a night, at which time he personated and feigned himself to be St. *Francis*, and was taken in bed with her; and it was earnestly pressed by the King's Advocates, that he might receive fourteen blows with a three corded whip, which is constantly used for such castigations, because it was an abominable wickedness: but the Judges would not suffer him to have above thirteen blows, because *amplianda sunt favores*, favours are to be enlarged. And in doubtful matters it must always be presumed for clemency and gentleness, according to which account, Mr. *Lilburn* received 10,000 stripes: for in every blow there was twenty stripes, by reason of the twenty knots, which being multiplied is 10,000, and in every stripe there was shame and pain, compression of the flesh, bruisings and effusion of blood.

(3.) The Pillory, a punishment something penal, but exceeding shameful, and most terrible to a generous nature, to stand two hours in open view of all men, as if he had been unworthy to tread upon the earth, the Sun shining very hot upon him, and not suffered to keep on his hat, and this immediately after his cruel whipping, that so they might put him to all the torture and pain that they could, argues abundance of wrath and malice.

This punishment of standing upon the Pillory, was first invented for Mountebanks and Cheats, that having gotten upon banks and [illegible], to wrong and abuse the people, were exalted in the same kind, to [illegible] [illegible] to the view and open shame of the people; but for a Gentleman to be so served, was never heard of, unless by that cruel Court.

(4.) Gagging, an unmanly and barbarous cruelty, to be exercised upon beasts, not men, for man differs from brutes, both [illegible], in reason and speech; a punishment never heard of in any age [illegible] out of tongues, and perforations in cases of blasphemy have been [illegible], but

never

never in a matter of ſuch a nature; and this to continue for above an hour, till the blood guſh'd out of his mouth, as if they would have pluck'd his jaws in pieces, and all this for nothing; O inſufferable torments!

So that by his impriſonment he was made a ſtock, a dead trunk, or picture of a man, that hath eyes and ſees not, hands and handles not, *&c.* By whipping they endeavoured to make him a rogue, or a ſlave; by the third puniſhment of the pillory, to make him a cheater, guilty of forgery and perjury; and by gagging, to make him a beaſt, and ſo upon the whole matter to deprive him of his reaſonable ſoul, ſuch cruelties that were never invented but by *Tygers* and *Wolves* in human ſhapes, *ferocitas Luporum, in humana figura.* But then the perſons that were ſo cruel and tyrannical aggravates the offence.

1. This cruelty was commanded to be executed by an eminent Court of Juſtice, profeſſing Chriſtianity, *peſſima eſt injuſtitia quæ fit ſub colore juſtitiæ:* 'tis the greateſt injuſtice to oppreſs and do injury, under a pretence of Juſtice. How often was it reſolved in that Court, that for a Juſtice of Peace or Conſtable to commit a riot, was ten times more ſeverely puniſhable than in a common perſon, becauſe it is to uſe, or rather abuſe that ſword of authority, to commit or countenance an unlawful action, which was ordained and put into their hands to ſuppreſs it.

2. The Eminency of the perſons augments the offence, *qualitas perſonæ auget peccatum*; for a Gentleman to act againſt the rule of the Law and Gentility, is more reprehenſible than in vulgar perſons. It was called the *Court of Star-Chamber*, from the eminency of the perſons, which were Judges: Stars of the greater magnitudes, as being the higheſt Court of ordinary Juſtice; but Mr. *Lilburn*'s Judges, inſtead of putting on the garment of Juſtice, were cloathed from head to feet, and their conſcience oiled and moiſtened, with cruelty and injuſtice mixed with the moſt poiſoned malice that ever entered into the hearts of any Judges.

And though ſome of them be dead, yet Juſtice lives though the party be dead; whatſoever becomes of them, their eſtates ought to make ſatisfaction according to their own rules, *qui non luet in corpore, ſolvit in burſa*; he that ſuffers not in his body, muſt ſuffer in his purſe.

A principal actor in this bloody tragedy, was the Lord-Keeper *Coventry*, not leſs eminent in cruelty than in place, Judge of the higheſt ſeat of mercy, the *Chancery*, which abated the edge of the Law, when it is too keen; for the chief Judge of mercy to degenerate into a ſavage cruelty, not heard of amongſt the *Barbarians*, how heinous is it? Not to ſpeak any thing of the decapitated Archbiſhop, that monſter of cruelty, and ſubtlety, whoſe eſtate we fear is dead with him, and therefore little can be expected from it.

The Biſhop of *London*, then Lord-Treaſurer, was a principal ſentencer of Mr. *Lilburn*; by their own Canons, no Biſhop ought to have a hand in blood, becauſe they pretend to be mild ſhepherds, but cruelty was their genius.

The Earl of *Arundel* was of an imbittered ſpirit againſt Mr. *Lilburn*, nothing but corporal puniſhment would allay the heat of his malice; who being Earl-Marſhal, could not be ignorant that *John Lilburn* was a Gentleman: for him that by his place was to protect all Gentlemen from injuries, and ſhould ſcorn to be active in the inflicting ſuch corporal, ignominious, cruel puniſhments upon a Gentleman, is a tranſcendent tranſgreſſion againſt the laws of ſtate and honour. It hath been cenſurable in that Court, to ſpeak contemptuous words of a Gentleman; and how often had he ordered ſatisfaction, for ſaying ſuch a one is no Gentlemen? And yet the ſame court and perſons not only to ſay a Gentleman is a rogue, but ſo to uſe him, as Mr. *Lilburn* was, is the greateſt ſcandal to the public Juſtice of the Kingdom, that hath been heard of.

The Judges aſſiſtants, that are called the *Fathers of the Law*, and are ſaid to carry Law in their breaſts, for them to begin and promote ſuch an unjuſt and illegal ſentence, for them that are ſet as Centinels to watch over and preſerve the people's liberties, to betray a poor Gentleman into the hands of merciless men, was an offence of an exceeding high nature: for had they declared the illegality of thoſe proceedings, and proteſted againſt it, as by virtue of their places (in duty) they ought to have done, it might have prevented the ſentence. If the proceeding had been regular by informations, and examinations, or *ore tenus*, as it was not, unleſs there had been ſome direct proof or ſpeaking circumſtance or very probable preſumption, that Mr. *Lilburn* had been guilty of ſome high crime; it had been a grievous thing in them to have aſſiſted in ſo cruel puniſhments. But when the pretence was no other, but concerning ſome of Dr. *Baſtwick*'s, Mr. *Burton*'s, or Mr. *Prynne*'s Books, which they knew could not be any breach of the peace, and that in the *Star-Chamber*, where there was no information, as in Mr. *Lilburn*'s caſe, to adminiſter an Oath, was all one with the High-Commiſſion, and directly contrary to the petition of right, in 3 *Car.* and Juſtice *Jones* had no reaſon for inflicting the corporal puniſhment.

But becauſe Mr. *Lilburn* was a young man, therefore it was fit he ſhould be puniſhed: Is not this to turn Juſtice into Wormood? Such Judges have ever been the moſt dangerous peſts to a State and Kingdom, and in former times, for leſs offence, moſt ſeverely puniſhed in their perſons and eſtates. The Lord *Cottington* thirſted exceedingly after the blood of this poor Gentleman, and the High-Commiſſioners had their hands as deep as any of the reſt, in regard that by their warrant he was firſt committed: the moſt unjuſt and tyrannical that ever was heard of, to command a poor Gentleman to be ſent to priſon, without conventing him before them, or aſking him whether he was guilty of any miſdemeanor; a mere uſurpation of authority, taking the ſword of Juſtice into their own hands, not caring to deſtroy a poor Gentleman, ſo as they might curry favour with the Prelates their grand patrons; thoſe High-Commiſſioners making themſelves Judges, Gaolers, and Executioners, and what not, to deſtroy the innocent.

It is conſiderable what puniſhment the Gaolers and Executioners of this cruel ſentence have deſerved. for however if a writ be directed to a Sheriff, commanding him to take the body of one who is a Peer of the Realm, or a privileged perſon, the Officer is excuſed by his warrant; yet when puniſhments are clearly againſt the Law of God, Nature, and Nations, which prohibit all ſuch cruelties and inhumanities; to make them bleed for the blood of Mr. *Lilburn*, would be an honourable piece of Juſtice, and a precedent of much ſafety to the ſubjects in after-times, and Officers would not dare to be ſo unmercifully cruel; as the Sheriffs ſmarted for the Ship-money, though they had proceſs from the *Exchequer*.

Mr. *Lilburn*'s ſufferings are beyond expreſſion, and no honeſt heart but is feelingly ſenſible of every blow that was given him; in his impriſonment, Whipping, Pillory, Gagging, Beatings, Hunger-bitings, and the Irons laid upon him, every true-hearted *Engliſhman*, that ſtands for the laws and liberties of the ſubject, was ſo uſed, and abuſed; for it might have been any ſuch man's caſe, as well as his. His eſtate quite exhauſted by their cruelties, his trade loſt, whereby he gained his livelihood, being before that time in a hopeful way of a Merchant, and well known to be very induſtrious in his calling; a man active for the Public, and by his merits hath procured the title of Lieutenant-Colonel in the preſent wars: What damages the Parliament will be pleaſed to adjudge and order him, he humbly ſubmits to their great Wiſdoms and honourable Juſtice: certainly not any of them would have ſuffered ſo much for ten thouſand pounds.

It is the Lord's great mercy that he is yet alive, having conflicted with, and gone through ſuch a ſea of puniſhments and miſeries. True it is, that in point of reparations, there is no proportion between money and ſuch corporal puniſhments, to a generous ſpirit: yet as there was never more indignity and a greater diſhonour to the Juſtice of the Kingdom, than by this wicked ſentence, and the cruel execution thereof, thereby proclaiming it to all the world that an *Engliſh* Gentleman muſt be made a ſlave, to ſatisfy the malicious and virulent humours of a tyrannical Court of Juſtice:

So it will be a very great honour and reparation to the public Juſtice of this Land, to give and adjudge Mr. *Lilburn* exemplary and proportionable damages, to be levied out of the eſtates of his unjuſt and malicious Judges, through whoſe injuſtice he not only ſuffered ſuch cruelties for three years, that not one of them would have ſuffered the like, nor received one of his ſtripes for many thouſands; but loſt his trade and livelihood.

The judicial law was blood for blood, an eye for an eye, tooth for tooth, *&c.* *Daniel*'s accuſers were caſt into the den of Lions, with their wives and children, though *Daniel* had no hurt by a miracle of mercy; by the equity and morality whereof, Mr. *Lilburn* ought to have good and proportionable reparation out of the eſtates of his unjuſt Judges and Tormentors, who ſought for his blood: but that God preſerved him by his extraordinary love and favour.

That all drooping ſpirits may chear up and be incouraged, that Juſtice will run down like a mighty ſtream, when it ſhall be executed upon the greateſt offenders: as now there is good hopes that Mr. *Lilburn* ſhall by ordinance of Parliament have ſpeedily good damages, anſwerable to his great ſufferings, ordered and adjudged him, to be raiſed out of the eſtates of his unjuſt Judges, that may be paid unto him without further expence, who hath been at ſuch extraordinary charges about the ſame, that ſo his reparation may be not only juſt, but ſeaſonable, by which he ſhall be obliged to venture his life, and all that is dear to him as formerly he hath done, for his honourable Judges in Parliament aſſembled.

Whereupon the Lords made the following Order.

Die Veneris, 13 *Feb.* 1645.

"Whereas the cauſe of *John Lilburn*, Gent. came this day to a hearing "at the Bar by his Counſel, being tranſmitted from the Houſe of Com-"mons, concerning a ſentence pronounced againſt him in the *Star-Cham-"ber*, 13 *Feb. Anno* 13. *Car. Reg.* and after an examination of the whole "proceedings, and a due conſideration of the ſaid ſentence; it is this day "adjudged, ordered, and determined by the Lords in Parliament aſſem-"bled, That the ſaid ſentence, and all proceedings thereupon, ſhall forth-"with be for ever totally vacated, obliterated, and taken off the file in all "Courts where they are yet remaining, as illegal, and moſt unjuſt, againſt "the liberty of the ſubject, and law of the land and *Magna Charta*, and "unfit to continue upon record. And that the ſaid *Lilburn* ſhall be for "ever abſolutely freed, and totally diſcharged from the ſaid ſentence, and "all proceedings thereupon, as fully and amply, as though never any "ſuch thing had been. And that all eſtreat and proceſs in the Court of "*Exchequer*, for levying of any fine, (if any ſuch be) ſhall be wholly can-"celled and made void; any thing to the contrary in any wiſe notwith-"ſtanding."

Joh. Browne, Cleric. Parliamentor.

But not aſſigning me any reparations in that Decree (the doing of which the Houſe of Commons left unto them, and the Lords according to former cuſtom looked upon to be their right in law to do), I prayed their aſſigning me particular reparations according to Law and Juſtice, out of the eſtates of my unjuſt Judges, that had done me ſo much wrong; upon which new addreſs to them, they did upon the 5th of *March*, 1645, order and decree, and aſſigned to be paid unto the ſaid *John Lilburn*, the ſum of 2000*l.* for his reparations, which for many reaſons (as their being aiding in the wars to the King, *&c.*), they fixed upon the Eſtates real and perſonal of *Francis* Lord *Cottington*, Sir *Francis Windebank*, and *James Ingram*, late Deputy Warden of the *Fleet*; and afterwards by another decree for the preſent levying thereof, out of their lands, at eight years purchaſe (as they were before the wars,) with the allowance of Intereſt at 8*l. per centum, per annum*, in caſe of obſtruction; for all or any part of it. and to this purpoſe cauſed an ordinance to be drawn up, which fully paſſed their Houſe the 15, 20, and 27*th* of *April*, 1646. and afterwards tranſmitted it to the Houſe of Commons, where by reaſon of my bloody adverſary old Sir *Henry Vane*'s Intereſts, and of my impriſonment by *Mancheſter*'s means in the *Tower* of *London*, it lay aſleep till the 1ſt of *Auguſt* 1648. at which time 7 or 8000 of my true friends in *London*, ſigned and cauſed to be delivered a Petition to the Houſe of Commons for my liberty, and the paſſing of the ſaid Ordinance. Whereupon the Houſe made this Order.

Die Martis, 1 *Auguſti* 1648.

Sir *John Maynard*, Sir *Peter Wentworth*, Lord *Carre*, Col. *Boſwel*, Col. *Ludlow*, Mr. *Holland*, Mr. *Copley*.

"It is referred to this Committee, or any five of them, to conſider how "Colonel *John Lilburn* may have ſuch ſatisfaction and allowance for his "ſufferings and loſſes, as was formerly intended him by this Houſe."

Henry Elſynge, Cler. Parl. Dom. Com.

Upon

Upon which Order I got the Committee to meet, and preferred a Petition to them. Upon which Petition, the Parliament having disposed of all that Part of the Lord *Cottington*'s Estate that I should have had, unto the Lord *Say*, and also compounded with Sir *Francis Windebank*'s Heir; the said Committee were pleased to fix it entirely upon the Lord-Keeper's Estate, as the principal guilty Man; of which, when the young Lord *Coventry*, his Son and Heir, heard thereof in *France*, he came posting to *England* as in Amaze, fearing what such a Precedent might bring upon him, if his Father's Estate [then dead] should be compelled to make me Satisfaction; he being so capital in Injustice, that if that Course should be taken, his Estate left him by his Father [if it were trebled] would not satisfy for his Father's palpable Injustice committed in his Life-time. And *Manchester* being in the said Bryers with his Father, being as unjust as the other, and having a Brother (*viz. George Montague*) and other considerable Interests in the House of Commons, so plied their Friends there, that they put a Stop to the second reading of the aforesaid Ordinance. Which I first fully understood by the Speaker's Means, then my great pretended Friend, who one Day began to reason with a Member of the House [and my special Friend] about the unreasonableness to fix my Reparations upon the Estate of the deceased Lord *Coventry*; nay, or to give me any Reparations at all out of the Estates of those Persons that did me wrong, for fear the Precedent in time might reach to themselves: "For, "Sir, said the Speaker, [as the Member told me] if my Son and Heir "should be liable in Law, to make Satisfaction to all those Men [out of "that Estate I should leave him] that I have in the Eye of the Law wrong'd "[by signing Warrants, Orders, and Decrees, by the Command of my "Superiors] he would soon be a Beggar, although I should leave him 5 or "6000 *l. per annum*; and therefore desired the said Member's Concur-"rence with him. And for the clamorous Importunity [as they called "it] of me and my Friends, to give me Reparations, but yet to do it in "such a Way, that the Precedent might not in future make themselves "smart for their Injustice to particular Men." Of which, when the said Member told me, he said, they were resolved to make the Commonwealth my Pay-master out of the publick Treasury, and colour over the Justness of it with this Pretence, "That *Cottington*'s Estate, *&c.* formerly assigned "me, they had since disposed of for the Commonwealth's use, to the "Lord *Say*; and therefore now it would be no Injustice to the Common-"wealth [although in the *Star-Chamber* it never wronged me] to pay me "my Reparation." And so finding I was like to be baffled, I delivered the under-written to every individual Member of the Honourable House of Commons.

The Humble Remembrance of Lieutenant Colonel John Lilburn, Sept. 4, 1648.

Honoured Sir,

VOuchsafe to take Notice, and seriously to consider, That the first Week this present Parliament sat, which is now almost full eight Years ago, I presented an humble Petition to the House of Commons, for Justice and Right against the cruel Judges of the *High-Commission-Court*, and the *Star-Chamber*; and I had the Honour [the same Day it was presented] to be one of the first Prisoners in *England* that was set at Liberty by this Parliament, and also received a speedy, full, fair, and candid Proceeding, in the hearing and examining my tyrannical Sufferings: But by reason of Multiplicity of publick Business, and other great Obstructions, I have not as yet been able to attain to the full End of my legal and just Expectation and Right, *viz.* Reparations for my long, sad, and tormenting Sufferings, by the foresaid unjust and unrighteous Judges.

Be pleased also favourably to take Notice, That upon the first of *August* last, there was an humble Petition presented to the Honourable House of Commons, subscribed by many Thousands of honest Citizens, *&c.* humbly to desire you to put me in full Possession of all your by-past just Votes about my foresaid Sufferings: Upon reading and debating of which Petition, as in Answer to that particular of it, your House were pleased to make this ensuing Order:

Die Martis, 1 Augusti, 1648.

Lord *Carre*, Sir *John Maynard*, Sir *Peter Wentworth*, Col. *Boswel*, Col. *Ludlow*, Mr. *Copley*, Mr. *Holland*.

"It is referred to this Committee, or any five of them, to consider "how Colonel *John Lilburn* may have Satisfaction and Allowance for his "Sufferings and Losses, as was formerly intended him by this House."

Henry Elsynge, Cler. Dom. Com.

Unto which said Committee at their first Sitting, I presented a Petition; the Copy of which thus followeth:

To the Honourable the Committee of the House of Commons, appointed to consider of Lieut. Col. Lilburn's *Business, in reference to the* Star-Chamber;

The Humble Petition of Lieut. Col. John Lilburn

Sheweth,

THAT besides your Petitioner's Sufferings by reason of his Banishment into the *Low-Countries*, he was first committed by Dr. *Lamb*, *Gwyn*, *Aylet*, 1637, and afterwards had three Years Imprisonment, in the Common Gaol of the *Fleet*, being whipped from *Fleet-Bridge* to *Westminster*, and enduring the cruel Torment of above five hundred Stripes with knotted Cords. Afterwards being set in the Pillory for the Space of two Hours, and by *James Ingram*, Deputy-Warden of the *Fleet*, gagged, tearing his Jaws almost in Pieces, without Order; which Sentence was given by Lord-Keeper *Coventry*, Earl of *Manchester*, Lord Privy-Seal, Lord *Newburgh*, Sir *Henry Vane*, sen. Lord Chief-Justice *Bramston*, and Judge *Jones*. And after the barbarous Execution of this Sentence, being *April* 18, 1638, the said Lord *Coventry*, Archbishop of *Canterbury*, Bishop of *London*, Earl of *Manchester*, Earl of *Arundel*, Earl of *Salisbury*, Lord *Cottington*, Lord *Newburgh*, Secretary *Coke*, and *Windebank*, passed another Sentence, in effect for the starving of your Petitioner, and for the tormenting of him with Irons upon Hands and Legs both Night and Day; and by keeping him close in the common Gaol of the *Fleet*, from the Speech of any of his Friends. All which was executed with the greatest Cruelty that could be, for the Space of almost three Years together, to the apparent Hazard of his Life, both by starving him [which was with all Art and Industry several ways attempted], and also by several Assaults made upon him by the said Warden's Man [instigated thereunto by the said Deputy-Warden, to the maiming and wounding him, whereby to this Day he is totally deprived of the Use of two of his Fingers]: All which, with much more, too tedious to be here inserted, was fully proved by sufficient Witnesses, before a Committee of your House, whereof Mr. *Francis Rouse* had the Chair; upon whose Report made, *May* 4, 1641, your House voted, "That the Sentence in the *Star-Chamber* given against the said "*John Lilburn*, and all the Proceedings thereupon, was illegal, and "against the Liberty of the Subject, and also bloody, wicked, cruel, bar-"barous, and tyrannical; and that he ought to have good Reparations "therefore." Which Votes (by reason of Multiplicity of Business in your House) cost your Petitioner some Years of importunate and chargeable Attendance to get them transmitted to the Lords; which was obtained in *February*, 1645, the 13th Day of which Month, your Petitioner's whole Cause was effectually opened at the Lords Bar, by his learned Counsel, Mr. *John Bradshaw* and Mr. *John Cook*; and there every particular again proved upon Oath, by Testimony of People of very good Quality. Whereupon they concurred in all things with the House of Commons, saving in the Matter of Reparation; but upon the Delivery of a true Narrative, (which your Petitioner with his own Hands in the same Month delivered unto every individual Lord) they made a further Decree, that your Petitioner should have 2000*l.* Reparations out of the Estates of the said Lord *Cottington*, Sir *Francis Windebank*, and *James Ingram*, for the Reasons alledged in an Ordinance which they passed in *April*, 1646, and transmitted to your House; where it hath lain dormant ever since, and is now referred to the Consideration of this honourable Committee.

Now, forasmuch as by the Judicial Laws of God (which are the pure Laws of right Reason), he that wilfully hurteth his Neighbour is bound to the Performance of these five things. *First*, "If it be a Blemish or "Wound, like for like, or to redeem it with Money, thereby to satisfy "him for his Wound. *Secondly*, For his Pain and Torment. *Thirdly*, "For the healing. *Fourthly*, For his Loss of Time in his Calling. *Fifth-*"*ly*, For the Shame and Disgrace:" All which are to be considered according to the Quality of the Person damnified: Which Reparations are to be paid out of the best of the Goods of him that damnified him, and that without Delay.

And as the Law of God, so the Laws of this Nation do abhor, and have severely punished (above all Persons) Judges, many times with the Loss of their Lives and Estates, who under Colour of Law have violated their Oaths, and destroyed the Lives, Liberties and Properties of the People, whom by Law they should have preserved: as may be instanced by the forty-four Judges and Justices hanged in one Year by King *Alfred*; divers of them for less Crimes than hath been done in the Case of your Petitioner; as may be read in the Law-Book called, *The Mirrour of Justice*, Page 239, 240, 241, *&c.* translated and reprinted this very Parliament: And by Justice *Thorp*, in *Edw.* III.'s Time, who was condemned to Death for the Violation of his Oath, for taking small Sums of Money in Causes depending before him; as appears in the third Part of *Coke's Institutes*, *fol.* 155, 156.

And by the Lord Chief-Justice *Tresilian*, &c. who in full Parliament in *Rich.* II.'s Time, was attached as a Traitor in the Forenoon, and had his Throat cut at *Tyburn* in the Afternoon, *because he had given it under his Hand, that the King might create unto himself, at his Pleasure, another rule to walk by, than the Law of the Land prescribes him*; as appears by the Parliament Records in the *Tower*, by many of your own Declarations, and also by the Chronicles of *England*.

Now, for as much as your Petitioner's Sufferings have been unparalleled, and his Prejudice sustained thereby altogether unrepairable, having lost his Limbs, *&c.* And forasmuch as by the Law of God, Nature, and Nations, Reparations for Hurts and Damages received, ought to be satisfied as far as may be in all Persons, though done by Accident, and not intentionally, and though through Ignorance: much more when the Persons offending did it knowingly, and on Purpose, in the Face, nay, in spite of the fundamental Laws of the Land, which they were sworn to preserve: And for that the Reparations in the said Ordinance assigned do scarce amount to what your Petitioner spent in his three Years sad Captivity, and his now almost eight Years chargeable Attendance, in suing for it, besides the Loss of a rich and profitable Trade for eleven Years together, and his Wounds, Torments, Smart and Disgrace, sustained by his said tyrannical Sentences:

He therefore humbly prayeth the Favour and Justice of this honourable Committee for some considerable Augmentation of his said Reparations; and the rather, because his Fellow-sufferer, Dr. *Bastwick*, had 4000*l.* Reparations allotted him, whose Sufferings (he submissively conceiveth) was nothing nigh so great, in Torment, Pain, and Shame, as your Petitioner's. And forasmuch as the now Lord *Coventry*, Son and Heir to the aforesaid Lord *Coventry*, hath walked in his Father's Steps, in Enmity to the Laws, Liberties, and Freedom of the Nation: By being in Arms at the Beginning of the Wars against the Parliament, and made his Peace with the Earl of *Essex* for a small Matter, and hath since deserted the Kingdom, living in *France* privately, receiving the Profits of a vast Estate which his Father left him: And forasmuch as his said Father (the late Lord *Coventry*) was the activest Man in infringing the Laws and Liberties of the Nation; although a Lawyer and Judge, sitting on the supreme Seat of Justice, and a Person (as is groundedly conceived) who got a great Estate by Corruption, and particularly a Man that principally passed, as Chief Judge of the Court, both the aforesaid Sentences against your Petitioner: And in regard the Estates of the said Lord *Cottington*, and Sir *Francis Windebank*, by subsequent Orders of both Houses upon urgent Occasions, are much intangled and altered from the Condition they were in in 1646, when the Lords ordered your Petitioner 2000 Marks out of them, and for that the Estate of *James Ingram* cannot be found, nor at present comes by: Your Petitioner, therefore, most humbly prayeth, that the greatest Part, if not all your Petitioner's Reparations may be fixed upon the said now Lord *Coventry*'s Estate, to be immediately paid your Petitioner, or else that his Rents, and the Profits of his Woods and Goods may be be ſeized in the reſpective Counties where they lie, for the ſatisfying thereof; that your Petitioner may no longer run the hazard of ruin to him and his, by tedious delays, having already contracted the debts of many hundred pounds, occaſioned by the chargeable proſecution hereof. And that if you ſhall think fit to conjoin any other with him, that it may be principally the Judges of the Law; who ought to have been pilots and guides unto the reſt of the Judges of that Court, who were Lords, and perſons not knowing the Law.

And your Petitioner ſhall ever pray, &c.

JOHN LILBURN.

After the reading of which, they entered into a ſerious debate of the whole buſineſs, and thereupon paſſed ſeveral Votes to be heads of an Ordinance, to be drawn up and reported to the Houſe, by the Right Honourable the Lord *Carr* Chairman to the ſaid Committee; who accordingly reported the Proceedings and Votes of the ſaid Committee to your Houſe, who approved of the ſaid Votes, and ordered an Ordinance to be preſented to the Houſe conſonant thereunto, which was accordingly done by the Lord *Carr*; which ordinance hath been once read in your Houſe: The Copy of which thus follows:

An Ordinance of the Lords and Commons aſſembled in Parliament, for the raiſing of three thouſand pounds out of the real Eſtate of the late Thomas *Lord* Coventry, *late Lord Keeper of the Great Seal of* England, *for and towards the reparation and damages of* John Lilburn, *Gent. which he ſuſtained by virtue and colour of two Sentences given and made againſt him, in the late Court of* Star-Chamber, *the one the* 13th *of* Febr. 1637. *the other the* 18th *of* April, 1638.

WHereas the cauſe of *John Lilburn* Gent. concerning two ſentences pronounced againſt him in the late Court of *Star-Chamber*, 13th of *February*, 13 *Car. Regis*, and 18th of *April*, 14 *Car. Regis*, were voted the 4th of *May* 1641, by the Houſe of Commons to be illegal, and againſt the liberty of the ſubject, and alſo bloody, wicked, cruel, barbarous, and tyrannical, which were tranſmitted from the ſaid Houſe of Commons unto the Houſe of Lords; who thereupon, by an order or decree, by them made 13th of *February* 1645, adjudged and declared the ſaid proceedings of the ſaid *Star-Chamber*, againſt the ſaid *John Lilburn*, to be illegal and moſt unjuſt, and againſt the liberty of the ſubject, and *Magna Charta*, and unfit to continue upon record, &c. And by another order or decree, made by them the ſaid Lords the 5th of *March* 1645, they aſſigned to be paid unto the ſaid *John Lilburn* the ſum of two thouſand pounds for his reparations; and the ſaid Houſe of Peers then fixed that ſum upon the eſtates real and perſonal of *Francis* Lord *Cottington*, Sir *Francis Windebank*, and *James Ingram* *, late Deputy-Warden of the *Fleet*: and afterwards for the preſent levying thereof, with allowance of Intereſt, in caſe of obſtructions, while the ſame ſhould be in levying, and of ſuch parts as ſhould not be forthwith levied; the ſaid Houſe of Peers did cauſe an ordinance to be drawn up, and paſſed the ſame in their Houſe, the 27th of *April* 1646, and afterwards tranſmitted the ſame to the Houſe of Commons for their concurrence; with whom it yet dependeth. And foraſmuch as ſince that tranſmiſſion, all, or the greateſt, of the eſtates of the ſaid Lord *Cottington*, and Sir *Francis Windebank*, is ſince by both Houſes diſpoſed of to other uſes; and the eſtate of the ſaid *James Ingram* is ſo ſmall and weak, and ſo entangled with former incumbrances, that it can afford little or no part unto the ſaid *John Lilburn* of the ſaid reparations: And for that the ſaid late Lord *Coventry* was the principal Judge, and chief Actor, in giving of both the ſaid illegal ſentences in the ſaid Court of *Star-Chamber*; and for the barbarous inflicting of puniſhments thereupon.

Therefore, and for ſatisfaction of the ſaid 2000*l.* and for the increaſe of reparation unto the ſaid *John Lilburn* for his extraordinary wrongs, ſufferings and loſſes thereby ſuſtained, and the long time hitherto elapſed without any ſatisfaction; the Lords and Commons aſſembled in Parliament do ordain, and be it hereby ordained by the ſaid Lords and Commons, and by authority of the ſame; That the ſaid *John Lilburn* ſhall receive the ſum of 3000*l.* out of all, or any the Manors, Meſſuages, Lands, Tenements and Hereditaments, whereof he, the ſaid late *Thomas* Lord *Coventry*, or any other perſon or perſons to or for his uſe, or in truſt for him, was or were ſeized in fee-ſimple, or fee-tail, or otherwiſe, at the time of the ſaid ſentences or decrees, or of either of them, in the ſaid late Court of *Star-Chamber*, or ſince within the Kingdom of *England*, or Dominion of *Wales*, any order or ordinance heretofore made by either or both Houſes of Parliament for the employment of the eſtate of the ſaid late *Thomas* Lord *Coventry* to the contrary hereof, in any wiſe notwithſtanding. And for the more ſpeedy levying of the ſaid ſum of three thouſand pounds, it is further ordered and ordained, that the ſeveral and reſpective Sheriffs, of the ſeveral and reſpective Counties within *England* and *Wales*, wherein any of the ſaid Lands, Tenements, or Hereditaments do lie, ſhall forthwith upon ſight, and by virtue of this ordinance, cauſe an inquiſition to be made and taken, by the Oaths of twelve or more lawful men, where the ſame lands do lie, and what the ſame are and do contain, and of the clear yearly value thereof, over and above all charges and repriſes: and after ſuch inquiſition ſo made and taken, the ſeveral and reſpective Sheriffs ſhall deliver unto the ſaid *John Lilburn* true copies in Parchment of the ſame inquiſitions by them taken, and ſhall then alſo deliver unto the ſaid *John Lilburn* the ſaid Lands, Tenements and Hereditaments, which ſhall be ſo compriſed or mentioned in the ſaid inquiſitions, to have and to hold, to him the ſaid *John Lilburn*, and his aſſigns, without impeachment of waſte; and until he ſhall have received out of the iſſues and profits thereof (to be eſtimated according to the yearly values contained in the ſaid inquiſitions) the ſaid ſum of three thouſand pounds; together with all reaſonable charges and expences to be ſuſtained from henceforth for obtaining the ſaid ſum of three thouſand pounds. And all and every the ſaid ſeveral and reſpective Sheriffs, and all other perſon and perſons whatſoever, that ſhall any ways act or aſſiſt in obedience to this ordinance, according to the true intent and meaning thereof, ſhall be therefore defended and kept harmleſs, by the authority of both Houſes of Parliament.

Be pleaſed to take further notice, that after the foreſaid ordinance was once read, it came to a debate in your Houſe for to be read the ſecond time, which was carried in the negative by a majority of voices; and I cannot but apprehend that there were divers in the Houſe unſatisfied in the ordinance itſelf, in regard the Houſe was divided upon the Debate and Vote, which I cannot but apprehend muſt flow from one of theſe two conſiderations:

Firſt, Either becauſe that the whole reparations is fixed upon the Lord *Coventry*'s eſtate ſingly, who had many co-partners in the ſentences, and who alſo it may be ſuppoſed hath expiated his crime by his death. Or elſe, ſecondly, Becauſe in ſome men's thoughts, ſome of my late actions are, or have been ſo evil in themſelves, that they may ſeem to them to overbalance the merits of all my ancient ſufferings.

However, on my preſenting my reaſons to the Houſe for reading it, my ordinance was called for to be read the ſecond time, which *Elſynge* the Clerk pretended he had laid ready upon the table before him; but what betwixt his knavery, old *Henry Vane*'s, the Speaker's, and young *Montague*'s, my ordinance was ſtol'n, and could never after be found: ſo that I was ſent to out of the Houſe to get another fair copy writ over preſently; which being long in doing, my friends went away, not expecting it would any more be meddled with that day, ſo that when moſt of them were gone, my adverſaries took the advantage to call for it, and in a thin Houſe read it the ſecond time, and upon debate threw it out of doors; and at preſent to ſtop my mouth, voted me 300*l.* ready-money (as they pretended) out of Sir *Charles Kemiſſes*'s compoſition, to enable me for preſent ſubſiſtance, and to follow my buſineſs; and alſo made this further order:

Die Martis, Septemb. 5, 1648.

ORdered by the Commons aſſembled in Parliament, that the ſum of three thouſand pounds be allowed and paid unto Lieutenant Colonel *John Lilburn*, for reparation of his damages ſuſtained by colour of the ſentences given againſt him in the late Court of *Star-Chamber*, where Lord *Carr* had the Chair, with the addition of Sir *John Danvers*, and Colonel *Rigby*, to conſider of, and preſent to this Houſe an Ordinance for ſettling of lands to him and his heirs, to the value of 3000*l.* at twelve years purchaſe, out of the eſtates of new Delinquents in the Inſurrections, not yet ſequeſtered.

H. Elſynge, Cler. Parl. Com. Dom.

Of which when I fully underſtood, I was troubled, but knew not how to help myſelf; and having already met with ſo many difficulties, and received ſo many baffles as I had done, I thought it was better (being almoſt wearied out with ſtruggling) to take half a loaf, than to go away without any bread at all. So after many Petitions and Letters to the Sequeſtrators, &c. the Committee cauſed an ordinance to be drawn up.

But when my ordinance came to the Lords, they diſabled me to cut down any more timber-trees than what were already fell'd, which I judged fitter for me to content myſelf with, than to ſtruggle any longer to get it paſs, as the Houſe of Commons had ſent it up. So the Lords in two or three days diſpatched it, and ſent it down to the Houſe of Commons for their concurrence, according to thoſe abridgements they had made in it; and taking my opportunity to ſpeak to thoſe in the Houſe of Commons I had intereſt in, I intreated them to diſpute it no more, but paſs it as the Lords had gelded it; and accordingly they did; the Copy of which thus followeth:

Die Jovis, 21 *Decemb.* 1648.

An Ordinance of the Lords and Commons aſſembled in Parliament, for raiſing of three thouſand pounds, out of the ſequeſtered eſtates and compoſitions of Sir Henry Gibb, *Knight; and Sir* Henry Bellingham, *Knight and Baronet; and* Thomas Bowes, *Eſquire; lying and being within the County of* Durham; *to be paid unto Lieut. Col.* John Lilburn, *by the Committee of Sequeſtrations of the ſaid County, for and towards the reparation and damages of the ſaid* John Lilburn, *which he ſuſtained by virtue and colour of two unjuſt Sentences, or Decrees; given and made againſt him in the late Court of* Star-Chamber, *the one the* 13th *of* February, 1637; *the other the* 18th *of* April, 1638.

WHereas the cauſe of Lieut. Col. *John Lilburn*, concerning two ſentences pronounced againſt him in the late Court of *Star-Chamber*, the 13th of *February, decimo tertio Caroli Regis*, and the 18th of *April, decimo quarto Caroli Regis*, (which were voted the 4th of *May*, 1641, by the Houſe of Commons to be illegal, and againſt the liberty of the ſubject, and alſo bloody, wicked, cruel, barbarous and tyrannical) were tranſmitted from the ſaid Houſe of Commons unto the Houſe of Lords; in which the Houſe of Peers concurred in judgment; and the 13th of *February* 1645, declared the ſaid proceedings of the ſaid *Star-Chamber*, againſt the ſaid *John Lilburn*, to be illegal, moſt unjuſt, and againſt the liberty of the ſubject, and law of the land, and *Magna Charta*, and unfit to continue upon record, &c. The ſaid Lords and Commons taking into their ſerious conſideration, the extraordinary ſufferings and barbarous tyranny, that by colour of the ſaid unjuſt decrees were inflicted upon the ſaid Lieut. Col. *John Lilburn*; and the long time hitherto elapſed without any ſatisfaction, do conceive it moſt juſt, equitable and reaſonable, to repair him in ſome conſiderable manner; and therefore, in purſuance of two orders of the Houſe of Commons, one of the 22d of *Auguſt* 1648, and the other of the 5th of *September* 1648, have ordained; and be it hereby ordained by the Lords and Commons aſſembled in Parliament, and by the authority of the ſame; That the ſaid *John Lilburn* ſhall have and receive the ſum of 3000*l.* to be paid unto him or his aſſigns, by the Committee of Sequeſtrations for the County of *Durham*, out of the firſt profits of the ſequeſtered eſtates, both lands and goods of Sir *Henry Gibb*, Knight; Sir *Henry Bellingham*, Knight and Baronet; and *Thomas Bowes*, Eſquire; lying and being in the County of *Durham*, having all been active in the late *Northern* Inſurrections, and aiding and aſſiſting to the moſt wicked invaſion of Duke *Hamilton*. And the ſaid Committee are hereby authoriſed to fell all ſuch woods (except timber-trees now ſtanding) as may conveniently be ſpared, and now ſtanding upon the ſaid lands (or already felled), or any of them. And

* 'But the Lord *Roberts*, the Lord *Wharton* &c. told me ſeveral times, if their eſtates had not been under ſequeſtration by Ordinance of Parliament, they would never 'have gone about to fix my reparations by Ordinance, (which they muſt needs then do, to take off the Sequeſtration) but have iſſued out a decree and extent under the 'Great Seal, immediately to have put me in preſent poſſeſſion of my 2000*l.* which they ſaid was their right by Law to do.'

if

And if the said Sir *Henry Gibb*, Sir *Henry Bellingham*, and *Thomas Bowes*, or any of them shall compound for their estate, so much of the said three thousand pounds as then shall remain unsatisfied shall be paid unto the said *John Lilburn*, or his assignees, out of their, or the first of their compositions. And this Ordinance or Copy thereof, attested under the hand or hands of the Clerk, or Clerks, of one or both Houses of Parliament, shall be a sufficient Warrant to the said Committee of Sequestrations in the said County of *Durham*, to pay the said 3000 *l.* as is before expressed, unto the said *John Lilburn* or his assigns; and likewise to indemnify and save harmless, all and every person or persons, that shall any way act in the performance of the true intent and meaning of this Ordinance.

Joh. Brown, Cler. Parliamentor.
H. Elsynge, Cler. Parl Dom. Com.

However, Lieut. Col. *Lilburn*, after great trouble, and much expence, got but little of the money ordered him.

XXI. Proceedings in Parliament against Sir *John Finch*, Baron of *Fordwich*, Lord Keeper, for High-Treason, 1640. 16 *Car.* I *.

THE House of Commons having secur'd that great Statesman the Earl of *Strafford*, and that zealous Churchman Archbishop *Laud*; began to prepare an Impeachment against the great Officer of the Law, the Lord-Keeper *Finch*, of High-Treason.

December 14th, a Committee was appointed to prepare a Charge against him; of which he having notice, sent to the House of Commons a Letter, desiring to be admitted to speak for himself, before any Vote past against him. Upon this Letter there arose a great debate in the House, and after some time spent therein, it was granted him; and *Monday*, *December* the 21st, was appointed for the hearing of him.

On *Monday* he was admitted in this manner; there was a Chair set for him to make use of if he pleased, and a Stool to lay the Purse upon, a little on the side of the Bar on the left hand as you come in; he himself brought in the Purse, and laid it in the Chair, but would not sit down himself, nor put on his Hat, though he was mov'd to it by Mr. Speaker, but spake all the while bare-headed and standing; the Serjeant at Arms attending on the House, standing by him with the Mace on his shoulder: And spake as follows.

Mr. Speaker,

I DO first present my most humble thanks to this Honourable Assembly for this favour vouchsafed me, in granting me admittance to their presence, and do humbly beseech them to believe it is no desire to preserve myself or my fortune, but to deserve the good opinions of those that have drawn me hither.

I do profess, in the presence of him that knoweth all hearts, that I had rather go from door to door, and crave *Da obolum Belizario, &c.* with the good opinion of this Assembly, than live and enjoy all the honours and fortunes I am capable of.

I do not come hither with an intention to justify my words, my actions, or my opinions; but to make a plain and clear narration for myself, and then humbly to submit to the wisdom and justice of this House myself, and all that concerns me.

I do well understand (*Mr. Speaker*) with what disadvantage any man can speak in his own cause, and if I could have told how to have transmitted my thoughts and actions, by a clearer representation of another (I do so much defy my own judgment in working, and my ways in expressing), that I should have been a most humble suitor another might have done it. But this House will not take words, but with clear and ingenuous dealing; and therefore I shall beseech them to think, I come not hither with a set or studied speech, I come to speak my heart, and to speak it clearly and plainly, and then leave it to your clemency and justice: and I hope if any thing shall slip from me, to work contrary to my meaning, or intention, disorderly or ill-placed, you will be pleased to make a favourable construction, and leave me the liberty of explanation, if there shall be any; but I hope there shall be no cause for it.

I hope, for my affection in Religion no man doubteth me; what my education, what, and under whom for many years, is well known; I lived near thirty years in the Society of *Gray's-Inn*: and if one that was a reverend Preacher in my time (Dr. *Sibbs*) were now alive, he were able to give testimony to this House, that when a party ill-affected in Religion sought to weary him, and tire him out, he had his chiefest encouragement from me.

I have now (*Mr. Speaker*) been fifteen years of the King's Council; from the first hour to this minute, no man is able to say that ever I was author, adviser, or consenter to any project.

It pleased the King (my gracious Master), after I had served him divers years, to prefer me to two places; to be Chief-Justice of the *CommonPleas*, and then Keeper of his Great-Seal: I say it in the presence of God, I was so far from the thought of the one, and from the ambition of the other, that if my Master's grace and goodness had not been, I had never enjoyed those honours.

I cannot tell (*Mr. Speaker*), nor I do not know what particulars there are, that may draw me into your disfavour or ill opinion, and therefore I shall come very weakly arm'd; yet to those that either in my own knowledge, or by such a knowledge as is given me, and not from any in this House, I shall speak somewhat, that I hope being truth, and accompanied with clearness and ingenuity, will at last procure some allay of that ill opinion which may perhaps be conceived of me.

Mr. Speaker, I had once the honour to sit in the place that you do: from the first time I came thither, to this unfortunate time, I do appeal to all that were here then, if I served you not with candor. Ill office I never did to any of the House, good offices I have witnesses enough I did many; I was so happy, that upon an occasion which once happened, I received an expression and testimony of the good affection of this House towards me.

For the last unhappy day, I had great share in the unhappiness and sorrow of it. I hope there are enough do remember, no man within the walls of this House did express more symptoms of sorrow, grief, and distraction than I did.

After an adjournment for two or three days, it pleased his Majesty to send for me, to let me know that he could not so resolve of things as he desired, and therefore was desirous that there might be an adjournment for some few days more. I protest I did not then discern in his Majesty, and I believe it was not in his thoughts, to think of the dissolving of this Assembly; but was pleased, in the first place, to give me a command to deliver his pleasure to the House for an adjournment for some few days, till the *Monday* following, as I remember, and commanded me withal to deliver his pleasure, that there should be no further speeches, but forthwith upon the delivery of the message come and wait upon him: he likewise commanded me, if questions were offered to be put, upon my Allegiance I should not dare to do it. How much I did then in all humbleness reason with his Majesty, is not for me here to speak; only thus much let me say, I was no Author of any counsel in it. I was only a person in receiving Commission; I speak not this, as any thing I now produce or do invent, or take up for my own excuse, but that which is known to divers, and some honourable persons in this House, to be most true. All that I will say for that, is humbly to beseech you all to consider, that if it had been any man's case, as it was mine, between the displeasure of a gracious King, and the ill opinion of an honourable Assembly; I beseech you lay all together, lay my first actions and behaviour with the last, I shall submit to your honourable and favourable constructions.

For the Shipping business, my opinion of that cause hath lain heavy upon me; I shall clearly and truly present unto you what every thing is, with this protestation, that if in reckoning up my own opinion what I was of, or what I delivered, any thing of it be displeasing, or contrary to the opinion of this House, that I am far from justifying of it, but submit that and all other my actions to your wisdom and goodness.

Mr. Speaker, the first Writs that were sent out about the Shipping-business, I had no more knowledge of, and was as ignorant as any one Member of this House, or any man in the Kingdom. I was never the Author nor Adviser of it, and will boldly say, from the first to this hour, I did never advise nor counsel the setting forth of any Ship-Writs in my life.

Mr. Speaker, it is true that I was made Chief-Justice of the *Common-Pleas* some four days before the Ship-Writs went out to the Ports and Maritime Places; as I do remember, the 20th of *October* 1634, they do bear *teste*, and I was sworn Justice the 16th of *October*: so as they went out in that time, but without my knowledge or privity, the God of Heaven knows this to be true.

Mr. Speaker, afterwards his Majesty was pleased to command my Lord Chief-Justice of the *King's-Bench*, that then was, Sir *Thomas Richardson*, and Chief-Baron of the *Exchequer* that now is, and myself, then Chief-Justice of the *Common-Pleas*, to take into consideration the Precedents then brought unto us; which we did, and after returned to his Majesty, what we had found out of those precedents.

It is true, that afterwards his Majesty did take into consideration, that if the whole Kingdom were concerned, that it was not reason to lay the whole burthen upon the Cinque Ports and Maritime Towns.

Thereupon, upon what ground his Majesty took that into his consideration, I do confess I do know nothing of it.

His Majesty did command my Lord Chief-Justice that now is, my Lord Chief-Baron, and myself, to return our opinions; Whether, when the whole Kingdom is in danger, and the Kingdom in general is concerned, it be not according to Law and Reason, that the whole Kingdom, and his Majesty, and all interested therein, should join in defending and preserving thereof?

This was, in time, about 1634.

In *Michaelmas*-Term following, his Majesty commanded me to go to all the Judges, and require their opinions in particular.

He commanded me to do it to every one, and to charge them upon their duty and allegiance to keep it secret.

Mr. Speaker, it was never intended by his Majesty (so professed by him) at that time, and so declared to all the Judges, that it was not required by him, to be such a binding opinion to the Subject, as to hinder him from calling it in question, nor be binding to themselves, but that upon better reason and advice they may alter it; but desired their opinions, for his own private reason.

I know very well, that extrajudicial opinions of Judges ought not to be binding.

But I did think, and speak my Heart and Conscience freely; myself, and the rest of the Judges being sworn, and by our Oaths tied to counsel the King, when he should require advice of us, that we were bound by our Oaths and Duties to return our opinions.

I did obey his Majesty's command, and do here before the God of Heaven avow it.

* This Proceeding explains the manner of obtaining the Judges opinions in Mr. *Hampden*'s Case about *Ship-Money*, Vol. I. *pag.* 483. as also the Lord Keeper's Reasons for what he did as Speaker in the Parliament 1629, for which see, *ante Page* [illegible]. Else this had not been inserted. His Lordship not putting in any Answer to the Articles exhibited against him.

I did

I did never use the least promise of preferment or reward to any, nor did use the least menace; I did leave it freely to their own Consciences and Liberty; for I was left to the liberty of my own by his Majesty, and had reason to leave them the liberty of their own Consciences.

And I beseech you be pleased to have some belief, that I would not say this, but that I know the God of Heaven will make it appear; and I beseech you that extravagant speeches may not move against that which is a positive and clear truth.

Mr. Speaker, in the discourse of this (as is between Judges) some small discourses sometimes arose, yet never was any cause wherein any Judges conferred, that were so little conference as between me and them.

Mr. Speaker, against a Negative, I can say nothing; but I shall affirm nothing unto you, but by the grace of God, as I affirm it to be true, so I make no doubt of making it appear to be so.

This opinion was subscribed without solicitation; there was not any man of us, did make any doubt of subscribing our opinion, but two, Mr. Justice *Hutton*, and Mr. Justice *Croke*.

Mr. Justice *Croke* made not a scruple of the thing, but of the introduction; for it was thus:

That whereas the Ports and the Maritime Towns were concerned, there according to the precedents in former times, the charge lay on them.

So when the Kingdom was in danger, of which his Majesty was the sole Judge; whether it was not agreeable to Law and Reason, the whole Kingdom to bear the charge?

I left this case with Judge *Croke*.

The next Term I spake with him, he could give me no resolution, because he had not seen the Writs in former times: but did give his opinion, that when the whole Kingdom was in danger, the charge of the defence ought to be borne by all.

So of that opinion of his, there was no need of a solicitation.

I speak no more here, than I did openly in my argument in the *Exchequer-Chamber*.

This is the naked truth: for Mr. Justice *Hutton*, he did never subscribe at all.

I will only say this, that I was so far from pressing him to give his opinion, because he did ask time to consider of it, that I will boldly say, and make it good, that when his Majesty would have had him sometimes sent for, to give his opinion, I beseeched his Majesty to leave him to himself and his conscience: and that was the ill office I did.

The Judges did subscribe in *November* or *December*, 1635.

I had no conference, nor (truly I think) by accident any discourse with any of the Judges touching their opinions: for till *February*, 1636, there was no speech of it, for when they had delivered their opinions, I did return according to my duty to my Master the King, and delivered them to him; in whose custody they be.

In *February*, 1636, upon a command that came from his Majesty, by one of the then Secretaries of State, the Judges all assembled in *Gray's-Inn*; we did then fall into a debate of the case then sent unto us, and we did then return our opinion unto his Majesty; there was then much discourse and great debate about it.

Mine opinion and conscience at that time was agreeable to that opinion I then delivered.

I did use the best arguments I could, for the maintenance of my opinion; and that was all I did.

It is true, that then at that time, Mr. Justice *Hutton*, and Mr. Justice *Croke*, did not differ in the main point, which was this:

When the Kingdom was in danger, the charge ought to be borne by the whole Kingdom.

But in this point, whether the King was the sole Judge of the danger, they differed.

So as there was between the first subscription, and this debate and consultation, some fifteen months difference.

It is true, that all of them did then subscribe, both Justice *Hutton*, and Justice *Croke*, which was returned to his Majesty, and after published by my Lord-Keeper (my predecessor) in the *Star-Chamber*.

For the manner of publishing it I will say nothing, but leave it to those, whose memories will call to mind what was then done.

The Reason of the subscription of Justice *Hutton*, and Justice *Croke*, (though they differed in opinion) grew from this, that was told them, from the rest of the Judges;

That where the greater number did agree in their vote, the rest were involved and included.

And now I have faithfully delivered what I did in that business, till I came (which was afterwards) to my argument in the *Exchequer-Chamber*: for the question was, *A scire facias* issued out of the *Exchequer* in that case of Mr. *Hampden's*; of which I can say nothing, for it was there begun, and afterwards rejourned, to have advice of all the Judges.

Mr. Speaker, amongst the rest (according to my duty) I argued the case. I shall not trouble you, to tell you what my argument was, I presume there are copies enough of it; only I will tell you there are four things, very briefly, that I then declared.

First, concerning the matter of danger, and necessity of the whole Kingdom.

I profess that there was never a Judge in the Kingdom did deliver an opinion, but that it must be in a case of apparent danger.

When we came to an argument of the case, it was not upon a matter of issue, but it was upon a demurrer;

Whether the danger was sufficiently admitted in pleading, and therefore was not the thing that was in dispute, that was the first degree and step that led unto it.

I did deliver myself as free and as clear as any man did, that the King ought to govern by the positive Laws of the Kingdom; that he could not alter nor change, nor innovate in matters of Law, but by common consent in Parliament.

I did further deliver, that if this were used to make a further revenue or benefit to the King, or in any other way but in case of necessity, and for the preservation of the Kingdom, the judgment did warrant no such thing:

My opinion in this business, I did in my conclusion of my argument submit to the judgment of the House.

I never delivered my opinion, that money ought to be raised, but Ships provided for the defence of this Kingdom, and in that the writ was performed.

And that the charge ought not to be in any case, but where the whole Kingdom was in danger.

And Mr. Justice *Hutton*, and Mr. Justice *Croke*, were of the same opinion with me.

I do humbly submit, having related unto you my whole carriage in this business; humbly submitting myself to your grave and favourable censures, beseeching you not to think that I delivered these things with the least intention to subvert or subject the Common Law of the Kingdom, or to bring in, or to introduce any new way of Government; it hath been far from my thoughts, as any thing under the Heavens.

Mr. Speaker, I have heard too that there hath been some ill opinion conceived of me about Forest business, which was a thing far out of the way of my study, as any thing I know toward the Law.

But it pleased his Majesty, in the sickness of Mr. *Noy*, to give some short warning to prepare myself for that employment.

When I came there, I did both the King and Commonwealth acceptable service; for I did and dare be bold to say, with extreme danger to myself and fortune, (some do understand my meaning herein) run thro' that business, and left the Forest as much as was there.

A thing in my judgment, considerable for the advantage of the Commonwealth, as could be undertaken.

When I went down about that employment, I satisfied myself about the matter of perambulation.

There were great difficulties of opinions, what perambulation was.

I did arm myself as well as I could, before I did any thing in it.

I did acquaint those that were then Judges, in the presence of the noble Lords, with such objections as I thought it my duty to offer unto them.

If they thought they were not objections of such weight as were fit to stir them, I would not do the King that disservice.

They thought the objections had such answers as might well induce the like upon a conference with the whole Country; admitting me to come and confer with them, the Country did unanimously subscribe.

It fell out afterwards, that the King commanded me, and all this before I was Chief-Justice, to go into *Essex*, and did then tell me he had been informed, that the bounds of the Forest were narrower than in truth they ought to be; and I did according to his command.

I will here profess that which is known to many, I had no thought or intention of enlarging the bounds of the Forest, further than *H.* and that part about it, for which there was a perambulation about 26 *Edw.* IV.

I desired the Country to confer with me about it, if they were pleased to do it; and then according to my duty, I did produce those Records which I thought fit for his Majesty's service, leaving them to discharge themselves as by Law and Justice they might do.

I did never, in the least kind, go about to overthrow the Charter of the Forest.

And did publish and maintain *Charta de Foresta*, as a sacred thing, and no man to violate it, and ought to be preserved for the King and Commonwealth.

I do in this humbly submit, and what I have done, to the Goodness and Justice of this House.

[Mr. *Rushworth* says, many were exceedingly taken with his Eloquence and Carriage, and it was a sad sight to see a Person of his greatness, parts and favour, to appear in such a posture, before such an Assembly, to plead for his Life and Fortunes.]

After his Lordship was retired, it was moved that this admission of the Lord-Keeper, might not be drawn into precedent; and in answer to what his Lordship said, Mr. *Rigby* made this following speech.

Mr. Speaker,

Though my judgment prompts me to sit still and be silent, yet the duty I owe to my King, my Country and my Conscience, move me to stand up and speak.

Mr. *Speaker*, had not this Syren so sweet a tongue, surely he could never have effected so much mischief to this Kingdom: you know, Sir, *optimorum putrefactio pessima*, the best things putrefied become the worst: and as it is in the natural, so in the body politick; and what's to be done then, Mr. *Speaker*? We all know *ense recidendum est*, the sword, Justice must strike, *ne pars sincera trahatur*.

Mr. *Speaker*, it is not the voice, *non vox sed votum*, not the tongue, but the heart and actions that are to be suspected: for doth not our Saviour say it, *Shew me thy faith by thy works, O man?* (St. *James*, not our Saviour saith it.) Now, Mr. *Speaker*, hath not this Kingdom seen, (seen, say I?) nay felt and smarted under the cruelty of this man's Justice? so malicious as to record it in every Court of *Westminster*; as if he had not been contented with inslaving of us all, unless he entailed it to all posterity. Why shall I believe words now, *cum factum videam*? Shall we be so weak men, as when we have been injured and abused, will be gained again with fair words and compliments? Or, like little children, when we have been whipt and beaten, be pleased again with sweetmeats? Oh no, there be some birds in the summer of Parliament will sing sweetly, who in the winter of persecution, will for their prey ravenously fly at all, upon our goods, nay seize upon our persons; and hath it not been with this man so, with some in this Assembly?

Mr. *Speaker*, it hath been objected unto us, that in judgment you should think of mercy, and *be ye merciful as your heavenly Father is merciful*; now God Almighty grant that we may be so, and that our hearts and judgments may be truly rectified to know truly what is mercy: I say to know what is mercy; for there is the point, Mr. *Speaker*: I have heard of foolish pity, foolish pity; do we not all know the effects of it? And I have met with this epithet to mercy, *crudelis misericordia*; and in some kind I think there may be a cruel mercy: I am sure that the Spirit of God said, Be not pitiful in judgment; nay it saith, be not pitiful of the poor in judgment, if not of the poor, then, *à latiori*, not of the rich; there's the emphasis. We see by the set and solemn appointment of our Courts of Justice, what provision the wisdom of our ancestors hath made for the preservation, honour, and esteem of Justice, witness our frequent Terms, Sessions, and Assizes, and in what pomp and state the Judges, in their Circuits, by the Sheriffs, Knights and Justices, and all the Country, are attended oft-times for the hanging of a poor Thief for the stealing of a Hog or a Sheep, nay in some cases for the stealing of a penny, and Justice too, *in terrorem*; and now shall not some of them be hanged that have robbed us of all our property, and thieved at once all our Sheep and

and all we have away, and would have made us indeed poor *Belizarios* to have begged for half-pennies, when they would not have left us one penny that we could have called our own?

Let us therefore now, Mr. *Speaker*, not be so pitiful as that we become remiss; not so pitiful in judgment, as to have no judgment; but set the deplorable estate of *Great Britain* now before our eyes, and consider how our most gracious Sovereign hath been abused, and both his Majesty and all his Subjects injured by these wicked instruments, for which my humble motion is, that with these particulars we become not so merciful as to the generality (the whole Kingdom) to grow merciless.

Fiat Justitia.

Whereupon he was the same day voted a Traitor, upon the following particulars:

1. For refusing to read the remonstrance against the Lord-Treasurer *Weston*, 4 *Car.* when the Parliament desired it.
2. For solliciting, persuading, and threatening the Judges to deliver their opinion for the levying of Ship-money *.
3. For several illegal actions in Forest-matters.
4. For ill offices done, in making the King dissolve the last Parliament, and causing his declaration thereupon to be put forth.

Whereupon it was resolved upon the question,

That *John* Lord *Finch*, Baron of *Fordwich*, Lord-Keeper of the Great Seal of *England*, shall be accused in this House, in the name of all the Commons of *England*, of High-Treason, and other great Misdemeanors.

Resolved,

That a message be sent by the Lord *Falkland*, to accuse *John* Lord *Finch*, Baron of *Fordwich*, Lord-Keeper of the Great Seal of *England*, in the name of this House, and all the Commons of *England*, of High-Treason, and other great Crimes and Misdemeanors; and to desire that he may be forthwith sequestred from Parliament, and be committed; and that in some convenient time this House will resort to their Lordships, with particular Accusations and Articles against him.

The next morning, the 22d, the Lord-Keeper (considering with what impetuosity and violence every thing was managed) got up early, and escaped in disguise into *Holland*, from whence he wrote a Letter to the Lord-Chamberlain, dated from the *Hague*, *January* 3, 1640.

My most well beloved Lord,

THE Interest your Lordship hath ever had in the best of my fortunes and affections, gives me the privilege of troubling your Lordship with these few lines, from one that hath nothing left to serve you withal but his prayers; these your Lordship shall never fail of, with an heart as full of true affection to your Lordship as ever any was. My Lord, it was not the loss of my place, and with that of my fortunes, nor being exiled from my dear Country and Friends, though many of them were cause of sorrow, that afflicts me; but that which I most suffer under is, that displeasure of the House of Commons conceived against me. I know a true heart I have ever born towards them, and your Lordship can witness in part, what ways I have gone in: but silence and patience best becomes me, with which I must leave myself and my actions to the favourable constructions of my noble Friends, in which number your Lordship hath a prime place. I am now at the *Hague*, where I arrived on *Thursday* the last of the last month, where I purpose to live in a fashion agreeable to the poorness of my fortunes, for my humbling in this World, I have utterly cast off the thoughts of it, and my aim shall be to learn to number my days, that I may apply my heart to wisdom, that wisdom that shall wipe away all tears from my eyes and heart, and lead me by the hand to true happiness, which can never be taken from me. I pray God of Heaven to bless this Parliament, both with a happy progress and conclusion; if my ruin may conduce but the least to it, I shall not repine at it. I truly pray for your Lordship and your noble Family, that God would give an increase of all worldly blessings, and in the fulness of days to receive you to his Glory; if I were capable of serving any body, I would tell your Lordship, that no man should be readier to make known his devotion and true gratitude to your Lordship, than

Your Lordship's most humble,
and most affectionate,
poor Kinsman and Servant,
J. FINCH.

Jan. 14. The Committee having prepared Articles of Impeachment against the Lord-Keeper, they were presented to the House, and are as follow:

The Accusation and Impeachment of John † *Lord* Finch, *Baron of* Fordwich, *Lord-Keeper of the Great Seal of* England, *by the House of Commons.*

Imprimis, THAT the said *John* Lord *Finch*, Baron of *Fordwich*, Lord-Keeper, &c. hath traitorously and wickedly endeavoured to subvert the fundamental Laws and established Government of the Realm of *England*, and instead thereof to introduce an arbitrary, tyrannical Government against Law, which he hath declared by traitorous and wicked words, counsels, opinions, judgments, practices and actions.

II. That in pursuance of those his traitorous and wicked purposes, he did in the third and fourth year of his Majesty's reign, or one of them, being then Speaker of the Commons House of Parliament, contrary to the commands of the House then assembled and sitting, deny and hinder the reading of some things which the said House of Commons required to be read, for the safety of the King and Kingdom, and preservation of the Religion of this Realm; and did forbid all the Members of the House to speak, and said that if any did offer to speak, he would rise and go away, and said nothing should be done in the House; and did offer to rise and go away, and did thereby and otherwise, as much as in him lay, endeavour to subvert the ancient and undoubted rights and course of Parliament.

III. That he being of his Majesty's Council at the Justice Seat, held for the County of *Essex*, in the month of *October*, in the 10th year of his now Majesty's reign, at *Stratford-Langton* in the same County, being then of his Majesty's Council, in that service did practise by unlawful means to enlarge the Forest of that County many Miles beyond the known bounds thereof, as they had been enjoyed near 300 years, contrary to the Law and to the Charter of the liberties of the Forest, and other Charters and divers Acts of Parliament: and for effecting the same did unlawfully cause and procure undue return to be made of Jurors, and great numbers of other persons who were unsworn, to be joined to them of the Jury, and threatened and awed the said Jurors to give a verdict for the King, and by unlawful means did surprize the County, that they might not make defence, and did use several menacing wicked speeches and actions to the Jury and others, for obtaining his unjust purpose aforesaid. And after verdict obtained for the King in the month of *April* following (at which time the said Justice-seat was called by adjournment), the said *John Finch*, then Lord Chief-Justice of his Majesty's Court of *Common-Pleas*, and one of the Judges assistants for them; he continued by farther unlawful and unjust practices, to maintain and confirm the said verdict, and did then and there, being assistant to the Justice in *Eyre*, advise the refusal of the traverse offered by the County, and all their evidences, but only what they should verbally deliver; which was refused accordingly.

IV. That he about the month of *November*, 1635, being then Lord Chief-Justice of the *Common-Pleas*, and having taken an Oath for due administration of Justice to his Majesty's liege people, according to the Laws and Statutes of the Realm, contrived an opinion *in hæc verba*, (when the good and safety, &c. *Vide State-Trials*, Vol. I.) and did subscribe his name to that opinion, and by persuasions, threats, and false suggestions, did solicit and procure Sir *John Bramstone*, Knight, then and now Lord Chief-Justice of *England*; Sir *Humphrey Davenport*, Knight, Lord Chief-Baron of his Majesty's Court of *Exchequer*; Sir *Richard Hutton*, Knight, late one of the Justices of his Majesty's Court of *Common-Pleas*; Sir *John Denham*, Knight, late one of the Barons of his Majesty's Court of *Exchequer*; Sir *William Jones*, Knight, late one of the Justices of the said Court of *King's-Bench*; Sir *George Croke*, Knight, then and now one of the Judges of the said Court of *King's Bench*; Sir *Thomas Trevor*, Knight, then and now one of the Barons of the *Exchequer*; Sir *George Vernon*, Knight, late one of the Justices of the said Court of *Common-Pleas*, Sir *Robert Berkley*, Knight, then and now one of the Justices of the said Court of *King's-Bench*; Sir *Francis Crawley*, Knight, then and now one of the Justices of the said Court of *Common-Pleas*; Sir *Richard Weston*, Knight, then and now one of the Barons of the said Court of *Exchequer*; some or one of them to subscribe, with their names, the said opinion presently, and enjoined them severally some or one of them secrecy, upon their Allegiance.

V. That he the fifth day of *June*, then being Lord Chief-Justice of the said Court of *Common-Pleas*, subscribed an extrajudicial opinion in answer to questions in a Letter from his Majesty, *in hæc verba*, &c. Vol. I. *page* 487.

And that he contrived the said questions; and procured the said Letter from his Majesty. And whereas the said Justice *Hutton* and Justice *Croke* declared to him their opinions to the contrary; yet he required and pressed them to subscribe, upon his promise that he would let his Majesty know the truth of their opinions, notwithstanding such subscriptions, which nevertheless he did not make known to his Majesty, but delivered the same to his Majesty as the opinion of all the Judges.

VI. That he being Lord Chief-Justice of the said Court of *Common-Pleas*, delivered his opinion in the *Exchequer-Chamber* against Mr. *Hampden* in the case of Ship-money, that he the said Mr. *Hampden* upon the matter and substance of the case was chargeable with the money then in question; a Copy of which proceedings the Commons will deliver to your Lordships: and did solicit and threaten the said Judges, some or one of them, to deliver their opinions in like manner against Mr. *Hampden*. And after the said Baron *Denham* had delivered his opinion for Mr. *Hampden*; the said Lord *Finch* repaired purposely to the said Baron *Denham*'s chamber in *Serjeants-Inn* in *Fleet-street*; and after the said Mr. Baron *Denham* had declared and expressed his opinion, urged him to retract the said opinion; which he refusing, was threatened by the said Lord *Finch*, because he refused.

VII. That he being then Lord Chief-Justice of the Court of *Common-Pleas* declared and published in the *Exchequer-Chamber* and *Western* Circuit where he went Judge; that the King's right to Ship-money, as aforesaid, was so inherent a right to the Crown, as an Act of Parliament could not take it away; and with divers malicious speeches inveighed against, and threatned all such as refused to pay Ship-money: all which opinions contained in the fourth, fifth and sixth Articles, are against the Law of the Realm, the Subjects right of property, and contrary to former resolutions in Parliament, and to the Petition of Right: which said resolutions and Petition of Right were well known to him resolved and enacted in Parliament, when he was Speaker of the Commons House of Parliament.

VIII. That he being Lord Chief-Justice of the Court of *Common-Pleas* did take the general practice of that Court to his private chamber; and that he sent warrants into all or many Shires of *England* to several men, as to *Francis Giles* of the County of *Devon*, *Robert Benson* of the County of *York*, Attornies of that Court, and to divers others, to release all persons arrested on any outlawry for about forty shillings fees; whereas none by Law so arrested can be bailed or released without supersedeas under seal, or reversal.

* Lord *Clarendon* in his History, Vol I. *pag.* [illegible] (8vo Edition) says, Undoubtedly my Lord *Finch*'s Speech in the *Exchequer-Chamber* made Ship-money [illegible] and formidable than all the Commitments by the Council-Table, and all the Distresses taken by the Sheriffs in *England*. And [illegible] he took it up [illegible] Mr. *Noy* left it, and being a Judge carried it up to that Pinnacle, from whence he almost broke his own Neck, having in his journey [illegible] Brethren to induce them to concur in a Judgment they had all cause to repent. To which is Declaration, [illegible] Keeper of the Great Seal of *England* [illegible] upon Demurrer put in to a Bill before him, which had no other Equity in it, than an order of the Lords of the Council, "That [illegible] so far [illegible] as to dispute those Orders, but that the wisdom of that Board should be always ground enough for [illegible]

† Sir *John Finch* was a man exceedingly obnoxious to the People, upon the business of Ship-money, [illegible] and advance the King's Service. Lord *Clarendon*'s History, Vol I. *pag.* 131 in 8vo

IX. That he being Lord Chief-Juftice of the Court of *Common-Pleas*, upon a pretended fuit begun in *Michaelmas*-Term, in the 11th year of his Majefty's reign, although there was no plaint or declaration againft him, did notoriouſly, and contrary to all Law and Juftice, by threats, menaces, and impriſonment, compel *Thomas Laurence*, an Executor, to pay nineteen pound twelve fhillings; and likewife caufed *Richard Bernard*, being only Overfeer of the laft Will of that Teftator, to be arrefted for the payment of the faid money, contrary to the advice of the reft of the Judges of that Court, and againft the known and ordinary courfe of Juftice, and his faid Oath and Knowledge: and denied his Majefty's fubjects, the common and ordinary Juftice of this Realm, as to Mr. *Limerick*, and others; and for his private benefit endamaged and ruined the eftates of very many of his Majefty's fubjects, contrary to his Oath and Knowledge.

X. That he being Lord-Keeper of the Great Seal of *England*, and fworn one of his Majefty's Privy-Council, did by falfe and malicious flanders labour to incenfe his Majefty againft Parliaments, and did frame and advife the publifhing the Declaration after the diffolution of the laft Parliament.

All which Treafons and Mifdemeanors above-mentioned, were done and committed by the faid *John* Lord *Finch*, Baron of *Fordwich*, Lord-Keeper of the Great Seal of *England*; and thereby he the aforefaid *Finch* hath traitorouſly, and contrary to his Allegiance laboured to lay imputations and fcandals upon his Majefty's Government, and to alienate the hearts of his Majefty's liege People from his Majefty, and to fet a divifion between them, and to ruin and deftroy his Majefty's Realm of *England*; for which they do impeach him the faid Lord *Finch*, Baron of *Fordwich*, Lord-Keeper of the Great Seal of *England*, of High-Treafon againft our fovereign Lord the King, his Crown and Dignity, of the Mifdemeanors above-mentioned. *And the faid Commons by proteftation, faving to themfelves the liberty of exhibiting, at any time hereafter, any other accufation or impeachment againft the faid Lord* Finch, *and alfo of replying to the anfwer, that the faid* John *Lord* Finch *fhall make unto the faid Articles, or to any of them, and of offering proof of the premiffes, or any of their impeachments or accufations that fhall be exhibited by them, as the cafe fhall, according to the courfe of Parliament, require; do pray, that the faid* John *Lord* Finch, *Baron of* Fordwich, *Lord-Keeper of the Great Seal of* England, *may be put to anfwer to all and every of the premiffes, and fuch Proceedings, Examinations, Trials, and Judgments, as may be upon every of them, had and ufed, as is agreeable to Law and Juftice.*

After reading thefe Articles, refolv'd upon the Queftion,

That thefe Articles thus read and ingrofs'd fhall be fent to the Lords, in maintenance of the Commons charge againft *John* Lord *Finch* of *Fordwich*, late Lord-Keeper of the Great Seal of *England*.

Mr *Arthur Goodwin* is appointed to go up with a meffage to the Lords to a conference with their Lordfhips, by a Committee of both Houfes, concerning Articles to be deliver'd in maintenance of the Commons accufation of *John* Lord *Finch* of *Fordwich*, late Lord-Keeper of the Great Seal of *England*; and concerning the liberty and property of the fubject.

At the requeft of the Lord *Falkland*, Mr. *Hyde* is appointed to be affiftant unto him, for the reading of the Articles to be deliver'd againft the late Lord-Keeper.

Mr *Goodwin* brought anfwer, that according to the order of this Houfe, he had deliver'd the meffage to their Lordfhips, and their Lordfhips will give a meeting to-morrow morning, at nine of the Clock, by a Committee of the whole Houfe, as is defired.

Accordingly the Articles againft the Lord-Keeper were prefented to the Lords; and after reading the fame, the Lord *Falkland* fpoke as follows:

My Lords,

THESE Articles againft my Lord *Finch* being read, I may be bold to apply that of the Poet, *Nil refert tales verfus qua voce legantur*; and I doubt not but your Lordfhips muft be of the fame opinion, of which the Houfe of Commons appears to have been, by the choice they have made of me, that the charge I have brought is fuch, as needs no affiftance from the bringer, leaving not fo much as the colour of a colour for any defence, including all poffible evidence, and all poffible aggravation (that addition alone excepted) which he alone could make, and hath made; I mean, his confeffion, included in his flight.

Here are many and mighty Crimes, *Crimes of Supererogation*, (fo that High-Treafon is but a part of his charge) purfuing him fervently in every feveral condition, (being a filent Speaker, an unjuft Judge, and an unconfcionable Keeper). That his life appears a perpetual warfare (by mines, and by battery, by battle, and by ftratagem,) againft our fundamental Laws, which (by his own confeffion) feveral Conquefts had left untouch'd, againft the excellent conftitution of this Kingdom, which hath made it appear unto ftrangers rather an Idea, than a real Commonwealth, and produced the honour and happinefs of this to be a wonder of every other Nation; and this with fuch unfortunate fuccefs, that as he always intended to make our ruins a ground of his advancement, fo his advancement the means of our further ruin.

After that, contrary to the further end of his place, and the ending of that meeting in which he held his place, he had, as it were, gagg'd the Commonwealth, taking away (to his power) all power of fpeech from that Body, of which he ought to have been the mouth, and which alone can perfectly reprefent the condition of the People, whom they only reprefent: which if he had not done, in all probability, what fo grave and judicious an Affembly might have offered to the confideration of fo gracious and juft a Prince, had occafioned the redrefs of the grievances they then fuffered, and prevented thofe which they have fince endured, according to the ancient maxim, *Odiffe quos læferis*. He purfued this offence towards the Parliament, by inveighing againft the Members, by fcandalizing their proceedings, by trampling upon their Acts and Declarations, by ufurping and devolving the right, by diminifhing and abrogating the power, both of that and other Parliaments, and making them (as much as in him lay) both ufelefs and odious to his Majefty; and purfued his hatred to this fountain of Juftice by corrupting the ftreams of it, the Laws; and perverting the conduit-pipes, the Judges.

He practifed the annihilating of ancient and notorious perambulations of particular Forefts, the better to prepare himfelf to annihilate the ancient and notorious perambulation of the whole Kingdom, the meres and boundaries between the liberties of the fubject and fovereign power; he endeavoured to have all tenures *durante beneplacito*, to bring all Law from his Majefty's Courts into his Majefty's breaft; he gave our goods to the King, our lands to the Deer, our liberties to his Sheriffs; fo that there was no way by which we had not been oppreft, and deftroyed, if the power of this perfon had been equal with his will, or that the will of his Majefty had been equal to his power.

He not only by this means made us liable to all the effect of an Invafion from without, but (by deftruction of our liberties, which included the deftruction of our propriety, which included the deftruction of our induftry) made us liable to the terribleft of all Invafions, that of want and poverty. So that if what he plotted had taken root, and he made it, as fure as his Declaration could make it, (what himfelf was not, Parliament-proof) in this wealthy and happy Kingdom, there could have been left no abundance but of grievances and difcontentment, no fatisfaction but amongft the guilty. It is generally obferved of the Plague, that the infection of others is an earneft, and conftant defire of all that are feized by it and as this defign refembles that difeafe, in the ruin, deftruction, and defolation it would have wrought, fo it feems no lefs like it in this effect: he having fo laboured to make others fhare in that guilt, that his folicitation was not only his action, but his works, making ufe both of his authority, his intereft, and importunity, to perfuade; and in his Majefty's name (whofe Piety is known to give that excellent prerogative to his Perfon, that the Law gives to his place, not to be able to do wrong) to threaten the reft of the Judges, to fign opinions contrary to Law, to affign anfwer contrary to their opinions, to give Judgment which they ought not to have given, and to recant Judgment when they had given it as they ought: fo that whofoever confiders his care of, and concernment, both in the growth and in the immorality of this project, cannot but by the fame way, by which the wifeft judgment found the true mother of the Child, difcover him not only to have been the fofterer, but the father of this moft pernicious and envious defign.

I fhall not need to obferve, that this was plotted and purfued by an *Englifhman* againft *England*, (which increafeth the Crime in no lefs degree than Parricide is beyond Murder) that this was done in the greateft matter joined to the greateft bond, being againft the general Liberty, and public propriety, by a fworn Judge (and at that falt itfelf, becaufe unfavoury, the Gofpel hath defign'd whither it muft be caft) that he poifoned our very antidotes, and turned our guard into a deftruction, making Law the ground of illegality, that he ufed this Law not only againft us, but againft itfelf, making it, as I may fay, *Felo de fe*, making the pretence (for I can fcarce fay the appearance of it) fo to contribute to the utter ruin of itfelf.

I fhall not need to fay, that either this is (or can be) of the higheft kind, and in the higheft degree of Parliamentary Treafon, a Treafon which needs not a computation of many feveral actions, which alone were not Treafon, to prove a Treafon all together, and by that demonftration of the intention, to make that formally Treafon which were materially but a mifdemeanor: this is a Treafon as well againft the King, as againft the Kingdom; for whatfoever is againft the whole, is undoubtedly againft the Head, which takes from his Majefty the ground of his rule, the Laws, (for if foundations be deftroyed, the pinnacles are moft endangered) which takes from his Majefty the principal honour of his rule; the ruling over Freemen, a power as much nobler than that over Villeins, as that is than that over Beafts; which endeavoured to take from his Majefty the principal fupport of his rule, their hearts and affections over whom he rules; (a better and furer ftrength and wall to the King, than the fea is to the Kingdom;) and by begetting a mutual diftruft, and by that a mutual difaffection between them, to hazard the danger even of the deftruction of both.

My Lords,

I fhall the lefs need to prefs this, becaufe as it were unreafonable in any cafe to fufpect your Juftice, fo here efpecially, where your intereft fo nearly unites you; your great fhare in poffeffions, giving you an equal concernment in propriety, the care and pains ufed by your noble Anceftors in the founding and afferting of our common liberties rendering the juft defence of them your moft proper and peculiar inheritance, and both exciting to oppofe and extirpate all fuch defigns as did introduce, and would have fettled an arbitrary, that is, an intolerable form of Government, and have made even your Lordfhips and your pofterity but Right Honourable Slaves.

My Lords,

I will fpend no more words, *luctando cum larva*, in accufing the Ghoft of a departed perfon, whom his Crimes accufe more than I can do, and his abfence accufeth no lefs than his Crime. Neither will I excufe the length of what I have faid, becaufe I cannot add to an excufe, without adding to the fault, or my own imperfections, either in the matter or manner of it; which I know muft appear the greater, by being compared with that learned Gentleman's great ability, who hath preceded me at this time: I will only defire, by the command, and in the behalf of the Houfe of Commons, that thefe proceedings againft the Lord *Finch* may be put in fo fpeedy a way of difpatch, as in fuch cafes the courfe of Parliament will allow.

The fame day, the Commons order'd thanks to be returned from the Houfe to Mr. *St. John*, Mr. *Whitlock*, the Lord *Falkland*, and Mr. *Hyde*, for the great fervice they have perform'd to the honour of the Houfe, and good of the Commonwealth, in the transferring the Articles againft the late Lord-Keeper.

Jan. 30. It was ordered by the Lords, that fuch Judges as the Houfe of Commons fhall defire, are to be examined in the cafe of the Lord *Finch*, by the fame deputed Lords as were appointed in the Earl of *Strafford*'s cafe: but the Judges are not to be examin'd upon any thing to accufe themfelves.

Feb. 15. The Houfe of Lords thought fit, that a Proclamation do iffue out to fummon the Lord *Finch*, late Lord-Keeper, perfonally to appear before the Lords in Parliament; to answer an Accusation of High-Treason brought against him by the Commons.

But his Lordship never thought fit to surrender himself, and the Civil War soon after breaking out, there was no further Proceedings against him, and he endured eight Years Banishment, and Compositions amounting to about 7000 *l.* But lived to see the horrid Murder of King *Charles* I. and the happy Restoration of King *Charles* II.

XXII. Two Judgments of the Lords assembled in Parliament, in 1647, against *John Morris*, alias *Poyntz*, *Mary* his Wife, *Isabel Smith*, *Leonard Darby*, and *John Harris*, for forging, framing, and publishing a Copy of a pretended Act of Parliament.

Die Martis, 21 *Septemb.* 1647.

WHEREAS *John Brown*, Esq. Clerk of the Parliaments, did the 25th Day of *June*, 1647, exhibit a Charge before the Lords in Parliament, against *John Morris*, alias *Poyntz*, *Mary* his Wife, *Isabel Smith*, *Leonard Darby*, and *John Harris*, for forging, framing, and publishing a Copy of a pretended Act of Parliament, alledged to have been made in the 43d of *Elizabeth*, and entitled, *An Act to enable and make good a Conveyance and Assurance made of the Manors of* Chipping-Onger, Northokenden, Southokenden, *and other Lands in the County of* Essex, *and* Beaves-Marks, *alias* Buries-Marks, *in* London, *by* James Morris, *Esq* *and* Gabriel Poyntz, *Esq. to* John Morris, *alias* Poyntz, *and his Heirs*; *and to establish the said Manors upon the said* John Morris, *alias* Poyntz, *and his Heirs*, *according to the said Conveyance*: Whereas in Truth there neither is, nor ever was any such Act of Parliament. And for forging and counterfeiting his Hand-writing, and subscribing to the said Copy, *John Brown*, *Cleric. Parliamentorum*. And the better to colour their leud Practices, have charged the said *John Brown* with the Loss of the said Record, and denying of his own Hand. And whereas Sir *Adam Littleton*, Bart. who had good Title to Part of the said Manors and Lands, as in right of Dame *Audery*, his Wife, whose Inheritance thereunto was sought to be impeached by the said Copy of the said pretended Act of Parliament, complained likewise against the said Persons before their Lordships, for the said Forgery and Publication; in that the said *John Morris*, *Leonard Darby*, *John Harris*, and *Isabel Smith*, did produce the said Copy at *Chelmsford*, at *Lent*-Assizes, in 1646, for the County of *Essex*; at a Trial in an *Ejectione Firmæ*, brought by *Thomas Smith*, Husband of the said *Isabel*, and Lessee of the said *John Morris*, against *Josias Clarke*, Tenant to the said Sir *Adam Littleton*, of Part of the said Lands contained in the said pretended Act, and did plead and affirm the same to be a true Copy of an Act of Parliament: And the said *Darby* and *Harris* did falsely and perjuriously swear in open Court at the said Trial, that they had examined the said Copy, by them produced, with the Record of the said pretended Act, in the Office of the Clerk of the Parliament; and did there also falsly and perjuriously swear, that they did shew that Writing to the Clerk of the Parliament, and that he did acknowledge the said Writing to be his own Hand; whereas in Truth the said Subscription to the said pretended Act of Parliament is counterfeit, and none of the said Clerk of the Parliament's Hand. And the said Sir *Adam* further complained of an Exemplification under the Great Seal of *England*, for countenancing the said forged Copy of the said pretended Act, by some undue Means by the said Parties thereunto affixed, of the Parties shewing, whereof Proof was made before their Lordships.

All which being Crimes of a very high and transcendant Nature, and do concern the publick Justice of the Kingdom, and of this honourable House, the supremest Judicatory of this Kingdom; that Acts of Parliament, the highest Records in this Kingdom, should be framed, invented, forged, and given in Evidence, and published as true Acts of Parliament; and the Hand of the Clerk of the Parliament, a sworn Officer, forged, counterfeited, and subscribed to the same; as that if such a bold and audacious Act should not be severely punished, no Man can be safe in his Life, Person or Estate: The said *John Brown*, and Sir *Adam Littleton*, desired that the Persons aforesaid might forthwith answer the said Charges; and that their Lordships would inflict such exemplary Punishment upon the Offenders, as may deter the like Attempts and leud Practices in others, and give such fitting Reparations as their Lordships in their Wisdom should think meet.

Whereupon the Persons aforesaid put in their Answers to the Premises, and pleaded Not Guilty; and after the Case had been divers Days fully heard by Counsel on both Sides, and Witnesses produced at this Bar, and the whole Matter after thoroughly weighed, debated, and fully considered of by the House; the Lords in Parliament assembled, being fully satisfied of the Guilt of the said Persons, for the aforesaid high Crimes charged against them, do award and adjudge,

1. That the said *John Morris*, alias *Poyntz*, shall pay as a Fine to our Sovereign Lord the King the Sum of 1000 *l.* *Isabel Smith* 200 *l.* *Leonard Darby* 400 *l.* and *John Harris* 400 *l.*

2. That the said Parties shall pay to *John Brown*, Esq. Clerk of the Parliament, for his Damages, 500 *l.*

3. That all the said Parties shall, before their Enlargement out of Prison, be bound to their good Behaviour during their Lives, before some one of his Majesty's Justices of his Bench at *Westminster*, with good Sureties.

4. That the said Copy of the pretended Act of Parliament, falsly affirmed upon Oath, to have been subscribed with the Name of the said Clerk of the Parliament, entitled, *An Act to enable and make good a Conveyance and Assurance, made of the Manors of* Chipping-Onger, Northokenden, Southokenden, *and other Lands in the County of* Essex; *and* Beaves Marks, *alias* Buries Marks, *in* London; *by* James Morris, *Esq.* Gabriel Poyntz, *Esq. to* John Morris, *alias* Poyntz, *and his Heirs, and to establish the said Manors upon the said* John Morris, *alias* Poyntz, *and his Heirs, according to the said Conveyance*, is hereby declared to be forged and counterfeit; and is by their Lordships adjudged and decreed to be for ever damned and cancelled, and never to be pleaded in any Court or Cause whatsoever; nor to be admitted to be given in Evidence, there being no Record of such pretended Act of Parliament to warrant the same.

5. That all the said several Persons hereby adjudged guilty of the said Crimes, shall ever hereafter be made uncapable to be Witnesses in any Cause whatsoever.

6. That *John Brown*, Esq. Clerk of the Parliament, is, in the Judgment of this House, free and clear of and from all and every the Aspersions, Falsities, and Charges of the said *John Morris*, alias *Poyntz*, *Isabel Smith*, *Leonard Darby*, and *John Harris*, charged, uttered, divulged, and given out by them against him, concerning the Matters herein mentioned. And that this Judgment shall be openly read and published in the Face of the County of *Essex*, at the next Assizes to be held for that County.

7. That the said Parties shall bring, or cause to be brought into this House by the first Day of *October* next, one Exemplification under the Great Seal of *England*, concerning the Manor of *Little Munden*, in the County of *Hertford*; and the aforesaid Exemplification of the said counterfeit Act of Parliament, to which the Great Seal of *England* is charged to have been unduly and fraudulently affixed, that so the foresaid forged Exemplification may be cancelled and vacated.

8. That they shall be imprisoned during the Pleasure of this House.

Joh. Brown, Cler. Parliamentorum.

Die Martis, 2d *Die Novemb.* 1647.

WHEREAS the Lords in Parliament assembled, upon the 21st of *September* last, gave Judgment concerning a Copy of a pretended Act of Parliament, entitled, *An Act to enable and make good a Conveyance and Assurance, made of the Manors of* Chipping-Onger, Northokenden, Southokenden, *and other Lands in the County of* Essex; *and* Beaves-Marks, *alias* Buries-Marks, *in* London, *by* James Morris, *Esq.* Gabriel Poyntz, *Esq. to* John Morris, *alias* Poyntz, *and his Heirs, and to establish the said Manors upon the said* John Morris, *alias* Poyntz, *and his Heirs, according to the said Conveyance*; and declared the same to be forged and counterfeit, and there to be for ever damned and cancelled, as by the said Judgment more at large appeareth.

And whereas Dame *Audery Littleton*, late Wife of Sir *Adam Littleton*, deceased, Sir *Folke Grevil*, Knt. and *Maurice Barrow*, Esq. by their Petition exhibited before the Lords in Parliament, complained, that notwithstanding the said Judgment, one *Isabel Smith* (a Person sentenced by their Lordships, and committed to *Newgate* for the said Forgery) having procured the said forged Act of Parliament, and other forged Writings, *viz.* three Fines of the Lands contained in the said forged Act, and a forged Pleading, setting forth the Uses of the said forged Fines, to be written in Parchment; and having by some slight made them to seem as if they had been written long since, did foist and shuffle in the same amongst other Evidences, and Writings remaining in the Treasury of the late Court of Wards; and pretending the same to be found there, obtained Copies thereof under the Hand of Mr. *Audely*, Clerk of the said Court, hoping thereby to gain some Credit and Authority to the said Forgeries, and further to impeach the Titles of the Petitioners.

To which Petition the said *Isabel Smith* put in her Answer, and a Day was appointed for hearing the same. At which Day the said *Isabel Smith*, being present at the Bar, and not making good any of the Particulars in her said Answer, nor giving any Satisfaction to such Questions as were by their Lordships demanded of her concerning the same: And the said several Writings, after full Examination by hearing of Counsel, and Witnesses produced; and also upon View of the said Writings (being by their Lordships Order brought into the House) manifestly appearing to their Lordships to be gross Forgeries: The Lords in Parliament assembled to declare, and adjudge;

That the said Parchment Writings, one whereof purporteth a Fine pretended to be levied at *St. Albans*, *a die sancti Martini in quindecim dies*, *Anno* 37 *Eliz.* between *James Morris*, Esq. and *John Morris*, alias *Poyntz*, his Son, Plaintiffs, and *Gabriel Poyntz*, Esq. and *William Cutts*, Defendants; of the Manor of *Chipping-Onger*, and other Lands and Tenements, with the Appurtenances, in *Chipping-Onger*, in the County of *Essex*: One other whereof purporteth a Fine pretended to be levied at *St. Albans*, *a die sancti Martini in quindecim dies*, *Anno* 37 *Eliz.* between *James Morris*, Esq. and *John Morris*, alias *Poyntz*, his Son, Plaintiffs; and *Gabriel Poyntz*, Esq. and *William Cutts*, Defendants, of the Manors of *Northokenden*, *Poyntz*, and *Greves*, with the Appurtenances, and of divers Messuages, Cottages, Mills, Lands, Meadows, Pastures, and other Hereditaments in *Northwokenden*, alias *Northokenden*, *Southwokenden*, alias *Southokenden*, *Avely*, *Upminster*, alias *Upmyster*, *Southweal*, *Brentwood*, alias *Burntwood*, *Warley*, alias *Warley Magna*, *Childerditch*, *Bulfan*, *Bownton*, alias *Bunton*, *East Thornedon*, *West Thornedon*, *West Thurrock*, *Grays Thurrock*, *Chawdwell*, *Styfford*, alias *Stiford*, *Horne-church*, *Basselden*, and *Cranham*, and of the Rectory of *Northwokenden*, alias *Northokenden*, with the Appurtenances, in the said County of *Essex*.

One

One other whereof purporteth a fine pretended to be levied at *St. Albans a die Sancti Martini in quindecim dies, Anno* 37 *Eliz.* between *James Morris*, Esq *John Morris* alias *Poyntz*, his Son, Plaintiffs; and *Gabriel Poyntz*, Esq. and *William Cutts*, Esq. Defendants; of four Messuages, six Gardens, and two Acres of Land with the appurtenances, in the Parish of St. *Katherine Cree-Church, London.*

One other of the said Parchment writings purporteth a pleading, setting forth the uses of the said fines, and beginning in these words, (viz.) Essex. ss. *In memorandum de Banco, Anno tricesimo octavo* Elizabeth, viz. *inter Record. Termini sancti Trinitatis Rollo* xxi. *ex parte Recordationum in Ter. manen. inter alia continetur ut sequitur, viz. Memorandum quod nuper invenitur in quodam Rollo extract. de finibus & issuis Banci in Termino Sancti Michaelis annis Regni Dominæ nostræ* Elizabethæ, *tricesimo sexto & septimo, quod* Gabriel Poyntz, *Esq. &c.*

And one other whereof purporteth a Copy of a pretended Act of Parliament, intitled, *An Act to enable and make good a conveyance and assurance, made of the Manors of* Chipping-Onger, Northokenden, Southokenden, *and other Lands in the County of* Essex; *and* Beaves-Marks *alias* Buries-Marks *in* London; *by* James Morris, *Esq*; *and* Gabriel Poyntz, *Esq*; *to* John Morris *alias* Poyntz, *and his Heirs, and to establish the said Manors upon the said* John Morris *alias* Poyntz, *and his Heirs, according to the said conveyance:* Are hereby declared to be forged and counterfeit, and are by their Lordships adjudged and decreed to be for ever damned and cancelled, and never to be pleaded, or admitted to be given in evidence in any Court, or Cause whatsoever: there being no Record of any such Fines, Pleading, or Act of Parliament to warrant the same; nor any Term then held at *St. Albans*, when the said fines were pretended to be levied there.

And it is further ordered by the Lords in Parliament assembled, that the said *Isabel Smith* shall by the 27th of *November* next bring, or cause to be brought into this House, the Copies of the said Parchment writings, (pretended to be found in the Treasury of the Court of Wards) subscribed by the said Mr. *Awdely*, that so the same may be cancelled and vacated.

John Brown, Cler. Parliamentorum.

Essex ss. *In memorandum de Banco, Anno tricesimo octavo* Elizabeth, viz. *inter Record. Termini Sancti Trinitatis Rollo* xxi. *ex parte Recordationum in Thesaurum manen. inter alia continetur ut sequitur, viz.*

" MEmorandum quod nuper invenitur in quodam Rollo extract. de finibus & issuis Banci & Termini Sancti Michaelis annis Regni Dominæ nostræ *Elizabethæ* tricesimo sexto & septimo, quod *Gabriel Poyntz*, Esq; fecit cum prædicta Domina Regina finem pro concordia cum *Jacobi Morris*, Esq; & aliis de Pl'ito condic. de Manor *Chipping-Onger*, alias *Anger* ad Castrum, cum appurtenanc. *&c.*"

5 *Novemb.* 1647.

I have searched the Records of the *Common-Pleas, de Termino Sancti Trinitat. Anno tricesimo octavo Reg. Eliz. Rollo vicesimo primo*, and do find that there is no inrollment of any such Record there, as is above-mentioned.

Per Johannem Cocks, Cleric.
Thesaur. de Com. Banco.

I have searched in the Treasurer's Remembrancer's Office in the *Exchequer*, amongst the Records of *Trinity*-Term, *Anno* xxxviii. *Reginæ Elizabeth. Roll.* xxi. but do not find that there is any such Record or Inrollment, as is above-mentioned.

T. Osborne.

6 *May*, 1647.

MEmorandum, that I *Francis Blake*, Keeper of the Books for the searchers of fines, and of the Records thereof in the Chirographer's Office, have made diligent search in the said Books, and amongst the said Records of *Michaelmas*-Term, 35 and 36 *Eliz.* and all the Terms after, till *Hillary* 38 *Eliz.* and I can find no fine at all from *Gabriel Poyntz* and *William Cutts*, or either of them, to any person whatsoever, of any Lands in the Counties of *Essex* or *London*. And moreover, I find by the said Records, that *Michaelmas*-Term, 36 and 37 *Eliz.* was held at the City of *Westminster*, and not at the Town of *St. Albans*. All which I do hereby (at the request of Sir *Adam Poyntz*, alias *Littleton*, Bart.) certify to all whom it may concern.

F. Blake.

Here ends the Proceedings of the Lords against them.

Soon after a short Breviate of Mr. *John Morris*'s case was drawn up, and delivered to his Excellency Sir *Thomas Fairfax*, by divers of the Parliament's Agents.

May it please your Excellency,

BEING deeply oppressed in our spirits, and overburdened in ourselves, at the manifold and doleful outcries and complaints of the people, in all parts of our quarters where we come, uttered against the daily pressures and inroads that are made by prerogative and arbitrary violence upon their common rights; and in particular, the cry and miserable moan of certain oppressed Commoners, to wit, of *John Poyntz*, alias *Morris*, Esq; *Isabel Smith*, *John Harris*, and *Leonard Darby*, coming unto our ears, that we could not, but (as in duty we are bound) deeply represent their miserable condition, as fellow-ferlers of their oppressions, and persons liable (when we come into their single capacity of Commons) to the said mischief; and therefore conceiving it our duty to contribute our utmost endeavours for the remedy of the same, we could not but unburden in some measure our spirits unto your Excellency in their behalfs, who in such a horrid and barbarous manner have been abused and supplanted of their common rights, by acts of violence and force, committed by *John Brown*, Clerk unto the House of Lords, and his accomplices, under the colour of several orders surreptitiously by misinformations gained from the said House, to the high usurpation and abuse of the name and authority of Parliament, in permitting the image thereof upon his own prerogative, outrage and violence, to the total ruin and supplantation of the just freedoms, and birthright inheritance of the said persons, as the several papers thereunto subjoined, for the full information of your Excellency, do demonstrate. And for more certain confirmation of our premises, represented by the same, be pleased to consider, that whereas the abovesaid persons are accused, condemned, and sentenced by the Lords (surprized by *Brown*'s misrepresentations and delusions) to pay 2500 *l.* fine, and suffer imprisonment, contrary to the regular course of the Laws, during the pleasure of the said House, for forging and framing a copy of an Act of Parliament, touching the estate of the said *John Poyntz* alias *Morris*, pretended to be taken out of the Office of the said *John Brown*, with his hand thereunto; no such original Record as *Brown* pretendeth is to be found in his Office: that since the said accusation, another original Record of the said Act of Parliament, with other writings and evidences for the said estate, is found in the Court of Wards, and they have gained copies thereof, examined and subscribed by the Master of the said Court and his Clerks, the which, with their hands thereunto, are herewith presented; and concerning the truth thereof, three of us can also give it upon Oath, that the wife of one *Godfrey Cade*, now prisoner in the *Fleet*, did declare unto us, that the said *John Brown* went to the *Fleet* unto her husband, and gave him twenty-five shillings in hand, and promised him five pounds more, and his inlargement, to swear at the Lords Bar, that he forged the copy of the said Act of Parliament, and counterfeited the Clerk's hand unto it; and the said *Cade* did also confess the same.

Wherefore we humbly implore that your Excellency would be pleased to grant the said distressed persons your letter of request unto the Parliament, according to their Petition, herewith directed to your Excellency, that the said persons, and their adversaries, may be left to the free course and trial at Common Law; and that in the mean time, till the controversy concerning the estate be decided at Law, the said persons may enjoy their enlargement upon bail, without any further trouble or durance, and the execution of their severe sentence be suspended, and the said *Poyntz*, alias *Morris*, enjoy peaceable possession of the said estate, like as all his ancestors, from the days of Queen *Elizabeth*, have done before him. Which request is so reasonable and just, and their condition so miserable, desperate, and dangerous, and of such concernment to the whole Commonwealth, that no man, if such exorbitances be not stopp'd and curb'd, can have any security in his estate or liberty, that we cannot but promise to ourselves your Excellency's commiseration of their condition, and readily assent unto their just suit. Thus we humbly take our leave, beseeching your favourable construction upon our boldness, and remain

Your Excellency's most humble
Servants and Soldiers,

Lieut. Gen. *R.* { *Robert Everard.* / *George Sadler.*

Com. Gen. *R.* { *George Garret.* / *Thomas Beverly.*

Col. *Whaley*'s. { *Matthew Wealy.* / *William Russel.* / *William Sampson.* / *Richard Daley.*

Col. *Rich*'s. { *William Hudson.* / *John Dober.*

Col. *Fleetwood*'s. { *William Prior.* / *William Bryan.*

But I don't find any thing farther done in this business.

XXIII. The Trial of Col. John Morris Governor of *Pontefract* Castle; at the Assizes at the Castle of *York*, before Mr. *John Puleston*, and Mr. Baron *Thorpe*, Justices of Assize, the 16th of *August*, *Anno Dom.* 1649, for High-Treason.

COLONEL *Morris* being demanded to hold up his hand, refused, and the Indictment was read against him for Treason, for levying War against the late King and the Parliament, upon *Stat.* 25 *Ed.* III. The Court desired him to plead *Guilty*, or not *Not Guilty*.

Col. *Morris*. My Lords, under correction, I conceive this Court hath not power to try me in this case, I being a martial man, I ought to be tried by a Council of War.

Court. Sir, What do you say, *are you guilty or not Guilty?* This is the second time you have been asked. Sir, if you will not answer the third time, we shall know what to do. *Are you guilty or not guilty?*

Col. *Morris*. My Lords, I still conceive I ought not to be tried here; if I have done any thing worthy of death, I appeal to a martial Court, to my Lord *Fairfax*, Major-General, or a general Council of War: you have not any precedent for it, either for you to try me in this way, or me to suffer by it.

Court. Are you guilty or not guilty? This is the third time.

Col. *Morris*. My Lords, if your Honours will force me to plead, I conceive I am not guilty.

Court. How will you be tryed?

Col. *Morris*. My Lords, I was never at any Bar before, I am ignorant herein.

Court. Tell him what to say. [*Upon that, some near him, told him*, by God and his Country.]

Col. *Morris*. By God and my Country. (After that, challenge is made for Col. *Morris* to except against any of the Jury.) [*Mr.* Brooke, *a great man for the cause, comes first returned, to be sworn as Foreman of the Jury.*]

Col. *Morris*. My Lords, I except against this *Brooke*.

Court. Sir, he is sworn, and you speak too late.

Col. *Morris*. My Lord, I appeal to himself, whether he be sworn or no.

Mr. *Brooke*. Sir, I am not to answer you, but the Court. My Lord, I did not kiss the Book.

Court. Sir, that is no matter, it's but a ceremony.

Col. *Morris*. My Lords, I beseech your Honours that I may except against him; I know him, as well as I know my right hand, to be my enemy.

Clerk of Assize. Sir, he is recorded sworn, there is no disputing against the Record.

Col. *Morris*. My Lords, I must submit to your Honours. (After that Col. *Morris* challenged 16 men, and my Lord *Puleston*, thinking Col. *Morris* tedious in excepting against so many, answer'd, Sir, Keep within your compass, or I will give you such a blow as will strike off your head.)

Col. *Morris*. My Lords, I desire nothing but Justice; for by the Statute of 14 *Hen*. VII. *fol*. 19. I may lawfully challenge thirty-five men, without shewing any cause to the contrary.

Court. It is granted. After a full Jury, the Indictment read, and Evidence for the State very full, that Col. *Morris* was Governor of *Pontefract*; which, *Morris* being very modest and civil, did not contradict any thing, until his time of answer.

Col. *Morris*. My Lords, I humbly desire a Copy of my Indictment, that I may know what to answer; I conceive I may plead special as well as general.

Court. Sir, you cannot by Law.

Col. *Morris*. My Lords, I conceive there is a point of Law in it, and I humbly desire to have Counsel; for I conceive by the Law, being attainted for High-Treason, I ought to have Counsel by the Statute 1 *Hen*. VII. *fol*. 23.

Court. Sir, I tell you, you cannot have it.

Col. *Morris*. Then, my Lords, I conceive I am not any way guilty of the Indictment for Treason: my Lords, it is said to be against the King, his Crown, and against his Peace; whereas, my Lords, I can make it appear, I have acted only for the King, and nothing against him, which may appear here by my Commission. The Court looks upon it, and answers,

Court. Sir, you are deceived, this is false, it is from the Prince.

Col. *Morris*. My Lords, it is very well known, my Lord *Fairfax* hath his Commmission derived from the Parliament, and upon that he grants Commission to his Officers, which is all one and the same. The Prince hath his from his Father, and I have mine from the Prince, which is full power, he being Captain-General of his Majesty's Forces.

Court. Sir, have you nothing else to say?

Col. *Morris*. My Lords, under correction, I conceive it is sufficient; for by the same power, all Judges, Justices of Peace, your Lordships, your Predecessors, and all other Officers, did act by the same power, and all process and writs of Law were acted, and executed in his name, and by his authority.

Court. His power was not in him, but the Kingdom, for he was in trust for the Kingdom; the King's Highway, and the King's Coin being so called, is not his own, but his Subjects; and his natural power, and legal power, are different.

Col. *Morris* My Lords, under correction, I conceive his legal and personal power are undivisible, all one, and cannot be separated.

Court. Sir, all is one, if the King bid me kill a man, is this a sufficient warrant for me to plead? No Sir, it is unlawful. Sir, have you no more?

Col. *Morris*. I beseech your Honours give me leave, I am upon my life.

Court. Speak what you will, Sir, you shall be heard.

Col. *Morris*. Your servant, my Lord; then, my Lords, I conceive I have acted nothing against the Parliament, for that which I acted, it was for the King: and since the abolishing of regal power, I have not meddled with any thing against the Parliament, for that Act was but enacted the 14th of *July* last, and before that Time and Act of abolishing Kingly-Government, that princely Palace which I kept by his Commission was demolished. My Lords, I beseech your Honours, that my Commission may be read, to give satisfaction to the Court.

Lord *Puleston*. Sir, it will do you no good, you may as well shew a Commission from the Pope, all is one.

Col. *Morris*. My Lords, I desire your Lordships to do me that Justice.

Lord *Thorpe*. For my part I am willing, if my Brother be not against it.

Lord *Puleston*. Sir, we hold it for Law to be void, it is to no purpose.

Col. *Morris*. Then if your Lordships be not pleased to do me that Justice that it may be read, I desire it may be restored me again. [*Upon that, Col.* Morris *received his Commission unread.*] My Lords, it seemeth strange, that your Honours should do that which was never done the like before, never any of your Predecessors ever did the like; I wish it may not be to your own and your friends wrong, that you make yourselves precedents of your acting, and myself of suffering. But, my Lords, I do not speak for saving my own life, for (I thank my God) I am prepared, and very willing to part with this lump of clay; I have had a large time of repentance, it being twenty-two weeks since my imprisonment; and I am sorry for those which are like to undergo the same sufferings, if your Lordships take away my life. And though I do not speak any way in glory, indeed at this present there is a cloud hanging over our heads, I desire there may be a fair Sunshine to dispel it. And though there were a world of plots in the Kingdom when I took the Castle, there is not wanting the same now, only the time is not yet come; and as I was to be the firebrand to *Scarborough*, so he (meaning *Bointon*) to *Tinmouth*, and that to others; and though you take away my life, there will be others which will take up the Lintstock to give fire, though I be gone.

Court. Sir, you have little hopes to talk of any fire to be given here, having received such a total rout in *Ireland*.

Col. *Morris*. My Lords, I should have been unwilling to have contradicted your late news concerning *Ireland*; but since you have given me a hint of it, you must give me leave to let your Honours know, that I received Letters from the Marquis of *Ormond* dated the 3d of *August*, and yours is but the 2d; wherein he pleases to let me understand of the great care he hath of me, and that whatsoever shall befall me here, the like shall be to those which he hath prisoners there, which (as he saith) are good store. Therefore if your Lordships did not at all value my person, yet methinks you should have some care of it for your own friends good.

Court. Sir, have you no more to say?

Col. *Morris*. My Lords, still I appeal to my Commission, which I conceive is sufficient to defend me withal, in what I have done, notwithstanding your power to the contrary.

Court. It is nothing at all, we have power to try you here.

Col. *Morris*. Then my Lords, (under correction) Laymen may as well be tried at a Martial Court: which if granted, those excellent Acts of *Magna Charta*, and the Petition of Right, would be destroyed.

Court. But you are not looked on here as a Soldier; we shall do what in Justice belongs to us.

Col. *Morris*. My Lords, still (under correction) I have taken the Oath of Allegiance, and I conceive in that I was bound to do as much as I did or have done, though I had not had any Commission at all. And I beseech your Lordships that you will do me Justice, and not incline to the right-hand of affection, or the left to hatred; but to have an ear for the accused as well as for the accuser: neither have I acted any thing contrary to my Allegiance, which Allegiance I was willing to pay to the Son, as well as to the Father. Now for the Allegiance, I owe to any person or authority but to these, I know none.

Lord *Thorpe*. Sir, if you have any thing else to say, speak for yourself, for this is not much to the purpose.

Col. *Morris*. My Lord, 'tis true, since you have rejected that authority which I acted by, I might as well have held my tongue at the first, and spake nothing, were it not for the satisfaction of the hearers; but if it must be so, that you will make me a precedent, you must do with me as you did with my dear and honoured Lord [*meaning my Lord of* Strafford] making an Act for the future, that this my suffering shall not be a precedent to any Soldiers hereafter. Besides, my Lord, this same Statute which you alledge against me is, if that any shall act against the King, 'tis Treason; which I have not done, but contrary, for him, and by his authority. And there is an Act of 11 *H*. VII *cap*. 1. *That whosoever they are that shall aid or assist the King at home or abroad, shall not be questioned at all.*

Lord *Thorpe*. 'Tis true, Sir, but *Hen*. VII. then stood in a fickle condition, and being an Usurper, made that Act for his own safety; sometimes the Duke of *York* ruling, sometimes the Duke of *Lancaster*, and others contending, therefore it was enacted.

Col. *Morris*. My Lord, but this same Act of *H*. VII. was later than that of *Ed*. III. which you have laid against me; and as yet was never repealed, until this last Act of 14 of *July*, before which time I had delivered up the place.

Lord *Thorpe*. Well, Sir, it seems you have not any more to say. After he had answered, the Court commanded Irons to be laid on them. (Cornet *Blackston* being condemned at the same time.)

Col. *Morris*. My Lord, I humbly desire that we may not be manacled; if you make any doubt of us, that we may have a greater guard upon us.

Lord *Puleston*. Sir, you that have made such attempts through such guards, as were of purpose set to receive you, ought to be look'd to now. Yet, if Mr. Sheriff please, I am content.

Col. *Morris*. Mr. Sheriff, I desire that this manacling may be forborn; if you please to clap a guard of an hundred men upon us, I shall pay for it. This is not only a disgrace to me, but in general to all Soldiers; which doth more trouble me than the loss of my life. Mr. Sheriff, what do you say?—*Mr. Sheriff*. Sir, Irons are the safest guards.

Col. *Morris*. My Lords, hitherto (I thank God) I have not done any unsoldiery or base act, and to begin now, I will not do it to save my life; and though you look upon me *Samson*-wise, I vow to God, I would not touch the pillars, though it lay in my power to injure you; therefore I still beg pardon, that I may not be manacled.

Under-Sheriff. Come, Sir, it cannot be help'd, we are commanded.

Col. *Morris*. My Lord, I beseech you grant me this favour; it is not my life I beg, but to forbear this manacling, which shame and dishonour doth more trouble me, than the loss of my life.

Under-Sheriff. It must be done. And upon that, did it, and carried him away. After dinner the Jury brought in their verdict, guilty of Treason *.

* Letters from *York*, "That one *Morris*, and one *Blackston*, were arraign'd before Baron *Thorpe*, and Judge *Puleston*, *for levying War against the Kingdom*; they pleaded "*not guilty, but desired, as they were martial men, that they might be tried by martial Law*: which was denied them.
"*Morris* at last said, *He would be tried by God and the Country*, and seventeen Witnesses proved foul Crimes against him." He had two sheets of paper written with matters of Law, and Statutes, many of which he pleaded, "and urged the cause of the War betwixt the two Houses of *York* and *Lancaster*, the difference of which from his "case was shewed by the Judges."
Then he produced a Commission from the King when he was Prince; the Judges told him, that the Prince was a Subject as well as he, and must be tried by the same Law.
"He was found guilty of Treason, and manacled with Irons, at which he said, *What, a martial Man Ironed? The like precedent was never before known.*
"He desired to have a strong Guard, saying, *Let me be damned if I escape*; but it was denied, so was a Copy of his Indictment, and to have Counsel, or to be exchanged
"He and *Blackston* were both condemn'd." *Whitlock*'s Memorials of the *English* Affairs, Page 411. *Edit*. 1732.

Col. *Morris.* My Lord, I am here found guilty of Treafon by that villain *Brooke*, whom I know to be mine enemy, and the firft man that I did except againft: in which I conceive I have received hard meafure, for none could have found me guilty of Treafon, had they gone according to the Letter of the Law, which they did not.

Lord *Pulefton.* Sir, you fpeak too late, you are not to difpute it now.

Col. *Morris.* Neither would I, my Lord, if this were a Court of *Chancery*, but being a Court of Law, bound up in exprefs words and letter, I conceive I ought to difpute it, and my bufinefs better weighed.

Lord *Pulefton.* Well, Sir, you are found guilty, therefore hold your peace.

Col. *Morris.* If I muft fuffer, I receive it with all alacrity and chearfulnefs, and I thank God I fhall die for a good Caufe, and the teftimony of a good Confcience; for which, had I as many Lives as there are Stars in the Firmament, I would facrifice them all for the fame.

Court. Sheriff, Gaoler take them away.

Col. *Morris.* Well, I befeech God blefs King *Charles*, and fight for all thofe that fight for him, or have fought for him.

After he was condemned, Colonel *Bethel* writ to the General and his Council of War, that *Morris* might be reprieved; but Colonel *Pride* opposed it, urging, *That it would not ftand with the Juftice of the Army, nor the Safety of the Commonwealth, to let fuch Enemies live, the Parliament having adjudged him worthy of Death, and given Inftructions to the Judges accordingly.*

The Speech of Col. John Morris, *Governor of* Pontefract-Caftle, *at the Place of Execution at* York, Auguft 23, 1649.

'WHEN he was brought out of prifon, looking upon the fledge 'that was there fet for him, lifting up his eyes to Heaven, 'knocking upon his breaft, he faid, I am as willing to go to my death, 'as to put off my doublet to go to bed; I defpife the fhame as well as the 'Crofs; I know I am going to a joyful place:' with many like expreffions.

When the Poft met him about St. *James*'s Church, that was fent to the Parliament to mediate for a reprieve; and told him he could not prevail in it, he faid, 'Sir, I pray God reward you for your pains, I 'hope, and am well affured to find a better pardon than any they can 'give; my hope is not in man, but in the living God.'

At the place of Execution he made this profeffion of his faith, his breeding, and the caufe he had fought in.

'*Gentlemen*, Firft I was bred up in the true Proteftant Religion, having my education and breeding from that honourable Houfe, my dear 'Lord and Mafter *Stafford*'s, which place, I dare boldly fay, was as well-'governed and ruled as ever any yet was before it; I much doubt, better 'than any will be after it, unlefs it pleafe God to put a period to thefe 'diftracted times; this Faith and Religion, I fay, I have been bred in, 'and I thank God I have hitherto lived in, without the leaft wavering, 'and now I am refolved by God's affiftance to die in.

'Thefe pains are nothing, if compared to thofe dolors and pains, 'which *Jefus Chrift* our Saviour hath fuffered for us; when in a bloody-'fweat he endured the wrath of God, the pain of Hell, and the curfed 'and fhameful death which was due to our fins; therefore I praife the 'Lord that I am not plagued with far more grievous punifhment; that 'the like hath befallen others, who undoubtedly are moft glorious and 'bleffed Saints with *Chrift* in Heaven. It is the Lord's affliction, and 'who will not take any affliction in good part when it comes from the 'hand of God? And what, Shall we receive good from the hands of 'God, and not receive evil? And though I defire, as I am carnal, that 'this Cup may depart from me, yet not my will, but thy will be done. 'Death brings unto the godly an end of finning, and of all miferies due 'unto fin: fo that after death there fhall be no more forrow, nor cry, 'nor pain, for *God fhall wipe away all tears from our eyes*; by death our 'fouls fhall be delivered from thraldom; and this *corruptible body fhall put on incorruption, and this mortal immortality.*

'Therefore bleffed are they that are delivered out of fo vile a world, 'and freed from fuch a body of bondage and corruption; the foul fhall 'enjoy immediate communion with God in everlafting blifs and glory; 'it takes us from the miferies of this world, and the fociety of finners, 'to the city of the living God, the celeftial *Jerufalem*.

'I blefs God I am thought worthy to fuffer for his name, and for fo 'good a caufe; and if I had a thoufand lives, I would willingly lay 'them down for the caufe of my King, the Lord's anointed; the Scripture commands us to fear God and honour the King, to be fubject to 'every Ordinance of man for the Lord's fake; whether to the King as 'fupreme, or to thofe that are in authority under him. I have been always faithful to my truft: and, though I have been moft bafely accufed for betraying *Liverpool*; yet I take God to witnefs, it is a moft 'falfe afperfion, for I was then fick in my bed, and knew not of the delivering of it, till the Officers and Soldiers had done it without my 'confent, and then I was carried prifoner to Sir *John Meldrum*. Afterwards I came down into the Country, and feeing I could not live 'quietly at home, I was perfuaded by Col. *Forbes*, Col. *Overton*, Lieut. 'Col. *Fairfax*, whom I took for my good friends, to march in their 'Troops: which I did, but with intention ftill to do my King the beft 'fervice when occafion was, and fo I did: and I pray God to turn the 'hearts of all the Soldiers to their lawful Sovereign, that this Land may 'enjoy peace, which till then it will never do: and though thou kill me, 'yet will I put my truft in thee; wherefore I truft in God he will not 'fail me nor forfake me.' Then he took his Bible, and read divers Pfalms fit for his own occafion and confolation, and then put up divers prayers, fome publickly, and fome privately; which being ended he was executed.

XXIV. The Proceedings, Examination, and Trial of Col. EUSEBIUS ANDREWE, (a Barrifter of *Gray's-Inn*,) before the High-Court of Juftice, *Aug.* 16, 1650, for High-Treafon.

Publifhed by *Francis Buckley*, Gent. who was Affiftant to Mr. *Andrewe* in the time of his Imprifonment, and an Eye-witnefs of all the bloody and execrable Proceedings.

ON *Monday* the 24th of *March*, 1649, Col. *Andrewe* was taken prifoner at *Gravefend* by Major *Parker*.

The next day, he was convented before the Lord-Prefident *Bradfhaw*, Sir *Henry Mildmay*, Knt. and *Thomas Scot*, Efq. three of the Members of State, delegated by the Council for the taking of the examination of him, and of Sir *Henry Chicl'ey*, Knt. Dr. *Henry Edwards*, and Mr. *Clark*, cafually found in the fame inn with Mr. *Andrewe*.

Thofe Gentlemen examined him fo punctually to every action and circumftance that had paffed on his part fince he took up arms, and efpecially fince the furrender of *Worcefter*, and his return from thence to *London*, and alfo concerning his feveral Lodgings, Names, Acquaintances, Removes, Abodes in the Country, Correfpondencies by Letters, and Intereft in places and perfons, as if they had kept a Diary for him. Which confidered, and that Sir *John Gell*, Bart. Major *Burnard*, Capt. *Smith*, Capt. *Benfon*, and Capt. *Allen*, (with whom he had the laft and moft queftionable correfpondence) were all in cuftody, he found himfelf to be betrayed, but could not at prefent guefs by whom, but well faw that he had better be full in his confeffion, than to deny what he faw by the perfectnefs of his examiners, would be proved againft him, by the difcovery of fome of thofe formerly fecured, and examined before his coming up.

In his Anfwers, he would have been circumftantial, but was kept clofe to the Queftions: at his departure he defired that he might fet down his own Narrative, according to his own fenfe, which was granted him to prepare, and to fend or bring to them as there was opportunity. And having totally, as much as in him lay, excufed his fellow-prifoners as to any thing relating to his Delinquency, he was with them committed to the *Gatehoufe*.

Wednefday following, he was re-convented and re-examined.

On *Friday*, he was again convented, and delivered in his Narrative to the Lord-Prefident, and the Houfe. But bufinefs happening, detaining the other two examiners, he was by the Prefident returned.

On *Saturday* he was recalled, and then, as at all times before, ufed and treated with civility, and no little preffure to difcover fome great perfons, his fuppofed confederates: the aim, as he conjectur'd (and that upon ftrong inference, and fome expreffions) was at Sir *Guy Palmes*, Sir *John Curfon*, and Sir *Thomas Whitmore*, &c. But he accounted it a great bleffing in his unhappinefs, that his misfortune was not fatal to any of his friends or familiars, who yet knew nothing of the reafon of his Imprifonment, more than for what they were beholden to common fame.

On *Sunday*, he was called out of his bed, and by two Meffengers, his Keeper, and his Men, brought into a boat at *King's-bridge*, at *Weftminfter*, and thence carried to the *Tower*. The warrant, which at the Lieutenant's houfe was read, imported, that he was committed clofe prifoner for High-Treafon, in endeavouring to fubvert the prefent Government, &c. to be kept till delivered by Law.

The Narrative follows.

To the Right Honourable the Council of State;

The humble Narrative * *of Col.* Eufebius Andrewe, *as to the Queftions and Matters of charge, whereupon he was examined before Prefident* Bradfhaw, *Sir* Henry Mildmay, *and* Thomas Scot, *Efq. in that behalf delegated by the Council the 27th of* March, 1650.

May it pleafe your Lordfhips,

BEING unfortunately, and by a treacherous practice feduced into an action which renders me obnoxious to your Lordfhips Difpleafure and Juftice, and thereupon convented and brought to examination, I affured your Lordfhips delegates that I came with a refolution to deal candidly, and not to preferve my life by framing a lye, or denying a truth. The fame purpofe I ftill retain, cafting myfelf wholly at your Lordfhips feet, humbly praying leave, that while I anfwer to matter of fact, I may be permitted to cloath it with pertinent circumftances; that while the one lays me liable to

* The Narrative is here printed at large, being the Evidence urged againft him at his Trial.

your Justice, the other may bring me within the capacity of your mercy; which in case it be afforded, I shall embrace with all humility and thankfulness. And if denied, I shall find cause within my bosom to justify God Almighty in his permission of my ruin; and I hope Charity enough to forgive whosoever have, or shall be instrumental to it, and bear the burden of my folly, with a sober confidence of God's reserved favour.

My engagement for his late Majesty began soon after *Hillary Term*, 1642, and continued until the surrender of *Worcester*, in *July* 1645.

I have omitted to make my composition, not having a considerable, and not willing to own an inconsiderable estate.

I have not taken the protestation, solemn league and covenant, negative Oath, nor subscribed the present engagement.

John Barnard, sometime a Major under me, and by reason of his good parts and sober demeanor, being in my good opinion, at my return to a private practice in my calling for my necessary support, frequently visited me, and imparted to me such occurrences as he met abroad in discourse, and did often intimate the discontent of the Reformades, the factions of the Levellers and Agitators, and the proceeding of a certain Committee, or select Council of Officers, of which Col. *Cook* was chief, and himself their Clerk, upon a printed charge against some for oppression, and against others for conceal'd delinquency; to the penning, promoting or counselling in which I was originally a stranger, nor did ever interest myself therein further than the hearing his discourse; neither did ever mediately or immediately meddle with any of the persons or actions of the Reformades, Levellers, or Agitators upon any of his discourses.

About * *Trinity-Term* last, Major *Barnard* obtruded to my acquaintance one Capt. *Holmes*, who soon after brought with him one *John Benson*, (who pretended to have had command under Sir *John Gell*, was anciently his servant, and until this time his dependant,) who, uninvited frequently produced to me transcripts of Letters, (with the copying of which he pretended to be entrusted under Mr. *Rushworth*) which did appear to purport the occurrences in reference to the affairs of State, and their concernments at home and abroad, from their several agents; which I only read in his sight, and immediately delivered them back, he pretending that he was to carry them to Mr. *Thomas Bushel* to be transmitted over sea.

Capt. *Holmes*, and *John Benson*, in their discourses did insinuate that their interest was great in the Reformades, and that by them great advantage would upon any importunity be done for the Royal Party, and magnified Sir *John Gell*'s interest in his Country, his reluctance at what he had done in the Parliament's service, and his willingness to expiate his former fault with a beneficial service to the Prince. And Major *Barnard* propounded, that a former design in the time of the war laid by me for the taking of the Isle of *Ely*, might by their help, and the conjuncture of some strength to be raised by Sir *John Gell*, then to me a stranger, and by *Holmes* and *Benson*, pretended to be willing and able to raise considerable numbers, be revived and executed; and thereupon it was concluded, that I should with *Benson* try who in *Cambridgeshire* would engage in it, and then ride down to Sir *John Gell*, to see if his strength and purpose were such as pretended; and this not to be executed but upon the contingency of successes in *Ireland*, and *Scotland*, was let fall as soon as conceived.

About the middle of *December*, Capt. *Holmes* brought me instructions, to draw a petition for Sir *John Gell*, for the getting of his arrears, which I drew accordingly; and not long after, I was invited to give him a meeting, till then having not seen or corresponded with him, and received an invitation and instruction to arbitrate between him and his Lady, with Sir *Thomas Priestwich*. And amongst other discourses, Sir *John Gell* did take notice of his irrequital of his service, and his losses, and the misapplication of his, and other services, to an end they intended not, and that he desired to be so understood, and when opportunity should be, to be so represented to the Prince; and did intimate, that if ever he took up arms again, it should be for the Prince: and at several other subsequent meetings the discourses were general, and much to this purpose, but no particular design laid or contrived.

The time limited by the Act for departure, *&c.* being near expired, and myself being purposed to withdraw into the Country, until the Summer Voyage, into some of the Plantations, and to that purpose being in treaty with Sir *Edmund Plowden*, about the conditions of *New Albion* plantation, of which he writes himself Count Palatine, and Proprietor; on *Saturday* 16 *Martii*, I was unexpectedly visited by Major *Barnard* and *John Benson*, and they enquiring my resolution concerning my leaving the Town in obedience to the Act, I signified my purpose to go to *New Albion* or to *Virginia*: upon which they took an opportunity to make a proposal to me in effect, that they had a considerable design laid, and friends and money to set on foot and back it, and that I should have two hundred pounds in hand, and power to draw money by Bills of Exchange, for what more should be necessary for my support, and management of what should concern the said design in *Holland*, if I would undertake to go over, and promote it to the Prince. And they did then in general terms signify, that it was an easy matter, especially the Cavaliers going out of the Town, by correspondence in all Counties, to surprize the horse of the army in their several quarters; and did intimate, that Major *Barnard* had a design in draught, which as I remember he produced, and I believe was concerning such surprizal but was not read, but referred to further time of consideration. My answer was, that if the money were ready, I would divert my former purpose from any Plantation, and entertain the motion.

Sunday morning they came again and informed me, that several persons of quality and fortune in *Kent*, *Buckingham*, and *Dorset*, were, or would then presently come up near the Town, and would join in an engagement, and advance money, and that Sir *John Gell* would also engage, and might with a word of his mouth bring in his friends, and Sir *Andrew Kniveton*, Sir *Guy Palmes*, and Mr. *Fitzherbert*, and a fourth person, whose name I remember not, and therefore desired me to draw an engagement, (which I did in a loose paper, after the sense of them or one of them, the said *Barnard*, or *Benson*, instructed) and to move Sir *John Gell* to join in such an engagement, but did press me to join in the same at that present, for the encouraging of their before mentioned friends, amongst whom, I remember only these Surnames *Boys*, *Thatch*, *Baker*, all to me absolute strangers.

That day I spake with Sir *John Gell*, and acquainted him with their offer and proposal to me, and desire from him: He answered, that he would not meddle with acting in that design (which he took upon him to be acquainted withal), for which he was as then in no capacity, nor would be engaged under his hand and seal, to be bound to, by any future action for them; for that *Benson* was a fellow given to drink, and lavish of his tongue: but entrusted me, that if I went over upon this occasion, to possess the Prince with a good opinion of him, and that he would do nothing against him; and if he were at all in command, he would be so to his advantage, or to that effect.

I returned to them Sir *John Gell*'s answer, with which they were not, or seemed not altogether unsatisfied, and appointed on *Monday* at five of the clock, that the persons of the Counties of *Kent*, *Buckingham* and *Dorset*, or some of each County from the rest, should give a meeting at the *Three Cranes*, at the *Savoy-Gate*, and be all satisfied in the design, and agree their respective portions of money to be paid in present, and raised for the future; desiring me to take care to move, that they might be also provided for, to be able to hold intelligence, and ride about from place to place to lay the design.

At the time I came; and Major *Barnard* produced two letters, one subscribed by *Smith*, another by *Thatcher*, purporting that the *Kentish* Gentlemen were come as far as *Rochester*, and would that night be within twelve miles of *London*, and lie there all day, and then in the evening, on *Tuesday* by eight of the clock, would at any place give meeting to himself, and his Colonel; and that they had sent a special guide to bring *Barnard* to them that night, whither he was instantly desired to repair, and that they durst come no nearer, in fear of the watchfulness of Colonel *Blunt*; and that the two hundred and fifty pounds were ready to be laid down to perform their undertaking: No man of any County giving any meeting according to the first appointment at the *Cranes*, but the said *Barnard* and *Benson*, and one who calls himself Captain *Ashley*, only known in face to me, who pretended to be privy and knowing of the truth of all that their former discourse and these letters tended to; and *Barnard* pretending to go instantly to horse from *Westminster*, I brought him and *Benson* to the water-side, and in the walk they importun'd me again to obtain Sir *John Gell*'s signature and seal to the engagement, which *Benson* had then ready engrossed, and that I would go presently to *Westminster* with them about it; which I refused, and told them, that I was able to satisfy any man of quality, discretion, and secrecy, concerning Sir *John*'s reality, though not actually engag'd; and so left them.

That night, about eight of the clock, one *Smith* came to me (till then) an absolute Stranger, and Capt. *Ashley* came to me, and brought me a letter from Major *Barnard*, highly reproving me and Sir *John Gell* of backwardness, in with-holding our own hands from the engagement, and that we intended our own honours upon their dangers, without giving them assurance of our secrecy and constancy; and that unless the engagement were subscribed by Sir *John Gell*, his *Kentish* friends would not proceed further. I was known to Mr. *Smith*, who took upon him to come as from them for satisfaction in that point. And in answer, I under a vow of secrecy told him, that I was satisfied concerning Sir *John Gell*, and presumed, that if any Gentleman of quality in whose judgment the rest would abide, should address to Sir *John*, that under an Oath of secrecy he would satisfy him, but durst not trust *Benson*, and *Barnard* was to him a stranger. With this they departed, assuring me that they thought no more would be expected from Sir *John*, and that they would, or one of them, away that night to the company; and that the next day being *Tuesday*, the money should be paid at the *Palsgrave's-head*.

They broke their time, and my occasions prest me into *London*, being next day to be gone by the Act; and about nine of the clock at night, I was sent for by Captain *Ashley* and *Benson*, who delivered me a letter from *Barnard*, pressing me to subscribe the engagement which *Benson* engrossed; and that being done, he would go with me the next day to *Gravesend*, and the Gentlemen of *Kent* should meet there, and there the money to be paid.

The tide being fit for passage on *Wednesday*, *Barnard* came not, but *Benson* pretended him to be at *Tottenham-Court* with the *Buckinghamshire* Gentlemen, and that he was well-hors'd, and would come presently, and should follow; and so Captain *Ashley* and myself, with no more than fifty shillings in my purse, presuming upon the money there, went to *Gravesend*, and expected till *Thursday* night, but found no *Kentish* men, and no one from *London* coming. Capt. *Ashley* went that night with the evening-tide for *London*, to enquire the reason; and on *Friday* morning early came Major *Barnard*, and Mr. *Smith* with a letter from *Benson*, purporting that if Sir *John Gell* would not co-ingage under his hand and seal, with those whose names were subscribed (of which I only know *Barnard*, *Smith*, *Benson*, and *Ashley*,) they would go over themselves (meaning himself and *Barnard*) to the Prince, and spoil both mine and Sir *John*'s credit with him, and disappoint all that I intended in his favour: and that he had letters from Sir *John*, which he could produce, should make him repent his refusal, or to such effect; and therefore desired me to write to Sir *John Gell*, to let him see his danger; which I did, laying the case before him, and not pressing him, but leaving him to do as God should direct him, and his judgment lead him. With which letter *Barnard* and *Smith* went away, with assurance that whether Sir *John Gell* engaged or not, I should hear next day from them, and if he did engage, they would come down and go for *Rochester*, where their former undertaking should be performed to me, and if he did not, I should be disengag'd, and have my subscription and seal sent me, and the design should fall. I expected till *Saturday* night, and finding no answer, resolved on *Monday* to intend my privacy in the Country, upon my first purpose for *New Albion*, and in the morning early was seized by a party of horse, and brought to *London*.

My Lords,

In that Narrative you will see a believing nature wrought upon by treacherous men, such who cannot be true to any, whilst false to parties.

The pretended design vanish'd, as never being more than a phantasm, and not worth your regard, the real design effected, so far as they had power or opportunity, that is, to bring the game into the toil, and there leave them to be entangled and made a quarry.

* This Error in time, as some others both of substance and circumstance, are rectified upon better memory, by some following papers sent to the Lord-President.

You

You will find me passively active, being prompted and enticed by their insinuation, and not once but hearkening to them.

It lies in your Lordships power to cut me off, by extending which, you can arrive to no honour amongst men; and possibly, by an Act of lenity, you may do an office acceptable to God.

Cujus fiat voluntas, modo in ruinâ meâ.

Whosoever shall be present at my Trial, or into whose hands this Narrative shall fall, will easily conclude with me,

Quos vult perdi Deus, hos dementat prius.

Eus. Andrewe.

On *Tuesday* the first of *April*, after his remove to the *Tower*, he was called to be further examined, and at his return writ back to them some particulars, (*viz.*) concerning Captain *Holmes*, by want of memory not before signified. And in case the state should have suffered aught by the said *Holmes*, it might have made Mr. *Andrewe* incapable of lawful favour by reason of his tenacity concerning the said *Holmes*, who (for aught Mr. *Andrewe* knew) was guilty of his being betrayed; and if so, might as well intimate his knowledge of *Holmes*'s purposes, to the end that Mr. *Andrewe*'s concealment of them might augment his crime; and also concerning Mr. *Thomas Barnard*, who being at large and unquestioned, Mr. *Andrewe* had cause to have the like jealousy of.

On *Friday* sevennight following, being the 11th of *April*, he was called again, and was confronted with Sir *John Gell*, and avowed what he did indeed neither directly deny, nor was troubled that he did aver; freely telling the President, that howbeit he did not remember some things in point, yet he was confident that he would not do him, nor any man wrong: and then declared to the President, that he look'd upon Sir *John Gell*, as upon himself, as a betrayed man; but as concerning others, he knew not by whom, he had been free in his confessions, though to his own injury.

He then acquainted their Lordships, that he had something to rectify in his former examinations and papers, upon better memory, in point of material circumstances. They directed him to put them into writing, and to send them, and they called for his hand to the former examinations and papers; which he gave them, and the same day writ to them as followeth:

To the Right Honourable the Lord-President and Council of State.

May it please your Lordships,

ACcording to the favourable licence by your Lorships to me given, I have digested into writing those matters of circumstance, wherein my Examinations and Narrative are in defect of my memory only incertain and short; humbly praying, that they may be received and made a part of that relation, which I must abide by at my Trial; and that the former errors may be rectified, and defects supplied so far, as by this supplementary account upon my serious recollections given, may be done. And I shall then be confident, I shall appear not to have wilfully concealed (however guilty) or misrendered any thing pertinent, whether the same carry with it my condemnation, or excuse.

What passed between myself and Mr. *Barnard*, before my acquaintance with *Holmes* and *Benson*, and which is exprest in my Answers and Narrative, was in time before *Easter-Term* last, when there was an order for departure of persons in my condition, from this Town; and I, in obedience thereunto, did leave this city on *Saturday* the 6th of *May*, and came to Mr. *Osborn*'s house at *Carlton-Hall* in *Suffolk*, on *Thursday* following; from whence I stirred not at any time more than five miles, until the sixth of *August*, when I was sent for to make assurances between a Kinswoman and her husband in point of jointure, by them to me mutually referred: in which business, and in other matters between another Kinswoman, and a Merchant of *London*, being under reference to arbitrement; as also in endeavouring to get some friend to contract in the behalf of my daughter, for the reversion of a Lease holden of the Dean and Chapter of *Ely*, in which she is interested for a life in being, I continued in and near the City until the third day of *September*; in which time *Barnard* voluntarily brought to my acquaintance *Holmes* and *Benson*, upon the pretences in my Answers and Narrative set forth, to which I humbly refer.

The note which mentions *Benson*'s going with me to *Cambridgeshire*, and so to Sir *John Gell*, which in my Answers I have expounded, was drawn from me by *Barnard*'s importunity, and written at his request; but what use he made of it, (other than to lay it up, and reserve it for his present purpose) I know not, nor had any account of it, but went away the third of *September*, there being no conclusion of any thing to be done in substance, or circumstance positive. But Mr. *Barnard*, who knew how to direct to me, promised by Letter to intimate further to me; from whom after that, I never received any Letter or Message to that, or any other purpose, until my return near *Michaelmas-Term*; when he told me, that the unsuccessfulness of things in *Ireland* had been the impediment.

As to the day, *viz.* the 18th of *October*, being the Fair-day at *Ely*, it was only in discourse mentioned to be an opportune time, in case the Isle were (as indeed it was not) garrisoned. Neither any solemn, or serious design or conclusion, there-to-fore or there-after made or laid, other than in transient communication; nor any person engaged so much as by word or promise, until this fresh stratagem was set on foot by *Barnard*.

I drew Sir *John Gell*'s petition before *Christmas*, and had several complements from him by *Holmes*, (at least pretended) before I saw him, and I believe, after Twelf-tide I was invited to him, and entrusted by him in the composing the differences between him and his Lady: in the last Term I drew his answer, and in the several times of our casual or occasional meetings, the discourses have amounted to what I have before signified, and in your presence and his avowed; and how more exactly to give your Lordships an account in time, I cannot.

As to the matter of the engagement, I abide by what I have formerly said, with this only, that at my engaging, which was late in the night, before my going out of Town, in obedience to the Act, I was promised by *Benson* that if Sir *John Gell*, and their pretended friends of the Country did not co-engage, I should be disengaged; and in the hour of my going away, *Barnard* being not ready according to promise, but by *Benson* pretended to be at *Tottenham-Court* with some *Buckinghamshire* men, and that he would undoubtedly follow, I told *Benson*, as I remember, in the presence of Captain *Ashley*, that whether he came or not, I must for the present remove to *Gravesend*, not having convenience of horse to go elsewhere so suddenly. And if there were performance on *Barnard*'s part with me, I should be ready on mine; and if not, I desire to be disengaged, and left to pursue my private occasions into *Surry*. And I did really carry with me deeds of my Clients to have employed myself upon, in case of their failure with me.

I humbly beg your Lordships pardon for a favourable interpretation of this trouble, which is a duty to truth, and right to others and myself; which could not be omitted by

(My Lords)

Your Lordships humble prisoner, and servant,

Eus. Andrewe.

This, together with a petition for allowance and liberty of friends resorts, being the same day sign'd in the presence of the Lieutenant, were seal'd up, and sent to the Lord President's own hand.

This was his second petition, which with a former to the same effect, (and not of moment to subscribe) did never receive any answer.

At the same time he writ to Sir *Henry Mildmay* on the behalf of the Gentlemen who were taken with him.

Mr. *Andrewe* at several times took upon him to aver to the Committee of State, that they had spies upon him for some years, and particularly *Barnard*; which the Lord-President did not deny, but justified the State, by the practice of all States, to set watches upon persons of ill affections to them.

This day the Lord *Grey* was with the other three of the State.

His third petition sent about *Easter*, being by Sir *Henry Mildmay* and Mr. *Scot* put upon it, to submit himself, with promise of favour if he sought the State in such manner; which for his relations sake he did, but with some caution, in these words:

To the Right Honourable the Lord-President, and Council;

The humble Petition of Eusebius Andrewe,

Sheweth,

THAT your Petitioner is seriously sensible, and humbly acknowledgeth, that for his high delinquency against the State he is become forfeited to their Justice.

That he hath not in the least prevaricated with your Lordships, in the confession of his proper faults and follies, nor hath kept aught reserved concerning himself, or any person, or thing, which may satisfy your Lordships, and more secure the State; and is not hopeless to be look'd upon as capable of your present favour and future mercy, which he now doth, and shall always implore.

That his present, deserved condition is made more uncomfortable, by his wants, and the exclusion of his friends and relations; without a supply, in which life itself becomes a punishment.

Your Petitioner casting himself at the feet of your Lordships, humbly prays,

That his being prosecuted before the HighCourt of Justice, may be suspended.

That by your order, his past and future charge of necessaries may be discharged, whilst he remains your prisoner.

That his friends and kindred may have recourse to him, and that he may have the freedom of his pen.

And in case your Petitioner shall be found in the least to misapply those favours, he shall adjudge himself worthy of a total deprivation of them, and of your future goodness towards him.

And your Petitioner, &c.

This was less than was look'd for, though as much as he could venture on; in which his desire for respite of his Trial was inserted, to prevent only his being the first, and exasperating them by giving others aim in the scrupling the Court.

This petition was solicited thirty-three days, but no answer could be obtained; and his wants growing upon him daily, he put in the Lieutenant's hands this following petition:

The Petition, (with stile as formerly, &c.*)*

Sheweth,

THAT your Petitioner hath been twelve weeks close prisoner, his friends neither permitted to visit, nor daring to relieve him, his score for necessaries swoln beyond his ability to discharge, his credit protested, and nothing more visible to him than his immediate perishing.

That he hath not been wanting to pray your favours, having three petitions lodged with your Lordships, constantly solicited, but unanswered.

That he hath in his confessions spared nothing which can more conduce to the State's security, or his own condemnation.

Your Petitioner therefore humbly prays,

That if at all he must, he may speedily receive his Trial, he being ready to submit to the will of God in the issue.

That if mercy be reserved for him, which he hath, and doth implore, your Lordships would please to admit him to sue out his pardon, and to a free conversation in this Commonwealth, upon security given for his future good demeanor.

That in the mean time he may have the liberty of the Church and *Tower*, and the freedom of his friends retort, and that order may be given for the debt incurred there in the time of his close restraint to be discharged. *And your Petitioner*, &c.

The Warrant of Commitment, which I could not get a Copy of till the 14th of July, *is as followeth:*

THESE are to will and requre you, herewith to receive into your custody the body of *Eusebius Andrewe*, Esq. and him you are safely to keep in close imprisonment in the *Tower* of *London*, in order to his further examination, he being committed unto you for High-Treason, in plotting and endeavouring the subversion and alteration of the present Government. Of this you are not to fail; and for so doing, this shall be your Warrant.

Given at the Council of State sitting at Whitehall, *this 30th day of* May, 1650.

Signed in the name and by the order of the Council of State appointed by Authority of Parliament.

To the Lieutenant of the Tower of London.

John Bradshaw, *President.*

This

This Warrant is vicious in itself, for two Reasons, which make a right Warrant of Commitment, *Coke's 2d* Part Instit. *fol.* 52, 590, 591. allowed by the Parliament.

1. That it is not done by due Process of Law.

2. That it hath not a Conclusion, *viz.* 'And safely to keep until he 'be delivered by due Course of Law.'

But leaves it indefinite, and is rather a Condemnation to perpetual, at least, to arbitrary Imprisonment, which is worse.

The close Imprisonment is but in order to his further Examination, and he had been twice since examined, and signed his Examinations before *Easter*, and did not refuse to answer any Question demanded of him.

The Warrant is dated from the Council of State sitting at *Whitehall*, the 30*th* of *May*; whereas he was brought to the *Tower* the 30*th* of *March*, being *Sunday*, by seven in the Morning, at the opening of the Gate (no Council sitting) and the Warrant signed on *Saturday* the 29*th* of *March*.

Having attended a Month in Expectation of an Answer to his last Petition, he petitioned the Parliament again.

To the High and Honourable the Parliament of *England*;

The humble Petition of Eusebius Andrewe, *Esq. close Prisoner in the* Tower *of* London,

Sheweth,

THAT your Petitioner hath been, by a confederate Pack of Setters, wrought into Actions, which (abstracted from their Circumstances) render him liable to your Justice; and this done, not without their further Hope, that your Petitioner, as they supposed, had Interest to have drawn divers Persons of Quality and Fortune into the same Entanglement.

That failing of that Part of their Aim, the said Confederates did betray your Petitioner to the honourable Council of State, by whose Warrant he hath been fifteen Weeks a strictly close Prisoner, without a Fortune of his own, the Access of Friends, or Means of Subsistence allowed; and is to perish by his Wants, before it be distinguished by a publick Trial, whether he be a fitter Object for the applying of your Justice, or your Mercy.

That he is hereby disabled to be accountable to the Service of God, the Duty to his Family and Friends, and to those who give him Credit for Bread. And in case he should be called from such his close Restraint to his Trial, must be destitute and deprived of all fair Means of making his reasonable Defence; which, however it may suit with Policy, will not be consistent with Religion and Honour.

Your Petitioner having for Relief in the Premises, by all opportune Addresses, and by four Petitions importunely solicited and sought the said Council of State without Answer; in the deep Sense of his pressing Sufferings humbly appealeth to this high Court, casting himself wholly thereupon, and as humbly prayeth,

1. That you would prevent your Justice by your Mercy, and admit him to sue out his Pardon, upon Security given for his future good Demeanor to the State in this Commonwealth.

2. That if that be too great a Favour, you would grant him Licence to depart the Commonwealth, he engaging not to act, or contrive aught to the disservice of the State.

3. That if he be not thought capable of either, but that he must receive a publick Trial, he may have a convenient time of Preparation, after a qualifying of his Imprisonment.

4. That in the mean time he may have the Liberty of the *Tower*, and resort of his Friends; and that by your Order, his Debt for Livelihood, incurred in his close Restraint, may be discharged.

In all which your Petitioner is ready to submit to the Will of God, whose Providence hath put Justice and Mercy into your present dispensing.

And shall ever pray.

Notwithstanding his Petitions and Letters, he was brought before the High Court of Justice (in *August*), of which *John Bradshaw* was President, and his own Narrative was urged against him as a Confession; and Attorney-General *Prideaux* used him with very ill Language. But he put into Court his Answers in writing, which were as follow:

The humble Answer of Eusebius Andrewe, *Esq. in his Defence, to the Proceeding against him before the Honourable the High Court of Justice, presented the 16th Day of* Aug. 1650.

THE said Respondent (with the Favour of this honourable Court) reserving and praying to be allowed the Benefit and Liberty of making further Answer, offereth to this honourable Court;

First, That by the Statute or Charter, stiled *Magna Charta*, which is the fundamental Law, and ought to be the Standard of the Laws of *England*, confirmed above thirty times, and yet unrepealed, it is in the 29th Chapter thereof granted and enacted,

1. That no Freeman shall be taken, or imprisoned, or be disseised of his Freehold or Liberties, or free Custom, or be outlawed, or exiled, or be any otherwise destroyed, nor will we pass upon him, nor condemn him, but by a lawful Judgment of his Peers, and by the Laws of the Land.

2. We shall sell to no Man, nor defer to any Man Justice or Right.

Secondly, That by the Statute of 42 of *Edw.* III. *chap.* 1.

1. The Great Charter is commanded to be kept in all the Points. And,

2. It is enacted, that if any Statute be made to the contrary, that shall be holden for none; which Statute is unrepealed.

The Respondent observeth, That by an Act of the 26th of *March*, 1650, entitled, *An Act for establishing an High Court of Justice*, Power is given to this Court to try, condemn, and cause Execution of Death to be done upon the Freemen of *England*, according as the major Number of any twelve of the Members thereof shall judge to appertain to Justice.

And thereupon the Respondent doth humbly infer and offereth for Law,

That the said Act is diametrically contrary unto, and utterly inconsistent with the said Great Charter, and is therefore by the said recited Statute to be holden for none.

That it can with no more Reason, Equity, or Justice, hold the Value and Reputation of a Law (the said Statute before recited being in Force), than it, contrary to the second Clause in the 29th *Chap.* of *Magna Charta*,

it had been also enacted, that Justice and Right shall be deferred to all Freemen, and sold to all that will buy it.

Thirdly, That upon premising, by the Petition of Right, 3 *Car.* that contrary to the Great Charter, Trials and Executions had been had and done against the Subjects by Commissions Martial, *&c.* it was therefore prayed, and by the Commission enacted, That,

1. No Commissions of the like Nature might be thenceforth issued, *&c.* And that done,

2. To prevent, lest any of the Subjects should be put to Death, contrary to the Laws and Franchise of the Land.

The Respondent humbly observeth and affirmeth, That

This Court is (though under a different Stile) in nature, and in the Proceedings thereof, directly the same with the Commission-Martial; the Freemen thereby being to be tried for Life, and adjudged by the major Number of the Commissioners sitting (as in Courts of Commissioners Martial was practised, and was agreeable to their Constitution), and consequently against the Petition of Right; in which he, and all the Freemen of *England* (if it be granted there be any such) hath, and have Right and Interest; and he humbly claims his Right accordingly.

Fourthly, That by the Remonstrance of the 15th of *December*, and the Declaration the 17th of *January*, 1641, the Benefit of the Laws and ordinary Courts of Justice are the Subjects Birth-rights.

By the Declarations of the 12th of *July*, and the 16th of *October*, 1642, the Preservation of the Laws, and the due Administration of Justice, are owned to be the justifying Cause of the War; and the Ends of the Parliament's Affairs managed by their Swords and Councils. And God's Curse is by them imprecated, in case they should ever decline those Ends.

By the Declaration of the 17th of *April*, 1646, Promise was made not to interrupt the Course of Justice in the ordinary Courts thereof.

By the Ordinance or Votes of Non-addresses, *Jan.* 1648, it is assured on the Parliament's behalf, That

Though they lay the King aside, yet they will govern by the Laws, and not interrupt the Course of Justice in the ordinary Courts thereof.

And thereupon the Respondent humbly inferreth and affirmeth, That

The Constitution of this Court is a Breach of that publick Faith of the Parliament, exhibited and pledged in the Declarations and Votes to the Freemen of *England*.

And upon the whole Matter, the Respondent (saving as aforesaid) doth humbly affirm for Law, and claim as his Right,

1. That this Court, in defect of the Validity of the Act, by which it is constituted, hath not Power against him, or to press him to a further Answer.

2. That by Virtue of *Magna Charta*, the Petition of Right, and the before-recited Remonstrance and Declarations, he ought not to be proceeded against by this Court, but by an ordinary Court of Justice, and to be tried by his Peers.

And prays, that this present Answer and Salvo may be accepted, and registered, and that he may be tried by his Peers accordingly.

EUS. ANDREWE.

The farther and second Answer of Eus. Andrewe, *Esq. to the Honourable the High Court of Justice, presented the 16th Day of* Aug. 1650.

THE said Respondent (with the Favour of this Honourable Court) reserving and praying to be allowed the Benefit and Liberty of making further Answer (if it shall be adjudged necessary), in all Humbleness for present Answer, offereth to this honourable Court,

That by the Letter and genuine Sense of the Act, entitled, *An Act for establishing an High Court of Justice*, the said Court is not qualified to try a Freeman of *England* (and such the Respondent averreth to be) for Life in Case of Treason.

First, For that, 1. The said Court is not constituted a Court of Record, and (but upon Record) cannot at all have that Account of their Freemen, which Kings were wont to have of their Ministers of Justice.

2. The Freemen, and such who are and may be concerned in him, can have no Record to resort unto, by which to preserve the Rights due to him and them respectively, *viz.* of

1. A Writ of Error, in case of erroneous Judgment, due by the Precedents.	*Pasch.* 39 *Ed.* III. *fol.* of *Gaunt's* Case. 4 *Ed.* III. *Rot. Par. Num.* 13. *Count de Arundel's* Case. 42 *Ed.* III. *Rot. Par. Nu.* 23. Sir *John* of *Lee's* Case.
2. A Plea of Autersoys acquit, in case of new Question for the same Fact; the Right to which, and the Necessity of such Record, appears by	*Wetherel* and *Darley's* Case, 4 *Rep.* 35 *Eliz.* *Vaux's* Case, *ibid.* 33 *Eliz.*
3. A being enlarged upon Acquittal, as is the Freeman's Due, by the Stat. 14 *Hen.* VI. *C.* 1. and the Case thereupon grounded.	*Dyer fol.* 120. and *Abridg. fol.* 33. The Year Book of *Edw.* VI. 10. *fol.* 19.
4. A Writ of Conspiracy against those who have practised the betraying the Life of the Respondent not to be brought before Acquittal, and no Acquittal but upon Record, as appeareth by	The *Poulterer's* Case, 9 *Rep. fol.* 55.

This Court is to determine at a Day, without account of their Proceedings, have Power to try, judge, and cause Execution, but not to acquit or to give Enlargement; so that the nocent are thereby punishable, the innocent not preservable; the injured and betrayed not vindicable; which are Defects incompatible with a Court of Justice, and inconsistent with Justice itself, and with the Honours of a Christian Nation and Commonwealth.

Secondly, For that the Members of this Court are by the Act directed to be sworn,

1. Not *in conspectu populi*, for the Freemen's Satisfaction.

2. Not in Words of Indifferency, and obliging to Equity.

3. In Words of manifest Partiality, *viz.*

You

You shall swear that you shall well and truly, according to the best of your skill and knowledge, execute the several powers given unto you by this Act.

The Respondent humbly offers, That

1. The Court in their capacity of Triers ought (in reason) to have been appointed by their constitution, to have been sworn as Triers in full Court, according to the practice in all equal ways of Trial.

2. The Court as Commissioners of Oyer and Terminer, (being authorized by the Act to hear and determine) should in like reason be appointed by an Oath, such as is usual for persons so qualified, as provided by 18 *Edw.* III. *viz.*

You shall swear, that well and lawfully you shall serve our Lord the King, and his People (mutatis mutandis) *in the office of Justice,* &c. *and that you deny to no man common right,* &c.

Or some Oath equivalent at least to that of a Justice of Peace, *Dalton, fol.* 13.

I A. B. do swear, that I will do equal right; and according to my best wit, cunning and power, after the Laws and Customs of the land, and the Statutes thereof made, &c.

3. The Court in the capacity of Triers should (in reason) be obliged by an Oath, of as equitable sense as that usually administered to Jurors, *viz.*

You shall well and truly try, and true deliverance make between our Sovereign Lord the King, (mutatis mutandis) *and the prisoner at the bar; so help you God.*

Whereas when this Court shall (as it is now constituted) have condemned the Freeman, the Respondent, or other, by applying their skill and knowledge, to their power, whether justly or not, the Oath by them taken is not in the letter broken; as to be exactable by man, though God will probably have a better account.

And therefore upon the whole matter premised, the Respondent (saving as before) offers for law and reason, that the honourable Court, the High Court of Justice, is not, by the letter and proper sense of the words of the Act, by which it is constituted, qualified in respect of the pre-objected defects to pass upon him for his life, upon a charge or crimination of High-Treason.

And humbly prays, that this his second Answer, and Salvo, may be received, and registered; and that he may be tried, as in his former Answer be prayed.

EUS. ANDREWE.

The farther and third Answer of Eusebius Andrewe, *Esq. to the Honourable the High Court of Justice, presented the 16th day of* Aug. 1650.

THE said Respondent (with the favour of this honourable Court) reserving and praying to be allowed the benefit and liberty of making further answer, (if it shall be adjudged necessary) in all humbleness for present Answer, offereth to this honourable Court,

That, *First,* It is his right (if he must admit this Court to be duly and legally established and constituted, as to their being a Court) to be tried by his Peers, men of his own condition and neighbourhood.

Secondly, It is within the power of the Court by the Letter and Sense of the Act, or at least as being not repugnant to the Act, to try him by such his Peers, &c.

First, That it is his right to be so, and only so tried, appears by *Magna Charta, cap.* 29. 25 *Edw.* I. *cap.* 1, and 2. 25 *Edw.* III. *cap.* 4. 25 *Edw.* III. *cap.* 2, and 4. 28 *Edw.* III. *cap.* 4. 37 *Edw.* III. *cap.* 18. 42 *Edw.* III. *cap.* 3.

By all which Statutes made in full Parliament, consisting of the head, and all the members actually, as well as virtually, this the Respondent's right is maintainable, and demandable, and the contrary proceedings thereunto are to be held for none, and redressed, &c. to be held for void, and error, &c.

So that, if the Laws and Courts were not obstructed, (in the cases of some sort of Freemen of *England,*) the whole proceeding contrary to these Laws, without a Jury of his Peers, were avoidable, and reservable by Writ of Error, as appears also by the precedents vouched by the Respondent in his second Answer.

Secondly, That it is in the Court's power to try the Freeman, and consequently the Respondent, by a Jury of his Equals; the Court is humbly desired to consider the words of qualification.

The Court is,

First, Required to hear and determine; and so, if at all Commissioners, then Commissioners of Oyer and Terminer, and such Commissioners, in their natural constitution and practical execution, do proceed against the Freemen according to Law, by a Jury of his Equals, and not otherwise.

Secondly, Authorized to proceed to trial, condemnation, and execution, &c. But not restrained to the manner of Trial, *limitative,* as to trial by the Court's opinion as Triers, *non exclusive,* as to trial *per Pares*; but is left in the manner, as in the judgment itself, to the opinion of the major number of twelve; and if they shall think fit to try by a Jury, it will be no offence against the Act, there being no clause or prohibition to the contrary.

And therefore the Respondent humbly claimeth his said Right, as consisting with the said Power.

And the more to induce the Court to grant him such his right, and the benefit thereof, the Respondent humbly representeth the manifest wrong, and multiplied disherison, done to him, and in him to the *Freemanry of England,* in the following particulars of their like just right (depending upon such trial to be allowed) if denied him, by this honourable Court.

First, The benefit of

Challenge to the Triers, thirty-five peremptorily, and for Treason *sans* number. } *Stampf. pl. Cor. fol.* 150. *Tit. Challenge, Poyning's* case. 32 *Hen.* VI. *Fitz. fol.* 26. *Allowed Hill.* 1 *Jacobi* to Sir *Wal. Raleigh* and *Brooks.*

Secondly, The liberty of

seeing, hearing, and counter-questioning the witnesses, for clearing the evidence in matter of circumstance, as well as in matter of fact, which appears to be the Respondent's right by

Stampf. pl. Cor. fol. 163, 164. the Statute of } 1 and 2 *Phil.* and *Mary, cap.* 10 and 11. 1 *Edw.* VI. *cap.* 12.

The Authority of (the Law's Oracle) *Coke* 2 part *Inst. fol.* 12. commenting upon the words in 25 *Edw.* III. *cap.* 2. *Provablement Attaint,* because the punishment was heavy, the proof to be punctual, and not upon presumptions, or inferences, or strains of wit, but upon good and sufficient proofs: also by the Statute of 1 *Eliz. cap.* 6. 13 *Eliz. cap.* 1.

Thirdly, The being

Convinced, or acquitted by a full, free, and fully-consented verdict. For,

First, A verdict by a Jury passeth from all, or not at all. In the proceeding by voices, a sentence passeth by way of concurrence, with which the *Star-Chamber, High-Commission,* and *Courts-Martial,* were branded, and condemned of *Inequality.*

Secondly, A verdict passeth upon a Jury before discharged, upon their affairs of Estate, or supplies of Nature, to prevent corruption of money and power; but as this Court proceeds (if it will proceed by voices), a Trial may be had this day, and a sentence may be given at leisure; when the will of those by whom the Freeman is prosecuted, be first known.

And upon the whole matter,

The Respondent humbly claims the benefit and right of being tried (if before this honourable Court) *per Pares,* men of his own condition, and of his neighbourhood, and that he may hear and see all the witnesses produced against him, *viva voce & aperto vultu*; and may have power, liberty, and time to produce witnesses in his defence.

And (saving as formerly) humbly prays that this his Answer, and Salvo, may be received and registered.

EUS. ANDREWE.

The several Arguments of Col. *Andrewe* at his Trial.

The First Argument.

My Lords, and you Gentlemen, Members of this Honourable Court,

I Have (as becomes me) been attentive to the charge which has been read against me. It appears in that dress it is put already, (though I presume it shall be clad in other apparel by Mr. Attorney) so specious, and so great as that my friends (if I have any here) begin to fear, the indifferent to doubt, and the partial to desire, and join in my condemnation; myself (I hope I am not partial to myself) believe, that it will be no more than the mountain's labour, and when it shall come to be dissected, will prove to be *inane aliquid*; like the Apples of *Sodom,* that however they take the first sense, the eye, as this the ear, do rather foul the fingers that touch them, than satisfy the appetite in its expectation upon them.

My Lord,

I am at an unusual bar, and engaged in a great cause of a far extendable concernment, my fee is life, and my duty is self-preservation; which in itself were less considerable, if by a precedent of my suffering, the consequence would not prove mischievously epidemical.

I do not wilfully refuse to plead to the charge, but humbly crave leave to offer my reasons for the suspending of my Plea. And if I be importunate (yet within the bounds of civility) I beg your pardon, and that I may have a full, free, and an uninterrupted hearing.

My Lord,

When the *Jews* pressed *Pilate* to sentence *Christ,* they obtruded to him that they had a Law, and by that Law he ought to die. What they thought reasonable to claim, when it served their turn to vent their malice, will be, I hope, warrantable for me to lay hold on in a better sense, for the vindication of *Christ,* who suffers when Justice is a sufferer. We have a Law too, and by that Law, I ought not to plead, not to be tried, not to be judged.

The Laws of *England* were not unknown, but mispractised, when the Barons fought King *John* into a consent to the (not new making, but) restorement of the ancient Laws.

And * *Magna Charta* itself is but a confirmation or restitution of the Common Law, and is become the standard by which Laws are reducible, and is the foundation of all other Acts of Parliament.

It hath been at no time dismembered; no part abrogated by any repeal.

It hath been confirmed above thirty times, and commanded as often to be observed and put in execution.

In the Act called *Confirmatio* † *Chartarum,* it is directed to be allowed as the Common Law in judgment, in all points, by all the ‖ Judges and Dispensers of Law, or which have the Law to guide.

It hath in former ages gained an honourable esteem in the old books: ‡ *Charta libertatum communis Libertas Angliæ, Charta de Libertatibus,* &c. these are the Appellations.

It was a *Noli me tangere,* and for seeking a reversal or avoidance of it, *Hubert de Burgh* was sentenced by the Barons, and the sentence confirmed by § King *Hen.* III.

The great *Hugh Spencer,* in the reign of *Edw.* II. was banished, but for rashly counselling against the ** *Encounter la forme de la grande Chartre.*

And to draw downwards yet one King's reign, and to the point to which I would apply; I find in the 42d †† of *Edw.* III. this great Charter was not only barely confirmed and commanded to be kept in all the points, for those are the words; but to prevent any alteration of it, it is enacted, That if any Statute be made to the contrary, that shall be holden for none.

By this ‖‖ *Magna Charta* it is granted, and enacted too; if my Lord *Coke* say true, who saith it is a Statute, as well as a Charter, being made by assent and authority of Parliament; That

No Freeman shall be taken or imprisoned, or be disseised of his freehold, or liberties, or free customs, or be out-law'd, or exiled, or any otherwise destroyed, nor will we pass upon him, nor condemn him, but by lawful judgment of his Peers, and by the Law of the Land.

* Coke [illegible] fol. 80, 81. † 25 Edw. I. cap. 1. ‖ Bracton 414, 431. Fleta lib. 2. cap. 48. lib. 5. cap. 3. ‡ Mirror cap. 2. 18. Britton fol. 177. § [illegible] Rot. [illegible] num. 1. 2. Pro utrius. M. [illegible] ** 14 Edw. II. †† 42 Edw. III. cap. 1. ‖‖ Coke [illegible]

We

We shall sell to no man, nor defer to any man either Justice or Right.

If this be truth and Law, which I have in these particulars premised to you; then, my Lords, give me leave to take notice,

That by that Act by which you are constituted a Court of Justice, you are authorized to try the Freemen of *England*; not *per Pares*, upon or for offences against articles, and the punishment to reach to life, as the major part of any twelve of the Commissioners shall judge to appertain to Justice.

Laying these together, a posting rider may read, that these Laws are diametrically opposite, and consequently inconsistent.

The latter hath its doom inherent by its innate contrariety to the former, and is a building, a superstructure so unsuitable to the foundation, that if it had not a double-edged support, it need no help to be demolish'd, but would fall, I know not whether to say, *sua mole*, or *sua penetitate*.

The Constitutors of this Law are *Gladiis dncti*; and therefore as I am not in opportune place to speak to them, so there is something of danger to speak too freely to them, but, my Lord, your Lordship, as you are in this place, are (I am sure ought to be) like the Escutcheons of Princes, with their adopted supporters, Knowledge and Conscience: and if you are, I am confident you will doubt of your Commission or Warrant to proceed against me, and compel me to preserve an inch of life, by giving away mine and my Countrymen's liberty, in condescending to a Plea and Trial, in this contra-legal way, and by power of this Act.

The Second Argument.

My Lord,

I Shall further beg leave to call to your memory the Petition of Right; which was made the business of the Parliament, at the time when it was preferred, and received the Royal Assent; must never be forgotten by those who hold in esteem the care of Parliaments, and gracious concessions of Kings.

In the Proem, or leading part of that Petition, the Statute of *Magna Charta* is instanced as to this particular, Trial for life by proper Courts, with other the Laws and Statutes, (some of which I have cited, and the rest shall upon another point in their place) and as it is complained, that proceedings had been by Commissioners martial, when and where, if by the Laws and Statutes of the Land they had deserved death, by the same Laws and Statutes also they might, and by no other Laws ought to have been judged; so it is prayed, and accordingly enacted, That no Commissions of like nature may be henceforth issued to any person or persons whatsoever to be executed, &c. and this to prevent, lest by colour of them, any of the subjects should be destroyed or put to death, contrary to the Laws and Franchise of the Land.

My Lord,

1. The Commissioners Martial were not evil in respect of the persons commissioned, being as this power is to you, so those always given to persons of quality and learning; but the evils of them were their proceedings by their own will and opinion, being themselves the Judges and the Jury; offices incompatible and inconsistent with the people's liberties; by the former Laws become their rights. When your Lordships shall read the Act by which you now sit, I am confident you will grant this power to be of the same nature, though not under the same name; and consequently in that petition complained of, in supposition that such might be, and enacted against *in Terminis*; that none such should be.

2. For that you are called by the Act, Commissioners, and yet have no Commission, but the Act itself; whereas you should, in regard you are not a Court of Record in yourselves, have Commissions returnable at a day, into some Court of Record, where your proceedings might be extant and visible, and as you are now constituted, you have a day prefixed to determine in; but that being come, you are to vanish, and your *vestigia* will be as imperceptible to the times and men to come, as the trace of a Swallow in the Air; which is inconsistent with the Honour and Justice of any Kingdom, or of any Christian Commonwealth.

For that you have only by this Act, a bare and single power to adjudge, and cause execution to be done, in case you shall judge it to appertain to Justice; but you have no power, if you think it appertain to Justice, to acquit, and upon acquittal to discharge the person tried, as is the Law expresly in my * Lord *Dyer*, and in the Year-book of *Edw.* IV. grounded upon the Statute of † *Hen.* VI. 14 of his reign, *cap.* 1. That

Justices of *Nisi prius* (who are Commissionary Justices) shall have power of all the cases of Felony and of Treason, to give their judgment, as well where a man is acquit of Felony, and of Treason; as where he is thereof attainted, at the day and place where the Inquisition, Inquest, and Jury shall be taken; and then from thenceforth to award execution to be made by force of the same judgments, which in an acquitted man's case can only be an enlargement.

But, my Lord, you have only power, if you can, to reach my life, if in your opinion deserving it. but not to reach me out of prison; so that if you kill me not here with the sword of Justice, you must leave me in worse hands, to be buried alive in restraint and want.

Which all is against the Laws of Nature and Nations, and particularly of this land. that are all so balanced and poised, as that they have equal regard to the delivery and freeing the Innocent, as to the Condemnation of the Nocent.

And *Isidore* in his Etymologies says of a Law, thus,

Erit autem lex honesta, justa, possibilis, secundum naturam & consuetudinem patriæ, loco, temporique conveniens, necessaria, & utilis; manifesta quoque, ne aliquid in captionem per obscuritatem captione contineat, nullo privato commodo, sed pro communi civium utilitate conscripta.

And as Laws should be, so should Courts and the Dispensers of Laws be.

But, my Lord, if this Court must be granted to be a Court, yourselves can make no more of it than a Court, *ex parte*, and set up to serve a particular end with the privation of the common utility and liberty, howsoever ushered in with a preamble of another stile, of preservation of peace, and prevention of war; but *Thucidides* will tell you, my Lord, in his fourth book, That

Turpius est his qui impia tenent insidiâre honesto prætextu, quam insidiosâ malevolentiâ uti; nam violentia videtur aliquid Juris habere, propter potentiam à fortunâ datam, sed fraus tantum ab injustitiâ oritur.

The Third Argument.

BUT, my Lord, if your Lordship be in your judgment and conscience satisfied, that the Act itself, in and as to its constitution, is good and valuable, and impowereth you sufficiently to proceed against me some way; then *Argumenti ergo dato, sed non juris ergo concesso*, that it is a Law, or an Act, and that all those Ordinances are out of doors; yet I pray your Lordship's leave, that I may make evident to your Lordship, that you are not hereby constituted a Court capable, in defect of the very letter of the Act, to pass upon any man, and consequently not upon me, in matter of life, or where life may be the concernment.

1. For Reason, you are not constituted a Court of Record ‡, which is absolutely necessary, having life and forfeiture of lands in your charge.

First, For the State, that they may have an account, (not in their Council-Chamber, but upon Record) what is become of the matter in issue, and of the person put upon his Trial.

2. For the Freeman of *England*, that in case he be acquitted of the crime wherewith he shall stand charged before this Court, he might at all times resort to the Record, upon any new question for the same fact, in any other Court holding Pleas of that nature, by which Record to plead his Auterfoys Acquit, and to make his defence, as also to preserve his estate, *si non legalement acquitte en le Poulteres's case*, 9. *R. Benegist demant acquittal nul req. si non de Record.* as also my benefit, a writ of Conspiracy.

To come nearer our own times, the like cause to complain, and the same redress is given in the Act § for abolishing of the *Star-Chamber*, upon the grounds and reasons drawn from these Laws; the Innovations and Invadings, upon which (as being fundamentals) was a great part of the substance of the grand remonstrance, committed to the whole World against the late King by the press: The ‖ charges against the Earl of *Strafford*, and the Archbishop of *Canterbury*.

The Interest of the Subject in these Laws was cryed up to be so precious, as that it had influence even to the absolving of all old Oaths, and the imposing of new, and to bring to adventure estate, and life, and soul, rather than to be usurped, or in the least intrenched upon.

Four ** several Declarations of the present Parliament have entitled the subject to them, and to the benefit of the ordinary Courts of Justice, as their birth-right. They have owned the preservation of them to be the cause of the war, and the ends of their affairs managed by their Swords or Councils; and God's curse is by them imprecated, in case they should ever decline the ends.

My Lord,

We have the Parliament's word and †† promise, not to interrupt the course of Justice in the ordinary Courts.

And in the ordinance of *Non-addresses* to the late King, they say, *Though they lay the King aside*, yet they will govern by the Laws, and not interrupt the course of Justice in the ordinary Courts thereof.

My Lord,

I am entitled to all these Laws, and these Promises and Declarations; and if this Court proceed against me, those notwithstanding, (the ordinary Courts of Justice being open and unobstructed) I am robb'd, and divested of them all, and in me the Freemanry of *England* are all despoiled, and may the Parliament's will (according to this precedent) despoilable; and may with Mr. *Stampford*, in his Pleas of the Crown, take up this saying, it will serve for a lamentation, *Misera servitus est, ubi jus est vagum & incognitum.*

Attorney-General *Prideaux*. Take heed you scandal not the Court.

The Fourth Argument.

THomas Aquinas (who, though a Papist, is not the less worthy to be vouched, where not Religion, but Policy, is the thing in question) saith, That *Lex est regula & mensura actuum agendorum vel omittendorum*, not *Actorum* and *Omissorum*.

And St. Paul says, *Rom.* vii. 7. *Concupiscentiam nesciebam, nisi lex diceret non concupisces.*

My Lord, your authority is in two several places to proceed against, as Traitors, such who have broken articles before they were made, viz.

Whosoever hath, or shall plot, contrive, or endeavour, &c.

Whatsoever Officer, &c. hath, or shall desert their trust, &c. shall die without mercy.

And thus, my Lord, the end of Laws and Law-making is perverted; which are not merely to punish offenders, but to prevent offences, which amongst Christian Men was never otherwise done, but by way of premonition; by Laws first interdictory, and then subpenatory.

The Earl of *Strafford* did (and very reasonably) take it unkindly, and so express'd himself upon his Trial, that a neglected Law should lie moulding amongst old parchments 200 years unused and unexercised, and be at last brought out to measure his past actions by; or to use his own words, *To be like a Coal raked up in the ashes*, to be at pleasure blown into a flame, and to make him and his family the first fuel to feed it. Truly if he had seen these articles (as he felt after somewhat like them), he would have cried out, and but modestly enough, that it is not mending of the faults, but the destruction of the person, which is manifestly designed in these Articles of *Retrospection.*

Disusage of Law, is some excuse for him who falls into a transgression; but the *non-existence* of a Law is a justification of the greatest offence.

And, my Lord, as you are to look backward to actions done before the Law made, so you are to take cognizance of offences against two former Acts, which make the Crimes therein certain in the matters of fact, fault and punishment; and if they be Laws, they must be deemed part of the Laws of the land, and definable and dispensable by the ordinary Courts of the land, in cases criminal: for extraordinary Courts

* Peacock's case, Dyer fol 120. 10 Edw. IV. fol. 19.

† 14 Hen VI. c. 1. Oath of a Juror.

‡ Withers and Davey's case, 35 Eliz. 14 Fort. Reurda.

§ 17 Car. Act for abolishing the *Star-Chamber*.

‖ Articles contra Strafford. Art. 1, 2 partes 1.

** Declar Dec 15. 1641 Jan. 17. 1641. July 12 1642. Oct. 2. 1642.

†† Declars April 17. 1646. Jan. 1648.

of

of that kind, have long since (even by the Parliament, of which this is the surviving part) been denied.

And although it is true, that when some particular fact is committed by some one or more particular persons against the Laws criminal, it often falls (and properly enough) that especial Commissions of Oyer and Terminer are for some urgent and expedient reason issued to try the matter and men; yet those Commissions do not restrain the Commissioners to proceed only against those persons, and upon those particular crimes, which the common fame hath rendred *hac vice*, to be triable; but run in general terms, and with general enablement to try all manner of Treasons, Felonies, *&c.*

And the Reason is,

1. For that it might possibly fall out, that a grand Jury will not find the bill against *John a Stile*; and if not, the Commissioners are sent down without their errand, if only directed to try *J. S.*

2. It may fall out, that where there are Treasons or Felonies committed by *J. S.* they may be accompanied with misprisions and misdemeanours in *J. O.* And if the particular crime of Treason, and the particular person of *J. S.* be only authorized to be enquired of, then the Commissioners can do but half their work: and therefore this commissionary power of yours, my Lord (the ordinary Courts being not obstructed, and you limited to particulars), is so far against the Common Law and Usage, that it is against common and vulgar reason; and (pardon that I must say it) savours more of a Snare, than of a Law; and more of a warrant of arbitrary execution, than of an enablement, to and for a judicial and legal Proceeding or Trial.

The Fifth Argument.

My Lord,

IN all Courts of Justice, as there is supposed to be an equality intended to such as shall fall under their cognizance and inquiry, which is a principle of morality innate, as well as a practical policy; so there have always in this Nation, at least beyond memory, or indeed record to the contrary, been certain Oaths obligatory, and of indifference administered to persons either enquiring of, or passing judgment against, or upon the subjects in all cases whatsoever. And the same thing is but necessary in your Lordships and this Court to be done (if at all you will proceed in so weighty a matter as life), against which I make this exception,

1. If you are at all sworn, you are not sworn *in conspectu*; and if you will be my Jury and my Judges also, I ought to have satisfaction that you are so sworn. Had you been only my Judges, and constituted after the ordinary manner, and to ordinary ends, I would have taken your being sworn for granted.

2. If you are sworn, and to no other words of Oath than what are comprized in the Act (which myself and all men else will easily believe you are not), then you are not sworn to any manner of equality.

The words are,

You * shall swear, that you shall well and truly, according to the best of your skill and knowledge, execute the several powers given unto you by this Act.

I beseech your Lordship, † that I may compare these words with the Oaths of Judges in *England*, when it was a Kingdom.

The words pertinent are only these,

You ‡ shall swear, that well and lawfully you shall serve our Lord the King, and his People in the office of Justice, *&c.*

And that you deny to no man common right, by the King's letters, or none other man's, nor for none other cause, *&c.*

I § *A. B.* do swear, that I will do equal right, *&c.* according to my best wit, cunning and power, after the Laws and Customs of the Land, and the Statutes thereof made, *&c.*

My Lord, these will concern you as my Judges, to consider how little the stiles agree, and how far your Oath is in respect of these unobligatory, and consequently unsatisfactory, to the persons which are or shall be concerned.

1. As to the first, yours contains no such words of equality.

2. As to the second Oath, yours hath such words as skill and knowledge, holding some resemblance with those of wit, cunning and power. But, my Lord, if your words were as well usher'd, and as well paged as those, it were some satisfaction, *viz.*

To do equal right, according, *&c.*

After the Laws and Customs of the Land, and the Statutes thereof made.

My Lord, as you are my Triers also, as well as my Judges, I beseech you to observe the Oath of a Juror, and the difference in sense (in letter, I know for the dignity sake it ought to differ).

You ‖ *shall well and truly try, and true deliverance make between our sovereign Lord the King, and the prisoner at the bar,* &c. I presume it is still the same (*mutatis mutandis*).

Truly, my Lord, when I look upon your enablement to try the matters and persons, which, and whom you are to try: you have power to destroy, and not to save; though to spare, yet not to acquit, or discharge; and your obligation by Oath to execute that power, according to your best skill and knowledge. I must needs say, and it is apparent, that when you have destroyed me, you have discharged all the duty that man can exact from you (though God will have a better reckoning), and instead of being tried by sworn Jurors, and adjudged by sworn Justices, myself and all who are or may fall into my condition, are to be tried by our sworn adversaries, I might have said sworn enemies. and we cannot in reason expect more Justice, than when the Son lays the wager, the Mother keeps stakes, and the Father is Judge, in a point of controversy.

More and better you may do, more or better we cannot by any light of reason expect.

The Sixth Argument.

BUT, my Lord, if all this be but a wind against a Rock, and move you to no declining of the exercise of your power, though against my right; yet certainly, my Lord, where your power and my right may be consistent, you will not stretch your power to the taking away my right; but rather by giving me my right, magnify your power.

This I may reasonably expect.

It is my right (granting you to be my Judges) to be tried by my Peers, the good men of my neighbourhood, and it is in your power (if your power be not inward) to try me so.

That this is my right, I must revisit ** *Magna Charta, Nisi per legale Judicium parium suorum.*

The Law of *Ed.* I. having confirmed the great Charter, †† saith, 'And 'we will, that if any judgment hereafter be given contrary to the point of 'the Charter aforesaid, by the Justices, or by any other our Ministers that 'hold Plea before them against the points of the Charter, it shall be un'done and holden for nought.'

And upon this very Law or Clause, a writ of error was brought by the ‡‡ Earl of *Lancaster*, for the misattainder of his brother, whose heir he was; and in that the points were two, and upon them both, judgment given for a reversal.

1. *Quod non fuit araniatus & ad responsionem positus tempore pacis, eo quod cancellaria, & aliæ curiæ Regis fuerant apertæ, in quo lex fiebat unicuique prout fieri consuevit.*

Attinctus.

2. *Quod condemnatus sive adjudicatus fuit absque araniamento seu responsione, seu legali judicio parium, contra legem, & contra tenorem Magnæ Chartæ.*

The like reversals, and upon the like reasons, have been had,

In the §§ Count *de Arundel*'s case.

In Sir *John* of *Lee*'s case,

It is provided, that no man from thenceforth should be attached by any accusation, nor forejudged of life, nor of limb, nor his lands, *&c.* against the form of the great Charter, and the Law of the land ‖‖.

My Lord,

Our fathers saw a Parliament (and reaped the blessing of it), which was called *Benedictum Parliamentum* (which hath circumscribed the loose interpreters of Treasons to a standard, and not left it to be *Individuum vagum*); and there it is said, that persons guilty of High-Treason (and my charge is not for less) must be provably attaint of open deed, by people of their own condition.

And again it is accorded, assented and established, that from henceforth none shall be taken by petition, or suggestion made to the King, or his Council, unless it be by indictment, or presentment of his good and lawful people of his neighbourhood where such deeds be done, in due manner, or by process made by writ original at the Common Law; Nor *** that none be ousted of his franchises, or of his freehold, unless he be duly brought to answer, and fore-judged of the same by the course of Law; and if any thing be done against the same, it shall be redressed, and holden for none.

It is assented and established (for the good governance of the Commons), that no man be put to answer without presentment before Justices, or matter of Record, or by due Process and Writ original, according to the old Law of the Land; and if any thing from henceforth be done contrary, it shall be void in Law, and holden for error.

My Lord,

That it is my right to be tried by a Jury of twelve men *de vicineto*, is evident; and it is as evident, that if you otherwise proceed with me (if Law were not out of fashion), you would but weave *Penelope*'s web, and one day's judgment would be unravel'd by the next day's writ of error.

But after-games for life are dangerous; and for estate, I have no great cause to be solicitous: but my right is my duty to preserve, as in relation to myself, and my honour to keep it, if it may be, from being in my precedent taken also from my Countrymen, the Freemen (if any such be now) of *England*, who have equal reason, though they may be wanting (some of them) of the same reasons wherewith to defend it.

That your Lordship may proceed by Jury, for aught is said, or contained in your Act to the contrary;

1. I pray consider the before-recited Laws are all unrepealed; and therefore if this Law intend to oppose those Laws, it should have repealed them, or at least have afforded a slight *Non-obstante*, or have given the subject the comfort of a *hac vice tantum*, that we might not have thought ourselves robb'd of all, but only plundered of a part of our right for necessity and experience sake, or at least have given us the favour of the Earl of *Strafford*'s Act, that it should never be drawn into example. but I am sure in this Act, that proceeding against him is super-exampled.

2. I desire you would consider your qualification; you are made Commissioners, and that of Oyer and Terminer, and those are not Proceeders in their own proper, natural and habitual constitution and practices, upon and according to their own judgments in matters of fact: you are in these words, *viz.*

Required to hear and determine, *&c.* constituted Commissioners of Oyer and Terminer.

3. You are authorized to proceed to Trial, Condemnation and execution, *&c.* but you are not restrained to the manner of such proceedings to Trial exclusively, as to Trial *per pares*, but left to do the manner of the Trial, as well as the judgment or execution, as you, or the major part of you, or twelve of you shall judge to appertain to Justice: And if such major part shall think fit to proceed by presentment and Jury, doubtless such your proceeding is no *Præmunire* against the power given you by the Act; but it is justifiable to fall within the letter of the Act, and that without a strained construction.

4. And if when you may lawfully (I mean by your own Law, if, *Argumenti ergo*, it be granted a Law) try me by a Jury, and will not, then, my Lord, pardon me, that I must aver, that you take from me, and in me from the commonalty of *England*, three great privileges, franchise and rights, to which I and they are, by the known, ancient, and unabrogated, unrepealed, and constantly practised Laws, entitled; which will be neither equitable nor honourable for you to do.

1. You take away the benefit of challenge, which I might make to a Jury or Jurors.

And that is contrary to my right, which is given me by the ††† Common Law, *in favorem vitæ*, to challenge in case of High-Treason, (for

* The Oath of the Commissioners. † 18 Edw. III. ‡ Oath of Justices. § Dalton's Justice of Peace, fol. 13. ‖ Oath of a Juror. ** Magna Charta, 9 Hen III 29. †† 25 Edw. I. cap. 1 and 2. ‡‡ Pasch. 39. Edw. III. John of Gaunt's case. §§ 4 Edw. III. Num. 13. Rot. Parl 42 Edw. III. Num. 23. Rot Parl. 5 Edw. III. 9. ‖‖ 52 Edw. III. 2 cap. 4. ejusd. *** The like in effect in 28 Edw. III. 3. 37 Edw. III. 18. 42 Edw. III. 3. ††† Stamp pl. Cor. T. Chaleng fol. 150.

I go to no less) thirty-five peremptorily, and for reason of challenge *sans* number.

This was judged in 32 *Hen.* VI. abridged by * *Fitz-Herbert, fol.* 26. *per challeng.* where eight Jurors were sworn, and the rest challenged, a new return made; and those eight returned, and though formerly allowed and sworn, yet challenged, and adjudged good.

The like allowed in *Hill.* 1 *Jac.* in the cases of Sir *Walter Raleigh* and *Brook*.

If this benefit were allowed me, my Lord, to except or challenge the whole Court, who are in number and quality my Triers, as a Jury are, I should not need to be peremptory in my challenge, being furnished with abundant reason.

(Here he was interrupted by *Keeble*, who said, those Statutes and Cases were out of date now).

My Lord,

A Jury of *Middlesex* will be no more nor less, if what I am accused of, to have endeavoured, should take effect, and therefore are not less concerned: I cannot say the same of the Court (or if I should, I should not be believed), and he that but whispers against † *Diana* at *Ephesus*, makes all the Craftsmen his enemies.

2. The second benefit and right, which by denying me a Trial *per pares*, you take from me, is the benefit of seeing, hearing, and counter-questioning the witnesses produced against me; which, in such way of Trials, ought to be *viva voce*.

That such is the Law, ‡ Mr. *Stamford* averreth in his Pleas of the Crown. And,

In Treason, two *sufficient* witnesses by the Statute ** of *Edw.* VI. are requisite; *sufficient* in relation to their quality, and to the fulness of their testimony.

Sir †† *Edward Coke* (an Author as authentick as any) puts this for Law in his expositions of the words in the Statutes for Treason, *Provablement attaint*; because the punishment was great, the proof should be punctual; not upon presumptions or inferences, or strains of wit, but upon good and sufficient proofs. And this he makes good by the Authority of ‖‖ *Stamford*, and the several Statutes of *Philip* and *Mary*, and of Queen *Elizabeth*, and of *Edw.* VI.

Now, my Lord, an evidence either taken in writing, as the person will voluntarily give it, or cautiously taken as the examiner will ask it (who is not sworn to take it indifferently, no more than the framers of the questions are to propound them fairly), may be a seeming fair, apposite, and a full testimony; or concerning the person giving testimony, or concerning the *modus*, the *ubi*, the *quando*, &c. the whole laid together may prove either nothing, or a malicious thing.

The case of Sir *Thomas More*, Lord-Chancellor, accused for bribery, is common; and I hope, if mine have fair play, it will prove no worse.

3. The third and last right and privilege you take from me, is the main of all the rest, and to the making of which (as it should be made up) all the rest are but conducing, and leading; that is, of a fair verdict.

My Lord,

By a Jury a verdict passeth from all, or not at all; and one knowing and conscientious man may preserve that innocent man, whom eleven either ignorant or careless men would destroy.

This Court's sentence is to be stated by number of voices, and some of them possibly not judging their own judgments, but concurring where their opinion of another's judgment shall lead them; which, as it was the great evil of the late Court of *Star-Chamber*, so wheresoever it is used (in Trials of Life especially) it is and can be no other than an evil.

My Lord,

By and from a Jury a verdict passeth before their discharge upon their necessary affairs, nay affairs of nature; and therefore they will give it both the righter, because their evidence is fresh in memory, without the intervention of other matters, as also for that they are without opportunity to be perverted by money or friendship. If this Court receive the evidence to-day, they may at any time (before the 29th of *September* next) give their sentence; for *vere-dictum* I never expect but from a Jury: and in the mean time, how much their own affairs may put the remembrance of me out of their heads, and how much the State's power may put my safety out of their hearts, I have just cause to suspect. For fear, I will not, being resolved never to be in love with that life which the Common Law of *England* cannot protect; and had rather die the Law's Martyr, than live the State's Slave.

The Close.

My Lord,

I have said; and now it only remains that I tell your Lordship, that I desire you to take into consideration what I have said; and that you would not suddenly, but deliberately give your judgment, whether I ought to plead before you as Judges, and to the charge in the Articles, and not in a Presentment or Indictment? Whether to be tried without a Jury, and condemn'd upon evidence unseen? Which this is (and I desire it may be recorded). As I do not now wilfully refuse to plead or answer, but offer my reasons for the suspension of my Plea, until your judgment in the points be known and pronounced, so, if I be in them over-ruled, I shall then give such answer to the charge, as shall become a man in my condition.

Fiat voluntas Dei, modo in ruinâ meâ.

Eus. Andrewe.

3. 7. 2. 1650.

Here the Attorney-General *Prideaux* put a stop to Mr. *Andrewe*, telling him, that the Court was not at leisure to take notice of those Law-Cases, but of his confession; *That he had an affection to act, though nothing acted, was sufficient Treason, and for that affection he deserved death.* And thereupon the Court pronounced sentence against him, That he should be hang'd, ‡‡ drawn and quarter'd. but on his Petition to the Parliament, an Act pass'd authorizing Commissioners of the High Court of Justice to issue their warrant for the beheading him according to his Petition.

Col. *Andrewe.* If I be over-rul'd by the Court, that I must either answer or be sentenced for my wilfulness, then I move that I may have a Copy of my charge, and a day assigned me to deliver my Answer under my hand.

Upon these Reasons:

1. If the Court proceed upon Articles, they cannot in reason conceive that I can plead the general issue to particulars; for in so doing, in case I be convicted of any one Article, I shall receive the doom of all.

2. For that *de facto* some of the Articles may be true, yet *de modo* they may not be available against me; and upon the general issue, I shall not be received to qualify fact with circumstance, and so instead of being allowed the freedom of my defence, which is allowed to every Thief in *Newgate*, I shall be tried and snared by such confession, or proof, as will serve the turn of my prosecutors, and not preserve myself, by making myself and actions understood.

The Articles are of several kinds and crimes; and as one single Plea will not be applicable to them all, so it is but requisite that I have a Copy of them, to give thereby to each one its proper Answer; which though in Indictments is not allowed, yet in this way of proceeding was never denied in the most arbitrary Courts.

The Council-Table gave a charge, and received answer in writing, in cases of Contempt against themselves or commands.

The *Star-Chamber* afforded the Defendant a Copy of the Bill, and liberty to examine and cross-examine witnesses, in case the fact charged were denied by the Answer.

The High-Commission the like, by their Articles and Proceedings upon them.

My Answer, if not in writing, may either not be understood, or misapprehended, or mis-set down by the Clerk, to my prejudice.

If this be denied me, then I must conclude they intend to wipe off my head, with the smooth glazed sword of pretended Justice; and must apply myself to my memory, in reference to the charge, and shall hear it read, which by my own knowledge of what has passed between the State and me, I may conjecture; and therefore prepare these following heads to help my memory, which in a case of so much concernment, is not totally to be relied upon.

First, As to what may be alledged against me in general terms, as a disaffected person, an oppugner of the State, or otherwise, &c.

There are two things which draw subjection, and oblige persons to a Commonwealth.

(1.) Protection in the State.

(2.) Personal engagement, or fealty in the subject.

(1.) Protection I have received none, but stand in the condition of a proscribed person.

1. Estate (if any) sequestrable, and not permitted by the Laws of the Nation to vindicate it.

2. Calling taken away, which the *Turk* would not have done, had he been Conqueror.

3. Dwelling not permitted where I can subsist, but where I may be obnoxious to want, and to the State's infliction of punishment, when they shall take occasion to repeat upon me any thing they shall call a crime, in reference to my past actions for the late King, and my Sovereign.

4. Right I can have none, unless I will damn my soul to preserve my estate, or repair my wrong by a contra-legal and contra-evangelical engagement.

This was sufficient reason, owned and justified by the Parliament, for their substraction of obedience, ὁ Βασιλεὺς [illegible] by their § Declarations, and Ordinances.

(2.) Fealty or personal engagement I have given none, *viz.*

1. I have not taken the protestation of *May* 1642.

2. I have not taken the solemn Oath and Covenant; yet if I had, I might have justified my actions by them.

3. I have not taken the negative Oath, because my Oath of Allegiance (from which no man can absolve me) is a negative to that, &c.

4. I have not taken the present engagement, much more against my Oath of Allegiance than the negative Oath.

If I had had so little conscience as to have taken them, I would have had so much as to have kept them; and the State cannot in reason expect from me, or any other, that we should take a second, when we see no conscience made of keeping the first; nor to take a third, the first and second being broken, without other dispensation than power, which, like *Alexander*'s sword, cuts the *Gordian* knot which it cannot untie.

Neither hath any man assurance, if he should take the last engagement, that he should have liberty to keep it longer than the fancy of the State held to the now new fashion of Government.

And therefore I stand clear as a down-right subject of *England*, to stand or fall by the Common Laws of *England*, and if they will deny me that, they deny me my Birth-right, which is equally right to [illegible], and no more than to deny me my estate, my calling, my abode, my means of right.

Secondly, As to my action at *Lichfield*, I justify myself,

1. By the late King's Commission, which my accuser knows I had, and under which he was by the same King constituted my Major.

2. *** What was done, was so done, when he who gave me the Commission was in being, and oppressed by injurious imprisonment, and what I did, was in order to his inlargement from his thraldom, and restorement to his lawful power; which was that to which my duty as a subject, by my Oath of Allegiance did bind me in general terms, and the duty of my qualification laid me under a particular obligation.

It was done before the now reputed Parliament were, or pretended to be the supreme authority of the Nation, or had assumed the power of Government, or were fram'd into a State, and consequently I am not answerable to them for any opposition to them, further than the Common

* Poyning's case. † Acts cap. 19. ‡ Stam. P. C. fol 163, 164. Stat. Philip and Mary 1, and 2. cap. 10. ** 1 Edw. VI. cap. 11. Clause ult. †† Coke 3 Inst. fol. 12. ‖‖ Stam. P. C. 164, 89. 1 Ed. VI. cap. 12. 1 and 2 Philip and Mary, 10 11. 1 Edw. VI and 16 Eliz. 1.

‡‡ [illegible]

§ Declaration [illegible] Ordinance of [illegible] in June 1642.

*** [illegible] that the Subjects [illegible] by reason of their allegiance, to serve the Prince for the time being in his Wars for the defence of him and the [illegible] against every rebellion or foreign power, within the land or without; and ought not to suffer in life, member, estate or otherwise for so doing.

Law binds to Parliaments without their head and hand, or defective in their members; and as to fuch offence (if it be one) this Court is not qualified to take any cognizance.

Thirdly, As to the defign concerning the furprife of the Ifle of *Ely*, it was but a bare difcourfe or communication, and no formal defign laid, agreed unto, nor perfon engaged in it, fo much as by promife.

And in cafes of confpiracy againft the Lives of Kings there were fome Statutes made, that very words and communication fhould be reputed Treafon; but all repealed, or expired;

And not thought fit by wifdom of Law-makers (having indifputable power to make Laws) to be revived fince the days of Queen *Mary*, notwithftanding thofe very many Treafons hatched and defigned againft Queen *Elizabeth*, and King *James*, &c.

If in the higheft point of Treafon, communication be not Treafon againft lawful Princes, certainly an affection, where the offence (fuch as it is) is of a far inferior nature of itfelf, fo it had a far inferior object, or fubject, concerning whom fuch difcourfe was holden.

Fourthly, As to my fuppofed correfponding with the King, the Lord *Hopton*, and the Earl of *Cleveland*, (if true) it was fo long fince, as that it falls not within compafs of this Court's Commiffion to try, *being confined to infant matters of a year old*, and my charge not exhibited to the Court of Juftice, before *Monday* the 15th of *July*. My laft letter received from Lord *Hopton*, bears date at the *Hague*, 18th or 28th of *June*, and was received in two days into *Suffex*.

Fifthly, As to the drawing, figning, or fealing of the engagement, it confifts of feveral branches.

That *de facto* I did it, and muft not deny it, becaufe I have confeffed it, which was more than needed, to them who knew it without enquiry; for I dare aver, that they had their inftrument by them employed, and cherifh'd in betraying me to it: And have fome years paft had a man in my bofom to watch me and my motions, which I did affirm to the Lord-Prefident, and he not denied it, but faid, it was no more than did become any State to do, who had fo much caufe to hold an active man in fufpect, as they had me, having never come in, and laid down the Cudgels, but held to my principles, and was ready upon every occafion to take fire.

And this I will prove, if I have legal (or becaufe that word is worn out of ufe), fair dealing from the Court. And,

Out of that I may juftly infer, what will be vifible enough, that it is the State's Act, and but my Confent, and they in no danger of me, but that I fhould preferve myfelf from their new Laws, into the lapfe of which I was not otherwife, or by any other action fallen.

As to the parts of it,

1. It confifts of an Oath of fecrecy.
2. An owning of King *Charles* II. to be fuch.
3. A refolution to endeavour to make him fuch.
4. A crimination of the State, under the names of rebels, and oppofers, who would not have him to be fuch.

To thefe, as they are rank'd,

The Oath of fecrecy hath relation only as to the not difcovering the coengagers in that refolution, and the refolution itfelf being not Treafon, the Oath of keeping fecret that refolution is not greater than the thing refolved.

1. The thing refolved was to endeavour, but was not an actual endeavouring.

2. If it were an actual endeavouring, yet it can only be fuppofed, that it muft be endeavoured by a war to be levied; and the endeavour to levy a war never actually levied, is not Treafon againft the King, againft whom only, and his relations, by our old Laws, which are Laws, a Treafon can be committed; and Petty-Treafon I am not accufed for.

That a bare intention, refolution, or engagement to levy a war is not Treafon, I refer myfelf to my * Lord *Coke*, who tells us, (and he is a man of credit) in his Book (printed and allowed for Law by the Houfes when they were two) that a confpiracy (and this engagement amounts not to fo much, but rather to an intention only to confpire) to raife a war, (as hath been faid, and fo refolv'd) is no Treafon by the † Act of *Edw.* III. until the War levied, as within, or to be reached by thofe words in that Law (Overt Act): and if it were not Treafon in thofe words in the original, it falls not within the words of the tranflation of this new-born Law, *viz.* by any open deed.

As to the firft and third branches of the engagement, which are interwoven, I conclude that neither of them, that is to fay, neither the Oath, nor the Refolution, are Treafons either within the old, or the new Laws, either in refpect of the perfons againft whom, or the progrefs made in the thing itfelf.

2. As to the owning of *Charles* II. it falls not within your Law; for that it is not a Publifhing, Proclaiming, or publickly Declaring his Title. The words of the Act are, [*proclaim, declare, publifh, or any way promote*] which promoting is matter of action more than a private owning.

And this by the Oath itfelf was not to be publifh'd, nor could, without publifhing the engagement itfelf, which was contrary to the Oath.

And though it may be objected, that the raifing the war could not be done, but by publifhing his Title, and the Engagement at laft; yet that, if it be granted, was no forwarder than an intendment; no more was this publifhing, and being not done, falls not within your Act.

The crimination of the State is but gueffed at by implication (for they are not named) to be meant, and I believe your Law reaches only to things literal, and not conftructive only; and for the word Rebels, I hope they will not take that to themfelves, and the word Oppofers is a very innocent expreffion, and at the worft is all but a fcandal.

Laftly, Be this engagement what it will, yet the terms upon which I figned and fealed it were fuch, as that it was my act not abfolute, but upon condition, and to be undone and avoided, in cafe of the *non-co-engaging* of others, by the State's decoy affured to be ready to do it; and at whofe inftance, and for whofe fatisfaction, it was pretended to be defired at my hands.

If the Court proceeds by way of Indictment, then I fhall move, that thofe perfons may be confronted, whom in my Narrative, Examinations and Letters I have named; and that I may demand of them, &c.

* Coke 3. Inft. fol. 14, and 38. † 25 Edw. III. cap. 2.

As alfo that Major *Parker* may be produced to be likewife demanded of, as a perfon by me lately, and fince my papers fent to the State, difcovered to be of the Plot to betray me.

If the Court proceed by way of Articles, and upon Examinations taken againft me; I defire, and that is but reafon, that I may examine my defence, as in all Courts, where fuch proceedings were ufed, was allowed.

If it be objected, That it was not ufed in cafes of Treafon, I anfwer, it is true; if they hold the ancient way of Trials, not; but if they proceed this way, it is but juft; and otherwife the Court are at liberty to ufe all means, public or private, to catch me; but I have none to defend myfelf: fo that it appears, that they feek not to do Juftice, but Execution.

And whether they be confronted or examined, thefe queftions are to be propounded, either *viva voce*, or by Interrogatory; and if by Interrogatory, I muft ftand upon a fair way of examination, *viz.*

That fome one from me, as well as one for the State's behalf, may be prefent, and fet down the examinations or depofitions; and that I may have a Copy of them as well againft me, as for me, as well taken already by the State, or to be taken upon my motion.

The Queftions.

1. Whether he knows Major *Barnard*, how long? &c. What communication and correfpondence concerning me, or my actions held between them? Whether he knew of the fuppofed defign againft the Ifle of *Ely*, and of the late engagement? How he knew them, and upon what reafon, and to what end difcovered to him, and by whom?

2. Whether he did inform the State (or any Member of the Council) of them, and how long he hath fo informed?

3. Whether he ever had in his cuftody the engagement under the hands and feals, and my letter to Sir *John Gell*? If fo, where, and whether not at *Gravefend* at my being there? Whether he were fent to watch me, and knew of my being there, before my being apprehended?

The fame queftions (*mutatis mutandis*) to be propounded to *Barnard*; and farther to him, and to *Benfon*, *Holmes*, *Afhley*, *Smith*, as they are marked.

4. Whether he did propound in both defigns to me, or I to him? Whether I fought him, or he me? In what difpofition he found me, upon the time by the Act limited for departure? &c.

5. Whether he were real to me in the particulars of perfons, confederates or money, ready to engage and to be advanced; and if not, then to what end he feigned thefe to me?

6. Whether the letters by him to me produced from *Smith*, and *Thatch* or *Thatcher*, were true, or feigned; and if feigned, to what end, and by whom fet on work?

7. Whether he were fet upon me, to watch my ways and motions? And whether he were not promifed, or did defign unto himfelf profit for the difcovering of me, and fuch whom I fhould bring in?

8. Whether I fram'd, or ever read the faid fuppofed defign? Or was to be *de futuro* acquainted with it?

9. Whether he brought, or I fought *Benfon*, or *Holmes*? And whether confederates with him, or defigned upon by him?

10. Whether my engagement were abfolute, or conditional, and what I fignified at my departure, and upon *Barnard*'s not coming; and where *Barnard* was pretended to be, and where he really was? What promife I had concerning the return of my engagement, in cafe Sir *John Gell* did not engage at *Gravefend*?

11. Whether copies of Letters weekly fhewed to me were real or feigned? And if feigned, why pretended to be real?

12. Whether there were really any *Kentifh*, *Dorfet*, or *Buckinghamfhire* men, and who, confederates? &c.

Thefe preparations formerly made in rough notes, were tranfcribed and put into form, and finifhed the 8th day of *July* 1650, by God's good affiftance; notwithftanding my abundant difadvantages of clofe imprifonment, and want of Books, or Advice; and I commit and fubmit the iffue to God, whom I befeech to fortify my fpirit, and enlarge my underftanding, when they fhall come to be made ufe of, myfelf refolving to be the Law's Confeffor while I live, and (if called to it) to be the Law's Martyr, when I die by the hand of the impending violence, under the fpecious name of Juftice.

Sed terras Aftræa reliquit,
&
Judica me, Domine, ne in furore, &c.

Eus. Andrewe.
8. 7. 2. 1650. *Domini.*

His Exceptions to his Triers.

John Hurft, Efq. a man who hath had his hand in blood, *viz.* Mr. *Bartin Hazelrigge* in a duel, for which arraigned, &c.

A perfon trying, *viz.* a Juror, and in this way of Trial he is fuch, ought to be a Freeman, *viz.* not in perfon, but in his pre-judicating opinion; which he is not, having publifhed that the Refpondent was the greateft Traitor in *England*, and that there was enough under his hand to hang him the Refpondent.

Sir *William Roe*, Captain *John Stone*, two of my Triers, were employed to examine the Refpondent, on the 2d of *July* 1650, and brought with them all the evidence againft him; and therefore in their capacity of my Triers, by the rule in challenges, they are challengeable, and incapable to fit.

But no regard was had to any of his Exceptions, or any Anfwer returned to his Queftions; and he was ordered to be beheaded.

The laft Speech of Col. Eufcebius Andrewe, *on the Scaffold on* Tower-Hill, Auguft 22, 1650.

THE Lieutenant of the *Tower* delivering the Colonel to the Sheriff, faid, He had brought him thus far on his journey. The Colonel replied, I hope I fhall neither tire in the way, nor go out of it.

When he came on the Scaffold (kiffing the block) he faid, I hope there is no more but this block between me and Heaven. After he had been fome while on the Scaffold, he fpake to the people as followeth:

Chriftian

Christian Gentlemen and good People,

Your business here this day is to see a sad spectacle, a man brought in a moment to be unmann'd, cut off in the prime of his years, taken from further opportunity of doing service to Himself, his Friends, the Common-wealth, or especially to God. It seldom happens but upon very great cause, and though, truly, if my general known course of life were enquired into, I may modestly say, there is such a moral honesty, as some may be so forward as to expostulate, why this great judgment is fallen upon me? But know, I am able to give them and myself an answer; and out of this breast, to give a better account of my judgment and Execution, than my Judges themselves, or you. It's God's just displeasure towards me, for my sins long unrepented of; many judgments withstood, and mercies slighted; therefore doth my gracious Father chastise me with this correction, that he may not lose me; and I pray you assist me with your prayers, that this rod may not be fruitless: that when under his rod I have laid down my life, by his staff I may be comforted, and received into Glory.

I am very confident, by what I have heard since my sentence, there are more exceptions made against the proceedings against me, than ever I made, my Triers had a Law, and the validity of that Law is indisputable, for me to say against it, or to make a question of it, I should but shame myself and my discretion. In the strictness of the Law, something is done by me, that is appliable to some clause therein, by which I stand condemned; the means by which I was brought under that interpretation, of that which was not in myself intended maliciously, being testimony given by persons whom I pity, so false, yet so positive, that I cannot condemn my Judges for passing sentence against me according to legal Justice; for equity lies in higher breasts. For my accusers, or rather betrayers, I pity, and am sorry for them; they have committed *Judas*'s crime, I wish and pray for them St *Peter*'s tears; and I wish other people so happy, they may be taken up betimes, before they have drunk more blood of Christian men, possibly, less deserving than myself.

It is true, there have been several addresses made for mercy, and I will lay the obstructions to nothing more than my own sins; and seeing God sees it fit, (I having not glorified him in my life) I shall do it in my death, I am content.

I profess, in the face of God, particular malice to any one of the State or Parliament, to do them a personal injury, I had never, for the cause in which I had a great while waded, I must say, my engagements and pursuance in it, hath laid no scruple upon my conscience; it was upon principles of Law, whereof I am a Professor, and upon principles of Religion, my judgment rectified, and my conscience satisfied, that I have pursued these ways; for which (I bless God) I find no blackness upon my conscience, nor have I put this into the bead-roll of my sins.

I presume not to decide controversies, I desire God to glorify himself in prospering that side that hath right with it, and that you may enjoy peace and plenty here, when I shall enjoy my God.

In my conversation in the world, I do not know where I have an enemy with cause, or that there is a person to whom I have regret; but if there be any whom I cannot recollect, under the notion of Christian men, I pardon them as freely as if I had named them; yea, I forgive all the world, as I desire my heavenly Father for his Christ's sake to forgive me.

For the business of Death, it is a sad sentence in itself, if men consult with flesh and blood: But, truly, without boasting I say it, or if I do boast, it is in the Lord, I have not to this minute had one consultation with flesh about the blow of the Axe, or one thought of it, more than my passport to Glory.

I take it as an honour, and I owe a thankfulness to those under whose power I am, that they have sent me hither to a place, however of punishment, yet of some honour, to die a death somewhat worthy my blood; and this courtesy of theirs hath much helped towards the satisfaction of my mind.

I shall desire God, that those Gentlemen in that sad bead-roll to be tried by the High Court of Justice, that they may find that really there, that is nominal in the Act, *An High Court of Justice, or Court of High Justice*; high in its Righteousness, not in its Severity: no more clouded with the testimony of folks that sell blood for gain. *Father, forgive them, and I forgive them, as I desire thee to forgive me.*

I desire you now to pray for me, and not give over praying until my last moment; that as I have a very great load of sins, so I may have the wings of your prayers assisting those Angels that shall convey my soul to Heaven. And I doubt not but I shall there see my blessed Saviour, and my gallant Master the King of *England*, and another Master which I much honour, my Lord *Capel*; hoping this day to see Christ in the presence of the Father, the King in the presence of him, my Lord *Capel* in the presence of them all, and myself with them, and all Saints, to rejoice for evermore.

Dr. *Swadling*. You have this morning, in the presence of a few, given some account of your Religion, and under general notions or words, have given account of your Faith, Charity and Repentance: (then speaking to the standers-by) if you please to hear the same questions asked here, you shall, that it may be a general testimony to you all, that he dieth in the favour of God.

(To the Colonel.) Now, Sir, I begin to deal with you; you do acknowledge, that this stroke you are by and bye to suffer, is a just punishment laid upon you by God for your former sins.

Col. *Andrewe*. I dare not only not deny it, but dare not but confess it. I have no opportunity of glorifying God more, than by taking shame to myself; and I have a reason of Justice for justifying God in my own bosom, which I have intrusted to yours.

Dr. You acknowledge you deserve more than this stroke of the Axe, and that a far greater misery is due to you, even the pains and torments of Hell, that the Damned there endure.

Col. I know it is due in righteous judgment; but I know again, I have a satisfaction made by my elder brother Christ Jesus, and then I say it is not due; it's due to me, but acquitted by his mediation.

Dr. Do you believe to be saved by that mediation, and no other?

Col. By that, and that only, renouncing all secondary causes.

Dr. Are you truly and unfeignedly sorry before God, as you appear to us, for all these sins that have brought you hither?

Col. I am sorry, and can never be sorrowful enough, and am sorry that I cannot be more sorry.

Dr. If God should by a miracle, not to put you to a vain hope, but if God should, as he did to *Hezekiah*, renew your days, what life do you resolve to lead hereafter?

Col. It is a question of great length, requires a great time to answer; men in such streights would promise great things; but I would first call some friends to limit how far I should make a vow, that I should not make a rash one, and so offer the sacrifice of fools: but a vow I would make, and by God's help endeavour to keep it.

Dr. Do you wish health and happiness upon all lawful Authority and Government?

Col. I do prize all obedience to lawful Government, and the adventuring against them is sinful; and I do not justify myself (whatever my judgment be) for my thus venturing against the present Government; I leave it to God to judge whether it be righteous; if it be, it must stand.

Dr. Are you now in love and charity with all men? Do you freely forgive them?

Col. With all the World freely; and the Lord forgive them, and forgive me, as I freely forgive them.

Dr. You have for some late years laid down the Gown, and took up the Sword, and you were a man of note in these parts where you had your residence; I have nothing to accuse you for want of diligence in hindering the doing of injuries; yet possibly there might be some wrong done by your Officers, or those under you, to some particular men; if you had your estate in your hands, would you make restitution?

Col. The wrongs themselves you bring to my mind are not great nor many; some things of no great moment; but such as they are, my desire is to make restitution, but have not wherewithal.

Dr. If you had ability, you would likewise leave a legacy of thankfulness to Almighty God; something to his poor servants, to his lame members, to his deaf members, to his dumb members.

Col. My will hath been always better than my ability that way.

Dr. Sir, I shall trouble you very little farther; I thank you for all those heavenly *Colloquies* I have enjoyed by being in your company these three days; and truly I am very sorry I must part with so heavenly an associate: we have known one another heretofore, but never to Christianity before; I have rather been a Scholar to learn from you, than an Instructor.

I wish this stage whereon you are made a spectacle to God, Angels and the World, may be a School to all about you, for though I will not diminish your sins, nor shall conceal or hypocrize my own, for they are great ones between God and myself, but I think there are few here have a lighter load upon them than you have, if we consider things well, and I only wish them your repentance, and that measure of faith God hath given you, and that measure of courage you have attained from God, and that constant perseverance God hath crowned you hitherto with.

Col. His Name be praised!

Here the Doctor prayed with him almost a quarter of an hour, after which the Colonel turning himself again to the people, spake as followeth:

One thing more I desire to be clear in; there lieth a common imputation upon the Cavaliers, that they are Papists, and under that name we are made odious to those of the contrary opinion. I am not a Papist, but renounce the Pope with all his dependencies. When the distractions in Religion first sprung up, I might have been thought apt to turn off from this Church to the *Romish*, but was utterly unsatisfied in their Doctrine in point of Faith, and very much as to their Discipline. The Religion I profess, is that which passeth under the name of *Protestant*, though that be rather a name of distinction, than properly essential to Religion: but that Religion found out in the Reformation, purged from all the Errors of *Rome*, in the Reign of *Edw.* VI. practised in the Reign of Queen *Elizabeth*, King *James*, and King *Charles*, that blessed Prince deceased; that Religion, before it was defaced, I am of, which I take to be Christ's Catholick, though not the *Roman* Catholick Religion.

Then he turned himself to the Executioner: I have no reason to quarrel with thee; thou art not the hand that throws the stone: I am not of such estate to be liberal, but here is 3*l.* for thee, which is all I have; now tell me what I lack?

Executioner. Your hair to be turned up.

Col. Shew me how to fit myself for the block.

After which, his doublet off, his hair turned up, he turned himself about to the people, and prayed a good while. Before he lay down to the block, he spake to the people as followeth:

There is none that looks upon me, though many faces, and perhaps different from me in opinion and practice, but hath something of pity in it; and may that mercy that is in your hearts, fall into your own bosoms when you have need of it: and may you never find such a block of sin to stand in the way of your mercy as I have met with.

I beseech you join with me in Prayer. Then he prayed, leaning on the Scaffold, half a quarter of an hour. Having done, he had some private conference with Dr. *Swadling*; then he taking his leave of the Sheriff and his friends, kissing them, and saluting him next him, he prepared himself for the block, kneeling down, said, let me try the block; which he did. After casting his eyes, and fixing them very intentively above, he said, when I say, *Lord* Jesus *receive me*, Executioner then do thy office. Then kissing the Axe, he lay down, and with as much undaunted, yet Christian Courage as possibly could be in man, did he expose his Throat to the fatal Axe, his Life to the Executioner, and commended his Soul into the hands of God, as into the hands of a faithful and merciful Creator, through the meritorious passion of a gracious Redeemer. Saying the fore-mentioned words, his head was stricken off at one blow.

Vera copia exam.

He died very resolutely *.

* Mr *Whitlock* in his Memorials, *page* 47[illegible], says, The High Court of Justice (afterwards) proceeded against Sir *John Gell*, and he was sentenced by the High Court for Misprision of High-Treason, to forfeit his Estate, and to be imprisoned during his Life.

Page 47[illegible] Capt. *Ashley* was sentenced by the High Court of Justice to have his Head cut off, and one *Benson* to be hanged, [illegible] the Commonwealth, in the treasonable engagement of Col. *Andrewe*.

Mr. *Benson* was executed at *Tyburn* (the 7th of Octob. 1650,) according to the Sentence of the High Court of Justice; but in regard that Capt. *Ashley* only [illegible] the engagement, but acted nothing in it, he was pardoned by the Parliament.

XXV. The

XXV. *The Trial of* RICHARD FAULCONER, *at the* King's-Bench, *in* Term. Pasch. 1652. *for* Perjury.

ON the 12th day of *July*, 1652, an Indictment of Perjury was delivered to the Grand-Jury at *Guildhall*, *London*, the Copy of which Indictment was as followeth:

London. *ss.* Be it remembered, that at the general Quarter-Sessions of the public Peace holden for the City of *London*, at the *Guildhall* of the same City, on *Monday* the 12th day of *July*, in the year of our Lord one thousand six hundred and fifty-two, before *John Kenrick*, Mayor of the City of *London*, *Thomas Atkin*, *Thomas Andrewe*, and *Thomas Foot*, Aldermen of the same City, and others their Fellow-Justices, assigned to keep the publick Peace in the City aforesaid; and also to hear and determine divers felonies, trespasses, and other misdemeanors committed within the same City; by the Oaths of *Robert Dawkes*, *John Harvey*, *William Pitcher*, *Pelham Moore*, *George Boddington*, *Thomas Pierson*, *Joseph Ruthe n*, *Samuel Coleman*, *Richard Payn*, *John Drasgate*, *Robert Trolasse*, *Richard Bartholomew*, *John Robinson*, *Robert Alington*, and *Thomas Wilmer*, good and lawful men of the City of *London*, then and there sworn, and charged to enquire for the Keepers of the Liberty of *England*, by the Authority of Parliament, and the Body of the City aforesaid, it is presented that the Bill following is true.

London, *ss.* The Jurors for the Keepers of the Liberty of *England*, by authority of Parliament, upon their Oath do present, That *Richard Faulconer*, of *Westbury*, in the County of *Southampton*, Gent. not having the fear of God before his eyes, but moved and seduced by the instigation of the Devil; and minding and endeavouring to bring the Right Honourable *William* Lord *Craven*, Baron of *Hampstead-Marshal*, in the County of *Berks*, in danger of the loss of his life, and of the sequestration, confiscation, forfeiture of all his Lands, Goods, and Chattels within this Commonwealth of *England*; the 10th day of *February*, in the year of our Lord God, one thousand six hundred and fifty, at the Parish of *Mary-Stanings*, in the Ward of *Cripplegate*, *London*, before *Samuel Moyer*, Esq. *James Russel*, Esq. *Edward Winslow*, Esq. *Josias Barners*, Esq. and *Arthur Squib*, Esq. then being Commissioners for compounding with Delinquents, and for managing of all and every the Estates of Delinquents, and *Popish* Recusants, that the 15th Day of *April*, in the said Year of our Lord, One thousand six hundred and fifty, were, or then after should, be under sequestration, did, upon the Holy Evangelists, corruptly, wilfully, falsely, and maliciously, of his own proper act, consent and agreement, swear, and upon his corporal Oath before the Commissioners aforesaid, on the said 10th day of *February*, in the said Year, one thousand six hundred and fifty, then having power to administer the said Oath, then and there depose concerning the said Lord *Craven*, in these *English* words following; that is to say, that about a fortnight before the conclusion of the Treaty at *Breda*, the Lord *Craven*, the Queen of *Bohemia* and her two Daughters came to *Breda* to the *Scots* King *Charles*, and went not thence till the King went to *Honsla'rdike*, a house of the Prince of *Orange*. That during that time, this Informant saw the Lord *Craven* divers times in presence with the said King, and every Day with the said King at the Court there, he being there with the Queen of *Bohemia*, and her two Daughters, to take their leave (as they said) of the King of *Scots*, before he went to *Scotland*. That several Officers, about thirty in number, made a Petition to the said King, to entertain them to fight for him against the Commonwealth of *England*, by the name of *barbarous and inhuman Rebels* either in *England* or *Scotland* for the recovering of his just rights, and reinstating him in his Throne; and deputed this Informant and Colonel *Drury* to present the said Petition, who indeed drew the same. That when this Informant and some other Officers came to the Court at *Breda*, intending to present the said Petition immediately to the King's hand; but finding the Lord *Craven* very near to him, likewise the Marquis of *Newcastle* (who presented his brother Sir *Charles Cavendish*, to kiss the said King's hand the evening before the said King's departure, who this Informant saw kiss the King's hand accordingly;) the Lord *Wilmot*, the Earl of *Cleveland*, the Queen of *Bohemia*, the Lord *Gerrard*, &c. and a great bustle of business; this Informant, with Colonel *Drury*, applied then selves to the Lord *Craven*, intreating him to present the Petition to the Queen of *Bohemia*, to present it to the King of *Scots*. The said Lord *Craven* taking the Petition and reading the same, chearfully said to Colonel *Drury* and this Informant, *There is the Queen of* Bohemia, *deliver it to her, and I will speak for you.* Upon which they applied themselves to the said Queen; and she presented the Petition; after which, the King of *Scots*, the Lord *Craven*, the Marquis of *Newcastle*, and the Queen of *Bohemia*, with some other Lords, went into a withdrawing Room, where this Informant and company could not enter. But the Lord *Craven* came forth of the withdrawing Chamber, and told this Informant and Company, *That they should receive an Answer from the Queen of* Bohemia *to their Petition, and that he had spoken to the Queen of* Bohemia *in their behalf*: who afterwards came and told this Informant and company, that she had delivered their Petition, and that the King had taken order for it. The next Morning at three of the clock, the King departed, but this Informant and Company had their quarters satisfied by the Princess of *Orange*, according to the said King's order upon their Petition; and thereby to enable them to follow the said King in the prosecution of those wars against the Parliament of *England*, which was the effect of their aforesaid Petition: That this Informant saw the Lord *Craven* very often and familiar with the said King, and enter with the said King into the withdrawing Chamber, and staid there the last Night the said King was at *Breda*, very late. which said Oath was, the said 10th day of *February*, in the year of our Lord one thousand six hundred and fifty, at the Parish and Ward aforesaid, reduced into writing, and taken before the said Commissioners, then having sufficient and lawful power to administer the said Oath, and to take the testimony and depositions of witnesses upon their Oaths in such cases. Whereas in truth neither did the several Officers, or any Officer make a Petition to the said King, to entertain him or them, to fight for him against the Commonwealth of *England*. Nor did several Officers, or any Officer, make a Petition to the said King to entertain him or them, to fight for him against the Commonwealth of *England*, by the name of *barbarous and inhuman Rebels*, either in *England* or *Scotland*; for the recovering of his just Rights, or re-instating him on his Throne: nor deputed he the said *Richard Faulconer*, and Colonel *Drury*, to present the said Petition, in the said Oath mentioned; nor did the said *Richard Faulconer*, with the said Colonel *Drury*, apply themselves to the said Lord *Craven*, intreating him to present the said Petition to the said Queen of *Bohemia* to present it to the said King of *Scots*. Nor did the said *Richard Faulconer*, with the said Colonel *Drury*, intreat him, the said Lord *Craven*, to present the said Petition to the said Queen of *Bohemia*, to present it to the said King of *Scots*. Nor did the said Lord *Craven* take the said Petition, or read the same; nor said unto the said *Richard Faulconer* and Colonel *Drury*, *There is the Queen of* Bohemia, *deliver it to her, and I will speak for you.* Nor did the said Lord *Craven* tell the said *Richard Faulconer* and company, in the said deposition mentioned, that they should receive an answer to their said Petition, or that he had spoken to the Queen *of Bohemia* in their behalf; as the said *Richard Faulconer* in and by the said deposition hath deposed. And so the Jurors aforesaid, upon their Oaths aforesaid, do say, that the said *Richard Faulconer*, in manner and form aforesaid, corruptly, wilfully, falsely, and maliciously, of his own proper act, consent and agreement, did commit wilful, false, and corrupt Perjury; to the great dishonour of Almighty God, and to the great damage, loss and infamy of the said *William* Lord *Craven*, and in contempt of the Laws of this Commonwealth; to the evil example of all others in the like case offending, and against the publick peace, &c.

SADLER.

This Indictment, upon the Testimony then produced upon Oath, was accordingly found by the Grand Jury.

The same day that this Indictment was found, Colonel *Drury*, who had given Evidence to the Grand Jury, repaired to *Whitehall*, to Captain *Bishop* (having been formerly examined by him concerning the Lord *Craven*, and told him, that as he was that morning going down *Holbornhill*, he was served with a *Subpœna* to appear that day at *Guildhall*, *London*; and that he was examined there concerning the Information given by *Faulconer* against the Lord *Craven*: and that after he was sworn before the Lord-Mayor, he gave the same Evidence to the Grand Jury, which he had formerly given to Captain *Bishop* upon his examination. Whereupon the said Captain *Bishop* took the Writ under seal out of his hand, with which he was served to appear, and said to *Dury*, How durst you be examined against the Commonwealth, and not acquaint me first therewith? And said further, Mr. Mayor (meaning the Lord-Mayor) had better have done something else than to have suffered that Indictment to be found; and immediately calls for a Messenger, and commits the said *Drury* to the Custody of one *Middleton*, a messenger to the Council of State; who forthwith carried *Drury* away Prisoner into the *Strand*, to the house of the said *Middleton*, where the said *Drury* was kept by him in strict custody, from *Monday* that the Indictment was found, and the Sessions begun, till *Saturday*, that the Sessions was past; by which restraint of *Drury*, who had *Faulconer*'s own hand-writing to produce against himself; and being otherwise the most material witness against *Faulconer*, there could be no further prosecution upon that Indictment that Sessions.

In *Michael-Term*, course was taken to remove the Indictment by a *Certiorari* into the Upper-bench, to the end the said *Faulconer* might be outlawed for Perjury. The Record being accordingly removed, a *Capias* in order to an Outlawry was taken out against the said *Faulconer*, who for several Sessions before had refused to appear. At last the said *Faulconer* was taken upon the said *Capias*, and carried to *Newgate*, where he lay for some time, but would not appear, nor plead to the Indictment; whereupon the Prosecutors for the Commonwealth were enforced to move the Court for a *Habeas Corpus*, to bring him to the Bar, that he might be enjoined to plead; and accordingly the Court required him to plead; whereupon he pleaded *Not guilty* to the Indictment.

In *Hillary-Term* following, a day was appointed for Trial upon the Indictment, at *Guildhall*, *London*, before the Lord Chief-Justice *Rolls*, where the said Captain *Bishop* and *Faulconer* appeared with their Counsel and Witnesses; and Mr. *Rushworth* also appeared in behalf of the Commonwealth with Counsel and Witnesses, and had given in the Record to have the Jury called: but it so fell out, that a person of Integrity then in Court, who had gotten certain knowledge when and where the said Oath was taken, gave Mr. *Rushworth* notice, that the Oath given to *Faulconer*, was administered unto him at *Whitehall* in *Middlesex*, and not at *Haberdashers-hall* in *London*; and therefore the place being mislaid in the Indictment, a *London* Jury could not find a fact done in *Middlesex*: whereupon Mr. *Rushworth* immediately withdrew the Record for that time, and gave a stop to the Trial.

No time was mis-spent to recover this Mistake; for within two Days a new Indictment was drawn, and preferred to the Grand Jury in *Middlesex* (Sir *Henry Blunt* being Foreman), where the Indictment was found; and was as followeth:

Hillary Term, 1652.

Middlesex. Before this time, that is to say, upon *Tuesday* next after the Morrow of the Purification of the Virgin *Mary*, this same Term, before the Keepers of the Liberty of *England*, by Authority of Parliament, in the Upper-Bench at *Westminster*, by the Oaths of twelve honest and lawful Men, it is presented, That *Richard Faulconer*, late of *Westbury*, in the County of *Southampton*, Gent. not having the Fear of God before his Eyes, but moved and seduced by the Instigation of the Devil; and minding and endeavouring to bring the Right Honourable *William* Lord *Craven*, Baron of *Hampstead-Marshal*, in the County of *Berks*, in Danger of the Loss of his Life, and of the Sequestration, Confiscation, and Forfeiture of all his Goods and Chattels, Lands and Tenements, within this Commonwealth of *England*; the 10th Day of *February*, in the Year of our Lord God, one thousand six hundred and fifty, at *Whitehall*, in the Parish of *Martins in the Fields*, in the County of *Middlesex*, before *Samuel Moyer*, Esq. *James Russel*, Esq. *Edward Winslow*, Esq. *Josias Barners*, Esq. and *Arthur Squib*, Esq. then being Commissioners for compounding with Delinquents, and for managing of all and every the Estates of Delinquents, and Popish Recusants, that the 15th Day of *April*, in the said Year of our Lord God, one thousand six hundred and fifty, were, or then after should be under Sequestration, did, upon the Holy Evangelists, corruptly, wilfully, falsely, and maliciously, of his own proper Act, Consent, and Agreement, swear, and upon his corporal Oath, before the Commissioners aforesaid, on the said 10th Day of *February*, in the said Year one thousand six hundred and fifty, then having sufficient and lawful Power to administer the said Oath, and to take the Testimony and Depositions of Witnesses upon their Oaths in such Cases, then and there deposed, That several Officers, about thirty in Number, made a Petition to the *Scots* King, *Charles*, to entertain them to fight for him against the Commonwealth of *England*, by the Name of *barbarous and inhuman Rebels*, either in *England* or *Scotland*, for the recovering of his just Rights, and re-instating him in his Throne. And did also then and there, corruptly, wilfully, falsely, and maliciously, before the said Commissioners, swear, that the said Officers deputed him, the said *Richard Faulconer*, and Colonel *Drury*, to present the said Petition; who, as the said *Richard Faulconer*, then and there, corruptly, wilfully, falsely, and maliciously, before the said commissioners did swear, indeed drew the same; and did also then and there, corruptly, wilfully, falsely, and maliciously, before the said Commissioners, swear, that he the said *Richard Faulconer*, with Colonel *Drury*, applied themselves to the Lord *Craven* (meaning the aforesaid *William* Lord *Craven*), intreating him to present the said Petition to the Queen of *Bohemia*, to present it to the King of *Scots*; and did also then and there, corruptly, wilfully, falsely, and maliciously, before the said Commissioners, swear, That the said Lord *Craven* taking the said Petition, and reading the same chearfully, said to Colonel *Drury*, and him the said *Richard Faulconer*, *There is the Queen of* Bohemia, *deliver it to her, and I will speak for you*. And that the said Queen of *Bohemia* did present the said Petition; and did also then and there, corruptly, wilfully, falsely, and maliciously, before the said Commissioners swear, That the said Lord *Craven* after told him the said *Richard Faulconer*, and Company, *That they should receive an Answer from the Queen of* Bohemia *to their Petition, and that he* (meaning the said *William* Lord *Craven*) *had spoken to the Queen of* Bohemia *in their behalf*. Whereas in Truth neither did several Officers, or any Officer, make a Petition to the said King, to entertain him or them, to fight for him against the Commonwealth of *England*. Nor did several Officers, or any Officer, make a Petition to the said King, to entertain him or them to fight for him against the Commonwealth of *England*, by the Name of *barbarous and inhuman Rebels*, either in *England* or *Scotland*. Nor did several Officers, or any Officer, make a Petition to the said King, to entertain him or them, to fight for him against the Commonwealth of *England*, by the Name of *barbarous and inhuman Rebels*, either in *England* or *Scotland*, for the recovering of his just Rights, or re-instating him on his Throne. And whereas in Truth, the said *Richard Faulconer*, and Colonel *Drury*, were not deputed by the said Officers to present the said Petition, in the said Oath mentioned; and whereas in Truth, he the said *Richard Faulconer*, with Colonel *Drury*, did not apply themselves to the said Lord *Craven*, intreating him to present the said Petition to the Queen of *Bohemia*, to present it to the said King of *Scots*. Nor did he the said *Richard Faulconer*, with the said Colonel *Drury*, intreat him the said Lord *Craven*, to present the said Petition to the said Queen of *Bohemia*, to present it to the said King of *Scots*. And whereas in Truth, the said Lord *Craven* did not take the said Petition, nor read the same, nor say unto the said Colonel *Drury*, and him the said *Richard Faulconer*, *There is the Queen of* Bohemia, *deliver it to her, and I will speak for you*. And whereas in Truth, the said Lord *Craven* did not tell him the said *Richard Faulconer*, and Company, in the said Deposition mentioned, that they should receive an Answer from the said Queen of *Bohemia* to the said Petition, nor that he said Lord *Craven* had spoken to the Queen of *Bohemia* in their Behalf; as the said *Richard Faulconer* in and by the said Deposition hath deposed. And so the Jurors aforesaid, upon their Oaths aforesaid, do say, That the said *Richard Faulconer*, in Manner and Form aforesaid, corruptly, wilfully, falsely, and maliciously, of his own proper Act, Consent, and Agreement, did commit wilful, false and corrupt Perjury, to the great Dishonour of Almighty God, and to the great Damage, Loss, and Infamy of the said *William* Lord *Craven*, and in Contempt of the Laws of this Commonwealth; to the evil Example of all others in the like Case offending, and against the public Peace, &c.

[The Reason wherefore this Indictment did not recite the Oath *in hæc verba*, as in the former Indictment, but assigned the Perjury in the material Parts of the Oath, was by Reason it came lately to Knowledge, that the original Oath could not be found, and therefore the Oath was to be proved by the Entries in the Book of Parliament, and at *Haberdashers-Hall*, and by the Testimony of the Persons who administered the Oath.]

The next Day after the Indictment was found, the Prosecutors for the Lord *Craven* moved the Court for a *Habeas Corpus*, to bring *Faulconer* to the Bar to plead to the Indictment; who being brought into Court, desired Time to plead till the next Term; Whereupon the Court made this Order:

That the said Faulconer, *having now in Court appeared unto the Indictment, should have Time to plead unto the same, until the Beginning of the next Term, so that the Issue thereupon may be tried at the Bar in open Court the same Term.*

Term. *Pasch.* 1652.

Faulconer having all this Vacation neglected to appear, or plead to the Indictment, the Prosecutors for the Lord *Craven* were enforced again to move for another *Habeas Corpus* to bring *Faulconer* to the Bar, to appear, or plead to the Indictment; who appearing, desired longer Time to attend his Counsel, which the Court granted accordingly: And the ordinary Rules of Court were given unto him for the peremptory Days of pleading, or Judgment to be entered against him; and the very last Day, when the last Rule was out, and not before, he pleaded *Not Guilty*. And the Court ordered, That the Issue upon the Indictment of Perjury against the Defendant, be tried at the Bar upon *Friday* on the Morrow of the *Ascension* of our Lord, and that the Sheriff of *Middlesex* do attend *Andrew Broughton*, Esq. with the Book of Freeholders forthwith; so that an indifferent Jury may be returned between the said Keepers, and the said Defendant, to try the Issue aforesaid, by Consent of the Parties on both Sides.

Mr. *Broughton* accordingly appointed the Sheriff to attend him the next Day in the Afternoon with the Book of Freeholders, who accordingly named the Jury, and Notice was given by the Sheriff, requiring them to appear at the Day of Trial.

Friday, May 20, 1652.

THE Jury appearing according to Summons, and *Faulconer* being brought in Custody, the Court proceeded to Trial, and ordered the Indictment to be read; which being afterwards opened by Mr. *Boynton*, the Evidence was managed by Mr. *Maynard*, Mr. *Hales*, Mr. *Twisden*, Mr. *Wilde*, Mr. *Philips*, Mr. *Baldwin*, and Mr. *Drury*; who were of Counsel for the Commonwealth against the said *Faulconer*.

Before the Counsel for the Commonwealth proceeded to produce any Witnesses, they offered unto the Court and the Jury something in general concerning the Indictment. That the Indictment was for the Crime of Perjury, wilfully and corruptly committed; that *Faulconer* makes an Oath, that there was a Petition delivered, in which there was a very sharp Reflection (as he swears) upon the Parliament, by the Name of *barbarous and inhuman Rebels*, he swears he was deputed to deliver it, being drawn by himself and *Drury*, and subscribed by thirty Officers; that in order to the Delivery thereof, they did require the Assistance of the Lord *Craven*, that he promised to speak for them, and brought them an Answer: But they hoped to prove unto the Jury, that this Oath which *Faulconer* did take was very false, that it was by Design, a Design for Money; that the Consequence of it was very notorious, the Ruin of that Gentleman, of his Estate, Fame and Fortune; that Witnesses will be produced to prove what in Truth the Petition was. There was a Petition delivered, but not a Petition to this Effect at all, and *Faulconer* knew the contrary. We shall produce what it was, and that under his own Hand, whereby it will appear that there was no such Matter in it as he had deposed; the Witnesses themselves will best speak the Particulars.

For the opening of some things concerning this Oath of *Faulconer*, it is to be observed, he took this Oath before the Commissioners of *Haberdashers-Hall*, at *Whitehall*, and it was there reduced into Writing, and a Transcript was made of the original; which Transcript was sent to the Council of State, and they ordered the same to be reported to the Parliament; and being reported there, is entered in the Journal-Book, and there remains a Record in Parliament.

The first thing, therefore, insisted upon by the Counsel for the Commonwealth, was the proving of a true Copy of *Faulconer*'s Deposition, in respect the original was lost, or rather imbezzled by *Faulconer*. To prove the same,

A Copy thereof was produced in Court, which agreed *verbatim* with that Deposition of his, which was filed upon Record at *Haberdashers-Hall* (the proper Court where it ought to remain): And though that upon the File was but a Copy, yet it was filed as Evidence of that Deposition he was sworn unto by them. But this was opposed by the Counsel for *Faulconer* as not sufficient Proof; and thereupon a Copy of an Order of the Council of State, of *March* 6, 1650, was produced unto the Court, whereby it did appear, that the Depositions against the Lord *Craven* had been transmitted to the Council of State by the Commissioners at *Haberdashers-Hall*. And it appeared further by the said Order, that Mr. Attorney-General was appointed by the Council of State to report these Depositions to the Parliament, so transmitted to that Council by the Commissioners at *Haberdashers-Hall*. And the Attorney-General being sworn in Court, did declare, that he reported no other Depositions to the Parliament, than what he received from the Council of State; and that the Depositions produced to him in Court (whereof the said *Faulconer*'s was one), were endorsed with the Hand-writing of the Lord *Bradshaw*, then Lord President of the Council of State; and that the Votes of Confiscation of the Lord *Craven*'s Estate did pass upon the Report of the said Depositions, which he presented to the Parliament from the Council of State.

Mr. *Fermin*, Chief-Clerk to Mr. *Scobel*, Clerk of the Parliament, did depose in Court, That the very same Depositions shewed in Court to Mr. Attorney-General, endorsed with the Lord *Bradshaw*'s Hand-writing, were entered in the Journal-Book, as read in Parliament that Day, when Mr. Attorney-general did make his Report unto the Parliament; which he knew the better to be true, for that he received the same from the Hands of Mr. *Scobel*, or Mr. *Darnel*, the Clerk-Assistant in Parliament, the same Day they were read in Parliament, to be entered in the Journal-Book: And that he did enter the same accordingly with the Votes of Confiscation, which passed upon the reading of those Depositions. And afterwards he and Mr. *Darnel* did examine the said Depositions, whereof the said *Faulconer*'s was one, after the same were so entered into the Journal-Book.

And for the further ſatisfaction of the Court, he produced the Journal of Parliament, wherein the ſaid depoſitions (and particularly that of *Faulconer*) were entered, which were read in Court out of the Journal; whereby it did appear that the depoſitions of the ſaid *Faulconer*, *Kitchingman* and *Reyley* were entered into the ſaid Journal, and did agree *verbatim* with the Copy of *Faulconer*'s and their depoſitions remaining at *Haberdaſhers Hall*, and with the Copy reported by Mr. Attorney-General from the Council of State to the Parliament.

Mr *Winſlow*, one of the Commiſſioners at *Haberdaſhers-hall*, being one before whom the ſaid *Faulconer* was ſworn, did teſtify upon Oath in Court, that the depoſition of *Faulconer* produced unto him, and whereupon there was an endorſement of the Lord *Bradſhaw*'s hand-writing; was, as he did believe, a true Copy of that depoſition to which the ſaid *Faulconer* was ſworn at *Whitehall*, for that he findeth his own hand ſubſcribed thereunto *(as examined by him to be a true Copy)*, and ſaid it was uſual with the Commiſſioners at *Haberdaſhers-hall*, when they take examinations concerning any Perſon of Quality, to appoint one of themſelves to go from the Table to examine the Copy by the Original: but whether, when he ſubſcribed his name to the Copy produced unto him, he did examine the ſame by the original depoſition before it was ſent for away by the Council of State, or afterwards, or by the Tranſcript remaining upon the file as a Record at *Haberdaſhert-hall*, he could not poſitively remember; but conceives that the Copy, to which his hand is ſubſcribed, as examined by him, to be a true Copy, was taken when they had the original in cuſtody; but cannot certainly ſay it.

Mr. *Barners*, another of the Commiſſioners at *Haberdaſhers-hall*, before whom alſo the ſaid Oath was taken, did teſtify upon Oath, that to the beſt of his remembrance, the particulars mentioned in *Faulconer*'s depoſitions then read in Court, were the ſame to which the ſaid *Faulconer* was ſworn unto by himſelf and the reſt of the Commiſſioners, though he could not remember every Syllable and Letter.

Mr. *Winſlow* and Mr. *Barners* were again produced to declare, what they did remember concerning this clauſe in the depoſition of the ſaid *Faulconer*'s (viz.) *That ſeveral Officers, about thirty in number, made a Petition to the King of* Scots, *to entertain them to fight for him againſt the Commonwealth of* England, *by the name of* barbarous and inhuman Rebels, *either in* England *or* Scotland, *&c.* And thereupon Mr. *Winſlow* did declare unto the Court, that he did well remember that clauſe in *Faulconer*'s depoſition when he was ſworn thereunto; but whether the number of Officers were thirty or no, he could not tell, but a certain number of Officers were named.

Mr. *Barners* did declare the like, but whether the word *inhuman* was in he could not poſitively ſay; but was certain that *barbarous Rebels* was contained in that clauſe; and that when *Faulconer* was ſworn unto the ſame, it was firſt read unto him, and amended in ſeveral places, and then he ſwore it to be true. And Mr. *Barners* ſaid, that he did remember his depoſition the better, for that himſelf and the reſt of the Commiſſioners had ſeveral debates upon it at *Haberdaſhers-hall*, whether they ſhould thereupon ſeize, ſequeſter, or ſecure the Lord *Craven*'s eſtate.

Having thus traced this Oath of *Faulconer*'s, which was taken at *Whitehall*, and brought to *Haberdaſhers-hall*, afterwards brought from *Haberdaſhers-hall* back again to *Whitehall*, and from *Whitehall* to the Parliament, and there entered in the Journal-Book, as the grounds upon which the Votes of Confiſcation did paſs; and having withal proved that particular clauſe of *barbarous and inhuman Rebels*, &c. the Counſel for the Commonwealth concluded as to that point, and left it to the Jury to judge, and to *Faulconer* to produce the original, which he hath got into his cuſtody, if he can find any variance in it from the depoſition recited in the Indictment.

And to prove that *Faulconer* had got the original Oath into his cuſtody, Mr. *Knight*, a Witneſs, was produced, who did teſtify upon Oath, that being in the company of *Faulconer* he did ſhew him a writing written with Captain *Biſhop*'s own hand (ſo far as he could judge one man's hand to be like another), and that *Faulconer*'s name was ſubſcribed thereunto; and that *Faulconer* told him, the ſaid *Knight*, that that writing was the original depoſition he was ſworn unto againſt the Lord *Craven*, and which he kept on purpoſe to keep Mr. *Biſhop* in awe (*Faulconer* being then in neceſſity and want); and that the ſaid *Faulconer* further ſaid unto him, the ſaid *Knight*, that he had received 20*l.* for the buſineſs of the Lord *Craven*, and was to have more; but ſaid he deſerved 2000*l.* for what he had done.

In the next place, the Counſel for the Commonwealth did apply themſelves to prove the falſity of the Oath (*viz.*) That there was no ſuch thing in the Petition mentioned by *Faulconer* in his depoſition, [*as that thirty Officers did petition to be entertained to fight for the King of* Scots *againſt the Commonwealth of* England, *by the name of* barbarous and inhuman rebels, *&c.*] And being to prove a Negative, they applied their proof to a certain time and place, which *Faulconer* in his own depoſition did prove for them; for he ſwears, that the Petition was delivered the Evening before the King of *Scots* went from *Breda*, and that the ſaid King went away the next morning at three a-clock. He ſwears further, that he and *Drury* drew the Petition, and were deputed to deliver the ſame; accordingly they applied their evidence.

Proofs as to the Falſity of Faulconer's *Oath.*

MR. *Horſnel* being produced, did teſtify, that the night before the King of *Scots* went from *Breda*, Colonel *Drury*, Capt. *Briſco*, and divers others, were with a little ſhort Petition to remember the King of a former Petition which they had delivered, that ſome courſe might be taken, that their arrears which they owed in the Town might be paid, that their Landlords where they lodged might not ſuffer, for they were not able themſelves to pay them; that he went along with them to the great window juſt over the moat, and there he, the ſaid *Horſnel*, did ſet his hand unto the ſame, and that he was in the Chamber when *Drury* and *Briſco* came in to deliver the Petition, in which there was not a word that concerned any thing, but only the relief of their preſent neceſſities. Being aſked by the Court, if there were not a mention of *barbarous and inhuman Rebels*; he anſwered, not any thing of that nature was in it. He further ſaid, that this Petition had reference to a former Petition he was not acquainted withal, nor was his hand ſet to the former Petition.

Captain *Briſco* being produced did teſtify, that there were divers Gentlemen in great diſtreſs met together in Colonel *Drury*'s Chamber, at the time of the Treaty of the *Scots* King with the Commiſſioners at *Breda*, and among other things it was agreed to draw a Petition to the King; which was drawn in Colonel *Drury*'s Chamber, expreſſing their neceſſities, that the People of the Town might be relieved, and that the Petitioners might not be left to periſh: that going to deliver it, they met with Secretary *Long* by the way, who told them it was to no purpoſe, for there was no moneys come in. Afterwards the Petitioners had notice the King was to depart from *Breda*; whereupon they met together again, and went into the further end of the Gallery, to draw a ſhort Petition, to put the King in mind of his Promiſe to Secretary *Long*, concerning the People of the Town of *Breda*, that they might be ſatisfied, and the Petitioners relieved, which Paper he the ſaid *Briſco* delivered to the *Scots* King, who threw it on a Table; and doing ſo, they ſtood all amazed, being likely to be left in diſtreſs; and unexpectedly came in the Lord *Craven*, whereupon he, the ſaid *Briſco*, having long ſerved in the Country, and knowing him to be a lover of Soldiers, he ſpoke unto him, and ſaid, Sir, we are a company of poor diſtreſſed Gentlemen, likely to be left here in miſery (he ſaid, *Well*); and the next morning the King went away, without giving any relief unto the Petitioners. The Court demanded of *Briſco*, whether there were no ſuch matter in it as *barbarous and inhuman Rebels?* He anſwered, that he read it, and was ſure there was no ſuch thing in it, the whole ſcope of it being to relieve their neceſſities, which was the occaſion of that Petition. Being demanded again by the Court, if *barbarous and inhuman Rebels* were not in the Petition? he anſwered, No, not any ſuch words at all, nor ſo much as any mention of the Parliament.

Colonel *Drury* was in the next place produced, who teſtified, that being at *Breda*, Lieutenant-Colonel *Bardſey*, Major *Faulconer*, Major *Hall*, Captain *Kitchingman*, and divers others came to his lodging, and told him that they were in a condition of ſtarving, and deſired him that he would aſſiſt them to draw a Petition to the King of *Scots*, to relieve their neceſſities, or elſe they muſt periſh; that the ſaid *Drury* being in their condition conſented unto it, and in his Chamber, in his ſon's paper-book, the Petition was drawn, Major *Faulconer* writ it with his own hand; which, ſaith *Drury*, I have here to ſhew, and ſo preſented the original under *Faulconer*'s hand unto the Court: in which Petition (ſaid *Drury*) we deſired ſome relief from his Majeſty, ſhewing how we had ſerved the former King, and in what neceſſities we were. That they were adviſed to deliver it to Secretary *Long*, for that they were told that the King had not a Piſtole to relieve himſelf, and it would be a vain thing, ſaid *Long*, to deliver it. That they followed Secretary *Long*, and ſolicited him daily for three weeks together, and ſtill he put them off; and the day before the King went from *Breda*, they drew a ſhort Petition to mind the King of his promiſe to Secretary *Long*, and to deſire that the Inhabitants of *Breda* that had relieved them, might not be undone; that *Briſco* was deputed with him to deliver it, and he accordingly delivered it to the King: that the King laid it down upon the Table: in ſteps the Lord *Craven*; then Captain *Briſco*, having trailed a Pike under the Lord *Craven*, went to him, and told him there were many Gentlemen ready to ſtarve, and deſired him to ſpeak a favourable word to the Queen of *Bohemia*. To which the Lord *Craven* anſwered, *Well*, as *Briſco* then told him. The next morning the King of *Scots* went away, and ſo nothing at all was done for the Petitioners; that original Petition, which *Drury* produced unto the Court, of *Faulconer*'s own hand-writing, and in the preſence of *Faulconer*, was publickly read in Court, and was as followeth, *viz.*

May it pleaſe your Majeſty,

"THE great ſenſe we have always had of your Majeſty's preſent condition hath been the prime cauſe of our long ſilence; but now our neceſſities are grown ſo great and inſupportable, that we are inforced either to petition or periſh: Moſt humbly deſiring your Majeſty, to take into your princely conſideration their extremities, who have been ever ready to proſtrate their Lives in your Majeſty's Royal Father's ſervice: nor no leſs willing and ready to proſecute the ſame in what your Majeſty ſhall command: Moſt humbly petitioning your Royal Order, that ſome courſe may be taken for our preſent ſubſiſtence, that our future endeavours may not be buried in that unavoidable calamity, which our Loyalty hath reduced us unto."

And we ſhall cordially pray for your Majeſty.

The Court demanding of Colonel *Drury*, if the ſaid Petition was *Faulconer*'s own hand-writing; he ſaid Yea, and looking back upon *Faulconer*, ſaid, he cannot deny it: I did dictate unto him, and *Faulconer* did write it in my Chamber; and that is the very original that was ſo drawn, and being fair written was afterwards delivered to Secretary *Long*: the other that was delivered was a memorial, to put the King in mind of his promiſe when money came in. And *Drury* further ſaid, that when he was examined by Mr. *Biſhop*, he did give in his Examination the contents of the firſt and latter Petition; and ſaid, he did expreſs himſelf at that time of his Examination by Mr. *Biſhop*, to the ſame effect which he had now done in Court. Being aſked by the Court, if the words *barbarous and inhuman Rebels* were in that firſt petition? the ſaid *Drury* anſwered, that *Faulconer* moved to have *barbarous and inhuman Rebels* inſerted into that Petition ſo drawn by himſelf, but was anſwered by the Petitioners, that as they were Soldiers of fortune, it was uncivil language, and ſo they would not give way unto it. Being demanded by the Court, who was deputed to deliver the laſt Petition, he ſaid, Captain *Briſco* was one, in regard he had many wounds at *Cannon-Froom*, that the King might commiſerate his caſe the more; and that he, the ſaid *Drury*, was alſo deputed with *Briſco* to deliver the ſame, becauſe he was known to the Queen of *Bohemia*, and ſome other perſons of quality, and *Faulconer* was not at all deputed. Being aſked, if the Lord *Craven* was preſent at the delivery of the firſt Petition? he anſwered No, the Petition was delivered three weeks before: but the Lord *Craven* was preſent when the laſt Petition was delivered, to mind the King of his promiſe. The ſaid *Drury* further informed the Court, that afterwards *Faulconer* being diſcontented that he got no money, ſaid, as he was going into Town, *This is a horrid Thing, that we ſhould be in this caſe, to follow a thing they call a King* (God damn me). *I will go into* England, *and do all the miſchief I can.*

Proofs as to the Credit of Faulconer.

IN the next place, the Counſel for the Commonwealth did apply themſelves to offer proof as to the credit of *Faulconer*. Mr. *Wooldridge* of *Clements-Inn*, Attorney at the Common-Law, being ſworn, did teſtify to this purpoſe;

purpose; That being in his chamber at *Clement's-Inn*, about this time twelve-month, *Faulconer* came to him, asked how some of his Countrymen near *Petersfield* did? That he asked *Faulconer* where he had been of so long a time? Who answered, he had been in the *Low Countries*; had seen some Lords sit in Council for the King; that he had been sworn against the Lord *Craven*, which would bring a great deal of advantage to the State; that he had money for the doing of it; and said, that he had received already 80 *l.* (it was that sum here mentioned, said Mr. *Wooldridge*, to the best [illegible] his remembrance), but *Faulconer* said, he did expect a greater reward; that the said *Faulconer* hath been as wicked a man as any in *England*; [illegible]hat he spent his Estate, and left the Country, did wicked acts while he was there: that being at *Petersfield*, he drank an health to the Devil in the middle of the Street, of which information being given, we sent to the Justice of the Peace in the Town, and had him bound over to the [illegible]ssions for doing of it; but said, he did not see him drink the health to the Devil.

Mr. *Jack*[illegible] of *Petersfield* being produced, testified, about five years ago, *Faulconer* w[illegible] ranting and drinking of healths, that he did drink a health to the Dev[illegible] and said this, *I have spent my Brother's Estate and my own; I will never want money, for whilst there is any in the Nation, I will get it one way or other, and I will do something of Infamy to be talked of, that the name of Faulconer shall never die.* Being asked in what manner he did drink the health? He answered, in the Street, down upon his knees; that he was present and thousands can witness it; that he was had before a Justice of Peace for it.

James G[illegible]*ham* being sworn, did testify, that in *May* 1647, after the Siege at *Ex*[illegible]*er*, it was his fortune to fall into the company of *Faulconer*, and as he [illegible]s with him in the cellar, he was swearing *damn him, blood and wounds*; ta[illegible]s a two-and-twenty shilling piece of Gold, put it into his hand, and [illegible]id, *God damn him, blood and wounds*, he would *bugger his Soul to Hell*; and these words he used frequently to Man, Woman, and Child, *bugger, bug*[illegible]*er, bugger*; and correct him for it, he would say, *damn him, blood and wo*[illegible]*nds*, he would do it. Being asked by the Court, if *Faulconer* did any thi[illegible] upon him? He answered, No, *he was able to deal with as good a man as he.*

Mr. *Hig*[illegible]s hath often heard *Faulconer* swear, *damn him* and *sink him*, and such wi[illegible]ked expressions.

Mr. *Brad*[illegible]y did testify, that he heard *Faulconer* say, *our Saviour Christ was a Bast*[illegible]*rd, and a Carpenter's Son, and carried a basket of Tools after his Father.*

Mr. *Dyer* being produced, did declare, that *Faulconer* confessed to him, that he had [illegible]ten pound of a man, by procuring one to personate Captain *Bishop*, it w[illegible]s thus (as *Faulconer* told him): That a Citizen, as he remembered *Faulco*[illegible] said, did desire *Faulconer* to get Captain *Bishop* to do a business for him, which Citizen did promise him twenty pound, ten in hand, and ten afterwards: whereupon *Faulconer* said he got one to personate Captain *Bishop*, and to go along with him to the Citizen: which man so personating Captain *Bishop*, promised the Citizen, upon the account of Major *Faulconer*'s good services for the publick, to afford him his best assistance in the effecting of what was desired in his Petition, which story *Faulconer* himself told. And *Faulconer* further said, that Captain *Bishop* had used him ill, in keeping him so low in money; that he had it one time in his thoughts, as Captain *Bishop* came from the Committee-chamber, through the Guard-chamber, down the stairs, to have cut his throat. Being asked by the Court, what money *Faulconer* had of Captain *Bishop*? He answered, he paid to *Faulconer* with his own hands, by Captain *Bishop*'s direction, twenty pound at one time, and about thirty pound more at other times, in several portions; that *Faulconer* confessed to him he had twenty pound afterwards. Being demanded what it was for he gave that money? He said, *I will not speak to that, I cannot speak to that.*

Captain *Ballard* being produced, did testify, that about three or four years ago, he came to *Faulconer*'s lodging, and saw him write a letter in his chamber, and that he writ it as if it had come from Colonel *Burgess* from *Jersey*, and set *Burgess*'s name to it; and *Faulconer* would have had him, the said *Ballard*, to carry this letter to one Capt. *Bishop* that belonged to the Council of State, and to say he had the letter from one of *Bristol*, and get some money of *Bishop* for that intelligence mentioned in the letter, of which the said *Ballard* was to have half. but he, the said *Ballard*, refused to go with the same, knowing it to be unjust.

Mr. *Powel*, a Justice of Peace of the County of *Middlesex*, did testify to the Court, that this *Faulconer* was brought before him upon suspicion of Felony, and committed, which *Mittimus* he produced in Court; and that afterwards the Lord Chief-Justice *Rolls* did send for him out of *New-Prison* to *Newgate*; that *Faulconer* hath a common name for a Robber on the highway.

Mr. *Goodman*, Goaler of *Ailesbury*, did testify unto the Court, that the said *Faulconer*, the 20th of *March* 1648, was committed to *Ailesbury* Gaol, by Sir *Thomas Saunders*, Mr. *Bulstrode*, and two other Justices of the Peace, upon suspicion of Felony, Robbery and Murder, and tendered a Certificate thereof in writing unto the Court.

The Defence made on the behalf of Faulconer.

THE evidence being given on the behalf of the Commonwealth, Mr. *Windham*, Mr. *Latch*, Mr. *Lechmere*, and Mr. *Haggat*, of Counsel for *Faulconer*, did offer something to the consideration of the Court, before they did produce their Witnesses; *viz.* that although it concerns every man that Perjury should be punished; for every man's life, liberty, fortune and estate depends upon an Oath, and in these times it is somewhat dangerous if they should be forsworn; so on the other side, if *Faulconer* be not forsworn, it is but just he should be acquitted. That the Council for the Commonwealth have endeavoured to prove that there was a Petition, but that there was no such words in the Petition as are suggested, and have endeavoured to impeach the credit of *Faulconer*: that they have produced a copy of *Faulconer*'s Oath, which ought not to be admitted; because it is but a Transcript of a Transcript, a Copy of a Copy, brought from *Haberdashers-hall* to the Council of State, and from the Council of State to the Parliament, and there the Copy is entered in the Journal-book. And the Witnesses that have been produced, do not swear positively to the Oath as it is in writing, and one particle may turn the whole sense of an Oath; and though these words *barbarous and inhuman Rebels* were in it, yet how it is applied, and how the sense of it falls, it cannot be judged, but by the original writing itself, and it concerns the Counsel for the Keepers to produce it. How it should come into *Faulconer*'s hands, there is no account given, but by one *Knight*, who saith *Faulconer* shewed him a thing, which *Faulconer* said was his [original] deposition against the Lord *Craven*; but the credit of *Knight*'s testimony is left to the Jury. It is sworn, that that copy produced in Court was examined; but Mr. *Winslow* doth not positively say it was examined by the original, when in their custody.

That as to the Witnesses produced against the credit of *Faulconer*, they did hope to counterpoise his life to be, as of a man that might be credited: that in the Petition delivered at *Breda* there is something of those words, though there be not *barbarous and inhuman Rebels*, which was but a nominal thing; yet the prostrating of themselves to prosecute the cause, is desired, may be observed; though the actual words be not there, yet the sense doth bear it: that the case is somewhat hard with *Faulconer*, who was employed at the Court of *Breda* as an emissary, as a spy: and at his return in giving an account of his observations at *Breda*, let something fall concerning the Lord *Craven*, without any design in him; and that what *Faulconer* delivered in his deposition was with qualifications, as he did believe, to his best remembrance, and the like.

Hereupon Captain *Bishop* was produced on the behalf of *Faulconer*, as a Witness, whose discourse was long, and consisted of three parts.

1. It took notice how the Council of State sent for him from his habitation at *Bristol*, to be employed in matters of great trust; and afterwards what trust was reposed in him and Mr. *Scot*, in order to the safety of the Nation.

2. By way of argument on behalf of *Faulconer*, he did declare what services *Faulconer* had done for the Commonwealth, and that *Faulconer* was one by whom this Commonwealth sat safe at this hour, and by whom he enjoyed his life: and what an ill requital this was to be thus proceeded against.

The third part of his discourse was, to declare what particular designs the State formerly had in hand, and what designs the enemy had against the State; and what service he did to countermine the enemy in their designs: the last of the three being not (as was conceived) so advisedly spoken in publick, and which would be more unfit to be in print, shall therefore here be past over in silence, as also what Captain *Bishop* said at large concerning the two first particulars, in respect they are no proofs pertinently to be applied, as to the perjury in question.

An account only shall be therefore given what Captain *Bishop* properly spoke as a Witness.

As a Witness, Captain *Bishop* said, he had never seen *Faulconer* in drink, or misbehave himself, but ever observed him as a sober man; that he drew *Faulconer*'s information [which *Faulconer* did deliver as the substance] and that he must say, that the words [*or to that effect*] should have been put in, and that it was his fault they were not in, and he could not tell but that they were in, that the Commissioners at *Haberdashers-hall* were desired to come to *Whitehall* to administer an Oath to the said *Faulconer* privately, lest danger should befal the Witnesses if they were discovered.

That *Horsnel* was formerly an Agent for the Prince, and was to receive orders from *Tom Cook* in the *Tower*, and was ordered to be tried by the High Court of Justice: that Colonel *Drury* was a Papist in arms, and being brought before him to be examined, still had the Lord *Craven* in his mouth, before he was asked a question.

The like of *Brisco*. He said, that before *Drury* and *Brisco* came from beyond seas, his Agent gave him notice of their coming, and thereupon he laid wait for them, and caught them; that *Drury* said, when he was examined, that he had not a penny of money; that he did not commit him to prison, but took his parole, and in commiseration gave him two shillings and six-pence for his supper. He said further, that *Drury* did contradict himself in what he had formerly informed the Council of State, and to that end produced in Court the copy of *Drury*'s Information; which being read in Court, agreed with the testimony which *Drury* then gave to the Jury.

[By way of digression observe, *That* Drury'*s and* Brisco'*s Informations, which Captain* Bishop *had taken above twelve months since, and which tended to clear the Lord* Craven, *he concealed till this hour that he produced the same in Court, and never transmitted those two Men's Examinations to the Parliament; though before the Bill of Sale did pass, he did transmit* Bardsey'*s and* Kitchingman'*s Re-examination taken by himself, and which he apprehended made against the Lord* Craven.]

Captain *Bishop* further said, that whereas it was objected that *Faulconer* had money; he answered, that it is great reason he should have money, for there was a real effect of the safety of the Commonwealth by his services: that notwithstanding any thing hath been sworn against *Faulconer*, he believes what he swore was truth.

Captain *Bishop* speaking again of *Faulconer*'s deposition, that the words [*or to that effect*] should have been added; the Court asked him, whether *Faulconer* gave any directions to express these words in his Examination? To which Captain *Bishop* made answer, That the deposition he made, was the substance of things, and he put it in words, and that [*or to that effect*] if they were not in, should have been in. The Court again asked him, if *Faulconer* did direct him to put in these words [*or to that effect?*] He replied again, he did deliver the whole, *as the effect of it*.

Captain *Bishop* being further asked by the Court, if he were present when the Commissioners gave the Oath, and took what *Faulconer* said in way of Information? He answered, *That he prepared it before the Commissioners were sent for*, and then they had only the administring the Oath; and said again, *I prepared the Information which he made Oath of.* Hereupon Mr. *Winslow* desired leave to inform the Court, that when he and the rest of the Commissioners came to *Whitehall* to administer this Oath, being sent for to that end, the Information was ready prepared by Captain *Bishop*, and having no Register with them, they made use of Captain *Bishop*, being well skilled in the use of his pen, to write over the deposition: for though he had prepared the deposition, the Commissioners did see occasion to alter much of it; and it was writ over again, and then read to *Faulconer*, and attested by him, and subscribed unto by the hands of all the Commissioners then present; and the Oath which we gave him was this, *Whether the deposition thus drawn, and that which he*

was

was examined unto, was the Truth, the whole Truth, and nothing but the Truth; Mr *Barners* attested the like: then Captain *Bishop* sat down.

After this Lieutenant-Colonel *Joyce* was produced, who likewise spoke of very great designs, and of matters of State, and what discoveries were made by *Faulconer*; which being not pertinent to the Perjury, shall be here omitted: but as a Witness he said, that *Harsnel* was formerly an Agent for the Prince. That *Faulconer* was a *Hampshire* man, a Gentleman well-bred, that he was an enemy to himself in spending his Estate, that he was always faithful to the Parliament; that he believes *Faulconer* hath cussed some of the Witnesses produced against him for their malignancy, and that nothing could be expected to come from them to the credit of *Faulconer*: that *Faulconer* was sent over by him as a spy into *Holland*, upon account of his faithfulness.

Lieutenant-Colonel *Bardsey* was produced in the next place, on the behalf of *Faulconer*, who testified, that he put his hand to the Petition at *Breda*; that the Lord *Craven* was desired to deliver it to the King of *Scots*; that the Lord *Craven* said he was no Courtier, but a Servant to the States of *Holland*; that it was fitter for the Princess Royal to deliver it, than himself, and so returned the Petition again. That the Queen of *Bohemia* told the Petitioners, the King would do for them what he was able; but about four o'clock in the morning he went away, and they had no other answer: that the contents of it was to put the King in mind of his promise, that some money might be delivered to the Petitioners for discharge of their quarters at *Breda*. Being asked by the Court, if there were any such expressions in it as *barbarous and inhuman Rebels*, he answered No. Being asked, if to that Petition which *Faulconer* drew, he would have had *barbarous and inhuman Rebels* added, he answered Yea, *Faulconer* did move to have those words in, but was refused it: that he the said *Bardsey* read over that Petition, and set his hand to it, and was at the penning of it, and *Faulconer* wrote it.

Captain *Kitchingman* being produced, did testify, that a Petition was drawn at *Breda*, and signed by him, *Faulconer*, and others, to be presented to the King of *Scots*; that it was in pursuance of gaining money to discharge their quarters, and to enable them to serve the King, but knows not by whom it was delivered; that Secretary *Long* was to issue out money unto them, but they never had any; and in order to the gaining of that money, there was another Petition drawn, but by whom delivered he knew not; only he saw a paper in the Queen of *Bohemia*'s hand, which was told him was the Petition; and after a quarter of an hour's discourse with the King, she delivered it to the King, but they never received any money upon that neither: that he did not read the last Petition at all, nor heard it read; that it was the first Petition which he signed.

Colonel *Deve* was produced in Court on the behalf of *Faulconer*, who said, he knew nothing of his birth, he only knew his Father and Mother, that they lived in good fashion and credit; but how this *Faulconer* hath been brought up, and where he hath inhabited for these ten or twelve years, he knew not: and that this was as much as he could say.

Michael, an Alehouse-keeper, was then produced, who said he knew nothing of *Faulconer*, but that he was a very honest man, *Faulconer* having lain in his house a year and three quarters; that he knows nothing to the contrary, but that he was a good Scholar, an honest man, and brought up at the University.

Captain *Moubrey* being produced as a Witness, did testify, that *Anno* 1649, in *Amsterdam*, he met accidentally with Captain *Brisco*, who said to him and others, Gentlemen, I see you are in a sad condition, I will set you in a way to get money; here are *Dutchmen* taking up Men to go to Plantations, and you shall have twelve stivers a-piece a-day, but I will warrant you, I will force them to leave you behind: and accordingly they received twelve stivers a-day, and *Brisco* would have had them on shipboard; but one *Church*, an *Englishman*, bid them take heed what they did, for he served some *Englishmen* so before, clapt them under decks, and received so many six Dollars a-piece for them, and so left them: that he hath known *Faulconer* five years, and he hath behaved himself civilly for aught he ever knew.

Mr. *Carey* did testify something to this purpose, in reference to *Brisco*'s sending men to Plantations; who said further, he had no more to say against *Brisco*, but that he was a man would drink, and sometimes swear, as well as other men that are accustomed to it: that he knows nothing to the contrary, but that he came to *Breda* to wait for employment: in the mean time, whilst he was there, he did as other men did, strive to seek for relief.

After the Court had with much patience heard Captain *Bishop*, and the rest of the Witnesses on the behalf of *Faulconer*, the Counsel for *Faulconer* summ'd up the Evidence, and left it to the Jury, with some further observations, *viz.*

That though the words *barbarous and inhuman Rebels* were not in the Petition, yet there were words of tender of service, as the King should command, and to prosecute his cause, which was the substance of the thing informed by *Faulconer*; that Captain *Bishop*, and Lieutenant-Colonel *Joyce*, who have testified of *Faulconer*'s services, were Witnesses to be preferred before any witnesses produced against *Faulconer*; that the endeavour is not only to convict this man, but by conviction and disabling of his credit, to undermine that which hath been acted by the Parliament, upon his testimony, and other concurrent testimonies, not only in passing Votes, but in passing an Act of Parliament to sell an Estate.

That there was nothing objected against the credit of this Witness, so long as there was any other stone to turn, tho' there were other endeavours used in Parliament to prevent the sale of the Lord *Craven*'s Estate, so that when all other stones fail'd, they then make use of this Indictment of Perjury, and so hope to undermine the Act of Parliament. Tho' *Faulconer* might have some extravagance, yet you see what his part was to act, to dissemble that he was not what he was, and it may be, when he was amongst the *Cavaliers*, and such kind of men, it was his part to be what might conduce to his end [illegible] for a man, as he was employed, must turn himself into all shapes, and tho' not drink a health, yet sometimes [illegible] *a curse to the Devil*, that they acknowledge the charge in part, but would lay it in words, not in substance, and therefore not strictly in the indictment.

That it was proved that the first Petition was to serve the King, as they formerly had served his Father, and they served his Father against the Parliament: so their offer must needs be, to be entertained to serve the King against the Parliament.

That it is a sad case, that this man for so many services performed by him for the Commonwealth, and settlements grounded upon his information, must be blasted here by an artificial Indictment a great while after.

And if he shall, after all this, be convicted of Perjury, it will be a discouragement for all men to undertake the like employment for the future.

And lastly, the Counsel for *Faulconer* did offer, that if there be a mistake in what he hath sworn, yet it appears not to be maliciously or corruptly done, and that therefore the Jury ought to find for *Faulconer*.

The Reply by the Counsel, on the behalf of the Commonwealth, against Faulconer *was to this purpose following:*

GENTLEMEN of the Jury, you have heard the defence that *Faulconer* hath made; we have charged him, that he did take the Oath that was set down in the Indictment. They say, *First*, We have not proved it; *Secondly*, That he did not take it, but did take it in effect; and *Thirdly*, If he did, it was not maliciously, nor corruptly: but not one of them hath said it is not false, no not one of their own Counsel. The evidence that hath been given, for the most part, hath been to magnify the service of this man, that is now in question before you: we shall admit his services to be true; but this we shall be bold to say, that a man that is employed beyond sea, and gives good return of his service in some kind, that that will not give him licence to make a false accusation in another kind: and it is no argument to say, that because this man was a spy beyond the sea, and did good service as a spy, that therefore he did not give a false information; in this he must not take a liberty to ruin any man by a false Oath: his service must not excuse him, if what he hath said be false.

As for what Mr. *Bishop* said concerning his Oath; Mr. *Bishop* tells you, it is his fault if the words [*or to that effect*] were not put down; if it were not, whose fault was it? It was mended by those whose judgments and consciences induced them to it. the Information he took was done by the judgment of the Committee, and not by the direction of him that was a Minister, a Scribe to write, and not a Judge to dictate and correct. You have here two men of unquestionable truth and honesty every way, (meaning Mr. *Winslow*, and Mr. *Barners*) that say positively, he did swear it; and God forbid that we should live to that day, that any man should be ruined upon a deposition, taken by the judgment of a Clerk, to such or such effect. If we should come to such a piece of Justice, that a deposition to such and such effect, and that taken by a Clerk, should come to cast a man, it is beyond an Oath of *&c.* For it is the Judges that must say, what is the effect of an Oath, and not the Clerk that writes it. If a Clerk shall take an Oath, and he shall come and say, *it is to this effect*, never shall any man be free from him, that by Perjury will ruin another man. It is proved unto you, it was read over to *Faulconer*, expresly mended in his sight, and sworn by him, and let the *effect* go with the *&c.* that went before it.

They objected to our Witnesses, that *Brisco* had sold his companions for twelve stivers a-day: that information had no other foundation, than the saying of a *Dutchmen*, that said so, or of an *Englishman* in a *Dutch* bottom; and what was testified, was what was said, and not what was known or sworn. They objected, that *Brisco* would swear as well as another; that takes not off his testimony. But what do they say, concerning their own Witness, *Bardsey*, whom they have produced? He hath sworn *in terminis*, in effect with *Drury*, which you will not forget: he swore, that when the first Petition was drawing, it was moved by *Faulconer*, that the words *barbarous and inhuman Rebels* should be put in; but it was rejected by them that were there as a thing uncivil: so their own Witness concurs with *Drury*.

As for the deposition on record at *Haberdashers hall*, which being filed there, it is proof of itself, which no man may aver against, when it is recorded; we have shewed it there, traced it here, brought a copy of it endorsed with the Lord *Bradshaw*'s hand; shall it be believed that a man shall be confiscated and lose his estate, and not so much as an Oath taken against him? It is apparent there was an Oath, and it is hoped you will believe that which the Parliament hath recorded, and expresly proved by the Gentlemen of *Haberdashers-hall* here present; which you will believe before any imaginations that can be made on the other side.

They have endeavoured to say something touching the conversation of this man, to uphold his credit, but, Gentlemen of the Jury, you are to consider of the man, what *damnable blasphemy* hath come out of his mouth, you have heard it. If a man will go so high, as to kneel down to *drink a health to the Devil*, I hope there is no excuse for that, his good services must not plead for him to comply with *God-dammes*; that will not justify him, he was not sent to do any such thing. But we have not rested there, have we not proved him a personator of other men, a decoy, and things that a man should be ashamed to name: the two-and-twenty shillings piece he took out, and what base wild words he spake, not fit to be repeated? That will not be palliated by any service whatsoever. And for that which Mr. *Bishop* hath said, nothing shall be said against him, but what appears to you, that Mr. *Bishop* hath gone beyond a Witness; for when he hath done his testimony, he seeketh and manageth the business, and in that is not equal to others that do not. For his expression, that *Faulconer* is one of them by which the Commonwealth of *England* sits safe at this hour, it is God we sit safe by, and not by him: I blame him not for his service, but when we are upon a question of truth, I say truth and righteousness is beyond all the service in the world.

They say my Lord *Craven* furthered the Petition, and promised to second it. Gentlemen, you must distinguish that which my Lord *Craven* knew, and that which he knew not. *There is not one Witness from beginning to ending, that can ever speak one word, that my Lord* Craven *knew what the first Petition was.* In that Petition was the expression of venturing their Lives, which was three weeks before the latter, which was singly to desire they might have money for their quarters. The first Petition had some expressions relating to their former service, and some expressions of their readiness for the future; but that Petition my Lord *Craven* never saw, but was delivered to one *Long* three weeks before, and *Drury* did put it down in his deposition, when he was examined by Mr. *Bishop*, which agrees with that which was read in Court.

But

But the particular time when the latter Petition, or Memorial, was delivered, with which the Lord *Craven* is charged, was the evening before the King [illegible] went from *Breda*.

They say that here is no corruption proved, and a man cannot be guilty without corruption: but certainly he that swears a thing that is false, it must of necessity be corrupt.

Faulconer [illegible] swears, that thirty Officers did subscribe the Petition: Doth he bring any one to confirm his testimony, or the least colour of evidence to what he hath sworn?

It was further pressed by the Counsel for the Commonwealth, that the Jury would distinguish these two things, between the Petition framed and dictated by *Drury*, and writ by *Faulconer*; and that other Petition delivered the night before the King went from *Breda*; the first is produced, and proved to be *Faulconer*'s own hand: that Petition was three weeks before, which begs for maintenance, and proffers service, the copy of which was brought forth before any evidence was given by them; for *Drury* upon his examination before the Council of State made the same known, and [illegible] which agrees *verbatim* with that read in Court. So the dictating of the Petition was by *Drury*, the writing by *Faulconer*, the delivery was to Secretary *Long*, and that was the thing whereof they did expect an account; but that was not the Petition to which the testimony of *Faulconer* at all goes. That Petition of which this Oath is spoken, and to which it is apply'd, is the Petition which was drawn the evening before the *Scots* King went from *Breda*; that is the Petition talked of in the deposition, that is the Petition upon which we pitch, and therefore if in that Petition there be none of these words, that which he hath sworn unto is false; for in that Petition we say there was no such words as *barbarous and inhuman Rebels*; nor such words of proffer of service or malignity, but mere desire of supply; and they have not offered the least proof to the contrary. And *secondly*, that it was not promoted by the Lord *Craven*, for the Petition was delivered by them to the *Scots* King, before such time as the Lord *Craven* came into the room, so that my Lord *Craven* was no promoter of the Petition; and had he been a promoter of it, there was no such thing in it, as might give offence: no, not the least mention of the Parliament, nor any thing that might offend. And whereas they object, that this Oath was not corrupt, the very words of his expression are very considerable, for he doth remarkably fix the words in his deposition, *To fight against the Commonwealth of* England by the name of *barbarous and inhuman Rebels*: Why would he fix such an *emphasis* upon it as that was? It could not be a bare mistake: nor the words *to this effect*, as Mr. *Bishop* would have had in, could never have served the turn; for to say he would fight against *the barbarous and inhuman Rebels*, or to that effect, there is no such effect in the one Petition nor in the other. Then a second thing is, that this *Faulconer* being, as he deposeth, the contriver of the Petition, it could not be a mere oversight and mistake in him; and then when he could not have his desire beyond seas to get monies, he said, *He would come here, and do what mischief he could.*

The Counsel urged further: Gentlemen of the Jury, what is become of the original deposition, it concerns not us to know, no more than the original of depositions taken in the Country: it lies upon them that are for the Oath to make it out. It cannot be presumed that the Parliament would confiscate a Nobleman's estate, and order it to be sold: would they enter it into the Journal-book, and make it a record, should it come and be transmitted from *Haberdashers-Hall* (the proper Judicatory for that business) to the Council of State, and from the Council of State to the Parliament, and then not to be a true Oath, or false copy? That is not to be borne, that a false Copy should sell a Gentleman's Estate, that a false Copy should be recorded to stand to all Eternity.

After the reply was made; every Judge in Court spoke what they in their judgment thought fit, for the better direction of the Jury: whereupon the Jury withdrew, and the next day brought in their Verdict, That they found the said *Faulconer* guilty of the Perjury mentioned in the Indictment. The Order following was thereupon made, viz.

By the Court:

The Defendant was this Day brought into Court, under the Custody of the Marshal of this Court, upon an Indictment for Perjury, whereunto he had formerly pleaded Not Guilty; *and the Jury thereupon being impannelled, and sworn, found him Guilty of the Perjury in the Indictment mentioned: and thereupon the said* Faulconer *is committed to the Custody of the said Marshal; there to remain until,* &c.

XXVI. The Trial of Mr. JOHN LILBURN, at the Sessions of the Peace held for the City of *London*, at Justice-Hall in the *Old-Bailey*, upon *Wednesday, Thursday, Friday* and *Saturday*, the 13th, 14th, 15th, and 16th Days of *July*, 1653, for returning into *England*, being banished by Act of Parliament.

[Written (the chief Part) by the said *John Lilburn.*]

I Was Counsel or Proctor for my Uncle, *George Lilburn*, Esq. and one Mr. *Josiah Primate*, &c. about a Colliery taken from them in the County of *Durham*, by force and violence, by Sir *Arthur Haslerig*; which he by his certificate computes to be worth five thousand pounds Sterling *per Annum*. About which Colliery the said Mr. *Primate* preferred a Petition to the Parliament, upon the 23d of *December*, 1651. in the delivery and management of which I appeared, as by the declared Law of *England* I might justifiably do.

Which Petition being by the Parliament referred to a Committee to examine it, who spent twelve or thirteen large hearings thereupon; and upon the 15th of *January*, 1651, new stile, the Chairman thereof, Mr. *Hill*, made his report to the House: but what it was, we never were permitted to see nor to hear read. And as some Members of Parliament have since told me, he made his report quite contrary to, or short of the evidence which was given in: whereupon the Parliament, the said 15th day of *January*, voted the foresaid Mr. *Primate*'s Petition to be false, malicious, and scandalous; and that Sir *Arthur Haslerig* is not guilty either of Oppression or Tyranny, in the Carriage and Prosecution of this business; and that all the Copies of the said Petition (which, relating only to *Primate*, is not here inserted) should be burnt by the hands of the Common-Hangman. And voted Mr. *Primate* to pay seven thousand pound, or to lie in prison till he pay it; which is all his punishment. And then the same day they passed certain Votes against me, which as they themselves, by special order of the 17th of *January*, have printed them, *verbatim* thus follow:

Resolved,

That the Fine of three thousand pounds be imposed upon Lieutenant Colonel *John Lilburn*, to be paid to the use of the Commonwealth.

That he be fined two thousand pounds more, to be paid to Sir *Arthur Haslerig*, for his damages; and two thousand pounds more, to be paid to *James Russel, Edward Winslow, William Molins*, and *Arthur Squib*, Esqrs. four of the Commissioners for compounding; that is to say, to each of them five hundred pounds for their damages.

Resolved, &c.

That Lieut. Col. *John Lilburn* be banished out of *England, Scotland*, and *Ireland*, and the Islands and Territories thereunto belonging; and not to return into any of them, upon pain of being proceeded against as a Felon, and in case of such return, shall suffer death accordingly.

Resolved, &c.

That Lieut. Col. *John Lilburn* do depart out of *England, Scotland*, and *Ireland*, and the Islands and Territories thereof, within thirty days now next coming; and in case the said *John Lilburn* shall, after the said thirty days, be found within *England, Scotland*, or *Ireland*, or the Islands and Territories thereunto belonging, or any of them, the said Lieut. Col. *John Lilburn* shall be proceeded against as a Felon, and shall suffer the pains of death accordingly.

Resolved, &c.

That the Serjeant at Arms attending the Parliament, do apprehend the said Lieut. Col. *John Lilburn*, and bring him to the bar of this House, upon *Tuesday* morning next, to receive the judgment of Parliament aforesaid, and that Mr. *Speaker* do direct a warrant to the Serjeant at Arms accordingly.

But being myself at the Parliament-door when these Votes past, and understanding what they had done, although they sate (to my remembrance) a good while after candle-light, I staid: and when the Serjeant at Arms came forth with his mace, and the *Speaker*, I spoke to him in these words, or to this effect: Mr. *Serjeant*, I understand the House hath this day passed some Votes against me, in which regard I staid on purpose, to see if you have any thing to say to me. Unto which he replied, No, Sir, I have no warrant yet to meddle with you, and therefore

therefore you may go whither you please. Well, Sir, if you have none to-night, I will promise you, to wait upon you to-morrow morning, to see whether then you will have any or no. And being as good as my word, the next day being *Friday*, *January* the 16th, he committed me to the custody of his Deputy, Mr. *Parsons*, where I remained till *Tuesday* morning next (as it was ordered in the last Vote) which was *January* the 20th; and coming to the Parliament-door, I was ushered into the Bar by the *Serjeant at Arms*, having his mace upon his shoulder; where Mr. *Speaker*, as the mouth of the House, expressed himself in these words, or to this effect:

Lieutenant-Colonel *Lilburn*, you are commanded by this House to kneel: unto which I answered in these words, or to this effect; Sir, with all Submission to this honourable House, I desire first a little liberty to speak. No, Sir, said he, you are not permitted to speak at all, but commanded to kneel. Well then, Sir, said I, with all submission, I stoop unto your sentence, that you have already past upon me, but I cannot kneel.

Lieutenant-Colonel *Lilburn*, said he, the House commands you to kneel. Well then, Sir, said I, to be short with you, I neither can kneel, nor will I kneel. Withdraw then, said he; which I did accordingly, making them two or three congées at my going out, the which also I did as I came in. Whereupon, as I was informed, seeing that I would not kneel at their Bar to receive my sentence, they voted to draw up an Act of Parliament to banish me; and passed another Vote by way of punishment, to take off ten days of the time they had formerly given me to depart the land in. Altho' upon the *Friday* at night before, I with my Keeper went to the *Serjeant*'s House, and spoke to him to this purpose: Mr. *Serjeant*, I understand the Parliament sits to-morrow, to chuse the Commissioners for regulating the Law, and I know it is their usual manner to command all men that come to their Bar (that they look upon as delinquents or offenders) to receive their sentence at their Bar kneeling. And truly, Sir, I have no desire at all to affront them, or to vex them more than they are, for I believe they are vexed enough already at me. And therefore I beseech you, oblige me so far unto you, as to tell the *Speaker* and some other Members, whom you please, from me, That when upon *Tuesday* I shall come to their Bar, to receive their sentence, I shall not kneel, although they should order you with your mace at their Bar to knock my brains out: and, Sir, if you please to give me leave, I will render you my reason, and it is this: I know when any kneels at your Bar to receive a sentence, the Parliament looks upon that action or gesture of kneeling, as a demonstration of a man's own convincement in his own conscience that he is guilty, and thereby does deserve such a punishment as by that sentence is past upon him; the which if I should do, I were in my own understanding the veriest rogue in the world, because my conscience and soul tells me, that I have done no evil, nor broke none of the Parliament's Laws, but followed (as by the Laws of *England* I may justifiably do) an honest, just and righteous business, in a just and honest way, without using any base or wicked ungodly means to effect my design in it. And whatever Mr. *Hill* hath reported to the House, I am sure of it, we have fully proved every clause and circumstance contained in our Petition, save only that clause of Sir *Arthur Haslerig*'s private corresponding with some of the Commissioners of *Haberdashers-hall*. But if we had not proved the Petition, there is no Law extant in *England* to enable the Parliament in the least to pass such a sentence upon me: and therefore for me in words, actions, or gesture, to do the least circumstance, to make the Parliament believe that I in mine own conscience was convinced that they had passed a just sentence upon me; I had rather, Mr. *Serjeant*, be cut in ten thousand pieces, than be such a *rogue* and *traitor* to mine own liberties and the nation's; and therefore I beg of you beforehand to tell them as much from me, that so they may avoid, if they please, their forcing me on *Tuesday* next to affront them. And he afterwards assured me, that the next day, being *Saturday*, he told twenty or thirty of the Members of Parliament of it; so that they put the affront upon themselves, and not I. But upon the said *Tuesday*, after that I was withdrawn out of the House, and set at liberty to be gone as soon as I pleased, there being great store of Citizens, my very good friends, at the door (who were persons that had always faithfully adhered to the Parliament's cause), with a Petition for the revoking of my banishment; the Petition being called for in, was read and debated, but laid aside, without giving any answer to the Petitioners. The Copy of which Petition, as since it is printed in *England*, thus followeth:

To the supreme Authority, the Parliament of the Commonwealth of *England*,

The Humble Petition of many well-affected People, inhabiting the City of London, Westminster, Southwark, *and parts adjacent, in behalf of the just Liberties of the free People of* England, *highly concerned in the sentence against Lieutenant-Colonel* John Lilburn *,

HUMBLY SHEWETH,

THAT if the manifold services, and extreme sufferings of Lieutenant-Col. *John Lilburn*, in opposition to tyranny and oppression, and how instrumental he hath been in the removal of divers sorts of oppressors, his wonderful deliverances, and clear acquitments by legal trials, from all former accusations, without the least stain to his reputation; if all these could be forgotten, and that he stood in our thoughts, but as the meanest of well-affected persons (and such at the least we must allow him, having in all times adhered to Parliaments), yet in your late proceedings towards him, and heavy censure upon him, we apprehend our native rights so much concerned, that we never conceived a greater cause of speedy application to you for redress, than upon this sad occasion.

For certainly it cannot be denied, but if he be really an offender, he is such by the breach of some Law, made and published before the fact, and ought by due process of Law, and verdict of twelve men, to be thereof convict, and found guilty of such crime; unto which the Law also hath prescribed such a punishment agreeable to that our fundamental liberty; which enjoineth that no Freeman of *England* should be adjudged of life, limb, liberty, or estate, but by Juries; a freedom which Parliaments in all ages contended to preserve from violation; as the birthright and chief inheritance of the people, as may appear most remarkably in the Petition of Right, which you have stiled, that most excellent Law.

And therefore we trust upon second thoughts (being the Parliament of *England*) you will be so far from bereaving us (who have never forfeited our right) of this our native right, and way of trials by Juries (for what is done unto any one, may be done unto every one), that you will preserve them entire to us, and to posterity, from the encroachments of any that would innovate upon them. And if the original of the unhappy differences between Sir *Arthur Haslerig* and Mr. *Lilburn* be duly weighed (being as we are informed), it will appear, that Sir *Arthur*'s stoppage of monies due to Mr. *Lilburn*, without legal process, was the first occasion thereof.

And it is believed, that if Mr. *Primate*'s cause [wherein Sir *Arthur* and Mr. *Lilburn* have been engaged] had at any time either at first or last been admitted to a trial at Law, and had passed any way by verdict of twelve sworn men; all the trouble and inconveniences arising thereupon had been prevented: the way of determination by major votes of Committees, being neither so certain nor so satisfactory in any case as by way of Juries, the benefit of challenges and exceptions, and unanimous consent, being all essential privileges in the latter: whereas Committees are tied to no such rules, but are at liberty to be present or absent at pleasure. Besides, Juries being birthright, and the other but new and temporary, men do not, nor [as we humbly conceive] ever will acquiesce in the one as in the other; from whence it is not altogether so much to be wondered at, if upon dissatisfactions, there have been such frequent printing of men's cases, and dealings of Committees, as there have been; and such harsh and inordinate heats and expressions between parties interested, such sudden and importunate appeals to your authority, being indeed all alike out of the true *English* road, and leading into nothing but trouble and perplexity, breeding hatred and enmities between worthy families, affronts and disgust between persons of the same publick affection and interest, and to the rejoicing of none but publick adversaries. All which, and many more inconveniences, can only be avoided, by referring all such cases to the usual trials and final determinations of Law.

And whereas you have censured Mr. *Lilburn* seven thousand pounds fine, and to perpetual banishment, and to die as a Felon if he return; we are exceedingly afflicted in our spirits thereby, not only because he hath not had the usual way of trial by Jury, which yet weighs very much with us; nor for that we believe he hath followed Mr. *Primate*'s cause, out of strong persuasion of the justness thereof (the cause in itself, as we have been informed, being very intricate and hard to be understood, and so did not wilfully or intentionally carry it out against his conscience, some of the Commissioners wishing to God it had therefore never came before them), nor for that we believe him innocent of any wilful breach of Parliament privilege, in delivering printed Petitions, before the original was presented unto you [that being never before published, to be a breach], though all these add to our grief, yet the main of our affliction ariseth from the destructiveness of the sentence, as being therein contrary to that other our fundamental native right, which injoins that fines should have regard to the qualities of the persons; a plowman saving his wainage, and a merchant his merchandise. Whereas this, if relating to his estate, we believe, is so far from preserving him in his quality, as that it leaves himself, his wife, and children, without sustenance; if in relation to his person, his affection to Parliaments, and zeal to publick freedom, renders all foreign Nations so unsafe to him, as that in effect he is banished into a wilderness, and exposed naked to the fury of bears and lions.

The premises duly weighed, and for that (as we are informed) the parties accused and censured have had no means to see what report hath been made by the honourable Committee, nor have had the liberty of exceptions thereunto, in like cases granted; and in that many well-affected people that heard the debates, and evidences on both sides, are unsatisfied, both in point of possession, and title to the colliery in question; that the honour of Parliament may stand immaculate, our native, fundamental rights inviolable, and all those gentlemen concerned in this cause left without any the least grudging, or just complaint;

We have deemed ourselves bound in conscience in most humble manner to intreat,

I. That you will be pleased to recal your fore-mentioned grievous sentence upon Lieutenant-Col. *John Lilburn*, and the rest concerned therein.

II. To give free Liberty to Mr. *Primate* to prosecute his cause, both for title and possession at the Common Law; and therein to make use of what Counsel he shall think fit.

III. That Sir *Arthur Haslerig* be referred to take his course at Law, for whatsoever injuries conceived to be done unto him by Lieutenant-Colonel *John Lilburn*, or any others, as was granted in Mr. *Primate*'s case with the said Sir *Arthur*; and that Mr. *Lilburn*, or any others, may have the same liberty against Sir *Arthur*, if they conceive any cause.

After which, the said friends of mine drew up another, as they hoped, much more effectual than that foregoing. And upon the *Tuesday* after, being *January* the seven-and-twentieth, went up with it to the Parliament-house, but could not that day get it read. Upon which I that night supped with about two hundred of them, at an house behind the *Exchange* in *London*; and the next morning went to the *Speaker* of the Parliament, and told him, that on the morrow, being *Thursday*, I intended, by God's assistance, to take my journey for beyond sea, and therefore intreated him to give me his Pass; but he told me he durst not for his hanging give me a Pass. Unto which I replied; Sir, that is very strange, that your House will command me, upon pain of death, to leave *England* by such a day, [which I am willing to do] and yet you will not enable me by your Pass to be gone. For want of which, it is very probable, when I come at the sea-side, your Officers of the Custom-house will stop me: and yet, because I am not gone out of *England* before such a day, I must be hanged. What is this else, but to lay a snare for my life? For you

* This Petition shewing the esteem and veneration *Lilburn* was in among the People, and the sentiments those times had of his Case, and the value they set on *Trials by Juries*, as the birthright of ENGLISHMEN; is the reason 'tis here inserted.

command

command me upon pain of death to be gone, and yet you will not give me your Pass to enable me to go, although it be almost impossible without it for me to get away.

Well, said the *Speaker*, I dare not for my Life give it you. So I was forced to depart without it. And the next Morning, being *Thursday*, *January* 29th, I took Horse at *Finsbury-stables*, by *Moor-fields*, and rid thro' *London* and *Southwark*, being accompanied with great Store of my Friends on Horse-back [illegible] who brought me divers Miles on my Journey. And the next day I came to *Dover*.

And being [illegible]ced at *Dover* to make use of the Parliament's printed Votes [illegible]ment, for my Pass, I was by the Officers let go, and in about my B[illegible]ne I arrived safe at *Ostend*; and upon the 8th of *February* a few Hours [illegible] last arrived (by God's Blessing) at *Amsterdam*, the Place of my desired Rest and Abode, where, within a few Days after, I found a printed Act of Parliament, which thus followeth:

An Act for the Execution of a Judgment given in Parliament against Lieutenant-Colonel *John Lilburn*.

'WHEREAS, upon the fifteenth Day of *January*, in the Year of our 'Lord 1651, a Judgment was given in Parliament against the said 'Lieutenant-Colonel *John Lilburn*, for high Crimes and Misdemeanors 'by him committed, relating to a false, malicious, and scandalous Pe'tition heretofore presented to the Parliament, by one *Josiah Primate*, of '*London*, Leatherseller, as by the due Proceedings had upon the said Pe'tition, and the Judgment thereupon given at large appeareth: Be it 'therefore enacted by this present Parliament, and by the Authority of 'the same, That the Fine of three thousand Pounds imposed upon the 'said *John Lilburn*, to the Use of the Commonwealth, by the Judgment 'aforesaid, shall be forthwith levied by due Process of Law, to the Use 'of the Commonwealth accordingly. And be it further enacted, That 'the Sum of two thousand Pounds imposed by the said Judgment upon 'the said *John Lilburn*, to be paid to Sir *Arthur Haslerig* for Damages, 'and the Sum of two thousand Pounds likewise imposed by the said Judg'ment upon the said *John Lilburn*, to be paid to *James Russel*, *Edward* '*Winslow*, *William Molins*, and *Arthur Squib*, in the said Judgment 'named; that is to say, to each of them five hundred Pounds for their 'Damages, shall be forthwith paid accordingly: And that the said Sir '*Arthur Haslerig*, *James Russel*, *Edward Winslow*, *William Molins*, and '*Arthur Squib*, their Executors and Administrators, shall have the like 'Remedy and Proceedings at Law respectively against the said *John Lil*'*burn*, his Heirs, Executors, Administrators, and Assigns, for the Re'covery of the respective Sums so given to them by the said Judgment, as 'if the said respective Sums had been due by several Recognizances in the 'Nature of a Statute Staple, acknowledged unto them severally by the 'said *John Lilburn*, upon the said 15th Day of *January*, in the Year of 'our Lord 1651. And be it likewise enacted by the Authority aforesaid, 'That the said *John Lilburn* shall, within twenty Days, to be accounted 'from the said 15th Day of *January*, 1651, depart out of *England*, *Scot*'*land*, *Ireland*, and the Islands, Territories, and Dominions thereof: 'And in case the said *John Lilburn*, at any time after the Expiration of the 'said twenty Days, to be accounted as aforesaid, shall be found, or shall 'be remaining within *England*, *Scotland*, *Ireland*, or within any of the 'Islands, Territories, or Dominions thereof; the said *John Lilburn* shall 'be, and is hereby adjudged a Felon, and shall be executed as a Felon, 'without Benefit of Clergy. And it is lastly enacted, by the Authority 'aforesaid, That all, and every Person and Persons, who shall, after the 'Expiration of the said twenty Days, wittingly relieve, harbour, or con'ceal the said *John Lilburn*, he being in *England*, *Scotland*, or *Ireland*, or 'any the Territories, Islands, or Dominions thereof, shall be hereby ad'judged accessary of Felony after the Fact. And all Judges, Justices, 'Mayors, Bailiffs, Sheriffs, and all other Officers, as well Military as 'Civil, in their respective Places, are hereby required to be aiding and 'assisting in apprehending the said *John Lilburn*, and in putting this Act 'in due Execution.'

Friday, the 30th of *January*, 1651. Ordered by the Parliament, That this Act be forthwith printed and published.

Henry Scobell, Cleric. Parliamenti.

But the said *John Lilburn* returning to his native Country in *June*, 1653, was apprehended, and committed to *Newgate*, as appears by the following *Mittimus*:

The (illegal) Mittimus *of the Lord Mayor.*

"Whereas it was enacted by a late Act of Parliament, (entitled, *An* "*Act for the Execution of a Judgment given in Parliament against Lieutenant*-"*Colonel* John Lilburn) That the said *John Lilburn* should, within twenty "Days, to be accounted from the 15th Day of *January*, 1651, depart "out of *England*, *Scotland*, *Ireland*, and the Islands, Territories, and Do"minions thereof. And that in case the said *John Lilburn*, at any Time "after the Expiration of the said twenty Days, to be accounted as afore"said, should be found, or should be remaining within *England*, *Scotland*, "*Ireland*, or within any of the Islands, Territories, or Dominions there"of; the said *John Lilburn is hereby adjudged a Felon, and to be executed as* "*a Felon*, as in the said Act was mentioned: And whereas the said *John* "*Lilburn* hath been remaining, and found since the Expiration of the said "twenty Days, within the Liberties of the City of *London*, in the Com"monwealth of *England*, contrary to the said Act: These are therefore, "in the Name of the *Keepers of the Liberties of* England, *by Authority of* "*Parliament*, to will and require you forthwith, upon Receipt hereof, "to receive into your Custody the Body of the said *John Lilburn*, whom "I send unto you herewith for the Felony aforesaid, and him safely to "keep, until he shall be delivered by due Course of Law; and this shall "be your Warrant." Given under my Hand and Seal, dated this 16th Day of *June*, in the Year of our Lord 1653.

John Fowk, Mayor.

To the Keepers of the Gaol of *Newgate*.

Before the Sessions began, *John Lilburn* petitioned the Parliament, but they taking no Notice of his Petition, he was brought to his Trial, *July* 13th, as follows:

The Keepers of the Liberties of *England*, by Authority of Parliament, against *John Lilburn*, now Prisoner at the Bar.

MR. *Lilburn* was brought to the Bar upon *Wednesday*, the 13th of *July*, where, after Silence being made in the Court, the Clerk commanded him to hold up his Hand at the Bar: Mr. *Lilburn* applying his Speech to the Lord Chief-Baron *Wylde*, desired his Honour to explain what was meant by holding up the Hand at the Bar, that so by doing that Act, Ceremony, or Form, he might not run himself into Snares and Dangers. And after a large Dispute betwixt the Court and him upon that Point, he saith, *Then, my Lord, my Name I must acknowledge to be* John Lilburn, *Gent. Son of* Richard Lilburn *of* Thickley-Punchardon, *in the County of* Durham, *Esq. and I am here ready to answer any thing any Man hath to lay to my Charge.* And the Indictment being read, Mr. *Lee*, the Clerk of the Court, demanded of him, whether he was *Guilty*, *or Not Guilty?* But Mr. *Lilburn*, the Prisoner at the Bar, applied himself to the Court, and said,

My Lord Chief-Baron Wylde,

I humbly desire as my Right by Law, to speak freely against the Insufficiency and Illegality of the Indictment, before I join Issue to it. Which being (with a little Struggling) granted him, he said, *Well then, my Lord, now is the Time, or never, for me to assign my Errors against the Indictment, before I plead to it: For if once I should plead to it, it will then be too late to assign the Errors; but if I do it before, then of Right and Justice you ought to grant me a Copy of my Indictment, and assign me learned Counsel in the Law to consult with, and a convenient time to return in my Answer unto the said Indictment: All which* (said the Prisoner) *is fully declared for good Law by the Lord* Coke, *in his 3d Institute, fol.* 29, 34. 137, 230. *which Book was published by two special Orders of the House of Commons in their Virginity and Purity, in* Anno 1641, *and* 1642, *for good Law.* The pregnant and pertinent Passages of which Places were distinctly read by the Prisoner at the Bar, and pressed with all the Earnestness and Reason he possibly could to enjoy the Benefit thereof. And to the Apprehension of the Prisoner, and Multitudes of the By-standers, the Court expresly ordered, that he should have Counsel assigned, and the Copy of the Indictment; but withal, he was ordered under his Hand to send in his Exceptions: Upon which the Prisoner was carried into the Garden, on the Backside of the Court, to draw them up; where, having remained some Space, during the dining of the Court, he writ a Letter, the Copy of which thus followeth:

For the Right Honourable the Lord Chief-Baron *Wylde*, and the rest of the Honourable Bench, these humbly present.

My Lord, and the Honourable Bench,

'SINCE I departed the Court, I have seriously considered, that I 'cannot legally make any Exceptions concerning the Errors in the 'Indictment, without a true Copy thereof, to compare with the Act 'against Lieutenant-Colonel *John Lilburn*, and therefore I humbly pray, 'that you would be pleased so far to do me that Right in Point of Life, 'that I may have a true Copy thereof, and I shall speedily present my Ex'ceptions under my Hand, and thankfully remain,

'Your Lordship's most humble Servant,

'JOHN LILBURN.'

Which Letter being delivered by one of the Officers, as the Judge was at Dinner; as soon as the Court sat again, the Prisoner, contrary to his Expectation, was called to the Bar again, and Mr. *Lee*, the Clerk of the Court, pressed very hard to him to plead to the Indictment, *Guilty*, *or Not Guilty*: But the Prisoner at the Bar applying himself to the Lord Chief-Baron *Wylde*, very much wondered why he should be called to the Bar any more, before he had enjoyed the Benefit of their own Order, for a Copy of his Indictment, and the Assignation of learned Counsel in the Law to consult with. Judge *Warburton* with some Heat falls upon the Prisoner, and undervalues the Works of that learned Man in the Law of *England*, Sir *Edward Coke*, and the Parliament's Orders, that had caused his second, third, and fourth Part of his Institutes to be printed; and highly extols the Absoluteness of Parliaments. Upon which the Prisoner at the Bar replies with a great deal of Zeal, Earnestness, Reason, Understanding, and Length of Time. And after a long and tedious Struggling, he could obtain no more that Night, but a lame Order to have Counsel assigned him only to one individual Point. And taking out the Order by his Friends the next Morning, being *Thursday*, *July* 14, 1653, he sent a Letter to the Court, the true Copy of which thus followeth:

For the Right Honourable the Lord Chief-Baron *Wylde*, and the rest of the Honourable Bench, for the Gaol Delivery of the *Old Baily*.

My Lord,

'VOUCHSAFE me Liberty to acquaint you, that immediately upon 'my getting to my Lodging in *Newgate*, I dispatched away this 'Bearer, Mr. *Overton*, with another Friend, to the Court for their Or'der, which was given unto them; and by it Mr. Serjeant *Glynn*, Mr. 'Serjeant *Earl*, Mr. *Maynard*, Mr. *Hales*, Mr. *Twisden*, Mr. *Wylde*, 'Mr. *Chute*, and Mr. *Norbury*, should be assigned of Counsel with *John* '*Lilburn*, Gentleman, to advise with him, whether he shall insist upon 'his Plea in Law, or whether he be the same *John Lilburn* named in the 'Act, or not, before ten of the Clock To-morrow in the Forenoon. Sir, 'the Parties who took the Order, posted away to seek the Counsel, and 'spent several Hours, but could find none of them but Mr. *Maynard*, 'who was sick; and Mr. *Chute*, who was just a-going out of Town: 'And besides, my Lord, give me Leave to acquaint your Honour, that 'in a private Way, I have got the Opinion of some well versed in the 'Law, and really, my Lord, when they read the Order of the Court, 'and are told, that I cannot get a Copy of the Indictment, they stand 'amazed at it, and know not what to advise: Therefore, being that 'really and in seriousness I have done the utmost to get the Advice of 'Counsel according to the said Order, and cannot obtain it to any pur'pose; neither can those that are willing privately to help me, do 'me any good (as they say) for want of the Copy of the Indictment, 'which they say in Law and Reason ought not to be denied 'to me; therefore I humbly continue my Suit to your Ho'nour,

'nour, and the honourable Bench, that you would not require impoſſibi-'lities from me, that am no Lawyer, in an abſolute unprecedented caſe, 'wherein I have no footſteps at all to tread in, or any other guide to walk 'by, but only the natural reaſon of an ignorant and illiterate Man in the 'practick part of the Law of *England*. And therefore do moſt humbly pray 'and beſeech your Honour, and the honourable Bench, as you are Chriſ-'tians, and men of honour and conſcience, to afford me a Copy of my 'Indictment, and time till the next Seſſions, to conſult with the Counſel 'that you have aſſigned me. for which favour and juſtice, I ſhall be very 'much obliged to remain,

Newgate, *July* 14, 1653.

'*Yours in ſincerity and heartineſs to ſerve you,*

'JOHN LILBURN.'

But for all the aforeſaid Letter, he was called to the Bar upon *Thurſday* in the forenoon, where he again ſtruggled very earneſtly for a Copy of his Indictment, as his right by Law; and the Lord Chief-Baron *Wylde* ſitting upon the Bench, the Recorder and the Priſoner had a long and hot encounter each with other; and about two a-clock in the afternoon the Priſoner was diſmiſſed, with a promiſe of the Copy of his Indictment, being thereupon ordered to bring in his Exceptions by two a-clock the next day in the afternoon. but the Priſoner, ſeveral hours after his diſmiſſion, apprehending himſelf wronged with thoſe delays or denials (of right and juſtice) that were put upon him, writ a third Letter, the Copy of which thus followeth:

For the Right Honourable the Lord Chief-Baron *Wylde*, and the Honourable the Court of Gaol-delivery, ſitting in the *Old-Bailey*, theſe humbly with ſpeed preſent.

'My Lord,

'I STAND amazed when I am denied a Copy of my Indictment, which 'I apprehended the Court granted me at the Bar as my right; I did 'therefore ſend my father and father-in-law, with my brother-in-law, and 'my couſin-german, humbly to deſire it as my right, but they returned me 'your denial of it: in which regard, in all humility, tho' much of my 'time be expired, I have by theſe few lines once again ſent my father and 'brother to wait upon you for a Copy of it (to leave you without excuſe), 'which is my abſolute right by Law; and do therefore humbly intreat you 'it may be ſent to me preſently, without which I am not bound in Law 'to draw up a Plea, nor cannot. But if I muſt be murdered and deſtroy-'ed without Law, my innocent blood be upon the heads of thoſe that ſhall 'be guilty of it, by will to take it from me. So humbly craving your 'Lordſhip's legal, ſpeedy, and juſt anſwer, I reſt

Thurſday, *July* 14, 1653. Paſt 5 a-clock at night.

'*Your Lordſhip's moſt humble Servant, ſo* '*far as you are a maintainer of the People* '*of* England's *fundamental Laws and* '*Liberties,*

'JOHN LILBURN.'

But receiving no benefit by the ſaid letter, the next morning, being *Friday*, his father went to the Lord Chief-Baron's Chamber, but he being preparing to go out of Town, he could not be permitted to ſpeak with him. After which, the old Gentleman came back to the *Old-Bailey*, to complain of his ſon's hard uſage; and from them with a meſſenger went back again to the Lord Chief-Baron's Chamber, and from thence to Attorney-General *Prideaux*'s Chamber, to get a Warrant from him to enjoy the Copy of the Indictment: and then coming to the Court again, about ten of the clock he received it from the hand of Mr. *Lee*; the Copy whereof thus followeth:

At the Seſſions of Peace held for the City of *London*, at Juſtice-Hall in the *Old-Bailey*, now ſitting, this preſent 16th day of *July*, 1653.

'*London, ſſ.* THE Jurors for the Keepers of the Liberty of *England*, by 'authority of Parliament, upon their Oaths do preſent, that 'in, and by a Statute made in the Parliament of this Commonwealth of '*England*, holden at *Weſtminſter*, in the County of *Middleſex*, the 30th of '*January*, in the year of our Lord, 1651, intitled *An Act for the execution of a judgment given in Parliament againſt Lieut. Col.* John Lilburn; it was en-'acted by the ſaid Parliament, and by the authority of the ſame, that the 'ſaid *John Lilburn* ſhould (within twenty days, to be accounted from the '15th day of *January*, 1651) depart out of *England*, *Scotland*, *Ireland*, and 'the Iſlands, Territories and Dominions thereof. And in caſe the ſaid '*John Lilburn*, at any time after the expiration of the ſaid twenty days, to 'be accounted as aforeſaid, ſhould be found, or ſhould be remaining with-'in *England*, *Scotland*, *Ireland*, or within any of the Iſlands, Territories or 'Dominions thereof; the ſaid *John Lilburn* ſhould be, and was thereby 'adjudged a Felon, and ſhould be executed as a Felon without benefit of 'Clergy. And it was alſo enacted by the authority aforeſaid, that all and 'every perſon and perſons, who ſhould, after the expiration of the ſaid 'twenty days, wittingly relieve, harbour, or conceal the ſaid *John Lil-'burn*, he being in *England*, *Scotland*, or *Ireland*, or any the Territories, 'Iſlands, or Dominions thereof, ſhould be thereby adjudged acceſſary of 'Felony after the fact. And all Judges, Juſtices, Mayors, Bailiffs, She-'riffs, and all other Officers, as well Military as Civil, in their reſpective 'places, are thereby required to be aiding and aſſiſting in apprehending 'the ſaid *John Lilburn*, and in putting the ſaid Act in due execution, as in 'and by the ſaid Act of Parliament appeareth. And that the ſaid *John 'Lilburn*, late of *London*, Gentleman, the Statute aforeſaid not weighing, 'nor the Puniſhments therein contained any whit fearing, after the expi-'ration of the ſaid twenty days, to be accounted from the ſaid 15th day of '*January*, 1651, as aforeſaid, to-wit, the 15th day of *June*, in the year of 'our Lord, 1653, was found, and was feloniouſly remaining within *Eng-'land* aforeſaid; that is to ſay, at *London*, to-wit, in the Pariſh of *Giles* 'without *Cripplegate*, in the Ward of *Cripplegate*, *London* aforeſaid, againſt 'the form of the Statute aforeſaid, and againſt the public peace, *&c.*'

SADLER.

And bringing it to his ſon, who, with the beſt Counſel that he had, reading it, his work was all of-new to begin again; ſo that he was forced firſt to poſt away his own father and others, to let the Court know, that although it was their order in Court, that he ſhould have had the Copy of his Indictment the day before, being *Thurſday*, about two a-clock in the afternoon; yet it was ten a-clock upon *Friday* forenoon, before he could get it. And at two a-clock in the afternoon upon the ſaid *Friday*, he was to appear at the Bar; and all his work, upon the ſerious viewing the Indictment, was to begin a-new, ſo that it was impoſſible that in three or four hours time he could be ready. And therefore his father and Mr. *Overton* preſs'd the Court to give him time till the next morning, being *Saturday* the 16th of *July*, to make his Exceptions ready, and put them in; but it would no ways be granted, nor no longer time than two hours to be added to the former. At the underſtanding of which, he intreated his father-in-law, and Mr. *Thomas Prince*, to go down to the Court again, and tell them that it was altogether impoſſible that the Priſoner could make his Exceptions ready by four a-clock in the afternoon of the ſaid *Friday*, it being ten in the forenoon, before he could get the Copy of the Indictment; although it was their order, that he ſhould have had it by two a-clock in the afternoon the day before: and therefore they preſſed hard at the Bar to the Court, to have till the next morning, being *Saturday*, for the Priſoner to bring in his Exceptions, but they alſo returned with a Negative. The Priſoner and ſuch as he had at work, followed his papers as for their lives; and about ſix or ſeven at night, came the meſſengers from the Court for Mr. *Lilburn* the Priſoner, who being come to the Bar, Mr. *Lee*, the Clerk, preſſed him again to plead *guilty or not guilty* to the ſaid Indictment; but the Priſoner little regarding him, addreſſed himſelf to the Lord-Mayor, as the then Preſident of the Court, and gave him an exact Narrative of what delays he had had about the getting of the Copy of the Indictment; being delayed from two a-clock in the afternoon upon *Thurſday*, till ten a-clock in the forenoon that preſent *Friday*: and that as ſoon as he had got it, he had taken all the pains, and uſed all the induſtry, that it was poſſible to be expected from an ignorant man in the formalities and niceties of the Law of *England*. That he had ſent ſeveral meſſengers truly to acquaint the Court, that he could not poſſibly get the ſaid Exceptions deliberately perfected before the morrow morning, being *Saturday*. That they were weighty things, and the failing in one word, might coſt him his life. That he was (when Mr. *Briſco* came for him) but newly begun to read, examine, and compare the ingroſſed copy with the original, to ſee whether there was any fault in it or no; that he nothing nigh had read over one quarter of it, when he was called away to come to the Court. That he hoped they would not compel him to put in uncorrected Exceptions for his life, eſpecially ſeeing the miſtake of one word might deſtroy him, and eſpecially ſeeing procraſtination of time was no part of his fault, but the Court's only and ſolely, who had cauſeleſly ſpent ſo much time, before they would give him that, the Copy of his Indictment, which was in Law (he having already made his verbal Exceptions) ſo eſſentially and legally his right, and without which he neither was bound, nor could make legally and formally in Law his Exceptions againſt the Indictment read unto him in Court. And therefore humbly prayed, that he might enjoy the honourable Court's favour till to-morrow morning, to make them ready, and put them in: which being granted, he the Priſoner departed to his lodging, and poſted away to ſeveral of his Counſel, ſome of which coming to him that night, he had a large diſcourſe with them, and they read much of his papers, and very highly approved of his Exceptions; but withal told him, he had fallen far ſhort in demanding his right and due.

So upon *Saturday*, about eight a-clock in the forenoon, he was brought to the Bar again, and he was preſſed again by Mr. *Lee*, to plead, *guilty*, or *not guilty*, to the Indictment.

But Mr. *Lilburn*, the Priſoner at the Bar, regarded not him, but addreſſed himſelf to the Lord-Mayor and the Court, acquainting them where they left off the laſt night; and that in obedience to their commands, he had brought in his Exceptions againſt the ſufficiency of the Indictment read unto him in the Court, fairly ingroſſed in Parchment according to Law, and humbly prayed that it might be accepted, recorded and read: ſo handing it into the Court, the Recorder, Mr. *Steele*, took it in his hand, looked upon it, and ſaid, Mr. *Lilburn*, this is not under your Counſel's hands.

Mr. *Lilburn*. No, Sir, it is not, I am ſure ſome of them tell me it needs not; but it is under my own hand, and I muſt and will juſtify, and make good thoſe Exceptions with my life.

Recorder. Wherefore did we aſſign Counſel? One cauſe was, that they might ſign your Exceptions.

Lilburn. My Lord, with your favour thus; be pleaſed to take notice, that in your aſſigning me Counſel, you have only done it to one individual point; which is not only a ſnare to me, but alſo to my Counſel. *Firſt*, To me, in cooping me up to one plea for my life; whereas the inſufficiency of the Indictment, and the illegal, contradictory things upon which it is grounded, and my right in Law, leaves me ſufficiently at elbow-room to have plurality of Pleas or Exceptions. and therefore in your aſſigning me Counſel in one point only; if they ſhould ſet their hands to any more but that one point alone, they tell me, they run themſelves into ſnares and dangers. But, my Lord, they likewiſe tell me, if you, and this honourable Court, pleaſe to aſſign them of my Counſel at large, they will not only ſign my Exceptions, but will venture their All at the Bar of Juſtice to maintain them to be good Law. And not only ſo, but they tell me, and bid me tell the Court, if I pleaſed, that if they have any underſtanding in the Law, and that their Law-books ſpeak truth, they are very confident that all the Judges and Lawyers in *England*, put together in one, ſhall never be able, while they breathe, to draw up a legal Indictment upon the Act of Baniſhment of the 30th of *January*, 1651, and the Votes or Judgment (as 'tis called) of the 15th of *January*, 1651, upon which it is grounded, if theſe printed copies of them be true copies, becauſe, my Lord, they ſay, a judgment, and the execution of a judgment, ought to be like a pair of Indentures exactly even in all things, the one neither to be above nor below the other, but even with it in all circumſtances; but in the pretended judgment, and the Act for execution thereof, there are theſe three eſſential differences:

Firſt, The judgment (as it's called) ſaith, Lieutenant-Colonel *John Lilburn* ſhall be baniſhed and depart out of *England*, within thirty days next after the ſaid 15th day of *January*, 1651; but the Act for executing the ſaid Judgment, expreſly ſaith, he ſhall not ſtay in *England* above twenty days next after the ſaid 15th day of *January*, 1651: So that, my Lord, here is ten days difference betwixt the

Judgment

Judgment itself, and the Act for the pretended execution thereof; which makes an essential nullity in it, and all proceedings that are founded upon it.

Secondly, The pretended Judgment banisheth one Lieutenant-Colonel *John Lilburn* out of *England*, *Scotland*, and *Ireland*, and the Islands and Territories thereunto belonging, but banisheth him not in the least out of their Dominions; so that *Wales* being stiled, distinguished, and denominated in Law to be a Dominion, the said banished Lieutenant-Colonel *John Lilburn*, by any words contained in the said banishing Votes or Judgment, might legally and securely have lived in *Wales* all his days. But then comes the said Act of *January* 30th, 1651, which is called An Act for the execution of the said Judgment of the 15th of *January*, 1651, given in Parliament against Lieutenant-Colonel *John Lilburn*, and it banisheth the said Lieutenant-Colonel out of *England*, *Scotland*, *Ireland*, and the Islands, Territories and Dominions thereof; so that here is a main essential difference betwixt the pretended Judgment, and the Act for the execution thereof.

The third difference betwixt them is this; the pretended Judgment of the 15th of *January*, 1651, saith, That if the said banished Lieutenant-Colonel *John Lilburn* shall return into *England*, &c. at any time after the expiration of the said thirty days, he shall be proceeded against as a Felon, and shall suffer death accordingly.

But the said pretended Act of the 30th of *January*, 1651, made on pretence for the execution thereof, expresly saith, by way of addition, that if the said Lieut. Col. *John Lilburn* shall return into *England*, &c. after his banishment, he shall be, and is hereby adjudged a Felon, and shall be executed as a Felon, without benefit of Clergy; so that, my Lord, they say it is impossible to draw up a legal Indictment upon the fore-mentioned contradicting Act, Votes, or pretended Judgment.

Mr. *Recorder*. Well then, Mr. *Lilburn*, seeing your Counsel are so willing, as you say they are, to sign your Exceptions for good Law, the Court will give you time till six of the clock at night, to get their hands to it, and will assign you Counsel at large. Unto which Mr. *Lilburn* replied, My Lord, I am put upon a great streight.

First, In that the Sessions are holden a week after they should usually have been held; by means of which length of time, most of the great and chiefest, ablest, and most learned Counsel of *England* are gone out of Town.

Secondly, Your Honour and the Court hath exhausted and spent from *Wednesday* morning till this hour, before you would fully grant me that which is my absolute right by Law; by means of which delay of time, I am afraid, I have by this lost all my Counsel, that you have assigned me, that I can fully rest upon, that were in Town, when I named them for my Counsel, and whom, if you pleased to have ordered it so, I could have often conferred with since, though now truly, I am afraid they are all gone out of Town upon the Circuit; and if they be, is it possible that I should get their hands to my Exceptions by six-a-clock? And therefore that we may delay no longer time in this Trial, I beseech you, without any more ado, accept of my own Exceptions under my own hand. I am sure I am the most concerned in them, and my life must pay for the faults in them, if there be any. And therefore I pray accept of them without any more ado, under my own hand alone. I am sure my Counsel tell me, you ought in Law to do it.

Recorder. Well, Mr. *Lilburn*, in short, the Court tells you they cannot in Law, nor will not accept them, without your Counsel sign them.

Lilburn. Really, Mr. *Recorder*, you drive me to very great streights, in delaying me so long my right by Law, before you will fully grant it me; it is an apparent hazard, and a very great probability my Counsel are already gone out of Town. and then after you have so delayed me, to tie me up to an unnecessary and unrequired in Law Punctilio, for me to get my Counsels hands to my Exceptions in so short a time, when in probability it is impossible it shall or can be done.

Besides, my Lord-Mayor, consider of the inconveniency that Mr. *Recorder* would tie me to, which is this; I stand here to plead for my life, and I am commanded to put in my Exceptions against the illegality of an Indictment read unto me, and it may be, it is evidently seen, known, or at least believed, that I have several of the now-present greatest men in *England* for my grand and chiefest adversaries; and therefore to tie me up in my case at all, to bring in any thing under my Counsels hands, is a snare and danger to me: for we all know by experience, my Lord, how easy it is for the great men in power, right or wrong, to crush and destroy any man that they in good earnest set themselves against; and it is apparent their Indignation is heated seven-fold against me (but I must avow it, without any the least just ground or cause), and it cannot chuse but burn in a very great degree against my Counsellors, that shall help me in Law to preserve my life, against their inraged and big-swollen malice. And, my Lord, I am sure, almost all those Counsellors that you have assigned me, are not only men of great estates, but also men of great practice, which is their livelihood; and 'tis possible my condition, before my Trial is done, will compel and necessitate me to speak that high, and yet legal language, that may ruin and destroy my Counsel, either to plead it, or set their hands to it: and for me to expect or desire that from them, that shall apparently tend to the ruin and destruction of them and their families, when I am in such a mean, low, and poor condition, as that I am able in no nature in the least to make them any part of amends for that ruin or loss they shall or may sustain, by too deep ingaging for my preservation, I were an irrational, unjust, beastly man to do it. My Lord, it is my person at present now at the Bar, that is in hazard and jeopardy, and none else. And, my Lord, I am long since robbed of all my estate, by the tyrannical will and arbitrary pleasure of Sir *Arthur Haslerig*, and have long since nothing left to buy me bread, but what I borrow. And, my Lord, I have now nothing to lose but my Wife and tender Babes, and my skin, and to die to me is gain, so I be not *felo de se*, a murderer of myself: and, therefore, I beseech you, my Lord, let me put in my Exceptions under my own hand.

Mr. *Recorder*. Mr. *Lilburn*, if you be so earnest thus to do, wherefore do you so much press for Counsel learned in the Law to be assigned you?

Mr. *Lilburn*. I will tell you presently, my Lord: In the *Italian History* of a Nobleman of *Italy*, and otherwise, I have read and heard of *Gustavus Adolphus*, that valiant and wise late King of *Sweden*; that although he was a most expert Soldier, yet in all difficult and knotty enterprizes that he did endeavour to undertake, he would call all his able, discreet and understanding Officers together. And because, as *Solomon* saith, two is better than one, and a three-fold cord is not easily broken; he would advise and consult with them all: but yet, being he was, and did apprehend himself most concerned, and had the far greatest stock to adventure in the affair he went about, he would not absolutely be tied up in every punctilio to their advice; but being a very wise, righteous, just, and withal valiant man, it is therefore said of him, when he had heard with mature deliberation all their advices, he would after that, with a serious consultation with his own reason and understanding, draw his own inferences and conclusions, and with mettle and gallantry put them only in execution. Even so, my Lord, my Life being at stake, although I have a little competency of understanding, and mettle enough to execute a thing; yet being I am ignorant of the punctilios, formalities or practick part of the Law; and being that the Scripture saith, *Woe to him that is alone*, for two is better than one, and a three-fold cord is not easily broken, on those considerations I am desirous to consult with learned Counsel in the Law, especially since it is my right by Law so to do. But I do assure you, my Lord, seeing God hath endowed me with a good proportion of judgment and understanding to discern of things, and seeing my adventure is abundantly the greatest, I will not absolutely be tied up to follow my Counsels advice in all things, neither will I do it, unless I like it very well; but in most knotty, difficult and high cases, that is not safe for them too deeply to engage in, for fear of their own ruin, and my absolute inability in any proportionable measure to requite them; I will therefore draw my inference and conclusions from their advice and counsel, and manage them myself in my own way, for the safety and preservation of my own life. And therefore, my Lord, I pray you again to accept of my Exceptions under my own hand, without any more ado, that so we may speedily come to some issue of this tedious, jangling business.

Recorder. Mr. *Lilburn*, I tell you again, the Court will not, nor cannot receive your Exceptions without being signed by your Counsel; and therefore to enable you to procure their hands, we will give you an order at large, that so you may fully be ready by six a-clock.

Mr. *Lilburn*. My Lord, I pray deliver the order speedily to my father there in Court, lest if it be never so little delayed, my Counsel be all gone out of Town: which being by the Court assented unto, the Copy of the order thus followeth:

" *London*. AT the Gaol-delivery of *Newgate*, *July* 16, 1653. Mr. Serjeant *Glynne*, Mr. Serjeant *Earle*, Mr. *Maynard*, Mr.
" *Hale*, Mr. *Twisden*, Mr. *Wilde*, Mr. *Chute*, Mr. *Norbury*, and Mr.
" *Webb*, are by this Court assigned of Counsel, with *John Lilburn*, Gent.
" to perfect his Plea in Law, and deliver the same under the hands of
" them, or one of them, before six of the clock this day in the after-
" noon." SADLER.

Whereupon the Prisoner withdrew to his lodging, and being brought to the Bar about six a-clock at night, Mr. *Lee*, the Clerk of the Court, pressed very hard to him, to answer and plead to the Indictment, *guilty or not guilty*; besides whom, stept up another Gentleman in the Court, and he in a mumbling manner prest something, as hard as his slender abilities would enable him. Whereupon Mr. *Lilburn* demanded to know of the Lord-Mayor, what that newly-come Gentleman was, that was so far afraid to speak out his mind, that he could not understand what he said. Whereupon answer was returned, it was Mr. *Hall*, the Attorney of the Dutchy, who was come thither to be a Prosecutor for the State or Commonwealth.

But Mr. *Lilburn*'s chiefest business being with the Court, he accordingly applied himself to the Lord-Mayor:

My Lord, I desire to give your Honour a true and real account of all my transactions, since I was last before you, which is this: You may remember at my being last at the Bar, I told you, I did verily believe my Counsel were all upon the point of going out of Town; in which regard I earnestly intreated you without more delay to deliver your order to my father, that so he might not fall short of getting to my Counsel before they were gone; but, my Lord, at my departure from the Bar, as soon as I came to my lodging, I all on post-haste dispatched my cousin-germans, *George* and *William Lilburn*, to Mr. *Norbury*, who they found just ready to mount on horseback, to be gone out of Town, and acquaint him by word of mouth, with the order the Court had made, to assign him my Counsel at large: and he was pleased, without any delay, in his riding habit, to hasten to me, and seriously read over my Exceptions, and sign them, and so bid me farewel, and is gone out of Town. But, my Lord, that which I desire your Honour to take notice of, is, That if I had stay'd till my father came forth of the Court with your order, I had totally lost Mr. *Norbury*, and he had absolutely been gone out of Town a good while before he could have got to him.

In the second place, having sent my said kinsmen post-haste before to my Counsel, as soon as my father came with your order, I posted him and my brother-in-law away to Mr. *Maynard*; with whom speaking at his own chamber, they found him sickly and ill, and altogether unfit and unable to come to me, by reason of that little time he had to stay in Town, those several things he had to do at his chamber during his staying, and the weakness of his body, and the absolute necessity of his being at a place by a fix'd hour, or to run the hazard of losing six hundred pound upon his own score: and if you doubt any thing of this relation, they are here in Court to declare the truth of it upon their Oaths themselves. But, my Lord, though Mr. *Maynard* could not well come to me, yet he was pleased to stay at his chamber, till my father fetch'd my Papers and Exceptions from me, which, with seriousness reading, he hath also signed them, which I have now in my hand. But, my Lords, from both my Counsellors, especially Mr *Maynard*, I perceive I am very much blamed for my ignorance and folly, in not, when I demanded the *Copy of my Indictment*, as my right by Law, demanding *Oyer*, *or hearing in open Court, of the Act of Parliament, the Judgment upon which it is grounded, and the Crimes upon which the Judgment is grounded*; which, I understand from them, should be exemplified under the Great Seal of *England*, and ought so to be here remaining in Court.

Mr. Recorder replied, Mr. *Lilburn*, we know of no ſuch thing, the Records of the Acts of Parliament are at *Weſtminſter*, in the Clerk of the Parliament's hands, and there you may have them.

Mr. *Lilburn.* Good Mr. Recorder, interrupt me not, but let me go on; I ſay, my Counſel tells me, I ought, as my right by Law, to have demanded *Oyer of the ſaid Act, Judgment and Crimes*, and after I had ſeen them under the Broad Seal of *England*, and heard them read in open Court, I ought, as my right by Law, to have demanded copies of them all three, and they ought not to have been denied me, that ſo I might have been fully enabled all at once to have returned Exceptions at large to the Indictment, the Act upon which it is grounded, the Judgment upon which the Act is grounded, and the Crimes, which is the original of all. And if no legal Act can be produced, they tell me the Indictment, and all proceedings upon it, are void and null. And they alſo ſay, if no legal Judgment can be produced, they tell me the Act for the execution of it is null, and falls to the ground. And they alſo ſay, if no Crimes in Law can be produced upon which the Judgment is legally founded, all is at an end, becauſe what is not good nor found in its original in Law, can never be made ſo by tract of time; and what is not ſound and ſubſtantial in its foundation, can never be made ſo in its fabrick or building. But yet, my Lord, they ſay it is not too late for me yet to inſiſt upon the *Oyer* as my right by Law: I confeſs, my Lord, their time would not permit either of them to ſtay in the Town, to draw me up the formal draught of ſuch a claim, much leſs would it permit them to ſtay in Town till it was engroſſed in parchment, that ſo they might ſet their hands unto it. But, my Lord, according to thoſe legal inſtructions that I have largely received from my Counſel, I have got ſuch a Paper formally in Law drawn up, and it is here ingroſſed in Parchment, and ſigned with my own hand. And, my Lord, I here tender it unto the Court, with two ſhillings as the Clerk's fee, to enter it upon Record at his peril. The Copy of which Parchment thus followeth:

At the Seſſions of Peace held for the City of *London*, at Juſtice-Hall in the *Old-Bailey*, now ſitting this preſent 16th day of *July*, 1653.

The Keepers of the Liberties of England, *by Authority of Parliament, againſt* John Lilburn, *now Priſoner at the Bar.*

THE ſaid *John Lilburn*, Gent. the now Priſoner at the Bar, ſuppoſed to be indicted by that name, brought to the Bar, and now appearing in perſon, having heard the ſaid Indictment read in theſe words, to wit:

London ſſ. The Jurors for the Keepers of the Liberties of *England*, by authority of Parliament upon their oaths do preſent, that in and by a Statute made in the Parliament of this Commonwealth of *England*, holden at *Weſtminſter* in the County of *Middleſex*, the 30th day of *January*, in the year of our Lord 1651, intitled, *An Act for the Execution of a Judgment given in Parliament againſt Lieutenant-Colonel* John Lilburn; and it was enacted by the ſaid Parliament, and by the authority of the ſame, That the ſaid *John Lilburn* ſhould (within twenty days, to be accounted from the 15th day of *January*, 1651), depart out of *England, Scotland, Ireland*, and the Iſlands, Territories, and Dominions thereof. And in caſe the ſaid *John Lilburn*, at any time after the expiration of the ſaid twenty days, to be accounted as aforeſaid, ſhould be found, or ſhould be remaining within *England, Scotland, Ireland*, or within any of the Iſlands, Territories, or Dominions thereof, the ſaid *John Lilburn* ſhould be, and was thereby adjudged a Felon, and ſhould be executed as a Felon, without benefit of Clergy.

And it was alſo enacted by the authority aforeſaid, That all and every perſon and perſons, who ſhould, after the expiration of the ſaid twenty days, wittingly relieve, harbour, or conceal the ſaid *John Lilburn*, he being in *England, Scotland, Ireland*, or any the Territories, Iſlands, or Dominions thereof, ſhould be thereby adjudged acceſſary of Felony after the fact. And all Judges, Juſtices, Mayors, Bayliffs, Sheriffs, and all other Officers, as well military as civil, in their reſpective places, are thereby required to be aiding and aſſiſting in apprehending the ſaid *John Lilburn*, and in putting the ſaid Act in due execution, as in and by the ſaid Act of Parliament appeareth. And that the ſaid *John Lilburn*, late of *London*, Gentleman, the Statute aforeſaid not weighing, nor the puniſhments therein contained any whit fearing, after the expiration of the ſaid twenty days, to be accounted from the ſaid 15th day of *January*, 1651, as aforeſaid; to wit, the 15th day of *June*, in the year of our Lord 1653, was found, and was feloniouſly remaining within *England* aforeſaid; that is to ſay, at *London*, to wit, in the Pariſh of *Giles* without *Cripplegate*, in the Ward of *Cripplegate, London* aforeſaid, againſt the form of the Statute aforeſaid, and againſt the publick Peace, *&c.*

Sadler.

Which being heard and read, he ſaith, that it appears by the ſaid Indictment, that he ſtands indicted by the name of *John Lilburn of London*, Gentleman, by virtue of an Act of Parliament made the 30th day of *January*, 1651; grounded upon a ſuppoſed Judgment given in Parliament againſt him the ſaid *John*, or one Lieutenant-Colonel *John Lilburn*, for ſeveral crimes and miſdemeanors therein contained. And therefore he the now Priſoner at the Bar, doth humbly pray *Oyer*, or hearing of the ſaid Act, Judgment, and ſuppoſed Crimes mentioned in the ſaid Act, according to Law, and under the Great Seal of *England*, to enable him to plead thereunto. And he will ever pray for your Honours and Bench.

John Lilburn.

Which being handed into the Court, Mr. Recorder looked upon it, and ſaid, Mr. *Lilburn*, this is not ſigned under your Counſel's hand; the thing that we expect is, your Exceptions ſign'd by your Counſel: what call you this Parchment?

Mr. *Lilburn.* I know not, Sir, what more properly to call it, than my legal demand of *Oyer*, or hearing in open Court the Act of Parliament upon which the Indictment is grounded, and the Judgment upon which the Act is grounded, and the Crimes which is the foundation of all. And, Sir, let me tell you, my Counſel commands me to inſiſt, and dwell upon the demand of *Oyer* as my right, and as the chiefeſt ſhield and buckler I have to [illegible]. for they ſay, if no legal crimes can be produced upon which the Judgment was grounded, all is at an end, and there can be no more proceedings againſt me. And I am ſure, there can be no felonious crimes in Law produced againſt me, for I never committed any in all my days, never was any legally ſo much as pretended to be laid unto my charge: therefore, my Lord, as my Birthright, and Inheritance, I demand the benefit of the Law, which is *Oyer*, or hearing of the Act, Judgment, and Crimes. But the Recorder, the Lord Mayor, and ſeveral others endeavoured to interrupt him.

Whereupon he cried out again and again, My Lord, Rob me not of my Birthright, the benefit of the Law, but let me have *Oyer*; which again and again I demand as my right, and inheritance. But four or five in the Court again interrupting him, *viz.* the Lord-Mayor, Mr. Recorder, Mr. Attorney-General *Prideaux*, and mumbling Mr. *Hall*; My Lord, Rob me not of my Birthright, the benefit of the Law, nor interrupt me not, but give me free liberty to ſpeak for my life. And, my Lord, if you will be ſo audacious and unjuſt in the face of this great auditory of People, to deny me, and rob me of all the rules of Juſtice and Right, and will forcibly ſtop my mouth, and not ſuffer me freely to ſpeak for my life according to Law, I will cry out and appeal to the People, and do cry out, and appeal to all the People that hear me this day, how that my Lord-Mayor, and this Court, by violence rob me of my Birthright by Law, and will not ſuffer me to ſpeak for my life. At which the Court being in a great heat and rage, Mr. Recorder ſent the Priſoner his parchment, and money out of the Court again; but he would have none of it, but commanded the Clerk again to receive it, and enter it upon Record at his Peril.

Mr. Attorney-General *Prideaux* being very buſy to hold the Priſoner to queſtions to inſnare himſelf, as whether he was that *John Lilburn* meant, and intended in the Indictment and Act, or no, and to ſtave him off from purſuing his juſt demand of *Oyer*; which the Priſoner perceiving, falls upon the ſaid Mr. *Prideaux* to this effect:

My Lord,

I had thought the other day I had ſaid enough to have ſilenced that Gentleman at this place, but, my Lord, ſeeing he will needs be doing, and ſpeaking, I beſeech you, my Lord, let me deſire to be ſatisfied, and to know in what capacity that Gentleman is here at this place; for I am ſure, my Lord, he is no Judge of the Law, nor no Citizen, and therefore cannot, as a Juſtice of Peace, ſit upon the Bench as one of my Judges. And, my Lord, if he be my proſecutor, as he is Attorney-General, he can be no more; and if ſo, my Lord, it is an amazement to me, that your Lordſhip and the Court will ſo diſhonour yourſelves, as to ſuffer a bare Proſecutor to ſit amongſt you upon the Bench, as one of the chiefeſt of you, with his hat on his head. My Lord, do that which becomes you, and thruſt him down to the Bar, and there let him (as I do) ſtand with his hat in his hand, and know his office and duty, and prate there. But, my Lord, whether he ſits as my Judge, or my Proſecutor, he is no competent man to be in either place; becauſe, my Lord, he is legally an impeached Traitor, by one Eſquire *Elliot*, now Priſoner in *Newgate*; who, my Lord, avows to me, that he hath long ſince, before the Lord Chief-Juſtice *Rolls*, and the reſt of the Judges of the Upper-Bench, legally and formally in Law exhibited a charge of High-Treaſon againſt him; which he avows the Court hath accepted of, and recorded as formal in Law, and required of him to enter into great bonds to proſecute it, and make it good: and, my Lord, here is a duplicate of the ſaid charge of High-Treaſon, which the Eſquire's own hand gave unto me as a true copy. And beſides, my Lord, he further vows to me, that the Attorney-General, by reaſon of his late power and greatneſs in Parliament, the ſaid Attorney-General ſtands out in contempt, and ſcorn of the law, and neither will, nor dare anſwer his ſaid charge of High-Treaſon; in which regard of his contempt of the Law of *England*, through his own acknowledged guilt thereby, he hath almoſt brought him at Law to be outlawed as a Traitor: which he avows, as ſoon as it is perfected, whenever he can meet the ſaid Attorney-General, and apprehend him, he will without any more ado execute him as a Traitor.

In all which regards, my Lord, I do avow Mr. Attorney-General, in Law, to be altogether uncompetent, either for my Judge, or Proſecutor, or any man's elſe whatſoever; or ſo much as to be at liberty, to converſe with the honeſt and untainted People of *England* till he hath yielded conformity to the Law, and anſwered to his ſaid charge of High-Treaſon. Unto which Mr. Recorder ſeemed to make ſome anſwer in the Attorney-General's behalf (which the penman hereof not well hearing, cannot ſet down).

But Mr. Recorder fell upon the Priſoner, and told him how he had trifled away the time of that Court, and had had more favour than any Priſoner ever had.

Mr. *Lilburn* endeavouring to reply, the Court over and over again and again interrupted him; but he would go on, and crying out ſaid to this effect: Mr. Recorder, I wonder you are not aſhamed to tax me with trifling away time, when it is only yourſelf and the Court that are truly guilty of it, in making me ſpend my lungs and my ſpirits for two or three days together, to plead and conteſt with you, before you would grant me that which is ſo abſolutely my right by Law, as a Copy of my Indictment is. ſo that, Sir, with your favour, it is you that trifle away time, and not I. And whereas you ſay, I have had more favour than ever Priſoner had; I wonder, Mr. Recorder, you are not aſhamed ſo to ſay: for what favour at all have I had, when I have not yet enjoyed ſo much as the Law allows me? Sir, let me tell you, the learned men of the Law, the Lord Chief-Juſtice *Rolls*, and the Judges of the King's or Upper-Bench, allowed the Lord *Macguire*, that arch bloody *Iriſh* Rebel and Traitor, who was indicted before them for his life, a thouſand times more favour than you do me. for although his crimes were notoriouſly wicked, even in the eye of the common or known Law of *England*, and obvious and perſpicuous almoſt to the ſight of every eye; yet when he made, as my information hath often told me, but one ſingle exception in a punctilio, or formality about his Peerage, againſt his Indictment, the Judges aſſigned him learned Counſel in the Law to plead it, and time enough for him and them to ſtudy and frame their Arguments in Law upon it.

Mr. *Recorder.* Mr. *Lilburn*, you tell us much of the advice your Counſel has given you about the *Oyer*, can you ſhew us their advice under their hands?——*Lilburn.* Yes, Sir, that I can.

Recorder

Recorder. Well, produce it.

Lilburn. Sir, do ye mean to the point of the *Oyer*?

Recorder. Yes.

Lilburn. Well then, Sir, it may be as to the punctilio of a word I have mistaken you; but I am sure I have it under one of their hands, and two Witnesses at the Bar to depose it upon Oath, that the other expresly advised it, as the ma[illegible]n essential thing to my life and well-being.

Recorder. Mr. *Lilburn*, for all your pretence of integrity, the auditors may take notice [illegible] hat you aver a falshood in the open Court that you are not able to make [illegible]ood.

Mr. *Lilburn.* [illegible] the midst of those many and eager interruptions that I meet with from [illegible]ree or four of you at a time, it is easy for a stronger memory than mine, to let a slip fall in the punctilio of a word; but, Sir, to the utmost of [illegible]y disparagement, and disadvantage, make the worst of [illegible] you can; and [illegible]ee what it can amount unto. For in the first place, I do avow with my life, that I saw Mr. *Norbury*, with his own hand, write these very words upon the back of the Copy of the Indictment, which is [illegible]ere in my hand, and are as followeth:

Mr. Lilburn [illegible]ught to see the Certiorari, *and the Return of the* Certiorari; *and if the Act be certified without the Judgment, which is recited therein, all [illegible] invalid for the Commonwealth.*

Mr. *Steele* was pleased to spend some time upon cavilling at Mr. *Lilburn*'s mispro[illegible]ncing the word *Certiorari*; although he had formerly told the Recorder, [illegible] neither understood *Latin*, nor *French*, nor could well read either of [illegible]em. And then he told them, that most Lawyers hands were very ill to [illegible]read by persons that were not well acquainted with them; but, Sir, saith he, here is Mr. *Norbury*'s own hand, and I do avow it upon my life for a truth, that my eyes saw his own hand and pen write it.

Secondly, If [illegible]ny memory mistake not, I have Mr. *Maynard*'s hand to the same thing also: in those instructions that Mr. *Maynard* under his hand sent me [illegible]y my father and brother this day, both of whom are here present in Court, upon their Oaths to justify, that if it be not plainly expressed under his hand, that by word of mouth, it was the principal instruction he gave unto them, to give unto me to insist upon, as my right, to demand the *Oyer*, &c. But, Sir, as for the paper itself, there it is, read it, which paper followeth in these words:

It said, that John Lilburn *the 15th of* June 1653, *was found, and was feloniously remaining in* England. *This is insufficient, for it is not said that he was feloniously found; so that the being found in* England *is not laid within the Indictment.* Secondly, *And was feloniously remaining; it should be said, was then and there feloniously remaining. So there is no Felony charged in his being found. There is no time charged of that which is laid as a Felony.* John Maynard, *the 16th of* July 1653.

And by way of postscript in the same hand, there are these words, *That the Prisoner at the Bar is to desire, that he may have Counsel to plead his Exceptions.* And in the same paper, in somewhat a different hand, there are these very words, *I pray the Oyer of the Act of Parliament the Indictment is grounded upon; pray enter it upon Record, accept of no Copy but the sight of the Record under the Broad Seal.* Which paper the Recorder reading, and seriously viewing, said, Mr. *Lilburn*, this paper will not reach your purposes; for those lines that seem to be Mr. *Maynard*'s, are not home to the thing in hand, and those lines that are for your purpose are in a quite different hand.

Mr. *Lilburn.* Well, Mr. *Recorder*, it matters not much, for I am sure the paper is not in the least of my writing; for I had it as it is from my brother, that I sent to Mr. *Maynard* with my father about my business, and I am sure it either all is Mr. *Maynard*'s hand, or my brother's; who writ down from the words of Mr. *Maynard*'s own mouth, those instructions that he gave unto him and my father for me to dwell and insist upon, and to venture and cast my life upon. There they both are, I pray administer unto them both their Oaths, that they may freely speak before the Court, what Mr. *Maynard* said unto them in this particular point about the *Oyer*, &c.

Whereupon old Mr. *Richard Lilburn*, the Prisoner's father, with his son-in-law Mr. *Thomas Gore*, began to speak, and to justify what the Prisoner had alledged; but the Court interrupted them, and commanded them to be silent, and would not let them go on. But Mr. *Recorder*, taking liberty to speak as long and as often as he pleased, took the liberty several times to calumniate, and render odious the Prisoner at the Bar, for averring a falshood in the open Court, and so sometimes did the Lord-Mayor also, although his Honour was pleased to shew Mr. *Lilburn* a printed Petition a day or two before, and did solemnly in the face of all the Court aver, that the Woman, pointing to Mrs. *Dormer*, then a Prisoner at the Bar, had avowed that she had the said printed Petition, and others of the same kind, from Mr. *Lilburn*. Upon which the said Mrs. *Dormer* openly cried out, That's false, my Lord, I never said any such thing in my life.

Upon these furious hurley-burleys, that happened betwixt the Lord-Mayor, Mr. Recorder, the Attorney-General, and mumbling Mr *Hall* the Attorney of the Dutchy, and Mr. *Lilburn* Prisoner at the Bar; Mr. *Lilburn*'s father, and his brother-in-law Mr. *Gore*, and one Mr. *Thomas Haws*, but especially Mr. *Thomas Prince*, pressed to speak; but could not be permitted, but were again and again interrupted and silenced.

But Mr. *Prince* pressed hard on, and told the Lord-Mayor to this purpose; That it was the known Law of *England*, that any by-stander whatsoever might speak for the Prisoner's benefit at the Bar, especially when they apprehended the Prisoner was like to be wronged, and denied his birthright, the benefit of the Law; and this privilege, my Lord, by order of the Court, you have granted me, and other of Mr. *Lilburn*'s friends as our right by Law, to speak in his behalf, when we see things urged against him against reason and right; and therefore, my Lord, the thing that Mr. *Lilburn* demands about his *Oyer*, or hearing read the Act of Parliament, upon which the Indictment is grounded, and the Judgment upon which the Act is grounded, and the crimes that ought to be the original of all, is so essentially his right, that it is an amazement to me to see it disputed: and also it is a wonder to me, that any man that pretends so much as to know the very first Rudiments, or the very first footsteps of the Law, as Mr Recorder doth, should endeavour to deny such a thing so commonly practised in every ordinary Court of Justice, in the case of every ordinary Bond and Bill that a suit is commenced upon.

The Court with violence and fury interrupting him, and silencing him; and Mr. Recorder commanding the Prisoner at the Bar at his peril to deliver in his Exceptions before it was too late to receive them, and Mr. *Hall* mumblingly pressing again and again to pass sentence of condemnation upon him; and the Attorney-General upon the Bench closely pressing to hold him to the point, and not let the Prisoner have any elbow-room to go from it, and Mr. *Lee* the Clerk of the Court, (like a most detestable Tyrant) pressing to gagg the Prisoner at the Bar, that so he should speak no more, and immediately pass sentence of condemnation upon him, and take him away: the Prisoner clearly perceiving the violence and fury of the Court, with an extreme, earnest, ardent and fierce, and shrill, loud voice, cried out;

My Lord, will you murder me without right of Law, by robbing me of my Birthright, and denying me of *Oyer*, which is as much my right by Law, as the blood that runs in my veins? My Lord, are you afraid, and ashamed to produce that *Act of Parliament* upon which you pretend to ground your Indictment, upon which you would take away my life? My Lord, if you thus proceed, you will give me and the people cause to believe, that there never was such an Act of Parliament as you pretend, nor such a Judgment as it pretends to be the executor of; nor no such crime ever committed or acted, as any Judgment of Felony can be imagined to be grounded upon; but that rather all your proceedings against me, from first to last, is a malicious pack'd conspiracy against me to murder me, and without ground or cause to take away my life. For whose life have I feloniously taken away, or endanger'd? And if none of all these things in the least can be laid unto my charge, or never were, where is the act of Felony that I have committed, upon which I am endeavoured to be hanged?

But the Officers crying out, *Hear the Court*; and the said mumbling Mr. *Hall* still singing his pitiful ill-tuned song of pressing for Judgment against the Prisoner; and so many of the Court fell upon him at once, to deliver in his Exceptions before it was too late, as made the proceedings of the Court full of confusion.

Mr. *Lilburn.* My Lord, I may not part with my Exceptions till my demand of *Oyer* be read. My Lord, my able and honest Counsel, both of them, in both of whom I have found a great deal of faithfulness and truth to me, have commanded me to dwell upon my demand of *Oyer*, as upon my life, and as upon a thing that is my undoubted right by Law, that cannot, nor ought not to be denied me. My Lord, the security of my life lies in it; and if it be granted me, I am for ever out of all danger of gunshot, because it is possible you cannot produce one line of a legal Act of Parliament, nor one syllable of a legal Judgment, nor, I am sure of it, so much as any shadow of pretence of a legal crime of Felony to be the foundation of all: and if so, they tell me absolutely all your proceedings against me are at an end, and I am safe and secure. Therefore, my Lord, I again and again press, to leave the Court without excuse, and do demand before all these people *Oyer*, or hearing of the Act, Judgment and Crimes upon which your Indictment is grounded, as a thing that is as much my right by Law, as the blood that runs in my veins; therefore, my Lord, deny it me not.

Mr. *Lilburn*, saith the Recorder, *it is late, and we cannot spend much more time about your business; and the Court hath already told you, they neither will nor can receive in your parchment for* Oyer, *without your Counsel sign it.*

Mr. *Lilburn.* Alas, Sir, I have dealt faithfully and truly with you, and told you, that it is drawn up by their instructions: but really and truly they were both gone out of *London*, before pen could be put to paper to draw the rough draught of it; and therefore it was impossible to get their hands to the ingrossed copy. Wherefore I beseech the Court to give me time but till *Monday* morning, and I will send after them for their hands; and engage not only to get their hands to the parchment, but to bring one or both of them to this Bar, to justify their instructions to me, and that their instructions are Law. Therefore, my Lord, be pleased to grant me but till *Monday* morning, and I will have them here, although I borrow money to send two Coaches with six horses a-piece to fetch them back.

Lord-Mayor. *No, the Court breaks up to-night, and therefore we cannot give you till* Monday.

Recorder. *Mr.* Lilburn, *seeing you insist so stiffly upon it for your* Oyer, *I will tell you what we will do with you: put in your Exceptions to-night, which you have under your Counsel's hands, and the Court will assure you that in case your Counsel at our next meeting about your business, will avow that your parchment for the demand of* Oyer *is Law, we will grant it you; and your putting in your Exceptions now, shall be no prejudice to you in any kind.*

Mr. *Lilburn* endeavouring to speak, to close with him, several of his honest and true friends that stood by him, cried out, there was a snare laid for him, and bid him rather die than go an inch from his Counsel's honest, just, and safe instructions. At which the Court grew very angry, and judgment again began to be pressed against the Prisoner at the Bar; and the Court required the Exceptions, without any more ado, to be delivered in.

Mr. *Lilburn.* Well then, my Lord, seeing I have done my utmost to obtain my right by Law, which is to have the *Oyer* of the Act, Judgment, and Crimes, upon which the Indictment is grounded, and it will not be granted me, but the Court hath over-ruled me; therefore, my Lord, to let all the world know that I am no baffler, nor procrastinator of time, nor have any thing of guilt, fear, or dread within me, although it be never so much to my wrong, and tend never so much to my apparent disadvantage or my ruin, I will close with Mr. Recorder, and immediately deliver in the Exceptions that I have in my hand already, signed by my Counsel, as a part of my Exceptions; provided he will distinctly repeat over the promise of the Court, and enter it upon record in the Court's Books, and order the Clerk immediately to draw up an order upon it, as large as it is in itself, and give it me legally signed before I stir from the Bar.

No, saith Mr. Recorder Steele, *Mr.* Lilburn, *the doing of that that you require, would take up too much time, and therefore the Court cannot do it: but they will make good what I have said unto you.*

Whereupon, Mr. *Lilburn* repeated what Mr. Recorder (in the name of the Court) had promised, and said, Sir, is not this that the Court will stand to? Yes, saith the Recorder. Then, Sir, I beseech you, in the audience of all these people, (that they may bear witness) repeat it over again yourself.

yourself. Which he did: and Mr. *Lilburn* closed with him, and accordingly delivered in his Exceptions.

And at his coming to his Lodging, some of his friends drew up the promise of the Court in writing, and set their hands to it; which thus followeth.

That if Mr. Lilburn *would deliver in the copy of his Exceptions, the not granting at this time his* Oyer *should be no prejudice to him.* And further, *That the Court was to consider of a time to have the Exceptions debated by Counsel: and if the Counsel of* John Lilburn, *Gentleman, when they came to plead to the Exceptions, conceived it necessary and right to have the* Oyer, *that then it should be granted him, before any proceeding upon the Exceptions should be, as if the Exceptions were not delivered into the Court.*

Witness, Richard Lilburn, George Wade, Thomas Webbe, George Lilburn, *jun.* William Lilburn.

Mr. *Lilburn.* My Lord, I here deliver your Lordship and this honourable Court, part of my Exceptions under my own and my Counsellors hands: but, my Lord, I have many more to make, when I shall hear the *Oyer*, and have copies of the Act, Judgment, and Crimes, according to my right, that your Indictment is grounded upon. And then spoke as follows:

My Lord,

I Have given into the Court my demand for *Oyer*, fairly ingrossed in parchment under my hand, and part of my Exceptions against the Indictment, which are very difficult points in Law, and beyond my reading and skill fully to argue, and therefore I must depend upon my learned Counsel for that.

It was never denied the worst of Traitors to have copies of their Indictments, and Counsel to argue the points of Law for them. The Lord *Macguire*, the great bloody Rebel of *Ireland*, indicted for Treason lately at the Upper Bench, had his Counsel to argue before the learned Judges thereof, when he was indicted for High-Treason, and spent much time only about his title of Baron. Duke *Hamilton*, Lord *Capel* of late, and the Lord *Castlehaven* formerly, were never denied it, nor the Earl of *Strafford:* yet all these persons were tried for facts that were crimes in the Common Law, for treachery, and bloodshed, and foul offences, such as the Law of Nature forbids and abhors (and had Laws made before their facts to be their guide). But my only crimes are, that my name is *John Lilburn*, and that I am in *England*, my native country: and the matter of Law that rose in their cases, was only upon the formality of the Indictment of charges against them, and consequently less need of serious arguments in Law; yet the Law is so tender of blood and life, that it takes away no advantage from any man whose life is in question or danger.

But, my Lord, I beseech you consider the difficulty of my case; the very crimes whereof I am accused, have no foundation in the Common Law, I am only accused for being in my native country; and the pretended Law against me lays no crime to my charge: I have wronged no man in his property; I have designed no evil against my country; I have hurt no man in his liberty, nor life, nor member.

The very crime laid to my charge, may be called a point of Law: it is supposed to arise upon the breach of a pretended Act of Parliament, so that it is not in matter of form, or in the formality, or nicety of proceedings against me, that the point in Law arises in my case: it is about the nature of the crime itself whereof I am accused, and therefore Counsel learned in the Law is more necessary in my case, deliberately and maturely to argue it before all the learned Judges of the Law in *England*, than in any case that hath been tried in *England* this five hundred years: here is no light to lead my Judges in their judgment, but the very light of the Law itself, being a strange kind of single Act made in a strange kind, or unknown and unheard-of manner. Here is no precedent, no example to help them: the like case, I dare avow it, was never tried in *England* before, and all *England*, and their posterities, yea the babes in their mothers wombs, are concerned in the event of my Trial. Whatsoever is the issue of my Trial, will hereafter be drawn into a precedent, either for the good or evil of all the people of *England*. Besides, the shedding of my blood without cause or reason, must needs bring guilt, punishment, and misery upon the causers and permitters thereof. Remember righteous *Abel's* case, *Naboth* and *Uriah* · therefore I hope much caution will be used in determining the difficult points of Law in my case. My Lord, not for my own sake, for the sparing of my blood, though I am bound to preserve it, if I can, by the great Law of Nature; yet, my Lord, if my life were only at the stake, I could contemn it, if I saw my contempt of it might serve my Country, and restore it to its liberty and freedom. But when the liberties of millions of persons already in being, and yet unborn, which consist and subsist in being ruled by written Laws and Rules; when these are at the stake, I hope the difficulties of the Law in this case, shall be seriously weighed, and solemnly debated by the most experienced men in the Law in the whole Nation.

The Copy of the fore-recited Exceptions thus followeth:

The Exceptions of *John Lilburn*, Gent. Prisoner at the Bar, to a Bill of Indictment preferred against him, grounded upon a pretended Act, intitled, *An Act for the Execution of a Judgment given in Parliament against Lieutenant-Colonel* John Lilburn; which Judgment is by the said Act supposed to be given the 15th day of *January*, 1651.

THE said *John Lilburn*, Prisoner at the Bar, saith, That the said Indictment is insufficient, in the Law, in matter, substance and form. And he humbly offereth these Exceptions following against the same.

Exception 1. For that the said Indictment is grounded only upon an Act intitled, *An Act for the Execution of a Judgment given in Parliament against Lieutenant-Colonel* John Lilburn. And it doth not appear, either by the title of the said Act recited in the Indictment, or by any thing contained in the said Act, that either the said Act itself is an Act of the Parliament of the Commonwealth of *England*, or of the Parliament sitting at *Westminster*, or that the said supposed Judgment, for the execution whereof the said Act is supposed to be made, was given in the Parliament of the Commonwealth of *England*, or in the Parliament sitting at *Westminster*; nor yet when the said Parliament did commence or end, or whether the same was held by prorogation or otherwise. And it is evident in Law, that no Law could at that time be made, but by the Parliament of the Commonwealth of *England*; for by the Law then in being, the power of making Laws was only in those persons which were known and distinguished by that title of the Parliament of the Commonwealth of *England:* and in that name only Addresses were made to them, both by the people of *England*, and by all foreign States and Princes, and all Addresses refused that wanted that title. Now for aught that appears in the said Act, whereupon the said Indictment is grounded, it may be as well an Act of Parliament in *France*, or *Scotland*, or *Naples*, as an Act of the Parliament of the Commonwealth of *England*; so that it doth not appear, that the said Indictment is grounded upon any Law of *England*; or that *John Lilburn*, Prisoner at the Bar, is indicted for any fact that is a Crime by any Law of *England*, and then the same is void in Law.

Exception 2. The said Indictment is grounded upon the fore-recited Act, intitled, *An Act for the Execution of a Judgment given in Parliament against Lieutenant-Colonel* John Lilburn; and so relates only to some Judgment supposed to be given in Parliament against the said Lieutenant-Colonel *John Lilburn*; and if no such Judgment were given, the Act were void, and the Judgment also. Now it doth not appear that any Judgment, for any Crime whatsoever, was given in Parliament against the said Lieutenant-Colonel *John Lilburn.* 1. Before any Judgment can be given in Law against any *Englishman*, for any Crime, there must be either an Indictment, Presentment, or some Information or Accusation against him, to that Court that judgeth him, for some Crime supposed to be committed by him. 2. The party accused must either appear before that Court, or be out-lawed for not appearing. 3. If the party appears, he must either confess the Crimes or Misdemeanors whereof he is accused, or else plead to the Indictment, Presentment, or Information, or Accusation against him, and come to Trial thereupon. And as some of these ought in Law to precede a Judgment against any *Englishman*, so also some of these afore-mentioned proceedings, in order to a lawful Judgment, ought to be entered upon such Record, wherein any such Judgment is entered; and unless it doth appear upon the Record, wherein any Judgment is entered against any *Englishman* for any Crime, that some such proceeding as abovesaid, hath been made before the Judgment passed against him, the Judgment is to be holden for erroneous and void, and ought so to be reputed. Now it doth not appear either by the said pretended Act, as it is recited in the Indictment, nor by any Record of the supposed Judgment produced, nor any otherwise, that there was any Indictment, Presentment, or Information to the Parliament of the Commonwealth of *England* against the said Lieutenant-Colonel *John Lilburn*; or if there were, it doth not appear, that he ever appeared to the same, nor that he was ever outlawed for not appearing: neither doth any pleading by the said Lieutenant-Colonel *John Lilburn* to any such Indictment or Information appear, nor any Trial of him for the same. And therefore if any such pretended Judgment be entered, as the said supposed Act, and the Indictment of *John Lilburn*, Prisoner at the Bar, thereupon doth relate unto, the same is erroneous and void in Law; and by consequence the said Indictment is void.

Exception 3. The said Indictment is erroneous and insufficient in Law, for that it is only grounded upon, and recites an Act, which Act is declared to be made for the execution of a Judgment passed in Parliament against Lieutenant-Colonel *John Lilburn*, the 15th day of *January*, 1651; when in truth there was no such Judgment, either in matter or form, passed in Parliament on the said 15th day of *January*, 1651; as is enacted by the said supposed Act, to be executed against the said Lieutenant-Colonel *John Lilburn*; and as is also recited in the said Indictment, to be enacted by the said Act, to be put in execution against him. *First*, There was no Judgment passed in Parliament upon the said 15th of *January*, 1651, that the said Lieutenant-Colonel *John Lilburn* should depart out of *England* within twenty days, after the said 15th day of *January*, 1651, as is mentioned in the said Indictment. *Secondly*, There was no Judgment passed in Parliament, upon the said 15th day of *January*, 1651, that the said Lieutenant-Colonel *John Lilburn* should depart out of *England*, *Scotland* and *Ireland*, or the Islands, Territories, or Dominions thereof, within any limited time whatsoever, or under any penalty whatsoever, as is mentioned in the said Indictment. *Thirdly*, There never was any Judgment passed in Parliament, the said 15th day of *January*, 1651, that the said Lieutenant-Colonel *John Lilburn* should be executed as a Felon, without benefit of Clergy, in case the said Lieutenant-Colonel *John Lilburn* should be found, or be remaining in *England*, *Scotland*, or *Ireland*, after the expiration of twenty days, or any other time whatsoever, to be accounted from the said 15th day of *January*, 1651. And if no such Judgment doth appear to have been passed against the said Lieutenant-Colonel *John Lilburn*, as is aforesaid, and as is recited by the said Indictment, to be enacted to be put in execution against him; then the original ground of the said Indictment is null and void: Which is a Judgment supposed to be passed in Parliament against the said Lieutenant-Colonel *John Lilburn*, in matter, substance, and form, as aforesaid, upon the 15th day of *January*, 1651, which is enacted by the said Act recited in the said Indictment to be put in execution whereas no such Judgment ever passed; and therefore cannot be supposed or admitted by the Law to be enacted to be put in execution: And upon these reasons and causes the Prisoner at the Bar conceives the said Indictment to be insufficient in the Law.

Exception 4. The said *John Lilburn* further excepts against the said Indictment, as insufficient in the Law, in regard of the uncertainty of the same; the Law requiring all allegations against any man to be certain; for that the said Indictment doth recite and ground itself upon an Act, made for the execution of a Judgment passed in Parliament against Lieutenant-Colonel *John Lilburn*; and then chargeth *John Lilburn*, late of *London*, Gentleman, to have been found in *England*; that is to say, in *London*, contrary to the said Act: but averreth not that the said *John Lilburn*, now Prisoner at the Bar, indicted by the name of *John Lilburn*, late of *London*, Gentleman, is one and the self-same person, with the said Lieutenant-Colonel *John Lilburn*, meant and intended by the said Act; and not other or divers: by reason whereof, [illegible]

are

are several per[illegible]sons known and distinguished by the name of *John Lilburn*, of *Lon*[illegible]*don*, Gentleman. And for that the said *John Lilburn*, Prisoner at the [illegible] Bar, doth not acknowledge that he now is, or at the making of the [illegible] said Act, or passing the said supposed Judgment, was a Lieutenant-[illegible]Colonel, or that he could be notified and distinguished by that title [illegible]; he, the said *John Lilburn*, Prisoner at the Bar, cannot join any [illegible] certain issue with the Keepers of the Liberties of *England* upon the [illegible] said Indictment. For the said Indictment not averring the said *John Lilbur*[illegible]*n*, now Prisoner at the Bar, to be the same Person, and not other, or [illegible] verse from that *John Lilburn*, intended and meant in the said Act, and [illegible] stinguished from all others of the same name, by the title of a Lieuten[illegible] Colonel; if the Prisoner at the Bar should plead the general issue of N[illegible] guilty, he should confess himself to be the same *John Lilburn*, intended [illegible] by the said Act; else he is not concerned to plead to the said Indictme[illegible]. And by consequence, if the Prisoner at the Bar should plead Not gu[illegible]y to the said Indictment; the only issue to be tried in point of fact betw[illegible] the Keepers of the Liberties of *England* and the Prisoner would be, wh[illegible]ther *J.hn Lilburn*, Prisoner at the Bar, was found in *England*, upon [illegible] 15th day of *June*, 1653? and by consequence, the Prisoner at the [illegible]ar, though he be not the person intended by the said Act, might be e[illegible]ared and condemned as a Felon, only because his name is *John Lilburn* [illegible] and if any other *John Lilburn* should in like manner plead to the said I[illegible]ctment, he should suffer, because he is called *John Lilburn*. For all wh[illegible]h errors and insufficiencies in the Law, in the said Indictment, Act, [illegible]nd supposed Judgment, appearing, the said *John Lilburn*, Prisoner at [illegible] Bar, humbly prayeth, that the said Indictment may be quashed, an[illegible] in case the honourable Court be not fully satisfied in the said errors [illegible]d insufficiencies of the said Indictment, he prayeth that Counsel lear[illegible]ed in the Law may be assigned him, and a competent time given for hi[illegible] to advise with them, and for them to prepare their arguments upon [illegible]l the said matters of Law. And that the case being of very great difficu[illegible]y, and much concernment to the liberty of all the people of *England*; an[illegible] being a case without any precedent; and the shedding or sparing of in[illegible]ocent blood, depending upon a resolution thereof: he humbly prayeth [illegible]hat the said difficult points of Law, arising upon the case, may be argu[illegible]d before the reverend Judges of the Law, as hath been accustom[illegible] in [illegible]uch cases, that their opinions may be had thereupon.

Signed *Jo*[illegible]*n Norbury, John Maynard*; and presented to, and accepted by the [illegible]ord-Mayor, and the honourable Bench, *July* 16, 1653.

JOHN LILBURN.

But the Co[illegible]urt being eager to see the Exceptions, the Cryer commanded silence, and [illegible]o hear the Court, who had commanded their Clerk with a low voice to read them the title of the Exceptions amongst themselves. Whereupon [illegible]as soon as the Prisoner at the Bar perceived the Court had heard the title, he desired them to read them all over with an audible voice. But withal, my Lord, said he, I beseech you and the Court to take notice, that they are but part of my Exceptions, which the Court hath forced, and compelled me to deliver in.

At which the Lord-Mayor was very angry, and said, Mr. *Lilburn*, you are very much to blame, thus to abuse and scandalize the Court, in saying we have compelled you: you may take your Exceptions again, if you are not free to deliver them in. Give him them again.

Lilburn. No, my Lord, I will have none of them; for seeing they are in, they are in; and I will stand to them, and maintain them with my life: and I hope, and doubt not but my honest and learned Counsel will back them with strong and unresistible arguments of Law. But, my Lord, hereafter I shall endeavour to keep the Court close to their promise, made unto me by their mouth, Mr. Recorder, about the *Oyer*: for, my Lord, here are witnesses enough of it. But, my Lord, whereas you say I have abused the Court, in declaring that they forced and compelled me to deliver in my Exceptions; my Lord, I absolutely deny it, that that averment is any abuse at all to the Court. You know, my Lord, you have over-ruled me in point of reading my Parchment about the *Oyer*, and you have ordered me to deliver in my Exceptions to the Indictment, which you know I have averred by Law, I ought not to be compelled to, till I have legally the *Oyer*: so that, my Lord, I must yet aver, that in the eye of the Law you have committed a force and compulsion upon me. But, my Lord, I have done with it.

They spent some time in reading the beginning of the Exceptions; which (an observant man might easily see) did very much trouble both the Lord-Mayor and the Recorder. But the Prisoner withdrew; and by several of those that sat nigher the Lord-Mayor and Recorder than he stood, he was certainly informed that the Attorney-General *Prideaux*, who sat upon the Bench, although he would not speak much openly and publickly, yet he constantly, in a whispering or clandestine way, press'd the Court to keep the Prisoner close to the question; *Whether he was the* John Lilburn *meant in the Act or no?* and to give him no elbow-room to let him get off it: And that Mr. Alderman *Atkins* was in a pitiful frighted condition, when the Prisoner appealed to the people against their injustice. And that the pitiful Alderman most lamentably cried out to Colonel *Okey*, presently to send for some troops of horse, to secure his worshipful person. And that Mr. *Lee*, the Clerk, was extreme earnest to have the Prisoner gagged at the Bar, that he should speak no more; and privately press'd very hard, immediately to have him condemned and taken away. And that the Lord-Mayor, at the reading of the title, in which the Act is called, *A pretended Act of Parliament*, said unto the Recorder, We are undone, if we receive in this; for we shall be adjudged betrayers of our trust. And at their reading the first Exception, the Recorder was amazed, and said, he wondered how Mr. *Lilburn* could get learned men in the Law to sign such Exceptions. And the Lord-Mayor asking him, what that Mr. *Norbury* was, whose hand was first to the Exceptions; the Recorder told him, he had lately been a Judge in *Wales*. My Lord, I do not so much wonder at his setting his hand to the Exceptions (for I have known him for many years to be a man of principles something in affinity to Mr. *Lilburn*); but for Mr. *John Maynard*, one of the greatest Lawyers of *England*, and one of the greatest practitioners of the Nation, for him to set his hand to such Exceptions, is that (my Lord) amazeth me. For if this very first Exception of Mr. *Lilburn*'s be good in Law, then all the late Acts of Parliament are totally invalidated, as well as that which he speaks against.

Then the Court broke up.

Notwithstanding the strictest enquiry, we can't find that *Lilburn*, or his friends, or any one else, ever published the remainder of his Trial. Mr. *Whitlock*, in his Memorials of the *English* affairs, *p.* 560, says no more than this:

July 13, 1653, Lieut. Col. *Lilburn* was arraigned at the Sessions in the *Old-Bailey*, upon the late Act for his Banishment.

July 14. Lieut. Col. *Lilburn* was brought again to his Trial, but he urg'd for further time in regard the Counsel assigned him refus'd to appear for him, only Serjeant *Maynard*, who was sick; and he had an order for a Copy of his Indictment.

July 17, (16) *Lilburn* was brought to his Trial, but nothing done in his business, and *page* 563. says, *Aug.* 11. *Lilburn*'s Trial proceeded at the Sessions-house.

16. Mr. *Lilburn*'s Trial at the Sessions-House proceeded.

20. The Jury found *Lilburn* not guilty; he pleaded long for himself.

Nothing of these three last days Proceedings are printed.

In a Book, entitled *Lieut. Col* John Lilburn *Tried and Cast, or his Case and Craft discovered*, 4to, 1653. is recited some of his speeches at his Trial, and Animadversions on them; which shews that the Colonel made a notable Defence. His Speeches, as mentioned in that Book, *page* 125, *&c.* are as follow:

Concerning the Act whereupon he was indicted, this he said, It was a lye and a falshood: an Act that hath no reason in it, no Law for it, it was done as *Pharaoh* did; resolved upon the question, that all the male children should be murdered. That if he died upon this Act, he died upon the same score that *Abel* did, being murdered by *Cain*. That the Act was a void Act, a printed thing, there being no one punctilio or clause in it, grounded on the Law of *England*, and that it was an unjust, unrighteous, and treacherous Act, and that he doubted not to shatter that Act in pieces. That they could not make an Act of Parliament, since the King's Head was cut off.

By the same Law they voted him to death, they might vote his honest twelve Jurymen.

He said, The Parliament before the King's head was cut off, and the Members taken out, were, in their purity, a gallant Parliament, who were tender of the liberties and welfare of the Nation, and walked in the steps of their ancestors and fore-fathers; then were the days of their virginity, they made good and righteous Laws, and then they had no force upon them: But since 1640, and 1641, there have been no good Laws made.

He affirms, that it was no lawful Parliament, that made that Act. Again, the Parliament that made this Act of Banishment was no Parliament, I will prove it: And the Parliament was rather transgressors than I. Again, admit the Parliament legal, *they had no power to send for me.* If there were any Judicatory in Parliament, it was the Lords House, not the Commons.

As for all Parliaments in general, he said Parliaments were a delegated Power, and ought to give a reason of all they do; and that it was not in their power, (as he had proved in his Plea at large, before the Lord Chief Justice *Rolls* and Mr. Justice *Bacon*, *May* 18, 1647;) nor had they the least jurisdiction, to sentence him, or any of the least free-born *Englishmen*; unless it be their own Members. That all crimes whatever were to be heard, determined, and judg'd at the Common-Law, and no where else. Acts of Attainder were not lawful.

Speaking to the Lord-Mayor; This is the strangest thing (saith he) that ever I saw, that a man must be cheated of his life. Good my Lord-Mayor, you have made yourself a party in my case, and taken a wrong *John Lilburn*; and if you do not make me hang, you are afraid of yourself. You make the land groan under your burthens and oppressions; I desire you will not deny me my right, that I may not lose my life in the resolve of a question, That *John Lilburn* shall be hanged, which in time may come to murder your posterity, and the posterity of those that hear me this day.

He told the Lord *Keeble*, that he had nothing to do to judge him, being a party, and had a salary of a thousand pounds *per annum* from the State.

To Mr. *Prideaux*, Attorney-General, he said, You are a blood-thirsty man, and you come here to justify your unrighteous Act; and I hope the Jury will take notice of all your violence. It is the admiration of my soul, that he should be a Judge in his own case; to have a Man sit as my Judge that thirsteth after my blood.

He said, that the army (many of them) have been very good instruments for the good of the Nation, to deliver us from Tyranny. I wish there is not a greater than they delivered us from.

For the Jury, he called them his honourable Jury, and said they were the Keepers of the Liberties of *England*; and will make it appear that the Jury are the Judges of the Law, as well as of the Fact.

Moreover, he charged them to consider, whether if I die on the *Monday*, the Parliament on *Tuesday* may not pass such a sentence against every one of you Twelve; and upon your wives and children, and all your relations; and then upon the rest of this City, and then upon the whole County of *Middlesex*, and then upon *Hertfordshire*, and so by degrees there be no people to inhabit *England*, but themselves?

I call *Jehovah* to witness (saith he), and do here protest before God, Angels and Men, I am not the person intended to be banished by that Act; speaking of the Act whereupon he was indicted.

The Jury having acquitted him, were summoned before the Council of State, on the 23d of *August*, 1653; in pursuance of an order of Parliament, of the 21st, to answer for their conduct.

The examination of which Jury is printed in *State-Trials*, Vol. I. *page* 81, 82. *Edit.* 1730, after his Trial at *Guildhall* in 1649, for High-Treason; to which the Reader is referr'd. But for what reason the examination of his Jury in 1653 is there inserted (having no relation to that Trial) would be difficult to tell.

XXVII. The Trial of MILES SINDERCOME, *alias* FISH, at the Upper-Bench, *Weſtminſter*, *Feb.* 9, 1656. for High-Treaſon.

Before the Lord Chief-Juſtice *Glynn*, and Mr. Juſtice *Warburton*.

JANUARY 1656, *Miles Sindercome* was committed cloſe Priſoner to the *Tower* of *London*, for High-Treaſon, and Sir *John Barkſtead*, Knight, Lieutenant of the *Tower*, gave order to Mr. *David Steer*, one of the Warders of the *Tower*, to be his Keeper; with ſtrict orders from the Lieutenant to be moſt careful of him. But Mr. *Steer* perceiving the deſperateneſs of his diſpoſition, by many violent and threatening ſpeeches, which he often uſed, acquainted Sir *John Barkſtead* therewith, and deſired more aſſiſtance, as well for the ſecurity of his own Perſon, as of the ſaid Priſoner. Wherefore, from that time forward, a guard of a Commiſſion Officer and Soldiers, were ordered to aſſiſt the ſaid Keeper, and ſecure the Priſoner, ſo that *Sindercome* finding no means poſſible for him to make an eſcape by force, endeavoured afterwards to corrupt his Keeper, offering him two hundred pounds, or ſo much as his place ſhou'd be worth, to aſſiſt him in making his eſcape, and deſired him, if he would undertake the matter, to furniſh him with a black ſuit of clothes, a peruke, and a ſhort dagger, to paſs him through the Water-gate, within the *Tower*, and ſaid, that then he would trouble him no further, but kill any man that ſhould oppoſe him in going. But his Keeper faithfully diſcharging his truſt, not only refuſed this proffer, but acquainted the Lieutenant therewith; who was therefore more vigilant and careful for his ſecurity. The Officers and Soldiers that daily attended in his chamber with him, would often adviſe him to make his peace with God, and to look after the eternal concernments of his Soul; which diſcourſe he would always divert by the ſpeaking of his own valour and courage, and how many he had ſlain while he was a Soldier, boaſting greatly therein, and of his knowledge in the Law of this Nation: And would often ſay, That he doubted not to make a very good defence, if he might be tried by a Jury, according to the ancient Law of *England*, and to come off as well as *John Lilburn*.

February 6, 1656, *Miles Sindercome* had notice of his Trial to be the next *Monday* following, and had liberty given to prepare himſelf for it; and for that purpoſe to ſend for, and converſe with, what perſons he would; and to have the uſe of pen, ink, and paper, and to write as he pleaſed; which he had, and did uſe accordingly.

February 9, 1656, *Sindercome* was brought to his Trial at the Upper-Bench Bar in *Weſtminſter-hall*, the particulars whereof are as follow.

The Indictment was for High-Treaſon, to this effect, *viz.*

THAT Miles Sindercome, *alias* Fiſh *, *and one* William Boyes, *with divers other Rebels and Traitors, againſt the Lord Protector, and Government of the Commonwealth, not having the fear of God in their hearts, but moved and ſeduced by the inſtigation of the Devil; on the 17th of* September, 1656, *and divers other days and times, as well before as after, at* Weſtminſter, *and divers other places in the County of* Middleſex, *falſely, maliciouſly and traiterouſly did conſpire, compaſs, and imagine the death of the ſaid Lord Protector, and to ſubvert and alter the Government of the Commonwealth, and to raiſe War within the ſame.*

For effecting whereof,

1. *They took a room in the Houſe of one* Edward Hilton, *and divers rooms in the houſe of one* James Midhope, *in* Weſtminſter; *whither they brought Guns, Harquebuſſes and Piſtols, charged with laden Bulets, and iron Slugs, to ſhoot, kill and murder him.*

2. January 1, 1656. *They provided Horſes and Weapons of War; and,*

3. *Took a houſe and banqueting-houſe at* Hammerſmith, *of one* Henry Buſby, *for the ſame purpoſe.*

4. January 9, 1656. *They conſpired to burn* Whitehall, *where his Highneſs was in his own perſon; and to that end brought a basket filled with Match, Brimſtone, Gunpowder, and other combuſtible Stuff and Materials, and ſet the ſame on fire in the Chapel there; to the great danger and diſquietment of his Highneſs, and ill example of others, in contempt of the Law, againſt their due obedience to his Highneſs and Government, againſt the Peace, and form of the Statute.* &c.

Thus far the Indictment.

Whereupon being arraigned, he pleaded *Not Guilty*, and for his Trial put himſelf upon his Country; and the iſſue being joined, there was immediately impannell'd a Jury of Gentlemen of worth and quality to paſs upon his Life and Death: he challenged ſeveral of them; and twelve being ſworn (with his own conſent), his Highneſs's Attorney-General (the Indictment being opened) proceeded to the Evidence, which was very full and clear, and two Witneſſes at the leaſt to all the points of the Indictment, with many aggravating circumſtances: the particulars whereof are herein after mentioned.

The Evidence to prove the Indictment.

THERE was one *Toope* of his Highneſs's Lifeguard, who was drawn into the buſineſs, and he proved fully, 1. What perſon *Sindercome* is, how he inveigled him, the ſaid *Toope*, with money in hand, and promiſes of more, and great preferment, to join with him to murder his Highneſs; ſaying, *Spain* could never obtain a peace with us, till he were taken out of the way. 2. The circumſtances of time, place, means and manner deſigned for this murder. 3. That he, the ſaid *Toope*, was to give notice when his Highneſs went forth; and at what end of the Coach he ſat. 4. Their buying and keeping of fleet horſes. 5. Their intent to fire *Whitehall*, the fire-work placed in the Chapel, and other circumſtances. 6. *Sindercome*'s reſolution, if the fire did not take, to kill the Protector, whatever came of it.

Alſo one *John Cecil* proved the whole deſign of *Sindercome* and *Boyes*, how long it was in hand, that *Sindercome* engaged him, the ſaid *Cecil*, in it; what words were uſed, how it ſhould be done; what the conſequence of the murder would be; the money provided, and that when it ſhould have been done, he, the ſaid *Cecil*, was deſigned to go to Col. *Sexby*, and to ſhare with *Sindercome* in his honour and profit. That the firſt thing agreed on, was to provide good horſes. What moneys were paid by *Sindercome*; *Sindercome*'s reſolution to aſſaſſinate his Highneſs when he went abroad; and the manner how. That they were upon the road five or ſix times on purpoſe; and in *Hyde-park* with ſwords, and piſtols charged, and had notice given them by *Toope* of his Highneſs's coming. That the hinges of *Hyde-park* Gate were filed off, in order to their eſcape. That they took an houſe with a banqueting-houſe at *Hammerſmith*, to ſhoot him with Guns, made on purpoſe to carry ten or twelve bullets at a time. That *Toope* was to give notice of his Highneſs's paſſing that way, and at which end of the Coach he ſat. That he, the ſaid *Cecil*, ſaw one of the Guns provided, which would carry twelve carbine bullets and a ſlug. He ſpake fully to the deſign of firing *Whitehall*; deſcribed the fire-work prepared, and the nature and intention it, and other circumſtances. Moreover, that *Boyes* aſſur'd them, that when the Protector ſhould be diſpatched, forces would come from *Spain* and *Flanders*; and a great part of the Fleet would fall off. And that he believed *Sexby* to be the main agent herein at *Bruſſels* †. He proved alſo the diſcourſe *Boyes* had about ſeizing *Portſmouth*, or ſome other port in the *Weſt*, and of a great ſum for that purpoſe. That thirty or forty are engaged in this deſign to kill the Protector, and it was ſo ordered, that not above two ſhould know each other, until the matter ſhould be ripe for execution; and that *Boyes* knew the whole number.

He ſpoke fully to that deſign to kill his Highneſs the firſt day of the Parliament; and their taking houſes for that purpoſe at *Weſtminſter*; and bringing arms thither, and other circumſtances ‡.

That *Boyes* goes by ſeveral names, and in ſeveral habits; ſometimes as a poor Prieſt in ragged clothes; ſometimes well clad as a Gentleman.

It was further proved by the ſaid *John Cecil*, and Col. *James Midhope*, that in order to the deſtroying of his Highneſs, he, the ſaid *Cecil*, *Sindercome*, and *Boyes*, took the ſaid *Midhope*'s houſe near the Abbey at *Weſtminſter*; and when they took it, *Sindercome* called himſelf *John Fiſh*, Clerk to one Mr. *Havers*, a pretended Gentleman of *Norfolk*; and *Cecil* went by the name of Mr. *Havers*'s Coachman.

It was proved likewiſe, that the firſt day of the Parliament, after they had taken *Midhope*'s houſe, he being there; *Sindercome* and *Cecil* went thither to him, from one *Edward Hilton*, a Sempſter's houſe in *King-ſtreet*, *Weſtminſter*, where they left a great trunk full of arms, brought from *Flanders*; and carried with them in a viol-caſe, one harquebuſs, and ſome piſtols, charged with leaden bullets, and ſlugs, about Sermon-time, to *Midhope*'s houſe; which they found very convenient for their purpoſe, and reſolved to buy it, and to build a room in the yard next the ſtreet; there being ſeveral back-yards and doors: and reſolved alſo to ſecure *Midhope*, or otherwiſe to deal with him that he might not diſcover them, nor hinder their deſign §.

It was proved, moreover, by *Cecil* and *Midhope*, that Sermon being ended, all three of them, *viz.* he, the ſaid *Cecil*, *Sindercome*, and *Boyes*, went into the yard of the houſe next the Abbey, to ſhoot his Highneſs, as he paſſed from the Abbey to meet the Parliament in the painted Chamber;

* The principal Perſon employ'd in the traitorous deſign, for the deſtruction of his Highneſs's Perſon, was a notable deſperate Fellow, named *Sindercome*, one who heretofore had been a Quarter-Maſter under Sir *John Reynolds* in the Army, and was about two years ago caſhier'd by General *Monk*, among others in *Scotland*. He aſſociated to himſelf one *Cecil*, and many others were engag'd in the Buſineſs. For the carrying on their work, they held correſpondence with ſome in *Flanders*, received directions thence from time to time, and for their encouragement, *Don Alonſo*, the late Ambaſſador of *Spain* in *England*, return'd them over Sums of Money, with which they were enabled to proceed. See a *Brief Relation of the late dangerous Plot.* Printed in a *further Narrative of the Paſſages of theſe Times in the Commonwealth of* England, pag. 7.

† In Col. *Edward Sexby*'s Narrative, which he delivered to Sir *John Barkſtead*, Lieutenant of the *Tower*, *Oct.* 12, 1657. printed in *A further Narrative of the Paſſages of theſe Times in the Commonwealth of* England, *pag.* 21. he ſays, "Sir *John*, I ſent to you to tell you, that I am guilty of the whole buſineſs of *Sindercome*, as to the deſign of "killing the Lord Protector, &c. and to that purpoſe I furniſh'd *Sindercome* with about 500*l.* in Money, and alſo with Arms, and tied him to an Engagement, that he ſhould "not reveal the deſign." *And further he ſaid*, "The Letters they have of mine, they could not prove them to be mine; but by my own Confeſſion, which I now confeſs, "and acknowledge that they are mine. And that I was with *Charles Stuart*, and acquainted him, that I was an enemy to the Lord Protector; and I alſo declare that I re"ceived a large ſum of Money from the *Spaniard* to carry on my ſaid deſign, and to make what Confuſion I could in *England*, by endeavouring the killing of the Lord [illegible] touching [illegible]

‡ [illegible]

§ [illegible]

and

and to that end, he, the said Cecil stood on the wall with his pistol charged, and Sindercome walked in the yard, but other company coming in thither, they were prevented, and Boyes went out of the yard into the throng of People.

It was further proved by Cecil, that this enterprize not succeeding, they resolved to murder his Highness some other way, to wit, to furnish themselves with fleet horses, to kill him as he rode forth. That Sindercome engaged Toope, who constantly gave him notice of the Life-guards going abroad, or the sadling of the Pad Nags.

That the first time they rode forth to kill him, was the latter end of September last (viz.) the Saturday after he had left going to Hampton-court.

That the second time was when he rode to Kensington, and thence, the back way to London.

The third time, when he went to Hyde-park in his Coach.

The fourth time, when he went to Turnham Green, and so by Acton home; at which time they rode forth to kill him, and resolved to break through all difficulties to effect it.

The fifth time, when he rode into Hyde-park, where his Highness alighting, walked him, the said Cecil, whose horse that was he rode on, being then on the out-side of the Park; and then Cecil was ready to have done it, but doubted his horse, having at that time got a cold.

That Sindercome rode forth once himself to kill his Highness, and told Cecil of it.

That all these attempts proving ineffectual, they resolved to desist till the Spring, and in the mean time to fire Whitehall.

That the said Cecil put on a thin holland shirt, and thin clothes, for his better escape when he rode forth to kill his Highness; and prepared his horse as if he had been to run a race.

To prove the taking of the house and banqueting-house at Hammersmith, of Henry Busby, Coachman to the Earl of Salisbury, there was beside Cecil, the testimony of Henry Busby himself, William Page, and William Neal, Sindercome's servant.

To prove the basket of stuff for firing the Chapel, there was the testimony of Cecil and Toope, and others who were persons of quality.

To prove the buying and keeping of the horses, there was the testimony of Henry Busby, who sold them one horse for fourscore pounds, also of William Page, and William Neal, Sindercome's servant.

To prove the hinges of Hyde-park gate being filed off, and the pales cut, there was the testimony of John Cecil, and Thomas Shell.

The Prisoner seeing the Evidence so clear against him, had nothing material to say for himself by way of defence, yet carried himself very insolent at the Bar; and when the Court asked him touching any of the matters proved against him, he would confidently deny what was laid to his charge. And after all the Evidence given, and the Prisoner heard what he had to say for himself; the Court summed up the whole to the Jury of Life and Death, and declared, that by the Common-Law, to compass or imagine the death of the chief Magistrate of the Land, by what name soever he was called, whether Lord-Protector or otherwise, is High-Treason, he being the chief Magistrate, and the Spring of Justice, in whose name all Writs run, all Commissions and Grants are made. and that the Statutes of Treason made 25 *Ed.* III. as to this, did only declare what the Common Law was before the making of that Statute, and was not introductive of a new Law*: and more to that effect; and then proceeded to Judgment against the Prisoner in this manner.

The SENTENCE.

It is considered by the Court, that the said Miles Sindercome, *alias* Fish, *be sent from hence to the Prison in the* Tower *of* London, *from whence he came, and from thence be drawn upon a hurdle through the streets of* London *to* Tyburn; *there to be hanged on the Gallows until he be half dead, and then to be cut down, and his intrails and bowels taken out, and burnt in his own sight, and his body divided into four quarters, and be disposed of as his Highness the Lord Protector shall think fit.*

The same day, after he was brought back again to the *Tower*, he was much inraged, and in a great passion; his Keeper, and *Elizabeth Herring*, one of his Sisters, being in the chamber with him, he did swear, *That they should never have his life*, and then desired his Keeper to help him to some poison, that he might make away himself. which he refusing, *Sindercome* then desired his Sister to buy him some for the same purpose. But she crying at that present, gave him no answer; but taking her opportunity (when the Keeper did not so much mind them) had some private discourse with him (which cannot be known what it was about). Presently after, his said Sister left him, and before her going, spake to his Keeper, saying, *Lord, what shall I do? Did you hear what my Brother said of the Poison?* Thereupon, the Keeper charged her not to bring him any, telling her, if her Brother were poisoned in his house, he would accuse her for assisting him in it.

The Lieutenant of the *Tower* then being fully acquainted with the desperateness of *Sindercome*, commanded a file of Soldiers to watch in the room below his chamber, and a Guard of Officers to be with him in his chamber, that all means for the making his escape might be prevented.

Sindercome the same day endeavoured to corrupt his Keeper, as formerly, and with much earnestness prest him to be helpful to him in his greatest distress; and asked, if it were not possible for him to make an escape, telling him, if he would assist him in it, he would make good to him two hundred pounds that night: and if he would go along with him, he would make that two hundred pounds, seven hundred pounds, or what more he should desire; farther requesting him to furnish him with a black suit, peruque, and dagger, for that purpose. But by reason that the Officers aforesaid were in the chamber with him, he had not liberty so freely to discourse with his Keeper about this business as he desired, and therefore earnestly desired the said Guard of Officers, and all in the chamber with him, to withdraw; in which time he wrote and delivered privately to his Keeper a note, whereof the next following words is a copy:

Mr. Steer,

YOU see my condition, it is no time to dally with it; I have already provided two hundred pounds for you; and if you will let me make my escape, and that you will go with me, or set me forth, I shall give you, were it five hundred pounds more, I do not care: if you will do any thing, let me know your mind; I hope God will work my deliverance by your means; let me hear your judgment, that we may conclude; for if you and I do conclude, I will have other clothes brought into the room below, with a peruque, and I will take up a board (meaning, as is conceived, one of the boards of his chamber, to go down into the room below it, where his black clothes should lie; though therein he would have been frustrated, by reason of the file of Soldiers, which the Lieutenant had commanded to watch there), *and I do judge that must be the way. For God's sake do what you can, and do not distrust my not performing to give you the money; for I can this night order you two hundred pounds to any body that you shall appoint: but if you should*—

You may observe, that the reason of his breaking off so abruptly, was, that the Guard of Officers, whom he had for that time desired to withdraw, finding that he made them stay somewhat longer than ordinary, prest in upon him, so that he had not time to write further. His Keeper for answer, endeavoured to take him off from those thoughts, telling him the impossibility of it, and desired him to consider his present condition, and prepare himself for another world; whereupon *Sindercome* finding he could no ways prevail, moved these things no more afterwards.

From which time, several pious and able Divines, some of which were appointed by his Highness, and others that were desired by the Lieutenant of the *Tower*, daily came to him; as Mr. *George Griffith*, Mr. *Thomas Brooks*, Mr. *John Hodges*, Mr. *Slater*, Mr. *Barker*, and others. But before they or any others entered into discourse with him, he would wave all questioning of him about the business for which he was condemned: they laboured much with him for his soul's good, but with no satisfaction to the greatest part, and with very little to others of them, he having before declared his judgment, or rather opinion, by reason of his inconstancy and unsettledness in them, sometimes owning the *universal point of redemption*, at other times, *that the soul died with the body, or slept with the body till the Resurrection, and then it may be it should rise; that by the grave Hell was meant*; with several other detestable tenets. And indeed there is scarce any erroneous opinion known in our times, that he had not a general notion of, and would pretend unto. In several of his discourses with those Ministers, he would not hear but that *Judas* was in as good a condition as *Peter*; and of that in the xviith of *John*, *v.* 12. where Christ saith, *While I was with them in the world, I kept them in thy name; those that thou gavest me I have kept, and none of them is lost but the Son of Perdition, that the Scripture might be fulfilled*: he would say, it was meant to all men, who as they were sinners, were Sons of destruction and perdition. And as to that Text, speaking of the disciples, which saith, *one of them was a Devil*, he would startle and say, it was a rugged and harsh saying. He would often put it as a case to them, whether for any person to contrive the death of another, and not to act it, were punishable by man? And being as often resolved, and told of the Laws made in that case; he would answer, that which they alledged was but the Law of man, and that Thoughts were not to be punished by man, but God who alone knew them.

Friday 13th of February.

Afterwards he had notice given him, that the next day was appointed for his Execution; and about eight o'clock that night, the Guard of Officers in his chamber, were Captain *Henry Sharp*, Captain-Lieutenant *William Fister*, Ensign *Philip Brown*, Serjeant *Nicholas Stock*, and his said Keeper. And presently after they came into the chamber, three Women came to him, two whereof were *Sindercome*'s Sisters, and the other one said to be his Sweetheart, who expressed trouble and sorrow, lamenting his condition. And one of his said Sisters, named *Elizabeth Herring*, told him, *She had rather see him die before she went from him, than he should die so barbarous a death as was intended him*, or to that effect: whereupon the Officers minding her expressions, took what care they could to prevent her in giving him any thing; and as soon as the said women were gone carefully searched the room. Then *Sindercome* desired the Officers and his Keeper to withdraw, that he might be private; in which privacy, he continued about a quarter of an hour, then came to the chamber-door, saying to the said Officers that stood without, *They might come in, for he had now done*; which words being not usual with him, were observed by most of them. The first that went in, found him rubbing his hands with his handkerchief, and wiping his nose and mouth therewith; and he walked a turn or two about the room, and then took the Bible, and sat down reading therein. A while after, he started up suddenly, saying, *He must go to bed*. and therewithal he undrest himself, and went into his bed. The said Guard of Officers in his chamber, being then discoursing together, *Sindercome* (a quarter of an hour after he had lain still) discoursed very freely with them of what they were talking. About which instant of time, orders were sent from Sir *John Barkstead*, to the said Officers, to be careful that he should not make away himself † by poison, in regard it was the last night he was to be there; and they should diligently search all places of his chamber, and about his bed to prevent it. But presently after, *Sindercome* fell asleep (as was thought), and snorting somewhat unusually, one of the Officers desired his Keeper to take a candle and look upon him; which he did, and found him almost dead there, which prevented their further search. Whereupon a Surgeon was immediately sent for, who applied medicines to him; notwithstanding which, after he had continued in that condition speechless about two hours, he died §.

* Mr. *Whitlock*, in his Memorials, *Page* 654. *Feb.* 9, 1656. *Sindercome* was tried at the Upper-Bench Bar, found guilty, and condemned to be hanged, drawn, and quartered: The Court declared, *That by the Common Law, to compass or imagine the Death of the Chief Magistrate, by what name soever he was called, whether Lord Protector, or otherwise, is High-Treason, and that the Statute* 25 Edw. III *was only declaratory of the Common Law.*

† *Sindercome* had been an Apprentice to a Chirurgeon, near St. *Catherine*'s at the *Tower*, and so it was probable had more than ordinary knowledge of Poisons.

§ Lord *Clarendon*, in his History of the Rebellion, Vol. III. Part 2 (8vo. *Edition*) *Page* 646, 647 says, *Sindercome* was a very stout Man, and one who had been much in his (*Cromwell*'s) favour, and who had twice or thrice, by wonderful and unexpected Accidents, been disappointed in the minute he made sure to kill him, and (that *Cromwell*) had caused him to be apprehended; his behaviour was so resolute in his Examination and Trial, as if he thought he should still be able to do it; and it was manifest that he had

February 14, 1656.

The Coroner's Inquest, consisting of Merchants, and other substantial Housekeepers of the *Tower* Liberty, had in charge to inquire of the manner of *Sindercome*'s death, which they diligently attended, and all such witnesses as could speak materially thereunto were examined by the Coroner. And although there were then very strong presumptions that he had poisoned himself; yet in regard the Surgeons, who had then only opened his body, and finding no usual symptoms accompanying the taking of sharp poisons, could not positively deliver their opinions, otherwise than hereafter is expressed, the Jury desired the giving up their verdict till *Monday* following.

The same day afterwards, at the desire of the Lieutenant of the *Tower*, Sir *Richard Napier*, Doctor of Physick, and Doctor *Fern*, Reader of Anatomy at *Gresham* College, opened *Sindercome*'s head, and gave their opinions thereof also. Which was likewise afterward viewed by Mr. *Charles Stamford*, Mr. *Nicholas Brethers*, Wardens to the Company of Surgeons, and Mr. *Laurence Loe*; all able and knowing persons in their profession, which remain with the said Coroner under their hands.

February 14, 1656.

Being then desired by Sir *John Barkstead*, Knt. Lieutenant of the *Tower*, to see the head of *Miles Sindercome* opened, his body having been opened before our coming by the Surgeons, and to give him our observations and sense thereof:

WE found the Brain much inflamed, red, and distended with Blood, swollen as full as the Skull could well hold; besides much grumous and clodded Blood out of the Veins, which must be the effect of some very violent and preternatural cause. Yet are we not able positively to determine what that is, or whence it did proceed, the motion being much more sudden and violent than that of Apoplexies, and other known diseases of the Brain, except when caused by contusion, and other the like extraordinary violences.

Richard Napier,
Christopher Fern.

WE, whose names are here subscribed, being ordered to open the body of Mils Sindercome, *Prisoner in the* Tower *of* London, *do hereby declare, according to the best of our judgments and experiences, That we could not find out or discover any, the usual or common symptoms or effects, accompanying the taking of known and sharp poisons causing sudden death; but by the distention and swelling of the Brain, and Vessels in the Head, with much coagulated blood which we found there, more than in ordinary diseases, our opinions are, that the said Prisoner hath caused the same by some extraordinary means, for the hastening of his death.*

Charles Stamford, }
Nicholas Brethers, } *Wardens.*
Laurence Loe.

February 15, 1656.

Being Sabbath-day, *Sindercome*'s Keeper, with others, having removed the body out of the chamber where he died, into a more airy place, and taken several things out of that chamber, removed the Close-stool, and under it was found a Paper subscribed with his own hand as followeth:

GOD knoweth my heart, I do take this course, because I would not have all the open shame of the World executed upon my body. I desire all good people not to judge amiss of me, for I do not fear my Life, but do trust God with my Soul. I did this thing without the privity of any person in the world: I do, before God and the world, clear my Keeper, my Sisters, Mother, or Brother, or any other of my Relations, but it was done alone by myself. I say by me,

The 13th day, 1656.

Miles Sindercome.

February 16, 1656.

The Jury sate again according to adjournment, to whom the aforesaid testimonies of the Physicians and Surgeons, and also *Sindercome*'s own note were apparent; so that they did then unanimously resolve and agree, that he, by some extraordinary means, had caused his own death, and that they verily believed the same to be by poison. But for their further direction, as to the formal part of their verdict, they at that time deferred the giving of it, and adjourned till seven o'clock the next morning, at the Lord Chief-Justice's house, where they accordingly met; and having received his Lordship's direction touching matter of form, did all unanimously agree on, and give up their verdict, to the effect following:

February 17, 1656.

Middlesex ss. WE find that upon the 13th day of *February*, in the year of our Lord, 1656, about the hour of nine in the night, *Miles Sindercome*, otherwise *Fish*, late of the Parish of *Peter in Bonds*, in the County of *Middlesex*; God not having before his eyes, but by the instigation of the Devil being moved and seduced, at the *Tower of London*, in the Parish and County aforesaid, feloniously, wilfully, and of his malice towards himself aforethought, as a Felon against himself, then and there feloniously upon himself did make an assault. And that the said *Miles Sindercome*, otherwise *Fish*, then and there, certain poisoned powder, hrough the nose of him the said *Miles*, into the head of him the said *Miles*, feloniously, wilfully, and of his malice towards himself aforethought, as a Felon of himself, feloniously did snuff and draw. By reason of which snuffing and drawing of the poison aforesaid, so as aforesaid, into the head of him the said *Miles Sindercome*; he the said *Miles Sindercome*, by the strength and operation of the poison aforesaid, himself did mortally poison; of which said mortal poisoning, he the said *Miles Sindercome*, otherwise *Fish*, within three hours after died. And so we find that the aforesaid *Miles Sindercome*, otherwise *Fish*, the said 13th day of *February*, in the year aforesaid, at the *Tower* of *London* aforesaid, in the Parish and County aforesaid, in manner and form aforesaid, feloniously, wilfully, and of his malice towards himself aforethought, as a Felon against himself, feloniously himself did kill and murder. We find no Goods or Chattels, that the said *Miles Sindercome*, otherwise *Fish* had, at the time of the felony and murder aforesaid, in manner and form aforesaid, upon himself done and committed. In witness hereof, we have hereunto set our hand, this 17th day of *February*, 1656, &c.

And thereupon the said Coroner issued forth his Warrant for the burial of *Sindercome*, the Copy whereof followeth:

Middlesex ss. WHereas the Jury impannel'd and sworn to inquire of the death of *Miles Sindercome*, otherwise *Fish*, did present upon their Oaths, that the said *Miles*, the 13th of this instant *February*, did feloniously poison himself: These are therefore in the name of his Highness, the Lord Protector of the Commonwealth of *England*, *Scotland*, and *Ireland*, to require you to bury the corpse of the said *Miles Sindercome*, according to Law, in the next common Highway. Hereof you are not to fail, as you will answer the contrary at your perils, dated the 17th day of *February*, 1656.

Thomas Evans, Coroner.

To the Constables and Headboroughs within the Liberty of the Tower of London.

On the same day, *February* 17, *Miles Sindercome* aforesaid, being found to have murdered himself, his body was according to Law drawn to the open place upon *Tower-hill*, at a horse's tail, with his head forward, and there under the Scaffold of common execution a hole being digged, he was turned in stark naked, and a stake spiked with Iron, was driven through him into the earth; that part of the stake which remained above ground being all plated with iron.

The Examination of Elizabeth Herring, *the Wife of* William Herring, *of the Precinct of* St. Katherine's, *Mariner; taken upon Oath, the* 14*th of* February, 1656.

SHE saith, that *Miles Sindercome* now dead was her brother, and that he was a Prisoner in the *Tower* of *London* the space of three weeks last past, or thereabouts, to her knowledge; and that for the space of a fortnight she was at the *Tower* several times to see the said *Miles*, and could be admitted but once to see him, until the 5th day of *February*, she this Informant was sent for to come to the said *Miles*. When she came to the said *Miles*, she found two Gentlemen in the room with him; who, as soon as this Informant came in, did say unto the said *Miles Sindercome*, that he was not to speak any thing in private to this Informant; then this Informant came away. And that she came several times after to the said *Miles*; that on *Monday* the 9th of this instant *February*, she came to the said *Miles* after he had received sentence to die; and lamenting his condition, she said, that he would bring his Mother's gray hairs with sorrow to the grave, and what an open shame it would be to him and all his friends. The said *Miles Sindercome* then did answer, saying, that before they should have his life so shamefully (meaning his Highness the Lord Protector, as this Informant believeth) he would poison himself first, and desired her, this Informant, to buy him some poison, which she refused. And that at times when this Informant hath been with the said *Miles*, she did see some strange faces which she did not know, and that she came every day since *Monday*, once a day or more to the said *Miles*: and saith, that he the said *Miles* did not speak any more words to her of any poison, or any other words of discontent, as if he intended to destroy himself; and that he never did complain to this Informant of any sickness or diseases that he was troubled withal. And that on *Friday*, the 13th of this instant *February*, she being alone with the said *Miles Sindercome*, did persuade him to confess who had a hand with him in the plot against his Highness the Lord Protector; that if he would confess, his Highness would grant him his life, and wished him to trust to God and man; and the said *Miles* answered, he would have it under black and white, and that he would trust no man. And that about eight of the clock at night she parted from the said *Miles*, and left him in good health, being prepared to die, as she thought; and that he found in his own conscience he had made his peace with the Lord. and this Informant denieth that she ever brought him any poison, or did buy any other thing to destroy him; yet confesseth that on *Friday* night she did say unto the said *Miles*, that she desired with all her heart, to see him die a natural death in that chamber. And further saith not.

The Mark of 2 *Elizabeth Herring*.

The Information of Martha Wickham, *Spinster, taken upon Oath, as aforesaid.*

SHE saith, that she hath known *Miles Sindercome* for the space of four years last past, and that he lodged at the house of *Daniel Stockwel*, Haberdasher of Hats on *London-Bridge*, where this Informant lived; and that the night before he was taken into custody, and imprisoned, he lay at his lodging in the said house. And this Informant denieth, and saith, that she doth not know any of the company that used to come to the said *Miles*, while he lodged there; and saith, that she hath been several times to see the said *Miles* at the *Tower* of *London*, while he remained there; and saith, that she doth not know of any poison, or any other violent thing, which was brought or sent to the said *Miles Sindercome*, to destroy himself; and further saith not.

Martha Wickham.

had more Associates, who were undiscovered and as resolute as himself; and though he (*Cromwell*) had got him condemned to die, the Fellow's carriage and words were such, as if he knew well how to avoid the Judgment; which made *Cromwell* believe that a Party in the Army would attempt his rescue. Whereupon he gave strict charge that he should be carefully looked to in the *Tower*, and three or four of the Guard always with him day and night. At the day appointed for his Execution, those troops *Cromwell* was most confident of were placed upon *Tower-hill*, where the Gallows was erected. But when the Guard called *Sindercome* to arise in the Morning, they found him dead in his bed, which gave [illegible] to *Cromwell*; for besides that he hoped that, at his Death, to avoid the utmost rigour of it, he would have confessed many of his Confederates; he now found himself under the reproach of having caused him to be poisoned, as not daring to bring him to publick Justice; nor could he suppress that scandal. It appeared upon Examination, that the night before, when he was going to bed in the presence of his Guard, his sister came to take her leave of him; and upon her going away, he put off his clothes, and leaped into his bed, and said, "This was the last bed he should ever go into." His body was drawn by a horse to the gallows where he should have been hanged, and buried under it, with a stake driven through him, as is usual in the case of self-murther. Yet this action perplexed *Cromwell* very much, and though he was without the particular discovery which he expected, he made a general discovery by it, that he himself was more odious in his army than he believed he had been.

The Information of Anne Pierce, *Wife of* Stephen Pierce, *of* Deptford, *in the County of* Kent, *Mariner, taken upon Oath, as aforesaid.*

SHE saith, That she was several times to see *Miles Sindercome*, the time he was in the *Tower*: Saith, That she doth not know of any Poison, or any other violent Thing that was brought to the said *Miles* to destroy himself; and she did never hear the said *Miles* speak any Words, as if he intended to destroy himself by Poison, or any other way: And further saith not.

The Mark of A *Anne Pierce.*

Middlesex ss. *The Information of* William Foster, *taken upon Oath, the 14th Day of February*, 1656, *before* Thomas Evans, *Gent. one of the Coroners of the County of* Middlesex.

HE saith, That on *Friday*, the 13th of *February*, about nine of the Clock at Night, he was in the Chamber where *Miles Sindercome*, otherwise *Fish*, lodged, within the *Tower* of *London*; saith, That the said *Miles Sindercome* did desire this Informant, and four more that were with him, that they would withdraw out of the Chamber whilst he went to Prayers; and within less than a Quarter of an Hour after, he called in this Informant, and those that were with him, into the Chamber again; and a Quarter of an Hour after that, the said *Miles* did take a Book into his Hands to read, and said, that he would go to bed, and that that was the last Night he should go into a Bed, and the last Bed he should go into. And then he lay down in his Bed, and, to this Informant's thinking, fell asleep, and snored. And this Informant desired *Daniel Steer*, *Miles Sindercome*'s Keeper, to take a Candle, and to see how the said *Miles* did lie in his Bed; and the said *Daniel Steer* did tell this Informant, that the said *Miles Sindercome*, alias *Fish*, was almost dead as he lay in the Bed, but the said *Miles Sindercome* did lie in that Condition speechless the Space of two Hours, and then died.

The Mark of F *William Foster.*

The Information of Philip Brown, *taken upon Oath, as aforesaid.*

HE saith, That on *Friday*, the 13th Day of *February*, about ten of the Clock in the Forenoon, he was with *Miles Sindercome*, otherwise *Fish*, in his Chamber, and staid there at Dinner; and in the same time, while that they were at Dinner, the said *Miles Sindercome* did say these Words, That that was the last Meal's Meat that ever he should eat, as he thought. And after, two of the said *Miles*'s Sisters, a Cousin, and another Gentlewoman with them, came to see the said *Miles*, and did then persuade him, the said *Miles*, to confess to them, and to declare whom they were, who had brought him into those Troubles and Sorrows that he was like to undergo. And he answered them, saying, To whom should he confess? He could not expect Mercy from him, who was resolved to give him none; saying, that *Cromwell* said to him, when he was taken and brought before him, *Sindercome*, have I caught you? you that have sought many Ways to take away my Life, I will have no Consideration at all of thy Life. And when he had uttered these Words, he was in a great Passion, and said, That he might go and declare against the Lord *Fleetwood*, the Lord *Lambert*, Sir *John Barkstead*, Sir *Thomas Pride*, or any other Member of the Army, if he were minded to destroy innocent Blood. And about seven of the Clock that Day, Orders were brought to this Informant from the Major, that the said *Miles Sindercome* might have some time allowed him apart, to prepare himself, if he desired it. And this Informant went out of the Chamber, and left the said *Miles* alone; and a Quarter of an Hour after, this Informant standing at the Chamber Door, did see the said *Miles* kneeling on his Knees on the Ground by the Bed-side, and presently after one of the Centinels that stood at his Chamber-door, did tell this Informant, that the said *Miles* did cough and kick, as if he was a-vomiting; and this Informant opened the Chamber-door, and went in, and found the said *Miles* walking about the Chamber. And Capt. *Foster*, and Capt. *Sharp*, who were ordered to be there that Night, then came into the Room; and about nine of the Clock at Night, the said *Miles* did desire this Informant, and the other Company that were there, to withdraw out of the Room, and about a Quarter of an Hour after, he called them in again; and the said *Miles* did then take a Book into his Hand to read, and said, that he would go to Bed, and that that was the last Night he should ever go to Bed, and the last Bed he should lie in; and then laid him down in his Bed. And then Capt. *Sharp* did desire *Daniel Steer*, the said *Miles*'s Keeper, to see how he did lie in his Bed; and the said *Daniel Steer* looking upon the said *Miles*, did say unto this Informant, and the rest there, that the said *Miles* was almost dead: And yet the said *Miles Sindercome* did lie in that Condition the Space of two Hours, and then died.

The Mark of B *Philip Brown.*

Middlesex ss. *The Information of* Daniel Steer, *Gent. taken upon Oath, as aforesaid.*

SAITH, That about the End of *January*, *Miles Sindercome*, alias *Fish*, being a Prisoner in the *Tower* of *London*, under the Custody of Sir *John Barkstead*, Knight, having some Discourse with this Informant, who was his Keeper, did then say unto this Informant, that if he would be faithful to him, the said *Miles*, he would give him to the Value of his Place, what it was worth, were it a hundred or two of Pounds; and desired him, this Informant, if he would undertake the Business, and accept of his Proffer, to provide him the said *Miles* a black Suit of Clothes, a Peruque, and also a short Dagger, and to pass him out of the Water-gate, and he would kill any Man that should oppose him; and the same Day that he was at his Trial, being the 9th of this instant *February*, after he came back again to the *Tower*, the said *Miles* was in a great Passion, his Sister *Elizabeth Herring* being then in his Company; he the said *Miles* then did swear, that they should not have their Ends (meaning, as this Informant believeth, that the Sentence pronounced against him that Day should not be executed). And then the said *Miles Sindercome* did desire this Informant to help him to some Poison, that he might make away with himself; and this Informant refusing to do any of those Things which he desired, the said *Miles* then did speak to the said *Elizabeth Herring*, his Sister, who was there, to bring him some Poison; but she the said *Elizabeth* crying, gave him no Answer. And afterwards the said *Miles*, and the said *Elizabeth*, had some private Discourse together in the Room, which this Informant did not hear. And the said *Elizabeth* parting from the said *Miles*, came down Stairs, and did speak to this Informant, saying, Lord, what shall I do, did you hear him what he said of the Poison? And this Informant answered, That he did hear what he said, and wished her not to bring him any; and further said to the said *Elizabeth Herring*, that if the said *Miles* was poisoned while he continued in this Informant's House, that he this Informant answered, he would charge her the said *Elizabeth* with helping the said *Miles* to Poison. And then the said *Elizabeth* went away from this Informant; and this Informant went up into the Chamber to the said *Miles Sindercome*; who asked this Informant, if it was not possible for him to help the said *Miles* to make an Escape now in his great Distress: and further said, that if this Informant would do it, he would make good to him 200 *l.* this Night: And then said, that if he this Informant would go along with the said *Miles*, when he escaped, he would make that 200 *l.* 700 *l.* or what more he should desire; further requiring earnestly, this Informant to help him to a black Suit, and a Peruque. This Informant then said to the said *Miles Sindercome*, that it was impossible for him to make an Escape, there being such strict Guard kept about him; and had no further Discourse at that time. And that on *Friday*, the 13th Day of *February*, about ten of the Clock at Night, this Informant then was with the said *Miles* in his Chamber, together with Captain *Henry Sharp*, Captain-Lieutenant *William Foster*, Ensign *Philip Browne*, Serjeant *Nicholas Stock*: And the said *Miles* did desire this Informant, and the rest of the Company, to withdraw out of the Room, which they did; and about a Quarter of an Hour after, he the said *Miles* did desire them to come again into his Chamber; he walking a Turn or two about the Room, did take into his Hand a Bible to read in; and a while after, he started up suddenly from the Place where he sat, saying, He would go to Bed, that that was the last Time he should go to Bed, and the last Bed he should lie in. And when the said *Miles* had lain a while in his Bed, he fell asleep, and snorted, and after that he had a rattling in his Throat; and this Informant was bid to take a Candle, and see the said *Miles* as he lay in his Bed; and when this Informant had looked upon the said *Miles*, he found him almost dead as he lay in his Bed. And this Informant being further asked, if he knew of any Poison, or other Means, which the said *Miles* did use to take away his Life, saith, That he did not see any, neither doth he know any more touching the said *Miles*'s Death, but what he hath already declared in this Information.

Daniel Steer.

The Information of Henry Sharp, *Gent. taken upon Oath, as aforesaid.*

SAITH, That between seven and eight of the Clock on *Friday* Night, being the 13th Day of *February*, being in the Chamber with *Miles Sindercome*, otherwise *Fish*, three Women, whose Names this Informant doth not know, came crying into the Chamber to the said *Miles*, lamenting his Condition; the said *Sindercome* then reading in a Bible, did so continue reading about Half an Hour, while the said three Women were there. One of the said Women said to him, the said *Miles*, that she would be glad to see him dead in the Room before she went from thence, rather than to have him die such a barbarous Death as was appointed for him to die. And after they were gone out of the Room, this Informant caused *Daniel Steer*, the said *Miles*'s Keeper, to search the Bed and the Room, lest any thing might be left there for the said *Miles* to hurt himself withal; and the Room being searched, nothing was found. And also upon Enquiry of the said *Steer*, this Informant found that all Instruments were taken from him; only the said *Steer* brought him up a Knife to cut his Meat withal, and carried it away when he had done. And that about Half an Hour after, he the said *Miles* desired this Informant, and the rest of the Company that were with him, to withdraw out of the Room; and about a Quarter of an Hour after, he called them into the Chamber again, and took a Book into his Hand to read in it, and after a little Time, he said he would go to Bed, and lie down in his Bed; and he hearing this Informant and Capt. *Foster* talking together, the said *Miles* talked very freely with him; and in the Time of their Discourse together, there came a Messenger to this Informant from Sir *John Barkstead*, requiring this Informant to have a special Care of the said *Miles Sindercome*, otherwise *Fish*, that he did not poison himself. This Informant did declare unto the other that were there, what Order he had received for the said *Miles*; and about a Quarter of an Hour after, this Informant hearing him the said *Miles* snore, desired *Daniel Steer*, the said *Miles*'s Keeper, to see how the said *Miles* did then. The said *Daniel* taking a Candle to look on the said *Miles Sindercome*, did tell this Informant that he was almost dead; yet the said *Miles* did live in that Condition, speechless, the Space of two Hours after, and then died.

Henry Sharp.

The Information of Elizabeth Sindercome, *of* Deptford, *in the County of* Kent, *Widow, taken upon Oath, the 14th of* February, 1656.

SHE saith, That she was three several Times to see *Miles Sindercome*, her Son, while he was Prisoner in the *Tower* of *London*; and saith, she doth not know of any violent Means or Ways used by the said *Miles Sindercome*, or any other, to hasten his Death; neither did she ever hear him speak any Words to that purpose: And that the last time she was with the said *Miles*, he did then tell her, this Informant, that he was prepared to die. And that two Ministers being then in the Chamber with him, she had no further Discourse with him, or did see him any more, until on *Friday* Night, about twelve of the Clock, she did hear she was sent for; and did hear that he was very sick and weak, of which Sickness he died presently after; and further saith not.

The Mark of 2 *Elizabeth Sindercome.*

XXVIII. Proceedings against ARCHIBALD, Marquis of *Argyle*, 13 *Car.* II. 1661, for High-Treason.

The Grand Indictment * of High-Treason, exhibited against the Marquis of *Argyle*, by his Majesty's Advocate, to the Parliament of *Scotland*.

ARCHIBALD, Marquis of *Argyle*, you are indicted and accused, and are to answer at the instance of Sir *John Fletcher*, Knight, his Majesty's Advocate for his Majesty's Interest, That whereas by the Laws of God, expressed in holy Writ, by the Laws of Nations, by the Common Law, and by the municipal Laws and Practice of this Kingdom; especially by the third Act of the fifth Parliament of King *James* I. and by the first Act of King *James* VI. of blessed memory, and by several other Acts of Parliament, all good and loyal Subjects of this Kingdom are bound and obliged perpetually to acknowlege, obey, maintain, defend and advance the Life, Honour, Safety, Dignity, Sovereign Authority, and Prerogative Royal of their Sovereign Lord and King, their Heirs and Successors, and Privilege of their Crown, with their lives, lands and goods, to the utmost of their power, constantly and faithfully to withstand all, and whatsoever persons or estates, who shall presume, press, or intend any ways to impugn, prejudice, or impair the same; and shall no way intend, attempt, engage, act or do any thing to the violation, hurt, derogation, impairing or prejudice of his Highness's sovereignty, prerogative, and privilege of his Crown, or any point or part thereof: and whosoever doth the contrary, to be punished as Traitors, and to forfeit their lives, lands and goods. Likewise by the 25th Act of the 6th Parliament of King *James* II. and by the 75th Act of the 9th Parliament of Queen *Mary*; all rising in fear of war against the King's Person or Majesty; all attempting to raise any band of men of war, horse or foot, in warlike posture, without special licence of the King's Majesty, and all suppliers of them, in help, redress or counsel, are punishable as Traitors. Likewise by the 43d Act of the 3d Parliament of King *James* I. and by the 134th Act of the 8th Parliament; and by Act the 10th, of the 10th Parliament; and by the 205th Act of the 14th Parliament of King *James* VI. it is statute and ordained, that no Subject, of whatsoever function, degree or quality, shall presume to take upon him publickly or privately to declaim, speak or write any purpose of reproach, slander, disdain or contempt of his Majesty's Person, Estate or Government, or tending to the dishonour, hurt or prejudice of his Highness, his Parents or Progenitors; or to meddle in the affairs of his Highness, his Estate present, by-gone, or in time coming; nor to deprave his Laws and Acts of Parliaments, nor misconstrue his proceedings, whereby any misliking may be moved betwixt the King's Majesty, his Nobility and loving Subjects, under the pain of losing their lives, lands and goods, and others therein contained. As also all hearers of any such leasings, slanderous speeches or words, and concealers thereof, without apprehending of the Authors (if it lie in their power), and reveal not the same to his Majesty, or some of his Judges or Officers, and are mentioned in the said Acts, are liable to the like punishment, as the principal offenders.

Likewise by the 130th Act of the 8th Parliament of King *James* VI. it is statute and ordained, that none of his Majesty's Lieges and Subjects do presume or take upon him to impugn the Dignity and Authority of the Estates of Parliament; or to speak or procure the innovation or diminution of the power and authority of the same, under the pain of Treason.

Likewise by the last Act of the 3d Parliament of King *James* V. and by the 33d Act of the first Parliament of King *James* VI. all burning of houses or corn, and wilful fire-rising, is declared Treason, and the committers thereof are to be punished.

Likewise by the 51st Act of the 11th Parliament of King *James* VI. it is statute and ordained, that the murder and slaughter of whatsoever his Majesty's Lieges, where the party slain is under the trust, credit, assurance and power of the slayer, all such murder and slaughter shall be Treason, and the persons found culpable shall forfeit life, lands and goods.

Likewise by the 37th Act of the 3d Parliament of King *James* I. and by the 144th Act of the 12th Parliament of King *James* VI. all receivers, suppliers, or inter-commoners with any Traitors, are punishable by forfeiture, as the Traitors themselves.

Likewise by Common Laws and Practice of this Kingdom, all concealers and not revealers of any malicious purpose, of putting any violent hands on the sacred person of your dread Sovereign the King's Majesty, or purpose of killing or putting him to death; and all advisers, counsellors, siders, abettors or havers of any accession thereto, are punishable as Traitors.

Nevertheless, 'tis of verity, that you the said Marquis of *Argyle*, having laid aside all fear of God, loyalty to his Majesty, and to his royal Father, of ever blessed memory, natural duty and affection to your native Country and Country-men, and respect and obedience to the Laws of all well-governed Realms, the Common-Law, and the Laws, Statutes, Acts of Parliament, and Practices of this Kingdom, and having traitorously intended and purposed the eradicating and subverting the fundamental Government of this Kingdom; at least the enervating, violating, derogating, or impairing the sovereign Authority, royal Prerogative of his Majesty, and Privilege of the Crown You, for carrying on of your said wicked purpose, having gathered and convocated together, in a hostile manner, a great many of your Friends, Servants, Vassals, Followers and other of his Majesty's Lieges, without any warrant, licence or command from his Majesty, and therewith, under pretence of opposing such as by you were then nick-named *Anti-Covenanters*, and opposing the work of Reformation (but who indeed were faithful assertors of his Majesty's lawful Authority), having marched to the ford of *Lyon* in *Athol*, in the month of 1640, there did in your tent, and in presence of a great many Gentlemen and others publickly declare, *That it was the opinion and judgment of many Divines and Lawyers, that a King may be deposed for desertions, venditions and invasions*: And that howbeit that your words were *in abstracto* from any King, yet that the sense and meaning thereof might appear to be of the then King's Majesty, your dread Sovereign, you did subjoin and say to the late Mr. *John Stuart*, of *Ladiwel*; *And, Mr.* John, *you understand Latin*.

Likewise considering the condition of the Kingdom, and the oppositions that a great many of the people were in to his Majesty; particularly you the said Marquis, and your three Complices and Followers; it is clear that the said words did not only treasonably reflect upon kingly Government, as being subject to the people, who might in the cause aforesaid depose a King; but also it is clear, that your meaning also and intention thereby was, that the King's Majesty, your dread Sovereign, might be so destroyed: And the said treasonable speeches were so vented by you, of design to usher in your many treasonable actions and practices done by you unto his sacred Person, Dignity, and Authority; which, doubtless, did occasion, and was mainly instrumental both in his deposition and cruel murder: Which wicked and treasonable speeches the said Mr. *John* having thereafter reported, you most cruelly and tyrannously did prosecute him to death, as a Leasing-maker betwixt the King's Majesty and his good Subjects, howbeit you could not but be conscious of the truth of what he had reported.

Secondly, In prosecution of your aforesaid wicked and treasonable purposes, you having marched with the said forces to the house of *Airlie*, belonging to his Majesty's right trusty and well beloved Cousin and chief Councillor *James* Earl of *Airlie*, which was then kept for his Majesty's service and authority; after you had forced the rendition of the said house, and destroyed the woods and plantings of the same, and wearied and destroyed the said Earl's friends and tenants, his Majesty's good Subjects, you did slight and demolish the said house; and to express your hatred to the said Earl, merely for his loyalty to his Majesty, did seize, or by those under you did seize upon the house of *Forther* in *Glenyla* belonging also to the said Earl; and without any colour or pretence of offence did wilfully, most treasonably, and contrary to the aforesaid Acts of Parliament, raise fire in the said house, and thereby burnt and destroyed the same, and all furniture therein.

Thirdly, In further prosecution of your treasonable plots and machinations against his Majesty's Person and Authority, contrary to the aforesaid Laws and Acts of Parliament *in Anno* 1640, you in an hostile manner, did most treasonably lay siege to his Majesty's Fort and Castle of *Dunbarton*, then fortified and kept for his Majesty's service by Col *Henderson*, having his Majesty's command and commission for that effect, and forced the said Colonel to render the said Castle to you; out of which most treasonably you caused to be transported and carried away a great many of his Majesty's cannon and other ammunition, appointed for defence and security of the said Castle.

Fourthly, Notwithstanding that his then Majesty had *in Anno* 1641 come himself in person to this Kingdom, and most graciously condescended to all such Acts as were required of him (how unjust soever) for securing and pleasing the people, and settling a peace; and that he had past one Act of Oblivion, to indemnify all such as had formerly been in opposition to his Majesty within this Kingdom, and that he had conferred upon you the title and dignity of Marquis, as a mark of his royal favour, and put you in places of greatest trust in the Kingdom; and that you had sworn and promised, in the Abbey of *Holyroodhouse*, that in case any trouble or commotions should happen to be raised in *England*, by any of his discontented Subjects against him, you would assist and defend him against all such, to the hazard of your life and fortunes: and that his Majesty had parted from this his ancient Kingdom, as was said and acknowledged by all, a contented Prince from a contented People: yet nevertheless his Majesty being forced and necessitated *in anno* 1642, to leave his Parliament in *England* then sitting at *Westminster*, and his royal Palace of *Whitehall*, and betake himself to defensive arms, for maintenance of his royal person, dignity and authority, and to protect the same against an army of Sectaries, who maliciously, traitorously, cruelly and treasonably did invade the same; you, contrary to your allegiance, obligations and recent Promise aforesaid, did by yourself and complices, to fortify and strengthen the said Rebels and Sectaries, and in direct opposition to his Majesty's person and dignity, call, or cause to be called a pretended convention of Estates *in Anno* 1643, without any shadow or colour of lawful authority; and you and they so convocated did take upon you the supreme authority of the Kingdom, enter in league with his Majesty's enemies, impose subsidies and excise upon the people, and raise an army of his Majesty's own subjects, and therewith entered his Majesty's Kingdom of *England*, seized upon his Majesty's Towns and Forts there; and killed, murdered, plundered and destroyed his good subjects, and in open and pitched fields fought for, with and in behalf of the

* [illegible] *Grand Indictment of High-Treason*, because there was another Charge exhibited against the Marquis, at the instance of Sir *James Lamond*; and there [illegible] Answers of the Marquis's to this Grand Indictment, which imperfect Proceedings are inserted in *State-Trials*, Vol. II. from *page* 413. [illegible] Bishop *Burnet*'s Account of his Trial, with his method of this Trial here inserted, not of that Indictment against the Marquis [illegible] And in *page* 430, is inserted the Marquis's Speech on the Scaffold, for which reason it is here omitted.

said Rebels, against his Majesty's forces, which in effect was the rise and cause of all our subsequent ruins and disasters that befel his Majesty or his loyal and good subjects thereafter.

Fifthly, In *Anno* 1645, after your return from *England*, to shew your implacable malice and hatred to all such as had any dependence upon, or affection to his Majesty, you by yourself, and others under your command, or at your direction, did most treasonably raise wilful fire, and burn the house of [illegible]ess *Lysvented*, inhabited by the Countess of *Sterling*, and in her possession, and all the moveables and furniture, they extending to a great value; notwithstanding that the said Countess was an honourable aged woman; and who, and her dearest husband, the Earl of *Sterling*, by all observances and dutiful respects obliged you, so far as in them lay; thereby adding to the said Act of Treason, the height of oppression and ingratitude.

Sixthly, In the year 1646, you by yourself, or those under your command, or for whom you were answerable, or whom you might have stopped or impeded, did [illegible]ke in the house of *Taward*, belonging to the Laird of *Salmond*, and the house of *Oscoge*, belonging to *Lamond* of *Oscoge*, and after articles of capitulation drawn and subscribed by the Laird of *Ardkinglass*, and other Officers under your command, did most treasonably, in manner aforesaid, under trust and assurance, as is said, burn the said house of *Oscoge*, cruelly hang, kill and murther a great many of the said Lairds of *Salmond* and *Oscoge's* friends and followers; as is more fully exprest in the Summons raised at their instance and mine, for his Majesty's interest against you, and which is repeated in a part of this article.

Seventhly, You having traitorously intended the utter ruin and extirpation of all faithful and loyal subjects, who had given testimony of their faithfulness to his Majesty's dearest Father, of ever-blessed memory, and having with an army of your complices, associates, vassals, servants, tenants and followers in *Anno* 1646, marched to *Kentire*, where a great many of his Majesty's well affected subjects of the name of *Mac-Donald*, *Mac-Cow*, and others, whose names are not particularly known, to the number of 3 or 400, had fortified themselves for their security, and against your oppression and violence, in the house of *Lochbehead* and *Donavertie*: And you with the said forces having marched to the said house of *Lochbehead*; the Gentlemen and others therein, without making the least opposition, and declaring that they had refuged themselves to the said place for shelter and protection, did render up the said house and themselves, upon assurance, that they might really and quietly return and live at their own homes; according thereto, they were dismissed and sent home, where they remained in peaceable manner by the space of days. Notwithstanding, thereafter, you and the forces aforesaid having besieged the Castle of *Donavertie*, during the said siege, there were several rendezvouzes appointed for the said Gentlemen to make their appearance; which frequently they did, and were still dismissed, until such time as those who were within the said house of *Donavertie* had rendered up the said house and themselves, to be disposed of at the mercy of the Kingdom, or pretended Committee of Estates: And that notwithstanding thereof, you and your said complices had most perfidiously, treacherously and treasonably (and for which also you are here indicted) slaughtered and murdered, or caused to be slaughtered and murdered, the number of 260 of them or 300, they being under your trust, assurance, credit, or power; and did dispose of the rest of them at your own hand, without any lawful warrant, to Captains *William Hay*, and *Archibald Campbell*, to serve in the *French* wars. Then and hereafter you caused, and appointed a new rendezvous of the said Gentlemen, who were in the house of *Lochebead*, and their followers; who having appeared in frequent manner, you caused to be singled out fifteen or sixteen of the said Gentlemen, who were that night sent to the said house of *Lochebead*, and the next morning brought forth by you, or such as were under your command, and most perfidiously, cruelly and inhumanly, without any order of Law, or form of Process civil or military, hanged and murdered. And to aggravate the said cruel and barbarous crime, 'tis of verity, That one of the said Persons being an old man, and having one son, of age not above sixteen or seventeen years; the father immediately before his death did depone, that his said son had never done any crimes offensive all his life-time, but that he had still been at Schools; and that some few days before, he had come from *Glascow*, the place of his education, to visit his Parents; and therefore did earnestly supplicate, in regard of his innocency, his life might be spared. Notwithstanding you, and the bloody actors of your purposes, were so unmerciful, as not to hearken to the said so just desire of the said dying old man, but forthwith the said young innocent boy was cruelly also hanged to death. Likewise not content with the aforesaid unheard-of horrid Acts of cruelty, in the month of 1640, or one or other of the months thereof, by yourself and followers, or such whom you might have stopt or lett, caused to be transported from the Isle of *Ila*, to the Isle of *Inwa*, to the number of two hundred persons of all sexes and ages; where all means of livelihood and subsistence being withdrawn from them, they in a most miserable manner were pined and starved to death by famine, except some very few, who had out-lived the rest, and were relieved and carried out of the said Isle by boats accidentally coming by: Likewise the person of *Macdonald*, alias *Coalmac Gilespy*, or *Ceawkittoche*, being *in Anno* ordained by the Parliament, or Committee of Estates thereof, to have been brought from prison out of the house of where he then was, and there had been kept by you and others in your time, many years before, to *Edinburgh*, that the causes for which he had been kept, and so detained in prison, might have been known; and he having for that end been brought in a ship the length of the road of *Leith*; you, for preventing such Information of your cruelty and oppression exercised towards him, and many of his friends and relations, which he was able to have given and made out; you in manifest contempt and scorn of that Committee of Parliament, under which you yourself acted, caused to take the person of the said *Cawkittoche* forth of the said ship, and after you had carried him to your own lands and bounds, cruelly caused to hang him to death.

Eighthly, Notwithstanding of the manifold acts of mercy and favour, dignity, honour and trust conferred upon you by your then dread Sovereign, for reclaiming of you from your disloyal and treasonable practices, plots and machinations, against his sacred person, dignity and authority; he being sore pressed and reduced to great straits and extremities by that army of Sectaries before-mentioned, with whom you had formerly joined, as is said; and having in that exigence and difficulty rather chosen, from an innate principle of affection of his Countrymen, to cast himself over in the hands of the army of his Majesty's subjects of his ancient Kingdom of *Scotland*, for shelter and preservation of his Royal Person; nevertheless, you, the said Marquis, being the chief ring-leader of that factious party, who then swayed the estate and affairs both in Council and Armies in the said Kingdom, did so contrive and complot, and by your influence so prevail, that after all fair offers made by his Majesty, and his earnest desire to have come and lived in *Scotland*, until such time as all differences in both Kingdoms had been settled: That a pretended Act of Parliament was made for abandoning and leaving his Majesty in the disposal and mercy of the inveterate enemies of his Majesty and Government, the said armies of Sectaries. And that your acting in, and accessions to, the said affair might be the more evident and clear, and to aggravate your eminent and singular guilt therein, you yourself went to *London*, where you basely, under pretext of satisfaction for the arrears of the said army, raised by the pretended authority of the pretended Convention of Estates, *in Anno* 1643, as is said, treacherously and treasonably gave up, at least condescended to the upgiving of your dread Sovereign and Master, and that as being impowered so to do by the Kingdom of *Scotland*; and thereby did rub an indelible mark of reproach and infamy upon the whole nation to all generations, so far as in you lay. And further, to clear your aforesaid treasonable dealings, accessions to, and correspondency with that infamous party of the said army, who carried on the said abominable and detestable act, you being at the same time in a pretended joint Committee of both Kingdoms, whiles as the *English* therein did call in question whether the *Scots* army would sincerely concur with them in their said treason and treachery; you, after many arguments used in their favours, earnestly desired them to have patience for a little time, and it would appear by somewhat of the officers of the army, how far they intended to concur and go along with them. Likewise within few days after there was a vindication and declaration emitted in name of the said armies, whereby it was held forth, that in case his Majesty would not condescend to all the desires of both Kingdoms, which was no less than the divesting himself of all regal power, civil, ecclesiastical, or military in state, church, or armies, they would deliver him up, which immediately after the payment of 200,000*l.* basely and treasonably was done by you and them.

Ninthly, *In Anno* 1648, his Majesty's Royal Father being, contrary to all Laws, divine and human, most unchristianly, barbarously and treasonably detained and kept prisoner within the Castle of *Carisbrook*, in the Isle of *Wight*, by a party of factious, disloyal and rebellious Sectaries; the Estates of Parliament then convened by his Majesty's authority, having taken the said inhuman, treasonable and cruel usage into serious consideration, they found this Kingdom engaged in honour and duty to resent so horrid and unheard-of cruelty and lese-majesty, and obliged to use their utmost endeavours to relieve him out of the hands of such wicked Usurpers, and to restore him to the exercise of his Royal authority in freedom, honour and safety; for effecting thereof, after all other fair ways essayed, upon mature consultation had, they found that the only probable means was the raising of an army of his Majesty's good subjects, which was accordingly statute and ordained by Act of the said Parliament. Against the carrying on of which, so just, laudable and necessary a duty, you did most violently and eminently oppose yourself, not only by arguing, voting against, and using all other means in your power to obstruct the same; but also, after the same was past into an Act of Parliament, you did most contemptuously and treasonably publickly dissent from, and enter a Protestation against the same; and not being therewith content, after the said army in pursuance of their duty and allegiance had marched into the said Kingdom, you shortly after in the month of in contempt of the aforesaid authority, and against the preservation of his Majesty's person and authority, did most treasonably convocate an army of factious, seditious and rebellious subjects, in opposition to the said army, and therewith committed divers and sundry outrages, murders, slaughters, plunders and vastations upon the persons and estates of divers of his Majesty's good subjects, and therewith invaded several of the cities and castles, seized thereupon, and upon the magazine with arms and ammunition therein: And at that time the said rebellious army of Sectaries of *England*, being upon the borders, you fearing and apprehending that the force and power raised by you should not be able to withstand his Majesty's good and loyal subjects who were then risen and ready to rise in arms for asserting and vindicating his Majesty's just authority, you did most basely, treacherously and treasonably call in to your aid and assistance the said armies of Sectaries. Likewise you yourself went in person to the house of *Mordington*, within a mile of the *English* borders, to the end aforesaid; and you did meet with the vile Usurper *Oliver Cromwell*, commander of the said army, with whom you had several private meetings and consultations, and thereby persuaded, and so prevailed with the said Traitor, that he thereafter marched with the said army to *Edinburgh* and the places thereabout; and which march and incoming of the said *Oliver* you might have undoubtedly hindered; in so far as it can be made appear by clear proof and testimonies of famous persons, That it having been complained upon to him at the said house of *Mordington*, that by reason of his being there with such a great number of Soldiers, the Lord *Mordington's* tenants would undoubtedly be ruined; he the said *Oliver* made answer, That he could not help the same, for his staying and going did depend upon you, and that he was ready, if you desired, to march back to *England*. At least, you did contrive, advise or consent to the raising and convocating of the said seditious, factious, and rebellious armies; at least was one of the number yourself, and with, and assisting to them in arms; at least, did vote, counsel or persuade the in-calling of the said army of Sectaries. And they being so brought in, you did countenance, assist, concur and consult with them, or their Commanders, or some of them, in publick or in private at *Edinburgh*, and in the *Canongate*, in the house called *Lady Home's Lodgings*, and in divers other places. As also, you did most villainously and traitorously contrive, counsel or vote for the drawing up of a Letter directed to the Traitor and abominable Usurper, wherein you and your complices did engage yourselves, in the name of of the Kingdom of *Scotland*, to employ your utmost endeavours, that none who have been active in, or consenting to the engagement against the said Sectaries, or had been in arms at *Sterling*, or elsewhere, in maintenance or pursuance of that engagement, should be employed in any publick place or trust within this Kingdom whatsoever, without advice or consent of the Kingdom of *England*; as the said Letter, dated the 6th day of *October*, 1648, more fully bears. As also, you did draw up, at least did counsel, advise or vote, to the up-drawing of certain Instructions given to Sir *John Chiesly*, who was sent by you and your complices, as Commissioner to the pretended House of Parliament of *England*, dated *October* 17, the year aforesaid; wherein you desire, that the noblemen, gentlemen of quality, and considerable officers of the army, that went into *England*, under the command of Duke *Hamilton*, and who were then prisoners, might be kept as pledges for the peace of that Kingdom; by which not only have you endeavoured most unnaturally to enslave your fellow-subjects and countrymen to the power of strangers, but most treacherously and treasonably, as an unworthy, ungrate Patriot, done what in you lay to destroy the life of your own dread Sovereign, and the Royal Authority in him and his succession, and to subject the honour, liberty, power and government of this his Majesty's ancient and free Kingdom, to the command, lust and tyranny of foreign traitors and usurpers. As also, you, upon the 4th day of *May* thereafter, having taken upon you most treasonably the supreme authority of this Kingdom, gave warrant under your hand for issuing out a Proclamation, declaring that the wives, children and families of *James* Lord *Ogilvy*, Lord *Rea*, *Lewis* Marquis of *Huntley* therein designant, *Lewis Gordon*, son to the Marquis of *Huntley*, *John* now Earl of *Middleton*, therein designant, *J.hn Middleton* of sometime designant General-Major, should be no longer under the protection of this Kingdom, and that such course should be taken for transporting them out of their country to foreign parts, as the Estates of Parliament, or their Committee, should think fit.

Tenthly, After his Majesty's dearest and most royal father, of eternal and most blessed memory, had been most unchristianly, inhumanly, horridly and barbarously murdered, by the said abominable traitor and usurper *Oliver Cromwel*, and his wicked complices, the devilish and treasonable courses, plots, contrivings and actings of yours did not yet terminate: For there being some motions for address to be made to his Majesty, by some of his good subjects of this his ancient Kingdom, as undoubted and rightful Successor to his deceased royal father in the imperial crown thereof, that his Majesty might come to his said antient Kingdom, for exercising his royal power and authority; the said motion and purpose being so just and lawful, you, notwithstanding of your great impudence and daring, always fearing, that a direct opposing thereof would prove altogether ineffectual; you, in a most indirect way, procured the application made for inviting his Majesty, to be so clogged with limitations, restrictions and conditions, to have been condescended to by his Majesty, before his admission to the exercise of his royal Government, as were most destructive to his Majesty's dignity and authority, and most derogatory to monarchical Government; as are more fully expressed in the several commissions, instructions and addresses sent and made to his Majesty to that effect, and publick proclamation of his Majesty at the mercat-cross of *Edinburgh*, by you and your complices, commissioners at *Breda*; all which are here repeated as a part of the Libel, *brevitatis causa*. And his Majesty, upon consideration, that the said unreasonable, unlawful and treasonable conditions were exacted of his Majesty by you, and a few number of factious subjects, who had, by the assistance of the usurper and tyrant *Oliver Cromwel*, thrust yourself into the government of his Majesty's ancient Kingdom; and trusting to the fidelity, the loyalty and good affection of his other good subjects, having, notwithstanding the said hard and unjust conditions, resolved to cast himself upon the loyalty and affections of his other good and faithful subjects; you, to obstruct his Majesty's purpose and resolution, yea, and so far as in you lay, to fright and terrify him therefrom by you and your complices cruel execution upon the Marquis of *Montross*, his Majesty's commissioner, and who represented his person in his said ancient kingdom; caused to be most horridly and inhumanly murdered the said Marquis, at the Mercat-cross, upon the 21st day of *May*, 1650, with all the circumstances of disgrace and dishonour: which so much reflected upon his Majesty's person, dignity and authority, and upon the honour of all true nobility; and is so recent and fresh, with detestation, in the memories of all good subjects and generous spirits, at home and abroad, that it is not fit to be mentioned or repeated here. But his Majesty still continuing in his former purpose and resolution, and after a most tedious and dangerous voyage at sea, having, by the providence of Almighty God, happily and safely arrived in his said ancient Kingdom; shortly thereafter, the cruel bloody murderer and usurper *Oliver Cromwel*, in pursuance of his Majesty, with a powerful army of Sectaries, by sea and land, invaded his said Majesty's ancient Kingdom. For opposing of whom, an army being raised; while both the said armies were in the field, you most treacherously and treasonably kept correspondency, and had intelligence with the said usurper, by writing to, and receiving letters from him, without his Majesty's private consent or warrant; at least, by sending to, and receiving messages from him by word of mouth. And further, to advance the designs of that abominable Regicide, after you had by your indirect means, plots, advices or contrivances, gotten his Majesty removed from his army at *Leith*; you by your influence upon a few number of the Commissioners of the General Assembly, yourself being one of the number then met at St. *Cuthbert*'s church, commonly called the West-Kirk, prevailed so, that for the weakening of the hands of friends, and strengthening the enemies, there was in a most clandestine and surreptitious manner an Act, as of the said commission of the Kirk, made, printed and published; wherein, besides many reproachful and slanderous expressions of his Majesty and his royal ancestors, more fully expressed in the said pretended Act, bearing date *August* 13, 1650, it was declared, that you disclaimed, and would not own his Majesty's interest, because of his refusal to subscribe and emit a declaration offered to him; and which declaration was contrived and drawn up by you, and contains many scandalous, seditious, imperious, reproachful and treasonable expressions, not only against his Majesty's authority and government, but also against his royal father and mother, and others his royal progenitors, as is more at large expressed in the aforesaid Act of the date above-written, and declaration bearing date the day the same year: of which declaration there needs no more be said, than that the circumstances by which his Majesty was enforced to sign the same, are enough known to the world; and that the worthiest and greatest part of his Majesty's ancient Kingdom did even detest and abhor the evil usage of his Majesty in that particular, when the same tyranny was exercised there by the power of you and a few evil men your complices, which at that time had spread itself over his Majesty's Kingdom of *England*; at least you and your complices did ratify and approve the said Act of the West-Kirk, and consent thereto; and at least you did deal with, and press and force his Majesty to sign and subscribe the declaration aforesaid; at least you were author or contriver, adviser or counsellor, persuader or voter, or assenter, assister, aider or abettor of the aforesaid restrictions, limitations and conditions, and of the aforesaid murder of his said Majesty's Commissioner, and manner thereof, and of the keeping of the said correspondence with the said invader and usurper, and of the said Act and Declarations, or any or other of them, or all or part thereof, or one or other of them.

Eleventhly, After it had pleased God to suffer that monster of men and cruel Regicide, *Oliver Cromwel*, so far to prevail against all his Majesty's endeavours for recovering his just right and interest in this and in his other Kingdoms, and over all the armies and forces raised by him for that end, so that he was necessitated to refugeate himself with foreign Princes and Estates: howbeit, at his Majesty's coronation, you, in the presence of God, and a great many of the Nobility of this Kingdom, and others therein convened at *Schoon*, the 1st of *January*, 1651, did swear to be faithful to the Crown, and true liege-men to his Majesty: yet nevertheless, contrary to the said oath, and notwithstanding the many favours, honours, benefits and acts of indemnity conferred upon you, and contrary to the Laws and Acts of Parliament, as is expressed; you did most perfidiously, ungratefully and treasonably, in *anno* 1653, or 1654, not only according to your bounden duty, not rise in arms, and join with the Earls of *Glencairn* and *Middleton*, who were commissioned from his Majesty for hindering the further progress of the usurpers, and expelling them forth of this Kingdom; but did in open hostility join with the said usurpers their forces; especially with the Colonels *Overton*, *Cobbet* and *Twisleton*; at least with the said Colonels *Cobbet* and *Twisleton*; at least with Colonel *Twisleton*, when he was in the Highlands in opposition to the said Earl of *Glencairn*; at least joined with one or other of them in counsel; did take and relieve prisoners, did furnish several pieces of great cannon, to the number of fourteen, in *anno* 1653, or 1654, to Colonel *Aldred*, then governor of *Air*: which cannon, or a great many of them, were taken out by you of his Majesty's castle of *Dunbarton*, at the time and in the manner above expressed. And likewise you did take pay from the said usurpers for a company of foot under them and in their service, thereby openly and clearly making it appear what you did intend by all your more covered and private machinations, plottings and treasonable actings against his Majesty's dearest father and himself. Likewise to make it appear what intimacy and power you had with the usurper, you not only did term and call the actings of his Majesty's forces against you and the usurpers, rebellion, but also you in *anno* 1654, did take upon you power to bring off such as were in that service, and to give remissions therefore under your own hand; particularly to *John Mac-Dowgaw* of *Dunolick*, as the same under your hand, the said *John*, will verify.

Twelfthly, The said *Oliver Cromwel*, that monster of men, vilest of traitors, most cruel murderer, bloody tyrant and usurper, having reached, as he thought, the end of all his devilish plots and treasonable machinations, by usurping the dominion and authority of his Majesty's three Kingdoms, and settling the same, so far as in him lay, upon him and his family; you conceiving the same so fixed and riveted, that in human probability it was not possible to be removed or shaken; that you might avowedly reap the fruits of your former more covered, vile and damnable plottings, contrivings and actings for the said arch-tyrant and traitor, you then pulled off and laid aside the mask of pretended loyalty and religion, under which you had all along formerly lurked, thereby having deceived and cheated a great many of his Majesty's good subjects from their due allegiance and loyalty under hypocritical fair pretences of your affection and zeal for Religion, Prince, and Country, to the utter ruin (if not of souls) of many of their bodies, estates and fortunes; and did openly, in face of the world, discover yourself in your own colours, appearing in a thing professedly and publickly in behalf of the said usurper against his Majesty's person and authority: in so far as in the month of 1657, after the decease of the said usurper, the succeeding usurper, his son, being most treasonably and tyrannically proclaimed Chief Magistrate and sole Protector of all his Majesty's dominions and territories thereto belonging, at the mercat-cross of his Majesty's cities of *Edinburgh* and *Dunbarton*, you having apparently, for such like services done or to be done, received from the said usurper *Oliver* one precept due upon the Exchequer of *Scotland*, for payment to you of 12,000*l. sterling*, or thereabout, did with your personal presence countenance the said tyrannical and treasonable proclamation; thereby, so far as in you lay, divesting his Majesty of his just and royal interest and right, and establishing the same on the persons and families of the said usurpers. Likewise not long after the said usurper, the more to establish himself in his usurped government, having called a pretended Parliament, consisting of a pretended new-coined House of Peers, and certain persons of his Majesty's three Kingdoms as a House of Commons to sit in *Westminster*; you did procure yourself elected Commissioner for the shire of *Aberdeen*, at least did accept of a commission from them; albeit both by the nobility of your birth, and your non-residence within the said shire, you was in law incapable to be so elected; at least ought and might have refused to accept any commission. Nevertheless having voluntarily, and of your own accord, embraced the said charge and employment; you thereupon took journey, and went to *London*, and most basely, perfidiously and treasonably, sate, voted, and otherwise acted in the said usurper's pretended Parliament, by whom his Majesty's right and interest was disclaimed and abjured, and the same owned only in the said

Usurper's Person as a Member of the said pretended House of Commons, to the high Indignity and Contempt of his Majesty's sacred Person and Authority, the utter Destruction of monarchical Government, the Dishonour of this Kingdom, and the great Disgrace of your own Family and Posterity.

Thirteenthly, You the said Marquis, to make it further appear to the World, that it was always your Purpose and Intention to destroy his Majesty's Authority and Government, and to oppose his Restauration to his just Right and Interest to his three Kingdoms, at a provincial Assembly holden at *Innerary* a little after the Defeat of his Majesty's Army at *Worcester*, the Ministers praying for his Majesty after the accustomed Manner, you did most villainously and treasonably rebuke them, saying, *That they were but Fools to pray for a malignant and wicked King, whom God had rejected, and would never restore him again*; or some such-like Words to that Purpose. And also, you being at *London*, in the Time of the Usurper *Oliver*, you said in Presence of divers Persons of Quality, *That you wondered how People could be so mad, as to call home a Family whom God had rejected*, or such Words to that Purpose: Likewise after your home-coming to *Scotland*, yea, openly in a publick Meeting at *James Maustertonne's*, in *Niddrey's* Winde, in Presence of several Noblemen and Gentlemen, you boasted, *That you would own any thing you had done in these things by-gone; and that if it were to do, you would do it again; howbeit you had known that all that had, would have come:* Thereby presumptuously taking upon you, by outward Success, to give Judgment upon the hidden and secret Counsels and Determinations of Almighty God, and thereby to alienate the Affections, Duties, and Allegiance of his Majesty's good Subjects, and to harden and confirm others, such as are otherways disposed in their wicked Courses towards his Majesty's Person and Authority.

Lastly, That your monstrous and execrable Treason may appear to all the World, it is of Verity, that in the Year 1648, at a private Conference betwixt you, *Oliver Cromwell*, and Col. *Ireton*, the said *Oliver* complaining of the many Difficulties that attended their Affairs, by reason of the divers Designs which his Majesty had on Foot from time to time against them; you the said Marquis made Answer, *That their Danger was great indeed, in regard that if any of these Designs should take effect, they were all ruined.* And thereupon gave your positive Advice, that they should proceed to the questioning of the King for his Life; assuring them, that they could never be safe until they had taken away his Majesty's Life. At least, you did know of the horrible and treasonable Design of murdering his said Majesty; and did most treasonably conceal, and not reveal the same till after the said horrid Deed was committed, and so past Prevention or Remedy. At which time, *in Anno* 1649, publickly in the Face of the pretended Parliament then sitting, you said, that the Usurper *Cromwell* had told you, *That* England *and* Scotland *would never be at Peace, until the King were put to Death.* By all which Particulars respectively, above rehearsed, it is clearly evinced, that you were, and are Author, Contriver, Deviser, Consulter, Adviser, of all or Part of all the aforesaid Crimes of Treason, and other above libelled, or other of them, in Manner above declared. And thereby has incurred the Pains and Punishments of High-Treason, and others contained in the Laws and Acts of Parliament above-written; which must and should be inflicted upon you with all Rigour, in Example to others in all time coming.

Sic subscrib. *Jo. Fletcher.*

31 *January*, 1661.

Ordered, That the above-written Dittay be given to the Marquis of *Argyle*, by a Herald or Pursuivant, and he to answer thereto, upon the 13th Day of *February* next to come.

The Marquis of *Argyle*'s Petition to the Parliament of *Scotland*, craving a Precognition of his Case, containing many weighty Reasons urging the Necessity thereof. Presented to the Parliament, *February* 12, 1661.

To my Lord Commissioner his Grace, and Honourable Estates of Parliament,

The humble Petition of Archibald *Marquis of* Argyle,

Humbly sheweth,

THAT for as much as the Petitioner can with a safe Conscience affirm, and solemnly protest, That whatever his Actings or Accession has been in relation to publick Business since the Beginning of the Troubles, till his Majesty's Departure hence in the Year 1651, though he will not purge himself of Errors, Failings, and Mistakes, both in Judgment and Practice, incident to human Frailty, and common to him, if not with the whole, at least with the greatest Part of the Nation; yet in one thing, though he were to die, he would still avouch and retain his Innocency, that he never intended any thing treasonably, out of any pernicious Design against his Majesty's late Royal Father of ever-glorious Memory, or his present Majesty (whom God may long preserve), their Persons or Government; but endeavoured always to his uttermost for settling the Differences betwixt their Majesties and the People. And as to any Actings before the Year 1641, or from the said Year, till his Majesty being in the Parliament at *Perth* and *Sterling*, your Petitioner did with a full Assurance rely upon his gracious Majesty, and his Royal Father, their Treaties, Approbation, Oblivion, and Indemnity, for what was past, and firmly believed that the same should never have risen in Judgment, or that the Petitioner should have been drawn in question therefore. And during his Majesty's Absence, and being forced from the Exercise of his Royal Government by the late Usurpers, and long after that the Nation, by their Deputies, had accepted of their Authority and Government, and they in Possession, the Petitioner was forced to Capitulation with them, being in their Hands, and under Sickness, and the same was, after all Endeavours used, according to the Duty of a good Subject; and upon the Petitioner's Part, so innocent and necessary for Self-preservation, without the least Intention, Action, or Effect to his Majesty's Prejudice: That albeit upon Mis-information (as the Petitioner humbly conceives) his Actings and Compliance both in their Designs and Quality have been mis-represented, as particularly singular and personal, stating the Petitioner in a degree of guilt beyond others, and incapable of pardon; the same have so far prevailed upon his Majesty, as to cloud and damp the propitious and comfortable rays of his Royal Grace and Favour, and have strained his gracious inclination beyond its natural disposition of clemency express'd to his other Subjects, to commit the Petitioner's person, and give way to the trial of his carriage and actings: Yet so firmly rooted is the Petitioner's persuasion of his Majesty's Justice and Clemency, and that he intends the reclaiming, and not the ruin of the meanest of his Subjects, who retain their loyalty, duty, and good affection to his Person and Government; that upon true and right representation of the Petitioner's carriage and actings, he shall be able to vindicate himself of these aspersions, and shall give his Majesty satisfaction; at least so far to extenuate his guilt, as may render him a fit object of that Royal Clemency, which is of that depth, that having swallowed and past by, not only personal but national guiltiness, of much more a deeper dye than any the Petitioner can be charged with, or made out against him; and so will not strain to pass by and pardon the faults and failings of a person, who never acted but in a publick joint way, without any sinister or treasonable design against his Majesty or his Royal Father; and against which he can defend himself either by acts of approbation and oblivion *in verbo principis*, which he conceives to be the supreme, sacred, and inviolable security, or which he was forced to, much against his inclination, by an insuperable necessity. And albeit his Majesty's grace and favour is strictly tied to no other rule but his royal will and pleasure; yet his Majesty's so innate, essential, and inseparable a quality of his royal nature, that the Petitioner is persuaded in all human certainty, that the leaving and committing to his Parliament (as is express'd in his Majesty's Declaration of *October* 12th last by-past) the trying and judging of the carriage of his subjects during the late troubles, as indeed it is in its own nature, and ought to be so accepted of all, as an undoubted evidence of his Majesty's affection to, and confidence in his people; so no other trial or judging is therein meaned, but a fair, just, legal and usual Trial, without any prejudice, passion, or prelimitation, or precipitation; like as by the said Declaration there was a freedom for all the people interested, to make their application to the Parliament, or in the mean time to the Committee, from whom only his Majesty is pleased to declare he would receive address and information. And seeing it was the Petitioner's misfortune, during the sitting of the said Committee, to be prisoner in *England*; whereas if he had been prisoner here in *Scotland*, he would have made application to them, and would have craved, and in justice expected that precognition might have been taken by them, to whom the preparing and ordering of that affair (to wit, anent the Trial of the Subjects carriage during the troubles) was recommended, that the Petitioner's absence, which was his punishment, not his fault, may not be prejudicial, seeing the Petitioner has lately received two several Dittays, wherein there be many crimes grossly false, with all the aspersions and aggravations imaginable laid to his charge; importing no less than the loss of his life, fame, and estate, and the ruin of him and his posterity; which he is confident is not intended by his Majesty. And that by the Law and Practice of this Kingdom, consonant to all reason and equity, the Petitioner ought to have upon his desire a precognition, for taking the deposition of certain persons, which being frequently and usually practised in this country, when any person is defamed for any crime, and therefore incarcerate before he was brought to a Trial, at his desire, precognition was taken in all business relating thereto; which the Petitioner in all humility conceives, ought much more not to be denied to him, not only by reason of respect to his quality, and of the importance and consequence thereof to all his Majesty's Subjects of all quality in all time coming; but also in regard it has been so meaned and intended by his Majesty's Declaration aforesaid; like as the manner of the crimes objected, being actings in times of wars and troubles, the guilt thereof was not personal and particular, but rather national and universal, and veiled and covered with acts of indempnity and oblivion; and so tender and ticklish, that if duly pondered, after a hearing allowed to the Petitioner, in prudence and policy, will not be found expedient to be tossed in public, or touched with every hand, but rather to be precognosced upon by some wise, sober, noble, and judicious persons, for thir and several other reasons in the paper hereto annexed. Nor does the Petitioner desire the same *animo protelandi*, nor needs the same breed any longer delay; nor is it sought without an end of zeal to his Majesty's power, and vindication of the Petitioner's innocency, as to many particulars wherewith he is aspersed; and it would be seriously pondered, that seeing *Cunctatio nulla longa ubi agitur de vita hominis*, far less can this small delay, which is usual, and in this case most expedient, if not absolutely necessary, be refused, *ubi agitur non solum de vita, sed de fama*, and of all worldly interests that can be dear or of value to any man.

Upon consideration of the premises, it is humbly craved, That your Grace, and the Honourable Estates of Parliament, may grant the Petitioner's desire, and to give Warrant to cite persons to depone before your Grace, and the Estates of Parliament, upon such interrogatories as your Petitioner shall give in, for clearing of several things concerning his intention and loyalty during the troubles. And for such as are out of the Country, and Strangers, residenters in England, *Commissions may be directed to such as your Grace and the Parliament shall think fit, to take their depositions upon Oath, and to return the same.*

And your Petitioner shall ever pray, &c.

Edinburgh, February 12, 1661.

This Petition being read, was refused:

Edinburgh, at the Parliament-House, *February* 13, 1661.

THE Marquis of *Argyle* (being accused of High-Treason, at the instance of Sir *John Fletcher*, his Majesty's Advocate for his Interest) was brought to the Bar. His Lordship humbly desired but to speak a few words before reading the Indictment; assuring to speak nothing in the cause itself.

itself. Whereupon he was removed a little, and after some debate, the House resolved that the said Indictment should be first read. Then his Lordship desired that a Bill which he had caused his Advocates to give in to the Lords of the Articles, (desiring a precognition, with many reasons urging the necessity of it) to which he had received no answer, might be read before the said Indictment: which being likewise refused, the said Indictment was first read; and after the reading thereof, the Marquis (being put off his first thoughts) was compelled to this extemporary discourse following, as it was faithfully writ when his Lordship spoke.

May it please your Grace,

MY Lord-Chancellor, before I speak any thing, I shall humbly protest my words may not be wrested, but that I may have charity to be believed; and I shall, with God's assistance, speak truth from my heart.

I shall, my Lord, resume *Mephibosheth*'s answer to *David* (after a great Rebellion, and himself evil reported of). Saith he, *Yea, let him take all, for as much as my Lord the King is come home again in peace into his own house*; 2 Sam. xix. 30. So say I, since it has pleased God Almighty graciously to return his sacred Majesty to the Royal Exercise of his Government over these Nations, to which he has undoubted right, and was most unjustly and violently thrust therefrom by the late tyrannizing Usurpers.

It is, my Lord, exceeding matter of joy to us all, that the iron yoke of Usurpation (under which we have these many years sadly groaned) is now broke, and with much freedom this High and Honourable Court of Parliament are meeting together under the refreshing warm beams of his Majesty's Royal Government (so much longed for by our almost starved expectations): and I do earnestly wish his Royal Presence upon his Royal Throne amongst us. But since at this time that great happiness cannot probably be expected, I am glad that his Majesty's prudence has singled out such a qualified and worthy person (as my Lord Commissioner his Grace) to represent himself; whose unspotted loyalty to his Majesty we can all witness.

I cannot, my Lord, but acknowledge these two grand mercies, which comfortably attends my present condition. One is, the high thoughts I deservedly entertain of that transcendent and princely clemency wherewith his sacred Majesty is so admirably delighted; abundantly evidenced by many noted and signal testimonies in all the steps of his Majesty's carriage; as those most gracious Letters, Declarations, and that free and most ample Act of Indempnity granted to all his Majesty's Subjects, (excepting some of the immediate murderers of his Royal Father) to eradicate any timorous jealousies of his Majesty's gracious pardon, (which might haply arise by serious reflectings) convincing them forcibly of their own miscarriages, in these unhappy times of distraction. The effects, my Lord, of which princely deportment (I am confidently hopeful) his Majesty has experimentally, and shall find, prove one effectual cement to conciliate the most anti-monarchick and disaffected persons (excepting some of those barbarous phanaticks) in all his Majesty's Dominions, most willingly to the subjection of his Majesty's Royal Scepter; and with a perfect hatred abominate all disloyal practices in themselves and others, in all time coming.

The second is, my Lord, when I consider that my Judges are not such as we had of late, strangers, but my own countrymen; both which jointly (together with the real sense and solid convictions I have of my innocency of those calumnies most unjustly charged upon me) encourages my hopes the rather, to expect such dealing as will most sympathize with that clement humour (to which his sacred Majesty has a natural propensity), and such equal administration of Justice (void of all biassing prejudices) as will be most suitable to such a high and honourable Meeting.

I shall therefore, my Lord, desire to use *Paul*'s answer for himself, (being accused of his Countrymen) he having a learned Orator, *Tertullus*, accusing him, as I have in my Lord-Advocate; *Paul*'s was heresy, mine of another nature; but I must say with him, that the things they alledge against me cannot be proved: but this I confess, in the way allowed by solemn Oaths and Covenants, I have served God, my King, and Country, (as he said) which they themselves also allow.

I shall, my Lord, remember (not with repining, but for information) my hard usage, never having had my hearing, nor allowance of pen, ink, nor paper, nor the comfort of seeing my friends freely, until I received this summons, which was in effect a load above a burden; enemies, both *Scots* and *English*, out of malice calumniating me for all the same things, excepting what relates to his Majesty's most Royal Father, of ever-glorious memory.

Therefore, my Lord, I beg charity and patient hearing, not doubting but the wisdom and goodness of the Parliament will be so favourable, and not as the inconsiderate multitude (as a learned and able man writes, Sir *Walter Raleigh*, in his Preface to the History of the World). As we see in experience, that dogs always bark at them they know not; and that is their nature, to accompany one another in those clamours; so it is with the inconsiderate multitude, who wanting that virtue which we call honesty in all men, and that special gift of God, which we call Charity in Christian men, condemn without hearing, and wound without offence given, led thereunto by uncertain Report only; which his Majesty King *James* only acknowledges to be the father of lyes. I shall not desire to be in the least mistaken by any that hear me; but sure I am, it is pertinently applicable to my case.

I intreat your Lordship likewise to consider the words of another notable man, (*Speed*, in his History) who says, As the tongues of Parasites are ill balances to weigh the virtues of Princes and great men, so neither should theirs, nor other men's blemishes be looked upon as they are drawn with the deformed pencil of envy or rancour, which do always attend eminency, whether in place or virtue. I shall not, my Lord, be so presumptuous as to arrogate any thing to myself in this, only I want not the two companions, for I am but a weak man, subject to many failings and infirmities, (whereof I do not purge myself) for as we must confess to God Almighty, if he should mark iniquity, who can stand? Neither shall I say, that there cannot a hole be discovered (as the Proverb is) in my coat; and it cannot but be so with any, specially such as have labour'd in such times and business. But I bless the Lord, that in these things which have been, and are here cast upon me, I am able to make the falshood and misconstruction of them palpably appear.

My Lord, before I mention any thing in particular, I must shew this honourable Meeting of Parliament, and all that hear me (who doubtless have various apprehensions of my being present in this condition), that I am here rather as my misfortune, not my injury; wherein I desire to explain the difference, as *Plato* and *Aristotle* do very well; calling injuries such things as are done purposely with a wicked mind; and misfortunes, such things as are done with a good mind, though the events prove bad, yet we could not foresee them.

So my Lord, I shall take God to record (who must judge me one day) upon my Conscience, that what I did, flowed not from any injurious principle to any, though I acknowledge the events were not still so successful (which was my misfortune) indeed; but it has been my lot often in these times (wherein I and many others have been inevitably involved) to be by the malicious tongues of my calumniating enemies misconstructed for the worst; yea, even in many things that the Lord was pleased to make successful. For the truth of this, I may, I hope safely appeal to many in this honourable House, who can abundantly witness, my faithful and loyal endeavours for both my King and native Country; whereof I should be very sparing to be an Herald myself, were not the contrary so impudently affirmed. There are five main calumnies that I desire, my Lord, to satisfy all that hear me a little in; to the end that the rest of less moment may be likewise in their own due time heard, afterward abstracted more from personal prejudice.

The first calumny is, my Lord, concerning that horrid and unparalleled murder of his late Royal Majesty of eternally blessed memory. I do here publickly declare that I neither desire, nor deserve the least countenance or favour, if I was either accessary to it, or on the counsel or knowledge of it: which to make clearly appear, is under oath in the Parliament-Books 1649; whereof I was the first starter myself, to the intent that we might both vindicate ourselves, and endeavour a discovery, if any amongst us had any accession to that horrid and villainous crime; as also in my latter Will, which I made going to *England*, *in Anno* 1655, or 1656, fearing what possibly might hereafter be obtruded by any upon me or my family upon that account, I set it down to clear my posterity; that I was altogether free of that detestable and execrable crime, or of any prejudice to his Majesty, in either Person or Government. I left this with a very worthy Gentleman, I believe well known to your Lordship, and never saw it since; so your Lordship may be pleased if ye will to call for it; and try the truth. Whatsoever other thing may be in it, I hope, my Lord, this opportunity is a mercy to me to have that vile calumny (amongst many others) against me to be cleared.

And, my Lord, to make this particular yet more evident, I did still, and do positively assert, that I never saw that monstrous Usurper *Oliver Cromwel* in the face, nor ever had the least correspondence with him, or any of that Sectarian Army, until the commands of the Committee of Estates sent me, with some other Noblemen and Gentlemen, to the border *in anno* 1648, to stop his march into *Scotland*, after those who retired from *Preston* fight; neither after he left the border, in the year 1648, did I ever correspond with him, or any of that Sectarian Army, so unsatisfied was I with their way, after the wicked and sinister courses he and they were upon, afforded evident presumptions for us to apprehend that he and they intended prejudice to his Royal Majesty. Only one letter I received from Sir *Arthur Ha[illegible]ig*, to which I returned answer, that he might spare his pains in writing to me, for I blessed the Lord, who had taught me by his word, *to fear G[illegible], and honour the King, and not to meddle with them that were given to change.* Though Sir *Arthur* be now dead, yet he acknowledged to several in the *Tower*, that he still had my letter: and when I was there, I often desired he might be posed and examined about it; which I can presently instruct. And during, my Lord, my being in *England*, neither in *London* nor *Newcastle*, *in anno* 1647, there was not any thing so much as mentioned concerning his late Majesty's Person; all that ever I heard of, was in publick Parliament 1647. The Commissioners Papers at *London*, and Committee Books at *Newcastle*, will clear this fully.

The second calumny is anent the inhuman murder of Duke *James Hamilton*: my Lord, it's well known my great respect to that truly noble and worthy Person, whereof (upon all occasions) I gave ample testimonies, and can yet convince any of his friends with the reality of it; and evidenced my true sorrow for the wicked cruelty committed upon him. But indeed I cannot deny I refused to compliment *Cromwel* on his behalf (he having, my Lord, been immediately preceding, so instrumental, and so very active in that most horrid and lamentable murder of his late sacred Majesty); and if I had done otherwise, undoubtedly it had been a more black Article in that Libel now read, than any that is in it.

The third calumny is, that which breeds a great part of these groundless clamours, (though it be not in the Indictment) is my Lord Marquis of *Huntley*'s death; wherein I may truly say, I was as earnest to preserve him, as possibly I could, (which is very well known to many in this honourable House) and my not prevailing may sufficiently evidence I had not so great a stroke nor power in the Parliament as is libelled. And, my Lord, for his Estate, I had nothing in that, but for my own absolutely necessary relief, and was ever most willing to part with any Interest I had therein, getting his friends (who professed much zeal for the standing of the Family) engaged for warrandize to me, of any portion that should happen to fall to my satisfaction. And to evidence that I was no means to harm the Family, I stood with my right betwixt all fines and forfeitures of Bonds, and accounted for any thing I could receive. And to manifest yet further, that the burden of that Family was not from any extrinsick cause to themselves, I have under the old Marquis's own hand, and his Son, *George* Lord *Gordon*, (who was a very worthy young Nobleman) the just Inventory of their debts, amounting to about one million of marks, *in anno* 1640. It would, I fear, my Lord, consume too much of the Parliament's precious time, to hear many other circumstances, to make this particular more clear, which I shall at this time forbear.

The fourth calumny is, the death of the Marquis of *Montrose*. There are many in this House, my Lord, who know very well I refused to meddle either in the matter or manner of it: and so far were we from having any

any particular quarrels at one another; that *in Anno* 1645, he and I were fully agreed upon Articles and Conditions contained in a Treaty past betwixt us: the Gentleman is yet alive who carried the messages both by word and writing betwixt us, and it was neither his fault nor mine that the business did not end at that time, which ('tis known to all) proved very obnoxious to the Kingdom thereafter.

The fifth calumny is concerning my dealing with the *English* after *Worcester* fight. It is well known, my Lord, to many, that myself, and the Gentlemen of *Argyleshire* (my Kinsmen, Vassals, and Tenants) endeavoured cordially to engage all their neighbours about them on all hands against the *English* (which they did not prevail in), but was most unhappily made known to the *English* Commanders for the time; which they caused immediately to be published (as a very notable discovery) in their News-books; which occasioned two sad disadvantages to us: For they not only crushed our attempts in the infancy, but also determined the severer resolutions against us; whereby two strong Regiments of Foot, (*Overton*'s and *Read*'s) and very near the number of one of Horse (under the command of one *Blackamoor*) were sent to *Argyle*; and when *Dean* came there, it pleased God to visit me with a great distemper of sickness (as Dr. *Cunningham*, and many others who were with me, can witness). What, my Lord, I was prest to, when I was violently in their hands, may be instructed by the paper itself (written by *Dean*'s man's own hand, yet extant to shew), which I did absolutely refuse, upon all the hazard of the uttermost of their malice; as also what I was necessitated to do, is likewise ready to be shewn, whereby I was still continued their Prisoner upon demand.

I shall, my Lord, add one reason more to clear this (besides many other weighty publick reasons and considerations, which I shall forbear to mention at this time, it being more natural to bring them in by way of defences afterward), my own Interest, and of all Noblemen and Superiors in *Scotland*. It may rationally be presumed, that I had been a very senseless fool, if ever I had been for promoting such an Authority and Interest over me, as levelled all, and was so totally destructive to all that differenced, myself and other Noblemen, from their own Vassals, (which many say I was too earnest in) yea, it being absurdly derogative to all true Nobility; and my Ancestors and I (as it is said in that libel) having had so many titles of honour, dignity, and eminent places of trust, conferred upon us by his Majesty's Royal Predecessors and himself (all for our constant Loyalty and Adherence to the Crown on all occasions), as the Records and Histories of this ancient Kingdom hold forth, besides the narratives of all our grants, and asserting the just privileges thereof, against all opposers. I did, my Lord, ever (even when the *English* were at the intolerable height of Usurpation) declare my true abhorrence to a Commonwealth Government, which was well known to them all. I was not indeed, my Lord, very dissatisfied, when there were rumours spread abroad of *Cromwel*'s being made a King (as some here present can witness); for I told them it was a most probable way for his Majesty; and the more it were encouraged, would tend the more to *Cromwel*'s, and their deformed Commonwealth's Government's ruin, and promote his Majesty's just Interest the more. My Lord, I shall not much blame my Lord-Advocate for doing his endeavour, (it being an essential part of his function to accuse) but I must say, that it is very hard measure, that so able a man has taken near as many months, in taking pains to prompt as many enemies as his persuasions could possibly invite, to vent out the highest notes of their malice; and laying out search by them for, and collecting all the bad reports, or rather (to give them their genuine term) I may call them a confused mass of the common clashes of the Country, thereby to advise misconstructions of all the publick actings of both Parliaments and Committees during the late troubles, and with strange and remote inferences to adduce all those to the channel of my particular actings; he has taken, I say, my Lord, as many months, as I have had days to answer them, being an exceeding disadvantage. But, my Lord, that's not all, I am likewise extremely troubled, that he labours in that libel all along to draw an obscure veil of perpetual oblivion over all my good services; and specially my faithful and loyal endeavours in restoring of his sacred Majesty to the Crown of this his most ancient Kingdom of *Scotland*, and the exercise of his Majesty's royal authority therein, with my cordial endeavours for his Majesty's restitution to the rest of his Dominions also; which his Majesty both knows, and has been pleased often to acknowledge it to have been good service. Yea, and many present in this honourable House know, that I extended both my zeal and affection to the utmost of my power for his Majesty's service in that particular; which I willingly acknowledge nothing, my Lord, but my duty, whereunto I was tied both by natural, civil, and christian bands to my Sovereign; and specially such a King, of whom I may say well, (as I have often affirmed) That he is a King in whom the Lord has been pleased to take such pleasure, as to possess his Majesty with so many superlative degrees of excellency, that will certainly exalt his Majesty's fame, both in our age, and to subsequent posterity, above all the Monarchs in the world. So that, my Lord, we may consequently discover a high demonstration of the Lord's singular kindness and special providential care for us his Majesty's Subjects, in preserving such a rich blessing as his sacred Majesty, (in whom the happiness of these Nations is wrapt up) under the safe wings of his divine Protection; I may say, even when the extravagant malice of men would have swallowed him up.

After my Lord had ended this discourse (being heard by all very attentively, without any interruptions), thus the Lord Advocate spoke to my Lord Chancellor:

My Lord, what can the Marquis of *Argyle* say to the opposition at *Stirling*, *in Anno* 1648?

The Marquis replied, that he found my Lord Advocate endeavoured to bring him to debate the particulars, (which he hoped should be cleared at another more convenient time) and waved answering the thing itself, but insisted thus:

My Lord Chancellor,

I have (*informative* only) hinted a little at the main things which I am often charged with, my memory cannot fully reach all, neither will time permit to circumstantiate these particulars, which I have only touched in the general; nor is it my purpose at present to fall on the debate of any of that Libel (not having yet consulted the process) by reason these Advocates your Lordship was pleased to allow me, have not yet all embraced, and the excuses of my ordinary Advocates (in whom I had confidence) being admitted as relevant. And these Gentlemen, that have been pleased (in obedience to your Lordship's command) to come here with me, not being much acquainted with matters of this weight, and not having unbraced till within these two or three days, so that they are strangers altogether to my case; I shall, therefore, my Lord, humbly desire, that a competent time may be allowed me, that I may prepare my defences, and I shall (God willing) abundantly clear every particular in that Libel. And also, my Lord, I humbly desire, that these other Advocates, who were ordained by your Lordships to assist me (and after the honourable Lords of Articles had heard them, rejected their excuses), may be now re-ordained to consult and appear for me.

The Marquis's Advocates entered a protestation, that what should happen to escape them in pleading (either by word or writ) for the life, honour, and estate of the said noble Marquis, their client, might not thereafter be obtruded to them as treasonable; whereupon they took instruments.

The Marquis assured my Lord Chancellor, that he knew not of any such protestation to be presented, and that it flowed simply of themselves: Whereupon the Lord Chancellor desired the Marquis and his Advocates to remove, till the House should consider both of my Lord's desire, and the Advocates protestation.

The Marquis and his Advocates being removed, the House (after some small debate) resolved, as to my Lord Marquis's desires, his Lordship should have till the 26th of *February* to give in his defences in writ, and ordained Mr. *Andrew Ker* to be one of his Advocates.

As to the Advocates protestation, the House resolved, that they could not be allowed to speak in cases of treason either by word or writ, but upon their peril; only allowed them in the general, as much as in such cases was indulged to any.

The Marquis and his Advocates being called in, my Lord Chancellor intimated the aforesaid resolutions of the House, both in reference to my Lord Marquis, and to the Advocates protestation.

When my Lord Chancellor had done, the Marquis spoke as followeth:

My Lord Chancellor,

THere is one thing that had almost escaped me, anent that opposition at *Sterling*, 1648, that my Lord Advocate was speaking of; that it may not stick with any of this honourable Meeting, I shall ingenuously declare, That after the defeat at *Preston*, I was desired to come and meet with the Committee of Estates (meaning those who were in the then Government), and being come with some of my friends to *Sterling*, fearing no man, and suspecting nothing, I was invaded by Sir *George Munro*, where several of my friends were killed, and myself hardly escaped, which is all that can be said I acted in arms, as many here know.

My Lord, not that I am any ways diffident, but I shall in due time clear every particular of that Libel, yet I am not a little troubled that some who have heard the calumnies therein, may let them have such an impression (being asserted with such confidence) as to conceive a possibility, if not a probability of their being true; I shall therefore desire so much charity from this honourable Meeting, that there be no hard thoughts entertained till I be fully heard.

The Marquis therefore, with the joint concurrence of his Advocates, humbly desired, That the Bill (containing many pungent reasons) for a precognition of his process, given to the honourable Lords of Articles, might be read and considered in plain Parliament.

To which my Lord Chancellor replied, That it had been formerly refused at the Articles, and that it would not be granted.

So his Lordship was carried back to the Castle.

Edinburgh, *March* 5, 1661, *at the Parliament House.*

The Marquis of Argyle being called in, gave in a Bill, containing several weighty Reasons, craving a continuation till the meeting of Parliament to-morrow. His Lordship being removed, after long debate it was carried against him by two or three votes, and his Lordship being called in, my Lord Chancellor told him it was refused, and ordered his Lordship to produce his defences; whereupon he spoke as followeth.

May it please your Grace,

MY Lord Chancellor, this business is of very great concernment to me, and not small in the preparative of it to the whole Nation, yea, it may concern many of your Lordships who are sitting here, and your posterity: and therefore I desire to have your Grace (my Lord Commissioner) and the remanent Members of this honourable Meeting, your patience to hear me a few words without prejudice or mis-construction, which any thing I can say is often obnoxious to.

I shall, my Lord, begin with the words of that godly King *Jehoshaphat*, that good King of *Judah* (after he was come back in peace to *Jerusalem*) in his instructions to his Judges, he desires them to take heed what they do, for they judge not for men, but for the Lord, who is with them in the judgment.

My Lord, I shall speak another word to many young men, who were either not born, or so young that it is impossible they could know the beginning of these businesses, which are contained in the Libel against me, (being all that hath been done since the year 1638) so that they might have heard by report what was done; but not why, or upon what grounds; and what some have suffered, but not what they have deserved.—Therefore I desire your Lordship's charity, until all the particulars, and several circumstances of every particular be heard, without which no man can judge rightly of any action. For as it is well observed by that incomparable *Grotius*, that *Aristotle* asserts, That there is more certainty in the mathematicks than morals; for as *Grotius* says it, the [illegible] forms from matters, as betwixt straight and crook [illegible] there is no medium, but in morals, even the least circumstance varies the matter, so that they are wont to have something betwixt them, with such latitude, that they can come sometime to this, sometime to the other extreme, so that betwixt that which ought to be done, and that which ought not to be done, is interposed that which may be done, but is nearer now to this than to the other extremity, or part, whence

whence ambiguity often ariſeth. The particular circumſtances are ſo obvious to every underſtanding man, that I need only to mention them.

Polybius, my Lord, makes much of his hiſtory depend upon theſe three, *concilia, cauſa, & eventus*; and there are likewiſe other three, *tempus, locus, & perſonæ*, the change whereof makes that which is lawful duty unlawful, and on the contrary: So likewiſe in ſpeaking or repeating words, the adding or paring from them will quite alter the ſenſe and meaning; as alſo in writing, the placing of commas or points, will change the ſentence to a quite other purpoſe than it was intended.

There is, my Lord, another maxim, which I do not mention as always undeniable; but when there is no lawful Magiſtrate exerciſing power and authority in a Nation, but an invading Uſurper in poſſeſſion, eſteeming former laws crimes; in ſuch a caſe, I ſay, the ſafety of the people is the ſupreme Law.

There is another maxim which is not queſtioned by any, and it is, Neceſſity has no law; for even the moral law of God yields to it, and Chriſt's diſciples, in *David*'s example: For this *Seneca* ſays, Neceſſity (the defence of human imbecillity) breaks every law; *Nam neceſſitas legum irridet vincula*, neceſſity ſcorns the fetters of law. So he that anſwers that Libel, *The Long Parliament revived*, ſpeaking of this laſt Parliament (which his Majeſty calls a bleſſed, healing Parliament), he ſays, the neceſſity to have it, may diſpenſe with ſome formalities: So *Ravenella* (ſo much eſteemed in matters of Scripture), after he has divided neceſſity into abſolute and hypothetick, makes that of ſubmitting to Powers of abſolute neceſſity. *Joſephus* alſo, my Lord, that famous hiſtorian, when he mentioned *David*'s ſpeech to his children, after he had made *Solomon* (being but younger Brother) King, he exhorts them to unity among themſelves, and ſubmiſſion to him and his authority; for if it ſhould pleaſe God to bring a foreign ſword amongſt you, you muſt ſubmit to them; much more then to him who is your brother, and one of your own Nation.

There is another maxim, my Lord, *Inter arma ſilent leges*; and it is well known, that divers retours and other things in *Scotland* were done in conſideration of times of peace, and times of war.

Another maxim, *Ex duobus malis minimum eligendum eſt, cum unum eorum non poteſt evitari*; ſays *Ariſtotle, Cicero*, and *Quintilian*, *cum diverſa mala inter ſe comparantur, minimum eorum locum boni occupat.*

There is another maxim, No man's intention muſt be judged by the event of any action, there being oftentimes ſo wide a difference betwixt the condition of a work, and the intention of the worker.

I ſhall only add another maxim, It cannot be eſteemed virtue to abſtain from vice, but where it is in our power to commit the vice, and we meet with a temptation.

As I have named ſhortly ſome few maxims, my Lord, I ſhall humbly tender ſome weighty conſiderations to your Lordſhip's thoughts.

The firſt conſideration is, That there are different conſiderations to be had of ſubjects actions when their lawful Magiſtrate is in the exerciſe of his authority by himſelf, or others lawfully conſtituted by him, and when there is no King in *Iſrael*.

The ſecond is, That there is a different conſideration betwixt the ſubjects actions when the lawful Magiſtrate is in the Nation, and when he is put from it, and ſo forced to leave the people to the prevalent power of a foreign ſword, and the invader in poſſeſſion of authority.

Thirdly, That there is a difference betwixt ſubjects actions, even with the invading Uſurper, after the repreſentatives of a Nation have ſubmitted to, and accepted of their authority and government, and they in poſſeſſion ſeveral years; the Nation acknowledging their conſtitutions, and all the lawyers preſſing and pleading them as laws.

Fourthly, The actions of ſubjects are to be conſidered, when aſſiſting the lawful Magiſtrate to their power, and never ſubmitting to the invading Uſurper until they were priſoners, and could do no better.

Fifthly, That there is likewiſe conſideration to be had of the actions of ſuch ſubjects, being ſtill priſoners upon demand under articles to that purpoſe.

Sixthly, It is to be conſidered likewiſe of the actions of ſuch a ſubject, who was particularly noticed and perſecuted by the invaders, for his affection to the lawful Magiſtrate and his government.

Seventhly, It is to be conſidered, that there is a great difference betwixt actions done *ad lucrum captandum*, and thoſe done *ad damnum evitandum*; that is to ſay, actions to procure benefit, and actions to ſhun detriment.

Eighthly, It is to be conſidered, that there hath ever been a favourable conſideration had, by any Prince, of any perſon coming voluntarily, and caſting himſelf upon a Prince's clemency.

Ninthly, It is to be conſidered, that his Majeſty himſelf hath a gracious, natural inclination unto clemency and mercy, which hath been ſo abundantly manifeſted to his ſubjects in *England*, even to all (except to ſome of the immediate murderers of his royal father) that it cannot be doubted, that the ſame will be wanting to his people in *Scotland*, who ſuffered by them (whom his Majeſty hath graciouſly pardoned) even for their dutiful ſervice, and affection to his Majeſty.

Therefore without thought of any prejudice to the Parliament, or this honourable Meeting, I muſt make uſe of my Lord Chancellor of *England* his words, though in another caſe, ſaying, *There cannot too much evil befal thoſe who do the beſt they can to corrupt his Majeſty's good-nature, and to extinguiſh his clemency*: For his Majeſty's ſelf declared his natural inclination to clemency, in his ſpeech to both his Houſes of Parliament in *England*, whom he hath, with all his people, conjured, deſired, and commanded, to aboliſh all notes of diſcord, ſeparations and difference of parties, and to lay aſide all other animoſities, and the memory of paſt provocations, and to return to a perfect unity amongſt themſelves under his Majeſty's protection; which is hoped all your Lordſhips will concur in, having ſo worthy a pattern to follow: And as theſe are his Majeſty's inclinations expreſs'd, ſo it is ſuitable to the arms he bears as King of *Scotland*, which is the Lion, whoſe motto is known to all:

——— Nobilis eſt ira Leonis,
Parcere ſubjectis, & debellare ſuperbos.

Which is to ſay, to vanquiſh and ſubdue the proud, and ſpare ſuch as are ſubmiſſive; of the which number I am one, and for that effect, in all humility preſent this humble ſubmiſſion to his Majeſty, and your Grace, my Lord Commiſſioner, in his Majeſty's name.

To my Lord Commiſſioner his Grace, and High Court of P
March 5, 1661.

FOraſmuch as I *Archibald*, Marquis of *Argyle*, am accuſed of the inſtance of his Majeſty's Advocate, before the high Cou liament; and being altogether unwilling to appear any way i tion to his ſacred Majeſty; conſidering alſo that this is the fir ment called by his Majeſty after his happy return to his King Government, for healing and repairing the diſtempers and breac by the late and long troubles: I have therefore reſolved that t ſultations and debates about the great affairs and concernment of jeſty and this Kingdom ſhall have no interruption upon occaſic proceſs againſt me. I will not repreſent the fatality and cont thoſe times, wherein I, with many others in theſe three Kingdc been involved; which have produced many ſad conſequences an far contrary to our intentions. Nor will I inſiſt upon the defenc actings in this Kingdom before the prevailing of the late Uſurpers if examined according to the ſtricteſt interpretation, and ſevereſt of Law, may be eſteemed a treſpaſs of his Majeſty's royal con and a tranſgreſſion of the Law: But, notwithſtanding thereof, ar Majeſty's clemency covered with the veil of oblivion by divers Parliament, and others, to that purpoſe, for the ſafety and ſecurit Majeſty's ſubjects: And that my actings ſince, and any com with ſo prevalent a power (which had wholly ſubdued this, and Majeſty's other dominions, and was univerſally acknowledged) looked upon as acts of mere neceſſity, which hath no law; an known, that during that time I had no favour from theſe Uſurpe

It was inconſiſtent with, and repugnant to my Intereſt, and ca thought (unleſs I had been demented and void of reaſon) that I have had freedom or affection to be for them, who being conſpir mies to monarchy, could never be expected to befriend or tolerate lity. And whereas that moſt horrid and abominable crime of away the precious life of the late King of ever-glorious memory, i maliciouſly and falſly charged upon me; if I had the leaſt acceſſion moſt vile and heinous crime, I would eſteem myſelf unworthy to liv that all higheſt puniſhments ſhould be inflicted upon me: but my w is in heaven, and my record on high, that no ſuch wicked or d thought ever entered into my heart. But chuſing to ſhun all debat ther than to uſe any words or arguments to reaſon with his M whom though I were righteous, yet would I not anſwer, but would my ſupplication to my Judge; and therefore (without any exc vindication) I do, in all humility, throw myſelf down at his Maj feet (and before his Grace his Majeſty's Commiſſioner, and the ho able Eſtates of Parliament), and do ſubmit and betake myſelf to his jeſty's mercy: and though it be the great unhappineſs of theſe times diſtempers and failings of theſe Kingdoms being ſo epidemick and un ſal), that his Majeſty ſhould have had ſo much occaſion and ſubject royal clemency; yet it is our great happineſs, and his Majeſty's honour, that he has expreſſed and given ſo ample teſtimony thereof, to thoſe who did invade his Majeſty and this Nation, for no other than for their faithful and loyal adherence to his Majeſty, and his royal intereſts: which renders his Majeſty's goodneſs incomparable, without parallel, and gives me confidence, that his Grace his Maje Commiſſioner, and the honourable Parliament, of their own goodneſs, in imitation of ſo great and excellent a pattern, will compaſſionate condition. And ſeeing it is a ſpecial part of his Majeſty's ſoverei and royal prerogative, to diſpenſe with the ſeverity of the Laws, and it is a part of the juſt liberty and privilege of the ſubjects, that in c of greateſt extremity and danger, they may have recourſe to his M jeſty as to a ſanctuary and refuge:

It is in all humility ſupplicated, that the Lord Commiſſioner's Gr and the honourable Parliament, would be pleaſed favourably to repreſent caſe to his Majeſty, and that the door of his royal mercy and bounty, wh is ſo large and patent to many, may not be ſhut upon one, whoſe anceſtors many ages (without the leaſt ſtain) have had the honour, by many ſig proofs of their loyalty, to be reputed ſerviceable to his Majeſty's ro progenitors in the defence of the Crown, and this his ancient Kingdo And if his Majeſty ſhall deign to hold out the golden ſceptre of his c mency, as an indelible character of his Majeſty's royal favour, it will a perpetual obligation of all poſſible gratitude upon me and my poſteri and will ever engage and devote us entirely to his Majeſty's ſervi And the interceſſion of this honourable Parliament on my behalf to gracious Majeſty, will be a real evidence of their moderation, and th ſhall be truly called a healing Parliament; and God, whoſe mercy above all his works, ſhall have the honour and glory which is due to h great name, when mercy triumphs over juſtice.

The aforeſaid ſubmiſſion being read, the Lords of Articles would give him present anſwer; but reſolved to report the ſame to the Parliament the morrow.

Edinburgh, Martii 6, 1661; *at the Parliament.*

MY Lord Chancellor having reported what had been done the forme day before the Lords of Articles anent the Marquis of *Argyle*'s proceſs, preſented his ſubmiſſion, which was immediately read; and after long debate, the firſt queſtion was ſtated;

If it was ſatisfactory, or ſhould be accepted or not?

The ſecond queſtion was, Whether they ſhould proceed preſently in his proceſs, without regard to his ſubmiſſion or not?

Both which were carried in the negative againſt him. Then he was brought to the bar, and the Lord Chancellor told him, that his ſubmiſſion was rejected, and that notwithſtanding thereof, the Parliament commanded him to give in his defences.

He replied, That his caſe was very hard, to be debarred from that which was his juſt privilege, and of all ſubjects, in ſuch extremities to refuge themſelves at his Majeſty's mercy and clemency; and that as it was the undeniable privilege of the ſubject, ſo alſo it was a ſpecial prerogative of his Majeſty, and the grandeur of it conſiſted much in the eminency of the subject, whom his Majesty should graciously be pleased to extend his mercy unto: And besides many other strong persuasions that encouraged his submission, his Majesty's own Proclamation (which he acquiesces in), wherein his Majesty is graciously pleased to declare, *That his just interest and royal prerogative being first asserted, and trial only taken of his subjects carriages, then he is most willing to pass an Act of Indemnity to secure them.* And the like being already done in our neighbouring Nation, and his Majesty having performed his royal promise there already, he desired that their study might be to imitate his royal pattern; considering, that as it was a practice most agreeable to his Majesty's clement inclination, so also, that as *Solomon* that wise King said, That *the King's throne is established by righteousness and mercy:* He entreated therefore their Lordships seriously to consider his condition, and not to single him out, and aim at his ruin; and not only his, but also, he feared, both his family and name, their ruins also.

As for giving in his defences presently, he said, That the confidence and firm hope he had that his humble submission should have been accepted, and so cut off totally all further trouble either to their Lordships or himself, made him the more secure and slack, not resolving to lean to them, or any way (as he had express'd in his submission) make use of them, though he were altogether innocent: and if he were necessitated to make use of his defences (as he declared he was most unwilling to do), it should be simply in obedience to their Lordships commands, and no otherwise.

Not having fully ended,

The Chancellor told him, if his Lordship had them not in readiness at that time, to have them ready to give in to the Lords of Articles the morrow.

So he was returned to the Castle.

March 7, 1661, *at the Lords of Articles.*

THE Marquis being called before the Lords of Articles to give in his defences,

He declared, that he had seen their Lordships Order, that he might forbear his coming, if he would produce his defences; therefore he told their Lordships ingenuously, that if he had them in readiness, he would neither have troubled their Lordships nor himself; for having a petition ready to desire a delay, he thought it rather his duty to come and propose it himself, hoping their Lordships would consider that his presenting his defences either lame and wanting something, or blotted so as they could not well be read, was a very great prejudice to him; but a delay of a few days was no prejudice at all to any thing my Lord Advocate could say; and therefore hoped their Lordships would not refuse him some competent time, whereby he might have them in readiness.

Upon the which he was removed; and after some debate, being called in again, my Lord Chancellor told his Lordship, That he was ordered to give in his defences before *Monday* at ten o'clock to my Lord Advocate, otherwise the Lords of Articles would take the whole business to their consideration, without regard to any thing he could say.

The Advocate told his Lordship, that he must give in his whole defences.

To which he answered,

That that was a new form to give in peremptory defences before the discussing of relevances.

Whereupon Sir *John Bychmore* did rise up, and told his Lordship, That he was commanded to inform him, that there was a different way betwixt a process in writ, and the ordinary way before the Session, or Chief-Justice.

To which his Lordship answered, That he was very ill-yoked with so able men; but he must tell them, that he had once the honour to sit as Chief-Justice in this city, and he knew the process before them was in writ, and yet the relevance was always first answered, before any peremptor proponed; for relevance is most to be considered in criminals.

Sir *John Therester* said, and so did the Advocate, That it was his Lordship's advantage to give in as strongly his defences as he could, otherwise the Advocate might refer the whole business to the Judge, and make no other answer.

His Lordship replied, That he would do in that by advice of his lawyers, and hoped any order of their Lordships at present, was without prejudice to his giving in more defences afterwards, since he was so straitned with time, and commanded to give in what was ready: His Lordship likewise added, if their Lordships and the Parliament had been pleased to grant his desire of a Precognition, which was agreeable, as he humbly conceived, both to Law and Practice, and his Majesty's Proclamation, which he acquiesced in, it could not but have been the readiest way for trying his carriage during the late troubles, where now of necessity he must in the process, which he hopes will not be refused, crave one way for exculpation in many particulars; for he both was resolved, and is resolved to deal very ingenuously as to matter of fact. And if that had been first tried, which he was most desirous of, both from the Committee, and since from the Parliament, he is hopeful there would not remain so much prejudice against him in the most part of things of greatest concernment in this Libel; and for his own part, he desired nothing more than the truth to have place, and to do with his person what they pleased; for by the course of nature he could not expect a long time to live, and he should not think his life ill bestowed, to be sacrificed for all that had been done in these Nations, if that were all.

Thereafter he was returned to the Castle.

The Marquis of Argyle's *Defences against the grand Indictment of High-Treason exhibited against him to the Parliament in* Scotland.

THE defender professes his sense of the mercy and happiness of the land, that we are delivered from the lawless arbitrary power of the armed force of cruel usurpers, and have restored to us our only lawful Sovereign Lord, and in his sacred person, the authority of law, the order of legal judgment, and in them the liberty of legal defences: thereupon depend the great security of the liberties, lives and estates of the subject; this gives the defender confidence to appear in judgment, nothing doubting of a fair procedure and full hearing, compleat time being allowed in all the dyets of the process, and all things therein so ordered, as may be suitable to the justice and gravity of this high and honourable Court, and the importance of the cause; justice, not only as to the defender, but justice as to the preparative and consequence. And he with much confidence expects all justice from his most gracious Sovereign, the justest of Princes, and who is represented and acting by so truly noble a person as my Lord Commissioner's Grace, also hoping the honourable Court of Parliament will without all prejudice impartially consider his legal and just defences, and that they will proceed so far without all ground of suspicion therein, that any who is within degrees to persons against whom he is libelled to have committed any of the deeds which are made the ground of his dittay; or if any are conscious to themselves of capital enmity, or has been any ways informer against the defender, or have predetermined by uttering the judgment already of his cause, conscience and honour will make them abstain sitting and voting therein: so much the more, that they see how unwilling he is to propone any recusatory against any Member of the House upon these or other grounds in law; so confident is he of the vindication of his own carriage, so much he defers to the ingenuity or generosity, and so high is the honour he bears to this honourable Court.

First, It is alledged, that there be no process, nor is the defender holden to answer, till the whole Libel and all the parts thereof be given him up to see: also it is the Commissioner's instructions, and addresses sent and made to his Majesty by the defender, as is alledged, and the Commissioners at *Breda* are expresly repeated, as a part of the libel, *brevitatis causa*, in the tenth article, and yet the same has not been produced nor given to the defender to see and advise with; till which be done, he cannot be held in to answer: like as, where points of the dittay are founded upon writ, the defender craves that he may have up the writs whereupon the same are founded, to see before he be holden to answer to the dittay, which is very consonant to law, *l.* 1. Sect. 3. *F. de edendo ubi edenda sunt omnia quæ actor editurus est, apud iudicem,* & *l.* 3. *cod. eodem.* whereby the pursuer is ordained to shew to the defender all that he will use against the defender before the Judge: Otherwise the defender cannot prepare himself for his defence, which is the reason given in these laws, *Paulus, lib.* 5. cent. 16. and the doctors throughout the said laws, & *l. unius,* Sect. 9 *F. de quest. post alios* to *l.* 2. *Mun.* 3. 4. 5. 6. *eo dedendo Bart. ad leg. ubi min.* 8. *F. de quest.* But so it is, there are several articles in this dittay founded upon writ, not produced; as in the first articles in the prosecution of Mr. *John Steward* to death, as a leasing-maker between the King and his subjects libelled, and yet neither libel nor sentence against Mr. *John* produced.

Item, Colonel *Henderson*'s commission for keeping *Dunbarton* castle is libelled, and the Commission not produced.

Item, In the sixth article a capitulation alledged, made and subscribed by the Laird of *Arkinglas* and other officers under the defender's command, with the Laird of *Lamond* and *Escoge*.

Item, The assurance alledged given to the persons within the house of *Lochhead*, mentioned in the seventh article, the defender craves, *ante omnia*, it may be produced.

Item, That ordinance of Parliament or Committee of Estates, whereby it is libelled in the same seventh article, that *Cailkitoch* was ordained to be brought from the prison where he was for the time, &c. to the town of *Edinburgh*.

Item, In the ninth article the defender's protestation, Parliam. *anno* 1648.

Item, In the same article the letter written to *Cromwell*, libelled as being dated the 6th of *October*, 1648, whereby it is libelled, that the defender and his complices wrote to *Cromwell*, &c.

Item, In the same article Sir *John Cheesly*'s instructions libelled, as being dated the 17th of *October*, 1648, desiring the persons taken in the engagement to be detained as pledges of that Kingdom's peace.

Item, Eod. art. the warrant alledged to be under the defender's hand for a proclamation against the families of *Ogilvie* and *Rea*.

Item, Art. 10. the letter alledged written to *Cromwell*, *anno* 1650, after his invasion.

Item, Eod. art. the act of the West-Kirk, with the declaration whereunto it relates.

Item, Art 11. the remission alledged given to *John Mac-Dougal* of *Dimolich*, under the defender's hand.

All which the defender humbly alledges ought to be given up to see, before he be held in to answer; especially *post tanti temporis intervallum*, so long a time having intervened between the Intention of this pursuit, and the dates of the said Act and papers aforesaid libelled on; some of them being twenty years ago, some fifteen, and the latest ten or eleven years; as has always been the practice in such cases, and may be instanced in my Lord *Balmerino*'s process, and was found by this honourable court in Mr. *James Guthrie*'s process.

Second, Under protestation that the former exceptation may be the first discussed, that the papers therein mentioned, *ante omnia*, be given up to the defender to see, it is alledged, that it has been always the princely care of his Majesty's royal ancestors to keep the Laws of this Realm certain, *Ne dum incerto utemur jure, fluctuaret respublica*; and lest Law, which is introduced for the lieges security, should become their snare: Therefore, by King *James* I. (that illustrious Prince) Parliament 7, *cap.* 107. all the interpretation of his Majesty's statutes, otherwise than the same bear, is forbidden; and if forbidden, can be no ground of dittay: and in effect to found a dittay upon Statutes otherwise than they bear, were to found it upon such Statutes we have not; but so it is in the proposition of this libel. The Acts of Parliament whereupon the same is founded, are otherwise repeated than they bear: for, 1. The first part of the proposition of the dittay founded upon the two first Acts of Parliament libelled, *viz.* the third Act of the 5th Parliament of King *James* I. and the first Act of King *James* VI. doth upon the said Acts conclude the pain of Forfeiture and Treason. The same is most irrelevant, because in the said Acts, there is no mention made of any crimes of the nature and quality libelled; the said third Act of the 5th Parliament of King *James* I. being anent the fees of Craftsmen, and the price of the work; and the first Act of King *James* VI. being anent the constitution of the Earl of *Murray*, Regent; and in neither of the said Acts is there any pain or punishment inferred, and so far less can the pain of Forfeiture or Treason be from the said Acts concluded against the defender. And if it should be said, the 5th Parliament of King *James* I. is mistaken in the writing for the first Parliament, and in citing the first Act of King *James* VI. the citation of the number of the Parliament is also omitted, *viz.* the number 18: The dittay

dittay repeats these two Acts otherways than they bear, for the words of the said 3d Act of the first Parliament of King *James* I. statutes and ordains, *That no man openly or notoriously rebel against the King's person, under the pain and forfeiting of life, lands and goods*; which is not at all in the libel repeated. And as to the said 1st Act of the 18th Parliament of King *James* VI. the words thereof are cited, yet with some difference and transposition libelled; but thereto is added the sanction and pain, *That whosoever doth in the contrary, they are to be punished as Traitors, and to forfeit their life, lands and goods*; whereas there is no sanction or pain in the said Act, only it is declarative of his Majesty's prerogative, and of his three Estates to maintain the same.

Item, In the second part of the proposition of the dittay, founded upon the 25th Act of the 6th Parliament of King *James* II. and 75th Act of the 9th Parliament of Queen *Mary*; is not repeated as it bears as to punishment, for therein they who attempt to do, or raise any bands of men of war, horse or foot, without any special licence of his Majesty, and his Successors, are only declared punishable by death; whereas they are libelled to be punishable as Traitors, while it is the pain only of the said 25th Act of the 6th Parliament of King *James* II.

Item, In the next part of the proposition of the dittay, founded upon the 43d Act of the 2d Parliament of King *James* I. and the 134th Act of the 8th Parliament, and the 10th Act of the 10th Parliament, and 205th Act of the 14th Parliament of King *James* VI. none of these Acts are repeated as they bear, but confounded, both as to the crimes and pains therein contained, to a very far different sense (as is humbly conceived) from that which the said Acts severally propose; transferring the pains of the said several Acts and Crimes therein contained from one to another, as may appear by what follows. For the first of these Acts, being the 43d Act of the 2d Parliament of King *James* I. is only of leasing-makers and tellers of them, which may engender strife between the King and his People; and the pain of the Act is tinsel of life and goods to the King, as is clear both by the title and body of the Act. The second Act, *viz.* the 134th Act of the 8th Parliament of King *James* VI. is also the same crime, *viz.* against those that utter false, slanderous and untrue speeches, to the disdain, reproach or contempt of his Majesty, his Council or Proceedings, or to the dishonour of his Majesty's parents and progenitors: adding also those that meddle in the affairs of his Majesty and his Estates, and the pain is the pain contained in the Acts of Parliament made against Leasing-makers and tellers of them. The third is the 10th Act of the 10th Parliament of King *James* VI. against those who speak or write any purpose of reproach or slander against his Majesty's Person, Estates or Government, or deprave his Laws or Acts of Parliament, or misconstrue his Majesty's proceedings, whereby any misbelieving may be moved between his Majesty and Nobility, and his loving Subjects: And the pain thereof is only the pain of death. And by the 205th Act of the 14th Parliament of King *James* VI. those that hear the said words Leasings, and do not apprehend and reveal the Authors thereof, shall incur the like punishment with the principal offenders; and yet Leasing-making, and telling, which is the crime punishable by the first of these Acts, *viz.* the 43d Act of the 2d Parliament of King *James* I. is punishable, but the loss of life and goods to the King is omitted. And false slanders, which is the crime contained in the 134th Act of the 8th Parliament of King *James* VI. and only speaking to the dishonour of his Majesty's Parents and Progenitors, and meddling with the affairs of his Highness's estate, is repeated out of the said 134th Act; and joined to the crime contained in the said Acts, 10th Parliament, 10 *James* VI. And to both, the pains added of losing life, lands and goods, whereas the pain of the said 10th Act is only of death. And the pain of the said 134th Act of the 8th Parliament of King *James* VI. is only the pain contained in the Acts against Leasing-makers, which in the said 43d Act of the 2d Parliament of King *James* I. is only the loss of life and goods, and not of life, lands and goods: but allanerly the escheats of goods moveable: as may appear, *First*, Because whenever the pain of tinsel of life and goods is found either in the Acts of Parliament or old Laws, goods are understood moveable, as is clear from the crimes that are ordained to be so punished: As man-slaughter, by the 42d Statute of *Robert* III. is prohibited under the pain of tinsel of life and goods; where *Skein* explains, that the goods are to be understood of moveables. And by the 90th Act of the 6th Parliament of King *James* I. the receipt of him who is fugitive for slaughter, is forbidden under the pain of tinsel of life and goods. (Where *Skein* expounds goods to be goods moveable, in his Tractate of Crimes, tit. 2. *cap.* 6. Parl. 4.) And so it is clear in the other Acts of Parliament, that their whole pains are distinct, *viz.* tinsel of life and goods alike, is only extended to moveables; and tinsel of life, lands and goods, which latter pain in the stile of our Acts of Parliament is commonly thus expressed: That he who incurs it shall die, and forfeit life, lands and goods, as the 31st Act of the 7th Parliament of King *James* II. & *passim alibi* forfeiture properly relating to lands; and in the common signification of our said goods, to be understood of goods moveable.

More especially it may appear, that the pain of the said 43d Act of the 2d Parliament of King *James* I. given to the said 134th Act of the 8th Parliament of King *James* VI. is only the pain of escheat of moveables, because the pain of forfeiting of life, lands and goods, is the proper pain of the crimes that by our laws are declared Treason. And therefore *Skein*, both in his Index of the Acts of Parliament on the word Treason, refers the crimes that are so punishable to the head of Treason; as also in his tract upon crimes in the end of *Reg. Maj.* but doth not at all mention therein the crime of the said 43d Act of the 2d Parliament of King *James* I. nor of the 134th Act of the 8th Parliament of King *James* VI. nor of the other Acts whereupon this part of the proposition is founded. But in his Index has the crime of Leasing-making between the King and his people under a head by itself, and therein expresly mentions both the said 43d Act of King *James* I. and 134th Act of King *James* VI. like as in the said tract of crimes after the chapters of Treason and points thereof, *cap.* 1. and pain of the same, which, *cap.* 2. he expresly says, is the tinsel of life, lands and goods; and declares, that he understands by goods, moveable goods. And anent the Process and Judge of the crime of Treason, *cap.* 3. when he comes to other crimes capital, of all which the pains are either

the tinsel of life and moveable goods, or life only, or of some
body or goods, but never of life, lands and goods, as is clear
whole tract that follows. And in his 12 *cap.* anent the crime
he has the crime of Leasing-making between the King and
And the same Acts of Parliament, *viz.* Act 43d of the 2d Pa
King *James* I. and the 205th Act of the 14th of King *James*
his 25th *cap.* has the crime of infamous and seditious libels; a
10th Act of the 10th Parliament of King *James* VI. cited there

Item, in the last two Acts of Parliament whereupon the pro
the dittay is founded, *viz.* the 37th Act of the 2d Parliament
James I. and 144th Act of the 12th Parliament of King *James*
libelled, That all recepters, supplyers or intercommoners with
tors, are punishable by forfeiture, as the Traitors themselves
not as the Act bears, for both the crime and pain libelled out
144th Act of the 12th Parliament of King *James* VI. the
simply against those who intercommon with Traitors and Rebels
such as are declared Rebels and Traitors. From all which it foll
the proposition of the libel founded upon the Acts as they are li
not relevant; and therefore the Defendant ought to be assoilzi
libello.

Tertio, As to the last part of the proposition of the dittay, th
der abhors so much the crime therein mentioned, that he thinks a
who will conceal any malicious purpose, wronging in the least,
in putting violent hands on the inviolable sacred person of his
Lord, were unworthy to breathe in common air, let alone to be d
and is so conscious to himself of his own innocency in any suc
that he needs no other defence, but the confident denial of any
therein, either less or more. But before a practice pass in this ho
Court of Parliament, of founding a dittay of Treason upon comm
and Practice; it is under protestation aforesaid, and with all hun
ledged against the relevancy of that part of the proposition, as found
the said Common Law and Practice, That it is not relevantly
thereon, in so far as by the 28th Act of Parliament 1640 it is
found and declared Traitors, but after Trial by the Parliament o
ordinary; and finding that the said Persons have contravened a
Act of Parliament, made under the pain of Treason: and the
person cannot be declared guilty of Treason on a Dittay founded o
mon Law and Practice. 2. *Pœna* being *legis sanctio*; and the C
Law is known with us, to have only *vim rationis, non legis*; and t
no pain, but especially the highest of pains cannot be founded the
And 3. specially as the practice beside the reason aforesaid; becau
4. *fad. senat. Consult. Turpilianum, facti quidem quæstio in arbitrio*
cantis, pœnæ vero persecutio non ejus voluntati mandatur, sed legis au
asservatur. Whence *Menochius* lib. 5. Presumpt. cap. 29. *in*
saith expresly, *pœna indici non potest nisi expresso jure sit cautum pe*
quis divus fad. reli. & sumptibus funerum. And it is the common
of the Doctors, That ever when punishment is not expresly de
the Law, but is permitted *arbitrio judicis*, it cannot be extended to
far less to the pain of Treason. And the foresaid Act of Parli
28th Act, *anno* 1640, takes away the relevancy of founding Treaso
Common Law and Practice, as said is.

If a Dittay to infer the crime of Treason might be founded on p
either of the Justice-Court or Parliament, which are two Courts,
which crimes of Treason are judged; yet our practice is *consuetudo*
ita judicatarum, as *Craig* defines it, *lib.* 1. *de feudis dig.* 8. And th
to it, as to the introducing of all other consuetudes, there must be
frequentia, reiterated acts and practices, *per l. de quibus ff. de legi*
Cart. Jason, and other Doctors on that Law; *& per l. Cod. quæ si*
consuetudo, & L. & in totum 3. *c. de cres. dif. privat.* 2. *illud explor*
an contradictio aliquo judicio sit firmata; that is, it would be tried if
in foro contradictorio have been given thereupon. As also saith *Craig*
disg. 8. *in fine*; and if in any case, that ought to be far more in c
and if in crimes, yet more in the highest of crimes; and in all co
ments of one of the most eminent Peers of the land, which is

For in matters civil (how small soever) before the session, a practic
never be founded on some decrees given either for non-compearan
on compearance where there is little or no dispute, or it may be gre
equality in Advocates of the two parties. And if in civils, where th
terest is only pecuniary, this ought to be much more in libels of Tr
as hath been said; but so it is, neither in Justice-Court nor Parli
will be found, that it hath been frequently judged, nor *in foro contradic*
on a dispute where this defence hath been propounded. Yea, it m
well alledged, that there can be no practice shewed of either of
Courts, that any hath been found guilty of Treason, but on some A
Parliament under the pain of Treason, as is said; but however the
28th Act of Parliament 1640 is most clear, which is most agreeab
reason, and the Law of *England*, very laudable in that point; as *Co*
it in his chapter of Treason, and therefore the libel as founded on pra
is noways relevant, and the defender ought to be assoilzied therefrom.

Quarto, Every libel both of civil Law and our Law ought to be
distinct and special; but especially criminal libels, because of the
importance of them, ought to be most clear, distinct and special, *li*
bellus in criminalibus debet esse clarissimus, saith *Dambeud, prax. crim*
num. 3. And therefore, *Libellus Criminalis obscurus parte etiam non*
piente extenditur favore rei, *Baldus in lege addita, num.* 10. *c. de ed*
Alex. Consil. 72. *col. versic. & licet volum.* 1 *hip. Consil.* 49. *& Ranta*
prax. Crim. Reg. 6. *f.* 3 *&* 4. *nec enim debet accusator cum existimationis*
enæ jactura, & discrimine vagari licet. L. si in rem ff. de rei vum. So
any obscure criminal libel is inept, and the defender ought to be assoil
therefrom, though he did not oppone his defence for that effect.
so it is, this Dittay is most unclear and undistinct, in so far as in the
position of the Dittay, there are many Acts of Parliament libelled
being Statutes anent diverse crimes of very different natures, and in
ring different punishments, according to the article of the com
and in the subsumption the Pannel is indicted for several crimes alled
committed by him, contrary to the said Laws and Acts of Parliam
in general, without condescending on the particular Acts of Parliam

4

that the Pannel has contravened by committing the particular deeds libelled, and ſo leaving him to great uncertainty. Whereas in all Law, Reaſon, and form of proceſs, the defendant ought to be certified what Acts and Laws he has contravened, by committing ſuch deeds that are in a multiplicity of crimes. After propoſing all the Statutes relating to the ſame crimes, all the deeds immediately ought to be ſubſumed, falling under the compaſs of ſuch Statutes, and thereafter the Acts relating to another indifferent crime ought to be propoſed, and the deeds falling under the compaſs of theſe Acts immediately ſubſumed, and throughout the libel, which is no way done here; but firſt, by many different Acts accumulated together in the propoſition, and then the moſt different facts accumulated together indiſtinctly in the ſubſumption, not condeſcending on the Acts by them contravened: and therefore the libel is inept, and the defendant ought to be aſſoilzied therefrom.

This defence is further confirmed in law; 2. Becauſe a libel being *ſyllogiſmus quidem practicus*, *Jaſon* and the *Doct. inſtit. de act.* in criminal dittays the propoſition conſiſts *in jure conſtitutionis*, in the laws whereupon the libel is founded. The manner is in the ſubſumption of the facts or crimes under theſe laws, and the concluſion inferring the pain: Becauſe of ſuch a crime, as falling under the law libelled, on a very eſſential part of every libel, is *quo jure petatur*; and a libel being uncertain in this, is unclear and uncertain in a very eſſential point, and inept. 3. In law, a libel ought ſo to be conceived as the defender may know *actionis ſpeciem*, otherwiſe it is inept. l. f. *de edendo*, l. 3. *c. eodem*, and may alſo know *actiones jus*, and that he may deliberate how to defend; but in our caſe, that ariſes from the diſtinct application of the laws to the facts, *ex quibus jus oritur*. 4. If ſuch uncertain libel were admitted, the defender, becauſe of the obſcurity and uncertainty of the libel, ſhould be prejudged of a certain defence he could make againſt the relevancy of the ſame, becauſe the relevancy of it conſiſts in the ſubſumption of the facts and crimes libelled under ſome certain law: which being condeſcended on by a diſtinct ſubſumption, under each law, of the crimes that were libelled properly to fall under the ſame, the defendant would alledge why ſuch crimes cannot be ſubſumed relevantly under ſuch laws and acts, which he otherwiſe cannot do in ſuch multiplicity both of different acts and crimes as are libelled in this dittay. there being not only in divers articles, but even in every article, a great diverſity of the crimes therein libelled, and yet the defender left in uncertainty under which of all the acts libelled on, the purſuer intends the ſubſumption thereof; and ſo in uncertainty altogether how to conceive his defence. And if this be not *maxime vagari, cum maximo alienæ vitæ et fortunarum periculo*; it is hoped, as it will be found very evident ſo it was never the practice heretofore uſed in criminal libels; and which, that it ſhould not be now ſuſtained, is of univerſal concernment. and if ſuſtained, might prove of very dangerous conſequence. And the libel, as it is now conceived, is inept, and the defender ought to be aſſoilzied therefrom.

BEFORE the defender come to his particular anſwer to the ſeveral articles of the dittay, to the effect the defender's caſe, in his acceſſion to the publick actings of this kingdom, during the unhappy troubles till the treaty of *Breda*, and his Majeſty's home-coming, may be truly ſtated; it is humbly craved that the Commiſſioner's Grace and honourable Eſtates of Parliament may be pleaſed to remember, that the Kirk and whole body of this Kingdom entered at firſt into the national covenant, for defence of religion and his Majeſty's perſon and authority, and mutual defence one of another in maintaining the ſame; wherein, and in what followed in proſecution thereof till the treaty with his late Majeſty, and Act of oblivion, ſet down at length and ratified in the 6th Act of the 2d Parliament, *anno* 1641; his late Majeſty did ſo far acknowledge and approve their loyalty, that in the ſeventh article of the ſaid large treaty his Majeſty was pleaſed to appoint, that at the cloſe of that treaty, their ſaid loyalty ſhould be made known at the time of publick thankſgiving in all places, particularly in the pariſh churches of his Majeſty's dominions. And in the ſaid Act of pacification and oblivion, is pleaſed to declare, that their conſtant loyalty in their intentions and proceedings ſhould not be hereafter called in queſtion; and that whatſoever fell forth in thoſe tumultuous times, whether prejudicial to his Majeſty's honour and authority, to the laws and liberty of the church, or the particular intereſt of the ſubject, might be buried in perpetual oblivion; and whatever had enſued thereon, no mention ſhould be made thereof in judgment or without: like as his Majeſty for himſelf and his ſucceſſors, promiſes, *in verbo Principis*, never to come in contrary to the ſaid ſtatute, nor any thing therein contained; but to hold the ſame firm and ſtable, and to cauſe it to be truly obſerved, and theſe preſents to have the full force and ſtrength of a perfect and true ſecurity. Like as thereafter *in anno* 1643, the league and covenant was entered in with the two Houſes of Parliament, upon the ground of the large treaty, by the Church and whole body of this Kingdom, purporting the ſame ends of the Covenant, for maintenance of Religion, King and Kingdom; which was thereafter approved by the Parliament, 1644, and fifth Act thereof, and proſecuted by wars both within and without the Kingdom, by the authority of divers ſucceeding Parliaments; church and ſtate going unanimouſly along together, without any apparent publick difference till the year 1648. And even then that Parliament, 1648, ſo highly homologate the ſaid league and covenant, that they declare the breaches thereof to be the grounds of their reſolutions of that war, Act 4, 7 and 8; and their deſires for preventing thereof to be the fulfilling of the ſame, *Ibidem*. The neceſſary qualification required in all with whom they would join either in their armies or committees, is, that they be ſuch who were of known faithfulneſs to the cauſe and covenant in the ſaid Act 7, and that they would oppoſe, and endeavour to ſuppreſs the enemies to the cauſe and covenant on all hands, *Ibid.* Witneſſing to the world that they ſwerved not from the principles contained in the national covenant and league and covenant, and that they reſolved cloſely and conſtantly to adhere thereunto, and to all the ends thereof. So that at that time there was ſtill no difference as to the cauſe and covenant, any difference being only in the manner, and not in the matter of that engagement.

Thereafter what ſtraits this poor Kingdom was reduced to, by the defeat of that engagement, and how unable it was to make reſiſtance to that *Engliſh* army, who, in proſecution of their victory, came to the borders, and entered the ſame, is notorious to all; wherewith the whole Kingdom being ſurprized with amazement, and in evident hazard, it was hard in that juncture of affairs to reſolve upon any courſe for preventing the ſame, or rather incumbent hazard of the Kingdom. Whereupon a *Quorum* of the Committee of Eſtates appointed by the ſaid Parliament, 1648, were neceſſitated to take upon them the managing of affairs, and to ſue for conditions of peace, not being able to reſiſt by force (the flower and ſtrength of the Nation being broke by the ſaid defeat) and to accept the ſame upon the eaſieſt terms that could be had for the time; which as it was endeavoured upon no other intention, or for any other end but that which they were conſtrained to by inevitable neceſſity; ſo at that time it was generally looked upon as good ſervice, and which at that time was moſt neceſſary to evite very great, and otherwiſe inevitable evils, being either neceſſitate to condeſcend to their demands at that time, or otherwiſe to have delivered the perſons of all that did proſecute the ſaid engagements, according to the obleaſment of the large treaty, together with the forts and ſtrength of the Kingdom. The ſucceeding Parliament for the time, in the year 1649, after proclamation of his preſent Majeſty, did ſend Commiſſioners to *Holland*, and afterwards, according to his Majeſty's deſire, to *Breda*, where there was a treaty concluded by his ſacred Majeſty; wherein he was graciouſly pleaſed to approve of the ſaid Parliament, *in anno* 1644, and remanent Parliaments, and their proceedings from the year 1641, preceding the ſaid treaty, which was thereafter ratified by his ſacred Majeſty and his Parliament at *Perth* and *Sterling*; and, after the royal example of his ever-glorious Father, an act of oblivion was indulged, whereby all that might be ground of queſtion was buried in oblivion, and pardoned by a general Act of oblivion in a moſt full and ample form.

This being the ſtate of publick affairs during the time aforeſaid, albeit by the firſt ten articles of the dittay, the defender is charged with deeds and publick actings, coming within the compaſs of the ſaid approbation and oblivion aforeſaid; yet ſuch firm reliance hath he of his Majeſty's perſiſting in his gracious clemency, which does in his royal heart ſo much abound, that albeit his Majeſty by his proclamation, dated the 12th of *October*, 1660, is pleaſed graciouſly to declare, that he has remitted to his Parliament the trial of the carriage of his ſubjects in *Scotland* during the late troubles: That the late troubles have only reſpect to the time during the Uſurper's poſſeſſion, and that trial ſhould be taken during that time of the ſubject's carriage: The defender in all humility conceiving, that it is no ways to be ſuppoſed, that his gracious Majeſty did thereby intend to rip up or revive, or to inſtitute any new trial of old offences, forgotten and forgiven, as is ſaid; eſpecially ſeeing it is not to be ſuppoſed that the bowels of his mercies ſhould be ſo ſtraitned to this his ancient Kingdom, to which he has upon all occaſions given ſo many ſignal and recent teſtimonies of his ſuperabundant favour, than they are, and have been to his ſubjects of his other dominions; to whom, according to his Majeſty's declarations, he hath granted a full and free pardon, from which few, and theſe only the unpardonable murderers of his royal Father, are excluded; for whom, or any guilty thereof, no puniſhment can be ſufficient. And therefore the defender in all humility conceives the ſaid articles, though libelled, are not to be inſiſted on.

The ſolemnity of the oaths, both of covenant and league, will be, as the defender hopes, pregnant preſumptions to put an end to all controverſy, anent the ſincerity of his (as of the Church and Kingdom) their loyal intentions for the maintenance of the perſon and authority of our dread Sovereign, whereunto they were thereby ſo religiouſly engaged; and the conſtant tenour of his acting ſtill by virtue of publick orders and warrants of Parliament, and their Committees, wherein his faithfulneſs in the execution was alſo in the like manner approved, will witneſs, that what he did was not for any private intereſt, but for the publick ends; whereunto he conceived himſelf engaged in manner aforeſaid. Nor was the defender for continuing of theſe unnatural civil diſcords, as he did witneſs by his inclination to an accommodation with *Montroſs*, in the year 1645, mentioned after in anſwer to the tenth article; which albeit fully agreed to betwixt him and the defender, yet he could not obtain the Committee's approbation thereof: which is an evidence, that the defender had not the chief ſway of affairs, and was always inclinable to peace, religion being ſecured; like as the carrying on the engagement in the year 1648, though the defender differed in his judgment as to the way and manner, upon the grounds and reaſons thereafter expreſs'd in anſwer to the ninth article, doth clearly evince, that he had not the chief ſway in publick actings. And what power and intereſt he had in the year 1649, he did faithfully, according to his bond duty, improve the ſame for removing theſe differences betwixt his Majeſty and his ſubjects, wherein he was paſſionately earneſt, as ſhall be made appear in anſwer to the ſaid tenth article. And after his Majeſty's home-coming, and during his being in this Kingdom; and thereafter, till the enemy had fully prevailed, and that by his articles of agreement he was there priſoner, he faithfully ſerved his Majeſty, and even during his Majeſty's abſence, did always, and ſtill ſhall, return loyal duty and good affection to his perſon, government, and poſterity.

And whatever theſe who are grown up may judge, who only ſee the unhappy and accidental events that are the effects of the corruption of men, but have not known the counſels and cauſes which are the two parts of theſe things neceſſary to be known to all who would judge of human actions aright; events being for the moſt part uncertain, and the worſt of events of times, through the corruption of agents, or other extrinſical circumſtances following upon the beſt of actions, yet had they been intimately acquainted with the grounds, cauſes, and nature of the actings while a-doing, the defender is confident that they would have concurred and been of the ſame judgment, as being clear, that theſe proceedings had no native connexion with the ſad and unexpected conſequences that have enſued.

And now to come to the particular defences to the ſeveral points of the ſubſumption, of the dittay. And firſt as to the article of the ſubſumption, anent the words alledged, ſpoken at the ford of *Lions*, which are libelled to have been, That it was the opinion and judgment of many lawyers and divines, that a King might be depoſed for deſertion, vendition, or invaſion; and which is alledged to have been meaned by the pannel of the then King's Majeſty; and the preſumptions adduced for inforcing that to have been the defender's meaning, are ſome

words

words alledged subjoined, to wit, *Mr.* John, *you understand Latin.* It is alledged for the defender, no ways acknowledging, to the best of his memory, that he uttered any such words; 1. All criminal dittays should contain in them at least year, month and place, otherwise they are inept; *Bartol. & D. D. ad L. libellorum ff. de accusatione*, because amongst other reasons, *diversitas loci varia argueret facinora*, saith *Buttand Reg.* 6. *Prax. cum postangel.* &c. But so it is, there is no month condescended on, when the defender should have spoken these words, and therefore the dittay in this article is inept. 2. There is no particular Act of Parliament in the Act libelled upon in the proposition condescended on, which is contravened by the words libelled; therefore the libel in this article of the subsumption is general and obscure, and till the particular law contravened be condescended on, one can receive no answer. 3. The speeches as they are libelled fall not under the compass of the acts libelled on in the proposition of the Libel, to infer any of the pains therein contained; because they are but libelled as the narration of the opinion of others, which is not relevant to infer so much, that the narrator is of the same opinion, except it were also libelled, that he did declare his homologation, and that he was of the same judgment, which neither is, nor can be libelled; far less then is it relevant to infer a crime, and so high a crime as treason. For suppone the defender had said, that they are very learned, both divines and lawyers, whose opinion it is, that the Pope is the head of the church, and that he has power to dispense with the article of faith, to depose Kings, a horrid opinion, &c and that it is their opinion also we may merit heaven by good works, and that all Hugonots or Protestants are damnable hereticks, and that he had related their words in *Latin*, as the *Latin* of that verse of the gloss of the common law, *cap. sicut de excess. prælat.*

Restituit Papa salus deponit, &c.
articulus solvit.

And had said to Mr. *John Stewart* thereupon, Mr. *John*, you understand *Latin*; albeit these opinions of these divines and lawyers be execrably heretical, yet nobody will say, that the defender's relation of them would have inferred him to have been guilty of the same, no more in our case can the relation libelled infer him to have been of that opinion with these divines and lawyers, or in any way thereby to have contravened any act of Parliament libelled. 2. The aforesaid opinion is libelled only to have been related *in abstracto* (nothing of our King's Majesty who then was). And whereas it is libelled, that it appears the sense and meaning thereof appeared to have been of the then King's Majesty, in so far as the defender subjoined to Mr. *John Stewart*, the words aforesaid, that he understood *Latin*: 1. The libel in this part is ambiguous; for this may be interpreted, either that it was the meaning of the opinion of these divines which he related, (this seems to be most consonant to the words) or else that his own meaning was, That it was the judgment that the then King's Majesty our Sovereign might be so dealt with, as is libelled in the latter part of this article, and so the article in this part thereof is ambiguous and inept, and there ought to be no process thereupon. *Nam libellus (in criminalibus præsertim) nihil ambiguitatis vel obscuritatis continere debet, per cap. Constitut.* 6. *extr. derig. don. Bet.* 3. If it be understood in the former sense, it is but still relative of the opinion of others; and if in this latter sense, to wit, that it was his own judgment, the presumption libelled of what he spake to Mr. *John Stewart* is no way relevant to infer it. 1. Because they held a more obvious meaning, *viz.* That it might have been, the opinion of these divines and lawyers was related in *Latin*; and indeed *Grotius* and *Barclaius*, who writ of that subject, are both in *Latin*, and that he had subjoined to Mr. *John Stewart*, *Mr.* John, *you understand* Latin. 2. That such opinions being rather the fancy of notional schoolmen, (otherwise not unlearned in their own art) or of such as are Doctors notional in the law, if there be any of such opinions, rather than of solid jurisconsults, who for most part do not so much as move these questions, not to be moved. 3. If any such words had been spoken to Mr. *John Stewart*, they might have had this more proverbial sense: some lawyers and divines are of that opinion, but the subtilty of these questions or opinions is *Latin* to me, that is, I understand it not; as we say commonly of things we understand not, *It is Latin to me*; but, Mr. *John*, you are a Scholar, and you understand it. Now it is a Rule in law, that where the meaning is doubtful or obscure, that which is the most favourable sense should be followed. *L.* 9. *ff. de reg. juris*, and *Matheus de afflictis, decisione* 265. *n.* 68, 69. *& decis.* 307. *n.* 15. And when these words are ambiguous, the declaration of him who uttered them should be acquiesced unto, *Menochius, consilio* 197. And the defender is ready to declare, that if he had ever spoken such words, he was very far from any such meaning as is libelled against him. Nor 4. is it any way presumable, that any rational man, who had the honour to know his late Majesty, could have made application of any of these three causes to so worthy and illustrious a Prince, seeing the said *Grotius*, *Barclay*, and others that write upon that subject acknowledge, yea, it is obvious to common sense, that hardly can they fall out in the worst of princes, if he be but *compos mentis*. And as to the presumption that follows, that the defender meaned by the late King's Majesty, because of the condition wherein the Kingdom was for the time; 1. It is far more presumable that the Kingdom was in such a condition of affection to his Majesty's sacred person and authority, as at that time none durst have uttered what might reflect thereupon, seeing it is libelled to have been shortly after the subscribing of the Covenant, wherein they had solemnly bound themselves by the oath of God to maintain his Majesty's person and authority. 2. His Majesty by his Royal judgment in the Act of oblivion, 1641, has presumed the loyalty of his subjects, both in their intentions and proceedings in these times, which is *presumptio juris, & de pre.* As for the defender's prosecuting of Mr. *John Stewart*, 1. It was a judicial process and legal act, and so can be no imputation to him, wherein the process was laid in so fair a course of law, that he was condemned, not only upon clear probation, but his own confession: and yet the words whereupon he was indicted and convicted were far different from these words, as they are here libelled, otherwise the defender would never have pursued it.

Ultimo, Adhering always to the alledgance above propounded, humbly protesting, that they may be first discussed: and whereupon it is craved, he may be assoilzied *in hoc libello*, because by Act of Parliament *in anno* 1641, amongst the imprinted Acts *anno* 70. the same service and he exonered. It is alledged, that the Defender ought to from the whole crimes in the first article, because after the time the alledged committing of the same, his late Majesty of glori granted that never-to-be-forgotten Act of Indemnity and *anno* 1641; which did proceed upon the preceding Treaty wi jesty, and which is solemnly confirmed by his Majesty himsel and his three Estates in his Parliament, 1641, 6th Act thereo his Majesty, for himself and his successors, does promise *in verb* never to come in the contrary of that Statute and sanction, o therein contained; but to hold the same in all points firm and and to cause it to be truly observed by all his Majesty's lieg Hereupon the Defender doth confidently rely, for all that is committed by him in this article, or any other preceding that t ing confident it is the greatest imaginable security that he and the lieges of the land can have.

As to the second article, and whole head thereof, 1. N month nor year of God are condescended on; and therefore so ge it is inept. *Nam generalitas parit obscuritatem, Marent. part.* 6. *libel oblat. quomodo concin. & per textus ibi citatos.* 2. It is scended which of the Acts of Parliament libelled this article, veral heads thereof, contravenes, which is a general ineptitude in this libel. 3. As to the first point; if that article anent the i the house of *Airly*, cutting and destroying the planting, and d the houses; 1. It is not relevantly libelled, in so far as it was l the house was kept for his Majesty's service, but doth not cond service now. 2. Is it libelled that there was any in it had a from his Majesty, without which it has not any colour of relevanc Defender never had any private quarrel, nor personal prejudi the noble Lord *James* Earl of *Airly*; but if his marching to be meaned of that which was *in anno* 1640, it was by virtue obedience to, a commission put upon him by the Committee for the time: nor was the said house, at his arrival thereat, ke Majesty's Service, as is (though wrongfully) libelled. But time was surrendered to the Earl of *Montrose*, who had put Col. keep the same for the King and Country's use, and which Co upon sight of the Defender's commission, did abandon the said h if there was any planting cut, it was allenarly some few shrubs a which the Defender could not hinder, for hurting to the sold though the Defender's commission bear power and warrant to the house, he was so far from stretching or fully executing the s he did not only slight the house, and delayed a long time to do in expectation that the Lord *Ogilvy* should have procured a cou from the Committee, and did slight it till he was past all hope ing the same; and this as is hoped will be acknowledged by the Earl; neither did, so far as the Defender knew or could hinder, his friends and followers, sustain any other prejudice than what and what all places are ordinarily obnoxious to, where armies of soldiers come: but however it is not relevant, as said is.

Tertio, That part of the said article, though it were true (as i is no ways relevant to infer the conclusion of the Dittay, there Law nor Statute libelled on; that for cutting of timber, or der the houses of private persons (though done upon private quarrel was not) infers the pain of Treason.

As to that part of the article, anent the burning of the house of beside the exceptions against both the points thereof, alledged the beginning, it is not relevant to say, that the Defender seized t to infer any crime, except it were libelled he seized by force, for have entered *in vacuam possessionem*. 2. *Non relevat* to libel, that t der him did seize thereupon, or raise fire therein, except it were that the Defender had given express order or warrant to raise th fire; who, as he gave not order therefore, so he was not present the place, nor knew any thing thereof, till after the house was bu *noxia caput sequitur*. 3. In the Acts of Parliament libelled on burning and wilful fire-raising, the same can only be understood o ing and raising of fire on private feuds, and for particular revenge of peace, and is not to be extended to such deeds done in the heat of wars, seeing *inter arma silent leges.*

And as to the aggravation of the Defender's hatred against th merely for his loyalty to his Majesty, it is *gratis dictum*, and aga presumption, *qua unusquisque præsumitur bonus*, and against that to his Majesty, that is hoped shall more and more appear in t fender.

Lastly, The Defender ought to be assoilzied from the said article, deeds therein mentioned. Because the same preceded the Act of *in anno* 1641, whereby all things that did fall forth in these tum times, whether prejudicial to his Majesty's honour and safety, o Laws and Practices of the Church and Kingdom, or to the partic terests of the subject, are buried in perpetual oblivion, as more contained in the said Act.

3. As to the third article, anent the besieging of *Dunbarton* and transporting Cannon and Ammunition out thereof.

It is alledged for the Defender, That the assaulting of the said not relevant to infer the conclusion of the Dittay, because, as is be ledged, none can be declared Traitors, but those who have contrav special Act made under the pain of Treason. But so it is, that the particular Acts of Parliament, whereupon the proposition is f mentions any thing against those who assault the King's Castle, n any of them infer the pain of Treason therefore. But only the 25 of Parliament, 6 *Jac.* VI. intitled *Sundry Points of Treason*, by th Acts they only are to be punished as Traitors, who assault the C places where the King's person is, and that without warrant of E but it is neither libelled, nor was the King's person in the said C the time of the alledged assaults thereof; nor did the Defender assa lay siege to the same without warrant from the Estates, but by their order and commission. And the truth is, the Defender himself did not before the said house, till the said Sir *John Henderson* being straitned w siege, sent for the Defender, and offered to surrender the house upon h able conditions, which the Defender suffered him to make himsel which were accordingly kept, not without ſome difficulty, the Inhabitants of the town, by reaſon of prejudice done to them, being highly incenſed againſt the ſaid Colonel.

As to that part of the ſaid article, anent the tranſporting of the King's Cannon and Ammunition, not relevant to infer the Concluſion, none of the Acts libelled on concluding againſt any ſuch fact, the ſaid crime of Treaſon; and the truth is, the Defender did never tranſport any Cannon or Ammunition out of the ſaid Caſtle, but two Cannons, which the Duke of *Richmond*, heritable Keeper thereof, gifted to the Defender, and which he would never have gifted, if they had not been his own, and not the King's. 2. The Defender ought to be aſſoilzied from the ſaid article, and all deeds therein contained, the ſame having alſo preceded the ſaid Act of oblivion, *in anno* 1641.

4. And as to the fourth article of the Dittay, anent the Defender's calling, or cauſing to be called a convention of Eſtates, *in anno* 1643, entering in league with his Majeſty's enemies, impoſing exciſe and ſubſidies on the Kingdom, raiſing an army, entering *England* therewith, fighting for and with the Rebels there; it is anſwered, That the whole points of this article of the Dittay are charged perſonally on the Defender, ſo contrary to the notoriety of the matter of the fact known to both Kingdoms, and to his Majeſty's Commiſſioner's Grace, and to the whole Parliament; yea, to the fifth Act of Parliament, 1644, relating and approving all the Acts that are made points of this article; that there needs no more but propone as known to all, and to repeat out of the ſaid publick Law and Act of Parliament, what is therein libelled, to evince that they are not the Defender's perſonal deeds: but the Committees (Commiſſioners eſtabliſhed by his Majeſty), Convention of Eſtates, and of the whole Church and Kingdom of *Scotland*, and approved by Parliament, 1644, in the ſaid fifth Act thereof. Firſt then as it is notorious, ſo it is clear by that Act, that the ſaid Convention of Eſtates was called not by the Defender, as is libelled, but by his Majeſty's Privy-Council, Commiſſioners for conſerving the Articles of the Treaty therein mentioned, and Commiſſioners of common burdens, all eſtabliſh'd by his Majeſty's authority *in anno* 1641, which Conſervators concerning that article in the large Treaty, bearing the Kingdom of *Scotland* their deſire for unity in Religion, and conformity in Church-Government, as a ſpecial means for conſerving of peace betwixt the two Kingdoms, in anſwer thereto his Majeſty, with advice of both Houſes of Parliament in *England*, doth declare his approbation of their affection in their deſire of having conformity of Church-Government between the Nations; and as the Parliament had already taken to conſideration the reformation of Church-Government; ſo they would proceed therein in due time: and this was one of the main grounds whereupon both Houſes entered the ſaid league. (2.) That the enacting and entering the League and Covenant, was an Act of that Convention of Eſtates, not the Defender's perſonal act. (3.) That the League and Covenant was entered in with the two Houſes of the Long Parliament, and aſſiſtance given to them in fighting with or for their army, or otherwiſe, which is libelled fighting with Rebels. The point of fact being thus cleared in oppoſition to the Dittay. 2. It is alledged, That the firſt two Members of this article are ſubſumed under none of the Acts of Parliament libelled on in the propoſition; there being no Act of Parliament libelled againſt meetings, bands or leagues in general; or in ſpecial betwixt the two Nations or Eſtates thereof. 3. As to the remanent members of the article, they can no ways be relevant (with all ſubmiſſion) except it were qualified, that the two Houſes of the Long Parliament, to whom the aſſiſtance libelled was given, that they were Enemies and Rebels; but that the Defender is confident it will not be ſaid, becauſe by his Majeſty's Act of Oblivion, 25 *April*, 1660, his Majeſty, after his happy Reſtoration, declares, that what was acted even againſt his Majeſty, and his Royal Father, by his Subjects in *England* during theſe times, thereafter ſhall not be called in queſtion at all, ſo much as to the prejudice of their reputation, in manner at length contained in that gracious Act. And how loyal the Long Parliament was, did appear in that the Uſurper durſt never attempt any thing againſt his late Majeſty's perſon, till they were broken, as alſo what loyalty the ſecluded Members of that Parliament have (as became them) ſhewed to his Majeſty in his juſt and glorious Reſtoration, is known to all *Europe*, to their eternal commendation and renown: No doubt as from conſcience of their oath of duty and allegiance, ſo of the oath of God whereunto they bound themſelves to maintain his Majeſty's perſon, authority and greatneſs, as well as Religion, in that Covenant. 4. All the foreſaid deeds, which are the members of this article, *viz.* The calling the foreſaid Convention of Eſtates, as being the Act of the foreſaid Council and Commiſſioners, the entering in the League and Covenant, raiſing of the army for aſſiſting the two Houſes of Parliament of *England*, impoſing Exciſe, *&c.* as all being acts of the ſaid Convention of Eſtates, together with the ſame Convention of Eſtates, are all approved by the ſaid 5th Act of Parliament, 1644. In reſpect whereof the Defender ought to be aſſoilzied from this whole article, and all the crimes contained therein. 5. Not only is the ſaid calling of the ſaid Convention of Eſtates, and the ſaid Convention entering in the League and Covenant, impoſing of Exciſe, raiſing of Forces for the Parliament of *England*, and remanent Acts of the ſaid Convention approved by the ſaid 5th Act of Parliament of 1644; but by his Majeſty's Treaty of *Breda*, and the Act of Oblivion, in the Parliament holden at *St. Johnſton* and *Sterling*, *in anno* 1650 and 1651, or either of them, all things done during theſe tumultuous times, intervening betwixt the ſaid Act of Oblivion 1641, and his Majeſty's home-coming 1650, whether prejudicial to his Majeſty's honour and authority, or to the Laws and Liberties of the Church and Kingdom, or to the particular intereſt of the ſubject, are buried in perpetual oblivion. And by the ſaid Treaty and Act of Ratification of the ſaid Parliament, or one or other of them, the ſaid Parliament 1644, and all Acts thereof are ratified; and ſo amongſt the reſt, this which is the 5th Act, which approves all the Acts, whereupon this 4th article of the Dittay is founded, and therefore the Defendant ought to be aſſoilzied therefrom.

5. As to the 5th Article, anent the burning of the houſe of *Menſtrie*, *in anno* 1645, the Defender is ſo innocent thereof, that if it were libelled relevantly, he needed no other defence but a ſimple denial; but the truth is, that it hath been burnt by ſome of the ſoldiers, commanded by Major-General *Bailey*, for the time, upon the greateſt provocations that could be, two pariſhes; *viz.* *Muckart* and *Doller*, having been burnt the night before, and ſeveral, both men, women and children, cruelly killed by the concourſe of thoſe that were in that houſe. But it is no way relevantly libelled, in ſo far as it is libelled, that the Defender, or others under his command, burnt it: 1. Becauſe there is no Act of Parliament, of all the Acts libelled upon in the propoſition, whereupon this can be ſubſumed; eſpecially the Acts anent the raiſing of fire, upon which (if upon any) it ſeems it is particularly founded, there is no ſuch odd extenſion of that ſo high a crime, as to make any guilty of it, by committing of it by others, who are under their command. And this were a very univerſal, terrible concernment; and in the preſent caſe were moſt dangerous and unjuſt, that a Commander ſhould be holden to anſwer for all the illegal deeds done by his ſoldiers. 2. It is againſt common reaſon, the Common Law, by which this therefore is well eſtabliſhed, that *delicta proprios tenent authores, & noxa caput ſequitur*; and therefore is not relevant that the Defender burnt it by himſelf, or others by his ſpecial direction, or particular order for that effect.

4. Though it were made relevant in manner foreſaid, yet the Dittay is inept as to this article, and the Defender ought yet to be aſſoilzied therefrom, becauſe the year of God is only libelled, to-wit, the year 1645; whereas not only the month, as in all criminal libels, *per L. libellorum ff. de accuſationibus*, and the Doctors treating thereupon, but the very day ought to be condeſcended on; for the omiſſion of the day prejudges the Defender of his defence; ſpecially his *alibi*, which he might and would propone, if the day were condeſcended on; that being required, the day ought to be condeſcended on, otherwiſe the libel is inept. *Nam Libellus debet continere non tantum annum & menſem, ſed & diem ſi reus id requiſierit cum probaturus ſuum alibi.* Damhaud, cap. 3. num. 4. 5. & Battander *Reg.* 6. *num.* 4. *Maranta in ſpec. de bel. Obl.* 3. *num.* 12. *per bart. in L. Si quis reus Column.* 3. *in fin. de publ. judic. & Jaſon. in L. Ubitraria* 2 *ſect. Si quis occiſi ff. de eo quod Crito loco.* But ſo it is, that if the day were condeſcended on of the ſaid burning, the Defender might, and if need were, would offer to prove, that he was that day, during all the time of the burning, *alibi*, at a conſiderable diſtance from the ſame place.

3. *Abſolvitur*, Becauſe Lieutenant-General *Bailey*, at that time when the houſe was burnt, had the command of the ſaid forces (adhering always to the former defences againſt the aptitude and relevancy of this part of the Dittay, and expreſſing the ſame that may be diſcuſs'd *ante omnia*): In reſpect whereof the Defender ought to be aſſoilzied *ab hoc libello*, at leaſt there can be no proceſs upon that part of the Dittay, as it is now libelled. 4. Albeit the Defender had burnt, or given direction only to burn the ſaid houſe, as he had not; yet by ſpecial Act and commiſſion of Lieutenancy, granted him by the Parliament 1644, he was empowered to purſue the *Macdonalds*, and their adherents and acceſſaries, with all kind of hoſtility, by fire and ſword, (with a diſpenſation) with ſlaughter, mutilations, raiſings of fire, aſſailing of houſes, taking of priſoners, and other inconvenements whatſoever, that ſhould fall out in the execution of that Commiſſion in purſuing of them; as the ſaid Act and Commiſſion may at length bear, and which commiſſion is ratified by his Majeſty in the Treaty at *Breda*, his ratification of that Seſſion of Parliament 1644, among the other Parliaments and Seſſions thereof ratified by his Majeſty, all after 1641, and preceding his return. But ſo it is, that the ſaid *Macdonalds* were at that time, at the burning of the ſaid houſe, joined with *Montroſs*; and it was in purſuance of both that the ſaid houſe was burnt, as is notorious, (and, if need be, the Defender will prove) and therefore though he had burnt, or given direction for the burning thereof, he ought to be aſſoilzied.

5. By Act of Parliament, 30th Act, 22 *March*, 1647, it is ſtatute and ordained, that all his Majeſty's good Subjects ſhall be altogether freed, and liberate in all time coming, from being any ways called, convened, purſued, troubled or moleſted in judgment, civil or criminal, or out with the ſame, for any deed done, or to be done by them, againſt the perſons, lands or goods, of ſuch as have, or ſhall be in the rebellion; (by which it is notorious, that the ſame armed oppoſition, made by the deceaſed Marquis of *Montroſs* and the ſaid *Macdonald*, and others under his command, to the Eſtates, is underſtood) during the time of their being in the ſaid rebellion, or have been, or ſhall be guilty with the rebels in their wicked courſes, or of any of them, who came under the firſt or ſecond Claſſes of delinquents, contained in the 5th Act of the 5th Seſſion of that Parliament holden at *St. Andrew*'s in the month of *January*, 1646. But ſo it is, the Defender offers to prove, if need be, that a ſon of the Earl of *Sterling*, named *Charles* or *John Alexander*, who had, or either of them had right to *Menſtrie*, had joined with *Montroſs* and thoſe under him; and ſo came under the ſecond claſs of the ſaid 5th Act of the 5th Seſſion of Parliament, 1646: Or at leaſt, went or ſent into their leaguer, or without compulſion entertained them in the ſaid houſe; and therefore the Defender ought not to be purſued, even though he had burnt, or given direction to burn the ſaid houſe (as he no ways did), and being purſued, ought to be aſſoilzied from this article; like as it is *conjunctim* alledged for the Defender in fortification of the ſaid Act, That the ſame is ratified by his Majeſty's large Treaty at *Breda*, as being one of the Acts of that Seſſion of Parliament, 1647, which amongſt the other Seſſions of Parliament, and Acts thereof, ſince the year 1641, and preceding his Majeſty's return, *in anno* 1650, are ratified by the ſaid Treaty, as alſo by the Act of ratification, at *St. Johnſton*'s or *Sterling*, in *anno* 1650 and 1651. By which ratification (or ratification of his Majeſty by the Treaty aforeſaid) the ſaid Act of Parliament 30, *in anno* 1647, comes (as a moſt ſolemn remiſſion granted by his Majeſty, and whole Eſtates of Parliament, to the perſons therein contained); and ſo like as if every one of them had got a particular remiſſion ſo ſolemn, it had been an uncontrovertible remiſſion for what were therein contained; ſo muſt it now be, being in effect of the ſame nature and virtue, albeit many be included in one.

6. By the Act of Oblivion at *St. Johnſton*'s or *Sterling*, in the year 1650 or 1651, all acts of hoſtility, whether between the King and his Subjects, or between Subject and Subject, and what things fell out in theſe times, betwixt the year 1641, and his Majeſty's return, whether prejudicial to his Majeſty's honour and authority, or to the Laws of the Kingdom, or

or the particular interest of his Subjects, are buried in oblivion. In respect whereof, though the Defender were accessary to the said burning, as he is not, yet he ought to be assoilzied.

As to the sixth article, anent the taking of the house of *Towart*, belonging to the Laird of *Lamond*, and the house of *Oscoge*, belonging to *Oscoge*; and after articles of capitulation drawn and subscribed by *Ardkinglas*, and others under his command, trust and assurance, murdering a great many of *Lamond*'s and *Oscoge*'s friends: As this is no way true, (the Defender being altogether innocent thereof) so it is no ways relevantly libelled. For, 1. Neither day nor month of these deeds are condescended on. 2. The alternity, by others under his command, not relevant to infer a crime, far less Treason against the Defender, for the reason contained in the first answer to the former article, *viz.* That there is neither Act of Parliament libelled, nor Common Law, ordaining a man to be liable to a pain, far less the highest of pains, for deeds or crimes by those under his command, except he gave them special direction. But every one is to suffer for his own fault, as more at length is contained in the said answer, which is here repeated. 3. *Non relevat* those for whom he is answerable, for the same reasons, because every one is answerable for his own fault and crime. 4. *Non relevat*, that others whom he might stop, did it; because there is neither any Act of Parliament libelled on, ordaining any to be answerable for all the deeds of those he might stop (specially the Act against murder under trust, bearing no such thing); nor is there any Law nor reason for the same, but *delicta proprios, tenent authores*, as hath been said; and no ways granting the Defender could have stopped them: for the truth is, he could not, and was not near them, when what is libelled was done: and albeit indeed, it be *contra officium charitatis*, not to stop any doing of mischief, if any one may safely do it, yet that it comes under the compass of Law to infer a crime, especially Treason, cannot be affirmed. 5. Taking of the house of *Towart* and *Oscoge*, is not subsumed upon any of the Acts of Parliament libelled, there being none of them, anent the taking in of houses belonging to the lieges, and so is not relevant to infer any of the crimes contained therein. 6. The alledged killing a great many of *Lamond*'s and *Oscoge*'s friends, after the assurance given by *Ardkinglas*, is no ways relevantly libelled, to infer the crime of slaughter under trust, because by the Act of Parliament, *Jac.* VI. *par.* 11. *cap.* 51. of slaughter under trust, upon the which it is founded, slaughter under trust, is only when the party slain is under the trust and assurance of the slayer, which is no way here libelled; but that the persons who are libelled to have been slain by the Defender, were under the trust of another, to-wit, *Ardkinglas*; who if he, or any other under the Defender's command, have done any thing against their own assurance, they are to answer for it.

7. The Defender adhering to these defences, and craving that they being against the relevancy be first discuss'd, repeats his former answer founded upon his Commission of Lieutenancy therein mentioned; for they who are designed *Lamond*'s and *Oscoge*'s friends, were the *Macdonalds*, or their adherents and accessaries, (as is notorious, and the Defender, if need shall be, offers to prove it) whom by the aforesaid Commission he had power to prosecute with fire and sword, with dispensation of slaughter, and raisings of fire, in manner at length contained in the Commission; which amongst the other Acts of Parliament, 1644, is ratified by his Majesty in his Treaty at *Breda*, as is alledged in the said answer, which is holden herein repeated; and therefore the Defender ought to be assoilzied from this article. And truly what cruelty was exercised, was by the Laird of *Lamond* himself, against the heritors and other inhabitants in the Sheriffdom of *Argyle*, for the which, upon a supplication given in to the King's Majesty and Committee of Estates at *Sterling*, in *August* 1651, he was imprisoned within the Castle of *Sterling*, till after Trial, Justice should have been done upon him; but was released by the *English* when they took the Castle, with the other prisoners. However, the Defender is confident, as it is known, so he shall make it appear, if need be, in the other process whereunto this relates, and wherein it will be more pertinent; and yet the day and time of the committing of the deeds mentioned in this article not being condescended on, as it ought to be when required by the Defender, that he may propone his *alibi*, he offers to prove, if need be, that he was *alibi* the time of the committing of the said deeds, at a very great distance, to-wit, in *England*. Like as his Majesty, by his Treaty at *Breda*, hath ratified and approved the Acts of Parliament; and his Majesty, and Estates of Parliament have ratified the said Treaty, and past an Act of Oblivion, of all former deeds done by the Subjects, which secures and indemnifies them for any former actings, in respect whereof he ought to be assoilzied.

As to the seventh article made up of several members or parts; as, 1. Anent the men alledged murdered at *Lockhead* and *Dunnaverty*. 2. Anent the aggravation added thereto; anent an old man begging his son's life, and denied him. 3. Anent the sending two hundred men from *Ila* to starve in *Jura*. 4. Anent the taking of the person of Col. *Kittoch* out of a Ship in *Leith* road, wherein it is libelled, that he had been brought by order of Parliament.

It is alledged against the seventh article, that, 1. The first part thereof (anent the men alledged murdered at *Lockhead* and *Dunnaverty*) is no ways relevant, not only in respect that the particular month and days whereupon the same should have been done, are not condescended upon, but also in respect there is not one particular person by name, and surname, whereby he might be known, condescended upon, against whom the deeds libelled should have been committed; without the which, this part of the article cannot be sustained as relevant; it being contrary to all Law and Practice, that murder in general, without naming the persons murdered, should be sustained as a relevant Dittay against any. 2. The slaughter alledged, committed upon those in the house of *Lockhead*, is not relevantly subsumed upon the Acts of Parliament libelled, in so far as there is no assurance libelled to have been given to them, to bring it under the Act of murder under trust, and there is no other Act libelled under which it can fall. 3. It is alledged, that the Defender cannot be charged with any of the deeds libelled in the said first part of the article (though they were true

and relevantly libelled, as they are not), because the expedition n
the Rebels in *Kintyre*, in the year libelled, was by *David Lesle*
under his command, against each, who, contrary to his Maj
sent to them at that time, commanding them to lay down arms
trary to their own engagements not to join with *Alister Mac*
notwithstanding continue in arms rebelliously, (as was then decl
Estates of Parliament) resisted *David Lesley* in the execution of hi
mission against them; who therefore after defeating of them ir
who took them out of the said houses of *Lockhead* and *Dunnaver*
any capitulation, and disposed of them, as the Council of War
sent with him thought fit, (which is notorious, and the Defen
to prove, if need be;) for which, and other his services, the
Lesley got the Parliament's approbation *in Anno* 1648, as the said
tion and exoneration bears date; which will clearly prove any
is herein alledged. And therefore the Defender, nor any in his
at that time, cannot be charged with any deeds libelled in the fi
this article, but ought to be assoilzied therefrom. 4. The Def
peats his third defence made to the fifth article founded upon his
sion of Lieutenancy; the persons mentioned in this article, agai
the deeds are libelled to have been committed, having been th
nalds, or the Adherents and Accessaries, which is notorious, (an
fender offers to prove, if need be) to prosecute whom he had the
sion containing dispensation, and which was ratified in manner m
in the said answer; like as he repeats the fourth and fifth answer
the said article, in respect whereof he ought to be assoilzied there

It is alledged against the second, third and fourth members o
venth article, that they are no ways subsumed, nor cannot be f
under any of the Acts of Parliament libelled, and therefore th
herein is inept, and the Defender ought to be assoilzied therefrom
in point of fact they are but mere calumnies). As to the second pa
the said old man and his son) it is no ways relevant, not con
ing on the persons names, and therefore can receive no other answ
that it is a mere fiction to make the Defender more odious, who
ously professes, that he never heard of such a thing till he saw it i
bel. The third part of this article hath no better ground than the
and the Defender desires, that for clearing his innocency of the fac
led therein (anent the sending of two hundred men from *Ila* to
Jura), that the Gentlemen in the said Isles may be examined upon t
of the matter. It is alledged, that the fourth part of this article
Col. *Kittoch*, is of the same nature with the former two, and there
simple relation of the truth is sufficient to refute the falsehood t
which is shortly this, *viz.* That Col. *Kittoch* was not brought to
either by order of the Committee of Estates or Parliament; but be
ken prisoner in *Ila*, by the forces under the command of *David Les*
delivered to the Defender, the Defender put him aboard in Captain
ship, who undertook to deliver him at *Dunstaffnage*. But Captain
finding the opportunity of a fair wind to *Leith*, to which he intend
not willing to lose the same, did not go to *Dunstaffnage*, but came
to *Leith* road; and immediately gave the Defender notice, that he
prisoner aboard; whom therefore the Defender received from hi
sent him to *Dunstaffnage*. And the Defender desires that Captain
who lives at *Weems*, may be examined upon the truth of this matt
whom he offers to prove this, if need were.

And whereas it is libelled, that Col. *Kittoch* was hanged, it is true
it is also true, that he was condemned to die in a Justice or Lieut
Court judicially; which is notorious, and the Defender offers to pr
need shall be: so that this can be a ground of no Crime nor Dittay
soever; but however the Defender ought to be assoilzied therefrom.

8. To the first member of the eighth article, that notwithstandi
manifold acts of dignity, favour and honour conferred upon him
then dread Sovereign; his Majesty being reduced to great straits by th
my of Sectaries, and having cast himself over in the hands of the ar
his *Scots* Subjects for shelter and preservation of his royal person; n
theless, the said Marquis being chief ring-leader of that factious party
then swayed the estate of affairs both in Council and Army, did so co
and complot, and by his influence so prevail, that after all fair offers
by his Majesty, and his desire to have come and lived in *Scotland*, ti
differences in both Kingdoms had been settled, an Act of Parliamen
made, for abandoning his Majesty to the mercy of his inveterate ene
the said army of Sectaries.

It is answered, that as he must continually acknowledge the late K
and his present Majesty's acts of favour, honour and trust; so must he
deny (as he safely may in the presence of God, who is the Searcher
hearts, and of all men) that he never entertained any disloyal thought
contrived any treasonable plot or machination against the sacred per
dignity or authority of his late Sovereign, or of his present most sacred
jesty; and therefore with a clear conscience may answer this Dittay:

1. That the same is not special nor clear, but very obscure and gen
how and in what manner he was chief ring-leader of any factious party
2. Who that factious party were; nor,
3. By what deeds, and how he swayed the state of affairs: nor,
4. Those means, by which, and upon whom, he procured his influe
to prevail.
5. The alledged offers made by his Majesty are not express'd;
therefore the said articles are altogether general and inept.

The Act of Parliament, which the Defendant is alledged to have p
cured to have been made, is not produced, nor indicated by number
rubrick, nor does the Defender know any Act of the tenor and title lib
led.

And the Defender in humility conceives, that it is not consistent wi
the Act libelled on, in the opposition of the Dittay, discharging persons
impugn the authority of the Estates of Parliament, to term the membe
thereof, especially in making an Act (which being carried by plurality
voices, as the deed of the whole, and especially such an Act as is me
tioned in the Libel, where there were none, or very few of a contra
judgment) a factious party.

13. The cause of the first member of the said eighth article, anent the pretended Act of Parliament, as is libelled, for abandoning and leaving his Majesty to the disposal and mercy of his enemies, the Sectarian army, does arise from the Acts of Parliament (as clearly appears), and can be subsumed on under none of the Acts of Parliament libelled: For if the tenth Act of Parliament, 1647, be understood and meaned as the Act libelled, that being an Act of Parliament, the defender humbly alledges, That an Act of an acknowledged lawful Parliament should be made a crime of accession, whereunto a Member of Parliament shall be indicted, especially for so high a crime as treason, is without ground of law or practice, and is hoped the honourable Parliament will no ways sustain it; and therefore, that he needs say no more now in confirmation hereof.

14. Likewise, all that is in that Act and substance thereof, being the Estates of Parliament their declaring their concurrence for his Majesty's going to *Holmby-House*, or some other of his houses in and about *London*; and that expresly to satisfy the desire both of his Majesty himself, and of his two Houses of Parliament in *England*; and there to remain, not under the power of Sectaries, but with such attendance about him as both Houses should think fit to appoint, with respect also had to the safety and preservation of his Royal person. And the Estates therein do also declare against all harm and prejudice, violence or injury to be done to the same (as indeed it was horrid to think that any on earth should have done), or prejudice to his Majesty's posterity: But thereafter it is clear from the fourth and seventh Acts of the Parliament, 1648, that the Sectarian army disobeyed, and threatened the Houses of Parliament, imprisoned and banished faithful Members, and by a sudden surprize, violently seized upon the person of the King's Majesty, carried him from his house at *Holmby* against his own will, and declared resolutions of both Kingdoms, and kept him under their guards; till at length, by their power and prevalency, he was committed, and kept close prisoner at the Isle of *Wight*: this being the true case out of the express words of the Acts before cited.

As to that declaration, Act 10. Parl. 1647, the defender alledges, 1. The Act bears express, that it was to satisfy his Majesty's own desire. 2. That it is homologate and approved by the Parliament, 1648, in so far as by their fourth Act, intitled, *Anent their resolutions concerning the breaches of covenant and treaties betwixt the Kingdom of* Scotland *and* England, *and demands for reparation thereof*; finds the violent seizing on his sacred Majesty's person, and taking him away from *Holmby-house*, (as appears by Act 7.) by that army, against the resolutions of both Kingdoms, a breach: And amongst the Reparations, they desire expresly, that conform to the former desires of this Kingdom, the King's Majesty may come with honour, freedom and safety to some of his Houses in or near *London*, that the Parliaments of both Kingdoms may make applications to him. And in their seventh Act, intitled, *A declaration of the Parliament of* Scotland, *to all his Majesty's good subjects of this Kingdom, concerning their resolutions for Religion, King and Kingdom*, &c. after they declare, that violently seizing on his Majesty's person, and carrying him away by that army, against the resolutions of both Kingdoms, to be a breach: And they declare, they intend to send to the two Houses of the Parliament of *England* the desires following; which they call necessary and just desires for Religion, his Majesty's good, and peace of these Kingdoms: whereof this is one, That conform to the former desires of this Kingdom, the King's Majesty may come with honour, freedom and safety to some of his Houses in or near *London*; and declares, that thereafter they will endeavour it: And Act 8. in their desires to both Houses of Parliament in *England*, the same desire is repeated, conform to the former desires of this Kingdom. By all which it is clear, that the seizing upon his sacred Majesty's person, was the violent deed of that wicked army, done with a violent surprisal against the declared resolutions of both Kingdoms. And that his Majesty's coming to some of his Houses in or about *London*, where both Kingdoms might make application to him, conform to his Kingdom's desire; which is, that wherein the Estates declare their concurrence with his Majesty and both Houses of Parliament in *England*'s desire in the said tenth Act, is approved as a just and necessary desire for his Majesty, and accordingly enacted among that Parliament, 1648, their desires to the said Houses; and declare it should be endeavoured, if refused: so highly it is approved by the said Parliament. In respect whereof, especially of the standing Acts of Parliament, 1648, the Defender humbly craves, That albeit the article was relevantly, distinctly and clearly libelled and subsumed on some of the Acts of Parliament in the proposition condescended on, (as he humbly conceives it is not) yet he ought to be assoilzied therefrom.

And for further clearing what was the ground and occasion of that Act, and the reasons inducing the Defender and the Parliament at that time to go along therein, and how little ground there is for challenging him thereon, it would be considered, That when the late King came to the army before *Newcastle*, the Defender was in *Ireland*, by commission from the Parliament, 1646; and that his Majesty's declarations anent the grounds of his resolution in coming to the *Scots*, was sent both to the Committee of Estates in *Scotland*, and to the Parliament of *England*; so that the same being printed before the Defender came to *Newcastle*, he neither did, nor could know, any other ground of his coming, nor what was contained in his declaration, *viz.* his gracious resolution to comply with his Parliaments in both Nations, and those entrusted by them, in every thing, for settling of truth and peace; and that he would totally commit himself to their Councils and Advice. Upon which terms, both the Committee of *Scotland*, and Officers of the army, declared to his Majesty, and to the Parliament of *England*, that they received him, and all this before the Defender came from *Ireland* to *Newcastle*, from whence his Majesty sent him with instructions to the Commissioners at *London* (of which Commissioners the Defender was one also) to hasten the Propositions; and privately commanded the Defender to take the advice of the Duke of *Richmond*, and Marquis of *Hertford*, anent what might concern his Majesty, and particularly, if it was fit that the *Scots* army should declare for his Majesty, whose judgment and opinion was (which they conjured him to tell his Majesty), that such a course was the only way at present to ruin his Majesty, for that he himself knew, that neither the Nobility nor Gentry of *England*, who attended him at *Oxford*, wished him to prevail over his Parliament by the sword, and much less would they endure the *Scots* army to do it, and that it would make all *England* as one man against him. And that it was their earnest request to his Majesty, by any means to give way to the Propositions. Which advice he not only faithfully told to his Majesty at *Newcastle*, and many others there, and to our gracious Sovereign who now is, when he was in *Scotland*; but also being in the Tower, he intreated the Lieutenant thereof to propose for him, that the Marquis of *Hertford*, who was then alive, might be examined in this matter, which was put off from time to time, because of his Majesty's great affairs. And as it is most certain, that neither Independent nor Sectary was able to carry one vote in the House at that time; so it is notorious, that they who tendered his Majesty most in *England*, were for disbanding the *Scots* army, and his Majesty's staying in *England*: wherein the Defender appeals to the particular knowledge of the Earl of *Lauderdale*, *Loudon*, Sir *Charles Erskine*, and the rest of the Commissioners then there. And it is of truth, which all know, that so little fear, suspicion and jealousy there was of what follow'd, that the great fear of his Majesty's friends in both Kingdoms was, that if he fixed on his subjects in *Scotland*, all *England* would be against him, and probably cast off his Government and Interest for ever: So that under what representation soever the matter may now appear, because of the sad sequels, yet to them who know the matter, as it was there stated, what declarations and assurances there were from the Parliament of *England*, and how little fear of the prevalency of Sectaries, it did appear to be an Act, if not of necessity, at least an Act very expedient and convenient for the time, otherwise many who did dissent thereto, would never have condescended; and consequently the Defender's concurring therein, upon such probable grounds, can be no such crime as is libelled; nor is it relevant to answer the conclusion of the dittay.

To the second member of this Article, bearing, that under pretext for satisfaction for the arrears of the army, he went to *London*; and there treasonably gave up, at least condescended to the up-giving of his dread Sovereign and Master, as being impowered so to do by the Kingdom of *Scotland*:

It is answered, 1. This member is not relevant, because neither the time of his going to *London*, nor of his being there, or the persons to whom he condescended to give up, are particularly mentioned and set down.

By which generality he is precluded from several defences which might arise to him if the dittay were clear; and it is a principle in common law, and of constant practice, That *non est vagandum in crimine, sed debet certum & speciatim dici*: for that *dolus & error versantur in generalibus.*

2. No ways acknowledging the relevancy of the subsumption herein, upon any of the acts of the Proposition, till the same be clearly condescended on; and craving the same may be first done, oppones the Act of Parliament: And the truth is, while the Defender was at *London*, there was nothing spoken at all by him of leaving his Majesty in *England*, except what he was expresly commanded by his Majesty to speak to *Richmond* and *Hertford*, as aforesaid.

To the third member of the eighth Article, bearing, That in a joint Committee of both Kingdoms, where the *English* questioned, whether the *Scots* army would concur with them in theirsaid treason and treachery; the Defender after many arguments used in their favour, earnestly requested them to have patience for a little time, and that it would appear how far they intended to concur. And that within few days thereafter there was a declaration and vindication emitted in name of the said army, holding forth, That in case his Majesty did not condescend to all the desires of both Kingdoms, which were no less than divesting himself of all regal power, civil, ecclesiastical and military, they would deliver him up; which immediately upon the receipt of two hundred thousand pounds the Defender and they did:

It is answered, That adhering to the former defences anent the subsumption, and repeating it here, this member, although it were rightly subsumed, as it is not, is most irrelevant and general in time, place, person and speeches; mention being made of many arguments, and never a one produced, and of a question and answer, out of which (even as libelled) Treason cannot be inferred, *viz.* That the Defender requested them to have patience a while, and it would appear how far the army intended to concur, but within few days after, the army declared themselves in manner as aforesaid: seeing these alledged words of the Defender, as they are indefinite and general, so the most they could infer is, That in a short time it would appear whether the army would concur or not. And what can from thence be inferred, as to any thing the army did? If they have outshot their duty, as it was in regard of him, with the speaking of these words, a future contingent, wherein the Defender had no casualty; so they must answer for themselves, and not the Defender.

And for aught he knows, there never was any such declaration emitted; neither should there be any captious use made of words, if there had been any such words spoken, as there never was, especially to infer his Treason; for that *lubricum linguæ* is oftener a frailty than a fault, and that by all Doctors of both Laws it is constantly held, that *verba debent intelligi ne sonent in delictum.* And that *in dubio* they should be interpreted *à proferenti.* And therefore no ways acknowledging the words and deeds libelled, except in so far as concerns the Defender's vote to the declaration, and as the circumstance libelled, That the delivery of his Majesty was immediately after the payment of 200,000 *l.* it is clear that there was no respect to that money in what was done therein, by the Act of 7 Parl. 1648, wherein the Estates there declare, That money was never the cause nor motive of any of our undertakings and resolutions, whatever our enemies had falsly suggested of that kind. And lastly, adhering to his former defences, oppones to this whole Article, the treaty at *Breda*, and the Acts of Parliament of oblivion and ratification.

As to the ninth Article, and whole first member thereof, bearing, That the Defender opposed the proceedings of Parliament, 1648, by arguing, voting, and after the Resolutions of Parliament were pass'd in an Act, in protesting against the same.

It is alledged for the Defender, 1. It is not condescended, under which of the Acts of Parliament libelled on in the Proposition, this Article is subsumed; and therefore the libel, as to that member of the Article, for arguing, voting and protesting, is inept, and the Defender hath just reason in such an incertitude to deny, that it can be relevantly subsumed on any of the said Acts of Parliament.

2. Arguing,

2. Arguing and voting is no ways relevant to infer the conclusion of the ditty; because by divine law, Law of Nations, statutes and practices of this Kingdom, *in deliberando*, a Member of Parliament or other Council, should give advice or suffrage, according to his persuasion of the good or ill of the subject debated on, and under consideration; wherein if his reason cannot bring him up, nor his conscience admit him the length of others in such public Councils, he ought to have charity for the one, and excuse for the other.

Like as by the 5th Act, Parl. 2. K. *Charles* I. it is expresly statute, That every Member of Parliament shall faithfully and freely speak, answer and express themselves upon all and every thing which is propounded, in so far as they think in their conscience may conduce to the glory of God, the peace of the Church and State, and employ their best endeavours to promote the same. Under which oath, (read in the audience of the late King, and by him approved in the Parliament, 1641) the defender, as a Peer of that Parliament, *in anno* 1648, was solemnly tied to the dictates of his reason, and prescripts of his conscience, and cannot be called in question as a Member, having freedom therein; and conform thereto is the oath of this present Parliament, bearing, that every Member shall faithfully and freely, according to their best judgment, give their advice and vote in Parliament.

To the second part of the first member of the said Article, anent the defender's protesting and dissenting from the said Act, 1648, it is alledged for the defender, The protestation is not produced as it ought to be, whereby it will appear, that if any was, the same was before the Act of Parliament pass'd, and that they did only protest and enter their dissent against proceeding to the determination of the question then in hand, which evinces the same to have been before the Act was made. Like as the defender offers himself to prove by the Members of Parliament then present, That being asked if they would renew the protestation after the Act, they shunned to do the same, the Act being now pass'd.

2. *Absolvitur*, (tho' the same were produced) because it is offered to be proved, that the same was ratified in the fourth Act, Parl. 2. Sess. 2. *Char*. II. which was approved at the treaty at *Breda*, and confirmed at *Perth* and *Sterling*, as is said. But for the honourable Parliament, their more full clearing, anent the defender's carriage in the said particular, it is offered to be proved, if need be, That the defender (before the Commissioners return from the said Isle of *Wight*, in the said year), when he heard that his Majesty had satisfied his people's desires concerning religion, in presence of divers persons of honour, he express'd himself passionately earnest to engage for his Majesty's freedom. Like as the only difference of the opinion anent the engagement was in the manner the grounds of those that were dissatisfied; being as they are express'd in the said protestation, *viz*. That the Parliament should not proceed till the commission of the Church were consulted; and adding also, (which is not therein express'd) till advertisement and three month's warning were given, conform to the large treaty; until all means of peace had been first essayed, and while first the lawfulness and necessity of that war should be found by the Parliament, conform to the 7th Act thereof. And it is humbly conceived, that many in this present Parliament do remember, how unanimous all were, that his Majesty should be brought out of the hands of the Sectaries, to some of his houses in or about *London*: And all they differed in was, that the Church should be consulted anent the securing of Religion, all means of peace should first have been essayed, and warning given in manner aforesaid, conform to the large Treaty; the breach whereof was made one of the grounds of that declaration, Act 7. And it cannot be refuted, but that at several meetings, the dissenters debated the dangerousness of that war (especially if the army should be defeated), from the sad consequences that might thereupon ensue to the King, Kingdom and Religion; as immediately thereafter fell out. Whereas had the Nation been intire and whole in their power and force, that army of Sectaries, in probability, would not have dared to have attempted those matters which afterwards they did. So that the case being truly stated, there will appear no malice against his Majesty's person, authority, and restitution thereof; but an unclearness to enter into a war of such danger and hazard, and the respect they had to the security of Religion (as all then professed) according to the Covenant.

To the second member of the ninth Article, whereby it is alledged, That in contempt of the authority of that Parliament, and against the preservation of his Majesty's person and authority, that the defender convocated an army of rebellious Subjects, and therewith committed divers and sundry outrages, slaughters and vastations, upon the persons and estates of his Majesty's Subjects; invaded cities and castles, seized upon magazines, arms and ammunition, and called in an army of Sectaries to his assistance:

It is answered, first, That the same is not relevantly subsumed upon any act of the proposition; at least till the Advocate condescend upon which act thereof the same is founded, the defender is not bound to make answer.

Secondly, The defender denies that he did convocate these forces, or gave counsel or command therefore: And as to his being with them, he must be assoilzied,

1. Because by a treaty at *Sterling*, betwixt the chief Officers of the army then alive, and out of prison; and a *Quorum* of Members of the Committee by authority of Parliament, 1648; who had power to order the incident affairs of the Nation, the said meeting, and all acts of hostility, and others thereby committed, are expresly discharged, *hinc inde*, and a mutual oblivion and indempnity therefore.

2. Any meeting he had with them, was by a call of those of the Committee of Estates, who joined with those forces, and who in the Treaty is acknowledged the Committee of Estates.

3. The said meeting and acting thereof, together with the Treaty and Articles thereof, is ratified and approved by the third Act, 2 Parl. 2. Sess. *Charles* II.

The third member of the ninth Article, bearing, That apprehending his power was not able to withstand his Majesty's good subjects, the defender called in to his assistance the army of Sectaries; and that he went into *Mordington*, and met with the commander of that army, had private consultations with him, and prevailed with him to come to *Edinburgh* with his army, whose coming he might have hindered; because *Oliver* [illegible] could not help his lying upon the tenants of *Mordington*, for [illegible] ing and going depended upon the defender; and that he did and consult with the Sectaries and their commanders, in *Edin* *Canongate*, in the house called the Lady *Hume*'s Lodging:

It is answered, That as to speeches and consultations in [illegible] relevant except they were condescended on; and as to the w[illegible] by *Cromwel*, if spoken by him, it was a lye, and can infer not the defender: and the occasion of his stay was till he got *Berw* *liste*, which could not be restored till the Treaty of *Sterling* was [illegible] as to his meeting and treating with him, *absolvitur*, because h[illegible] did the same by warrant of the Committee, and which Treaty in the aforesaid Act of Parliament thereafter.

To the fourth member, That he concealed and voted to the [illegible] of a letter, directed to *Cromwel*, wherein he and his complic[illegible] themselves, in the name of the Kingdom of *Scotland*, to do [illegible] endeavours, that none who had been accessary to the engage[illegible] arms at *Sterling*, in pursuance thereof, should be employed in [illegible] Trust, without the advice and consent of the Parliament:

It is answered, 1. No such letter produced.

2. Though it were produced, yet consenting and voting no[illegible] because a vote in the Committee of Estates can infer no crime [illegible] defender, nor any member thereof, nor any Act pass'd in the [illegible] mittee: especially seeing,

3. The Acts of the said Committee were ratified in the fou[illegible] the Parliament aforesaid; all ratified thereafter by the Treaty at [illegible] Acts of ratification at *Perth* and *Sterling*: and the necessity the[illegible] be also considered in respect of the large Treaty, both Kingdo[illegible] given their publick faith, that the breakers should be rendered up [illegible] servers; and that the *English* army then upon the borders, r[illegible] performance thereof against the engagers, and for farther securit[illegible] and places of strength. It was at that time counted a great favo[illegible] dering their power to have made their own terms) when they n[illegible] imposed and forced what they pleased more, yet they did accept [illegible]

To the fifth member of this article, bearing, That he did dr[illegible] least did counsel the drawing of certain instructions, given to [illegible] *Chiesly*, purporting, That the Noblemen, Gentlemen of quality, [illegible] siderable Officers, who went into *England* under Duke *Hamilton*, [illegible] there prisoners, should be kept as pledges for the peace of the Ki[illegible]

It is answered, 1. Not produced as it ought to be, that it ma[illegible] appear whether he subscribed the same or not.

2. Not relevant (one of the Committee) except it were libelle[illegible] and voted at that time; for *noxa caput sequitur*.

3. Not relevant, voted *quia in senatu nemo tenetur de consilio*.

4. Oppones the authority of the Committee, Treaty, Acts [illegible] ment, and Ratifications aforesaid.

To the last member of this Article, bearing, That he gave wa[illegible] der his hand for issuing of a proclamation against the families of [illegible] of *Rea* and *Vyres*:

It is alledged for the defender, 1. No such warrant produced [illegible] such a warrant were produced under the defender's hand, it will [illegible] appear to be as President of some Committee, and so not his person[illegible] nor such a deed as can infer any crime against him.

2. No such proclamation ensued.

3. Although ensued, yet that took no effect, and so was *minæ ta[illegible] animus ad effectum non perductus*.

4. Oppones the Act of the Committee, and Act of Parliament [illegible] aforesaid; which Parliament, and the whole Act thereof, is ratifi[illegible] Treaty at *Breda*, and approved in the Parliament at *St. Johns*[illegible] *Sterling*; wherein was also made an Act of oblivion, oftentimes b[illegible] ledged on: in respect whereof the defender ought to be assoilzied [illegible] said ninth Article, and whole member thereof, and all therein co[illegible] And because the defender has in his defences so oft alledged the Act [illegible] liament, 1649, for his vindication, he desires that it may be [illegible] (which is very observable) that by the printed Treaty at *Edinb*[illegible] *Sterling*, *September*, 1648, it is agreed and appointed by those of th[illegible] mittee at *Sterling*, 1648, that a Parliament should sit down before [illegible] of *January* next; conform thereunto, they did convene and sit d[illegible] fourth of the month of *January*, as by the said Treaty, and the [illegible] third Acts of the Parliament doth appear: whereby it is clear, [illegible] said Parliament, 1649, was appointed to sit by the Committee of [illegible] liament, 1648; who had power by the last Act of the said Parlia[illegible] convene the Parliament before the first *Thursday* in *March*, 1650, [illegible] thought fit: as also that Session of the Parliament, 1649, by the [illegible] thereof continues the same to the first *Thursday* in *March*, 1650. A[illegible] day they convened in the next Sessions, and therein ratified the Act [illegible] liament made in the former Session; and which day was the Dyet t[illegible] the Parliament, 1640, continued the same, with power to the Com[illegible] of Estates to convene the same sooner, if they thought fit, as [illegible] Whence it is evident, that the said Parliament, 1649, whether as ap[illegible] ed by the uncontroverted Committee, 1648, at *Sterling*, in the fi[illegible] sion, or as it is continued to the first *Tuesday* of *March*, 1650, in [illegible] cond Session, (both conform to the last Act of the Parliament, 1648 [illegible] subsist and sway the said defender his just reason, to found his defenc[illegible] on the acts thereof. It is also further considerable, as to the loyalty [illegible] Parliament, that therein the murder of his late Majesty was declared a[illegible] his present Majesty proclaimed and brought home, his subjects of thi[illegible] tion reconciled to him, and taken into favour, an army appointed [illegible] pose his enemies, the crown set upon his head; and that Session of [illegible] wherein the whole preceding proceedings were approved, was dignifi[illegible] the presence of his royal person.

And to the tenth Article, and that part thereof where it is libelled, the defender, *in anno* 1649, not daring to oppose in public, or in a[illegible] way, his Majesty's home-coming, he procured the application made, clogged with such limitations and restrictions, as were most derogat[illegible] monarchical Government, as is alledged to be more fully express'd i[illegible] Commission, Instructions and addresses, which are repeated as a pa[illegible] the Libel.

It is alledged for the defender, 1. Seeing the said commission, instructions and addresses are libelled on, and repeated as a part of the dittay; in all law and form of process, they ought to be produced with the libel, for the reason adduced in the defence, against the revelancy of the proposition of the dittay; and till which be produced, it cannot be consistent with the said limitations and restrictions, and how far they are derogatory to monarchical Government; and therefore till then there can be no process.

2. It is not condescended nor cleared, on which of the acts libelled on in the proposition, this Article and Members thereof are subsumed; and therefore it is obscure and inept · and in that incertitude, the defender has just reason to deny, that it can be subsumed on any of the said Acts, to infer the crime and pain libelled against the defender, none of the said Statutes making any mention of treating or in erring any pain therefore. Likewise after ruptures and differences betwixt a King and his subjects, all Lawyers and Politicians do agree, that the best and safest way of removing the same, is by Treaty; and that being concluded on, it is also their opinions, that the same are to be observed, at least so far as to exempt the subjects from punishment, to whom indemnity has been thereby premised. And in this, *Grotius de jure belli & pacis, lib.* 3. *cap.* 19. is most clear; and many others who write on that subject. And therefore the said Treaty being concluded, and after ratified by his Majesty and his Parliament, the defender cannot be called in question for his accession thereto, nor the pain of treason thereupon inferred. For the said Treaty and conditions thereof being accepted and agreed by his Majesty's voluntary contract, cannot be like as a crime, far less so high a crime as treason, against the defender.

3. *Absolvitur* from that member of the said Article; because not only after the said Treaty did his Majesty tacitly remit any crime, if any was, in the said Treaty, by admitting the defender to places of trust, by receiving the crown from his hand at the coronation, and by admitting him to take the oath of allegiance, and to be a Member of his Majesty's Privy-Council; but also after the said Treaty was ratified, there was an Act of pardon and oblivion by his Majesty and Estates of Parliament, oft-times before alledged, and is here repeated.

Though the above-written defences be relevant in law, as to the said member; yet for the defender's further vindication, the honourable Parliament would take notice, that all along the preceding Articles, all the publick actings from the year of God 1640, to the year 1648, (wherein the Generality and Representatives, both civil and ecclesiastick in the Kingdom, concurred) are charged upon the defender as his particular actings, or as if the defender had been the special author; whereas in this article anent the treating with, and bringing home of his Majesty, therein it is known the defender, according to his bounden duty, was most active and zealous; and therein he wrestled with all his might, and by his pains and God's blessing thereon, overcame many difficulties, and did effectuate the same. The libeller does so far detract from the defender's faithful discharge of his duty in this so glorious action, and without libelling the least presumption of any circumstance to make the same probable; the defender is accused, as if he had in his judgment been against his Majesty's home-coming; which because he durst not avow publickly, therefore he betook himself to underhand dealing, to clog the Treaty with limitations and restrictions, excluding the defender from all accession to the said duty, in so far as it was good, *viz.* to bring home the King, and making him to be the sole author of all libelled to be evil therein, to wit, of the limitations and restrictions. Whereas the truth is, he was active in the King's home-bringing, and was passive in the other; having laboured what he could, that there should be as few conditions, and the same as satisfactory to his Majesty as was possible at that time to obtain; which is known to all that did transact the said affair, and which, if need be, is offered to be proved. And for further clearing hereof, if this Article shall be further insisted on, my Lord Advocate will be pleased to condescend to declare who the Parties were that made the motion for addresses to his Majesty, of whom the defender should have been afraid, if he had been of a contrary judgment, to have opposed openly. For if the defender had so great sway in affairs, as all along the preceding Articles he is allowed to have had; and also if he had intended, (as is broadly and with foul mouth alledged) in the said Libel all along alledged, to have extirpated and evacuated the King's Majesty's authority, government and posterity; and had such correspondence with those abominable Regicides, as all are persuaded by the said libel to believe, in the said year of God, 1649; when the said traytors were strong, and both this land thro' divisions and otherwise, very low; and when the power was in the defender's and his complices hands, (as my Lord Advocate is pleased to libel and term them) who at that time had the managing of affairs; then was the fittest time and best opportunity, if they had any such disloyal thoughts, to have shaken off that Government. But so far did they abhor any such treachery, that they not only proclaimed his Majesty, and according to their duty owned his interest, even with the hazard of their lives and fortunes, there being none so shallow, but easily might have seen, that the discharge of the said duty would bring upon themselves and the Nation the power of *England*, (the only power of arms and armies being at that time in the abominable Regicides their hands) who did immediately thereafter invade this Kingdom.

As to the other member of the tenth Article, whereby it is libelled, That the defender, (to obstruct his Majesty's purpose, yea, in so far as in him lay, and to terrify him therefrom; by his and his complices cruelty executed upon the Marquis of *Montross*, who as his Majesty's Commissioner did represent his Majesty's person) caused to murder the said Marquis, *in anno* 1650, in manner, *&c.*

1. It is no way relevantly libelled, that the defender in general caused to murder him, except it were condescended, *quo modo* he caused; and if thereby be meant his voicing in Parliament, 1649, in the said matter; *non relevat*, because a Vote, Act, or Sentence of Parliament, is no way relevant to infer a crime against any particular member therein, as hath been oft before alledged.

Likewise, 2. The sentence of the forfeiture of the life and estate of the said Marquis, was no decree of the Parliament 1649, but of the Parliament 1645, which was homologate by several other Acts of Parliament, excepting the said Marquis among other excepted persons, as specially by and by the 22d Act of the Parliament 1648.

And yet, 3. the Defender did not vote in the business of *Montross*, as he can prove, if need be, by the members there present 1649. And as to the aggravations of the said murder, the said Marquis being his Majesty's Commissioner for the time; it is no way a relevant circumstance to aggravate the same, except it had been libelled, that the said commission had been shown to the Parliament, which nobody can affirm; but on the contrary, the said Parliament conceived they had just reason to presume that there could be no such commission for his coming against them at that time; because his Majesty, after the murder of his royal Father, very graciously had admitted their gracious applications to him.

Like as before *Montross*'s coming at that time to *Scotland*, and always thereafter, his Majesty had a Committee of the said Parliament, under the name and title of the Committee of Estates of his Majesty's Kingdom of *Scotland*.

As to the Defender, his alledged keeping correspondency with *Cromwel* in the year 1650, as the same is irrevelantly libelled, no deeds nor acts of correspondency being condescended on; so there was never any such thing. And there was one named *Hamilton*, who vented this untruth, hanged at *Sterling*, and at his death did declare, *That the same was a most unjust calumny*; and it is not to be believed that at that time he would have charged his soul with a Lye; and in Law, the words of a dying man are oraculously believed.

As to the Act of the *West Kirk*, the Defender (noways acknowledging the relevancy of the said article, as it is libelled) was so free from having the least accession to the said Act or Declaration; that so soon as he got knowledge thereof, to evidence his fidelity to his Majesty, it is offered to be proved by witnesses (for their loyalty above all exception), that when the first news came, that the Commissioners were about the drawing of the said Act, the Defender gave advice to his Majesty, to draw a fair Declaration, and to go such a length, as in freedom he could, that thereby he might prevent the said Act, and obviate the pressing thereof. But as for the other that was pressed, he was altogether against the same, and dealt with the Minister who came from the Commissioners of the Kirk, to forbear pressing his Majesty therewith, which also, if need were, might be proved.

As to the eleventh article, and subsequent articles, because the same are for deeds of compliance after the Usurpers had prevailed and were in possession; before the Defender make particular answer, it is necessary to premise in general, that it being notoriously known to the world (to the eternal honour of this Kingdom) as for that damnable usurpation of *Oliver*, not only we were not active in establishing the same, but according to our bound allegiance to our Sovereign, were to the utmost possibility of our power in arms under his Majesty; and otherways active against him, and in opposition thereto, many lost their estates, many their lives, and all of us our liberties: and when we could do no more, being oppressed by the force of the said Usurper, (as a chaste forced Virgin) we cried to God and Man, attesting Heaven and Earth against Usurpers, (even when their bloody swords were at our throats) he and his army, amongst many other execrable mischiefs, were also guilty of this usurpation. We have suffered, and been only passive under that irresistable force. And as this was the condition of the Kingdom, so specially the Defender, who as he had been most active and instrumental in his Majesty's home-bringing, (which was the only ground of the quarrel, and for which he was looked upon by them as one of their capital enemies) even so after it pleased God for our exercise and punishment, to suffer their power to prevail over all his Majesty's forces and over this Kingdom, such aversion had the Defender, even so much as to live under their power, much less to comply actively with them, that after *Worcester* fight, the Defender offered to Mr. *David Dick*, if he could get his company, or the company of any other honest Minister, that he would never capitulate with any *Englishman*, so long as he could subsist in any part of *Scotland*, either in his lands, or isles thereupon. It is humbly craved that Mr. *David Dick* may be examined. Neither did the Defender ever capitulate with them, in *August* 1652; having before that, endeavoured all that in him lay, to have persuaded those of *Athol*, *Monteith*, and others, his neighbours in the Highlands to have concurred with him, that they might have jointly made some probable force, for resisting the over-spreading power of the Usurper; but all in vain. Likewise, long before that time, the whole forces and strength of the Kingdom were surrendered, yea, the whole Kingdom, by their Deputies and Representatives (who met at *Dalkeith*, with the Commissioners of the Parliament of *England*, so called) was forced to submit to their power, and accept the tender of the Union of this Nation with *England*, proffered by them. Neither did he at the said time, in *August* 1652, voluntarily come in, and capitulate with the said *English*; but was surprized, (several Regiments of their forces, horse and foot, having suddenly come about his house, where he was for the time lying deadly sick) as can be testified by Dr. *Cunningham*, who was with him for the time, and is humbly craved to be examined thereon As also, notwithstanding the said surprizal, and the Defender's condition, though they threatened (notwithstanding his sickness) to carry him away prisoner, yet all their threatening could not prevail with him, but he did absolutely refuse to subscribe the articles first offered, which contained the tender of the union, and an obligement upon his part to promote the same, and the Government as then established, and to live peaceably; yea, such jealousy had they of the Defender, that by his capitulation he was prisoner upon demand. Neither during all the time of their power over this Kingdom, had he ever any favour of the said *English*, but was always looked upon by them with a most jealous eye. And for evidencing hereof, the Defender humbly craves, that there be a commission granted for examining of Lieutenant-Colonel *Utter*, (anent what was deponed by *Macnachtan*, and several others) *viz.* of the Defender's small affection to the *English*, or any other authority but the King's. Likewise, it is notorious how unjustly he was persecuted before the *Exchequer* here for the time, for payment of 4000*l. Sterling*, alledged to be due for by-gone feu-duties. This being the Defender's true case, it is hoped, that

that the honourable Court of Parliament will take consideration how the Defender stood out as long as he could, till he was prisoner; and will have a different consideration of Subjects acting under the lawful Magistrate in exercise of his authority by himself, or others lawfully constituted by him; and of the actions under cruel usurpation and tyranny, the lawful Magistrate being forced, for his own safety, to abandon his Dominions and People to the lust and oppression of the unjust Usurper (who was master not only of their fortunes and persons, but their lives and all that was dear to them); and had for a long time detained the possession of his unjust usurpation, and devoured the lawful Magistrate. Which case is not only differenced by all who write on that subject, but also *Coke* in the third part of the Institutes of the Laws of *England*, *cap.* 10. anent Treason, in expounding the Statute of the 25 *Edw.* III. upon the words of the Statute *le Roy*, puts such a weight upon the King's being in possession, or one of the same, that he expresly affirms, the Statute is to be understood of a King regnant, and in possession of the Crown and Kingdom; as also, that in such cases, a favourable consideration is to be had of the actions of a subject, who was particularly noticed, and jealously looked upon by the Usurper, for his affection to the lawful Magistrate and his Government. All which being remitted to the Commissioner his Grace, and the honourable Parliament their consideration, he now comes to answer to the eleventh article: against which eleventh article, and all the members thereof, as libelled, it is alledged, the said article is general, not condescending on the day or month, nor on the particular year of God, of the committing of the deeds therein libelled, but only alternative *in anno* 1653, or 1654, and therefore (as has been oft before alledged) the same is inept, and there can be no process thereon. 2. It is not condescended on, nor cleared, which of the Acts of Parliament libelled on in the proposition, this article, and several members thereof, are subsumed; and therefore it is obscure and general, and in that incertitude the Defender has reason to deny, that it can be subsumed on any of the said Acts to infer the said crime and pain.

As to that which is first libelled in this article, *That the Defender did not rise in arms with the Commissioner his Grace, and the Earl of* Glencairn, *who were commissioned by his Majesty*; the Defender repeats the two exceptions aforesaid, against the whole article, being confident this cannot be subsumed on none of the Acts libelled on. And further alledges, that it is not relevantly libelled, to infer *(vel minimam culpam)* against the Defender, far less so high a crime, except it were libelled, that your Lordship's commission had been shewed him, and he required, which was never done. And herein he may refer himself to the Commissioner his Grace's Declaration; and if his Grace does not remember, that the Defender sent him word, shewing his desire to have met with his Grace, and to have spoke with him about the business; but had never the honour to have his Grace's answer or appointment.

2. For further clearing, that his not joining, except he had been required, is no crime, it is evident from the fourth Act of the first Parliament *Jac.* I. that those only are punishable, who do not assist the King's host, being required thereto. And *Craig*, *page* 365, says, that because the King has so many Vassals, they are not obliged, nor cannot be punished; except the particular pain to be inflicted upon the away-stayer, be particularly express'd in the edict, by which they are commanded to appear. And *page* 365, he says, that those who come not, being warned by an edict, shall be punished; and *page* 370, he says, that the Vassals should not be obliged to appear at any such services, except they be desired; which commands shall be proved by his Peers. These edicts were particularly required by the fundamental Law, and were called *heri bona*, which is defined by *Cujas*, to be the calling and citation of the army, and is *lib.* 3. *cap.* 10. *quart. leg. franc.* to be the punishment of him who comes not to the King's host, when he is called: and this assertion is clearly proved from *Rague*, in his Treatise *de Jur. Reg. pag.* 53. Likewise by the said Act of the first Parliament of King *James* I. it is expresly ordained, that those who disobey to defend the King against notorious Rebels shall be challenged:

1. If they be required by the King, as is said;

2. And except they have for themselves reasonable excuses. But sure it is, the Defender not only was never required, as has been alledged, but there were even pregnant reasons, as he humbly conceives, the which seemed very probable at that time. Albeit it be the duty of all his Majesty's Subjects, to rise for his Majesty's Interest, in opposition to Usurpers; yet it was not seasonable, as affairs then stood, till either they had been defeated by sea in the engagement, that they then had with *Holland*, (whereby both the forces might have been diverted, and the transportation of Victuals and Ammunition from *England*, *Ireland*, and the parts of *Scotland* under their command, and their army in *Scotland*, might have been intercluded;) or that *Spain* and *France* had concluded that peace, whereof there was then several reports: and thereupon his Majesty's subjects in *Scotland* might have had hopes of some probable assistance in the undertakings in his Majesty's service; or that division, and, in consequence, confusion, had fallen out in the *English* army amongst themselves; whereof there seemed to be but little hope, so long as the appearance for his Majesty should meet them as against a common enemy, as it was. Like as it would be thought it should have no other effect; and as in effect the event proved, that that army never divided till they had no common enemy, against whom mutual preservation doth necessitate a mutual concourse, but all at amity one with another. And albeit a particular command had not been absolutely necessary, (if his Majesty had been there in person) yet in a juncture of time, wherein such a war was improbable for many state reasons (which induces the Defender to believe, that there was no commission granted at that time), which presumptions *excusant à dolo*; and without dole (as has been said formerly) there can be no crime. And though he had been required, yet could not have been punished for his not obeying, seeing in effect he was the enemies prisoner upon demand.

But this is conceived only to be libelled as an aggravation of what followed, which is, *That he joined in open hostility with the Usurper's forces, especially with the Colonels* Overton *and* Twisleton, *at the least* Cobbet *and* Twisleton, *at the least* Twisleton, *when he was in the Highlands, and in opposition to the said Earls*.

It is answered, 1. This member is general, not condescending upon the
particular deeds of hostility, and therefore inept; for crimin
ought to be most clear, as is affirmed by *Damhaud*, *cap.* 30.
num. 4. and should contain all the qualities of the crime alledge
ted. And as to the alternative, that he joined with one or othe
it is most lax and obscure, and therefore in that also this Ditt
And for the alternative added (at the least he gave counsel) *non r*
cause general), except the counsel were condescended on, and t
such as might fall under the Acts libelled on; and the most tha
ledged, if the time were condescended on of his alledged joinin
he was in company (it may be) with *Twisleton*; and if it was, h
ly going along with him to General *Monk* (being sent for by
that when the Earl of *Glencairn* was under treaty with him; if n
treaty was concluded, which he conceives will not be denied), an
fender being their prisoner upon demand, by his capitulation wi
General *Dean*.

It is alledged first, that a prisoner should go in company (be
manded) with, and to those whose prisoner he is, is nothing like

2. Though that had not been, yet he alledges in answer to t
ber of the alternative, anent his furnishing of several pieces of
non to *Alured*, Governor of *Air*, *viz.* That the Defender and al
his, or in his possession, being under the absolute power of the
they might command him to go, or call him where they wo
whom to go along, or to bring whatever he had to them, had i
his back, had he been able to carry it: and that cannot be imput
for any crime (otherwise who should be innocent) when subdu
they not give to their enemy of their goods, whatever he will ha
who in *Scotland* should be innocent? Behoved not all to bring th
is, in effect, did they not take what they pleased? But as for volu
ing, or joining in action with *Twisleton*, or any of the others
their service, the Defender absolutely denies the same.

Item, For his taking and relieving prisoners, *non relevat*, excep
soner was specially condescended on: specially relieving of prison
relevant to infer any crime, but on the contrary is a good office t
sons and parties; except it is libelled that he, as an Officer under
lish service, took and relieved prisoners, which can never be mad
whatever the same might import. But the truth is, the Defender
with no such things; and the Defender shall truly relate the poi
which he conceives hereby to be meant, which is as follows: Th
der hearing that his Isle and County of *Roisnaith* was pillaged, a
up the river *Clyde*, the boat wherein he was being followed by
boat; and the Defender having asked what they were? they alled
did belong to the Earl of *Glencairn*, but could shew no warrant; a
upon the Defender having some suspicion that they were rather
than soldiers belonging to the Earl, and fearing that General *Mon*
the Defender was then going to, and whom he had never seen
time, might get notice thereof, and make use of the same as a sn
Defender advised them to secure their money and arms in the han
of his servants, upon assurance that the same should be delivered t
after he should be certified what they were; and thereafter recom
them (fearing to incur the danger of a private prison) to the Ga
Dumbarton, not under the notion of soldiers under the Earl of *Glenca*
as common Delinquents for injury done to the Country. And a
turn after a few days (being tender that they should incur no dang
cured their releasement, and their names were never enrolled as p
to be exchanged; and according to his promise, he caused to be
vered their money and arms.

As to the following member of that article, *viz.* *That the Defender*
from the Usurpers, for a company of Scots *under them, and in their servi*

Adhering to the several exceptions against the relevancy of the
tions of the Dittay, and exceptions against this whole article, in the
ning of the answer thereto, specially that it is not condescended,
which of the Acts libelled on this member is subsumed, till which b
the Defender has reason to deny that it falls under any of them.
is it relevantly libelled, to infer any crime, unless it had been l
that the Defender, having commission for that pretended company
English service at that time, had levied that company, or enrolle
names as a formed company, under the *English* and their Regiment
engaged them to the Commonwealth and their service; because th
required in a soldier in any service.

1. That he be *relatus in numeros*, that is to say, inrolled, *per lex e*
Y. de Test. milit.

2. *Ut præstet Sacramentum*, that is, that they gave the oath, *ex m*
F. eod. & Veget. 2. *cap.* 6. or that the Defender had imployed them
English military service, or in execution of their orders, all which
fender absolutely denies; they never having been inrolled, given an
or engagement, or imployed in their service, as is said.

But on the contrary, and the truth is, there used to be in the said
and all other places in the *Highlands* in broken times, watches to ke
depredations, masterful reifs, and other oppressions amongst the co
people themselves and their neighbours in such times. And accord
in the year of God 1653, or thereabout, the shire of *Argyle* not bein
to entertain their watch, and pay cess also, (not being as yet well p
after the burning) General *Monk* was prevailed with, to help to ent
the said watch (like as at the same time, also several other shires bor
upon the *Highlands*, as *Inverness*, *Perthshire*, *Aberdeenshire*, *Sterling*,
barton, all of them had watches at the said times, and allowance the
from General *Monk*), who within two months did withdraw the said a
ance from the said watch of *Argyleshire*, because they refused to e
against those that were then in the hills, under the Defender's fo
others, whom the said General *Monk* also alledged they favoured
thereupon withdrew his help and allowance for the said watch, and
of the Defender what his Grace pleased.

And to evince that this was nothing but a watch, the men were no
formed company, but several Gentlemen in the shire had the ordering o
vers numbers of them at convenient and needful places of the shire,
proportionable entertainment, and without subordination as ordinar
diers; all which is notorious, and, if need be, the Defender offers to
And the Duke of *Albemarle* it is hoped will remember, how much

he was, that the Defender would not engage the said watch against the said Lord *Lorne* and his parties; and what prejudice he did still entertain against the Defender upon the said publick account. As also Colonel *Robert Lilburn*, when the Lord *Lorne* and *Kenmure* went to *Kentyre* in the year 1653, the said *Lilburn*, immediately upon the notice thereof, having come with a considerable party of the *English* army to *Dumbarton*; and sent to the Defender to meet him, and to go along with him in *Argyle* towards *Kentyre*; if the said Colonel does not know and perfectly remember, that the Defender shunned the meeting, and would not go; whereupon he returned back with the forces, after he was at the length of *Lochlomond*; whereupon the Defender humbly craves that he may be urged to declare. As also that the Countess of *Balcarras* may be examined, if the Defender did not assist her and her husband, in their passage through *Argyleshire*, as they were going to a meeting at *Finlarig* for the business in the hills, in the year 1653. Neither can it be alledged, that the Defender or any of his people did the least prejudice to any person or party that professed to be for his Majesty's service; albeit if he had been so disposed, he had, and might have had several opportunities to have done the same.

As for the member following, *That the Defender called the actings of his Majesty's forces against the Usurper, rebellion*:

It is most general, neither condescending on time nor place, and therefore irrelevant and inept; but when condescended on, he nothing doubts, but that it shall appear he spoke no such things, nor had he ever any such construction thereof.

As to the last deed in the said article, *That the Defender* in anno 1654 *took upon him power to bring off such as were in that service, and to give remissions therefore, and particularly to* John Macdowgall:

It is general, neither condescended on time nor person brought off, and therefore inept and irrelevant. And if it be meant only of the person named, *viz. John Macdougall* of *Dunolich*; it will never be made out that he was in that service, when the Commissioner his Grace and the Earl of *Glencairn* were in the field; nor that there ever was a remission granted by the Defender to him, or any other, in relation to that service.

As to the twelfth article and first member thereof, anent the Defender's *countenancing and assisting, by his personal presence, the tyrannical and treasonable Proclamation of* Richard *the Usurper and Protector of his Majesty's dominions, at the Market-Cross of* Edinburgh *and* Dumbarton:

The Defender is so notoriously innocent of this member of the article, that he might with much confidence (in place of all other defence) simply deny it. But he will do no more for defence and clearing of his innocency, than where he is to propone his defence of *alibi*, that there month and day must be condescended on, whereof none is condescended on in this member of the article; and till this be condescended on, it is inept, and the Defender ought to be assoilzied therefrom. But the days of the said Proclamation at *Edinburgh* and *Dumbarton* being condescended on; the Defender offers him to prove, that during these days he was *alibi*, and neither at the city of *Edinburgh* nor *Dumbarton* all these days.

As to the second member, *anent the Defender's procuring himself elected a Commissioner for the shire of* Aberdeen; *and accepting a Commission from them, to* Richard's *pretended Parliament, and sitting and voting therein as a Member of his pretended House of Commons*:

That the *English* usurpation was one of the most horrid usurpations that ever has been in *Europe*, against all divine and human Law, against the most uncontroverted right of the most illustrious of Kings, our dread Sovereign, and his most Royal Father of eternal, glorious memory, which none of common sense or honesty will controvert. Next, the said Usurpers having nothing but an unparalleled, unjust detention of that power, whereunto no manner of way they had the least right to, or any title whatsoever; but in place of a title, armed violence and force: the only mean (for title they had none) whereby they both *de facto* attained, and violently detained that possession unjustly, of that power whereof the only right was, and possession ought to have been our dread Sovereign's: Whosoever by arms, counsel, or otherways, aided or abetted that armed force, in establishing *de facto*, of the power in the persons of the monsters of men, and so in setting up of that abominable usurpation; that he is guilty of the highest Treason, is heartily acknowledged. But the Usurpers having treasonably thrust their and our Sovereign, his Majesty, from all possession of his just right, and having taken upon them the supreme power; and being possessed (though most unjustly) yet most peaceably therein, and keeping the same by force, as they had taken it; the case then became most singular, as to what the poor oppressed subjects under their force might do, *hoc rerum statu posito*, in this state of affairs, wherein the Usurper had treasonably put them. *Lucklama*, a most acute *Juris Consult. Ecclog.* 6. *membran. in L.* 3. *de Officiis prætorum* observes, learnedly, that *Distinctio fieri debet inter personam ejus qui Magistratum gerit (cum tamen jus ad Magistratum non habeat) & ipsum Magistratum quem gesserit; persona enim ejus est privata, hic publicus; & in publicis non tanta personæ quam utilitatis hic publicæ habenda est ratio, ut enim tutela, ait Cicero, p.* 1. *Offic. Sic procurato reipub. ad utilitatem eorum qui commissi sunt, non ad eorum quibus commissa gerenda est, & sapientes definiunt nihil aliud esse imperium nisi curam rei alienæ, ut ait Ammianus Marcellinus lib.* 29. that is, *ipsius reipub.* So *Lucklama* distinguishes betwixt the person of him who unjustly *de facto* attains the Magistracy (whose person is still but in effect private, and in the case of usurpation, a Traitor), and the Magistracy which he carries, which is publick.

Likewise, it should be distinguished betwixt acts concurring with the Usurper, transferring *de facto* in his person the power he usurps, (which are treasonable against the lawful Sovereign) and acts, whereby the oppressed subjects make use of the power now usurped; wherein the utility, not of the Usurper, but of the subjects, is respected, as *Lucklama* observes, *ubi sup.* And then *Grotius, lib.* 1. *de Jure belli & pacis, cap.* 4. *num.* 15. speaking *de invasore imperii*, of an unjust invader, while his possession remains unjust, says, the act of power is binding for the good of the Commonweal, and because it is probable the lawful Governor's will is, rather the Usurper's command should be obeyed, or take effect, than that Laws and Judgments should fail in confusion in their terms; *Restat ut de invasore imperii videamus nunc postquam longa possessione vel pacto jus nactus est, sed quamdiu durat in justæ possidendæ causa, & quidem dum possidet actus imperii quos exercet vim habere possunt obligandi, non ex ipsius jure, quod nullum, sed ex eo quod omnino probabile sit, eum qui jus imperandi habet sive est Populus ipse, sive Rex, sive Senatus, se malle interim rata esse quæ imperat quam legibus sub tali summam induci confusionem.* And *Lessius*, who is one of the Authors *Grotius* cites upon the place, says, in the place cited, *viz. Lib.* 2. *de Justitia & Jure, cap.* 29. *dub.* 9. *F.* 37. That *Tyranni usurpatione potestatis manantis ob temperandum propter bonum commune*; which is, that the Tyrant and Usurper is to be obeyed, even from the law of nature, for the publick good, in such a state of affairs; and adds, *alioque omnia essent plena latrociniis & furtis*; that is, all would be full of robberies, thefts and confusion, in that state of affairs, because of the Usurper's force the use of no other Government can be had. So that the necessity of the benefit of Government for the good of the subjects or common-wealth, especially in what relates *ad republicæ statum*, in things necessary for the standing of the common-wealth, or to evite the ruin thereof; and the interpretative and presumed consent thereupon of the Prince, who has the right to the authority which the Usurper has usurped, but is excluded by the Usurper from benefiting the subjects by it himself for the time, are the two grounds whereupon the making use of the power now in the hands of the Usurper is founded, as is said. Whereupon it is subsumed, that in our case the Invader and Usurper *Oliver* having violently taken upon him the power, after he had put his and our Sovereign from the possession thereof, oppressed by his armed force this Nation, and amongst others the defender, and *Oliver* having kept the possession all his time, and *Richard* continuing the same, the benefit of that power, which now he had usurped, and whereof he was in possession, was, as always it is, so necessary for the standing of the common-wealth, that without it men become but as fish in the sea, the lesser a prey to the oppression of the great: but especially, the said *Richard* having called a pretended Parliament, and commanded the Shires to send Commissioners thereto. Meetings and Representatives of the Nation, as they are of great use at any time, for treating common affairs of common consent, so transcendently at that time, for moderating the arbitrary tyranny of a Usurper; and that not being able to expugn his force, they might by strength of common-counsel overcome and persuade his reason to things absolutely necessary for the subsistence, at least for the preventing the ruin of the whole body of the Kingdom, and of his Majesty's Lieges therein: as was the stopping that miserable union, which the defender knew that it would be, as it had been before, at even other Parliaments, so, at that, strongly attempted, as indeed thereafter it was. Which union was that vortex wherein our Religion, our ancient Government, monarchick in his Majesty's person and family, and the interest of the nobility and our liberties were wholly swallowed up; and under pretext of being united, we were really enslaved to that pretended Common-wealth. The easing, if they could not persuade him to the taking off of the maintenance and cess, (which upon *Scotland* was sixtuple more than the proportion of *England*, and in itself so heavy, with the excise and other publick burthens laid by the Usurper on it, that more was exacted in one month, than his Majesty's royal Predecessors would have imposed or taken of taxation for an age, so that the Country could not subsist under it;) as also taking off some of the forces under which we were kept in bondage, if that at least could have been obtained: The prevention of the alteration and change of our whole laws, which was vehemently threatened, yea, and in general the confounding, and, *dolo optimo*, circumventing and defeating of the counsels, by which the event proved, it was more hopeful and easy to overcome that force, than by might or power. And as the liberty of the election of the members in *England*, at the time of *Richard*'s Parliament, made it serviceable to his Majesty in it, and hopeful to all his Majesty's friends and loyal subjects, so was it no small encouragement to the defender to go there for the same end: And at the meeting in the Committee of *Scots* affairs, and several other meetings, when they were upon the debate of the said union, the defender, on purpose to stop the same, did propone, that there could be no union, except it were agreed, that we might enjoy our Religion in *Scotland* without alteration, as it was established by our own laws: and that we might be ruled and judged according to the same laws, and except our cess were proportioned according to theirs in *England*. All which concerns the defender knew would never be granted, and were indeed so utterly improbable at that time, that the proposition thereof was construed for no other end, than for the end aforesaid, to stop the said union: likewise it did so well succeed, as in effect it did obstruct it, as the several persons of quality that were present can, and, if need be, will declare. And at that meeting, the actings and usurpation of the Usurper *Oliver*, and the oppressions of that army were of purpose much called in question to make that government and them odious, which accordingly happily followed; and such a breach and confusion amongst them was made, that their affairs thereafter could never come to any consistency, which made considerably and evidently a way to his Majesty's happy and glorious Restauration. To all which joining, that the call and command of the armed force has *parentis necessitatem*, a necessity of obeying lying upon persons under their power; it will follow from what is alledged out of these above-cited Authors, founded strongly on reason, the defender in that state of affairs had necessity and some obligation to go and essay what could be done by counsel, wisdom and prudence, since now there was no strength nor might left, effective for the standing; at least, to evite the ruin of the Country, in the particulars above-mentioned, and others of that nature, at least, the defender, as all of us, was under their force; and for eviting of his own and the Country's ruin, *habuit parentis necessitatem*: and by consequence there was no design of treason therein, but by the contrary, most loyal intentions, upon good ground of hope, and very probable appearance. And therefore it is hoped the Commissioner's Grace and the Estates of Parliament will not find this member relevant to infer so high a crime against the defender; *hoc maxime attento*, that beside publick ends, it was even a necessary self-preservative act, for the Defender had several other things of personal interest; as that they had ordained him to pay to them about 40 000 *l. sterling*, for alledged feu-duties, and in time coming so much, that both joined, he was not able to bear, and if need be, be, it is offered to be proved, and that he was most rigorously persecuted for the same; not only threatning to use real execution against his Estate, but also to imprison his person.

For eviting whereof, he was behoved to go at that time to *London*, and could not have his person secured from arrestments there, but by going in commission: And it is known that his Majesty is so gracious, as in not a few, to excuse what they did of that nature, to evite though but their own personal ruin, not imputing it to unfaithfulness in them at such a time; according to whose glorious and imitable example, it is with much confidence hoped, that the Commissioner's Grace, and honourable Estates of Parliament, will have a favourable construction of what the defender did in that particular, being necessitated thereto both for publick and private interest; without any deceit or fraud, either in the intention or event, there being nothing at that time, while the defender was there, done, for confirming the usurpation, or excluding his Majesty's Interest.

Likewise it may appear, that it was only the concourse both of publick and private interests and necessities aforesaid, that moved the defender to go at that time; because, though he was desired oft-times before to go, yet he still refused till then: He was one of the last that went to that, being the very last pretended Parliament under their power; not till long after that commissioners had gone for the Nation for several years, and that all had submitted to their constitutions, and were of necessity made use of as laws for the time.

As for the aggravations of this member, and to the first, That because of the defendant's nobility, he was incapable to have been elected, at least might have refused:

It is answered, That it is notorious, nobility was not then respected at all, nor was any ground of excuse, the meetings to the elections being commanded to all, as heretofore (and so noblemen and others heretofore met promiscuously through all the Nation) as is notoriously to all known.

And whereas it is libelled, That he had not his residence within the Shire; it ought to be repelled as irrelevant, because it is true, and was known to the Usurpers, and their Ministers and underlings, that he had land within the said Shire, and that considerable. So that he could not decline the said employment without prejudice, the will and lust of the Usurper at that time being uncontroulable, and tied to no rules of law or justice.

And whereas it is inferred, That sitting and voting in that pretended Parliament, he acknowledged his Majesty's power and interest to be in the Usurper's person: It is answered,

1. He acknowledged the same no otherwise but as all the kingdom did, to wit, *de facto*, for *de facto* the Usurper had taken or possess'd himself of the power; as his Majesty is pleased to speak of it in his proclamation anent commerce with *Portugal*, in *October* last, and had obtained the same for a long time: But neither the defender, nor any other loyal subject, ever did, or will acknowledge, that *de jure* the same belonged to him, or that he had any just right or lawful title thereto: as also *Lessius* says in the above-written place, speaking of them that seek from Usurpers that use of Government; whereunto, he says, they are holden in and obliged, once taking on them the Government, (though sinfully and unlawfully) they seek the benefit of it, says he, not absolutely, but under a tacit condition, *viz.* if the Usurpers will take upon them the Government: *Petunt*, says he, *sub tacita quadam conditione, si velit se pro principe gerere*; speaking of the Usurper. And that the Usurper would not give the use of the power he had taken upon him, but in the way he pleased, was his crime, which he continued during his usurpation. In respect of all which, it is humbly craved, that the defender may be assoilzied from the crime of treason, libelled thereupon.

Like as for the defender's further clearing in this particular, it is humbly desired, that certain ministers and others above exception, whom the defender shall condescend on, may be examined, if after his return from *England, in anno* 1658, he did not express with great joy his hopes, that business in *England* did tend toward his Majesty's advantage.

Item, That a commission be directed for examining Sir *Anthony Ashley Cowper*, and several other *Englishmen* above all exception; how the defender express'd himself in private anent his disaffection to that usurpation, during his being there the time of the said Parliament, even though to his very great hazard at that time.

Item, That certain persons, upon whose names also he shall condescend, may be examin'd, if the defender to their certain knowledge, at the time of Sir *George Booth*'s rising (which fell out immediately after the defender's return from the said Parliament) did not put himself out of the way, being informed that he was to be secured, and thereupon delay'd his journey to *Caithness*, and so be the readier to have laid hold of any opportunity that should have offered for his Majesty's service and restitution; that time being the most probable that ever offered after *Worcester* fight.

As for the precept of twelve thousand pound sterling, which is alledged the defender got from the Usurpers;

It is answered, The defender did indeed obtain a precept, but not as a reward of any service (which he never did, nor desired to deserve from them), but for what they had wrongfully intromitted with, of the half of the excise of wine and strong waters, whereunto the defender had right by Act of Parliament, before they had any power in *Scotland*.

And as to the thirteenth Article, first, for the whole Article, it is not consented on what Act of Parliament the same, consisting of three different members, is subsumed; and till it be condescended on, there can be no process thereupon.

And as to the first member thereof, anent the words alledged spoken at *Innerary*:

1. No time is condescended on, and therefore the libel in that part is inept for the reasons afore-mentioned, for which a criminal dittay ought to be special in the time, at least year and month.

2. Whereas it is libelled, he rebuked the Ministers for praying for the King, in the words libelled, or some such like words; *non relevat* as to the ministers, except the persons were condescended on, whom he rebuked.

3. *Non relevat*, some such-like words; some such-like being most general, except the words were particularly libelled, alledged to be such-like whereby the defender might advise his defences, and alledge why they were not such-like, as he would, if any words ever he spoke were c on; for the truth is, he never spoke any such words; an from rebuking any for praying for the King's Majesty, that aft at *Worcester* (which is the general time libelled, wherein he sho buked the ministers for praying for the King), he himself caus praying for his Majesty both in his Parish-Church and Family, presence and audience of the *English* when they came there, th to his great hazard so to do.

As to the second member anent the words libelled and allec been spoken by the defender at *London*, That he wondered hov should be so mad as to call home a family whom God had rejected never restore; or some such-like words:

First, This is also general; neither time, that is, year nor mon ticular place, condescended on.

Secondly, It is libelled, That it was in the presence of quality, they ought to be condescended on.

Thirdly, In so far as it is libelled the defender said, The peop to call home his Majesty; it is general and inept, not condesce people, and what was the occasion; if there was any motion mad home the King, whereupon that should have been spoken, whom it was. And *Dambaud, cap.* 30. *prax. com. num.* 4. and A criminal dittay should be most clear, and contain *omnes crim qualitates, lib.* 30. *F. de accus.* and *Bart.* and others, *ibid.* tha contain all the qualities of crimes alledged to be committed.

Fourthly, Some such-like words *non relevat*, except the word cially condescended on: which if they were, the defender would evince they were no-wise such-like: for the truth is, he never such words, but on the contrary did all that he could there to ma his Majesty's happy Restauration; as has been at length cleared

And was a very suspected person, in so far as in the year one th hundred fifty-seven, *Oliver* was so jealous of the defender, tha manded him to stay at *London*, and not to return to *Scotland*, till as he was pleased to express, were settled. So that not without culty, by the mediation of the Lord *Broughil* and *Charles Fleetwo* tained his liberty: Whereupon the defender desires the said *Cha wood* may be examined, which he also desired at *London*. And was suspected, as odious to the *English* for his known affection t as is notorious, and has also before been expressed.

As to the third member of the said article, anent the alledged *Mastertonne*'s;

1. Neither the year nor month condescended on, and therefore g to the time, and inept.

2. As to the first member thereof, That he would own any thi done;

First, It is exceedingly general, and not relevant; except what things he had owned were specially condescended, and what time, month: It is an unparalleled generality, and therefore till made sp process thereupon.

Secondly, It can import nothing in common sense, wherein thing is to acknowledge it for a man's own; but what he had ledged to be his own, whether word or deed, he would yet ackno which is an expression of ingenuity, and no crime: And this be received sense of owning, the word cannot be strained to any othe or if occasion should be taken so to do, and that another sense coul on that expression, yet being *more interpretatio capienda est*, the mo interpretation is to be taken, *Perd. ea quæ S. I.* 1. *F. de reg. juris* ing both justest and safest by that law. And in ambiguous speec such as may receive two senses, every man is the best expounde own mind, and his interpretation ought to be admitted, *per leg. in a F. de reg. juris*, and other laws. But the sense aforesaid is so plai there is no place for caption.

As to what follows in the said member, That if what he had ow done were to do, he would do it again, albeit he had known that all t been would have come.

1. As to what is alledged against the first part of this member, T is exceedingly general as to the time and month he should have spoke

2. As to what the things are that he would do if they were to be and that time the things were done, or owned to be done, or that the that he would do if they were to do, is a crime.

3. What were those things in particular that are understood, or subsumed under the general of all things that have come to pass; upon it may be inferred, that that were a crime for the defender to said, that notwithstanding of them he would do what he had done, i were to do; and therefore the libel in this part of the member is also ral, obscure and inept. And to evince the ineptitude of this generality pose the defender were thus indicted; You are indicted for all th have done the times by-gone, preceding your being in *James Master* house, after your coming for *London*: were not that dittay witho controversy irrelevant? Then is it not also irrelevant to be indict owning in general that he had owned, or saying in general, that he do that he had owned during that time, if that were to do again, wi any farther particular condescendance?

Like as, 4. There is a very clear, obvious and benign sense these may have, (if ever he spake, as he truly never remembers that he spak such words) that if it had been possible that times could have retu and actions to be done under the same circumstances and representa they had then, it is probable these same might be the defender's actions a though he had known what had come thereafter, not having conne with, or necessary dependance on these actings, each does not so muc import his present thoughts or approbation thereof, but is very cons with a present disapprobation of the same. And is it not ordinary to that if such times were as have been, or such motives or circumstanc actions as have been, that it is very like I would be engaged in as well as others, or as I have been myself; and yet to say great consistence I ought not so to do, like as truly it is kn and if need be, is offered to be proved, that the defender, o just contrary, had said to one of *Cromwel*'s Councillors, an many other famous Gentlemen, that things had been done wher would have been very far from engaging in, if he had seen what followed, which was the product of the corruption of evil men, that had abused what was well intended, for accomplishing of their wicked ends, and (till they brake forth and could not be resisted) unknown designs. And the Defender hopes the sense aforesaid is very clear, and even though it were not so obvious, yet *rapiendu est occasio quæ benignum præbet responsum, L. Rapiend.* 168. *F. de reg. juris.* That is, any occasion should be even taken, as it were, though there were some violence done to the words for a benign interpretation; and therefore by all means that interpretation of the words that may seem to infer a crime ought to be eschewed. Or if the word might be drawn to any other sense, yet *in dubiis benigniora præferenda sunt*, as has been said, in speeches dubious, the most benign sense is to be preferred, *præt. semp.* 56. *F. de reg. juris*; or where words are obscure, or may suffer two senses, the party's own interpretation is to be taken as the best interpreter of his own mind; *Per ea quæ ff.* 1. *F. de reg. juris.* And *odia sunt restringenda, favores ampliandi*; what is odious, (as that which may infer a crime against any) should be restricted, and favour amplified; and in general, the Judge is always to be more inclined to absolve than condemn, and so consequently take the sense that may absolve, rather than that which may condemn, *Leg. Corianus F. de oblig.* & 47. *act.*

5. The Doctors say, that *voluntas & propositum delinquentis distinguunt facinora per legem expressam, leg. qui in jur.* 53. *F. de furtis in præ.* that is, the will and purpose of him that commits a crime, distinguisheth it; but *velleitas*, or *voluntas inefficax*, as it is called, not a will, but a would, is no purpose to do, and can be the cause of no crime; especially being about things past, and qualified with an impossible condition, if things already done were to do, which is altogether impossible, that a deed done can return to have a new Being, and so to be done. And even there is some presumption of that mistake may be in this, from the place libelled, in which it is alledged to have been spoken, it being such as it is not improbable, that men may be very apt to fail both in judgment and memory, and so both wrong themselves and misconstrue others. And as for the aggravations that follow, that by speaking these words the defender took upon him by outward success, to give judgment upon the secret Counsel of the Almighty: 1. As it is in no wise true that the defender spoke any of the words libelled; so this does, as he humbly conceives, in no wise follow upon the words immediately going before, alledged spoken in *Mastertonne*'s, *viz.* That the Defender owned what he had done, or would do the same if it were to do again; for that is not any judgment given of any hidden counsels of the Lord's, but an expression at most of his own actions. And as for the words before these, albeit he had been so presumptuous as to say them, as he blesses the Lord he never was, yet it is not libelled, that any thing that is therein alledged to have been spoken, either at *Innerary* or *London*, was spoken or inferred from Providence and success. For the Defender blesses the Lord, he has been otherwise taught than to use, or rather to abuse so *Turkish* an argument, and which the Lord has by his Majesty's happy restoration so signally refuted.

And as to the last aggravation, that the Defender thereby hardened others, such as otherwise were not ill disposed, in their wicked courses towards his Majesty; it is indeed a sad reflection upon others herein not called. However, 1. It is so general, both as to these others and their courses, that it cannot, and the Defender hopes it shall have no weight; especially considering that, 2. The Defender oppones his defences before alledged, against all the members of this Article; whereby it is clear, that as they are libelled, they can infer no such thing, in respect of all which the Defender ought to be assoilzied also from this Article of the Dittay.

As to the last Article, 1. It is not condescended under which of the Acts of Parliament libelled on, it is subsumed; and till then, it is ineptly libelled, and there can be no process thereupon. Moreover, the Defender has the testimony of his own conscience, yea, and of an higher, that nothing libelled therein is true. Albeit if he had said, that the Usurper's hazard was great from his Majesty, and if his Majesty's designs took effect they were ruined, the same were notorious truths, and it ought to have been so; that is, it ought to be, and it was good, they were in hazard from his Majesty's designs; and it was most just that his Majesty's designs should take effect to their ruin. And what crime could be in so saying, he cannot apprehend: however, he never spoke any such words to *Cromwell* or *Ireton*, which *Ireton* he never saw with his eyes; and did far more abhor the least thought of giving counsel to challenge, or question his late Majesty upon his precious life; and his innocency shall rest confident, absolutely to deny the same.

And as to the last part of this Article, whereby it is libelled, that *in anno* 1649, in face of the Parliament then sitting, he told, that the Usurper *Cromwell* had told him, that *England* and *Scotland* would never be at peace till the King were put to death; the Defender adheres, as to this part, to the general exception against all this Article.

That it is not condescended under which of the Acts of Parliament libelled on it is subsumed, till which be done, there can be no process; and if it be intended that it be subsumed under the 43d Act, 2 Parl. *Jam.* I. and the 134th Act, Parl. 1. and 10th Act and 10th Parl. and 205th Act, 14th Parl. K. *Jam.* VI. all these Acts, as both by their titles and tenours, and by *Skene* in his Index on the words Leasing-makers, appears; and it seems by their conjunction in this libel, they are understood also therein of lying and slandering his Majesty and his Progenitors: and the words libelled, though very horrid, yet seem to be of another nature. And 2. To that Act 205, Parl. 14. *Jam.* VI. whereon only any thing can be subsumed against him for concealing and not apprehending; 1 It is general as to the time when *Cromwell* should have told it to him, and therefore inept till the time be condescended on, which must be; especially seeing, if it be not condescended on to have been after the engagement was broken, nothing can be subsumed on the said Act thereupon against the Defender, nor on his not apprehending him; for he was not holden thereto by that Act expresly, except (according to Law it had been in his power. But so it is, it is known, that at that time it was not in the power of the whole Kingdom to apprehend him, whether his victory or strength be considered, or the Kingdom's low and weak condition at that time, wherein they lay open to ruin by him, if the Lord had not restrained him more than their power could effectuate. And as to the concealing and not revealing, the Defender ought to be assoilzied; because by the express words of the Act, that revealing is declared to be such a revealing to some of his Majesty's Privy-Council, or some under-officer, &c. as that there-through the authors of slanderous speeches may be called, tried, and punished: But that cannot be subsumed, except it were subsumed that the speeches were spoken before witness, otherwise could not have been proved, and without probation could not have been so urged, as that sentence could have been given thereupon, and the Author punished according to the words of the Act, which is also according to Common Law, and which is hereafter cleared. Like as if the words thereafter should have been found treasonable, and the Defender not being found able to have proved them, he should have brought himself under the crime of treason, for accusing another of treason, and not being able to prove it, and therefore could not be holden so to do. As also, albeit the Defender had heard any such words as is libelled, (which he altogether denies) and that before witness, yet through his revealing thereof, the Author could not be tried or punished; for it is notoriously known, it was above the power of the Kingdoms at that time, as is said, or for many years thereafter, to punish him; and therefore the Defender's not revealing cannot be subsumed upon the said Act of Parliament, to infer the pain contained therein, or related unto.

Lastly, the pains of the said Act, and other Acts before-mentioned together therewith, is not the pain of treason, as has been oft before evinced; and therefore the Defender cannot be convened for treason, or the pain thereof, upon the said Acts, but ought to be assoilzied therefrom.

But if this member of this Article be intended to be subsumed under the last part of the proposition of the Dittay, whereby it is alledged, that by Common Law and Practice of this Kingdom, all concealers and not revealers of any malicious purpose of putting violent hands on the sacred person of his Majesty, or purposing of killing and putting him to death, are guilty of treason; the defender protesting his innocence in never concealing any such purpose, nor the words aforesaid libelled, which he abhors, he is so far from justifying thereof, judging the horrid murder of his Majesty to have been the very ruin of our peace and happiness: Yet as to the relevancy of that part of the proposition, in so far as is founded upon Common Law and Practice only, the Defender, because of the preparative, repeats what was before alledged in the answer to the proposition, in that part thereof: And adds further, *In crimine læsæ Majestatis*, in the crime of lese Majesty, *Num sciens tractatum proditionis contra principem vel patriam, & illum non relevans, sit puniendus pœna mortis*; that is, whether he that knows a treaty about treason against his Prince and Country, be punishable by death. *Clarus, l.* 5. *S. fus. pract. crim. quest.* 57. says, that many hold he is punishable by death: And that *Cagnol.* in his *lib. Culpa caret F. de reg juris num.* 2. that it is the common opinion, citing *Alciat. in lib. tacere F. de verb. sig. & m. l. bona fide, num.* 20. *F. de poss.* & *in lib.* 4. of *Cato num.* 30. *F. de verb. oblig.* related also by *Gigas, de crimine læsæ Majestatis fol.* 180. *num.* 10. *Roll. Cons* 88. *num.* 10. *lib.* 2. *Carol prac. crim. fol.* 253. *num.* 29, saith, that all others follow this opinion. And *Baldus* cries out in one certain counsel, that because *Bartol* held otherwise, therefore his soul for that, as a crime, is tormented in hell. Where it is clear, that even by *Clarus*'s acknowledgement (which is very high treason) is not Treason, by the common opinion of the Doctors, according as is asserted by the famous Authors he cites, and whom he contradicts not therein. 2. And *Clarus* nothing contradicting, but this is the common opinion, albeit he be of another mind with *Bartol*, that it is capital to conceal, and not reveal, yet it is only in two cases; to wit, *In tractatu qui fiat contra ejus personam vel statum*; that is, where he has been conscious to, and known any treaty or consultation against the Prince's Estate or Person. But as for other causes, he holds expresly, that the concealer, and not revealer, is not punishable by death, in these words; *In aliis autem casibus etsi sint comprehensi in crimine læsæ Majestatis non putarem esse puniendum pœna mortis subditum qui non revelaverit*: And that he counsels Princes even in these cases, to use clemency and humanity, rather than severity; and to excuse their subjects upon any probable cause, from the pain of death. Whence, 3. It is alledged, even according to *Clarus*'s opinion, concealing not relevant to infer the pain of death, except where the concealer has been conscious to, and heard some treaty, that is, deliberate consultation against the Prince or his Estate. But so it is, the words libelled, especially what is alledged to have been heard in Parliament, 1649, seems not to import that, being, as would appear, but *volitantia verba*, if any such thing had been heard, which the Defender absolutely denies; and importing indeed the Author *Cromwell*'s thought or opinion, that there would be troubles still so long as his Majesty *(horrendum dictum)* were not put to death. But *Clarus, lib.* 5. *prax. crim. F fin. num* 87. distinguishing betwixt *cogitationem nudam*, a naked thought, and *tractatum*, a treaty or consulting; he affirms that a naked or sole thought is not punishable in any crime, no, not in Lese-Majesty, except only heresy, when guilt is perfected in the mind. And thereafter, *num.* 2. he moves the question, *Sed pone quis non steterit in meris terminis cogitationis, sed ulterius etiam processerit ad tractatum cum aliquo de ipso maleficio committendo.* But, says he, put the case that any has not contained himself within the bounds of a thought, but has proceeded further to treat with any for committing the crime, &c. thereby making a clear difference betwixt a clear, sole thought, and a treaty about committing the crime. Now the words, as they are libelled, do not import any treaty with any for committing that horrid murder, but the signification only of *Cromwell*'s damnable thought, what might be the consequence of not taking the life of our dread Sovereign.

And hence, 3. It will follow, that these words cannot be subsumed relevantly, under that part of the proposition of the Libel; because that any sense these words seemed to have, as they are libelled, would appear only to import his naked thought of what might be the consequence of taking the life of our then dread Sovereign, but no purpose of his to take the same. Neither could any presume, albeit his thought anent that consequence had been true, (as it is most contrary to the truth) that yet any man, in whom there had been the least sparkle of common reason, or conscience, would have purposed to commit, or committed one of the highest evils of sin, to evite, though very great evils of punishment, it being a received rule among men, at least among Christian men, that the least of the evils of sin should not be committed, to evite the greatest of the evils of punishment.

4. *Gomez*, a most excellent Lawyer, is clear in his third *tom. variar. resolv. de crimine læsæ majestatis, num.* 8. that concealing even of treason, is only then punishable, when the concealer might prove it otherwise; not *per text. leg. nostris, in fine cap. de calumniat. & L. quæ accus. capite, cap. de edendo*: whereby it is said, that whosoever counsels to accuse, should have his proofs ready, and who accuseth falsely shall be punished as the party accused would be, if the accusation were proved. *Gomez* citeth the canon law, *Platla, Hippolatus*, and others for their exception, which *à fortiori* holds in our law, whereby the 49th Act Parl. 11. *Jam.* VI. accusing any of treason, not being able to prove, so that the party accused be acquit, being so far reprobate by our law, that it is declared, that thereby the accuser shall incur the same crime of treason whereof he accused the other; is a sufficient warrant to the defender not to have revealed that of *Cromwel*, if there had been any such speech, as the defender never heard any such, except he had witness to have proved it; which neither is libelled, nor can be alledged, and therefore he ought also to be assoilzied therefrom.

5. All these laws anent concealing and not revealing, (as the defender humbly conceives) must be understood where the treason is privately plotted, and the execution thereof is carried on by secret conveyance, and which by revealing might be crushed and prevented. But it is notorious that the Usurper, as he had the power of armed force, so he had the unparalleled boldness to carry on his execrable treason most openly; and that his power was such, as it was impossible for his Majesty's poor subjects of this Kingdom to resist (nor yet his Majesty's other Kingdoms, though far more powerful, and that many thousands of them from their souls abhorred the said act) or prevent and impede the same. And if the defender had heard any such words of the Usurper (as he has just reason to deny he ever heard), whatever they should import; what probable reason might have been for not revealing it at that time, from the prevalency and power of that enemy, the condition of our poor Country, and utter impossibility to bring him to punishment, beside the want of probation: and so what place there were to *Clarus*'s counsel of humanity, the defender leaves to the Commissioner's Grace, and the honourable Estates of Parliament to judge.

6. Whatever relevancy there were in the defender's concealing, yet his acknowledgment thereof in Parliament, 1649, as libelled, *non relevat*, to infer or prove it. 1. Because a confession that prejudgeth a party must be prejudicial, that is, *In judicio, idque utroque jure & civili & canonico*; as says *Panormitan. C. ex parte decret, de confess. num.* 16 that it must be in judgment in a process, wherein he who confesseth is convened, as is clear by *Leg.* 6. *F. de confess.* where the words are, *Si dum quis convenitur, confiteatur*, that is, If any be convened, confess, *&c.* and *Panormitan. dicto loco* saith, That to the end a confession may prejudge him, who confesseth, it must be among other requisites, *super re litigiosa*, that is, on any thing litigious, or any thing in dependance or process, *per L. in confessionibus, F. de Interrog. ait*, the words are, *Confessionibus falsis respondentes, ita obligantur, si ejus nomine de quo quis interrogatus sit, cum aliquo sit actio*; that is, any in making answer is obliged by false confessions, if there be any action or dependance against him, upon that whereupon he was interrogate and confessed: and *Panormitan* is express, *ubi supra*, That *non valet confessio, facta coram Judice, tanquam in judicio, nisi Judex ad hoc sedeat, per Bartol. in l·b. si confessus, F. de custod. reor.* That is, a confession is not valid, though made before a Judge, as in judgment, except the Judge be sitting on that business. Whence it is clear, that the acknowledgment libelled is no ways relevant to infer against the Defender what is libelled to have been thereby acknowledged, except it were libelled, that he had been in judgment convened thereupon, or that there was a process depending against the said defender, wherein he had confessed what was libelled in judgment, and the Parliament had been sitting on that process. But so it is, that neither is it, nor can be libelled, and therefore his naked acknowledgment not relevant; and in effect, if in any discourse before the Parliament, any such word had escaped the defender, (which he in no wise acknowledges) yet that such a passing and indeliberate word should infer or prove a crime, or so high a crime against him, he is hopeful the honourable Court of Parliament will be very far from ever finding: For the very reason, why confession has so much weight, is because it is presumed that no man will confess against himself in Judgment, that whereupon he is convened and processed, without great deliberation: which holds not, if the acknowledgment be giv[illegible] cess, there being no dependant action or process upon t[illegible] And therefore the defender is confident that he need no[illegible] nourable Court with more legal dispute against the rele[illegible] ledged acknowledgment.

7. The words or acknowledgment libelled as spoke[illegible] 1649, can never be obtruded to the defender; nor that [illegible] to the Counsel of that horrid murder of his late Majesty: [illegible] torious, and he offers to prove, if need be, that the whol[illegible] said Parliament, 1649, and he himself, amongst others [illegible] ment, were purged by their solemn oaths of all knowled[illegible] to that wicked design in relation to the King's Majesty a[illegible] liament.

8. And yet he is so confident he never spake any such [illegible] ment, that the day being condescended on, and dyet of [illegible] ment, as by all doctors is agreed it ought to be, then th[illegible] to prove his *alibi*: He offers to prove, (if need be) he was [illegible] et, and so not in Parliament, where he is alledged to h[illegible] words. And yet that the defender's innocency, as to the ac[illegible] ledge of that horrid murder, may yet further appear, it is [illegible] persons, and to some of the Members of this present Parlia[illegible] *Cromwel* was in *Scotland, in anno* 1650, notwithstanding it [illegible] malice he had to the defender at that time, in this particu[illegible] himself concerning the Marquis of *Argyle, That he thought hi[illegible] neither courage nor honour to have been upon such a business.* A[illegible] thanks God he had so much honour and honesty, as in no [illegible] cessary thereunto, and to abhor the same.

9 The defender ought to be assoilzied from the two last A[illegible] all the other, from the year 1641, to his Majesty's coming [illegible] *land, in anno* 1650, because of the ratification and oblivion [illegible] Majesty's treaty at *Breda*, and most full and ample Act of [illegible] oblivion at St. *Johnston* and *Sterling, anno* 1650 and 1651.

And in regard the deeds libelled are either such as preced[illegible] and Act of oblivion, *in anno* 1641, and were thereby pardon[illegible] in oblivion; for such as intervened after the year 1641, befor[illegible] home-coming, in the year 1650, during which time he [illegible] charged with several deeds which are irrelevant, and where[illegible] der is most innocent. And for such public actings as the defe[illegible] ed with, and had accession to, the defender is also secured an[illegible] his Majesty's treaty, and gracious condescendance at *Breda*, [illegible] so thereafter ratified in Parliament, or are deeds of necessary [illegible] both for the public and self-preservation in that unhappy jun[illegible] compliance, as it was sore against his inclination, if it ha[illegible] power to have helped it, so it is not more th[illegible] whole Kingd[illegible] far less than many condescended to: It is in all humility ex[illegible] the defender should not be brought under the compass of law [illegible] which were as to make him the singular sufferer in so universa[illegible] there can be no precedent therefore instanced, either out of S[illegible] Holy Writ, the Histories of our own, or of other Nations, t[illegible] not having contributed to the said usurpation, but to his powe[illegible] same, when the said unjust usurpation prevailed, expelled the [illegible] gistrate, detained the unjust usurpation for many years, and tyra[illegible] the people when the lawful Magistrate could not rule for the [illegible] tect or help; that the said subject for his compliance, and using [illegible] for necessary, public, and self-preservation, should be indicted [illegible] crime, is in all humility conceived without precedent or parale[illegible] contrary to the current of example and practice, that may be [illegible] ture and other Histories adduced, and not so suitable to that g[illegible] natural clemency, whereof his Majesty hath given so abunda[illegible] others, even the Usurpers and Invaders, and who aided and [illegible] without envy be it spoken; and which is not only most agre[illegible] Majesty's gracious inclination, but very suitable to that advice [illegible] royal Father to him; in whose words, in one section, there a[illegible] *Your Prerogative is best shewed and exercised in remitting, rather th[illegible] ing the rigour of the Law, than which nothing is worse.* In respe[illegible] and of the defences above-mentioned, the defender ought to be [illegible] from this Libel, and the whole Articles therein contained.

See *State-Trials, Vol.* II. *page* 428, 429, 430, and 431. for B[illegible] *net*'s Account of the further Proceedings on this Trial *, an[illegible] quis's speech on the Scaffold.

* The Author of *an Apologetical Relation of the particular Sufferings of the faithful Ministry and Professors of the Church of* Scotland, *since* August, 1660, in *page* 81, and 82, gives the following Account of the Proceedings against this Nobleman.

This his compliance with them, at that time, by sitting in their Judicatories, and their concurring with his advice and counsel, for the good of the land that under their feet, is the only particular ground upon which his sentence is founded, and the particular, special cause pretended, for which he was condemned [illegible] as a Traitor, and to have his head put on the top of the Tolbooth as an eminent Traitor. A sentence which, questionless, at first view, may make all men standing astonished, and to wonder how ever it could have entered into the mind of the Parliament of *Scotland*, to sentence unto death such a Peer of the Land, [illegible] ful Member of the Kingdom, and an Ornament, upon such a ground, and for such a cause. But if these four particulars be considered, the matter will yet appear [illegible] derful.

1. The matter of compliance with the *English* at that time, was so far from being accounted treasonable, that several of the Lawyers, (among whom was [illegible] *Fletcher*, who was now advanced to be his Majesty's Advocate, and did accuse this worthy Nobleman of Treason) did swear and subscribe an oath, to be faithful [illegible] Government, as it was then established, without King and House of Lords. Now if there had been treason really in this deed, either by the civil law, or by the laws of the land, would not the lawyers have perceived it, whose daily work and study the laws are?

2. If this had been the deed of this nobleman alone, the matter had been less to have been wondered at; but it being such a deed whereof few of the Nobles [illegible] were altogether free, yea, whereof many of the Members of Parliament his Judges were guilty, the matter is beyond a parallel. It is hard to make *fores crim*[illegible] and condemn the accused, reason would require that the table should be purged. Is it not strange for a Parliament to condemn one for such a fault, for whic[illegible] their own Members might with as much justice and equity be condemned? And is it not strange, how they being, by their own confession, Traitors in the highest deg[illegible] sit and judge others? It is true, it will be replied, That his Majesty might pardon whom he pleased: But then it will evidently appear, that not this, but some [illegible] was the cause of this worthy nobleman's death. Whatever may be said in point of law, yet it will be a dispute in point of conscience, If Kings may pardon such [illegible] do deserve death by the law of God, or if such crimes which Kings may pardon, of their own accord, and according to their own good pleasure, do before the L[illegible] death?

3. If the Parliament had thought this particular worthy to bear so much stress, why would they have spent so much of their time in searching for other grounds [illegible] on? and why did they not make use of this at the first? But it is like this had never once been mentioned, if they had been able to fasten treason upon any other [illegible] tions. And this makes it so much the more to be wondered at, that they would condemn such a nobleman for such a particular, which they would never once na[illegible] if they could have done their intended work otherwise.

4. Is it not strange, that of all the compliers of *Scotland*, there was not one, except this nobleman, impannelled upon this account, much less put to death; yea, strange that those noblemen were never once questioned, who being desired by General *Monk*, when he was entering *England* with his army to encounter *Lambert* [illegible] jure King *Charles* and his interest, and this nobleman must die? Yea, is it not yet more strange that one *William Purves*, who by complying had occasioned almost [illegible] many noblemen, burghs and gentlemen, should have been absolved by Act of Parliament, (as might be cleared, if there were a table of the unprinted Acts set down [illegible] [illegible] and yet th[illegible] nobleman must be sentenced to death, for complying for the good of the Country?

But to [illegible] in point of law, [illegible] particular Queries be considered, and then any shall be able to perceive the [illegible]

[illegible] By what Act of Parliament is such a deed [illegible] treasonable? By what municipal law can any Member of the Kingdom be charged [illegible] of treason for [illegible] with a conqueror for life and liberty; [illegible] sitting in his councils for the good of the country, after that he, with the rest of the [illegible] [illegible] after the whole land had been overcome in several battles, and wholly over[illegible] [illegible] the King and Country, before the victory obtained; but in all points had carried [illegible] [illegible] What Act of Parliament declareth such a deed as this treasonable, and such [illegible]

2. Was there ever ſuch a *Practique* in *Scotland* ſince ever there was a King in it? Several times was the Kingdom of *Scotland* over-run by the Kingdom of *England*, particularly in the days of *Baliol*, and at that time King *Edward* cauſed the Nobles of *Scotland* to ſwear allegiance unto him. But when *Bruce* came to be King, was there any of the Nobles queſtioned for treaſon upon that account? And ſeeing there can no inſtance be produced out of the Hiſtory of *Scotland*, ſince ever it was a Kingdom, that any ſubject, nobleman or other, was accuſed of high-treaſon, for ſuch a cauſe, ſurely this nobleman's caſe is unparallel'd.

3. Is not this ſtrange, conſidering what the principle of Royaliſts is? They ſay, *That conqueſt giveth a juſt title to a crown*; ſo ſayeth *D. Ferne*, *Arniſæus*, and *Maxwell*, in his *Sacro-Sancta Regum Majeſtas, cap.* 17. And by this principle *Cromwell* was the lawful ſupreme Governor of the Kingdom of *Scotland*, and had juſt title and right to the crown thereof, having now conquered the ſame. And if this principle of theirs be true (which is much queſtioned by their oppoſites), no compliance with him could, by any law in the world, be treaſon againſt any Prince whatſoever; for obedience unto, and concurrence with a lawful ſupreme Magiſtrate, can be treaſon againſt no man living: How then could this nobleman be challenged upon the account of treaſon for compliance? Let all the Royaliſts anſwer this, without contradicting themſelves, if they can.

4. Is there any Lawyer who can produce ſuch a definition of treaſon againſt a Prince, or a ſupreme Magiſtrate, out of the Civil Law, as will condemn the deed of this worthy nobleman, and make compliance with a Conqueror for the good and ſafety of the Country, after all means of Defence are broken and loſt, an Act of Treaſon? And ſince the Civil Law can condemn no ſuch deed as treaſonable, the ſentence given out againſt this nobleman muſt be without all warrant of law.

5. Are there not many Countries, Kingdoms and Cities that have been over-run by their enemies, and have had their own lawful Governors put from them, and ſo have been forced to live under the feet of ſtrangers? And hath it not been uſual for them to comply with ſuch as had the preſent power in their hand, for their own ſafety and the good of the place? And was it ever yet heard, that ſuch were accuſed and condemned of treaſon againſt their own lawful Governors, thruſt from them ſore againſt their wills, for any ſuch compliance? And is it not wonderful that this eminent nobleman ſhould become a preparative to all the world.

XXIX. The Trial of the Lord Morley, for Murder, *April* 30, 1666. 18 *Car.* II. before the Houſe of Lords.

MEMORANDUM*, That upon *Saturday* the 28th of *April*, 1666, *Anno* 18 *Car.* II. all the Judges of *England*, *viz* myſelf, *J. K.* Lord Chief-Juſtice of the *King's-Bench*; Sir *Orlando Bridgman*, Lord Chief-Juſtice of the *Common-Pleas*; Sir *Matthew Hales*, Chief-Baron of the *Exchequer*, my brother *Atkins*, brother *Twiſden*, brother *Tyrell*, brother *Turner*, brother *Browne*, brother *Windham*, brother *Archer*, brother *Raynsford*, and brother *Morton*, met together at *Serjeants-Inn* in *Fleet-ſtreet*, to conſider of ſuch things as might in point of Law, fall out in the Trial of the Lord *Morley* †; who was on the *Monday* to be tried by his Peers for a murder: and we did all, *una voce*, reſolve ſeveral things following, *par.* 1. Firſt it was agreed, That upon the letter of the Lord High-Steward directed to us, we were to attend at the Trial in our ſcarlet Robes, and the Chief-Judges in their Collars of SS, which I did accordingly. But my Lord *Bridgman* was abſent, being ſuddenly taken with the Gout; the Chief-Baron had not his Collar of SS, having left it behind him in the Country, but we all were in ſcarlet, but no body then had a Collar of SS, but myſelf, for the reaſons aforeſaid.

2. It was reſolved, That in caſe the Peers who are Triers, after the evidence given, and the Priſoner withdrawn, and they gone to conſult of their verdict, ſhould deſire to ſpeak with any of the Judges to have their opinion upon any point of Law, that if the Lord Steward ſpoke to us to go, we ſhould go to them, but when the Lords aſked us any queſtion, we ſhould not deliver any opinion, but let them know we were not to deliver any private opinion, without conference with the reſt of the Judges, and that to be openly done in Court. And this notwithſtanding the precedent in the caſe of the Earl of *Caſtlehaven*, was thought prudent in regard of ourſelves, as well as for the avoiding ſuſpicion, which might grow by private opinions, all reſolutions of Judges being always done in publick.

3. Although we were not all agreed in the precedent of the Lord *Dacre's* caſe, cited by Sir *Edw. Coke*, in the Pleas of the Crown, *p.* 29. & 30. that the Judges may deliver any opinion in open Court, in the abſence of the Priſoner, yet it was agreed, that if the Lord Steward ſhould in open Court, demand any of our opinions in any thing, though in the abſence of the Priſoner, we were to give anſwer to the queſtion, the Lord High-Steward ſhould demand of us; we being call'd to aſſiſt the Court, and the demand of any queſtion in ſuch caſe being referr'd to the diſcretion of the High-Steward.

4. It was reſolved by us all, That in caſe any of the Witneſſes which were examined before the Coroner were dead, or unable to travel, and oath made thereof, that then the examinations of ſuch Witneſſes, ſo dead or unable to travel, might be read; the Coroner firſt making oath that ſuch examinations are the ſame which he took upon oath, without any addition or alteration whatſoever.

5. That in caſe oath ſhould be made, that any Witneſs who had been examined by the Coroner, and was then abſent, was detained by the means or procurement of the Priſoner, and the opinion of the Judges aſked whether ſuch examination might be read; we ſhould anſwer, that if their Lordſhips were ſatisfied by the evidence they had heard, that the Witneſs was detained by means or procurement of the Priſoner, then the examination might be read, but whether he was detained by the means or procurement of the Priſoner, was matter of fact of which we were not Judges, but their Lordſhips.

6. Agreed, That if a Witneſs who was examined by the Coroner be abſent, and oath is made that they have uſed all their endeavours to find him, and cannot find him, that is not ſufficient to authorize the reading of ſuch examination.

7. Agreed, That no words, be they what they will, are in Law ſuch a provocation, as if a man kill another for words only, will diminiſh the offence of killing a man, from murder to be manſlaughter. As ſuppoſe one call another ſon of a whore, or give him the lye, and thereupon he to whom the words are given kill the other, this is murder; but if upon ill words, both the parties ſuddenly fight, and one kill the other, this is but manſlaughter, for it is a combat betwixt two upon a ſudden heat, which is the legal deſcription of manſlaughter ‡: and we were all of opinion that the Statute of 1 *Jac.* for ſtabbing a man, not having firſt ſtruck, nor having any weapon drawn, was only a declaration of the Common Law, and made to prevent the inconveniencies of Juries, who were apt to believe that to be a provocation to extenuate a murder, which in Law was not.

8 Agreed, that if upon words two men grow to anger, and afterwards they ſuppreſs that anger, and then fall into other diſcourſes, or have other diverſions for ſuch a ſpace of time as, in reaſonable intendment, their heat might be cooled, and ſome time after they draw one upon another, and fight ‖, and one is killed, this is murder; becauſe being attended with ſuch circumſtances as is reaſonably ſuppoſed to be a deliberate act, and a premeditated revenge upon the firſt quarrel, but the circumſtances of ſuch an act being matter of fact, the Jury are Judges of thoſe circumſtances.

Lord High-Steward's Commiſſion.

CAROLUS ſecundus Dei gratia Ang. Scot. Fran. & Hiber. Rex, fidei Defenſor. &c. Clariſſimo Conſanguineo & Conciliario noſtro Edwardo Comiti Clarendon Dom. Cancellar. Angliæ Salutem. Sciatis quod cum Thomas Dom Morley & Mounteagle nuper de parochia S. Egidii in campis in Com. Midd. coram nobis apud Weſtm. de felonia & murdr. per ipſum Thom. Dom. Morley & Mounteagle commiſſ. & perpetrat. per Sacram. probor. & legal. Hom. Com. præd. indictat. exiſtit. Nos conſiderantes quod Juſtitia eſt Virtus excellens & Altiſſimo complacens, eaq; præ omnibus uti volumus, ac pro eo quod officium Seneſcalli Angliæ cujus preſentia pro Adminiſtratione Juſticiæ & executione ejuſdem in hac parte firm. requiritur (ut accepimus) jam vacat, de fidelitate, prudentia provida, Circumſpectione & Induſtria veſtris plurim. confidentes, ordinavimus & conſtituimus vos ex hac cauſa Seneſcallum Angliæ ad officium illud cum omnibus eodem officio in hac parte debit. & pertinen. (hac vice) gerend. occupand. & exercend. Dantes & Concedentes vob. tenore preſentium plenam & ſufficientem poteſtatem & authoritatem & mandat. ſpeciale indictament. præd. eundem Thomæ Dom Morley & Mounteagle concernen. cum omnibus illud tangen. a delect. & fidel. noſtro Joh. Kelyng Milite Capital. Juſticiario noſtro ad placita coram nob. tenend. & aſſign. in cujus Cuſtodia remanent, recipiend. & illud inſpiciend. & ad certos diem & locum quos ad hoc providetis ipſum Thomæ Dom. Morley & Mounteagle coram vobis evocand. & ipſum ſuperinde audiend. & examinand. & reſpond. compellend. ac fine debito terminand. Nec non tot & toties Dom. Proceres & Magnates hujus regni noſtri Angl. ejuſd. Thomæ Dom. Morley & Mounteagle pares per quos rei veritas in hac parte melius ſciri poterit ad diem & locum præd. ex cauſa præd. coram vobis comparare aſtringend. veritateq; inde comperta ad Judicium per vos inde Seneſcall. noſtrum Angl. in hac parte reddend. ſecundum Legem & Conſuetudinem regni noſtri Angliæ (hac vice) verſus præfat. Thomam Dom. Morley & Mounteagle procedend. ſententiend. adjudicand. & Executionem inde fieri præcipiend. Ceteraq; omnia & ſingula quæ ad officium Seneſcalli Angliæ in hac parte pertinent & requiruntur (hac vice) faciend. exercend. & exequend. Et ideo vob. mandamus quod circa præmiſſa diligenter intendatis ac ea fac. & exequamini in forma præd. Damus autem univerſis & ſingulis Ducibus, Marchionibus, Comitibus, Vicecomitibus Baronibus, & aliis Officiariis, Miniſtris & Ligeis noſtris quibuſcunq; tenore preſentium firmiter in Mandatis quod vobis in executione præmiſſorum intendentes ſint conſulentes, aſſiſtentes, obedientes & auxiliantes in omnibus prout decet. Mandavimus enim prætat. Capital. Juſticiar. noſtro pred. quod Indictament. præd. cum omnibus illud tangen. ex cauſa præd. vobis deliber. Mandavimus etiam Locumtenenti noſtro Turris noſtr. London. ſive ejus Deputat. ibidem quod ad certos diem & locum quos ei ſcire fac. prætat. Thomam Dom. Morley & Mounteagle coram vobis venire fac. In cujus rei Teſtimonium has literas noſtras fieri fecimus patentes, teſte meipſo apud Weſtm. duodecimo die Aprilis Anno Regni noſtri decimo octavo.

Per ipſum Regem propria manu ſignat.

BARKER.

Breve de Certiorari.

CAROLUS ſecundus Dei gratia dilect. & fidel. noſtro Joh. Kelyng Milit. Capital. Juſtic. noſtro ad placita coram nobis tenend. aſſign. Salutem. Vob. mandamus quod quoddam Indictament. de Felonia & Murdro unde Thomas Dom. Morley & Mounteagle nuper de parechia S. Egidii in Campis in com. noſtro Midd. in noſtra curia coram nobis apud Weſt. indictat. exiſtit, & penes vos in cur. noſtra jam remanen. cum omnibus ill. tangen. Clariſſimo

* *Kelyng's Reports, page* 53.

† *Vide Moore's Reports*, 621. Reſolved by all the Judges, that on a Trial by Peers, the Priſoner cannot challenge any of the Peers that are returned on his Jury.

‡ *Vide Crompton's Juſtice* 23. *a. b.* Two play at tables, and fall out ſuddenly, and one with a Dagger kill the other. If there be a quarrel, and a reaſonable time before they fight, it is murder.

‖ Two fall out ſuddenly, and fight preſently, and one kill the other, it is but manſlaughter. So if after they have quarrelled, they preſently go into the field and fight, one kills the other, 'tis but manſlaughter; for all is one continued act of fury. But if two fall out ſuddenly, and before any blows, preſently appoint to go to the field and fight, and one kill the other, this is murder, becauſe it appeareth by chooſing a fit place to fight, their reaſon was above their paſſion, and ſo a deliberate act. *Vide Crompton's Juſtice, page* 23.

Consanguineo & Consiliar. nostro Edwardo Comiti Clarendon, Cancellar. nostro Angl. & hac vice Senescallo Angl. sub sigillo nostro deliberetis indilate, una cum hac brevi ut ipse Senescallus inspectit Indictament. præd. & ceteris ill. tangen. ulterius inde (hac vice) fieri fac. quod de jure & secundum Legem & Consuetudinem regni nostri Angl. firmit. faciend. Teste, &c.

BARKER.

Breve de venire fac.

CArolus secundus, &c. dilecto & fidel. nostro Joh. Robinson Militi & Baronetto Locumtenenti Turris nostr. London. vel deputat. suo ibidem Salutem. Vobis mandamus quod Thomam Dom. Morley & Mounteagle nuper de parochia S. Egidii in Campis in com. nostro Midd. de Felonia & Murdro indictat. & vestra in Custodia infra Turrem nostram London. præd. detent. coram Charissimo Consanguineo & Consiliar. nostro Edwardo Comiti Clarendon Dom. Cancellar. nostro Angl. & hac vice Senescallo Angliæ ad certum diem & locum quos idem Senescallus vobis scire fac. super præmissis responsur. salvo & secure venire fac. Et hoc nullatenus omittatis. Teste, &c.

BARKER.

EDwardus Comes Clarendon Dom. Cancellar. Angl. & hac vice Senescallus Angl. Joh. Kelyng Militi Capitali Justic. Dom. Regis ad placita coram ipso Rege tenend. assign. Salutem. Virtute Literarum Dom. Regis Patentium mihi direct. vobis mando firmiter injungend. quod quoddam Indictamentum de Felonia & Murdro unde Thomas Dom. Morley & Mounteagle nuper de parochia S. Egidii in Campis in com. Midd. in cur. Dom. Regis coram ipso Rege apud Westm. indictat. existit, & penes vos in cur. præd. jam remanen. cum omnibus ill. tangen. adeo plane & integre prout coram dicto Dom. Rege nuper capt. fuit quocunq; nomine præd. Thomas Dom. Morley & Mounteagle nuncupetur, in eodem coram me præfat. Senescallo sub sigillo vestro apud Westm. in magna Aula placitor. ibidem die Lunæ (viz.) tricesimo die instantis mensis Aprilis ad horam octavam ante meridiem, ejusq; diei liberetis una cum hoc præcepto ut ulterius inde fieri faciam, quod de jure ad secundum Legem & Consuetud. Regni Angl. fuerit faciend. Dat. sub sigillo meo apud Westm. 14 Die Aprilis Anno Regni Dom. Caroli secundi, Dei gratia Angl. Scot. Fran. & Hiber. Regis fidei Defensoris, &c. decimo octavo.

Per Senescallum,

FANSHAW.

EDwardus Comes Clarendon Dom. Cancellar. Angl. hac vice Senescallus Angliæ Joh. Robinson Militi & Baronetto Locumtenenti Dom. Regis Turris suæ London. vel Deputat. suo ibidem Salutem. Virtute Literar. Dom. Regis Patent. mihi direct. tibi mando firmiter injungendo quod Corpus Thomæ Dom. Morley & Mounteagle nuper de parochia S. Egidii in Campis in com. Midd. in Prisona Dom. Regis sub Custodia tua detent. ut dicitur, una cum causa detentionis suæ quocunque nomine idem Thomas Dom. Morley & Mounteagle in eodem censeatur, habes coram me præfato Senescallo, apud Westm. in magna Aula placitor. ibidem die Lunæ (viz.) 30. die instantis mensis Aprilis, ad horam octavam ante meridiem ejusdem diei, ad subjiciend. & recipiend. ea omnia quæ Cur. Dom. Regis de eo tunc ibidem consideraverit: in hac parte, & habeas ibi tunc hoc præceptum. Dat. sub sigillo meo apud Westm. 14 die Aprilis, Anno Regni Dom. Car. secundi Dei gratia Angl. Scot. Fran. & Hiber. Regis Fidei Defensoris, &c. 18.

Per Senescallum,

FANSHAW.

EDwardus Comes Clarendon Cancellar. Angl. hac vice Senescallus Angliæ Rogero Harsnett Arm' servien. Dom. Regis ad Arma Salutem. Virtute Literar. Dom. Regis Patent. mihi direct. tibi mando firmiter injungendo quod summoneas tot & toties Dom. Proceres & Magnates hujus Regni Angl. Thomæ Dom. Morley & Mounteagle nuper de parochia S. Egidii in Campis in Com. Midd. Pares per quos rei veritas de Felonia & Murdro unde idem Thomas Dom. Morley & Mounteagle indictat. existit melius sciri potuit quod ipsi personalit. compereant coram me præfat. Senescallo apud Westm. in Com. Midd. in Magna Aula placitor. ibidem die Lunæ (viz.) 30 die instantis Mensis Aprilis ad horam octavam ante meridiem ejusdem diei ad faciend. tunc & ibidem ea quæ in hac parte fuerint faciend. & habeas ibi tunc nomina prædictor. Dom. procerum, & Magnat. & hoc præcept. Dat. sub sigillo meo apud Westm. &c.

Per Senescallum,

FANSHAW.

THE Lord-Chancellor being then Lord Steward, came from *Worcester-house* in his coach, having (besides his usual attendance) Sir *John Eaton*, his Majesty's chief Gentleman-Usher, carrying a white staff nine foot long; and Sir *Edward Walker*, Garter King at Arms in his Coat of Office, attending on him. And he was met at *Westminster-hall-gate* with five Maces more, who all went before him into the Court, where he took his place in a Chair of State; the five Maces placed themselves on each side of the State; and Serjeant *Lee* went into the body of the Court, and there laid down his Mace; and he supplied the place of Marshal or Crier of the Court. Sir *John Eaton* with the white Staff, and Sir *Edward Walker* stood at the lower-end of the State; Sir *John Eaton* on the right-hand of the Lord-Steward, and Sir *Edward Walker* on the left.

The Clerk of the Crown in Chancery, standing at the lower-end of the Court, with three obeisances coming up to the Lord-Steward, on his knee presented the Commission unto him.

Sir *Thomas Fanshaw*, Clerk of the Crown in the *King's-Bench*, with the like reverence, came and received the Commission from the Lord-Steward, and returned to his place in the midst of the Court.

Serjeant *Lee*, after an O-yes, made Proclamation, *viz.* the L[ord High] Steward of *England* doth command all persons to keep silence, [while his] Majesty's Commission is reading.

Sir *Thomas Fanshaw* read the Commission.

Then Sir *John Eaton* and Sir *Edward Walker* carrying the wh[ite staff] between them, on the knee presented it to my Lord Steward, a[nd he de]livered it back to Sir *John Eaton*, who placed himself with it on t[he lower] end of the State, on the right-hand of the Lord-Steward, and Si[r Edward] *Walker* on the left, on a seat even with the body of the Court, [leaving a] space between them for the Lord-Steward to see the Prisoner; [on that] seat also sat the Clerk of the Crown in *Chancery*, and Mr. *Kips*, [the Seal-]bearer, the Seal being laid at the lower-end of the State before [the Lord] Steward.

O-yes again, and Proclamation made; The Lord High-S[teward of] *England* doth command all persons whatsoever, except Peer[s, Privy-]Councillors, and Judges, to be uncovered.

Serjeant *Barcroft* called to make return of the precept to him, who came into the body of the Court, and delivered it to Sir *Tho[mas Fan]shaw*, and he read the return on the backside of the precept.

O-yes again, and the Lords required to answer to their names.

The Lords Triers called by the list, Mr. *Waterhouse*, assistan[t to Sir] *Thomas Fanshaw*, reading their names, and Serjeant *Lee* calling,

John Lord *Roberts*, Keeper of the Privy-Seal.
Edward Earl of *Manchester*, Lord-Chamberlain.
Henry Lord *Arlington*, Secretary of State.

Aubery Earl of *Oxford*.
William Earl of *Bedford*.
James Earl of *Suffolk*.
Richard Earl of *Dorset*.
John Earl of *Exeter*.
John Earl of *Bridgwater*.
James Earl of *Northampton*.
Henry Earl of *Peterborough*.
—— Earl of *Thanet*.
Nicholas Earl of *Scarsdale*.
John Earl of *Bath*.
William Earl of *Craven*.
Thomas Viscount *Falconbridg[e]*.
John Viscount *Mordaunt*.
Philip Lord *Wharton*.
William Lord *Paget*.
William Lord *Maynard*.
Francis Lord *Newport*.
John Lord *Lucas*.
Charles Lord *Gerrard*.
John Lord *Berkley*.
Horatio Lord *Townshend*.
Anthony Lord *Ashley*.
John Lord *Freshevile*.

O-yes again, and the Lieutenant of the *Tower* called, to make [return] of his Precept, and bring in his Prisoner.

The Prisoner brought to the Bar, and the precept delivered to S[erjeant] *Lee*, and by him to Sir *Thomas Fanshaw*, who read the return [on the] backside of the precept.

Then the Lord-Steward made a speech to the Prisoner, telling h[im the] cause of his being brought thither.

The Indictment read by Sir *Thomas Fanshaw*, and the Plea made [in the] *King's-Bench*, where he had pleaded *Not guilty*, and put himself u[pon his] Peers.

Then the Lord-Steward made a speech (by way of charge) [to the] Peers.

O-yes, and Proclamation made; If any will give evidence f[or our] sovereign Lord the King, against *Thomas* Lord *Morley* and *Mou[nteagle]*, they shall be heard; the Prisoner stands at the Bar upon his deliver[ance].

Lord-Steward said, he heard the Lord *Morley* was lame, and th[erefore] bid the Lieutenant of the *Tower* set a chair for him to ease himself.

Lord *Morley* desired to be heard; but the Lord-Steward told him it was usual to hear the evidence first, and after that he might and be heard any thing he had to offer; whereupon he sat down.

Serjeant *Glynn*, the King's eldest Serjeant, opened the Indictmen[t, and] Mr. Attorney-General *Palmer*.

Several Witnesses examined; the Prisoner asking them what qu[estions] he pleased.

Two Witnesses swore, that the Lord *Morley* run him into the h[ead].

One Witness swore a former grudge *.

Another, that when he had run Mr. *Hastings* through the hea[d, he] swore, *God-damme*, I promised thee this, and now I have given it [thee]. And that the quarrel begun at the *Fleece-Tavern* about an Half C[rown] that the Lord *Morley* said he had laid down.

Mr. Sollicitor-General *Finch* desired the depositions of some Wit[nesses] taken before the Coroner (who were since dead) might be read; [which] the Prisoner opposed, desiring that no evidence might be given a[gainst] him, but face to face.

The Lord-Steward demanded the opinion of the Judges, who [by the] Lord Chief-Justice *Kelyng* delivered their opinion; that upon proof that the Witnesses were dead, and oath by the Coroner, that the [depo]sitions were unaltered, they ought to be read; which was done.

The depositions of three Witnesses read.

Serjeant *Maynard* desired, that the depositions of a material W[itness] taken at the Coroner's Inquest (who had now absented himself, so [that] they could not find him) might be read.

The Prisoner opposed it, and the opinion of the Judges bein[g re]quired; the Lord Chief-Justice delivered the opinion, That if the [Court] upon any evidence were satisfied, the Witness was withdrawn b[y the] procurement of the Prisoner, the deposition ought to be read, othe[rwise] not. Whereupon

Thomas Harding sworn, deposed, That *Thomas Snell*, his appre[ntice,] was lately run away from him, and that his fellows said, he told t[hem] before he went away, that the Lord *Morley*'s Trial was to be sh[ortly,] but he would not be there.

The Court not thinking this evidence sufficient, the depositio[n was] not read.

Lord *Morley* desired some witnesses might be heard on his side, o[n his] behalf, who were admitted, but not upon oath.

Lord *Morley* heard to say what he pleased for himself.

Mr. Sollicitor summed up the evidence as follows, *viz.*

* Mr. *Hastings* and his brother had some time before met Lord *Morley* in the street, and grossly affronted him; whereupon Lord *Morley* complained to the House of [Lords,] who ordered them first into custody, and then committed them to the *Tower*, from whence they petitioned the Lords, who discharged them upon their entering into R[ecog]nizances for their good behaviour. *Vide* Lords Journals of that time.

April 30, 1666.

The Speech of Sir *Heneage Finch*, Knt. the King's Sollicitor-General, at the Trial of the Lord *Morley* (the Earl of *Clarendon*, Lord Chancellor, being then Lord High-Steward of *England*, *Pro tempore*) who summ'd up the Evidence, &c. *

THAT a man is slain is not denied by my Lord *Morley*: the manner how it came to pass we have proved for the King. His Lordship hath endeavoured by his witnesses to difference the case in some circumstances: the question will now be reduced to this; Whether this fact be murder, as it is charged upon him in the Indictment, or any less offence than that; in which I see, my Lord *Morley* placeth his hopes, that it will fall? My Lord, because that this is a question of Law, arising from fact; I will, with your Grace's permission, and the favour of my Lords the Peers, presume in the first place, to lay down some principles or conclusions in Law, wherein, I think, I am not deceived; and would be loth to prevaricate in a case of blood. And when I have laid down the conclusions, I shall proceed to apply them to the fact now in proof before you, and compare it to such a proof as his Lordship hath produced. There are in Law but three cases imaginable, which are any way capable of excuse for the death of a man. These are, *First*, when a man kills another in his own defence. *Secondly*, when he doth it upon misadventure and meer accident. *Third*, when he doth it in heat of passion, or any sudden adventure (for that which is done in prosecution of Justice hath no affinity with the present question). The two first of these do excuse *à Toto*, 'tis not so much as felony; the last *à Tanto*, 'tis felony, but within Clergy. But yet, my Lord, the Common Law, the ancient Common Law of *England*, would not endure to hear of any excuse at all for the death of a man. By the antient Law, before the Statute of *Marlbridge*, he that killed a man in his own defence; and after that till the Statute of *Gloucester*, he that had killed a man by the most innocent misfortune in the world (the glance of an arrow, or any thing else than that) must have died for it, as a murderer. For murder is a sin so contrary to the genius and temper of the *English* nation, that whosoever looks but like it, hath ever been prosecuted by our Law, by a most strict and speedy vengeance. When the Law began to let in some kind of excuses in these cases, yet they were circled in with as wary cautions and observations; and bound and limited with as nice distinctions and differences as could be. And therefore, he that kills a man *se defendendo*, must not plead that he did it so; but he must plead *not guilty*: for it is a maxim in the Law, that the death of a man can never be justified; nay, the Jury cannot find him to be *se defendendo*, but they must find the special fact, and leave it to the Court to judge, whether it were *se defendendo*, as in circumstances. For if the fact be so, that the man did not fly to the wall, or his last refuge, before he did give the mortal wound, he is a felon still. He that kills a man by accident or misadventure, must take care that the action he was about were absolutely lawful and necessary too: for if there were an unnecessary meddling with edge-tools, or fire-arms; if there were unnecessary recreation in the act which produced this event, he is responsible to the Law for the utmost consequence. And at this day, if a man that kills another in the city escapes out of the city, the city is to be amerced for letting a notorious malefactor escape. Hitherto your Lordships see, that in these two cases, which are most pardonable of any, yet the Law is very severe; and therefore in cases of an higher nature, it is still more rigorous. Now, because the hope of this case is, that it will end in manslaughter, and because that manslaughter is only distinguished from murder, in that it is not designed, but otherwise, it is in itself an act as wilful and as violent, (though not so malicious) and so borders upon murder: I shall proceed to shew your Lordships how the Law watches upon manslaughter, with all the jealousies and circumspections imaginable; and therefore it is an undoubted principle of Law (and all the men in *England* hold their lives upon very miserable terms, if it were otherwise), if any man shall meet a man in the street, and kill him without any visible provocation, the Law supposeth there was malice precedent, and judgeth this act murder. *Secondly*, As it is murder, to kill without any provocation, so if the provocation be slight and trivial, it is all one in Law, as if there were none. For the Law of *England* allows no man to value himself at such a rate, as if the blood of his neighbour were a fit sacrifice to expiate every mean and slight affront. This was the case that fell out in the time of the most reverend Chief-Justice, the Lord *Popham*: A Gentleman of *Kent* came by another, and made wry mouths and laughed, and made such signs as usually put men into passion; the other presently fell upon him and killed him: and my Lord Chief-Justice *Popham* and his brethren delivered their opinions, that it was murder: for this was not a competent provocation; and the man was hanged upon an appeal of murder. *Thirdly*, As no provocation makes it murder, and a slight one, is all one with none; so if the provocation be great and high, and such as might be capable of excuse in itself, yet if a man be not slain in the very heat and bent of passion; if there be any interval of time, as a night's rest, and sleeping upon it, the Law knows no such period: but if there be such an interval, that the Law supposes the blood might, and ought to have been cooled again; that a man might have come to himself, and then he falls on the person that gave him the provocation, that which was passion at the first, is malice at the last; and that which would have been manslaughter then, is murder now. This I submit to your Lordships judgments, who hear me now; and if I did not think the Law was clear in these points, I would not presume to affirm it in so great and solemn an Assembly. To come to the matter of fact, I desire your Lordships to consider what Mr. *Hastings* hath done, and what he hath suffered. *First*, There appears to be so little of provocation, that the poor Gentleman that is murdered, offered any man five pound to tell him what the quarrel was. His Lordship makes his defence, that he hopes his Peers will consider, that there is no other provocation than the half-crown. I am sorry for it. I am sure the Laws of *England* allow no man to take away another's life for half-a-crown, without being guilty of murder. The first thing that is said Mr. *Hastings* should do is this: he is in a manner suspected, and hears my Lord quarrel about an half crown, and saith, I wonder a person of honour should make such a-do about an half crown, and then throws down four half crowns upon the table to make satisfaction: presently swords are drawn, and Mr. *Brommidge* draws his first, and hectors it for my Lord; then they are put up again: there is one interval and recollection of time. My Lord proceeds to quarrel with Mr. *Hastings*, and calls his sins to remembrance; and knowing that Mr. *Hastings* had been guilty of killing a man not long before, presently tells him, We come not here to stab folks; which was a bitter reply. Mr. *Hastings* is grieved to see himself so openly reproached by my Lord, and could not chuse but tell him, he was a Gentleman (and surely *Hastings* is a confessed Gentleman, and a noble name in this Kingdom, and always must be); but at last goes a little further, and saith, As good a Gentleman as my Lord. This is not comparable to laughing at my Lord, nor to making wry mouths; and yet if *Hastings* had done this, and his Lordship had killed him for it, he had stood guilty of murder. Observe, I beseech your Lordships, how Mr. *Hastings* is treated; he is four times drawn upon, twice by *Brommidge* in the house; in the street, *Brommidge* draws upon him again; and just under the arch in *Lincolns-Inn-Fields* he draws the fourth time. Now saith Mr. *Hastings*, I have no quarrel to you, Captain; if there be any, it must be disputed between me and my Lord. This is not such a speech to make a quarrel, but to prevent one: What could a Gentleman do less, that found himself four times assaulted? For if he would decline the quarrel, the best way was to put *Brommidge* out of the case, as a likely expedient. When that would not do, to the field they come. And here, my Lord *Morley* hath produced some witnesses, who being not to be sworn, have said freely, that Mr. *Hastings* pressed my Lord to fight, and saw him draw, and attack with the three on the other side. *Street* said, he resolved to fight my Lord; and another, that my Lord said he would not fight. This they bring, to make my Lord *Morley* purely passive, and only drawn to fight. Under favour, we must submit to the judgment of your Grace and your Lordships his Peers. The thing that is said here is not probable. 'Tis plain, Mr. *Hastings* had said, he would give any man five pounds that would tell him what the quarrel was: Would he that knew no quarrel have the blood of my Lord *Morley*? But then, compare this with the witnesses, which we have brought and sworn; all three expresly say, they saw the fight and the beginning of it. But with submission to your Grace, a fight it cannot be called; in truth, it is a direct assassination: for three witnesses swore, there were two upon one all the while; viz. upon Mr. *Hastings*. And Mr. *Hastings* being thus pressed steps back to get a little ground; then my Lord takes him at the advantage, and shortens his sword, and runs him in the head. Now they that say, my Lord *Morley* went away first towards his own house, have forgot that he came back again and killed the man. I press this case upon the bare want of provocation, because the consequence is great in Law: I press it, as if the proof were to be set here, and no more were to be said; and do presume to affirm, it is malice in the Law, and murder in his Lordship. But yet we shall not rest here; but if we go a little farther, your Lordships will see, here is malice apparent, malice confessed and most evident. As soon as Mr. *Hastings* was slain, my Lord *Morley*, with a most desperate imprecation, throws the sword upon him, *God damn me*, there you lie. Another swears his Lordship said, I have promised, and now you have it. Can your Lordships doubt now, whether my Lord killed Mr. *Hastings* with a deliberate hatred? You see, he confesseth it was in discharge of a promise; and my Lord is to be believed against himself. And the brother of the Gentleman hath made a sad comment upon these words, and tells us, how the promise arose, and how it came to be performed. Mr. *Hastings* tells his brother, that he once had the unhappiness to have a quarrel with my Lord many years ago, almost ten, and that fighting with my Lord, he had the misfortune to give him an hurt; and though the witness speaks only out of his brother's mouth, yet he testifies, that his brother told it him in the anguish of his spirit, as a secret that troubled him, and which he did not tell out of design, but by way of lamentation. And yet if Mr. *Hastings* had been found bleeding in the field, and been asked who killed him, and had said, my Lord *Morley* had slain him; it had been good evidence, though no other witnesses were, and though it came out of his own mouth. The brother swears farther, that my Lord *Morley* coming by, and his brother paying his Lordship due respect, my Lord received it with so much contempt, that his brother said presently, he knew not what it meant, I doubt he bears me a grudge. This was a year and an half before his death; but within a quarter of a year before, the witnesses say, his brother, his father, and my Lord, were at an ale-house; no sooner was his brother gone down stairs, but when he came up again he finds my Lord with a sword drawn, and swears that his brother then told him, that my Lord was always urging him to drink; and then would seek all occasions he could to give and take offence. So then, it seems, it was my Lord's custom to urge Mr *Hastings*, and to give him frequent provocations, as if he had sought an occasion for manslaughter, that he might kill him within the protection of the Law. This is the most desperate complication of malice that can be. To this purpose, I shall presume to put a case (which our books speak), and which will highly concern the point in this case. If my Lord *Morley* had fled to the wall, and had slain Mr. *Hastings* when he had fled to the wall, that would not have served his turn, as this case is; for our books tell us of one, who bore malice to another, and then provoked him to draw his sword; seeing the sword drawn, he fled away, to tempt the adversary to pursue, and still retired till he came to the wall; now seeing himself at his last refuge, he thought to kill him legally and safely in his own defence. But since the pretence of Law was but an art to disguise the malice of his heart, which he now executed freely, the book says it was murder: so 'twill be here. Your Lordships will give me leave on this occasion to tell you, that it is either the misfortune or the just reproach of some governments in foreign states, that there are places abroad, where murder is a cheaper sin than theft; and the same people, that will rise up in arms as one man to pursue a pilferer, will yet make a lane through the midst of them,

* Taken from the *Norfolk* Collection in the Royal Society Library.

them, for the Man-slayer to escape. Hence it comes to pass, that Men are slain every day for any thing, for nothing; insomuch that a learned Civilian writing of those Republicks, tells us plainly, *Frequentiores sunt hominum cædes, quam nativitates.* But however it be in these Commonwealths, yet we, who have the happiness to live under a monarchy, (the best of Governments) and under a King, (the best of monarchs) have all our lives secur'd to us, by his Majesty's own royal and immediate protection; and therefore no corruption of manners will ever be able to bring this sin into fashion and credit amongst us, nothing will ever naturalize it here. I do acknowledge to your Lordships (for why should I conceal any thing that makes for my Lord *Morley*'s advantage?) I do confess that an affront, or indignity offered to a Peer, is much more heinous, than that which is offered to a private Gentleman. But I must needs say withal, that the Law hath provided another manner of reparation for a Peer, than that which it gives a Gentleman. The same words that being spoken of a Gentleman, will bear no kind of action; when they are spoken to a Peer, become *Scandalum Magnatum.* The Peer recovers great damage; the King inflicts fine or imprisonment: so that upon the matter the offender is bound in chains, and brought and laid at my Lord's feet. Now for him, whose honour is thus guarded by the Law, to avenge himself by his sword, is a most unpardonable excuse. I do not pretend, I do not offer to say, that the killing of a man, is more capital in case of a Peer, than would be in the case of a private Gentleman: but I do presume to affirm, that no provocation in the world, can make that to be but manslaughter in the case of a Peer, that would be murder in the case of a Gentleman; that is this case. Will your Lordships therefore give me leave to turn the tables, and suppose Mr. *Hastings* had killed my Lord *Morley*, upon so slight and groundless a pretence; as suppose, my Lord *Morley*, in his life-time, had with grief of heart complained to his brother, that Mr. *Hastings* did bear him a secret hatred, because in a former combat his Lordship had worsted Mr. *Hastings*, and given him an hurt: Suppose, my Lord *Morley* had long before this complained farther, that he saw the effect of Mr. *Hastings*'s malice upon every occasion, and when his Lordship did but offer to salute Mr. *Hastings*, and give him a respect, Mr. *Hastings* receiv'd it sullenly and unmannerly, and return'd it with contempt; suppose that his Lordship had complain'd farther, that Mr. *Hastings* did nothing but seek occasions and pretences of a quarrel; and suppose that within a quarter of a year of my Lord *Morley*'s death, Mr. *Hastings* had been found in an alehouse, with my Lord *Morley*, and had there drawn his sword upon my Lord; and then my Lord had complain'd to his Brother, that he did believe Mr. *Hastings* would do him some mischief some time or other: And suppose, after all this, that my Lord *Morley* had been slain just in such a manner, as Mr. *Hastings* hath been, would your Lordship, would the Kingdom have thought this a sufficient account for noble blood, if Mr. *Hastings* had been only found guilty of Manslaughter, and escap'd by his Clergy, and a burning in the hand? My Lords, the quality of an offender may serve to inhance the crime; but since the world stood, it never was counted any abatement. The same duty to the King, the same obedience to his Laws, the same reverence to human nature, the same care to avoid effusion of Christian blood is expected from a Lord, which is required from the meanest Commoner of *England*. 'Tis the case of all the people of *England*, who are highly concern'd in the present example; if they put their trust in the Law, as the great avenger of blood in the world, and once find themselves deceived, who knows the consequence that may follow? Wh private families? What massacres it may produce at last? And no doubt, but all the Kingdom will observe, and mark the issue ‹ and will be curious to know, what will become of a Lord, in the blood of a Gentleman hath been so vile and inconsiderable: possible, I say, if it were possible, that so great a Tribunal as t either mistake the fact, or misunderstand the Law, what Ju there left on this side Heaven for mankind to rely on? I pret aggravate the matter: this is the place where no detestation of no passion of the Prosecutor, and no compassion of your Lordshi a Peer of the Realm, is to have any ingredient in the verdict. fore, having observ'd to your Lordships, that there is malice i the Law, and in a manner confess'd by the party, besides the formal malice which hath been prov'd; I shall now submit Judgment, which the Law hath wisely placed in your Lordi noble breasts; with this only consideration, 'tis the voice of l creth, I know your Lordships will give it such an audience as to have; such an audience as may quiet it, and keep it from c more; such an audience as may cleanse the land from blood, means to continue to your Lordships that due veneration, whic have to your Lordships most righteous and impartial proceedings

After him Serjeant *Maynard* spoke.

Lord-Steward desired the Lords to withdraw into the Court o and consider of their evidence; but he did not sum up the eviden Lieutenant of the *Tower* bid to withdraw his Prisoner.

The Lords and the Prisoner being withdrawn; Serjeant *Le* wine and biscuits to the Lord-Steward, and then round the Cour

The Lords stayed about three hours, and then returned into th and took their places.

Sir *Thomas Fanshaw* first called them according to their precede all being present, he then called them again, beginning with the who answering to his name,

The Lord-Steward asked him, saying, my Lord *Fresnevile*, is r *Morley Guilty or not Guilty?* Who laying his hand on his breast, ar *Not Guilty of Murder, but Guilty of Manslaughter.*

And in the same manner asking them all severally, they all g same answer, except two, the Lord *Wharton*, and Lord *Ashle* answered, *Guilty of Murder.*

The Lords having delivered their verdict, the Lieutenant of th was commanded to bring in his Prisoner.

The Lord-Steward told him, his Peers had found him *Guilty o slaughter*, and asked him, what he could say for himself?

He answered, he desired the benefit of the Clergy, and the ber the Statute.

Lord-Steward said, he must have the benefit of the Clergy: ar he conceived the Statute was clear in his behalf; and asking the c of the Judges, they all bowed in token of consent.

The Lord-Steward making a short speech of admonishment Prisoner, told him he was discharged, paying his Fees; and the miss'd the Court, and broke his Staff.

XXX. The Proceedings in the Court of *King's-Bench, Exchequer*, and *House of Peers*, in the (of Sir Samuel Barnardiston, Bart. against Sir William Soame, Sheriff of *Suffolk*, concerr the Election of Members to Parliament, 1674, 26 *Car.* II.

A Copy of the Record *inter Soame* and *Barnardiston.*

Placita coram Domino Rege apud Westmonasterium de Termino Sancte Trinitatis Anno Regni Domini Caroli Secundi nunc Regis Anglie, &c. *vicesimo sexto, Rotulo* 1577.

Midd. ss. MEmorandum quod alias scilicet Termino Pasche ultimo preterito coram Domino Rege apud Westmonast. venit Samuel Barnardiston Baronet. per Tho. Ditchfield Attornatum suum & protulit hic in curia dicti Domini Regis tunc ibidem quandam Billam suam versus Willielmum Soame Militem nuper Vicecomitem Comitatus Suffolcie in custodia Marrescalli, &c. de placito transgressione super casum & sunt pleg. de pros. scilicet Johannes Doe & Ricardus Roe. Que quidem Billa sequitur in hæc verba ss. Middl. Samuel Barnardiston Baronettus queritur de Willielmo Soame Milite nuper Vicecomite Comitatus Suffolcie in custodia Mar. Marrescal. Domini Regis coram ipso Rege existentem pro eo, videlicet, quod cum Dominus Rex nunc octavo die Februarii Anno Regni dicti Domini Regis nunc vicesimo quinto per breve suum gerend. dat. eisdem die & anno emanans extra Cancellariam suam apud Westmonasterium predict. in dicto Com. Middl. adtunc existent. tunc Vicecomit. Com. Suffolcie predict. directum, recitando per idem breve, quod cum Henricus North Baronettus nuper elect. fuerat unus Mil. Com. predict. pro adtunc present. Parliamento dicti Domini Regis inchoat. apud Civitatem suam Westmonasterii octavo die Maii Anno Regni dicti Domini Regis tertio decimo, & ab inde per diversas Prorogationes usq; tricesimum diem Octobris Anno Regni ejusdem nunc Regis vicesimo quarto continuat. & ab eodem tricesimo die Octobris idem Parliamentum usq; quartum diem tunc instantis Februarii ulterius prorogat. fuerat, ibidem tunc tenend. & pro sequend. Quodque ipse sic elect. & debito modo retornat. juxta formam Statuti in hujusmodi casu edit. & provis. in domo interiori communitate Regni dicti Domini Regis Anglie constitut. fuerat, prout per Record. dicti Parliamenti sui in Cance sua residend. plenius constabat, ac idem Henricus North unus Militu Com. predict. existend. diem suum clausit extremum ut dictus Don Rex acceperat, cujus pretextu subditi dicti Domini Regis Com. Suff pred. de uno Milite ad tractandum pro utilitate ejusdem Com. destitu eiunt, idem Dom. Rex nolens tamen quod Communitas Regni s dicto Parliamento suo ad negotia dicti Domini Regis & statum Regn & Ecclesie Anglicane aggregat. ex causa predicta immoraretur seu tenuaretur, quo minus negotia illa debitum sorcierentur, effectum ei Vicecomit. dicti Com. Suff. per breve ill. precepisset quod loco pre Henrici in pleno Com. suo immediate post receptum brevis illius u alium militem gladio cinctum idoneum & discretum Com. predict. (clamatione prius de premissis ac de die & loco facta) libere & indiffere per illos qui hujusmodi proclamation. ill. interessent juxta formam Sta inde editi & provisi eligi faceret, & nomen ejusdem Militis in quibus indenturis inter predict. Vicecomitem & illos qui hujusmodi Electioni teressint inde conficiend. (licet hujusmodi eligend. presens esset vel abse inseri eumq; ad dictum Parliamentum venire faceret, ita quod idem M sic eligend. plenam & sufficientem potestatem pro se & Communi Com. predict. haberet ad faciend. & consentiend. hiis que in Parliame de communi consilio dicti regni sui (favente Deo) contingerent ordir super negotiis ante dictis (noluit dictus Dominus Rex tamen, quod dictus Vic. Suff. nec aliquis alius Vicecomes dicti Regni sui aliqual esset electus) & Electionem illam sic factam distincte & aperte sub sig ejusdem Vic. & sigillis eorum qui Electioni ill. interessent dicto Dom Regi in Cancellariam suam certificaret indilate remittend. Dicto Domi Regi alteram partem Indenture predicte eidem brevi consuetam, una ci eodem brevi prout in eodem brevi plenius continetur. Quod quidem br postea scilicet duodecimo die Februarii Anno Regno dicti Domini Re nunc vicesimo quinto supradict. apud Gippovicum in dicto Com. Su

pret:

prefato Willielmo Soame tunc Vic. dicti Com. Suff existens deliberatum fuit in forma juris exequendum quodq; predictus Will. Vic. Com. predicti tunc existend. ad prox Com. suum ejusdem Com. Suff. post receptionem dicti brevis, scilicet, vicesimo quarto die Februarii Anno Regni dicti Domini Regis nunc vicesimo quinto suuradicto, ac vigore brevis illius in pleno Com. suo tunc tent. apud Gippovicum predict. in dict. Com. Suff. coram eodem Williel. adtunc Vic. ejusdem Com. breve illum legi fecisset nec non publicam Proclamationem de die & loco in brevi predicto in ea parte content. fecisset nec non de uno milite gladio cincto magis idoneo & discreto Com. predict. juxta formam & exigentiam brevis illius eligend. adveniend. ad Parliamentum predictum in pleno Com. ill. prout ill. per breve ill. precept. fuit & secundum formam ill. precept. fuit, videlicet int. horam octavam & horam undecimam antea meridiem ejusdem vicesimi quarti die Februarii Anno vicesimo quinto supradicto super quo processum fuit tunc ibidem in pleno Com. ill. ad Electionem unius alius Militis pro eodem Com. in loco predicti Henrici, per Gentes in Com. illius residentes ac eidem Proclamationi interessentes, ac licet idem Samuel in eodem pleno Com. tent. apud Gippovicum predict. (qui tunc & diu antea fuit Miles gladio cinctus in predicto Com. videlicet apud Brightwell commorans & conversans & in eodem Com Suff. natus) secundum exigentiam brevis predicti debite electus & nominatus fuit eodem vicesimo quarto die Februarii inter horam octavam & horam undecimam fore Militem Com. illius in loco predicti Henrici North pro predicto Parliamento adveniend. pro eodem Com ad idem Parliamentum per majorem numerum Gentium tunc residentium infra dictum Com. Suffolciæ, predicto tempore Proclamationis predicti tunc & ibidem present. eidem Proclamationi interessentium quorum tunc quilibet expendere potuit quadraginta solidos liberi tenementi & ultra per annum infra Com. ill. Ac licet predictus Willielmus adtunc Vict. dicti Com. Suffolciæ existens premissa satis sciens, postea scilicet eodem vicesimo quarto die Februarii anno regni dicti domini Regis nunc vicesimo quinto in Cancellarium dicti domini Regis nunc apud Westmonasterium predictum in dicto Com. Middl. breve predict. retornabit simul cum quadam Indentura inter ipsum Vicecomitem & predict. Electores ipsius Sam. de pred. Electione ipsius Sam. fact. secundum exigentiam brevis pred. Predictus tamen Williel. adtunc Vicecomes predicti Com. Suff. existens Officii sui debitum minime ponderans, sed machinans & malitiose intendens ipsum Sam. in hac parte minus rite pregravare ac eundem Samuelem de fiducia & officii unius Militis Comitatus predict. in dicto Parliamento exercend. omnia frustrare & deprivare, & predictum Samuel. ad diversas magnas & grandes pecuniarum summas expendend. causare, contra debitum officii sui predicti falso, malitiose & deceptive adtunc in eandem Cancellariam apud Westmonasterium predictam retornavit, una cum Indentura predicta quandam aliam Indenturam eidem brevi similiter annex. specifican. ill. fore fact. inter prefatum Willielmum adtunc existen. Vicecom. dicti Comitatus Suffol. ex una parte & diversas alias personas dicti Comitatus in Indentura illa specificata & continens, quod dicte alie persone ut major pars totius Comitatus predicti in predicto pleno Comitatu Suffol. apud Gippovicum predictum dicto vicesimo quarto die Februarii anno supradicto elegerunt quendam Lionel. Talamach Baronettum alias dictum Dominum Huntingtowre in Regno Scotie in loco predicti Henrici North un. Militem Comitatus Suffol. predicti pro Parliamento predicto adveniend. eidem Parliamento pro Comitatu illo ubi (re vera) predictus Lionel. non fuit elect. per majorem partem Comitatus illius fore Mil. in loco predicti Henrici pro Comitatu predicto, prout per ultimam Indenturam predictam falso supponitur, ratione cujus quidem falsi retorn. de predicta alia Indentura per predictum Willielmum Vicecomitem dicti Comitatus Suffol. existen. in forma predicta fact. idem Samuel in domo inferiori pro Communitate hujus regni Anglie in dicto Parliamento ad predict. retorn. predicti brevis & diversa tempora postea assemblat. apud Westmonasterium pred. constitut. admitti non potuit, quousque idem Samuel suppetitionem suam Communitati dicti Parliamenti pro remedio suo congruo in ea parte exhibit. & post diversas ingentes denar. summas in & circa manifestationem & verificationem dicte Electionis ipsius Samuelis coram dicta Communitate expend. & diversos labores in ea parte per ipsum Samuelem susten. postea scilicet vicesimo die Februarii anno regni Domini regis nunc vicesimo sexto per Communitat. dicti Parliamenti in domo Communitat. præd. admissus fuit, & electio ipsius Samuelis præd. per Communitat. præd. declarat. fuit fore bona, unde idem Samuel dicit quod ipse deterioratus est & dampnum habet ad valentiam trium mille librarum & inde producit sectam, &c. Et modo ad hunc diem, scilicet diem Veneris proximam post craftinum sancte Trinitatis isto eodem Termino usque quem diem præd. Williel. habuit licentiam ad billam præd. interloquendi & tunc ad respondendum, &c. coram Domino Rege apud Westmonasterium venit tam præd. Samuel per Attornatum suum præd. quam præd. Willielmus per Johannem Needham Attornatum suum, & idem Willielmus defendit vim & injuriam quando, &c. & dicit quod ipse non est inde culpabilis, & de hoc ponit se super patriam, & præd. Samuel similiter, &c. Ideo ven' inde Juratores coram Domino Rege apud Westmonasterium die Veneris proximo post tres septimanas sancti Michaelis & qui nec, &c. ad recogn. &c. quia tam, &c. idem dies datus est partibus præd. ibidem, &c. De quo die jurata præd. inter partes prædictas de placito præd. posita fuit inde inter eas in respectum coram Domino Rege apud Westmonasterium usque diem Jovis in craftino sancti Martini ex tunc proximo sequente pro defectu Juratorum, &c. Ad quem diem coram Domino Rege apud West. venit tam præd. Samuel quam præd. Williel. per Attornatos suos præd. & Juratores jurat. illius exact. similiter ven. qui ad veritatem de & super premissis dicend. elect. triat. & jurat. dicunt super Sacramentum suum quod præd. Williel. est culpabilis de præmissis præd. modo & forma prout præd. Samuel superius versus eum queritur & assidunt dampna ipsius Samuelis occasione premissorum præd. ultra misas & custagia sua per ipsum circa sectam suam in hac parte apposita ad octingentas libras, & pro misis & custagiis illis ad quadraginta solidos. Sed quia curia dicti Domini Regis nunc hic de judicio suo de & super premissis reddendum nondum advisatur dies inde ulterior datus est partibus præd. coram Domino Rege apud Westm. usque diem Veneris proximum post Octobas Purificat. beate Marie de judicio suo inde audiend. eo quod curia dicti Domini Regis hic inde nondum, &c. Ad quem diem coram Domino Rege apud Westm. venit tam præd. Samuel quam præd. Williel. per Attornatos suos præd. super quo visis & per curiam dicti Domini Regis nunc hic plene intellectis omnibus & singulis premissis matutaque deliberatione inde habita, consideratum est quod præd. Samuel Barnardiston recuperet versus prætatum Williel. Soame dampna sua præd. per Juratores præd in forma predicta assess. necnon nonaginta & octo libras pro misis & custagiis suis præd. eidem Samuel per curiam dicti Domini Regis nunc hic assensu suo de incremento adjudicat. Que quidem dampna in toto se attingunt ad noningentas libras & præd. Williel. in misericordia, &c. Postea scilicet die Sabbati vicesimo quarto die Aprilis Anno Regni Domini Regis nunc, &c. vicesimo septimo transcript. Record. & processſ. præd inter partes predictas de placito præd. cum omnibus ea tangentibus pretextu cujusdam brevis dicti Domini Regis de errore corrigend. per prefat. Williel. Soame in premissis prosecut. coram Justiciariis Domini Regis de Communi Banco & Baronibus de Scaccario dicti Domini Regis de gradu de le Coise in Cameram Scaccarii juxta formam Statuti in Parliamento Domine Elizabethe nuper Regine Anglie apud West. vicesimo tertio die Novembris Anno Regni sui vicesimo septimo tent' edit. a predicta curia dicti Domini Regis hic coram ipso Rege transmissa fuerunt, predictusque Williel. Soame in eadem curia Camere Scaccarii comparen' diversas causas & materias pro errore in Recordo & Processu præd. pro revocatione & adnullatione Judicii præd. assignavit, ad quas præd. Samuel Barnardiston in eadem curia Camere Scaccarii præd. similiter comparend. placitavit, quod nec in Recordo nec in Processu præd. nec in redditione Judicii præd. in ullo fuit errat. Postmodumq; scilicet die Sabbati decimo die Junii Anno Regni dicti Domini Regis nunc vicesimo octavo visis premissis & per curiam Camere Scac. præd. diligent. examinat. & plenis intellectis tam Record. & Process. præd. quam Judicio præd. super eisdem reddit. videbatur curia Camere Scac. præd. quod judicium præd. vitiosum & defectivum in lege existit. Ideo adtunc & ibidem per eandem curiam consideratum fuit quod judicium præd. in omnibus reversetur, adnulletur & penitus pro nullo habeatur, & quod præd. Williel. ad omnia que occasione judicii præd. amisit restituatur, super quo Record. præd. nec non process. præd. justiciar. dicti Dom. Regis de Communi Banco Baron. de Scacc. dicti Dom. Regis coram eis in premissis habit. coram Domino Rege ubicunq; &c. remittebantur secund. formam Statuti præd. & in eadem curia dicti Dom. Regis hic coram ipso Rege jam resident, &c. Postea scilicet vicesimo quarto die Maii Anno Regni Domini Gulielmi & Marie nunc Regis & Regine Anglie primo Record. & Process. præd. inter partes præd. cum omnibus ea tangentibus pretextu cujusdam brevis de errore corrigend. per prefat. Samuel. Barnardiston in premissis præd. prosecut. dicto Domino Reg. & Regine in present Parl. à præd. curia dicti Dom. Reg. & Regine hic transmis. fuit, predictusq; Samuel in eadem curia Parl. comparens, diversas causas & materias pro erroribus in Recordo & processu præd. pro revocatione & adnullatione Judicii præd. assignavit; & postea, scilicet vicesimo quinto die Junii Anno dictorum Dom. & Dom. Reg. & Regine supradict. in præd. curia Parliamenti visis & per curiam ibidem diligenter examinat. & plenius intellectis tam Record. & Process. præd. judicio super eisdem reddit quam præd. errore superius assignat. pro eo quod videtur curie Parl. præd. quod Record. ill. in nullo vitiosum aut defectivum existit & quod Record. ill. in nullo fuit erratum. Ideo adtunc & ibidem consideratum est per eandem curiam Parl. præ quod Judicium præd. in omnibus affirmetur & in omni suo robore stet & effect.

Sir *Samuel Barnardiston* against Sir *William Soame*, late Sheriff of *Suffolk*, in B. R *.

CASE, and declares that a writ issued out of Chancery to the defendant, then Sheriff of *Suffolk*, to elect a Knight of the County for the Parliament: and that the Plaintiff was chosen by the majority of Freeholders, and that the Defendant returned the Writ with an Indenture of the said Election, but maliciously intending to deprive the Plaintiff, *de fiducia & officio præd' falso & deceptive, una cum indentura præd' retornavit unam alteram indenturam in cancellaria præd' specificant' quod aliæ personæ liberi tenentes vel major pars liberorum tenentium elegerunt quendam Lionellum Tolmach, ubi re vera præd' Lionellus non fuit electus per majorem numerum liberorum tenentium; ratione cujus*, the Plaintiff was kept out of the House of Commons, and put to great charge to prove his election in the House of Commons. The Defendant pleaded *non culp.* and upon trial at bar, *Twisden*, *Rainsford*, and *Wylde* held, and so directed the Jury, That if this double return was made maliciously, they ought to find for the Plaintiff, which accordingly they did, and gave him 800*l.* damages; though the evidence, as to the malice and falsity, was very slender. For the Poll was granted; upon which the matter seeming doubtful, whether some of them who voted for the Plaintiff had sufficient freehold to qualify them to give their votes; the Sheriff, by advice of Counsel then present, and of some Members of Parliament there also, made this double return, to prevent an action for a false return, in case it should appear that some Freeholders that voted for the Plaintiff had sufficient freehold. And after, upon examination in Parliament, the election of the Plaintiff was adjudged good, and the Defendant committed by them for making this double return: And now 'twas moved in arrest of judgment by *North*, Attorney-General, and *Scroggs*, King's Serjeant, that this Action lies not, and that no such Action was ever yet maintained in this case; for the case of *Nevil* and *Stroud* was never resolved, but in respect of difficulty sent to Parliament, where it never received a determination. And the reasons they urged against the Action, were, *First*, Because the falsity or verity of the return is only examinable in the House of Commons, who are the sole Judges, and will punish such falsities; and accordingly they have so done in this case, by committing the Sheriff, and he ought not to be twice punished for the same fault. And before the Statute of *H.* VI. no Action lay for a false return, and that only gives an action of debt for 100*l.* *Secondly*, The right of the party is not considerable in this case; for this is not an office of profit, but of trust, concerning the State. *Thirdly*, What the Sheriff does in this case, he doth as a Judge; for he is Judge of the election, and therefore no action lies against him. *Fourthly*, What the Sheriff doth in this case is *propter difficultatem*, upon his doubtfulness of the matter, and Judges of Assize may, *propter difficultatem*, adjourn an Assize: the Sheriff hath done no more in this case than laid the matter before the House of Commons, that the validity of the votes may be there deliberately examined. To which 'twas answer'd by *Maynard*

* *Levinz*'s Reports, Part. II, 114. *Keble*'s Reports, Vol. III. 365, 369, 389, 419, 428, 442, 664.

King's

King's Serjeant, and Sir *William Jones*, Sollicitor; *First*, That here was malice and falsity in the Sheriff, and thereby damage and charge to the plaintiff, and all this found by the Jury, which is sufficient to maintain an action in all cases, whether there has been a like action in such case or not before; for actions upon the case are founded upon the particular case, which is mostly new. And the case of *Nevil* and *Stroud* was not for a double return, but for making no return; for there two were elected, and the Sheriff made no return as to one, and for that he brought the action. *Secondly*, The commitment by the Parliament is only to punish the contempt of the Sheriff, as to them and the State, but not to repair the party for the damage he sustained; and thus in several respects, one may be twice punished *pro uno delicto*. As it falls out often in many cases, particularly in criminal matters, wherein the party is punished for the King by indictment, and by the party for the special damage he sustained. *Thirdly*, The Sheriff is not a Judge of the election in this case, but a minister to take the polls; of which, in point of sufficiency, the House of Commons is Judge. *Fourthly*, Though the Statute of *H.* VI. gives to the party the 100*l.* penalty, that will not prove this action does not lie at Common Law. The Parliament intended only to give a certain penalty to the party, which was considerable then, though not so considerable now, and not leave them to a Jury's discretion altogether for damages. *Et adjornatur ad proximum terminum*, when *Hale* being in Court, he, *Twysden* and *Wylde*; forasmuch as the return is said to be *falso & malitiose & ea intentione*, to put the plaintiff to charge and expence, and so found by the Jury; held the action lay, and gave Judgment for the plaintiff; *Rainsford* doubting.

Upon this a writ of Error was brought in the Chequer Chamber, where six Judges were for reversing the Judgment, and two for affirming it.

Their Arguments here follow.

Barnardiston versus *Soame*. *In Case*.

The Case.

ON the death of Sir *Henry North*, one of the Knights for *Suffolk*, a writ was issued forth for the election of a new Member; and Sir *Samuel Barnardiston*, and my Lord *Huntingtowre*, were the two candidates; but Sir *Samuel* carried it by 78 voices, and was returned: And my Lord *Huntingtowre* having made an interest with the Sheriff, got the Sheriff to return him too; and he sat in the House till the election was there determined for Sir *Samuel*. Whereupon Sir *Samuel Barnardiston*, for this double Return, brought an action upon the case against the Sheriff, and tried it at the *King's-Bench* bar, 12 *Nov.* 1674, before my Lord Chief-Justice *Hale*, and recovered 1000*l.* damages: and afterwards a writ of Error was brought in the *Exchequer* Chamber, and there the Judgment in the *King's-Bench* was reversed; only *Atkins* and *Ellis* were for affirming it.

Judge *Ellis*'s Argument is as followeth:

First, The Declaration does consist of the writ to the Sheriff, his Return, and the Averment of the plaintiff's damage.

The writ does shew the great import of what was to be done, and what he should do.

Now as to the Return:

1. It is impossible to be a true Return, but it is a false Return; for that *simul & semel*, both should be chosen at the same time, that can't be: So then he hath not observed the writ.

2. The writ requires that the House should be full, and have a Member of Parliament, but by this Return neither can sit in Parliament; for it appears, that from the 24th of *February*, 25 *Car.* II. until the confirmation, he was kept out. So the end of the writ not at all observed, and the business of the Parliament retarded as much as could be.

3. It may be said, This may be done by mistake, he may mistake the law; but when the plaintiff comes and says, That he knowing the Plaintiff was duly elected, and on purpose to keep him out of the House, did *falso & malitiose* make this Return; then here is a false and malicious Return, and made knowingly upon him: Then an Action lies.

Then to consider the Case,

1. At Common Law; and I conceive it will lie.

2. The Acts of Parliament have not taken away the Remedy which the Common Law gave.

1. That the Common Law gave remedy; for that it was falsely and maliciously done, we must not doubt it: It is a matter of fact, and the Jury have found it so, and that there was a wrong done to *Barnardiston*, and it is of the Sheriff's own knowledge: Then,

2. When I suffer an injury, joined with a loss, the Common Law gives me a remedy for it.

Cooper and *Andrews*'s case, *Hob.* 43.

Then take it as done by an Officer of Justice, and a sworn Officer, and of the greatest in the Kingdom: If it should not lie in that case, there would be a failure of Justice, but no failure of wrong.

Second, That in cases of far less concern, as to Officers, it will lie, and then we shall see in this case what it will do.

Powle and *Godfrey*'s case, *Rolls*, lib. 1. 63. Co. lib. 12. 128. In that case, because there was a temporal loss to the party, though for a spiritual wrong, the law gave him damages.

Rolls 1 lib. 1. 108. 24. *Ford* and *Hoskbin*'s case against an Archdeacon, F. N. B. 47. and yet an Archdeacon is a spiritual Officer: So that if he do not induct the Parson, he may have his remedy; for where he suffers a loss, the Law gives him his remedy.

Now here is *injuria & dampnum*, he does complain about the nature of his election, and the undue return of an election; and to a Court that never yet did give damages to the party.

3. Then when there is a colour of Justice, and a man does proceed in a legal way, yet *falso & malitiose*, an action lies, *Hob.* 266. *Waterer* and *Freeman*'s case. If a man will arrest one, and put him to special bail, a special action of the case lies against him.

Cro. 3. 130. *Windham* and *Clere*'s case against a Justice of Peace; Whereas in truth the Justice never had any complaint. An lie against him, because he did *falso & malitiose*.

Id. 21 *E.* IV. 22, 23. If a misinformation be in a Court of action lies against him. Now here is a very great misinform to the Chancery upon this return.

Obj. This is a new case, and a case of a great deal of d therefore we must have a great deal of care of making new laws

Answ. It were endless to put cases where there never was a c yet an action will lie, if damage: there was no precedent for a the case for falsely and maliciously accusing one of treason, be and *Crashaw*'s case. *Rolls Abr.* l. 1. 1131.

Bulstr. 2. 270. *Jones* 93. *Cro.* 1. 15. Though there it wa that never any precedents were, that this action was brought f ously and falsely accusing one of treason, and the danger of t would lie, yet the Judges resolved otherwise, being falsely a ously; and though never any precedents could be shewn, yet judgment expressly that the action would lie.

2 *Cro.* 534. *Moor* and *Blackwell*'s case: Objected, That no could be found where insufficient returns have been amended Court said, If there never was a precedent, they would make a thereof. The first precedent had a beginning, and there was nor

2. There is a great difference where the Law is silent in the

Before *Stade*'s case they never could shew any action of the an *Indebitatus assumpsit*; multitudes of actions of debt, but no case, yet adjudged it would lie: For where there is *eadem ratio eadem lex*: and will any man doubt where there is a false return, an action will lie? In actions of the case there is less reason precedents than in other things; they grow as the invention grows; according as new frauds and new deceits arise, so shoul medies.

Obj Never an action brought for such a return; and *Littleton*' That if such an action could be brought, it would have been bro fore now.

Answ. 1. My Lord *Coke* says, The not user of an action does away the action, but ye may bring the action if ye have cause.

2. May it not be said as it was said to the former cases? Th accusations of treason, and false ones too, and no actions brought fore no action ought to lie now. I cannot see, if ye reverse th ment, ye must reverse many more of the same nature.

'Tis true, there is a great difference, that if the nature of the such as it cannot be falsely and maliciously, the adding these wo not change the nature; but if the nature of the thing be so, and do find *falso & malitiose*, the action will lie. As for the first part, false accusation of stealing an apple off a tree, an action will though the declaration is *falso & malitiose*, for the nature of the will not permit it; so *Moor*, 491. *Palmer* and *Porter*'s case, th action will lie upon that reason: But in our case, the nature thing is of such a wrong, that an action may lie.

Then though the Acts of Parliament may give remedy, yet th not away the remedy at Common Law, which was his ancient r *Plow.* 113. puts many cases to that purpose; and the difference is for if it were no crime and offence at Common Law, but given Act, then no action could lie but upon the Act; but where there w other remedy, he may take either that at Common Law, or the upon the Act.

The Common Law gave an action of the case upon too little iss turned by the Sheriff, the Statute gives an averment, yet he may ta action still.

Now consider the remedy this Act gives, and see whether it be s a remedy: For first, He must bring his action within the time limi the Act, or else he is out of the Act; now if there be a double retu pending in the House, no man will bring an action, depending th turn undecided, and the Judges will not countenance such an actio the party is quite deprived of his remedy. Then, secondly, As thi is, the Sheriff is not within the Act at all, for he has returned the tiff. Now if this should be suffered, there would be an evasion o the Statute, and the Statute would give no remedy at all. Thirdl is the same mischief to the plaintiff, if my Lord had been singl turned, he might have vindicated his election as much as in this d return, and have been in the House as soon.

Obj. This is a general matter, and all the subjects of *England* are cerned in it; and *Co. Rep.* 3. *Williams*'s case, where there is a ge nuisance, every man shall not have an action.

Resp. Where there is a general concern, and no particular dan every man shall not have an action; but when there is particular dan there he may. Here is a particular damage to the Plaintiff, and so well intitled to his action. *Rep.* 9. *Marie*'s case. 1 *Inst.* 59. *Po* case. 3 *Cro.* 664. *Fineux* and *Hoveden*'s case.

Obj. This matter is matter proper to be determined in Parliament, a hard case the Sheriff should be condemned for that he could not hel

Resp. As to the Right of election that is determinable there, and it so; but for his damage, it neither was, nor could be examined there the House of Commons had given damages, and the Parliament broken up, how should he have recovered them?

1. Here is no action brought against a Member.

2. No action brought for any thing done in Parliament.

3. The return is into Chancery; the Sheriff's work was ende Chancery; it was filed in Chancery, and there remains, and there remain. So that all the malice and falsity was done in Chancery; the action is not brought for any right of election, but for what was d to put him to charges.

If there had been an equality of voices, he must have returned so; is here a little mistake; but what is done, is done falsely and maliciou and with an intent to put him to charges.

Obj. The Sheriff is not concerned himself for what was done in Commons House.

Answ. He was not charged with it there; this action is not brou purely for a double return; yet if so, and he does it knowingly, an act will lie, the return is plain, for the Sheriff is a great Officer, and the does give that credit to him, that it will not suffer any averment agai his return, but an action of the case will lie, *Rep.* 11. *Bagg's* case; and the Sheriff is a sworn Officer, and the law imposes this Man upon me, and the law is my caution in that case, and gives me a remedy.

Obj. Here is no double return, for it is no return at all, it not being under seal, and the Statute says, all returns shall be under the seal of the Electors: So here is no harm at all; he might have gone into the House, if he had pleased.

Answ. At the Common Law there was no necessity the return should have been under the seal of the Electors: So it is a good return until avoided, and not a void return. If it were not good unless under the seal of all those that elect, what will become of those that sit now? It was never done yet, if he makes a return without seal, it is good, *primâ facie*.

As to the exceptions taken to the declaration, it is well laid in strictness of pleading; he says, *secundum exigentiam brevis*; and tho' he says *per aliam indenturam factam*, it was as much as *factum indentatum*, 1 *Inst.* 103 *Leo.* 310. *Maydwell* and *Andrewe's* case. How should it be a return, unless it be as it should be? And ye must intend so as it should be, 3 *Cro.* 737.

The pleading of *Bulkley's* case is the same with this, and no exception taken to it: But if it had been upon a demurrer, there might have been more said for the exception; but now it is an exception upon a verdict, and it shall be intended, that they that tried it had the right of the return. 2 *Bulst.* 41. *Yelv.* 247. after a verdict a vicious plea shall be made good, *Allen* and *Naske's* case, 3 *Cro.* 53 *ibid.* 371. *Southwell* and *Brown's* case, and *Fulwood's* case, 4 *Rep.* is a stronger case than has been cited, and yet adjudged good.

Though there be no seal, yet when he returns this, and a man suffers damage by it, and all the mischief that may happen, who is the party would take advantage of it? he that has done the wrong? No, he cannot, 21 *E.* IV. 22. 15 *E.* IV. 18, 19.

So therefore, both because the declaration is well laid, and the party well entitled to his action,

The Judgment ought to be affirmed.

An Argument in the great Case concerning Election of Members to Parliament, by Sir Robert Atkins, *Knight of the honourable Order of the* Bath, *and late one of the Judges of the Court of* Common-Pleas.

Trin. 26 *Car.* II. *In the Court of* King's-Bench, Rot. 577.

Sir *Samuel Barnardiston*, Bart. Plaintiff; Sir *William Soame*, Defendant. *In Trespass upon the Case.*

THAT whereas the King, 8 *Feb.* 25. of his reign, by a writ out of the Chancery, directed to the then Sheriff of *Suffolk*, commanded that he should cause an election to be made of another Knight for the said Shire, in the place of Sir *Henry North*, lately dead; and that he should certify the election under his own seal, and the seals of those that were present at the election, into the Chancery.

Which writ, 12 *Feb.* 25 *Car.* II. was delivered to the defendant, then Sheriff.

And, 24 *Feb.* 25 *Car.* II. in full County, by the people resident in that County, the writ was read.

And altho' the plaintiff was duly elected to be Knight for that County, by the greater number of the people then resident in the said County, every one whereof could spend 40 *s. per annum* within that County:

And altho' the defendant, then Sheriff of the said County, *premissa satis sciens*, afterwards the same 24 *Feb.* 25 *Car.* II. returned the said writ into the Chancery; together with an Indenture between him the said Sheriff, and the aforesaid Electors of the plaintiff, of the aforesaid Election of the plaintiff, made according as the said writ requires.

Yet the defendant, then Sheriff, *Officii sui debitum minime ponderans, sed machinans & malitiose intendans ipsum Samuelem in hac parte minus rite praegravare*, and to deprive the plaintiff of the trust and office of one of the Knights of the Shire, to be exercised in Parliament, and to cause the plaintiff to expend great sums of money against the duty of his office:

Falsely, maliciously and deceitfully returned into the Chancery, together with the aforesaid Indenture, another Indenture annex'd to the said writ, purporting the same to be made between him the said defendant, then Sheriff, of the one part, and divers other persons; containing, That the said other persons, as the greater part of the said County, did chuse one Sir *Lionel Tolmache*, Bart. otherwise *Lionel* Lord *Huntingtowre*, as Knight of the Shire, to come to Parliament.

Whereas in truth, the said *Lionel* was not chosen by the greater part.

By reason of which false return of the said other Indenture, the plaintiff could not be admitted into the Lower House at the return of the said writ, and a long time after.

Till the plaintiff, upon his petition to the Commons, and till after he had spent divers great sums of money about the proving of his election, and divers pains and labours in that behalf sustain'd, afterwards, *scil.* 20. *Feb.* 26 *Car.* II. he was admitted, and his election was declared to be good.

To his damage of 3000 *l.*

Plea. Not guilty.

Verdict. *Pro quer' dam.* 800 *l.*

Judgment. *Pro quer'* Sir *Samuel Barnardiston*, in the *King's-Bench*, for the 800 *l.* damages, and for the 98 *l.* costs.

The defendant, Sir *William Soame*, sued a writ of Error before the Justices of the *Common-Bench*, and the Barons of the *Exchequer*, in the *Exchequer-Chamber*, to reverse the said judgment given by the Judges of the *King's-Bench*.

And two of the Justices of the *Common Bench*, viz. Sir *Robert Atkins*, and Sir *William Elis*, upon argument, were of opinion, That the said judgment was good in law, and were for affirming that judgment.

But the other two Judges of the *Common Bench*, and the four Barons of the *Exchequer*, holding the said judgment in the *King's-Bench* erroneous, were for reversing the said Judgment.

And the said Judgment still stands revers'd; but needs a redress by error in Parliament.

Sir *Samuel Barnardiston*, Bart. Plaintiff, Sir *William Soame*, Defendant, *in an Action upon the Case.*

I Shall divide the Record into the several parts of it:

1. There is first, the occasion, or as we commonly call it, the inducement to the action, that is, Sir *Henry North*, who served in Parliament as Knight of the Shire for *Suffolk*, died; and a new writ issued to chuse another in his place.

2. In the next place, the right that accrued to the plaintiff, Sir *Samuel Barnardiston*, he was duly elected Knight of the Shire.

3. The injury done him by the defendant, with the aggravations of it, *viz.* Although the defendant well knew the plaintiff was duly elected, and tho' he did return him; yet contrary to the duty of his office as Sheriff, and intending to oppress him, and to deprive him of the right he had, and on purpose to put him to great expence and charges,

He did falsely, maliciously, and deceitfully return another Indenture with the former; importing, that another person was chosen by the greater part of the County.

4. The damage sustained by the plaintiff, after the writ was returned.
1. He could not for a long time be admitted to sit to do his duty, and discharge his trust.
2. He was put to great charges to prove his election.
3. He did sustain great pains and labour.

5. The right done him at last, and the satisfaction and amends made him;
1. By the House of Commons. His election was declared good, and he was admitted to sit.
2. By the Jury. They have found the wrong done by the defendant, and the damage sustained by the plaintiff; and they have repair'd him with 800 *l.* damages.
3. By the Court of *King's-Bench*. They have given judgment for the plaintiff.

And the question before us, is, whether this judgment be erroneous? I hold the judgment not to be erroneous. I am for affirming of the judgment.

1. I conceive the matter set forth in the plaintiff's declaration, to be actionable. 2. That the wrong and injury complained of, is such for which the Law gives him a remedy. And 3. That he has taken his proper remedy, by bringing this action upon the case.

All this being in the affirmative, the proof of it lies upon me.

My ground and foundation is this, That where one person does injury to another, and the person to whom the wrong is done sustains particular damage and loss by the injury, there the Law gives a remedy, by action, to the party injur'd.

But here is an injury done.
And here is a particular damage sustain'd.
Therefore an action lies.

I shall first prove the ground or foundation, which is the major proposition, That where a wrong or injury is done, and a particular damage sustained, there the Law gives a remedy by action.

1. From the nature and quality of the Law; which is to do right to all, and to give relief and redress to those that receive wrongs. And should there be any case where a person might receive an injury and damage, and yet have no remedy nor redress, the Law would be defective; which would be a reproach to the Law and Government.

The Law has appointed several Courts, and given them several powers and jurisdictions; so that in the one or the other, every person that has suffered injury and damage may make his complaint, and have right done him.

Sir *Edw. Coke*, in his *Mag. Chart. fol.* 405. in his *Expos.* upon the *Stat.* of *W.* II *c.* 14. says, It is an ancient maxim of the Common Law, *Non recedant quaerentes a curia Regis sine remedio.* Whoever has just cause to complain, shall have their just remedy. And *curia Regis non debet deficere in justitia exhibenda.*

Both these rules and maxims, which have one and the same sense, are remembered in that *Stat.* of *Mag. Chart. c.* 24.

In *Pinchon's* case, 9 *Rep. fol.* 88. *b. adjud.* That an action upon the case lies against executors for a debt, due by the testator upon a simple contract. And in the argument of that case it is said, That by that resolution, *Justice and right is advanced*, and the creditor paid his just debt; and if the debt should be discharged by the death of the debtor, it would (say the Judges) be a great defect in the Law, that there should be a right, and no remedy for it. And the Judges urge the maxim I mention'd but now, *curia Domini Regis deficere non debet conquerentibus in justitia exhibenda.*

In *Meriel Tresham's* case, 9 *Rep. fol.* 3. it is urged as an absurd thing in law, that a man should have wrong done him, and yet should be without remedy: And the reporter does observe, that the Judges in all ages have endeavoured to put the rule of *W.* II. in execution, *Curia domini Regis non debet deficere conquerentibus in justitia exhibenda.*

Nay, the Law has so great a zeal for redressing of wrongs, that as sacred as the maxims and rules of the Law are, yet if there were any rules or maxims that stood in our way to hinder, the Law would break through those rules and maxims, rather than suffer an injury to be without remedy. 4 *Inst fol.* 71. about the middle, *No wrong or injury, either public or private, can be done, but it shall be reform'd or punish'd in one Court or other, by due course of Law.* And in the lower end of that folio, *A failure of Justice is abhorred in Law.*

Sir *Fran. Bacon*, amongst the elements of the Law, *fol.* 51. delivers this as a principle, *Receditur a placitis juris potius quam injuria & delicta remaneant impunita*; which he himself expounds in this sense, The Law will dispense with some maxims, rather than wrongs should be unpunished.

2. My next argument to prove this position, *That where an injury is done, and damage sustained, the Law gives remedy*, shall be taken from the nature of an action, which is the ordinary remedy the Law gives for the repairing of a private wrong.

Now what the nature and definition of an action is, we learn from the most ancient authors of the Law, as *Bracton*, and *Fleta*, and the *Mirror* of the Justices, as they are collected by Sir *E. C.* 2 *Inst. fol.* 40. and they all agree almost in the same words

Actio nihil aliud est quam jus prosequendi in judicio, quod alicui debetur, & quod nascitur ex maleficio, vel quod provenit ex delicto vel injuria.

It is nothing else but a means or remedy for a man to have right done him, that has suffered wrong and injury.

It is the argument commonly used, and the reason given to maintain an action, and in particular an action upon the case, *viz.* That there is an injury done, and a damage sustained.

Sir *E. C.* 12 *Rep. fol.* 128. *ref. p. tot. cur.* If a *Sumner* return one summoned, or cited into the *Spiritual Court*, where in truth he was never summoned, and he is pronounced *contumax*, and thereupon excommunicate; he shall have an action upon the case against the Sumner: And the reason given is, because there is *injuria & damnum.* 'Tis the same case that is reported in *Rolls* 1 *Rep. fol.* 63. by the name of *Powle* and *Godfrey:* which I shall have further occasion to mention before I have done. You have the same case reported by Sir *Francis Moor*, *fol.* 835.

This may suffice to prove the major proposition, *That where wrong and injury is done to any man, and particular damage sustained by it, there the Law entitles him to an action.*

For the minor proposition, That in the case before us, there is a wrong and injury done to the plaintiff, and a particular damage sustained by him. To make this out, I shall need to do no more than barely to relate the very fact; and put it as a question to any plain man, that has but a common capacity, and no learning, nor acquired parts, and to stand to his judgment in the case.

And the case is no more than this: The plaintiff had the honour to be chosen to that great trust and employment, of a Knight of the Shire, by his Countrymen, to serve in Parliament; by which he was justly entitled to several great privileges, and to wages for the time he served. And 'tis an honour and employment we all know is highly esteemed, and generally desired and sought after; and he that desires it, desires a good office. The defendant having the office of a Sheriff, and being bound by his office and oath to do justly and truly, *Et præmissa satis sciens*; that is, well knowing the Plaintiff had the only right to be returned, and that no other had the least colour for it, and where there was not the least doubt or difficulty in the case:

Yet falsely, deceitfully, and maliciously to deprive him of his trust and office, on purpose to put him to great charges, he returned another person with him.

And after all, the Question is, Whether he has done him any wrong or no?

By occasion of this, the plaintiff was hindered from sitting in the House, and was put to great expence, and underwent great trouble and labour. And the Question is, Whether the Plaintiff has been at any particular damage?

Shall I have my action for a halfpenny trespass *pedibus ambulando?* Does the Law give me an action of assault and battery, if a man does but lift up his hand to strike me? Or for a few ill words, that will break no bones? And shall I recover damage for these petty things, and shall no action lie for so notorious an injury as is done in this case?

But our greatest work is to answer the many objections that have been made against this action; which yet, I will be bold to say, have much more of wit than of weight in them.

And the difficulty rather lies in the great power and interest of the parties to the action, and of those that concern themselves in the example and consequence of it, upon a politick account, than from any uncertainty of the Law: that is, there is a design to model the Parliament to the humour of the Court.

Sir *Ed. Coke*, in his preface to *Rep. fol.* 6. in the beginning of the *folio*, affirms, That he never saw any case of great value proceed quietly, without many exceptions in arrest of judgment.

Object. 1. This is a matter that concerns the Government, and is of a publick nature; the employment of a Parliament-man, consisting *in negotiis regem, statum, & defensionem Regni & Ecclesiæ concernentibus:* And therefore the punishment of an offence committed, in reference to this, should be by a publick prosecution, and not to be appropriated to any particular private person; nor the amends and satisfaction made to any one man.

Answ. It must be agreed, That publick injuries wherein all, or very many are concerned, are proper for a publick prosecution; as in the name of the King, or by a presentment at a Leet, or Quarter-Sessions, &c. But if any particular man receive a particular damage by the publick offence or injury, he shall have his action; and this is consistent enough with the prosecution for the publick. As the case of 27 *H.* VIII. *fol.* 26, 27. *Br. Abr. Act. Sr. Ca. Pl.* 6. If a man make a ditch upon the King's highway, this is a wrong to every man that has a right to pass that way, and he is presentable at a Leet for this offence; but if I and my horse happen to fall into the ditch, riding along the way, and so receive a particular damage, I may have an action upon the case against him that made the ditch. 9 *Rep.* 113. 5 *Rep.* [illegible]2, 73. It is the ordinary case, *A* makes an assault and battery upon *B.* this is but one single act, *but it has a double aspect.* 'Tis a breach of the King's peace, and for that *A* is indictable, and may be fined to the King, and imprisoned. *It is a particular wrong to B.* for which *B.* may have an action of assault and battery, and recover damages, and both of them consistent.

So in our case, this false and malicious double return, it was an injury to the King and Kingdom, and to the House of Commons, in that while the election by this means was under dispute, they wanted the plaintiff's service and assistance. It was a wrong to the County of *Suffolk*, for the Knight of a Shire has *plenam potestatem pro se & communitate comitatus ad faciendum & consentiendum*; but it was more particularly an injury to the plaintiff, in that he was for some time deprived of the honour done him by his Country; who by their electing of him, settled this character upon him, that he was *magis idoneus & discretus*; for the writ commands such to be chosen.

He was hindered from discharging his trust, committed to him by his own County; hindered from doing service to the King and Kingdom; hindered of his wages.

The *Stat.* of 27 *H.* VIII. *c.* 26. which unites *England* to *Wales*, enacts, That for every Shire in *Wales* there shall be chosen one Knight to serve in Parliament, and one Burgess for every Borough; and that the Knights and Burgesses shall have like dignity, pre-eminence, and privilege, and shall be allowed such fees as other Knights and Burgesses of the Parliament have, and are allowed: By which it appears there are dignities, pre-eminences, privileges and fees, belonging to such as serve in Parlia[ment;] all which the plaintiff, for a time, was hindered by this false ret[urn.]

And that it does concern the Government, it argues the great[er wrong] done to the plaintiff; for every member of Parliament, for the [time he] serves there, is instrumental in carrying on the Government. [It is] an high honour to him. *Tu regere imperio populos, Hæ tibi eru[nt artes].* 'Tis a noble employment.

And since it does so nearly concern the Government, we [think the] Judges should be the more careful to discourage all abuses comm[itted by] Sheriffs in elections: It is of vast concernment to the Kingd[om, that] elections should be fair, and returns duly made, without partia[lity or] indirect means used. And we, by Judgments, should encourage a[ll reme]dies against such abuses and practices.

Besides all this, the plaintiff has been put to great expences, [and un]dergone great labour and trouble; which is a private and partic[ular da]mage, and therefore entitles him to his particular action.

A Justice of peace may have an action of slander in relatio[n to his] office, yet that was not an offence at Common Law neither; a[nd that] concerns the Government.

The *Stat.* of 7 *H.* IV. *cap.* 1. recites, That the Commons [made] grievous complaint to the King, of the undue elections of the Kn[ights of] the Counties, *which* (says the Preamble) *be sometimes made by aff[ection of] the Sheriffs*, to the great slander of the Counties, and hindrance [of the] business of the Commonalty of the said Counties.

By which it appears, how great the mischief was in those da[ys, and] whence it came principally, *viz.* from the partiality of the Sherif[fs; and] that *Stat.* to prevent the abuses, does appoint the return of Ind[entures] under the Seal of the Sheriff, and the seals of the Electors: But [the de]fendant in our case has practised an abuse even in the very remedy[, by re]turning several Indentures, and so evading the good provision [made by] that Statute.

The *Stat.* of 11 *H.* IV *c.* 1. observes, That *no pain is set in [that]* that *Stat.* of 7 *H.* IV. upon Sheriffs, if they make returns con[trary to] that Statute, and give power to Judges of Assize to punish them, [and to] inflict the penalty of 100*l.* upon the Sheriff; and the Knights un[duly re]turned are to lose their wages. And all this depends upon the [inquiry] made by the Judges of Assize. At this time surely this matter o[f electi]ons, and the examining and determining of the right, was not [so] sacred and so incommunicable a thing as some would have it n[ow; for] by this *Statute* 'tis referred to the Judges of the Assize.

But the principal *Statute* in this matter, is that of 23 *H.* V[I.] which sets out the great abuses by Sheriffs committed in elections[; and re]cites, That of late divers Sheriffs, *for their singular avail and luc[re]*, [had] not made due elections of the Knights. One would think by tho[se words] *(for their lucre)*, that there was money stirring upon these occasio[ns even] in those times; and that some men paid dear to be chosen Par[liament]men: Or else, how could a Sheriff make profit to himself by an e[lection?] And to be a Parliament-man, it seems, was a very desirable [thing in] those days.

And forasmuch (says that Statute) *as a sufficient pain, and conve[nient re]medy* for the party in such case grieved, is not ordained in the said [Statute] against the Sheriffs: It therefore provides a better remedy.

But let us, to our purpose, observe by the way, that it men[tions a] *Party grieved*, so that *there is a Party grieved:* It is not merely a [publick] offence, but an injury to some particular persons, and to some [per]son; for it says the party grieved, but it does not mention who th[e party] grieved is. So that it may be objected, that those words (t[he party] grieved) refer to every Elector, as well as the Knight elected.

But the enacting Clause expounds the words, and declares w[hat the] makers of that Law meant; for it makes the first offer of the f[orfeiture] to every person chosen Knight, and not duly returned: So then 't[is plain] that the *Knight elected, and not returned, is the Party grieved.* If [there be a] particular wrong done him, then it follows he ought to have a p[articular] remedy and satisfaction: And he was a party grieved before these [Statutes] made, and this penalty and remedy given; for these Statutes do [not] make him a party grieved, but mention him as being so before[. If he] were so before, surely the Law gave him some remedy, or else t[here was] a *Gravamen* without *Remedium*; which would have been a defe[ct in the] same.

Object. 2. Is that which I think is most relied upon, and that [the most] weight laid upon it, *viz.* *That this action concerns an election of a [Member of] the Parliament, and therefore belongs to the jurisdiction of the Parlia[ment, and] ought to be determined there, and not by any Court inferior to it.*

Answ. To this it has been truly answered, That though in th[is case we] have often occasion to speak of the Parliament, and to mention [elections] to Parliament, yet the right of election is not called in question, [nor is] it to be tried in this action, but was determined by the House [of Com]mons; and this action is pursuant to that decision of the right of [election] by the Parliament, and grounds itself upon it.

I shall, however, take this occasion, in the first place, to sh[ew that in] matters that concern the Parliament, the Judges of *Westminster* [have] in all times, and must meddle, and take cognizance of them[; and in] the next place, what they have declined and left to the Parliament.

1. They have debated and resolved, *what is a good Session of P[arliament,] and what is not, and what makes a Session*, as in 11. 12 [illegible] in *L*[illegible] *Rep.* 29. There were several Acts of Parliament that had [been made in a] former Parliament, which were continued only to the first Se[ssion of the] next Parliament; and in that case they held those acts then [illegible] for though the Parliament had met, yet no Act passing, the[y] adjudged it was no Session, and there was a necessity that the[y] should determine this. For though the King and Parliament [illegible] yet the Courts in *Westminster-hall* put those Acts in execution, [and there]fore must first satisfy themselves.

2. Whether they are in force or not so, in the Prince['s case,] whether the charter made by King *Ed.* III to the Prince, w[as an Act] of Parliament or not, is here argued and resolved. So 4 *H.* [illegible] 6 and 7 *H.* VII. 14, 15.

3. In *Roll's Ab.* 1 *part. fol.* 93. *cr.* 19 under the Title of [illegible] *Case*, there is cited 17 *E.* III. in *B. R. Rot.* 60, where [illegible] brought by *John Botchard*, Knight of [illegible], against the Sheri[ff of that] county, for not levying 10*l.* [illegible] Now, in order to the [illegible] [rela]ting to the Parliament, as, When the [illegible]

his attendance was? and divers other questions relating to the Parliament, must of necessity be incident.

10 *Eliz. Dy. fol.* 275. The very lower end of that *folio*, there is an action brought against the Keeper, for letting a Burgess of Parliament go at large by writ *de privilegio Parliamenti*, who was in execution: The Lord *Dyer* says nothing there, what became of it; but Sir *Francis Moor*, in his *Rep. fol.* 57. at the lower end of that *fol.* reports, that it was held by *Dyer*, that if one condemn'd in debt or trespass be chosen to the Parliament, and after taken in execution, that he shall not have his privilege of Parliament. And, as he says, it was so held by the Sages of the Law, in the case of *Ferrers*; and that tho' his privilege was indeed allow'd, yet, (as they held) it was *minus juste*; which case of *Ferrers* was the same here mentioned before to be in *Dy. fol.* 275. as appears by Mr. *Crompton* in his *jurisdiction* of Courts, *fol.* 8. *b.*

So that some things relating to the Parliament, the Courts of *Westminster-hall* must determine; and the Judges cannot avoid it, if they will do justice.

2. But some things there are concerning the Parliament, which the Courts of *Westminster-hall* may determine if they think fit, or they may at the discretion of the Judges suspend their further proceeding, and refer them till the Parliament meets to determine them.

33 *H.* VI. *fol.* 17, 18. It is there debated by the Judges, whether it were a perfect and *legal Act* that pass'd in Parliament against Sir *John Pilkington*, for a rape committed by him, and it depended upon the course of the two Houses, in their transmitting of Bills from one to another, and of indorsing the Bills; and they sent for the Clerk of the Parliament and consulted with him about it; and there, *Fortescue*, Chief-Justice, held the Act in question to be a good Act of Parliament; but, says he, peradventure the matter, or question, shall wait till the next Parliament meet, and then we may be certified by them of the certainty of the matter. By this it appears, that the Judges did not disown the jurisdiction of that cause, that was so nearly depending upon the usage of Parliament, but that it belonged to them, and not to the Parliament; yet it was convenient to be advised by the Parliament, and to wait till then.

And Sir *Ed. Coke*, in his 2 *Inst.* 408. tells us, that matters of difficulty were usually adjourned to Parliament.

3. Some things there are that concern the Parliament, wherein the Courts of *Westminster-hall* must not intermeddle, but the jurisdiction belongs to the Parliament only.

By the Statute of 4 *H.* VIII. *c.* 8. tho' all in that Act that concerns one *Richard Strode* is a private Act, yet there is one clause which is a general Act, and is declaratory of the ancient law and custom of Parliament, *viz.* It is enacted, *That all Suits, Accusements, Condemnations, Executions, Fines, Amerciaments, Punishments, Corrections, Charges, and Impositions, at any time from thenceforth, to be put or had upon any Member, for any Bill, speaking, reasoning, or declaring of any matter concerning the Parliament, to be communed or treated of, be utterly void and of none effect.* This concerns none but Members of Parliament, and it provides for freedom of debates in matters that are proper to be treated of in Parliament.

The Lords, for themselves only, and for their own House, made claim of this privilege and jurisdiction, 11 *R.* II. *numb.* 7. Sir *Robert Cotton's Abr. fol.* 321. but it is limited only to matters moved in Parliament, and the King allowed it in full Parliament.

And Sir *Ed. Coke*, in his 2 *Inst. fol.* 15. says, That *pari ratione*, the like belongs to the House of Commons*: And this is the reason, says Sir *E. C.* that Judges ought not to give any opinion of a matter of Parliament, because it is not to be decided by the common Laws used in other Courts, but *secundum legem & consuetudinem Parliamenti.*

So likewise in case of the privilege of a Member of Parliament, against suits and executions, sitting the Parliament, the Judges have refused to give their opinion, tho' demanded by the Lords; as they did in the case of *Thorp*, Speaker of the House of Commons, who was taken in execution between two Sessions of Parliament, of which the Commons made Complaint to the Lords, and the Lords asked the advice of the Judges, whether the Speaker ought to be delivered by privilege of Parliament? The Judges answered, *That they ought not to determine the privilege of the High Court of Parliament*: the case is 31 *H.* VI. *fol.*--- *Rolls Ab.* 2d *part.* 94. *ca.* 1. See 39 *H.* VI. Sir *Robert Cotton's Abridg. num* 6.

Concerning departure from Parliament, (sitting the Parliament) and not attending according to their duty; the case seems doubtful, whether any other Court than the Parliament can determine of that offence, it seeming to be of a middle nature. For tho' it be an offence committed by a Member, and that in Parliament-time, which argues for their privilege, and against the jurisdiction of any inferior Court, especially while the Parliament sits, who undoubtedly may take cognizance of it, and punish it: Yet on the other side, when the Parliament has not taken cognizance of it, and the Parliament is risen, why should not that offence, at the King's suit, be punished in the Star-chamber, while that was a Court, and now in the *King's-Bench*? And why should privilege protect against non-attendance, when the true ground of privilege is by reason of attendance. And Mr. *Plowden*, who was a very learned Lawyer, submits to the jurisdiction, but traverses his departure; as the case of the Bishop of *Winchester*, 3 *E.* III. remembered by Sir *Ed Coke*, in his 2 *Inst.* in his *Chapter of Parliament*, (as far as he reports it) seems rather to be an authority against the jurisdiction of any other Court besides the Parliament itself, in such case of proceeding against a Member to punish him for non-attendance: For the Bishop being impleaded by original writ at the King's suit, (which I suppose was in the *King's-Bench*) *quia recessit à Parliamento sine licentia Regis.*

The Bishop pleaded *quod ipse est unus de paribus, & dicit, quod si quis eorum deliquerit in Dominum Regem in aliquo Parliamento, in Parliamento debet corrigi & emendari, & non alibi in minori curia.* And so Sir *E. C.* seems to leave the victory on the Bishop's side, and that his plea succeeded. But Sir *Francis Moor*, 779, 780 reports the case of the Lord *Sturton*, and the Lord *Mordant*, how they were deeply fined in the Star-chamber, 4 *Jac.* for absenting from Parliament, at the complaint of the Attorney General, *ore tenus.* And there were then present in the Star-chamber, the Lord-Chancellor, Chief-Justice *Popham*, *Fleming*, and *Walmsly*. And for precedents to justify the proceeding against them in that Court, they cite the case of the Earl of *Cornwal*, 4 *H* III and the Bishop of *Winchester's* case, (which I mentioned out now) 3 *E.* III how that for departing from Parliament, without licence, their lands were seized.

But the objection in our case is, *concerning a matter of election of a Knight of a Shire* to serve in Parliament that no other Court but the Parliament must meddle in it, as the objectors would have it.

Answ. It is not impertinent, therefore, to enquire briefly of the true Jurisdiction in this matter.

Sir *Robert Cotton* affirms, that writs of Summons for Knights of the Shire to serve in Parliament, began 49 *H* III. and that the admittance of Commoners into the Parliament, was purposely to lessen and curb the power of the Lords, after the daring Earl of *Leicester* was slain in the battle of *Evesham* (which was that very year), and the Barons were totally routed by Prince *Edward*, (afterwards King *E.* I.) and K. *H.* III. was rescued out of their hands. And to back that opinion, it is observed, that the first writ to the Sheriffs, to summon two Knights out of every Shire that is to be found upon record, is that of the close Roll 49 *H.* III. (the very same year) *dorso* 10 and 11. Thus Mr. *Prynne* affirms, in his preface to the Abridgment of the Records of the Tower, *fol.* 11. in the beginning of that *fol.* and *fol.* 13. *b.* in the middle of that *fol.*

But we must not be governed by Historians in matters of law; and therefore, notwithstanding this observation of Sir *Robert Cotton's* and Mr *Prynne's*, we must presume that the House of Commons, and elections of Knights of the Shire, are as ancient as the Common Law, and have been time immemorial; because we find no written law that does first begin any such Institution.

But to come closer to the objection, and to enquire who are the proper Judges of the right of elections?

Mr. *Prynne*, in the same Preface, *fol.* 14. *b.* in the middle of it, (as I myself have folio'd it, for the print has no *folios* to the Preface,) "The "King and Lords (says he) were anciently sole Judges of the legality "of elections of Members of the House of Commons, till the time of "King *Henry* VII."

And in Sir *Robert Cotton's* Abridgment, *fol.* 392. the year 1 *H.* IV. *num.* 80. at the prayer of the Commons, the King declares, that the Commons were only petitioners, and that all judgments apertain to the King and Lords, unless it were in Statutes, Grants, Subsidies, or such like; the which order the King would from that time to be observed.

But we know that the House of Commons is now possess'd of the jurisdiction of determining all questions concerning the election of their own Members; so far at least, as is in order to their being admitted or excluded from sitting there. But how far their judgment is concluding to all others to other purposes, I have now no just occasion to examine; for, as has been observ'd, the Plaintiff in this case grounds his action upon his original right of election, and mentions the determination of the House on his side, and not only alleges that he was duly elected, but so returned by the Defendant himself. And that tho' he were for some time hindered from sitting, by occasion of the false return, made by the Defendant on purpose, and the election was under question by it, yet he prov'd it clearly to the House, and was admitted, and his election declared good; and taking it for granted that he was duly elected, he sues in the *King's-Bench*, by this action to recover damages for the injury done him by the Defendant, for which the House of Commons could not have help'd him. For to that purpose they have no jurisdiction, for they cannot examine a witness upon oath, nor can they act the part of a Jury to give damages, nor have they any power to award a trial, or to cause the Sheriff to impannel a Jury.

Obj. 3. This is an action of a new invention, and *primæ impressionis*, and never any such was brought before, save that of *Nevil* against *Stroud*; which never had any determination.

Answ. 'Tis true 'tis new, in the particular circumstances, but not in the main, nor in the substance; 'tis new, in that 'tis brought by one elected Knight of a Shire against the Sheriff, for a false and malicious return of another Indenture, whereby the plaintiff was put to great expence and trouble; *but 'tis not new in the general nature of the action* For nothing is more frequent then actions upon the case, where an injury is done and damage sustained; nay, 'tis very frequent for actions upon the case to be brought against Sheriffs, for mere false returns, and that where there is no malice, nor any of those great aggravations that appear in this case.

For this I refer you to the case in *Rolls's Abr.* 1. *part. fol.* 99. *Grin, Palmer* and *Marshal*, in the *King's-Bench*, where the Bailiff of a Franchise was newly removed; but tho' he were removed, took upon him to answer, but made a false answer to the Sheriff's warrant, to execute a *Fieri fac'* against an Administrator, and the Sheriff made that Return to the Court; and thereupon an action upon the case brought against the Sheriff, and adjudged it lies. And that the Sheriff at his peril must take notice who is the rightful Bailiff of the Franchise, and accept of no answer to his warrant from any other.

19 *H.* VI. 29. An Action upon the case against a deputy Sheriff, for *embezzelling a Writ.*

19 *H.* VI. 38. by *Paston.* If a Sheriff upon a *Venire fac'* return a Jury that is insufficient to pay issues, the next Sheriff to whom the issues are estreated to be levied, must charge himself with the issues, and must not return a *Nihil*, but shall have an action upon the case against his Predecessor, for his false return; yet here is no malice, but at the most a neglect, or a mistake only.

39 *E.* III. 7. *Brook.* action upon the case, 67.

An action upon the case against a Sheriff for not summoning and warning a man in due time, upon a writ of *Præmunire* or attachment, whereby he sustained damage, as judgment given against him, or the like. This is but a bare neglect or omission, and seems to be the least or lowest sort of injuries; and yet being accompanied with a particular damage to the party, tho' without any malice on the Sheriff's part, the action will lie.

3 *E.* IV. 20. *Brook.* action upon the case, *pl.* 91. by *Danby* and *Pigot*, for a false return only.

If a *Nihil* be returned against me who have land, *F. N. B.* 93. 31 *E.* III. *Fitz. Abr Process* 55.

So for not returning a writ of second deliverance, which is a mere neglect and *non-feasance*, tho' there be no malice, 21 *E.* III. 43. *Br. Act. s. ca. pl.* 48. 5 *Rep.* 32 *b.* 91. 7 *Rep.* 1.

So against a Bishop, if he falsely return, that an executor has not refused the executorship, when *re vera* he has refused it, 2 *Leon.* 221.

So against an Escheator, 9 *H* VI 60. 21 *E.* IV. 23. 27.

Much more shall the action upon the case lie against the Sheriff, as the circumstances of this case are, where the return is not only false, but he

* Sir *John Eliot*, and *Denzil Holles*, pleaded the like Plea to the jurisdiction of the *King's-Bench.* *Ante p.* 243.

knew

knew it to be false, and he did it maliciously, with a purpose to hinder the plaintiff from sitting, and to put him to expence, and where the plaintiff has had so great a damage. And the Sheriff by his oath is oblig'd to do right as well to poor as to rich, in all that belongeth to his office. 2. To do no wrong to any man for favour nor hate. 3. To disturb no man's right. 4. Truly to return, and truly to serve all the King's writs, as far forth as shall be within his cunning. And the Jury by their verdict in this case, have found the defendant to fail in every one of these clauses of his oath. And tho' the circumstances that do diversify all cases are new in this case; yet 'tis very frequent in actions upon the case, to have new cases and new circumstances; and there is nothing more frequent than this variety and novelty.

Sir *Fran. Bacon*, in his Book of advancement of learning, speaking of cases omitted in law, *fol.* 38. says, *That the narrow compass of man's wisdom cannot comprehend all cases which time hath found out*; and therefore cases omitted and new, do often present themselves, but every new case does not require a new law; for then the legislative power must be continually exercis'd: But tho' it differs from former cases in circumstances, yet it may fall under a general rule, or be proceeded upon by parity of reason; *ubi est eadem ratio, ibi idem est jus.*

And the Statute of *W.* 21. *cap.* 24. has made ample provision for all such new cases that fall under a general rule, but have no formed writ, or writ of course, that fits it in all the particulars and circumstances. *In consimili casu, simili remedio indigente, fiat breve*, says that Statute.

In the 8th *Rep. fol.* 48. *Jehu Webb*'s case, there you have the distinction of writs; some are *brevia formata seu de cursu*, and from thence the Cursitors have their name, because they have the drawing of those writs.

Some are *brevia Magistralia quæ nec sunt de cursu nec formata*, i. e. *de aliqua certa forma, sed sæpius variant secundum varietatem casuum, factorum & querularum*; as are actions upon the case, *&c.* which have not any certain form, but are upon occasion drawn by the Masters of the Chancery, and from thence are called *Magistralia*; all this is by virtue of the words of the Statute of *W.* II. *c.* 24. *Concordant clerici in Cancellaria de brevi faciendo.* 2 *Inst.* 405, 406, 407.

And many new cases may be put, that have no parallel cases to be found in our Books, if all the particulars and circumstances be regarded, as the case, 8 *Car. Croke* 291. in the King's Bench, where an action upon the case is brought against an *Apparitor*, for what he did in his office, *viz.* for falsely and maliciously presenting one, and that in the *Spiritual Court*, for incontinency. This was against an officer for what he did in his office, and to which his oath obliged him; and this was for a thing done in the Spiritual Court, *viz.* the Consistory Court at *Exeter*, and for a matter merely of ecclesiastical cognisance, *viz.* incontinency, wherein the Common Law had nothing to do; and this case had no parallel nor precedent before it: and yet being an injury and damage to the party presented, and done falsely and maliciously, and without colour, and for which the party injured could have no recompence in any other Court, but at Common Law, it was adjudged the action lay. This case, tho' it had no parallel before it in all the circumstances, yet in many respects it is a parallel to the case before us. There is the like action against constables for making a false presentment, *Croke Car.* 467. and the case I cited before against a Sumner, 12 *Rep.* 128.

And for that objection and observation concerning the novelty of this action, this more may be said in answer to it; That till of late years Sheriffs have given no occasion for the like action of this; for double returns, upon elections to Parliament, have not been in ancient times.

Mr. *Prynne*, in his *Brevia Parliamentaria Rediviva, fol.* 137. observes, that there were not above two or three cases of elections questioned from 49 *H.* III. till 22 *E.* IV. for aught appears by the returns, or Parliament-Rolls, and not so much as one double return or indenture.

And the common law does comply with, and conform to the general opinion and genius of the Kingdom, and values what they generally esteem and value, and disesteems what they value not.

Heretofore an election to serve in Parliament was not a thing so desirable, and so much sought after as now-a-days it is; and it is not the desire or seeking after it that is to be dislik'd or condemn'd, for he that desireth the office of a Bishop (says the *Apostle*) desires a good office; but it is the undue means used, or the ill ends for which it is desired, that makes the seeking bad.

Mr. *Prynne, ut supra, fol.* 165. *anno* 1 *E.* III. a writ issued to elect two Knights for the county of *Northumberland*, and the Sheriff returned this answer, *communitas comit. Northumbriæ sic respondet, quod ipsi per inimicos Scotiæ adeo sunt destructi, quod non habent unde solvere expensa duobus militibus proficiscentis ad consilium apud Lincoln. tenendum.*

In his fourth part of his Register of Parliamentary writs, is mentioned a Patent of exemption granted 42 *E.* I. to the town of *Torrington* in *Devonshire*; which Patent recites in its preamble, *that the men of that town never used to send Burgesses to Parliament*, till the Sheriff, 21 *E.* I. *summonitas fuisse malitiose returnavit.*

So that a malicious return to Parliament is no new thing, but has been formerly done; and as the plaintiff in this action has well sued the Sheriff for returning another with him, so I make no doubt but as the case then stood with the general humour and opinion of the people, those of *Torrington* might have had their remedy against the then Sheriff for returning them summoned.

And the Law is still the same, in that it still sets a price and esteem upon that which the people generally esteem and value.

And several cases have been put to prove, that new Statutes have given occasion to new actions upon the case, which actions could not have been sued at the Common Law; and yet those new Laws and statutes do not give those new actions, but only occasioned them.

Barnes vers. Carey 12 *Jac.* King's-Bench, *Rolls*'s *Rep. fol.* 47.

The plaintiff there brought an action upon the case against the Sheriff of *Bristol*, for suffering *J. S.* to escape out of his custody, *J. S.* being committed by the Commissioners of bankrupts, for refusing to answer Interrogatories, the plaintiff being one of the creditors, and *J. S.* a bankrupt; and after many exceptions taken to the declaration, the Court gave judgment for the plaintiff. And yet there was no such thing as a commission of bankrupt at the common Law; but the common Law takes occasion by the statutes of bankrupt, to give such an action upon th[e] before those statutes could not have been sued.

In like manner the common Law takes occasion by thos[e] give the action of waste against tenant for life, or years, ag[ainst] lay not by common Law, to give an action upon the case ag[ainst te]nants, if they will not permit their Lessors to enter upon th[e] sed, to view whether waste be done or not. *Croke* 2 *part*, 47[...]

Object. 4. That there is not one case in Law parallel to t[...] Sheriff to be sued for returning the whole truth, and somethi[ng] the truth: tho' actions for false returns are frequent.

Answ. This is an action for a false return, and something [...] it is for a false return, appears by that allegation, that he di[d] his return, and the Jury have found it so, and we must belie[ve] was false in this, in that he returned an Indenture pretende[d] the hands and seals of divers persons, as the greater part of t[...] ty, purporting the choice of another than the plaintiff to be [...] Shire. The plaintiff does not alledge, that there ever was [...] denture sealed by any person; but that the defendant did fals[ely] other Indenture, purporting the same to be made by divers [...] So that we may reasonably understand it, that in truth there [...] such Indenture sealed by any but the Sheriff himself, and not [...] that were present at the election. 2*dly*, Tho' the Sheriff [...] the whole truth, yet together with that truth he returned a fa[...] till it was re-examined, it could not appear which was the t[...] the mean time the plaintiff sustained all his damage.

Object. 5. That the Sheriff acted herein as a Judge, and t[...] err, he is not to be sued for it, but his error may be reformed; [...] will not suffer an averment tending to the discredit of a Ju[dg]*ment.* 491. *b.* and *Dy.* 89. *b.*

Answ. All this is true, as to one that is a Judge of Record. [...] the greatness of his authority, and the great trust the King an[d] pose in a Judge of Record; but the Sheriff is no Judge at a[...] acts in the election of Knights for the Shire, but is only an [...] Record, 9 *H.* VI. 53. and 60. *Br. Ab. Tit. Act. s. ca. plac.* 6. [...] particular cases indeed, the Sheriff is a Judge, as in a *Justici[es] ad. fin.* and a Judge of Record, as in a *Re-disseisin*, by the Statute of [...]

Object. 6. The Statute of 23 *H.* VI. *c.* 15. has provided a r[...] the Sheriff for any abuse committed by him in elections, *viz* [...] of an hundred pound, in case of Knights of the Shire, to th[e in]jured: And it does recite in the preamble, that a convenien[t ...] the party grieved is not ordained in the former statutes; an[d] it is inferred, that there was no remedy for the party grieve[d at com]mon Law, nor before this statute.

Answ. I have already proved, that there was a remedy at [...] Law, and before this statute; and this statute is an argumen[t ...] for this statute mentions a party grieved, and there could be [...] out a remedy, otherwise the Law would have been defective. [...] not be denied, but that if there were a remedy at the comm[on Law ...] statute being in the affirmative does not take it away, only it [...] remedy.

And for the words of this statute of 23 *H.* VI. that *a conven[ient ...]* the party grieved is not ordained by the formed statutes; thi[s ...] gue that there was no remedy at the Common Law, nor doe[s ...] there was no remedy at all; but that there was no *conveni[ent ...]* those former statutes, and thereupon the statute of 23 *H.* VI. [...] dred pound to the Knight injured by an undue return.

I shall put some like cases where Acts of Parliament g[...] where yet there were other remedies before at common Law, [...] may sue for either; *Rolls' Ab.* 1. *part. fol.* 93. *case* 20.

A *Distringas* is awarded to the Sheriff to distrain the defen[dant ...] tion, and the Sheriff returns too small issues, tho' an averme[nt ...] statute of *W.* II. *c.* 43. yet the plaintiff may well have his ac[tion upon the] case against the Sheriff, because it appears by the words of th[...] it is a false return. Observe the argument there used, *viz.*

If the action upon the case did not lie, in such case the pl[aintiff ...] any remedy at the common Law, which was greatly mischie[vous ...] statute (as is there observed) tho' it gives a new remedy, and [...] tice of any remedy that was before in the case, yet it does n[ot ...] plaintiff from any remedy that he had at the common Law [...] indeed made a *Quære*; but Serjeant *Rolls* has this Note upon [...] 3 *Car.* one Mrs. *Bennet*, upon good advice, brought such an ac[tion upon the] case against the Sheriff of *London*, for returning too small issu[es ...] Mayor and Commonalty of *London*.

The statute of *W.* II. *c.* 24. (Sir *E. C.* 2 *Inst. fol.* 404, 4[...] an assize of *nusance* against the Alienee of him that levied tha[t ...] that statute seems (as Sir *E. C.* observes) to understand that t[he ...] ed was without any remedy before; for it provides in these w[ords ...] *non recedant quærentes a curia Regis sine remedio*: yet Sir *E. C.* [...] *fol.* 405. of his 2. *Inst.* at the lower end of that *folio*, upon [...] *ria*) *That the makers of that Act knew well that the party injured* [...] might enter upon the ground of the wrong-doer, not only w[...] his hands, but after it was aliened too, and abate the nusan[ce ...] vent himself of the remedy by assize of nusance given by this [...] sides this, he had another remedy by action, *viz.* If he had [...] damage (says Sir *E. C.*) he might bring his action upon the [case to re]cover damage, *ne quærentes recederent a curia sine remedio.*

Object. The ground of this action against the Sheriff is [...] double return. Now the declaration sets forth only one perfe[ct ...] that is of the plaintiff's election, which the declaration says, [...] *exigentiam brevis*; and it was by Indenture, under the seal[s ...] and Electors: And tho' the plaintiff alledges, that the late [...] Electors returned another Indenture of the election of an[...] (which is the *gravamen* that he complains of) yet that appear[s ...] turn; for it was not said, *that that Indenture was under any se[als ...]* statutes of 7 *H.* IV. *c.* 15. and 8 *H.* VI. *c.* 7. require Indentu[res ...] the Electors to be tack'd to the writ, which Indentures so se[al]ed, shall be holden for the Sheriff's return.

Answ. This other Indenture last mentioned, must be und[er ...] denture ensealed, in like manner as the former; for the declara[tion ...]

mentions the first Indenture, whereby the Plaintiff was returned to be chosen, and that it is said to be so ensealed, as the Statutes require, and then the declaration says, that the Sheriff, together with that Indenture, return'd another Indenture: so that it must be reasonably understood, to be an Indenture, in like manner ensealed.

And then 'tis said by the declaration of this last Indenture, that it was annexed to the Writ, and so return'd by the Defendant the Sheriff, which must therefore be presum'd to be an Indenture ensealed, or else to what purpose did the Defendant annex it to the Writ, and return it?

And further the declaration says, that by reason of the false return, the Plaintiff could not be admitted into the Lower House, till he had made proof of his Election. Now, if that other Indenture were not ensealed, it could not be said to be a false return; for it would indeed have been no return, and it could not have hindered the Plaintiff from being admitted, nor put him to the proof of his Election.

And that the Indenture must be understood an Indenture ensealed, by those that were present at the Election, appears by the Writ; the form whereof you will find in *Crompt. Jurisdiction of Courts, fol.* 1. *b.* the Clause is this; *Et nomina eorundem militum, sic electorum, in quibusdam Indenturis, inter te & illos qui hujusmodi Electioni interfuerint inde conficiendis, inseri.* And in another Clause, *Et Electionem illam sub sigillo tuo & sigillis eorum qui Electioni illi interfuerint nobis in Cancellariam certifices, remittens nobis alteram partem Indenturar. prædictar. præsentibus consutam una cum hoc breve.*

The Lord Chief-Justice *North*'s Argument, in the Case between Sir *William Soame*, Sheriff of *Suffolk*, and Sir *Samuel Barnardiston*, Bart. adjudged in the Court of *Exchequer-Chamber*, upon a Writ of Error, containing the Reasons of that Judgment.

SIR *Samuel Barnardiston*, the Plaintiff, brings an action upon the case in *Banco Regis* against the Defendant, Sir *William Soame*, late Sheriff of *Suffolk*, setting forth, that a Writ issued for the chusing of a Knight for that County, to serve in the then Parliament, instead of Sir *Henry North*, deceased; that at the next County Court the Freeholders proceeded to an Election, and altho' the Plaintiff was duly chosen *per majorem numerum gentium tunc resident. infra dict. Comitat. quorum tunc quilibet expendere potuit* 40s. *libri ten'ti & ultra per annum infra Comitat. illud, ac licet prædictus* Willielmus, *præmissa satis sciens, postea brevem præd. in cur. Cancellar. retornavit, simul cum quadam Indentura inter ipsum Vicecomitem & prædict. Electores ipsius* Samuelis *de prædicta Electione ipsius* Samuelis *fact. secund. Exigentiam brevis prædict. Prædictus tamen* Willielmus *adtunc Vicecomes Officii sui debitum minime ponderans, sed machinans & malitiose intendens ipsum* Samuelem *in hac parte minus rite prægravare, ac eundem* Samuelem *de fiducia & officio unius Mil. Comitat. prædict. in dict. Parliamento exercend omnino frustrare, & deprivare & prædict.* Samuelem *ad diversas magnas & grandes pecuniarum summas expend. causare, contra debitum officii sui prad. false, malitiose, scienter & deceptive, adtunc in ead. Cancellar. apud* Westmonast. *prædict retornavit una cum Indentura prædict. quandam aliam Indenturam eidem brevi similiter annex. specificat. illam fore fact inter præfat.* Willielmum, *&c. una parte, & diversas alias personas dict. Comitat. in Indentura illa specificat. & continent. quod dictæ al. personæ, ut major pars totius Comitat. prædict in prædicto pleno Comitat. elegerunt quend.* Lionellum Talmash, *Bar. alias dict.* Lionel *Dom* Huntingtowre, *in Regno* Scotiæ, *in loco prædicti* Henrici North *un. Mil. Com.* Suffolk *prædict. pro Parliamento prædicto adveniend. eidem Parliamento pro Com. il. Ubi re vera prædictus* Lionellus *non fuit electus par majorem partem, prout per eadt. Indent. falso supponitur. Ratione cujus quidem falsi retorn. de prædicta al. Indent. &c. idem* Samuel *in Dominum inferiorem pro Comitat. hujus Regni* Angliæ, *&c. assemblat. admitti non potuit, quousque idem* Samuel *per petitionem suam Comitat. dicti Parliamenti pro remedio congruo exhibet; & post diversas ingentes denar. summas in & circa manifestationem & verificationem dictæ Electionis coram dict. Comitat. expendit, & diversos labores in ea parte sustent. Postea scil. &c. per Comitat. in Domum Comitat. prædict. admissus fuit & electio ipsius* Samuelis *per Comitat. declarat. fuit, fore bona, unde deterior est, & damnum habet ad Valenc.* 3000*l.*

There is a Verdict given for the Plaintiff, and damages found to the value of 800*l.* and Judgment thereupon, and a Writ of Error is brought to reverse that Judgment.

I have but a little Time left me to say what I have to offer, it being very late, and yet I must desire leave to produce those reasons I have in maintenance of my opinion: I will be careful not to detain you longer than will be necessary.

And therefore, I will not trouble you with starting the case again, nor will I speak of any exceptions that have been made to the declaration, for I love not the niceties of the Law, in cases where they do prevail: and in this case I have only considered the foundations of the action; which if I had found well established upon reason, or the grounds of the Law, I would have examined what has been objected to the forms of the declaration, which must have brought great weight to have overturned those Proceedings.

But as the point of the action, upon the most serious consideration I could have of it, and weighing what has been before now, and also at this time, said in support of it; I am of opinion, that the Judgment ought to be reversed; for that no such action as this, at Bar, does lie by the Common Law.

Because this is a cause of considerable value, great damages being recovered, because it is a Judgment of great authority, being upon a cause tried at the *King's-Bench* Bar, and given upon deliberation there, because it is a case of an extraordinary nature, and of great import, each party pretending benefit to the Parliament by it; because it is an action *Primæ Impressionis*, that never was before adjudged, the report of which will be listened after: I have taken pains to collect and set down the reasons that I must go upon in determining this case, that as the Judgment had the countenance of some deliberation in the Court where it was given, so the reversal being with greater deliberation, may appear grounded upon reasons that ought to prevail.

I can say with my brother *Wyndham*, that I love rather to affirm Judgments than to reverse them, but I can attribute no more of authority to the Judgment, tho' it were given in a superior Court, and upon deliberation. I must judge of it as if the case came to be judged originally by me:

the argument to support a Judgment from the authority of itself, is, *Exceptio ejusdem rei cujus petitur Dissolutio*, which must not be admitted in cases of Writs of Error. We are entrusted to examine and correct the errors of that Court, and for that purpose we are made superior to it; we must proceed according to our own knowledge and discretion, or else we do not perform the trust reposed in us.

I must needs say, this is a cause that imports it more than any cause I have known to come before us, for it is a cause *Primæ Impressionis*, and the question is, Whether by this Judgment a change of the Common Law be introduced? It is the principal use of Writs of Error, and Appeals, to hinder the change of the Law; therefore do Writs of Error in our Law, and Appeals in the Civil Law, carry Judgments and Decrees to be examin'd by superior Courts until they come to the highest, who are entrusted that they will not change the Law.

Therefore do Writs of Error lie from *Ireland*, which is a subordinate Kingdom to *England*, by whose Laws it is governed, that they might not be able to change the Law by their Judgments, and not so much for the particular right of the party.

For otherwise it would be very easy for Judges, by construction and interpretation, to change even a written Law; and it would be most easy for the Judges of the Common Laws of *England*, which are not written, but depend upon usage, to make a change in them, especially if they may justify themselves by such a rule as my brother *Atkins* lays down to support this case, *viz.* that the Common Law complies with the genius of the Nation. I admit that the Laws are fitted to the genius of the Nation; but when that genius changes, the Parliament is only entrusted to judge of it, and by changing the Law to make it suitable to it. But if the Judges shall say it is Common Law, because it suits with the genius of the Nation, they may take upon them to change the whole as well as any part of it, the consequence whereof may easily be seen; I wish we had not found it by sad experience.

If the case at the Bar be a change of the Law, it is happy that it comes to be questioned in the first instance; for if this cause had been any way agreed and quitted, and a second case of this nature had been question'd, there would have been a precedent urg'd, which cannot be spoke of here; for this case hath no fellow, there never having been the like Judgment before.

The method I shall take in what I have to say, shall be,

1st, To remove some prejudice the Case is under.

2dly, Give my reasons against the Action.

3dly, Weigh what has been said to maintain the Action.

1st, The case is under this prejudice, that an action of the case lies for false returns of Sheriffs, and why should it not lie in this case as well as any other?

To remove this prejudice, I shall shew some material differences betwixt the nature of ordinary returns and this return.

In ordinary returns the party is concluded, and absolutely without remedy; for the Court must take the return as the Sheriff makes it. In ordinary cases the Sheriff may, and frequently does, take security of the Plaintiff, or the Sheriff hath means by Law to be secure; as, if he doubts the property of the goods, he may return a *Fieri facias, Nulius venit ad monstrandum bona.* In some cases he may, for his safety, impannel a Jury, as upon an *Elegit*; or he may resort to the Court, and pray reasonable time to prepare his return, if the matter be difficult; and hath other shelters, that if he be wary, will save him from danger.

But in this case the party is not concluded, for upon a Petition to the Parliament, it they see it just, they will cause the return to be altered by the Clerk of the Crown, if the Sheriff be not in the way; in this case, the Sheriff may not take security, it were criminal in him to make such a return by Compact, nor can the Sheriff make a fruitless return or obtain delay to consult his safety.

These differences are of that nature, that they change the case in the reason of it, as I shall hereafter make appear: and no man can infer, because an action lies for false returns in ordinary cases; therefore it lies in case of a return to Parliament, where the Sheriff is clearly upon terms.

My reasons against this action are applicable to this case, and make it different from all the cases, that have been put by my brothers that argued for the action: I observe they argued only upon generals, without any other application to this case than by the topick of concluding, *à Minori ad Majus*, because an action lies in cases of inferior nature, therefore it will lie in this; which rule holds not in diverse cases, where there are particular reasons to the contrary, as I shall by-and-bye shew to be in this.

2dly, I shall give you my reasons against this action, which are as follow:

(1.) My first reason is this, because the Sheriff as to the declaring the majority is Judge; and no action will lie against a Judge, for what he does judicially, tho' it should be laid *falso, malitiose & scienter*; as appears in *Co.* 12. *Rep. fol.* 24. *They who are intrusted to judge, ought to be free from vexation, that they may determine without fear; the Law requires courage in a Judge, and therefore provides security for the support of that courage.* But,

1. Is the Sheriff a Judge in this case? And,

2. Is there the same reason he should be freed from all actions?

As to the first it is of necessity, that as to the declaring the majority, he should be Judge upon the place: in other cases, in the County Court, the Freeholders are the Judges, and he is the Minister. When we say the Freeholders, we mean the major part of them is to judge; but when the question is, Which is the major part? they cannot determine the question; but of necessity the Sheriff must determine that, the nature of the thing speaks it.

Therefore it was held rightly in *Letchmere*'s case, 13 and 14. *Car.* II. that as to the Election of Knights to the Parliament, the Court is properly the Sheriff's Court, and the Writ is in the nature of a special Commission, *Elegi facias.*

I know a Judge may have many ministerial Acts incumbent upon him, as the Chief-Justices have to certify Records upon Writs of Error, therefore it is necessary for me to observe, that the [illegible] here is for what he does as a Judge, and not for any thing [illegible] which appears by the [illegible], that the Sheriff [illegible] another Indenture, specifying it to be made by the major part of the Freeholders, and containing that the Lord *Huntingtower* was chosen, *ubi re vera* the Lord *Huntingtowre* was not chosen by the major part of the Freeholders. If it had been said *ubi re vera* the Freeholders supposed to seal the same, never did seal the same, there had been a falsity in his ministerial part of sending in the Indenture; but his sending his two Indentures, which were really sealed by the Freeholders, as they import; wherein the Freeholders of each Indenture (and not the Sheriff) say, that they are the major part, is no falsity in his ministerial part, but only deferring to judge between them, which is the major part; or more properly judging that they are both equal in number.

They object, that the matter of this question is not matter of Judgment, 'tis but counting the Poll, which requires Arithmetick, but not Judgment; but certainly if it be rightly considered, it will be thought this question of Majority is not barely a question of fact, but a question of judgment, a question of difficult judgment, there are so many qualifications of Electors,

1. They must have 40 *s. per annum*, there the value must be judged.
2. It must be Freehold; there the Title.
3. It must be their own; there colourable and fraudulent gifts made many times on purpose to get voices, must be judged.
4. The Electors must be resident; here the settlement of the party must be determined.
5. There are many things that incapacitate voices, as bribery, force, *&c.* and many other questions arise, that are of such difficulty in debate of them, much time is spent in Parliament; and sometimes a Committee determines one way, and the House another. Is not this then a question that refers to Judgment?

They object again, the Sheriff may give an oath concerning all the qualifications, and he is to look no farther.

I answer, the Statute has given the Sheriff power to give an oath in assistance of him; but the Statute does not say that whosoever takes that oath shall have a voice: neither does the Statute 23 *Hen.* VI. say, that the Sheriff shall not be charged with a false return, that pursues that way: so that although he may use those means for his direction, yet he must consider his own safety, and not make a false return. If a man, upon taking such an oath, give the Sheriff a special answer, or if it should be known to the Sheriff he swears false, the Sheriff must determine according to his own judgment, and not by what is sworn.

It may hence be concluded, that the Sheriff, as to declaring a majority, is a Judge; and if so, my next assertion is, that there is the same reason he should be free from actions, as any Judge in *Westminster-hall*, or any other Judge. Does it not import the Publick, that the Sheriff should deal uprightly and impartially? Ought he not to have courage, and for that end should not the Law provide him security?

Consider his disadvantages, what a noise and croud accompany such elections; what importunity, nay, what violence there is upon him from the contesting parties.

We may say, no other Judge has more need of courage and resolution to manage himself, and determine uprightly, than he. No other Judge determines in a case of greater consequence to the publick, or difficulty, than he; expose him to such actions, and in most Elections he must have trouble, for commonly each party is confident of his strength, his conduct, and his friends; that let the Sheriff return never so uprightly, the party that is rejected will revenge it by a suit, especially if he may sue at Common Law, to have boundless damages, without running any hazard himself, but of the loss of his costs.

If we Judges, that find ourselves secure from actions, should not be tender of others that are in the same circumstances; it may well be said, *Wo unto you, for you impose heavy burthens upon others, but will not bear the least of them yourselves.*

2. My second reason is, because it is *alieni fori*, either to examine the right of the Election, or behaviour of the Sheriff; both which are incident, and indeed the only considerations that can guide in the Trial of such causes, if they be allowed.

It is admitted, that the Parliament is the only proper Judicature to determine the right of Election, and to censure the behaviour of the Sheriff. How then can the Common Law try a cause, that cannot determine of those things, without which the cause cannot be tried?

No action upon the case will lie for breach of a trust, because the determination of the principal thing, the trust, does not belong to the Common Law, but to the Court of *Chancery*: certainly the reason of the case at Bar is stronger, as the Parliament ought to have more reverence than the Court of *Chancery*.

They object, that it may be tried after the Parliament hath decided the Election; for then that which the Common Law would not try is determined, and the Parliament cannot give the party the costs he is put unto.

Then I perceive they would have the determination of the Parliament binding to the Sheriff in the action, which it cannot be; for that is between other parties to which the Sheriff is not called: it is against the course of Law, that any Judgment, Decree or Proceeding betwixt other parties should bind the interest of, or any way conclude a third person; no more ought it to do here: it may be easy for parties combining to represent a case so to the Parliament, that the right of Election may appear either way as the parties please. Is it fit the Sheriff, who is not admitted to controvert such determination, should be concluded by it, in an action brought against him, to make him pay the reckoning?

Did the Parliament believe, when they determined this Election, that they passed Sentence against the Sheriff, upon which he must pay 800 *l.*? Sure if they had imagined so, they would, nay, in Justice, they ought to have heard his defence, before they determined it.

And yet that was the measure of this case, the Sheriff was not heard in Parliament, indeed he was not blamed there: and yet upon the Trial, which concerned him so deeply, he was not allowed to defend himself, by shewing any majority or equality of voices, the Parliament having determined the Election.

I do not by these reflections tax the Law of Injustice, or the course of Parliament of Inconvenience, I am an admirer of the methods of both: it is from the Excellency of them, I conclude this Proceeding in this new-fangled action, being absurd, unjust and unreasonable, cannot be legal.

To answer the other branch of this objection, I say, it does not follow, that because the Parliament cannot give costs, therefore this new-devised action must lie, to help the party to them.

4

For then such an action might as well lie in all cases, wh[...] wrong to be remedied by course of Law, and no costs are gi[...]

At the Common Law no costs were given in any case, and remain at this day, where the Statutes have given no costs. [...] hibition, *Scire facias*, and *Quare impedit*, and divers other ca[...] no action will lie to recover those costs, and why should it li[...] at Bar?

In this case the Parliament have already had it under th[...] ration in the Statute 23 *Hen.* VI. and have appointed what [...] by the Sheriff that offends, *viz.* 100 *l.* to the party, 100 *l.* [...] and imprisonment; the Parliament have stated what shall [...] compensation, and what for punishment, and would have [...] costs, if they had thought fit.

3. My third reason is, because a double return is a law[...] the Sheriff to perform his duty in doubtful cases.

If this be so, then all aggravations of *falso, malitiose & s[...]* make the thing actionable; for whatever a man may do fo[...] cannot be the ground of an action.

There is sometimes *Damnum absque injuria*, though the t[...] on purpose to bring a loss upon another, without any design [...] himself, as if a new house be erected contiguous to my gr[...] build any thing on purpose to blind the lights of that new h[...] action will accrue, though the malice were never so grea[...] will it lie, when a man acts for his own safety.

If a Jury will find a special verdict; if a Judge will adv[...] time to consider; if a Bishop will delay a Patron, and imp[...] to enquire of the Right of Patronage; you cannot bring a[...] these delays, though you suppose it to be done maliciously, [...] pose to put you to charges; though you suppose it to be d[...] knowing the Law to be clear: for they take but the liberty [...] provided for their safety, and there can be no demonstrati[...] have not real doubts, for these are within their own breasts; [...] very mischievous, that a man might not have leave to doub[...] great peril.

The course of Parliament makes out the ground of this [...] true in fact, so that a double return is lawful when the She[...] for if the Parliament did not allow a double return in do[...] they ought never to accept a double return: if it were in itse[...] unlawful return, they ought not to endure it a moment, but [...] Sheriff, and compel him forthwith to make a single return. [...] where there is doubt, the Parliament sends not for the S[...] they have examined the case, and given particular directio[...]

And it must of necessity be the course: for suppose th[...] equal: suppose the Election is void for force; suppose the S[...] upon the validity of some voices, shall he transmit his dou[...] to Parliament? Was there ever any such thing done? W[...] any other way but to make a double return, and leave it [...] decision of Parliament?

It was said by my brother *Ellis*, that if the Sheriff had ret[...] nature of a special verdict, the special matter, and had conc[...] manner, *viz.* if the Parliament shall adjudge Sir *Samuel Barn[...]* chosen, then he returns him; and if the Parliament shall [...] Lord *Huntingtowre* to be chosen, then he returns him; th[...] turn as this had been safe, and could not have borne an acti[...]

This is a pretty invention, found out for argument sake, I [...] it furnishes no force at all to the part for which it is brough[...] shews the right to be the other way: for let any man of reas[...] ther a double return, as it is now used, be not the same th[...] quence? Is not a double return, as if the Sheriff should say [...] ament, "The right of Election is between these two, I a[...] "which of them I shall reject, and expect your directions." [...] import of a double return, and is the same in effect, as if it h[...] like a special verdict; and so my brother *Ellis*'s instance [...] actionable, though he concluded otherwise.

That other new-fangled way could not be received.—For

1. *The Freeholders would never join in such a return.*
2. *Such a return is not capable of being amended by the Sheriff.*

But the judgment of the Parliament must be entered upo[...] make it any return, it concluding nothing of itself, as a sp[...] concludes nothing, till the judgment of the Court be ente[...] roll with it.

3. *The Parliament will not, as I believe, admit of new device [...] of their Proceedings, whatever we do at Law.*

But the double return is practicable in the County, for th[...] of each part will tender their Indentures; and it is easily am[...] liament, by rejecting the Indenture of those Freeholders that [...] major part, which way has been practised in doubtful ca[...] years.

So that I apprehend the case at Bar to be more regular [...] able, than that case, which my brother *Ellis* put as a ca[...] bear an action.

Again, suppose the Sheriff had informed the Parliament [...] and that he could not readily determine where the majority [...] was betwixt two persons, *A.* and *B.* and thereupon desired [...] either to grant him time to determine it, if they pleased to c[...] so to do, or else, that they would decide it themselves, a[...] obey what directions they should make in it; and thereupo[...] ment had taken upon themselves to determine it.

This most clearly had not been actionable, for it is not acti[...] lay a return to any Court of Justice, where the Sheriff had l[...] Court so to do.

A double return, in my understanding, speaks the same [...] Parliament; and upon it they may either direct the Sheriff t[...] gle return, which is to cause him to decide it, or they may [...] selves.

And here, I must needs reflect upon the second reason I [...] this action, that the matter of it is *alieni fori*, I find my [...] brothers that argued for the action, engaged in a di[...] nature of a double return, and the course of Parl[...] it, which, as a Judge, I cannot so well speak to. I [...] to be of this House of Commons, and whilst I wa[...]

fidered as well as I could the course of the Proceedings of the House, and am therefore able to speak something of them, and I am brought into this discourse necessarily by this action: but I must needs say, it is an improper discourse for Judges, for they know not what is the course of Parliament, nor the privilege of Parliament. When the Lords in Parliament, whom they are bound to assist with their advice, ask the Judges any thing, concerning the course or privilege of Parliament, they have answer'd, that they know them not, nor can advise concerning them.

If in Parliament we do not know, nor can advise concerning these things; how can we judge upon them out of Parliament? We ought to know before we judge, and therefore we cannot judge of things we cannot know.

Our being engaged in a discourse improper for Judges, shews the action to be improper, as much as any other argument that can be made; and this argument arises from my brothers that argued for the action.

But now I am in this discourse, I must go a little farther; my observation from the course of Parliament has been, that they will not permit the Sheriff to delay his return, to deliberate, and he cannot take security of either party, and if a single return be not justified by the Committee of Elections, he is in danger of the Statute of 23 *Hen.* VI.

It follows, that there is no way for an innocent Sheriff to be safe, where he conceives doubt, but in making a double return; and if that should be actionable too, the service of the Parliament would be the most ungrateful service in the world.

It seems ridiculous to me, that it should be objected, that this course of Law is necessary to prevent the great mischief arising from double returns; whenas, if it be a mischief, or dislik'd by the Parliament, either in general or any particular case, they may reject them when they please, and command the Sheriff to make a single return; so that they may remedy it by their practice, without their Legislative Power.

Their practice hitherto has been to receive double returns, which therefore in some cases must be lawful, and in this very case the double return was accepted, and the Sheriff no way punish'd for it; which he ought to have been, if he had been blameable.

If double returns are accepted by Parliament, they are allow'd, and we must say they are lawful, which is the ground of my third reason; for which I hold this action not maintainable.

4. My fourth reason is, That there is no legal damages occasioned by the Sheriff. The damages laid in the declaration are,

1. *Being kept from sitting in the House.*

2. *The pains and charges he was put unto, to get his admittance into the House.*

1. That of his being kept from sitting in the House, is as much every man's damage in the whole County, nay, in the whole Kingdom, and any man else might as well have an action for it, as the Member chosen.

To sit in Parliament is a service in the Member, for the benefit of the King and Kingdom; and not for the particular profit of the Member.

It is a rule in Law, that no particular man may bring an action for a nusance to the King's high-way; because all the men in *England* might as well have actions, which would be infinite · and therefore such an offence is punishable only by Indictment, except there be special loss occasion'd by that nusance.

For the same reason, the exclusion of a Member from the House, being as much damage to all men in *England*, as to himself, he, nor any man else in *England*, can have an action for it; but it is punishable upon the public score, and not otherwise.

For this reason was the Statute 23 *Hen.* VI. wisely consider'd: by that Statute the action is not given to the party for his particular damage; but the action given is a popular action, only the party griev'd hath a preference for six months: but if he do not sue in that time, every man else is at liberty to recover the same sum.

2. The other point of damage, is the pains and charges he was put unto, and that is not occasion'd by the Sheriff, but by the deliberation of the House. Why should the Sheriff pay for that? It may be, if the Parliament had sent for the Sheriff the first day, and blamed the double return, he would have ventur'd to determine the matter speedily, and there should have been no cause of complaint for delay: but the Parliament saw so much cause of doubt, that they think it not fit to put the Sheriff to determine, but to resolve to examine the matter, and give him directions that may guide him in mending his return; thereupon they give a day to the parties on both sides, and finding the matter of long examination, and withal difficult, they deliberate upon it.

It seems very unreasonable the Sheriff should be made pay for this, which he did not occasion; but was a course taken by the Parliament for their own satisfaction, who found no fault in the Sheriff for putting them to all that trouble.

Suppose Sir *Samuel Barnardiston* had been return'd alone, and the Lord *Huntingtowre* had petitioned against that return, there had been the same charge to have defended that return; so that it was the contest of the opposite party that occasioned the charge, the deliberation of the Parliament that occasioned the delay; but neither of them can be imputed to the Sheriff.

I cannot difference this case, from the case of bringing an action against a Jury, for maliciously, knowingly, and on purpose, to put the party to charges, finding a matter specially, whereby great delay and great expences were, before the party could obtain judgment; and yet I think no man will affirm that an action will lie in that case.

In this case the damages are found entire, so that if both parts, *viz.* the not sitting in the House, and the pains and charges are not actionable causes of damages; it will be intended the Jury gave for both, and so the judgment is for that cause erroneous.

I suppose the wages of Parliament will not be mentioned for damages, for in most places they are only imaginary, being not demanded; but if there were to be any consideration of them, it will not alter this case; for upon this return they are due as from the first day, and so no damage can be pretended upon that score.

5. My fifth reason is drawn from the Statute of 23 *Hen.* VI. which has been so often mention'd, that Statute is a great evidence to me, that no action lay by the Common Law against a Sheriff, for a false return of a writ of Election to the Parliament; and this evidence is much strengthened by the observation that hath been made, that never any action was brought otherwise than upon that Statute.

I must admit, that if an action lay by the Common Law, this Statute hath not taken it away, for there are no negative words in the Statute; but it is not likely that the Parliament would have made that Law, if there had been any remedy for the party before.

The Statute observes, that some Laws had been made before, for preventing false returns, but there was not convenient remedy provided for the party griev'd; and therefore gives him an action for 100 *l.* If the Courts of Justice had, by the Common Law, jurisdiction to examine misdemeanors concerning the returns of Sheriffs to the Parliament; what needed the Parliament to be so elaborate, to provide Law after Law, to give them power therein, and at last to give the party griev'd an action? Can any man imagine but that the Parliament took the Law to be, that the party was without remedy? I know preambles of Acts of Parliament are not always Gospel; but it becomes us, I am sure, to have respect to them, and not to impute any falsity or failing to them, especially where constant usage speaks for them.

It has been objected, that in those times, it was reckoned a damage to be return'd to serve in Parliament, which is the reason that no man then did bring his action against the Sheriff for returning another in his stead. This cannot be true, for the Statute calls him the party griev'd, and is careful in providing convenient remedy for him; and we see by the many Statutes about those times, that it was a mischief very frequent, and there wanted no occasion for those actions; which does extremely strengthen the argument of the non-user of this pretended Common Law.

An action upon the case, where it may be brought, is a plaster that fits itself for all times and all sores; and if such an action might then have been brought, there was no need for the Parliament to provide a convenient remedy.

By *Littleton*'s rule, often mentioned by my brothers, we may conclude this action will not lie; for if such an action had lain, it would have been brought before this time.

In the case of *Buckley* against *Rice Thomas*, in *Plowden*'s *Commentaries*, 118, which appears to be so elaborately argued both at Bar and Bench; if this Common Law had been thought upon, they might have prevented the question, whether the Sheriffs of *Wales* were bound by the Statute 23 *Hen.* VI.

It seems plain to me, that the makers of the said Statute were ignorant of this Common Law; and yet my brother *Thurland* observes, the Judges, in those times, usually assisted in the penning of the Laws.

The Judges and Counsel in the time of *Buckley*'s case were ignorant of this Common Law, else it would have been mention'd in the argument of that case.

This Common Law was never reveal'd, that I find, until a time that there were divers other new lights: I mean those times, when *Nevil* brought an action for a false return against *Stroud*, during the late troubles; but in those times it could never obtain Judgment. I have heard that the Court of *Common-Pleas* sent the Record to the Parliament, as a case too difficult for the Courts of Common Law to determine.

The Statute of 23 *Hen.* VI. is not only evidence, that no such action lay at the Common Law; but, in my opinion, is not consistent with any remedy at the Common Law, unless it be allowed that the party should be doubly punished.

If the party griev'd has brought his action upon the Statute, and recover'd, it was admitted by the Counsel, that no action can be brought at the Common Law; nor *e contra*, can he recover by the Statute, after he has recovered by the Common Law, because *Nemo bis punitur pro eodem delicto.*

So far it stands well; but suppose the party griev'd has let slip his time of three months, and then a third person brings a popular action, and recovers 100 *l.* upon the Statute; there is nothing can bar the party griev'd from his action at Common Law, for his sitting still will not conclude him; no Statute of Limitations extending to this case. And if it be so, then must the party, besides his Fine and Imprisonment, be doubly punished by this Statute; which was made, as the Letter of it imports, because there wanted convenient remedy.

And now I am discoursing of this Statute, I must observe the great wisdom of the course of Parliament in these cases, which hath in great measure prevented the bringing actions against Sheriffs, even upon this Statute.

Where the Sheriff mistakes the person in his return, he incurs the penalty of 23 *Hen.* VI. tho' it be without malice: and it may happen that any where there are 21 Electors of one side, and 20 of the other, the Sheriff returns him that hath 21, and the Parliament adjudging an incapacity in two of the 21, may determine he that had the 20 voices was duly chosen. In such case the Sheriff had made a false return, within the penalty of the Statute 23 *Hen.* VI. and no evidence shall be given against the determination of the Parliament.

This was a very hard case for the Sheriff; and if we were liable to such a mischief, many a past Sheriff might be awaken'd, that takes himself to be secure.

But the course of Parliament prevents this, as it is reason; for immediately upon their determination, they send for the Sheriff, and cause him to amend his return; and thenceforward the amended return is the Sheriff's return, and there is no record that can warrant any action to be brought for a false return: as when the Marshal of the *King's-Bench* or Warden of the *Fleet* have made an improvident return, omitting some causes wherewith the Prisoner stood charg'd in their custody, whereby they became liable to action, they frequently move the Court to amend the return; and when the return is amended, all is set right, for there is no averring against a Record: in like manner, when the Sheriff hath amended his return, he is secure from any action upon that occasion.

By this means, there has of late years been no recovery upon the Statute, because all persons chuse rather to compel the Sheriff to amend his return, that they might be admitted to sit in the House, than to take their remedy upon the Statute, and no man can recover upon the Statute first, and have afterwards their return amended: for I have been told, that by the course of Parliament, unless the Petition be lodged within some few days after the return, it cannot be received afterwards. So that a man cannot upon that

Statute

Statute have remedy at Law, and alſo in Parliament: which ſeems to be wiſely provided, to prevent any contrariety of determinations.

This Statute of 23 *H.* VI. furniſhed thoſe that argued for this action, with one argument, which doth now vaniſh: They ſaid that all the inconveniences that could be objected to this action, were the ſame upon the Statute of 23 *H.* VI. *viz.* That upon that Statute, the right of election muſt be examined upon a trial, where there might be a contrariety of determinations; for it appears by what I have ſaid, that there can be no contrariety of determinations.

And there are other inconveniences in this remedy by the Common Law, which are not in the remedy given by the Statute; for by the Statute the ſum to be recovered is limited; the informer hath a time prefixed, ſo that there are bounds ſet which cannot be exceeded: but the remedy by the Common Law is without limitation of time, which is conſiderable, for all Sheriffs that ever made any return otherwiſe than the Parliament determined, will be liable, during their whole lives, to them that will call them to account for it. I ſay, this is without limitation of time, without meaſure of damages, or any rules contained in a written law It depends upon a general notion of remedy, which may be enlarged by conſtruction, as it is now introduced without precedent.

To finiſh my obſervation upon this Statute, I ſay it is great wiſdom in the Parliament to call the Sheriff to amend the return, and ſo prevent any remedy againſt him upon the Statute 23 *H.* VI. for I do not ſee that the rules of law concerning elections, are ſo manifeſtly clear and known, that it is fit that the Sheriff ſhould, upon all returns that are corrected by the Parliament, pay the reckoning of the conteſt.

6. I have a ſixth reaſon againſt this action; which is, becauſe the Sheriff is not admitted to take ſecurity to ſave him harmleſs in ſuch caſes; I take this reaſon to be *inſtar omnium*, and there needs no other in the caſe.

It were the moſt unreaſonable and grievous thing in the world, that the Sheriffs ſhould be bound to act without any deliberation, and not to be allowed to take any ſecurity; and yet be liable to an action, which way ſoever he takes: There is no courſe can avoid it but this of a double return, as I have before ſhewn.

It has not been ſaid, by any that argued the other way, that the Sheriff may take ſecurity: and, I ſuppoſe, will not be ſaid; for it would be a dangerous courſe for Parliaments, for then the moſt litigious man muſt be returned, and not he who is truly choſen.

If the Sheriff may not take ſecurity, the law muſt be his ſecurity. It was an argument uſed by my brother *Ellis*, That becauſe the law impoſes an officer, to wit, the Sheriff, therefore the law muſt give the party an action againſt that officer, if he miſdemean himſelf. The argument does not hold univerſally, for the law impoſes a Judge, and yet no action lies againſt him. But the reaſon of that argument, if turned the other way, is irreſiagable; as thus, The law will not ſuffer the Sheriff to take a ſecurity, therefore the law muſt be his ſecurity, elſe it were a moſt unreaſonable law. This reaſon of itſelf is ſufficient to bear the whole caſe; for no caſe can be put in our law, nay, no caſe can be in any reaſonable law, where a man is compelled to judge without deliberation, and cannot take ſecurity, and yet ſhall be liable to an action.

I have two more reaſons to add, upon which I lay great weight, tho' they depend not upon any particular circumſtances of this caſe, but the general conſideration of it.

1. *That it is a new invention.*
2. *That it relates to the Parliament.*

1. As it is a *new invention*, it ought to be examined very ſtrictly, and have no allowance of favour at the end; and it will have the ſame fortune that many other novelties, heretofore attempted in our law, have had.

Actions upon the caſe have ſometimes been received in new caſes, where it ſtands with the rules of law, and no inconvenience appears; but they have been more often rejected. I ſhall inſtance ſome caſes that have been rejected, becauſe it will be manifeſted by them, that all the arguments and poſitions laid down by my brothers that would ſupport the action, are as well applicable to ſeveral caſes that have been already rejected, as to the caſe at bar.

An action upon the caſe was brought againſt a grand-jury-man, for falſely and maliciouſly conſpiring to indict another, and adjudged it would not lie.

Againſt a witneſs for teſtifying falſely and maliciouſly; and an action was brought againſt a Judge, for acting falſely and maliciouſly; but adjudged that no action would lie in thoſe caſes.

Theſe three inſtances are applicable to every argument urged for this action. The arguments my brothers made in depreſſing falſity and malice, thoſe which they made from the compariſon of other actions upon the caſe *à minori ad majus*; the argument, that becauſe the law impoſes the officer, it will puniſh the malice, has the ſame force in the caſe of a Judge, Juror, or Witneſs; and yet my brothers admit in thoſe caſes, an action will not lie, which ſhews the invalidity of thoſe arguments.

Now I ſhall give other inſtances where actions upon the caſe have been rejected for novelty and reaſons of inconvenience.

An action of the caſe was brought againſt the Lord of a Manor for not admitting a copy-holder, and it was adjudged it would not lie. *Cro. Jac.* 368.

There was a verdict found, and damages given by the jury in that caſe: the Lord is compellable in Chancery to admit a copy-holder; and what harm would it have been, if there might have been a remedy given by the Common Law, there being a cuſtom broken by which the Lord was bound? The reaſons of the books are, becauſe it was a novelty, and it would be vexatious, if every copy-holder ſhould have an action againſt the Lord, when he refuſed to admit him upon his own terms.

It has been adjudged, that an action upon the caſe will not lie for the breach of a truſt, becauſe the Common Law cannot try what a truſt is; but if ſuch actions were allowed, the law might declare that to be a truſt, which the Court of Chancery, that properly judges of truſts, might ſay is none; and where the Common Law cannot examine the principal matter, the damages that were but dependant upon it ſhall not be regarded

Anthony Maddiſon brought an action againſt *Skipwith*, for maliciouſly killing Sir *Tho. Wortley*: the caſe was thus, The plaintiff was a young lawyer that had expended all his gains in the purchaſe of a r[...] determinable upon the death of Sir *Tho. Wortley*, *Skipwit[h]* with Sir *Thomas Wortley* in the ſtreets, about a miſtreſs, a[...] whereby *Maddiſon* loſt his rent. It was held the action wo[...] though it were laid to be done maliciouſly, on purpoſe to d[...] plaintiff's rent.

I obſerved in that caſe, that although Mr. *Maddiſon* kne[w] that there was a miſtreſs in the caſe, and that the rent was [...] yet he would fain try his fortune in the ſuit, thinking th[at] [per]haps, out of compaſſion to him, or to diſcourage the like [...] make the manſlayer pay him for his loſs: but the Judges wo[...] it to go on, it being a mere device and a new-fangled a[...]

It hath been held, that an action will not lie againſt a Par[ſon] for tithes in-kind, knowing that there was a *modus*, becauſe i[t] [...] be perilous for any Parſon to inſiſt upon his right.

It was held by the Court of *Common-Pleas*, that no ac[tion] [...] ſuing an Attorney, knowingly, in any other Court againſt [...] for his means to enjoy his privilege, is to claim it by writ [...] and he is not bound to claim his privilege, nor can his [...] he will claim it.

An action was lately brought in the *King's-Bench*, (as I ha[...] delaying a poſt-letter maliciouſly, whereby the plaintiff w[...] gence that might have been of great advantage to him. Th[...] countenanced the action, ſo that it proceeded no farther. It [...] (as I heard) to this effect; That if ſuch precedents were ad[...] could hardly be any dealing or correſpondence, but migh[t] [...] actions at law: and although the caſe depended upon proof [...] malice, and the defendant will be acquitted if his caſe be no[...] we muſt conſider that there is both charge and vexation of [...] tends the defence of a juſt cauſe, and we muſt not ſubject [...] their actions to ſuch trouble and hazard.

Theſe inſtances ſhew, that although an action upon the ca[ſe] [...] ed a catholicon, yet when actions have been applied to nev[...] have always been ſtrictly examined, and upon conſideration[...] inconvenience they have been many times rejected.

For though the law advances remedies, as my brothers ob[...] is with conſideration that vexation be not more advanced th[...]

It is my opinion, that no new device ever was, or can b[e] [...] into the law, but abſurdities and difficulties ariſe upon it, wh[...] foreſeen: which makes me very jealous of admitting novelti[es].

2. In matters relating to the Parliament (which is my ſec[ond]) there is no need of introducing novelties; for the Parliamen[t] [...] new laws to anſwer any miſchiefs that ariſe, and it ought [...] them to do it.

Eſpecially in a caſe of this nature, concerning election[s] [...] Parliament have already taken care of, and preſcribed reme[dies] [...] veral Statutes that have been made concerning them; I [...] caſe, there is little need to ſtrain the law.

The Judges in all times have been very tender of meddli[ng] [...] ters relating to Parliament. I do not find that ever they t[...] but where Statutes give them expreſs power; or that they e[...] the behaviour of a Sheriff, or any officer of the Parliamen[t] [...] to any ſervice performed to the Parliament, but upon th[...] And in *Braunker*'s caſe, *Dyer* 168. the Statute was their rul[e] [...] *Chamber*, and they inflicted the ſame puniſhment that is app[ointed] [...] Statute.

If we ſhall allow general remedies (as an action upon the [...] applied to caſes relating to the Parliament, we ſhall at l[a]ſt [...] lege of Parliament, and that great privilege of judging of t[...] vileges.

Suppoſe an action ſhould be brought in time of proroga[tion] [...] Member of Parliament, for that he falſely and maliciouſly [...] complaint of breach of privilege to the Parliament, where[...] was ſent for in cuſtody, and loſt his liberty, and was put to [...] to acquit himſelf, and was acquitted by the Parliament.

If upon ſuch a caſe the jury ſhould find the defendant [...] ſhould not that action be maintained as well as this at ba[r] [...] ſaid for that action, that the judgment of the Parliament [...] and the privilege is not tried at Law, but determined, 1. I[...] 2. It may be ſaid, the party has no other way to recover hi[...]

It would be dangerous to admit ſuch an action, for then t[...] peril in claiming privilege; for if the party complained of, [...] tune to be acquitted by the Houſe, the Member that made t[...] would be at the mercy of the jury, as to the point of mali[ce] [...] tity of damages. Such a precedent, I ſuppoſe, would n[...] Parliament; and yet it may with more juſtice be the ſecond c[...] at the bar the firſt.

Actions may be brought for giving Parliament protection[s] [...] Actions may be brought againſt the Clerk of the Parliament [...] Arms, and Speaker, for aught I know, for executing the[ir] [...] with averments of malice and damage, and then muſt Jud[ges] [...] determine what they ought to do by their officers. This is [...] ſcribing rules to the Parliament for them to act by.

It cannot be ſeen whither we ſhall be drawn, if we meddle [...] of Parliament in actions at law. Therefore, in my judgm[ent] [...] ſafety is in thoſe bounds that are warranted by Acts of P[...] conſtant practice.

Suppoſe this action had been brought before the election [...] cided in the Houſe, and the jury had found one way, and t[...] had determined contrary; how inconſiſtent had this been?

But it was ſaid in the *King's-Bench* that the Court wou[ld] [...] before the Parliament had determined the election, and the[...] be conteſted, but the judgment of the Parliament muſt be fo[...] my brother *Ellis* but now ſaid, *Surely no man will be ſo indiſcr[eet]* [...] *ſuch an action before the Parliament hath determined [...]* [...] *try it, before ſuch time as the election be determined [...]*

In my opinion this was not rightly conſidered, for [...] any ſuit, to expect the determination of the Parliament [...] or juſtice is there, that the Sheriff, who is no p[...] the Parliament, ſhould be concluded in any th[...]

other parties, to defend himſelf from a demand of damages in a Court of law, where witneſſes are examined upon oath, which they cannot be in the Commons Houſe?

There is no reaſon the ſuit of law ſhould ſtay till the Houſe have determined the election, if the determination of the Houſe be not concluſive in that ſuit.

And for the diſcretion of the parties that are like to bring ſuch actions, I cannot depend upon it: for I ſee in this age, ſome men will inſiſt upon their private rights to the hindrance of publick Affairs of higher conſequence than any that can come before the Courts in *Weſtminſter-hall.*

It may be, there will not want men that will preſs us to judge in ſuch caſes; and not only before the Parliament have determined, but againſt what the Parliament have determined; and will tell us, that the Sheriff was no party, that witneſſes were not there examined upon oath, and produce Arguments from Antiquity which we ſhall be very loath to judge of.

I can ſee no other way to avoid conſequences derogatory to the honour of the Parliament, but to reject the action; and all others that ſhall relate either to the proceedings or privilege of Parliament, as our Predeceſſors have done.

For if we ſhould admit general remedies in matters relating to the Parliament, we muſt ſet bounds how far they ſhall go, which is a dangerous province; for if we err, privilege of Parliament will be invaded, which we ought not any way to endamage.

This I ſpeak of general remedies: Now I will conſider this particular caſe, which, in my opinion, would bring great danger and diſhonour to the Parliament.

It is diſhonourable to the Parliament that there ſhould be no protection in their ſervice; I have ſhewn that the Sheriff can be ſafe in no caſe, if he ſhall be ſued in ſuch a caſe as this: And can there be a greater reproach, than that there is no ſafety in their ſervice? Nobody can ſerve them chearfully and willingly at that rate.

It has been objected that the Sheriff is not their officer, but is the officer of the Court of *Chancery*, which ſends forth the writs, and receives the returns. The Argument is plauſible, but will not paſs in the Parliament; for they ſay the Court of *Chancery* is the Repoſitory for their writs, but will not allow them to iſſue without warrant from the Houſe: They will not ſuffer the Court of *Chancery* to meddle with the returns of the Sheriff. The Parliament ſends immediate order to the Sheriff; if the return be too ſlow, they direct the Sheriff to amend his return, and they puniſh the Sheriff where they find him faulty; ſo that it appears they exerciſe an immediate juriſdiction over the Sheriff. And I ſuppoſe they would judge it very falſe doctrine to ſay, that the Court of *Chancery*, or us, can any way meddle with the returns or the officer.

Admitting the Sheriff to act in returns as the Officer of the Parliament, it concerns them that he ſhould be liable to no other puniſhment but what they inflict, otherwiſe they cannot expect to be obeyed.

To have others judge when their ſervants do well, will be to have others give rules to their ſervants and ſervice, which they will think inconvenient.

Let it be conſidered how hard a taſk Sheriffs have in the elections of Knights to the Parliament: The appearance commonly is very numerous, the parties conteſting very violent, the proceeding tumultuous, the polling ſometimes is at ſeveral places at once; ſo that the Sheriff can hardly be a witneſs of the action: and if the diſpute be in the Houſe of Commons, he is no party to it. If after all this, the Sheriff, who cannot indemnify himſelf by ſecurity, ſtill be liable to an action, the ſervice of the Parliament may be reckoned a miſerable ſlavery; which is not for their honour.

As this is diſhonourable, ſo it is dangerous to Parliaments; it concerns the Kingdom that returns to the Parliament ſhould be upright and impartial, and that they may be ſo, the Sheriff ſhould be ſecure from all fears.

Judges are not liable to actions, that they may proceed uprightly and impartially; if they were ſubject to ſuits for their judgments, there is that earneſtneſs and confidence on both ſides, that one ſide would be diſſatisfied and trouble them, and they could not diſcharge their duty without apprehenſions of diſquiet.

If the Sheriff be expoſed to actions thus, let us conſider what and whom he is to fear: He may fear the ſuit of the party, and he may fear the ſuit of the King. And it follows neceſſarily, that if an action lies, an information for the King will alſo lie for the miſdemeanor in his office: If it be not a caſe privileged by the complexion of it, as Parliamentary, from being examined in *Weſtminſter-hall*, but that he may be puniſhed at the ſuit of the Party, he may certainly as well be puniſhed at the ſuit of the King: If ſo, Where is the Sheriff's ſecurity? Will his own innocence ſecure him? That muſt be tried by a jury of the County where the Parliament ſits; who are, it may be, ſtrangers to him as well as to the matter; or by a jury of the County where the election was, where, it may be, they will be of an oppoſite party; the plaintiff may wait his opportunity, and queſtion him twenty years after: And if he be condemned, his puniſhment is unlimited, a fine may be ſet to any height for the King, and damages may be given to any value for the party. Where is his ſecurity upon ſuch proceedings? Will he not be more afraid of ſuch puniſhment out of Parliament, than of any puniſhment in Parliament? Will not, nay, may not his terror make him deſire to pleaſe them that can puniſh him out of Parliament, rather than to do right? Will not that be dangerous to the conſtitution of Parliaments?

As the puniſhment out of Parliament may be a terror to thoſe who mean well, ſo colourable puniſhments may be as miſchievous on the other ſide; for they may prevent any puniſhment in Parliament, for *nemo bis punitur pro eodem delicto*; they may ſerve for protection of men that do ill. When it is ſeriouſly weigh'd, of what conſequence this may be, the caſe at Bar will not be thought a caſe fit to be received by the Judges without the countenance of a new law.

They object, here is malice found by the verdict, and that there can be no danger or inconveniency that malice ſhould be puniſhed.

This objection fortifies my opinion; for malice, upon which they would have the ſcales turn in this caſe, is not a thing demonſtrative, but interpretative, and lies in opinion; ſo that it may give an handle to any man to puniſh another by.

The inſtance of this very caſe ſhews, that a good man may reaſonably be afraid of the event of his defence in ſuch a caſe.

For altho' the matter was of great examination in Parliament, and at laſt decided but by few voices, and no obſervation of the Sheriff's miſcarriage there; tho' it appeared upon the trial (which I may ſay, being preſent there), that the Sheriff was guided by the advice of his friends, of Counſel, and of Parliament-men, that told him the only ſafe courſe was to make a double return; yet the Jury condemned him to pay 800*l.* againſt the expectation of the Court: for the Judges that were preſent at the trial did all declare publickly, that they would not have given that verdict.

The Judges heard all the evidence the Jury could go upon; for being of a remote County to the place of election, the Jury could know nothing of their own knowledge, and yet the Judges concurred not with the Jury in their opinion.

I know we are not to examine the truth of the verdict, we muſt take it for goſpel; neither doth any partiality in this particular lead me in judgment: but I ſhew it as an inſtance that malice is not demonſtrative; men's minds may be miſtaken, and innocent men may therefore have reaſon to be afraid, eſpecially in ill times, and may uſe ſuch means for their ſafety as may not be convenient for Parliaments.

But there can be no danger or inconvenience in the cenſure of the Parliament, that repreſents the whole Kingdom, who hitherto have alone exerciſed this power, and who may at any time reform the law, if the preſent practice be any way inconvenient.

Upon theſe reaſons which I have produced, I ground my opinion: Now it will be neceſſary to weigh what hath been ſaid in oppoſition to it.

The Arguments urged on the other ſide, related either to the ingredients or circumſtances of this action, or to the foundation or ſubſtance of it.

I call the ingredients and circumſtances of the action, that it is laid with theſe words, *Falſo, malitioſe, deceptive, & ſcienter:* And that there is a verdict in this caſe, and damages are found.

The words *falſo, malitioſe, & deceptive*, will ſometimes make a thing actionable, which is not ſo in itſelf, without malice proved, tho' there be the ſame damage to the party.

As where a man cauſes another to be falſely indicted, yet if it be not *malitioſe*, no action lies; tho' there be the ſame trouble, charge and damage in one caſe as the other.

But it is only where a man is a voluntary Agent; for if a man be compellable to act, you cannot moleſt him upon any averment of malice: As if a grand-jury-man cauſes another to be indicted, tho' you aver malice, you cannot have an action againſt him; ſo for a witneſs that doth teſtify, or a Judge that judgeth.

In the caſe at Bar, the Sheriff is compellable to act, and not barely as a Miniſter to ſend the Indenture, but as a Judge to ſay which is the major part of the due Electors; and if he miſtakes, there is no reaſon it ſhould ſubject him to an action upon an artificial averment of malice.

I remember in *Shepherd* and *Wakeman*'s caſe in the *King's Bench*, Mr. Juſtice *Wyndham* ſaid well, that the words *falſo & malitioſe* were grown words of courſe, and put into every action: So that to his knowledge Juries many times had no regard to them, that he looked upon them as words of form.

If we ſhould make the words *falſo & malitioſe* ſupport an action without a fit ſubject matter, all the actions of mankind would be liable to ſuit and vexation: they that have the cooking (as we call it) of declarations in actions of the caſe, if they be ſkilful in their art, will be ſure to put in the words *falſo & malitioſe*, let the caſe be what it will; they are here pepper and vinegar in a Cook's hand, that help to make ſauce for any meat, but will not make a diſh of themſelves.

Falſo & malitioſe will not enable an action againſt a Judge.

Nor againſt an indictor or witneſs, nor where words are not actionable, tho' the plaintiff hath a verdict and damages found; nor for a breach of truſt, which is *aliens fori.*

The reaſon of every one of theſe caſes holds in the caſe at Bar: Therefore it ought to have the ſame Reſolution.

As to the word *ſcienter*, it hath weight ſometimes; and if an action be brought for keeping a dog that worried another's ſheep, *ſciens canem ad mordend' oves eſſe conſuetud.* or for detaining the ſervant or wife of another, *ſcienter:* In theſe caſes, if the defendant hath been told that the dog did worry ſheep, or that it was the ſervant or wife of another, tho' it may be he did not believe it, yet it was *ſcienter*; for the word implies no more than having notice: And in thoſe actions he muſt inform himſelf at his peril, and may, if he doubts, avoid danger by putting away thoſe things which give offence. But in this caſe he could receive information by none, and is not to believe or diſbelieve any body, but is bound to judge of the thing himſelf, and to act according to his judgment; ſo that no proof could be made of the *ſcienter*, for one ſide tells him the Election was one way, and the other ſide tells him it is the other way; but he being preſent to the whole action, muſt follow the dictates of his own judgment. Hence it appears, *ſcienter* in this caſe is an empty word, not referring to notice of a fact, but a matter of judgment, which cannot any way be proved.

It has been often urged, that this caſe is ſtronger by being after a verdict and damages found by the jury; and it has been ſaid, that perhaps upon a demurrer, it might have been found more doubtful.

The caſe is the ſame to me upon a verdict, that it would have been upon a general demurrer, and no ſtronger; for a demurrer is the confeſſion of the party, of all that can be proved, or can poſſibly be found upon that declaration.

It is my Lord *Coke*'s advice in *Cromwel*'s caſe, *4th part*, 14. *a.* never to demur to a declaration, if there be any hopes of the matter of fact; for the matter in law will as well ſerve after a verdict as upon a demurrer.

It had been a very odious caſe, if the Sheriff ſhould have admitted all this fact to be true by a demurrer.

The finding the Plaintiff's damages adds no ſtrength to the caſe; for we ſee every day upon actions for words, tho' the jury find the defendant guilty for ſpeaking words *falſo & malitioſe*, and find it to be to the Plaintiff's great damages; yet if the words are not ſuch as will bear an action, the Court ſtays judgment: and if judgment happens to be given, it is reverſable for error; which ſhews that the finding damages by the jury cannot make an action better than if it were to be adjudged upon demurrer.

I shall now consider what hath been said to maintain this action upon the main substance and foundation of it. They say, this is a case within the general reason of the Common Law, for here is malice, falsity and damage; and where they concur, there ought to be remedy. And altho' this be a new case, yet it ought not for that reason to be rejected; for other kind of actions have been newly introduced, and this is as fit to be entertained as any.

My brothers that argued even now for the action, shewed great learning and great pains; and certainly have said all that can be invented in support of this case: But as far as I could perceive, they have spoken only upon general notions to that purpose I just now mentioned; but nothing that I could observe applicable to the reasons and differences I go upon.

As for the rule they go upon, that where falsity, malice and damage do concur, there must be remedy; I confess it is true generally, but not universally, for it holds not in the case of a Judge, nor an Indictor, nor a Witness, nor of words that import not legal slander, tho' they are found to bring damage, as I have shewn before. And the reasons that exempt these cases from the general rule, have the same force in the case at bar.

I must confess the Judges have sometimes entertained new kinds of actions, but it was upon great deliberation, and with great discretion, where a general inconvenience requir'd it.

If *Slane*'s case were new (for my brother *Thurland* observed truly it was said in that case, that there were infinite numbers of precedents) that case imported the common course of justice. Actions for words that are said to be new, tho' they have been used some hundreds of years, are a necessary means to preserve the peace of the Kingdom. The case of *Smith* and *Crashaw*, *Cro. Car.* 15. was a case of general concern, being that prosecutions for treasons may be against any man, and at any time.

But in the case at bar, neither the peace of the Kingdom, nor the course of justice is concerned in general, but only the administration of officers of the Parliament, in the execution of Parliamentary Writs; and can never happen but in time of Parliament, and must of necessity fall under the notice of the Parliament; so that if the law were deficient, it is to be presumed the Parliament would take care to supply it: Discretion requires us rather to attend that, than to introduce new precedents upon such general notions that cannot govern the course of Parliament.

My brother *Atkins* said, the Common Law complied with the genius of the Nation; I do not understand the Argument: Does the Common Law change? Are we to judge of the changes of the genius of the Nation? Whither may general notions carry us at this rate? For my own part, I think, tho the Common Law be not written, yet it is certain, and not arbitrary. We are sworn to observe the laws as they are, and I see not how we can change them by our Judgments and as for the genius of the Nation, it will be best considered by the Parliament, who have power of the laws, and may bring us to a compliance with it.

In the case at bar, I look upon the Sheriff as a particular officer of the Parliament for the managing elections, and as if he were not Sheriff. I look upon the writ as if it were an order of Parliament, and had not the name of a writ: I look upon the course of Parliament, which we pretend not to know, to be incident to the consideration of it; so that it stands not upon the general notion of remedy in the common course of justice.

The Arguments of the falling of the value of money, whereby the penalty of 100*l.* provided by the 23 *H.* VI. is become inconsiderable, and the increase of the estimation of being a Member of Parliament; if they were true, are arguments to the Parliament to change the law by increasing the penalty, but we cannot do it.

My brother *Maynard*, in his Argument, would embolden us; telling us we are not to think the case too hard for us, because of the name or course of Parliament, for Judges have punished Absentees: They may determine what is a Parliament, what is an Act of Parliament, how long an ordinance of Parliament shall continue, and may punish trespasses done in the very Parliament.

I will not dispute the truth of what he said in this, but if his Arguments were artificial, he might have spared them, for they have no manner of effect to draw me beyond my sphere.

I will not be afraid to determine any thing that I think proper for me to judge; but seeing I cannot find the Courts of Justice have at any time meddled with cases of this nature, but upon express power given them by Acts of Parliament, I cannot consent to this precedent; I am confident when there is need, the Parliament will discern it, and make laws to enlarge our power, so far as they shall think convenient.

I see no harm that Sheriffs in the mean time should be safe from this new-devised action, which they call the Common Law, if they misdemean themselves, they are answerable to the Parliament, whose officers they be, or may be punished by the Statute, made for regulating Elections.

It is time for me to conclude, which I shall do by repeating the opinion I at first delivered, *viz.* That this judgment is not warranted by the rules of law; That it introduceth novelty of dangerous consequence, and therefore ought to be reversed. *Sæpe viatorem nova, non vetus orbita, fallit.*

North, Chief-Justice, and five other Judges (against *Ellis* and *Atkins*) reversed the judgment upon the matter in Law, That the action lies not.

[Note, The Lord Chief-Justice *Vaughan*, and Lord Chief-Baron *Turner*, both deceased, who in their lives were eminent Members of Parliament, were of the same opinion.]

Soon after the Revolution, Sir *Samuel Barnardiston* brought his Writ of Error into the House of Peers, to reverse the reversal of the judgment given in the Exchequer; but the House affirmed the reversal of the said judgment, as appears by the following Resolutions.

Veneris, 24 Maii, 1689.

THIS Day the Lord Chief-Justice of the Court of *King's-Bench* brought into this House a transcript of a Writ of Error, to reverse a judgment given against *Barnardiston* at the suit of *Soame*.

Sabbati, 25 Maii, 1689.

Whereas Sir *Samuel Barnardiston* brought his Writ of Error into this House, and hath assigned errors thereupon, to which Sir *William Soame* was Defendant, who left Dame *Catherine Soame*, his widow, his executrix: and the House being moved, that the said Dame *Catherine Soame* may join issue thereupon, it is ordered by the Lords Spiritual and Temporal in Parliament assembled, that the said Dame *Catherine Soame* be, and is ed to join issue to the said Writ, on or before *Thursday* next, instant, at ten of the clock in the forenoon; whereof the *Barnardiston* is to cause notice to be given to the said Dame end she join issue accordingly.

Sabbati, 1 Junii, 1689.

The House being moved, that they would be pleased to for hearing the errors argued upon the Writ of Error bro House, wherein Sir *Samuel Barnardiston* is Plaintiff, and D *Soame*, widow, executrix of Sir *William Soame*, Defendant: by the Lords Spiritual and Temporal in Parliament assembl House will hear the said errors argued by Counsel on bot bar, on *Saturday* next, being the 8th instant, at ten of th forenoon; and in the mean time she may join issue if she p of the said Sir *Samuel Barnardiston* is to cause notice to be gi Dame *Catherine Soame*, to the end she attend accordingly.

Sabbati, 8 die Junii, 1689.

This day being appointed for hearing errors argued by the Writ of Error between Sir *Samuel Barnardiston* and th the Counsel for the Plaintiff appeared, but none appeared f dant: And upon oath made at the bar by *Nicholas Baker*, S he served the order of this House at the house of the Lady by giving notice, that the cause was to be heard this day; House heard the Counsel of the Plaintiff, and made the e *viz.*

After hearing Counsel this day, upon the Writ of Error this House, wherein Sir *Samuel Barnardiston* is Plaintiff, a *therine Soame* is Defendant; It is ordered by the Lords Spirit poral in Parliament assembled, the giving judgment on this be, and is hereby suspended, until *Monday* next; and thos were Judges, and now in Town, do attend this House that the House of their reasons and grounds for their judgmen of the judgment in Sir *Samuel Barnardiston*'s case.

Ordered, That all the Judges be present on *Monday* mo this House in this business of Sir *Samuel Barnardiston*.

Lunæ, 10 Junii, 1689.

William Muntague, Esq. was called in, and the Speak That the House desired to hear from him, upon what grou nions he gave his opinion for the reversal of the judgm eight hundred pounds to Sir *Samuel Barnardiston*?

He taking notice that there was Counsel present for Sir *S diston*, but no Counsel for the Lady *Soame*, he said, seeing did not appear with Counsel, he desired he might not be Counsel for the Defendant, upon that the company was withdraw: And the House ordered Mr. *Mountague* should come in alone; who being come in, said, he would, for th satisfaction, (as well as he can remember) acquaint them wit and reasons which induced him to give his opinion for the judgment; and so he proceeded to give the heads of what being ended, he withdrew.

And after consideration thereof, it was moved that the *Samuel Barnardiston* should be called in, and the Speaker to with the effect of what Mr. *Mountague* had said; that so the be able thereby to reply, for the better information of their the Judges then present. And after some debate, the que whether the Counsel shall be called in? It was resolved in t

Then it was moved to make use of proxies, which was op cerning their not being admitted in preliminary cases of ju

After hearing *William Mountague*, Esq. for his judgment *Barnardiston*'s case, and debate thereupon, it is ordere Clerk do inspect the books concerning proxies; and whe been used in cases of judicature, and give an account to-mo what he finds therein: And that all the Judges do attend morrow.

Martis, 11 Junii, 1689.

The Clerk of the Parliament, in pursuance of the Order y ed several instances where proxies have been used in prelim vate causes: It is ordered by the Lords Spiritual and Tem ment assembled, That proxies may be used in such prelimi not in giving judgment, and that this order be added t standing Orders.

Ordered, That the Counsel of Sir *Samuel Barnardiston* sh *Friday* next, to reply to what Mr. *Mountague* gave for his versal of Sir *Samuel Barnardiston*'s judgment, and that all attend at the same time.

Veneris, 14 die Junii, 1689.

After hearing Counsel in Sir *Samuel Barnardiston*'s case ply to what Mr. *William Mountague* said for his reason judgment given in the *Exchequer*; It is ordered, That t hear all the Judges give their opinions in this case on *Tu* this Instant *June*, at ten of the clock in the forenoon.

Martis, 25 die Junii, 1689.

The House heard the opinion of all the Judges in the *muel Barnardiston*, upon his Writ of Error depending in t

And the question being put, Whether to go on in the b siness now? It was resolved in the affirmative.

After debate, the question being put, Whether to reverse the judgment given between Sir *Samuel Barnardiston* a *Soame*? It was resolved in the negative.

Leave is given to several Lords to enter their dissent t question, and accordingly do enter their dissent for the rea

1. Because it is a denying Sir *Samuel Barnardiston* the which gives relief in all wrong and injury And tho' this the first impression, yet there being a damage to the Plaintif Law gives him this action to repair himself; and if it we would be a failure of justice, which cannot be admitted.

2. Because the allowing this reversal tends towards the giving the power and encouragement to Sheriffs to make false and double returns; by which means the right of Elections will be avoided, and it tends thereby to the packing of a House of Commons, which may overturn the whole frame of the Government, and establish what Religion and Governments a pack'd Parliament shall think fit.

Bolton, *S. Stamford,*
Macclesfield, *Herbert.*
P. Wharton,

Whereas by virtue of their Majesties Writ of Error, returnable into the House of Peers, a record of the Court of *King's-Bench* was brought into this House the 24th of *May*, 1689, with the transcript thereof, wherein judgment is entered for Sir *Samuel Barnardiston* against Sir *William Soame*: upon which Writ, Errors being assigned, after hearing Counsel at the Bar, to argue the said Errors assigned, and due consideration had of what was offered thereupon, the Lords Spiritual and Temporal in Parliament assembled, do order and adjudge, that the Judgment given in the *Exchequer* Chamber, for the reversal of the Judgment given in the Court of *King's-Bench* for Sir *Samuel Barnardiston* against Sir *William Soame*, be, and is hereby affirmed: And that the said Writ of Error, and transcript annexed, be remitted to the Court of *King's-Bench*.

The Tenor of which Judgment to be affixed to the Transcript to be remitted, follows;

ET postea, scilicet quarto die Maii Anno Regni Domini Gulielmi & Dnæ. Mariæ nunc Regis & Reginæ Angl. primo transcript. Record. & processſ. præd. inter partes præd. cum omnibus ea tangent. pretext. cujusdam brev. de Error corrigend. & præfat. Samuel. Barnardiston, in premiſſ. perſecut. dict. Dom. Reg. & Dom. Reginæ in present. Parliament. à pred. curia dict. Dom. & Dominæ Regis & Reginæ hic transmiſſ. fuit pred. Samuel. in eadem curia Parliament. comparens, diversas causas & materias per Erroribus in Record. & processſ. pred. pro revocatione & adnullatione Judicii pred. assignaverit; & postea scilicet 25 die Junii Anno dict. Dom. & Dominæ Regis & Reginæ, supradict. in pred. cur Parliament. pred. visis, & per cur. ibidem diligenter examinat. & plenius intellect. Sam. Recordo & Processſ. pred. ac Judicio super iisdem reddit. qua Errore superius assignat. pro eo quod videtur cur. Parl. pred. quod Record. illum in nullo vitiosum aut defectum existit, & quod in Record. ill. in nullo erratum, adtunc & ibidem consideratum est per eandem curiam Parliament. pred. quod Judic. pred. in omnibus affirmetur & in omni suo robore stet & effectu.

XXXI. Proceedings in the *House of Commons*, on an Appeal being brought in the *House of Lords*, by Dr. SHIRLEY, against Sir JOHN FAGG, and others, their Members, *May* 1675, 27 *Car.* II.

Martis, 4 Maii, 1675.

SIR *John Fagg*, Bart. this day informed the House, that he was summon'd to appear to a Petition in the House of Lords; a Committee was thereupon appointed to search for precedents to that purpose.

Mercurii, 5 Maii.

Resolved, That a Message be sent to the Lords, to acquaint them that this House hath received information, That there is a Petition of Appeal depending before them, at the suit of *Thomas Shirley*, Esq. against Sir *John Fagg*, a Member of this House; to which Petition, he is, by order of the House of Lords, directed to answer on *Friday* next; and to desire the Lords to have a regard to the privileges of this House; and that Sir *Trevor Williams* do go up with the Message to the Lords.

Sir *Trevor Williams* reports, that he had attended the Lords with the Message of this House, concerning Sir *John Fagg*; and that the Lords will return an answer by Messengers of their own.

Veneris, 7 Maii.

A Message from the Lords by Sir *William Beversham*, and Sir *Samuel Clarke*.

Mr. Speaker,

The Lords have considered of the Message received from the House of Commons, concerning privilege in the case of Sir *John Fagg*, and do return this answer, That the House of Commons need not doubt, but that the Lords will have a regard to the privileges of the House of Commons, as they have of their own.

Sabbati, 8 Maii.

A Committee was appointed to inspect the Lords Journals, to see what entries are therein made against Sir *John Fagg*, a Member of this House, and to report the same.

Mercurii, 12 Maii.

Dr. *Thomas Shirley* ordered to be sent for in custody, to answer his breach of the privileges of this House, in prosecuting a suit by petition of Appeal in the Lords House, against Sir *John Fagg*, a Member of this House, during the session and privilege of Parliament.

And a Committee is also appointed to inspect the Lords Journals, to see what has been done in like cases; and the said Sir *John Fagg* is ordered not to proceed, or make any answer to the said Appeal, without the licence of this House.

Veneris, 14 Maii.

Sir *Thomas Lee* reports from the Committee appointed to inspect the Journals of the House of Lords, and the entries therein, in the case between Dr. *Thomas Shirley* and Sir *John Fagg*, a Member of this House, That the Committee had perused the Journals of the Lords House, and found the entries to be as follow:

April *the* 30*th.*

Thomas Shirley, Esq. presented a Petition to the Lords.

Ordered, That the said Sir *John Fagg* may have a copy of the said Petition, and put in his answer thereunto, in writing, on *Friday* the 7th day of *May* next, at ten of the clock in the forenoon, if he thinks fit.

May *the* 5*th.*

The Commons send a Message by Sir *Trevor Williams*:

The Knights, Citizens, and Burgesses of the House of Commons, in Parliament assembled, have been informed, that there is a Petition of Appeal depending before their Lordships, at the suit of *Thomas Shirley*, Esq. against Sir *John Fagg*, a Member of their House. To which Petition he is, by their Lordships order, directed to answer on *Friday* next, and desire their Lordships to take care of their privileges.

Answer, That this House have considered of their Message, and will send answer by Messengers of their own.

Ordered, That the Committee for Privileges do meet this afternoon, to consider of the Message received from the House of Commons this day, concerning *Thomas Shirley*, Esq. and Sir *John Fagg*, a Member of the House, and search precedents in the case, and report to the House tomorrow morning.

May *the* 6*th.*

The Earl of *Berks* reported, That the Committee of Privileges having met and considered of what was referred to them in the case between *Thomas Shirley*, Esq. and Sir *John Fagg*, a Member of the House of Commons, and the Message from the House of Commons thereupon; have ordered him to report, That the Committee have found that the House did refer the business of Mr. *Hale* and Mr. *Slingsby*, upon the like Message of the House of Commons, to the Committee of Privileges; who did report to the House, That it is the undoubted right of the Lords in judicature, to receive and determine in time of Parliament, Appeals from inferior Courts, though a Member of either House be concerned, that there may be no failure of justice in the land; and the House did agree with the Committee therein: And thereupon the Committee do humbly offer to their Lordships, upon this occasion, to take the same course, and to insist upon their just rights in this particular, which their Lordships will be pleased to signify to the House of Commons, in such manner as they shall think fit.

The House agreed with the Committee in this declaration, and ordered the same to be entered into the Journal-book of this House, as their declaration, *viz.*

"That it is the undoubted right of the Lords in Judicature, to receive "and determine in time of Parliament, Appeals from inferior Courts, "though a Member of either House be concerned, that there may be no "failure of justice in the land."

Then it was moved, that the former answer sent to the House of Commons, in the case of Mr. *Slingsby* and Mr. *Hale*, might be given now to the House of Commons, in this case of Sir *John Fagg*, and that the declaration and report agreed to this day, might be added to it.

The Declaration aforesaid was read, and the question being put, Whether this shall be as a part of the answer to be given to the House of Commons? It was resolved in the negative.

The answer returned formerly to the House of Commons, in the case of Mr. *Slingsby* and Mr *Hale*, was in these words; *That the House of Commons need not doubt but that their Lordships will have a regard to the privileges of the House of Commons, as they have of their own.*

The question being put, Whether this answer shall be now returned to the Message from the House of Commons? It was resolved in the affirmative.

May the 7th, it was sent accordingly.

Maii 7.

Whereas this day was appointed for Sir *John Fagg* to put in an answer to the Petition and Appeal of *Thomas Shirley*, Esq. depending in this House, if he thought fit; the said Sir *John Fagg* appearing personally this day at the Bar, and desiring longer time to put in an answer thereunto;

It is thereupon ordered, That the said Sir *John Fagg* hath hereby further time given him for putting in his answer, till *Wednesday* next, being the 12th day of this instant *May*, at ten o'clock in the forenoon.

Maii 12.

Sir *John Fagg* put in his answer to the petition of Mr. *Shirley*.

A debate arising thereupon, touching the privilege of their House;

Resolved, &c. That the Appeal brought by Dr. *Shirley* in the House of Lords, against Sir *John Fagg*, a Member of this House, and the proceedings thereupon, are a breach of the undoubted rights and privileges of this House.

The House being informed, that the Warrant of this House for taking of the said Dr. *Shirley* into custody, was forcibly taken away and detained from the Serjeant at Arms his Deputy, attending this House, by the Lord *Mohun*: And the Serjeant's Deputy being called in and examined as to the matter of fact, gave this testimony:

That he found Dr. *Shirley* in the inner Lobby of the House of Lords, and that he came to him, and desired to speak with him, and acquainted him that he had a Warrant from the House of Commons to apprehend him, and desired to know, whether he could shew him any reason to excuse him, that

that he might not ſerve the warrant on him: And that he likewiſe told him, that he would not execute the warrant on him in that place, but deſired of him, that he would go along with him freely; and that in caſe he would not, he would take his opportunity in another place.

And that the ſaid Lord *Mohun* coming in, in the mean time, required him to ſhew his warrant; which he producing, the Lord *Mohun* laid hands on it, and held it ſo faſt, that it was in danger of being torn, and that therefore he was forced to part with it, and deſiring to have it again, the Lord *Mohun* refuſed it, but carried the warrant into the Houſe of Lords. That Dr. *Shirley* afterwards refuſed to go along with him, ſaying, that he was not then his priſoner; and that ſeveral perſons interpoſing, the Doctor eſcaped from them. And a debate ariſing thereupon,

Reſolved, That a Meſſage be ſent to the Lords to complain of the Lord *Mohun*, for forcibly taking away and detaining the warrant of this Houſe, from the Deputy Serjeant at Arms, for taking of Dr. *Shirley* into cuſtody; and to demand the juſtice of the Lords Houſe againſt the ſaid Lord *Mohun*.

And that the Lord *Antram* do go up to the Lords with the Meſſage.

Ordered, That Mr. Speaker do iſſue forth a new warrant to the Serjeant at Arms attending this Houſe, for apprehending Dr. *Thomas Shirley*, to anſwer his breach of privilege, for proſecuting a ſuit by petition of Appeal in the Lords Houſe, againſt Sir *John Fagg*, a Member of this Houſe, during the ſeſſion and privilege of Parliament.

Sabbati, 15 *Maii* 1675.

The Lord *Antram* reports from the Lords, that he had, in obedience to the commands of this Houſe, attended the Lords, and delivered the Meſſage concerning the Lord *Mohun*'s taking away and detaining the warrant for apprehending Dr. *Shirley*, and that the Lords had returned this anſwer;

Gentlemen of the Houſe of Commons,

The Lords have conſidered of your Meſſage, and of the complaint therein; and they return you this anſwer, That they find the Lord Mohun *hath done nothing but what is according to his duty.*

The Houſe then reſumed the debate of the matter concerning the privileges of this Houſe; and the matter being debated,

Reſolved, &c. That the Appeal brought by Dr. *Shirley* in the Houſe of Lords againſt Sir *John Fagg*, a Member of this Houſe of Commons, and the proceedings thereupon, is a breach of the undoubted rights and privileges of the Houſe of Commons; and therefore the Commons deſire, that there be no further proceedings in that cauſe, before their Lordſhips.

Ordered, That a conference be deſired with the Lords concerning the privileges of this Houſe, in the caſe of Sir *John Fagg*; and that Sir *Thomas Lee* do go up to the Lords to deſire a conference.

A Meſſage from the Lords by Sir *Mondeford Bramſton*, and Sir *William Gluſcock*:

Mr. Speaker,

We are commanded to let this Houſe know, that the Lords ſpiritual and temporal aſſembled in Parliament, have received a warrant, ſigned Edward Seymour, *which they have appointed us to ſhew you; and deſire to know, whether it be a warrant ordered by this Houſe?*

The matter of the Meſſage being debated, the queſtion being put, That the word *unparliamentary*, be part of the anſwer to the Lords Meſſage,

It paſſed in the negative.

Reſolved, That the meſſengers be called in, and that this Anſwer be returned, *That this Houſe will conſider of the Meſſage.*

The meſſengers being called in, *Mr. Speaker* does acquaint them, that the Houſe will conſider of the Meſſage.

Reſolved, That the Meſſage laſt received from the Lords, is an unparliamentary Meſſage.

Reſolved, That a conference be deſired to be had with the Lords upon the ſubject-matter of the laſt Meſſage received from the Houſe of Lords.

Reſolved, That it be referred to Mr. *Garraway*, *&c.* to draw up reaſons to be offered at the ſaid conference.

Then the Houſe being informed, that there is a cauſe upon an Appeal brought up by Sir *Nicholas Stoughton*, againſt Mr. *Onſlow*, a Member of this Houſe, appointed to be heard at the bar of the Lords Houſe:

Reſolved, That a Meſſage be ſent to the Lords to acquaint them, that this Houſe has received information, that there is a cauſe upon an Appeal brought by Sir *Nicholas Stoughton* againſt Mr. *Onſlow*, a Member of this Houſe, appointed to be heard at the bar of their Houſe, on *Monday* next; and to deſire their Lordſhips to have regard to the privileges of this Houſe: And that Sir *Richard Temple* do go up with the Meſſage to the Lords.

Ordered, That Mr. *Onſlow* do not appear any further in the proſecution of the Appeal brought againſt him by Sir *Nicholas Stoughton*, in the Houſe of Lords.

Ordered, That Sir *Nicholas Stoughton* be ſent for in cuſtody of the Serjeant at Arms attending this Houſe, to anſwer his breach of privilege in proſecuting a ſuit in the Houſe of Lords, againſt *Arthur Onſlow*, Eſq. a Member of this Houſe, during the ſeſſion and privilege of Parliament.

Reſolved, That whoever ſhall appear at the bar of the Lords Houſe, to proſecute any ſuit againſt any Member of this Houſe, ſhall be deemed a breaker and infringer of the rights and privileges of this Houſe.

Lunæ, 17 *Maii*, 1675.

Sir *Richard Temple* reports, That the perſon appointed had attended the Lords, and delivered the vote of this Houſe, concerning the Appeal brought by Dr. *Shirley* againſt Sir *John Fagg*.

Sir *Thomas Lee* reports from the Committee appointed to draw up reaſons for the conference to be had with the Lords, Reaſons agreed by the Committee, which are as follow, *viz.*

For that the Meſſage is by way of interrogatory upon the proceedings of the Houſe of Commons, in a caſe concerning the privilege of a Member of that Houſe, of which they are proper Judges.

For that the matter of the Meſſage carries in it an undue reflection upon the *Speaker* of the Houſe of Commons.

For that the matter of the Meſſage doth highly reflect upon the whole Houſe of Commons, in their Lordſhips queſtioning that Houſe concerning their own orders; which they have the more reaſon to apprehend, becauſe the day before this Meſſage was brought to them, the warrant was owned by the complaint of the Houſe of Commons to their Lord ſhips ſame was taken and detained from a ſervant of theirs, by a Pe imports, that the queſtion in that Meſſage could not be for inform ly, and ſo tends to interrupt that mutual good correſpondenc y, wh to be preſerved inviolably between the two Houſes of Parlia ment

Martis, 18 *Maii*, 1675.

Sir *Richard Temple* reports from the Lords, That he had atte Lordſhips, according to the command of this Houſe, with the m the caſe of Mr. *Onſlow*; to which the Lords returned an anſwer, ing in writing, was delivered in at the Clerk's table, and read; followeth:

The Lords do declare, *That it is the undoubted right of the Lords ture, to receive and determine in time of Parliament Appeals from infer though a Member of either Houſe be concerned, that there may be no fai tice in the land: And from this right, and the exerciſe thereof, their will not depart.*

The matter of the Lords anſwer being debated, *Reſolved*, " " the undoubted right of this Houſe, that none of their Member " moned to attend the Houſe of Lords, during the ſitting or pr " Parliament."

Reſolved, That a conference be deſired with the Lords, upon leges of this Houſe, contained in the Lords anſwer to the laſt M this Houſe, in the caſe of Mr. *Onſlow*.

Ordered, That Sir *Henry Ford* do go up to the Lords, to deſire ence upon the ſubject-matter of their Meſſage, concerning the w apprehending Dr. *Shirley*.

Jovis, 20 *Maii*, 1675.

Sir *Thomas Lee* reports, from the Committee appointed to draw ſons to be offered at the conference to be had with the Lords upon vileges of this Houſe, contained in the Lords anſwer to the laſt M this Houſe, in the caſe of Mr. *Onſlow*; which reaſons were twice with ſome alterations at the Clerk's table (upon the queſtion ſever agreed to: which are as follow, *viz.*

1. That by the laws and uſage of Parliament, privilege of P. belongs to every Member of the Houſe of Commons, in all caſe Treaſon, Felony, and breach of the Peace; which hath often be red in Parliament, without any exception of Appeals before the L

2. That the reaſon of that privilege is, that the Members of th of Commons may freely attend the public affairs of that Houſe, wit turbance or interruption; which doth extend as well to Appeals b Houſe of Peers, as to proceedings in other Courts.

3. That by the conſtant courſe and uſage of Parliament, no M the Houſe of Commons can attend the Houſe of Lords, without cial leave of that Houſe firſt obtained, much leſs be ſummoned or led ſo to do.

4. If the Lords ſhall proceed to hear and determine any Appe the party neither can, nor ought to attend, ſuch proceedings would trary to the rules of juſtice.

5. That the not determining of an Appeal againſt a Member of th of Commons, is not a failure of juſtice, but only a ſuſpenſion of ings in a particular caſe, during the continuance of that Parliamen is but temporary.

6. That in caſe it were a failure of juſtice, it is not to be rem the Houſe of Lords alone, but it may be by Act of Parliament.

[Here Sir *Thomas Littleton* reported from the Committee appointe pare the further addreſs of this Houſe to his Majeſty, for the recall of his ſubjects as are in the *French* King's ſervice; which the Hou red the further conſideration of till *Wedneſday* next.]

Then Sir *Trevor Williams* reports from the Lords, that he had a and deſired a conference with the Lords on the privilege of this Hou tained in the Lords anſwer to the Meſſage of this Houſe, in the caſe *Onſlow*: And that the Lords will return an anſwer by Meſſengers of th

Mr. *Powle* reports, from the conference had with the Lords upon ject-matter of the former conference, concerning the warrant fo hending Dr. *Shirley*, That the Lords had returned an anſwer to the of this Houſe, delivered at the former Conference, and are as follo

" The Lords have appointed this conference, upon the ſubject " of the laſt conference, and have commanded us to give theſe anſ " the reaſons and other matters then delivered by the Houſe of Com

" To the firſt queſtion, the Lords conceive, that the moſt natu " of being informed, is by way of queſtion; and ſeeing a paper her " did reflect upon the privileges of the Lords Houſe, their Lordſhips " not proceed upon it till they were aſſured it was owned by the H " Commons: But the Lords had no occaſion at that time, nor do th " think fit to enter into the debate of the Houſe of Commons being " being proper Judges in the caſe concerning the privilege of a Me " that Houſe; their Lordſhips neceſſary conſideration upon ſight " paper, being only, how far the Houſe of Commons ordering (" paper were theirs) the apprehenſion of Dr. *Shirley*, for proſecut " Appeal before the Lords, did entrench upon their Lordſhips both " lege and undoubted rights of judicature in the conſequence of it, e " ting all the Members of both Houſes from the judicature of this th " eſt Court of the Kingdom; which would cauſe a failure of that ſ " juſtice, not adminiſtrable in any other Court, and which their Lo " will never admit.

" As to the ſecond reaſon, the Lords anſwer, That they do not " hend how the Matter of this Meſſage is any reflection upon the " of the Houſe of Commons.

" To the third reaſon, The Lords cannot imagine how it can be " hended in the leaſt to reflect upon the Houſe of Commons, for the " of Peers, upon a paper produced to their Lordſhips, in form of " rant of that Houſe, whereof doubt was made among the Lords, " ther any ſuch thing had been ordered by that Houſe, to enquire " Commons, whether ſuch warrant was ordered there or no? And " out ſuch Liberty uſed by the Lords, it will be very hard for their " ſhips to be rightly informed, ſo as to preſerve a good correſponden " tween the two Houſes, which their Lordſhips ſhall endeavour; or to " when warrants in the name of that Houſe are true or pretended: " is ſo ungrounded an apprehenſion, that their Lordſhips intended a

I

" S

" flection in asking that question, and not taking notice in their message of " the complaint of the House of Commons owning that warrant, that the " Lords had sent their message concerning that paper to the House of Com- " mons, before the Lords had received the said Commons complaint.

" But their Lordships have great cause to except against the unjust and " strained reflection of that House upon their Lordships, in asserting that " the question in the Lords message could not be for information, as we " affirm, but tending to interrupt the mutual correspondence between the " two Houses; which we deny, and had not the least thought of.

" The Lords have further commanded us to say, That they doubt not " when the House of Commons have received what we have delivered at " this conference, they will be sensible of their error, in calling our " message strange, unusual, or unparliamentary. Though we cannot but " take notice, that their answer to our message, That they would con- " sider of it, was the first of that kind that we can find to have come from " that House."

The question being put, Whether the House be satisfied with the reasons delivered by the Lords at the last conference? it passed in the negative.

Resolved, That a free conference be desired with the Lords upon the matter delivered at the last conference: and that the former Managers do attend, and manage the free conference.

May 21. The House resolved on *Wednesday* next to proceed in *Friday*, the further consideration of that part of the message relating to Appeals from inferior Courts. Sir *Trevor Williams* ordered to go up to the Lords, to desire a conference upon the privileges of this House, contained in their answer to the message touching Mr. *Onslow*'s case, which he accordingly did; and reports, That the Lords will return an answer thereto by messengers of their own.

May 27. A message ordered to be sent to the Lords to remind them of the former message; and again to desire a conference upon the privileges of this House, in the case of Mr. *Onslow*. And ordered the matter of the jurisdiction of the Lords, in cases of Appeal, be taken into consideration to-morrow morning.

Veneris, 28 Maii, 1675.

Sir *Thomas Lee* reports, from the Committee to whom it was referred to draw up reasons to be offered at a conference to be had with the Lords upon the subject-matter of their answer to the last message of this House, in the case of Mr. *Onslow*, several reasons agreed by the said Committee; which he read in his place, and afterwards delivered the same in at the Clerk's table; where the same being twice read, were, upon the question, severally agreed unto, and are as follow, *viz.*

" For that the Commons desired a conference upon their privileges " concerned by the Lords answer to a message sent to the Lords the 18th " of *May*, in the case of Mr. *Onslow*; their Lordships have not agreed any " conference in the case of Mr. *Onslow*; but have only agreed a confe- " rence concerning their privileges in general, without reference to the " case of the said Mr. *Onslow*; which was the only subject-matter of the " desired conference.

" The limitation in the Lords agreement to a conference, with proviso " that nothing be offered at the conference that may any way concern " their Lordships judicature, is in effect a denial of any conference at all, " upon the subject on which it was desired; which ought not to be: the " judicature which their Lordships claim in Appeals against a Member of " the House of Commons, and the privilege of that House being in that " case so involved, that there can be no conference upon the latter, with- " out some way touching upon the former.

" That this manner of agreeing to a conference with any limitation or " proviso, is against the course of Proceedings betwixt the two Houses " of Parliament, in coming to conference; and doth seem to place a power " in the Managers of such conferences, to judge whether such proviso's " be broken or not, and accordingly to proceed, or break off the confe- " rence upon their own judgments."

Lunæ, 31 Maii, 1675.

Sir *Leoline Jenkins* reports, that he had attended the Lords, with the message of this House, for a conference upon the subject-matter of the Lords answer to the last message of this House, in the case of Mr. *Onslow*; and that the Lords had sent answer, that they would return answer by messengers of their own.

A message from the Lords by Sir *Mondeford Brampston*, and Sir *William Beversham.*

" *Mr. Speaker*,

" The Lords have commanded us to acquaint you, that they desire a " conference presently in the Painted-Chamber, with the House of Com- " mons, upon their not coming to the conference desired by them on " *Thursday* last, and by the Lords appointed to be at ten of the clock in " the Painted-Chamber, on *Friday* the 28th of this instant *May*."

The messengers being withdrawn, and the message debated, a present conference upon the question was agreed.

And the messengers being called in, Mr. Speaker acquaints them, that the House had agreed to a present conference.

Ordered, That the former Members that were appointed to manage the former conference in the case of Mr. *Onslow*, do attend and manage this conference.

Sir *John Trevor* reports, from the conference, that the Lords had declared the intent of this conference, to the effect following, *viz.* " That " the Lords have appointed this conference, out of that constant desire and " resolution that they have to continue a fair correspondence between the " two Houses; which is of the essence of Parliamentary Proceedings.

" For this end their Lordships have commanded us to tell you, that they " cannot but take notice of the House of Commons failing to be on *Friday* " last, at a conference desired by themselves, and appointed by the Lords " at ten of the clock in the Painted-Chamber.

" That they conceive it tends to an interruption of all Parliamentary " Proceedings, and to evade the right of the Lords to appoint time and " place for a conference."

Ordered, That it be referred to the former Committee, who are appointed to draw up reasons, to be offered at a conference to be had with the Lords, upon the subject-matter of their answer to the message of this House, in the case of Mr. *Onslow*; to consider of the matter delivered by the Lords at the last conference; and to prepare and draw up further reasons, to be offered at another conference to be had with the Lords, upon the subject-matter of the last conference. And that the Committee do meet this afternoon at five of the clock in the Speaker's Chamber. And Mr. Serjeant *Maynard*, and Mr. *Sawyer*, are to have notice to attend the same.

Martis, 1 Junii, 1675.

Sir *Thomas Lee* reports, from the Committee appointed to inspect the Journals of the House of Lords, and to see what Proceedings have been entered, in the case of Mr. *Dalmahoy* and Mr. *Onslow*; that they had inspected the Lords Journals, as to the case of Mr. *Dalmahoy*, and collected what Proceedings had been in that case, but had no opportunity or time, yet to do it in the case of Mr. *Onslow*. Which Proceedings being reported, were read, and delivered in at the Clerk's table; and are as follow, *viz.*

19 *April*, 1675.

The Appeal brought by *Crispe* and *Crispe*, complaining against a Decree in *Chancery* made, wherein Mr. *Dalmahoy* is recited to be one of the Petitioners; *Cranbourne* and *Bowyer* are ordered to put in an answer, and *Dalmahoy*, if he please.

Maii 12, 1675.

Ordered, That this House will hear Counsel at the Bar, upon the Petition and Appeal of Sir *Nicholas Crispe* and others, against the Lady Viscountess *Cranbourne*, the Lady *Anne Bowyer*, and *Thomas Dalmahoy*, Esq; and their answer thereunto, depending in this House, on *Wednesday* the 19th of this instant *May*, at ten of the clock in the forenoon; whereof the Petitioners are to cause timely notice to be given to the said Defendants, or their Agents in the said cause, for that purpose.

Maii 16, 1675.

Whereas Sir *Nicholas Crispe*, Bart having an Appeal depending in this House, against the Lady *Cranbourne*, Lady *Bowyer*, and *Thomas Dalmahoy*, Esq; a Member of the House of Commons; hath prayed that Counsel may be assigned him to plead his cause upon the said Appeal, and hath named Counsel for that purpose:

It is ordered, That Sir *John Churchill*, Serjeant *Peck*, Serjeant *Pemberton*, and Mr. *Porter*, named by the said Sir *Nicholas Crispe*, be, and are hereby appointed to open, and manage the said cause, on the part and behalf of the said Sir *Nicholas Crispe*, on *Thursday* the 27th day of this instant *May*, at ten of the clock in the forenoon; and at such other times, as it shall be depending in this House.

Upon reading the Petition of Sir *Nicholas Crispe*, Bart. *Thomas Crispe* and *John Crispe*, Esqrs. shewing, that having an Appeal depending in this House against *Thomas Dalmahoy*, Esq; a Member of the House of Commons, and others; they are in danger of being arrested by an order of the House of Commons; and therefore pray the protection of this House, that they may have liberty to prosecute their said Appeal with Freedom:

It is thereupon ordered, That the said Sir *Nicholas Crispe*, Bart. *John Crispe*, and *Thomas Crispe*, or any of them, their or any of their Counsel, Agents or Sollicitors, or such other person or persons as they shall employ, in prosecuting the said Appeal before this House, be, and are hereby privileged, and protected accordingly by this House, until the matter upon the Appeal be determined by their Lordships. And all persons whatsoever are hereby prohibited from arresting, imprisoning, or otherwise molesting the said Sir *Nicholas Crispe*, *John Crispe*, and *Thomas Crispe*, or any of them, their or any of their Counsel, Agents, or Sollicitors, upon any pretence whatsoever, during the time prefixed, as they or such of them will answer the contrary to this House.

Maii 26, 1675.

The cause between Sir *Nicholas Crispe*, &c. plaintiffs, and *Thomas Dalmahoy*, Esq; defendant, appointed to be heard the 27th, was ordered to be heard the 28th *Maii*.

Maii 27.

Upon reading the petition of Sir *Nicholas Crispe*, complaining, that the Counsel assigned him by this House, to plead his cause at the bar, wherein Mr. *Dalmahoy* is one of the defendants, do refuse to plead for him in this case, in regard of a vote of the House of Commons; Sir *Nicholas Crispe* was called in, and testified, that he shewed the order of this House to Serjeant *Peck*, Serjeant *Pemberton*, Sir *John Churchill*, and Mr. *Porter*

Whereupon it is ordered, That whereas Sir *John Churchill*, Serjeant *Peck*, Serjeant *Pemberton*, and Mr. *Porter*, were by order of this House, dated on the 19th instant, assigned to be of Counsel for Sir *Nicholas Crispe*, *John Crispe*, and *Thomas Crispe*, in their cause depending in this House against *Thomas Dalmahoy*, Esq; a Member of the House of Commons, and other defendants, at such time as the said cause shall be appointed to be pleaded at the bar of this House; having appointed to hear the said cause by Counsel on both sides, to-morrow at three of the clock in the afternoon:

It is this day ordered, That the said Sir *John Churchill*, Serjeant *Peck*, Serjeant *Pemberton*, and Mr. *Porter*, be, and are hereby required, to appear at the bar of this House, to-morrow, at three of the clock in the afternoon, as Counsel to plead in the said cause, on the behalf of the said Sir *Nicholas Crispe*, *John* and *Thomas Crispe*, as they will answer the contrary to this House.

Maii 28, 1675.

Counsel heard at the bar on both parts, upon the Petition and Appeal of Sir *Nicholas Crispe*, &c. and the answer of *Diana* Viscountess *Cranbourne*, &c. and *Thomas Dalmahoy*, Esq; put in thereunto, concerning a decree in *Chancery*: *Resolved*, the Petition and Decree be dismissed.

Maii 28.

This day the House heard the Counsel of Sir *Nicholas Crispe*, *John Crispe*, and *Thomas Crispe*, upon their Petition and Appeal depending in this House; and also the Counsel of the Lady *Bowyer*, and Mr. *Dalmahoy*, upon their answer thereunto; and after a serious consideration thereof, the question being put, Whether this Petition and Appeal shall be dismissed this House?

It was resolved in the affirmative.

Mr.

Mr. Serjeant *Pemberton*, Sir *John Churchill*, Mr. Serjeant *Peck*, and Mr. *Porter* attending at the door, in obedience to the order of the House of Commons; and being severally called in, Mr. *Speaker* did severally acquaint them, that they were summoned to give an account to the House, of their appearing as Counsel at the Bar of the House of Lords, in the prosecution of a cause depending upon an appeal, wherein Mr. *Dalmahoy*, a Member of this House, is concerned, in the manifest breach of the order of this House; and giving up, as much as in them lies, the rights and privileges of the Commons of *England:* And they having answered and made their excuses to the effect following: That they had no notice of the order or vote of this House, but what they have heard in common discourse abroad; and because they conceived Mr. *Dalmahoy*, a Member of this House, might be concerned, they refused several times to appear as Counsel, or to accept their fees; but being assigned of Counsel for Sir *Nicholas Crispe*, and an order of the House of Lords being served on them to attend at their peril, and that then attending, and Mr. *Dalmahoy* having put in his answer in the Lords House, and not insisting on his privilege afterwards, and the Counsel for the Lady *Bowyer*, who was the principal party concerned, denying to be of counsel for Mr. *Dalmahoy*, they conceived they might safely appear as Counsel without breach of the order, or invading the rights and privileges of this House, which was not intended by them; and Sir *John Churchill*, by way of further excuse for himself, said, that he had witnesses ready to prove, that Mr. *Dalmahoy* was willing and desirous to have the business go forward. And the said Mr. Serjeant *Pemberton*, Sir *John Churchill*, Mr. Serjeant *Peck*, and Mr. *Porter*, did all of them humbly submit themselves to the pleasure of the House, if they had in any thing misbehaved themselves; and being withdrawn, and the matter debated: The question being put, That Serjeant *Pemberton* be taken into the custody of the Serjeant at Arms attending this House?

It was resolved in the affirmative.

Ordered, That Serjeant *Pemberton*, Sir *John Churchill*, Mr. Serjeant *Peck*, and *Charles Porter*, Esq. be taken into the custody of the Serjeant at Arms attending this House, for their breach of privilege of this House.

Mercurii, 2 die Junii.

Ordered, That Sir *Richard Temple*, Mr. *Vaughan*, and Sir *Thomas Lee* do withdraw, and amend the reasons upon the debates of the House, which was done; and the reasons agreed to are as follow:

"The House of Commons do agree with the Lords, that conferences between the two Houses of Parliament are essential to Parliamentary Proceedings, when they are agreed in the usual and Parliamentary way; but the manner of the Lords agreement to the conference, to have been on *Friday* the 28th of *May* last, at ten of the clock, in the Painted Chamber, with limitation and proviso, did necessitate the House of Commons to forbear to meet at that conference, and gave the first interruption to parliamentary Proceedings in conferences between the two Houses.

"For that the conference desired by the Commons, was upon their privileges, concerned in the answer of the Lords to a message of the House of Commons, sent to the Lords the 17th of *May*, in the case of Mr. *Onslow*, to the which the Lords did not agree, but did only agree to a conference concerning their privileges in general, without reference to the case of the said Mr. *Onslow*; which was the only subject-matter of the desired conference.

"The limitations in the Lords agreement to a conference, with proviso that nothing be offered at the conference that may any ways concern the Lords judicature, is in effect a denial of any conference at all upon the subject upon which it was desired; which ought not to be.

"The judicature which the Lords claim in Appeals against a Member of the House of Commons, and the privilege of that House in that case, is so involved, that no conference can be upon the matter without some way touching the former.

"That this manner of agreeing to a conference with any limitation or proviso, is against the course of proceedings between the two Houses of Parliament, in coming to conferences; and doth seem to place a power in the Managers of such conferences to judge, whether such proviso's be broken or not; and accordingly to proceed or break off the conference upon their own judgments.

"The House of Commons doubt not, but that when the Lords have considered of what is delivered at this conference, the good correspondence which the Lords express they desire to continue between the two Houses, (which the Commons also are no less careful to maintain) will induce them to remove the present interruption of coming to conferences; and therefore to agree to the conference, as it was desired by the House of Commons, upon the privileges of their House, concerned in the Lords answer to the message of the House of Commons, in the case of Mr. *Onslow:* That the particular limitation, that nothing be offered at the conference, that may any way concern the judicature of the Lords, appears unreasonable; for that their Lordships judicature in Parliament is circumscribed by the laws of the land, as to their proceedings and judgments; and is, as well as all other Courts, subjected to Parliament."

Jovis, 3 die Junii, 1675.

Mr. *Vaughan* reports, That the Lord Privy-Seal did manage the conference, and had delivered the intent and occasion of the conference; which Mr. *Vaughan* did report to the House, to the effect following, *viz.*

"The Lords do take notice of the House of Commons, their ordering into custody of their Serjeant, Mr. Serjeant *Peck*, Sir *John Churchill*, Mr. Serjeant *Pemberton*, and Mr. *Charles Porter*, Counsellors at Law; assigned by their Lordships to be of Counsel in an Appeal heard at their Lordships Bar, in the case of Sir *Nicholas Crispe*, against the Lady *Bowyer*, Mr. *Dalmahoy*, and others; the Lords in Parliament, where his Majesty is highest in his royal estate, and where the last resort of judging upon Writs of Error, and Appeals in Equity, in all causes, and over all persons, is undoubtedly fixed, and permanently lodged.

"It is an unexampled usurpation and breach of privilege against the House of Peers, that their orders or judgments should be disputed, or endeavoured to be controuled, or the execution thereof obstructed by the Lower House of Parliament; who are no Court, nor have authority to
"ster an oath, or give any judgment.

"It is a transcendent invasion on the right and liberty of the sub
"against *Magna Charta, the Petition of Right*, and many other law
"have provided, *That no Freeman shall be imprisoned, or otherwise*
"*of his liberty, but by due process of Law.*

"This tends to the subversion of the Government of this King
"to the introducing of arbitrariness and disorder.

"Because it is in the nature of an injunction from the Lower Ho
"have no authority or power of judicature over inferior subjects, n
"over the King and Lords) against the orders and judgments of
"preme Court.

"We are further commanded to acquaint you, That the Lo
"therefore, out of that justice which they are dispensers of, against
"sion and breach of laws, by judgment of this Court, set at libert
"Gentleman-Usher of the Black Rod, all the said Serjeants and
"lors; and prohibited the Lieutenant of the Tower, and all othe
"ers of prisons, and Gaolers, and all persons whatsoever, from
"and imprisoning, detaining, or otherwise molesting, or charging
"Gentlemen, or any of them in this case: And if any person, of
"gree soever, shall presume to the contrary, their Lordships will
"the authority with them intrusted for putting the laws in executi

"And we are further commanded to read to you, a Roll of Par
"in the first year of the reign of King *Henry* the IVth, whereof
"brought the original with us."

And a debate arising thereupon,

Resolved, That a conference be desired with the Lords upon the
matter of the last conference; and that these Members following
pointed to prepare and draw up reasons upon the debates of the Ho
offered at the conference; Mr. Secretary *Coventry*, &c.

Ordered, That the officer in whose custody is the Record of th
Henry the IVth, mentioned at the conference with the Lords, do a
Committee appointed to draw up reasons for another conference t
noon: And they are to meet at three of the clock, in the Speaker'
ber, and to send for Persons, Papers, and Records.

Ordered, That no Member of this House do attend the Lords H
on any summons from the Lords, without leave of the House.

Veneris, 4 Junii, 1675.

Ordered, That the thanks of the House be returned to Mr. *Spea*
causing Mr. Serjeant *Pemberton*, formerly committed by order of thi
to the custody of the Serjeant at Arms attending this House, for a b
privilege, to be seized and taken into custody in *Westminster-hall*,
breach of privilege.

The House being informed, that Sir *John Churchill*, Mr. Serjea
and Mr. *Charles Porter*, who were ordered to be taken into the cu
the Serjeant at Arms attending this House, are now in *Westminster-*

Ordered, That the Serjeant at Arms now attending this House
with his Mace into *Westminster-hall*, and do execute the order of this
and the warrant of Mr. *Speaker* thereupon; for seizing and bringing
tody Mr. Serjeant *Peck*, Sir *John Churchill*, and Mr. *Charles Po*
their breach of the privilege of this House.

The Serjeant returning, gave an account, that he had executed t
of this House, and Mr. *Speaker*'s warrant thereupon, and had brou
said Mr. Serjeant *Peck*, Sir *John Churchill*, and Mr. *Charles Porter*,
tody, into the *Speaker*'s chamber.

The question being put, That Sir *John Churchill*, Mr. Serjea
Mr. Serjeant *Pemberton*, and Mr. *Charles Porter*, be sent to the To
their breach of privilege, and contempt of the authority of this Hou

It was resolved in the affirmative.

Ordered, That Mr. *Speaker* do issue his warrant to the Lieutena
Tower, to receive them into his custody.

Ordered, That *John Popham*, Esq. the now Serjeant at Arms at
this House, be protected against all persons that shall any ways n
hinder him from executing his office.

Sir *Thomas Lee* reports from the Committee, the reasons agreed t
fered at the conference to be had with the Lords upon the matters d
at the last conference; which were twice read, and with some ame
made at the table, severally agreed; and are as follow, *viz.*

"Your Lordships having desired the last conference, upon ma
"high importance concerning the dignity of the King, and the
"the Government, the Commons did not expect to hear from you
"ships at that conference, things so contrary to, and inconsiste
"the matter upon which the said conference was desired, as were
"livered by your Lordships.

"It was much below the expectation of the Commons, that after
"sentation of your Lordships Message of matters of so high importa
"particular upon which the conference was grounded, should be
"commitment of four Lawyers to the custody of their own Serjeant a
"for a manifest violation of the privileges of their House.

"But the Commons were much more surprised, when your L
"had introduced the conference with an assurance, that it was in
"a good correspondency between the two Houses, that your Lordship
"immediately assume a power to judge the orders of the House of Co
"for imprisonment of Mr. Serjeant *Pemberton*, Mr. Serjeant *Peck*, S
"*Churchill*, and Mr. *Charles Porter*, to be illegal and arbitrary; and
"ecution thereof a great indignity to the King's Majesty; with man
"high reflections upon the House of Commons throughout the wh
"ference; whereby your Lordships have condemned the whole H
"Commons as criminal, which is without precedent or example,
"ground or reason so to do.

"It is not against the King's dignity for the House of Commons
"nish by imprisonment, a Commoner that is guilty of violating th
"vileges, that being according to the known laws and customs of
"ment; and the right of their privileges declared by the King's roy
"decessors in former Parliaments, and by himself in this.

"But your Lordſhips claiming to be the ſupreme Court, and that his "Majeſty is higheſt in his royal eſtate in the Court of judicature there, "is a diminution of the dignity of the King, who is higheſt in his royal "eſtate in full Parliament; and is derogatory to the authority of the "whole Parliament, by appropriating it to yourſelves.

"The Commons did not by this impriſonment infringe any privileges "of the Houſe of Peers, but only defend and maintain their own: On the "other ſide, your Lordſhips do highly intrench upon the rights and pri- "vileges of the Houſe of Commons, by denying them to be a court, or "to have any authority or power of judicature; which, if admitted, will "leave them without any power or authority to preſerve themſelves.

"As to what your Lordſhips call a tranſcendent invaſion of the rights "and liberty of the ſubject, and againſt *Magna Charta*, the *Petition of* "*Right*, and many other laws; the Houſe of Commons preſume that your "Lordſhips know, that neither the *Great Charter*, *Petition of Right*, or "any other laws, do take away the law and cuſtom of Parliament, or of "either Houſe of Parliament, or elſe your Lordſhips have much forgot- "ten the *Great Charter*, and thoſe other laws, in the ſeveral judgments "your Lordſhips have paſſed upon the King's ſubjects in caſes of privi- "lege. But the Commons cannot find by *Magna Charta*, or by any other "law or ancient cuſtom of Parliament, that your Lordſhips have any ju- "riſdiction in caſes of Appeals from the Courts of Equity.

"We are further commanded to acquaint you, that the enlargement of "thoſe perſons in priſon, by order of the Houſe of Commons, by the "Gentleman-Uſher of the Black-Rod, and the prohibition which threa- "tens all officers and other perſons whatſoever, not to receive or detain "them, is an apparent breach of the rights and privileges of the Houſe of "Commons: And they have therefore cauſed them to be retaken into "the cuſtody of the Serjeant at Arms attending this Houſe, and have "committed them to the Tower.

"As for the Parliament-Roll of the firſt of King *Henry* the IVth, "cauſed to be read by your Lordſhips at the laſt conference, but "not applied, the Commons apprehend it doth not concern the caſe in "queſtion: For that this Record was made upon occaſion of judgments "given by the Lords, to depoſe and impriſon their lawful King; to "which the Commons were not willing to be made Parties. And there- "fore the Commons conceive it will not be for the honour of your Lord- "ſhips to make further uſe of that Record.

"But we are commanded to read to your Lordſhips the Parliament- "Roll of 4 *Ed.* III. *N.* 6. which, if your Lordſhips pleaſe to conſider, "they doubt not but your Lordſhips will find occaſion to apply it to the "preſent purpoſe."

Ordered, The Thanks of the Houſe be given to the Speaker, for his care in iſſuing the Warrant for retaking the perſons committed yeſterday into cuſtody.

The Serjeant at Arms ordered to be ſent to the Tower; and the other Serjeant at Arms attending, was ordered to apprehend him for betraying his truſt, in not executing his office, in bringing the perſons committed yeſterday to his cuſtody, to the bar of the Houſe.

An Addreſs ordered to be prepared to be preſented to his Majeſty, to deſire a new Serjeant at Arms to attend the Houſe.

Saturday, June 5, 1675.

Mr. Secretary *Coventry* acquainted the Houſe, that it was his Majeſty's deſire, that the Houſe would adjourn till four of the clock in the afternoon, and that both Houſes ſhould at that time attend him in the Banquetting-houſe at *Whitehall*.

A debate ariſing touching the removal of *John Popham*, Eſq. Serjeant at Arms in ordinary, attending the Houſe yeſterday, the further debate thereof was adjourned till five of the clock in the afternoon. And then the Houſe adjourned till four in the afternoon.

In the Afternoon,

The Houſe then met at the time they adjourn'd to, and went in a body to his Majeſty at *Whitehall*; and the Houſe of Lords being alſo preſent, his Majeſty made the following Speech.

My Lords and Gentlemen,

YOU may remember, that at the meeting of this Seſſion I told you, no endeavours would be wanting to make the continuance of this Parliament unpracticable. I am ſorry that experience hath ſo quickly ſhewed you the truth of what I then ſaid, but I hope that you are well convinced, that the intent of all theſe contrivances is only to procure a diſſolution. I confeſs I look upon it as a moſt malicious deſign of thoſe who are enemies to me and the Church of England; *and were the contrivers known, I ſhould not doubt but the diſlike of their practices would alone be a means of bringing the Houſes to a good underſtanding. But ſince I cannot preſcribe any way how to arrive to the diſcovery of it, I muſt tell you plainly my opinion, that the means of coming to any compoſure between yourſelves, cannot be without admitting of ſuch free conferences as may convince one another by the reaſons then offered, or enable me to judge rightly of the differences, when all hath been ſaid on both ſides which the matter will afford: for I am not to ſuffer theſe differences to grow to diſorders in the whole Kingdom, if I can prevent it; and I am ſure my judgment ſhall always be impartial between my two Houſes of Parliament. But I muſt let you know, that whilſt you are in debate about your privileges, I will not ſuffer my own to be invaded. I have nothing more to ſay to you at this time, but to deſire, as I did when we met firſt, that you would yet conſider, and not ſuffer ill men's deſigns to hinder the Seſſions from a happy concluſion.*

[The Houſe of Lords preſented an Addreſs to his Majeſty, to remove the Lieutenant of the *Tower*; whereupon the Lord-Treaſurer reported his Majeſty's anſwer, *viz.* "That his Majeſty hath conſidered the cir- "cumſtances of the matter, and is not ſatisfied how with juſtice he can "remove him."]

The Houſe then took into conſideration his Majeſty's Speech, and reſolved, *nemine contradicente*, That the humble Thanks of this Houſe be returned to his Majeſty, for the gracious expreſſions in his Speech this day made to both Houſes of Parliament; and ſuch Members of this Houſe as are of his Majeſty's Privy-Council are deſired to preſent the humble Thanks of this Houſe to his Majeſty.

Reſolved, That it doth not appear to this Houſe, that any Member thereof hath either contrived or promoted the difference between the two Houſes of Parliament; or in aſſerting the Rights of the Commons of *England*, and the privileges of this Houſe; or to have done any thing inconſiſtent with his duty, or the truſt repoſed in him. And then adjourned to *Monday, June* 7.

On *Monday, June* 7, the Houſe reſolved, That what Serjeant *Popham* did in retaking the four Lawyers into his cuſtody, and conducting them to the *Tower* of *London*, was in purſuance of his duty, and by the order of the Houſe; and the further debate concerning the ſaid Serjeant at Arms was adjourned till *Wedneſday* morning.

A copy of an order from the Houſe of Lords for the hearing Counſel in the caſe of Sir *John Fagg*, a Member of this Houſe, to-morrow morning, was then read and debated: And,

Reſolved, That as to the caſe of appeal brought againſt Sir *John Fagg*, in the Houſe of Lords, he ſhall have the protection and aſſiſtance of this Houſe.

Reſolved, nem. con. That if any perſon or perſons ſhall be aiding or aſſiſting in putting in execution any ſentence or judgment that ſhall be given by the Houſe of Lords, upon the Appeal brought by Dr. *Shirley* againſt Sir *John Fagg*, a Member of this Houſe, ſuch perſon or perſons ſhall be adjudged and taken to be betrayers of the rights and liberties of the Commons of *England*, and the privileges of this Houſe; and ſhall be proceeded againſt accordingly.

Ordered, That theſe Votes be made publick, by ſetting them up in *Weſtminſter-hall*, and in the Lobby of this Houſe; and the Clerk of the Houſe to take care to ſee it done.

In the afternoon the Houſe proceeded in the further conſideration of effectual means for the preſervation of their rights and privileges, and reſolved, *nem. con.* That no perſon committed by order or warrant of this Houſe, for breach of the privileges or contempt of the authority of the Houſe, ought to be diſcharged during the Seſſion of Parliament, without the order or warrant of this Houſe.

Reſolved, nem. con. That the Lieutenant of the *Tower* of *London*, in receiving and detaining in cuſtody, Sir *John Churchill*, Serjeant *Peck*, Serjeant *Pemberton*, and Mr. *Porter*, hath performed his duty according to law; and for his ſo doing, he ſhall have the aſſiſtance and protection of this Houſe.

Reſolved, That the Lieutenant of the *Tower*, in caſe he hath, or ſhall receive any writ, warrant, order, or command, to remove or deliver any perſon or perſons committed to his charge, for breach of the privileges or contempt of the authority of the Houſe of Commons, by order or warrant of the Houſe; ſhall not make any return thereof, or yield any obedience thereto, before he hath firſt acquainted the Houſe therewith, and received their order and direction how to proceed therein.

Ordered, That theſe reſolutions be immediately ſent to the Lieutenant of the *Tower*; and then the Houſe adjourned.

Tueſday, June 8, 1675.

A meſſage ſent to the Lords to remind them of the laſt conference; and for a conference upon the ſubject-matter delivered by the Lords at the laſt conference.

Sir *John Robinſon* informing the Houſe, that he had received the four Lawyers committed to his cuſtody by this Houſe, and denied to deliver them to the Gentleman-Uſher of the Black-Rod; and that he was ſerved laſt night with four Writs of *Habeas Corpus*, to bring the ſaid four Lawyers before the King and his Parliament at *Weſtminſter*, this morning, and craved the advice of the Houſe what to do therein:

Ordered, The Thanks of the Houſe be given to the ſaid Sir *John Robinſon* for his behaviour therein; and Mr. *Speaker* intimated to him, that he ſhould forbear to return the ſaid Writs of *Habeas Corpus*, which were read and debated; and the further debate thereof was adjourned till to-morrow morning, and a Committee appointed to ſearch the Lords Journals to ſee what hath been done in the caſe of the four Lawyers, the Writs of *Habeas Corpus*, and Mr. Serjeant *Popham*; and to ſearch for precedents on the Writs of *Habeas Corpus*. and adjourn'd.

Mercurii, 9 die Junii.

Sir *Thomas Clarges* reports from the Committee, to whom it was referred to ſearch for precedents touching Writs of *Habeas Corpus* returnable in Parliament; that the Committee had found ſeveral precedents of Writs of *Habeas Corpus* returnable in Parliament, and conſidered of them: And that the Committee thereupon had agreed upon four Reſolves to be preſented to the Houſe, which he read in his place, and afterwards delivered the ſame in at the Clerk's table, where they being twice read, were upon the queſtion ſeverally agreed to, and are as follow:

"*Reſolved, nem. con.* 1. That no Commoners of *England*, committed "by the order or warrant of the Houſe of Commons, for breach of privi- "lege, or contempt of the authority of the ſaid Houſe, ought, without or- "der of this Houſe to be by any Writ of *Habeas Corpus*, or any other autho- "rity whatſoever, made to appear and anſwer, or receive any determination "in the Houſe of Peers, during that Seſſion of Parliament wherein ſuch "perſons were ſo committed.

"*Reſolved, nem. con.* 2. That the order of the Houſe of Peers for the "iſſuing out the Writs of *Habeas Corpus* concerning Mr. Serjeant *Pem-* "*berton*, Mr. Serjeant *Peck*, Sir *John Churchill*, and Mr. *Charles Porter*, "is inſufficient and illegal; for that it is general, and expreſſes no parti- "cular cauſe of privilege, and commands the King's Great Seal to be "put to writs not returnable before the ſaid Houſe of Peers.

"*Reſolved, nem. con* 3. That the Lord-Keeper be acquainted with theſe "reſolutions, to the end that the ſaid Writs of *Habeas Corpus* be ſuper- "ſeded, as contrary to law and the privileges of this Houſe.

"*Reſolved, nem. con.* 4. That a meſſage be ſent to the Lords to ac- "quaint their Lordſhips, that Mr. Serjeant *Peck*, Sir *John Churchill*, Mr. "Serjeant *Pemberton*, and Mr. *Charles Porter*, were committed by order "and warrant of this Houſe for manifeſt breach of the privilege, and "contempt of the authority of this Houſe."

Ordered, That Col. *Birch* do go up to the Lords with a meſſage, that a conference be deſired upon the ſubject-matter of the laſt conference.

A meſſage was this day ſent from his Majeſty in the Houſe of Lords, by Sir *Edward Carteret*, Uſher of the Black-Rod, commanding this honourable Houſe to attend his Majeſty forthwith in the Houſe of Peers, and accordingly Mr. *Speaker* went up with the Houſe, where his Majeſty was pleaſed to make the following Speech to them:

My

My Lords and Gentlemen,

'I Think I have given sufficient Evidence to the World, that I have 'not been wanting on my Part, in my Endeavours to procure the full 'satisfaction of all my Subjects, in the Matters both of Religion and 'Property: I have not only invited you to those Considerations at our 'first Meeting, but I have been careful, through this whole Session, that 'no concern of my own should divert you from them.

'Besides, as I had only designed the Matter of it to be the procuring 'of good Laws, so for the gaining of them, I have already waited much 'longer than I intended; and should have been contented still to have 'continued my Expectation, had there any Hopes remained of a good 'Conclusion. But I must confess, the ill Designs of our Enemies have 'been too prevalent against those good ones I had proposed to myself, in 'behalf of my People; and those unhappy Differences between my two '*Houses* are grown to such a Height, that I find no possible means of put'ting an End to them, but by a Prorogation. It is with great unwilling'ness that I make use of this Expedient, having always intended an Ad'journment for the preserving of such Bills as were unfinished. But my 'Hopes are, that by this Means the present Occasion of Differences be'ing taken away, you will be so careful hereafter of the Public, as not 'to seek new ones, nor to revive the old.

'I intend to meet you here again in Winter, and have directed my 'Lord-Keeper to prorogue you till the thirteenth Day of *October* next.'

October 13, 1675, the King came to the House, and began thus:

My Lords and Gentlemen,

'I Meet you now with more than an usual Concern for the event of this 'Sessions; and I know it's but what may be reasonably expected from 'the Care I have for the Preservation of the Government. The Causes of 'the last prorogation, as I for my Part do not desire to remember, so I 'hope no Man else will, unless it be to learn from thence how to avoid 'the like Occasion for the future: And I pray consider how fatal the 'Consequences may be, and how little Benefit is like to redound to the 'People by it. However, if any of that Kind shall arise, I desire you 'would defer those Debates, till you have brought such publick Bills to 'Perfection, as may conduce to the Good and Safety of the Kingdom.'

[The rest of the Speech relates to his Majesty's recommending the Security of the Protestant Religion, the Supply for building Ships, and publick Debts, *&c.*]

Then the Lord *Finch*, by his Majesty's Order, made a Speech to both Houses, recommending Unanimity, and making good Laws, and the Care of Religion, *&c.*

The Earl of *Shaftesbury*'s Speech in the House of Lords, upon the Debate of appointing a Day for the hearing Dr. *Shirley*'s Cause, the 20th of *October*, 1675.

My Lords,

OUR All is at Stake, and therefore you must give me Leave to speak freely before we part with it. My Lord Bishop of *Salisbury* is of Opinion, *That we should rather appoint a Day to consider what to do upon the Petition, than to appoint a Day of hearing*; and my Lord-Keeper, for I may name them at a Committee of the whole House, tells us in very eloquent and studied language, *That he will propose us a Way far less liable to Exception, and much less offensive and injurious to our own Privileges, than that of appointing a Day of hearing.* And I beseech your Lordships, did you not after all these fine Words expect some admirable Proposal? But it ended in this, *That your Lordships should appoint a Day, nay, a very long Day, to consider what you would do in it*: And my Lord hath undertaken to convince you, that this is your only Course, by several undeniable Reasons, the first of which is, *That 'tis against your Judicature to have this Cause, which is not proper, before us, nor ought to be relieved by us.* To this, my Lords, give me Leave to answer, That I did not expect from a Man professing the Law, that after an Answer by Order of the Court was put in, and a Day had been appointed for hearing, which by some Accident was set aside; and the Plaintiff moving for a second Day to be assigned, that ever, without hearing Counsel of both Sides, the Court did enter into the Merits of the Cause. And if your Lordships should do it here in a Cause attended with the Circumstances this is, it would not only be an apparent Injustice, but a plain *Subterfuge*, to avoid a Point you durst not maintain.

But my Lord's second Reason speaks the Matter more clearly; for that is, *Because 'tis a doubtful Case, whether the Commons have not Privilege*, and therefore my Lord would have you *to appoint a further, and a very long Day to consider of it*: Which, in plain *English* is, that your Lordships should confess upon your Books, that you conceive it on second Thoughts a doubtful Case; for so your appointing a Day to consider will do, and that for no other Reason, but because my Lord-Keeper thinks it so: which I hope will not be a Reason to prevail with your Lordships, since we cannot yet, by Experience, tell that his Lordship is capable of thinking your Lordships in the right, in any Matter against the Judgment of the House of Commons; 'tis so hard a Thing even for the ablest of Men to change ill Habits.

But my Lord's third Reason is the most admirable of all, which he stiles unanswerable, *viz. That your Lordships are all convinced in your Consciences, that this (if prosecuted) will cause a Breach.* I beseech your Lordships consider, whether this Argument, thus applied, would not overthrow the Law of Nature, and all the Laws of Right and Property in the World. For 'tis an Argument, and a very good one, that you should not stand or insist on Claims, where you have not a clear Right, or where the Question is not of Consequence and Moment, in a Matter that may produce a dangerous and pernicious Breach between Relations, Persons, or Bodies Politick, joined in Interest and high Concerns together. So, on the other Hand, if the Obstinacy of the Party in the wrong, shall be made an unanswerable Argument for the other Party to recede and give up his just Rights; how long shall the People keep their Liberties, or the Princes or Governors of the World their Prerogatives? How long shall the Husband maintain his Dominion, or any Man his Property, from his Friend's or his Neighbour's Obstinacy? But, my Lords, when I hear my Lord-Keeper open so eloquently the fatal Consequences of a Breach, I cannot forbear to fall into some Admiration how it comes to pass, that (if the Consequences be so fatal) the King's Ministers in the House of Commons, of which there are several that are of the Cabinet, and have daily Resort to his Majesty, and have the Direction and Trust of his Affairs; I say, that none of these should press these Cons there; or give the least Stop to the Career of that House in this but that all the Votes concerning this Affair, nay, even that ve *That no Appeal from any Court of Equity is cognizable by the House* should pass *nemine contradicente*. And yet all the great Minister here, the Bishops and other Lords of greatest Dependance on th contend this Point, as if it were *pro Aris & Focis*. I hear his M *Scotland* hath been pleased to declare against Appeals in Parlia cannot much blame the Court, if they think (the Lord-Keeper Judges being of the King's naming, and in his Power to change) Justice of the Nation is safe enough, and I, my Lords, may thi during this King's Time, though I hear *Scotland*, not withou complain already. Yet how future Princes may use this Power, Judges may be made not Men of Ability or Integrity, but Men tion and Dependance, and who will do what they are comman all Men's Causes come to be judged, and Estates disposed on, Men at Court please.

My Lords, the Constitution of our Government hath provid for us; and I can never believe so wise a Body as the House of C will prove that foolish Woman which plucks down her House Hands.

My Lords, I must presume in the next Place, to say something was offered by my Lord Bishop of *Salisbury*, a Man of great Lear Abilities, and always versed in a stronger and closer Way of reason the Business of that noble Lord I answered before did accustom and that Reverend Prelate hath stated the Matter very fair upon tw

The first, *Whether the hearing of Causes and Appeals, and especial Point, where the Members have Privilege, be so material to us, that it to give way to the Reason of State, of greater Affairs that pressed us at th*

The second was, *If this Business be of that Moment, yet whethe pointing a Day to consider of this Petition, would prove of that Conseq Prejudice to your Cause?*

My Lords, to these give me Leave in the first Place to say, Matter is no less than your whole Judicature; and your Judicatu Life and Soul of the Dignity of the Peerage of *England*, you will grow burdensome, if you grow useless: You have now the gre most useful End of Parliaments principally in you, which is not new Laws, but to redress Grievances, and to maintain the ol Marks. The House of Commons Business is to complain, your L to redress, not only the Complaints from them that are the Eyes Nation, but all other particular Persons that address to you. may groan under a Multitude of Laws, and I believe ours do when Laws grow so multiplied, they prove oftener Snares than tions and Security to the People. I look upon it as the Ignora Weakness of the latter Age, if not worse, the Effect of the Desig Men; that it is grown a general Opinion, that where there is no ticular Direction in some Act of Parliament, the Law is defecti the Common Law had not provided much better, shorter, and pla the Peace and Quiet of the Nation, than intricate, long perplex tutes do; which has made Work for the Lawyers, given Powe Judges, lessened your Lordships Power, and in a good Measure u the Security of the People.

My Lord Bishop tells us, *That your whole Judicature is not in but only the Privilege of the House of Commons, of their Members not at your Bar*: My Lords, were it no more, yet that for Justice People's Sake you ought not to part with. How far a Privileg House of Commons, their Servants, and those they own, doth *Westminster-Hall* may with grief tell your Lordships. And the Pri vilege of their Members being not sued, must be allowed by you ships as well; and what a Failure of Justice this would prove, wi are Lords for Life, and you for Inheritance, let the World jud my Part, I am willing to come to Conference whenever the Disp begin again; and dare undertake to your Lordships, that they h ther Precedent, Reason, nor any justifiable Pretence to shew ag and therefore, my Lords, if you part with this undoubted Righ for asking, where will the asking stop? And, my Lords, we ar doth not stop here, for they have already, *Nemine Contradicent* against your Lordships Power of Appeals from any Court of Eq that you may plainly see where this Caution and Reason of State to stop; not one Jot short of laying your whole Judicature aside, same Reason of passing the King's Money, of not interrupting goo and whatever else must of Necessity avoid all Breach, upon what S ever; and your Lordships plainly see the Breach will be as we upon your Judicature in general, as upon this; so that when you ships have appointed a Day, a very long Day, for to consider Dr. *Shirley*'s Cause be not too hot to handle; and when you ha the same for Sir *Nicholas Stanton*, whose Petition I hear is coming Lordships must proceed to a Vote, to lay all private Business aside Weeks: For that Phrase of private Business hath obtained upon Age, upon that which is your most publick Duty and Business; the Administration of Justice. And I can tell your Lordships, be Reason that leads to it, that I have some Intelligence of the design a Vote. For on the second Day of your Sitting, at the Rising Lords House, there came a Gentleman into the Lobby, belongi very great Person, and asked in very great Haste, *Are the Lords up they passed the Vote?* And being asked, *What Vote?* He answered, *of no private Business for six Weeks.*

My Lords, if this be your Business, see where you are; if w postpone our Judicature for fear of offending the House of Comm six Weeks, that they in the interim may pass the Money, and o ceptable Bills that his Majesty thinks of Importance; are so ma Men in the House of Commons to be laid asleep, and to pass all t ceptable Things; and when they have done, to let us be let loo them?

Will they not remember this next time there is want of Mo may not they rather be assured by those Ministers that are among and go on so unanimously with them, that the King is on their Sid Controversy? And when the public Businesses are over, our time too short to make a Breach, or vindicate ourselves in the Matte then I beg your Lordships, where are you, after you have asle the last Sessions your right of Judicature, so highly, even in this point; and after the House of Commons had gone so high against you on the other hand, as to post up their declaration and remonstrances on *Westminster-Hall* doors; the very next Session after, you postpone the very same causes; and not only those, but all Judicatures whatsoever? I beseech your Lordships, will not this prove a fatal precedent and confession against yourselves? 'Tis a Maxim, and a rational one among the Lawyers, *That one precedent where the Case hath been contested, is worth a thousand where there hath been no contest.* My Lords, in saying this, I humbly suppose I have given a sufficient answer to my Lord Bishop's second question; *Whether the appointing a day to consider what you will do with this Petition, be of that consequence to your right?* For it is a plain confession, that it is a doubtful case, and that infinitely stronger than if it were a new thing to you, never heard of before: for it is the very same case, and the very same thing desired in that case, that you formerly ordered, and so strongly asserted; so that upon time, and all the deliberation imaginable, you declare yourselves to become doubtful, and you put yourselves out of your own hands, into that power that you have no reason to believe on your side in this question.

My Lords, I have all the duty imaginable to his Majesty, and shall with all submission give way to any thing he should think of importance to his affairs: but in this point it is to alter the constitution of the Government, if you are asked to lay this aside, and there is no reason of State can be an argument to your Lordships to turn yourselves out of that interest you have in the constitution of the Government; 'tis not only your concern that you maintain yourselves in't, but 'tis the concern of the poorest man in *England*, that you keep your station: 'tis your Lordships concern, and that so highly, that I will be bold to say, the King can give none of you a requital or recompence for it. What are empty titles? What is present power, or riches, and a great estate, wherein I have no firm nor fixed property? 'Tis the constitution of the Government, and maintaining it, that secures your Lordships and every man else in what he hath: the poorest Lord, if the birth-right of the Peerage be maintained, has a fair prospect before him for himself or his posterity; but the greatest title, with the greatest present power and riches, is but a mean creature, and maintains those in absolute Monarchies, no otherwise than by servile and low flatteries, and upon uncertain terms.

My Lords, 'tis not only your Interest, but the Interest of the Nation, that you maintain your rights; for let the House of Commons and Gentry of *England* think what they please, there is no Prince that ever govern'd without Nobility or an Army: if you will not have one, you must have t'other, or the Monarchy cannot long support, or keep itself from tumbling into a Democratical Republic. Your Lordships and the People have the same cause, and the same enemies. My Lords, would you be in favour with the King? 'Tis a very ill way to it, to put yourselves out of a future capacity, to be considerable in his service. I do not find in story, or in modern experience, but that 'tis better, and a man is much more regarded that is still in a capacity, and opportunity to serve, than he that hath wholly deprived himself of all for his Prince's service. And I therefore declare, that I will serve my Prince as a Peer, but will not destroy the Peerage to serve him.

My Lords, I have heard of twenty foolish models and expedients to secure the Justice of the Nation, and yet to take this right from your Lordships, as the King by his commission appointing Commoners to hear Appeals; or that the Twelve Judges should be the persons, or that persons should be appointed by Act of Parliament, which are all not only to take away your Lordships just right, that ought not to be altered any more than any other part of the Government, but are in themselves, when well weighed, ridiculous: I must deal freely with your Lordships, these things could never have risen in men's minds, but that there have been some kind of provocation that has given the first rise to it. Pray, my Lords, forgive me, if on this occasion I put you in mind of Committee-dinners, and the scandal of it, those droves of Ladies that attended all causes; 'twas come to that pass, that men even hired or borrowed of their friends handsome sisters or daughters to deliver their Petitions: but yet for all this, I must say that your judgments have been sacred, unless in one or two causes; and those we owe most to that Bench, from whence we now apprehend most danger.

There is one thing I had almost forgot to speak to, *which is the conjuncture of time, the hinge upon which our reason of State turns*; and to that, my Lords, give me leave to say, if this be not a time of leisure for you to vindicate your privileges, you must never expect one. I could almost say, that the harmony, good agreement, and concord that is to be prayed for at most other times, may be fatal to us now; we owe the peace of these last two years, and the disengagement from the *French* Interest, to the two Houses differing from the sense and opinion of *Whitehall*: so at this time, the thing in the world this Nation has most reason to apprehend, is a general peace, which cannot now happen without very advantageous terms to the *French*, and disadvantageous to the House of *Austria*. We are the King's great Counsellors, and if so, have a right to differ, and give contrary counsels to those few that are nearest about him: I fear they would advance a general peace, I am sure I would advise against it, and hinder it at this time by all the ways imaginable. I heartily wish nothing from you may add weight and reputation to those counsels who would assist the *French*. No money for ships, nor preparations you can make, nor personal assurances our Prince can have, can secure us from the *French*, if they are at leisure. He is grown the most potent of us all at sea. he has built 24 ships this last year, and has 30 more in number than we; besides the advantage, that our ships are all out of order, and his so exquisitely provided for, that every ship has his particular store-house. 'Tis incredible the money he hath, and is bestowing in making harbours; he makes Nature itself give way to the vastness of his expence: and after all this, shall a Prince so wise, so intent upon his affairs, be thought to make all these preparations to sail over land, and fall on the back of *Hungary*, and batter the walls of *Kaminitz*? Or is it possible he should oversee his Interest in seizing of *Ireland*, a thing so feasible to him, if he be master of the Seas, as he certainly now is, and which, when attained, gives him all the *Streights Mediterranean*, *East* and *West-India* Trade, and renders him both by situation, and excellent harbours, perpetual Master of the Seas without dispute?

My Lords, to conclude this point, I fear the Court of *England* is greatly mistaken in it, and I do not wish them the reputation of the concurrence of the Kingdom: and this out of the most sincere loyalty to his Majesty, and love to my Nation.

My Lords, I have but one thing more to trouble you with, and that peradventure is a consideration of the greatest weight and concern, both to your Lordships and the whole Nation. I have often seen in this House, that the arguments, with strongest reason, and most convincing to the Lay-Lords in general, have not had the same effect upon the Bishops bench; but that they have unanimously gone against us in matters, that many of us have thought essential and undoubted rights: and I consider, that 'tis not possible that men of great learning, piety, and reason, as their Lordships are, should not have the same care of doing right, and the same conviction what is right, upon clear reason offered, that other your Lordships have. And therefore, my Lords, I must necessarily think we differ in principles; and then 'tis very easy to apprehend, what is the clearest sense to men of my principle, may not at all persuade or affect the conscience of the best man of a different one. I put your Lordships the case plainly, as 'tis now before us. My principle is, *That the King is King by Law, and by the same Law that the poor man enjoys his cottage*; and so it becomes the concern of every man in *England*, that has but his liberty, to maintain and defend, to his utmost, the King in all his rights and prerogatives. My principle is also, *That the Lords House, and the Judicature and Rights belonging to it, are an essential part of the Government, and established by the same Law*: the King governing and administring Justice by his House of Lords, and advising with both his Houses of Parliament in all important matters, is the Government I own, I am born under, and am obliged to. If ever there should happen in future ages (which God forbid) a King governing by an Army, without his Parliament, 'tis a Government I own not, am not obliged to, nor was born under. According to this principle, every honest man that holds it, must endeavour equally to preserve the frame of the Government, in all the parts of it, and cannot satisfy his conscience to give up the Lords House for the service of the Crown, or to take away the just rights and privileges of the House of Commons to please the Lords. But there is another principle got into the world, my Lords, that hath not been long there; for Archbishop *Laud* was the first author that I remember of it; and I cannot find that the Jesuits, or indeed the *Popish* Clergy, have ever own'd it, but some of the Episcopal Clergy of our *British* Isle; and 'tis withal, as 'tis new, so the most dangerous, destructive Doctrine to our Government and Law, that ever was. 'Tis the first of the Canons published by the Convocation 1640. *That Monarchy is of Divine Right.* This Doctrine was then preached up, and maintained by *Sibthorp*, *Manwaring*, and others, and of later years, by a book published by Dr. *Sanderson*, Bishop of *Lincoln*, under the name of Archbishop *Usher*, and how much it is spread amongst our dignified Clergy, is very easily known. We all agree, *That the King and his Government is to be obeyed for Conscience sake*, and that the divine precepts require not only here, but in all parts of the world, obedience to lawful Governours. But that this family are our Kings, and this particular frame of Government is our lawful constitution, and obliges us, is owing only to the particular Laws of our Country. This *Laudean* Doctrine was the root that produced the Bill of Test last Session, and some very perplexed Oaths, that are of the same nature with that, and yet imposed by several Acts of this Parliament.

In a word, if this Doctrine be true, our *Magna Charta* is of no use, our Laws are but rules amongst ourselves during the King's pleasure. Monarchy, if of divine right, cannot be bounded or limited by human Laws; nay, what's more, cannot bind itself: and all our claims of right by the Law, or constitution of the Government, all the jurisdiction and privilege of this House, all the rights and privileges of the House of Commons, all the properties and liberties of the people, are to give way not only to the Interest, but the will and pleasure of the Crown. And the best and worthiest of men, holding this principle, must vote to deliver up all we have, not only when reason of State, and the separate Interest of the Crown require it; but when the will and pleasure of the King is known would have it so. For that must be, to a man of that principle, the only rule and measure of Right and Justice. Therefore, my Lords, you see how necessary it is, that our principles be known; and how fatal to us all it is, that this principle should be suffered to spread any further.

My Lords, to conclude, your Lordships have seen of what consequence this matter is to you, and that the appointing a day to consider, is no less than declaring yourselves doubtful, upon second and deliberate thoughts, that you put yourselves out of your own hands, into a more than a moral probability of having this Session made a precedent against you. You see your duty to yourselves and the people; and that 'tis really not the Interest of the House of Commons, but may be the inclination of the Court, that you lose the power of Appeals: but I beg our House may not be *Felo de se*, but that your Lordships would take in this affair the only course to preserve yourselves, and appoint a day, this day three weeks, for the hearing of Dr. *Shirley*'s cause, which is my humble motion.

Saturday, *Nov.* 13, 1675. An order from the Lords to hear Sir *John Fagg*'s cause to-morrow morning, was this day read in the House of Commons, and debated, and the farther debate thereof adjourned till *Monday* morning next.

Monday, *Nov.* 15. The House resolved, That the prosecuting Appeals in the Lords House, by Dr. *Thomas Shirley* against Sir *John Fagg*, a Member of this House, is a breach of the privileges of this House; and that the said Sir *John Fagg* do not make any defence at the Lords Bar, in the said Appeal; and the further debate thereof was adjourned till to-morrow morning.

Tuesday, *Nov.* 16. Adjourned the further debate of Sir *John Fagg*'s business till to-morrow morning; and on *Wednesday*, adjourned the further debate till *Thursday*, when Sir *John Fagg*'s business was resumed, and resolved, That a conference be desired of the Lords, for avoiding differences between the two Houses, and then adjourned till *Friday* morning.

Veneris, 19 die Novembris.

Sir *William Coventry* reports from the Committee, to whom it was referred to prepare and draw up reasons to be offered at the conference, to be desired with the Lords, for avoiding the occasions of reviving the differences between the two Houses; and a paper of reasons agreed by the said Committee, to be reported to the House, being read; and the same being agreed to, is as followeth, *viz.*

His Majesty having recommended to us, at the opening of this Sessions of Parliament, the avoiding this difference, if possible: and if it could not be prevented, that then we should defer these debates till we had brought such publick bills to perfection, as may conduce to the good and safety of the Kingdom. The Commons esteem it a great misfortune, that contrary to that most excellent advice, the proceedings in the Appeal, brought the last Session against Sir *John Fagg*, by Dr. *Shirley*, hath been renewed, and a day set for hearing the cause; and therefore the Commons have judged it the best way, before they enter into the argument of defence of their rights in this matter, to propose to your Lordships the putting off the proceedings in that matter for some short time; that so they may, according to his Majesty's advice, give a dispatch to some bills now before them, of great importance to the King and Kingdom, which being finished, the Commons will be ready to give your Lordships such reasons against those proceedings, and in defence of their rights, as we hope may satisfy your Lordships that no such proceedings ought to have been.

Resolved, That a message be sent to the Lords, to desire a conference, to preserve the good correspondence between the two Houses.

Resolved, That whosoever shall prosecute any Appeal before the Lords, against any Commoner of *England*, from any Court of Equity, shall be deemed a betrayer of the rights and privileges of the Commons of *England*; and shall be proceeded against accordingly: and the resolution ordered to be affixed in the *Lobby*, *Westminster-hall-gate*, and all Inns of Court and *Chancery*; and then adjourned till next morning, *Nov* the 20th.

Die Sab. Nov. 20.

Ordered, That Dr. *Thomas Shirley* be taken into custody by the Serjeant at Arms attending this House, as also Sir *Nicholas Stanton*, for serving Mr. *Onslow* with an order to attend the Lords; and then adjourned to *Monday Nov.* 22.

On *Saturday Nov.* 20. 1675, Dr. *Thomas Shirley* appeared at the bar of the House of Lords, and his Counsel Mr. *Wallop* appearing, who would have excused himself, but was ordered to appear again on *Monday* morning next to plead the cause; and the other two Counsel (one being in the country, and the other sick) were excused; and the said Dr. *Shirley*, Sir *Nicholas Stanton*, and Mr. *Wallop* were ordered to have the protection of the House: And upon Debate of the Commons Vote made yesterday,

Ordered, That the paper posted up in several places, signed by *William Goldsbro*, Cler. Dom. Com. against the Judicature of the House of Peers, in cases of Appeals from Courts of Equity, is illegal, unparliamentary, and tending to the dissolution of the Government. And then upon consideration of the said vote of the Commons, it was proposed by Lord *Mohun* to make an Address to his Majesty to dissolve the Parliament, and call another and frequent Parliaments; and upon debate thereof, about eight o'clock at night they came to this question, and carried it by two votes only, That there should be no Address, the numbers being fifty and forty-eight: and then adjourned to *Monday*.

On which day the House being met, a message was sent by his Majesty, for the House to attend him forthwith in the House of Peers, which the House accordingly did, when his Majesty passed three Bills, and the Lord-Keeper, by his Majesty's order, prorogued both Houses of Parliament, till the 15th day of *February* come twelvemonth, 1676, which enc pute.

The Protestation, with reasons of several Lords for th tion of this Parliament, entered in the Lords Jour *vember* 22, 1675, the day the Parliament was proroge

WE whose names are under-written, Peers of this Realm, h posed, *That an humble Address might be made to his Majest House, that he would be graciously pleased to dissolve this Parliamen* House having carried it in the negative: for the justification of intentions towards his Majesty's service, and of our true respe rence to this honourable House; and to shew that we had no i indirect ends in this our humble proposal, do with all humility forth the grounds and reasons why we were of opinion, that the Address should have been made.

1. We do humbly conceive, that it is according to the an and Statutes of this Realm, that there should be frequent an ments, and that the practice of several years hath been accordi

2. It seems not reasonable that any particular number of for many years ingross so great a trust of the people, as to be sentatives in the House of Commons: and all other the Gent Members of Corporations of the same degree and quality should be so long excluded. Neither, as we humbly conceive, tageous to the Government, that the Counties, Cities and should be confined for so long a time to such Members as they chosen to serve for them; the mutual Correspondence and those who chuse and are chosen, admitting of great variations of time.

3. The long continuance of any such as are entrusted for who have so great a power over the purse of the Nation, m humble opinion, naturally endanger the producing of factions and the carrying on of particular Interests and Designs, rathe publick Good.

And we are the more confirmed in our desires for the said h dress, by reason of this unhappy breach fallen out betwixt the t of which the House of Peers hath not given the least occ having done nothing but what their ancestors and predecessors times done, and what is according to their duty, and for the Inte People that they should do. which notwithstanding, the Hou mons have proceeded in such an unprecedented and extraordinar it is, in our humble opinion, become altogether unpracticable Houses, as the case stands, jointly to pursue those great and gc which they were called.

For these reasons, we do enter our protestation against, and diss said Vote.

Buckingham,	Chesterfield,	Hallifax,	Mc
Winchester,	Stamford,	Yarmouth,	De
Salisbury,	Berks,	Newport,	Tc
Bridgwater,	Clarendon,	Sandys,	Gr
Dorset,	Shaftesbury,	Wharton,	
Westmorland,	Faulconbridge,	Petre,	

These were all the Lords that were in the House early enough to testation before the Parliament was prorogued.

XXXII. Proceedings against Mr. *Francis Jenkes*, for a Speech made by him on the *Husti Guildhall*, on *Midsummer-day*, 1676, 27 Car. II.

[Published by his Friends.]

MR. *Jenkes* having been a Trader for many years, and observing the daily decay of trade in the City, occasioned by such mischiefs, as lay not in the industry of its inhabitants, but only in the power of the Government to redress; and that did require a more speedy redress than a Parliament prorogued for fifteen months could afford: after having in vain solicited the Lord-Mayor for a Common-Council, that might consider of a Petition about trade, out of a hearty zeal for the good of the City, as well as encouraged by the consent and desire of many sober Citizens, the liberty reserved to the Lord-Mayor, Aldermen and Common-Council, by the Statute of the 13th of this King, concerning Petitions, the votes of a majority of temporal Lords at the last Sessions, together with the unanswerable reasons given in their protestation, did at the Folk-mote (or Common-hall) holden the 24th of *June* last past, in the *Guildhall* of *London*, thus deliver himself:

Mr. *Common Serjeant*,

" IT seems a vain thing for this Court to be serious about the choice of " Magistrates and Officers for the well government of this city; except " they first take care to remedy those many mischiefs and grievances, which " this city now groans under, and which seem so to threaten the ruin and " destruction of the whole, that if there be not some speedy redress, there " will be little need of Magistrates and Officers, for there will be no city " or people left here to be governed.

" *London* hath once already been burn'd to ashes, and firing is now become " such a trade, that not only *London*, the Burrough of *Southwark*, and " the places adjoining, but all the Cities, Burroughs, Towns corporate, " and places of principal trade throughout the whole Kingdom, are per- " petually in danger; so that no rational or considerate man amongst us " can promise himself, his wife, his children, or estate one " curity, but they may all be devour'd in the consuming " cept some speedy and effectual course be taken.

" But this is not all; for were our houses secure from fire, " the general decay of trade, if not remedied, as must unavoi " the whole city to poverty and ruin: and it is conceived, " very much occasion'd by the *French*, who have laid such gr " tions upon our Woollen Cloth, Stuffs and other Manufactu " have almost lost our trade with *France*. They have spoiled ou " *Holland*, *Flanders*, and *Germany*, by a destructive war. " ruined our trade at home, and beggar'd many thousands of " and industrious Weavers, and other *English* Manufacturers a " by the vast quantity of their Silks, and other unnecessary c " imported hither. So that upon an exact balance of the tra " us and them taken, it has been demonstrated, that this city " dom doth lose eleven hundred thousand pounds every year " whereof, they who in Queen *Elizabeth*'s time might not b " build men of war, are now grown so powerful at Sea, as to " beat both *Dutch* and *Spaniard*, and have made themselves i " sole masters of the *Mediterranean* Sea. And they are grown " tuous, as daily to affront our *English* Merchants, and some " Majesty's own ports. The Privateers daily take our Mer " plunder others, strip, imprison and torment our seamen, " discouragement of our *English* Navigation, and almost rui " chant

" I shall instance in but one thing more, but that is worse " rest, that is, the just apprehension that is upon the m " men, of danger to his Majesty's person, and the Prot " I had not spoken this at this time and place, but having "serve the City in Common-Council, I have endeavoured at several times "to bring these things before the Court, but could not. In the end "of the last Common-Council I did desire my Lord-Mayor, that a "Common-Council might speedily be held, to hear and consider of a "petition about trade, subscribed by a great number of citizens of good "quality; and his Lordship did then promise, that a Common-Council should speedily be held: But it is a good time since, and there "have been many fires and losses, but no Common-Council.

"Wherefore methinks it does become the wisdom and gravity of this "Court, not to admit of any longer delay in a matter wherein their All "is concerned. And I do humbly move, (and I conceive it is not only "my sense, but the sense of the far greater part of this Court) that some "Members of this Court may accompany the Sheriffs and Mr. Common-"Serjeant, before we proceed to any other matter, to wait upon my "Lord Mayor and the Court of Aldermen, to desire that a Common-"Council might speedily be held, humbly to petition his Majesty, that "for the quieting and satisfying the minds of his liege people, and for "remedy of the many mischiefs and grievances we now groan under, he "would graciously be pleased (according to the Statutes of the 4th and "36th of Ed. III.) timely to call a new Parliament."

Scarcely were the words, *a new Parliament*, pronounced, but the greatest part of the Assembly cried out, *Well moved, well moved!* And tho' none spake up formally to the Sheriffs, yet several amongst them spake enough to shew a high approbation of what had been said, and not one word was spoken in contradiction: which when the Common-Serjeant saw, to prevent (as is conceived) others speaking to the same matter, he spake to this purpose:

"That what had been moved, seemed to be the general sense of the "whole Court; and since the Gentleman that made the motion was "pleased to join him with the Sheriffs, and that he must offer his opi-"nion in the matter, it was this, That it was not so proper to carry up "that message before they did proceed to their elections, as first to deter-"mine their elections, and then carry up an account of these and that "together."

But many in the Court did insist upon the motion, and desired a message might be sent up immediately; whereupon one of the Sheriffs spake, and did acknowledge, "That what had been said by the Gentleman that "spake first, was true; but that he was an old citizen, and had long "known Common Halls, and he did believe that the proper work of the "day was the election of officers; and therefore he did desire that the "Court would proceed, and not to carry up the message till after that "was done." To which one replied, "That according to his utmost "understanding, that Court was one of the antientest, greatest, and "most powerful Courts of this City; and although the customary busi-"ness of this day were the choice of officers, yet that Court had cogni-"zance of any thing whatever that did relate to the good of the City; "and therefore it was conceived, that nothing was more proper at that "time, than this which concerned the preservation of the City from "utter ruin."

Upon which the other Sheriff directing his discourse to the Assembly, said, "That what the Gentlemen had moved there, was true, and not "unknown to most of the persons there present; but that he was of his "brother's opinion, that it was fit first to go on to the work of the day, "and not to carry up that message till after the election."

Many persons being still dissatisfied, and calling for a present message to be sent up, the Gentleman who first moved the business, made it his request, "That since there seemed a difference touching the circum-"stance of time, that they would proceed to election, and carry up the "message with the persons elected, as the Sheriffs desired;" to which the Common Hall unanimously agreed. Upon which, silence being made, the Common Hall proceeded to election of Sheriffs; and made their election, and sent up an account thereof to the Lord Mayor and Aldermen by the Sheriffs and Common-Serjeant, as is usual in such cases.

The Lord Mayor and Aldermen presently came down, and took their Seats in the Court of *Hustings*, according to custom, upon which, the Common-Serjeant came forth to the front of the Court, and declared the names of the persons elected, and immediately gave back. Whereupon the Common Hall called out for an answer to their message; upon which, the Common-Serjeant stepping forward again in the presence of the Lord Mayor, Aldermen and Sheriffs, said, "That he had acquainted his "Lordship and the Aldermen with their request, and that his Lordship "had commanded him to declare unto them, That he would be ready "to join with them in that or any other thing for the good of the City." And with that the Lord Mayor and Aldermen, &c. left the Court of *Hustings*, and dismissed the Assembly.

After dinner, the Recorder, Sir *John Howel*, out of a great pretence of loyalty, but indeed a personal grudge against Mr. *Jenkes*, conveyed the news to *Whitehall*; where, with his usual strain of *Rhetorick*, he made such a dismal representation of the matter, and was so powerful in his eloquence, as to occasion both the Sheriffs and some other of the City-officers to be sent for; who were examined by the Lord Chief Justice *Rainsford*, in the presence of the King, the Lord Chancellor, Lord Treasurer, Duke *Lauderdale*, and other Lords.

The Sheriffs and two others made affidavits; but a copy of them could never be obtained.

Upon the 27th of *June*, Mr. *Jenkes* was summoned by a messenger to appear at the Council-board the next day; accompanied with many of his friends, he attended in the Lobby, near the Council-Chamber, according to his summons, and after some time was called in; but his friends pressing to follow him, (as is usual on such occasions) were kept out, and not one suffered to go in with him.

The King sitting in Council, the Lord Chancellor, Duke *Lauderdale*, and other Lords about him, the Clerk read an affidavit made by the two Sheriffs, the Common Crier, and one *John Green*, an Attorney; the substance whereof was,

That Fr. Jenkes, *at a Common Hall, in* London, *the 24th of* June *last past, did complain of grievances; and did desire, that before they went upon any other business, certain Members of that Court might accompany the Sheriffs and the Common Serjeant to wait upon the Lord Mayor, then in the chamber, to desire that a Common-Council might be called to petition his Majesty, in the name of the City, to call a* new Parliament,

The affidavit being read, the Council-board proceeded to this effect:

Lord Chancellor. Sir, What say you to this matter?

Mr. *Jenkes.* I desire to know if this be all you have to charge against me?

A Lord. Then you make little of this, you will find it to be enough.

L. Chan. Sir, did you move for a Common-Council to petition for a new Parliament?

Mr. *Jenkes.* Is it any crime to petition for a new Parliament?

To which his Lordship not thinking fit to give answer, proceeded,

L. Chan. Answer to the matter in charge.

Mr. *Jenkes.* With the liberty of his Majesty and this Board, I will.

The King. Go on.

Mr. *Jenkes.* May it please your Majesty, of all the subjects you have—

A Lord. (interrupting him) Answer to the matter.

Mr. *Jenkes.* If his Majesty will be pleased to hear me, I hope you will.

King. Let him go on.

Mr. *Jenkes.* May it please your Majesty, of all the subjects you have, none are more loyal than your City of *London*, and in the City none more loyal than myself: And no man there did more desire, and, in my circumstances, act more, in order to your Majesty's Restoration, than myself. And I do defy any citizen, or other whomsoever, to say I have forfeited my loyalty by any one individual act——

King. (interrupting him) Sir, you are not Lord-Mayor, and I am very well satisfied with the loyalty of the City, and that it needs no such vouchers.

L. Chan. Speak to the matter.

Mr. *Jenkes.* May it please your Majesty, being summoned to a Court of Common Hall in *London*, which is a Court that consists of the main body of the City—

L. Chan. (interrupting him) Sir, you are under a double mistake; for first, it was not a Court; and next, it did not consist of the main body of the City of *London*.

Mr. *Jenkes.* With your Lordship's leave, it was a Court which did consist of all the Livery of the City of *London*; which, if I understand any thing, is the main body of the City of *London*. And every Member of that Court hath freedom to propose and debate any such matter or thing as he believes is for the service of his Majesty, and the good of the City; and no man can use more understanding than God hath given him. And I assure your Lordship, what I then moved was according to the utmost of my understanding for his Majesty's service, and the good of the City. And, my Lord, if I were under a mistake, I had the fortune to have good company; for what I moved was approved by the whole Court.

King. It was not so.

Secretary. We have a deposition to the contrary.

Mr. *Jenkes.* It was so.

Other Lords. It was not so.

Mr. *Jenkes.* May it please your Majesty, if you have a hundred depositions to the contrary, if the matter of fact were so, it was so, and I do affirm it was approved by the whole Court.

A Lord. How came you to be a Privy-Councillor?

Mr. *Jenkes.* I never had any such ambitious thought in my head.

A Lord. How came you then to meddle with matters of State?

Mr. *Jenkes.* I thought any of his Majesty's subjects, in an humble manner, might petition his Majesty for a remedy of any grievance whatsoever.

A Lord. Do you think any one may petition for a Parliament?

Mr. *Jenkes.* I believe they may.

The King. I know whose scholar you are, and I'll take care that none such as you shall have to do with the Government.

Several Lords. What was't you moved? What was't you moved?

Mr. *Jenkes.* My Lords, what I spake was not in a corner, but openly in the face of a multitude, and therefore cannot want a witness to attest it.

A Lord. Just now it was a Court, and now it is a multitude.

Mr. *Jenkes.* We Citizens pretend not to place our words so exactly in form, but that there may be some mistake in them; but I think my expression was no great absurdity: For though it were a Court, yet the persons there were so numerous, that it may not be very improper to term them a multitude. Yet, if I have failed in due expression, I beg his Majesty's pardon. I know somewhat of the customs of the City of *London*, and the powers and privileges of the Courts there; and somewhat also of the laws of *England*; but what the powers and customs of this Court are, I know not, and therefore shall desire to say little, lest I should unwillingly offend.

L. Chan. Sir, pray tell us, who advised you in this matter?

The King. Who advised you?

Mr. *Jenkes.* What I then proposed was consented to by the whole Court, and so became their Act, as I said before.

L. Chan. and others. Answer directly to the question, or declare you will not.

Mr. *Jenkes.* Since I see your Majesty and the Lords are angry, though I am not sensible that I have given you any just cause for it; I must not say I did it without advice, lest you should be more angry; and to name any particular person (if there were such) would be a mean and unworthy thing, therefore I desire to be excused all farther answer to such questions; since the law doth provide, that no man be put to answer to his own prejudice.

King. We will take that for an answer.

L. Chan. Since you name the law, by the law you shall be tried.

Mr. *Jenkes.* I thank you and this Board.

L. Chan. You may withdraw.

He immediately withdrew, and the room being cleared of all his friends, and other company; Mr. *Jenkes* was kept there for the space of an hour and an half; and, after that, without being called in any more, was, by a warrant of the Council, sent to the prison of the Gatehouse within the liberties of *Westminster*. Soon after his commitment, he demanded of the Keeper a copy of the warrant by which he was committed; as he might, and by law ought to have. The Keeper gave him a promise of it, but delaying the performance for two days, Mr. *Jenkes* resolutely demanded it of him as his duty, but could not yet obtain it. Some time after, the Keeper sent him one voluntarily, by his man, with this excuse, That before he had positive order to deny him one, and now had to give it him.

The

The Copy of the Warrant.

WHereas it appears to his Majesty in Council, by the examination of Sir *Thomas Gold*, Sir *John Shorter*, Knights, Sheriffs of the City of *London*, *John Wells*, Common-Crier of the said City, and *John Green*, one of the Attorneys of the Lord-Mayor's Court, taken upon oath before the Lord-Chief-Justice *Rainsford*, That *Francis Jenkes*, of the said City, Linen-Draper, did, on the 24th of this instant *June*, at a Common-Hall, then assembled at the *Guildhall* of the said City, for chusing Officers for the ensuing year, in a most seditious and mutinous manner, openly move and stir the persons then present, that before they did go on to the choice of new Officers (which was the only occasion of that assembly) they should go to the Lord-Mayor, and desire him to call a Common-Council, that might make an address to his Majesty in the name of the City, to call a new Parliament. And whereas the said *Francis Jenkes*, being now called in, and heard before his Majesty in Council, was so far from denying or extenuating his offence, that he did in a presumptuous and arrogant manner endeavour to justify the same:

These are therefore to command you, to take into your custody the body of the said *Francis Jenkes*, herewith sent you, and him to keep safely, until he shall be delivered by due course of law; for which this shall be your warrant.

Dated at the Council-Chamber in *Whitehall*, this 28th day of *June*, 1676.

To the Keeper of the Gatehouse, *Westminster*, or his Deputy.

Lindsey. *W. Maynard.* *R. Carr.*
Peterborough. *Tho. Chichely.* *Finch.*
C Craven. *Danby.* *Ormond.*
G. Carter. *Anglesey.* *Bridgwater.*
Lauderdale. *Arlington.* *Hen. Coventry.*
Northampton. *Bathe.* *J. Ernle.*
Carbery. *J. Williamson.* *Robert Southwell.*

Next day being the 29th of *June*, divers of Mr. *Jenkes*'s friends waited upon Mr. Secretary *Williamson*, and desired to become bail for him; but Mr. Secretary refused to take any bail. but told them, if they did mind him of it on *Wednesday* morning, he would move it at the Council. But Mr. *Jenkes* believing that to be (as it proved) but a delay, ordered some of his friends to wait upon the Lord Chief-Justice *Rainsford*, and moved him for an *Habeas Corpus ad Subjiciend. & Recipiend. &c.* which accordingly was done, but his Lordship denied to grant it, alledging no other reason, but that it was Vacation. though his Lordship could not but know that writ to be the Subject's right at all times, as well out of Term as in Term; and Mr. *Jenkes*'s friends were ready to offer him multitudes of precedents when it had been granted out of Term, both anciently, and since his Majesty's Restoration.

Mr. *Jenkes* resolving to leave no legal course to attain his liberty untried; upon *Friday*, the 30th of *June*, at a general Seal, did by his Counsel move the Lord-Chancellor for an *Habeas Corpus*. At first his Lordship did seem much surprized, and did refuse to hear his Counsel; but after a little pause, his Lordship bid Mr. *Jenkes*'s Counsel to move it again the next Seal, and ordered the Seal to be put off from *Tuesday* the 4th, until *Thursday* the 6th of *July*.

Upon *Wednesday* the 5th of *July*, Mr. *Jenkes*'s friends waited upon Mr. Secretary *Williamson*, and desired him, according to his promise, to move in Council, that Mr. *Jenkes* might be bailed; but he said he had spoke with the King, and could do nothing without a Petition. So upon *Thursday* the 6th of *July*, being a publick Seal, Mr. *Jenkes*'s Counsel did again move the Lord-Chancellor (according to his Lordship's order), and asserted the authority of the Lord *Coke*, who is most clear in the case, 2 *part, Inst. fol.* 53. speaking of the Writ of *Habeas Corpus* in the *King's-Bench*, he saith, The like Writ is to be granted out of the Chancery, either in Term (as in the *King's-Bench*) or in the Vacation; for the Court of Chancery is *Officina Justitiæ*, and is ever opened, and never adjourned: So as the Subject being wrongfully imprisoned, may have Justice for the liberty of his person, as well in the Vacation time as in Term.

And in the 4th *Inst. fol.* 88. speaking of the Court of Chancery, he saith, And this Court is the rather always open, for that if a man be wrongfully imprisoned in the Vacation, the Lord-Chancellor may grant an *Habeas Corpus*, and do him Justice according to law; *vid.* 4 *Inst. fol.* 182, 190. Thus the Lord *Coke*.

Mr. *Jenkes*'s Counsel did likewise offer a precedent or two; but the Lord Chancellor making light of the Lord *Coke*'s opinion, saying, *The Lord* Coke *was not infallible*; and slighting all that Mr. *Jenkes*'s Counsel offered, over-rul'd the matter, denying to grant the Writ.

On *Tuesday* morning, *July* 11, at the Quarter-Sessions, holden for the liberty of *Westminster*, Mr. *Jenkes* being still a prisoner in the Gatehouse, did move by his Counsel to be bailed; where this was the substance of what passed, as it was taken by a person present.

Court. We have no such name in our Calendar; and we sitting here by a limited commission, can take no notice of any person that is not in our Calendar.

Counsel. Every Keeper of a Prison, either in County or Franchise, ought by the Statute of 3 *Hen.* VII. *cap.* 3. to certify the names of every prisoner in their custody, at the next general Gaol-delivery there, to be calendar'd before the Justice of Gaol-delivery, that the parties may be delivered according to law, upon pain of 100*l.* for every default there recorded. And I demand that this default of the Gaoler may be recorded according to that Statute; and that you would, as you may, command him to calendar him now.

The Statute was read.

Court. We are no general Gaol-delivery, for we cannot try several felons, but they must be tried at the general Gaol-delivery for the County.

Coun. You are a general Gaol-delivery for all offences within the cognizance of your Franchise; and therefore, unless the fact for which he is committed be such as is above your cognizance, he ought to be tried here; and if it be such a fact, he ought notwithstanding to be calenda that you may send him to the County-Gaol, where he may be t

Gaoler. I never did calendar any man that was committed by t cil-table.

Coun. The neglect hath not taken away your duty; and as oft have omitted so to do, so oft have you deserved to be fined. again demand of this Court, that this default of yours may be r

The Court inclined to the Gaoler, and would not record whereupon the Counsel proceeded.

Coun. Since you exclude him from the benefit of your pref mission, I apply myself to you, without respect to that, as you tices of Peace in general; and as such, you have power to bail bailable by law, except in some particular cases, where you are ed by Statute.

Court. By whom is he committed?

Coun. By the Council-board.

Court. Do you believe the Council-board can commit to priso

Coun. I admit it.

Court. We don't know for what offence he is committed.

Coun. I have here a Copy of the Commitment, and desire it may

But the Gaoler refusing to own it for a true copy, tho' given by and the Court requiring a nicer proof that it was a true Copy, th at that time be made, they ordered the Counsel to attend in the aft and in the mean time the Gaoler to give a true Copy. In the a the Counsel appearing, the Court called to him, and asked him had to say.

Coun. I have now a Copy given and signed by the Gaoler f Copy, and desire it may be read.

The Gaoler, who was to prove it a true Copy, upon the Coun ing into the Court, took an occasion to slink away; and the Co it had been by design) were ready to take hold of that opport evade the business; but Mr. *Jenkes*'s friends fetched him back. swearing it to be a true Copy, it was read.

Court. What is it you demand?

Coun. What I did before; That there being nothing in this V for which he is not bailable by law, I demand that he may be ba

Court. You have taken a wrong course in coming to us.

Coun. I presume he applies himself properly to you; for he prisoner within your Liberty, you are the most proper persons to As Justices of the Peace, you have power to bail any man witl jurisdiction, bailable by law, and where you may bail by the law, y to do. and I demand it for Mr. *Jenkes*.

Court. Where do you find such power given to Justices of the

Coun. By the same Statute of *Hen.* VII. that I cited against the the enacting part whereof saith, *That the Justices of the Peace Shire, City or Town, or two of them at the least, whereof one to be of* rum, *have authority or power to let any such prisoner or persons, mai by the law, that have been imprisoned within their several Counties Town, to bail or mainprize, unto their next general Sessions; or unto Gaol-delivery of the same Gaols of every Shire, City or Town, as we Franchises as without, where any Gaols be, or hereafter shall be, &c.*

The whole Statute was read, and the Court taking hold of the p said, This Statute was made for the prevention of bailing felons able by law, and enables us only to bail felons bailable by law.

Coun. The preamble of the Act recites the mischief occasione Statute of 1 *R.* III. but the enacting part repeals that Act, and g a general power of letting any person, mainpernable by the law, and I am sure no Statutes made for the liberty of the Subject, receive such a strait construction.

Court. Do you consider by whom he is committed? The Privy-C

Coun. I do, and think that alters not the case.

Court. He is committed by a superior Court, and we, who ar ferior one, cannot bail him.

Coun. It is not the Court that commits, but the fact for which t is committed, ought to direct you in bail. The Statute of *H.* hath no such exception in it; nor hath any other since put any straint upon you.

Court. Would you have us bail him, after the Lord-Chance the Lord Chief-Justice have refused to grant a *Habeas Corpus*?

Coun. They did not deny the *Habeas Corpus* because he was not by law, but because the course of their Courts, in their opinions, not admit it: But, however, if you ought to bail him, (as by tute, I think, you ought) their refusal does not lessen your duty.

Court. We doubt very much that any inferior Court can bail committed by a superior one.

Coun. Scruples and fears do not alter the law: This doubt w made in the *King's-Bench*, in the great case of *Selden*, and others; law was for the prisoner before that time, and was sufficiently then; and this case differs nothing from that in reason.

Court. It does, for that was upon a *Habeas Corpus* out of the *Bench.*

Coun. That is but a circumstantial difference. The *Habeas Corp* that Court is only to remove the Prisoner, and the cause before that justice may be done to him: Mr. *Jenkes* is already within y risdiction, and the Statute gives you authority to bail him; and thority makes it your duty, and I rely upon that.

Court. We considered upon it at dinner, and do believe it a ra and fit to be advised upon; and we will advise.

Why did you not move yesterday when my Lord Chief-Justice Town? Now there are no Judges in Town to advise with.

Coun. That we did not come yesterday was no design, for he fond of a Gaol; and if it be an indiscretion, yet that is no suffici son to detain a man in prison. However, if you have power (wh ought to know) you have it as well when they are not in Town, as when they are. Is he bailable by law, or not?

Court. There is nothing in the warrant, for which he is not bailable by law.

Coun. For what reason then do you deny him?

Court. We do not deny him, but we will advise, because he is committed by a superior Court.

Coun. No man ought to be imprisoned for any misdemeanour before conviction, without bail; and it is against the Petition of Right, that any man bailable by Law, should be detained in Gaol without it. I don't know how, by such denials as this, the being committed by a superior Court may grow to be reason; but at present I think the Petition of Right spoils it for being a good one.

Court. You can give us no precedent of any one being bailed by Justices at the Sessions, who was committed by the Council-board.

Coun. I believe it is a rare case that a man should be forced to apply himself to such, but I think I can furnish you with an instance; and that is of one *Cannon*, a Quaker, who was committed by the Privy-Council about *Christmas* last, and was bailed at the Sessions of the *Old-Bailey*.

A pert By-stander, no ways concerned, suggested to the Court, and the Court repeated after him,

Court. He was committed to *Newgate*-prison, and was calendar'd there.

Coun. If you stick to the reason of being committed by a superior Court, that is no answer; but if it must be an answer, Mr. *Jenkes* is committed to the prison of this liberty, and ought to have been calendar'd here; and then I do again demand that the Gaoler be fined.

Court. We think it a rare case, and fit to be advised upon; and our Commission we here sit by, directs us to do so in difficult cases.

Coun. I told you before, I had nothing to do with the Commission you here sit by; and you yourselves excluded me from it: but I apply myself to you as Justices of the Peace merely, and as such you ought to take upon you the knowledge of your office.

Court. In the great case of *Selden*, that you cited, the Judges took two Terms to advise.

Coun. You very well know what opinion was had of their doing so. Will you advise upon it to-night with the King's Counsel, and I'll attend you to-morrow morning?

Court. We think fit to advise with the Judges about it, till next Sessions.

Coun. I can easily interpret what such advising means.

Court. You say you apply yourself to us as Justices of the Peace merely, then you may come to any two of us a fortnight hence, or more, and perhaps we may advise in the mean time.

Coun. I believe it will be a difficult matter to get any two of you together upon this occasion.

Mr *Jenkes* finding all these Common Doors to liberty shut against him, did by advice betake himself to another method, not less legal than the former; tho' the power granted by the Statutes to Justices of Peace, and the constant issuing of the Writ of *Habeas Corpus* upon demand (both more easy courses) have occasioned it to be of more seldom use.

Justice *Fitzherbert*, in his *Natura Brevium* (an Author, and a Book of justly venerable authority in our law), in his Chapter of *Main-prize*, declares, That if a man be taken by the King's commission, and kept in prison for felony or misdemeanours, he may by his friends put in sureties in the Chancery, that he will appear before the Justices, &c. and be of good behaviour, &c. and that body for body; and thereupon he shall have a Writ out of the Chancery, unto the Sheriff, or unto the Constable of the castle where he is imprisoned, to set him at liberty, if he be imprisoned for that cause and no other.

Which words seem plainly to declare the Writ of *Main-prize* to be the subject's right, and not to leave a discretional power to the Officers of Chancery in granting it. But the scarcity of precedents being the great objection against the *Habeas Corpus* out of Chancery, Mr. *Jenkes* resolved to offend no more in that kind, and therefore caused a search to be made in the *Rolls* in the *Tower*, for the Writs of *Main-prize*, where a multitude of them was found, and many in the case of a commitment by the King's command. A copy of one, and a note of several others were taken out, to back the authority of *Fitzherbert*. With this provision, on *Monday*, *July* 17, four of Mr. *Jenkes*'s friends, substantial Merchants, attended by a Counsel, went to the Lord Chancellor; and tho' upon tender of themselves as bail for him, they might have demanded their Writ of *Main-prize* as the subject's right, without other formality, yet they addressed themselves to him in a more respectful manner, by way of petition, thus:

To the Right Honourable *Henry* Lord *Finch*, Baron of *Daventry*, and Lord High-Chancellor of *England*; the humble Petition of *A. B. C. D.* of *London*, Merchants, friends to *Francis Jenkes*, now a Prisoner in the Gatehouse of *Westminster*, sheweth,

THAT the said *Francis Jenkes* was committed to the said Prison, by virtue of a warrant, a true copy whereof is hereunto annexed, for a fact bailable by law; for which, and no other cause, he yet remains there a Prisoner: And that in this and all other cases of like nature, your Petitioners are advised, upon putting in bail in the Court of Chancery, according to the ancient course and usage thereof, a Writ of *Main-prize* ought to issue under the Great Seal, to be directed to the Sheriff or Keeper of the Prison where such prisoner stands committed, to deliver the prisoner so committed.

That your Petitioners being men of good estates, (as shall, if your Lordship require, be made out to your Lordship) do desire, and are ready to become bail for the said *Francis Jenkes*; according to the course of the Chancery, and according to the Law.

The Petitioners therefore pray, that your Lordship would accept of bail accordingly, and that thereupon your Lordship would order a Writ to be made forthwith, to be directed to the Keeper of the Gatehouse, for the discharge of the said *Francis Jenkes*. And your Petitioners shall always pray, &c.

The Petition being sent in to, and read by his Lordship, was returned by the Secretary with this answer; "That his Lordship did very well approve of the Petition, but since Mr. *Jenkes* was committed by the Council-board, he thought fit that they should be petitioned, and should bail him."

But Mr. *Jenkes*'s friends not being satisfied with that answer, pressed to speak to his Lordship, and were by his Lordship's order called in, who coming towards them, spake to this effect.

Lord Chan. Who is't that puts you on these improper methods?

Coun. We presume this address to your Lordship to be a proper course in our case, and is such as we have precedent for.

Lord Chan. Are you a Lawyer? — *Coun.* Yes, my Lord.

Lord Chan. Have you read *Fitzherbert's Nat. Brevium*? Look in his Writ *de Homine replegiando*.

Coun. We have nothing to do with that Writ, but it is by *Fitzherbert* that we are directed to this course, in his Chapter of *Main-prize*, where he saith (what is before cited); and we are confirmed in his opinion by a multitude of precedents out of the close Rolls in the *Tower*: I have the copy of one here, and the Number and Roll of many more.

The precedent shewn to his Lordship was this:

Ex Rol. claus. de Anno Regni Regis *Ed.* III. XI. parte prima, membr. 28.

De Deliberand. Ric. Monyword *à prisona.*

REX Senescallo & Marescallo Hospitii nostri, salutem; cum *Ric. Monyword*, in Prisona Marescallæ nostræ per præceptum nostrum, pro quibusdam transgressionibus & contemptibus nobis factis ut dicitur detentus, existat sub custodia Janitoris nostri, &c. *Williel. Stury*, Chivalier, *Tho. Pride*, de Comitat. *Salop. Olivertus* de *Bourdeaux*, de Com. *Berk. Andreas Aubray*, *Johannes Pissflan*, & *Petrus Fan*, de London, *coram nobis in Cancellaria nostra, personaliter constituti manuceperunt predictum* Richard. viz. *quilibet eorum corpus pro corpore habere coram nobis, vel Justiciariis nostris, aut consilio nostro, quandocunq; & ubicunq; voluerimus ad mandatum nostrum ad stand. rect. de transgressionibus & contemptibus & aliis excessibus quibuscunq; unde indictatus vel rectatus est, & quod bene & fideliter erga nos, & populum nostrum, de cætero se gerit, vobis mandamus, quod prefatum* Richard. *a Pris. prædicta, si ea occasione, & non alia, detineatur, in eadem deliberari faciatis, per manucaptionem supradictam.*

Teste Rege *apud* Westmonast. *decimo nono die* Martii, *Per istum Regem.*
Convenit cum *Recordo*, *Laur. Halsted*, Deput. *Algernon May*, militis.

The Note of the Number and Roll of several Writs of *Main-prize*, upon surety put into Chancery, shewn to his Lordship, was this

2 *Ed.* III. *part.* 1. To the Constable of the *Tower*, to deliver *John Bri e*.

2 *Ed* III. *part* 1. *mem.* 29. To the Constable of the *Tower*, to deliver *Bernard Pouch*.

2 *Ed.* III. *part.* 1. *mem.* 28. To the Constable of the *Tower*, to deliver *Henry Compton*. Teste 26 *Martii*.

Eodem Rot. 23. To the Constable of the *Tower*, to deliver *John de Wassenham*. Teste 18 *Aprilis*.

44 *Ed.* III. *part* 1. *mem.* 6. *custod. Forest.* For delivery of several persons committed for hunting in Forests since the *Stat.* 28. *Ed.* III. *cap.* 9.

Eodem Rot. mem. 10. The like. Teste 20 *Aug.*

Eodem Rot. mem. 17. The like.

Eodem Rot. mem. 25. The like for *Will. de Clark*.

3 *Rich.* II. *mem.* 3. To the Sheriff of *London*, to deliver *Nich. de Swederton* and *John Deye*. Teste 5 *December*.

Eodem Rot. mem. 22. To the Justices of *North Wales*, to deliver *Llyd*.

Lord Chan. One precedent of discretion is worth a thousand of these precedents.

His Lordship read the precedent, and observing it to bear Teste the 19th day of *March*, which could never be in Term, asked, When it was returnable? and said, it must be returnable in some Court at *Westminster*.

Coun. This precedent hath no return, neither doth the nature of the Writ in this case require one; for it is only a mandate to the Gaoler, to set him at liberty upon sureties first taken in Chancery for his appearance before the Justices; which Justices, and the time of his appearance, I suppose, are to be named in the Recognizance.

Lord Chan. Whether there ought to be a return, is the question; besides, this is a Writ directed immediately to the Marshal of the Houshold, and is a different case.

Coun. With submission to your Lordship, it makes no difference who is the Gaoler; and those I have given your Lordship the Number and Roll of, are to several Gaolers.

Then *Fitzherbert*'s *Nat. Brevium* was shewn to his Lordship, and upon reading the words there, *If a man be imprisoned by the King's commission*, &c. his Lordship said, That it was intended of one imprisoned by virtue of a Commission out of Chancery.

Coun. I humbly presume, that is not the sense of the Book; the precedents I have shewn your Lordship seem to interpret it, and are upon other Comments, and *Fitzherbert*, in his *Abridgement*, *Tit. Main-prize*, *pl.* 23. cites a Book-case, that shews this to have been a course in the Chancery; but we submit it to your Lordship's judgment.

Lord Chan. A little submission in a proper place will do, but he hath a mind to come out with a high hand.

Coun. He has a mind to be discharged by law, as the warrant for his commitment directs.

Lord Chan. I am not to controul any Act of the Privy-Council.

Coun. At the last motion for a *Habeas Corpus*, your Lordship was pleased to say, That though that was not a proper method for Mr. *Jenkes* to obtain his liberty by, yet there was one: and upon that encouragement from your Lordship, search has been made, and this course we have now taken, found to have been the ancient course; and we did presume, the same that your Lordship meant.

Lord Chan. You have used a great deal of industry to miss the right way. Your precedents of *Edw.* III. and *Rich.* II. (three hundred years old) I'll consider of till next Term. Upon which answer, Mr. *Jenkes*'s friends withdrew.

Now the plenty of precedents proved as great a fault as want of them did before, and their Age, which used to add to their authority, and give them a greater respect, made them contemned. Such always is the fate, where *stat pro ratione voluntas*. In the afternoon, the Secretary sent first carried

carried in the Petition, came to Mr. *Jenkes* in a dissembled confusion, and told him, That he had committed a mistake in returning the Petition; That his Lordship had asked him for it, and would be very angry with him if he had it not; That he had left his Lordship looking over some papers, and had taken that opportunity of coming for it; and desired that he might have it, to preserve him from his Lordship's displeasure.

Note, That he returned it by his Lordship's Order.

Tho' the Morning's action gave Mr. *Jenkes* a great deal of reason to suspect the Secretary's tale to be a mere contrivance, and easy to surmise the truth; yet he took no notice of what had then passed, but sent the Petition (which was then in some of his friends hands) that evening to him. Upon the second thoughts which his Lordship bestowed upon the matter of the Petition, he was better reconciled to it, and proved better than his word in considering the precedents; for instead of pausing upon them till the next Term, he was pleased to carry them and the Petition to the Privy-Council, the next *Wednesday*; where, tho' all the particulars are not known, upon credible information, this was the substance of what passed:

His Lordship acquainted the Board with the Address that had been made to him; and moved, that the Petition might be there read. After it was read, his Lordship told them, that it had some appearance of law, and desired that the Attorney-General might give his opinion. Mr. Attorney told him, if it were law, his Lordship ought to grant it, if it were not law, then to deny it; if it were of such difficulty as he could not satisfy himself, that then he should advise with the Judges.

His Lordship then moved for an order of Council for his direction in the matter; to which some of the Lords replied, That they were a Court of State, and not of Law, and that it did belong to him, as Lord Chancellor, to inform them of matters of law: Thereupon his Lordship, clapping his hands to his breast, said, I thank God I have courage enough to serve his Majesty.

About the latter end of *July*, some of Mr. *Jenkes*'s friends attended his Lordship again, and offered him bail; insisting upon the Writ of *Main-prize* as the subject's right; alledging to his Lordship the hazards that his health, his family, and his trade were exposed to by his confinement His Lordship asked them, why they had not petitioned the King and Council? and told them, if Mr. *Jenkes* thought it better to lie in prison and complain, than petition and be bailed, he might do as he pleased.

They told him they had tendered bail to Mr. Secretary *Williamson*, who promised them to move the King in Council in it: But when they reminded him of it upon the next Council-day, he was pleased to excuse himself. His Lordship toldt hem, he'never heard they had tender'd bail; but the Writ of *Main-prize* was forgotten in all his answer.

They then told him, that the general report was, that the King and Council had referred it to his Lordship; but his Lordship would take no notice of that likewise, but said, the King would advise with the Judges when they came to Town. His Lordship withdrew from them; and they left word with his Secretary, That Mr. *Jenkes* looked upon himself to be his Lordship's Prisoner.

On the — of *August*, Mr. *Jenkes*'s friends went again to my Lord Chancellor's; but his Secretary told them, his Lordship could not be spoke with.

They prevailed with his Secretary to go up to him, and remind his Lordship of his last answer of advising with the Judges; and tell him, that several of the Judges had been in Town, and they did now desire his Lordship's Resolution.

The Secretary at his return told them, that as soon as he began to mention the business, his Lordship fell into a fit of the Stone; but when that was over, he would mention it to him. About two hours after, they returned; and the Secretary being absent, another of his Lordship's servants came to them, and told them that his Lordship was not well, and could not be spoke with; but had ordered him to tell them, that Mr. *Jenkes* might advise with his Counsel what was fit to be done, for he was none of his Counsel; and if he would petition the King and Council, he might; and that That was his answer.

On the 11th of *August*, being the last Council-day that was to be before the 3d of *October*, Mr. *Jenkes* thought fit again to tender bail to the Council; and that the Lord Chancellor, who disowned all knowledge of his doing so before, and that the whole Council might know of it, he sent this Letter by his bail to the Lord Privy-Seal, then President of the Council, which was publicky read.

" *My Lord,*

" I Have been imprisoned since the 28th of *June*, to my great loss, " charge, and prejudice of my health. I have hitherto been deni- " ed bail, *Habeas Corpus*, and the Writ of *Main-prize*; which I am in- " formed, were never before denied to any of his Majesty's subjects in " the like case: And this only for moving in a lawful Court, and in a " quiet and peaceable manner, that which I did believe to be for his Ma- " jesty's service, and the good of the City and Kingdom, and the preser- " vation of the Protestant Religion; and which I conceive I can " appear to be according to the Laws and Statutes of this Realm " am publickly called thereto. Wherefore I do not beg a discharg " I desire nothing more than to clear my Innocence by a public trial " since Mr. *Murrel* and others, committed to this prison for matt " a far other nature, are daily bailed out; my humble request t " Lordship is, that you would be pleased to move his Majesty, t " as well as any other of his Majesty's subjects, may enjoy the b " of the Laws; and that the Writ of *Main-prize* may be granted t " or that my bail, which now attend, may be taken: Your Lordshi " very much oblige

" *Your Lordship's humble Servant,*

" FRANCIS JENKE

This Letter was by some improved into a Petition; and when the given it that name, (tho' that was the only thing wanting to please the Chancellor) yet it could not procure the acceptance of bail; but the m proposed by his Lordship, proved as ineffectual as those that were der ed of him. The Lord Chancellor's Resolutions being sufficiently vered, Mr. *Jenkes*'s friends forbore all farther sollicitation of his Lo and made fresh application to the Lord Chief-Justice *Rainsford*, o *gust* 18, then just returned from the Circuit.

The time of Sessions at the *Old-Bailey* drawing on, they cause Writs of *Habeas Corpus* to be made (the common course of removin soners from one Gaol to another); one, *ad deliberandum*, directed Keeper at the Gate-house; and the other, *ad recipiendum*, directed Sheriffs of *London*, and desired his Lordship to sign them, that Mr. might be removed and brought to trial; for that the Keeper of the house not calendaring any State-Prisoner, (as he called him) at the sions for *Westminster*, he might lie there all his life-time without which no subject ought to do. His Lordship excused himself upo late return to Town, which had not yet afforded him leisure to a and sent them to the Attorney-General, to know whether he were for a trial, before he would give them any answer.

Mr. Attorney, upon their coming to him, very worthily told That he had no order in it, but that he would not oppose the granting of Writs: adding, God forbid but that the Law should have its due cou

They returned to the Lord Chief-Justice with this answer, and o to make oath that it was Mr. Attorney's answer; but he would give dit to nothing, but a note under Mr. Attorney's own hand. The him, it was hard that a man should lie in prison, who was willi bring himself upon trial; that Writs of this nature were every day g ed, and did presume, could not reasonably be denied. His Lordshi swered, he would know whether Mr. Attorney were ready for a They replied, That they did not know when Mr. Attorney would b dy, and Mr. *Jenkes* must stay for his Trial till then.

They then moved his Lordship, as they had done formerly, Th would grant a *Habeas Corpus* to bring him before his Lordship, an he would accept of substantial Citizens for bail, who should rende whensoever Mr. Attorney should call for him; alledging, that such had been frequently granted by the Lord Chief-Justice *Keeling*, an of the now Justices of the *King's-Bench*.

His Lordship returned, That he did not doubt the security they offer him; but he had never granted such a Writ, and he knew not what authority others had done it: And in short, refused to grant that or the other Writs.

After all these denials of right, Mr. *Jenkes* resolved to sit still, wi satisfaction, that his ill success was not imputable to the injustice cause; but to the pleasure or fear of those that had the power of ing it otherwise: And with patience to expect it till the Term shou open the prison-doors; which will not brook the denial of a *Habeas pus*, tho' a long Vacation must.

No further address was therefore made to either of their Lordships themselves, after they had taken the pleasure of denying him, were p to condescend to intercede for him: for as we heard, by very credibl formation, the Lord Chief-Justice went to the Lord Chancellor and him, " That the Writs demanded of him, were according to Law " could not be denied; and that he had only taken time till he ha " quainted his Lordship with it."

The Lord Chancellor directed him to the Lord Treasurer for fu advice; who sent him to the King. As soon as his Majesty under that what was demanded was the subject's right, he immediately manded that the laws should have their due course, which their Lord had stopped: And accordingly he was bailed.

[He was afterwards, in 1683, tried with *Thomas Pilkington*, *Henry nish*, Esqrs. and others, for a Riot at *Guildhall*, and fined 300 m See *State-Trials*, *Vol.* III. *p.* 541.

XXXIII. Articles of High Misdemeanours, humbly offered and presented to the Consideratior his most Sacred Majesty, and his most Honourable Privy-Council, against Sir WILLIAM SCROG Lord Chief-Justice of the *King's-Bench*; exhibited by Dr. *Oates*, and Captain *Bed* 31 *Car.* II.

I. THAT the said Lord Chief Justice, contrary to his oath, the duty of his place, in contempt of the King, his Crown and Dignity, did set at liberty several persons accused upon oath before him of High-Treason, without their being ever tried, or otherwise acquitted; as namely, the Lord *Brudenell*, &c

II. That at the Trial of Sir *George Wakeman* and others at the Sessions-House in the *Old-Bailey*, for High-Treason, the said Chief-Justice (according to the Dignity of his place) man the said Trial, did brow-beat and curb Dr. *Titus Oates*, and *William Bedlow*, two of the principal Witnesses for the Ki that case; and encourage the Jury impannelled and sworn to tr malefactors, against the said witnesses, by his publickly speaking flightly and abusively against them and their evidence, and the misrepeating and omitting of material parts of their evidence; whereby the parties indicted were by the said Jury acquitted of the fact then charged against them, and fully proved by the said witnesses *.

III. That the said Lord Chief-Justice, after the Trial of the said Sir *George Wakeman*, and others for High-Treason, as aforesaid, in the further abuse of the said Dr *Titus Oates*, and Mr. *William Bedlow*, and in their great disparagement speaking of them; said, that before the Trial of Sir *George Wakeman* (meaning the aforesaid Trial) the witnesses (meaning the aforesaid Dr. *Titus Oates*, and the said Mr. *William Bedlow*) were to be believed; but that at and after the said Trial, they were not to be believed by him, nor should not be believed by him; or to that very effect.

IV. That the said Lord Chief-Justice, by reason of his office, hath taken upon him the power to oppress by imprisonment, his Majesty's loyal subjects; namely, *Henry Care*, for writing and causing to be printed divers single-sheet Books in *English*, called *The Packet of Advice from Rome*; for the information and discovery of the idolatrous errors and impieties of the *Romish* Church, to his Majesty's loyal and obedient Protestant Subjects (in this conjuncture of time very useful): although the said Lord Chief-Justice neither did, nor could alledge or charge the said *Care* with any thing contained in the said Book, that was any ways criminal or derogatory to his Majesty's Laws, Crown or Dignity; and refused to take very good Bail for him, though offered, and afterwards less bail taken for him upon his *Habeas Corpus* in Court; but by the said Lord Chief-Justice's means, he was continued bound all the Term to his good behaviour; and at the end thereof until the next Term; although no particular crime was, or could be proved against or laid to his charge.

V. That to the great oppression of his Majesty's loyal Subjects, the said Lord Chief-Justice, contrary to Law, and in manifest breach of his oath, hath, without any reasonable cause, imprisoned a Feme-Covert, and divers others his Majesty's said Subjects, and refused to take bail, though tendered, and the matter bailable, as in the case of Mrs. *Jane Curtis*, Mr. *Francis Smith*, &c.

VI. That the said Lord Chief-Justice is very much addicted to swearing and cursing in his common discourse; and to drink to excess, to the great disparagement of the dignity and gravity of his said place. He did in his common discourse at dinner at a Gentleman's house of Quality, publickly and openly use and utter many oaths and curses, and there drank to excess.

VII. That *Charles Price* being accused upon oath, before the said Lord Chief-Justice, to be a *Popish* Priest and Jesuit, and imprisoned for the same, and also divers other persons accused upon oath for High-Treason; as namely, Sir *Francis Mannock*, *Richard Vaughan*, Esq. and *Daniel Arthur*, Merchant; the said Lord Chief-Justice set them at large upon bail, without consulting his Majesty's Counsel, or his witnesses, and against their consent; divers of which persons have not since appeared, but have forfeited their recognizances, and the persons not to be found.

VIII. That the said Lord Chief-Justice, to the great discouragement of his Majesty's loyal Protestant Subjects; to the manifest encouragement of the Roman Catholick Subjects, when information hath been duly and legally given to him of the abode, or person of a Popish Priest or Jesuit, and a warrant desired from him to take or search for such Priests or Jesuits, he hath in a slighting and scornful manner refused the same, and bid the Informer go to Sir *William Waller*, who busied himself in such matters mainly.

IX. That the Trial of *Knox* and *Lane*, at the Bar of the *King's-Bench* Court for their misdemeanours, in endeavouring to take away the credit of Dr. *Titus Oates*, and Mr *William Bedlow*, two of the principal witnesses for his Majesty, in the proving of the Conspiracy and Conspirators against his Majesty's Life, and Government of these Kingdoms of *England*, *Scotland*, and *Ireland*, the destruction of the Protestants and Protestant Religion, and introducing and settling of Popery there; although the evidence was so full and clear against them, that the Jury found them guilty without going from the bar; yet the said Lord Chief-Justice, in further discouragement and disparaging the evidence of the said Dr. *Titus Oates*, and Mr. *William Bedlow*, would not, nor did not give any charge to the Jury therein, but rose up suddenly, after the evidence closed by the Counsel, and left the said Court abruptly, before the said Jury had given in their verdict.

X. That the said Lord Chief-Justice, knowing that one *William Osborn* was in the conspiracy and contrivance with the said *Knox* and *Lane*, in the last article mentioned, to take away the credit of the said Dr. *Titus Oates*, and Mr. *William Bedlow*; and knowing the said Dr. *Titus Oates*, and Mr. *William Bedlow*, to be material witnesses for his Majesty, in proving of the conspiracy and conspirators, in the said last article mentioned, and had been so against several of the said conspirators that had been tried, and were to be so against several others of the said conspirators that were impeached or accused for the said High-Treason, and were to be tried for the same; and knowing the said *William Osborn* had been detected before the Lords in Parliament assembled, for his said conspiracy and contrivance with the said *Knox* and *Lane*; and that upon his own oath, thereupon denying the fact in their said conspiracy and contrivance to be true: yet out of his malice to the said Dr. *Titus Oates*, and Mr. *William Bedlow*; and as much as in him lay to endeavour the disparagement, if not the suppressing of the further discovery of that hellish and damnable plot; the said Lord Chief-Justice, without the knowledge, consent or approbation of his Majesty, or any of his learned Counsel in the Law, or the said Dr. *Titus Oates*, or Mr. *William Bedlow*; did voluntarily give the said *Osborn* liberty to make an affidavit before him upon oath, of the truth of the said fact, he had before, as aforesaid, denied upon his oath; with intent that the same might be made use of against the said Dr. *Titus Oates*, and Mr. *William Bedlow*, to their disparagement, and the apparent prejudice of his Majesty, against the said conspirators, in the said High-Treason.

XI. That he the said Lord Chief-Justice, to manifest his slighting opinion of the evidence of the said Dr. *Titus Oates*, and Mr. *William Bedlow*, in the presence of his most sacred Majesty, and the Right Honourable the Lords and others of his Majesty's most Honourable Privy-Council; did dare to say, that he had thought that Dr. *Titus Oates*, and Mr. *William Bedlow*, always had an accusation ready against any body.

XII. That at the assize holden at *Monmouth* last, the said Lord Chief-Justice, in the presence of several Justices of the Peace for the said County, did say to Mr. *William Bedlow*, that he did believe in his conscience, that *Richard Langhorn*, whom he condemned, died wrongfully, to the great disparagement of his Majesty's Crown and Dignity, the Justice of the Court, the Jury and Evidence.

XIII. That the said Lord Chief-Justice, contrary to the dignity of his place, did make merchandize of the Trials of certain Priests to be tried in *Staffordshire*, and took twenty guineas in earnest; then sold the said Trials to other persons, refusing to return the said twenty guineas to those from whom he had received them. And furthermore, before the Trial of Sir *George Wakeman*; he the said Lord Chief-Justice did bargain with two Booksellers for one hundred and fifty guineas, for them to print the Trials; and in case they would not lay down the money before he went into the Court, he would not go into the Court, but would go into the Country: and if the said Trial, by reason of its length, could not be finished in one day, he would have a hundred guineas more, or to that very effect.

The Answer of Sir *William Scroggs*, Knt. Lord Chief-Justice of the *King's-Bench*, to the Articles of Mr. *Titus Oates*, and Mr. *William Bedlow*.

I. TO the first he saith, that the Lord *Brudenell* was bailed by the Court of *King's-Bench* in open Court, and afterwards by the Court discharged; with this, that *William Bedlow* did importune the Lord *Westmorland* to get the said Lord *Brudenell* discharged, for that he had nothing to say against him, as he said to the Lord *Westmorland*.

See the Rules of Court.

II. To the second, he saith, That as to his omitting or misrepeating the evidence at Sir *George Wakeman's* Trial, it is a reflection upon the whole Court to suppose it true, and that they should let it pass. But he saith, that Mr. *Oates* being asked at that Trial, why he did not charge Sir *George Wakeman* at the Council-Table with a letter under his own hand concerning the death of the King? He answered, He did not know but that he did. to which it was replied, It is plain he did not; for then the Council would have committed him. To which Mr. *Oates* replied, That that Council would commit nobody for the plot; which might be the cause of the misdemeanour of frowning in the articles mentioned.

III. To the third, he saith, he doth not remember that ever he expressed much concerning their credit before their Trial; but that there were some passages at that Trial which gave him great cause of doubt; which he hopes he might do, without making it an article of misdemeanour.

IV. and V. To the fourth and fifth, he saith, That the persons in the articles mentioned, were committed by him for publishing several libellous and scandalous papers, which were proved against them upon oath: which commitments, even of a *Feme-Covert* also, notwithstanding Mr. *Oates* and Mr. *Bedlow's* skill, were according to Law: though there is no Law for these persons to call me to account for judicial acts done upon other men.

VI. To the sixth, which is an insolent scandal, he referreth himself to the testimony of that Gentleman of Quality, whoever he be.

VII. To the seventh, he saith, That the persons in this article were bailed and discharged by the Court, where the Attorney-General was first called, but indeed Mr. *Oates* and Mr. *Bedlow's* consent was not asked.

VIII. To the eighth, he saith, he conceives himself not obliged to do all the business that Justices of the Peace may do; and though without an offence he might have given such an answer as is mentioned, yet he did not, but a servant of his did.

IX. To the ninth, he saith, That when the cause was tried, he told the Jury the matter was plain, and so did the rest of the Court; upon which he went away, without any compliment to Mr. *Oates*, to try causes in *London*.

X. To the tenth, he saith, That *Osborn* made only two affidavits before him: the substance of one was, that one *Bowring*, a servant to Mr. *Oates*, had said, that he had heard Mr. *Oates* say, that the Kingdom of *England* would never flourish, until it became elective, and the Kings chosen by the People. The other affidavit was when he was sent to him by an order of Council to be examined; wherein amongst other things he swears, that though at the Trial of *Knox* and *Lane*, it was asked where *Osborn* was, and Mr. *Oates's* Counsel answered, that he was fled; yet *Osborn* swears, that he at that time was at his father's house in the country, and that Mr. *Oates* knew it; that he took his leave of him the day before he went, and told whither he went, and saw a letter wrote by Mr. *Oates* to his father to send for him. Notwithstanding it was carried at the Trial, as if he had been fled no man knew whither; so that the affidavit which the article chargeth me for permitting to be made, was not sworn before me.

XI. He saith, it is more to be wondered how Mr. *Oates* should dare to charge that as an article of misdemeanour, which was said in the King's presence, and yet repeated false too.

XII. That at *Monmouth Assizes* he did tell Mr. *Bedlow*, that he was more unsatisfied about Mr. *Langhorn's* Trial than all the rest; and the rather, for that he was credibly informed since the Trial, that Mr. *Langhorn's* study was so situated, that he that walked in his Chamber

* Sir *Francis Winnington* in his Speech in the Parliament, 1680, printed in the *Faithful Register*, or, *the Debates of the House of Commons, in four several Parliaments*, says, at *Wakeman's* Trial, those persons who at former Trials had been treated with that respect that is due to the King's Evidence, and whose Credit and Reputation had stood clear without exception in all other Trials, were now not only brow-beaten, but their Evidence presented to the Jury as doubtful and not to be depended on, and so at all other Trials of Papists from that time forward. By which many of the greatest offenders were quitted and cleared as to the Plot, and those that were brought for defaming the King's Evidence and suborning Witnesses, in order thereto, very kindly treated, and discharged with easy sentences, especially if Papists; but if Protestants, though only for [illegible] some unlicensed Book, were imprisoned and largely fined. But I beg leave to particularize in the case of one Care, who was indicted for printing a Weekly Intelligence, called *The Packet of Advice from Rome, or the History of Popery*. This man had a strange knack of writing extraordinary well upon that [illegible] very useful at this time for the information of the people, because it laid open very [illegible] of that Church. However, upon an information given to the Court of *King's-Bench* against this *Care*, this Rule was made,

Ordinatum est quod Liber intitulat. The Weekly Packet, &c. *non ulterius imprimatur, vel publicetur per aliquam personam quamcunque. Per Cur.*

I think this amounts to little less than a total prohibition of printing any thing against Popery.

could

could not see Mr. *Langhorn* write in his study: which was Mr. *Bedlow*'s evidence.

XIII. He saith, the matter complained of is a mere contract with other men, of which he thinks himself not bound to give Mr. *Oates* and Mr. *Bedlow* any other account, but that by the taking of twenty guineas he lost forty; and that his backwardness to go into the Court at *Wakeman*'s Trial, makes it look as if he had not had ten thousand pounds to favour *Wakeman* in his Trial.

If these Articles shall appear to your Majesty to be frivolous, or scandalous, or not true; I humbly pray your Majesty's just resentment thereo[r] nour to your Courts and Government.

And that such an unknown Attempt may not go unpunished; th[e] moters may be left to be proceeded against according to Law.

The Articles of Mr. *Titus Oates*, and Mr. *William Bedlow*, a[gainst] Lord Chief-Justice *Scroggs*, were heard this 21st of *January*; 16[80] the King and Counsel; and upon the hearing of both sides, M[r. Oates] and Captain *Bedlow* are left to be proceeded against according to

But I don't find the Chief-Justice recover'd any damages.

XXXIV. Proceedings against Sir WILLIAM SCROGGS, Knt. Lord Chief-Justice of the K[ing's] *Bench*, and other Judges, in Parliament, 1680. 32 *Car.* II.

Novem. 13, 1680.

Several Persons were examined in the House of Commons about the dismissing of a Grand-Jury in Middlesex. *After which, several Members of the House spoke as follows*; viz.

Sir *William Jones*.

MR. *Speaker*, Sir, the preservation of the Government in general, as well as our particular safeties, have a dependance upon the matter that is now before you, in which there are so many miscarriages so complicated, as there ariseth some difficulty how to examine them. I cannot but observe, how the Proclamation is here again mentioned; by which you may conclude, there lieth a great weight upon the people's right to petition by means thereof, and that the best way to remove it, is to find out the advisers and contrivers of that Proclamation, in order to proceed against them according to their deserts. Without which, what you have done in asserting the Right of Petitioning, will remain with some doubt; and those that advised the proclaiming to the people, that it is seditious to petition the King, without that chastisement they deserve. And therefore, I humbly conceive, you will do well to consider of it as soon as you can. It is not strange, that the Proclamation should be made use of with Country Gentlemen, to get abhorrers to petitioning, seeing the Judges themselves have made use of it to that purpose. *They should have known, that though a Proclamation might be of great use, to intimate the observation of a Law, yet that it had never been used instead of a Law.* But yet I do not admire so much at this as I do at the discharge of the Grand Jury, before they had finished their presentments. *It tends so much to the subversion of the established Laws of this Land, that I dare pronounce, that all the Laws you have already, and all that you can make, will signify nothing against any great man, unless you can remedy it for the future.* I observe, there were two reasons why this Grand-Jury were so extrajudicially discharged; one, because they would otherwise have presented the Duke of *York* for a Papist; the other, because they presented a Petition to be deliver'd to the King for the sitting of the Parliament, which they said it was not their business to deliver. Though I cannot but observe, how upon other occasions they did receive Petitions, and delivered them to the King; *and all the difference was, that the Petitions so delivered were against sittings of Parliaments.* The truth is, I cannot much condemn them for it; for if they were guilty of such crimes as the witnesses have this day given you information of, I think they had no reason to further Petitions for the sitting of a Parliament. But, Sir, this business will need a further Information, and therefore, I humbly pray it may be referred to a Committee.

Sir *Francis Winnington*.

Mr. Speaker, Sir, I think we are come to the old times again, *When the Judges pretended they had a rule of Government, as well as a rule of Law*; and they have acted accordingly. If they did never read *Magna Charta*, I think they are not fit to be Judges; if they have read *Magna Charta*, and do thus so contrary, they deserve a severe chastisement. To discharge Grand-Juries of purpose to disappoint them of making their presentments, is to deprive the Subject of the greatest benefit and security the Law hath provided for them. *If the Judges, instead of acting by Law, shall be acted by their ambition, and endeavour to get promotions rather by worshipping the rising Sun, than by doing Justice*, this Nation will soon be reduced to a miserable condition. Suppose that after the discharge of this Grand-Jury, some Person had offered to present some Murder, Treason, or other capital crime, for want of the Grand-Jury, there would have been a failure of Justice. As faults committed by Judges are of more dangerous consequence than others to the Public, so there do not want precedents of severer chastisements for them than for others. I humbly move you first to pass a Vote upon this business of discharging Grand-Juries, and then to appoint a Committee to examine the miscarriages of the Judges in *Westminster-hall*, and to report the same with all speed to you.

Mr. *S. Titus*.

Mr. Speaker, Sir, As it hath been observed that this business has some reference to the Proclamation, so I believe there is something of the plot in it too, and therefore, *I think if this Plot do not go on, it would have the worst luck that ever Plot had*, seeing the Judges, as well as most other persons in public places, have given it as much assistance as they could. But whereas some have spoken ill of these Judges, I desire to speak well of them in one thing. I am confident they have herein shewed themselves grateful to their benefactors; for I do believe that some of them were preferr'd to their places of purpose, because they should do what they have done. Laws of themselves are but dead letters: unless you can secure the execution as well of those you have already, as of those you are now making, we shall spen[d] our time to little purpose. Therefore I second the motion that h[ath been] made for a Vote, to declare the sense of the House as to the disch[arging] Grand-Juries, and for referring the further examination to a Com[mittee].

Mr. *W. Sacheverel*.

Mr. Speaker, Sir, the business of this debate is a great instanc[e of our] sick and languishing condition. As our Ships, Forts, and Castle[s are for] securing us from the danger of our Enemies from abroad, so our L[aws against] our enemies at home; and if committed to such persons as will t[urn their] strength upon us, are equally dangerous. Sir, *We all know ho[w the Go]vernment of* Scotland *hath been quite altered since his Majesty's Restaur[ation, by] some Laws made there; pray let us have a care that ours be not alt[er]ed [by the cor]rupt proceedings of Judges, lest we be reduced to the same weak condition [of defend]ing ourselves against Popery and arbitrary Government here, that they* If Judges can thus prevent the penalties of the Law, by discharging Juries before they have made their presentments, and can make their Rules of Court, I think the Government may soon be [su]and therefore, that it is high time for this House to speak with those men. In former times several Judges have been impeached, an[d] too, for less crimes than these; and the reason was, because they h[ad broken] the King's oath as well as their own. If what hath been said of these Judges be fully proved, they shall not want my Vote to [punish] them the same chastisement. The truth is, Sir, I know not ho[w the] consequences we justly fear from Judges, can be prevented, as lon[g as they] are made *durante beneplacito*, and have such dependencies as they ha[ve; but] this must be a work of time. In order to remedy our present gri[evances] let us pass a Vote upon this business of discharging Grand-Juries, it may be penn'd as the case deserves. If you please, let it be draw[n by] a Committee, that may withdraw for that purpose; and let there be appointed to examine the miscarriage of the Judges.

Mr. *H. Powell*.

Mr. Speaker, Sir, I would beg leave to observe to you, because it may be necessary to be considered by your Committee, what in[formation] was given not long since by some of these Judges about Printing[; it] was, that Printing of News might be prohibited by Law; and acc[ordingly] a Proclamation issued out. I will not take on me to censure the o[pinion as] illegal, but leave it to your further consideration. *But I remember a consultation held by the Judges a little before, and they gave their opin[ion, that] they knew not of any way to prevent Printing by Law, because the Act [for that] purpose was expired. Upon which, some Judges were put out, and new [ones put] in, and then this other opinion was given.* These things are worthy [of a se]rious examination: for if Treasurers may raise money by shuttin[g up the] *Exchequer*, borrowing of the Bankers, or retrenchments, and the[Judges] make new Laws by an ill construction, or an ill execution of the o[ld ones,] I conclude, that Parliaments will soon be found useless, and the [sitting of] the people an inconvenience to the Government. And therefore, Sir, you have been well moved to endeavour to pass your censure of these illegal proceedings by a Vote, and to refer the farther co[nsidera]tion to a Committee.

Sir *Francis Winnington*.

Mr. Speaker, In the front of *Magna Charta* it is said, *Nulli ne[gabimus,] nulli deferemus Justitiam*; we will defer or deny Justice to no man the King is sworn, and with this the Judges are entrusted by the[ir oaths;] I admire what they can say for themselves: if they have not read i[t,] they are not fit to sit upon the Bench; and if they have, I had alr[eady said] they deserve to lose their heads.

Mr. Speaker, The state of this poor Nation is to be deplored, th[at in al]most all ages, the Judges, who ought to be preservers of the Laws, [have en]deavour'd to destroy them; and that to please a Court-faction, they [have by] treachery attempted to break the bonds asunder of *Magna Charta*, t[he great] treasury of our peace. It was no sooner pass'd, but a Chief-Justice [(Hubert *de*] *Burg*) in that day, persuades the King he was not bound by it, [because] he was under age, when it was pass'd. But this sort of insolence [the] Parliament resented, to the ruin of the pernicious Chief-Justice. In [the time] of *Richard* II. an unthinking, dissolute Prince, there were Judges [that] insinuate into the King, that the Parliament were only his creatu[res, and de]pended on his will, and not on the fundamental constitutions [of the] Land, which treacherous advice proved the ruin of the King; [for] which all those evil Instruments were brought to Justice. In [the late] Majesty's time, his misfortunes were occasioned chiefly by the [opinions] of the Long Robe; his Judges by an extrajudicial opinion [gave] the King power to raise money upon an extraordinary occasi[on with]out Parliament, and made the King Judge of such o[ccasions.] Charity prompts me to think they thought this a service [to the] King, but the sad consequences of it may convince all m[en] that every illegal act weakens the Royal Interest; and to endeavour to introduce absolute Dominion in these Realms, is the worst of Treasons: because whilst it bears the face of friendship to the King, and designs to be for his service, it never fails of the contrary effect.

The two great Pillars of the Government, are Parliaments and Juries; it is this gives us the title of freeborn *Englishmen.* For my notion of free *Englishmen* is this, that they are ruled by Laws of their own making, and tried by men of the same condition with themselves. The two great and undoubted privileges of the people, have been lately invaded by the Judges that now sit in *Westminster-hall*, they have espoused Proclamation against Law; they have discountenanced and opposed several legal Acts, that tended to the sitting of this honourable House; they have grasped the legislative Power into their own hands, as in that instance of Printing; the Parliament was considering that matter, but they, in the interim, made their private opinion to be law, to supersede the judgment of this House: They have discharged Grand Juries, on purpose to quell their presentments, and shelter great Criminals from Justice, and when Juries have presented their opinion for the sitting of this Parliament, they have in disdain thrown them at their feet, and told them they would be no messengers to carry such Petitions; and yet, in a few days after, have encouraged all that would spit their venom against the Government: they have served an ignorant and arbitrary faction, and been the messengers of abhorrences to the King.

Mr. Speaker, What we have now to do, is to load them with shame, who bid defiance to the Law; they are guilty of crimes against Nature, against the King, against their Knowledge, and against Posterity. The whole frame of Nature doth loudly and daily petition to God their Creator; and Kings, like God, may be addressed to in like manner, by petition, not command. They likewise knew it was lawful to petition; ignorance can be no Plea, and their knowledge aggravates their crimes; the children unborn are bound to curse such proceedings, for 'twas not Petitioning, but Parliaments they abhorred. The Atheist pleads against a God, not that he disbelieves a Deity, but would have it so. *Tresilian* and *Belknap* were Judges too; their Learning gave them honour, but their Villainies made their exit by a Rope. The end of my motion therefore is, that we may address warmly to our Prince against them, let us settle a Committee to enquire into their crimes, and not fail of doing Justice upon them that have perverted it; let us purge the Fountain, and the Streams will issue pure.

Then the House agreed to the following Resolutions.

Resolved, *That the discharging of a Grand-Jury by any Judge, before the end of the Term, Assizes, or Sessions, while matters are under their consideration, and not presented, is arbitrary, illegal, destructive to public Justice, a manifest violation of his Oath, and is a means to subvert the fundamental Laws of this Kingdom.*

Resolved, *That a Committee be appointed to examine the Proceedings of the Judges in* Westminster-Hall, *and report the same, with their opinion therein to the House.*

Whereupon a Committee was appointed, and they sat several days, and then made the following Report:

The Report of the Committee of the House of Commons, appointed to examine the Proceedings of the Judges, &c. *Thursday, Dec.* 23, 1680 *.

THIS Committee being informed, that in *Trinity*-Term last, the Court of *King's-Bench* discharged the Grand-Jury, that served for the hundred of *Ossulston*, in the County of *Middlesex*, in a very unusual manner; proceeded to enquire into the same, and found by the information of *Charles Umfreville*, Esq; Foreman of the said Jury, *Edward Proby*, *Henry Gerard*, and *John Smith*, Gentlemen, also of the said Jury, That on the 21st of *June* last, the Constables attending the said Jury were found defective, in not presenting the Papists as they ought, and thereupon were ordered by the said Jury to make further presentments of them on the 26th following, on which day the Jury met for that purpose; when several Peers of this Realm, and other persons of honour and quality, brought them a bill against *James*, Duke of *York*, for not coming to Church: but some exceptions being taken to that bill, in that it did not set forth the said Duke to be a Papist, some of the Jury attended the said persons of quality to receive satisfaction therein In the mean time, and about an hour after they had received the said bill, some of the Jury attended the Court of *King's-Bench* with a Petition, which they desired the Court to present in their name unto his Majesty for the sitting of this Parliament. Upon which, the Lord-Chief-Justice *Scroggs* raised many scruples, and on pretence that they were not all in Court (tho' twenty of the Jury had subscribed the Petition), sent for them, saying, He would dispatch them presently. The Jury being come, and their names called over, they renewed their desire that the Court would present their Petition: but the Chief-Justice asked, if they had any bills? They answered, they had, but the Clerks were drawing them into form. Upon which, the Chief-Justice said, they would not make two works of one business. And the Petition being read, he said this was no article of their charge, nor was there any Act of Parliament that required the Court to deliver the Grand Jury's Petitions. That there was a Proclamation about them; and that it was not reasonable the Court should be obliged to run on their errands; and he thought it much, that they should come with a Petition to alter the King's mind declared in the News-Book. The Jury said, they did it not to impose on the Court, but (as other Juries had done) with all submission they desired it: but the Court refused, bidding the Cryer return them their Petition. And Mr. Justice *Jones* told them, they had meddled with matters of State, not given them in charge, but presented no bills of the matters given in charge. They answered as before, they had many before them, that would be ready in due time. Notwithstanding which, the said Justice *Jones* told them, they were discharged from further service. But *Philip Ward* (the Clerk that attended the said Jury) cried out, No, no, they have many bills before them, for which the Court understanding (as it seems to this Committee) a secret reason, which the Clerk did not, reproved him, asking, if he or they were to give the rule there? The Cryer then told the Court, they would not receive their Petition; the Chief-Justice bid him let it alone, so it was left there; and the Jury returned to the Court-house, and there found several Constables with Presentments of Papists and other offenders, as the Jury had directed them on the 21st before, but could not now receive the said presentments, being discharged; whereby much business was obstructed, tho' none of the said Informants ever knew the said Jury discharged before the last day of the Term, which was not till four days after. And it further appeareth to the Committee, by the evidences of *Samuel Astry*, *Jasper Waterhouse*, and *Philip Ward*, Clerks, that have long served in the said Court, that they were much surprized at the said discharging of the Jury, in that it was never done in their memory before; and the rather, because the said *Waterhouse*, as Secondary, constantly enters on that Grand-Jury's paper, that the last day of the Term is given them to return their verdict on, as the last day but one is given to the other two Grand-Juries of that County, which entry is as followeth:

Trinit. 32 Car. II.

Juratores habent diem ad veredictum suum reddendum usq; diem Mercurii proxime post tres Septimanas sanctæ Trinitatis. Middlesex. Ossulston Hundred.

Being the last day of the Term, and so in all the other Terms the last day is given; which makes it appear to this Committee, that they were not in truth discharged for not having their presentments ready, since the Court had given them a longer day, but only to obstruct their further proceedings; and it appeareth by the evidence aforesaid to this Committee, that the four Judges of that Court were present at the discharging of the said Jury, and it did not appear that any of them did dissent therein; upon consideration whereof, the Committee came to this resolution:

Resolved, That it is the opinion of this Committee, that the discharging of the Grand-Jury of the hundred of *Ossulston*, in the County of *Middlesex*, by the Court of *King's-Bench*, in *Trinity* Term last, before the last day of the Term, and before they had finished their presentments, was illegal, arbitrary, and a high misdemeanour.

This Committee proceeded also to enquire into a rule of the Court of *King's-Bench*, lately made against the publishing of a Book, called *The Weekly Packet of Advice from* Rome; or, *The History of Popery*: and *Samuel Astry*, Gent. examined thereupon, informed this Committee, that the Author of the said Book, *Henry Carr*, had been informed against for the same, and had pleaded to the Information; but before it was tried, a rule was made on a motion, as he supposeth, against the said Book; all the Judges of that Court (as he remembers) being present, and none dissenting. The copy of which rule he gave in to this Committee, and is as followeth:

Dies Mercurii proxime post tres Septimanas sanctæ Trinitatis, *Anno* 32. Car. II. *Regis*.

Ordinatum est quod liber intitulat. The Weekly Packet of Advice from *Rome*; *or*, The History of Popery, *non ulterius imprimatur vel publicetur per aliquam Personam quamcunq;* *Per Cur.*

And this Committee admiring that Protestant Judges should take offence against a Book, whose chief design was to expose the cheats and foppery of Popery, enquired further into it, and found by the evidence of *Jane Curtis*, that the said Book had been licensed for several months, that her husband paid for the copy, and entered it in the Hall-book of the Company. But for all this, she could not prevail by these reasons, with the Lord Chief-Justice *Scroggs*, to permit it any longer; who said, 'twas a scandalous Libel, and against the King's Proclamation, and he would ruin her if ever she printed it any more. And soon after she was served with the said rule, as the Author, and other Printers were; and by the Author's evidence it appears, that he was taken and brought before the said Chief-Justice by his warrant above a year since, and upon his owning he writ part of that Book, the Chief-Justice called him rogue and other ill names; saying, he would fill all the gaols in *England* with such rogues, and pile them up as men do faggots; and so committed him to prison, refusing sufficient bail, and saying he would gaol him, to put him to charges, and his Lordship observed his word punctually therein, forcing him to his *Habeas Corpus*, and then taking the same bail he refused before. Upon which, this Committee came to this resolution:

Resolved, That it is the opinion of the Committee, that the rule made by the Court of *King's-Bench*, in *Trinity* Term last, against printing a Book, called, *The Weekly Packet of Advice from* Rome, is illegal and arbitrary.

And the Committee proceeded further, and upon Information that a very great latitude had been taken of late by the Judges, in imposing fines on the persons found guilty before them, caused a transcript of all the fines imposed by the *King's-Bench* since *Easter* Term, in the 28th of his Majesty's Reign, to be brought before them, from the said Court, by *Samuel Astry*, Gent. By perusal of which, it appeared to this Committee, that the quality of the offence, and the ability of the person found guilty, have not been the measures that have determined the quantity of many of these fines; which being so very numerous, the Committee refer themselves to those Records as to the general, instancing in some particulars as follow:

Upon *Joseph Brown*, of *London*, Gent. on an Information for publishing a printed Book, called *The Long Parliament dissolved*; in which is set forth these words: *Nor let any man think it strange, that we account it Treason for you to sit and act contrary to our Laws; for if in the first Parliament of* Richard II. Grimes *and* Weston, *for lack of courage only were adjudged guilty of High-Treason for surrendering the places committed to their trust; how much more you, if you turn Renegadoes to the people that intrusted you, and as much as in you lie surrender not a little pitiful Castle or two, but all the legal defence the people of* England *have for their lives, liberties and properties at once! Neither let the vain persuasion delude you, that no precedent can be found, that one* English *Parliament hath hanged up another; though peradventure even that may be proved a mistake: for an unprecedented crime calls for an unprecedented punishment; and if you shall be so wicked to do the one, or rather endeavour to do, (for now you are no longer a Parliament) what ground of confidence you can have that none will be found so worthy to do the other, we cannot understand and do faithfully* Trinit. 29. Car. II.

* This Report is printed in State-Trials, Vol. III. page [illegible]. but without the Impeachment and Answer of the Lord Chief-Justice *Scroggs*, or the Debates in Parliament, so that to make this Proceeding complete, we have printed the Report here again, that Gentlemen may see the whole at one view.

promise if your unworthiness provoke us to it, that we will use our honest and utmost Endeavours (whenever a new Parliament shall be called) to chuse such as may convince you of your Mistake: The old and infallible Observation, That Parliaments are the Pulse of the People, *shall lose its Esteem; or you will find, that this your Presumption was over-fond; however, it argues but a bad Mind to sin, because it's believed it shall not be punished.* The Judgment was, that he be fined 1000 Marks, be bound to the good Behaviour for seven Years, and his Name struck out of the Roll of the Attorneys, without any Offence alledged in his said Vocation. And the publishing the Libel consisted only in superscribing a Pacquet, with this inclosed, to the *East-Indies*. Which Fine he not being able to pay, (living only upon his Practice) he lay in Prison for three Years, till his Majesty graciously pardoned him, and recommended him to be restored to his Place again of Attorney, by his Warrant dated the 15th of *December*, 1679. Notwithstanding which, he has not yet obtained the said Restoration from the Court of *King's-Bench*.

Hil. 29 & 30. Car. II.

Upon *John Harrington* of *London*, Gent. for speaking these Words laid in *Latin* thus: *Quod nostra Gubernatio de tribus statibus consistebat, & si Rebellio eveniret in Regno, & non accideret contra omnes tres status non est Rebellio.* A Fine of 1000*l.* Sureties for the good Behaviour for seven Years, and to recant the Words in open Court; which Fine he was in no Capacity of ever paying.

Hil. 31 & 32. Car II.

Upon *Benjamin Harris* of *London*, Stationer, on an Information for printing a Book, called *An Appeal from the Country to the City*, setting forth these Words: *We in the Country have done our Parts, in chusing for the generality good Members to serve in Parliament: But if (as our two last Parliaments were) they must be dissolved or prorogued whenever they come to redress the Grievances of the Subject, we may be pitied, not blamed, if the Plot takes effect; and in all Probability it will. Our Parliaments are not then to be condemned, for that their not being suffered to sit, occasioned it.* Judgment to pay 500*l.* Fine, stand on the Pillory an Hour, and give Sureties for the good Behaviour for three Years. And the said *Benjamin Harris* informed this Committee, That the Lord Chief-Justice *Scroggs* pressed the Court then to add to this Judgment, his being publickly whipt; but Mr. Justice *Pemberton* holding up his Hands in Admiration at their Severity therein, Mr. Justice *Jones* pronounced the Judgment aforesaid; and he remains yet in Prison, unable to pay the said Fine.

Notwithstanding which Severity in the Cases fore-mentioned, this Committee has observed the said Court has not wanted in any other Cases an extraordinary Compassion and Mercy, tho' there appeared no publick Reason judicially in the Trial; as in particular:

Hil. 31 & 32. Car. II.

Upon *Thomas Knox*, Principal, on an Indictment of Subornation and Conspiracy against the Testimony and Life of Dr. *Oates*, for Sodomy; and also against the Testimony of *William Bedloe*; a Fine of 200 Marks, a Year's Imprisonment, and to find Sureties for the good Behaviour for three Years.

Eod. Ter.

Upon *John Lane*, for the same Offence, a Fine of 100 Marks, to stand in the Pillory for an Hour, and to be imprisoned for one Year.

Par. 32 Car. II.

Upon *John Tasborough*, Gent. on an Indictment for Subornation of *Stephen Dugdale*, tending to overthrow the whole Discovery of the Plot: The said *Tasborough* being affirmed to be a Person of good Quality, a Fine of 100*l.*

Upon *Anne Price*, for the same Offence, 200*l.*

Eod. Ter. Trin. 32 Car. II.

Upon *Nathaniel Thompson* and *William Badcock*, on an Information for printing and publishing a weekly Libel, called *The True Domestic Intelligence, or, News both from City and Country*, and known to be Popishly affected, a Fine of 3*l.* 6*s.* 8*d.* on each of them.

Eod. Ter.

Upon *Matthew Turner*, Stationer, on an Information for vending and publishing a Book, called *The Compendium*; wherein the Justice of the Nation in the late Trials of the Popish Conspirators, even by some of these Judges themselves, is highly arraigned; and all the Witnesses for the King horribly aspersed: And this being the common notorious Popish Bookseller of the Town, Judgment to pay a Fine of 100 Marks, and is said to be out of Prison already.

Trin. 32. Car. II

Upon ——— *Loveland*, on an Indictment for a notorious Conspiracy and Subornation against the Life and Honour of the Duke of *Buckingham*, for Sodomy, a Fine of 5*l.* and to stand an Hour in the Pillory.

Mich. 32 Car. II

Upon *Edward Christian*, Esq. for the same Offence, a Fine of 100 Marks, and to stand an Hour in the Pillory. And upon *Arthur Obrian*, for the same Offence, a Fine of 20 Marks, and to stand an Hour in the Pillory.

Upon Consideration whereof, this Committee came to this Resolution:

Resolved, That it is the Opinion of this Committee, that the Court of *King's-Bench* (in the Imposition of Fines on Offenders of late Years) hath acted arbitrarily, illegally, and partially, favouring Papists, and Persons Popishly affected, and excessively oppressing his Majesty's Protestant Subjects.

And this Committee being informed, That several of his Majesty's Subjects had been committed for Crimes bailable by Law, although they then tendered sufficient Sureties, which were refused, only to put them to Vexation and Charge, proceeded to enquire into the same, and found that not only the fore-mentioned *Henry Carr* had been so refused the common Right of a Subject, as is above-said, but that *George Broome*, being a Constable last Year in *London*, and committing some of the Lord Chief-Justice *Scroggs*'s Servants, for great Disorders, according to his Duty, he was in a few Days arrested by a Tipstaff, without any *London* Constable, and carried before the said Chief-Justice, by his Warrant, to answer for the said committing of those Persons abovesaid, but being there, was accused of having spoken irreverently of the said Chief-Justice, and an Affidavit read to him to that Purpose; and was falsely (as the said *George Broome* affirms) sworn against, by two Persons that use to be common Bail in that Court, and of very ill Reputation. Upon which he was committed to the *King's-Bench*, though he then tendered two able Citizens and

Common-Council-men of *London* to be his Bail: And he was
bring his *Habeas Corpus*, to his great Charge, before he came ou
the Marshal, Mr. *Cooling*, exacted 5*l.* of him, of which he co
to the Chief-Justice; but had no other Answer, but he might as
medy at Law. But the said Marshal fearing he should be questio
stored him two Guineas of it.

And further, this Committee was informed by *Francis Smith*,
ler, That about *Michaelmas* was Twelve-month he was brought b
said Chief-Justice, by his Warrant, and charged by the Messenge
Stephens, That he had seen some Parcels of a Pamphlet, called *Ob*
on Sir George Wakeman's *Trial*, in his Shop: Upon which t
Justice told him, he would make him an Example, use him like
France, and pile him and all the Booksellers and Printers up i
like Faggots: And so committed him to the *King's-Bench*, swe
cursing at him in great Fury. And when he tendered three suffi
tizens of *London* for his Bail, alledging, Imprisonment in his Circu
would be his utter Ruin; the Chief-Justice replied, The Citize
like sufficient Persons, but he would take no Bail: And so he w
to come out by a *Habeas Corpus*, and was afterwards informed a
the same Matter, to his great Charge and Vexation. And a w
Francis (the Son of the said *Francis Smith*) was committed by
Chief-Justice, and Bail refused, for selling a Pamphlet, called
Year's Gift for the said Chief-Justice, to a Coffee-house; and he
to them he would take no Bail, for he would ruin them all.

And further it appeared to this Committee, that the said Chie
(about *October* was Twelve-month) committed in like manner *Ja*
she having a Husband and Children, for selling a Book, called
against Injustice; which his Lordship called a Libel against him.
Friends tendering sufficient Bail, and desiring him to have Me
her Poverty and Condition, he swore by the Name of God she
to Prison, and he would shew her no more Mercy, than they
pect from a Wolf that came to devour them; and she might
Habeas Corpus, and come out so; which she was forced to do;
informed against and prosecuted, to her utter Ruin, four or fi
after.

In like manner it appeared to this Committee, that about that
Edward Berry, Stationer, of *Gray's-Inn*, was committed by
Chief-Justice, being accused of selling *The Observations on Si*
Wakeman's *Trial*: And though he tendered 1000*l.* bail, yet t
Justice said, He would take no Bail, he should go to Prison, and
according to Law. And after he, with much Trouble and Ch
out by a *Habeas Corpus*, he was forced by himself, or his Att
attend five Terms before he could be discharged, though no In
was exhibited against him in all that time. In Consideration
and of others of the like Nature (too tedious here to relate), t
mittee came to this Resolution:

Resolved, That it is the Opinion of this Committee, that th
sufficient Bail in these Cases, wherein the Persons committed
able by Law, was illegal, and a high Breach of the Liberty of th

And this Committee being informed of an extraordinary Kind o
given at the last Assizes at *Kingston*, in the County of *Surry*, by
ron *Weston*, and proceeding to examine several Persons then
present, it was made appear to this Committee, by the Testimo
Cole, *Richard Mayo*, and *John Pierce*, Gentlemen, and other
whom put down the said Baron's Words in writing, immedia
Part of the said Charge was to this Effect: He inveighed v
against *Farel*, *Luther*, *Calvin*, and *Zuinglius*, condemning the
thors of the Reformation, which was against their Princes Mi
then adding to this Purpose; "*Zuinglius* set up his Fanaticism,
"*vin* built on that blessed Foundation; and, to speak Tru
"Disciples are seasoned with such a Sharpness of Spirit, tha
"concerns Magistrates to keep a strait Hand over them; and
"are restless, amusing us with Fears, and nothing will serve t
"Parliament. For my Part, I know no Representative of t
"but the King; all Power centers in him: 'Tis true, he does
"with his Ministers, but he *is* the sole Representative; and
"has Wisdom enough to intrust it no more in these Men,
"given us such late Examples of their Wisdom and Faithfulne
this Committee taking the said Matter into their Consideration
this Resolution,

Resolved, That it is the Opinion of this Committee, that the
pressions in the Charge given by the said Baron *Weston*, were a S
the Reformation, in derogation of the Rights and Privileges o
ments, and tending to raise Discord between his Majesty and his

And this Committee being informed by several Printers and B
of great Trouble and Vexation given them unjustly, by o
Stephens, called a Messenger of the Press; the said *Stephens* being
ed by this Committee, by what Authority he had proceeded in t
ner, produced two Warrants under the Hand and Seal of the Ch
Scroggs, which were *in hæc verba*:

'*Angl. ss.* WHEREAS there are divers ill disposed Persons
' daily print and publish many seditious and t
' Books and Pamphlets, endeavouring thereby to dispose the
' his Majesty's Subjects to Sedition and Rebellion. And also
' Libels, reflecting upon particular Persons, to the great Sca
' Majesty's Government. For suppressing whereof, his Ma
' lately issued out his Royal Proclamation: And for the more ef
' pressing the said seditious Books, Libels, and Pamphlets, and to
' that the Authors and Publishers thereof may be brought to th
' ment:

' These are to will and require you, and in his Majesty's
' charge and command you, and every of you, upon Sight her
' aiding and assisting to *Robert Stephens*, Messenger of the Pre
' seizing on all such Books and Pamphlets as aforesaid, as he th
' formed of, in any Booksellers or Printers Shops or Wa
' elsewhere, whatsoever; to the End they may be disposed as to
' appertain. Also if you shall be informed of the Authors, Pr
' Publishers of such Books or Pamphlets as are above-mentione

'to apprehend them, and have them before one of his Majesty's Justices 'of the Peace, to be proceeded against according to Law. Dated this '29th day of *November*, 1679.'

To *Robert Stephens*, Messenger of the Press, and to all Mayors, Sheriffs, Bailiffs, Constables, and all other Officers and Ministers whom these may concern. *W. SCROGGS.*

Angl. ss. 'WHEREAS the King's Majesty hath lately issued out his 'Proclamation for suppressing the Printing and Publishing unlicensed News-Books, and Pamphlets of News: Notwithstanding which, there are divers persons who do daily print and publish such 'unlicensed Books and Pamphlets:

'These are therefore to will and require you, and in his Majesty's Name 'to charge and command you, and every of you, from time to time, and 'at all times, so often as you shall be thereunto required, to be aiding and 'assisting to *Robert Stephens*, Messenger of the Press, in the seizing of all 'such Books and Pamphlets as aforesaid, as he shall be informed of, in 'any Bookseller's Shop, or Printer's Shop or Ware-houses, or elsewhere 'whatsoever, to the end they may be disposed of as to Law shall appertain. 'Likewise, if you shall be informed of the Authors, Printers or Publishers 'of such Books or Pamphlets, you are to apprehend them, and have them 'before Me, or one of his Majesty's Justices of the Peace, to be proceeded 'against as to Law shall appertain. Dated this 28th Day of *May*, '*Anno Dom.* 1680.'

To all Mayors, Sheriffs, Bailiffs, Constables, and all other Officers and Ministers whom these may concern. *W. SCROGGS.*

To *Robert Stephens*, Messenger of the Press.

Upon view whereof this Committee came to this Resolution:

Resolved, That it is the Opinion of this Committee, that the said Warrants are arbitrary and illegal.

And this Committee being informed of certain scandalous discourses, said to be uttered in public places by the Lord Chief Justice *Scroggs*, proceeded to examine Sir *Robert Atkins*, late one of the Justices of the *Common-Pleas*, concerning the same; by whom it appears, That at a Sessions-dinner at the *Old-Bailey*, in the Mayoralty of Sir *Robert Clayton*, who was then present; the said Chief Justice took occasion to speak very much against petitioning, condemning it as resembling 41, as factious and tending to Rebellion, or to that effect; to which the said Sir *Robert Atkins* made no reply, suspecting he waited for some advantage over him. But the Chief Justice continuing and pressing him with the said discourse, he began to justify petitioning as the right of the people; especially for the sitting of a Parliament, which the Law requires, if it be done with modesty and respect. Upon which the Chief Justice fell into a great passion; and there is some reason to believe, that soon after he made an ill representation of what the said Sir *Robert* had then spoke, unto his Majesty. And this Committee was further informed, that the said Sir *Robert Atkins* being in circuit with the said Chief Justice, at Summer Assizes was twelve-month, at *Monmouth*, (Mr. *Arnold*, Mr. *Price*, and Mr. *Bedloe* being then in company) the Chief Justice fell severely, in publick, upon Mr. *Bedloe*; taking off the credit of his evidence, and alledging he had over-shot himself in it, or to that effect, very much to the disparagement of his testimony. And the said Sir *Robert* defending Mr. *Bedloe*'s evidence and credit, he grew extreme angry and loud; saying to this effect, *That he verily believed* Langhorn *died innocently*. To which the said Sir *Robert* replied, He wondered how he could think so, who had condemned him himself, and had not moved the King for a reprieve for him. All which matters of discourse, this Committee humbly submit to the wisdom and consideration of this House, without taking upon them to give any opinion therein.

And this Committee proceeded further to inquire into some passages that happened at *Lent* Assizes last for the County of *Somerset*, at the trial of *Thomas Dare*, Gent. there, upon an Indictment for saying falsly and seditiously, *That the Subjects had but two means to redress their grievances, one by petitioning, the other by rebellion*. and found, that though by his other discourse, when he said so, that it appeared plainly he had no rebellious intent in that he said, *Then God forbid there should be a rebellion, he would be the first man to draw the sword against a Rebel*; yet he was prosecuted with great violence. And having pleaded, Not guilty, he moved Mr. Justice *Jones*, (who then sat Judge there) that he might try it at the next Assizes; for that Mr. *Searle* (who was by at the speaking of the words, and a material witness for his defence) was not then to be had, and an affidavit to that purpose was made and received; but the said Justice *Jones* told him, That was a favour of the Court only, and he had not deserved any favour, and so forced him to try it presently. But the Jury, appearing to be an extraordinary one, provided on purpose, being all of persons that had highly opposed petitioning for the sitting of this Parliament, he was advised to withdraw his plea; and the said Justice *Jones* encouraging him so to do, he confest the words, denying any evil intention, and gave the said Justice an account in writing, of the truth of the whole matter, and made a submission in Court, as he was directed by the said Justice, who promised to recommend him to his Majesty; but imposed a fine of 500*l.* on him, and to be bound to good behaviour for three years: Declaring also, That he was turned out from being a Common-Counsellor of the Corporation of *Taunton*, in the said County, on pretence of a clause in their Charter, giving such a power to a Judge of Assize. And the said *Thomas Dare* remains yet in prison for the said Fine; in which matter of the Trial aforesaid, this Committee desireth to refer itself to the judgment of this House.

The Resolutions of the House of Commons upon the said Report.

1. That it is the Opinion of this House, that the discharging of the Grand Jury of the hundred of *Ossulston*, in the County of *Middlesex*, by the Court of *King's-Bench*, in *Trinity* Term last, before the last day of the Term; and before they had finished their presentments, was arbitrary and illegal, destructive to publick Justice, a manifest violation of the Oaths of the Judges of that Court, and a means to subvert the fundamental Laws of this Kingdom, and to introduce Popery.

2. That it is the Opinion of this House, that the rule made by the Court of *King's Bench*, in *Trinity* Term last, against printing of a Book, called, *The Weekly Pacquet of Advice from Rome*, is illegal and arbitrary; thereby usurping to themselves legislative power, to the great discouragement of the Protestants, and for the countenancing of Popery.

3. That it is the Opinion of this House, that the Court of *King's Bench*, in the imposition of fines on offenders of late years, have acted arbitrarily, illegally and partially, favouring Papists, and persons popishly affected, and excessively oppressing his Majesty's Protestant Subjects.

4. That it is the opinion of this House, that the refusing sufficient bail in these Cases, wherein the persons committed were bailable by law, was illegal, and a high breach of the Liberties of the Subject.

5. That it is the Opinion of this House, that the said expressions in the charge given by the said Baron *Weston*, were a scandal to the Reformation; and tending to raise discord between his Majesty and his Subjects, and to the subversion of the ancient constitution of Parliaments, and of the Government of this Kingdom.

6. That it is the opinion of this House, that the said Warrants are arbitrary and illegal.

The Resolutions of the Commons, for the Impeachment of the said Judges.

Resolved, That Sir *William Scroggs*, Knt. Chief Justice of the Court of *King's Bench*, be impeached upon the said Report, and the Resolutions of the House thereupon.

Resolved, That Sir *Thomas Jones*, one of the Justices of the said Court of *King's Bench*, be impeached upon the said Report, and Resolutions of the House thereupon.

Resolved, That Sir *Richard Weston*, one of the Barons of the Court of *Exchequer*, be impeached upon the said Report, and Resolutions of the House thereupon.

Ordered, That the Committee appointed to prepare an impeachment against Sir *Francis North*, Chief Justice of the Court of *Common-Pleas*, do prepare impeachments against the said Sir *William Scroggs*, Sir *Thomas Jones*, and Sir *Richard Weston*, upon the said Report and Resolutions.

Ordered, That the said Report, and several Resolutions of this House thereupon, be printed; and that Mr. *Speaker* take care in the printing thereof a-part from this day's other Votes.

January 5, 168⁰⁄₁. *The Articles against Sir* William Scroggs, *Chief Justice of the* King's Bench, *were read as follow:*

Articles of Impeachment of High-Treason, and other great Crimes and Misdemeanours, against Sir *William Scroggs*, Chief Justice of the Court of *King's-Bench*, by the Commons in Parliament assembled, in their own Name, and in the Name of all the Commons of *England*.

1. THAT he the said Sir *William Scroggs*, then being Chief Justice of the Court of *King's Bench*, hath traitorously and wickedly endeavoured to subvert the fundamental Laws, and the established Religion and Government of this Kingdom of *England*, and instead thereof, to introduce Popery and an arbitrary and tyrannical Government, against Law, which he has declared by divers traitorous and wicked Words, Opinions, Judgments, Practices and Actions.

2. That the said Sir *William Scroggs*, in *Trinity* Term last, being then Chief Justice of the said Court, and having taken an oath duly to administer Justice, according to the Laws and Statutes of this Realm; in pursuance of his said traitorous purposes did, together with the rest of the said Justices of the same Court, several days before the end of the said Term, in an arbitrary manner discharge the Grand Jury, which then served for the Hundred of *Ossulston*, in the County of *Middlesex*, before they had made their Presentments, or had found several Bills of Indictment which were then before them; whereof the said Sir *William Scroggs* was then fully informed: and that the same would be tendered to the Court upon the last day of the said Term; which day then was, and by the known course of the said Court hath always heretofore been given unto the said Jury for the delivering in of their Bills and Presentments: By which sudden and illegal discharge of the said Jury, the course of Justice was stopped maliciously and designedly, the Presentments of many Papists and other offenders were obstructed, and in particular, a Bill of Indictment against *James* Duke of *York*, for absenting himself from Church, which was then before them, was prevented from being proceeded upon.

3. That whereas one *Henry Carr* had, for some time before, published every week a certain Book, intitled, *The Weekly Pacquet of Advice from* Rome, *or, the History of Popery*; wherein the superstitions and cheats of the Church of *Rome* were from time to time exposed; he the said Sir *William Scroggs*, then Chief Justice of the Court of *King's Bench*, together with the other Judges of the said Court, before any legal conviction of the said *Carr* of any crime, did in the same *Trinity* Term, in a most illegal and arbitrary manner, make, and cause to be entered, a certain rule of that Court, against the printing of the said Book, *in hæc Verba:*

Dies Mercurii proxime post tres Septimanas Sanctæ Trinitatis, Anno 32 *Car.* II. *Regis.*

ORdinatum est quod Liber intitulat' The Weekly Pacquet of Advice from *Rome*, or, The History of Popery, *non ulterius imprimatur vel publicetur per aliquam personam quamcunque.*

Per Cur'

And did cause the said *Carr*, and divers Printers and other persons to be served with the same; which said Rule and other Proceedings were most apparently contrary to all Justice, in condemning not only what had been written without hearing the Parties, but also all that might for the future be written on that subject; a manifest countenancing of Popery and discouragement of Protestants, an open invasion upon the right of the Subject, and an encroaching and assuming to themselves a legislative power and authority.

4. That the said Sir *William Scroggs*, since he was made Chief Justice of the *King's-Bench*, hath, together with the other Judges of the said Court, most notoriously departed from all rules of justice and equality, in the imposition

impofition of fines upon perfons convicted of Mifdemeanours in the faid Court; and particularly in the Term of *Eafter* laft paft, did openly declare in the faid Court, in the cafe of one *Jeffop*, who was convicted of publifhing falfe News, and was then to be fined, That he would have regard to perfons and their principles in impofing of fines, and would fet a fine of 500 *l.* on one perfon for the fame offence, for the which he would not fine another 100 *l.* And according to his faid unjuft and arbitrary declaration, he the faid Sir *William Scroggs*, together with the faid other Juftices, did then impofe a fine of 100 *l.* upon the faid *Jeffop*; although the faid *Jeffop* had before that time proved one *Hewit* to be convicted as Author of the faid falfe News; and afterwards, in the fame Term, did fine the faid *Hewit* upon his faid conviction, only five marks: Nor hath the faid Sir *William Scroggs*, together with the other Judges of the faid Court, had any regard to the nature of the offences, or the ability of the perfons, in the impofing of fines; but have been manifeftly partial and favourable to Papifts, and perfons affected to, and promoting the Popifh Intereft, in this time of imminent danger from them: And at the fame time have moft feverely and grievoufly oppreffed his Majefty's Proteftant fubjects, as will appear upon view of the feveral Records of fines fet in the faid Court. By which arbitrary, unjuft, and partial proceedings, many of his Majefty's liege-people have been ruined, and Popery countenanced under colour of juftice, and all the mifchiefs and exceffes of the Court of *Star-Chamber*, by Act of Parliament fuppreffed, have been again, in direct oppofition of the faid Law, introduced.

5. That he the faid Sir *William Scroggs*, for the further accomplifhing of his faid traitorous and wicked purpofes, and defigning to fubject the Perfons, as well as the Eftates of his Majefty's liege people, to his lawlefs will and pleafure, hath frequently refufed to accept of bail, though the fame were fufficient, and legally tendered to him by many perfons accufed before him only of fuch crimes for which by law bail ought to have been taken, and divers of the faid perfons being only accufed of offences againft himfelf; declaring at the fame time, that he refufed bail, and committed them to gaol only to put them to charges; and ufing fuch furious threats as were to the terrour of his Majefty's fubjects, and fuch fcandalous expreffions as were a difhonour to the Government, and to the dignity of his office. And, particularly, that he the faid Sir *William Scroggs* did, in the year 1679, commit and detain in prifon, in fuch unlawful manner, among others, *Henry Carr*, *George Broome*, *Edward Berry*, *Benjamin Harris*, *Francis Smith*, fen. *Francis Smith*, jun. and *Jane Curtis*, citizens of *London*: Which proceedings of the faid Sir *William Scroggs*, are a high breach of the liberty of the fubject, deftructive to the fundamental laws of this Realm, contrary to the Petition of Right, and other Statutes; and do manifeftly tend to the introducing of arbitrary power.

6. That he the faid Sir *William Scroggs*, in further oppreffion of his Majefty's liege-people, hath, fince his being made Chief-Juftice of the faid Court of *King's-Bench*, in an arbitrary manner, granted divers general warrants for attaching the perfons and feizing the goods of his Majefty's fubjects, not named or defcribed particularly in the faid warrants: By means whereof, many of his Majefty's fubjects have been vexed, their houfes entered into, and they themfelves grievoufly oppreffed, contrary to Law.

7. Whereas there hath been a horrid and damnable Plot contrived and carried on by the Papifts, for the murthering the King, the fubverfion of the Laws and Government of this Kingdom, and for the deftruction of the Proteftant Religion in the fame; all which the faid Sir *William Scroggs* well knew, having himfelf not only tried, but given judgment againft feveral of the offenders: Neverthelefs, the faid Sir *William Scroggs* did, at divers times and places, as well fitting in Court, as otherwife, openly defame and fcandalize feveral of the witneffes, who had proved the faid treafons againft divers of the confpirators, and had given evidence againft divers other perfons, who were then untried, and did endeavour to difparage their evidence, and take off their credit; whereby, as much as in him lay, he did traitoroufly and wickedly fupprefs and ftifle the difcovery of the faid Popifh Plot, and encourage the confpirators to proceed in the fame, to the great and apparent danger of his Majefty's facred life, and of the well-eftablifhed Government, and Religion of this Realm of *England*.

8. Whereas the faid Sir *William Scroggs*, being advanced to be Chief-Juftice of the Court of *King's-Bench*, ought by a fober, grave and virtuous converfation, to have given a good example to the King's liege-people, and to demean himfelf anfwerable to the dignity of fo eminent a Station; yet he the faid Sir *William Scroggs*, on the contrary, by his frequent and notorious Exceffes and Debaucheries, and his prophane and atheiftical Difcourfes, doth daily affront Almighty God, difhonour his Majefty, give countenance and encouragement to all manner of vice and wickednefs, and bring the higheft fcandal on the public Juftice of the Kingdom.

All which Words, Opinions and Actions of the faid Sir *William Scroggs*, were by him fpoken and done, traitoroufly, wickedly, falfly, and malicioufly, to alienate the hearts of the King's fubjects from his Majefty, and to fet a divifion between him and them; and to fubvert the fundamental Laws, and the eftablifhed Religion and Government of this Kingdom, and to introduce Popery, and an arbitrary and tyrannical Government, contrary to his own knowledge, and the known Laws of the Realm of *England*. And thereby he the faid Sir *William Scroggs* hath not only broken his own oath, but alfo, as far as in him lay, hath broken the King's oath to his people; whereof he the faid Sir *William Scroggs*, reprefenting his Majefty in fo high an office of Juftice, had the cuftody; for which the faid Commons do impeach him the faid Sir *William Scroggs*, of the High-Treafon againft our Sovereign Lord the King, and his Crown and Dignity, and other the high Crimes and Mifdemeanors aforefaid.

And the faid Commons, by proteftation faving to themfelves the liberty of exhibiting at any time hereafter, any other accufation or impeachment againft the faid Sir *William Scroggs*, and alfo of replying to the anfwer that he fhall make thereunto, and of offering proofs of the premiffes, or of any other impeachments or accufations that fhall be by them exhibited againft him, as the cafe fhall (according to the courfe of Parliament) require, do pray that the faid Sir *William Scroggs*, Chief-Juftice of the Court of *King's-Bench*, may be put to anfwer to all and every the Premiffes, and may be committed to fafe cuftody; and that fuch proceedings, examinations, trials, and judgments may be upon him had and ufed, as is
Law and Juftice, and the courfe of Parliaments.

Refolved, That the faid Sir *William Scroggs* be impeach
faid Articles.

Upon which the following Speeches were made.

Sir *Thomas Lee.*

Mr. Speaker, Sir, in my opinion, the matter contained in t
Articles, doth not anfwer the firft Article nor the Title; for
accufe Sir *William Scroggs* in general words, of High-Treafon
of crimes; and when you come to particulars, you inftance th
of Grand-Juries, prohibiting the Printing of Pamphlets, i
levying of fines, and the like. Sir, I would not be underfto
Advocate for the Lord-Chief-Juftice *Scroggs*; but I hope that
fit here, you will always give me leave to be an Advocate for
which I cannot more fignally demonftrate, than by offering
againft every thing which I think will reflect upon the Juftice
of the Houfe, or prove any hinderance to the finifhing of thofe g
you have under debate.

Sir, I am of opinion, that though all thefe things contai
Articles fhould be fully proved, they will not amount to T
although it be true that you do but impeach, and that the I
judge, yet it is not agreeable to the Juftice of this Houfe, that
fhould be for *Treafon*, unlefs you are well fatisfied that you ca
that the matter contained in the Articles is fo: which I very n
And therefore I am of opinion, that the Articles ought on
High Crimes and Mifdemeanours, which I am the more forw
you earneftly to, becaufe I am afraid if thefe Articles fhould g
Treafon, it may occafion fome difpute with the Lords, wh
they do not conclude that the matter contained in the Articl
to Treafon, will not commit him, notwithftanding their Ord
the Earl of *Danby*'s cafe: And that may occafion fuch mif-und
as may hinder all other bufinefs. And alfo if you fend it up
Treafon, it may occafion another difpute with the Bifhops, wh
fhall withdraw or no, when the Cafe comes to be tried. Upon
matter, I think it will be much fafer that you make the Impeac
High Crimes and Mifdemeanours only.

Mr. *Daniel Finch* (afterwards Earl of *Nottingham*).

Mr. Speaker, Sir, my obligation to ferve my Country, call
give you my opinion in this matter, and not any kindnefs to my L
Juftice; for I can fafely declare, that I do not think him f
eminent place now, becaufe indeed I never thought he was fit
what I fhall fay, proceeds from my kindnefs to the Publick, and
obligations to this Houfe. I think we ought to be cautious h
creafe Laws to take away our lives; our fore-fathers were very
it, as may appear by the Statute of 25 *Ed.* III. which was ma
vent the Judges from taking on them any power to declare
Treafon but what was exprefs'd within that Statute; referving a
crimes of that nature to the judgement of the Nation in Parlian
no doubt may declare other things Treafon which are not w
Statute. But it is a queftion with me, whether it can be done
way than by Bill, that fo it may be an Act of King, Lords and C
and not for the Houfe of Lords only, the Commons only profec
the King not concerned. That the Lords alone are proper
many cafes, when perfons are profecuted upon fome known La
to be doubted: But I much queftion if they ought to be fo
declarative Treafon, though upon an Impeachment from the Houfe of
For that were to allow the Lords alone a power of making a L
cafes of the higheft Nature, even of life and death. Sir, our f
thought not good to intruft their lives nor liberties with any o
alone; they thought with a multitude of Counfellors there
fafety: And therefore I hope we fhall be very cautious how w
precedent in the cafe. And I am the more earneft in moving yo
becaufe I am very confident that no precedent can be offered
good, that there was ever any thing declared Treafon in Parliamen
was not felony by fome exprefs, known law before. And I hope
be fo careful of ourfelves and our pofterity, as not to go about t
breach upon the conftitution of the Government in this partic
rather make the Impeachment only for High Crimes and Mifdeme

Sir *Francis Winnington.*

Mr. Speaker, Sir, I cannot agree with that honourable Mem
fpoke laft, as to his notion that the Parliament cannot declare a
to be Treafon, which was not before Felony by fome known l
Statute of 25 *Ed.* III. leaves the power at large to Parliaments wit
fuch reftriction. And I am of opinion, that any thing that ten
deftruction or alteration of the Government, hath always been, a
to be declared in Parliament, Treafon, if brought there to be
The *Parliament doth not in this make new Crimes, and then conden*
but *only declares that to be a Crime which was fo before, and wante*
but condemnation. And it may confift with the prudence of this
as well to be careful how to weaken thofe Laws and Cuftoms wh
fo much to the prefervation of the Government, as how to incr
that may tend to the deftruction of any one Man, by multiplyin
dents for chaftizing of Treafon; the crimes for which *Trefilian*
reft at that time were impeached, were not Felony by any know
and yet they were condemned in Parliament. *Empfon* and *D.*
accufed in general, for endeavouring to fubvert the Government,
being in general words, was not Felony by any known Law,
Judges having recourfe to Parliament, they were condemned.
Articles againft *Finch*, *Berkley*, and the reft, were all for High-T
and the matter contained in their Articles amounted to no mo
what is now contained in this. And there is fo little weight
cafes that have been offered againft this, that I think they are
rather for ornament than argument. *The Chancellor is the K*
the King's confcience, and the Judges of his coronation-oath. A
are in great places, and have a great power, fo they ought to
more careful how they behave themfelves: And as they have
encouragements, fo to be fubject to more fevere chaftifements than

the publick being more concerned in their actions; and therefore the custom of Parliaments hath made that treason in them, which is not so in other persons. The words of Judges and Privy-Councillors, in some cases, are *Overt-Acts* of themselves, I think it will become the wisdom of the Nation, to make all the defence and provision they can, against the corrupt doings of Men in such places. And I do not see what danger can arise to our posterities by such proceedings. Is it not with the Parliament we entrust this power? Who can imagine that a Parliament can ever be so constituted, as not to be carefully concerned in their proceedings as to life and death; and only to concern themselves therein, when some extraordinary exigencies in which the Government is much concerned, requires it? What Man would desire to live after he was thought worthy of death by such an assembly? And notwithstanding what hath been said to extenuate the crimes mentioned in these Articles, I think, the Order that was made in the King's-Bench about Printing, by the Judges, was taking on them a legislative Power; which hath formerly been judged treason: And I think we live now in as dangerous times as ever, *and under as great a necessity to have a care of the mischiefs that may happen to the Nation by ill Judges, as ever.* And I see no reason to doubt our being able to make good these Articles; and therefore I pray that the Articles may be ingrossed as they are.

Mr. *Powell.*

Mr Speaker, Sir, I agree that it will become this House very well, to be very cautious how they make precedents in cases of treason, which are the proceedings of life and death: as also how they weaken parliamentary Sheet-Anchors that are necessary to preserve the Government. And I hope that nothing but the true merits of the cause will lead us in a matter of so great importance, and neither wit nor oratory, nor any forced explanation of the laws. I see it agreed by all, that Parliaments have a power of declaring treason. The question is, Which is most customary and securest, to have it done by Bill, that so, King, Lords and Commons may join therein? or whether by an impeachment from the Commons, the Lords being only the Judges? or whether any thing ought or can be declared treason by Parliament, which was not felony by some known law before?

Sir, I am of opinion that it is safest and most agreeable to the policy of this Government, that the declaring of any thing treason in Parliament should be by Bill, that King, Lords and Commons may join therein, that so such a precious thing as the life of the subject should have the greatest security imaginable. However, it is not to be doubted, but it hath been practised otherways, and that many persons have been condemned in Parliament upon impeachment from the Commons, for facts which were not treason by any known Law. And the reason may be, thereby to *prevent the dangers that might arise from some Ministers of State growing so great with the King, as that they should be able to secure him from ever giving his consent to a Bill.* In such a case, by giving ill counsel and other secret courses, (happily as far as treason, yet not known by any law) they would be secure from punishment, if this way of proceeding against such a person, where the King's concurrence is not necessary, were not allowed of. And the preserving of this right is so far from being contrary to the wisdom of our Ancestors, that it is very agreeable to all their proceedings in the constitution of this Government, in order to balance it the better, and preserve it against the designs of great ill Men. And as to the other objection, whether the Parliament can declare any thing treason that was not felony before by some known law; I am quite of another opinion, and do believe that the practice hath been otherways. The Judges in *Rich.* the IId's time were condemned for giving extrajudicial opinions, which, I think, was not felony by any Statute-Law. A Knight of *Cheshire* was condemned in Parliament, for conspiring the death of the King's uncle: an Earl of *Northumberland*, for giving liveries to so many persons as were judged a little army; and many other cases which I have read of, in which persons have been condemned in Parliament, when their crimes were not felony by any known law. But I do not take any delight in ripping-up old Statutes or Precedents about treasons. I am sorry the misfortunes of our times should make it now necessary. But if the Parliament, as I conclude, have often declared such things as these treason, and the Commons have impeached persons guilty of such crimes for High-Treason, I see no just objection why these Articles should go up as they are drawn: For notwithstanding what hath been said to mitigate the crimes contained in these Articles, I am of opinion, that the order made in the *King's-Bench*, about *Printing, their Warrants for seizing of Books, their dismissing of Grand Juries, doth tend to the subversion of the Government; and hath been, and ever ought to be, in Judges, judged High-Treason.* And therefore, that it cannot consist with the prudence of this House, nor the security of the Nation, that this person should be impeached of less than High-Treason: And therefore I move you, that the Articles may be engrossed.

Mr. *Paul Foley.*

Mr. Speaker, Sir, we are not going about to declare any thing treason, but to offer our Articles, and leave it to the Lords; therefore most of these arguments would be more proper there: for we only impeach, they are to be the Judges, whether the matter be treason or no. It is true, we ought to be cautious what we do in it, because it is not proper that this House should impeach a man for treason, without having good grounds for it. But is not the *Order about Printing a kind of an Act of State to serve instead of a Law?* Is not the use of Grand-Juries a very essential part of this Government? And *is not the dismissing of them, as this Judge did,* a way to render them useless? Are not his *Warrants to seize Books and Papers arbitrary?* and doth not all tend to the subversion of the Government? and what better grounds should we have for our proceedings? I think the Articles are well drawn; and ought to be engrossed as they are.

Sir *Richard Temple.*

Mr. Speaker, Sir, I cannot admit that Parliaments, by impeachments before the Lords, can make any thing treason, but only such matters as were treason by common law, before the Statute of *Edward* the Third. And, I think, we ought to be so cautious of our posterities, as not to press for such precedents, lest you put into the hands of the Lords a power, for which we may have cause to repent hereafter, but never get back again: For the Lords do not use to part with those Powers they once get. There are precedents by which it appears, that the Lords have attempted to make declarative treasons alone, without any impeachment from the Commons. Have a care how you give them encouragement to proceed therein; better keep to the other way of making no declarative treasons but by Bill.

The Articles were read, and Question put:

Resolved, That the said Sir *William Scroggs* be impeached upon the said Articles; and that the said Articles be ingrossed, and carried up to the Lords by my Lord *Cavendish*.

Ordered, That the Committee appointed to examine the proceedings of the Judges in *Westminster-hall*, and to prepare impeachments against Sir *Francis North*, Chief-Justice of the *Common-Pleas*; Sir *Thomas Jones*, one of the Justices of the Court of *King's-Bench*; and Sir *Richard W*[illegible], one of the Barons of the Court of *Exchequer*, do bring in such impeachments with all convenient speed.

After the Articles were brought into the House of Lords; the Lord Chief-Justice put in the following Answer; viz.

The Answer of Sir *William Scroggs*, Knt. Chief-Justice of his Majesty's Court of *King's-Bench*, to the Articles of Impeachment exhibited against him by the Commons of *England*, in the late Parliament assembled:

"THE said Sir *William Scroggs*, by, and under protestation, that there is "no manner of High-Treason, nor by any Overt-Act of High-Treason particularly alledged or expressed in the said Articles of Impeachment, "to which the said Sir *William Scroggs* can, or is bound by Law to make "any answer unto; and saving to himself, (and which he prayeth may "be saved to him), both now and at all times hereafter, all, and all manner of benefit and advantage of exception to the insufficiency of the "said Articles, in point of law; as well for that there is no overt-act "of treason expressed therein, as for all other the defects therein appearing; for the Plea thereto he saith, That he is in no wise guilty of "all or any the crimes, offences, or misdemeanours, of what nature, kind, "or quality soever, by the said Articles of Impeachment charged upon "him, in manner and form, as in and by the said Articles is supposed; "which he is ready to aver and prove, as this honourable House shall "award, and humbly submitteth himself, and the justice of his cause, "to this most honourable House: and prayeth to be discharged of the "premisses, and to be hence dismissed and acquitted of all the matters, "crimes, misdemeanours, and offences, in and by the said Articles of "Impeachment charged upon him, &c.

"W. Scroggs."

After this, a Petition of Sir *William Scroggs* was read.

To the Right Honourable the Lords Spiritual and Temporal, in this present Parliament assembled; The humble Petition of Sir William Scroggs, *Knt. Chief-Justice of his Majesty's Court of* King's-Bench; *sheweth,*

"THAT your Petitioner, the last Parliament, was impeached before your Lordships, by the House of Commons, of several "Articles stiled High-Treason, and other great Crimes and Misdemeanours.

"To which your Petitioner hath now, with the first opportunity, "put in his answer to this honourable House.

"Your Petitioner humbly prays, that your Lordships would be "pleased to appoint the House of Commons to reply, that so a convenient day may be appointed for the hearing of the Cause; that "your Petitioner may no longer lie under the reproach of the word "High-Treason.

"*And your Petitioner, as in duty bound, shall ever pray,* &c.

"W. Scroggs."

Ordered, That the copy of this Answer and Petition shall be sent to the House of Commons.

But the Parliament being soon after prorogued, this affair was dropped. However, the Lord Chief-Justice was removed from his high Station, and allowed a pension for life.

XXXV. The Report from the Committee of the Commons in Parliament, appointed by th nourable House of Commons, to consider the Petition of *Richard Thompson* of *Bristol*, Clerk to examine Complaints against him. And the Resolution of the Commons in Parliament this Report, for his Impeachment of High Crimes and Misdemeanours; *Friday, Decemb* 1680. 32 *Car.* II.

The Report from the Committee of the Commons in Parliament, appointed to consider the Petition of *Richard Thompson*, and to examine Complaints against him.

At the Committee appointed to take into consideration the Petition of Richard Thompson, *Clerk; and to examine the Complaints against him.*

IN the first place, the Committee read unto the said *Thompson*, the heads of the Complaints against him; which (for the most part) he denying, desired to have his accusers brought face to face: Whereupon the Committee proceeded to the examination of witnesses, to prove the said complaint.

The *first* Witness examined, saith, That there being a great noise and rumour, that Mr. *Thompson* had prepared a Sermon to be preached on the thirtieth of *January*, 1679, the said witness went to the said Sermon, and did hear Mr. *Thompson* publickly declare, that the Presbyterians were such persons, as the very Devil blush'd at them; and that the villain *Hampden* grudged, and made it more scruple of conscience, to give twenty shillings to the King, for supplying his necessities by Ship-money and Loan, which was his right by Law, than to raise Rebellion against him. And that the Presbyterians are worse (and far more intolerable) than either Priests or Jesuits.

The second saith, That hearing a great talk and noise spread of a Sermon to be preached by Mr. *Thompson*, on the 30th of *January*, 1679; he was minded to hear the same, and accordingly did; at which he writ some notes: amongst which, he saith, that Mr. *Thompson* openly preached, that the Devil blush'd at the Presbyterians; and that the villain *Hampden* grudged more to give the King twenty shillings, which was his just due by Law (Ship-money and Loan), than to raise Rebellion against him; and that a Presbyterian Brother, *qua talis*, was as great a Traitor by the Statute, as any Priest or Jesuit whatsoever.

That he heard, that Mr. *Thompson* said, that he hoped the Presbyterians would be pulled out of their houses, and the Gaols filled with them: and wish'd their houses burnt.

The third saith, That he was cited to the Bishop's Court, to receive the Sacrament last *Easter*; but being out of town at that time, did receive it at a place called *Purl* in *Wiltshire*; and that a month after he came home, was again cited to the said Court; and he did accordingly appear, and told the Court, that he hoped his absence and business might be accepted for a lawful excuse; upon which Mr. *Thompson* immediately said, that they would proceed to excommunicate him. Upon which, this Informant produced his certificate, of which the Chancellor approved, and said it was lawful. Hereupon Mr. *Thompson* said, that his receiving the Sacrament from any other Minister, than the Minister of the Parish wherein he dwelled, was damnation to his Soul; and that he would maintain this Doctrine.

The fourth saith, That being at *Bristol*-Fair, he heard a great talk and noise of a Satyr-Sermon prepared, and designed to be preached by Mr. *Thompson* against the Presbyterians, on the 30th of *January*, 1679; and that very many resorted to hear him: in which Sermon, the said Mr. *Thompson* declared and said, that there was a great talk of a plot: but (says he) a Presbyterian is the man; and further added, that the villain *Hampden* scrupled to give the King 20*s.* upon Ship-money and Loan, which was due by Law, but did not scruple to raise Rebellion against him.

The fifth saith, That Mr. *Thompson*, in a Sermon preached the 30th of *January*, 1679, did say, that the Presbyterians did seem to out-vie *Mariana*, and that *Calvin* was the first that preached the *King-killing Doctrine*, and that after he had quoted *Calvin* often, said, if this be true then, a Presbyterian Brother, *qua talis*, is as great a Traitor as any Priest or Jesuit: and that then he condemned all the Proceedings of Parliament.

The sixth saith, That he the said Mr. *Thompson*, had utter'd many scandalous words concerning the Act for *burying in Woollen*; affirming, that the makers of that Law were a company of *old Fools and Fanaticks, and that he would bring a School-boy should make a better Act than that, and construe it when he had done.*

The seventh saith, That Mr. *Thompson* in a Sermon by him preached (while Petitions for the sitting of this Parliament were on foot) speaking of a second Rebellion by the *Scotch*, who had framed a formidable Army, and came as far as *Durham*, to deliver a Petition forsooth, and that they seemed rather to command than petition their Sovereign to grant; and comparing that Petition with the then Petition on foot, greatly inveighed against it, and scoffed much at it.

The eighth saith, That Mr. *Thompson* (when the Petition was on foot for the sitting of this Parliament) used at the Funeral Sermon of one Mr. *Wharton* these words (pointing at the dead, said), that he was no Schismatical petitioning Rebel, and that by his instigations, the Grand-Jury of *Bristol* made a presentment of their detestation against petitioning for the sitting of the Parliament; that the said Mr. *Thompson* had told him, that he was Governor to Mr *Narbor*, when he was beyond Sea; and said, that he had been very often (and above one hundred times) at Mass, in the great Church at *Paris*, and usually gave Half a Crown to get a place to hear a certain Doctor of that Church, and that he was like to be brought over to that Religion, and that when he went beyond Sea, did not know but that he might be of that Religion before his return. That he is very censorious, and frequently casts evil aspersions against several Di *Bristol* of great note, *viz.* Mr. *Chetwind*, Mr. *Standfast*, Mr. (Mr. *Palmer*, and others, saying, that such as went to their Lectur the brats of the Devil.

The ninth saith, That Mr. *Thompson* in his preaching inveighed against subscribing Petitions for sitting of this Parliament, saying, was the seed of Rebellion, and like to Forty-one; and that the L them on work, and the Devil would pay them their wages; sayir before he would set his hand to such Petitions, he would cut it and cut them off.

The tenth saith, That about two years since, being in the Ch St. *Thomas*'s Church in *Bristol*, where Queen *Elizabeth*'s Effigies *Thompson* pointing his finger to it, said, that she was the worst of and a most leud and infamous woman; upon which this Inform plied, he never heard any speak ill of her: thereupon Mr. *Thomps* she was no better than a Church-robber, and that *Hen.* VIII. beg and that she finish'd it.

The eleventh, *Rowe*, saith, That in the year, 1678, he waited Mayor to Church, and that Mr. *Thompson*, who was there, ra *Hen.* VIII. saying, he did more hurt in robbing the Abbey-lands, t did good by the Reformation. That after dinner, Mr. *Thompson* c this Informant, and claps his hands on his shoulders, saying, Hah had Queen *Elizabeth* been living, you needed not to have been bearer of *Bristol*. The said *Rowe* asked him Why? He replied, sh such a lusty Rogue (so well) as he was; and he would have been for her drudgery at *Whitehall*.

The twelfth saith, That he heard a great noise of a Sermon to be preac Mr. *Thompson* on the 30th of *January*, 1679, to the second part of th Tune; and that he was present at the same Sermon, in which Mr. *son* said, there was a great noise of a Popish Plot, but, says he, here thing in it but a Presbyterian Plot; for here they are going about tion for the sitting of the Parliament, but the end of it will be to the King's head to the block, as they have done his father.

The thirteenth saith, That in *January* last, or thereabouts, there Petition going about for the sitting of this Parliament, when Mr. *son*, in *Redcliff* Church, in his Sermon said, it was a seditious and r ous Petition, and rather than he would sign it, his hand should be c

The fourteenth saith, The 8th day of *April*, he going to pay Mr. *son* his dues, speaking concerning the Meeters in private; Mr. *Th* said, he would haul them out, and fill the Gaols with them, and to see their houses a-fire about their ears in a short time; and this said *Thompson*, doubled again and again.

The fifteenth saith, That about *December*, 1679, Mr. *Thompson* ca visit his mother, being sick; and discoursing of Religion, *Thompson* if he were as well satisfied of other things, as he was of justificatio ricular confession, penance, extreme unction, and crism in baptis would not have been so long separated from the Catholick Church. further affirmed, that the Church of *Rome* was the true Catholick Ch He further endeavoured to prove extreme unction, and auricular c sion, as well as he could, out of the Epistles. Further, he hath hear say, the King was a person of a mean and soft temper, and could easily to any thing, but yet a *Solomon* in vices; but that the Duke o was a Prince of a brave Spirit, would be faithful to his Friends, an it was our own faults that he was a *Roman* Catholick, in that we him to fly into *France*, where he embraced that Religion. About the time, he the said *Thompson* said the Church would be militant; but g commended the decency of solemnizing the Mass in *France*; and t was performed with much more reverence and devotion than any Religion doth use. He further heard him say, in a Sermon, abou time of petitioning, he would rather cut off his hand than sign it, an many bad expressions of it; that it was the seed of Rebellion, an Forty and Forty-one. And further, the said Mr. *Thompson*, at one *ford*'s shop-door in *Bristol*, speaking of *Bedloe*, said, that he was not believed, because *Bedloe* had said he, meaning Mr. *Thompson*, was *Omer*'s, where Mr. *Thompson* said he was not; and that *Bedloe* was of life, and in many Plots, and not to be credited in any thing he said. that in another discourse he commended the *Romish* Clergy for their life, and is himself so; and did at the same time vilify and rail at the *lish* Clergy for marrying; saying, it was better for a Clergyman to be than to marry; and that the *Calvinists* in *France* were lecherous tell and could scarce be two years a Priest without a wife. About the t and after the Election of Sir *John Knight* to this Parliament, Mr. *Th son* said, he was not fit to be believed, and as bad as any Fanatick. further said in the Pulpit at St. *Thomas*'s, that after excommunicati the Bishop, without absolution from the Spiritual Court, such a one surely damned; and he would pawn his Soul for the truth of it.

Evidence ended, Mr. *Thompson*, after the Evidence given by every ticular Person, Face to Face, was asked to every one, if he had any q tions to ask before they called another? Who answer'd, he should say any thing at present. When the Witnesses before-ment were all examined, Mr. *Thompson* being desired to make his defe and declare whether he were guilty of the matters laid to his cha did for the greatest part confess words spoken to that effect, an other things endeavoured to turn the words with more favour tow

h

himself; but the witnesses being of great credit, and many more being ready to have made good the same things, the Committee looked upon the business to be of a high nature, and therefore ordered the matter to be reported specially, leaving it to the wisdom of the House.

The Resolution of the House of Commons, upon the said Report.

Resolved, Nemine contradicente,

THAT *Richard Thompson*, Clerk, hath publickly defamed his sacred Majesty, preached Sedition, vilified the Reformation, promoted Popery, by asserting Popish Principles, decrying the Popish Plot, and turning the same upon the Protestants; and endeavoured to subvert the Liberty and Property of the Subject, and the Rights and Privileges of Parliaments; and that he is a scandal and reproach to his function.

And that the said Richard Thompson, *be impeached upon the said Report and Resolution of the House. And a Committee is appointed to prepare the said Impeachment, and to receive further instructions against him; and to send for Persons, Papers, and Records.*

Mercurii, 5 die Januarii, 1680.

A Petition of *Richard Thompson*, Clerk, in custody of the Serjeant at Arms attending this House, was read.

Ordered, That the said Serjeant at Arms be impowered to receive sufficient security, for the forth-coming of the said *Richard Thompson*, to answer to the Impeachment against him.

Jan. 10. 1680. The House was prorogued, which put an end to the intended Impeachment.

XXXVI. The Great Case of MONOPOLIES, between the *East-India* Company, Plaintiffs, and THO. SANDYS, Defendant: Whether their Patent for Trading to the *East-Indies*, exclusive of all others, is good? 35 *Car.* II. 1683.

THE *East-India* Company having a Patent granted them of the sole Trade to the *East-Indies* exclusive of all others, commenced a suit against Mr. *Sandys* for trading thither without licence; in which case, the following Arguments were made, *viz.*

Mr. *Holt* * (afterwards Lord Chief Justice) his Argument.

The Governor and Company of Merchants of *London*, trading to the *East-Indies*, against *Thomas Sandys*, *de Term. Mich.* 35 *Caroli 2di, Rs. Rot.* 126.

THE Defendant comes and prays *Oyer* of the Letters Patent, which are set forth, as we have declared and pleaded.

To this Plea the Plaintiffs have demurred. My Lord, I do conceive the general question in this case, will be this, Whether or no an action lies by the Company upon this Charter; for that the Defendant not being a member of the Company, has traded into the *East-Indies* without licence of the Company? My Lord, I think there may be two questions made in this case, first, Whether or no this Grant of the King to the Company, to have the sole trade to the *Indies*, exclusive of all others his Subjects, whether that be a good Grant? *Secondly*, Supposing it to be a good Grant, yet whether or no it does rest such an interest, liberty or franchise in the Company, that an action may be brought and maintained by them against any person trading to the *East-Indies*; who is not qualified by this Charter? My Lord, for the first, I do humbly conceive that this Charter granted to the Company to have the sole trade to the *Indies* exclusive of all others is a good Grant; and, My Lord, I shall endeavour to make it appear to be a good Grant, from these considerations: *First*, My Lord, from the consideration of the persons that are to be traded withal, and they are infidels, and not Christians. *Secondly*, My Lord, from the consideration of Foreign Trade itself, how and in what nature by Law, it may be restrained by the King's Royal Power. And in the *third* place, consider the circumstances and particulars of this Grant made to the Company in this case.

My Lord, for the first, that does relate to the persons to be traded with, they being Infidels and not Christians; I do conceive that by the law of the land, no subject of *England* can trade with Infidels, without licence from the King; or at least it is in the power of the King to prohibit it, and for this very reason, because Infidels are by the Law taken notice of, and the Law hath adjudged them to be perpetual enemies; the Law hath set a mark upon them, and they are used as all other enemies are. And so, 7 *Rep.* 17. 6. the express words of my Lord *Coke* are in *Calvin's* case; says he, Infidels are perpetual enemies. *Reg.* 282. That sets forth the Writ of Protection, that was given to the Prior and Brothers of the Hospital of St. *John* at *Jerusalem*, that it was used for the defence of the Church, *contra Christi & omnium Christianorum inimicos*, 12 *H.* VIII. 4. If a man do beat a man outlawed, a Traitor, or a Pagan, and they bring an action, he may plead his being a Pagan; and in abatement of his action: I mention this, my Lord, to shew what opinion the Law has of these people, judging of them to be enemies as they are Infidels, and for that reason has excluded them from the benefit of the Law, and the common Justice the Nation affords: and from that it may be inferred, that since the Law hath excluded them from common Justice, surely the Law will not allow an intercourse or intimate correspondence with such persons to the subjects of *England*. And, my Lord, this is grounded upon the care that the Government hath, or ought to have, by the constitution of the Government itself, of the Christian Religion, which I conceive is the main end of Government. The profession and preservation of Christianity is of so high a nature, that of itself it supersedes all Law. if any Law be made against any point of the Christian Religion, that Law is *ipso facto* void. Why? Because it is made against the prime and original end of Government. If the King conquer a Christian Country, their Law continues till it be altered by the King; but if he conquers a Pagan country, the Law ceases *ipso facto* to be Law; for the Law of Infidels is contrary and repugnant to the Christian Religion. Why then, if the Christian Religion have the prevalence in Christian countries, there must be some means provided by the Law, whereby the King may have a power to preserve it: and there is nothing more dangerous to the right Religion, than for the Professors of that Religion to have commerce with Pagans; we read how the Children of *Israel* were perverted from the true Religion, by converse with the Nations round about them, in the book of *Judges*.

And *Grotius de bello & pace, Lib.* 2. *Chap.* 15. *Parag.* 11. says, *Cavendum est enim ne nimia commixturatio contagium adferat infirmis, quamobrem utile erit, Sedes distingui sicut Israelitæ seorsim ab Ægyptiis habitarunt.*

The Government is to take care that there is not an infection, by correspondence with Infidels; my Lord, 'tis not to be doubted but that the King is to have a care of the Christian Religion. In old times of Popery. *Bracton, Lib.* 2. *Ch.* 24. the King of *England*, says he, is *Dei Minister & Vicarius*: & 5. *ch. Bracton, Jus publicum est quod ad Statum.*

This is looked upon to be part of the *Jus publicum*, the care of Religion and sacred things, and the propagation thereof; why then, my Lord, if this be true, then 'tis lawful for the King to take care and use his Royal Authority, to prevent all his subjects from being perverted. My Lord, I think 'tis plain by the Writ of *Ne Exeat Regnum*, that says the King may prohibit any person from going beyond Sea. Why? For the defence of the Realm; that is a sufficient reason, it is not in the power of the party to litigate it with the King, but he must submit. Now always Religion is first to be regarded; *secondly*, The defence of the Kingdom; and *thirdly*, The Trade thereof. Now, my Lord, the subjects of a Christian Prince going to trade with Infidels, being in their company, that may be dangerous to the State and Religion; so that it must necessarily be in the power of the King to controul it. *Hob.* 217. *Courteen's* case, it was adjudged that an Information did lie at the Common Law, before any Statute, against any persons that should transport Coin, because 'tis against the Policy and State of Government that money should be transported; now if it be against the Policy of State to trade with Infidels, by the same reason that ought to be restrained. In the next place, I will consider foreign trade, and whether the subjects of *England* have right to such a foreign trade, that they can *ad libitum* trade without any controul; and I conceive they have not.

First, My Lord, I conceive that the liberty and right of a foreign trade, depends upon agreement and contract with foreign Princes, in whose country the trade is; and if so be it do depend upon agreement and amity with the Prince; then have not the subjects of *England* such an uncontrolable right of trading, because it depends upon the accidents of Peace and War; which, if there were such a right, it could not. 30. *ch. Magna Charta, omnes Mercatores, nisi publice antea prohibiti fuerunt, habeant salvum & securum conductum exire de Anglia & venire in Angliam, & morari & ire per Angliam præterquam in tempore guerræ.* Then he goes on further, if there happen to be War with a foreign Prince, and the Kingdom of *England*, and the Merchants of that Country be found in *England*; this shews that War is an interruption of the Commerce. 12 *H.* VII. *ch.* 6. my Lord, that Statute recites, that the Merchants-Adventurers inhabiting within the city of *London*, and divers parts of *England*, had free passage, &c. into divers parts of *Spain* and other places, that were in league and amity with our Kingdom and Sovereign; so that it appears that league and amity is the foundation of Commerce.

Selden, in his *Mare clausum*, says, the rights of trades are founded on the covenants of Princes; What is the reason? Lest the manners and morals of the people should be corrupted by the example of foreign Nations. My Lord, 2 *Rolls Abr.* 214. mentions the Parliament-roll of 1 *H.* V. wherein it is said, that the Commons did petition the King that the Merchants of *England*, paying their customs and other duties, might have liberty to export their goods to any place or country, notwithstanding any proclamation to the contrary: and the King says he will be advised, he would advise with his Council. My Lord, from that time to this it appears that there was no complaint of the King's proclamation as illegal, that did prohibit their trade; but they only pray that he would make an alteration of the Law. But there were several proclamations at that time to restrain the subject from trading with foreigners (therefore they desire he would consent they might trade); but the King in that

* The Six following Arguments in this *Great Case*, were copied from the MSS. of *Samuel Pepys*, Esq. (Secretary to the Admiralty) in *Magdalen* College, *Cambridge*. These Arguments are of great concern to the Publick in general, and to every individual Man in this Kingdom, either immediately or by consequences, since Trade is the Life of a Nation; and must be of great service to the Professors of the Law, to shew on what grounds and reasons the Case was adjudged. And the Proceedings on the *Quo Warranto*, in *State Trials*, Vol. IV. P. 769. having been found useful to the gentlemen of the Law, is the reason why these Arguments, (tho' not so properly a Trial) spoke by some of the greatest Men that ever appeared at the Bar, are here inserted.

The Arguments of *Holt*, *Treby*, *Finch*, *Pollexfen*, and *Sawyer*, are very briefly abridged in *Skinner's Reports*. But the Arguments of Mr *Williams*, and the Lord Chief Justice *Jeffreys*, are not mentioned there.

case did think fit to part with his power, but gives the usual answer in such cases. My Lord, in the next place it is necessary for the King to have power to restrain a foreign trade, because a foreign trade, as the case may be, may be very inconvenient and mischievous: for 'tis well known, that if so be the importation of foreign Commodities do exceed the exportation of domestic, that trade is rather a grievance than a benefit; so 'tis said, 2 *Inst.* 325. and, my Lord, there has been sufficient appearance of this matter of late days.

My Lord, the importation of *Irish* cattle, by the 18th of this King, *chap* 2. was declared to be a nuisance. So the 29th of King *Charles* I. the importation of *French* Commodities: why this, my Lord, is declared, the Statute does not enact it, but declares it to be in itself a common nuisance: why now, if so be a trade come to be a nuisance, that it is rather hurtful than advantageous; the King, by virtue of his prerogative, is to defend the Nation, and protect his Subjects from these evils; he has a power to restrain these evils, especially when we have the judgment of the Parliament, by whom these things have been declared to be nuisances, 10 *Rep.* 141. In the case of the Isle of *Ely*, the first Statute that was made concerning Sewers, was in *H.* VI's time; there was a question, that since there was a thing so necessary as the taking care of the Inundation with remedy there before any Statute, says the book, the King by his prerogative, as the Fountain of Justice, might take care of it, though there was no Statute then. My Lord, when foreign commodities come to be an annoyance to the people, the Law must be defective, if the King had not a power to restrain them. But in this case here 'tis only a regulation of Trade, a grant of it to the Company, and 'tis only specified how they shall manage that Trade, to the intent all people might trade under the Government as they ought to do: and I think, my Lord, it is well known, that if this Company had not settled and established a Trade in the *Indies*, Mr. *Sandys*, nor none of these Gentlemen could have had an opportunity to do it. And if they have liberty to interfere with the Company, they would ruin the Company, and they themselves could not trade; but I know what objections will be made against me, even by the Defendants Plea. My Lord, that 18 *E.* III. *ch.* 3. to-wit, that the Sea shall be open to all Merchants to part with their Merchandize where they please; which, with submission to your Lordships, cannot be taken so universally as they themselves would have it. For if you will take the words to be so large, without any manner of restraint, you will make this Statute to give liberty of trade to the King's enemies, for they are Merchants. But, my Lord, the next answer I give to it is this; I conceive the true meaning of the Statute is, that the Sea should be open without paying any extraordinary duties but what might justly be imposed: that is, that none should pay any duty or custom for Navigation, but only the due custom, that is, when they come into Port. And so I must compare that Statute with *Magna Charta*, 30 *ch. omnes Mercatores nisi publicè antea prohibiti fuerint, habeant salvum & securum conductum exire de Anglia & venire in Angliam*, &c. *sine malis tolnetis*; so that they have liberty allowed in this case to trade without unlawful exactions. But, my Lord, in the third place, supposing this Statute to be taken as general, as I know the other side endeavours it should, yet it cannot extend to this case; for I think they can hardly make it out, that at that time there was any trade drove with Infidels, but the trade was drove with Christians: why now, if there was not such a trade had at the making of that Statute, we must not extend the Law to this case, which differs from the reason of trade in other cases. That there was none, I think appears plainly by History; *Hollingshed*'s History of *England*, 163, whereas, says he, in times past, the chief trade was in *Holland*, *Portugal*, &c. now, says he, men not being content with those journeys, they have sought out the *East* and *West-Indies*, and have made now and then suspicious Voyages. And it appears by the Statute of *H.* VII. that I mentioned before, that the ancient trade of *England* consisted with near Countries, and so the trade was at the time of the making of this Statute.

My Lord, I do observe as to the Case I reported before, when the Commons did petition the King, that they might have liberty to trade notwithstanding any proclamation, *Rolls Abr.* 214. they were not of an opinion at that time, that this Statute did extend to Merchants, to give them liberty to trade every where at their will and pleasure; if they had, they would have insisted upon it, and urged it to the King, that whereas there was a Statute gave them free liberty, therefore desire the law might be observed: but they do not deny, no, they tacitly acknowledge the King had such a power.

My Lord, it does appear what the ancient trade of *England* was by the Customs; for at the Common Law there was no Custom but in three things, Wool, Woolfell and Leather; these are the Customs that were due to the King by Common Law: indeed, there was foreign Custom, but that was for a foreign commodity, and was prize; *Dyer* 165. 2 *Inst.* 52, & 43. *Davies*, *Rep.* 8.

Now, my Lord, if so be the trade of the Nation had consisted of other commodities, it may be supposed, there would have been custom paid for them afterwards, in *Ed.* III's time. when new Trades were introduced, we find Acts of Parliament made for raising new Custom; therefore since no Custom was paid, but these ancient Customs, we may suppose the trade of the Nation mostly consisted of these commodities. *Dalton*, [illegible] 85. *Dyer* 165. Merchants as well as others may be prohibited from going out of the land, or any person whatsoever and *Davies*, *Rep. fol.* 9 *b.* gives one reason why the King did permit the Merchants to trade, when it was in his power by Writ of *Ne exeat Regnum*, or proclamation, to put a stop to them.

My Lord, in many cases, when the doing of an Act may be to the public detriment, the King hath power to restrain it, and it cannot be done without the King's licence. *Co. Litt. fol.* 5. a Subject can't build a Castle, or other fortress defensible, without licence of the King; why? because it may be dangerous. Why then should a Subject trade with an Infidel Country, without licence from the King? for by trading with Infidels they endanger their Religion. And therefore, as it requires licence to build a Castle, tho' a man otherwise might lawfully do it upon his own ground, so for the same reason does it to trade with Infidels. 11 *Rep.* 87. *b.* 2 *Inst.* 199. A man cannot inclose his ground to make a Park without licence of the King, tho' in that case he takes nothing from any body, but such inclosing and turning profitable ground into a place of pleasure, may be of public conse-

quence, and therefore cannot be done without the Ki[ng] 11 *H.* VII 23. If two men play at sword and buckler, an[d] other, that is felony; but if they play with licence of the Ki[ng] felony; so that the King hath power to prohibit, and by [his] make that unlawful, that otherwise would be lawful. For t[he] command a man, by his Writ, to stay in the Kingdom, and if h[e] to the King's Writ or Proclamation, in that case the King m[ay] Lands for the contempt, as in the case of Sir *Francis Inglefi[eld]* the King may govern the trade of the Nation in regard it m[ay] vous, the King may hinder it, when it will be apparently m[ischievous].

In the third place, I shall consider the Grant; and the Gr[ant] things in it: 'Tis a Grant to a Company, that they and their trade to the *Indies*, notwithstanding any statute or diversity of [re]ligion; and that they should have the sole commerce and trade is a prohibition to any of the King's subjects to trade there wit[hout] Now, my Lord, this Grant I take to be good; for, my Lord not in itself be lawful without the King's licence, yet it is in the King to make it so. And for this reason can the King ma[ke a] denizen.

The reason of the Law, why an Alien is uncapable to pu[rchase] here, is because 'tis against the policy of the Land for to suffer to come into *England*, and enrich himself with the lands and g[oods of the] Kingdom, yet the King may cure this incapacity; but notwit[hstanding he] be made a Denizen, yet does he remain an Alien still, and sub[ject to the] Prince from whence he came; *Dyer*, 3 *ch. B.* So that notwit[hstanding it] may be dangerous for an Alien to have land, yet the King is en[abled to do] it, and he may give this Alien liberty to purchase land.

My Lord, it is, as I have observed, unlawful to transport [money out of] *England*; yet the King may give leave to transport Coin, as th[e pre]cedent 5 *Car.* I. of a licence to transport 10,000 *l.* So, my L[ord,] trading with Infidels, tho' in itself it's against the policy of t[he Govern]ment; that is, for the subject to have an uncontroulable liberty [to trade at] their pleasure; yet the King, who is entrusted with the admi[nistration of] the Government, may give authority to do it. And there is a g[reat] difference between trading in a Company, and trading out of a [Company;] if they trade in a Company, they trade under the Government [of England;] if they trade out of a Company, then they trade out of the Gov[ernment of] *England*, and out of its protection. This Company is incorporate[d] to have the Government of this trade; they being Christians, n[ay] are to take care of the Christian Religion; and to take care th[eir A]gents and Factors that trade under this constitution, keep up to [their Reli]gion they profess; but certainly it is quite another thing when p[ersons go] of their own head; there they converse only with Infidels, they c[annot have] Divine Offices.

My Lord, it has been objected; Oh, but say they, if the King [may give li]cence to some, tho' they cannot do it without the King's licenc[e; the] King having dispensed with this Law, this dispensation shall ha[ve a uni]versal influence, and give licence to others.

My Lord, it seems to me a very strange inference; they ack[nowledge] that make this objection, that without the King's licence, beyo[nd this, the case] is, where the King hath qualified his Grant solely to the Com[pany and] their Factors, they would have it extend to all the people of *E[ngland].* [I] think 'tis the first time that ever the King's licence, or authori[ty the King] gives, should be extended beyond itself. But, my Lord, the gr[eat objec]tion will be, that this is a Monopoly, and therefore the Grant [against] Law; with submission, I think it is none; and I hope I have said [enough] already to prove it to be none, and it does not come within the de[finition of] a Monopoly, 3 *Instit.* 181. A Monopoly is an institution or all[owance by] the King, by his Grant, Commission or otherwise, to any person o[r persons,] bodies politick or corporate, of or for the sole buying, selling, [making,] working or using of any thing; whereby any person or persons, b[odies po]litic or corporate, are sought to be restrained of any freedom or li[berty that] they had before, or hindered in their lawful trade: restrained of th[at which] they had before, that I think they cannot make out, that they eve[r had] such freedom. They cannot make out that they were in possessi[on of this] trade before, therefore this Charter does not restrain them of any [liberty] they had; then say they, it hinders others lawful trade.

My Lord, I have made it appear, that the trading with Infidels [without] licence of the King is not a lawful trade. But to go further, tho' [the proof] lies on their side, they having the affirmation; yet I hope to give [evi]dence, as is even as much as can be expected in any case. In th[e 43d of] Queen *Elizabeth*, a Parliament was sitting at *Westminster*, and at [that] time there was a Charter granted to this Company; and a Charter [with] these very words, of having the sole trade exclusive of others; and [there had] been another Charter granted before of having the sole trade, 27 [of the] Queen. Now in this Parliament, 43d of the said Queen, the Pa[rliament] fell very vigorously against Monopolies, and brought in a great cat[alogue of] them. But, my Lord, I do observe, that in all the catalogue, [and in all] the debates of Parliament at that time, there's not one word men[tioned of] the *East India* Company's Charter, neither of the Charter of t[he 27th of] the Queen, nor of the Charter of that very Parliament, nay, th[ere] is much as mention made of the Charter granted to any other C[ompany.] My Lord, I have this from a Book that is lately come out, *Town[shend's Col]lection of Proceedings in Parliament*, 244, 245. there is the whole c[atalogue of] Monopolies, and the full debate of them; but as for any Charter[s of Cor]porations, tho' there were many at that time, there is not the least [mention.]

My Lord, between the 43d of the Queen, and the 20th of King [James, was] about twenty-three years; in the 43d of the Queen, the discourse of [Mono]polies first began in Parliament; and they were considering, it may [be sup]posed, all this time, how to settle the matter of Monopolies, and to [define] what were Monopolies. And after all this long consideration, and [so much] agitation as it had, they came to make the Statute of 21 *Jac.* wh[ich was] to be a settling and bounding the prerogative of the Crown, and rig[ht of the] subject, it does condemn Monopolies, and has these words, all M[onopo]lies, and all Commissions for the sole buying, &c. or using of any thi[ng with]in the King's Dominions, why that is condemned. But, my Lord [it does] appear that the Parliament were so far from condemning the Charte[r of this] Company, or the Charter of any other Company, that there is an proviso that the Statute of Monopolies should not extend to any Company for the ordering or managing of trade, tho' I think the words of the Statute did not reach this case, yet they were so careful, that they would have a proviso to save this and all other Companies. And, my Lord, there is a Statute, 3 *Jac. cap.* 6. by the preamble of which Statute it appears that the King had granted a Charter to divers Merchants to be a Company, and to have the sole trade into *Spain* and *Portugal*, excluding all others that were not members. The Statute recites the mischief of liberty to all the King's subjects to trade there: I observe, the Parliament did not condemn the Charter to be unlawful, but took it to be good, and that nothing less than an Act of Parliament could restore the liberty of trade to the subjects against the Charter; for they do say, notwithstanding the Charter had given the sole right of trade to the Company, yet it should be lawful for all people to trade there, notwithstanding that Charter. Now, my Lord, I do think that practice and usage is a great evidence of the Law: I shall shew your Lordship some precedents of some Charters, that have been granted to persons of a sole trade exclusive of others. 6 *Feb.* 26 *Eliz.* she granted to *Abraham Gilbert* and his associates the sole trade to *China*, prohibiting others. 6 *March*, 27 *Eliz.* there is a Patent to Sir *Walter Raleigh* to discover new Countries that were heathenish and under Infidels. 11 *Sept.* 23 of her Reign, there was a Patent to divers *Turkey*-Merchants to have the sole trade to *Turkey*, excluding all others. 1*st* of *Jan.* 34th of the Queen, a Charter granted to the *Turkey*-Company. 5 *July*, 27th of the Queen, there were Letters Patents granted to certain Noblemen and Gentlemen to trade into *Barbary*, and that during twelve years none should trade there, but they, their Agents and Assigns. 30 *Eliz.* a Patent made to the Merchants of *Exeter* to have the sole trade to Rivers of in *Guinea*; 34th of the Queen, another Patent to *Gregory* and *Pope*, to have the sole trade to *Guinea*. My Lord, all these I have now quoted, I have caused to be examined on the Rolls, and are to be found there. 2. *Brownlow*, 296. there it was held by my Lord *Coke*, that no subject ought to trade to an Infidel Country without licence of the King, for fear of being perverted from the Christian Religion; this my Lord *Coke* says, and he says he had seen an ancient precedent of a licence. *More* 675, *Darcy* and *Allen*. Justice *Dodderidge* (that I think was only then Serjeant) argues against the Patent, but he did agree that a Grant to a Company to have the sole trade with Infidels is a good Grant, and the King by his prerogative might restrain his subjects from it: he admits a Patent for sole Printing was good; why, because the Publick was concerned; My Lord, the Parliament of late time have been so far from looking upon the *East-India* Company to be a Monopoly, that they have declared it to be for the good of the Kingdom; 14th of this King, *chap.* 24. in the preamble 'tis recited.

Now, my Lord, I hope I have made good, that the King has this power both by precedents, by authorities, and opinions of Lawyers; and also the judgment and the opinion of the Parliament: And that it was never condemned, and so I conclude this first point. The second point, my Lord, in the next place, which I shall be very short upon, for that it will be consequential to what I have endeavoured to prove before; that is supposing it to be a good Grant, whether if any person do trade to the damage of the Company, 'tis a good ground for an action.

First, I do think the Company have, and 'tis very plain they have an inheritance, and 'tis a franchise and liberty they could not have, unless they had the King's Grant, and others excluded from it; then it does agree with all the cases of this nature; wherever the King grants a franchise to one, and another person violates the franchise, the King's Patentee may have an action of the case, against the person that does interfere or violate the franchise. 22 *H.* VI. 14. 11 *H.* IV. 47. supposing the King grant a man a Fair or Market, if any man set up another Fair or Market, tho' with the licence of the King, yet he that has the Grant shall have an action. Now the *East-India* Company are to be at great charges, nay, there is a trust reposed in them, that they shall trade, and carry on this trade for the good of the Company; so that they are put into a trade, and are obliged to carry it on. The Defendant hath no right; if they have a right, they shall have a remedy against any that invade it. And for these reasons

I pray your Judgment for the Plaintiffs.

Sir *George Treby* (afterwards Lord Chief-Justice) his Argument.

The Governor, and Company of Merchants of *London*, trading into the *East-Indies*, against *Thomas Sandys*. *Trin.* 35 *Caroli Secundi Reg. Rot.* 126.

May it please your Lordship,

I AM of Counsel in this case with *Thomas Sandys*, the Defendant. The Case arises upon a Charter set forth by the Plaintiffs, and a Statute pleaded by us; and it is as Mr. *Holt* has opened it. Only I shall, for my purpose, open it a little more than he did.

It is a special action on the case, declarative; wherein the Plaintiffs declare, that King *Charles* II. our present King, by his Letters Patents, bearing date the 3d of *April*, in the 13th year of his reign, reciting that the Governor and Company of Merchants trading into the *East-Indies*, had been of long time a corporation, and enjoyed divers liberties, privileges and immunities, by virtue of divers Letters Patents, and Charters, granted to them by Q. *Elizabeth* and King *James*; and the King being informed, that divers disorders and inconveniencies were then lately committed, to the great prejudice of the said Company, and interruption of their trade: Whereupon they had humbly besought the King, to grant and confirm their said Charter, with some alterations and additions, tending to the advancement and benefit of their trade.

The King gives and grants to them, that they shall be a corporation perpetual, to have succession and capacity, &c. And further willed and granted, that they, and every one that was, or should be of the Company, and their sons at their several ages of 21, and their apprentices, factors, and servants employed by them, might and should freely traffick, and use the trade of merchandize by sea, by such ways and passages then found and discovered, as they should think fittest, into and from the *East-Indies*; and into and from the Islands, Ports, Havens, Cities, Creeks, Towns and Places of *Asia*, *Africa*, or *America*, or any of them, beyond the Cape of *Bona Esperanza*, to the Streights of *Magellan*, as by the Court of the Company shall from time to time be limited and agreed, without any molestation, impeachment or disturbance; any statute, usage, diversity of religion or faith, or any other cause or matter whatsoever notwithstanding, so always the same trade be not undertaken, or addressed, to any Country, Island, Port, Haven, City, Creek, Town, or Place, already in the lawful and actual possession of any such Christian Prince or State, as at this present is, or at any time hereafter shal be in league or amity with the King, his heirs or successors, and who doth not, or will not accept of such trade.

And further grants, That they and their successors, and their factors, servants, and assignees, in the trade of merchandize for them, and in their behalf, shall for ever hereafter have, use and enjoy, the whole, entire and only trade and traffick, and the whole, entire, and only liberty, use and privilege of trading and trafficking, and using the feat and trade of merchandizing, to and from the said *East-Indies*; and to and from all the Islands, Ports, Havens, Cities, Towns and Places aforesaid.

And further grants to them, that the said *East-Indies*, or the Islands, &c. shall not be visited, frequented or haunted by any of his subjects, during the time that these Letters Patents remain in force, contrary to the true meaning of the said Letters Patents, and the virtue of the prerogative Royal. Charging also and commanding, and prohibiting all other subjects, that none of them visit, haunt, frequent, or trade, traffick or adventure by way of merchandizing into or from any part of the said *East-Indies*, &c. unless it be by and with the licence and agreement of the Company, in writing first had and obtained under the common seal.

Here the declaration makes a break, or stop, and so it would seem as if the restraint and prohibition were absolute and general; but upon *Oyer* prayed of the Letters Patents, they being set forth *in hæc verba*, it appears to be, *sub modo*, under the following penalty, *viz.* Upon pain that every such other person or persons, that shall trade to or from the *East-Indies*, shall incur the King's Indignation, and forfeiture and loss of the goods, merchandizes, and other things whatsoever, which so shall be brought into this Realm of *England*, or any the dominions of the same. As also the Ship and Ships, with the furniture thereof, wherein such goods, merchandizes and other things, shall be brought or found, the one half of all the said forfeitures to be to the King, his heirs and successors; the other half to the Company. And further, all and every the said offenders, for the said contempt, to suffer imprisonment during the King's pleasure; and such other punishments as to the King, his heirs and successors, for so high a contempt, shall seem meet and convenient; and not to be in any wise delivered, until they and every of them shall become bound to the Governor, in the sum of 1000*l.* at least; at no time then after to sail or traffick into any part of the said *East-Indies*, &c. And further grants, That the Company may grant and give licence under the common seal, to any persons to sail and traffick to the *East-Indies*; and that the King, his heirs and successors, will not, during the Letters Patents, give licence to any person to sail or trade there.

By virtue of which Letters Patents they alledge they have been, and are a corporation; and have had, established and managed, and do still manage a great trade of merchandize to the said *East-Indies*, with the inhabitants there; who at the time of making the said Letters Patents, or since, were not Christians, nor subjects to any Christian Prince or State; but were, and are infidels and enemies of the Christian faith; and have spent and laid out many and great sums of money on that occasion.

And further say, that the commerce and trade aforesaid cannot be established, managed or carried on but *per hujusmodi Corpus Corporatum*, by such a Corporation; and that they ought to have and enjoy the sole trade there, according to the form and effect of the said Letters Patents.

But the said *Thomas Sandys* being a subject of the King, and no member of the Company, nor son, apprentice, factor, servant, or assignee, sufficiently knowing the premises, and designing to prejudice the Company, contrary to the form and effect of the said Letters Patents, after the making the same, and after the Company had settled their trade, 19 *Jan.* 34 *Reg.* did trade into the *East-Indies*, within the Parts, Regions, and Places above-specified, beyond the promontory of *Good-Hope*, on this side the Streights of *Magellan* aforesaid, in certain Ports and Places, called *Atcheen*, *Mechlopotan*, and *Porto Nova*, with a certain Ship, called the *Expectation*, without the licence, and against the will of the Governor and Company, and to the prejudice, impoverishment, and manifest grievance, and against the form and effect of the said Letters Patents; to the damage of the plaintiffs 1000*l.*

The Defendant prays *Oyer* of the Letters Patents; whereupon they are set forth *in hæc verba*.

And thereupon the Defendant pleads the Statute, 18 *Ed.* III. *Cap.* 3. whereby 'tis enacted, *That the Sea be open to all manner of Merchants, to pass with their merchandize where it shall please them.*

Upon this the Plaintiffs demur.

My Lord, I shall not differ with Mr. *Holt* in the state of the controversy, but make the same two points, *viz.* 1. Whether this Patent, as it purports an exclusion of all other subjects from this trade, be good or void? 2. Whether here be an apt suit brought?

In the first place, I shall not question but the Patent is good, to make these persons a corporation, and all the privileges and benefits they can derive from being a body corporate, they may enjoy, and apply them to trade if they will. Yet as to this particular, I shall observe thus much, that when such Charters of Incorporation were first taken notice of in Q. *Elizabeth*'s and K. *James*'s time, they did not escape the censure of learned men, who foresaw the ill use of them. *Co. Mag. Char.* 540. Three things which have fair pretences are mischievous: 1. New Courts; 2. New Offices; 3. New Corporations trading into foreign Parts, or at home; which under the fair pretence of order and government, in conclusion tend to the hindrance of trade and traffick, and in the end produce Monoplies.

1. *Rolls Rep.* 126. Justice *Dodderidge* says, these things would overthrow the Realm.

In this argument I am sensible I am to speak of a tender point, *the King's Prerogative:* But I shall treat it with that regard and deference that I ought, and as our Books teach us.

The prerogative is great; but it has this general and just limitation, That nothing is to be done thereby that is mischievous or injurious to the subject.

Finch's Law, 81, 83, 84. speaks highly of it, as a matter divine: *The King* (says he) *carries God's stamp, and has the shadow of God's excellencies given him; the power of God is always joined with justice; for to do wrong, is not omnipotence, but weakness. So it is with the King; he can be no wrong-doer, he is all justice; therefore he has a prerogative in all things that are not injurious to the subject, as he may create Corporations,* &c. (says he). And so say I, he may create Corporations, and this Corporation; but for the same reason, he cannot add a restraint to all other subjects from exercising this trade.

I shall lay for my foundation, that this Patent, as to restraining the trade, and excluding all other subjects, has the nature of a Monopoly, and is therefore void in that particular.

Mr. *Holt* and I are agreed on the description of a Monopoly, which is made by my Lord *Coke, Pla. Coron.* 181, *viz.* an Institution by the King, by his grant, commission, or otherwise, to any person, or corporations, of or for the sole buying, selling, making, working or using of any thing whereby any persons or corporations are sought to be restrained of any freedom or liberty they had before, or hindered in their lawful trade.

And the like description is made in the preamble of the Act concerning Monopolies, 21 *Jac. cap.* 3. where it is also declared, That all grants of Monopolies, and all other matters or things whatsoever, any way tending to the instituting, erecting, strengthening, furthering or countenancing of the same, are altogether contrary to the laws of this Realm, and utterly void, and of no effect; and in no wise to be put in use or execution.

If therefore this trade to the *East-Indies* be a lawful trade, then this Patent for the restraining it must be a Monopoly. The nature of a Monopoly consists in restraining a common right; it appropriates to one, or a few, what others had the lawful use of before.

I confess, I did a little wonder to hear merchandizing to the *East-Indies* objected against as an unlawful trade, and did not expect so much divinity in the argument; but to that I shall endeavour to answer by and bye.

Generally speaking, merchandizing was always reckoned a lawful trade; every man might use the sea, and trade with other Nations as freely as he might use the air.

And for this trade to the *East-Indies*, it was lawfully used before there was a Company, or else there had never been a Company. This trade has been long, but this Company is made by these Letters Patents 22 years ago.

This is not distinguished, nor distinguishable from the reasons and rules laid down in the other cases of Monopolies.

I shall chiefly insist upon two cases in one Book, *Coke* 11 *Rep.* the Taylor of *Ipswich* his case, *fol.* 53. and *Darcy* and *Allen*'s case, called the case of Monopolies, *fol.* 86. It is the main ground of both those cases, that at Common-Law no man could be prohibited to exercise his trade, for that is an avoidance of Idleness, it helps to provide sustenance for a man and his family; and 'tis a service to the King: and the consequences of restraining trade are pernicious, as raising prices of commodities and impoverishing men, bad commodities, &c.

Now that foreign trade was understood to be comprehended under this general resolution, I desire your Lordship to look upon the report of the Taylor of *Ipswich*'s case, in 1 *Rolls rep.* 4. where it is said, that no trade of Merchandize can be hindered by Patent, and a Charter to hinder trade at Sea is void; as that a hundred men shall have the sole trade, or the like.

The King's prerogative cannot make this good; it is not lawful for a man to restrain himself from his trade, 5 *Moor* 242. 2 *Leon.* 210. a bond not to use his trade of a Dyer or a Smith is void, so a bond not to plough his land.

And so a bond that a man shall not go out of his house, for a man must serve the King, and do his duty with his liberty and his labour; and if Merchants and Mariners should enter into a bond or a covenant not to trade, or not to trade to the *East-Indies*, it were void. And if it be unlawful for a man to restrain himself from it, the King cannot restrain him.

Another reason is, the King cannot by his Letters Patents take away the subjects property, and I do not know a greater property than freedom of trade and labour; the King cannot take away six-pence that a man has got by his trade, much less can he take away his whole trade: if the profit which a man gets by his trade be his own, the liberty whereby he acquires it is his own, otherwise the whole property of traders were precarious.

Mr. *Holt* would expound the Statutes that are pleaded, to signify that the King shall not lay an imposition upon Merchandize. Though that be not the true meaning of the Statute, yet even that were sufficient for our purpose, and will prove that the King cannot totally prohibit a man to trade, for if he can prohibit absolutely, he can prohibit *sub modo*, and require that none shall trade unless they pay so much and so much for licence; and so by that means he might lay that imposition, which, it is agreed, he cannot.

In *Darcy*'s Patent there was a rent of a hundred marks *per annum* reserved to the Queen; and they that drew, and they that argued that Patent, supposing the Grant of the sole trade to have been good, made no doubt of the consequence, that the reservation was good.

It is truly said by my Lord *Coke, Co. Mag. Cha* 47, & 63. that all Monopolies concerning trade and traffick, are against the Common Law, and divers Statutes; and 'tis as truly said by him, *Co. Placita Coronæ*, 182. that though these Monopolies were ever without Law, yet they were never without friends.

Several attempts have been made for them; Mr. *Holt* has cited some; for the most part, they lurked private, sometimes they have appeared in Courts of Justice, but there they have always been disappointed.

Rot. Parl. 50 *Ed.* III. *nu.* 33. It appears there had been a Patent granted to one *Peachy* for the sole selling sweet Wine in *London:* this concerned a thing of delicacy, and was a matter of small moment then; yet the Patent was brought into Parliament, and adjudged vo party punished.

Co. Mag. Charta 61. and *Pla. Cor.* 182. A Patent granted and *Mary* (in respect of *Philip*'s landing there) that all Malm be imported at *Southampton*, and not elsewhere, adjudged void. was the College of Physicians erected by Letters Patents; wh was a clause, that none without their allowance, should practi in, or within seven Miles compass of *London*. *Coke*'s 8. *Rep* Dr. *Bonham*'s case, but they were well advised that that cla Letters Patents was void; and therefore 16 *H.* VIII. they pr Act of Parliament to make good their Letters Patents; and reason of making that Act, was to give that force to that restra could not be by the Letters Patents only.

15th *Jacobi*, was granted a Patent for sole printing of Law- validity of which happened to come in question in 1668, in between the Patentees and some Booksellers, who had acquired Law-books to be printed, and it was referred to all the Judges.

Many specious reasons were given to maintain it; as, that t tion of Printing was new, that it concerned the State, and w of public care; that it was in the nature of a Proclamation, could make Proclamations but the King. That the King had ing of Serjeants and Officers, and Judges of Law; that they we in a particular language and character, with abbreviations, &c. was the opinion of all the Judges certified to my Lord-Keeper, t persons who had acquired Copies since the Patent, could not be by the Patent from printing them.

Lord Chief-Justice. It received another Judgment in the House

Sir *George Treby*. Not this case, my Lord.

But besides the Common-Law, our point is most strongly e by particular Statutes, and it has been the wisdom and care of and Parliaments in all times to assert this freedom of trade.

Magna Charta, cap. 30. All Merchants (if they were not ope hibited before) shall have their safe and sure conduct to depart, c tarry, to buy and sell without any manner of evil toll, by the rightful customs, except in time of War.

It is true, as Mr. *Holt* says, that this provides against *Mal* but 'tis plain too, that it establishes their liberty of trading, and and going with their Merchandize.

My Lord *Coke* says, indeed, that this respects Aliens only, b strongly proves that the *English* had this liberty; for they wou have extended it to Aliens, and have left the *English* without it.

From this exception *(nisi antea publicè prohibiti fuerint)* it canno ferred that the King may restrain his subjects from trade; for n *Coke*, in his *Comment. fol.* 57. says, that this prohibition must be i by Act of Parliament, for that it concerns the whole Realm, an plied by the word *publicè*.

Besides that, this prohibition must relate to Aliens only, a likely in respect of War too.

Subsequent Statutes make it most clear. 2 *Edw.* III. *cap.* 9. chants, Strangers shall go and come with their Merchandize. 6 *(Stat.* 1.) *cap.* 1. all Merchants, Strangers and others, may fre and sell their commodities, from whencesoever they come, with terruption; notwithstanding Charters or Usage to the contrary. Charters and Usage (if any be) the King, Lords and Commons be of no force, as being to the damage of the King and his grea and the oppression of the Commons.

14 *Ed.* III. (*Stat.* 2) *cap.* 2. All Merchants, Aliens, Denize Foreigners (except those which be of enmity) may without let, with their Merchandize, tarry and return.

25 *Edw.* III. (*Stat.* 4.) *cap.* 2. If any Charter, Proclamation, mand, Usage, Allowance or Judgment be made to the contrary, i be void.

28 *Ed.* III. *(Stat.* 1.) *cap.* 2. establishes the like freedom, as time of that King's Progenitors, and there is used the word *English* chants, as in other Statutes the word Denizens.

I observe that it was then looked upon as an ancient right, it been in the time of his Progenitors.

2 *R.* II. *cap.* 1. 11 *R.* II. *cap.* 7. and 16 *R.* II. *cap.* 1. are like purpose.

When there has been occasion to prohibit any Merchandize, been done by Acts of Parliament.

27 *H.* VI. *cap.* 1. confirmed 28 *H.* VI. *cap.* 1. prohibits Mer dize, growing or wrought within the Dominions of the Duke of *gundy*, and the like, 4 *E.* IV. *cap.* 5. till that Duke revoked his P mation concerning our cloths.

3 *E.* IV. *cap.* 4. Forbids importing woollen caps, cloths, laces and many other Statutes of like nature; whereof some in his p Majesty's reign, as concerning *Irish* cattle, *French* goods, and conce our Foreign Plantations. all which were vain and needless, if the alone could have restrained the same.

26 *H.* VIII. *cap.* 10. Gives power to the King, during his life, strain or set at liberty traffick beyond Sea for certain Countries. *Henry* the VIIIth. as my Lord *Coke* (*Inst. co.* 361.) observes, sto high upon his prerogative, as ever any King had done; and would have accepted his power from a Grant of Parliament, if he had h prerogative of this nature before.

35 *Eliz. cap.* 7. It is enacted that the Queen may prohibit transpo of corn by proclamation; and so it is 1 *Jac. cap.* 25. which shews t proclamation, which is an Act of Prerogative, was not sufficient fo purpose, without the authority that was derived upon it from the Ac Parliament.

My Lord, I shall now answer Mr. *Holt*'s Arguments and Allegatio

First, He says, that, by the Law of the land, no subject can trade Infidels without the King's licence.

But I say, this is *gratis dictum*, and I must deny the Law to be He cannot find any Statute, Judgment or Resolution in all our books to this purpose.

All the authority he has is a casual saying of a single Judge in *M born*'s case.

For in *Darcy* and *Allen*'s case, there is not a word spoken by *Dodderi* or any other, concerning trade with Infidels.

Dodderidge says nothing of foreign trade; cites and affirms the Law of *Mag. Charta*, *cap.* 30.

Michelborn's case is in 2*d Brownlow* 296. and it is in these words: *Hill.* 7 *Jacobi*, in the Common Bench, upon a motion made for consultation, upon a prohibition awarded, it was said by the Lord *Coke*, that no subject of the King may trade with any Infidels without licence of the King; and the reason of that is, he may relinquish the Catholick Faith and adhere to Infidelism. And he said, he had seen a licence made in the time of *Edw.* III. where the King recited, that he having a special trust and confidence that his subjects will not decline from his Faith and Religion, licensed him *ut supra*; and this did arise upon a recital of a licence, made to a Merchant to trade to the *East-Indies*.

First, To this slender authority I answer,

If the Law had been according to this conceit, there would have been much said and done about it in divers cases; there would have been proceedings against persons that had traded to *Granada*; (of which the *Moors* lost the Dominion within these 200 years) to *Barbary*, to *Turky*, and other Infidel places in *Asia*, *Africa*, or *America*, but we never heard or read of any till now.

Secondly, 'Tis an apocryphal case; that Book, called *Brownlow*, is of little authority; it was printed without approbation of the Judges, or any legal licence.

And the conceipt is of less authority, it is reported as *dictum obiter*, upon a motion, a casual saying of the Judge; which the Clerk took, and likely mistook, for it is nowhere said in my Lord *Coke*'s own Books, though they are voluminous. And the ground of his saying (if he did say) it is, that he had seen a licence in *Edw.* III's time, but I cannot learn that it has been seen by any man else. Neither Mr. *Holt* nor I can find it, nor does my Lord *Coke* tell us where it was; perhaps it was taken upon trust, and mistaken, perhaps not authentick, and perhaps a sufficient answer to it would have been found in it; however, it was but one, and certainly, if the Law had required it, there would have been more than one licence from the beginning of our Records till that day.

Una Hirundo, &c.

Thirdly, The reason there given makes strongly against this Charter; the reason is, lest men should decline from the Faith; so that it seems there is a special trust in the King, that he should suffer none to go into Infidel parts, but such as are orthodox, sound and firm in Religion, such of whom the King is specially assured that they will not fall from the Faith, which is to be exercised by the King only; and he is to grant licence to particular and known persons of whom he has this confidence, the King cannot grant his royal care to the Company.

But now this Charter would have this trust deputed and transferred, for it contains a licence not only for the then Members of the Company (who were twenty-two or twenty-three years ago), but their unknown successors, and to their sons begotten, and to be begotten, and their Servants, Factors, Apprentices, and Licensees.

Mr. *Holt* also gives a reason for this trade being unlawful, namely, That the Law has judged Infidels to be perpetual enemies, for which he relies upon another singular saying of my Lord *Coke* in *Calvin*'s case, *fol.* 17. and recites two authorities cited there, namely, the *Register*, 282. and 12 *H.* VIII. 4.

And he takes notice that the children of *Israel* were perverted from the true Religion by converse with the Nations round about them. And he cites *Grotius de jure belli & pacis*, *lib.* 2. *cap.* 15. *par.* 11. where he says, *Cavendum est ne nimia commixtio contagium adferat Infirmis.*

As to this singular opinion of Infidels being perpetual enemies, it is not easy to understand what my Lord *Coke* means by it, his words are these:

All Infidels are in Law *perpetui inimici*, for between them, as with the Devil, whose subjects they are, and the Christian, there is perpetual hostility, and can be no peace; for as the Apostle says, 2*d Corinthians* 15. *What agreement is there of* Christ *with* Belial, *or what part has the Believer with the Infidel?*

It seems by these words, that it is to be understood of a spiritual discord in respect of Religion, and not a temporal between the Nations: for he says, 'tis because they are the Devil's subjects, and he relies upon the Texts of Scripture: and if this perpetual hostility be taken in a political and proper sense, and the Law be so, it destroys the licence and privilege of the Company, and their action brought, and all possibility of such a thing for them. There is not nor can be any peace, treaty or intercourse between the *English* and the *Indians*, but a constant never-ceasing state of war; and especially if it be founded upon a Divine Precept for whatsoever prerogative the King may have, he cannot have a prerogative to dispense with the Canon of the Scripture.

But my Lord *Coke* himself does much clear this matter, *Jur. Co.* 155. where he says, that there may be peace and leagues of commerce with Infidels. All that the Register says, is that the Hospitallers were instituted for defence *contra Christi & Christianorum inimicos*; which is an expression of the enemies of Religion, not of the State. In the book of *Henry* the VIII. he said indeed *obiter*, that a person outlawed, a Traitor, or a Pagan being beaten, shall not have an action; it is true in case of an Out-law, or a Traitor, it may be pleaded in abatement: but no other Book says, nor can any man maintain that the Law is so in case of a Pagan.

A Pagan, Turk or Jew, may maintain an action of debt or battery, or other personal action here, were it otherwise, there could be no trading of the Jews here, nor of the Turks; the contrary whereof is implied and admitted in the Act of Navigation, 12 *Caroli* II. *cap* 18. *paragr.* 18.

By the like reason that there should be no trading with Infidels, there ought to be no foreign trade at all, for there is no Country where the Religion does not differ in somewhat or other from the religion established in the Church of *England*.

And whatever he says of the Children of *Israel*, I think there are many instances in the Old Testament of commerce with the Heathen, though I, not foreseeing such use of Divinity here, am not so well furnished.

As to the citation out of *Grotius*, it is by way of caution only; but the whole drift of that chapter demonstrates, that commerce and leagues with Infidels are lawful, and he expounds that text of 2 *Cor.* which my Lord *Coke* bottoms upon, to refer only to joining with them in Idol-worship. And to shew clearly the mind of that Author, he has writ a whole Book, intituled, *Mare Liberum*, to manifest the right and lawfulness of trade to the *Indies*; and he says, that God in nature appointed all people to resort to, and trade with others, for that he hath given several commodities to some, which others stand in need of.

I must take leave to say, that this notion of Christians not to have commerce with Infidels is a conceit absurd, monkish, phantastical and phanatical.

'Tis a-kin to *Dominium fundatur in Gratia.*

The *Indians* have a right to trade here, and we there, and this is a right natural and human, which the Christian Faith doth not alter.

I agree with Mr. *Holt*, that an Act of Parliament made against the Christian Religion is void; but I think a Charter against natural and civil right is as certainly void.

Mr. *Holt* further says, that public safety and policy are concerned in this trade, and therefore it should be restrainable by the Common Law; and he cites *Courteen*'s case, *Hob* 270. where several Merchants were punished for buying and transporting great sums of money, because (the Book says) it was against the State-Policy and safety of the Kingdom; and so punishable, and not permitted by the Common Law: and Mr *Holt* says, that trading with Infidels is in like manner against the State-Policy too

Answ. That was in the *Star-Chamber*, and perhaps it was one of the errors for which that Court was dissolved, 16 *Car.* I. *cap* 10. in which Act it is said, that the Judges of that Court had undertaken to punish where no Law did warrant.

If transporting of money had been prohibited by Common Law, the Statutes 9 *E.* III. *cap.* 1. and 5 *R.* II. *cap.* 2, &c. had been needless; but before those Statutes every man might dispose of his own private money as he would. And in that case of *Courteen*'s the offence seems to have consisted in ingrossing great quantities; and so it more fully appears in a contemporary report of the same case, in the select cases added to *Popham*, 149 and 150. where it is said, that as one shall be punished for ingrossing commodities, so another for great quantities of money, all other commodities being thereby ingrossed. And this point of *Courteen*'s case is a good authority against the privilege claimed by the Company, which in truth is nothing else but to ingross to themselves all the commodities of *India*, &c.

But if the Common Law would have all the treasure kept within the Realm, it does not follow that we must keep all other commodities, and have no trade at all; at least without special licence, I know no State-Policy or Law for that.

In the next place, Mr. *Holt* considers foreign trade, and says, the subjects have not a right to trade abroad, *ad libitum*.

Answ. This is against the former argument and the ground of the Plaintiff's declaration, for that was, there should be no trade to those places, for a special cause, (*viz.*) because they were Infidels; but this argument imports, that there ought not to be any trade at all abroad, no not with Christian countries, without the King's licence.

The reason with which he would support this argument is, because trade depends upon treaties, and upon the accidents of peace and war, which the King has the power of.

But this too thwarts the former argument, for Infidels he says are perpetual enemies; and if so, there is no peace nor treaty with them, and therefore no trade to be (as not by the Company) with them.

Besides, allowing there may be peace and treaties with them, I cannot see how this consideration can conduce to the present question; for it cannot be pretended, that the King makes leagues with *Indian* Princes, that one part of his subjects should trade thither, and the rest should not, or that the King is or can be in amity with them, as to one part of his subjects (namely the Company), and in enmity with them, as to the other of his subjects.

The King has, and is to preserve, the highways, but it is to keep them for the passage of himself and his people; not to shut them up against any of his people at least, except in case of war.

He cites the Statute 12 *H.* VII. *cap.* 6. where the Merchant-Adventurers say, they had commerce with *Spain* and *Portugal*, and other places in league and amity with the King.

No doubt they had, and beyond this is truly said in the same Statute, that of right they ought to have it, which shews that it was not by the King's grant or licence. And in like manner the Defendant of right ought to have trade with the *Indians*, there being no war betwixt this Realm and them.

He cites out of *Roll*'s Abridgment, 2 *Pars*, 214. a note of *Rot. Parl.* 1 *H.* V. *nu.* 41. where the Commons pray that all Merchants may export and import to and from any place, any goods at their pleasure, paying the customs and other dues, any proclamation notwithstanding; the King answers, that he will be advised by his Council.

And Mr. *Holt* takes this to be an acknowledgment by them of the legality of the Proclamation.

Answ. It is not so, for it was the course then, to propose and pass declaratory and confirming (as well as other) Laws, by way of Petitions to the King; and though they thought the proclamation illegal, yet it was more proper for them to endeavour to obtain redress by prayer than contest. But their Petition was a Petition of Right, and the Proclamation (especially if there was no war a-foot) was void, being against the Common and Statute Law. And to cite and set up such a Proclamation, is to set up grievance to the Law: and yet I take it there was an extraordinary occasion at that time, *Hen.* V. having occasion to lay an embargo on ships, in order to his proceeding to his great war in *France*.

He says that foreign trade may be mischievous, it may be a nuisance, so the importing *Irish* cattle and *French* goods have been declared to be by the Parliament, and the King may restrain such evils.

Answ. These Acts of Parliament were enacting, and they enact it shall be adjudged a common nuisance. They did not find and declare it to have been one before.

If it had been so, there had been no need of these Acts, and we know the reason of that clause was to make the matter dispensable.

If the importing *East-India* commodities be a nuisance, it is not licenseable, and the Company cannot maintain their trade, much less their action; unless it should be thought that the bringing in of those commodities by the Defendant is a nuisance, but the bringing in the same by the Plaintiffs is not.

He inforces this with a reason, that there may be mischief from the abundance of the importation exceeding our exportation, and resembling it to what

ly

is said 10 *Rep.* 141. that by the Common Law the King ought to save and defend his Realm as well against the Sea as against enemies; that it should not be drowned nor wasted; and as the King may prevent inundation of water, so he says, he may as to trade.

Answ. This is a similitude in words, but not as to the nature of things, and if there be any force in it, it is against the Plaintiffs; for there is not in their Charter any limitation, the Company may bring in as much as they will, nay, it seems by their allegation, that this trade is to be managed most largely by means of the Company, and therefore thence is rather the danger of the glut.

Mr. *Holt* makes it a great argument to maintain the Charter, that it is a necessary regulation of the trade, and that the trade could not have been settled but by such a Company; and says, if it should be laid open, it would ruin the trade both of the Company and the Defendant.

And it is averred in the declaration, that this trade cannot be managed, but *per hujusmodi Corpus Corporatum.*

Answ. This contradicts *Michelborn*'s case, for that was upon a licence granted to a single Merchant to trade to the *East-Indies*; and it is known that this trade has been managed by private persons before, and since there was a Company.

And this is to set up convenience or pretence of convenience against Law; the Statute, which we have pleaded, says, that all trade shall be open; the Plaintiffs say, it shall be open to them only, because they can manage it best.

If other men should say that they could manage it better, the pretence were as fair for them to exclude the Company from the trade.

But I except against this averment, it is a frivolous and impossible averment, no issue can be taken upon it, unless issue should be taken upon a similitude, (*viz.*) *hujusmodi Corpus Corporatum.*

If a licence were granted (as it is said to be in *Michelborn*'s case) to one man to trade to the *East-Indies*, and he should bring such an action, and aver that the trade could not be managed but by such an one as he, it would not be good, and yet as good as this is. In an action for words, it is not allowable to alledge that the Defendant spoke such words, or *hujus similia.*

Moreover, the declaration, as it is penned, contradicts itself; for it says, that the trade cannot be managed but by the Company, and yet charges the Defendant that he did manage a trade there; which is not possible, and it is penal enough upon the Defendant that he attempts to manage trade where he cannot.

Mr. *Holt* objects, that the Statute we plead, ought not to be taken universally, that the Sea shall be open to all Merchants; for then it would extend to give liberty of trade to the King's enemies who are Merchants.

Answ. True it is, neither this, nor any such Law extends further than to Alien Armies and Subjects, there are *jura belli*, as well as *jura pacis*; and it is understood, that enemies who are foreigners may be taken and proceeded against according to Martial Law; but the Defendant is a subject, and cannot be an enemy.

He says further, that this Statute should not extend to this trade, because that in *Edw.* III's time, when it was made, trade was driven with Christians only, and not with Infidels.

If this be so, it destroys the only authority he has (*viz.*) *Michelborn*'s case, where the only ground of the opinion is, that there was a licence granted to trade with Infidels, in the time of the said *Ed.* III.

But this Statute must be taken as it is penned, universally, and not confined to those countries, places and parts which were then used; the Statute does not distinguish, & *ubi lex non distinguit, ne nos distinguimus*, otherwise no man must trade, but to those few places that he can prove were traded to before, 18 *E.* III.

He says (as *ff. n. b.* 85.) that the King may restrain men, by *Ne Exeat Regnum*, from going beyond Sea: and cites *Davis*, 9. *b.* that one reason of the King's being intitled by prescription to the great custom, was for his leave to Merchants to go and carry goods out of the Realm.

Answ. It is true, that Book of *Davis* does say so, but he cites to prove the opinion, *Dyer* 165. and this Statute, 18 *E.* III. which we have pleaded; so that that Book is of no further use, than the authorities upon which it is founded do warrant: which if we examine, we shall find that in *Dyer* it is, among other things, made a *quære*, in a case referred to the Judges concerning a new imposition set by Queen *Mary* on Merchandize, whether by Common Law Merchants were, or might be restrained from going out of the Kingdom, without leave of the King or Queen, to which the Judges give no resolution: which shews, they thought the Law was, that there was no such restraint or need of leave; for when Judges give no resolution, in the case of the King, it is a sign that in their opinion the Law is against him, and for the Statute, 18 *E.* III. which we plead, it is flat against [illegible].

F. N. B. 85. *a.* is express, that by Common Law, every subject may go out of the Kingdom for Merchandize, or Travel, or other causes as he pleases, without leave, *V. Co.* [illegible] *Car.* 180.

5 *R.* II. *cap.* 2. Restrains people passing out, but it excepts Merchants, and even that Statute is repealed. [illegible] *cap.* 1. is clear that the King may restrain his subjects from going out of the Realm, by his Writ of *Ne Exeat Regnum.* But that Writ was originally for the Clergy only, and is properly granted for matter of State only, and the words of it are, *Quam plurima* [illegible] *tendis.* Of late indeed it has been extended to command a person to abide the Justice of a Court here, but I think no further. It is always to restrain a man from something unlawful, and against the duty of a subject; never to restrain from a lawful Act, as trade is.

Neither is it general or universal, but always particular, and granted upon oath, made concerning a particular person, and since there needs such a special Writ to restrain an obnoxious person, it proves the Law to be, that all other persons are at liberty to go.

And there is no *Ne Exeat Regnum* against the Defendant, nor cause for any, and if there had been, and he had gone against it, though it were in contempt to the King, it would not give cause of action to the Plaintiffs.

He cites *Co. Lit.* 5. *a.* That no subject can build a castle or a fortress without the King's licence, and 11 *Rep.* 87. *a.* and *Co.* [illegible] 169. that no man can make a park without the King's licence; and 11 *H.* VII. 13. that the King may licence, where [illegible] it is felony.

Answ. These instances agree not to our case: a man may [illegible] castles without the King's licence, any more than raise forces. [illegible] priate beasts, which are *feræ naturæ*, and the King's game; [illegible] take away the lives of the King's subjects; but there is no pa[illegible] son, that a man should not use an innocent trade.

It is more suitable thereto, to instance, that a man may with[illegible] build a house, or make a hedge, and inclose a garden or field, a[illegible] preserve the lives of himself and his family.

In the next place, Mr. *Holt* says, there's a great deal of dif[illegible] tween trading in a Company, and trading out of a Company [illegible] Charter is good because it gives the trade to a Company, ar[illegible] Company, and Christians, they will take care that their A[illegible] Factors keep up to the Christian Religion; but other people [illegible] verse only with Infidels, and cannot have Divine Offices.

Answ. It is not required by the Charter, that the Members [illegible] the Company, should be Christians, and their sons, servants, a[illegible] may be no Christians, nor are they bound to have Divine Offic[illegible] the Defendant and others are likewise Christians, and may ha[illegible] Offices as well as they; and in this trade, the Defendant and [illegible] him converse with the same persons, as the Company and the[illegible] do, or if not, then there is no interfering, no cause of compl[illegible]

He observes out of the Journal of the House of Commons, 43 [illegible] the House of Commons fell vigorously upon Monopolies; and [illegible] brought in a catalogue of them, but therein is nothing of the [illegible] trade, tho' there was such a Charter then in being.

Answ. I know not whether there was such a Charter then i[illegible] but if there were, possibly it was not taken notice of, or p[illegible] grievance then appeared from it; and likely that Company was [illegible] used, than to endeavour to restrain others from trade.

Besides, I have heard a Vote of the House of Commons cited f[illegible] but never knew the silence of the House of Commons cited for [illegible] before; doubtless in that Parliament, as in others, the Meml[illegible] plained of those grievances, which then affected the Boroughs a[illegible] they served for: they undertake not to enumerate all the M[illegible] that were or might be, and it is most prudent, in order to obtai[illegible] to limit their complaints to the present occasion.

First, Mr. *Holt* mentions three Statutes, 3 *Jacobi, cap.* 6. th[illegible] been a Charter obtained by some Merchants for sole trade into t[illegible] nions of *Spain* and *Portugal.* It is enacted, that it shall and ma[illegible] ful, for all subjects to trade thither, notwithstanding that Char[illegible] other; and thereupon he infers, that the Parliament takes the C[illegible] be good, and therefore enact that the trade shall be laid open.

Answ. There is no just ground for this inference.

First, It were a strain beyond the Plaintiff's own foundation [illegible] it related to a trade to *Spain* or *Portugal*, which are Christian Co[illegible]

Secondly, The preamble of the Act sets forth reasons enough [illegible] the Patent at Common Law, (*viz.*) that all subjects ought [illegible] equally the benefit of peace and free trade; that otherwise the s[illegible] *England* would be in a worse condition than those of *Scotland* an[illegible] that it was attended with the impoverishing of Merchants, Mar[illegible] Manufacturers, lessening the price of their commodities, and e[illegible] foreign, &c.

Thirdly, The Act calls it a common traffick, and does not o[illegible] shall be lawful, but that there shall be free liberty to trade there [illegible] sort and manner as was accustomed: so that the Act did not [illegible] Charter illegal, but found it so, as being an innovation agains[illegible] used and ought to be.

Also he mentions the Statute of Monopolies, 21 *Jacobi, cap.* [illegible] in he observes, there is a proviso to save the Companies or So[illegible] Merchants. And the Statute 14 *Caroli* II. *cap.* 24. which in [illegible] amble declares the putting in of Stock into the *East-India* Co[illegible] be for publick good.

Answ. That last Statute [illegible] in the preamble says, it is for [illegible] good, but it is the publick good of the Company, and the [illegible] He says, that divers Noblemen, Gentlemen, and other person[illegible] lity, not bred to trade or merchandize, did put in Stock [illegible] that they shall not in that respect be reckoned Traders, a[illegible] to a Commission of Bankrupt: whereupon I might observe [illegible] Company is not to be reckoned a Company of Merchants, and [illegible] not within the proviso, 21 *Jacobi*, above-mentioned.

But I give this further answer concerning that proviso [illegible] it are, Provided also, and it is hereby further enacted, [illegible] ected, that this Act, or any thing therein contained, shall [illegible] extend, or be prejudicial to the City of *London*, &c. or to any [illegible] or Societies of Merchants within this Realm, erected f[illegible] [illegible] enlargement or ordering of any trade, or merchandize, [illegible] the same, and their liberties, privileges, powers and immun[illegible] and continue of such force and effect, as they were before the [illegible] this Act, and of none other, any thing before in this Act to the [illegible]

Now *first*, this is but a general saying, and supposing, at [illegible] that there was such an *East-India* Company then in being, [illegible] ment had had as favourable an opinion of their Charter, as [illegible] *Muscovy* or *Merchants* [illegible], or the other there mentioned, they [illegible] it by particular mention, as they did those, which would [illegible] some countenance to such a Charter.

Secondly, Admitting it saved generally or particularly [illegible] that does not make it better, the proviso only says, it shall [illegible] such force and effect, as it was before of the making the Act, [illegible] *i. e.* If notwithstanding the body of the Act, if it were [illegible] and void before, it shall remain so, and if it were good [illegible] shall remain so, notwithstanding the proviso.

If it be asked, to what purpose the proviso was made, it is [illegible] thus, the Statute giving an additional penalty of [illegible] double costs against any person, that should, after forty [illegible] at Session of Parliament, hinder, grieve, disturb or [illegible] or any ways seize, attach, distrain, take, carry [illegible] goods, by occasion or pretext of any Monopoly, or [illegible] mission, Grant, Licence, Power, Faculty, Letter Patents, [illegible]

Now the proviso appointed that nothing in this Act shall [illegible] any Society or Company of Merchants; it saves persons [illegible] hinder, grieve, disturb or disquiet others by occasion or prete[illegible] a society or Company from the penalty, so that the Plaintiffs [illegible] advantage from the proviso (if they are at all within it), that they shall not be liable to the Defendant's treble Damages and double costs for bringing this present Suit against him.

6 *Car. Jones* 231. *Mounson versus Lister*, was a case concerning an office granted by Letters Patent, 4 *Jacobi*, for sole making all Bills, Informations and Letters missive in the Council of *York*. Now the next proviso in the Statute does save Officers in the same manner as this proviso does Societies or Companies of Merchants. It was adjudged, that though this grant of this office were saved by the proviso, yet it was still a Monopoly, and void; it being unreasonable that one person should have the making of all bills, &c. which is proper work for Counsel or Attornies, and that (in case of cross-bill) both parties should be obliged to disclose their evidence to that person; but by reason of this proviso, this Grantee should not be liable to the treble damages and double costs; the proviso saves us against that Statute, but does not establish against the Common Law.

Besides, this proviso does not at all extend to this Charter; it only concerns such as were then in being, and says, they shall continue in such force, as they were before the making of that Statute. But this Company that is now Plaintiff was made not long since, *viz.* by Charter 13 of this King.

Mr. *Holt* cites seven precedents of Grants by Queen *Eliz.* of sole trading to several Infidel parts.

To which I answer, That the more there are of this kind, the stronger the argument is for us; for the greater occasion has been administered to bring actions or informations of this nature, but none was ever brought; and the reason why none has been brought is, because none could be upon this score.

The clauses in this Charter, for forfeiting ship and goods, and imprisonment, &c. may as well be cited for precedents hereafter, and yet it will not be denied, that at least some of these clauses are void. it has been frequent to insert clauses in Charters, which will not hold water, they serve for a flourish, and *in terrorem*, like the penalty of 100*l.* in a *Subpœna*.

Also these Charters were temporary, and they were bottomed upon some new discovery of a trade or a passage; and in truth that is the only good foundation upon which such a Charter can be granted, *Godb.* 254. when a new invention or discovery has been made, or is making by any person, by his skill, charge, and perhaps peril of his life, the King may remunerate him with such a Grant; but that must be only for a reasonable number of years, and no further by the Common Law: and before the Statute of Monopolies, 21 *Jacobi*, adjusted that reasonable time to fourteen years. And I take it that the first Grant made in *England* to persons for sole trade to the *East-Indies*, was upon suggestion and consideration of their being first traders there, and that was for fifteen years, which is long since expired. Though it seems, trade to the *East-Indies* was known to other *Europeans* many hundred years ago.

Impiger extremos currit Mercator ad Indos
Per Mare. Hor.

I shall mention two or three Act of Parliament, which do countenance and encourage free trade by any person to the *East-Indies*.

17 *Caroli* I. *cap.* 21. It is made a Premunire to hinder any persons from importing Salt-Petre; the Defendant did import Salt-Petre in this Ship, and so do all Ships that come from the *East-Indies*; it is their usual ballast.

12 *Caroli* II. *cap.* 18. *parag.* 3. (confirmed and re-enacted 13 *Car.* II. *cap.* 14.) forbids the bringing in of any goods of *Africa*, *Asia*, or *America*. and in any Vessel, but such as belong to the people of *England*, *Ireland*, *Wales*, and *Berwick*, or of the King's foreign Plantations, and *paragr.* 13. mentions *East-India* commodities. Here was just occasion for the Parliament to take notice of the Company (for this present charter was in being in 13, when the last Act passed, and a like former Charter in being in 12, when the first passed), and so they would, if they had thought the trade restrained to the Company. But they seem to allow, that these goods may be imported in any *English* or *Irish* Vessels, whether of the Company or of other persons.

22 and 23 *Car.* II. *cap.* 11. It is enacted, That all and every person or persons, that shall build or cause to be built any ship or vessel of three decks, with a fore-castle, and five foot between each deck, mounted with thirty pieces of ordnance, and other ammunition proportionable, shall, for the first two voyages, which the said ship or ships make from his Majesty's Dominions to any foreign port, have and receive to their own proper use and benefit one tenth part: and all persons that shall build any ships of two decks, above three hundred tuns and thirty guns, shall have one twentieth part of the Customs, that shall be paid to his Majesty for all such goods or merchandize, as shall be exported or imported on the said ship or ships, to and from this Kingdom.

'Tis known, that such ships used to be built and employed for the *East-India* trade, and not for trade to any Christian Country; but the Act takes no notice of this Company, or of a licence to be from the King; but allows and declares, that all and every person or persons may build any ship of three decks, and make a voyage with her to any foreign part, and encourage people so to do, with a reward; to which reward (if the Defendant's ship be within the circumstances) the Defendant might be entitled for this voyage for which he is now sued. And certainly no Law appoints a reward and a punishment for the same thing.

I will establish this point with two authorities, not of a private nature, like dormant Patents, but the judgment of Parliaments, and of the Court of *King's-Bench*.

1 & 2 *Ph.* & *Mar.* the *Muscovy* Company was erected by Letters Patent, and therein a clause, to restrain all others from trading upon a like penalty, as here; but notwithstanding that, other people did trade thither: and thereupon, 8 *Eliz.* an Act of Parliament was made, reciting the Charter, and that other persons did trade thither notwithstanding; and therefore enacts that the Charter shall stand, and no other person shall trade thither; which shews the judgment of the Parliament, that without this Act the restraint was not good.

The other concerned the late *Canary* Company.

It is *Mich.* 20 *Car.* II. *Rot.* 403. *Banco Regis*, *Horn.* 118, &c. *Ivy.*

They had a Charter with like restraint and penalties as in this; and in trespass brought for seizing the ship, the Defendant justified by virtue of the Charter, and judgment was given for the Plaintiff against the Charter, by the uniform opinion of the whole Court.

That case indeed was not the same with this, as to the manner; but as to the matter and substance it is the same.

I shall conclude this point with an observation of my Lord *Coke*, *Jur. Co.* 31. that Acts of Parliament against the freedom of merchandize never hold long.

If that be the fate of Acts of Parliament, which are Laws, certainly a Charter made to such purpose, ought not to be allowed.

The Second Point.

I take the Law to be clear with *F. N. B.* 85. *a.* that every subject may go out of the Kingdom for merchandize as he pleases, and whither he pleases, without asking leave of the King, and shall not be punished for it.

But now taking it by admission, that persons are restrained, and that the Defendant ought not to have traded to the *East-Indies* without licence; yet I conceive this action upon the case can never be maintained.

In maintenance of it, Mr. *Holt* says, that this privilege of trade granted to the Company is a franchise; and if another violates it, the Grantee may have an action of the case against that person, as 22 *H.* VI. 14. and 11 *H.* IV. 47. where the King has granted a Fair or Market; if a man set up another Fair or Market to the damage of the former, he that has the Grant shall have an action in the case.

I observe, that in the arguing of the first point, Mr. *Holt* all along called this a licence, which now (to support this second point) he would have a franchise; but these two things differ greatly. A franchise (understood properly) is an Hereditament, a thing of interest, and assignable and transferrable; but a Licence is only *Relaxatio Juris*, a dispensation with the Law, a privilege to certain persons to do an Act with impunity. When the King grants a market, he creates or grants a real thing; but when he gives liberty to trade, he does not create or grant a real thing, but only discharges or prevents a penalty inflictable for trading without such leave.

When the King creates or grants a Market to any person, if he makes a Grant of another Market to another person, to the damage of the first, it will be void, because the Grantee has a franchise that is a real interest; and the Grantee may have an action of the case against him that sets up a Market under pretence of such a Grant, as well as he may against a man that sets up a Market without any pretence of Grant.

But if the King license any person to trade, he may notwithstanding license others too, although that be to the damage of the first; for he has not conveyed any interest to the first, that should hinder him from dispensing with others.

There is no bottom for this action to stand upon; there are but two things in the Charter towards it; *first*, a licence to the Company to trade; *secondly*, a prohibition and restraint to others, whereby the Company is to have the sole trade.

If the King had only granted a licence to the Company to trade to the *East-Indies*; the Company could not thereupon have an action against the Defendant for trading thither. Now when the King, in the same Charter, adds a restraint and prohibition to the Defendant and all other subjects; this Mr. *Holt* would have to be no more than the Law said before; but if it be more, this does not add any real interest to the Company, or better entitle them to an action.

Suppose it to be an offence, and punishable for the Defendant to trade to the *East-Indies* without the King's licence; the King dispenses to the Plaintiffs, so that they may trade there freely, then the Defendant trades there without licence, this may (according to that supposition) subject him to penalty at the suit of the King, but this gives no title to levy money upon the Defendant for trading without licence, there is no privity, no cause of action.

The resolution at the end of the Case of Monopolies, 11 *Rep.* 88. *b.* is a clear authority to this purpose. Cards were prohibited by Act of Parliament to be imported; and the Queen grants to *Darcy* that he should have the sole importation of Cards, *non obstante* that Statute, and during that Grant, another man imported Cards, against whom *Darcy* brought an action on the Case for it, and therein alledged too that he had been at great charge to make and provide Cards sufficient. But resolved that the action would not lie; but for punishing the party, the remedy which the Statute appointed against importing must be followed.

It is insisted upon, that the Plaintiffs have been at great charge to carry on this trade, and by others interloping they should lose the fruits of it.

The Defendant has as much to say, that he has been at great charge, and by restraining and prosecuting him he should be a loser.

But I say, this is *damnum sine injuria*. In the mentioned Books of 22 *H.* VI. 14. and 11 *H* IV 47. it is held, that the action on the case would not lie, which was brought by a Schoolmaster (or two), for that he had an ancient school in a town, and one set up another near, so that whereas before he had two shillings a quarter for a boy, now he could have but one shilling: so for erecting a mill, that withdraws custom from a former mill, no action lies.

In every action on the case, there must be *damnum & injuria*, there must be a wrong to the party plaintiff: It is no wrong to the Plaintiffs here that another offends against that Law, which is dispensed with to them.

If the Defendant's trading without the King's leave be an offence against the King, it is punishable by the King still, and that way of punishment must be followed, if there is to be any; besides, all the foundation the Plaintiffs should stand upon is the Charter, but they do not follow that; the Charter appoints the penalty to be forfeiture of ship and goods, whereof one half to the King; but no action on the case is given, or meant, wherein the carriage may be more or less, and wherein the King is excluded from any share.

If an Act of Parliament prohibit under forfeiture of ship and goods, the one half to the King, the other to the party, that must be followed, there shall never be an action on the case; for the Common Law shuts it up with a strong negative, and says, there shall be no other penalty. And in all cases of Statutes, By-Laws and Charters, the method of punishment prescribed must be observed.

To obviate this the Plaintiffs have been cautelous, and have misrecited the Charter in their declaration; they, to let in a pretence for their action, recite the prohibition or restraint, and stop there, as if the prohibition were absolute and general; whereas it is *sub modo*, under a special penalty of forfeiture.

And this appears upon *Oyer*, and therefore for this variance, judgment ought to be for the Defendant, if there were nothing else in the case.

But waving this concerning the form of the Suit, I insist upon the main matter.

There is a natural necessity that every man that will live must eat, and thence a necessity and obligation to labour; and there is a property in this means of livelihood as well as in life.

The King's power and prerogative is to establish and preserve this to all his Subjects.

Traffick is one of the honestest and justest sorts of industry, and is more especially proper for an Island.

The King cannot prohibit merchandize, nor lay a penny imposition upon it; therefore our Kings have received tunnage and poundage from the Grants of Parliaments: whereas if they had such a power (as the Plaintiffs Counsel speak of) over all trade, they might by the means of that, have made an undeniable title to such a revenue, without the consent of the Lords and Commons.

Restraining of trade (though but for a time or place) is one of the great things which has been always reserved to, and exercised by authority of Parliament, as we find almost in every Sessions.

This which is now before your Lordship, is the greatest Monopoly that has been attempted. It monopolizes *Africa*, *Asia*, and *America*, at least on the *South*; it devours above half the trade of the Nation, the trade of Linnens from *Hamburgh*, *Flanders*, and *Holland*; Silks from *Italy* and *Turky*, and when the prohibition expires, from *France*; and affects our Manufactures at home, upon all which the livelihood of many thousands depends.

It is against the Common Law and many express Statutes.

No man was ever punished, in any Court, for using foreign trade; no, not in the *Star-Chamber*, which extends the prerogative most. It is *Casus primæ impressionis*, although there has been occasion to have had precedents, if any such accident could have lain.

But as this is the first that has been brought, I shall presume it will receive that just discouragement from your Lordships, that it will be the last. And

I pray your Judgment for the Defendant.

Mr. Sollicitor-General *Finch* (afterwards Earl of *Nottingham*) his Argument.

De Term. Pasch. Anno Regni Regis Caroli Secundi xxxvi. *Die Sabbati* xix *Aprilis, Anno Dom.* 1684. *Banco Regis.*

The *East-India* Company against *Thomas Sandys*.

MR. Justice *Withins*. Mr. Sollicitor-General, do you argue that case to-day?

Mr. *Sollicitor General*. Yes, Sir.

Mr. Justice *Withins*. Mr. *Pollexfen*, do you argue on the other side?

Mr. *Pollexfen*. I do, Sir.

Mr. Justice *Withins*. Then, Gentlemen, let him come down to the Bar.

Mr. *Sollicitor General*. My Lord, this is an Action upon the case, brought by the *East-India* Company against *Sandys*; wherein they do set forth that the King, reciting former Letters Patents granted to this Company to incorporate it, did grant a Charter to such particular men, and made them a Corporation by the name of the Governor, &c. and did grant to them the sole trade in all the parts upon the Coasts of *Asia*, *Africa*, and *America*, from the *Cape of Good-Hope* to the *Streights of Magellan*. And further, that he did likewise grant to this Company and successors the sole trade; and granted to them, that no other of the King's subjects should trade within those limits, and did expresly prohibit all his subjects, to trade thither, not being of the Company without a licence from them. Then they say, that Mr. *Sandys*, being one of the King's subjects, did take upon him to trade within the limits of those Letters Patents, to wit, at *Messapotan*, not having a licence from their Company, or any other authority to do it. And this they lay to their damage of 1000*l*.

Mr. *Sandys* to this, after he prayed *Oyer* of the Letters Patents, which are set forth *in hæc verba*, pleads the Statute of 18 *E*. III. which says, that the Sea shall be open, and all Merchants shall go with their merchandize, where they please. To this Plea we have demurred.

Upon this Record, the Questions will be these two:

First, Whether or no the Patent to the *East-India* Company, with a prohibition to all others to trade within their limits, therein set forth, be a good Patent? The next is,

Secondly, Whether, admitting it to be a good Patent, this action will lie; that is, whether it be a bare licence to the Company, or whether it pass such an Interest to the Company with that licence, as will entitle them to an action against any that shall intrude or incroach upon their trade?

First, My Lord, I am to prove that this Grant is good; and here these considerations will fall in.

First, Whether the King had power at Common Law to have made such a Grant?

Secondly, Whether that power be any ways abridged by any Act of Parliament, as it is much insisted upon by the other side?

Answ. First, That the King had such a power at Common Law, I conceive is plain, for these reasons:

First, Because no subject at the Common Law had a right to trade with Infidels, no nor to go thither, without licence from the King first had and obtained.

Secondly, No such trade can be established without precedent treaties, and no such treaties can be made by subjects, without licence from the King to make them. If therefore this Patent does not restrain any natural liberty or right that the subject had, but is introductive of a new one, they had not before; it will not fall out to be within the definition of a Monopoly, in which it is one essential part that it restrains people from that liberty they had before.

Now that no subject had a right at Common Law to trade with Infidels, or go into an Infidel Country, without licence from the Ki
evident thus. And,

First, It will be very considerable, before we enter upon tha
particularly, to see how all right in general to trade stands c
tiated; and there it is plain,

First, That there is no trade, but what depends upon the
and pleasure of the foreign Prince with whom it is, whether he
it or no; that is pretty clear.

Secondly, This may be restrained by a total prohibition of any
with that Prince or Nation, by the King here.

Thirdly, Tho' every man now, and Merchants always were at
go abroad without licence, yet the King may restrain any ma
Writ *Ne Exeat Regnum*, from going out of the Kingdom; and tha
shewing any particular cause why, or alledging any matter that
sable and triable with the King. And,

Fourthly and *Lastly*, If any foreign Prince, upon concluding a
or treaty with the King, should restrain trade to any number of p
any particular qualification of manner of proceeding in it; I see
any man can pretend to a right, to act contrary to that, in breac
a league or treaty made with the King by such a foreign Prince.

Then we say further, by the Statute of 3 and 4 *Jacobi*, which
trade to *Spain* and *Portugal*, that does show plainly that that trade
fore inclosed; and it does not show that the Inclosure of it was ill
gives a right that was restrained before: and yet I am far from affir
the subject has no right to trade, tho' it has been objected that t
it, and makes it as none; and therefore, they held it absolutely
to disaffirm that power and prerogative, which the Law, for th
good, does repose in the King, and that upon reasons that will not b
are so fit to be urged in decency: for I take it, the possibility of t
of power, is no objection against that power. For by this argum
the King has a power and prerogative by Law to restrain subjects fr
beyond Sea, by a *Ne Exeat Regnum*, no, say they, he cannot; for the
restrain all his subjects from going out of the Kingdom, and so i
and hinder every one from going out of the Nation. It is the sa
ment with this, that they urge the King claims a prerogative to rest
trade upon occasion; they say this argument cannot hold, for by
he may restrain all commerce and trade whatsoever: so that this w
guing does strike at all power, and I need give no other reason fo
there can be no power at all, which is not accompanied with som
and there is no trust, but it possibly (morally speaking) may be bro
that this is no argument against the right of the subject to trade on
side, nor against the prerogative of the King on the other, in whom
has reposed a trust to regulate and qualify trade.

But, My Lord, in this case the question is not of so large an exte
so general as this is: but only here it is a question, how that righ
with respect to Infidels, and that is the question before your Lordsh

And I cannot but observe, in my entrance into the question, tha
the Law had once been held clear in this matter, this could not ha
to be any subject of debate now, for no such trade as this, could ev
been gained to the Nation; for none could have ventured upon so
ous an enterprize, or so chargeable a project as this was, if it had b
doubt whether those that run no such adventure should be admitted
the first fruits of it.

So that this question, as it tends to overthrow this trade, if the I
taken to be as they would have it, so it overthrows the *Turky* trade too.
stands upon the same foundation, with respect to the prohibition by
Patents as this does: for the question is not, upon how easy terms th
leges are to be obtain'd, as it is confessed the terms are easier in the
Company, than in the *East-India* Company; but whether any term
are requisite: if any terms can be impos'd upon it, then those are g
none, then that will overthrow the *Turky* trade, and all the trade of t
tion. And surely if they can prevail in this question, the subjects, for
right they pretend so much to stand up, will have little cause to than
for standing up for a right, as they call it, against the very Interest
Nation. But to return to our argument:

The subject can have no such right to trade with Infidels with
cence from the King; for they are looked upon as enemies, not onl
spiritual sense, as they are of a contrary Faith and Religion, but they
treated in Law; and the resolutions of the Law are such as we may
Calvin's case, and the 12 *H*. VIII. which is a Book they cited, and wa
ted here before, upon the first argument of this case; where it is held
a Pagan, tho' he be beaten, cannot have or maintain any action at al
cause he is *perpetuus inimicus*: so an Alien Enemy can neither maintain
or personal Action, as it is said in the *1st Inst*. 129. *B*. so a Jewess, t
born here, and marrying a converted Jew, shall not be endowed; an
the same Book 32, so that they are look'd upon no more than co
Aliens; for we see that tho' they are born here, yet they have not the
cities so much as of Denizens, for they shall not be endowed, as De
may. And tho' my Lord *Coke*, by the way, says, in that Book, no Ali
be endowed; yet I find in the Parliament Rolls a Petition of the Com
it is in 8 *H*. *V*. *m*. 16. they pray that Female Aliens may be endowed
the King's answer is, Let it be as it is desired. But I mention that o
the bye, for it is not at all relating to our question, but for that the
resolution goes to it, that an Infidel is always to be treated as an ene

But, my Lord, further, that all Infidels are likewise Aliens and Ene
in respect of their properties which they gain here; it is to be ga
from what I find in *Rot*. *finium* 50 *H*. III. *m*. 5. the King releases a
that was owing to a Jew; and in the same *Roll*, 49 *H*. III. *Rot*. *f*
there are divers pardons of debts owing to Jews, some in recompence fo
vice done, and others in compassion of the poor, that they had drawn
be engaged for great sums to them.

Rot. *Parl*. 13 *E*. I. *m*. 4. A Jew died, and the King granted aw
goods, and his Widow redeem'd them for 1000*l*. and the King grant
the Jewess, that he would not discharge any debts, that were owing t
This shews their properties were all at the King's mercy; and some
the King granted licence to them, and gave them leave to assign their d
Rot. *Parl*. 3 *E*. I. *m*. 6. which recites that it was provided by King *H*
that no Jew should sell his goods without licence. The King grants
cence to *Judeo Nostro* to sell a debt of 20*l*. that was owing him fron

B

Bishop of *Bath* and *Wells*; and doubtless the reason of that Law in *Hen.* IIId's time, was, that the King might prevent any mischief, that might follow upon an unlicensed commerce between his subjects and those Infidels: and this appears plainly by considering, that by the ancient Law of the Land, no Jew could inhabit any where within the Kingdom, but where by custom they were permitted to dwell; and so is *Rot. Claus.* 1 *E.* I. *m.* 7. *in dorso*; they had gone and inhabited at *Winchester*; but they were removed thence, and the Record tells you the reason why, *Amoti*, &c.

They had particular Justices assigned over to them, to determine their causes, and that you see *Rot. Claus.* 49 *H.* III. *m.* 4. the King constitutes two Justices *ad Custod. Judæorum*, and gives them power to determine their Pleas in the places where they were accustomed to inhabit.

And there is in *R.t. Parl.* 13 *E.* I. *m.* 7. a very remarkable Record to this purpose, *Rex dilectis*, &c.

My Lord, I find another Record like this in the Patent-Rolls of that year; for we see what care the Law took, that Christians should not be circumvented by the Jews; and the Government had an eye upon them, that they should not have commerce one with another; that recognizances shou'd be enter'd in the presence of Christians. That Record is thus, *Rex omnibus*, &c.

We see a man here, that deals with a Jew, and buys things of him without Licence, and the King grants that he would not trouble him, or proceed against him by Law for that offence.

By the ancient Law it appears, that if a Christian marry'd to a Jew, it was felony, and the party offending was to be burnt; so is the 3*d Inst. fol.* 89. and there my Lord *Coke* cites *Fleta* for his authority in it.

From all this it appears, that Infidels have no right to trade and traffic here, and surely then no subject has a right to trade with them in their country; for the restraint certainly must be mutual. And, my Lord, for this, I must remember you of a case that has been before cited in this case, and that is *Michelborne*'s case in *Brownlow*, where my Lord *Coke* declares the Law to be as we say, and that he hath seen a Licence in *Edw.* III's time, and that he says was for the safety of Religion.

And surely, my Lord, it is upon some such grounds as this, that the Law provides that no excommunicate person shall bring an action, no not *in auter droit*, because no person must converse with them; therefore, they cannot sue as Executor to any person. Then if the Law be cautious for the safety of Religion, as to restrain converse in our country; *à fortiori* it may restrain the Subjects liberty of trading in an Infidel country, where they must be under the Laws of the place; and the inconveniencies in the one case are sure much greater than in the other.

For we see in *Calvin*'s case, if the King conquers an Infidel country, their Laws actually cease till the King gives them new ones. But 'tis otherwise of a Christian country, for there the Laws remain till the King is pleased to alter them.

Another reason, my Lord, is this, the King's prerogative in making leagues and truces, is sure as large and unlimited as the subjects right to trade; and yet in the case of Infidels that is restrain'd, as to some sort of leagues that a Christian Prince cannot make with them, &c. For that you may see in the 4*th Inst.* 155. where my Lord *Coke* says that the Law of *England* is so, that the King can't make *Fœdus mutui auxilii aut amicitiæ*, with an Infidel Prince. And there he reckons up four sorts of leagues; three of which he says may be had with Infidels, that is, *Fœdus Pacis, Fœdus Congratulationis*, & *Fœdus Commercii*; but *Fœdus mutui Auxilii*, he says, by Law is not allowable: and herein these leagues are grounded upon the Law of God.

Therefore, my Lord, the Law surely does not give the subject an unlimited freedom to trade, but it must depend upon such cautions and security, as nothing but such leagues can provide for; which leagues I am sure none but the King is capable of making.

This then, one would think, were enough to clear our Patent from that objection, that 'tis a Monopoly. But there are no other things, that make it yet more evident it is not so. As first, in all the complaints that have been of Monopolies, this Patent was never counted to be one among them, nor thought to be illegal; if it ever had been thought so, the Statute of 21 *Jacobi*, *cap.* 3. which is a Statute made for regulating of trade, would never have been made.

In the next place, I say either the first Patent for this trade was a Monopoly, or this is none: the first was none, not only for the reasons I gave before, but because it was a new trade. Patents for new Inventions are not made good by the Statute of 21 of King *James*, but left as they were before; only they are restrain'd to a number of years, and were always good, because they were for the incouragement of trade, and of useful inventions to increase them.

A fortiori therefore in this case, what is of much greater consequence to the Nation is a point of trade, than any little slight Invention of a particular thing, must be allowed to be good; then I say, sure if the first Patent be not a Monopoly, then neither can this Patent be a Monopoly, for there is no Law that hath declared how long such a trade as this is may be inclosed, as the Statute of 21 King *James* has set limits for, as new Inventions.

And again, this Company is for the advantage and benefit of the Nation, which a Monopoly can never be: and that it is for the benefit of the Nation, appears by the Statute of the 14th of this King, *cap.* 24. which recites it to be of great advantage to the Publick, and for the encouragement of the Publick Trade and Navigation. Here then, my Lord, is both the Judgment of the Parliament concerning Companies of this kind, and an incouragement of this particular Company by the whole Parliament.

And again, they are taken notice of in another Statute, made in the 29th of this King, *ch.* 1. where they are taxed 20*s.* for every 100*l.* capital Stock in the Company.

Another reason is this, because of the absolute necessity of a Company to manage this trade, not only in respect of the *Indians* themselves, but also in respect of other foreign Nations, who are rivals to us in this trade, and are ready to take all advantages against us about it. But this part of the Case is much more fit to be discoursed of by Merchants and Statesmen, than Lawyers.

Yet thus far the Law falls in to consider this matter, as they are a Corporation under stipulations and leagues with other Countries for the carrying on of their trade; and so are in the nature almost of foreign Plantations, under a regulated and Christian Government within themselves, whereby those mischiefs are prevented, that would have fallen upon an unlimited and unregulated trade with Infidels, that are enemies to our Religion and Nation; which the Law, as I have already shewn, takes so much care to prevent.

For other considerations, whether this trade be driven to the full extent of it, or may be more advantageous to be enlarged, as it is proper here to be discoursed of in a Court of Law, so the Application for that must be made elsewhere; for I do not know any Law that hath made the Defendant a Reformer among us.

My Lord, in the next place, the next question is, whether this prerogative of the King is abridged, or restrain'd by any Act of Parliament, as is insisted on by the Defendant's Counsel? I think not. For,

First, In general, the chief trade of this Nation consisted anciently most in Wool, Wool-Fell and Leather, and with our neighbouring Nations only; and yet,

Secondly, Even that trade was restrain'd in the exercise of it; for none must buy and sell, but he must do it at the Staple, as appears by 2 *Ed.* III. *chap.* 9. that abrogates the Staple, and afterwards it was erected again. And then in the

Third place, there was no such trade as this or any other ever establish'd with Infidels in those days, and so there was no occasion for such a Law to restrain them.

The best rule therefore to interpret this Act of Parliament, will be to apply the remedy to the inconvenience and mischief that was before it. If then there was no such inconvenience as this complain'd of, the restriction of the trade with Infidels; then all may reasonably conclude and insist upon it, there was no such remedy as the laying open of a trade, as they alledge, intended to be introduced. But if we consider the Act itself, we shall see some particular reason for the making of it, either for the taking off some cloggs, that were upon the trade then in use, or the providing some remedies which were introduced to obviate the present inconveniences and mischiefs.

First then, for *Magna Charta*, which hath been cited *chap.* 30. that gives liberty to Merchants, *Quod nisi publicè antea prohibiti fuerint, habeant salvum* & *securum conductum exire de Anglia* & *venire in Angliam*, & *morari* & *ire per Angliam, tam per terram quam per aquam, ad emendum* & *vendendum sine omnibus malis tolnetis*, &c. *præterquam in tempore guerræ*.

This helped Merchant-Strangers in this particular, because before that they could come but at four times in the year, and must stay here but forty days at a time; as my Lord *Coke* observes in his Comment upon that Statute, and cites the *Mirror of Justice* for it. And if this Law proves any thing relating to this question, it is, that before that Act, Merchants could not go out of the Kingdom, and still they may be prohibited publickly; which, tho' my Lord *Coke* says must be by Act of Parliament, yet he cites no Law for that opinion; and with submission, the word Publick doth not necessarily import that it shou'd be by Act of Parliament. My Lord, that Law that comes nearest in words to this case here before you, is that of 1 *E.* III. which is pleaded by the Defendant, that is part of the Act, the latter clause of it, that the Sea be open to all manner of Merchants, to pass with their merchandize whither they please.

This is part of that Law; but, my Lord, the meaning of this Law is quite and clear another thing, as I shall shew with submission most plainly: and I will beg leave, my Lord, a little to introduce it, by giving you a History of this Law, how it comes to be made; for it is but a short one, and 'tis only the last clause of it that is pleaded by the Defendant.

By the Statute of the 11th of *Edw.* III. it was made felony to transport Wool, and this my Lord *Coke* observes in his Comment upon *Magna Charta*, upon *chap.* 30. King *Edw.* III. took advantage of it, for exacting money of the Merchants, for dispensations with the Law, and for licences for transporting of Wool. Hereupon several complaints were made in the Parliament; and particularly, in the 17th year of *Edw.* III. *Rot. Par. nu.* 28. the Commons complain, that the Grant of 40*s.* upon a Sack of Wool made by the Merchants only, was not to bind the Commons, and therefore pray it may be revoked. The King answer'd, This cannot tend to charge the Commons; for that there was set a certain price upon Wool in every County, which the King willed should stand; and that all Wool sold under that price should be forfeited in the hands of the buyer.

This was in 17 *E.* III. and this matter, my Lord, among other things, was represented to the same Parliament, by the same Merchants, by way of advice, as a thing fit, 17 *E* III. *in dorso nu.* 58. of the Parliament-Rolls of that year. And they set forth, Whereas they were summon'd to *Nottingham*, to inform the price of Wools, which they did not, regarding the times to come as they say, and that was abused; they pray liberty to buy Wools as freely as other merchandizes, as they can agree between buyer and seller; and that all Indictments and Proceedings contrary to that Law might be stayed, and further they add their advice, that the King would ordain the Staple in some place in *England*, rather than beyond the seas.

Then comes the 18 *E.* III. *Rot. Parl. nu.* 12. among other Petitions of the Commons, there are these which refer to the first part of the Act of Parliament: That the prices set upon the sorts of Wools in every County, which run more to the damage than advantage of the people, might be ousted, and that every one may buy freely, as he can agree with the seller, and none be accused for doing the contrary.

This, my Lord, explains the first part of that Act of Parliament; that the ordinances before this time made upon taking sorts of Wool, which was imprinted in *Rastall*, and all the Statute-Books, (for the Roll is, *sur pris*,) and defeated, and that every man, as well Stranger as Denizen, may henceforth buy Wool as he can agree with the seller, as they were wont to do before the said ordinances.

Now, my Lord, you shall see the latter part of the Act, which is that they plead: among the Petitions of the Commons in the said Roll, there the 5th Petition is, reciting, *That whereas the King had granted to them of* Flanders, *that the Staple for Wool should be held at* Bruges, at the time of which Grant, all manner of Merchants, that is, *Lombards, Genoese, Catalonians, Spaniards*, and others, who used to buy the greatest part of the Wool, and carry them out of *Flanders* by land and sea where they would, to the great profit and increase of the price of Wool, thither coming: yet the Towns of *Bruges, Gent*, and *Ipres*, have of late ordained, That

That no wools coming to the Staple, be sold to strangers, nor carried out of the said Country of *Flanders*, as they used to be, to the damage of the merchants of *England*, and of all the commonalty; and therefore they pray remedy hereof.

This is granted by the King, that they may buy wool as they were wont to do; and that a Writ should be sent to the Sheriff to make Proclamation accordingly. Then they pray, that the effect of these answers may be put into writing, in the manner of a Patent under the Great Seal; and this is done, in which there is this very Statute of 18 *E.* III. *in terminis*, as it is printed. And this plainly shews, that the Sea being to be open, and Merchants to pass wherever they please, was only in answer to that petition and representation, and to redress the mischief; that they might buy here, and go where they would, and not be necessitated to go and buy at the staple; which was so abused by those of *Bruges*: And this is likewise pursuant to the advice and petitions of Merchants before the 17th *E.* III. That the King would establish a staple somewhere in *England*, and not in parts beyond the Seas.

My Lord, for the rest of the Acts of Parliament that have been cited on the other side, I shall not enter upon them particularly; but this every body at the first sight may see, they carry their own answer along with them, and the occasion of their making does appear in themselves, tho' this did not, and very few of them come up to this Question now before you, or any thing like it, as will appear plainly upon the bare reading of them.

The only Question then, my Lord, that remains, is, whether the action lies for the Company? For I think I have made it out, that the King had such a prerogative at Common Law, and no Act of Parliament hath taken it away. Then I say, the Question is, Whether an action lies for the Company; that is, whether it be a bare licence, or coupled with an Interest? And as to that point, I shall be very short, for to me it seems to be no Question at all. For,

First, They are at a great charge and expence to support this trade, and therefore surely they ought to profit by it.

Secondly, They are looked upon by the Parliament to have an interest in this trade, or else they had never been taxed so high as twenty Shillings for every 100*l.* in their stock. Then if they have an interest in the trade, this trading of the defendant is an encroachment upon that interest, and then here is *damnum & injuria*; which will intitle them to an action.

For so it is in other things: A Fair, in some sense, is but a licence to hold a market at such a time, in such a place; but because of the profit that tends to that liberty, and the charge that the party is at in keeping of it, an action does lie against any Man that sets up another Fair, to the prejudice of him that had the first Grant.

In the common case of Patents for new inventions, an action lies for using the invention without licence, because of the interest conveyed by the Grant, and the charge that the party that invents, is at. So that I think, my Lord, with submission, we have here an interest in this trade; and an interest, I say, as well as a licence, well founded upon the King's Letters Patent; which the King had power to make by prerogative at the Common Law, and that power not restrained by any Act of Parliament. And therefore I humbly pray your judgment for the Plaintiffs.

Mr. Pollexfen, *(afterwards Lord Chief Justice) his Argument.*

De Term. Pasch. Anno Regni Regis Caroli Secundi xxxvi. *Die Lunæ* xxi. *Aprilis, Anno Dom.* 1684, *Banco Regis. The* East-India *Company against* Thomas Sandys.

Mr. *Pollexfen.*

MAY it please your Lordship, the Governor and Company of Merchants of *London*, trading to the *East-Indies*, they are plaintiffs, and *Thomas Sandys* is the defendant. If your Lordship please, I will open a little more of the Record than has yet been opened: And the Case upon the Record stands thus:

These plaintiffs bring their actions against the defendant, and do declare, That the King by his Letters Patent, in the 13th year of his reign, did grant to them the sole trade, between the Cape of *Good Hope* and the Streights of *Magellan*, in the *East-Indies*. And did also grant unto them, that they, and nobody else, should come thither, nor trade there, and they do say, the defendant did come thither, and did trade; and that this is to the plaintiffs damage.

This defendant has prayed *Oyer* of the Letters Patent; and there are some things that are not mentioned in the Declaration: but not being upon the Record, and appearing upon the *Oyer*, I crave leave to open them, that I may make use of them in the discourse I am to make; and I desire your Lordship would please to take notice of them.

In the Letters Patent, when they come to the Prohibition and Restraint, the Prohibition and Restraint is in this manner, which they have left out in their declaration. The Letters Patent do prohibit the trading without a licence, upon pain that every such person that shall trade to or from the *East-Indies*, shall incur the forfeiture of his merchandize, and also of the Ship; one moiety to the King, and the other moiety to the *East-India* Company.

And then there follows another clause, which is omitted also out of the Declaration; and that is a clause of Grant to the Company, that for any consideration of benefit to their own use, they may grant licence to strangers or others, to trade to and from the *East-Indies*.

And then there is another clause that is omitted also, and that is this, That the King grants to the Company, that the King will not, without consent of the Company, give licence to any persons besides the Company to trade thither.

And there is likewise another clause which I would take notice of, That nobody of the Company should have a vote in the Company, unless he have a stock of 500*l.*

These clauses now being in the Letters Patent, and the Letters Patent being set forth upon the Record, they are become parts of the Cause.

The defendant has pleaded the Statute of 18 *E.* III. and thereupon there is a demurrer.

My Lord, the Questions that are in the Cause are only these two:

First, Whether or no this Grant of the sole trade to the plaint[illegible] good grant or not? And next,

Secondly, Supposing it should be a good Grant, Whether [illegible] plaintiffs can maintain this action, as now it is brought?

My Lord, in the argument of this Case divers Things have [illegible] in which I shall differ from the other side; but only take notice [illegible] they may be of force in point of argument, to make the Quest[illegible] are in the Case to turn, as to the Law, one way or other.

My Lord, it is no Question but that the King, by Law, car[illegible] any of his subjects from going out of the Kingdom: For the K[illegible] a particular interest in the services of his subjects; and theref[illegible] most reasonable and an undoubted Rule, I think, in the Law, [illegible] King may restrain any particular subject *pro hic & nunc*, as the K[illegible] it to be most necessary and convenient for his service to restrain.

Next, my Lord, I do not deny, but think it also to be a La[illegible] the King may restrain all his subjects from a trade to such a p[illegible] Country or City, upon some reasons or occasions; as in times [illegible] and times of plague, that I reckon by law may be done very wel[illegible]

But, my Lord, that is not the Question in our Case; for the [illegible] in our Case is a Question concerning a sole trade granted to a p[illegible] person, or body politick, (which is but one particular person in [illegible] ration of Law) with a restraint upon, and excluding all his ot[illegible] jects. Now from what has been granted already, to argue [illegible] King may grant such a sole trade, is no consequence at all from [illegible] sitions that have been agreed, *i. e.* from the authority and power [illegible] has to restrain his subjects from going out of the Kingdom, or t[illegible] them from trading in such a place. For,

First, As to the power the King has by Law to restrain his [illegible] from going out of the Kingdom; though by Law his power be [illegible] first of all it is not a power universal to restrain all his people [illegible] restrain this or that man for his particular service, for this or t[illegible] cular Time. But to make a universal restraint, that none sha[illegible] but you *J. S.* or you such a body politick, will go a great dea[illegible] than ever it has been before, or can be conceived.

Next, my Lord, That because the King can restrain trade in [illegible] war, or in time of plague, that therefore he can restrain all his [illegible] and for ever; except such and such particular Men, or a Corpo[illegible] that must needs be further than ever any thing I have heard y[illegible] Law, or could find any footsteps of.

So that I think there are no inferences can be drawn fro[illegible] things, that can conclude any thing as to its particular point t[illegible] we are upon, *i. e.* That the King can grant a sole trade to any pa[illegible] person and body politick, and their successors for ever; and restr[illegible] exclude all his other subjects from that trade. My Lord, that [illegible] be, I think, a consequence that can be drawn from any of the p[illegible] that I have laid down.

And, My Lord, further I would observe this in the arguing [illegible] Case, That when they lay down this as a general position, T[illegible] King can restrain his subjects; there is no distinction, nor is t[illegible] foundation in Law for it, betwixt going to an Infidel Country, o[illegible] to a Christian Country. For it is as undoubted, the King may [illegible] any of his subjects, as the King's pleasure shall be, or as there [illegible] war or plague, and such other occasions as may require it, fro[illegible] into a Christian country, as well as he may from going into an [illegible] one; and therefore if the argument have weight in it in this p[illegible] hath weight as well to affect Christian Countries, and the who[illegible] abroad with them, as Infidel Countries, and trading with them.

And there is no difference at all from this reason or foundatio[illegible] can be inferred, as I can make.

Next, my Lord, when they argue and make use of the Sta[illegible] 3 *Jac. Cap.* 6. which enacts, *That the King's subjects shall freely* [illegible] Spain *and* Portugal, *notwithstanding the Charters of incorporation to some Merchants, and the prohibitions in those Charters*: If they [illegible] that those Charters of restraint were lawfully granted, then they d[illegible] for a power in the King to restrain trade even to Christian Cou[illegible] which is a thing, under favour, that never was yet affirmed, a[illegible] member, but rather the contrary admitted: And if they say, [illegible] Charters that were granted for restraint of trade to *Spain* and [illegible] were not lawful, because they were Christian Countries, then the[illegible] makes nothing for them: for sure it is no argument, that because [illegible] lawful Charter was granted, therefore another unlawful Charter [illegible] granted; or because that was void, therefore the other should [illegible] void; no, rather the contrary.

My Lord, these things I have taken notice of, because they a[illegible] ters that have been insisted on in the argument on the other side; [illegible] would lay what is not necessary out of the Case. And I now c[illegible] the great point of this Case, and which indeed is a great poin[illegible] consequence of it.

First, Whether the Grant of sole trade to the Plaintiffs, be[illegible] Grant or not?

And I humbly conceive, such a Grant of a sole trade to any pa[illegible] person, or body politick, with a restraint to all others, is agai[illegible] Law of the land, and by the Common Law void; and this I shall [illegible] vour to prove from good authorities.

1. By the Common Law, trade is free and open for the King[illegible] jects; and for that the Books that I shall cite are these, 3 *Inst.* 18[illegible] *mercium Jure Gentium commune esse debet, & non in Monopolium & p[illegible] pauculorum Quæstum convertendum; iniquum est alios permittere, ali[illegible] bere Mercaturam.*

The next Book, my Lord, is *Fitzh. Nat. Br. fo.* 85. that says *Note, That by the course of Common Law, every Man may at his ple[illegible] out of the Realm for merchandize, or to travel, or other cause, as sha[illegible] him, without demanding licence of the King; and shall not be punished* [illegible] And the *Stat.* of 5 *R.* II. *c.* 2. which prohibited all but the gre[illegible] and Merchants, to pass out of the Realm without licence, has declared the Law, when it excepted Merchants, that they had a [illegible] go without licence: But this Statute is repealed afterwards by the [illegible] of 4 *Jac. cap.* 1.

Then, my Lord, there is *Rolls*, 1 *Rep. fol.* 41 the Taylor of *Ipswich's* Case against *Sherring*. The words and sense of the Books are, *That no Trade, Mechanick, or Merchant, can be hindered by the King's Patent.* A Patent to hinder trade at sea, is a void Patent; a Patent that only a hundred persons shall use such a trade, is not good.

Dyer 165. *That every one may at his pleasure go with his Goods*; and cites *F. N. B.* for it. And *F. N. B.* 85. saith thus, *Note, That by the Common Law, every Man may at his pleasure go out of the Realm for merchandize, or to travel, without demanding licence of the King.*

These, my Lord, are the Books, and thus they speak generally at the Common Law: and I offer it to your Lordship as a further reason, That the Common Law is such, notwithstanding all their arguments, in regard that the Common Law, as far as it is against ingrossing, is also against all sole trade. For, my Lord, all sole trade is ingrossing, as I take it, with submission; appropriating trade and merchandize to a particular person or persons, or body politick, excluding others, is ingrossing such trade. Now that ingrossing is against the Common Law, and against the very fundamentals and principles of the Common Law; that, I think I need not labour much to prove, nor shall I go about to cite many Books to prove that.

That ingrossing any sort of merchandize is an offence at Common Law, *vide* 3 *Inst.* 196. And in the Case *Dominus Rex vers. Crispe & al.* here was lately an agreement betwixt copperas makers and copperas-merchants, for the buying of all copperas. These copperas-makers should for three years make at so much a Ton; and restraining them from selling to any others. It was here adjudged an ingrossing, upon an information.

And if a Company of Merchants shall buy up here, in like manner, all the merchandize of *Spain*, or *Portugal*, or the *Canaries*, or other town or place, for three years to come; this, I think, would be an ingrossing, and the contract against law.

But then, my Lord, to prove that sole trade is ingrossing, that the nature of the thing must speak; for whosoever has the sole trade of buying and selling of such a sort of commodity, or whosoever has the sole trade to any particular Country or Place, has thereby the sole ingrossing, and sole having of all the commodities of that place; so likewise has he the sole buying. and all the people that have to deal about the commodities that are to be vended and vented in that Country or Place, are at his will and pleasure; and thereby he makes all those his own, and he makes what price he pleases, and orders and disposes of them, both as to value and every thing else, as his own. And thereby, my Lord, I take it, it must be ingrossing; and every monopolizing of buying and selling, or of trade, is ingrossing. But that only ingrossing is by particular agreement and contracts between particular men, among one another, without the King's authority, or help of his Letters Patent; but monopolizing is ingrossing under colour of authority, by help of those Letters Patent that create them: for the consequence of it must be, that they would sell at their own prices, and thereby exact upon the King's Subjects: And their Patent for the sole trade to the *East-Indies*, invests them in all the merchandizes of these Countries, and ingrosseth all in their hands. Then if ingrossing by the Common Law be forbidden, and it is unlawful to do it, all Letters Patent to authorize and help Men to ingross, must needs be as void as that, which is the end of ingrossing; and that is monopolizing.

My Lord, in the 3d *Inst.* 181. the Case of *John Peachy*, in 50 *E.* III. who was severely punished for procuring a Grant or Licence under the Great Seal, that he only might sell sweet Wines in *London*, is a strong case for us. For, my Lord, this was ingrossing by colour of the King's Grant, and punished as a great offence: And the case of Monopolies, that are reported 11 *Co.* 84. *Moor* 673. and in *Noy*, do prove that monopolizing is ingrossing, and the same law that is against ingrossing is against monopolizing; and the same law that makes the one void, makes the other void.

In *Darcy's* case, where a Grant by Patent was made to him for the sole importing from beyond sea, and the selling of cards under a rent, and prohibiting all others to sell; there it was adjudged a void Grant.

And the *Stat.* of 21 *Jac. cap.* 3. does declare all Monopolies to be void at Common Law; so then if this Grant be a Grant to you, to ingross or monopolize, I think it will be easily concluded to be against the Common Law, and made void thereby.

Next, my Lord, that this Grant of the sole trade to the *East-Indies* is against the ancient Statute-Laws of this Land, I think is plain also. As for the Statute of Monopolies, I shall crave leave to speak of it by itself, by-and-bye. But I say it is against the ancient Statutes of this Kingdom. *Magna Charta*, 9 *H.* III *cap.* 30. all Merchants, if they were not prohibited before, should have their sure and safe conduct to depart out of *England*, and come into *England*, and stay, and go thro' *England*, as well by land as by water, to buy and sell without any evil tolls, by the ancient and just custom, except in time of war. And my Lord *Coke* says, That in this Act, *Nisi publice prohibiti fuerint*, is intended of a prohibition by the publick Council of the Kingdom, by Act of Parliament. So that this Act does in these words make our case: It says, *They shall, if not openly prohibited, have safe and sure conduct:* And if that open or public prohibition must be by Act of Parliament, so it is probably a declaration of the Common Law. Then here is no such in this case, no prohibition by Act of Parliament to restrain from going to the *East-Indies*, but the Defendant may go thither if he please. The *Stat.* of 2 *Ed.* III. *cap.* 9. *That all Merchants, Strangers, &c. may go and come with their Merchandize into* England, *after the tenor of the* Great Charter

The Statute that is pleaded 18 *E.* III. *cap.* 3. *That all Merchants, Strangers, and Denizens, and all other and every of them, of what estate and condition soever they be, shall sell their merchandizes from whencesoever they come, freely, without interruption; and shall have the Sea open to them, to pass with their merchandize where they shall please, without interruption, excepting to the King's enemies; and that this Act shall be observed and performed notwithstanding any Charter to the contrary; and that Charters to the contrary are of no force, but are to the King's damage, and to the oppression of the Commons.*

Stat. 14 *E.* III. *cap.* 2. recites *Magna Charta*, and enacts, *That all Merchants, Aliens, and Denizens, may without Lett, safely come with their merchandize, safely tarry, and safely return.*

Now, if so be, all Merchants, Strangers, &c. shall sell their merchandize wherever they come, without interruption, and that enacting clause be large enough, as sure it is; then it has an express clause, That all Charters and Patents to the contrary are void, as being to the King's damage, and the oppression of the people, and therefore they are all by the Parliament declared to be void.

The *Stat.* of 25 *E.* III. *cap.* 2 confirms the former *Stat.* of 9 *E.* III. and has the same clause in effect; *If any Proclamation or Commission be to the contrary, it shall be void.* The Statutes of 2 *R.* II. *cap.* 1. and 11 *R.* II. *cap.* 7. confirms the two former Acts, and enact, *That all Charters, Letters Patent, and Commands to the contrary, shall be void.* So that, my Lord, those many Statutes, as most of the old ones, being penned in general (but short) words, and being in favour of trade, have been taken to extend generally, for the general and most large advantage of trade; tho' perhaps some particular trades were by construction mostly concerned, as the Statutes of the Staple might be the occasion of making some part of them. But they do enact, as your Lordship sees, in general words, *That all Grants and Letters Patent to the contrary shall be void*; and surely this would have never been put in, but that in all times Grants have been made, which the King has been received in, and found them contrary to his real advantage, though they have been otherwise pretended, and were to the oppression of the people, and therefore void.

In the 2 *Inst.* 63. my Lord *Coke*, in his observation upon the consideration of *Magna Charta*, and the several Statutes that were after that made in reference to trade, says, That upon this *Chap.* of *Mag. Chart.* (to wit) the 30th, this conclusion is necessarily gathered, *That all Monopolies concerning trade and traffick are against the liberty and freedom granted and declared by his Great Charter, and against divers other Acts of Parliament, which are good Commentaries upon it.* So that, my Lord, I do not offer it only as my present thoughts, but what has been taken for Law heretofore; that those Acts are of general extent, and all Charters made to the contrary, are *ipso facto* void, and of no force.

Obj. My Lord, they say it is true, if we are a Monopoly, then the Law is against us; but we are no Monopoly.

Resp. My Lord, to prove they are a Monopoly, that is the next thing, which, with your Lordship's favour, I shall go about.

And for that I shall first take the description that is of a Monopoly, made by my Lord *Coke*, in his *chap.* of Monopolies, in the 3d *Inst.* 181. and if it is possible to exempt them out of that description, I confess then they have a stronger Case than I do hope they have.

A Monopoly (says he) is an institution, or an allowance by the King, by his Grant, Commission, or otherwise, to any person or persons, bodies politic or corporate, of or for the sole buying, selling, making, working, or using of any thing, whereby any person or persons, bodies politick or corporate, are sought to be restrained of any freedom or liberty that they had before, or hindered in their lawful trade.

First, My Lord, I think by their Patent, they have the sole trade granted to them; that is, the sole buying and selling (for merchandizing consists in buying and selling), and therefore they have the sole buying and selling in the *East-Indies*; and they have consequently the sole selling of the commodities when they come home; for none else can bring them home but them, if their Charter be good.

The sole using of any thing is a general word; and another part of this description, sole trading, is sole using of merchandizes, in a particular place to which they trade, and so they are within all the words sole selling, sole buying, sole using

Secondly, They are also within the latter part; whereby any person is hindered or restrained from any freedom or liberty they had before, or in their lawful trade: For that it is lawful for them, as I hope I shall make it appear, as I think, upon the Patent granted to seize the Ships and Goods of those that trade thither; and the bringing of this action is a sufficient proof that you were hinderers of this trade, and people's going thither to traffick. So I think, my Lord, they come within every part of the description that's given in that Book of a Monopoly.

Next, my Lord, I think that all the evils and mischiefs that are in the Books taken notice of to be in Monopolies, are also in this case; and whatsoever hath the evils and mischiefs attending Monopolies, it is a great and shrewd argument, that that which hath the effect, hath also the cause.

The evils and mischiefs that attend Monopolies, are, *first*, That the price of the commodities they sell shall be kept up, and raised higher than otherwise it would be. He that hath the sole sale will keep up the price as high as he pleases; this is one of the evils mentioned in the case of Monopolies, reported by my Lord *Coke*, *lib.* 11. *fo.* 86. *b.* the truth whereof I think is evident enough in that Company; for the price and value of things they bring from thence, are of their own setting, and at their own disposal. Nothing among men is more evident than that; and indeed it must be a most wonderful virtue, and a mighty contempt of riches, that a Man, who hath the sole commodity in his hands, will not sell it for the most he can; or not keep up the price, and make the most of it; and in things that he buys, to be sure he will buy as cheap as he can, and in things that he sells, he will sell as dear as he can; and I think that he that has such a power must be a man of an extraordinary virtue, if he do not execute it.

Secondly, Another evil of Monopoly is, that it is *pro privato paucularum quæstu*, which is likewise mentioned in the margin of the Book cited before, 3 *Inst.* 181. Now whether this trade be for particular private gain of a few or no, I think any man that knows any thing will be satisfied about it in his own mind, who considers the present state and condition of this Company. It is not upon Record indeed, but sure it is easily gathered as a consequence, and it will appear plainly by this reason to be *pro privato pauculorum quæstu*: for trade is not in its own nature fixed and stable, but varying and altering, sometimes better, sometimes worse, sometimes beneficial, sometimes detrimental, according as the times of war and peace, sickness, scarcity of this or that commodity in this or that Country; or the modes and customs of the Country, or the manners and habits of men do occasion it: And the Merchants by their education and observation, are those that govern and manage this trade for the maintenance of themselves and their families, and the general good of Men; and direct and employ

their

their Eſtates and Traffick into this or that part of the World, as time and occaſion ſhall give them beſt encouragement.

But a ſole trade granted into this or that part of the World to one Company, and of another part to another, ſets up particular men that head that Company, but deſtroys all other Merchants and inferior people; all ſhipping muſt be ſubject to the prices theſe Impropriators of trade will allow them, or elſe lie ſtill and be deſtroy'd, for none elſe muſt employ them, nor can do it; and ſo muſt all Maſters of Ships, for it is neceſſary to them, in order for their livelihood, that they go ſuch Voyages, and theſe cannot go, except upon the terms that the Company will allow of. So all Mariners, Artificers, Factors, and all other perſons, whoſe employments depend upon this trade, muſt be ſubject to their will and pleaſure: and of how great conſequence that may be to the Kingdom, my Lord, does deſerve conſideration.

Thirdly, A third evil and miſchief in Monopolies is, that they are to the oppreſſion of the King's people; and any body, I think, that has known any thing of late years about this Company, that is, that knows their dealings with, and handling of their factors and ſervants, that get any thing in their ſervice; and other people that they employ, will find inſtances enough of their oppreſſion; and that will be enough to ſatisfy any man, what kind of people they are: for what a work is there, when they have any factor or ſervant, or any body elſe that has got any thing in their ſervice? Thoſe things indeed are not upon the Record, but they are conſequences that are viſible to every body: and the truth of it is, in all Patents for ſole trade, ſo it will be. So that if the evils and miſchiefs, which the Common Law forbids, and endeavours to prevent, by judging all Monopolies, Ingroſſings and ſole Trade unlawful, be to be avoided, the evils and miſchefs attending their Patent and ſole Trade are perhaps the greater, becauſe their Trade is the greateſt that ever *England* knew.

My Lord, in *Fitzherbert*'s *Natura Brevium*, 222. there is this ſaid, and I urge it for this reaſon; becauſe if ſo be theſe are conſequences of a ſole trade, it cannot be denied but theſe are oppreſſions of all the King's people. Now there it is ſaid, that every Grant of the King has a condition implied in it, *Quod Patria per Donationem non magis ſolito oneretur ſeu gravetur*; ſo the Book of 13 *H.* IV. 14. Grant *le Roy*, to the charge or prejudice of the ſubjects, is void: and therefore the King is deceived in this Grant; and the Grant is as well by the Common Law, as all theſe ancient Statutes, void.

Obj. Ay, but ſay they, this is not a Patent granted to the advantage of a few, or for the raiſing of the prizes and monopolizing of commodities, but for good government and order, and the preſervation of this trade, that otherwiſe would be deſtroyed: and ſay they, there have been ſuch Grants heretofore to *Turky*, *Barbary*, and other places.

Rep. It is true, my Lord, this is ſaid; and that Patent does ſay, that it is for good order and government, and the advantage of trade. But I pray, my Lord will alſo remember what our Books ſay concerning ſuch Grants and Monopolies, in 2 *Inſt.* 540 that new Corporations trading into foreign parts and at home, tho' under the fair pretence of order and government, yet in concluſion tend to the hindrance of trade and traffick, and in the end produce Monopolies. This is an old obſervation, for in the 11*th Rep.* 88. *b.* in the end of the caſe of Monopolies, there are theſe words: *Privilegia quæ re vera ſunt in Prajudicium, Reip. magis tamen ſpecioſa habent Frontiſpicia, & boni publici prætextum, quam bonæ & legales Conceſſiones, ſed prætextu licito non debent admitti illicitum.* Thoſe are the words of that Book; and there it is alſo taken notice of, that *Darcy*'s Patent had a moſt glorious and ſpecious preamble; for there it is mention'd, that the ſubjects might exerciſe themſelves in huſbandry and lawful employments, and that Cards-making had made Cards-playing more frequent, and principally among Servants and Apprentices; and therefore the ſole making, and trade of Cards-ſelling, was granted to *Darcy*. Obſerve, ſays the Book, what a glorious pretext and preamble this odious Monopoly had.

There is the caſe of *Horn* and *Ivy*, *Mich.* 20. *Car.* II. *Rot.* 403. A Patent made three years after the Patent given to the Company, and in imitation thereof, the Patent is to the *Canary* Company; and recites, that the trade to the *Canaries* was of great advantage to the King's ſubjects at that time; and by reaſon of too much exceſs in trading of ſubjects there, our merchandizes were decreaſed in their value; ſo that the King's ſubjects were forced to carry Silver there to get Wines; and all this happened for want of regulation and good government, and thereupon the Patent did conſtitute Sir *Arthur Ingram*, and about ſixty perſons more by name. And all thoſe, that had been traders there within ſeven years, for the value of 1000*l.* a-year, ſhould be a Company and Body politick and corporate by ſuch a name; that there ſhould be a Governor, a Deputy-Governor, and twelve Aſſiſtants, and names them, but to be continued by election, and ſhould have the ſole trade to theſe Iſlands; that no other ſhou'd haunt or viſit theſe Iſlands, and prohibits all others under pain of forfeiture and impriſonment, and indeed follows very much the frame of this Patent, with a *non-obſtante* to the Statute of Monopolies. But notwithſtanding this glorious preamble, this Patent was ſoon afterwards condemn'd, both in this Court, and afterwards in the Parliament for the abuſe of trade, and the regulation of it for the general good, which is the thing that is pretended; but few men can doubt what is really intended by that; and no one I think can doubt, what is the real intention of this Patent under the name of regulation and government: to ingroſs all into the hands of ten or twelve men is moſt excellent regulation and government.

My Lord, as to the other Companies and Charters that have been granted, ſuppoſing that all theſe Grants were ſuch as this, and uſed and practiſed as this is, it is no argument that they are legal, or that this was good. For, my Lord, it is well known, both by the ancient Statutes that I have cited, and by common experience, that there have been in all ages and times Patents granted, that were not by Law grantable, but the King was deceived in them, and thoſe Patents were void and of no force; and therefore it is no argument, becauſe there have been many ſuch Grants and Patents in former times, that this ſhould be good.

I agree, my Lord, if ever this Grant, or any Grant like this, had come in queſtion, and had receiv'd any judicial allowance to be good, it had been ſo nething; but otherwiſe it can be no inference at all, becauſe there are others this is a good one.

But, my Lord, to keep myſelf cloſe to the point of Monopo
polies have been granted in the beſt of times; in Queen *Eliz*
there was *Darcy*'s Patent granted then; and it appears th
grants to divers others of the ſole making and ſelling of Card
it was queſtion'd, it was condemn'd. Statute 9 *E.* III. *cap.* 1.
Statutes before-cited, the clauſes that ſay, all Patents granted o
ed contrary to the freedom of trade in theſe Statutes mentio

Firſt, That ſuch Patents have been.

Secondly, That they did foreſee, and provided againſt, thoſ
be.

The Proviſo in the Statute of 43 *Eliz. cap.* 1. *ſect.* 9. ſhe
Monopolies were granted; but ſo far were they from receiving
ance, or approbation, that that Statute that was made in the
reign, for confirmation of the Queen's Grants by a ſpecial Prov
cept and provide that it ſhould not extend to make good any
tent that did concern any licences, powers or privileges, comn
Monopolies.

The Statute of Monopolies and this Statute ſufficiently ſhev
were ſuch Grants, and that they were not allowed; ſo that ev
Elizabeth's time, and during her reign, divers ſuch Grants it
been made. But, my Lord, if ſo be there had never been any
lowance in times paſt for any ſole trade, or ſole buying or ſ
there have been in all times ſuch Grants made, yet that will b
ment that they were good, but on the contrary; and further t
of theſe Companies have been to the contrary, till within lat
ſole trade practiſed among them.

But, my Lord, on the contrary, ſince that Patents have been
ſince that there is no judicial allowance of ſuch; I would app
to ſhew whether there has been any practice of theſe things. I
poſe, but that in *Turky* and *Barbary*, perſons have traded tha
been licenſed by the Companies, and that continually in all
yet I think no-body will find any judicial opinion that has
againſt them for it, or that ever any ſuch Patent was of force
the ſubjects freedom of trade in thoſe places.

My Lord, I am apt to think, that the Grants to thoſe Comp
is, the *Turky*-Company, the *Barbary*-Company, and the *Ruſſia*-
are like to this of ſole trade; but yet if it never has been praci
ſtrain others in this manner, it is rather an argument againſt t
other ſide; but they have never dealt thus, nor uſed the clauſe of p
as theſe men do. For, my Lord, whoever thinks to make any
for the preſervation of ſuch a ſole trade by a Company, with
of others, becauſe ſuch Patents and Charters have been grante
Companies, will have but little reaſon ſo to do, if he conſider wh
rence there is between this Company and them: for, my Lord, t
panies did never ſet up for a ſole trade, tho' there be ſuch wo
Patents, they never uſed them, but have always uſed their
contrary, and in another method in a commendable way, and I
legal way; but not ſo as to warrant any thing of this, that is
tended. Therefore if your Lordſhip pleaſe to give me leave, I
ſerve the difference betwixt the way of trading, that thoſe o
panies have, and the trade of the *Eaſt-India* Company. The
of *Turky*, *Barbary*, *Ruſſia*, *Muſcovy* and *Hamburgh*, nor any ot
late years, did ever trade with a Joint-Stock; but the Memb
ſaid Company, every man uſed his own trade, bought and ſol
commodity, uſed and employed his own factors and ſervants; and
pany took ſome care to ſend out a Conſul, or ſome one to be their
preſerve the trade, and by ſmall impoſts upon the commodities
to provide for ſuch Officers: which Impoſts or Aſſeſſments we
By-Laws and Regulations among themſelves. They take care th
ſhall not be over-clogged by the Commodities they ſend out, w
do alſo by their own Orders and By-Laws that are made am
ſelves; they only order what Ships ſhall go, but leave the partic
bers of the Company, every man to ſend what he will upon hi
count, and appoint who he will to be his factor, and to bring
commodity he pleaſes: they trade not upon any Joint-Stock, o
of the Body-Politick. If you deal with any of them, you know
ticular perſon you have to deal with: no man is refuſed to b
Company, that has a mind, paying ſome ſmall ſum of mon
freedom; and whoever is of the Company, has a Vote in orderi
fairs of the Company. But now you of the *Eaſt-India* Compa
the ſole trade into the Body-Politick; you have a Joint-Stock,
whether Merchant or not, if he can buy ſuch a ſhare in their S
their Company. The Committee manage, and the reſt muſt ſub
pleaſures and diſtribution: thoſe few of them which have the m
have the diſpoſal of the whole Stock, no Member trades, buys
has any thing that he calls his own, but only ſuch a ſhare in the S
ſuffer not the Members to trade with their own money, at thei
cretion; or to employ whom they pleaſe, this you do not do; yo
man to have a Vote among you (and your Letters Patent have ſu
that none ſhall) but he who has 500*l.* ſtock; which 500*l.* no m
quire, unleſs he pays 14*l.* or 15*l.* for it, two and a half *per Cen*
great ſum. So that by the very foundation, they can have no mo
in their Company, than they that have 500*l.* ſhares; and theſe
ing ingroſſed into few hands, they have all, and call themſelves
pany. So that man that will not be deceived by words, but
things different one from another, will diſtinguiſh between one
and Society, and another; who are Ingroſſers, Monopolizers, an

The *Turky* Company, and the reſt like it, may be truly ſaid
nagers, Regulators and Improvers of Trade. They have no Jo
that they trade upon, they ingroſs not, they admit every man
to be free of their Company, to trade with his own money, his
dit, and buy and ſell his own, and to employ whom he pleaſeth.
among them, under pretence of government, regulation and p
of trade, makes unreaſonable advantages.

But this inviſible *Eaſt-India* Merchant, the Body-Politick,
countenances ſome few men among them to ingroſs, buy and ſ
own rates, and that exclude all others for the great and exceſſ
tages of the few.

The other Companies, as the *Turky* Company, &c. have not any sole buying or selling, nor exercising any sole trade or ingrossing.

Every Member of these Companies, which are a multitude, and every one that is not, may, if he will, be a Member, and no man is excluded.

But this Company is quite contrary, and therefore (if ever any was) are great Ingrossers and Monopolizers of trade. I do not argue nor speak against Companies, nor regulating, nor managing trade, which was the true intent of the Patent; such as I have mentioned, and is virtuously and commendably practised in the great Companies of *Turky*, *Muscovy*, *Hamburgh*, and others; where the Members of the Companies trade upon their own particular Stock and Estates, and no Merchant hindered or denied to be a Member, that desires it, paying its ordinary fees of admission: but against the invisible Merchant, this politick capacity trading in Joint-Stock.

Suppose a like Patent to any one, or two, or three men, Farmers or Partners in their private capacity of this sole trade; and they had the management of it, and hereby possessors of such vast wealth and merchandize:

What would this Politick Body (I mean the principal Members, for the Body cannot think or have sense) judge of this?

Perhaps yours is much worse; there a man should know with whom he dealt, who were his debtors, and how to come at them; but dealing with you is a kind of dealing with spirits, an invisible body, only subsisting *in Intelligentia Legis*.

Therefore being so unlike the other Companies, and so contrary to them, you have no countenance from them; but though they are good and commendable, you are Ingrossers and Monopolizers.

This shews the great and vast difference between the one and the other; this shews that you, that are the *East-India* Company, have the sole trade as a Company; and whoever buys in many Stocks, has as many votes as he has 500 *l.* in the Stock.

There is no such thing in any other Company, but quite otherwise in all these respects; but hereby it comes to pass, that he that has so many shares in the Stock, has an absolute power, by having so many votes.

The invisible Body or Corporation perhaps trade for 1,000,000 *l. per Ann.* they get into their hands to sell 7 or 800,000*l.* worth of merchandize at a time; the three last sales they made came to 1,8000,000 *l.* nobody hath these commodities but they. Is this trading, and no ingrossing or monopolizing? It is their wonderful virtue then, hatred and contempt of riches, that makes them not to raise and increase values and prices, and be as rich as they please, if they do not do it. Never was there such an instance of so great trade in *England*, but none of your Members buys or trades at all; any man among you, whether he be Merchant or not Merchant, Citizen or Gentleman, or what he will, if he has a Stock, his Stock goes on by this joint-trade, but it is a few men that manage the whole as they see best; no man employs ships or workmen as he thinks most convenient; but you are one great trader in this vast trade, which is indeed one quarter part of the trade of the whole World.

My Lord, this being then the great difference between this trade by a Joint-Stock, and in the Company as a Body Politick, which is but as one entire person, having the trade entire to himself, and the trade of particular Members, under orderly regulations:

It is quite a different and distinct thing from any thing, in any of the other Companies, that they would be likened unto to obtain their own ends: nor is there any reason to make them like one another, for the whole matter is carried on distinct in both; the one is a sole trade by a Body Politick, the other dispersed through the Members, according to their own discretion and occasion, under regulation. No man, if he comes into the *East-India* Company, can trade among you, or vote among you, unless he have 500*l.* Stock; and if he do not come in, (since it is according to your constitution, that every man should have as many votes as he has 500*l.*) his vote is like to do him little good, if some few men in the Company agree against it.

And besides this, my Lord, in the *Turky* Company, where they trade as distinct Members, every man knows his creditor and his debtor, because they deal in their natural capacities; but you trading in capacity of a Body Politick, every man that trades with you has a creditor or a debtor, he knows not whom.

And it is a great mischief, when persons know not how to sue or how to deal with them; for take them all a-part, they are as just and as good people to deal with, as can be; but take them together as a body, what more hard to deal with than a Corporation?

My Lord, we have seen the instance of these things in this Company, in a few days they having so great power, that none could contend with them, and soon after so invisible, as well as low that no Dun can find them. This we all know very well, my Lord; and I instance in this to show, that whereas they would be likened to other Companies, which were created for the preservation and benefit of trade; and the Members of it are under the regulation and government of the Company, but not as you are; they are traders, your Members are none, you are only the Body Politick, the invisible Merchant, that no one knows where to find; and a Body Politick, in judgment of Law, has neither Soul nor Conscience, and yet forsooth are traders.

I only instance in these things, to shew that signifies nothing which you did insist upon, that there are other Companies for trade, for I say, that they are good and regular, and not Monopolizers, for they do not trade in such a manner by sole buying and selling, but every one trades as a particular Merchant; but you are otherwise, your Body Politick is the sole Merchant, and none of your Members can trade, unless a particular servant, perhaps to save charges, you give him leave to buy or deal in some little things; but all others are quite excluded.

My Lord, having thus shewed you the way of their trade in sole buying and sole selling, I shall now, in the next place, come to the Statute of Monopolies, which is the Statute of 21 King *James*, *chap.* 3. and I hope I shall plainly shew you, that they are within the words and meaning of that Statute.

By that Statute, my Lord, it is enacted, that all Monopolies, Commissions, Grants, Licences, Charters and Letters Patent granted, or to be granted to any particular persons, Bodies Politick or Corporate, of, or for the sole buying, selling, making, working, or using of any thing within this Realm; and all Proclamations, Inhibitions, Restraints, Warrants of Assistance; and all other matters and things whatsoever, tending to the instituting, erecting, strengthening, furthering, or countenancing the same contrary to the Laws of this Realm, are and shall be utterly void and of none effect.

And that all Persons, Bodies Politick and Corporate, which now are; or hereafter shall be, shall stand and be disabled to have use, exercise, or put in use any Monopoly, or such Commission, Grant, Licence, Charter, Letters Patent, Proclamations, Inhibitions, Restraint or other matter, or thing tending as aforesaid; or any liberty, power or faculty, grounded or pretended to be grounded upon them.

Then, my Lord, there follows the clauses of forfeiture of treble damages to the party grieved, by the using of any such Monopoly; then there is the clause about new Inventions and some other things; then comes the *Proviso* concerning Corporations, of which some use being made in this case, I shall crave leave to consider it distinctly.

Provided also, and it is hereby enacted, That this Act, or any thing therein contained, shall not in any wise extend or be prejudicial to the City of *London*, &c. or any Corporation, Company or Fellowship of any Art, Trade, Occupation or Mystery, or to any Companies or Societies of Merchants, within the Realm, erected for the maintenance, enlarging, or ordering of any trade or merchandize; but that the same Charters, Corporations, Companies, Fellowships and Societies, and their Liberties, Privileges, Powers and Immunities shall be and continue of like force and effect, as they were before the making of this Act, and no other, any thing in this Act to the contrary notwithstanding.

The next Proviso extends to Patents granted, or to be granted for Printing, making of Salt-Petre, and Offices, which do not concern the case in question.

By the description of a Monopoly, which I have before, out of my Lord *Coke*, stated and expressed, this sole trade granted to you, and the exclusion of all others, is a Monopoly within that description, as I have before shewn that their Charter is directly contrary to this Act. My Lord, *first*. That they are within the enacting clause of this Act; this, I think, by comparing what they claim with the enacting clause, will plainly appear. I need not now stand so much upon the word Monopoly, whether by what I have said, I have proved them a Monopoly or no; but by the other words of the Statute, supposing that word Monopoly was out of the Act, yet they are within it: for the Act of Parliament having the words of sole selling, or sole buying, or sole using of any thing; if they have the sole buying or sole selling, or sole using of this trade, then they are most plainly, I think, within the enacting words of this Act of Parliament.

Now, my Lord, that their Charter is directly contrary to the enacting words, I must also therein refer myself to the words of the Charter, which has sole buying; for all others are prohibited so much as to come and go from and to the *East-Indies* without their licence. It has also sole selling; for all others are prohibited to import any commodity from thence into the Realm; and they cannot sell them, except they import them. They have likewise the sole using; for they have granted to them the sole trade, which includes all buying, selling, sole using, that appropriates all to themselves, and excludes all others.

How then, my Lord, can any man read this Act of Parliament and their Charter, and compare them togeher, but he must at the same time conclude, that their Charter is contrary to what is enacted there? For the Act of Parliament does say, That all Letters Patent granted to any Person, or Body Politick, for the sole buying, sole selling, or sole using any thing, and all Proclamations, Restraints and Inhibitions to the contrary, and all other matters and things touching thereunto, are contrary to law, and utterly void, and of none effect; why then they have by their Grant, the sole buying, sole selling, and sole using of this trade; therefore they are quite contrary to what is in the enacting words of this Act of Parliament. Then, my Lord, if they are contrary to the enacting clause of the Act, then their hopes must be, that they are saved by the *Proviso*.

My Lord *Coke*, in his Comment upon this Act, in 3 *Inst.* 182. does say this Act is forcibly and vehemently penned for the suppression of all Monopolies; and the word sole using, is there said to be so general, as no Monopoly can be raised but will be within the reach of this Statute.

The word, *any-thing*, shews also the general scope and intent, that nothing should be excluded that was a Monopoly. For Monopolies, in times past, were ever without Law, but never without friends. And if it be so penned for the suppression of all, it ought to have a large and general construction.

Obj. But then let us see whether they are in the saving of this *Proviso*.

The *Proviso* excepts Charters to Companies or Societies of Merchants within this Realm, erected for the maintenance, inlargement, or ordering of trade or merchandize.

Resp. This *Proviso* extends not to this Charter, or any Letters Patent that were not at the time of the making of this Act; and that is the first thing that I offer, why they are not within the reach of the *Proviso*. Because this *Proviso* does not extend to any Letters Patent after the Act of Parliament made, but only the Letters Patent before. For the *Proviso* says, *It shall not extend, or be prejudicial to any Town Corporate*, concerning any Charter granted to them, &c. or Customs used by them, or to Societies erected for the maintenance, inlargement or ordering any trade or merchandize. This does extend to those that were granted or erected at the time of the making of the Act; and there are no words of saving, for any that should hereafter be erected. And the word hereafter would as well have been in the clause of saving, as in the enacting clause, if it had been intended. But the following words, concluding this *Proviso*, shew it further, for the *Proviso* goes on, and says, That the same Charters, Customs, Corporations, Fellowships and Societies, and their Liberties, &c. shall be and continue of such force and effect, as they were before the making of this Act, and no other. This shews, that that which is within the *Proviso*, was that which was before the making of the Act only; and this governs and concludes the whole *Proviso*. Now that only extending to those that then were, and to leave them as they were, to leave their Charters and Companies, their Powers and Privileges, in the same state and condition as they were before the Act, can never have any reference to what should be after.

 The

The Beginning of the *Proviso* says, this Act shall not prejudice them: The Conclusion says, they shall be as they were before the Act was made; therefore they must have had a Being before the Act, but no Words herein extend to those that then had not a Being.

And, my Lord, the next *Proviso* for Printing, Salt-petre, Offices, &c. that is to this, further shews this to be the Meaning of this *Proviso*; for that expresly provides, That this Act, or any thing therein contained, shall not extend to any Grant or Privilege heretofore made, or hereafter to be made, of, for, or concerning Printing. If then the former Clause had intended to include any Letters Patent that were after to be granted, it would have had these Words, *To be granted as well here as in the Clause that comes afterwards.*

But, my Lord, suppose this not to be a sufficient Answer to this *Proviso*, but that this *Proviso* shall be construed to extend to Companies, Charters, Privileges, and Immunities, granted after this Act; yet the Plaintiffs are not within this *Proviso*, nor the saving of it: For it extends only to Companies that are for the Maintenance, Inlargement, or ordering of any Trade or Merchandize, and to their Powers, &c. that they have to that End not two Companies, that are erected to have a sole Trade by a joint Stock, or Stock of the Corporation, to exclude all others from having any thing to do in that Trade. It does, and reasonably may be intended to extend to all Companies that are for the Maintenance, increase, and well-ordering of Trade; as the *Turky* Company, the *Muscovy* Company, the *Russia* Company, and *Hamborough* Company, and those that I have been speaking of, that trade not as Bodies Politic, or a joint Stock, but every Merchant that will, may be thereof a Member, and every Member thereof trades upon his own private Stock and Account as a Merchant; but not to this Company, who, instead of ordering the Trade, endeavour to bring the sole Trade unto themselves.

Therefore, my Lord, these are the Companies that are within the Exception saved from the Penalties of this Act; but we must be as silly as the Infidels they deal with in these Matters, not to distinguish betwixt these Corporations, and their Management and yours; they exclude none from Trade, they trade not in a politick Capacity in a sole Stock, but every Man is a Trader upon his own peculiar, but you take upon you in your politick Capacity, as you have expressed it in your Declaration, *totum, integrum & solum Commercium & Negotiationem habere, uti & gaudere*; and to exclude not only all Strangers, but all your own Members, to have any distinct or separate Trade upon his own Account, except a little to pay and excuse you of Charges, and thereby ingross all that vast Quantity of Merchandizes, the many hundred thousand Pounds worth you bring in or carry out. In whom is the Property? In the Corporation. Who buys and sells all? The Corporation. Who are the Debtors for the Money that buys and provides these Merchandizes? The Body Politick, the Corporation, the invisible Body. Who shall be sued for all these Debts? The Body Politick; sue them as you can, they will either be too great and too rich to contend with, or else in that Condition as you know not how or where to have them.

An invisible Body, subsisting only in *Intelligentiâ legis*, a Body Politick without Soul or Conscience, as the Law says it to be.

We have seen them in a Year's Time, in both these Qualifications, so great as scarce any Man would contend with them, so invisible at another time, as a Dun would scarce find them; this surely cannot be for the Maintenance or Inlargement of Trade, to deal with I know not whom, where no Security or Person subsists.

It is indeed for the Maintenance of the Company's Trade, to enable some of them to get 10 or 20,000 *l. per Annum* by it, and to keep this vast Trade in a few Hands.

But sure that is not of the Trade the *Proviso* intends; restraining to the Body Politick, which is but one Person, or many in Partnership, is quite contrary to the Enlargement of the *Proviso* mentioned.

And therefore to say you are within the saving by this *Proviso*, a Company erected for the Maintenance and Inlargement of Trade, when you restrain all but yourselves to trade, seems to be a Contradiction.

And for the following Words in the *Proviso*, *Or ordering of any Trade or Merchandize*; if you say you are saved within the Extent of these Words, then you must make a Construction of these Words in this Sense:

That ordering Trade or Merchandize, is excluding all others, and taking the whole to ourselves. A most excellent *Ordering* that is.

But the Sense of these Words in the *Proviso* is, to save to the Corporations and Fellowships of Arts, Trades, Occupations and Mysteries, and to Companies of Merchants, the Powers and Authorities that they had for the Maintenance, Inlargement, or ordering of Trade;

By taking care that Commodities were honestly and rightly made, without Fraud or Deceit, as to the Goodness or Excellency of the Commodity, or Deceit in their Measures or Quantity;

That the Servants and younger Sort were honestly and industriously educated in their Trades and Mysteries, by the Masters and elder Sort;

To place and keep good Order and Decorum amongst those of the same Mystery and Trade;

For assembling and consulting for the common Good and Management of their respective Trades and Employments.

This is that which the *Proviso* excepts and provides for, not for a sole Trade in a Company, in a joint Stock, excluding all others, as this is.

For the same Exception is also for the Manufactures that are mentioned just before, as new Inventions, and the Society of any Craft or Mystery, these also are under the Exception, which does still expound them to be meant of that regular, due Order and Government in Companies, for the due regulating of Trades and Mysteries, that is, by making By-laws to take care that their Wares be well and substantially made, that the younger Sort be obedient to the elder, and the elder instruct the younger, and not oppress them. These are the Laws that they have Power (and 'tis fit they should have) to make for the Management and Increase of Trade. But to have a sole Power over Trade, and an Interest in it by a joint Stock, to ingross it into one Man's Hands, or into the Hands of a Body Politick, which is but as one Person in Law, and in this Manner to trade under the Pretence of Order or good Government, this, under Favour, was never meant or intended by this Exception in this Act. Therefore that which I have before expressed, is the Sense and Meaning of this *Proviso*, and not the having the sole Trade, excluding all others, as here is endeavoured and designed to have.

My Lord, in the Taylor of *Ipswich*'s Case, 11 *Co.* 54. tha[illegible] of Taylors made a By-law, to exclude Taylors from exerci[illegible] their Trade within the Town of *Ipswich*, unless they present[illegible] to the Master and Wardens of the Company, and three of [illegible] them to be sufficient Workmen, and proved they have served [illegible] at least as Apprentices, and then admitted by the Master, and W[illegible] Company, and if any did offend in any Part, they should forf[illegible] to the Company. In this Case there seemed to be a good End an[illegible] to exclude insufficient Workmen, and to encourage good on[illegible] Order one might think. Yet so zealous and careful were the J[illegible] lest under any Pretence they should exclude Men from th[illegible] Trades, that they adjudged this a void By-law, as tending in t[illegible] of it, to restrain Men of their Freedom in using their Trades, [illegible] ducing Oppression of the young Tradesmen by the old and ri[illegible] men, and to subvert the Liberty the Law gives. And in that [illegible] it was adjudged, *fo.* 54. That Ordinances for the good Orde[illegible] vernment of Men, of Trades and Mysteries, are good; but not [illegible] any in their lawful Mystery. *Norris* and *Stap*'s Case, *Hob.* 2[illegible] same Purpose.

Therefore, my Lord, this is the Sense and Meaning of that [illegible] that is in the Statute of Monopolies, That it saves such as w[illegible] ordering of Men in their Trades and good Government, but [illegible] able a Corporation to have a sole Trade, to hinder or exclude o[illegible] using it. That is the true Sense of the *Proviso*: But for the o[illegible] that they would have, 'tis the way to make it the most repugnant [illegible] tradictory Act that can be: For, my Lord, to shew that it i[illegible] me Leave to compare them.

The Sense they would have is, That it should save to Bodie[illegible] the having the sole buying, selling, and using any Merchandize [illegible] as a Corporation, that such should be excepted out of this Act.

Now let us compare the *Proviso* with the enacting Clause, a[illegible] the *Proviso* in that Sense they would have it, that a Body Poli[illegible] have the sole buying and selling, or using any Merchandize or [illegible] a Corporation, then the enacting Part, with the *Proviso*, will [illegible] enacted, *That Letters Patent to any Person or Body Politick, for th[illegible] ing, sole making or using of any thing within this Realm, or contrar[illegible] and void; and no Body Politick shall be capable of having, using, or [illegible] of any such Letters Patent, Inhibition or Restraint, provided that B[illegible] litick may have the sole buying, selling, and using of any Trade or Me[illegible]*

Is there any thing can be put in Words and Terms more cont[illegible] than this is? And yet thus it must be if their Sense prevail: So [illegible] Lord, there is not a more repugnant and contradictory thing can [illegible] than this *Proviso* to the Body of the Act, if you take it in the S[illegible] would have it.

Suppose the Statute of   that enacts, That no M[illegible] use a Trade that he has not served an Apprenticeship to by the [illegible] seven Years, had a *Proviso*, that a Man may chuse a Trade tha[illegible] not served an Apprenticeship to by the Space of seven Years; this [illegible] a void repugnant *Proviso*. This is as plainly repugnant, that [illegible] Politick shall be capable of having a sole Trade. Repugnant *Pr[illegible]* in Law void.

My Lord, If so be a *Proviso* be repugnant and contradictory [illegible] will be void; and so are all our Books, 1 *Co.* 46. *Plowd. Com.* [illegible] Statute gives the Lands of *J. S.* to the King, and then a *Prov[illegible]* to save the Right of all Persons: This shall be construed, all [illegible] besides *J. S.* not to destroy the Premises.

Therefore when this Act says, That all Patents granted to a B[illegible] litick, of the sole buying, selling, and using of any thing wi[illegible] Realm, shall be void; and a *Proviso* says, that it shall not exten[illegible] prejudicial to any Company of Merchants erected for the ordering [illegible] tenance, and Increase of any Trade or Merchandize, if construed [illegible] Sense, to give the Company sole buying, selling, and using of an[illegible] is directly contradictory and void; then that cannot be the Sen[illegible] taking it in the other, which I apprehend to be the true Sense, th[illegible] and Government is provided for; that is the meaning of the *Prov[illegible]* nothing else: and this is the general Practice of the Societies and [illegible] nies allowed in all times. But a sole Trade, under the Pretence [illegible] lour of Order and Management, never, as I believe, had any judi[illegible] lowance: And then you are within the enacting Clause of th[illegible] Parliament, and are a Monopoly; or because, it may be, you do [illegible] that Word, you have the sole buying, and sole selling, and sole [illegible] this Trade, which is contrary to the express Words of this Act of [illegible] ment, and so your Patent and Charter is void.

But, my Lord, they endeavour to answer this Objection with [illegible] Sort of Answer. They say the *Proviso* is, That the Act shall not [illegible] to Companies of Merchants erected for Government and Order of [illegible] but that their Charters, Privileges, and Immunities, shall be of lik[illegible] and Effect as they were before the making this Act; and theref[illegible] they, Patents to Companies of Merchants for ordering of Trade, [illegible] before this Act, shall be good still, and therefore, say they, this [illegible] not hurt us.

My Lord, the Objection is nice, as I apprehend, but so it is, [illegible] them right, this, under favour, is but the same thing again [illegible] Words; for the Conclusion of this *Proviso* extends no further t[illegible] Charter mentioned in the Beginning of it, it extends but to t[illegible] Charters (so are the very Words) shall be of a good Force, &c. [illegible] then what Charter or Patent is it that shall remain as th[illegible] the Act? Why those that are excepted. What are excepted? [illegible] are for Order and Management, as I have before shewn, [illegible] are for a Body Politick, to use a sole Trade, that is repugnant [illegible] acting Clause, therefore these, as I have said, are not excepted [illegible] the *Proviso*, and so we come back again where we were: [illegible] cepted out of the Act? If you are, I agree the Act hurts [illegible] are not excepted, then you cannot be in the same Condition [illegible] before, or as such Charters were before the making the Act; [illegible] Conclusion and latter Part of the *Proviso* is to be taken in no [illegible] than the Words that went before in the Beginning, nor can [illegible] ther than these Words extend; so that I see it resorts [illegible] where it was. If they be excepted, they be not within the A[illegible] the *Proviso* will be repugnant, as I have said before, and cont[illegible] if they are not excepted, they have no Benefit by the *P[illegible]*.

So, my Lord, taking it upon what I have said, I do hope that the words of the Act of Parliament plainly do extend to bodies politick, and to inhibit the ingrossing sole trade by bodies politick. They say themselves, and it appears they are a body politick, and they have this sole trade; and so the enacting clause extends to them.

Next, I say, the *Proviso* extends to Charters granted before, not to Charters to be granted after the Act of Parliament: and as to those Charters that are excepted, it leaves them just as they were before; but if their sense takes place, then it is, as I conceive, with submission, most palpably contradictory and repugnant to the Act; and then it is as lawful at this day to grant to any Corporation any sole trade or manufacture, yea, downright to grant them a Monopoly, as it is to make any other Grant; and so this would be rather a countenance, than an Act made against them.

But then, my Lord, they come to another thing; this is an Infidel Country, this is a sole trade with Infidels, and such a trade the subjects never had any right to have without the King's licence; and now being so, that differences the cause: and to prove it, they cite *Michelborn*'s Case, in 2 *Brownl.* 296. wherein Mr. *Brownlow* being Prothonotary, recites what my Lord *Coke* said in that Case, That no subject might trade into Infidel Countries without the King's licence; and his reason was, because he might relinquish the Catholic faith, and adhere to Infidelism: and that he had seen a licence in the time of *Ed.* III. wherein the King recites the confidence that he had in his subject, that he would not decline his Religion, and licensed him; and that this did arise upon the recital of a licence made to trade to the *East-Indies*.

And they do cite *Calvin*'s Case, in *Co.* 7. *Rep. fo.* 17. wherein 'tis said, That Infidels are, in law, *perpetui inimici*, and between them and Christians there is perpetual hostility, there can be no peace; and 12 *H.* VIII. *fol.* 4. where it is holden, that a Pagan cannot have or maintain any action at all, nor have any thing within this Realm; and to prove this, *Register* 282. and 12 *H.* VIII. *fo.* 4. are there cited.

My Lord, I have the more fully recited what this is, because I hope I shall give very full answers to all: But, my Lord, before I do answer those Books;

First, Let us see what the consequence of it will be: Supposing the Law to be as these Books say, and as these Gentlemen would have it; and the consequence will be, that the plaintiffs cannot maintain their action, but the Charters granted to them will be void.

First, Upon the reasons given in these Books; for if the Books are of authority, the reasons there given must be of authority (says that Book of *Brownlow*'s). The King has the care and preservation of Religion, by the Law vested and reposed in him, that the subject should not trade with Infidels without licence, that they may not renounce their faith; and the King will take care to give licence to traffick, to such only as he can have confidence will never waver from their profession.

Supposing this to be true, then their Patent must be nought; for then it is only grantable to persons in whom such confidence may be. My Lord, then see how this will stand with their Charter. Their corporation and body politick is indefinite, as to persons, and the members changed continually; some sell their stocks, and go out, or die; others buy their stocks, and come in that way to be members of the company, or as executors to those that die, and many new members are every year. I doubt they do not much examine, or take care to be satisfied, how fixed those are in their Religion they daily take in; and how then can there be confidence in a body politick, which the law says has neither soul nor conscience? What confidence can be reposed in such a person about Religion?

Secondly, Besides, it is not only the members of the Company, that at the time of the incorporation were incorporated, and their successors, that are thus privileged; but their sons and apprentices, their factors and servants, have licence by this Patent to trade there: and what security can there be, that such may not (by conversing with Infidels) change their Religion? If this Licence be a trust and prerogative in the King, to be given to such persons in whom the King can have confidence, that they will not, by converse with Infidels, change or prejudice their religion, *&c.* this cannot be granted to a body politick and their successors, which may have continuance for ever; and to their sons, factors, apprentices and servants, persons altogether unknown, not born, nor *in rerum natura* when these Letters Patent were made.

Suppose such a licence to you, to trade with enemies, and supposing that the Law has established such a power and prerogative in the King, in the preservation of religion, to license; the King cannot grant this prerogative to you of the *East-India* Company, that you should have a power to grant licences to whom you will: yet all this is done by your Patent; for you have thereby power granted you for your sons, apprentices, factors and servants, which are persons that you yourselves nominate and appoint at your discretions, and undoubtedly very religious, and others that you bring into your Company.

Next, besides this power that you have expressed for those that are your apprentices, *&c.* which are at your discretion, to make whom you please; there is another express clause, That the Company for any consideration, or benefit to themselves, may grant licence to any servant, stranger or other, to use this trade. So the Patent expresses what the meaning was of the word Consideration, by adding the Words, *or benefit to themselves*; and that the King, without consent of the Company, will not grant licence to any other to trade there.

Can this then be a good Grant? Can the King grant from himself his kingly care, and the trust in him reposed for the care of Religion to you, to manage it as you will, and that he will not use it himself without your consent? Surely, you cannot say so. So that supposing by law there is such a trust reposed in the King for preservation of religion, as you would have, to give licence to his subjects to trade with Infidels; and that none without his licence can do it: yet this grant to you will be void in itself, and then you have no more right than we, and can maintain no action against us.

But then a little to consider the authorities upon which this great matter relies, to prove this religious point or piece of law.

First, That Book of *Brownl.* is a Book that was printed in the late times, and not licensed by any Judge or Person whatsoever; but truly I have got a copy, and a note of the Roll of the Case there reported; and it is this, *Mich.* 7 *Jac. B. C. Rot.* 3107. *Michelborn* against *Bathurst*; it is in a prohibition, setting forth, That the King had granted to the plaintiff his commission to go with the ship *Tyger* to the *Indies*, to spoil and suppress the Infidels, and to take from them what he could; that the plaintiff, in the Prohibition, having this commission from the King, did enter into Articles with the defendant, to give him a share of what he should get in the adventure: and thereupon there was a suit in the Admiralty by the defendant, against the plaintiff, and he comes and moves for a Prohibition, suggesting that the articles were made upon the land, and not upon the high sea, and so the Court had no jurisdiction. Now upon the debate of this Case, it did appear, there was a kind of Letters of mart, a commission from the King, in a warlike manner to spoil the Infidels, and get what he could from them. But now, how this would come in debate to make a resolution about the business of trade, I do not know; probably it might be as is there related; but what is in the Book is only an occasional saying of my Lord *Coke*'s, upon the motion for this prohibition. So that a man that will lay any great stress upon such an authority, must be mighty willing; for it is only an occasional saying, and nothing relating to what was there brought in judgment, which was about a commission to take away goods, perhaps from enemies, by Letters of mart, not about trade; and so I hope there is no great matter in that Report.

The next Case, my Lord, is that of *Calvin*, where it is said, that an Infidel is *perpetuus inimicus*, can maintain no action, or have any thing; and that there is perpetual hostilities between Christians and such, and no peace can be made with them.

My Lord, 'tis true, that this is said in *Calvin*'s case, but I must also say, as there was no occasion in the former Report for saying of that, no more is there in *Calvin*'s case for saying of this; for it made nothing to the matter in question about the *Post-nati*, or were they any wise led to it, in the debate of that case; there was nothing there in judgment that gave occasion for it, so that I cannot think it was much considered of before it was spoken.

The Books that are there cited, I have looked upon, to see if they would prove any such thing as they are there cited for, and I think they do it not by any means.

There is first the Register 282. and all that I find there is, that in a writ of protection granted to the Prior and Brethren of the Hospital of St. *John* at *Jerusalem*, and their agents, it is said, That that Hospital was founded in defence of Holy Church, against the enemies of Christ and Christians: but truly, how to conclude out of that Book this, that Infidels should not have any property in trade, or be *perpetui inimici*, with whom no peace can be had, I know not, or that can maintain no action.

Then *fo.* 12 *H.* VIII. 4. they also cited, that is only this, The original case in an action of trespass for beating his servant, taking away his dog, called a blood-hound: And there it is said, If a Lord beat his villein, or an husband beat his wife, or a man beat one out-law'd, or a traitor, or a Pagan; they shall have no action, because they are not able to sue an action. I must confess, my Lord, this comes in very oddly, from a dog to a Pagan, and there is nothing to lead to it in all that case, that I can see; and yet this is all the authority that is cited in *Calvin*'s case, to prove that they can have no action. So that all that a man can make of this is only discourse, and sudden thoughts and opinions, and sayings of Counsel; nothing of debate or judgment in the case.

It is true, my Lord, the Christian Religion and Paganism are so contrary to one another, that it is impossible they should be reconciled any more than contradictions can be reconciled; but because the religions cannot be reconciled, that therefore there should be a partition-wall between us, as to property and commerce, perhaps is a doctrine as irreligious as can be, and does destroy all means of coming to convince and reduce them to the faith. But now, besides these extrajudicial and occasional sayings in these Books cited, which are of little authority, I cannot find any Books or Cases, much less judgment or authority, for such opinions in so great a point as this is: but on the other side, if a man considers the general cause and practice of trade and commerce, and legal proceedings in all times and ages, one would think my Lord *Coke* could not be in earnest in what he has said in *Calvin*'s case about Infidels. Let a man consider what a great part of the world we have commerce with are Infidels, at this day, as the *Turks*, the *Persians*, the *Moors*; and other places in *Spain* and *Portugal* were possessed by the *Moors*, who were Infidels, till about 200 years since: for till the year 1474, the *Moors* had possession of both these Countries for the space of near 700 years before, and have we not always had trading with all those? Have we not leagues and treaties with the Princes of Infidel Countries? Do we not receive Ambassadors from them, and send Ambassadors to them, and Ministers residing with them? Have we not, from time to time, and this in all times and ages, and that in Q. *Elizabeth*'s time, in the best and most religious time, for many hundred years? Have we not likewise war and peace with them, in like manner as with Christian Kings and Countries?

And let a man consider the consequences of this doctrine. If they are *perpetui inimici*, then we may justify killing of them, as those we are in hostility with, wheresoever we meet them, and justify the taking away what they have from them, as 17 *E.* IV. *fo.* 13, 14. it is adjudged, that a man may seize and take to his own use the goods of an alien enemy, wherever he can find them; for it is the price of his adventure to take them, and of his victory over his enemy, if he have taken him. And 2 *H.* VII. 15. if an Infidel be an alien enemy, then any man may take away the goods of an Infidel, and have them to his own use; and this would be a good trade, if this be so; any man may kill and beat him, if this be so.

Mr. Sollicitor, in his argument, was pleased to use many ancient Rolls and Records out of *H.* III. and *Ed.* I. and about those times, concerning these Princes dealing with and handling of the *Jews*; and I believe he might have cited many more.

Mr. *Prynne*, in his Book which he calls *The second Part of a short Demurrer to the* Jews, *discontinued and barred Remitter into* England, printed in the year 1656, has a long treatise, in which I believe an hundred Records and Histories are cited to this purpose, That the *Jews* did exact and enrich themselves by usury, to the great impoverishing of the people; and that the Princes of those times polled them, taxed them, and

and took away the eſtates of the *Jews* from time to time; and thereby a man might think that theſe Kings uſed them but as ſpunges, to make them gripe what they could from others, and then ſqueezed it from them into their own treaſury: and it muſt in all probability be ſo. The Story is true, my Lord, as he relates it, and in the Rolls there are a multitude of them cited to that purpoſe.

But beſides Mr. *Prynne*, there is a Statute of *Morton*, *ch.* 5. made 20 *H.* III. my Lord *Coke* in the 2d *Inſt.* 89 ſays, was principally deſigned againſt the uſurious *Jews*. The Statute de *Judaiſmo*, 18 *E.* I. relates, that the King's people had been diſinherited, much injured and impoveriſhed by the uſury of the *Jews*, and enacts, *That no Jew thereafter ſhould take uſury upon Lands, Rents, or other Things*. And in the 2d *Inſt.* 507. my Lord *Coke*, in his Comment upon that Statute, ſays, That 15,060 *Jews* thereupon went out of the Realm.

So that, my Lord, we do not diſpute but that the fact alledged may be true; that the *Jews* were extorſive, and the King took away their eſtates: But the matter is the uſe and application of that fact.

For, *firſt*, I think if it be known aw, and taken to be according to any known law which we have, that they were as alien enemies, then as the King might take away their eſtates ſo the ſubjects may take them away too; ſo there is no ſuch uſe to be made of it as the other ſide would have, as I perceive. They ſay as Infidels the King would take away their eſtates, becauſe they are *perpetui inimici*; and I ſay, if they were alien enemies, then the ſubjects might take them away too; for ſo the Book ſays.

But next, my Lord, I do uſe it another way; That all theſe dealings with the *Jews* ſhew, that they were not alien enemies, but treated as alien amies, ſo long as the King pleaſed. For, my Lord, if they were alien enemies, and the Books they cite are true, as *Calvin's* caſe mentions them, all their contracts and dealings were all abſolutely void, they could never have any property. How could they then be guilty of uſury? How could any man living be extorted upon by them, to pay any money due to them upon contracts or bargains, unleſs theſe men were treated as alien amies? How could they have the benefit of their contracts, as other alien amies have? So that I take it, that is a ſtrong evidence that they were treated as alien amies; otherwiſe it is impoſſible that which you ſay could be true, That they could hurt the King's people by extortion and uſurious contracts; when, according to your law, they were not able to make any contracts, or have any property at all: Is it poſſible the King could take away their eſtates that had none? And they had none, if your doctrine be true. If any man owed them money, they could not recover it, becauſe they could not bring any action; and the King could not have it, becauſe it was a void contract made with one not capable of making a contract. So that, my Lord, the inſtances they make uſe of, are, I hope, inſtruments and ſtrong arguments againſt them, not for them. They were taken notice of as alien amies, capable of making contracts, which the King's ſubjects were never bound to perform, unleſs they were legal, and they obliged by them by law. As for theſe ancient Records in general, time had hidden the knowledge of the laws, and tranſactions of thoſe times. It is not poſſible to know what the laws and tranſactions of thoſe times were, or rightly to diſtinguiſh between legal and violent acts.

And ſo being references from thence to conclude in judgment now, is *notum per ignotius*; or like dependencies, which unleſs latter times have concurred or agreed with, are only fit to make diſorder and confuſion.

Secondly, But that which is deducible from hence, is not, as I conceive, what has been endeavoured;

That they had no property, becauſe the Princes of thoſe times took from them their eſtates when they pleaſed, and taxed them how or in what manner they pleaſed.

But perhaps the reaſon was, that theſe people being under the curſe, and being a vagrant people, without Head, Prince, Governor or Country, it was no difficulty to tax or take from them at pleaſure, being hated of the people where they lived.

But it could not be as they would have it, that they ſhould be amongſt us alien enemies; for an alien enemy can neither make bargain nor contract, nor be capable of property;

But the ſubject may, at will and pleaſure, fall upon and take all that he has to his own uſe, as upon the King's enemy; and what he can take from him is his own acquiſition, as the price of his adventure, and conqueſt over his enemy.

The Books cited 17 *E.* IV. 2, & 7. prove this.

But by what is admitted by them, that they were great uſurers, and had great eſtates, it is evident, that they were here treated as alien amies: How could they elſe in ſuch multitudes live amongſt us? How could they be uſurers, and get eſtates, if they could not make contracts? How is it poſſible they could preſerve their bodies or eſtates againſt the King's ſubjects, unleſs they had the King's protection, and were treated as alien amies? And of latter times, how many of them have lived amongſt us, driven great trades, have had, and have at this time, conſiderable eſtates?

Let it now be adjudged, that any man that will, may take away their eſtates: that they can have no remedy or action for their debts owing to them, but inſtead thereof may be beaten or impriſoned as enemies to the King;

And we ſhall probably ſee, what the ſucceſs of ſuch a judgment will be.

My Lord, that they are taken notice of and handled as other aliens, without any diſtinction between alien enemy and alien Infidel, I would offer this as an argument. The queſtion, I confeſs, is new, and ſo there is not much that I can find in our Books about it; but the Act of *Navigation* made in the 12th year of this King, a year before this Charter now in judgment before you, concerning trade, ſhews, that Infidels have the ſame liberty of trade as Chriſtians, that Act being made for increaſe of ſhipping and navigation (it is *ch.* 18.) prohibiting goods to be imported by any foreign ſhips, except ſhips of that ſame Country where the goods do grow; and diſtinguiſhes not between Infidel and Chriſtian Countries, but expreſsly ſays, *That no currants, nor commodities of the growth, product, or manufacture of any of the Countries, Iſlands, Dominions or Territories, in the* Ottoman *or* Turkiſh *Empire* And does enact, *That no goods ſhall be imported from that Country, but in our Ships, or Ships of the Country of which the Goods are, and thoſe Ships to be navigated by a Maſter, and three-*

urths of the ſame Country. This muſt be an admittance and a ance, that the maſters and mariners of that Country have the f dom and privilege of trade that other foreign aliens have; and they ly, that the Infidels of the *Turkiſh* Empire have liberty of trade

My Lord, the Act for tonnage and poundage has general rates poſitions ſet upon the commodities of all Infidel Countries, with ing, brought in by, or with any manner of diſtinction. So that that this opinion of a difference between alien Infidels and alien Cl was not taken notice of, nor known, nor thought of, till now: Lord, if it had, it is unlikely the Act of *Navigation* ſhould pro give allowance, for the maſters and mariners of Infidel Countries hither with Goods, when by Law they could never come in, b enemies, and to be knocked on the head if they did.

My Lord, pray let us conſider of late times what a number of *J* lived among us; ſhould we declare this for Law at this day, people ought to uſe them as alien enemies, ſtrip them, plunder them them on the head, kill them and flay them, what would be the quence! What work would this make! For if this be true, w aſſert that they are perpetual enemies, then we can have no pe them; whoever owes a *Jew* any thing may play the *Jew* with hi pay him, whoever has a mind to any thing he has, may take from him; if he has a mind to beat him, and knock him on t he may, there is no protection for him, nor peace with him.

My Lord, I do believe that 'tis true, that the *Jews* being un curſe, and having been a vagrant people for ſo long a time, and no Prince to defend them, it is probable, they have been made of, and our Kings and Princes have made bold to do with them ing to their own pleaſures; though what is recorded of it, is ſo l that it is hard to know the whole truth: But I think they are n dents to be followed now, unleſs they had been followed by a ſu of practice and authority in our Books of Law: for otherwiſe ma a man might argue of old Books from dark things to darker, as he will, and never make any thing clear. In the caſe of *Sout. How*, there was occaſion for this to be taken notice of, if this had been true Law. It is reported in 2 *Cro. fo.* 469. A man e another to ſell Jewels in *Barbary* for him, and the other perſon them as true Jewels, when indeed they were counterfeit, and nc 100*l.* value, to the King of *Barbary* for 800*l.* and thereupon t finding himſelf cheated, impriſoned the plaintiff that ſold them til he repayed him his money, and he brought an action againſt ſon that employed him to ſell them. It would have been of uſ caſe, if the contract and ſale, and the lawfulneſs of converſing in Chriſtians with Infidels had been queſtionable, for the Defendan action to have urged againſt the Plaintiff, What reaſon had h him? For what had he to do to go amongſt the King's enemies ought not to recover damages for any ſuch thing. I ſay, it wou been of uſe, if any ſuch point of Law had at that time been thoug

In that caſe, it was of all ſides admitted, and not ſo much as that this contract was void, becauſe the King of *Barbary* was an

So that this opinion, that Infidels are perpetual enemies, and petual hoſtility, can maintain no action, nor have any property us, has no authority for its foundation, but only ſome extrajudi ings, without debate or conſideration; and it is againſt the c practices of Princes and People at all times.

Perhaps it is no ſmall part of religion, that men ſhould ſpeak, plainly and uprightly one with another.

We know that religion too often has been made a cloak and other ends and purpoſes. It ſhould not be ſo, and I hope will uſed in this caſe.

My Lord, the Statutes that I have cited, they have made no of diſtinction between Infidels and Chriſtians in matter of trade; hardly to be thought, eſpecially as to ſome of the latter ones, there was trade with Infidels then: For it is ſcarce to be thought Princes ſhould go thither only with ſwords in their hands, to m upon them, and afterwards to make peace with them, and no n taken of the law about trade concerning Infidels.

The Statutes I have cited of *Magna Charta*, *cap.* 9 *E.* III. 25 2 and 11 *R.* II. all declare and enact the freedom of trade, in all words, except only ſuch as are in war with the King: In them is there any exception of trade with Infidels.

Can it be imagined that in thoſe days we had no trade with *Barbary*? Our Kings went with armies to the *Holy Land*, and had made war and peace with the *Turks*. Had we no trade there our ſwords?

But to look nearer home, *Spain* and *Portugal* were Infidels, an hands of the *Moors*, in the year 1494, which was 14 *E.* IV. C thought that in all theſe times between *Magna Charta*, *H.* III. an we had no trade with *Spain* and *Portugal*?

Stat. 12. *H.* VII. *cap.* 6. was made in the year 1497, which 23 years after the *Moors* were driven out; and in that Statute 'tis that the Merchant adventurers, dwelling in divers parts of *Engl* of *London*, did ſhew, *That whereas they had their free paſſage, courſ courſe, with their Goods, Wares and Merchandizes, in divers coaſts beyond the Seas, as well into* Spain, Portugal, Venice, Dantzic land, *and* Frieſland, *and divers and many other Regions and Coun league and amity with the King; that they were impoſed upon by a Co Merchants in* London, *and forced to pay duties*.

I only make uſe of the recital, to prove the free paſſage the tioned to *Spain* and *Portugal*, and to other Regions and Countri

There is no diſtinction of Infidel Countries from Chriſtian Co though *Spain* and *Portugal* had been ſo lately Infidels.

'Tis moſt probable the trade they had then was with *Turky* a *bary*, as well as with *Venice*: The words *other Regions and Countr* to imply as much, and the freedom equal.

So that, I think, as to this objection, That Infidels are perpet mies, that we can have no peace with them, nor they maintain or have any property by our law; I think the authority to none at all. The conſtant practice, as well by Princes as P conſtantly againſt it.

The Charters that they have cited to *Barbary* and other places, some of them are before the last of these Statutes, that is the Statute of K. *James*; and yet there is no difference taken notice of there between Christian and Infidel Countries: So that, my Lord, taking all together the light, or at least the weak authority of these sayings and occasional discourses, for this distinction of Infidel or Christian, in point of trade, will signify but little; and the constant practice of all our time, wherein we have any sort of trade; and the arguments drawn from the Records that have been cited of the *Jews* having property and allowance to live amongst us, and our dealings with foreign nations taken notice of in our Acts of Parliament, without such distinction, seems to be a practice so quite contrary to those sayings, that are perhaps taken out of some zealous Catholick Authors of those superstitious times, rather than consonant to the rules of Law, that they can be no foundation for this distinction; especially considering that *Spain* and *Portugal*, as I said, 'till the middle of *Edward* IVth's time, were possessed by Infidels: and yet I cannot but think they must be traded with, and no man can find any thing of the distinction but only out of these occasional sayings in *Calvin*'s case.

But be that point of trading with or without licence (which I mentioned before) how it will, yet I conceive that point will never be sufficient to ground this same sole trade, or to found a Monopoly upon; that cannot warrant a Grant of a sole trade, sole buying and sole selling, to be granted to you and your successors, your sons, servants, apprentices, factors, and such as you shall license for ever: There is a licence and grant in perpetuity, not only to those that then were, but to their sons and successors, and those whom they shall license; and this into a very great part of the World.

And by the same reason all *Turky* and *Barbary*, a great part of the *West-Indies*, and other places of the World, may be monopolized; and perhaps all Christian Countries.

The Statute of Monopolies has no allowance or exception for Monopolies to Infidel Countries; that is, against all sole buying, sole selling, or sole using of any thing.

And the *Turky* trade was used long before that time, as by Charter, granted 23 *Eliz.* So was the *Bourbon* trade, as by the Charter thereof; and I believe to the *East-Indies* also.

And the Statute of Monopolies being so general (the *Proviso* not reasonably construable to except this Company out of the extent of that Statute, unless all Patents that may be granted to Companies of Monopolies, are by that exception or *Proviso* out of the Statute) and deserving for the suppressing so great evils as Monopolies are, and always have been accounted:

I hope it will not be avoided upon any imaginary difference in Law, betwixt Infidel and Christian Countries to monopolize thereby the trade, perhaps of the greater part of the World, as *Turky*, *Persia*, *Barbary*, *East* and *West-Indies*; for the *West-Indies*, I think, the greater part are Pagans.

My Lord, I have looked over the cases that were here, and the debates that have been printed in 3d and 4th of King *Charles* I. about the King's Power of imposing rates and subsidies, and impositions upon merchandizes, in *Bates*'s case in the *Exchequer*, 4 *Car.* I. 2 *Inst.* 63. and Mr. *Rushworth*'s account of the debates in Parliament at that time about that matter: many things are there said concerning the King's Power of restraining and prohibiting of trade, and the Writ *Ne Exeat Regnum*. And from these reasons, they that argued for the King, urge reasonableness of impositions upon merchandize. That case arose from an imposition upon Currants, and methinks if there had been known any such distinction, as they would here insinuate, it had been of great use in that case as well as this; but throughout the Arguments and Reasons there debated, they did never make any distinction between Infidel and Christian, but native and foreign commodities; and did endeavour to have a prerogative to impose rates upon them: and the reasons were these, and all the Arguments run thus: The King can prohibit and restrain any Merchant to go out of the country by Writ, *Ne Exeat Regnum*; the King can prohibit any foreign commodities to be imported; then none can go out without licence, nor import without licence, and consequently it is a legal thing, when this licence is granted upon the payment of such a duty or imposition, or under such a rate as can be agreed on between the King and the Merchant; and therefore such an imposition or farm is lawful.

These were the arguments in that case, and in these arguments it appears that a restraint in consequence does import a tax, rate or farm, for a dispensation with that restraint.

For if licences be requisite, it is worth consideration, whether that will not introduce the imposing of rates without Parliament, or otherwise than in a parliamentary way. This, I say, is worthy consideration. Suppose it true; there have been licences to go into Infidel Countries to trade; so there have been to go beyond the Seas, and have been to other trade besides this: yet it does not follow as a true consequence, that it is unlawful to go or trade without licences, much less does it follow from thence, that such a Patent as this to any one or few Subjects, or to such a Corporation, to have the whole and sole trade into any place, and power of licensing others, can be warranted by it.

I do not question but the King may restrain the passage of Merchants and Merchandize in some cases, and to embargo Ships in some cases.

But these are upon special reasons; as,

First, In the case of War.

Secondly, In the case of such Merchandizes as are necessary for the defence or safety of the Kingdom, to restrain their Exportation.

Thirdly, In case of a plague from particular places to import.

But then these prohibitions are general, and their particular reasons and grounds are apparent.

But if under any pretence any sole trade to some one person, Body Politick or Natural, be granted, excluding all others; that Grant, I conceive, is in deceit of the King, and to the prejudice of his Subjects, and void.

Never has such a Grant hitherto had any judicial allowance; nay, so far from that, that as far as I could observe, no opinion has been till within four or five years, that such Grants were good to exclude others, nor any action or suit ever adventured before now, to be brought upon any such ground.

So that, my Lord, as to this great point, both the old Common Law, and the old Statute Law, and the Statute of Monopolies, with submission, are against this Grant of the sole trade; and the distinction between Infidel Countries and Christian, is so thin, and upon so weak a bottom, that I hope it will never be strong enough to bear the weight of so great a consequence as this is. For though at present Infidels be distinguished from Christians; yet from their arguments and kind of reasoning about restraint of going beyond Sea and trading, *Spain* and *Portugal* may be brought in, and *France* too; and so the argument will run from Infidel to Christian at length, and I know not where it will stop.

So I humbly leave that point to your Lordship's judgment, whether such a Grant of a sole trade, appears to be such a Grant, as is good according to Law; and whether or no, notwithstanding what they have said, it does not appear by the old Common Law, and the old Statute Law, and by all our late Acts of Parliament, to be in Law a void Grant?

The next thing, my Lord, I come unto, is the second point, which I shall be but short in: about the first, I have taken up most of your time, and I beg your Lordship's pardon for it; because, if I mistake not, it is a most weighty point in the consequence of it. But then supposing and admitting their Grant to be a good Grant, whether or no, can you maintain this action? If the Law should be so, that the Defendant ought not to have traded there without licence, then he may be punishable at the King's suit, by fine and imprisonment; but that you should maintain an action against him, what cause of action, what damage or loss to you, have you laid in your declaration? You say in your declaration, that the Defendant *Sandys*, not being a Member of your Company, nor a Son, Factor or Servant, nor Assign of your Company, traded into the *East-Indies* in the places within the limits of your Charter; and has there bought wares, and bargained and sold merchandizes, and imported and sold them in *England*, against the will of the Company, and to their prejudice and impoverishment, against the form of their Charter, and to the Company's damage 1000 *l*.

First, You have not alledged in all your declaration, whether or no he had a licence from the King, and that is nought: for I think, tho' the King is pleased to say in his Letters Patent, he will not grant licences without leave of the Company, yet he may do so, if he please, notwithstanding that Grant.

Secondly, Then you have not shewn any loss or damage you have had by his trading thither: did he buy so much of the merchandize of the country, as not to leave there sufficient for you to furnish your Ships withal, so that they came home empty? No such thing is alledged. Did he hence export to sell there so much merchandize, as not sufficient left for you here to buy? Or, did he bring home here so much, as that there were not buyers sufficient for his Goods and yours also? There are no such things alledged; or is the truth so, as that hereby your imposing your prices upon your commodities, selling at your own prices, and exacting what you thought fit, was hindered; and for this you would maintain an action.

I think it will be the first time, that ever a man recovered damages for being hindered from imposing and exacting his own prices, or having the advantage of his Monopoly, or for another's having an earlier or a quicker trade, and under-selling his own commodities and merchandizes lower than the Plaintiffs can afford them.

You agree by your own declaration, that there are many others that are concerned as well as you: you say, you have the sole trade to yourselves; your Factors, your Servants and your Sons, as soon as they come to twenty-one; all that are of your Company, all that you grant licences to, all that you shall assign your trade to, all those have an interest, if you can maintain an action. Other people have trade there as well as you, can they maintain an action?

A Commoner may bring an action upon the case against a stranger, for putting his Cattle into the Common, provided that the Common thereby be impaired, and the Commoner have not sufficient Common as before, and have a damage, otherwise he can maintain no action.

In *Robert Mary*'s case, 9 *Co.* 113. it is there resolved, That for every feeding of the beasts of a stranger in a Common, the Commoner shall not have an assize or action upon the case; but an action does lie, if the feeding be such, that the Commoner cannot have common pasture for his own beasts; and then it is the consequence, the loss of his Common, that gives him cause of action.

It is not alledged in the declaration, that your trade was any thing the worse. No damage appears to you by it: What reason, that you should recover damages, where you have not sustained any loss? And you have alledged none in your declaration; how can your declaration be good? It then contains no cause of action.

You should now, if you would have made a declaration, that should have intitled you to a cause of action, have shewn how you suffered by *Sandys*, a stranger trading to the *East-Indies*; that he bought up all, and you could have nothing; for if he left enough for you, what hurt have you? What reason is there you should recover damage, if you have not sustained any loss? And if you alledge none in your declaration: How is your declaration, that shews no cause of action, maintainable?

In the case of Monopolies, 11 *Co.* 88. *b. Rolls Abr. 1st part. fol.* 106. The last point in that case is a full authority in this point. That admitting the Patent to be good, for the sole making and selling of Cards, that was granted to *Darcy* for 12 years, yet no action would lie in that case, though the Defendant did, contrary to this Patent, sell Cards. Adjudged that it was a Monopoly, and Patent void: that if the Patent had been good, yet no action would have lain against the Defendant upon it.

My Lord, If that be so as it is declared to be in that case, in the last point resolved by the Judges, if that action would not lie there, this will not lie; supposing his Charter to be never so good, and the Defendant has done contrary to it.

My Lord, there is only one other reason for which the action will not lie; and that is grounded upon the Letters Patent, as they are granted to you. For by the Letters Patent, it is not absolutely, but *sub modo* granted, that you shall have the sole trade; and that no other person shall trade there, under pain of forfeiting ship and goods; one half to the King, another half to the Company. So that, my Lord, the words of restraint are not absolute, but only under such a penalty and forfeiture.

Now, my Lord, if I should suppose this Patent to have all the force and strength that they can desire; supposing that this Patent were in an Act of Parliament, penned in this manner, that did restrain all persons from trading to the *East-Indies*, except the Company, under pain of forfeiture of ship and goods; under favour, you that will have advan-

advantage of this restraint, must take it in that manner as the Act does give it; you shall not have any other penalty or punishment, but what the Act gives. For when any new Law is made, you must take it as it is, and no otherwise, till another new Law be made. And so is the Rule in 7 *Co.* 37. 11. *Co.* 56, & 59. *Plowd. Com.* 206. It cannot be altered without a new Law.

And I would but only suppose upon the Statute of *Edw.* VI. that gives the owner of tithes treble damages against him that sets them not forth; a man brings an action upon the case, would that be well? No, he must take the Law as it is; such an action never was brought, nor if brought, could be maintain'd; yet here the damages are given to the party.

The like of all other penal Statutes, a man must only forfeit the Penalty the Statute inflicts; so that this action cannot, as I conceive, be maintain'd. So that, my Lord, taking all together, admitting (tho' I hope it is not so) that this Patent is a good Patent; yet you are not the sole persons interested, there are others besides you, your Grantees, Factors and Servants, and Sons are to trade there. You have not laid any particular damage; therefore you cannot, by the reason of the case of Monopolies, maintain any such action as this.

And if you will take advantage of this Grant, it is reasonable you should take it as the Grant gives it, proceed for the forfeiture of ship and goods; but for the action of the case, your Charter does not give it; nor, if an Act of Parliament had been penned after this manner, would such an action have lain.

So that to conclude,

First, That that which this Company claims in this case by this Patent, to have the sole trade to the *East-Indies* in their politick capacity, excluding others, is a Monopoly, and ingrossing, against the Common Law, and the antient Statutes, and the Statute of Monopolies, 21 *Jacobi*, and therefore they have no right to have what they claim.

Secondly, That what the Defendant has done in this case, he has lawfully done, and therefore not to be punish'd.

Thirdly, That tho' the Company had a lawful claim to the trade in such manner, as in their declaration is set forth, and the Defendant done what he ought not, yet they cannot maintain this action.

And upon the whole matter, whether best for the Company to have judgment for them or against them, may deserve their thoughts.

But this being so great in the consequence, as the whole trade of the Kingdom depending upon it, I have laboured the more.

The antient Laws, the antient ways, is what I endeavour, and against new ways upon any pretence whatsoever.

And therefore, my Lord, I humbly beg your judgment for the Defendant.

Lord Chief-Justice. Do you intend to have another Argument in it, Gentlemen?

Mr. Sollic'tor-General. What your Lordship pleases.

Lord Chief-Justice. It is a case of great weight and consequence, perhaps, as ever any case, that has come into *Westminster-hall.* I must needs say, it has been extraordinarily well argued on both sides; and it must be necessarily taken notice of as a point of great consequence, wherein the King's prerogative, and the privileges of the *East-India* Company, and this joint trade, are concern'd on the one side: and the benefit of particular persons, and the liberty of free, uncontroulable trading is concern'd on the other: and it is fit there should be all the consideration, and all the deliberation upon a matter of this great moment, that possibly can be. I cannot be so wonderfully captivated with the differences, that have been made between the Charter to the *East-India* Company, and those to the *Turky* Company and the others; and tho' I have heard much in the defence of Charters and Corporations, I am of opinion there is no such great matter of commendation due to them: but I take the Common Law to be the best Law in the World. For that Charter, that you Mr. *Pollexfen* defended here so strongly after judgment given against it, the Corporation became as invisible within a few days, as you say this was, no duns could see it; tho' there were duns that went to wait upon that Corporation, but came away as empty as they went: and I wish the duns were like to be as well satisfied from the one, as they are from the other; and therefore there can be no great matter in that. But there is another thing that very much deserves consideration, it is a question wherein trade is mightily concern'd: we know we have a potent Neighbour, who has both experience and industry, and are our rival in this trade, I wish we had as much industry, and were as diligent as they; they have found by long experience, that a Joint-Stock is the only way to carry on their trade, I mean *Holland.* And it is very well known, if it had not been for a Joint-Stock, the trade had never been so beneficial as it is. And Mr. *Sandys* would not have had such a desire to the trade, for it would not have been so well settled and fixed, and therefore, I take it to be a wonderful thing, and to carry a great consequence in it upon that account, that we should consider how this trade comes to be so great, and so desirable. Now that by the Joint-stock, and Industry and expence of the Company, the thing is become facile and valuable, for particular persons to come and sweep away the advantage of it, that ought to be well consider'd. Mr. *Sandys* and his partners are very zealous now to reap the fruits of the Company's labours. But suppose this question should be asked, Will you be contented to come in and pay your proportion of all the charge these people have been at, to put the trade into this capacity it is in? But is it fair, after they have reduced it into so good a condition, at a vast expence and trouble, for other particular persons to come and say, Let us have the benefit of it, that have had nothing of the burthen and charge? And then there is another consequence of great concern; peace and war, no one doubts, are actually in the power of that Prince and People with whom the trade is. I would desire to know, supposing an injury should be committed by any particular person to the Infidels, and the Ship get away; will not all the rest of the Company's stock, being of the same Nation, be in danger of suffering by it? Certainly it would; and therefore since they are likely to answer for the wrong, is it not fit they should have the management of it? So we may, if we come to argue by consequences, easily find out a great many inconveniencies on both sides, but they are not to over-rule the Law one way or the other; they are specious pretences by way of argument, but the Law is a certain rule, and consequences are
or other to over-rule it. The main point truly is a point c
sideration and weight; perhaps as considerable as ever any th
in debate here, and therefore it is fit, that all due deliberati
to have it debated.

Mr. Justice *Withins.* Mr. *Pollexfen*, you seem to argue tha
Grant to them is a void Grant, and against Common Law,
Monopoly in granting them the sole trade; then that does
the point in *Michelborne*'s case, about trading without Licen
fidels; and therefore you go upon another ground, than wh.
citor did.

Mr. *Pollexfen.* I go upon the particular case here before yo

Mr. Justice *Withins.* And you have not given any answer
tion of the Commons, cited by *Mr. Sollicitor.*

Mr. *Pollexfen.* Truly, Sir, I think, it does not need any a
go chiefly against this Grant, which is against Law, and voi

Lord-Chief-Justice. Truly, Mr. *Pollexfen*, I am not much in
with your other point about the action; for what became, pr.
actions that have been brought upon that Statute of Monop
Patentees of new inventions, as there has been multitudes
Hales's time, and at all times?

Mr. *Pollexfen.* In that case there's no-body but the particu
that has that invention; and he brings the action. But h
own shewing, you have intitled others to the trade, as the se
factors, and children; and therefore you can never have such

Lord-Chief-Justice. When will you have it argued again?

Mr. *Pollexfen.* We shall be ready for the Defendant next

Lord-Chief-Justice. That is a little too soon, there's but
Vacation, and that is but a short Term; I think you had be
other argument in *Michaelmas*-Term.

Mr. Sollicitor-General. Yes, if your Lordship please.

Mr. *Pollexfen.* What your Lordship pleases; we shall be re
Lordship pleases to hear us next Term.

Lord-Chief-Justice. I know Mr. *Sandys* is in very great ha
zeal and transport of any particular person must not think to
go hand over head in a case of this great weight and mome
great consideration to be had of the length of time that this C
continued; there has been an *East-India* Company in King J
in the late King's time, and in this King's time.

Mr. Justice *Holloway.* And here is a great trade settled, w
destroy it presently.

Lord-Chief-Justice. We must not gratify the zeal and tran
Sandys, by being over-hasty in this matter.

Mr. *Pollexfen.* My Lord, we shall be well content to stay t
mas-Term.

Lord-Chief-Justice. Ay, I know the Counsel will, but w
Client will or no, I cannot well tell, nor do not much care.
will consider of it, and hear another argument in *Michaelmas*-

Mr. Attorney-General (Sir *Robert Sawyer*) his Arg

The Governor and Company of Merchants of *Lond*
to the *East-Indies*, Plaintiffs. *Thomas Sandys*, Defe

De termino S. Michaelis, *Anno Regni Regis* 36 Car. II. xxxi.
1684.

IN an action upon the case brought by the Company against
dant, for trading into the *East-Indies* contrary to their Gra
judice of their trade, and to their damage of 1000 *l*

It comes before the Court upon the Plaintiffs demurrer to
dant's Plea of the Statute of 15 *E.* III.

The Record having been so often opened at large, I sh
as a Case upon the Record.

The King by his Letters Patent, 3tio *Aprilis*, 13 *Car.* II. r
the Company had long been a Company, and enjoyed divers
privileges under the Charters of Queen *Elizabeth* and King *Ja*
the Company the sole trade and traffick to the *East-Indies*, be
del country, with a prohibition to all others of his subjects to
ther, without the leave and licence of the Company.

The Defendant not qualified as the Charter directs, withou
of the Company, and against their wills, trades to the *East-I*
prejudice and damage of the Company's trade.

Upon this case, the points which have been moved and
two.

First, Whether the Letters Patent giving licence to the C
trade into the *East-Indies*, and to exercise the sole trade there,
hibition to other subjects to trade there, be good in Law?

Secondly, Whether admitting the Patent good, this action
the Company?

In debating of the first point, I shall not go about to main
lidity of these Letters Patent, or any such of like nature, to
King from granting licence to other of his subjects as he shal
shall content myself, to shew that all the subject not licensed
not authorized by the Company (as the Defendant is not) are
these Letters Patent.

Where the question will be between the King's prerogative
one of the highest points thereof, which concerns the defenc
tection of his Kingdom), and the intercourse with foreign Nati
one side; and the general liberty of trade, which is a tender
meerly concerns the interest of his subjects, on the other side.

It therefore being a question of great consequence, and g
sequence than difficulty, as I hope to shew, I shall, in examini
point, use the utmost caution, by asserting the King's just pre
this matter, and not to depress the subjects true liberty of trad

The subject matter of this question, only relating to a for
with Infidels, not in amity with the King of *England*,
necessarily oblige me to enter into the consideration of

trade, or of the King's prerogative, or the subjects liberty in relation thereto.

Which would much shorten my task in supporting these Letters Patent, and the trouble the Court is like to receive thereby.

But because the great force of the arguments, made use of on the other side against these Letters Patent, have been drawn from principles and precedents of Law, which concern as well the inland trade and traffick of this Kingdom, as with other Christian Nations in amity with the King of *England*, with whom leagues of commerce have been made by our Kings; or to whom a common trade hath been laid open by several particular laws:

It is made necessary for me, from the other side, a little to consider these trades, and how far the subjects liberty or the King's prerogative be concern'd in them.

Whereby it will appear, that the arguments and authorities produced by the defendant's Counsel, will be of no great force to impeach these Letters Patent for the management of a foreign trade with Infidels.

I shall therefore briefly consider the inland or native trade within the Kingdom, and then the foreign trade with other Nations.

The inland trade is either for manufactures or merchandize.

Under the trade of manufactures falls in the husbandman, and all sorts of artificers; who have full right by the Common Law, to exercise what, and as many trades as they please; so as no annoyance happen to the neighbourhood: And with these the King's prerogative is little concerned, it cannot restrain them, it being their livelihood.

Nor is the public weal otherwise concerned therein, than that all its members should live by their honest labour and industry. As to the trade of merchandize, or inland commerce, every man (generally speaking) might buy of any man, whether native or foreign, and as many kinds or sorts of merchandize as he pleaseth, which I take to have been the Common Law before 37 *Ed.* III. *cap.* 5. whereby all trading Merchants were restrained to one sort of merchandize.

But that Act continued not long, being repealed 38 *Ed.* III. *cap.* 2.

Yet this trade of inland merchandize lay under several restrictions at Common Law. 1. Notwithstanding such general liberty of buying and selling, no man could ingross any one commodity. 2. The ancient Common Law confined this sort of trade to certain places, as Towns, Cities, or other public places appointed by the King, *Co.* 3 *Inst. fo.* 196. *in the Chap. Forestalling.*

It was punishable to buy above the value of twenty-pence elsewhere, or to anticipate merchandizes before they arrived at these places.

3. No assemblies could be held for the traffick of buying or selling, without the King's licence; for tho' some Markets and Fairs are held by prescription, (the original Grants not appearing) yet these were derived from the Crown, by some royal licence before time of memory: they all depend upon the same Crown, and may be forfeited to the Crown.

This is so frequent in our Books, I need not cite the authorities.

And here the prerogative of the Crown had a great stroke.

The inland traders, in buying and selling, might buy and sell in private places, and could not be restrained: But they could not hold assemblies for trade without the King's leave and licence; Marts, Fairs and Markets, in their true notion, being no other than royal licences to assemble for trade and traffick.

And these, when granted, cannot be resumed without cause of forfeiture: For I do admit, that a licence to trade or traffick carries an interest with it, being a matter of profit.

And I take the Law to be the same, whether the Fair or Market be erected only, and not granted to any one; and where it is granted to a subject, all the King's subjects have a liberty and right of trafficking there, and cannot be prohibited by the Lord of the Fair or Market.

The reason of these restrictions of the inland trade of merchandize, and the King's prerogative therein, is from the concern the public peace and justice of the Kingdom hath in this sort of trade, more than in the former of the manufactures, *viz.* to prevent all manner of cheats by false weights and measures, corrupt merchandizes, and too great enhancing of the prices, and breaches of the peace, occasioned by public concourses, tho' under colour of trade and traffick.

And upon this ground the Common Law provides, That to all such licences for public Marts, which the King may grant when and where he pleases, being not to the damage of others before granted, a Court of Justice is incident of common right, for preservation of the public peace and correction of such deceits which generally attend the trade of merchandizing.

Fourthly, There was another restriction upon the inland merchandize taken notice of in our Books, which was more particular, and to certain places, *viz.*

The claim of foreign bought and foreign sold, by several Cities, Towns and Ports, some by custom, and others by Charters; and there is no great question to be made, but before 9 *E.* III. *cap.* 1. the Charters as well as Customs did prevail for that Liberty, but both were taken away by the Statute, and divers subsequent laws taken notice of in the case of the City of *London*, *Co.* 8. *fo.* 128.

And between that and 9 *H.* IV. there were great strugglings in Parliament between the foreign Merchants and the City of *London*, and other Towns, about that Custom.

'Till at length, *London* prevailed for a private Act of Parliament for establishing of the Customs, which they have enjoyed ever since 9 *H.* IV. 30.

By an ancient Record of *Henry* III. it appears, that the abbots, and others the religious of the County of *Lincoln*, under colour of selling their wool, which arose upon their demesne lands, turned Merchants, and bought up wools, and sold them with their own wools: They were prohibited to do it by a Writ out of the Chancery.

And upon the complaint of the Merchants of *Lincoln*, in the time of *Edward* I. the like Writ of Prohibition issued, *Pla. Parl.* in the Appendix, 609. By all which it appears, that the inland traffick of the Kingdom, which was within the care and cognizance of the Common Law, was not unlimited, nor the subjects liberty therein never so large as it is now insisted upon, to all foreign parts whatsoever.

And that the managery of the principal part of the home traffick, which consists in the Marts, Fairs, and Markets of the Kingdom, depends upon the King's prerogative, and is managed under it, the Law having entrusted the King with that power for the benefit of his people, and the peace of the Kingdom.

In the next place, I will take a view of the foreign trade.

The Common Law, and our Law-books, take notice of but two sorts of Foreigners, alien friends, and alien enemies; *Calvin's* Case, *Co.* 7. 17.

Neither can there be any other sort of Foreigners, generally speaking: for if the question arise, whether alien Friend, or alien Enemy, it must be tried by the leagues with the Prince, whose subject he is; which is, or ought to be enrolled in *Chancery*. And tho' there be not actual war or fighting between the two Princes and their Subjects, yet they are *in statu belli*, and may assume arms when they please, and seize the goods and persons of each other's Subjects.

I shall first consider what the Common Law determined as to the Subjects trade and traffick with alien Friends beyond the seas, and upon what foot that trade stands; and then particularly consider how it determines in case of Commerce with alien Enemies, and incidentally of Infidels.

I conceive the Common Law hath made no express provision, nor given any absolute right for the Subjects to trade with any Foreigners beyond the Seas.

It will be of little use to discourse how far the Law of Nations interposes in this matter: whether every Nation be obliged to entertain Trade and Commerce with another Nation.

And antecedent to all leagues and treaties for Commerce, little will be found besides the laws of hospitality, which do not give any demandable right.

Bodinus, in his Book *de Repub. lib.* 1. *cap.* 6, 7. says, *Quæ tametsi jure gentium esse videantur prohiberi, tamen sæpe a Principibus videmus.*

And in his Book *de Repub. lib.* 1. *cap.* 6. holds, *That it is lawful to forbid Foreigners from entering the borders, not only if a war be on foot, but in time of peace, that the manners of the Inhabitants may not be corrupted by converse with Strangers.*

And in his Book *de Repub. lib.* 1. *cap.* 6, 7. *That the Laws of Commerce are contained in the particular compacts and agreements of people and Princes.*

What *Bodinus* declares to be the Law of Nations, exactly agrees with the Laws of this Kingdom; for all Strangers came hither under safe-conducts, which contained both the King's licence and protection of them.

The King might inhibit Foreigners from coming into the Realm, and might remand them when here.

Magna Charta, *cap.* 30. which is a general safe-conduct to Merchants-strangers, reserves this prerogative to the King, *nisi publice prohibiti.*

My Lord *Coke*, in his Comment upon this Chapter, 2 *Inst.* 5. 7. admits they might have been prohibited before this Statute, but construes the saving of this Prohibition by Act of Parliament.

Which Construction, as it is without any former Precedent or Authority, so it is against the constant stream of Precedents and Practice ever since.

Rot. Claus. 24 *H.* III. *dorso*, which was after this Statute, the King sent his writs to several Mayors, commanding that all the Merchants, *ultra montem*, should depart the Kingdom within a month.

And in the same Roll, *dorso*, there is another Writ to the Mayor of *London*, giving leave to *Roman*, *Florentine*, and some other Merchants, to stay till the feast of St. *Martin* in the year following.

And the constant practice in every King's reign since, hath been both by proclamation and orders of Council, to command foreigners to depart the Realm.

Besides, the construction my Lord *Coke* puts upon it, makes the clause idle and elusory.

That one Act of Parliament should provide for a saving by a subsequent Act, which of itself would be repealed by the former.

So where an Act of Parliament prohibited foreigners to come in, the King by his safe-conducts might license them.

The Commons, in the Parliament 1 *H.* V. pray, That the Statute made by *Henry* IV. for avoiding of strangers out of the Realm, might be put in execution. The King grants it, saving his prerogative to license whom he pleases. The Commons replied, *Their intention was no otherwise, nor ever should be by the Grace of God*, 1 *H.* V. *No.* 15. *Rolls Prerogative*, 180.

This might further appear by the several Statutes made for the inviolable observation of the King's safe-conducts, which are in express words mentioned to extend to alien enemies, as well as alien friends; 2 *H.* V. *cap.* 6. and 20 *H.* VI. *cap.* 1.

It is held in *Horn* and *Ivy*'s Case, *Hill.* 21 and 22 *Car. Secundi*, *Banco Regis*, *Syderfin.* That at Common Law the King might prohibit the importation of foreign commodities, before the Statutes therefore made.

So then as the case stood at Common Law, foreign Princes and Nations might prohibit the subjects of *England* to trade with them, as the King might prohibit foreigners to trade here.

The King might inhibit any of his subjects from going beyond sea: And this might have been by particular Writ or general Proclamation.

Our Books and Precedents are so full in this point, that it was admitted on the other side; for there could not be produced any authority that renders it the least questionable, but multitudes are for it.

Rot. Claus. 7 *Ed.* II. *mem.* 10. A Writ to the Sheriff of *York*, to seize the bodies and lands of such as had gone beyond sea, contrary to the King's Inhibition.

Rot. Claus. 41 *Ed.* III. *mem.* 24. *dorso*, Writs to all the maritime towns to take care that a Proclamation prohibiting all his subjects (except noted Merchants, and those unarmed) be put in execution.

Hereby it is evident, that it was penal to go beyond sea, contrary to the King's Inhibition, before the Statute of 5 *R.* II. *cap.* 2.

All that that Statute adds to strengthen the King's Inhibition, is only a point of further penalty, *viz.* A forfeiture of the Goods of the passenger, and of the Vessel of the Master exporting: And tho' there be three sorts of persons excepted out of that Statute, *viz.* Lords and other great Men, true and notable Merchants, and the King's soldiers; yet that Law gave those persons no other liberty than they had before, only leaves them out of the Penalty provided by that Statute.

That before this Statute, Noblemen and other great Men might be prohibited, appears by my Lord *Coke*'s opinion, 3 *Inst.* 179. in the case of fugitives; and the Records there mentioned, especially that of the 25th of *Ed* III. *Rot. claus. memb.* 15. *dorso*, where the King, by his proclamation, prohibits, that *Nequis Comes, Baro, Miles religiosus, sagittarius aut operarius, extra Regnum se transferret, sub pœna Arrestationis, et Incarcerationis.*

And for the King's soldiers, it is plain they could not depart the Realm without the King's leave: but his raising of them for his foreign service, was a sufficient licence for them to depart the Realm with their several Captains.

And for the true and notable Merchants excepted in the Statute, they are the same with the noted Merchants excepted in the Proclamation of 41 *E.* III. who were the Merchants of the Staple, who were admitted and sworn to observe the laws of the Staple; and were bound to repair thither, and not elsewhere, without the King's special licence, as I shall afterwards shew.

By the Statute of 27 *Ed.* III. which settled the laws of the Staple, *cap.* 23. all Merchants, as well aliens as denizens, repairing to the Staple, are required to be sworn before the Mayor and Constable of the Staple. After the Staple was at *Calais*, as it was 41 *E.* III. & 5 *R.* II. the same laws of the Staple continued; and these Merchants are in many Records taken notice of.

37 *H* VIII. *cap.* 15. All persons are prohibited to buy wool in *Kent*, and some other Counties, except the Merchants of the Staple.

And 1 *Eliz. cap.* 13. provides, It shall be lawful for the Merchants, called *Merchant-Adventurers*, and *Merchants of the Staple*, out of the River of *Thames* only, and twice in the year at most, to ship out and in foreign bottoms.

Now 41 *E.* III. & 5 *R.* II. the Staple was at *Calais*, and all the Merchants of the Staple were bound to repair thither only, and had a general licence so to do, without taking of Passports, as the form of the Statute of 5 *R.* II. directed.

But these notable Merchants were restrained to trade to any other place than the Staple, as I shall after shew.

As the King may inhibit any of his subjects going beyond sea, so he may at any time recall any of his subjects, under penalty of forfeiture of Goods and Lands, during life, *Dyer* 12. 8. *parag.* 10. & 276. & 375. 3 *Inst.* 179. in the chapter of fugitives, & 25 & 26 *Eliz. Cater*'s case in the *Exchequer Chamber*, *Leon. fo.* 9.

Upon these grounds it is evident, that the Common Law did not give any absolute right to the subjects to trade beyond sea with foreigners; for no man can have a full right by law to any thing which others have a right by the same law to hinder him of, or to obstruct him in the using or enjoyment of it.

And Mr. *Pollexfen* did rightly observe, that this fundamental right of the King, of prohibiting his subjects from going beyond sea, equally respects the trade with Christian Nations as with Infidels; for both have a right to debar the *English* from trading with them, as the King of *England* had a right, at Common Law, to restrain his subjects within the Realm from passing over the sea to trade with them.

Which is founded upon the King's right of protecting his Kingdom, which could not be discharged if the subjects had such general right as is pretended, of withdrawing their persons and estates as well to Infidel as Christian Countries.

And if such general right were by the Common Law, it is marvelous; and that no Record or Book-case can be found, where it was ever so resolved.

Notwithstanding great occasion has been given in all times, by prohibition, for the subject to have asserted such right;

The only authority produced is the opinion of *Fitzherbert* in *Nat. Brev. fo.* 85. where the words of *Fitzherbert* are, *That by the course of the Common Law, every man may go out of the Realm for merchandize, or travel, or any other cause, as he pleases, without demanding licence of the King, and shall not be punished for it.*

By this opinion, the liberty the subject had to travel, or to go for any other cause beyond sea, is the same as to trade.

And this opinion imports no more than a bare impunity, that the Common Law made no express provision against it, so as to punish it as an offence at Common Law, but left it to the discretion of the King to prohibit, or permit, as he should see cause.

That this was the meaning of *Fitzherbert*, and that he did not intend any right the Common Law gave the subjects to go beyond sea, but only that the Common Law was silent therein, and left it as a thing indifferent, antecedent to the King's Inhibition; is evident both by *Fitzherbert*, in the same place, and the co-temporary opinions of the Sages of that time.

For immediately *Fitzherbert* explains his opinion, That because every subject is bound to defend the King and the Realm, the King at his pleasure may command the subject not to go out of the Realm without his licence, and if they do contrary thereto, they shall be fined for their disobedience.

Here, by *Fitzherbert*, that liberty which he had asserted for the subject to trade or travel, as it was equal, so it might be equally restrained by the King, at his pleasure.

All the Judges at that time were of the same opinion.

Mich. 1 *Eliz. Dyer* 165. in an assembly of the Judges and others, the question is fully stated, Whether a subject generally might withdraw his person out of the Kingdom, for merchandize, travel, or other cause, by the sole licence or permission of the Common Law?

The question is not put upon any right the subject had to go, but upon a bare permission at Common Law.

For all the Judges agreed with *Fitzherbert*, that the King might prohibit them.

And *Fitzherbert*'s opinion for such permission only is urged; and at that time left with a *Quære* upon it, without any allowance of such permission from the Judges, but seemingly to the contrary.

But afterwards *Mich.* 12 & 13. *Eliz. Dyer* 296. a particular case of a Merchant that went beyond sea to live, and not for merchandize, without the King's licence, came before the Judges; and 'twas debated before the Judges of both Benches, and the Chief Baron, upon this point,

Whether it were an offence punishable at Common Law?

Two of the Judges held it to be an offence, and that the Common Law did prohibit it.

The rest of the Judges concurred with *Fitzherbert*, and an express prohibition by the King, by Proclamation or an offence of contempt, but left by the Common Law a rent, which imports no right, but a bare impunity.

But all the Judges, after a Prohibition, held it an off[illegible] punishable at Common Law; whereby that point is [illegible] nion of *Fitzherbert* and the Judges of that time, That Law licence was but a bare permission, importing only i[illegible] the Law was silent before an express Prohibition of the K[illegible] lowest degree of permission taken notice of in Books of L[illegible]

Grotius, in his Book *De Jure Belli & Pacis, lib. fo.* [illegible] permission, properly so called, *Permissio autem proprie,* [illegible] *sed actionis negatio, nisi quatenus aliud ab eo, cui permittitur* [illegible] *dimentum ponat.*

But this permission of the Common Law goes not so fa[illegible] debar others from obstructing the action, which may be i[illegible] the King and other Nations, as I have shewn.

It carries only impunity with it, and this liberty of hau[illegible] strangers in amity, something resembles that liberty whi[illegible] Law allows one subject towards another, *viz.* a free pass[illegible] to speak or treat with him, which sounds only in excuse may be prohibited by the owner.

9 *Ed.* IV. *fo.* 4. *par.* 15. In trespass for breaking his [illegible] fendant pleaded a licence from the Plaintiff; who repli[illegible] the Licence he prohibited the defendant to come.

For be the licence express from the party, or implied b[illegible] owner might determine it by an express Prohibition.

But tho' the Common Law did not expressly prohibit th[illegible] sea without licence, so as to punish it as an offence crimin[illegible] discountenance all going beyond sea without the King[illegible] adjudging their issue born there, after such a departure, [illegible] inheritable to the *English* Laws; as was resolved *inter Hide* [illegible] 25 *Eliz. B. Rs.*

3 *Cro.* 3. That if Baron and Feme go beyond sea with[illegible] tarry there after the time limited by the licence, and have is[illegible] shall be aliens, and not inheritable.

Besides those Powers or Prerogatives wherewith the [illegible] entrusts the King for the defence of the Realm, *viz.* to p[illegible] move aliens, to restrain them from going, and to recall hi[illegible] when gone beyond sea;

The Law rests the sole power of making leagues with for[illegible] King alone,

Which is the first step towards a foreign trade,

The Common Law admitting of no trade with and enemi[illegible] made friends only by publick leagues to be made capable of bein[illegible]

And as the making of all leagues, so the modelling a[illegible] such leagues, are by the King alone.

As it is to be observed, that no leagues were ever yet ma[illegible] limited and universal trade, but in all leagues the particul[illegible] laws of each Country are excepted; as for example, salt c[illegible] ported into *France*; and most *French* commodities are re[illegible] being imported hither:

So it was resolved, *Pasch.* 36. *Eliz.* (4 *Inst.* 5.) 3 *Inst. Hen*[illegible] *Tomlinson*, upon a seizure of *French* Goods, and a complaint t[illegible] upon it, That the Laws of either Kingdom were excepted i[illegible]

Much less doth the King in any league conclude or buil[illegible] prerogative towards his own subjects, in granting them licen[illegible] or in restraining of them from going beyond sea, tho' in orde[illegible]

Moreover, the rules of the Common Law are not adapted [illegible] matters of foreign trade, neither can foreigners be presumed [illegible] nizance of the municipal laws of this Kingdom.

The principal part of foreign trade is transacted beyond se[illegible] Common Law can have no cognizance, but is confined within [illegible] of the four seas.

The Law was so strict, that an obligation bearing date at a [illegible] beyond sea, could not be tried in *England*, 21 *E.* IV. *fol.* 74.

Service of a Privy Seal upon a subject beyond sea, comman[illegible] return, when certified, into *Chancery*, and sent by *Mittimus* [illegible] *chequer* for seizing of Goods and Lands, is not traversable, triable in *England*, 2 *Eliz. Dyer* 176.

In the Case of the King and *Cusack*, 17 *Jacobi*, *Rolls* [illegible] *fol.* 112. Serjeant *Davies* argues, that the municipal [illegible] are not sufficient for ordering the affairs and traffick of Mercha[illegible]

And upon this ground, when the Staple was removed from [illegible] to several Towns in *England*, by the Statute of [illegible] III. it [illegible] That the trade should be governed by the same law, it was be[illegible]

And by 7 *Chap.* it is enacted, *That all Merchants* [illegible] *shall be ruled by the Law-Merchant of all things touching the S*[illegible] *by the Common Law of the Land.*

Whereby, in negative words, the Common Law was exc[illegible] intermeddling in the affairs of Merchants, as not proper to d[illegible] controversies, and whereof foreigners could have no cognizan[illegible]

By all which it appears, that the Common Law made no p[illegible] foreign trade.

The Common Law therefore having given no right to th[illegible] trade beyond the seas with foreigners, nor prefer[illegible] managing of that trade, but left that matter solely to the Ki[illegible] best profit of his people:

It may be proper to consider upon what foundations the [illegible] stands.

The foundations are two

1. Leagues made by the Kings of *England* with foreign Princes;
2. Royal licences, which are either solely by Grant, or Parliament.

For all Acts of Parliament in matters of prerogative and [illegible] from the King, are by the King's Grants in Parliament [illegible]

By leagues, foreigners are bound by publick compact to [illegible] King's subjects to a freedom to trade with foreigners beyond [illegible]

I have already spoken of leagues, as the [illegible] foreign trade, and without which no foreign [illegible] by the subject.

4

What I shall add, is only concerning the necessary dependance of that trade upon leagues, in its continuance and regulation; if the league be broken, let the subjects right be what it will, to trade either singly by Grant, or by Act of Parliament, it is suspended, and after Proclamation made, becomes unlawful and punishable, as trading with enemies.

The leagues and treaties with foreign Princes for trade and commerce, whereof the sole power is in the King, to bind the subjects of *England*.

They are the only Laws betwixt Nation and Nation to direct their trade and commerce by.

And by the said leagues, trade may be limited to certain places and commodities, or other restrictions, as the two Princes shall agree upon, who are the only masters of their leagues.

A clear and full instance of this, is in the leagues for trade with *Flanders* and the *Low-Countries*, between the Kings of *England* and the Dukes of *Burgundy*; whereby the Staple was settled at *Bruges*; and that no Wools should be sold in *Flanders*, but what came out of *England*; and that no *English* Cloth should be sold in *Flanders*, on pain of forfeiture.

21 E. III. Complaint was made in Parliament by the Merchants of several abuses committed by the men of *Bruges*, in restraining our Merchants from selling their Wools to whom they pleas'd at *Bruges*; and pray'd remedy.

The King's answer was, that the ordinance of the Staple should be view'd, and that *Thomas Michelborne*, with whom the Patent touching that ordinance was, be call'd to bring the same with him, and some of the Merchants of the country, who best understood this matter: and the King by advice of his Council would provide remedy; *Rot. Parl.* 21 *E.* III. *nu.* 10.

22 E. III. Another complaint is made in Parliament against the men of *Bruges*, for prohibiting the Merchants to buy staple Wares here, and pray redress.

The King answers that he will speak with the *Flemish* Ambassador about it, 22 *E.* III. *nu.* 13.

8 H. V. A grievous complaint made in Parliament against the men of *Flanders*, that tho' *English* Merchants observed the ancient league, that no Wools but *English* should be sold in *Flanders*, and no *English* Cloth sold there; yet they permitted the Wools of *Scotland*, *Catalonia*, *Arragon* and *Spain*, to be sold there, and pray remedy.

The King answers, that search shall be made for the alliance.

And upon the like complaint, 9 *H.* V. the Commons pray, the King would please to treat with the Duke of *Burgundy*, that no other than *English* Wools should be manufactur'd there, or that the *English* might sell their Cloth there,

The King answers, he would treat that the *English* Cloths might be there sold. *Rolls Prerogative*, 1 *fo.* 14. *title, League.*

But this treaty came to little purpose, till after the Acts of Parliament were made, 27 *H.* VI. *cap.* 1. (20 *H.* VI. *cap.* 4.) 4 *E.* IV. *cap.* 5. for excluding all the commodities of *Flanders*, until the Duke of *Burgundy* recall'd his proclamation for banishing Cloths out of his Dominions.

Those Statutes produced a firm league between the Kings and the Duke of *Burgundy*; who in the Record is call'd the Duke of *Hans*, or of the Still-yard, from the Merchants his subjects, who had long in *England* obtain'd those names.

By that league a free trade for Cloth was agreed upon for the *English* Merchants in *Flanders*, to continue for ever; and the King confirm'd to the subjects of the Duke, as well the liberties granted by *Edw.* I. to Merchants-Strangers in general, by his *Charta Mercatoria*; as those granted by *Edw.* II. to the Merchants of the Still-yard in particular: which league was confirm'd in Parliament, 13 *E.* IV. *nu.* 2.

These leagues may suffice to shew the dependance foreign trade hath upon leagues, as to its continuance and regulation.

By this league the Staple at *Bruges* was taken off, and liberty granted to the *English* Merchants to sell their Cloths in any part of the Duke's Dominions.

Who these *English* Merchants were, I shall in this place only make a short remark; That they were the Company of Merchant-Adventurers, erected and licensed for the better regulation of trade for Wool and Cloth, beyond the Seas, by Letters Patent, 1 *Feb.* 8 *H.* IV. and confirm'd by other Letters Patent, 1 *Oct.* 1 *H.* V. which I shall speak more largely to, when I come to shew the constant possession the Crown hath had of licensing Corporations for foreign trade, exclusive to others.

The other foundation, upon which all foreign trade stands, are royal licences.

I before shew'd that the licence, which the Common Law gave to trade with foreigners, was no sure foundation of trade; because it might by Law be interrupted by the King, and did in its nature import no more than a bare impunity.

But where the King grants licences to his subjects to trade with foreigners, they gain a right or interest to trade according to such licences;

Which are either by Grant only, or by Act of Parliament. I will first consider those, that are singly by the King's Grants.

That as the King may at Common Law prohibit any of his subjects to go beyond sea, so that he may licence them to go for trade or otherwise, is unquestionable.

The Writ of *Ne Exeat Regnum*, and several forms of licences in the *Register*, *fol.* 190. and multitudes of other authorities make it out.

The King may grant such licences, not only where himself may prohibit, but where the Common Law, and Acts of Parliament do prohibit.

Alien Enemies are prohibited by the Common Law to come within the Realm; yet the King may license them to come by his safe-conduct, as fully appears by the Statutes made for the observation of safe-conducts.

And it is observable, that such safe-conducts put the Alien Enemy into the condition of an Alien Amy, as fully under the King's protection, during the continuance of his safe-conducts.

No subject could seize his goods or injure his person, but he was punishable for it, both at the suit of the King, and of the party.

For before the Statutes made, conservators for truces and safe-conducts were appointed, appears by a Record of this Court, *Pasch.* 13 *E.* III. *Banco Regis*, *Rot.* 12. which I shall have occasion to make use of to another purpose.

And that such an Alien Enemy may bring his personal action for debt, or any injury, appears by the case of *John Douglas*, a *Scotchman*, 20 *E.* IV. *fol.* 6. *Pl.* 6. and *Moore* 431.

The King may license his subjects to trade with enemies prohibited by Common Law.

And for licences to come, go and trade both within and without the Realm, against express Acts of Parliaments, the instances are infinite

But for the better methodizing of these, I shall make use of precedents and authorities, to make out the exercise of the King's prerogative in all times, as to matters relating to Foreign Trade.

I shall reduce what I have to offer under these heads;

First, That the Staples, which were the publick Marts for all Merchants to resort to, were at first settled only by the Kings of this Realm, antecedent to any Act of Parliament.

Secondly, That after the Staple was established at *Calais* by Act of Parliament; the King gave licence to trade to other places, which no subject could do without such licence.

Thirdly, That the regulation and managery of Foreign Trade in all cases, where Acts of Parliament have not particularly interpos'd, have been guided and governed by the King's prerogative, both in point of licence and inhibition.

First Head; As to settling the Staple in the Dominions of foreign Princes, as in the instance of *Bruges*; that must be done by leagues, nor can it otherwise be.

But the appointing of the Staples in *England*, or in the Foreign Dominions of the King, was at first by the King alone.

This is expresly so declared in the recital of the Statute, 2 *E.* III. *cap.* 9. whereby Merchants-Strangers, &c. have liberty granted them to trade in *England*, according to the form of the Great Charter.

By Merchants-Privy, distinguished from Merchants-Strangers, in this Law, are plainly intended the Merchants of the King's foreign Dominions.

The *Irish*, who by *Ordinatio pro Statu Hiberniæ*, 17 *E.* I. had liberty granted them to traffick into *England*, so as they gave security not to go unto, nor commerce with *Scotland*, nor other the King's Enemies.

And the *Gascoigners*, and other the King's subjects in *France*, who had divers liberties of trade granted them by the King; as appears by a difference between them and the *Londoners*, decided judicially in Parliament, 20 *E.* I. *Parl. fol.* 180, and 130.

That by Merchants-Privy is to be understood of the King's foreign subjects, I collect from the reference this Law hath to *Magna Charta*, which concern'd only foreign Merchants; whereby the King's power to restrain them was reserv'd, and consequently was reserv'd by this Law; as is taken notice of by an Act not printed, 8 *E.* III. *num.* 20. that the Staple was during the King's pleasure, and the King revoked the Staple, giving Merchant-strangers liberty to buy any Staple-wares, 1 *E.* III. *Parl. Rot. pars* 2 and 3. *Mem.* 24.

A Commission issues to the Mayor of *London* to put in execution the orders made by *E.* II. for establishing the Staple in several Counties of *England*, and for the rule and government of Merchants.

By 27 *E.* III. *cap.* 1. the Staple was settled in several Towns in *England*.

But that Law had no words to bind the King's prerogative to remove it; and of that opinion was the Parliament, 38 *E.* III. where the Commons pray that the Staple may always continue in *England*.

The King answers, it shall continue till the next Parliament.

The first of *March* in the same year, the King remised it to *Calais*; but 43 *E.* III. *cap* 1. because of a war that broke out with *France*, it is brought back: the Act recites, that it had been removed to *Calais* by the King, for the profit of the Realm and ease of the Merchants of *England*.

47 *E.* III. *nu.* 17. The Commons pray that the Staple may be only kept at *Calais*, and that no Grant be made to the contrary.

The King answers, that he will appoint the Staple, as by the Council he shall think best.

1 *R.* II *nu.* 98. The Commons pray to know where the Staple shall be, if *Calais* haply be besieged.

The King answers, in such places of the Realm, as were last used.

By the constitution of these Staples, Merchants were not only licensed, but obliged to repair thither, and restrained to export their Staple-wares to any other place.

And altho' many Statutes were made to fortify and strengthen the Staple, by creating a forfeiture of all Staple-wares, if carried to any other place; yet by the Records I have produced, it is manifest that the sole appointment and ordering of the Staples was in the King, and that by the acknowledgment of several Parliaments.

2 *H.* V. *cap.* 6. provides, that merchandizes of the Staple shall not be exported to any other place without the King's licence, before brought to the Staple, on pain of forfeiture.

2 *H.* VI *cap.* 4 provides, that all Staple wares shall be carried to *Calais*, so long as the Staple is there.

And 8 *H.* VI. *cap.* 17. provides, that if Merchants export the merchandizes of the Staple to any other place, the merchandizes shall be forfeited; except the Merchants of *Jeane* and *Venice*. And *cap.* 27. several licences granted by the King to export to other places are revoked.

What these Staple-wares were, is fit to be known, they comprehending the greatest part of the native commodities of this Realm, that were merchandizable in foreign parts.

By the Statute of the Staple, 27 *E.* III. the Staple-wares are Wools, Leather, Woolfels and Lead; to these are added, by a Statute made 50 *E.* III. Tin, Worsted, Butter, Cheese, Feathers, and many other commodities.

This Statute, tho' it be not printed, yet is taken notice of as a Statute and a Law of the Staple, by the Statute of 3 *H.* VI. *cap.* 4. whereby Butter and Cheese are recited to have been made Staple-wares by this Law.

The Record is 50 *E.* III. *nu.* 20. (or 200.) where the Commons of the Town of *Calais* pray that the Staple may be holden only there:

Which the King grants, that it shall be holden only there, and no where else beyond sea, as well of all ancient Staple-wares, as of Tin, Worsted, Butter, Cheese, Feathers, &c.

The Staple was several times remov'd by *R.* II. but from 21 *R.* II. it continued at *Calais*, till that Town was taken by the *French*.

By all which it is manifest, upon what slender grounds the Statute of 15 *E.* III. *cap.* 3. that the Seas be open to all Merchants to pass where they please, was urged and insisted upon to be a Law in force, or to have any influence upon this case.

For

For besides what Mr. Sollicitor truly observ'd, that it was made for a special purpose, to take off the present Staple; to which all Merchants, as well foreign as *English*, were confin'd to carry their goods, and was of the same purport, as the Statute of 8 *E.* III. *nu.* 20. I before mention'd, which open'd the then present Staple.

For by the several Laws I have mention'd for fixing and strengthening of the Staples, the Statute of 15 *E.* III. was absolutely repeal'd and set aside.

As to all *English*, *Welsh* and *Irish*, by the Statute of 27 *E.* III. for settling the Staple in *England*, by *chap.* 1. whereof all *Englishmen*, *Irishmen*, and *Welshmen* are expresly prohibited to export any Staple-wares; and liberty given only to Merchants-strangers to do it.

And by 3. *chap.* it is made felony for the *English*, *Irish* or *Welsh* to export.

And when the Staple was return'd to *Calais*, it was a forfeiture, as I have shewn, to export those wares to any other place without express licence; for that the *Mare Liberum*, by the Statute 15 *E.* III. became *Mare Clausum* long since by many subsequent Laws, and not to be open'd but by a royal licence.

1 *H.* V. *nu.* 40. The Commons pray all Merchants may export to any place beyond the Seas, or import any goods except goods of the Staple.

The King answers, he will advise with his Council.

The Parliament did not insist upon any right, by 15 *E.* III. but pray'd it as an act of Grace, and were modest in their request, that the general licence desired might be restrain'd to merchandizes, which were not Staple Commodities, yet it was denied by the King.

17 *R.* II. *nu.* 15. Several Towns in the *West* prayed they might carry their Wool into *Normandy*.

The King answers, let them repair to *Calais*, as is appointed.

18 *H.* VI. *nu.* 50. The Commons pray that every Merchant may lawfully transport all manner of Hides, Calves Skins, Coney Felts and Tallow, to what place him liketh, other than to *Calais*.

Which is denied by the King.

By 18 *H.* VI. *cap.* 6. Liberty is given to export Butter and Cheese to any other place besides the Staple, in amity with the King, provided the King may restrain the same when it shall please him.

Where was the force of 15 *E.* III. if so minute a thing as Butter and Cheese could not be freely exported without an express Statute?

And that is obtain'd upon such urgent reasons as are mention'd in the Statute, and granted too but conditionally, with a saving of the King's right to restrain.

This may suffice for making out the first head, that the Staples to which all Merchants are obliged to repair, were principally instituted and appointed by the King alone; and that the Statute of 15 *E.* III. is wholly repealed by the Laws for settling the Staples.

Second Head; In the next place, I shall offer some authority to make out the King's undoubted right to grant liberty of trade to other places, after the Staple was fixed at *Calais*.

My Lord *Coke* in 4 *Inst.* 282. is much in the right, in affirming the Staple was continued at *Calais* above 200 years, though he be mistaken in another assertion, as I have fully shewed,

That it could not be removed but by Act of Parliament.

But I will admit the Staple at last fixed at *Calais*, by 21 *R.* II. and strengthen'd and fenced under the penalty of forfeiture of the goods, by the Statutes, 2 *H.* V. and 8 *H.* VI.

Yet the Kings, by their prerogative, did and might lawfully grant licences to trade to other places.

I will not here trouble you with the general learning of dispensations with penal Laws, tho' our Books are full of it, and determine in favour of the Crown.

But I shall confine myself to instances of foreign trade, wherein it will appear, by what I have already said, and shall farther offer, that the Crown had a peculiar prerogative not disputed, or drawn into question in any times till of late.

The men of *Berwick* and *Newcastle* have had such licences granted them, which being found detrimental to the King's revenue, arising at the Staple, were revoked by Act of Parliament, 8 *H.* VI. *cap.* 31.

20 *H.* VI. *cap.* 4. Denizens, who shall take licences to export to any place but the Staple, shall pay Alien duties.

Here the King's right to grant such licences is acknowledged by the Parliament; 27 *H.* VI. *cap.* 1. upon complaint of the King's Officers in Parliament, that by the multitude of licences to export elsewhere than the Staple, the revenue of the Staple was sunk from 68000 *l. per Ann.* to 12000 *l. per Ann.* all licences before granted are vacated.

In the Year-book, 2 *R.* II. *fol.* 12. *Parl.* 16. and 1 *H.* VII. *fol.* 3. A licence granted to the Town of *Waterford*, to carry goods of the Staple where they pleased, is allow'd; the *Irish* being bound to the Staple as well as the *English*.

1 *H.* V. *n.* 15. which I before mention'd, the Commons allowed of the King's prerogative to license strangers to come into *England*, tho' prohibited by Act of Parliament.

Where the Statute 15 *H. cap.* 3. prescribed a form of safe-conduct, yet it was resolved the King might grant them, as before at Common Law: *Edw.* IV. *fol.* 33. *L.* 340. and 13 *E.* IV. *fol.* 9.

Where by 31 *E.* III. *cap.* 20. the exportation of all sorts of Corn was prohibited, except to *Calais* and *Gascoign*.

Several Indictments were preferred, 36 *Edw.* III. against *John Lamb*, *Andrew Taverner*, and several other Merchants, for exporting great quantities of Corn and Grain. They severally pleaded the King's licences, mentioning the quantities, and in some of them the certain places to which the Corn was to be carried; but in others generally, *ad quascunque Partes exteras, præter illas, quæ de Munitia Regis existunt.*

Which are allowed, Treasury, *Int. Pl. Coronæ & totum*, 36 *E.* III.

Whereas 5 *Eliz.* prohibited the exportation of Sheep-skins.

Hillary, 3 *Jac.* I. *Shaw* brings his action against *Hawes* upon that Statute.

The Defendant pleads a licence, 19 *May*, 31 *Eliz.* to *Gilbert Lee*, his factors, executors, deputies and assignees, to export Sheep-skins for ten years, not exceeding 200,000 in any one year; if it happen'd by any restraint, or any other cause, they should not export that number; and pleads that *Lee* assigned to, and nominated *Scot* to execute the Letters Patent, with the contingent clauses: And,

That *Scot* assigns to the Defendant, with
contingent clause, and pleads he was hinde
tifies for the exportation afterwards.

All the Court held, that this was a disp
to *Lee*, the first Patentee.

But judgment was given against *Hawes* th
First, Because being a dispensation, it i
Secondly, That though *Scot* might have
nated, yet he could not nominate over.
Thirdly, The advantage of the future con
lar. 3. & *Pasch.* 4 *Jac. Banco Regis*, *Ro.*
Monop. cu. 3.

Third Head; In the last place I shall shew
nagery of the foreign trade, in all cases wh
particularly interposed, hath been guided a
of the Crown, both in point of licence and

That the foreign trade was at first transac
ers, is most evident from *Magna Charta*, wh
only for foreign Merchants.

And if any *English* had at that time exerc
least pretence thereto; no doubt can be, b
liberties would have made some provision for
which it doth not.

The Statute of *Acton Burnell* 13 *E.* I. intr
for the benefit of Merchant-strangers, for
their debts.

For the only mischief the Statute takes noti
withdrew themselves from coming into the R
because there was no speedy Law provided f

I have not met with any footsteps of any
in the Reigns of *E.* I. or *E.* II. or before, an
terprized the foreign trade.

But in those Kings reigns, the foreign trad
Charters to foreigners; for though *Magna Ch*
duct to Merchant-strangers, yet the King n
ter such prohibition might license, as I have

And therefore the foreign Merchants had a
ters, *viz. Charta Mercatoria*, by *E.* I. and th
of the *Hans*, or the *Still-yard*, which I have

And 6 *E.* II. the *Gascoignes* founded th
with the City of *London*, 20 *E.* I. upon their
the Kings of *England*.

Indeed the men of *Guernsey*, 32 *H.* III. obta
to them and their heirs, freely to fish and to
King's Dominions thrice in the week, betwe
and *Easter*; *Par. Roll.* 32 *H.* III. *mem.*

The earliest attempt towards a foreign trad
English, is the fishing trade upon the seas, 11

At which time the King granted licences t
borough, *Whitby* and *Dunwich*, to them and oth
to fish, to fish in the sea with vessels of thirty
tion' seu Mandatis MS. in contrarium factis n
11. *E.* III. *pars secunda*, *Membr.* 35.

Though these licences were intended only t
whereof the Dominion was in the King;

Yet by colour of these licences, the *Engl*
H. IV's reign, made fishing voyages to *Iceland*

Whereupon *H.* V. at the instance of the su
mark, prohibited the *English* to fish there.

And thereupon the Parliament, 3 *H.* V. pra
ed, that the *English* might freely fish there.

Which was denied by the King, 3 *H.* V.
whereby it is evident, they had no right to do
prohibit them, it being a foreign traffick, wh
had made any provision.

Afterwards the same King, in the 5th year
cences to *Geoffery Pamping* and *John Hastings* of
Richard Pais of *Winterton*; *William James* and
mere; to go *versus Partes exteras* to take fish.

That every one of them might employ two f
fish and bring it into *England* by themselves, A
Rot. 5 *H.* V. *membr.* 34.

E. I. Before any Statute made therefore by
the exportation of Horses, Arms, Money, Gold
men of *Dartmouth* were proceeded against by
Bench, for exporting Money contrary to the Pro
Rot. 38. amongst the Records in the Treasury.

The Crime in the Information is said to be
Contemptum & Inobedientiam Coronæque suæ pl. jud
bationem manifestam.

To which, those of the Defendants that were
of whom one afterwards died, and another was in
Scotland. So the Record ends with a continuan

Rot. Clauso, 41 *E.* III. *membr.* 25. A Writ issu
that he permit no Alien Ship to be freighted th
Town were freighted.

It is evident upon what I produced under the
cords of Parliament, 1 *H.* V. *nu.* 41. and 18
English Merchants had not then any right or ge
what places they pleased any sort of merchandize

But such Petitions were denied in both these K
time there was a Company of Merchants-Adven
into *Holland*, *Zealand*, *Brabant*, *Flanders*, and othe
erected for the rule and government of all *English*
those parts; and all who should trade there, enjoi
rules of the Company.

But it was not objected to those Kings, that some
unless they would be subject to the rules of the Co

The Company was erected by Letters Patent, 5
firm'd by *H.* V. 1 *Oct.* 1 *H.* V. and confirm'd by

I

That the Merchant-Adventurers enjoyed their privileges, and permitted none to trade within their limits, who submitted not to the rule of the Company, and who should not be contributors to their publick charges, is evident from the *Stat.* 12 *H.* VII. *cap.* 6. insisted on by Mr. *Pollexfen*; but was made use of by him, only for the historical part of it contained in the petition presented by the Merchants to the Parliament for their liberty of trade; which, by what I have already shewed, could not be true as to the staple wares, unless they have licences from the King (which in all probability they had) to certain places.

And what is it they pretend to in their Petition? Only freedom to repair to, and trade at the four general Marts, which being annually held and proclaimed, was an invitation to all neighbouring Nations to repair thither; and all *English* Merchants, as well as others, if they had lain under no restraint from the Company's Charter, or other Prohibition of the King, might have repaired thither with their cloth or other wares, not being staple wares, without offence, as I before admitted.

In case there had been such a right to a free trade to all Nations in amity, as the Petition suggests (for as yet the Merchants retain some Modesty, not to pretend to a free trade with aliens, not in amity, much less with Infidels, whom the laws of all Christian Countries adjudge alien enemies):

This had been the proper time for the Parliament to have asserted that right, and adjudged the Patent illegal, as Parliaments have frequently done with Patents which have been against Law. But the Parliament knew no such right, and therefore by the enacting clause, allowance is given to the Charter; only their immoderate demands of admittance-fines are restrained, and the fine limited to 10 Marks. And accordingly in their Charter afterwards renewed by *H.* VII. they are obliged to take no more of any person admitted into their Company than 10 marks.

Ph. & Mary, 26 *Feb.* 1 & 2 *P & M.* erected a Corporation of Merchants-Adventurers to *Russia*, and Parts adjacent, with licence to trade, and prohibition to others, upon pain of forfeiture of Ship and Goods.

That this forfeiture might be effected, the Charter is confirmed by Parliament, 8 *Eliz.*

This Act takes notice, that several persons, after the trade was found beneficial at the cost of the Company, for their peculiar gain, utterly to decay the trade of the Company, contrary to the tenor of the Letters Patent, in great disorder traded into those parts, to the great detriment of the commonwealth.

Here is a full description (*mutato nomine*) of the defendant and his interloping companions.

By the Judgment of the Parliament then, a limited trade, under the order and rule of a Company, as settled by the Crown, was thought most beneficial to the King.

And those that traded contrary to the tenor of the Letters Patent, are reckoned disorderly traders, in prejudice of the commonwealth.

So far was the Parliament from thinking all the subjects had a right to trade there.

After the taking of *Calais*, in the latter end of Q. *Mary*'s reign, Q. *Elizabeth* and the *English* Merchants were no doubt in great straights what to do.

For by the *Stat.* 2 *H.* VI. all merchandizes of the Staple were to be carried to *Calais*, while the Staple was there, which ceased by the taking of *Calais*.

But by 2 *H.* V. no merchandizes of the Staple could be exported without the King's licence, till brought to the Staple.

The Queen had no place convenient left for erecting the Staple at, beyond the seas. And though in *R.* II's time, when the Parliament demanded where the Staple should be, if *Calais* were besieged? The King's answer was ready (viz.) *At such places in* England *it was last at*:

Yet now when *Calais* was taken, such answer would not serve the turn; but the placing of it in *England* would be useless and ineffectual, and destructive to the Queen's revenues in her customs.

For by several laws made by *E.* IV. *R.* III. & *H.* VII. most foreign manufactures were prohibited, and great discouragements put upon all foreign Merchants coming into *England*, but those of the *Hans* and *Stillyard*.

And few foreign Merchants would repair into *England* to fetch our commodities, when they can bring little to barter with but ready money.

And to have granted to every Merchant a several licence, as it would be chargeable to the subject, so it might prove mischievous to the Kingdom, the subjects trading severally, without any rule or government, in foreign parts, upon the account of the general law of reprizals, which obtains in all Nations.

Whereby every subject and his goods are liable for the injuries and wrongs committed by any one; which, in the more barbarous Countries, is executed with great barbarity.

And therefore Q. *Elizabeth* in the direction of foreign trade, instead of Staples, for the rule, order and government of Merchants, at certain places, followed the precedents of the Merchants-Adventurers and *Russia* Companies, by erecting Corporations of Merchants for the rule and government of the foreign trade.

Which Companies as they are presumed to have a better State to answer for injuries done in foreign Parts, than any single person can be presumed to have:

So in their very constitution are more responsible to the Law for their misdemeanour, by *Quo Warrantos*, whereby they may lose their liberty of trade.

It is very doubtful whether licences granted for trade to single persons, may be forfeited, they passing an interest, if the licence to go beyond sea, to trade or otherwise, be for a certain time, as most licences were. It is held by the Judges, 2 *Eliz. Dyer*, 176. in the Case of Mr. *Barnes* and the Dutchess of *Somerset*, that the licence is not revocable.

The Queen, in her reign, erected many Corporations for foreign trade: I shall mention only some, which have been publickly taken notice of, and received allowance.

17 *June*, 2 *Eliz.* The Queen, by Letters Patent, incorporated several Merchants of *Exeter*, and gave them licence to trade into *France*; and that no artificer should be admitted of the Companies.

The Prohibition was not general to her other subjects, but only to the men of *Exeter*.

The Company enjoyed their liberties all the Queen's reign, and flourished under them till 3 *Jac.*

When by Act of Parliament the trade was opened, and general licence given to trade with *France*, *Spain* and *Portugal*, and the dominions thereof.

Whereupon a question arose, Whether their Charter was not set aside by the general words of 3 *Jac.* and therefore 4 *Jac. cap.* 9. it is enacted, and declared, *That the said general Act doth not nor shall dissolve, annihilate, or impeach the said Charter, or the said Company, in any of their privileges, liberties or immunities, granted to them by the said Charter; any thing in the said general Act to the contrary notwithstanding.*

This Act added no new force to the Charter, but enacted and declared it to be out of the provision of 3 *Jac.* for general licence to trade into those Countries.

Where, by the Judgment of the Parliament, the Queen's power to grant such Charters is admitted. For if the Patent had been void in Law, before 3 *Jac.* to make an Act of Parliament only to declare it out of the provision of that Law, were idle and illusory.

The Queen's subjects, for their licence to fish at *Iceland*, paid the Queen a quantity of fish, called composition-fish, by the Act of Parliament made 5 *Eliz. cap.* 5.

Whereby, for the encouragement of the fishing trade, the purveyors are prohibited to take purveyance of sea-fish; the composition-fish, payable by the Queen's subjects travelling to *Iceland*, are excepted.

The Patent of the *Greenland* Company to fish there, was held good, *Rolls*, 1 *pt. fo.* 5. in the Case of the Taylors of *Ipswich*.

This trade, notwithstanding the privileges granted to the Company, was almost lost.

And thereupon 25 *Car.* II. *cap.* 7. that trade is opened, not only to the *English*, but to all foreigners residing in *England*.

The *East-India* Company was erected by Queen *Elizabeth*, 31 *Dec.* 43 *Eliz.* and renewed to them and successors, 13 *May*, 7 *Jac.* with prohibition to all others to trade there, and confirmed to them by this King, 3 *Apr.* 13 *Car.* II. upon which Patent the question ariseth about a foreign trade, which hath been enjoyed by the Company above 80 years.

And its consequence concerned the prerogative of the Crown, in all the Charters for foreign trade which have been granted.

Whereas I have shewn, the most considerable part of the foreign trade hath in all times been managed under Grants from the Crown, in appointing the Staples for Merchants to repair to, in licensing trade to other places, notwithstanding those Staples; and in licensing and prohibiting foreign trade in such Cases where Acts of Parliament had not made special provision.

I now proceed to consider of Royal Licences by Act of Parliament.

It will be infinite to take notice of the several Statutes made relating to foreign trade.

And therefore I shall at this time offer some general observations upon them.

Observ. 1. Upon examining into the ancient laws for foreign trade, it will be found that there are far more laws for restraining the exercise of foreign trade, by *Englishmen*, than there are for opening of it.

So much, that for a long time whilst the Staple was in *England*, they were prohibited, under severe penalties, not to export any Staple wares; and when the Staple was removed beyond sea, they were confined to *Calais*, and such liberty of trade to other places as the Kings from time to time had granted to Corporations, and single persons were frequently taken off, though the King's prerogative to grant them was never yet impeached by any Statute.

The great discouragement to them by foreigners first began in the reigns of *Ed.* IV. *R.* III. and *H.* VII. But in those Kings reigns, the *English* were strictly held to the Staple, unless licensed by the Kings.

This observation is made out of the several laws I have touched upon, and many others, which are in the Statutes at large that are printed.

Observ. 2 There was never yet any Statute made, that gave a general liberty of trade to *Englishmen* to or with all Nations; but what were made, were special and particular.

The only law that had any resemblance to any such purpose, was 15 *Ed.* III. so much insisted on, which has been sufficiently already shewn to import no such thing; and the several attempts in Parliament to have introduced a greater liberty of trade with foreign Nations, in amity, and the particular laws that have been made for licensing some trades, do fully argue that the law was never understood to intend any such matter, as a general licence to trade every where.

Observ. 3. The several special statutes that have been made for liberty of foreign trade to particular Countries, or for particular commodities, are introductive of a new law, and not declaratory; and do plainly argue the King's right before to prohibit some of them in express terms, others by necessary implication.

I shall instance in some of them, the *Stat.* 17 *Ed.* I. *Ordinatio pro Statu, &c Hiberniæ*, opens the trade from *Ireland* to *England* and *Wales*, for the *Irish* commodities.

Whereby all Merchants have liberty granted them to import their Merchandize into *England*, but so that they give good security, that they shall not go unto, nor commerce with our enemies of *Scotland*, nor others of our enemies.

This law restrained the subject of no liberty he had before; and therefore, if the Merchant had before such general liberty, or right to import those commodities, his right of trading would have excused his giving any security, which is not imposed by law, otherwise than as a precedent condition to a right conferred by the Statute.

This law opened the trade from *Ireland* to *England*, as well to foreigners as *Englishmen*, but it extended only to *Irish* commodities: for the exporting of *English* commodities into *Ireland*, continued to be managed under the King's licences till *Edward* III.

And if any did to the contrary, he was subject to fine and ransom for his contempt, as appeared by 34 *Ed.* III. *cap.* 17. whereby the trade is opened for *English* and other commodities into *Ireland*.

By that law it is accorded, That all Merchants, as well aliens as denizens, may come into *Ireland* with their merchandize, and from thence freely to return without fine or ransom.

This law extended not to the *English* Merchants, but only to the aliens and denizens.

In

In the next Chapter, *cap.* 18. the *Engliſh* are provided for, who had not ſo large a liberty granted them as the aliens and denizens had. The 18 *chap.* provides, *That the People of* England *who have heritage and poſſeſſions in* Ireland, *may bring their corn, beaſts, and victuals, to the ſaid land of* Ireland, *and from thence to re-carry their goods and merchandizes into* England *freely, without impeachment.*

The liberty of exporting into *Ireland*, granted to the *Engliſh*, is reſtrained both to ſuch *Engliſh* only who had lands in *Ireland*, as alſo in the ſorts of the commodities, *viz.* corn, beaſts, and victuals only.

But the liberty to export from *Ireland* is larger, extending to all commodities, according to the latitude of *Ordinatio Hiberniæ*, which took in all *Iriſh* commodities.

38 *E.* III. *cap.* 11. The King wills of his grace and ſufferance, *That all Merchants-denizens, that be not artificers, ſhall paſs into* Gaſcoign *to fetch wines; and that the* Gaſcoigners, *and other aliens, may import; always ſaved to the King, that it may be lawful to him, whenſoever it is adviſed by his Council, to ordain of this Article, as beſt ſhall ſeem to him for the profit of him and his C mmons.*

This is expreſſed to be an Act of Grace, and contains a ſaving of the King's ancient prerogative, 18 *H.* VI. *cap.* 3. which I before mentioned: for liberty of exportation of butter and cheeſe, expreſly ſaves the King's right, provided the King may reſtrain the ſame when it ſhall pleaſe him.

To paſs by many ancient Statutes of like nature, the Act of tonnage and poundage, 12 *C* II. which gives liberty of exporting divers commodities, which the Kings of *England* might in all times prohibit, as to gunpowder, arms and ammunition, expreſly ſaves the King's right, to prohibit by Proclamation.

3 *J. cap.* 6. which is the largeſt licence for foreign trade that was ever given to any *Engliſhmen* in Parliament, by opening of the trade to *Spain, Portugal*, and *France*, and the dominions thereof, fully proves the King's prerogative in this matter, both in the title and body of the Act.

The title of the Act is, *An Act to enable all his Majeſty's loving Subjects of* England *and* Wales, *to trade freely into the dominions of* Spain, Portugal, *and* France.

A very improper Title, if ſo be the King's ſubjects were before enabled to do it, and had a right to do it by the Common Law, as is pretended; and would not be reſtrained from it by the King.

And no doubt can be made, if ſuch right had been, but the Parliament would have ſeen it, being very inquiſitive at this time into all the ſubjects rights, and very jealous leſt any of the ancient rights of *Engliſhmen* ſhould be invaded by K. *James* coming from another Nation, and would not have complimented the King with the title of an enabling law.

The reaſons from the body of the Act are ſtrong; the reaſons offered for ſuch general liberty are only politick, none drawn from the right or any ancient uſage the *Engliſh* could pretend to.

The Act in its recital admits, *That by the Letters Patent for incorporating the Company to trade into* Spain *and* Portugal, *his Majeſty's other ſubjects were diſabled and debarred from the free enlargement of common traffick into thoſe dominions.*

Which were not true, if the other ſubjects had before a right to trade there, but the patent would have been void againſt them.

3. There are no declarative words of any former right, but only of enacting, and proviſional for a future liberty, *viz.*

That it ſhall, and may be lawful from henceforth.

4. The Act, in expreſs words, provides only againſt the miſchief and inconveniencies which may grow or redound upon the Patent, and to redreſs any injury done by the Patent.

5. The liberty granted, is reſtrained to be in ſuch ſort, and in as free a manner, as was at any time accuſtomed ſince the beginning of the King's reign, and before the late Charter of Incorporation.

Whereby it appears, that the uſage to trade freely into theſe Countries without licences, was but from the entrance of K. *James*;

The Statute referring to no other free uſage: And therefore this Act did not over-reach any Charter granted by Queen *Elizabeth*, as was afterwards declared in the next Parliaments, 4 *J. cap.* 9. in the caſe of the Charter to the Merchants of *Exeter*, for the *French* trade granted 2 *Eliz.* which I before mentioned.

*Obſerv.*4. That all Acts of Parliament which grant licence of trade, do ſuppoſe the other foundation of foreign trade to have continuance, *viz.* according to leagues with foreign Princes.

For no Act of Parliament ever gave licence to trade with aliens not in amity; and if the leave be determined, the liberty is ſuſpended, tho' granted by Parliament, till the leave be renewed.

Obſerv 5. The laſt thing I ſhall obſerve upon the laws that give licence of trade, is, that where liberty of trade is given by Act of Parliament, without any reſervation to the King of his ancient right, the King in ſuch caſe hath ſo bound up himſelf, that he cannot generally prohibit or reſtrain that trade wherein he hath granted his ſubjects an intereſt by a law.

For a general prohibition or reſtraint would amount to a repeal of a law, which the King cannot do without an Act of Parliament.

The law will be the ſame here as in the caſes where Acts of Parliament do generally prohibit, where general licences would be void, becauſe they tend to repeal a law.

Upon this ground the licence in *Darcy*'s caſe, for that part which concerned the importation of foreign cards, was judged void in law, becauſe too general, not limited to any certainty.

But the King may in particular, and certainly, diſpenſe and licenſe againſt prohibiting Statutes.

And ſo he may in particular reſtrain the perſons of his ſubjects from going beyond the ſeas, notwithſtanding any of the laws which give licence of trade:

But cannot grant a reſtraint or prohibition generally, where Acts of Parliament have given a general licence, unleſs it be in ſpecial caſes, and for a time, where the intereſt of the Publick requires it; as of the plague, and furniſhing out of the King's Navies, in time of war with any Prince. And therefore I ſhall admit, that if any publick law can be produced, which gives liberty of trade for all the King's ſubjects, to the Judges, that this Patent will be void, as a reſtraint of that liberty againſt law.

Upon this ground the *Canary* Patent was held void, becauſe againſt the expreſs liberty granted by 3 *Jac* and therein ſaved; or of the Common

Law Monopoly, by reſtraining the right
for the benefit of a few.

Upon the ſame reaſon, the Grant of P
ſhould be landed at *Southampton*, was aga
the rights of ſeveral free ports, before gra
London, and others, as 27 *Ed.* III. *cap.*
had liberty granted to bring their wines
43 *Ed.* III. whereby the *Engliſh, Iriſh*,
fetch their wines and bring them to any p

And therefore was repealed in Parl.a
whereby it appears, that the Parliament
lant enough to take notice of Patents a

The like in the caſe of *John Peachy*,
by retail, 50 *Ed.* III. the Parliament le
that Grant an Inhibition under the Gr
Citizens of *London* to ſell ſweet wines i
voked, 50 *Ed.* III. *No.* 13. and *Peachy*
of the Grant, 50 *Ed.* III. *N.* 33.

This Grant was not only againſt ma
have been cited in the arguments in th
Importers liberty to ſell their wines
pleaſed; and many expreſs Grants to t
were confirmed in Parliament; but w
Law, being a reſtraint and monopol
wines in *London* and other parts of *En*

For when foreign merchandizes are
with, they fall under the rules and go
the retailing of them here becomes an

In *Lambard*, 43 *Ed* III. *lib. aſſ. f*
when foreign merchandizes are brough
prices is puniſhable.

At Common Law in like manner, a
wiſe to debaſe the prices of our inlan

The reaſons of theſe caſes, which
the arguments of the other ſide, prov
produce ſome clearer Statute than 15
to the *Eaſt-Indies*.

Having conſidered of foreign trade
been managed in all times, I procee
the law determines of trade and com
quently with Infidels. Here the co
it was in the former; in that, the C
preſs Prohibition by the King.

But here the Common Law is a
war with alien enemies.

Whether the commerce with alie
the extent of aiding and comforting
within 25 *Ed.* III. I ſhall not at t
while for the interlopers who traffi
with the King of *England*, withou
but before the Statute at Common

Paſc. 13 *Ed.* II. *Rot.* 13. *B. R*
againſt three perſons for trading
King of *England*; the Defendants
in the Marches of *Scotland*; which
but the King: thereupon they obt
Rolls Prerogative, tit. Gaver reſſo. 1

I need not labour to clear a point
dant's Counſel, but their endeavour
mies; wherein they have a difficu
the laws of all Chriſtian Countrie

In the great Inſtance of the *Je*
eſtates ſeized, as of enemies almoſt

They call for authorities, but o
the opinion of any one learned ma
between the *Engliſh* laws and Infi
the Court to repeat the authoritie
the enmity between Infidels and
than ſufficient, after ſuch ſolemn
the Iſt's Reign.

All which have received a ver
obſcure.

That time hath hid the Law
whether they were Acts of Law,

And that the reaſon why Prin
be, is becauſe they are under no

But why the Records ſhould b
eminent a caſe as that of the *Je*
the Common Law, in the diviſi
could not hear any good reaſon

For I take it, the principles o
againſt, are as clearly laid down
we have.

For the caſe of the *Jews* ſt
ſtrangers, of ſeveral Countries i
ral Kings, and under the gene
they were under the King's pr
as any other Merchant-ſtrang
might grant, as I have ſhewn,
them were indenized, others
lands, as well as leaſes and per

Then they are baniſhed by t
that were never indemnified up
and enemies to the Chriſtian r

To whom then will their la
ſonal eſtates as they had not li

The Law adjudged it all to t
about their eſtates, did not fal
Jews, (as the Defendant's Co
the King and ſeveral Doctors
were able to defend their righ

To the dark Records (as they were stiled) I will add a case solemnly adjudged between the King and a potent Subject, the Archbishop of *York*, 21 *Edw.* I. where the case was;

The Prior of *Pidlington* was indebted to a *Jew* in 300 *l.* After the banishment of the *Jews*, the *Jew* met with the Archbishop in *France*, and prevailed with him to help him to the money; that Archbishop persuaded the Prior, that he was bound in conscience to pay the money to the *Jew's* Attorney; who did it accordingly.

And all this was after a Proclamation issued for discovery of the *Jews* debts.

For this concealment and trespass, the Archbishop was sued by the King, before the Council in Parliament, and laid it to his damage of 1000 *l.* To which the Archbishop appeared and pleaded, and to avoid a Trial by a Country Jury, as the Record mentions, he was put upon his allegiance to tell the truth.

Whereupon he confess'd the Information, and Judgment was given against him, and the taxing the fine referred to the King.

The reasons of the Judgment fully declare what the Law was; *Quia idem Episcopus bene cognovit quod post exilium Judæorum a prædicto Judæo intellexit, quod pecunia prædicta sibi in regno debebatur, & post eorum exilium omnia quæ sua fuerunt, & in regno remanserunt, tam debita quam alia bona quæcunque, ipsi Domino Regi remanserunt, & catella sua fuerunt.*

That he did not only conceal, but contrary to his faith, wherein he was bound to the King, persuaded the Prior and Convent, for saving of their souls, to pay. *Pla. Parl.* 173.

The Archbishop did not doubt of the Law, tho' the Defendant's Counsel do; but a recourse to Conscience against Law, in deceit of the King, against his faith and allegiance.

This I hope will be allowed to be a Judgment, and a Judgment that declares the Law as plainly as ever Judgment did, and of a higher nature than any Judgment in *Westminster-hall*.

In the same year several mean Lords petition the King in Council for the arrearages, in rent and services, of the lands the *Jews* held of them before their banishment.

The Council answered, That for the time *Jews* held it, it was their fault not to collect them; for so long as the King held them, he would pay them; for the time they were in any Grantees hands, they should have recourse to his Grantees. *Pla. Parl. Riley, fol.* 129.

Here the King's title to the real and personal estates of the *Jews* in *England*, is asserted by Judgment of the highest Court of Judicature in *England*.

The principles of Law, upon which the Judgment past against the *Jews*, are frequently laid down in our Book.

If an Alien Amy or Enemy purchase lands, the King shall have them, and may seize them at any time; and tho' the Alien died seized upon Office found, the King shall have them, and not the Lord, by Escheat.

This my Lord *Coke* reports to have been resolv'd by all the Judges, *Pasch.* 29 *Eliz.* in Sir *James Croft's* case, 1 *Inst. fol.* 2.

There it was also held indeed, that if a Denizen died seized without heir, the Lord, by Escheat should have the land, and not the King; but that is in case of a compleated Denization, where the issue of the Denizen is capable of inheriting. But in case of *Jews* or Infidels, the Denization was void, being made to them as strangers, without taking notice of their enmity to the Christian Religion; and so the King deceiv'd in the Grant.

And an Infidel, though born in *England*, is not inheritable to the Laws of the land; if he should, the land might soon be over-run with *Jews* and Infidels, and no redress to be had: so that neither denization nor birth did alter the state of the *Jews* as to Inheritances within *England*, but they remain'd Aliens under safe-conduct only.

If an Alien Enemy had a lease of lands, or of a house for habitation, the King should have it, within the same resolution in Sir *James Croft's* case, and not any subject that should enter upon him.

Nay, if an Alien Friend, who should take a house for habitation, should die, or leave the lands, the King should have the lease.

But then, how stands the Law for the goods of an Alien Enemy without the Realm?

Mr. *Pollexfen*, to argue Infidels to be no Alien enemies, urged from the mischief that might ensue, that then every man might seize the persons or estates of *Jews* and Infidels, because by Law every person might seize the persons and goods of Alien enemies: and for that, cited the authority of 7 *E.* IV. *fol.* 13. *Co.* 2 *H.* VII. *fol.* 15. *b* which are but the same case, the authority of 7 *E.* IV. being only mention'd in course; argument in the Book of *H.* VII. The authority of 7 *E.* IV. is good Law, but misapplied, in not observing the difference between the times of the enemy's, or his goods coming into the Realm.

After open War proclaim'd, whereby all the subjects have notice whom the King hath declared his enemies, and against whom they are to join in defence of themselves and the Kingdom, if the persons or goods of such enemies come into the Kingdom, any subject may seize them, and gain a property in the goods, as a prize taken in open War, according to the authority of 7 *E.* IV. And indeed the Laws of all Nations; and that not only of enemies goods, but of *Englishmen's* goods taken by the enemies; (whereby the property was left) and brought hither by the same authority of 7 *E.* IV.

Which plainly shews the meaning of the Book, to be of goods taken in open War; whereby the property of the goods rests in the Captor as lawful prize.

But when the persons or goods of Aliens are in, or come into *England* under safe-conduct; and the safe-conduct be not determined by the King, either by Proclamation of open War, or otherwise, no subject can seize the person or goods of such Alien enemies.

Upon this difference the Law was settled, 36 *H.* VIII. by the Judges, *Bro. Propert.* 38. in the abridgment of the case, 7 *E.* IV.

That where a *Frenchman* inhabited in *England*, and a War was afterwards proclaimed, no subject could seize his goods, because they were here before.

But if he came after the War, any man may seize his person and goods, and shall have a property in them, and in such case the King shall not have them.

And so was it put in practice, saith the Book, 'tween the *English* and the *Scots*.

And when *Eulloign* was taken by the King's subjects, 19 *Ed* IV. *fol* 6. *pl.* 4. where a debt was owing by a subject of the King of *Denmark's*, and a war breaks out, the subject shall not retain the debt, but the King shall have it.

22 or 2 *E.* IV. *fol.* 4, 5. *pl.* 9. In false imprisonment, the Defendant justifies under the King's Commission for apprehending a *Scotchman*, there being a war between the King of *England*, and the King of *Scotland*.

I before shewed, that an Alien enemy, which came over by the King's safe-conduct, was as much under the protection of the Laws, as any Alien Amy whatsoever, and no subject could seize or molest his person or goods.

And the determining the safe-conduct by the King, left the Alien enemy in the same condition as other Alien enemies, after war proclaimed, who were here before under the general safe-conduct of the Laws.

In which case the subjects had no liberty to seize either the persons or goods of Alien enemies; but that power was reserved by Law expresly to the King.

Which, besides the authorities I have produced, expresly appears by *Magna Charta*, *chap.* 30. which provides, that if the Merchant-strangers be of a land which makes a war against us, and be found in our Realm at the beginning of the war, they shall be attached, without harm of body or goods until it be known to us or our Chief-Justice how our Merchants be intreated there.

So that the disposal of their persons and goods was wholly in the King. And the liberty the subjects had to intermeddle with foreign enemies, extended only to such who came here after a war proclaimed.

By all which, the King's title to the lands, debts and personal estates of the Jews, after the King had determined their safe-conduct, by banishing them out of the Realm as Infidels, evidently appears; and those dark Records refined in some measure from their obscurity, by the constant tenor of the Common Law, practised ever since.

But doth not the making leagues with, and sending of Ambassadors to some Infidel Countries, argue that Infidels are not Alien enemies? No, certainly.

But the practice of the Kings of *England*, and other Christian Princes, fully argues the contrary; for the making such treaties, in order to trade, proves that no trade could be managed with them, before the treaty concluded.

My Lord *Coke* (who was of opinion that an Infidel is *perpetuus inimicus*) yet agrees with other learned men, that a league of peace, (which is only a cessation of all hostility) and a league of commerce (which amounts to no more than a reciprocal and general safe-conduct to each other's subjects) may be made with an Infidel Prince, 4 *Inst. fol.* 155.

But he is called *perpetuus inimicus*, from the practice of the Kings of *England*, and other Kings and Princes, not to make any leagues of friendship or alliance with Infidel Princes, whether restrained from making such leagues by the Municipal Laws of the several Christian Countries, or the general Rights of Christianity, is not to my purpose to determine.

But either a cessation of open hostility, or a general safe-conduct, by a treaty of commerce, binds up the subjects hands from intermeddling with the goods or persons of Infidels.

And therefore the Act of Navigation, that mentions the goods of the *Ottoman* Country, makes nothing to the Case.

For by the treaty of commerce with the *Ottoman* Empire, they might be brought in, and by his subjects before, under a general safe-conduct. But as to the *Mogul* and other *Indian* Princes, there is no league of peace or commerce between them and the Kings of *England*.

Which makes the case of the *East-India* Company stronger yet, than that of the *Turky* Company.

Though I conceive, that upon these principles I have laid down Law strong enough.

And herein the case of the *East India* Company is particular, for the King hath made no league for them.

But by the Letters Patent, hath given them special power to make war or peace with any Infidel Prince for the benefit and better advantage of their trade.

So that all other subjects are merely precarious, and have no pretence of taking any advantage of any peace made by the Company.

So as to them, the *Indians* remain to all purposes Alien Enemies.

Having now shewn, that all foreign trade depends upon, and hath been managed by leagues and royal licences, either by Letters Patent, or special Acts of Parliament; and

That the King may prohibit generally, where no Act of Parliament hath intervened to the contrary, and the Common Law prohibits trade with Infidels, and no Act of Parliament has provided for it.

That that trade cannot be managed but by the King's licence, in some such manner as is directed by these Letters Patent to the Company.

That the answers to all the authorities and arguments made use of by the Defendant's Counsel, which I have not answer'd, lie open for the authority of the Taylors of *Ipswich* case; and the several other authorities of mechanick trades, and of inland merchandize, to which the subjects have a right by Common Law, make nothing against our case of foreign trade, and to an Infidel country, to which I have argued the subjects have no right, but were prohibited.

The opinion of the Taylors in *Ipswich* case, that a Patent to hinder trade at sea is void; that generally to hinder all trade at sea, is no doubt good Law: because many licences then in being, and several Acts of Parliament in many cases had granted liberty of trade.

But in the same case the restraining of trade to a particular country, for which no Act of Parliament had made provision, is allow'd of in the case of the *Greenland* Patent.

There was no authority produced, and I believe cannot be, that gives the least countenance for liberty of trade with Infidels, or to impeach the King's prerogative of prohibiting trade to foreign countries, whereto licence for trade had not been granted by the King's Letters Patent, or by Acts of Parliament.

The arguments drawn from the reason of the Common Law were two:

First, From the liberty the subject had to go and trade into all foreign parts, for which were cited *Fitzherbert* and *Dyer*.

That liberty, and those authorities, I have already examined, and shewed that the subject had no liberty, but was prohibited by the Common Law to trade with Infidel countries.

And the liberty to trade with foreigners in amity, was but a bare permission, till the King prohibited.

Secondly, The other ground insisted on was, that all ingrossing of merchandize was unlawful at Common Law: and therefore a Patent leading to authorize an unlawful ingrossing is void, as a Monopoly at Common Law, and declared so by 21 *Jac.*

Here I will join issue with Mr. *Pollexfen*, and do admit, that if it be an unlawful ingrossing, whether by the Common Law, or any Statute in force, the Patent will be void.

And he must admit unto me, that if it be no unlawful ingrossing, it is no Monopoly at Common Law.

As he did in his argument ingenuously admit, that if it were no Monopoly at Common Law, it is not within the Statute 21 *Jacobi*; so that the question between us will turn upon this single point:

Whether the ingrossing the foreign merchandize of *India* be unlawful?

Upon what I have already said, it appears it is not. For I have shewn that the Common Law regarded, and made provision only for, merchandizes within the land; and though when foreign merchandizes came thither, they fell under the rules of the Common Law; yet the ingrossing, or sole buying of foreign commodities beyond the seas, and selling in gross, or by the Merchant-Importer, was no offence at Common Law.

Neither is there any Statute that makes it an offence at this day.

It is true, the Statute of 37 *E.* III. *cap.* 5. prohibited *English* Merchants to ingross merchandizes.

But the Merchant-stranger was not bound by that Law: and that Statute was the next year repealed, as to the *English* Merchants, 38 *E.* III. *cap.* 2. And that at present the Law is, that any Merchant may buy in gross, and sell in gross, appears by the resolution of all the Judges, *Mich.* 39 & 40 *Eliz. Co.* 3 *Inst.* 196. in the chapter of ingrossing.

And the resolution goes a step further than the Merchant-Importer.

That any person may buy in gross of the Merchant-Importer, and sell by retail.

And it follows by a clear consequence, that if *English* Merchants in such places, where by Law they have a right to trade, may ingross the commodity of the place without offence; the ingrossing foreign commodities of any place, where the subject cannot trade without licence, can be no argument to invalidate such licence.

Because ingrossing of foreign Merchandize, by any Merchant-Importer, is no crime, but lawful for every trader.

And then the consequence of all ingrossing will be the raising the price of the commodity.

Yet it being a commodity of foreign growth, and not such as the Law hath any where determined necessary for the support of life, as victuals and such like;

The Common Law hath no regard to the price, but leaves the Merchant free to make his advantage of his dangerous adventure.

The advantages that some subjects may receive by the trade, and others may be debarred from, which are alike hazardous, and depend upon a multitude of accidents, are no measures of right or wrong, to pass a legal judgment upon.

But if the Company have a right to trade, and others have not, as I have argued, whatever their advantage may be, which cannot be estimated till they have wound up their bottom:

The ingrossing of the *Indian* commodities cannot be infected with the taint of a Monopoly, which always supposes something done against common right, which is altogether inconsistent with having a right due to the King.

For it is of the essence of a Monopoly, according to the definition thereof proposed by Mr. *Pollexfen*, and taken out of my Lord *Coke*, *viz.* that it tends to restrain such liberty and freedom the subject had before, or to hinder him in his lawful trade.

So that every sole buying and selling a commodity, if it be lawful, can be no Monopoly, in the legal sense of the word; which is evident in several land commodities, where the sole buying and selling is coupled with a right.

The King may grant to farm his pre-emption of Tin, whereby the Grantee hath the sole buying and selling, if he pleaseth, of the whole commodity.

Such a grant to *Tidman* a foreigner was complained of in Parliament, 21 *E.* III. and prayed by the Commons, that no such merchandize be sold, but to the commonalty of Merchants.

The King answers, that it was a profit belonging to the Prince, and every Lord may make his profit of his own; 21 *E.* III. *nu.* 29.

That this sole right of buying and selling was ever enjoyed, appears by the case of the Stannaries, 4 *J. Co.* 12. *fol.* 10 & 11.

So of all Gold and Silver dug within the Realm, and of all royal fishes taken; the King and his Grantees shall have the sole disposal, or right of selling them.

It is no just answer to these instances, that they are inheritances and rights vested in the Dukes of *Cornwall* and the Crown:

Which they may dispose to whom they please. So is his prerogative of licensing foreign trade. And as to the question of a Monopoly, which implies a wrong in restraining the rights of others; there is no difference between having a right existing, which may be granted, and having a power or prerogative to confer a right on others.

For 'tis the having the right to do the thing that makes it no Monopoly.

And therefore, if the King have a right to license some of his subjects to do a thing, which other of his subjects cannot do, or are rightfully prohibited to do; whether the thing granted were before *in esse* or *de novo* constituted, it is all as one to the validity of the Grant. This is proved by the instance of Fairs and Markets.

Whether anciently in the Crown, or *de novo* erected and granted to any subject, the case will be the same, as to the subjects sole right of holding the Fair and Market exclusive of others.

And rights conferred by the King's prerogative, are every whit as strong as any right granted out of the Crown, which was before *in esse* there.

So that the Pretence of an unlawful Ingrossment and Monopoly being removed, by Mr. *Pollexfen*'s admittance, 'tis not within 21 *Jacobi*.

And it is plain, it is not within the words of the enacting part of the Statute, without the aid of the Proviso: for it is expresly limited to grants made, or to be made, for the sole buying and selling, or using of any thing within the Realm. So that it was only the liberty of the inland trade and traffick, to which the subjects had right before, that was fenced and secured

by this Statute. And this Patent is not
within the Realm; and though the sellin
and is lawful, notwithstanding any Law

And the Proviso was only added, to
Parliament, not to intermeddle with a
which he might, and lawfully had exerc
subjects.

Besides, to put it past all scruple, th
words of the Proviso.

It was a Company in the reign of Qu
is recited in the declaration.

And by their Charter 7 *Jac.* had the s
sive clauses to others.

And if the Parliament had not adjud
maintenance and enlargement, or order
other Companies, they would undoubted
them, upon that Charter of 7 *Jac.*

For this very Parliament was inquisiti
in the least tended towards a Monopoly.

And if they had thought that Charter
tender of the point at that time.

The objection made from the different
stocks, is of no great weight, because it to
whether a Company may have a sole trade

For every Company draws a charge
Company are not liable to.

And if the subject have a right to trade
he can be no more compelled to be of the
trades upon separate Stocks, than of one w

And the objection, that ordering of tra
intended of licensing of some, with excl
force; for it could not be intended of any

All the Patents for foreign trade befor
were Patents of exclusion of others than th

And if it be well considered, all the aut
Companies erected for well-governing and
mit, they may be exclusive to others;

It not being possible that a foreign trade
vernment, by any Letters Patent whatsoeve
subject to that rule and government.

And it is evident, that no rule of any C
of the Company; and if every man, not c
trade will not be under any rules made for
pany.

So that such Patent will be only for k
rule and government, but not at all of the

Which of necessity must produce the rui
probability of the trade itself.

For if others trade without limitation, d
Company, and not be liable to the charg
trade must be supported; they may and wi
and forestall and anticipate the Markets, t
more effectually towards the destruction o
both to King and Kingdom.

Besides, the Factories and Stock of the
obnoxious and liable for all injuries comm
Government of the place, by any Interlope
general Law of reprizals.

I will not further pursue the arguments of
but do rest upon the right, which I have en
steps.

First, That the subject had no right to th
a foreign trade, but might be prohibited.

Secondly, That no league or royal licence
general right.

Thirdly, That foreign trade hath in all ti
by the undoubted prerogative of the Crown
biting others. And that in all cases not pro

And that such Grants and Licences have
Parliaments.

Fourthly, That no Act of Parliament
trade, much less to trade with Infidels.

Fifthly, That the Common Law prohibi
with Alien Enemies.

Sixthly, In the last place, I have applied a
and arguments made use of to impeach the C

Upon all which, I conclude the chief poi

First, That the Grant to the Company, of
sive to others, is good in Law.

Secondly, As to the second point, whether th
Company have a right to the sole trade there,

I shall spend but a little of your time abou

Because if the Company have by Law t
Law will give them a remedy to redress inju
recovery of their damages.

Which is properly by an action of the C
medy to redress themselves. For a prosecutio
cannot be in satisfaction of the Company's d

I shall therefore rest that point upon the
by the Plaintiff's Counsel.

I shall only apply answers to the objections

Obj. 1. 'Tis not alledged the Defendant ha

Ans. The Complainants case is sufficientl
sole trade to the *Indies* granted to them, and
tice thereof, and yet traded contrary to their

If the Defendant had had the King's li
Plea, then the validity thereof, as against th
into question; but he rests upon the licence,

Obj. 2. They have shewn no special loss o

Answ. Neither need any be shewn, no mo
the case, where the right of any person is inju

2

of a Commoner who hath no eſtate in the land, nor the ſole right in the profit *apprender*, comes not to the caſe; the Law denies ſuch Commoner liberty of bringing his action, without a ſpecial damage, to prevent a multiplicity of actions, which upon the ſame ground every Commoner would be intitled to.

But otherwiſe it is, where any hath the ſole Piſcary or Profit *apprender*; after ſetting forth the ſpecial caſe, and wherein his right is invaded, a general declaration to his damage is ſufficient, and the examination of the particulars will belong to the Jury.

Obj. 3. That the action is grounded upon the reſtraints in the Letters Patent; and that reſtraint is not abſolute, but upon pain of forfeiture of ſhips and goods.

Anſ. The firſt part is miſtaken; for the action is grounded upon the grant of the whole, entire and only trade and traffick to the *Indies*, inforc'd with the King's covenant, not to grant licence to any others.

And beſides this clauſe of the prohibition, there is a diſtinct clauſe of Grant, that none of theſe countries or places ſhall be viſited, frequented or haunted by any of the King's ſubjects, during the continuance of this Patent, which hath no penalty annexed to it.

Upon theſe Grants the action is grounded; and if there were no clauſe of prohibition, the trading to theſe Infidels by others without licence from the King, is enterprizing a trade not only againſt the prohibition of the Common Law, but the King's expreſs prohibition.

But the action is not founded upon this clauſe, but upon other clauſes of conferring a right to the ſole trade.

The authority cited by Mr. *Pollexfen*, as an authority in point, againſt the action out of 11 *Rep.* 88. and *Rolls Abridgment*, *fol.* 106. *nu.* 6. in *Darcy*'s caſe, that admitting the grant or diſpenſation to *Darcy* were good, for importing foreign Cards contrary to the Statute of *Ed.* IV. yet the action would not lie, reacheth not our caſe of a right conferred by the King's prerogative, and not of any diſpenſation from a penal law.

Before the Statute of *Edw.* VI. every Subject might import foreign Cards; the Statute reſtrains that liberty under penalty of forfeiture.

The diſpenſation of one ſubject from the Law, works no Intereſt but a bare exemption from the penalty;

Which in the caſe of *Shaw* and *Hawes*, was held could not be aſſigned over; and therefore Grants that are merely Diſpenſations, convey no Intereſt againſt any other Subject, who is no otherwiſe reſtrain'd from doing the thing, than by the Statute under a penalty.

But where the King by his prerogative may grant the ſole uſe of a thing,* (as in caſe of new Inventions) the Grantee hath an Intereſt ſufficient to ſupport an action upon the caſe, as *Rolls* is of opinion. The next paragraph, *fol.* 106. *nu.* 17. That if the King grant that none ſhall uſe ſuch a thing (whereof the King hath power to grant), but the Grantee, reſerving a rent, if another uſe it, an action upon the caſe will lie;

Which is a ſtronger authority in point for the action, than that of *Darcy*'s caſe of a mere diſpenſation, is againſt it.

And therefore having proved the Grant of the ſole trade to be good, the action is well brought for damages;

And pray Judgment for the Plaintiffs.

Mr. *Williams*'s Argument.

De termino S. Michaelis, *Anno Regni Regis* Car. *Secundi* xxxvi. *Annoq; Domini* 1684.

The Eaſt-India *Company againſt* Thomas Sandys.

THE Queſtions in this Caſe, are two.

1. Whether this Grant of ſole trading to this Company, excluding all others his Majeſty's ſubjects who are not members of this Company, or within the qualifications of this Grant, be a legal Grant?

2. Admitting it a legal Grant, if this action be maintainable by the Company againſt the Defendant?

That this Grant is legal in all its parts, I do not find that the Counſel that argued for it, have endeavoured to maintain.

Mr. Attorney hath admitted in his argument, it is not.

That ſome parts of it are againſt law, is manifeſt, *viz.* it inflicts illegal penalties upon perſons offending againſt it, by creating a forfeiture of their goods and merchandize, which ſhall be brought into the Realm, or any of the dominions thereof, contrary to this Grant.

It alſo creates a forfeiture of the Ships, with the furniture thereof, wherein ſuch goods ſhall be imported or found; the one half to the King, the other half to the Company.

It grants, That the offenders againſt it ſhall be impriſoned during the King's pleaſure, and not to be delivered out of priſon until the offenders become bound to the Governor in the ſum of 1000 *l.* at leaſt, that ſuch perſon ſhall not at any time after ſail or traffick into any places mentioned in the Grant.

It gives the Company liberty to licenſe perſons to trade within the limits of this Grant; and that the King, his heirs and ſucceſſors, ſhall not, during theſe Letters Patent, licenſe any perſon to ſail or trade there.

In theſe things the property and liberty of the ſubjects, are put into the power of the Company; and they are to diſpoſe of the liberty and property to ſerve their own Company, and not the Publick.

If this Company may ſeize Goods and Ships, and impriſon the King's ſubjects, according to their Grant, they will have a greater prerogative over the ſubject than his Majeſty hath; they have power to ſeize goods, and impriſon perſons, without trial, without legal proceeding, which the King cannot do; and I humbly conceive, cannot grant to any ſubject or corporation.

The Judgment upon the *Canary* Patent, which I ſhall have occaſion to mention more largely herein, by the opinion of all the Judges, damned the penalties of that, agreeing in ſubſtance with theſe. The ſubſtance of this was admitted, at leaſt not defended, by Mr. Attorney General.

This Grant does not only give this Company dominion over the properties and liberties of the ſubject, and inveſt the Company with the prerogative of the Crown to licenſe men and ſhips to trade in theſe limits, but it doth diveſt the Crown, the King, his heirs and ſucceſſors, of a high prerogative; That the King ſhall not licenſe, as I take it, the King ſhall not trade in theſe limits without the licence of this Company. For as this great and mighty Charter is penned, it doth not only inveſt the Company, but diveſt the King of his prerogative.

Mr. Attorney and the King's Counſel could not argue for the Company in this matter, without arguing againſt the prerogative of the King. They are of the King's Counſel that argued for this Grant, but 'tis not to be believed they were of the King's Counſel, or friends, that drew it or adviſed it.

We that argue for Mr. *Sandys*, argue for the King's prerogative: That the King, notwithſtanding this Grant to this Company, may licenſe Mr. *Sandys*, or any other ſubject, to trade in theſe limits; and it doth not appear upon this Record but Mr. *Sandys* hath the King's licence to trade in thoſe places; he may licenſe any other ſubject to trade there.

And that the King by his Grant cannot exclude himſelf of his prerogative.

It will ſerve our turn, for the defendant in this caſe to avoid the plaintiffs action. If the plaintiffs ought not by law to have the ſole licenſing of traders in theſe limits; for the ſtinging part of their declaration is laid in this, *That the Defendant traded without their Licence.*

There was greater care had to greaten this Company, than to preſerve the prerogative of the King in this Grant; and the prerogative is named in this caſe, to ſerve the Company, and not the King: and they that drew this Grant, did neither conſult the honour nor prerogative of the King, the liberty or property of the Subject, the trade of the Kingdom, nor the law of the land: But their buſineſs was to greaten this Company, to the detriment of the King, the Law, and the Subject; as I hope to make out in this caſe.

In my way to the particular Queſtions in this caſe, I ſhall obſerve,

1. That the plaintiffs in their declaration do alledge, That they have eſtabliſhed and managed, and do manage a great trade of merchandize to the *Eaſt-Indies*, with the inhabitants there, who at the time of the making the Letters Patent, were not, and ever ſince are not Chriſtians; but then were, and now are infidels, and enemies to the Chriſtian faith.

Yet they do not alledge, nor can ſay that theſe *Indians* are in enmity with the Crown of *England*, or that they are alien enemies to *England*.

2. Tho' the preſent inhabitants of theſe places are Infidels, and enemies to the Chriſtian Faith, yet it may be, and we hope there may be an univerſal converſion to the Chriſtian Faith; and we are taught by the Church to pray for it, and to uſe all manner of means to bring it to paſs.

Why may not theſe places, or ſome of them, become inhabited with Chriſtians, as *Spain* and *Portugal* are now inhabited by Chriſtians, where Infidels did inhabit about 200 years ago?

3. This Grant doth not exclude a trade with Infidels only in theſe places, but with all perſons in theſe places.

I do not obſerve, that any of the Company's Counſel that argued before Mr. Attorney, have denied *Engliſhmen* the liberty of trading with Chriſtians in any part of the World, without licence from the King. Herein I take him to be alone.

4. They ſay, this trade cannot be managed but *per corpus corporatum*.

Yet have they an excluſion of all perſons, and bodies politick and corporate, to trade, or manage a trade in theſe places without their licence; and by this means exclude the King from conſtituting any other Company within the limits of their Grant, or in any part of it, which may be very neceſſary for the Government, and publick trade of the King.

1. It may be, the *Indians* may inſiſt upon ſome ſuch Company to be inſtituted by the King, by ſome treaty of commerce.

Now hath the King by this means, not only excluded his ſubjects from the trade of this Place; but he hath excluded himſelf of the liberty of making or conſtituting any other Company for trade or commerce, in all, or any of theſe places.

2. Perhaps the government and good management of trade in theſe places, may in time require more Companies to be inſtituted, in all, or ſome of theſe places; and the Company's Counſel, except Mr. Attorney, are now arguing the King by his prerogative, out of his prerogative:

That the King had prerogative enough to make this glorious Company the ſole traders, and managers of trade in theſe places, and to exclude himſelf and his ſucceſſors, and all the reſt of his ſubjects, from this trade and management:

3. And by this means conſtitute a ſort of Republick for the management of trade in theſe places, borrowing perhaps from *Hamborough* and other republican places, the ways and methods of managing trade upon a common ſtock, in fraternities and companies; and by this experiment alter the conſtitution of *England* in the management of trade, by altering the nature of our *Engliſh* properties in our goods veſted and placed in perſons, and placing our properties in companies and fraternities; and by fixing the myſtery of trade in companies, to the prejudice of ſingle perſons, and may in time turn to ill example, and endanger the Government in its other parts, as well as the trade of *England*.

The main queſtion in this caſe doth turn upon the power of the King;

If the King by his royal power may appropriate this trade in theſe infidel places to this Company?

Firſt, That the King hath power to do this, by the advice of his great Council, the Parliament, is not doubted. So there is no defect or want of power in the King to do this by the Law of *England*; the exceptions in the Statute of 21 *Jac. cap.* 3. do except ſuch Grants out of that Statute.

The queſtion is only a queſtion of the manner of doing this by the King.

Secondly, Whether he may do it, without the advice of his Great Council in Parliament?

As there is no defect or want of power in the King, ſo there is no defect in the Law of *England*.

Thirdly, But if there be a neceſſity or a conveniency to the doing of this for the Crown, or for the government, for the ſubject or for trade?

Fourthly, It is not to be ſuppoſed but that the Lords and Commons in Parliament, will and ought to aſſent to ſuch a Grant in Parliament as much as the Privy-Council, or any other of the King's Counſel, are obliged to adviſe it out of Parliament; and it ought to be ſo preſumed by the conſtitution of *England*.

And I take this to be one of the *Ardua Regni*, which is a ſubject matter fit and proper for the conſideration and deliberation of a Parliament, and ought not to paſs by any Grant without them.

The trade of *England*, the property and liberty of the ſubject, the King's revenue by Tonnage, Poundage and Cuſtoms, the prerogative of the King, are under great reſtrictions by this Grant.

This

This work is too heavy for the pen of an Attorney, or Sollicitor, to put into a Bill for the Great Seal, without the deliberation of a Parliament.

The King cannot naturalize an Alien; but by Act of Parliament, the Law doth intrust the King by his Letters Patent, to make Denizens of Aliens, but not to naturalize them.

It may be too much for me to give the reason of this, why the King hath not power to naturalize Aliens, as well as to denizenize them.

I humbly take the reason to proceed from the interest of the Subject, that the right of the Subject is immediately concerned in letting in Aliens to have the same right, liberty and freedom with *English* Subjects in *England*, and that this ought not to be granted to Aliens, not by the King under his Great Seal, without the consent of the Lords and Commons, the Representatives of the Subjects in Parliament.

There may be high State-Policy, sometimes to naturalize an Alien, and that perhaps it cannot always wait the meeting of a Parliament; yet hath the Law placed this trust in the King, to be exercised by the King, with the advice of the Lords and Commons in Parliament, and no otherwise.

The right of every *Englishman* in his freedom of trade in these parts, is concerned in this Grant, and every *Englishman* not admitted to trade by this Grant, is excluded of his freedom; and the King disables himself to license any other *English* Subjects to trade in these parts.

If the King had made such a Grant to Aliens, and excluded all his *English* Subjects from trading in these places, or if the King had granted only to his *Irish* or *Scotch* Subjects, and excluded his *English* Subjects, had these been good Grants or legal?

If the King has the prerogative, the Company's Counsel urge in this case, all this might have been done, and these Grants had been legal, tho' exclusive of all his *English* Subjects.

It is enough, I humbly conceive, the King hath the prerogative of granting and constituting such Companies, and making such Grants in Parliament; and the Law allows no more in cases of this nature, which concern the right of every Subject in *England*, and therefore ought not to be taken from him, but by his consent in Parliament.

I think it may be admitted, the King may by his Great Seal, without the advice of the Lords and Commons in Parliament, constitute a Company for the good management of trade in these parts, or any part of the world:

But he cannot, as I humbly conceive, by any Grant under his Great Seal, totally exclude his Subjects of their right and liberty of trading in any place upon the seas or beyond the seas.

Rolls 1. *Rep. fol.* 4. The Taylors of *Ipswich* case; the King may grant a Charter for good ordering of trade; this is for the benefit of the Subject, 2 *Ed.*III. *Britton*'s case.

The good management of trade is for the benefit of the Subject.

I shall endeavour to maintain, that the Subjects of *England* had a right to trade in these parts, before the making of this Grant, or the constituting any Company by the Crown in the *East-Indies*, and without any licence from the Crown; and by consequence this Grant appropriating this trade to this Company, and excluding the rest of the King's Subjects from their right and liberty of trade there, is an illegal Monopoly in trade, condemned both by the Common Law and Statute Law of *England*: and the Infidelism of the Inhabitants of these places, is no bar nor impediment to the trade and commerce of *English* Subjects in these places, without leave or licence from the Crown, no more than in Christian Countries.

That the prerogative of the Crown, to grant and issue out Writs of *Ne Exeat Regnum*, against this or that Subject, is no argument for this power to make such a Grant as this, or to exclude his Subjects from trading in Infidel Countries.

The *Ne Exeat Regnum* is a Writ that may be granted by the Keeper of the Great Seal, without any express Warrant or Command from the King, upon some suggestion, that the party may be required to give caution not to leave the Kingdom, till he answers such a suit, or the like.

This Writ is never granted without some special reason or cause in a particular case; the Subject complained of may appear in *Chancery*, and answering the Cause, may discharge the Writ.

Such a Grant under the Great Seal, for some of the King's Subjects to go abroad, and for the rest to stay at home, I conceive, would not be good in Law. No parity of reason, because the King may, by his Writ of *Ne Exeat Regnum*, stay a Subject from going out of the Kingdom, that therefore the King may by his Grant hinder him to trade out of the Kingdom. Men may, and do trade by their factors and correspondents, and do not stir out of the Kingdom; their personal attendance in their trade in places remote is not necessary.

The Subjects of *England* trading in merchandize, have, and always had a right to trade upon the seas, and beyond the seas, without licence from the Crown.

That they had such liberty to trade with all Christian Countries, I do not find it denied by any of the Company's Counsel, but Mr. Attorney; he hath yielded something the other Counsel have denied, and denied what others have admitted; and in something in his argument, he is, as I conceive, inconsistent with himself.

That trade is as free to all men as the air, that the seas are like the highways, free and open to all passengers.

Grotius *de Mari libero, Mare & littora Maris jure gentium sunt communia.*

Grotius *de jure belli & pacis, cap.* 3. *par.* 12. *Illud certum est, etiam qui Mare occupaverit, Navigationem impedire non posse inermem & innoxiam, quando nec per terram talis transitus probiberi potest, qui & minus esse solet necessarius & magis noxius.*

Cap. 3. *Ad Reges potestas omnium pertinet, ad singulos proprietas.*

Welwood's Abridgment of Sea-Laws, in his Epistle to the Duke of *Lenox*, and Earls of *Northampton* and *Nottingham*, Lord Admirals of *England*, *Scotland*, *Ireland*, and the Isles, he presses them to maintain the privileges due for the maintenance of the Admiralty, and the jurisdiction thereof, and that they would vindicate the same from all sort of encroaching and usurping; but above all, the conservancy of the seas (as the chief point of the Office) requires security and safety in common for all loyal Subjects, traders on sea.

By his opinion there's a community for
the seas, and not to be appropriated to a f
Britton, cap. 33. *De Purchas.* he disting
not corporeal, of things in common and t
Choses communes sicome la meer, & le eyr,
sicome & de pecher en flos, & en meer, & en co
The King I admit hath a sovereignty in
in the *British* seas is exclusive of other Prin
Mr. *Jo. Burroughs*'s sovereignty of th
utriusque Reipublicæ when he had *Normandy*
Julius Cæsar de bello Gallico, lib. 4. King
rerum, Insularum Oceani, quæ Britanniam ci
quæ infra eam includantur, Imperator & Domi
Bal. de rerum Dominiis, videmus de jure
Dominia sicut in terrâ. Mare ipsum ad cent
distinctaque illius Regionis, cui proxima approp
I do agree that the King hath a prerogati
within the King's liegeance; and that, by
Sturgeon, and other great fish in the sea belon
cap. 11.

And that the Statute *de prerogativo Regis*, a
Wrecks, Whales and great Sturgeons to be
gative.

And that the King hath his old customs,
and great Fish, by his conservancy of the se
lib. 5. *fol.* 108. *b.* 5. *Ri.* 2. *pars* 2. The Ki
age, *pro defensione Maris.*

But the King hath not any prerogative t
Subject from the benefit of his right of Con
and trade.

As the King hath his sovereignty upon t
him liegeance there; so have they their rig
the seas, and they are not to be invaded.

And the King hath the care and conserva
care, guard and conservancy of his Subjects
the seas, he hath his Tunnage, Poundage a
Rolls Abridgment, Tit. Prerogative. The sub
age are granted to the King for the safe-gua
Stat. 1. *Ed.* IV. *cap.* 13. recites, that *H.*
Kings, had granted to them, by the Comm
fence of the Realm, for the keeping and
intercourse of Merchandize safely to come
out of the same, a subsidy of all manner
coming in, and going out of the Realm.

And if any one be afterwards robbed by
misfortune, he shall ship as many more with
Stat. 1. *Mary, cap.* 18. and *Eliz.* 19. the
Stat. 45 *Ed.* III. *cap.* 4. And all rates and
and traffick upon the seas, and beyond the
Parliament, and can't be laid by the King al
of Parliament. 3 *Inst. fol.* 181. *Commercium*
& non in Monopolium & privatum pauculorum
alios permittere, alios inhibere Mercaturam.

Dyer, fol. 296. 13 *Eliz.* That a subject of
may depart out of the Realm without the Q
tho' not to merchandize; and such going o
tempt to the Queen, before a *Ne Exeat Reg*
or proclamation issue.

Stat. 5 *R.* II. *cap.* 2. doth affirm this by
Dyer, fol. 165 & 296. agrees with *Nat. B*
Merchant pays at the Common Law any C
chandize whatsoever, except three, *viz.* Wool
press for all Merchants, and confirmed by *Sta*
Rolls 1. *Rep. fol.* 4. Taylors of *Ipswich* cas
trade mechanick or merchandizing ought t
Patent in any sort, but by Act of Parliament
9 *H.* III. *cap.* 30. A Charter to hinder tr
that only 100 persons shall trade is void in itse
at this time. 2 *Inst.* 57. The Patent to *Greenl*
trade was found at the peril of the party's life
Taylors of *Ipswich* case, where there is no
his Charter cannot hinder trade.

The Patent to the College of Physicians,
Physick without their licence, would have be
firmed by Act of Parliament; yet this concer
England. and is a mystery, and the Professors
by persons of skill in it.

It may be admitted, that the King for spec
or that Subject, perhaps, to trade in some cer
As the King may inhibit a Subject's going
person goes beyond the seas after such an inhi
Subject, for which he is punishable.

But it is hard to infer from such particular i
sons, to trade in particular places or countries,
sons from going beyond the seas, to infer un
inhibit all his Subjects to go beyond the seas,
his Subjects except some few to trade.

There is a great difference between an inhi
this or that person to go beyond the seas, and
sons to trade, except such a Company.

This Grant imports a restraint upon trade
liberty of the Subjects, for the benefit of some
out any benefit to the Crown, or security to th
of *Ne Exeat Regnum.*

The Company may license Aliens only, a
trust is placed in the Company, which the Law
For the allay that is offered to this exclusion
and *English* Merchants in these places;

Obj. That they are excluded only from trading in the *East-Indies* with Infidels, and the Inhabitants there, who are enemies to the Christian Faith and Religion.

And that it is for the common safety of the Christian Religion, that this is done to avoid the danger of corrupting and perverting Christians to Infidelism.

I do not meet with any authority for this power given to the King.

But that *English* subjects have the same freedom of trade with Infidels as they have with Christians in places beyond the seas; so they be not in enmity with the Crown of *England*.

Michelborne's case, *Brownlow 2d Rep.* 296. That case hath been observed already to have no authority, nor the Book authentick, and at best but some saying of my Lord *Coke*, in a matter not then in judgment before the Court, and that perhaps mistaken by the Prothonotary.

I oppose to the probability of this saying, the report of the Taylors of *Ipswich* case, in *Rolls Rep. fol.* 4. 12 *Jac.* The Lord *Coke* was then Chief-Justice of the *King's-Bench*, and says in the resolution in that case, that no trade mechanick or merchantable can be hindered by the King's Patent, not in any place, without an Act of Parliament; a Charter to hinder trade at sea is void.

How can this stand with what is published in *Brownlow*, that my Lord *Coke* should say in the *Common-Pleas*, before this time, that an *English* subject cannot trade with Infidels, without licence from the King; and that he had seen a licence in the time of *Edw.* III. to that purpose?

The reason given for that saying, is as weak, because they are common enemies to the Christian Faith.

They may be enemies to the Christian Religion, and not enemies to the Crown of *England*, or to the trade of *England*.

The Law denies trade and commerce only with enemies to the Crown, not with enemies to the Christian Religion.

It is sufficiently observed already, by the Counsel that have argued on this side, that there are treaties of trade and commerce between the Crown of *England*, and these places of Infidels, and that there are leagues and embassies between them. 4 *Inst.* 155. allows leagues of commerce, and trade, and peace with Infidels.

And what may be the consequence, to declare that to be Law, that they are incapable of the benefit of the Law of *England*, allowed to other Aliens, and that they are not to be protected from personal injuries by our Law?

12 *H.* VIII. 4. A Pagan beaten in *England* cannot sue, *quia perpetuus inimicus.*

And to put them in the same condition with outlawed and excommunicated persons, how doth this consist with the common justice of Nations, or with the policy of trade in an Island?

Obj. By Mr. Sollicitor, 5 *Inst. fol.* 32. A Jewess born in *England*, marrying a converted Jew, not dowable.

Mr. Sollicitor hath cited many cases and Records out of Mr. *Prynne*'s Collections, and from the *Rolls* themselves, how the Jews were treated in *England* in trade; what restraints and taxes were laid upon them by the Crown.

I do not take it that any of these Records reach the reason of restraint of trade, imposed upon *English* subjects by this Grant.

There's no restraint but that *English* subjects might trade with Jews in their own countries.

That Jews were used thus in *England*, is no argument that the *East-India* Company may use *English* subjects like Jews abroad in other Countries.

St. *Paul*'s first Epistle to the *Corinthians*, *chap.* 6. reprehends the Christians for going to Law one with another before Infidel Judges, who were their enemies; calling it a fault, and he speaks it to their shame, that they would not rather receive wrong, or make Arbiters of their own to judge between the brethren, than to go to Law one with another, and that before unbelievers; but there's no reproof to the Christians for conversing or trading with Infidels.

4 *Inst. fol.* 155. *Darcy* and *Allen*'s case, *Moor*'s *Rep. fol.* 674, and 675. are Authorities for leagues and commerce with Pagans, which signify leagues of commerce with Infidels.

Lord *Coke* cites several texts out of the holy Writ to justify it, out of the Books of *Joshua*, *Kings* and *Chronicles*.

If it be true, there was such freedom of trade by the Common Law for all *English* subjects with Infidels and Christians in all parts of the World, and that without licence from the King:

To restrain this freedom of trade to a Company of *English* subjects, excluding all others the King's subjects from their ancient liberty and freedom of trade, I take to be a Monopoly, and comes within the description and reason of the odiousness of Monopolies, so largely argued by Mr. *Pollexfen*, that I shall not take up the time of the Court in repeating what he hath said, and I cannot add to it.

Neither will I trouble the Court with mentioning the authorities he hath cited for that purpose; but refer myself to the same authority in that matter.

Yet I take it, under correction, that it is fit to be very well considered, if this Patent be not a Monopoly, and an ingrossing and appropriating of trade to few persons, which did belong and was common to all *Englishmen*, though a licence from the Crown was necessary for their exercise of this trade; yet every *Englishman* was capable of such licence, and was intitled to such licence from the Crown, and had a right to it.

Now hath this Grant put it out of the King's power to grant such licences, and hath placed this power, and the exercise of it in this Company, and by this means hath by this Patent granted and appropriated a trade to this Company, which was common to all his subjects; and hath given to this Company the sole licensing of traders in these parts, excluding all the subjects of *England*, which shall not be licensed by this Company, to trade in these parts: I conceive this makes this Patent and Grant illegal and void;

And makes this restraint in trade, which was common to all with the King's licence, now peculiar to this Company; and doth monopolize the trade and the means of trading, by placing it in the sole hands and power of the Company, even the sole licensing of traders, and they may by this Grant license Aliens only to exclude *English* subjects.

My Lord *Coke*'s description of Monopolies and Monopolists, Projectors and Propounders, doth sufficiently illustrate this, with reflecting upon what Mr. *Pollexfen* hath said in his argument, without repetition of them to the Court.

The Statute of *Magna Charta* declares the liberty and freedom Merchants have to buy and sell without restraint, by the old and rightful customs, except in time of war.

2 *Inst. cap.* 29 & 30. *Stat.* 9 *H.* III. 30. *Nisi publicè prohibentur*, saith my Lord *Coke*, is intended a prohibition by Act of Parliament.

Yelverton, 10 *Jac.* is of the same opinion with Lord *Coke* in his book about impositions upon trade; as I have it from a Gentleman in our profession. *Vide* his Manuscripts.

21 *Jac. cap.* 3. declares all Monopolies to be against Common Law.

Coke 11. Case of Monopolies, 84 *Moor*'s *Rep.* 673. nay, *Darcy*'s Grant for the sole importing of Cards from beyond the seas, and selling them for twenty-one years, 44 *Eliz.* prohibited and judged a void Grant.

Stat. 2 *E.* III. *cap.* 9. confirms *Magna Charta*, for going and coming with merchandize to and from *England*, according to *Magna Charta.*

9 *E.* III. *cap.* 1. damns all Charters to the contrary, as illegal and oppressive to the people. 4 *E* III. *cap.* 2. confirms also *Magna Charta*. 25 *E*. III. *cap.* 2. doth the same, and makes Letters Patent to the contrary void.

11 *R*. II. *cap.* 7. 12 *H*. VII. 6. for free passage, &c. such Letters Patent restraining trade have been pursued in Parliament, with hue and cry, in all Parliaments and Ages.

Obj. This Grant is made to a Company for good government, and for the ordering of trade, and no Monopoly, and it is within the Proviso of the Statute 21 *Jac.*

Ans. Allowed in *Darcy*'s case by the arguments for that Grant, and if it be not for public good, the Grant is illegal.

If this Grant be neither good for the King, nor for the subject, nor for the trade of *England*, it cannot be said to be for the public good.

It cannot be good for the King, for it restrains him in his prerogative, as you would have it the King had power to license every subject; by this Grant he hath excluded himself of all power of licensing. He can license no subject to trade in these parts.

The King suffers in his Customs and in his Navigation.

The subject is excluded from trading in these places, without the licence of this Company.

Trade itself is restrained, for it is reduced and appropriated to a Company, and to few persons, which was common to all the King's subjects.

2 *Inst. fol.* 57. Lord *Coke*'s reason against it, for all the subjects are concerned in trade, therefore all ought to consent to it in Parliament.

Tho' they are a Company, they are not constituted by this Grant, to regulate and manage trade for *England*, but for themselves and their Company.

The heightening, the lowering of commodities, the raising, the lessening the rates of all the commodities of these places, the ingrossing of all the trade of these places, is in their power and in their pleasure.

There are no rules or qualifications in this Grant, injoining to admit numbers into this Company, or directing or requiring their licences for this trade. They have the trade in themselves, without any check or controul from his Majesty or the Government; they are independent from the Government by this Grant, they are without appeal.

Obj. That they are a Company, and that this Grant to them is within the exception of the *Stat.* 21 *Jac cap.* 3.

Answ. 1. Because that exception doth not reach to Letters Patent made to Corporations, after the making of that Act.

No words of saving to any Corporation, that should be afterwards erected or granted.

2. This Proviso doth not make them better than they were before the making of the Act, only leaves them as they were before, and as it found them.

If they were legal before, they continue so; if illegal, they are so notwithstanding this Act.

Obj. That many Grants of this nature have been made to several Companies; to the *Turky* Company, *Muscovy* and *Hamborough* Companies.

Ans. They do not trade in Joint-Stock, and monopolize, as this Company doth; they do not exclude persons from their Company, as this doth. Mr. *Pollexfen* hath differenced them at large.

That there have been many Monopoly Grants in all Ages from the Crown, appears by the Statute of *Magna Charta*, by other Statutes made in *E.* IIId's time, *R.* II. *H.* VII. and King *James*'s time; and by the judgments given on Monopoly Patents in all ages.

In the case of Monopolies. In the Taylors of *Ipswich* case.

Peachy's case, 5 *E.* III. severely punished for procuring a licence under the Great Seal, that he only should sell sweet Wines in *London*, &c.

Inst. 3. *fol.* 181. *Darcy* and *Allen*'s, *Mar. Rep.* 44 *Eliz.* Oppression is older than the Law made to punish it; Monopolies are as old as the Laws made to punish them; it is no argument to justify injuries by their ages.

Sir *Arthur Ingram*'s Patent, 17 *Car.* II. for the *Canary* Company, granting them the sole trade there. There are glorious recitals in that Patent, of advantage to the King's subjects, and for the regulation of trade; making the Company a body politick, that they should have the sole trade to those Islands, excluding all others under pains and forfeitures, with a *non obstante* to the Statute against Monopolies; Judgment was given against this Patent, *Mich.* 20 *Car.* II.

11 *Rep. fol.* 54. Taylors of *Ipswich* case. Compare this case with the Company of Taylors case; for the good of Trade and Company, and the Orders and By-laws fair and plausible, yet damned, because a restraint on trade.

The Company had the profit of the reformation. No other difference between the cases, than that This is a mighty, That a petty Company.

14 *Car.* II. *cap.* 24. That Statute provides, that persons by having Stocks in this Company, shall not be adjudged traders within the Statutes against Bankrupts, which is called by Mr. Sollicitor the Judgment of the Parliament for this Grant.

Says Mr. Sollicitor, *Stat.* 14 *Car.* II. *cap.* 24. takes notice of this Company, and that it is an advantage to the Nation and Trade of it.

Stat. 29 *Car.* II. 1. takes notice of this Company, and taxes every Capital Stock in the Company at 20*s.* for every 100*l.* Capital Stock in the Company.

Ans. This Poll-Act taxes all Guilds and Fraternities, Bodies Politick and Corporate; this doth not make them legal Corporations, Guilds or Fraternities.

The

The Judgment the Parliament had of this Grant doth better appear upon the Journals of the Houses of Parliament, of the complaints made to the Parliament, that this grant was a grievance.

It is no new thing to mention proceedings upon Journals of Parliament: and the Judges take notice of them. *Hob. Rep. & Rolls.*

And in a cause of this consequence it may be proper to adjourn it to Parliament, where it may receive the Judgment of his Majesty in Parliament.

This will be a safe establishment of the Law in this great case, which concerns the King's prerogative, the right of the subject, and of the whole Kingdom in the trade of the Nation.

It will meet there with a Judgment that will certainly establish it, if it be for the Interest of the King and Kingdom; but if for the enlarging of this Great Company, it will meet with the common fate of projecting Patents against the interest of the King and Subject.

It is a mighty argument for the reputation this Patent had with the Parliament, and the opinion they had of it, by taxing their Capital-Stock at 20 *s. per Cent.*

So they do reputed Esquires, at 5 *l.* by the head.

Sollicitors, Attorneys, and oppressive Usurers, have the like esteem with this Act of Parliament.

Stat. 3 *Jac. cap.* 6. This Statute is but declaratory of the Common Law, and made to avoid questions and suits in Law; which might be occasioned by Charters of impropriating the trade of *Spain* and *Portugal*, and then in making for the trade of *France*.

If the mischiefs recited in that Statute, and the evils happening to *England*, and the King's subjects be true, without all hesitation,

Those Charters mentioned in that Statute, and condemned by that Statute, were not only grievous, but illegal, and Monopolies;

It appropriating the trade of these dominions to few Merchants, and excluding all other his Majesty's subjects from the trade;

Debarring the King's subjects in *England* from that free and common traffick, which his subjects in *Ireland* and *Scotland* had;

To the manifest impoverishing of Masters, Owners of Ships, Mariners, Fishermen, Clothiers, Tuckers, Spinsters, and many thousands of handicrafts-men;

The decrease of his Majesty's Customs, Subsidies, and other Impositions;

The ruin and decay of Navigation;

The abating of the prices of our Wool, Cloth, Corn, and such like commodities;

The enhancing of all *French* and *Spanish* commodities, that all Owners and Mariners, with divers others, shall be cut off from the ordinary means of maintenance, and preserving their estates,

And all *French* and *Spanish* commodities shall be in a few hands;

To the hurt and prejudice of all the subjects, therefore enacts, it shall be lawful for all his Majesty's subjects in *England* and *Wales*, to have free liberty to trade into, and from *Spain*, *France* and *Portugal*, in such sort as was accustomed at any time in his Majesty's time.

Stat. 4 *Jac. cap.* 9. Made to confirm the Charter to the Company of *Exeter* Merchants, upon singular reasons recited in the Act of Parliament, declaring the *Stat.* 30 *Jac. cap.* 6. should not impeach that Charter, being for publick good.

Stat. 45. *Ed.* III. *cap.* 4. That no imposition shall be charged upon Wool in no sort, without the assent of the Parliament: this *Stat.* was not made out of necessity, for it was the Common Law; yet it was thought fit by the Parliament at that time, to declare the Law by an Act of Parliament.

Stat. 1. *H.* IV. *cap.* 16, 17. Against Letters Patent made to ingross trades, &c.

So ancient was the Monopoly, and ingrossing of trades by illegal Letters Patent.

When illegal things turn to a grievance, 'tis usual to suppress them by Acts of Parliament, and not to leave their Judgment to the ordinary Courts of Justice, without declaration first had in Parliament.

Stat. 21 *Jac. cap.* 3. This Statute takes notice, tho' the King's Disposition, Judgment and Declaration was, that all Monopolies were against Law; and that no Suitors should move for such Grants yet upon misinformations and untrue pretences of publick good, many such Grants have been unduly obtained, and unlawfully put in execution, to the great grievance and inconvenience of the subject, contrary to the Laws of the Realm.

For the avoiding whereof, that Statute is made against all Grants to any person or persons, bodies politick or corporate, of any Monopoly; and declares the same illegal.

This Statute doth quadrate with the description of a Monopoly.

So doth the *East-India* Company's Charter in all its points and parts, and in the exercise of it, quadrate with these Monopolies, and their descriptions in our Law-Books and Cases;

With my Lord *Coke*'s description of a Monopoly, in his 3d *Inst. cap.* Monopolies.

If Mr. *Sandys* be pictured in Mr. Attorney's argument, I take it the *East-India* Charter is pictured in this Statute.

The Act of Tunnage and Poundage, 12 *Car.* II. says, The Commons in Parliament reposing trust and confidence in your Majesty, in and for the safe-guard of the seas, against all persons intending, or that shall intend the disturbance of your Commons, in the intercourse of trade, and the invading of this your Realm, give and grant for every Tun of Wine of the growth of *France*, that shall come into the Port of *London*, by your natural-born subjects, 4 *l.* 10 *s.* by strangers and aliens, 6 *l.*

The like notice taken of Poundage, to be paid by subjects and aliens.

Fol. 67. Rates in Wares, Silks imported in Ships *English*-built, directly from the *East-Indies*, the pound weight containing sixteen ounces; Subsidy duty 15 *s.*

Of the Manufacture of *Italy*, imported from thence in *English*-built Ships, the pound weight containing sixteen ounces; duty 1 *l.* 13 *s.* 4 *d.*

This Act distinguishes between Subjects and Alien Importers, between *English* and Foreign Ships, not between the *East-India* Company only and Aliens: shall this Law made for *England*, be now appropriated to this Company, and the rest of *England* excluded by this Grant against this Statute?

This Law is made for all the King's subjects and their *English*-built Ships.

The consideration of this Subsidy moves from all the subjects, the Grant is by all, and the benefit ought to be for all the subjects of *England*.

The Law is the same as to fore[...]
importation from *Italy*, to which [...]
The Act for encouraging and in[...]
12 *Car.* II. the best Law that ever[...]
ment, except the Laws for the pre[...]
The Proviso in it follows: Provi[...]
in contained, extend not, or be m[...]
East-India commodities, laden in *En*[...]
ter and three-fourths of the Marin[...]
place or places of loading them, in [...]
or *Eastward* of *Cabo Bona Speranza* [...]
places of their growth.

This Law made for the increase [...]
doth this Company invade; and app[...]
to themselves, by excluding all oth[...]
Is this for increase or decrease of [...]
confine it to few hands, excluding [...]
There is neither Common nor St[...]
I hope the Judgment of this Cour[...]
Parliament will prevail against this [...]
The Proviso is, for all *Englishmen* [...]
East-India commodities brought fro[...]
The Charter says, this Company [...]
ly carry. Which shall prevail, th[...]
These last mentioned Acts of Parlia[...]
Alien Importers, between *English* a[...]
Not between the *East-India* Com[...]
Laws made for *England*, be now ap[...]
Shall they have the benefit of it [...]
subjects the advantages given by A[...]
some what is granted to all?

I crave leave to observe some thi[...]
ney's positions and inferences in his [...]
He distinguishes between inland a[...]
ject the benefit of a home trade with[...]
That the Husbandman might plo[...]
That one *Englishman* might priv[...]
Law, without licence from the Cro[...]
Yet one subject could not buy, sel[...]
open fair or market, without licence [...]
servation of the peace, to prevent pu[...]
no Fair or Market could be kept, b[...]
I think there are Fairs, Markets, a[...]
tion, and their beginning is not kno[...]
And prescriptions are compared [...]
be discover'd.

And that such ancient prescripti[...]
Kings or Inhabitants in the World [...]
And for foreign trade: He laid it d[...]
trade abroad without the King's lice[...]
I do not find any authority for th[...]
The rest of the Counsel that arg[...]
on it; nay, they did seem to adm[...]
Alien Christians, without the Kin[...]
This is against the authority of [...]
Lord *Coke*'s opinion, *Rolls Rep.* Ta[...]
Magna Charta, 2 *E.* III. *cap.* 9. [...]
38 *E.* III. *cap.* 2. 5 *R.* II. *cap.* 2. [...]
Stat. 26 *H.* VIII. *cap.* 10. *Rast.* [...]
mited time power to license trade [...]
parts, in some commodities. *Vide* [...]
His distinction for Merchants t[...]
and therein he distinguishes betwe[...]
liged to come to the Staple.

What warrant hath he for this d[...]
to the King in Parliament: the P[...]
King's restraint of Merchants in th[...]
ment: the continuing of the Sta[...]
seeming to the contrary, give him [...]
1 *H.* V. 7. The Prayer of the [...]
Merchants out of the Kingdom [...]
2 *H.* V. *cap.* 5.

Those were Bills in Parliament [...]
sent; so were many of the Rolls [...]
their royal assent, especially in th[...]
in his prerogative.

The Commons did not deman[...]
tition claim their right.

Such answers of *Roy advisera*, [...]
subject.

Neither is the Petition or Pray[...]
matter that is their right, to the C[...]
This was the usual method, an[...]
liament to the Kings, especially [...]
H. V. then corrected upon some [...]
and *H.* VI. which may be read [...]
It is their usual way to secur[...]
right in *Car.* I.

The Prince's case, *Co. Tit.* 8. [...]
Parliament, in the several reigns [...]
That the Staple did continue [...]
Stat. 2 *E.* III. *cap.* 9. That [...]
side the seas, ordained by Kings [...]
vided, shall cease, &c.

This Statute took away the [...]
But there was a Staple set up [...]
altered by several Acts of Par[...]
Act of 2 *E.* III.

But *English* Merchants are [...]
meaning of them.

And I do not find that Mr. Attorney gives any account how these Staples were taken away by Law, but vanished at the taking of *Calais*; he hath not told us the beginning or ending of the Staple by Law, I know no Common Law for them, or his distinction.

Rolls Abr. Prerogative, Title Proclamation, pl. 6. 27 *E.* III. by the Statute of the Staple, it was ordained, that Merchants-Aliens might bring from beyond seas merchandize of the Staple, but not Merchants-Denizens.

Because Merchants-Denizens doubted to be impeached in time to come for their merchandize, which they passed by virtue of such Grant and Proclamation, forasmuch as they were made out of Parliament.

Ideò it is granted in Parliament, 34 *E.* III. *cap.* 2.

Stat. 5 *R.* II *cap* 2. This Statute prohibits the exportation of Gold or Silver, and that no person other than Lords and great Men of the Realm, true and notable Merchants, and the King's soldiers, go out of the Realm, without the King's licence.

This is declared to be after publication of this ordinance, which implies such licence was not necessary before the making of this Statute.

Mr. Attorney was pleased to allow, licences to particular persons to trade were not revocable; but Companies having such licences may be dissolved by *Quo Warranto*.

Therefore more safe to fix trade in Companies than persons.

Then doth this Charter do the greater wrong to particular persons, who by Law may have such licences, which cannot be taken from them.

And it doth not appear, but *Sandys* hath such licence, or may have, and ought not to be restrained therein by any Grant.

Mr. Attorney did turn this matter upon a question of fact, which will, or will not make this Company and their Grant a Monopoly:

Viz. Whether this Company and their Grant be a publick good and advantage to the trade of *England?*

This is a matter not to be decided in this Court, I suppose, and we cannot come at this question in this case; therefore not fit, safe or wise to determine the Law in this case, till the fact be cleared and settled, and that in such a Judicature where this question may be determined and settled, and the Law thereupon declared and established.

It appears to the Court, there are many illegal things in this Grant.

That the Grant is a restraint to the trade of *English* Merchants.

That it is a new Grant.

That it may be dangerous to establish such Grants by Judgment in a Court of Law.

That there are some things in the *Canary* Patent, in *Darcy*'s Patent, nay, in the Patent for sweet Wines, that were commendable and useful; yet that little good did not prevail, but the whole perished, and was poisoned in the Monopoly of those Grants.

It is adviseable how this Court, in this action, can adjudge for the Plaintiffs upon this Record, where the whole Grant is set forth upon Record in pleading; and it appearing to the Court, that some parts of this Grant are manifestly illegal, and may occasion oppression to the subject, and that the best parts of this Grant are doubtful, if good or useful for *England*, or the trade of it:

It cannot appear upon this Roll, for what part of this Grant the Court shall adjudge for the Plaintiffs, and against the Defendant.

And it cannot appear what part of it doth appear to the Court to be illegal.

This may turn to a precedent for the whole Grant in after-ages, since we judge by precedents: And this precedent may occasion more Monopoly-Patents, and this Judgment give them sanction.

As for the second point in this case; whether this action be maintainable by the Company against the Defendant *Sandys*, admitting their Grant to be good:

1. To allow such an action in a Court of Law for this Company against a single subject, will be to give them opportunity to ruin any subject, that shall oppose them in trade.

They that are too great for all other Companies in *England*, must be too strong for any private subject in contest.

2. If their Grant be a legal Grant, they have sufficient pains and penalties in it to reduce any person to compliance with their Grant, without the aid of actions in *Westminster-hall*.

And the Grant which makes them a Company, and doth constitute them and their power, doth direct the remedies, ways and methods to support and maintain them in their power and Company, in all the things granted them; and there being no remedy given them by action, I think it may be hard to adjudge, that an action will lie for them in this case, against the Defendant.

In cases of new Injuries created by Grants, or by Act of Parliament, and remedies created to repair such injuries in the Grants and Acts that create them, such remedies are to be pursued, and not new remedies to be given in Courts for such new-created Injuries.

This is an action brought upon the Grant, where no such remedy is provided by the Grant, and other penalties are provided by the Grant.

The Grant directs and gives forfeiture of all the goods imported against it, and the Ship wherein they are imported; but the Grant doth not express the offender to answer damages to the Company, which is required by this Action, and no special damages are laid in the declaration.

This is like a penal Statute, which creates an offence, and adds a penalty.

The party ought to sue for such penalties, and not to sue for damages in an action upon the case.

This may be the case upon the Statute, 2 E. VI. for tithes, it gives debts and no damages; so the case doth not lie upon that Statute.

Upon the Statute for forcible entries, and upon all other Penal Laws, which give penalties by single, double, or treble damages;

It was never practised to bring actions upon the case, upon such Statutes, unless in *Darcy*'s case, which action miscarried, *Moor* 671.

I humbly conceive this action is not like actions upon the Custom of *London*, or upon Duties to the City of *London*, which have been brought by way of Indebitants for the duty.

In all these cases there was a certain duty created by the Grant, Custom or Charter, which made the party Debtor to the Corporation; but in this case here is no duty created;

Only an injury declared, and a penalty directed, which ought not to be turned to an action upon the case, in my opinion.

I hope the Court will not make a precedent, for the Company to multiply actions against all persons that they conceive to be interlopers or aggressors upon their Grant, Company or Trade.

There is no special damages laid in the declaration to accrue to the Company:

Only in general, that the Defendant, contrary to the form and effect of these Letters Patent, did trade within the limits of their Grant, without licence of the Company, with a Ship called The *Expectation*, to the prejudice of the Company.

Williams's case, 2 *Co.* 5. *fol.* 72. Defendant being Vicar of *Alderbury* in Com. *Salop*, is obliged by himself, or his Chaplain, to celebrate divine service at *Woolaston*, and within the parish of *Alterbury* every *Sunday*, and to administer the sacrament to the Plaintiff, his servants and tenants within his said Manor, time out of mind:

And that the Defendant had not celebrated divine service, or administered the sacrament to the Plaintiff, his servants and tenants for a certain time, *ad damnum* of the Plaintiff. *Non cul.* pleaded, verdict for the Plaintiff, moved in arrest of Judgment, that an action upon the case doth not lie. Had this been a private Chapel for himself and family, an action upon the case had lain; for then no other person could have brought an action but himself; his servants could not.

But in this action, his tenants might bring their actions.

Which may occasion multitudes of suits, for one default in the Plaintiff.

The same may happen in this case; every Member of this Company may bring the like action against this Defendant.

And as in that case the Plaintiff had his remedy in the Ecclesiastical Courts;—so hath the Company their remedy, as the King had against offenders, in trade without licence.

If licence was necessary by Law, by contempt to his royal prerogative, or proclamation:

Compare it to the case of a nuisance in the highway, no action lies for it, without special damages.

They do not aver in the declaration, that this trade cannot be managed without their Company.

If there be any legal punishment provided for such offenders, such punishments are to be pursued, and not new remedies by actions created, to the grievance and oppression of the subject.

Darcy and *Allen*, Action on the case, brought by *Darcy* against *Allen*, for selling Cards, contrary to his Patent; Judgment *pro Def.*

Williams's case, 5 *Co. p* 72. *Mary*'s case, *lib.* 9. *publicum damnum* is not to be reformed by action upon the case, but by publick proceedings by indictment: or the like case lies *pro privato damno*.

The proceeding of the Company in this action, is supposed to be to right the Publick in the name of the Company, not for the reparation of private damage, but to repair the Publick in their Company.

The Company is in the nature of the late fancied *Custodes Libertatis Angliæ*, a notion to serve the Publick, as they would have it;

And not to be used to recover damages for private injuries, but to support and save the trade in publick actions.

This Charter restrains the King in his prerogative, the Kingdom in its trade, the subjects in their freedom to trade; the King is concerned in his revenue, the subject in his right, in this question.

What the Company cannot accomplish by the forfeitures, powers and penalties of their Charter; they design to establish by the Judgment of the Court, in this action for the Company.

I know the Justice of this Court is superior to this Company, and it is placed in safer and better hands than trade or regulation of it in the Company for *England*.

I therefore pray your Judgment against the Company, and their action, for the Defendant.

Term Hill. 36 & 37 *Car.* II.

This Term the Judges * delivered their opinions *seriatim* in this great cause. *Walcot* was but short, and his reasons being included in those of *Holloway*'s, &c. who spoke after, I have omitted them, to avoid repetition.

Holloway said, all might be reduced to one single point, which was, whether the Charter granting a sole trade to this Company, exclusive to all others, be good?

That this was a great point, both in regard of the King's prerogative, and the People's liberty.

He divided all trade, *ut supra* was done *per Sawyer*, Attorney-General.

Foreign trade with Christians hath been opened by several Acts of Parliament; and at Common Law 'twas an inherent prerogative in the Crown, that none should trade with foreigners without the King's licence. And the King having this prerogative at Common Law, an Act of Parliament is necessary to divest him of it; which none hath done but to some particular places.

Michelborn's case, cited by those that argued for the Company, hath not in any sort been answered by the other side.

This is a trade not to be carried on but by a Company; and none can erect a Company but the King.

The King hath the sole power of this trade, as of war and peace; and by declaring a war, he may determine a publick trade, tho' settled by Act of Parliament.

No Parliament ever look'd on this as a Monopoly, nay, so far from it, as in the 14 *Car.* II. *cap.* 24. this Company, &c. are said to be an advantage to the Publick; and that Act was made, that the persons of this Company, &c. should not be discouraged in those honourable endeavours, for promoting publick undertakings; then how can this be a Monopoly?

It never hath been questioned as such by Parliament, though they have look'd narrowly into the King's prerogative, even to the questioning some things that were his undoubted right; and concludes *pro Quer.*

Withins. Here are two points;

First, Whether Letters Patent giving a sole trade to a Company, exclusive to others, be good?

Secondly, Whether, in case if they be good, an action lies?

He thinks there is but one question, and that whether the action will lie or not, as the Company hath an interest or not. For if they have an interest by these Letters Patent, then the action will unquestionably lie.

* Skinner's Reports, p. 223, 224, 225, 226.

The

The case depending solely on foreign trade with Infidels, he shall apply to that, and not meddle with inland trade.

'Tis a great point as to the King's prerogative, and the people's liberty.

First, He takes it, that by the Common Law the King has a prerogative to restrain all his subjects from going beyond sea, as *F. N. B.* 85. 'Tis true *F.* says, every subject may go out of the Realm to merchandize, *&c.* but that is to be understood, he shall not be punished for so doing, but the King may prohibit him, as appears by the same Book; and that three ways, (*i. e.*) by the Great-Seal, the Privy-Seal or Signet, or by Proclamation. And tho' in *Dyer* 165. cited by Mr. *Williams*, 'tis said, that before *R.* II. subjects may go beyond sea, yet 'tis there agreed, the King may prohibit; and a *quære* is made, if a going over without a licence be not a contempt, though there was no prohibition. Afterwards in the same Book 296. 'tis holden such departure before express prohibition is no contempt; but all the Books say, when there is a prohibition, then it is a contempt.

As none may go against or without the King's licence; so if they are gone, the King may recal them, as appears by *Dyer* 375.

'Tis *objected*, the King may prohibit some particular persons by writ; but he cannot prohibit all his subjects.

Answered, There are several ways of prohibiting by writ, which is directed to particular persons; and by proclamation, which is general.

And all the King's subjects are bound to take notice of the King's Great-Seal and Privy Seal.

Secondly, The King hath the controuling power over all trade with Infidels; he may say, over all foreign trade in general: he saith, *Michelborne*'s case goes farther than *Fitzherbert*'s *N. B.* and he hath not heard any authority offered against *Michelborne*'s case, as to trade with Infidels, and the opinion in that case seems to be given upon such a question as this. So that it is the judgment of the Court in a like case, for he who was then Chief-Justice delivered it, and none of the Court opposed it.

The prerogative of making leagues is in the King, and he may make them as he pleases; then it would be hard, the Law should give the King a power to make leagues, and yet the subjects should have a right to do such things to break them. But though the subjects may not trade with Infidels, yet the King may license them, or trade himself; as the *Jews* were prohibited commerce with the Nations, yet *Solomon* traded with *Hiram* King of *Tyre* for Gold.

The several Licences and Petitions, cited and shewn by the Plaintiffs Counsel, though they prove no right in the Crown, yet are evidences of it; for to what purpose should there be so many licences from the Crown, and petitions from the Commons to the King, for liberty to trade, unless the King had such a right? Therefore, unless where the Parliament hath opened it, the King hath power to controul all foreign trade, especially with Infidels.

Objection. But though the King had such right, yet now the prohibiting part of the Patent is void by the Statute of *E.* III. which is pleaded; and the enabling part of the Patent is void by the Statute of Monopolies.

Answer. As to the first, that Statute relates not to this trade.

First, Because no such trade then in being; so that the Parliament could have no regard to it, unless by prophecy, neither could they know whether it would prove hurtful or beneficial to the Kingdom. But take the Act at the largest, yet you must take it to relate to the subject matter, which was for Wool, so that the words *shall be open* may be taken *free from Custom*, and to have no other impositions upon them.

As to the *second*, whether a Monopoly: he says, a Monopoly is no Immoral Act, but only against the politick part of our Law; which if it happen to be of advantage to the Publick, as this trade is; then it ceases a so to be against the prohibiting part of the Law, and so not within the Law of Monopolies.

The Company hath been in possession of this trade near one hundred years, and that possession will in time give a right: and cited *Grotius de Jure Pacis*, &c. and concludes *pro Quer.*

The Argument of the Lord Chief-Justice *Jefferies*, at the Court of *King's-Bench*, concerning the Great Case of Monopolies.

The *East-India* Company Plaintiffs, and *Thomas Sandys* Defendant; wherein their Patent for trading to the *East-Indies*, exclusive of all others, is adjudged good.

Entered *Trin.* 35 *Car.* II. *B. R. Rot* 126. and adjudged *Termino S. Hilar. Annis* 36 & 37 *Car.* II. & *Primo Jac.* II.

P L E A.

1. DEfendant demands *Oyer* of the Letters Patent which are set forth *in hæc verba*: In which (as it hath been observed) the penalty of forfeiture of ship and goods, one moiety to the King, and the other to the Company, and imprisonment, is omitted.

2. There is a clause, that the Company may license strangers or others, and that the King will not without the consent of the Company give licences, *&c.*

3. That none shall have a Vote in the General Assembly, but he that hath 500*l.* stock.

4. And there is another clause, which hath not been mentioned by the Counsel on either side; that if it should hereafter appear to his Majesty or his successors, that that Grant, or the continuance thereof, shall not be profitable to his Majesty, his heirs and successors, or to this Realm, that after three years warning, under the Privy-Seal or Sign Manual, the same should be utterly void

For Plea, the Defendant says, by an Act of Parliament, made 15 *E.* III. it is enacted, that the sea shall be open for all Merchants to pass with their merchandizes where they please; and that the Defendant, by virtue of that Act, and according to the Common Law of *England*, did traffick within these places mentioned in the declaration, without any licence, and against the will of the Company, as the Plaintiffs have declared, *prout ei bene licuit.*

Plaintiffs demur.

In the debate of this case, at the Bar, there were several matters discoursed of; but at length by the consent
case was resolved into these two points

1. Whether these Letters Patent givi
the Plaintiffs, to exercise the sole trade
their Grant, with prohibition to all oth

2. Admitting the Grant good, wheth
the Plaintiffs?

Now to let me into the debate of the
to remember some things that have been
think are no ways in question.

I. At this time I conceive, therefore
hibit his subjects from going beyond se
solute prerogative, without giving any
sure was it ever thought a question,
For the writ in *Fitz. N. B.* 85. and th
and our Books say, the surmises mentio
able. so is *Dyer* 165 & 296. For sur
jects from going beyond sea, and is not
doing, but that is not now in question

II. In the next place, I do not con
much discourse hath been about *India*
Indies were, at the time of the Grant
tians or *Infidels*; tho' by the way, in th
perhaps that matter may in some meas
not at all affect the Grant to the Plaint
ther this country or place, or any othe
that is not otherwise provided for by A
same question.

III. Whether every clause and ar
touching forfeiture of ship and good
clauses contained in the Charter, be le
For surely it would be hard to maintai
tiffs Counsel have avoided those quest
tho' the Defendant's Counsel have me
intended to sully the cause, and not th
question.

IV. Nor is it the question, whether
King has fettered or confined his prer
exclude himself from granting licence
within the limits of the Plaintiffs Ch
friend to the King's prerogative), in te
be surprized by the inconsiderate extr
have us believe, that he was afflicted
must necessarily ensue by the King's
and that either by the advice, consent,
General, and the rest of his Counsel
East-India Company for the sake of
King in discharge of their duty. To a
dilemma, I am of opinion, though it
now before us, the King may grant li
to the *East-Indies*, notwithstanding th
condition therein contained, to the
caution or advertisement, that in his
reflection that he made upon his Co
hasty inadvertency in the passing of t
duced to be of that persuasion, for th
whose opinions have been quoted by
the Defendant's side, were then of th
and advised both these Letters Pate
that have been granted for these hund
fit to say, that I believe Mr. Attorne
Counsel, have discharged their duty a
this Grant, as Mr. *Williams* has in
by endeavouring to destroy it. In sh
clause in this Charter is not to be mai
the question now to be determined.

V. Whereas it has been objected,
agreed, that the Defendant never was
nor had any licence from them to tra
licence from the King; which, as I
grant by any clause in the Letters Pa
Defendant had any such licence, it o
which not being done, it ought to b
of the fact is, the Defendant never h

VI. It was observed, that the Plai
that this trade could not be managed
and by this means they had exclude
Companies to trade within their limi
Kingdom might hereafter require it.
further treaty of commerce, or that
more Companies to be erected; yet
Plaintiffs a mere Republick, and th
England, in the management of tra
in Companies, who (were they ind
so called. Yet in as much as I did
this Grant either excluded from mak
or from making any Corporations,
the rest of his subjects, notwithstan
so I am of opinion that that objectio
to be determined: and for that rea
improper to mention that Clause in
Bar, which the King has annexed
should hereafter appear to his Majesty
the continuance thereof, in the who
ble to his Majesty, his heirs and succe
years warning by warrant, under the
made utterly void. So that it appea
himself of the power, nor at the time
to shew his inclination for the prom
has given himself scope enough to

2

by the way I cannot but obſerve that Mr. *Williams*, to ſhew his diſlike to a Commonwealth, declared it to be abſolutely oppoſite to the intereſt of a ſingle perſon; but the ſingle perſon he concern'd himſelf for, was not the King and his prerogative, but his Client the Defendant, and his trade; who tho' I cannot in propriety of ſpeech call a Commonwealth, yet I cannot but think this oppoſition of his ſeems to proceed from a Republican principle. For he by his interloping has been the firſt ſubject that within this Kingdom, for near an hundred years laſt paſt, hath in *Weſtminſter-hall* publickly oppoſed himſelf againſt the King's undoubted prerogative in the Grant now before us: and I hope, by this example, the reſt of his Majeſty's ſubjects will be deterred from the like diſobedience.

There were ſome other ſuperfluous objections made againſt the clauſes in the Charter, and againſt the formality of the pleadings, which I think not neceſſary to remember; and therefore having thus premiſed, I ſhall now deſcend to thoſe points I think only material in this cauſe.

1. The firſt and great point in this cauſe, is, Whether this Grant of the ſole trade to the *Indies*, to the *Eaſt-India* Company, excluſive of all others, be a good Grant in Law or not? And I am of opinion it is. And by the way, I cannot but make the ſame remark in this caſe, as my Lord Chief-Baron Fleming made in the great caſe of *Bates* in the *Exchequer*, *Lane*, *f.* 27. that it is a great grace and eminent act of condeſcenſion in the King to this Defendant, that he does permit this great point of his prerogative to be diſputed in *Weſtminſter-hall*; but by this he does ſufficiently ſignify to all his ſubjects, that he will perſiſt in nothing, tho' it ſeem never ſo much for his advantage, but according to the Laws of the Land. I ſhall therefore endeavour to make it appear, that he is inveſted with this prerogative by the Law of this Nation: but by the Law I do not only mean the cuſtomary Common Law or Statutes of this Realm, which are native and peculiar to this Nation, which, as Mr. Attorney well obſerved, are not adapted to this purpoſe; but ſuch other Laws alſo as be common to other Nations, as well as ours, and have been received and uſed time out of mind, by the King and People of *England* in divers caſes, and by ſuch ancient uſage are become the Laws of *England* in thoſe caſes; namely, the general Laws of Nations, the Law-Merchant, the Imperial or Civil Law; every of which Laws, ſo far forth as the ſame have been receiv'd and us'd in *England* time out of mind, may be properly ſaid to be Laws of *England*.

And for the better communicating my thoughts upon this ſubject, I will proceed by theſe ſteps:

1. I will very briefly conſider of the inland trade within this Kingdom, and the foreign trade with other Nations; and therein obſerve, that the King's prerogative is concerned in both, and that there is a great difference between both, allow'd by the Municipal Laws of this Kingdom.

2. I ſhall ſhew that the liberty of foreign trade may be reſtrain'd.

3. That foreign trade and commerce being introduc'd by the Law of Nations, ought to be govern'd and judg'd according to thoſe laws.

4. That by the Laws of Nations, the regulation and reſtraint of trade and commerce is reckon'd *inter Juris Regalia*; *i. e.* the prerogative of the ſupreme Magiſtrate.

5. That tho' by the Laws of this Land, and by the Laws of all other Nations, Monopolies are prohibited, yet Societies to trade, ſuch as the Plaintiffs, to certain places excluſive of others, are no Monopolies by the Laws of this Land, but are allow'd to be erected both here, and in other countries, and are ſtrengthen'd by the uſage and practice of both in all times.

6. I ſhall ſhew the authorities that are extant in our Books, together with precedents, and reaſons both publick and politick; for, as my Lord *Fleming* ſays, that ſuch reaſons are good directions for our judgment in ſuch caſes as theſe, being demonſtrations of the courſe of antiquity; and therein alſo obſerve the neceſſity and advantage of ſuch Societies, and by the way endeavour to anſwer the ſeveral Acts of Parliament, precedents and authorities, with all other the objections that have been made againſt my concluſion.

Firſt, then, to conſider the difference between the inland and the foreign trade allow'd of in our Books, and that the King's prerogative doth affect both. As to Manufactures, under which all ſorts of Artificers are concern'd, I think they remain with the moſt liberty by the Common Law; and as Mr. Attorney obſerv'd, the publick weal is little concern'd therein, only to preſerve every one in the quiet enjoyment of the fruits of his own labour and induſtry, yet even in that the King's prerogative hath not been totally excluded for as it is taken notice of in our Books, all things that are at this day enjoy'd by cuſtom or preſcription, had their commencement by royal Grant; and by that means no Artificer within the City of *London* can at this day uſe two trades, *i. e.* a *Carpenter* cannot uſe the trade of a *Joyner*, or a *Brick'ayer* of a *Plaiſterer*.

2. As to the trade of merchandize or inland commerce, generally ſpeaking, it had the next freedom by the Common Law, but was ſubject nevertheleſs to be limited or reſtrain'd by the King's prerogative in ſeveral particulars; as for inſtance, to prevent all foreſtalling and ingroſſing. So Mr. Attorney did well obſerve, that numbers of people could not meet to traffick or merchandize, without being in danger of being puniſh'd as unlawful aſſemblies. the Crown therefore granted the liberties of Fairs and Markets, for the ſake of commerce and trade, all which did originally proceed from the Crown, and therefore by abuſing thoſe liberties may ſtill be forfeited to the Crown, and paſſing by all other inſtances, I ſhall only inſtance one taken notice of in our Books, which well conſider'd may go a great way in the caſe at the Bar. *Regiſter*, *fol* 107. the King grants to the Abbot of *Weſtminſter* and his ſucceſſors, that they ſhould hold a Fair at *Weſtminſter* thirty odd days together, with a prohibition that no man ſhould buy or ſell within ſeven miles of that Fair during that time; and the King does there command the Sheriffs of *London* by his writ to ſeize the body of an inhabitant of *Saliſbury*, for ſelling cloths in *London* within the time of the Fair. Now here is a Charter granted to a particular perſon excluſive of others, for a time ſubject to more objections than the Charter now in queſtion, yet approved of by our Books. Hence it came that Corporations were erected, and trade confined to places and perſons excluſive of others, for all ſuch came originally from the Crown: And as I ſaid before in the caſe of Fairs, ſo I may now ſay in the caſe of Corporations, that tho' they claim liberties and privileges by preſcription, yet theſe originally proceeded from the Crown, and are therefore forfeitable to the Crown: an eminent inſtance hereof is that caſe of the City of *London*, for abuſing their liberties, which they claimed by preſcription, confirmed by divers Charters and Acts of Parliament; by Judgment of this Court, their liberties and franchiſes were ſeized into the King's hands, and therefore remain as a Vill to all intents and purpoſes, till his Majeſty ſhall be pleaſed of his bounty to reſtore them Now that the inland traffick is moſt concern'd, either in Corporations, Markets, or Fairs, which all proceed from the Crown, does plainly evince that the King's prerogative has a more immediate influence over dealings in merchandizes, than it has over other mechanick crafts and myſteries: and that, as Mr. Attorney did well obſerve, to prevent frauds, deceits, and other abuſes either in weight, meaſures, or otherwiſe, which would certainly interrupt ſuch commerce. But our Law goes yet a ſtep further, and allows further difference between inland merchandize and foreign, and allows a different way of determining controverſies that ariſe thereupon; the Common Law and Statutes of this Realm, allowing the Law-Merchant, which is part of the Law of Nations, ſhould decide ſuch controverſies. *Decimo tertio H.* IV. *fol.* 19. a complaint made to the King and Council of ſome goods taken away from a Merchant; it was moved in that caſe, that the matter might be determined at the Common Law: but the Lord-Chancellor ſaid, that the ſuit being brought by a Merchant, who is not bound to ſue according to the Common Law, to have his cauſe tried by twelve men, and to obſerve the other ſolemnities of our Law; but ſhall ſue in *Chancery* according to the Law of Nature, which is the Univerſal Law of the World. And it is in that caſe agreed by all the Judges, that if foreign merchandize were ſtol'n or waiſed, they could not be ſeized, as other *Engliſh* merchandizes might be by the Rule of the Common Law, as waifs and ſtrays. which ſhews plainly there is a difference in the conſideration of our Law, between foreign merchandizes that croſs the ſeas, and other inland goods and commodities. If two Merchants be partners in merchandizes, one ſhall have an action of accompt againſt the other, *ſecundum Legem Mercatoriam*, ſays the *Regiſter*, *fol.* 135. and *F. N. B.* 117. *D.* And yet by the rule of the Common Law, if two men be jointly poſſeſſed of other goods, which are no merchandize, the one cannot bring an action of account againſt the other; if one of the Merchants die, the Executor may bring his account againſt the ſurvivor for his moiety, *Reg.* 135. *F. N. B.* 177. But if it were a copartnerſhip for other goods, it would ſurvive *per jus accreſcendi*, according to the rules of the Common Law.

In an action of Debt upon a ſimple Contract, the Defendant may wage his Law, but it is otherwiſe in a Contract about Merchandize, in *Lane*'s Reports, *Bates*'s Caſe agreed, *Reg.* 260. *A.* at Common Law, the goods of Eccleſiaſtical Perſons were excuſed from toll; but ſays the writ, *Dum tamen Merchandizas aliquas non exercitat de iiſdem.* It ſhews, that then they fall under another conſideration. If one man wrongs another man of his goods, here an action of treſpaſs will lie: But if a Merchant's Goods be taken upon or beyond the Seas, there muſt be a Writ of Reprizal to obtain ſatisfaction; the *Parl. Roll.* 3 *Ed.* I. *M* 19. *in Archivi Turris Londini*, where the Bailiffs of *Southampton* are commanded by Writ, *quod omnes Mercatores Leodienſes ad partes Angliæ accidentes per bona & catella ſua diſtringantur ſecundum Legem Mercatorum & Conſuetudinem Regni, ad ſatisfaciendum Mercatoribus Florentinis*, &c. When, by the way, obſerve, that *Lex Mercatoria*, which differs from the ordinary Common Law, is ſaid to be *Conſuetudo regni Angliæ*; by which we may obſerve, that foreign merchandizes and trades differ from others in the eye of Law, even by the allowance of Common Law itſelf.

Several Acts of Parliament have been alſo made for the more ſpeedy recovery of debts contracted for merchandizes, as the Statute of *Acton Burnel*, the Statute *de Mercatoribus*, and the Statute *Viceſimo Septim. Ed.* III. *cap.* 2. amongſt other things it is enacted, *That for merchandizes taken away, the Party ſhall be arreſted, and ſpeedy and ready Proceſs ſhall be againſt him from day to day, and from hour to hour, according to the Law-Merchant, and not at the Common Law.* So the Statute for erecting the Court of Inſurance, deſigned for the ſpeedy eaſe of Merchants, has left the determination according to the Law of Merchants; and therefore hath ordered the Judge of the Admiralty Court always to preſide in thoſe Commiſſions. By all which I think I may fairly conclude, there is a great difference allowed of, between the inland and foreign commerce, and that.

2. I ſhall endeavour to prove, that the liberty of foreign trade may be reſtrained.

And here I muſt premiſe, that as at firſt all things were promiſcuouſly common and undivided to all, ſo the free exerciſe of this univerſal right, was then inſtead of property, but as ſoon as the number of men increaſed, and they found by experience the inconveniency of holding all things in common, things were reduced into property by agreement and compact; either expreſs, as by partition; or implied, by *premier Occupancy*.

After this Government was eſtabliſhed, and laws were made, even for the ordering thoſe things to which no man had any right; as for example, deſerts, places uninhabited, iſlands in the ſeas, wild beaſts, fiſhes, and birds; the former were uſually gained and diſpoſed of by him that had the ſovereignty over the People; the latter, by him that had the dominion over the Lands and Waters, who might forbid others from hunting, fiſhing, &c.

And in virtue of this univerſal Law, his Majeſty and his Predeceſſors have always diſpoſed of the ſeveral Plantations abroad, that have been diſcovered or gained by any of their ſubjects, and may do for the future, in caſe any other be diſcovered and acquired. For tho' the laws of Nations can command nothing which the law of Nature forbids, yet they may bound and circumſcribe that which the Law of Nature leaves free, and forbid that which naturally may be lawful. Now to apply this to our preſent purpoſe of trade and commerce, Mr. *Williams* quoted that common ſaying, *Commercia debent eſſe libera*; from whence he infers, that by the law of Nature and Nations, the ſea and trade, and traffic ought to be free as the air; and for that he has cited *Grotius de Jure Belli ac Pacis*, *cap.* 3. *Welwood*'s Abridgm. of the Sea-laws, in his Epiſtle to the Lord Admiral; *Grotius de Mari libero*, where he ſays, *Mare & Littora Maris Jure Gentium ſunt communia. Britton*, *cap.* 33. *De purchoſ le Mere & le air ſunt tho s Common*; Sir *John Burrough* his Sovereignty of the Seas; *Baldus de rerum Dominis.* But I think none of thoſe Books can warrant his concluſion; for ſurely that expreſſion, *Commercia ſunt libera*, cannot poſſibly be underſtood in ſuch

a literal

a literal ſenſe, That every man in every Nation ſhould be at liberty to trade, either in what commodities, or to what place, or at what time ſoever he ſhall think fit. For I took it to be granted by all that argued for the Defendant, that trade and commerce muſt be ſubject to ſome laws; and *Grotius*, in his book *de Mari libero*, propoſes this main deſign, to prove, that any one Nation had not power to hinder another Nation from free commerce; and that the *Spaniards* therefore had no right to prohibit the *Dutch* from trading into ſuch parts of the *Indies*, whereof the *Spaniards* were not poſſeſſed, upon pretence that they had the dominion of thoſe ſeas: *Inter nos & Hiſpanos*, ſays he, *hæc controverſia eſt, ſitne immenſum & vaſtum Mare regni unius nec maritimi acceſſio? Populóne unquam jus ſit volentes populos prohibere ne vendant, ne permutent, ne denique commeent inter ſeſe.* And for the benefit of his Countrymen he doth therefore aſſert, *licere cuivis genti quamvis alteram adire, cumque ea negotiare*; which, taking that to be true, which by the law of Nations is certainly otherwiſe, yet nothing can be inferred from thence, but only the queſtion of commerce between one Nation and another. And how that was before leagues and treaties were made, little may perhaps be found, as Mr. Attorney well obſerved, beſides the laws of hoſpitality, which do not give any demandable right; but ſurely *Grotius* there hath no particular reſpect to particular ſubjects of this or any other Nation, how far the ſupreme power of any Nation may erect a ſociety of trade to a certain place, and for certain commodities, excluſive of all other ſubjects of their own.

And that plainly appears, both from the ſcope of his Book, as alſo for that for ſeveral years, both before and at the time of publiſhing that Treatiſe, the *Dutch Eaſt-India* Company was eſtabliſhed; which I ſhall have farther occaſion to diſcourſe of by-and-bye.

As for *Welwood*'s Epiſtle, I have ſeldom obſerved that Epiſtles have been cited in *Weſtminſter-hall* as authorities: Yet ſuppoſing it to be ſo, That all loyal ſubjects ſhall have their Petitions granted to ſafety and ſecurity in their trade, I ſuppoſe *Welwood* little dreamt of Interlopers, when he talk'd of loyal ſubjects: if it can be meant only of ſuch who may trade by Law, that is to beg the queſtion in reſpect of the Plaintiff and Defendant. As to that of *Britton*, That the ſea is common, it is anſwer'd by what hath been ſaid before; and *Welwood*, pag. 66. ſays, That by *Commune* or *Publicum*, is meant, a thing common for the uſe of any one ſort of People, according to that Saying, *Roma Communis Patria eſt*, but not for all of all Nations; *Welwood*, *pag.* 66. That paſſage of *Burrough* is only obſerved to prove the King's prerogative within the four ſeas; and though Mr. *Williams* would have inſinuated, as if the Sturgeons and other great fiſh, and wrecks, and the like, had come to the King by the *Stat.* of 17 *E* III. *c.* 2. that Act was but a declaration of the Common Law; for he had it by the right of his prerogative; *Plowden*'s Commentaries, in the caſe of *Mines*; *Coke* 5. Sir *Henry Conſtable*'s caſe; theſe things were veſted in the King by his prerogative by the Common Law. Yet I cannot but obſerve, that the Treatiſe of *Mare Liberum*, on which Mr. *Williams* ſo much relies, was craftily writ, to overthrow the King's prerogative in that beneficial part thereof, relating to the fiſhing on the *Engliſh* coaſts; and contains a plain Proclamation for all perſons of any Nation, indifferently to fiſh in all kinds of ſeas; for, ſays *cap.* 5. *fol.* 10. *Quæ autem navigationis eadem Piſcatus habenda eſt ratio, ut communis maneat omnibus.* And herein tho' Mr. *Williams* intends to make good the premiſſes, I preſume that Mr. *Pollexfen*, that argued on the ſame ſide, has a greater concern for his friends in the *Weſt*, than to join with him to make good that concluſion. And before I go off from this point, I think it not amiſs, the better to clear the way to my concluſions, to give ſome inſtances wherein other Nations, as well as our own, have not only thought it legal, but neceſſary for their ſeveral publick advantages, to put reſtrictions upon trade, and did not think it injurious to natural equity, and the freedom of mankind, ſo much diſcourſed of on the other ſide. To give ſome few inſtances; *Videmus Jura Commerciorum*, ſays *Bodin de Repub. lib.* 1. *cap.* 7. *non ſolum omnibus populorum principumque inter ſe conventis, verum etiam ſingularum Statutis*, &c. And after he has enumerated the compacts for trade between the Pope and the *Venetians*, between the citizens of the *Hans* Towns, and the Kings of *England*, *France*, and *Spain*, and ſeveral other Countries; *Ibi*, ſays he, *inter ſe Commercium multis modis perſonarum, mercium, locorum, temporum atque omni alia ratione coarctarunt.* So is *Marguardus*, *fol.* 155. and *Buchanan* in his 7th Book *de Rebus Scotiæ*; and in all Countries, the importation and exportation of ſome commodities are prohibited, as ſalt from *France*, horſes from other Countries, wool from hence. In whomſoever that power of reſtraint does remain, the power of licenſing ſome, and reſtraining of others, ſurely does alſo remain by parity of reaſon; but of that more by and bye. And as Mr. Attorney did truly obſerve, upon peruſal of the Statutes that are now in print relating to trade, the Parliaments have in all ages, even to this King's reign, ſince his reſtoration, thought fit to make more laws to prohibit foreign trade, than to increaſe it; as looking upon it more advantageous to the common weal. And thus having obſerved that other Nations, as well as we, have not only thought it legal, but neceſſary, to make laws for the reſtraint of trade: and thereby thought they did no injuſtice to the liberty of mankind:

3. I proceed to the next ſtep. I ſhall therefore, *thirdly*, endeavour to prove, that foreign trade and commerce, being introduced by the Laws of Nations, ought to be governed and adjudged according to thoſe Laws; and I do not know of any Statute or Book of the Common Law now in print, that doth oppoſe this aſſertion. *Coke* 3 *Inſt. fol.* 181. in the margin, cited by the Defendant's Counſel at the Bar: *Commercium*, ſays he, *Jure Gentium eſſe debet*; nay, it is the expreſs text of Law. *ex Jure Gentium Commercia ſunt introducta*: which being laid down as undeniably true, and ſo admitted to be by the Defendant's Counſel; I would infer from thence, ſince commerce and traffick are founded upon the Law of Nations by the natural reaſons of things, all controverſies ariſing about the ſame, ſhall be determined by the ſame Laws, eſpecially where there is no poſitive and expreſs Law in that Country where ſuch controverſies do ariſe, to determine them by; and Mr. *Williams* ſeems to allow, that there are no ſuch Laws in this Kingdom, for he thinks that the controverſy now before us, is not to be decided but by Parliament.

All other Nations have governed themſelves by this principle; and upon this ground ſtands the Court of Admiralty in this Kingdom, *viz.* That

there might be uniform Judgments giv
World, in cauſes relating to commerce,
much as the Common and Statute Lav
narrow to govern and decide difference
and can never be thought to bear any
Law of all Nations, as the intereſts of
to contend for; it will become us that
the better determining this caſe, to obſ
deceſſors in determining ſuch like cauſ
Nations.

The Common Law, by the ſeveral a
tice of the Law-Merchant; and as the
it is part of the Law of Nations, and
cording to that Law; the ſeveral Acts
a particular proviſion, that matters of
according to the Law-Merchant, whicl
Nations; and is univerſal, and one an
World. And therefore *Cicero* ſpeakin
Lex Romæ, alia Athenis, alia nunc, alia
omni tempore una eademque Lex obtinebit.
obliged, more induſtriouſly to ſearch in
to enable me to give judgment in this ca
affect the King's ſubjects in all parts o
thereof, particularly, by my Lord Chi
Judgment of the great caſe of *Bates*, ab
Lane, *fol.* 27. and does not only affirm
practices of all Judges, in all Ages.

Do not we leave the determination of
according to the Eccleſiaſtical Laws; fo
tion, leagues, truces, embaſſies; nay eve
ping of the Defendant's Ship by an Adr
opinion of all this Court, and afterward
and *Exchequer*, to be decided in the Adm
out of that Court, his Ship is detained t
Court proceeds according to the Law of
ſpecified are not to be controuled by the

And if cuſtoms make a Law, then the
Law of Nations; which brings me to m
main thing upon which this cauſe will t

Therefore, 4*thly*, I conceive, that bo
by the Common Law of *England*, the r
ment of foreign trade and commerce, is
is in the power of the King: and 'tis h
not abridged or controuled, by any Act

This queſtion is not concerning the c
inconveniencies that may happen thereu
cies ariſing, the King is to be ſupplicate
farther take notice of, when I come to
made againſt this Grant.

Commerciorum Jura ſunt privilegiata, a
dorum Mercatorum licentiam Principis indu
very expreſs Text of the Civil Law; and
dinus de Republica, lib. 1. *c.* 7. ſays, *Quæ*
tur prohibere, tametſi ſæpe à Principibus v
Mr. Attorney, That the Laws of Comm
cular compacts and agreements of Princes
236. *Mercatura eſt res indifferens, in q*
permittendo ſuam pro Commodo Reipublicæ
Carpzovius, a famous *German* Lawyer,
N. 13, & 14. *Exempla haud rara ſunt, u*
commercia ad certas perſonas certave loca re
and Principles, aſſerted to be the Laws o
ciples of our Laws. Mr. Attorney, in hi
many Records and Precedents to make go
he did with great clearneſs. I therefore
of them as I can; and only remind you o
ceſſary to make good my aſſertion, which
ceive the King had an abſolute power to f
chants or others, from coming within h
war and in times of peace, according to h
therefore gave ſafe-conducts to Merchant
ages, and at his pleaſure commanded them
or Order of Council; of which there is
inſtances. And the Statute of *Mag. Char*
the Defendant's Counſel, is but a general
niſi publice ante prohibiti fuerint, habeant ſa
Where by the way I muſt obſerve, that
in his Comment upon the Chapter, is onl
gers; for I cannot find, that in thoſe d
Kingdom did apply themſelves to foreign
not ſo conſiderable, as to be taken notice
can meet with. And before the making
2 *Inſt fol.* 57. does agree, that the King
gers at his pleaſure. But he conceives, and
to his memory, I think without any colo
words, *niſi publicè prohibeantur*, to inten
ment, and his reaſon is, for that it conce
the coming in of ſtrangers concern the R
more than it did before? Surely no. D
and peace, abſolutely belong to the King
that of publick concern to the Kingdom
ſtrangers a natural dependant upon that
there had been out, there had been no
ſurely the King's proclamation will make
Act of Parliament can do: nay, and I m
ment anciently were made publick by P
we have many inſtances of Writs dire
to cauſe Acts of Parliament to be publi

was the conſtant and ancient uſage. And is it not more natural for ſtrangers that are abroad, to take notice of the King's publick Edicts, which are known to be of great importance in all Countries, more than they would of an Act of Parliament that affects the King's own dominions only? Beſides, it appears more impertinent, if you turn thoſe words into a *Proviſo*; and then it will amount to no more in plain *Engliſh* than this, *provided that this Law ſhall continue, except it be hereafter repealed*, which ſurely would be very ridiculous.

Mr. Attorney and Mr. Sollicitor both, in their arguments, quoted ſeveral Records and Precedents, where the King, in all times after the making of that Act, did prohibit ſtrangers from coming in, and did command them out when they were here, at pleaſure. I ſhall not trouble you with the repetition of the Records, for they were many; nay, the King, when Acts of Parliament had prohibited, did grant ſafe-conduct; and of that ſort, in *Rolls Prerogative*, 180. you will find ſeveral inſtances; and in the ſeveral Acts of Parliament cited by Mr. Attorney, to confirm the King's prerogative, as to ſafe conducts, it doth appear. *Syderfin. fol.* 441. it is ſaid, that the King by the Common Law, might prohibit the importation of foreign goods; and whoever acted againſt ſuch Prohibition, forfeited his Ship.

The King might prohibit any of his ſubjects from going beyond the ſeas at pleaſure, and recal them again as he thought fit; and that, as I have ſaid before, without giving any reaſon. The Books of *Fitzherbert*'s N. B. and *Regiſter*, before recited, make this evident. Mr. Attorney indeed cited many inſtances wherein the Kings had made uſe of their prerogatives, as 7 *Ed.* II. *M.* 10. *Quadrogeſimo Ed.* III. *M.* 24. *Stat.* 5 *R.* 2. *cap.* 2. which confirms it, 3 *Inſt.* 179. *Viceſimo quinto Ed.* III. *M.* 10. with many more *; and indeed I think it was not denied, but that after a Prohibition, it was an offence admitted of by the Defendant's Counſel for any ſubjects to go beyond the ſeas, *Dy.* 165 & 296. agrees it.

And that is ſufficient for the preſent purpoſe, there being a Prohibition in the Charter in queſtion, to all perſons that are not there mentioned. What influence the King's prerogative muſt neceſſarily have upon foreign trade and commerce, appears by his frequent granting Letters of Mart and Repriſal: Theſe are not allowed of by the Law of Nature, Civil or Common Law; for thereby no man is bound by another's act, without his conſent, but by the general conſent of Nations, *humana neceſſitate exigente*. The King only has the power of making leagues and truces with foreign Princes, upon which only all foreign trade does depend; and thoſe leagues are made upon ſuch terms and conditions, and under ſuch limitations, as both Princes think fit: Many inſtances to this purpoſe were alſo cited by Mr. Attorney, to which I refer myſelf; and the differences that ariſe from Merchants beyond the ſeas, are to be determined according to thoſe leagues, and cannot be decided by the municipal laws of this Realm, which cannot be put in execution in foreign parts.

Fourthly, The King is abſolutely Maſter of War and Peace; which he could not be, in caſe he had not a power to lay reſtraint upon his own ſubjects in relation to foreign commerce; ſince *eo ipſo*, that war is proclaimed, all publick commerce is prohibited: and the Counſel that argued for the Defendant, admitted, That the King might prohibit his ſubjects to go or trade beyond the ſeas in caſes of wars or plagues. How ſtrangely prepoſterous then would it be for a man to imagine, that the King ſhould have an abſolute power of War and Peace, and yet be denied the means to preſerve the one, and prevent the other! Is not that therefore the great reaſon why the King is at ſo great expence in maintaining Ambaſſadors and Envoys in all the trading parts of the World, without which we ſhould be in a perpetual ſtate of War? Would it not be monſtrous, that when the King is entered into league with any ſovereign Prince, in a matter of trade very advantageous to his People, to have it in the power of any one of his ſubjects to deſtroy it? As for inſtance, ſuppoſe a league between our King and the Emperor of *Morrocco*, for a trade to *Tangier*, were made upon condition, That no *Engliſh* Ship coming there for commerce, ſhould be above a hundred ton, and a fleet of merchant ſhips within that condition, were in Port at *Tangier*; and Mr. *Sandys*, with the ſame obſtinacy as he ſeems to appear in this caſe, ſhould have gone with a Ship of above a hundred ton to *Tangier*; that would have been an abſolute breach of the league; we ſhould have been immediately in a ſtate of war, the merchant-ſhips and goods abſolutely forfeited to the Emperor by the Law of Nations, and they and their families thereby undone, without any remedy, till Mr. *Sandys* ſhould be pleaſed to return into *England*; and alſo bring with him an Eſtate ſufficient to make them a recompence: and then alſo perhaps it would be difficult to contrive ſuch an action in our Law, to compel Mr. *Sandys* to do it. Beſides, the King has no other way, if his Ambaſſadors and Miniſters in foreign parts cannot prevail that right ſhould be done to his ſubjects; or if Mr. *Sandys*'s interloping Ship, and all its cargo, had been wrongfully taken away from him by any foreign Prince, but by the King's declaring of a War, and compelling them to make reſtitution by force; the conſequence whereof will affect more than foreign traders, who would be then concerned, both in their perſons and purſes; and it would be very hard for all the King's ſubjects to lie under the burthen and charge, and the profits and advantages accrue only to a few. And here, by the way, I think it not improper to take notice of an objection that was made by the defendant's Counſel, of the unreaſonableneſs that the King ſhould be entruſted with this prerogative: for as well as he may reſtrain perſons trading to the *Indies*, he may alſo reſtrain them from trading into any other part of the World. The very objection ſeems to carry an unſavoury, as well as unreaſonable miſtruſt in a ſubject to his Prince. For as it is a maxim in our Law, the King cannot be preſumed to do wrong; and I am ſure the conſtant practice of our preſent King has not given us the leaſt umbrage for ſuch diffidence; and I think I may truly ſay, we are as ſafe by our Prince's own natural inclinations, as we can be by any law in this particular. The King has the abſolute power of pardoning all offenders by his inherent prerogative, which an Act of Parliament cannot deprive him of, the caſe of murder is a full inſtance of that; nor was that prerogative ever diſputed in any age, tho' never ſo troubleſome; ſaving in that ſingle caſe of the Earl of *Danby*, and that without any reaſon, that I could ever hear of. Is it therefore to be objected and preſumed, that the King will pardon all the traitors, murtherers and robbers, and other felons, and make uſe of his prerogative to let all malefactors eſcape?

The King is the Fountain of Honour, as well as of Juſtice, and in virtue of that prerogative, may ennoble as many of his ſubjects as he pleaſes; and thereby exempt them from arreſts, and other common proceſſes of the Law, by means whereof men do more ſpeedily recover their juſt debts, and have redreſs for injuries. Is it therefore to be preſumed the King will make ſuch a glut of Noblemen, becauſe he may do it? And as this is againſt his inclination, ſo certainly it is againſt his intereſt, to make ſuch Grants as the defendant's Counſel ſeem to fear; for it is more for the King's benefit than it can be for his ſubjects, the greater the importation of foreign commodities is; for from thence ariſe his cuſtoms and Impoſitions, thoſe neceſſary ſupports of the Crown: and therefore, in ſome ſenſe, the King is the only perſon truly concerned in this queſtion; for this Iſland ſupported its Inhabitants in many ages without any foreign trade at all, having in it all things neceſſary for the life of man.

Terra ſuis contenta bonis, non indiga mercis, ſays the Poet. And truly, I think, if at this day moſt of the *Eaſt-India* commodities were abſolutely prohibited, tho' it might be injurious as to the profit of ſome few traders, it would not be ſo to the generality of the Inhabitants of this Realm. And therefore, as I have offered theſe few inſtances to prove the King ſhould have ſuch a prerogative, in the next place I come to ſhew, that the Kings of *England* have exerciſed this their prerogative in all ages: and as the King has the power of reſtraint of foreign trade, ſo he is the only Judge when it is proper to uſe that power, which ſeems plainly to be for the ſame reaſon. And I think Mr. *Williams*'s remark of the difficulty of this caſe, that it ſhould neceſſitate the King to call a Parliament to aſſiſt him with power to determine this queſtion, is not to be paſſed by without ſome obſervation.

God be praiſed, 'tis in the King's power to call and diſſolve Parliaments, when and how he pleaſes; and he is the only Judge of theſe *Ardua Regni*, that he ſhould think fit to conſult with the Parliament about. And Mr. *Williams* would do well to ſave himſelf the trouble of adviſing the King of what things are fit for him to conſult with his Parliament about, 'till ſuch time as he be thereunto called. But it hath been too much practiſed at this and other bars in *Weſtminſter-Hall*, of late years, to captivate the *Lay Gens*, by leſſening the power of the King, and advancing, I had almoſt ſaid, the prerogative of the People: and from hence comes the many miſchiefs to the King's ſubjects in parts abroad, by making the power of the King thought ſo inconſiderable, as though he were a mere Duke of *Venice*, being abſolutely dependant upon his Parliament. Would it not be mightily for the honour and dignity of the Crown of *England*, think ye, that the Emperor of *Fez* and *Morocco*, or any Prince of the remote parts of the World, ſhould be told, That Mr. *Sandys*, one of the King of *Great Britain*'s ſubjects, came into the Emperor's Territories againſt his Prince's conſent, and that he had no power to hinder him, unleſs he would conſult with all his Nobles, and the Repreſentatives of all his common ſubjects, to aſſiſt therein? Would not the Emperor believe *Sandys* to be the greater Prince of the two? But tho' ſuch ſort of declamations are ſo much for the ſervice of the Crown, and for the honour of the Kingdom, as they would have it believed; yet I think they have the ſame tendency of duty and ſervice to the King, with ſome other matters that of late have happened amongſt us, *viz.* Some have been ſo concerned, as well for the ſafety and ſecurity of his Majeſty's ſacred Perſon, and to make him formidable to his rebellious ſubjects at home, as to deſire that his Guards might be diſcharged, becauſe it looked as though he deſigned to rule by a ſtanding army; and to ſhew their tenderneſs to his ſacred Life, would have him removed from the aſſiſtance of evil Councillors, as they called them; and put himſelf into the hands of aſſaſſinates, as tho' one murdered Prince were not ſufficient to ſatisfy that piece of ſtate-policy in one and the ſame age. And in order that he might have ſufficient to ſupport the neceſſity, as well as the dignity of a Crown, which all good ſubjects are zealous for; ſome, of late, have induſtriouſly endeavoured to have prevented him from being able to borrow any money upon the credit of any part of his revenue, a privilege that the meaneſt of the perſons concerned in that queſtion would think themſelves highly injured to be debarred of.

Theſe and the like attempts, if not prevented, will render the King and his Government low and deſpicable in all other parts of the World. And as for the inſtance between a Denizen and a man naturalized, I think it rather makes againſt, than for Mr. *Williams*'s concluſion, as to the main queſtion. For tho' the King cannot naturalize a man, and thereby give him inheritable blood, as a natural-born ſubject, to inherit lands; yet he may make an Alien a Denizen; and by that means he becomes to have as much privilege as any of the King's natural ſubjects hath as to trade and commerce, which is the only queſtion now before us: And I cannot help being of opinion, that this Kingdom was in greater regard abroad, and the Inhabitants thereof more proſperous at home, when the prerogative of the Crown was more abſolute than now it is: therefore it is our duty as good Judges, as well as good Subjects, to endeavour to ſupport it as much as we can by Law. And ſo I proceed to mention ſome precedents and authorities, whereby the Kings of *England* have in all ages exerciſed this part of their prerogative, of reſtraining, diſpoſing, and ordering matters of commerce and foreign trade, by Royal Licences, Charters, and Diſpenſations.

And herein I ſhall content myſelf with as much brevity as I can, only in producing ſome few of thoſe many inſtances, which were with great care and induſtry found out by Mr. Attorney, and Mr. Sollicitor; and by them ſo learnedly and properly applied to the caſe in queſtion.

1. Therefore it has been well obſerved, that the Staples, which were the common and publick Marts for all Merchants to reſort to, were firſt erected by the King's prerogative, without any Act of Parliament; as it doth plainly appear by the ſeveral Acts of Parliament mentioned at the Bar, either for ſetting the places, or enlarging the commodities that were permitted to be brought to the Staple; for ſurely in all times, when

* *Rolls Abr.* 2. *fo* 214. The Commons pray leave to export and import foreign Goods at their pleaſure, except Goods of the Staple, notwithſtanding any Proclamation to the contrary. *Reſp. Le Roy voet eſtre adviſe par ſon Counſel.*

the Staple was fixed in the Dominions of any other Prince, that muſt be done by league, which none can make but the King. To inſtance one authority for all, the *Stat.* 2 *Ed.* III. *cap.* 9. expreſly ſays, *It is enacted, That the Staples beyond the ſeas, and on this ſide, ordained by Kings in time paſt,* &c. Mr. Attorney and Mr. Sollicitor cited ſeveral Records, and other Acts of Parliament, that allow this to be the King's prerogative abſolutely; which I ſhall only name, they having opened the particulars at large, *viz. Viceſimo E.* III. *Plac. Parl. Rolls Abr. fol.* 108, 130. *Octavo. E.* III. *num.* 20 27 *E.* III. *cap.* 1. 43 *E.* III. *c.* 1. 47 *E.* III. *N.* 17. *Prim. R.* 2. *N.* 98. with many more; which did not only licenſe Merchants to repair to their ſeveral Staples, but prohibited them from carrying their ſtaple commodities to any other places, and the ſeveral Acts of Parliament made touching the Staple, only inflicted greater forfeitures upon the perſons offending, more than the King by his prerogative did inflict; but neither added to, or diminiſhed any part of the power of the Crown: the truth whereof will alſo farther appear by the conſent of the Parliament, plainly declared in ſeveral Statutes following, *viz.* 2 *H.* V. *c.* 6. 2 *H.* VI. *c.* 4. 8 *H.* VI. *c.* 17 & 27. by which, and ſeveral other inſtances, both by Mr. Sollicitor and Mr. Attorney, I do conceive it does plainly appear, that the Statute of 2 *Ed.* III. *c.* 9. *Nono Ed.* III. *c.* 1. *decimo-quarto Ed.* III. *c.* 2. the *Stat.* of *decimo-quinto Ed.* III. mentioned in the Defendant's Plea, *decimo* 8 *Ed.* III. *c.* 3. which the Defendant's Counſel have much inſiſted on, for the opening the liberty of trade only concerned Merchants of the Staples; and by the Acts of Parliaments made relating to that trade, ſince particularly mentioned by Mr. Attorney, ſtand now repealed.

And tho' the place of the Staple, as well as the commodities, were aſcertained by Acts of Parliament, yet the King granted to merchants licences to trade elſewhere; which prerogative is allowed of by Acts of Parliament, and other authorities in our Books: for inſtance, amongſt many others, the *Stat.* 8 *H.* VI. 21 22 *Hen.* VI. *chap.* 4. 15 *Hen.* VI. *c.* 3. 27 *H.* VI. *c.* 1. 1 *H.* VII. *fol.* 3. *A.* 13 *Ed.* IV. *fol.* 3. *l.* 5 *E.* IV. 33.

And as the King, before thoſe Acts of Parliament mentioned, ordered the merchandizes of the Staple; ſo all other foreign trade, not taken notice of by Acts of Parliament, were begun and abſolutely diſpoſed of by the King's prerogative, for as my Lord *Coke*, in his Comment upon *Mag. Chart. c.* 30. does truly obſerve, That by *Mercatores* there, only is meant Merchant-Strangers; for as I ſaid, I do not find that any of the Subjects of this King meddled in foreign trade, in many years after the making of that Act: The firſt inſtance I meet with, is in *Malin's Lex Mercatoria, fol.* 150, of the ſociety of Merchants, which is the Staples-Adventurers, made by a Grant from K. *Ed.* III. and were called the Brotherhood of *St. Thomas a Becket* of *Canterbury*, 'till the time of *Hen.* VII. who confirmed their Charter, but changed their name to that of Merchant-Adventurers, by which name they continued a Corporation.

And that the King did ſhut and open foreign trade at his pleaſure, by many inſtances mentioned by Mr. Attorney and Mr. Sollicitor, does farther appear, 33 *Hen.* III. *mem.* 1. 2 *E.* III. *pars ſecunda memb.* 35. 3 *H.* III. *N.* 33. *Rolls Prerogative* 170 & 214. before cited, *primo H.* V. 41. *decimo-octavo H.* VI. *N.* 60. and the *Stat.* of 12 *H.* VII. *c.* 6. which I have cauſed to be ſearched. And in *Plowden*'s Commentaries, in the great Caſe of *Mines Royal* it is ſet down as a Rule, That ancient Charters and Grants of the Crown, are the beſt evidences of the Prerogative. *Phil.* and *Mary* erected the Corporation of *Ruſſia* Merchants, by Charter, with a prohibition to others, with the like conditions within mentioned in the Charter at the Bar; and was afterwards approved of in Parliament in 8 *Eliz.* and the forfeiture mentioned in the Letters Patent made more effectual. And as Mr. Attorney did truly obſerve, that when *Calais* was taken, and thereby the Staples unſettled, Queen *Elizabeth* thought, according to the precedent of the *Ruſſia* and other Companies, it was moſt advantageous for the carrying on of Trade and foreign Commerce, to erect Societies and Corporations; which was well approved of in thoſe times, and ſo has continued ever ſince undiſturbed, until this preſent queſtion; which I ſhall more particularly inſiſt upon, when I come to diſcourſe of the next Head.

And here by the way, I ſhall only remember, that there were many Records and Books cited by the Counſel at the Bar, to prove the difference between alien enemies, and alien amies; and how theſe infidels are in law looked upon as perpetual enemies, and the many caſes that were cited about the Jews, and others, I think will not be neceſſary to be farther inſiſted upon; for I conceive they do not concern the queſtion that is now before us. For were not the Charter now in queſtion in being, it would be worth while for Mr. *Sandys* to conſider, how far he might be obnoxious to puniſhment, for trading with Infidels, who are in law called *perpetui inimici.* And therefore I conceive, it is as penal for any of the King's Subjects to trade with Infidels, who are alien enemies, without a Royal Licence, as it is to trade with aliens amies, contrary to a Royal prohibition. And I cannot conjecture how he will avoid this rock, notwithſtanding his pretended ſkill in navigation, without making uſe of this Charter as a ſafe-conduct to him, by implication: though he ſeems here ſo much to ſtruggle againſt it. and how far that would prevail for his benefit, may be alſo conſidered. But as I ſaid before,

4. The true Queſtion is, Whether this be a good Grant to the Plaintiffs, of a ſole trade to the *Indies*, were the Inhabitants thereof Chriſtians or Infidels, excluſive of others?

And therefore I proceed to the next ſtep, That though unlawful Engroſſing, and Monopolies, are prohibited by the laws of this, and all other Nations; yet I do conceive, that the Charter now in queſtion, of a ſole trade excluſive of others, is no ſuch unlawful engroſſing, or Monopoly, but is ſupported and encouraged, as conducing to publick benefit by the Law, Practice, and Uſage of this and other Countries And herein, by the way, though the word *Monopoly*, or *Engroſſing*, generally ſpoken of is odious in the eye of our Law, yet ſome Engroſſings, and ſo ſome Monopolies, are allowed of in our Books; and ſo I deſire to be underſtood, when I ſay a lawful or unlawful Monopoly, or a lawful or unlawful Engroſſing And in as much as this is the great, and as I think, the only objection that either hath, or can be made againſt the preſent Charter, I ſhall be the more particular in giving my opinion therein, with the reaſons and authorities that have induced me thereunto.

I premiſe only this, that in all thoſe Cou[...]
are erected by the ſupreme Power, excluſiv[...]
the Bar, Monopolies are forbidden; and ar[...]
Laws, as they can be by the Common and S[...]
in *Holand, Germany, France* and *Spain*, &c.

And ſo wherever the Civil Law prevails,
confiſcation of Goods, and baniſhment. *C.*
part 1. *fol.* 497.

Now though Monopolies are forbidden, [...]
to be ſo univerſally true, (as no general La[...]
in no reſpect, and upon no occaſion or eme[...]
any exception or limitation.

The exceptions thereof may be ſuch as th[...]

1. Though no private Perſons can have t[...]
their own private authority, yet this may be
by the prerogative of the Prince; if,

2. It be upon good cauſe, and for the publ[...]

3. From the neceſſity of beginning and [...]
foreign commerce, which can be only done [...]

4. Such Companies and Societies ought t[...]
upon the natural equity and juſtice, that no
mitted either to reap the profit, or to endang[...]
begun, and been carried on by them, with g[...]

Now in as much as foreign trade can never
dom, except the balance be kept equal betwe[...]
which can never be done, but by keeping u[...]
the regulation thereof with the other Countr[...]
before, the municipal Laws of this Realm ſe[...]
poſe, I will therefore firſt conſider how this q[...]
of Nations; and then how it is conſidered by
rities in both to make good my aſſertion.
former more natural and effectual for the de[...]
me more inquiſitive than otherwiſe I ſhould [...]
Obſer. 23. diſtinguiſhes *inter Monopolia licita* [...]

Licitum Monopolium, ſays he, *eſt, ſi certis p*[...]
Collegio conceſſerit Princeps ut ei ſoli jus ſit vende[...]
fore recites a Law of the Emperors *Theodoſiu*[...]
certain Governors of Commerce were appoin[...]
nulli Mercatori niſi ad deſignata loca temporibus p[...]
ſpecies diſtrahendas paſſim liceret accedere.

Carpzovius, in his deciſions before-mentio[...]
& 14. makes this no new caſe; *Et certe (non*[...]
(quæ tamen liberrima eſſe debent) pone ex cauſa n[...]
neceſſitatis, ex quo Monopolia alias prohibita jure [...]

And again, *Exempla haud rara ſunt ubi* neceſſi[...]
nopolia quandoque probari: *Commercia* ad certa[...]
videmus.

Idem, *Deciſ.* 4. *N.* 10. & *N.* 13. *Nimirum*
nopoliorum à Principis *arbitrio dependet, &c.*
fol. 301. *N.* 15. *Hoc non procedit in Monopo*[...]
Reipub. contracto, quia ſicut monopolia, privatá a[...]
pernicioſa: Ita hæc quæ Legis Autoritate, ex juſt[...]
valde utilia ſunt.

Grotius de J. B. & P. lib. 2. *cap.* 12. *Sect.* 1[...]
Jure naturæ pugnant: nam poſſunt interdum à ſu[...]
cauſa & pretio.

He gives amongſt others theſe two Example[...]

1. From the Hiſtory of *Joſeph*, when he was
is, ſays he, an illuſtrious inſtance of this matt[...]

2. That under the *Romans*, the *Alexandrian*
Indian and *Ethiopick* commodities.

So *Thuanus, lib.* 32. gives an inſtance of a G[...]
Ann. 1604. for the ſole trade into *Canada*, or
gives this reaſon, *Ne gravis eſſet ærario ad ſuble*[...]
ſtitutæ ſumptus.

Which I conceive will go a great way in ſu[...]
Companies as cannot be begun but by a public[...]

C. de monopoliis, the prohibition is expreſsly
vel alia conſuetudo *in utilitatem publicam vergen*[...]

Mercatura eſt res indifferens, in qua Magiſtra[...]
mittendo ſuam pro Commodo Reipub. poteſt interpon[...]
Fœn. Trapezit. fo. 236. *Hoc ſolum permiſſum e*[...]
aliis vendat ſalem. Alciat. in Q. *inter publica* 17. [...]
it is at this day practiſed in *France, Touan. lib.*

Sic in Sale Vendenſi, Monopolia etiam hodie in [...]
orum permiſſione. Scacca de Mercat. part 4. *N.* 3[...]

Sic in Repub. Lubecenſi, certis quibuſdam Merca[...]
jus coquendi ſacchari, & ſalis ſpeciali Privilegio conc[...]
[...] 7. *N.* 24.

And then as to the uſage:

Hæc eſt communiſſima omnium, nullo prorſus re[...]
quod jura hujuſmodi Emporalia & Regalia poſſunt [...]
ceſſionem ſummi Principis, ſed etiam Conſuetudine [...]
Juſtitia, lib. 2. *c.* 22. *Dub.* 21.

By the Imperial Laws commerce and traffick
limitations; ſometimes the Subjects of the Em[...]
to trade to certain places, particularly named, a[...]
ſtitutions, forbidden to export coin, gold, or [...]
Nations.

And that the Law or cuſtoms of Nations is ſo,

And firſt in *Germany*, where the Law prohib[...]
ſee how the Law there ſtands in reſpect of o[...]

Circa Monopolia autem, quæ exercentur [illegible]
eſſe illicitum, ſi non cuivis quodvis negotiationis [illegible]
illis duntaxat qui ad idem exercendum juxta inſtitut[...]
runt, quemadmodum in rebus pub. Europæis te[illegible]
eum, qui mercatorium aut opificium aliquod [illegible]

This as to Corporations.

As to trading Societies thus:

Sed & fieri potest, ut à summa potestate Societati mercatorum indulgeatur certum genus Mercium & certis locis advehere, exclusis reliquis, cujus privilegii concedendi variæ possunt esse causæ.

I. *Nam Commercia quæ ad loca remotissima instituerentur, priusquam rite stabiliantur magnos requirant sumptus, & ancipiti eventui initio sunt obnoxia, ergo Authoribus talium Commerciorum cavendum est, ne quod ab ipsis constitutum magno cum periculo, & sumptu sunt, alii gratis intercipiant.*

II. *Ac præterea ejusmodi Societates privilegiatæ opibus suis Reipub. exigente necessitate, felicius possunt quam singula succurrere.*

III. *Videntur etiam meliori fide Commercia tractari, ac majorem Copiam Mercium hoc modo posse advehi, neque de tot fraudibus & compendiis cogitare necessum habent, quorum lucrum in commune velut ærarium reductum æqualibus portionibus distribuitur.*

Puffendorff de Jure Naturæ & Gentium. lib. 5. *fol.* 655.

A learned Author does more at large describe it.

It has been a question sometimes debated, whether the Society entered into by the *Hans* Towns were not against Law? *Quippe quod speciem Monopolii præ se ferre videtur, ut certis locis merces emant confœderati quæ rursus pretio eo, quo volunt, vendant.*

This is the same objection now made against the Charter at the Bar.

But the answer given was twofold, and will come home to this case.

I. That the Emperor, *Charles* IV. has given his approbation, and made it lawful by his authority.

II. That they had continued in possession of this Society so long, that now the length of time (together with the Prince's consent) removed all doubt whatsoever; *Carpzovius de lege Regia Germanorum, cap.* 6. *sect.* 10. And the Charter now in question, and other Charters of like nature granted by the Kings of *England*, which I shall have occasion to remember by and bye, remain undisturbed without the least interruption, as long as this Society did before this question was stated.

And though, according to the rules of our Laws, such a length of time does not obtain the credit of a prescription; yet by the Law of Nations, and the practices of all other countries, which are only adapted for this purpose, it is otherwise. *Præscriptio enim tam longi temporis vim legis obtinet, imo tollit omne vitium.*

Præscriptio temporis immemorialis, quæ privilegiata est, & ex vitioso etiam titulo dominium & jus tribuit, omnesque Solemnitates, etiam extrinsecus, negotio accessiss. præsumit tanti temporis Antiquitas, num. 10. *n. Atque omnem Monopolii respectum consuetudo immemorialis vel Cæsarum approbatio excludit, n.* 10.26.

Quia consuetudo immemorialis Cæsarum situ & concessu hæc antiqua Societas fulcitur, omnis Monopolii respectus etiam minimus læserat. Marg. lib. 4. *cap.* 7. *n.* 50.

And as these *Hans* Towns were one of the first Corporations of trade I have read of, so was it thought the interest of *England* to support and encourage them. I find above sixty (some say eighty) Towns and Cities united their Stocks, making *Lubeck*, *Brunswick*, *Dantzick*, and *Cullen*, the chief places of their residence; and so great was their trade and credit under that constitution, that many Princes granted them large privileges, and they kept Courts by their Deputies and Councils at *Bergen*.

By the Laws of *Spain*, all Monopolies are forbidden, and under the same penalties appointed by the Civil Law: yet there also a right may be acquired to a sole trade, by licence obtained from the King, or by Prescription.

Quinta partida Tit. 7. *leg.* 2. *membris hoc Commercium Maritimum exclusis cæteris ad* 20. *annos concederetur. Neque ulla re se magis prodidit Imperii odium Batavicæ nostris diebus, (Deo ita volente) constituti magnitudo, & felicitas, quam Navigationum in Indias Orientales susceptarum constantia & successus, ad quas ut ærario parceretur, Societates institutæ, cautumque tandem, ut sub unam Societatem omnes coirent, quod alioque experimento constitisset, Aromatum pretia ab insularis ob emptorum frequentiam augeri, & cum alii aliis prævertere, & lucrum ad se aliorum damno derivare satagerent, ubi concordia maxima est opus, æmulationum & dissidii semina spargi.*

I come in the next place to make it appear, that as the Law of Nations, and the practice of all other Countries, warrants the like Grants and restrictions with the case at the Bar; so I conceive this Charter of sole trade to the *Indies*, excluding others, is neither opposed by the Common Law, or prohibited by any Act of Parliament; but is supported by both, as will more evidently appear by the practice and constant usage in all times.

Therefore, though ingrossing be a crime, odious in the Law, and punishable, yet all manner of ingrossing is not.

Therefore in the case of foreign trade, which is only applicable to the case at the Bar, it was resolved by all the Judges of *England*, 3 *Instit.* 196. That Merchants may buy beyond sea in gross, and sell here again in gross also. I say, that all Monopolies are not unlawful. Generally speaking they are, and therefore, I will admit the description of an unlawful Monopoly, made by my Lord *Coke*, 3 *Instit.* 181.

A Monopoly is an institution or allowance by the King, by his Grant, Commission, or otherwise, to any person or persons, bodies politick or corporate, of, or for the sole buying, selling, making, working, or using any thing; whereby any person or persons, bodies politic or corporate, are sought to be restrained of any freedom or liberty they had before, or hindered in their lawful trade.

Now if the subjects of *England* had not, before this Grant, a freedom and liberty to trade to the *Indies*, against the King's royal pleasure, the Charter at the Bar will be no Monopoly within that rule.

Now that they had no such liberty, hath been sufficiently proved by the several prohibitions mentioned before; and the many more instances thereof, cited by Mr. Attorney and Mr. Sollicitor; and it would be very strange, that the King might prohibit Foreigners from coming here into *England*, and not prohibit his own subjects from going into foreign Countries.

And it is not denied, but if the King should proclaim a war with the *Indians*, that then it would be a prohibition to all his subjects to have any commerce with them; nay, and he might continue that war as long as he pleases; and by that means all his subjects would be as well prevented of any of the commodities of that country, and also of exporting any of our commodities thither. So that surely this Charter, with these restrictions, is much better than a total exclusion; and therefore foreign trade is not like our home trade, to which the word Monopolies is properly applicable; for that cannot be totally excluded for any time, tho' never so small, by any Act of Prerogative.

Object. Ay, but, say the Defendant's Counsel, though the King can by his prerogative prohibit all trade to any country, upon such great emergencies as war and plague, *&c.* yet to grant liberty to some, and exclude others, that makes the Grant at the Bar be thought a Monopoly. Which is still begging the question; for if the King by his prerogative, have the power of restraining and disposing foreign trade, where Acts of Parliament have not interposed; as by the precedents already cited I conceive clearly he has, as inherent to his Crown; therefore, as he may restrain all, so he may restrain any part by the same parity of reason.

If the King proclaims a war with any country, which is a general prohibition of trade, and should order that *John a Style*, or a dozen, or any greater number of his subjects, *&c.* and give them instructions to treat for a peace, and the persons so appointed should carry on a trade; would not Mr. *Sandys*, do you think, have as much reason to murmur that he was none of those Ambassadors, as he has now by being not comprized within the Charter? And would it not be thought an arrogancy and sauciness in him, to demand an account of the instruction given by the King to such Ambassadors? Or durst he trade there till a peace were proclaimed with that country?

And the gloss of that Law says, *Mercatores non faciant inter Monopolium de re non vendenda nisi pro certo pretio, vel de non exercendo officium nisi per eos recipiatur Officiales & Socios: Possunt tamen hæc facere cum concensu & scientia Regis & contra facientes perpetuo exulabunt, & eorum bona Regi applicantur. Ex privilegio ergo Regis possunt similiter & consuetudine vel prescriptione, quia quod privilegio acquiritur, etiam præscriptione acquiri potest.*

And there quotes *ubi dicitur, quod potest concedi privilegium; quod quis solus piscetur in certa parte Maris, & aliis potest prohiberi.*

In *France* Monopolies are prohibited also, *Sub pœna Confiscationis corporis & bonorum indict. Const. Fr.* 1. *Art.* 191.

Notwithstanding which, there are established several Corporations for trade; I will name but two. *Anno.* 1657, the *French* King makes a grant of the sole fishery in his Dominions to a Society, excluding others upon pain that Interlopers shall incur the penalty, *de Confiscation des Vaisseaux & Merchandizes & de dix mille Livres d' Amende. Aytz. vol.* 4. *pag.* 207. And in the year 1664, the *East-India* Company, by his declaration, with an exclusion to all others, like our *East-India* Company, *page* 74, 75.

In the *United Provinces*, the Laws against Monopolies are the same, yet there always were several trading Corporations exclusive of all others. 3 *June* 1621: in the Charter of the *Dutch West-India* Company it is granted thus: And in case any one shall go to, or negotiate in any of the aforesaid places granted to this Company, and without consent of the said Company, it shall be upon pain and forfeiture of such ship and goods, as shall be found to trade in those Coasts and Places, which being presently and on all sides, on the behalf of the said Company, set upon, taken, and forfeited, shall be and remain to the use of the said Company, *Aytz. vol.* 1. *p.* 62. *sect.* 1.

And in case such ships or goods be sold, or fly into lands or havens, the Riggers and Part-owners thereof shall and may be distrained to the value of the said ship and goods.

That the aforesaid Company shall within the said limits make Governors, Officers of War and Justice; and for the other necessary services for the preservation of the places, and maintaining of good order, policy and justice, and the advancement of their trade, shall appoint, dispose and displace, and substitute others in their places, as they shall find their affairs do require.

All ships coming to any place where the Company have their Garrison and Government, shall not transport thence any men, goods, or money, without leave and consent of the Council, upon the pain and forfeiture of six months wages, &c.

In the Grant to the *Dutch India* Company, 20 *Mar.* 1602. that nobody, of what quality or condition soever, shall for the space of twenty-one years pass *Eastwards* of the *Cape of Good Hope*, upon forfeiture of ships and goods, *Aytz.* 1 *vol. fol.* 157.

That the said Company may appoint Governors and Officers of war and justice, and for other necessary services, for the preservation of their places, and maintenance of good order, policy and justice.

The said officers to take the oath of supremacy to the States-General; and of fidelity, as to what concerns trade and traffick, to the Company.

And afterwards, the 9th of *Sept.* 1606. a *Placart* was published, that nobody, directly or indirectly, shall pass or trade beyond the *Cape of Good Hope*, upon pain of death, and forfeiture of their ships or goods, which shall be found to have done or to do so. And though they should absent themselves out of the *United Provinces*, yet the sentence shall go on, and be decreed and executed, with the present confiscation and selling of their goods, actions, and credits.

Idem, page 158. And surely the *Dutch* have been always by us esteemed as our greatest and most dangerous rivals in trade.

And as for the reason and necessity of establishing this way of trading by Companies, see the judgment of *Thuanus, lib. Hist.* 124 and 130, where making mention of the *East-Indies*, he saith thus: *Diversis itinerious hujus Regionis Incolarumque Ingeniis cognitis tanta frequentiâ à privatis hæc ipsa Navigatio & Commercium exercitum fuit, ut alter alterum fere ivisset perditum. Ad obviandum itaque huic malo visum fuit, An.* 1602. *quibusdam hujus Navigationis mercatoribus, præpotentum ordinum consensu certum constituere corpus, cujus tantummodo*, &c.

The *Indians* being Infidels are by law esteemed common enemies; and the opinion of my Lord *Coke* in *Michelborne*'s case, I think, therefore, to be Law, notwithstanding the objections that have been made against it, which none of our books warrant; now the King by his Charter makes the Plaintiffs as it were his Ambassadors to concert a peace, and Mr. *Sandys* murmurs because he is not one of them.

The King may grant a Fair or Market to every subject he has; but because he grants that privilege to some of his subjects, have the rest any just ground of complaint? Because the King may pardon every offender, but will not pardon any Highwayman now in *Newgate*, must those gaol-birds, therefore, think themselves injured in their liberty and property? Because the King granted to his town of *Hull*,

that

that no other Ships should be there freighted for foreign Parts, till the Ships of that Town were first freighted; as he did, *Rot. Clauf.* 41 *E.* III. *memb.* 25. did *London*, *Dover*, or any other Town of Trade complain? Would any of these Gentlemen that contend for this Liberty of Trade, adventure with their Fortunes to *Algiers*, and when they are seized upon be the *Algerines*, tell them we are *Englishmen*, and we have by the Common Law of *England*, and many Statutes of our Kingdom, which support the Liberty of the Subject, a Freedom to trade wherever we please? Or would not they rather say, we have a Pass from the King of *England*, and rely upon that, which presumes Treaties, Leagues, and Truces between Princes; and in case that will not prevail, the King will see them righted? And in the Charter that is now before us, there is a particular Restriction and Limitation of Trade to any Prince in amity with our King. Now as the constant Usage and Practice of other Countries warrants such Societies as these, so does ours too: For, as I said, the *Hans* Towns were some of the first Corporations of Trade that we read of in History; so was it thought the Interest of *England* to support and encourage them.

King *H.* III. gave them great Privileges, and the *Still-yards* for their Residence, which they enjoyed near 300 Years, managing their Trade by an Alderman and Counsel, called *The Guild of the Hans*, ingrossing the Trade of *England* for Grain, Cables, Masts, Pitch, Tar, *&c.* and under that Colour the *Jacobsons* at this Day claim several Privileges.

It is observed by many Historians, that the most flourishing Trades have been begun by united Stocks and Policies.

In this Kingdom a Patent was first obtained for the erecting the Staple, from *E.* III. before any Act of Parliament intermeddled in that Trade, and proceeded under several Regulations till the Time of Queen *Elizabeth*. In the Book I cited before, *Malyn*'s *Lex Mercatoria*, *fol.* 150. says, This Company of Merchants are above 400 Years standing, as that Book reckons from 1248, when the said Merchants obtained Privileges of *John* Duke of *Brabant*, and were called the Brotherhood of St. *Thomas Becket* of *Canterbury*: Which were confirmed by King *E.* III. *H.* IV. *H.* V. *H.* VI. *E.* IV. *R.* III. *H.* VII. who gave them the Name of *Merchant-Adventurers*; and after him confirmed by *H.* VIII. *E.* VI. *Q. M.* Q *Eliz.* and King *James*, not without many Enemies and Opposers; especially, says that Book, of late taxing them to be Monopolies, and unprofitable to the Commonwealth, being that all our Cloths are not dressed and dyed in *England*; yet it still prevailed, as being thought for the publick good.

And 'tis observable, that Queen *Elizabeth* did not only confirm what was done by her Predecessors, but augmented and greatly enlarged the Privileges of this ancient Company; and confirmed the Charter of the *Muscovy* Company, granted by *Philip* and *Mary*; and set up several other Companies, as that of *Exeter*, mentioned at the Bar; the *East-India* Company, and the *Levant* and the *Eastland* Company. And although that ancient and beneficial Company of Staplers was often opposed by particular Persons, and complained of as a Monopoly intrenching upon the Liberty of the Subject, in several Parliaments, in the Time of *H.* IV. *H.* VII. *E.* VI. and Queen *Mary*: Yet all Parties being heard, these Complaints were fully answered, and the Company's Privileges ratified and enlarged.

Again, in Queen *Elizabeth*'s Time, the Clothiers having prevailed against the Company, the clothing Countries were almost quickly ruined, and reduced to that Extremity, that in 29 *Eliz.* the Lords of the Council sent for the Members of that Company, desiring them to reassume their Privileges, and chearfully to proceed in their Society; with Assurance of all Countenance and Assistance from the Government. And in the Reign of King *James*, after several Interlopers had endeavoured to destroy the Company, the King published his Proclamation to restore the Company to its ancient Privileges.

So did King *Charles* I. 7 *Dec.* 1634, reciting, "Whereas we have "taken into our princely Consideration the manifold Benefits that re-"dound to this Kingdom; and finding how much Order and Govern-"ment will conduce to the Encrease and Advancement of the same, we "have thought fit, with the Advice of our Privy-Council, *&c.*" There he gives an Establishment to the Company, and prohibits any to intrude upon their Privileges, upon pain of such Punishments as the *Star-Chamber* shall inflict.

Since this, it may be worth Consideration, whether the breaking of this Company, has not occasioned the great Decay of our Trade in Wool: It being agreeable to Reason, that as no Law can be effectual without Courts of Justice to put them in Execution; nor a straggling Army subsist without Discipline: So a straggling Trade managed by particular Persons, whilst every one strives to advance his own private Interest, will ruin the Trade in general, especially such a hazardous Trade as this to the *East-Indies*, which already hath been so chargeable, and can only be prevented by the Conduct and Government of a public Society: And surely to look after and settle these Matters, properly belongs to the Care and Prudence of our Governors.

Now I shall observe, how the Practice has been both in Queen *Elizabeth*'s Time, and ever since, and that although many Charters like ours at the Bar have been granted; and none ever demanded by a Judgment in *Westminster-hall*, or so much as objected against, save only that of the *Canary* Patent, till this Cause at the Bar: And though several Attempts have been made both in Parliament, and in the Courts at *Westminster-hall*, against Monopolies; yet this Charter, and others of the like Nature, were never looked upon under that Character. For instance,

1. A Charter was granted 2 *Eliz.* to the Merchants of *Exeter* for the sole Trade to *France*, excluding all other Merchants of *Exeter* not of that Company, continued undisturbed, and prevailed against a great Opposition that was made against it in Parliament. King *Edward* VI. and King *Philip* and *Mary*, having granted a Charter like ours to the *Russia* Company, which continued in Peace till the eighth of Queen *Elizabeth*; when the Parliament taking Notice of that Patent, thought fit to confirm it with all the Commendations imaginable; and was so far from thinking it a Monopoly, that it says, the Commonwealth before that time had received great Advantages by it; and grants, and inflicts greater and other Penalties than were or could be inflicted by the Letters Patent: And it is observable, that there were some Interlopers upon that Trade in those Days, and had been liable to the Forfeitures inflicted by those Letters Patent, and were therefore forced to apply themselves to that Parliament,

and did obtain a special Proviso to e
not that Act of Parliament been made
take to be an Authority full, as to th
Queen *Elizabeth*, during her Reig
like Nature, which passed the Peru
learned Men in our Profession. In t
Chief-Baron *Weston* was Sollicitor, S
and passed those Patents both to the *R*
my Lord Chief-Justice *Popham* was
Egerton Sollicitor, in whose Time som
like to this at the Bar. And then m
and my Lord Chief Baron *Fleming*
thereof; and it is observable, that
Parliament took Notice of many Pat
the Book cited at the Bar, *Townsen*
Parliament seemed to be as high as ev
particularly were incensed by those
in by Mr. Secretary *Cecil*, that were
Commonwealth; and though there
amongst whom that of *Darcy* is one,
complained of any Charter granted
undisturbed. And by the way it is n
tent was not immediately damned in
Fate in *Westminster-hall*; the great
was, the Restraint that was put upon
in *More's Reports*, 672. And thus st
ter, the *Turky* Company, the *Barba*
all Charters of sole Trade, excluding
all Queen *Elizabeth*'s Time.

But in the third Year of King *Ja*
ing a general Trade to *Spain*, *Port*
Subjects; which could not be done
Preamble to that Act; nor does that
or open a free Trade to any other Pa
ters of foreign Trade, save to *Spain*
they did before. And in the 4th o
particularly of the Charter granted
Trade to *France*, and because it wa
neral Words of that Statute *E.* III.
That the said Statute of Patents, ne
late or impeach the said Charter, o
Privileges, Liberties, or Immunitie
Charter, any thing contained in that
standing; and from this Act of Parl
I. That the Parliament thought
Trade to *France*, exclusive of others
Weal of that City.

II. That the Letters Patent were
Assistance of an Act of Parliament to
confirm those Letters Patent, but p
should not by general Words be th
Now had the Parliament thought th
have confirmed or strengthened it, as
cluded, that had it not been for tr
good to all Intents and Purposes: A
the Case at the Bar. But to proceed
ing, exclusive of others, granted by
Part 5. *fol.* 3. Taylors of *Ipswich*'s
Westminster, is agreed to be Law; i
Justice *Dodderidge*: And by the way
that dispute the King's Prerogative;
Sandys, and others that are now in
I shall read the very Words of the Bo
Chips will fall into his Eyes; *Et qui*
metur splendore ejus.

In King *James*'s Time, many Gr
ticularly in 7 *Jac.* the Patent gran
Queen *Elizabeth*, was, by the Advic
Lord *Hobart*, then Attorney-Genera
General, confirmed and allowed wi
the Bar; and so remained undisturb
Reign, and was not thought to be
Proviso in the Statute, 43 *Eliz. cap.*
the Monopoly Patents complained
Queen, which I mentioned before.
insisted on by the Defendant's Cou
Monopolies, *Stat.* 21 *Jac. cap.* 3 v
the Case at the Bar. For first, Th
the sole buying, selling, making, u
which are the very Words of the A
East-India Company Licence or To
thing against the Tenor or Purport o
only things provided against by that
ed to take the same general Care of a
the Parliament did in 3 *Jac.* of tha
therefore, to the End that those W
Monopolies might not be thought to
for Trade, there is a Proviso, *Sect.* 9
any Corporations, Companies, or Fe
tainance, Enlargement, or ordering
leaves the same as they were before
And it is observable, that the Parlia
sufficient to support those Charters t
tions for Trade and Merchandize;
saving of Patents for Inland Commod
Ordnance, Shot, and the like.

So that this Company was in full
Trade, exclusive of others, all King
till all the Prerogatives of the Cro
Head too was taken off by Traitors

God having restored us our King, and re-invested him with all h s undoubted prerogatives, as well as restored us to our ancient rights and privileges, and scarce, as I may say, warm in his Throne, but amongst the other considerations that he had for the publick weal of his subjects, he considers the publick advantage of this Kingdom arising by trade, and amongst them, one of his first thoughts are fixed upon this Company. For 3d of *April*, 1661, he by his Letters Patent taking notice of the Charters of Queen *Elizabeth*, and King *James*, granted to the *East-India* Company, all of the injuries that were done to them by the late troubles; with the advice of his Council, and approbation of Mr. Attorney *Palmer*, and my Lord-Chancellor *Finch*, he granted and confirmed to them all their privileges. The 27th of *May*, in the 20th of his reign, Lord-Chancellor *Finch* being Attorney, and my Lord-Keeper, that now is, Sollicitor, he confirms this Charter; and grants to the *East-India* Company other privileges, by another Charter in the 28th year of his reign, at which time the Lord-Keeper was Attorney, and Sir *William Jones*, Sollicitor; he confirms the former, and grants more privileges: and in the 25th year of his reign, by the Charter now in question, passed with the approbation of the present Attorney and Solicitor, men of great ability in their professions, and of whom, were they not present, I should say much more; the Charter to this Company was confirmed with additional privileges.

Nor has this Charter passed only the approbation of his Majesty and Council, since his happy Restauration, but the Parliament has likewise taken notice of it; the Statute 14 *Car.* II. *cap.* 14 takes notice of it to be of great advantage to the publick. The *Stat.* of the 29th of this King for poll-money, taxes them with twenty shillings for every hundred pound in Stock. In the great case between *Skinner* and the *East-India* Company, the House of Commons defended them, even to an eruption between the two Houses.

Mr. *Jenks* and some other Linnen-Drapers and Tradesmen of *London*, taking the advantage of the heats that too frequently possessed the House of Commons of late years, especially against the point of prerogative, did furiously attack the *East-India* Company, but without any success. and this Company was never assaulted in *Westminster-Hall* till this cause at the Bar. I cannot help therefore this observation, that as the King by his Charter 1667, takes notice, that the Charters granted by Queen *Elizabeth* and King *James* remained uninterrupted till the late rebellion; so the Interlopers against the King's prerogative in this particular, and the horrid conspirators against the King's life in this last hellish conspiracy, first appeared in *Westminster-Hall* about the same time.

As to the objections I have not yet given answer to, I think they are but few: my Lord *Coke's* opinion, cited by Mr. *Pollexfen*, 2 *Inst.* 540. where my Lord observes new things, which with fair pretences prove hurtful to the Commonwealth; and amongst them reckons, that new Corporations trading into foreign parts and at home, which under the fair pretences of order and government, in conclusion tend to the hindrance of trade and traffick, and in the end produce Monopolies, does not all concern the case at the Bar. For this Charter that hath continued for an 100 years without any interruption till of late, can neither be thought a new Corporation or hindrance of trade, and Sir *Edward Coke*, when he was Attorney-General, and past this Charter, was as learned in the Law, as he was when he published that Book, and was turned out of being Chief-Justice, did not think this Charter needed that caution.

As to the case of the *Canary* Patent between *Horn* and *Ivy*, that cannot affect the case at the Bar.

I. For first, the Judgment in that case was given upon the point of pleading, and not upon the validity of the Patent.

II. That Patent was in perfect oppostition to the Statute, 3 *Jac.* that opened a free trade to *Spain*, and therefore could not be restrained by the King's Letters Patent, but there is no such objection to our case.

The Counsel that argued for the Defendant seemed to allow the Charters to the *Virginia*, *Turky*, and *Eastland* Companies, which are exclusive of others, to be good, because they are managed by a Regulation, and not by a Joint-Stock, which surely can make no difference: for it is a Grant of a sole trade to them, exclusive of others, as well as the case at the Bar. And 'tis as hard to get into the *Turky* Company, as it is into this; and may be more chargeable: for you cannot be a Member of the *Turky* Company, but you must be a *Freeman of the City of London*; and makes you liable to all the great offices of charge in that Government. But a freedom of the *East-India* Company may be purchased at a much easier rate; the Members of the *East-India* Company are as visible as those of the *Turky*. And though it was said, the *East-India* Company were sometimes invisible, yet, were the *Turky* Company infested with so many Interlopers as the *East-India* Company have, they would not appear so glorious and splendid as they now do, and as I heartily wish they may long continue. But the King by this Charter has reserved to himself a power to destroy and alter the whole Charter, or any part thereof, so as to put it into a way of regulation instead of a Joint-stock, in such manner as he shall in his great wisdom think fit; therefore it becomes us in duty and modesty to wait till we receive his further royal pleasure therein. And whereas it was objected at the Bar, because the King cannot lay any imposition upon foreign trade, therefore he cannot restrain it:

I do not know to what end that objection was made, because it does not affect the question at the Bar; but lest it may obtain the effect, that I presume was aimed at, I think it not amiss to say, that even at this day there is much more may be said in the maintenance of the King's prerogative in *Westminster-Hall*, in that case, than can be offered against his prerogative in this. But in as much as that and several other objections against the Charter proceeded from an unreasonable, as well as unmannerly mistrust they have of the Crown, I cannot but remember that his sacred Majesty was not so mistrustful of them. For he since his restauration has bestowed upon his subjects more than all his predecessors, put them all together, since the conquest, ever did. Nay, he in a moment frankly bestowed upon us more than ever he desires he should be trusted with again, for by his act of indempnity he bestowed upon his subjects their lives, liberties and estates, which were all justly and legally forfeited to him by the late rebellion; the consideration whereof will prevent all fear, and jealousies, and promote in all loyal hearts a firm resolution to sacrifice their lives and fortunes, so freely bestowed upon us by him, to maintain the Crown and just Prerogatives thereof; so that it may have a perpetual continuance in that Royal Family, in a lawful succession, which I heartily pray may be so long as the sun and moon endures.

From what has been said, I hope it doth plainly appear, that since the Law of this Land, and the Law of Nature and Nations, allow the power of making Companies to manage traffick, exclusive to all others, to be in the Prince, that this is reckoned to be *inter Jura Regalia*; that no Act of Parliament does restrain this Prerogative, that the practice of all *Europe* has been accordingly; that particularly such Companies have been erected in *England*, and those Companies have been in quiet possession of their privileges for such a number of years; that they have passed the approbation of many learned men; that they have been thought for the publick advantage of the Nation, by so many Kings and Princes, with the advice of their Council, both in and out of Parliament; that all Statutes and Authorities of Law that we can meet with in our Books affirm it, and none that I can meet with oppose it.

That the *East-India* Company have solely run the hazard, and been at great expences,

In discovering places,
Erecting Forts, and keeping Forces,
Settling Factories,
And making leagues and treaties abroad;

It would be against natural justice and equity, (which no municipal law can take away) for others to reap the benefit and advantage of all this:

Especially since all this has been occasioned by an Act of the publick, and by the just prerogative of the Crown, under which they claim.

So that now, supposing the matter had been doubtful at the beginning (as yet the contrary is evident), yet after so many years undisputed and uninterrupted prerogative of the King, and the possession of the Companies pursuant thereunto; and yet the laws having always been open to any subjects who conceived themselves grieved; that speech which *Josephus* records of King *Agrippa*, to those Jews who after many years endeavoured to recover their lost pretence, may be applied to these clamorous Interlopers:

Intempestivum est nunc libertatem concupiscere, olim ne amitteretur certatum oportuit. Non amantes libertatis ascendi estis, sed subditi contumaces.

And so the *Romans* answered *Antiochus* (to shew the injustice of his demands), *That he required those Cities which his Predecessors for so many years had never enjoyed.*

And Queen *Elizabeth* pleaded against the King of *Denmark*, for the rights of fishing upon the coasts of *Norway* and *New-Island*, That neither his great-grandfather, grandfather, nor father, had exacted any thing for it; and therefore concluded it to be unjust. *Cambd. Eliz. sub. ann* 1600.

So that I conclude the first, and, as I conceive, the only point in this case, that Letters Patent which give licence and liberty to the Plaintiffs to exercise their sole trade to the *Indies*, within the limits of their Grant, exclusive of all others, is a good Grant in law.

2. I do conceive, that the Defendant trading to the *Indies*, contrary to this Charter, may be punished by information at the suit of the King; and that this action by the Plaintiffs is also well brought; but in as much as I have detained you so long upon the first point, I shall trespass upon your patience but a few words to this.

1. Therefore I conceive, the Plaintiff need not alledge any special damage, no more than the Grantee of a fair, market, or any other franchise.

2. The action is brought, and grounded upon the Grant of the sole and entire trade; which, as I conceive, is a franchise the King may grant, and is like the case of new inventions; upon which Letters Patent actions are brought by every day's experience; and the prohibiting clause is added, only to make the thing more notorious, and that Interlopers, in case they should be prosecuted at the King's suit, should be more inexcusable. And until you can imagine there be as many *East-India* Companies, as there are commoners and school-masters in *England*, *Mary's* case, *Coke* 9. can never be thought an objection. As to the objection in the 11 *Rep.* 88. *Rolls Abridg. part* 1. *p.* 106. *Darcy's* case, that admitting the Grant or Dispensation to *Darcy* had been good, for the sole importing of foreign Cards; yet that being only a Dispensation to the *Stat.* of *Ed.* IV. and did only exclude *Darcy* from the penalty of that Act, he could not maintain the action: But if in case that Grant had vested an interest, as our Grant at the Bar does, he might have brought an action, as, my Lord *Rolls* says in the next paragraph, may be collected out of *Darcy's* case

The case upon Patents of new inventions, are full authorities in the case at the Bar: And so is that case of the Abbot of *Westminster*, wherein the Grant of the market for thirty days, exclusive of others, is particularly set forth in the action. And the *Salisbury* man that brought cloth to *London*, and sold the same contrary to that Charter, is prosecuted in an action of trespass upon the case, at the suit of the Abbot; and the writ concludes, (supposing the Grant good) *In nostri contemptum & prædicti Abbatis grave damnum ac Fr. & libertatum suarum prædictarum læsionem manifestam*; which is an authority full as to this point.

Upon the whole matter, I am of the same opinion with my brothers; and do conceive, that that Grant to the Plaintiffs of the sole trade to the *Indies*, exclusive of others, is a good Grant, and that the action is well brought:

And therefore let the Plaintiff take his Judgment.

XXXVII. The Lady *Ivy*'s Trial, for great Part of *Shadwell*, in the Cou *Martis* 3 *Junii*, 1684. *Ter. Trin.* 36 *Car.* II. *B. R.* Before the Lord C

Elam Mossom, Plaintiff; *versus* Dame *Theodosia Iva*, Defendant.

This Day this Cause came to be tried at the Bar of the Court of King's-Bench, *by a special Jury of the County of* Middlesex; *whose Names follow:*

Middlesex Jury.

Sir *Reginald Forster*, Bart.	*Richard Reynell*, Esq;
Sir *John Cutler*, Kt. and Bart.	*Ralph Bucknall*, Esq;
Sir *Goddard Nelthorp*, Bart.	*Thomas Austin*, Esq;
Sir *Michael Heneage*, Knt.	*Joseph Dawson*, Esq;
Sir *William Gulston*, Knt.	*Thomas Cleve*, Esq;
Sir *Richard Downton*, Knt.	*Richard White*, Esq;

Who being counted, the Record was read to them by the Clerk of the Papers, in *English*; and opened by Mr. *Holloway*, for the Plaintiff.

Mr. Serj. *Stringer.* MAY it please your Lordship, and you Gentlemen of the Jury, I am of Counsel in this Case for the Plaintiff; and the Question will be, whether the Lessor or the Plaintiff hath a good title to the Tenements in question, which are about three or four hundred tenements, near *Radcliffe*, in *Shadwell* Parish; and the ground thereof is, say we, the ancient Inheritance of the Church of St. *Paul's*, who have had the possession thereof for four or five hundred years *. We shall prove leases down for some hundreds of years, till we come to that made to the Lessor of the Plaintiff; under whom we claim. We will begin with the last lease of Dean *Stillingfleet*, 30 *Sept.* 1678, upon the surrender of the lease made by Dean *Sancroft*, now Lord Archbishop of *Canterbury*.

Swear *Jeoffrey Willan (which was done)*; it is a Church-lease, but yet he is a witness to it.

The Lease of 30 Sept. 1678, *was read.*

Mr. Serj. *Stringer. (Shewing to him another Deed)* Did you see that Deed sealed and delivered?

Willan. Yes, Sir.

An Indenture quadripartite made the 25th of March, 1679, 31 Car. II. *between* Thomas Neale, *Esq;* *the Lady* Gold, &c. *Read.*

Mr. Att. Gen. We admit the Assignment.

Mr. Serj. *Stringer.* Then we shall prove the Lands in question were always held of the Dean of *Paul's*.

Mr. Att. Gen. Ay do, shew that these lands in question were so, if you can.

L. C. J. I would not interrupt you, Gentlemen, pray go your own way; but if I mistake not, you had as good begin with 5 *Ed.* VI. as you did last time, as I remember; I have not indeed my Book I had then, here, I fear we have not overmuch time to waste: we shall want time at the latter end of the cause, therefore pray come close to the merits of the cause.

Mr. Serj. *Stringer.* We will shew it, if they require, they know it well enough.

Mr. Att. Gen. Shew what you can.

Mr. Serj. *Stringer.* In 5 *H.* VIII. the Dean of *Paul's*, *Collet*, leases to one *John Hall*.

L. C. J. But it is 5 of *Ed* VI. I ask for.

Mr. Serj. *Stringer.* 23 *Feb.* 5 *Ed.* VI. Dean *May* doth make a lease to *Joan Hall*, and *Marcellus Hall*. Then Dean *Fecknam*, 10 *Dec.* 2 and 3 *Phil.* and *Mar.* in consideration of a surrender of that lease, letts another lease to *Marcellus Hall*; and so it continued till *May*, 1630, and then Dean *Donne* made a lease for three lives; and upon the surrender of that in 1636, Dean *Winneff* made a lease to *Moor*, and in 1640, he made another lease to *Winterburn*, which was sold to Mr *Neale*, and so came to the Lessor of the Plaintiff. First read this book.

Mr. Att. Gen. What Book is it, Mr. Serjeant?

L. C. J. Ay, tell us what it is; open it before you read it.

Clerk reads.] A tenement with a water-mill, *cum Pertinentiis*——

L. C. J. What is it you read there?

Mr. Serj. *Stringer.* It is a Book that belongs to the Dean and Chapter of St. *Paul's*.

L. C. J. What Book is it? How do you prove it to belong to the Dean and Chapter of *Paul's*?

(Then Mr. Spencer *was called, but could not readily come in by reason of the Crowd.* Mr. Porter *was sworn.)*

Mr. Serj. *Stringer.* Mr. *Porter*, What say you to this Book?

Porter. Since the beginning of this Suit, this Book was found among the Writings of the Dean and Chapter of *Paul's*.

Mr. Att. Gen. How long ago, Sir, upon your oath?

Porter. About a year ago.

L. C. J. That is but a slovenly account of such a Book as this.

Mr. *Williams.* It is plain, my Lord, it is not a new Book made on purpose.

L. C. J. It is plain, that in this slippery age we live in, it is very easy to make a Book look as old as you would have it.

Mr. Serj. *Stringer.* We will go on to the lease made to *Marcellus Hall.*

(Then Mr. Spencer *came in and was sworn.)*

Mr. *Williams.* Pray, Sir, when first saw you that Book?

Spencer. Seven years ago.

Mr. Att. Gen. Where, Sir?

Spencer. Among the evidences of the Dean and Chapter of *Paul's*.

L. C. J. What is it you would read in it? An entire lease, or what?

Mr. Serj. *Stringer.* 'Tis a short note of a lease.

Clerk reads.] A tenement with a water-mill——

L. C. J. See if the Book have any title.

Clerk. No, my Lord.

L. C. J. Let me see it. *(Which was*

Mr. Serj. *Stringer.* The 23d of *Feb.*

L. C. J. You, *Spencer*, have you se any lease made by Dean *Collet*?

Spencer. I have not observed that I h

L. C. J. Have you seen any lease ma *Henry* VIII. about any of the Church's cause I observe here in this Paper, in t *Collet*, writ with another hand than that with the same hand as the other. And for the maker of this lease, as being pu was not Dean till long after. Upon yo lease lett that is here spoken of?

Spencer. I know not, my Lord; that

L. C. J. Is this lease in your Book

Mr. Att. Gen. Pray, Gentlemen, yo nal Deed of purchase, where is it now?

Mr. *Williams.* That Book was produ

L. C. J. What first trial? Not that

Mr *Williams.* It was in Court at tha

L. C. J. I believe not, you are mist the notes I took then, and I find no suc

Mr. Att. Gen. They produced then t

L. C. J. Is there any lease of *Henry*

Spencer. I do not remember any leas land; but I have seen that Book ever si ness.

L. C. J. Have you not a Book of the was *Collet* Dean?

Mr. *Williams.* In 1505.

L. C. J. When was *Nowell* Dean?

Mr. *Williams.* In 1560.

L. C. J. Then I assure you this Boo

Mr. Att. Gen. They threaten us with I believe it will be found on Mr. *Neale*'s

L. C. J. If in case you come and yourselves upon the antiquity of it, as long to the Dean and Chapter, and lea that Book *Nowell* is written by the same Dean then; but because you find *Collet* till threescore years after, *Nowell* is turn draws a great suspicion certainly upon pose.

Mr. *Williams.* It is true, my Lord. thing; but we find an old Book amo and we produce it as such; we have be done for our purpose.

L. C. J. Who knows who did it? B

Mr. Att. Gen. And your title is u *Paul's*.

L. C. J. Who keeps the evidences th ter of *Paul's*?

Spencer. They are kept in the Chapt

L. C. J. I am persuaded there may be be such an one; but it looks a little un *Spencer*, did you look upon those two pa

Spencer. No; I did not observe it.

Mr. Serj. *Stringer.* My Lord, our n made by *Collet*.

Mr. Att. Gen. Come, upon your Oa *Neale*, come to search in this Book?

Spencer. Yes, they did.

Mr. Serj. *Lutwich.* How long ago wa

Spencer. As to Mr. *Baron* or Mr. N them come to search; but some for then

Mr. *Williams.* Do you believe the Bo you came at first to it?

Mr. Serj. *Lutwich.* You say they did come for then, to drink?

Spencer. They have come to the Offic them search.

Mr. *Williams.* But I ask you again, w

Spencer. I believe it was, I know of n

Mr. Serj. *Stringer.* But to put it out lease, which does recite this lease of *Coll*

Mr. *North.* Nay, my Lord, we have a fortify that Book to be true, as to the fo was then made as the Book says: for Catalogue of the evidences of the Dea writing——And in this there is ment made in 5 *H.* VIII. Pray, Sir, look upo

Spencer. I have seen this among the re and Chapter of *Paul's*.

Mr. Att. Gen. How long ago?

Spencer. I cannot directly tell.

Mr. *Pollexfen.* How long do you think

Spencer. Two years ago.

Mr. Att. Gen. That is since this conte

L. C. J. Ay, that is a little too lately

* The State of the question being, Whether the seven acres in *Shadwell*, was part of the ancient Inheritance of the Dean of St. *Pau*[illegible] so now Lessor of the Plaintiff; or part of *Wapping* Marsh, that had been drained by one [illegible], and after sold to the *Stephens*'s, un[illegible]

Mr. Serj *Lutwich.* Did you ſee it before Mr. *Neale* or Mr. *Baron* ordered a ſearch there?

Spencer. I cannot ſay particularly I did: I have ſeen this paper——

Mr. Att. Gen. Paper, man? It is a Parchment; pr'ythee mind what thou ſay'ſt: How long is it ſince you firſt ſaw that Parchment?

Spencer I believe I have ſeen it this ſeven years; but not that I can ſwear to have taken any particular notice of it.

Mr. Att. Gen. Where did you ſee it firſt, upon your oath?

Spencer. Among the reſt of the Deeds and Evidences that belong to the Dean and Chapter of *Paul's*.

Mr. Att. Gen. Upon what occaſion did you take notice of it firſt?

Spencer. Upon ſearching among the writings.

Mr. Att. Gen. Who did ſearch with you at that time, upon your oath?

Spencer. Mr. *Porter*.

L. C. J. Read it.

Mr. Att. Gen. Was it delivered to Mr. *Neale* before it was brought hither?

Spencer. It is brought here now among the Dean's other writings, we never uſe to deliver any out.

Clerk reads.] This is dated 2 *Eliz.* 1559. Books and other writings appertaining.

Mr. Serj. *Stringer.* Now we will read the leaſe to *Marcellus Hall*; wherein this is recited to have been made.

(*The leaſe in the Book was read, dated* 23 Feb. 5 Ed. VI. *for five-and-forty years, at* 10*l. rent.*)

Mr. Serj. *Stringer.* Then the next leaſe is in 2 & 3 *Phil. & Mar.*

[*Which was read.*

10 Dec. 2 & 3 Phil. & Mar. *from Dean* Fecknam *to* Marcellus Hall *for ninety years from* Michaelmas *before.*

Mr. Att. Gen. There is a licence to alter the Mill, which we ſhall prove he afterwards did.

Mr. Serj. *Stringer.* Your Lordſhip obſerves here were grounds and ſeveral houſes at this time lett, with the Mill and Ponds, and ditches to receive the water. After this, *Marcellus Hall* aſſigned to *Adrian Moor*, he in the year 1618, deviſeth it to his Wife *Mary Moor*; and in 1630, ſhe ſurrenders, and hath a new leaſe for lives.

Mr. Att. Gen. Shew your aſſignments, Mr. Serjeant, from *Marcellus Hall.*

Mr. Serj. *Stringer.* That we cannot do, nor need we, for we are not to derive our title that way, but the Church's title is ours. We will ſhew you Dean *Donne's* leaſe to *Mary Moor*, upon her ſurrender.

[*Which leaſe, dated* 14 May, 1630. 6 Car I. *for three lives, at* 10*l.* &c. *was read.*]

Mr. Serj. *Stringer.* Then *Mary Moor*, ſix years after, ſurrenders this leaſe, and takes a new leaſe for three lives in Dean *Winneff's* time, at 10*l.* a year rent, and 40*s* increaſe.

[*Which leaſe dated* 5 Aug. 1636. 6 Car. I. *was read.*]

Then another leaſe dated 5 March, 1640, 16 Car. I. *by Dean* Winneff *to* Samuel Whitwick, *and* John Winterburn, at 10*l. the ancient rent,* 40*s. before increaſed, and* 4*l. more now increaſed.*

Mr. Serj. *Stringer.* Thus far it ſtood upon leaſes for lives: this leaſe continued till 1669, till Mr. *Neale* bought this land, and then he renewed it from the now Archbiſhop, then Dean *Sancroft*, who raiſed the rent to 80*l.* during the life of *Freak*, who was the ſurviving life, and to 100*l.* after.

[*Which leaſe, dated* 12 July, 21 Car. II. 1669. *was read.*]

Mr. Serj. *Stringer.* We have brought it home now, my Lord, to the Leſſor of the Plaintiff: For we have ſhewn this leaſe was ſurrendered to Dean *Stillingfleet*; and thereupon he made a leaſe to *Garrard* and *Cratford*, which we have given an account of before. And ſo we have ſhewn a ſucceſſion of leaſes from the Church, for 130 odd years.

L. C. J. The laſt leaſe is at the rent of 240*l.* a-year, I think.

Mr. Serj. *Stringer.* Yes, my Lord.

Mr. Serj. *Maynard.* Have you done, Gentlemen?

Mr. Serj. *Stringer.* Yes, we have, till you give us farther occaſion, Brother.

Mr. Serj. *Maynard.* Then, may it pleaſe your Lordſhip, and you Gentlemen of the Jury, I am of Counſel in this cauſe for the Defendant, my Lady *Ivy*. The Plaintiffs have given you a ſort of evidence for a title; but the truth of it is, all that they ſay will not make a concluſion, ſuch as they would have from their Premiſes: For all that they have proved, is, that the Deans of *Paul's*, ſucceſſively one after another, have made leaſes. They did in the beginning tell you, they had had this land hundreds of years: But what have they had? and what leaſes have they made? But only a mill, a bakehouſe, a trough of lead, and all houſes, lands, meadows and paſtures thereto belonging. We do not deny but that they are to have a mill; their leaſes are alſo, even the new ones do moſtly follow the track and words that were uſed in Queen *Mary* and *Henry* the Eighth's times. But here is the truth of our caſe: That the Dean and Chapter had a mill, we agree; nay, more than that, we agree that they have eighteen acres that lie on the North ſide of *Ratcliffe* high-way; and alſo that they have another parcel of land, called the *Lynches*. That this may be underſtood, we now crave leave to deliver maps to the Court and the Jury.

Mr. Serj. *Stringer.* And we deſire ours may be ſeen too.

Mr. *J. Withins.* Aye, deliver in your maps, this is the only fit place for them.

(*Which was done on both ſides.*)

Mr. Serj. *Maynard.* Then, my Lord, I will go on. We agree, I ſay, they had a mill, which is now taken down and put in another place: We ſhall ſhew them where it did ſtand, and that was no part of the land now in queſtion. The Jury have ſeen the place, and I hope have had a ſatisfactory view of it. There was once a mill ſtanding, and there was once a pond, but that mill and pond do ſtand elſewhere. The land in queſtion, we ſay, was anciently marſh ground, and ſubject to the overflowing of the Water, and it is ſo to this day. In *H.* VIII's time, it was by one *Vanderdelf*, a *Dutchman*, drained. This, by Act of Parliament, *Richard Hill* was made owner of, and he convey'd it to *Stephins*, who was the Defendant's anceſtor, and whoſe heir ſhe is. And the boundaries are ſet down in that, and the ſubſequent conveyances, which cannot poſſibly ſtand with thoſe that their mill is ſaid to ſtand in. We ſhall ſhew by ſeveral Records the Queen had a title to it by a conveyance in way of mortgage to her; and this afterwards was conveyed back again to the anceſtor of my Lady *Ivy*. We yield they had a mill, and they have increaſed the rent ſufficiently upon it, not to need other men's land. They have houſes built upon it; I know not indeed how much, but I think it is near 1000*l.* a-year that it yields to them. If then we can demonſtratively ſhew you where our ground is, and where their's is, and if we affirm our title by Records and good Conveyances; then by a pretence to a mill, I hope they ſhall not grind us, or take away all our land.

Mr. Att. Gen. My Lord, and Gentlemen of the Jury, I crave leave to anſwer the Evidence that has been given, before I enter upon our title. They have ſpent a great deal of time to derive down a title to the Dean and Chapter of *Paul's*, to a mill, a bake-houſe, and ſome little ground thereto belonging. And truly, as Mr. Serjeant ſays, no man ever queſtioned the Dean and Chapter for their mill, and bake-houſe, and leaden trough. But the thing in queſtion is, ſeven acres and an half of land, which in the memory of man was marſh-ground; if you obſerved it. Gentlemen, upon the view how it lies, you know the *North* bound is the Dean's *Lynches*, the *South* bound is the *Thames Wall*, the *Weſt* bound *Foxe's-lane*, and the *Eaſt* bound is the *Hilly ground* that is called *Cock-hill*. And we ſay as to all this land, it is none of the Dean and Chapter's, nor ever did paſs, or was enjoyed by this leaſe; but we ſhall ſhew you it was under another leaſe. I muſt obſerve, that it is very ſtrange upon their own evidence, that a mill, *cum Pertinentiis*, ſhould paſs ſeven acres of ground; and a mill that was demoliſhed ſo long ago as in Queen *Mary's* time, (for ſo we ſhall plainly ſhew you it was) and that theſe lands, containing ſo conſiderable a revenue, ſhould not have a ſurvey taken of them, or a boundary made of the land, that they might know what was theirs, and what their neighbours. For your Lordſhip and the Jury may obſerve, in all the leaſes and conveyances down to this time, in Dean *Collet's* leaſe, and onward, there was nothing mentioned but a mill with the appurtenances, or a tenement with the appurtenances. But they have not one fixed boundary of their lands; and really it cannot be preſumed the Dean and Chapter ſhould be ſo ignorant. Beſides, in the ancient leaſe that they produced of *Ed.* VIth's time, there was a covenant to pay the quit-rent, as for lands holden of the manor of *Stepney*. And we did expect that they would have brought ſome of the Rolls and Records of that manor; and out of ſome ſurvey, there remaining, would have given a particular teſtimony of what lands belong to the Dean, and what do not. But in truth, we ſay this is properly marſh-land; for that will be your queſtion, Gentlemen, that you are to try, I believe, at laſt: Whether theſe ſeven acres, thus bounded on *Foxe's-lane*, *Weſt*; on the *Thames*, *South*; on the *Hilly-way*, called *Cock-hill*, or *Mill-ditch*, *Eaſt*; and on the Dean and Chapter's *Lynches*, *North*, be marſh-ground? The Dean and Chapter have given evidence of ſome leaſes, which upon the ſurrenders were delivered up to them; but there are none produced, they only read the entries in their Books. Now we ſhall demonſtrate that this mill of theirs was an overſhot-mill; for there is mention made of a leaden trough, which is the only proper inſtrument of an overſhot-mill. Therefore we will firſt ſettle (becauſe they themſelves will not) what is theirs; and then we doubt not to give you ſatisfaction that this was never any of theirs, but the undoubted Inheritance of the *Stepkins*; and not a foot of it belongs to any other man living. But further, ſince they will not, we ſhall produce a piece of evidence, which indeed we muſt thank Mr. *Neale* for; for he blabbing it about that he had a ſurvey of the manor of *Stepney*, which would do our work, put us upon ſearching there for it; and we have it here, and there you will find a particular of all the Dean's lands, under 33*s.* and 4*d.* quit-rent. And the particulars are thus deſcribed in that Book, (which ſhews that there was a tenement that ſtood by the mill, and that paid a quit-rent, and the other lands came under that quit-rent) Twenty acres, called *Shadwell-field*, that lieth on the North-ſide of *Ratcliff* high-way, known at this day; and all this piece of ground, of twenty acres, is built upon and improved; which was one part of the land that came under a quit-rent, but not pretended to be any part of this. The next is five acres, called the *Lynches*, and it appears by the Record to be but five acres, and ſo it is meaſured now. *Ratcliff* high-way went on the top of the hill, and this is called the *Lynch way*, not improved nor built upon; and is exactly abutted according to our Records, and decyphered by acres to an acre. Then comes the third parcel, and that only concerns you to enquire of, whether theſe ſeven acres and an half be parcel of that? And that is deſcribed in the Record to be a tenement, called *Derrick-hills*, which is a bake-houſe with a mill, and the leaden trough, the appurtenances of the mill, at the rent of 33*s.* and 4*d.* Theſe are all the parcels named of the Dean and Chapter's lands. And at the laſt trial when they produced the deed of purchaſe, whereby this was conveyed to the Dean, which I think was in *H.* III's time, it yielded but 3*l.* a-year in the whole, and now in time it is come to 2000*l.* a year, without this great gobbet, which they intend now, if they can, to ſwallow up. And now as to this parcel, all they can claim is but a mill, and in the latter leaſes, it is a houſe where the mill ſtood, and that we ſhall ſhew by Records where it ſtood; and it is ſaid to be called *Derrick-hills*, and ſituate on the *Eaſt* end of the marſh now in queſtion. And to go a ſtep farther, we ſhall ſhew that this was altered in Queen *Mary's* time; for in 5 *E.* IV. the Book wherein their leaſes is, makes mention of the mill as ſtanding, then in 10 *Dec.* 2 & 3 *Ph. & M.* there is a kind of myſtery which we ſhall by our evidence unriddle: For then though the tenant had above forty years in being, and to come, he muſt renew his leaſe from Dean *Fecknam* at that time. Now we ſhall ſhew that the 20th of the ſame *December*, this place where the mill then lately ſtood, was lett to *John Carter*, Oar-maker. There are in that place, at this day, lands and houſes that yield the Dean and Chapter an hundred pounds a-year, diſtinct from the *Lynches* and the *North* ground of *Ratcliff* high-way, and that is a very good improvement for a mill, and a bake-houſe, and a leaden trough, and a ditch for the water. Now by their leaſe in 1630, they recite that the mill was not worth the keeping up, and according to the power given them by the leaſe, 2 & 3 *Phil. & Mar.* to pull down the mill, it was pull'd down and built upon, and it came to yield them 100*l.* a-year, as it doth at this day. After this we ſhall call witneſſes to ſet forth, that in this place, in the *Eaſt* end of *Cock-hill*, in the memory of man, there was found the floor of the old mill, and there are thoſe living that can atteſt it. So we ſhall ſhew they are fiſhing in a wrong pool; they have ſufficient to anſwer their deed of purchaſe; and all the evidence that hath been given you, will appear to be be only to entertain the Court with an amusing nothing; and to take up the time. But we shall go yet a step further, and shew beyond all peradventure, that this land in question was marsh-ground: And the other side must admit, that if it be marsh-ground, the Dean and Chapter have nothing to do with it, never pretended to a foot of it, nor doth any tittle of their evidence mention marsh-ground. And truly we will admit it to them, if it be not marsh-ground we have nothing to do with it. So that, Gentlemen, your great question is, Whether this be marsh-ground, or not? And thereupon the main of the question will be about the *East* boundary alone, and no other: For that *Wapping-marsh* bounded *South* on the *Thames*, *North* on the *Lynches*, and *West* on St. *Catherine*'s, is no question, nor ever was in all the trials that have been. Therefore the only point that the evidence is to be applied unto, is about the Eastern boundary. That we lay to be *Cock-Hill*, anciently called the *Hilly-way*, or *Millbank*, now *Cock-Hill*; and in the Records of *Stepney* manor, it is called *Cornhill*: And it is a rising hilly ground, it appears to be so to this day; I appeal to the Jury who have seen it. Now that this was marsh-ground, and the Inheritance of the *Stepkins*'s, we shall prove by these steps: *First*, We shall produce an Act of Parliament made in 27 *Hen.* VIII. wherein the bounds appear to be plainly the same as now we say they are at this day; only now it is all built, that is all the difference, and the marsh doth thereby contain 130 acres. Now by that Act, the whole marsh is vested, as to one moiety, in *Richard Hill*, as assignee of *Vanderdelf* the *Dutchman*, who had drained it, and for his pains was to have one half, and he agreed with the participators, among whom *Stepkins* was one, and had 53 acres, and particularly this land. So that the Dean of *Paul*'s must derive a title from this Act, if he will have the land. But we shall shew how they colour their possession. Afterwards *Richard Hill*, 11 *Nov.* 37 *H.* VIII. he doth make a lease to the Dean and Chapter's miller, and that for thirty-four years, wherein you will exactly see the boundaries of the Act are pursued. After he had leased it to the Dean's miller, he passeth away the inheritance to *Thomas Stepkins*, in time, 16 *Apr.* 6. *Ed.* VI. *Marcellus Hall* the *miller*, after *Stepkins* had obtained the inheritance upon agreement between them, gets a lease from *Stepkins* of 128 years of the lands in question, as you may see by the bounds they are exactly the same; and this was in time 20 *Apr.* 6. *Ed.* VI. So the miller had now ground on both sides the way that is called *Cock-Hill*; on the *East* side by lease from *Hill*, on the *West* side by lease from *Stepkins*. Then in point of time we shall come to shew the lease made to *Roper*. For *Marcellus Hall*, after he had taken this long lease from *Stepkins*, 30 *Nov.* 2 & 3 *Phil* & *Mar.* doth demise the land in question to *Richard Roper*, for twenty-four years: and we shall shew that in all the Queen's time *Roper* was tenant. Then *Jasper Hill*, who was the Heir of *Richard Hill*, in 12 *Nov.* 5 & 6. *Ph.* & *M.* by deed, and afterwards 3 *Eliz.* by fine and common recovery, conveys all these lands particularly by name, and re-leaseth them to *John* and *Macheline Stepkins*, and the heirs of *John*; and so lodged the inheritance in the *Stepkins*'s, all but that which was thus out in a long lease to *Marcellus Hall*. We shall prove that before *Richard Hill* died, he entered into a Statute to *Vrvold* and *Salvago* for a great sum of money; and this statute comes to be extended 3 *Eliz.* and there this land, notwithstanding these leases, is seized and extended as *Hill*'s lands. We shall shew all this land upon a commission of sewers, had a survey taken of it. When we have shewn all these Records, and proved that this is marsh-ground, and not a witness of theirs but must acknowledge it to be marsh-ground (for that part of *Fox's-lane*, was raised at least nine foot, and so proportionably was the rest of the ground; and it appears at this day, that upon a high tide all their cellars are overflown), I think then you will make no doubt, whether this be our land or no. And to proceed in this order that I have opened, we will first shew you the survey. There was one thing I forgot about the eleven acres—

Mr. Serj. *Stringer.* What is it you read first, Sir?

L. C. J. What do you begin with, Mr. Attorney?

Mr. Att. Gen. Your Lordship observes they shew a lease from Dean *Feckman*, the 10 *Dec.* 2 & 3 of *Ph.* & *M.* Now on the 22 *Dec.* in the same year, we shall shew *Marcellus Hall*, by lease to *Carter*, butts it upon the *East* side of the mill.

L. C. J. I took the notes the last time of your evidence, and it began in *H.* VIIIth's time.

Mr. Att. Gen. My Lord, when we come to our title, we shall go on in the same method we did then; but now we are only shewing where the lands are.

L. C. J. Go your own way.

Clerk reads.] This Indenture, made the 22d day of *December*, in the second and third years of the reigns of our sovereign Lord and Lady *Philip* and *Mary*, by the Grace of God, King and Queen of *England*, *Spain*, *France*, both the *Sicilies*, *Jerusalem*, and *Ireland*, Defenders of the faith, Arch-Dukes of *Austria*, Dukes of *Burgundy*, *Millain* and *Brabant*; Counts of *Haspurg*, *Flanders*, and *Tyrol*; between *Marcellus Hall* of *Ratcliff*, miller, of the one part, and *John Carter* of *Ratcliffe*, oar-maker of *Stebunheath*, of the other part; witnesseth, That the said *Marcellus Hall* hath demised, granted, and to farm lett unto the said *John Carter*, that his wharf lying in *Ratcliff*, where late the mill stood, called *Ratcliff-mill*, adjoining on the *West* upon the *East* side of the mill-ditch, *alias* the mill-dam, reaching from thence *Eastward* 30 foot; and from the *North-east* corner of the said mill-dam, Southward to the River of *Thames*, 20 foot; to have and to hold all and whole the said wharf, as is before specified, with all commodities and profits belonging to the same, to the said *John Carter*, to his heirs, executors, and assigns, from the feast of St. *Mary* the Virgin, immediately following the date of these presents, until the end and term of 30 years.——

L. C. J. This lease was read the last time.

Mr. Serj. *Stringer.* Yes, it was so, my Lord.

Clerk reads.]———to be fully complete and ended, yielding and paying therefore for the same, unto the said *Marcellus Hall*, his heirs, executors, and assigns, ten shillings of lawful money of *England* yearly; that is to say, at the feast of the Annunciation of St. *Mary* the Virgin. And if it happen the said rent to be behind and unpaid at the said feast, in part or in all, by the space of one fortnight, and lawfully asked of the said *John Carter*, his executors, and assigns, then it shall be lawful to the said *Marcellus Hall*, his heirs, executors, and assigns, to distrain for his said rent so being behind, and the distress so taken, to keep until such time as the said rent with the arrearages, be fully satisfied and paid.——

L. C. J. For how many years is that?—*Mr. Att. Gen.* Thirty years.

L. C. J. Wha
Mr. Att. Gen.
Sir *J. Trevor.* I
lease, that so it m
cellent art at findi
L. C. J. Ay, c
Mr. Att. Gen.
L. C. J. But th
account of it on th
Mr. Att. Gen.
When did you first
Mr. *Williams.* A
Knowles. My Lo
foot long, and three
among other writing
L. C. J. How c
Knowles. As I wa
Mr. *Powis.* Pray,
looked there and fou
Mr. Serj. *Pemb.*
Knowles. My Lord
ever saw my Lady *Ivy*
Vicarer, that I had sev
my Lady desired me t
concerned *Stepkins*'s e
look them all over, fo
would do her a great k
And upon the fourth o
L. C. J. How was
Mr. Att. Gen. They
Mr. *Williams.* Did y
L. C. J. I ask you ag
Knowles. He was part
Mr. Sol. Gen. Wright
his Executor, and so he
Mr. Att. Gen. But pr
shewn to Mr. *Neale*?
Knowles. In the year
Uncle *Wright*, the writi
Neale's request, all the wr
Gray's-Inn, one *Cage*, I
there they were left three
among them.
Mr. Att. Gen. Were th
Knowles. There were tw
Mr. Att. Gen. Had you a
Knowles. I was arrested
presently after came and go
Knowles, I am sorry you w
Sir, said I; said he, I do b
Sir, said I: But says he, pra
That I will, two or three,
Ivy, or *Banister*, foist the D
ever I saw either of them,
said he.
Mr. *Williams.* Who was
you and Mr. *Neale*?---*Know*
Mr. *Williams.* It was at th
ny this.
L. J. C. Will he not? W
Knowles. I do say, I found
L. C. J. Read it; *read the*
a question or two. As I unders
look among *Winterburn*'s wri
Estate?---*Knowles.* Yes, my L
L. C. J. Where was that?--
L. C. J. And when did you
Knowles. I found the deed in
with me, or was in the *place* w
L. C. J. Was there any body
Knowles. No.
L. C. J. Then you found it
L. C. J. Did you read it?
Knowles. I did the outside; w
L. C. J. Nay, do not be angr
est so fast a man can scarce unde
you say you read it, what part wa
Knowles. The backside, the ou
Mr. *Williams.* There is noth
L. C. J. How did you gather b
my Lady *Ivy*?---*Knowles.* I only r
L. C. J. *Stepkins*'s name, you
Knowles What deed do you ask
L. C. J. That deed, the only de
Christian name?
Knowles. *Stephen Knowles.*
L. C. J. If I mistook you, I beg
ing this very deed now shewn to yo
Knowles. I thought you had mean
L. C. J. Well then, let that pass
now something concerning this deed
upon your oath, when saw you that
Knowles. I cannot say what day it
L. C. J. But, look you, if I mistoo
again), did not you say you found tha
writings of *Winterburn*'s, in a room,
foot wide, in your garret? Did not y
Lady *Ivy* first, upon the 2d of *Aug*
in *September* following? And did not
in your conscience, that in the year
among others, sent to the Chamber of

that they remained ethre there months, and then were brought back again to you; and you believe in your conſcience this was one of them? And did not you ſay, when I aſked you, how you came to know this belonged to my Lady *Ivy*; you ſaid, becauſe my Lady *Ivy* had ſpoke to you, to look if there was any thing belonging to *Stepkins*, and you read the outſide of the deed, and found *Stepkins*'s name, and ſo you knew it to concern her? Did not you ſay all this?

Knowles. I believe I did.

L. C. J. Now tell me then by the outſide of that deed, how thou canſt tell that it belonged to *Stepkins*? For if thou canſt, thou art more crafty than any body here, I believe.

Knowles. I thought it had been the long leaſe, for that has *Stepkins* on the outſide.

L. C. J. Well, let that paſs for a miſtake; we muſt now begin again upon a new matter. When firſt ſaw you that deed?

Knowles. In *September*, 1682.

L. C. J. How do you know that?--*Knowles*. I put my hand to it.

L. C. J. Did you read the inſide of that deed?

Knowles. No, I did not.

L. C. J. Look you then, we aſk you how you came to know it was a deed belonging to *Stepkins*?

Knowles. I read the backſide, and put my hand to it.

L. C. J. How came you to put your hand to this deed as belonging to *Stepkins*, when you never looked into the deed?

Knowles. When I found this deed to have written upon it *Marcellus Hall*, I did believe it was ſomething that concerned the *Stepkins*'s.

L. C. J. Let us ſee the deed now---(*which was done*) --You ſay that was the reaſon upon your oath?----*Knowles*. Yes, it was.

L. C. J. Then look upon it again, and do not be ſurprized, but let us have the truth come out, in God's name. Was that the reaſon?

Knowles. It was, my Lord

L. C. J. I would fain ſee Mr. *Sutton*, I have a queſtion to aſk him.

Mr. Att. Gen. He is here, my Lord.

L. C. J. Give Mr. *Sutton* his oath---(*which was done*)---Look upon the outſide of that deed, and upon your oath tell us whoſe hand-writing that is.

Sutton. All but the word (*Lett.*) is my hand-writing.

L. C. J. Are not the words *Marcellus Hall* all of of your hand-writing?

Sutton. It is.

L. C. J. Then how couldſt thou know this to belong to the *Stepkins*'s by the words *Marcellus Hall*, when you firſt diſcovered this deed in *September*, 1682, and you found it by yourſelf, and put your hand to it; and yet that *Marcellus Hall* be written by Mr. *Sutton*, which muſt be after that time?

Mr. Att. Gen. He ſays he knows it, becauſe he put his hand to it; I ſuppoſe he read ſomewhat of the inſide.

L. C. J. He ſaid the backſide, the outſide; he did not read the inſide.

Mr. Att. Gen. My Lord, I deſire our evidence may not be anticipated.

L. C. J. Mr. Attorney, I would not anticipate your evidence; but I muſt tell you by the way, your evidence anticipate themſelves: And this fellow, *Knowles*, without any more ado, has proved himſelf an errant, notorious knave. And if your evidence will blunder and ſpoil themſelves, I cannot tell how to help it. I knew, as ſoon as I ſaw the deed, that that was *Sutton*'s hand, I know his hand, as well as that you are Mr. Attorney.

Mr Sol. Gen. Pray, my Lord, give me leave to aſk him a queſtion, which I hope may clear all this matter, for it is plain the man is miſtaken.

L. C. J. Miſtaken! Yes, I aſſure you very groſly. Aſk him what queſtions you will; but if he ſhould ſwear as long as Sir *John Falſtaffe* fought, I would never believe a word he ſays.

Mr. Sol. Gen. Did you look into the middle of one of the deeds?

Knowles. Yes, I did.

Mr. Sol. Gen. Can you tell which you looked into the inſide of, and which you did not?

Knowles. The leaſe and ſome others I did, but I cannot particularly tell.

Mr. Sol. Gen. Then, my Lord, here is the caſe: Here are multitudes of deeds, and a man looks on the inſide of ſome, and the outſide of others; is it poſſible for a man to ſpeak poſitively to all the particular deeds, without being liable to miſtake?

L. C. J. Mr. Sollicitor, you ſay well; if he had ſaid, I looked upon the outſide of ſome, and the inſide of others, and wherever I ſaw either on the outſide, or in the inſide the name of *Stepkins*, or *Marcellus Hall*, I laid them by, and thought they might concern my Lady *Ivy*; that had been ſomething. But when he comes to be aſked about this particular deed, and he upon his oath ſhall declare that to be the reaſon why he thought it belonged to *Stepkins*, becauſe of the name of *Marcellus Hall* on the outſide, and never read any part of the inſide, when *Sutton* ſwears *Marcellus Hall* was written by him, what would you have a man ſay?

Mr. Sol. Gen. My Lord, I have but this to ſay; if there were never a deed delivered by *Knowles* to my Lady *Ivy*, or *Sutton*, where *Marcellus Hall*'s name was written on the backſide of it, but by Mr *Sutton*; I confeſs it were a ſtrong objection. But where there are other deeds, and a great many, a man may eaſily be miſtaken. It is impoſſible for any man, in a multitude of deeds that he finds among a great parcel, and delivers many of them out, to take it upon his memory particularly, which he looked on the inſide of, and which he looked on the backſide or outſide of.

L. C. J. Did he not give it as a particular reaſon of his knowledge, that they belonged to my Lady *Ivy*? For wherever he ſaw *Marcellus Hall* or *Stepkins*, he thought that belonged to her.

Mr. Sol. Gen. Wherever he ſaw thoſe names, that is either in the inſide or outſide.

L. C. J. Under favour, Sir, he did not ſay ſo; but poſitively ſaid, he knew it by that name. And you ſhall never argue me into a belief, that it is impoſſible for a man to give a true reaſon, if he have one, for his remembrance of a thing.

Mr. Sol. Gen. I beg your pardon, my Lord; as I apprehend him, he ſwore he looked into the inſide of ſome, and the outſide of others, and there were a great many of them.

L. C. J. And I beg your pardon, Mr. Sollicitor, I know what he ſwore as well as any body elſe: If indeed he had ſworn cautiouſly, and with care, it might have been taken for a ſlip, or a miſtake.

Mr. Att. Gen. My Lord, we muſt leave it upon its own weight; but we are not come to our title yet: I have the deed in my hand, which is a very old one, and therefore needs not ſuch exact proof He is miſtaken, we do own it, and I muſt appeal to the Court, whether a man may not be miſtaken in a great multitude of deeds.

L. C. J. Well now, after all this is done, let him give an account how he came to know this to belong to *Stepkins*, or my Lady *Ivy*, if he can. I ſpeak it not to prejudice your cauſe, but only to have the truth come out. But for the witneſs that ſwears, it may affect him I aſſure you. Give him the deed, and let him look upon it.—Look upon the inſide; and look upon the outſide too.

Knowles. I believe, my Lord, upon better conſideration, I have read this deed before now.

L. C. J. Very well; and yet you ſwore the contrary juſt now.

Knowles. I was in a maze, my Lord.

L. C. J. I am ſure thou ſworeſt wildly.

Mr. Sol. Gen. Pray what deed did you take it to be at firſt?

Knowles. The leaſe of 128 Years.

L. C. J. Pr'thee read it now to us.

Knowles Reads.---This Indenture made the 22d day of *Dec.*----

L. C. J. Between whom?

Knowles Reads.---Between *Marcellus Hall* of *Radcliff*, miller, of the one part, and *John Carter*, oar-maker, of the other part, witneſſeth, that the ſaid *Marcellus Hall* hath demiſed, granted, and to farm letten to the ſaid *John Carter*, all that wharf lying in *Radcliff*, where late a mill ſtood, called *Ratcliff-mill*.----

L. C. J. Can you ſay you ever read ſo much before?

Knowles. I believe I did.

L. C. J. When was it?----*Knowles*. In *September*, 1682.

L. C. J. Then you read it before you ſhewed it to my Lady *Ivy*?

Knowles. Yes, my Lord.

L. C. J. And you found what the contents were by reading?

Knowles. Yes, my Lord.

L. C. J. Did you read it through?---*Knowles*. No, I did not, I believe.

L. C. J. How far do you think you read?

Knowles As far as I have read now.

L. C. J. Did you find any thing there of the name of *Stepkins*?

Knowles. No, not in that I did not.

L. C. J. I would deſire to know of you, who it was that came to my Lady *Ivy*, to inform her you had ſuch and ſuch writings?

Knowles It was one Mr. *Vicarer*, about a trial that was to have been two or three years ago, at the Bar of the Court of *King's-Bench* here; but the cauſe did not then go on: After that Mr. *Vicarer* did tell my Lady, that one *Knowles* had a great company of writings that were *Winterburn*'s; and ſhe deſired him that he would pleaſe to talk with me, to ſee if I could do her any kindneſs or ſervice in any of thoſe deeds. The firſt time that I ſaw her was the 2d of *Auguſt*, as near as I can remember, and then I told her, I was Executor to *Winterburn*, and had a great many writings. Said ſhe, do you know the hand of *Stepkins*? if you do, and can find any writings that relate to *Stepkins*, you will do me a great kindneſs.

L. C. J. Did ſhe name any body elſe to you?

Knowles. She named one *Lun*, and one *Barker*, and one *Holder*, and ſeveral others; I do not remember all.

L. C. J. Was there any mention made of one *Collet*?—*Knowles*. No.

L. C. J. Was there of one *Donne*?---*Knowles*. Of one *Lun* there was.

L. C. J. Of one *Fecknam*?——*Knowles*. No.

L. C. J. Of one *May*?—*Knowles*. No.

L. C. J. One *Joan Hall*?----*Knowles*. No.

L. C. J. Was there any mention made of any *Hall*?

Knowles. Yes, there was.

L. C. J. What *Hall* did ſhe ſpeak of?

Knowles. I am not certain whether any *Hall* was named or no.

Mr. Att. Gen. He ſays, he is ſure there was of *Stepkins*, and ſeveral others, but not of any *Hall*.

L. C. J. He does ſo, Mr. Attorney. But now I would aſk him this queſtion, If there were no mention of any *Hall*, how came you to find out that this leaſe from *Marcellus Hall* to *Carter* ſhould affect *Stepkins*, or my Lady *Ivy*?

Knowles. My Lord, I will give you an account of that.

L. C. J. Ay, do if you can.

Knowles. This was at the firſt time that I ſaw my Lady *Ivy*, that this diſcourſe was between us; upon another diſcourſe, at another time, *Hall* was mentioned to me.

L. C. J. How many names did ſhe tell you of at firſt?

Knowles. I cannot remember them all.

L. C. J. He remembers as punctually as can be the 2d of *Auguſt* to be the firſt time that ever he ſaw my Lady *Ivy*; and then ſhe ſpoke to him of looking for writings that concerned *Stephins*, and *Lun*, and *Barker*; and he remembers ſuch a day, the fourth of *Sept.* 1682, he found the deeds; but he will not give any account how he came to know, by *Hall*'s name, that this belonged to *Stepkins*. I would fain know when you firſt heard of the name of the *Halls*?---*Knowles*. It was all within a month's time.

L. C. J. Who was it firſt ſpoke to you to enquire about the *Halls*?

Knowles. My Lady *Ivy* ſpoke to me about *Hall* when I gave her account of ſome deeds I had found.

L. C. J. How often did you look over the writings?

Knowles. Several times.

L. C. J. The firſt time, did you give my Lady *Ivy* an account that you had found any thing?

Knowles. Yes, I gave her an account of the leaſe of 128 years.

L. C. J. Did you find nothing elſe but that?

Knowles. Yes.

L. C. J. What did you find elſe?

Knowles. Several: I cannot give an account of all.

L. C. J. Did you find that leaſe, or this deed firſt?---*Knowles*. The leaſe.

L. C. J. When did you firſt find this deed?

Knowles. The 4th of *September* I found the leaſe, and within fourteen or fifteen days after I found the reſt.

L. C. J. How many deeds did you find out?----*Knowles*. Half a ſcore.

L. C. J. Who was by when you found the deeds the ſecond time?

Knowles

Knowles When I had found the leafe for 128 years, I laid it by, and looked further for other things, and found a mortgage which concerned myfelf, and that made me more eager to look for what might concern me befides; that I was not fo careful as I fhould have been of the leafe of 128 years, but mixed it among the writings again: but I told my Lady I had found fuch a deed, and fhe ordered Mr. *Banifter* to help me to find it again.

L C. J. Prythee anfwer me once more. Who firft put you in mind of looking after the *Halls*?---*Knowles*. My Lady *Ivy*.

L. C. J. Was any body by, when fhe fpoke to you to look after the *Halls*?---*Knowles*. Yes, Mr. *Banifter* was by.

L. C. J. Who elfe?---*Knowles*. Several of my Lady's fervants.

L. C. J. Name fome of them that were by.

Knowles. There was Mr. *Banifter*'s wife and his daughter by.

L. C. J. What day was it my Lady *Ivy* firft fpoke to you to look after the *Halls*?---*Knowles*. Within a week after I firft faw her.

L. C. J. Was it before you found the leafe you fpeak of?

Knowles. Yes, it was before.

L. C. J. How comes it to pafs then, that you did not find it at the firft looking, which was the 4th of *September*, when you found that leafe, you fay?

Mr. Att. Gen. We muft lay afide the teftimony of this man.

L. C. J. Ay, fo you had need.

Mr. Sol. Gen. Pray leave the deed in Court, we fhall have Mr. *Neale* too bufy with it elfe.

Mr. Att Gen. We fhall defire your Lordfhip to confider all the ufe we make of this deed is to prove, that the mill was removed to another place.

L. C. J. I do not know what it proves, but if you had kept your witnefs *Knowles* in the mill, I think you had done better than brought him hither.

Mr. Att. Gen: Swear Mr. *Banifter* and Mr. *Clerk*. (*Which was done.*)

Mr. Sol. Gen. Did you examine that with the Roll, Sir? (*Shewing him a paper.*)

Mr. *Clerk*. Yes Sir, I did examine that with the Book that Mr. *Northy* fhewed me; I think they fay he is fteward of the manor of *Stepney*; he read in the book, and I read the copy; and it is a true copy of a furvey of that manor, taken 25 *Eliz.*

Mr. Att. Gen. I heard fay you have the books of the manor here; pray let them be produced.

Mr. *Williams*. You are merry, Mr. Attorney; if it is a true copy, pray let it be read.

Clerk reads.] The Dean of St. *Paul*'s holds freely of fee or field, containing by eftimation- -

L C. J. Who is Lord of the manor of *Stepney* now?

Mr. *Powis*. My Lady *Wentworth* is Lady of the manor.

Clerk reads.] The Dean of St. *Paul*'s holds—

L. C. J. This bounds it on the Eaft, on the Dean and Chapter of *Paul*'s lands, and fo doth you no good.

Mr. *Williams*. Let them go on, my Lord.

Mr. Att. Gen. With fubmiffion, thefe are our exact boundaries.

L. C. J. Well, go on.

Mr. Att. Gen. We fhall go on; and with fubmiffion thefe bounds exactly agree with the bounds that are fet by the Act of Parliament for draining the marfh. Here is nothing that we can fee that they can claim but a mill and bake-houfe, and they are all bounded on the *Weft* by *Wall-Marfh*; and the *Lynches* are bounded in, part upon the *North*, and in part upon the *Weft*, and there was a little part of the marfh did run into the *North* bounds. But now we fhall come to our evidence; and firft we fhall fhew the Act of Parliament.

Which being Anno 22 *H.* VIII. *was read.*

Mr. Att. Gen. Next we fhall fhew *Richard Hill*'s conveyance by mortgage, to *Vivold* and *Salvago*.

Which Indenture of Mortgage was read.

Clerk reads.] This Indenture made the eighth day of *November*, in the 32d year of our Sovereign Lord King *Henry* the eighth, between *Richard Hill* citizen and mercer of *London*, on the one party, and *Anthony Vivold* and *Henry Salvago*, Merchants, of of the other party; witneffeth, That where the faid *Richard* before time was indebted unto the faid *Anthony Vivold* and *H. Salvago* in the fum of 560*l.* of lawful money of *England*, whereof they are of their free will have pardoned 280*l.* The faid *Richard Hill* by thefe prefents All that moiety of marfh ground being 130 acres, lying and being that is to fay, from *Ratcliffe* mill, that joins to the *Hilly Lynch* to *Ratcliffe* Town, on the party of the Eaft; to *Grafh Mill* by the *Hermitage*, on the party of the Weft; on the high-way, leading from *London* to *Ratcliffe* on the party of the North; and on the river of *Thames*, on the party of the South given and affured to the faid *Richard Hill*, by authority of Parliament, in the 27th year of the moft noble Reign to have and to hold---

Mr. Att. Gen. This doth veft the lands in queftion with others in *Vivold* and *Salvago*, as a fecurity for their money.

Mr. Sol. Gen. Now we fhall fhew a leafe from *Hill* to *Marcellus Hall*.

Clerk reads.] This Indenture made the eleventh day of *November*, in the 37th year of the reign of *Henry* the eighth; between *Richard Hill*, citizen and mercer of *London*, of the one party, and *Marcellus Hall* of *Ratcliffe*, miller, of the other party, witneffeth, that the faid *Richard Hill*, for the fum of fix pounds of lawful money of *England*, to him in hand paid, at the enfealing and delivery hereof, whereof the faid *Richard Hill* hereby acknowledgeth himfelf to be fully fatisfied, contented and paid; and whereof he doth clearly acquit and difcharge the faid *Marcellus Hall*, his Executors and Adminiftrators by thefe prefents, hath demifed, granted, and to farm letten, and by thefe prefents doth demife, grant, and to farm lett unto, the faid *Marcellus Hall*, a parcel of marfh-ground, lying and being at the Eaft end of the marfh that butts on *Ratcliffe* hilly marfh wall-bank, or wall belonging and the well *Shadwell*, containing by eftimation eleven acres and a half, more or lefs, abutting on *Thames* Wall, on the party of the South; to the lands called the *Dean*'s *Lynches*, on the party of the North; and on the wall that reaches from the *Lynches* to the Ifland, by the pond on the Weft, with all the foreland and foil. All which marfh-land is in the Parifh of *Stebunheath* to have and to hold

the marfh-land fo
Hall, from the feaft of the
coming, for thirty and fou

Mr. Att. Gen. This wa
ven acres and half an acre,
of our land. Next then v
Stepkins, which will bring

L. C. J. Read the refer

Clerk reads.] Yielding a
the faid *Richard Hill*, his h
lawful money of *England*,
of the Nativity of St. *Joh*
Birth of our Lord, and th

Mr. S. *Pemberton*. Pray
count of this leafe, where

Mr. Att. Gen. You hav

Mr. S. *Pemberton*. Yes
about it, becaufe we find

Mr Att. Gen. We can
for; but that will let you
have to fay for yourfelves.

Mr. S. *Pemberton*. You
account where you had it
ftion, Whether my Lady

Mr. Att. Gen. My Lor
intire; they would fain
quarrelling with our witn
impeach the validity of th
doubt not but we fhall g
give an account of the de

L. C. J. Nay, nay, G
dialogues and little heats.
fhall not hinder you whe

Clerk. This deed hath
marked fo.

Mr. Att. Gen. It has
L. C. J. Well, will y
Mr. Sol. Gen. Then
Clerk. This is alfo ma
dated 16 *Apr.* in the 6th

To all faithful Peopl
chard Hill, citizen and m
everlafting. Know ye
hundred and thirty pou
kins, alias *Stipkin*, of th
in the County of *Middl*
in hand paid, wherewit

L. C. J. Upon who
here?

Mr. S. *Stringer*. My
Plaintiff to be here; an
him fome queftions: if
we can.

Mr. Att. Gen. Nay,
fhould be examined no

Mr Bar. *Gregory*. I a
a while, and not break i

L. C. J. If you plea
may be long.

Mr. Bar. *Gregory*. I

L C. J. Nay, we w
remember we would ha
it; now you are like to

Clerk reads] And d
Stepkins alias *Stipkin*, hi
by this my prefent writ
twenty acres and a hal
in *Wapping-marfh*
joining on the weft fid
leading to *Ratcliff* To
thereunto belonging, a
the *Lynches*, called *Sha*
the next piece Weft a
acre, and the pond an
lying in the bottom of
that reaches from the
ven acres and a half of
miller; and alfo the
faid eleven acres and
acres; and alfo all th
tenure of *Richard Hi*
acres; and alfo all tha
faid *Richard Hill* hold
to fay, all that parce
Pond, containing by e
acres I bought of, and
St. All
lefs, of marfh-land, ab
to the lands of the D
Paul, called the *Lynch*
on the part of the Ea
on the part of the wef
to the faid four-and-
piece or parcel of wal
on par
ing of *William Kneve*
bank or wall are in
aforefaid hill and h
Town of *Ratcliff*
are part and parcel

was heretofore continually for the most part overflown and drowned with the water of the River of *Thames*, and all and singular messuages, cottages, houses, edifices, orchards, tofts foreland and soil, which were the said *Thomas Stepkins*'s before the overflowing and all and singular messuages, edifices, cottages cellars, sollars, orchards woods and underwoods, and all other the rest of my hereditaments whatsoever, in the Parish and Manor of *Stepney*, in the County of *Middlesex*.

Mr Att. Gen. Now we shall produce a lease from *Stepkins* to *Marcellus Hall*.

Mr. Serj. *Pemberton*. I hope they will give some account of this deed first.

Mr. Att Gen. When you say any thing against it, Mr. Serjeant, we will; but we desire now to go on with our evidence. Read that deed.

Clerk reads.] This has been read before, and is marked.

This Indenture made the twentieth day of *April*, in the sixth year of the Reign of our sovereign Lord King *Edward* the Sixth, by the Grace of God King of *England*, *France*, and *Ireland*; betwixt *Thomas Stepkins*, otherwise *Stipkin*, of the Parish of St. *Mary Matfelton*, in the County of *Middlesex*, without *Aldgate* beer-brewer, of the one part; and *Marcellus Hall* of *Ratcliff*, miller, of the other part; witnesseth, That the said *Thomas Stepkins*, otherwise *Stipkin*, for the sum of 50*l* of lawful money of *England*, to the said *Thomas Stepkins*, otherwise *Stipkin*, by the said *Marcellus Hall* at the ensealing hereof, well and truly paid and satisfied, and of the same doth clearly acquit and discharge the said *Marcellus Hall*, his Executors and Assigns, and every of them, by these presents hath demised, granted, betaken, and to farm letten; and by these presents doth demise, grant, betake, and to farm lett unto the said *Marcellus Hall*, all those his parcels of marsh-land lying and joining on the west side of hilly bank, or way called *Ratcliff-way* and the well adjoining to the way that goeth up to the *Lynches*, called *Shadwell*, lying in the east end of the marsh, containing by estimation of measure, three acres and a half, and all the next piece west, adjoining to the same, containing by estimation of measure, six acres and the pond, and two acres adjoining on the west side of the six acres, lying on the bottom of the hilly *Lynches*, adjoining north-west on the wall, which reacheth from the *Lynches* to the Island by the pond; all which eleven acres and a half, little more or less, abutteth on the *Thames* wall on the party of the south; to the Dean and Chapter of the Cathedral Church of St. *Paul*, called the *Lynches*, on the party of the north; and on the wall by the pond on the party of the west, and also all the *Thames* wall belonging to the said eleven acres and a half of meadow or marsh-land · which said piece or parcel of bank or wall, doth abutt on the south end of the aforesaid *hilly Bank*, or way reaching to the east side of it, which leadeth to *Ratcliff* Town on the party of the east, and on the wall in the occupation of *John Everard*, on the party of the west; and also all the foreland and soil down to the low-water mark of the River *Thames* belonging to the premises; all which in the east end of *Wapping* marsh, abutting on the aforesaid mill, and the *hilly Bank*, or way leading as aforesaid in the Parish and Manor of *Stebunheath*, otherwise *Stepney*, in the County of *Middlesex*, and now in the holding of the said *Marcellus Hall*, to have and to hold all the said parcels of marsh-land, foreland and soil, and every part and parcel thereof, to the said *Marcellus Hall*, his Executors and Assigns, from the feast of the Annunciation of St. *Mary* the Virgin, before the date hereof, to the end and term of one hundred twenty-eight years, thence next ensuing, yielding—

Mr. Sol. Gen. Read the Proviso.

L. C. J. Read the reservation of the rent.

Clerk reads.] Yielding and paying therefore yearly for the same, to the said *Thomas Stepkins*, his Heirs and Assigns, one pepper-corn, at the feast of the Annunciation—

Mr. Sol. Gen. Now read the Proviso.

Clerk reads.] And the said *Marcellus Hall* for himself, his Executors, and Assigns covenanteth and granteth to and with the said *Thomas Stepkins*, his Heirs and Assigns, that he the said *Marcellus Hall*, his Executors and Assigns, shall and will bear all manner of charges.—And it is further covenanted, granted, and agreed between the said parties, that it shall not be lawful for the said *Marcellus Hall*, his Executors or Assigns, to alienate or assign this present term of years, or any part thereof, without the special licence and consent of the said *Thomas Stepkins*, his Heirs and Assigns—

Mr. *Williams*. Pray, my Lord, will you give me leave to ask a question of Mr. *Banister*?

Mr. Att. Gen. My Lord, he has not been examined yet, they cannot, under favour, ask him any questions.

Mr. *Williams*. You have sworn him, and so he is under an oath, and we may doubtless examine him as your witness to this deed that you have read. Is that your name, Sir? *(Shewing the deed of* 16 April).

Banister. This is my name, written by my own hand.

Mr. *Williams*. When did you write your hand there, Mr. *Banister*?

Banister. The 16th of *April*, 1682.

Mr. *Williams*. Pray, Sir, look upon it again.

Banister. This is my hand, and I writ it myself when the deed was found; I writ a paper of such deeds as were found at the same instant of time.

Mr. *Williams*. And you writ it when you found it?

Banister. I writ that name at that instant of time.

Mr. S. *Pemberton*. When was it, do you say?

Banister. The 16th of *Sept* 1682.

Mr. *Williams*. Are you sure of it?

Banister. Yes, I am sure of it.

Mr. S. *Pemberton*. Just now it was *April*.

Banister. It was in *September*, 1682. I writ this paper at the same time.

L. C. J. Where did you write this name to this deed?

Banister. At. Mr. *Knowles*'s house.

L. C. J. When was the first time that you saw that deed?

Banister. The very same day that I writ my name on this paper.

L. C. J. Did he find the deed, or you? Let me see it. *(Which was done.)*

Banister. He had found that deed before, but had misplaid it, and desired my assistance to find it again.

L. C. J. Where did you find it?

Banister. In a garret in Mr. *Knowles*'s house.

Mr. Sol. Gen. Were there not a great many deeds there?

Banister. Yes, there were a great many.

L. C. J. Prythee look upon it again, and consider what thou say'st.

Banister. This is my name.

L. C. J. Very well; and how came thy name there?

Banister. This is the very deed I looked upon at that time.

L. C. J. Where did you first see that deed?

Banister. I was at the finding of it in a garret at Mr. *Knowles*'s house.

L. C. J. That was in *Sept.* 1682; you say.

Banister. Yes, in *Sept.* 1682. I never saw it before.

L. C. J. Pray, who are parties to that deed?

Mr. *Williams*. My Lord, it is the purchase of the Inheritance.

L. C. J. It is so, and how should that come to be in the possession of *Knowles*?

Banister. I never saw it before that time.

L. C. J. Read it again.

Clerk reads.] ---This is dated the 16th of *April*, in the sixth year of *Edward* the sixth. To all faithful---

Mr. Sol Gen. Certainly, my Lord he is under a mistake.

L. C. J. Ay, so is he sure enough, but a very foul one upon my word. But let us see if we can bring him out of it. Mr. *Banister*, let me ask you a question.

Banister. Yes, my Lord, if you please.

L. C. J. Then pray mind what I say, and consider of it. The 16th of *September*, 1682, was the time that you went on purpose to look for deeds at Mr. *Knowles*'s house?

Banister. I was there on the seventh day of *September*, and that was the first day that ever I came into Mr. *Knowles*'s house in my life.

L. C. J. There were some deeds, it seems, that Mr. *Knowles* had found before?

Banister. So Mr. *Knowles* said.

L. C. J. What became of those deeds he had found before?

Banister. As he told me he had mislaid them.

L. C. J. And when did you come to have an account that he had found those deeds first?

Banister. It was after I had paid him 3*l*. for water.

L. C. J. When was the first time that he spoke of it?

Banister. It was the fifth or fourth of *September*.

L. C. J. And when did you first go thither?

Banister. On the 7th of *September*, he desired me to come and help him, and assist him in finding out the deeds that he had mislaid.

L. C. J. What do you know of this deed?

Banister. We found one deed---

L. C. J. Look upon that carefully, is that your hand?

Banister. That is my hand.

L. C. J. Do you remember when you put your hand to that deed?

Banister. The paper I have in my hand was written at the same time.

L. C. J. Look upon that paper, and consider it well; and now tell us whether you found that deed first, or Mr. *Knowles*?

Banister. Mr. *Knowles*.

L. C. J. Now look upon it, and look upon it carefully, when was it?

Banister. This deed came into my hands the same day that I writ this note

Mr. Att. Gen. My Lord, we desire we may go on with our evidence, and not have them break in upon us to examine any such thing till their time comes; if they have any thing to object against our witnesses, let them take their time.

Mr S. *Pemberton*. Mr. Attorney, we are very regular sure in what we do; you produce a deed, and we desire an account how you came by that deed, and finding Mr. *Banister*'s name, who is your witness, and sworn by you, we would know of him what he knows of it.

L. C. J. Ay, ay, let truth come out, in God's name. Look upon it, Mr. *Banister*, once more. What say you to it?

Banister. This is the same deed, and my hand.

L. C. J. Upon your oath, Sir, when did you first see that deed?

Banister. This deed I saw the 7th of *Sept.* 1682.

L. C. J. Where?

Banister. In the garret at Mr. *Knowles*'s house.

L. C. J. Did you find it first, or Mr. *Knowles*?

Banister. I cannot tell, it may be I might.

L. C. J. Are you sure you then put your name to that deed?

Banister I did put my hand upon this same deed the 7th of *Sept.* 1682.

L. C. J. Prythee look upon it again, and look very carefully upon it. [*Which he did for a good while together.*

L. C. J. Now look upon your note again.

Mr. Att. Gen. Pray do so, and peruse it carefully, and see whether that Deed be in your note.

L. C. J. Nay, good Mr. Attorney, let us have no directions. What say you?

Banister. I set my hand to several deeds that I found there, to some writings on the 7th of *September*, and to others on the 16th.

L. C. J. Now tell us, which of them it was that thou didst put thy hand upon this deed?

Banister. I believe it might be the 7th.

L. C. J. Didst thou not see that deed before the 7th of *September*, 1682, upon thy oath?

Banister. No, never.

L. C. J. Who was with you when you first found that deed?

Mr. Att. Gen. Pray my Lord, let this note be read, and that will clear all.

L. C. J. No, by no means Mr. Attorney; he may make use of what notes he pleases, to refresh his own memory; but we will never support or prop up a perjury at that rate, I assure you, by a note. Was Mr. *Knowles* with you when you found that deed?

Banister. He was.

L. C. J. Do you take it upon your oath that that deed was found the 7th of *September*, 1682, in the garret at Mr. *Knowles*'s house?

Banister. I cannot tell which of the two it was, the seventh or the sixteenth.

L. C. J. Was it one of the two, upon your oath?

Banister. It was one of the two.

L. C. J. Now call Mr. *Knowles* again.

Mr. *Williams*. There he is, my Lord; if your Lordship please to look upon the deed---*Knowles*'s name was to it likewise, but scraped out.

L. C. J. Well, we will ask him about it But, Mr. *Banister* positively swears he was at the finding of this deed. What say you, *Knowles*?

Knowles. I know nothing of it, my name is not to it.

Mr.

Mr. *Williams*. Was your name ever to it, or not?

Knowles. No, never.

Mr. *Dobbins*. But it was to it at the trial in *Michaelmas* term.

L. C. J. Did you set your name to all the deeds you found in the garret?

Knowles. Yes, I did.

L. C. J. Upon your Oath, *Banister*, did you set your name to any deeds that he did not, that were found there?

Banister. I believe I might do so, I would not swear punctually to it.

L. C. J. Was he with you?

Banister. He was with me in the very same chamber.

Knowles. I do not know that ever I put my hand to that deed in my life.

L. C. J. Did you ever see that deed?

Knowles. I cannot say I did; I remember nothing of it.

L. C. J. I ask you once again, when you found this deed, was he with you?—*Banister*. Yes, Sir.

L. C. J. You, *Knowles*, did you ever trust him to look and search any deeds in your garret, but when you were by yourself?

Knowles. No, my Lord.

L. C. J. Then I would ask you upon your oath, because you are the persons that had these deeds in your custody; was there any deeds delivered out of your hand that you did not set your hand to?

Knowles. I believe there was never an one.

L. C. J. How came this deed, which he swears was found there, not to have your hand to it?—*Knowles*. I do not know that ever I saw it.

Mr. Att. Gen. Did Mr. *Knowles* say he was looking for deeds of his own concern, when he found the first deed?

Banister. He did say he had looked before, and had found some of these deeds, and then mislaid them, and desired my assistance to find them again.

L. C. J. What did he say to you at first?

Banister. He said he had been spoken unto by my Lady *Ivy*, to look for deeds that might concern her ancestors, and he had found some; but finding some also that concerned himself, he had mislaid my Lady's, and desired me to help him to find them again.

L. C. J. What employment have you under my Lady *Ivy*?

Banister. I am her rent-gatherer.

L. C. J. Her bailiff, I suppose: But now you speak of what my Lady *Ivy* desired of *Knowles*, I would ask you a question, lest it slip out of my memory, Were you present at any time when my Lady *Ivy* spoke to Mr. *Knowles* to look after any deeds?—*Banister*. Yes, I was.

L. C. J. Pray tell us whose deeds she desired him to look?

Banister. The deeds he said he had mislaid.

L. C. J. What were they?—*Banister*. The deed of *Richard Hill*, and the deeds belonging to *Stepney* and *Shadwell*.

L. C. J. What names did she mention to him, that she would have looked after?—*Banister*. She did mention some.

L. C. J. Upon your oath, did she mention any deeds made by Dr. *Donne*, Dean of St. *Paul*'s?—*Banister*. No.

L. C. J. By one *May*, Dean of St. *Paul*'s?—*Banister*. No.

L. C. J. Was one *Lun* named?—*Banister*. No.

L. C. J. Or one *Holder*?—*Banister*. Not that I know of.

L. C. J. Did she mention one *Joan Hall*?

Banister. I do not know that my Lady *Ivy* gave particular order for any of these names.

L. C. J. Did she, upon your oath, name *Marcellus Hall* to you?

Banister. No, my Lord.

L. C. J. Upon your oath, *Knowles*, was not he by when my Lady named *Marcellus Hall* to you?—*Knowles*. He was, my Lord.

Banister. I did not hear my Lady name that name at all.

L. C. J. No; he heard her give order for no particular deeds, neither for *Holder*, nor *Lun*, nor *Marcellus Hall*, but only concerning *Stepney* and *Shadwell*.

Sir *Edw. Herbert*. *Banister*, did he say he had before found them, and mislaid them?—*Banister*. Yes.

Mr. Att. Gen. Upon your oath, what deed do you take that to be which is produced?

Mr. *Powis*. Can you read it, yea, or no?

L. C. J. Mr. *Powis*, do you think my Lady *Ivy* sent *Banister* to look after deeds that he could not read? that were very pretty!

Mr. Att. Gen. What deed do you take it to be?

Mr. Sol. Gen. Let me ask you one question, Mr. *Banister*; Did you ever set your hand to any deeds that were not found at Mr. *Knowles*'s?

Banister. Yes I have.

Mr. *Lutwich*. Upon what occasion did you put your hand to them?

Banister. Because they were ancient deeds, and I was to look out where the hands were that they did concern.

Mr. Att. Gen. Pray now answer my question; look upon it, and tell me what deed do you take it to be?—*Banister*. It is a deed of sale to *Stepkins*.

L. C. J. It is so, you are in the right of it; and now upon your oath, where did you find that deed of sale?

Banister. My hand is to it, and this is one of the deeds, I take it to be so, that was found in the garret at Mr. *Knowles*'s house.

L. C. J. He has said so, I know not how often.

Mr. Att. Gen. He is not himself.

L. C. J. How can I help that, Mr. Attorney? But what he says, is plain.

Mr. Sol. Gen. Pray read over the note you have in your hand to yourself, and remember all the deeds that are particularly therein contained.

L. C. J. Let him read his note, (*which he did*) and now ask him what you will.

Mr. Att. Gen Is there any deed of the 16th of *April*, 6 *Edw.* VI. from *Hill* to *Stepkins*, in that note?

L. C. J. That is no fair question, Mr. Attorney.

Mr. Att. Gen With your favour, my Lord, I conceive it is; for that will make it plain that he is mistaken.

L. C. J. I believe he is; but with your favour, it is not a fair question; you are only to ask him, whether that deed given in evidence be there?

Mr. Sol. Gen. I would ask him one short question, my Lord, and I think it is a fair one.

L. C. J. Ay, in God's name, ask what fair questions you will, but no leading ones.

Mr. Sol. Gen. Now, Mr. *Baniſter*, you have conſidered of it; pray once more look upon the deed again---*(which he did,)*---Was that deed one that you ſigned then or no?

Baniſter. This is my name, but I cannot find the date of this deed in my paper. I cannot tell now whether it be one I found then or no.

Mr. Sol. Gen. Did you ſet your hand to any deeds that were found there, which you did not ſet down in your paper?

Baniſter. No, not that I know of, I do not know I did.

L. C. J. Prithee where didſt thou ſet thy hand to that deed?

Baniſter. I ſet my hand to the deeds that were found there at the houſe.

L. C. J. Did you ſet your hand to none elſe but what were found there?

Baniſter. I have ſet my hand to divers deeds beſide, but they are none of thoſe deeds that are in my paper.

L. C. J. Where did you ſet your hand to any deeds beſides?

Baniſter. To divers deeds I have ſet my hand at home.

L. C. J. Have you to any relating to the lands in queſtion?

Baniſter. I do not know that I have ſet my hand to any deeds relating to the lands in queſtion, but at Mr. *Knowles*'s.

L. C. J. To what purpoſe did you ſet your hand and name to the deeds you found at *Knowles*'s?

Baniſter. To the ſame intent to teſtify that I was at the finding of them.

L. C. J. To what end did you ſet your hand to any other deeds?

Baniſter. To the intent that I knew better where the lands did lie than ſhe did; and when my Lady found any deeds, I ſet my hand to them, and then found the places where the lands lay.

L. C. J. Thou haſt had a fair time to conſider of that deed; canſt thou ſee here to what place that deed relates, by this mark?

Baniſter. I cannot find the date of the deed in my paper.

L. C. J. But where do you think you did put your name to that deed?

Baniſter. I cannot tell whether I did it at that time or no, but this is my name.

L. C. J. I know thy name is there, man; I read it two hours ago. but did you put your hand to that as one of the deeds that you found in *September*, 1682, when you were at Mr. *Knowles*'s, or not?----*Baniſter.* I cannot tell.

L. C. J. Doſt thou believe thou didſt not?----*Baniſter.* I cannot tell.

L. C. J. Canſt thou tell the reaſon why thou didſt ſet thy hand to it?

Baniſter. Certainly becauſe I was at the finding of it; I know no otherwiſe.

Mr. S. *Pemberton.* Now pray look upon this deed *(ſhewing him another)* and ſee whether that be your name or not?

Baniſter. Yes, my Lord, I will.

Mr. S. *Pemberton.* Is that your name?

Baniſter. Yes, it is; this is one of the deeds that was found at Mr. *Knowles*'s.

Mr. S. *Pemberton.* You ſaid ſo as to the other two.

Mr. Att. Gen. But he was not ſo poſitive in it.

Baniſter. This is rat-eaten, and ſo I know it again; and there is a rat-eaten deed ſet down in my paper.

L. C. J. Let him be as poſitive as he will, he has been forſworn five times.

Mr. Sol. Gen. He was confounded with a miſtake of the deeds, he having ſet his hand to ſo many.

L. C. J. They are perjured both of them plainly; that is the truth of the matter.

Mr. Att. Gen. I hope the folly of our witneſſes in ſuch circumſtances, ſhall not rob us of our own land, and that it appears to be plainly.

L. C. J. God forbid but you ſhould have your own land; but by the Grace of God, if I can help it, you ſhall never have a foot of land by forſwearing and perjury.

Mr. *Williams.* When did you find that deed?

Baniſter. The 16th of *September*.

Mr. *Williams.* Where?---*Baniſter.* In the garret at Mr. *Knowles*'s.

Mr. *Williams.* Are you ſure of it?

Baniſter. Yes, I am ſure of that deed, becauſe it is rat-eaten.

Mr. *Williams. Knowles*, pray, do you look upon it, what ſay you to that deed?

Knowles. This is my hand, and this is one of the deeds that was found there at that time.

Mr. *Williams.* Pray read the date of that deed there.

Clerk reads.] This indenture, made the 13th day of *November*, in the 2d and 3d years of *Philip* and *Mary*---

Mr. S. *Pemberton.* That is a deed from *Marcellus Hall* to *Roper*; how ſhould that come to be at *Knowles*'s?

L. C. J. They have ſworn it.

Mr. Att. Gen. They go about to blemiſh our deeds by the folly of our witneſſes, which we cannot help. We however leave the deeds to the Jury, and let them ſee if thoſe ſeals and other things look like counterfeit.

L. C. J. Well, go on, the Jury will have the deeds with them.

Mr. Att. Gen. My Lord, we did before produce a conveyance from *Richard Hill* to *Stepkins*. It reſted not there, that conveyance had no legal execution; thereupon there was a fine and recovery by the heir of *Hill*; and what was the occaſion of that, will appear by the deed.

Clerk reads.] This Indenture made the 12th day of *November*, in the 5th and 6th years of the Reigns of our ſovereign Lord and Lady, *Philip* and *Mary*, by the Grace of God King and Queen of *England*, *Spain*, *France*, both the *Sicilies*, *Jeruſalem*, and *Ireland*, Defenders of the Faith; Arch-Dukes of *Auſtria*, Dukes of *Burgundy*, *Millan* and *Brabant*; Counts of *Haſpurg*, *Flanders* and *Tyrol*: between *Jaſper Hill*, ſon and heir of *Richard Hill*, late Citizen and Mercer of *London*, of the one party; and *Macheline Stepkins*, late wife and executrix of the laſt will and teſtament of *Thomas Stepkins*, and *John Stepkins*, ſon and heir apparent of the ſaid *Thomas*, of the other party, witneſſeth, That whereas the ſaid *Richard Hill*, father of the ſaid *Jaſper* amounting in the whole to the ſum of 200*l* by the ſaid *Macheline* And where variance concerning all that parcel of marſh-land unto St. *Katherine*'s, which the ſaid *Richard Hill* bought of *Cornelius Vanderdelf* for the aſſuring all that *Wapping-marſh*, the ſaid *Richard Hill* ſtands bound in an obligation of which condition, that he ſhould make by a certain day, a good, ſure, ſufficient, indefeaſible of and in all thoſe parcels of marſh-land, lying in *Wapping*-marſh; that is to ſay, all that with ſix acres of marſh, now in the tenure or occupation of one *Knevett*, or his aſſigns, and all thoſe lying in the Eaſt and in the tenure of one *Miller*; that is ſay, all the bank, containing by eſtimation three acres and an half; and all thoſe next adjoining, by meaſure ſix acres or more and two acres by eſtimation of meaſure lying in the bottom of the *Lynches*, and reacheth from the *Lynches* to the Iſland by the pond; and alſo that parcel divided into twain ſix acres; and alſo that holds in his own hands; that is to ſay, all that parcel with the iſland and pond, containing by eſtimation of meaſure, five acres and of, and in all thoſe parcels lying on the weſt ſide of the pond, containing in the whole fixteen acres by meaſure; all which ſaid fixteen acres to *Gravel-lane*, the ſaid *Robert Hill* had in his own occupation reaching to *Gravel-lane*, ſometime plowed and ſown by one *Richard Clayton*, and now in the occupation of one *Cooper*, butcher, and lying on the eaſt ſide of *Gravel-lane* towards *London* fields, which was conveyed to him from one *Richard Tyrrell*; and alſo all that marſh in the tenure of one *Clayton*, butcher, one *William Cound*, butcher, ſeventeen acres and of *Edward Aſh*, four acres; and alſo all the lands, tenements, rents, houſes, ponds, fiſhings, mills, to the low-water-mark of the River *Thames*, and all trees For the appeaſing all variances and ſuits, the ſaid parties to this Indenture have fully condeſcended and agreed in form following; that is to ſay; The ſaid *Jaſper Hill*, for the ſum of 1200*l.* of lawful money of *England*, in which he acknowledgeth himſelf to be truly indebted to the ſaid *Macheline* and *John Stepkins*, doth give, grant, bargain, ſell to the ſaid *Macheline* and *John Stepkins* all the ſaid marſh-ground lying in *Wapping*-marſh, with all manner of lands, tenements forelands, ways, trees to the low-water-mark with the appurtenances lying and being in without or elſewhere within the pariſhes their heirs and aſſigns for ever, all the right, title together with all evidences and writings diſcharged of all former charges, incumbrances by the ſaid *Jaſper Hill*.---

Mr. Att. Gen. Next we ſhall ſhew that *Marcellus Hall*, that had this long leaſe, and had demiſed the ſeven acres down from *Shadwell* to *Roper*, doth on the 14th of *November*, in the 5th and 6th years of *Philip* and *Mary*, ſurrender the remaining four acres to *Thomas Stepkins*; and then we ſhall ſhew it was demiſed to *Fox*, who was the firſt builder and made *Fox's-lane*.

Mr. Sol. Gen. Your Lordſhip doth obſerve, that the licence was to aſſign the whole eleven acres and an half, but he did aſſign but ſeven.

Clerk reads.] This is dated on the 14th of *November*, in the 5th and 6th years of King *Philip* and Queen *Mary*.

To all whom this preſent writing ſhall come; I *Marcellus Hall* of *Ratcliff*, miller, ſend greeting in our Lord God everlaſting. Whereas *Thomas Stepkins* hath by his Indenture, dated the 20th day of *April*, in the 6th year of King *Edward* VI lett to me the ſaid *Marcellus Hall* on the weſt ſide with the *Thames* wall thereto belonging, with the foreland and ſoil for one hundred and twenty and eight years: know ye that I the ſaid *Marcellus Hall*, for the ſum of 30*l.* of good and lawful money of *England* in hand paid have by theſe preſents remiſed, releaſed, and abſolutely confirmed, to the ſaid *John Stepkins*, his heirs, executors and aſſigns, all ſuch eſtate, right, title, intereſt, term of years, eſtate, property, claim and demand, which I, or any perſon to my uſe, have, or ought to have, or at any time ſhall to have in, or to four acres of marſh-ground, abutting eaſt on the green bank, or way through, ſix acres leading up to *Ratcliff* way, which way adjoineth to the weſt ſide of the lands in the occupying of *Roper*; which ſaid lands was made over with the leave and licence of the ſaid *Thomas Stepkins*, to the right worſhipful for the term of ninety-three years; and weſt on the field, in the occupying of *John* north on the *Lynches*, and ſouth of, in, or to the *Thames* wall abutting eaſt on the ſouth-weſt way, as aforeſaid down to the low-water-mark of the River of *Thames* So that neither I, my executors or aſſigns, any right, claim, demand or any part thereof but from all ſhall be utterly excluded and debarred for ever---

Mr. Att. Gen. Here is a fine levied, *Quin' Trin'* 3 *Eliz.* they had beſt aſk where that was found too! Is not that forged?

[*The Fine was read.*]

Mr. Sol. Gen. Here is a recovery alſo, and a deed to lead the Uſes: in which recovery the tenants vouch *Jaſper Hill*, who voucheth over the common vouchee. [*The Recovery was read.*]

L. C. J. Read your deed to lead the uſes.

Clerk reads.] This Indenture made the 12th day of *May*, in the fourth year of the reign of our ſovereign Lady *Elizabeth*, by the Grace of God, Queen of *England*, *France*, and *Ireland*; Defender of the Faith, &c. between *Macheline Stepkins* of the one party, and *Edward Buggin* Where it was concluded, fully condeſcended and agreed between the parties to this Indenture, that they the ſaid *Edward Buggin* ſhould in the term of the *Holy Trinity* recover to them by writ of *Entry ſur Diſſeiſin in le Poſt*, to be had againſt the ſaid *Macheline* and *John*, before the Queen's Majeſty's Juſtices of the Common-Pleas at *Weſtminſter*, for that time, being according to the uſe of former recoveries one hundred acres of freſh marſh, within the pariſhes, towns, fields And it was fully agreed between the ſaid parties, that the ſaid recovery ſhould be to the uſes---

Mr *Williams.* Mr. *Baniſter*, pray, Sir, look upon this deed, and ſee whether your name be to that deed or no? *(Shewing him the Surrender of* Hall.)

Baniſter. This is my name.

Mr. *Williams.* Was Mr. *Knowles*'s hand to that deed?

Baniſter. I cannot tell.

Mr. S. *Pemberton.* Did not he and you put your hands together to it?

Baniſter. I did not make it, I did not forge it.

Mr. S. *Pemberton.* No, I do not think you did, you have not brains to o it.

Mr. *Williams.* Where did you find that deed?

Mr. S. *Pemberton.* How came you to put your hand to it?

L C. J. Is it one of the deeds of purchaſe?

Mr. S. *Pemberton.* Yes, it is; and therefore we would know, ſince Mr. *Knowles*'s name is to it, how it came there.

L. C. J. Is it the ſurrender made by *Marcellus Hall* to *John Stepkins*?

Mr. *Williams.* Yes, my Lord, it is.

L. C. J. Let me ſee it---His name, I believe, has been there.

Mr. *Williams.* Do you know any thing of the raſing of it out?

Baniſter. No, not I.

Mr. *Williams.* You, *Knowles*, were you at the finding of that deed?

Knowles. I ſet my hand to none but what I found.

L. C. J. But what do you ſay to that deed?

Knowles. I do not remember this deed at all; I cannot ſay any thing to it.

L. C. J. Was your name to it?

Knowles. Here is my name, but I do not know who put it there.

L. C. J. Is that your writing, *Baniſter*?

Baniſter. That on the backſide is.

Mr. *Williams.* Look into your note, that you may not out-run yourſelf. Why did you ſet your hand to it?

Baniſter. I ſuppoſe it was one of the deeds found there.

Mr. *Williams.* How ſhould it come there? It belonged to the purchaſer.

Mr. Att. Gen. Now we ſhall go to matter of record again. *Richard Hill*, it ſeems, before the leaſe made to *Marcellus Hall*, entered into a Recognizance in 4 *Eliz.* this is extended, and that will ſhew it to be *Richard Hill*'s eſtate.

Mr. *Powis* Can you object any forgery of Records, pray?

Mr. Sol Gen. Pray Sir, look upon that *(to the Witneſs)*; where did you examine that?

Witneſs. I examined this at the *Rolls*.

Mr. *Williams.* Is it a true copy, upon your oath?---*Witneſs.* It is.

L. C. J. Read it.

Clerk. This is teſted at *Weſtminſter*, 17 *Jan.* 4 *Eliz.* And here is an inquiſition taken the 6th of *April*, in the ſame year.

Mr. Att. Gen. We will read that part of the Inquiſition that concerns our queſtion; for the eaſt bound is only in queſtion now. *(It was read.)*

Mr. Att. Gen. Was this produced at the former trial, the firſt trial?

Sutton. No, I think not in *Michaelmas* Term.

Mr. Sol. Gen. Then we ſhall ſhew an Inquiſition upon a commiſſion of ſewers.

Mr. Att. Gen. The land in queſtion is every foot of it in the marſh; and that they muſt acknowledge they have no title to.

Mr. *Williams.* This is an inquiſition which they produce, taken before a commiſſion of ſewers. I deſire to know how that comes to lie in a private hand, for it is the original Inquiſition, and ought to remain with the officer.

Mr. Att. Gen. The whole intereſt of the marſh was ours, therefore it might well be left with us.

Mr. S. *Pemberton.* Under favour, good Mr. Attorney, ſuch things ſhould be kept by the Clerk to the Commiſſioners.

Mr. Att. Gen. How many trials has this been produced at?

Mr. S. *Pemberton.* With ſubmiſſion, my Lord, this that they produce being an Original, may very well come under great ſuſpicion, in regard it ought to be brought in by the officer, in whoſe cuſtody it ought to remain.

Mr. *Williams.* It is not a thing of bare intereſt between party and party, but a thing that concerns the publick, and therefore ſhould be brought in the officer's cuſtody.

L. C. J. Read it *de bene eſſe*; let us ſee what it is.

Mr. Att. Gen. My Lord, I would aſk Mr. *Sutton*, was not this produced and read before the trial in *Michaelmas*-Term laſt?

Sutton. It was produced in Court twelve years ago.

Mr. Sol. Gen. Was it allowed as evidence?---*Sutton.* Yes, conſtantly.

Mr. Att. Gen. Pray read it.

Mr. *Williams.* Pray who has had it in keeping all this while?

Sutton. My Lady *Ivy* brought it to me among her writings at firſt.

L. C. J. Read it.

Clerk reads.] The verdict and preſentment of us the Jurors, as well of all defects, annoyances, within the limits or bounds of *Wapping*, and *Wapping*-marſh, from *Graſh*-mill to the mill at *Ratcliff*, that is to ſay, the 20th of *December*, *Anno Dom.* 1572, and in the 14th year of the Queen's Majeſty's Reign that now is.

The names of the Freeholders within *Wapping*-marſh, and the number of acres contained within the ſame marſh, with all the names of the occupiers thereof.

Firſt, *John Stepkins*, Gent. Free-holder, for a parcel containing twenty-two acres, in the tenure of *Richard Ew* *Benedict* Gent.

Mr. Att. Gen. You may ſkip over a great deal, and read only that which conduces to the queſtion.

Clerk. No one can read it very well, I think. *(Reads)* On the weſt ſide of *Gravel lane*, containing 68 acres---Is that it?

Mr. Att. Gen. No, go to the eaſt ſide.

Clerk reads.] ---Freeholders; one parcel containing ten acres, in the tenure of *John Hodges* and *John Gee*, *John Stepkins*, Gent. two parcels, containing twenty acres, in the tenure of *John Cooper*, and *John Harding*, *John Stepkins*, Gent. One parcel, containing four acres, in the tenure of *John Stepkins*. One parcel, containing twelve acres, in the tenure of *John* *Roger James*, Freeholder. Two parcels, containing ſix acres, *Robert Hemmings* and *John Stepkins*. One parcel, containing one acre and an half, *Richard Roper*. One parcel, containing ſix acres, in the tenure of *Richard Roper*.

All which parcels be on the eaſt part of *Gravel-lane*, containing ſixty acres--- Then here is ſomewhat interlined and ſtruck out again.

Mr. *Williams.* This doth not concern the Church.

Mr. Att. Gen. No more it doth not, as you ſay, indeed, for they cannot claim any of the marſh. Now we ſhall ſhew a warrant three years after, from the Commiſſioners to ſurvey.

Clerk reads.] ---This is dated the 18th of *July*, in the 17th year of the

moſt proſper
God, *&c.*

To our wel
as, the Quee
day of *April*,
vey and view
near the Tow
not only to c
order for the
ſhall ſeem goo
your wiſdom a
commanding y
ther the work
and decrees as
appoint; and t
made expendit

and further, w
to provide for a
workmen

your ſo doing, t

Mr. Att. Gen.
ginning, and ſhe
a fine was levied

Clerk reads.] T
of the Reign of o
nourable Sir *Will*
ſurer of *England*;
Highneſs's moſt h
her Majeſty's Att
jeſty, and to her
Whereas *William*
the determination
cember

hath commanded t
and Sir *Thomas Bro*

ſhould be owing
of the ſaid ſum of 7
with them the ſaid
heirs, executors
the ſaid ſum into the
ment

of, and in one cloſe
manor of *Yewel*; and
tenement, with the ap
of *John Stout*; and 19
ſaid manor

Mr. Att. Gen. Wh
Clerk reads.] This
Mr. Sol. Gen. This
there is the Re-grant.

(Which being und
Regis, *was rea*

Mr. Att. Gen. Part of
L. C. J. Ay, I have
laſt trial.

Mr. Att. Gen. Mr. S
Mr. *Williams.* A cop
Sutton. At the *Rolls* C
Mr. Att. Gen. It is a
Record is forged, Mr. *I*
Mr. *Williams.* I kno
it, let us ſee what it is.

(The Copy of a deed
L. C. J. Then the nex
25th of *January*, 4 *Eliz.*
Adminiſtrator of *Vivold* an
Mr. Att. Gen. We did
find, I think: Here how
Clerk. This is ſigned
Feb 1561.
Mr. Att. Gen. Here is
not material.
L. C. J. That is true;
Clerk. This is a bond o
ſuch, That whereas one R
Hill 3 *Dec*
taken and acknowledged---
Mr. Att. Gen. There is
but to confirm the belief of
ceipt of the purchaſe-mone
Clerk reads.] This is date
Elizabeth. Be it known unt
of *Wormly* have ha
John Stepkins for
the full ſum of 1338*l.* of law
payment of all ſuch purchaſ
Mr. Att. Gen Then the
John Stepkins; but that is le
L. C. J. Well, then there
Mr. Att. Gen. We have d
cords, and now we ſhall com
And firſt we ſhall begin wi h
the land by the rents, and pa
L. C. J. Prove what you w

Mr. Att Gen. Mr. *Knowles*, have you received the Dean's rents?

Knowles. For the uſe of Mr. *Neale* I have.

Mr. Att. Gen. What are the rents of the eaſt ſide of *Cock-hill?*

Knowles. About 100*l.* a year.

Mr. Sol. Gen. What are they?—*Knowles.* Houſes.

Mr. Att. Gen. All houſes?—*Knowles.* Some houſes, ſome ground-rents.

Mr. Att. Gen. What is the rack-rent?—*Knowles.* About 100*l.* a year.

Mr. *Williams.* Which houſes do you ſpeak of, Mr. *Knowles?*

Knowles. On the eaſt ſide of *Cock-hill.*

Mr. Att. Gen. Do you know the *Lynches?*—*Knowles.* Yes, I do.

Mr. Att. Gen. Who receives the rents of that ground?

Knowles. Mr. *Neale* did.

Mr. Att. Gen. Have you received the rents of the twenty acres?

Knowles. Yes, for Mr. *Neale* I have.

Mr. Att. Gen. Theſe three together, what are they all?

Knowles. About 2000*l.* a year.

Mr. Att. Gen. All this the Church of *Paul*'s has, beſides the lands in queſtion.

Mr. *Williams.* You ſay that part is worth 100*l.* a year?—*Knowles.* Yes.

Mr. S. *Stringer.* How much land might it contain?

Knowles. It is a matter of the length of the hall.

L. C. J. And how broad is it?—*Knowles.* Not very broad.

Mr. Att. Gen. Now then to come to the lands in queſtion; Do you know *Mariner's-ſtreet?*—*Knowles.* Yes.

Mr. Att. Gen. Who is in poſſeſſion of that, and receives the rents of it?

Knowles. Mr. *Neale.*

Mr. Att. Gen. What ſay you to *Griffin's-Alley?*

Knowles. Some of it is in mortgage; Mr. *Babington* had it, but for Mr. *Neale*'s uſe.

Mr. Att. Gen. What ſay you to the water-houſe?

Knowles. That Mr. *Neale* himſelf has.

Mr. Att. Gen. Theſe are the things in queſtion; do you know that which is called *New———?*—*Knowles.* That is Mr. *Neale*'s too.

Mr. Sol. Gen. Our leaſe of 128 years expired but in the year 1680; and we could not come at it till then, and we had it not till 1682, and that anſwereth their poſſeſſion.

Mr. Att. Gen. Now we ſhall call our witneſſes to prove it marſh-ground. Swear *Thomas Hughes.* (*Which was done.*)—Do you know *Wapping*-marſh?—*Hughes.* Yes.

Mr. Sol. Gen. Do you know the houſes in queſtion?

Hughes. Which houſes?

Mr. Sol. Gen. The houſes now in ſuit for?—*Hughes.* Yes, I do.

Mr. Att. Gen. How long have you known them?

Hughes. There was no houſes when I knew it firſt.

Mr. Att. Gen. Do you know *Cock-hill?*—*Hughes.* Yes.

Mr. Att. Gen. Do you know *Foxe's-lane?*

Hughes. Yes; I did know it before it was built.

Mr. Att. Gen. Did you know the houſes that lay on the eaſt ſide of *Foxe's-Lane?*—*Hughes.* What houſes there?

Mr. Att. Gen. Did you know any houſes there formerly?

Hughes. I know not what you mean.

Mr. Att. Gen. I aſk you again, do you know *Foxe's-Lane?*

Hughes. Yes; it was a bank before it was built.

Mr. *Powis.* Do you know the *Lynches?*

Mr. Att. Gen. Nay, let us aſk but one at once, pray. I will aſk you a plain queſtion; Did you know the marſh before it was built upon?

Hughes. Yes, Sir, that I did.

Mr. Att. Gen. How far did the marſh-ground go?

Hughes. To *Cock-Hill* Eaſtward, as far as the broad bridge; Weſtward, as far as *Foxe's-Lane.*

Mr. Att. Gen. Was all that marſh-ground?

Hughes. The River of *Thames* did flow round about it, and there were bogs, trees and buſhes, and ſuch things.

Mr. S. *Lutwich.* Did you know the place where *Ratcliff* mill ſtood?

Hughes. According to report I did.

Mr. S. *Lutwich.* Ay, where was that?—*Hughes.* Juſt at *Bell-wharf.*

Mr. S. *Lutwich.* Upon which ſide of *Cock-hill?*

Hughes. In *Shadwell Hamlet.*

Mr. Att. Gen. That is right.

Mr. *Powis.* Was that like the other end of the marſh?

Huges. The River came in there wholly.

Mr. S. *Lutwich* At high flood does the water come in there at this time?

Hughes. It did at every tide high and low formerly, now it is dam'd up.

L.C.J. Did the tide come up to that you call *Foxe's-lane?*—*Hughes.* Yes.

L.C.J. Then that makes an end of the queſtion: It cannot be as you ſay.

Mr. Att. Gen. How ſo, my Lord?

L. C. J. How could it be an overſhot-mill? How could the mill be turned but with the tide?

Mr. Att. Gen. Their evidence makes it appear ſuch by the leaden trough, which is an inſtrument belonging only to an overſhot-mill?

L. C. J. Tell not me of the leaden trough, Mr. Attorney; look you upon the ſurvey you produced, and take notice of the laſt paragraph, and there you will find the words, *Prox' adjacent' cuidam tenemento, &c.* what make you of that?

Mr. *Att. Gen.* Pray, my Lord, let it be read.

L. C. J. I will in the mean time aſk your witneſs a queſtion. Friend, thou ſeemeſt to be a man that underſtands ſomething. Thou ſayeſt *Foxe's-lane* was a bank before it was built, and the tide before that time came up to that bank, both high and low. Now ſuppoſe there had been a mill in that ground, how ſhould it have been driven?

Hughes. I will tell your Honour: My Lord, by report, and I ſuppoſe it may be true, the mill ſtood all the tide of flood, and when the flood was at high water, there was a dam which kept it in, and it went out again at ebb-tide, and ſo the mill was drove.

L. C. J. There is your overſhot-mill gone then, Mr. Attorney.

Mr. Att. Gen. If ever ſeven or eight acres of ground can be the appurtenances of a mill, I ſhould much wonder

L. C. J. Mr. Attorney, I can tell you of a mill over againſt this place, which I myſelf, and we all can remember. All the eſtate about it was in the *Traps* family, he was a Gentleman of our houſe; all the water that drives that Mill, and two or three Mills that ſerve that ſide of the river, is taken in as the tide comes in, and is pent in as he ſays by a dam; and when they open that, the Mill turns back again. For I would fain have all theſe things, that ſeem to be dark, cleared by the way as they go. I will ſuppoſe all the Records you have read to be right, and that it is called *Ratcliff-Mill*, and then there is the *Mill bank*, and the *Hilly-bank*, and the *Hilly-way*; it is plain then, there was a *Mill-bank*, or a *Hilly-bank*, or whatever you call it. It ſo falls out that the thing now in queſtion is made plain upon your own evidence, there was really ponds and gutters, and thoſe things that were to ſatisfy the Mill. This Mill comes to be plucked down, and the ponds and all the ſluices come now to be built upon. this is not like your Marſh-ground that is on the weſtern part of the bank, but it is a parcel of meare or marſh, as the pond and the reſt ſtifled up by thoſe things, that till ſuch time as the Mill was taken away were receptacles for to pen up the water that came in with the tide. What is the meaning of thoſe words in the ſurvey that I ſpoke of before, and the ſeveral tenements and orchards, and ponds, and ſewers, *&c.* and all thoſe things? Would you have it that this ſhould all point to the ſcite of the Mill, as though all the boundaries ſhould extend to the eaſt-end of the Mill?

Mr. S. *Stringer.* That was the reaſon why I aſked but now, how big the whole was?

L. C. J. And will, what you would have, Mr. Attorney, a ditch or two, ever anſwer the words in the ſurvey?

Mr. Att. Gen. Nor will all their words amount to divers cloſes of ground, as this muſt make in the whole.

Mr. Sol. Gen. Their twenty acres elſewhere anſwers all they can claim.

L. C. J. But this you yourſelf ſay is the *Derricks-hills*, in the ſurvey; and you do take it, as ſoon as the Mill was pulled down in one place, it was ſet up in another.

Mr. Att. Gen. After he had taken our long leaſe he erected one, we ſay, upon our ground; for he had pulled down the old Mill, and lett that to *Carter.*

Mr. Sol. Gen. My Lord it is plain, that the old Mill and the new Mill were not upon the ſame ground, from *Carter*'s leaſe.

L. C. J. Mr. Solicitor, you indeed agree among yourſelves that it is plain, but alas! the fact is quite contrary.

Mr. S. *Maynard.* My Lord, we do make our argument for the Defendant's title as your Lordſhip does apprehend it. The boundaries towards the eaſt is made the Mill and *Ratcliff-Town.* This place that contains ſeven acres, though it had paſſages for the water, is not the Mill, and it can never be, that ſo much ground can be reckoned to be lands belonging to the Mill: it is the Mill itſelf that is the eaſt bound.

L. C. J. No, it is the Mill and the Mill-bank, Brother.

Mr. S. *Maynard.* With ſubmiſſion, my Lord, it is *Ratcliff-Mill.*

L. C. J. Is there no Mill-bank in any of the deeds?

Mr. S. *Maynard.* Not that I remember.

L. C. J. At the peril of my diſcretion be that, Brother.

Mr. S. *Maynard.* Take it to be ſo as your Lordſhip ſays, that there is mention of a Mill-bank, that cannot lie eaſt, for it lieth in a little pond.

L. C. J. Good Brother let us not puzzle that which is as plain as that the ſun ſhines. The controverſy is about all the weſt part of *Foxe's-lane.*

Mr. Att. Gen. No, it is the eaſt bound that we contend for.

L. C. J. Mr. Attorney, if you will miſtake the point, I cannot help it, I aſſure you I do not. Pray take notice of it, it is called 130 acres in your Act of Parliament.

Mr. Att. Gen. Yes, my Lord, 130 acres.

L. C. J. Now then the eaſt of your land by your own ſhewing is Mill-bank; the eaſt of Mill-bank is the Mill, whereas the weſt part is St *Katherine*'s, ſo all your deeds and records ſay; but the eaſt part of the land is Mill-bank.

Mr. S. *Maynard.* No, my Lord, *Ratcliff-Mill.*

L.C.J. But I ſay, Ay, Brother. Then how broad doth *Foxe's-lane* extend?

Mr. Att. Gen. 'Tis reckoned 30 foot in *Carter*'s leaſe, I think.

L. C. J. That is a leaſe that I perceive there is ſome controverſy about, therefore I do not ſo much mind that: it is a perch of land, I think, in ſome of your evidences.

Mr. Att. Gen. Where *Foxe's-lane* is, is the four acres that were ſurrendered; now that being the weſt bound of the eleven acres, where then are the other ſeven?

L. C. J. Read the deed-poll again, the particulars and bounds only.

Clerk. [*Reads.*] All thoſe my four-and-twenty acres and an half—

Mr. Att. Gen. The eaſt bound your Lordſhip ſees is the Mill: now your Lordſhip makes an objection, that if it were as we ſay, an overſhot Mill, it could not have been driven——

L. C. J. Do not, pray, make any ſilly objection for me, and then think to anſwer it. I tell you I do ſay, that it is impoſſible there could be any Mill there but a Tide-Mill: the thing is as plain, Mr. Attorney, as any thing in the world can be; go on with your evidence.

Mr. Sol. Gen. Pray ſwear *John Somerly.*——[*Which was done.*]——How long have you known the place in queſtion?

Somerly. I have known it about 27 or 28 years.

Mr. Att. Gen. Do you know where the Mill ſtood, or was reported to ſtand?

Somerly. I know where it was reported to ſtand, but I never knew the Mill myſelf, it was demoliſhed before my time.

Mr. Att. Gen. Where was it reported to ſtand?

Somerly. As it was reported, it ſtood about half the length of the hall off the bank, rather leaning to the river of *Thames* than the highway.

Mr. Att. Gen. Where was the way to the Mill?—*Somerly.* At *Cock-hill.*

L. C. J. That your own evidence ſay, was on the weſt-ſide of the Mill.

Mr. Att. Gen. Did you know *Shadwell?*

Somerly. I know that that is called *Shadwell.* Do you mean the Well?

Mr. Att. Gen. Yes; how far is the Well from *Cock-hill?*

Somerly Half the length of the hall.

Mr. *Williams.* How far is it eaſt of *Foxe's-lane?*

Somerly. Truly I cannot well tell.

L. C. J.

L. C. J. The question is, whether that be the well that is mentioned in the evidences?

Somerly. I never knew any other well; I paid for filling of it up.

Mr. *Williams.* What was it? Was it not a pond formerly?

Somerly. It was a well.

Mr. Att. Gen. What was it called?

Somerly. *Shadwell* it was called, I knew no other name it had; and that well was wharfed about, and there was a piece of wood about six foot long put into it, and it was on the side of the hill; a Cooper had it in his possession, and he us'd to put his hoops into it——

Mr. Att. Gen. Do you remember the ditch that run under the *Lynches*?

Somerly. I remember there was a ditch that run a long way; there were three or four bridges over it.

Mr. *Williams.* Was that a wide ditch?

Somerly. It had planks to go over, and it was a deep ditch.

Mr. Att. Gen. When you knew it, did cattle feed there?

Somerly. Not in my time.

Mr. Sol. Gen. When you first knew that well, was it reputed an ancient well?---*Somerly.* I knew it not till I came to buy it.

Mr. Att. Gen. What do you know of the raising of *Fox's-lane*?

Somerly. I lived there 26 years ago, and in the time since I lived in it, it is raised the length of my stick and more: for when the tide came in strong, it used to drive stones and planks in at the windows. There was a Waterhouse erected upon *Wapping-wall*, and they went to lay pipes along the street, but they could not lay them there, for they found great pieces of timber, and other things in the ground that hindered it; and upon that they raised the ground.

Mr. *Williams.* Was not there a dam made at the end of *Fox's lane* to keep out the tide?---*Somerly.* I never knew of any.

L. C. J. Was not *Fox's-lane* reputed an ancient way?

Somerly. I suppose they were continually paving it to raise it higher and higher.

Mr. Att. Gen. When you knew it first, was it higher than the marsh?

Somerly. It was all built when I came thither. It is six yards higher at one end than the other.

Mr. Att. Gen. Swear *John Holmes.*——[*Which was done.*]——Do you know the houses in question, between *Foxe's-lane* and *Cock-hill*?

Holmes. Yes.

Mr. Att. Gen. How long have you known it?

Holmes. I have known the place a matter of 28 years or more.

Mr. Att. Gen. Did you know it before it was built?

Holmes. No, I did not take notice of it, to say notice.

Mr. Att. Gen. Do you know that place that is called *Shadwell*?

Holmes. No.

Mr. Sol. Gen. What do you know of the raising of *Fox's-lane*?

Holmes. I never did know of raising the lane.

Mr. Att. Gen. Not at all?

L. C. J. Was it not all the time you knew it a common passage?

Holmes. Yes, a common highway.

L. C. J. Shew, if you can, that there was any highway from North to South, but *Fox's-lane*.

Mr. Att. Gen. Do you know *Cock-hill*?

Holmes. That is quite off from it.

L. C. J. Let me ask you a question. Suppose you were to go for the purpose from *Shadwell* down to the river of *Thames*, would you go to *Cock-hill* or *Fox's-lane*?

Holmes. If I had occasion to go down to *Pelican-stairs*, then I would go to *Fox's-lane*; but if I were to go to *Bell-wharf*, I would go to *Cock-hill*.

L. C. J. That is quite another way.

Mr. Sol. Gen. It is southward of *Cock-hill*, where the Mill stood.

Mr. Att. Gen. That adjoined just upon the way.

Mr. Sol. Gen. Doth not *Cock-hill* lead to the *Thames*?

Holmes. *Cock-hill* is the first beginning of the going down to *Bell-wharf*.

Mr. Sol. Gen. Swear *Eleanor Barefoot* and *Mary Day.* [Eleanor Barefoot *was sworn.*] Do you know *Fox's-lane*?

Barefoot. Yes, I know it very well.

Mr. Att. Gen. How long have you known it?

Barefoot. Threescore and almost six years.

Mr. Att. Gen. Then you knew it before it was built?---*Barefoot.* Yes.

Mr. Att. Gen. Did you know the old Mill?---*Barefoot.* Who, Sir?

Mr. Att. Gen. Do you remember who first built there?

Barefoot. I cannot tell.

Mr. Att. Gen. Pray, when you knew it first, what was it, and who's?

Barefoot. It was a Marsh-ground from *Cock-hill* to *Fenner's-field*, it was counted and known to be Mr. *Stephins*'s; he was a great Freeholder, and Owner of all the ground up to *East-Smithfield*.

L. C. J. How? Why is not the *Lynches* between *Cock-hill* and St. *Katherine's*?---*Barefoot.* The upper ground was only belonging to the Dean of St. *Paul's*.

L. C. J. Do you remember that which is now called *Fox's-lane*?

Barefoot. Yes.

L. C. J. Was it a lane at that time?---*Barefoot.* Yes, it was.

Mr. Att. Gen. Do you remember how the water came in there?

Barefoot. Yes.

Mr. Att. Gen. Did it come up to the bank?

Barefoot. At high tides it came over, so that none could pass.

L. C. J. But at common tides?

Barefoot. It came at common tides till it was raised.

L. C. J. But it was an usual passage for Carts and Carriages?

Barefoot. Yes.

Mr. Att. Gen. How was the Mill driven that was there?

Barefoot. There was a Mill in my time that went with the tide, and all the water that came down from that Mill came into a pond, and so to the Mill-dam, and so drove this Mill.

L. C. J. Which Mill dost thou speak of? Didst thou know *Ratcliff-Mill*?

Mr. Att. Gen. Did you know *Cock-hill Mill*?

Barefoot. Yes, that I speak of.

L. C. J. And h

Barefoot. It was

L. C. J. It cam

L. C. J. How d

Mr. *Williams.* W

Barefoot. It ran i

Mr. Att. Gen. W

Barefoot. In *New*

Mr. Att. Gen. W

Barefoot. It went

Mr. *Williams.* W

Mr. Att. Gen. H

Barefoot. A quart

Mr. *Williams.* W

Mr. Att. Gen. Do

Mr. Att. Gen. Ho

Barefoot. Half a m

Mr. Att. Gen. Di

Barefoot. Yes, I d

Mr. Sol. Gen. On

Barefoot. It was

Broad-bridge.

Mr. Att. Gen. Ho

Barefoot. A pretty

Mr. Att. Gen. How

Barefoot. About 4 and *Broad-Bridge*; *F*

L. C. J. When yo *Lynches* on the north,

Barefoot. A place fo

Mr. Att. Gen. And St. *Katherines*?---*Bare*

Mr. Att. Gen. Who

Barefoot. Mr. *Stephi*

Mr. Att. Gen. Had t

Barefoot. The uppe ground was Mr. *Stephi*

Mr. *Williams.* Was *Fox's lane*?---*Barefoot.*

L. C. J. Do you kn *lane*? Did it ever lie u

Barefoot. At high tid

L. C. J. But at com

Barefoot. I cannot te much lower; but I am

Mr. Att. Gen. When by the *Lynch* ditch?---*B*

L. C. J. Do you rem well?---*Barefoot.* The was the mill.

L. C. J. But answe *Lynches* by the well?

Barefoot. There was n

Mr. Att. Gen. Was th

L. C. J. That is fart

M. Att. Gen. *Shadwell*

L. C. J. But where is remember what the woma wells as there were panes well. But that will not

Mr. Att. Gen. Swear know *Cock-hill*?---*Cope.*

Mr. Att. Gen. Did you

Cope. There was one at

L. C. J. How long ago

Cope. Threescore years

L. C. J. How was that

Mr. Att. Gen. Where d

Cope. At *Frying-pan sta*

Mr. Att. Gen. Whither

Cope. It went into the iron-mill built by one *Whi*

L. C. J. How far did the

Mr. Att. Gen. As near a the tide?

L. C. J. Ay, how far di

Cope. Almost as far as *Ne*

L. C. J. Did the tide con

Cope. It flowed over at fo

L. C. J. What did it at

Cope. It never came so hig

Mr. Att. Gen. How high

Mr. Att. Gen. How near

Cope. Within forty foot up

Mr. Att. Gen. And did th

Cope. Yes; it went to the

L. C. J. Where was your

Cope. At *Fox's-lane.*

Mr. Att. Gen. Was there a to the lane, under which the

L. C. J. What is it that l

Cope. *Ratcliff-Town.*

L. C. J. Which was furth

Cope. *Cock-hill.*

L. C. J. So it is by your ow be but *Fox's-lane*?

Mr. Att. Gen. *Shadwell* is o

L. C. J. *Robin Hood* upon *Greendale* ſtood; therefore this muſt be your land: that is all the argument I can make of it. Your boundaries do make it as plain as the noſe in a man's face.

Mr. Att. Gen. Swear Mr. *Holwell.*---[*Which was done.*]---How long have you known this place, the lands in queſtion?---*Hol.* Not above a year.

L. C. J. He is your Surveyor, I think.

Mr. Att. Gen. He is ſo, my Lord. Pray, you *Cope*, which way did the water go?----*Cope.* Weſtward.

L. C. J. But which way did you uſe to go to the river from the *Lynches*?

Cope. We ſometimes went the lower way, and ſometimes the higher way.

L. C. J. Which was the higher way?----*Cope.* *Ratcliff-Highway.*

L. C. J. And which was the lower way?

Cope. Through *Wapping* and *Shadwell*: *Shadwell* is the lower way.

L. C. J. Thou talkeſt of the north-weſt way; but if you were to go directly from north to ſouth, which way would you have gone?

Cope. Down *Cock-hill*, or down *Broad-bridge.*

L. C. J. Where is that?---*Cope.* Beyond *Cock-hill.*

L. C. J. Whereabouts is it?---*Cope.* Within a little of *Fox's-lane.*

L. C. J. When you went down *Cock-hill*, upon which hand did you leave the mill?

Cope. If I went the lower way, I left the mill on the left-hand.

L. C. J. But when you went the higher way down *Cock-hill*?

Cope. Then we left the mill behind us.

L. C. J. What doſt thou mean by behind thee?---*Cope.* I left it north.

L. C. J. That could never be, man.

Mr. Att. Gen. Yes, my Lord, he is right.

L. C. J. But I ſay he is not right, Mr. Attorney, for *Cock-hill* is north of the mill.

Mr. Att. Gen. *Cope*, do you know *Fox's-lane*?---*Cope.* Yes, very well.

Mr. Att. Gen. Is it raiſed?---*Cope.* Yes; eight or nine foot.

Mr. Att. Gen. What was the reaſon of its being raiſed?

Cope. It was not fitting for carts to go over.

L. C. J. Why ſo?---*Cope.* The Water came upon it.

Mr. Att. Gen. And then to come to the admeaſurement, taking in the place in queſtion, it makes juſt 130 acres, which is our number, and no more.

L. C. J. Then you will leave the Dean nothing.

Mr. Att. Gen. Yes, he has 2000*l.* a-year.

L. C. J. Where?

Mr. Att. Gen. In the eaſt, beyond this place.

L. C. J. Why, would you have any of the land that belongs to the mill?

Mr. Att. Gen. We claim this as marſh-land; which they have nothing to do with, and the number of acres will not be anſwered without it. Mr. *Holwell*, have you admeaſured the marſh?----Mr. *Hol.* Yes; I have, Sir.

Mr. Att. Gen. From whence did you begin?---*Hol.* From *Hermitage-Dock.*

Mr. Att. Gen. Within what bounds?

Hol. That which they call the *Lynches* and the marſh to St. *Katherine's* from the well?

Mr. Att. Gen. And how much doth it make?

Hol. Beſides the well and the *Lynches*, I find it ſomething above 130 acres.

L. C. J. Somewhat above, how much pr'ythee?--*Hol.* Not an acre above.

Mr. *Will.* Pray, Sir, how many acres lies eaſt of *Gravel-lane.*

Hol. Beſides the well and the *Lynches*, I can make but fifty acres and an half.

L. C. J. Where did you reckon up the whole?

Mr. Att. Gen. To make up the 130 acres he took in the mill and all.

L. C. J. That is very well.

Mr. Att. Gen. Why, my Lord, it is no more than 130 acres, and ſo much we muſt have.

L. C. J. Look into the ſurvey that you produced, and ſee what that ſays; Beſides all---

Mr. Att. Gen. Thoſe lie eaſtward of the mill.

L. C. J. Pray, did you meaſure the wall?

Hol. *Wapping* wall is 20 acres.

Mr. Att. Gen. If they will conſent, the Jury ſhall have the ſurvey with them.

Mr. *Will.* With all our hearts, let them have it.

L. C. J. Gentlemen, both ſides conſent, you ſhall have the ſurvey with you; but without that conſent you could not have had it, it not being under ſeal.

Mr. Att. Gen. Then we deſire our laſt verdict may be read. Mr. *Sutton*, was it a verdict upon full evidence?---*Sutton.* Yes, Sir.

Mr. Att. Gen. How many hours did it laſt?---*Sutton.* Five or Six.

Mr. Att. Gen. Was there a view in it?---*Sutton.* There was ſo.

L. C. J. Read it.---(*Which was done*)---Mr. *Holwell*, how much, pray, is the land between *Fox's-lane* and the mill?

Hol. Below the *Lynches* I find it to be ſeven acres and an half.

L. C. J. Can you expect then that all thoſe words of gardens, orchards, &c. ſhould be anſwered under ſeven acres and an half? Beſides, the firſt and ancient reſervation of rent was 10*l.* a-year; after, it was increaſed to 16*l.* a-year, and it doth appear the mill turned to ſo little account, that it was pulled down, and ſo the land was to anſwer the rent; which, for a ground-rent upon a Church-leaſe, in thoſe days, was very great. Have you done now?

Mr. Att. Gen. We have done for the preſent, my Lord.

L. C. J. What ſay you to it then for the Plaintiff, Gentlemen?

Mr. S. *Stringer.* May it pleaſe your Lordſhip, and you Gentlemen of the Jury; if we ſhould give no further evidence at all than what we have already given, but leave it upon this, I dare affirm it plainly appears that they have no title at all to this land. As to their laſt piece of evidence I would firſt give an anſwer to that, and that is their verdict; and that which I would obſerve upon it, and ſay to it, is this; it was a verdict obtained upon forged Deeds: Deeds found, as is pretended, and as you have heard from their two ſpecial witneſſes, in a very extraordinary manner, found in a garret. But by what art prepared, and that they are forged, I queſtion not but we ſhall give you ſatisfaction. But beſides, as to their admeaſurement, it ſeems as they would have it, 130 acres is the queſtion about the extent of the marſh. So much they claim; and we ſhall bring two Surveyors that will give you an account upon their oaths, that between *Fox's lane*, which we ſay is the weſt boundary of our land, and the eaſt of theirs, and *Hermitage Dock*, where the marſh ends, there is above 130 acres; and ſo they do not want their number. For all the evidence that they have given out of Records, we agree them to be as they ſay; and by that agreement ſhall do ourſelves no harm at all, for they all do confirm our aſſertion. They place the eaſtern bound of the marſh at *Ratcliff-Town*; now at *Fox's-lane* doth *Ratcliff-town* begin. The art has been to confound the Cauſe by puzzling boundaries, when it is a plain apparent miſtake thy run upon; and indeed I may very well ſay, a wilful one too. They would have us confine all to a mill and a little ditch, when there are at leaſt ſeven acres always enjoyed with it, and all called the mill; which had a pond, gardens, orchards, tenements, &c. And now there are very large drains neceſſarily made, to keep the water from annoying the Inhabitants, and to carry it away. But for a further evidence of our title, we ſhall firſt prove, that upon a bill exhibited in the *Exchequer* by Mr. Attorney General, againſt *Stepkins* their anceſtor, to know what incroachments had been made, what belonged to the Dean of *Paul's*, and what to Mr. *Stepkins*, are fully ſet out. There it is proved, that the bounds of the marſh were *Wapping-wall*, alias *Fox's-lane.* The marſh was continually overflown with water; but now in our ground there was a great many ditches and places to keep the water for the ſervice of the mill. When we came to build upon our ground, which was 15 *Jacobi*, (then it began) then he brought an action, and did pretend that we did incroach the wall ſomewhat into the marſh; there we had a verdict upon a view, and after a non-ſuit upon full evidence. There was likewiſe a Bill exhibited in Chancery againſt *Stepkins* the father; wherein the bounds are ſet forth, and he in his anſwer particularly enumerates the boundaries. And it has been conſtantly the reputation of the place, that this was the Dean's lands, ſurveyed as the Dean's lands, ſold in the late times of uſurpation as the Dean's lands. The firſt thing, my Lord, which they produced, and that we did then, and do now controvert, is *Carter's* leaſe: This, they ſay, was found in the garret; and they bring two witneſſes for it: But how they have behaved themſelves! What confuſion there is in their evidence! You ſee---

L. C. J. Brother *Stringer*, if you have any evidence to give, pray give that firſt, and leave your remarks till the laſt; you ſhall then ſay what you will; but firſt give your evidence.

Mr. S. *Stringer.* My Lord, we ſhall purſue your direction: We ſay, upon *Fox's* building, *Stepkins* ſurmiſing that the wall belonged to him, comes and brings an action of ejectment againſt *Fox's* tenants for this wall, and upon trial the verdict went againſt him. Then there was another action brought, and he was non-ſuited upon that. Afterwards there was a bill preferred againſt him, and in his anſwer he confeſſeth that his wall-marſh bounded upon *Fox's-lane.* Here are the Bill and Anſwer,

(*Which were read.*)

As likewiſe Copies of two Records, one in the Common-Pleas; *the other in the* King's-Bench.

Hill. 12 Jacobi *Ejectment*; George Boſwell, *Plaintiff, againſt* Tho. Fox, *Defendant*; *not guilty, pleaded a verdict for the Defendant.*

Mich. 14 Jacobi, *Ejectment*; William Sorrel, *Plaintiff, againſt* Tho. Fox; *Not guilty pleaded, and the Plaintiff became Nonſuit.*

Sir *John Trevor.* My Lord, we have this further piece of evidence; we have here a leaſe made by *Stepkins*, of ſeven acres of lands, weſtward of *Fox's-lane*, which divides the marſh from the mill-ditches, and there is a covenant, that if he recover any part of the wall, marſh-wall, the tenant ſhall have the advantage of it, and increaſe his rent.

(*Which Leaſe bearing date*, 16 Aug. 13 Jac. Anno Dom. 1615, *was read.*)

Mr. *Williams.* This was in time between the non-ſuit and the verdict.

Mr. S. *Stringer.* My Lord, as I did open it, there was an information exhibited by Mr. Attorney Gen. *Noy*, 7 *Car.* I. againſt our tenants and theirs, and upon that information there were examinations of witneſſes, and all the bounds of both parties particularly ſet out; which make it all as plain and clear as can be. This cannot be ſet up to ſerve a turn; it was in 7 *Car.* I. ſo long ago; and when that ſhews the wall to be the inheritance of the Dean of *Paul's*, it anſwers all their pretence of a leaſe----

L. C. J. Look you, Brother, that cannot be given in evidence, and I will tell you why; if it were an information againſt *Stepkins* himſelf, he being the party under whom they claim, no doubt it were evidence; but it is againſt the tenants of the one, and the tenants of the other; who only could ſupport their own tenancies, but they could not know their landlords particular titles, and then this cannot be evidence to bind their inheritance.

Mr. S. *Stringer.* We ſubmit it to you, my Lord. Then we ſhall offer you a ſurvey. In the year 1649, this was expoſed to ſale as Church-lands, and a ſurvey taken, and found to be the inheritance of the Church of *Paul's*; and as ſuch ſold for 9500*l.* and enjoyed by the Purchaſers till the Reſtoration.

Mr. *Williams.* Yes, and to that very perſon ſold from whom they ſay they had theſe leaſes which they have produced: That is, to *Winterburn*, whoſe Executor *Knowles* was, as he ſays; and if he had ſuch a leaſe, which then had been forty years in being, would he have given ſo much money, or ventured to purchaſe it as the inheritance of the Church?

Mr. S. *Stringer.* Here is the ſurvey then taken.

Mr. Att. Gen. We oppoſe the reading of your ſurvey, becauſe it had not any authority to warrant it.

L. C. J. Nay, Mr. Attorney, tho' there was no ſufficient authority, yet ſuch things have always been allowed as evidence. You cannot but remember it was done in the caſe of *Finſbury Rotten-Row*, as they call it, *Whitecroſs-ſtreet.*

Mr. Att. Gen. Then let them read the commiſſion it was made upon.

Mr. S. *Pemberton.* We have none; there were many things done then of this nature, without commiſſion under ſeal.

L. C. J. Ay, they did them by orders from Committees. Read it.

(*It was read, dated* Dec. An. 1649.)

Mr. S. *Stringer.* Now we will ſhew the deeds of purchaſe, which was by deed enrolled.

Dated 22 Nov. An. 1650. *for* 9540*l.*

Mr. S. *Stringer.* My Lord, becauſe they pretend this to be an over-ſhot-mill, as they call it; though it be plain it could not be by the place, yet we have three tide-millers that we would trouble you with a little: but firſt here are ſome others, *Bland*, *Marr*, and *Leyburn*, who

who will give an Account of it.—*(They were ſworn.)*—*Bland*, Do you know the Houſes in queſtion?——*Bland.* Yes.

Mr. *Williams.* How long have you known them?

Bland. Thirty Years.

Mr. S. *Pemberton.* Pray, what is the common Reputation whoſe the Lands were?—*Bland.* It was always taken to be the Dean's Lands.

Mr. *Williams.* Who were the Tenants?

Bland. Mr. *Woitwick* and Mr. *Winterburn*.

L. C. J. Prithee, canſt thou tell what was taken to be the Eaſt Boundary of *Wapping*-marſh?—*Bland. Fox's-Lane.*

L. C. J. Was that the Reputation, upon your Oath, in all your Time?

Bland. Yes, ever ſince I knew it.

Mr. *Williams. Bland*, Pray, do you know the Pond?

Bland. The Ponds were filled up; but there were Ditches in my Time.

L. C. J. How near were the Ditches to *Fox's-Lane*?

Bland. Within ten Foot.

Mr. *Williams.* What was the uſe of thoſe Ditches?

Bland. The Water came in at *Bell-wharf*, and filled up the Ditches with the Tide, and ſo it went back again.

Mr. S. *Stringer.* Can you tell who purchaſed theſe Lands of the State in the late Times?——*Bland. Whitwick* and *Winterburn*.

Sir *John Trevor.* Swear *William Kemp* and *Curtlett*. *(Which was done.)*

Mr. *Williams.* Hark you, Mr. *Curtlett*, we would aſk you a Queſtion. My Lord, your Lordſhip obſerves, there is a Well called *Shadwell*, that is at the Eaſt End of their Marſh. We ſhall ſhew where that Well is: There was a Well very lately juſt by *Wall-marſh*, hard by the Place where the Church is now built, which was called *Shadwell*, and from which the Church has its Name. *Curtlett*, do you know *Fox's-Lane*?

Curtlett. Yes, I do.

Mr. *Williams.* How long have you known it?

Curtlett. I have known it ſixty Years.

Mr. *Williams.* When you firſt knew it, whoſe Land was it?

Curtlett. I am ignorant of the original Title, or the derivative Title, I know not whoſe it was, or is.

Mr. S. *Pemberton.* But whoſe was it reputed to be? That we mean.

Curtlett. Sometimes it was reputed Mrs. *Moor*'s, ſometimes *Winterburn*'s, ſometimes one's, ſometimes another's.

Mr. *Williams.* Do you remember the Mill that was in this Ground in Queſtion?—*Curtlett.* Yes, very well.

Mr. *Williams.* How was that Mill driven?

Curtlett. The Water came in at *Bell wharf*, Eaſtward, out of the *Thames*, into the Pond, and ſo run beyond *Broad-bridge*, and vented itſelf into divers Ditches; and when the Tide went out, it returned back again, and employed the Mill.

Mr. *Williams.* How far went the Ditches?

Curtlett. Some of them to *Fox's-Lane*; and one principal Ditch turned up half way the Lane, that People were forced to have Boards and Planks to go over it.

L. C. J. The Thing is very plain; had it been, as they ſay, an Overſhot Mill, this Proviſion that was made of Water for it, for aught I ſee, would have drowned all the Ground round about it.

Curtlett. When I was a Boy, we uſed to ſwim in that Place that was near *Shadwell*, in the Eddy; there I have ſeen the Water as it went out, and the Mill wrought with it as it went back again.

L. C. J. Was there not a Way, when you knew it firſt, from North to South?—*Curtlett.* I cannot well tell.

Mr. Att. Gen. Was there not a Way from *Ratcliff-High-Way*, at *Cock-hill*, to the River of *Thames*?

Curtlett. There was a common Way for Carts and Horſes down to the *Ballaſt-wharf*, and there was a great vacant Place——

Mr. Att. Gen. Pray, let me aſk you, Did you ever hear theſe Lands reputed to be *Stepkins*'s when you knew them firſt?

Curtlett. We have heard talk of that Gentleman.

Mr. Att. Gen. How long ago?

Curtlett. I have not heard of him this twenty Years.

Mr. Att. Gen. Have you above twenty Years ago?

Curtlett. If I did hear of him, I do not believe then it was in his Poſſeſſion; I cannot tell whoſe Title is beſt: You have, I ſuppoſe, both of you better Witneſſes than I, Conveyances and Deeds.

Mr. Att. Gen. He is a wiſe Witneſs, he will not ſwear whoſe it is.

L. C. J. He is ſo, Mr. *Attorney*; I wiſh yours were ſo too.

Mr. *Williams.* Pray, what was it beyond *Shadwell*, and how near was *Shadwell* to *Marſh-wall*?

Curtlett. Shadwell was on the further Side, near *Fox's-lane*.

Mr. *Williams.* To the Eaſt or Weſt of *Fox's-lane*?

Curtlett. To the Weſt.

Mr. *Williams.* Did you know the Well that is called *Shadwell*?

Curtlett. I know there was ſuch a ſmall Spring.

L. C. J. Did it lie Eaſt of *Fox's-lane*, or Weſt, do you ſay?

Curtlett. Weſt, it lay.

Mr. *Williams.* Pray, did the Place where you uſed to ſwim come up as far as the Wall?——*Curtlett.* Oh, no.

L. C. J. I believe that was within the *Thames* only.

Mr. *Williams.* How near have you ſwam to *Fox's-lane*?

Curtlett. It was in the *Thames*, in an Eddy, there the Water went underneath the Mill.

Mr. Att. Gen. In whoſe Ground was that Well that you call *Shadwell*?

Curtlett. I cannot tell in whoſe Ground it was.

Mr. Att. Gen. Was it in the *Lynches*, or in the Marſh-ground, upon your Oath?—*Curtlett.* I cannot tell indeed whoſe Ground it was in.

Mr. Att. Gen. Did it riſe very high?

Curtlett. It was out of the high Ground where the Church is built.

Mr. S. *Lutwich.* Did you ever hear of any Well but what lay between *Fox's-lane* and the Mill?

Curtlett. Sir, I can only give an Account where that Well lies that was called *Shadwell*, where the Church is now.

Mr. Att. Gen. How many Wells have you known?

Curtlett. None but that, Sir.

L. C. J. He does not know as many as there are Panes of Glaſs in the Window, Mr. *Attorney*.

Mill to be there: For I kept Part of a Tide-mill myſelf, and have done ſo this forty Years; and I know the Water muſt riſe at leaſt ten, twelve, or fourteen Foot higher than it needs in a Tide-mill. For we take in our Water as the Tide comes in, and we have a Pair of Gates that are hung with hinges at the top, which open as the tide comes in, but the water, as it goeth out, ſhuts it again, and that keeps the water to ſtand three or four hours in ſome mills, and then we have only guts that belong to the wheel, and when we draw up the gates, the water goes out. We have no water that comes above the ſhaft, which is half the heighth of the wheel, which is ſixteen foot high. To talk of an over-ſhot mill, the water muſt riſe ſo high as to go over the whole marſh.

L. C. J. And muſt drown all the town and country too. It is plainly ſo, Mr. *Attorney*, talk as long as you will.

Mr. Att. Gen. Friend, I aſk you but one ſhort, plain queſtion: I would know, can they uſe a leaden trough with thoſe Tide-mills, as you call them?

Grindy. We can uſe none, nor do we make any ſuch thing.

Mr. Att. Gen. Would not the ſprings in the *Lynches* carry an over-ſhot mill?

Grindy. Sir, I have ſeen the place all about many times; and I will lay any man 20*l.* to 20*s.* that all the ſprings thereabouts ſhall not produce a quarter enough water.

Mr. *Williams.* Where is *George Care?* Swear him—[*Which was done.*]---Do you know *Fox's-lane?*—*Care.* Very well.

Mr. *Williams.* How long have you known it?

Care. Eight-and-fifty years.

Mr. *Williams.* Did you know *Shadwell*, the well ſo called?

Care. That I did, Sir.

Mr. *Williams.* Where ſtood it, pray?

Care. At the upper end of *Fox's-lane* as we go weſtward, and juſt at the ſide of the Church-yard there is one now, and brick'd over head, where they uſed to fetch water: I never knew any other.

Mr. *Williams.* Was that called *Shadwell?*

Care. I never knew any other but what I tell you of.

Mr. *S. Stringer.* Pray, what was uſually taken to be the eaſt-bound of *Wapping-marſh?*

Care. The weſt ſide of *Fox's-lane* was called *Marſh-wall*, or *Wall-marſh*, and that was the boundary to *Stepkins*'s lands; and eaſtward was always the lands of the Dean of *Paul*'s, and I have known it this eight-and-fifty years, nay, I was the firſt that ever built an houſe in *Fox's-lane.*

Mr. Att. Gen. Do you know the *Lynches*, or the high ground northward?

Care. I know it not by that name.

Mr. Att. Gen. This Well you ſpeak of, did it not riſe out of that ground?

Care. It was by the Church-yard that is now.

Mr. Att. Gen. You have claim'd the inheritance of it.

Mr. *Williams.* Sir, we hope we ſhall not need to be taught which is our inheritance; where is Mr. *Marr?* We ſhall now, my Lord, anſwer the admeaſurement made by her Surveyor *Holwell.* Pray, will you, Mr. *Marr*, tell the Court how many acres it is?

Marr. The land which is counted *Wapping-marſh*, which is bounded on *Fox's-lane* eaſt, on the Dean's land weſt, upon *Graſh mill, Well-cloſe, Nightingale-lane*, &c. if we take it to the upper ground, doth contain 130 acres; but take in that which is in queſtion too, and it makes 141 acres.

Mr. *Williams.* Did you meaſure it too, Mr. *Leyburn?*

Leyburn. I did ſo too, Sir; and it is as he ſays.

L. C. J. How much is it?

Leyburn. I took the whole, from St. *Katherine*'s to *Fox's-lane*, and it makes 130 acres beſides the upland and foreland, and the like between *Graſh-mill* and *Wall-marſh-wall:* it is at leaſt ſo much; it is, I think, ſomewhat more, the ditches being undetermined.

L. C. J. Well, what is it all this while you keep my brother *Gregory* for?

Mr. *Williams.* If your Lordſhip pleaſe, we have only a ſhort queſtion to aſk Mr. Baron *Gregory*; if he pleaſe to be ſworn—[*Which was done*]——Where is Mr. *Knowles?* Sir, you were pleaſed to ſay that the writings were carried to Mr. *Neale*'s Counſel in *Gray's Inn*, and that that writing was among them?—*Knowles.* They were ſo, and I believe it was among them.

Mr. *Williams.* My Lord, Mr. Baron *Gregory* had the peruſal of the writings.

L. C. J. But, Mr. *Williams*, my Brother *Gregory* was not named to be the Counſellor in *Gray's-Inn.*

Knowles. No, one *Gage*, or ſome ſuch name.

L. C. J. I ſuppoſe it was to Mr. *Cage*'s chamber, that married *Okey*'s widow.

Mr. S. *Stringer.* I believe it was, and I am ſorry we have kept Mr. Baron *Gregory* ſo long. *Knowles*, pray, did you know they were with Mr. Baron *Gregory?*

L. C. J. Did you know that they were with my Brother *Gregory?*

Knowles. No, my Lord, that I remember.

L. C. J. Well, Brother, we cannot help your ſtaying now; but remember you had an offer made you at firſt, and you are puniſhed for refuſing it. Go on, Brother *Stringer.*

Mr. S. *Pemberton.* My Lord, that which we were ſurprized with the laſt Trial, was the newneſs of theſe deeds to us. It look'd to us to be ſo ſtrange a thing, ſo amazing a thing to us, that we knew not how to give an anſwer to it. We have ſince conſidered of theſe things, and your Lordſhip doth ſee what account they themſelves have given of them; and what an improbability it is that theſe deeds ſhould be found, as they ſay. Here was a poſſeſſion which we have proved under the Dean of *Paul*'s leaſe for ſo long; this they would ſtrip us of; theſe deeds they have trumped up. It made us look into it more warily, and we cannot conceive it probable, or any thing likely, that the Deed of Purchaſe, whereby this land is pretended to be purchaſed into the family of the *Stepkins*'s, ſhould be found in the hands of the Dean of *Paul*'s Leſſee, who likewiſe purchaſed it of the State, as the inheritance of the Dean of *Paul*'s. How could the Deed of Purchaſe from *Hill* be in our Leſſee's houſe?

Mr. Att. Gen. It was not, that is a miſtake.

Mr. S. *Pemberton.* Good Mr. Attorney, do not interrupt me. We muſt rely upon it, that they ſwore it the laſt time, and that the Deed of Inheritance was made four days before our Deed, on purpoſe to warrant the trick. Here is likewiſe a ſurrender made between *Hall* and *Stepkins* produced. How ſhould the Dean's Leſſees come to have that Deed of ſurrender? But to ſatisfy your Lordſhip in this matter, we ſhall give a full and fair evidence that theſe deeds are forged.

Mr. *Bradbury.* My Lord, we have had a violent ſuſpicion, that theſe

a

Deeds were forged. But we ſuſpect it now no longer, for we have detected it, and will ſhew as palpable, ſelf-evident forgery upon the face of theſe deeds as ever was. I deſire to ſee the Deed of the 13th of *November*, in the 2d and 3d years of *Philip* and *Mary*, from *Marcellus Hall* to *Roper*: and that of the 22d of *December*, in the ſame years, from *Marcelus Hall* to *Carter*, I deſire to ſee too. Your Lordſhip ſees the uſe of theſe deeds. The one is grafted upon our leaſe from Dean *Feckenham*, where it is recited, that the mill is demoliſhed, and a new one erected in another place (ſays their deed); and upon that they ſet up the notion of an over-ſhot mill, and all the puzzling matter brought into this cauſe. But I dare undertake to prove them plainly forged.

Mr. Att. Gen. That is an undertaking indeed.

Mr. *Bradbury.* It is an undertaking indeed to detect the Defendant's artifice; but I will venture upon it, and ſhall demonſtrate it ſo evidently, that Mr. Attorney himſelf ſhall be convinced they are forged.

Mr. Att. Gen. Come on, let us ſee this demonſtration.

Mr. *Bradbury.* The Deeds have brought that evidence upon their own faces, that is 1000 witneſſes.

Mr. *Williams.* Prithee open the exception.

Mr. *Bradbury.* If your Lordſhip pleaſe to look upon them, the ſtile of the King and Queen in both run thus: The one is, This Indenture, made the 13th day of *November*, in the ſecond and third years of the reigns of our ſovereign Lord and Lady *Philip* and *Mary*, by the grace of God, King and Queen of *England, Spain, France*, both *Sicilies, Jeruſalem*, and *Ireland*, Defenders of the Faith, Archdukes of *Auſtria*, Dukes of *Burgundy, Millan* and *Brabant*, Counts of *Haſpurg, Flanders* and *Tyroll.* The other is, This Indenture made the 22d day of *December* in the ſame year. Now in *November* and *December*, ſecond and third of *Philip* and *Mary*, it was impoſſible for any man in the world to draw a deed in this form that thoſe two writings are—

Mr. Att. Gen. Is that your demonſtration?

L. C. J. Pray, let him go on, methinks it is very ingenious.

Mr. *Bradbury.* My Lord, I had the hint from my Lord *Coke* in his firſt Inſtitutes; not as to this particular ſtile, for I know he is miſtaken there, but for the detecting of forgeries in general.

L. C. J. It is very well; pray go on.

Mr. *Bradbury.* My Lord, at that time King *Philip* and Queen *Mary* were, among other ſtiles, ſtiled King and Queen of *Naples*, Princes of *Spain* and *Sicily*; they never were called King and Queen of *Spain*, and both the *Sicilies* then; and laſtly, *Burgundy* was never put before *Millan.* Now to prove all this that I ſay, I have here all the Records of that time, which will prove their ſtile to be otherwiſe. *Firſt*, We ſhall ſhew the Acts of Parliament of that time. The ſitting began the 21ſt of *October*, in that year, which was before their Deeds, and ended the 9th of *December* after. We ſhall firſt read the titles of the Acts of Parliament, and you will find them juſt as I have opened them. Read the Statute-Book.

Clerk reads.] Acts made at a Parliament begun and holden at *Weſtminſter*, the one-and-twentieth day of *October*, in the ſecond and third years of the reign of our moſt gracious Sovereign Lord and Lady *Philip* and *Mary*, by the Grace of God, King and Queen of *England, France, Naples, Jeruſalem* and *Ireland*, Defenders of the Faith, Princes of *Spain* and *Sicily*, Archdukes of *Auſtria*, Dukes of *Millan, Burgundy* and *Brabant*, Counts of *Haſpurg, Flanders* and *Tyroll:* and there continued and kept until the diſſolution of the ſame, being the ninth day of *December* then next enſuing.

Mr. *Bradbury.* Here in the Acts made by the publick Council of the Kingdom, the ſtile is in the ancient manner. And your Lordſhip obſerves theſe no ſmall differences. Here firſt *Spain* is left out in the enumeration of the kingdoms, and ſo *Sicily* and *Naples* is inſtead of them. In the Deeds, *Spain* is put in before *France*, and the *Sicilies* made a kingdom too. *Secondly*, Here in the ſtile of the Act they are called but Princes of *Spain* and *Sicily*, that in the Deeds is quite left out. And then in the Acts of Parliament, *Millan* is put before *Burgundy*; in the Deeds *Burgundy* before *Millan.* And how this great alteration of the ſtile ſhould come to be put in a Miller's leaſe, is ſtrange. We have next an account of all the fines of *Hillary* Term, which was the next Term following; for their firſt Deeds happen to be in *Michaelmas* Term, and then the Parliament ſate too. (*Many of which were read.*)

Mr. *Bradbury.* Here are likewiſe the Fines of the *Eaſter*-Term following, which ſhew that ſtill the old ſtile continued in all the publick Records. And if we could as eaſily have brought all the enrolments of Deeds, that would prove the ſame. (*The Fines of* Eaſter *Term read.*)

Mr. *Bradbury.* Now, my Lord, we ſhall ſhew when the ſtile turned, that was in *Trinity*-Term after. (*The Fines read.*)

Mr. *Bradbury.* But I cannot ſee how theſe Deeds could be truly made at that time, when they ſtand ſingle, and none like them can be ſhewn, except they come from the ſame forge that theſe do. I cannot believe the Miller alone, or he that drew his leaſes for him, could ſo long before propheſy what manner of ſtile ſhould hereafter be uſed.

Mr. *Williams.* Your Lordſhip has heard our Deed of the 10th of *December*, in the ſame year, read already: but we having here the Ledger-Book of the Church of St. *Paul*'s, which cannot be made for a turn, but was written at that time; we deſire the ſtile may be read there.——(*Which was done.*)——But to go a little further, to ſatisfy your Lordſhip that they are very likely to be forged, we ſhall give ſome evidence that this is not an unuſual thing with ſome people concerned in this cauſe. The witneſſes will name them to you, and give you an account of it. Swear this Lady and Sir *Charles Cotterel.* (*Which was done.*)

L. C. J. Well, what is it you call theſe perſons to?

Sir *John Trevor.* To ſpeak plain, my Lord, we call them to give an account of my Lady *Ivy*'s forging a Mortgage from one Sir *William Salkhill* for 1500*l.* of a houſe in St. *Martin's-lane*, to which forgery Mr. *Duffett*, that Lady's huſband, was privy, and what benefit he ſhould have by it, you will hear. Sir *Charles Cotterel*, pray, will you tell what you know of my Lady *Ivy* in this matter?

Sir *Ch. Cotterel.* My Lord, that which I have to ſay is this; my Lord, I am tenant to my Lady *Salkhill*, Sir *William Salkhill*'s widow, in a houſe in St. *Martin's-lane*, and was ſo to her huſband a year and a half before he died. The houſe hath been built backward, and the garden ſide they kept to themſelves; but all the houſe that was firſt built, I took, and have it ſtill.

My

My Lady *Ivy* did come to the houſe about three months before Sir *William* died, parting from her huſband Sir *Thomas Ivy*: ſhe came thither as a refuge; where ſhe had been before, and was received very kindly. He died, as I ſaid, about three months after, and my Lady then deſired to know how accounts ſtood between Sir *William* and her about moneys he had lent her, and ſupplied her with. And upon the account ſhe appeared to owe Sir *William* 96*l.* ſhe then took 4*l.* more out of my Lady *Salkbill*'s money, and told her, now, Madam, I owe you 100*l.* She had been entertained as a gueſt there without paying any thing for it, and at his death ſhe continued with my Lady *Salkbill* three quarters of a year after. And being there (as ſhe pretended), in great kindneſs to me, ſhe perſuaded my Lady and me, that the leaſe of my Lady's houſe ſhould be turned over to me, in truſt for a debt of fourſcore pounds that was owing to me by Sir *William Salkbill*. Said I to my Lady *Salkbill*, Madam, I am in no doubt of my money, I pay as much rent as this in a year and more, I can pay myſelf that way, pray let me not meddle with any ſuch thing, Mr. *Duffett* will be perſuaded I intend to cheat them if I ſhould. But ſtill my Lady *Ivy* was at it, and prevailed upon my Lady *Salkbill* to preſs me to it. At laſt, upon their importunity, ſaid I, if it be neceſſary for my Lady's ſervice, let it be done what you think fit. She therefore gave direction to Mr. *Sutton*, and he came to me, and I directed him to draw a writing to turn over the houſe to me as a ſecurity. He aſked me how much my debt was? Fourſcore pounds, ſaid I. Said he, I ſhould ſee my Lord of *Saliſbury*'s leaſe to my Lady, for he muſt take out ſome things to draw this by. He did ſee it, and took as much by note out of it as he thought fit, to make the other by. Then a writing was drawn, this was in *June* 1670, or 1671, I am not certain particularly which; but ſhe brings this writing, and my Lady *Salkbill* ſigned it by her deſire; and my Lady *Ivy* and Mr. *Sutton* were both witneſſes to it. About a year after I heard that ſhe ſet on foot a Mortgage of her own upon this houſe from Sir *William Salkbill*. I wondered at it, becauſe when the account was made up, ſhe appeared to be in Sir *William*'s debt; and I told thoſe that told me of it, I would believe it when I did ſee it. I was then informed the writing was at *Malmeſbury*. She after went out of town, and comes back again in a little while, and this writing, as I heard, was ſhown to ſeveral perſons of my acquaintance, that came to me and told me they had ſeen it; but ſaid I, ſo have not I, but when I ſee it I will believe it. At laſt Serjeant *Weſt*, who was a relation of mine, I married his aunt, one day brought over this writing to me; and told me he had got this writing at laſt, and leave from my Lady *Ivy* to let me ſee it. I looked upon it, and there I did ſee at the bottom, where the ſeal was, *William Salkbill*, and then I turned to look upon the witneſſes names. No, ſays he, you muſt not ſee that, who are witneſſes to the Deed; for my Lady *Ivy* made me promiſe, before ſhe let me have it to ſhew you, that you ſhould not ſee the witneſſes names. Then ſaid I again, I have ſeen enough to give me ſatisfaction· I was a little the more confirmed that the thing was not a reality but fiction, and ſo I told him. My Lady ſaw that would not paſs; ſhe offered, provided Mrs. *Duffett*, my Lady's daughter, might have the advantage of the houſe, to releaſe the matter.

L. C. J. Pray, Sir, for how much was the pretended Mortgage?

Sir *Charles Cotterel*. For 1500*l.* that Sir *William Salkbill* owed her; which I thought ſomewhat ſtrange, ſeeing, as I ſaid, ſhe owed Sir *William* ſo much at his death. At laſt I came to produce my writing, (for ſhe told me I might give Mrs. *Duffett* a right to the houſe). Now I had not read over the writing made me; but now when I came to look upon it, inſtead of a Mortgage for ſecuring my debt, mine was a Deed of Sale from my Lady *Salkbill*, whereby the houſe and the leaſe from my Lord of *Saliſbury* were ſold me for fourſcore pounds; at which I was a little amazed. My Lady was then pleaſed to ſay I was a cheat, tho' I had no hand in it, nor indeed would have had any thing at all done; but upon my Lady *Ivy*'s importunity, and my Lady *Salkbill*'s, I gave direction only for a Mortgage.

L. C. J. What was it that *Sutton* took out of my Lord of *Saliſbury*'s leaſe?

Sir *C. Cot.* He was to take notes to draw a Mortgage of that leaſe by.

L. C. J. He got the notes tho', for aught I perceive, to draw another Mortgage by. A very trick, it ſmells rank of the Knave.

Mr. S. *Stringer*. Pray, Sir *Charles*, did you ever pay any money by my Lady's order?

Sir *C. Cot.* I did lend my Lady *Ivy* 50*l.* ſhe being in diſtreſs for money, afterwards it was made up 100*l.* About *February* 1671, it was made up 1250*l.* and by agreement among them my Lady *Ivy* did relinquiſh that ſaid Mortgage ſhe had thus ſet on foot: and there was a Deed Tripartite made between me of the firſt, my Lady *Ivy* of the ſecond part, and ſome Truſtees for Mrs. *Duffett* of the third part, whereby the reverſion was given to Mrs. *Duffett*, and my Lady confirm'd it, and gave my Lady *Salkbill* a Bond of 1000*l.* in which Colonel *Gravener* was bound for her, that ſhe ſhould not trouble my Lady about the houſe; yet notwithſtanding did ſhe afterwards write to Mr. *Duffett*, as I have heard, that ſhe would ſet it on foot again, and ſhe ſhould have half of what ſhe had recovered.

L. C. J. The Inheritance of the houſe, it ſeems, is in my Lord of *Saliſbury*.

Sir *C. Cot.* Yes, my Lord; Sir *William Salkbill* had the original leaſe from my Lord of *Saliſbury*.

L. C. J. What direction did you give *Sutton* about it?

Sir *C. Cot.* To make a Mortgage only to ſecure fourſcore pound.

L. C. J. And what did he make?

Sir *C. Cot.* An abſolute Deed of Sale.

L. C. J. Was there no proviſo in it, to be void upon payment of money?

Sir *C. Cot.* No, nothing but an actual Sale for ſo much money.

L. C. J. You ſay my Lady *Ivy* afterwards did relinquiſh her pretended Mortgage, pray had ſhe nothing for it?

Sir *C. Cot.* Nothing that I know of; ſhe joined in that Deed Tripartite.

Mr. *Williams*. What ſhould diſpoſe her to give Mrs. *Duffett* 1500*l.* if it were really owing her?

L. C. J. Is that Mortgage here among your writings, Mr. Attorney?

Lady *Ivy*. Indeed, my Lord, I would have brought it, if they had given the leaſt notice of what they now talk of.

Mr. Att. Gen.
forged that Deed
Sir *C. Cot.* N
what I found an
Lady *Ivy*. Y
L. C. J. Na
what he has ſaid
Lady *Ivy* If
L. C. J. Na
Mr. *Williams*.
may be we ſhall g
Pray, ſwear that
the Jury, what y
tion, in making
Mrs. *Duffett*.
ſeveral Deeds for
L. C. J. Do
Mr. Att. Gen.
L. C. J. Trul
ſaid. Pray, Miſtr
Mrs. *Duffett*.
terfeit ſeveral De
ber was in the T
her order counter
ſeveral letters pr
were counterfeit.
writing upon a p
ſwered me, He w
would get many h
I deſired him to c
accounted a very h
pique to my moth
tended to have o
father. She did o
real, but that it
Malmeſbury. Said
it, if you do not
and would not hav
advantage. But
writing, in my fig
L. C. J. Was n
Mrs. *Duffett*. S
Ink he ſhould uſe
Ink, and to fetch
Mr. S. *Stringer*.
L. C. J. Miſtr
while theſe things
give you any inter
Mrs. *Duffett*. M
times ſtand at the
come and diſturb t
but one Mr. *Sutton*
L. C. J. Did h
Mrs. *Duffett*. I
came in, they ſome
upon them; and ſo
Mr. *Duffett* was co
L. C. J. When
Mrs. *Duffett*. C
L. C. J. No, how
L. C. J. You are m
Mrs. *Duffett*. I
Mr. *Stringer*. P
make them look lik
Mrs. *Duffett*. F
uſed to rub them o
their pockets to cre
intended to make uſ
Mr. Att. Gen. M
of, called *Glover*'s
L. C. J. Ay, I
in *Weſtminſter-Hall*.
Mr. Att. Gen. Her
Mrs. *Duffett*. As
have been ſo many
he told me was one
Mr. *Williams*. M
their Deeds they ma
Balconies, and all y
L. C. J. Ay, ho
Mrs. *Duffett*. W
them look dirty, and
ſtanding, it was uſe
the rain to come upo
day they were expoſe
they might be ſhrivel
L. C. J. Is your h
Mr. Att. Gen. Ho
Mrs. *Duffett*. I w
L. C. J. Was your
Mrs. *Duffett*. Yes
L. C. J. Yes, I k
remember all that bu
Mrs. *Duffett*. I w
would not let me ſwe
L. C. J. Pray, Mi
Mr. *Williams*. Had I
Mrs. *Duffett*. My
Cotterel's money.
Mr. *Williams*. Do

Mrs. *Duffett*. The Attorney had 200*l*. of the fame money too.

L. C. J. What Attorney do you mean?----Mrs. *Duffett*. Mr. *Sutton*.

L. C. J. Had he fo, how came he to deferve it?

Mr. *Dobbins*. Pray, Madam, what do you know of counterfeiting any feals?

Mrs. *Duffett*. Mr. *Duffett* once had the impreffion of a feal in his hand, with which he faid he was going to one Mr. *Dryden*, to have it counterfeited, but I do not remember what the feal was.

Mr. *Williams*. When the deeds were written, how did he ufe to put the names to them?

Mrs. *Duffett*. I have feen my Lady herfelf write fome great Letters of the names firft upon other papers, which Mr. *Duffett* could not fo well hit, and he has writ the reft.

Mr. *Williams*. Can you tell the names?

Mrs. *Duffett*. Truly, I do not remember what names.

Mr. *Williams*. We have another witnefs who will give you an account of fome Letters of my Lady's, which we fhall defire to be read. Swear Mrs. *Elizabeth Rycott*. (*Which was done.*)

Mr. Att Gen. She talks of *Glover*'s leafe.——

L. C. J. She fays, fhe doth not know whether that be the deed, there were fo many forged, Mr. Attorney. But fhe fwears thus, my Hufband did forge a writing he called *Glover*'s leafe.—

Mrs. *Duffett*. She had two or three mortgages forged.

Mr. *Williams*. Come, Miftrefs, where had you thefe Letters?

Mrs *Rycott*. I had thefe Letters from Mr *Duffett*.

Mr. *Williams*. Pray, where had you thefe bottles?

Mrs. *Rycott*. This is the ink I faw Mr. *Duffett* write for my Lady *Ivy* with, at Mrs. *Lee*'s Houfe, at the table in the kitchen.

L. C. J. Who did he write for?

Mrs. *Rycott*. For my Lady *Ivy*; I did not know what they were that were written, but he faid they were forged; and with ink out of thefe bottles he faid he could make new-written writings look like old ones very foon.

Mr. *Williams*. Did you ever fpeak with my Lady *Ivy*? Do you know her hand?

Mrs. *Rycott*. I do not know thefe Letters to be her hand, but Mr. *Duffett* gave me them as her Letters.

Mr. *Williams*. Sir *Charles Cotterel*, pray, will you look upon them; you know my Lady *Ivy*'s hand.

Sir *Charles Cotterel*. I do fo---they are all of a hand, and I think they are my Lady's: I believe it truly.

Clerk reads.] This is figned *T. I.* [*All the Letters were read.*]

Mr. *Williams*. Your Lordfhip fees one of thefe Letters tells Mr. *Duffett*, fhe intends to fet Sir *William Salkbill*'s mortgage on foot, and he fhould have half what fhe recovered. If it were a true mortgage, why fhould fhe have give him half?

L. C. J. They were very great together, that is plain; they were very familiar. What were Mr. *Duffett*'s merits towards my Lady, I cannot tell. Will you go on? It is late.

Mr. *Williams*. This is all we fhall offer at prefent, 'till we have occafion further from them.

L. C. J. Well, what fay you to this, Mr. Attorney?

Mr. Att Gen. If they have done----

L. C. J. They have, they fay.

Mr. Att. Gen. Then may it pleafe your Lordfhip, and you Gentlemen They of the Jury, I fhall begin to anfwer their evidence about the firft. have produced fome argumentative evidence out of many Records, to convict our deeds of forgery. In truth, if they had not bragg'd of this very thing, it had been a fhrewd objection, becaufe we could not have been prepared to have given an anfwer to what we could not have forefeen we fhould have been accufed of. But upon their boafts they have put us upon the fearch as well as they, and we can give as good an account of it. They tell you they had their hint from my Lord *Coke*; but that hint has led them into a great error; for he is miftaken himfelf in the computation of this time, as he is in a great many other things.

Mr *Bradbury*. I know he is miftaken; but I depend not upon his remarks of that time. I faid only, I had the general hint about detecting forgeries from thence.

Mr. Att. Gen. But yet for all your confidence of the demonftration, your foundation fails: For, my Lord, to fettle the fact, we fhall fhew that the King of *Spain*, *Charles* V. who was likewife Emperor, refigned his Crown the 25th of *October*, in the 2d and 3d years of *Philip* and *Mary*. It is true, the Parliament-Rolls, in the title of them relating to the firft day of the feffion, there the ftile that was ufed at firft could not be altered. But the fact of their being the King and Queen of *Spain*, was fo notorious to all the World, that we fhall fhew you in multitudes of the Rolls of that year, the ftile was as in our deeds; fo that the ufe might be various: But that will not prove our deeds forged. It may be, the Courts of Law might not take notice of it, as to alter the ftile 'till *Trinity* term; though we have not fearched fo far among them, but in the common conveyances which are upon Record in the Rolls, there it is altered. And as to the time of their becoming King and Queen of *Spain*, we have an Hiftory that tells you the very day when the King refigned, which was the 25th of *October*.

L. C. J. I tell you, Gentlemen, methinks Mr. Attorney has been very fortunate to day, in giving very fatisfactory anfwers to two objections: Firft, they would quite deftroy Mr. *Neale*'s title to this land, by a piece of evidence that they had never had, but that Mr. *Neale* had bragged of it; and that was the furvey, which, with much confidence of the victory, was produced. and yet, when it was fo, to me it feemed the ftabbingeft enemy the defendant's Caufe had; but that you are to have with you, and muft judge upon it. Now he tells you again, Mr *Neale* has been a blabb of his tongue, and could not keep the fecret to himfelf, but muft brag that the deeds were forged, for the ftile of the Queen's reign is changed, and by this bragging they have fmoked the bufinefs, and can fhew Records for it But now inftead of Records, the up fhot is a little loufy Hiftory. Can that be an anfwer to thofe great numbers of Records brought by the other fide? Is a printed Hiftory, written by I know not who, an evidence in a Court of Law?

Mr. Att. Gen. My Lord, befides that, which we muft fubmit to your Judgment, whether, upon fuch a point of fact in a foreign Country, to be determined by a foreigner's Hiftory, not printed for this purpofe, fhall be a fort of evidence; but I fay, befides that, here is a Gentleman, Mr. *Clerk*, that fearched the Roll, and he will tell you what they are in this point.

Mr. *Clarke*. I did fearch in the Rolls, and find many in that year like thefe. And my Lord *Coke* is utterly miftaken; he fays it was not altered 'till the 4th and 5th years of *Phil.* and *Mary*.

L. C. J. I care not what my Lord *Coke* fays, but what the Records fay, let us fee them.

Mr. *Clerk*. I faw a great many in that year.

L. C. J. Lord, Gentlemen, what do you make of us, to keep us here with I do not know what! Mr. Attorney, he tells us that Mr. *Neale* was fo great a blockhead to brag of this, and fo we were prepared for an anfwer; but all the anfwer is, my Lord *Coke* is miftaken, and there are many Records, but we have none of them, *Præmoniti*, *Præmuniti* If he did brag fo, and you knew it, and would not bring records to wipe off the objection, it is ten times worfe than if it had been anfwered only with the unexpectednefs of it.

Mr. *Bradbury*. My Lord, I dare affirm that there are none of the Rolls of that year fo, till after *Eafter*-Term—

L. C. J. Lord, Sir, you muft be cackling too; we told you your objection was very ingenious, but that muft not make you troublefome; you cannot lay an egg, but you muft be cackling over it. The objection is now upon them, let them anfwer it if they can. Have you any of the Records here?

Mr. Sol. Gen. We have not, it feems, my Lord.

L. C. J. Then this muft pafs unanfwered, and muft be left to the Jury.

Mr. Sol. Gen. But, my Lord, they have gone a little farther in this cafe, and indeed farther than becomes them, I think, to lay afperfions upon my Lady *Ivy*, as if fhe were frequently guilty of forgery. And for that Sir *Charles Cotterel* fwears, that fhe did pretend fhe had a mortgage of a houfe in St. *Martin's-lane* for 1500*l*. and this mortgage, he fays, he was told of by fome that did fee it; whereupon he did likewife defire to fee it; and without feeing of it, he declared, he would never be fatisfied of the reality of the thing: and thereupon Mr. Serjeant *Weft* brought it him, and he faw it, but was not permitted to fee the witneffes names, and thereupon he was more diffatisfied than before about it. But if Sir *Charles Cotterel* had given any the leaft intimation of fuch a thing, now we would have gratified them with a fight of it in Court, where he fhould have had his full view; for my Lady has it ftill, and it is a true mortgage, and for a real confideration. But he fays this is releafed, and fhe did that, as is fuppofed, to fupprefs any inquiry after it. But with reverence to Sir *Charles Cotterel*, the fact is otherwife. My Lady *Salkbill* pretended to a debt from my Lady *Ivy*, for nine years diet for four Perfons; and the reckoning being made according to my Lady *Ivy*'s quality, was made fo high, that it paid off the mortgage: But fhe has the deed ftill—

L. C. J. But what fay you to the deed of fale, and my friend *Sutton*'s notes out of the leafe; and the debt of 96*l*. and 4*l*. but a little before acknowledged by my Lady *Ivy*—

Mr. Sol Gen. My Lord, in anfwer to that, we fay, he has been pleafed to give it a great deal of garniture; and as he is mafter of the ceremonies, to adorn the ftory with abundance of flourifhes of his own kindnefs and interefts----

L. C. J. Mr. Sollicitor, you are not to judge of that, whether it be flourifh only or fubftance; the Court and the Jury are the Judges of that, and truly I think it very material to the Caufe, I affure you I do, let the dirt be taken off as it can, it fticks very much, I muft fpeak my mind.

Mr. Sol. Gen. When I am over-ruled, I acquiefce in the Judgment of the Court.

L. C. J. Pray, Sir, apply yourfelf to anfwer the evidence.

Mr. Sol. Gen. So I do, my Lord, as well as I can. The next witnefs is this Gentlewoman, Mrs. *Duffett*; fhe fwears, that fhe faw her hufband, Mr. *Duffett*, counterfeit many deeds, fhe does not particularize them: And here have been likewife feveral Letters read, that did import a tranfaction and correfpondence between my Lady *Ivy* and him.

L. C. J. Pray, Mr. Sollicitor, remember fhe fwears fhe faw that leafe of *Salkbill*'s, and that called *Glover*'s leafe.

Mr. Sol. Gen. My Lord, this witnefs that fwears this, is not only a Perfon unfit to be believed, but is contradicted by a Record, and for that, my Lord, it ftands thus: Mr. *Johnfon*, as is well known, had his trial for the matter about which fhe now fwears: for Mr. *Johnfon*, on the behalf of Alderman *Ireton*, undertook to pay 500*l*. to Mr. *Duffett*, to procure fomebody to fwear the deed, called *Glover*'s leafe, to be forged. Upon this there was an information exhibited in this Court againft Mr. *Johnfon*, for fubornation; and upon full evidence *Johnfon* was convicted for his endeavour. And the Record of that conviction we have here, and defire to have produced and read.

L. C. J. And I tell you, Mr. Sollicitor, that is no evidence in this Cafe.

Mr. Sol. Gen. Why, pray, good my Lord, did not they here juft now fwear her?

L. C. J. But the Information put in by Mr. Attorney *Noy*, pray, remember, was not fuffered to be read, becaufe not againft any of the Parties, but third Perfons.

Mr. *Sol. Gen*. But pray, my Lord, give me leave to apply it to the objection here made in our cafe, to the credit of our deeds. They fay it is fufpicious, becaufe my Lady *Ivy* ufed to forge deeds; and particularly *Duffett*, they fay, did once forge for her *Glover*'s leafe. Now to anfwer that, we come to fhew that my Lady *Ivy* did not forge *Glover*'s leafe, but there was indeed an art ufed to perfuade *Duffett* to fwear it forged, when indeed it was not; for which trick *Johnfon*, that was the agent, or inftrument, was convicted, and that conviction is, I think, a good evidence that it was not forged.

L. C. J. None in the world, Mr. Sollicitor, and that from the very evidence that has been given in this Caufe this day: For it is plain, if you will believe this woman, (and I yet fee no Caufe to the contrary) that fhe was coming into the Court to have fworn the truth, which would have perhaps cleared *Johnfon*; but my Lady *Ivy* would needs keep her away. Now if *Duffett* were fo great a rogue as to forge, he would not ftick to fwear, to protect that forgery: And then how eafy a thing was it, had *Johnfon* been the greateft Saint in the World, to have got him convicted upon what *Duffett* came to fwear againft him; though, had fhe come then in, *Duffett* would have appeared one not at all fit to be credited.

Mr. Sol Gen. My Lord, I have then one thing more to offer; I cannot tell indeed whether it be material, for it feems I have been fo unhappy as to offer fome things that have not been thought material.

L. C. J.

L. C. J. You have so indeed, Mr. Sollicitor, I must speak the truth; there have been several things offered as evidence, which in another Cause and Place, would not, I am sure, have been offered.

Mr. Sol. Gen. My Lord, I submit what I offer for my Client to the judgment of the Court. But that which I would say now, is this: We have here the husband's oath concerning this matter, that this woman who now takes upon her to swear these forgeries and things, told him she could have 500 *l.* if she would swear against my Lady *Ivy*.

L. C. J. Is that evidence against the wife?

Mr. Sollicitor. He is now dead, it seems; but here is his oath.

L. C. J. Pray, consider with yourself, could the husband have been a witness against the wife about what she told him upon an information for that offence of subornation?

Mr. Sol. Gen. No, my Lord, I think not.

L. C. J. Could the wife be an evidence against the husband for the forgery?---*Mr. Sol. Gen.* No, my Lord, she could not, and yet she swears it upon him here.

L. C. J. That is not against him, man; he is out of the case, but against my Lady *Ivy*; and how can the oath of the husband be evidence here?

Mr. Att. Gen. Cryer, call Mr. *Gibson*, to give an account of this Gentlewoman.

Mr. Sol. Gen. Suppose, my Lord, that both husband and wife were brought as evidence against my Lady *Ivy*, were that good?

L. C. J. Certainly that were very good.

Mr. Sol. Gen. Why then, my Lord, one of them says, that she saw such and such things done by Lady *Ivy*, and by him for her; and the other says, such things were not done, but she confessed she could have 500 *l* to swear they were done: Shall not this evidence be admitted to contradict the other?

L. C. J. Why, good Lord! Gentlemen, is the philosophy of this so witty, that it need be so confidently urged? Is it good Logick, that because they both were good witnesses against my Lady *Ivy*, therefore either of them is a good witness against the other? Shall the husband's oath be read against the wife, to fix a crime upon her? Sure you do not intend this shall pass for argument, but to spend time.

Cryer. Here is *Gibson* now, Sir.

Mr. Att. Gen. Swear him. *(Which was done.)*

Mr. Sol. Gen. We are not now, my Lord, examining what *Duffett* swore about forgery or not forgery; but is not this confession of hers an argument against the credit of her testimony, who now says, she saw my Lady *Ivy* do so and so, when she has confessed she could have money to swear against my Lady *Ivy*.

L. C. J. But, Mr. Sollicitor, if you will not apprehend the question, I cannot help it; Is it not the husband that swears against the wife?

Mr. Att. Gen. Do you know that Gentlewoman there, *Gibson*?

Gibson. I have heard of her.

L. C. J. Nay, be not angry, Mr. Sollicitor; for if you be, we cannot help that neither. The Law is the Law for you as well as me.

Mr. Sol. Gen. My Lord, I must take the Rule from you now.

L. C. J. And so you shall, Sir, from the Court, as long as I sit here; and so shall every body else, by the Grace of God. I assure you I care not whether it please or displease; we must not have our time taken up with impertinent things; for I must say, there have been as many offered in this Cause to-day, as ever were in any Cause that ever I heard; and if all be not as some would have it, then they must be in passion presently. The Court gives all due respects, and expects them.

Mr. Att. Gen. Have you any acquaintance with that woman?

Gibson. I have seen her a great while ago.

Mr. Att. Gen. What do you know of her? What reputation is she of?

Gibson. I know nothing of her reputation, I know she was Mr. *Duffett*'s wife.

L. C. J. And so do we, she tells us so. What then?

Gibson. I have seen her a-bed with Mr. *Frogmorton*, and she told me she had then a frog in her belly.

Mr. *Williams.* It seems then by having this Gentleman so ready, they were aware of this too: I suppose Mr. *Neale* bragg'd of this too, or else the guilty conscience put them upon preparing for it. But yet I think they do us no great harm by it.

Mr. Att. Gen. You will give our evidence an answer I suppose by and bye: But we will go on to the rest of yours. As to the bill and answer in the year 1629, in that of *John Stepkins*, it is said, he makes the bounds eastward to be *Fox's-lane*; but it is plain, he that gives in that answer was not acquainted with the transactions of the Estate before his own time. And if you consider the time of that answer, there was near fourscore years then past since the lease made, and so long it had been out of the family, rendering a pepper-corn rent; and so the profitable interest was only the four acres surrendered to him by the tenant, before the licence to aliene: and it appears not that he had any notice of the reversion. But I observe in the answer there is one passage remarkable; that there was a way, time out of mind, that did part this land, and that which was reputed the Dean and Chapter's land. Now that doth not tie it up to make *Fox's-lane* that same way, but only says generally, there was an old way, which must be understood of the way down from *Cock-hill* to *Bell-wharf*: So that I take it, that this is no conclusion upon us. Nor upon the same ground is that lease made 13 *Jacobi*, by *John Stepkins*, where he abutts his land upon that wall which is called *Wall-marsh-wall*, and covenants to have the rent increased, if any thing beyond that be recovered; for there was near threescore years to come then of this lease, and he had no pretence of title to contest it at that time, and so the verdicts are all answered that way, the lease expired not till the year 1680.

Mr. Sol. Gen. Then, my Lord, for the survey that they produce of the late times, by order of the Committee of Parliament for sale of Church-lands, how that should give a title, I do not understand. It is the first time I ever heard of a particular of Dean and Chapter's lands to be an evidence, when at that time there was no Dean and Chapter. But that which is a clear answer to it is this: *Winterburn* who had the lease from the Church, did also claim under *Marcellus Hall*, who had a lease for ninety years; that in time expired in the year 1640. That interest being then determined, he gets these put into the survey (which it was his interest to do) as the inheritance of the Church, which would gain him a fee-simple upon his purchase, he concealing the long lease, and they being so long

in possession;
and it appears
witnesses that
deration, upon
Lord, taking
Hall be a good
and do explain
are afterwards
render to be th
acres; but wh
given no accou
survey, I take i
For that saith,
Now then, it
reacheth up to
ours: and upo
both sides the J
our bounds and
Defendant. W

Mr. Att. Gen.
bill and answer
last trial?---*Sut*

Mr. Att. Gen
now.

L. C. J. Hav
the Plaintiff?---
Lordship and th

L. C. J. The
long: I think t
ed in *Westminste*
years. I think
long: That ind
Colt, in this Co
length before.

But, Gentlem
and consideration
of circumstances,
evidence that hat
assistance I am al
Some of you I ha
you some trouble
question. And i
had a view of the
tion of mine.

The question ir
built upon to a ve
on the east side of
twixt that and the
merly belonged to
not part of the D
the Dean and Ch
Plaintiff: but if
marsh-land, and
issue is with the D

The Plaintiff c
enjoyed under the
receive the rents o
tion, says, in his
behalf of Mr. *Neal*

That is not suff
original; and in p
made a lease of the
Book is produced
takes no notice at
of a mill in *Shadw*
cing that Writing.
objection, and a m
there were two pla
mour an evidence o
inserted, who happ
Nowell was original
the other part of th
to, how it came to
put in? That seem
shoar up an eviden
gined that *Nowell* s
was not Dean till
Now had this obje
the evidence lame,
leg forwards. But
ment scroll, which
cer, *Spencer*, says h
be a new thing for t
in time, in some s
Dean *Collet*, 5 *H.* V
and supports the cre
an answer to that ob
this will shew that it

The next piece of
they come and produ
leases; and those are
ways read and allow
Dr. *May*, then Dean
lands in question to *J*
and Chapter of *Paul'*

Then they tell you
Dean *Fecknam* takes
Hall, and that is for
of, and some increase
pair the mill, and th
the present question,

cence to remove the mill. You, Gentlemen, will have the deeds with you, and are to judge of them.

The leases from 5 *H* VIII. to this Dean *Fecknam* are only leases made for years; and by reason of these leases for years, and the long lease which they pretend to, the Defendant's Counsel insist upon it, that they could not be let in to controvert the Plaintiff's title, for the last lease for 128 years, from *Stepkins* to *Hall*, expired in time but in the year 1680.

Now say the Plaintiff's Counsel, (and they produce that which is very material in the Case) 5 *Aug.* 1636, this was then lett to one *Mary More*, the relict of one *Adrian More*, formerly the assignee of the lease that came from Dean *Fecknam* to *Marcellus Hall.* And there, instead of continuing it a lease for years, he letts to *Mary More*, in consideration of the former leases, and turns it into an Estate for three Lives. So far then was the Dean of *Paul's* from apprehending himself to be but Lessee for years, that he takes upon him to create freeholds, which only he that has the inheritance can do

They go on further, and tell you, that in 1640, the same Dean of St. *Paul's*, she having sold her interest to one *Whitwick* and *Winterburn*, there is a new Estate made to them for three Lives. These continue in possession under that lease, till Mr. *Neale* purchased in their interest: and his Grace of *Canterbury*, then Dean *Sancroft*, he made another lease to the said Mr. *Neale* for three Lives, and there is a great increase of rent, 80*l.* during the life of one of the former surviving Lives, and then to 100*l.* Then comes the lease made to the now Lessors of the Plaintiff, by this reverend Divine that is here, now Dr. *Stillingfleet*, the present Dean of St. *Paul's* at yearly 240*l.* And this is the substance of the evidence first given by the Plaintiff, for his title which is underneath that last lease of Dean *Stillingfleet*, which they say is a good title: and in case it doth appear that the lands are the inheritance of the Dean of *Paul's*, it is not controverted by the Defendants, but that the Plaintiff must have a verdict for him.

But say they which are for the Defendants, this is not their inheritance, but the Defendant's: and to prove their objection, they produce abundance of deeds, of which, as well as I can, I will give you a punctual and particular account. For with all the faith and fidelity I can, I will give you the substance of what has been said on both sides.

First, It is not to be doubted, for it is beyond all contradiction plain, there were 130 acres of marsh-lands, lands covered with water, which one *Vanderdelf*, a *Dutchman*, undertook to drain, and had an Act of Parliament made, *anno* 27 *H.* VIII. to encourage him for his endeavours to drain it, giving him the one half. That Act of Parliament is produced, and it is there said to be 130 acres.

Now you are to take notice of the boundaries of this marsh-land, as making the state of this question. The Act of Parliament bounds the marsh upon the *Hermitage*, or such a mill called *Grash-mill*, upon the West. It is bounded on the high-way leading to *Ratcliff*, on the North, which is called *Ratcliff* high-way to this day: It is bounded to the river *Thames* on the South; and it is bounded upon the Town of *Ratcliff* towards the East.

Afterwards, in *H.* VIII's time, comes in *Richard Hill*, who was owner of some part of this marsh (*Vanderdelf's* moiety), and he in time, 23 *H.* VIII. became indebted to one *Salvago* and another, and there he comes and acknowledges a Statute to them for their debt. And (because I would have you have all things before your view that were done at one time) in the same year there is a mortgage made of the lands of *Richard Hill*, (among which, they for the Defendant apprehend, are comprized the lands in question, as marsh-land, to *Salvago*, for the payment of their money) and in that mortgage the same words are made use of for the boundaries, as are in the draining Act. This, to derive their title, they produce to shew, that there was such an ownership, and such a mortgage.

Then they tell you, that in 37 *H.* VIII. the same *Richard Hill*, he goes and divides some part of these lands, that is to say, eleven acres and an half, and that he conveys away by lease for 34 years to *Marcellus Hall*; whom I name the more particularly, because it is a name that has been much canvassed, and gives a countenance to the title on both sides. Now in that deed, whereby this is thus conveyed to *Marcellus Hall*, there is no notice taken particularly of the eastern boundary to be the mill, or the mill-bank, or the hilly-bank. Now, say they, the mill was just upon the point, hard by that place that is called now by the name of *Cock-hill*; and so that boundary doth take in the thing in question, the seven acres and a half, because that deed takes notice of the mill, hilly-bank, or way.

In the next place, they offer you this for evidence, that in 6 *Ed.* VI. the same *Richard Hill*, for 130*l.* sells his land to *Thomas Stepkins*. And when it comes to convey the inheritance to him, it is laid to be under the same boundaries as are mentioned there, bounded on the hilly-bank or mill-bank, eastward. Now, say they, that sheweth plainly, that still the mill was the thing that was intended to be the boundary; and there being seven acres and an half of land between the mill and the western bounds, those seven acres cannot be construed to extend to a mill with the appurtenances, but rather it is to bound upon the mill and include the lands, than to have the lands go with the mill.

They proceed further and say, that *Thomas Stepkins*, the same year, did for 50*l.* lett this to *Marcellus Hall*, for 128 years, at a pepper-corn rent, which lease expired but in 1680, and till now we could not come to litigate that matter, because he had made such a lease. But then I am to take notice by the way, and so must you into the bargain; there is another boundary made there, abutting on the Well there, called *Shadwell*, and the way leading from *Shadwell* to the *Lynches*.

After this they come to tell you further, that *Marcellus Hall*, 22 *Dec.* 2 and 3 *Phil.* and *Mar.* lett a lease to *Carter*, and that was for 20 years. Now you are to take notice, that in this lease of *Carter's*, there is notice taken of a mill, and about an acre of land thereunto belonging, very carefully put in; and that, say they, sheweth that your boundary could not extend to so much as seven acres.

And to back that evidence, they shew you a certain survey, taken in Queen *Elizabeth's* time, concerning the manor of *Stepney*, which you are by consent to have with you; and you will do well to consider it well in your perusal of it.

And now comes the main deed. Say the Defendant's Counsel, it falls out that you are but Lessee under *Marcellus Hall*, who was Lessee under us, and was obliged in a particular covenant, that he should not lett any part of this land without the licence of our ancestor *Stepkins*, who made him such a long lease. But it happened he had a mind to lett some part of this land to the Dean of *Paul's*, from whom he had a lease of the mill. And accordingly he had a licence from *Stepkins* so to do; which, say they, is the reason why they come to lay claim to our land. This they take notice to be in time, 16 *Nov.* 2 and 3 *Phil.* and *Mar.* when I must tell you by the way, that the first lease, pretended by them to be made to *Marcellus Hall*, is the long one, 6 *Ed.* VI. by *Thomas Stepkins*; so that *Marcellus Hall* came to be Lessee under the Dean and Chapter, before he had any authority or interest from *Stepkins*, nay before he had any lease from *Hill*.

Mr Att. Gen My Lord, if your Lordship pleases to remember, *Marcellus Hall* did first take by lease from *Richard Hill*, in 37 *H.* VIII

L. C. J. Pardon me, Mr. Attorney, I did not mis-repeat it; I say, he first had a lease from the Dean and Chapter.

Mr. Att. Gen. That was of the mill only—

L. C. J. That is contested, and the very gist of the question; Mr. Attorney, how much is comprehended in that lease?

But to go on with the Defendant's evidence. Then in *Nov.* 2 and 3 *Phil.* and *Mar.* is the deed to *Roper*, of which I shall have occasion to say more anon.

In 5 and 6 *Phil.* and *Mar.* comes *Jasper Hill* the Son of *Richard Hill*, (the first owner of the land, and that entered into the Statute to *Salvago*) he makes a conveyance to *Macheline Stepkins*, *Thomas's* widow, and *John Stepkins*, his heir, mother and son; upon which, afterwards there is a surrender made by *Marcellus Hall* to *John Stepkins*, son and heir of *Thomas*, of four acres; which say they was not assigned with the other seven to the Dean of *Paul's*.

Then in 3 *Elizabeth*, pursuant to the conveyance made by *Jasper Hill* to the *Stepkins's*, there is a fine and recovery suffered; and 4 *Elizabeth*, a deed to lead the uses of that fine which are to *John Stepkins* and his mother, and the heirs of *John*. But still, in all these deeds and conveyances, there is mention made of the mill, mill-bank, or hilly-bank, or hilly-way, to be the boundaries; and likewise of *Shadwell*.

After that, they produced a bond, wherein *Spinola* is bound to *Stepkins* to take off the Statute entered into 32 *H.* VIII. by *Richard Hill*.

Then 14 *Elizabeth*, they produce a commission of sewers, where notice is taken of the several land-holders of *Wapping*-marsh, who were liable to make satisfaction for any want of repairs or defects in the marsh There *Roper* is taken notice of as a tenant, and one *James* and *Stepkins* too: and they do infer from hence, that *James* and *Roper's* land is part of this, and was under *Stepkins*, and is enjoyed to this day under the title of the *Stepkins's*.

They go on further, and tell you, that 15 *Eliz.* *Stepkins* became indebted to the Crown, by taking a teller's debt upon him, and had a mind to secure the debt, and therefore conveys his land to the then Treasurer, Attorney-General and Sollicitor-General, to secure a great sum of money; and this land they would have to pass among the rest.

Afterwards, 17 *Eliz.* the commissioners sit again, and there is a Return made of all those that were land-holders, the same named before.

Then 7 *Jacobi*, was there a re-grant out of the Crown made to *Stepkins* of all his land. Wherein, generally speaking, the bounds of the lands belonging to *Stepkins* are called the *Mill-bank*, &c. This must, say they, of necessity take in the lands in question, otherwise it is impossible that should be the boundary. And they make use of this further argument: Say they, we have taken a survey of all the lands, those in question and the other marsh-lands, from *Hermitage-dock*, alias St. *Katherine's*, even to this mill; and it doth just humour the number of Acres in the Act for draining *Wapping*-marsh; that is to say, it makes just 130 acres. All which, they say, plainly belongs to the *Stepkins's*.

They then come to examine their living witnesses, and they have produced them in this order as I name them: their witnesses have been as they are in my paper. One *Hughs*, and *Somerly*, and *Holmes*, and *Barefoot*, and *Cope*, and *Holewell*. And the substance of what they say is this The old woman, *Barefoot*, says, she has known the place in question these threescore and odd years; she remembers well the situation of it, and that the water drove another mill first, and did not come near to *Fox's-lane* by a quarter of a mile, but run more to the North. And this land, she says, was always reckoned to be *Stepkins's*, and she never knew any one have any thing to do there but they And in as much as there was some discourse concerning a well; she says, she doth remember there was a well between *Fox's-lane* and the mill, and that was half a mile off *Fox's-lane*, and was called *Shadwell*. She remembers it so well, that if there were as many wells as there are panes in the glass window before you, that was the right well, and there was no other well called *Shadwell*, but that.

Then *Hughs* tells you, he remembered the land before it was built upon; that at common ordinary tides the water used to come up to *Fox's-lane*, and at high tides over it; but the land has been raised much higher since that.

Then *Cope*, he gives an account of his knowing it above threescore years ago; and he in general says, he did not know how far westward the water went that drove the mill; but *Fox's-lane*, he says, was the way from North to South, westward of the mill, and he knew not any way eastward of the mill but *Fox's-lane*, for *Cock-hill* is eastward of the mill. And much like to this was the testimony of the other witnesses; which being done, they concluded with the evidence of the surveyor *Holewell*, about the admeasurement. And this, as I remember, or can recollect, is the substance of the Defendant's evidence, before the Plaintiff's reply.

And then as to that which was offered by the Defendants, as evidence of the boundaries, the Plaintiffs give this answer; and it is that which will be the pinching question in this Cause to all eternity: Whether or no, *Mill-bank*, or *Mill-hill*, or the *Hilly-way*, or whatsoever else it is called in their old Deeds, be not that which is now called *Fox's-lane*.

Say they, *first*, by your own evidence, (that same ancient survey that you produced, and which, by consent, you Gentlemen of the Jury are to have with you) there is notice taken of 130 acres that belong to the marsh; there is notice taken of the *Lynches*, as belonging to the Dean and Chapter of *Paul's*. But then in the last paragraph of the back-side of the leaf, (so we call the second side, for distinction sake) you will find this taken notice of, which said marsh doth bound

on

on the lands hereaſter mentioned on the Eaſt. And what are the lands thereaſter mentioned? Theſe you will find; *Item*, holden by the Dean and Chapter of *Paul*'s, one meſſuage, called *Derrick-hils*, another tenement called ſo and ſo, and ſeveral orchards, gardens, ponds, &c. and a water-mill thereunto belonging. So that there was on the Eaſt part of the marſh-land, orchards, gardens, a meſſuage, a tenement, waters, ponds, fiſhings, and a mill, and ſeveral other things. Now, if in caſe the Eaſtern boundaries of the marſh came up to the mill you ſpeak of, how comes it to paſs that you yourſelf, in your own ſurvey, make the Eaſtern bounds to be upon theſe lands, and all theſe belonging to the Dean and Chapter of *Paul*'s? And when they come to read the particulars of what belonged to the Dean and Chapter, that ſurvey bounds to the Dean and Chapter's land upon the marſh-land. You that have been upon the view, may the better underſtand it; and you ſee the Eaſtern part of the mill was the waſte ground, and made a lane to carry down ballaſt, as the witneſſes ſay. This doth juſt humour all the old boundaries.

Nay, to ſhew that this is really ſo, they ſay, that in time, in the year 1615, there was an action commenced before my Lord Chief Juſtice *Coke*, when he ſate in this Court, wherein this controverſy aroſe. *Fox*, who was as well tenant to the Dean and Chapter of *Paul*'s, as he was to *Stepkins*, he comes, and he builds upon that old wall, called *Wall-marſh-wall*, which begot a conteſt betwixt *Stepkins*, who was the anceſtor of my Lady *Ivy* and this *Fox*; and upon that conteſt this was the queſtion, Whether there had been any incroachment upon the marſh? Not but that the wall was reckoned, even by *Stepkins*, to be the boundary, though running, as *Stepkins* ſaid, twenty foot into the Eaſt part of the marſh; and there *Stepkins* was non-ſuited. Afterwards it came into the Common-Pleas, and there was a verdict, whereby it was ſettled, that the whole wall belonged to the Dean and Chapter of *Paul*'s.

But afterwards Mrs. *Moor*, the Leſſee of the Church, would not be quiet with this, but exhibits a bill againſt *John Stepkins*, and others, and to ſettle the boundaries, becauſe he pretended incroachments upon his ground: they therefore require him to aſcertain the matter upon his oath. He in his anſwer confeſſeth, he had heard of the verdict before-mentioned, but knew nothing of it himſelf, but when he comes to ſet forth the boundaries, he is ſo far from taking notice that the boundaries take in the lands in queſtion, that he tells you there was an ancient bank, which was the ordinary bounds between his land and the land of the Church; and this is a high-way a common high-way. But it was true, as he believed, they had incroached, though ſuch a verdict and nonſuit were obtained by them. Not that ever he pretended to any thing on the Eaſtern part of that paſſage or bank, called *Fox's-lane*; but he pretended to twenty foot on the Weſtern part of it, as an incroachment.

They ſay further too, that notwithſtanding all this, *John Stepkins* was not ſo confident of his title to even thoſe twenty foot on the Weſt part; but that he comes and makes a bargain with another man. I will lett you this Eaſt part of the marſh-land, and if I recover any of the wall, you ſhall pay ſuch a rent for it; but if not, you ſhall hold it as you did before. So jealous he was of his title, even to that which he thought was incroached upon.

And they fix it thus, to humour and explain the particulars mentioned of orchards, ponds, gardens, &c. for here were a great many ſluices and cuts for the water to be received in, and ſo all may well be comprehended under the name of a mill with the appurtenances; and that they ſay goeth a great way in the queſtion. You are to conſider of it, Gentlemen.

Then they further ſhew, that whereas the other ſide ſurmiſe the boundary to be *Shadwell*, which they would have to be placed a great way higher, by the place called *Cock hill*; here comes an old man that tells you, he knew the place ſixty years ago and above, and there was no other well called *Shadwell*, but that which was where the Church now ſtands, and that is on the Weſt part of *Fox's-lane*. Now I muſt tell you, upon the evidence it is pretty ſtrong, becauſe he gives ſuch an account of it that it was bricked over, and a common well to all People, which muſt make the thing very notorious, and he never heard of any other well called *Shadwell*. It is true, there might be a ſpring on the one ſide of this ground in queſtion, and the other; you have heard the evidence on both ſides, I muſt leave it at large to you.

Then to make the thing more plain, they offer to you that this was a tide-mill, and not as the Defendant pretends, an overſhot-mill, and that is notoriouſly plain it is ſo, and it is againſt ſenſe it ſhould be otherwiſe. Here was one that wrought at the mill, and his father before him, ſixty years; nay, it appears that to have water to drive an overſhot-mill in that place muſt drown the whole level, becauſe it muſt be raiſed ſo much higher than the wheel; and if ſo, that ſtands higher than the place, were it raiſed never ſo high, of late called *Fox's-lane*. But there were tides that came within twenty foot of it; and you muſt give me leave to tell you, I underſtand ſo much of it, that a tide-mill is never ſuffered to have the water juſt ſwim up and back again; but they have cuts to retain the water a while, that it may go the eaſier off. And ſo the great number and length of the cuts and ponds, and ditches here, were but only receptacles and baſons to receive the tide, which did not riſe (as they tell you it ſhould not) above half the wheel. The nature of the thing itſelf ſpeaks againſt what they would have it to be; and to ſtrengthen the argument, they have called five or ſix, or more witneſſes, that have known it all along ſo to be: And yet this I apprehend, the other ſide take to be their moſt material point to make it marſh-ground.

But the Counſel for the Plaintiff ſay this further to you: They have a ſurvey taken in *Oliver*'s time, which they produced, but were oppoſed by the Counſel of the other ſide; and I muſt confeſs I did wonder to hear the objection, that it was ſtrange this ſhould be ſurveyed as Dean and Chapter's lands, in a time when there were no Deans and Chapters; whereas it was ſurveyed as that which was ſo, while there were ſuch things as Deans and Chapters, and it was in order to be ſold as ſuch. And upon my word, if the lands of the Dean and Chapter's Inheritance were no bigger than the Defendant would have them, there was a good round ſum paid to the State for the mill only. But alas! you have a witneſs that tells you (there being in the ſurvey mention of one *Craven*), that there was a *Craven* on the Eaſt part of the ground, that had a large orchard and garden, and ground.

4

And upon this p
the Plaintiff's (
the Church's I
had a leaſe in b
ſion, and that t
fine houſes wer
tance under the
he had the long
was not theirs
a trivial rent of
lumping penny

But then the
narrowly obſerv
Carter's leaſe,
that of *Roper*, v
are forged. A

The firſt par
of this nature,
Books of Law,
in ſuch a time,
made to them i
at that time, t
true deeds. An
the deſign be la
will appear o
upon Juſtice fo
ſion and ſhame
care to have bc
you call *Philip*
you put *Burgu*
of both deeds,
forgery in the
themſelves Kin
ſecond and thi
November befor
were but Prince
fore that time,

For inſtances
Acts of Parliam
ſhew you the fi
Term; till whi
coveries, bore
not enrolled of
Defendant's Co
of your own ma
ſay, we have fo
this purpoſe, wh

And in truth
and it is made th
was pleaſed to r
bragging of this
prepared to giv
very one thing

But ſtill, ſay
and evince the l
the Defendant,
evidence.

Firſt of all, S
which doth not
bad upon my F
is a very knave.
law her forge t
he gives a ſhrew
you, upon Sir
any debt from
and her, ſhe w
from her huſban
beſides his relie
preſent when ſh
knowledged her
out the ſeeking
ſhe, Does not
fourſcore pound
But, ſays my L
as a ſecurity to
cerned for Sir
himſelf? Nay,
rity upon that h
ſelf. If her m
of honeſty or v
that obſervation
Cotterel yielded
intruſted to dra
Saliſbury's leaſe
poſe it was rec
notes out of it,
Sir *Charles Cott*
otherwiſe, Sir
Sutton, are wit
ſolute deed of fa
Cotterel underſt
debt of 1500*l.*
houſe.

Sir *Charles C*

L. C. J. Fi
ſuch a ſecurity
as a ſecurity f
prior mortgage

indebted 100*l.* upon her taking the four pounds from my Lady *Salkhill*, if she had so great a sum owing her. And what a slovenly answer is that given by the Counsel for my Lady *Ivy*, that she and others were called upon for nine years diet? Whereas Sir *Charles Cotterel* swears, she owned herself upon the account indebted 100*l.* and there was no bartering for diet, but that she had gratis for three quarters of a year after Sir *William*'s death, as she had it several times before.

And now, while it is in my memory, I would remind you of one thing more before we come to the other witnesses, there is a thing that to me cramps this business very home upon my Lady *Ivy*. How comes it to pass my Lady *Ivy* should be so wonderful kind to my Lady *Salkhill*'s daughter, as to part with 1500*l.* so secured, to have the house settled upon her, without any consideration in the World that I can hear of? That is such a melting piece of kindness, that they would do well to find out some flam to authorize it. It seems upon Sir *Charles Cotterel*'s desire to see this pretended mortgage, and its being brought him by my Brother *West*, who is now dead, she was wonderful careful that he should not see the witnesses to it, it was so precious and tender a thing: But, alas! it is all melted down and gone of a sudden, without any consideration at all whatsoever, and she can readily join with Sir *Charles Cotterel* to settle this upon Mrs. *Duffett*, the Lady *Salkhill*'s daughter, and enter into bond not to disturb the enjoyment.

Then there comes another evidence, and that is the Gentlewoman Mrs. *Duffett*, who it seems they would have to be a loose sort of creature; but methinks she has a good round oath upon her tongue: for she does directly swear that she was present, and saw Mr. *Duffett* her husband forge that very mortgage Sir *Charles Cotterel* speaks of, that my Lady *Ivy* directed it, and gave her order to put saffron in the ink to make it look old; that she saw him writing in a parchment, which he told her was *Glover*'s lease, and other things, and all for my Lady *Ivy*. Nay, she tells you my Lady *Ivy* was so extraordinary an artist at the managing of such an affair, that this master-workman, *Duffett*, was not so dextrous at it as she; for he could not write the first great Letters of the names that were to be put to the forged deeds, but she did that herself, and the rest he did. How far she is to be believed, I must leave to you; you hear what is objected against her about the frog in her belly; and I do not know what; whether that will take off the credibility of her testimony, I leave to you. She doth give a very free and large account how they used to order their matters to make the ink look old, (as I said) they put saffron in it; then they rubbed the outsides of the deeds in dirty windows, and after that used to lay them in a balcony for the rain to come upon them in the nights, and to dry them in the sun, or by the fire, to shrivel them up. And this she says was their method, and process they used. All which the Plaintiff's Counsel urge, to shew the probability that these deeds of theirs are forged.

Then they tell you, which is yet somewhat more to strengthen her evidence, there is a woman, that though she speaks out of Mr. *Duffett*'s mouth, and that can be no evidence against my Lady *Ivy*, yet says, she received from him a parcel of Letters, which are sworn by Sir *Charles Cotterel* to be all of my Lady *Ivy*'s own hand-writing; which Letters have been read to you: and they shew a great familiarity between my Lady *Ivy* and Mr. *Duffett*, a great care and concern for the promotion of this *Duffett*, the Gentlewoman's husband, and of some deeds that were likely to be thought new and suspected. And she tells him at the latter end of one, that she is sollicitous till the trouble be over. But she was resolved to set on foot Sir *William Salkhill*'s mortgage, and if that thing did go well, he should have half.

That supports the credibility of the woman's testimony: But besides that, there is another thing that looks very untoward, because Mrs. *Duffett* doth directly swear, that out of the 1000*l.* paid my Lady *Ivy* by Sir *Charles Cotterel*, 200*l.* was paid and given to her husband, and Mr. *Sutton* forsooth had 200*l.* more. For what service, I wonder, must my Lady *Ivy* be so liberal to Mr. *Sutton* and Mr. *Duffett*? Let Mr. *Sutton* shuffle and rouse himself as he pleaseth, it will stick upon him, and I must confess it looks untowardly, his getting my Lord of *Salisbury*'s lease to pick notes out of it, and then to have such a mortgage trumped up in this manner. It is very rank, I assure you.

This is the substance of the evidence that has been offered by the Plaintiff, to prove and induce you to believe these deeds forged.

Now, in answer to this, they on the other side would offer, that Sir *Charles Cotterel*'s evidence is a surprize upon them. They say they have such a Writing, and such and such Deeds, *Glover*'s lease, and *Salkhill*'s mortgage; but they are not prepared to give such an answer as they would have done, had they had notice. Here has been likewise great struggling and striving to have the verdict read to overthrow Mrs. *Duffett*'s testimony; but that cannot be allowed to be given in evidence between these parties. Then they would have read her husband's oath, he being dead: but that is no point of evidence at all neither; for in case the man were alive, it would not be evidence what he should have heard his own wife say. If both of them indeed had been heard together, and testified against my Lady *Ivy*, it had been good evidence; or they both might have testified for her. But by the Law the husband cannot be a witness against his wife, nor a wife against her husband, to charge them with any thing criminal, except only in cases of high-treason. This is so known a common rule, that I thought it could never have borne any question or debate.

This is the substance of the evidence on both sides, as near as I can recollect it; save only that which indeed I should have mentioned before, the Defendant had produced an exemplification of a verdict obtained the last *Michaelmas* Term. To which they for the Plaintiff answer, We were not then prepared to answer your deeds, which were very new, surprizing and unexpected to us: We have now given new evidence that we never gave then, and it was a verdict obtained by surprize: We now shew our boundaries better than we could then; and so that they make to be the result of the whole matter.

Now upon the main, after this very long evidence, though the Case has been darkened as much as ever any Case could be endeavoured to be; and though the event of it be a matter of considerable value, yet the matter of fact is as clear as the sun at noon-day; and a plain point of fact it is, and must depend upon. If we do admit all their deeds to be good deeds, without any consideration of the forgery, *pro* or *con*, yet if the mill-ponds, ditches, orchards, gardens, &c. can be taken to be seven acres; then the boundaries upon the mill or hilly-bank, which may well be *Foxe's-lane*, that will answer both the deeds of the Plaintiff and of the Defendant, and though never so many houses be built upon it, it will signify nothing in the Case. And that it is so, whereas the Defendant's surveyor swears, that 130 acres will not be made up without the lands in question; the Plaintiff has brought two surveyors, that swear there is full 130 acres, and more, without them. So you have two surveyors on the one side, and one on the other; and you yourselves have viewed it.

After this long evidence, Gentlemen, you have had as good an account of the substance of it, as I can by my notes and memory recollect. If any of the Gentlemen that are of the Counsel for the Plaintiff, or for the Defendant, do think I have omitted any thing that is material, on either side, they have free liberty to remind the Court of it. You are the Judges of this fact, whether this land do of right belong to the Plaintiff or to the Defendant: And I leave it to your consideration.

After which, the Jury withdrew to consider of their Verdict, and the Court arose. That Evening the Jury gave in a private Verdict before a Judge; and appearing the next morning at the Bar, were called over, and demanded if they did abide by the Verdict they had given the night before; to which they answered, Yes: which being declared by the Secondary to be for the Plaintiff, the Jury were discharged.

Then a motion was made by the Plaintiff's Counsel, that several deeds produced by the Defendant, that were detected of forgery, might be left in Court, in order to have them pursued, and convicted of the forgery. The Court, upon debate of the matter, and the Plaintiff's Counsel declaring they would prosecute an Information of forgery, the deeds of the 13th of *November*, and the 22d of *December*, 2 and 3 *Phil.* and *Mary*, were ordered to be left with the Clerk of the Crown till further Order, and in the mean time the Plaintiff to have Copies of them from the Clerk; and by Rule of Court a Trial at Bar is ordered in *Michaelmas* Term.

In Trinity-Term there was an Information against Lady Ivy, *for forging and publishing the said two Indentures, as follows.*

Rex *versus* Ivy.

Information against the Lady Ivy, *for forging and publishing two Indentures*, Trin. 36 Car. Secund. Rot. 48.

ss. QUod Theodosia Bryan, de, &c. alias dict' Theodosia Ivy, de, &c. vid. die anno, &c. Vi & Armis, &c. apud Westm. in Com. Midd' ex suo propr. capite & imaginatione subtilit' falso & fraudulent' fabricavit & fecit & fieri & fabricari causavit quoddam falsum factum continen' Materiam sequen' videlicet, *This Indenture made the* 13th *Day of* November, *in the 2d and 3d year of the Reign of our Lord and Lady*, Philip *and* Mary, *by the Grace of God, King and Queen of* England, Spain, France *and* Ireland; *Defenders of the Faith, Arch-Dukes of* Austria, *Dukes of* Burgundy, Milan, *and* Brabant; *Counts of* Hasburgh, Flanders *and* Tyrol: *Between* Marcellus Hall *of* Radcliff, *miller, on the one Part, and* Richard Roper, *Citizen and Salter of* London, *of the other Part, witnesseth*, &c. prout per pred' falsum & controfact' factum plenius liquet & apparet Quodq; pred' Theodosia Bryan alias dict' Domina T. Ivy postea, scilicet die, anno, &c. apud, &c. scient' subtilit' & falso pred' falsum & fabricatum factum publicavit & publicari causavit ut verum factum pred' Marcelli Hall sigillat' & deliberat' p. prefat' M. H. ubi revera eadem T. B. alias dict' Domina T. I. adtunc & ibidem bene scivit & intellexit dictum factum fore falsum controfact' & fabricat' Anglice *Forged*, & non fuisse factum pred' M. H. nec p. ipsum sigillat' & deliberat' Et ulterius pred' Coron' & Attorn' dicti Dom' Regis pro eodem Domino Rege dat' Cur' hic intelligi & informari quod eadem T. B. alias, &c. die & anno suprad' &c. vi & armis, &c. apud, &c. ex suo proprio capite & imaginatione scient' subtilit' falso & fraudulent' fabricavit & fecit & fieri & fabricari causavit quoddam al' falsum factum continen' materiam sequen' videlicet, *This Indenture, made*, &c. prout per pred' ult' mentionat' falsum & controfactum factum plenius liquet & apparet Et pred' T. B. alias, &c. postea scilicet die anno suprad', &c. apud, &c. scient' subtilit' & falso pred' falsum & fabricatum factum ult' mentionat' publicavit & publicari causavit ut verum factum pred' M. H. sigillat' & deliberat' per prefat' M. H. ubi revera eadem T. B. alias, &c. adtunc & ibid. bene scivit & intellexit dictum ult' mentionat' factum fore falsum controfact' & fabricat' Anglice *Forged*, & non fuisse factum pred' M. H. nec per ipsum sigillat' aut deliberat' Ad grave dampn' ejusdem G. B. in contempt' dicti Domini Regis nunc Legumq; suar' in malum & perniciosum exemplum omn' al' in tali casu delinquen' ac contra pacem dicti Domini Regis nunc Coron' & Dignitat' suas, &c.

XXXVIII. The Trial of *William Difney*, Efq. by the King *Terminer*, held at the *Marfhalfea* in *Southwark*, on *Thurfday*

A SPECIAL Commiffion of *Oyer* and *Terminer* for the County of *Surrey*, being appointed for the trying of Mr. *Difney*, before the Lord Chief Juftice of *England*, and other his Majefty's Juftices; he was brought before the King's Commiffioners at the *Marfhalfea*, in *Southwark*, on *June* 21, in order to his Trial upon an Indictment for High-Treafon: "For printing and publifhing a moft vile and traitorous Paper "againft his moft facred Majefty and his Government, intituled, *The* "*Declaration of* James *Duke of* Monmouth, *and the Noblemen, Gentlemen,* "*and others now in Arms*, &c." And being arraign'd thereupon, he pleaded Not guilty, and defir'd he might have Counfel granted him, but was denied; the Court telling him it was not allowable in capital Cafes: yet upon his farther requeft, he had leave to make ufe of what Books he thought fit to prepare for his defence, and allowed till the 25th.

On *Thurfday* the 25th, he was brought to his Trial; when the Meffenger depofed, that having a Warrant for the apprehending of *William Difney*, Efq. he took fome files of Mufqueteers, and two or three Gentlemen to his affiftance; when approaching to the houfe of one *Tyrrel*, a Gardener in the parifh of *Lambeth*, on *Monday June* the 15th, 1685, between twelve and one of the clock in the morning, he broke into the apartment of Mr. *Difney*; where entering his chamber, he found the prifoner in his fhirt, who crav'd his breeches: but the Meffenger replied No, faying, if he had a Night-Gown he might put it on. Immediately after viewing his breeches, there was found a dagger in his pocket, and alfo fome other things, likewife a brace of piftols, and a great hanger in the nature of a Scimeter.

His maid *Mary Allett* was fuppofed to be in bed with him, by reafon her cloaths were upon his bed: his daughter about eleven years of age or thereabouts was in another part of the room a-bed alone. The Meffenger farther depofed, that getting into the Printing-houfe, he there found the Forms (as Printers call them) of the traitorous Declaration in the Printing-room, there being by computation about 750 of them printed on one fide, and about five of the faid traitorous Declarations perfect. Upon the Meffenger's queftioning how they came there, he pretended ignorance.

The evidence appearing very plain, and he making little or no defence for himfelf, was found guilty of High-Treafon; fentenced to be drawn, hanged, and quarter'd; which was accordingly done at *Kenningtom-Common* in the County of *Surrey*, on *Monday* the 29th of *June*, 1685, and his quarters fet upon the City-gates.

A true and full Account given by the Minifter of St. George, *concerning the Behaviour and laft dying Speech of* William Difney, *Efq.* June *29th*, 1685.

BEtween nine and ten of the clock in the morning, I was fent for by the High Sheriff of *Surrey*, to officiate as Ordinary at the execution of the prifoner at the *Marfhalfea*. Before he was brought out, a neighbouring Minifter and I (upon the Sheriff's motion) went into the room where he was; when the reverend Parfon (having feen him the night before) afk'd him whether he had confidered of thofe things which he had formerly offer'd him; and did very pathetically prefs him that he would give glory to God, by a full and ingenuous confeffion of his crime, intimating to him the fatal confequences that might have followed, if he had perfected that evil work: how many men's lives might have been loft in the quarrel; whofe blood he was fo far guilty of, as he contributed to the increafe of the rebellion, by his printing the traitorous paper (or words

to the fame effect
difcontent) to th
did not come to
to fay that migh
fo he defired not
paffed ere we par
I only told him,
he thanked me.

When he cam
afked him, how
were yet to come
for yourfelf, or I
fire you to pray f
I fhewed him the
remember out of
Jefus Chrift cam
And then he pro
finner againft Go
that he had confe
God's pardon; a
Jefus Chrift parc
hopes that he f
merits, but the r
if his hopes were
the Scriptures, w
upon I recounte
Penitents; as tha
ednefs, and doeth t
After which he m
him all his fins,
to blefs the King
as well as juft to
to him in giving
have taken him o
And then (he fai
given me time to
fhame of this dea
may fomewhat d
Afterwards he de
ing to his mind a
he anfwered ever
lived in, and did
which he repeate
After Prayer, I a
He anfwer'd No.
do or fay? He ar
for your care of r
for me, and mine
left him going to

This, accordin
and, as near as I
ney and me.

XXXIX. The Trial of Sir *Edward Hales*, Bart. for neglecti and Allegiance, with his Plea thereto, upon the King's and the Opinion of the Judges thereupon, 1686.

Pafchæ, 2 *Jac.* II. In the *King's-Bench.*

Arthur Godden *Plaintiff, in an Action of Debt of* 500*l. grounded upon the Act of* 25 Car. II. *for preventing Dangers from* Popifh *Recufants.*

Sir Edward Hales, *Bart. Defendant.*

THE Plaintiff declares, That the Defendant, after the firft day of *Eafter-Term* 1673. *fc.* 28 *Nov.* 1 *Jac.* II. at *Hackington* in *Kent*, was admitted to the office of a Colonel of a Foot-Regiment.

That being a military office, and a place of truft under the King, and by authority from the King.

And the Defendant held that office by the fpace of three months, next after the 28 *Nov.* 1 *Jac.* II.

And from the
is an inhabitant

And the Plain
three months nex
not receive the S
to receive it;

Avers, that th
and Allegiance,
Quarter-Seffions
next Term after
after.

And that the I
Hackington in *Ke*
to the Statute of
fants.

* 25 *Car.* II. *cap.* 2. *An Act for preventing Dangers which may happen from* Popifh *Recufants.*] For preventi the minds of his Majefty's good Subjects, be it enacted, &c. That every perfon that fhall bear any office, from or under his Majefty, &c. within the Realm of *England*, &c. fhall perfonally appear in the Co Quarter-Seffions in that County where he fhall refide, within three Months next after his admittance into Oaths of Supremacy and Allegiance, and fhall alfo receive the Sacrament of the Lord's Supper, according upon fome Lord's-day, immediately after Divine Service.

Whereupon the Defendant at *Rochester*, at the Assizes held 29th *Mar.* 2 *Jac.* II. was duly indicted for such his neglect, and for executing the said office contrary to the said Statute.

And thereupon duly convict, as by the Record thereof appears; whereupon the Plaintiff became entitled to this 500*l.* as forfeited by the Defendant.

The Defendant pleads, that the King within the three months, in the declaration mentioned, and before the next Term or Quarter-Sessions, after his admittance to the said office, and before his suit began, *sc.* 9 *Jan.* 1 *Jac.* II. by his Letters Patent under the Great Seal, and here produced in Court, did dispense with, pardon, remit and discharge (among others) the Defendant from taking the said oaths, and from receiving the Sacrament, and from subscribing the declaration against Transubstantiation or tests in the Act of 25 *Car.* II. for preventing dangers from *Popish* Recusants, or in any other Act, and from all crimes, convictions, penalties, forfeitures, damages, disabilities, by him incurred by his exercising the office of Colonel.

Or by the Act intituled, *An Act for the preserving of the King's Person and Government, by disabling Papists from sitting in either House of Parliament.* Or by the Acts made in the first or third years of King *James* I. or the Acts made 5 *Eliz.* or 23, or 29, or 35 *Eliz.*

And the King, by his Letters Patent, granted, that the Defendant should be enabled to hold that office in any place in *England*, or *Wales*, or *Berwick*, or in the Fleet, or in *Jersey* or *Guernsey*, and to receive his pay or wages;

Any clause in the said Acts, or in any other Act notwithstanding, & *non obstante*, that the Defendant was or should be a Recusant convict,

As by the said Letters Patent doth appear.

Whereupon the Defendant prays judgment of the Court, whether the Plaintiff ought to maintain this action.

The Plaintiff demurred generally to this Plea.

The Defendant joined in demurrer.

The questions are two, 1. Whether the Defendant ought to have pleaded this pardon and dispensation to the indictment, or whether he may not plead it in bar to the action?

2. Admitting he may plead it to the action, whether it be a good bar, and whether the King by his prerogative may dispense with the Statute?

Mr. *Northey*, who argued for the Plaintiff, held that the Defendant may not be permitted to plead this matter in bar of the action, because he ought to have pleaded it to the indictment; and he having not pleaded it then, the Law will construe it to be waving of it, as the case in *Brook's Abridgment*, Charter of Pardon, 15. That in case of an indictment for murder, one that has pleaded Not guilty, cannot plead the pardon after, unless dated since this plea of not guilty. So 3 *Crooke* in a *Fieri Facias*, if the Defendant appears, and has a release, and does not plead it, he has lost the benefit of it, and shall not be released by *Audita Querela*: now the Defendant shall not be permitted to plead it against the Plaintiff, no more than he could have pleaded it against the King; for this action is in the nature of an execution upon a judgment, and may be likened to this case; an administrator *de bonis non*, by 17 Car. II. is enabled to sue forth an execution upon a judgment, recovered by an executor of the first testator, and the Statute doth put the administrator in the same case as the executor was; and the Defendant in that case can allege no other matter against the administrator, than he could have done against the executor, neither can he avoid this execution by any plea that he might have pleaded to the first action. And if this Defendant shall be received to plead this plea now, he will falsify the indictment, that was found against him, for if the offence be pardoned, he ought not to have been indicted: but admit this Defendant may well plead this plea, yet I hold it no bar to the Plaintiff's action.

I do allow that the King may dispense with several penal Laws in some cases, but that prerogative of the King is bounded, so that with some Statutes he cannot dispense, wherein the subject is interested, as in 4 *Instit.* (135) So the King cannot license a man to make a nuisance or commit a murder, as 11 *Henry* VII. 11, 12. And that this is an Act wherein all the subjects have an interest, I humbly submit to the Judgment of the Court.

The King cannot dispense with the Statute 31 of *Eliz. chap.* 6. against Simony, nor with the Statute 17 *Edw.* VI. 1. against buying and selling of offices, as appears by the 1 *Instit.* 12. *a.* 30. *Instit.* 154. 20. *Crooke* 385. *Hobart* 75. 1 *Instit.* 234. *a.* A man that is disabled by Law to take such an office, the King cannot capacitate him: as if the King should grant to one to sell an office, within the Statute *Edw.* VI. and to another to buy that office, these Grants would be void, as in *Vaughan* 534. in the case of *Thomas* and *Sorrel*, there are several cases put, wherein the King cannot dispense with a Statute.

Now by this Statute that we are upon, it is enacted, that every officer shall take the oaths, that every person that does neglect, shall be disabled to hold the said office; now this Act does not work upon the taking, but upon the holding; and if such conditions be not performed, he is thereby rendered uncapable to hold his office, and the King can never enable a man whom the Law hath disabled, 3 *Instit.* 154. But I foresee the case in 12 *Coke* 18. will be objected against me, where it is said, that no Act of Parliament can bind the King from any prerogative which is solely and inseparably annexed to his person, but that he may dispense with it by a *non obstante*; and the Book doth instance in the case of Sheriffs, upon the Statute 23 *Hen.* VI. which does enact, that all Patents made or to be made of any office of a Sheriff, &c. for term of years, &c. within any County of *England*, &c. shall forfeit 200*l.* Yet, says that Book, the King may dispense with that Statute, and cites 2 *Hen.* VII. 66. to be there so adjudged by all the Judges of *England*; and that this is the only authority that seems to countenance this case. But this is the opinion only of my Lord *Coke*, for the Book which he cites and depends upon was never adjudged, as appears by *Brook* 5 *pt.* 45, 109 and what was said in that case, was only said by one Judge, and never judicially determined, nor so much as spoken to by any other Judge; therefore the foundation that my Lord *Coke* has laid, failing, the superstructure must needs fall, and so, with submission, that single opinion in 12 *Coke*, *fol.* 18. is not law. But admitting the case to be Law, that can be no rule to guide this case by, for that Statute was made, rather to deprive the King of his power of making Sheriffs, and so consequently commanding his Sheriffs not to serve him, than to disable the subject, and thereby restraining the King's prerogative, which is so inherent in him. But by the Statute 25 *Car.* II. 2. the prerogative of the King is not touched, for the King may grant the office to any of his subjects, and it is only a direction to the subject to qualify himself for the King's service; and if he be uncapable to serve the King, 'tis through his own fault and neglect, and may be punishable for the same, as in the case of Sir *John Reade*, in 27 and 28 *Car.* II. in the *Exchequer* he was made and sworn Sheriff of *Hertfordshire*, and neglected to take the oaths according to this Statute; by reason of which, the office became void, and afterwards there was an information exhibited against him upon this Statute we are now upon, for neglecting to take the said oaths, and executing his office, and upon this he was convicted and fined. And the Court was of opinion that no subject could put himself out of a capacity to serve the King, but for so doing he is punishable; and in the Law of the Sheriffs the dispensation is in the Patent, but in our case the dispensation is after the Patent, and so a difference between the two cases: and for these reasons, I pray your Lordship's judgment for the Plaintiff.

Arguments for the Defendant.

Sir *Thomas Powys*, the King's Solicitor, argued for the Defendant.

AS to the first point, that supposing the Defendant ought to have pleaded the dispensation to the Indictment, it does not appear by this Record, but that he did; for the declaration is, that he was *Legitime Modo Convictus*, and does not say whether he pleaded Not guilty, or how he pleaded; and for any thing that appears, he did plead it against the King, yet he may be admitted to plead it against the Plaintiff who is a stranger.

If they stand upon this as an estople, they ought to have relied upon it, and replied, that he had the dispensation at the time of the Indictment, and refused to plead it; for he that pleads an estople, must rely upon it, as the authorities are which treat of estoples. And therefore as to the first point, I think, with submission, we have very well pleaded the pardon and dispensation in bar of the action.

As to the second point, whether the King can dispense with the Statute or no; I humbly conceive, with submission, the King may very well dispense with the Statute; 'tis admitted that the King may in many cases dispense with an Act of Parliament, and let us consider why not this? It's well observed in 2 *Instit.* 496. that the King's prerogative is as much the Law of *England* as any other Law whatsoever; and the King may upon any cause moving him in respect of time, place, or person, by a *non obstante* dispense with any particular person, and that he shall not incur the penalty of the Statute, 7 *Coke* 36, 37. *Vaughan* 333. 347. *Glanvil* in his argument *ante P.* 205. doth admit a power in the King to dispense with *Penal Laws*, and yet he was no friend to the prerogative. Though the consent of the Lords and Commons be requisite to the making of the Act of Parliament, yet it is the King that gives the sanction to the said Laws, and most of the ancient Statutes began in form of Charters, as it appears in 8 *Coke* 19. and the intents and meanings of Acts of Parliament, are every day by the Judges extended, and changed according to a better rule of Reason and Justice than the words will bear, *Hobart* 229 and the Judges have an authority over the Statute-Laws, to mould them according to the truest and best sense, *Hobart* 346. and Statutes which have been made against common right, have been construed void, 8 *Coke* 118.

There is a distinction taken in our Books between Malum in se, *and* Malum prohibitum.

The former the King cannot dispense with, the latter he may; as where the Statute generally prohibits any thing upon a penalty, which was lawful before, (the Subject receiving no Injury by such a Dispensation) the King there may dispense with such an Act. *Vaughan* 343. *Dyer* 5. 2. The King granted a licence to carry Bell-metal out of the Realm, notwithstanding the Statute, *Dyer* 54. It was enacted by Statute, 4 *Hobart* 9. that none should convey wine into *England* out of *Gascoigne*, but in *English* ships; and the King granted a licence to a man, that he, his deputies and factors might convey, &c. in any ship, notwithstanding the Statute, 28 *Coke* 32 *Vaughan* 352, 353, 354. Now to apply the cases to the case in question, this is *Malum Prohibitum*, whether is the dispensation any damage to the subject? If it were any wrong, it were to the King himself, and sure the King may very well dispense with that, which only relates to himself.

I must distinguish between those Acts of Parliament which concern Property, and those which concern Government. Acts of Parliament which concern Property, the King cannot dispense with; but those which concern Government he may; and this for the great inconveniencies which may happen, or urgencies of State which may force him to it, and those unforeseen at the time of making the Law: for it may happen, by a vicissitude of times, those Laws that were made for the preservation of Government, should turn to the destruction of it, if the King could not dispense with them.

The Common Law in some cases does so very much respect the prerogative, that it leaves the private interest of the subject unregarded, and the King may dig in any of his subjects land for Saltpetre to make Gun-powder. Now this Statute 25 *Car.* II. was made to diminish the King's

And every the person aforesaid, that doth or shall neglect or refuse to take the said Oaths and the Sacrament in the said Courts, and at the respective times aforesaid, shall be *ipso facto* adjudged uncapable, and disabled in Law to all intents and purposes whatsoever, to have, occupy or enjoy, the said office or employment, and every such office and place shall be void, *and is hereby adjudged void.*

And every person that shall neglect or refuse to take the said Oaths or the Sacrament as aforesaid, and yet after such neglect or refusal, shall execute any of the said offices, after the said times expired, wherein he ought to have taken the same, and being thereupon lawfully convicted upon any information, &c. in any of the King's Courts at *Westminster*, or at the Assizes, every such person shall forfeit 500*l* to be recovered by him that shall sue for the same.

And at the same time when the persons concerned in this Act shall take the said Oaths, they shall likewise subscribe the Petition against the belief of Transubstantiation under the same penalties as by this Act is appointed.

prerogative, but to secure him from his enemies, and for the preservation of the Government; and the King is best judge what will be most for his own security, and the Government's preservation. No Act of Parliament can discharge the subject from his allegiance which he owes to the King. every one is bound by his allegiance to serve his Prince when he shall be required. Therefore no Act of Parliament can disable any man to serve the King. But they object, that this Act doth make no one incapable, but at his own election.

If this were so, it would be in the election of some or all the subjects to incapacitate themselves to serve the King, and the King would be unserved: for if it were not in the power of the King to force the subject, he would not (it may be not) be served at all; as in the case of Sir *John Reade*, cited by the other side; he neglected to take the oaths, and thereby the office became void; so that the next elected might refuse, and the next. In the mean time the King's service lies neglected, and no business of the County can proceed, for want of a Sheriff. To pardon murder, is a prerogative solely and inseparably incident to the King, who may dispense with Statutes restraining it, 12 *Coke* 18. He may dispense with *non residente*. *Hobart* 146. 3 *Institut.* 339. In 3 *Instit.* the Lord *Coke* speaking of Acts of Parliament that were made to restrain the King's power of pardoning murder, says, that such Acts are good for King's to follow, but not binding, *Coke* 18, 19. There are several Statutes cited, with which the King by his prerogative may dispense, as the Statute 36 *Hen.* VI. which does enact, that no man shall be Sheriff of one County two years together. Yet it was adjudged by all the Judges of *England*, says that Book, that the King may dispense with it; the Statute of 4 *Hen.* IV. 31. that no *Welshman* shall be Justice, or other Officer whatsoever in any part of *Wales*; and yet the King may dispense with it. The Statute 8 *Rich.* 22. and 33 *Hen.* VIII. 24. do enact, that none shall be Justice of the Assize in the County where he was born, and yet the King with a special *non obstante* may dispense with that Statute. And in *Plowden* 502. 13. the King may grant to a man to be an Escheater for life, notwithstanding that Statute.

To answer the Statutes which have been cited, which the King cannot dispense with: I say, as to the Statutes of Simony and Usury, the King cannot dispense with them; but what is that to the matter in hand? For there is no restriction of the subjects service, but the King may have the benefit notwithstanding. Then as to the Statute 5 *Ed.* VI. 16. against buying and selling of judicial offices, of which Statute, there is a clause in the 1*st Institut.* 134. that the King may not dispense with that Statute: There is a difference between that Statute and this; for that does enact, that if any person shall bargain and sell any office, &c. shall lose the office, &c. and all such bargains and contracts shall be void; and that he that shall give any sum of money, &c. for any such office, &c. shall be a disabled person in Law, to have, occupy, or enjoy the said office, &c.

Now the Statute doth disable the party upon doing such an act, to take the office; for the making the bargain is prior to taking the office, and thereby he is disabled to take it, so that he can never have the office legally vested in him, if the King cannot dispense with a conditional subsequent, and so that does not come near this. And for this reason I humbly pray Judgment for the Defendant.

Then the Lord Chief-Justice Herbert *spake thus:*

Chief-Justice. THIS is a case of great consequence, but of as little difficulty as ever any case was, that raised so great an expectation, for if the King cannot dispense with this Statute, he cannot dispense with any *Penal Law* whatsoever.

As to the first point, whether he shall be admitted to plead this dispensation, and pardon to this action of debt; (having not pleaded it to the Indictment) I think he may: for this Court shall not be bound by the finding of the Jury below, for he (for any thing that does appear) did plead it there, and the Jury might have gone against the direction of the Court, yet that shall not conclude us; but if the party has good matter to discharge himself, we may shew it: as if a man be convicted of an assault and battery against the Defendant, the Plaintiff may give the former conviction in evidence, but yet he must also prove the battery, or else he shall not recover.

And this being an estople, it shall not bind, because the Plaintiff was not party to the first suit.

As to the second point, whether the King can dispense with the Act or no, I think it a question of little difficulty. There is no Law whatsoever but may be dispensed with by the supreme Law-giver; as the Laws of God may be dispensed with by God himself; as it appears by God's command to *Abraham*, to offer up his son *Isaac*: So likewise the Law of Man may be dispensed with by the Legislator, for a Law may either be too wide or too narrow, and there may be many cases which may be out of the conveniencies which did induce the Law to be made; for it is impossible for the wisest Law-maker to foresee all the cases that may be, or are to be remedied, and therefore there must be a power somewhere, able to dispense with these Laws. But as to the case of Simony, that is objected by the other side, that is against the Law of God, and a special offence, and therefore *malum in se*, which I do agree the King cannot dispense with. And as to the cases of Usury and Non-Residence, those cases do come in under that rule, that the King cannot dispense with them, because the subject has a benefit by them; for in case of Usury the Bond is made void by the Statute, and therefore if the King should dispense with it, the subject would lose the benefit of the avoiding the Bond. And as to the cases of buying and selling of offices, which are objected, there is no need of resolving, whether the King could dispense with that Statute or no, because the party was disabled to take any such office by the contract, and

the disability was
the King could n
have been in this
take the oaths, re
dispensation; for
tacked, it does pr

The case of the
to it in every part
and the King to g
says, that the Pat
contrary; and ther
Opinion of all the
with that Statute;
dispense with it by
in it that it should n
that made it, may r
at the time of grant
the time of granting
oaths, for doing of
the case of the Sheriff
time, and is cited fo
questioned; for the
to it: then I defy all
that and this, only th
ticulars. But becau
it does concern us to
of so great consequen
some Sheriffs that be
Juries, and then we
offenders; and it also
vice of it: for if that
to 23 *Hen.* VIII. 24.
go the Circuits; and
as well in that case as

On *Monday* the 21
Judges, his Lordship
"In the Case of *Go*
"pensation from the K
"such a Prerogative?
"as clear a Case as eve
"I know not what diffi
"to give so much coun
"advice of all the Jud
"*jeant's-Inn*, and this c
"Sheriffs was put, whe
"cause upon that depen
"And I must tell you,
"delivered their opinion
"and that all the Attain
"returned by such Sher
"quently that men need
"And in the next place,
"ginable difference betw
"were the much cleare
"tions.

"My Brother *Powel* f
"but he would rather hav
"since sent by my Broth
"with us. To these t
"*Street*; who yet continu
"in this Case: But that
"opinion of eleven. W
"having the concurrence
"well declare the opinion
"in this Case: And the J
"1. That the Kings of
"2. That the laws of
"3. That therefore 't
"*England*, to dispense with
"ticular necessary Reason
"4. That of those reason
"judge: And then, which
"5. That this is not a t
"People, but the ancient r
"of the Kings of *England*;
"be. And therefore such a
"time enough to save him fr
"for the Defendant †,

Quod querens nil cap

This Judgment making a
fication of his opinion, publ

A Short Account of the Authori
Sir Edward Hales's *Case*:
of the Common-Pleas, in vin

HAVING been called to a pl
my most sincere resolut
the duty of that place, wit

* See *Comberbach's* Reports, *page* 21, &c *seq.* where this Case is largely reported.

† Bishop *Burnet*, in his History of his own Time, *Vol.* I. *pag.* 669. says: Sir *Edward Hales*, a Gentleman of a noble
had long disguised it; and had once to myself so solemnly denied it, that I was led from thence to see, there was no credit
or Religion was concerned. He had an Employment, and not taking the Test, his coachman was set up to inform against
the Informer: When this was to be brought to trial, the Judges were secretly asked their opinions; and such as were not
ed out; and upon two or three canvassings, the half of them were dismissed, and others of more pliable and obedient under
were weak and ignorant to a scandal. The Suit went on in a feeble prosecution, and in *Trinity*-Term Judgment was given.

And in *page* 671. the Bishop says,

But Judges, who are before-hand determined how to give their opinions, will not be much moved, even by the stronges
cation at the bar, were rather a farce, fitter for a mock-trial in a Play, than such as became men of Learning in so import
hear with what arguments the Judges would maintain the Judgment that they should give; but they made nothing of it:
Defendant, as if it had been in a Cause of course.

hard fortune to fall under the greatest infamy and reproach that is possible for any man to lie under, of perjury and breach of trust; in giving a Judgment in Sir *Edward Hales*'s Case, contrary to Law, and contrary to my knowledge and opinion (for that only can make it criminal); and which, they say, tends to the subversion of all our Laws, contrary to the oath that every Judge takes, and to that high trust reposed in him, to judge to the best of his understanding, according to Law: Although I cannot hope to wipe off that universal ill impression that the malice of some people, who understand the nature of this Case very well, has made upon most men who do not understand it; yet in order to clear myself to all just and disinterested persons who are only my enemies by mistake, I think myself obliged to give some short account of that Judgment, and the grounds upon which it was given: and this I will do, not by making an elaborate and legal argument, to make out by reasons of my own, that the Judgment then given is consonant to Law; which whether it be or no, is like to be considered in Parliament, and to whose determination I shall as entirely and chearfully submit, as any other person in the Nation. But I shall set down, not all the variety of Cases that we meet with in our Books, touching the King's power of dispensing with Acts of Parliament; for that would swell this Paper to an unreasonable length, and discourage many from reading any part of it; but only some few of the chiefest and plainest authorities in Law, upon which the resolution in the Case of Sir *Edward Hales* was grounded. I shall not only cite the Books and Pages where those Cases are to be found, but transcribe the very words, that every body may be convinced, that if we were in a mistake, it was no wilful mistake, but that we had the authority of former Judgments given by great men that went before us (and for which they were never questioned) to lead us into it.

The Case (for I must state it upon my memory, not having any Copy of the Record by me) was shortly this:

An action popular was brought against Sir *Edward Hales*, upon the Statute 25 *Car.* II. *c.* 2. for the penalty of 500*l.* wherein the Plaintiff declares, that whereas it was provided by the Statute, *&c.* (setting forth the Statute): Notwithstanding which, the Defendant having a commission to serve the King as a Colonel of Foot, and not having received the Sacrament, nor taken the oaths and tests, *&c.* within the times prescribed by the Act, and after the times expired wherein he ought to have received the Sacrament, and taken the oaths and tests as aforesaid, he did execute the said Office, and continued to act by colour of the said commission; of which he was indicted and convicted at the Assizes in *Kent, &c.* whereby the action accrues to the Plaintiff for the penalty of 500*l.* The Defendant pleads, that before the time expired, *&c.* he had a dispensation under the broad Seal to act, *non obstante* that Statute.

To which the Plaintiff demurs.

And Judgment was given for the Defendant, that his Plea was good.

And first, it will be necessary to shew what this dispensing Power is, which is warranted by our Judgment; and that will best appear by the definition of it, which is given in the 11th Report of my Lord *Coke, page* 88. in the Case of Monopolies; *Dispensatio mali prohibiti est de jure Domino Regi concessa propter impossibilitatem prævidendi de omnibus particularibus; & dispensatio est mali prohibiti provida relaxatio, utilitate seu necessitate pensatâ.* "For true it is (says the Book) that in as much as an Act of "Parliament, which generally prohibits any thing upon a penalty that is "popular, or only given to the King, may be inconvenient to divers particular persons, in respect of person, time, or place; for this purpose "the Law [illegible] a power to the King to dispense with particular persons."

And in the [illegible] *Rep. p.* 63. in the Case of penal Statutes, which was the opinion of all the Judges of *England*, 2 *Jacobi*, it is resolved, 'That 'the King may dispense with any particular person; that he shall not incur 'the penalty of the Statute, tho' it be an Act made *pro bono publico*; and 'that this is a trust and confidence inseparably annexed to the royal per'son of the King.' I cite these two first cases, chiefly to shew, that a Dispensation in its nature is particular, and given to particular persons by name; which is all the power that is attributed to the King by our Judgment. And this I mention, because of an unreasonable mistake of most People that talk of the dispensing Power, as though the King's declaration of *Liberty of Conscience*, whereby all the Laws that concern Religion are at once totally suspended and laid asleep, were warranted by it: Let that declaration stand or fall upon its own bottom, I am sure the Case I am now speaking of has nothing to do with it. And having by these Cases cleared the nature of all dispensations, which are always granted to particular persons (as Sir *Edward Hales*'s was in our Case, who was the first, and I think the only, person who then had such a Dispensation), I shall now cite some of the chief authorities upon which our Judgment was given in that case: And the first and great case that I cite, wherein the King's dispensing Power is described and limited, is in the Year-book of *Hen.* VII. *fol.* 11. & *H.* VII. *fol.* 12. in these words: "There is a diversity (says "the Book) between *malum prohibitum* and *malum in se*, as a Statute for"bids any man to coin money, and if he does he shall be hanged; this "is *malum prohibitum*; for before the Statute coining money was lawful, "but now it is not so, and therefore the King can dispense with it. So "if a man ship wool in any place but *Calais*, it is *malum prohibitum*; because "it is prohibited by Act of Parliament, and the King can dispense with "it, and so in like cases: But that which is *malum in se*, the King, nor "no other person can dispense with; as if the King would give a man "power to kill another, or license one to make a nusance in a high"way, this were void; and yet the King can pardon these things when "they are done." These are the very words of that Book; and my Lord *Vaughan* discoursing of, and explaining this case in the case of *Thomas* and *Sorrell*, in his *Rep. p.* 333. first shews, how a Dispensation differs from a Pardon. For a Dispensation does *jus dare*, and makes the thing prohibited (to all others) lawful to be done by him that has it. And therefore the King cannot dispense with *mala in se*, because they never were, and never can be, made lawful: But even these (says the Year-book) may be pardoned after they are done.

From these Cases results this plain Syllogism; Whatever is not prohibited by the Law of God, but was lawful before any Act of Parliament made to forbid it, the King, by his Dispensation, granted to a particular person, may make lawful again, to that person who has such Dispensation, though it continues unlawful to every body else.

But to execute any office without taking the oaths and the tests antecedent to any Acts of Parliament made to forbid it, was lawful.

Therefore the Dispensation granted to Sir *Edward Hales*, did make it lawful for him to do so, though it continued unlawful for any body else.

In this argument the premises are none of our own; we have them out of our law books; and the authority of those books have never yet been questioned. I appeal then to any indifferent person, whether it can be criminal in Judges, to draw a necessary conclusion from premises, and book-cases that have been taken for Law for so many ages together.

The next great Case is the resolution of all the Judges of *England*, in 2 *Hen.* VII. in the *Exchequer-Chamber*, upon the King's Power of dispensing with the Statute of 23 *Hen.* VI. *cap.* 8. *That no man should be Sheriff for above one year.* The recital in the preamble, and the whole Purview, if compared with our Statute of 25 *Car.* II. *cap.* 2. equals it in every particular, and in some goes beyond it: for the mischiefs recited in this latter Statute are only in these words, *For preventing dangers which may happen from Popish Recusants, and quieting the minds of his Majesty's good Subjects.* The cause of making the Statute of 23 *Hen.* VI. is for preventing the importable damage of the King and his People, perjury, manslaughter and great oppression. The Purview enacts,

1. *That no man shall be Sheriff for above a year.*
2. *That all Letters Patent made for years or lives shall be void.*
3. *That no* Non obstante *shall make them good* (which shews that the Parliament thought the King could otherwise have dispensed with this Act by a *Non obstante*).
4. *Whoever acts by colour of such Letters Patent shall forfeit* 200*l.*
5. *He shall be utterly disabled to bear the office of Sheriff in any County of* England.
6. *That every Pardon for such offence shall be void.*

Notwithstanding all this, it was adjudged in that Case before-cited by all the Judges of *England*, (who were at that time as learned as ever sate upon the Bench); I say, it was adjudged by all the Judges in the Exchequer Chamber, that the King's Dispensation with that Statute was good.

Having then this Case before us, if we should have judged the Dispensation not good in Sir *Edward Hales*'s Case, it must have been upon one of these two grounds: that is, either, 1. In the first place, we must have found some difference between the King's power in that case and in this, which I confess, after the wisest enquiry, does not appear to me, and I wish any man would shew me any such difference if he can: or else, 2. We must have adjudged that solemn resolution given in the Exchequer Chamber by all the Judges of *England* so long ago, and which has been taken for good Law ever since, we must adjudge no Law: whereas the known rule is, that after any point of Law has been solemnly settled in the Exchequer-chamber by all the Judges, we never suffer it to be disputed or drawn in question again.

But our enemies seeing the force of this argument, have had the confidence to say, that that point is not resolved in that case; they might with as much modesty affirm, *Thou shalt not bear false Witness against thy Neighbour*, to be none of the Ten Commandments; we can only reply in this case as in that, that if we have eyes to read, and common sense to judge, it is there resolved. Indeed there is another point about the Sheriff's passing his accounts, which the Judges were divided in; but in the point of the dispensation they all agreed; or else, that other point could never have come in question.

But to put this beyond all controversy, we have two things to offer.

First, That it has been cited as adjudged in several books of great authority.

Secondly, It has been the constant practice to have such dispensations in all Kings reigns ever since that resolution.

As to the first, though I might cite many books, yet I will only cite three or four of the clearest and greatest authorities: and the first shall be *Fitzherbert*, in his abridgment of this very case, *Tit. Grant.* 33. who lived near this time, and could not easily be mistaken in the sense of the Year-book: *The patent*, says he, *was adjudged good by all the Justices; but the Statute says expresly, it shall be void*; therefore it is only made good by the King's dispensing.

2. Next to him shall be *Plowden*, who, as all Lawyers will confess, is as little like to be mistaken in the sense of the Year-books, as any Reporter we have; and he, in his *Commentaries, p.* 502. in the case between *Greendon* and the Bishop of *Lincoln*, after citing the case both out of Year-book, and out of *Fitzherbert*'s abridgment, has these very words where the Statute was, *That the King's grant to any man to be Sheriff of any County for longer time than a year shall be void, notwithstanding any clause of* non obstante *to be put into the patent*: There it is held, *that the King's grant to the Earl of* Northumberland, *to be Sheriff during life must have a clause of* Non-obstante, *because of the precise words of the Statute before-mentioned; and with such a clause of* Non-obstante, *the patent to the Earl was good.*

3. Next is my Lord *Coke*, who asserts the King's prerogative touching this matter in much higher terms than we could presume to do, in giving Judgment in Sir *Edward Hales*'s case: for in his twelfth report, page 18, he has these words: 'No Act can bind the King from any Prerogative 'which is sole and inseparable to his person, but that he may dispense 'with it by a *Non-obstante*, as a sovereign power to command any of his 'subjects to serve him for the publick weal; and this solely and insepa'rably is annext to his person: and his royal power cannot be restrained 'by any Act of Parliament, neither in *Thesi* nor in *Hypothesi*, but that 'the King by his royal Prerogative may dispense with it: For upon the 'Commandment of the King, and Obedience of the subject, does his Go'vernment consist; as is provided by the Statute of 23 *Hen.* VI. *cap.* 8. 'That all Patents made or to be made of any office of Sheriff, *&c.* for 'term of years, for life, in fee simple or in tail, are void and of none ef'fect, any clause or parol *de non obstante*, put or to be put into such pa'tents to be made notwithstanding. And further, whosoever shall take 'upon him or them, to accept or occupy such office of Sheriff, by virtue 'of such grants or patents, shall stand perpetually disabled to be or bear 'the office of Sheriff within any County of *England*, by the same autho'rity. And notwithstanding that by this Act, *First*, The Patent is made 'void. *Secondly*, The King is restrained to grant *non obstante*. *Thirdly*, 'The grantee disabled to take the office; yet the King by his royal sove'reign power of commanding, may command by his patent (for such causes, 'as he in his wisdom doth think meet and profitable for himself and the

'Commonwealth, of which he himself is solely Judge) to serve him and 'the weal Publick as Sheriff of such a County for Years, or for Life, *&c.* 'And so it was resolved by all the Justices of *England* in the *Exchequer-Chamber*, 2 *H.* VII. And after some other Cases to this Point of the 'King's Prerogative, he has this farther (*says he*) see 4 *Hen.* IV. *cap.* 31. 'in which it is ordained, that no *Welshman* be *Justice*, *Chamberlain*, *Treasurer*, *Sheriff*, *Steward*, *Constable* of a Castle, *Escheator*, *Coroner*, or chief '*Forester*, nor other Officer whatsoever, nor Keeper of *Records*, &c in any 'Part of *Wales*, notwithstanding any Patent made to the contrary, with 'Clause of *Non obstante licet sit Wallicus natus:* And yet without question 'the King may grant with a *Non obstante*.' Thus far that Book, and I have transcribed the Book at large, that every Body may see that the King's Power of dispensing with such Acts of Parliament as restrain his granting Offices, stands upon a peculiar Reason, besides the general one upon which his Power of dispensing with other penal Laws is founded. And that if this be a pernicious Opinion, we are not to suffer as the first Authors of it. But lest it should be objected, that this is my Lord *Coke*'s single Opinion, or that the twelfth Report is not of so great Authority as the rest of his Reports are; the same is resolved by all the Judges of *England*, (if my Lord *Coke* be a faithful Reporter) in *Calvin*'s Case, in the seventh Report, p. 14. in these Words. *Every Subject is by his natural Allegiance bound to serve and obey his Sovereign, &c. It is enacted by the Parliament of* 23 H. VI. *That no Man should serve the King as Sheriff of any County above one Year, and that notwithstanding any Clause of* Non obstante *to the contrary; that is to say, notwithstanding that the King should expresly dispense with the said Act; howbeit it is agreed,* 2 H. VII. *that against the express Purview of that Act the King may by a special* Non obstante *dispense with that Act.* For that the Act could not bar the King of the Service of his Subject, *which the Law of Nature did give unto him.* This is reported (unless my Lord *Coke* had a mind to deceive the succeeding Judges, and draw them in to give pernicious Opinions) as the Sense of all the Judges of *England* in King *James*'s Time, in the Exchequer-chamber.

And now I would ask, These Cases thus solemnly resolved, are they Law? Or are they not? If it shall be said, that they are not Law, what Foundations have the Judges to stand upon? or what certain Measures can they take in giving Judgment, either between the King and his Subjects, or between Party and Party; if so many solemn Resolutions by all the Judges in *England*, in the Exchequer-chamber, are not to be relied upon? If they are Law, then I appeal to all Mankind, whether our Case does not come up in every Tittle to the Reason of those Resolutions: Whether the Act of 25 *Car.* II do not bar the King of the Service of some of his Subjects; and whether therefore for great Reasons, and in particular Cases, he may not dispense with it?

But besides the Authority of this Case, we have the constant Practice, that this Statute of Sheriffs has been constantly dispensed with ever since it was made; and if those Dispensations were not good, then all Persons convicted upon Indictments found by Grand Juries, returned by such Sheriffs, are legally attainted; then all Pannels of Juries returned, and other Process executed in Civil Causes, by such Sheriffs, was altogether erroneous; and it is strange that Nobody in so long a Time should hit that Blot.

Obj. The only Objection that I hear is made to this, by eminent Men of our Profession, (who freely acknowledge the Authority of these Cases, and the Resolution in them, that no Act of Parliament can debar the King of the Service of his Subjects which the Law of Nature gives him, to be good Law;) is this, that say they, It is not the Act of Parliament that debars the King of the Service of his Subjects in this Case, but it is the Default of those Subjects who will not qualify themselves for his Service, by doing those Things that the Statute requires. But for a full and plain Answer to this, I say,

First, We are not now considering these Grants of Offices, as they are beneficial to the Subjects, on whom they are conferred, but as the King has an Interest in the Service of those Subjects; and it is a known Rule in Law, that among common Persons, no Man shall suffer by the Default of another; much less shall the King be prejudiced by the Default of any of his People.

But, secondly, Pray, where is the Difference between an Act of Parliament's barring the King directly of the Service of his Subject, and doing of it by necessary and inevitable Consequence? As, if an Act of Parliament were made, that no Man that is lame or deaf should serve the King in any Office, though they were otherwise well qualified for it; the King were as effectually debarred of the Service of such Subjects, as tho' they had been expressed by Name. I know it will be said, that these are natural Defects, which the Subject cannot help; but the others are wilful Impediments, that may be removed if they please.

But to prove that this is not so: I ask, whether when the Act requires Declarations and Subscriptions to be made, it should be done *contrary* to a Man's Opinion, or *according* to it? Certainly no Man will say, *contrary* to a Man's Opinion; for that would be high Dissimulation, and more elude the Ends of the Act, than not doing it at all. If then it must be done *according* to a Man's Opinion, it is no more in any Man's Power to change his Opinion, than to cure himself of Deafness or Lameness. Every Man believes, not because he will, but because he must believe. Error is a Disease of the Mind, as much as those before-mentioned are of the Body. It is true, a Man may seek for Instruction, and use all Means to be better informed; and so may a Man, in the other Case, try all proper Remedies to cure his Distempers, but proper Remedies do not always effect the Cure, and often when they do, there is much Time taken up in the Operation: And the King, who is in no Default at all, loses the Service of his Subject in the mean time. And if this Prerogative be, as my Lord *Coke* says, *Proprium quarto modo*, and that it belongs to our Kings, as he says, *Omni, soli & semper*, the King can be no more debarred of the Service of his Subject for a Month or a Year, than he can be debarred of it for ever; especially since in that Month or Year may happen such Occasions, which afterwards, during the joint Lives of the King that is to command, and of the Subject to be commanded, may probably never happen again.

Many other Cases of Acts of Parliament might be cited, as 8 *R.* II. 2. That no Man should go Judge of Assize into his own County. And 10 *E.* III. 3. That whoever has a Pardon of Felony, shall find Sureties

for the good Behaviou
been constantly dispe
not to heap up all th
those that were, as t
giving Judgment in
some Objections, I ha
be of the greatest weig
the Commons of *Engl.*
dispensing to be in the

But first, To answe

1. *Obj.* This Act was
of 11 *H.* VII. the King
case dispensed with, wou
sance.

Answ. Tho' this will
in words or reasons of m
would be suspected an
Vaughan; whom I cite
and it is very well kno
Prerogative too high. I
the King can't dispense w
cause every particular Per
his Action, which the K
Page 335. *why the King ma*
has a Right to a particula
against a penal Law, by w
whence it follows, that if an
whence no particular Damage
the King may dispense with su

Now to apply this to our
the test, no particular pers
person can have any damag
not meant, that being the c
King may dispense with it,
he explains this very well:
be dispensed with, if the Reason
tra bonum publicum; *for a*
Though such Laws are pro bo
lorum populi, (which are th
as will appear at large in the
I will cite by and bye), *but*
Discretion shall think fit to order
tion the Estate of every Pater-f
his Family, which yet is but
they have no Interest in it, but l

Obj. 2. But it is again obje
leo, in a less Degree, the K
highly necessary for the Public

Answ. To which my Lord
Page 344.

1. *All penal Laws, when mar*
Things necessary, there is no Gra

2. *If any penal Laws were p*
penal were less dispensible than
Money of right Alloy, in Imitation
Licence; but it may be licensed,
the Statute 5 H. IV. c. 4. *but n*
tempore *H.* VI. The Dispe
may be seen, *Coke, Placita Coro.*

Obj. 3. But if the King hav
dispense with twenty, with an
of little Force.

Answ. From the Abuse of a T
Thing itself, is no Consequence
above cited, a high trust repose
his Trust, there is never a one o
the Ruin of his People. To t

1. Every body will grant, that
bery; yet if he should pardon e
committed, it were better to live
our native Country; and the hun
Crimes, would be rendered of as
the Law in our Case would be by

2. There is no Doubt but th
England, and thereby give him a
should abuse his Power so far as
this Honour upon every body th
struction of the legislative Power of
Cases, (or in any other Branch of
should judge the King had such a
Objection to say, these Prerogatives
given a pernicious Judgment

When we were to give Judgment
neither know, nor hinder, it we
this Power; we were only to
such a Power or no, and for that
cited, and two much greater tha
Concessions of all the Commons o
this dispensing Power to be in the K
plying Temper, but when
(especially in the latter Case) abo

And the first of these is *Rot. P*
Roll's second Abridgment, Tit. *P*
Words. *The Commons pray, that the*
Kingdom, may be kept and executed
rogative, that he may dispense with
mons answered, that their Intent was no
of God. There were a great Appre
cies from Aliens then, as there is
And afterwards, in the same P
n. 22.] when the Commons prayed

of the same nature with this in our case; (for they were made against the Court of *Rome*'s encroaching Jurisdiction in *England*); I say, when they made the like Prayer, that these may be put in execution, being admonished by the King's answer in the former case, they themselves insert in their very Prayer, a saving for this Prerogative of the King, and then the King agrees to it.

But the plainest Concession of the Commons of *England* assembled in Parliament, was that 3 *Caroli*, upon a Debate between the two Houses, upon the Petition of Right; *ante p.* 204, 205. as it was delivered by Mr. *Glanvil*, in a full Committee of both Houses of Parliament, 23 *May*, 1628. in the Painted Chamber: and that what he says as to this matter, may not pass for the single opinion of Mr. *Glanvil*, (though he was a learned man) he in the presence of the Commons, addresses himself to the Lords in these words, *p.* 204. *Having thus reduced to your Lordships memory the effects of your own reasons; I will now, with your Lordships favour, come to the points of our reply, wherein I most humbly beseech your Lordships to weigh the reasons which I shall present, not as the sense of myself, the weakest Member of our House, but as the genuine and true sense of the whole House of Commons, conceived in a business debated there with the greatest Gravity and Solemnity, with the greatest concurrence of Opinions, and Unanimity, that ever was in any business maturely agitated in that House.* And then coming to speak of the Point in question, he delivers the sense of the Commons in these words: (*ante* page 205.) *There is a trust inseparably reposed in the persons of the Kings of* England, *but that Trust is regulated by Law; for example, when Statutes are made to prohibit things not* mala in se, *but only* mala quia prohibita, *under certain forfeitures and penalties to accrue to the King, and to the Informers that shall sue for the breach of them: the Commons must, and ever will acknowledge a regal and sovereign Prerogative in the King, touching such Statutes, that it is in his Majesty's absolute and undoubted Power, to grant dispensations to particular persons, with the clauses of* non obstante, *to do as they might have done before those Statutes, wherein his Majesty conferring grace and favour upon some, doth not do wrong to others. But there is a difference between those Statutes and the Laws and Statutes whereon the petition is grounded: By those Statutes the subject has no interest in the Penalties, which are all the fruit such Statutes can produce (that is, to such Informer) until by Suit or Information commenced, he become entitled to the particular forfeitures, whereas the laws and Statutes mentioned in our Petition are of another nature. There shall your Lordships find us to rely upon the good old Statute called* Magna Charta, *which declareth and confirmeth the ancient Common Laws of the Liberties of* England. *There shall your Lordships also find us to insist upon divers other most material Statutes, made in the time of King* Edward III. *and King* Edward IV. *and other famous Kings, for explanation and ratification of the lawful Rights and Privileges belonging to the Subjects of this Realm: Laws not inflicting Penalties upon offenders* in malis prohibitis, *but Laws declarative or positive, conferring or confirming,* ipso facto, *an inherent right and interest of liberty and freedom in the subjects of this Realm, as their birthrights and inheritances descendable to their Heirs and Posterity: Statutes incorporate into the body of the Common Law, over which (with reverence be it spoken) there is no trust in the King's sovereign power or prerogative royal, to enable him to dispense with them, or to take from his subjects that birthright or inheritance which they have in their Liberties, by virtue of the Common Law, and of these Statutes.*

I have the rather cited this at large, because it is a clear acknowledgment of the King's dispensing Power in as large a manner as we have adjudged it, and does at the same time vindicate it from one of the most clamorous, the most malicious, but withal, the weakest objections that ever was made against it. By this Judgment, say they, you have cancelled all our Laws, and given up our lives, liberties, and estates, to be disposed of at the King's pleasure. It is plain, that this is no consequence at all; for the Commons here in Parliament, at the same time that they expresly grant that the King has undoubted Power of dispensing with laws prohibiting things that are not *mala in se*, but only *mala quia prohibita*; laws that are made, as my Lord *Vaughan* expresses it, *pro bono populi complicati*; yet they utterly deny, as they had good reason to do, that the King can dispense with one tittle of *Magna Charta*, or any of those other laws whereby the lives, the liberties, the interests of any of the subjects are conferred upon, or confirmed to them; for these are Laws *pro bono singulorum populi*, which the King can never dispense with. And as to this matter, I do not know whether it will be proper, but any man, so sensibly touched in his reputation, may be provoked to commit some indecencies. I must appeal to all men that have observed my actions and behaviour since I have had the honour to sit upon the Bench, whether I use to be guilty, in Laws of this kind, to strain the construction of them for the King's Interest. First, in such Laws wherein the lives of men have been concerned, I confess, I have been scrupulous even to a fault; for in some cases upon Statutes that had been adjudged felony by wiser and better Judges than myself, and it was highly for the King's service they should be so; yet I could never give Judgment of Death, because I could not satisfy my own conscience that those Statutes were now in force. And in other cases, wherein the rights of the subjects have been brought in question, how strictly I have kept to that substantial difference taken by the House of Commons, that though the King in Laws of Government, in penal Laws of public nature, has a power to dispense in particular cases, yet he cannot dispense with Laws which vest any the least right or property in any of his subjects, will appear by the opinion I gave in the case of *Magdalen College*, (for the truth of which, I appeal to all that know any thing of the transactions in that case) wherein, when the King's right against the College was endeavoured to be asserted by a dispensation granted by himself, I utterly denied that dispensation to be of any force at all, because there was a particular right and interest vested in the Members of that College, as there is in the Members of many other Corporations, of chusing their own head. So far have I been from giving up all Men's lives, liberties, and properties to the King's pleasure.

I had forgot to take notice of two or three objections more that are usually made.

Obj. First, here is a disability, and the King cannot dispense with a disability. As the Statute against buying offices, the King, say they, cannot dispense with for that reason.

Answ. There is the same disability in the case of Sheriffs; and yet resolved that the King can dispense in that case; and the reason in the Statute of buying offices, or sitting in Parliament without taking the oaths, is because there is a disability actually incurred; and when any person is actually disabled, he cannot have his disability taken off but by Act of Parliament. But in the Statute dispensed with, in the case of Sir *E. Hales*, there is no disability actually laid upon any man; but certain things are required to be done, and as a penalty for disobeying the said Act, and omitting the doing those things required by it; the disability with the other forfeitures are to be incurr'd after conviction. Now the nature of dispensations being, as was shewed before, to make the thing lawful to him who has it, which is unlawful to every body else; it does plainly prevent the committing any offence by that person, and consequently the incurring any penalty or disability at all. But in the case of buying offices the person is disabled before the dispensation comes; for he is disabled, *ipso facto*, by contracting or dealing for the office. So the true difference between the case of Sheriffs, and the case of buying offices, is this, *That the King in the one case can prevent the incurring a disability, but cannot purge it in the other after it is incurred.* To illustrate this by a case of the like nature, *The King may prevent an attainder, but he cannot purge an attainder.* If a man has committed Treason or Felony, *the King by granting his pardon may infallibly prevent the Offender's ever being attainted; but after he is once actually attainted, the King can by no means take off that attainder, or purge the corruption of blood, but by Act of Parliament; provided the Judgment by which he is attainted be not erroneous.*

Obj. But it is objected, that these Laws were made for the interest of Religion, and all offences against Religion are *mala in se*, and therefore not to be dispensed with.

Answ. I answer, that true it is, all offences that are directly against Religion, as it is constituted such by the Divine Law, are *mala in se*, and not to be dispensed with, and in this case the Parliament is bound, as well as the King; for an Act of Parliament made against Religion in that sense is utterly void, as is instanced in *Doctor* and *Student*, of an Act, *That should forbid the giving of Alms upon any occasion*, &c. But human and politick Constitutions, though made for the interest of Religion, as they had a beginning, so they are alterable by the same power that made them; and therefore the breaches of them are in their nature *mala prohibita*, as was resolved in the great Case of dispensations, in 11 *H.* VII. above cited, and instances given; *as the King may dispense with a Priest holding of two Benefices*, though the Laws against pluralities were made for the interest of Religion, and the better edification of the people. *So the King may dispense with a Bastard's entering into Priest's orders*, &c. These instances are taken for Law in that Year-book.

But to all this I know it is said, that these high trusts and prerogatives might be always safe, and sometimes useful in a Protestant Prince's hands, who would faithfully discharge the duty of one that ought to be *custos utriusque tabulæ*; but when these prerogatives are asserted to a Prince who is of a contrary religion to that established by Law, there would be always danger of their being abused to the prejudice or destruction of the established Religion.

To which I answer, that it cannot be forgotten, that the promoters of the Bill of Exclusion used the same argument: If you leave him King, say they, he will have all the prerogatives of a King, and those prerogatives may be made instrumental to the ruin of your religion; which could not be denied by the gentlemen on the other side, who opposed that Bill. Their only reply was, *fiat justitia, ruat cœlum*, it is his right, and we must not do evil that good may come; we must not do wrong, no not to promote the interest of religion itself. The same argument that weighed with them to assert the right of succession to the Crown of *England*, and consequently to all the prerogatives together, was the rule we had to guide us in giving Judgment in this case concerning a particular branch of them. We must not break our oath, nor give Judgment contrary to what seemed to us to be Law, let the consequence be what it will.

But it has been farther objected to me, by some of my friends, that, though I could not in conscience have given Judgment against the King, being of the opinion that I was, yet I should rather have parted with my place, than to have given a Judgment, even according to Law, which might be so prejudicial to that excellent religion that I profess; and of which when I cease to be, let me cease to be at all.

I answer, That neither in prudence nor in conscience I could have taken that course.

First. Not in prudence; for I confess that saying, *Omnia dat, qui Justa negat*, had great weight with me in the case: and that I was of opinion, since an incroachment of Jurisdiction was feared, there could not be a greater, nor more dangerous provocation to it, than for Protestant Judges to refuse to give Judgment for a Prince of a different persuasion, in that which we could not deny to be his right.

And next, in conscience, I could not decline giving Judgment in this case; for by our oaths we are as much obliged to give Judgment one way or other, as we are to give what we think a righteous Judgment in all cases that come before us.

It has been objected, that all this was a contrivance, an informer set up, and all but a feigned action.

As to this matter, I can truly say, that I don't remember that I ever heard of this Action, 'till after it was actually brought; but in this there seems to be no hurt or inconvenience at all. The Law is as well tried and settled in a feign'd Action, as in a true. There are feigned Actions directed every day out of Chancery to this very purpose, that great and difficult points of Law may be settled by them; and why the King might not direct such an Action to be brought to satisfy himself whether he had such a power, and if he had, that the people might be satisfied, and acquiesce in it; I confess I see no difference at all. If there were indirect means used for procuring opinions, or the like, I have nothing to say to it. I stand upon my innocence, and challenge all the world to lay any thing of that kind to my charge. My part was only to give my own opinion, in which, if either by misunderstanding the books that I have cited, or by drawing weak conclusions from them, I have erred in the Judgment that I gave; How can I for this be charged as a criminal? The law neither supposes, nor requires an infallibility in any of his Majesty's Courts of Justice; it were very uneasy sitting in them, if it did. We can but judge according to the books that lie before us, and according to the measure of our understanding of those books:

we

we have not always ſo much light to guide us, as we thought we had in this caſe. We often meet with caſes new and rare, and very ill ſettled by former Judgments, where we are forced to dig truth, as it were, out of the mine, to compare and diſtinguiſh, to ſkreen and ſift, and gather the ſenſe of the Law out of the confuſion of diſagreeing, and very often contradictory opinions, as well as we can. and if after all our labour and our pains, we happen to be miſtaken, it was never yet imputed as a crime. The Judgment is reverſed in a writ of error, not only without any accuſation, but without the leaſt reflection upon him that gave it. Nor can a miſtake in Judgment be more criminal in a matter of a greater concernment, than it is in matters of the leaſt conſequence: It would be very miſchievous and very dangerous, if it ſhould. For if in queſtions of Prerogative, any miſtake ſhall be made capital on the one hand, when Judgment is given for the King; why ſucceeding Princes may not be as angry at any miſtakes on the other hand, I cannot imagine. And when once affairs are come to that paſs, there will be great encouragement for any man, that can make the leaſt ſhift to live without it, to undertake thoſe very neceſſary, but very difficult, and very troubleſome employments; great freedom for men to give Judgment according to their opinion and their conſcience; and great reliance upon the reſolutions of thoſe, who know they ſhall be ſure to pay with their lives and fortunes for any miſtake of theirs, either to the King or the People, as either of them ſhall happen to get the upper hand. For my own part, I thank God, I can ſay theſe two things: Firſt, That for theſe ten years together, wherein (with very little intermiſſion) I have ſate as a Judge in ſeveral Courts, though I may be juſtly accuſed of many weakneſſes and miſtakes, yet I have never given Judgment in any one Caſe againſt the clear dictates of my reaſon and my conſcience. And the ſecond thing is, that I never gave Judgment in any controverted Point, wherein I had ſo many, and ſo great authorities to warrant it, as I have to warrant that Judgment which was given in Sir *Edward Hales*'s Caſe. And this I ſay, not to ſet up that opinion again in a Pamphlet, which was ſo ill reliſhed in a Court of Juſtice, nor to oppoſe my Senſe to the Judgment of the Nation; for I think it is very fit that this dark Learning (as my Lord *Vaughan* calls it) of *Diſpenſations*, ſhould receive ſome light from a determination in Parliament; that Judges for the time to come, may judge by more certain Rules, which Acts of Parliament the King may, and which he may not diſpenſe with. But I have cited thoſe authorities at this time in my own defence, and for theſe particular purpoſes; in the firſt place, to ſhew,

1. That we are not the firſt inventors of this diſpenſing Power, but that it has been allowed without controverſy, to the Kings of *England* in all ages, that they might diſpenſe with many Acts of Parliament.

2. That if our Judgment was erroneous, and that the King could not diſpenſe with that Act of Parliament; yet that error was but an error in that ſingle Caſe, and had no ſuch large and miſchievous conſequences as is pretended. For that, becauſe we judged that the King could diſpenſe with that Statute, for others to conclude from thence, that therefore he had a Power to diſpenſe with all other Statutes; eſpecially ſuch as confer, or veſt in any of the ſubjects any manner of intereſt whatſoever, in their lives, liberties, or eſtates; or that, becauſe the King may diſpenſe with a penal Law, wherein a diſability is annexed to the breach of it as a penalty, and that penalty not to be incurred before a legal conviction, and where the King's diſpenſation makes the thing diſpenſed with lawful, and conſequently prevents any conviction or penalty at all: For others to conclude from thence, that therefore the King may diſpenſe with ſuch Statutes, where a precedent diſability is actually laid upon any man, as there is upon the Members of both Houſes, till they have taken the oaths and teſts preſcribed, and therefore without queſtion, is not in the King's power to diſpenſe. I ſay, theſe are conſequences which may flow from the heated imaginations of angry men, but have no warrant or foundation at all from the Judgment given by us.

I have one thing more to ſay in my juſtification, which is, that if I have been guilty of ſo heinous offences as I am accuſed of, where is the temptation or the reward? If it was to keep in my Judge's place, which otherwiſe I might have loſt, I can only anſwer, That if that were the caſe, I then became the worſt man in the world, only to keep that, which it is pretty well known, I was with much difficulty, with the perſuaſion of my friends, prevailed with to accept: and for any other reward, whoever is acquainted with the circumſtances of my fortune, will, I am confident, notwithſtanding the falſe and idle reports, of I know not what great reverſions lately fallen to me, as eaſily acquit me of having been corrupted by the King, to give a pernicious Judgment in this Caſe, as of having enriched myſelf by taking bribes in caſes between party and party.

All that I have to add more, is, that howſoever this that I have ſaid in my defence may happen to be underſtood at preſent, yet I could not deny myſelf the ſatisfaction of having put in a Plea of Innocence at leaſt; that whatſoever ſhall happen to me now, may perhaps meet with a more equal Judgment in after-times; ſince it ought to be much leſs uneaſy to me to loſe my life, if any body be very fond of taking it, than to let the aſperſions that are every day caſt upon me, to paſs in ſilence; or ſuffer myſelf to be tranſmitted to poſterity under the character of a betrayer of my Religion, or a ſubverter of the laws and liberties of my country.

Sir Robert Atkins, *at the End of his* Enquiry into the Power of diſpenſing with Penal Statutes, *makes the following ſhort Argument upon the Pleadings of the afore-mentioned Caſe of Sir* Edward Hales.

THE firſt Point argued by the Plaintiff's Counſel was, That it appears by the Declaration, and it is now confeſſed by the Defendant's joining demurrer, that the Defendant had been indicted for this offence, in exerciſing the Office of a Colonel without having taken the Teſts.

And upon the Indictment he either did plead this Diſpenſation, or might have pleaded it. And he is now convict, according to the direction of the Act of 25 *Car.* II. ſo that he now comes too late to plead it to this Action: For he cannot falſify the conviction, nor aver any thing againſt the Record of it, and bring the fact to be tried over again in this Action; but is

concluded and eſtopped in Law t
Record, by which he is found g
Parliament.

The Defendant either did plead
dictment, in diſcharge of the Ind
the Judges at the Aſſizes (as by L
Or he might have pleaded it, if he h
And not having done it, he had e
to plead it, being convict of the c

To this it was objected (as I he
advantage of an Eſtoppel, ought tc
the Defendant's Plea, and to hav

For the Rule is, That he that
an Eſtoppel.

It is true, if a man will plead a

But in this Caſe the Plaintiff do
pel appears by the Declaration, an
that there was no need for the Pla
tion, which doth ſufficiently app
That he did not take the Teſts wit
conviction is confeſſed by his Plea

If a man recover a debt upon a
Executor ſue a *Scire facias* upon
plead any Plea that he might have
Dureſs, or the like: for he is conc

In *Jeſon* and *Kete*'s Caſe, in *Syde*
Juſtice, a man ſhall never help hi
equitable ſuit at Law) for any mat

There is no Eſtoppel in this Caſ
ment, which is the King's ſuit:
now Plaintiffs, and ſo they are tw

The conviction upon the Indict
dant himſelf, of which any man n
ſhall never be admitted to aver again
firſt part, *fol.* 3.

An attainder for treaſon is an uni
may take the advantage, not only
his wife too, if ſhe ſue for dower.
Manw. Ch. Bar.

Where a man is attainted by his
not eſtopped to ſay he was not g
after enfeoff *J. S.* of his land; and
verdict, there *J. S.* is eſtopped, an
becauſe he claims under him: muc
verdict, that he is not guilty †.

If a man be acquitted of felony,
Rep. 81. *b.* is eſtopped to ſay the c
vict, by the ſame reaſon §.

As to that which is objected, tha
(which is the King's ſuit); but this
dict ſhall not conclude the Defend

This is not another ſuit, but in e
and grounded upon that Record, a
a dependant action; as a Writ of e
Facias upon a Record, are dependa
Judgment.

The Act of 25 *Car.* II. *c.* 2. hat
his neglect of taking the two Oaths
mitted, to execute any ſuch office
hath made him indictable at the Aſſ
der incurs (among other penalties)
any one that will ſue for it in an ac

So the Statute hath directed the
convicting the offender, by Indictm

And if he that ſues for the forfeit
over again, then the conviction at t
all in vain. And ſuch constructio
makers; for they intended this for
trials: For ſuppoſe it ſhould be trie
paſs for the Defendant, here ſhall b
verdict: and ſuch conſtruction oug
as may not elude, but agree with the
that no words, clauſe or ſentence, ſh

And this conviction upon the Indi
of debt brought by the now Plaintif
being thereupon lawfully convicted upo
from thenceforth forfeit 500 *l.*

So that till there be ſuch a conv if
500 *l.* nor no action can be brought
proved and determined before any a
the proof of the offence, whereof the
made in this action over again: if it

Suppoſe the Plaintiff here had bro
the Defendant of taking the Oaths,
his acting in his office after ſuch negl
Indictment, and had only averr'd, th
yet acted, would this action have be
had been a conviction, but the Plain
ration, but had only averr'd the offe
a good declaration? Surely it would
the conviction is the very ground an
action would not lie without ſuch
new action, but a dependant action.

And the uſual difference is where
pending upon a Record, and ground
teral ſuit, not depending upon that F

* 7 *E.* 4. 1. Br. Eſtoppel 163. † *Knoil* and *Haymor*'s caſe, third Kebl. 528. by Chief-Juſtice *Hale.* ‡ *Rol. Abr.* firſt Part, 36

I

An Action against the Sheriff for an escape of one taken in execution; this is a dependant Action, and is grounded upon the Record of the Judgment given against the party that escaped. The Sheriff cannot aver any thing against that Record, and examine it over again, nor can he take any advantage of error, or erroneous proceeding, in obtaining that Judgment. *Saunders's Rep.* 2 *part.* 101 *.

So in an Action of debt grounded upon a Judgment, or in an *Audita querela*, to be relieved upon a Judgment.

And so in our Case, this Action of debt for the 500*l.* is grounded upon the conviction; which must stand for truth as long as it remains in force, not avoided by error or attaint

A Writ of Error to reverse a Judgment, is a dependant Action. In error, the Plaintiff may not aver any thing against the Record. *Mullens versus Weidy. Syderfin's* 1*st part*, 94. Error was sued in the *King's-Bench* to reverse a Judgment given in the *Palace-Court*. And the Plaintiff in error assigned for error, that the Duke of *Ormond* (who is principal Judge of that Court by Patent) was not there It was agreed by the Court, that it might not be assigned for error, for it was contrary to the Record.

But *per Cur.* in an Action of trespass, or false imprisonment, which, (says that Report) are collateral Actions, he may falsify and assign that, if he be taken upon such Judgment.

So if a man be indicted and convict of an assault and battery, and afterwards the person so assaulted brings his Action for the battery, this hath no dependance upon the Indictment or Conviction; for it may be sued, tho' there were no Indictment, but is a distinct and collateral suit. The Indictment and Verdict is no estoppel, nor can so much as be given in evidence: as is held by the whole Court, in the Case of *Samson* versus *Yardley*, and *Totbill*, 10 *Car.* II. B. R. *Keble's* 2 *part*, 384. The like in an appeal of murder, *Keble's* 2 *part*, 223.

Another penalty upon the offender against this Statute of 25 *Car.* II. is, that he shall be disabled to sue in any Action Now suppose a person convict at the Assizes, sues an Action, may not the Defendant in that Action take the advantage of that disability, and plead the conviction? As in case of an Outlawry pleaded in disability; there need not be set forth all the proceedings in that suit wherein the Plaintiff was outlawed, but he may plead the Record of the Outlawry and rely upon it; and it shall not be examined whether there was any just cause to sue him to the Outlawry, or not.

The Indictment, the Defendant's Plea to it, and the Verdict upon it, have determined the matter of fact, that the Defendant is guilty of the offence against this Act of Parliament.

The Act itself hath pronounced the Judgment, which consists of many particulars; one whereof is, that the Defendant shall forfeit 500*l.* to him that will sue for it; and the action of debt for the 500*l.* brought by the Plaintiff, grounded upon all these, is in the nature of an execution.

And all these put together, are not several and distinct suits, but in effect all but one suit and process, one depending upon the other.

The second Point is, Whether the Dispensation pleaded by the Defendant be a good bar to the Action of debt? And this is properly called, The great Point of the Case.

For which the Reader is referred to Sir Robert Atkins's *Large Pamphlet, of* The Enquiry into the Power of dispensing with Penal Statutes.

Then Sir Robert *adds a Postscript: Being some Animadversions upon a Book writ by Sir* Edward Herbert, *Lord-Chief-Justice of the* Common-Pleas, *entituled*, A short Account of the Authorities in Law, upon which Judgment was given in Sir *Edward Hales's* Case.

[*After a short Apology for making some Animadversions upon the said Book, he proceeds thus:*

THE Chief-Justice *Herbert*, *ante pag.* 617. gives us the definition of a dispensation out of Sir *Edward Coke's* 11*th Rep. fol.* 88. viz. *Dispensatio mali probibiti est de jure Domino Regi concessa, propter impossibilitatem prævidendi de omnibus particularibus.*

And again, *Dispensatio est mali probibiti provida relaxatio utilitate seu necessitate compensata.*

Upon the word *Concessa*, I would gladly be satisfied, when, or by whom that Power was ever granted to the King; where shall we find that Grant?

It is clear, that whoever hath the entire power of making a Law, may justly dispense with that Law. And therefore Almighty God, being the sole and supreme Law-giver, might dispense even with the moral Law, as he did with the sixth Commandment, when he commanded *Abraham* to sacrifice his son *Isaac*; and with the eighth Commandment, when he commanded the *Israelites* to borrow the jewels of the *Egyptians*, and to go away without restoring of them.

But it stands not with reason, that he who hath but a share with others in making of a Law, (as the King hath no more) should have the power, by himself alone to dispense with the Law, unless that power were expresly intrusted with him by the rest of the Law-makers; as sometimes hath been done.

Sir *Edward Coke*, in his 7*th Rep.* in the case of *Penal Statutes*, *fol.* 36. towards the lower end, does affirm, that this dispensing Power is committed to the King, by all his subjects. So that it is not claimed *Jure Divino*, but by grant from the People. But where to find any such Grant we know not.

I have, as I conceive, made it appear in my larger argument, *p.* 14. that
the first invention of Dispensation with Laws, began with the Pope, about
the time of *Innocent* III. and by our King *Henry* III. in imitation, and by
encouragement from the Pope; so that it was not by the Grant of the People, but ever exclaimed against by all good men, and generally by all the
People, and ever fenced against by a multitude of Acts of Parliament.
It is true, the dispensing with laws hath ever since been practised; and
they began at first here in *England* to be used only in Cases where the King
alone was concerned, in Statutes made for his own profit, wherein he
might have done what he pleased. But it is but of later times that they
have been stretched to Cases that concern the whole Realm. See my Argument, *fol.* 13. Hence it evidently appears, it cannot be a legal prerogative in the King; for that must ever be by prescription, and restrained
to those cases that have been used time immemorial, and must not be extended to new cases.

Now there hath been no such usage as will warrant the dispensing with such an Act of Parliament as is now before us, that of 25 *Car.* II. *c.* 2.

The Chief-Justice *Herbert*, from the definition before recited, and those two authorities of Sir *Edward Coke*, in his Case of Monopolies, and that other of penal Statutes, frames an argument to prove, that the Dispensation granted to Sir *Edward Hales*, was good in Law.

Because a Dispensation is properly and only in case of a *Malum Prohibitum*, he thence infers, that the King can dispense in all cases of *mala prohibita*.

Which is a wrong inference, and that which Logicians call, *Fallacia à dicto secundum quid ad dictum simpliciter*. Because he can dispense with some, that therefore he can dispense with all, is no good consequence.

It appears by the late Chief-Justice *Vaughan's* Reports, in the Case of *Thomas* and *Sorrel*, (so often cited by the Chief Justice *Herbert*) *Vaughan's Rep. fol.* 333. the fourth Paragraph, that his opinion is, That the King cannot dispense with every *Malum Probibitum*; and he gives many instances of such *Mala Prohibita* that are not dispensable, *fol.* 342, and 334. *parag.* 4.

Therefore the Lord-Chief-Justice *Herbert* should, as I conceive, regularly first have given us the distinction of *Mala Probibita*, into such as are dispensable, and such as are not dispensable; and then have shewn, that the Dispensation granted to Sir *Edward Hales*, fell under the first part: But that learned Reporter, the Chief-Justice *Vaughan* (so often cited by our now Lord-Chief-Justice) in the aforesaid case of *Thomas* and *Sorrel*, *fol* 332. *the last Paragraph save one*, quarrels with the very distinction of *Malum Probibitum*, and *Malum in se*, and says it is confounding.

From whence I would observe, and from the whole Report in *Thomas* and *Sorrel's* case, that the notion of dispensation is as yet but crude and undigested, and not fully shaped and formed by the Judges.

The Pope was the Inventor of it, our Kings have borrowed it from them; and the Judges from time to time have nursed and dressed it up, and given it countenance. And it is still upon the growth and encroaching, till it hath almost subverted all Law, and made the regal power absolute, if not dissolute.

I must agree, that our Books of late have run much upon a distinction, *viz.* Where the breach of a penal Statute is to the particular damage of any person, for which such person may have his Action against the breaker of that law; there, tho' it be but *Malum Probibitum*, yet the King cannot dispense with that penal Law, according to the rule in *Bracton*:

Rex non potest gratiam facere cum injuriâ & damno alterius.

As for instance, there are several Statutes that prohibit one man from maintaining another's suit, though in a just cause. See *Poulton de pace Regis & Regni*, in his *chap. of Maintenance*, *fol.* 55.

Now it is held that the King cannot dispense with those Laws, because it would be to the prejudice and damage of that particular person, against whom the suit is so maintained by another; for there can be no maintenance, but it is to the wrong of a particular person.

So of carrying a distress out of the Hundred.

But there are many other penal laws, where, by the transgressing of them, no subject can have any particular damage, and therefore no particular Action for the breach of them.

As upon the Statute that prohibits the transportation of wool, under a penalty. By the breach of this Law, that is, by the exportation of wool, no one particular man hath any damage, more than every other man hath, but it is only against the publick good.

And the breach of such a penal law is punishable only at the King's suit, by indictment or presentment.

And the like where such a penal Statute gives an Action popular, to him that will sue for the penalty, who hath no right to it more than another, till his suit be commenced.

In these cases, it is commonly held, that the King may dispense with such penal Statutes, as to some particular persons, and for some limited time, (whereof they make the King the sole Judge;) because, as the reason is given in the Chief-Justice *Vaughan's Reports*, *fol.* 344. *parag.* 2. such offence wrongs none but the King. This is now the common received opinion and distinction. And the breach of such kind of Statutes, are said to be only the King's damage in his publick capacity, as supreme Governor, and wronging none but himself. Lord *Vaugh. Rep.* 342. *parag.* 3.

But if we will narrowly search into this distinction, and weigh the reasons so given, we shall find it is without any just ground.

The damage done to the particular person in the Cases past, in the first part of this distinction, are merely his own proper and peculiar damage; and he is intitled to his particular action for it, in his own proper personal right, and therefore if he discharge and dispense with them, it is no wrong to any other man: he may do what he will with his own.

But the Cases in the second part of this distinction, are where the King hath a right to the suit, and the offence and damage are said to be to him only.

But are they so (as the former) in his own personal right, as his Lands and other Revenues are? Or are they to him but as a trustee for the Publick, for which reason he is called *Creditor Pœnæ?* And may he therefore, upon the like reason dispense with them, or dispose of them, as a subject may do with his own particular Interests?

Again, shall a publick damage and injury to the whole Nation, be more dispensable by the King, than the loss of one private man?

——fuit hæc sapientia quondam
Publica privatis secernere——

And therefore, in my apprehension, the King cannot, in such cases of Dispensations, be truly said to wrong none but himself, and it is not agreeable to the definition before given, *Utilitate Compensata*, for the King wrongs the whole Realm by it. Whereas if he grants a dispensation with a Penal Law of the first sort of this distinction, he only wrongs some particular persons.

The cases and authorities for dispensations in our Books that were granted in ancient times, will generally be found to be only where the Penal Statutes were made for the King's own proper interest and benefit at his dispen-

* *Jaques* versus *Cæsar*. And Dr. *Drury's* Case, 8 *R.* 142. And *Mackally's* Case, 9 *R.* 68.

ſing with the Statute of *Mortmain*. For in ſuch caſes it was to the King's own loſs only, in caſes where the King might by Law have given away his lands or ſervices. So the King may in his Patent of grant of lands, diſpenſe with the Statutes, 1 *Hen.* IV. *cap.* 6. that require there ſhall be mention of the true values of them. And by a *non obſtante* to thoſe Statutes (which is now generally uſed) the King doth in effect declare, that it is his pleaſure to grant thoſe lands, whatever the value of them be, more or leſs: and the Statute does by expreſs words ſave a liberty to the King in that caſe.

The King is not a truſtee for others in ſuch caſes, nor can theſe diſpenſations be ſaid to be *directly* to the damage of the Public. And ſuch Penal Laws as merely concern the King's own revenue or profit, may juſtly be thought to be intended, to be made only to put the King's matters into an ordinary method and courſe, and ſo ſave the King a labour, as the Lord *Hobart* ſays; and ſo prevent the King's being ſurpriz'd or miſ-inform'd, when Patents are gain'd from him, and not deſign'd to tie the King's hands, or to reſtrain his power; as out of all doubt was done and intended by the Law-makers in our Act of 25 *Car.* II.

But in all the late caſes and authorities which we meet with in our Books concerning *non obſtante's*, and diſpenſations, as in the time of King *Hen.* VII. and ſo downward to this day, we ſhall find them practiſing upon ſuch Penal Statutes as merely concern the publick good and benefit, and the Laws of ſuch a nature, by the breach of which the whole Nation ſuffers: while ſome particular perſons, it may be, by giving a large fine, or a yearly ſum, obtain the favour to be diſpens'd with and exempt from a Penal Law, while all others continue to be bound by it.

As for example; where a Statute forbids the exportation of Wool, or of Cloth undyed or undreſs'd, under a penalty; ſuch a Law is greatly for the publick good, and it takes care that our own people ſhall have employment and maintenance. Yet this is ſuch a Law, as according to the receiv'd diſtinction, the King may diſpenſe with, there being no particular damage to one man more than to another, by breach of ſuch a Law, although it be a mighty damage to the whole Nation: for by ſuch a diſpenſation, the perſon ſo diſpens'd with to export ſuch white Cloth undyed, will have the ſole trade, which before the making of that Penal Statute was equal and common to all. I wiſh the Houſe of Commons would enquire what vaſt riches have been heretofore gotten by ſuch as have obtained the diſpenſations with this Penal Statute, beſides the ſums they paid to the Crown for them. Theſe are mere Monopolies.

In ſuch a caſe it may rightly be applied, *That Sin taketh occaſion by the Law*. It had been better for the Nation, that ſuch Laws were never made, being no better obſerv'd: For here again the diſpenſation is neither *Utilitate*, nor *Neceſſitate penſata*.

Look into the caſe of *Thomas* and *Sorrel*, and you will find few or no caſes of diſpenſations cited out of our Books, but of the time of King *Henry* VII. and much more of very late times: ſo that the ill practice is ſtill improving and ſtretching.

The Lord Chief-Juſtice *Herbert*, in the next place, *page* 618. proceeds to mention the great caſe of 2 *Hen.* VII. a reſolution of all the Judges in the *Exchequer-chamber*, upon the King's diſpenſing with the Statute of 23 *Hen.* VI. *cap.* 8. *That no man ſhould be Sheriff above one year.* This is the great leading caſe and authority, upon which the main ſtreſs is laid to juſtify the Judgment given in Sir *Edward Hales*'s caſe.

I would avoid repeating what I have already ſo largely ſaid to this authority, to which I muſt refer my Reader, by which I hope it is moſt evidently made out, that the King neither hath, nor never had any juſt right or power to elect Sheriffs: but the right of electing was anciently and originally belonging to the Freeholders of the ſeveral Counties: and ſince it was unjuſtly taken from them as they have ever been on the loſing hand; it hath been lodged in the great Officers of the Realm, as the Lord-Chancellor, Lord-Treaſurer, Lord Privy-Seal, and the Judges, *&c.* as appears by the ſeveral Statutes.

And they are to make ſuch choice every year in the *Exchequer*, on a day appointed by the Statute for that purpoſe. So that the Sheriffs are by thoſe Statutes to continue in their offices for one year only; and the King cannot hinder ſuch election.

Only by his Patent or Commiſſion to the Sheriff, hath he uſed to ſignify to the Sheriff himſelf that is ſo choſen; and to publiſh to all others who the perſon is that is ſo choſen. This is all the uſe of the Patent; but it is the proper election of thoſe great Officers that truly veſts them in their Office.

And it does as clearly appear, that when former Kings have diſpens'd with a Sheriff's continuing in his Office for longer than one year, contrary to the ſeveral Statutes ſo forbidding it, the King hath ſo done it by virtue (not of his prerogative, but) of a ſpecial Act of Parliament enabling him to do it, for ſome extraordinary occaſions, and for ſome limited time only. See for this the Statute of 9 *Hen.* V. *cap.* 5. in the Statutes at large, and my larger argument, *fol.* 34.

The truth is, the power of diſpenſing is originally in the Legiſlators. He only can diſpenſe with a Law, that can make a Law. The power is equal; and the Legiſlators can confer the ſame power upon the King or any others, for ſome convenient time, *&c.* as appears by the laſt inſtance of the Sheriff, and divers other like caſes, mentioned in my foregoing argument, where I have alſo obſerved many other things upon that reſolution of 2 *Hen.* VII. concerning Sheriffs.

The Chief-Juſtice *Herbert* ſuppoſes the miſchiefs recited in the preamble of that Statute of 23 *H.* VI. *cap.* 8. concerning Sheriffs continuing in their offices longer than one year, to be equal, if not greater (as he judges) than the miſchiefs recited in the Statute of 25 *Car.* II. by Papiſts being in offices; and from thence, I preſume, would infer, that the caſe of Sir *Edward Hales* is not ſo fatal in the conſequence, as the caſe of a Sheriff.

I may appeal to any ordinary judgment, and to the ſad experience and trial we have ſo lately had, and to the danger we were ſo lately in (from which Almighty God, by no leſs than a miracle, hath in great mercy delivered the Nation), whether the miſchiefs that could any way poſſibly ariſe from the diſpenſing with the former (I mean the Statute concerning Sheriffs) be comparable to the infinite miſchiefs ariſing from putting Papiſts into office, and intruſting them with our Religion, and all our Civil Rights.

The Chief-Juſtice, upon thoſe words of the Statute concerning She-

riffs, *viz. Tha*
thoſe words do
ing Sheriffs, w
could otherwi
Anſw. This
from ſhewing
that had not t
might have do
diſpenſations u
prevent for the
of doing it. *E*
demns a contra
I heartily d
gument) caref
ſeveral caſes ar
warrant that re
which the Kin
certain ſtaple,
between thoſe
this weighty in
tion of 2 *Hen.*
inferior and mi
It is true, Sir
be truly his) h
new and differe
fore I preſume
Judges, who g
Thus ſays Si
the weſt parts o
neſs, wealth an
Canons of thei
ments to maint
Sir *Edward C*
this ground, *viz*
ſubjects to ſerve h
pa aby annexed t
Act of Parliamen
That it is no
ral Acts of Par
argument, *fol.*
Acts, was give
ſome ſhort time
ſelves exercis'd
Judge of the
Coke, by that on
fol. 19. which (
of Parliament.
Yet we have
which in the jud
in Law) may th
And is the K
ſerve him for th
riffs to continue
25 *Car.* II. that
ſome very unfit,
fices of truſt and
and by the advic
whole Realm?
Does the Ki
choice of hi perſ
this reſtraint? I
ant ſubjects eno
count Proteſtant
whom they hold
continually plot
defence of the P
are all concern'd
And are thoſe
of *Rome*, and a
Nation, with t
Is not this to
This Act tha
a reſtraint upon
by the wrong h
lution, by advic
of truſt, but ſu
ſ... the great
tion of the Prote
And this agre
granted to one t
King himſelf.
fol. 37.
The Lord C
ſo many ſolemn
chamber, are no
were ten times a
expreſs poſitive
words could th
to the purpoſe,
Grant of ſuch a
and *ipſo facto* a
And is not a Ju
higheſt authorit
But (ſays the
diſpenſe with th
quent practice t
none of the num
Treaſurer, Judg
may ſo do, thou

Twelve Judges, to be an error in the King. See Sir *Edward Coke*'s 2 *Instit.* or *Magna Charta*, *fol.* 559. and yet it is practis'd to this very day.

The Chief-Justice, *page* 619. seems to excuse *Popish* Recusants for not qualifying themselves for offices, by taking the oaths and the test, *&c.* for that no man (saith he) hath it in his power to change his opinion in Religion as he pleaseth, and therefore it is not their fault. It is an error of the mind, *&c.*

Ans. Here is no occasion taken to find fault with them for their opinion; let them keep their Religion still, if they like it so well, who hinders them. This Act of 25 *Car.* II. imposes no penalty upon them for their opinion; but is there any necessity of their being in offices? Must they needs be Guardians of the Protestant Religion? The penalty upon them by this Act, is not for their opinion, but for their presuming to undertake offices and trusts, for which they are by King and Parliament adjudg'd and declar'd unfit.

Page 620. The Chief-Justice *Vaughan* is brought in, arguing for the King's power of dispensing with (*Nominal*) nuisances (as he is pleas'd to call and distinguish nuisances). The word nominal, as there understood, imports, that though a Parliament declares any thing to be a nuisance, (as sometimes they do in Acts of Parliament, to render them indispensable) which yet in its proper nature would not otherwise be so conceiv'd to be; that such a nominal nuisance (as he holds) may however be dispens'd with by the King, though regularly by Law the King may not dispense with any nuisance.

Answ. Shall any singular or particular person, though a Chief-Justice, presume to call that a mere *nominal nuisance*, which a Parliament by a solemn Act and Law have adjudg'd and declared to be a real nuisance? Are we not all concluded by what a Law says? This arrogance is the mischief now complain'd of.

The Chief-Justice *Herbert*, *page* 620. says, that from the abuse of a thing, an argument cannot be drawn against the thing itself. I agree this is regularly true; yet we have an instance to the contrary in the Scripture, in that point of the *Brazen Serpent*. But in our case the abuse doth arise from the very nature of the thing itself, from the constitution of it.

For the King practises no more in dispensing, than what these resolutions of the Judges allow him to do by this pretended prerogative. The error is the foundation.

They have made his power to be unlimited, either as to number of persons, or as to the time, how long the dispensation shall continue. Sir *Edward Coke* says, and so the other Books, That the King is the sole Judge of these.

Nec metas Rerum, nec Tempora ponunt.

The Chief-Justice *Herbert*, *fol.* 620. cites two clear concessions (as he is pleas'd to call them) of all the Commons of *England* in Parliament, which he esteems much greater authorities than the several resolutions of all the Twelve Judges.

But how far these are from concessions, will easily appear to an indifferent Reader. They are no more than prudent and patient avoiding of disputes with the several Kings. And there are multitudes of the like in the old Parliament-Rolls.

It is but an humble clearing of themselves from any purpose in general, to abridge the King of any of his prerogatives (which have always been touchy and tender things); but it is no clear nor direct allowance of that dispensing there mention'd, to be any such prerogative in him.

However, I am glad to see an House of Commons to be in so great request with the Judges. It will be so at some times, more than at others.

Yet I do not remember, that in any argument I have hitherto met with, a vote, or order, or opinion of the House of Commons hath been cited for an authority in Law, before now. Will the House of Peers allow of this authority for Law?

It will be said, that this is but the acknowledgment of parties concern'd in Interest; which is allowed for a good testimony, and strongest against themselves.

Answ. I do not like to have the King and his people to have divided interests. Prerogative and the people's liberties should not be look'd upon as opposites. The prerogative is given by Law to the King, the better to enable him to protect and preserve the subjects rights. Therefore, it truly concerns the people to maintain prerogative.

I could cite several Parliament-Records wherein the poor House of Commons have been forced to submit themselves, and humbly beg pardon of the King, for doing no more than their duty, merely to avert his displeasure. See the case of Sir *Thomas Haxley*, whom the King adjudg'd a Traitor, for exhibiting a Bill to the Commons for the avoiding of the outrageous expences of the King's house, 20 *R.* II. *num.* 14, 15, 16, 17, and 23, and the Commons were driven to discover his name to the King, and the whole House in a mournful manner craving pardon for their entertaining of that Bill.

No doubt, as good an authority against the Commons for so saucily meddling in a matter so sacred, and so far above them. Yet afterwards, 1 *Hen.* IV. *num.* 91. that Judgment against Sir *Thomas Haxley* was revers'd.

As for the distinction, *page* 622. of a disability actually incurr'd before the meddling in an office, and where the disability is prevented by the coming of a dispensation; I answer, that its being so prevented, is but *Petitio Principii*, and a begging of the question. And to this distinction I have (I think) fully spoken in my larger argument, *fol.* 40.

The late Parliament, in making this Act of 25 *Car.* II. had, no doubt, a prospect that probably the Crown would descend upon a *Popish* Successor; and they levelled this Act against the dangers that might then befal our Religion and Liberties, and they thought it a good security: but it is all vanished and come to nothing, by occasion of this Judgment in the case of Sir *Edward Hales*. And that must be justified by a *Fiat Justitia*.

As to the objection that the Chief-Justice fancies might have been made against him, or advice given him that he should rather have parted with his place, than to have given a Judgment so prejudicial to the Religion he professes, *pag.* 622.

This, I say, that for my part I should never have advis'd him to have parted with his place, much less to have given a Judgment against his own opinion. But let his opinion be what it was, yet seeing the clear intention of the makers of the Law contrary to that his opinion, and knowing the desperate effects and consequences that would follow upon the dispensing with that Act, (for we were upon the brink of destruction by it) and taking notice (as this Chief-Justice and the rest of the Judges needs must) that the King had first endeavour'd to have gain'd a dispensing power in this matter from both Houses (which was the fair and legal course), and that yet that very Parliament which, out of too great a compliance with those times, had over-look'd so many grievances, and conniv'd at the King's taking and collecting of the Customs, (tho' in truth the Collectors, and all that had any hand in the receiving of them, incurr'd a *Præmunire* by it) not to mention the ill artifice used in gaining the Excise; yet that Parliament of the King's boggled at the dispensing with the Act of 25 *Car.* II. knowing the mighty importance of it.

And though they could not but take notice that so many Judges at once had been remov'd, because they could not swallow this *Bitter Pill*, and others brought into their places, as might be justly suspected, to serve a turn, and the King's learned Counsel could not at first find out this prerogative to do his work with, till so many ways had been attempted, and all prov'd ineffectual; sure in such circumstances it had been prudence, nay the duty of the Judges to have referr'd the determination of it to a Parliament; and the rather, because it was to expound a Law newly made, and the consequences so dreadful, and the intent of the Law-makers so evident.

And this hath been frequently practis'd by Judges, in cases of far less difficulty and concernment. This I have also enlarged upon in my large argument, *pag.* 26.

Object. But it might have been a long time before any Parliament had been called.

Answ. We ought to have Parliaments once a-year, and oftener if need be; and *eadem præsumitur esse mens Regis, quæ Legis*; and we then stood in great need of a Parliament even for the sake of this very case.

And these hasty Judgments are one ill cause why Parliaments meet no oftener; the work of Parliaments is taken out of their hands by the Judges. And it is the interest of some great Officers, that Parliaments should not be called, or else be hastily prorogu'd or adjourn'd.

As to the point of the feigned Action, which the Lord Chief-Justice seems to justify, I conceive he mistakes the force of the objection. Feigned Actions may be useful; but this Action against Sir *Edward Hales*, is suspected not only to have been feign'd and brought by *Covin* between him and his servant and friend, but it was feignedly and faintly prosecuted, and not heartily and stoutly defended.

This solemn resolution was given upon a few short arguments at the Bar, and without any at the Bench, and upon other reasons (as I have heard) which were then made use of, are now given by the Chief-Justice; but the times will not bear them.

After all, I intend not by this to do the office of an accuser, nor to charge it as a crime. But as I think myself bound in duty, on the behalf of the whole Nation, of myself, (though a small part and member of it) and of my friends, I humbly propose, that the Judgment given in Sir *Edward Hales*'s case, may, after a due examination, (if there be found cause) be legally revers'd by the House of Lords, and that reversal approv'd of and confirm'd by a special Act of Parliament.

But as that Judgment of the Lord-Chief-Justice's was of the utmost consequence, and his Vindication far from satisfying the People; Mr. *Atwood*, a very considerable man in his profession, at that time, undertook the answering the Chief-Justice: Therefore to set the whole matter in a true light, and to observe an exact impartiality, Mr. *Atwood*'s Examination of the Chief-Justice's Account, is here inserted, as follows.

The Lord Chief-Justice Herbert's *Account examin'd by* William Atwood, *Esq. Barrister at Law, wherein is shewn, That those Authorities in Law, whereby he would excuse the Judgment in Sir* Edward Hales's *case, are very unfairly cited, and as ill applied.*

WERE it not the reproach of our times, to have had men advanc'd to Courts of Judicature for other merits besides Integrity and Learning in the Laws of their Country; it might seem a great piece of vanity in me, to answer a Book stamp'd with the name and authority of a Chief-Justice.

Yet, perhaps, I might be thought, not without cause, to take this as my more immediate Province; having been the first of the profession who ventur'd in public companies to shew, how wofully that innocent Book-case, 2 *Hen.* VII. in relation to Sheriffs, has been mistook, or wrested, to serve for colour to that hasty Judgment in Sir *Edward Hales*'s feigned case.

Wherefore, how needful soever the Chief-Justice may find it, to make protestations of his sincerity, *vid. Account*, *p.* 616. this may supersede any such from me. Nor would I willingly call his a protestation contrary to apparent fact (especially considering that weakness of Judgment manifested by this defence), did he not give too great occasion for it. 1. From the large steps which he took to precipitate, and, as I am well assured, to sollicit that resolution. 2d. The manner in which he delivered it, widely differing from what he now prints. 3. The unfairness of his present quotations. And, 4. The unhappiness, not to say worse, of those instances which he is pleased to give of his sincerity.

I shall not dispute, or repeat his Lordship's state of the case: but the question upon it being, Whether the King may by his prerogative dispense with the Statute 25 *Car.* II. *cap.* 2. requiring all persons in any office under the King, to take the test against Popery, I shall enquire,

1. Whether those Books, which he relies on as authorities for his Judgment, give any colour to it?

2. Whether, admit they did, they would countenance the resolution as he delivered it?

3. Whether those Instances which he offers of his sincerity, may reasonably be taken for such?

4. Whether he in any measure clears himself from the imputation of being highly criminal?

His Lordship, like a master-disputant, begins, as he thinks, with a definition of a Dispensation, which he says, *Account*, *p.* 617. is given by the Lord *Coke* *: *Dispensatio mali prohibiti est de jure Domino Regi concessa, propter impossibilitatem prævidendi de omnibus particularibus; & dispensatio est mali prohibiti provida relaxatio, utilitate, seu necessitate pensata.*

Where, I must say, he very unlearnedly clogs the definition of a dispensing power, with the person in whom 'tis supposed to be lodged; nay, and

* *Coke* 11. *Rep. fol.* 88.

and the reaſon too why it ſhould be ſo, which neither the Lord *Coke*, nor common ſenſe, gives him any warrant to bring into the definition. However it ſeems, according to this, a diſpenſing Power, in ſome caſe or other, is veſted in the King; which yet is far from proving any thing to his purpoſe; for either the King may in all caſes diſpenſe as to particular perſons, and then his diſtinction of *malum prohibitum*, *v. p.* 617. and *malum in ſe*, falls to the ground, or elſe it reaches only to thoſe caſes, in which the judgment or flattery of Judges have aſcribed it to him.

He adds out of the Lord *Coke*, (*p.* 617.) 11 *Rep f.* 88. as an enlargement upon what he calls the definition, *Inaſmuch as an Act of Parliament, which generally prohibits any thing upon a penalty that is popular, or only given to the King, may be inconvenient to divers particular perſons, in reſpect of perſon, time, or place; for this purpoſe the Law gives a Power to the King to diſpenſe with particular perſons.* Where the Lord *Coke* manifeſtly reſtrains the penalty, to ſuch as is given the King as Head of the People, upon which account only he calls it popular: nor, indeed, can be thought to take in what is granted to any ſubject that will inform; it being mentioned without diſtinction, whether before or after an Information commenced.

And that the Lord *Coke*'s words here, 7 *Rep. f.* 36. ought not to be reſtrained farther, is yet more evident, from the caſe of *Penal Statutes*, on which Sir *Edward Herbert*'s miſ-repreſentations will occaſion my more particular Remarks.

As Sir *Edward*, conſidering what intereſt he has ſerv'd, may be preſumed ſomething converſant with Prieſts and Jeſuits, he might, among others of leſs uſe, have conſulted the learned *Suarez* (*a*), who after the definition, which he makes to be *Legis humanæ relaxatio*, in a diſtinct Chapter ſhews, with whom the ordinary power of diſpenſing (which he diſtinguiſhes from that which is delegated) is lodged, where he ſays, *ib. c.* 14. *f.* 395. *Certum eſt eum habere ordinariam poteſtatem diſpenſandi, qui legem tulit:* And he gives the reaſon, *Quia ab ejus voluntate & potentia pendet.* So that none can have this power, but he, or they who are veſted with the legiſlative excluſive of others, or ſuch as have it delegated from thence. That the King has not the legiſlative excluſive of others, is what I have formerly proved at large (*b*); and it lies on the other ſide to ſhew, that the diſpenſing power has been delegated to him. Yet thus much may be ſaid on the contrary:

Firſt, That the King could not in Law be preſumed to have exerciſed ſuch a power by himſelf; for that the ancient Law provided, that he ſhould have a Council choſe in Parliament, who (as the Charter affirm'd to be declaratory of the ancient Law, and ſworn at the Coronation of *Hen.* III. has it (*c*)) were ſworn *quod negotia Domini Regis & Regni fideliter tractabunt, & ſine acceptatione perſonarum omnibus juſtitiam exhibebunt:* and that it was accounted the Law long after that, appears by the impeachment of *Roger Mortimer*, 4 *E.* III. part of which was, that *Whereas it was ordained in the Parliament next after the King's Coronation, that four Biſhops, four Earls, and four Barons, ſhould ſtand by the King*, Pur luy Counſeiller; *without whoſe aſſent* Nul gros Buſoign ne ſe Feuſt: nevertheleſs *Mortimer* would undertake to manage all by himſelf, accroaching royal Power (*d*). And it is eaſily to be ſhewn, that ſuch a Council was in uſe, or continually inſiſted on, as the right of the Kingdom, from the time of the Charter, confirm'd 28 *Hen.* III. till the end of the Reign of *Hen.* VI.

2. A Power to grant *non obſtante's* to Statutes, could not have been a right in the Crown at Common Law; for we have clear proofs of its odious and condemned beginning from the ſulphureous fountain of *Rome*, as an honeſt popiſh lawyer confeſs'd with a deep ſigh, 35 *Hen.* III. This *non obſtante Matthew Paris* calls, *a deteſtable addition againſt all Reaſon and Juſtice:* And when, the year after, King *Henry* urged the example of the Pope for *non obſtante's*, the Prior of *Jeruſalem* ſays, *God forbid you ſhould uſe this unpleaſant and abſurd word, as long as you obſerve Juſtice you may be King, and as ſoon as you violate it, you will ceaſe to be King*; which ſhews how little foundation in Law it then was thought to have; and what the whole Nation thought of the Pope's uſe of it, may be ſeen at large in *Matthew Paris*, and Mr. *Prynne*'s Animadverſions on the 4th *Inſtitute* (*e*).

Farther, the reaſons given why the King ought to have this power, fail here upon many accounts.

1. In that the intereſt of the whole, of which the Legiſlators are the beſt Judges, when they make the Law without exception, ought to outweigh all private inconveniencies.

2. The Law has provided a more certain and equal remedy; having taken as ſufficient care for the meeting of Parliaments, once a year at leaſt, and I may ſay, (*f*) ſitting too, as it has for the ſitting of the common Courts of Juſtice; as appears from the ſeveral Statutes in print, and others in the Rolls, which avoid the common cavil upon the words, *oftener if need be.*

And theſe were, like the famous triennial Act, proviſions for the greater certainty of meeting ſo often at leaſt, but no receſſions from the old Law; which, as appears both by the *Mirrour*, and the life of King *Alſred* (*g*), was for the great Council to meet twice a year at *London*.

3. The great reaſon aſſigned in the *Latin* quotation from the Lord *Coke*, *propter impoſſibilitatem prævidendi de omnibus particularibus*, which is after diſtinguiſhed, as to perſon, time, and place, can by no means be applied to the caſe in queſtion: For, 1. The Law was made but very few years before their Lordſhips reſolution, and not grown more inconvenient by length of time, to any particular perſon, than it was at the making of the Act. 2. The Law-makers had in their immediate proſpect every particular perſon of the *Romiſh* communion; and the time when, and place where the danger would happen, if any ſuch were commiſſioned.

Let us now ſee what help he can have from his ſecond quotation from

the Lord *Coke*, which is 7 *Rep.* *j*
and would have it believed, tha
England, 2 *Jac.* I. that the Kin
that he ſhall not incur the penal
pro bono publico; and that this is a
the royal perſon of the King, *Ac*
throws his diſtinction of *malum*
at large, in relation to any St.
perverts the Lord *Coke*'s ſenſe,
Statute is made pro bono public
and the fountain of Juſtice and M
is a truſt and confidence inſeparab
ſo high a point of Sovereignty, th
power of any private perſon, or to
King, by all his ſubjects, for th
King can, upon any cauſe moving h
make a non obſtante *to diſpenſe*
incur the penalty of this Statute.

Where the ſole queſtion was
the King, as entruſted by all the
by inflicting the penalty. Th
to be transferred over; but tha
penalty granted to himſelf · up
has made a very foul ſtretch; (
cerning which the queſtion bei
difference betwen theſe two pr
" truſted the King with a Stat
" inſeparable, and cannot be
" intruſted, may be diſpenſed
ed from my Lord *Coke*. And th
" good, yet the King may diſ
" dence inſeparably annexed t
Sir *Edward Herbert*'s perverſe c
the King is entruſted with the ex
he may diſpenſe with that Statut
with any Statute made for the pub
that the queſtion in the Lord
over the penalty; which pena
the other would make it of diſp
and not to be transferred; ſo a

His next ſtep is to the Year-
leaves us to ſeek the year, whi
caſe which he cites, wherein th
limited.

" There is a diverſity, ſays t
" *prohibitum*, and *malum in ſe*;
" and if he does, he ſhall be ha
" the Statute, coining money
" fore the King can diſpenſe v
" but *Calais*, it is *malum proh*
" Parliament. But that wh
" perſon can diſpenſe with:
" kill another; or licenſe one
" were void, and yet the King c
Upon this caſe 'tis obſervable,
ed in relation to things, and i
taken in Sir *Edward Herbert*'s
to all in general, where the m.
himſelf owns, that the nature
particular perſons by name.
moſt, are but *mala prohibita*: a
with; when he himſelf owns
tittle of *Magna Charta*: And
tradiction. Wherefore the ru
as it was not, being only ſpok
applied only to ſuch caſes as a
money, which goes upon the
ſaid, that *ſuch Statutes as give*
that of ſhipping wool at *Calai*
and both ſufficiently ſhew the
in ſe, to relate barely to ſuch
are againſt an accidental prero
rights of the ſubjects in gener.

And I much wonder that
Vaughan, in the caſe of *Thoma*
infer from the Year-book, wh
Rule has more confounded men's
and *fol* 333. himſelf denies th
prohibitum by Statute, though

Oh, but my Lord *Vaughan* ſ
makes the thing prohibited to a
it. Does he ſay this of every *m*
we muſt apply it to the caſe then
about which the King had a Pre
with that, falls within the rule i
the caſe of *Penal Statutes* (*l*). Y
Prerogative, ſince the 1ſt of *E*

(*a*) *Suarez de Legibus, lib.* 6. *cap.* 10. *fol.* 384. *ib. cap.* 14. *fol.* 395. (*b*) V. *Jus Angl. ab Antiquo.* & *Jani. Angl. fa.*

(*c*) Vid. *Mat. Par. de anno* 28 *H.* III. So *Rot. Par.* 42 *H* III. *m.* 4. *m.* 10. V. *Jan. An. fa. Nov. p.* 244. *Rot Par.* 4 *E*

(*d*) Vid. *Rot. Par.* 5 *E.* II *Ryley pl. parl. f.* 317. *Rot. Par.* 8 *E.* II. *n.* 35. 4 *E.* III. *n.* 16. 17 *E.* *n.* 12. *Walſingham, f.* 243
Vid. *etiam* 5 *H.* IV. *n.* 37 11 *H.* IV. *n.* 15. 1 *H.* VI. *n.* 16. 24. 30. 11 *H.* VI. *n.* 17. 31 *H.* VI. *n.* 38 Vid. *Rolls Ab.* 2 part
827. *illepidum.* (*e*) *Prynne*'s Animad. *f.* 129, 130. Vid. *etiam* Sir *John Davis* 's *Rep. f.* 69. *b.*

(*f*) Vid. *Mod. ten. Parl. Parliamentum ſeparari non debet, dummodo aliqua Petitio pendeat indiſcuſſa vel ad minus ad quam*
trarium permittat, perjurius eſt. As I find it in an ancient MS. of the *Modus.* Vid. *etiam* 4 *Inſt. fol.* 11. Vid. 50 *E.* III. *n.* 17;
in the King's Name, 2 *R.* II. *n.* 4.

(*g*) Vid. *Spelm. Vit. Ælfredi, f* 115. *Mirrour, p.* 282. Where 'tis placed among the abuſes of the Law, That Parliam

(*h*) Chief-Juſtice *Fineaux*, 11 *H* VII. *f.* 12 2.

(*i*) *Moor's Rep. f.* 714. Indeed the Book ſpeaks alſo of diſpenſing with Statutes, re[illegible]ing the Prerogative; but that
Subject for the limitation of that Power, *vid. infra.*

(*k*) *Sup. f.* 714. (*l*) 7 *Rep. f.* 36. *b.*

4

the Judges of *England*, in the *Exchequer-Chamber*, and adjourned over for the difficulty (*a*), Whether the King could licenſe the ſhipping wools elſewhere than at *Calais*, one of the very inſtances which Sir *Edward Herbert* relies on. And Chief-Juſtice *Huſſey* was poſitive that the King could not licenſe; tho' indeed the Chief-Baron, and ſome others, held as *Fineux* did afterwards. Wherefore nobody of leſs aſſurance than our Chief-Juſtice can ſay, from theſe Caſes reſults this plain ſyllogiſm:

Whatever is not prohibited by the Law of God, but was lawful before any Act of Parliament made to forbid it, the King by his diſpenſation may make lawful again, to that perſon who has ſuch diſpenſation, tho' it continues unlawful to any body elſe, &c. *Acc. p.* 617. In which, if we grant his major, I will own, the concluſion to bring it to Sir *Edward Hales*'s caſe is not criminal. Yet the propoſition is ſo pernicious, ſtriking at the very foundation of our government, that if there were a reſolution, inſtead of an extra-judicial opinion, giving that countenance which even that looſe opinion does not; yet it ought to be rejected: for if all Acts of Parliament, contrary to *Magna Charta*, are void, as ſome have held, I am ſure much more ſo would ſuch Reſolutions of Judges be. And that ſuch an one would be contrary to that *Great Charter*, is evident: for no man can ſay, that all things prohibited by *Magna Charta*, are prohibited by the law of God.

To come to Sir *Edward*'s next great caſe, as he calls it, *Acc. p.* 618, but indeed the only one which has coloured the reſolution to the world; which is that 2 *H.* VII. Notwithſtanding his promiſe, he, *p.* 617, has not been ſo far to give the words of that caſe, or ſo much of them as is material, leſt every body might judge of how little uſe it would be to him; nay, leſt men ſhould be for ſatisfying their own eyes, he has not directed to the *folio*.

The *Engliſh* of the material part is thus (*b*): "In the *Exchequer-Chamber* all the Juſtices were ſhewn for the King, how King *Edward* the Fourth, by his Letters Patent, had conſtituted the Earl of *N*—— Sheriff of the ſame County; and had granted the ſaid Earl the office of Sheriff of the ſaid County for the term of his life, with all the other offices tended, thereto belonging; rendering to the King at his Exchequer, annually, 100*l.* without any account, or any other thing to be given for it, *&c.*

"Now, 1. Whether this Patent was good? And alſo, 2. How this Patent ſhall be intended? were the points in queſtion. And as to the firſt point, the Juſtices held the Patent good; for it is a thing which may well be granted for term of life or inheritance; as divers Counties have a Sheriff by inheritance; and this commenced by a Grant of the King. Then was ſhewn a Reſumption: and then was ſhewn a Proviſo for *H.* Earl of *N.* ſo that the Patent remains in its force. *Radcliff* ſhews the Statute of 28 *E.* III. *c.* 7. and 24 *E.* III. *c.* 5. That no Sheriff ſhall be more than one year, *&c.* altho' he had a *non obſtante.* And notwithſtanding this, that the King ſhall always have his Prerogative, as of the value and certainty of the land, and other things granted by the King, and of wools ſhipped, and of Charters of murder, and many other caſes where the Statutes are, That Patents that want theſe things ſhall be void; yet the Patents are good with a *non obſtante*: But without a *non obſtante* the Patents are void, by reaſon of the Statutes. So here the Patent, with a *non obſtante*, *&c.*"

This is all that is ſaid in the Book upon the firſt point, upon which it is obſervable,

1. By the Book it would ſeem, that this *Radcliff* was but a Serjeant at Law, for at the end of the caſe *Brian Juſtice* demands of *Brian Radcliffe*, *&c.* Yet indeed I find upon ſearch, that he was a Baron of the Exchequer.

2. What *Radcliff* ſays, is after the reſolution of the Judges is over, and no way influenced that.

3. Whereas Sir *Edward Herbert* ſays, the reſolution was upon 23 *H.* VI. *c.* 1. *Radcliff*, who ſhould better know the ſubject of debate, diſcourſes only concerning the Statutes, 28 *E.* III. *c.* 7. (*c*) and 12 *E.* III. *c.* 5 which are barely prohibitory, without any mention of *non obſtante's*, or any avoiding or diſabling clauſe. Indeed *Radcliff*, it being upon a ſudden diſcourſe, as the Book ſhews, miſtakes the Statutes, as if they had ſuch clauſes. and *Brook* (*d*), who cites part of the Patent, which it ſeems he had ſeen, ſays, there was in it a *non obſtante* to the Statutes 28 *E* III. *c.* 7 and 12 *E.* III. *c.* 9.

Fitzherbert (*e*) indeed ſays, *R.* objected the 23 *H.* VI. but for that *ſit liber judex.*

4. But above all, tho' our Chief Juſtice calls them the Judges enemies, *Acc. p.* 618 who ſay, the point of *non obſtante* is not reſolved in this caſe, which he calls confidence; and that they may as well deny one of the ten Commandments: 'Tis manifeſt beyond contradiction, that the reſolution ended at *iſſint que le Patent demurr en ſa force*: after which comes *Radcliff*'s diſcourſe, and the reſolution went upon two grounds.

1. That this was a thing grantable for inheritance, or for life; which if it were, it could not be preſumed to be touched by the prohibitory Statutes. And beſides, if the queſtion had been upon the other, the caſe had been an exception out of the Statute, for the (*f*) Statute excepts *ſuch Counties in which divers of the King's Liege People be inheritable to the office of Sheriff at the making of the Statute; and alſo ſuch perſons who have Eſtate of freehold in the Office of Sheriff, at the making of the Letters Patent made to them of the office of Sheriffs*, *&c.* Now whether this were really a County ſo inheritable, or of an Eſtate of freehold, at the time, or no, is not ſo very material, being at leaſt it was ſo look'd upon by the Judges, nay, and by the Parliament too, as will appear by their ſecond ground.

But that this County was ſuch an one, I take to be alſo true in fact: for it is to be conſidered, that this was the County of *Northumberland* (*g*), which was a *Palatinate*; upon which reaſon this, with other Counties under it, was left out of the Survey in *Doomſday-Book*, as being *penſitationibus liberi*. This *Palatinate* comprized *Cumberland* and *Weſtmoreland*, among other Counties. in the laſt of which, the Sheriffwick is at this day enjoyed in fee. Indeed *Northumberland* came ſoon into the Crown, as early as the time of *William* the Second, upon the rebellion of *Mowbray*, conſtituted Earl thereof in the time of *William* the Firſt: But the authority in law is much clearer, that this Sheriffwick, if ever held in fee, would remain in the Crown as an inheritance in groſs, and was not merged, than any Sir *Edward Herbert* has produced on his ſide: for which we may obſerve the rule taken in the Caſe of the Abbot of *Strata Mercella*, 9 *Rep. f.* 25. *b.* which is this: "When a Liberty, Franchiſe, or Juriſdiction was at the beginning erected and created by the King, and there was no ſuch Flower in the Crown before, there, by the acceſſion of them again to the Crown, they are not extinct."

Where inſtances are given of the caſes of Markets, Hundreds, and Earldoms; nor can any one ſay, that Sheriffwicks are ancient Flowers of the Crown. But more directly to our caſe, is that between Sir *Robert Atkins* and *Robert Holford* (*h*), which, though not in our Books, is well known. The Caſe was of the Grant of the Seven Hundreds of *Cirenceſter*, with the returns of Writs to the Abbot and Convent of *Cirenceſter*. This came to the Crown by the diſſolution of Monaſteries, 31 *H.* VIII. but yet that it was not merged thereby, but remained as an inheritance in groſs, without the help of any Statute, was the opinion of the great *Hales*, then Chief-Baron, and of two other *Barons*, *Windham* and *Turner*. Part of *Hales*'s words, as I find them excellently well reported, and full to this point, are:

"Such Hundreds as were anciently ſever'd from the Counties, and come again to the Crown by eſcheat or forfeiture, were ſometimes, but rarely committed to the Sheriff, and rejoined to the County, but for the moſt part kept as diſtinct: *Rot. Brevium*, and the Hundred to which it was annexed, without an actual and ſpecial re-annexion to the County, remains in the King in groſs; for the *Rot Brevium* is a thing created *de novo*. Suppoſe it were a Court of Juriſdiction merely created by the King, and the Hundred itſelf, tho' ancient, yet by return to the Crown it is not merged or annexed: This I know in the caſe of the Courts belonging to the Honours of *Glouceſter* and *Hereford*, that came to *H.* V. by marriage of a coheir, it is ſtill *in eſſe*."

This were enough to ſhew, that the Judges reſolution 2 *H.* VII. had a better legal foundation than what Sir *Edward Herbert* would ſuggeſt.

2. But then, beſides that, there was another ground mentioned in the Book, which was, That a reſumption was ſhewn before the Judges; and then was ſhewn a Proviſo for *H.* Earl of *N.* and ſo (ſays the Book) the Patent remains in its force. This reſumption was an Act of Reſumption 1 *H.* VII. and if this Act provided for that Earl's Grant, as the Judges, it ſeems, thought it did, who can doubt but the Grant was good? The Act of Reſumption is to be ſeen upon Record, *Rot. Parl.* 1 *H.* VII. *part* 2. It is a reſumption of Grants made by *Edward* the Fourth; and among others of the *Yefts*, that is, *Gifts of offices*; The Proviſo runs thus.

"Provided always, that this Act of Reſumption, or any other Act made, or to be made, in this preſent Parliament, be not in any wiſe prejudicial or hurtful to the ſeveral Grants and Letters Patents made to *Henry* Earl of *Northumberland*, *&c.*" Which indeed does not make good any void Grant, but ſuppoſes all the Grants to him to be good in Law; nor would the Judges diſpute their ſuppoſal.

I admit with him, *Acc. p.* 618, that *Fitzherbert* ſays, and that truly, that the Patent was adjudged good; but the reaſon he gives agrees with what I have ſhewn: his words are, *for ſuch a thing may be grantable for Inheritance, or for Life.* And then I am ſure that the Statute does not ſay expreſsly, the Patent ſhall be void, though Sir *Edward* affirms that it does. *Vid Acc. p.* 618.

Obj. It may be objected, that the exception in the Statute relates to eſtates in the ſubject; but if this were an intereſt in groſs in the King, that it could not be taken from him without expreſs words, cannot be denied me.

What he cites from *Plowden*, *Acc. p.* 618. can be of no more ſervice; for he only ſays, *there it is held*, and I agree it is held by *Radcliff*, *Acc. p.* 618. with a miſtake of the Statute, That the King can grant a Sheriffwick for more than a year: Yet whereas he magnifies this as cited by *Plowden*, who, as he ſuppoſes, well underſtood the ſenſe of the Year-book:

It does not (*i*) appear that it was *Plowden*, but one who was of Councill in the Caſe for the Defendant, who mentions this.

2. He mentions it only as a Caſe in *Fitzherbert*, *Plowden*, *f.* 502. without referring to the Book, 2 *H.* VII.

But the ſecond point raiſed before the Judges, 2 *H.* VII. which occaſioned the main debate in that caſe, as appears by the Book, ſhews, that the reſolution could not be upon the point of Prerogative; for they queſtioned whether the King could diſpenſe with his own profit. And all the Judges, except *Brian* and *Cateſby*, held, that the Patentee ſhall account for the green wax, and other things, notwithſtanding the clauſe of *abſque reddendo computum*: But the debate concerning other things ariſing upon that ſecond point was adjourned; the firſt reſolved upon the grounds above.

Tho' hitherto there is no Proof, that any one of authority in the Law has taken the Book 2 *H.* VII. in Sir *Edward Herbert*'s ſenſe, which yet would be of no moment if they were expreſs, being the Book is to be ſeen, and clearly otherwiſe; yet he thinks my Lord *Coke* will bear him out, and to this purpoſe he cites two places one, where he ſuppoſes that the Lord *Coke* not only authorizes this ſenſe of the caſe, but aſſerts the Prerogative, *Acc p.* 618. in much higher terms than they would preſume to do: and by the ſecond he would have it believed, that if the Lord *Coke* be a faithful Reporter, all the Judges of *England* took that caſe in the ſame ſenſe.

The firſt is the caſe of cuſtoms, 24 *Eliz.* which is pregnant with many objections againſt its being of any force in this caſe.

1. The Book, 12 *Rep. f.* 17. is of ſuſpected authority, being printed in the late times, and what the Lord *Coke* never owned, or thought fit to print in his life-time.

2. This comes foiſted in among caſes in the time of King *James*, without any parallel caſe which might occaſion the placing of it there.

3. It was when the Lord *Coke* was but a young Reporter, it being ten years before he was King's Sollicitor (*k*).

4. It is not only no point in queſtion relating to the caſe where 'tis cited, and ſo extrajudicial, but wholly foreign to it: For the queſtion

(*a*) 1 *H.* VII. *f.* 2. b. & 3. d. (*b*) 2 *H* VII. *f.* 6. b. & 7 a. (*c*) It ſhould be *c.* 9. (*d*) *F.* 7. a. *Brook's* Patents, *n* 45. (*e*) *Fitz Ab.* tit. Grant, *n.* 22.
(*f*) 13 *H.* VI. *c* 8 (*g*) Vid. *Camb Brit f.* 115. Vid. *Dugdale's Baron. f* 2. *Brompton*, a. *f.* 779. *ad* 798 *de Regno Northumb.*
(*h*) Sir *Rob Atkins*, v. *Rob Holford in Scaccbario*, *Hil* 22 & 23 *Car* II. Vid *Rep penes doctiſſimum Dominum Ward.*
(*i*) *Grendon*, v. *eveſque de Lincoln.* (*k*) Was made Sollicitor 16 *June*, 34 *Eliz. Dudg. Chron, Series*, *f.* 99.

was, Whether goods sold before they were landed, were to pay custom within the Statute 1 *Eliz. c.* 11. Wherefore being barely a *memorandum* of a young Reporter, no way occasioned by what went before, it cannot possibly have any weight.

5. The fancy'd reason here given why the King may dispense with the Statute of Sheriffs, is none at all: for whereas it says, 12 *Rep. f.* 18. *That the King has a sovereign Power to command any of his Subjects to serve him for the publick weal, and this solely and inseparably annexed to his person: and this Royal Power cannot be restrained by any Act of Parliament*: There is no authority cited for this, but the case 2 *H.* VII. which, as appears to any body that reads it, neither has that reason been mentioned so much as by any one Judge, nor in the least goes upon the point of the prerogative. Besides, if the King can command any Subject to serve him for the publick weal, either he is to be Judge, or the Laws: If the latter, then no person, not qualified by law, is obliged to act; nor tho' qualified, to do any thing forbid by the laws: If the former, as the words imply, then the King's commands may be pleaded to justify any ill Minister who has rendered himself obnoxious to the laws. But that this cannot be, is sufficiently evinced by necessary examples in all ages. And this, by the way, may shew how false, as well as pernicious, that doctrine is which tell us, that *ἐξουσία* in the *New Testament*, always signifies the authority of a Person, not of a Law. Or, as another has it to the same purpose, *By higher Powers, it is evident, we are to understand the persons of sovereign Princes, or Governors, not the Laws and Constitutions, as our Republican Doctors pretend.*

Of the same batch is another memorable position, *That the King's most illegal Acts, tho' they have not the authority of the Law* (for indeed, to say they have, would be a blunder with a witness), *yet they have the authority of Sovereign Power*. Some will say, that this is qualified by what follows, *which is irresistible and unaccountable*: as if the King had this power only so far as it is irresistible and unaccountable. Whereas it is evident the proposition is entire before, being the medium whereby he would prove, that the King's illegal Acts are not unauthoritative; in proof of which medium, he afterwards affirms, that the sovereign Power which made the laws, and can repeal and dispense with them, is inseparable from the Person of the Prince.

Reduc'd to a Syllogism, it runs thus; *The authority of sovereign Power is irresistible and unaccountable*; *but the King's most illegal Acts have the authority of sovereign Power*. This is an entire proposition upon which he concludes, *Ergo, the King's most illegal Acts are irresistible and unaccountable*. This assumption he goes on to prove from the supposition, that such a Sovereign Power as he describes, is inseparable from the person of the Prince; upon which, or the like Doctrine, another raises this comfortable use: *In all sovereign Governments* (and such he at large endeavours to shew *England* to be) *Subjects must be slaves as to this particular*; *they must trust their lives and liberties with their Sovereign.*

But for the honour of our Gown, this may be said, That such Hereticks never appeared among Lawyers, till Divines began first to wrest the laws and scriptures to their own damnation. But as the former quotation out of the Lord *Coke* can do Sir *Edward Herbert* no service, upon the reasons above shewn; much less can the other, which is one of Sir *Edward*'s usual perversions. He tells us, *Acc. ante* p. 619. That it is resolved by all the Judges (if my Lord *Coke* be a faithful Reporter), that it is agreed 2 *H.* VII. that the King may, against the express provision of the Act 23 *H.* VI. dispense with that Act; for that the Act could not bar the King of the service of his Subjects, which the law of nature did give unto him. He adds, *This is reported (unless my Lord* Coke *had a mind to deceive the succeeding Judges, and draw them in to give pernicious opinions) as the sense of all the Judges of* England, *in King* James's *time, in the Exchequer-Chamber*. Whereas the Lord *Coke*, on purpose to prevent such an abuse of his words, says in the beginning of the Case, 7 *Rep. f.* 4. "I shall give no just offence to any, "if I challenge that which of right is due to every Reporter; that is, to "reduce the sum and effect of all to such a method, as upon consideration "had of all the arguments, he himself thinketh to be fittest and clearest "for the right understanding of the true reasons and causes of the Judg-"ment, and resolution of the case in question."

Upon which it is evident, that if any one of the Judges mentioned this, the Lord *Coke* is a faithful Reporter; but had he been silent as to this matter, no man could suppose, that such a tedious argument as that in *Calvin*'s case was the resolution in which the Judges concurred in every expression.

But Sir *Edward Herbert*'s own eyes might, and ought to have satisfied him, that the Judges 2 *H.* VII gave no determination upon the 23 *H.* VI. nor does the Book say, that so much as any one person spoke to that Statute, or mentioned the reason devised in *Calvin*'s case; *For that the Act could not bar the King of the service of his Subject, which the Law of Nature did give unto him.* Nor could Sir *Edward* chuse but know the absurdity of that ground: for according to that, all ought to be left in the state of nature, as it was before any Law made; so that not only any person might act, tho' prohibited by subsequent Laws, but he might act any thing forbid by any positive Law; which would make a mad world. And this would come of a natural allegiance due to the person of a King, without respect to the Laws of his Government *(a)*. And the resolution of the Judges in *Calvin*'s case is quite contrary to this supposal; for it is there resolved, That they who were born under King *James*'s allegiance, before he had the Crown of *England*, were aliens here, notwithstanding that accession *(b)*.

But my Lord *Coke* is so far from giving any real countenance to such a resolution, as that in Sir *Edward Hales*'s case, that he, in concurrence with all the Judges of *England*, is express to the contrary; for in relation to the Court of Admiralty, he and the rest of the Judges declare, 4 *Inst f.* 135. "That the Statutes of 13 *R.* II. *c.* 3. 15 *R.* II. *c.* 5. and 2 *H.* IV. *c.* 11. "being Statutes declaring the jurisdiction of the Court of the Admiral, "[illegible] all the Subjects of the Realm have interest, cannot be dis-"pens'd with by any [illegible]." Nay, he gives another resolution of Judges, tho' not so solemn as the former, yet what he says is warranted in the Books, and the resolution came up to our case *in terminis*, 3 *Inst. f.* 154. his words are, "When an Act of Parliament is made, that disabled any

"Person, or maketh any thing void. "or Common-wealth; in that law "and therefore the King cannot di[s-] "the Common Law."

All the chimerical foundation of [...] I need not concern myself with the [...] vanish *in fumo*; and instead of the A[...] *resolutions may not? Acc. ante p.* 619. [...] senses are not sufficient Judges agai[nst] any subject, mere transubstantiatio[n] for a resolution which never was to [...]

But we are told, That besides the [...] practice that this Statute has been d[...] not so, the consequences would be [...] *ante p.* 619. But to this I say,

1. *A facto ad jus non valet argumen[tum]* on the side of the fact.

2. The fact cannot be shewn, fo[r] for more than one year by the same [...]

3. However the consequences wo[uld] know, even Laws made by Kings *de* [...] binding, and so have the admittanc[e] seisors, and others without title. [...] stress upon precedents of our own [...] and we well know, that notwithstan[ding] in the City of *London*, yet no challe[nge] Sheriffs *de facto*.

That I may not be here unnecess[arily] real or fancied objections; I shall ha[...] and shall begin with his last, as havi[ng] cases above-cited, and which he fee[...] Serjeant *Glanvil*'s argument, deliver[ed] and Commons; wherein he owns, th[...] *prohibita, Acc. ante p.* 621. under ce[...] King, and the Informer, there the [...] more than appears from any case tha[...] have shewn above; yet is no more tha[n] immediately after he had denied that [...] *for the good of the Church or Commonw[ealth] Subjects have an Interest, and therefor[e] more than with the Common Law.*

All that is more, in Serjeant *Glan[vil]* Laws which were then insisted upon; [...] be an evidence of the opinion of the [...] being the point put to the question, t[...] is of the opinion of all the Judges. [...] not be stretch'd farther than *mala pr[ohibita]* is, in relation to new prerogatives, o[...] in general have no interest vested in t[...] such cases, *wherein his Majesty, by con[...] not do wrong to others*; *Acc. p.* as it [...] *Moor (e)*, where 'tis held, that Stat[...] strain the prerogative, may be dispen[...] pose of Interests. And as to what r[...] within the *mala prohibita*, tho' it fal[...] we may observe the difference taken [...] is made to ease the Sovereign of labo[ur] the first case the King may dispense, [...]

And I think no Man can doubt [...] which only requires officers to take t[...] from Papists, but disables them that [...] vests an interest, not only in several [...] versioners, but in all the Subjects in [...] Statutes insisted on in the Petition o[...] *Glanvil*, *Acc. ante p.* 621. "Not La[ws] "[illegible], but Laws declarative, [illegible] "*an inherent Right and interest of th[e]* "*Realm, as their birth-right, and* [...] "*posterity.*" A freedom, I may a[...] *Statutes incorporate into the body of th[e]* [...] *verence be it spoken, there is no trust in* [...] *tive royal, to enable him to dispense with t[...] right, or inheritance which they have in* [...] *Law, and of these Statutes*: I may say, [...]

And such a Statute it is, that no m[...] Interest, not only here, but thro' *Ch[ristendom]* [...] gating or impairing the force of it, [...] storing the ancient constitution, both [...] tellors, among other things, as might [...] *Apostles*; than any other means, ne[...] Highness the Prince of *Orange*, wh[...] the subject of present admiration, bu[t] ages, and will be celebrated in all fu[ture] [...]

But to return from this short dig[ression] *Glanvil* speaks as well of such Laws [...] clarative; such as confer an inheren[t] [...] Statute, as well as common Law, not [...] manifestly on our side, and seems not [...] Lord *Coke*, where he makes so express [...] dispensing power which he allows. [...] no more, considering the import of [...] herent, and inseparable [illegible] rived. [illegible] inherent, and [illegible] the true meaning [illegible] not to be separated and transferred

(a) [illegible] Exceptions to S[illegible] Serm. *Rights* part 1 *f.* 439 & 441 [illegible] Gen[illegible] Quest [illegible] 212 to 214. [illegible] *f.* 58. *b.* (d) Vid. *supra*, 3 *Inst f.* 154. [illegible] of Lord [illegible] Judgment, which is always accurate for the reason of the Law. (c) [illegible] *Rep. f.* 27 [illegible] (e) Vid. Lord Coke's Cap. of [illegible]

Man will doubt the Power of a Parliament, in relation even to them; and if they cannot be receded from in particular, at least they may in gross; when a King does *cedere imperio*, or *abdicare Regnum*, which most prerogative-casuists (*a*) own may be, not only by actual Cession from the Government, but by Acts amounting to an Abdication, and shewing a fixed Intention no longer to treat his People as Subjects. Nor perhaps could there be greater Evidence of such Intention, than the dispensing at a Lump, not barely by Retail to particular Persons, with those Laws which were made by the united Wisdom of the Nation to secure it, as much as they thought human Means could, or at least the Court would yield to against those real Dangers which were in their immediate Prospect. Nor in all Probability had this Enclosure been laid waste, if the dispensing Judges had not made the first Gap.

As to Sir *Edward*'s supposed clear Concessions of this Power from all the Commons of *England*, 1 *H. V. Acc. ante p.* 620. they are quite otherwise than he represents them, nor would be conclusive to his Point however.

In the first, says Sir *Edward*, " The Commons pray, that the Statutes " for voiding of Aliens out of the Kingdom may be kept and executed; " to which the King agrees, saving his Prerogative, that he may dispense " with whom he pleases; and upon this the Commons answered, that " their Intent was no other."

But the Recorder says, *Sauvant a luy sa prerogative*, " saving to him " his Prerogative." Whatever that was, they declared they never intended to injure it. Then it goes on with the Copulative *and*, which adds new Matter, and is dishonestly left out by Sir *Edward*, *Et quil purra dispenser avesque ceux queux luy plerra*, " And that he may dispense with " whom he pleases." Which is an additional Grant or Licence to that King; but that this saving is but a general saving of the Prerogative, appears by the very next Record, which he cites of the same Parliament.

Sir *Edward*'s Words are, " In the same Parliament, when the Com- " mons pray, That the Statutes of Provisors, Statutes of the same Na- " ture with this in our Case (for they were made against the Court of " *Rome*'s encroaching Jurisdiction in *England*), I say, when they make " the like Prayer, that these may be put in Execution; being admonish- " ed by the King's Answer in the former Case, they themselves insert in " their very Prayer, a saving for this Prerogative of the King's, and then " the King agrees to it." Where he would insinuate, that this Prerogative of dispensing with particular Persons is there saved, when the Record is express to the contrary: The Words in *English* are,

" Also the Commons pray, for the good and Profit of the Realm, that " all the Statutes made against Provisors, in the Times of the most noble " King, *E*. III. *R*. II. *H*. IV. (*b*) your Father, whom God be mer- " ciful to, may stand in their Force, and may be held and executed in all " Points, and that no Protection, nor other Grant, to any Person, by " our Lord the King, working to the contrary, in forbearance of the " Execution of the said Statutes, be allowable or available to any Person " whatsoever in this Matter. And if any thing be done to the contrary, " let it be held for null or void; saving all times the Prerogative of the " King."

The King answers, " Let the Statutes thereof made, be held and " kept." Which is plainly meant according to their Prayer, without the King's impeding the Execution of them by any Protection, or other Grant to any Person whatsoever; and if such Grant be, that it shall be void. Is not this as much as to say, (*Vid. Acc. ante p.* 618.) *That no non obstante shall make any such Grant good?* Or, but Sir *Edward* will tell us, *That this shews that the Parliament thought the King could otherwise have dispensed with these Acts*. By no Means; it only argues an Abuse crept in (which *Matthew Paris* shews to have been as early as the Time of *H*. III.) and likely to be allowed of by the Judges, but the Parliament would prevent even that; and surely they would never provide, that a *non obstante*, or Grant to a particular Person shall be void, if they thought the King had a Prerogative to defeat this when he pleased: Much less, when they had a Prerogative to defeat this when he pleased: Much less, when they expressly pray against such an Abuse, can they be thought to contradict themselves, and in the same Breath that they desire that no Person whatever may be dispensed with, yet leave the King a Prerogative to dispense with whom he pleases. The Absurdity of which Reasoning he might have seen in that excellent Speech of Serjeant *Glanvil* (*c*), which he himself receives as the Sense *of the Commons of* England, *assembled in Parliament*.

Wherefore the saving in both the Records *Acc. ante, p.* 621. can be but general savings, of such Prerogative as the Kings had, whatever it were, which the Kings, as they began to encroach upon the People, or to be jealous of their Encroachments, would have inserted out of abundant Caution, before they would yield to several Acts. And these being Acts of Parliament, which could pass but as the King consented, the People were forced often to gild the Pills with such Savings; but it was otherwise of Judgments in Parliaments to which no Consent of the King was requisite.

Farther yet, admit the King had a Prerogative of dispensing with particular Persons, both as to Aliens and Provisions; yet there could no general Rule be taken from thence, because it would only argue, that the fondness for Aliens, and fear of displeasing the Court of *Rome*, had at first occasioned the reserving the Power of easing some particular Persons, without which the King would pass no Act against them. However it was, the frequent Complaints of the Commons (*d*), and Acts made against both the one and the other, shews that those Laws were little regarded or executed, and yet that the King had not a Prerogative allowed him any more for particular Persons, than for all in general.

Sir *Edward* has five other trivial Instances of the dispensing Power, which, however, I shall not omit. One is the dispensing with the Statute, 8 *R*. II. *c*. 2. *Account, p.* 619 [illegible] requires, that no Man should [illegible] *Assize* [illegible] County. But for this there is only Practice, which his [illegible], and so could be of no Authority in Law. Besides, the Statute is barely prohibitory, and does not render the Patents void if otherwise; yet I cannot say but an Information would lie, though there were a *non obstante* in the Case.

The second is of dispensing with the Statute 10 *Ed*. III. *cap*. 3. *Acc. ante, p.* 619. which provides, *That whoever has a Pardon of Felony, shall find Sureties for the good Behaviour*; of which he says, as of the other, *That it has been constantly dispensed with ever since it was made*. But if the Practice had been so, which he does not prove, it would not avail, unless it had come in question judicially, whether the Pardon would be valid to one who had not given, or at least tendered Sureties. Indeed there is a Case in our Books, where the Court did not require Sureties, because of a particular Clause in the Pardon dispensing with it: But this was no earlier than 16 *Car*. I. (*e*) the Judges of which Time paid sufficient Deference to Prerogative; but that Case seems to be not only *primæ impressionis*, and without any Reason given, but in effect condemned by the Reporter, as he shews that the Court abused their Discretion, if they had any, in the Matter. 'Twas the Case of Sir *Matthew Mints*, who appeared to be guilty of several Misdemeanors, for which he deserved to be bound to the good Behaviour, committed after the Time to which he was pardoned.

The third and fourth Instances, scattered from the rest, are of dispensing with Pluralities, and Bastards entering in Priests Orders; *Acc. ante, p.* 622. which, if possible, will be less serviceable to him: For,

1. Such dispensations are never granted by the King (*f*), but by the Archbishop; and the King only licenses, or confirms, the Archbishop's Dispensation in unusual Cases.

2. That the King's Licence or Confirmation in *Cases unwont*, as the Statute has it, is of any Force, is owing to the Statute, 25 *Hen*. VIII. *cap*. 21.

3. Even in usual Cases, where the Archbishop might dispense, though the King's Confirmation be added, yet unless it come in due time, it will not prevent a Lapse incurred upon the Statute 21 *Hen*. VIII. *cap*. 13. against Pluralities; as was adjudged in *Digby*'s Case (*g*), though the Dispensation came before Induction. And this comes up fully to one of the Points in Sir *Edward Hales*'s Case, which our Chief-Justice has not been so fair as in the least to mention to be a Point in the Case. Nay, quite contrary, he supposes it to be a Case, *Acc. ante, p* 623. *where a Disability is annexed as a Penalty, and that Penalty is not to be incurred before legal Conviction, and where the King's Dispensation makes the Thing dispensed with lawful, and consequently prevents any Conviction or Penalty at all*; forgetting, that in the very State of the Case, he owns there was a Conviction before the Dispensation came. So that here was a Disability actually incurred, and that upon Record, as appears in the Pleadings; and while that Record remains, there is no falsifying of it, though in fact the Conviction were before the three Months given in the Statute to prevent a Disability (*h*); and he had no other Means, than either to plead no such Record, or to bring his Writ of Error. Wherefore this Dispensation comes clearly within *Digby*'s Case, as being too late, supposing otherwise it were valid.

As Sir *Edward* shews that he has read *Thomas* and *Sorrel*'s Case, he might have known another Reason of these two Cases, *viz*. (*i*) " That " the King may dispense with a Bastard to take Holy Orders, or with a " Clerk to have two Benefices with Cure, which were *mala prohibita* by " the Canon Law, and by the Council of *Lateran*, not by Act of Par- " liament;" which is most true. For these are mentioned in the Book of *Hen*. VII. before any Act made against Pluralities.

There is another Instance in that wild Annotation, upon the Case of Customs in the 12 *Rep*. where 'tis said, " See (*Acc. p.* 619.) 4 *Hen*. IV. " *cap*. 31. in which 'tis ordained, that no *Welshman* be Justice, *&c*. in " any Part of *Wales*, notwithstanding any Patent to the contrary, with " Clause of *non obstante licet sit Wallicus*: And yet without Question the " King may grant with a *non obstante*."

Nor do I question it neither, even before 21 *Jac*. I. *cap*. 38 when that Statute was repealed, provided the *Welshman use not Welsh Speech*; and this by 27 *H*. VIII. *cap*. 26.

But as to these three last Instances, it might be said further, that if they were stronger than they prove, yet they might fall under the Difference received by him from Lord *Vaughan*, where he says, the King may dispense with Laws made *pro bono publico complicati*, but not with such as were made *pro bono singulorum populi*; in which the Lord *Vaughan* is not so absurd, as to mean, that though the King cannot dispense with a Law in which any Man in particular is so far interested, as to be entitled to an Action for himself alone, yet he may with those in which all the subjects are interested. But his Meaning, to make him consistent with himself, must be restrained to Lord *Coke*'s Sense upon the Penal Statute, which makes this Power to be only where *the King, as Head of the Commonwealth, is trusted by all the Realm* (*k*); in which Sense he alone is to look after the Interest of the *populus complicatus* under him as Head. Thus Lord *Vaughan*, 1. Expresly, (*Acc. p.* 620) qualifies it, when he says, " They are *pro* " *bono populi complicati*, as the King in his Discretion shall think fit to or- " der them for the good of the whole." 2 He illustrates it by the Example of a *Pater familias* (*l*); " Whose Estate, he tells us, may be said " to be *pro bono communi* of his Family, which yet is but at his Discre- " tion and Management of it, and they have no Interest in it, but have Benefit by it." 3. Both he and Sir *Edward Herbert* allow Instances, where every particular Man is not entitled to his Action, and yet the Statutes are owned to be *pro bono singulorum populi*, and not to be dispensed with; *Account, p.* 620. and such are *Magna Charta*, and those other Laws mentioned by Serjeant *Glanvil* and Sir *Edward*. *Acc. p.* 620. And if some Difference can be found between the Interest *singulorum populi* in all those Statutes, and in ours, to use his Words, I wish any Man would shew me any such Difference, or else we must say, that not only the former Resolutions, but Lord *Vaughan* here, as well as where I before observed, is full against him, nay, he is even against himself

(*a*) Vid. Grot. de Jure Belli & Pacis [illegible] p. 344, 345 [illegible] Mastere, &c. But if ever any such strange Cases [illegible] proposed [illegible] Reformed [illegible] Foundation [illegible] Commonwealth, which they [illegible] when they first consented to have a King.

(*b*) Rot. Parl. 11 H. V. [illegible] (*c*) Vid. Serjeant Glanvil's Speech, [illegible] (*d*) Vid. Dr. Stillingfleet against [illegible] from p. 42 [illegible] (*e*) Sir Matthew Mints's Case, [illegible] 4 Rep. [illegible] *Oxford* [illegible]

(*l*) Vaughan, [illegible] (*k*) Vid. 7 Rep. [illegible] Vaughan [illegible] himfelf: which I would be loth to think that Lord *Vaughan* is (*a*), who owns, *That the King cannot difpenfe in any cafe but with his own right, and not with the right of any other*, which he confines not to individual perfons, confidered fingly; for he fays exprefsly (*b*), "*If the wifdom of the Parlia-*" *ment hath made an Act to reftrain, pro bono publico*, the importation of "foreign manufactures, that the fubjects of the Realm may apply them-" felves to the making of the faid manufactures for their fupport and "livelihood, to grant to one or more the importation of fuch manufac-" ture, without any limitation, *non obftante* the faid Act, is a Mono-" poly, and void" For this I am fure, particular perfons are not entitled to actions upon their own accounts. Indeed he fuppofes the King may licenfe, limiting the quantity, and that for private ufes (*c*), not by way of merchandize, as not being againft the end of the Act. Wherefore in our cafe all fubjects being interefted as Proteftants, their fupport and encouragement being provided for by the Act, and the letting Papifts into the Government againft the end of it, who can doubt but Lord *Vaughan* would have pronounced Sir *Edward Hales*'s difpenfation void?

And whereas our Judge pleads in his excufe, *Account, p.* 622. That though this Law was made for the intereft of Religion, the offence is not directly againft Religion, but againft a politick Conftitution, tho' made for the intereft of Religion; he might not only have learnt from Lord *Coke*, that the fubjects have fuch an intereft as the King cannot difpenfe with, in what is made void or tortious, that is, unlawful, for the good of the Church; but Lord *Vaughan* fhews (*d*), that there are *mala politica* not to be difpenfed with, and inftances in fome things, which are nuifances *in fpecie*.

Now, befides what already has been fhewn, to difable thefe three laft inftances urged by Sir *Edward*, that they are not *pro bono fingulorum populi*, as that rule is vindicated from mifapplications, may appear, in that neither of them affect all the people in general. As to the Clergymen, they can only do injury in their refpective parifhes where they are beneficed, and the *Welfhman* in that part of *Wales* where he is an officer; nor befides, can the Clergymen be fuppofed much to prejudice the intereft of Religion, being the Pluralift cannot fupply his Cure but by one qualified, and the Baftard might be a good man, and good Preacher. And yet even thefe would fall within Lord *Vaughan*'s acceptation of his own rule (*e*); for he fhews that laws made for the benefit of but part of the Kingdom, Artificers and Hufbandmen, cannot be difpenfed with to any one perfon, to fruftrate the ends of the Statutes.

This leads to another flourifh which he makes with the Lord *Vaughan*'s authority, in anfwer to the objection, that the Law was made *pro bono publico, Acc. p.* 620. and it was highly neceffary for the publick. Indeed Lord *Vaughan* will have it, that the fole reafon why a Statute cannot be difpenfed with, is not, that the Law was made *pro bono publico*, becaufe all Laws were made for publick good, and yet difpenfations had been allowed in fome, nor was the degree of publick good that which altered the cafe; yet he fhews that the extent of it does. and feems ftill to keep to Lord *Coke*'s rule, where the People had entrufted the King with the Law, as Head of the complicated body, there the truft was entirely in him; but when the law extended in intereft not only to individual perfons, but to a confiderable part of the Nation, much more when to all, in either of which cafes the Statute is *pro bono fingulorum populi*, in neither of thefe can the King difpenfe. And that the Statute in queftion is of the largeft extent, appears as the Nation is a Proteftant Nation, this the religion eftablifhed by Law, and thefe provifions neceffary means to preferve it; and therefore though the Papifts have no benefit by it, they are not in Law, in this refpect, any part of the people; for people always is taken for them that have legal interefts. Thus when the Statute provides (*f*) that the People of Counties fhall choofe their Sheriffs, it relates not to all the People in general, but only to Freeholders.

Secondly, Having thus fhewn, that thofe grounds which our Judge pretends to have gone upon, afford no countenance even to his palliation of the Judgment, they will appear much lefs to countenance it as it was delivered, which to evince, I fhall here fet it down *ipfiffimis verbis*, from that faithful reporter Mr. *Blaney*.

It was on that memorable day, when, as another mark of his fincerity, he directed the willing Jury, and concurred in the infamous fentence againft that excellent Author Mr. *Johnfon*; when the Jury was gone out, the Chief-Juftice took occafion to inveigh againft fpreading of fcandalous reports about cafes depending in the Court; and to prevent any thing of that nature in the cafe of Sir *Edward Hales*, he thought fit to deliver the opinion of the Judges in this manner:

Chief-Juftice. "In the cafe of *Godwin* and *Hales*, wherein the Defend-" ant pleads a difpenfation from the King, it is doubted, whether or no "the King had fuch a prerogative? Truly, upon the argument before us, "it appeared as clear a cafe as ever came before this Court: But becaufe "men fancy I know not what difficulty, when really there is none, we "were willing to give fo much countenance to the queftion in the cafe, "as to take the advice of all the Judges in *England*. They were all af-" fembled at *Serjeant's-Inn*, and this cafe was put them, and the great "cafe of the Sheriffs was put; whether the difpenfation in that cafe were "legal, becaufe upon that depended the execution of all the Law of the "Nation? And, I muft tell you that there were then ten upon the place, "that clearly delivered their opinions, that the cafe of the Sheriffs was "good Law, and that all the Attainders grounded upon Indictments "found by Juries returned by fuch Sheriffs, were good, and not erro-" neous; and confequently, that men need not have any fears or fcruples "about that matter. And in the next place, they did clearly declare, "that there was no imaginable difference between that cafe and this, un-" lefs it were, that this were the much clearer cafe of the two, and lia-" ble to the fewer exceptions. My Brother *Powel* faid, he was inclined "to be of the fame opinion, but he would rather have fome more time to

"confider of it; but he has fin
"know that he does concur wi
"one diffenter, Brother *Street*,
"King cannot difpenfe in this ca
"Judge, againft the opinion o
"judgments before, and having
"we think we may very well
"that the King may difpenfe in
"grounds:
"1. That the Kings of *Eng*
"2. That the Laws of *Eng*
"3. That therefore, 'tis a
"*England*, to difpenfe with P
"particular neceffary reafons.
"4. That of thofe reafons,
"fole Judge: and then, whi
"5. That this is not a truft
"people; but the ancient rem
"tive of the Kings of *Engla*
"nor can be. And therefore
"Defendant in this cafe, and
"to come time enough to
"ought to be given for the D
'Tis evident, that thefe pr
he has, or could have urged
famy has been fet upon the J
feveral ages, one would have
tion; yet indeed, he might
the other Gown, who, I t
notions. Whatever power of
it to be entrufted by the peo
down from Heaven the Lord
pofition of an abfolute fover
perfon, as fuch will have it,
it are but caftles in the air:
tution, to fee what that pow
fays, is, *à populo effluxa*, "
have no occafion, from any
nor can any be offered bu
money Judges, which fee
fhort of it: for though the
dom's neceffity, yet they
danger to be prevented by t
is abufed to the bringing in
But I muft obferve, *vide*
Herbert owns the difpen
it is very fit it fhould receiv
that Judges may judge, by m
may, and which he may not
can be no darknefs in it;
the legiflative does; and
Account, p. 617. when he
be difpenfible by the King
prohibitum, that is not *ma*
fhewn ought to be, it w
who never difpenfes with
are founded upon etern
and Man would be fubj
taken it out of the pow
extravagant power: for,
from the Crown, nor ca
the fovereign power and p
the way, there is an im
this implies, that 'tis bu
3. His printed and parol
vious by the comparifon
'tis a dark learning; th
the Court.
Thirdly, Tho' his inf
his defence, yet it may
be followed to thofe in
enough for him to fhe
lows the multitude to
does, he can no more
Account, p. 616. than
In matters of blood,
tendernefs, and thinks
he, *in fome cafes upon*
better Judges than myfel
be fo, yet I would never
confcience, that thofe St
to give judgment agai
Court exacts it, and
tenance it: But we
diers (*k*), of which
fuch judgment, as is
admit of any queftio
London, Sir *John Ho*
But I wifh our C
Lord *Brandon*. The
warded; and the fon
to tear brave fpirits,

(*a*) Thomas v. Sorrel, *f.* 350. (*b*) Ib. *f.* 347. (*c*) Vaugh. *f.* 34
(*e*) Lord *Vaughan*, *f.* 344, 345, 346, 347. (*f*) 2 Inft. *f.* 559. (*g*) So *Sibthorp*,
(*h*) Vid. *Cafe of Refiftance*, p. 200. See there fuch a Sovereignty as makes Laws, can repeal and difpenfe w *ac eorum corporum & bonorum rex hujufmodi erectus eft, & ad hanc poteftatem a populo effluxam ipfe habet quo ei no* 13 & 14 *Car* II *cap.* 29. Vid. Rufhworth, part 2. *fol.* 608.
(*i*) Vid. Grot. de Jure Belli & Pacis, l. 1. c. 1. *Sicut ut bis duo non fint quatuor, ne a Deo quidem effici poteft non fit*
(*k*) The cafe *Crook, Car.* 15. & *Hutton* 134. is of one preft to ferve beyond Sea.

father was obliged to change his soil, till it might become more equal, not unmindful of our Saviour's advice, or rather precept, ***When persecuted in one Country, to flee into another***; that tho' he contemned Death, he might not provoke it. The son falling into their hands, both his life and honour, which the severest trials approved to be most valued by him, were designed for a sacrifice. In subserviency to which, our Chief-Justice directed the willing Jury to find him guilty of high-treason, chiefly upon a supposed conspiracy to seize the Castle of *Chester*; which, if true, were but felony by a Statute *(a)*, as to that part, yet in force, and so could be no evidence of treason. Nor would he suffer the fact to be found specially, tho' he pretended not to answer the Cases and Records, which were cited to shew, that the matter alledged could not be treason: nor did the then Sollicitor undertake the task, notwithstanding that shew of reasoning, with which he laboured to set aside the authority of Lord *Coke (b)*, pleading expresly and unanswerably for that injured Hero, (of whom the Age was not worthy) the Lord *Russel*.

Nor was the proof in Lord *Brandon*'s case less defective than the matter; for besides the scandalous *Sexton*, who swore to designs against another King, there was but one witness in the eye of the law: he indeed is so far legal, as that he might be heard, being an *Approver (c)*; but no way credible, considering how far he had been drawn with his fetters about his heels, even to *(d)* contradict himself. The other by no means legal, being under an outlawry for High-Treason, unreversed: For though the execution of that Judgment (for so in law it is) was pardoned by the King, yet the crime was by no means purged, to set him right as to fame; which though the Counsel offered to make good, they were not suffered to speak to it: and yet the point is very *(e)* clear by ancient authorities, and confirmed by later, without any thing really to the contrary. Nay, farther, though besides all these things, another matter was urged in arrest of Judgment, upon which Judgment had *(f)* formerly been arrested; yet, without enquiring whether the fact were true, or the Book law, that, with the rest, was over-ruled, to come at the life of a person obnoxious to the Government, as some called themselves. Such was Sir *Edward*'s great scrupulousness and tenderness where the life of man was concerned.

He adds a scruple in a case before himself, and the other Usurpers of the High-commission-Court; but his singularity therein can be no excuse for his acting at all upon a commission apparently against the Statute; which took away not only the power of fining and imprisoning, which that Court illegally pretended to, but the spiritual authority which it really had: and such a commission it was, as never received countenance till the Act *(g)* long since repealed; which not only made *H.* VIII. Head of the Church, but gave him power, which he afterwards delegated to Lord *Cromwell*, (*V.* 31 *H.* VIII. *c.* 10.) to redress all errors, heresies and abuses, by spiritual authority.

Fourthly, I suppose it is by this time pretty evident, that Sir *Edward*'s crime will admit of no extenuation; but the aggravations are many, it appearing,

1. That he (*Acc. p.* 623.) and his brethren were the inventors of this dispensing Power, in such extent as he contends for in the Print; but much more in his real resolution.

2. That the error (*V. ib.*) was an error in that single case, but of large and mischievous consequences: and if the King could dispense with that Statute upon the reasons given, and circumstances appearing in Sir *Edw. Hales*'s case, others may well conclude from thence, that therefore he has a power to dispense with all other Statutes, even such as confer or vest in any of the subjects any manner of interest whatsoever, in their lives, liberties, and estates, *Acc. p.* 623. And there being a conviction, and consequently a disability actually incurred before the dispensation, therefore, by reason of this case, the King may dispense with such Statutes where a precedent disability is actually laid upon a man, as there is upon the Members of both Houses, till they have taken the oaths and tests prescribed. These are not consequences which may flow from the heated imaginations of angry men, but such as have warrant and foundation from their Judgment.

3. His so far undervaluing the wisdom of the Nation, as to make the benefit of a law against the undue continuance of Sheriffs, equal, nay, go beyond what they could devise for the security of their religion; or rather, so to undervalue the holy religion, which I think he yet professes, when however it would not come up to the point, according to the differences which himself receives. *Acc. p.* 618. speaking of the Statute 23 *H.* VI. *c.* 1. He says, ' The recital in the preamble, and the whole purview, if compared with our Statute of 25 *Car.* II. *c.* 2. equals it in every ' particular, and in some goes beyond it: For the mischiefs recited in this ' latter-Statute are only in these words, " For preventing dangers which " may happen from Popish Recusants, and quieting the minds of his Majesty's good subjects:" The other, " For preventing the importable da- " mage of the King and his People, by perjury, manslaughter, and great " oppression." Then he goes on to the purview, express against *non obstante's*, and creating a disability: but, according to his usual haste, he stays not here to make the comparison, but hastens to his sham resolution, as has been sufficiently evinced already. The questions here will be, 1. Whether the mischiefs intended to be prevented are equal in both? 2. Admit they were equal in degree, whether they are in extent? Which if they are not, still the resolution, if real, will fail him; according to the difference which he himself receives, of *pro bono populi complicati*, and *singulorum populi*.

1. For the first, I suppose he thinks the Epithet *importable* gives the odds; as if Popery wanted an Epithet to represent it to Protestants, for what they ought to do their utmost to prevent; as if it did not carry in the belly of it perjuries, manslaughters, and great oppressions, by wholesale; or that mischiefs more remote and accidental, as the continuance of Sheriffs, may habituate to corruption, and that occasion the other fatal train, could equal the more immediate and certain consequences, unless by good laws prevented, of *French* conversions, proceeding from fixed principles. But then to give Judgment to frustrate this necessary law, at a time when the Papists had a King of their own superstition to head them, is to make the King as much above the law as our ancient Lawyers tell us, the Law and his Court by way of eminence, that is, the great Council, or Parliament, are above him *(b)*.

2. As this proves the interest of the subject in the law about Sheriffs, to be neither equal, nor so immediate as in our Statute, there needs not many words to shew the difference of the extent: The peace only of particular Counties, and that by small insensible degrees, is there concerned. Nay, admit the King had this power, and should so violate that trust which Sir *Edward* will have to be reposed in him, (*Acc. p.* 620.) as to extend it to all Counties, where he puts in the Sheriffs, yet this could not affect all the People; because there might be a retreat to *London*, *Middlesex*, and *Westmoreland*; in neither of which has it been pretended that the King had such a power, till the late violence of some, and treachery of others, gave that unhappy inlet of perjury, manslaughter, I may say murder and oppression; before which, *London* was a perfect *Goshen* in an *Egyptian* Kingdom.

3. But what can excuse our Chief Justice's so apparent falsifying both Records and Law-books? Or if not, at least, his shameful negligence in not going to the fountain-heads, but setting up the recitals of cases against the cases themselves; and the extrajudicial opinions or arguments of Judges, nay the very annotations of Reporters, foreign to any matter in question, against solemn resolutions; which, either wilful falsifications or criminal negligence has occasioned the answering objections with a case which never had a resolution, but what he and his brethren gave, when it was brought in by head and shoulders, only to be a leading case to this.

4. He could not but know, that the case was faintly argued against Sir *Edward Hales*; either he, or the late *Empson* and *Dudley*, having given the fees on both sides: wherefore 'twas comical for the Chief-Justice to say, *that the Case appeared clear upon the argument*. I am sure he is inexcusable, that when causes of less consequence, and of less dark learning used to be argued twice at least; this was but once: And the learned Mr. *Wallop*, who could have set it in the truest light, was refused to be heard to it, though he required it.

5. Our Chief-Justice might easily have found, that the beginning of *non obstante's* was within time of memory, which would not be enough to entitle the King to a prerogative: For as 'tis in *Plowden*, every prerogative contains a prescription, for it rests in usage *(i)*; that is, such as are not derived from known Grants of the People. And he might have learnt from that great man, whom he would fain draw to his side, That *Precedents are useful to decide Questions*; ***but in such Cases as these, which depend upon fundamental principles, from which demonstrations may be drawn, millions of Precedents are to no purpose (k).***

Time of legal memory is well known to extend to the Reign of *R.* I. *(l)*
And though *non obstante's*, as I observed before, are complained of within
that time, as early as 35 *H.* III. yet that diligent and faithful searcher
into antiquity, Mr. *Prynne*, shews, That they were then made use of, only
to revoke some indiscreet grants or privileges, but not to elude, subvert,
or dispense with any penal Laws; or Acts of Parliament, till they were
introduced by religious persons; after the Statute of *Mortmain*, 7 *E.* I. to
elude and frustrate the Act. And if this be true, I am sure thus far there
is no colour for the late resolution; for they might have seen in Lord *Vaughan*
f. 356. that the King in that case dispenses only with his own right,
and concludes not the mean Lords.

Though successive resolutions of Judges are but evidences of the law;
and such as are to be examined and rectified by the constitution and fundamental maxims of the inherent rights and liberties of a free-born People;
yet if Sir *Edward* had had the diligence to read what might have occurred
on this subject, or the honesty to hear it from others, he might have known,
that it is far from being a settled point, that the King might dispense with
particular persons, as to whatever is not prohibited by the law of God;
and that his dispensation makes the thing prohibited lawful to be done by
him that has it *(m)*. The farther we look back since this power has come
in question, the less does it seem allowed.

Edward III. *(n)* with the assent of that Council, which, as I observed
before, was chosen in Parliament, had granted to merchants-denizens, for
a time, the same liberty about staple commodities which merchants-aliens
had: though this was not by the King alone, and for the benefit of natives,
yet the merchants, fearing that they might be impeached in time to come
for their merchandize, which they so had passed by virtue of such grants,
forasmuch as they were made out of Parliament, for their surety, obtained
a ratification and confirmation in Parliament.

(a) Vid. 14 *Eliz. c.* 1. *Rastal. f.* 411. "To conspire to levy War is an Overt-Act to testify the design of the death of the King; and the error of my Lord *Coke* has possibly
(b) L. *Russel's Trial, f.* 57. *Sol.* " To conspire to levy War is an Overt-Act to testify the design of the death of the King; which were not of levying War within the Kingdom, and besides were expressed by
" misled my Lord." This he goes to refute by the cases of *Story* and Lord *Cobbam*, which were not of levying War within the Kingdom, *Saunderson*'s Hist. of K. *James, f.* 283.
the Overt-Act of Writing. Vid. 3 *Inst. f.* 14. *Hales*'s Pleas of the Crown, *p.* 13. *Dyer, f.* 298. b.

(c) *Lib. Ass.* 27. *pl.* 20. Of an Approver shared, says, *Il ne duist passer sans estre duement purge, car tout sont en male.* At Mr. *Cornish*'s, *è contra.*
(d) At Lord *Russel*'s Trial, I am not certain whether I did hear something about a Declaration, &c. *Trial. f.* 59.
(e) That such are not *probi & legales*, for Witnesses or Juries, *vid.* 2. *Rolls. f.* 144. *alias* 154. 1 *Brownlow. p.* 34. *part* 2. 47. *Roll's Ab. tit. Chal.* 657. *Brook tit. Testmoins*, *pl.* ult. *Fitzher. tit. Process*, 208. *Dyer, f.* 32. 2. *Owen, f.* 22. *Cassiemain*'s Trial, *f.* 8. 11 *H.* IV. 41. b. *Godbolt* 288. *Fortescue, p.* 60. b. *Fleta, lib.* 4. *c.* 8. *Bratton de Corona*, 109. 3. *p.* 118. b. *Roll's Ab. tit. Prer. f.* 221. Vid. *de eodem Baluzium, tom.* 1. *f.* 887. 2. 362.
(f) *Arundel's Case*, 6 *Rep. f.* 14. *(g)* 26 *H.* VIII. *c.* 1. repealed 1 & 2 *P.* & *M.*
(h) *Bratton, l.* 1. *c.* 16. *Rex habet Superiorem, Deum S. item legem per quam factus est Rex, item Curiam suam, viz. Comites, Barones, qui Comites dicuntur quasi socii, &c.* supposed to be Dr. *Ashton*'s.
Fleta, l. 1. *c.* 17. *p.* 17. 2. has *Superiores.* Which avoids the Cavil in the *Royal Apol. ed. Anno* 1684. *p.* 36. the sending Process into *Wales.*
(i) *Plowden* of Mines, *f.* 322. 10. *(k)* *Vaughan, f.* 419. *Nota*, This was in a Case of less consequence,
(l) *Brook Prescrip. n.* 6. *Stat. West.* 1. 3 *E.* I. *c.* 39. *Stat. de quo Warranto*, 18 *E.* I. *Prynne's Animad. f.* 133.
(m) Vid. *Conr.* Dr. *Brady's Compleat Hist.* dedicated to King *James* II. *Pref.* All the Liberties and Privileges the People can pretend to, were the Grants and Concessions of the Kings of this Nation, and were derived from the Crown: Founded upon his supposed Proofs, that *W.* I. obtained this land by conquest, and governed it accordingly. Vid. *Brady*'s first book, *p.* 22. *in marg.* refuted in *Jus Anglorum.*
(n) V. *Roll's abr. tit. Prer. f.* 180. 34 *E.* III. *c.* 21.

But the *vexata quæstio* (*a*) was about licensing the shipping of wool elsewhere than at *Calais* that the King might do this, the pretence was specious. *Calais* was no part of the antient demesne of the Crown, but a new acquisition, whose interests the King seemed to have more absolutely at his disposal; according to the resolution of our Judges, *anno* 1667, before the House of Lords, who declared, That though the *Canaries* were the Dominion of the King of *Spain* (*b*), they were no part of the Dominion of *Spain*. And if Sir *Edward* had taken notice of Lord *Coke*, where he is against, as well as where he seems to favour him, he ought to have observed, 3 *Inst. f.* 186. that one *Lyons*, a merchant, and Lord *Latimer*, were sentenced in Parliament, for procuring of Licences and Dispensations for transporting of wool. And this they laid to the destruction of the staple, and of the money of *Calais*, to the great damage of the King and Realm (*c*). Indeed the year after the Lord *Latimer*'s sentence is remitted at the request of the Commons, alledging that the charge against him was not true, not for defect of matter; 51 *E.* III. *n.* 75. So that here is a Judgment of the House of Lords in point, against one of those very cases, upon which Court-Judges have since founded their distinction of *malum prohibitum*, and *malum in se*: *Acc. p.* 617. And it is an easy thing to know which ought to turn the scale.

After this, 37 *H.* VI. *f.* 4. it came to be a question before all the Judges in the *Exchequer-Chamber*, Whether this offence, being pardoned, (which that the King might do after it was committed, has not been disputed) the pardon, before an information brought, would defeat the informer of his share? There the Court held, That if the suit were the party's, the pardon should not bar him: But the sole question was, Whether the party was entitled to any suit, being the advantage was given to the discoverer, which he might have by a suggestion in the *Exchequer*, but the Statute gives no action (*d*)? However, this received no determination at that time.

But if the question had then been of a dispensation, and whether that would bar the Informer's action given by Statute, can any man doubt but that they would have adjudged it could not; when, notwithstanding a pardon, and that an case where an action was not expresly given? Yet it was so doubtful, that they would not determine against the Informer. But that the dispensation would not have availed with them; or at least, they would not have looked upon it to authorize what was prohibited by any Statute, appears from other passages there: as where it is said (*e*), That in a recognizance of the peace, (which is not confined to one entered into at the request of a subject) the King cannot pardon or release, till the peace is broken. And where a man ought to repair a bridge, the King can pardon only for the fine due to himself: But however the party shall be obliged to repair the bridge, because this is to the damage of all the People. And to the same purpose is that 3 *H.* VII. (*f*) that though the King may pardon, or free from a pecuniary mulct before the occasion happen, yet he cannot pardon or discharge the trespass itself: an instance is given in voluntary escapes. So far were they from believing that the King, in remitting the pecuniary mulct, could make the thing lawful: Nor could this in the least be inferred from the other, because, however, an Act may be made void or tortious. Indeed in the Reign of *R.* III. (2 *R.* III. *f.* 12.) whose character blemishes the Judgments of his time; it was held by all the Judges in the *Exchequer-Chamber*, that the King might license the shipping of wool elsewhere than at the staple; yet even they were not of opinion that the licence made the thing lawful, for then the discoverer could not have had his share, which they agreed that he ought to have, and so the licence was only as far as it concerned the King. They also settled the other point, which before was a doubt (*g*), That a pardon before an information brought, would defeat the informer. But then the authority of the first point is suspended by a doubt remaining before all the Judges, afterwards assembled upon a re-hearing of this cause, in a more settled time. Indeed they agreed the other, of an information after a pardon; but hitherto there is no manner of proof of any case, wherein the King by his dispensation could discharge the penalty given not only to himself, but also to an Informer, who has his action given by Statute. But for this we must take a leap downwards, as far as 13 *Jac.* I. which we may balance with the 7th of his Reign, when it is held by Lord *Coke*, 3 *Inst.* 154. that where a Statute concerns the benefit of the King alone, he may dispense with it by a *non obstante*: And by the Court, *That where it concerns the benefit of the subject, the King cannot dispense. Rolls's Ab. tit. Prer. f.* 179.

7. Whereas our Chief-Justice thinks, that a Statute's providing against *non obstante's*, shews that the King could otherwise have dispensed with the Act by a *non obstante*, *Acc. p.* 618. it is not only unconcluding, because it might be no more than an argument of an abuse of the law; but turns very strong against him. For, admit the resolution of the Judges, 2 *H.* VII. were as he contends, yet he, who makes so much of a concession of the Commons of *England*, assembled in Parliament, *Acc. p.* 621. when he thinks it of his side, ought surely to yield, that the Judgment of King, Lords and Commons, is of uncontroulable authority. Wherefore, when not only one, but several Parliaments provide, that all *non obstante's* shall be void, is it not plain that their Judgment was, that such *non obstante's* could not be set up by any resolution of Judges? And for this we have the Judgment of King, Lords and Commons, and that of but late days, That even where a Grant is made to the King, where 'twill be said he is solely entrusted for the publick good, yet it may be out of his power to defeat it by a *non obstante*. This appears by the Statute 19 *Car.* II. *c.* 8. (*h*) which provides, *That no Letters Patent granted to any person, of exemptions from subsidies*, &c. *shall free them from the charges of*

any sum granted by that Act: Ana
or to be made in bar of any Act or
ance of his Majesty, are thereby de
And even where Statutes have
though the Statutes were such a
prerogative; yet if we receive th
has no prerogative warranting n
ticles against King *Richard* the
King, contrary to the Laws and I
tinue longer than one Year, &c.

This were enough to set asi
though, as Sir *Edward Herbert*
resolved there, That that was r
tioned till after the resolution.
mons in competition with that
if the concessions of the Commo
weight with him, I know not w
urged against him; which it we
reasonings in *Calvin*'s case (*k*),
justly called mere Court-law. S
of Commons, 4 *Jac.* I. (*l*) woul
arguments of those learned men
Lords upon the question of the
see how inexcusable the Judges c
ment in *Calvin*'s case, after they
but know, that the then Parlia
not so complying as the Judges
wards. But they secured their c
father of the present Lord *Ossu*,
and had a swinging fine imposed
after, upon pretence of extortion
ground was, his disrelishing Spe
well known, some Princes used t
altâ mente repostum, &c.

8. *Non obstante's* having no oth
of Princes, and servility of Judge
ing the King alone; they ought
advice of *Bracton* (*n*) will rise u
tells them, *If such things never h*
out light from former Cases, and
Court. According to which,
have been frequent in former
Judges; and that as often for t
cacy of the points.

9. But for the closing aggrava
Justice denies all indirect means f
his innocence, challenging the w
charge; I think, by this time, f
his assurance: if either threats or
the world will judge either of the
informed, if both cannot be justly

If after all, he can excuse hi
Acc. p. 623. and making assevera
his conscience, I must say, Judg
and been made examples to little
reputation of his Justice, in hang
liaments have been very barbarou
who yet, either were so ingenuous
so provoking as to justify them.

It is well known in story (*p*), t
Counsel at law, suffered for treas
11 *R.* II. for delivering their opi
traitors, who hindered the King from
over a Statute, and an Ordinance and
ment (*q*). The substance of thei
power to defeat the provisions of t
tion; and is a direct precedent, a
Nor can it avail them, that the ex
c. 2. do not condemn them, since
sons to the Judgment of Parliamen
that power untouched. And who
that justified in print, and publishe
son, as it tends to the subverting t
Nor can they have any colour for a
is the Bury? when they see so many

Nor ought Sir *Edward* to wonde
though not directly against the pers
or his coin; nor yet an actual levy
hering to his enemies (*r*); for he
the Lord *Kimbolton*, and others, ex
Attorney-General,

"That they have traitorously en
"and Beings of Parliaments."

But since Sir *Edward* pleads con
and might have urged the authority
the scripture-notion of higher powe
ment; I shall conclude with the g
famous *Bilson*, afterwards Bishop o

(*a*) *Nota*, This is one of the Cases mentioned by *Fineux ante*. (*b*) Vid. 3 *Jac c.* 6. forbidding Trade to the Dominions of *Spa*
(*d*) This is not rightly abridged by *Brook*, *tit. Charter de Pardon*, *n.* 24. 37 *H.* VI *f.* 5. *adjournatur*.
(*e*) 37 *H* VI. 46. V. 5 *E.* IV. *f.* 34. a. Where a Statute concerns only the King himself, which the King may chuse to use at his
(*f*) 3 *H.* VII. *f.* 15. b. Chief-Justice *Hussey* citing *Fortescue*. (*g*) 1 *H.* VII. *f.* 2. b. & 3. a. (*h*) According t
(*i*) *Vid.* the Stat. barely prohibitory. 28 *E.* III. *c.* 7. & 12 *E.* III. *c.* 9. V. *Knighton*. (*k*) See them censured in *Va*
(*l*) *Moor*, a. *f.* 790 to 805. (*m*) *Vid.* his Censure. 4 *Inst. f.* 336.
(*n*) 2 *Inst. f.* 408. *l.* 1. *c.* 2. *Si autem talia nunquam prius evenerint, & obscurum & difficile sit eorum judicium, tunc ponantur* [illegible] Vid. [illegible] E. III. [illegible] 33 *H.* VI. 18 a. *C'est un Act de Parlement & nos volumus estre bien avis devant que nous* [illegible] *attendre en prochein Parlement.*
(*o*) Vid. [illegible] *a p.* 2?0 to 300. (*p*) *Tresilian*, *Belknappe* V. *Vol.* 1 *p.* 1. (*q*) *Knighton*, *f.* 2726, 272?. [illegible]
(*r*) Vid. *Glanvill*, [illegible] *Crimen Læsæ Majestatis, ut de nece vel seditione personæ Domini Regis vel Regni.* *Rymer. Collect.* [illegible]
(*s*) *Bilson of Christian Subjection*, *p.* 280.

"By superior powers ordain'd of God, we understand not only Princes, but all politick States and Regimens; some where the People, some where the Nobles have the same interest to the sword that Princes have in their Kingdoms: And in Kingdoms where Princes bear rule by the sword, we do not mean the Prince's private will against his Laws, but his precept derived from his Laws, and agreeing with his Laws *."

XL. The Proceedings against Mr. SAMUEL JOHNSON; who was tried at the *King's-Bench* Bar, *Westminster*, for High-Misdemeanours (and found guilty of writing and publishing two seditious and scandalous Libels against the Government); on *Monday* the 21st of *June*, 1686. 2 *Jac.* II.

SAMUEL JOHNSON having been arraigned upon an Information for high misdemeanours, in writing, printing and publishing two scandalous and seditious Libels, &c and thereto pleading *Not Guilty*, was, by a rule of Court, brought again to the Court of *King's-Bench*, *Westminster*, on *Monday*, *June* the 21st, in order to take his trial: when a Jury of Knights and Gentlemen of the County of *Surry* being sworn, the Information was read; the substance of which was, "That he, the Prisoner, had, in the Parish of *St. George's*, *Southwark*, on the 25th of *May*, in the second year of his Majesty's reign, maliciously and designedly published two pernicious, scandalous and seditious libels, to raise and stir up sedition and rebellion in his Majesty's liege-subjects, &c." The title of one being, *An Humble and Hearty Address to all the* English *Protestants in this present Army*. Which is as follows:

An Humble and Hearty Address to all the English *Protestants in this present Army*.

Gentlemen,

NEXT to the duty which we owe to God, which ought to be the principal care of men, of your profession especially, because you carry your lives in your hands, and often look death in the face: the second thing that deserves your consideration, is the service of your native Country, wherein you drew your first breath, and breathed a free *English* air. Now I would desire you to consider, how well you comply with these two main points, by engaging in this present service.

Is it in the name of God, and for his service, that you have joined yourselves with Papists; who will indeed fight for the Mass-book, but burn the Bible: and who seek to extirpate the Protestant Religion with your swords, because they cannot do it with their own? And will you be aiding and assisting to set up Mass-houses, to erect that Popish Kingdom of darkness and desolation amongst us, and to train up all our children in Popery? How can you do these things, and yet call yourselves Protestants?

And then what service can be done your Country by being under the command of *French* and *Irish* Papists, and by bringing the Nation under a foreign yoke? Will you help them to make forcible entry into the houses of your countrymen, under the name of *Quartering*, directly contrary to *Magna Charta*, and the *Petition of Right*? Will you be aiding and assisting to all the murders and outrages which they shall commit by their void commissions? Which were declared illegal, and sufficiently blasted by both Houses of Parliament (if there had been any need of it), for it was very well known before, that a Papist cannot have a commission, but by the law is utterly disabled and disarmed. Will you exchange your birth-right of *English* laws and liberties for martial, or club-law, and help to destroy all others, only to be eaten last yourselves? If I know you well, as you are *Englishmen*, you hate and scorn these things. And therefore be not unequally yoked with idolatrous and bloody Papists. *Be valiant for the truth, and shew yourselves men.*

The same considerations are likewise humbly offered to all the *English* Seamen, who have been the bulwark of this Nation against *Popery* and *Slavery*, ever since *Eighty-Eight*.

And the other, *viz. The Opinion is this, that Resistance may be used, in case our Religion and Rights should be invaded* †: "Tending to withdraw them from their duty and allegiance, and to excite and stir up the soldiers, &c. to mutiny and rebellion, &c." After this, the Information was, by the King's Counsel, opened to the Jury, as to the nature and circumstances, together with the evil consequences that might attend such bold and dangerous attempts: which being rendered largely and exactly, as to the particulars mentioned in the said information, wherewith the Prisoner was charged, they proceeded to call their witnesses to prove the fact.

And *First*, Mr. *Belamy*, at the *Three Brushes* in *Southwark*, being sworn, gave evidence, That coming acquainted some time since with the Prisoner, and about a fortnight before *Whitsuntide* last, discoursing with him, the second of these Libels was mentioned: And soon after he sent him a box with some rheams of them in it, to be dispersed, and gave him notice that he had a second Paper in the Press; and withal, a caution not to publish those he had sent before, till he had received that which proved to be the former Libel before-mentioned. And further, that about six or eight months before that, the Prisoner had sent him other Libels to disperse: and being shewed the Libels mentioned in the Information, he deposed, they were the same that had been sent him. His man likewise gave evidence, That he had received a box nailed up, but could give no account of what was in it, as to particulars.

Ann Whitney, sometime servant to the Prisoner, being sworn, gave evidence, That by her master's or mistress's direction, she was not certain which, she took a porter, and caused him to carry a box, wherein one of the Libels mentioned, *viz* the second, was inclosed to Mr. *Belamy*: And that she had, by the like order, carried other papers loose; some of which were the Address, &c. And being asked by the Prisoner, how she knew that? Her reply was, That she knew it, insomuch that she had read the title, and very well remembered it.

The Porter that carried the box gave evidence, That the maid had hired him to carry a box to the *Three Brushes*, and that she went with him, and paid him according to agreement, and that he took it up in *Spital-fields*. After this, the messenger, who searched the Prisoner's lodging with the Right Honourable the Earl of *Sunderland*'s warrant, being sworn, gave evidence, That he found a Paper in writing, upon a table or shelf, which appeared in Court to be part of the copy, or the same with the paper, entitled *The Opinion*, &c. he swearing, upon sight thereof, that it was the same he found in the prisoner's lodging. Then was the Book of the Vestry, or Parish affairs of *St. Paul's*, *Covent-garden*, produced; wherein the Prisoner, sometime past, had given an acquittance for money received, as an assistant Curate, &c. which being compared with the paper, seemed not to differ in the hand. But no other evidence appeared in that case, than that the Book had been always kept in the Vestry, and for the most part under lock and key, and it being put to the prisoner, he did not greatly deny it. When for a further confirmation, *John Darby*, a Printer, and his wife, were sworn: The former deposing, That he had printed a book for the prisoner from a manuscript, and that hand was very like that of the Libel produced in Court: but he had never seen him write, and therefore could not be positive that that manuscript was his own hand.

As for his wife, her evidence was, that the prisoner paying her some money, she had given him an acquittance; but that, as she conceived, he wrote all but her name, for going up stairs, he soon returned with an acquittance, which she subscribed.

This being what materially was given in evidence for the King, the Prisoner had leave to make his defence, who after some discourse, alledged, That he had been confined, and had not had opportunity to prepare for his defence, as not having leave to go to his Counsel. To which the Court replied, That he had leave upon the motion made on his behalf, to send for Counsel; and that they ought not to be refused coming to him. Then he urged several other matters, which being over-ruled by the Court, he proceeded to intimate, that he hoped, that seeing he was indicted for a seditious and scandalous Libel, &c. the Jury would consider whether those papers they had heard read, were so or no? But was told, that the Jury ought to consider it only as to the matter of fact, whether he was guilty of writing or publishing them, &c.? and that the rest lay in the breast of the Court to consider. Thereupon he urged, That though they might be sent, yet it was no publication, as it was laid in the indictment, because the box was nailed. But being fully answered in that point, and loose papers appearing likewise to be sent, the Counsel for the King summed up their evidence to the Jury, none appearing on the behalf of the prisoner.

After which, the Court gave the charge, putting the Prisoner, as well as the Jury, in mind of the great mischief that such Libels might occasion: And minded him likewise, that it was within a small matter of High-Treason; and might have been raised to that degree, were not the laws, and those who managed them, tender of life, &c.

After the charge was given, the Jury withdrew; and returning within a quarter of an hour, brought in the Prisoner guilty of the High Misdemeanour.

Nov. 16, following, Mr. *Johnson*'s sentence was pronounced by Sir *Francis Withins*, as follows; To pay 500 marks to the King, and to lie in prison till it was paid; to stand three times in the pillory, on the *Monday* following, in the *Palace-yard*, *Westminster*; on *Wednesday*, at *Charing-Cross*; and the *Monday* after at the *Royal-Exchange*; and to be whipt by the common Hangman from *Newgate* to *Tyburn* ‡.

After Sentence was past upon him, in order to load him with the greater ignominy, the Courtiers, on pretence of respect to the Church, moved, That before the execution of the sentence, he should be degraded from the order of Priesthood. This ought to have been done, according to the Canons, by his own Diocesan, the Bishop of *London*, but that Prelate was then under a suspension himself, because he would not obey the King's Orders to suspend Dr *Sharp*, now Archbishop of *York*, for preaching against Popery in his own Parish Church of *St. Giles's in the Fields*. Dr. *Carew*, Bishop of *Durham*, Dr. *Sprat*, Bishop of *Rochester*, and Dr. *White*, Bishop of *Peterborough*, being then Commissioners for the diocese of *London*, in the place

* *Glanvil. Prol. Bracton, vol.* III *c* 9. *Fleta, lib* 1. *c.* 17. *Fortescue, c.* 9. *Mir. p.* 9.

† This is printed in Mr. *Johnson's* Works, *p.* 159, to 166, which being too long to insert here, the Reader is referred to it.

‡ Mr. *Johnson*, 1683, was tried on an Information, in the *King's-Bench*, for writing *Julian the Apostate*, and fined 500 marks, and committed Prisoner to the *King's-Bench* till he should pay it; which they knew was the same with perpetual imprisonment, since he was not able to pay that sum. Thus he was condemned and committed, to the great Joy of the Papists; when in him they saw the Laws of England condemned by the Judges, who study'd more to oblige the Court than to do their duty. *See some Memoirs of Mr* S. Johnson, *p.* 7. *in his Works.*

of

of the suspended Bishop, were appointed to degrade Mr. *Johnson*; which they performed in the Chapter-house of St. *Paul*'s, where Dr. *Sherlock* and other Clergymen attended: but Dr. *Stillingfleet*, then Dean of St. *Paul*'s, refused to have any hand in it.

When they came to the formality of putting a Bible in his hand, and taking it from him again, he was much affected, and parted with it with difficulty, kissing it, and saying with tears, *that they could not however deprive him of the use and benefit of that sacred Depositum.* It happened that they were guilty of an omission, in not stripping him of his cassock; which, as slight a particular as it might seem, render'd his degradation imperfect, and afterwards saved him his benefice.

On the 1st of *December*, 1686, the sentence was put in execution; which Mr. *Johnson* endured with as firm a courage, and as Christian a behaviour as ever was discover'd on any such occasion: tho' at the same time he had a quick sense of every stripe which was given him, with a whip of nine cords knotted, to the number of 317.

In the first Parliament after the Revolution, when the House of Commons was preparing an Act of Indemnity, Mr. *Johnson* was advised by his friends to get a clause put into it, that he might have his remedy at Law against such as had been his illegal oppressors. They seemed to be sensible that they were obnoxious, and could not justify what they had done. About that time the Lord Bishop of *Durham* gave Mr. *Johnson* and his lawyer a meeting, and made his peace with him, to their mutual satisfaction.

Sir *Francis Withirs*, who pronounced the Sentence against him, sent a relation of Mrs. *Johnson*'s to tell him a feign'd story, that Sir *Francis* lay dangerously ill, and could not die in peace, unless Mr. *Johnson* would forgive him. To which he reply'd, That he heartily forgave him what injury he had done to him. Some few days after, the same person brought Sir *Francis* to Mr. *Johnson*, as he was walking in *Westminster-hall*; where Sir *Francis* saluted him, and told him, *That his Christian and kind answer had prov'd a reviving Cordial to him.* To which Mr. *Johnson* reply'd, That he heartily forgave the injury done to himself; but as he had been an enemy to his country, he hoped he would be made accountable for it: it being a common saying with him, *That he was obliged to forgive his own enemies, but not the enemies of his Country.*

The Parliament taking Mr. *Johnson*'s case into consideration, resolved, *June* 11, 1689, That the Judgment given against him in the *King's-Bench*, upon an information for a misdemeanor, was cruel and illegal.

A Committee was at the same time appointed to bring in a Bill for reversing that Judgment: and being also ordered to enquire how Mr. *Johnson* came to be degraded, and by what authority it was done; Mr. *Christy*, the Chairman, some days after, reported his case to this purpose:

"That in *Trinity-Term*, 1686, an information was exhibited against "Mr. *Johnson*, in the name of Sir *Robert Sawyer*, Attorney-General, for "writing and publishing a scandalous and seditious Libel, intitled, *An* "*humble and hearty Address*, &c. That the same Term they forced him "to plead, got a Jury to find him guilty, and Sir *Francis Withins* pro-"nounced the following Sentence upon him: *To pay five hundred marks* "*to the King, and to lie in prison till 'twas paid: To stand thrice in the pil-*"*lory, in the* Palace-yard, *at* Charing-cross, *and at the* Old-Exchange: "*and to be whipt by the Common Hangman from* Newgate *to* Tyburn. That "the Judges then in Court, were the Lord Chief-Justice *Herbert*, Sir "*Francis Withins*, Sir *Robert Wright*, and Sir *Richard Holloway*. That

" apprehending 'twou
" punishment inflicte
" first degraded: In o
" in the diocese of the
" the 20th of *Novembe*
" diocese of *London*, h
" thither by *Habeas Co*
" *chester*, and *Peterbor*
" the Bishop of *London*
" and many Spectator
" him with great mil
" That Mr. *Johnson* de
" which the Bishops de
" *he should be declared a*
" *Rectory, that he should*
" *all right and privilege*
" *and of all vestments a*
" Mr. *Johnson* protested
" being done by his ow
" was also his appeal to
" After which, they
" on his head, and then
" which he demanded as
" they promised to send l
" shillings. Then they
" with readily, they took
" *vember*, the Judgment
" great rigour and cruelt
" his cassok on the pillor
" whipp'd with a whip c
" Committee. That M
" against her, for the like
" On all which, the C
" which, on the report, v
" *ment against Mr.* Johns
" *Commission was illegal, a*
" don, *and the authority co*
" *Mr.* Johnson *not being*
" *it, was illegal: That a*
" *to declare all the proceedi*
" *that an Address be made t*
" *Ecclesiastical Preferment,*

The House likewise orde
the Ecclesiastical Commissi
The House presented two
son: But tho' his Majesty
their request, Mr. *Johnson*
Mr. *Johnson*, however, being
without a reward; for the K
of the *Post-office*, for his an
money, and likewise bestow
on his son.

XLI. The Trial of *Rowland Walters*, *Dearing Bradshaw*, and *Ambro* of Sir *Charles Pymm*, Bart.) at the Sessions held at the *Old-Bailey*, o 1688, before the Right Honourable Sir *John Shorter*, Knt. Lord-l and Sir *Bartholomew Shower*, Knt. Recorder of the same City; toge Justices of the Peace for the City of *London*, and County of *Middle*

Clerk. CRYER, make Proclamation.

Cryer. Oyes, Oyes, Oyes!

Clerk. Keeper of *Newgate*, bring the Prisoners to the Bar. (*Which was done*).

Clerk. You the prisoners at the Bar, those men whom you shall hear called, and personally appear, are to try between our sovereign Lord the King, and you who are arraigned, upon your several lives and death: if you shall except against any one of them, you must speak before they be sworn.

Clerk. Cryer, call *Henry Dyer*.

The *Jurors* sworn are as followeth:

Henry Dyer,	*Richard Chase*,	*John Hill*,
Giles Baggs,	*Samuel Burgess*,	*Obadiah Hickman*,
Matthew Jerman,	*William Villiers*,	*John Read*,
Timothy Waldoe,	*John Frith*,	*Francis Willis*.

Who were all sworn.

Clerk. Cryer, count these, twelve good men and true.

Clerk. Cryer, make proclamation. (*Which was done*).

Clerk. *You Gentlemen of the Jury, look upon the Prisoners at the Bar, and hearken to their Charge; they stand indicted by the names of* Rowland Walters, Dearing Bradshaw, *and* Ambrose Cave, *Gents. for that they not having the fear of God before their eyes, but being instigated and seduced by the Devil, and their own wicked Hearts, on the fourth Day of* May, *in the fourth year of the reign of our sovereign Lord King* James II. *in the Parish of St.* Nicholas Cole-Abby, *in and upon Sir* Charles Pymm, *Bart feloniously, wilfully, and of their malice fore-thought, did make an assault; and that he the said* Rowland Walters, *having then and there in his right-hand, a certain Rapier made of iron or steel, of the value of about 5s. and him the said Sir* Charles Pymm *in*

and upon the right side of him th
right pap, did strike and thrust
Pymm, *a little above the right*
inch, of the depth of ten inches.
Ambrose Cave, *were present,*
Rowland Walters, *in the perp*
said Sir Charles Pymm. *So th*
malice fore-thought, did intentio
the said Sir Charles Pymm, *ag*
his Crown, and Dignity, and ag
and provided. Upon this Indict
unto pleaded Not Guilty, and for
their Country, which Country you
they, or either of them committed
them, or either of them, guilty of t
goods and chattels they, or either
the said wilful murder; but if yo
hear your evidence.

Mr. *Walters.* My Lord, I hu
before me.

Court. That cannot be, Mr.
one Indictment.

Counsel for the King. My Lor
am here retained a Counsel for
Bar, who all three stand indict
Bart. in the Parish of St. *Nichol*
body near the right pap, giving
and there instantly died. Th
aiding, abetting, and assisting h

Another Counsel for the King. My Lords, this Murder fell out on the fourth day of *May* last, after this manner, *viz.* The said Sir *Charles Pymm*, one Mr. *Mirriday*, Mr. *Neale*, and Sir *Thomas Middleton*, and others, dined at the *Swan-Tavern* upon *Fish-street-Hill*; after they were come into the house they went up stairs; after which the Prisoners at the bar came into the house, and took another room to dine of beef and other things. But one of Sir *Charles*'s company desired to have a plate of it; upon which Mr. *Cloudsley* told them some Gentlemen had bespoke it for dinner; but he said he would get them a plate of it, which was sent up, and ordered to be reckoned into Mr. *Walters* the prisoner's bill. After dinner they drank their healths, and returned them thanks for their beef; and towards the evening Sir *Charles Pymm* and his friends came down stairs, and met the prisoners at the bottom, and Mr. *Cave* asked them how they liked the beef that was sent up? upon which one in the company answered, and told them, They did not send it, for they had paid for it. Upon which farther words arose, and Mr. *Bradshaw* drew his sword, and fell upon Sir *Charles Pymm*; but he got out into the street. After which Mr. *Walters* came forth, and plucked Sir *Charles Pymm* by the arms, and forced him to fight with him, saying, Here is my hand, and here is my sword; and as soon as he was in the street, he received this mortal wound, and so fell down dead. After this, Mr. *Walters* took him by the nape of the neck, and dash'd his head upon the ground, and cried out, *God damn you, you are dead:* and said farther, *Let the sword alone in his body.* My Lord, this shall be proved to be done without any manner of provocation; and if so, I hope you, Gentlemen of the Jury, will find him guilty of wilful murder

Clerk. Call Mr. *Mirriday*, Mr. *Neale*, Mr. *Palms*, and Mr. *Bruges*. (*Who were sworn.*)

Mr. *Mirriday* My Lord, on the fourth day of *May* last, on a *Friday*, Sir *Charles Pymm*, myself, and these Gentlemen here in Court, came to dine at the *Swan-Tavern* in *Old Fish-street*. We asked for meat, and Mr. *Cloudsley*, the man of the house, told us, we might have fish, for he had no meat, but what was bespoke by Mr *Walters* and his company. We desired him to help us to a plate of it, if it might be got, which we had brought up stairs; after dinner we drank the Gentlemen's healths that sent it, and returned them thanks for it. A while after Sir *Thomas Middleton* went away, and about an hour after that, or thereabouts, Sir *Charles Pymm* and the rest of us came down to go away; and when we were in the entry, Mr. *Cave* met us, and asked Sir *Charles* how he liked the beef that was sent up; who answered, We did not know you sent it, for we have paid for it. Then the boy that kept the bar told us, that he did not reckon it in the bill; upon which Mr. *Cave* seemed to take it ill: But, my Lord, I cannot be positive whether Mr. *Bradshaw* and Mr. *Palms* were at any words. Then I took Mr. *Cave* to one side into the entry, and he thought that I had a mind to fight him, but I did what I could to make an end of the quarrel. [*Upon which the Court highly commended Mr.* Mirriday.]

Court This was in the entry, but where was Sir *Charles Pymm*?

Mr. *Mirriday*. He was then in the entry.

Court. Where was Mr. *Walters*?

Mr. *Mirriday*. He was at the door, my Lord; but I cannot swear positively to any particular passage as to the murder; but Mr. *Walters* called Sir *Charles Pymm* rogue, and gave him very ill words, and I saw him take him by the neck, and forced his head downwards, and said, *God damn him, he is dead*, to the best of my remembrance, my Lord. Then, I took Sir *Charles* up in my arms, and pulled the sword out of his body, and then Mr. *Walters* said, *God damn him, let it stay in his guts, or in his body*, or words to that effect.

Court. Was Mr. *Cave* or Mr. *Bradshaw* at the place where Sir *Charles* fell?

Mr. *Mirriday*. No, my Lord, they were in the entry scuffling there.

Court. What came of Mr. *Walters* afterwards?

Mr. *Mirriday*. My Lord, he stay'd a little till I had pulled the sword out of his body, then he ran away.

Court. Did they draw their swords in the entry?

Mr. *Mirriday*. I cannot tell that?

Court. Did you see them draw their swords?

Mr. *Mirriday*. I cannot say Sir *Charles Pymm*'s sword was drawn, but I saw Mr. *Walters* draw his sword in the street.

Court. Do you know whether Mr. *Walters* was wounded or no?

Mr. *Mirriday*. I do not know that, for I did not see the wound given.

Court. Mr. *Walters*, will you ask him any questions?

Mr. *Walters*. Yes, my Lord: Mr. *Mirriday*, what did you say to Sir *Charles Pymm* in the Fish-monger's shop? Did you not say, Go, and fight him, and I will be your Second?

Mr *Mirriday*. My Lord, I do not remember one word of that.

Court. Mr. *Mirriday*, were you in any Fishmonger's shop?

Mr. *Mirriday*. Yes, my Lord, I was there, but I do not remember one word between Mr. *Walters* and Sir *Charles*, and, as I hope for salvation, I said no such thing; and that's all I have to say.

Clerk. Cryer, call Mr. *Neale*.

Mr. *Neale*. My Lord, I went and met with these Gentlemen that dined with us at the aforesaid Tavern, and we had fish and two beef marrow-bones, and a plate of beef for dinner; and when we came down to go away, these Gentlemen met us, and said, *God damn you, how did you like the beef?* which raised a quarrel among us; but immediately, after I thought it was all over, I saw Mr. *Walters* run Sir *Charles Pymm* thorough.

Court. Was his sword drawn?

Mr. *Neale*. Yes both of their swords were drawn.

Court. Where was Mr. *Bradshaw*?

Mr. *Neale*. I cannot tell where he was directly: but, my Lord, I heard Sir *Charles Pymm* say nothing to Mr. *Walters*.

Clerk. Cryer, call Mr. *Palms*.

Mr. *Palms*. My Lord, after the reckoning was paid, we came down stairs, and called for a coach, and because it rained, there was none to be had; and these Gentlemen followed us into the entry, and so words to the same purpose as aforesaid passed between them; after which, I met Mr. *Bradshaw*, and we fell out in the Fishmonger's shop.

Court. Who began?—Mr. *Palms*. I know not, I cannot remember that.

Court. Were you not in drink?

Mr. *Palms*. My Lord, we drank nine or ten bottles among six of us; after which Mr. *Bradshaw* and I drew our swords, and then Mr. *Mirriday* came and took him away from me into the entry, and in the mean time, while we were talking in the entry, the business was done.

Court. Were your swords put up again?

Palms. I had put up mine.

Counsel for the King. Did you take notice of what passed between Mr. *Walters* and Sir *Charles Pymm*?

Mr. *Palms*. I heard nothing of high words.

Court. Yes, yes, it was all about the beef.

Clerk. Cryer, call for Mr. *Presland*, the Bar-keeper.

Presland My Lord, I made the bill for the reckoning.

Court. Did you put the beef into the bill?

Presland. No, I did not, when they came down stairs, the coach was fetch'd for them, *viz.* for Sir *Charles Pymm* and his company, and the reckoning was paid. When Sir *Charles Pymm* and the rest of his company came down into the entry, Mr. *Walters* came out of the room, &c. and I heard them argue about their dinner, and they came to me, and asked me what was to pay for beef, and I told them nothing.

Court. Did you see the man killed?

Presland. My Lord, I did not see him killed, not I.

Court. Who was it that quarrelled with the coachman?

Presland. My Lord, Mr. *Neale* quarrelled with the Coachman about his staying: the Coachman refused going with him, because his Horses were hot.

Clerk. Cryer, call Mr. *Brummidge*.

Mr. *Brummidge*. My Lord, between eleven and twelve a-clock in the morning on the fourth of *May* last, Sir *Charles Pymm* came to Mr. *Cloudsley*'s door in a coach, and asked him what he might have for dinner; who told him that he might have a mullet and some smelts, and I sold a mullet to Mr. *Cloudsley* so Sir *Charles* went to the *Exchange*, and I saw no more of him till I saw him kill'd. While I was in the house, came in one Mr. *Allen* and others, to enquire for Sir *Charles Pymm*, and Mr. *Cloudsley* told them that he had bespoke a dinner, and was gone to the *Exchange*, *viz.* a mullet and some smelts; but one of the Gentlemen desired a bit of the beef that was at the fire, so Mr. *Cloudsley* said he would get a plate for him. So I went to the door, and the Coachman came, and his horses being hot, he desired to go away because it rain'd; but Mr. *Neale* put his foot-boy into the coach, and the Coachman after pulled his Boy out of the coach, and drove away. And after that, I saw Mr. *Cave* and others come to the door, and jostled each other into the next shop, and were at very high words, and so afterwards they went into the entry again, and Sir *Charles Pymm* and Mr. *Walters* came out without the door, the latter of which said, *Here is my hand, and here is my sword*; but they returned both in again into the Tavern, and within two minutes came out again, and I saw Mr. *Walters* thrust Sir *Charles Pymm* through his back.

Court. Did you see him do any thing to him after he was down?

Mr. *Brummidge*. No, my Lord, I did not.

Court. Did you not say, that *Walters* went over the kennel, and drew his sword, and stood upon his guard, and then you say, that you saw Sir *Charles Pymm* come out with his sword drawn; Was his sword drawn?

Mr. *Brummidge*. I did not see him draw it; but it was drawn.

Court. Where did he receive his wound?

Brummidge. Within a foot of the kennel; I was but a little way off, but I did not see him beat his head against the ground.

Clerk. Cryer, call Mr *Fletcher*.

Mr. *Fletcher*. My Lord, on *Friday* in the evening on the fourth of *May*, I was going by the Tavern-door about seven a-clock at night, and I heard a noise, and a talking of going to the other end of the town to be merry, and turning myself back to hearken further, I saw Mr. *Walters* come out of the door and draw his sword, and Sir *Charles Pymm* came out, and drew his sword; and presently Mr. *Walters*'s sword was through Sir *Charles Pymm*'s body almost a foot; and he fell down crinkling immediately; and when he was down, I saw Mr. *Walters* hit him in the kennel, and take him by the nape of the neck, and after cried, *God damn him, let the sword stick in his body*, and afterwards I saw Mr. *Mirriday* pull the sword out of his body.

Court. Did you see Mr. *Bradshaw* there when Sir *Charles* fell?

Mr. *Fletcher*. No, my Lord, I saw none there but Mr. *Walters* and Sir *Charles*, they were out of doors, and the rest were in the entry

Mary White and *Sarah Webb* were called, who could give little or no evidence as to matter of fact, as concerning the death of Sir *Charles*; and being timorous, could not see what they might have seen.

Clerk. Cryer, call Mr. *Allen*.

Mr. *Allen*. I know but very little of the matter, but that there was a plate of beef sent up to us, but we knew not from whence it came, till afterwards the Drawer brought us word that the Gentlemen below had sent it up; after which, we drank their healths, and returned them thanks for it. After which, I went to the Coffee-house hard by, and sat about half an hour, and presently heard a cry of murder, and I came down, and saw Sir *Charles Pymm* lying with a wound in his body, and another in his head, but I did not know who it was, not then; but I asked who did this business, and exhorted the people to take them as soon as they could.

Court. I think you said that Mr. *Bradshaw*'s sword was drawn?

Mr. *Allen*. Yes, it was, but I believe that he did not know that Sir *Charles Pymm* was kill'd.

Mrs. *Sheepwash* was called, but could depose nothing material.

Court. Mr. *Walters*, you have been here indicted, together with Mr. *Bradshaw* and Mr. *Cave*, for the murder of Sir *Charles Pymm*, Knt. and Bart. you have heard what charge hath been laid against you, which hath been a very strong one, and now it behoves you to make your defence as well as you can.

Mr. *Walters*. My Lord, I was no way the occasion of the quarrel; when I came thither, I asked for some meat, and having not eaten all the day before, we had a piece of beef, of which Sir *Charles Pymm* and his company had some, who afterwards drank our healths, as I was informed. For my part, my Lord, I never saw the Gentleman before in my days: my Lord, I am very sorry it should be my misfortune to kill him in the quarrel. Sir *Charles Pymm* asked me, saying, *God damn you, Sir, what have you to do to meddle?* I went presently, my Lord, to a Fishmonger's, where Mr. *Mirriday* was, and Sir *Charles Pymm* came, and Mr. *Mirriday* said to him, Sir *Charles*, *Damn you, Sir, go and fight him, and I will be your Second.* And presently they came upon me, and I drew my sword in my own defence, and he ran me eight inches into the thigh, and at the same pass, I had the misfortune, my Lord, to run him into the body.

Court. Would you ask Mr. *Mirriday* any question?

Walters. Yes, my Lord. Mr. *Mirriday*, did you see me strike Sir *Charles*'s head upon the ground?

Mirriday. No, Sir, I did not see that; neither did I say any such thing in the Fishmonger's shop, as to bid Sir *Charles* fight you.

Clerk. Cryer, call *Matthew Perin.*

Perin. My Lord, all that I saw of the business was, that when the Coachman was called to the door, Mr. *Neale* came and threatened him if he did not stay; then Mr. *Cave* and Mr. *Bradshaw* were in the entry, and I heard them discourse about beef; and some of them said, You give us beef, and make us pay for it; and there was answer made, they were Rascals that said so, for they did not. There was one of the Gentlemen in our shop hearing of it, said, Let me come to him, I will fight him.

Court. Do you know the man?

Perin. No, I do not know who it was.

Mr. *Walters.* I was wounded at the same time, my Lord.

Court. That is admitted of.

Mr. *Walters.* Let him be asked, whether I beat the head against the ground,

Perin. No, my Lord, I did not see him do that.

Court. He had a wound, the question is how he came by it; whether he might not fall upon it himself, it was a slanting wound?

Mr *Walters.* Pray, my Lord, let Sir *Charles*'s sword be seen, all blood. [But that gave no satisfaction on either side.]

Court. Mr. *Bradshaw*, what have you to say for yourself?

Mr. *Bradshaw.* My Lord, I was there, but I know nothing of the death of Sir *Charles Pymm*, nor how he came by it; there were some words arose amongst us, and I desired them to cease, for fear a further quarrel should ensue upon it.

Court. Mr. *Cave*, what have you to say?

Mr. *Cave.* I know no more of the matter than this Gentleman saith: I saw not Sir *Charles Pymm* killed.

Clerk. Cryer, make proclamation.

Cryer. All people are commanded to keep silence upon pain of imprisonment.

Then Mr. Baron *Jenner* summ'd up the evidence as followeth:

Baron *Jenner.* Gentlemen of the Jury, you have three persons indicted, *viz.* Mr. *Walters*, Mr. *Bradshaw* and Mr. *Cave*, for murdering Sir *Charles Pymm*, Bart. and have had several witnesses called for the King, against the prisoners at the Bar; the first of which was Mr. *Mirriday*; and he gives you this account, and 'tis all that each and every one gives, and it agrees on all sides; and he tells you, that all those Gentlemen were to dine at Mr. *Cloudsley*'s, at the *Swan-Tavern* in *Old Fish-street*; and that they were there at dinner, it is very plainly prov'd. And being there, it seems that some of those Gentlemen had bespoke a fish-dinner, some flesh, and had some, *viz.* a plate of beef; and he tells you also, that when dinner was over, some words did arise concerning the reckoning, and that one of the companies were got down stairs in the entry, where a further quarrel did arise. Mr. *Mirriday* tells you further, that Mr. *Bradshaw* and he quarrelled, so there was a scuffle in the entry; after which things were pretty well quieted there: in comes Mr. *Walters* and Sir *Charles Pymm*, and while Mr. *Mirriday* was securing the first quarrel, they, *viz.* Sir *Charles Pymm* and Mr. *Walters* were got out at the door, and Sir *Charles* was stooping down, and Mr. *Walters* was pushing upon his neck and throwing him down.

So said Mr. *Mirriday*, and when he went to take the sword out of his body, he saw him a dying man.

The next evidence was Mr. *Neale*, and he observes to you, that one of the Gentlemen did say, that the quarrel was not intended against them; and he gives an account of the story, how that it was about the beef; how that Sir *Charles* was run through by *Walters*, but he did not see him knock his head against the ground.

Mr. *Palms* gives the like account, and saith, that whilst they were a scuffling in the entry, Sir *Charles* was kill'd at the door.

The next evidence is the Drawer, who tells you of a squabble that Mr. *Neale* had with the Coachman at the door, and how that there was left four of the Gentlemen behind, and that the Coachman was unwilling to wait because it rained, his horses being hot, they might catch cold; whereupon

he put his foot-boy into th
went away · this was befor

The next evidence was o
same account, how that a
Walters was on one side of
side, and there they stood v
came close, they wounded
but he did not see his head

Comes *Fletcher*, my Lor
was going by the door hom
wounded stooping down; a
nape of his neck, and knoc
swear, *Let the sword stick in*
it to be in the like manner
ling Sir *Charles Pymm* out

Last of all, Gentlemen
who went away to the C
came and found Sir *Charle*
men, is the evidence that

Now, for the prisoner
Sir *Charles* had struck him b
it: likewise speaks of Mr. *F*
Pymm struck him before he
quarrel, in which that hor
Pymm, lost his Life.

Now for Mr. *Bradshaw*,
saith, that he did not kno
and for Mr. *Cave*, I do not
of them.

Now, Gentlemen, I mu
of all, to begin with Mr. *W*
may be guided to deal with
appear by any of the evide
premeditated malice betwee
fore, and knew not each ot
lice from him in particular.

The next step, Gentleme
ral malice upon Mr. *Walte*
kill another with whom I
ditated malice, but I rath
amongst them: and this
but by a hot and sudden fro
on such a worthy Gentlem
premeditated, then he can b
and as for the other two, th
in the summing up of these
Here are my Brothers to hel

Then the Gentlemen of
an hour, and returned int
amongst them spoke to the

Juryman. My Lord, we a
the death of Sir *Charles Pym*
after he had run the sword
that, but must knock his hea
the said Sir *Charles Pymm* w

Mr. Justice *Allibone.* Ge
rect you in this case, and te
reach a man's life, where no
proved, appears very plain t
been proved that those Gent
deceased, had never been in

Gentlemen, you are upo
and I, as a Judge, am upon
of the living as the dead. So
can be called nothing else
men are subject to; so that
quent passion; which sad p
Charles Pymm in the midst o

Then the Jury went out a
turning, brought in Mr. *W*
two were acquitted.

THE END OF THE SEVENTH V

... a that there was a quarrel, but ...
or how Sir *Charles Pymm* was kill...
y thing objected against him, ...

...u what the Law is in this case. ...
so as it fares with Mr. *Walters*, ...
her two. Now it hath not been ...
t you have heard, that there was ...
for they were never in ...
that there could be no ...

...ere is nothing that can impute ...
if I had no design to kill a man, ...
quarrel, that cannot be any ...
k that there was a little heat ...
...ction was carried on by nothing ...
d I am very sorry that it should fall ...
e was. And if there was no ...
guilty of nothing but Manslaughter, ...
t be totally acquitted. If I have ...
ces, or mistaken my self in any par...

...y withdrew for about the space ...
t upon a scruple of conscience ...
s followeth:

...atisfied in our consciences concerning ...
...ard on it malice fore-thought, ...
h his body, he was not ...
...ift the ground, so we do ...
...iously murdered.
... of the Jury, I shall endeavour ...
what the Law saith, That ...
...se malice is proved; that there ...
...u I hope also to you, because ...
viz. the prisoners at the Bar, ...
... before.
...oaths to serve the King as Jurymen, ...
... to try the cause as well on ...
...on the whole matter, Gentlemen, ...
...orm, an ungoverned storm ...
...ot reach precedent malice, but ...
...as continued to that height, that ...
... his life.

... about a quarter of an hour, and ...
...uilty of manslaughter, but the ...

CPSIA information can be obtained at www.ICGtesting.com
Printed in the USA
LVOW01s1201251014

410415LV00006B/55/P